PAGE 36

ON THE ROAD

YOUR COMPLETE DESTINATION GUIDE
In-depth reviews, detailed listings and insider tips

THIS EDITION WRITTEN AND RESEARCHED BY

Regis St Louis,
Sandra Bao, Greg Benchwick, Celeste Brash,
Gregor Clark, Alex Egerton, Bridget Gleeson, Beth Kohn,
Carolyn McCarthy, Kevin Raub, Paul Smith, Lucas Vidgen

welcome to South America

Setting for Big Adventures

From the snowcapped peaks of the Andes to the undulating waterways of the Amazon, South America spreads a dazzling array of natural wonders. This is a continent of lush rainforests, towering volcanoes, misty cloud forests, bone-dry deserts, red-rock canyons, ice-blue glaciers and sun-kissed beaches. As landscapes go, there aren't many other places on earth that offer so much range – or so many opportunities for adventure.

You can hike past ancient temples first laid down by the Incas, contemplate the awe-inspiring power of Iguazú Falls or spend the day watching wildlife from a dugout canoe on one of the Amazon's countless *igarapés* (narrow waterways). You can barrel down Andean roads by mountain bike, go whitewater rafting on class V rivers and surf amazing breaks off both coasts. And once you think you've experienced it all, head to the dramatic landscapes in Tierra del Fuego, go eye-to-eye with extraordinary creatures in the Galápagos, and scramble up tableland mountains in the Gran Sabana for a panorama that seems straight out of the Mesozoic era.

Cultural Treasures

South America's great diversity doesn't end with geography. Across the continent

Andean peaks, Amazonian rainforest, Patagonian glaciers, Incan ruins, colonial towns, white-sand beaches and vertiginous nightlife: the wonders of South America set the stage for incredible adventures.

(left) Patagonia's Cerro Fitz Roy (p146)
(below) Festival in Cuenca, Ecuador (p671)

you'll find magnificent colonial towns where cobblestone streets lead past gilded churches and stately plazas – a scene little changed since the 18th century. Elsewhere, you can haggle over colorful textiles at indigenous markets, share meals with traditional dwellers of the rainforest and follow the pounding rhythms laid down by Afro-Brazilian drum corps. South America is home to an astounding variety of living and ancient cultures, and experiencing it all firsthand is as easy as showing up.

La Vida Musical

Welcome to one of the world's great music destinations. Colombian salsa, Brazilian samba, Argentine tango and Andean folk music all receive airtime across the globe, but nothing quite compares to hearing those rhythms in the place where they were born. Sultry *milongas* (dance halls) in Buenos Aires, simmering samba clubs in Rio, *salsotecas* (salsa clubs) in Quito – all great places to chase the heart of Saturday night. Yet this is only the beginning of a great musical odyssey that encompasses poetic Peruvian *trovas*, soulful Ecuadorian *pasillos*, fast-stepping Brazilian *forró*, whirling Venezuelan merengue, steel-pan Guyanese drumming, Paraguayan harp music and scores of other regional styles. The best way to experience it is to simply plunge in – though you might want to take a dance class along the way!

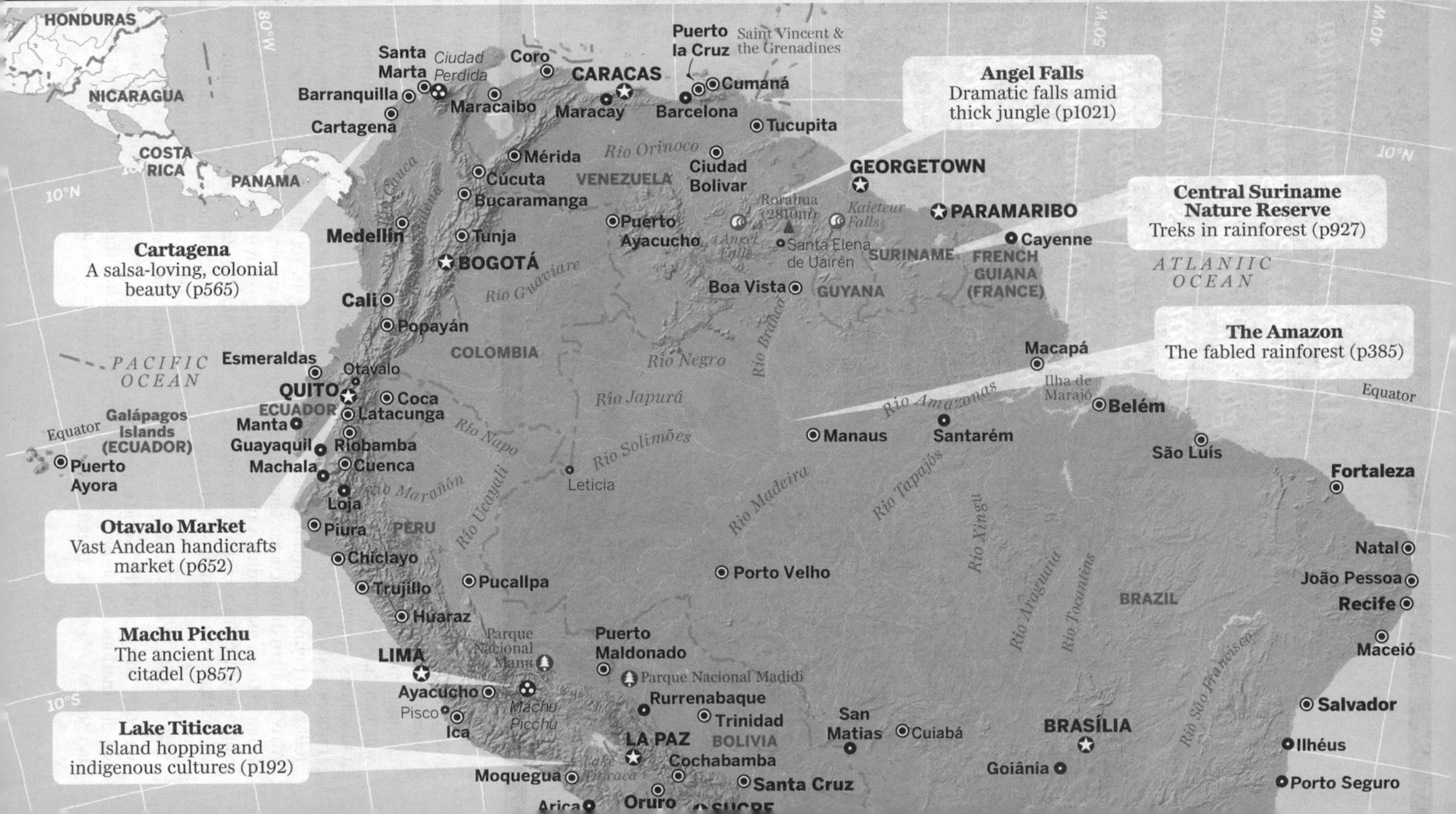
Angel Falls
Dramatic falls amid thick jungle (p1021)
Central Suriname Nature Reserve
Treks in rainforest (p927)
The Amazon
The fabled rainforest (p385)
Cartagena
A salsa-loving, colonial beauty (p565)
Otavalo Market
Vast Andean handicrafts market (p652)
Machu Picchu
The ancient Inca citadel (p857)
Lake Titicaca
Island hopping and indigenous cultures (p192)
HONDURAS
NICARAGUA
COSTA RICA
PANAMA
10°N
80°W
50°W
40°W
10°S
PACIFIC OCEAN
ATLANTIC OCEAN
Equator
Galápagos Islands (ECUADOR)
Puerto Ayora
Santa Marta
Ciudad Perdida
Coro
CARACAS
Puerto la Cruz
Saint Vincent & the Grenadines
Cumaná
Barranquilla
Maracaibo
Maracay
Barcelona
Tucupita
Cartagena
Mérida
Río Orinoco
Ciudad Bolivar
Cúcuta
VENEZUELA
Bucaramanga
GEORGETOWN
Roraima (2810m)
Kaieteur Falls
PARAMARIBO
Medellín
Tunja
Puerto Ayacucho
Angel Falls
Santa Elena de Uairén
SURINAME
Cayenne
FRENCH GUIANA (FRANCE)
BOGOTÁ
Río Guaviare
Boa Vista
GUYANA
Cali
Popayán
COLOMBIA
Río Negro
Río Branco
Macapá
Esmeraldas
Otavalo
QUITO
ECUADOR
Coca
Latacunga
Río Japurá
Río Amazonas
Ilha de Marajó
Belém
Manta
Guayaquil
Riobamba
Río Napo
Manaus
Santarém
Machala
Cuenca
Río Solimões
São Luís
Loja
Río Marañón
Leticia
Río Madeira
Río Tapajós
Fortaleza
Piura
PERU
Río Ucayali
Río Xingu
Chiclayo
Natal
Trujillo
Pucallpa
Porto Velho
João Pessoa
Río Araguaia
Río Tocantins
BRAZIL
Recife
Huaraz
Parque Nacional Manu
Puerto Maldonado
Maceió
LIMA
Parque Nacional Madidi
Río São Francisco
Ayacucho
Machu Picchu
Rurrenabaque
Salvador
Pisco
Ica
Trinidad
San Matias
Cuiabá
BRASÍLIA
LA PAZ
BOLIVIA
Ilhéus
Lake Titicaca
Cochabamba
Goiânia
Moquegua
Santa Cruz
Porto Seguro
Arica
Oruro

Salar de Uyuni
Otherworldly salt flats (p212)
Buenos Aires
Blazing nightlife, colorful neighborhoods (p41)
Rio de Janeiro
Beaches, caipirinhas and samba (p266)
Iguazú Falls
One of earth's mightiest falls (p83)
Encarnación
Paraguay's most captivating city (p776)
Colonia del Sacramento
Photogenic 18th-century charmer (p943)
Glaciar Perito Moreno
Massive, dramatically set glacier (p151)
Torres del Paine
Granite peaks soaring over Patagonia (p508)
Uyuni
Potosí
Iquique
Tupiza
Tarija
Calama
Villazón
San Pedro de Atacama
Antofagasta
San Salvador de Jujuy
Salta
Tucumán
Tropic of Capricorn
Campo Grande
PARAGUAY
Ciudad del Este
Foz do Iguaçu
Puerto Iguazú
ASUNCIÓN
Corrientes
Encarnación
Posadas
Belo Horizonte
Ouro Prêto
São Paolo
Rio de Janeiro
Curitiba
Florianópolis
Caxias do Sul
Porto Alegre
Pelotas
Río Paraná
Río Uruguay
La Serena
Córdoba
Santa Fe
URUGUAY
Rosario
Punta del Diablo
Punta del Este
MONTEVIDEO
BUENOS AIRES
Mendoza
Viña del Mar
Valparaíso
SANTIAGO
ARGENTINA
Archipiélago Juan Fernández (CHILE)
PACIFIC OCEAN
Concepción
Chillan
Mar del Plata
Temuco
Pucón
Valdivia
Osorno
Bariloche
Puerto Montt
El Bolsón
Ilha Grande de Chiloé
Puerto Madryn
ATLANIIC OCEAN
Coyhaique
CHILE
Parque Nacional Los Glaciares
El Calafate
Falkland Islands (Islas Malvinas)
Stanley
Parque Nacional Torres del Paine
Río Gallegos
Puerto Natales
Punta Arenas
Ushuaia
0 1,000 km
0 500 miles
20°S
30°S
40°S
50°S
80°W
60°W
50°W
40°W
30°W
Rapa Nui (CHILE)
Rapa Nui (Easter Island)

15 TOP EXPERIENCES

Machu Picchu

1 A fantastic Inca citadel lost to the world until its early 20th-century discovery, Peru's Machu Picchu (p857) stands as a ruin among ruins. With its emerald terraces and steep peaks that echo on the horizon, the sight simply surpasses the imagination. This marvel of engineering has withstood half a dozen centuries of earthquakes, foreign invasion and howling weather. Discover it for yourself, wander through its stone temples and scale the dizzying heights of Wayna Picchu.

The Amazon

2 Home to the greatest collection of plant and animal life on earth, the awe-inspiring Amazon encompasses more than seven million square kilometers. There are countless ways to experience its astounding biodiversity: trekking through dense jungle, visiting indigenous villages, flying over the vast green expanse of undulating waterways, slow-boating between river towns or lounging in a jungle lodge after a day spent wildlife-watching. Nine countries share a bit of the famous rainforest, and all of them have excellent bases to experience it firsthand. Emperor tamarin

1

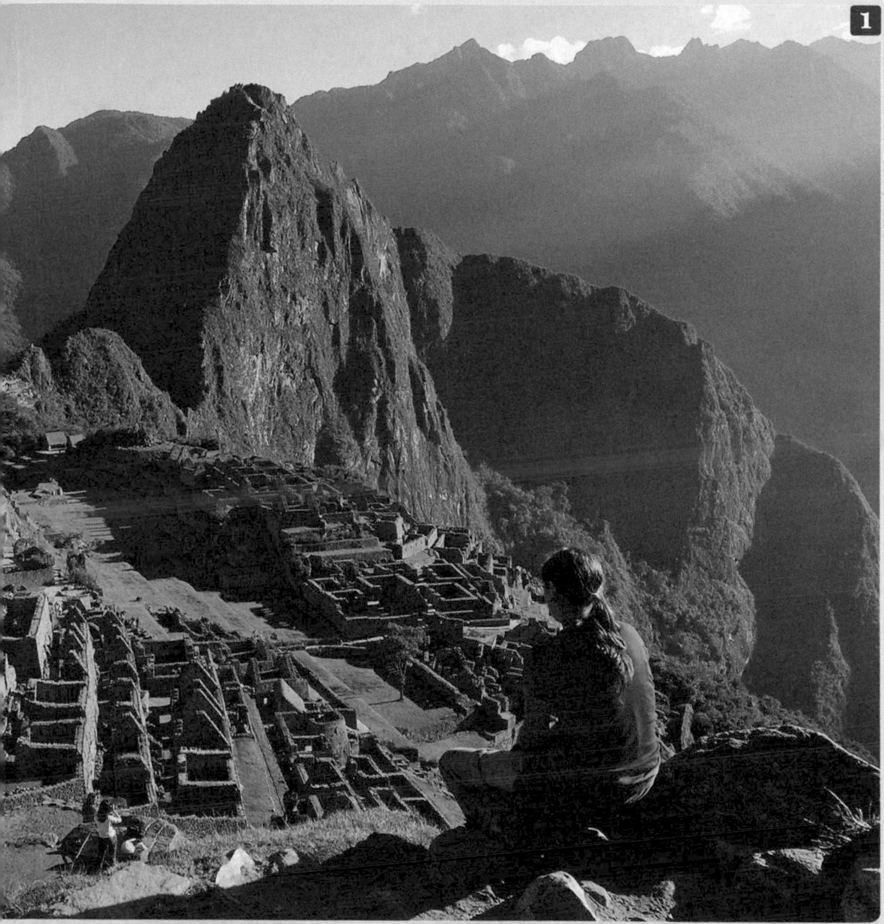

JUERGEN RITTERBACH / GETTY IMAGES ©

2

CARRIE VONDERHAAR/OCEAN FUTURES SOCIETY A / GETTY IMAGES ©

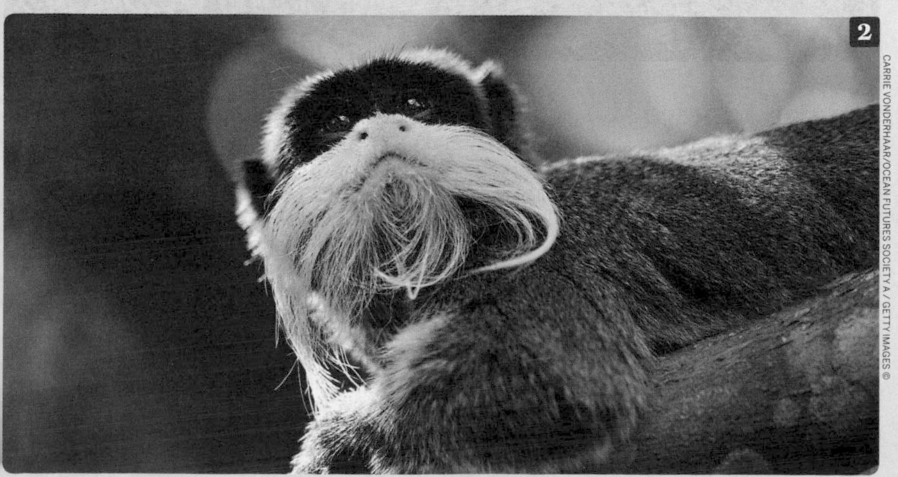

3

4

Rio de Janeiro

3 Few cities in the world enjoy more seductive charm than Brazil's Cidade Maravilhosa (Marvelous City), but calling it merely marvelous doesn't quite cut it. On privileged real estate flanked by striking Atlantic-blue waters, sugary white sands and a mountainous backdrop of Crayola-green rainforest, Rio's (p266) cinematic cityscape has few rivals. And once its soundtrack kicks in – a high-on-life siren's song of bossa nova and samba – Rio's raw energy seizes you with the come-hither allure of a tropical fantasy. You'll have no choice but to follow.

Lake Titicaca

4 Less a lake than a highland ocean, Lake Titicaca (p192) in Bolivia is the highest navigable body of water in the world. In Andean tradition it's the birthplace of the sun. Here, banner-blue skies turn to bitterly cold nights. Among its fantastical sights are the surreal floating islands crafted entirely of tightly woven *totora* reeds. Enthralling and in many ways singular, the shimmering deep-blue Lake Titicaca is the longtime home of highland cultures steeped in the old ways.

KEREN SU / GETTY IMAGES ©

ANGEL HERRERO DE FRUTOS / GETTY IMAGES ©

Buenos Aires

5 Whip together a beautiful Argentine metropolis with gourmet cuisine, awesome shopping, frenzied nightlife and gorgeous locals, and you get Buenos Aires (p41). It's a European-like, cosmopolitan city encompassing both slick neighborhoods and downtrodden ghettos, but that's the appeal. You can experience classic cafes, amazing steaks, surprising architecture, energizing *fútbol* games and, of course, that sultry tango. Buenos Aires is elegant, seductive, emotional, confounding, frustrating and chock-full of attitude – there's absolutely no other place like it in the world.

Salar de Uyuni

6 Who knew feeling this cold could feel so good? While the three- to four-day jeep tour through the world's largest salt flat (p212) will leave your bones chattering, it quite possibly could be the singular experience that defines your Bolivian adventure. The salt flat in its vastness, austerity and crystalline perfection will inspire you, while your early morning exploration of rock gardens, geyser fields and piping hot springs – along with the camaraderie of three days on the road with your fellow 'Salterians' – will create a kinship not likely to fade anytime soon.

Colonia del Sacramento

7 Take a step back in time as you explore the winding cobbled streets and fascinating history of Uruguay's former smugglers' haven (p943). Then check out the great bar and restaurant scene and the gorgeous position on a peninsula of the Río de la Plata. All this, and its superaccessible location just a short hop away from both Montevideo and Buenos Aires, makes 'Colonia' a classic tourist destination, but even on weekends it's worth dodging the crowds and letting yourself get seduced by the town's eternal charms.

Torres del Paine

8 The wind is whipping and dark clouds form overhead as the hiking trail suddenly opens to reveal a stunning vista of rugged granite spires soaring high over the Patagonian steppe. These are the Torres del Paine (p508), the proud centerpiece of Chile's famous national park. Trekking through this Unesco Biosphere Reserve isn't for the faint of heart – guides say the park sees all four seasons in a single day – but hiking the 'W' remains a rite of passage for generations of adventurous travelers.

7

VIVIANE PONTI / GETTY IMAGES ©

8

JOSEF FRIEDHUBER / GETTY IMAGES ©

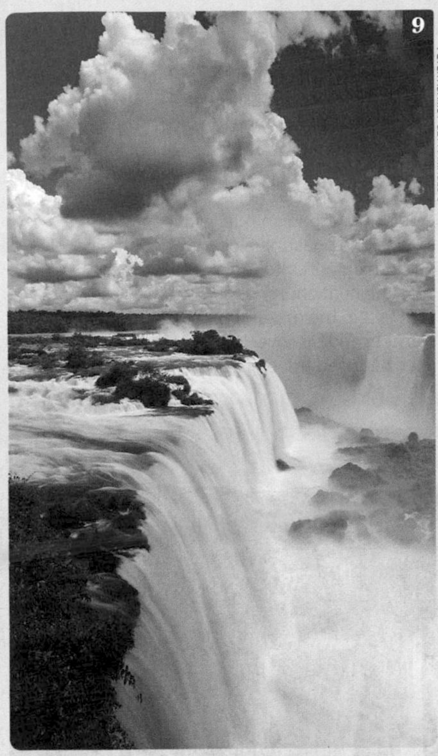
9
PETER ADAMS / GETTY IMAGES ©

10
NIGEL PAVITT / GETTY IMAGES

11
DANITA DELIMONT / GETTY IMAGES ©

Iguazú Falls

9 The thunderous roar, the dramatic cascades, the refreshing sprays, the absolute miraculous work of Mother Nature – nothing prepares you for that flooring first moment you set eyes upon Iguazú Falls. On the Brazilian side (p318), the wide-eyed view of the whole astounding scene stretches out before you in all its panoramic wonder. In Argentina (p83), get up close and personal with the deafening Devil's Throat, which provides the fall's single most mind-blowing moment. In all, the 275 falls deliver one of the world's best 'wow' moments in unforgettable fashion.

Otavalo Market

10 Every Saturday the world seems to converge on the bustling Ecuadorian town of Otavalo in the Andes, where a huge market (p652) spreads out from the Plaza de Ponchos throughout the town. The choice is enormous, the quality immensely change-able and the crowds can be a drag, but you'll find some incredible bargains here among the brightly colored rugs, traditional crafts, clothing, Tigua folk art and quality straw hats. Nearby, the squawks and squeals of livestock drown out the chatter of Quichua-speaking farmers at Otavalo's equally famous animal market.

Central Suriname Nature Reserve

11 Cascading rapids rush past smooth boulders and forested islands lined with white-sand beaches. The sun-dappled jungle is hot and muggy, but the beauty of the foliage, birdsong and musky scents outweigh the discomforts. In one of Suriname's largest nature reserves (p927), you can trek to plateaus with views over never-ending pristine forest, then cool off in a waterfall at the end of the day. At night dance to African drums before gazing at shooting stars in the deep black sky, in near-mosquito-free bliss.

Blue poison dart frog

Salto Ángel (Angel Falls)

12 Fly over a surreal landscape of flat-topped *tepuis* to Venezuela's Parque Nacional Canaima, and touch down alongside the pink-tinted cascades of Canaima lagoon. Your next step is a five-hour river journey through lush jungle. From the Mirador Laime, witness the cascade of Salto Ángel (p1021), the world's tallest waterfall, as it thunders 979m from the plateau of Auyantepui. Swim while gazing up at the water flow, and then sleep in a hammock camp, serenaded by the evening jungle.

Cartagena

13 Stroll through the perfectly preserved streets of Cartagena's old town (p565) and be swept away by the grace, romance and legend of one of the continent's finest colonial settlements. Inside its imposing walls, much of this Colombian city still looks as it did during Spanish rule, with pastel-hued mansions boasting elegant wooden balconies that open out onto majestic plazas shaded by magnificent churches. Throw away the map, get lost in the maze of narrow cobblestoned streets and discover why this magical place has seduced travelers for centuries.

KRZYSZTOF DYDYNSKI / GETTY IMAGES ©

ALFREDO MAIQUEZ / GETTY IMAGES ©

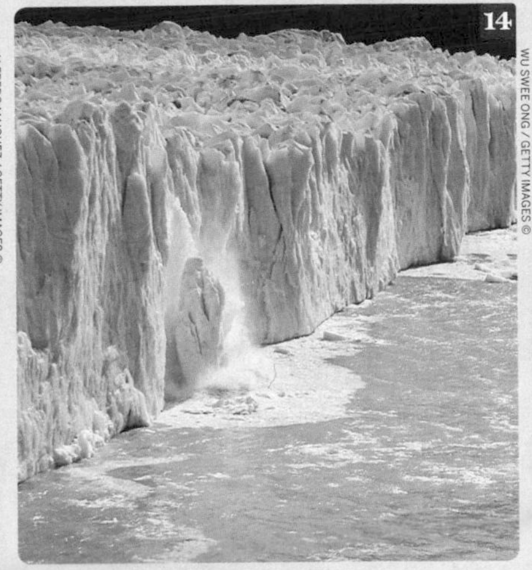

WU SWEE ONG / GETTY IMAGES ©

AFP / GETTY IMAGES ©

Glaciar Perito Moreno

14 Possibly the world's most dynamic glacier, the Perito Moreno (p151) in Argentina advances up to 2m per day, which means plenty of exciting, spine-tingling calving. It's supremely accessible, too – you can get very close to the action via a complex network of steel boardwalks, perfectly situated near (but not too near!) the glacier's face. Everyone stands there, watching in suspense, for the next building-size chunk to sheer off and slowly tip into the water below, creating thunderous crashes and huge waves. Trust us, it's awesome.

Encarnación

15 With its new beach, sparkling coastal promenade and wildly energetic Carnaval, Paraguay's 'Pearl of the South' (p776) is billing itself as the local answer to Rio de Janeiro. Though some might find that a bit ambitious, there is no doubt that Encarnación's unique take on Carnaval is a whole lot of fun – the crowd dances as much as the participants, spray snow fills the hot summer air and the party goes on well into the early hours of the morning.

need to know

Planes

» Flying between countries is quite expensive, although pre-purchased air passes provide decent value. Domestic flights are generally more affordable.

Buses

» Amazonia aside, buses go everywhere and come in all types, from slow local options to comfy international buses connecting major towns of neighboring countries.

When to Go

May–Sep

» In the Andes of Ecuador, Peru and Bolivia, these are generally the driest months and the best time to go trekking.

» The dry season in the Pantanal, and the best time to see wildlife there.

Oct–Nov

» The driest months in the Amazon are generally July to November.

» Fewer crowds and lower prices make this a good time to visit Buenos Aires, Rio and other coastal destinations.

Dec–Mar

» It's high season in Brazil and the Altantic coast; beaches and festivals (like Carnaval) are big draws.

» The best time to visit Patagonia, although expect higher prices.

Your Daily Budget

Budget less than $30

» Cheapest in Bolivia, Paraguay, Ecuador and Colombia

» Dorm beds from $7, double rooms from $20

» Shopping at markets, eating inexpensive set meals: from $2.50

Midrange $30-$80

» Budget jungle lodge in the Amazon: $50 to $80 per day

» Excursions: hiking-, cycling-, birdwatching tours: from $40 per day

» 3½-day boat trip from Manaus to Belém: $110 (hammock fare)

Top end over $80

» Hiking the Inca Trail (4-day trek): $500 per person

» Multiday Galápagos cruise: around $200 per day

Cars

» Car hire can be pricey and crossing borders is a hassle. However, a car is handy for exploring remote areas and national parks.

Trains

» There are few trains in operation, although some scenic lines operate in Argentina, Bolivia, Brazil, Ecuador and Peru.

Boat

» The prime mode of travel in the Amazon, with slow, crowded boats making multiday journeys between towns.

Bicycle

» Daunting but highly rewarding for the intrepid. Challenges: poor roads, reckless drivers and high altitudes.

Websites

» **Lonely Planet** (www.lonelyplanet.com) Thorn Tree forum, destination information and hotel bookings.

» **Latin American Network Information Center** (www.lanic.utexas.edu) Links to all things Latin American.

» **South American Explorers** (www.saexplorers.org) Country profiles; travel discounts for members.

» **UK Foreign & Commonwealth Office** (www.fco.gov.uk) Travel advisories.

» **US State Department** (www.state.gov) Travel advice and warnings.

Money

» ATMs are available in major towns and cities, and are generally the best way of getting cash. Stock up on funds before visiting remote areas.

» Most hostels and budget hotels accept cash only.

» Hone your bargaining skills before visiting markets.

» Keep an emergency stash of US dollars (the easiest currency to exchange).

» Be careful changing money at borders; read up on exchange rates and scams before you arrive.

Visas

Visitors from the USA and some other countries require visas (best arranged in advance) when visiting Brazil, Bolivia, Paraguay and Suriname. Make sure you have enough blank pages in your passport, and that it will be valid for six months beyond your proposed entry date to each country.

Arriving in South America

» **Aeropuerto Internacional de Ezeiza, Buenos Aires**
Shuttle bus frequent to downtown (AR$60-70)
Taxi AR$180

» **Aeropuerto Internacional Jorge Chávez, Lima**
Combi: take 'La S' (S2-3); find it southbound along Av Elmer Faucett
Taxi S45

» **Aeropuerto El Dorado, Bogotá**
Shuttle bus to Portal El Dorado; transfer to TransMilenio bus (COP$1700)
Taxi COP$21,000

Get Inspired

Poets, revolutionaries and adventurers have all contributed to the ever-expanding genre of Latin American literature.

Mario Vargas Llosa and Gabriel García Márquez – both Nobel Prize winners and sometime rivals – are considered the continent's best living writers. Recommended reads: Márquez' *Love in the Time of Cholera* and Llosa's *War of the End of the World*.

Jorge Luis Borges, another giant of modern literature, is best known for his labyrinthine tales, and playful melding of myth and truth in works like *Ficciones*.

Less esoteric are the novels of Brazil's Jorge Amado, who wrote colorful, ribald stories set in Bahía. *Dona Flor and Her Two Husbands* is a classic.

The Motorcycle Diaries, by Ernesto 'Che' Guevara, is a breezy travelogue written by the Argentine-born revolutionary.

More poignant is Bruce Chatwin's *In Patagonia*, a beautifully written travel narrative that blends fact and fable.

if you like...

Colonial Splendor

South America has a stunning array of architectural wonders, where cobblestone streets lead past magnificent cathedrals, photogenic plazas and brightly painted townhouses – some of which date back to the 16th century. But don't just take our word for it: the following destinations are also Unesco World Heritage Sites.

Quito Wandering the buzzing streets of the *centro histórico* (old town) presents dramatic scenery at every turn (p628)

Colonia del Sacramento Uruguay's delightfully picturesque riverfront town is a short ferry ride from Buenos Aires (p943)

Ouro Preto One of Brazil's most alluring colonial towns, hilly Ouro Preto is packed with 18th-century treasures (p303)

Cartagena Colombia's comeliest coastal town has a beautifully preserved center scenically set on the Caribbean (p565)

Arequipa A Peruvian charmer with striking colonial *sillar* architecture and spicy salt-of-the-earth eateries (p826)

Paramaribo A strange and exotic blend of colonial Dutch buildings and grassy squares in oft-overlooked Suriname (p920)

Big Cities

South America's cities are home to first-rate museums, foodie-loving restaurants and rocking nightlife. You can shop atmospheric markets, cozy up at an art-filled cafe or spend the day exploring charming neighborhoods.

Rio de Janeiro The Cidade Maravilhosa (Marvelous City) lives up to its name with lovely beaches, samba-fueled nightlife and jaw-dropping scenery (p266)

Buenos Aires A place that's hard to leave, with colorful neighborhoods, late-night dining, old-world cafes, sultry tango clubs and French and Italianate architecture (p41)

Lima Sure, it's chaotic, but Lima is a great place for seafood feasts and late night bar-hopping in bohemian Barranco; its museums also house Peru's best pre-Columbian collections (p802)

Bogotá The Colombian capital has salsa-fueled nightclubs and an intriguing colonial center – plus fascinating nearby sights like the surreal underground salt cathedral at Zipaquira (p532)

Valparaíso A bohemian city and Unesco World Heritage Site that's often considered Chile's cultural capital (p429)

Ancient Ruins

Pre-Columbian peoples left behind a wide-ranging legacy: the awe-inspiring monuments and artfully crafted works in ceramic, gold and stone comprise but a fraction of the great works in existence before the Europeans arrived.

Machu Picchu The godfather of great ruins, this mountaintop Inca citadel is best enjoyed as the finale of a multiday trek (p857)

Cuzco The continent's oldest continuously inhabited city, where you can still find flawless Inca-built walls lining cobblestone streets (p841)

Kuélap Perched atop a limestone mountain, this monumental stone-fortified city is a relic of a fierce cloud-forest-dwelling civilization (p891)

San Agustín In southwest Colombia, the mysterious San Agustín culture left behind hundreds of statues carved from volcanic rock (p601)

Rapa Nui Better known as Easter Island, this Polynesian outpost is home to utterly mystifying *moai* (statues; p513)

Nazca Lines Mysterious carvings in the sand spread across hundreds of square kilometers; scenic flights are the best way to see it (p822)

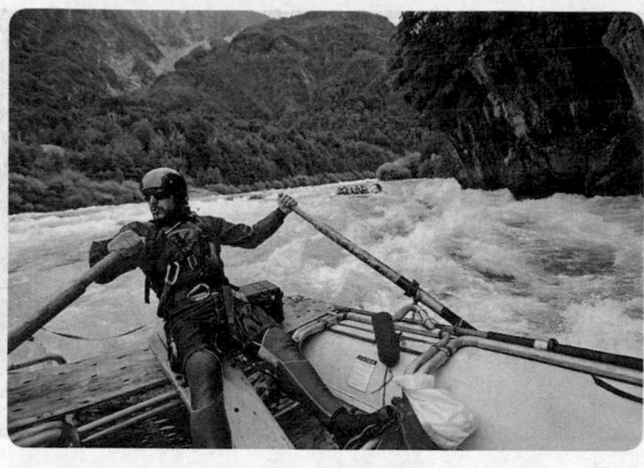

» Rafting on the Río Futaleufú, Chile (p498)

Beaches

Shimmering beaches wedged between tropical rainforest and deep blue sea: South America spreads some mighty enticing destinations for sun-lovers. Remote island getaways, party-loving surf towns and glittering sands just steps away from big city allure... this is just the beginning.

Archipiélago Los Roques Straight north of Caracas, 300 pristine islands make a magnificent setting for beach-combing, snorkeling and diving (p989)

Arraial d'Ajuda Brazil is spoiled for choice when it comes to world-class beaches; this peaceful town in the northeast is gateway to some of Bahia's prettiest coastline (p348)

Punta del Diablo Forget the over-hyped mayhem of Punta del Este; Uruguay's more tranquil summertime getaway is this coastal beauty just south of the Brazilian border (p957)

Parque Nacional Natural Tayrona Fronting the Caribbean Sea, this pristine national park in Colombia has gorgeous beaches and does a fine imitation of paradise lost (p560)

Outdoor Adventures

Adrenaline junkies can get their fix negotiating snow-capped peaks, rushing rivers and pounding surf. Rafting, rock climbing, mountain biking, hang-gliding, sand-boarding and zip-lining: there are hundreds of ways to get your heart racing.

Whitewater rafting The enchanting Argentine city of Mendoza is the gateway to thrilling river adventures (p114)

Mountain biking The World's Most Dangerous Road: the name says it all – this 64km mountain bike trip outside La Paz takes in perilous descents, so make sure your brakes (and travel insurance!) are top notch (p189)

Hang-gliding Sail high above the forest-covered hills of Rio to a beachside landing on a fantastic tandem flight (p270)

Sandboarding Take a wild ride down 150m high sand dunes just outside a desert oasis town in northern Chile (p453)

Mountain climbing Strap on your crampons and make your way up 5897m Volcán Cotopaxi, one of Ecuador's most popular climbs (p657)

Dramatic Scenery

Thundering waterfalls, cone-shaped volcanoes and red-rock canyons – the only thing missing are the pterodactyls. When gazing upon these natural wonders, you might feel like you've stepped back a few million years.

Parque Nacional da Chapada Diamantina Head to Brazil's northeast to hike across dramatic plateaus and swim in refreshing waterfalls (p342)

Iguazú Falls Spread between Argentina and Brazil, these are some of the most spectacular waterfalls on earth (p83)

Cañón del Cotahuasi Hard to reach but immensely rewarding is this Central Andean icon, the world's deepest canyon (p827)

Salar de Uyuni The world's largest salt flats are a dazzling remnant of a vast prehistoric lake (p212)

Roraima In southeastern Venezuela, you'll find otherworldly landscapes of tableland mountains, wind-carved gorges, ribbon waterfalls and carnivorous plants (p1024)

Parque Nacional Torres del Paine In southern Patagonia, sparkling glaciers, topaz lakes and sheer granite cliff-faces defy the imagination (p508)

» Hiking in the Parque Nacional Los Glaciares, Argentina (p151)

Festivals & Events

Whether you prefer the colorful pageantry of Semana Santa (Holy Week) or the unbridled revelry of Carnaval, the continent has you covered. From the traditional to the downright surreal, here are a few events worth planning a trip around.

Carnaval Many towns in Brazil throw a wild pre-Lenten bash, but Salvador and Rio are the best places to celebrate a few sleepless nights (p270)

Fiesta de la Mamá Negra This Ecuadorian fest features processions, witches, whole roast pigs, a bit of cross-dressing and plenty of alcohol (p658)

Festival y Mundial de Baile Learn some new moves at this massive tango festival in Buenos Aires in August (p51)

Fiesta de la Virgen de la Candelaria In Puno, Peru gives a thunderous street party for its patron saint (p836)

Fiesta del Santo Patrono de Moxos One of Bolivia's biggest bashes includes fireworks, dancing, feasts and wild costumes (p20)

Hiking & Trekking

Against a backdrop of Andean peaks, misty cloud forests and Amazonian jungle, trekking here is world class. Whether you're out for a short day's hike or a multiday journey, you'll find limitless options.

Quilotoa Avid walkers shouldn't miss this scenic multiday Ecuadorian journey, overnighting at simple village guesthouses along the way (p659)

Choro Traversing Bolivia's Parque Nacional Cotopata, the four-day Choro Trek begins amid alpine scenery before descending into the lush, subtropical Yungas region (p203)

Cordillera Huayhuash circuit Rivaling the big Himalayan treks, this 10-day Peruvian odyssey takes you among alpine lakes with condors circling the nearby 6000m peaks (p886)

El Chaltén In Argentine Patagonia, El Chaltén offers unparalleled trekking amid glaciers, alpine lakes and craggy mountains (p146)

Ciudad Perdida Like a scene torn from an Indiana Jones film, the trek to Colombia's 'Lost City' is a challenging six-day (return) journey to the overgrown ruins of a large pre-Columbian town (p562)

Wildlife

South America is home to more plant and animal species than any other place on earth and there are countless settings to watch wildlife.

The Amazon Manaus is still one of the top gateways for a journey into the mother of all rainforests (p381)

The Pantanal You're likely to see even more animal species here than in the Amazon at these wildlife-rich wetlands; Cuiabá is one of the top spots to plan a trip (p329)

The Galápagos Needing little introduction, these volcanic islands are home to creatures so tame, you'll practically be tripping over all the sea lions you come across (p704)

Cloud forests With over 400 recorded bird species in the area, Mindo's cloud forests are a mecca for birders (p651)

Parque Nacional San Rafael Paraguay's verdant strand of Atlantic Forest has refreshing lakes, forest paths and superb bird-watching (p780)

month by month

Top Events

1. **Carnaval** February
2. **Fiesta de la Virgen de la Candelaria** February
3. **Semana Santa** March/April
4. **Inti Raymi** June
5. **Festival Mundial de Tango** August

January

It's peak season in Brazil and Argentina. Expect higher prices, bigger crowds and sweltering temperatures as city dwellers head to the coast. This is also the most popular time to travel to Patagonia.

Santiago a Mil

This long-running theater and dance fest features dozens of shows and events around the Chilean capital, staged by international and local companies. The 17-day event begins in early January (www.santiagoamil.cl) and is held throughout the city, including in free outdoor venues.

Festival Nacional del Folklore

Near the city of Córdoba, the town of Cosquín hosts Argentina's National Festival of Folk Music (www.aquicosquin.org) during the last week of January. It's the country's largest and best known folk festival.

February

The sizzling summer is still in full swing in the southern half of the continent, with exorbitant prices and sparse accommodation during Brazilian Carnaval. Elsewhere, it's fairly wet in the Andes and the Amazon region.

Carnaval

The famous bacchanalian event happens all across South America, though the pre-Lenten revelry is most famous in Brazil. Rio and Salvador throw the liveliest bashes, with street parades, costume parties and round-the-clock merriment. Carnaval runs from Friday to Tuesday before Ash Wednesday in February or early March.

Carnaval Encarnaceno

Although its northern neighbor hogs all the attention, Paraguay is also a great place to celebrate Carnaval, especially in Encarnación, which throws a riotous fest on every weekend in February. Come for the costumed parades, pounding rhythms and partying through the late hours (www.carnaval.com.py).

Fiesta de la Virgen de la Candelaria

Celebrated across the highlands in Bolivia and Peru, this festival features music, drinking, eating, dancing, processions, water balloons (in Bolivia) and fireworks. The biggest celebrations take place in Copacabana (Bolivia) and Puno (Peru). The big day is February 2.

March

While the weather is still warm in the south, the crowds thin and prices fall a bit at beach destinations. It's still rainy in the Andes.

Semana Santa

Throughout Latin America, Holy Week is celebrated with fervor. In Quito (Ecuador), purple-robed penitents parade through the streets on Good Friday, while Ouro Preto (Brazil) features streets 'painted' with flowers. Ayacucho hosts Peru's most colorful Semana Santa, culminating in an all-night street party before Easter.

Fiesta Nacional de la Vendimia

In Argentina's wine country, Mendoza hosts a renowned five-day harvest festival (www.vendimia.mendoza.gov.ar) with parades, folkloric events, fireworks, the blessing of the fruit and a royal coronation – all in honor of Mendoza's intoxicating produce.

Pujillay

Celebrated in Tarabuco (Bolivia) on the second Sunday in March, hordes of indigenous folks gather to celebrate the 1816 victory of local armies over Spanish troops with ritual dancing, song, music and *chicha* (corn beer) drinking.

Rupununi Rodeo

In Lethem (Guyana), Easter weekend means good fun at the rodeo. Some 10,000 visitors come to watch the blend of Wild West meets Amerindian traditions. There's roping, saddle- and bareback riding (broncos, bulls) and a beauty pageant.

Lollapalooza Chile

Chile's biggest rock fest (www.lollapaloozacl.com) kicks off in Santiago in late March or early April, and features an impressive line-up of homegrown and international groups on par with the North American version of Lollapalooza. Buy tickets early for the best deals.

Semana Criolla

After Carnaval, this is Montevideo's liveliest fest, and is essentially a celebration of gaucho culture – those tough-looking, leather boot-wearing cowboys from Uruguay's interior who manage to make oversized belt buckles look cool. Come for rodeo events, concerts, open-air barbecues and craft fairs.

May

Buenos Aires and Rio head into low season, with cooler weather and lower prices; the rain begins to taper off in the Andes, making it a fine time to go trekking.

Diablos Danzantes

In Caracas, Diablos Danzantes (Dancing Devils), features hundreds of diabolically clothed dancers parading through the streets to the sounds of pounding drums. The Venezuelan fest, which blends Spanish and African traditions, takes place on Corpus Christi, 60 days after Easter (May or June).

Q'oyoriti

A fascinating indigenous pilgrimage to the holy mountain of Ausangate, outside of Cuzco, takes place around Corpus Christi (May or June). Though relatively unknown outside Peru, it's well worth checking out.

June

High season in the Andean nations corresponds with the North American summer (June to August), when the weather is also sunniest and driest. Book major tours (like hiking the Inca Trail) well in advance.

Inti Raymi

This millennia-old indigenous celebration of the summer solstice and harvest is celebrated in many Andean towns. In Cuzco it's the event of the year, attracting thousands of visitors who come for street fairs, open-air concerts and historical re-enactmetns. In Ecuador, Otavalo is the place to be.

Bumba Meu Boi

This folkloric fest, celebrated all across Brazil's Maranhão region in late June, blends African, indigenous and Portuguese traditions. Hundreds of troupes take to the streets in São Luís, dancing, singing and re-enacting one of the region's great creation myths.

São Paulo Pride

It's official: São Paulo throws the largest gay pride parade on the planet, attracting some four million people. There are street fairs, concerts, film screenings and exhibitions in the days leading up to the big parade – which usually happens on Sunday in mid-June.

July

July is among the coldest months in the far south (not a good time to visit Patagonia or Buenos Aires). It is, however, a great time to plan a wildlife-watching trip in the Pantanal.

Fiesta del Santo Patrono de Moxos

Running from July 22 to the end of the month, this spirited festival transforms sleepy San Ignacio de Moxos into a hard-partying town. Expect processions, outrageous costumes (including locals dressed as Amazon warriors), fireworks and plenty of drinking.

Founding of Guayaquil

Street dancing, fireworks and processions are all part of the celebration on the nights leading up to the anniversary of Guayaquil's founding (July 25). Along with the national holiday on July 24 (Simón Bolívar's birthday), Ecuador's largest city closes down and celebrates with abandon.

August

It's dry in many parts of the continent, making August a fine time to visit the Amazon, the Pantanal or the Andes. It's chilly to freezing south of the Tropic of Capricorn.

Festival y Mundial de Baile

World-class tango dancers perform throughout Buenos Aires during this two-week festival (www.tangobuenosaires.gob.ar). Competition is fierce for the title of 'world's best tango dancer.' You can also hone your own moves at classes and workshops.

Festival de Música del Pacífico Petronio Álvarez

In Cali, one of Colombia's best fests celebrates Afro-Colombian music and culture over five days in mid-August (www.festivalpetronioalvarez.com), when over 100 groups light up the city. You'll find infectious rhythms and welcoming, dance-happy crowds.

La Virgen del Cisne

In Ecuador's southern highlands, thousands of colorfully garbed pilgrims take to the roads each year around August 15 in the extraordinary 70km procession to Loja, carrying the Virgen del Cisne (Virgin of the Swan).

Feria de las Flores

In Medellín, the Flower Festival (www.feriadelasfloresmedellin.gov.co) brings sweet smells to the spring-like Colombian city. Highlights include concerts, a gastronomy fair, a horse parade, orchid exhibits and the Desfile de Silleteros, when farmers parade through the streets laden with enormous baskets of flowers.

September

The weather remains dry and sunny (but chilly) in the Andes, though you'll find fewer crowds. September is also a good (less rainy) time to visit the Amazon.

Bienal de São Paulo

One of the world's most important arts events showcases some 3000 works by over 100 artists from across the globe. It runs from September to December in even numbered years, and is principally based in Parque do Ibirapuera (www.bienal.org.br).

Fiesta de la Mamá Negra

Latacunga (Ecuador) hosts one of the highlands' most famous celebrations, in honor of La Virgen de las Mercedes. La Mamá Negra, played by a man dressed as a black woman, pays tribute to the liberation of African slaves during the 19th century.

October

Heavy rains make for tough traveling in Colombia, while the Andes generally have milder weather. In Bolivia, Brazil, Chile and Argentina, temperatures are mild, making it a pleasant time to visit.

Oktoberfest

Celebrating the historical legacy of Brazil's substantial German immigrants, Oktoberfest features 17 days of folk music, dancing and beer drinking. It's considered the largest German fest in the Americas and goes down in mid-October in Blumenau (www.oktoberfestblumenau.com.br).

Círio de Nazaré

Belém's enormous annual event, Círio de Nazaré brings around one million people to the streets to take part in the procession of one of Brazil's most important icons. Fireworks, hymns and one massive flower-bedecked carriage creaking through the throngs are all part of this massive, wild spiritual gathering.

November

Rainier days are on the horizon in the Amazon. Generally November nets better prices, good weather and fewer crowds than December in most parts of South America.

Puno Day

One of Peru's folkloric capitals, Puno hosts dozens of colorful fiestas throughout the year. One of the best is Puno Day, where costumed dancers, military parades and folk bands celebrate the legendary emergence of the first Inca, Manco Cápac, from Lake Titicaca.

Festival Internacional de Cine de Mar del Plata

Launched in 1950, this cinematic event is one of the most important film festivals in Latin America (www.mardelplatafilmfest.com). Running for nine days in mid-November, the fest screens an international lineup of features, shorts, documentaries and experimental works.

Hmong New Year

For something completely different, head to the small village of Cacao (French Guyana) to celebrate the Hmong New Year with a thriving community of Laotians. Traditional singing and dancing, Laotian cuisine and beautifully embroidered costumes are all part of the experience. Held in November or December.

December

December marks the beginning of summer, with beach days (and higher prices) on both the Atlantic and Pacific coasts. It's fairly rainy in the Andes.

Buenos Aires Jazz Festival Internacional

BA's big jazz festival (www.buenosairesjazz.gob.ar) showcases the talents of over 200 musicians to play in 70 different concerts around town. Jazz musicians of all kinds are featured – emerging and established, avant-garde and mainstream, national and international.

Fiestas de Quito

Quito's biggest bash is a much anticipated event, with parades and street dances throughout the first week of December. Open-air stages all across town fill the Ecuadorian capital with music, while colorful *chivas* (open-topped buses) full of revelers maneuver through the streets.

Carnatal

Brazil's biggest 'off-season Carnaval' is this Salvador-style festival held in Natal in December. It features raucous street parties and thumping *trios eletricos* (amplified bands playing atop mobile-speaker trucks). You can get in on the fun by joining one of the *blocos* (drumming and dancing processions).

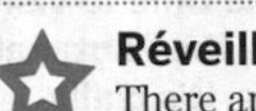

Réveillon

There are many great spots in South America to celebrate New Year's Eve, but Rio is a perennial favorite. Some two million revelers, dressed in white to bring good luck, pack the sands of Copacabana Beach to watch fireworks light up the night sky.

Itineraries

Pelourinho, the historic center of Salvador, Brazil (p337)

PETER ADAMS / GETTY IMAGES ©

The Big Loop

Four to Six Months

This classic South American journey takes in some of the continent's most famous sites, including Andean peaks, Amazonian rainforest, Machu Picchu, Iguazú Falls and the Galápagos Islands. The journey begins and ends in Buenos Aires.

CREDIT/LONELY PLANET IMAGES ©

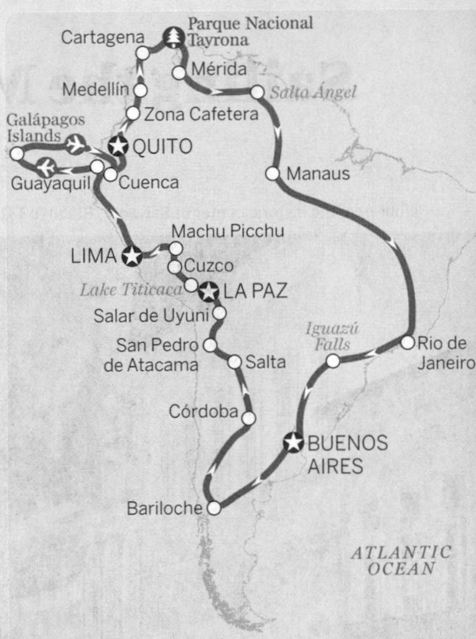

» Start off in **Buenos Aires**. Spend several days exploring the mesmerizing Argentine capital.

» Go east to **Bariloche** for spectacular scenery then north to historic **Córdoba** and gorgeous **Salta** before crossing over to Chile's desert oasis of **San Pedro de Atacama**.

» Head into Bolivia to experience the surreal **Salar de Uyuni**.

» Continue to **La Paz** and on to Peru via **Lake Titicaca**.

» Linger in ancient **Cuzco** and at mystical **Machu Picchu** before going to **Lima** and on to Ecuador.

» From **Guayaquil**, fly to the otherworldly **Galápagos Islands**.

» Back on the mainland, visit colonial **Cuenca** and historic **Quito**.

» Pass into Colombia to see the spectacular **Zona Cafetera** and bustling **Medellín**, then go to **Cartagena** to chill out on the Caribbean.

» See beautiful **Parque Nacional Tayrona** and then hang out for a couple of days in **Mérida**, Venezuela, before visiting **Salto Ángel**.

» Cross into Brazil and onto **Manaus** for a jungle trip before flying down to **Rio de Janeiro** for beaches and nightlife.

» Visit thundering **Iguazú Falls** before returning to **Buenos Aires**.

Clockwise from top left

1 Children in Cuzco, Peru (p841) **2** Plaza de Armas, Cuzco (p841) **3** Volcán Licancábur, Chile (p451) **4** Quito, Ecuador (p628)

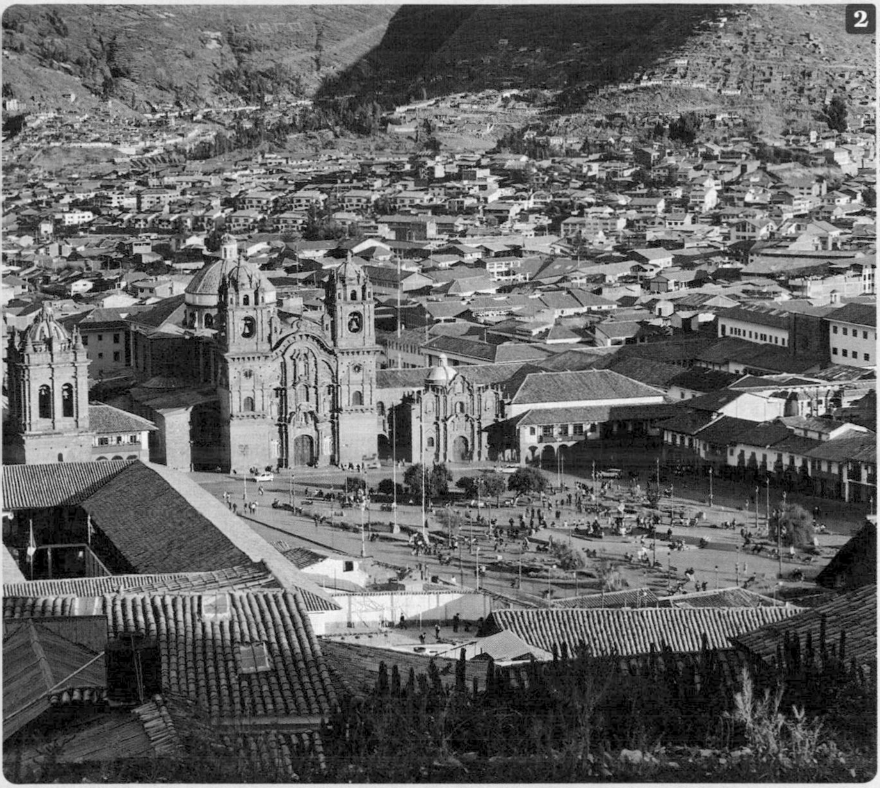

2

YINYANG / GETTY IMAGES ©

3

LEONID PLOTKIN / GETTY IMAGES ©

Andean High

Two Months

For rugged adventure, unparalleled alpine vistas, rich indigenous cultures and colorful market towns journey down the Andes from Colombia to Argentina. Along the way, you'll pass through colonial towns, cloud forests and surreal desert landscapes.

AXEL FASSIO / GETTY IMAGES ©

» Fly into **Bogotá**, taking in the old historic center and lively nightlife.

» Continue south to **San Agustín** to explore pre-Columbian ruins, and on to **Parque Nacional Puracé**, for Andean treks.

» Then go to **Pasto** and on to the beautifully set **Laguna de la Cocha**.

» Cross into Ecuador and visit **Otavalo**, for markets and day trips to alpine lakes.

» Head west to **Mindo** for misty cloud-forest adventures.

» Continue south through **Quito** and on to **Volcán Cotopaxi**, for hikes and majestic scenery.

» Visit colonial **Cuenca**, relax in laid-back **Vilcabamba**, then continue into Peru and down to **Huaraz** for trekking in the Cordillera Blanca.

» Spend a few days in **Cuzco**, then hike the **Inca Trail** to **Machu Picchu**.

» Head across shimmering **Lake Titicaca** into Bolivia for more hiking in the **Cordillera Real**.

» Continue south to the **Salar de Uyuni**, before crossing to Argentina by way of the spectacular **Quebrada de Humahuaca**.

» Continue into Argentina toward enchanting **Mendoza**, near massive **Cerro Aconcagua**, the western hemisphere's highest peak.

Clockwise from top left

1 Street food in Bogotá, Colombia (p532) **2** Highlands around Mindo, Ecuador (p651) **3** Plaza de Bolívar, Bogotá (p532) **4** Parque Nacional Huascarán, Peru (p884)

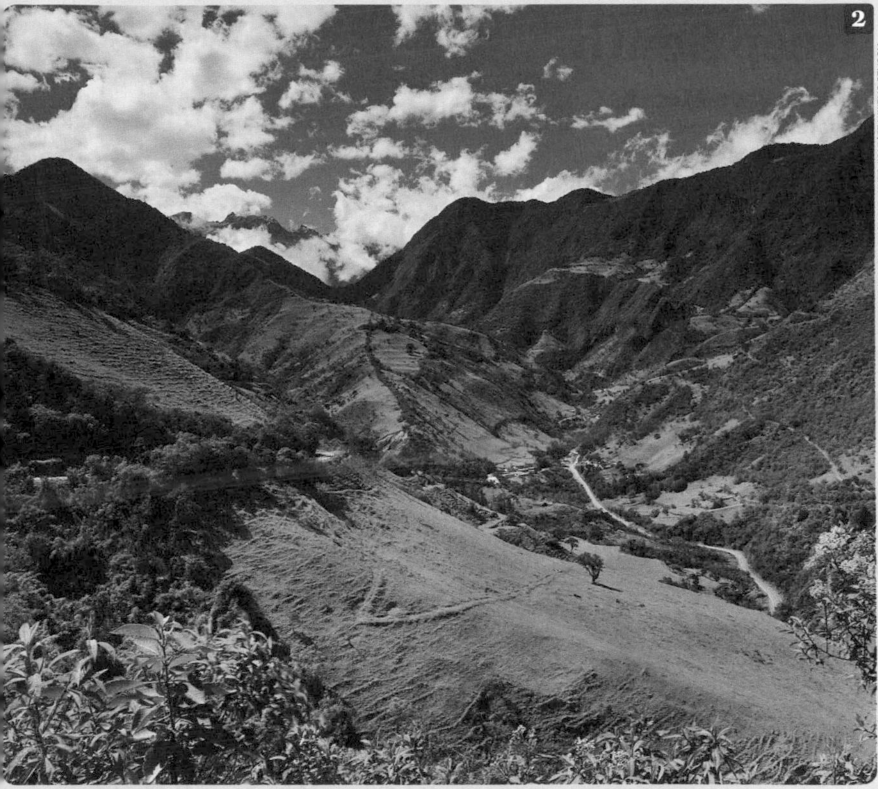

VISUALS UNLIMITED, INC./GERRY BISHOP Y / GETTY IMAGES ©

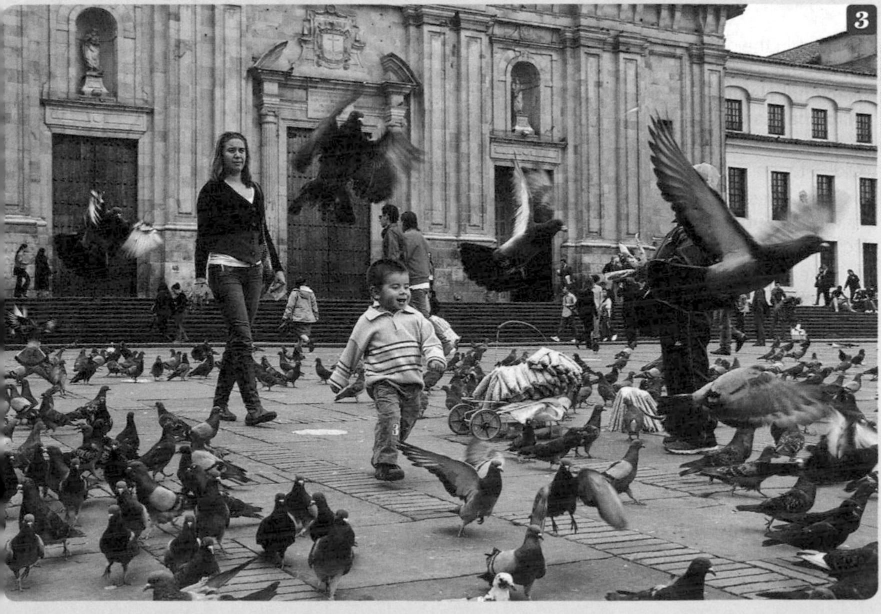

MARGIE POLITZER / GETTY IMAGES ©

Deep South

One to Two Months

Mysterious, windswept, glacier-riddled Patagonia is one of South America's most magical destinations. Patagonia – and the archipelago of Tierra del Fuego – is best visited November through March, and you can see more for cheaper if you camp.

1

4

DAN FAIRCHILD / GETTY IMAGES ©

» Start in the outdoors-loving town of **Bariloche**. Take in the stunning **Parque Nacional Nahuel Huapi** and **Parque Nacional Lanín**.

» Head south to **Esquel**, for a taste of the Old Patagonian Express.

» Travel west into Chile to the Andean hamlet of **Futaleufú** for some of the continent's best rafting.

» Take the scenic Carretera Austral to **Coyhaique** and on to **Lago General Carrera**, and visit the caves of **Capilla de Mármol**.

» Head to the windswept **Chile Chico**, then cross into Argentina to **Los Antiguos**.

» Bounce down to **El Chaltén** in spectacular **Parque Nacional Los Glaciares**, and on to the wondrous **Glaciar Perito Moreno** near El Calafate.

» Cross back into Chile to hike beneath the granite spires of **Torres del Paine**.

» Head to **Punta Arenas**, then south into Argentina's **Tierra del Fuego** and bottom out at **Ushuaia**, the southernmost city in the world.

» Work back north along the Atlantic, stopping for penguins in **Reserva Provincial Punta Tombo** and whales in **Reserva Faunística Península Valdés**.

» End the trip in **Buenos Aires**.

Clockwise from top left

1 Parque Nacional Lanín, Argentina (p127) **2** Fitz Roy range, Argentina (p146) **3** Glaciar Perito Moreno, Argentina (p151) **4** Ushuaia, Argentina (p153)

2

PICAVET / GETTY IMAGES ©

3

TIM MAKINS / GETTY IMAGES ©

Sailing the Mighty Amazon

One to Two Months

The mightiest river on the planet makes a fabled setting for adventure. This tough but rewarding journey travels its length, taking in wildlife-watching, historic cities and beautiful river beaches.

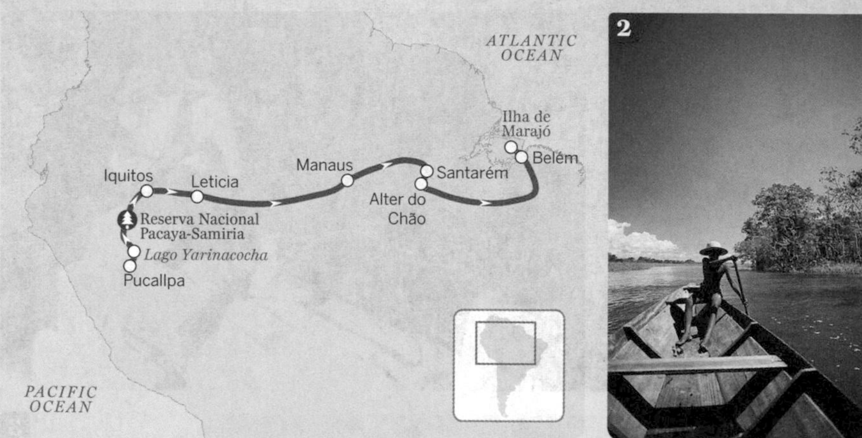

» Start in **Pucallpa**, Peru (a flight or long bus ride from Lima).

» Before hitting the river, visit nearby **Lago Yarinacocha**, a lovely oxbow lake ringed by tribal villages.

» From Pucallpa, begin the classic slow riverboat journey north along the Río Ucayali to Lagunas, where you can continue on to the wildlife-rich **Reserva Nacional Pacaya-Samiria**. Afterwards, spend a day exploring the bustling city of **Iquitos**.

» From here, get a boat to the tri-border region of Peru, Colombia and Brazil, and take a break in Colombia's **Leticia**.

» From Leticia, it's three more arduous days to the bustling city of **Manaus**, which is famed for its 19th-century opera house and buzzing markets. This is also a great base for jungle excursions.

» Chug east to **Santarém**, where you can visit the white-sand beaches of **Alter do Chão**.

» Another 3½ days further, and you'll reach culturally rich **Belém**, a good spot for sampling traditional Amazonian cuisine.

» Cross over to **Ilha de Marajó**, a massive river island dotted with friendly towns, wandering buffaloes and pleasant beaches.

Above
1 Toucan **2** Canoeing on Rio Solimões, Brazil (p381)

Atlantic Coast

One to Two Months

Colonial towns, Afro-Brazilian culture, gorgeous beaches and buzzing nightlife set the stage for an epic 7400km ramble up the Atlantic coast. Surfing, snorkeling, forest treks and urban exploring are all essential experiences along the way.

CREDIT/LONELY PLANET IMAGES ©

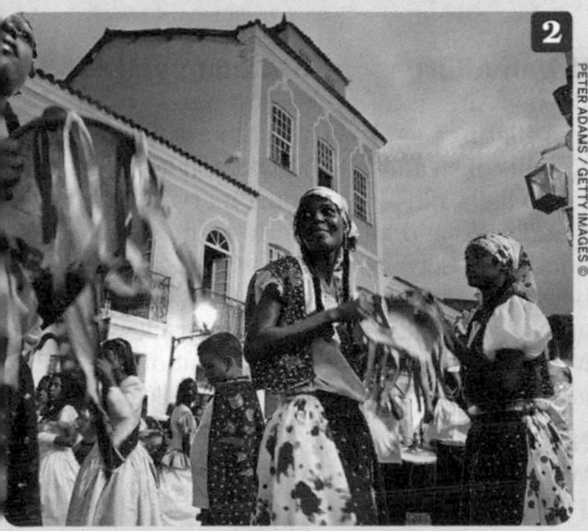

PETER ADAMS / GETTY IMAGES ©

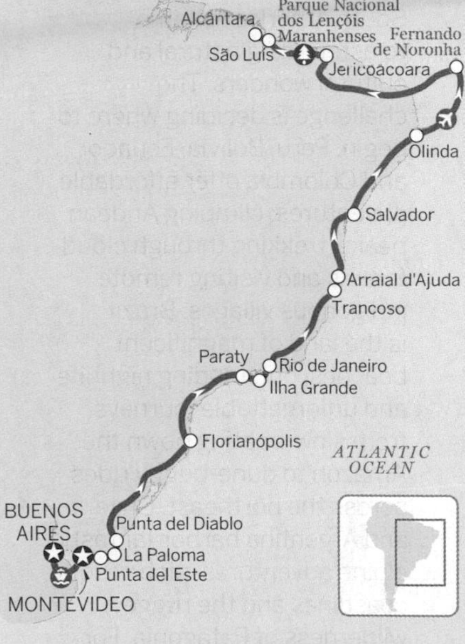

» Start off in Argentina, spending a few days taking in the charms of **Buenos Aires** before ferrying over to historic **Montevideo**.

» Stop in Uruguay's pretty beach towns – **Punta del Este**, **La Paloma** and **Punta del Diablo** – en route to Brazil.

» Make your way to **Florianópolis**, gateway to secluded beaches and stunning scenery, then head up the coast to the scenic colonial town of **Paraty**, and get your island fix on rainforest-covered **Ilha Grande**.

» Northeast of there await the pretty beaches, lush scenery and samba-fueled nightlife of **Rio de Janeiro**.

» Fly to Porto Seguro and continue to **Trancoso** and **Arraial d'Ajuda** – both enticing, laid-back towns near cliff-backed beaches.

» Spend a few days in **Salvador**, Brazil's mesmerizing Afro-Brazilian gem.

» Further up the coast, visit pretty **Olinda**, then catch a flight from Recife to the spectacular archipelago of **Fernando de Noronha**.

» Back on the mainland, travel north, stopping at the backpackers' paradise of **Jericoacoara** and the surreal dunes of **Parque Nacional dos Lençóis Maranhenses**.

» The final stops are reggae-charged **São Luís** and untouristy colonial **Alcântara**.

Above
1 Jericoacoara, Brazil (p365) **2** Festival in Salvador, Brazil (p334)

countries at a glance

Thirteen countries strong, South America is home to astounding natural and cultural wonders. The challenge is deciding where to begin. Peru, Bolivia, Ecuador and Colombia offer affordable adventures: climbing Andean peaks, trekking through cloud forests and visiting remote indigenous villages. Brazil is the land of magnificent beaches, outstanding nightlife and unforgettable journeys, from slow-boating down the Amazon to dune-buggy rides across the northeast. Chile and Argentina harbor fantastic alpine adventures, picturesque coastlines and the rugged wilderness of Patagonia. For off-the-beaten-path travel, explore the jungle-lined interior of the Guianas.

All over the continent you'll find colonial towns and laid-back seaside villages – just the antidote after a few days (or weeks) of taking in South America's jaw-dropping sights.

Argentina

Big Cities ✓✓✓
Scenery ✓✓✓
Outdoors ✓✓✓

Urban Allure

Buenos Aires is a scintillating metropolis of steamy tango halls, old-world cafes and hip boutiques. Córdoba boasts a flourishing arts scene, while Mendoza is for adventure seekers.

Natural Wonders

The Moreno glacier is awe-inspiring. The Peninsula Valdes is home to whales, penguins and other wildlife. Witness spectacular rock formations in Quebrada de Humahuaca and nature's raw power at Iguazú Falls.

Great Outdoors

You'll find magnificent hiking in Patagonia, the Mendoza area and the Lake District, superb white-water rafting near Bariloche and Mendoza, and skiing at Las Leñas, Cerro Castor and Cerro Catedral.

p38

Bolivia

Scenery ✓✓✓
Trekking ✓✓✓
Wildlife ✓✓✓

Stunning Vistas

As you travel across this remarkable remote wilderness, you'll marvel at the world's largest salt flat, whimsical rock formations, cacti-encrusted valleys straight out of the Old West, volcanic peaks, Technicolor lakes and a sky that seems to stretch forever.

Inca Trails

For long hauls and shorter day trips along ancient Inca paving, down cloud-encased valleys and through vast swaths of wilderness, you can't beat Bolivia's treks.

Wild Exploration

Nature is everywhere, making Bolivia a hands-down favorite for nature lovers. A series of large national parks and nature preserves protect (to a certain degree) the country's endemic and at-risk species.

p174

Brazil

Beaches ✓✓✓
Wildlife ✓✓✓
Culture ✓✓✓

Captivating Coastlines
Synonymous with paradise, Brazil boasts nearly 7500km of perfect-palmed coastline to prove it. For idyllic sands, start with Fernando de Noronha, Maranhão or Rio Grande do Sul.

Unrivaled Biodiversity
The world's most biodiverse country is home to a lifetime's worth of wildlife, most famously found in the Amazon and the Pantanal, but from Bonito to Belém, you'll be floored.

The Melting Pot
Portuguese colonists; Japanese, African, Arab and European immigrants; and a healthy indigenous population shaped the Brazil melting pot. From food to film, *isso é Brasil* (this is Brazil)!

p262

Chile

Outdoors ✓✓✓
Landscape ✓✓✓
Wine & Pisco ✓✓

Trekking in Chilean Patagonia
Strong winds, sudden rain, rustic *refugios* (shelters) and striking landscapes – hiking the classic 'W' is an unforgettable adventure in Torres del Paine.

Dreamy Desertscapes
The driest desert in the world, the Atacama is an otherworldly place of salt caves, eerie moonlike surfaces and powerful geysers circled by snow-tipped volcanoes.

House of Spirits (& Wine)
Chile is still battling Peru over the ownership of *pisco*; the potent grape brandy is produced in Valle del Elqui. But no one can contest Chile's mastery of Carmenere, a full-bodied red wine – it's the toast of the nation.

p408

Colombia

Landscape ✓✓✓
Outdoors ✓✓✓
Coffee ✓✓

Nature's Bounty
From the towering sand dunes near Punta Gallinas to the glaciers of Parque Nacional El Cocuy and flooded forests of the Amazonas, Colombia's phenomenal landscapes make for your very own nature documentary.

Endless Adventures
The small city of San Gil is a one-stop adventure playground with rafting, climbing, paragliding and more – just a fraction of the adventures on offer around the country to keep your adrenaline pumping.

Black Gold
Learn to pick and grade coffee beans (and sample the final product) at award-winning plantations around Manizales and Armenia in the Zona Cafetera.

p528

Ecuador

Architecture ✓✓✓
Landscape ✓✓✓
Ecotourism ✓✓✓

Cultural Exploration
The picturesque colonial centers of Quito and Cuenca are packed with architectural treasures. Quito and Guayaquil have outstanding collections of pre-Columbian art and modern works by Oswaldo Guayasamín.

Dramatic Landscapes
Get a taste of the Amazon in jungle lodges, and stunning Andean scenery in Quilotoa. Or take a cruise around the otherworldly Galápagos.

Ecotourism
Top outdoor experiences include climbing Andean peaks (Cotopaxi is popular), mountain biking down them (try Chimborazo), ecotourism in the cloud forests of Mindo and whitewater rafting near Tena.

p624

French Guiana

History ✓✓
Food ✓✓
Wildlife ✓✓

Haunted Prisons

Between 1852 and 1938 around 70,000 prisoners were sent to French Guiana from France. Today, the old structures are eerily crumbling into the jungles; the most interesting are offshore on the now-relaxing Îles du Salut.

Spicy Mix

African, Hmong, French, Javanese and Brazilian culinary traditions plus local spices and fresh jungle produce equals the most interesting food in the region.

Turtles & Sloths

Cuddle a sloth at Chou-Aï sloth rehabilitation center or take a trip to the coast during turtle season to watch crowds of turtles laying eggs in the sand.

p728

Guyana

Wildlife ✓✓✓
Culture ✓✓✓
Architecture ✓

Amazonian Monsters

You want big? Track the world's largest scaled freshwater fish (arapaima), anteaters, caimans and more. The best part: they're all relatively easy to find.

Amerindian Eco-Trail

Hop from one village-run Amerindian lodge to the next through the Rupununi savannas. Bird-watch and learn to shoot a bow and arrow while supporting sustainable businesses.

Dilapidated Gems

Nothing is shined up in colonial Georgetown, but that's part of its charm. Marvel at the ingenious natural cooling system even as the paint seems to chip off before your eyes.

p747

Paraguay

History ✓
Culture ✓✓
Wildlife ✓✓✓

Colonial Relics

The Jesuit revolution began and ended in the jungles of eastern Paraguay, and though the social experiment is long gone, the wonderful churches the Jesuits left behind stand in silent testament.

Indigenous Influences

Paraguayan culture has been shaped by a history of corrupt dictatorships and a strong indigenous influence – a cultural cocktail that makes it a strange and fascinating country to explore.

Biodiversity in the Chaco

Paraguay's arid Chaco positively teems with wildlife, and though the dusty surroundings look inhospitable, it's arguably the best place to see tapir, puma and the endangered chaco peccary.

p765

Peru

Culture ✓✓✓
Ruins ✓✓✓
Landscape ✓✓✓

Indigenous Lore

In Peru, culture isn't something you enter a dusty museum to find. It's all around you. The strong traditions of indigenous cultures are easily witnessed in many religious or seasonal festivals.

Civilization of the Incas

From the heights of Machu Picchu to the cloud forest of Kuélap, Peru's ruins garner due fame, but that doesn't always mean crowds. Many are reached by gorgeous hikes, attractions in their own right.

The Andes to the Amazon

From the ample sands of the coast to verdant Amazonian rainforest, lost canyon villages and the majestic peaks of the Cordillera Blanca, Peru features stark and stunning scenery.

p798

Suriname

Culture ✓✓✓
Wildlife ✓✓
Architecture ✓✓

Maroon Adventures

Boat down the Upper Suriname River to find myriad lodges run by Maroon tribes who have retained a distinctive African-Amazonian culture. Lodging ranges from luxurious bungalows to simple hammock shelters.

Vast Jungles

Deep in the Central Suriname Nature Reserve you'll see troupes of monkeys, tons of birds, caimans and maybe even a jaguar or harpy eagle.

Unesco City

Paramaribo's heritage district is unlike anywhere else in the world. Imagine colonial Dutch lines in a Wild West setting doused in all the colors and culture of the Caribbean.

p917

Uruguay

Beaches ✓✓✓
Architecture ✓✓
Landscape ✓✓

Sun, Sand & Surf

With more than 300km of quality coastline, Uruguay pretty much guarantees you'll find a spot to lay your towel.

Colonial Riches

Colonia del Sacramento's the superstar, of course, and Montevideo's Old Town has its fans, too. But visit pretty much any plaza in the country for gorgeous Spanish-influenced streetscapes.

Inland Adventures

While everyone's chuckling it up beachside, those in the know head for Uruguay's interior – a beautiful rolling hillscape that's the epitome of getting off the gringo trail.

p933

Venezuela

Beaches ✓✓
Outdoors ✓✓✓
Wildlife ✓✓✓

Caribbean Beauty

Find solitude on a tiny island among the aquamarine waters in Los Roques or on the remote beaches of Isla de Margarita and the Península de Paria.

Adrenaline Adventures

Take your pick from surfing the sand dunes near Coro, kitesurfing along the Caribbean or paragliding in Mérida. Or grab your pack and summit the mysterious Roraima *tepui*.

All Creatures Great & Small

From bird-watching in Parque Nacional Henri Pittier, the anacondas, anteaters and capybaras around Los Llanos, to howler monkeys, caimans and piranhas in the Orinoco Delta, the landscape invites discovery.

p968

Every listing is recommended by our authors, and their favorite places are listed first

Look out for these icons:

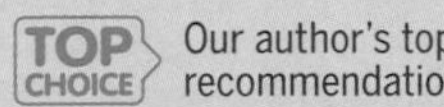

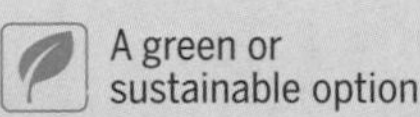

FREE No payment required

See the Index for a full list of destinations covered in this book.

On the Road

Argentina

Includes »

Best Places to Eat

- » Sarkis (p55)
- » La Nieta (p88)
- » Don José (p102)
- » Kalma Resto (p153)

Best Places to Stay

- » Hostel Alamo (p118)
- » Rusty-K Hostal (p95)
- » La Casona de Odile (p135)
- » Nothofagus B&B (p147)

Why Go?

With its gorgeous landscapes, cosmopolitan cities and lively culture, Argentina is a traveler's paradise. It stretches almost 3500km from Bolivia to the tip of South America, encompassing a wide array of geography and climates. Nature lovers can traverse the Patagonian steppe, climb South America's highest peak, walk among thousands of penguins and witness the world's most amazing waterfalls. Hikers can sample the stunning scenery of the lush Lake District – with its glorious lakes and white-tipped mountains – and revel in Patagonia's glacier-carved landscapes and painted Andean deserts. City slickers will adore fabulous Buenos Aires, where they can dance the sexy tango, shop for designer clothes, sample a wide range of ethnic cuisine and party at nightclubs all night long.

Argentina is a safe, friendly and spirited destination to explore. Now is a great time to visit, so get your spirit in gear and prepare for an unforgettable adventure!

When to Go

Buenos Aires

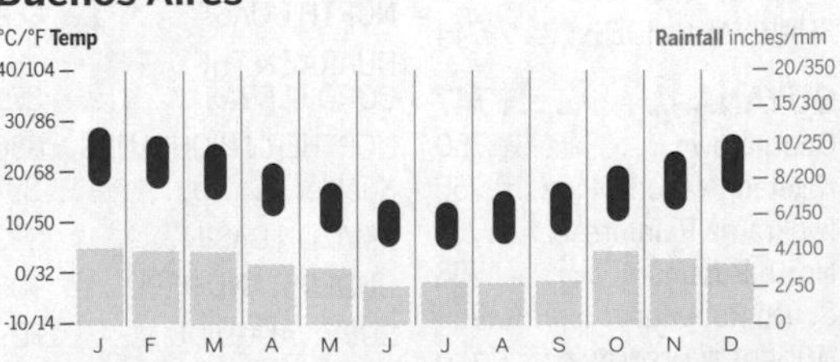

Dec–Feb Best for Patagonia and beaches. Buenos Aires and the north are hot.

Mar–May & Sep–Nov Great months for Buenos Aires, the Lake District and Mendoza.

Jun–Aug Peak ski season. A good time to visit the north. Beaches shut down.

Connections

Buenos Aires is linked by air to most other country capitals in South America. Overland, Argentina has a few border crossings each with Bolivia, Paraguay, Brazil and Uruguay, and many, many border crossings with Chile. Generally, border formalities are staightforward if your documents are in order. When crossing into Chile by air or land, don't take fresh fruits or vegetables (even in sandwiches), dairy products or meat; fines are steep.

ITINERARIES

Two Weeks

Spend your first few days taking in Buenos Aires, then head to Mendoza (for wine tasting and outdoor adventures) and Bariloche (for hiking in summer and skiing in winter). If you love summertime hiking, however, make the Patagonian hamlet of El Chaltén your priority instead; once here you can't miss the nearby destination of El Calafate for its amazing Perito Moreno glacier.

One Month

Seeing all of Argentina in one month will likely require a few key airplane flights. Or, depending on the season you'll be there, concentrate on the north or south. First, take a few days to explore the wonders of Buenos Aires. Spectacular Iguazú Falls is worth a couple of days any time of year. Colonial Salta is best April to November, while Córdoba, Mendoza and the Lake District can be visited year-round. Some Patagonian destinations, such as El Chaltén and Ushuaia, have limited services from June to August (except for skiing).

Essential Food & Drink

» **Beef** Argentines have perfected grilling beef, instilling a smoky, salty outer layer to their delectable steaks

» **Wine** Exploring Argentina by the glass will take you from the malbecs of Mendoza to the *torrontés* of Cafayate to the syrahs of San Juan

» **Maté** Although most first-time maté drinkers can barely choke the stuff down, this bitter, grassy tea is an important social bonding experience

» **Ice cream** Argentina makes some of the world's best *helado*, swirled into a miniature peaked mountain with a spoon stuck in the side

» **Italian food** You'll find pizza and pasta at so many restaurants, it's a wonder the locals can consume it all

» **Dulce de leche** Argentina has turned milk and sugar into the world's best caramel sauce; find it in most of the country's sweetest concoctions

AT A GLANCE

» **Currency** Argentine peso (AR$)

» **Language** Spanish

» **Money** ATMs widespread; credit cards at higher-end places

» **Visas** Usually not required; some countries pay a 'reciprocity fee'

» **Time** GMT minus three hours

Fast Facts

» **Area** 2.8 million sq km

» **Population** 42 million

» **Capital** Buenos Aires

» **Emergency** ☎101

» **Country code** ☎54

Exchange Rates

Australia	A$1	AR$5.2
Canada	C$1	AR$5.0
Euro zone	€1	AR$6.6
New Zealand	NZ$1	AR$4.2
UK	UK£1	AR$7.6
USA	US$1	AR$5.1

Set Your Budget

» **Hostel bed** AR$70-90, doubles AR$200-350

» **Two-course evening meal** AR$60-70

» **Beer in a bar** AR$30

» **Four-hour bus ticket** AR$100

Resources

» **Blogs** (www.bloggersinargentina.blogspot.com)

» **News** (www.argentinaindependent.com)

» **Politics, culture, economy** (www.argentinepost.com)

Argentina Highlights

❶ Eat, shop, tango and party all night long in Argentina's sophisticated capital, **Buenos Aires** (p41)

❷ Take in **Iguazú Falls** (p83), the world's most amazing waterfall, stretching almost 3km long

❸ Explore **Córdoba** (p84), Argentina's attractive second-largest city, along with its alternative culture

❹ Hike, trek and camp to your heart's content in **El Chaltén** (p146), where the scenery's not bad either

❺ Fish, ski, hike and go whitewater rafting among gorgeous mountains and lakes at **Bariloche** (p130)

❻ Sip world-class wines and partake in outdoor adventures at **Mendoza** (p114)

❼ Check out the amazing and constantly calving Perito Moreno glacier in the **Parque Nacional Los Glaciares** (p151) from El Calafate

❽ Ogle whales, elephant seals and penguins at the wildlife mecca of **Península Valdés** (p143)

❾ Set your sights on lovely, vivid and harsh cacti-dotted mountainscapes at **Quebrada de Humahuaca** (p105)

BUENOS AIRES

☎011 / POP 13 MILLION (GREATER BA)

Believe everything you've heard – Buenos Aires is one of South America's most electrifying cities, graced with European architecture, atmospheric neighborhoods and bustling nightlife. BA's passionate residents are proud and even haughty, but once you get to know them they'll bend over backwards to help.

After Argentina's economic collapse in 2002, BA bounced back and created a re naissance that's still keeping the city aglow today. Argentines found the 'outside' world prohibitively expensive, so turned their energy inwards, with impressive results. New restaurants, boutiques and businesses keep popping up, not only to serve the locals and their pesos, but also to cater to the influx of foreign tourists bringing hard currency.

Yet every great metropolis has a poor side. Cracked sidewalks, ubiquitous graffiti and rough edges – even in the wealthiest neighborhoods – speak volumes about this city. Poverty and beggars exist, and at night the *cartoneros* (garbage recyclers) appear. There's a deep melancholy here: an acknowledgement of Argentina's riches coupled with the despair of not realizing its full potential. The undeniable reality is that BA comes with a darker side.

So throw yourself into this heady mix and hold on tight, because you're going for a wild ride. Don't be surprised if you fall in love with this amazing and sexy city – you won't be the first, or the last.

Sights

At Buenos Aires' heart is its *microcentro*, which holds many of the city's historical buildings and museums. To the north lies upper-crust Recoleta, with its famous cemetery, and park-filled Palermo, home to many great restaurants and bars. Down south is where the blue-colllar class hangs: this includes tango mecca San Telmo and colorful, roughhousing La Boca. There's enough bustle in this city to keep you trotting around all day and all night.

CITY CENTER

Buenos Aires' *microcentro* holds many 19th-century European buildings, which surprises many travelers expecting a more Latin American feel. The liveliest street here is pedestrian street Florida, packed with masses of harried businesspeople, curious tourists, angling leather salespeople and shady money changers. Make sure to stop at Galerías Pacífico, one of BA's most gorgeous shopping malls and home to some amazing ceiling paintings.

South of Florida is busy Av Corrientes, and if you head west on this thoroughfare you'll cross superbroad Av 9 de Julio (run!). It's decisively punctuated by the famously phallic *Obelisco*, a major symbol of Buenos Aires. Just beyond is the city's traditional theater district, also full of many cheap bookstores.

East of the city center is BA's newest *barrio* (neighborhood), Puerto Madero. This renovated docklands area is lined with pleasant pedestrian walkways, expensive lofts, trendy restaurants and bars and some of the city's priciest hotels.

TOP CHOICE Plaza de Mayo PLAZA

(Map p44; cnr Av de Mayo & San Martín) The heart and soul of BA is Plaza de Mayo, which attracts souvenir salesmen, curious tourists and sometimes vehement activists. Over toward the east you'll see rosy **Casa Rosada** (Pink House; Map p44), home to the president's offices as well as the balconies from where Evita Perón preached to her thousands; free tours are available on Saturday and Sunday from 10am to 6pm. Just behind is the **Museo del Bicentennario** (Map p44; ☎4344-3802; Avs Paseo Colón & Hipólito Yrigoyen; ⏲10am-6pm Wed-Sun), an airy museum highlighting Argentina's tumultuous history. Across from the Casa Rosada is the **Cabildo** (Map p44; Bolívar 65; admission AR$1; ⏲10:30am-5pm Wed-Fri, 11:30am-6pm Sat & Sun), a mid-18th-century town hall building and all that's left of the colonial arches that once surrounded Plaza de Mayo. The museum inside offers scanty exhibits, but the cafe in back is a great place to relax. Finally, the baroque **Catedral Metropolitana** (Map p44; ⏲7:30am-6:30pm Mon-Fri, 9am-7pm Sat & Sun) contains the tomb of General José de San Martín, Argentina's most revered hero; outside you'll see a flame keeping his spirit alive.

Teatro Colón NOTABLE BUILDING

(Map p44; ☎4378-7127; www.teatrocolon.org.ar; Cerrito 628) Since its opening in 1908, visitors have marveled at magnificent Teatro Colón, a luxurious seven-story building and world-class facility for opera, ballet and classical

Greater Buenos Aires

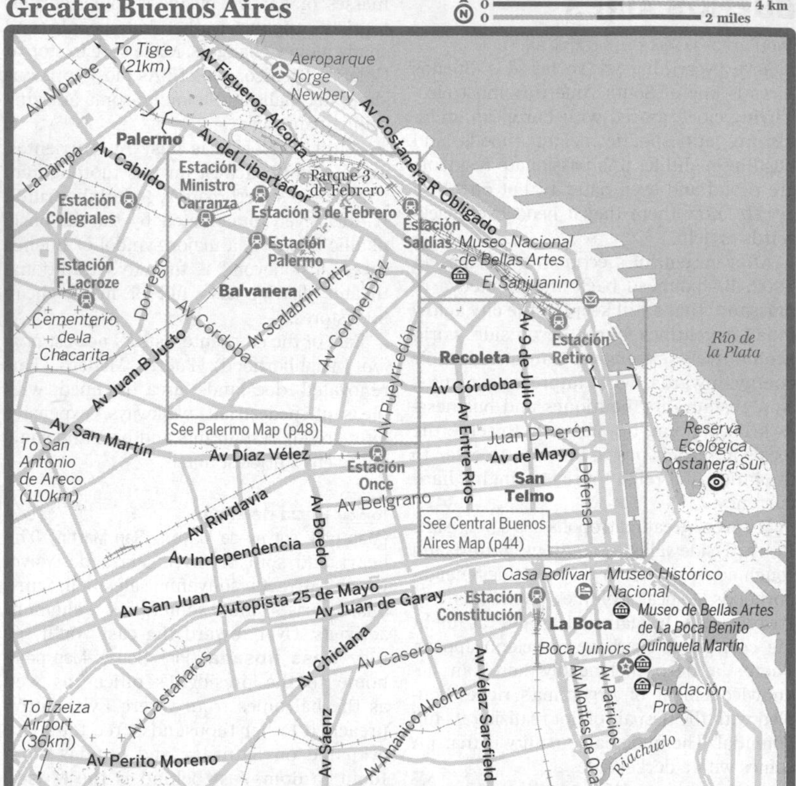

music. It was the southern hemisphere's largest theater until the Sydney Opera House was built in 1973. Opening night featured Verdi's *Aïda,* and visitors have been wowed ever since. Today the theater seats 2500 spectators on plush red-velvet chairs while surrounding them with tiers of gilded balconies. Good backstage tours are available (call or arrive early to reserve); enter via Tucumán.

Museo Fortabat MUSEUM
(Map p44; ☎4310-6600; www.coleccionfortabat.org.ar; Olga Cossettini 141; admission AR$35; ⏲noon-9pm Tue-Sun) Located in Puerto Madero, this cutting-edge art museum shows off the collection of multimillionaire Amalia Lacroze de Fortabat, Argentina's wealthiest woman. Airy salons exhibit works by famous Argentine and international artists – look for Warhol's take on Fortabat herself. Call ahead for tours in English.

Reserva Ecológica Costanera Sur NATURE RESERVE
(Av Rodríguez 1550; ⏲8am-7pm Tue-Sun) Surprisingly close to downtown, the beautifully marshy land of this ecological preserve makes it a popular destination for nature lovers, who come for fresh air and green views. Bird-watchers will adore the 200-plus bird species here, and on sunny weekends cyclists can rent bikes just outside the park's main (southern) entrance.

Manzana de las Luces NOTABLE BUILDING
(Map p44; Perú 272) A block south of Plaza de Mayo is this 'Block of Enlightenment', a solid square of 18th-century buildings that includes Iglesia San Ignacio, Buenos Aires' oldest church, and Colegio Nacional, an elite secondary school. During colonial times this was BA's center of learning, and today it still symbolizes high culture in the capital. **Tours** (☎4331-9534; Perú 272; AR$12) in Spanish are available; drop by for a schedule.

Palacio del Congreso NOTABLE BUILDING

(Map p44; Hipólito Yrigoyen 1849) Colossal and topped with a green dome, the Palacio del Congreso (Congress building) was modeled on the Capitol Building in Washington, DC, and was completed in 1906. It faces pigeon-filled Plaza del Congreso and its Monumento a los Dos Congresos, the granite steps of which symbolize the Andes.

SAN TELMO

Six blocks south of Plaza de Mayo, San Telmo – home of BA's main tango culture – is full of cobbled streets, aging mansions and antique shops. Historically, its low rents have attracted artists, but these days you'll see more boutiques than studios. The neighborhood was a fashionable place until 1870, when a series of epidemics over 20 years drove the rich elite northwards; many houses were then subdivided and turned into cramped immigrant shelters.

TOP CHOICE **Plaza Dorrego** PLAZA

(Map p44) On Sundays, Plaza Dorrego, and the street it's on (Defensa), packs in the crowds with its famous antiques fair. Hordes of tourists bump elbows for rusty pocket watches, old crystal ware and coins, along with plenty of modern knickknacks. Donation tango shows and buskers offer photo ops, while nearby are pleasant cafes where you can sip anything from cognac to cappuccino. To avoid the madness, visit Plaza Dorrego from Monday to Saturday; tables are set up within the plaza itself for peaceful dining.

El Zanjón de Granados ARCHAEOLOGICAL SITE

(Map p44; ☎4361-3002; www.elzanjon.com.ar; Defensa 755; Mon-Fri 1hr tour AR$60, Sun 30min tour AR$30; ⊙tours on the hour 11am-3pm Mon-Fri, every 30min 1-6pm Sun) This amazing archaeological site is one of the more unusual places in Buenos Aires. Below the remains of a mansion, a series of old tunnels, sewers and water wells going back to 1730 were discovered. All have been meticulously reconstructed, brick by brick, and attractively lit, offering a fascinating glimpse into the city's past.

Museo de Arte Moderno de Buenos Aires (Mamba) MUSEUM

(Map p44; ☎4342-3001; www.museodeartemoderno.buenosaires.gob.ar; Av San Juan 350; admission AR$2; ⊙11am-7pm Tue-Fri, to 8pm Sat & Sun) Housed in a former tobacco warehouse, this spacious and newly remodeled museum shows off the works of both national and international contemporary artists. Expect temporary exhibitions showcasing everything from photography to industrial design, and from figurative to conceptual art.

FREE **Museo Histórico Nacional** MUSEUM

(☎4307-1182; Defensa 1600; admission free; ⊙11am-6pm Wed-Sun) This national historical museum is located in Parque Lezama, the supposed site of Pedro de Mendoza's original founding of the city in 1536. Major figures of Argentine historical periods, such as San Martín, Rosas and Sarmiento, are represented, along with a few artifacts and paintings. Exhibits are a bit sparse, but the security is great – be prepared to hand over your bag while you look around.

LA BOCA

Vivid, working-class La Boca, situated along the old port and at the *boca* (mouth) of the Río Riachuelo, was built by Italian immigrants from Genoa. Its main attraction is colorful Caminito, a short pedestrian walk lined with corrugated-metal buildings. Local artists display their brightly colored paintings, adding to the vibrant ambience. The neighborhood is also home to the Boca Juniors soccer team.

Be aware that this is one of the poorer *barrios* of Buenos Aires and, whether day or night, you shouldn't wander from the beaten path of tourist hangouts. Buses 29, 130 and 152 run to La Boca.

Fundación Proa MUSEUM

(☎4104-1000; www.proa.org; Av Don Pedro de Mendoza 1929; admission AR$12; ⊙11am-7pm Tue-Sun) This excellent and modern art museum

DON'T MISS

» Shopping and eating in Palermo Viejo.

» Looking for finds at San Telmo's bustling Sunday antiques fair.

» Wandering through Recoleta's amazing cemetery.

» Experiencing a *fútbol* game's passion.

» Taking in the high kicks at a tango show.

» Soaking up Buenos Aires' second-to-none nightlife.

Central Buenos Aires

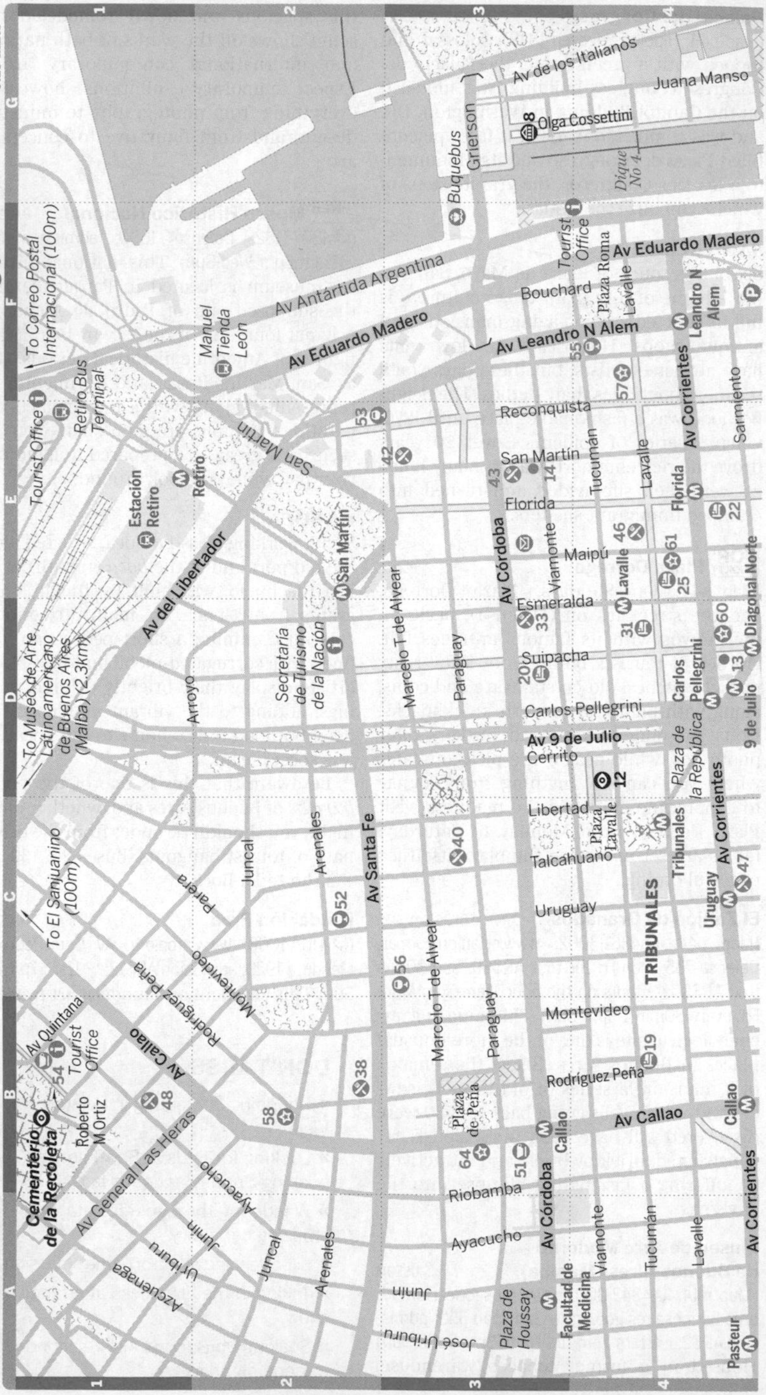

0 500 m
0 0.25 miles

Cementerio de la Recoleta
54
Av Quintana
Tourist Office
Roberto M Ortiz
To El Sanjuanino (100m)
To Museo de Arte Latinoamericano de Buenos Aires (Malba) (2.3km)
Tourist Office
To Correo Postal Internacional (100m)
Retiro Bus Terminal
Estación Retiro
Retiro
Av General Las Heras
Av Callao
48
Azcuénaga
Uriburu
Junín
Ayacucho
Rodríguez Peña
Montevideo
Parera
Arroyo
Av del Libertador
Manuel Tienda León
Juncal
58
Secretaría de Turismo de la Nación
San Martín
Arenales
52
38
San Martín
Av Santa Fe
53
42
Av Eduardo Madero
Av Antártida Argentina
56
Marcelo T de Alvear
José Uriburu
Junín
Ayacucho
Riobamba
64
Plaza de Peña
40
Paraguay
Buquebus
Grierson
Plaza de Houssay
51
Av Córdoba
43
Av Córdoba
Callao
Facultad de Medicina
Viamonte
Rodríguez Peña
Montevideo
Uruguay
Talcahuano
Libertad
Cerrito
Av 9 de Julio
Carlos Pellegrini
20
Suipacha
33
Esmeralda
Viamonte
Maipú
Florida
San Martín
14
Reconquista
Av Leandro N Alem
Bouchard
Tourist Office
8
Olga Cossettini
Av de los Italianos
55
Plaza Lavalle
12
Tucumán
Plaza Roma
Dique No 4
Av Callao
19
TRIBUNALES
31
Lavalle
46
57
Lavalle
Tucumán
Lavalle
Tribunales
Plaza de la República
Carlos Pellegrini
25
61
Florida
Av Corrientes
Leandro N Alem
Juana Manso
Pasteur
Av Corrientes
Callao
Uruguay
Av Corrientes
47
9 de Julio
13
60
Diagonal Norte
22
Sarmiento

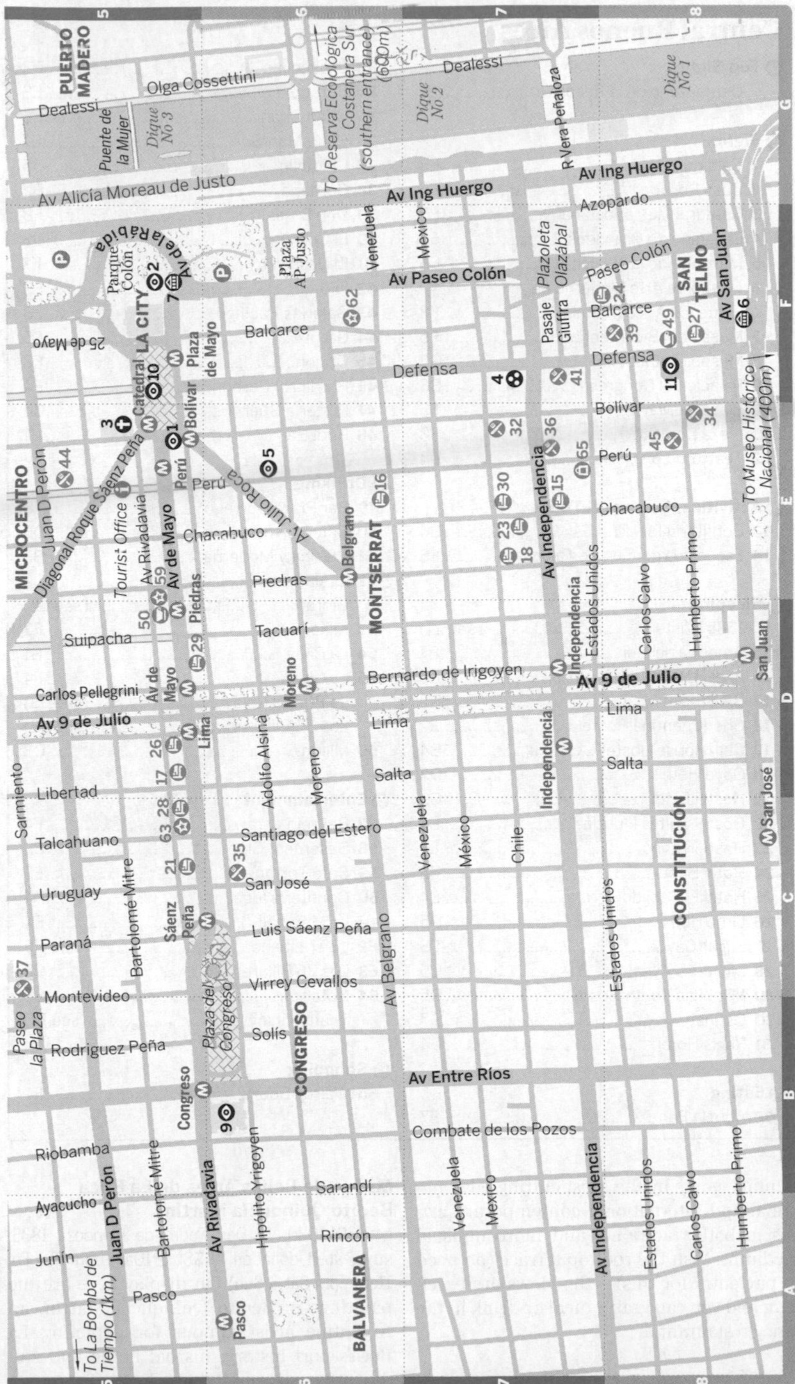
PUERTO MADERO
Olga Cossettini
Dealessi
Puente de la Mujer
Dique No 3
Dique No 2
Dique No 1
To Reserva Ecológica Costanera Sur (southern entrance) (600m)
Av Alicia Moreau de Justo
Av Ing Huergo
R Vera Peñaloza
Azopardo
Av de la Rábida
Parque Colón
Plaza AP Justo
Venezuela
Mexico
Plazoleta Olazábal
Av Paseo Colón
Paseo Colón
SAN TELMO
Av San Juan
LA CITY
25 de Mayo
Balcarce
Pasaje Giuffra
Defensa
Catedral
Plaza de Mayo
Bolívar
Perú
MICROCENTRO
Juan D Perón
Diagonal Roque Sáenz Peña
Tourist Office
Av Rivadavia
Av de Mayo
Av Julio Roca
Chacabuco
Piedras
Tacuarí
Belgrano
MONTSERRAT
Av Independencia
Independencia
Estados Unidos
Carlos Calvo
Humberto Primo
To Museo Histórico Nacional (400m)
Suipacha
Carlos Pellegrini
Av 9 de Julio
Moreno
Bernardo de Irigoyen
San Juan
Lima
Salta
Sarmiento
Libertad
Talcahuano
Uruguay
Paraná
Montevideo
Rodriguez Peña
Paseo la Plaza
Bartolomé Mitre
Adolfo Alsina
Santiago del Estero
San José
Luis Sáenz Peña
Virrey Cevallos
Solís
Sáenz Peña
Plaza del Congreso
CONGRESO
Congreso
Av Belgrano
México
Chile
CONSTITUCIÓN
Av Entre Ríos
Combate de los Pozos
Riobamba
Ayacucho
Junín
Pasco
Sarandí
Rincón
Hipólito Yrigoyen
Av Rivadavia
BALVANERA
To La Bomba de Tiempo (1km)

Central Buenos Aires

Top Sights
Cementerio de la Recoleta B1

Sights
1 Cabildo E5
2 Casa Rosada F5
3 Catedral Metropolitana E5
4 El Zanjón de Granados F7
5 Manzana de las Luces E6
6 Museo de Arte Moderno de Buenos Aires (Mamba) F8
7 Museo del Bicentennario F5
8 Museo Fortabat G3
9 Palacio del Congreso B6
10 Plaza de Mayo F5
11 Plaza Dorrego F8
12 Teatro Colón D4

Activities, Courses & Tours
13 Confitería Ideal D4
14 Escuela Argentina de Tango E3

Sleeping
1385 Hostel .... (see 21)
15 America del Sur E7
16 Axel Hotel E6
17 BA Stop D5
18 Che Argentina Hostel E7
19 Chill House Hostel B4
20 Goya Hotel D3
21 Hostel Estoril C5
22 Hostel Suites Florida E4
23 Hostel Tango E7
24 Hotel Babel F8
25 Hotel El Cabildo E4
26 Lime House D5
27 Lugar Gay F8
28 Milhouse Avenue C5
29 Milhouse Youth Hostel D5
30 Ostinatto E7
31 Regis Hotel D4

Eating
32 Abuela Pan E7
33 Broccolino D3
34 Caracol E8
35 Chan Chan C6
36 Chifa Man-San E7
37 Chiquilín C5
38 Cumaná B2
39 Don Ernesto F8
40 El Cuartito C3
41 El Desnivel F7
42 Filo E3
43 Galerías Pacífico E3
44 Granix E5
45 Origen E8
46 Parrilla al Carbón E4
47 Pizzería Güerrín C4
48 Rodi Bar B1

Drinking
49 Bar Plaza Dorrego F8
50 Café Tortoni D5
51 Clásica y Moderna B3
52 El Alamo C2
Gibraltar .... (see 65)
53 Kilkenny E2
54 La Biela B1
55 La Cigale F4
La Puerta Roja .... (see 23)
Los 36 Billares .... (see 28)
56 Milión C3

Entertainment
57 Bahrein F4
58 Basement Club B2
59 Café Tortoni E5
60 Confitería Ideal D4
61 La Marshall E4
62 La Trastienda F6
63 Los 36 Billares C5
64 Notorious B3
Teatro Colón .... (see 12)

Shopping
65 Walrus Books E7

exhibits works by the most cutting-edge national and international contemporary artists in both traditional and more unusual mediums. Visit the rooftop terrace (no need to pay entry for this) – the views are excellent, and you can grab a meal or drink in the fancy restaurant.

Museo de Bellas Artes de La Boca Benito Quinquela Martín MUSEUM
(☎4301-1080; Av Don Pedro de Mendoza 1835; suggested donation AR$8; ⊙10am-6pm Tue-Fri, 11am-6pm Sat & Sun) On display here are the paintings of Benito Quinquela Martín, an Argentine artist famous for depicting La Boca's port history; his old home and studio are also maintained here. There are

also works by more contemporary artists, along with a small but excellent collection of painted wood figureheads (carved statues decorating the bows of ships).

RECOLETA

The plushest of Buenos Aires' neighborhoods is ritzy Recoleta, filled with gorgeous European-style buildings and international boutiques. It also holds some pleasant green spaces, like Plaza Intendente Alvear, where a crafts fair takes place on weekends. Sit at a cafe nearby, note the giant *ombú* trees and if you're lucky you'll spot a *paseaperros* (professional dog-walker) strolling with 15 or so leashed canines of all shapes and tails.

TOP CHOICE Cementerio de la Recoleta CEMETERY

(Map p44; ☎0800-444-2363 x1451; cnr Junín & Guido; admission free; ⊙7am-6pm) Possibly Buenos Aires' top tourist attraction is this amazing necropolis where, in death just as in life, generations of Argentina's elite rest in ornate splendor. It's fascinating to wander around for hours and explore this extensive mini-city of lofty statues, detailed marble facades and earthy-smelling sarcophagi. Crypts hold the remains of the city's elite: past presidents, military heroes, influential politicians and the rich and famous. Hunt down Evita's grave (follow the crowds), and bring your camera – there are some great photo ops here.

FREE Museo Nacional de Bellas Artes MUSEUM

(☎5288-9900; www.mnba.org.ar; Av del Libertador 1473; ⊙12:30pm-8:30pm Tue-Fri, 9:30am-8:30pm Sat & Sun) Arguably Argentina's top fine-arts museum, this destination is a must-see for art lovers. It showcases works by Renoir, Monet, Gauguin, Cézanne and Picasso, along with many classic Argentine artists such as Xul Solar and Eduardo Sívori. There are also temporary exhibits and a small gift shop.

PALERMO

Full of grassy parks, imposing statues and elegant embassies, Palermo on a sunny weekend afternoon is a *porteño* (people from Buenos Aires) yuppie dream. On weekends a ring road around Parque 3 de Febrero is closed to motor vehicles, and you can rent bikes or inline skates (among other things) and do some serious people-watching while on wheels. Palermo also contains the Campo de Polo (Polo Grounds), where polo matches are played, Hipódromo (Racetrack) and Planetario (Planetarium).

Make sure to stroll through the subneighborhood of Palermo Viejo, just south of the parks. It's further divided into Palermo Soho and Palermo Hollywood. Here you'll find BA's hippest restaurants, trendiest boutiques and liveliest nightlife. Its beautiful old buildings make for some great wanderings too.

TOP CHOICE Museo de Arte Latinoamericano de Buenos Aires (Malba) MUSEUM

(Map p48; ☎4808-6511; www.malba.org.ar; Av Figueroa Alcorta 3415; admission AR$30, Wed AR$15; ⊙noon-8pm Thu-Mon, to 9pm Wed) Sparkling inside glass walls is this airy, cutting-edge museum. Art patron Eduardo Costantini displays his limited but fine collection, which includes work by Argentines Xul Solar and Antonio Berni, plus some pieces by Mexicans Diego Rivera and Frida Kahlo. A cinema screens art-house films, and there's an excellent cafe for watching the beautiful people.

Jardín Zoológico ZOO

(Map p48; ☎4011-9900; www.zoobuenosaires.com.ar; cnr Avs Las Heras & Sarmiento; admission AR$30-47; ⊙10am-6pm Tue-Sun Oct-Mar, to 5pm Apr-Sep) Artificial lakes, pleasant walking paths and over 350 species of animal entertain the crowds at this relatively good zoo. Most of the enclosures offer decent space and some buildings are impressive in themselves – check out the elephant house. An aquarium, a monkey island, a petting zoo and a large aviary are other highlights.

Jardín Japonés GARDENS

(Map p48; ☎4804-4922; www.jardinjapones.org.ar; cnr Avs Casares & Berro; admission AR$16; ⊙10am-6pm) This peaceful paradise is one of the capital's best-kept gardens, where you can enjoy lovely ponds filled with koi and spanned by pretty bridges. The teahouse and restaurant make for good breaks, and Japanese culture can be experienced through occasional exhibitions and workshops.

Museo Evita MUSEUM

(Map p48; ☎4807-0306; www.museoevita.org; Lafinur 2988; local/foreigner AR$5/15; ⊙11am-7pm Tue-Sun) Evita Perón's legendary and effervescent life has been immortalized in this museum through videos, historical photos, books, old posters and newspaper headlines;

Palermo

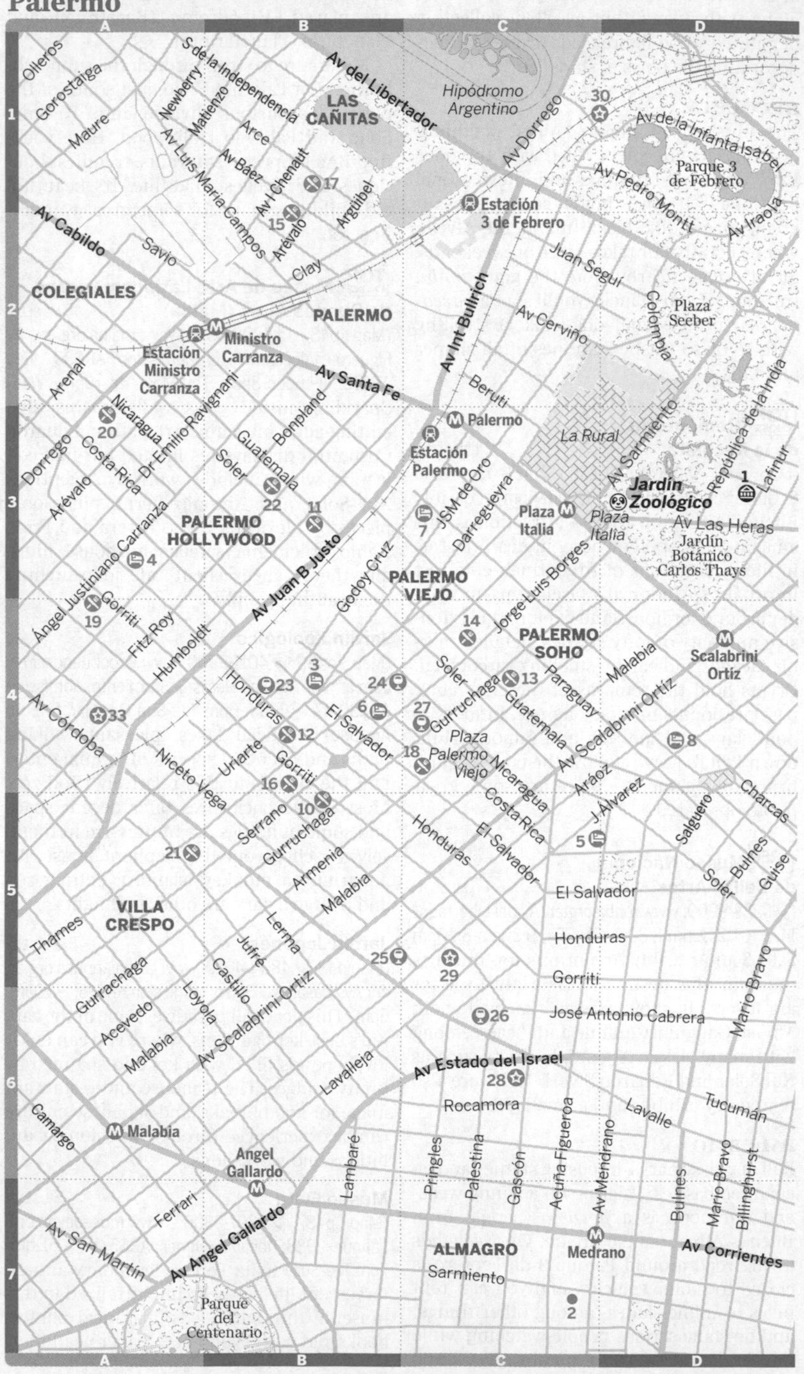

A
B
C
D
1
2
3
4
5
6
7
Olleros
Gorostiaga
Maure
S de la Independencia
Newberry
Matienzo
Arce
Av Luis María Campos
Av Báez
Av I Chenaut
Arguibel
Arévalo
Clay
Av del Libertador
LAS CAÑITAS
Hipódromo Argentino
Av Dorrego
30
Av de la Infanta Isabel
Parque 3 de Febrero
Av Pedro Montt
Av Iraola
Estación 3 de Febrero
17
15
Av Cabildo
Savio
COLEGIALES
Juan Seguí
Colombia
Plaza Seeber
Av Cerviño
Av Int Bullrich
PALERMO
Ministro Carranza
Estación Ministro Carranza
Av Santa Fe
Arenal
Nicaragua
Dr Emilio Ravignani
20
Costa Rica
Dorrego
Arévalo
Bonpland
Guatemala
Soler
Beruti
Palermo
Estación Palermo
La Rural
Av Sarmiento
República de la India
Lafinur
1
Jardín Zoológico
22
11
PALERMO HOLLYWOOD
Carranza
JSM de Oro
7
Darregueyra
Plaza Italia
Plaza Italia
Av Las Heras
Jardín Botánico Carlos Thays
4
Ángel Justiniano Carranza
Av Juan B Justo
Godoy Cruz
PALERMO VIEJO
Gorriti
19
Fitz Roy
Humboldt
Jorge Luis Borges
14
PALERMO SOHO
Malabia
Scalabrini Ortiz
3
23
24
Honduras
Soler
13
Gurruchaga
Paraguay
Av Scalabrini Ortiz
Av Córdoba
33
6
27
El Salvador
Guatemala
8
12
Plaza Palermo Viejo
18
Niceto Vega
Uriarte
Gorriti
Nicaragua
Aráoz
Charcas
16
10
Serrano
Gurruchaga
Costa Rica
J Álvarez
Salguero
Honduras
El Salvador
5
21
Armenia
Malabia
Bulnes
Soler
Guise
VILLA CRESPO
Thames
El Salvador
Lerma
Honduras
Jufré
25
29
Gorriti
Gurruchaga
Castillo
Mario Bravo
Acevedo
Loyola
Av Scalabrini Ortiz
26
José Antonio Cabrera
Malabia
Lavalleja
Av Estado del Israel
28
Rocamora
Lavalle
Tucumán
Camargo
Malabia
Angel Gallardo
Lambaré
Pringles
Palestina
Gascón
Acuña Figueroa
Av Mendrano
Bulnes
Mario Bravo
Billinghurst
Ferrari
Av Angel Gallardo
Av San Martín
ALMAGRO
Medrano
Av Corrientes
Sarmiento
2
Parque del Centenario

Palermo

Top Sights

Sights

Activities, Courses & Tours

Sleeping

Eating

Drinking

Entertainment

even her fingerprints are recorded. The prize memorabilia, however, would have to be her wardrobe: dresses, shoes, handbags, hats and blouses stand proudly behind shining glass, forever pressed and pristine.

Activities

Porteños' main activities are walking, shopping and dancing tango. Those searching for greener pastures, however, head to Palermo's parks, where joggers run past strolling families and young men playing *fútbol* (soccer – join in only if you're very confident of your skills).

Safe cycling is possible in BA, and protected bike lanes have popped up on certain streets. Good places to pedal are Palermo's parks (weekend rentals on Av de la Infanta Isabel near Av Pedro Montt), along with Puerto Madero and its nearby Reserva Ecológica Costanera Sur (weekend rentals outside the main entrance). Bike-tour companies rent bikes and also do guided tours.

Unless you stay at a fancy hotel or join a gym, swimming pools are hard to come by; to cool off, try **Parque Norte** (☎4787-1382; www.parquenorte.com; Avs Cantilo & Guiraldes; admission Mon-Fri AR$50, Sat & Sun AR$65; ⊙9am-8pm Mon-Fri, 8am-8pm Sat & Sun), a fun water park. Soccer players should check out **Buenos Aires Fútbol Amigos** (www.fcbafa.com), while yoga aficionados can try **Buena Onda Yoga** (www.buenaondayoga.com).

Some companies like Tangol (p61) offer activities such as skydiving, helicopter tours and *estancia* (extensive grazing establishment, either for cattle or sheep, with dominating owner or manager and dependent resident labor force) visits, which often include horse riding. For something totally different, learn to play polo with **Argentina Polo Day** (www.argentinapoloday.com.ar).

Courses

Language

Buenos Aires is a popular destination for Spanish-language students. There are plenty of schools and even more private teachers, so ask around for recommendations (or check out www.123teachme.com). All schools offer social excursions and can help with accommodations; some have volunteer opportunities. For something fun and different, join www.spanglishexchange.com – sort of a speed-dating concept, but with language.

Tango

Tango classes are available everywhere – even your own hostel may offer them. Many inexpensive classes are available at *milongas* (dance halls), which can put you in touch with private teachers, some of whom speak English. Cultural centers and dance academies often have affordable classes as well.

La Catedral COURSE
(Map p48; ☎15-5325-1630; www.lacatedralclub.com; Sarmiento 4006, 1st fl) Casual warehouse space with bohemian vibe and nightly *milongas*. Check website for class schedule.

Confitería Ideal COURSE
(Map p44; ☎4328-7750; www.confiteriaideal.com; Suipacha 384) One of BA's biggest tango meccas, with lots of classes (some in English) and frequent *milongas*.

Escuela Argentina de Tango COURSE
(Map p44; ☎4312-4990; www.eatango.org; cnr Av Córdoba & Florida) Large range of classes and teachers, plus a central location in Galerías Pacífico.

Tours

If you want to take a tour, plenty of creative choices exist. Tangol (p61) is a travel agency that brokers many kinds of city tours, while www.LandingPadBA.com has some interesting options as well.

BA Free Tour WALKING TOUR
(☎15-6395-3000; www.bafreetour.com; donation recommended) Free (well, donation) walking tours given by enthusiastic young guides.

Biking Buenos Aires BICYCLE TOUR
(☎4040-8989; www.bikingbuenosaires.com) Bike tours guided by English-speaking expats.

Buenos Aires Bus BUS TOUR
(☎5239-5160; www.buenosairesbus.com) Hop-on, hop-off topless bus with 24 stops.

Cultour WALKING TOUR
(☎15-6365-6892; www.cultour.com.ar) Walks guided by university students and teachers.

Foto Ruta PHOTOGRAPHY
(☎6030-8881; www.foto-ruta.com) More like a photography workshop, but you'll certainly get to know BA in a different way.

Graffitimundo ART TOUR
(☎15-3683-3219; www.graffitimundo.com) Expat-run tours of BA's best graffiti and stencil art,

with proceeds benefitting the artists and art scene.

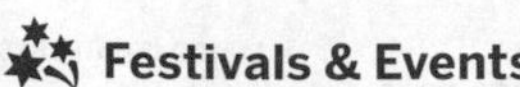

Festivals & Events

A few of Buenos Aires' biggest celebrations include the following.

Fashion BA CULTURE
(www.bafweek.com.ar) High fashion in February and August.

Festival Internacional de Cine Independiente FILM
(www.bafici.gov.ar) Independent film festival in April.

Arte BA ART
(www.arteba.com) Art show in May.

Exposición Rural CULTURE
(www.exposicionrural.com.ar) Agricultural and livestock fair in late July.

Festival y Mundial de Baile DANCE
(www.tangobuenosaires.gob.ar) Huge tango festival in August.

Vinos y Bodegas WINE
(www.expovinosybodegas.com.ar) Wine festival in September.

Sleeping

Buenos Aires' *microcentro* is close to many sights and services, though it's busy and noisy during the day. San Telmo is about 15 minutes' walk south and good for those seeking old colonial atmosphere, cobbled streets, proximity to some tango venues and a blue-collar flavor around the edges. Palermo Viejo is northwest of the center and about a 10-minute taxi ride. It's a pretty area full of wonderful old buildings and dotted with the city's best ethnic restaurants, trendiest boutiques and liveliest bars.

Private rooms in some hostels don't always come with private bathroom, though they can cost more than rooms in a cheap hotel. All hostels listed here include kitchen access, light breakfast and free internet; most have free wi-fi and lockers (bring your own lock). The bigger ones offer more services and activities, and many take credit cards. Hostelling International cards are available at any HI hostel or BA's Hostelling International office (p166).

BA has some good budget hotel choices. Most offer a simple breakfast and cable TV; some take credit cards (which might incur a fee of up to 10% – ask beforehand). Most listings also have internet and/or wi-fi available for guests.

CITY CENTER

Goya Hotel HOTEL $$
(Map p44; ☎4322-9269; www.goyahotel.com.ar; Suipacha 748; s AR$300-350, d AR$350-400; ❄@📶) A good midrange choice with 40 modern, comfortable and carpeted rooms. Located on a pedestrian street, so no traffic noise. 'Classic' rooms are older and have open showers; 'superior' rooms are slicker and have bathtubs. Beautiful breakfast room with patio. Mention Lonely Planet for a 10% discount.

Hostel Estoril HOSTEL $$
(Map p44; ☎4382-9073; www.hostelestoril.com.ar; Av de Mayo 1385, 1st & 6th fl; dm AR$80-90, s AR$250, d AR$300-360; ❄@📶) This is one of BA's best hostels, located in an old building and spread across two separate floors. It's stylish and clean, with pleasant, good-sized dorms and hotel-quality doubles. There's a nice kitchen and internal patio. The awesome rooftop terrace has amazing views of Av de Mayo.

Milhouse Avenue HOSTEL $$
(Map p44; ☎4383-9383; www.milhousehostel.com; Av de Mayo 1245; dm AR$70-80, d/tr/q AR$330/370/420; ❄@📶) This is a huge party hostel in a beautiful old building. All the services you could ask for, and more: bar with draught beer, rooftop terrace, basement TV lounge/kitchen area and DJ parties. Good dorms, and doubles are beautiful – some have original claw-foot tubs. Wheelchair accessible; HI discount.

Milhouse Youth Hostel HOSTEL $$
(Map p44; ☎4345-9604; www.milhousehostel.com; Hipólito Yrigoyen 959; dm AR$70-80, d/tr/q AR$330/370/420; ❄@📶) BA's premiere party hostel, this large and central spot offers a plethora of activities and services. Dorms are good and private rooms very pleasant; most surround a pleasant open patio. There's a bar-cafe (with pool table), TV lounge and rooftop terrace. HI discount.

Regis Hotel HOTEL $$$
(Map p44; ☎4327-2605; www.hotel-regis.com.ar; Lavalle 813; s/d AR$540/580; ❄📶) Quiet and central upscale choice on pedestrian Lavalle, with attentive service and old-style atmosphere. Comfortable, carpeted rooms come with fridge and cable TV, and some have balconies. Breakfast buffet.

Hostel Suites Florida HOSTEL $$
(Map p44; ☎4325-0969; www.hostelsuites.com; Av Florida 328; dm/d/tr AR$80/340/385; ❄@📶) Argentina's largest hostel, with some 340 beds and an awesome location on pedestrian Florida. Offers plenty of services, large common spaces (including a pool table area and movie room), good dorms and lovely contemporary doubles. Bike rentals and HI Discount too, though the kitchen is tiny.

Hotel El Cabildo HOTEL $$
(Map p44; ☎4322-6745; Lavalle 748; s/d AR$320/340; ❄@📶) Forty-six nice, clean rooms centrally located right on pedestrian Lavalle. Superior doubles, larger and with views, are best. Breakfast is served next door. Reserve ahead; 10% cash discount.

1385 Hostel HOSTEL $
(Map p44; ☎4383-9668; Av de Mayo 1385, 2nd & 3rd fl; dm AR$50-60, s AR$90, d AR$150-160; @📶) Economical but good hostel owned by the same family as Hostel Estoril (a more upscale hostel in the same building). Pleasant living room, with internal patio available. Dorms are six to eight beds.

BA Stop HOSTEL $
(Map p44; ☎4382-7406; www.bastop.com; Av Rivadavia 1194; dm AR$60-90, s AR$195-280, d AR$260-350; @📶) Decent but darkish hostel in old building. Art murals on walls and tranquil back room with table tennis. Nice modern doubles in the newer upstairs section; beware the cheap but 10-bed dorm (bring earplugs).

Lime House HOSTEL $
(Map p44; ☎4383-4561; www.limehouse.com.ar; Lima 11; dm/d AR$80/300; @📶) Funky, rustic hostel in an old, outdated building that's centrally located but next to busy Av 9 de Julio – expect some noise. There's a nice pool room (popular with smokers) and upstairs is a rooftop with views. Undergoing a gradual remodel.

SAN TELMO

TOP CHOICE **America del Sur** HOSTEL $$
(Map p44; ☎4300-5525; www.americahostel.com.ar; Chacabuco 718; dm/d AR$85/400; ❄@📶) Gorgeous, prize-winning hostel with bar-cafe area near reception and elegant wood patio in back. Clean dorms with four beds all have well-designed bathrooms, while private rooms are tastefully done. There are great services and cheap *asado* (barbecue) dinners on Fridays.

Hotel Babel BOUTIQUE HOTEL $$$
(Map p44; ☎4300-8300; www.hotelbabel.com.ar; Balcarce 946; d AR$520-600; ❄@📶) Just nine beautiful rooms are available at this colorful boutique hotel. Standard rooms have queen beds; superior rooms have two twins or a king. All are arranged around a bright patio (though some rooms don't have windows). Good breakfast included, and discounts offered for cash payment.

Che Argentina Hostel HOSTEL $
(Map p44; ☎4307-6287; www.cheargentinahostel.com.ar; Piedras 708; dm/s/d AR$70/220, d AR$280-300, tr AR$330-350; ❄@📶) Good small hostel in a charming old building. There are just seven rooms (three dorms and four privates), along with a large terrace and pleasant dining area. Best for those seeking a nonparty atmosphere, though it's located on a noisy street corner.

Ostinatto HOSTEL $$
(Map p44; ☎4362-9639; www.ostinatto.com; Chile 680; dm AR$70-80, d AR$290-320; ❄@📶) Snazzy hostel with ground-floor bar-lounge, catwalks in its airy central well, a small rooftop terrace and a slick penthouse (AR$440). Free tango, Spanish and yoga classes.

Hostel Tango HOSTEL $
(Map p44; ☎4300-2420; www.hosteltangoargentina.com; Chacabuco 747; dm AR$55-100, d AR$230-260; @📶) Popular hostel with an upscale reception area where backpackers hang out. Open hallways and patios are great in summer, but wet during rainstorms. Good dorms come either with or without attached bathroom.

PALERMO VIEJO

Cypress In GUESTHOUSE $$$
(Map p48; ☎4833-5834; www.cypressin.com; Costa Rica 4828; s AR$380, d AR$480-520, tr AR$640; ❄@📶) This neat contemporary guesthouse boasts a slick lounge-lobby area, and though the 13 small rooms are comparatively plain, they're good and comfortable (some share bathrooms). A rooftop patio makes for a great hangout area, and the best room is located up here.

Chill House Hostel HOSTEL $
(Map p44; ☎4861-6175; www.chillhouse.com.ar; Agüero 781; dm AR$70-85, d AR$245-270; @📶) Cool-vibe hostel in a wonderful remodeled

old house with high ceilings and rustic artsy style. Dorms and private rooms are great, and there's an awesome rooftop terrace where weekly *asados* take place. French spoken; free bike rentals too. Located just south of Palermo, in Abasto.

Back in BA HOSTEL $
(Map p48; ☎4774-2859; www.backinba.com; El Salvador 5115; dm/d/tr AR$70/210/280; @) Intimate, friendly and casual hostel with *buena onda* (good vibes). Reception is an upstairs bar counter and there's a small central patio for Thursday-night *asados* and other events. It's the kind of place where you're likely to make some new friends.

Casa Esmeralda HOSTEL $
(Map p48; ☎4772-2446; www.casaesmeralda.com.ar; Honduras 5765; dm/d AR$70/210; @) Homey, small and rustic hostel with a casual vibe and a pleasant garden area. There's also a sunny rooftop patio and a friendly dog on the premises, and you can't beat its Palermo location. Bike rentals available.

Reina Madre Hostel HOSTEL $
(Map p48; ☎4962 5553; www.hostelreinamadre.com.ar; Anchorena 1118; dm AR$85-90, s/d AR$190/200; @; underground rail Línea D Pueyrredón) Wonderful family-run hostel in an old remodeled building on the southern fringe of Recoleta. It's clean and well managed, with a decent kitchen-dining area, plus a TV room with flatscreen. Best of all, there's a nice wooden rooftop deck for occasional *asados*.

Hostel Suites Palermo HOSTEL $
(Map p48; ☎4773-0806; www.hostelsuites.com; Charcas 4752; dm AR$80-90, r AR$260-350; @) Somewhat upscale hostel in a beautiful renovated old building. High ceilings, nice interior patio and great rooftop terrace. Most rooms have their own bathroom; the best are the two doubles with balcony. There are nightly events, and HI discount is available.

Costa Rica Hotel HOTEL $$$
(Map p48; ☎4864-7390; www.hotelcostarica.com.ar; Costa Rica 4137; d AR$350-825; @) Upscale on a small scale is this 30-room boutique-feel hotel. Rooms are small but comfortable, some lining a pleasant rooftop terrace. Semi outdoor halls and stairs are narrow, however, and breakfast costs extra.

Mansilla 3935 B&B B&B $$
(Map p48; ☎4833-3821; www.mansilla3935.com; Mansilla 3935; s/d AR$220/320; @) Family-run B&B offering a great deal. Each of the six simple but lovely rooms comes with its own bathroom. Ceilings are high, and a few tiny patios add some charm. There's a dog on the premises.

 Eating

Buenos Aires is overflowing with excellent food, and you'll dine well at all budget levels. Typical restaurants serve a standard fare of *parrilla* (grilled meats), pastas, pizzas and *minutas* (short orders), but for something different head to Palermo, home to a large number of ethnic eateries. Another food-oriented neighborhood is Puerto Madero, but most of the restaurants here cater to the business set and are consequently very fancy and relatively expensive, and lean more toward steaks than stir-fries.

Vegetarians rejoice: unlike in the rest of Argentina, there is a good range of meat-free restaurants in BA – you just have to know where to look. Most nonvegetarian restaurants offer a few pastas, salads and pizzas – but not much else is meat-free.

CITY CENTER

Chan Chan PERUVIAN $
(Map p44; ☎4382-8492; Hipólito Yrigoyen 1390; mains AR$30-45; ⊙lunch & dinner Tue-Sun) Very popular and artsy Peruvian joint serving seafood (including *ceviche* – marinated raw seafood) and rice dishes, along with more exotic duck and rabbit (but no guinea pig!). Try the *chicha morada* (a tasty corn-based fruity drink) or go for a *pisco sour* (grape brandy with lemon juice, egg white and powdered sugar), and be prepared to wait.

Filo ITALIAN $$
(Map p44; ☎4311-0312; San Martín 975; pizzas AR$40-60, mains AR$45-70; ⊙lunch & dinner) Hip and artsy restaurant offering a mind-boggling selection of meats, salads, sandwiches, pizzas, pastas and desserts – all of it good.

Chiquilín PARRILLA $$
(Map p44; ☎4373-5163; Sarmiento 1599; mains AR$40-85; ⊙lunch & dinner Wed-Mon) Popular and long-running *parrilla* (grillhouse) with an upscale atmosphere, hanging hams for decoration and suited waiters offering good service.

Broccolino ITALIAN $$
(Map p44; ☎4322-7754; Esmeralda 776; mains AR$45-70; ⊙lunch & dinner) Excellent pasta, with way too many topping choices (you order the pasta and toppings separately). Also plenty of pizzas, salads, meats and house-made bread.

Pizzería Güerrín PIZZERIA $
(Map p44; ☎4371-8141; Av Corrientes 1368; slices AR$6-8; ⊙11am-1am Sun-Thu, to 2am Fri & Sat) Great for good, fast and cheap pizza slices; you can eat standing up, like the thrifty locals, or sit down for a rest.

Granix VEGETARIAN $$
(Map p44; ☎4343-4020; Florida 165; all-you-can-eat AR$57; ⊙11am-3:30pm Mon-Fri; ✎) Large, popular vegetarian cafeteria on the 1st floor in Galería Güemes. Buffet includes juice and dessert. You can also buy food to go.

Parrilla al Carbón PARRILLA $
(Map p44; ☎4328-0824; Lavalle 663; mains AR$25-64; ⊙lunch & dinner) For fast, cheap and tasty grilled meats in the city center you won't do much better than this hole-in-the-wall joint. Grab a steak for AR$44 or a *choripan* (sausage sandwich) for a ridiculous AR$12. It's next to Balcarce cafe.

El Cuartito PIZZERIA $
(Map p44; Talcahuano 937; slices AR$10; ⊙closed Mon) Another excellent, inexpensive stand-up or sit-down pizzeria, and a BA institution in business for over 80 years. Check out the cool old sports posters.

Galerías Pacífico FAST FOOD $$
(Map p44; cnr Avs Florida & Córdoba; meals AR$40-60) Downstairs food court in a fancy mall; a good place to go with a large group, as there's something for everyone.

SAN TELMO

El Desnivel PARRILLA $$
(Map p44; Defensa 855; mains AR$30-85; ⊙closed Mon lunch) Hugely popular with both locals and tourists. Get a table in the original room in front for the best atmosphere, and ask for the *menu del día* (daily menu) for cheaper options.

Chifa Man-San PERUVIAN-CHINESE $$
(Map p44; Perú 832; Mains AR$25-75; ⊙noon-4:30pm & 7-11:30pm Mon-Fri, noon-midnight Sat & Sun) Very casual Peruvian-Chinese restaurant with huge menu: wonton soup, omelets, *ceviche* and all sorts of meat and seafood dishes. Weekday lunch specials cost under AR$28.

Don Ernesto PARRILLA $$
(Map p44; Carlos Calvo 375; mains AR$25-70) Good *parrilla* popular with both tourists and locals (even John Cusack once ate here). Good-quality meats, plus homemade pastas and seafood. Huge *ojo de bife* (eye of round steak) and cool graffiti on the walls.

Caracol ARGENTINE $
(Map p44; Bolívar 1101; mains AR$25-50) Very popular with locals for its well-priced, abundant dishes. Typical Argentine fare and traditional service, plus good lunch specials under AR$35.

Origen INTERNATIONAL $
(Map p44; Primo 599; mains AR$30-60; ⊙8am-10pm Mon-Fri, 8:30am-10pm Sat, 9am-10pm Sun) Smart corner cafe with a small menu highlighted by fancy sandwiches, salads, pizzas and stir-fries. *Licuados* (fruit shakes) available, plus lots of desserts. Grab a sidewalk table for people-watching.

Abuela Pan VEGETARIAN $
(Map p44; Chile 518; daily menu AR$32; ⊙8am-7pm Mon-Fri, 9am-4pm Sun; ✎) Small, atmospheric cafe with just a handful of tables. The vegetarian special changes daily – expect things like eggplant tarts, Thai risotto and quinoa burgers.

RECOLETA

Cumaná ARGENTINE $
(Map p44; ☎4813-9207; Rodriguez Peña 1149; mains AR$25-40; ⊙lunch & dinner) The low-priced pizzas, empanadas and *cazuelas* (a soupy stew of broth, rice, a half ear of corn and some meat) pack in the crowds at this casual, upscale-rustic eatery, which serves northern specialties. Get here early to avoid a wait.

Rodi Bar ARGENTINE $$
(Map p44; ☎4801-5230; Vicente López 1900; mains AR$38-80; ⊙6am-2am) Traditional restaurant with fine old-world atmosphere and extensive menu offering something for everyone. A great option for well-priced, unpretentious food in upscale Recoleta. Note the lunch specials.

El Sanjuanino ARGENTINE $
(☎4805-2683; Posadas 1515; mains AR$33-50; ⊙lunch & dinner) Cheap Recoleta eats – *locro* (traditional hearty stew), tamales and empanadas. It's crowded inside, so get takeout and head to a nearby park.

PALERMO VIEJO

TOP CHOICE Sarkis MIDDLE EASTERN $$
(Map p48; ☎4772-4911; Thames 1101; mains AR$28-58; ⊙lunch & dinner) The food is so awesome at this long-standing Middle Eastern restaurant that you'll wait for hours on weekends. For appetizers try *boquerones* (marinated sardines), then order the lamb in yogurt sauce. Order many small plates if you want to try it all.

TOP CHOICE Don Julio PARRILLA $$
(Map p48; ☎4832-6058; Guatemala 4699; mains AR$55-85; ⊙lunch & dinner) A *parrilla* highly recommended for its exceptional meat dishes – it's as good as its fancier neighbors, but with a much more traditional feel. Nice corner location with sidewalk tables, and the wine list is also better than average.

Sudestada ASIAN $$$
(Map p48; ☎4776-3777; Guatemala 5602; mains AR$85-90; ⊙lunch Mon-Fri, dinner Mon-Sat) Upscale corner restaurant serving magnificent dishes from Thailand, Vietnam, Malaysia and Singapore (such as barbecued rabbit or grilled pork in tamarind sauce). A refreshing change: the spicy food here really is spicy! The weekday lunch menu is a good deal (AR$42).

Bio VEGETARIAN $$
(Map p48; ☎4774-3880; Humboldt 2199; mains AR$42-55; ⊙lunch daily, dinner Tue-Sun; ☑) Small corner bistro serving tasty and creative vegetarian fare, like seitan curry, quinoa risotto and great salads. Organic ingredients are used when possible. The ginger lemonade is a must on a hot day.

Oui Oui INTERNATIONAL $
(Map p48; Nicaragua 6068; mains AR$40-50; ⊙8am-8pm Tue-Fri, 10am-8pm Sat & Sun) Cute as a bug is this tiny French bistro serving mostly gourmet salads and outstanding sandwiches. Weekend brunch is awesome – arrive early to get a table. There's an annex, Almacén Oui Oui, on the corner at Nicaragua 6099.

El Primo PARRILLA $$
(Map p48; ☎4772-8441; Baéz 302; mains AR$40-65; ⊙dinner daily, lunch Fri-Sun) Popular and classic corner *parrilla* in happenin' Las Cañitas. Try the *vacío* (preferably *jugoso* – it'll come medium rare); it's a tasty, chewy cut and the half-portion is enough for most people. The *brochettes* (shish kebabs) are house specialties.

Baraka INTERNATIONAL $$
(Map p48; ☎4834-6427; Gurruchaga 1450; mains AR$32-58; ⊙10am-9pm Tue, Wed & Sun, to midnight Thu, Fri & Sat) Trendy and casual cafe with a creative menu highlighted by exotic choices: Thai chicken curry, squash *ñoquis* (gnocchi) and arugula risotto. Great homemade pastries, along with *licuados* and many exotic teas.

Meraviglia VEGETARIAN $
(Map p48; ☎4775-7949; cnr Gorriti & Carranza; mains AR$35-45; ⊙9:30am-7pm Mon-Fri, 10:30am-7pm Sat & Sun; ☑) Airy and bright vegetarian cafe with small but high-quality menu. There's homemade granola and yogurt for breakfast or well-prepared salads, tarts and sandwiches for lunch or a late-afternoon snack. Everything is freshly made, with mostly organic ingredients.

La Fábrica del Taco MEXICAN $$
(Map p48; ☎4833-3534; Gorriti 5062; tacos AR$10-20; ⊙noon-6pm & 7pm-1am Tue, Wed & Sun, noon-6pm & 7pm-3am Thu-Sat) Super-popular, casual and colorful taco joint. Authentic Mexican cooks slap together tasty tacos, which you should wash down with an *agua fresca* (fresh fruit juice). Come off-hours for a table.

Mark's Deli & Coffeehouse INTERNATIONAL $$
(Map p48; El Salvador 4701; mains AR$40-55) Very popular cafe-deli serving excellent soups, salads and sandwiches, with iced coffee for hot days. Modern decor, pleasant outside seating and a guaranteed wait on sunny weekends.

El Preferido de Palermo ARGENTINE $$
(Map p48; ☎4774-6585; cnr Borges & Guatemala; mains AR$30-70; ⊙lunch & dinner Mon-Sat) This local joint has an old general-store atmosphere, with jars of olives in the window and tall tables *not* made for comfort. Great varied menu, however: homemade pastas, Cuban rice, Spanish veal, tripe and *puchero* (a meat and vegetable stew).

Club Eros ARGENTINE $
(Map p48; ☎4832-1313; Uriarte 1609; mains under AR$36; ⊙lunch & dinner) Very casual eatery stuffed with mostly older male diners watching sports on TV. It's a great place to pick up on local flavor, and the food is dirt cheap. Cool indoor soccer pitch next door.

Las Cholas ARGENTINE $

(Map p48; ☎4899-0094; Arce 306; mains AR$32-54; ⏰lunch & dinner) Good-value northern Argentine food in hip Las Cañitas, good for *cazuelas*, *pasteles* (vegetable tarts) and empanadas. Also lots of meats, sandwiches and desserts. Upscale rustic and very popular, so get here early.

Drinking

Buenos Aires is all about the night, and there are plenty of cafes, bars and live-music venues in which to drink the dark away. Cafes have very long hours: they're usually open early morning until late into the night. Bars and live-music venues open late and stay open even later; on weekends they'll often be hopping until 6am.

Cafes

Buenos Aires has a big cafe culture, which is obvious once you see the number of cafes in the city. Some are famous institutions, full of elegant old atmosphere and rich history; most are modern and trendy. *Porteños* will spend hours solving the world's problems over *medialunas* (croissants) and a *cortado* (coffee with a little milk). Most cafes have a long list of drinks and serve breakfast, lunch and dinner too.

TOP CHOICE **Bar Plaza Dorrego** CAFE

(Map p44; Defensa 1098) One of San Telmo's most atmospheric cafes. The dark wood surroundings (check out the graffiti) and old-world ambience can't be beat; grab a window seat and try to avoid staring at Starbucks across the street. Large food and drink menu.

La Biela CAFE

(Map p44; Av Quintana 600) The upper-crust elite dawdle for hours at this classy joint in Recoleta. Prices are relatively high, and the outside-seating menu costs even more, but it's great for people-watching and simply irresistible on a warm sunny day.

Café Tortoni CAFE

(Map p44; ☎4342-4328; Av de Mayo 825) The Cadillac of BA's cafes is too popular for its own good – it's expensive, the waiters are surly, there's a souvenir counter inside and sometimes you have to wait in line *to get in*. Still, it has a charming old atmosphere and relatively affordable nightly tango shows.

Clásica y Moderna CAFE

(Map p44; ☎4812-8707; Av Callao 892) Classic, cozy cafe with a heavy bohemian vibe. These brick walls have seen famous poets, philosophers and singers; these days it's a venue for intimate music shows. There's a small bookstore inside, and usually a Spanish-language newspaper or two.

Los 36 Billares BAR, CAFE

(Map p44; Av de Mayo 1265) A long-running spot, with wood details and classic surroundings. It's popular as a billiards hall, with plenty of tables and occasional competitions. Tango shows take place in the evenings.

Bars

Palermo Viejo has BA's highest concentration of trendy and upscale bars, though there are a few good ones downtown and in San Telmo as well. *Porteños* aren't big drinkers, and getting smashed is generally frowned upon. For a very happening scene, hang out with the masses in Plaza Serrano (in Palermo Viejo) on a weekend night – there are plenty of bars with sidewalk tables.

Pub Crawl PUB CRAWL

(☎15-5464-1886; www.pubcrawlba.com) For a night of rowdy drinking, join the expat-run Pub Crawl. For AR$120 you get food, drinks, transport to several bars and one nightclub, plus dozens of instant friends.

Magdalena's Party BAR

(Map p48; Thames 1795) Popular bar with an international mix of owners. A bit upscale but still laid-back, with good service and *buena onda*. DJs spin from Thursday to Saturday nights, with cheap drinks making this a good preclub bar; try the vodka lemonade by the pitcher.

La Puerta Roja BAR

(Map p44; ☎4362-5649; Chacabuco 733) Hit the buzzer to get into this San Telmo joint; there's no sign. Upstairs is a good bar area, a pool table in back and a smoking room overlooking the street. Come early for good, cheap food and mellower vibe – it gets busy later on. Expat-run; look for the red door.

Sugar BAR

(Map p48; Costa Rica 4619) From 7pm to midnight it's happy hour at this megapopular Palermo Viejo bar, which attracts a youthful mix of students, expats and Argentines. Tuesday is the Hype preparty, Thursday women drink free (after the AR$50 entry) and on weekends you'll wait in line to get in.

Milión COCKTAIL BAR
(Map p44; Paraná 1048) Bar-restaurant located in a richly renovated old mansion. The drinking happens on the 2nd and 3rd floors, and happy hour is 6pm to 9pm weekdays (starting 8pm weekends). It's elegant and very popular, with a nice terrace overlooking the leafy garden.

La Cigale BAR
(Map p44; 25 de Mayo 597; closed Sun) A hip downtown lounge in an airy upstairs space. Known for its tasty cocktails (happy hour from 6pm to 10pm; try the mojito), and has lunch specials for the business set. Near-nightly DJs, and is especially popular for its Tuesday DJ 'French Night.'

Antares BAR
(Map p48; Arévalo 2876) Modern, trendy and spacious bar-restaurant named after its Mar del Plata-based brewery. Unsurprisingly, it's best for its beer: try the seven-taste sampler (the Scotch ale is especially good). They usually have eight beers on tap. Also in Palermo Soho at Armenia 1447.

Gibraltar PUB
(Map p44; Perú 895) One of BA's most popular expat pubs that also attracts a heady mix of backpackers and locals. It has a good, unpretentious atmosphere and serves tasty international foods like roast beef with gravy and green Thai curry, plus plenty of whiskeys. There's a pool table in the back.

Shanghai Dragon PUB
(Map p48; Aráoz 1199) Newest entry by the owners of the highly successful Gibraltar and Bangalore pubs, but with affordable Chinese food instead of Indian. More proud of their nine beers on tap, mostly Argentine brands, rather than fancy cocktails. Come early if you like quiet as it gets pumped later at night.

Congo COCKTAIL BAR
(Map p48; Honduras 5329) A great Palermo Viejo drinking den, best on warm nights when you can relax out back in one of BA's best patio gardens. Cool, superhip and upscale; be prepared to wait in line on weekends, when there are DJs and a drink minimum to enter.

El Alamo SPORTS BAR
(Map p44; 4813-7324; Uruguay 1175) American-run bar unsurprisingly popular with expats, since it shows lots of US sports on TV. There are huge pitchers of cheap beer during happy hour, and women drink 'free' beer after paying AR$40 entry (until 10pm, 11pm or midnight depending on the day).

Kilkenny PUB
(Map p44; Marcelo T de Alvear 399;) The city's most famous Irish pub is fashionable with businesspeople on weekdays after work, and crammed full of everyone else on weekend nights. Good, dark atmosphere, but on weekends it's uncomfortably packed inside – try for a sidewalk table.

Post Street Bar BAR
(Map p48; Thames 1885) Very casual and funky bar with colorful stencils covering the walls from top to bottom. This makes you feel like you're hanging out drinking in an artsy ghetto. Head to the back and upstairs, where a rooftop patio is perfect on warm nights.

☆ Entertainment

Buenos Aires never sleeps, so you'll find something to do every night of the week. There are continuous theater and musical performances, and tango shows are everywhere. On weekends (and even some weeknights) the nightclubs shift into high gear.

Every modern shopping center has its multiscreen cinema complex; most movies are shown in their original language, with subtitles. Check the **Argentina Independent** (www.argentinaindependent.com) for screening times and general event information.

Discount ticket vendors (selling tickets for select theater, tango and movie performances) include **Cartelera Vea Más** (6320-5319; www.veamasdigital.com.ar; Av Corrientes 1660, Local 2), **Cartelera Baires** (www.cartelerabaires.com; Av Corrientes 1382) and **Cartelera Espectáculos** (4322-1559; www.123info.com.ar; Lavalle 742)

Ticketek (☎5237-7200; www.ticketek.com.ar) has outlets throughout the city and sells tickets for large venues.

Tango Shows

Most travelers will want to take in a tango show in BA, as they should. It's a bit futile to look for 'nontouristy' shows, however, as tango is a participatory dance and so its shows are geared toward voyeurs. If you want less sensationalism, then look for cheaper shows; they'll tend to be more traditional. *Milongas* are where dancers strut their stuff, but spectators don't really belong there (though a few *milonga* venues might put on the occasional spectator show).

There are many dinner-tango shows oriented to wealthier tourists. Some have a Las Vegas-like feel and often involve costume changes, dry ice and plenty of high kicks. aThe physical dancing feats can be spectacular, though this is not considered authentic tango (which is much more subtle). Reservations are usually necessary, and transportation is sometimes available.

There are 'free' (donation) street tango shows on Sunday at San Telmo's antiques fair and by chance in front of Galerías Pacífico in the *microcentro*. You might also see it on weekends on El Caminito in La Boca, or on Calle Florida near Lavalle. Schedules can be hit-or-miss, so catching them is a matter of luck. Some restaurants (especially in San Telmo and La Boca) offer free tango shows while you eat. Cultural centers are also good places to search for affordable shows, especially **Centro Cultural Borges** (www.ccborges.org.ar).

The following venues are mainly cafes that also offer affordable tango shows. To choose one of the pricier, more upscale

GAY & LESBIAN BUENOS AIRES

Buenos Aires is one of South America's top gay destinations and offers a vibrant range of gay bars, cafes and clubs. You'll have to know where to look, however; despite general tolerance for homosexuality, this ain't San Francisco or Sydney yet. The city's lesbian scene also definitely exists, though it's not nearly as overt as the boys' (but is it ever?).

Look up current sweetheart spots in free booklets such as *La Otra Guía* (www.laotraguia.com.ar), *The Ronda* (www.theronda.com.ar) and *Gay Map* (www.gaymapbuenosaires.com), all available at tourist or gay destinations. A good website with general information is www.thegayguide.com.ar.

San Telmo is a popular neighborhood for gay-run hotels and B&Bs, including **Axel Hotel** (Map p44; ☎4136 9393; www.axelhotels.com/buenosaires; Venezuela 649; r AR$560-640; ❄@📶; underground rail Línea E Belgrano) and **Lugar Gay** (Map p44; www.lugargay.com.ar). And if you're here in November, don't miss the **gay pride parade** (www.marchadelorgullo.org.ar) and **gay tango festival** (www.festivaltangoqueer.com.ar). Speaking of gay tango, for classes and *milongas* (dance halls) there's **La Marshall** (Map p44; ☎4300-3487; www.lamarshall.com.ar; Av Independencia 572) and **Tango Queer** (www.tangoqueer.com).

To explore new gay destinations and make new friends, check out www.outandaboutpubcrawl.com.

Popular gay nightspots:

Amerika (Map p48; www.ameri-k.com.ar; Gascón 1040) All-you-can-drink madness; large crowds, dark corners and thumping music. Sunday is gayest.

Bach Bar (Map p48; ☎15-5184-0137; www.bach-bar.com.ar; JA Cabrera 4390) Rowdy fun, especially for lesbians. Intimate and packed, with occasional stripper shows.

Glam (Map p48; www.glambsas.com.ar; José Antonio Cabrera 3046) A fun and crowded gay club in a big old mansion. Plenty of lounges, bars and young pretty boys.

Fiesta Dorothy! (www.fiestadorothy.com) Once (occasionally twice) a month but sooo worth it. Check the facebook page for dates.

Fiesta Plop (Map p48; www.facebook.com/fiestaplop; cnr Federico Lacroze & Álvarez Thomas) Popular Friday night party with a young crowd; at the same venue but on Saturday is **Fiesta Puerca** (www.facebook.com/fiestapuerca).

Rheo (p59) One of BA's best Saturday night parties, located at the Crobar nightclub in Palermo (www.rheo.com.ar).

dinner-tango shows, of which there are many, ask around for recommendations; prices and quality tend to be comparable and a show-only option is often included.

Café Tortoni TANGO SHOW
(Map p44; ☎4342-4328; www.cafetortoni.com.ar; Av de Mayo 829; show AR$100-120) Tango in the back of a historic, elegant cafe. Shows are 1¼ hours long and run three times nightly (4 time on Saturday nights); the less expensive one has more singing, and the more expensive one more dancing. Reserve in person from noon to 5pm, one day in advance; cash payment only.

Los 36 Billares CAFE, BAR
(Map p44; ☎4381-5696; www.los36billares.com.ar; Av de Mayo 1265; shows AR$50) A combination restaurant-cafe-bar-billiards hall, this atmospheric old place has been around for nearly 100 years. It offers affordable tango shows a couple of times per week, often on weeknights. Call ahead for a schedule or check the website. Minimum purchase of food and drinks are usually required.

Confitería Ideal TANGO SHOW
(Map p44; ☎5265-8069; www.confiteriaideal.com; Suipacha 384, 1st fl; dinner-show AR$170) The mother of all tango venues offers several passable shows throughout the week, along with plenty of classes and *milongas* (of many kinds) daily.

Nightclubs

Buenos Aires is all about the night, and clubbing is no exception. The action doesn't even start until 2am, and the later, the better. Those in the know take a nap before dinner, then stay up till the early- morning light – or even until noon the next day!

Porteños are fickle and hot spots change, so it's always best to ask where the hottest night spots are during your stay and double-check the hours/days.

Niceto Club CLUB
(Map p48; www.nicetoclub.com; Niceto Vega 5510; ⏲Thu-Sat) One of BA's biggest crowd-pullers. Best on Thursday nights, when theater company Club 69 takes over and puts on a raucous transvestite show that's popular with gays, hets and everything in between. Get here early to avoid long lines.

Crobar CLUB
(Map p48; www.crobar.com.ar; cnr Av de la Infanta Isabell & Freyre; ⏲Fri & Sat) This perennially popular club dishes up some of BA's best electronic music, spun by both resident and international guest DJs. Expect a good mix of partygoers with money and style, though the atmosphere isn't as snobby as you'd think. Mezzanines and walkways are perfect viewpoints for the beautiful crowds. Best on Fridays.

Bahrein NIGHTCLUB
(Map p44; www.bahreinba.com; Lavalle 345; ⏲Tue, Wed, Fri & Sat) On Tuesday this popular downtown spot offers up the best drum 'n' bass in town, while Saturday means international DJs. Chill-out spaces and eclectic decor add to the cool-vibe mix, and each floor has a different beat. Check out the old vault in the basement; the building used to be a bank.

Kika CLUB
(Map p48; www.kikaclub.com.ar; Honduras 5339; ⏲Tue-Sat) Well located near the heart of Palermo Viejo's bar scene, making Kika's Tuesday-night popular 'Hype' party (www.hype-ba.com) easily accessible for the trendy crowds. It's a mix of electro, indie, hip-hop, drum 'n' bass and dubstep, all spun by both local and international DJs. Other nights see electronica, reggaeton, Latin beats and live bands ruling the roost.

Basement Club CLUB
(Map p44; Rodriguez Peña 1220; ⏲Thu-Sat) This cool but unpretentious subterranean club is known for first-rate DJ lineups spinning electronica and tech-minimal-funky house beats to a diverse young crowd. Thanks to the Shamrock, the ever-popular Irish pub on the same premises, the place sees plenty of traffic throughout the night; just descend the stairs after enjoying a few pints at ground level.

Live Music

Some bars have live music too.

TOP CHOICE **La Bomba de Tiempo** LIVE MUSIC
(Map p48; www.labombadetiempo.com; Sarmiento 3131; AR$50; ⏲Mon 7pm) For one of BA's biggest and most unique parties, check out the eclectic drumming show La Bomba de Tiempo; it's at Ciudad Cultural Konex.

Teatro Colón CLASSICAL MUSIC
(Map p44; ☎4378-7100; www.teatrocolon.org.ar; Cerrito 628) Buenos Aires' premier venue for the arts, Teatro Colón has hosted prominent figures such as Placido Domingo and Luciano Pavarotti.

Notorious JAZZ
(Map p44; ☎4813-6888; www.notorious.com.ar; Av Callao 966) Small place with great intimate feel, and one of BA's premier venues for live jazz music. Other offerings include Brazilian, piano and tango. Dinner available; up front is a CD shop where you can listen before buying.

La Trastienda LIVE MUSIC
(Map p44; ☎5170-5483; www.latrastienda.com; Balcarce 460) International acts specializing in salsa, merengue, blues, Latin pop and tango play at this large venue (600 seats, plus 150 standing room), but rock rules the roost. Check website for schedules. There's a restaurant in front.

Spectator Sports

If you're lucky enough to witness a *fútbol* match, you'll encounter a passion unrivaled in any other sport. The most popular teams are **Boca Juniors** (☎4362-2260; www.bocajuniors.com.ar; Brandsen 805) in La Boca and **River Plate** (☎4789-1200; www.cariverplate.com; Alcorta 7597) in Belgrano, northwest of Aeroparque Jorge Newberry.

Ticket prices ultimately depend on the teams playing and the demand. In general, however, *entradas populares* (bleachers) are the cheapest seats and attract the more emotional fans of the game; don't show any signs of wealth in this section, including watches, necklaces or fancy cameras. *Plateas* (fixed seats) are a safer bet. There are also tour companies, such as Tangol (p61), that can take you to games.

Polo in Buenos Aires is most popular from October to December, and games take place at Campo de Polo in Palermo. Rugby, horse racing and *pato* (a traditional Argentine game played on horseback) are some other spectator possibilities.

Shopping

Buenos Aires has its share of modern shopping malls, along with flashy store-lined streets like Calle Florida and Av Santa Fe. You'll find decent-quality clothes, shoes, leather, accessories, electronics, music and homewares, but anything imported (like electronics) will be very expensive.

Palermo Viejo is the best neighborhood for boutiques and creative fashions. Av Alvear, toward the Recoleta cemetery, means designer labels. Defensa in San Telmo is full of pricey antique shops. There are several weekend crafts markets, such as the hippy *feria artesanal* in front of Recoleta's cemetery. The famous San Telmo antiques fair takes place on Sunday. Leather jackets and bags are sold in stores on Calle Murillo (599-600 blocks) in the neighborhood of Villa Crespo. For cheap third-world imports, head to Av Pueyrredón near Estación Once (Once train station); you can find just about anything there.

Walrus Books (Map p44; ☎4300-7135; Estados Unidos 617; ⏲noon-8pm Tue-Sun) is run by an American-Argentine couple, and carries new and used books in English (including Lonely Planet titles).

Information

Dangers & Annoyances

Petty crime exists in Buenos Aires like in any big city. In general, BA is pretty safe. You can walk around at all hours of the night in many places, even as a lone woman (people stay out late, and there are often other pedestrians on the streets). Most tourists leave unscathed – they tend to be travel-smart and don't wear fancy jewelry or go around with their wallets hanging out or purses left carelessly on a chair. They're cautious of pickpockets in crowded places, aware of their surroundings and at least *pretend* to know where they're going.

If anything, BA is besieged more by minor nuisances. When buying anything, count your change and keep an eye out for fake bills, especially in dark places like taxis and nightclubs (search for clear lines and a good watermark). Watch carefully for traffic when crossing streets, and look out for the piles of dog droppings underfoot. Note that fresh air is often lacking – air pollution and smoking are big issues. Dealing with taxis can be interesting to say the least (see Taxi & Remise, p63).

Every city has its edgy neighborhoods, and in BA these include Constitución Estación (train station), the eastern border of San Telmo and La Boca (where, outside tourist streets, you should be careful even during the day). Av Florida can be edgy only very, very late at night.

Immigration Offices

Immigration (☎4317-0234; www.migraciones.gov.ar; Av Antártida Argentina 1355; ⏲7:30am-2pm Mon-Fri)

Internet Access

Internet access is everywhere and connections are generally fast and affordable.

Money

There is a gray market for US dollars, and you may hear people on pedestrian Av Florida call out '*cambio, cambio.*' However, it's wiser to change money at a bank or *cambio* (exchange house) – scams and counterfeit bills do exist. Most transactions require ID, and lines can be long at banks. *Cambios* have slightly poorer exchange rates, but are quicker and have fewer limitations. You can get a pretty fair rate for US dollars at many retail establishments.

Traveler's checks are very hard to cash (try exchange houses rather than banks) and incur bad exchange rates; one exception is **American Express** (☎4310-3000; Arenales 707).

You'll find that ATMs are commonplace, though there are withdrawal limits that depend on your banking system. Visa and MasterCard holders can get cash advances, but check with your bank before traveling.

Post

National post branches are all over the city.

Correo Postal Internacional (☎4891-9191; www.correoargentino.com.ar; Av Antártida Argentina) For international parcels 2kg to 20kg; see website for rates. Contents must be checked. Boxes sold here.

FedEx (☎0810-333-3339; www.fedex.com; Maipú 753) Has several branches across the city.

Telephone

The easiest way to make a call is from a *locutorio* (small telephone office), where you enter a booth and make calls in a safe, quiet environment. Costs are comparable to street telephones and you don't need change. Most *locutorios* offer reasonably priced fax and internet services as well.

Public phones are numerous; use coins, or buy a magnetic phone card from any kiosk.

Tourist Information

Buenos Aires' small tourist offices are spread out in key tourist locations throughout the city. Hours vary throughout the year.

Secretaría de Turismo de la Nación (☎0800-555-0016, 4312-2232; www.turismo.gov.ar; Av Santa Fe 883; ⏲9am-5pm Mon-Fri) Mostly info on Argentina but helps with BA.

Tourist offices (www.bue.gov.ar) Florida (Tourist Kiosk; cnr Avs Florida & Diagonal Roque Sáenz Peña); Puerto Madero (Tourist Kiosk; Av Alicia Moreau de Justo, Dique 4); Recoleta (Tourist Kiosk; cnr Av Quintana & Ortiz); Retiro bus station (Retiro bus station, across from bus slot 36; ⏲7:30am-1pm Mon-Fri & Sun).

Tourist police (Comisaría del Turista; ☎0800-999-5000, 4346-5748; Av Corrientes 436; ⏲24hr) Provides interpreters and helps victims of robberies and rip-offs.

Travel Agencies

Say Hueque (☎5258-8740; www.sayhueque.com) Downtown (☎5199-2517; Viamonte 749, 6th fl); Palermo Viejo (☎5258-8740; Thames 2062); San Telmo (☎5352-9321; Chile 557) Recommended travel agency that customizes and books adventure trips for travelers around Argentina and Chile. Also helps reserve accommodations.

Tangol (☎4363-6000; www.tangol.com; Av Florida 971, Suite 31) Helpful travel agency that books activities such as skydiving, *estancia* visits, night tours of BA and guided soccer games. Also organizes plenty of travel packages around the country. Also at Defensa 831.

ℹ Getting There & Away

Air

Most international flights leave from **Ezeiza Airport** (☎5480-6111; www.aa2000.com.ar). For more information on how to get into town from Ezeiza, see boxed text, p63.

Manuel Tienda León (MTL; www.tiendaleon.com) charges AR$25 for the 15-minute ride from downtown to **Aeroparque Jorge Newbery** (☎5480-6111; www.aa2000.com.ar). Or take city bus 45 from Plaza San Martín (AR$2). Taxis cost around AR$50.

Boat

Buquebus (☎4316-6500; www.buquebus.com; cnr Avs Antártida Argentina & Córdoba), which has several offices around town, has several daily ferries to Colonia via a fast boat (one hour) or a slow boat (three hours). One boat daily also goes directly to Montevideo (three hours), though boat/bus combinations via Colonia are cheaper. There are also seasonally available boat-bus services to Punta del Este, Uruguay's top beach resort. There are more services in the summer season, when it's a good idea to buy your ticket in advance. Ticket prices vary throughout the year.

SUBE CARD

If you're planning on staying in Buenos Aires for more than a few days, getting a **SUBE** (www.sube.gob.ar) card might be worthwhile. It's a rechargeable card that you can use for the Subte, local buses and some trains, saving you ticket costs and time waiting in line. Get it at some shops, post offices or OCA offices around the city (check the website); you'll need your passport and the cost is AR$15. Charging the card can be done at certain kiosks and Subte or train stations.

Bus

Retiro (www.tebasa.com.ar; Av Antártida Argentina) is a huge three-story bus terminal with slots for 75 buses. Inside are cafeterias, shops, bathrooms, luggage storage, telephone offices with internet, ATMs, and a 24-hour information kiosk to help you navigate the terminal. There's also a **tourist information office** (Suite 83; ⌚7:30am-1pm Mon-Fri); look for it across from bus slot 36.

The following lists are a small sample of very extensive services. Prices will vary widely depending on the season, the company and the economy. During holidays, prices rise; buy your ticket in advance.

DOMESTIC SERVICES

DESTINATION	COST (AR$)	DURATION (HR)
Bariloche	700-800	21
Comodoro Rivadavia	725	24
Córdoba	320	10
Mar del Plata	220	6
Mendoza	500	15
Puerto Iguazú	700	19
Puerto Madryn	500-600	18
Rosario	150	5
Salta	800	21
Tucumán	650	16

INTERNATIONAL SERVICES

DESTINATION	COST (AR$)	DURATION (HR)
Asunción, Paraguay	550	18
Foz do Iguazú, Brazil	700	19
Montevideo, Uruguay	250	10
Rio de Janeiro, Brazil	900	42
Santiago, Chile	600	20
São Paulo, Brazil	750	34

Train

With very few exceptions, rail travel in Argentina is limited to Buenos Aires' suburbs and provincial cities. It's cheaper but not nearly as fast, frequent or comfortable as hopping on a bus.

Each of BA's train stations has its own Subte stop. Useful stations include the following:

Estación Constitución Services by Metropolitano (☎0800-122-358736) and Ferrobaires (☎0810-666-8736; www.ferrobaires.gba.gov.ar) to Bahía Blanca and Atlantic beach towns.

Estación Retiro (☎4317-4400) Service by Metropolitano and Ferrovias (☎0800-777-3377; www.ferrovias.com.ar) to Tigre and Rosario.

 Getting Around

Bicycle

Buenos Aires has several companies that offer guided bike tours, such as Biking Buenos Aires (p50). They also rent out bikes, but be aware that motor vehicles in this city consider bikes a pest – ride defensively and use the bike lanes set aside on some streets. Safer biking neighborhoods are San Telmo and Palermo (both with some cobbled streets), as well as Puerto Madero and its Reserva Ecológica Costanera Sur (p42).

Note that BA has a bike-share program, but it's meant for Argentine residents (and requires local ID).

Bus

Sold at many kiosks, the Guía T (pocket version around AR$10) details some 200 bus routes. Fares depend on the distance, but most rides cost AR$2; place coins (bills not accepted) in the machine behind the driver. If you're in town for a long while, it might be worth getting a SUBE (p61) card to save money. Offer front seats to elderly passengers or those with kids.

Check out www.omnilineas.com and click on 'City Buses' to figure out what local bus to take.

Car & Motorcycle

We don't recommend you rent a car to drive around Buenos Aires. *Porteño* drivers turn crazy behind the wheel and you shouldn't compete with them. Also, public transport is excellent. Cars are good to explore the countryside, however. Try **Avis** (☎4326-5542; www.avis.com.ar; Cerrito 1535), **New Way** (☎4515-0331; www.newwayrentacar.com; Marcelo T de Alvear 773) or **Hertz** (☎4816-8001; www.hertz.com.ar; Paraguay 1138) Rentals cost around AR$260 per day with 200 free kilometers.

For motorcycle rentals contact **Motocare** (☎4761-2696; www.motocare.com.ar/rental; Echeverria 738, Vicente Lopez) in the *barrio* of Vicente Lopez.

Subway

Buenos Aires' **Subte** (www.subte.com.ar) is fast, efficient and costs AR$2.50 per ride. The most useful lines for travelers are Líneas A, B, D and E (which run from the *microcentro* to the capital's western and northern outskirts) and Línea C (which links Estación Retiro and Constitución).

Trains operate from approximately 5am to 10:30pm except Sunday and holidays (when hours are 8am to 10pm); they run frequently on weekdays, less so on weekends.

GETTING INTO TOWN

If you fly into Buenos Aires from outside Argentina, you'll probably land at Ezeiza Airport (p61), 35km south of the city center (about a 40-minute ride from downtown). Ezeiza is clean and modern and has food services, shops, internet access and luggage storage. There's also an **information counter** (☎5480-6111; ⏲24hr).

To enter Argentina, some nationalities are charged a 'reciprocity fee' equivalent to what Argentines pay to visit those countries. This fee applies to Americans (US$160, valid for 10 years), Australians (US$100, valid for one year) and Canadians (US$75 for one entry, or US$150 for five years). You must pay this fee online, with a credit card, before arriving in Argentina. For instructions, see www.migraciones.gov.ar/accesible; you'll have to click on 'Pay your reciprocity fee' and then sign up at the 'Log In'. Remember to print out a receipt and bring it with you while traveling to prove payment.

One way into town is the frequent, comfortable shuttle service by **Manuel Tienda León** (MTL; ☎4315-5115; www.tiendaleon.com; Av Madero 1299; AR$65); its booth is just outside customs. Another option is **Hostel Shuttle** (☎4511-8723; www.hostelshuttle.com.ar; AR$40), which goes five times daily from Ezeiza to certain downtown hostels, but you'll likely need to reserve in advance. Those seeking luxury should investigate **Silver Star Transport** (☎in Argentina 011-15-6826-8876, in the USA 214-502-1605; www.silverstarcar.com).

For taxis, avoid the shuttle companies' hiked-up prices and head behind the shuttle booths to the city taxi booth, which charges around AR$200 (including tolls). Or save a few pesos and go outside the airport doors to the yellow taxi booth (AR$178). Important: *do not* go with a taxi tout – find the booths. Hard-core penny-pinchers can take bus 8 (AR$4 in coins, two hours) from outside the Aerolíneas Argentinas (domestic) terminal, which is a short walk away. Get small change in bills and coins at the bank before getting on the bus.

If you need to change money, avoid the *cambios* (exchange houses) as their rates are bad. Instead, head to the nearby Banco de la Nación, which has fair rates and is open 24 hours. There are several ATMS in Ezeiza (withdraw uneven denominations – ie AR$690 instead of AR$700 – to get change).

Most domestic flights land at Aeroparque Jorge Newbery (p61), only a few kilometers north of the city center. Manuel Tienda León shuttles to the city center take 15 minutes and cost AR$25. Bus 45 also goes to the center; take it going south (to the right as you leave the airport; AR$2). Taxis to downtown cost about AR$50.

Shuttle transfers from Ezeiza to Aeroparque cost AR$75.

Retiro bus station is about 1km north of the city center; it has shops, cafes, telephone and internet services and luggage storage (don't leave luggage unattended). Dozens of BA's local bus lines converge here; outside, it's a seething mass and not to be figured out after a 10-hour bus ride. You can take the Subte if your destination is near a stop, or head to one of the *remise* (a type of taxi) booths near the bus slots. There's a tourist information office.

Taxi & Remise

Black-and-yellow cabs are ubiquitous on BA's streets, though their prices seem to go up every six months (and cost 20% more from 10pm-6am). Tips are unnecessary, but rounding up to the nearest peso is common. If you're taking a taxi into town from Ezeiza airport, head to the city taxi counter (blue sign, with posted prices), a little behind the first row of transport booths. This is important – don't just go with any driver who calls to you.

Some people might warn you it's not safe to take street taxis in Buenos Aires because of robbery. For the most part, however, it's safe to hail a street taxi. In fact, taxi drivers are much better at ripping you off. Make sure the driver uses the meter: it's good to have an idea of where you're going, and make sure the meter doesn't run fast (it should change every 200 meters, or about every three blocks). Know your money: fake bills feel fake and either don't have watermarks or have a bad one. Finally, try to pay with exact change or at least with low-denomination bills: some drivers deftly replace high bills with low ones, or switch your real bill for a fake one. And if you do experience a problem with a taxi, get the taxi's permit number (hanging in every licensed taxi) or license plate number – and call the **tourist assistance line** (☎0800-999-2838).

If you want to play it safest, however, call a *remise* (a type of taxi). They're considered safer than street taxis, since an established company sends them out. Any business should be able to phone a *remise* for you. And remember that most taxi and *remise* drivers are honest people just making a living.

AROUND BUENOS AIRES

Day trips to charming, cobbled Colonia del Sacramento (p943) in Uruguay are popular, and it's also easy to reach Montevideo (Uruguay's capital; p936), and the beach resort of Punta del Este (p954), only a few hours away from Buenos Aires.

Tigre

About an hour north of Buenos Aires is this favorite *porteño* weekend destination. You can check out the popular **riverfront**, take a relaxing boat ride in the **Delta del Paraná** and shop at **Mercado de Frutos** (a daily crafts market that's best on weekends).

Tigre's **tourist office** (☎4512-4497; Mitre 305) is behind McDonald's. Nearby are ticket counters for commuter boats that cruise the waterways; the tourist office is good and can recommend a destination.

The quickest, cheapest way to get to Tigre is by taking the 'Mitre line—Ramal Tigre' from Retiro train station (AR$1.35, 50 minutes, frequent). The most scenic way is to take either the same train mentioned above, or buses 59, 60 or 152 directly to where the **Tren de la Costa** (www.trendelacosta.com.ar) begins, in the suburb of Olivos. This is a pleasant electric train; the final station is in Tigre.

San Antonio de Areco

☎02326 / POP 23,000

Dating from the early 18th century, this serene village northwest of Buenos Aires is the symbolic center of Argentina's diminishing *gaucho* (cowboy) culture. It's also host to the country's biggest *gaucho* celebration, **Día de la Tradición**, on November 10. The village has a cute plaza surrounded by historic buildings, and local artisans are known for producing maté paraphernalia, *rastras* (silver-studded belts) and *facones* (long-bladed knives). Buses run regularly from BA's Retiro bus terminal (AR$40, two hours).

NORTHEAST ARGENTINA

From the spectacular natural wilderness of Iguazú Falls in the north to the chic sophistication of Rosario in the south, the northeast is one of Argentina's most diverse regions. Wedged between the Ríos Paraná and Uruguay (thus earning it the nickname 'Mesopotamia'), the region relies heavily on those rivers for fun and its livelihood. In contrast, the neighbouring Chaco is sparsely populated, and often called Argentina's 'empty quarter.'

The northeast was one of the Jesuits' Argentinean power bases until their expulsion from the Americas in 1767, the legacy of which can be seen in the remains of the many missions in the region's northeast.

Rosario

☎0341 / POP 1,523,400

So, you dig the vibe of the Buenos Aires, but the sheer size of it is sending you a little loco in the coco? Rosario may be the place for you.

Located just a few hours north, this is in many ways Argentina's second city – not in terms of population, but culturally, financially and aesthetically. Its roaring port trade and growing population even made it a candidate for national capital status for a while there.

These days the city's backpacker scene is growing slowly, and the huge university and corresponding population of students, artists and musicians give it a solid foundation.

Nighttime, the streets come alive and the bars and clubs pack out. In the day, once everybody wakes up, they shuffle down to the river beaches for more music, drinks and a bit of a lie-down.

It's not all fun and games, though. Culture-vultures won't be disappointed by the wealth of museums and galleries, and Che Guevara fans will want to check out his birthplace.

Sights & Activities

Prices, dates and hours change throughout the year. Check with the tourist office to be sure.

Northeast Argentina

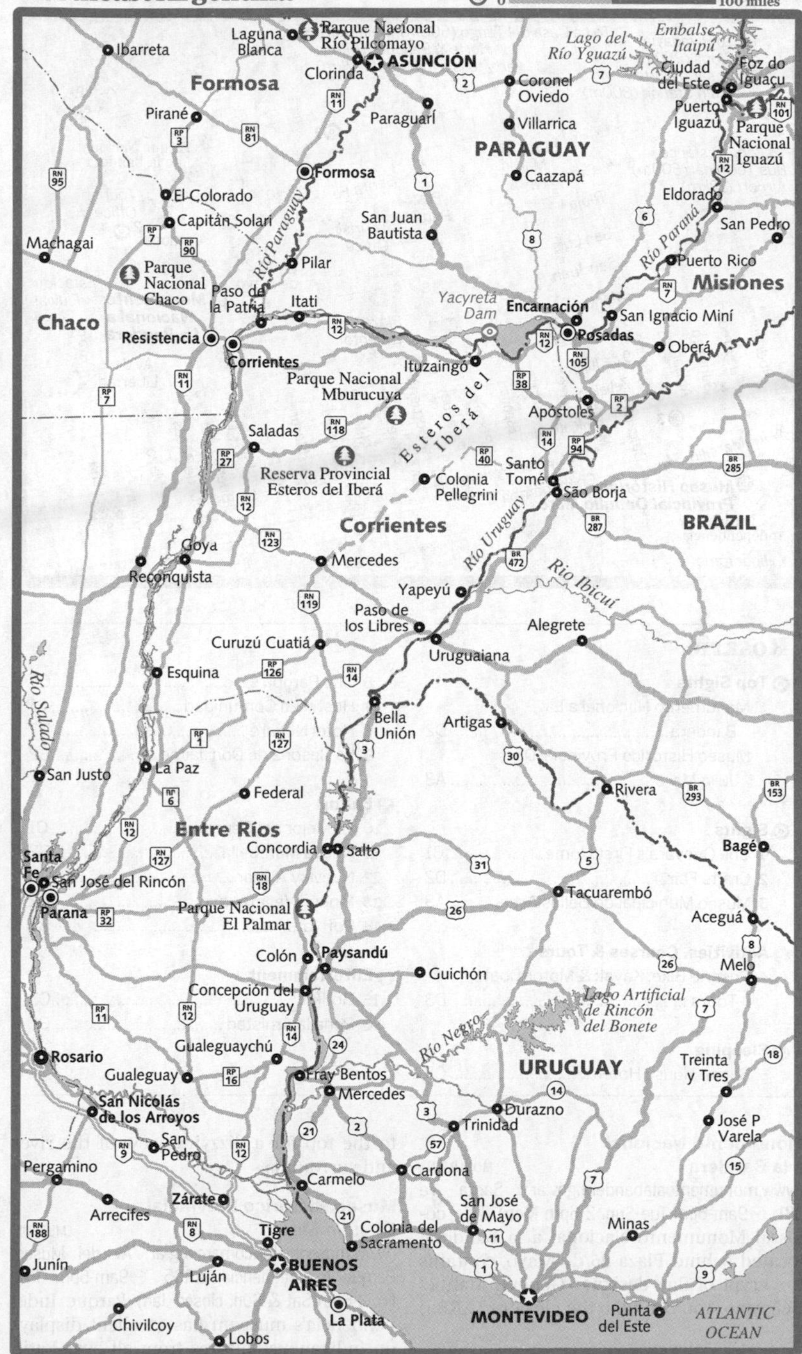

Rosario

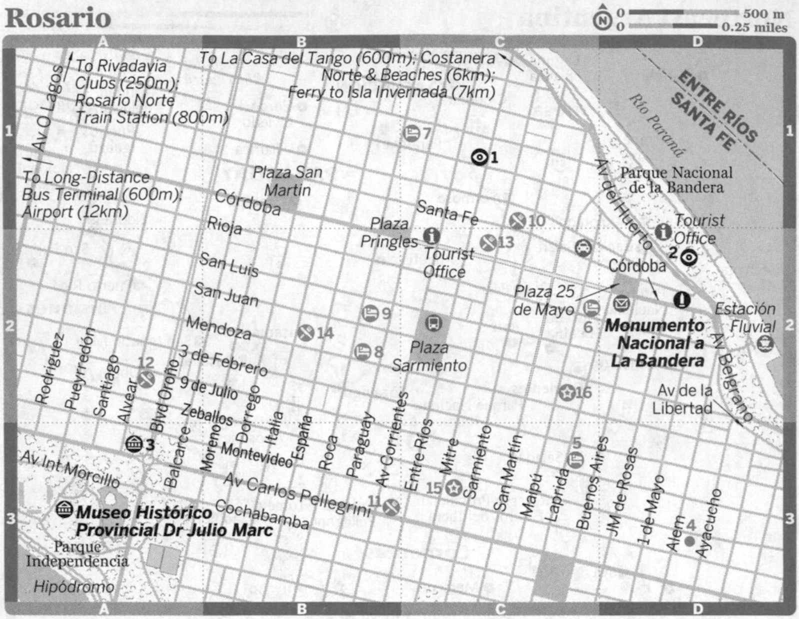

Rosario

Top Sights
- Monumento Nacional a La Bandera D2
- Museo Histórico Provincial Dr Julio Marc A3

Sights
1. Che Guevara's First Home C1
2. Crafts Fair D2
3. Museo Municipal de Bellas Artes A3

Activities, Courses & Tours

4. Rosario Bike, Kayak & Motor Boat Tours D3

Sleeping

5. Barisit House Hotel C3
6. Che Pampa's C2
7. Hostel La Comunidad C1
8. Hotel Nogaré B2
9. La Casona de Don Jaime B2

Eating

10. Lo Mejor del Centro C1
11. Nueva Marabella B3
12. Nueve y Alvear A2
13. Rincón Vegetariano C2
14. Softya B2

Entertainment

15. Gotika C3
16. Peña la Amistad C2

Monumento Nacional a la Bandera MONUMENT

(www.monumentoalabandera.gov.ar; Santa Fe 581; ⏲9am-6pm Tue-Sun, 2-6pm Mon) The colossal Monumento Nacional a la Bandera, located behind Plaza 25 de Mayo, contains the crypt of flag designer General Manuel Belgrano. You can take the elevator (AR$3) to the top for a dizzying view of the river and surrounds.

Museo Histórico Provincial Dr Julio Marc MUSEUM

(www.museohistoricomarc.org.ar; Av del Museo, Parque Independencia; AR$5; ⏲9am-5pm Tue-Fri, 2-6pm Sat & Sun, closed Jan) Parque Independencia's museum has excellent displays on indigenous cultures from all over Latin

America, colonial and religious artifacts and the most ornate collection of maté paraphernalia you ever did see.

Museo Municipal de Bellas Artes MUSEUM
(www.museocastagnino.org.ar; cnr Av Carlos Pellegrini & Blvd Oroño; admission AR$5; ⌚3-8pm, closed Tue) Lovingly curated and featuring some world-class pieces, Rosario's fine-art museum focuses on Argentine and European artists.

Che Guevara's First Home NOTABLE BUILDING
(Entre Ríos 480) Renowned architect Alejandro Bustillo designed the apartment building at Entre Ríos 480 where, in 1928, Ernesto Guevara Lynch and Celia de la Serna resided after the birth of their son Ernesto Guevara de la Serna, popularly known today as El Che.

Crafts Fair MARKET
(Av Belgrano; ⌚8am-5pm Sat & Sun) This weekend crafts fair is located south of the tourist office.

Paracaidismo Rosario ADVENTURE SPORTS
(☎15-617-8100; www.paracaidismorosario.com.ar) Out at the airfield, 15km west of town, Paracaidismo Rosario offers one-off tandem skydives as well as longer certification courses.

Rosario Bike, Kayak & Motor Boat Tours BOAT TOUR, CYCLING
(☎15-571-3812; www.bikerosario.com.ar; Zeballos 327) Offers bike hire (per half-/full day AR$50/60), and guided bike and kayak tours.

Beaches

For a more relaxed, family-oriented scene, take the red 153 bus from the corner of Corrientes and Córdoba 6km north to Av Puccio (from here the bus turns inland). Stroll up the boardwalk along **Catalunya beach** and look for a spot to lay the towel. There are plenty of restaurants around. Keep walking and in 20 minutes you'll hit a private beach, **Av Florida**, which charges AR$8 for access to a wider stretch of sand. Beyond it is Estación Costa Alta (the boat dock), where you can take a 15-minute ride across the Paraná (return AR$8) to **Isla Invernada**, land of woodsier, more natural beaches (camping possible). To get to the boat dock without the stroll, take bus 103 from the local bus terminal on San Luis; it stops close by.

For a younger, noisier experience, catch a ferry (one way AR$20) from the Estación Fluvial (Ferry Station) to **Isla Espinillo**, where you'll find a selection of restaurants and bars, music, hammock space and water sports on offer, such as water skiing, Jet Skiing and windsurfing.

 Courses

Spanish in Rosario LANGUAGE COURSE
(☎437-2860; www.spanishinrosario.com; Catamarca 3095) Rosario's is a great place to hang out for a while, and this set-up offers enjoyable language programs to help you put that time to good use. It can also arrange family stays and volunteer work placements.

 Festivals & Events

Every June Rosario celebrates **Semana de la Bandera** (Flag Week), climaxing in ceremonies on June 20, the anniversary of the death of Manuel Belgrano, the Argentinian flag's designer. In early October the **Semana del Arte** includes a poetry festival and theater, comedy and dance performances. From mid-October to early November, the **Festival de Jazz** takes place in various venues around town. Also in November, the national **Encuentro de las Colectividades**, a tribute to the country's immigrants, is celebrated with fancy dress, music and food stalls.

Sleeping

Che Pampa's HOSTEL $
(☎424-5202; www.chepampas.com; Rioja 812; dm AR$60-70, d AR$220; ❄@📶) Centrally located and decked out in deep reds and low-slung furniture, this is one of the city's better hostels. The kitchen's cramped, but the excellent hangout areas more than compensate.

La Casona de Don Jaime HOSTEL $
(☎527-9964; www.youthhostelrosario.com.ar; Roca 1051; dm AR$48, s/d without bathroom AR$120/220) Rosario's first hostel is basic but well set up. There are comfy sitting areas and an attached bar. There's also a small, clean kitchen, lockers and a variety of activities on offer.

Hotel Nogaré HOTEL $
(Mendoza 1578; s/d AR$160/240; 📶) A straight-up, no frills budget hotel. Rooms vary wildly, so take a look at a few – and check the sponge factor on your mattress – before deciding.

Hostel La Comunidad HOSTEL $
(☎424-5302; www.lacomunidadhostel.com; Roca 453; dm/d AR$60/150; @📶) Occupying a gorgeous old Rosario building, this spot has lofty ceilings and a light, airy feel. The dorms have handsome wooden bunks and floorboards; a cute private room is also available. The hostel has a bar and lounge area, and a peaceful vibe.

Barisit House Hotel HOTEL $$
(☎447-6464; www.barisit.com.ar; Laprida 1311; s/d AR$300/400; ❄@📶) Some pleasingly Zen touches in the lobby and patio area as well as large, modern rooms make this a stand-out.

Camping Municipal CAMPGROUND $
(☎471-4381; Lisandro deTorre 1620, Granadero Baigorria; campsites per person AR$5 plus per tent AR$10) Camping Municipal is 9km north of the city; take bus 35 or 143 from the center to Barra 9.

Isla Invernada CAMPGROUND
(☎455-0285) The most natural campsites are on Isla Invernada, but there are no facilities.

Eating

If you feel like exploring, take a wander along Av Carlos Pelligrini between Maipú and Moreno. This is Rosario's restaurant strip – 10 blocks dedicated to the pillars of Argentine cuisine: pizza, *parrilla*, pasta, *tenedores libres* (all-you-can-eat restaurants) and ice cream, sometimes all gloriously available in the one location. Otherwise, there's a *confitería* (cafe/snack bar) on just about every street corner.

TOP CHOICE **Nueva Marabella** PIZZERIA $
(Av Carlos Pelligrini 1385; AR$35-60; ⏰lunch & dinner) Tired of that doughy mess that often passes for pizza around these parts? Slip into this no-frills pizza joint for crunchy stone-baked pizzas. The all-you-can-eat deal (AR$34) should please the big eaters.

Lo Mejor del Centro PARRILLA $
(Santa Fe 1171; mains AR$30-60; ⏰lunch & dinner) When this *parrilla* went bust, the staff were left jobless, but the local government let them reopen it as a cooperative. The meat's as good as you'll taste in Rosario, but you can also enjoy homemade pasta, creative salads and a warm, convivial buzz at the tightly packed tables.

Softya MIDDLE EASTERN $
(Italia 1069; mains AR$30-50; ⏰lunch & dinner) Good, authentic Middle Eastern food, and a delicious range of Syrian desserts.

Nueve y Alvear PARRILLA $$
(cnr 9 de Julio & Alvear; mains AR$60-80; ⏰lunch & dinner) A better-than-average neighborhood *parrilla*. It's a bit pricier than its downtown counterparts, but the food is several steps up in quality.

Rincón Vegetariano VEGETARIAN $
(www.turinconvegetariano.blogspot.com; Mitre 720; mains AR$20-35; ⏰breakfast, lunch & dinner Mon-Sat; 🥕) With more than 50 dishes to choose from and a tad more atmosphere than your average all-you-can-eat joint, this is Rosario's best bet for staying meat-free. There are a couple of chicken and *parrilla* dishes on offer, just in case.

☆ Entertainment

For the complete lowdown on the tango scene, look for the free monthly magazine *Rosario de Tango* (www.rosariodetango.com.ar), which lists classes, *milongas* (dance halls) and other tango-related news. For general cultural events, the monthly Agenda Cultural (AC) magazine is the one to look for. Both these magazines are available in hostels and the tourist office.

For the megadisco scene, make your way northwest of downtown along Rivadavia. Clubs here open their doors shortly after midnight, but remain deserted until after 2am, when lines begin to form. Any taxi driver will know where you're going, and the fare from the center should be about AR$35. A more central option is at the Estación Fluvial, where there are a couple of bars and clubs.

La Casa del Tango DANCE
(www.lacasadeltangorosario.com; riverbank at España) This tango center has info on performances around town, offers fun, very cheap evening lessons, and stages various events. It also has a good cafe and restaurant.

Gotika GAY
(www.gotikacityclub.com.ar; Mitre 1539; ⏰Fri-Sun) Rosario's best downtown dance club is set up in a renovated church. Music varies, but concentrates on break beat and drum and bass.

REMOTE NATIONAL PARKS IN NORTHEAST ARGENTINA

Northeast Argentina is home to some incredible parks that take some getting to, but are well worthwhile. Here are a few. For more information, log on to www.parquesnacionales.gov.ar.

Parque Nacional El Palmar (☎03447-49-3049; www.elpalmarapn.com.ar; RN 14, Km 199; Argentine/foreigner AR$20/40; ⊙8am-6pm) Home to capybara, *ñandú* (rhea; large flightless bird resembling the ostrich) and poisonous pit vipers, this 8500-hectare park protects the endangered yatay palm. The park also has cheap camping, good walking trails and swimming holes. It lies between Colón and Concordia, on the Uruguayan border; both are easily accessible from Gualeguaychú.

Parque Nacional Chaco (☎03725-499-161; www.parquesnacionales.gov.ar; admission free; ⊙visitors center 9am-7pm) This park protects 15,000 hectares of marshes, palm savannas and strands of the disappearing *quebracho colorado* tree. Birds far outnumber mammals – there are plenty of rhea, jabiru, roseate spoonbills, cormorants and common caracaras – but mosquitoes outnumber them all. Bring repellent. Camping is free, but facilities are basic. Capitán Solari (5km from the park entrance) is the nearest town, and is easily accessed from Resistencia.

Parque Nacional Río Pilcomayo (☎03718-470-045; www.parquesnacionales.gov.ar; RN 86; ⊙8am-6pm) This 600-sq-km park is home to caiman, tapirs, anteaters, maned wolves and an abundance of birdlife, particularly around the centerpiece, Laguna Blanca (where piranha make swimming a bad idea). Access is via the small town of Laguna Blanca (9km east of the actual lagoon), which can be reached from Formosa.

Peña la Amistad TRADITIONAL MUSIC
(www.folklorerosario.com; Maipú 1111; ⊙Fri & Sat) *Peñas* (clubs/bars that host informal folk-music gatherings) have been enjoying a resurgence of popularity among young Argentines of late, and if you haven't checked one out, this is a fine place to start. It's one of Rosario's oldest and best respected.

Information

The informative **tourist office** (☎480-2230; www.rosarioturismo.com; Av del Huerto; ⊙9am-7pm) is on the waterfront. There's a more **central branch** (cnr Corrientes & Córdoba; ⊙9am-8pm) downtown.

Cambios along San Martín and Córdoba change traveler's checks; there are many banks and ATMs on Santa Fe between Mitre and Entre Ríos.

The **post office** (Córdoba 721) is near Plaza Sarmiento.

Getting There & Around

Aerolíneas Argentinas (☎420-8138; Córdoba 852) flies four times weekly to Buenos Aires. **Sol** (☎0810-444-4765; www.sol.com.ar) flies daily to Buenos Aires (AR$230) and Córdoba (AR$280). A *remise* to/from the airport (8km from town) should cost around AR$30.

The **long-distance bus terminal** (☎437-3030; www.terminalrosario.com.ar; Cafferata & Santa Fe) is 4km west of the center. Services include Buenos Aires (AR$160, four hours), Córdoba (AR$190, six hours), Santa Fe (AR$81, 2½ hours), Mendoza (AR$480, 12 hours) and Montevideo, Uruguay (AR$450, 10 hours). Many local buses go to the **center** (☎437-2384; Cafferata 702); buy magnetic cards (AR$2.70) at kiosks beforehand. Bus 138 leaves from the train station.

Manuel Tienda León (☎409-8000; www.mtlrosario.com.ar; San Lorenzo 935) offers door-to-door shuttle service to Buenos Aires hotels and airports (AR$290, four hours).

The **Rosario Norte train station** (www.ferrocentralsa.com.ar; Av del Valle 2750), 3km northwest of the center, has services to Buenos Aires, Tucumán and Córdoba. Due to the poor condition of tracks and carriages and frequent delays, you'd have to be a true train buff to appreciate these services.

Santa Fe

☎0342 / POP 518,100

Santa Fe would be a fairly dull town if not for the university population. Thanks to this, there's a healthy bar and club scene, and plenty of fun to be had during the day.

Relocated during the mid-17th century because of hostile indigenous groups, floods and isolation, the city duplicates the original plan of Santa Fe La Vieja (Old Santa Fe). But

Santa Fe

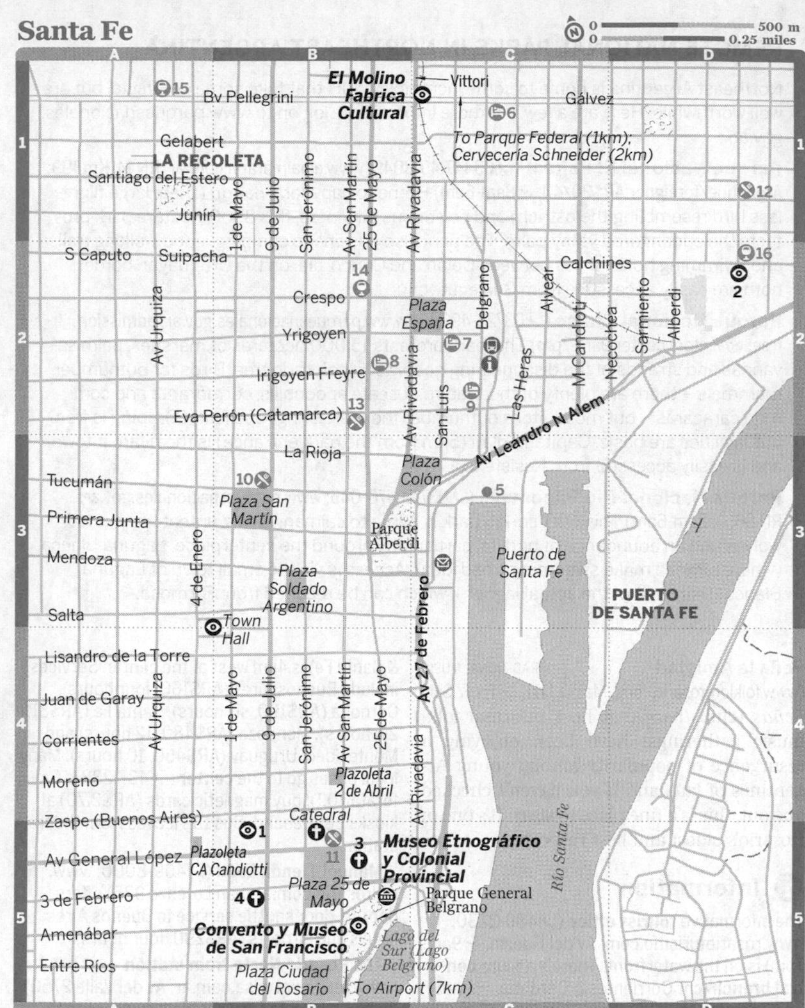

a 19th-century neo-Parisian building boom and more recent construction have left only isolated colonial buildings, mostly near Plaza 25 de Mayo.

Sights & Activities

Some colonial buildings are museums, but churches still serve their ecclesiastical functions, such as the mid-17th-century **Templo de Santo Domingo** (cnr 3 de Febrero & 9 de Julio). The exterior simplicity of the 1696 Jesuit **Iglesia de la Compañía** (Plaza 25 de Mayo) masks an ornate interior. The restored, two-story **Casa de los Aldao** (Buenos Aires 2861) dates from the early 18th century.

Convento y Museo de San Francisco MONASTERY

(Amenábar 2257; admission by donation; ⌚9am-12:30pm & 3-7pm Tue-Sun) Built in 1680, the Convento y Museo de San Francisco, south of Plaza 25 de Mayo, is Santa Fe's most important landmark. Its meter-thick walls support a roof of Paraguayan cedar and hardwood beams fitted with wooden spikes rather than nails. The doors are hand-worked originals, while the baroque pulpit is laminated in gold. Its museum covers

Santa Fe

Top Sights
- Convento y Museo de San Francisco B5
- El Molino Fabrica Cultural C1
- Museo Etnográfico y Colonial Provincial B5

Sights
1. Casa de los Aldao B5
2. Cervecería Schneider D2
3. Iglesia de la Compañía B5
4. Templo de Santo Domingo B5

Activities, Courses & Tours
5. Costa Litoral C3

Sleeping
6. Hostel Santa Fe C1
7. Hotel Constituyentes C2
8. Hotel Emperatriz B2
9. Hotel Galeón C2

Eating
10. Diáafah Makánun B3
11. Merengo B5
12. Oh! Resto D1
13. Restaurante España B2

Drinking
14. Monte Libano Bar B2
15. Mula Pub A1
16. Patio de la Ceveza D2

Entertainment
- Casa España .... (see 8)

secular and religious topics from colonial and republican eras.

Museo Etnográfico y Colonial Provincial MUSEUM
(25 de Mayo 1470; admission by donation; ⌚9am-12:30pm & 3-7pm Tue-Sun) The Museo Etnográfico y Colonial Juan de Garay has a scale model of Santa Fe La Vieja, but the real showstopper is the *gaucho* 'camp chair', made entirely of cow bones and leather. Gruesome – but comfortable! There are also colonial artifacts, indigenous basketry, Spanish ceramics and a stuffed horse.

FREE **El Molino Fabrica Cultural** ARTS CENTER
(cnr Gálvez & Vittori; ⌚4-7pm Thu-Sun) Santa Fe is undergoing a small cultural revolution, thanks to the provincial government converting abandoned buildings into cultural spaces. This one, in an ex–flour mill, offers free paper, wood and textiles craft classes. You're welcome to drop in on a class or just see the students' work on display.

Cervecería Schneider BREWERY
(☎450-2237; www.cervezaschneider.com; Calchines 1401) Santa Fe has its own brewery, Cervecería Schneider, and brand of beer (called, uh, Santa Fe). Free guided tours of the ultramodern facility culminate in a tasting session, which consists of one glass per person, regardless of wheedling. Reservations are necessary and you must wear long pants and closed shoes.

Costa Litoral BOAT TOUR
(☎456-4381; www.costalitoral.net; Dique 1) Offers two-hour riverboat cruises (AR$46 per person).

Festivals & Events

Santa Fe's **beer festival** takes place on the last weekend in January and first weekend in February in the Parque Federal, about 1.5km north of town. Festivities include plenty of live music and a certain carbonated alcoholic beverage.

Sleeping

The surprisingly seedy area around the bus terminal is the budget hotel zone. It's not dangerous – just the town center for various unsavory transactions.

Hostel Santa Fe HOSTEL $
(☎455-4000; www.santafe-hostel.com; Gálvez 2173; dm/d AR$65/220; @) Santa Fe's most conveniently located hostel has spacious dorms, one reasonably priced double and an on-site travel agency.

Hotel Constituyentes HOTEL $
(☎452-1586; www.hotelconstituyentes.com.ar; San Luis 2862; s/d AR$180/250, without bathroom AR$100/160; @) A block from the bus terminal, this hotel has large carpeted rooms with TV. Get one at the back to avoid street noise.

Hotel Galeón HOTEL $$
(☎454-1788; www.hotelgaleon.com.ar; Belgrano 2759; s/d AR$320/405; ❄@🛜) Bright and unusual, all curved surfaces and weird angles, this cheery place is a breath of fresh air. There's a variety of room types, none of which is a conventional shape. The beds are seriously comfortable and the bathrooms pleasant. It's handy for the bus too.

Hotel Emperatriz HOTEL $
(☎453-0061; emperatrizhotel.wordpress.com; Irigoyen Freyre 2440; s/d AR$150/200; ❄🛜) The lobby, with its fabulous Moorish tiling, may raise hopes unfairly, but the rooms are OK.

Eating

On Belgrano, across from the bus terminal, several places serve Argentine staples such as empanadas, pizza and *parrillada* (mixed grill). The bus terminal sports a 24-hour snack bar serving huge portions of decent grub.

Oh! Resto INTERNATIONAL $$
(cnr Lavalle & Candiotti; mains AR$50-70; ⊙dinner Tue-Sun) Gourmet pizzas, some interesting meals and a whole heap of ambience are what's on offer at Santa Fe's hippest bar-restaurant.

Diáafah Makánun MIDDLE EASTERN $
(cnr Tucumán & 9 de Julio; dishes AR$8-20) Excellent value, supertasty Lebanese food. You'll probably want to order a few dishes to fill up, but you'll walk away happy.

El Quincho de Chiquito SEAFOOD $$
(cnr Brown & Obispo Vieytes; set menu AR$67) Think you like fish? Put that to the test at this local-favorite restaurant, 6km north of downtown, where a few fish-based starters are followed by seven different fish dishes. Still hungry? Unlikely, but you can reorder any of the dishes, as many times as you like. Take bus 16 on Pellegrini and tell the driver where you're going.

Merengo BAKERY $
(Av General López 2634; alfajores from AR$3) In 1851 Merengo stuck two biscuits together with *dulce de leche* (milk caramel) and invented the *alfajor*, now Argentina's favorite snack. They're still going strong: delicious.

Restaurante España ARGENTINE $$
(Av San Martín 2644; mains AR$40-80; 🛜) A huge menu covers the range of seafood, steaks, pasta, chicken and crepes, with a few Spanish dishes thrown in to justify the name. The wine list is a winner too.

Drinking & Entertainment

Santa Fe's rock-steady nightlife once centered on the intersection of Av San Martín and Santiago del Estero, an area known as La Recoleta, but is now starting to spread through town.

Patio de la Ceveza BREWERY
(cnr Calchines & Lavalle; ⊙2pm-1am) Summer nights, drop into this oversized beer garden, which has it's own *cerveducto*, piping in the good stuff direct from the brewery next door.

Mula Pub PUB
(Pellegrini 3090; ⊙10pm-late Thu-Sun) Downstairs is a laid-back bar; upstairs things heat up with a good dance floor playing hip hop and electronica.

Monte Libano Bar BAR
(cnr Crespo & 25 de Mayo; ⊙8pm-late Wed-Sun) Headquarters for Santa Fe's boho crowd, once it fills up, this corner bar is well worth a stop for a few drinks.

Casa España CULTURAL CENTER
(☎456-6538; www.ate.org.ar; Rivadavia 2871; ⊙4-9pm Wed-Sat) One of the best cultural centers in town, hosting live theater, exhibitions and concerts.

Information

There are several ATMs along the San Martín *peatonal* (pedestrian mall).

Municipal tourist office (☎457-4123; www.santafe-turistica.com.ar; Belgrano 2910; ⊙8am-9pm) In the bus terminal.

Post office (Av 27 de Febrero 2331)

Tourfe (Av San Martín 2500) Collects 3% commission on traveler's checks.

Getting There & Around

Aerolíneas Argentinas (☎0810-222-86527; 25 de Mayo 2287) flies regularly from Santa Fe to Buenos Aires and **Sol** (☎0810-444-4765; www.sol.com.ar) flies daily to Rosario.

The bus information office at the **bus terminal** (☎457-4124; www.terminalsantafe.com; Belgrano 2910) posts fares for all destinations.

Buses leave hourly for Paraná (AR$18, one hour). Other services include Rosario (AR$56, 2½ hours), Buenos Aires (AR$235, six hours), Corrientes (AR$302, nine hours) and Posadas (AR$552, 10 hours).

International services include Asunción, Paraguay (AR$370, 13 hours); and Montevideo, Uruguay (AR$428, 11 hours).

Paraná

☎0343 / POP 281,000

Although less famous than Santa Fe, Paraná is, in many ways, a more attractive place.

Built on the hilly banks of its namesake river, the historical center is largely intact, and the city boasts a couple of majestic plazas. As is the rule in this part of the world, fun-seekers hit the riverbanks at night to choose from an array of restaurants, clubs and bars.

Sights & Activities

From Plaza Primero de Mayo, the town center, San Martín is a *peatonal* for six blocks. Plaza Primero de Mayo has had an **Iglesia Catedral** since 1730, but the current building dates from 1885. When Paraná was capital of the confederation, the Senate deliberated at the **Colegio del Huerto**, at the corner of 9 de Julio and 25 de Mayo.

Museo Histórico de Entre Ríos Martín Leguizamón MUSEUM
(Plaza Alvear; voluntary contribution AR$1; ⊙8am-12:30pm & 3-8pm Tue-Fri, 9am-noon Sat) At the west end of the San Martín *peatonal,* this museum flaunts provincial pride, as knowledgeable guides go to rhetorical extremes extolling the role of local *caudillos* (local strongmen) in Argentine history.

Museo de Bellas Artes Pedro E Martínez GALLERY
(voluntary contribution AR$1.; ⊙9am-noon & 4-9pm Mon-Fri, 10:30am-12:30pm & 5:30-8pm Sat, 10:30am-12:30pm Sun) Adjacent to Museo Histórico de Entre Ríos Martín Leguizamón, this subterranean gallery displays works by provincial artists.

Museo de la Ciudad MUSEUM
(Parque Urquiza; ⊙8am-noon & 4-8pm Mon-Fri) The modern Museo de la Ciudad focuses on Paraná's urban past and surroundings. Winter opening hours are slightly shorter.

Costanera 241 BOAT TOUR
(☎423-4385; www.costanera241.com.ar; Buenos Aires 212) Offers river tours, fishing trips and kayak safaris.

Paraná en Kayak KAYAKING
(☎422-7143; www.paranaenkayak.com.ar) Offers easy kayak trips on the river as well as longer routes.

Medano's Bikes BICYCLE RENTAL
(☎424-0613; www.medanosbikes.com.ar) Rents bikes and offers bike tours of the city.

Sleeping

Paraná Hostel HOSTEL $
(☎422-8233; www.paranahostel.com.ar; Pazos 159; dm/d AR$70/155; @📶) In a new and improved location, Paraná's best hostel is all class – central, clean, spacious and well equipped.

Paraná Hotel Plaza Jardín HOTEL $
(☎423-1700; www.hotelesparana.com.ar; Av 9 de Julio 60; s/d from AR$199/255; ❄@📶) Set in a lovely old colonial building, this hotel has a peaceful patio that's great for a break from the midday heat. Prices drop significantly outside of summer.

Eating

Bugatti INTERNATIONAL $
(☎15-504-0770; Portside; mains AR$35-60) No surprises on the menu here – meat, chicken, pasta and fish – but the elegance of the dining room in this renovated post office makes the trip worthwhile. Even if you're not hungry, the balcony bar is a great place to take a breather.

El Viejo Marino II SEAFOOD $$
(Av Laurencina 341; mains AR$50-110) Spend five minutes in this town and people will be telling you that you have to try the fish. Stay another couple of minutes and they'll be telling you to check this place out. They're right, too – the atmosphere is loud and fun, the servings huge, and the specials, such as *surubí milanesa* (river fish fried in breadcrumbs, AR$32), keep the locals coming back.

Drinking & Entertainment

Weekends are the real party nights in Paraná, and most of the action centers on the eastern end of the riverfront, by the port. Here, **Kravitz** (Figueroa s/n; ⊙10pm-late Fri & Sat) plays the usual mix of mainstream *marcha* (Argentine dance music), house and salsa. **Anderson** (Lineal 334; ⊙Thu-Sat) is a spot for a drink or a dance, but only if you're 25 or over. There are many other bars and discos in the area.

Information

There are several ATMs along the San Martín *peatonal*.

Municipal tourist office (☎0800-555-9575, 423-0183; Buenos Aires 132; ⏲8am-6pm) Paraná's municipal tourist office has branches at the bus terminal and at the Oficina Parque on the riverfront. The free-call number is handy if you find yourself in need of on-the-spot tourist information.

Post office (cnr 25 de Mayo & Monte Caseros)

Provincial tourist office (☎422-3384; Laprida 5; ⏲8am-9pm Mon-Sat, 9am-6pm Sun)

Getting There & Around

The **bus terminal** (☎422-1282) is on Ramírez between Posadas and Moreno. Buses leave hourly for Santa Fe (AR$18, one hour). Other services and fares closely resemble those to and from Santa Fe. Bus 1 goes from the bus terminal past the center to the riverside (AR$1.80).

Gualeguaychú

☎03446 / POP 85,500

Gualeguaychú is a summertime river resort for families. As such, you're likely to see several men who have taken their tops off who really shouldn't have. It's also the site for some of the country's most outrageous Carnaval celebrations in February, featuring young people who have taken their tops off.

Sights & Activities

Corsódromo STADIUM
(Blvd Irazusta) Alongside the station, the Corsódromo is the main site for Gualeguaychú's lively Carnaval.

Termas de Gualeguaychú HEATH & FITNESS
(☎49-9167; www.gualeguaychutermal.com.ar; RP 42, Km 2.5; admission AR$40; ⏲8am-midnight) Cross the river bridge and follow signs 2km for the Termas de Gualeguaychú, a popular complex of shallow thermal pools at various temperatures.

Sleeping & Eating

Confiterías and snack bars line Av 25 de Mayo, while the *costanera* has shoulder-to-shoulder *parrillas* between Bolívar and Concordia.

Hostel Gualeguaychú HOSTEL $
(☎42-4371; www.hostelgualeguaychu.com.ar; Méndez 290; dm incl breakfast AR$34-98; @☎) The best hostel in town by a long, long margin. If this one fills up, it has another couple close by. Prices vary according to time of year; check the website for details.

Aguay Hotel HOTEL $$
(☎42-2099; www.hotelaguay.com.ar; Av Costanera 130; s/d AR$370/550; ❄@☒) The town's best-looking (and best-located) hotel drops its rates considerably in the low season. Check out the fantastic river views from the 3rd-floor cafe-bar.

Hotel Brutti HOTEL $
(☎42-6048; Bolívar 591; s/d AR$80/160; ☎) One of the cheaper and more reliable choices in town. The rooms facing the front are lighter, but there's a bit of morning noise from the market opposite.

Campo Alto PARILLA $$
(cnr Costanera Nte & Concordia; mains AR$50-100; ⏲lunch & dinner) With its tree-shaded terrace and occasional live music, this casual restaurant has a better atmosphere than most.

Samba INTERNATIONAL $
(cnr Costanera & Bolívar; mains AR$35-60; ⏲lunch & dinner Tue-Sun) Right down on the riverfront with an excellent raised outdoor deck. Tends to open only in summer.

Information

The **tourist office** (☎42-2900) is on the Plazoleta de los Artesanos. There's another at the bus terminal. Several banks have ATMs.

Getting There & Around

The **bus terminal** (☎44-0688; cnr Blvd Jurado & Artigas) is 1km southwest of downtown. Departures include Buenos Aires (AR$70, three hours), Paraná (AR$90, four hours) and Corrientes (AR$280, 10 hours). There's one bus a day to Fray Bentos, Uruguay (AR$35, one hour).

Bicitour (☎42-7810; Caballería 871) rents bikes for AR$5/40 per hour/day.

Yapeyú

☎03772 / POP 2400

Mellow little Yapeyú lies 72km north of Paso de los Libres and has exactly two attractions: the birthplace of national hero General José de San Martín and some remnants from its Jesuit mission past. It once had a population of 8000 Guaraní, who tended up to 80,000 cattle. After the Jesuits' expulsion, the Gua-raní dispersed and the mission fell into ruins. Tiny Yapeyú is trying its hardest. What few sights exist are well signposted in Spanish, English, Portuguese and Guaraní.

The **Museo de Cultura Jesuítica**, consisting of several modern kiosks on the foundations of mission buildings, has a sundial, a few other mission relics and interesting photographs.

It's a measure of the esteem that Argentines hold for the Liberator that they have built a building to protect the **Casa de San Martín**, the house where José de San Martín was born, even though it's mostly been eroded to its foundations.

Near the river, **Camping Paraíso** (☎49-3056; www.paraisoyapeyu.com.ar; cnr Paso de los Patos & San Martín; campsites per person AR$20, bungalows for 2/4 people AR$200/340) has good hot showers for campers and some excellent bungalows. Insects can be abundant, and low-lying sites can flood in heavy rain. **Hotel San Martín** (☎03772-49-3120; Sargento Cabral 712; s/d AR$140/200; ❄) has cheerful rooms that face an inner courtyard.

Comedor El Paraíso (Matorras s/n; mains AR$30-50; ⏲breakfast, lunch & dinner) serves passable meals and has good river views. It's next to the Casa de San Martín.

Buses stop three times daily at the small **bus terminal** (cnr Av del Libertador & Chacabuco), en route between Paso de los Libres and Posadas.

Reserva Provincial Esteros del Iberá

Esteros del Iberá is a wildlife cornucopia comparable to Brazil's Pantanal do Mato Grosso. Aquatic plants and grasses, including 'floating islands,' dominate this wetlands wilderness covering 13,000 sq km. The most notable wildlife species are reptiles such as the caiman and anaconda, mammals such as the maned wolf, howler monkey, neotropical otter, pampas and swamp deer, and capybara, and more than 350 bird species.

Bird-watchers and nature nuts from all over the world converge on the village of Colonia Pellegrini, 120km northeast of Mercedes, to take advantage of the ease of access to the park (Colonia Pellegrini lies within the park's boundaries). It's a charming enough place in its own right: dirt roads, little traffic and plenty of trees. There is a visitors center across the causeway from Colonia Pellegrini with information on the reserve and a couple of short self-guided walking trails. The **tourist office** (info.turismo@ibera.gov.ar; ⏲8am-7pm) at the entrance to the village is helpful and also rents bikes for AR$25/90 per hour/day. Two-hour **launch tours** (AR$100-120) are good value. Horse tours (AR$90 per hour) are pleasant, but you'll see more wildlife from the boat.

Many hotel operators in Mercedes (the gateway town) will try to railroad you into buying a package tour with tales of overbooking, closed hotels etc. If you want to book ahead and go all-inclusive, fine, but there's really no need to panic – there are way more beds available than there will ever be tourists and it's easy (and much cheaper) to organize your room, food and tours on the spot. The tourist office in Colonia Pellegrini has a complete list of accommodations and eateries in town, and www.camaraturismoibera.com is an excellent source of information.

Camping is possible at the **municipal campground** (☎03773-15-62-9656; www.ibera.gov.ar; Mbiguá s/n; per person 1st/subsequent days AR$50/40, vehicle AR$20) in Colonia Pellegrini, which has excellent, grassy waterfront sites.

A number of *hospedajes* (basic hotels) offer rooms with private bathroom for around AR$60 per person, the best of which is probably **Posada de la Luna** (☎03773-15-628823; cnr Capivára & Ysypá; s/d AR$60/100), down by the waterfront.

On the lake near the causeway, **Irupé Lodge** (☎0376-443-8312; www.ibera-argentina.com; Yacaré s/n; s/d from AR$350/520; ❄📶🏊) has a great rustic feel, a decent swimming pool and good views across the water.

Buses run from Corrientes and Paso de los Libres to Mercedes, where *combis* (small buses) to Colonia Pellegrini (AR$35, four hours) leave at noon Monday to Friday and 9:30am Saturday, and return to Mercedes at 5am Monday to Saturday. Heading north is complicated. There may be a weekly bus (ask at the tourist office); otherwise, try to get a group together to pay for a private transfer to Virasoro (AR$650, three hours) for onward buses to Posadas.

Corrientes

☎03783 / POP 368,400

It's hard to love Corrientes, but you're welcome to try. It's a big, serious city with a couple of decent museums and a reputation for being very budget-unfriendly. Once the sun starts setting, a walk along the riverfront might make you feel a bit happier about being here. The once-moribund **Carnaval Correntino** (www.carnavalescorrentinos.com) has experienced a revival and now attracts crowds of up to 80,000.

GETTING TO BRAZIL

The small, largely uninteresting town of **Paso de los Libres** is the gateway to the Brazilian town of Uruguaiana. The border crossing is marked by a bridge about 10 blocks southwest of central Plaza Independencia. Taxis charge about AR$60 to take you through to Uruguaiana. The border is open 24 hours. Once in Brazil, the nearest town to the border we recommend is **Porto Alegre**.

Between Paso's bus terminal and the center are some very dodgy neighborhoods – it's well worth investing in the AR$2.25/20 bus/taxi fare to get you through.

Across from the bus terminal, **Hotel Capri** (☎03722-42-1260; Llanes s/n; s/d AR$80/130) is the place to be if you need a lie-down between buses. More central and much more comfortable is **Hotel Las Vegas** (☎03722-42-3490; Sarmiento 554; s/d AR$160/250; ❄📶). There are resto-bars all along Colón between Mitre and Sitja Nia. The best restaurant in town is **El Nuevo Mesón** (Colón 587; mains AR$30-50).

Moving on from Paso de los Libres, there are regular buses to Mercedes (AR$25, two hours), Buenos Aires (AR$356, nine hours), Corrientes (AR$120, five hours), Santa Fe (AR$285, eight hours) and many other destinations.

Sights

The commercial center of Corrientes is the Junín *peatonal,* between Salta and Catamarca, but the most attractive area is the shady riverside along Av Costanera General San Martín. The east side of San Juan, between Plácido Martínez and Quintana, is a shady, attractive area. The **Monumento a la Gloria** there honors the Italian community; a series of striking **murals** chronicles local history since colonial times.

FREE Museo de Bellas Artes Dr Juan Ramón Vidal GALLERY
(www.culturacorrientes.gov.ar; San Juan 634; ⏲9am-1pm & 4-8pm) The Museo de Bellas Artes Dr Juan Ramón Vidal emphasizes sculpture and oil paintings from local artists and hosts the occasional international exhibition.

FREE Museo de Artesanías Tradicionales Folclóricas MUSEUM
(Quintana 905; ⏲8am-9pm Mon-Sat) This intriguing museum offers a couple of small displays of fine traditional *artesanía* (handicrafts) as well as a good shop selling craft products. The highlight, though, is watching students being taught to work leather, silver, bone and wood by master craftspeople.

Sleeping

Corrientes is finally catching on to the hostelling scene, and actually features one of the best in the country. The hotel scene is still rather dispiriting – what there is isn't cheap, and what's relatively cheap isn't very good. Cheaper, better hotels are on offer across the river in Resistencia. During Carnaval, the tourist office maintains a list of *casas de familia* (modest family accommodations) offering rooms.

TOP CHOICE Bienvenida Golondrina HOSTEL $
(☎443-5316; www.bienvenidagolondrina.com; La Rioja 455; dm/s/d AR$200/280/85; ❄@📶) Occupying a marvelous centenarian building, with high ceilings, stained glass and artistic flourishes, this hostel makes a great base a few steps from the *costanera.* Dorms are spacious, facilities are great and there are free bikes for guests.

Corrientes Plaza Hotel HOTEL $
(☎446-6500; www.hotel-corrientes.com.ar; Junín 1549; s/d AR$250/310; ❄@📶🏊) A good deal on the square in the heart of modern Corrientes, the Plaza has spacious, faultless modern rooms with LCD television and most with minibar. The staff is friendly and there's a good breakfast spread.

Hotel Dora HOTEL $
(☎42-1053; hoteldora@hotmail.com; España 1050; r AR$180; ❄) Vaguely acceptable, with somewhat clean rooms in a good location.

Eating & Drinking

Be on the lookout for *chipas* (crunchy, cheesy scones) and *sopa paraguaya* (a flour-based, quichelike pie). They occasionally turn up on restaurant menus, but your best bet are the street vendors around the bus terminal.

The main nightlife area is around the intersection of Junín and Buenos Aires, where several bars and clubs get going on weekends. The *costanera* west of the bridge also sees some action.

TOP CHOICE **Enófilos** ARGENTINE $$
(☎443-9271; Junín 1260; mains AR$55-80; ⏰lunch & dinner Mon-Sat; 📶) Some call this excellent restaurant Corrientes' one saving grace. It offers carefully prepared food and a great wine cellar. Weekday set lunches (AR$45) are a bargain.

☆ Entertainment

Parrilla Puente Pexoa TRADITIONAL MUSIC
(☎445-1687; RN 12 at Virgen de Itatí roundabout; ⏰from 8:30pm Fri & Sat) This relaxed restaurant is a great place to check out *chamamé,* which is a sort of Guaraní version of polka dancing. Sound deadly? It actually gets very rowdy and is sometimes hilarious. People show up in full *gaucho* regalia, and up to four bands play each night. From downtown, take bus 102 marked '17 de Agosto' 7km out of town to the Virgen de Itatí roundabout. It's just off the roundabout; the driver will point it out. A taxi back costs around AR$35.

ℹ Information

There are several banks with ATMs around 9 de Julio.

Cambio El Dorado (9 de Julio 1341) Changes cash and traveler's checks.

Post office (cnr San Juan & San Martín)

Provincial tourist office (☎442-7200; www.turismocorrientes.gov.ar; 25 de Mayo 1330; ⏰8am-2pm, 3-9pm) The best tourist office in town.

ℹ Getting There & Around

Aerolíneas Argentinas (☎442-3918; Junín 1301) flies daily to Buenos Aires from Corrientes. Local bus 105 (AR$2) goes to the **airport** (☎445-8358; RN 12), about 15km east of town. A *remise* should cost around AR$40.

Frequent buses (AR$3) and shared taxis (AR$7) to Resistencia leave from the **local bus terminal** (cnr Av Costanera General San Martín & La Rioja). Shared taxis also leave from the corner of Santa Fe and 3 de Abril. The **long-distance bus terminal** (☎441-4839; Av Maipú 2400) has departures for Paso de los Libres (AR$120, five hours) via Mercedes (AR$78, 3½ hours) for access to Esteros del Iberá; Posadas (AR$150, four hours); Formosa (AR$122, three hours); Puerto Iguazú (AR$334, nine hours); Buenos Aires (AR$593, 11 hours); and Asunción, Paraguay (AR$120, six hours).

Bus 106 runs between San Lorenzo downtown and the bus terminal.

Resistencia

☎03722 / POP 404,400

Sculpture lovers wallow like pigs in mud in Resistencia. A joint project between the local council and various arts organizations has led to the placement of more than 500 sculptures in the city streets and parks, free for everyone to see. Delightful Plaza 25 de Mayo, a riot of tall palms and comical *palo borracho* trees, marks the city center.

👁 Sights

There's insufficient space here to detail the number of **sculptures** in city parks and on the sidewalks, but the tourist office distributes a map with their locations that makes a good introduction to the city. The best starting point is the **Museo de Escultura** (Parque 2 de Febrero; ⏰8am-noon & 3-8pm Mon-Sat), an open-air workshop on the north side of Parque 2 de Febrero. Several of the most impressive pieces are on display here, and this is where, during the **Bienal de Escultura** (www.bienaldelchaco.com), held on the third week of July in even years, you can catch sculptors at work.

El Fogón de los Arrieros ARTS CENTER, MUSEUM
(Brown 350; admission AR$5; ⏰museum 8am-noon, 3:30-7:30pm Mon-Fri, 8am-1pm Sat) El Fogón de los Arrieros is the driving force behind the city's progressive displays of public art and is famous for its eclectic assemblage of art objects from around the Chaco province, Argentina and the world.

FREE **Museo del Hombre Chaqueño** MUSEUM
(JB Justo 280; ⏰10am-6pm Mon-Fri, 3-6pm Sat) Focuses on the colonization of the Chaco and has exhibits and information on the Guaraní, Mocoví, Komlek and Mataco provincial indigenous cultures.

🛏 Sleeping

Residencial Bariloche HOTEL $
(☎442-1412; Obligado 239; s/d AR$100/150; ❄📶) A good deal: spacious, clean and quiet rooms with cable TV. Pay an extra AR$10 for air-con or just get blown away by the industrial-sized room fans.

Hotel Colón HOTEL $$
(442-2277; www.colonhotelyapart.com; Santa María de Oro 143; s/d AR$230/340;) A slick lobby leads onto large, unrenovated rooms a half block from the main plaza.

Hotel Alfil HOTEL $
(442-0882; Santa María de Oro 495; s/d AR$90/130;) A few blocks south of the plaza, the old-fashioned Alfil is a reasonable budget choice. The interior rooms are dark but worthwhile if the significant street noise in the exterior rooms will bother you. Air-con is AR$10 extra, but overall a decent deal despite the lack of breakfast.

Hotel Luxor HOTEL $
(444-7252; camorsluxor@hotmail.com; Remedios de Escalada 19; s/d AR$85/130;) About as basic as you want to get, but you can't argue with the price. Breakfast, TV and air-con all cost extra.

Camping Parque 2 de Febrero CAMPGROUND $
(445-8366; Avalos 1100; campsites per person AR$20) Has excellent facilities.

Eating

Several attractive *confiterías* and ice-cream parlors have rejuvenated the area north and northwest of Plaza 25 de Mayo.

Fenix Bar ARGENTINE $
(Don Bosco 133; meals AR$30-50) The menu includes the usual gamut of pizza, meats and pastas, but the food is well presented, the decor atmospheric and the wine selection excellent.

El Viejo Café ARGENTINE $
(Pellegrini 109; mains AR$30-50; 7am-late Sun-Thu, 1pm-late Fri & Sat) Not a hugely imaginative menu, but has a wonderful, rustic atmosphere and is popular with the locals Thursday to Saturday for the live jazz shows.

La Bianca ARGENTINE $
(Colón 102; dishes AR$30-55; lunch & dinner Wed-Mon) Busy and bustling, this long-time local split-level favorite keeps 'em coming for its well-priced pasta, pizza and soufflés. There's also meat and salad dishes in generous quantities. A cheap and cheerful option.

Pizza Party PIZZERIA $
(cnr Obligado & San Martín; pizzas from AR$40) Despite the name, this is the most popular pizzeria in town, with excellent thin-crust pies and shady courtyard seating.

Drinking & Entertainment

Weather permitting, there are often free folk concerts in the Plaza 25 de Mayo on Sunday nights.

Zingara BAR
(Güemes; 6pm-late Wed-Sat) This hip, minimally decorated bar wouldn't be out of place somewhere like Milan or Paris. Cocktails feature heavily on the drinks menu.

Centro Cultural Guido Mirada PERFORMING ARTS
(442-5421; Colón 146; open for performances) The Centro Cultural Guido Mirada shows art-house films and hosts live theater and dance performances.

Information

There are ATMs near Plaza 25 de Mayo.

Cambio El Dorado (Paz 36; 9am-6pm Mon-Fri, to 1pm Sat) Changes traveler's checks at reasonable rates.

Post office (cnr Sarmiento & Yrigoyen; 9am-6pm Mon-Fri) Faces the plaza.

Tourist kiosk (445-8289; Plaza 25 de Mayo; 9am-6pm) About 450m away from the tourist office. Handy.

Tourist office (442-3547; Santa Fe 178; 9am-6pm) Well stocked.

Getting There & Around

Aerolíneas Argentinas (444-5551; JB Justo 184) has daily flights to/from Resistencia to Buenos Aires and **Aero Chaco** (0810-444-2376; www.aerochaco.com.ar; Av Sarmiento 715) flies to Cordoba.

Bus

The **bus terminal** (446-1098; cnr MacLean & Islas Malvinas) has an urban service (marked 'Chaco-Corrientes') between Resistencia and Corrientes for AR$3. You can catch it in front of the post office on Plaza 25 de Mayo.

You can save yourself a trip out to the bus terminal by buying tickets in advance at the **telecentro** (cnr Brown & López y Planes).

Buses 3 and 10 run between the bus terminal and Plaza 25 de Mayo (AR$2.70).

BUSES FROM RESISTENCIA

La Estrella buses service Capitán Solari, near Parque Nacional Chaco, four times daily (AR$32, 2½ hours). Other destinations include the following:

DESTINATION	COST (AR$)	DURATION (HR)
Asunción (Paraguay)	110	5
Buenos Aires	590	13
Córdoba	414	12
Formosa	111	2½
Posadas	155	5
Puerto Iguazú	344	10
Rosario	390	9
Santa Fe	291	7
Salta	441	10

Formosa

03717 / POP 246,700

Way out here on the Río Paraguay, this town has a much more Paraguayan feel than others in the region. The riverfront has been tastefully restored and makes for an excellent place to go for a wander once the sun starts to go down.

Hotel del Litoral (442-3893; Rivadavia 1102; s/d AR$180/220; ❄) has tidy little rooms a few blocks from both the main drag and the waterfront. Even in winter months you might be thankful for the air-con.

One bus a day leaves Formosa's terminal at 10am for Clorinda, Laguna Naick-Neck and Laguna Blanca (Parque Nacional Río Pilcomayo). There are regular services to Resistencia (AR$90), Buenos Aires (AR$698) and other destinations.

Posadas

03752 / POP 344,800

If you're heading north, now's about the time that things start to feel very tropical, and the jungle begins to creep into the edges of the picture. Posadas is mainly interesting as an access point, both to Paraguay and the Jesuit mission sites north of here, but it's a cool little city in its own right, with some sweet plazas and a well-developed eating, drinking and partying scene down on the waterfront.

GETTING TO PARAGUAY

Buses from Posadas to Encarnación (AR$10) leave every 20 minutes from the south side of plaza San Martín, passing through downtown before crossing the bridge (get off for immigration procedures and hang on to your ticket; you'll be able to catch another bus continuing in the same direction).

Buses also go from Puerto Iguazú to Ciudad del Este (AR$10).

Both borders are open 24 hours. Most non-EU citizens require a visa to enter Paraguay.

Sights & Activities

Museo de Ciencias Naturales e Historia MUSEUM

(San Luis 384; admission AR$7; 9am-1pm & 3-6pm Mon-Fri, 9am-1pm Sat) The natural history section of the Museo de Ciencias Naturales e Historia focuses on fauna and the geology and mineralogy of the province. The museum also has an excellent serpentarium, an aviary, an aquarium, and a historical section that stresses prehistory, the Jesuit missions and modern colonization.

FREE **Fundación Artesanías Misioneras** GALLERY

(cnr Alvarez & Arrechea; 9am-12:30pm & 5-8pm Mon-Sat) Guaraní culture is strong in this part of Argentina, and you'll see Guaraní artists selling their wares throughout the center. Particularly fine pieces are displayed and sold here.

Costanera WATERFRONT

In the cool of the afternoon, the *costanera* comes alive. It's a favorite spot for everyone from joggers, cyclists, dog walkers, maté sippers, hot-dog vendors to young couples staring wistfully at the lights of Paraguay across the water.

Sleeping

Posadeña Linda HOSTEL $

(443-9238; posadenalindahostel@hotmail.com; Bolívar 1439; dm/d AR$75/AR$200; @ 🛜 ≋) Run with a caring attitude, this excellent, narrow hostel a short walk from the square offers a genuine welcome, comfortable bunks and a patio with tiny plunge pool.

City Hotel HOTEL $

(443-9401; www.misionescityhotel.com.ar; Colón 1754; s/d AR$160/208; ❄ @ 🛜) A surprisingly good deal for the smack-on-the-plaza location. Rooms are nothing special, but comfortable enough.

Posadas Hotel HOTEL $$
(☎444-0888; www.hotelposadas.com.ar; Bolívar 1949; s/d from AR$345/390; ❄@☕) With by far the best-looking interiors of any hotel in town, the Posadas' rooms are spacious, comfortable and well decorated.

Eating & Drinking

For cheap eats with few surprises, head for the semipedestrian intersection of Bolívar and San Lorenzo, where there's a range of pizza and pasta joints with sidewalk seating.

La Italia ITALIAN $
(Bolivar 1738; mains AR$30-50; ⊙lunch & dinner) A relaxed atmosphere and wide menu covering pretty much every corner of pizza, pasta, steak and seafood territory makes this a local favorite.

Café Vitrage CAFE $
(cnr Bolívar & Colón; mains AR$25-50) With its brass fittings and dark wood features, the Vitrage oozes style. Mostly a bar-cafe, it can also whip up a juicy steak any time of the day or night.

El Rayo CAFETERIA $
(Bolívar 2089; light meals AR$20-35) No-frills and effective, this joint is thronged at lunchtime for its delicious empanadas, *lomitos* (steak sandwiches) and good-value pizza. Service comes with a smile too. Thumbs up.

El Viejo Pinar ARGENTINE $
(San Lorenzo 1782; mains AR$30-50; ⊙lunch & dinner) Good-value set meals, and excellent people-watching opportunities from the 2nd-floor balcony.

Bohemia Karaoke Pub BAR
(San Lorenzo 1551; ⊙9pm-late Wed-Sat) Offers pretty much what the name says.

Shopping

Mercado La Placita MARKET
(cnr Sarmiento & Av Roque Sánez Peña) There's something for everyone at the indoor Mercado La Placita, from counterfeit sneakers to Paraguayan handicrafts and homemade cigars.

Information

There are several downtown ATMs.

Cambios Mazza (Bolívar; ⊙9am-6pm Mon-Fri, to 1pm Sat) Changes traveler's checks.

Post office (cnr Bolívar & Ayacucho; ⊙9am-6pm Mon-Fri)

Tourist office (☎444-7539; www.turismo.misiones.gov.ar; Colón 1985; ⊙8am-8pm Mon-Fri, 8am-noon & 4-8pm Sat & Sun) Has well-informed staff. There's another office at the bus terminal, open the same hours.

Getting There & Around

Bus 28 from San Lorenzo between La Rioja and Entre Ríos goes to the airport, 12km southwest of town, and **Aerolíneas Argentinas** (☎442-2036; Ayacucho 1724) runs its own shuttle service. A *remise* costs about AR$40.

The bus terminal is almost 6km from the downtown area. Buses 8, 15 and 24 travel between the two (AR$1.70). A taxi costs about AR$25. Destinations include Corrientes (AR$145, four hours), Resistencia (AR$155, five hours), Puerto Iguazú (AR$98, 5½ hours) and Buenos Aires (AR$546, 13 hours). Buses to San Ignacio Miní (AR$20, one hour) leave frequently.

Trains run on Wednesdays and Saturdays from nearby Garupá to Buenos Aires (AR$130 to AR$240, 24 hours). Shuttle services leave from Posadas' **railway station** (☎443-6076; www.trenesdellitoral.com.ar; cnr Madariaga & Estación) about 15 minutes before departures.

San Ignacio Miní

☎03752 / POP 8420

A mellow little town between Posadas and Puerto Iguazú, San Ignacio attracts most visitors for the large, well-preserved ruins of the Jesuit mission that give the town its name. If you're staying here and have some time to kill, it's well worth checking out the Casa de Quiroga too. If you're just passing through, you can leave your bags in the ticket office at the bus terminal while you check out the ruins.

Sights

Mission of San Ignacio Miní RUIN
(admission AR$60; ⊙7am-6pm) At its peak, in 1733, the mission of San Ignacio Miní had an indigenous population of nearly 4500. The enormous red-sandstone church, embellished with bas-relief sculptures, was designed in 'Guaraní baroque' style (a mixture of Spanish baroque style and indigenous themes). Adjacent to the tile-roofed church were the cemetery and cloisters; the same complex held classrooms, a kitchen, a prison and workshops. On all sides of the Plaza de Armas were the living quarters. There is a sound and light show (AR$60) at 7pm nightly and a set of fairly bizarre museum exhibits as you enter. Note

that you must present your passport to enter here.

Casa de Quiroga NOTABLE BUILDING
(Quiroga s/n; admission AR$15; ⏲9am-5pm) Casa de Quiroga is at the southern end of town, offering grand views of the Río Paraná. A small museum contains photos and some of the famous Uruguayan writer's possessions and first editions.

Sleeping & Eating

Rivadavia between the bus stop and the ruins is lined with small restaurants serving *milanesas* (breaded steaks), pizzas etc.

Adventure Hostel HOSTEL $
(☎447-0955; www.sihostel.com; Independencia 469; dm AR$56-63, d AR$200; ❄@🛜≋) A beautifully set up hostel with air-con dorms, a great pool area, a huge kitchen and plenty of hammock action. More like this, please.

Hotel La Toscana HOTEL $
(☎447-0777; www.hotellatoscana.com.ar; cnr H Irigoyen & Uruguay; s/d AR$120/180; ❄🛜≋) In a quiet location a couple of blocks back from the highway, this welcoming Italian-run place offers cool, spacious rooms surrounding a great pool, deck and garden area.

La Aldea ARGENTINE $
(cnr Rivadavia & Morena; mains AR$30-50, set meals AR$35; ⏲breakfast, lunch & dinner) The menu at La Aldea holds few surprises, but it has a lovely rear deck and is one of the only late-night eating options in town.

Getting There & Away

The new **bus terminal** (RN 12) is out on the highway, about a 1km walk to the ruins. There are regular services between Posadas (AR$20, one hour) and Puerto Iguazú (AR$80, 4 to 6 hours).

Puerto Iguazú

☎03757 / POP 34,000

With a world-class attraction just down the road, Puerto Iguazú should feel overrun by tourists, but it absorbs the crowds well and manages to retain some of its relaxed, small-town atmosphere. The falls are definitely the drawcard here: you'll meet your share of people who have come straight from Buenos Aires, and are heading straight back again. There's a steady backpacker population, and a lively hostel and restaurant scene.

Sights

Güirá Oga ZOO
(www.guiraoga.com.ar; RN 12, Km 5; admission AR$40; ⏲9am-6pm, last entry 4:30pm) Five kilometers out of town on the way to the national park, this is an animal hospital and center for rehabilitation of injured wildlife. It also carries out valuable research into the Iguazú forest environment and has a breeding program for endangered species. You get walked around the park by one of the biologists and get to meet the creatures. The visit takes about 80 minutes.

La Casa Ecológica de Botellas NOTABLE BUILDING
(http://lacasadebotellas.googlepages.com; RN 12, Km 5; admission AR$20; ⏲8:30am-7pm) About 200m down a side road just before Güirá Oga, this fascinating place is well worth a visit. The owners have taken used packaging materials – plastic bottles, juice cartons and the like – to build not only an impressive house, but furnishings and a bunch of original handicrafts that make unusual gifts. The guided visit will talk you through their techniques.

Sleeping

Marco Polo Inn HOSTEL $
(☎42-5559; www.marcopoloinniguazu.com; Av Córdoba 158; dm/d AR$90/340; ❄@🛜≋) Huge complex with a good pool and bar. Book ahead.

Timbó Posada HOSTEL $$
(☎42-2698; www.timboiguazu.com.ar; Av Misiones 147; dm AR$52, d from AR$248; ❄@🛜≋) A cute little downtown hostel. The central location, lush pool area and spacious dorms make it a standout.

Hostel Guembe HOSTEL $
(☎42-1035; www.elguembehostelhouse.com.ar; Av Guaraní s/n; dm AR$70, r without bathroom AR$290; ❄@🛜) Mellower than most hostels in town, with OK dorms and a pretty garden area.

Residencial Lola GUESTHOUSE $
(☎42-3954; residenciallola@hotmail.com; Av Córdoba 255; s/d AR$120/200; @🛜) No-frills budget rooms that may well be the cheapest in town.

Puerto Iguazú

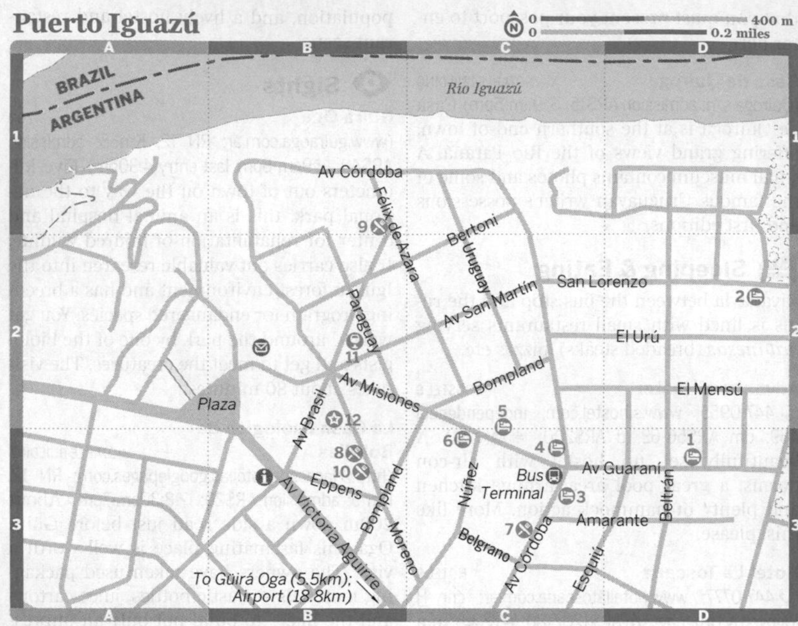

Puerto Iguazú

Sleeping

1 Hostel Guembe.......D3
2 Jasy Hotel.......D2
3 Marco Polo Inn.......C3
4 Residencial Lola.......C3
5 Residencial Los Ríos.......C2
6 Timbó Posada.......C3

Eating

7 Color.......C3
8 El Andariego.......B3
9 La Feirinha.......B1
10 La Misionera.......B3

Drinking

11 Cuba Libre.......B2

Entertainment

12 La Barranca.......B2

Jasy Hotel HOTEL $$
(☎42-4337; www.jasyhotel.com; San Lorenzo 154; r AR$400; ❄📶🏊) Excellent rooms for two to five people a short walk from the bus terminal. The leafy setting and excellent pool/deck area make up for the removed location.

Residencial Los Ríos HOTEL $
(☎42-5465; Av Misiones 70; s/d AR$220/280; ❄📶) Big modern rooms by the bus terminal. Prices drop in the low season, making this a good budget deal.

Camping Costa Ramón CAMPGROUND $
(☎42-1358; www.campingcostaramon.blogspot.com; Irupé & Rosa Blanca; campsites per person AR$50; 📶🏊) Excellent services down by the riverside out on the edge of town.

Eating

El Andariego PARRILLA $
(Moreno 229; mains AR$40-70) This no-frills neighborhood *parrilla* does good, cheap meat and pasta dishes.

La Feirinha MARKET $
(cnr Brasil & Azara; mains AR$25-60; ⊙dinner) A pleasingly downbeat selection of food stalls, outdoor eateries, wine shops and delicatessens. Live music weekend nights.

Color PARRILLA, PIZZERIA $$
(☎42-0206; www.parrillapizzacolor.com; Av Córdoba 135; mains AR$35-78) This remodeled pizza 'n' *parrilla* packs them into its tightly spaced tables, but the prices are fair for this strip, and the meat comes out redolent of wood smoke; try the *picaña*, a tender rump cut.

La Misionera BAKERY $
(P Moreno 207; empanadas AR$4; ⏲10am-midnight) Decent pizza and excellent empanadas with a variety of fillings from this well-regarded central bakery.

Drinking & Entertainment

Going out in Puerto Iguazú is so much fun that even Brazilians come here to dance. Imagine that. Most of the action revolves around the six-way intersection of Avs Brazil and San Martín. Keep an eye out for **Cuba Libre** (cnr Av Brasil & Paraguay), which has long happy hours and occasional live music, and **La Barranca** (Moreno s/n), for all your megadisco requirements.

Information

Brazilian Consulate (☎42-0192; Córdoba 264) Arranges visas in half a day, much better than the week it takes their Buenos Aires counterparts to do the same job.

Post office (Av San Martín 780)

Tourist office (☎42-0800; Av Victoria Aguirre 311; ⏲8am-8pm) This is the main office. There's also a tourist kiosk downstairs at the bus terminal.

Getting There & Around

AIR Aerolíneas Argentinas (☎420168; Av Victoria Aguirre 316) flies daily to Buenos Aires. *Remises* to the airport, 18km southeast of town, cost about AR$120. Various companies offer shuttle service for AR$60. Ask at your hotel.

BICYCLE IAT Turismo (☎420-317; www.iguazena.com.ar; Aguirre 262 loc 7) rents mountain bikes for AR$50 per day.

BUS The **bus terminal** (☎42-3006; cnr Avs Córdoba & Misiones) has departures for Posadas (AR$98, 5½ hours), Buenos Aires (AR$828, 20 hours) and intermediate points. Frequent buses also leave for Parque Nacional Iguazú (AR$10, 30 minutes).

TAXI For groups of three or more hoping to see both sides of the falls as well as Ciudad del Este and the Itaipú hydroelectric project, a shared cab or *remise* can be a good idea; figure about AR$650 for a full day's sightseeing, but make sure you account for visa costs. Tour operators inside the bus terminal offer this tour for AR$100 per person.

Parque Nacional Iguazú

People who doubt the theory that negative ions generated by waterfalls make people happier might have to reconsider after visiting the **Iguazú Falls**. Moods just seem to improve the closer you get to the falls, until eventually people degenerate into a giggling, shrieking mess. And this is grown adults we're talking about.

But getting happy isn't the only reason to come here. The power, size and sheer noise of the falls have to be experienced to be believed. You could try coming early, or later in the day (tour groups tend to leave by 3pm), but you're unlikely ever to have the place to yourself. The **park** (☎49-1469; www.iguazuargentina.com; admission Argentine/foreigner AR$65/170; ⏲8am-6pm) quickly fills with Argentines, backpackers, families and tour groups – but who cares? Get up close to the Garganta del Diablo (Devil's Throat) and the whole world seems to drop away.

Guaraní legend says that Iguazú Falls originated when a jealous forest god, enraged by a warrior escaping downriver by canoe with a young girl, caused the riverbed to collapse in front of the lovers, producing precipitous falls over which the girl fell and, at their base, turned into a rock. The warrior survived as a tree overlooking his fallen lover.

The geological origins of the falls are more prosaic. In southern Brazil, the Río Iguazú passes over a basalt plateau that ends just above its confluence with the Paraná. Before reaching the edge, the river divides into many channels to form several distinctive *cataratas* (cataracts).

The most awesome is the semicircular Garganta del Diablo, a deafening and dampening part of the experience, approached by launch and via a system of *pasarelas* (catwalks). There's no doubt that it's spectacular – there's only one question: where's the bungee jump?

Despite development pressures, the 55,000-hectare park is a natural wonderland

GETTING TO BRAZIL & PARAGUAY

Buses to Foz do Iguaçu, Brazil (AR$25, one hour) leave regularly from Puerto Iguazú's bus terminal. The bus will wait as you complete immigration procedures. The border is open 24 hours, but buses only run in daylight hours.

Frequent buses go from Puerto Iguazú's bus terminal to Ciudad del Este, Paraguay (AR$10, one hour) and wait at the border as you complete customs formalities.

of subtropical rainforest, with more than 2000 identified plant species, countless insects, 400 bird species, and many mammals and reptiles.

If you've got the time (and the money for a visa), it's worth checking out the Brazilian side of the falls too, for a few different angles, plus the grand overview.

Dangers & Annoyances

The Río Iguazú's currents are strong and swift; more than one tourist has been swept downriver and drowned near Isla San Martín.

The wildlife is potentially dangerous: in 1997 a jaguar killed a park ranger's infant son. Visitors should respect the big cats and, in case you encounter one, it's important not to panic. Speak calmly but loudly, do not run or turn your back, and try to appear bigger than you are by waving your arms or clothing.

Sights

Before seeing Iguazú Falls themselves, grab a map, look around the **museum**, and climb the nearby **tower** for a good overall view. Plan hikes before the mid-morning tour-bus invasion. Descending from the visitors center, you can cross by free launch to **Isla Grande San Martín**, which offers unique views and a refuge from the masses on the mainland.

Several *pasarelas* give good views of smaller falls, and, in the distance, the **Garganta del Diablo**. A train from the visitors center operates regularly to shuttle visitors from site to site. At the last stop, follow the trail to the lookout perched right on the edge of the mighty falls.

Activities

Best in the early morning, the Sendero Macuco nature trail leads through dense forest, where a steep sidetrack goes to the base of a hidden waterfall. Another trail goes to the *bañado,* a marsh abounding in birdlife. Allow about 2½ hours return (6km) for the entire Sendero Macuco trail.

To get elsewhere in the forest, you can hitchhike or hire a car to take you out along RN 101 toward the village of Bernardo de Irigoyen. Few visitors explore this part of the park, and it is still nearly pristine forest.

Iguazú Jungle Explorer BOAT TOUR
(☎42-1696; www.iguazujungle.com; Argentina) Iguazú Jungle Explorer, based at the visitors center, can arrange thrilling 12-minute speedboat trips below the falls (AR$130), as well as 4WD excursions on the Yacaratía trail to Puerto Macuco.

Moonlight Walks WALKING TOUR
(☎03757-49-1469; www.iguazuargentina.com; guided walks with/without dinner AR$270/200) Offers walks to the falls at 8pm, 8:45pm and 9:30pm on the five nights around the full moon. Call to reserve a place.

Information

Buses from Puerto Iguazú drop passengers at the Centro de Informes, where there's a small natural-history museum. There's also a photo-developing lab, a gift shop, a bar and many other services, including restaurants and snack bars.

Getting There & Away

Regular buses run to Puerto Iguazú (AR$10, 30 minutes).

NORTHWEST ARGENTINA

With a very tangible sense of history, the northwest is Argentina's most indigenous region, and the sights and people here show much closer links with the country's Andean neighbors than the European character of its urban centers.

Córdoba

☎0351 / POP 1,895,800

Argentina's second city is everything it should be – vibrant, fun, manageable in size and (in places) gorgeous to look at. Culture-vultures beware: you may get stuck here. Music, theater, film, dance: whatever you want, you can be pretty sure it's going on somewhere in town. The city also rocks out with seven universities, and has a buzz that some say is unmatched in the whole country.

Sights

To see Córdoba's colonial buildings and monuments, start at the **cabildo** (colonial town council) on Plaza San Martín. At the plaza's southwest corner, crowned by a Romanesque dome, the **Iglesia Catedral** (cnr Independencia & 27 de Abril; ⏰9:30am-3:15pm), begun in 1577, mixes a variety of styles.

Northwest Argentina

0 200 km
0 100 miles

BOLIVIA
CHILE
Villazón
La Quiaca
Yavi
Laguna Pozuelos
Monumento Natural Laguna de los Pozuelos
Parque Nacional Baritú
Pocitos
Río Pilcomayo
Tartagal
Abra Pampa
Aguas Blancas
Tres Cruces
Jujuy
Humahuaca
Orán
Susques
Río Martín
Formosa
Humahuaca
Parque Nacional Calilegua
Tilcara
Purmamarca
San Salvador de Jujuy
Termas de Reyes
San Antonio de los Cobres
San Pedro de Jujuy
Salta
General Güemes
La Poma
Salta
Parque Nacional Finca El Rey
Payogasta
Cachi
Parque Nacional Los Cardones
JV González
Chaco
Molinos
Valles Calchaquíes
Quebrada de Cafayate
Metán
Angastaco
Rosario de la Frontera
San Carlos
Antofagasta de la Sierra
Cafayate
Trancas
Quilmes (Ruines Indígenas)
Tucumán
Río Salado
Santa María
Tucumán
Catamarca
Tafí del Valle
Santiago del Estero
Famaillá
Hualfín
Concepcíon
Termas de Río Hondo
Belén
Santiago del Estero
Suncho Corral
San Pedro
Tinogasta
Las Juntas
Catamarca
Añatuya
San Blas
Río Dulce
Vinchina
Frías
Aminga
Huillapima
Chilecito
Vientos del Señor
Villa Unión
La Rioja
Villa Ojo de Agua
La Rioja
Parque Nacional Talampaya
Salinas Grandes
Patquía
Parque Provincial Ischigualasto
Chamical
Laguna Mar Chiquita
Capilla del Monte
Cruz del Eje
San Agustín de Valle Fértil
Malanzán
La Cumbre
Jesús María
La Falda
Salsacate
Cosquín
Córdoba
San Juan
Chepes
Villa Carlos Paz
Alta Gracia
Mina Clavero
Ulapes
Pilar
Villa General Belgrano
San Luis
Córdoba
Mendoza

RN 9, RN 40, RP 16, RN 34, RN 81, RP 5, RN 66, RN 51, RP 27, RN 9, RN 34, RP 17, RP 33, RN 40, RP 5, RN 16, RN 68, RP 43, RN 16, RP 307, RN 9, RP 303, 31, RN 40, RN 60, RP 46, RP 3, RN 38, RN 64, RN 64, RN 89, RN 40, RN 9, RN 38, RN 157, RN 98, RP 26, RP 5, RN 60, RN 34, RP 26, RN 74, RN 40, RN 79, RN 150, RN 60, RP 27, RN 38, RP 28, RP 17, RP 510, RP 29, RP 10, RP 20, RN 19, RN 141, RN 40, RN 79, RN 9, RN 36, RN 158, RN 9

Córdoba

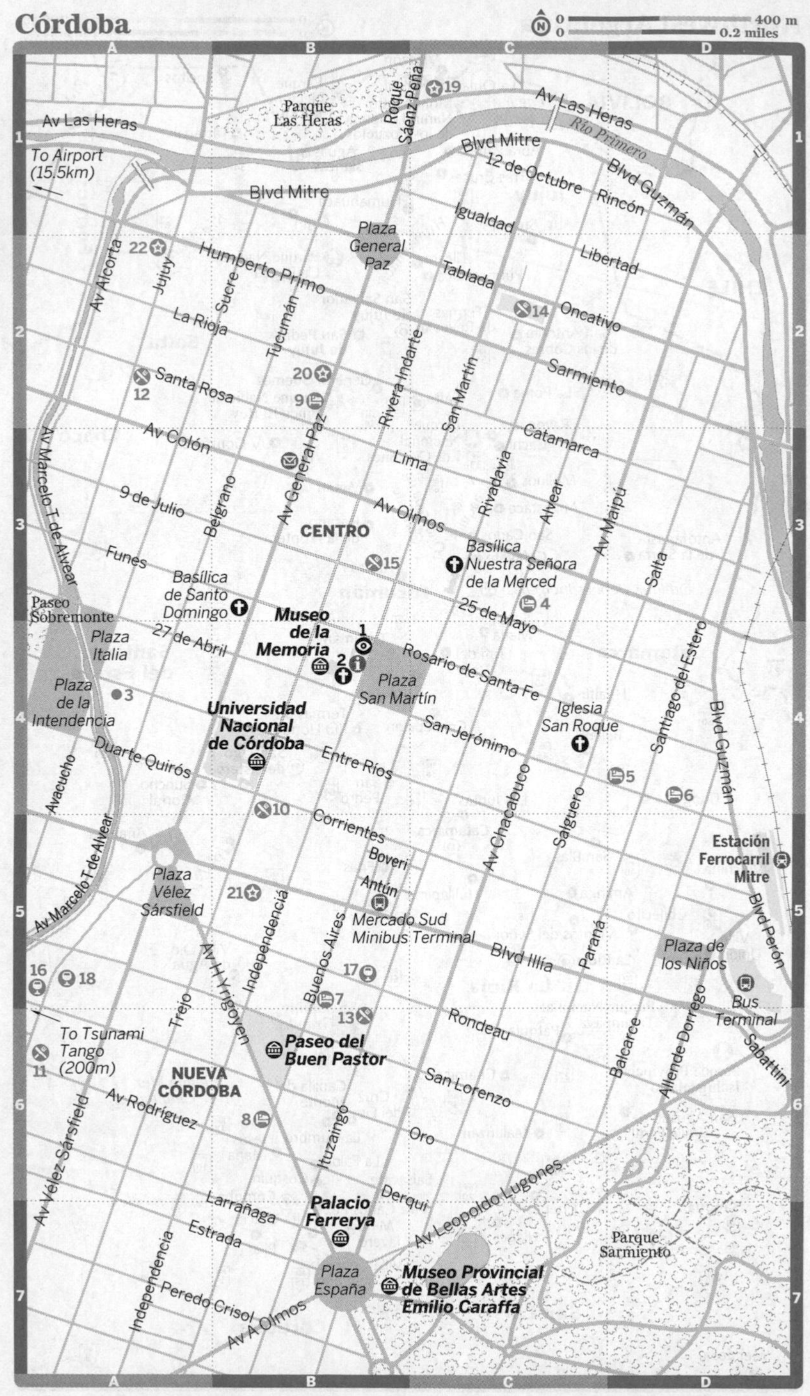

0 400 m
0 0.2 miles
Av Las Heras
Parque Las Heras
Roque Sáenz Peña
19
Río Primero
Blvd Mitre
12 de Octubre
Rincón
Blvd Guzmán
To Airport (15.5km)
Igualdad
Plaza General Paz
Libertad
22
Humberto Primo
Tablada
Av Alcorta
Jujuy
Sucre
Tucumán
14
Oncativo
La Rioja
Rivera Indarte
20
Sarmiento
12
Santa Rosa
San Martín
9
Catamarca
Av Colón
Av General Paz
Lima
9 de Julio
Belgrano
Rivadavia
Alvear
Av Maipú
Av Olmos
CENTRO
Av Marcelo T de Alvear
Funes
15
Basílica Nuestra Señora de la Merced
Salta
Basílica de Santo Domingo
4
Paseo Sobremonte
25 de Mayo
Museo de la Memoria
1
Plaza Italia
27 de Abril
2
Rosario de Santa Fe
Plaza San Martín
Santiago del Estero
Plaza de la Intendencia
3
Universidad Nacional de Córdoba
Iglesia San Roque
San Jerónimo
Duarte Quirós
Entre Ríos
5
6
Blvd Guzmán
Avacucho
Av Chacabuco
10
Salguero
Corrientes
Estación Ferrocarril Mitre
Boveri
Av Marcelo T de Alvear
Plaza Vélez Sársfield
21
Antún
Mercado Sud Minibus Terminal
Blvd Perón
Independencia
Buenos Aires
Blvd Illía
Paraná
Plaza de los Niños
16
18
17
Av H Yrigoyen
7
Bus Terminal
Trejo
13
Rondeau
To Tsunami Tango (200m)
Paseo del Buen Pastor
Sabattini
11
NUEVA CÓRDOBA
San Lorenzo
Balcarce
Allende Dorrego
Av Rodríguez
8
Oro
Av Vélez Sársfield
Ituzaingó
Av Leopoldo Lugones
Derqui
Palacio Ferrerya
Larrañaga
Estrada
Parque Sarmiento
Independencia
Plaza España
Museo Provincial de Bellas Artes Emilio Caraffa
Peredo Crisol
Av A Olmos

Córdoba

Top Sights
- Museo de la Memoria B4
- Museo Provincial de Bellas Artes Emilio Caraffa B7
- Palacio Ferrerya B7
- Paseo del Buen Pastor B6
- Universidad Nacional de Córdoba B4

Sights
- 1 Cabildo B4
- 2 Iglesia Catedral B4

Activities, Courses & Tours
- 3 Able Spanish School A4

Sleeping
- 4 Hostel Alvear C3
- 5 Hotel Helvetia D4
- 6 Hotel Quetzal D4
- 7 Le Grand Hostel B5
- 8 Mundo Nomade B6
- 9 Palenque Hostel B2

Eating
- 10 La Candela B4
- 11 La Nieta A6
- 12 La Parrilla de Raul A2
- 13 Mega Doner B6
- 14 Mercado Norte C2
- 15 Verde Siempre Verde B3

Drinking
- 16 But Mitre A5
- 17 Canario Negro B5
- 18 Los Infernadas A5

Entertainment
- 19 Captain Blue C1
- 20 Centro Cultural Casona Municipal B2
- 21 Cineclub Municipal Hugo del Carril B5
- 22 La Sala del Rey A2
- Patio del Tango .... (see 1)

Universidad Nacional de Córdoba HISTORIC BUILDING
(Obispo Trejo 242; tours AR$10; ⊙in English 1am & 5pm Mon-Sat, in Spanish 11am & 3pm Mon-Sat) While guided tours of the Universidad Nacional de Córdoba may sound a little dry, they get rave reviews. The tour takes you on a whirlwind ride through the ages, encompassing the history of Córdoba, Argentina, the Jesuits, and the university's museum and library.

FREE **Museo de la Memoria** MUSEUM
(San Jerónimo s/n; ⊙10am-6pm Tue-Sat) There's not a whole lot of joy at the Museo de la Memoria, but that's kind of the whole point. Set in a former detention/torture facility, it's a somber documentation of Dirty War atrocities told through photographs of the (often startlingly young) 'disappeared' of the era.

South of the center is Córdoba's **Milla Cultural** (Cultural Mile) – 1.6km of theaters, art galleries and art schools. The highlights here are the **Paseo del Buen Pastor** (Av H Yrigoyen 325; admission free; ⊙10am-8pm), which showcases work by Córdoba's young and emerging artists; the **Palacio Ferrerya** (Av H Yrigoyen 551; admission AR$10; ⊙8am-8pm Tue-Sun), housing 400 works of fine art; and the **Museo Provincial de Bellas Artes Emilio Caraffa** (Av H Yrigoyen 651; admission AR$10; ⊙10am-8pm Tue-Sun), which features a rotating collection of top-shelf contemporary art.

Activities

There's plenty to do in and around Córdoba: paragliding, skydiving, trekking, rafting, rock climbing, horse riding and mountain biking, to name a few options. The hostels are the best source of information on who's currently offering what.

Courses

Able Spanish School LANGUAGE COURSE
(☎422-4692; www.ablespanish.com.ar; Caseros 45) Offers accommodation and afternoon activities at extra cost, and discounts for extended study.

Tsunami Tango DANCE
(☎15-313-8746; www.tsunamitango.blogspot.com; Laprida 453) Tango classes and *milongas* Tuesday to Saturday. Check the website for times.

Sleeping

Palenque Hostel HOSTEL $
(☎423-7588; www.palenquehostel.com.ar; Av General Paz 371; dm from AR$60, d without bathroom AR$180; ❄@) In a classy and atmospheric old building.

WORTH A TRIP

COSQUÍN

Up in the hills, 55km outside Córdoba, this sleepy little town springs to life once a year for the world-famous nine-day **Festival Nacional del Folklore** (www.aquicosquin.org), held every January since 1961. Aside from that, there's not a whole lot going on, but the **aerosilla** (chairlift; return AR$45; ⏲10am-5pm) up Cerro Pan de Azúcar (1260m), 15km out of town, gives some great views over the valley. A taxi there costs AR$65, including waiting time.

Hotels in town include the basic **Hospedaje Remanso** (☎03541-45-2681; Paz 38; s/d AR$120/180) and the more comfortable **Hospedaje Siempreverde** (☎03541-45-0093; www.hosteriasiempreverde.com; Santa Fe 525; s/d AR$200/260; 📶). Accommodation can get tricky during festival time – book early or consider commuting from Córdoba.

San Martín between the plaza and the stadium is lined with cafes, restaurants and *parrillas*. **La Casona** (San Martín & Corrientes; mains AR$40-70; ⏲lunch & dinner) has good homemade pastas plus the standard *parrilla* offerings.

Frequent buses run to Córdoba (AR$25, 1½ hours).

Mundo Nomade HOSTEL $
(☎554-8047; www.mundonomade.com.ar; Buenos Aires 768; dm AR$50-65, s/d without bathroom AR$70/150; @📶) Set in an old house with funky decor, mural- and graffiti-covered walls etc, this cozy hostel doubles as a student residence, so there's always a crowd around.

Hostel Alvear HOSTEL $
(☎421-6502; www.alvearhostel.com.ar; Alvear 158; dm/d AR$60/180; @) The best of the downtown hostels, Hostel Alvear is set in a rambling building with good common areas, pool table, foosball etc.

Le Grand Hostel HOSTEL $
(☎422-7115; www.legrandshostel.com; Buenos Aires 547; dm AR$60-80, d without bathroom AR$180; ❄@📶) The best-looking hostel in town would be a madhouse if it ever hit its 108-bed capacity, but until then it's an excellent option. Need a good night's sleep? Look elsewhere.

Hotel Quetzal HOTEL $
(☎426-5117; www.hotelquetzal.com.ar; San Jerónimo 579; s/d AR$180/260; ❄@📶) The neighborhood's a bit run-down, but the prices on these clean and spacious modern rooms are excellent.

Hotel Helvetia HOTEL $
(☎421-7297; San Jerónimo 479; s/d AR$120/180) Nothing fancy going on here, but if you're looking for an old-school budget hotel, the big, plain, slightly crumbling rooms should fit the bill.

Camping San Martín CAMPGROUND $
(☎433-8400; per person AR$22) Spacious but basic, in the Parque General San Martín, 13km west of downtown. Bus 1 from Plaza San Martín goes to the Complejo Ferial, about 1km from the park.

Eating

TOP CHOICE **La Nieta** FUSION $$
(☎468-1920; Belgrano 783; mains AR$60-100; ⏲dinner Tue-Fri, 4:30pm-1am Sat & Sun) An excellent menu of delectable regional specialties, creative pastas and house recipes. Grab a table on the lovely upstairs terrace.

La Candela ARGENTINE $
(Duarte Quirós 67; empanadas AR$4.50, locro AR$30; ⏲lunch & dinner) A rustic student hangout featuring tasty and cheap empanadas and *locro*.

La Parrilla de Raul PARRILLA $
(cnr Jujuy & Santa Rosa; mains AR$25-40; ⏲lunch & dinner) Of Córdoba's *parrillas*, this is probably one of the most famous. *Parrillada* for two costs only AR$60, not including extras such as drinks or salad.

Mercado Norte MARKET $
(cnr Rivadavia & Oncativo; ⏲Mon-Sat) Cheap set lunches can be found in and around the Mercado Norte. On weekends *choripan* vendors sell juicy Spanish chorizo in a bun for AR$12.

Mega Doner MIDDLE EASTERN $
(Ituzaingó 528; set meals AR$30-50; ⏲lunch & dinner) Conveniently located in Nueva Cór-

doba's bar district, this place specializes in real giro *doners*. Daily lunch specials are an excellent deal and there's outdoor seating.

Verde Siempre Verde VEGETARIAN $
(9 de Julio 36; set meals AR$42; lunch & dinner;) Delicious, fresh, mostly vegetarian food, homemade bread and wholemeal pastas.

Drinking

Córdoba's drink of choice is Fernet (a strong, medicinal tasting, herbed liquor from Italy), almost always mixed with Coke.

For barhopping, head straight to Calle Rondeau, between Independencia and Ituzaingo – two blocks packed with bars. If you can get a spot at **Boca de Lobo** (Rondeau 157), that'll make a fine start.

The other area to check out is in the neighborhood of Güemes, alongside the Cañada. **But Mitre** (www.butmitre.com; Av Marcelo T de Alvear 635) and **Los Infernadas** (Belgrano 631) are the standbys here, but go for a wander – you're sure to find plenty of others.

Entertainment

Discos are mostly north of the center, along Av Las Heras. Music styles vary – listen for something you like and look for people handing out free passes. **Captain Blue** (Las Heras 124) gets seriously crowded, especially when bands play; there are plenty of others in this area.

Cuarteto music (Argentina's original pop, a Córdoba invention) is predictably big here and played live in many venues. But it's also the gangsta rap of Argentine folk music and tends to attract undesirable crowds. **La Sala del Rey** (Humberto Primero 439) is a respectable venue and the best place to catch a *cuarteto* show.

Patio del Tango DANCE
(on the outdoor Patio Mayor, Cabildo; admission AR$5, with dance lessons AR$20) Friday nights, the city hosts the Patio del Tango in the historic *cabildo* (weather permitting), kicking off with two-hour tango lessons at 7pm.

Cineclub Municipal Hugo del Carril CINEMA
(433-2463; www.cineclubmunicipal.org.ar; Blvd San Juan 49; admission AR$10; box office 9am-late) For art-house flicks at rock-bottom prices, check out the Cineclub Municipal Hugo del Carril.

Centro Cultural Casona Municipal CULTURAL CENTER
(cnr Av General Paz & La Rioja; 8am-8pm Sun-Fri, 10am-10pm Sat) Shows contemporary and avante-garde art, hosts concerts, and offers month-long art and music courses.

Information

There are ATMs near Plaza San Martín.

Cambio Barujel (cnr Rivadavia & 25 de Mayo; 9am-6pm Mon-Fri, 9am-2pm Sat) For changing traveler's checks.

Main post office (Av General Paz 201)

Provincial tourist office (433-1982; 8am-9pm) In the historic *cabildo* on Plaza San Martín.

Getting There & Around

AIR Aerolíneas Argentinas/Austral (482-1025; Av Colón 520) and **LAN** (0810-999-9526; www.lan.com.ar; San Lorenzo 309) fly to Buenos Aires.

Sol (0810-122-7765; www.sol.com.ar) flies to Rosario, Mendoza, Buenos Aires and other regional destinations.

The **airport** (434-8390) is about 15km north of town. Bus A5 (marked 'Aeropuerto') leaves from Plaza San Martín. You'll either need a magnetic card or *cospel* (token) – both available from kiosks. Taxis to the airport cost about AR$60.

BUS Local buses don't serve the bus terminal, but it's an easy eight-block walk to the center; just keep moving toward the big steeple. A taxi shouldn't cost more than AR$20.

Córdoba's **bus terminal** (NETOC; 423-0532, 423-4199; Blvd Perón 300) has departures for Tucumán (AR$290, 11 hours), Buenos Aires (AR$320, 10 hours), Mendoza (AR$330, 10 hours), Posadas (AR$660, 15 hours) and Salta (AR$450, 13 hours). There are various international departures, including Montevideo, Uruguay (AR$509, 16 hours).

Frequent minibuses leave from the **Mercado Sud Minibus Terminal** (Blvd Illia near Buenos Aires) to Cosquín, Jesús María and Alta Gracia.

TRAIN Córdoba's **Estación Ferrocarril Mitre** (426-3565; Blvd Perón s/n) has departures for Buenos Aires (AR$30 to AR$300, 15 hours) via Rosario. Book tickets well in advance.

Trains to Cosquín (AR$6.50, two hours) leave from **Estación Rodriguez del Busto** (477-6195; Cardeñosa 3500) on the northwest outskirts of town daily at 10:25am and 4:25pm. Buses A4 and A7 from the central plaza go to the station or it's an AR$25 taxi ride.

Around Córdoba

JESÚS MARÍA

☎03525 / POP 53,100

After losing their operating funds to pirates off the coast of Brazil, the Jesuits produced and sold wine from Jesús María to support their university in colonial Córdoba. The town is located 51km north of Córdoba via RN 9.

If you're only planning on seeing one Jesuit mission, **Museo Jesuítico Nacional de Jesús María** (☎42-0126; admission AR$15; ⏲8am-7pm Mon-Fri, 10am-noon & 2-6pm Sat & Sun) should probably be it. Easily accessed, but in a peaceful rural setting, it's been wonderfully preserved and restored, and is crammed full of artifacts. For some reason there's a contemporary art exhibition on the top floor. Go around the back to check out the antique winemaking gear.

Buses run between Córdoba and Jesús María (AR$20, one hour).

ALTA GRACIA

☎03547 / POP 48,300

Only 35km southwest of Córdoba, the colonial mountain town of Alta Gracia is steeped in history. Its illustrious residents have ranged from Jesuit pioneers to Viceroy Santiago Liniers, Spanish composer Manuel de Falla and revolutionary Ernesto 'Che' Guevara. The tourist office, located in the clocktower opposite the museum Virrey Liniers, has a good town map.

From 1643 to 1762, Jesuit fathers built the **Iglesia Parroquial Nuestra Señora de la Merced** on the west side of the central Plaza Manuel Solares; the nearby Jesuit workshops of **El Obraje** (1643) are now a public school. Liniers, one of the last officials to occupy the post of viceroy of the Río de la Plata, resided in what is now the **Museo Histórico Nacional del Virrey Liniers** (☎42-1303; www.museoliniers.org.ar; admission AR$10, Wed free; ⏲9am-1pm & 3-7pm Tue-Fri, 9:30am-12:30pm & 3:30-6:30pm Sat, Sun & holidays), alongside the church.

Though the Guevaras lived in several houses in the 1930s, their primary residence was **Villa Beatriz**, which has now been converted into the **Museo Casa Ernesto 'Che' Guevara** (Avellaneda 501; admission AR$75; ⏲2-7pm Mon, from 9am Tue-Sun). The museum focuses heavily on the legend's early life, and, judging by the photographs, Che was a pretty intense guy by the time he was 16, and definitely had his cool look down by his early 20s. Particularly touching are some of Che's letters that he wrote to his parents and children towards the end of his life.

The **Altagracia Hostel** (☎42-8810; www.altagraciahostel.com.ar; Paraguay 218; dm/r AR$60/180) offers spacious, clean dorms a few blocks downhill from the clocktower.

The long, narrow rooms at **Hostal Hispania** (☎42-6555; Vélez Sársfield 57; s/d AR$180/300; ❄📶🏊) are supermodern and set around a lovely garden area featuring a beautifully tiled swimming pool. Many of the rooms have balconies.

Parrillas and sidewalk cafes line Av Belgrano in the few blocks downhill from the *estancia*. Out by Che's house, **Sol de Polen**

QUIRKY TOWNS IN CÓRDOBA'S SIERRAS

For some reason, Córdoba's Sierras region is one of the quirkiest in Argentina, and the great thing about traveling in the region is that every once in a while you stumble upon something truly wonderful and unexpected. Here are a few of our favorites:

Capilla del Monte This otherwise sleepy little hill town is world-famous among UFO watchers, who come here in the hope of communing with the extraterrestrials from on top of the mystical Cerro Uritorco.

Villa General Belgrano (www.elsitiodelavilla.com/oktoberfest) The town's strong German heritage gives it a very European flavor, which really takes off as the beer starts flowing in Oktoberfest.

Villa Carlos Paz (www.villacarlospaz.gov.ar/turismo) Like a mix between Vegas and Disneyland, this lakeside getaway is dotted with theme hotels (the Great Pyramids, the Kremlin) and centered around a massive cuckoo clock.

Museo Rocsen (www.museorocsen.org) Near the tiny town of Nono, outside of Mina Clavero, the 11,000-plus pieces on display form probably the most eclectic collection of trash/treasure you're ever likely to see.

(42-7332; Avellenada 529; mains AR$35-60) has good Cuban-inspired set lunches and a couple of basic rooms (doubles AR$100) out back.

From the **bus terminal** (Tacuarí at Perón), buses run every 15 minutes to and from Córdoba (AR$9, one hour). You can flag them down as they pass through town.

La Rioja

03822 / POP 189,400

This is siesta country, folks. Between noon and 5pm *everything* shuts down (except, for some reason, bookstores). Once the sun starts dipping behind the surrounding mountains, people emerge from their houses, and the city and its three gorgeous central plazas take on a lively, refreshed feel. There's some stuff to do around here – most notably visiting the Vientos del Señor and the remote Parque Nacional Talampaya. Most people, however, use the town as a comfy break in the long-haul journey between Mendoza and Salta.

In 1591 Juan Ramírez de Velasco founded Todos los Santos de la Nueva Rioja, at the base of the Sierra del Velasco, 154km south of Catamarca. The 1894 earthquake destroyed many buildings, but the restored commercial center, near Plaza 25 de Mayo, replicates colonial style.

Sights

Museo Folklórico MUSEUM
(Pelagio Luna 811; admission by donation; 9am-1pm & 5-9pm Tue-Fri) The Museo Folklórico is set in a wonderful 19th-century house and displays ceramic reproductions of mythological figures from local folklore, as well as *gaucho* paraphernalia and colorful weavings.

FREE **El Paseo Cultural** ARTS CENTER
(cnr Luna & Belgrano; 10am-8pm) It's worth stopping in at this massive downtown cultural center to see what's going on. It has a regularly changing program of contemporary art and photography exhibitions, film screenings, concerts etc.

Museo Inca Huasi MUSEUM
(Alberdi 650; admission by donation; 9am-1pm & 4-8pm Tue-Fri, 9am-1pm Sat) The Museo Inca Huasi exhibits more than 12,000 pieces, from tools and artifacts to Diaguita ceramics and weavings.

Convento de San Francisco CHURCH
(cnr 25 de Mayo & Bazán y Bustos; 7am-9pm) This church houses the Niño Alcalde, a Christ-child icon symbolically recognized as the city's mayor.

Festivals & Events

El Tinkunako FOLKLORE
The December 31 ceremony El Tinkunako re-enacts San Francisco Solano's mediation between the Diaguitas and the Spaniards in 1593. When accepting peace, the Diaguitas imposed two conditions: resignation of the Spanish mayor and his replacement by the Niño Alcalde.

Sleeping

Accommodation in La Rioja suffers from two problems: it's overpriced and often booked out. The tourist office keeps a list of homestays.

Hostel Apacheta HOSTEL $
(15-444-5445; www.apachetahostel.com.ar; San Nicolás de Bari 669; dm AR$65;) Treading that fine line between cool and grungy, La Rioja's only real hostel has a great central location and decent amenities. You can rent bikes here.

Hotel Mirasol HOTEL $
(442-0760; Rivadavia 941; s/d AR$80/130;) Nothing fancy, but a good budget choice in an excellent downtown location.

Gran Hotel Embajador HOTEL $
(443-8580; www.granhotelembajador.com.ar; San Martín 250; s/d AR$175/250;) A great-value option in town. Some upstairs rooms have balconies.

Country Las Vegas CAMPGROUND $
(RN 75, Km 31.5; campsites per person AR$20) A decent campground on the western edge of town; to get there, catch city bus 1 southbound on Perón.

Eating

Rivadavia east of Plaza 9 de Julio is lined with cafes, restaurants and *parrillas*.

La Aldea de la Virgen de Luján ARGENTINE $
(Rivadavia 756; lunches AR$30-50; 7am-3pm & 7-11pm Mon-Sat, 10am-3pm Sun) Serves excellent homemade pasta and, very occasionally, regional specialties.

Marhaba MIDDLE EASTERN $
(Vega 22; mains AR$30-60; ⌚lunch & dinner) Seriously good Middle Eastern food like you may not expect in La Rioja. Choose from a decent range of dishes or go for the trusty *schwarma*, made with fresh-baked pita bread.

Stanzza ITALIAN $$
(Dorrego 160; mains AR$40-60) Arguably La Rioja's finest dining. The steaks and pastas are good – creatively and carefully prepared – but the seafood dishes are the standouts.

Café del Paseo CAFE $
(cnr Pelagio Luna & 25 de Mayo; light meals AR$20-40) The coziest cafe in town offers great people-watching opportunities.

Information

La Rioja's handiest information source is the **tourist kiosk** (Plaza 25 de Mayo; ⌚8am-9:30pm) on the plaza. They have a decent city map, good accommodation information and many kilos worth of brochures covering other provincial destinations.

Several banks have ATMs.

The **post office** is at Perón 764.

Getting There & Away

Aerolíneas Argentinas (☎442-6307; Belgrano 63) flies Monday to Saturday to Buenos Aires.

La Rioja's new **bus terminal** (Barrio Evita s/n) is 5km from the center. Bus 8 (AR$2) runs between the two. A taxi costs around AR$20. There are departures for Chilecito (AR$35, three hours), Tucumán (AR$220, six hours), Córdoba (AR$208, 6½ hours), San Juan (AR$260, six hours), Mendoza (AR$360, eight hours), Salta (AR$395, 10 hours) and Buenos Aires (AR$650, 16 hours).

Santiago del Estero

☎0385 / POP 374,600

Due to its central location, Santiago is a major transportation hub, but unfortunately for 'modern' Argentina's oldest city, its list of charms pretty much ends there.

Sleeping & Eating

Hotel Savoy HOTEL $$
(☎421-1234; www.savoysantiago.com.ar; Tucumán 39; s/d AR$230/350; ❄📶) The eye-popping grandeur of the facade and lobby here make up for the fairly ordinary rooms. Pay an extra AR$30 for a balcony and wi-fi.

Residencial Emaus GUESTHOUSE $
(☎421-5893; Av Moreno Sur 675; s/d AR$100/160; 📶) Light and airy rooms with TV and benevolent management.

Bruno's INTERNATIONAL $
(Independencia 40; mains AR$30-50; ⌚breakfast, lunch & dinner) Of the various restaurants ringing the plaza, this one gets the tick for good sandwiches and its wide upstairs balcony that overlooks the plaza.

Information

The provincial **tourist office** (☎421-3253; Libertad 417) is on the plaza. Several banks have ATMs. The post office is at the corner of Buenos Aires and Urquiza.

Getting There & Away

Aerolíneas Argentinas (☎422-4335; 24 de Septiembre 547) flies daily to Buenos Aires.

The **bus terminal** (www.tosde.com.ar; cnr Perú & Chacabuco) has frequent departures to Tucumán (AR$77, two hours) and Buenos Aires (AR$666, 12 hours).

Trains leave from **Estación la Banda** (☎427-3918), 7km out of town, for Tucumán (AR$20 to AR$38, 3½ hours) at 7am on Tuesdays and Saturdays, and Buenos Aires (AR$45 to AR$400, 21 hours) at 8pm Wednesdays and 11pm Saturdays.

Tucumán

☎0381 / POP 850,100

A big city with a small-town feel, Tucumán is definitely improving in terms of the backpacking scene. There are some good hostels, a pumping nightlife and some excellent adventures to be had in the surrounding hills. Independence Day (July 9) celebrations are especially vigorous in Tucumán, which hosted the congress that declared Argentine independence in 1816.

Sights & Activities

Casa de Gobierno NOTABLE BUILDING
Spectacularly lit up at night, Tucumán's most imposing landmark is the Casa de Gobierno, which replaced the colonial *cabildo* on Plaza Independencia in 1912.

FREE **Museo Folclórico Manuel Belgrano** MUSEUM
(Av 24 de Septiembre 565) Although closed at the time of research, this fascinating museum usually displays horse gear, indigenous

WORTH A TRIP

VIENTOS DEL SEÑOR

The plan was to start a community tourism project to promote kite buggying out on the Vientos del Señor salt flats, some 90km northwest of La Rioja. But one thing didn't lead to another and the money ran out. But the guys running the project liked it so much they wanted to stay on. And the town council decided to donate the equipment to them, provided they allow visitors to use it for free.

What all this means for us is the biggest bargain in the world of kite buggying. As long as you can get out there, you're pretty much guaranteed to have the place to yourself, and you can doodle around on the carts and buggies to your heart's content. All for the cost of how much you decide to tip the caretakers.

For more information, check with the tourist office or Hostel Apacheta, both in La Rioja. Tours (AR$244 per person) run to Vientos del Señor from La Rioja but stop everywhere along the way first, leaving you very little time at the site. The best way to go is to catch a minibus from La Rioja's **minibus terminal** (☎446-8562; Artigas 750) heading for Aimogasta (AR$35, one hour). Ask the driver to let you off at the turnoff to Vientos del Señor. It's about a 1km walk from the turnoff to the site.

musical instruments, weavings, woodcarvings and Quilmes pottery.

FREE **Casa del Obispo Colombres** MUSEUM
(⌚8am-1pm & 2:30-8pm Mon-Fri, 9am-8pm Sat & Sun) Casa del Obispo Colombres is an 18th-century house that preserves the first ox-powered *trapiche* (sugar mill) of Tucumán's postindependence industry. Guided tours (in Spanish) explain the mill's operations.

Sleeping

Tucumán Hostel HOSTEL $
(☎420-1584; www.tucumanhostel.com; Buenos Aires 669; dm AR$55-60, d with/without bathroom AR$195/165; ❄@🛜≋) Despite the rash of newcomers, it's still one of the best, with spacious dorms, good doubles, great common areas and a leafy garden in a beautiful old building.

Hostel Oh! HOSTEL $
(☎430-8849; www.hosteloh.com.ar; Santa Fe 930; dm AR$70-90, s/d without bathroom AR$170/190; @🛜≋) In nearly every way a wonderful hostel – spacious, friendly and atmospheric. The one downfall? The bed-to-bathroom ratio is heavily skewed in favor of long waits.

King Hotel HOTEL $
(☎431-0211; Chacabuco 18; s/d AR$145/210; ❄🛜) About as good as it gets budget-hotel-wise in this town. Rooms are plain but clean and spacious enough. It often fills up by mid-afternoon, so you might want to book ahead.

Backpacker's Tucumán HOSTEL $
(☎430-2716; www.backpackerstucuman.com; Laprida 456; dm AR$70, s/d without bathroom AR$125/180; @🛜) An excellent downtown location, good atmosphere and spacious dorms. Has tourist info and cheap meals.

Hotel Versailles HOTEL $
(☎422-9760; www.hotelversaillestuc.com.ar; Alvarez 481; s/d AR$222/270; ❄@🛜) Tucumán's hotels tend to lack style, but this one has a few classy touches. Not many, but a few. Good location too.

Eating & Drinking

Plaza de Almas CAFE $
(www.plazadealmas.com; Maipú 791; mains AR$40-60; ⌚8pm-late) Although it can seat well over a hundred people, the well-designed spaces here, spread out over three levels indoors and out, maintain an intimate atmosphere. The menu is simple but creative, with a range of kebabs, meat dishes and salads on offer.

Mercado del Norte MARKET $
Stalls at the Mercado del Norte, with an entrance at the corner of Mendoza and Maipú, serve good cheap food and great pizza.

Costumbres Argentinos ARGENTINE $
(San Juan 666; mains AR$30-50) The food here is decent enough, but the real reason to come is the atmosphere: there's a sweet beer garden out back and live music Thursday to Sunday nights.

El Portal ARGENTINE $
(☎422-6024; Av 24 de Septiembre 351; empanadas AR$4.50, mains AR$45; ⏰10am-11pm) This is a rustic indoor-outdoor eatery offering a simple menu. It's an excellent place to try regional specialties sucah as *humitas* (corn dumplings).

The stretch of Calle Lillo to the west of the market between La Madrid and San Lorenzo – known as El Abasto – was Tucumán's nightlife zone until 'early closing' (4am) laws put the area into decline. Some venues are hanging on, but most of the action has moved to smaller downtown bars such as **Managua** (San Juan 1015; ⏰8pm-late) and **Pangea** (Laprida 289; ⏰9pm-late Tue-Sun), which are good fun, lively enough and offer simple food.

Information

ATMs are numerous.

Maguitur (San Martín 765; ⏰8am-6pm Mon-Sat) Cashes traveler's checks (2% commission).

Post office (cnr 25 de Mayo & Córdoba; ⏰9am-6pm Mon-Fri)

Tourist office (☎430-3644; www.tucumanturismo.gob.ar; 24 de Septiembre 484; ⏰8am-10pm Mon-Fri, 9am-9pm Sat & Sun) On Plaza Independencia. There's also a booth at the bus terminal.

Getting There & Around

Tucumán's **airport** (☎426-4906) is 8km east of downtown. To get there, catch bus 121, which passes the center and the bus terminal (AR$2), or take a taxi (AR$55). **Aerolíneas Argentinas** (☎431-1030; 9 de Julio 110) flies daily to Buenos Aires.

Tucumán's **bus terminal** (Brígido Terán 350) is a few blocks from the center, a decent walk if you don't want to fork out the AR$6 cab fare. It has a post office, *locutorios* (small telephone offices), a supermarket, bars and restaurants – all blissfully air-conditioned.

Aconquija services Tafí del Valle (AR$40, 2½ hours) and Cafayate (AR$130, six hours).

Long-distance destinations include Santiago del Estero (AR$75, two hours), Córdoba (AR$293, 11 hours), Salta (AR$175, four hours), Corrientes (AR$415, 12 hours), La Rioja (AR$190, six hours) and Buenos Aires (AR$767, 15 hours).

Trains run from **Estación Ferrocarril Mitre** (☎430-9220; www.ferrocentralsa.com.ar) to Buenos Aires Wednesdays at 5pm and Saturdays at 7:40pm (AR$45 to AR$400, 25 hours).

Tafí del Valle

☎03867 / POP 4200

Set in a pretty valley overlooking a lake, Tafí is where folks from Tucumán come to escape the heat in summer. In the low season it's much mellower (which isn't to imply that there's any sort of frenzy here in summertime), but still gorgeous, and makes a good base for exploring the surrounding countryside and ruins at Quilmes.

Sights & Activities

Parque Los Menhires ARCHAEOLOGICAL SITE
(admission AR$3; ⏰9am-7pm) At Parque Los Menhires, at the south end of La Angostura reservoir, stand more than 80 indigenous granite monuments collected from nearby archaeological sites. Take any bus passing El Mollar or a taxi (AR$25) or walk the 12km downhill toward the lake.

Festivals & Events

At 2000m, Tafí, a temperate island in a subtropical sea, produces some exceedingly good handmade cheese. The **cheese festival**, held during the second week in February, is well worth a look (and, possibly, a nibble).

Sleeping & Eating

Numerous *parrillas,* specializing in *lechón* (suckling pig) and *chivito* (goat), line Av Perón.

Nomade Hostel HOSTEL $
(☎0381-15-440-0686; www.nomadehostel.com.ar; Los Castaños s/n; dm AR$60 d with/without bathroom AR$200/160; @📶) A relaxed and welcoming place a 10-minute walk from the bus terminal. Turn right, follow the tarmac road, and you'll see it signposted on the right. Prices include home-cooked breakfast and dinner. Bike hire available.

TOP CHOICE **Estancia Los Cuartos** LODGE $$
(☎0381-15-587-4230; www.estancialoscuartos.com; Critto s/n; s/d AR$290/320; 📶) It's hard to stress what a bargain the beautiful rooms in this historic homestead right by the bus terminal are. Breakfast includes a platter of cheese, made on the premises.

Hospedaje Celia GUESTHOUSE $
(☎42-1170; Belgrano 443; r per person AR$70) Set back from the road 100m uphill from the

church, this place offers bright, white and comfortable rooms with private bathroom. There are inconveniences – no sockets in the rooms, for example – but the price is right.

Camping Los Sauzales CAMPGROUND $
(☎42-1880; Los Palenques s/n; per person/tent AR$15/20, per car AR$10-20) Run-down but pleasant grassy campsite about 750m west of the plaza. Also has simple cabins and bungalows (AR$90 to AR$150).

Don Pepito PARRILLA $
(www.donpepitodetafi.com.ar; Perón 193; mains AR$40-60) Don Pepino is the coziest of the bunch of *parillas* on Av Perón and usually has live entertainment at mealtimes.

Kkechuwa BAR
(Perón s/n) Friendly place with an excellent range of artisanal beers and food options ranging from sandwiches to llama dishes.

Information

Banco Tucumán (Av Miguel Critto) Has an ATM.

Casa del Turista (☎42-1084; Av Miguel Critto; ⏲9am-7pm Mon-Sat, to 5pm Sun) Helpful tourist office in Tafí's central plaza.

Getting There & Around

Tafí's **bus terminal** (Av Miguel Critto) is an easy walk from the center. Departures include Cafayate (AR$90, four hours) and Tucumán (AR$40, 2½ hours). Mountain bikes can be rented from Nomade Hostel for AR$10/50 per hour/day.

IT'S ALL DOWNHILL FROM HERE

One of the best day trips you can do from Tafí del Valle needs no guide at all. Hire a bike, and start off downhill past the lake and out onto the road to Tucumán. It's a 40km (mostly) downhill cruise, following the course of the Río Los Sosa, with literally hundreds of gorgeous swimming holes and picnic spots right by the roadside.

Once you lose sight of the river and houses start appearing, you know the best part of the ride is over. You can hail any Tafí-bound bus (make sure you choose a safe place for them to pull over), stash your bike underneath and ride home in style.

There's no food or water anywhere along this route, so come prepared. And check your brakes before leaving too – you'll definitely be using them.

Cafayate

☎03868 / POP 13,700

Set at the entrance to the Quebrada de Cafayate, 1600m above sea level and surrounded by some of the Argentina's best vineyards, Cafayate provides the opportunity to indulge in two of life's great pleasures: drinking wine and exploring nature. If you're pressed for time, you can combine the two and take a bottle out into the Quebrada with you, in which case we would recommend a local *torrontés*, provided you can keep it chilled.

February's **La Serenata** (www.serenatacafayate.com.ar) music festival draws big crowds.

Sights & Activities

From 25 de Mayo, two blocks south of Colón, a 5km walk southwest leads you to the **Río Colorado**. Follow the river upstream for about two hours to get to a 10m **waterfall**, where you can swim. Look out for hidden **rock paintings** on the way (for a couple of pesos, local children will guide you).

Several operators around the plaza offer tours of the Quebrada for AR$90 per person. Try to go in the late afternoon, when it's cooler and the colors and photo ops are better.

Museo de Vitivinicultura MUSEUM
(Av Gral Güemes; admission AR$30; ⏲10am-7:30pm Tue-Sun) The Museo de Vitivinicultura, near Colón, details the history of local wines. There are 14 wineries in and around Cafayate that offer visits and tastings – the tourist office has a list of opening hours and prices. Make sure you try the fruity white *torrontés*.

Puna Turismo BICYCLE RENTAL
(☎42-2038; www.punaturismo.com; San Martín 80) Offers quad-bike tours from AR$270 and rents mountain bikes (AR$60/80 per half-/full day).

Sleeping

TOP CHOICE **Rusty-K Hostal** HOSTEL $
(☎42-2031; www.rustykhostal.com.ar; Rivadavia 281; dm AR$50, d with/without bathroom AR$200/150; @☎) A wonderfully atmospheric hostel

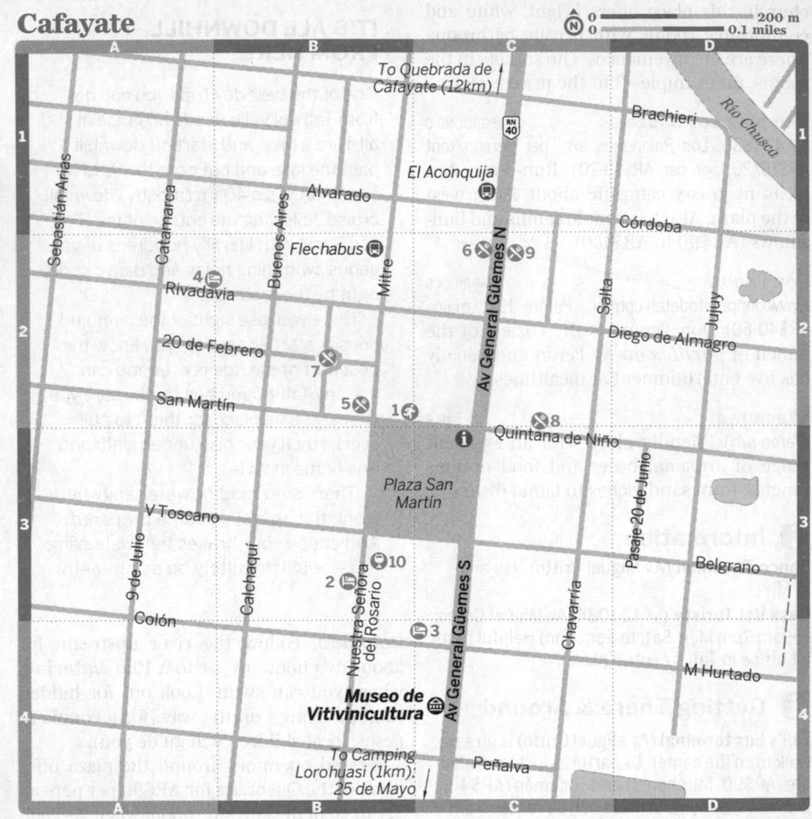

Cafayate

Top Sights
Museo de Vitivinicultura C4

Activities, Courses & Tours
1 Puna Turismo B2

Sleeping
2 El Portal de las Viñas B3
3 Killa C4
4 Rusty-K Hostal A2

Eating
5 Casa de las Empanadas B2
6 Heladería Miranda C2
7 Mercado Central B2
8 Quilla Huasi C2
9 Santa Barbara C2

Drinking
10 Chato's Wine Bar B3

with some good common areas and a big backyard.

El Portal de las Viñas GUESTHOUSE $
(☎42-1098; www.portalvinias.com.ar; Nuestra Señora del Rosario 155; d/q AR$250/400; ❄📶) An excellent-value budget spot just off the plaza. Rooms have terracotta-tile floors and spacious bathrooms, and are set around a vine-shaded courtyard.

Killa BOUTIQUE HOTEL $$
(☎42-2254; www.killacafayate.com.ar; Colón 47; s/d AR$360/450; ❄@📶🏊) Not nearly as dangerous as it sounds, this small hotel has the feel of a country inn despite its location one block off the plaza. Rooms are spacious and stylish, and service is top notch.

Camping Lorohuasi CAMPGROUND $
(☎42-2292; RN 40 Sur; campsites per person AR$20; 🏊) Located 1km south of town. It

has hot showers, a swimming pool and a grocery store.

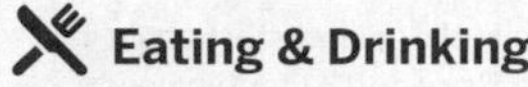

Eating & Drinking

Heladería Miranda ICE CREAM **$**
(Av Gral Güemes; per scoop AR$8; ⏲10am-10pm) This place sells imaginative wine-flavored ice cream with a considerable alcoholic kick.

Santa Barbara PARRILLA **$**
(Av Gral Güemes 145; mains AR$30-55; ⏲lunch & dinner) There's nothing fancy going on here - just your straight-down-the-line *parrilla* offerings. The roaring open fire is a welcome sight in winter.

Casa de las Empanadas ARGENTINE **$**
(Mitre 24; dozen empanadas AR$40; ⏲lunch & dinner) Decorated with the scrawls of contented customers, this no-frills place has a wide selection of empanadas that are all absolutely delicious. Local wine in ceramic jugs and *humitas, locro* and tamales round out the meal.

Quilla Huasi ARGENTINE **$**
(Quintana de Niño 70; mains AR$40-60; ⏲lunch & dinner) A cute little place specializing in home-style versions of regional favorites such as *humitas*, tamales and *locro*. The goat stew is a standout.

Mercado Central MARKET **$**
(cnr San Martín & 11 de Noviembre) Cheap eats can be found at the various *comedores* (eateries) inside the Mercado Central. Restaurants around the plaza do good regional dishes at reasonable prices.

Chato's Wine Bar WINE BAR
(Nuestra Señora del Rosario 132; ⏲7pm-midnight) Strangely, this is the only proper wine bar in Cafayate. It has a list of some 200 available by the glass. It's a great place for a tasting session, a drink in friendly surroundings, or a chat about wine.

Information

Tourist information kiosk (☎42-2442; Plaza San Martín; ⏲8am-8pm) At the northeast corner of Plaza San Martín.

Getting There & Around

Flechabus (Mitre s/n) has buses to Salta (AR$58, four hours) and up the Valle Calchaquíes to Angastaco (AR$25, two hours) via San Carlos.

El Aconquija (cnr Av Gral Güemes & Alvarado) has departures to Tucumán (AR$130, six hours), passing through Tafí del Valle (AR$90, five hours). Take one of the daily buses to Santa María to visit the ruins at Quilmes, in Tucumán province (AR$16, one hour).

Getting between Cafayate and Cachi can mean a tough but rewarding backroad trip, up the Valles Calchaquíes (see boxed text, p98).

Around Cafayate

QUEBRADA DE CAFAYATE

From Cafayate, RN 68 slices through the Martian-like landscape of the Quebrada de Cafayate on its way to Salta. About 50km north of Cafayate, the eastern Sierra de Carahuasi is the backdrop for distinctive sandstone landforms such as the Garganta del Diablo (Devil's Throat), El Anfiteatro (Amphitheater), El Sapo (Toad), El Fraile (Friar), El Obelisco (Obelisk) and Los Castillos (Castles).

Other than car rental or organized tours, the best way to see the Quebrada is by bike or on foot. Bring plenty of water and go in the morning, as unpleasant, strong winds kick up in the afternoon. At Cafayate, cyclists can load their bikes onto any bus heading to Salta and disembark at the impressive box canyon of Garganta del Diablo. From here, the 50-odd kilometers back to Cafayate can be biked in about four hours, but it's too far on foot. When you've had enough, walkers should simply hail down another bus on its way back to Cafayate.

VALLES CALCHAQUÍES

In this valley north and south of Cafayate, once a principal route across the Andes, the Calchaquí people resisted Spanish attempts to impose forced labor obligations. Tired of having to protect their pack trains, the Spaniards relocated many Calchaquí to Buenos Aires, and the land fell to Spaniards, who formed large rural estates.

CACHI

☎03868 / POP 3145

Cachi is a spectacularly beautiful town and by far the most visually impressive of those along the Valles Calchaquíes. There's not a whole lot to do here, but that's all part of the charm. The **tourist office** (☎49-1902; oficinadeturismo.cachi@gmail.com; Güemes s/n; ⏲9am-8pm) is in the municipal building on the plaza. It have an atrocious city map but good info on hotels and attractions.

THE BACK ROAD: CACHI TO CAFAYATE

If you're in Cachi and heading towards Cafayate, buses reach Molinos and start again in Angastaco, leaving a 42km stretch of gorgeous, lonely road unserviced. Hitchhiking is common in these parts, but traffic is rare and even the towns that have bus service have infrequent departures.

It's hard, but not impossible. The last thing you want to do is stand on the roadside with your thumb out. The best thing to do is, when you hit town, start asking around literally everywhere – the police station, hospital, *kioskos* – to see if anybody knows anyone who is going your way. Somebody will and you won't get stuck for long. If you do, there are decent, cheap places to stay and eat in Molinos, Angastaco and San Carlos.

You may end up in the back of a pickup truck with the wind in your hair and the mountains in your face. But really – this is the sort of adventure you probably had in mind when you booked your airfare.

Sound like too much? You can always ask at the *remisería* (*remise* office) in front of Cachi's bus terminal if there's a group going that you can join. *Remises* seat four passengers and cost AR$650 from Cafayate to Cachi. The stretch from Molinos to Angastaco should cost about AR$200.

While you're here, definitely stop in at the **Museo Arqueológico** (admission AR$5 or AR$10 donation; ⏲10am-7pm Mon-Fri, to 6pm Sat, to 1pm Sun), a slickly presented collection of area finds, including an impressive array of petroglyphs.

Various companies offer excurions and activities in the surrounding hills. **Urkupiña** (☎49-1317; uk_cachi@hotmail.com; Zorrilla s/n) offers cycling trips, quad-bike excursions and reasonably priced transportation to Cafayate along the RN40.

For accommodations, check out the municipal **campground & hostel** (☎49-1902; oficinadeturismo.cachi@gmail.com; campsites AR$15-25, dm/cabin AR$12/125; 🏊) or **Hospedaje Don Arturo** (☎49-1087; www.hospedajedonarturo.blogspot.com; Bustamante s/n; s/d AR$120/200, without bathroom AR$90/160), where the killer views off the back deck make up for the humbleness of the facilities. One of the better hotels in town is the **Hostería Cachi** (☎49-1105; www.soldelvalle.com.ar; Av ACA s/n; s/d AR$282/438; ❄@📶🏊), which has an excellent hilltop location and stylish, modern rooms.

Some cheap restaurants surround the plaza. The most interesting restaurant in town is **Ashpamanta** (☎0387-15-451-4267; www.ashpamantarestaurante.com; Bustamante s/n; dishes AR$28-55), just off the plaza, where all ingredients are locally grown.

It's difficult but not impossible to get directly from Cachi to Cafayate. It's easier to take a bus back to Salta (AR$45, 4½ hours), via the scenic Cuesta del Obispo route past Parque Nacional Los Cardones.

QUILMES

This pre-Hispanic **pucará** (indigenous Andean fortress; admission AR$10; ⏲8am-7pm), in Tucumán province, 50km south of Cafayate, is Argentina's most extensive preserved ruin. Dating from about AD 1000, this complex urban settlement covered about 30 hectares and housed perhaps 5000 people. The Quilmes people abided contact with the Incas but could not outlast the Spaniards, who, in 1667, deported the last 2000 to Buenos Aires.

Quilmes' thick walls underscore its defensive functions, but evidence of dense occupation sprawls north and south of the nucleus.

Parador Ruinas de Quilmes (☎03892-42-1075) is a hotel-restaurant beside the ruins that has been closed for some time now due to a local legal dispute. Call ahead or ask at any tourist office for the latest update.

Buses from Cafayate to Santa María pass the Quilmes junction, but from there, it's 5km to the ruins by foot or thumb.

Salta

☎0387 / POP 566,700

Salta has experienced a huge surge in popularity as a backpacking destination over the last few years, and rightly so – the setting's gorgeous, the hostels are attractive, the nightlife pumps and there's plenty to do in and around town.

Sights

Salta owes much of its reputation for beauty to the various churches scattered around the downtown area. The 19th-century **Iglesia Catedral** (España 596) guards the ashes of General Martín Miguel de Güemes, a hero of the wars of independence. So ornate it's almost gaudy, the **Iglesia San Francisco** (cnr Caseros & Córdoba; ⏲8am-noon & 5-9pm) is a Salta landmark. Only Carmelite nuns can enter the 16th-century adobe **Convento de San Bernardo** (cnr Caseros & Santa Fe), but anyone can admire its carved *algarrobo* (carob wood) door or peek inside the chapel during Mass, held at 8am daily.

Cerro San Bernardo HILL

For spectacular views of Salta and the Lerma valley, take the **teleférico** (cable car; ☎431-0641; one way/round trip AR$15/30; ⏲10am-7pm) from Parque San Martín, or climb the winding staircase trail that starts behind the Güemes monument. You can hire a mountain bike up top and roll back down for AR$60.

Museo de Arqueología de Alta Montaña (MAAM) MUSEUM

(www.maam.org.ar; B Mitre 77; Argentines/foreigners AR$30/40; ⏲11am-7:30pm Tue-Sun) Documents the amazing discovery of three mummies found at an altitude of 6700m on the Llullailaco volcano. The climate kept the bodies and a collection of textiles and sacred objects found alongside them almost perfectly preserved.

Pajcha – Museo de Arte Étnico Americano MUSEUM

(www.museopajchasalta.com.ar; 20 de Febrero 831; admission AR$20; ⏲10am-1pm & 4-8pm Mon-Sat) This eye-opening private museum is a must-see for anyone interested in indigenous art and culture. Six exquisitely presented rooms showcase contemporary and recent artisanal work from all over Latin America. The quality of the pieces exhibited is extraordinarily high, testament to decades of study and collection by the anthropologist founder.

FREE **Museo de Arte Contemporáneo** GALLERY

(Zuviría 90; ⏲9am-8pm Tue-Sat, 4-8pm Sun) Displays the work of contemporary artists from Salta, as well as other parts of Argentina and the world. The space is well lit and expertly curated. Exhibitions change regularly and are usually of high quality.

Museo Antropológico MUSEUM

(www.antropologico.com.ar; cnr Ejército del Norte & Polo Sur; admission AR$5; ⏲8am-7pm Mon-Fri, 10am-6pm Sat) Just above the Güemes monument, on the lower slopes of Cerro San Bernardo, this welcoming museum has good representations of local ceramics, especially from the Tastil ruins (Argentina's largest pre-Inca town), and some well-designed displays in its attractive, purpose-built spaces.

Activities

Whitewater rafting outside of town is available with various companies along Buenos Aires, near the Plaza 9 de Julio. **Salta Rafting** (☎421-3216; www.saltarafting.com; Caseros 177) can take care of all your rafting, ziplining, mountain biking, trekking and horse-riding requirements.

If that all sounds a bit much for you, **pedal boats** (per 20 minutes AR$30) are available on the lake in Parque San Martín.

El Tren a las Nubes TOUR

(☎422-3033; www.trenalasnubes.com.ar; cnr Ameghino & Balcarce; from AR$830) From Salta, the Tren a las Nubes (Train to the Clouds) makes countless switchbacks and spirals to ascend the Quebrada del Toro and reach the high *puna* (Andean plateau). The La Polvorilla viaduct, crossing a broad desert canyon, is a magnificent engineering achievement at 4220m above sea level. The tracks have been plagued by maintenance issues in recent years and departures are not at all guaranteed. When it is running, most trips take place on Saturday only from April to November but can be more frequent during July holidays. Contact Tren a las Nubes to get the latest news.

Sleeping

Hostel los Cordones HOSTEL $

(☎431-4026; www.loscordones.todowebsalta.com.ar; Entre Ríos 454; dm AR$60-70, d with/without bathroom AR$200/150; @☁) A sweet little hostel offering a good range of rooms. The location near the Balcarce nightlife zone is a bonus for party people.

Sol Huasi HOSTEL $

(☎422-2508; www.abaco.ya.com/solhuasiweb; Belgrano 671; dm/d AR$50/150; @☁) This is a basic hostel located in a cool old house. The

Salta

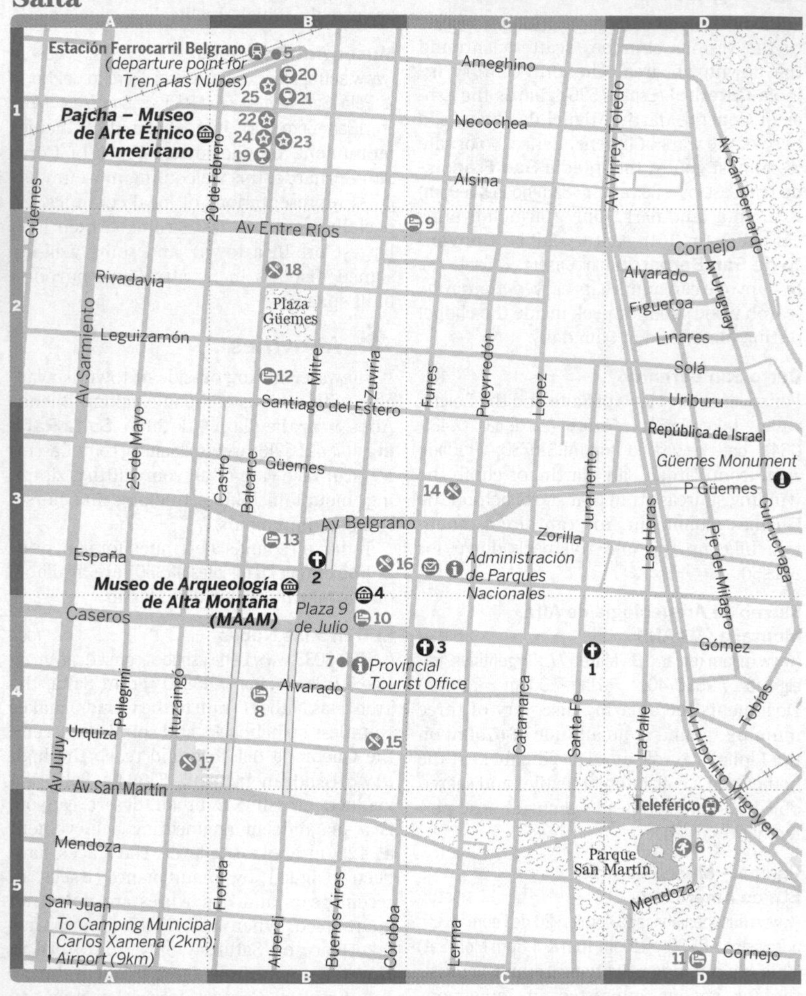

traveler-run vibe and supercentral location are pluses.

Inti Huasi HOSTEL $
(☎431-0167; www.intihuasihostel.com.ar; Abraham Cornejo 120; dm/d AR$50/150; @☎) A short stroll from the bus terminal, this hostel has an appealing atmosphere, with plenty of socializing in the good kitchen and grassy patio area. Dorms are spacious and comfortable.

Hotel Colonial HOTEL $$
(☎421-1740; www.saltahotelcolonial.com.ar; Zuviría 6; s/d from AR$300/350; ❄☎) The biggest bargain in this price range is this classic old number right on Plaza 9 de Julio. It's a bit rough around the edges, and you'd want to pay the extra AR$100 for a balcony, but it's got a style and romanticism that can't be beat.

Ferienhaus HOSTEL $
(☎431-6476; www.ferienhaushostelsalta.com; Alvarado 751; dm AR$45; @☎) A couple of blocks from Plaza 9 de Julio, this is a great location. The spacious dorms, good hangout areas and friendly staff add to the appeal.

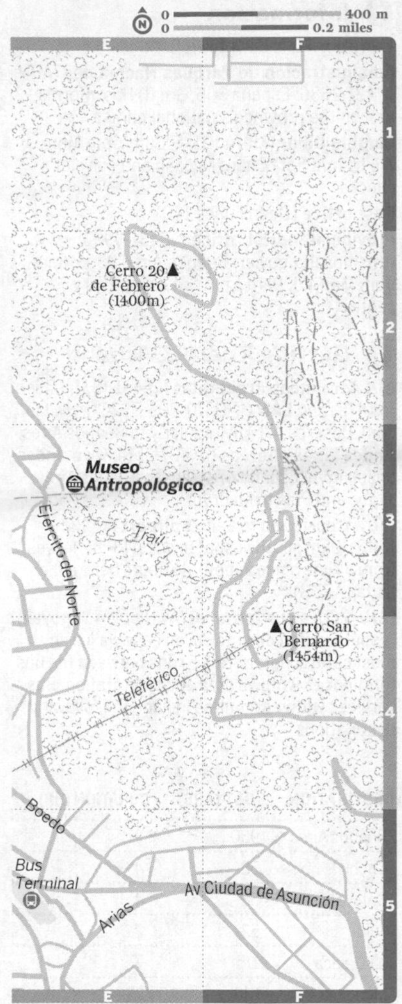

Salta

Top Sights
- Museo Antropológico E3
- Museo de Arqueología de Alta Montaña (MAAM) B3
- Pajcha – Museo de Arte Étnico Americano A1

Sights
1. Convento de San Bernardo C4
2. Iglesia Catedral B3
3. Iglesia San Francisco C4
4. Museo de Arte Contemporáneo B3

Activities, Courses & Tours
5. El Tren a las Nubes B1
6. Pedal Boats D5
7. Salta Rafting B4

Sleeping
8. Ferienhaus B4
9. Hostel los Cordones C2
10. Hotel Colonial B4
11. Inti Huasi D5
12. Residencial Balcarce B2
13. Sol Huasi B3

Eating
14. Bio's Diet C3
15. Don José B4
16. La Chueca B3
17. Mercado Central A4
18. Pashionaria B2

Drinking
19. Ksa Tomada B1
20. Macondo B1
21. Wasabi B1

Entertainment
22. Amnesia B1
23. La Estación B1
24. La Vieja Estación B1
25. Pachamama B1

Residencial Balcarce GUESTHOUSE $
(☎431-8135; www.residencialbalcarce.com.ar; Balcarce 460; s/d AR$140/200, without bathroom AR$100/140; wifi) An honest little budget hotel in a good spot. The beds aren't that great, but everything else is.

Camping Municipal Carlos Xamena CAMPGROUND $
(☎423-1341; Av Libano; per person/tent/car AR$10/25/25; pool) Features a gigantic swimming pool. Take bus 3B from the corner of Mendoza and Lerma near the Parque San Martín.

Eating & Drinking

The west side of Plaza 9 de Julio is lined with cafes and bars that have tables out on the plaza; there are some great spots for coffee, snacks or a few drinks.

Balcarce, south of the train station, is Salta's very happening *zona viva* – four blocks stacked with restaurants, bars and clubs.

TOP CHOICE **Don José** PARRILLA $

(Urquiza 484; mains AR$30-60; ⊙lunch & dinner) Bustling at all hours, this local-favorite *parrilla* has excellent prices and a menu that takes a couple of unexpected turns, including river fish and homemade pasta.

Pashionaria PARRILLA $$

(Balcarce 660; mains AR$45-80; ⊙lunch & dinner) Located at the start of the Balcarce strip, this old house turned *parrilla* has some interesting offerings on the menu, including llama steaks.

La Chueca ARGENTINE $

(España 476; empanadas AR$5, mains around AR$50; ⊙lunch & dinner) Salta's empanadas are famous countrywide and this is as good a place as any to find out why, alongside regional favorites such as *locro, humitas* and goat stew.

Bio's Diet VEGETARIAN $

(Güemes 321; lunch AR$25; ⊙lunch Mon-Sat;) A set menu that changes daily, plus tasty salads, soyburgers and options for special diets make this a welcome break from the steakhouse.

Mercado Central MARKET $

(Florida & Av San Martín; mains from AR$15) At this large, lively market you can supplement inexpensive pizza, empanadas and *humitas* with fresh fruit and vegetables.

In the Balcarce area, smaller bars include **Ksa Tomada** (Balcarce 821; ⊙9pm-late Wed-Sun), and the loungey cool of **Wasabi** (Balcarce 938; ⊙9pm-late Thu-Sat). **Macondo** (www.macondobar.com; Balcarce 980; ⊙8pm-late) is the place for a few quiet drinks (midweek, anyway).

Entertainment

Going out is easy in Salta, thanks to the compact nature of the nightlife zone – which is basically crammed into two blocks at the north end of Balcarce. Everything's here, from the megadisco experience at **La Estación** (Balcarce 872; ⊙Thu-Sat) and **Amnesia** (cnr Balcarce & Necochea; ⊙10pm-late Thu-Sat) to down-home *peñas* such as **La Vieja Estación** (☎421-7727; www.viejaestacion-salta.com.ar; Balcarce 885; shows AR$15-25; ⊙8pm-3am Tue-Sun) and **Pachamama** (Balcarce 931; ⊙8pm-2am Tue-Sun).

Information

There are ATMs downtown.

Administración de Parques Nacionales (APN; ☎431-2686; España 366, 3rd fl) Has information on the province's national parks.

Cambio Dinar (Mitre 101; ⊙8am-6pm Mon-Fri, to 1pm Sat) Changes cash and traveler's checks.

Post office (Deán Funes 140)

Provincial tourist office (☎431-0950; www.turismosalta.gov.ar; Buenos Aires 93; ⊙8am-9pm Mon-Fri, 9am-8pm Sat & Sun) Very central.

Getting There & Around

AIR **Aerolíneas Argentinas** (☎431-1331; Caseros 475) and **LAN** (☎0810-999-9526; www.lan.com; Caseros 476) fly regularly to Buenos Aires. **Andes Líneas Aéreas** (☎437-3514; www.andesonline.com; España 478) flies to Buenos Aires, Jujuy, and Puerto Madryn.

Transportation to Salta's **airport** (☎423-1648), 9km southwest of town on RP 51, leaves from airline offices about 1½ hours before the flight (AR$8).

BUS Salta's **bus terminal** (Av Hipólito Yrigoyen) is southeast of downtown, an easy walk from most central hotels. Bus 5 runs between the bus terminal, downtown area and train station. Bus services within Argentina include the following destinations:

DESTINATION	COST (AR$)	DURATION (HR)
Buenos Aires	930	21
Cachi	58	4
Cafayate	58	4
Jujuy	52	2
La Quiaca	115	7
Mendoza	619	18
Molinos	82	7
Resistencia	441	12
Rosario	754	16
Tucumán	167	4½

Géminis services the Chilean destinations of San Pedro de Atacama (AR$275, eight hours) and Calama (AR$285, 12 hours) on Mondays, Tuesdays, Thursdays and Saturdays, connecting to Antofagasta, Iquique and Arica.

BICYCLE **MTB Salta** (☎421-5971; www.mtbsalta.com; Güemes 569) rents bikes for AR$70/100 per half-/full day.

San Salvador de Jujuy

0388 / POP 340,000

If you're heading north, Jujuy is where you start to feel the proximity to Bolivia; you see it in people's faces, the chaotic street scenes, the markets that spill out onto sidewalks, and the restaurant menus that offer *locro, humitas* and *sopa de mani* (spicy peanut soup) as a matter of course, rather than as 'regional specialties.'

Originally a key stopover for colonial mule-traders en route to Potosí, Jujuy played an important part in the wars of independence when General Manuel Belgrano directed the evacuation of the entire city to avoid royalist capture; every August Jujuy's biggest event, the weeklong **Semana de Jujuy**, celebrates the *éxodo jujeño* (Jujuy exodus).

Sights & Activities

Plaza Belgrano PLAZA

As in many Argentine towns, the majority of impressive buildings are to be found around the central plaza. Opposite Plaza Belgrano, Jujuy's **Iglesia Catedral** (1763) features a gold-laminated Spanish baroque pulpit, built by local artisans under a European master. In a small square next to the church is the **Paseo de los Artesanos** (9am-12:30pm & 3-6pm), a colorful arts market. On the south side of Plaza Belgrano, the imposing **Casa de Gobierno** is built in the style of a French palace and houses Argentina's first national flag. On the north side of the plaza, the colonial **cabildo** (Plaza Belgrano) deserves more attention than the **Museo Policial** (8:30am-1pm & 3-9pm Mon-Fri, 9am-noon & 6-8pm Sat & Sun) within.

Museo Arqueológico Provincial MUSEUM

(Lavalle 434; admission AR$5; 8am-8pm Mon-Fri, 9am-1pm & 3-7pm Sat & Sun) If you have even a basic grasp of Spanish, the Museo Arqueológico Provincial is well worth your while: the guided tour is excellent, and the detailed descriptions of shamanism in the area are fascinating. If not, the poorly labeled exhibits may leave you a bit cold.

Hostería Termas de Reyes Thermal Baths HEALTH & FITNESS

(admission AR$20; 9am-7pm) Don't leave Jujuy without wallowing in the thermal baths at Termas de Reyes, 20km northwest of downtownoverlooking the scenic canyon of the Río Reyes. Look for the bus (AR$3, one hour) passing along Urquiza with 'Termas' on the placard. Take food – there's nothing to buy out there.

Noroeste TOUR

(423-7565; www.noroestevirtual.com.ar; San Martín 136) A recommended tour operator offering trips to provincial highlights, plus more offbeat options such as paragliding, snowboarding and community tourism.

Sleeping

Club Hostel HOSTEL $

(423-7565; www.clubhosteljujuy.com.ar; San Martín 134; dm/d AR$90/200;) Decent location, excellent rooms and friendly staff. The travel agency Noroeste is on-site.

Residencial Alvear GUESTHOUSE $

(422-2982; aurora627@wirenet.com.ar; Alvear 627; s/d AR$140/250, without bathroom AR$75/150;) This is the best budget hotel near the city center. Just make sure you're at the back, away from the noisy restaurant downstairs.

Dublin Hostel HOSTEL $

(422-9608; www.yokwahi.com/; Independencia 946; dm/d without bathroom AR$60/180;) Set in a big ol' classic house, this place has some stylish touches. The central location and on-site bar are bonuses.

Posada El Arribo BOUTIQUE HOTEL $$

(422-2539; www.elarribo.com; Belgrano 1263; s/d from AR$250/380;) An oasis in the heart of Jujuy, this highly impressive family-run place is a real visual feast. The renovated 19th-century mansion is wonderful, with high ceilings and wooden floors; there's patio space galore and a huge garden.

Hotel Internacional HOTEL $$

(423-1599; www.hinternacionaljujuy.com.ar; Belgrano 501; s/d AR$250/310;) Perched on a corner of the plaza, this high-rise has smallish but bright cream-colored rooms with good-looking clean bathrooms. Some have spectacular views out over the plaza, and nice touches include a morning paper put under your door. Good value.

Camping El Refugio CAMPGROUND $

(490-9344; www.elrefugiodeyala.com.ar; RN 9, Km 14; per person AR$20) Located about 3km west of downtown Jujuy. Bus 9 heads there from downtown or the bus terminal.

San Salvador de Jujuy

San Salvador de Jujuy

Top Sights
Museo Arqueológico Provincial C1
Paseo de los Artesanos D2

Sights
1 Cabildo D1
2 Casa de Gobierno D2
3 Iglesia Catedral D2
Museo Policial .... (see 1)

Sleeping
4 Dublin Hostel B2
5 Hotel Internacional D1
6 Posada El Arribo A2
7 Residencial Alvear C1

Eating
8 Madre Tierra C1
9 Manos Jujeñas B1
10 Mercado Municipal C1
11 Miralejos D2
12 Viracocha B2
13 Zorba C2

Drinking
14 Alto Belgrano C2

Entertainment
15 Voodoo C1

Shopping
16 Mercado del Sur C3

Eating & Drinking

As far as drinking in Jujuy goes, you have two options: shooting pool and singing karaoke at **Alto Belgrano** (Belgrano 724; 4pm-late) or flat out thumping disco at **Voodoo** (Alvear 546; Wed-Sat).

Manos Jujeñas ARGENTINE $
(Av Senador Pérez 381; mains AR$30-45; Tue-Sun) One of Jujuy's best addresses for no-frills traditional slow-food cooking, this place fills up with a contented buzz on weekend evenings. There are several classic northeastern dishes to choose from, but it's the *picante* – marinated chicken or tongue (or both) with onion, tomato, rice and Andean potatoes – that's the pride of the house.

Miralejos ARGENTINE $$
(Sarmiento 368; meals AR$40-60; breakfast, lunch & dinner) This is plazaside dining at

its finest. Miralejos offers the full gamut of steak and pasta (with a wide choice of interesting sauces), with a few local trout dishes thrown in. The outside tables are a great place for breakfast.

Madre Tierra BAKERY, CAFE **$$**
(Belgrano 619; 4-course lunch AR$60; ⏲7am-6pm Mon-Sat; ✍) The vegetarian food is excellent, and the salads, crepes and soups can be washed down with carrot or apple juice.

Viracocha ARGENTINE **$**
(cnr Independencia & Lamadrid; mains AR$24-38; ⏲lunch Wed-Mon, dinner Wed-Sat & Mon) Some other places say they offer regional food, but this one delivers, with plenty of quinoa, llama and spicy favorites to choose from alongside a good range of steak and fish dishes.

Zorba INTERNATIONAL **$$**
(cnr Necochea & Belgrano; mains AR$40-60; ⏲breakfast, lunch & dinner) Good news: the Greek food is back on the menu at this main-street cafe. Even better: the gut-busting Americano breakfast hasn't gone anywhere.

Mercado Municipal MARKET **$**
(cnr Alvear & Balcarce) Upstairs, several eateries serve inexpensive regional specialties that are generally spicier than elsewhere in Argentina; try *chicharrón con mote* (stir-fried pork with boiled maize).

Information

ATMs are common on Belgrano, and banks should be able to change traveler's checks.

Staff at the **municipal tourist office** (☎422-1326; Av Urquiza 354; ⏲8am-10pm) in the old railway station are helpful and have abundant maps and brochures on hand. There's another tourist information kiosk just outside the bus terminal and a **provincial tourist office** (☎422-1343; www.turismo.jujuy.gov.ar; Gorriti 295; ⏲7am-10pm Mon-Fri, 9am-9pm Sat & Sun) right on the plaza.

The **post office** (cnr Independencia & Lamadrid) is downtown.

Getting There & Around

Air

Aerolíneas Argentinas (☎422-2575; www.aerolineas.com; Av Pérez 341) flies to Buenos Aires regularly. **Andes Líneas Aéreas** (☎431-0279; www.andesonline.com; San Martín 1283) flies to Buenos Aires via Salta.

Jujuy's **airport** (☎491-1103) is 32km southeast of town. The airlines provide transportation to the airport.

Bus

Jujuy's scruffy **bus terminal** (☎422-1375; cnr Av Dorrego & Iguazú) blends in with the Mercado del Sur. It has long-distance and provincial bus services, although Salta has more alternatives. To get to the center from the terminal, walk north along Av Dorrego and across the river, keeping the hill at your back.

Chile-bound buses from Salta to Calama (AR$285, 13 hours) stop in Jujuy Tuesdays, Thursdays and Sundays. Make reservations in advance at the Plusultra Mercobus office at the terminal.

El Quiaqueño goes to La Quiaca (AR$50, five hours), Humahuaca (AR$30, 2½ hours) and Tilcara (AR$20, 1½ hours). Cota Norte goes daily to Libertador General San Martín (AR$50, two hours), for access to Parque Nacional Calilegua.

Long-distance services include Tucumán (AR$155, 5½ hours), Córdoba (AR$506, 12 hours), Mendoza (AR$633, 16 hours) and Buenos Aires (AR$994, 24 hours).

Quebrada de Humahuaca

North of Jujuy, RN 9 snakes its way through the Quebrada de Humahuaca, a painter's palette of color on barren hillsides, dwarfing hamlets where Quechua peasants scratch a living growing maize and raising scrawny livestock. On this colonial post route to Potosí, the architecture and other cultural features mirror Peru and Bolivia.

Various earthquakes leveled many of the adobe churches, but they were often rebuilt during the 17th and 18th centuries with solid walls, simple bell towers, and striking doors and wood paneling from the *cardón* cactus.

TILCARA

☎0388 / POP 6050

The most comfortable of the Quebrada towns, Tilcara is also one of the prettiest, and it hosts a number of fine eating and sleeping options.

Tilcara's hilltop *pucará,* a pre-Hispanic fortress with unobstructed views, is its most conspicuous attraction, but the village's museums and its reputation as an artists colony also help make it an appealing stopover for travelers.

Sights & Activities

Museo Arqueológico Dr Eduardo Casanova MUSEUM
(Belgrano 445; admission AR$30, Mon free; ⊙9am-6pm) This well-organized museum, run by the Universidad de Buenos Aires, features some artifacts from the site of the *pucará*. The room dedicated to ceremonial masks and their manufacture is particularly impressive. The museum is located in a striking colonial house on the south side of Plaza Prado. Admission also includes entry to El Pucará.

Museo José Antonio Terry GALLERY
(Rivadavia 459; admission AR$10; ⊙10am-6pm Tue-Sun) The Museo José Antonio Terry features the work of the Buenos Aires–born painter whose themes were largely rural and indigenous; his oils depict native weavers, market and street scenes, and portraits. Also featured is work from local and regional artists.

El Pucará RUIN
(admission AR$30; ⊙dawn-dusk-) Rising above the sediments of the Río Grande valley, an isolated hill is the site of El Pucará, located 1km south of central Tilcara. There are fantastic views of the valley from the top of the fort, which has been brilliantly reconstructed in parts. The admission fee includes entry to the Museo Arqueológico Dr Eduardo Casanova.

Maimará CEMETERY
Only a few kilometers south of Tilcara, the hillside cemetery of Maimará is a can't-miss photo opportunity.

Tilcara Mountain Bike BICYCLE RENTAL
(☎0388-15-500-8570; tilcarabikes@hotmail.com; Belgrano s/n; per 1/6 hours AR$20/60 ; ⊙9:30am-7pm) A friendly setup opposite the bus terminal that rents out well-maintained mountain bikes and has useful area maps for day trips.

Tilcara is full of trekking and tour operators. Check with the tourist office for flyers. **Caravana de Llamas** (☎495-5326; www.caravanadellamas.com; cnr Corte & Viltipico) offers llama trekking (the llamas carry luggage, not people) of varying lengths and difficulties from AR$250.

Sleeping & Eating

Cheap places to eat line Belgrano and Lavalle between the bus terminal and Plaza Prado.

Hostel Waira HOSTEL $
(Padilla 596; dm AR$40, s/d AR$120/160, without bathroom AR$80/120; @📶) A short walk up the hill from the main drag, this well set-up hostel offers decent dorms and great rooms, surrounding a large garden with shady trees.

Patio Alto HOTEL, HOSTEL $$
(☎495-5792; www.patioalto.com.ar; Torrico 675; dm/s/d AR$98/360/390; @) Great vistas from the coziness of your large bed are the high-

GETTING TO BOLIVIA

Cold, windy **La Quiaca** is a major crossing point to Bolivia. It has decent places to stay and eat, but little to detain the traveler. If you arrive late at night, however, it's best to stay here as services are much better than across the border in Villazón.

La Quiaca has no tourist office, but the ACA station on RN 9 has maps. **Hostel El Apolillo** (☎42-2388; www.elapolillohostel.blogspot.com; Arabe Siria 146; dm/s/d/tr AR$50/100/150/180; @📶) is one of the finer hostels in the country, and is full of information on what to do in the area and how to move on. In terms of hotels, the **Hotel de Turismo** (☎42-2243; hotelmun@laquiaca.com.ar; cnr Árabe Siria & San Martín; s/d AR$150/250; @📶) is about as good as it gets, and serves decent meals too.

From the **bus terminal** (cnr Belgrano & España), there are frequent connections to Jujuy (AR$50, five hours), Salta (AR$115, seven hours) and intermediate points, plus long-distance services.

The border is a 1km walk from the bus terminal. There is no public transportation, but if there's a taxi around, they should be able to take you for AR$8. The border is open 8am to 8pm daily, but the hours are subject to change – don't arrive too close to opening or closing time.

light of the handsome modern rooms here. There are also downstairs (but upmarket) dorms that are every bit as nice – the only thing missing is the view.

Uwa Wasi HOTEL $$
(☎495-5368; www.uwawasi.com.ar; Lavalle 564; d AR$350, s/d without bathroom AR$120/240) Beautiful, medium-sized rooms around a vine-shaded courtyard. The mountain views from out back alone are worth the price.

Autocamping El Jardín CAMPGROUND $
(☎495-5128; www.eljardintilcara.com.ar; Belgrano 700; campsites per person AR$25) At the west end of Belgrano, near the river. Good hot showers and attractive vegetable and flower gardens.

La Chacana ARGENTINE, FUSION $
(Belgrano 472; mains AR$18-30) This place is set in a sweet little courtyard and offers nouveau Andean dishes featuring quinoa, wild mushrooms and local herbs.

El Cafecito CAFE $
(cnr Belgrano & Rivadavia; ⌚breakfast & lunch) El Cafecito is the place for coffee and croissants. The homemade cakes (AR$8 to AR$10) are worth keeping an eye out for.

Entertainment

Nightlife is limited in Tilcara, but there are plenty of *peñas* around, hosting live folk music every night. **La Peña de Carlitos** (cnr Rivadavia & Lavalle; ⌚noon-1am) is probably the most consistent.

Information

The **tourist office** (☎0388 495-5135; mun_tilcara@cootepal.com.ar; Belgrano 366; ⌚8am-9pm Mon-Fri, 8am-1pm & 2-9pm Sat, 8am-noon Sun), in the municipal offices, distributes a useful map.

Banco Macro, on Plaza Prado, has an ATM.

Getting There & Around

Both northbound and southbound buses leave from the bus terminal on Exodo, three blocks west of Plaza Prado. Sample destinations include Jujuy (AR$20, 1½ hours), Humahuaca (AR$10, 40 minutes) and La Quiaca (AR$41, four hours).

HUMAHUACA

☎03887 / POP 8500

A popular stopover on the Salta–Bolivia route, Humahuaca is a mostly Quechuan village of narrow cobbled streets lined with adobe houses. There's plenty to do in the surrounding countryside, and the town provides some great photo opportunities.

Sights & Activities

Cabildo NOTABLE BUILDING
(Plaza Gómez) The *cabildo* is famous for its clocktower, where a life-size figure of San Francisco Solano emerges daily at noon to deliver a benediction. Be sure to arrive early; the clock is erratic and the figure appears only very briefly.

Iglesia de la Candelaria CHURCH
Humahuaca's patron saint resides in the colonial Iglesia de la Candelaria, which faces the plaza. It contains 18th-century oil paintings by Cuzco painter Marcos Sapaca.

Monumento a la Independencia MONUMENT
Overlooking the town is this monument by Tilcara sculptor Ernesto Soto Avendaño.

Museo Arqueológico Torres Aparicio MUSEUM
(Córdoba 249; admission AR$8; ⌚11am-2pm Thu-Sat) This museum has a small but interesting collection of local archaeological finds.

Coctaca RUIN
Ten kilometers north of Humahuaca by a dirt road, on the east side of the bridge over the Río Grande, northwestern Argentina's most extensive pre-Columbian ruins cover 40 hectares. Many appear to be broad agricultural terraces on an alluvial fan, but there are also obvious outlines of clusters of buildings.

Ser Andino OUTDOORS
(☎42-1659; www.serandino.com.ar; Jujuy 393) The best-established tour and trekking agency in town. It also rents mountain bikes for AR$30 per four hours.

Festivals & Events

Carnaval celebrations are particularly boisterous here.

On 2 February, the village holds a **festival** in honor of the town's patron saint, the Virgen de la Candelaria.

Sleeping & Eating

Many restaurants around town feature live folk music most nights.

Hostal Río Grande HOTEL $
(☎42-1908; Corrientes 480; s/d AR$80/160, without bathroom AR$40/80; @) Basic rooms out the back of a family home. The ones upstairs get some good views of the surrounding countryside.

Hostal La Soñada GUESTHOUSE $
(☎42-1228; www.hostallasoniada.com; San Martín s/n; s/d AR$200/250; ❄📶) Across the tracks from the center, this cute inn offers immaculate, tastefully decorated rooms, comfortable common areas and a charming backyard.

Hostería Naty GUESTHOUSE $
(☎42-1022; www.hosterianaty.com.ar; Buenos Aires 488; s/d AR$110/150; 📶) Right in the heart of town, with rooms of varying shapes and sizes at a fair price. The ones around the outside patio are quieter.

Casa Vieja ARGENTINE $$
(cnr Buenos Aires & Salta; mains AR$35-70; 🖉) One of the more appealing restaurants in town, featuring regional dishes alongside Argentine standards.

El Refugio ARGENTINE $
(Salta 159; mains AR$30-50; ⏲breakfast, lunch & dinner) A cute little place a couple of blocks off Plaza Gómez. Regional dishes (featuring llama, quinoa and corn) dominate the menu, with a couple of pasta dishes thrown in for good measure. Good salad selection, too.

Information

The **tourist office** (Plaza Gómez s/n; ⏲10am-9pm Mon-Fri) beneath the clock tower keeps irregular hours but has excellent information on accommodation and local attractions.

Getting There & Away

From the **bus terminal** (cnr Belgrano & Entre Ríos) there are several departures to Salta (AR$70, five hours) and Jujuy (AR$30, two hours), and northbound buses to La Quiaca (AR$32, two hours).

ATLANTIC COAST

The beaches along the Atlantic coast form Buenos Aires' backyard, and summer sees millions of *porteños* pouring into towns such as Mar del Plata and Pinamar for sun and fun. The rest of the year, and in smaller towns, the pace of life rarely approaches anything resembling hectic.

Mar del Plata

☎0223 / POP 575,100

On summer weekends, the beach in Mardel (as it's commonly known) gets really, seriously, comically crowded. We're talking people standing shoulder to shoulder, knee-deep in water. During the week, and in the nonsummer months, the crowds disperse, hotel prices drop and the place takes on a much more relaxed feel.

Founded in 1874, this most popular of Argentine beach destinations was originally a commercial and industrial center, then a resort for upper-class *porteño* families. Mardel now caters mostly to middle-class vacationers.

Sights & Activities

Museo del Mar MUSEUM
(Av Colón 1114; admission AR$30; ⏲10am-7pm) Museo del Mar is probably the most extensive seashell museum you'll ever see. Based around central cafes on two floors are a small tide pool and an aquarium. It's a good place to rest and have tea.

Aquarium Mar del Plata AQUARIUM
(☎467-0700; www.mdpaquarium.com.ar; Av Martínez de Hoz 5600; adult/child 3-10yr AR$98/70; ⏲10am-8pm) The excellent aquarium, 6km south of town, has all regular fishy attractions, plus dolphin shows, swimming with the sharks, and water-ski and wakeboard classes. Bus 221 from the center goes here.

Villa Normandy NOTABLE BUILDING
(Viamonte 2216) Now the Italian consulate, 1919 Villa Normandy is one of few surviving examples of the French style that was en vogue in the 1950s.

Iglesia Stella Maris CHURCH
Near the top of Stella Maris hill, this church has an impressive marble altar; its virgin is the patron saint of local fishers.

FREE **Torre Tanque** TOWER
(☎451-4681; Falucho 995; ⏲8am-4pm Mon-Fri) This medieval water storage tower on the summit of the hill offers outstanding views.

Intersub DIVING
(☎467-4081; Catamarca 3644) Offers scuba courses and dive trips and rents out scuba gear.

Arcangél EXTREME SPORTS
(☎463-1167; www.parapentes.com) Arcangél offers tandem parachute jumps for AR$250.

Bicicletería Madrid BICYCLE RENTAL
(☎494-1932; Yrigoyen 2249; per hour/day AR$20/80) You can rent bicycles from this place on Plaza Mitre.

MDP Surf School SURFING
(Balneario #8, Playa Grande) Offers surf classes, board and wetsuit hire.

Festivals & Events

Mar del Plata Film Festival FILM FESTIVAL
(www.mardelplatafilmfest.com) Held in November, this film festival attracts serious international attention, both for films that debut here and the celebrities that attend.

Sleeping

Prices are about 30% higher in January and February, so it's worth making reservations.

Rates at Mardel's crowded campgrounds, mostly south of town, are around AR$30 per person; the tourist office has information about their facilities.

La Pergola Hostel HOSTEL $
(493-3695; www.lapergolahostel.com.ar; Yrigoyen 1093; dm AR$75; @) Set in a beautiful 1929 stone house a block from the beach, this is one of the better-looking hostels in town.

Alta Esperanza Hostel HOSTEL $
(495-8650; www.altaesperanzahostel.com.ar; Av Peralta Ramos 1361; dm AR$85-125, r AR$320-350; @) Mardel's first waterfront hostel is located in a historic, Normandy-style building and offers six- to 12-bed dorms and a few private rooms. It's best for nonparty types – this is a place to relax. If you want a sea-view room, book ahead.

Hostel Playa Grande Suites HOSTEL $
(451-2396; www.hostelplayagrande.com.ar; Alem 3495; dm/d AR$50/200;) Smack in the middle of the bar street and a short hop from the beach, this is Mardel's ultimate surf/party hostel. Book ahead in summer.

Playa Varese Inn HOTEL $$
(451-1813; www.playavareseinn.com.ar; Gascón 715; s/d AR$350/400; @) Tucked away in a quiet neighborhood between Playa Grande and downtown, the Varese offers comfortable, cozy rooms with great beds. Reserve ahead in summer – it's popular.

Eating

There are many *tenedores libres* in the town center for AR$30 to AR$40, not including drinks – a great deal if you're a big eater.

TOP CHOICE **Mambru** BURGERS $
(Libertad 3321; mains AR$40-70; lunch & dinner) A burger joint with class? And sensational burgers? *And* good prices? Correcto. The pizzas and calzones are good, too, but the standout is the 20-deep burger menu, all of them winners.

Huijá PARRILLA $
(cnr Alem & Rodriguez; mains AR$40-70; lunch & dinner) Packed out day and night, Huijá offers good-value *parrilla* standards and the friendly neighborhood vibe you don't get downtown.

El Jamón INTERNATIONAL $$
(493-7447; Bolívar 2801; mains AR$40-60; lunch Mon-Sat, dinner Wed-Sat) A local neighborhood favorite that's short on atmosphere but long on value. You might be lucky enough to try the roasted *vacio*, shrimp kebab or mussels *provencal* – the menu changes daily.

Taberna Baska SPANISH $$
(480-0209; 12 de Octubre 3301; mains AR$35-90; lunch & dinner) Forget the overpriced tourist joints down by the port – the best seafood in town is at this authentic Basque restaurant a few blocks away.

Drinking

Weekends, the place to be is Alem, down near Playa Grande – a strip of bars, discos and restaurants.

The discos on Av Constitución heat up late on the weekends. Check out **Chocolate** (Av Constitución 4469; 10pm-late Tue-Sun summer) or **Sobremonte** (Av Constitución 6690; 10pm-late Wed-Sun), both of which charge AR$30 to AR$60 admission. Bus 551 runs from the center all night.

Check the monthly *Guía de Actividades*, available from the tourist office, for cultural happenings.

La Bodeguita del Medio BAR
(Castelli 1252; 7pm-late) This bar takes a fair stab at the whole Cuban thing, offering two-for-one-mojitos happy hours and a range of Cuban dishes.

Antares BAR
(Córdoba 3025; 8pm-late) This microbrewery serves up seven of its own brews, as well a range of German-influenced dishes and meat-and-beer stews.

Information

The **tourist office** (495-1777; Blvd Marítimo 2240) is near Plaza Colón.

Most *cambios*, banks and ATMs are near the intersections of San Martín and Córdoba, and Avs Independencia and Luro. Free walking tours of the city (in Spanish) leave from in front of the cathedral on Wednesday and Saturday at 5pm.

Getting There & Away

AIR **Aerolíneas Argentinas** (☎496-0101; Moreno 2442) and **Austral** (☎496-0101; Moreno 2442) scoot to Buenos Aires. **LADE** (☎491-1484; Corrientes 1537) is cheapest to Buenos Aires and also serves Patagonia.

BUS Mardel's **bus terminal** (☎561-3743; Luro 4500) is adjacent to the train station. There are departures to Buenos Aires (AR$246, 5½ hours), Pinamar (AR$56, 2½ hours), Villa Gesell (AR$45, two hours) and La Plata (AR$188, five hours).

TRAIN The **train station** (☎475-6076; www.sofse.gob.ar; Av Luro 4700 at Italia; ⏲6am-midnight) is about 20 blocks from the beach, but there's a **ticket office** (cnr Belgrano & San Luís, UCIP Building) downtown. In summer there are daily departures to Buenos Aires for AR$150 in *primera* and AR$250 in *superpullman* (those under 25 get a discount in the low season). The trip takes about seven hours.

Getting Around

The **airport** (☎478-0744) is 9km northwest of town (take bus 542 marked 'aeropuerto'); taxis there cost around AR$55.

Villa Gesell

☎02255 / POP 35,800

This laid-back dune community sleeps in the low season, but in summer it's a favorite for young *porteños*, who stream in to party the warm nights away. It's one of the prettiest coastal towns: small, with windy, sandy roads sporting charming summer cottages (and also grander retreats).

Sights & Activities

Gesell's long **beach** and boardwalk draw swimmers, sunbathers and horse riders. There's year-round **fishing** from the pier.

Feria Artesanal MARKET
(Regional y Artística; Av 3) Feria Artesanal, between Paseos 112 and 113, is an excellent arts and crafts fair that takes place every evening from mid-December to mid-March. The rest of the year it's a weekend-only event.

Windy SURFING
(☎47-4626; www.windyplayabar.com.ar; Paseo 104) Surf classes are available from Windy on the beachfront. Ask about kitesurfing classes – gear is rented to experienced kitesurfers only.

Casa Macca BICYCLE RENTAL
(☎46-8013; Av Buenos Aires; per hour/day AR$20/60) Bikes can be rented here. It's located between Paseo 101 & Av 5.

Aventura Faro Querandí TOUR
(☎46-8989; cnr Av 3 & Paseo 132) Offers exciting 4WD tours to the nearbly lighthouse, complete with some hair-raising dune bashing and excellent photo opportunities.

Sleeping

The most affordable *hospedajes* are north of Av 3. It's important to book ahead in summer, especially in the second half of January, when prices rise even more.

Gesell's campgrounds charge AR$10 to AR$20 per person. Most close for the low season, but **Autocamping Casablanca** (☎47-0771; www.autocampingcasablanca.com; Av 3) and **Camping Monte Bubi** (☎47-0732; www.montebubi.com.ar; Av 3), at the south end of town, are open all year.

La Deseada Hostel HOSTEL $
(☎47-3276; www.ladeseadahostel.com.ar; cnr Av 6 & Paseo 119; dm AR$150; @📶) One of the best-looking hostels on the coast, tucked away six blocks from the beach and a 15-minute walk from the center.

Los Médanos HOTEL $
(☎46-3205; Av 5 No 549 ; s/d AR$120/240) Basic rooms run by a friendly family. There are other, similarly priced hotels on the same block.

Hospedaje Villa Gesell HOTEL $
(☎46-6368; www.hospedajevillagesell.com.ar; Av 3 No 812; r AR$300) You really can't get more cheap or central than this family-run spot with 10 budget rooms, most located around a little patio area. There's also a garden at the back.

Hotel Royal HOTEL $$
(☎46-2411; www.hotelroyalgesell.com.ar; cnr Av 3 & Paseo 110bis; s/d AR$250/350) One of the few budget hotels open year-round, offering reasonable rooms on the main drag a few blocks from the beach.

Eating

Av 3 is the place to go for pizza, sandwiches, ice cream and *parrilla*.

The biggest concentration of bars is on Paseo 105, between Avs 2 and 3. The beachside restaurants are great places to have a few drinks and a snack at sunset, or have a meal if your wallet is up to the challenge.

Sutton 212 INTERNATIONAL **$$**
(cnr Paseo 105 & Av 2; mains AR$50-70; ⌚breakfast, lunch & dinner) With its fabric-covered ceilings and Rajasthani lamp shades, this is one of the hippest places along the coast. On top of that, surprisingly, the food, imported beers and cocktails are all reasonably priced.

Rias Baixes SEAFOOD **$$**
(Paseo 105 No 335; meals AR$50-80) The strip lighting and plastic chairs at this local *marisquería* (seafood restaurant) aren't about to win it any interior-design prizes, but it definitely serves some of the freshest, best-value seafood in town.

Las Margaritas ITALIAN **$$**
(☎45-6377; Av 2; mains AR$50-70; ⌚dinner) Charmingly cozy and quiet, this place between Paseos 104 and 105 serves excellent homemade pasta, including a shrimp and squid-ink ravioli. The tiramisu is excellent. Reserve in summer.

☆ Entertainment

Anfiteatro del Pinar CONCERT VENUE
(☎46-7123; cnr Av 10 & Paseo 102) Performances in January, February and at Semana Santa. Gesell's Encuentros Corales (a choir music festival) takes place annually in this lovely amphitheater.

Cine Teatro Atlas THEATER
(☎46-2969; Paseo 108) Such rock-and-roll greats as Charly García and Los Pericos have played at this small theater, situated between Avs 3 and 4, which doubles as a cinema during the low season.

Pueblo Límite CLUB
(☎45-2845; www.pueblolimite.com; Buenos Aires 2600; admission incl drink AR$30) A small-town megadisco, this complex has three dance clubs, two bars and a restaurant in summer. In the low season, it's just two discos – one for Latin pop, the other electronica.

Information

Banks and ATMs are on Av 3. There's a central **tourist office** (www.gesell.gov.ar; Paseo 107 btwn Avs 2 & 3; ⌚8am-8pm) just off the main street.

Getting There & Away

The main **bus terminal** (cnr Av 3 & Paseo 140) is south of town; bus 504 or an AR$25 taxi ride will get you to the center. Bus destinations include Buenos Aires (AR$206, five hours), Mar del Plata (AR$45, two hours) and Pinamar (AR$13, one hour).

Pinamar

☎02254 / POP 38,600

Rivaling Uruguay's Punta del Este in the fashion stakes, Pinamar and the surrounding towns are where wealthy Argentine families come to play in summertime.

Sights & Activities

Many places are only open on weekends and in summer, but at other times you can stroll peacefully in bordering pine forests and along the wide, attractive **beach** without being trampled by holidaymakers.

Skydiving, glider and balloon flights can be arranged at the **Aerodromo Pinamar** (☎49-3953). Bike hire is available from **Leo** (☎48-8855; Av Bunge 1111; ⌚9am-8pm). There are many more activities on offer, especially in the summer months, look for brochures in the tourist office.

Festivals & Events

The **Pinamar Film Festival** (www.pantallapinamar.com) draws crowds in early March.

Sleeping

Several campgrounds, charging AR$90 for two, line the coast between Ostende and Pinamar.

Hospedaje Acacia HOTEL **$**
(☎48-5175; Del Cangrejo 1358; s/d AR$150/300) A good, basic hotel, a few blocks from Pinamar's tourist office and about a 15-minute walk to the beach. There's a little garden patio at the back, but no breakfast on offer.

Albergue Bruno Valente HOSTEL **$**
(☎40-2783; info@aaaj.org.ar; cnr Mitre & Nuestras Malvinas, Ostende; dm AR$80) Although closed at the time of writing, this is generally a good, cheap option in summer, and a cold and dreary one in winter. It's close to the beach and far from the center, and some of the front rooms have balconies with sea views.

Eating & Drinking

Av Bunge is lined with restaurants, snack bars and ice cream parlors.

Cantina Tulumei SEAFOOD **$$**
(Bunge 64; mains AR$40-80; ⏲lunch & dinner) Pinamar's best seafood restaurant is still going strong. Check out the seafood *parrilla* for two (AR$108).

Jalisco MEXICAN **$**
(Bunge 456; mains AR$50-60; ⏲lunch & dinner) Adding just a touch of variety to your Pinamar diet, with Tex-Mex faves like fajitas and quesadillas and some OK pasta and seafood dishes too.

Acqua & Farina PIZZERIA **$$**
(cnr Cerezo & Boyero, Cariló; mains AR$30-60; ⏲lunch & dinner) Head to the neighboring village of Cariló for the best thin-crust pizza around, as well as fresh salads and homemade pastas. Located in Cariló plaza, the last stop for the local 'Montemar' bus.

Ojalá CAFÉ **$**
(cnr Bunge & Marco Polo; mains around AR$40; ⏲breakfast, lunch & dinner) Pinamar's classic corner coffee shop provides a cozy atmosphere and decent-value set lunches (AR$69).

During summer the restaurants along the beachfront turn into bars and discos (don't worry – you'll hear 'em) and generally go until the break of dawn. In the low season, check the area bounded by Avs Bunge, Libertador and de las Artes. Solid bets are **Antiek Bar** (Av Libertador 27) and **Paco** (cnr Avs de las Gaviotas & de las Artes). Not cool enough for you? Try **Black Cream** (cnr Jones & Av Libertador), possibly the Atlantic coast's only dedicated funk club.

Information

Libertador, roughly paralleling the beach, and perpendicular Av Bunge are the main drags. The **tourist office** (☎49-1680; Av Shaw 18) has a good map.

Getting There & Away

The **bus terminal** (cnr Shaw & Calle del Pejerrey) is 12 blocks from the beach and seven from the center. Bus destinations include Buenos Aires (AR$218, 4½ hours), Mar del Plata (AR$62, 2½ hours) and Villa Gesell (AR$13, one hour)

The train station is a couple of kilometers north of town, near Bunge. Trains run in summer to Buenos Aires on Sundays (AR$194, six hours). Purchase tickets at the bus terminal..

Bahía Blanca

☎0291 / POP 292,600

Mostly a stopover point for people headed elsewhere, Bahía Blanca is surprisingly cosmopolitan for its size, and boasts Argentina's worst-signposted museum.

Sights

On weekends there's a **feria artesanal** (crafts fair) on Plaza Rivadavia.

FREE **Museo del Puerto** MUSEUM
(☎457-3006; cnr Guillermo Torres & Cárrega; ⏲8:30am-12:30pm Mon-Fri, 4-8pm Sat & Sun) The most worthwhile sight is Museo del Puerto, a whimsical tribute to the immigrant population of Bahía Blanca. From downtown, buses 500 and 501 drop passengers a few blocks away – ask for plenty of directions.

Sleeping & Eating

Bahía Blanca Hostel HOSTEL **$**
(☎452-6802; www.hostelbahiablanca.com; Soler 701; dm/s AR$42/70, d with/without bathroom AR$120/85; @) A new hostel set up in an old-school way; what it lacks in charm it makes up for in value.

Hotel Victoria HOTEL **$**
(☎452-0522; www.hotelvictoriabb.com.ar; Gral Paz 84; s/d AR$150/260, without bathroom AR$100/180; ❄) This well-kept old building has a range of basic, comfortable rooms set around a leafy central courtyard.

Piazza ARGENTINE **$**
(cnr O'Higgins & Chiclana; mains AR$40-55; ⏲breakfast, lunch & dinner) A popular lunch spot right on the plaza, with an imaginative menu and a fully stocked bar. Chocoholics should not miss the chocolate mousse (AR$8).

Bambú BUFFET **$$**
(Chiclana 298; buffet AR$52-65; ⏲lunch & dinner) The best deal in town for the hungry is this *tenedor libre* efficiently run by a Chinese family. You can choose from heaps of cooked dishes (many with Asian flavors), along with Argentine *asado*. Drinks cost extra.

Information

For the lowdown on music, art and theater happenings around town, pick up a copy of the *Agenda Cultural*, available in the tourist office, restaurants and bars.

Post office (Moreno 34)

Pullman Cambio (San Martín 171) Changes traveler's checks.

Tourist office (☎459-4007; Alsina 45; ⊙8am-3pm Mon-Fri) Almost overwhelmingly helpful.

Getting There & Around

The airport is 15km east of town. **Aerolíneas Argentinas/Austral** (☎456-0561; San Martín 298) has flights to Buenos Aires.

The **bus terminal** (Brown 1700) is about 2km east of Plaza Rivadavia; there are many local buses heading into town (AR$1; buy magnetic cards from kiosks). To avoid the trek out to the terminal you can buy bus tickets at the handy downtown **office** (cnr Chiclana & Alsina) right on the plaza. Destinations include Sierra de la Ventana (AR$44, two hours), Buenos Aires (AR$430, nine hours), Santa Rosa (AR$170, six hours) and Neuquén (AR$248, seven hours).

The **train station** (☎452-9196; Cerri 750) has services to Buenos Aires Tuesday to Friday and Sundays. Fares cost AR$58/95 in *turista*/Pullman class.

Sierra de la Ventana

☎0291 / POP 3020

Sierra de la Ventana is where *porteños* come to escape the summer heat, hike around a bit and cool off in swimming holes. The nearby mountain range of the same name in Parque Provincial Ernesto Tornquist attracts hikers and climbers to its jagged peaks, which rise over 1300m.

For a nice walk, go to the end of Calle Tornquist and cross the small dam (which makes a local **swimming hole**). On the other side you'll see **Cerro del Amor**; hike to the top for good views of town and pampas.

El Tornillo (☎0291-15-431-1812; Roca 142; ⊙10am-7pm, closed in afternoons during hot weather) rents bikes for AR$15/70 per one/eight hours.

Sleeping & Eating

There are several free campsites along the river, with bathroom facilities nearby at the pleasant and grassy municipal swimming pool.

Hostería Maiten HOTEL $
(☎491-5073; hosteriamaiten@yahoo.com.ar; Iguazú 93; s/d AR$180/220; 📶) Spotless, older-style rooms around a lush courtyard. A good budget deal.

La Casa de Juani HOSTEL $
(☎0291-15-416-0931; hostellacasadejuani@hotmail.com; Camino de las Carretas s/n; dm/r AR$70/160; @📶) Next to fields on the edge of town, this tiny but beautiful hostel has just one private room and one four-bed dorm (camping and *cabañas* coming). Bike rentals are available. To get here, it's about a 10-minute dusty walk from the YPF gas station.

Hotel Atero HOTEL $
(☎491-5002; cnr Av San Martín & Güemes; s/d AR$250/300; ❄📶) One of the most comfortable options in town, with large, homey rooms right on the main street.

Camping El Paraíso CAMPGROUND $
(☎0291-15-407-4530; camping_elparaiso@yahoo.com.ar; Los Tilos 150; campsites per person AR$28, cabañas from AR$100) This decent campground is pretty centrally located, with dusty, shady sites and various services. Small *cabañas* with bunk beds and outside baths are available. It's located 2.5 blocks from the main street.

Parrilla Rali-Hué PARRILLA $
(☎491-5220; San Martín 307; mains AR$35-60; ⊙lunch & dinner) Good atmosphere and reasonable prices for a main-street tourist town *parrilla*.

Sol y Luna ARGENTINE $
(☎491-5316; Av San Martín 658; mains AR$35-60; ⊙lunch & dinner) This place has an excellent menu of carefully prepared dishes, and the trout with almond sauce (AR$45) is a standout.

Information

Tourist office (☎491-5303; www.sierradelaventana.org.ar; Av del Golf s/n; ⊙8am-8pm) Near the train station.

Getting There & Away

Sierra de la Ventana has no bus terminal; buses leave from the respective companies' offices. **Condor Estrella** (☎491-5091) leaves twice daily for Bahía Blanca (AR$44, 2½ hours), and has daily departures for La Plata (AR$261, 13 hours) and Buenos Aires (AR$262, nine hours). If times don't suit, there are various *combi* companies, including **Norte Bus** (☎0291-15-468-5101; San Martín 155), that run slightly quicker minibuses to Bahía Blanca for around AR$50.

The train station is located near the tourist office. Tuesdays to Saturdays, there's train service from here or nearby Tornquist to Bahía Blanca (AR$15 to AR$24, three hours) and Plaza Constitución in Buenos Aires (AR$49 to AR$79, 11 hours).

Around Sierra de la Ventana

Popular for ranger-guided walks and independent hiking, the 6700-hectare **Parque Provincial Ernesto Tornquist** (☎491-0039; admission AR$10; ⏰8am-5pm Dec-Mar, 9am-5pm Apr-Nov) is the starting point for the 1136m summit of **Cerro de la Ventana**. It's about two hours' routine hiking for anyone except the wheezing *porteño* tobacco addicts who struggle to the crest of what is probably the country's most climbed peak. Leave early: you can't climb after 11am in winter, noon in summer.

Friendly **Campamento Base** (☎0291-494-0999; www.comarcaturistica.com.ar/campamentobase; RP 76 Km 224; campsites per person AR$20, dm AR$50) provides shady campsites, clean bathrooms and excellent hot showers.

Buses traveling between Bahía Blanca and Sierra de la Ventana can drop you at the park entrance, and there are also buses directly to the park from the village (AR$17, one hour).

CENTRAL ARGENTINA

Containing the wine-producing centers of Mendoza, San Luis and San Juan (which themselves comprise an area known as Cuyo), there's no doubt what Central Argentina's main attraction is. But once you've polished off a few bottles, you won't be left twiddling your thumbs – this is also Argentina's adventure playground, and the opportunities for rafting, trekking, skiing and climbing are almost endless.

San Luis

☎02652 / POP 224,800

San Luis is coming up as a backpacking destination, but it still has a long way to go. Most people come here to visit the nearby Parque Nacional Sierra de las Quijadas. The commercial center is along the parallel streets of San Martín and Rivadavia, between Plaza Pringles in the north and Plaza Independencia to the south.

The large, multibed dorms at **San Luis Hostel** (☎442-4188; www.sanluishostel.com.ar; Falucho 646; dm/tw AR$65/160; @🛜🏊) are a bit of a turnoff, but the rest of the hostel is beautiful. Staff can arrange trips to Sierra de las Quijadas and tours of local gold mines.

Av Illia, which runs northwest from the delightful Plaza Pringles, is the center of San Luis' moderately hopping bar scene. There are plenty of fast-food options along this street. **Aranjuez** (cnr Pringles & Rivadavia; mains AR$30-55; ⏰breakfast, lunch & dinner) is a fairly standard cafe/bar/restaurant which gets a mention for its sidewalk tables, a great place to take a breather.

Several banks, mostly around Plaza Pringles, have ATMs. The **tourist office** (☎442-3957; www.turismo.sanluis.gov.ar; cnr Av Illia & Junín) has a huge amount of information on San Luis' surrounding areas.

Aerolineas Argentinas (☎442-5671; Av Illia 472) flies daily to Buenos Aires. The **bus terminal** (☎442-4021; España btwn San Martín & Rivadavia) has departures to Mendoza (AR$125, 3½ hours), San Juan (AR$185, five hours), Rosario (AR$310, 11 hours) and Buenos Aires (AR$380, 12 hours).

Mendoza

☎0261 / POP 933,600

In 1861 an earthquake leveled the city of Mendoza. This was a tragedy for the *mendocinos* (people from Mendoza), but rebuilding efforts created some of the city's most loved aspects: the authorities anticipated (somewhat pessimistically) the *next* earthquake by rebuilding the city with wide avenues (for the rubble to fall into) and spacious plazas (to use as evacuation points). The result is one of Argentina's most seductive cities – stunningly picturesque and a joy to walk around.

Add to this the fact that it's smack in the middle of many of the country's best vineyards (the region produces 70% of the country's wine) and that it's the base for any number of outdoor activities, and you know you'll be spending more than a couple of days here.

Early March's **Fiesta Nacional de la Vendimia** (wine harvest festival) attracts big crowds; book accommodation well ahead. The surrounding countryside offers wine tasting, mountaineering, cycling and whitewater rafting. Many different tours of the area are available.

Sights

Plaza Independencia has a **crafts fair** Thursday through Sunday night, while Plaza Pellegrini holds its own weekend **antiques market** with music and dancing.

Central Argentina

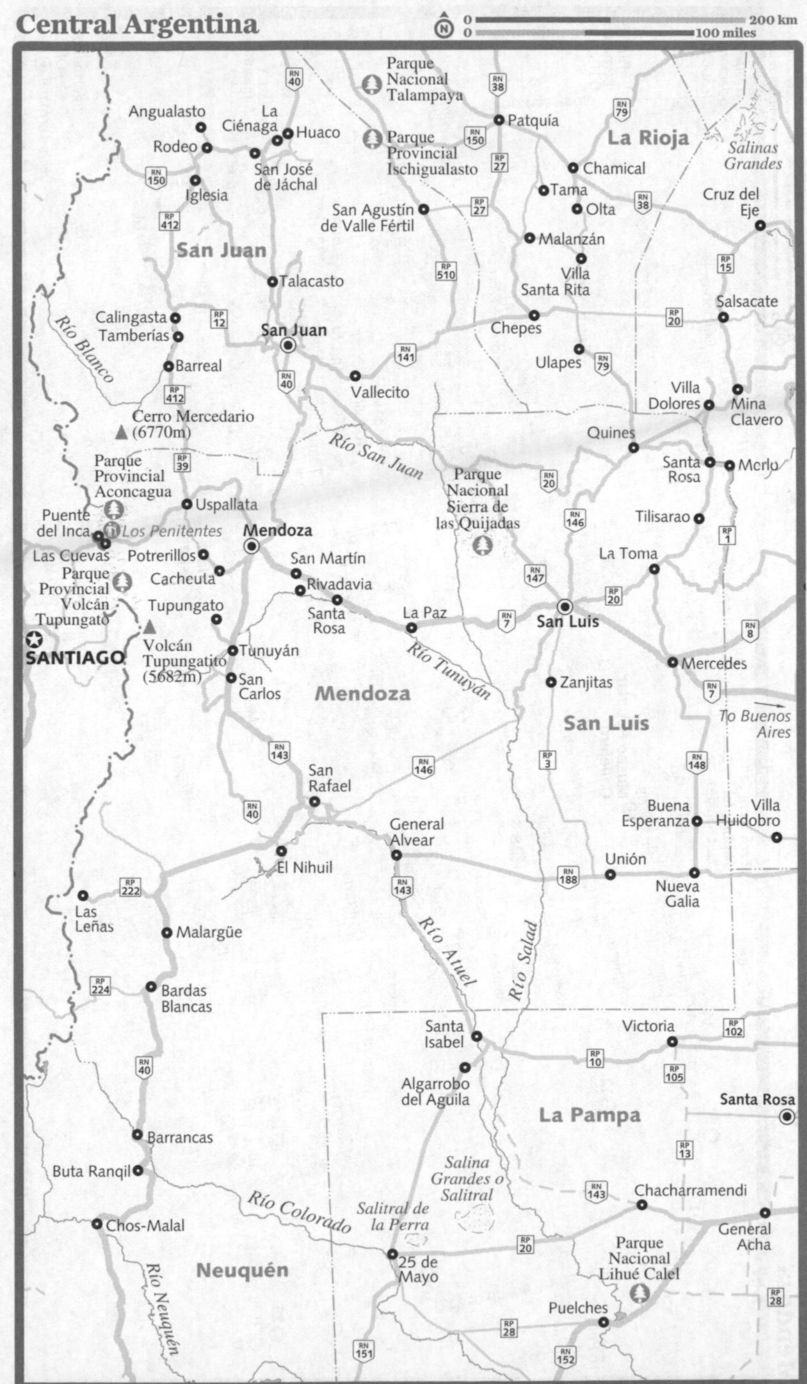

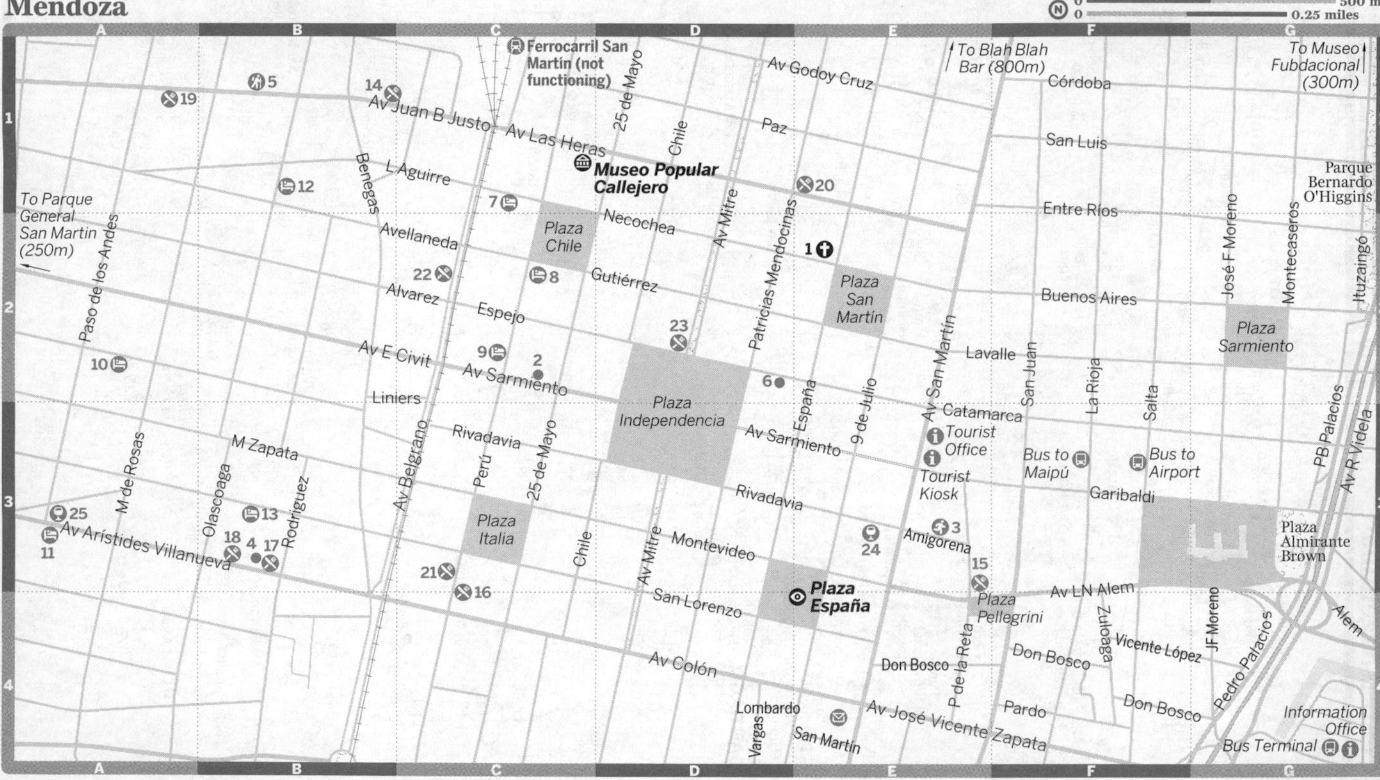
Mendoza
0
500 m
0
0.25 miles
Ferrocarril San Martín (not functioning)
To Blah Blah Bar (800m)
To Museo Fubdacional (300m)
Av Godoy Cruz
Córdoba
Av Juan B Justo
Av Las Heras
25 de Mayo
Chile
Paz
San Luis
Parque Bernardo O'Higgins
L Aguirre
Benegas
Museo Popular Callejero
Entre Ríos
To Parque General San Martin (250m)
Necochea
Av Mitre
Patricias Mendocinas
José F Moreno
Montecaseros
Itzuzaingó
Avellaneda
Plaza Chile
Gutiérrez
Plaza San Martín
Buenos Aires
Paso de los Andes
Alvarez
Espejo
Plaza Sarmiento
Av E Civit
Av Sarmiento
Lavalle
Av San Martín
San Juan
La Rioja
Salta
PB Palacios
Av R Videla
Liniers
Plaza Independencia
España
9 de Julio
Catamarca
Tourist Office
Tourist Kiosk
Bus to Maipú
Bus to Airport
Garibaldi
M Zapata
Rivadavia
M de Rosas
Olascoaga
Rodriguez
Av Belgrano
Perú
Plaza Italia
Amigorena
Plaza Almirante Brown
Av Arístides Villanueva
Montevideo
Plaza España
Av LN Alem
Plaza Pellegrini
San Lorenzo
Zuloaga
Vicente López
JF Moreno
Alem
Pedro Palacios
Av Colón
Don Bosco
P de la Reta
Pardo
Lombardo
Vargas
San Martín
Av José Vicente Zapata
Information Office
Bus Terminal
1
2
3
4
5
6
7
8
9
10
11
12
13
14
15
16
17
18
19
20
21
22
23
24
25
A
B
C
D
E
F
G

Mendoza

Top Sights
Museo Popular Callejero C1
Plaza España E4

Sights
1 Iglesia, Convento y Basílica de San Francisco E2

Activities, Courses & Tours
2 Ampora Wine Tours C2
3 Argentina Rafting E3
4 Fundación Brasilia B3
5 Inka Expediciones B1
6 Trout & Wine D2

Sleeping
7 Hostel Alamo C1
8 Hotel Casino C2
9 Hotel Zamora C2
10 La Escondida A2
11 Mendoza Inn A3
12 Plan B Hostel B1
13 Quinta Rufino B3

Eating
14 Anna Bistro B1
15 Arrope E3
16 Ciao Cuoco C4
17 Cocina Poblana B3
18 El Palenque B3
19 La Flor de la Canela A1
20 Mercado Central E1
21 Patancha C3
22 Pizza & Grill C2
23 Quinta Norte D2

Drinking
24 La Reserva E3
25 Por Acá A3

Museo Fundacional MUSEUM
(cnr Alberdi & Videla Castillo; admission AR$10; 8am-8pm) The spacious Museo Fundacional protects the foundations of the original *cabildo,* destroyed by the 1861 earthquake. There are also exhibits of items found at the site, and scale models of old and new Mendoza.

Parque General San Martín PARK
Parque General San Martín, 2km west of town, is a forested 420-hectare green space containing **Cerro de la Gloria** (nice views), several museums and a lake, among other things. There have been reports of muggings in this park. Don't go alone, near dark or carrying valuables. Bus 110 gets you here from Plaza Independencia.

Plaza España PLAZA
(cnr España & San Lorenzo) Check out the beautiful tile work in the plaza.

Museo Popular Callejero MUSEUM
(cnr Av Las Heras & 25 de Mayo) This unique museum, along the sidewalk at the corner of Av Las Heras and 25 de Mayo, features encased dioramas depicting the history of one of Mendoza's major avenues.

Bodega La Rural WINERY
(497-2013; www.bodegalarural.com.ar; Montecaseros 2625; 9am-1pm & 2-5pm Mon-Fri) Bodega La Rural, lying 17km southeast of downtown in Maipú, has a museum that displays winemaking tools used by 19th-century pioneers, as well as colonial religious sculptures from the Cuyo region. Tours run every half hour on weekdays and hourly on weekends, but less frequently in English. Take bus 173 from La Rioja between Garibaldi and Catamarca.

Di Tomasso WINERY
(587-8900; www.familiaditommaso.com; Urquiza 8136; tours AR$20) About 17km southeast of downtown in Maipú is Di Tomasso, a beautiful, historic vineyard dating back to the 1830s. The winery tour includes a quick pass through the original cellar section. Bus 173 leaves from La Rioja between Garibaldi and Catamarca and will get you here.

Iglesia, Convento y Basílica de San Francisco CHURCH
(Necochea 201; 9am-1pm Mon-Sat) The Virgen de Cuyo in the Iglesia, Convento y Basílica de San Francisco was the patron of San Martín's Army of the Andes.

Activities

Scaling nearby Aconcagua is one of the most popular activities here, but there are also plenty of operators offering rafting, climbing, mountain biking and trekking, among other things. Most hostels can organize these.

Ski rental places operate along Av Las Heras during winter.

Inka Expediciones HIKING
(☎425-0871; www.inka.com.ar; Av Juan B Justo 345) Offers fully serviced guided treks to the summit of Aconcagua as well as logistical support for independent climbers.

Cabaña la Guatana HORSE RIDING
(☎15-668-6801; www.criolloslaguatana.com.ar; Maza Sur 8001, Lulunta, Maipú) Horse-riding tours through the vineyards of Maipú.

Argentina Rafting ADVENTURE TOURS
(☎429-6325; www.argentinarafting.com; Amigorena 86) Rafting, mountain biking, kayaking, paragliding and rock climbing, among other activities.

Courses

Fundación Brasilia LANGUAGE COURSE
(☎423-6917; www.fundacionbrasilia.org; Av Arístides Villanueva 251) Offers individual and group Spanish classes.

Sleeping

Note that hotel prices rise from January to March, most notably during the wine festival in early March. Some hostels in Mendoza will only rent you a bed if you buy one of their tours. Needless to say, none of these are recommended here.

TOP CHOICE **Hostel Alamo** HOSTEL $
(☎429-5565; www.hostelalamo.com.ar; Necochea 740; dm AR$70, d with/without bathroom AR$220/160; @☎≋) An impeccable hostel in a great location, the Alamo offers roomy four-bed dorms, great hangout areas and a wonderful backyard with a small swimming pool.

Plan B Hostel HOSTEL $
(☎420-2869; www.hostelplanb.com; Olascoaga 1323; dm/d AR$68/160; @☎) Set in a quiet residential neighborhood just out of the center, this beautiful little hostel offers six-bed dorms with good mattresses, OK private rooms and a tranquil, friendly atmosphere.

La Escondida HOTEL $$
(☎425-5202; www.laescondidabb.com; Julio A Roca 344; s/d AR$280/320; ❄@☎≋) Set in a huge house in the quiet residential neighborhood known as La Quinta, rooms here aren't fancy but the place just feels right. Great value, run by a friendly family.

Quinta Rufino HOTEL $
(www.quintarufinohostel.com.ar; Ortega 142; s/d AR$150/180, without bathroom AR$120/160) Halfway between a hostel and a hotel, this place has OK rooms, fantastic hangout areas and a decent kitchen for guest use. It's set on a quiet street a couple of blocks from the Aristedes bar zone.

Hotel Zamora HOTEL $
(☎425-7537; Perú 1156; s/d AR$160/200; ❄☎) A sweet little family-run hotel offering comfortable rooms, a buffet breakfast and a charming courtyard with tinkling fountain and Spanish tile work.

Mendoza Inn HOSTEL $
(☎438-0818; www.mendozahostel.com; Av Arístides Villanueva 470; dm/d AR$70/240; @☎≋) With

REMOTE NATIONAL PARKS IN CENTRAL ARGENTINA

Central Argentina has an amazing range of landscapes, which is reflected in its national parks. For more information, log on to www.parquesnacionales.gov.ar. Following are a couple of hard-to-reach but extremely worthwhile examples:

Parque Nacional Lihué Calel (☎029-5243-6595; www.lihuecalel.com.ar; admission free) In a desertlike landscape in the middle of the pampa, this 32,000-hectare park is surprisingly biodiverse, playing host to puma, jaguarondi, armadillos and many birds of prey, such as the *carancho* (crested caracara), alongside flowering cacti and petroglyphs. Santa Rosa is the nearest town of any size – there are cheap hotels near the bus terminal and restaurants on the plaza, but it's still 226km away and access is complicated – hiring a car is the best way to see the park.

Parque Nacional Sierra de las Quijadas (☎02652-44-5141; usopublicoquijadas@apn.gov.ar; admission AR$20) Covering 150,000 hectares, this park features spectacular, surreal rock formations and dinosaur tracks and fossils. Hiking is excellent and camping is free, but be careful of flash flooding. The nearest town is San Luis; its park office can help with transportation and logistics.

THE GRAPE ESCAPE

It would be a crime to come to Mendoza and not visit at least one vineyard. A crime, people. Argentina's wines are constantly improving and, consequently, attracting international attention. Wine tasting is a popular activity at the many wineries in the area.

Depending on your budget and time frame, there are a few options:

» Bussing around Maipú and Luján.

» Bussing to Maipú, then renting a bike (AR$60) for a self-guided tour. Cyclists can consider biking a 40km circuit that would cover Di Tomasso (p117), Bodega la Rural (p117) and more. Call first to confirm opening hours. Established operators in Maipú include **Bikes & Wines** (☎410-6686; www.bikesandwines.com; cnr Urquiza & Montecaseros; bikes per day AR$60) and **Mr Hugo** (☎497-4067; www.mrhugobikes.com; Urquiza 2228; bikes per day AR$60). They provide basic maps and reasonable rides, but check your wheels (brakes, seat etc) before heading out. Tourist information offices in Mendoza also have area maps.

» A low-cost (around AR$120) tour, available through any hostel or tour operator. These are fine for your average Joe, but they can get crowded and rushed, and tastings certainly won't include any of the good stuff.

» A high-end wine tour with outfits such as **Trout & Wine** (☎425-5613; www.troutandwine.com; Espejo 266) or **Ampora Wine Tours** (☎429-2931; www.mendozawinetours.com; Av Sarmiento 647). These start at around AR$780, but you'll be visiting some exclusive wineries in small groups and be getting samples of some of the finest wines that the region has to offer.

a great location and friendly, bilingual staff, this is one of the city's better hostels. Common areas are spacious and the big shady backyard and pool are definite pluses.

Hotel Casino HOTEL $
(☎425-6666; www.nuevohotelcasino.com.ar; Gutiérrez 668; s/d AR$120/150; ❄📶) Some good, spacious rooms and some smallish, ordinary ones. They're all clean and comfortable, but take a look at a few before deciding.

Parque Suizo CAMPGROUND $
(☎444-1991; www.campingsuizo.com.ar; Av Champagnat; campsites AR$35; ⛄) About 6km northwest of town, in El Challao, this woody campground has hot showers, laundry facilities and a grocery. Get here on Bus 110, which leaves from Av LN Alem just east of Av San Martín and from Av Sarmiento.

Eating

Sidewalk restaurants on pedestrian Av Sarmiento are fine places to people-watch. The restaurants along Avs Las Heras and San Martín offer good-value set meals; see signboards for details.

Patancha INTERNATIONAL $$
(Perú 778; mains AR$50-70; ⏰lunch & dinner) A cute little place serving up some great tapas alongside traditional favorites such as *humitas* and the occasional surprise such as seafood stir-fry. The AR$45 set lunch is a bargain.

La Flor de la Canela PERUVIAN $
(Av Juan B Justo 426; mains AR$40-60; ⏰lunch & dinner Wed-Mon) Need something spicy? Check out this authentic, bare-bones Peruvian eatery a few blocks from the center. What it lacks in atmosphere it makes up for in flavor.

Anna Bistro FUSION $$
(Av Juan B Justo 161; mains AR$60-90; ⏰lunch & dinner) One of Mendoza's best-looking restaurants offers a wonderful garden area, cool music and carefully prepared dishes.

Quinta Norte ARGENTINE $
(Av Mitre & Espejo; set meals AR$40, mains AR$40-60; ⏰lunch & dinner) A good range of daily specials and shady sidewalk seating make this one a winner.

El Palenque ARGENTINE $$
(Av Arístides Villanueva 287; mains AR$45-60; ⏰lunch & dinner Mon-Sat) Popular for years and still going strong, this casual restaurant-bar serves up some good standards with a

few surprises thrown in. Come early or book ahead.

Pizza & Grill PIZZERIA $
(Av Belgrano 1210; mains AR$35-60; ⏲lunch & dinner) One of the city's better pizza joints, offering a wide range of toppings, a decent range of nonpizza items and good-value set lunches.

Ciao Cuoco ITALIAN $$$
(Perú 747; mains AR$50-70; ⏲lunch & dinner) The front courtyard of this charming pasta restaurant is the place to be on a sunny day. At night, enjoy the rustic decor inside. It has a good range of Italian-inspired dishes.

Arrope VEGETARIAN $
(Primitiva de la Reta 927; per 100g AR$5; ⏲breakfast & lunch;) Feeling a little meat-heavy? Slip into this cozy vegetarian cafe-restaurant and choose from a wide range of animal-free goodies on the buffet table.

Cocina Poblana MIDDLE EASTERN $
(Av Arístides Villanueva 217; dishes AR$35-50; ⏲lunch & dinner Mon-Sat) Tasty, inexpensive Middle Eastern food comes as a welcome break from all that steak.

Mercado Central MARKET $
(cnr Av Las Heras & Patricias Mendocinas; AR$25-50; ⏲breakfast, lunch & dinner) The renovated Mercado Central is a good hunting ground for cheap pizza, empanadas and sandwiches.

Drinking

Av Aristides Villanueva, west of the center, is ground zero in terms of Mendoza's happening bar scene. Going for a wander is your best bet, but here are a few to get you started.

Por Acá BAR
(420-0346; Av Arístides Villanueva 557) Purple and yellow outside and polka-dotted upstairs, this bar-cum-lounge gets packed after 2am, and by the end of the night, dancing on the tables is not uncommon. Good retro dance music.

Blah Blah Bar BAR
(Escalada 2307) An anchor point for the Tajamar nightlife zone, this is Mendoza's version of a dive bar. It's hip but restrained, with a casual atmosphere and plenty of outdoor seating.

La Reserva GAY
(Rivadavia 34; admission free-AR$25) This small, nominally gay bar packs in a mixed crowd and has outrageous drag shows at midnight every night, with hard-core techno later.

Information

Wine snobs and the wine-curious should pick up a free copy of the *Wine Republic* (www.wine-republic.com), an English-language magazine devoted to Mendoza's wining and dining scene.

Cambio Santiago (Av San Martín 1199; ⏲8am-6pm Mon-Fri, 9am-1pm Sat & Sun) Charges 2% for traveler's checks.

Information office (431-5000; ⏲8am-8pm) In the bus terminal.

Post office (Av San Martín at Colón)

Tourist kiosk (420-1333; Garibaldi; ⏲8am-6pm) This helpful kiosk near Av San Martín is the most convenient information source.

Tourist office (420-2800; www.turismo.mendoza.gov.ar; Av San Martín 1143; ⏲8am-10pm Mon-Fri) Mendoza's main tourist office has mounds of brochures and sells climbing and trekking permits for Aconcagua.

Getting There & Away

Air

Aerolíneas Argentinas/Austral (420-4185; Av Sarmiento 82) has daily flights to Buenos Aires.

LAN (425-7900; Rivadavia 135) flies twice daily to Santiago de Chile.

Sol (0810-444-4765; www.sol.com.ar) Sol flies to Córdoba, Rosario and Río Gallegos.

Bus

The **bus terminal** (431-1299) is about 10 blocks east of the town center.

DESTINATION	COST (AR$)	DURATION (HR)
Aconcagua	36	3½
Buenos Aires	460	14
Córdoba	330	9
Las Leñas	110	7
Los Penitentes	36	4
Malargüe	80	6
Neuquén	415	12
San Juan	95	2
San Luis	125	3½
Tucumán	581	14
Uspallata	30	2
Valparaíso	160	8

Getting Around

The bus terminal is about 15 minutes' walk from the center; catch the Villa Nueva trolley if you don't feel like walking. Mendoza's airport is 6km north of the city. Bus 60 (Aeropuerto) Salta, between Garibald & Catamarca) goes from Calle Salta straight there.

Mendoza buses take magnetic fare cards, sold at kiosks in multiple values of the AR$2.50 fare. Trolleys cost AR$2.50 in coins.

Uspallata

02624 / POP 4040

In an exceptionally beautiful valley surrounded by polychrome mountains, 105km west of Mendoza at an altitude of 1751m, this crossroads village along RN 7 is a good base for exploring the surrounding area, which served as a location for the Brad Pitt epic *Seven Years in Tibet*.

Sights

One kilometer north of the highway junction toward Villavicencio, a signed side road leads to ruins and a museum at the **Bóvedas Históricas Uspallata**, a metallurgical site since pre-Columbian times. About 4km north of Uspallata, in a volcanic outcrop near a small monument to San Ceferino Namuncurá, is a faded but still visible set of **petroglyphs**.

Sleeping & Eating

Hostel International Uspallata HOSTEL $
(15-466-7240; www.hosteluspallata.com.ar; RN 7 s/n; dm/d AR$50/150) A beautiful, spacious hostel set in breathtaking countryside 5km out of Uspallata (aka the middle of nowhere). From Mendoza or Uspallata, tell the driver you're getting off here. Otherwise it's a AR$20 *remise* ride from town.

El Portico del Valle HOTEL $
(42-0103; www.porticodelvalle.com; cnr Las Heras & RN 7; s/d AR$140/220;) Comfy and airy rooms by the junction. Further up Las Heras are a couple of good, cheaper hotels.

Camping Municipal CAMPGROUND $
(0261-15-664-5285; www.campinguspallata.com.ar; RN 52; campsites AR$20 per person;) Uspallata's poplar-shaded campground is 500m north of the Villavicencio junction.

El Rancho PARRILLA $$
(cnr RN7 & Cerro Chacay; mains AR$45-60; lunch & dinner) The coziest *parrilla* in town, serving all the usual, plus a good roasted *chivo* (goat).

Café Tibet CAFE $
(cnr RN 7 & Las Heras; mains AR$25-35; breakfast, lunch & dinner) No visit to Uspallata would be complete without at least a coffee in this little oddity. The food is nothing spectacular, but the decor, comprising leftover props from *Seven Years in Tibet*, is a must for fans of the surreal.

Information

Tourist information (42-0009; RN 7 s/n; 9am-8pm) Opposite the YPF station.

Getting There & Away

The bus terminal is tucked behind the new, rampantly ugly casino on the main drag. There are departures for Mendoza (AR$30, 2½ hours) and Puente del Inca (AR$20, one hour) and points in between. Santiago-bound buses will carry passengers to and across the border but are often full; in winter, the pass can close to all traffic for weeks at a time.

Around Uspallata

LOS PENITENTES

Both the terrain and snow cover can be excellent for downhill and Nordic skiing at **Los Penitentes** (0261-423-4848; www.lospenitentes.com), two hours southwest of Uspallata at an altitude of 2580m. Lifts and accommodations are very modern; the maximum vertical drop on its 21 runs exceeds 700m. A day ski pass costs AR$200 to AR$280, depending on the time of year. The season runs from June to September.

The cozy converted cabin of **Hostel Los Penitentes** (0261-425-5511; www.penitentes.com.ar; dm AR$140) accommodates 38 in very close quarters, and has a kitchen, wood-burning stove and three shared bathrooms. Meals are available for AR$30, and dorm rates are halved in summer. The hostel offers Nordic- and downhill-skiing trips in winter, and Aconcagua treks and expeditions in summer. If you're looking for a bit more comfort, the **Hotel Ayelén** (0261-427-1123; www.ayelenpenitentes.com.ar; s/d from AR$300/600) is open year-round; it has an excellent setup and offers good meals in its on-site restaurant.

From Mendoza, several buses pass daily through Uspallata to Los Penitentes (AR$36, four hours).

PUENTE DEL INCA

About 8km west of Los Penitentes, on the way to the Chilean border and near the turnoff to Aconcagua, you will find one of Argentina's most striking wonders. Situated 2720m above sea level, Puente del Inca is a natural stone bridge spanning the Río Mendoza. Underneath it, rock walls and the ruins of an old spa are stained yellow by warm, sulfurous thermal springs. You can hike into Parque Provincial Aconcagua from here.

The little, no-frills hostel of **La Vieja Estación** (☎0261-425-2110; campsites per person AR$20, dm AR$90) offers mountain climbing, glacier trekking and snowshoeing. There's a cheap restaurant and bar on the premises.

Cozy, wood-paneled rooms and a big dining hall give **Hostería Puente del Inca** (☎02624-42-0266; www.hosteriapdelinca.com.ar; s/d AR$345/400) a real ski-lodge feel.

Daily buses to Mendoza take about four hours (AR$52).

PARQUE PROVINCIAL ACONCAGUA

On the Chilean border, Parque Provincial Aconcagua protects 71,000 hectares of high country surrounding the western hemisphere's highest summit – 6962m **Cerro Aconcagua**. There are trekking possibilities to base camps and refuges beneath the permanent snow line.

Reaching Aconcagua's summit requires at least 13 to 15 days, including some time for acclimatization. Potential climbers should get RJ Secor's climbing guide, *Aconcagua,* and check www.aconcagua.com.ar and www.aconcagua.mendoza.gov.ar for more information.

Mid-November to mid-March, permits are mandatory for trekking and climbing; these permits vary from AR$380 to AR$800 for trekkers and AR$1200 to AR$3000 for climbers, depending on the date. Mid-December to late January is high season. Purchase permits in Mendoza from the main tourist office (p120).

Many adventure-travel agencies in and around Mendoza arrange excursions into the high mountains.

San Juan

☎0264 / POP 498,700

Smelling kerosene? Don't panic – that's just the proud folks of San Juan *polishing their sidewalks.* Uh-huh. An attractive enough place, San Juan's big claims to fame are the nearby wineries and access to Parque Provincial Ischigualasto.

Rather than changing names as they intersect the central plaza (which is what happens in most Argentine towns), streets in San Juan keep their name but are designated by compass points, with street numbers starting at zero at the plaza and rising from there. Thus there will be two Laprida 150s – one Laprida 150 Este and one Laprida 150 Oeste.

Sights & Activities

Museo de Vino Santiago Graffigna MUSEUM
(☎421-4227; www.graffignawines.com; Colón 1342 Norte; ⏲9am-5:30pm Mon-Sat, 1-5pm Sun) A wine museum that's well worth a visit if you're not planning on visiting any of the area wineries. Take bus 12A from in front of the tourist office on Sarmiento (AR$2.50, 15 minutes).

Triasico Turismo TOUR
(☎422-8566; www.triasico.com.ar; Sarmiento 42 Sur) Specializes in Ischigualasto tours (AR$420, minimum two people) – come here if you're struggling to get a group together.

Sleeping

San Juan Hostel HOSTEL $
(☎420-1835; www.sanjuanhostel.com; Av Córdoba 317 Este; dm AR$60-70, s/d AR$140/200, without bathroom AR$100/140; ❄@📶) Simple, spacious and friendly, this hostel is in a good spot between the terminal and center. Good info on tours and local attractions.

Argentia Hostel HOSTEL $
(☎408-4243; www.hostelargentia.com; Sarmiento 57 Norte; dm AR$60-70, r AR$160, s/d without bathroom AR$80/120, apt AR$220-280; ❄@📶🏊) Set in a huge, centrally located house, this is the best hostel in town, with roomy dorms, great common areas and a bargain-priced apartment out back.

Plaza Hotel HOTEL $
(☎422-5179; plazahotelsanjuan@hotmail.com; Sarmiento 344 Sur; s/d AR$180/240; ❄) There's no plaza in sight, but the large, unrenovated rooms here represent fair value. Check out a few for better ventilation and light.

Hotel Alhambra HOTEL **$**
(☎421-4780; www.alhambrahotel.com.ar; Gral Acha 180 Sur; s/d AR$200/290; ❄📶) Comfy, slightly cramped rooms in an excellent location just off the plaza.

Camping El Pinar CAMPGROUND **$**
(☎433-2374; RP 113, Km 14; campsites per person AR$20, per tent AR$20) Buses go to this woodsy municipal site on Benavídez Oeste, located about 6km west of downtown.

Eating

The pedestrian section of Rivadavia is crammed with sidewalk cafes and fast-food joints.

TOP CHOICE **Remolacha** PARRILLA **$$**
(cnr Av José Ignacio de la Roza & Sarmiento; mains AR$50-80; ⏰lunch & dinner) The best *parrilla* in town features a lovely garden area out front and a cheaper take-out counter around the side.

Baró INTERNATIONAL **$**
(Rivadavia 55 Oeste; mains AR$30-60; ⏰breakfast, lunch & dinner) This popular main-street cafe-restaurant has the best variety of pasta dishes in town, and a relaxed atmosphere that makes it a good stop for coffee or drinks at any time.

Soychú VEGETARIAN **$**
(Av José Ignacio de la Roza 223 Oeste; buffet AR$39; ⏰lunch & dinner Mon-Sat, lunch Sun; ✎) This friendly vegetarian eatery has a seriously good selection of food and fresh juices.

Information

Cambio Santiago (General Acha 52 Sur; ⏰8am-6pm Mon-Fri, 9am-1pm Sat & Sun) Change your dollars here.

Post Office (Av José Ignacio de la Roza 259 Este; ⏰9am-6pm Mon-Fri) Near the plaza.

Tourist Office (☎422-2431; www.turismo.sanjuan.gov.ar; Sarmiento 24 Sur; ⏰8am-7pm) Also has a smaller branch at the bus terminal.

Getting There & Away

Aerolíneas Argentinas/Austral (☎421-4158; Av San Martín 215 Oeste) flies daily to Buenos Aires.

The **bus terminal** (☎422-1604; Estados Unidos 492 Sur) has buses to Mendoza (AR$95, three hours), Córdoba (AR$285, nine hours), San Agustín de Valle Fértil (AR$65, four hours), La Rioja (AR$226, six hours) and Buenos Aires (AR$635, 15 hours).

For car rental, try **Classic** (☎422-4622; Av San Martín 163 Oeste). If you're heading to Ischigualasto, one of the cheapest ways to do it is to get a group together in your hostel and hire a car for the day.

Around San Juan

SAN AGUSTÍN DE VALLE FÉRTIL

This relaxed, green little village is 250km northeast of San Juan and set amid colorful hills and rivers. It relies on farming, animal husbandry, mining and tourism. Visitors to Parques Ischigualasto and Talampaya use San Agustín as a base, and there are also nearby **petroglyphs** and the Río Seco to explore.

The **tourist office** (Gral Acha; ⏰7am-1pm & 5-10pm Mon-Fri, 8am-1pm Sat), on the plaza, can help set you up with tours of the area. There's camping and cheap accommodation, and a couple of good *parrillas*. Change money before you get here.

Buses roll daily to and from San Juan (AR$65, four hours).

PARQUE PROVINCIAL ISCHIGUALASTO

At every meander in the canyon of **Parque Provincial Ischigualasto** (☎0264-49-1100; www.ischigualasto.org), a desert valley between sedimentary mountain ranges, the intermittent waters of the Río Ischigualasto have exposed a wealth of Triassic fossils and dinosaur bones (up to 180 million years old) and carved distinctive shapes in the monochrome clays, red sandstone and volcanic ash. The desert flora of *algarrobo* trees, shrubs and cacti complement the eerie moonscape, and fauna include guanacos, condors, Patagonian hares and foxes.

Camping is (unofficially) permitted at the visitors center near the entrance, which also has a *confitería* with simple meals and cold drinks. There are toilets and showers, but water shortages are frequent and there's no shade.

Ischigualasto is about 80km north of San Agustín. Given its size and isolation, the only practical way to visit the park is by vehicle. After you pay the AR$35 entrance fee, a ranger will accompany your vehicle on a two- or three-hour circuit over the park's unpaved roads, which may be impassable after rain.

If you have no transportation, ask the San Agustín tourist office about tours or hiring a car and driver, or contact the park. Tour operators in San Juan do tours here, but it's way cheaper to make your own way to San Agustín and line something up there. Some tours can be combined with **Parque Nacional Talampaya**, almost 100km northeast of Ischigualasto.

Malargüe

☎02627 / POP 20,600

From precolonial times, the Pehuenche people hunted and gathered in the valley of Malargüe, but the advance of European agricultural colonists dispossessed the original inhabitants of their land. Today petroleum is a principal industry, but Malargüe, 400km south of Mendoza, is also a year-round outdoor activity center: Las Leñas offers Argentina's best **skiing**, and there are archaeological sites and fauna reserves nearby, plus organized **caving** possibilities.

Sleeping & Eating

Restaurants line the five blocks of San Martín south of the plaza.

Hotel Remenso HOTEL $

(☎447-1360; Torres 15; s/d AR$180/260) As far as budget hotels go, this ticks all the right boxes – it's clean and central, and run by a doting señora.

Hostel La Caverna HOSTEL $

(☎442-7569; www.lacavernahostel.com.ar; Rodriguez 445; dm/d AR$60/180; @📶) This is the best hostel in town – mostly because the competition is slim.

Camping Municipal Malargüe CAMPGROUND $

(☎447-0691; Alfonso Capdevila s/n; campsites AR$40) Open all year, this campground is located at the north end of town.

TOP CHOICE **El Quincho de María** ARGENTINE $$

(Av San Martín 440; mains AR$40-70; ⊙lunch & dinner) El Quincho de María has arguably the best food in town.

Los Olivos ARGENTINE $

(San Martín 409; mains AR$30-60; ⊙lunch & dinner) Los Olivos is a laid-back main-street eatery that offers a succulent baked goat (AR$60).

Information

Tourist Office (☎447-1659; www.malargue.gov.ar; RN 40, Parque del Ayer; ⊙8am-8pm) At the northern end of town, directly on the highway.

Getting There & Away

The **bus terminal** (cnr Av General Roca & Aldao) has regular services to Mendoza (AR$80, six hours) and Las Leñas (AR$20, 1½ hours). There is a weekly summer service across the 2500m Paso Pehuenche and down the awesome canyon of the Río Maule to Talca, Chile.

If you're heading south, there is a daily bus to Buta Ranquil (AR$120, five hours) in Neuquén province, with connections further south from there. Book at least a day in advance at **Transportes Leader** (☎447-0519; San Martín 775), which operates out of the Club los Amigos pool hall.

Las Leñas

Wealthy Argentines and foreigners alike come to Las Leñas, the country's most prestigious ski resort, to look dazzling zooming down the slopes and then spend nights partying until the sun peeks over the snowy mountains. Summer activities include hiking, horse riding and mountain biking. Despite the fancy glitter, it's not completely out of reach for budget travelers.

Open from approximately July to October, Las Leñas is only 70km from Malargüe. Its 33 runs reach a peak of 3430m, with a maximum drop of 1230m. Lift tickets cost roughly from AR$268 to AR$393 (depending on the season) for a full day of skiing. The **ticket office** (☎02604-47-1281; www.laslenas.com; Cerrito 1186, 8th fl) can provide more information.

Budget travelers will find regular transportation from Malargüe, where accommodations are cheaper. Buses from Mendoza (AR$110) take seven hours.

THE LAKE DISTRICT

Extending from Neuquén down through Esquel, Argentina's Lake District is a gorgeous destination with lots of opportunities for adventure. There are lofty mountains to climb and ski down, rushing rivers to raft, clear lakes to boat or fish and beautiful national parks to explore. From big-city Bariloche to hippie El Bolsón, the Lake District's towns and cities each have their own distinct geography, architecture and cultural offerings. There's something fun to do every month of the year, so don't miss visiting this multifaceted region.

The Lake District

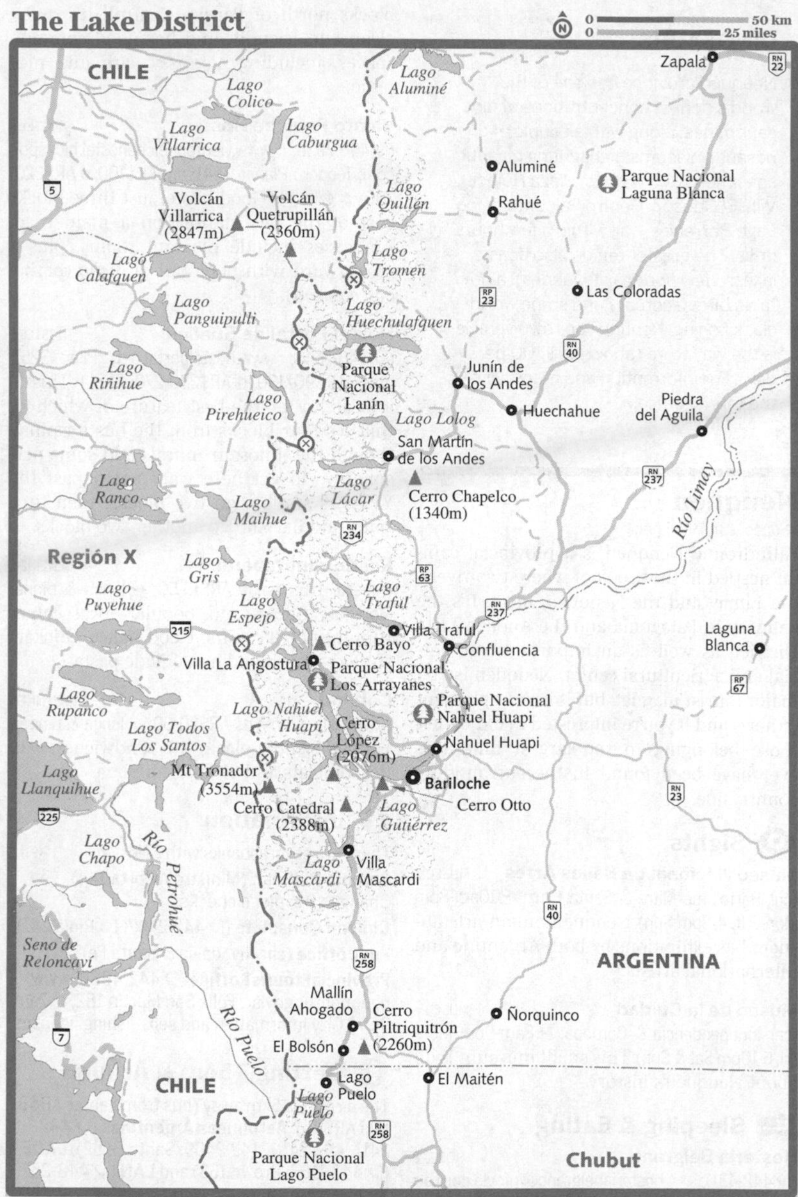

The Lake District's original inhabitants were the Puelches and Pehuenches, so named for their dependence on pine nuts from the *pehuén* (monkey-puzzle tree). Though Spaniards explored the area in the late 16th century, it was the Mapuche who dominated the region until the 19th century, when European settlers arrived. Today you can still see Mapuche living around here, especially on national park lands.

DINOSAURS

Neuquén province has one of the world's richest concentrations of dinosaur bones, along with a couple of dinosaur museums highlighting gigantic specimens. A few hints: Plaza Huincul, Villa El Chocón, Centro Paleontológico Lago Barreales – all within a few hours' drive. The greater region also boasts lakes, a few *bodegas* (wineries), a notable bird sanctuary and some world-class fishing. Renting your own vehicle is the way to go (about AR$400 per day). For information and maps, visit the tourist office.

Neuquén

☎0299 / POP 350,000

Palindromic Neuquén is a provincial capital nestled in the crook of where two rivers, the Limay and the Neuquén, meet. It's the gateway to Patagonia and the Andean Lake District, as well as an important commercial and agricultural center. Neuquén isn't a major tourist magnet, but it isn't unpleasant either – and if you're interested in old bones, those belonging to the largest dinosaurs ever have been found in the surrounding countryside.

Sights

Museo Nacional de Bellas Artes MUSEUM
(cnr Bartolomé Mitre & Santa Cruz; ⏰10am-8pm Mon-Sat, 4-8pm Sun) Neuquén's main art musuem has exhibitions by both Argentine and international artists.

Museo de la Cuidad MUSEUM
(cnr Independencia & Córdoba; ⏰8am-9pm Mon-Fri, 6-10pm Sat & Sun) This small museum is all about Neuquén's history.

Sleeping & Eating

Hostería Belgrano HOTEL $
(☎442-4311; hosteriabelgrano@infovia.com.ar; Rivadavia 283; s/d/tr AR$160/250/300; ❄📶) Small, central and friendly place to stay, with plant-filled lobby and guesthouse feel.

Punto Patagonico Hostel HOSTEL $
(☎447-9940; www.puntopatagonico.com; Periodistas Neuquinas 94; dm/d AR$80/210; @📶) Neuquen's best hostel is located about 10 blocks north of Parque Central. It's quiet, clean and friendly, and has good common spaces, including a grassy yard and nice patio.

Viento Puelche Hostel HOSTEL $
(☎446-7936; www.vientopuelchehostel.blogspot.com; Teodoro Planas 3841; dm AR$100, d AR$220-290; ❄@📶🏊) Good hostel just three blocks east of the bus station, on a main road. Amenities include pleasant rooms, plus a grassy yard with pool and *quincho* (barbecue *cabaña*).

Hostel Portal de Sueños HOSTEL $
(☎446-7643; www.hostelportal.net; Pilar 3257; dm/s AR$90/130, d AR$230-270; @📶) This is a basic hostel, the best feature of which is that it's four blocks from the bus terminal, though the dinosaur murals add some personality. To get here walk north past the YPF gas station, go two blocks, then turn right on Pilar and go another two blocks.

Restaurant Alberdi ARGENTINE $
(Alberdi 176; mains AR$15-50; ⏰lunch & dinner Mon-Sat) Cheap and popular local eatery running for 35 years. Good baked chicken, stuffed squash and homemade pastas.

Cabildo ARGENTINE $
(Rivadavia 72; mains AR$20-60; ⏰lunch & dinner) Family-friendly place with sandwiches, waffles, omelets and 27 kinds of pizza.

Information

There are several banks with ATMs.

Cambio Pullman (Ministro Alcorta 144) Changes traveler's checks.

Chilean Consulate (☎442-2447; La Rioja 241)

Post office (cnr Rivadavia & Santa Fe)

Provincial tourist office (☎442-4089; www.neuquentur.gov.ar; Félix San Martín 182; ⏰7am-9pm) City information and sells fishing licenses.

Getting There & Around

The airport is 5km away (bus from center AR$3, taxi AR$35). **Aerolíneas Argentinas** (☎442-2411, 442-2410, 442-2409; Santa Fe 52), **LADE** (☎443-1153; Brown 163) and **LAN** (☎448-2570; Yrigoyen 347) have services.

Neuquén's modern bus terminal is 4km west of the center; there's a tourist office inside. To get downtown take a frequent 'Pehueche' bus (AR$2) or a taxi (AR$25). Destinations include Bariloche (AR$200, six hours), Bahía Blanca (AR$220, seven hours), Buenos Aires (AR$500, 15 hours), Junín de los Andes (AR$100, six hours), Mendoza (AR$350, 10 hours), Viedma

(AR$110, 10 hours) and Temuco, Chile (AR$175, 10 hours). Most local buses take magnetic cards, bought at the terminal or at some kiosks. Also note that taxis charge 20% more between 11pm and 6am.

Junín de los Andes

☎02972 / POP 16,000

Cute and pleasant, Junín proclaims itself Argentina's 'trout capital' – and there are indeed some beautiful, trout-filled rivers in the area. It's a tranquil and slow-paced hamlet on the beautiful Río Chimehuín, 42km north of San Martín de los Andes. There's nothing much to do except wander around, explore the river or mountains and visit gorgeous Parque Nacional Lanín. If you're into churches, visit the cathedral's Christ figure, who sports a Mapuche visage.

Sights & Activities

Parque Vía Christi PARK
(☎15-470-6245; admission AR$30; ⏲8am-8pm daily) Walk 10 minutes from the western edge of town to hillside, pine-dotted Parque Vía Christi. Here you can wander the 22 (and counting) stations of the cross while getting good views of the area. It's a very creative, well-done effort fusing Christian themes with Mapuche struggles. Call ahead to arrange for a possible English-speaking guide.

Museo Mapuche MUSEUM
(Padre Milanesio 557; ⏲9am-8pm Mon-Fri, to 1pm Sat) For indigenous artifacts, visit Museo Mapuche. Hours can be sporadic.

Sleeping & Eating

Reencuentro Hostel HOSTEL $
(☎49-2220; www.elreencuentrohostel.blogspot.com; Pedro Illera 189; dm/s/d/tr AR$89/99/190/285; @📶) Your basic, casual hostel run by amiable host Alex. Good, colorful rooms all share bathrooms (bring a towel), and there's a tiny bar area that serves beer. Ask about bike rentals.

Tromen Hostel HOSTEL $
(☎49-1498; www.hosteltromen.com.ar; Lonquimay 195; dm/d/tr/q AR$60/180/230/270; @📶) Very homey, rustic hostel in a home with creaky floors. Rooms are small and most share bathrooms; there's one nine-bed dorm at the top. Small common spaces mean it can get crowded if full.

Laura Vicuña CAMPGROUND $
(☎49-1149; mallinlaura@gmail.com; Ponte 867; campsite per person AR$42, dm/cabaña AR$60/320) Pleasant and open all year, with sunny riverside campsites. Dorms and four-person cabañas also available, as is one two-bedroom apartment for up to six people (AR$480). Beware school groups from September to November.

Sigmund ARGENTINE $
(Juan M de Rosas 690; mains AR$30-65; ⏲lunch & dinner) Fabulous trendy eatery with colorful artsy decor, healthy food and great *onda*. Choose from dozens of pizzas, pasta, sandwiches and salads, all delivered with friendly service. Good music too.

Ruca Hueney PARRILLA $$
(☎49-1113; cnr Colonel Suárez & D Milanesio; mains AR$50-80; ⏲lunch & dinner) Junín's oldest and classiest restaurant, serving meats, homemade pastas and regional specialties like trout. Pick up something at the cheaper takeout counter next door and picnic at the park across the street.

Information

There's a bank (ATM) on the plaza.

Tourist office (☎49-1160; junindelosandes.gov.ar; cnr Milanesio & Suárez; ⏲8am-9pm) At the plaza; issues fishing permits. The National Park Office has a desk here too.

Getting There & Away

The airport is 19km south, toward San Martín de los Andes.

The bus station is three blocks west of the plaza. Destinations include San Martín de los Andes (AR$7, 45 minutes), Bariloche (AR$75, three hours) and Neuquén (AR$100, six hours).

Parque Nacional Lanín

At 3776m, snowcapped Volcán Lanín is the dominating centerpiece of this tranquil **national park** (www.parquenacionallanin.gov.ar; admission AR$50), where extensive stands of *lenga* (southern beech) and the curious monkey-puzzle tree flourish. Pleistocene glaciers left behind blue finger-shaped lakes, excellent for fishing and camping. For more information and maps, contact the National Park Office in Junín or San Martín.

In summer (January and February) **Lago Huechulafquen** is easily accessible from Junín; there are outstanding views of Volcán Lanín and several worthwhile hikes. Mapuche-run campgrounds include Raquithue, Piedra Mala and Bahía Cañicul; charges per person are AR$30 to AR$40. Free campsites around the park are also available; bring supplies from town. The forested **Lago Tromen** area also offers good hiking and camping.

From San Martín you can boat west on **Lago Lácar** to Paso Hua Hum and cross by road to Puerto Pirehueico (Chile); there's also bus service. Hua Hum has camping and hiking trails. Fifteen kilometers north of San Martín, serene **Lago Lolog** has good camping and fishing.

In summer vans from Junín's bus station go all along Lago Huechulafquen to Puerto Canoa and beyond (AR$25, two to three daily). There are also services to Lagos Tromen and Curruhué. Buses to Chile over the Hua Hum and Tromen passes also stop at intermediate points, but in summer are often full.

San Martín de los Andes

☎02972 / POP 35,000

Attractive San Martín is a small, fashionable destination crowded with rowdy Argentines in summer. Nestled between two verdant mountains on the shores of Lago Lácar, the town boasts many wood and stone chalet-style buildings, many of them chocolate shops, ice-cream stores and souvenir boutiques. But behind the touristy streets lie pleasant residential neighborhoods with pretty rose-filled gardens, and the surrounding area has wonderful forested trails perfect for hiking and biking.

Sights & Activities

Che Guevara fans can check out **La Pastera**, a small museum dedicated to this icon.

The 2.5km steep, dusty hike to **Mirador Bandurrias** (admission hikers AR$2, cyclists AR$5, collected Dec-Mar) ends with awesome views of Lago Lácar; be sure to take a snack or lunch. Tough cyclists can rent bikes at several shops in town and reach the *mirador* (lookout) in about an hour via dirt roads. **Playa la Islita** is a pleasant little beach located 2.5km further from the mirador.

In winter you can ski at **Cerro Chapelco**, a ski center 20km away.

From the pier there are seven-hour boat tours to Paso Hua Hum (round trip AR$250) to access walks and a waterfall. There's also boat transport to Quila Quina (round trip AR$90) for beaches and water sports.

Sleeping & Eating

Reserve accommodation ahead in high seasons (late December to March, Easter, and July to August).

Wesley Hostería GUESTHOUSE $$$
(☎42-7875; www.wesleyhouse.com.ar; Obeid 911; s/d/tr AR$410/460/590; @☎) Beautiful, peaceful and central guesthouse with just five wood-floored rooms, each with TV, fridge and private bathroom. There's a great loft area in which to hang out, plus a homemade breakfast.

Puma Youth Hostel HOSTEL $
(☎42-2443; www.pumahostel.com.ar; Fosbery 535; dm/s/d AR$97/180/290; @☎) This good, clean HI hostel has a pleasant dining area and spacious private rooms and dorms. Nearly all rooms have their own bathrooms. HI discount.

Secuoya Hostel HOSTEL $
(☎42-4485; Rivadavia 411; dm/d AR$85/240) Small 18-bed hostel in a plain house, with small rooms, creaky floors, dark kitchen and rustic dining area.

Ladera Norte Hostel HOSTEL $
(☎41-1481; www.ladera-norte.com.ar; Weber 531; dm/s/d AR$95/200/300; @☎) Rather impersonal 50-bed hostel with big main lobby (and table-tennis table) and industrial halls. Dorms are nice enough and most are carpeted, but avoid the 10-bed one.

Hostel Rukalhue HOSTEL $$
(☎42-7431; www.rukalhue.com.ar; Juez del Valle 682; dm AR$95, d AR$300-350; @☎) Large hostel with a variety of rooms. Choose from the older industrial wing, hosting small but good dorms. There's also a newer section with decent doubles, each with bathroom. For 'luxury' select a large apartment, each with kitchen and dining areas. The dusty garden out back has lots of trees – bring your hammock. Breakfast offered only in high season.

Camping ACA CAMPGROUND $
(☎42-7332; Av Koessler 2175; campsites with 2 person minimum per person AR$45) Spacious campground a 15-minute walk east of center, with shady dirt sites (avoid ones near the road). Get a *cabaña* for some luxury (worldwide AAA members only, AR$500 to AR$700). There's also good camping at Playa Catrite (campsites per person AR$30 to AR$50), 4km south of town.

El Mesón INTERNATIONAL $$$
(☎42-4970; Rivadavia 885; mains AR$65-80; ⊙lunch & dinner) Personally attended by the owners is this small, Spanish-influenced restaurant specializing in seafood. The generous dishes are well prepared: try the trout, paella or Patagonian lamb. Great service.

Corazón Contento CAFE $
(San Martín 467; mains AR$35-65; ⊙9am-11pm) Wonderful small, modern cafe serving healthy treats like vegetable tarts, plump empanadas, fruity *licuados* and baked goods. Basics like sandwiches, salads, burgers and pizzas available too. Order waffles for breakfast.

Dublin Pub PUB $
(San Martín 599; mains AR$30-60; ⊙9am-3am) Popular contemporary pub with great front patio and upper balcony. Cooks up mostly sandwiches, along with a few pastas, salads and meat dishes. Cocktails and local beers also, along with live bands on Friday and Saturday nights.

Information

There are several ATMs near Plaza San Martín.

Andina Internacional (☎42-7871; Capitán Drury 876) Changes traveler's checks.

National Park office (☎42-0664; Frey 479)

Post office (cnr Pérez & Roca)

Tourist office (☎42-7347; www.sanmartindelosandes.gov.ar; cnr San Martín & Rosas; ⊙8am-9pm) Near the plaza.

Getting There & Away

The airport is 23km north of town. Airlines include **Aerolíneas Argentinas** (☎41-0588; Belgrano 949) and **LADE** (☎42-7672).

The bus station is five blocks west of Plaza San Martín. Destinations include Junín de los Andes (AR$7, 45 minutes), Villa La Angostura (AR$42, 2½ hours) and Bariloche (AR$70, four hours). Chilean destinations include Pucon (AR$120, five hours) and Temuco (AR$120, six hours); from December to February, book these trips two days in advance.

Villa La Angostura

☎0294 / POP 11,000

Tiny Villa La Angostura is a darling chocolate-box town that takes its name from the *angosta* (narrow) 91m neck of land connecting it to the striking Península Quetrihué. There's no doubt that Villa is touristy, but it's also charming; wood-and-stone alpine buildings line the three-block-long main street. There's skiing at nearby Cerro Bayo in winter.

El Cruce is the main part of town and contains the bus terminal and most hotels and businesses; the main street is Arrayanes. Woodsy La Villa, with a few restaurants, hotels and a nice beach, is 3km southwest and on the shores of Lago Nahuel Huapi.

Sights & Activities

The cinnamon-barked *arrayán,* a myrtle relative, is protected in the small but beautiful **Parque Nacional Los Arrayanes** (admission AR$50) on the Península Quetrihué. The main *bosque* (forest) of *arrayanes* is situated at the southern tip of the peninsula; it's reachable by a 40- to 60-minute boat ride (one-way/round trip AR$95/170) or via hike on a relatively easy 12km trail from La Villa.

Experienced mountain-bike riders (there are stairs and hills!) should rent a bike to reach the *arrayán* forest. It's possible to boat either there or back, hiking or biking the other way (buy your return boat ticket in advance). Takc food and water; there's an ideal picnic spot next to a lake near the end of the trail.

At the start of the Arrayanes trail, near the beach, a steep 30- to 45-minute hike leads to a panoramic viewpoints over Lago Nahuel Huapi.

From the El Cruce part of town, a 3km walk north takes you to the **Mirador Belvedere** trailhead; hike another 30 minutes for good views. Nearby is **Cascada Inayacal**, a 50m waterfall, and a few hours' hike further on is **Cajón Negro**, a pretty valley (but get a map and directions beforehand from the tourist office, as trails and shortcuts around here can be confusing).

Sleeping & Eating

The following are all in or near El Cruce. Reserve ahead in January and February.

Residencial Río Bonito GUESTHOUSE $
(☎449-4110; www.riobonitopatagonia.com.ar; Topa Topa 260; d/tr AR$280/350; @wi-fi) Wonderful little guesthouse located on a residential street near the bus terminal. Garden roses greet you in front and the five rooms inside will be even better once they're all remodeled. Run by a friendly young couple.

Hostel La Angostura HOSTEL $
(☎449-4834; www.hostellaangostura.com.ar; Barbagelata 157; dm/d AR$90/290; @☎) Excellent central hostel with comfy lodgelike spaces and clean, modern rooms, each with its own bathroom. Spacious four- or five-bed dorms. There's a nice deck in front for smokers. HI discount.

Italian Hostel HOSTEL $
(☎449-4376; www.italianhostel.com.ar; Los Marquis 215; dm/d AR$90/250; @☎) Great-vibe hostel with decks, pleasant garden and friendly staff. The two dorms are very large (six and 10 beds) but good. There are three cozy private rooms with shared bathroom upstairs.

Hostal Bajo Cero HOSTEL $
(☎449-5454; www.bajocerohostel.com; Río Caleufu 88; dm/d/tr/q AR$100/350/380/480; @☎) About 1200m west of the bus terminal is this gorgeous hostel with large, well-designed dorms and lovely doubles. It has a nice garden and kitchen, plus airy common spaces.

Hostel Don Pilón HOSTEL $
(☎494-269; www.hosteldonpilon.com; Belvedere 204; dm/s/d AR$90/250/280; @☎) Decent friendly hostel located in an old *hostería* (guesthouse). Ground-floor rooms get more noise from the common spaces; upstairs rooms are quieter. Better-than-average breakfast.

Camping Unquehué CAMPGROUND $
(☎449-4103; www.campingunquehue.com.ar; Av Siete Lagos 727; campsites per person AR$46, tent AR$16, apt from AR$360) Attractive, well-run and family-friendly campground 500m west of the terminal. Great grassy sites, excellent facilities and a nearby supermarket. Modern studio apartments also available.

Hub INTERNATIONAL $$
(Av Arrayanes 256; mains AR$50-75; ⊙dinner Mon-Sat) Popular restaurant serving up not only the usual suspects (meat and pasta) but specialties like venison stew, seafood paella and mushroom-stuffed chicken. Gourmet salads too. Becomes a nightclub on Friday and Saturday nights.

El Viejo Fred INTERNATIONAL $$
(Arrayanes 167; mains AR$40-60; ⊙lunch & dinner) Modern restaurant good for traditional dishes like pizza and salads, though more exotic choices includes things like lamb goulash. Good music and vibe, along with a great front patio for people-watching.

Gran Nevada ARGENTINE $
(Av Arrayanes 106; mains AR$35-50; ⊙lunch & dinner) Family-friendly place megapopular for its cheap and plentiful meats, pizzas and pastas. Come early or be prepared to wait.

Information

ATMs are available around town.

Andina (Arrayanes 256) Changes traveler's checks.

National Park office (☎449-4152)

Post office (Las Fuschias 121) In a shopping gallery behind the bus terminal

Tourist office (☎449-4124; Arrayanes 9; ⊙8am-9pm)

Getting There & Around

From the bus terminal, buses depart for Bariloche (AR$27, 1¼ hours) and San Martín de los Andes (AR$42, 2½ hours, sit on left). If heading into Chile, reserve ahead for buses passing through. Buses to La Villa (where the boat docks and park entrance are located) leave every two hours.

There are several bike-rental places in town.

Bariloche

☎0294 / POP 110,000

The Argentine Lake District's largest city, San Carlos de Bariloche attracts scores of travelers in both summer and winter. It's finely located on the shores of beautiful Lago Nahuel Huapi, and lofty mountain peaks are visible from all around. While Bariloche's center bustles with tourists shopping at myriad chocolate shops, souvenir stores and trendy boutiques, the real attractions lie outside the city: Parque Nacional Nahuel Huapi offers spectacular hiking, and there's also great camping, trekking, rafting, fishing and skiing in the area. Despite the heavy touristy feel, Bariloche is a good place to stop, hang out, get errands done and, of course, have some fun.

Sights & Activities

The heart of town is the Centro Cívico, a group of well-kept public buildings built of log and stone (architect Ezequiel Bustillo originally adapted Middle European styles into this form of architecture, now associated with the Lake District area). The **Museo de la Patagonia** (☎442-2309; Centro Cívico; donation AR$20; ⊙10am-12:30pm & 2-5pm Tue-Fri, 10am-6pm Sat), located here, offers a history of the area, along with good displays of stuffed critters and archaeological artifacts.

Rafting trips on the Río Limay (easy class II) or Río Manso (class III to IV) are very popular. **Extremo Sur** (442-7301; www.extremosur.com; Morales 765) and **Aguas Blancas** (443-2799; www.aguasblancas.com.ar; Morales 564) have good tours.

For kayaking, a couple of good companies are **Cuadrante Sur** (15-451-1350; www.cuadrantesur.com) and **Tranqueando** (446-1905; www.tranqueando.com). Other activities include hiking, trekking, rock-climbing, biking, paragliding, horseriding, fishing and skiing.

Many agencies and hostels offer tours. One backpacker-oriented agency is **Lagos del Sur** (445-8410; www.lagosdelsur.tur.ar; Salta 355), with several interesting area offerings.

Courses

La Montaña LANGUAGE COURSE
(452-4212; www.lamontana.com; Elflein 251) Spanish school that also offers accommodations, volunteer work programs and social excursions.

Sleeping

Make reservations from late December to February, July and August and during holidays (especially Easter).

TOP CHOICE **Penthouse 1004** HOSTEL $
(443-2228; www.penthouse1004.com.ar; San Martín 127, 10th fl, Suite 1004; dm AR$90, d AR$250; @ wifi) Spectacular five-star views, both from the rooms and the awe-inspiring terrace. Great common areas including a large kitchen, friendly service and good atmosphere. All rooms share bathrooms.

La Barraca GUESTHOUSE $
(442-4102; www.labarracasuites.com; Av Los Pioneros 39; d/tr AR$350/390; @ wifi) Lovely guesthouse with only six simple but beautiful rooms, well run by a French-Argentine couple. It's peaceful, with grassy garden and views, and there's a giant fireplace in the living room. Kitchen use available.

Periko's HOSTEL $
(452-2326; www.perikos.com; Morales 555; dm AR$90, d AR$240-280; @ wifi) Beautiful, well-run hostel with pleasant atmosphere, grassy yard and wonderful kitchen. Well-thought-out dorms and exceptional, hotel-quality doubles.

BARILOCHE'S LOCAL BUSES

Most of Bariloche's local buses work with magnetic cards, or *cospeles*, that can only be purchased at the downtown **3 de Mayo bus office** (442-5648; www.3demayobariloche.com.ar; Moreno 480; 7:30am-8:30pm Mon-Fri, 8am-4pm Sat). Cards cost AR$17 (including AR$3 credit) and can be recharged at various places in town (the tourist office has a list and bus schedule). With this card, rides cost AR$3 each and can be used for several people at once. If you don't want to buy a card you can buy individual tickets, but this way most rides cost AR$6 each. Some hostels will loan cards, so ask.

The only local Bariloche bus that takes cash is the Cerro Catedral bus (AR$8).

Hostel 41 Below HOSTEL $
(443-6433; www.hostel41below.com; Juramento 94; dm AR$80-90, d without bathroom AR$250; @ wifi) Intimate hostel with clean dorms, fine doubles (with view) and a mellow vibe. Easy to meet others in the wonderful common room. Kiwi-run.

Hostería Portofino GUESTHOUSE $
(442-2795; www.hosteriaportofino.com; Morales 439; d/t/q AR$340/410/$475, 7-person apt AR$690; @ wifi) A young French-Argentine couple has breathed new life into this old guesthouse, which offers 13 simple, yet stylish and comfortable, rooms – most with private bathroom. Occasional dinners available.

Tango Inn Downtown HOSTEL $$
(440-0004; www.tangoinn.com; Salta 514; dm AR$90-100, s & d AR$320-370; @ wifi) Best for its superior doubles, which boast unbeatable views of the lake. Good large dorms, plus a purple lounge room with pool table. There's even a Jacuzzi! Its other hostel, Tango Inn Soho, is 500m from bus terminal at 12 de Octubre 1915. HI discount.

Greenhouse Hostel HOSTEL $
(444-2267; www.greenhousehostel.com.ar; Tronador 4651, Km 4.7; dm AR$70-90, d AR$200-230; @ wifi) If you're looking for a peaceful hostel outside Bariloche, try this spot. There are only 22 beds, a comfortable common area

Bariloche

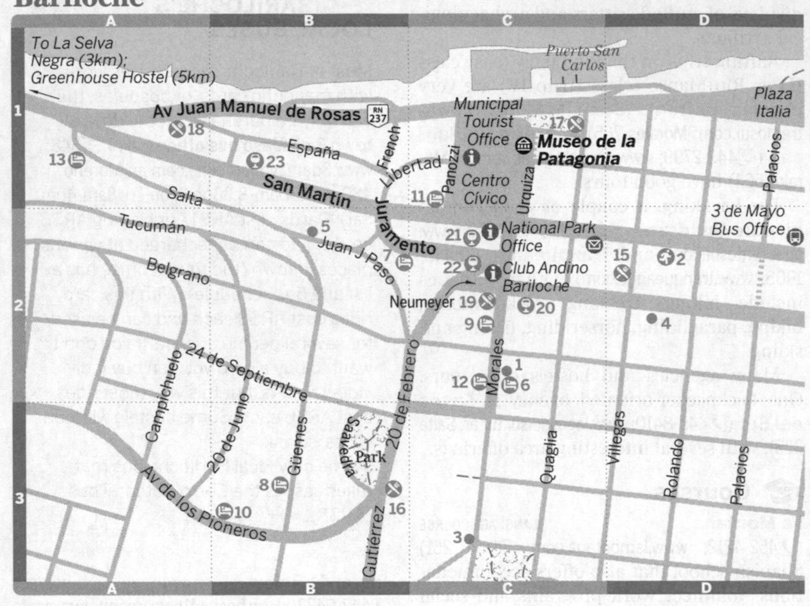

Bariloche

Top Sights
Museo de la Patagonia C1

Activities, Courses & Tours
1 Aguas Blancas C2
2 Bikeway D2
3 Extremo Sur C3
4 La Montaña D2
5 Lagos del Sur B2

Sleeping
6 Achalay C2
7 Hostel 41 Below B2
8 Hostería Güemes B3
9 Hostería Portofino C2
10 La Barraca B3
11 Penthouse 1004 .... C1
12 Periko's C2
13 Tango Inn Downtown A1

Eating
14 Covita E1
15 El Boliche de Alberto D2
16 El Vegetariano B3
17 Kostelo C1
18 La Trattoria de la Famiglia Bianchi A1
19 Manush C2

Drinking
20 Antares C2
21 Konna Bar C2
22 Los Vikingos C2
23 Wilkenny B1

and a grassy backyard with deck – some rooms even have partial water views. Call ahead for free pickup.

Hostería Güemes GUESTHOUSE $
(☎442-4785; Güemes 715; r AR$220; @📶) Quiet family guesthouse sporting plain but comfortable rooms. Nice airy living room with central fireplace and city views. Spanish-speaking owner Cholo is an expert on the area's fishing.

Achalay HOSTEL $$
(☎452-2556; www.hostelachalay.com; Morales 564; dm/d AR$90/300; @📶) Basic, no-frills hostel with supercasual vibe, located in an old house. Most rooms share bathrooms; nice sloping grassy front yard.

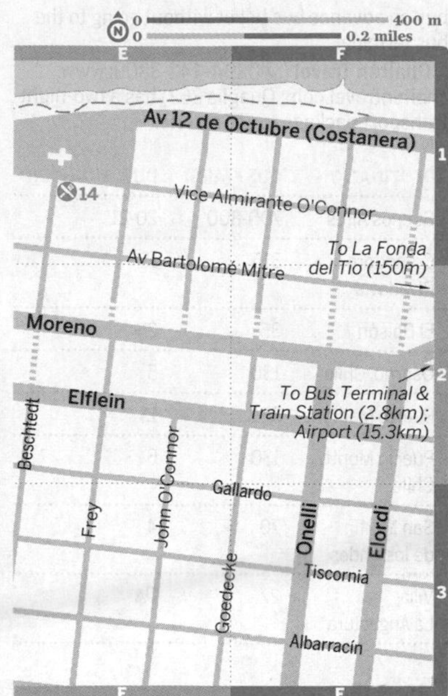

La Selva Negra CAMPGROUND $
(☎444-1013; campingselvanegra@speedy.com.ar; Av Bustillo, Km 2.9; campsites per person AR$50) Pleasant shady campsites. It's 3km west of town; take bus 10, 20 or 21.

Eating

Regional specialties include *jabali* (wild boar), *ciervo* (venison), and *trucha* (trout). Most bars serve food too.

TOP CHOICE **El Boliche de Alberto** PARRILLA $$
(☎443-1433; Villegas 347; mains AR$45-75; ⏰lunch & dinner) Bariloche's most famous *parrilla*, boasting excellent meats. There's another branch around the corner at Elflein 158, plus an equally good pasta restaurant at Elflein and Villegas.

Covita VEGETARIAN $
(☎442-1708; O'Conner 511; mains AR$30-60; ⏰lunch Mon-Sat, dinner Thu-Sat; ✎) Wonderfully healthy cafe that caters to macrobiotic, vegan and even raw food diets. Choose from salads, stir-fries, curries and sushi, among other things. Fresh organic juices too.

Manush PUB $
(☎442-8905; Neumeyer 20; mains AR$25-50; ⏰6pm-2am Mon-Thu, to 3am Fri & Sat) Intimate brewery pub-restaurant featuring good tapas, pizzas, *cazuelas* and cheese boards, along with daily specials. Wash it all down with a home-brewed pale ale.

Antares BAR
(☎443-1454; Elflein 47; mains AR$40-60) A popular modern bar-restaurant serving sandwiches, crepes, tapas and cheese/meat boards. The attractive copper-hued beer dispensers are decorative only - Antares' eight beers are brewed only in Mar del Plata and shipped from there. Occasional live music.

La Trattoria de la Famiglia Bianchi ITALIAN $$
(☎442-1596; España 590; mains AR$40-66; ⏰lunch & dinner) Excellent Italian restaurant serving up creative pastas like venison sorrentinos and risottos with seafood and wild mushrooms.

Kostelo INTERNATIONAL $$
(☎443-9697; Quaglia 111; mains AR$50-80; ⏰lunch & dinner Tue-Sun) Modern and upscale bar-restaurant best for its location right near the lake. The food is creative, well presented and comes in decent portions. Try to get a table with water view.

La Fonda del Tio ARGENTINE $
(Av Bartolomé Mitre 1130; mains AR$25-50) Where locals go for large portions of good, inexpensive food. Arrive early to avoid a wait.

El Vegetariano VEGETARIAN $
(20 de Febrero 730; set menus AR$35; ⏰closed Sun; ✎) Simple, fresh and healthy five-course vegetarian menu, which changes daily. A la carte, vegan choices and takeout also available.

Drinking

There are four small but popular bars on Juramento, just off San Martín. Most bars serve some food too.

Berlina BREWERY
(☎452-3336; Bustillo, Km 11.75) Great-vibe brewery started by three brothers, one of whom is an eccentric, German-educated brewmaster. Try the five-beer sampler with the thin-crust pizza. Nice grassy garden for sunny days. Located nearly 12km from Bariloche's center, but easily accessible by bus.

Konna Bar BAR
(Juramento 73) Tight and cozy brewery-bar with warm atmosphere, though often gets stuffed full of young patrons. Great beer.

Los Vikingos BAR
(cnr Juramento & 20 de Febrero) A laid-back little corner bar serving a good range of local microbrewery beers at excellent prices. The music's cool and the decor eclectic. DJs play on weekends.

Wilkenny BAR
(San Martín 435) Bariloche's biggest and loudest drinking attraction, this popular pub comes with a wraparound bar.

Information

Internet cafes and ATMs are common.

Cambio Sudamérica (Av Bartolomé Mitre 63) Changes traveler's checks.

Chilean Consulate (☎442-3050; España 275)

Club Andino Bariloche (☎442-2266; www.clubandino.com.ar; 20 de Febrero 30) Trekking, camping, hiking, topo maps and *refugio* (a usually rustic shelter in a national park or remote area) information. Also offers guides and transport to Pampa Linda (Mt Trondador).

Municipal tourist office (☎442-9850; www.barilochepatagonia.info; Centro Cívico; ⏲8am-9pm) Good and efficient; has information on magnetic bus cards and local bus schedules. Also at the bus terminal.

National Park office (☎442-3111; San Martín 24; ⏲8am-4pm Mon-Fri, 9am-3pm Sat & Sun) Hiking and camping information plus maps.

Post office (Moreno 175)

Getting There & Around

Air

The airport is 15km east of town; take bus 72 (AR$6) from the town center or a taxi (AR$75).

Aerolíneas Argentinas (☎443-3304; Av Bartolomé Mitre 185), **LAN** (☎0810-999-9526; www.lan.com; Av Bartolomé Mitre 523) and **LADE** (☎442-3562; www.lade.com.ar; O'Connor 214) provide services.

Bicycle

Bikeway (☎445-6571; www.bikeway.com.ar; Moreno 237) rents bicycles and does area bike excursions.

Bus

The bus terminal is 2.5km east of the center. To bus to the center, you'll need to buy a AR$6 ticket at the 3 de Mayo bus counter, then go outside and wait at the bus stop shelter (it's nearby, towards the train station). If you arrive outside the 9am to 7pm hours, however, you'll have to taxi (AR$35) as the bus counter will be closed.

Some long-distance bus companies have a ticket office downtown, so you might be able to buy an advance bus ticket without going to the bus terminal.

Chaltén Travel (☎0294-442-3809; www.chaltentravel.com; Quaglia 262) has a two-night transport package to El Calafate.

DESTINATION	COST (AR$)	DURATION (HR)
Buenos Aires	700-800	20-21
Comodoro Rivadavia	315	15
El Bolsón	35	2¼
Osorno, Chile	130	5
Puerto Madryn	350	13
Puerto Montt, Chile	130	6
San Martín de los Andes	70	4
Villa La Angostura	27	1¼

Car

There are plenty of car rental agencies in town; try **Correntoso** (☎442-7737; www.correntosorentacar.com; Mitre 106, 1st fl, Suite 5). Car rental rates are around AR$250 (with 200km) per day.

Train

The **train station** (☎42-3172)is next to the bus terminal. At time of writing there were no trains running, but check during your visit.

Parque Nacional Nahuel Huapi

Lago Nahuel Huapi, a glacial relic over 100km long, is the centerpiece of this gorgeous national park. To the west, 3554m Monte Tronador marks the Andean crest and Chilean border. Humid Valdivian forest covers its lower slopes, while summer wildflowers blanket alpine meadows.

The 60km **Circuito Chico** loop is a popular excursion. Every 20 minutes, bus 20 (from San Martín and Morales in Bariloche) heads along Lago Nahuel Huapi to end at Puerto Pañuelos, where boat trips leave a few times daily for beautiful **Puerto Blest**, touristy **Isla Victoria** and pretty **Península Quetrihué**. Bus 10 goes the other way, inland via **Colonia Suiza** (a small, woodsy Swiss community), and ends at Bahía López, where you can hike a short way to the tip of the peninsula Brazo de la Tristeza. In summer bus 11 does the whole Circuito, connecting Puerto Pañuelos with Bahía López, but in winter you can walk the 8km stretch along the nonbusy highway, with much of that being on a woodsy nature trail. There's a beautiful two-hour side hike to Villa Tacul, on the shores of Lago Nahuel Huapi. It's best to walk from Bahía López to Puerto Pañuelos rather than the other way around, since many more buses head back to Bariloche from Pañuelos. Be sure to confirm bus schedules in Bariloche's tourist office, as schedules vary from season to season.

Tough cyclists can hop a bus to Km 18.6 and rent a bike at **Bike Cordillera** (☎452-4828; www.cordillerabike.com). This way you'll bike less, avoid busy Av Bustillo and take advantage of the loop's more scenic sections. Be aware this is a hilly, 25km ride, but you can extend it to visit area attractions. Call ahead to reserve a bicycle.

Skiing is a popular winter activity from mid-June to October. **Cerro Catedral** (☎40-9000; www.catedralaltapatagonia.com), some 20km west of town, is one of the biggest ski centers in South America. It boasts dozens of runs, a cable car, gondola and plenty of services (including rentals). The best part, however, is the views: peaks surrounding the lakes are gloriously visible.

Area hikes include climbing up **Cerros Otto**, **Catedral** and **Campanario**; all have chairlifts as well. The six-hour hike up Monte Tronador flanks to Refugio Meiling usually involves an overnight stay as it's a 2½-hour drive to the trailhead (Pampa Linda) from Bariloche. Summiting Trondador requires technical expertise.

If trekking, check with Club Andino or National Park Office, both in Bariloche, for trail conditions; snow can block trails, even in summer.

El Bolsón

☎0294 / POP 40,000

Hippies rejoice: there's a must-see destination for you in Argentina, and it's called El Bolsoń. Within its liberal and artsy borders live alternate-lifestyle folks who've made their town a 'nonnuclear zone' and 'ecological municipality.' Located about 120km south of Bariloche, nondescript El Bolsón is surrounded by dramatically jagged mountain peaks. Its economic prosperity comes from a warm microclimate and fertile soil, both of which support a cadre of organic farms devoted to hops, cheese, soft fruits such as raspberries, and orchards. This, and El Bolsón's true personality, can be seen at its famous **feria artesanal** (craft market), where creative crafts and healthy food are sold; catch it during the day on Plaza Pagano on Tuesdays, Thursdays and weekends (best on Saturdays).

For summer activities such as rafting on Río Azul, paragliding and horse riding, contact **Grado 42** (☎4449-3124; www.grado42.com; Av Belgrano 406) or **Huara** (☎445-5000; www.huaraviajesyturismo.com.ar; Dorrego 410).

Sleeping

Surrounding mountains offer plenty of camping opportunities, plus *refugios* (bunks AR$50 to AR$60).

TOP CHOICE **La Casona de Odile Hostel** HOSTEL $
(☎449-2753; www.odile.com.ar; dm AR$90, d AR$280; @📶) Five kilometers north of the center is this amazing hostel, one of Argentina's best. It's on two gorgeous hectares of land near a lovely river, and the friendly young owners know area trails. Bike rentals, weekly *asados* and homemade snacks available. Lujancito bus stops nearby.

La Posada de Hamelin GUESTHOUSE $$
(☎449-2030; www.posadadehamelin.com.ar; Granollers 2179; s/d/tr AR$240/320/400; 📶) Just four cozy rooms in this sweet, friendly and vine-covered family home. Excellent breakfast (AR$30).

Residencial Los Helechos GUESTHOUSE $
(☎449-2262; www.posadaloshelechos.com.ar; San Martín 3248; s/d/apt AR$180/220/280) Family-run guesthouse with four clean, modern rooms and two apartments, a pretty flowery garden and kitchen access. Look for the 'Kioscón' sign.

Mandala Hostel HOSTEL $
(☎472-0219; www.hostelmandala.com.ar; cnr Los Maitenes & Amancay; dm/d AR$90/280; @📶) Beautiful, guesthouselike hostel located 3km north of the plaza (take the Golondrina bus). Private rooms are clean, modern and some have balconies, while dorms are comfortable and spacious. All rooms come with bathroom.

La Casa del Arbol HOSTEL $
(☎472-0176; www.hostelelbolson.com; Perito Moreno 3038; dm/d $90/240; @📶) Great central hostel

with amenities that include great kitchen, cheap communal meals, covered patio, grassy garden and good vibes.

La Casa del Viajero HOSTEL $
(☎449-3092; aporro@elbolson.com; near Libertad & Las Flores, Barrio Usina; dm/d AR$70/160;) Totally laid-back, very rustic and artsy backwater. Expect no luxuries – but that's the appeal. Kitchens available. Call for pickup as it's hard to find.

Posada Pehuenia HOSTEL $
(☎448-3010; www.hospedajepehuenia.com; Azcuenaga 140; dm/s/d AR$80/150/200, cabañas AR$320;) Friendly hostel with small, colorful rooms and great kitchen. Nice backyard *cabañas* (sleeping four to five) and bike rentals, plus weekly *asados*.

Camping Refugio Patagónico CAMPGROUND $
(☎448-3888; www.refugiopatagonico.com.ar; Falkland Islands s/n; campsites per person AR$40;) Grassy camping on four hectares with pleasant shady sites, mountain views and expansive fields. Don't confuse it with Refugio Patagónico, which is a decent hostel next door (they used to be owned by the same people).

Eating & Drinking

Food at the *feria artesanal* is tasty, healthy and good value.

Apunto PARRILLA $$
(☎448-3780; San Martín 2762; mains AR$60-85) Well-regarded *parrilla* with abundant portions of good-quality meat. Located across from tourist office.

Cervecería El Bolsón Centro PUB, RESTAURANT
(☎448-3014; cnr Av San Martín & Fernandez; mains AR$40-60) Relaxing place that brews about a dozen beers and also serves pizza, pastas and regional specialties. Great beer patio.

Patio Venzano ARGENTINE $$
(cnr Sarmiento & Pablo Hube; mains AR$40-60; ⊙lunch & dinner) Great cozy atmosphere and nice patio add to the tasty meat, burgers, omelets, crepes and homemade pasta offerings here.

Otto Tipp ARGENTINE $$
(☎449-3700; cnr Roca & Falkland Islands; mains AR$55-85; ⊙lunch & dinner Dec-Feb, dinner Wed-Sat Mar-Jan) Large brewery restaurant with plenty of pizzas, along with some homemade pastas and regional dishes.

Jauja ICE CREAM $
(Av San Martín 2867; cones AR$13-21; ⊙breakfast, lunch & dinner) Best for its famous ice-cream counter.

Information

The competent **tourist office** (☎449-2604; www.elbolson.gov.ar) is next to Plaza Pagano, and has good info on area hikes and bus schedules. There are no exchange houses and just two ATMs (where lines can get long). The post office is opposite the tourist office.

Getting There & Around

LADE (☎49-2206; Sarmiento 3238) occasionally flies to El Bolsoń.

There's no central bus terminal; several bus companies are spread around town, with Via Bariloche having the most departures to and from Bariloche. See the tourist office for schedules. Destinations include Bariloche (AR$35, 2½ hours), Esquel (AR$45, 2½ hours), Puerto Madryn (AR$310, 11 hours) and Buenos Aires (from AR$650, 23 hours).

Rent bikes at **Maputur** (☎449-1440; Perito Moreno 2331) or **El Tabano** (☎449-3093; Perito Moreno 2871).

Around El Bolsón

The spectacular granite ridge of 2260m **Cerro Piltriquitrón** looms to the east like the back of some prehistoric beast. From the 1100m level ('plataforma'), reached by *remise* (AR$240 round trip with 1½-hr wait), a further 40-minute hike leads to **Bosque Tallado** (admission AR$20, charged Jan, Feb & Easter), a shady grove of about 50 figures carved from logs. Another 20-minute walk uphill is **Refugio Piltriquitrón** (camping/dm free/AR$35), where you can have a drink or even sack down (bring your sleeping bag). From here it's 2½ hours to the summit. The weather is very changeable, so bring layers.

On a ridge 7km west of town is **Cabeza del Indio** (admission AR$4), a rock outcrop resembling a man's profile; the trail has great views of the Río Azul and Lago Puelo. There are also a couple of **waterfalls** (admission each AR$4) about 10km north of town. All these are most accessible by bus in January and February.

A good three-hour hike reaches the narrow canyon of pretty **Cajón del Azul**. At the end is a friendly *refugio* where you can eat or stay the night. From where the town buses (AR$10) drop you off, it's about a 15-minute steep walk to the Cajón del Azul trailhead.

About 18km south of El Bolsón is windy **Parque Nacional Lago Puelo** (admission AR$20). You can camp, swim, fish, hike or take a boat tour to the Chilean border. In summer regular buses run from El Bolsón (AR$5, 30 minutes).

Esquel

☎02945 / POP 40,000

Homely Esquel doesn't look like much at first glance, but it boasts a dramatic setting at the foothills of western Chubut province and is the transition point from Andean forest to the Patagonian steppe. It's also the starting gate for the Old Patagonian Express and gateway to Parque Nacional Los Alerces. There's good hiking, rafting, kayaking, horse riding, fishing and skiing in the area, and the pleasant Welsh stronghold of Trevelin is a good day trip away.

Sights & Activities

La Trochita (☎in Esquel 45-1403) is Argentina's famous narrow-gauge steam train. It does short tourist runs from the station near the corner of Brown and Roggero to Nahuel Pan, 20km east (AR$180, 2¾-hour tour). At the other end of the tracks, 140km away, is El Maitén; the railroad's workshops and a museum are here. El Maitén is accessible from El Bolsón; there is currently no regular train connection from Esquel. Check the tourist office for current schedules.

For adventure tours and activities try **EPA Expediciones** (☎45-7015; www.epaexpediciones.com; Fontana 482). Bike rentals are available at **Coyote Bikes** (☎45-5505; Rivadavia 887; ⌚9am-1pm & 3:30-8pm Mon-Fri, 9am-1pm Sat).

Sleeping

Sol Azul HOSTEL $
(☎45-5193; www.hostelsolazul.com.ar; Rivadavia 2869; dm AR$80; @📶) Wonderfully designed hostel with what is likely Argentina's best hostel kitchen. There are very pleasant dorms with floor heating, a sauna and two tent spaces (AR$40 per person). The downside is that it's located 1km northeast of the bus terminal (a 15-minute walk or AR$15 taxi ride).

Casa del Pueblo HOSTEL $
(☎45-0581; www.esquelcasadelpueblo.com.ar; San Martín 661; dm AR$80-95, d AR$240-280; @📶) Mazelike but good hostel with cozy common areas, solid kitchen and grassy garden with hammocks. Rooms are all different design and sizes. Occasional *asados* offered and bike rentals possible; HI discount is also available.

Planeta Hostel HOSTEL $
(☎45-6846; www.planetahostel.com; Roca 458; dm/d AR$80/200; 📶) Central hostel with a wide variety of decent, good-sized rooms. There's also a good kitchen and nice patio. HI discount.

Anochecer Andino HOSTEL $
(☎45-0498; www.anochecerandino.com.ar; Ameghino 482; dm/s/d AR$75/90/180; @📶) Rather homely and plain hostel, but it's clean and the owners are friendly and kind. Dorms hold four to eight beds, and there's a small barbecue patio. Homemade dinners are available.

Eating & Drinking

María Castaña CAFE $
(cnr 25 de Mayo & Rivadavia; mains AR$30-60; ⌚9am-late) Popular cafe with sidewalk tables and plenty of menu choices like sandwiches, pastas and cheese boards.

La Luna ARGENTINE $$
(Av Fontana 656; mains AR$40-75; ⌚noon-4pm & 7pm-1am) Great for its outdoor patio and pizzas; also serves craft beers.

Cheers PUB $
(☎45-7041; cnr Sarmiento & Av Alvear; mains AR$30-60; ⌚noon-late) Irish-pub wannabe serving up typical but good pub fare like meats, salads, pastas and pizza. Antares and Heineken beers too.

Hotel Argentino BAR
(25 de Mayo 862; ⌚4pm-5am) Old-time Wild West saloon bar and pool tables. Funky atmosphere worth checking out.

Information

Banks with ATMs are located on Alvear and on 25 de Mayo near Alvear.

Club Andino (☎45-3248; Ameghino 1346) Alpine club.

Post office (Av Alvear 1192) Near the tourist office.

Tourist office (☎45-1927; www.esquel.gov.ar; cnr Av Alvear & Sarmiento; ⌚7am-11pm)

Another tourist office branch is located at the bus terminal.

Getting There & Around

The airport is 24km east of town (taxi AR$80). **Aerolíneas Argentinas** (☎453-614; Av Fontana 406) and **LADE** (☎452-124; Alvear 1085) provide services.

Esquel's modern bus terminal is eight blocks north of the center, at the corner of Av Alvear and Brun. Destinations include El Bolsón (AR$45, 2½ hours), Bariloche (AR$88, 4½ hours), Puerto Madryn (AR$270, 10 hours) and Comodoro Rivadavia (AR$180, nine hours). Buses go to Trevelin (AR$5, 25 minutes) from the terminal, stopping along Av Alvear on their way south.

Trevelin

☎02945 / POP 10,000

Historic Trevelin is a calm, sunny and laid-back community located only 24km south of Esquel.

Landmarks include the historical **Museo Regional** (☎48-0189; cnr 25 de Mayo & Molino Viejo), housed in a restored brick mill, and **Capilla Bethel**, a Welsh chapel dating from 1910. **Tumba de Malacara** (☎48-0108; admission AR$20; ⏲10am-noon & 3-8pm), two blocks northeast of the plaza, is a monument dedicated to the horse that apparently saved John Evans, Trevelin's founder.

Hostel Casaverde (☎48-0091; www.casaverdehostel.com.ar; Los Alerces s/n; dm/d AR$75/240; wi-fi), sitting at the top of a small hill, is the best budget accommodation in town and is both friendly and serene. The rooms, kitchen, atmosphere and views are so welcoming that you'll be tempted to extend your stay. An HI discount applies.

You can have afternoon tea (served from 3pm to 8pm) and conquer a whole platter of pastries at **Nain Maggie** (☎48-0232; www.casadetenainmaggie.com; Perito Moreno 179; tea service AR$70; ⏲10am-12:30pm & 3-8:30pm) and **Las Mutisias** (☎48-0165; Av San Martín 170; tea service AR$55), while keeping your ears pricked for locals speaking not Spanish but Welsh.

For information, you can visit the **tourist office** (☎48-0120; www.trevelin.gov.ar) located on Plaza Fontana.

Half-hourly buses run from Esquel to Trevelin (AR$5, less frequently during off seasons).

Parque Nacional Los Alerces

Just 33km west of Esquel, the spacious Andean **Parque Nacional Los Alerces** (admission AR$50) protects extensive stands of *alerce (Fitzroya cupressoides)*, a large and long-lived conifer of humid Valdivian forests. Other common trees here include cypress, incense cedar, southern beeches and *arrayán*. The *colihue* (a bamboolike plant) undergrowth is almost impenetrable.

The receding glaciers of Los Alerces' peaks, which barely reach 2300m, have left nearly pristine lakes and streams with charming vistas and excellent fishing. Westerly storms drop nearly 3000mm of rain annually, but summers are mild and the park's eastern zone is much drier. A **visitors center** (☎47-1015; ⏲8am-9pm) can help you plan excursions.

A popular five-hour boat tour sails from Puerto Chucao (on Lago Menéndez) and heads to **El Alerzal**, an accessible stand of rare *alerces* (AR$230). A two-hour stopover permits a walk around a loop trail that passes Lago Cisne and an attractive waterfall to end up at **El Abuelo** (Grandfather), a 57m-tall, 2600-year-old *alerce*.

In the park there are organized **campgrounds** (campsites per person AR$30-54), along with some free sites. Lago Krüger, reached either by foot (17km, 12 hours) or by taxi boat from nearby Villa Futalaufquen, has a campground, a restaurant and expensive *hostería*. See Esquel's tourist office for a complete list of accommodations options.

From January to mid-March there are twice-daily buses from Esquel (AR$20, 25 minutes); outside summer there are four buses per week.

PATAGONIA

Few places in the world inspire the imagination like mystical Patagonia. You can cruise bleak RN 40 (South America's Route 66), watch an active glacier calve house-size icebergs, and hike among some of the most fantastic mountain scenery in the world. There are Welsh teahouses, petrified forests, quirky outpost towns, penguin colonies, huge sheep *estancias* and some of the world's largest trout. The sky is wide,

Patagonia

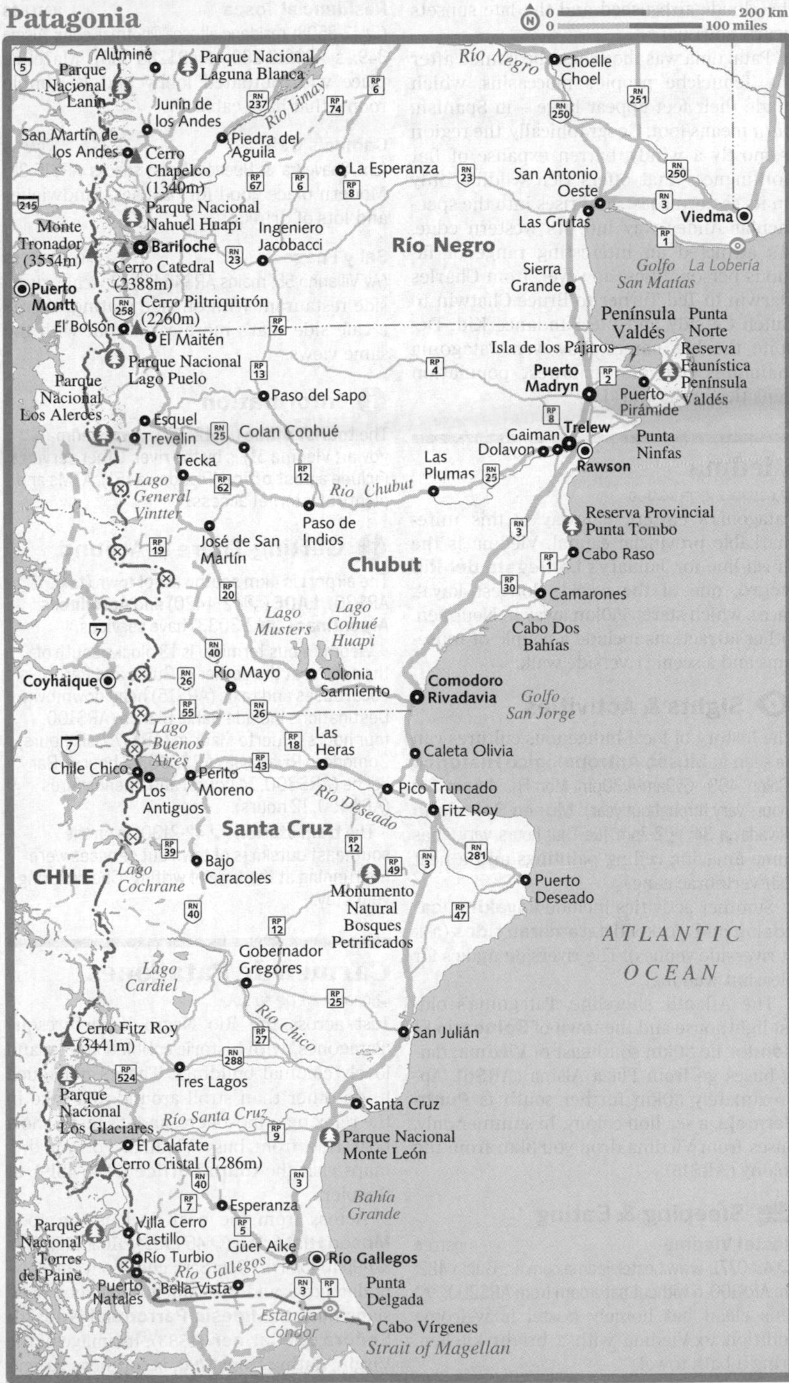
N
0 200 km
0 100 miles
Aluminé
Parque Nacional Laguna Blanca
Parque Nacional Lanín
Junín de los Andes
San Martín de los Andes
Cerro Chapelco (1340m)
Piedra del Aguila
Río Limay
Río Negro
Choelle Choel
La Esperanza
San Antonio Oeste
Las Grutas
Viedma
Parque Nacional Nahuel Huapi
Monte Tronador (3554m)
Bariloche
Ingeniero Jacobacci
Río Negro
Cerro Catedral (2388m)
Puerto Montt
Cerro Piltriquitrón (2260m)
El Bolsón
El Maitén
Golfo San Matías
La Lobería
Sierra Grande
Península Valdés
Punta Norte
Reserva Faunística Península Valdés
Isla de los Pájaros
Puerto Madryn
Puerto Pirámide
Parque Nacional Lago Puelo
Parque Nacional Los Alerces
Paso del Sapo
Esquel
Trevelin
Colan Conhué
Gaiman
Dolavon
Trelew
Rawson
Punta Ninfas
Tecka
Las Plumas
Lago General Vintter
Río Chubut
Paso de Indios
José de San Martín
Reserva Provincial Punta Tombo
Cabo Raso
Chubut
Camarones
Cabo Dos Bahías
Lago Musters
Lago Colhué Huapi
Coyhaique
Río Mayo
Colonia Sarmiento
Comodoro Rivadavia
Golfo San Jorge
Lago Buenos Aires
Las Heras
Caleta Olivia
Chile Chico
Los Antiguos
Perito Moreno
Pico Truncado
Río Deseado
Fitz Roy
Santa Cruz
CHILE
Lago Cochrane
Bajo Caracoles
Monumento Natural Bosques Petrificados
Puerto Deseado
ATLANTIC OCEAN
Gobernador Gregores
Lago Cardiel
Río Chico
Cerro Fitz Roy (3441m)
San Julián
Tres Lagos
Parque Nacional Los Glaciares
Río Santa Cruz
Santa Cruz
El Calafate
Parque Nacional Monte León
Cerro Cristal (1286m)
Esperanza
Bahía Grande
Parque Nacional Torres del Paine
Villa Cerro Castillo
Río Turbio
Güer Aike
Río Gallegos
Río Gallegos
Puerto Natales
Bella Vista
Punta Delgada
Estancia Cóndor
Cabo Vírgenes
Strait of Magellan
5
215
7
7
RN 237
RP 6
RP 74
RN 251
RN 250
RP 67
RP 6
RP 8
RN 23
RN 250
RN 3
RP 1
RN 23
RN 258
RP 76
RP 13
RP 4
RP 2
RP 8
RN 25
RP 12
RP 62
RN 25
RN 3
RP 19
RP 1
RP 30
RP 20
RN 40
RN 26
RP 55
RN 26
RP 18
RP 43
RP 12
RP 39
RP 49
RN 3
RN 281
RN 40
RP 12
RP 47
RP 25
RP 27
RN 288
RP 524
RP 9
RN 40
RN 3
RP 7
RP 5
RN 3
RP 1

the clouds airbrushed and the late sunsets nearly spiritual.

Patagonia was thought to be named after the Tehuelche people's moccasins, which made their feet appear huge – in Spanish, *pata* means foot. Geographically, the region is mostly a windy, barren expanse of flat nothingness that offers rich wildlife only on its eastern coast, and rises into the spectacular Andes way into its western edge. It's attracted an interesting range of famous personalities, however, from Charles Darwin to Ted Turner to Bruce Chatwin to Butch Cassidy and the Sundance Kid. Despite the big names, however, Patagonia maintains one of the lowest population densities in the world.

Viedma

☎02920 / POP 70,000

Patagonia's eastern gateway is this unremarkable provincial capital. Viedma is the finish line for January's **La Regata del Río Negro**, one of the world's longest kayak races, which starts 550km away in Neuquén. Other attractions include a couple of museums and a scenic riverside walk.

Sights & Activities

The history of local indigenous cultures can be seen at **Museo Antropológico Histórico** (Colón 498; ⏲9am-4:30pm Mon-Fri, 4-6pm Sat (hours vary throughout year). **Museo Salesiano** (Rivadavia 34; ⏲2-7pm Tue-Thu; hours vary) has some amazing ceiling paintings and a neat fish-vertebrae cane.

Summer activities include **kayaking**, **canoeing** and weekend **catamaran rides** (ask at riverside venues). The riverside makes for pleasant walking.

The Atlantic shoreline, Patagonia's oldest lighthouse and the town of **Balneario El Cóndor** lie 30km southeast of Viedma; daily buses go from Plaza Alsina (AR$6). Approximately 30km further south is **Punta Bermeja**, a sea lion colony. In summer only, buses from Viedma drop you 3km from the colony (AR$15).

Sleeping & Eating

Hostel Viedma HOSTEL $
(☎43-0771; www.hostelviedma.com.ar; Guido 482; dm AR$100, d without bathroom from AR$200; 📶) This clean but homely hostel is welcome addition to Viedma with a bright kitchen. bring a bath towel.

Residencial Tosca HOTEL $$
(☎42-8508; residencialtosca@hotmail.com; Alsina 349; s AR$210-280, d AR$280-380) Mazelike place with outdated lobby and 10 simple rooms that have cable TV.

Camila's Café CAFE $
(cnr Saavedra & Buenos Aires; snacks AR$15-22) Modern place good for pastries, sandwiches and lots of drinks.

Sal y Fuego ARGENTINE $$
(Av Villarino 55; mains AR$45-85) Upscale riverside restaurant with outside seating; there's a cafe side that's more casual but with the same views.

Information

The **tourist office** (☎42-7171; www.viedma.gov.ar; Viedma 51) is by the river. Other services include a **post office** (Rivadavia 151), ATMs and plenty of internet access.

Getting There & Around

The airport is 4km southwest of town (taxi AR$30). **LADE** (☎42-4420) and **Aerolíneas Argentinas** (☎42-3033) have services.

Viedma's bus terminal is 13 blocks south of the center, at the corner of Guido and Perón. Local buses and taxis (AR$15) head downtown. Destinations include Bahía Blanca (AR$100, four hours), Puerto Madryn (AR$175, six hours), Comodoro Rivadavia (AR$300, 12 hours), Bariloche (AR$300, 14 hours) and Buenos Aires (AR$450, 12 hours).

The **train station** (☎42-2130) is on the southeast outskirts of town but services were not running at the time of writing. Check during your stay.

Carmen de Patagones

☎02920 / POP 30,000

Just across the Río Negro is picturesque 'Patagones,' with historic cobbled streets and lovely colonial buildings. There's not much to do other than stroll around and take in the relaxing atmosphere, and it's just a short boat ride from busy Viedma. For walking maps visit the **tourist office** (☎46-4819), at the pier.

Across from the boat dock is the good **Museo Histórico** (☎46-2729; ⏲10am-12:30pm & 7-9pm Mon-Fri, 7-9pm Sat); check out the cow-udder bowl and old gaucho artifacts. Salesians built the **Iglesia Parroquial Nuestra Señora del Carmen** (1883); its image of the Virgin, dating from 1780, is southern Argentina's oldest. Note the flags captured in the 1827 victory over the Brazilians.

The bus terminal has services to Buenos Aires and Puerto Madryn (among other places), but long-distance buses are more frequent from Viedma.

Patagones is connected to Viedma by frequent buses, but the *balsa* (passenger boat) is more scenic. It crosses the river every few minutes (AR$2, two minutes).

Puerto Madryn

☎0280 / POP 100,000

Founded by Welsh settlers in 1886, this sheltered port city owes much of its popularity to the nearby wildlife sanctuary, Reserva Faunística Península Valdés. It holds its own as a modest beach destination, however, and boasts a lively tourist street scene and popular boardwalk. From June to mid-December visiting right whales take center stage.

Sights & Activities

The pretty **Museo Provincial del Hombre y el Mar** (☎445-1139; cnr García & Menéndez; admission AR$6, Tue free; ⊙hours vary widely by season/cruiseship schedule) has some small but fine natural history exhibits, especially on orcas. Well-done **EcoCentro** (☎445-7470; www.ecocentro.org.ar; J Verne 3784; admission AR$44) offers excellent exhibits of local sea life, complete with a touch pool and lofty glass tower. It's a pleasant 4km coastal walk from the center, or take the Linea 2 bus to the last stop, then walk 1km. Hours are erratic, so call beforehand.

Other area activities include kayaking, windsurfing, scuba diving and horse riding. You can pedal (or taxi) 17km southeast to **Punta Loma** (admission AR$25; ⊙dawn-dusk), a sea lion rookery, or 19km northwest to **Playa El Doradillo**, which offers super close-up whale-watching (especially at high tide) from June to September.

Tours

Countless agencies and nearly all hotels/hostels sell land tours to Península Valdés and Punta Tombo (both AR$350). Take water (and bring your own lunch, to save costs), as it's a very long drive to both reserves. Boat tours to see whales and dolphins are also available.

When choosing a tour agency, it's always best to get recommendations from fellow travelers. Ask questions such as: what was the group size, how much time did you spend at what destinations, and was there an English-speaking guide? One company you can try is **Fugu Tours** (☎447-5218; www.fugutours.com.ar; 28 de Julio 66).

Sleeping

Prices listed are for the high season, approximately October to March. In January it's a good idea to reserve ahead.

La Tosca HOSTEL **$**
(☎445-6133; www.latoscahostel.com; Sarmiento 437; dm/s AR$80/190, d AR$260-330; @📶) Small, friendly hostel with great common areas. Small, darkish dorms (doubles are brighter upstairs) line a grassy yard excellent for hanging out. Dinners are available.

La Casa de Tounens HOSTEL **$**
(☎447-2681; www.lacasadetounens.com; Passaje 1 de Marzo 432; dm AR$70, s AR$180-220, d AR$200-280; @📶) Cozy, friendly hostel just half a block from the bus terminal, run by a French-Argentine couple. It offers a wide variety of rooms, nice patio areas and free bike rental.

El Gualicho HOSTEL **$$**
(☎445-4163; www.elgualicho.com.ar; Marcos A Zar 480; dm/d/tr/q AR$95/420/485/540; @📶) Excellent, very large HI hostel with lots of services, including pool table and grassy garden. Spacious dorms and comfortable, hotel-quality doubles, triples and quads.

Hi! Patagonia Hostel HOSTEL **$**
(☎445-0155; www.hipatagonia.com; Av Roca 1040; dm AR$90, d AR$270-360, tr AR$360-420; @📶) Simple hostel best for its backyard bar-patio, which is great for socializing. Bike rentals and bouldering wall too.

El Retorno HOSTEL **$**
(☎445-6044; www.elretornohostel.com.ar; Mitre 798; dm from AR$70, d AR$ 250-350; @📶) Plain, mazelike hostel lacking a large common area, but with friendly and attentive owners. Free pickup.

Complejo Turístico Puerto Madryn HOTEL **$**
(☎447-4426; www.hostalmadryn.com.ar; 25 de Mayo 1136; d & tr AR$340, apt AR$480; 📶) Large fenced-in complex with five good, modern rooms (with kitchen access) and 12 large apartments that sleep four to six. Large grassy backyard; no breakfast. Run by a standoff-ish family.

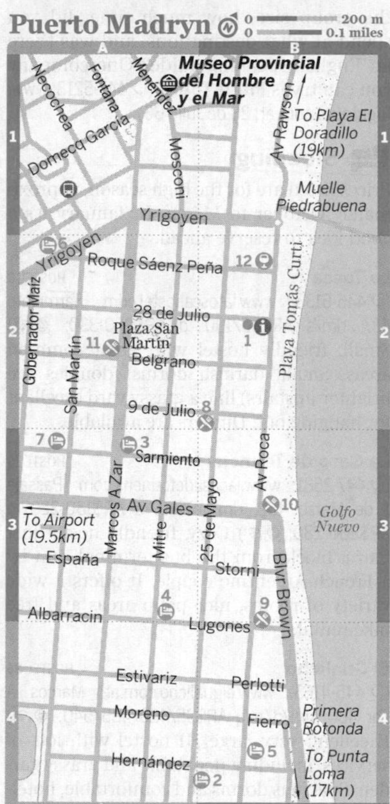

Puerto Madryn

Top Sights

Museo Provincial del Hombre y el Mar A1

Activities, Courses & Tours

1 Fugu Tours B2

Sleeping

2 Complejo Turístico Puerto Madryn B4
3 El Gualicho A3
4 El Retorno A3
5 Hi! Patagonia Hostel B4
6 La Casa de Tounens A2
7 La Tosca A3

Eating

8 Bodegón Bienvenidos B2
9 El Náutico B3
10 Lizard Café B3
Mr Jones .... (see 8)
11 Patagonia Resto-Bar A2

Drinking

12 Margarita Bar B2

ACA Camping CAMPGROUND $
(☎445-2952; campsites per 2 AR$75, d AR$180) Shady, sandy sites; simple bunk doubles. Some food is available (but it's best to take your own). It's located 4km south of the center; take Linea 2 bus to the last stop, then walk 800m (taxi AR$35). Open in high season only.

Eating & Drinking

Patagonia Resto-Bar SEAFOOD $$
(☎445-2249; Belgrano 323; mains AR$40-70; ⌚noon-3pm & 8pm-late, closed Mon) With circular faux-leather booths and giant marine murals, this upscale, blue-hued restaurant offers abundant, well-presented gourmet dishes. There's a nice patio, and late at night there's a good drinking atmosphere.

Mr Jones INTERNATIONAL $
(9 de Julio 116; mains AR$30-60; ⌚dinner) Popular spot with relatively exotic cuisine (goulash, pot pies, Asian fusion) along with 30 kinds of pizza and imported beers like Negro Modela, Guinness and Budweiser. Vegetarian options too.

Bodegón Bienvenidos ARGENTINE $$
(☎447-2547; 25 de Mayo 411; mains AR$46-60; ⌚lunch & dinner) Cozy, friendly restaurant with just a handful of tables and good ser vice. It's good for dishes like *cazuelas*, pastas, paella, seafood and salads. Creative, plus abundant portions.

El Náutico SEAFOOD $$
(☎447-1404; Av Roca 790; mains AR$40-55) Nearly 50 years running, this large seafood restaurant has good service and local atmosphere. The huge menu has something for everyone – try the three-course meal for AR$68.

Lizard Café ARGENTINE $$
(☎445-8333; cnr Avs Roca & Gales; mains AR$35-70; ⌚7am-2am) Good-value, casual eatery that's popular for its pizza, hamburgers, salads and sandwiches. Check out the two pool tables (with beach view) located on the 2nd floor.

Margarita Bar PUB
(Roque Sáenz Peña; mains 25-60; ⌚11am-4am) Hip brick-wall pub, food menu (good pizza), foreign cocktails and great atmosphere.

Information

There's a **tourist office** (☎45-3504; www.madryn.gov.ar/turismo; Av Roca 223; ⌚7am-10pm Dec-Mar, limited hours Apr-Nov) both in the center and at the bus terminal (p143). There are many internet cafes and banks with ATMs, and **Cambio Thaler** (☎445-5858; Av Roca 497; ⌚9:30am-1pm & 6-8pm Mon-Fri, 10am-1pm & 7-9pm Sat & Sun) changes traveler's checks.

Getting There & Around

Madryn has an airport, but most flights arrive 65km south at Trelew (door-to-door shuttle per person AR$50, taxi AR$200; buses between Puerto Madryn/Trelew can stop at airport). **Aerolíneas Argentinas** (☎445-1998; Av Roca 427), **LADE** (☎445-1256; Av Roca 119) and **Andes** (☎445-2355; www.andesonline.com; Av Roca 624) have services. The departure tax is AR$32.

From the **bus terminal** (cnr Ciudad de Nefyn & Dr Avila), destinations include Puerto Pirámide (AR$24, 1½ hours), Trelew (AR$16, one hour), Comodoro Rivadavia (AR$142, six hours), Viedma (AR$175, eight hours), Esquel (AR$260, 10 hours), Bariloche (AR$350, 13 hours) and Buenos Aires (from AR$500, 18 hours).

Rental cars are easily available; rates run about AR$400 per day with 400km. For bike rentals check out **Na Praia** (☎45-5633; Blvr Brown 860); it also rents kayaks and organizes windsurfing classes.

Reserva Faunística Península Valdés

☎0280

Gouged by two large bays, this oddly shaped peninsula is mostly a flat, bleak and dry landscape of unrelenting low shrubs, with the occasional guanacos or rheas (ostrichlike birds) to add interest. Once you get to the coastlines, however, the real celebrity wildlife awaits: sea lions, elephant seals, southern right whales, Commerson's dolphins, Magellanic penguins and – if you're very, very lucky – orcas (who have been filmed here beaching themselves to snatch pinnipeds). June to mid-December is whale-watching season, penguins waddle around from October to March, and elephant seals and sea lions lounge around all year. Commerson's dolphins and dusky dolphins are spotted year-round, while the orca phenomenon happens mostly during high tide from February to April.

As you enter the **Reserva Faunística Península Valdés** (admission AR$100; ⌚8am-8pm) you'll pass the thin 5km neck of the peninsula. If you're on a tour bus, it will stop at a good interpretation center and lookout. Squint northwards for a glimpse of **Isla de los Pájaros**. This small island inspired Antoine de Saint-Exupéry's description of a hat, or 'boa swallowing an elephant,' in his book *The Little Prince* (from 1929 to 1931 Saint-Exupéry flew as a postal manager in the area). Also, keep an eye out for salt flats **Salina Grande** and **Salina Chico** (42m below sea level) – South America's lowest spots.

Caleta Valdés is a bay sheltered by a long gravel spit and favored by elephant seals. Just north of here lives a substantial colony of burrowing Magellanic penguins. At **Punta Norte** a mixed group of sea lions and elephant seals snoozes, with the occasional orca pod keeping an eye out offshore.

Puerto Pirámide – a sunny, sandy, shrubby, one-street kinda town – is home to 500 souls. You can stay here, the peninsula's only sizable settlement, to enjoy a calm spot and be closer to wildlife attractions (if you're staying here, admission to the Reserva Faunística is good for two days). Services, however, are severely limited compared to Puerto Madryn's: for example, there's only one ATM in town (that may not work), and there are no car rentals. Scuba diving, horseback riding and some limited tours are available, however. Boat tours outside whale-watching season aren't really worth it unless you adore shorebirds and sea lions, though there's a chance of seeing dolphins. For information there's the **tourist office** (☎449-5048; www.puertopiramides.gov.ar; Primera bajada al mar s/n; ⌚9am-2pm; sometimes open later).

Sleeping & Eating

There are several accommodation options in Puerto Pirámide; in summer it's a good idea to reserve ahead.

Among food options, La Estación, across from the YPF gas station, has a nice deck and atmosphere. There are many restaurants by the water, down the first street to the right as you enter town; try Quimey Quipán, with a patio next to the beach.

La Casa de la Tía Alicia GUESTHOUSE $
(☎449-5046; Av de las Ballenas s/n; per person AR$100) Aunt Alicia's pink house, across from the 'plaza', is the best value in town. There are just four cute, small and peaceful rooms available; some share bathroom.

Hostel Bahía Ballenas HOSTEL $
(☎423-8766; www.bahiaballenas.com.ar; Av de las Ballenas s/n; dm AR$120; @) Basic hostel with two large 12-bed, sex-segregated dorms. Was closed at the time of writing, so call ahead for details.

Camping Puerto Pirámides CAMPGROUND $
(☎Municipalidad 449-5084; campsites per person AR$35, showers AR$20) Gravel sites sheltered by shrubs and dunes; beach access available.

Getting There & Away

Buses from Puerto Madryn leave for Puerto Pirámide two to three times daily in summer (AR$24, 1½ hours). Schedules are less frequent on weekends and in the off season.

Trelew

☎0280 / POP 99,000

Trelew is not an exciting city, but it does have a pleasant bustling center with leafy plaza and some historical buildings. There's an excellent dinosaur-oriented museum, and it's a convenient base for exploring the nearby Welsh villages of Gaiman and Dolavon, along with the noisy Punta Tombo penguin reserve.

Trelew's major cultural event is late October's **Eisteddfod de Chubut**, celebrating Welsh traditions.

Sights

In the former railway station, the nicely presented **Museo Pueblo de Luis** (☎442-4062; cnr Av Fontana & Lewis Jones; admission AR$2; ⏲8am-8pm Mon-Fri, 2-8pm Sat & Sun) has good Welsh and indigenous peoples' artifacts. Nearby is the excellent **Museo Paleontológico Egidio Feruglio**, (☎442-0012; www.mef.org.ar; Av Fontana 140; admission AR$38; ⏲9am-8pm Mon-Fri, 10am-7pm Sat & Sun) with realistic dinosaur exhibits, including crystallized dinosaur eggs.

Tours

Several travel agencies organize tours to Península Valdés and Punta Tombo. Tours are similarly priced to those from Puerto Madryn. There are also tours to see black-and-white Commerson's dolphins (AR$220, seen all year round but best viewed September to November).

Sleeping & Eating

Residencial Rivadavia GUESTHOUSE $
(☎443-4472; www.cpatagonia.com/rivadavia; Rivadavia 55; s AR$160, d AR$200-220, tr AR$280; @ 📶) Go for the upstairs rooms, which are newer and brighter, at this plain guesthouse. Breakfast costs extra.

Hotel Touring Club HOTEL $$
(☎443-3997; www.touringpatagonia.com.ar; Fontana 240; s/d/tr/q AR$230/360/460/550; 📶) An institution, with a downstairs cafe exuding classic atmosphere. Rooms upstairs vary widely; those on the inside can be depressing, so get one facing the pedestrian street.

Hostel El Agora HOSTEL $
(☎442-6899; www.hostelagora.com.ar; Edwin Roberts 33; dm AR$80; @ 📶) Five blocks northwest of the bus terminal is this improving hostel, with decent kitchen and dining areas. Tiny patio in back and bike rentals.

Confitería Touring Club ARGENTINE $
(Fontana 240; mains AR$20-60) Excellent for its old-time atmosphere and serious, suited waiters. Breakfast, sandwiches and lots of alcoholic drinks available; check out the dusty bottles behind the bar.

Boru Irish Pub & Restobar PUB $$
(Belgrano 351; mains AR$30-70) Good, modern pub-restaurant serving up the usual – pizzas, pastas, meats and salads. There's a nice front covered deck for people-watching.

Information

There's a **tourist office** (☎442-0139; cnr San Martín & Mitre; ⏲8:30am-8pm Mon-Fri, 9am-9pm Sat & Sun) on the plaza, where many banks with ATMs can be found, along with the **post office** (cnr Av 25 de Mayo & Mitre).

Getting There & Around

The airport is 6km north of town (take Puerto Madryn bus and walk 300m; taxi AR$30). **Aerolíneas Argentinas** (☎442-0222; Rivadavia 548) and **LADE** (☎443-5740), with offices at the bus station, fly here.

Trelew's bus station is six blocks northeast of downtown; there's a tourist information booth inside. Destinations include Puerto Madryn (AR$16, one hour), Gaiman (AR$5, 30 minutes), Comodoro Rivadavia (AR$144, five hours),

Bariloche (AR$335, 12 hours) and Buenos Aires (AR$625, 18 hours).

Car-rental stands are at the airport and in town; cheapest rentals run about AR$400 per day.

Around Trelew

GAIMAN

0280 / POP 11,000

For a taste of Wales in Patagonia, head 17km west of Trelew to Gaiman. The streets are calm and wide and the buildings are nondescript and low; on hot days the local boys swim in the nearby river. The real reason travelers visit Gaiman, however, is to down pastries at one of several good **Welsh teahouses**. Most open around 2pm and offer unlimited tea and homemade sweets for AR$75 to AR$85 (eat a very light lunch).

The small **Museo Histórico Regional Gales** (cnr Sarmiento & 28 de Julio; admission AR$3; 3-8pm Dec-Mar, 3-7pm Tue-Sun Apr-Nov) details Welsh colonization with old pioneer photographs and household items. And those who like spooky spots should explore the 300m old railroad tunnel near the tourist office.

Gaiman is an easy day trip from Trelew, but if you want to stay, try homey **Dyffryn Gwirdd** (449-1777; patagongales@yahoo.com.ar; Av Eugenio Tello 103; s/d AR$150/200;), with seven simple but good rooms (breakfast extra). Some teahouses also let rooms.

To get oriented visit the **tourist office** (449-1571; www.gaiman.gov.ar; cnr Rivadavia & Belgrano; 9am-8pm Dec-Mar, 9am-6pm Apr-Nov).

Frequent buses go to/from Trelew (AR$5, 30 minutes); you'll have to either pay in coins or buy a AR$10 bus card.

RESERVA PROVINCIAL PUNTA TOMBO

From September to April, up to a million Magellanic penguins breed at **Punta Tombo** (admission AR$60; 8am-8pm Aug-Apr), 110km south of Trelew and 1½ hours by road. It's the largest penguin colony outside Antarctica. Other area birds include rheas, cormorants, giant petrels, kelp gulls and oyster-catchers. You may also spy some land critters such as armadillos, foxes and guanacos on the way there.

You can get very close to the birds for photos, but don't try to touch them – they'll nip. To get there, arrange a tour in Trelew or Puerto Madryn (AR$350) or hire a taxi (AR$800 round trip; negotiate waiting fee). Car rentals are possible from Puerto Madryn or Trelew.

Comodoro Rivadavia

0297 / POP 180,000

Petroleum-rich Comodoro Rivadavia is popular only as a convenient pit stop along Argentina's long eastern coastline. It's a nondescript city with busy streets and the ugliest cathedral you'll likely ever see. If you're stuck here and are desperate, check out the **Museo del Petróleo** (Petroleum Museum; 455-9558; San Lorenzo 250; admission AR$20; 9am-5pm Tue-Fri, 3-6pm Sat), 3km north.

Sleeping & Eating

Hostería Rua Marina HOTEL **$$**

(406-9615; ruamarinapatagonia@yahoo.com.ar; Belgrano 738; s AR$160-260, d AR$300-345;) Worn, dark rooms, stuffy in hot weather and most facing an indoor hall. The best ones are rooms 18, 19 and 20 – they're in the back and upstairs, and boast outside windows.

25 de Mayo HOTEL **$$**

(447-2350; 25 de Mayo 989; s/d AR$220/340, without bathroom AR$160/220;) Very basic, with most rooms facing a small outdoor hallway. Kitchen access available.

Patio de Comidas FAST FOOD **$**

(cnr Güemes & San Martín; meals AR$20-40) Cafeteria-style food court. Next to La Anónima supermarket.

Information

Tourist Office (444-0664; 8am-8pm Mon-Fri, 9am-3pm Sat & Sun) From Monday to Friday, located in the Ceptur building at Moreno and Yrigoyen (two blocks east of the bus terminal). On Saturday and Sunday, located at the southwest corner of Rivadavia and Pellegrini (one block north of the bus terminal).

Getting There & Around

The airport is 8km east of the center (bus AR$1.75, taxi AR$63). **Aerolíneas Argentinas** (444-0050; Av Rivadavia 156) and **LADE** (447-0585; Av Rivadavia 360) operate flights here.

The bus terminal is in the center of town. Destinations include Puerto Madryn (AR$162, six hours), Los Antiguos (AR$185, 6½ hours), Esquel (AR$200, nine hours), Bariloche (AR$315, 14 hours), Río Gallegos (AR$375, 11 hours) and Buenos Aires (AR$725, 24 hours).

DESTINO SUR

So you arrive in Chaltén with high hopes of trekking, but it's raining sideways and bitterly cold. After some freezing hikes, what could be better than a long soak in a hot Jacuzzi? Check into **Destino Sur** (☎49-3360; www.hoteldestinosur.com; Lionel Terrey 370; r AR$735-800; @📶), a relatively luxurious hotel with beautiful spacious rooms and buffet breakfast – there's a sauna too if the Jacuzzi isn't enough.

Los Antiguos

☎02963 / POP 5000

Situated on the shores of Lago Buenos Aires, Los Antiguos is a calm little town with rows of poplar trees sheltering *chacras* (small, independent farms) of cherries, strawberries, apples, apricots and peaches. Travelers come to cross the border into Chile, and getting here via RN 40 can be an adventure in itself.

The **Fiesta de la Cereza** (cherry festival) occurs the first or second weekend in January, and the nearby countryside has good hiking, fishing and windsurfing.

A 20-minute walk east of the center is the cypress-sheltered **Camping Municipal** (☎49-1265; Av 11 de Julio s/n; tent site AR$20, cabin AR$120-180), which also has cabins. **Albergue Padilla** (☎49-1140; San Martín 44; dm/d AR$90/300) is a basic family-run hostel with one eight-bed dorm; Chaltén Travel buses can drop you here. For more comfort, try **Hotel Los Antiguos Cerezos** (☎49-1132; hotel_losantiguoscerezos@hotmail.com; Av 11 de Julio 850; s/d AR$230/300; 📶) or **Hostería Mora** (☎15-420-7472; Av Costanera 1064; dm/s/d AR$125/360/460), a combination upscale-hostel and hotel. A decent place to eat is the chalet-like **Viva El Viento** (☎49-1109; www.vivaelviento.com; Av 11 de Julio 447; mains AR$40-85; ⏲9am-9pm Oct-Apr; 📶). These places are all on or near the main drag, except for Hostería Mora.

The **tourist office** (☎49-1261; www.losantiguos.tur.ar; 11 de Julio 446; ⏲Jan-Feb 8am-midnight, Mar-Apr 8am-10pm, May-Dec 8am-8pm) has information on local activities. There's one bank with an ATM.

Los Antiguos' bus terminal is on Tehuelches 157, about a 10-minute walk to the center. Buses cross the border to Chile Chico, 12km away, a few times daily (AR$22). From November through March, **Chaltén Travel** (www.chaltentravel.com) goes to El Chaltén on even-numbered days (AR$320, 12 hours). Other destinations include Perito Moreno (AR$43, 45 minutes), Esquel (AR$320, 10 hours), El Bolsón (AR$367, 14 hours), Bariloche (AR$385, 13 hours) and Comodoro Rivadavia (AR$185, 6½ hours). The gradual paving of RN 40 and changing demand will keep transport options in flux, so make sure you get current information from the tourist office.

El Chaltén

☎02962 / POP 1200

Argentina's trekking capital and one of Patagonia's top traveler magnets, this small but growing village is set in a pretty river valley. Travelers come for the extraordinary snowcapped towers of the **Fitz Roy range**, offering world-class hiking and camping – along with astounding mountain scenery. Climbers from around the world make their bid to summit the premier peak **Cerro Fitz Roy** (3441m), among others. Pack for wind, rain and cold temperatures even in summer, when views of the peaks can be obscured. If the sun is out, however, El Chaltén is an outdoor lover's paradise.

Note that El Chaltén is within national park boundaries, and rules regarding fires and cleaning distances from rivers must be followed. The area's river waters are potable without filtration – please help keep them clean. El Chaltén mostly shuts down from April to October.

Activities

Hiking

One popular hike goes to **Laguna Torre** and the base camp for skilled technical climbers attempting the spire of **Cerro Torre** (3128m); it's 11km (three hours one way).

Another hike climbs from the end of town to a signed junction, where a side trail leads to backcountry campsites at Laguna Capri. The main trail continues gently to Río Blanco, base camp for the Cerro Fitz Roy climb, and then very steeply to **Laguna de los Tres** (12.5km; four hours one way).

The 15km hike to **Lago Toro** is seven hours one way, so most folks camp overnight.

Sleeping

Prices listed are for late December through February, when you should arrive with reservations. Not all accommodations include breakfast.

Note that the closest free campsites are at Laguna Capri, a two-hour hike from El Chaltén (no fires allowed).

TOP CHOICE Nothofagus B&B B&B $$
(☎49-3087; www.nothofagusbb.com.ar; cnr Hensen & Riquelme; s/d/tr AR$340/350/410, without bathroom AR$240/250/340; ⊙Oct-Apr; @📶) Wonderfully homey, friendly and cozy guesthouse with nine spotless rooms. Be prepared to separate your organic waste and recycle.

Cabañas Aires del Fitz GUESTHOUSE $$
(☎49-3134; www.airesdelfitz.com.ar; Arbilla 124; d/tr AR$440/520, q AR$580-630; 📶) Stay at one of the four cute and wonderful cabañas here – each is well stocked, and equipped with a kitchen, good mattresses, satellite TV and views of Fitzroy. Up to six people accomodated.

Latitud 49 GUESTHOUSE $$
(☎49-3347; www.latitud49.com; Arbilla 145; d/tr/q AR$420/460/500; 📶) Accommodations run by a friendly couple and split into two locations. On a residential street where the couple lives are two beautiful apartments with kitchen, sleeping up to four people. And near the center of town are three comfortable rooms, all sharing a pleasant front patio; inquire about them at Patagonicus pizzeria.

Hostería Lago Viedma GUESTHOUSE $$
(☎49-3089; www.elchalten.com/lagoviedma; Arbilla 71; d AR$350; 📶) Just four tidy and simply decorated rooms, all with private bathroom, at this dollhouselike place.

Rancho Grande Hostel HOSTEL $$
(☎49-3092; www.ranchograndehostel.com; Av San Martín 724; dm/s/d AR$100/390/450; @📶) Large hostel with spacious, modern dorms and nice common areas. Many services and busy atmosphere. Good doubles, all with bathroom. Takes credit cards; HI discount.

Albergue Patagonia HOSTEL $
(☎49-3019; www.patagoniahostel.com.ar; Av San Martín 392; dm AR$90, s/d from AR$240/260; ⊙Sep-May; @📶) An old, cozy hostel with small dorms and cramped bathrooms. The modern wing has larger, more comfortable (and more expensive) rooms. A *cabaña* sleeps up to five and has a kitchen. Bike rentals available; HI discount.

Condor de Los Andes HOSTEL $$
(☎49-3101; www.condordelosandes.com; cnr Río de las Vueltas & Halvor Halvorsen; dm AR$90-105, s/d AR$380; @📶) Medium-sized hostel with nice common spaces and good vibe. Nice private rooms have breakfast included (breakfast not included for dorms). HI discount.

Camping El Relincho CAMPGROUND $
(☎49-3007; www.elrelinchopatagonia.com.ar; Av San Martín 545; campsites per person AR$40) Large grassy complex with pleasant campsites near river. Rustic hangout building. Three large and comfortable *cabañas* available (AR$550 to AR$710).

Camping El Refugio CAMPGROUND $
(☎49-3221; Calle 3 s/n; campsites per person AR$25, dm with/without own sleeping bag AR$40/60) Campground with lovely riverside

CHILE THROUGH THE BACK DOOR

This one- or two-day trip can be completed between November and March. Bring provisions and Chilean pesos (if possible). Check boat schedules beforehand, as boats don't run every day.

From El Chaltén, get on the morning shuttle to Lago del Desierto (AR$130, one hour), where you can either take the **Patagonia Aventura boat** (☎49-3110; www.patagonia-aventura.com.ar; AR$110) for 45 minutes or hike along the eastern shore (15km, 4½ hours). At the northern end of the lake is Argentine immigration. From here it's a 22km, six-hour walk (vehicle and horse transportation available after 6km) to Candelario Mansilla and Chilean immigration; here you'll find basic accommodations, camping and meals.

Chilean boat **Hielo Sur** (www.hielosur.com) goes from Candelario Mansilla to Puerto Bahamondez (CH$40,000, three hours) thrice weekly. From Puerto Bahamondez you can bus to Villa O'Higgins (CH$2000, 15 minutes).

sites and rustic dorm building. Bathrooms are very basic and it can get crowded.

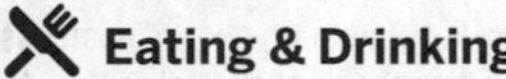

Eating & Drinking

Pack lunches are available at most hostels/hotels and at some restaurants.

Estepa PATAGONIAN $$$
(cnr Cerro Solo & Av Antonio Rojo; mains AR$60-85; ⌚noon-1am Mon-Sat) Well-prepared and tasty dishes like lamb with Calafate sauce and salmon ravioli. Plenty of pizzas; also makes lunch boxes.

El Muro ARGENTINE $$
(Av San Martín 912; mains AR$45-70; ⌚dinner) Go for the homemade pasta, a specialty lamb dish or pizza topped with venison or boar. Great desserts. It's located towards the end of town.

El Bodegón Cervecería PUB $$
(San Martín 564; mains AR$35-70; ⌚12:30pm-3am mid-Oct–late Apr) Wonderfully cozy pub with creative driftwood decor, good homemade brews and feisty female beer meister. Pizza, pastas and *locro* available.

Patagonicus PIZZERIA $$
(cnr Güemes & Madsen; pizzas AR$30-80; ⌚closed Wed & May-Sep) Popular pizzeria baking 20 kinds of pies, as well as pastas, salads and sandwiches.

Information

On the left just before the bridge into town, **park headquarters** (☎49-3004; ⌚8am-8pm Dec-Feb) has maps and hiking information (and videos for rainy days); day buses automatically stop here. The **tourist office** (☎49-3370; ⌚8am-10pm) is at the bus terminal.

Make sure you bring enough Argentine pesos (US dollars and euros are accepted at some places) for your stay in El Chaltén. There are no banks or exchange houses, and only one (unreliable) ATM. Few places take traveler's checks, credit cards or US dollars – and if they do, exchange rates are poor. Many travelers have left sooner than they wanted to because they ran out of money.

Locutorios and limited internet access (it can be slow and expensive) are available. A decent selection of camping food and supplies is readily available at the small supermarkets in town. Gear like stoves, fuel, sleeping bags, tents and warm clothes can be bought or rented from several businesses on San Martín (the main drag). Bike rentals and mountain-guide services are also available.

Getting There & Away

The following schedules are for December through February; during other months services are less frequent or nonexistent.

Chaltén's bus terminal is near the entrance to town. There are several daily buses to El Calafate (AR$90, three hours). Las Lengas goes a few times daily to Lago del Desierto (AR$130, one hour) and Hostería El Pilar (AR$50, 20 minutes).

Chaltén Travel (☎493-092; cnr Guemes & Lago del Desierto) provides transport to Los Antiguos (AR$320, 12 hours) and Bariloche (AR$640, two days, overnight accommodation not included) from mid-November to mid-April, but only on odd-numbered days.

El Calafate

☎02902 / POP 22,000

Years of fast growth have peaked in El Calafate, which, despite a tourist facade, remains a pleasant-enough pit stop for a few days. Its prime location between El Chaltén and Torres del Paine (Chile) means that most Patagonian travelers pass through here at some point or another, and fortunately, there is one incredible, unmissable attraction: the dynamic Glaciar Perito Moreno, located 80km away in Parque Nacional Los Glaciares.

Sights & Activities

Within town there's not much to do besides souvenir shopping and getting your business done, but a few distractions exist. Calafate's newest trophy is the **Glaciarium** (☎49-7912; www.glaciarium.com; adult/child AR$80/55; ⌚9am-8pm Sep-May, 11am-8pm May-Aug), a high-tech museum which explains the formation of icebergs and glaciers via fancy exhibits and videos. There's even an 'ice bar' in the basement (AR$70 includes drinks with glacial ice cubes!). It's 6km east of town; shuttle available (AR$30 round trip).

Just north of center you will find nicely presented **Centro de Interpretación Histórico** (☎49-2799; cnr Brown & Bonarelli; admission AR$40; ⌚10am-8pm Sept-May, 11am-5pm Jun-Aug), which explains the history of Patagonia via dinosaur replicas, diagrams and a video. Finally, **Laguna Nimez** (admission AR$25; ⌚9am-9pm) is a wetlands sanctuary 15 minutes' walk from town. Walk north on Alem, go over the small white bridge, and at the restaurant, jog right, then left.

El Calafate

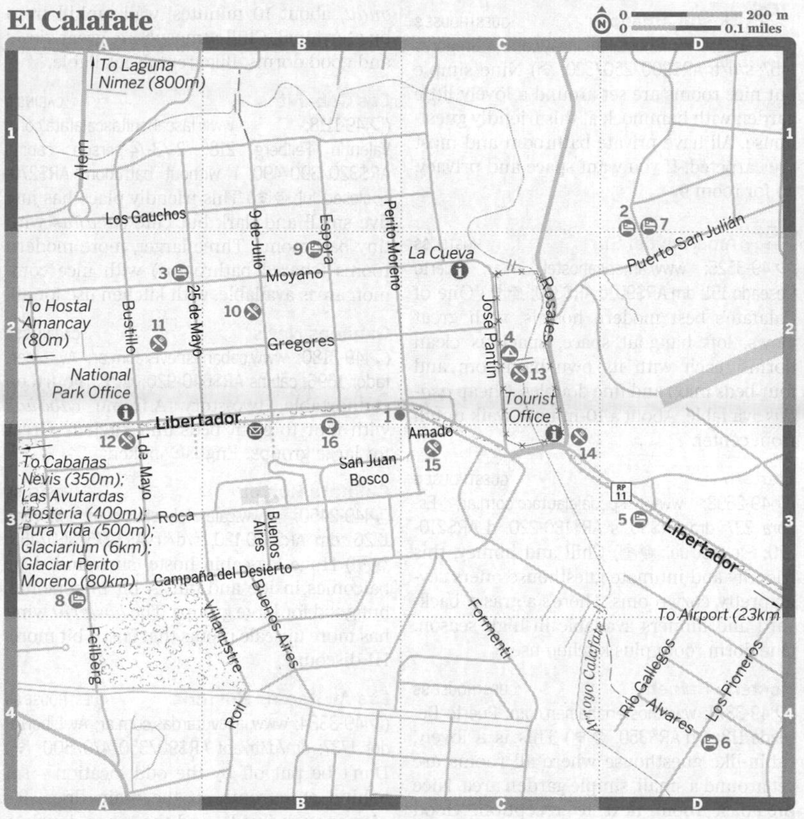

El Calafate

Activities, Courses & Tours

1 Hielo y Aventura B2

Sleeping

2 America del Sur D1
3 Calafate Hostel A2
4 Camping El Ovejero C2
5 Hostel del Glaciar Libertador D3
6 Hostel del Glaciar Pioneros D4
7 Hostería Hainen D1
8 Las Cabañitas A3
9 Lautaro B2

Eating

10 El Cucharón B2
11 Kau Kaleshen A2
12 La Lechuza A3
13 La Marca C2
14 La Tablita C3
15 Viva la Pepa C3

Drinking

16 Librobar B3

Various shops around Calafate's downtown rent outdoor clothing and camping gear.

Sleeping

Reserve ahead from late December through February.

TOP CHOICE **Hostal Amancay** GUESTHOUSE $
(☎49-1113; www.hostalamancay.com; Gregores 1457; s/d/tr AR$200/250/320;) Nine simple but nice rooms are set around a lovely little garden with hammock at this friendly guesthouse. All have private bathroom and most are carpeted. If you want space and privacy, go for room 9.

TOP CHOICE **America del Sur** HOSTEL $$
(☎49-3525; www.americahostel.com.ar; Puerto Deseado 151; dm AR$90, d AR$370; @) One of Calafate's best modern hostels, with great views, loft hangout space, spacious clean dorms (each with its own bathroom and four beds max) and fine doubles. Cheap *asados* available. About a 10-minute walk uphill from center.

Lautaro GUESTHOUSE $
(☎49-2698; www.hospedajelautaro.com.ar; Espora 237; dm AR$80, s AR$180-220, d AR$210-270; closed Jul; @) Chill and homey, this friendly and intimate guesthouse offers seven pretty, cozy rooms. There's a grassy backyard and dinners available in high season. One dorm room plus kitchen use.

Hostería Hainen GUESTHOUSE $$
(☎49-3874; www.hosteriahainen.com; Puerto Deseado 118; s/d AR$350; @) This is a lovely, cabin-like guesthouse where all rooms are set around a small, simple garden area. Nice breakfast room next to reception. Good value.

Hostel del Glaciar Libertador HOSTEL $$
(☎49-2492; www.glaciar.com; Av Libertador 587; dm AR$105, s/d AR$396/435; @) Big modern hostel with most rooms set around a pleasant central 'well' area, plus nice common spaces. Clean, well-thought-out dorms and lovely doubles. Many services and HI discount.

Hostel del Glaciar Pioneros HOSTEL $$
(☎49-1243; www.glaciar.com; Los Pioneros 251; dm AR$83, s AR$237-330, d AR$308-358; Nov-Mar; @) Good, long-running hostel with spacious common areas and cool hangout restaurant-pub. Dorms are small but clean; superior doubles are excellent. HI discount.

I Keu Ken Hostel HOSTEL $$
(☎49-5175; www.patagoniaikeuken.com.ar; FM Pontoriero 171; dm AR$90, d/tr AR$360/400; @) Pleasant and friendly small hostel with good *onda*, about 10 minutes' walk uphill from bus terminal. Chill atmosphere, great views and good dorms. Bike rentals available.

Las Cabañitas CABINS $
(☎49-1118; www.lascabanitascalafate.com; Valentín Feilberg 218; 2-/3-/4-person cabins AR$320/390/490, r without bathroom AR$270; closed Jul; @) This friendly place has just five small and dark but cute *cabañas* with tiny bathrooms. Three larger, more modern rooms (shared bathrooms) with nice common areas available, with kitchen use for all.

Cabañas Nevis CABINS $$$
(☎49-3180; www.cabanasnevis.com.ar; Av Libertador 1696; cabins AR$640-920; @) Fourteen comfortable, two-story A-frame *cabañas* with four to eight beds and kitchen. Great for large groups; English spoken.

Calafate Hostel HOSTEL $$
(☎49-2450; www.calafatehostels.com; Moyano 1226; dm AR$100-120, s/d/tr AR$275/360/450; @) Huge log-cabin hostel surrounded by balconies inside and out. A bit impersonal, but good for large groups. The *hostería* wing has more upscale rooms that cost a bit more. HI discount.

Las Avutardas Hostería GUESTHOUSE $$
(☎49-3384; www.lasavutardas.com.ar; Av Libertador 1737; dm/d/tr/apt AR$90/350/470/500;) Don't be put off by the odd location – set behind storefronts on the main drag. It's nice enough inside, and the tango-dancing, guitar-playing owner Andy is a plus. Slick modern rooms are lovely, and the apartments come with kitchen.

Camping El Ovejero CAMPGROUND $
(☎49-3422; www.campingelovejero.com.ar; José Pantín 64; campsites per person AR$25-35, dm AR$40-70; @) Central campground with shady, dusty creekside sites, picnic tables and fire pits. Two dorms and one private room (AR$280), along with cheap rustic trailer bunks, also available. Good inexpensive restaurant.

Eating & Drinking

Some cafes provide *viandas* (pack lunches). If going to large supermarkets, take bags or your backpack, as plastic bags have been banned in El Calafate.

Viva la Pepa CAFE $$
(Amado 833; mains AR$40-70; lunch & dinner) Delicious, creative and well-prepared dishes

like savory and sweet crepes, beautifully constructed salads and huge tasty sandwiches.

La Tablita PARRILLA **$$**
(Rosales 24; mains AR$40-80; ⊙lunch Thu-Tue, dinner daily) Excellent and popular for its great meat dishes. Reserve ahead in person, especially on weekends.

Pura Vida ARGENTINE **$$**
(☎49-3356; Av Libertador 1876; mains AR$50-66; ⊙dinner Thu-Tue; ☑) Creative healthy food and huge portions. Try the meat stew served in a squash, the eggplant tart, lamb pie or rabbit stew. There's even apple pie with ice cream for dessert.

El Cucharón ARGENTINE **$$$**
(9 de Julio 145; mains AR$60-80; ⊙lunch & dinner) Local, upscale restaurant and an excellent place to try the regional classic *cazuela de cordero* (lamb stew). There's also mushroom risotto, trout with lemon, homemade pastas and pumpkin soup.

La Lechuza PIZZERIA **$$**
(Av Libertador 1301; pizzas AR$50-90) Popular spot baking up dozens of excellent pizzas, both traditional and more exotic (try the pickled eggplant or Patagonian lamb). Sandwiches, salads and pasta too.

Kau Kaleshen VEGETARIAN **$**
(Gregores 1256; mains AR$30-40; ⊙4-11pm Mon-Sat; ☑) Healthy, tasty fare at this vegetarian joint includes wraps, stir-fries, soybean schnitzels, lentil burgers, whole-wheat pizza, sweet waffles, cheese fondue and vegan salads. Herbal teas, organic wine, local beers, juices, lassies and yogurt shakes too.

La Marca PARRILLA **$$**
(José Pantín 64; mains AR$45-70; ⊙lunch & dinner; limited hours outside Jan & Feb) Cheap but good parrilla that offers a AR$75 all-you-can-eat deal (including salad bar). Located at the Camping El Ovejero campground.

Librobar PUB
(Av Libertador 1015) Calafate's best hangout cafe-bar, with good people-watching views from its 2nd-floor loft. Offers a large drink selection, a few snacks and live music in summer. Front patio downstairs for sunny days.

ℹ Information

There are several banks with ATMs in town, though money can run out on busy weekends. If you're planning on visiting El Chaltén, withdraw enough money here.

Cambio Thaler (Av Libertador 963) Changes traveler's checks.

La Cueva (☎49-2417; jorgelemos322@hotmail.com; Moyano 839) Basic mountaineers' *refugio* that organizes area treks.

National Park office (☎49-1545; Av Libertador 1302) Issues trekking permits and fishing licenses. It's better to get information here than at the park.

Post office (Av Libertador 1133)

Tourist office (☎49-1090; www.elcalafate.gov.ar; cnr Av Libertador & Rosales; ⊙8am-8pm) Another branch is located at the bus terminal.

ℹ Getting There & Around

Book your flight into and out of El Calafate well ahead of time. The airport is 23km east of town; the departure tax is AR$38.

Ves Patagonia (☎49-4355; www.vespatagonia.com) has door-to-door shuttle services for AR$33; taxis cost AR$100. **Aerolineas Argentinas** (☎49-2816, 49-2814; Av Libertador 1361), **LADE** (☎49-1262; Jean Mermoz 168) and **LAN** (☎49-2155; 9 de Julio 81) operate flights here.

Calafate's bus terminal is a couple blocks above the main drag; there's a AR$5.20 tax on all bus tickets. Bus destinations include Río Gallegos (AR$150, 4½ hours), El Chaltén (AR$85, three hours) and Puerto Natales (Chile; AR$110, five hours).

In summer, **Chaltén Travel** (☎49-2480, 49-2212; www.chaltentravel.com; Av Libertador 1174) does the two-day trip from El Calafate to Bariloche via adventurous Ruta 40 (AR$700). Car rentals in El Calafate cost about AR$400 per day with 200km; try **Nunatek** (☎49-1987; www.nunatekrentacar.com; G Gregores 1075) car rental.

Parque Nacional Los Glaciares

Few glaciers can match the suspense and excitement of the blue-hued **Glaciar Perito Moreno**. Its 60m jagged ice peaks shear off and crash with huge splashes and thunderous rifle-cracks, birthing small tidal waves and large bobbing icebergs – all while your neck hairs rise a-tingling. It's the highlight of **Parque Nacional Los Glaciares** (admission AR$100, collected after 8am) and measures 35km in length, 5km in width and 60m in height. What makes this glacier exceptional is that it's advancing – up to 2m per day – and constantly dropping chunks of ice off its face. While most of the world's glaciers are receding, the Glaciar Perito Moreno is considered 'stable.' And every once in a while, part of its facade advances far enough to reach the Península de Magallanes to dam the Brazo Rico arm of Lago Argentino. This causes tremendous pressure to build up, and after a few years a river cuts through the dam and eventually collapses it – with spectacular results.

The Glaciar Perito Moreno was born to be a tourist attraction. The ideally located Península de Magallanes is close enough to the glacier to provide glorious panoramas, but far enough away to be safe. A long series of catwalks and platforms gives everyone a great view. Hanging around for a few hours, just looking at the glacier (or condors above) and waiting for the next great calving, can be an existential experience. And realize that since you're 800m away from the glacier, which is the equivalent of a 20-story building, what may seem like a small chunk of ice falling could actually be the size of a car!

Most tours from El Calafate cost AR$180 and up for transport (sit on the left), guide and a few hours at the glacier; Hostel del Glaciar Pioneros (p150) and Hostel del Glaciar Libertador (p150) offer an 'alternative' tour that includes a short hike and boat ride (AR$230). If you don't want a tour, head to El Calafate's bus station; round-trip transport costs AR$120 and gives you several hours at the glacier. Groups of up to four can hire a *remise* for about AR$450 with three hours wait time (negotiate!). Also, consider seeing the glacier later in the afternoon, when many of the crowds have gone and more ice falls after the heat of the day.

There's a cafeteria selling simple sandwiches and snacks at the site, but for best selection and price you should bring a lunch from El Calafate. Note also that the weather is very changeable and can be windy, so dress appropriately.

Boat tours to other glaciers are also available, but a more adventurous option is to take a tour with **Hielo y Aventura** (☎49-2094, 49-2205; www.hieloyaventura.com; Av Libertador 935; tours AR$460-690, not incl transport or park admission) and hike directly on the Moreno glacier in crampons.

Río Gallegos

☎02966 / POP 110,000

Río Gallegos is not a very interesting destination, but it's not terribly boring either. The main drag downtown is lively, the low tides are amazingly low and some of the continent's best fly-fishing is nearby. Still, most travelers stop here just long enough to catch the next bus to El Calafate, Puerto Natales or Ushuaia.

Sleeping

Hotel Covadonga HOTEL $
(☎42-0190; hotelcovadongargl@hotmail.com; Av Kirchner 1244; d with/without bathroom AR$300/270; 📶) This is an old hotel with some retro charm – and it's barely trying for style. Inside rooms are dark and some share bathrooms.

Casa de Familia Elcira Contreras HOSTEL $
(☎42-9856; Zuccarrino 431; dm/r AR$80/220; @📶) Simple home run by an elderly woman, with clean rooms and kitchen access. One eight-bed apartment available. It's about 10 blocks from the center and a 15-minute walk from the bus terminal (taxi AR$20).

Information

Provincial tourist office (☎42-2702; Av Kirchner 863) There's also a tourist office at the bus terminal.

Getting There & Away

The airport is 7km from the center (taxi AR$60). **Aerolíneas Argentinas** (☎0810-2228-6527; Av San Martín 545), **LAN** (☎45-7189; airport) and **LADE** (☎42-2316; Fagnano 53) operate services.

The bus terminal is about 2km from the center, on RN 3 (bus B or C AR$3, taxi AR$25). Destinations include El Calafate (AR$120, four hours), Ushuaia (AR$445, 12 hours), Comodoro Rivadavia (AR$375, 11 hours), Río Grande (AR$345, eight hours) and Buenos Aires (AR$1200, 36 hours). Buses to Punta Arenas (AR$95, six hours) run only twice weekly; try buying your ticket in advance. Buses to Puerto Natales (AR$110, six hours) often include a transfer and wait in Río Turbio.

TIERRA DEL FUEGO

Reluctantly shared by Argentina and Chile, the 'land of fire' really *is* the end of the world. The archipelago, surrounded by the stormy

South Atlantic and the Strait of Magellan, offers plenty of natural beauty: scenic glaciers, lush forests, astounding mountains, clear waterways and a dramatic coast. The largest city, Ushuaia, boasts the title 'southernmost city in the world' – and is the main gateway to Antarctica. Tierra del Fuego is isolated and hard to reach, but for true adventure-seekers it's a must.

Passing ships gave Tierra del Fuego its name: they spotted distant shoreline campfires that the Yámana (or Yahgan) people tended. In 1520 Magellan paid a visit, but he was seeking passage to the Asian spice islands. As ships sailed by, the indigenous Ona (or Selknam) and Haush continued hunting land animals, while the Yámana and Alacalufe lived on seafood and marine mammals. The early 1800s, however, brought on European settlement – and the demise of these indigenous peoples.

DON'T MISS

KALMA RESTO

Creating quite a stir, tiny **Kalma Resto** (☎42-5786; www.kalmaresto.com.ar; Antártida Argentina 57; mains AR$75-140; ⏲8pm-midnight Tue-Sun; lunch by reservation only) presents Fuegian staples, like crab and octopus, in a giddy new context. Black sea bass contrasts with a tart tomato sauce and the roast lamb stew revels in earthy pine mushrooms. Service is stellar, with young chef Jorge Monopoli making the rounds of the few black linen tables.

Ushuaia

☎02901 / POP 65,000

Nestled on the shores of the Beagle Channel (Canal de Beagle), as far south as roads go on earth, lies charismatic Ushuaia. Boasting 1500m Fuegan Andes peaks as a spectacular backdrop, this touristy yet pleasant city attracts all sorts of travelers: the independent backpackers, the cruisers, the Antarctica-bound and those who finally end their South American biking, motorcycling or driving journeys here – at the southernmost city in the world. But there's more than just this quirky novelty at hand, as adventurous souls also come to explore nearby pristine mountains, lakes and glaciers, as well as partake in the area's many other outdoor possibilities.

Originally established as a penal colony, Ushuaia became a key naval base in 1950. Gold, lumber, wool and fishing brought in revenue over the years, but today tourism drives this fast-growing city's economy. In the summer high season (December through March), cruise ships visit almost daily – and the main drag, Av San Martín, fills with Gore-Tex-wearing tourists. Like a star at her peak, Ushuaia's popularity won't be waning anytime soon.

Sights & Activities

The small but good **Museo del Fin del Mundo** (☎42-1863; www.museodelfindelmundo.org.ar; cnr Av Maipú & Rivadavia; admission AR$30; ⏲9am-8pm) explains Ushuaia's indigenous and natural histories; check out the bone implements and bird taxidermy room. It has a nearby annex in a historical building at Av Maipú 465. The excellent **Museo Marítimo** (☎43-7481; www.museomaritimo.com; cnr Yaganes & Paz; admission AR$70; ⏲9am-8pm) is located in an old prison that held up to 700 inmates in 380 small jail cells. There are interesting exhibits on expeditions to Antarctica, plus stuffed penguins and an art gallery. Tiny **Museo Yámana** (☎42-2874; Rivadavia 56; admission AR$35; ⏲10am-8pm) has some history on the area's indigenous people.

After seeing the Glaciar Perito Moreno in El Calafate, the **Glaciar Martial** here will seem like a piddly ice cube – but at least it's located in a beautiful valley with great views of Ushuaia and the Beagle Channel. Walk or taxi (AR$35) to a short chairlift 7km northwest of town; from here it's about two hours' walk up to the glacier (shorter if you take the chairlift, AR$50). There's a teahouse serving snacks near the chairlift.

Hop on a **boat tour** to *estancias*, a lighthouse, Puerto Williams, bird island and sea lion or penguin colonies. Ask about the size of the boat (smaller boats get closer to wildlife), whether there are bilingual guides and if there are any landings (only Pira Tour actually lands at the penguin colony, which is active October through March). Tours range from AR$200 to AR$385; tickets are available at the pier, travel agencies and hotels.

Founded by missionary Thomas Bridges and located 85km east of Ushuaia, **Estancia Harberton** (www.estanciaharberton.com;

Tierra del Fuego

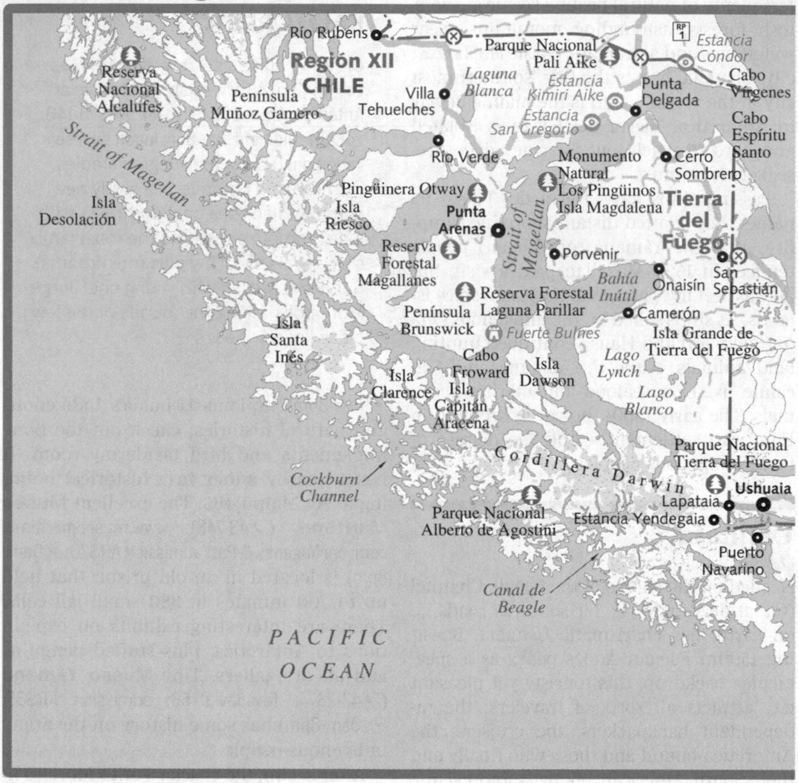

Río Rubens
Región XII
CHILE
Parque Nacional
Pali Aike
Estancia
Cóndor
Reserva
Nacional
Alcalufes
Península
Muñoz Gamero
Villa
Tehuelches
Laguna
Blanca
Estancia
Kimiri Aike
Punta
Delgada
Cabo
Vírgenes
Estancia
San Gregorio
Cabo
Espíritu
Santo
Strait of Magellan
Río Verde
Monumento
Natural
Los Pingüinos
Cerro
Sombrero
Isla
Desolación
Pingüinera Otway
Isla
Riesco
Punta
Arenas
Isla Magdalena
Tierra
del
Fuego
Reserva
Forestal
Magallanes
Strait of
Magellan
Porvenir
San
Sebastián
Bahía
Inútil
Onaisín
Reserva Forestal
Laguna Parillar
Península
Brunswick
Camerón
Isla
Santa
Inés
Fuerte Bulnes
Isla Grande de
Tierra del Fuego
Cabo
Froward
Lago
Lynch
Isla
Clarence
Isla
Capitán
Aracena
Isla
Dawson
Lago
Blanco
Cordillera Darwin
Parque Nacional
Tierra del Fuego
Cockburn
Channel
Ushuaia
Lapataia
Parque Nacional
Alberto de Agostini
Estancia Yendegaia
Puerto
Navarino
Canal de
Beagle
PACIFIC
OCEAN

admission AR$45; ⊙mid-Oct–mid-Apr) was Tierra del Fuego's first *estancia*. This 200-sq-km ranch boasts splendid scenery and alluring history. There's a good museum, and you can take an optional boat trip to the area's penguin colony. Get here by taxi, rental car or boat tour (the latter offering only a limited time at the estancia). Overnight stays are possible.

Hiking and trekking opportunities aren't limited to the national park: the entire mountain range behind Ushuaia, with its lakes and rivers, is an outdoor person's wonderland. However, many trails are poorly marked, so hire a guide from **Compañía de Guías** (☎43-7753; www.companiadeguias.com.ar; San Martín 654), which has guides for trekking, mountaineering, ice/rock climbing, horse riding and sailing; it also offers gear rental.

Plenty of ski resorts dot the nearby mountains, with both downhill and cross-country options. The largest resort is **Cerro Castor** (☎49-9301; www.cerrocastor.com; full-day lift ticket adult/child AR$240/165; ⊙mid-Jun–mid-Oct), about 27km from Ushuaia, with almost 20 slopes. The ski season runs from June to October.

Tours

Many travel agencies sell tours around the region. You can go horse riding, canoeing or mountain biking, visit nearby lakes, go looking for birds and beavers, and even get pulled by husky dogsleds during winter. **Canal Fun** (☎43-7395; www.canalfun.com; 9 de Julio 118) is one of the better adventure tour organizers, with prices to match.

For bike and gear rentals, try **Ushuaia Extremo** (☎43-4373; www.ushuaiaextremo.com; San Martín 1306).

Sleeping

Reservations are a good idea in December and January.

TOP CHOICE **Galeazzi-Basily B&B** B&B $$
(☎42-3213; www.avesdelsur.com.ar; Valdéz 323; s/d AR$210/320, cabin AR$450-630; @wi-fi) Wonderful B&B with friendly, polyglot hosts. Newer *cabañas* out back have private bathrooms and kitchens. Also has two dogs on premises.

TOP CHOICE **Antarctica Hostel** HOSTEL $
(☎43-5774; www.antarcticahostel.com; Antártida Argentina 270; dm/d/tr AR$100/300/350; @wi-fi) Popular, good-vibe hostel with relaxing reception lounge area, kitchen/eating loft and grassy backyard.

Alto Andino HOTEL $$$
(☎43-0920; www.altoandinohotel.com; Paz 868; d from AR$800; @wi-fi) Eighteen luxurious rooms and suites (with kitchenettes) with slick, minimalist design. Spectacular views from the top-floor breakfast/lounge area. Worth splashing out for.

Freestyle HOSTEL $
(☎43-2874; www.ushuaiafreestyle.com; Paz 866/868; dm AR$90-100; @wi-fi) Modern five-star hostel with fine spacious dorms and all the services. Top-floor lounge has awesome mountain and water views, faux-leather sofas and a pool table.

La Casa en Ushuaia GUESTHOUSE $$
(☎42-3202; www.lacasaenushuaia.com; Paz 1380; s/d without bathroom AR$300/350; @wi-fi) Wonderfully modern, stylish guesthouse with six comfortable and bright rooms with views (they share three bathrooms). Small common area; limited kitchen use. English and French spoken.

Los Calafates GUESTHOUSE $$
(☎43-5515; www.loscalafateshostal.com.ar; Fagnano 456; s/d/tr AR$300/350/400; wi-fi) Just five homey and warm rooms (each with private bathroom) are on offer at this clean and quiet guesthouse. Tiny kitchen and garden available.

Tango B&B B&B $$$
(☎42-2895; www.tangobyb.com.ar; Valdéz 950; d AR$450-520, tr AR$610; @wi-fi) Just four rooms, all with private bathroom, are on tap at this cozy home with views over the city. Your host Raúl puts on a tango music show twice a week.

Casa de Familia Zaprucki GUESTHOUSE $
(☎42-1316; zaprucki@hotmail.com; Deloquí 271; apt AR$300-500; ⊙Oct-Apr; wi-fi) A little garden of Eden run by an elderly woman. Four clean, homey and private apartments (all with kitchen) that hold up to six. One has three bedrooms. Breakfast extra.

Yakush HOSTEL $$
(☎43-5807; www.hostelyakush.com.ar; Piedrabuena 118; dm AR$130-140, d AR$340-400; ⊙mid-Oct–mid-Apr; @wi-fi) Colorful, clean hostel with good dorms, nice upstairs lounging loft and attractive kitchen-dining area.

Hostal Río Ona GUESTHOUSE $$
(☎42-1327; www.rioona.com.ar; Magallanes 196; s/d/tr AR$230/320/400; wi-fi) Ten comfortable rooms at this basic guesthouse, four with kitchenette. The breakfast room has a microwave and coffeemaker.

Ushuaia

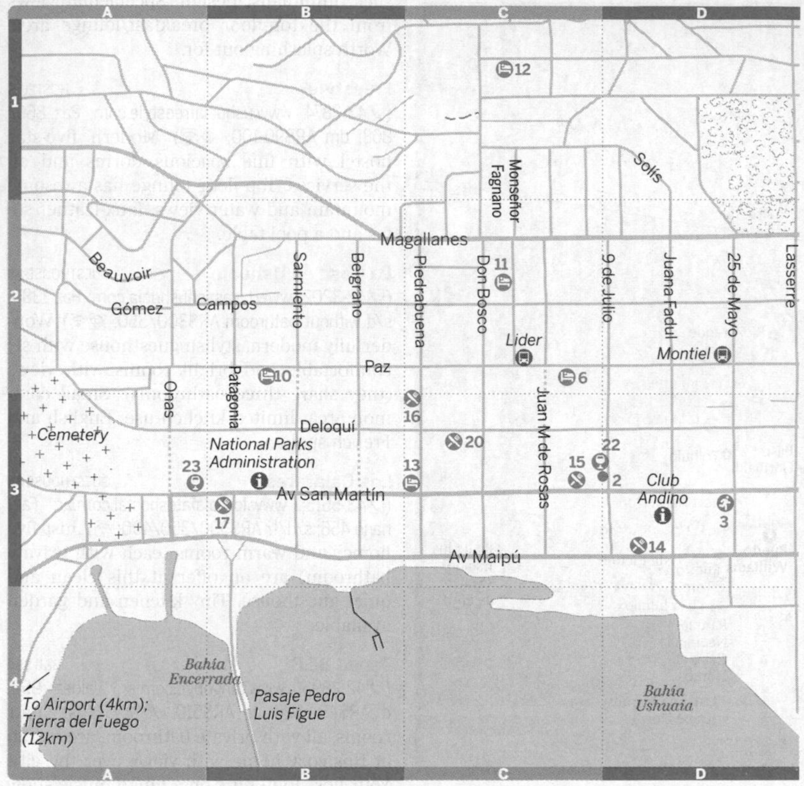

Los Cormoranes HOSTEL $$
(☎42-3459; www.loscormoranes.com; Kamshen 788; dm AR$135-160, d/tr/q AR$420/490/550; @☎) Hillside hostel with small six- and eight-bed dorms facing outdoor plank hallways. The best double is room 10. HI discount available. About a 15-minute walk to center.

Hostel Cruz del Sur HOSTEL $
(☎43-4099; www.xdelsur.com.ar; Deloquí 242; dm AR$80-85, d AR$260; @☎) Small mazelike hostel with small dorms and interesting, separate 'hangout room' in backyard. Just one private room.

Camping La Pista del Andino CAMPGROUND $
(☎43-5890; Alem 2873; campsites per person AR$45; ❄@☎) About 2km uphill from the center (taxi AR$20), this camping spot has pleasant sites with views. Cooking facilities, good common areas and drinks are available. Bring your own food.

Eating & Drinking

María Lola Restó ARGENTINE $$$
(☎42-1185; Deloquí 1048; mains AR$75-90; ⏲noon-midnight Mon-Sat) Upscale restaurant cooking up dishes such as seafood risotto and *cordero fueguino* (Patagonian lamb). Good service and views; you should reserve on weekends.

Almacen Ramos Generales CAFE $$
(☎42-7317; www.ramosgeneralesushuaia.com; Av Maipú 749; mains AR$35-75; ⏲9am-midnight) A wonderful old-time atmosphere here is reminiscent of an old general store. There's great bread, pastries and panini, plus a selection of exotic coffees and teas.

Placeres Patagónicos ARGENTINE $$
(☎43-3798; www.patagonicosweb.com.ar; 289 Deloquí; snacks AR$12-45, tablas AR$100-450) This homey joint serves tasty snacks – crepes, *milanesas* and homemade pastries. The

Ushuaia

Top Sights
- Museo del Fin del Mundo F3
- Museo Marítimo F2

Sights
- 1 Museo Yámana E3

Activities, Courses & Tours
- 2 Canal Fun D3
- 3 Compañía de Guías de Patagonia D3

Sleeping
- Alto Andino (see 6)
- 4 Antarctica Hostel F2
- 5 Casa de Familia Zaprucki E3
- 6 Freestyle C2
- 7 Galeazzi-Basily B&B E1
- 8 Hostal Río Ona F2
- 9 Hostel Cruz del Sur E3
- 10 La Casa en Ushuaia B2
- 11 Los Calafates C2
- 12 Tango B&B C1
- 13 Yakush C3

Eating
- 14 Almacen Ramos Generales D3
- 15 Bodegón Fueguino C3
- 16 El Bambú C3
- 17 El Turco B3
- 18 Kalma Resto F3
- 19 Lomitos Martinica F3
- 20 María Lola Restó C3
- 21 Placeres Patagónicos E3

Drinking
- 22 Dublin Irish Pub C3
- 23 Macario 1910 A3

specialty is *tablas*: wood cutting boards piled with bread, smoked trout and wild boar. Herbal teas and maté too.

Bodegón Fueguino PATAGONIAN $$
(43-1972; Av San Martín 859; mains AR$55-82; Tue-Sun) In a cute orange house, this place serves great homemade pizzas and pastas, along with nine kinds of *cordero* (lamb).

El Turco CAFE $$
(42-4711; Av San Martín 1410; mains AR$40-60; noon-3pm & 8pm-midnight) Popular with locals for its good-value meats, pizza and pasta.

Lomitos Martinica ARGENTINE $
(43-2134; Av San Martín 68; mains AR$25-48; 11:30am-3pm & 8:30pm-midnight Mon-Sat) Cheap, small *parrilla* also serving up a few pizzas and pastas, plus huge sandwiches.

El Bambú VEGETARIAN $
(43-7028; Piedrabuena 276; per kg AR$40; 11am-5pm Mon-Fri;) Good vegetarian food for takeout only (no tables).

Macario 1910 PUB
(42-2757; www.macario1910.com; Av San Martín 1485; 6pm-late) This pub serves locally made Beagle Beer on tap, while above-average pub fare includes fresh tuna sandwiches and homemade shoestring fries.

Dublin Irish Pub PUB
(43-0744; www.dublinushuaia.com; 9 de Julio 168) Intimate pub with good atmosphere and dim lighting. Popular with foreigners.

BEYOND THE EDGE OF THE WORLD – ANTARCTICA

A trip to awe-inspiring Antarctica is a once-in-a-lifetime adventure. It's expensive but worth every penny, and is so much more than just a continent to tick off your list. The land and ice shelves pile hundreds of meters thick with kilometers of undulating, untouched snow, while countless glaciers drape down mountainsides. Icebergs loom like tall buildings and come in shapes you didn't think possible, from triangles to dragon silhouettes to graceful sculptures with circular arches. The wildlife is magnificent; you'll see thousands of curious penguins and a wide variety of flying birds, seals and whales. Antarctica is an astounding place, and its tourism industry is growing fast as more and more people visit. We can only hope that careful management will assure that this glorious continent remains beautiful.

For the average person, cruising is the easiest and best way to visit the White Continent. The season runs from November through March; peak-season voyages often get sold out. Last-minute tickets might be available later in the season, but sailings on reasonably small ships (fewer than 100 passengers) will still cost at least US$4000. Regular tickets start from around US$5000. Ask how many days you will actually spend in Antarctica – as crossing the Southern Ocean takes up to two days each way – and how many landings will be included. The smaller the ship, the more landings per passenger (always depending on the weather).

Because of its relatively close location to the Antarctic peninsula (1000km), most cruises leave from Ushuaia. Travel agencies such as **Rumbo Sur** (☎42-2275; www.rumbosur.com.ar; Av San Martín 350), **All Patagonia** (☎43-3622; www.allpatagonia.com; Juana Fadul 60) and Canal Fun (p154) offer 'last-minute' packages, though there are many more. **Alicia Petiet** (☎58-6016; www.antarcticatravels.com; Av San Martín 1306) is a tour consultant who helps travelers with Antarctic cruises.

If booking from home, check that your company is a member of **IAATO** (International Association Antarctica Tour Operators; www.iaato.org), whose members must abide by strict guidelines for responsible travel to Antarctica. For basic info in Ushuaia, visit the **Antarctica tourist office** (☎43-0015; www.tierradelfuego.org/ar/antartida; Av Maipú 505) at Ushuaia's pier.

Lonely Planet's *Antarctica* guidebook is an indispensable guide to the region's history and wildlife, and has a section on various ways to reach the Big Ice.

One last thing: bring more film and/or extra memory cards than you think you'll need. You'll thank us later.

Information

Internet cafes are common. Most banks in town have ATMs.

Cambio Thaler (Av San Martín 209; ⏲10am-1pm & 5-8pm Mon-Sat, 5-8pm Sun) Changes traveler's checks.

Chilean Consulate (☎43-0909; Jainén 50)

Club Andino (☎42-2335; www.clubandinoushuaia.com.ar; Juana Fadul 50; ⏲9am-1pm & 3-8pm Mon-Fri) Provides trekking maps and guidebooks.

Municipal tourist office (☎43-7666; www.turismoushuaia.com; Prefectura Naval 470; ⏲9am-8pm Nov-Mar, to 6pm Apr-Oct) Located at the pier.

National Parks administration (☎42-1315; Av San Martín 1395)

Getting There & Around

In January and February, you should make bookings for your passage in and out of Ushuaia in advance.

Ushuaia's airport is located 4km south of the center (taxi AR$38); the departure tax is AR$28. **Aerolíneas Argentinas** (☎0810-2228-6527; cnr Av Maipú & 9 de Julio) and **LADE** (☎0810-810-5233; Av San Martín 542) provide services.

Ushuaia does not have a bus terminal, but the tourist office can help with transport options. **Taqsa** (☎43-5453; Godoy 41) and **Tecni-Austral** (☎43-1408, 43-1412; Roca 157), in the Tolkar travel agency, have daily services to Río Grande (AR$100, three hours) and Río Gallegos (AR$445, 12 hours); both also go to Punta Arenas (AR$280 to AR$335, 12 hours) a few times weekly. **Lider** (☎44-2264; Paz 921) and **Montiel** (☎42-1366; Paz 605) head to Río Grande (AR$110, three hours) up to eight times daily. Several companies go to Puerto Natales a few times weekly (AR$335, 12 hours). You can also connect to Puerto Natales via Río Gallegos.

Taxis around town are available. Rental cars will cost around AR$300 per day with 200km free. For bike rentals there's Ushuaia Extremo (p154).

Parque Nacional Tierra del Fuego

West of Ushuaia 12km lies beautiful **Parque Nacional Tierra del Fuego** (admission AR$85, collected 8am-8pm), which extends all the way from the Beagle Channel in the south to beyond Lago Fagnano in the north. Only a small part of the park is accessible to the public, however, and despite a tiny system of short trails, the views along the bays, rivers and forests are wonderfully scenic. You should keep your eyes peeled for *cauquén* (upland geese), cormorants and grebes. The most common land critters you'll see are the European rabbit and North American beaver – introduced species that have wreaked havoc on the ecosystem. Foxes and the occasional guanaco might also visit. Marine mammals are most common on offshore islands.

For information on the park's walks, you can get a map from the tourist office or National Parks office located in Ushuaia. There's also a nice visitors center in the park with an attached restaurant and a small museum. The only organized campground here is **Lago Roca** (☎15-41-2649; campsites per person AR$30, dm AR$55). A cafeteria and tiny grocery (note though that its stock is very limited and pretty expensive) are located nearby. Free campsites are also available in the park.

Minibuses to the park charge AR$85 per person round trip. They leave hourly from 9am to 6pm daily, from the corner of Av Maipú and Fadul. Taxis are cheaper for groups. You can also take **El Tren del Fin del Mundo** (☎43-1600; www.trendelfindemundo.com.ar; adult/child plus park entrance fee AR$155/50), a narrow-gauge steam train (just note that you'll have to get a taxi to the train station, which is located 8km west of Ushuaia).

UNDERSTAND ARGENTINA

Argentina Today

After years of boom, Argentina's inflation remains high and the economy continues to sputter. President Cristina Fernández de Kirchner's popularity has sunk since her landslide re-election in 2011. Kirchner has often been compared to Evita for her fight against poverty and her administration of generous social programs – but both have also shown authoritarian tendencies, such as trying to censor the media and rule by decree.

During her time in office, there have been countrywide transportation strikes, extensive roadblocks from unhappy unions, and several mass protests over higher crime rates and lower quality living standards. Her government has been accused of manipulating economic numbers – in March 2011, the *Economist* magazine stated that it no longer trusted inflation figures coming out of Argentina. Kirchner herself has been accused of challenging the Falkland Islands' sovereignty as a way to gain national popularity.

Despite her many detractors, however, this *presidenta* has made admirable strides – she's addressed the abuses of the military dictatorship, championed same-sex marriage laws and, over all, supported the blue-collar classes. There are some who love her for it, just like they did Evita. But many think the country's tilt toward socialism is a step back, and that another currency crash is on the horizon.

In March 2013, the former archbishop of Buenos Aires, Jorge Bergoglio, became Pope Francis I.

History

The Good Old Days

Before the Spanish hit the scene, nomadic hunter-gatherers roamed the wilds of ancient Argentina. The Yámana (or Yahgan) gathered shellfish in Patagonia, while on the pampas the Querandí used *boleadoras* (weights on cords) to snag rhea (ostrich-like birds) and guanaco (the llama's cousin). Up in the subtropical northeast, the Guaraní settled down long enough to cultivate maize, while in the arid northwest the Diaguita developed an irrigation system for crops.

In 1536 the Querandí were unfortunate enough to meet pushy Spaniards in search of silver. They eventually drove the explorers away to more welcoming Paraguay. (Left behind were cattle and horses, which multiplied and gave rise to the legendary *gaucho*). The Spanish were persistent, however, and in 1580 they returned and managed to establish Buenos Aires, though trade restrictions from Spain limited the new settlement's growth. The northern colonies of Tucumán, Córdoba and Salta, however, thrived by providing mules, cloth and foodstuffs for the booming silver mines of Bolivia. Meanwhile, Spaniards from Chile moved into the Andean Cuyo region, which produced wine and grain.

Cutting the Purse Strings

In 1776 Spain designated the bootlegger township of Buenos Aires as 'capital of the new viceroyalty of the Río de la Plata,' a nod to its strategic port location. A rogue British force, hoping to snag a piece of the trade pie, invaded in 1806 but was given the boot soon after by the rallied settlers. With newfound power, the confident colonists revolted against Spain, which they held a grudge against for the trade restrictions. Complete independence was their reward six years later in 1816.

Despite this unity, the provinces resisted Buenos Aires' authority. Argentina split allegiances between the inhabitants of Buenos Aires (Unitarists) and the country folk (Federalists). A civil war ensued, and the two parties' bloody, vindictive conflicts nearly exhausted the country.

In 1829 Juan Manuel de Rosas came into power as a Federalist, but applied his own brand of Unitarist principles to centralize control in Buenos Aires. He built a large army, created the *mazorca* (a ruthless secret police), institutionalized torture and forced overseas trade through the port city. Finally, in 1852, Justo José de Urquiza (once Rosas' supporter) led a Unitarist army that forced the dictator from power. Urquiza drew up a constitution and became Argentina's first president.

The Fleeting Golden Age

Argentina's new laws opened up the country to foreign investment, trade and immigration. In the following decades, sheep, cattle and cereal products were freely exported, while Spanish, Italian, French and other European immigrants came in search of a better life. Prosperity arrived at last, and Argentina became one of the richest countries in the world in the early 20th century.

The prosperity was tenuous, however, as global economic fluctuations brought about new foreign trade restrictions that mostly benefited rich producers of wheat, wine and sugar. After the 1880s poor immigrants continued flooding into the city, nearly doubling Buenos Aires' population to one million residents. The city's face changed: old colonial buildings were torn down, major streets were widened and urban services improved. The industrial sector couldn't absorb all the immigrants and their needs, however, and the gap between rich and poor widened. In 1929 the military took power from an ineffectual civilian government, but an obscure colonel – Juan Domingo Perón – was the first leader to really confront the looming social crisis.

The Peróns – Love 'em or Hate 'em

Today the Peróns have become Argentina's most revered – as well as most despised – political figures. Many people believe that Argentina has never recovered, either economically or spiritually, since Perón's first presidency.

From a minor post in the labor ministry, and with the help of his charismatic soon-to-be wife, Eva Duarte (Evita), Juan Perón won the presidency in 1946. His social welfare and new economic order programs helped the working class, which benefited from improved wages, job security and working conditions. His heavy control over the country, however, was tinged with fascism: he abused his presidential powers by using excessive intimidation and squelching free press. Dynamic Evita, meanwhile, had her own sometimes vindictive political ends, though she was mostly championed for her charitable work and women's rights campaigns.

Rising inflation and economic difficulties (due especially to a shortage of capital from war-torn Europe) undermined Perón's second presidency in 1952; Evita's death the same year was another blow. After a coup against him in 1955, Perón retreated to Spain to plot his return. The opportunity came almost two decades later when Héctor Cámpora resigned the presidency in 1973.

Perón won the elections easily, but his death in mid-1974 sucked the country back into the governmental coups and chaos that had plagued it since his exile. In 1976 military rule prevailed once again, and Argentina entered its darkest hour.

Dirty War (1976–83)

In the late 1960s, when antigovernment sentiment was rife, a left-wing, highly organized Peronist guerrilla group called the Montoneros was formed. The mostly educated, middle-class youths bombed foreign businesses, kidnapped executives for ransom and robbed banks to finance their armed struggle and spread their social messages. On March 24, 1976, a bloodless military coup led by General Jorge Videla took control of the Argentine government and ushered in a period of terror and brutality. Euphemistically called the Process of National Reorganization (aka El Proceso), this movement begat a period of state-sponsored violence and anarchy, and the primary target was the Montoneros.

Some estimate that up to 30,000 people died in the infamous Guerra Sucia (Dirty War). Zero tolerance was the theme: the dictatorship did not distinguish between the revolutionary guerrillas or those who simply expressed reservations about the dictatorship's indiscriminate brutality. To 'disappear' meant to be detained, tortured and probably killed, without legal process. Ironically, the Dirty War ended only when the Argentine military attempted a real military operation, the repossession of the Falkland Islands (Islas Malvinas).

Falklands War

Argentina's economy continued to decline during military rule and eventually collapsed into chaos. El Proceso was coming undone.

In late 1981 General Leopoldo Galtieri took the presidential hot seat. To stay in power amid a faltering economy, a desperate Galtieri played the nationalist card and launched an invasion in April 1982 to dislodge the British from the Falkland Islands (Islas Malvinas).

The brief occupation of the islands claimed by Argentina for 150 years, unleashed a wave of nationalist euphoria that lasted about a week. Then the Argentines realized that iron-clad British prime minister Margaret Thatcher was not a wallflower, especially when she had political troubles of her own. Britain fought back, sending a naval contingent to set things straight, and Argentina's mostly teenage, ill-trained and poorly motivated forces surrendered after 74 days. The military, stripped of its reputation, finally withdrew from government. In 1983 Argentina handed Raúl Alfonsín the presidency.

Crisis

Alfonsín brought democracy back to Argentina and solved some territorial disputes with Chile. He also managed to curb inflation a bit but couldn't pull the long-struggling country back onto its feet.

Carlos Menem, president from 1989 to 1999, brought brief prosperity to Argentina by selling off many private industries and borrowing heavily. He also practically stopped inflation in its tracks by pegging the peso with the US dollar, but this was only a quick fix. After a few years the peso became so overvalued that Argentine goods weren't competitive on the global market. Toward the end of Menem's rule unemployment spiraled steadily upwards.

In 1999 Fernando de la Rúa was sworn into office. He inherited an almost bankrupt government, which witnessed yet another economic downturn, even higher unemployment and a widespread lack of public confidence. By 2001 the economy teetered on the brink of collapse, and in December Fernando de la Rúa resigned. The country went through three more presidents within two weeks before finally putting Eduardo Duhalde in charge. Duhalde devalued the peso in January 2002, defaulting on AR$140 billion in debt.

Comeback

After some instability, the peso settled to around three to the US dollar, which, due to Argentina's suddenly cheap exports, created a booming economy. In 2003 the left-leaning Néstor Kirchner was handed the presidential reins and became an immensely popular leader. He kept the economy growing strong, paid some of Argentina's debts to the International Monetary Fund (IMF) and curbed corruption to a degree. Argentina was living high and there was optimism in the air.

In 2007 Kirchner's term was up, but he wasn't through with politics. His wife, Cristina Fernández de Kirchner, ran for and won the nation's highest office – becoming Argentina's first elected woman president. And despite a rocky first tenure that included the occasional corruption scandal and a major tax-hike conflict, Cristina easily won re-election in 2011 – probably helped by the the sympathy she gained after her husband passed away from a sudden heart attack in 2010.

Culture

Lifestyle

Nearly a third of Argentines are considered to be living in poverty. To save resources and maintain family ties, several generations often live under one roof.

Families are pretty close, and Sundays are often reserved for the family *asado* (barbecue). Friends are also highly valued and Argentines love to go out in large groups. They'll give each other kisses on the cheek every time they meet – even introduced strangers, men and women alike, will get a kiss.

Argentines like to stay out *late;* dinner is often at 10pm, and finishing dessert around midnight on a weekend is the norm. Bars and discos often stay open until 6am or so, even in smaller cities.

The important culture of maté is very visible in Argentina; you'll see folks sipping this bitter herb drink at home, work and play. They carry their gourds and hot-water thermoses while traveling and on picnics. Consider yourself honored if you're invited to partake in a maté-drinking ritual.

Population

About 90% of the country's population lives in urban areas. Argentina's literacy rate is over 97%.

Nineteenth-century immigration created a large population of Italians and Spanish, though many other European nationalities are represented. Newer mixes include Japanese, Koreans and Chinese (rarer outside the capital), and other South American nationalities, such as Peruvians, Bolivians, Paraguayans and Uruguayans.

Indigenous peoples make up less than 1% of Argentina's population, with the Mapuche of Patagonia being the largest group. Smaller groups of Guaraní, Tobas, Wichi and Tehuelche, among others, inhabit other northern pockets. Up to 15% of the country's population is *mestizo* (of mixed indigenous and Spanish descent); most *mestizo* reside up north.

Religion

Most of Argentina's population is Roman Catholic (the official state religion), with Protestants making up the second most popular group. Buenos Aires is home to one of the largest Jewish populations outside Israel, and also claims what is likely Latin America's largest mosque.

Spiritualism and veneration of the dead are widespread: visitors to Recoleta and Chacarita cemeteries will see pilgrims communing with icons like Juan and Evita Perón, Carlos Gardel and psychic Madre María. Cult beliefs like the Difunta Correa of San Juan province also attract hundreds of thousands of fans.

Arts

Literature

Argentina's biggest literary name is Jorge Luis Borges, famous for his short stories and poetry. Borges created alternative-reality worlds and elaborate time circles with vivid and imaginative style; check out his surreal compendiums *Labyrinths* or *Ficciones.* Internationally acclaimed Julio Cortázar wrote about seemingly normal people while using strange metaphors and whimsical descriptions of people's unseen realities. His big novel is *Hopscotch,* which requires more than one reading.

Ernesto Sábato is known for his intellectual novels and essays, many of which explore the chasm between good and evil. Sábato's notable works include *Sobre héroes y tumbas* (On Heroes and Tombs), popular with Argentine youth in the '60s, and the startling essay *Nunca más,* which describes Dirty War atrocities. Other famous Argentine writers include Manuel Puig *(Kiss of the Spider Woman),* Adolfo Bioy Casares *(The Invention of Morel),* Osvaldo Soriano *(Shadows),* Roberto Arlt *(The Seven Madmen)* and Silvina Ocampo (poetry and children's stories).

Contemporary writers include Juan José Saer, who penned short stories and complex crime novels, and novelist and journalist Rodrigo Fresán, who wrote the best-selling *The History of Argentina* and the psychedelic *Kensington Gardens.* Ricardo Piglia and Tomás Eloy Martínez are other distinguished Argentine writers who, in addition to their important works, have taught at prominent American universities.

Cinema

In the past, Argentine cinema has achieved international stature through such directors as Luis Puenzo (*The Official Story;* 1984) and Héctor Babenco (*Kiss of the Spider Woman;* 1985).

More recent notable works by Argentine directors include Fabián Bielinsky's witty and entertaining *Nueve reinas* (Nine Queens; 2000), Juan José Campanella's *El hijo de la novia* (The Son of the Bride; 2001), which got an Oscar nomination for Best Foreign Language Film, and Lucrecia Martel's sexual-awakening film *La niña santa* (The Holy Girl; 2004). Carlos Sorín's *Bombón el perro* (Bombón, the Dog; 2004) is a captivating tale of man's best friend and changing fortunes.

Pablo Trapero is one of Argentina's foremost filmmakers. Among his works are award-winning *Mundo Grúa* (Crane World; 1999), the comedy-drama *Familia rodante* (Rolling Family; 2004) and noir drama *Carancho,* which was played at the Cannes Film Festival in 2010. Daniel Burman is another bright directoral star whose oeuvre includes *Derecho de familia* (Family Law; 2006) and *Dos hermanos* (Brother and Sister; 2010).

Tristán Bauer's award-winning *Illuminados por el fuego* (Blessed by Fire; 2005) follows a soldier of the Falklands War, while Juan Diego Solanas won top prize at the Stockholm Film Festival for his well-executed and mature *Nordeste* (Northeast; 2005), which tackles social issues like child trafficking. Other recent Argentine films include Damián Szifron's hilarious *Tiempo de valientes* (On Probation; 2005), Adrián Caetano's *Crónica de una fuga* (Chronicle of an Escape; 2006), which chronicles an escape from a torture camp during Argentina's Dirty War, and Lucía Puenzo's *XXY* (2007), the story of a teenage hermaphrodite.

Mariano Cohn and Gastón Duprat's *El hombre de al lado* (The Man Next Door; 2009) is an award-winning moral drama that screened at Sundance Film Festival in 2010. Finally, Argentina's most recent Oscar-winning film is Campanella's crime thriller *El secreto de sus ojos* (The Secret in Their Eyes; 2009).

TANGO

Tango is Argentina's sultry dance, thought to have started in Buenos Aires' bordellos in the 1880s (though Montevideo in Uruguay also stakes a claim to the dance's origin). It wasn't mainstream until it was filtered through Europe, finally hitting high popularity in Argentina around 1913. Carlos Gardel is tango's most famous songbird.

Music

Legendary figures like Carlos Gardel and Astor Piazzolla popularized tango music, and contemporaries such as Susana Rinaldi, Adriana Varela and Osvaldo Pugliese carry on the tradition. Recent tango 'fusion' groups include Gotan Project, BajoFondo Tango Club and Tanghetto.

Mercedes Sosa, Leon Gieco, Horacio Guarany, Atahualpa Yupanqui and Los Chalchaleros have been very influential in the evolution of Argentine *música olklórica.*

Rock stars Charly García, Gustavo Cerati, Andrés Calamaro, Luis Alberto Spinetta and Fito Páez are some of Argentina's best-known musicians, while popular groups have included Soda Stereo, Sumo, Los Pericos, Babasónicos, Divididos, Sui Generis and Los Fabulosos Cadillacs.

Contemporary Argentine musical artists include wacky Bersuit Vergarabat, alternative Catupecu Machu, versatile Gazpacho and the multitalented Kevin Johansen.

Córdoba's edgy *cuarteto* is Argentina's original pop music, played in working-class bars throughout the country. Coarse *cumbia villera* was born in shantytowns, fusing cumbia with gangsta rap, reggae and punk. Finally, *murga* is a form of athletic musical theater composed of actors and percussionists; they often perform at Carnaval.

Cuisine

Food

As a whole, Argentina does not have a widely varied cuisine – most folks here seem to survive on meat, pasta and pizza – but the country's famous beef is often sublime. At a *parrilla* or *asado* you should try *bife de chorizo* (thick sirloin), *bife de lomo* (tenderloin) or a *parrillada.* Ask for *chimichurri,* a spicy sauce of garlic, parsley and olive oil.

Steaks tend to come medium *(a punto)*, so if you want it rare, say *jugoso*. You're on your own with well-done steak.

The Italian influence is apparent in dishes like pizza, spaghetti, ravioli and chewy *ñoquis* (gnocchi). Vegetarian fare is available in Buenos Aires and other large cities. *Tenedores libres* (all-you-can-eat buffets) are popular everywhere and often good value. Middle Eastern food is common in the north, while the northwest has spicy dishes like those of Bolivia or Peru. In Patagonia lamb is king, while specialties such as trout, boar and venison are served around the Lake District.

Confiterías usually grill sandwiches like *lomito* (steak), *milanesa* (a thin breaded steak) and hamburgers. *Restaurantes* have larger menus and professional waiters. Cafes are important social places for pretty much everything from marriage proposals to revolutions, and many also serve alcohol and simple meals.

Large supermarkets often have a counter with good, cheap takeout. Western fast-food chains exist in larger cities.

Breakfast is usually a simple affair of coffee, tea or maté with *tostadas* (toast), *manteca* (butter) and *mermelada* (jam). *Medialunas* (croissants) come either sweet or plain. Lunch is around 1pm, teatime around 5pm and dinner usually after 8pm (few restaurants open before this hour).

Empanadas are baked or fried turnovers with vegetables, beef, cheese or other fillings. *Sandwichitos de miga* (thin, crust-free sandwiches layered with ham and cheese) are great at teatime. Commonly sold at kiosks, *alfajores* are cookie sandwiches filled with *dulce de leche* (a thick milky caramel sauce) or *mermelada* and covered in chocolate.

Postres (desserts) include *ensalada de fruta* (fruit salad), pies and cakes, *facturas* (pastries) and flan, which can be topped with *crema* (whipped cream) or *dulce de leche*. Argentina's Italian-derived *helado* (ice cream) are South America's best.

The usual *propina* (tip) at restaurants is 10%. At fancier restaurants, a *cubierto* (a service charge separate from the tip) of a few pesos is often included in the bill to cover bread and 'use of utensils.'

Drinks

ALCOHOLIC DRINKS

Argentines like to drink (but not to excess), and you'll find lists of beer, wine, whiskey and gin at many cafes, restaurants and bars. Both Quilmes and Isenbeck are popular beers; ask for *chopp* (draft or lager). Microbrews are widely available in the Lake District.

Some Argentine wines are world-class; both *tintos* (reds) and *blancos* (whites) are excellent, but malbecs are especially well known. The major wine-producing areas are found near Mendoza, San Juan, La Rioja and Salta.

Note that in Argentina the legal drinking age is 18.

NONALCOHOLIC DRINKS

Soft drinks are available everywhere. For water, there's both *con gas* (carbonated) and *sin gas* (noncarbonated) mineral water. Or ask for Argentina's usually drinkable *agua de canilla* (tap water). For fresh-squeezed orange juice, ask for *jugo de naranja exprimido*. *Licuados* are water- or milk-blended fruit drinks.

Even in the smallest town, coffee will be espresso. *Café chico* is thick, dark coffee in a very small cup (try a *ristretto,* with even less water). *Café cortado* is a small coffee with a touch of milk; *cortado doble* is a larger portion. *Café con leche* (a latte) is served for breakfast only; after lunch or dinner, request a *cortado*.

Tea is commonplace. You shouldn't decline an invitation for grasslike maté, although it's definitely an acquired taste.

Sports

Rugby, tennis, basketball, polo, golf, motor racing, skiing and cycling are popular sports, but soccer is an obsession. The national team has twice won the World Cup, once in 1978 and again in 1986, after Diego Armando Maradona (Argentina's bad-boy, rags-to-riches soccer star) surreptitiously punched in a goal to beat England in the quarterfinals. Today, Lionel Messi is Argentina's biggest *fútbol* star.

The game between River Plate and Boca Juniors is a classic match not to be missed, as the rivalry between the two teams is famously intense.

Environment

The Land

Argentina is huge – it's the world's eighth-largest country. It stretches some 3500km north to south and encompasses a wide range of environments and terrain.

The glorious Andes line the edge of northwest Argentina, where only hardy cactus and scrubby vegetation survive. Here, soaring peaks and salt lakes give way to the subtropical lowland provinces of Salta and Santiago del Estero. To the south, the hot and scenic Tucumán, Catamarca and La Rioja provinces harbor agriculture and viticulture.

Drier thornlands of the western Andean foothills give way to the forked river valleys and hot lowlands of Formosa and Chaco provinces. Rainfall is heaviest to the northeast, where swampy forests and subtropical savannas thrive. Densely forested Misiones province contains the awe-inspiring Iguazú Falls. Rivers streaming off these immense cataracts lead to the alluvial grasslands of Corrientes and Entre Ríos provinces. Summers here are very hot and humid.

The west-central Cuyo region (Mendoza, San Juan and San Luis provinces) pumps out most of Argentina's world-class wine vintages. Central Argentina has the mountainous Córdoba and richly agricultural Santa Fe provinces. The Pampas is a flat, rich plain full of agriculture and livestock. Along the Atlantic Coast are many popular and attractive beaches.

Patagonia spans the lower third of Argentina. Most of this region is flat and arid, but toward the Andes rainfall is abundant and supports the lush Lake District. The southern Andes boasts huge glaciers, while down on the flats cool steppes pasture large flocks of sheep.

The Tierra del Fuego archipelago mostly belongs to Chile. Its northern half resembles the Patagonian steppe, while dense forests and glaciers cover the mountainous southern half. The climate can be relatively mild, even in winter (though temperatures can also drop below freezing). The weather in this region is very changeable throughout the year.

Like several other countries, Argentina lays claim to a section of Antarctica.

Wildlife

The famous Pampas are mostly sprawling grasslands and home to many birds of prey and introduced plant species; most of the region's remaining native vegetation survives up north along the Río Paraná. Also in the northern swamplands live the odd-looking capybara (the world's largest rodent), swamp deer, the alligator-like caiman and many large migratory birds.

The main forested areas of Argentina are found in subtropical Misiones province and on the eastward-sloping Andes from Neuquén province south, where southern beech species and coniferous woodlands predominate; look for the strange monkey-puzzle tree *(Araucaria araucana or pehuén)* around the Lake District. In the higher altitudes of the Andes and in much of Patagonia, pasture grasses are sparse. Northern Andean saline lakes harbor pink flamingos, and on the Patagonian steppe you're likely to see guanacos, rheas, Patagonian hares, armadillos, crested caracaras and gray foxes. Pumas and condors live in the southern Andean foothills, but sightings have sadly been rare.

Coastal Patagonia, especially around Península Valdés, has dense and viewable concentrations of marine fauna, including southern right whales, sea lions, southern elephant seals, Magellanic penguins and orcas.

National Parks

Argentina has a good range of national parks. A wide variety of climates is represented, such as swamp, desert and rainforest – and highlights include giant trees, waterfalls and glaciers.

Some of Argentina's best national parks include the following:

Parque Nacional Iguazú (p83) World-renowned for its waterfalls.

Parque Nacional Los Alerces (p138) Site of ancient *alerce* (false larch) forests.

Parque Nacional Los Glaciares (p151) Awesome for its glaciers and alpine towers.

Parque Nacional Nahuel Huapi (p134) Offers vivid alpine scenery.

Parque Nacional Tierra del Fuego (p159) Exceptional beech forests and fauna.

Parque Provincial Aconcagua (p122) Boasts the continent's highest peak.

Reserva Faunística Península Valdés (p143) Famous for coastal fauna.

Reserva Provincial Esteros del Iberá (p75) Home to various swamp-dwelling wildlife.

SURVIVAL GUIDE

Directory A–Z

Accommodations

There's an excellent range of affordable hostels throughout Argentina. Most hostels are friendly and offer tours and services. All include kitchen access and sheets; most have towel rental, internet access, free wi-fi, luggage storage, light breakfast and double rooms (book these ahead). Typical prices for dorm rooms are AR$70 to AR$90, while doubles usually run from about AR$200 at the cheapest (prices vary widely depending on the destination). Hostel organizations include **Hostelling International** (☎4511-8723; www.hostels.org.ar; Av Florida 835), **Minihostels** (www.minihostels.com) and **HoLa** (www.holahostels.com); membership is not required to stay at any of the participating hostels, but around 10% discounts are given to members.

Residenciales are small hotels, while *hospedajes* or *casas de familia* are usually family homes with extra bedrooms and shared bathrooms. Hotels can range from one to five stars, and rooms usually come with private bathroom and a light breakfast (coffee, tea and bread or croissants). In Buenos Aires, apartment rentals are popular and can be a money-saver if you're staying a long time.

Camping is cheap and popular in Argentina, though sites aren't always near the center of town. National parks usually have organized sites, and some offer distant *refugios* (basic shelters for trekkers).

Peak tourist months in Buenos Aires are July, August and November to January, when accommodation prices are at their highest. Patagonia is busiest during the summer (November to February), though ski resort towns fill up fast in July and August. Northern destinations and the Atlantic beach towns attract the most travelers in December and January (the latter are practically ghost towns the rest of the year). In peak season it's wise to make reservations ahead of time.

> **SLEEPING PRICE RANGES**
>
> Reviews are listed in order of preference. The following price ranges refer to a double room with bathroom in the high season.
>
> **$** less than AR$300
>
> **$$** AR$300 to AR$450
>
> **$$$** more than AR$450

Activities

Argentina has plenty for the adventurous traveler. A multitude of beautiful national parks offer awesome summer hiking and trekking, especially around Bariloche and Patagonia's Fitz Roy range. The highest peak outside Asia is lofty Aconcagua, at 6962m.

Skiing is world-class, with major resorts at Cerro Catedral, near Bariloche; Las Leñas, near Malargüe; Los Penitentes; and Chapelco, near San Martín de los Andes. The ski season runs from approximately mid-June to mid-October. In summer, these mountains turn into activity centers for mountain biking.

Cycling is a popular activity in Mendoza, the Andean northwest, the Lake District and Patagonia (where winds are fierce!). Mountain bikes are best for pedaling the sometimes remote and bad roads, many of which are gravel. Many tourist cities have bike rentals, though the quality is not up to Western standards.

The Lake District and Patagonia have some of the world's best fly-fishing, with introduced trout and landlocked Atlantic salmon reaching epic proportions. The season in these areas runs from November to mid-April. It's almost always catch-and-release.

Whitewater rafting can be enjoyed near Mendoza (as well as in the Lake District) and horse riding and paragliding are popular in many tourist areas.

Business Hours

Traditionally, businesses open by 9am, break at 1pm for lunch and then reopen at 4pm until 8pm or 9pm. This pattern is still common in the provinces, but government offices and many businesses in Buenos Aires have adopted the 9am to 6pm schedule.

Restaurants generally open noon to 3pm for lunch and 8pm to midnight for dinner. On weekends hours can be longer. Cafes are open all day long; most bars tend to open their doors late, around 9pm or 10pm.

Opening hours aren't listed in reviews throughout this chapter unless they vary widely from these standards.

Electricity

Argentina's electric current operates on 220V, 50Hz. Most plugs are either two rounded prongs (as in Europe) or three angled flat prongs (as in Australia).

Embassies & Consulates

The following is not a complete list:

Australian Embassy (011-4779-3500; www.argentina.embassy.gov.au; Villanueva 1400, Buenos Aires)

Bolivian Embassy Buenos Aires (011-4394-1463; www.embajadadebolivia.com.ar; Corrientes 545, 2nd fl) La Qiaca (03885-422-283; cnr San Juan & Árabe Siria); Salta (0387-421-1040; Boedo 34); San Salvador de Jujuy (0388-424-0501; Independencia 1098)

Brazilian Embassy Buenos Aires (011-4515-6500; www.brasil.org.ar; Carlos Pellegrini 1363, 5th fl) Paso de Los Libres (03772-425-444; Mitre 842); Puerto Iguazú (03757-420-192; Córdoba 264)

Canadian Embassy (011-4808-1000; www.canadainternational.gc.ca; Tagle 2828, Buenos Aires)

Chilean Embassy Buenos Aires (011-4331-6228; www.chileabroad.gov.cl/argentina; Diagonal Roque Sáenz Peña 547, 2nd fl) Bariloche (02944-523-050; Av Juan Manuel de Rosas 180); Esquel (02945-451-189; Molinari 754); Mendoza (0261-425-5024; Belgrano 1080); Neuquén (0299-442-2447; La Rioja 241); Rio Gallegos (02966-422-364; Moreno 148); Salta (0387-431-1857; Santiago del Estero 965); Ushuaia (02901-430-909; Jainén 50)

Dutch Embassy (011-4338-0050; www.embajadaholanda.int.ar; Olga Cossettini 831, 3rd fl, Buenos Aires)

French Embassy (011-4515-6900; www.embafrancia-argentina.org; Basavilvaso 1253, Buenos Aires)

German Embassy (011-4778-2500; www.buenos-aires.diplo.de; Villanueva 1055, Buenos Aires)

Irish Embassy (011-5787-0801; www.embassyofireland.org.ar; Av del Libertador 1068, 6th fl, Buenos Aires)

New Zealand Embassy (011-4328-0747; www.nzembassy.com/argentina; Carlos Pellegrini 1427, 5th fl, Buenos Aires)

Paraguayan Embassy (Buenos Aires 011-4814-4803; www.embajadadelparaguay.org.ar; Viamonte 1851, Buenos Aires) Posadas (03752-423-858; San Lorenzo 179); Puerto Iguazú (03757-424-230; Córdoba 370)

Uruguayan Embassy Buenos Aires (011-4807-3040; www.embajadadeluruguay.com.ar; Av Las Heras 1907) Gualeguaychú (03446-426-168; Rivadavia 510)

UK Embassy (011-4808-2200; www.ukinargentina.fco.gov.uk; Dr Luis Agote 2412, Buenos Aires)

USA Embassy (011-5777-4533; http://argentina.usembassy.gov; Colombia 4300, Buenos Aires)

FOOD PRICE RANGES

Reviews are listed in order of preference. The following price indicators apply for mains:

$ less than AR$50

$$ AR$50 to AR$70

$$$ more than AR$70

Gay & Lesbian Travelers

Argentina is a strongly Catholic country, but enclaves of tolerance toward gays and lesbians do exist. This is especially true in Buenos Aires, which is a top gay destination. BA was the first city in Latin America to accept civil unions between same-sex couples (in 2002).

Argentine men are more physically demonstrative than you may be used to, so behaviors such as cheek kisses or a vigorous embrace are commonplace. Lesbians walking hand in hand should attract little attention, as heterosexual Argentine women sometimes do this, but this would be suspicious behavior for males. In general, do your thing – but be discreet.

Health

Argentina requires no vaccinations. In 2009 there was a dengue outbreak in some parts of northern Argentina, and malaria is always a minor concern in the more rural, lowland border sections of Salta, Jujuy, Corrientes and Misiones provinces. In the high Andes, watch for signs of altitude sickness and use more sunscreen. For more information see http://wwwnc.cdc.gov/travel/destinations/argentina.htm.

Urban water supplies are usually potable, making salads and ice safe to consume. Many prescription drugs are available over

ELECTRONICS WARNING

Note that buying certain electronic products is now practically impossible in Argentina due to severe import restrictions. If you bring your smart phone, don't flash it around unnecessarily or leave it unprotected. This goes for tablet and laptop computers too.

the counter. Seek out an embassy recommendation if you need serious Western-type medical services.

Internet Access

Argentina is online: every city and town in the country, no matter how small, has internet cafes. In downtown Buenos Aires they're on practically every corner. Most *locutorios* (telephone offices) also offer internet access. Costs are very affordable.

To type the @ *(arroba)* symbol, hold down the Alt-key while typing 64 on the keypad. Or ask the attendant *'¿Cómo se hace la arroba?'*.

Language

Besides flamboyance, the unique pronunciation of *castellano* – Argentina's Italian-accented version of the Spanish language – readily identifies an Argentine elsewhere in Latin America or abroad. If you're in Buenos Aires you'll also hear *lunfardo,* the capital's colorful slang.

Some immigrants retain their language as a badge of identity. Quechua speakers, numerous in the northwest, tend to be bilingual in Spanish. Many Mapuche speakers live in the southern Andes, while most Guaraní speakers live in northeastern Argentina. English is understood by many Argentines in the tourist industry.

Pick up a copy of Lonely Planet's *Latin American Spanish* phrasebook to avoid cluelessness.

Argentina is a good destination in which to learn Spanish, and there are dozens of schools (and private instructors) to choose from in Buenos Aires. Other large cities, such as Bariloche, Mendoza and Córdoba, also have Spanish schools.

Legal Matters

Many drugs that are illegal in the US and most European countries are also illegal here. Constitutionally, a person is innocent until proven guilty, although people are regularly held for years without trial. If arrested, you have the constitutional right to a lawyer, a telephone call and to remain silent.

If you behave, it's unlikely you'll run into trouble with the police. Politely mention contacting your consulate if you do have a run-in. Drivers sometimes take care of matters on the spot by saying '*¿Cómo podemos arreglar esto más rapido?*' (How can we sort this out faster?). In all events, it's a good idea to carry identification (or copies in a pinch) and always be courteous and cooperative when dealing with police or government officials.

Money

Carrying a combination of US dollars, Argentine pesos and ATM/credit cards is best.

ATMS

Cajeros automáticos (ATMs) are the best way to go in Argentina, whether you're in a big city or small town. Practically every bank has one, transactions are straightforward and exchange rates are reasonable. Most ATMs have English instructions. Savvy travelers bring more than one card, in case.

One issue with ATMs is that there's a limit on how many pesos you can withdraw per transaction. This limit depends on your network system. You can usually make more than one transaction per day, but your bank may charge you a per-transaction fee – it's good to check with them before traveling. Local Argentine banks also charge a per-transaction fee, so withdrawing near your limit may be the best course of action if you want to save money.

When getting cash out, consider withdrawing an odd number like AR$790, instead of AR$800; this will guarantee you some small bills for change. Don't expect to be able to withdraw US dollars.

BARGAINING

Bargaining might be possible in the northwest and in craft fairs countrywide, especially if you buy several items, but it's not the sport that it is in some other countries in Latin America, and certainly not something you do in most stores in Argentina.

If you stay several days at a hotel, you can often negotiate a better rate. Many higher-range hotels will give discounts for cash payments.

CASH

Bills come in denominations of two, five, 10, 20, 50 and 100 pesos. One peso equals 100 centavos. Coins come in five, 10, 25 and 50 centavos as well as one and two pesos. Always carry small-denomination bills and coins.

US dollars are the easiest currency to exchange, though euros are also widely accepted at cambios (exchange houses).There is a black market for US dollars, which are highly desirable these days, but it's illegal to change money this way and not recommended – scams exist for the unwary. In Buenos Aires especially, beware fake bills, which tend to look and feel a little fake and either have bad watermarks or are missing them altogether. They're often given out in dark places like nightclubs or taxis; see http://landingpadba.com/ba-basics-counterfeit-money for more.

CREDIT CARDS

The larger a hotel is, the greater the chance it will accept credit cards. Ditto for stores and other services like bus tickets. Some businesses add a *recargo* (surcharge) of up to 10% to credit-card purchases; always ask before charging. Note that restaurant tips can't be added to the bill and must be paid in cash.

MasterCard and Visa are the main honchos, but American Express is also commonly accepted. Let your company know you'll be using your card(s) abroad. Limited cash advances are possible (try Banco de la Nación) but are difficult, involving paperwork and fees.

MONEYCHANGERS

US dollars and certain other currencies can be converted to Argentine pesos at most banks or *cambios* (exchange houses). *Cambios* offer slightly poorer rates but have fewer restrictions, and often shorter lines.

Buenos Aires' Av Florida is rife with shady figures offering '*cambio, cambio, cambio*' to passing pedestrians. Using these illegal street changers is not recommended; there are quite a few fake bills floating about, along with plenty of scams.

Traveler's checks are very difficult to cash (even at banks) and suffer poor exchange rates. They're not recommended as your main source of traveling money.

You should double-check the exchange rate when you travel, as Argentina's peso is highly volatile.

Post

Letters and postcards (up to 20g) can be sent to the US, Europe and Australia; even small towns usually have a post office. You can send packages under 2kg from any post office, but anything heavier needs to go through the *aduana* (customs office). Don't send anything too valuable.

Correo Argentino (www.correoargentino.com.ar) – the privatized postal service – has become more dependable over the years, but send essential mail *certificado* (registered). Private couriers, such as OCA and FedEx, are available in some larger cities – but are much more expensive.

Public Holidays

Government offices and businesses close on most national holidays, which are often moved to the nearest Monday or Friday to extend weekends. Provincial holidays are not listed here.

Año Nuevo (New Year's Day) January 1

Carnaval February/March (floating Monday and Tuesday)

Día de la Memoria (Memorial Day; anniversary of 1976's military coup) March 24

Semana Santa (Easter) March/April

Día de las Malvinas (Malvinas Day) April 2

Día del Trabajador (Labor Day) May 1

Revolución de Mayo (May Revolution of 1810) May 25

Día de la Bandera (Flag Day) June 20

Día de la Independencia (Independence Day) July 9

Día del Libertador San Martín (Anniversary of San Martín's death) Third Monday in August

Día del Respeto a la Diversidad Cultural (Cultural Diversity Day) October 12 (observed second Monday in October)

Dia de la Soberanía Nacional (National

PESKY INFLATION

While accurate at the time of writing, prices in this book are likely to rise rapidly due to Argentina's unofficial inflation of around 25% (officially it's 10%). Check before booking to avoid surprises.

TWO-TIER COSTS IN ARGENTINA

A few upscale hotels, some museums and tango shows, most national parks and one major airline have adopted a two-tier price system. Rates for foreigners are double (or more) locals' prices. While it's useless to complain to service personnel at government-run entities about this discrepancy, you can choose to stay at hotels that don't discriminate – just ask.

Sovereignty Day) November 20 (observed fourth Monday in November)

Día de la Concepción Inmaculada (Immaculate Conception Day) December 8

Navidad (Christmas Day; businesses close starting midday on Dec 24) December 25

Responsible Travel

Unlike Bolivia or Peru, modern Argentina doesn't have huge numbers of indigenous peoples with delicate cultures. Most responsible travel here includes how you behave in the country's more pristine areas, such as the village of El Chaltén (which is located inside a national park). Common sense rules: keep water sources potable by washing 100 steps away from rivers and lakes, don't litter (this includes cigarette butts) and avoid walking off-trail.

Safe Travel

Despite occasional crime waves, Argentina remains one of the safest countries in Latin America. Most alert tourists who visit Buenos Aires leave happy and unscathed (see Dangers & Annoyances, p60). Outside the big cities, serious crime is not common. Lock your valuables up in hostels, where, sadly enough, your own fellow travellers are occasionally to blame for thefts.

In general, the biggest dangers in Argentina are speeding cars and buses: *never* assume you have the right of way as a pedestrian. If you're sensitive to cigarette smoke, be aware that Argentines are truly addicted to nicotine: they'll light up almost anywhere.

Telephone

Telecom and Telefónica are the major Argentine phone companies. *Locutorios* are very common in any city; you enter private booths, make calls, then pay at the front counter. These are a better choice than street phones (which are relatively rare) as they offer privacy and quiet, and you won't run out of coins.

Calling the US, Europe and Australia from *locutorios* is best on evenings and weekends, when rates are lower. Least expensive is buying credit phone cards at kiosks or calling over the internet (eg via Skype).

Cell phone numbers start with ☎15. Toll-free numbers start with ☎0800.

To call someone in Argentina from outside Argentina, you'll need to dial your country's international access code, then Argentina's country code (☎54), then the city's area code (leaving out the first 0), then the number itself. (When dialing an Argentine cell phone from outside Argentina, dial your country's international access code, then ☎54, then ☎9, then the area code without the 0, then the number – leaving out the 15).

Argentina operates mainly on the GSM 850/1900 network. If you have an unlocked, tri- or quad-band GSM cell phone, you can buy a prepaid SIM chip in Argentina and insert it into your phone (adding credits as needed). You can also buy or rent cell phones in Argentina. Check websites like www.kropla.com for current information.

Toilets

Argentina's public toilets are better than most other South American countries, but not quite as good as those in the West. Head to restaurants, fast-food outlets, shopping malls and even large hotels to scout out a seat. Carry toilet paper and don't expect hot water, soap or paper towels to be available. In smaller towns, some public toilets charge a small fee for entry.

Tourist Information

All tourist-oriented cities in Argentina have a conveniently located tourist office, and many of them have English-speaking staff.

In Buenos Aires, each Argentine province has a tourist office. Also in BA is the excellent **Secretaría de Turismo de la Nación** (☎0800-555-0016, 4312-2232; www.turismo.gov.ar; Av Santa Fe 883; ⏲9am-5pm Mon-Fri), which dispenses information on all of Argentina.

Travelers with Disabilities

Mobility-impaired folks will have a tough time in big cities, where sidewalks are often busy, narrow and cracked. Ramps don't exist at every corner, and Argentine drivers have little patience for slow pedestrians (disabled or not). Higher-end hotels tend to have the best wheelchair access; with restaurants and tourist sights it's best to call ahead.

There are some kneeling buses in Buenos Aires (called *piso bajo*), but taxis are common and affordable so it's definitely best to use them. Call radio taxis or *remises* beforehand to ask for a proper-sized vehicle that can take a wheelchair.

Visas

Residents of Canada, the US, Australia and many western European countries do not need visas to enter Argentina; they receive an automatic 90-day stamp on arrival. Citizens from the US, Canada and Australia will, however, be charged a significant 'reciprocity fee' when they arrive in an airport in Buenos Aires (see Getting into Town, p63). It's smart to double-check all this information with your embassy before you leave, as changes often occur.

For visa extensions (90 days, AR$300), visit *migraciones* (immigration offices) in the provincial capitals. There's also an **immigration office** (☎4317-0234; www.migraciones.gov.ar; Av Antártida Argentina 1355; ⏲7:30am-2pm Mon-Fri) in Buenos Aires. For information on obtaining Argentine residency, see www.argentinaresidency.com.

Volunteering

Volunteer opportunities in Argentina include the following:

Conservación Patagonica (www.patagonialandtrust.org/makeadifference_v.htm) Help to create a national park.

Fundación Banco de Alimentos (www.bancodealimentos.org.ar) Short-term work at a food bank.

Idealists in Argentina (www.idealistsinargentina.wetpaint.com)

Life Argentina (www.lifeargentina.org)

Unión de los Pibes (www.uniondelospibes.blogspot.com) Buenos Aires' kids in need.

Volunteer South America (www.volunteersouthamerica.net) List of NGOs offering volunteer opportunities in South America.

Wander Argentina (www.wander-argentina.org/category/volunteer)

WWOOF Argentina (www.wwoofargentina.com) Organic farming in Argentina.

Women Travelers

Being a woman traveler in Argentina is not difficult, even if you're alone. In some ways Argentina is a safer place for a woman than Europe, the USA and most other Latin American countries. Argentina has a *machismo* culture, however, and some men will feel the need to comment on a woman's attractiveness. They'll try to get your attention by hissing, whistling, or making *piropos* (flirtatious comments). The best thing to do is completely ignore them – like Argentine women do. After all, most men don't mean to be rude, and many local women even consider *piropos* to be compliments.

On the plus side of *machismo,* expect men to hold a door open for you and let you enter first, including getting on buses; this gives you a better chance at grabbing an empty seat, so get in there quick.

Work

In Argentina, casual jobs are limited for foreigners. Teaching English is your best bet, especially in Buenos Aires and other major cities. However, most teachers make just enough to get by. A TESOL or TESL certificate will be an advantage in acquiring work. Foreigners also find work in traveler-oriented bars and hostels.

Many expats work illegally on tourist visas, which they must renew every three months (in BA this usually means hopping to Uruguay a few times per year). Work schedules drop off during the holiday months of January and February.

For job postings, check out http://buenosaires.en.craigslist.org or the classifieds in www.baexpats.org.

Getting There & Away

Air

Cosmopolitan Buenos Aires is linked to most of the capitals in South America. Argentina's main international airport is Buenos Aires' Aeropuerto Internacional Ministro Pistarini (known as Ezeiza). Aeroparque Jorge Newbery (known simply as Aeroparque) is the capital's domestic airport. A few other Argentine cities have 'international' airports, but they mostly serve domestic destinations. The national airline is Aerolíneas Argentinas.

Argentina no longer has a departure tax (the cost is now included in the ticket price).

Boat

Ferries link Buenos Aires to several points in Uruguay.

Bus

It's possible to cross into Argentina from Bolivia, Paraguay, Brazil, Uruguay and Chile.

Getting Around

Air

The airline situation in Argentina is in constant flux; minor airlines go in and out of business regularly. Ticket prices are unpredictable, though they are always highest during holiday times (July and late December to February). Certain flights in extensive Patagonia are comparable to bus fares when you consider time saved.

The major airlines in Argentina are **Aerolíneas Argentinas** (AR; www.aerolineasargentinas.com) and **LAN** (www.lan.com). Each airline has a principal office, as well as regional offices in various cities.

There may be special air-pass deals available; check with a travel agency specializing in Latin America, since deals come and go regularly. These passes may need to be purchased outside Argentina (sometimes in conjunction with an international ticket), you need to be a foreign resident to use them, and they're often limited to travel within a certain time period.

Bicycle

Cycling around the country has become popular among travelers. Beautiful routes in the north include the highway from Tucumán to Tafí del Valle and the Quebrada de Cafayate. Around Mendoza, there's touring that includes stops at wineries. The Lake District also has scenic roads, like the Siete Lagos route. Drawbacks include the wind (which can slow progress to a crawl in Patagonia) and reckless motorists. Less-traveled secondary roads with little traffic are good alternatives. Rental bikes are common in tourist areas and a great way to get around.

Bus

Long-distance buses are modern, fast, comfortable and usually the best budget way to get around (and overnight trips save accommodation costs). Journeys of more than six hours or so will either have pit stops for refreshments or serve drinks, sweet snacks and sometimes simple meals. All have bathrooms, though they're often grungy, lack water (bring toilet paper/wet wipes) and are sometimes for 'liquids only.' The most luxurious companies offer more expensive *coche-cama, ejecutivo* or *suite* seats, most of which can lay flat. But even regular buses are usually comfortable enough, even on long trips.

Bus terminals usually have kiosks, restrooms, cheap eats and luggage storage. In small towns be aware of the timetable for your next bus out (and possibly buy a ticket), since some routes run infrequently. In summer there are more departures. At holiday periods (January, February or July) buy advance tickets. If you know exact travel dates, you can often buy a ticket from any departure point to any destination, but it depends on the company. For bus ticket prices from Buenos Aires, check www.omnilineas.com.

Car

Renting a car in Argentina is not cheap, but can get you away from the beaten path and start you on some adventures. Figure AR$250 to AR$400 (depending on the destination) per day average for a cheap model with some free mileage. The minimum driving age in Argentina is 18.

Forget driving in Buenos Aires; traffic is unforgiving and parking is a headache, while public transport is great.

The **Automobile Club Argentina** (ACA; www.aca.org.ar) has offices, service stations and garages in major cities. If you're a member of an overseas affiliate (like AAA in the United States) you may be able to obtain vehicular services and discounts on maps –

GETTING TO CHILE

For most travelers, crossing the border from Argentina into Chile is a relatively quick, easy procedure. Usually the same bus takes you right through and there are no fees. Border outposts are open daylight hours; Dorotea (near Puerto Natales) is open 24 hours in summer. Just have your papers in order, don't take anything illegal (including fresh food) and you should be golden. And try to get your ticket as soon as possible, as Chile-bound buses often fill up quickly.

bring your card. The ACA's main headquarters is in Buenos Aires.

To rent a car you must be 21 years old and have a credit card and valid driver's license from your country. An International Driving Permit is useful but not always necessary.

Hitchhiking

Good places for a pickup are gas stations on the outskirts of large cities, where truckers refuel their vehicles. In Patagonia, distances are great and vehicles few, so expect long waits and carry snack foods and warm, windproof clothing. Carry extra water as well, especially in the desert north. Realize that many cars are full with families.

Haciendo dedo (hitchhiking) is fairly safe for women in Argentina; however, don't do it alone, don't get in a car with two men and don't do it at night. There is nothing especially unsafe about hitchhiking in rural Argentina, but don't hitchhike in Buenos Aires.

A sign will improve your chances for a pickup, especially something like *visitando Argentina de Canadá* (visiting Argentina from Canada), rather than just a destination. Argentines are fascinated by foreigners.

For more tips visit www.wander-argentina.com/10-tips-for-hitchhiking-in-argentina.

Local Transportation

Even small towns have good bus systems. A few cities use magnetic fare cards, which can usually be bought at kiosks (Buenos Aires uses both magnetic cards and coins). Pay attention to placards indicating the destination, since identically numbered buses may cover slightly different routes.

Taxis have digital-readout meters. Tipping isn't expected, but you can leave extra change. *Remises* are taxis that you book over the phone, or regular cars without meters; any hotel or restaurant should be able to call one for you. They're considered more secure than taxis since an established company sends them out. Ask the fare in advance.

Buenos Aires is the only city with a subway system, known as Subte.

Tours

Most of Argentina can be seen independently with just this guidebook (of course!). There are certain destinations, however, where it can be more informative and cost-effective to take a tour rather than rent a car. Visiting the Moreno Glacier outside El Calafate is one place; Peninsula Valdés and Punta Tombo, both near Puerto Madryn, are some others. Whitewater rafting, whale-watching and other adventures often require signing up for tours. Buenos Aires is full of interesting tours that give you deeper insight into that great city – these include biking tours, graffiti tours and even food tours.

Train

The British-built train system in Argentina is not as widespread as it once was, and bus travel is now faster, more flexible and reliable. There are long-distance services from Buenos Aires to Rosario, Córdoba, Tucumán, Posadas, Santiago del Estero, Bahía Blanca and Atlantic beach towns. There's also service from Viedma to Bariloche.

The very scenic, famous and expensive Tren a las Nubes chugs from Salta, in the north, toward Chile. It's notoriously undependable, so check and double-check the situation before getting your hopes up.

In Patagonia there are a couple of short touristy train rides (both narrow gauge) such as La Trochita, which originates in Esquel or El Maitén, and El Tren del Fin del Mundo, in Ushuaia.

Bolivia

Includes »

Best Adventures

- » El Choro Trek (p203)
- » Amazon tour (p237)
- » Trekking from tip-to-tail on Isla del Sol (p197)
- » Climbing in the Cordillera Real (p203)

Best Places to Stay

- » Las Olas (p195)
- » Hostal Sol y Luna (p201)
- » Casa Verde (p226)
- » La Posada del Sol (p236)
- » Chalalàn Ecolodge (p241)

Why Go?

Rough around the edges, superlative in its natural beauty, rugged, vexing and slightly nerve-racking, Bolivia is one of South America's most complex nations.

Just finding your way from summit to city can be a challenge in and of itself. Then there are the peaks, the rivers, the treks, the jungles, the gut-bursting mountain-bike descents, and the vast, impenetrable and remote expanses that tug you ever further into the wild.

For sky walkers, the steep-peaked mountains offer a lifetime's worth of adventure. Plunging down from the Andes to the edge of the Amazon, multiday romps follow ancient Inca paving, making this one of the world's top trekking destinations, while deep in the dark heart of the Amazon, river trips take you past the riotous barks of monkeys and a thriving mass of biodiversity that will leave you awestruck.

The cultural, historical and spiritual richness of the country with the highest percentage of indigenous peoples in Latin America make this a place to see, learn and experience.

When to Go

La Paz

°C/°F **Temp**
40/104
30/86
20/68
10/50
0/32
-10/14

Rainfall inches/mm
20/350
15/300
10/250
8/200
6/150
4/100
2/50
0

J F M A M J J A S O N D

May–Oct High season; expect sunny days and good hiking, biking and climbing conditions.

Nov–Apr Rainy season means tough travel; the lowlands can be miserable, but cities are still fun.

Feb–Apr Festivals across the nation put a smiley face on the rainy season.

Connections

Bolivia's border crossings include Guajará-Mirim and Corumbá (Brazil), La Quiaca and Pocitos (Argentina), Tambo Quemado and Hito Cajón near San Pedro de Atacama (Chile), Yunguyo and Desaguadero (Peru) and Fortín Infante Rivarola (Paraguay). Getting in and out of Bolivia is fairly straight-forward, though at some off-the-beaten-track border crossings you may be charged a small fee. Depending on the border crossing, you may also be asked to provide proof of yellow fever vaccination. The border crossing to San Pedro de Atacama is best done with a tour outfit from Uyuni.

ITINERARIES

Two Weeks

Start out with a day of acclimatization in La Paz, visiting the markets. From there, head to Lake Titicaca, then circle down the Altiplano to the Salar de Uyuni for a bone-chatteringly-cold three-day jeep tour. Swing up to Potosí, a starkly beautiful Unesco World Heritage city, then head to the white city of Sucre to hang out with students in grand plazas. Return to La Paz via Cochabamba, taking in the good views along the way. On your last day in La Paz, consider a mountain bike down to Coroico.

One Month

Start from where the two-week itinerary leaves off. From there, the adventurous can take on the Takesi or Choro treks, then puddle-jump their way to Rurrenabaque and Parque Nacional Madidi. City explorers could simply head over to Santa Cruz, where you'll kick off a multiday road trip through the Jesuit Missions Circuit, curling back around to the unique ruins and spectacular Parque Nacional e Área de Uso Mútiple Amboró near the tranquil village of Samaipata.

Essential Food & Drink

» **Salteñas, tucumanas, empanadas** Pastry shells stuffed with vegetable and meat goodness

» **Sopa** Soup starts every meal; for those with nut allergies, note that *maní* means peanut

» **Pollo** Chicken, either *frito* (fried), *a la broaster* (cooked on a spit), *asado* (barbecued) or *dorado* (broiled)

» **Carne** Beef – typically *asado* or *parrillada* (grilled)

» **Api** A yummy drink made from a ground purple corn

» **Mate de coca** An infusion of water and dried coca leaves

» **Singani** Grape brandy

AT A GLANCE

» **Currency** Boliviano (B$)

» **Languages** Spanish, Quechua, Aymará

» **Money** ATMs can be scarce; US dollars are best to exchange

» **Visas** US travelers have to pay

» **Time** GMT minus four hours

BOLIVIA

Fast Facts

» **Area** 1,098,580 sq km

» **Population** 9.8 million

» **Capital** Sucre (constitutional), La Paz (de facto)

» **Emergency** ☎119

» **Country code** ☎591

Exchange Rates

Australia	A$1	B$7
Canada	C$1	B$7
Euro zone	€1	B$9
New Zealand	NZ$1	B$6
UK	UK£1	B$11
USA	US$1	B$7

Set Your Budget

» **Hostel bed** US$4-7 (B$30-50)

» **Dinner** US$3-5 (B$20-35)

» **Bus** US$5 (B$35)

» **Beer** US$1 (B$7)

Resources

» **Bolivia Express** (www.bolivianexpress.org)

» **Bolivia Online** (www.bolivia-online.net)

» **Bolivia Web** (www.boliviaweb.com)

» **Bolivia Weekly** (www.boliviaweekly.com)

Bolivia Highlights

1. Explore **Potosí** (p228), the silver city of contrasts
2. Make your way through **Parque Nacional e Área de Uso Múltiple Amboró** (p236) for spectacular biodiversity and landscapes
3. Dive into history with a walking tour of **Sucre** (p223), where architecture and culture come to light
4. Discover the living history of Chiquitania along the **Jesuit Missions Circuit** (p236)
5. Kick back in **Samaipata** (p235) before exploring the nearby El Fuerte ruins
6. Jungle trek through **Parque Nacional Madidi** (p241) for ecotourism, howlers, birds and bugs at their best
7. Enjoy hiking, biking, climbing, rafting… The world is your playground in the **Cordillera Real** (p203)
8. Worship the sun and sand with visits to the ruins, lost coves and mini-treks around **Lake Titicaca** (p192)
9. Create your own requiem for a dream at the surreal **Salar de Uyuni** (p212)
10. Challenge yourself to extreme hammocking at its best in **Coroico** (p200)

0 200 km
0 100 miles

BRAZIL

Río Guaporé (Iténez)

Costa Marques

San Joaquín

Magdalena

Parque Nacional Noel Kempff Mercado

Serranía Huanchaca

Perseverancia

TRINIDAD

9

Concepción

Jesuit Missions Circuit

San Javier

San Ignacio de Velasco

4

Santa Ana de Velasco

San Miguel de Velasco

San Rafael de Velasco

Río Ichilo

4

Puerto Villarroel

Buena Vista

Parque Nacional e Área de Uso Múltiple Amboró

2

SANTA CRUZ

Puerto Pailas

San José de Chiquitos

Pantanal

5

Samaipata

Llanos de Chiquitos

Serranía de San José

Serranía de Santiago

Roboré

Bañados del Izozog

Río Grande o Guapay

Puerto Suárez

Corumbá

Quijarro

Tarabuco

Gran Chaco

Camiri

Boyuibe

6

Fortín General Eugenio A Garay

Río Paraguay

Villamontes

PARAGUAY

TARIJA

Río Pilcomayo

Yacuiba

Pocitos

Filadelfia

Tartagal

Aguas Blancas

LA PAZ

☎02 / POP 1.4 MILLION

La Paz is a city of Gothic proportions, world-class views and a multiethnic cultural imprint unique to the Americas. It's sinister and serendipitous – often at the same time. While there's plenty of petty crime, traffic and pollution, La Paz is somehow so unique and so odd that it very well could become the highlight of your trip.

Most of the city lies in a preposterously steep valley at around 3660m. Medieval-looking buildings ascend the slopes with haphazardness, finally spilling over the edge into the rough commerce hub of El Alto, while to the south the three-peaked Illimani (6402m) watches over the city in stately serenity.

A few days wandering the frenetic markets, high-quality museums, crafts stalls, cloistered nightclubs and coiling alleyways will not disappoint. This is also the staging center for many of the hikes, bikes and excursions into the fascinating Andean wilderness areas that surround the city.

Sights

The metropolitan area of La Paz is divided into three very distinct zones. North of the city center is the separate municipality of El Alto (where the airport is). This fast-growing commercial and industrial city is the center for Aymará culture, has fascinating markets and few tourist attractions. Down from here in the valley is the city of La Paz, where most travelers spend their time. On the west side of the valley are the notable commercial districts of Rosario, Belen, San Pedro and Sopocachi. To the east, the action centers on the Plaza Murillo, Santa Barbara and Miraflores neighborhoods. If you get lost in La Paz, head downhill. You'll soon enough find yourself somewhere along the main thoroughfare or El Prado. Further down valley to the south is the Zona Sur. This is where the city's wealthy live. With safety a concern in the town proper, many businesses (and businesspeople) are moving to the Zona Sur. There's a good collection of upscale restaurants and hotels here.

WEST OF EL PRADO

The areas west of the Prado include the fascinating markets around Rosario, Belen and San Pedro, the cemetery and the sophisticated Sopocachi neighborhood.

Markets MARKET

La Paz's buzzing, frenetic markets are easily the highlight of any trip. There are open-air markets from Plaza Pérez Velasco uphill to the cemetery – past Mercado Lanza, and Plazas Eguino and Garita de Lima.

North of Plaza San Francisco, on Calle Figueroa, **Mercado Lanza** (Map p186; ⏱6am-8pm) is one of La Paz's main food markets. It also houses the splendid **Flower Market**.

Iglesia de San Francisco CHURCH

(Map p186; Plaza San Francisco) The hewed stone basilica of San Francisco, on the plaza of the same name, reflects an appealing blend of 16th-century Spanish and *mestizo* (a person of mixed indigenous and Spanish descent) trends. The cloisters and garden of **Museo San Francisco** (Map p186; ☎231-8472; Plaza San Francisco; entrance B$20; ⏱9am-6pm Mon-Sat), adjacent to the basilica, beautifully revive the history and art of the city's landmark.

Museo de la Coca MUSEUM

(Coca Museum; Map p186; Linares 906, Rosario; admission B$10; ⏱10am-7pm daily) Chew on some facts inside the small, slightly tired Coca Museum.

Mercado de Hechicería MARKET

(Witches' Market; Map p186) The city's most unusual market, the Witches' Market, lies along Calles Jiménez and Linares between Sagárnaga and Santa Cruz, amid lively tourist *artesanías* (stores selling locally handcrafted items). Merchandise includes herbal and folk remedies, plus llama fetuses and dried toucan beaks, used in traditional Andean rituals.

Museo de Arte Contemporáneo Plaza MUSEUM

(MAC | Contemporary Art Museum; Map p182; Av 16 de Julio 1698, Prado; admission B$15; ⏱9am-9pm) Better modern art may be found in various other collections around town, but this private museum wins the gold star for the most interesting building: a restored 19th-century mansion (only one of four left on the Prado) with a glass roof and stained-glass panels designed by Gustave Eiffel.

La Paz Cemetery CEMETERY

Most interesting on the Día de los Muertos (Day of the Dead; November 2), when half the city turns out to honor their ancestors. Be aware that the area around the cemetery is a little unsafe, especially at night. Get here by walking uphill from the Mercado Negro.

La Paz

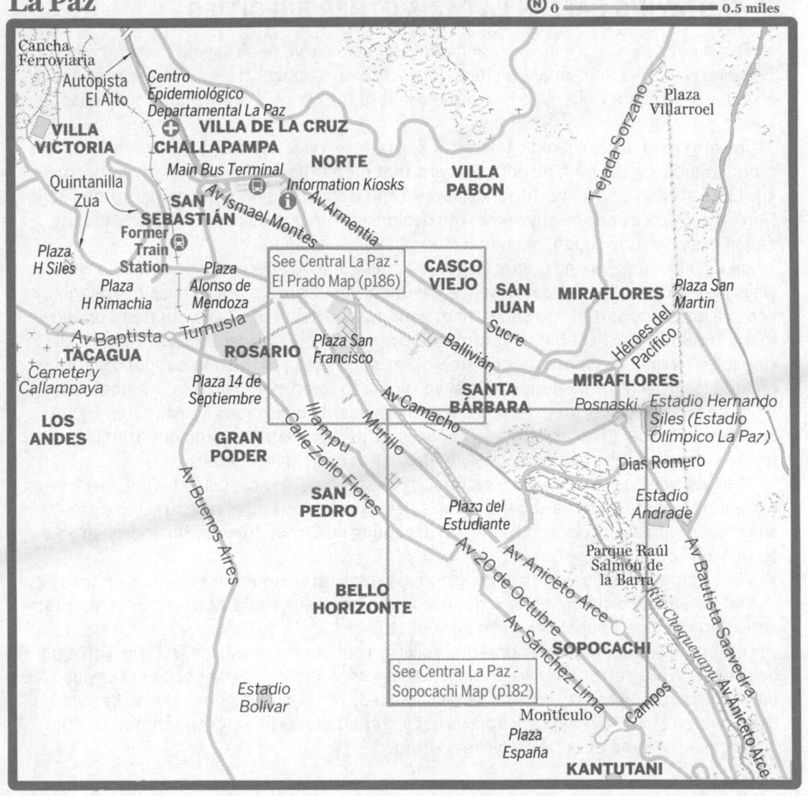

Sopocachi NEIGHBORHOOD
Sopocachi has some of La Paz's best restaurants and nightspots. You can spend a few hours people-watching on **Plaza Eduardo Avaroa**, before hoofing up to the wonderful views from **Monticulo Park**. A warning that express taxi robberies and muggings are common, especially at night near Plaza Eduardo Avaroa and Plaza España. Take a radio taxi.

EAST OF EL PRADO

Cathedral CHURCH
(Map p186; Plaza Murillo) Although it's a relatively recent addition to La Paz's collection of religious structures, the 1835 cathedral is an impressive structure – mostly because it is built on a steep hillside. Beside the cathedral is the **Presidential Palace**.

Museo Nacional del Arte MUSEUM
(National Art Museum; Map p186; www.mna.org.bo; cnr Comercio & Socabaya, Casco Viejo; admission B$15; ⌚9:30am-12:30pm & 3-7pm Tue-Fri, 10am-5:30pm Sat, 10am-1:30pm Sun) The various levels are dedicated to different eras, from pre-Hispanic works to contemporary art, with an emphasis on religious themes.

FREE **Museo de Etnografía y Folklore** MUSEUM
(Ethnography & Folklore Museum; Map p186; www.musef.org.bo; cnr Ingavi & Sanjinés, Casco Viejo; ⌚9am-12:30pm & 3-7pm Mon-Sat, 9am-12:30pm Sun) Anthropology buffs should check out this free museum.

TOP CHOICE **Calle Jaén Museums** MUSEUM
(Map p186; Calle Jaén, Casco Viejo; combination admission B$4; ⌚9am-12:30pm & 2:30am-7pm Tue-Fri, 9am-1pm Sat & Sun) These four, small, interesting museums are clustered together along Calle Jaén, La Paz's finest colonial street, and can generally be bundled into one visit. Buy tickets at the Museo

STAYING SAFE IN LA PAZ & OTHER BIG CITIES

La Paz is not a safe city, especially at night. For years we've been saying that crime in Bolivia is no worse than large US cities. Today, this is no longer true, and travelers should exercise precaution while in La Paz and the rest of the country. A little common sense goes a long way.

Travel in groups, take a radio taxi after 8pm (these have a radio in the car and a promo bubble on the roof; do not take cabs that merely have a 'taxi' sticker), carry small amounts of cash, and leave the fancy jewelry and electronics at home or in the hotel safe. Don't try to score cocaine anywhere; the dealers can be dangerous characters and the penalties for getting caught are harsh (see p255).

Fake police officers and bogus tourist officials exist. Authentic police officers will always be uniformed (undercover police are under strict orders not to hassle foreigners) and will never insist that you show them your passport, get in a taxi with them or allow them to search you in public. If confronted by an imposter, refuse to show them your valuables (wallet, passport, money etc), or insist on going to the nearest police station on foot. If physically threatened, it is always best to hand over valuables immediately.

In the last few years, there have been many incidents of 'express kidnappings' by taxi drivers, where the driver and his accomplices (who board later or jump out from the trunk) kidnap you and beat you until you provide your ATM PIN details.

The best way to prevent express kidnappings is to take a radio cab. At night, ask the restaurant or hotel to call a cab – the cab's details are recorded at a central base. Don't share cabs with strangers and beware of accepting lifts from drivers who approach you (especially around dodgy bus areas).

Violent attacks, including strangling and assault with weapons like clubs, is on the rise.

Petty theft and pickpocketing is not uncommon in restaurants, bus terminals, markets and internet cafes. Keep a close eye on your stuff.

One popular scam involves someone spilling a substance on you or spitting a phlegm ball at you. While you or they are wiping it off, another lifts your wallet or slashes your pack; the perpetrator may be an 'innocent' old lady or young girl. Similarly, make sure that you don't bend over to pick up a valuable item that has been 'dropped.' You risk being accused of theft, or of being pickpocketed.

Costumbrista. **Museo de Metales Preciosos** (Museum of Precious Metals; Map p186; Jaén 777) houses silver, gold and copper works from Tiwanaku. **Museo del Litoral** (Map p186; Jaén 798) incorporates relics from the 1884 war in which Bolivia became landlocked after losing its Litoral department to Chile. **Casa de Murillo** (Map p186; Jaén 790) displays collections of colonial art and furniture. And **Museo Costumbrista Juan de Vargas** (Map p186; cnr Jaén & Sucre) contains art and photos.

Museo de Instrumentos Musicales MUSEUM
(Museum of Musical Instruments; Map p186; Jaén 711, Casco Viejo; admission B$5; ⌚9:30am-1pm & 2-6:30pm daily) The exhaustive, hands-on collection of unique instruments at this museum is a must for musicians. You can also arrange *charango* (Andean stringed instrument) and wind instrument lessons here for around B$50 per hour.

Museo Nacional de Arqueología MUSEUM
(National Archaeology Museum; Map p182; Tiawanacu 93, Casco Viejo; admission B$10; ⌚9am-12:30pm & 3-7pm Mon-Fri, 9am-noon Sat) This museum (closed for renovations at press time) holds a small but well-sorted collection of artifacts that illustrate the most interesting aspects of Tiwanaku culture.

Parque Raúl Salmón de la Barra PARK
(Map p182; off Bolívar, Miraflores; ⌚daylight) La Paz's city park has interesting skyways and the **Laikakota Mirador**. Traveling circuses will often set up here too.

EL ALTO

La Ceja NEIGHBORHOOD
In the lively La Ceja (Brow) district, you can find everything under the sun. For an excellent market experience don't miss the massive **Mercado 16 de Julio** (⌚6am-3pm Thu & Sun), which stretches for many blocks along the main thoroughfare and across Plaza 16 de Julio.

Activities

Mountain Biking

There are tons of mountain biking options just outside of La Paz. Intermediate riders can take on a thrilling downhill ride on the **World's Most Dangerous Road** (see boxed text, p189), while advanced riders may wish to go for the less traveled **Chacaltaya to Zongo Route**, the rides near **Sorata**, or include a bit of single track on the top of the **Dangerous Road Route** for an extra B$100. Beginners should check out the **Balcón Andino** descent near the Zona Sur.

Gravity Assisted Mountain Biking MOUNTAIN BIKING
(Map p182; ☎231-3849; www.gravitybolivia.com; Av 16 de Julio 1490 No 10, Edificio Avenida, Prado) The best operation in town. Its Dangerous Road trip (B$750 per person) ends with hot showers, an all-you-can-eat buffet and a tour of La Senda Verde Refugio Natural animal refuge near Yolosa.

B-Side MOUNTAIN BIKING
(Map p186; ☎211-4225; Linares 943, Rosario) B-Side is recommended for the La Cumbre to Coroico trip (B$310 to B$690 per person).

Trekking & Climbing

La Paz is the staging ground for most of the climbs in the Cordilleras. From here novice climbers can arrange trips to Huayna Potosí (two to three days, B$900 to B$1100), while more experienced climbers may look to climb Illimani (four to five days, US$485), Sajama (five days, US$650), Parinacota (four days, US$530) and beyond.

Except for the altitude, La Paz and its environs are made for hiking. Many La Paz tour agencies offer daily 'hiking' tours to Chacaltaya, a rough 35km drive north of La Paz, and an easy way to bag a high peak. Head to Valle de la Luna, Valle de las Animas or Muela del Diablo for do-it-yourself day-hikes from La Paz. Other longer day trips or guided tours take you to the Hampaturi Valley and Cotapata National Park.

Andean Summits CLIMBING
(☎242-2106; www.andeansummits.com; Muñoz Cornejo 1009, Sopocachi) Quality agency that offers a variety of outdoor activities including mountaineering and trekking.

La Paz on Foot ECOTOUR
(☎7154-3918, 224-8350; www.lapazonfoot.com; 400 Prolongación Posnanski, Miraflores) A tip-top operation for day hikes and longer treks.

Courses

Pico Verde Languages LANGUAGE COURSE
(Map p186; ☎231-9828; www.pico-verde.com; Sagárnaga 363, 2nd fl, Rosario) Plan on paying around B$60 per hour for individual instruction and B$30 to B$50 for group lessons.

Tours

Many of Bolivia's tour agencies are based in La Paz. Most agencies run day tours (B$70 to B$500 per person) in and around La Paz, as well as to Lake Titicaca, Tiwanaku, Zongo Valley, Chacaltaya, Valle de la Luna and other sites.

America Tours GUIDED TOUR
(Map p182; ☎02-237-4204; www.america-ecotours.com; Av 16 de Julio 1490 No 9, Prado) This recommended English-speaking agency offers a wide range of ecotourism projects and tours.

Madidi Travel ECOTOUR
(Map p186; ☎231-8313; www.madidi-travel.com; Linares 968, Rosario) Specializes in trips to Parque Nacional Madidi.

Magri Turismo GUIDED TOUR
(Map p182; ☎244-2727; www.magriturismo.com; Ca-pitán Ravelo 2101, Prado) Organizes a range of tours around Bolivia.

Turisbus GUIDED TOUR
(Map p186; ☎244-1756; www.turisbus.com; Illampu 704, Hotel Rosario, Rosario) A large range of day and multiday tours organized for groups and individuals.

Festivals & Events

Of the major festivals and holidays during the year, Alasitas (January 24), the festival of abundance, and El Gran Poder (late May to early June) are the most interesting to visitors. The Fiestas Universitarias take place during the first week in December, accompanied by riotous merrymaking and plenty of water-balloon bombs.

Sleeping

Most backpackers beeline for central La Paz to find a bed. The area around Mercado de Hechicería (Witches' Market; between Illampu, Santa Cruz and Sagárnaga) is about as close as Bolivia gets to a travelers ghetto. If you want to live closer to movie theaters, a wider array of restaurants and a bar or two, consider staying closer to Sopocachi.

Central La Paz – Sopocachi

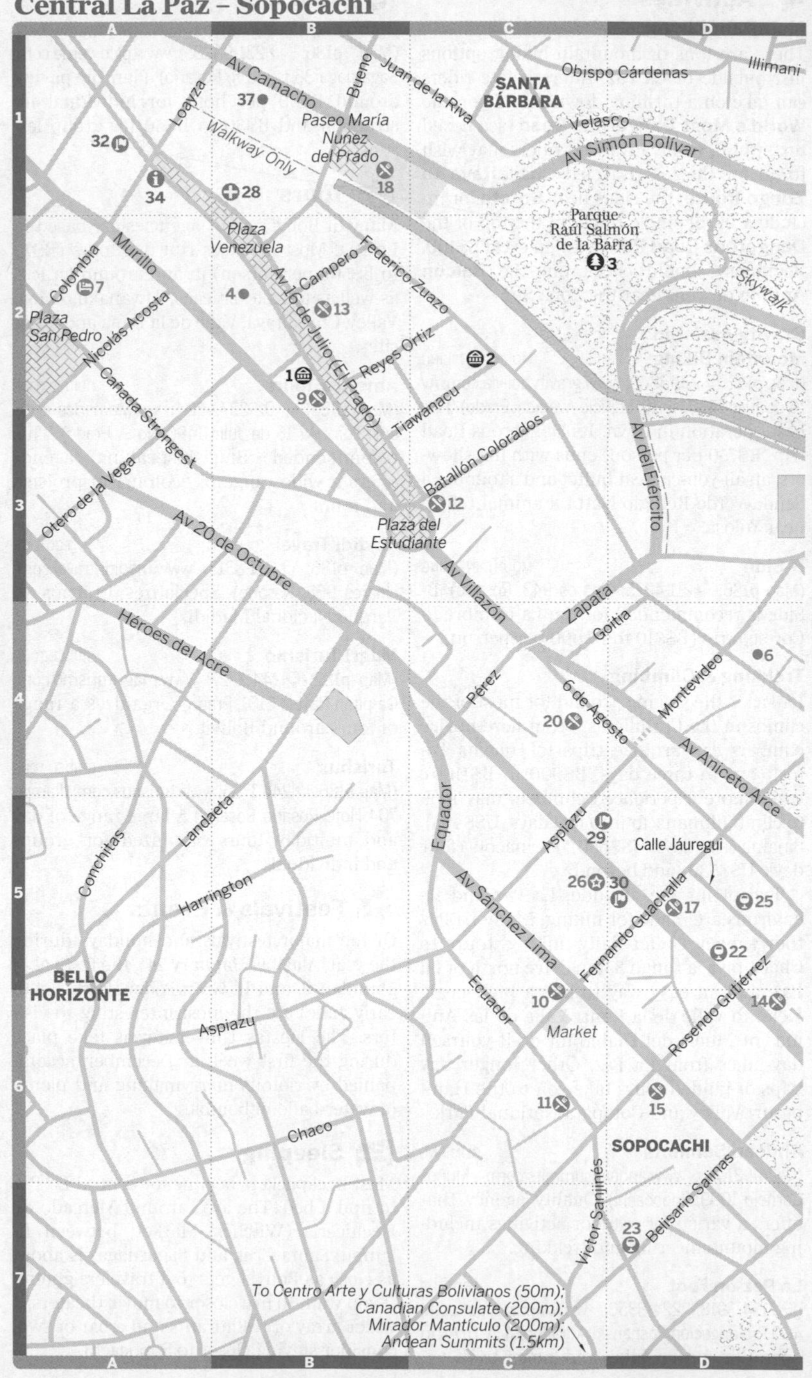

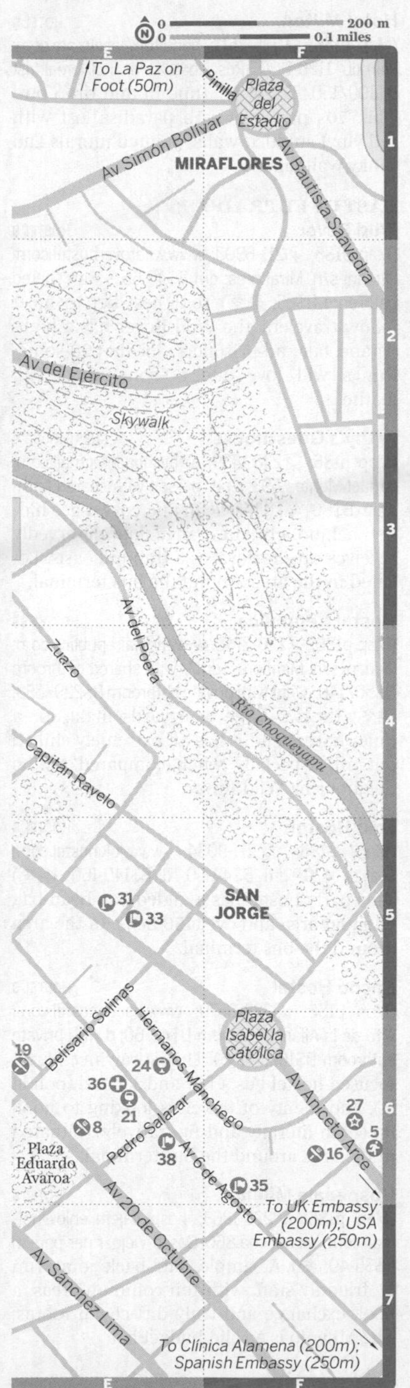

Central La Paz – Sopocachi

Sights

1 Museo de Arte Contemporáneo Plaza B2
2 Museo Nacional de Arqueología C2
3 Parque Raúl Salmón de la Barra C2

Activities, Courses & Tours

4 America Tours B2
5 Centro Boliviano-Americano F6
Gravity Assisted Mountain Biking .... (see 4)
6 Magri Turismo D4

Sleeping

7 Onkel Inn A2

Eating

8 Alexander Coffee & Pub E6
9 Alexander Coffee & Pub B2
10 Arco Iris C6
11 Armonía C6
12 Café Ciudad C3
13 Cafe La Terraza B2
14 Cafe La Terraza D6
15 Irupana D6
16 Ketal Hipermercado F6
17 La Guinguette D5
18 Mercado Camacho B1
19 Paceña La Salteña E6
20 Sergiu's Pizza C4

Drinking

21 Dead Stroke E6
22 Diesel Nacional D5
23 Green Bar D7
24 Mongo's E6
25 Reineke Fuchs D5

Entertainment

26 Thelonious Jazz Bar C5
27 Traffic Dance F6

Information

28 24-hour Pharmacy B1
29 Argentinian Embassy C5
30 Australian Consulate D5
31 Brazilian Embassy E5
32 Ecuadorian Embassy A1
33 German Embassy E5
34 InfoTur A1
35 Italian Embassy F6
36 Medicentro E6
37 Migración B1
38 Paraguayan Embassy E6

WEST OF EL PRADO

Onkel Inn HOSTEL $$
(Map p182; ☎249-0456; www.onkelinn.com; Colombia 257, Sopocachi; dm/s/d/tr incl breakfast B$60/200/250/300; @🛜) This bright, HI-affiliated place is in a fabulous spot between San Pedro and El Prado. It's less of a scene than the hostels up by the bus terminal, making it good for *tranquilo* travelers.

Hotel Las Brisas HOTEL $$
(Map p186; ☎246-3691; www.hotelbrisas.net; Illampu 742, Rosario; s/d/tr incl breakfast B$150/250/340; @🛜) A solid budget bet with a 'Bolivia *moderna*' style – think stark but neat rooms (some with internal windows), funky murals and crispy sheets.

Hotel Continental HOTEL $
(Map p186; ☎245-1176; www.hotelcontinentalbolivia.com; Illampu 626, Rosario; d/tr with private bathroom B$140/200, with shared bathroom B$120/170; 🛜) This dark and dreary downtown option is popular among thrift-sters.

Hostal Maya Inn HOTEL $
(Map p186; ☎231-1970; www.hostalmaya.com; Sagárnaga 339, Rosario; s/d incl breakfast B$90/160; @🛜) This is a friendly, if basic, place. The most appealing rooms have windows (note: a few don't), although rooms at the front can be a little noisy.

Hotel Sagárnaga HOTEL $
(Map p186; ☎235-0252; www.hotel-sagarnaga.com; Sagárnaga 326, Rosario; s/d/tr incl breakfast B$140/180/240; @🛜) East-facing rooms are the best, and decent solar showers should keep you warm come bath time.

EASY EATS

While they are a bit saccharine, these chain restaurants are a good spot if your stomach is easily upset.

Alexander Coffee & Pub (www.alexandercoffee.com; mains B$16-40; ⏲6am-11pm) Branches in Prado (Map p182; 16 de Julio 1832), Socabaya (Map p186; Calle Potosí 1091) and Sopocachi (Map p182; 20 de Octubre 2463).

Cafe La Terraza (mains B$10-40; ⏲until late) Branches in Prado (Map p182; 16 de Julio 1615) and Sopocachi (Map p182; 20 de Octubre 2331, Montenegro Bloque).

Hotel Milton HOTEL $
(Map p186; ☎235-3511; homilton@acelerate.com; Illampu 1126-1130, Rosario; s/d/tr incl breakfast B$100/150/225; @🛜) Tune in and drop out! This '70s pad truly is a paradise lost with red vinyl-studded walls, painted murals and funky wallpaper.

EAST OF EL PRADO

Wild Rover HOSTEL $
(Map p186; ☎211-6903; www.wildroverhostel.com; Illimani s/n, Miraflores; dm B$45-65, s with shared bathroom B$65; @🛜) Your best bet to meet fellow travelers, the Wild Rover has a high-octane, take-no-prisoners vibe that 20-somethings will love and 30-somethings will loathe.

Arthy's Guesthouse GUESTHOUSE $
(Map p186; ☎228-1439; arthyshouse@gmail.com; Ismael Montes 693; r per person with shared bathroom B$80; @) This clean and cozy place hidden behind a bright orange door deservedly receives rave reviews as a tranquil oasis. Located in the area around the bus terminal.

Hostal República HOSTEL $$
(Map p186; ☎220-2742; www.hostalrepublica.com; Illimani s/n, Miraflores; dm/s with shared bathroom B$50/140, d/apt with private bathroom B$229/553; @🛜) Its two large courtyards make for a quiet haven, and it has an extremely chilled out air, especially when compared to the neighboring Wild Rover.

Loki Hostel HOSTEL $
(Map p186; ☎211-9034; www.lokihostel.com; Loayza 420; dm B$44-60, d B$140-160; @🛜) This party hostel has a gilded bar, bean-bag hangout area and over 180 beds. In the area around the bus terminal.

Bacoo Hostel HOSTEL $
(Map p186; ☎228-0679; www.bacoohostel.com; Alto de la Alianza 693; dm B$40-60, d with private bathroom B$160; @🛜) This sprawling party-focused hostel has a bar and Jacuzzi (ooh la la), and plenty of travelers looking to hook up (both literally and figuratively). Situated in the area around the bus terminal.

Hospedaje Milenio HOTEL $
(Map p186; ☎228-1263; hospedajemilenio@hotmail.com; Yanacocha 860, Casco Viejo; r per person B$35-40; 🛜) A simple, laid-back joint run by friendly staff, with fun common areas, a book exchange and truly dirt-cheap rooms. The Milenio is a solid budget bet.

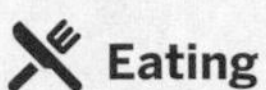

Eating

For local fare, your cheapest bets are the *almuerzos* (set lunches) in the countless hole-in-the-wall restaurants; look for the chalkboard menus out front. Street stalls and markets offer tasty morsels, and there are vegetarian restaurants around.

If you don't mind the hectic settings and questionable hygiene, your most interesting (and cheapest) food options are found in the markets. The *comedor* (dining hall) at **Mercado Uruguay** off Max Paredes, sells set meals (of varying standards and in basic surrounds), including tripe and *ispi* (similar to sardines), for less than B$8. Other areas to look for cheap and informal meals include the street markets around **Av Buenos Aires**, and the **Mercado Camacho** (Map p182; cnr Avs Simón Bolívar & Bueno), known for its juice stands, fresh breads and puffy *llauchas* (cheese pastries).

WEST OF EL PRADO

Ángelo Colonial INTERNATIONAL $$
(Map p186; ☎236-0199; Linares 922, Rosario; mains B$20-50) This quirky, dimly lit colonial-style restaurant features a ramshackle collection of antiquities, plus excellent soups, salads and luscious veggie lasagna.

La Guinguette FRENCH $$
(Map p182; Fernando Guachalla 399, Sopocachi; mains B$45-70; ⏲9am-11pm Mon-Sat) Hang out with the Sopocachi cool cats at this chic spot below the Alianza Francesa.

Star of India INDIAN $$
(Map p186; Cochabamba 170, Rosario; mains B$32-45; ✎) Worthy of a London curry-house (the owner is British), this place is hot.

Martiani Pizza PIZZERIA $
(Map p186; Illampu 738, Rosario; B$20-35; ⏲1-9:30pm Mon-Sat) This is a damn good pie, with crispy crust, fresh ingredients and plenty of savory thrust in the sauce.

Paceña La Salteña FAST FOOD $
(Map p182; Av 20 de Octubre 2379, Sopocachi; salteña B$5-10; ⏲8:30am-2pm) Eating a *salteña* (a baked stuffed pastry) is a not-to-be-missed local experience.

Armonía VEGETARIAN $
(Map p182; Ecuador 2284, Sopocachi; buffet B$29; ⏲lunch Mon-Sat; ✎) A recommended all-you-can-eat vegetarian lunch is found above Librería Armonía in Sopocachi. Organic products are served when possible.

Sergiu's Pizza PIZZERIA $
(Map p182; 6 de Agosto 2040, Prado; slices from B$12; ⏲from 5pm) Popular among students, this evening-only hole-in-the-wall near the Aspiazu steps serves up a reasonable NYC-style pizza and fast foods.

Pepe's Coffee Bar CAFE $
(Map p186; Jiménez 894, Rosario; snacks B$10-25) This cheery, inviting, artsy cafe is tucked away on a sunny bend in the Witches' Market.

Irupana SUPERMARKET
(Map p186; cnr Murillo 1014 & Tarija, Rosario) Locally made organic produce is sold at this health-food chain. There is another branch in **Sopocachi** (Map p182; cnr Fernando Guachalla & Av Sanchez Lima, Sopocachi).

Arco Iris SUPERMARKET
(Map p182; Fernando Guachalla 554, Sopocachi; ⏲8am-8pm Mon-Sat) Arco Iris has an extensive *pastelería* (cake shop) and deli featuring fine regional specialties.

Ketal Hipermercado SUPERMARKET
(Map p182; cnr Av Aniceto Arce & Pinilla, Sopocachi) Stock up at this supermarket.

EAST OF EL PRADO

Café Ciudad INTERNATIONAL $
(Map p182; Plaza del Estudiante, Prado; B$15-40; ⏲24hr daily; 📶) This La Paz institution serves up warm coffee, surly service, yummy pizzas, hamburgers and other international favorites, plus one of the best *pique machos* (Bolivian dish with sausages and french fries in a savory sauce) in town.

Confitería Club de La Paz CAFE $
(Map p186; cnr Avs Camacho & Mariscal Santa Cruz, Prado; mains B$10-30) For a quick coffee or empanada, join the well-dressed elderly patrons in their daily rituals. The cafe was formerly renowned as a literary cafe and haunt of politicians (and, formerly, of Nazi war criminals).

Confitería Manantial VEGETARIAN $
(Map p186; Potosí 909, Hotel Gloria, Casco Viejo; buffet B$25; ⏲lunch Mon-Sat; ✎) This place has a good-value, popular veggie buffet. Arrive before 12:30pm or you risk missing the best dishes.

Drinking

Bocaisapo PUB
(Map p186; Jaén, Casco Viejo; ⏲7pm-late Thu-Sat) This bohemian favorite has live music and a maddening elixir de coca drink.

Central La Paz – El Prado

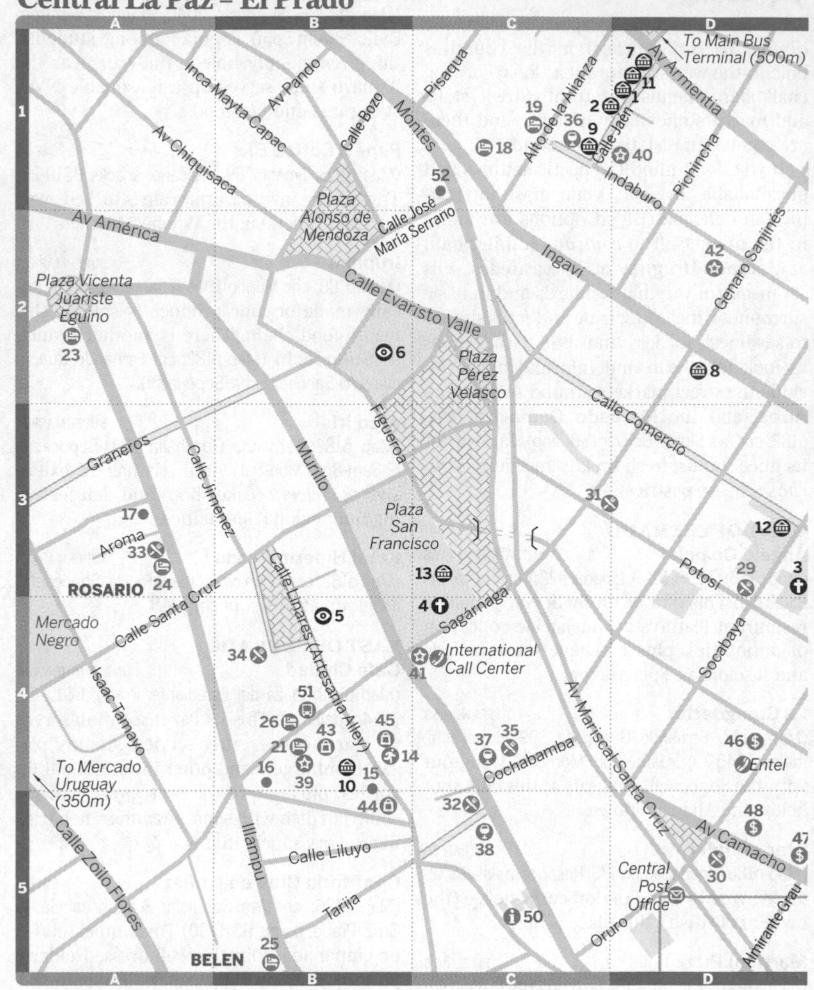

Mongo's PUB

(Map p182; Hermanos Manchego 2444, Sopocachi; ⏲6pm-3am) Mongo's is a perennial favorite. The experience includes dancing on the tables in addition to excellent pub grub (mains B$30 to B$60) and with a good mix of locals and tourists.

Café Sol y Luna PUB

(Map p186; cnr Murillo & Cochabamba, Rosario; ⏲9am-1am) A low-key, Dutch-run hangout offering cocktails, good coffee and tasty international meals.

Green Bar PUB

(Map p182; Belisario Salinas 596, Sopocachi) A cloistered pub setting with intellectual types.

Diesel Nacional LOUNGE

(Map p182; Av 20 de Octubre 2271, Sopocachi; ⏲from 7:30pm Mon-Sat) The postmodern reality escape for overpriced drinks with the rich kids.

Oliver's Travels PUB

(Map p186; cnr Murillo & Cochabamba, 2nd fl, Rosario) The worst (or best?) cultural experience in La Paz is to be had at this pub, thanks to its crowd of mainly foreign revelers.

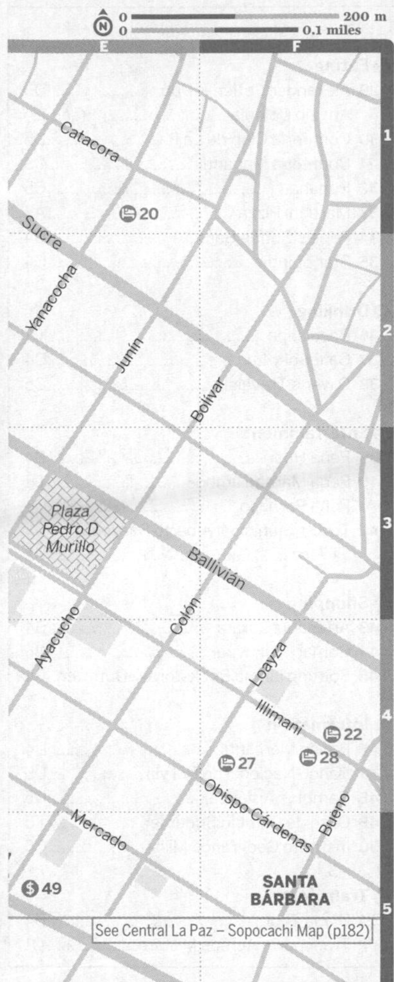

Reineke Fuchs BEER HALL
(Map p182; Jáuregui 2241, Sopocachi; ⏲from 6pm Mon-Sat) Sopocachi brewhaus featuring imported German beers.

Dead Stroke BAR
(Map p182; Av 6 de Agosto 2460; ⏲from 5pm Mon-Sat) An upbeat and marginally sleazy billiards bar with cable TV.

☆ Entertainment

Typical of La Paz (and most of Bolivia) are folk-music venues known as *peñas*. Most present traditional Andean music is rendered on *zampoñas* (pan flute), *quenas* (simple reed flute) and *charangos*, but also often include guitar shows and song recitals. Many *peñas* advertise nightly shows, but in reality most only have shows on Friday and Saturday nights, starting at 9pm or 10pm and lasting until 1am or 2am. Admission ranges from B$30 to B$80 and usually includes the first drink; meals cost extra.

Pick up a copy of the free monthly booklet *Kaos* (available in bars and cafes) for a day-by-day rundown of what's on in La Paz.

Soccer matches are played at Estadio Hernando Siles (Estadio Olímpico La Paz; Miraflores). Sunday (year-round) is the big game day, and Wednesday and Saturday also have games. Prices vary according to seats and whether it's a local or international game (B$20 to B$100).

Peña Marka Tambo TRADITIONAL MUSIC
(Map p186; ☎228-0041; Jaén 710, Casco Viejo; cover charge B$35; ⏲from 8pm Thu-Sat) A less expensive – and some claim more traditional – *peña*.

Peña Huari TRADITIONAL MUSIC
(Map p186; ☎231-6225; Sagárnaga 339, Rosario; cover charge B$105; ⏲show 8pm nightly) The city's best-known *peña* is aimed at tourists and Bolivian business people. The attached restaurant specializes in Bolivian cuisine; the buffet dinner costs B$100.

Peña Parnaso TRADITIONAL MUSIC
(Map p186; ☎231-6827; Sagárnaga 189, Rosario; cover charge B$80; ⏲show 8:30pm) Also open for lunch (B$35) with no show.

Centro Arte y Culturas Bolivianos LIVE MUSIC
(Ecuador 2582, Sopocachi) This arts complex has rotating exhibits, live music (Thursday through Saturday), a decent restaurant and terrace cafe. It's called the Luna Llena Rock Bar come 8pm.

Thelonious Jazz Bar JAZZ
(Map p182; Av 20 de Octubre 2172, Sopocachi; cover charge around B$25; ⏲7pm-3am Mon-Sat) Bebop fans love this charmingly low-key bar.

Traffic Dance DANCE
(Map p182; www.trafficsanjorge.com; Av Aniceto Arce 2549, Prado) Slightly cheesy dance spot.

Teatro Municipal Alberto Saavedra Pérez THEATER
(Map p186; cnr Sanjinés & Indaburo, Casco Viejo; tickets B$20-50) This theater has an ambitious

Central La Paz – El Prado

Sights

1	Calle Jaén Museums	D1
2	Casa de Murillo	C1
3	Cathedral	D3
4	Iglesia de San Francisco	C4
5	Mercado de Hechicería	B4
6	Mercado Lanza	B2
7	Museo Costumbrista Juan de Vargas	D1
8	Museo de Etnografía y Folklore	D2
9	Museo de Instrumentos Musicales	C1
10	Museo de la Coca	B4
11	Museo de Metales Preciosos	D1
	Museo del Litoral	(see 11)
12	Museo Nacional del Arte	D3
13	Museo San Francisco	C3

Activities, Courses & Tours

14	B-Side	B4
15	Madidi Travel	B4
16	Pico Verde Languages	B4
17	Turisbus	A3

Sleeping

18	Arthy's Guesthouse	C1
19	Bacoo Hostel	C1
20	Hospedaje Milenio	E1
21	Hostal Maya Inn	B4
22	Hostal República	F4
23	Hotel Continental	A2
24	Hotel Las Brisas	A3
25	Hotel Milton	B5
26	Hotel Sagárnaga	B4
27	Loki Hostel	F4
28	Wild Rover	F4

Eating

29	Alexander Coffee & Pub	D3
	Ángelo Colonial	(see 15)
30	Confitería Club de La Paz	D5
31	Confitería Manantial	C3
32	Irupana	C5
33	Martiani Pizza	A3
34	Pepe's Coffee Bar	B4
35	Star of India	C4

Drinking

36	Bocaisapo	C1
37	Café Sol y Luna	C4
38	Oliver's Travels	C5

Entertainment

39	Peña Huari	B4
40	Peña Marka Tambo	D1
41	Peña Parnaso	C4
42	Teatro Municipal Alberto Saavedra Pérez	D2

Shopping

43	Artesanía Sorata	B4
44	Comart Tukuypaj	B5
45	Spitting Llama Bookstore & Outfitter	B4

Information

46	Banco Mercantil	D4
47	Banco Nacional de Bolivia	D5
48	Cambios América	D5
49	Casa de Cambio Sudamer	E5
50	Instituto Geográfico Militar	C5

Transport

51	Diana Tours	B4
52	Transporte Aéreos Militares	C1

program of folklore shows, folk-music concerts and foreign theatrical presentations.

Shopping

La Paz is a shopper's paradise; not only are prices very reasonable, but the quality of what's offered can be astounding. The main tourist shopping area lies along the very steep and literally breathtaking Calle Sagárnaga between Santa Cruz and Tamayo, and spreads out along adjoining streets. Here, you'll also find Calle Linares, an alley chock-a-block with artisans' stores.

To trade books, the best library is Oliver's Travels bar. Or try Gravity Assisted Mountain Biking or Café Sol y Luna.

Artesanía Sorata ARTS & CRAFTS
(Map p186; www.artesaniasorata.com; Sagárnaga 363, Rosario) A community-focused project.

Comart Tukuypaj ARTS & CRAFTS
(Map p186; www.comart-tukuypaj.com; Linares 958, Rosario) Offers export-quality, fair-trade llama, alpaca and *artesanías* from around the country.

Spitting Llama Bookstore & Outfitter OUTDOOR EQUIPMENT
(Map p186; www.thespittingllama.com; Linares 947) Inside Posada de la Abuela, this friendly one-stop shop stocks everything from maps to gear, including tents, backpacks and hiking boots.

DEADLY TREADLIES & THE WORLD'S MOST DANGEROUS ROAD

Many agencies offering the La Cumbre to Coroico mountain-bike plunge give travelers T-shirts boasting about surviving the road. Keep in mind that the gravel road is narrow (just over 3.2m wide), with precipitous cliffs with up to 600m drops and few safety barriers.

In March 2007 a new replacement road opened. Prior to this, the road between La Paz and Coroico was identified as the World's Most Dangerous Road (WMDR) by an Inter-American Development Bank (IDB) report, citing an average of 26 vehicles per year that disappeared over the edge into the great abyss.

With the new road up and running, the old road – the WMDR – is now used almost exclusively by cyclists, support vehicles and the odd tourist bus.

Around 15 cyclists have died doing the 64km trip (with a 3600m vertical descent) and readers have reported close encounters and nasty accidents. Be careful when selecting your agency – talk with the guide, look at the bike, inspect brake pads and gears, and ask what they do to prevent accidents. Cheaper isn't always necessarily better.

Nuts & Bolts

The trip begins around 7am in La Paz. Your agency will arrange a hotel pickup. From there, you bus it up to the *cumbre* (summit), about 45 minutes outside La Paz. Trips cost anywhere from B$310 to B$750, but you get what you pay for. Advanced riders can include a fun section of single track up top for an extra B$100. Most operations provide a solid buffet lunch in Coroico, and some even have arrangements with hotels for showers/swimming pool rights. There is a B$25 surcharge to use the old road. Bring sunscreen, a swimsuit and dust-rag (if they don't provide one), and ask about water allotments. The bus picks you back up in the early evening. Expect to arrive back in La Paz at around 9pm.

Information

Dangers & Annoyances

La Paz has become increasingly dangerous; see p180 for tips on staying safe.

La Paz is a great city to explore on foot, but take the local advice '*camina lento, toma poco... y duerme solo*' (walk slowly, drink little... and sleep by your lonesome) to avoid feeling the effects of *soroche* (altitude sickness). *Soroche* pills are said to be ineffective, and can even increase altitude sickness. Acetaminophen (also known as Tylenol or paracetemol) does work, and drinking lots of water helps too.

In the last couple of years, it seems traffic has increased tenfold due in part to secondhand car imports – take care when crossing roads and avoid walking in busy streets at peak hours when fumes can be overwhelming.

Protests are not uncommon in La Paz (and they do sometimes turn violent). These center around Plazas San Francisco and Murillo.

Emergency

Fire & Ambulance (☎118)

Police (Radio Patrol; ☎110)

Tourist Police (Policía Turística; ☎800-140-071; Puerta 22, Plaza del Estadio, Miraflores) Report thefts here to obtain a *denuncia* (affidavit) for insurance purposes – they won't recover any stolen goods. They also have a kiosk in front of the bus terminal. English-speaking. Next to Disco Love City.

Immigration Offices

Migración (Map p182; ☎211-0960; www.migracion.gob.bo; Camacho 1468; ⏰8:30am-4pm Mon-Fri) Some call this place 'Migraine-ation,' but this is where you must obtain your visa extensions.

Internet Access

Charges range from B$1 to B$3 an hour. Many of the smarter cafes and most hotels now have wi-fi access.

Media

La Razón (www.la-razon.com), *El Diario* (www.eldiario.net) and *La Prensa* (www.laprensa.com.bo) are La Paz's major daily newspapers. National media chains **ATB** (www.bolivia.com) and **Grupo Fides** (www.radiofides.com) host the most up-to-date online news sites. *Bolivia Weekly* (www.boliviaweekly.com) for up-to-date English headlines.

Medical Services

For serious medical emergency conditions, contact your embassy for doctor recommendations.

24-hour Pharmacy (Farmacia 24 Horas; Map p182; cnr Av 16 de Julio; ⏰24hr) A good pharmacy on the Prado.

Clínica Alemana (☎432-521; Av 60 de Agosto; ⏲24hr) Twenty-four-hour service and German efficiency.

Centro Epidemiológico Departamental La Paz (Centro Pilote; ☎245-0166; Vásquez near Perú; ⏲8:30am-11:30am Mon-Fri) Antimalarials, and rabies and yellow fever vaccinations.

High Altitude Pathology Institute (☎7325-8026, 224-5394; www.altitudeclinic.com; Saavedra 2302, Miraflores) English spoken.

Medicentro (Map p182; ☎243-2521; Av 6 de Agosto 2821, Prado; ⏲24hr) Twenty-four-hour service recommended for general care.

Money

Cash withdrawals of bolivianos and US dollars are possible at numerous ATMs at major intersections around the city. For cash advances (bolivianos only; amount according to your limit in your home country) with no commission and little hassle, try the Lonely Planet–listed options.

Try Western Union/DHL, which has outlets scattered all around town, for urgent international money transfers.

Casas de cambio (exchange bureaux) in the city center can be quicker and more convenient than banks.

Be wary of counterfeit US dollars and bolivianos, especially with *cambistas* (street money changers) who loiter around the intersections of Colón, Camacho and Santa Cruz. Traveler's checks can be virtually impossible to change, except at money changers and banks.

Banco Mercantil (Map p186; cnr Mercado & Ayacucho)

Banco Nacional de Bolivia (Map p186; cnr Colón & Camacho)

Cambios América (Map p186; Camacho 1223, Casco Viejo) Money-changing bureau.

Casa de Cambio Sudamer (Map p186; Colón 206 near Camacho, Casco Viejo; ⏲8:30am-6:30pm Mon-Fri, 9:30am-12:30pm Sat) Also has Moneygram service for money transfers.

Post

Central Post Office (Ecobol; cnr Mariscal Santa Cruz & Oruro, Prado; ⏲8am-8pm Mon-Fri, 8:30am-6pm Sat, 9am-noon Sun) *Lista de correos* (*poste restante*) mail is held for two months for free here – bring your passport. A downstairs customs desk facilitates international parcel posting.

Telephone

Convenient *puntos* (privately run phone offices) of various carriers – Entel, Cotel, Tigo, Viva etc – are scattered throughout the city, and some mobile services now have wandering salesman who will allow you to make a call from their cell phone. Street kiosks, which are on nearly every corner, also sell phone cards, and offer brief local calls for around B$1 per minute. You can buy cell phone sim cards (known as *chips*) for around B$10 from Entel or any carrier outlet.

Entel (Ayacucho 267, Casco Viejo; ⏲8:30am-9pm Mon-Fri, to 8:30pm Sat, 9am-4pm Sun)

International Call Center (Galería Chuquiago, cnr Sagárnaga & Murillo; ⏲8:30am-8pm)

Tourist Information

Free city maps are available at the tourist offices and inside the central post office.

Information Kiosks (Main bus terminal) They have maps and may help you find a hotel.

InfoTur (Map p182; ☎265-1778; www.visitbolivia.org; cnr Avs Mariscal Santa Cruz & Colombia, Prado; ⏲8:30am-7pm Mon-Fri, 9:30am-1pm Sat & Sun) English is spoken by some staff.

Getting There & Away

Most travelers will arrive at either El Alto International Airport or the main bus terminal. Buses from within Bolivia may also drop you in Villa Fátima or the Plaza 1 de Mayo area.

Air

El Alto International Airport (LPB) is 10km via toll-road from the city center on the Altiplano. The domestic departure tax is B$15, while the international departure tax is US$25 (payable in cash-only in the airport lobby).

Minibus 212 runs frequently between Plaza Isabel la Católica and the airport between around 7am and 8pm. Heading into town from the airport, this service will drop you anywhere along the Prado.

Radio taxis (around B$50 for up to four people) will pick you up at your door; confirm the price when booking, or ask the driver to verify it when you climb in. For a fifth person, there is an additional B$10 charge. Transportes Aéreos Militares (TAM) flights leave from the military airport in El Alto. Catch a Río Seco *micro* (small bus or minibus) from the upper Prado. Taxi fares should be about the same as for the main El Alto airport.

Times and schedules change often. Check online and call ahead. See p259 for international airlines and p260 for domestic ones.

Bus

La Paz has three bus terminals/bus areas. You can use the main bus terminal for most national and international destinations. If you are going to the Yungas or the Amazon, you'll need to go to Villa Fátima. For Sorata, Titicaca and Tiwanaku, head to the Cemetery area. Most national destinations are serviced hourly for major cities and daily for less-visited spots. International departures generally leave once weekly; check ahead as schedules change. You can get to all the bus areas by *micro*, but radio taxis are recommended for your safety.

Tourist bus services to Copacabana, Puno (book with La Paz tour agencies), Tiwanaku, Uyuni and Valle de la Luna cut down on risk and up your comfort.

Bolivia en tus Manos (www.boliviaentusmanos.com/terminal)

Diana Tours (Map p186; www.diana-tours.com; Main Bus Terminal; B$60) Round-trip guided tour to Valle de la Luna, leaving at 8:30am.

Nuevo Continente (Main Bus Terminal; B$60) Round-trip guided tours to Tiwanaku, leaving at 9am and returning at 4pm.

Todo Turismo (www.todoturismo.bo; Main Bus Terminal; B$230) Direct overnight buses to Uyuni leaving at 9pm (10hrs).

MAIN TERMINAL

The **main bus terminal** (Terminal de Buses; Plaza Antofagasta) services all national destinations south and east of La Paz, as well as international destinations. It is a 15-minute uphill walk north of the city center. Fares are relatively uniform between companies. The station was designed by Gustave Eiffel.

DESTINATION	COST (B$)	DURATION (HR)
Arica	130	8
Buenos Aires	650	48-50
Copacabana	35	3-4
Cochabamba	43-90	7-8
Cuzco	130	12-17
Iquique	150	11-13
Lima	500-600	27
Oruro	23-60	3.5
Potosí	52-110	8
Puno	100	8
Santa Cruz (new road)	85-170	17
Santa Cruz (old road)	95-180	20
Sucre	69-135	14
Tarija	115-215	24
Tupiza	90	20
Uyuni	72-155	10
Villazón	90-200	23

CEMETERY AREA

Buses leaving the Cemetery (Baptista La Paz) offers cheap service to Tiwanaku, Titicaca and Sorata (via Desaguadero). This area is especially hairy at night, and you should watch your bags while boarding.

DESTINATION	COST (B$)	DURATION (HR)
Copacabana	15	3
Desaguadero	15	2
Huarina (for Cordillera Apolobamba)	10	3
Sorata	17	5
Tiwanaku	6-15	1.5

VILLA FÁTIMA

Villa Fátima (Tejada Sorzano) services Coroico, and other Yungas and Amazon destinations, mostly via microbus. It's about 1km uphill from Plaza Gualberto Villarroel. There's no central station, so ask around to find the buses servicing your particular destination. Offices on Yanacachi, by an old gas station, service Coroico; on Av Las Américas, also by a gas station, service the Amazon Basin; and on San Jorge, service Chulumani. There are more operations clustered along Virgen del Carmen, just west of Av Las Américas.

DESTINATION	COST ($B)	DURATION (HR)
Caranavi	15-25	8
Chulumani	20	4
Coroico	20-30	3
Cumbre	20	1
Rurrenabaque	120	18-20
Yolosita	20	3

Getting Around

MICRO & MINIBUS La Paz's sputtering and smoke-spewing *micros* (small bus or minibus) charge around B$2 per trip. Minibuses service most places as well, for a slightly higher cost. In addition to a route number or letter, *micros* plainly display their destination and route on a signboard posted in the front window. Minibuses usually have a young tout screaming the stops. Wave to catch the bus. They stop at signed *paradas* (official stops), or if the cops aren't watching, whenever you wave them down.

SHARED CARS & MINIBUSES *Trufis* are shared cars or minibuses that ply set routes. Destinations are identified on placards on the roof or windscreen. They charge approximately B$3 around town and B$4 to Zona Sur.

RADIO TAXI Radio taxis (with roof bubbles advertising their telephone numbers) are recommended. They charge about B$10 around the center, B$12 to B$14 (more in peak hours) from Sagárnaga to Sopocachi or Sopocachi to the Cemetery district, and B$15 to B$20 to Zona Sur. Charges are a little higher after 11pm. Normal taxi service (with just a taxi sign, no phone number and no bubble) works as a collective cabs, charging each passenger around B$6, but these are known for express kidnappings.

If possible, ask your hotel or restaurant to ring for a taxi. Otherwise, taxis can be waved down anywhere, except near intersections or in areas cordoned off by the police. Always confirm the fair before you go anywhere.

AROUND LA PAZ

Tiwanaku

While it's no Machu Picchu or Tikal, a visit to the ruins of Tiwanaku (sometimes spelled Tiahuanaco or Tihuanaco) makes for a good day trip from La Paz. The site itself is less than outstanding, with a few carved monoliths, archways and arcades, and a decent museum, but history buffs will love diving into the myths and mysteries of this lost civilization. In the eponymous village, there are a number of hotels, restaurants, a fun little plaza with excellent sculptures inspired by Tiwanaku styles and a 16th-century church, built, no doubt, with stones from the Tiwanaku site.

Little is actually known about the people who constructed the ceremonial center on the southern shore of Lake Titicaca more than a thousand years ago. Archaeologists generally agree that the civilization that spawned Tiwanaku rose around 600 BC. Construction on the ceremonial site was under way by about AD 700, but by around AD1200 the group had melted into obscurity, becoming another 'lost' civilization. Evidence of its influence, particularly its religion, has been found throughout the vast area that later became the Inca empire.

Visiting the Ruins

Entrance to the **site and museum** (B$80; ⏲tickets 9am-4pm, site open until 5pm) is paid opposite the visitors center. If you go on your own, start your visit in the museum to get a basic understanding of the history, then head to the ruins. Guided **tours** (✆7524-3141; tiwanakuguias_turismo@hotmail.com; B$80 for 1-6 people) are available in English and Spanish, and are highly recommended.

The star of the show at the on-site museum is the massive 7.3m Monolito Bennett Pachamama, rescued in 2002 from its former smoggy home at the outdoor Templete Semisubterráneo in La Paz.

Just 100m west of the site, **Hotel Akapana** (✆289-5104; www.hotelakapana; Ferrocarril; s/d incl breakfast B$80/150) has three levels, simple rooms with good views, hot water 24 hours a day, and a top-floor mirador with amazing views of the neighboring site.

Getting There & Away

Many La Paz agencies offer reasonably priced, guided, full- and half-day Tiwanaku tours (B$70 to B$140 per person), including transportation and a bilingual guide.

Nuevo Continente (Main Bus Terminal; B$60) has round-trip guided trips to Tiwanaku, leaving from La Paz's main bus terminal at 9am and returning at 4pm.

For those who prefer to go it alone, buses from La Paz's Cemetery leave every hour, and cost between B$6 and B$15.

Minibuses, which are often crowded, pass the museum near the entrance to the complex. To return to La Paz, catch a minibus from the village's main plaza. Make sure it says Cemeterio, otherwise, you'll get dropped off in El Alto's Ceja.

Empresa Ferroviaria Andina (FCA; ✆241-6545; www.fca.com.bo) has started a pilot program to run occasional return train trips from La Paz's El Alto to Tiwanaku (with a 1.5-hour stop) and to Guaqui on Lake Titicaca (with a two-hour stop). The train departs La Paz the second Sunday of each month at 8am (B$10 to B$40). Check the website or call ahead.

LAKE TITICACA

A visit to the world's largest high-altitude lake feels like a journey to the top of the world. Everything – and everyone – that sits beside this impressive body of water, from the traditional Aymará villages to the glacier-capped peaks of the Cordillera Real, seem to fall into the background, the singularity, power and sheer gravity of the lake pulling all eyes, all energy and all power to its massive depths.

Set between Peru and Bolivia at 3808m, the 8400-sq-km lake offers plenty of activities to keep you busy for at least a week. There are trips to the many islands that speckle the shore-line, hikes to lost coves and floating islands, parties in the tourist hub of Copacabana, and chance encounters with locals that will provide new insight into the culture and traditions of Bolivia's top attraction.

Lake Titicaca

Copacabana

☎02 / POP 54,300

Nestled between two hills and perched on the southern shore of Lake Titicaca, Copacabana (Copa) is a small, bright and enchanting town. For centuries it was the site of religious pilgrimages, and today, local and international pilgrims flock to its fiestas.

Although it can appear a little tourist-ready, the town is a pleasant place to wander around. It has scenic walks along the lake and beyond, is the launching pad for visiting Isla del Sol and Isla de la Luna, and makes a pleasant stopover between La Paz and Puno or Cuzco (Peru).

Sights & Activities

Much of the action in Copa centers around Plaza 2 de Febrero and 6 de Agosto, the main commercial drag, which runs east to west. The transportation hub is at Plaza Sucre. At its western end is the lake and a walkway (Costañera), which traces the lakeshore.

The sparkling Moorish-style **cathedral** (6 de Agosto) dominates the town with its domes and colourful azulejos (blue Portuguese-style ceramic tiles). The famous black Virgin de Candelaria statue is housed upstairs in the Camarín de la Virgen de Candelaria (open all day but hours are unreliable). The colorful Bendiciones de Movilidades (cha'lla; blessing of automobiles) occurs daily (though more reliably on weekends) during the festival season at 10am in front of the cathedral.

The hill north of town is **Cerro Calvario** and can be reached in 30 minutes on foot and is well worth the climb, particularly at sunset. The trail to the summit begins near the church at the end of Destacamento 211 and climbs past the 14 stations of the cross.

Other sights around town (all with sporadic opening hours) include the pre-Inca

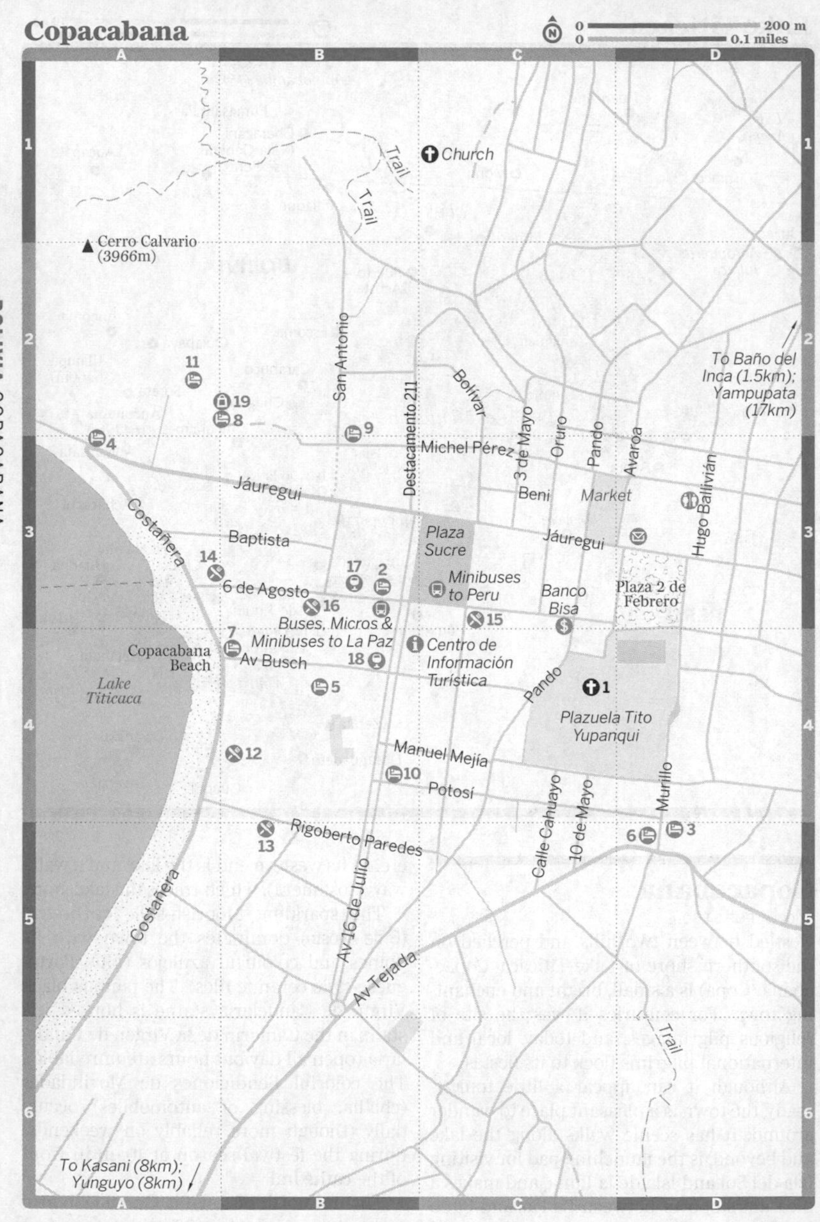

astronomical observatory at **Horca del Inca** (admission B$10); the neglected **Tribunal del Inca** (admission B$5) north of the cemetery; and the community of **Kusijata** (admission B$5) with a small archaeological display 3km northeast of town, with the **Baño del Inca** nearby.

Head to the lakeshore to rent all manner of boating craft, bicycles (B$70 per day) and motorbikes (B$50 per hour).

Copacabana

Sights

1 Cathedral C4

Sleeping

2 Hostal 6 de Agosto B3
3 Hostal Emperador D5
4 Hostal Flores del Lago A3
5 Hostal Los Andes B4
6 Hostal Sonia D5
7 Hostel Leyenda B4
8 Hotel La Cúpula B2
9 Hotel Utama B2
10 Hotel Wendy Mar B4
11 Las Olas A2

Eating

12 Beachfront Stalls B4
13 Kota Kahuaña B5
La Cúpula Restaurant .... (see 8)
14 La Orilla A3
15 Pensión Aransaya C3
16 Pueblo El Viejo B3

Drinking

17 Nemo's B3
18 Waykys B4

Shopping

19 Hotel La Cúpula B2

Hiking, biking or simply busing along the road from Copacabana to Yampupata, a small hamlet about 17km north of town, is a fun little adventure.

Festivals & Events

Alasitas Festival SPIRITUAL
A Bolivian tradition is the blessing of miniature objects, like cars or houses, at the Alasitas festival, as a prayer that the real thing will be obtained in the coming year.

Fiesta de la Virgen de Candelaria RELIGIOUS
Following Alasitas, the Fiesta de la Virgen de Candelaria is celebrated from February 2 to February 5. Pilgrims from Peru and Bolivia perform traditional Aymará dances amid much music, drinking and feasting.

Good Friday RELIGIOUS
The town fills with pilgrims, who join a solemn candlelit procession at dusk.

Independence Day FIESTA
(⏲first week in August) The biggest fiesta lasts for a week around Independence Day.

Sleeping

A host of budget options abound, charging around B$30 per person (significantly more in high season and during festivals), especially along Calle Jáuregui. Water is scarce here, so watch your shower time, and expect some cold water.

TOP CHOICE **Las Olas** BOUTIQUE HOTEL $$
(☎7250-8668; www.hostallasolas.com; Michel Pérez 1-3; s B$210-224, d B$266-294; @📶) In a few words: quirky, creative, stylish, ecofriendly, million-dollar vistas. Plus there are kitchens, private terraces with hammocks, and a solar-powered Jacuzzi. You get the idea – a once-in-a-lifetime experience, and well worth the splurge. Reserve one to two weeks ahead, and get here by passing by La Cúpula, the partner hotel.

Hotel La Cúpula HOTEL $$
(☎862-2029; www.hotelcupula.com; Michel Pérez 1-3; s/d/ste B$133/210/266; 📶) International travelers rave about this inviting oasis, marked by two gleaming white domes on the slopes of Cerro Calvario, with stupendous lake views. The rooms are pretty basic and the beds will be too soft for some.

Hostel Leyenda HOSTEL $
(☎7067-4097; hostel.leyenda@gmail.com; cnr Avs Busch & Constañera; s/d incl breakfast B$80/120; 📶) A solid bet for budgeteers, with views of the water, a lush garden and 'Bolivian boutique' rooms. The corner rooms have lots of space for the same price, and the top-story suite (also the same price) has a totora raft (reed boat) and its own terrace.

Hostal Flores del Lago HOTEL $
(☎862-2117; www.taypibolivia.com; Jáuregui; s/d/tr B$80/120/180; 📶) This large four-story option on the north side of the harbor is a top-tier budget buy. The clean rooms are slightly damp, but you'll love the views and the friendly lobby area.

Hostal Sonia HOTEL $
(☎862-2019; hostalsoniacopacabana@gmail.com; Murillo 256; s/d B$40/70; @📶) This lively spot has bright and cheery rooms, great views from the upstairs rooms and a top-floor terrace, making it one of the top budget bets in town.

Hostal Los Andes HOTEL $
(☎862-2103; fvelazquez@entelnet.bo; Av Busch s/n; s/d incl breakfast B$100/140; 📶) Although it's nothing fancy, this top-notch budget

ENTERING & LEAVING PERU

Most travelers enter/exit Peru via Copacabana (and the Tiquina Straits) or the scruffy town of Desaguadero (avoiding Copacabana altogether). Note that Peruvian time is one hour behind Bolivian time. Always keep your backpack with you when crossing the border.

Micros (small bus or minibus) to the Kasani–Yunguyo border leave Copacabana's Plaza Sucre regularly, usually when full (B$3, 15 minutes). At Kasani you obtain your exit stamp at passport control and head on foot across the border. Sometimes the border agent will charge you a nominal fee for the crossing (of around B$30). On the Peruvian side, *micros* and taxis will ferry you to Yunguyo (around 6 Peruvian soles, 15 minutes). From here, you can catch a bus heading to Puno. An efficient alternative is to catch a tourist bus from/to La Paz to Puno via Copacabana (from B$60); some allow you a couple of days' stay in Copacabana. Note: even if you've bought a ticket to Cuzco or elsewhere in Peru, you'll change buses in Puno. Here, buses to Cuzco depart from the international terminal; this is located about three blocks from the local terminal.

A quicker, if less interesting, route is via Desaguadero, on the southern side of the lake. Several bus companies head to/from this border from/to Peru. The crossing should be hassle-free: you obtain your exit stamp from the **Bolivian passport control** (possible fee of B$30; ⌚8:30am-8:30pm), walk across a bridge and get an entry stamp at *migración* in Peru. Frequent buses head to Puno hourly (around 3½ hours).

choice is neat and clean, light and breezy, polished and professional.

Hostal Emperador HOTEL **$**
(☎862-2083; Murillo 235; r per person B$20, with private bathroom B$30) This budget travelers' favorite is a basic, albeit lively and colorful, joint, with hot showers, a laundry service, a small shared kitchen and luggage storage.

Hotel Wendy Mar HOTEL **$**
(☎862-2124; hotelwendymar01@hotmail.com; Av 16 de Julio; r B$70-90; 📶) Everything about this excellent budget option is neat and orderly, from the hospital corner sheets to the spotless floors.

Hotel Utama HOTEL **$$**
(☎862-2013; www.utamahotel.com; cnr Michel Peréz & San Antonio; s/d incl breakfast B$105/175; P@📶) Set on the hill overlooking town, this clean reliable option has firm beds, a fun central terrace and sketchy electric showers.

Hostal 6 de Agosto HOTEL **$**
(Av 6 de Agosto; r per person B$30) A rosy and very central place with a sunny outlook over a garden. Clean, if standard, rooms at dirt-cheap prices.

Eating

The local specialty is *trucha criolla* (rainbow trout) and *pejerrey* (king fish) from Lake Titicaca. These are served along the **beachfront stalls** for as little as B$20. The bargain basement is the market *comedor*, where you can have an 'insulin shock' breakfast or afternoon tea of hot *api morado* (hot corn drink; B$2) and syrupy *buñuelos* (doughnuts or fritters; B$1).

La Orilla INTERNATIONAL **$$**
(☎862-2267; Av 6 de Agosto; mains B$25-45; ⌚4-9:30pm Mon-Sat; 🖉) Some say this cozy maritime-themed restaurant is the best restaurant in town, with fresh, crunchy-from-the-vine vegetables, crispy and super savory pizzas, and interesting trout creations that incorporate spinach and bacon (mmm, bacon).

La Cúpula Restaurant INTERNATIONAL **$$**
(www.hotelcupula.com; Michel Pérez 1-3; mains B$20-50; ⌚closed lunch Tue; 🖉) Inventive use of local ingredients make up an extensive international and local menu. The vegetarian range includes a tasty lasagna, and there's plenty for carnivores too.

Kota Kahuaña INTERNATIONAL **$$**
(☎862-2141; Rigoberto Paredes near Costañera; mains B$25-55) This hotel restaurant has excellent views of the lake, great service and well-prepared international dishes.

Pueblo El Viejo INTERNATIONAL **$$**
(Av 6 de Agosto 684; mains B$35-50) Pueblo El Viejo serves up a good burger and pizza, and is open until late. Service can be quite slow, so plan on being here a while.

Pensión Aransaya BOLIVIAN $
(Av 6 de Agosto 121; set lunch B$15, mains B$25-40; ⌚lunch) Super-friendly local favorite for a tall, cold beer and trout heaped with all the trimmings.

Drinking

Waykys BAR
(Av 16 de Julio) A friendly, warm den of a place with cozy corners, graffiti-covered walls, a billiards table, book exchange and a varying range of music.

Nemo's BAR
(Calle 6 de Agosto s/n; ⌚from 5pm daily) Offers no-frills decor, cool music, a short list of food and a long list of beer.

Shopping

The best book exchange is at **Hotel La Cúpula** (www.hotelcupula.com; Pérez 1-3).

Information

There are continuing reports of nasty incidents involving travelers on illegal minibuses and taxis that offer service between Copacabana and La Paz, especially on those who arrive in La Paz at night. The smaller minibuses are more dangerous – they tend to be packed with people and are prone to speed. Travelers are encouraged to take the formal tourist buses (or the larger buses), and schedule your trip to arrive by day.

The thin air, characteristically brilliant sunshine and reflection off the water combine to admit scorching levels of ultraviolet radiation. Wear a hat and sunscreen in this region, and drinks lots of water to avoid dehydration.

The ATMs in town often don't work. Calle 6 de Agosto is the Wall Street of Copacabana, and nearly every shop will exchange foreign currency. The **Banco Bisa ATM** (6 de Agosto & Pando) accepts most international cards, if it works at all. You can buy Peruvian soles at most *artesanías*, but you'll normally find better rates in Kasani, Bolivia, or Yuguyo, just beyond the Peruvian border.

Centro de Información Turística (Av 16 de Julio near Plaza Sucre; ⌚9am-1pm & 2-6pm Wed-Sun) There is a helpful English-speaking attendant, although only rudimentary information is available.

Copacabana Community Tourism Site (www.copacabana-bolivia.com) Has a good events calendar, and updated info on community tourism projects. Run by the tourism operator Turisbus.

Post Office (Calle 6 de Agosto s/n; ⌚10am-8pm Mon-Fri, 9am-noon Sat)

Getting There & Away

Bus

Most buses leave from near Plazas 2 de Febrero or Sucre. The more comfortable nonstop tour buses from La Paz to Copacabana – including Milton Tours and Combi Tours – cost from around B$25 to B$30 and are well worth the investment as night-time hijackings are not uncommon on this route. They depart from La Paz at around 8am and leave Copacabana at 1:30pm (B$30, 3½ hours). Tickets can be purchased from tour agencies. You will need to exit your bus at the Estrecho de Tiquina (Tiquina Straits), to cross via **ferry** (B$1.50 per person, B$35-40 per car; 5am-9pm) between the towns of San Pedro de Tiquina (tourist info office on the main plaza) to San Pablo de Tiquina.

Buses to Peru, including Arequipa (B$120, 8½ hours), Cuzco (B$110, 15 hours) and Puno (B$30, three to four hours), depart and arrive in Copacabana from Av 6 de Agosto. You can also get to Puno by catching a public minibus from Plaza Sucre to the border at Kasani (B$3, 15 minutes). Across the border there's frequent, if crowded, onward transportation to Yunguyo (five minutes) and Puno (2½ hours).

Boat

Buy your tickets for boat tours to Isla de la Luna and Isla del Sol from agencies on Av 6 de Agosto or from beachfront kiosks. Traveling in a big group? Consider renting a private boat through these operators for B$600 per day. Separate return service is available from both islands.

Isla del Sol

☎02 / POP 2500

Easily the highlight of any Lake Titicaca excursion (and perhaps your entire Bolivia romp), Isla del Sol (elevation 3808m) is a large island with several traditional communities, decent tourist infrastructure like hotels and restaurants, a few worthwhile pre-Colombian ruins, amazing views, great hikes and, well, lots of sun.

The large 70-sq-km island definitely merits a night or two – you can then devote a day each to the northern and southern ends. While the day tour gives you a decent introduction to the island (you can do a walking circuit of the main sights in a long day), whirlwind half-day tours are strictly for the been-there-done-that crowd.

The island's permanent residents – a mix of indigenous peoples and recent émigrés/escapers – are distributed between the main settlements of **Cha'llapampa**, near the island's northern end; **Cha'lla**, which backs

Isla del Sol

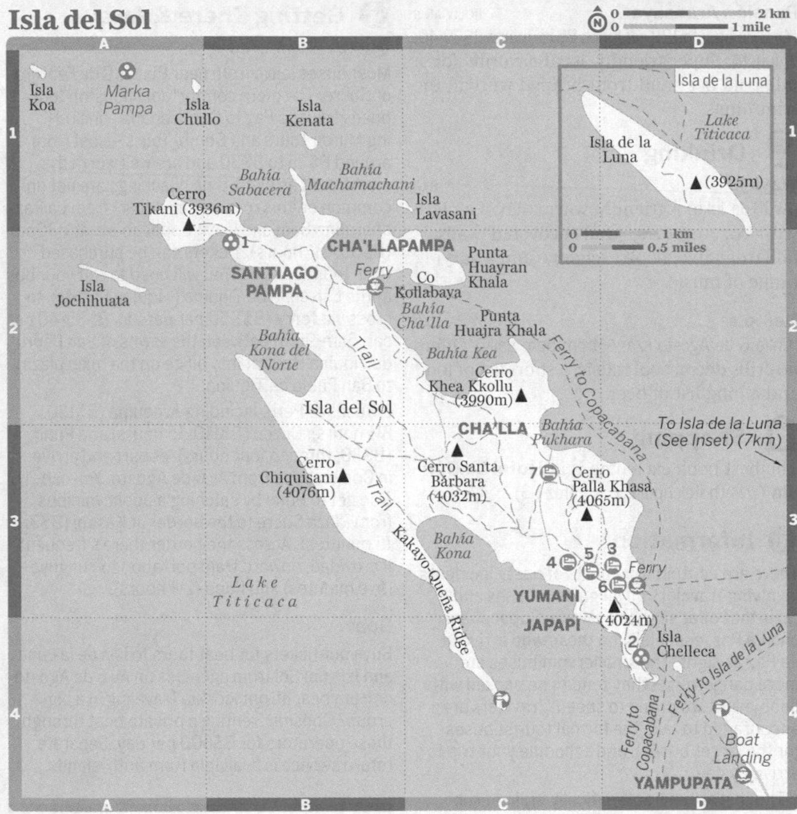

Isla del Sol

Sights

1	Chincana Ruins	B2
2	Pilko Kaina	D4

Sleeping

3	Hostal Illampu	D3
4	Hostal Puerta del Sol	C3
5	Hotel Imperio del Sol	C3
	Inti Wasi Lodge	(see 3)
6	Las Cabañas	D3
7	Palla Khasa	C3

up to a lovely sandy beach on the central east coast; and **Yumani**, which straddles the ridge above the Escalera del Inca on the south and is the biggest town on the island.

There are no vehicles on Isla del Sol, so visitors are limited to hiking along rocky trails (some are now paved in Inca style) or traveling by boat. The main ports are at **Pilko Kaina**, the **Escalera del Inca** in Yumani and near the **Templo del Inca** and **Chincana ruins** at Cha'llapampa. There's also a small port at **Japapi** on the southwest coast.

Sights

There's a B$5 fee to cross the island, and each site attracts its own admission fee.

Fuente del Inca & Escalera del Inca GARDENS
(admission B$5) Just uphill from the ferry dock at the village of Yumani, this lovely hanging garden and rolling waterfall is most people's introduction to Isla del Sol.

Pilko Kaina RUINS
(admission B$5) This prominent ruins complex near the southern tip of the island (about 30 minutes south by foot from Yumani) sits well camouflaged against a steep terraced slope.

Cha'lla VILLAGE
(admission B$5) This agreeable little village has a dusty **Museo Étnico** (admission free with Cha'lla trail fee).

Cha'llapampa VILLAGE
(museum admission incl Chicana Ruins entrance B$10) Most boat tours visiting the northern ruins land at Cha'llapampa, home to a **small museum.**

Chincana Ruins RUINS
(admission B$10) The island's most spectacular ruins complex, the Chincana ruins, lies near the island's northern tip. Its main feature is the **Palacio del Inca**. If you've the energy, climb nearby **Cerro Uma Qolla** for a great view.

Sleeping

The most scenic place to stay is Yumani. Ch'allapampa and Ch'alla have basic options. In high season (June to August and during festivals) prices listed here may double.

Palla Khasa CABIN $$
(☎7321-1585; palla-khasa@hotmail.com; s/d incl breakfast B$150/250) About 300m north of Yumani proper, this top choice has lovely grounds and simple but workable rooms – we like *numero* three the best.

Las Cabañas CABIN $$
(s/d incl breakfast B$80/160) Perched on the hill leading into town from the dock, these simple adobe bungalows afford great views, and have 24-hour hot water. The beds are nice and soft.

Hostal Puerta del Sol HOTEL $$
(☎7195-5101; s without/with bathroom B$40/150, cabin per person B$150, d B$200) On the promontory on top of the hill, this friendly option has nice views from most rooms (number 14 is awesome), clean sheets and a nice terrace.

Hotel Imperio del Sol HOTEL $
(r per person with/without bathroom B$60/30) This peachy and central place on the hillside running into town is a good bet, with clean rooms and reliable service.

Hostal Illampu HOTEL $
(r per person without bathroom B$25) Halfway up the hill into town, this budget option has excellent views and decent rooms.

Inti Wasi Lodge HOSTEL $
(☎7196-0223; museo_templodelsol@yahoo.es; dm per person B$25, cabins per person incl breakfast B$70) Four basic, but cozy cabins with en suites and great views and a recommended restaurant. To get here, turn right just before Hostal Illampu as you head up the hill.

Eating

There are more pizzerias in Yumani than Titicaca has *trucha*. Nearly all menus are identical; *almuerzos* and set dinners cost between B$25 and B$30.

Getting There & Away

Launches embark from Copacabana beach around 8:30am and 1:30pm daily. Depending on the season and the company, they may drop you off at a choice of the island's north or south (check with the agency). Return trips leave Yampupata at 10:30am and 4pm (B$20 one-way), and Cha'llapampa at 1pm (B$20).

Most full-day trips go directly north to Cha'llapampa (two to 2½ hours). Boats anchor for 1½ hours only – you'll have just enough time to hike up to the Chincana ruins, and return again to catch the boat at 1pm to the Escalera del Inca and Pilko Kaina in the island's south. Here, you'll spend around two hours before departing for Copa.

Half-day trips generally go to the south of Isla del Sol only.

Those who wish to hike the length of the island can get off at Cha'llapampa in the morning and walk south to the Escalera del Inca (Yumani) for the return boat in the afternoon.

Asociación Unión Marines (Costañera; one-way B$20, round-trip B$25; ⏲departs Copacabana 8:30am & 1:30pm) Ferry service to the north and south of Isla del Sol, with a stop on the return at a floating island.

Titicaca Tours (Costañera; round-trip B$35; ⏲departs Copacabana 8:30am) Offers a round-trip boat tour that stops at Isla de la Luna for an hour, continuing to the southern end of Isla del Sol for a two-hour stop before heading back to Copacabana.

THE CORDILLERAS & THE YUNGAS

Caught between the Andes and the Amazon, this rugged transition zone has just about everything you could ask for from your Bolivia adventure.

For the vertically inspired, there are glacier-capped 6000m peaks and adrenaline-charged mountain-bike descents. Nature lovers and the culturally curious will dig the cloud forests and hillside semi-tropical

Yungas towns of Chulumani, Coroico and Sorata. Here, you can kick off hikes to nearby waterfalls, start your river trip into the Amazon, mountain-bike until your bum is numb, or simply swing with the breeze from your mountain hideaway.

Coroico

02 / POP 2360

With warm weather, spectacular views, good resort-style hotels for all budgets and an infectious laid-back air, Coroico is the most-visited tourist town in the Yungas. Perched eyrie-like on the shoulder of Cerro Uchumachi, the village commands a far-ranging view across forested canyons, cloud-wreathed mountain peaks, patchwork agricultural lands, citrus orchards, coffee plantations and dozens of small settlements. When the weather clears, the view stretches to the snow-covered summits of Mururata, Huayna Potosí and Tiquimani, high in the Cordillera Real.

Yolosa is located about 7km from Coroico along the World's Most Dangerous Road. There are a few cool hangouts in town, an animal refuge, and a steady stream of dust-caked Dangerous Road bikers who generally end their rides here.

Sights & Activities

For pretty views, trek an easy 20 minutes up to **El Calvario**, where the stations of the cross lead to a grassy knoll and **chapel**. To get there, head uphill toward Hotel Esmeralda. There are two good trailheads from El Calvario. The one to the left leads to the **cascadas**, a trio of waterfalls 5km (two hours) beyond the chapel. The trail to the right leads up to **Cerro Uchumachi** (a five-hour round trip), which affords terrific views of the valley.

Solo travelers – especially women – should check with their hotels about the security situation before heading out.

About three hours north from Coroico is the **Río Coroico**, which flows through the Nor Yungas. This is the country's most popular commercially rafted river, and is the most convenient to La Paz.

La Paz agencies will take you down the World's Most Dangerous Road to Coroico. From town, you can rent bikes from most hotels to take you to some of the nearby attractions.

Asociación de Guias Turismo Local de Coroico GUIDED TOUR
(7306-9888; Plaza García Lanza; 8am-noon, 2:30am-7:30pm) A range of guide services including transit cost between B$280 and B$320 (for up to four people).

Tours 4x4 GUIDED TOUR
(7371-9251; cosingis@hotmail.com; Cuenca 22) As well as offering 4X4 tours, it also has fun trips to a zip-line (B$170), remote swimming holes (B$70) and the waterfalls.

Cross Country Coroico MOUNTAIN BIKING
(7157-3015; www.cxccoroico.lobopages.com; Pacheco 2058) Offers day trips to attractions in the region for all levels of riders from B$280 per person.

Courses

Siria León LANGUAGE COURSE
(7195-5431; siria_leon@yahoo.com; private lesson per hr B$40) A recommended teacher for Spanish language classes.

WORTH A TRIP

GREAT DAY TRIPS FROM COROICO

Coroico is a good launching point for day trips or longer excursions into the neighboring countryside.

Poza Esmeralda y Turquesa Book a trip with a Coroico agency for an afternoon swim in this 'secret' spot.

La Senda Verde Refugio Natural (7472-2825; www.sendaverde.com; Yolosa; admission B$49, reservations required, children under 10 not admitted; 10am-12:30pm) This 12-hectare animal refuge is located just 500m south of Yolosa and about 7km from Coroico.

Zzip the Flying Fox (2231-3849; www.ziplinebolivia.com; Yolosa; one trip B$255; 9-11am & 1-5pm) Three zip-line sections take you flying through the forest canopy near Yolosa at speeds up to 85km per hour.

Sleeping

On weekends from June to August hotels are often booked out. It's possible to make advance reservations, but there's no guarantee that all hotels will honor them. On holiday weekends prices may increase by as much as 100%. Around the tiny village of Yolosa (about 7km north of town) there are several ecolodges worth checking out.

Hostal Sol y Luna RESORT **$$**
(7373-1232, in La Paz 02-244-0588; www.solyluna-bolivia.com; campsite B$30, s/d with bathroom B$120/200, without bathroom B$70/100, d apt or cabañas with bathroom B$260-300;) Set on a jungly hill some way from town, this inspiring spot offers appealingly rustic accommodations in a variety of *cabañas* (cabins), simple dorms and camping spots. It's a 20-minute uphill walk from town, or a B$15 taxi gets you to and from the main plaza.

La Senda Verde Resort LODGE **$**
(7472-2825; www.sendaverde.com; r per person incl breakfast B$120-150;) This delightful spot is accessed from the Yolosa–La Paz road, a short walk from town (500m south of Yolosa). It has a verdant setting on the banks of two rivers and is a great spot to relax.

Hotel Esmeralda HOTEL **$$**
(213-6017; www.hotelesmeralda.com; Julio Suazo s/n; s/d with bathroom B$216/360, dm/s/d without bathroom B$75/120/200; @) A top pick for backpackers and the party set, this resort-style hotel set on the hillside overlooking the town has amazing grounds, tremendous views, a swimming pool and a fun traveler scene.

Hostal Kory HOTEL **$**
(7156-4050; Kennedy s/n; r per person with/without bathroom B$140/70;) Right in the center of town, this is one of your best budget bets.

Hostal Tunqui Eye HOTEL **$**
(7490-6666; coroico_eye@yahoo.com; Iturralde 4043; r per person with/without bathroom B$40/30;) In the ultra-budget spectrum, this recent entrant has newer beds, clean(ish) sheets and good views from the terrace.

Hostal 1866 HOTEL **$**
(259-6440; www.hostal1866.net; Cuenca s/n; r per person with/without bathroom B$65/45) This architecturally impossible building situated just up from the plaza is a solid bet for the budget set.

Eating

The plaza is ringed by a number of inexpensive local cafes and pizzerias.

Back-Stube Konditorei GERMAN **$$**
(Kennedy s/n; mains B$30-50; 9:30am-2:30pm & 6:30am-10pm Wed-Fri, 9:30am-10pm Sat & Sun;) One of the best places to eat in town, this welcoming bakery-restaurant has excellent breakfasts, tempting cakes and pastries, as well as pasta, vegetarian plates and memorable *sauerbraten* (marinated pot-roast beef).

El Cafetal INTERNATIONAL **$$**
(Miranda s/n; mains B$15-40) This secluded hotel restaurant has unbeatable views, where you can enjoy some of the Yungas' finest food.

Luna Llena INTERNATIONAL **$$**
(Hostal Sol y Luna; mains B$20-40;) The small outdoor restaurant at the Hostal Sol y Luna has a well-priced, tasty menu of Bolivian and European dishes including vegetarian options.

Bamboo's Café MEXICAN **$**
(Iturralde 1047; mains B$20-40) This friendly candlelit Mexican restaurant has pretty authentic guacamole, tacos, burritos and yumm-irrific refried beans.

Entertainment

Murcielaguitos DANCE
(Pacheco s/n; Fri & Sat night) After midnight, when the resto-bars shut, it's time for dancing at Murcielaguitos.

Information

There's a basic regional hospital near Hostal El Cafetal, on the upper road out of town, but for serious medical treatment you'll be happiest in La Paz. There are no foreign-card-accepting ATMs in Coroico, and not all hotels accept credit cards. For tourist information online, try www.coroico-info.com.

Prodem (213-6009; Plaza García Lanza; 8:30am-12:30pm & 2:30am-6pm Wed-Fri) Changes dollars at a fair rate and does cash advances for 5% commission.

Tourist Office (Bus Terminal; 8am-8pm) There's a small information kiosk at the bus terminal.

Getting There & Away

The La Paz–Coroico road is now open, replacing the World's Most Dangerous Road as the town's access route. It's asphalted along its whole length, but in the short time it's been open several landslides have cut up some sections. Buses and *micros* from La Paz arrive at the bus terminal on Av Manning. It's a steep walk uphill to the plaza, or you can hop in a taxi (B$5). **Turbus Totaí** (☎2289-5573) run comfortable taxi services to La Paz from the terminal, leaving when full (B$25, two hours).

From the Villa Fátima area in La Paz, buses and *micros* leave for Coroico (B$25, 3½ hours) at least hourly from 7:30am to 8:30pm, with extra runs on weekends and holidays. En route they stop in Yolosita, a dusty crossroads where you can connect with buses and *camiones* (open-bed trucks) north to Rurrenabaque (B$100, 15 to 18 hours) and further into Bolivian Amazonia.

For Chulumani, the quickest route is to backtrack to La Paz. Although the junction for the Chulumani road is at Unduavi, few passing *micros* have spare seats at this point.

The road to Caranavi was only open 3pm to 6am as of press time. Buses from the Coroico terminal will take you there (and on to other Amazonian destinations) for B$30.

Chulumani

☎02 / POP 3000

Perched scenically on the side of a hill, this peaceful little town is the capital of the Sud Yungas. It's a lot like Coroico, with a friendly town square, bustling market and tropical attitude, but receives next to no international visitors.

Sights & Activities

There are several lovely walks in the Chulumani area. A butterfly-clouded, five-hour (one-way) downhill hike will take you from Chulumani down to the Río Solacama; you can easily get a bus or *micro* back. In three to four hours you can also walk to Ocabaya, while other walks take you from the higher village of Villa Remedios to the lower one, or from Chicaloma down to Ocabaya. Another beautiful hike is the four-hour walk from Chulumani to Chirca, where there's the church of a revered local virgin.

Apa-Apa Reserva Ecológica WILDLIFE RESERVE
(☎7254-7770; apapayungas@hotmail.com) An interesting day trip is to the Apa-Apa Reserva Ecológica, 8km from town. The reserve runs four-hour guided forest walks (B$50 per person with a B$200 minimum), runs an ecolodge, and has a cafe serving meals and homemade ice cream. A taxi from Chulumani to the reserve costs B$15.

Sleeping & Eating

For cheap and tasty fried chicken, **Restaurant Rinconcito Chulameño** on Plaza Libertad is a friendly choice. **Snack San Bartolomé** is another decent option on the plaza.

Country House HOTEL $
(Tolopata 13; r per person with bathroom incl breakfast B$70;) Probably your best bet in town, this welcoming country home is 10 minutes west of the plaza by the basketball court and Mirador La Ladera. The rooms, decorated in an attractively rustic style, are spotless, and have hot-water bathrooms and fresh flowers.

Hostal Dion HOTEL $
(☎289-6034; hostaldion@hotmail.com; Bolívar s/n; r per person with/without bathroom incl breakfast B$70/50) A half block south of Plaza Libertad, this is the best of the central options.

Information

Chulumani's tourist office is in a kiosk on the main plaza. There's no ATM in Chulumani; Banco Fie on the main plaza and Prodem (two blocks West of the Plaza on Pando) give cash advances.

Getting There & Away

Yunga Cruz trekkers finish in Chulumani, and the town is readily accessed from Yanacachi at the end of the Takesi trek. From Yanacachi, walk down to the main road and wait for transportation headed downhill; it's about 1½ hours to Chulumani.

From Villa Fátima in La Paz, around the corner of Calles San Borja and 15 de Abril, different companies depart when full for Chulumani (B$20, four hours) from 8am to 4pm. From Chulumani, La Paz-bound buses wait around the *tranca* (police post). If you're coming from Coroico, get off at Unduavi and wait for another vehicle. It will likely be standing-room only; if a seat is a priority, you'll have to go all the way back to La Paz.

Sorata

☎02 / POP 2500

Sorata is the town that tourism forgot. Once rivaling Coroico for weekend visitors, this picturesque colonial village, perched on a hillside beneath the towering snow-capped peaks of Illampu and Ancohuma, is slowly falling into decay. Restaurants and hotels are going out of business, tour operators are jumping ship and trash isn't getting picked up. Everyday it's becoming less touristy and well... more Bolivian.

And while it doesn't have the shiny digs of its arch nemesis Coroico, this semi-tropical village sitting high above a verdant agricultural valley does offer great weather, access to some of Bolivia's best treks, kick-ass downhill mountain biking and an atavistic air that may just become intoxicating.

Activities

Hiking & Walking

Peak hiking season is May to September. Ambitious adventurers can do the seven-day **El Camino del Oro trek**, an ancient trading route between the *altiplano* and the Río Tipuani gold fields. Note that this is a rough part of Bolivia, and not many people are taking on this trek these days. With wildcat miners, it can be quite dangerous, plus, without regular traffic, you'll need to clear some trail with machetes. If you go here, it's highly recommended to travel with a local guide.

Alternatively, there's the steep climb up to **Laguna Chillata**, a long day trek with multiple trails (it's best to take a guide; you can't see the lake until you get there); **Laguna Glacial** (5100m), a two- to three-day high-altitude trek; the challenging five-day **Mapiri Trail**; or the seven-day **Illampu circuit**.

With Sorata's economy turning from tourism to mining and farming (coca, marijuana, you name it), there are fewer guides offering services here, and fewer pack animals for hire. Spattered reports indicate that this could be a dangerous area for trekking and many agencies are no longer offering treks in the region. Check with locals before you depart.

Asociación de Guías de Sorata GUIDED TOUR
(Sorata Guides & Porters Association; ☎213-6672; guiasorata@hotmail.com; Sucre 302) This guides association also rents equipment of varying quality and arranges many different treks. Expect to pay around B$300 to B$400 per day for a guide (and mule to carry your equipment). Cooking equipment is included in these prices, but food is extra. Clients are expected to pay for the guide's food.

Gruta de San Pedro WALKING
(San Pedro Cave; admission B$15; ⊙8am-5pm) A popular excursion is to the Gruta de San Pedro, 12km from town. The cave is approximately 400m deep with an enclosed lagoon, and though it is no longer possible to swim in it, it can be crossed with pedal boats.

Mountain Biking

Andean Epics MOUNTAIN BIKING
(☎7127-6685; www.andeanepics.com) This La Paz-based operator is your best bet for rides near Sorata. Its signature trip combines two days of riding with three days on motorized dugout canoe from Sorata to Rurrenabaque (B$2500 per person, all inclusive). They were moving as of press time, so check out the website for its new shopfront location.

Sleeping

TOP CHOICE **Altai Oasis** LODGE $$
(☎7151-9856; www.altaioasis.lobopages.com; campsite B$30, dm/s/d without bathroom B$84/125/250, s/d with bathroom B$245/315, cabin B$500-800;) This really does feel like an oasis, with a lush garden, hammocks, caged macaws, a pretty balcony cafe-restaurant and a range of accommodations options. To get here, follow the downhill track past the soccer field to the river, climb back up to the road and turn left before reaching Café Illampu.

Hotel Santa Lucia HOTEL $
(☎7151-3812; r per person with/without bathroom B$50/40) Located near the soccer field, this is the cleanest, neatest option in town. The bright yellow hotel does have a

TREKKING IN THE CORDILLERAS

Several worthwhile treks run between the *altiplano* and the Yungas. Most popular are the **Choro** (La Cumbre to Coroico; 70km), **Takesi** (Taquesi; 45km) and **Yunga Cruz** (114km). These two- to four-day treks all begin with a brief ascent, then head down from spectacular high-mountain landscapes into the riotous vegetation of the Yungas. This area is also home to **Huayna Potosí** (6088m), the most popular major peak to climb; many agencies in La Paz can organize the ascent.

The best time for these treks is during the May to September dry season. Security is a concern as nasty incidents, including robberies and assaults, have been reported, so it's best to check the situation ahead of time and avoid solo hiking.

slightly institutional feel, but in return you get excellent mattresses (by Sorata standards), crisp lines and tidy shared facilities.

Hostal Las Piedras HOTEL $
(☎7191-6341; laspiedras2002@yahoo.de; Ascarrunz s/n; s/d without bathroom B$50/80, s/d/tr with bathroom B$100/140/180) This German-owned joint has amazing views from most rooms, a cool vibe, shared kitchen and fun common area.

Hostal Paraíso HOTEL $
(☎7302-3447; Villavicencio s/n; r per person B$40) This central spot has a bright, flowery patio, a series of roof terraces with nice views, new beds and old carpets.

Eating

Small, inexpensive restaurants around the market and the plaza sell cheap and filling *almuerzos*.

Café Illampu BAKERY $
(snacks B$20-35; ⌚9am-6:30pm Wed-Mon) A 15-minute down-and-up walk from town, this lovely relaxing spot is en route to the San Pedro Cave.

Altai Oasis INTERNATIONAL $$
(mains B$20-50;) The peaceful balcony restaurant at this loveable retreat, 15 minutes' walk from town, serves coffee, drinks and a range of vegetarian dishes.

Mercado MARKET $
(Muñecas s/n; mains B$5-20) Head to the market to grab the goods for a picnic lunch. There are some food stands here too.

Information

Sunday is market day, and Tuesday, when many businesses are closed, is considered *domingo sorateño* (Sorata's Sunday). There's no tourist information center or ATM.

Getting There & Away

From near La Paz's cemetery, buses leave hourly between 4am and 5:30pm (B$17, three hours). From the plaza in Sorata, La Paz–bound *micros* depart when full and *flotas* (long-distance buses) leave on the hour between 4am and 5pm.

Sindicato de Transportes Unificada Sorata (Plaza Enrique Peñaranda s/n) has daily service to Copacabana (9am, B$40), Coroico via La Paz (9am, B$36), Achacachi (no set time, B$12), and Haurina (hourly, B$15). For Copacabana you can also get off at the junction town of Huarina and wait for another, probably packed, bus. They also service the town on the rough 4WD track to the gold mining settlement of Mapiri.

SOUTHERN ALTIPLANO

The harsh, at times almost primeval geography of the Southern Altiplano will tug at the heartstrings of those with a deep love of bleak and solitary places. Stretching southwards from La Paz, this high-plains wilderness is framed by majestic volcanic peaks, swathes of treeless wilderness and the white emptiness of the eerie *salares* (salt plains) almost devoid of life. At night, the starscapes are spectacular, and it's as cold as you could ever imagine.

The areas around Parque Nacional Sajama offer spectacular off-beat wilderness exploration, while revelers may wish to hit up the Carnaval celebration in the gritty, straight-talking mining city of Oruro. Further south, the Salar de Uyuni is the star attraction, and the three-day jeep tour makes it to the top of most travelers' lists. From there, you can head to the warmer cactus-studded valleys around Tupiza for horseback trips and mountain biking.

Oruro

☎02 / POP 260,000

Oruro is dirty and crowded, the food sucks and there's not much to do outside of Carnaval season. Yet there's something about this place – the largest berg in the region, a miners' city that takes no slack from no one – that endears it to visitors, making for an oddly atavistic experience that some may find thrilling.

While many visitors skip Oruro altogether, it does have decent museums, and there's plenty to see in the surrounding area. It's also culturally very colorful, with a rich dance and musical heritage that culminates in the riotous Carnaval celebrations.

Sights & Activities

The action around town tends to center around the Plaza 10 de Febrero and Plaza del Folklore. Bolívar is the main commercial drag and a fun evening people-watching walk.

Museo Sacro, Folklórico, Arqueológico y Minero MUSEUM
(Plaza del Folklore s/n; admission both museums B$10, camera/video use B$3/20; ⌚9-11:15am &

The Southwest

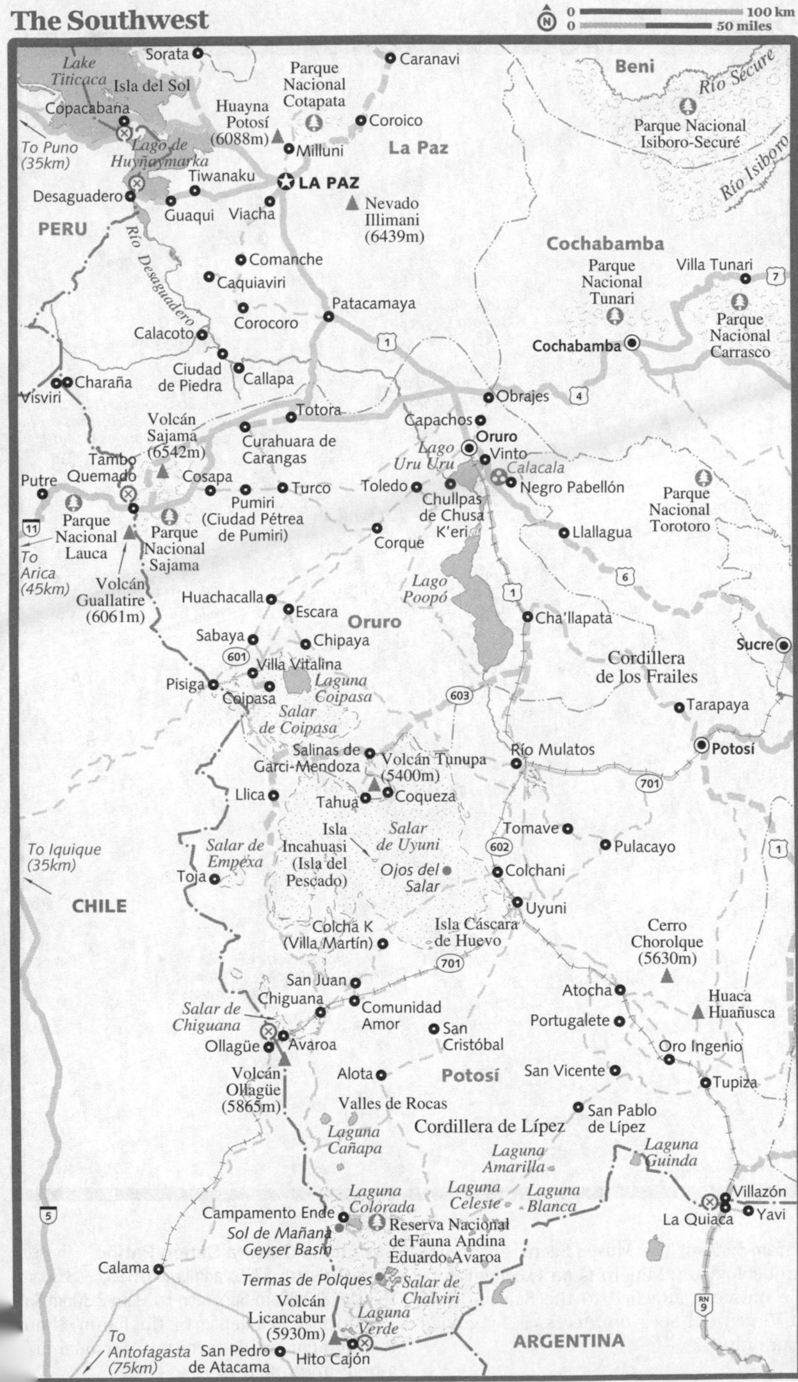

Oruro

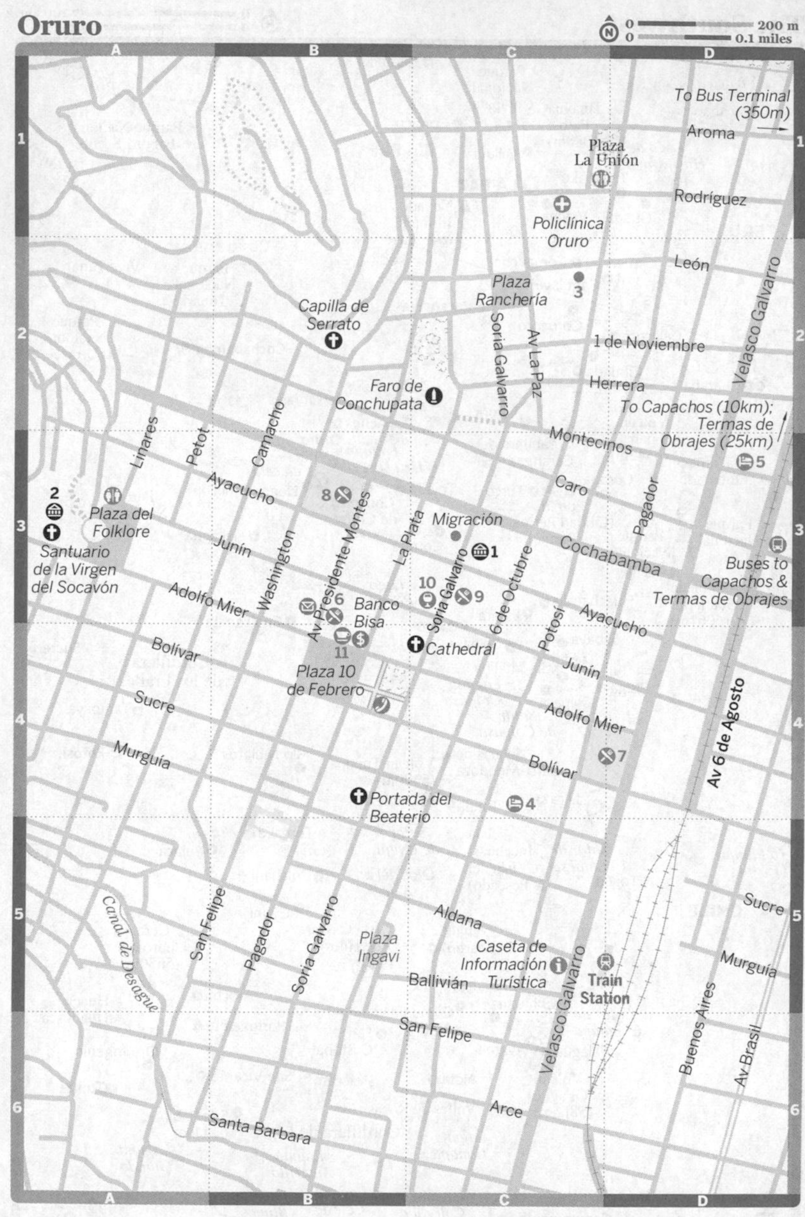

3:15am-5:30pm) The Museo Sacro, Folklórico, Arqueológico y Minero is an excellent double museum attached to the Santuario de la Virgen del Socavón. Access is by guided tour only.

Casa de la Cultura Simón Patiño MUSEUM
(Soria Galvarro 5755; admission B$8; ⏲8:30am-11:30am & 2:30am-6pm Mon-Fri, 9am-2:30pm Sat) The former residence of tin baron Simón Patiño includes his furniture, personal bric-a-brac, and fine toys.

Oruro

Sights

1 Casa de la Cultura Simón Patiño........C3
2 Museo Sacro, Folklórico, Arqueológico y Minero..................A3

Activities, Courses & Tours

3 Charlie Tours.......................................C2

Sleeping

4 Hotel Repostero..................................C4
5 Residencial 21 de Abril......................D3

Eating

6 La Casona..B3
7 Mercado Campero...............................D4
8 Mercado Fermín López.......................B3
9 Restaurant Ardentia............................C3

Drinking

10 Bar Huari..C3
11 Dali...B4

Museo Casa Arte Taller Cardozo Velasquez MUSEUM
(☎527-5245; juegueoruro@hotmail.com; Junín 738; admission B$8; ⏲no specific hours, call ahead) A family of seven artists open their whimsical little house and art studio to visitors. Check ahead to see if they are sponsoring other cultural activities in town.

Mina San José GUIDED TOUR
The tour lasts about three hours and costs B$50. To get there take a yellow *micro* (marked 'D' or 'San José') or the light-blue mini (B$5) from the northwest corner of Plaza 10 de Febrero. Note that mine tours can be dangerous – for information on safety, see boxed text, p230.

Termas de Obrajes HOT SPRINGS
(admission B$10) The Termas de Obrajes hot springs, 25km northeast of town, are a popular destination. It's a well-run complex, with a pool and private bathrooms with tubs, which you can reserve for half an hour and gradually fill up with the magnesium-rich water. From the corner of Caro and Av 6 de Agosto, catch an Obrajes *micro* (B$7, 30 minutes) from 7:30am to 5pm daily, which also passes the grungier **Capachos hot springs** (B$3), 10km east of town. The last *micro* to Oruro departs at 4pm.

Charlie Tours GUIDED TOUR
(☎524-0666; charlietours@yahoo.com) English-speaking guides take you on tours to the area's attractions. It is outside of town, so call or email. Prices vary.

Festivals & Events

Carnaval FESTIVAL
During the spectacular Carnaval, from the Saturday before Ash Wednesday, the city turns into a parade of party animals. Revelers – including proud locals, 90% of whom call themselves *quirquinchos* (armadillos) – pitch water at each other (which, frankly, can be downright tiresome). Several parades (including the Entrada and La Diablada) feature dancers in intricately garish masks and costumes.

Sleeping

There are quite a few handy, if not classy, *alojamientos* (very basic accommodations) near the train station on Velasco Galvarro.

Residencial 21 de Abril HOSTEL $
(☎527-9205; simon21deabril@bolivia.com; Montecinos 198; dm/r per person with shared bathroom B$40/50, d with private bathroom B$50; wi-fi) Probably your best budget bet, this friendly family-run spot is a short walk from the center with tidy bright rooms, TV and hot water available all day. There's a sauna for guest use.

Hotel Bernal HOTEL $
(☎527-9468; Brasil 701; s/d/tr B$85/130/170) Opposite the bus terminal, this budget option smells a bit like burnt cotton candy and has soft beds, limpid pillows and slightly dirty sheets.

Hotel Repostero HOTEL $
(☎525-8001; ph_tania@hotmail.com; Sucre 370; s/d/tr incl breakfast B$150/200/230; wi-fi) You'll love the sign at this faded but likeable old place, which has a variety of ever-so-slightly-smoky rooms in two wings, all with hot showers and cable TV.

Eating

Mercado Campero (food B$5-15; ⏲6am-8pm) and **Mercado Fermín López** (food B$5-15; ⏲6am-8pm) have rows of lunch spots.

Restaurant Ardentia INTERNATIONAL $
(Soria Galvarro; mains B$17-27; ⏲6:30am-11pm Mon-Sat) Serves thoughtfully prepared lasagna, simple but savory chicken and beef dishes, and international standards like hamburgers.

La Casona ITALIAN $
(Montes 5969; pizzas from B$20) Out-of-the-oven *salteñas* by day, quick sandwiches for lunch, and pizza and pasta at dinner keep this little place buzzing, especially at night when it gets really busy and hot, temperature-wise.

Drinking

Bar Huari BAR
(cnr Junín 608 & Soria Galvarro) Not much seems to have changed in this traditional bar since the 1930s.

Dali CAFE
(Plaza 10 de Febrero, 2nd fl; ⏲10am-2am) About as hoity-toity as you can get in Oruro, this stylish and popular cafe caters to Oruro's young set. Come for the drinks, not the food.

Information

There are a couple of ATMs on Plaza 10 de Febrero. Watch your cash stash – local pickpockets and bag-slashers are quite competent, especially during drunken festivals.

Banco Bisa (Plaza 10 de Febrero) Cashes Amex traveler's checks into bolivianos without commission (for US dollars, there's a US$6 fee).

Caseta de Información Turística (Tourist Information Office) This booth gives out city maps and leaflets, and tourist police are occasionally on hand. There is also a booth across from the bus station.

Migración (☎527-0239; S Galvarro, btwn Ayacucho & Cochabamba; ⏲8:30am-12:30pm & 2:30pm-6:30pm Mon-Fri) Extend your stay here (last door on the left).

Getting There & Away

Bus

All long-distance buses use the **bus terminal** (☎527-9535; Brasil s/n; terminal fee B$1.50), a 15-minute walk or short cab ride northeast of the center. There's a *casa de cambio* (money-changing office) on the upper level, luggage storage on the ground floor (B$5) and a sporadically open tourist information booth, which provides maps.

Buses to La Paz (B$20, three hours) depart every half-hour, and there are several departures for Cochabamba (B$20, four hours), Potosí (B$25, five hours) and Sucre (B$80, eight hours). For Santa Cruz, you must make a connection in Cochabamba. Night buses to Uyuni (B$30 to B$35, eight hours) leave between 7pm and 8pm – they are freezing cold, so bring a sleeping bag.

There is daily service to Arica (B$100, 10 hours), Calama (B$130, 20 hours) and Iquique (B$80, eight hours) in Chile, generally departing in the evening. There are also buses for Tarija (B$70, 20 hours) and Tupiza (B$60, 12 hours).

Train

Trains run from Oruro south to Villazón on the Argentina board, passing through Uyuni, Atocha and Tupiza along the way. The Expreso del Sur is slightly more luxurious, departing Oruro on Tuesday and Friday. Cheaper service is had on the Wara Wara line, leaving Oruro Wednesday and Sunday. There is return service from Villazón on Monday, Wednesday, Thursday and

TRAINS DEPARTING ORURO

Expreso del Sur Train: Departing Tuesday & Thursday

RUN	COST (B$ FIRST/COACH)*	SCHEDULE
Oruro-Uyuni	112/56	3:30-10:20pm
Uyuni-Atocha	168/77	10:40pm-12:45am
Atocha-Tupiza	224/101	12:55-4am
Tupiza-Villazón	261/119	4:10-7:05am

Wara Wara Train: Departing Wednesday & Sunday

RUN	COST (B$ FIRST/COACH/NORMAL)*	SCHEDULE
Oruro-Uyuni	95/44/32	7pm-2:20am
Uyuni-Atocha	126/57/42	2:50-5am
Atocha-Tupiza	170/75/56	5:20-8:35am
Tupiza-Villazón	205/94/67	9:05am-12:05pm

** Prices one-way from Oruro*

Saturday. From Uyuni, you can get slow trains to Calama (Chile). Buy tickets at least a day ahead from the **train station** (☎527-4605; www.fca.com.bo; ⏰8:15am-11:30am & 2:30pm-6pm Mon & Thu, 8:15am-6pm Tue & Fri, 8:15am-noon & 2:30pm-7pm Wed, 8:15am-11:30am & 3pm-7pm Sun); don't forget your passport. On train days, there's a left-luggage kiosk here. Watch your belongings on the train, and bring a sleeping bag.

Uyuni

☎02 / POP 20,000

Seemingly built in defiance of the desert-like landscape, Uyuni stands desolate yet undaunted in Bolivia's southwestern corner. Mention Uyuni to a Bolivian and they will whistle and emphasize '*harto frío*' – extreme cold. Yet, despite the icy conditions, Uyuni's got a cheerful buzz about it with hundreds of travelers passing through every week to kick off their tour of the Salar de Uyuni along the Southwest Circuit.

Sights

You can take day trips to the Salar de Uyuni from town, but most choose to head out on a three- or four-day tour.

FREE **Cemeterio de Trenes** HISTORIC SITE

(Train Cemetery) A large collection of historic steam locomotives and rail cars sit decaying in the yards about 3km southwest of the modern-day station along Av Ferroviaria.

Museo Arqueología y Antropológico de los Andes Meridionales MUSEUM

(Arce near Colón; admission B$5; ⏰8am-noon & 2:20pm-6:30pm Mon-Fri) A small affair featuring mummies, long skulls, fossils, ceramics and textiles.

Tours

While you can theoretically visit the Salar de Uyuni and the attractions of the Southwest Circuit independently, it is extremely challenging due to unreliable transport and the remoteness of the area. So the vast majority of people take an organized tour from either Uyuni or Tupiza. From the end of December to the end of March, the salt flat floods. During this time, many agencies shut down, and you can travel just 10km into the salt flat, but not beyond.

Costs

Tours cost B$700 to B$800 for three days at a standard agency, and B$800 to B$1000 at a high-end operation. Four-day and custom trips will run B$800 and up. Tours include a driver (who also serves as your guide, mechanic and cook, but probably doesn't speak English), two-nights accommodation (quality varies depending on the agency), three meals a day, and transit. You'll also need to pay a B$30 entrance fee to Isla Incahuasi and a B$150 fee to enter the nature reserve. Those traveling on to Chile will need B$21 to B$50 for the border. Many agencies don't accept credit cards.

Don't choose an agency solely on price: the cheaper operators can be unsafe. See p212 for more information.

What to Bring

You'll want to bring a couple liters of water, snacks, headlamp, sunscreen, sunglasses, sunhat and warm clothes, including gloves and a decent jacket. A sleeping bag is highly recommended. Ask your operator to include a free sleeping bag rental in your fee. Otherwise, they cost about B$50 to rent and are really worth it.

Sleeping & Eating

On a standard tour, you will stay in a hotel made of salt the first night (just on the edge of the salt flat). The next night, you'll stay in a basic lodge. None have heaters, some have hot showers (for B$10 extra), and you will be cold. They generally put your whole group in one room. If you are doing it yourself, these basic hotels cost about B$30 per night.

Your driver is generally your cook, and the quality of food varies. Vegetarians should make arrangements with the operator ahead of time.

Standard Tours

The most popular tour is the three-day circuit taking in the Salar de Uyuni, Laguna Colorada, Sol de Mañana, Laguna Verde and points in between. There are probably 20 to 50 people a day doing this trip. You can book a day trip for B$200 to Isla Incahuasi, but if you've come all this way, you'd better suffer with the rest of the pilgrims.

Sleeping

Only better hotels offer heating, and there are water rations in Uyuni year-round. Bring a sleeping bag.

Los Girasoles Hotel HOTEL $$$

(☎693-3323; girasoleshotel@hotmail.com; Santa Cruz 155; s/d/tr B$280/480/600) This spacious and handsome hotel offers helpful service

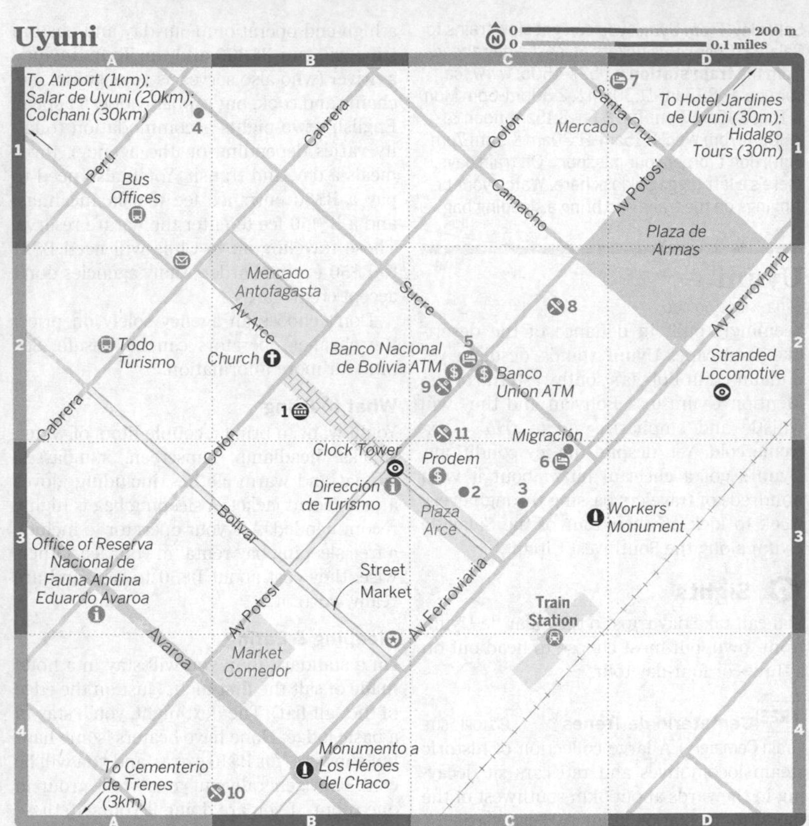

Uyuni

Sights

1 Museo Arqueología y Antropológico de los Andes Meridionales B2

Activities, Courses & Tours

2 Andrea Tours C3
3 Cordillera Tours C3
4 Fremen Tours A1

Sleeping

5 HI-Salar de Uyuni C2
6 Hotel Avenida C3
7 Los Girasoles Hotel D1
Piedra Blanca Backpackers Hostel .... (see 2)

Eating

8 La Loco C2
9 Lithium Club C2
10 Minuteman Revolutionary Pizza B4
11 Wiphala Pub C2

and attractive rooms with big comfortable beds, TV, cactus-wood paneling and gas-heated bathrooms.

Piedra Blanca Backpackers Hostel HOSTEL **$$**
(☎693-2517; piedrablanca_hostel@hotmail.com; Av Arce 27; dm B$55, r per person with/without bathroom incl breakfast B$200/150) This upstart hostel has fun common areas in a cool building that wraps around an interior courtyard. There are three dorm rooms that sleep six to 18 people, plus a handful of private rooms with or without attached bathrooms. You can leave your luggage here for B$3 per day.

Waiting for a train? Stop by for a hot shower (B$20) before you head on your way.

Hotel Avenida HOTEL **$**
(693-2078; Av Ferroviaria 11; s/d/tr with shared bathroom B$30/60/90, s/d with private bathroom B$50/100) Near the train station, this place is popular for its clean, renovated rooms, friendly staff, laundry sinks and hot showers.

HI-Salar de Uyuni HOSTEL **$**
(693-2228; cnr Potosí & Sucre; dm B$45, r per person with shared/private bathroom B$50/100) This HI affiliate offers good beds (no bunks) and all the typical hostel amenities.

Eating

For quick eats, cheap meals are on offer at the market *comedor* and nearby street food stalls. A fast-food kiosk next to the clock tower has a few tables outside and cheap bites (B$8 to B$35) like sandwiches and hamburgers. Nearly every restaurant doubles as a pub (hooray!).

TOP CHOICE **Minuteman Revolutionary Pizza** PIZZERIA **$$**
(Av Ferroviaria 60; pizzas B$30-40; breakfast & dinner) Inside Toñito Hotel, this convivial spot, run by Chris from Boston and his Bolivian wife Sussy, is a deserved travelers' favorite with the best pizzas in town.

Lithium Club BOLIVIAN **$$**
(Av Potosí; mains B$45-70) This upper-end choice has horrible service but great food.

La Loco INTERNATIONAL **$$**
(Av Potosí, btwn Sucre & Camacho; snacks B$9, mains B$25-30; 4pm-2am, closed low season) This friendly French-run restaurant and pub is a barn-like space that's lit low and furnished with comfortingly chunky wooden furniture around a log fire.

Wiphala Pub PUB **$$**
(Av Potosí 325; mains B$25-50) Named after the multicolored Aymará flag, this place has a welcoming feel with its wooden tables, earthy vibe and board games.

Information

Watch your cash stash, especially around the train and bus stations. There are cash machines in town, but they don't always work.

Banco Nacional de Bolivia ATM (Av Potosí)

Banco Union ATM (cnr Sucre & Av Potosí)

Dirección de Turismo (direccionturismo uyuni@hotmail.com; cnr Potosí & Arce; 8:30am-noon & 2-6:30pm Mon-Fri) Inside the clock tower.

Hospital (693-2025) Along Av Arce on the edge of town.

Migración (Av Ferroviaria btwn Av Arce & Sucre; 8:30am-noon & 2:30am-6pm Mon-Fri, 8:30am-noon Sat & Sun) For visa needs. If traveling to Chile, you are better off getting your exit stamp at the border.

Office of Reserva Nacional de Fauna Andina Eduardo Avaroa (REA; www.boliviarea.com; cnr Colón & Avaroa; 8:30am-12:30pm & 2:30am-6:30pm Mon-Fri) Somewhat helpful administrative office for the park of the same name. You can buy your park entry (B$150) here if going under your own steam.

Post Office (Av Arce s/n)

Prodem (Plaza Arce) Cash advances.

Getting There & Away

You can get to Uyuni by bus, plane or train. Buy your bus ticket the day before and your train ticket as far in advance as you can.

Bus

All buses leave from the west end of Av Arce, a couple of minutes' walk from the plaza. There's a choice of companies to most destinations, so ask around to get the best price, best time and best service.

Buses to Oruro (B$43 to B$117, seven to eight hours) and La Paz (B$71 to B$230, 10 to 12 hours) generally leave around at 7pm or 8pm. Buses south to Atocha (B$30, four hours), Tupiza (B$50, seven to eight hours) and Villazón (B$60, 10 hours) leave at 6am and 8pm. Buses to Potosí (B$30, six hours) leave at 9:30am and 6:30pm; for Sucre (B$60 to $70, nine hours) buses leave at 9:30am, noon and 7:30pm. There are also buses to Cochabamba (B$72 to B$155, 12 hours).

The most comfortable and safest terrestrial transport back to La Paz is with **Todo Turismo** (693-3337; www.todoturismo.bo; Cabrera 158 btwn Bolívar & Av Arce; B$230 one-way), which runs a heated bus service with friendly staff and an onboard meal, departing daily at 8pm.

There are buses at 3:30am on Monday and Thursday and at 5am on Sunday and Wednesday to Calama (B$100, nine hours) in Chile. You will have to change buses in Avaroa at the Chilean border; there are sometimes waits of up to two hours.

An alternative route to Chile is with an organized tour, which will leave you in San Pedro de Atacama. Some of the tour companies, including Cordillera Tours (p212), offer direct jeep transfers to San Pedro, which cost around B$300 per person. The jeeps typically leave at 4pm, there's a sleepover in Villa Mar, and you arrive

CHOOSING AN AGENCY

Operators are piled high in Uyuni: there are currently more than 80 agencies offering trips to the *salar* (salt plain). Competition has lowered prices but that cost-cutting leads to operators cutting corners at the expense of your safety and the environment. Fly-by-night operators are not uncommon – and at least 17 travelers have died on this trip, mostly from drunk-driving accidents. Ask to see the car you will be driving in (Toyota Landcruisers are the best) and to meet the driver ahead of time. If they try to switch drivers or trucks on you, call them on it. Along the way, make sure your driver is not drinking alcohol (and demand to switch cars if they are). It's also a good idea to ask to see photos of the hotel where you will be staying.

The following operators are among the better ones.

Cordillera Tours (☎693-3304; www.cordilleratraveller.com; Av Ferroviaria 314) Good choice for transfers to Chile.

Andrea Tours (☎693-2638; www.salar-andreatours.com; Av Arce 27) Another office is at Peru 200, behind the bus terminal.

Fremen Tours (☎693-3543; www.andes-amazonia.com; Sucre 325) Upmarket option. Their hotels are heated!

in San Pedro at noon the next day. From San Pedro, buses to Salta (Argentina) depart three times weekly (Tuesday, Friday and Saturday) at 10:30am. You can also get to Argentina via Villazón.

Air

The easiest way to get to town is by flying direct from La Paz to **Uyuni International Airport** (1km north of Uyuni). **Amaszonas** (☎222-0848; www.amaszonas.com; Potosí s/n) has Uyuni–La Paz flights Monday, Wednesday and Friday at 9am. La Paz–Uyuni flights leave Tuesday, Thursday, Saturday and Sunday at 7am (and possibly 1:40pm, depending on demand). Schedules change frequently, and tickets cost B$869 to B$975 one-way.

Train

Uyuni has a modern, well-organized **train station** (☎693-2320; www.fca.com.bo; Av Ferroviaria s/n). Trains take you north to Oruro, south to Villazón and east to Calama, Chile. Seats often sell out so buy your ticket several days in advance or get an agency to do it for you. There are numerous reports of slow-trains, cancelled trains, and large gaps in service – but that's all part of the adventure.

Depending on size, you may have to check your backpack/case into the luggage compartment. Look out for snatch thieves on the train just before it pulls out.

Expreso del Sur is the slightly more luxurious of the two services available, departing Uyuni on Thursday and Sunday at 12:05am for Oruro (first/coach B$112/56); and to Atocha, Tupiza and Villazón on Wednesday and Saturday (12:45am). Cheaper service is available on the Wara Wara line, leaving Uyuni Tuesday and Friday at 1:45am for Oruro (first/coach/normal B$95/44/32); and south to Atocha, Tupiza and Villazón on Thursday and Monday (2:50am).

On Monday at 3am a train trundles west for Avaroa (B$32, five hours) on the Chilean border, where you cross to Ollagüe and may have to wait a few hours to clear Chilean customs. From here, another train continues to Calama (B$91 from Uyuni, six hours from Ollagüe). The whole trip can take up to 24 hours but it's a spectacular, if uncomfortable, journey. Taking a bus to Calama is more reliable.

Southwest Circuit

Bolivia's southwestern corner is an awe-inspiring collection of harsh, diverse landscapes ranging from the blinding white Salar de Uyuni salt flat to the geothermal hotbed of Los Lípez, one of the world's harshest wilderness regions and an important refuge for many Andean wildlife species.

Much of the region is nominally protected in the **Reserva Nacional de Fauna Andina Eduardo Avaroa** (REA; www.boliviarea.com; admission B$150), which was created in 1973, covers an area of 7150 sq km and receives in excess of 50,000 visitors annually.

SALAR DE UYUNI

One of the globe's most evocative and eerie sights, the world's largest salt flat (12,106 sq km) sits at 3653m (11,984ft). When the surface is dry, the *salar* is a pure white expanse of the greatest nothingness imaginable – just the blue sky, the white ground and you. When there's a little water, the surface perfectly reflects the clouds and the blue Altiplano sky, and the horizon disappears.

THE STANDARD CIRCUIT

After stopping in the **Cemeterio de Trenes**, **Cochani salt extraction areas**, and a now-closed **Salt Hotel** (B$25 entrance), your tour will continue on to the spectacular **Isla Incahuasi** (admission B$30), better known as Isla del Pescado, in the heart of the *salar* 80km west of Colchani. This hilly outpost is covered in Trichoreus cactus and surrounded by a flat white sea of hexagonal salt tiles. At the base of the island, the **Museo Ritual** has some interesting Spanish-language displays on Aymará rituals, beliefs and cultures.

Most groups have their lunch here. There's also a **café-restaurant** (nyc0079@hotmail.com; mains B$14-48, set lunch B$40; ⏲lunch Jul-Oct) run by La Paz–based Mongo's; email to make a reservation.

Many tours stay the first night in the handful of salt hotels around the village of Chuvica, which sits on the eastern edge of the salt flat. A signed 1km **trail** just south of the village takes you up the hillside to a small cavern (make sure you get down before sunset). There's a basic store here. The **salt hotels** (☎7441-7357; B$30) in town are nearly identical, with no heat, salt floors, furniture and walls, and common dining rooms where you can eat dinner and shiver. An extra B$10 gets you a hot shower.

FAR SOUTHWEST

Several startlingly beautiful sights are hidden away in this remote corner, normally visited on your second and third day. The surreal landscape is nearly treeless, punctuated by gentle hills and volcanoes near the Chilean border. Wildlife in the area includes three types of flamingos (most notably the rare James species), plus plenty of llamas, vicuñas, emus and owls.

The following sites comprise the major stops on most tours. **Laguna Colorada** is a bright adobe-red lake fringed with cake-white minerals, 25km east of the Chilean border. The 4950m-high **Sol de Mañana geyser basin** has boiling mud pots and sulfurous fumaroles. Tread carefully when approaching the site; any damp or cracked earth is potentially dangerous. The nearby **Termas de Polques** hot springs spout comfortable 30°C (86°F) sulfurous water and provide a relaxing morning dip at 4200m.

Laguna Verde, a splendid aquamarine lake, lies in Bolivia's southwestern corner at 5000m. Behind the lake rises the dramatic 5930m cone of **Volcán Licancabur**, which can be climbed; take a local guide.

Getting There & Around

The easiest way to visit the far southwest is with a group from Uyuni; the above attractions are all visited on the standard three-day trip. Alternatively, you can set out from Tupiza and end up in Uyuni, a very worthwhile option.

Tupiza

☎02 / POP 22,300

The pace of things in tranquil Tupiza seems a few beats slower than in other Bolivian towns, making this a great place to peace out for a few days, head out for a rip-romping cowboy adventure like Butch Cassidy and Sundance did 100 years ago, or trundle out on the back road to the Salar de Uyuni.

Set in a spectacular 'Wild West' countryside, the capital of Sud Chichas corners itself into the Río Tupiza Valley, and is surrounded by rugged scenery – weird eroded rainbow-colored rocks cut by tortuous, gravelly *quebradas* (ravines, usually dry) and cactus-studded slopes.

Sights & Activities

Tupiza's main attraction is the spectacular surrounding countryside, best seen on foot or horseback. Recommended destinations in the vicinity, all less than 32km away, include the following canyons and rock formations: **Quebrada de Palala**, **Quebrada de Palmira**, **El Cañon del Duende**, **Quebrada Seca** and **El Sillar**.

CROSSING THE BORDER TO CHILE

Most agencies now offer cross-border connections to San Pedro de Atacama by arrangement with Chilean operators. You'll make the connection not long after passing Laguna Verde. Arrange this ahead of time with your operator. It may be wise to stop by the Migración (p211) office in Uyuni before doing this. The Hito Cajón border post is much more reliable than it used to be. They charge an exit tax of B$15 to B$30 here (B$21 is the standard), and supposedly operate 24 hours a day. Try to be there before 6pm just to be on the safe side.

A short trek up **Cerro Corazón de Jesús** reveals lovely views over the town, especially at sunset. Lively **street markets** convene on Thursday and Saturday morning near the train station. Hotel Mitru promotes its solar-heated **pool** (Chichas 187; B$20 for half-day).

Tours

There's an ever-increasing number of operators in Tupiza offering trips through the Southwest Circuit ending in Uyuni or back in Tupiza (or, in some cases, San Pedro de Atacama in Chile). Expect to pay between B$1200 and B$1350 per person for the standard four-day trip.

All agencies offer horse riding; there are jaunts of three (B$105), five (B$175) or seven hours (B$245), or even two or four days (B$380 to B$480). Also on offer by all the agencies is the triathlon, an active full-day tour of the surrounding area by jeep, horse and mountain bike. These range in price between B$200 and B$300 per person.

Recommended agencies include the following ones:

La Torre Tours GUIDED TOUR
(☎694-2633;www.latorretours-tupiza.com;Chichas 220, Hotel La Torre) Also rents bikes for B$70 per day.

Tupiza Tours GUIDED TOUR
(☎694-3003; www.tupizatours.com; Chichas 187, Hotel Mitru) This outfit pioneered many of the Tupiza-area routes now also offered by competitors.

Valle Hermoso Tours GUIDED TOUR
(☎694-4344; www.vallehermosatours.com; Arraya 478, Hostal Valle Hermoso) This agency gets mixed reviews and the owners tend to be pushy.

Sleeping

The cheapest options are basic *residenciales* (budget accommodations) opposite the train station.

TOP CHOICE **Hotel Mitru** HOTEL **$$**
(☎694-3001; www.hotelmitru.com; Chichas 187; r per person without bathroom B$60, s with bathroom B$180-220, d with bathroom B$200-300;) The best and most reliable hotel in town, the busy Mitru has been run by the same family for generations and is a relaxing choice built around a solar-heated swimming pool that's just the ticket after a dusty day out on horseback. Nonguests can enjoy the pool for B$20 per half-day.

Hotel La Torre HOTEL **$**
(☎694-2633;www.latorretours-tupiza.com;Chichas 220; r per person with shared bathroom B$50, s/d with bathroom inl breakfast B$70/140) This sound, central choice run by a retired nurse and doctor offers clean rooms with good beds and spotless bathrooms.

TRAINS DEPARTING TUPIZA

Expreso del Sur Train: Villazón to Oruro Wednesday & Saturday

RUN	COST (B$ FIRST/COACH)	SCHEDULE
Villazón-Tupiza	37/18	3:30-6:15pm
Tupiza-Atocha	56/24	6:25-9:30pm
Atocha-Uyuni	93/42	9:45-11:50pm
Uyuni-Oruro	224/101	12:05-7am

Wara Wara Train: Villazón to Oruro Monday & Thursday

RUN	COST (B$ FIRST/COACH/ NORMAL)	SCHEDULE
Villazón-Tupiza	35/19/11	3:30-6:15pm
Tupiza-Atocha	44/18/15	7:05-10:45pm
Atocha-Uyuni	75/31/24	9:45-11:50pm
Uyuni-Oruro	170/75/56	1:45-9:10am

** Prices one-way from Tupiza.*

Hostal Valle Hermoso HOSTEL $
(☎694-4344; www.vallehermosotours.com; Arraya 478; dm/r per person with shared bathroom B$40/40, s/d with bathroom B$60/120;) Set in two separate buildings a block apart, this is an old-school hostel with a book exchange, roof terrace and plenty of social space.

Tupiza Hostal HOTEL $
(☎694-5240; Florida 10; r per person with shared bathroom B$30) Budget seekers should check out this place. The rooms are pretty dark and the beds are pretty poor quality, but the sheets are clean and the courtyard is a great spot to hang out with fellow travelers.

Eating

Affordable street meals are served outside the train station and at the *comedores* around the market.

TOP CHOICE **Milan Center** PIZZERIA $$
(cnr Chichas & Chuquisaca; mains B$30-50, pizza B$27-30; 8am-10pm) For the best pizza in town, head over to Milan Center, which serves up crispy thin-crust pizzas and an amazing variety of topping options.

Il Bambino BOLIVIAN $
(Florida & Santa Cruz; set lunch B$12) This friendly corner eatery offers excellent *salteñas* (B$3) in the morning and is a popular spot with locals. The *almuerzo* is thought to be one of the best in town, and is a great kilo-per-boliviano value.

Alamo MEXICAN $
(Avaroa & Santa Cruz; snacks B$4-9, mains B$9-15) A green light outside marks this popular saloon-style spot where locals and tourists mingle in the funky two-floor space with a Mexican vibe and lots of knick-knacks.

Rinconcito Quilmes ARGENTINIAN $$
(Suipacha 14; set lunch B$10, mains B$25-35) You'll see few other gringos at this little spot known for cheap, filling lunches served in a spacious dining room and a couple of outside tables. It's popular on weekends for its *asados* (barbecues) with quality meat from Argentina.

Information

Most accommodations can do a load of washing for you and most agencies distribute small maps of the town and the surroundings.

Banco Union (cnr 7 de Noviembre & Sucre)

Latin America Cambio (Avaroa 160) Cash exchange and credit-card advances.

Getting There & Away

Bus

The **bus station** (Pedro Arraya) has buses to most major destinations or hubs in the region. There are multiple trips per day down to Villazón. Buses to other destinations tend to leave either in the morning or evening. Schedules change often so check ahead.

DESTINATION	COST (B$)	DURATION (HR)
Cochabamba	80	16-18
La Paz	70	13-15
Oruro	60	11
Potosí	50	6
Tarija	50	6-8
Villazón	15-22	3

Train

Unfortunately, if you travel by train you miss most of the brilliant scenery on the route to Uyuni, so you might consider the less comfortable bus service. The ticket window at the **train station** (☎694-2527) opens irregularly on days when there's a train, so it can be easier to have an agency buy your tickets for a small surcharge.

Tarija

☎04 / POP 153,000

Tarija's biggest drawcard is the vineyards on its doorstep and the city makes a great base for visiting the surrounding wineries in El Valle de la Concepción, home to the world's highest wines and the throat-tingling singani (distilled grape spirit).

Nothing much else happens in Tarija, but the city has some interesting colonial architecture and grows on those who stay a while to enjoy the pleasantly mild climate and take in the chilled atmosphere; this little city is as laid-back as they get, with palm-lined squares, sizzling Argentine barbecues, sprawling bar and cafe terraces, and tight streets with narrow pavements.

Sights & Activities

Casa Dorada MUSEUM
(Ingavi O-370; guided tour B$5; 9-11am & 3-5pm Mon-Fri, Sat 9-11am, guided visits only on the hour) The Gilded House dates back to 1930.

FREE **Museo de Arqueología y Paleontología** MUSEUM
(cnr Lema & Trigo; 8am-noon & 3-6pm Mon-Sat) The university-run Archaeology & Paleontology Museum provides a glimpse of the

CROSSING THE BORDER TO ARGENTINA

The Bolivian side of the main border crossing to Argentina in the town of Villazón is a sprawling, dusty, chaotic sort of place. The frontier and bus station are always busy as numerous Bolivians work in Argentina. Watch out for the usual scammers who tend to congregate at borders; dodgy banknotes and petty theft are not unknown.

The **Argentine consulate** (☎597-2011; Plaza 6 de Agosto 123; ⊙10am-1pm Mon-Fri) is on the main square. Numerous *casas de cambio* (exchange offices) near the bridge along Av República Argentina offer reasonable rates of exchange for US dollars and Argentine pesos, less for bolivianos. **Banco Mercantil** (JM Deheza 423) changes cash and has an ATM dispensing US dollars and bolivianos.

All northbound buses depart from the **Villazón bus terminal** (fee B$2). All except those bound for Tarija pass through Tupiza (B$15 to B$22, 2½ hours); it's a beautiful trip, so try to go in the daylight and grab a window seat – at night, it can be a very scary ride. Regular bus services also head to La Paz (B$140 to B$170, 21 hours) via Potosí (B$80 to B$120, 11 hours) and Oruro (B$140 to B$160, 17 hours). Daily evening buses along the rough but amazing route to Tarija (B$40, seven to eight hours) continue to Bermejo (there are four onward departures per day). Argentine bus companies have ticket offices opposite Villazón's terminal, but all Argentine buses leave from the La Quiaca bus terminal, across the border. You'll be hassled by ticket sellers for both Argentine and Bolivian bus services; don't be rushed into buying a ticket, as there may be a service leaving sooner. You can easily bargain down the price on longer routes; conversely, the sellers may try and overcharge you on shorter journeys.

The Villazón train station is 1.5km north of the border crossing – a taxi costs B$5.

To just visit La Quiaca briefly, there's no need to visit immigration; just walk straight across the bridge. Crossing the border is usually no problem, but avoid the line of traders getting their goods searched; otherwise it may take you hours to clear customs.

On the north side of the international bridge, **Bolivian customs & immigration** (⊙24hr) issues exit and entry stamps (the latter normally only for 30 days) – there is no official charge for these services, but a B$21 to B$50 'service fee' is sometimes leveraged. Argentine immigration and Argentine customs are open from 7am to 11pm. Formalities are minimal but the wait and exhaustive custom searches can be very long. In addition, those entering Argentina may be held up at several control points further south of the border by more customs searches.

prehistoric creatures and the lives of the early peoples who inhabited the Tarija area.

Viva Tours ECOTOUR
(☎663-8325; Bolívar 251, 2nd fl) For wine tours and adventurous ecotrips to Tarija's hinterlands – including four nearby national reserves – it's tough to beat Viva Tours.

Sur Bike HIKING, CYCLING
(☎7619-4200) Offers bike tours.

VTB Tours TOURS
(☎664-4341; Ingavi O-784) One of the city's longest established agencies with a reliable reputation.

Sleeping

Hostal del Sol HOTEL **$$**
(☎666-5259; www.hoteldelsol.com.bo; Sucre N-782; s/d B$250/350; ❄@) Among the nicest accommodations in town, Hostal del Sol has coffee-colored walls, flat-screen TVs, marble floors and a bright, modern design all round. Friendly service, good breakfasts and free internet make this a great place to stay.

Hostal Zeballos HOSTEL **$**
(☎664-2068; Sucre N-966; s/d B$120/160, s/d without bathroom B$60/120) Superficially the most attractive budget option, with dozens of potted plants and climbers giving the place a fresh, spring feel. However, make sure you see the room before you commit: the basement ones are grim and dark; go for something upstairs.

Gran Hotel Londres HOTEL **$**
(☎664-2369; Daniel Campos 1072; s/d B$80/120, s/d without bathroom B$45/80) This kind of retro style may once have looked very grand

in London (or maybe not), but these days wood-panelled walls and dated tourism posters might best be described as 'quirky.'

Residencial El Rosario PENSION **$**
(☎664-2942; Ingavi 777; s B$40-45, d B$80-90) It's rare to find a budget place that is so well-tended, with freshly painted and clean, though rather small, rooms looking onto a quiet patio. There are reliable gas-heated showers, laundry sinks and a common cable TV room.

Eating

You'll need to be brave to try *ranga ranga* (tripe with onion, tomato and chilli) and *chan faina* (lamb guts with greens), but even delicate stomachs will enjoy *sopa de maní* (peanut soup) or *saice* (diced meat and vegetables). Don't forget to sample the desserts too; *dulce de lacayote*, *pepitas de leche* (cinnamon fudge) and *tojori* (pancakes with cloves and aniseed) are all favorites. Get a hold of the *Guía Gastronomica* from the tourist office for more mouthwatering ideas.

TOP CHOICE **Pizza Pazza** PIZZERIA **$$$**
(Carlos Lazcano, cnr Belgrano & Pino; pizza B$40-110) Exuberant hostess Edith Paz Zamora has put together a really unique blend of art and, you guessed it, pizza. The walls are splashed with colorful paintings (many featuring giraffe-necked, bug-eyed women!) and those with a creative ilk take over on Thursday (art night) and Friday (bohemian night) when folklore, music and dancing are added to the tasty menu.

Taberna Gattopardo INTERNATIONAL **$$**
(Plaza Luis de Fuentes y Vargas; mains B$22-50) This welcoming European-run tavern is one of Tarija's most popular hangouts. There are good espressos and cappuccinos in the morning, well-prepared salads, burgers, pizzas and *ceviche* (marinated raw fish) at midday, and chicken fillets and fondue bourguignonne in the evening.

La Floresta BUFFET **$$**
(Carretera a San Jacintom, Barrio Germán Busch; buffet B$45-60; ⏰Fri-Sun) A great place for pitchers of fresh lemonade and all-you-can-eat buffets.

Café Campero SANDWICHES **$**
(Campero near Bolívar; mains B$10-30; ⏰dinner only Tue-Sun) Dive into the fabulous range of breads, cakes and pastries here.

Mercado Central MARKET **$**
(Sucre & Domingo Paz) At the northeast corner of the market, street vendors sell snacks and pastries unavailable in other parts of Bolivia.

Drinking & Entertainment

Keep an eye out for flyers advertising *peñas,* usually held at restaurants on weekends.

La Candela BAR
(Plaza Sucre; ⏰9am-midnight Mon-Fri, 9am-2am Sat & Sun) This thriving little French-owned bar-cafe has a bohemian atmosphere, as well as a great snack menu and live music at weekends.

Xoxo BAR
(Calle 15 de Abril; ⏰8am-midnight daily) Retro rock chic at this bar-cafe with walls adorned by pop art and drink cans from across the globe.

Information

There are numerous ATMs around the plaza.

Casas de cambio (Bolívar) change US dollars and Argentine pesos.

Infotur (☎667-2633; cnr 15 de Abril & Trigo; ⏰8am-noon & 2:30am-6:30pm Mon-Fri, 9am-noon & 4-7pm Sat & Sun) Distributes basic town maps.

Local Tourist Office (☎663-3581; cnr Bolívar & Sucre; ⏰2:30-6:30pm Mon-Fri) Not much material or information, but the staff is friendly.

Migración (☎664-3594; Ingavi 789) For entry/exit stamps or to extend your stay.

Getting There & Around

Air

The **Oriel Lea Plaza Airport** (☎664-2195) is 3km east of town off Av Victor Paz Estenssoro. **TAM** (☎664-2734; La Madrid O-470) has flights to Santa Cruz (B$558) every day except Thursday and regular flights to Sucre (B$477) with connections for La Paz (B$783) and Cochabamba (B$519). The short hop to Yacuiba (B$308) leaves daily except Tuesday and Thursday. **Aerocon** (☎665-8634; Ballivián 525) flies daily between Yacuiba and Santa Cruz (B$880) via Tarija.

Bus

The **bus terminal** (☎663-6508) is at the east end of town, a 20-minute walk from the center along Av Victor Paz Estenssoro. Annoyingly, if you are looking for a quick getaway, almost all services leave in the afternoon between 4:30pm and 8:30pm. Services to Santa Cruz pass through Villamontes from where there are connections to Yacuiba and Asunción (Paraguay), though frustratingly the latter pass through in the early hours of the morning, meaning you'll have to wait almost 20 hours for your onward ride.

DESTINATION	COST (B$)	DURATION (HR)
Cochabamba	90-115	26
Oruro	90	20
Potosí	60-70	12-15
Sucre	70-90	18
Santa Cruz	90-115	24
Villamontes	40-50	9

Around Tarija

San Lorenzo, 15km north of Tarija along the Tupiza road, is a quaint colonial village with cobbled streets and carved balconies. *Micros* and *trufis* (B$3, 30 minutes) leave from the corner of Av Domingo Paz and Saracho in Tarija approximately every 20 minutes during the day.

Tomatitas, with its natural swimming holes, three lovely rivers (the Sella, Guadalquivir and Erquis) and happy little eateries, is popular with day-trippers from Tarija. From here you can walk or hitch the 9km to **Coimata**, where there's more swimming and a walking track 40 minutes upstream to the base of the two-tiered **Coimata Falls**, which has a total drop of about 60m.

The **Sama Biological Reserve** protects representative samples of both the Altiplano and the inter-Andean valley ecosystems. Entry to the reserve is US$15; the fee is not included in the prices by tour companies.

To get to the reserve and Coimata, *micros A* and *B* to Tomatitas leave every 20 minutes from the corner of Av Domingo Paz and Saracho in Tarija (B$1.50), some continuing on to Jurina (B$5) via San Lorenzo. Get off near the school and then walk the rest of the way. For Coimata, similarly frequent departures leave from the corner of Campesino and Comercio (B$3), in Tarija.

El Valle de la Concepción, or simply 'El Valle,' is the heart of Bolivian wine and *singani* production.

For a guided visit to the valley's wineries, contact Viva Tours (p216) in Tarija. If you prefer to visit under your own steam, El Valle lies off the route toward Bermejo; take the right fork at the *tranca* east of Tarija. Taxis and *micro V* leave when full (B$5, 30 minutes) from the corner of Corrado and Trigo.

CENTRAL HIGHLANDS

Cochabamba

04 / POP 608,200

Busy, buzzy Cochabamba is one of Bolivia's boom cities, and it has a distinct, almost Mediterranean vitality that perhaps owes something to its clement climate. While much of the city's population is typically poor, parts of town have a notably prosperous feel. The spacious new-town avenues have a wide choice of restaurants, eagerly grazed by the food-crazy *cochabambinos*, and the bar life is lively, driven by students and young professionals.

Cochabamba was founded in January 1574 by Sebastián Barba de Padilla. During the height of Potosí's silver boom, the Cochabamba Valley developed into the primary source of food for the miners in agriculturally unproductive Potosí.

Sights & Activities

Convento de Santa Teresa CONVENT
(Baptista & Ecuador; admission B$20; tours hourly 9-11am & 2:30-4:30pm Mon-Fri, 2:30-4:30pm Sat) The most interesting building in town is the noble, timeworn Convento de Santa Teresa.

Palacio Portales PALACE
(Potosí 1450; admission incl guide B$10; gardens 3-6:30pm Tue-Fri, 9am-noon Sat & Sun; English tours 4pm & 5pm Mon-Fri, 10:30am & 11:30am Sat, 11:30am Sun) The Palacio Portales in the barrio of Queru Queru provides evidence of the extravagance of tin baron Simón Patiño. Take *micro E* north from east of Av San Martín.

Museo Arqueológico MUSEUM
(cnr Jordán E-199 & Aguirre; admission B$25; 8:30am-6pm Mon-Fri, 8am-noon Sat) The Archaeology Museum has an excellent overview of Bolivia's various indigenous cultures.

Cristo de la Concordia LANDMARK
This immense Christ statue standing atop Cerro de San Pedro behind Cochabamba is the second largest of its kind in the world. There's a footpath from the base of the mountain (1250 steps), but several robberies have been reported here. Take the **teleférico** (Cable Car; return B$8; closed Mon). The closest public transportation access is on *micro E* from Av San Martín and Sucre.

Tourist Bus BUS TOUR
(☎450-8920; per person B$25) A convenient tourist bus leaves from Plaza Colón at 10am and 3pm and visits all the city sights.

Courses

Cochabamba is a popular place to hole up for a few weeks of Spanish or Quechua lessons. Cultural centers offer courses for around B$50 per hour.

Centro Boliviano Americano LANGUAGE COURSE
(☎422-1288; 25 de Mayo N-365) Can recommend private language teachers.

Escuela Runawasí CULTURAL COURSE
(☎424-8923; www.runawasi.org; Blanco Galindo Km 4.5, Villa Juan XXIII) Offers a linguistic and cultural immersion from B$1200 per week.

Tours

Bolivia Cultura TOUR
(☎452-7272; www.boliviacultura.com; España 301) Professional trips to Parque Nacional Torotoro and other regional attractions.

Fremen Tours TOUR
(☎425-9392; www.andes-amazonia.com; Tumusla N-245) Organizes local excursions and high-quality trips to the Chapare, Amazon and Salar de Uyuni.

Sleeping

Don't be tempted by the rock-bottom prices for lodgings in the market areas and around the bus station. It's cheap for a reason – the area is positively dangerous after dark.

Hostal Sauna Internacional Inn HOTEL $
(☎452-5382; Junín near México; s/d B$70/140) HSII (it's much easier to say it like that!) is great value for basic but comfortable rooms with cable TV. Your boliviano goes a bit further here compared to other nearby hotels, and despite being a slightly odd addition to the services on offer, the weekend sauna (3pm to 6pm) may be an added bonus for some people.

Residencial Familiar PENSION $
(☎422-7988; Sucre E-554; s/d B$130/160, s/d without bathroom B$50/100) Set in a lovely old building, this budget place has lots of character. It's built around a secluded patio, complete with nude sculpture in the fountain.

Apart Hotel Concordia APARTMENT $$
(☎422-1518; Av Aniceto Arce 690; d/tr B$200/250;) This fading but likable place, with two- and three-person apartments, is family run and family oriented. It's north of town near the university (so often booked up with students) and accessible on *micro B*.

Hostal La Fontaine HOTEL $
(☎425-2838; Hamiraya N-181; s/d B$95/160; @) Decent value but it could do with a lick of paint and the odd religious images adorning the stairwells are slightly unnerving. Rooms are spacious, with cable TV and minibar, but those on the ground floor are too dark.

Hostal Colonial PENSION $
(☎458-3791; Junín N-134; s/d B$60/120, s/d without bathroom B$50/100) A travelers' favorite but somewhat over-rated considering the facilities and the other options in the price range. Rooms are a bit run down, but the best are upstairs overlooking the leafy courtyard gardens.

Eating

Cochabambinos pride themselves on being the most food-loving of Bolivians, and there is a dazzling array of local specialties for foodies to try including *lomo borracho* (beef with egg in a beer soup) and *picante de pollo* (chicken in spicy sauce). Ask at the tourist office for its *Cochabamba Gastronòmica* leaflet.

There's tasty street food and snacks all over Cochabamba – the *papas rellenas* (potatoes filled with meat or cheese) at the corner of Achá and Villazón are particularly delicious. Great *salteñas* and empanadas are ubiquitous; for the latter, try **Los Castores** (Ballivián 790; empanadas B$6), which has a range of delicious fillings both savory and sweet. Locals swear by the *anticuchos* (beef-heart shish kebabs) that sizzle all night at the corner of Avs Villaroel and América.

TOP CHOICE **Kabbab** ARABIC $$
(Potosí N-1392; mains B$30-60; dinner only) A thousand-and-one variations on Persian kebabs served in an intimate space adjacent to the Palacio de Portales. Highlights include clay-oven flat bread, Turkish coffee and decent baklava.

Páprika INTERNATIONAL $$$
(Chuquisaca; mains B$27-80) One of the 'in' spots, this is a swish resto-bar popular for its food. After dark it becomes a trendy spot for a late drink and is also a good place to meet up with young Bolivians.

Cochabamba

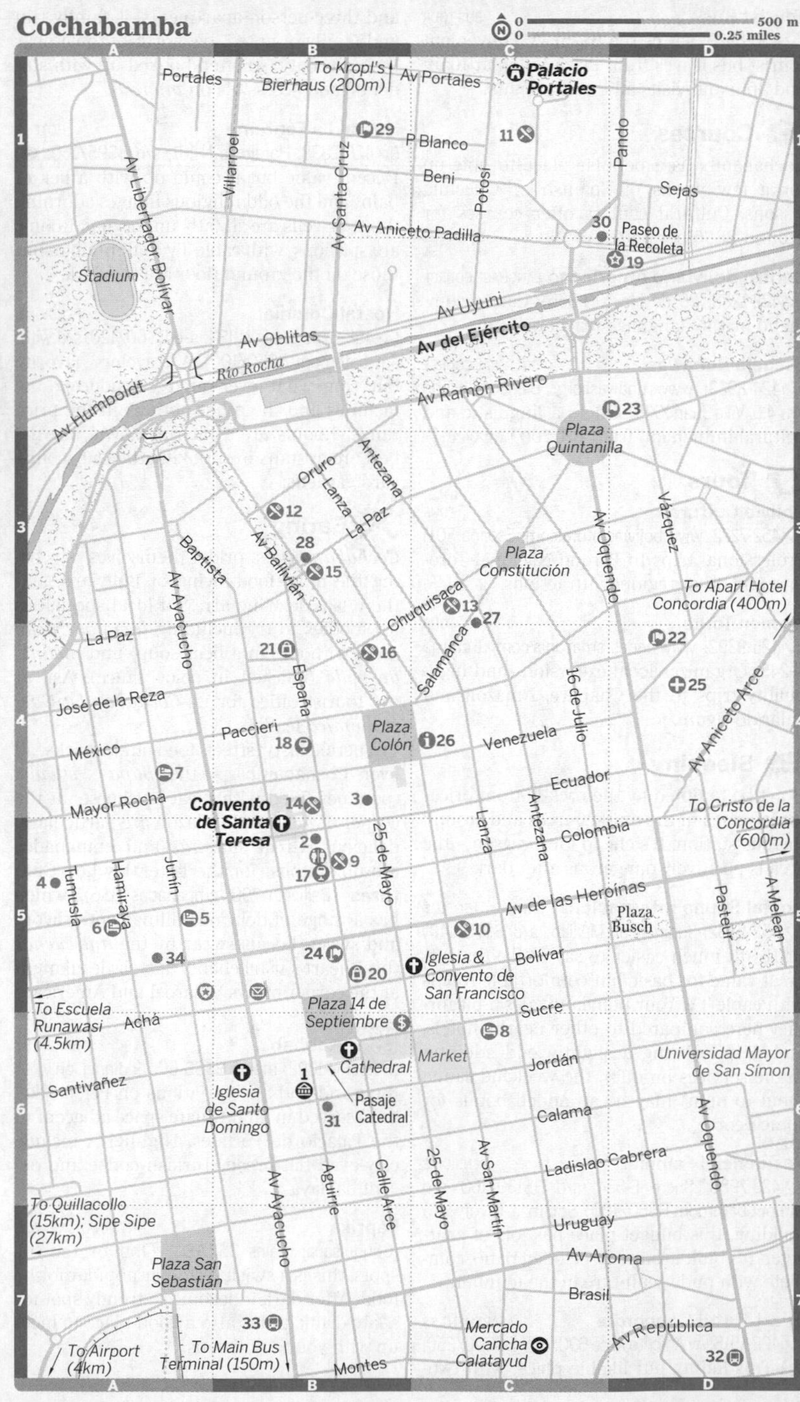
0 500 m
0 0.25 miles
To Kropl's Bierhaus (200m)
Portales
Av Portales
Palacio Portales
P Blanco
Beni
Villarroel
Av Santa Cruz
Potosí
Pando
Sejas
Av Aniceto Padilla
Paseo de la Recoleta
Av Libertador Bolívar
Stadium
Av Uyuni
Av del Ejército
Av Oblitas
Río Rocha
Av Humboldt
Av Ramón Rivero
Plaza Quintanilla
Oruro
Lanza
Antezana
La Paz
Baptista
Av Ballivián
Av Ayacucho
Vázquez
Av Oquendo
Plaza Constitución
Chuquisaca
Salamanca
To Apart Hotel Concordia (400m)
La Paz
España
José de la Reza
Paccieri
Plaza Colón
Venezuela
16 de Julio
Av Aniceto Arce
México
Mayor Rocha
Convento de Santa Teresa
Ecuador
Antezana
Lanza
25 de Mayo
Colombia
To Cristo de la Concordia (600m)
Tumusla
Hamiraya
Junín
Av de las Heroínas
Plaza Busch
Pasteur
A Melean
Iglesia & Convento de San Francisco
Bolívar
To Escuela Runawasi (4.5km)
Achá
Plaza 14 de Septiembre
Sucre
Market
Cathedral
Jordán
Universidad Mayor de San Símon
Santivañez
Iglesia de Santo Domingo
Pasaje Catedral
Calama
Av Oquendo
Av Ayacucho
Aguirre
Calle Arce
25 de Mayo
Av San Martín
Ladislao Cabrera
To Quillacollo (15km); Sipe Sipe (27km)
Uruguay
Av Aroma
Plaza San Sebastián
Brasil
Mercado Cancha Calatayud
Av República
To Airport (4km)
To Main Bus Terminal (150m)
Montes
1 2 3 4 5 6 7 8 9 10 11 12 13 14 15 16 17 18 19 20 21 22 23 24 25 26 27 28 29 30 31 32 33 34
A B C D

Cochabamba

Top Sights

	Convento de Santa Teresa	B5
	Palacio Portales	C1

Sights

1	Museo Arqueológico	B6

Activities, Courses & Tours

2	Bolivia Cultura	B5
3	Centro Boliviano Americano	B4
4	Fremen Tours	A5

Sleeping

5	Hostal Colonial	A5
6	Hostal La Fontaine	A5
7	Hostal Sauna Internacional Inn	A4
8	Residencial Familiar	C6

Eating

9	Gopal	B5
10	Gopinath Uno's	C5
11	Kabbab	C1
12	Los Castores	B3
13	Páprika	C3
14	Picasso's	B4
15	Savarín	B3
16	Sucremanta	B4

Drinking

17	Cerebritos	B5
18	Oásis de Dali	B4

Entertainment

19	Levoa	D2

Shopping

20	Los Amigos del Libro	B5
21	Spitting Llama	B4

Information

22	Argentinian Consulate	D4
23	Brazilian Consulate	D2
24	German Consulate	B5
25	Hospital Viedma	D4
26	Infotur	C4
27	Lavaya	C3
28	Migración	B3
29	Peruvian Consulate	B1

Transport

30	Aerocon	C1
31	BoA	B6
32	Micros & Buses to Chapare	D7
33	Micros to Quillacollo, Pahirumani & Sipe Sipe	B7
34	TAM	A5

Savarín LATIN AMERICAN $
(Av Ballivián 626; set lunch B$19) Despite lackluster service, this is a well-established, popular place on Av Ballivián, with a wide streetside terrace where people congregate at lunchtime for filling *almuerzos* and, in the evening, for a beer or three.

Sucremanta LATIN AMERICAN $
(Av Ballivián 510; mains from B$18; lunch only) A chain of *restaurantes típicos* where you can sample dependable local dishes, including *mondongo* (pork ribs) and *menudito* (pork, chicken and beef stew).

Gopal VEGETARIAN $$
(España N-250; mains B$20-40, buffet B$18; lunch daily, dinner Mon-Fri;) Half-decent vegetarian dishes, including soy-based conversions of Bolivian dishes, and a few curries.

Picasso's MEXICAN $$
(España & Mayor Rocha; mains B$12-49) As is the case with many of the places along España, Picasso's blurrs the boundaries between cafe, restaurant and bar, metamorphosing from one to the next, mostly depending on the time of day.

Gopinath Uno's VEGETARIAN $
(Av de las Heroínas 562 near Av San Martín; set lunch B$15; 8am-4pm Mon-Sat;) Tasty and remarkably cheap, with vegetarian buffet fare served on plastic, prison-style trays.

Drinking & Entertainment

There's plenty of drinking action along El Prado (Av Ballivián) and Calle España is also fertile territory, the latter with an ever changing parade of appealing, bohemian cafe-bars.

Many of the bars along El Prado and España turn into mini-discos after midnight throughout the week, but at weekends the in-crowd head to the Recoleta and Av Pando.

Kropl's Bierhaus BEER HALL
(Av América E-992) Home-brew beer, a lively atmosphere and Tex-Mex bar snacks make this a happening place to hang out.

Cerebritos BAR

(España N-251; ⊙6pm-late) A grungy, likable bar with cable drums for tables and loud rock and hip-hop music.

Oásis de Dali BAR

(España N-428) A popular *boliche* (nightclub) that successfully mixes alcohol consumption with an appreciation for art.

Levoa CLUB

(Paseo de la Recoleta) At weekends the cool kids head to the Recoleta to the trendy dancing place Levoa. Expect to pay more than B$30 to get in.

Shopping

Los Amigos del Libro BOOKS

(España cnr Bolívar) Stocks Lonely Planet guidebook titles.

Spitting Llama BOOKS

(España 615) Sells camping equipment and foreign-language books.

Information

According to locals the streets south of Av Aroma are best avoided and are positively dangerous at night – don't be tempted by the cheaper accommodation in this area. The bus station is around here, so don't be surprised if, when arriving in the early hours of the morning, you are not allowed off the bus until sunrise. Pickpocketing and petty thefts are common in the markets, so don't carry any more than you are likely to need. The Colina San Sebastián and Coronilla Hill near the bus station are both extremely dangerous throughout the day. Avoid them.

Money changers gather along Av de la Heroínas and near the market at 25 de Mayo. Their rates are competitive but some only accept US cash. There are numerous ATMs and cash advances are available at major banks; a handy cluster of ATMs is at the corner of Heroínas and Ayacucho. **Banco Unión** (25 de Mayo cnr Sucre) has one of several Western Union offices.

Hospital Viedma (☎453-3240; Venezuela) Full-service public hospital.

Infotur (☎466-2277; Plaza Colón; ⊙8am-noon & 2:30am-6:30pm Mon-Fri) Very welcoming, and hands out good city material.

Lavaya (Salamanca cnr Antezana; ⊙closed Sun) Most hotels offer laundry services, but for a commercial laundry try Lavaya.

Migración (☎452-4625; cnr La Paz & Av Ballivián; ⊙8:30am-4pm Mon-Fri) For visa and length-of-stay extensions.

Post Office & Entel (cnr Ayacucho & Heroínas; ⊙6:30am-10pm) International calls and post.

Tourist Police (☎120, 450-3880; Plaza 14 de Septiembre)

Getting There & Around

Air

The flight between La Paz and Cochabamba's **Jorge Wilstermann Airport** (domestic/international departure tax B$14/170) is amazing. Sit on the left coming from La Paz.

TAM (☎441-1545; Potosí cnr Buenos Aires) runs two or three daily flights between Santa Cruz and La Paz via Cochabamba and a couple of daily flights to Sucre. Except for Thursday, there is a daily flight to Trinidad and Tarija, the latter continuing on to Yacuiba on Tuesday and Saturday morning. **Aerocon** (☎448-9177; Aniceto Padilla 755) has a couple of daily flights to Trinidad with onward connections to the Amazon region, but places are limited. **BoA** (☎414-0873; Jordan 202) flies to the same destinations as TAM but prices are slightly higher, so they don't usually fill up as quickly.

Bus & Taxi

Cochabamba's **main bus terminal** (☎423-4600; Ayacucho near Tarata; terminal fee B$4) has an information kiosk, a branch of the tourist police, ATMs, luggage storage and a *cambio* (money exchange bureau).

Trufis (collective taxis) and *micros* to eastern Cochabamba Valley villages leave from along Av República at the corners of Barrientos or 6 de Agosto. Torotoro *micros* (B$25) depart daily at 6pm except Thursday, with an additional 6am service on Thursday and Sunday. To the western part of the valley, services leave from the corner of Ayacucho and Av Aroma. For Villa Tunari, *micros* leave from the corner of Av República and Oquendo.

DESTINATION	COST (B$)	DURATION (HR)
Buenos Aires (Argentina)	550	72
La Paz	45-100	20
Oruro	25	4
Santa Cruz	old road 54-110; new road 66-120	8-10
Sucre	50-70	12
Potosí	52-120	15
Villa Tunari	bus 15; *trufi* 35	bus 4; *trufi* 3

Around Cochabamba

Parque Nacional Tunari, an easily accessible, 3090 sq km park, was created in 1962 to protect the forested slopes above Cochabamba. It encompasses a wide diversity of habitats from dry inter-Andean valleys to the more humid and highly endangered Polylepis forests of the Cordillera Tunari.

The ruins of **Inka-Rakay** are a 2½ hour cross-country (but well-signed) walk from the village of **Sipe Sipe**, 27km southwest of Cochabamba. It makes a good side trip, but note that there have been several serious reports of campers being assaulted here. Sunday is market day in Sipe Sipe. Direct *micros* run on Wednesday and Saturday; otherwise go via **Quillacollo**, which is reached by *micro* from Cochabamba.

About 160km northeast of Cochabamba is the steamy, relaxed Chapare town of **Villa Tunari** and **Inti Wara Yassi** (Parque Machía; www.intiwarayassi.org), a wildlife refuge and mellow place to warm up after the *altiplano*.

Parque Nacional Torotoro is 135km southeast of Cochabamba in Potosí department. Here you'll find dinosaur tracks, cool geological formations and some excellent hikes, caves and ruins. The road has been improved in recent years, but can be tricky November to February.

Sucre

☎04 / POP 215,800

Proud, genteel Sucre is Bolivia's most beautiful city, and the symbolic heart of the nation. It was here that independence was proclaimed, and while La Paz is now the seat of government and treasury, Sucre is recognized in the constitution as the nation's capital. A glorious ensemble of whitewashed buildings sheltering pretty patios, it's a spruce place that preserves a wealth of colonial architecture. Sensibly, there are strict controls on development, which have kept Sucre as a real showpiece of Bolivia. It was declared a Unesco World Heritage Site in 1991.

Set in a valley surrounded by low mountains, Sucre enjoys a mild and comfortable climate. It's still a center of learning, and both the city and its university enjoy reputations as focal points of progressive thought within the country.

Sights

For the best view in town, inquire about climbing the cupula at the national police office inside the **Prefectura de Chuquisaca** (State Government Building), next to the cathedral.

Casa de la Libertad MUSEUM

(www.casadelalibertad.org.bo; Plaza 25 de Mayo 11; admission incl optional guided tour B$15; ⏲9am-noon & 2:30am-6:30pm Tue-Sat, 9am-noon Sun) For a dose of Bolivian history, it's hard to beat this museum, where the Bolivian declaration of independence was signed on August 6, 1825. It has been designated as a national memorial, and is the symbolic heart of the nation.

Museo de Arte Indígena MUSEUM

(www.asur.org.bo; Pasaje Iturricha 314; admission B$22; ⏲8:30am-noon & 2:30am-6pm daily) This superb museum of indigenous arts is a must for anyone interested in the indigenous groups of the Sucre area, focusing particularly on the woven textiles of the Jalq'a and Candelaria (Tarabuco) cultures.

COCA-LAND

About 1.2 million kilos of coca leaf are consumed monthly in Bolivia, leading President Evo Morales to declare it an intrinsic part of Bolivia's heritage in his 2009 constitution.

But not all the coca grown in the country is for traditional use. Bolivia is the world's second or third biggest cocaine producer, depending on whom you ask. They produce up to 290 tons of the white stuff each year. Between 24,000 and 30,000 hectares of coca are cultivated nationally (depending on eradication efforts). Legal production of coca is capped at 12,000 hectares.

If you get caught with the illegal stuff, your embassy will not help you, so don't buy it. It's also illegal to carry coca leaves into most countries, so chew them all before you leave the country.

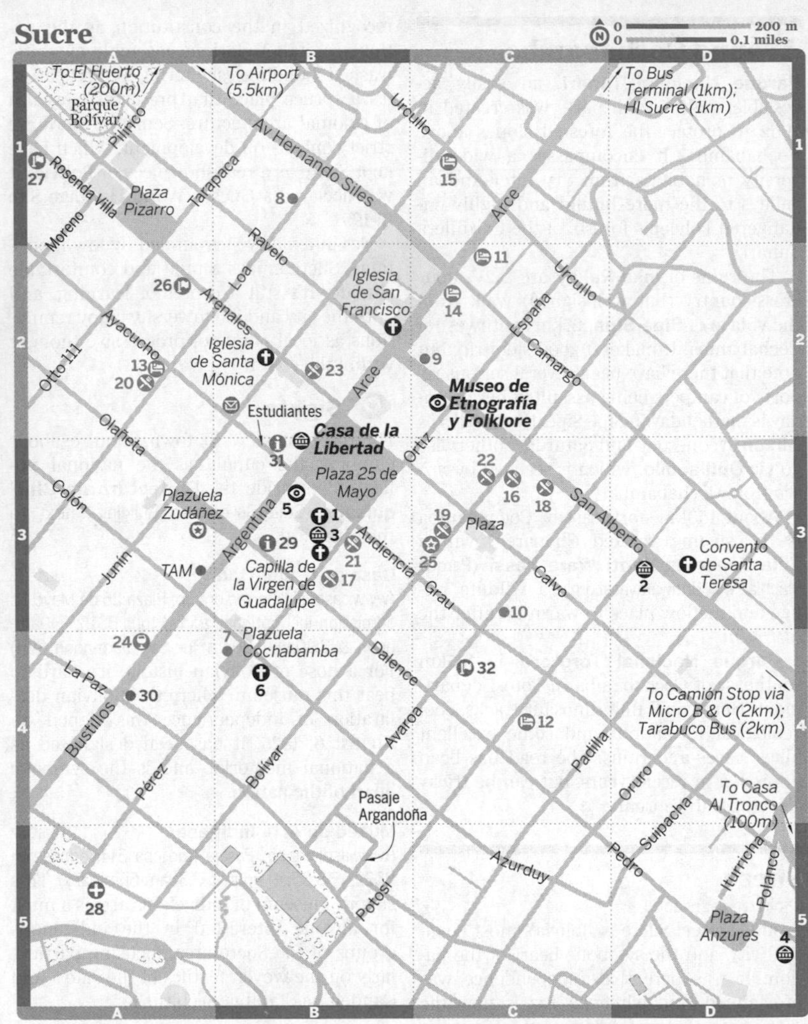

Museo de Etnografía y Folklore MUSEUM
(MUSEF; www.musef.org.bo; España 74; admission B$15; ⌚9:30am-12:30pm & 2:30am-6:30pm Mon-Fri, 9:30am-12:30pm Sat) The new Museum of Ethnography & Folklore, known locally as MUSEF, showcases a series of fascinating displays that vividly illustrate the great diversity of Bolivia's ethnic cultures.

Parque Cretácico (Cal Orck'o) ARCHAEOLOGICAL SITE
(Cretaceous Park; www.parquecretacicosucre.com; admission B$30; ⌚9am-5pm Mon-Fri, 10am-3pm Sat, 10am-5pm Sun) This slick theme park has a number of life-size models of dinosaurs, plus real dinosaur tracks. *Micro* 4 (B$1.50) runs from the city center past the site; tell the driver where you want to get off.

Templo Nuestra Señora de la Merced CHURCH
(Pérez 1; admission B$5; ⌚2-5pm Mon-Fri) This church is blessed with the most beautiful interior of any church in Sucre.

Catedral CHURCH
(Plaza 25 de Mayo; ⌚closed Mon-Sat) Sucre's cathedral dates from the middle of the 16th century and is a harmonious blend of

Sucre

Renaissance architecture with later baroque additions.

Museo de la Catedral MUSEUM
(☎645-2257; Ortiz 61; admission US$1.90; ⏰10am-noon & 3-5pm Mon-Fri, 10am-noon Sat) One by one the four sections in the museum reveal Bolivia's best collections of religious relics.

Museo de la Recoleta MUSEUM
(Plaza Anzures; admission B$10; ⏰9-11:30am & 2:30am-4:30pm Mon-Fri, 3-5pm Sat) Overlooking the city of Sucre from the top of Calle Polanco, La Recoleta was established by the Franciscan Order in 1601.

Activities

There are numerous agencies in town, and nearly all offer trips to Tarabuco (around B$40 per person) for the Sunday market; many hotels and *hostales* (small hotels) can also arrange this trip. Many also offer day trips to the Cordillera de los Frailes, but you will contribute more to the local communities by going for longer.

Bolivia Specialist GUIDED TOUR
(☎643-7389; www.boliviaspecialist.com; Ortiz 30) Tours organized all over Bolivia as well as in the local region.

Candelaria Tours TOUR
(☎644-0340; www.candelariatours.com; Plazuela Cochabamba) Intelligent and reliable agency running many types of trips.

Condor Trekkers WALKING TOUR
(☎7289-1740; www.condortrekkers.org; Loa 457) Organizes a series of multiday hikes and volunteer opportunities in local communities.

Joy Ride Bolivia TOUR
(☎642-5544; www.joyridebol.com; Ortiz 14) Popular hiking, biking and horse-riding tours, with groups leaving almost daily.

Courses

Fox Language Academy LANGUAGE COURSE
(☎644-0688; www.foxacademysucre.com; San Alberto 30) Fox Language Academy runs volunteer schemes and learning Spanish or Quechua here subsidizes English classes for underprivileged local kids.

Instituto Cultural Boliviano Alemán LANGUAGE COURSE
(ICBA; ☎645-2091; www.icba-sucre.edu.bo; Avaroa 326) Spanish and Quechua language classes.

Festivals & Events

Sucre loves an excuse for a celebration. It's worth checking out the list of many religious festivals at the tourist office.

Fiesta de la Virgen de Guadalupe RELIGIOUS
On the weekend closest to September 8, people from all over the country flock to join local *campesinos* (peasant farmers) in a celebration of the Fiesta de la Virgen de Guadalupe with traditional songs and dance.

Sleeping

Accommodations in Sucre are among the country's most expensive. The cheapest places cluster near the market and along Calles Ravelo and San Alberto.

Casa Verde B&B $$
(☎645-8291; Potosí 374; s/d/ste B$120/195/245, s/d without bathroom B$70/80; @≋) Treading the thin line between hotel and top-class hostel, the immaculate Casa Verde is a real home from home. Deservedly popular and frankly under-priced for the quality of service.

La Dolce Vita GUESTHOUSE $
(☎691-2014; www.dolcevitasucre.com; Urcullo 342; s/d/tr B$90/140/195; s/d without bathroom B$55/100; @) A delightfully friendly and spacious guesthouse, offering a variety of comfortable, honey-colored rooms for all budgets. Guests can use a kitchen, or catch some sun on the terraces.

Casa Al Tronco GUESTHOUSE $
(☎642-3195; Topater 57; s/d B$80/150) This charming guesthouse in the Recoleta district has just three rooms so book in advance. Glorious views of the city from two terraces, use of a kitchen and a welcoming reception might make you stay longer than planned.

HI Sucre HOSTEL $$
(☎644-0471; www.hostellingbolivia.org; Loayza 119; dm/s/d B$40/140/200, s/d without bathroom B$50/100; @) Set in a building with attractive original features, Sucre's HI hostel is one of Bolivia's few purpose-built hostels and thus has excellent amenities. It's clean and friendly and has a shared kitchen and even some private rooms with spa baths and cable TV.

Gringo's Rincón HOSTEL $
(Loa 743; dm B$50) A bit improvised (no phone yet!), this is a new dorm-only hostel for young, party-loving backpackers interested in meeting up with a like-minded crowd. It's clean, spacious and friendly, but can get noisy.

Hostal San Francisco PENSION $
(☎645-2117; Arce 191; s/d B$70/120) With a stunning entry hall and eye-catchingly ornamental staircase, this place belongs in a higher price range, but while the rooms don't quite live up to the initial impression, you won't feel you've wasted your bolivianos.

Casa de Huéspedes San Marcos PENSION $
(☎646-2087; Arce 233; s/d B$50/100, s/d without bathroom B$40/80) This place gets a good rap from travelers who appreciate its friendly owners and clean, quiet rooms, as well as kitchen and laundry access.

Eating

TOP CHOICE **Tentaciones** INTERNATIONAL $$
(Arenales 11; mains B$20-40) Though the gourmet pizza and pasta are advertised as the main draw here, this stylish contemporary cafe-restaurant is worth a visit if only to sample the fantastically inventive non-alcoholic fruit juice cocktails.

El Huerto INTERNATIONAL $$
(☎645-1538; Cabrera 86; mains B$25-40) Set in a lovely secluded garden, this is a favorite spot for Sucre's people in the know. It's got the atmosphere of a classy lawn party, with sunshades and grass underfoot.

Florín INTERNATIONAL $$
(Bolívar 567; mains B$35-45) One of the places to be seen in Sucre, this atmospheric bar-restaurant serves a mixture of typical Bolivian food and international dishes, including a 'Full English' breakfast. Popular with locals and gringos alike, who line up along the enormous 13m-long bar (surely the biggest in Bolivia?) at night to swill down the beers.

Joy Ride Café INTERNATIONAL $$
(Ortiz 14; mains B$25-50; ⏲7:30am-2am Mon-Fri, 9am-2am Sat & Sun) This wildly popular gringo-tastic cafe, restaurant and bar has everything, from dawn espressos to midnight vodkas, nightly movies to weekend dancing on tables. It's spacious, friendly, well-run

and you'll need an hour just to read through the menu.

Amsterdam INTERNATIONAL $

(Bolívar 426; sandwiches B$15-25) Founded with the aim of supporting the Centro Educativo Ñanta (a charity for street children), having a snack or two in Amsterdam gives something back to the community. It's Dutch-owned – but you guessed that already.

Locot's INTERNATIONAL $$

(Bolívar 465; mains B$20-42; ⊙8am-late; 🖉) Relaxed and attractive, this bar-restaurant is in an interesting old building, with original art on the walls. It offers a wide choice of Bolivian, Mexican and international food (also vegetarian), and has a gringo-friendly vibe.

Bibliocafé LATIN AMERICAN $$

(Ortiz 42 & 50; mains B$20-40; ⊙11am-3am) With two adjacent locations, this has something for everyone; one side is dark and cozy, the other a little smarter-looking.

Freya VEGETARIAN $

(Loa 751; set lunch B$20; ⊙noon-2pm Mon-Sat; 🖉) Part of the Freya Gym, this likable place serves up tasty vegetarian *almuerzos*, though the choice is very limited.

El Germen INTERNATIONAL $$

(San Alberto 237; mains B$25-40, vegetarian set lunch B$20; 🖉) This simply decorated, peaceful spot is a favorite for its tasty vegetarian dishes. There's a book exchange too.

Drinking & Entertainment

Check out the bar-restaurants in the Eating section for early parties. For *discotecas* (weekends only) you'll need to head north of the city center; it's easiest by taxi.

There's a monthly brochure detailing Sucre's cultural events; look for it at tourist offices or in bars and restaurants.

Mooy DISCO

(Pérez 331, inside Supermercado SAS; admission B$20-60) Upmarket disco-bar for young ravers with cash to splash.

Salfari PUB

(Bustillos 237; ⊙8pm-3am) This little gem of a pub has friendly service, a loyal local crowd, and lively games of poker and *cacho* (dice) usually going on.

Centro Cultural los Masis PERFORMING ARTS

(☎645-3403; Bolívar 561; ⊙10am-noon & 3:30am-9pm Mon-Fri) Centro Cultural los Masis hosts concerts and other cultural events. It also has a small museum of local musical instruments and offers Quechua classes.

Information

ATMs are located all around the city center but not at the bus station.

Head online to www.sucreturistico.gob.bo for good info.

Hospital Santa Bárbara (☎646-0133; cnr Ayacucho & René Moreno) Good hospital.

Infotur (☎645-5983; Dalence 1; ⊙8am-noon & 4-6pm Mon-Sat, 9am-noon & 2:30-6pm Sat-Sun) Up the stairs behind the Prefectura building.

Main Post Office (cnr Estudiantes & Junín) The tranquil main post office has an *aduana* (customs) office downstairs for *encomiendas* (parcels). It doesn't close for lunch and is open late.

Migración (☎645-3647; Bustillos 284; ⊙8:30am-4:30pm Mon-Fri) A no-fuss place to extend visas and lengths of stay.

Oficina Universitaria de Turismo (☎644-7644; Estudiantes 49; ⊙4-7pm Mon-Sat, 2-7pm Sun) Information office run by university students.

Tourist police (☎648-0467; Plazuela Zudáñez) Sucre has long enjoyed a reputation as one of Bolivia's safest towns, but occasionally visitors are harassed by bogus police or 'fake tourists.' If you have a problem, report it to the tourist police.

Getting There & Away

Air

The domestic departure tax is B$11. Sucre has daily flights to Tarija and Cochabamba with **TAM** (☎646-0944; Bustillos) and **Aerocon** (☎645-0007; Juana Azurduy Airport). Flights to Cochabamba connect with La Paz and Santa Cruz so they fill up fast and you will need to book ahead. **Juana Azurduy Airport** (☎645-4445) is frequently shut in bad weather, so check with the airline before heading out there.

Bus & Shared Taxi

The **bus terminal** (☎644-1292) is a 15-minute walk uphill from the center, and most easily accessed by *micros A* or *3* (B$1.50) from along Ravelo, or by taxi (as the *micros* are too crowded for lots of luggage). Unless you're headed for Potosí, it's wise to book long-distance buses a day in advance, in order to reserve a seat. There's a terminal tax of B$2.50. To save the trip to the bus station many central travel agents also sell tickets on selected services for a small commission.

DESTINATION	COST (B$)	DURATION (HR)
Camiri	100	14
Cochabamba	50-70	12
La Paz	70-135	14-16
Oruro	50-60	10
Potosí	15-30	3
Santa Cruz	94-105	15-20

Getting Around

Local *micros* (B$2) take circuitous routes around Sucre's one-way streets. Most seem to congregate at or near the market; they can be waved down virtually anywhere. You can reach the bus terminal on *micro A* or the airport on *micros F* or *1* (allow an hour) or by taxi (B$25).

Around Sucre

The small, predominantly indigenous village of **Tarabuco**, 65km southeast of Sucre, is known for its beautiful weavings, the colorful, sprawling **Sunday market** and the **Pujllay** festival on the third Sunday in March, when hundreds of indigenous people from the surrounding countryside descend on the town in local costumes.

The easiest way to get to Tarabuco is by charter bus (B$40 round-trip, two hours each way) from Sucre, which leaves from outside Hostal Charcas on Ravelo around 8:30am. Tickets must be bought in advance from bigger hotels or any travel agent. From Tarabuco, the buses return to Sucre anytime between 1pm and 3pm.

Alternatively, *micros* (B$10, two hours) leave when full from Av de las Américas in Sucre on Sunday between 6:30am and 9:30am. Returns to Sucre leave between 11am and 3:30pm.

For scenic trekking opportunities, head to **Cordillera de los Frailes**, a spectacular mountain range that runs through much of western Chuquisaca and northern Potosí departments. Home to the Quechua-speaking Jalq'a people, it has a string of sites worth visiting, including the rock paintings of **Pumamachay** and **Incamachay**, the weaving village of **Potolo**, the dramatic **Maragua Crater** and the **Talula hot springs**. There are plenty of hiking routes but they traverse little-visited areas; to minimize cultural impact and avoid getting hopelessly lost, hire a registered guide (around B$200 per day plus costs) in Sucre.

Potosí

02 / POP 145,000

The conquistadors never found El Dorado, the legendary city of gold, but they did get their hands on Potosí and its Cerro Rico, a 'Rich Hill' full of silver. The city was founded in 1545 as soon as the ore was discovered, and pretty soon the silver extracted here was bankrolling the Spanish empire. Even today, something very lucrative is said to *vale un Potosí* (be worth a Potosí).

Potosí's story is wholly tied to its silver. During the boom years, when the metal must have seemed inexhaustible, it became the largest and wealthiest city of the Americas. Once the silver more or less dried up however, the city went into decline and its citizens slipped into poverty. The ore is still being extracted by miners in some of the most abysmal conditions imaginable – a visit to see today's miners at work provokes disbelief at just how appalling the job is. But the rest of Potosí – its grand churches, ornate colonial architecture and down-to-earth, friendly inhabitants – is a real delight.

Sights

Potosí's central area contains a wealth of colonial architecture.

Casa Nacional de la Moneda MUSEUM

(Ayacucho near Bustillos; admission by mandatory 2hr guided tour B$40, camera B$20; 9am, 10:30am, 2:30pm & 4:30pm Tue-Sat, 9am & 10:30am Sun) Casa Nacional de la Moneda is worth its weight in silver; it's one of South America's finest museums. Constructed between 1753 and 1773 to control the minting of colonial coins, the restored building now houses religious art, ancient coins and wooden minting machines.

Los Ingenios HISTORICAL BUILDING

On the banks *(la ribera)* of the Río Huana Mayu, in the upper Potosí barrios of Cantumarca and San Antonio, are some fine ruined examples of the *ingenios* (smelters). These were formerly used to extract silver from the ore hauled out of Cerro Rico.

Museo & Convento de San Francisco MUSEUM

(cnr Tarija & Nogales; admission B$15; 9am-noon & 2:30am-6pm Mon-Fri, 9am-noon Sat) The San Francisco Convent was founded in 1547 by Fray Gaspar de Valverde, making it the oldest monastery in Bolivia. The museum has

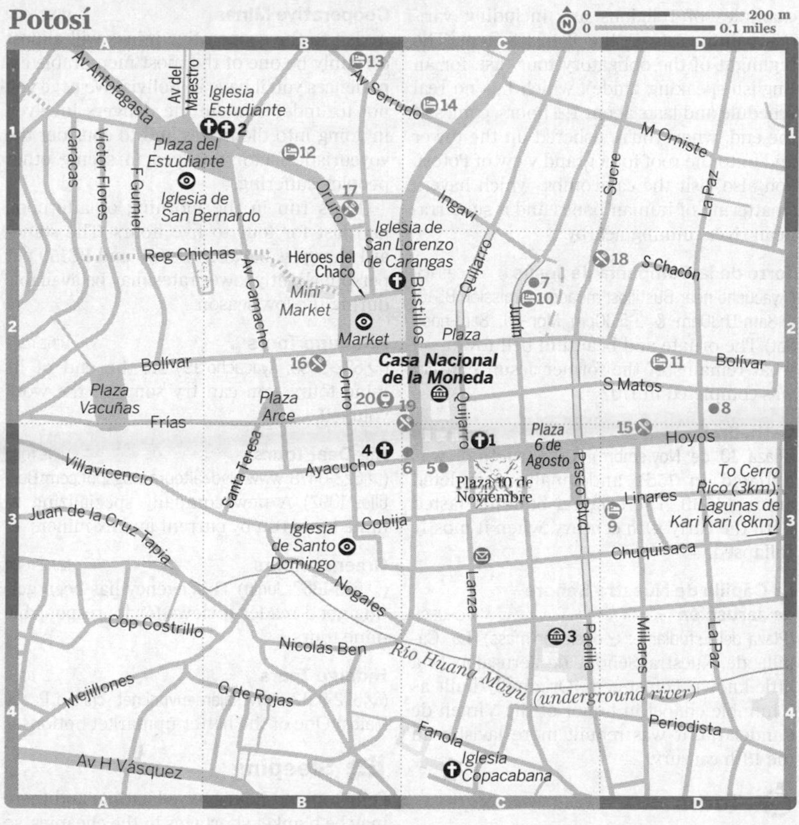

Potosí

Top Sights
Casa Nacional de la Moneda C2

Sights
1 Cathedral C3
Iglesia de la Merced .... (see 15)
2 La Capilla de Nuestra Señora de Jerusalén B1
3 Museo & Convento de San Francisco C4
4 Torre de la Compañía de Jesús B3

Activities, Courses & Tours
5 Altiplano Tours C3
6 Big Deal Tours C3
7 Greengo Tours C2
8 Hidalgo Tours D2

Sleeping
9 Hostal Carlos V Imperial D3
10 Hostal Felimar C2
11 Hostal Las Tres Portadas D2
12 Hostal San José B1
13 Residencial 10 de Noviembre B1
14 Residencial Felcar C1

Eating
15 Café de la Merced D3
16 Malpartida B2
17 Manzana Mágica B1
18 Phishqa Warmis D2
19 Pizzeria El Maná C2

Drinking
20 La Casona Pub B2

Information
Infotur .... (see 4)
Tourist Police .... (see 4)

examples of religious art, including various paintings from the Potosí School. The highlight of the obligatory tour (ask for an English-speaking guide), which has no real schedule and lasts about 1½ hours, comes at the end, when you're ushered up the tower and onto the roof for a grand view of Potosí. You also visit the catacombs, which have a smattering of human bones and a subterranean river running nearby.

Torre de la Compañía de Jesús CHURCH
(Ayacucho near Bustillos; mirador admission B$10; 8am-11:30am & 2-5:30pm Mon-Fri, 8am-noon Sat) The ornate and beautiful bell tower, on what remains of the former Jesuit church, was completed in 1707.

Cathedral CHURCH
(Plaza 10 de Noviembre) Construction was initiated in 1564 and finally completed around 1600. The original building lasted until the early 19th century, when it mostly collapsed.

La Capilla de Nuestra Señora de Jerusalén CHURCH
(Plaza del Estudiante; open for mass) La Capilla de Nuestra Señora de Jerusalén is a little-known Potosí gem. Originally built as a humble chapel in honor of the Virgen de Candelaria, it was rebuilt more lavishly in the 18th century.

Tours

In addition to mine tours, there are a variety of guided tours offered by the huge number of local agencies, including a three-hour city tour (B$70 to B$100 not including entry fees) of the museums and monuments. Other popular options include Tarapaya (B$50 to B$100); guided trekking trips around the **Lagunas de Kari Kari** (B$160 to B$280); and tours of colonial haciendas around Potosí (B$150).

Cooperative Mines MINE TOUR
A visit to the cooperative mines will almost certainly be one of the most memorable experiences you'll have in Bolivia. We urge you not to underestimate the dangers involved in going into the mines and to consider the voyeuristic factor involved in seeing other people's suffering.

Tours run in the morning or afternoon and last for four to five hours. The standard charge is between B$100 and B$150 per person; slightly lower rates may be available during the low season.

Altiplano Tours MINE TOUR
(622-5353; Ayacucho 19) At the end of its mine tours, you can try some of the work yourself.

Big Deal Tours MINE TOUR
(623-0478; www.bigdealtours.blogspot.com; Bustillos 1092) A new company specializing in mine tours run by current and ex-miners.

Greengo Tours MINE TOUR
(623-1362; Junín) This agency has been getting good reader reviews for its responsible mine tours.

Hidalgo Tours TOUR
(622-9512; www.salardeuyuni.net; cnr La Paz & Matos) One of the better upmarket options.

Sleeping

Only top-end hotels have heating, and there may be blanket shortages in the cheapies, so you'll want a sleeping bag. Hard-core budget places may charge extra for hot showers.

TOP CHOICE **Hostal Carlos V Imperial** HOTEL $$
(623-1010; Linares 42; d/ste B$180/200, s/d without bathroom B$70/140) In terms of value for money this is about your best bet in town, though the rooms with shared bathroom are a little cramped. The same can't be

WARNING: MINE TOURS

The cooperatives are not museums, but working mines and fairly nightmarish places. Anyone undertaking a tour needs to realize that there are risks involved. Anyone with doubts or medical problems – especially claustrophobes, asthmatics and others with respiratory conditions – should avoid these tours. Medical experts including the NHS note that limited exposure from a few hours' on a tour is extremely unlikely to cause any lasting health impacts. If you have any concerns whatsoever about exposure to asbestos or silica dust, you should not enter the mines. Accidents also happen – explosions, falling rocks, runaway trolleys etc. For these reasons, all tour companies make visitors sign a disclaimer absolving them completely from any responsibility for injury, illness or death – if your tour operator does not, choose another.

said for ensuite rooms though, and the extra space is money well spent.

Hostal San José PENSION **$$**
(☎622-4394; Oruro 171; s/d B$90/180, without bathroom B$70/140) This place has a cheery vibe and decent location; a 3rd floor was going up at research time. Ground floor rooms are pokey with low ceilings, so it's worth paying the extra for a better room: more warmth, an electric socket and a bigger bed with a less lumpy mattress.

Hostal Las Tres Portadas HOTEL **$**
(☎622-8919; www.tresportadas.com; Bolívar 1092; s/d/t/ste B$90/150/200/300, s without bathroom B$70; @) Situated in one of Potosí's most characterful buildings and based around two pretty patios, this blue-colored hotel is well run and adequately heated.

Hostal Felimar HOSTEL **$**
(☎622-4357; Junín 14; s/d/tr B$100/140/170, s/d without bathroom B$60/90) This pleasant, centrally located hostel has some low-ceilinged rooms and some nicer upstairs rooms with balconies affording views over the colonial street below.

Residencial 10 de Noviembre PENSION **$**
(☎622-3253; Av Serrudo 181; d B$120, per person without bathroom B$40) In a tall white building, with fresh paint outside and in. Rooms are perfectly decent, with impeccable shared bathrooms, reliable hot water, and a lovely covered terrace.

Residencial Felcar PENSION **$**
(☎622-4966; Av Serrudo 345; s/d B$70/140, without bathroom B$30/60) This friendly place makes for a sound option with its clean, simple rooms (you'll want a sleeping bag in the cheaper ones).

Eating

Stalls in the market *comedor* serve inexpensive breakfasts of bread, pastries and coffee. Downstairs there are some excellent juice stands. Cheese or meat empanadas are sold around the market until early afternoon, and in the evening, street vendors sell cornmeal and cheese *humitas* (corn dumplings).

TOP CHOICE **Malpartida** BOLIVIAN **$**
(Bolívar 644; salteñas B$5; ⌚morning only) Most Bolivians acknowledge, when pushed, that Potosí does the best *salteñas* – juicy, spicy and oh-so-tasty. In Potosí, if you ask around town where you can get the best *salteñas* this is where you'll be sent, presumably making it the best of the best.

Pizzeria El Maná PIZZERIA **$**
(Bustillos 1080; set lunch B$15, pizza B$14-26) You can't beat this family-style locals' favorite, right opposite Casa Nacional de la Moneda, for its great-value lunches. This yellow-painted spot is simple both in decor and cuisine. At night they only serve pizzas.

La Casona Pub PUB
(Frías 41; ⌚6pm-midnight Mon-Sat) The atmospheric La Casona Pub is tucked away in the historic 1775 home of the royal envoy sent to administer the mint. It's a memorable, friendly watering hole with pub grub. On Friday it stages live music performances.

Phishqa Warmis INTERNATIONAL **$$**
(Sucre 56; meals B$20-50, set lunch B$25) A pleasingly cozy little restaurant-lounge with colored walls and a vaulted ceiling. The pub-style à la carte food gets mixed reviews, but the buffet *almuerzo* is better.

Manzana Mágica VEGETARIAN **$**
(Oruro 239; mains B$12-25; ⌚8:30am-3pm & 5:30am-10pm Mon-Sat; 🖉) This is a worthwhile, strictly vegetarian spot known for its breakfast – muesli, juice, eggs and brown bread, and tasty soy steaks. The *almuerzo* (B$15) is ultra-healthy.

Café de la Merced CAFE **$**
(Iglesia de la Merced, Hoyos s/n; light meals B$15; ⌚11am-12:30pm & 2-6pm) You couldn't ask for a better location than this rooftop cafe: atop the Iglesia de la Merced, right by the bells, with stellar city views.

Information

ATMs are common in the center of town.

Infotur (☎623-1021; Ayacucho near Bustillos; ⌚8am-noon & 2-6pm Mon-Fri) Quite helpful and making a big effort to improve the standard of Potosí's services. At the time of writing, there were unconfirmed rumors that the office may move to the ex Hotel IV Centenario building on Plaza del Estudiante.

Migración (☎622-5989; Calama 188) For visa extensions.

Post Office (cnr Lanza & Chuquisaca; ⌚8am-8pm Mon-Fri, to 5:30pm Sat, 9am-11:30pm Sun) Close to the main square.

Tourist Police (☎622-7477; Ayacucho near Bustillos) Helpful; on the ground floor of the Torre de la Compañía de Jesús building, together with the tourist office. They also run a kiosk on Pasaje Boulevar, on the corner.

Getting There & Away

Timetables and contact details for all transport operators can be found online at www.potosy.com.bo.

Micros and minibuses (B$1.30) shuttle between the center and the Cerro Rico mines, as well to the bus terminal. Taxis charge B$4 per person around the center, slightly more at night and B$10 to the bus terminal.

Bus & Shared Taxi

All road routes into Potosí are quite scenic, and arriving by day will always provide a dramatic introduction to the city. The new bus terminal is about 2km north of the city center on Av Las Banderas and nearly all *flotas* now depart from here. *Micros I* or *A* run between the bus terminal and the cathedral.

There are direct *flotas* to La Paz, but in many cases it can be quicker to look for a connection in Oruro. Similarly for Sucre, shared taxis (B$50, two hours) are pricier than the *flotas*, but are faster and more comfortable and can pick you up at your hotel. Try **Cielito Express** (☎624-6040), **Infinito** (☎624-5040) or **Correcaminos** (☎624-3383), but expect speed.

For Uyuni (B$40, six hours) buses depart irregularly from the old terminal, 15 minutes downhill on foot from the center. The rugged route to Uyuni is quite breathtaking.

DESTINATION	COST (B$)	DURATION (HR)
Cochabamba	52-120	15
La Paz	52-135	8
Oruro	30-40	6
Sucre	15-30	3
Tarija	60-70	12-15
Tupiza	60-100	7
Villazón	60-80	9

Around Potosí

The **Lagunas de Kari Kari** are artificial lakes constructed in the late 16th and early 17th centuries by 20,000 indigenous slaves to provide water for the city and for hydropower to run the city's 82 *ingenios*. The easiest way to visit Lagunas de Kari Kari is with a Potosí tour agency, which charge around B$180 per person per day based on a group of three.

Belief in the curative powers of **Tarapaya** (3600m), the most frequently visited **hot springs** area around Potosí, dates back to Inca times. *Camiones* leave for Tarapaya (B$4, 30 minutes) from Plaza Chuquimia near the old bus terminal in Potosí roughly every half hour from 7am to 7pm. Taxis cost about B$50 one way. The last *micro* from Tarapaya back to Potosí leaves between 5pm and 6pm.

For a peaceful retreat or some comfortable hill walking, visit **Hacienda Cayara** (☎622-6380; www.hotelmuseocayara.com.bo; lunch & dinner B$50, tea B$20; r per person B$180), which lies 25km down the valley northwest of Potosí.

THE SOUTHEAST

The Bolivian Oriente is not what you generally see in Bolivian tourist brochures. This tropical region, the country's most prosperous, has a palpable desire to differentiate itself from Bolivia's traditional highland image.

Though Santa Cruz is Bolivia's most populous city, it manages to retain a small-town atmosphere despite its cosmopolitan population. From here you can visit the charming Jesuit mission towns, which contain the country's loveliest and most fascinating examples of Jesuit architecture. Pre-Inca ruins hide near the small town of Samaipata; revolutionaries can make a pilgrimage to where Che Guevara met his maker on the Che Trail around Vallegrande; and there are miles of trekking and tons of wildlife at the little-disturbed Parque Nacional e Área de Uso Mútiple Amboró.

Santa Cruz

☎03 / POP 1.13 MILLION

Santa Cruz may surprise you with its small-town feel, lack of high-rise blocks and a lightly buzzing, relaxed tropical atmosphere. The city center is vibrant and thriving, its narrow streets crowded with suited businessmen sipping *chicha* (corn beer) at street stalls, while taxis jostle with horses and carts for pole position at traffic lights. Locals still lounge on the main square listening to *camba* (Eastern Lowlands) music, restaurants close for siesta and little stores line the porch-fronted houses selling cheap local products.

It's well worth spending a few days here, wandering the streets, eating at the many international restaurants and checking out the rich kids' play area, Equipetrol, where nightlife is rife with naughtiness.

Alternatively, join the locals and chill out on the town square.

Sights & Activities

There are few attractions in Santa Cruz proper, but the shady **Plaza 24 de Septiembre** with its **cathedral** is an attractive place to relax by day or night. There are good city views from the **bell tower** (admission B$3; 10am-noon & 4-6pm Tue, Thu, Sat & Sun).

Parque El Arenal PARK
Locals relax around the lagoon at Parque El Arenal, but it's best not to dawdle here at night. On an island in the lagoon, a bas-relief mural by renowned Bolivian artist Lorgio Vaca depicts historic and modern-day aspects of Santa Cruz. There's a small folk **museum** (342-9939; admission free; 8am-noon & 2:30am-6:30pm Mon-Fri) here too.

Jardín Zoológico ZOO
(342-9939; adult/child B$10/5; 9am-6:30pm) Santa Cruz' zoo has a collection of native birds, mammals and reptiles kept in pleasingly humane conditions.

Take *micro 55* from Calle Vallegrande, *micro 76* from Calle Santa Bárbara or anything marked 'Zoológico.' Taxis for up to four people cost around B$15 from the center.

Museo Guaraní MUSEUM
(admission B$5; 8am-4pm Mon-Fri) A small but fascinating and professionally presented exhibition of Guaraní culture. Look for the animal masks and *tinajas* (huge clay pots) used for making *chicha*. You'll need to knock on the gate for entry.

Take *micro 55* from Calle Vallegrande or *micro 76* from Calle Santa Bárbara. It's around the corner from Jardín Zoológico.

Aqualand SWIMMING
(half day B$35-50, full day B$50-70; 10am-6pm Thu-Sun May-Sep) For a real splash, dive into this water park near Viru-Viru Airport, north of the city center. The best way to get here is by taxi (around B$30).

Tours

Amboró Tours TOUR
(339-0600; www.amborotours.com; Libertad 417, 2nd fl) Trips to Parque Nacional e Área de Uso Mútiple Amboró and Jesuit missions.

Bird Bolivia TOUR
(356-3636; www.birdbolivia.com) Professional bird-watching tours.

WORTH A TRIP

BIOCENTRO GÜEMBE

A great place for a day out of Santa Cruz, **Biocentro Güembe** (370-0700; www.biocentroguembe.com; Km 5, Camino Porongo, Zona Urubó; adult/child B$90/50)has a butterfly farm, orchid exhibitions and 15 natural pools. The best way to get out here is by taxi (B$40).

Misional Tours TOUR
(360-1985; www.misionaltours.com; Los Motojobobos 2515) For the Mission Circuit.

Sleeping

Los Aventureros HOSTEL $$
(343-4793; www.losaventureros.net; Pedro Rivera Méndez btwn Beni & Alemania; dm B$60, s/d B$120/200;) Run by a couple of *ex-mochilleros* (backpackers) from Sucre, this is a new breed of hostel offering great value rooms and little quirks such as Arabian tents for those who prefer to sleep under the stars.

Residencial Ikandire HOTEL $$
(339-3975; www.residencialikandire.com; Sucre 51; s/d/tr B$160/200/270, without bathroom B$110/160/240;) This converted colonial house retains a number of quaint original features, though the nausea-inducing bedspreads in some rooms are not among them. That said, this new place is excellent value and one of the best options in the center.

Jodanga Backpackers Hostel HOSTEL $$
(312-0033; www.jodanga.com; El Fuerte 1380, Zona Parque Urbano; dm B$70-85, d B$220, d without bathroom B$180;) The 'in' place for Santa Cruz backpackers, this superbly equipped hostel has a pool, Jacuzzi, pool table, free internet and seriously groovy, air-conditioned rooms, as well as a party atmosphere inspired by its own bar. They also organize great-value Spanish language classes.

Alojamiento Santa Bárbara PENSION $
(332-1817; Santa Bárbara 151; s/d B$40/60) This is a low-key place with a courtyard and bare rooms with hospital-like beds. It's much loved by backpackers and young Bolivians for being cheap and central.

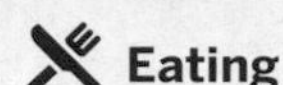

Eating

Av Monseñor Rivero is lined with snazzy cafes.

TOP CHOICE **Taj Mahal** INDIAN $$$
(Bumberque 365; mains B$55-110) Hallelujah! It's pretty hard to find an Indian restaurant in South America, and even harder to find a good one.

Naturalia ORGANIC
(www.naturalia.com.bo; Independencia 452) Organic grocery store.

Naïs INTERNATIONAL $$
(Av Alemania; mains B$23-49) This Chilean-owned place serves a bit of everything, from juicy grills with notable racks of ribs, to saucy chicken and fine fish dishes.

Vegetarian Center Cuerpomonte VEGETARIAN $
(Aroma 64; buffet per kg B$25; ⏲9am-6pm Mon-Sat; ✎) Basic and simple, this place has a buffet selection, including quinoa cake, mashed sweet potato, salad bar goodies, veggie soups and lots of other nice wholesome things to keep your body healthy.

Drinking

The hippest nightspots are along Av San Martin, between the second and third *anillos* (rings) in **Barrio Equipetrol**, a B$10 to B$15 taxi ride from the center. Admission is B$20 to B$70 and drinks are expensive.

A young beach crowd gathers on weekends at Río Pira'i. The area is potentially unsafe at other times though. Near the university, Av Busch is lined with places catering to serious drinkers.

Irish Pub IRISH PUB
(Plaza 24 de Septiembre) A travelers' second home in Santa Cruz, this place has pricey beers, delicious soups and comfort food.

Lorca BAR
(Moreno 20; ⏲8am-late) Meeting place of the city's arty crowd. Before the music starts, short films are screened.

Clapton's Blues Bar THEME BAR
(cnr Ballivián & Cochabamba; admission B$20; ⏲Sat & Sun) A dark jazz-and-blues bar.

Bar El Tapekuá LOUNGE
(cnr La Paz & Ballivián; ⏲from 7:30pm Wed-Sat) Good, earthy food and has live music most nights (B$15 to B$20 cover).

Kiwi's BAR
(Bolívar 208; snacks B$28-46) A laid-back place where you can sip on *bebidas extremas*.

Entertainment

Eleguá PERFORMING ARTS
(Libertad 651) During the week this is a Cuban cultural-center-cum-bar-cum-dance-school (it depends which day you visit!). At weekends it metamorphoses into a groovy Latino disco.

El Rincón Salteño TRADITIONAL MUSIC
(26 de Febrero at Charagua; ⏲from 10pm Fri-Sun) Traditional *peñas* are scarce in modern Santa Cruz. Positioned on the second *anillo.*

Information

Roughly oval in shape, Santa Cruz is laid out in *anillos* (rings), which form concentric circles around the city center, and *radiales* (spokes) that connect the rings. Radial 1, the road to Viru-Viru Airport, runs roughly north-south; the *radiales* progress clockwise up to Radial 27.

Within the *primer anillo*, Junín is the street with the most banks, ATMs and internet cafes, and Av René Moreno is lined with souvenir stores and bars. To the northwest of the center, Av San Martin, otherwise known as Barrio Equipetrol, is the main area for the party crowd, being full of bars and clubs.

Beware of bogus immigration officials and carefully check the credentials of anyone who demands to see your passport or other ID. No real police officer will ever ask to see your documents in the street; be especially wary of 'civilian' police who will most certainly turn out to be fraudsters.

Clínica Foianini (☎336-2211; Av Irala 468) Hospital used by embassies.

Entel Office (Warnes 82)

Fundación Amigos de la Naturaleza (FAN; ☎355-6800; www.fan-bo.org; Carretera a Samaipata, Km 7.5; ⏲8am-4:30pm Mon-Thu, to 2pm Fri) Though no longer in charge of the parks, FAN is still the best contact for national parks information. West of town *(micro 44)* off the old Cochabamba road.

Infotur (☎336-9681; Sucre; ⏲8am-noon & 3-7pm) Very well stocked with information for the whole region.

Migración (☎333-2136; ⏲8:30am-4:30pm Mon-Fri) Migración is north of the city center, opposite the zoo entrance. Visa extensions are available here. The most reliable office is at Viru-Viru Airport.

Tourist Police (☎800-14-0099; north side of Plaza 24 de Septiembre)

Getting There & Around

Air

Viru-Viru International Airport (VVI; ☎338-5000), 15km north of the center, handles some domestic and most international flights. The smaller **Aeropuerto El Trompillo** (☎351-1010), in the southeast of the city, receives the majority of the domestic flights.

TAM (☎353-2639) flies direct to La Paz daily, stopping en route in Cochabamba from where there are connections to Sucre. Flights to Tarija leave most days if there is sufficient demand, and morning flights to Trinidad depart four times a week. **TAM Mercosur** (☎339-1999; cnr of La Riva & Velasco) flies to Asunción (Paraguay) every day with connections to Buenos Aires, Santiago de Chile and several Brazilian cities. **Aerocon** (☎351-1200; Aeropuerto El Trompillo) flies several times daily to Trinidad with onward connections to Cobija and Riberalta from El Trompillo Airport.

Aerolíneas Argentinas (☎333-9776; Junín 22) has services several times a week to Buenos Aires.

Bus, Micro & Shared Taxi

The full-service **bimodal terminal** (☎348-8482; terminal fee B$3), the combined long-distance bus and train station, is located 1.5km east of the center, just before the third *anillo* at the end of Av Brasil.

The main part of the terminal is for *flotas* (long-distance buses) and the train; on the other side of the tunnel is the *micro* terminal for regional services. International routes have offices at the left-hand end of the main terminal as you enter. Most *flotas* leave in the morning before 10am and in the evening after 6pm. Taking a series of connecting *micros* or taxis can be a faster, if more complicated way, of reaching your destination, rather than waiting all day for an evening *flota*.

Heading for the Jesuit missions and Chiquitania, *flotas* leave in the morning and early evening (7pm to 9pm). *Micros* run throughout the day, every two hours or so, but only go as far as Concepción.

Smaller *micros* and *trufis* to regional destinations in Santa Cruz department leave regularly from outside the old bus terminal and less regularly from the *micro* platforms at the bimodal terminal. To Buena Vista (B$23, two hours), they wait on Izozog (Isoso), near the old bus terminal. To Samaipata (B$30, three hours), *trufis* leave on the opposite side of Av Cañoto, about two blocks from the old bus terminal. To Vallegrande (B$60, six hours) *trufi* departures are from the Plazuela Oruro on the third ring.

DESTINATION	COST (B$)	DURATION (HR)
Camiri	30	5-6
Cochabamba	old road 54-110; new road 66-120	8-10
Concepción	35	7
La Paz	old road 85-170; new road 95-180	15-23
Quijarro	70	12
San Javier	30	6
San José de Chiquitos	50	5
San Matías	150	20
Sucre	80-110	15-25
Tarija	90-115	24
Trinidad	53-125	8-10
Vallegrande	35	7-8
Yacuiba	50-110	15

Train

Trains depart from the bimodal terminal bound for Quijarro and Yacuiba. The rail service to Yacuiba on the Argentine border (via Villamontes; the connection point for buses to Paraguay) departs at 3:30pm on Thursday (B$47, 16½ hours) and returns on Friday at 5pm.

Around Santa Cruz

SAMAIPATA

The beautiful village of Samaipata (1650m) is set amid the stunning wilderness in the foothills of the Cordillera Oriental. One of the top gringo-trail spots in Bolivia and a popular weekend getaway for *cruceños,* it's brimming with foreign-run stylish hotels and restaurants. It's the perfect base to chill, hike or explore the numerous sights. Those include the mystical pre-Inca site of **El Furte** just uphill from the village, the **Che Guevara trail** (the iconic leader was assassinated in the nearby village of La Higuera) and Parque Nacional e Área de Uso Mútiple Amboró further afield.

Trufis run throughout the day when full between Santa Cruz and Samaipata (B$30, three hours). From Santa Cruz, services leave from the corner of Av Omar Chavez Ortíz and Solis de Olguin, a few blocks from the old terminal. From Samaipata, services depart from the main plaza.

CROSSING THE BORDER TO BRAZIL

The main border crossing to Brazil is at Quijarro at the end of the train line, with a second, minor crossing at San Matías, the access point to the northern Brazilian Pantanal.

You'll more than likely arrive in Quijarro by train between 7am and 9am to be greeted by a line of taxi drivers offering to take you the 3km to the border (B$10). **Customs offices** (8am-11am & 2-5pm Mon-Fri, 9am-1pm Sat & Sun) are on opposing sides of the bridge. Bolivian officials have been known to unofficially charge for the exit stamp, but stand your ground politely. Crossing this border you are generally asked to show a yellow-fever vaccination certificate. No exceptions are granted and you will be whisked off to a vaccination clinic if you fail to produce it. On the Brazilian side of the border yellow *canarinho* (city buses) will take you into Corumbá (R$2.50). Brazilian entry stamps are given at the border. Get your stamp as soon as possible to avoid later problems and make sure you have the necessary visas if you require them.

For a slightly more adventurous border crossing try San Matías. In the dry season, a Trans-Bolivia bus leaves at 7:45pm from Santa Cruz to Cáceres in Brazil (30 hours), via San Matías (B$150, 26 hours). Brazilian entry or exit stamps should be picked up from the Polícia Federal office at Rua Antônio João 160 in Cáceres; get your exit and entry stamps for Bolivia in Santa Cruz.

Tours

Jukumari Tours TOUR
(7262-7202; Bolívar) An excellent locally run agency; in addition to the local attractions it offers packages to the Che Trail and the Jesuit Mission Circuit.

Michael Blendinger Tours ECOTOUR
(944-6227; www.discoveringbolivia.com; Bolívar) Biologist-run Michael Blendinger Tours is best for orchid, birding and full-moon tours in English and German.

Sleeping

TOP CHOICE **La Posada del Sol** HOTEL $
(7211-0628; www.laposadadelsol.net; Zona Barrio Nuevo; dm/s/d B$60/120/140;) Hotel quality, hostel prices, this is the best value in town.

PARQUE NACIONAL E ÁREA DE USO MÚTIPLE AMBORÓ

This extraordinary park crosses two 'divides': the warmer northern Amazonian-type section, and the southern Yungas-type section, with cooler temperatures (and fewer mosquitoes). The village of Buena Vista, two hours (100km) northwest of Santa Cruz, is a staging point for trips into the spectacular forested lowland section of Parque Nacional e Área de Uso Mútiple Amboró.

By far the easiest and safest way to visit the park is by guided tour with one of the recommended tour agencies in Santa Cruz.

JESUIT MISSIONS CIRCUIT

From the late 17th century, Jesuits established settlements called *reducciones* in Bolivia's eastern lowlands, building churches, establishing farms and instructing the indigenous in religion, agriculture, music and crafts in return for conversion and manual labor. A circuit north and east of Santa Cruz takes in some mission sites, with buildings in various stages of reconstruction or decay. InfoTur offices, food and lodging are found in most of the towns.

Check out www.misionesjesuiticas.com.bo (in Spanish) and www.chiquitania.com.

Going clockwise from Santa Cruz:

San Xavier The oldest mission (1691) and popular getaway for wealthy *cruceños*.

Concepción An attractive town with a gaudy 1709 church and restoration studios.

San Ignacio de Velasco The commercial heart of the Jesuit mission district.

San Miguel de Velasco A sleepy town with a beautiful painstakingly restored church (1721).

Santa Ana de Velasco A tiny village with a rustic 1755 church.

San Rafael de Velasco The 1740s church is noted for its fine interior.

San José de Chiquitos Frontier town with the area's only stone church (restoration nearing completion at the time of research).

If you wish to travel the mission circuit on public transport, the bus schedules synchronize better going counterclockwise: that is starting the circuit at San José de Chiquitos. Travelling the opposite way, unsynchronized and irregular bus schedules make for a frustrating journey. A much less time-consuming way of doing it is by taking a guided tour from Santa Cruz or Samaipata, which costs around US$450 for a four-day package taking in all the major towns.

THE AMAZON BASIN

The Amazon Basin is one of Bolivia's largest and most mesmerizing regions. The rainforest is raucous with wildlife and spending a few days roaming the sweaty jungle is an experience you're unlikely to forget. But it's not only the forests that are enchanting: it's also the richness of the indigenous cultures, traditions and languages that exist throughout the region.

Mossy hills peak around the town of Rurrenabaque, most people's first point of entry into the region and the main base camp for visits to the fascinating Parque Nacional Madidi. This is home to a growing ethnoecotourism industry that looks to help local communities. The village of San Ignacio de Moxos is famous for its wild July fiesta and Trinidad, the region's biggest settlement and an active cattle ranching center, is the transit point toward Santa Cruz. North frontier towns of Riberalta and Cobija are in remote regions that few travelers dare to tread.

Rurrenabaque

☎03 / POP 13,700

The relaxing 'Rurre,' as the town is endearingly known, has a fabulous setting. Sliced by the deep Río Beni and surrounded by mossy green hills, the town's alluring sunsets turn the sky a burned orange, and a dense fog sneaks down the river among the lush, moist trees. Once darkness falls, the surrounding rainforest comes alive, and croaks, barks, buzzes and roars can be heard in the distance.

Rurre is a major traveler base. Backpackers fill the streets, and restaurants, cafes and hotels cater mainly to Western tastes. Some travelers spend their days relaxing in the ubiquitous hammocks, but at some stage the majority go off on riverboat adventures into the rainforest or pampas.

The area's original people, the Tacana, were one of the few lowland tribes that resisted Christianity. They are responsible for the name 'Beni,' which means 'wind,' as well as the curious name of 'Rurrenabaque,' which is derived from 'Arroyo Inambaque,' the Hispanicized version of the Tacana name 'Suse-Inambaque,' the 'Ravine of Ducks.'

Sights & Activities

El Chorro SPRING

A few kilometers upstream from the town, El Chorro is an idyllic spot with a waterfall and pool. You can reach it by boat only; inquire at the harbor.

Butterfly Pool El Mirador SWIMMING

(☎booking 7111 5324; admission US$2.50) Fab swim spot. Reservations can be made at the Butterfly Pub.

Biggest Canopy in Bolivia ADVENTURE SPORT

(☎892-2875; per person B$250) A community-run forest canopy zip-line in nearby Villa Alcira. Transport is included in the price.

Tours

Bala Tours TOUR

(☎892-2527; www.balatours.com; Santa Cruz near Comercio) Has its own jungle camp, Caracoles, a comfortable pampas lodge on Río Yacumo and a forest lodge at Tacuaral.

Fluvial Tours/Amazonia Adventures TOUR

(☎892-2372; www.fluvialtoursbolivia.com; Avaroa) This is Rurrenabaque's longest-running agency.

Sleeping

If you're willing to pay more, consider staying in an ecolodge in Madidi (see p241).

WORTH A TRIP

PARQUE NACIONAL NOEL KEMPFF MERCADO

The wonderfully remote and globally important Parque Nacional Noel Kempff Mercado is home to a broad spectrum of Amazonian flora and fauna.

An attempt to generate a tourist trail to the park appears to have failed. The park still remains an exciting off-the-beaten-track option for adventurous independent travelers – check with a Santa Cruz agency for visiting the park.

The Amazon Basin

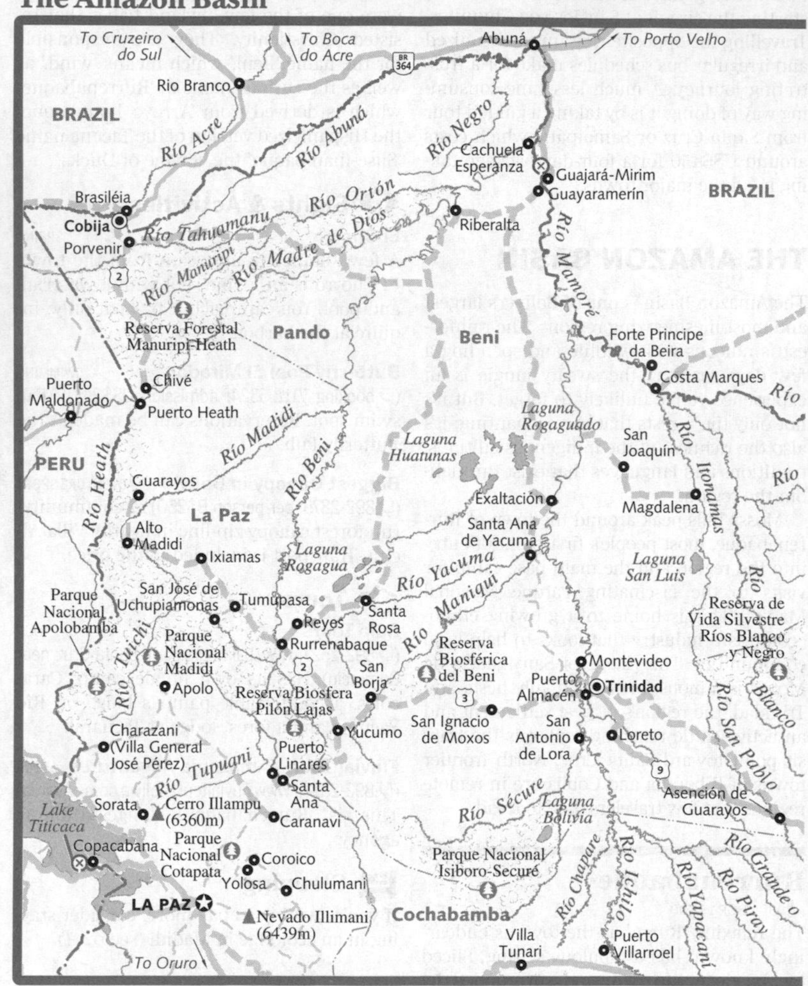

Hotel Oriental HOTEL $
(☎892-2401; Plaza 2 de Febrero; s/d B$100/150) If you meet people who are staying at the Oriental, right on the plaza, they'll invariably be raving about what an excellent place it is – and it really is. Comfy rooms, great showers, garden hammocks for snoozing, and big breakfasts, are included in the price.

Hostal Pahuichi HOSTEL $
(☎892-2558; Comercio; s/d/tr B$100/100/150) The newly renovated rooms here are tasteful, colorful and dare we say it stylish (almost!), with sleek wooden furniture and sparklingly tiled private bathrooms.

Hotel Los Tucanes de Rurre HOTEL $
(☎892-2039; Bolívar near Aniceto Arce; s/d with shared bathroom B$70/80, with private bathroom B$80/100) This big, thatched-roof house offers a sprawling garden, a roof terrace and sweeping views over the river. There are hammocks swinging on the patio, a pool table and clean simple rooms.

Centro de Recreación del Ejército PENSION $
(☎892-2377; Plaza 2 de Febrero; r per person B$80, without bathroom B$30) These old army barracks are a decent option.

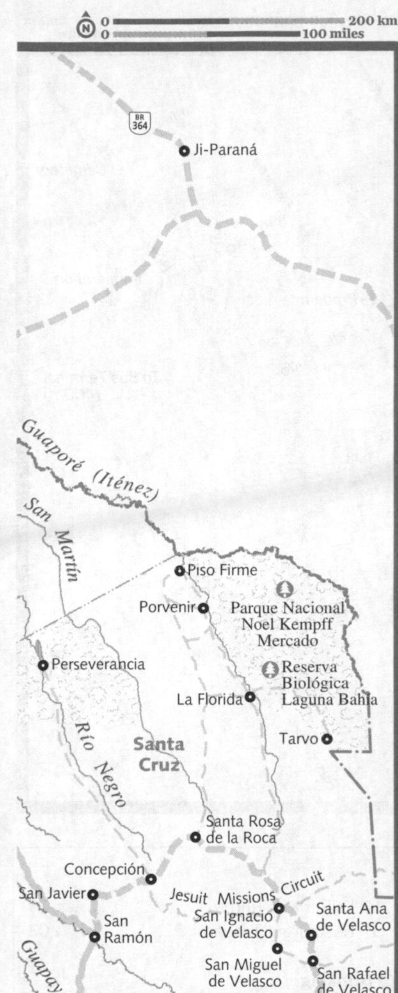

Hostal Rurrenabaque HOSTEL $
(☎892-2481; Vaca Diez near Bolívar 1490; s/d B$100/120, s without bathroom B$70; 📶) A mustard-colored, porticoed edifice, with muted wood-floored rooms. There are no frills here except for on the curtains.

Eating & Drinking

Several fish restaurants line the riverfront: candlelit **La Cabaña** and **Playa Azul** grill or fry up the catch of the day for around B$40. In addition to the Beni standard, *masaco* (mashed yucca or plantains, served with dried meat, rice, noodles, thin soup and bananas), try the excellent *pescado hecho en taquara* (fish baked in a special local pan) or *pescado en dunucuabi* (fish wrapped in a rainforest leaf and baked over a wood fire).

TOP CHOICE **La Perla de Rurre** LATIN AMERICAN $$
(Bolívar at Vaca Diez; mains B$40-50) Everyone in Rurre will tell you that this is their favorite restaurant and 'The Pearl' does indeed serve up some mean fresh fish and chicken dishes. The surroundings are simple but the service is excellent.

Casa de Campo HEALTH FOOD $$$
(Vaca Diez near Avaroa; breakfast B$20-65; ⏰8am-2pm & 6-10pm) Healthy food is the name of the game here, with all-day breakfasts, homemade pastries, vegetarian dishes, soups, salads, you name it.

Restaurant Tacuaral INTERNATIONAL $$
(Santa Cruz near Avaroa; mains B$18-38, sandwiches B$18) This open-air eatery with shaded sidewalk seating has an ambitious menu, covering breakfast to dinner. It's friendly and popular, especially for its lasagna.

Café Piraña INTERNATIONAL $$
(Santa Cruz near Avaroa s/n; mains B$15-50; 🌿) This Piraña has bite, with a great chill-out area, delicious vegetarian and meat dishes, yummy breakfasts, fresh juices, and a library and film screenings most nights upstairs.

Jungle Bar Moskkito BAR
(www.moskkito.com; Vaca Diez) There's a positive vibe, cheery service and the foliage that hangs from the roof makes you feel like you are in the jungle.

Luna Lounge BAR
(Avaroa near Santa Cruz) Bouncing atmosphere, good pizza and great cocktails.

Entertainment

Banana Club CLUB
(Comercio; admission incl 1 drink B$15) Head here if you want to try salsa dancing or Bolivian-style grooving.

Information

There is one ATM here, a block north of the plaza at **Banco Union** (Comercio), but it is wise to bring enough cash just in case it is out of order. For emergencies you can get cash advances at **Prodem** (Avaroa; ⏰8am-6pm Mon-Fri, to 2pm Sat), but only on Visa and Mastercard (including Visa debit cards). Tours can usually be paid for with credit cards.

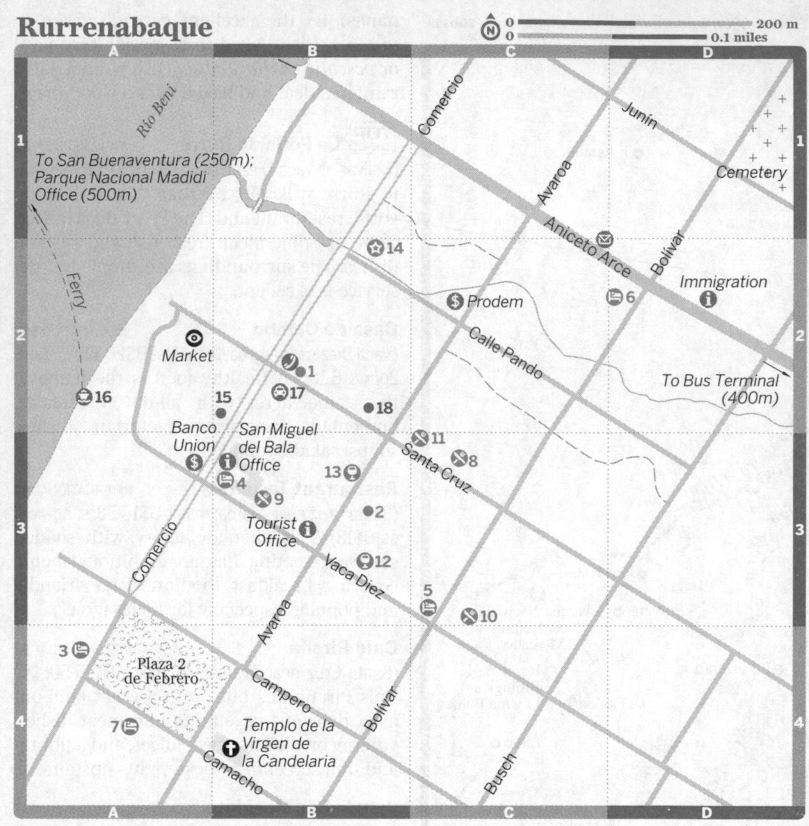

Rurrenabaque

Activities, Courses & Tours
1 Bala Tours B2
2 Fluvial Tours/Amazonia Adventures B3

Sleeping
3 Centro de Recreación del Ejército A4
4 Hostal Pahuichi B3
5 Hostal Rurrenabaque C3
6 Hotel Los Tucanes de Rurre D2
7 Hotel Oriental A4

Eating
8 Café Piraña C3
9 Casa de Campo B3
10 La Perla de Rurre C3
11 Restaurant Tacuaral C3

Drinking
12 Jungle Bar Moskkito B3
13 Luna Lounge B3

Entertainment
14 Banana Club B2

Transport
15 Amaszonas B2
16 Ferries to/from San Buenaventura A2
17 Moto-Taxi Parada B2
18 TAM B2

Immigration (892-2241; Aniceto Arce btwn Busch & Bolívar; 8:30am-12:30pm & 2:30am-6:30pm Mon-Fri) For visa extensions.

SERNAP Parque Nacional Madidi Office (892-2246, 892-2540; Libertad behind the market; 7am-3pm Mon-Sun) Across the river in San Buenaventura. Access to the park costs B$125 but should be included in tour quotes.

Post Office (Aniceto Arce)

Tourist Office (7138-3684; Vaca Diez near Avaroa; 8am-noon & 2:30am-6pm Mon-Fri) Happy to answer questions and keen to advise on responsible tourism, but short on material.

Getting There & Around

Air

Rurre's airport is a few kilometers north of town and there is a two-pronged terminal fee of B$15. Transfer in minibus to and from the airline offices costs an additional B$6. The brief flight to La Paz is an affordable way of avoiding the arduous 24-hour bus journey to the capital.

TAM (892-2398; Santa Cruz) flies between La Paz and Rurre (B$480, one hour) at least once a day, with additional services during peak periods. **Amaszonas** (892-2472; Comercio near Santa Cruz) has four daily flights to La Paz (B$650) and theoretically flies daily to Trinidad (B$581).

Boat

Thanks to the Guayaramerín road, there's little cargo transportation down the Río Beni to Riberalta these days and there's no traffic at all during periods of low water. You'll need a dose of luck to find something and will have to negotiate what you consider a fair price for the trip, which may take as long as 10 days.

Bus

The bus terminal is a good 20-minute walk northeast of the city center and all buses and shared taxis depart from here. Prices are standard and do not vary between companies.

Several daily services make the daunting trip from Rurrenabaque to La Paz (B$70, 18 to 24 hours), via Yolosita (B$65, 14 to 20 hours), the hop-off point for Coroico.

The route to Trinidad (B$150, 17 to 30 hours) via San Borja (taxi/bus B$80/50, nine to 18 hours) and San Ignacio de Moxos (B$100, 12 hours) remains one of the worst in the country and is typically closed during the rainy season. Buses now run year-round to Riberalta (B$110, 17 to 40 hours) and Guayaramerín (B$120, 18 hours to three days), but you need a healthy dose of stamina, insect repellent and food if you're going to attempt the journey in the wet season.

Parque Nacional Madidi

The Río Madidi watershed is one of South America's most intact ecosystems. Most of it is protected by the 1.8 million-hectare Parque Nacional Madidi, which takes in a range of habitats, from the steaming lowland rainforests to 5500m Andean peaks. This little-trodden utopia is home to an astonishing variety of Amazonian wildlife: 44% of all New World mammal species, 38% of neotropical amphibian species, almost 1000 species of bird and more threatened species than any park in the world.

The populated portions of the park along the Río Tuichi have been accorded a special Unesco designation permitting indigenous inhabitants to utilize traditional forest resources, but the park has also been considered for oil exploration and as a site for a major hydroelectric scheme in the past.

It is difficult to visit the park independently, but if you wish to do so the B$125 admission fee is payable at the SERNAP office in San Buenaventura – you must be accompanied by an authorized guide. By far the easiest and most responsible way to arrange access is by visiting one of the community projects listed by Lonely Planet.

Sleeping

TOP CHOICE **Chalalán Ecolodge** LODGE $$$
(892-2419, in La Paz 02-231-1451; www.chalalan.com; 3 nights & 4 days all inclusive per person US$390) Bolivia's oldest and most successful community-based ecotourism project. Set up in the early 1990s by the inhabitants of remote San José de Uchupiamonas, it has become a lifeline for villagers, and has so far generated money for a school and a small clinic.

TOP CHOICE **Sadiri** LODGE $$$
(6770-9087, in Santa Cruz 03-356-3636; full board including transfer & return to Rurrenabaque per person per day US$150) What sets Sadiri apart from the other Madidi lodges is its highland location (between 500 and 950m), resulting in a much cooler temperature than the sweaty lowlands.

San Miguel del Bala LODGE $$$
(892-2394; www.sanmigueldelbala.com; per person per day B$450) A glorious community ecolodge in its own patch of paradise right on Madidi's doorstep, 40 minutes upstream

CHOOSING A JUNGLE & PAMPAS TOUR

Jungle and pampas tours are Rurrenabaque's bread and butter, but the quality of service provided by the numerous tour agencies varies considerably and in the name of competition some operators are much less responsible than they ought to be.

Not all companies provide the same level of service, and cheaper most definitely does not mean better. Local authorities have set minimum prices at B$900 for a three-day, two-night excursion.

Use only operators authorized by the Servicio Nacional de Áreas Protegidas (SERNAP) as these are the only ones allowed to legally enter Parque Nacional Madidi.

Foreigners must be accompanied by a local guide, but not all speak English very well.

Jungle Tours

Most trips are by canoe upstream along the Río Beni, and some continue up the Río Tuichi, camping and taking shore and jungle walks along the way, with plenty of swimming opportunities and hammock time. Accommodations are generally at agencies' private camps.

Pampas Tours

It's easier to see wildlife in the wetland savannas northeast of town, but the sun is more oppressive, and the bugs can be worse.

by boat from Rurre. The price includes transportation, accommodations, food and guided tours. The **booking office** (☎892-2394; www.sanmigueldelbala.com; Comercio near Vaca Diez) is in Rurrenabaque.

Trinidad

☎03 / POP 80,000

Trinidad is the place you'll come to if you're after a trip down the long and deep Río Mamoré, or on your way between Santa Cruz and Rurrenabaque. Despite its colonial architecture and colonnaded streets, it's a modern town that is growing rapidly. Its most notable feature is the massive, green, tropical main square (Trinidad is only 14 degrees south of the equator), once home to a population of friendly sloths.

The city of La Santísima Trinidad (the Most Holy Trinity) was founded in 1686 by Padre Cipriano Barace as the second Jesuit mission in the flatlands of the southern Beni. It was originally constructed on the banks of the Río Mamoré, 14km from its present location, but floods and pestilence along the riverbanks necessitated relocation. In 1769 it was moved to the Arroyo de San Juan, which now divides the city in two.

Sights & Activities

Plaza Gral José Ballivián PLAZA

Trinidad's loveliest feature is Plaza Gral José Ballivián. On the south side of the plaza, the **cathedral**, built on the site of an earlier Jesuit church, is an unimpressive building.

Ken Lee Ethno Archaeological Museum MUSEUM

(Av Ganadera; admission B$5; ⏲8am-noon & 3-6pm) The city's top cultural attraction. It exhibits artifacts from the Trinidad region, including traditional instruments and tribal costumes.

FREE **Parque Pantanal** ZOO

(Av Laureano Villar; ⏲8am-6pm) There are several deer here and also some anacondas in the ponds, so watch your toes!

Fremen Tours TOUR

(☎462-2726; www.andes-amazonia.com; Cipriano Barace 332) Fremen Tours specializes in all-inclusive river cruises. Trips should be booked through the offices in Cochabamba.

Turismo Moxos TOUR

(☎462-1141; turmoxos@entelnet.bo; 6 de Agosto 114) Turismo Moxos organizes three-day dolphin cruises on the Río Ibare, visits to Sirionó villages, four-day canoe safaris into the jungle and one-day horse riding trips into remote areas.

Sleeping

TOP CHOICE **Hostal Sirari** HOSTEL $$

(☎462-4472; Av Santa Cruz 538; s/d B$100/160, with air-con s/d B$160/200; ❄) A step up in quality without the step up in price. Rooms are whitewashed, sparklingly new and in comparison to other Trinidad hostels worth more than what you pay.

Hostal El Tajibo HOTEL $
(☎462-2324; Av Santa Cruz 423; s/d B$100/150, with air-con B$200/250; ❄) One of Trinidad's better-value budget options, this hotel has attractive, almost stylish rooms and comfortable beds.

Hotel Colonial HOTEL $
(☎462-2864; Vaca Diez 76; s/d B$100/150, with air-con B$200/250; ❄) If Hostal El Tajibo is full, the same owners run the carbon-copy Colonial a couple of blocks further on from the plaza.

Residencial Santa Cruz PENSION $
(☎462-0711; Av Santa Cruz 537; s/d B$80/140, s without bathroom B$60) A budget place that makes a real effort to cheer up its rooms with colorful decor, hand-painted wall hangings and bright bedclothes. Rooms on the 1st floor are airier (and slightly pricier).

Eating & Drinking

Trinidad is cattle country, so beef is bountiful. If budget is the priority, hit the Mercado Municipal, where for a pittance you can try the local specialty, *arroz con queso* (rice with cheese), plus shish kebabs, *yuca* (cassava), plantains and salads. There are several decent places around the plaza.

TOP CHOICE **Churrasquería La Estancia** BARBECUE $$$
(Ibare near Velarde; mains B$40-120) Ask anybody in Trinidad where to get a good bit of beef and you will be sent here. With its palm roof and coal fire barbecue hamming up the ranch-house setting, the succulent and juicy cuts will make you wonder how other restaurants even dare to call themselves *churrasquerías* (grilled-meat restaurants).

Los Farroles INTERNATIONAL $$$
(Av 6 de Agosta near Av 18 de Noviembre; set lunch B$25, mains B$30-130) They serve salads here! In fact this upmarket (by Trinidad standards) restaurant serves a bit of everything from pizza and steak to chicken and fish.

El Tabano SEAFOOD $$
(Villavicencio near Mamoré; mains B$20-55) With cool beers and cocktails served in the courtyard, this grass-roofed resto-pub is a popular place with Trinidad's young crowd.

Information

Use bottled water for everything in Trinidad except your shower. The town water supply is contaminated.

Several Enlace ATMs near the main plaza accept international cards; this is a good spot to get some cash before heading out to the Amazon proper. Money changers gather on Av 6 de Agosto between Suárez and Av 18 de Noviembre.

Immigration Office (☎462-1449; Av Los Tajibos near Ibañez Carranza) Top floor of the white building a block from the bus terminal.

Tourist Office (☎462-1322; Felix Pinto; ⌚8:30am-12:30pm & 2:30am-6pm Mon-Fri)

Getting There & Around

Air

Departing air travelers must pay B$7 for use of the Jorge Heinrich Arauz Airport, which is just outside the northwest corner of town along Av Laureano Villar (moto-taxi B$7).

WORTH A TRIP

EXPLORING MORE OF THE AMAZON

San Ignacio de Moxos is a friendly, tranquil indigenous Moxos village, 92km west of Trinidad, that dedicates itself to agriculture and oozes an ambience quite distinct from any other Bolivian town. The best time to visit San Ignacio is for the annual festival on July 30 and 31. The easiest access is from Trinidad, with *camionetas* (pickups or small trucks) running when full from the *parada* at 1 de Mayo near Velarde (B$70, four hours).

North of Santa Ana de Yacuma is a cluster of 11 wonderful natural lakes flanked by wild rainforest and linked together by a network of weed-choked streams, which are known collectively as **Los Lagos**. This unique and enchanting region has hardly been explored by foreign tourists because of its remoteness. Chartering a plane from Trinidad or Santa Cruz is your safest bet if you want to get here as painlessly as possible. From July to November land transport can be arranged in Santa Ana de Yacuma. It's a spectacular six-hour drive.

CROSSING THE BORDER TO BRAZIL

Crossing to Brazil from the northern Bolivian towns of Cobija and Guayaramerín involves crossings of the Ríos Acre and Mamoré, respectively.

Popping into the Brazilian town of Guajará-Mirim for the day from Bolivian Guayaramerín is really easy. Day visits are encouraged, and you don't even need a visa. *Lanchas* (B$10) across the river leave from the port every half an hour from 6am to 6pm, and sporadically through the night. To travel further into Brazil or to enter Bolivia, you'll have to complete border formalities. The immigration offices in **Guajará-Mirim** (Av Quintina Bocaiúva; ⏲8am-noon & 2-6pm Mon-Fri) and **Guayaramerín** (Av Costanera) are in the respective port areas.

It's a long, hot slog across the bridge from Cobija to Brasiléia. Entry/exit stamps are available at immigration in Cobija at the Bolivian end of the bridge and from **Brasiléia's Polícia Federal** (Av Prefeito Moreira; ⏲8am-noon & 2-5pm). With some negotiation, taxis will take you to the Polícia Federal in Brasiléia, wait while you clear immigration, then take you on to the center or to the bus terminal. Alternatively, take the *lancha* (B$5) across the Río Acre; from there it's another 1.5km to the Polícia Federal.

Although officials don't always check, technically everyone needs to have a yellow-fever vaccination certificate to enter Brazil. If you don't have one, head for the convenient and relatively sanitary clinic at the port on the Brazilian side. For more information, check out Lonely Planet's *Brazil*.

Amaszonas (☎462-2426; Av 18 de Noviembre 267) shuttles daily to La Paz, sometimes via San Borja and has regular flights to Cobija, Riberalta and Guayaramerín. **Aerocon** (☎462-4442; Av 18 de Noviembre near Av 6 de Agosto) handles several daily flights to Santa Cruz, Riberalta and Cobija. **TAM** (☎462-2363; Av Bolívar near Av Santa Cruz) has a couple of flights a week to Cochabamba and La Paz.

Taxis to and from the airport charge around B$25, but if you don't have much luggage, mototaxis are cheaper (B$10) – you'll be surprised by how much luggage they can accommodate with a bit of creativity.

Bus & Camioneta

The rambling bus terminal is a 10-minute walk east of the center. Several *flotas* depart nightly between 6pm and 10pm for Santa Cruz (normal/*bus cama* B$53/125, eight to 10 hours). A number of companies theoretically serve Rurrenabaque (B$130, 17 to 30 hours) daily via San Borja (B$50, eight to 12 hours), though from November to May these services are typically suspended. There are also daily dry-season departures to Riberalta (B$200, 17 to 30 hours) and Guayaramerín (B$240, 22 to 35 hours).

Camionetas (pickups or small trucks) run to San Ignacio de Moxos (B$70, four hours) when full from the *parada* at 1 de Mayo near Velarde. Buses (B$50, six hours) occasionally run from the terminal around 9am but departures are increasingly sporadic.

UNDERSTAND BOLIVIA

Bolivia Today

In Bolivia, crisis is the status quo. Protests, poverty, inequality and slow economic progress are part of everyday life – as are movements toward greater social inclusion. At the center of it all is president Evo Morales and his constitution, institutional reforms, and broad policies that have marked the nation's revolutionary movement toward socialism.

Economically, the nationalization of energy and mining interests was applauded by Bolivia's poor, but has soured relations with foreign investors and some foreign governments. And despite sky-high commodity prices, Bolivia's economy hasn't grown as fast as it should. The export of raw materials remains the nation's bread and butter. And with the world's largest lithium deposits, plenty of natural gas and mineral wealth, Bolivia could very well continue to see moderate economic progress for the foreseeable future. The stumbling blocks will include environmental conditions (deforestation, desertification and climate change), depressed foreign markets, and the reluctance of foreign company's to invest their money and know-how in a country with a growing track record of nationalizations.

Despite modest economic growth, over half of Bolivians still live in poverty, and the social programs of the Evo Morales' administration outlined under the new constitution have only made minimal progress in remedying the nation's poverty traps.

These new measures have succeeded, however, in re-framing Bolivia's social structure. Despite having practically no escape from poverty (even today), there seems to be a sparkle of self-awareness and hope that's never been more evident among the nation's indigenous majority. And indigenous people today, especially highlands groups, are playing a significant role in politics and policy.

On the political front, conflict is on the rise. There are some 1000 standing conflicts across the nation over high food and energy prices, the use of natural resources, education, social inclusion, environmental degradation and more. People protest poor working conditions, mining operations that contaminate rivers and roads that displace communities and affect ecosystems – like the proposed Brazilian-financed road through the Amazon that brought about major national protests in 2012 and was later rejected by Morales. These protests regularly shut down the nation's roads and are having a detrimental effect on the economy. In addition, violence stemming from the ever-evolving drug trade is building throughout the region.

Evo Morales' moves to redistribute lands and redistribute wealth have met with strong opposition from Bolivia's gas and resource-rich eastern region (where autonomy movements are ongoing). Despite this opposition – and growing discontent over what many perceive as weak rule of law and widespread corruption – many expect that the numerous social entitlement programs sponsored by the Morales' administration, and paid for with the growing incomes from mining, agriculture and gas exports, will keep Morales' revolution moving forward.

Internationally, the Bolivian government has played a tight-rope act, a political two-step that balances foreign investment with national interests. At the heart of it is the concept of keeping the wealth from Bolivia's natural resources in Bolivia. No matter how you frame it, the political and social movements of today are coming together to create what will certainly be one of the most interesting chapters in Bolivian history.

History

Bolivia's living history is evident in every corner of daily life. And the significant events that shaped the past – from the rise of Tiwanaku and the Pax Incaica to the Spanish Conquest, independence movement, discovery of vast mineral wealth, loss of territories to neighbors on all sides, economic twists, flips and flops, and coup after coup after coup – have piled on top of each other to create the Bolivia you see today.

You can connect with the artistic threads of history in the country's Pre-Hispanic ruins, Colonial-era churches and in the museums, galleries and chaotic markets of the city centers. The cultural imprint that dates back more than 6000 years is seen in the language, dress, customs and traditions of indigenous peoples, and in the unique dual society that sorts Spanish-descendants, recent immigrants and indigenous peoples into difficult-to-escape archetypes: a dominant paradigm that is only now being challenged with the rise of the country's first self-declared indigenous president.

The economic wake from this dual society is viscerally palpable in the underclasses and indigenous majority, and in the sky-scraping edifices of La Paz and the broad haciendas around Santa Cruz.

From a purely economic standpoint, Bolivia is a country that never should have been. The country has vast natural resources, but a small, sparse population, meaning the country primarily produces raw goods. Politically, it has been pushed and pulled and bent out of shape by the stronger spheres of influence centering in Cuzco, Madrid, Lima, Buenos Aires and Washington, DC. And while much of Bolivia's history follows the macro-trends of the rest of South America, the country's spirit, character and context have come together to form a complex and intricate story unique unto itself.

Pre-Colonial Times

Advanced civilizations first developed along the Peruvian coast and in the valleys in the early AD period. Highland civilizations developed a little later on. Some archaeologists define the prehistory of the Central Andes in terms of 'horizons' – Early, Middle and Late – each of which was characterized by distinct architectural and artistic trends.

The so-called Early Horizon (1400–400 BC) was an era of architectural innovation and activity, most evident in the ruins of Chavín de Huantar, on the eastern slopes of the Andes in Peru. Chavín influences resounded far and wide, even after the decline of Chavín society, and spilled over into the Early Middle Horizon (400 BC–AD 500).

The Middle Horizon (AD 500–900) was marked by the imperial expansion of the Tiwanaku and Huari (of the Ayacucho Valley of present-day Peru) cultures. The Tiwanakans produced technically advanced work, most notably the city itself. They created impressive ceramics, gilded ornamentation, engraved pillars and slabs with calendar markings, and designs representing their bearded white leader and deity, Viracocha.

The period between AD 900 and 1475 is known as the Late Intermediate Horizon. After the fall of Tiwanaku, regionalized city-states like Chan-Chan in Peru and the Aymará Kingdoms around the southern shores of Lake Titicaca came to power. But it was the rise and fall of the Inca Empire that would truly define the pre-Colombian period.

Around 1440 the Inca started to expand their political boundaries. The eighth Inca king, Viracocha (not to be confused with the Tiwanaku deity of the same name), believed the mandate from their Sun God was not just to conquer, plunder and enslave, but to organize defeated tribes and absorb them into the realm of the benevolent Sun God.

Between 1476 and 1534 the Inca civilization was able to extend its influence over the Aymará Kingdoms around Lake Titicaca.

By the late 1520s internal rivalries began to take their toll on the empire with the sons of Inca Huayna Capac – Atahualpa and Huáscar – fighting a bloody civil war after the death of their father. Atahualpa (who controlled the northern reaches of the empire) won the war.

Conquistadors

The Spanish conquest of South America was remarkably quick. The power vacuum left by the Inca Civil War helped, as did the epidemics caused by European diseases.

Alto Perú (the area we now know as Bolivia) was aligned with Huáscar during the Inca Civil War, making its conquest rather easy for Diego de Almagro.

In 1544, Diego Huallpa revealed his discovery of silver at Cerro Rico in Potosí. By this time, Spanish conquerors had already firmly implanted their customs on the remnants of the Inca empire.

Potosí was officially founded in 1545, and in 1558 Alto Perú gained its autonomy from Lima with the placement of an Audiencia (Royal Court) in Sucre. Spider-webbing out from Potosí, transportation hubs, farming communities and other support centers sprung up. Due to the world's most prolific mine, Potosí's silver underwrote Spain's international ambitions – enabling the country to fight the Counter-Reformation in Europe – also supporting the extravagance of its monarchy for at least two centuries.

Independence

The early part of the 19th century was a time of revolution and independence in Bolivia (and much of the world for that matter). Harvest failures and epidemics severely affected the Bolivian economy between 1803 and 1805. And when the economy is bad, the conditions are good for revolution. To top it off, with the French Revolution, Napoleon's wars in Europe and British support for Latin America Independence movements, the colonists of the Americas were finally able to perceive what the world without royalty would look like.

By May 1809, Spanish America's first independence movement had gained momentum, and was well underway in Chuquisaca (later renamed Sucre), with other cities quick to follow suit.

By the early 1820s, General Simón Bolívar had succeeded in liberating both Venezuela and Colombia from Spanish domination. In 1822 he dispatched Mariscal (Field Marshall) Antonio José de Sucre to Ecuador to defeat the Royalists at the battle of Pichincha. In 1824, after years of guerrilla action against the Spanish and the victories of Bolívar and Sucre in the battles of Junín (August 6) and Ayacucho (December 9), Peru won its independence.

With both Argentina and Peru eying the prize of the Potosí mines, Sucre incited a declaration of independence from Peru and, in 1825, the new Republic of Bolivia was born. Bolívar (yep, the country was named after him) and Sucre served as Bolivia's first and second presidents, but after a brief attempt by the third president, Andrés Santa Cruz, to form a confederation with Peru, things began to go awry. Chilean opposition eventually broke up this potentially powerful nation, and thereafter Bolivia was relegated to a more secondary role in regional affairs with a period of caudillo rule dominating the national politics until the 1880s. Thereafter Bolivia was ruled by a civilian oligarchy divided into liberal and conservative groups until the 1930s, when the traditional political system again fell apart, leading to constant military intervention until the 1952 Revolution.

Shrinking Territory

At the time of independence Bolivia's boundaries encompassed well over 2 million sq km. But its neighbors soon moved to acquire its territory, removing coastal access and much of the area covered by its ancient Amazonian rubber trees.

The coastal loss occurred during the War of the Pacific, fought against Chile between 1879 and 1884. Many Bolivians believe that Chile stole the Atacama Desert's copper- and nitrate-rich sands and 850km of coastline from Peru and Bolivia by invading during Carnaval. Chile did attempt to compensate for the loss by building a railroad from La Paz to the ocean and allowing Bolivia free port privileges in Antofagasta, but Bolivians have never forgotten this devastating *enclaustramiento* (landlocked status).

The next major loss was in 1903 during the rubber boom when Brazil hacked away at Bolivia's inland expanse. Brazil and Bolivia had both been ransacking the forests of the Acre territory – it was so rich in rubber trees that Brazil engineered a dispute over sovereignty and sent in its army. Brazil then convinced the Acre region to secede from the Bolivian republic, and promptly annexed it.

There were two separate territory losses to Argentina. First, Argentina annexed a large slice of the Chaco in 1862. Then, in 1883, the territory of Puna de Atacama also went to Argentina. It had been offered to both Chile and Argentina, the former in exchange for return of the Litoral, the latter in exchange for clarification over Bolivia's ownership of Tarija.

After losing the War of the Pacific, Bolivia was desperate to have the Chaco, an inhospitable region beneath which rich oilfields were mooted to lie, as an outlet to the Atlantic via the Río Paraguay. Between 1932 and 1935, a particularly brutal war was waged between Bolivia and Paraguay over the disputed territory (more than 80,000 lives were lost). Though no decisive victory was reached, both nations had grown weary of fighting, and peace negotiations in 1938 awarded most of the disputed territory to Paraguay.

Continuing Political Strife

During the 20th century wealthy tin barons and landowners controlled Bolivian farming and mining interests, while the peasantry was relegated to a feudal system of peonage known as *pongueaje*. The beating Bolivia took in the Chaco War made way for reformist associations, civil unrest among the *cholos* (indigenous people who dress traditionally but live in cities – now referred to as *mestizos* with the term *cholo* being deemed pejorative), and a series of coups by reform-minded military leaders.

The most significant development was the emergence of the Movimiento Nacionalista Revolucionario (MNR) political party. They united the masses behind the common cause of popular reform, sparking friction between peasant miners and absentee tin bosses. Under the leadership of Víctor Paz Estenssoro, the MNR prevailed in the 1951 elections, but a last-minute military coup prevented it from actually taking power. What ensued was a period of serious combat, which ended with the defeat of the military and Paz Estenssoro's rise to power in what has been called the National Revolution of 1952. He immediately nationalized mines, evicted the tin barons, put an end to *pongueaje* and set up Comibol (Corporación Minera de Bolivia), the state entity in charge of mining interests.

The MNR remained in power for 12 years under various leaders. But even with US support, the MNR was unable to raise the standard of living or increase food production substantially. Its effectiveness and popularity ground to a halt and Víctor Paz Estenssoro became increasingly autocratic; in 1964 his government was overthrown by a military junta headed by General René Barrientos Ortuño. Five years later Barrientos died in a helicopter accident and a series of coups, military dictators and juntas followed.

It was in this context that right-wing coalition leader General Hugo Banzer Suárez eventually took over in 1971 and served a turbulent term through to 1978, punctuated by reactionary extremism and human rights abuses.

The next three years were filled with failed elections, appointed presidents, military coups and brutal regimes, a rash of tortures, arrests and disappearances, as well as a marked increase in cocaine production and trafficking.

In 1982 Congress elected Hernán Siles Zuazo, the civilian left-wing leader of the Communist-supported Movimiento de la Izquierda Revolucionaria (MIR), which began one of the longest democratic periods in Bolivian history to date. His term was beleaguered with labor disputes, ruthless government overspending and huge monetary devaluation, resulting in a truly staggering inflation rate that at one point reached 35,000% annually.

When Siles Zuazo gave up after three years and called general elections, Víctor Paz Estenssoro returned to politics to become president for the fourth time. He immediately enacted harsh measures to revive the shattered economy: he ousted labor unions, removed government restrictions on internal trade, slashed the government deficit, imposed a wage freeze, eliminated price subsidies, laid off workers at inefficient government-owned companies, allowed the peso to float against the US dollar and deployed armed forces to keep the peace.

Inflation was curtailed within weeks, but spiraling unemployment threatened the government's stability.

Chaos Prevails

The early '90s were characterized by political apathy, party politics, and the struggle between *capitalization* (the opening of state companies to international investment) and populist models. The free market won with the election of Gonzolo 'Goni' Sanchéz de Lozada, the MNR leader who had played a key role in the curtailing of inflation through 'shock therapy' during the Estenssoro government.

Overseas investors in formerly state-owned companies received 49% equity, total voting control, license to operate in Bolivia and up to 49% of the profits. The remaining 51% of the shares were distributed to Bolivians as pensions and through Participación Popular, a program meant to channel spending away from cities and into rural schools, clinics and other local infrastructure.

In late 1995 reform issues were overshadowed by violence and unrest surrounding US-directed coca eradication in the Chapare. In 1997 voters upset by the reforms cast 22.5% of the ballot in favor of comeback king and former dictator General Hugo Banzer Suárez. In the late 1990s Banzer faced swelling public discontent with his coca eradication measures and widespread corruption, and unrest in response to increasing gas prices, a serious water shortage and economic downturn in the department of Cochabamba.

Following a successful campaign advised by a team of US political consultants that he hired, 'Goni' was appointed president in August 2002. His economic policies were met with widespread demonstrations and the loss of 67 lives during a police lock-down in La Paz the following year. In October 2003 Goni resigned amid massive popular protests and fled to the US. He currently faces charges both in the US and Bolivia, and a formal extradition process is underway.

Protests, rising fuel prices and continued unrest pushed Goni's predecessor, Carlos Mesa to resign in 2005.

The Morales Era

In December 2005 Bolivians elected their country's first indigenous president. A former *cocalero* (coca grower) and representative from Cochabamba, Evo Morales of Movimiento al Socialismo (MAS) won nearly 54% of the vote, having promised to alter the traditional political class and to empower the nation's poor (mainly indigenous) majority. After the election, Morales quickly grabbed the lefty spotlight, touring the world and meeting with Venezuela's Hugo Chávez, Cuba's Fidel Castro, Brazil's Lula da Silva and members of South Africa's African National Congress. Symbolically, on May Day 2006, he nationalized Bolivia's natural gas reserves and raised taxes on energy investors in a move that would consolidate Bolivian resources in Bolivian hands. Nationalizations continue to this day.

In July 2006 Morales formed a National Constituent Assembly to set about rewriting the country's constitution. In January 2009 the new socially-focused constitution was approved by 67% of voters in a nationwide referendum. The first constitution in Bolivia approved by popular vote, it gave greater power to the country's indigenous majority and allowed Morales to seek a second five-year term, which he won that same year. The constitution also limited the size of landholdings in order to redistribute Bolivia's land from large ranchers and landowners to poor indigenous farmers.

Culture

The National Psyche

Bolivia is a remarkably stratified society. And while the archetypes defined by 500 years of Spanish-descendent rule are starting to slowly fade, who you are – where you fit in society and what opportunities you will have throughout life – is still largely defined by the color of your skin, the language you speak, the clothes you wear and the money you have.

Attitude depends on climate and altitude. *Cambas* (lowlanders) and *kollas* (highlanders) enjoy expounding on what makes them different (ie better) than the other. Lowlanders are said to be warmer, more casual and more generous to strangers; highlanders are supposedly harder working but less open-minded. While the jesting used to be good-natured, regional tensions have increased over the past few years, with Santa Cruz's threats of succession constantly in the news.

Life's not easy – it's actually really tough for most Bolivians – so many try to take joy from the little things: soccer, the rising of the sun, good rains and harvests, birthdays, religious festivals, coca, *cerveza* (beer), births and christenings.

Lifestyle

Life in this fiercely self-reliant nation begins with the family. No matter what tribe or class you come from, it's likely that you have close ties to your extended family. In the highlands, the concept of *ayllu* (the traditional peasant system of communal land ownership, management and decision making) that dates back to the Inca times is still important today.

Day-to-day life varies from Bolivian to Bolivian, mostly depending on whether they live in the city or in the country and whether they are rich or poor. Many *campesinos* (peasant farmers) live without running water, heat or electricity, and some wear clothing that has hardly changed in style since the Spanish arrived. But in the Bolivian cities, especially Santa Cruz (the country's richest city), La Paz, Cochabamba and Sucre, thousands of people enjoy the comforts of contemporary conveniences and live very modern lifestyles.

For Bolivia's poor, the day is about making enough money to eat, going to church, doing chores, study for the children, and a bit of laughter and forgetting. For the richer city class, there are distractions that come from economic surplus like theater, cuisine, the arts, and the ever-important country club.

Homosexuality is legal in Bolivia but isn't openly flaunted in this society of machismo. Despite a growing number of gay bars in

BOLIVIA'S INDIGENOUS GROUPS

Highlands

Aymará The Aymará culture emerged on the southern shores of Titicaca after the fall of Tiwanaku. Today, Aymará live in the areas surrounding the lake and in the Yungas, calling La Paz's El Alto the capital of Aymará culture.

Chipaya Perhaps the direct descendants of Tiwanaku.

Kallawaya A remote tribe with a dying language.

Quechua Descended from the Inca, there are some 9 to 14 million Quechua speakers in Bolivia, Peru, Ecuador, Chile, Colombia and Argentina today.

Lowlands

Chiquitano Living primarily in the Chiquitania tropical savannah outside Santa Cruz, but also in Beni and into Brazil, there's about 180,000 Chiquitanos in Bolivia. About a quarter of them speak Chiquitano.

Guaraní This tribe shares a common language and lives in Paraguay, Brazil and parts of Uruguay and Bolivia.

Mojeño From the Beni department, this significant ethnic group was quite large before the 17th century, with over 350,000 people.

some larger cities, gay culture remains fairly subtle.

Religion

Roughly 95% of Bolivia's population professes Roman Catholicism and practices it to varying degree. The remaining 5% are Protestant, agnostic and belonging to other religions. Strong evangelical movements are rapidly gaining followers with their fire-and-brimstone messages of the world's imminent end. Despite the political and economic strength of Western religions, it's clear that most religious activities have mixed Inca and Aymará belief systems with Christianity.

Population

Bolivia is a multiethnic society with a remarkable diversity of linguistic, cultural and artistic traditions. In fact, the country has the largest population of indigenous peoples in South America, with most sociologists and anthropologists saying that over 60% of the population is of indigenous descent.

Bolivia has 36 identified indigenous groups. The vast majority of those who identify themselves as indigenous are Aymará (about 25%) and Quechua (about 30%), many of whom live in the highlands. The remaining groups (including Guaraní and Chiquitano) are located almost entirely in the lowlands.

Mestizos (a person of mixed indigenous and Spanish descent), make up a substantial portion of the population. *Mestizos* sometimes fall into 'white society', while others retain their roots within the indigenous societal makeup.

Cuisine

Meat invariably dominates Bolivian cuisine and it is usually accompanied by rice, a starchy tuber (usually potato) and shredded lettuce. Often, the whole affair is drowned by *llajhua* (a fiery tomato-based salsa). The soups are a specialty.

Desayuno (breakfast) consists of little more than coffee and a bread roll, and is often followed by a mid-morning street snack such as a *salteña* (meat and vegetable pastie), *tucumana* (an empanada-like pastry) or an empanada.

Almuerzo (lunch) is the main meal of the day. The best-value meals are found in and around markets (often under B$10) and at no-frills restaurants offering set lunches (usually between B$15 and B$40). *La cena*, the evening meal, is mostly served à la carte.

Vegetarian options are on the rise, but you'll be stuck with lots of over-cooked vegetables, rice, potatoes, pizza and pasta. Quinoa is a super grain, perfect for vegetarians.

Arts

Music & Dance

While all Andean musical traditions have evolved from a series of pre-Inca, Inca, Spanish, Amazonian and even African influences, each region of Bolivia has developed distinctive musical traditions, dances and instruments.

The instrument Bolivia is most known for, and understandably proud of, is the *charango,* considered the king of all stringed instruments. Modeled after the Spanish *vihuela* and mandolin, it gained initial popularity in Potosí during the city's mining heyday. Another instrument commonplace in the gringo markets is the *quena,* a small flute made of cane, bone or ceramic. The instrument predates Europeans by many centuries and the earliest examples, made of stone, were found near Potosí. A curious instrument known as a jaguar-caller comes from the Amazon region. This hollowed-out calabash, with a small hole into which the player inserts his hand, seems to do the trick in calling the big cats to the hunt.

Traditional Altiplano dances celebrate war, fertility, hunting prowess, marriage and work. After the Spanish arrived, European dances and those of the African slaves were introduced, resulting in the hybrid dances that now characterize many Bolivian celebrations.

Oruro's Carnaval draws huge local and international crowds. Potosí is famed for *tinku,* a traditional festival that features ritual fighting, while La Paz is renowned for La Morenada, which re-enacts the dance of African slaves brought to the courts of Viceroy Felipe III.

Weaving

Bolivian textiles come in diverse patterns. The majority display a degree of skill that results from millennia of artistry and tradition. The most common piece is a *manta* or *aguayo,* a square shawl made of two handwoven strips joined edge to edge. Also common are the *chuspa* (coca pouch), *chullo* (knitted hat), the *falda* (skirt), woven belts and touristy items such as camera bags made from remnants.

Regional differences are manifested in weaving style, motif and use. Weavings from Tarabuco often feature intricate zoomorphic patterns, while distinctive red-and-black designs come from Potolo, northwest of Sucre. Zoomorphic patterns are also prominent in the wild Charazani country north of Lake Titicaca and in several Altiplano areas outside La Paz, including Lique and Calamarka.

Some extremely fine weavings originate in Sica Sica, one of the many dusty and nondescript villages between La Paz and Oruro, while in Calcha, southeast of Potosí, expert spinning and an extremely tight weave – more than 150 threads per inch – produce Bolivia's finest textiles.

Vicuña fibers, the finest and most expensive in the world, are produced in Apolobamba and in Parque Nacional Sajama.

Sports

Like many of its Latin American neighbors, Bolivia's national sport is *fútbol* (soccer). La Paz's Bolívar and The Strongest usually participate (albeit weakly) in the Copa Libertadores, the annual showdown of Latin America's top clubs. Professional *fútbol* matches are held every weekend in big cities, and impromptu street games are always happening. While small towns lack many basic services, you can be sure to find a well-tended *cancha* (soccer field) almost everywhere you go – and you'll be welcome to join in. Some communities still bar women from the field, but in the Altiplano, women's teams have started popping up, where they play clad in *polleras* (skirts) and jerseys.

In rural communities, volleyball is a sunset affair, with mostly adults playing a couple of times a week. Racquetball, billiards, chess and *cacho* (dice) are also popular. The unofficial national sport, however, has to be feasting and feting – the competition between dancers and drinkers knows no bounds.

Environment

When people think of Bolivia it generally conjures up images of somewhere high (La Paz), dry (Altiplano) and salty (Uyuni salt plains). While this may be true for large areas of the country, there's much more to the Bolivian landscape than just mountains. The range of altitude – from 130m above seal level in the jungles of the Amazon Basin to 6542m on the peaks of the rugged Andes – has resulted in a huge variety of ecological and geological niches supporting a bewildering variety of nature. Environmentally it is one of the most diverse countries on the continent.

The country's 1415 bird species and 5000 described plant species rank among the highest numbers in the world. It's also among the Neotropical countries with the highest level of endemism (species which exist only in Bolivia), with 21 birds, 28 reptiles, 72 amphibians and 25 mammals found nowhere else on earth.

But while it may seem obvious that Bolivia's natural resources are one of its greatest assets, not everybody values assets that don't have a direct monetary value. From the lush tropical forests of Parque Nacional e Área de Uso Mútiple Amboró to the wetlands of the Pantanal, the scrub that obscures the Chaco gas fields and the *Polylepis* woodlands of the Andes, the Bolivian environment is under constant threat from destruction for economic exploitation.

The Land

Two Andean mountain chains define the west of the country, with many peaks above 6000m. The western Cordillera Occidental stands between Bolivia and the Pacific coast. The eastern Cordillera Real runs southeast, then turns south across central Bolivia, joining the other chain to form the southern Cordillera Central.

The haunting Altiplano (altitude 3500m–4000m), is boxed in by these two great cordilleras. It's an immense, nearly treeless plain punctuated by mountains and solitary volcanic peaks. At the Altiplano's northern end, straddling the Peruvian border, Lake Titicaca is one of the world's highest navigable lakes. In the far southwestern corner, the land is drier and less populated. The salty remnants of two vast ancient lakes, the Salar de Uyuni and the Salar de Coipasa, are there as well.

East of the Cordillera Central are the Central Highlands, with scrubby hills, valleys and fertile basins with a Mediterranean-like climate. North of the Cordillera Real, the rainy Yungas form a transition zone between arid highlands and humid lowlands.

More than half of Bolivia's total area is in the Amazon Basin, with sweaty tropical rainforest in the western section, and flat cerrados and extensions of the Pantanal wetland in the east. In the country's southeastern corner is the nearly impenetrable scrubland of the Gran Chaco, an arid, thorny forest that experiences the highest temperatures in the country.

Wildlife

The distribution of wildlife is dictated by the country's geography and varies considerably from region to region. The Altiplano is home to vicuñas, flamingos and condors; the Chaco to secretive jaguars, pumas and peccaries; the Pantanal provides refuge for giant otters, marsh deer and waterbirds; while the Amazon Basin contains the richest density of species on earth, featuring an incredible variety of reptiles, parrots, monkeys, hummingbirds, butterflies, fish and bugs (by the zillions!).

Of course the animals that steal the show are the regional giants. The majestic jaguar, the continent's top predator; the elephant-nosed tapir (*anta*); and the walking vacuum cleaner that is the giant anteater. The continent's biggest bird is here too, the ostrich-like rhea or *ñandú,* and it can be surprisingly common in some areas; you may even be lucky enough to spot the breathtaking Andean condor, unsurprisingly revered by the Inca, soaring on mountain thermals.

River travelers are almost certain to spot capybaras (like giant aquatic guinea pigs) and caiman (alligators). It's not unusual to see anacondas in the rivers of the department of Beni and a spot of piranha fishing is virtually an obligation for anybody spending time in the Amazon.

Overland travelers frequently see armadillos, foxes, *jochis* (agoutis) and the grey-faced, llama-like guanaco. Similar, but more delicately-proportioned, is the fuzzy vicuña, once mercilessly hunted for its woolly coat but now recovering well. You won't have to work quite as hard to spot their domesticated relatives, the llama and the alpaca.

Many nonprofit groups are working on countrywide environmental conservation efforts. Besides the international conservation organizations, the following local groups are having a positive impact.

Asociación Armonía (www.armonia-bo.org) Everything you need to know about birding and bird conservation.

Fundación Amigos de la Naturaleza (p234) One of the most active of the local conservation groups, working at the national level.

Protección del Medioambiente del Tarija (www.elgranchaco.com/prometa) Works in the Gran Chaco region on a series of social and conservation initiatives.

National Parks

Our favorite national parks and protected areas – there are 22 in total – and what you'll see.

Amboró Near Santa Cruz, home to rare spectacled bears, jaguars and an astonishing variety of birdlife.

Apolobamba Excellent hiking in this remote mountain range abutting the Peruvian border, with Bolivia's densest condor population.

Cotapata Most of the Choro trek passes through here, midway between La Paz and Coroico in the Yungas.

Madidi Protects a wide range of wildlife habitats; home to more than 1100 bird species.

Noel Kempff Mercado Remote park on the Brazilian border; contains a variety of wildlife and some of Bolivia's most inspiring scenery.

Reserva Nacional de Fauna Andina Eduardo Avaroa A highlight of the Southwest Circuit tour, including wildlife-rich lagoons.

Sajama Adjoining Chile's magnificent Parque Nacional Lauca; contains Volcán Sajama (6542m), Bolivia's highest peak.

Torotoro Enormous rock formations with dinosaur tracks from the Cretaceous period, plus caves and ancient ruins.

Tunari Within hiking distance of Cochabamba; features lovely nature trails through mountain scenery.

SURVIVAL GUIDE

Directory A–Z

Accommodations

Bolivian accommodations are among South America's cheapest, though price and value are hardly uniform. The sleeping sections in this book are organized by author preference. You can sometimes negotiate the room price in cheaper places.

The Bolivian hotel-rating system divides accommodations into these categories: *posadas* (inns), *alojamientos, residenciales, casas de huéspedes, hostales* (hostels) and *hoteles* (hotels). Rock-bottom places are usually found around the bus and train stations, though these areas are often the most dangerous in town. Room availability is only a problem at popular weekend getaways such as Coroico and during fiestas (especially Carnaval in Oruro and festivals in Copacabana), when prices double.

In the Altiplano, heat and hot water often makes the difference in price, while in lowland areas, air-cons and fans are common delimiters.

Warning: several readers have alerted us to improper use of propane heaters in Bolivia. These are sometimes offered in cheaper accommodations but are not meant to be used in enclosed spaces so refrain from using them if supplied.

Bolivia offers excellent camping, especially along trekking routes and in remote mountain areas. Gear (of varying quality) is easily rented in La Paz and at popular trekking base camps like Sorata. It's always a good idea to ask for permission if somebody is around. Theft and assaults have been reported in some areas – always enquire locally about security before heading off to set up camp.

Activities

Bolivia is like a theme park for grownup adventurers. There are multiday treks, 'easy' day hikes, mountain-bike rides that'll leave your teeth chattering, climbs to lost Andean peaks, rivers for rafting and romping, rugged 4X4 journeys to the lost corners of the old Inca Empire, and just about anything you could ask for in between. While do-it-yourself expeditions add an element of adventure, bringing a local guide lowers your risk of incident (getting robbed, lost or just plain lonely), plus you're contributing to the local economy.

Hiking and trekking are arguably the most rewarding Andean activities – add a porter, llama train and experienced guide, and you have all the makings for a grand adventure. Some of the most popular hikes and treks in Bolivia begin near La Paz, traverse the Cordillera Real along ancient Inca routes and end in the Yungas.

SLEEPING PRICE RANGES

The following price ranges refer to a double room with bathroom in high season, including all taxes and fees.

La Paz

$ less than B$180

$$ B$180 to B$560

$$$ more than B$560

The Rest of the Country

$ less than B$160

$$ B$160 to B$400

$$$ more than B$400

Trekking in Bolivia by Yossi Brain and Lonely Planet's *Trekking in the Central Andes* are good resources.

Climbing in Bolivia is an exercise in extremes – like the country itself. In the dry southern winter (May to October) temperatures may fluctuate as much as 40.5°C in a single day. Once you're acclimatized to the Altiplano's relatively thin air (you'll need at least a week), there is still 2500m of even thinner air lurking above.

A plus for climbers is the access to mountains; although public transportation may not always be available, roads pass within easy striking distance of many fine peaks.

The **Asociación de Guias de Montaña** (☎214-7951; www.agmtb.org) in La Paz certifies climbing guides in Bolivia.

Bolivia is blessed with some of the most dramatic mountain-biking terrain in the world: seven months every year of near-perfect weather and relatively easy access to mountain ranges, magnificent lakes, pre-Hispanic ruins and trails, and myriad ecozones connected by an extensive network of footpaths and jeep roads.

One of Bolivia's greatest secrets is the number of whitewater rivers that drain the eastern slopes of the Andes between the Cordillera Apolobamba and the Chapare.

Some La Paz tour agencies can organize day trips on the **Río Coroico**. Other options include the **Río Unduavi** and numerous wild **Chapare rivers**.

Amazon canoe tours along the **Río Beni** are unforgettable as are the trips along the **Río Mamoré** from Trinidad.

Business Hours

Most businesses are closed on Sundays, save for restaurants.

Banks 9am to 4pm or 6pm Monday to Friday; 10am to noon or 5pm Saturday

Markets Stir as early as 6am and some are open on Sunday mornings

Restaurants Hours generally run from breakfast (8am to 10am), lunch (noon to 3pm) and dinner (6pm to 10pm or 11pm)

Shops Sometimes close from noon to 2pm for lunch on weekdays, and are open from 10am to noon or 5pm on Saturdays

Electricity

Most electricity currents are 220V AC, at 50Hz. Most plugs and sockets are the two-pin, round-prong variety, but a few anomalous American-style two-pin, parallel flat-pronged sockets exist.

Embassies & Consulates

For a full list of foreign diplomatic representation in Bolivia, see www.embassiesabroad.com/embassies-in/bolivia.

Argentinian Embassy (Map p182; ☎02-241-7737; www.mrecic.gov.ar; Aspiazu 475, La Paz) Cochabamba (☎04-425-5859; Federico Blanco 929); Villazón (☎02-596-5253; Saavedra 311); Santa Cruz (☎03-334-7133; Junín 22); Tarija (☎04-664-4273; Bolívar 696)

Australian Consulate (Map p182; ☎02-242-2957, 2-211-5655; Av 20 de Octubre 2396, 3rd fl, La Paz)

Brazilian Embassy (Map p182; ☎02-216-6400; www.brasil.org.bo; Arce 2739, Edificio Multicentro, La Paz) Cochabamba (☎04-425-5860; Av Oquendo N-1080); Guayaramerín (☎03-855-3766; Av 24 de Septiembre No 28); Santa Cruz (☎03-334-4400; Av Germán Busch 330); Sucre (☎04-645-2661; Arenales 212)

Canadian Consulate (☎800-10-0101; La Paz)

Chilean Consulate (☎02-279-7331; www.chileabroad.gov.cl; Calle 14 No 8024, Calacoto, La Paz) Santa Cruz (☎03-335-8989; René Moreno 551, 1st fl)

Ecuadorian Embassy (Map p182; ☎02-278-4422; Calle 10 No 8054, Calacoto, La Paz) Sucre (☎04-646-0622; Los Ceibos 2, Barrio Tucsupaya)

French Embassy (☎02-214-9900; www.ambafrance-bo.org; Fernando Siles 5390, Obrajes, La Paz)

German Embassy (Map p182; ☎02-244-0066; www.la-paz.diplo.de; Av Aniceto Arce 2395, La Paz) Cochabamba (☎04-425-4024; cnr España & Av de las Heroínas, Edificio La Promontora, 6th fl); Sucre (☎04-645-2091; Rosenda Villa 54)

Italian Embassy (Map p182; ☎02-278-8506; www.amblapaz.esteri.it; Calle 5 No 458, Obrajes, La Paz)

Paraguayan Embassy (Map p182; ☎02-243-3176; Pedro Salazar 351, Edificio Illimani, La Paz)

Peruvian Embassy (☎02-244-0631; www.conperlapaz.org; Av 6 de Agosto No 2455, Edificio Hilda, La Paz) Cochabamba (☎04-448-6556; Edificio Continental, Blanco N-1344); Santa Cruz (☎03-341-9091; Viador Pinto 84); Sucre (☎04-645-5592; Avaroa 472)

Spanish Embassy (☎02-211-7820; www.maec.es; Av 6 de Agosto 2827, La Paz) Santa Cruz (☎03-332-8921; Santiesteban 237); Santa Cruz (☎03-312-1349; Av Cañoto)

UK Embassy (☎02-243-3424; www.ukinbolivia.fco.gov.uk; Arce 2732, La Paz) Santa Cruz (☎03-353-5035; Santa Cruz International School, Km 7.5)

USA Embassy (☎02-216-8000; http://bolivia.usembassy.gov; Av Aniceto Arce 2780, La Paz) Santa Cruz (☎03-351-3477; Av Roque Aguilera 146)

Gay & Lesbian Travelers

Homosexuality is legal in Bolivia but still not widely accepted. In 2004 parliament attempted (unsuccessfully) to introduce Law 810, which would allow homosexual couples to marry and foster children.

Gay bars and venues are limited to the larger cities, especially Santa Cruz and La Paz, but these are still somewhat clandestine affairs. As for hotels, sharing a room is no problem – but discretion is still in order.

Gay rights lobby groups are active in La Paz (MGLP Libertad), Cochabamba (Dignidad) and most visibly in progressive Santa Cruz, which held Bolivia's first Gay Pride Festival in 2001. La Paz is known for La Familia Galan, the capital's most fabulous group of cross-dressing queens who aim to educate Bolivians around issues of sexuality and gender through theater performances. The feminist activist group **Mujeres Creando** (www.mujerescreando.org) in La Paz promotes the rights of oppressed groups.

Health

Sanitation and hygiene are not Bolivia's strong suits, so pay attention to what you eat. Most tap water isn't safe to drink; stick to bottled water if your budget allows. Carry iodine if you'll be trekking.

The *altiplano* lies between 3000m and 4000m, and many visitors to La Paz, Copacabana and Potosí will have problems with altitude sickness. Complications like cerebral edema have been the cause of death in otherwise fit, healthy travelers. Diabetics should note that only the Touch II blood glucose meter gives accurate readings at altitudes over 2000m.

Bolivia is officially in a yellow-fever zone, so a vaccination is recommended; it is in fact obligatory for US citizens requesting visas and for onward travel (such as Brazil, which requires the certificate). Anyone coming from a yellow-fever infected area needs a vaccination certificate to enter Bolivia. Take precautions against malaria in the lowlands.

While medical facilities might not be exactly what you're used to back home, there are decent hospitals in the biggest cities and passable clinics in most towns (but *not* in remote parts of the country).

Internet Access

Nearly every corner of Bolivia has a cyber cafe and wi-fi is now standard in most midrange and top-end hotels (and many cafes). Rates run from B$2 to B$5 per hour. In smaller towns, expect to pay more – check the local Entel offices and be ready for slow satellite connections.

Legal Matters

Regardless of its reputation as the major coca provider, drugs – including cocaine – are highly illegal in Bolivia, and possession and use brings a jail sentence. Foreign embassies are powerless to help (or won't want to know!). Don't even think about it.

Maps

Maps are available in La Paz, Cochabamba and Santa Cruz through Los Amigos del Libro and some bookstores. Government 1:50,000 topographical and specialty sheets are available from the **Instituto Geográfico Militar** (IGM; Map p186; Juan Pablo 23, Edificio Murillo, San Pedro; ⌚8:30am-12:30pm & 2:30am-6:30pm Mon-Fri), with offices in La Paz and in most other major cities.

International sources for hard-to-find maps include the US-based **Maplink** (www.maplink.com) and **Omnimap** (www.omnimap.com), and the UK-based **Stanfords** (www.stanfords.co.uk). In Germany, **Deutscher Alpenverein** (www.alpenverein.de) publishes a series of climbing maps.

Money

Bolivia uses the boliviano (B$). Most prices are pegged to the US dollar. Only crisp US dollar bills are accepted (they are the currency for savings).

The boliviano is divided into 100 centavos. Bolivianos come in 10, 20, 50, 100 and 200 denomination notes, with coins worth 1, 2 and 5 bolivianos as well as 10, 20 and 50 centavos. Often called pesos (the currency was changed from pesos to bolivianos in 1987), bolivianos are extremely difficult to unload outside the country.

Counterfeit bolivianos and US dollars are less common than they used to be, but it still happens more often than you'd like.

ATMS

Sizable towns have *cajeros automáticos* (ATMs) – usually Banco Nacional de Bolivia, Banco Bisa, Banco Mercantil Santa Cruz and Banco Unión. They dispense bolivianos in 50 and 100 notes (sometimes US dollars as well) on Visa, Mastercard, Plus and Cirrus cards; note that in the past, many Europeans have reported trouble using their cards.

In smaller towns, the local bank Prodem is a good option for cash advances on Visa and Mastercard (3% to 6% commission charged) and many branches are meant to be open on Saturday mornings; the hours and machines are unreliable. Don't rely on ATMs; always carry some cash with you, especially if venturing into rural areas.

CASH

Finding change for bills larger than B$10 is a national pastime, as change for larger notes is scarce outside big cities. When exchanging money or making big purchases, request the *cambio* (change) in small denominations. If you can stand the queues, most banks will break large bills. Also, check any larger bills for damage as you may not be able to change them if they're torn or taped together.

FOOD PRICE RANGES

The following price ranges refer to the cost of a main.

$ less than B$30

$$ B$30 to B$60

$$$ more than B$60

CREDIT CARDS

Brand-name plastic, such as Visa, Mastercard and (less often) American Express, may be used in larger cities at the better hotels, restaurants and tour agencies.

EXCHANGING MONEY

Visitors fare best with US dollars (travelers have reported that it's difficult to change euros). Currency may be exchanged at *casas de cambio* (exchange bureaux) and at some banks in larger cities. You can often change money in travel agencies, hotels and sometimes in stores selling touristy items. *Cambistas* (street money changers) operate in most cities but only change cash dollars, paying roughly the same as *casas de cambio*. They're convenient after hours, but guard against rip-offs and counterfeit notes.

The rate for cash doesn't vary much from place to place, and there is no black-market rate. Currencies of neighboring countries may be exchanged in border areas and at *casas de cambio* in La Paz. Beware of mangled notes: unless both halves of a repaired banknote bear identical serial numbers, it's worthless. Also note that US$100 bills of the CB-B2 series are not accepted anywhere, neither are US$50 bills of the AB-B2 series.

INTERNATIONAL TRANSFERS

The fastest way to have money transferred from abroad is with **Western Union** (www.westernunion.com). A newer, alternative option is through **Money Gram** (www.moneygram.com), which has offices in all major cities – watch the hefty fees, though. Your bank can also wire money to a cooperating Bolivian bank; it may take a couple of business days.

PayPal is increasingly used to make bank transfers to pay for hotels.

TIPPING

Formal tipping is haphazard except in the nicer restaurants. Elsewhere, locals leave coins amounting to a maximum of 10% of the total in recognition of good service.

Photography

While some Bolivians are willing photo subjects, others may be superstitious about your camera, suspicious of your motives or interested in payment. Many children will ask for payment, often after you've taken their photo. It's best to err on not taking such shots in the first place – be sensitive to the wishes of locals.

Post

Even the smallest towns have post offices – some are signposted 'Ecobol' (Empresa Correos de Bolivia). From major towns, the post is generally reliable (although often involving long delays), but when posting anything important, it's better to pay extra to have it registered or send it by courier. **DHL** (www.dhl.com) is the most reliable courier company with international service.

Airmail *postales* (postcards) or letters weighing up to 20g cost around B$7.50 to the USA, B$9 to Europe and B$10.50 to the rest of the world. Relatively reliable express-mail service is available for rates similar to those charged by private international couriers.

Public Holidays

On major holidays, banks, offices and other services are closed and public transport is often bursting at the seams; book ahead if possible.

New Year's Day January 1

Semana Santa (Easter Week) March/April

Día del Trabajo (Labor Day) May 1

Día de la Independencia (Independence Day) August 6

Día de Colón (Columbus Day) October 12

Día de los Muertos (All Souls' Day) November 2

Navidad (Christmas) December 25

Not about to be outdone by their neighbors, each department has its own holiday: February 10 in Oruro, November 10 in Potosí, April 15 in Tarija, May 25 in Chuquisaca, July 16 in La Paz, September 14 in Cochabamba, September 24 in Santa Cruz and Pando and November 18 in Beni.

Safe Travel

Crime against tourists is on the increase in Bolivia, especially in La Paz and, to a lesser extent, Cochabamba, Copacabana and Oruro. Scams are commonplace and fake police, false tourist police and 'helpful' tourists are on the rise.

There is a strong tradition of social protest in Bolivia: and with over 1000 ongoing conflicts, demonstrations are a regular occurrence and this can affect travelers. While generally peaceful, they can turn threatening in nature at times: agitated protestors throw stones and rocks and police occasionally use force and tear gas to disperse crowds. *Bloqueos* (roadblocks) and strikes by transportation workers often lead to long delays. Be careful using taxis during transportation strikes – you may end up at the receiving end of a rock, which people pelt at those who are not in sympathy with them.

The rainy season means flooding, landslides and road washouts, which in turn means more delays. Getting stuck overnight behind a landslide can happen; you'll be a happier camper with ample food, drink and warm clothes on hand.

Note that the mine tours in Potosí, bike trips outside La Paz and the 4x4 excursions around Salar de Uyuni have become so hugely popular that agencies are willing to forgo safety. Make sure you do your research before signing up for the tour.

As always when traveling, safety is in numbers; solo travelers should remain alert when traveling, especially at night.

Telephone

Bolivia's country code is ☎591. The international direct-dialing access code is ☎00. Calls from telephone offices are getting cheaper all the time, especially now that there's competition between the carriers – they can vary between B$1.50 and B$8 per minute. In La Paz the cheapest of cheap calls can be made from international calling centers around Calle Sagárnaga for around B$2 per minute.

Cell phones are everywhere and easy (as is internet calling).

Even Bolivians struggle with their own telephone network. Here's a quick kit to get you dialing.

NUMBERS

Numbers for *líneas fijas* (landlines) have seven digits; cellular numbers have eight digits. Numerous telecommunications carriers include, among others, Entel, Cotel, Tigo, Boliviatel and Viva. Each carrier has an individual code between ☎010 and ☎021.

AREA CODES

Each department (region) has its own single-digit area code that must be used when dialing from another region or to another city, regardless of whether it's the same area code as the one you're in. The department codes are: (☎2) La Paz, Oruro, Potosí; (☎3) Santa Cruz, Beni, Pando; (☎4) Cochabamba, Chuquisaca, Tarija.

PUBLIC PHONES

Dialing landlines from public phone booths is easy; ask the cashier for advice.

PLACING CALLS

To make a call to another landline within the same city, simply dial the seven-digit number. If you're calling another region, dial 0 plus the single-digit area code followed by the seven-digit number, eg ☎02-123-4567. If calling a cell phone, ask the cashier for instructions; most *puntos* (phone offices) have different phones for calls to cellulars and landlines, so you may have to swap cabins if calling both.

CELLULAR PHONES

Cellular to cellular calls within the same city are simple – just dial the eight-digit number. A recorded message (in Spanish) may prompt you for a carrier number, indicating that the person is either not within the same city or region (or has a SIM card from another region), in which case you must then redial using a 0 plus the two-digit carrier number plus the eight-digit cellular number. For cellular to landline calls within the same city, in most cases, you must dial the single-digit area code, and then the seven-digit number. For cellular to landline calls to another region, in most cases, you must dial a 0 plus the two-digit carrier code, followed by the single-digit area code, and then the seven-digit number, eg if dialing Sucre from La Paz, dial 0 plus ☎10 (or any one of the carrier codes; 10 is Entel's network carrier) + ☎4 (Sucre's area code) + the seven-digit number.

INTERNATIONAL CALLS

For international calls, you must first dial ☎00 followed by a country code, area code (without the first 0) and the phone number.

Toilets

» Poorly maintained *baños públicos* (public toilets) abound and charge around B$1 in populated areas and B$5 in the wilderness, like around the Salar de Uyuni.

» Carry toilet paper with you wherever you go, at all times.

» Toilet paper isn't flushed down Bolivian toilets – use the wastebaskets provided.

Tourist Information

There are often offices covering the *prefectura* (department) and *alcaldía* (local municipality) of a particular city. The major cities, such as Santa Cruz and La Paz, have offices for both, although the different tourism bodies range from helpful to useless, often flying under the new InfoTur banner. Servicio Nacional de Áreas Protegidas (SERNAP) is the best source of information about Bolivia's national parks.

Visas

Passports must be valid for six months beyond the date of entry. Entry or exit stamps are supposed to be free. In remote border areas, you will often be charged anywhere from B$15 to B$30 for an exit stamp. Personal documents – passports and visas – must be carried at all times, especially in lowland regions. It's safest to carry photocopies rather than originals.

Bolivian visa requirements can be arbitrarily changed and interpreted. Regulations, including entry stays, are likely to change. Each Bolivian consulate and border crossing may have its own entry procedures and idiosyncrasies.

In 2007, as an act of reciprocity, the Morales government introduced visas for US citizens visiting Bolivia (a 90-day visa valid for five years costs US$135). At the time of writing, it was possible to obtain the visa upon arrival in Bolivia; check with the **Bolivian embassy** (☎202-483-4410; www.bolivia-usa.org) before traveling.

Citizens of most South American and Western European countries can get a tourist card on entry for stays up to 90 days (depending on the nationality). Citizens of Canada, Australia, New Zealand and Japan are granted 30 days, while citizens of Israel are granted 90 days. This is subject to change; always check with your consulate prior to entry. If you want to stay longer, you have to extend your tourist card (accomplished at the immigration office in any major city with a letter requesting the extension; it's free for some nationalities – for others, it costs B$198 per 30-day extension). The maximum time travelers are permitted to stay in the country is 180 days in one year. Alternatively, you can apply for a visa. Visas are issued by Bolivian consular representatives, including those in neighboring South American countries. Brazilian visas can be complicated, so check ahead. Costs vary according to the consulate and the nationality of the applicant but hover around B$2500.

Overstayers can be fined B$14 per day (or more, depending on the nationality) – payable at the immigration office or airport – and may face ribbons of red tape at the border or airport when leaving the country.

In addition to a valid passport and visa, citizens of many Communist, African, Middle Eastern and Asian countries require 'official permission' from the Bolivian Ministry of Foreign Affairs before a visa will be issued.

Volunteering

Volunteer organizations in Bolivia include the following:

Animales SOS (☎02-230-8080; www.animalessos.org; Av Chacaltaya 1759, La Paz) An animal welfare group caring for mistreated or abused stray animals.

Senda Verde (☎7472-2825; www.sendaverde.com; Yolosa) Just outside of Coroico, this wildlife refuge has a two-week volunteer program.

Sustainable Bolivia (☎04-423-3786; www.sustainablebolivia.org; Julio Arauco Prado 230, Cochabamba) Cochabamba-based nonprofit organization.

Women Travelers

Despite the importance of women in Bolivian society and the elevation of females in public life (including a female president and women mayors), the machismo mindset still pervades in Bolivia. In the home, women rule, while external affairs are largely managed by men. As a female traveling alone, the mere fact that you appear to be unmarried and far from your home and family may cause you to appear suspiciously disreputable.

Bear in mind that modesty is expected of women in much of Spanish-speaking Latin America.

As a safety measure for a woman traveler, try to avoid arriving at a place at night. If you need to take a taxi at night, it's preferable to call for a radio taxi than to flag one down in the street. Note that during the period leading up to Carnaval and during the festivities, a woman traveling solo can be a popular target for water bombs, which can feel like quite a harassment or at least an annoyance.

Women should avoid hiking alone, and never walk alone at night.

Work

For paid work, qualified English teachers can try the professionally run **Centro**

Boliviano-Americano (CBA; Map p182; ☎243-0107; www.cba.edu.bo; Parque Zenón Iturralde 121) in La Paz; there are also offices in other cities. New, unqualified teachers must forfeit two months' salary in return for their training. Better paying are private school positions teaching math, science or social studies. Accredited teachers can expect to earn up to US$500 per month for a full-time position. Other travelers find work in gringo bars, tour operators or hostels. Keep in mind that you are likely taking the job from a Bolivian by doing this.

Getting There & Away

A landlocked country, Bolivia has numerous entry/exit points, and you can get here by boat, bus, train, plane, foot and bike. Some are easier and more accessible than others.

Flights, tours and rail tickets can be booked online at www.lonelyplanet.com/bookings.

Entering the Country

If you have your documents in order and you are willing to answer a few questions about the aim of your visit, entry into Bolivia should be a breeze. If crossing at a smaller border post, you might well be asked to pay an 'exit fee.' Unless otherwise noted in the text, these fees are strictly unofficial. Note that Bolivian border times can be unreliable at best; always check with a *migración* (immigration) office in the nearest major town. Also, if you plan to cross the border outside the stated hours, or at a point where there is no border post, you can usually do so by obtaining an exit/entry stamp from the nearest *migración* office on departure/arrival.

Air

There are only a few US and European airlines offering direct flights to Bolivia, so airfares are high. There are direct services to most major South American cities; the flights to/from Chile and Peru are the cheapest. Santa Cruz is an increasingly popular entry point from Western European hubs. Due to altitude-related costs, flying into La Paz is more expensive than into Santa Cruz. High season for most fares is from early June to late August, and mid-December to mid-February.

Bolivia's principal international airports are La Paz's **El Alto** (LPB), formerly known as John F Kennedy Memorial, and Santa Cruz's **Viru-Viru International** (VVI).

Aerolíneas Argentinas (☎02-333-9776; www.aerolineas.com.ar)

Amaszonas (☎02-222-0848; www.amaszonas.com)

American Airlines (☎02-334-1314; www.aa.com)

BOA (☎901-105-010; www.boa.bo) It is the new national airline but still has irregular service.

Grupo Taca (☎TACA 800-10-8222; www.taca.com)

LAN Airlines (☎800-100-521; www.lan.com)

TAM (☎02-244-3442; www.tam.com.br)

Boat

The Brazilian and Peruvian Amazon frontiers are accessible via irregular riverboats.

Bus

Daily *flotas* (long-distance buses) link La Paz with Buenos Aires (Argentina) via Bermejo or Yacuiba; Salta (Argentina) via Tupiza/Villazón; Corumbá (Brazil) via Quijarro; and Arica and Iquique (Chile) via Tambo Quemado. Increasingly popular is the crossing to San Pedro de Atacama (Chile) as a detour from Salar de Uyuni tours. The most popular overland route to and from Puno and Cuzco (Peru) is via Copacabana, but traveling via Desaguadero is quicker. Several bus services from Santa Cruz via Villamontes run the route to Asunción (Paraguay) on a daily basis.

Car & Motorcycle

Motoring in Bolivia is certain to try your patience (and mechanical skills!), but will be a trip of a lifetime. Most rental agencies accept national driver's licenses, but if you plan on doing a lot of motoring bring an International Driving Permit. For motorcycle

DEPARTURE TAX

Departure taxes vary on your airport and destination. All are payable at the airport (either at the counter or a separate window), and are not included in ticket prices. Domestic departure taxes range from B$11 to B$15. International departure tax is US$25. Some airports also levy a municipal tax of up to B$7.

and moped rentals, a passport is all that is normally required.

Train

Bolivia's only remaining international train route detours west from the Villazón–Oruro line at Uyuni. It passes through the Andes to the Chilean frontier at Avaroa/Ollagüe then descends precipitously to Calama, Chile. Other adventurous routes dead end at the Argentine frontier at Villazón/La Quiaca and Yacuiba/Pocitos and in the Brazilian Pantanal at Quijarro/Corumbá.

Getting Around

Bolivian roads are getting better, with several new paved routes popping up in the last few years. Air transit is also easier, slightly more cost effective and more prevalent, especially in the Lowlands. Most of Bolivia is covered by small bus, boat, train and airline companies. It still takes a while to get from place to place and roadblocks (by protesters) and closed roads due to construction or landslides are not uncommon, nor are flooded roads and rivers with too little water to traverse.

Air

Air travel in Bolivia is inexpensive and it's the quickest and most reliable means of reaching out-of-the-way places. It's also the only means of transportation that isn't washed out during the wet season. Although weather-related disruptions definitely occur, planes eventually get through even during summer flooding in northern Bolivia. Schedules tend to change frequently and cancellations are common, so plan ahead of time.

Aerocon (☎901-105-252; www.aerocon.bo) Connects the country's major cities as well as some more remote corners.

Amaszonas (☎02-222-0848; www.amaszonas.com) Flies small planes from La Paz to Uyuni, Rurrenabaque, Trinidad, Santa Cruz and other lowland destinations. Service to Cuzco (Peru) is on its way.

Transporte Aéreos Militares (Map p186; ☎268-1111; www.tam.bo; Ismael Montes 738, Prado) Flights to Cobija, Cochabamba, Guayamerín, Puerto Suárez, Riberalta, Rurrenabaque, Santa Cruz, Sucre, Tarija, Trinidad, Yacuiba, Ixiamas and Uyuni.

Boat

There's no scheduled passenger service on the Amazon, so travelers almost invariably wind up on some sort of cargo vessel. The most popular routes are from Puerto Villarroel to Trinidad and Trinidad to Guayaramerín. There are also much less frequented routes from Rurrenabaque or Puerto Heath to Riberalta. Journeys are harder and harder to arrange these days.

Bus

Buses and their various iterations are the most popular form of Bolivian transportation. It's cheap and relatively safe but also quite uncomfortable and nerve-racking at times. Long-distance bus lines in Bolivia are called *flotas,* large buses are known as *buses,* three-quarter (usually older) ones are called *micros,* and minibuses are just that. If looking for a bus terminal, ask for *la terminal terrestre* or *la terminal de buses.* Each terminal charges a small fee of a couple of bolivianos, which you pay to an agent upon boarding or when purchasing the ticket at the counter.

The only choices you'll have to make are on major, long-haul routes, where the better companies offer *coche* (or '*bus*'), *semi-cama* (half-sleepers with seats that recline a long way and have footrests) and *cama* (sleeper) service. The price can double for sleeper service, but could be worth it. Tourist buses to major destinations like Copacabana and Uyuni cost double, but are safer and more comfortable.

Keep your valuables with you on the bus (not in the overhead bin). You should padlock your bag if it's going on top. Take warm clothes and even a sleeping bag for anything in the Altiplano, and expect transit times to vary up to three hours. Getting stranded overnight is not that uncommon.

Hitchhiking

Thanks to relatively easy access to *camiones* and a profusion of buses, hitchhiking isn't really necessary or popular in Bolivia. Still, it's not unknown and drivers of *movilidades – coches* (cars), *camionetas* (pickup trucks), NGO vehicles, gas trucks and other vehicles – are usually happy to pick up passengers when they have room. Always ask the price, if any, before climbing aboard, even for short distances; if they do charge, it should amount to about half the bus fare for the equivalent distance.

Micro, Minibus & Trufi

Micros (small bus or minibus) are used in larger cities and serve as Bolivia's least expensive form of public transportation. They follow set routes, and the route numbers or letters are usually marked on a placard behind the windshield. This is often backed by a description of the route, including the streets that are followed to reach the end of the line. They can be hailed anywhere along their routes, though bus stops in some bigger cities are starting to pop up. When you want to disembark, move toward the front and tell the driver or assistant where you want them to stop.

Minibuses and *trufis* (which may be shared cars, vans or minibuses), also known as *colectivos*, are prevalent in the larger towns and cities, and follow set routes that are numbered and described on placards. They are always cheaper than taxis and nearly as convenient. As with *micros*, you can board or alight anywhere along their route.

Taxi

Urban taxis are relatively inexpensive. Few are equipped with meters but in most cities and towns there are standard per-person fares for short hauls. In some places taxis are collective and behave more like *trufis,* charging a set rate per person.

Radio taxis, on the other hand, always charge a set rate for up to four people; if you squeeze in five people, the fare increases by a small margin. When using taxis, try to have enough change to cover the fare; drivers often like to plead a lack of change in the hope that you'll give them the benefit of the difference. As a general rule, taxi drivers aren't tipped.

In larger cities, especially at night if traveling solo, it's advisable to go for a radio taxi instead of hailing one in the street; have your hotel or restaurant call for one.

Tours

Tours are a convenient way to visit a site when you're short on time or motivation, and are frequently the easiest way to visit remote areas. They're also relatively cheap, but the cost will depend on the number of people in your group. Popular organized tours include Tiwanaku, Uyuni, and excursions to remote attractions such as the Cordillera Apolobamba. Arrange organized tours in La Paz or the town closest to the attraction you wish to visit.

There are scores of outfits offering trekking, mountain-climbing and rainforest adventure packages. For climbing in the Cordilleras, operators offer customized expeditions including guides, transport, porters, cooks and equipment. Some also rent trekking equipment.

Train

Since privatization in the mid-1990s, passenger rail services have been cut back. The western network operated by **Empresa Ferroviaria Andina** (FCA; www.fca.com.bo) runs from Oruro to Villazón on the Argentine border; a branch line runs southwest from Uyuni to Avaroa (on the Chilean border).

The east is operated by **Ferroviaria Oriental** (www.ferroviariaoriental.com), which has a line from Santa Cruz to the Brazilian frontier at Quijarro, where you cross to the Pantanal. An infrequently used service goes south from Santa Cruz to Yacuiba on the Argentine border, and there's a pilot project running tourist trains from La Paz to Tiwanaku.

Brazil

Includes »

Best Places to Eat

» Espírito Santa (p280)

» Bráz Pizzaria (p298)

» A Portinha (p349)

» Tacacá da Gisela (p383)

» Vó Bertila (p320)

Best Beaches

» Baía de Sancho (p355)

» Praia do Espelho (p349)

» Lopes Mendes (p290)

» Praia de Jericoacoara (p365)

» Praia dos Golfinhos (p358)

Why Go?

Brazil. The mere whisper of its name awakens the senses with promises of paradise: cerulean waters giving way to 7500km of sun-kissed sands; music-filled metropolises and idyllic tropical islands; enchanting colonial towns and rugged red-rock canyons; majestic waterfalls and crystal-clear rivers; lush rainforests and dense jungles; gorgeous people and the Beautiful Game. It's all here in spectacular cinematic overload.

The country has enthralled for centuries for good reason: every bit of the hyperbole is unequivocally true. It all climaxes in Brazil's most famous celebration, Carnaval, which storms though the country's cities and towns like a best-of blitz of hip-shaking samba, dazzling costumes and carefree lust for life, but Brazilians hardly check their passion for revelry at Lent. The Brazilian Way – *O Jeito Brasileiro* – embodies the country's lust for life, and will seize you in its sensational clutches every day of the year.

When to Go

Rio de Janeiro

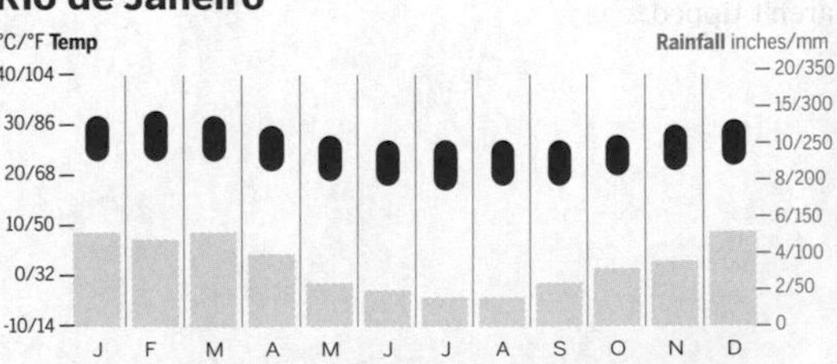

Dec–Feb Summer sizzles in the lead-up to Carnaval. Rainy season in the Amazon.

Sep–Nov Crowds dispel as spring brings serenity and pleasant temperatures.

Mar–Jun Affordable prices and Northeast sunshine beckon travelers.

Connections

Brazil shares land borders with every country on the continent except Chile and Ecuador. The most common land crossings for travelers include the epic Amazon river crossing from Belém or Manaus to Leticia (Colombia) or Iquitos (Peru); a trek through the Pantanal, the world's largest wetlands, and out through Corumbá into Bolivia via the daily train link with Santa Cruz; and the waterlogged tri-border linking Foz do Iguaçu with Ciudad del Este, Paraguay and Puerto Iguazú, Argentina. By air, you can reach most South American capitals directly, including Asunción, Buenos Aires, Caracas, Lima, Montevideo and Santiago (as well as Santa Cruz, Bolivia); and common overland bus routes reach Asunción, Buenos Aires, Montevideo, Santiago and Santa Cruz, Bolivia.

ITINERARIES

Two Weeks

Throw yourself into the thick of it in the Cidade Maravilhosa (Marvelous City – Rio de Janeiro's appropriate nickname), taking in the sights, sounds, seductions and samba of South America's most stunning city. Then spend a few days dazzled by nature in two of the world's most important ecological hot spots, the Amazon and the Pantanal, and get up close and personal with the world's most stupendous waterfall at Foz do Iguaçu.

One Month

Follow the two-week itinerary, but supplement Brazil's greatest hits with visits to some of the country's most cinematic destinations: beautifully preserved colonial towns in the states of Rio (Paraty) and Minas Gerais (Ouro Preto and Tiradentes); postcard-perfect beaches in Fernando de Noronha, Bahia or Florianópolis; miraculous dune desertscapes in Parque Nacional dos Lençóis Maranhenses; and the aquatic wonderland of Bonito.

Essential Food & Drink

» **Feijoada** The national dish: a beans, beef and/or pork stew

» **Açaí** Blended Amazon palm berries, usually mixed with banana, granola, honey and *guaraná* syrup

» **Moqueca** Seafood stew from Bahia (Bahiana) or Espírito Santo (Capixaba)

» **Picanha** Brazil's most succulent meat cut, roughly translated as 'rump cap'

» **Pão de queijo** Ubiquitous cheese bread made with *manioc* (cassava) flour, milk, eggs and cheese

» **Cachaça** Rumlike liquor made from fermented sugarcane juice

» **Caipirinha** The national cocktail: *cachaça*, lime and sugar

AT A GLANCE

» **Currency** Real (R$)

» **Languages** Portuguese and 180 indigenous languages

» **Money** ATMs widespread, credit cards widely accepted

» **Visas** Required for Americans, Australians and Canadians; not needed for most others

Fast Facts

» **Area** 8,456,510 sq km

» **Capital** Brasília

» **Emergency** ☎192

» **Country code** ☎55

Exchange Rates

Australia	A$1	R$2.07
Canada	C$1	R$1.98
Euro zone	€1	R$2.69
New Zealand	NZ$1	R$1.65
UK	UK£1	R$3.14
USA	US$1	R$1.98

Set Your Budget

» **Rio budget sleeps** US$20 (dorm) to US$100 (double)

» **Pay-by-weight lunch** US$8-14

» **Cocktail** US$4-12

» **Rio–Ouro Preto bus fare** US$55

Resources

» **Visit Brazil** (www.visitbrasil.com)

» **Brazilian Embassy in London** (www.brazil.org.uk)

» **Rio Times** (www.riotimesonline.com)

» **Brazzil** (www.brazzil.com)

Brazil Highlights

1. Fall under the seductive spell of **Rio de Janeiro** (p266) amid the whirlwind of wild samba clubs, sizzling sands, soaring peaks and sexy sunsets
2. Feel the breath of Mother Nature's ferocious roar at the jaw-dropping waterfalls of **Foz do Iguaçu** (p318)
3. Dig into some of the world's most pristine sands in **Fernando de Noronha** (p355)
4. Spy pointy-toothed piranhas and glowing caiman eyes while cruising the mighty **Amazon** (p371)
5. Meander along cobblestones in cinematic colonial towns like **Ouro Preto** (p303), **Paraty** (p291) and **Tiradentes** (p306)
6. Follow delirious drumbeats through the colonial center during regular evening street parties in **Salvador** (p334)
7. Shutter-stalk spectacular animals in the **Pantanal** (p326), followed by a dip into the nearby aquatic wonderland of **Bonito** (p332)
8. Hike surreal landscapes in dramatic national parks like **Lençóis Maranhenses** (p370) and **Chapada Diamantina** (p342)

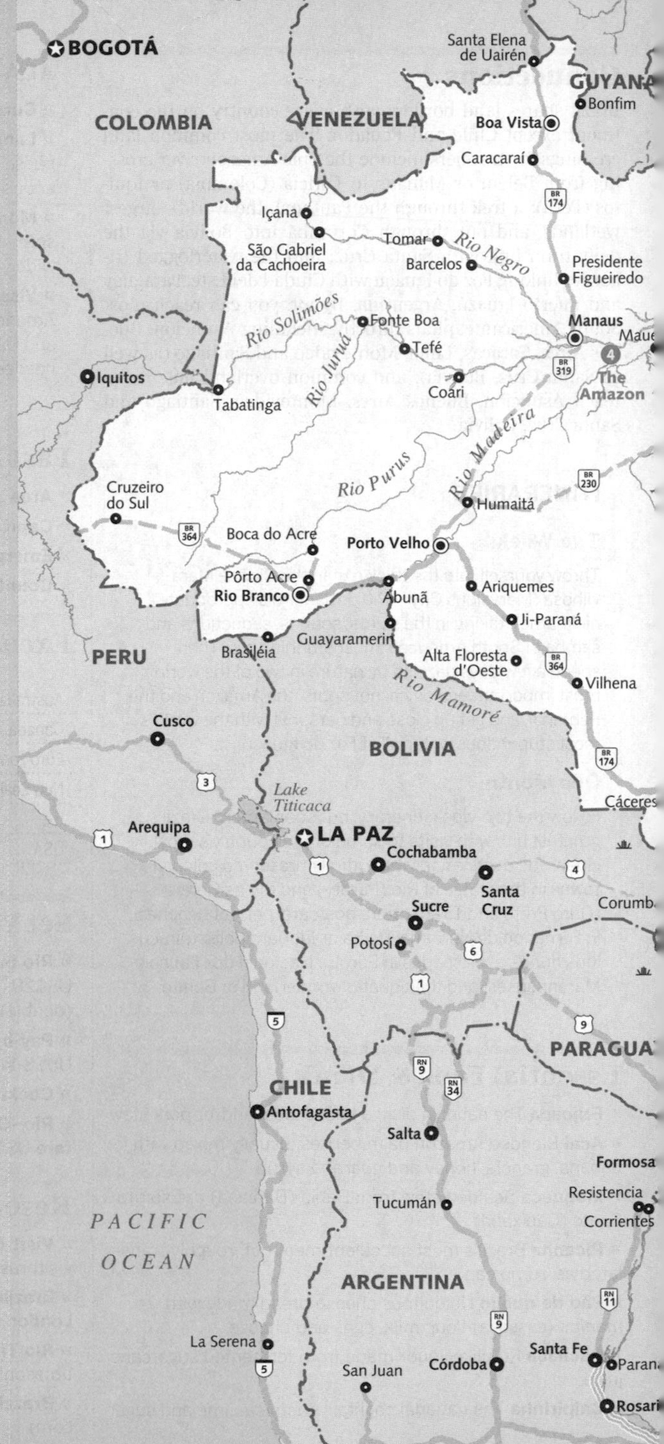

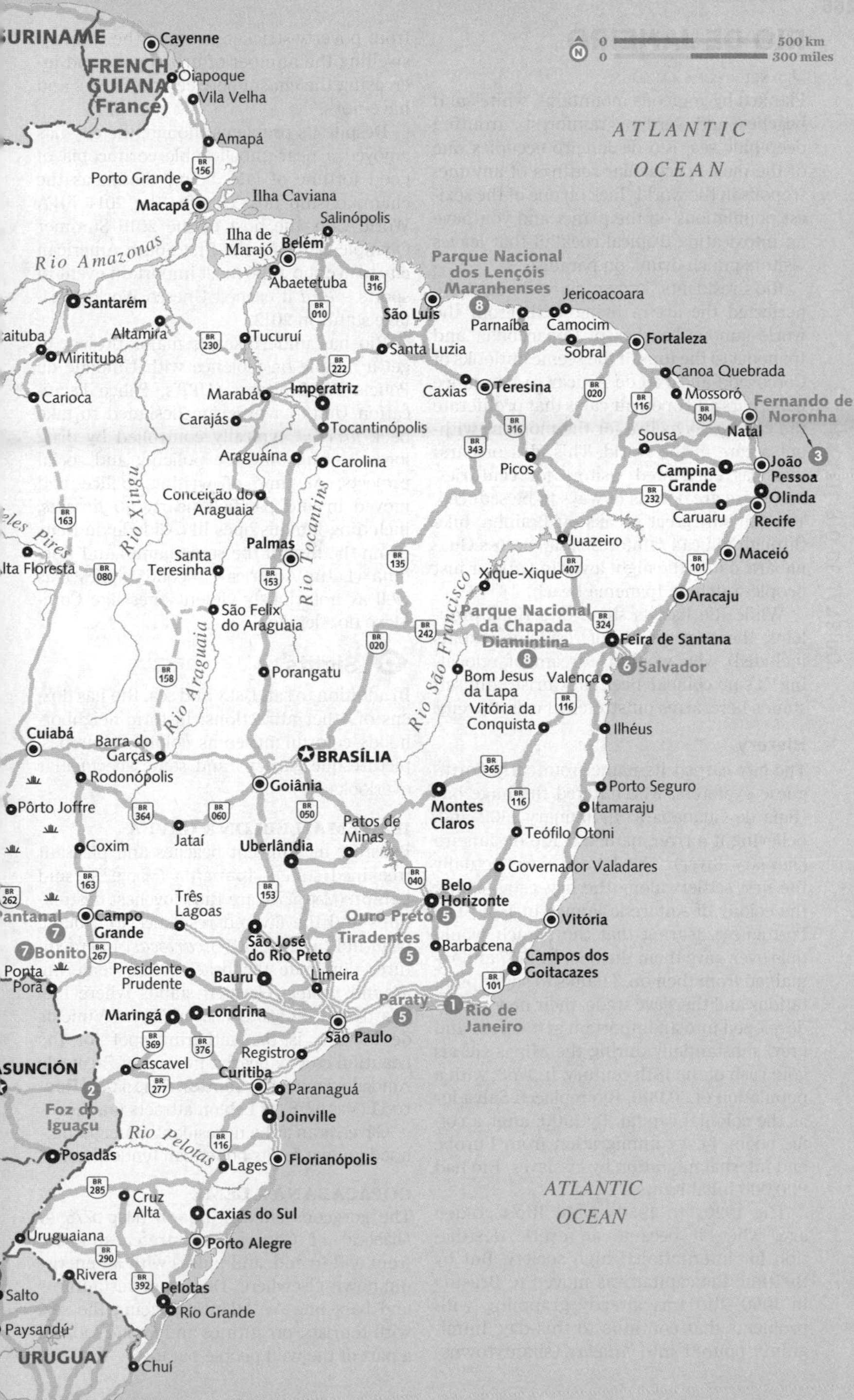
0 500 km
0 300 miles
ATLANTIC OCEAN
SURINAME
Cayenne
FRENCH GUIANA (France)
Oiapoque
Vila Velha
Amapá
Porto Grande
Macapá
Ilha Caviana
Salinópolis
Ilha de Marajó
Belém
Rio Amazonas
Abaetetuba
Santarém
Altamira
Tucuruí
São Luís
Santa Luzia
Parque Nacional dos Lençóis Maranhenses
Parnaíba
Camocim
Jericoacoara
Sobral
Fortaleza
Canoa Quebrada
Mossoró
Fernando de Noronha
Natal
Sousa
Caxias
Teresina
Imperatriz
Marabá
Carajás
Tocantinópolis
Araguaína
Carolina
Miritituba
Carioca
Picos
Campina Grande
João Pessoa
Olinda
Recife
Caruaru
Conceição do Araguaia
Rio Xingu
Rio Tocantins
Juazeiro
Maceió
Palmas
Santa Teresinha
Alta Floresta
Xique-Xique
Aracaju
São Felix do Araguaia
Parque Nacional da Chapada Diamantina
Feira de Santana
Salvador
Rio São Francisco
Rio Araguaia
Porangatu
Bom Jesus da Lapa
Valença
Vitória da Conquista
Ilhéus
Cuiabá
Barra do Garças
BRASÍLIA
Rodonópolis
Goiânia
Porto Seguro
Itamaraju
Montes Claros
Pôrto Joffre
Jataí
Patos de Minas
Teófilo Otoni
Coxim
Uberlândia
Governador Valadares
Belo Horizonte
Pantanal
Três Lagoas
Campo Grande
Ouro Preto
Vitória
Bonito
São José do Rio Preto
Tiradentes
Barbacena
Ponta Porã
Presidente Prudente
Bauru
Limeira
Campos dos Goitacazes
Maringá
Londrina
Paraty
Rio de Janeiro
São Paulo
Registro
ASUNCIÓN
Cascavel
Curitiba
Paranaguá
Foz do Iguaçu
Joinville
Rio Pelotas
Posadas
Lages
Florianópolis
Cruz Alta
Caxias do Sul
Uruguaiana
Porto Alegre
Rivera
Pelotas
Salto
Río Grande
Paysandú
URUGUAY
Chuí
ATLANTIC OCEAN

RIO DE JANEIRO

0XX21 / POP 6.4 MILLION

Flanked by gorgeous mountains, white-sand beaches and verdant rainforests fronting deep-blue sea, Rio de Janeiro occupies one of the most spectacular settings of any metropolis in the world. Tack on one of the sexiest populations on the planet and you have an intoxicating tropical cocktail that leaves visitors punch-drunk on paradise.

Rio's residents, known as *cariocas,* have perfected the art of living well. From the world-famous beaches of Copacabana and Ipanema to the tops of the scenic outlooks of Corcovado and Pão de Açúcar to the dance halls, bars and open-air cafes that proliferate the city, *cariocas* live for the moment without a care in the world. This idea of paradise has enchanted visitors for centuries, and there are dozens of ways to be seduced. You can surf great breaks off Prainha, hike through Tijuca's rainforests, sail across Guanabára, dance the night away in Lapa or just people-watch on Ipanema Beach.

While Rio has its share of serious problems, there are plenty of residents (expats included) who wouldn't dream of relocating. It's no coincidence that Christo himself stands here, arms outstretched over the city.

History

The city earned its name from early Portuguese explorers, who entered the huge bay (Baía de Guanabara) in January 1502 and, believing it a river, named it Rio de Janeiro (January River). The French were actually the first settlers along the bay, establishing the colony of Antarctic France in 1555. The Portuguese, fearing that the French would take over, gave them the boot in 1567 and remained from then on. Thanks to sugar plantations and the slave trade, their new colony developed into an important settlement and grew substantially during the Minas Gerais gold rush of the 18th century. In 1763, with a population of 50,000, Rio replaced Salvador as the colonial capital. By 1900, after a coffee boom, heavy immigration from Europe and internal migration by ex-slaves, Rio had 800,000 inhabitants.

The 1920s to 1950s were Rio's golden age, when it became an exotic destination for international high society. But by the time the capital was moved to Brasília in 1960, Rio was already grappling with problems that continue to this day. Immigrants poured into *favelas* (shantytowns) from poverty-stricken areas of the country, swelling the number of urban poor and increasing the chasm between the have's and have-not's.

Despite its problems though, the city has enjoyed a near-unbelievable cornucopia of good fortune of late, being chosen as the championship host city for the 2014 FIFA World Cup, the host of the 2016 Summer Olympic Games – the first South American city to ever host the most important event in sports – *and* it earned Unesco World Heritage status in 2012.

Rio has undertaken a major project to get a handle on violence with Unidade de Polícia Pacificadoras (UPP's; Police Pacification Units), a program designed to take back *favelas*, typically controlled by drug lords, through intense policing and social projects. At time of writing, police had moved in and pacified nearly 30 *favelas*, including famous ones like Cidade de Deus (from the film of the same name) and Rocinha (Latin America's second biggest) as well as notoriously violent ones like Complexo do Alemão.

Sights

In addition to sand, sky and sea, Rio has dozens of other attractions: historic neighborhoods, colorful museums, colonial churches, picturesque gardens and some spectacular overlooks.

IPANEMA, LEBLON & GÁVEA

Boasting magnificent beaches and pleasant tree-lined streets, **Ipanema** (Map p278) and **Leblon** (Map p278) are Rio's loveliest destinations and the favored residence for young, beautiful (and wealthy) *cariocas*. Microcultures dominate the beach, often centering around *postos* (elevated stands where lifeguards sit). **Posto 9** (Map p278), off Vinícius de Moraes, is the gathering spot for the beautiful crowd; nearby, in front of Farme de Amoedo, is the **gay section** (Map p278); **Posto 11** (Map p278) in Leblon attracts families.

Gávea is an affluent residential neighbourhood known for its bohemian tendencies.

COPACABANA & LEME

The gorgeous curving **beach** (Map p276; Av Atlântica) of Copacabana stretches 4.5km from end to end, and pulses with an energy unknown elsewhere. Dozens of restaurants and bars line Av Atlântica, facing the sea, with tourists, prostitutes and *favela* kids all a part of the wild people-parade.

Rio de Janeiro

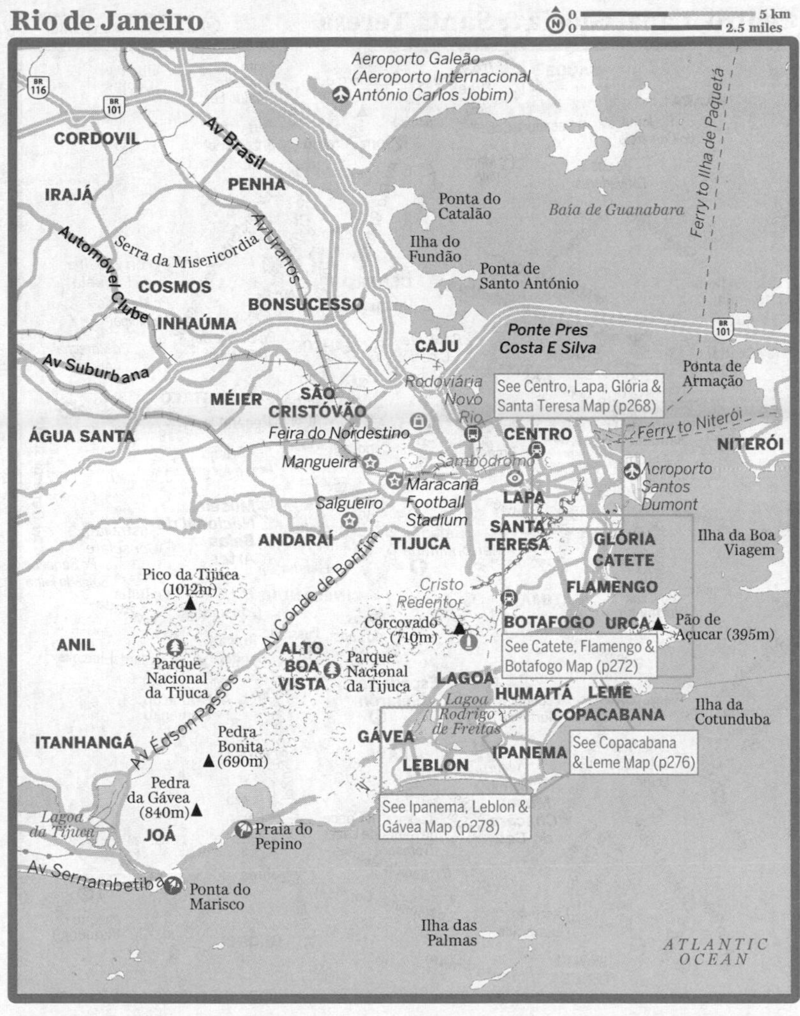

SANTA TERESA & LAPA

Set on a hill overlooking the city, Santa Teresa, with its cobbled streets and aging mansions, retains the charm of days past and presents Rio's most atmospheric neighborhood. Currently the residence of a whole new generation of artists and bohemians, Santa Teresa has colorful restaurants and bars as well as a lively weekend scene concentrated around Largo do Guimarães and Largo das Neves.

The *bondinho* (streetcar) traditionally used to reach Santa Teresa was closed at the time of writing after a deadly 2011 derailment. A R$110 million upgraded *bonde* was expected to relaunch in 2014. It leaves from the station on Professor Lélio Gama, behind Petrobras. Until then, catch a taxi from the Glória metro station (R$7) or buses 014 or 006 from Largo de Carioca downtown.

TOP CHOICE Escadaria Selarón LANDMARK

(Map p268; stairway btwn Joaquim Silva in Lapa & Pinto Martins in Santa Teresa) Rio's most famous staircase is the legacy of eccentric Chilean artist Selarón, who died at its foot in 2012 under mysterious circumstances (police eventually ruled he had doused himself in

Centro, Lapa, Glória & Santa Teresa

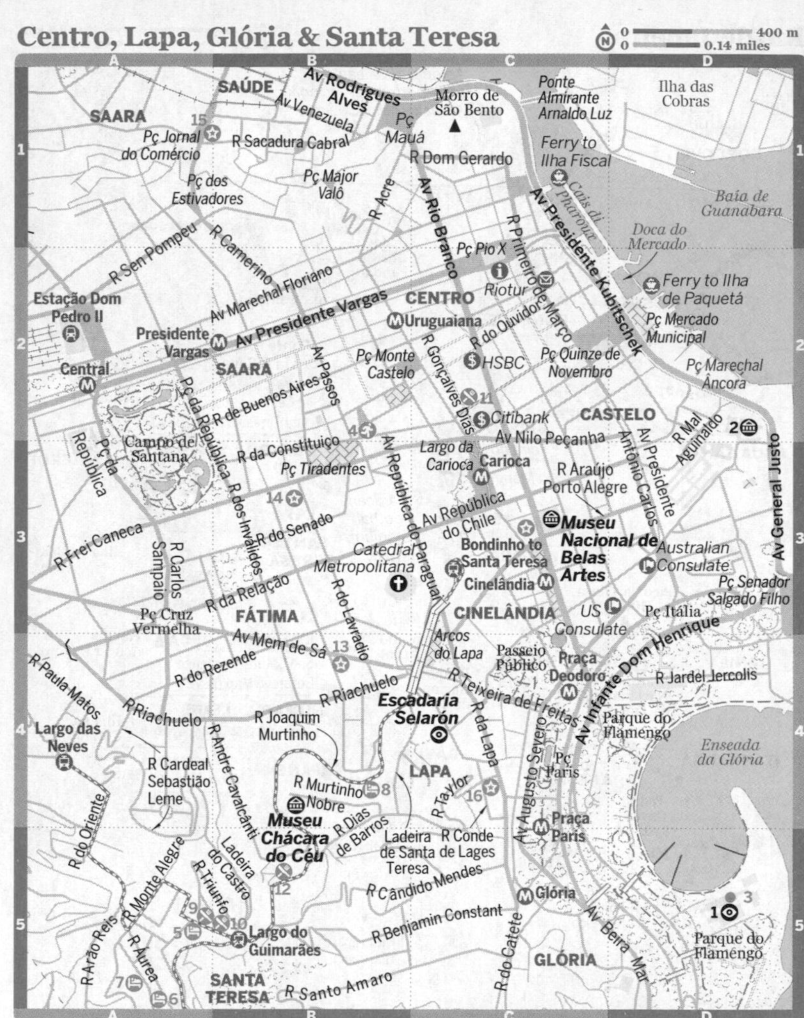

lighter fluid and set himself on fire). Since 1990, Selaró had covered some 215 steps, from Santa Teresa to Lapa, with over 2000 tiles from 120 countries in mosaic-like fashion. Beautiful.

Museu Chácara do Céu MUSEUM

(Map p268; ☎3970-1126; www.museuscastromaya.com.br; Murtinho Nobre 93, Lapa; admission R$2, Wed free; ⊙noon-5pm Wed-Mon) Museu Chácara do Céu is a delightful art and antiques museum in a former industrialist's mansion with beautiful gardens and great views.

URCA & BOTAFOGO

The peaceful streets of Urca offer a welcome escape from the urban bustle.

Pão de Açúcar MOUNTAIN

(Sugarloaf; Map p272; ☎2546-8400; www.bondinho.com.br; Av Pasteur 520, Urca; adult/child R$53/26; ⊙8am-7:50pm) Rio's iconic 396m mountain offers fabulous views over the city. To reach the summit you can go by cable car, changing lines at Morro da Urca (215m); or you can also climb up. To get there take an 'Urca' bus (bus 107 from Centro or Flamengo; bus 511 or 512 from the Zona Sul – the 'South Zone').

Centro, Lapa, Glória & Santa Teresa

COSME VELHO

TOP CHOICE Cristo Redentor MONUMENT
(Christ the Redeemer; ☎2558-1329; www.corcovado.com.br; Cosme Velho 513, cog station; adult/child R$46/23; ⏲8am-7pm) Atop the 710m-high peak known as Corcovado (Hunchback), the looming statue of Cristo Redentor (Christ the Redeemer), voted one of the New Seven Wonders of the World in 2007, offers fantastic views over Rio. To reach the train, take a taxi or a 'Cosme Velho' bus (180, 569, 583). If you want to take a vehicle up, vans depart every 15 minutes from Paineiras (R$18.52 to R$26.53 depending on weekends and holidays) from 8am to 7pm in summer (until 6pm otherwise).

CENTRO & GLÓRIA

Rio's bustling commercial district has many remnants of its once-magnificent past. Looming baroque churches, wide plazas and cobblestone streets lie scattered throughout the district.

Museu Nacional de Belas Artes MUSEUM
(Map p268; ☎2219-8474; www.mnba.gov.br; Rio Branco 199, Centro; adult/student R$8/4; ⏲10am-6pm Tue-Fri, noon-5pm Sat & Sun) This small museum houses fine art from the 17th to the 20th century, including Brazilian classics like Cândido Portinari's *Café*.

Museu Histórico Nacional MUSEUM
(Map p268; ☎2550-9224; www.museuhistoriconacional.com.br; off General Justo near Praça Marechal Âncora; admission R$8, Sun free; ⏲10am-5:30pm Tue-Fri, 2-6pm Sat & Sun) Occupying the former 18th-century colonial arsenal, the large Museu Histórico Nacional contains thousands of historic relics relating to the history of Brazil.

CATETE & FLAMENGO

Museu da República MUSEUM
(Map p272; ☎3235-3693; www.museudarepublica.org.br; Rua do Catete 153; admission R$6, Wed & Sun free; ⏲10am-noon & 1-5pm Tue-Fri, 2-6pm Sat & Sun) Museu da República occupies the beautiful 19th-century Palácio do Catete, which served as Brazil's presidential palace until 1954. It houses a collection of artifacts from the republican period and the eerily preserved room where President Getúlio Vargas killed himself. Located 100m north of Metro Catete.

FREE Parque do Catete PARK
(Map p272) Behind Parque do Catete, the former palace grounds contain a pleasant outdoor cafe and a small pond.

JARDIM BOTÂNICO & LAGOA

TOP CHOICE Jardim Botânico GARDENS
(Botanical Garden; Map p278; www.jbrj.com.br; Jardim Botânico 1008; admission R$6; ⏲8am-5pm) This verdant Botanical Garden, with over 5000 varieties of plants, is quiet and serene on weekdays and fills with families and music on weekends. To get there take a 'Jardim Botânico' bus, or any other bus marked 'via Jóquei.'

Lagoa Rodrigo de Freitas LAGOON
(Map p278) Just north of Ipanema stretches the Lagoa Rodrigo de Freitas, a picturesque saltwater lagoon ringed with a walking-biking trail. The lakeside kiosks provide a scenic spot for an outdoor meal, with live music on weekend nights.

PARQUE NACIONAL DA TIJUCA

Lush trails through tropical rainforest lie just 15 minutes from concrete Copacabana. The 120-sq-km refuge of the **Parque Nacional da Tijuca** (Map p272; www.parquedatijuca.com.br; ⌚8am-5pm), a remnant of the Atlantic rainforest, has excellently marked trails over small peaks and past waterfalls.

It's best to go by car, but if you can't, catch bus 233 or 234 or take the metro to Saens Peña, then catch a bus going to Barra da Tijuca and get off at Alta da Boa Vista, the small suburb close to the park entrance.

Activities

Rio's lush mountains and glimmering coastline just cry out for attention, and there are hundreds of ways to experience their magic on a sun-drenched afternoon.

The fantastic hang glide off 510m Pedra Bonita, one of the giant granite slabs towering over the city, is a highlight of any trip to Brazil. Many pilots offer tandem flights (from around R$250 including transportation, plus R$20 for insurance at the launch site), but reputable picks include **Just Fly** (☎2268-0565; http://justflyinrio.blogspot.com) and **SuperFly** (☎3322-2286; www.riosuperfly.com.br).

Bem Brasil CRUISE

(Map p268; www.bembrasilrio.com; Marina da Glória, Glória; R$50-70) Runs popular booze cruises in the bay from a two-floor sailboat soundtracked by well-known house DJ Andrew Gracie every Monday night at 11pm.

Centro Cultural Carioca Dança DANCE

(Map p268; ☎3176-1412; www.dancaccc.com.br; Sete de Setembro 237, 3rd fl, Centro; classes individual/monthly R$20/90) Offers one-hour classes in samba and *forró* (a type of Brazilian music), which meet around twice a week.

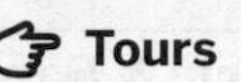

Tours

Rio Hiking HIKING

(☎2552-9204; www.riohiking.com.br; full-day tour from R$150) Offers highly rewarding climbs up Pão de Açúcar.

Favela Tour CULTURAL TOUR

(☎3322-2727; www.favelatour.com.br; R$65) Marcelo Armstrong's insightful tour pioneered *favela* tourism – his three-hour excursion takes in Rocinha and Vila Canoas and a portion of proceeds go toward the Para Ti NGO, which benefits local school children.

Special Adventure BICYCLE TOUR

(Map p272; ☎2266-3002; www.specialadventure.com.br; General Polidoro 174, Botafogo) Enthusiastic cycle guru Andre runs good time bike tours through Rio's *Zona Sul*, Lagoa or Centro (on Sundays) as well as renting bicycles.

Brazil Expedition NIGHTLIFE TOUR

(☎9998-2907; www.brazilexpedition.com) Popular Saturday-night tours to samba schools (R$60 to R$80) in season and Sunday *favela* funk parties (R$60).

Festivals & Events

One of the world's biggest and wildest parties, **Carnaval** in all its colorful, hedonistic bacchanalia is virtually synonymous with Rio. Although Carnaval is ostensibly just five days of revelry (Friday to Tuesday preceding Ash Wednesday), *cariocas* begin partying months in advance. The parade through the *sambódromo* (samba parade ground), featuring elaborate floats flanked by thousands of pounding drummers and twirling dancers, is the culmination of the festivities, though the real action is at the parties about town.

PORTO MARAVILHA

Rio's docklands, located north of Centro in the neighborhoods of Gamboa and Barrio Saúde (as well as stretching into Centro, São Cristóvão and Cidade Nova), will be transformed into the **Porto Maravilha** (Marvelous Port; www.portomaravilha.com.br), the most exciting and ambitious of the city's transformations for the Olympic stage. The massive urban waterfront revitalization project, clocking in at a area of 5 million square meters and a projected tally of R$8 billion over 15 years, will turn a historic but underused and dilapidated port into one of Rio's showcase attractions. It will include new cultural attractions like the Art Museum of Rio de Janeiro (MAR), the Museu da Amanha and the Jardim do Valongo hanging gardens, and 17km of bike paths, numerous parks, and squares dotted with 15,000 new trees. As the traditional birthplace for samba and *choro* (improvised samba), Rio's port will indeed be singing again by 2016.

FAVELA CHIC

Favela (slum or shanty town) sleeps are nothing new – intrepid travelers have been venturing into Rio's urban mazes for nearly a decade – but as more and more of Rio's *favelas* are pacified, hostels and *pousadas* (guesthouses) are popping up faster than the rudimentary constructions which make up the *favelas* themselves. Our favorites:

Maze Inn (Map p272; ☎2558-5547; www.jazzrio.info; Casa 66, Tavares Bastos 414, Catete; dm R$60, s/d from R$120/150) Owned by English renaissance man Bob Nadkarni, this *pousada* and jazz house in Tavares Bastos *favela* is almost legendary. Jazz nights are the first and third Friday of every month (R$30).

Vidigalbergue (☎7929-7999; www.vidigalbergue.com.br; Casa 2, Av Niemeyer 314, Vidigal; ❄@📶) Stunning seaviews are the coup at this friendly hostel at the bottom of Vidigal *favela*.

Pousada Favelinha (Map p272; ☎2556-5273; www.favelinha.com; Almirante Alexandrino 2023, Santa Teresa; dm/d R$45/110; @) This European-run inn in Santa Teresa's Pereirão da Silva *favela* was the first…way back in 2004.

Nightclubs and bars throw special costumed events. There are free live concerts throughout the city (Largo do Machado, Arcos do Lapa, Praça General Osório), while those seeking a bit of decadence can head to various balls about town. *Bandas,* also called *blocos,* are one of the best ways to celebrate *carioca*-style. These consist of a procession of drummers and vocalists followed by anyone who wants to dance through the streets of Rio. Check *Veja*'s 'Rio' insert or Riotur for times and locations. *Blocos* in Santa Teresa and Ipanema are highly recommended.

The spectacular main parade takes place in the **sambódromo** (Marques do Sapuçai) near Praça Onze metro station. Before an exuberant crowd of some 30,000, each of 12 samba schools has its hour to dazzle the audience. Top schools compete on Carnaval Sunday and Monday (March 2 and 3 in 2014, February 15 and 16 in 2015, February 7 and 8 in 2016). The safest way of reaching the *sambódromo* is by taxi or metro, which runs round the clock during Carnaval.

For information on buying *sambódromo* tickets at official prices (around R$120 to R$550 for the main parades), stop by Riotur or Carnaval's **Central de Atendimento** (☎2233-8151; www.liesa.globo.com; Alfândega 25, Centro; ⏲10am-4pm Mon-Fri Sept-Carnival); or visit the Carnaval site (www.rio-carnival.net). By Carnaval weekend most tickets are sold out, leaving you at the mercy of the scalpers (they will find you), or simply show up at the *sambódromo* around midnight when you can get grandstand tickets for 50% less or more, depending on the hour and location.

Keep in mind that Carnaval is costly: room rates can quadruple and some thieves keep in the spirit of things by robbing in costume.

Sleeping

Ipanema and Leblon are the most appealing *Zona Sul* neighborhoods to base yourself. The historic hillside bohemian quarter of Santa Teresa is Rio's most charming *bairro* (suburb). The upstart neighborhood of Botafogo is starting to emerge as Rio's next 'It' neighborhood and is the most centrally located to the majority of the city's most important attractions. Cheaper accommodation clusters around the working-class areas of Catete and Glória.

IPANEMA, LEBLON & GÁVEA

Ipanema Beach House HOSTEL **$$**
(Map p278; ☎3202-2693; www.ipanemahouse.com; Barão da Torre 485, Ipanema; dm R$60, d with/without bathroom from R$200/180; @📶🏊) This converted two-story house dating to 1918 is one of Rio's most atmospheric hostels, with six- and nine-bed dorms, private rooms, spacious indoor and outdoor lounges and a welcoming pool.

Mango Tree HOSTEL **$$**
(Map p278; ☎2287-9255; www.mangotreehostel.com; Prudente de Morais 594, Ipanema; dm from R$55, d with/without bathroom from R$190/170; ❄@📶) In a handsome villa, this popular hostel offers rooms with two-toned wood floors and a handful of new finely designed

Catete, Flamengo & Botafogo

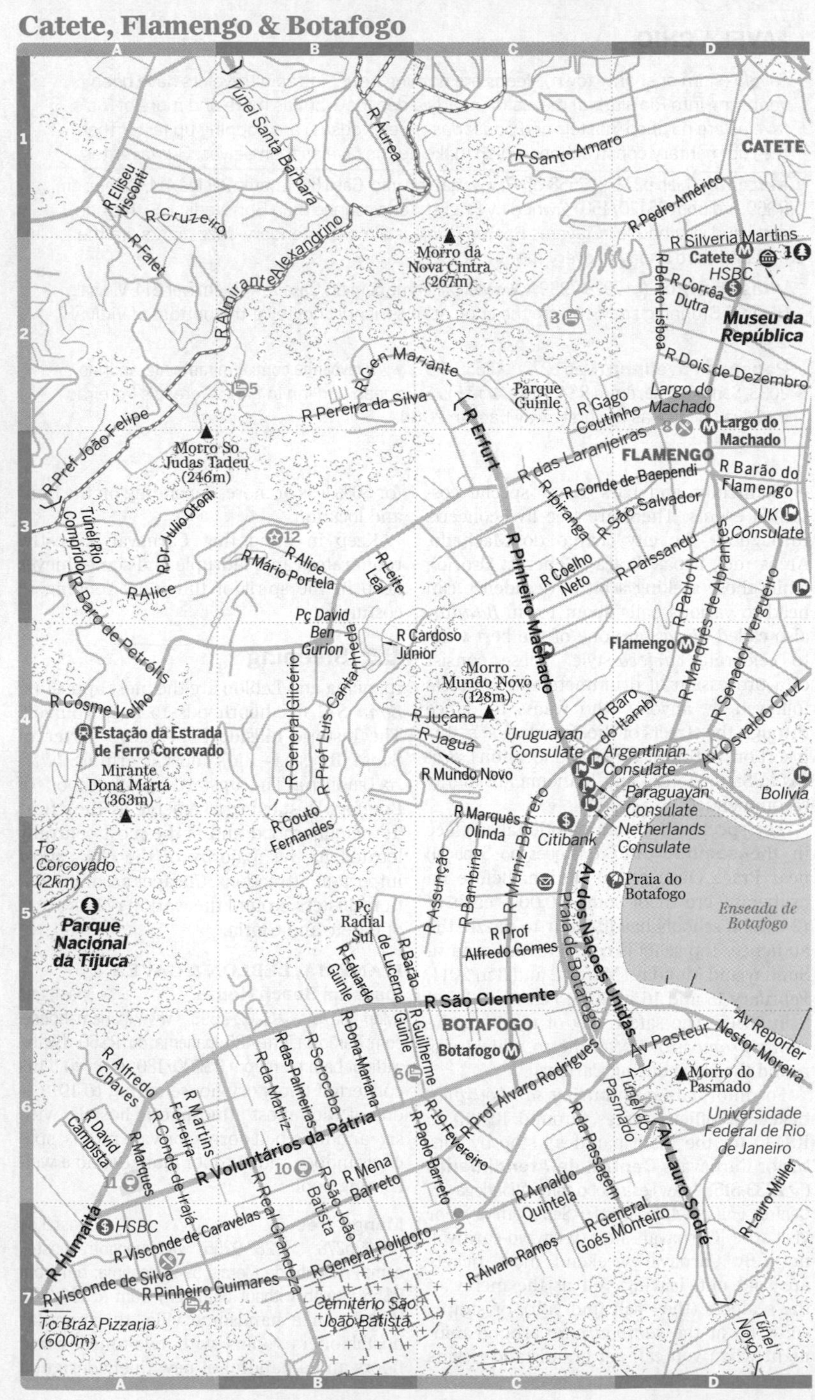

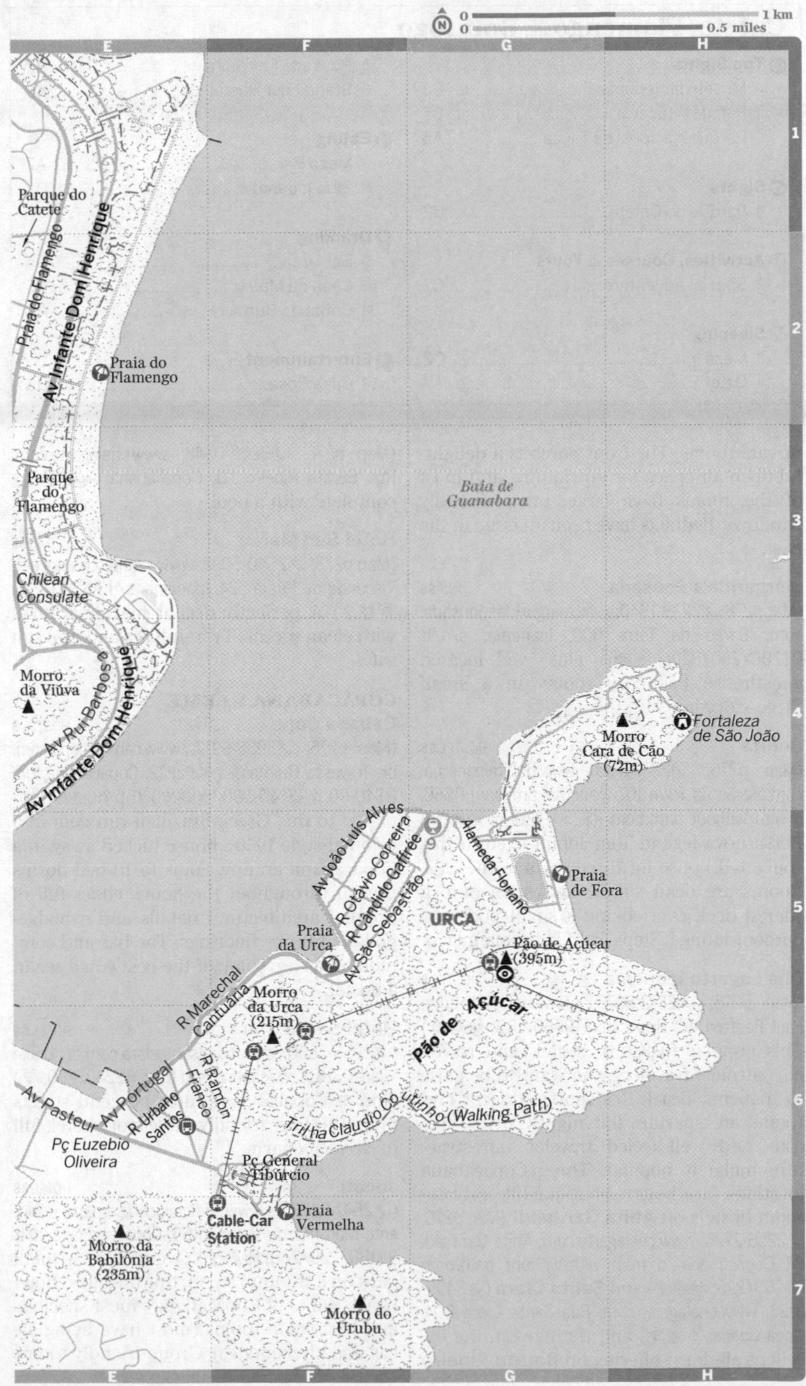
0
1 km
0
0.5 miles
Parque do Catete
Praia do Flamengo
Av Infante Dom Henrique
Praia do Flamengo
Parque do Flamengo
Chilean Consulate
Morro da Viúva
Av Rui Barbosa
Av Infante Dom Henrique
Baía de Guanabara
Morro Cara de Cão (72m)
Fortaleza de São João
Av João Luís Alves
R Otávio Correira
R Cândido Gaffrée
Av São Sebastião
Alameda Floriano
Praia de Fora
URCA
Praia da Urca
Pão de Açúcar (395m)
Morro da Urca (215m)
R Marechal Cantuária
Pão de Açúcar
R Ramon Franco
Av Portugal
R Urbano Santos
Av Pasteur
Pç Euzebio Oliveira
Trilha Claudio Coutinho (Walking Path)
Pç General Tibúrcio
Cable-Car Station
Praia Vermelha
Morro da Babilônia (235m)
Morro do Urubu

Catete, Flamengo & Botafogo

Top Sights
Museu da República D2
Pão de Açúcar G5
Parque Nacional da Tijuca A5

Sights
1 Parque do Catete D2

Activities, Courses & Tours
2 Special Adventure C7

Sleeping
3 Maze Inn C2
4 Oztel A7
5 Pousada Favelinha B2
6 Stand Fast Hostel B6

Eating
7 Meza Bar A7
8 Sírio Libaneza D2

Drinking
9 Bar Urca G5
10 Casa da Matriz B6
11 Cobal do Humaitá A6

Entertainment
12 Casa Rosa B3

private rooms. The front porch is a delightful open-air space for unwinding, and most of the rooms have large, breeze-friendly windows. Bedbugs have been an issue in the past.

Margarida's Pousada INN $$
(Map p278; 2239-1840; www.margaridaspousada.com; Barão da Torre 600, Ipanema; s/d/tr R$200/250/320;) This well-located guesthouse has cozy rooms in a small three-story house.

Bonita HOSTEL $$
(Map p276; 2227-1703; www.bonitaipanema.com; Barão da Torre 107, Ipanema; dm from R$60, d with/without bathroom R$250/220;) Bossa nova legend Tom Jobim lived in this converted house for three years in the '60s. Rooms are dead simple and open onto a shared deck overlooking a small pool and outdoor lounge. Steps from Ipanema metro.

Che Lagarto Ipanema HOSTEL $
(Map p278; 2512-8076; www.chelagarto.com; Paul Redfern 48; dm/d from R$60/180;) This popular five-story hostel (and rowdy bar) attracts travelers who want to be close to Ipanema Beach. It's short on decor and rooms are spartan, but nightly drink specials and well-heeled traveler infrastructure make it popular. Three Copacabana locations fare better: boutique-like private-room hostels on **Anita Garibaldi** (Map p276; 2256-2776; www.chelagarto.com; Anita Garibaldi 87, Copacabana; d from with/without bathroom R$258/225;) and **Santa Clara** (3495-3133; www.chelagarto.com; Rua Santa Clara 304, Copacabana;) and the newest, the excellent all-dorm offering on **Barata Ribeiro** (Map p276; 3209-0348; www.chelagarto.com; Rua Barata Ribeiro 111, Copacabana;), complete with a pool.

Hotel San Marco HOTEL $$
(Map p278; 2540-5032; www.sanmarcohotel.net; Visconde de Pirajá 524, Ipanema; s/d R$260/275;) A perfectly decent midrange hotel with clean rooms, TV, minibars and in-room safes.

COPACABANA & LEME

Cabana Copa HOSTEL $
(Map p276; 3988-9912; www.cabanacopa.com.br; Travessa Guimarães Natal 12, Copacabana; dm R$40-90, d R$140-200;) Top hostel honors go to this Greek-Brazilian-run gem in a colonial-style 1950's house tucked away in a Copacabana cranny. Four- to 10-bed dorms prevail throughout the home, chock-full of original architectural details and a hodgepodge of funky floorings. The bar and common areas are some of the best you'll see in a hostel.

Hotel Santa Clara HOTEL $$
(2256-2650; www.hotelsantaclara.com.br; Décio Vilares 316, Copacabana; s/d from R$240/260;) One of Copacabana's most peaceful streets hides this very friendly three-story hotel, full of *carioca* charm.

Jucati HOTEL $$
(2547-5422; www.edificiojucati.com.br; Tenente Marones de Gusmão 85, Copacabana; s/d/tr R$180/220/260;) Overlooking a small park on a tranquil street, this unsigned hotel boasts some of Copacabana's most spacious and best-value rooms (most have living areas and kitchenettes). Group-friendly rooms

start at R$180 for a single and rise just R$40 per person up to six. No breakfast.

Alex Rio Flats APARTMENT $$
(☎2287-7658; www.alexrioflats.com; studios R$160-200, apt R$250-400; ❄📶) For about the same as a double in most hostels, you can have your own apartment in Rio. This company rents out studios and one- and two-bedroom in Copacabana and Arpoador, all within striking distance of the beach. Three-day minimum.

Rio Backpackers HOSTEL $
(Map p276; ☎2236-3803; www.riobackpackers.com.br; Travessa Santa Leocádia 38, Copacabana; dm from R$40, r with/without bathroom R$160/150; ❄@📶) Young backpackers flock to this popular hostel in Copacabana run by a lovely hostel veteran named Adriana. They are opening a more chic all-private-room hostel, **Boulevard All Suites** (Map p276; Edmundo Lins 21, Copacabana), in Copa.

SANTA TERESA & LAPA

Casa Cool Beans GUESTHOUSE $$
(Map p268; ☎2262-0552; www.casacoolbeans.com; Laurinda Santos Lobo 136, Santa Teresa; d R$260-340; ❄@📶🏊) Expectations are exceeded at this discreet B&B where the American owner's mantra focuses around personalized service. Each colorful room in the renovated 1930's Spanish-style villa was designed by a different *carioca* artist and there's a spacious sun deck and breakfast area. It's pretty perfect.

Casa Áurea GUESTHOUSE $$
(Map p268; ☎2242-5830; www.casaaurea.com.br; Áurea 80, Santa Teresa; dm R$75, s/d R$200/250, without bathroom R$140/180) This charming 13-room *pousada* (guesthouse) oozes rustic goodness from one of the neighborhood's oldest homes, full of attention-grabbing knickknacks.

Cama e Café HOMESTAY $$
(Map p268; ☎2225-4366; www.camaecafe.com; Paschoal Carlos Magno 90, Santa Teresa; r R$130-300; ⏲9am-5:30pm Mon-Fri, to 2pm Sat) This excellent B&B network links travelers with local residents (musicians, poets, architects, chefs) who rent spare rooms in their homes. Accommodations range from modest to lavish and now include Copacabana and Ipanema as well.

Rio Hostel HOSTEL $
(Map p268; ☎3852-0827; www.riohostel.com; Joaquim Murtinho 361, Santa Teresa; dm R$40-45, d R$150-160; ❄@📶🏊) This welcoming hostel is ideally placed for exploring Rio's most bohemian neighborhood.

URCA & BOTAFOGO

Oztel HOSTEL $$$
(Map p272; ☎3042-1853; www.oztel.com.br; Pinheiro Guimarães 91, Botafogo; dm R$55-75, d R$240-290; ❄@📶) Evoking a Warholian aesthetic, Rio's coolest and most colorful hostel is like sleeping in an art gallery. The arty front deck and bar is an inviting hang lounge but the real coup are the R$270 private rooms: with a garden patio under the nose of Christo, you'll be hard-pressed to find a groovier room in Rio.

Stand Fast Hostel HOSTEL $
(Map p272; ☎2553-7420; www.standfasthostel.com; 19 de Fevereiro 52, Botafogo; dm from R$35, d without bathroom R$120; ❄@📶) An exciting new hostel run by a young Dutch-born, Brazilian-Scot whippersnapper named Cloud, whose first language is American English (don't ask us, ask her). Everything here is spotless and top quality, including marble bathrooms and a sunny front porch.

Eating

The best places for cheap dining are self-serve lunch buffets and juice bars. For fancier fare, Leblon has the best options. Another atmospheric choice is along Joaquim Murtinho in Santa Teresa, and the corner of Mem de Sá and Lavrádio in Lapa is full of pre-party *botecos* (neighborhood bars). Self-caterers should look out for the ubiquitous Rio grocery chain Zona Sul – named after the city's most coveted zone.

IPANEMA, LEBLON & GÁVEA

Delírio Tropical BRAZILIAN $
(Map p278; ☎3624-8162; www.delirio.com.br; Garcia D'Ávila 48; salads R$11-15; ⏲11am-9pm Mon-Sat, noon-7pm Sun; 🌿) Famed for delicious salads, vegetarian leanings and downhome comfort food, Delírio Tropical is one of the only

DON'T MISS...

- » Sunsets on Ipanema
- » Samba clubs in Lapa
- » The view from Pão de Açúcar
- » A stroll through Santa Teresa
- » The funicular ride to Cristo Redentor
- » Football madness at Maracanã

Copacabana & Leme

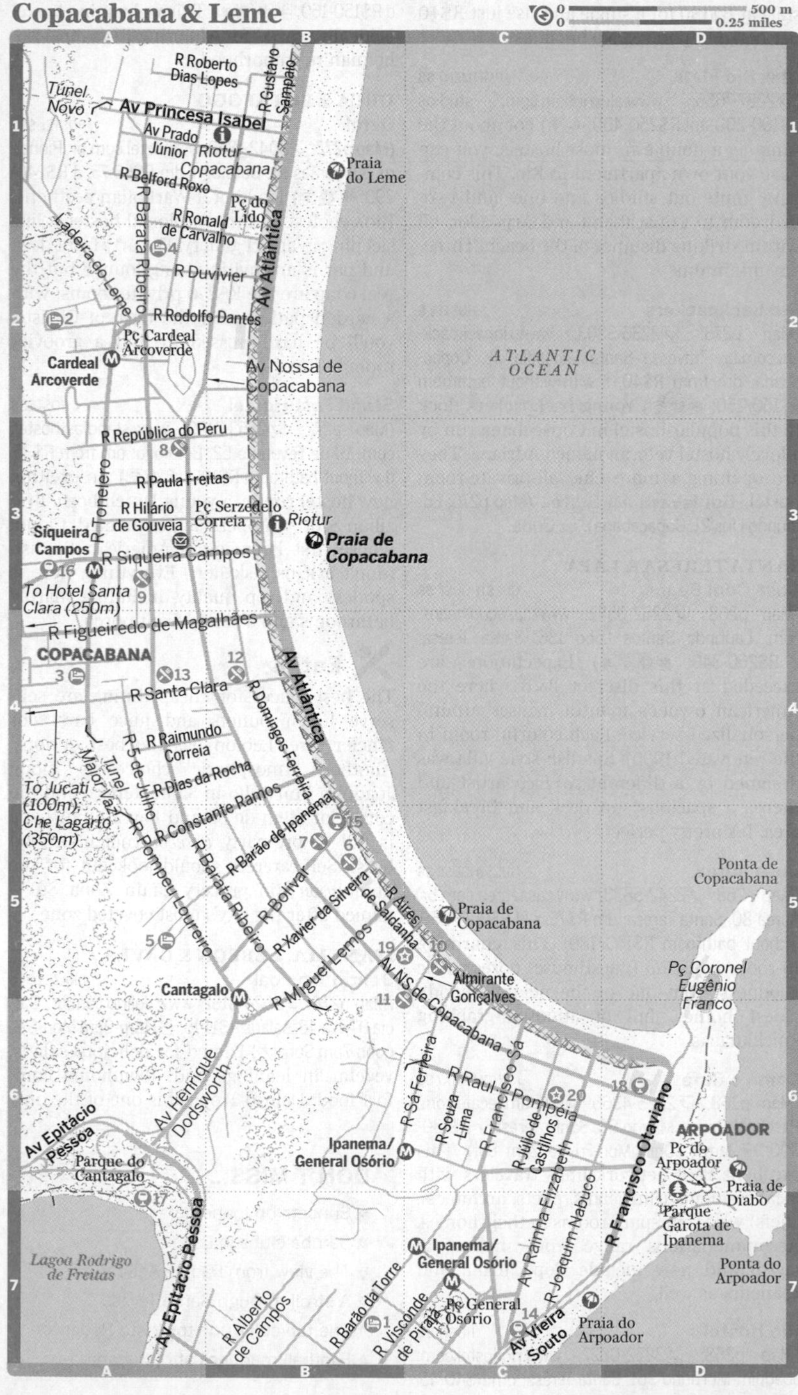

Copacabana & Leme

Top Sights

Praia de Copacabana ... B3

Sleeping

1 Bonita ... B7
2 Cabana Copa ... A2
3 Che Lagarto ... A4
4 Che Lagarto ... A2
5 Rio Backpackers ... A5

Eating

6 Blue Agave ... B5
7 Boteco Belmonte ... B5
8 Botequim Informal ... A3
9 Boulevard All Suites ... A3
10 Brasileirinho ... C5
11 Frontera ... B6
12 Santa Satisfação ... B4
13 The Bakers ... A4

Drinking

14 Bar Astor ... C7
15 Devassa ... B5
16 Fosfobox ... A3
17 Palaphita Kitch ... A7
18 TV Bar ... D6

Entertainment

19 Bip Bip ... C5
20 Le Boy ... C6

restaurants in Brazil we honestly think is too cheap. The fantastic flurry of home-cooked goodness changes daily (grab an English menu as you wait in the considerable sidewalk lines).

Zazá Bistrô Tropical FUSION **$$$**
(Map p278; ☎2247-9101; www.zazabistro.com.br; Joana Angélica 40; mains R$51-65; ⏱7:30pm-midnight Mon-Thu, 1:30pm-1am Fri & Sat, 12:30pm-6pm Sun) For a splurge, sexy Zazá sits inside a handsomely converted house in Ipanema with retro-tropical French-colonial decor. The often Brazilian/Asian-fused mains are a unanimously loved delight by *cariocas* and call on organic ingredients where possible, and the inventive cocktails (R$16 to R$23) are the perfect chaser. Reservations by internet only.

Braseiro da Gávea BRAZILIAN **$$**
(Map p278; ☎2239-7494; www.braseirodagavea.com.br; Praça Santos Dumont 116, Gávea; mains for 2 R$62-90; ⏱noon-1am Sun-Thu, to 3am Fri & Sat) This Baixo Gávea hot spot spent a chunk of the 2000s as *Veja Rio's* best place to flirt; indeed the singles scene commences here over brews and fabulous grills and it's the anchor for the street-party explosion that kicks off here on Monday, Thursday and Sunday nights.

Porcão Ipanema CHURRASCARIA **$$$**
(Map p278; www.porcao.com.br; Barão de Torre 218, Ipanema; all you can eat R$92) The Ipanema location of one of Rio's best *churrascarias* (restaurants featuring barbecued meat) is hipper, more convenient and R$28 less for the same food, while the one in Parque do Flamengo offers stunning views of Pão de Açúcar. Either way, it's meat overload and a quintessential Brazilian experience.

Bibi Sucos FAST FOOD **$**
(Map p278; ☎2259-4298; www.bibisucos.com.br; Ataúlfo de Paiva 591A; açaí R$6-14; ⏱8am-2am) Bibi does one of Brazil's best *açaís*. It also owns **Bibi Crepes** (Map p278; ☎2259-4948; Cupertino Durão 81; crepes R$16-28; ⏱noon-1am), which does good work around the corner.

Jobi BRAZILIAN **$$**
(Map p278; Ataulfo de Paiva 1166, Leblon; executive lunch specials R$18-30) This tiny, old-school *boteco* (neighborhood bar) has been a Rio institution for over 50 years and gets wild in the wee hours. The *picanha* (beef steak) is divine.

Brasileirinho BRAZILIAN **$$$**
(Map p278; ☎2523-5184; Jangadeiros 10; mains R$34-57; ⏱noon-11pm) With the same owners as the more formal Casa de Feijoada around the corner, here you get the same version of Rio's signature black bean and salted pork dish while saving a few reais, in a more colorful and rustic atmosphere. A second location in **Copacabana** (Map p276; Atlântica 3564, Copacabana; feijoada R$56) has opened with views.

Gringo Cafe CAFE **$$**
(Map p278; www.gringocafe.com; Barão da Torre 240, Ipanema; breakfast R$12.95-22.95, mains R$19-22.95; 📶) *Feijoada* not sitting well? This American-run diner dishes up homesick remedies in spades: waffles, pancakes, hash

Ipanema, Leblon & Gávea

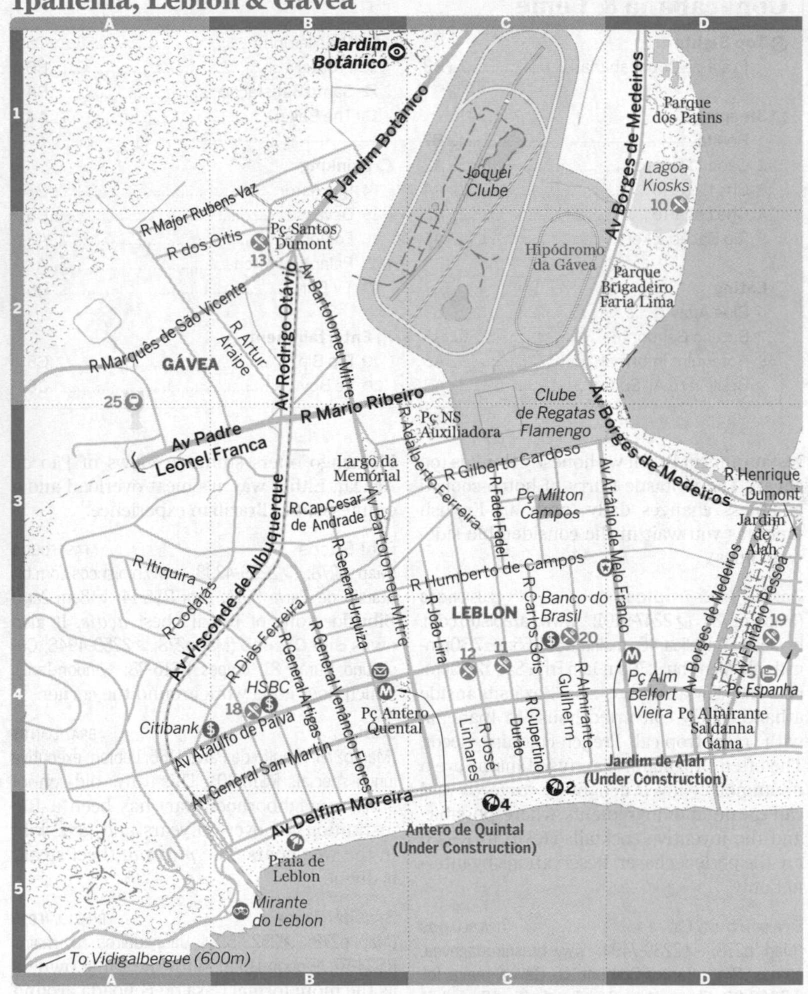

browns, mac and cheese, chili, tuna melts and so on.

Mil Frutas ICE CREAM $

(Map p278; ☎2521-1384; www.milfrutas.com.br; Garcia D'Ávila 134; ice cream from R$10; ⏰11am-1am) Beat the heat at Rio's top spot for ice cream. Of the ridiculous flavor options on offer, guava and cheese is the most popular.

Koni JAPANESE $

(Map p278; www.konistore.com.br; Altaufa de Paiva 320, Leblon; items R$9.50-11.50) This bright-orange Japazilian hot spot is all over Rio. It does fresh tuna or salmon in sushi cones *(temaki)*, the best of which is salmon with crunchy wasabi peas and shoestring leeks.

Kilograma BUFFET $

(Map p278; www.kilograma.com.br; Visconde de Pirajá 644, Ipanema; per kg weekend/weekday R$19.90/21.90) This is a well-regarded pay-by-weight option ideally located between Ipanema and Leblon.

COPACABANA & LEME

Santa Satisfação BRAZILIAN $$

(Map p276; ☎2255-9349; www.santasatisfacao.com; Santa Clara 36C, Copacabana; mains R$20-42; ⏰closed Sun) Oozing farmhouse charm, this

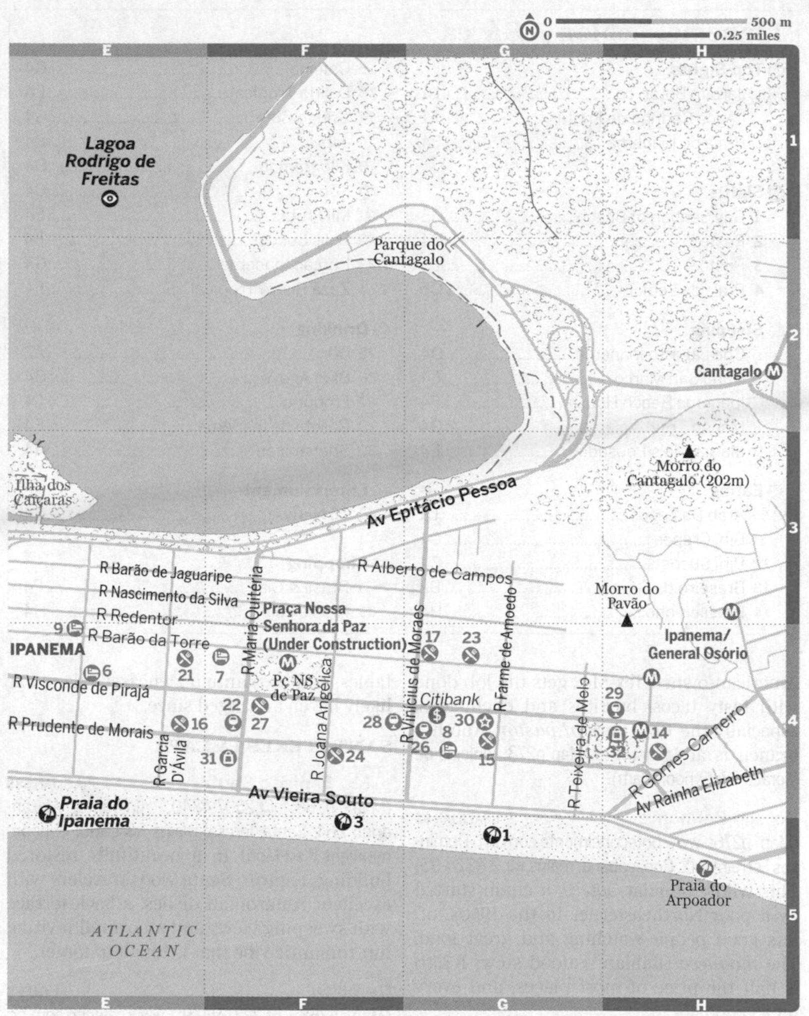

always-packed bistro is worth forking out a bit extra for outstanding daily lunch specials of upscale Brazilian comfort food and sophisticated sandwiches.

Botequim Informal BRAZILIAN **$$**
(Map p276; www.botequiminformal.com.br; NS de Copacabana 434, Copacabana; mains for 2 R$49.90-63.90;) With great food, ice-cold *chope* (draft beer) and (nearly) honest prices, this Rio chain *boteco* is a good-time option which doesn't require a run to the ATM. Mains for two, which usually involve some serious meat served on the table on a *chapa* (sizzling hot plate), are the best bet.

Bakers CAFE **$$**
(Map p276; 3209-1212; www.thebakers.com.br; Santa Clara 86, Copacabana; desserts R$7-10, lunch specials R$27-30; 9am-8pm) A sweet den of decadence long on colorful kitsch – even longer on sweets, coffee and good sandwiches.

Blue Agave MEXICAN **$**
(Map p276; Aires de Saldanha 21D, Copacabana; from 6pm, closed Mon;) Mexican can be hard going in Brazil, but this branch of

Ipanema, Leblon & Gávea

Top Sights

	Jardim Botânico	B1
	Lagoa Rodrigo de Freitas	E1
	Praia do Ipanema	E4

Sights

1	Gay Section of Beach	G5
2	Posto 11	C4
3	Posto 9	F5
4	Praia de Leblon	C5

Sleeping

5	Che Lagarto Ipanema	D4
6	Hotel San Marco	E4
7	Ipanema Beach House	F4
8	Mango Tree	G4
9	Margarida's Pousada	E4

Eating

10	Arab Da Lagoa	D1
11	Bibi Crepes	C4
12	Bibi Sucos	C4
13	Braseiro da Gávea	B2
14	Brasileirinho	H4
15	Cafeína	G4
16	Delírio Tropical	E4
17	Gringo Cafe	G4
18	Jobi	B4
19	Kilograma	D4
20	Koni	C4
21	Mil Frutas	E4
22	Polis Sucos	F4
23	Porcão Ipanema	G4
24	Zazá Bistrô Tropical	F4

Drinking

25	00	A2
26	Blue Agave	G4
27	Empório	F4
28	Garota de Ipanema	F4
29	Shenanigan's	H4

Entertainment

30	Tô Nem Aí	G4

Shopping

31	Brasil & Cia	F4
32	Hippie Fair	H4

American-owned Tex-Mex gets the job done with tasty tacos, burritos and enchiladas, especially the BBQ pork *al pastor*. Another branch is at **Ipanema** (Map p278; Vinícius de Moraes 68; ⏲noon-2am).

Boteco Belmonte BRAZILIAN **$$**
(Map p276; www.botecobelmonte.com.br; Domingos Ferreira 242, Copacabana; mains for 2 R$24-95) This wildly popular *boteco,* a chain started by a poor Northeasterner in the 1950s, offers good people-watching and great food. The *moqueca* (Bahian seafood stew; R$59) is half the price of most places, and every bit as good.

Frontera BUFFET **$**
(Map p276; www.frontera.com.br; NS de Copacabana 1144; per kg R$21.90-26.90; ⏲11am-11pm; Wi-Fi) Frontera offers more than 60 dishes at its delectable lunch buffet.

CENTRO

Confeitaria Colombo CAFE **$**
(Map p268; ☎2505-1500; www.confeitariacolombo.com.br; Gonçalves Dias 34, Centro; pastries around R$7; ⏲9am-8pm Mon-Fri, to 5pm Sat) Step back in time at this gorgeous belle epoque cafe that recalls Rio's colonial heyday. Opened in 1897, the cafe's massive mirrors, marble tables and gargantuan, encased glass bar likely haven't changed since.

SANTA TERESA & LAPA

TOP CHOICE **Espírito Santa** BRAZILIAN **$$$**
(Map p268; ☎2507-4840; Almirante Alexandrino 264, Santa Teresa; mains R$42-60; ⏲noon-midnight Wed-Mon) In a beautifully restored building, Espirito Santa woos travelers with excellent Amazonian dishes, a back terrace with sweeping views and an overall inviting hip/romantic vibe that is tough to forget.

Cafecito CAFÉ **$**
(Map p268; ☎2221-9439; www.cafecito.com.br; Paschoal Carlos Magno 121, Santa Teresa; sandwiches R$11-21; ⏲10am-10pm) This wildly charismatic open-air cafe serves great coffee, artisanal beers and very good gourmet sandwiches on ciabatta.

Bar do Mineiro BRAZILIAN **$$**
(Map p268; ☎2221-9227; Paschoal Carlos Magno 99, Santa Teresa; mains R$32-47; ⏲noon-2am Tue-Sat, to midnight Sun) A Santa Teresa favorite, with a menu of traditional Minas dishes like *carne seca* (dried meat with spices), *feijão tropeiro* with *pernil* (a mix of beans, eggs, kale and *yuca* flour with pork) and Saturday *feijoada*.

URCA & BOTAFOGO

Meza Bar TAPAS $$
(Map p272; www.mezabar.com.br; Capitão Salomão 69, Botafogo; tapas R$10-25; ⏲6pm-1am) Botafogo's see-and-be-seen hot spot serves up delectable, Brazilian-slanted tapas to a sophisticated and trendy crowd. Creative cocktails and delightful staff round out the fun.

CATETE & FLAMENGO

Sírio Libaneza MIDDLE EASTERN $
(Map p272; www.rotisseriasl.com.br; Largo do Machado 29, Loja 16-19, Flamengo; snacks R$7-22; ⏲8am-11pm Mon-Sat; 📶) It's shocking how many *cariocas* don't know about the awesome and cheap Syrian-Lebanese food offered here inside the Galleria Condor on Largo do Machado – yet it's still always a madhouse. Make sure you try the killer *kaftas* (kebabs) and hummus.

JARDIM BOTÂNICO & LAGOA

TOP CHOICE **Bráz Pizzaria** PIZZERIA $$
(www.brazpizzaria.com.br; Maria Angelica 129, Jardim Botânico; pizzas R$42-63.50) If you don't get a chance to sample *pizza paulistana* in São Paulo then don't miss this unforgettable pizzeria, one of only three outlets outside Sampa.

Arab Da Lagoa MIDDLE EASTERN $$
(Map p278; ☎2540-0747; www.restaurantearab.com.br; Borges de Medeiros, Parque dos Patins; mains R$22-40; ⏲9am-1:30am) One of numerous restaurants on the lake, this open-air place serves traditional Middle Eastern specialties such as hummus and kebabs in an outrageously scenic setting. Pick the right table and you can see Cristo up there.

Drinking

Few cities can rival the dynamism of Rio's nightlife. Samba clubs, jazz bars, open-air cafes, lounges and nightclubs are just one part of the scene, while the *boteco* is practically a *carioca* institution. If you can read a bit of Portuguese, there are many good sources of information: the *Veja Rio* insert in *Veja* magazine, Thursday and Friday editions of *O Globo* and *Jornal do Brasil* and the Rio Festa website (www.riofesta.com.br).

IPANEMA, LEBLON & GÁVEA

Cafes & Juice Bars

Rio's numerous juice bars are a must. For coffee culture and people-watching, head to the sidewalk cafes scattered about Ipanema and Leblon.

Polis Sucos JUICE BAR $
(Map p278; ☎2247-2518; Maria Quitéria 70; juices around R$6; ⏲7am-midnight) A top juice bar.

Cafeína CAFE $$
(Map p278; ☎2521-2194; www.cafeina.com.br; Farme de Amoedo 43; quiches R$7-9, sandwiches R$20-30; ⏲8am-11:30pm; 📶) This attractive cafe makes a fine spot for espresso and scrumptious desserts while the city strolls by.

WORTH A TRIP

PETRÓPOLIS

Tucked away in the Atlantic rainforest 65km above Rio de Janeiro, the airy mountain town of Petrópolis is an important epicenter in Brazilian history. Once the summer home of the Portuguese imperial family, Petrópolis has some striking vestiges of the past, including a former palace and streets lined with gorgeous colonial mansions. The city's top attraction is the **Museu Imperial** (www.museuimperial.gov.br; Rua da Imperatriz 220; adult/student R$8/4; ⏲11am-5:30pm Tue-Sun), which exhibits royal finery in the former palace of Dom Pedro II (including the astonishing 639-diamond, 77-pearl imperial crown). Nearby is the 19th-century **Catedral São Pedro de Alcântara** (Sao Pedro de Alcântara 60; adult/student R$8/4), housing the tombs of Brazil's last emperor, Dom Pedro II, his wife and daughter; and the city's newest attraction, the **Cervejaria Bohemia** (www.bohemia.com.br/ceverjaria; Rua Alfredo Pachá 166; adult/student R$39/19.50; ⏲11am-6pm Wed-Fri, 10am-8pm Sat & Sun), where tours include one of its specialty beers (Escura, Weiss or Confraria, which are only brewed here) and there's a small bar-restaurant on-site (the only spot in Brazil you can get Bohemia on draft).

Buses run between Rio and Petrópolis every half hour from 4:45am to midnight (R$18.05, one hour). There are six buses daily to Teresópolis (R$14.75, 1½ hours). The bus station is located in Bingen, 10km from town. From there, take bus 100 or 10 (R$2.50) and get off at Rua do Imperador 675 for the short walk to the museum.

Additional locations can be found in Leblon and Botafogo.

Bars

Empório BAR

(Map p278; ☎3813-2526; Maria Quitéria 37; ⏰8:30pm-late) An eclectic, alt-rock crowd of *cariocas* and eager gringos stirs things up at this battered Ipanema favorite.

Bar Astor BAR

(Map p276; www.barastor.com.br; Veira Souto 110; ⏰6pm-1am Mon-Fri, noon-3am Sat, noon-10pm Sun) One of São Paulo's best bars has arrived in Rio in spectacular fashion. This gorgeous art deco *boteco* on prime Ipanema real estate does meticulously prepared *caipirinhas* (R$16.50-21) – some 20 exotic flavors in all.

Palaphita Kitch LOUNGE

(Map p276; ☎2227-0837; www.palaphitakitch.com.br; Av Epitâcio Pessoa s/n, Lagoa; ⏰6pm-1am) Outstandingly atmospheric spot for a sundowner, this open-air, thatched-roof wonderland with rustic bamboo furniture and flickering tiki torches sits in a peaceful setting on the edge of the lake.

Garota de Ipanema BAR

(Map p278; ☎2523-3787; Vinícius de Moraes 49) Plenty of tourists pack this open-air bar, but it would be a sin not to mention the place where Jobim and Vinícius penned the famed song 'The Girl from Ipanema.'

Shenanigan's BAR

(Map p278; Visconde de Pirajá 112A; admission R$5 to R$25; ⏰6pm-2am) This Irish pub attracts a mix of sunburnt gringos and youngish *cariocas* for European soccer and US sports – if you can concentrate over the live rock music.

COPACABANA & LEME

Devassa BAR

(Map p276; www.cervejariadevassa.com.br; Bolivar 8A, Copacabana; 📶) Devassa (which kind of means 'promiscuous,' FYI) was one of Brazil's first microbrews *not* brewed in the south. This location has beach views.

URCA & BOTAFOGO

Bar Urca BAR

(Map p272; ☎2295-8744; Cândido Gaffrée 205, Urca; ⏰9am-11pm Mon-Sat, to 8pm Sun) After Sugar Loaf, after the beach, after whatever… as the sun sets, *cariocas* gather along the Urca seawall to take in views of the bay over thirst-quenching *chope*. Waiters dash back and forth between the bar and the crowds.

Cobal do Humaitá BAR

(Map p272; Voluntarios da Pátria 446, Humaitá; ⏰7am-2am Mon-Sat) On the western edge of Botafogo (technically in Humaitá), the Cobal is a a gourmet fresh-food market by day and transforms into a festive nightspot when the sun goes down.

☆ Entertainment

Live Music

Lapa's samba clubs are still a fantastic night out, but the underground scene here has moved on under the weight of a tourist onslaught – try Botafogo to escape fellow gringos. Sunday evenings in **Marina da**

BAR-HOPPING 101

When it comes to bars, nearly every neighborhood in Rio has its drinking clusters. While Ipanema has scattered options, Leblon has many trendy choices along the western end of General San Martin. Near Lagoa, a youthful population fills the bars around JJ Seabra, and there's almost always a fun crowd packing the bars facing Praça Santos Dumont. The lakeside kiosks (in Parque Brigadeiro Faria Lima) are a favorite date place, with live music in the open air. Copacabana's Av Atlântica packs many sidewalk bars and restaurants and good-time kiosks, especially on Sunday afternoon when the southeastern lanes are pedestrianized between 6am and 6pm. Botafogo has authentic *carioca* (Rio locals) bars, particularly around Visconde de Caravelas and in the Cobal market, while Baixo Botafogo, at the end of Voluntários da Pátria, is lined with sidewalk bars that go off on Thursdays and Saturdays. In Santa Teresa you'll find colorful bars around Largo do Guimarães and Largo das Neves. It all comes together in Rio's best nightlife neighborhood, Lapa, which turns into an all-night street and samba shindig on weekends, when its main thoroughfare, Mem de Sá, is closed to traffic after 10pm and its lively *botecos* (traditional neigborhood bars), samba clubs and street *barracas* (bar stalls) explode with spirited *cariocas* – a definite don't miss.

GAY & LESBIAN RIO

On the beaches, you'll find gay-friendly drink stands across from the Copacabana Palace Hotel in Copacabana and opposite Farme de Amoedo (Rio's gayest street) in Ipanema. On Ipanema Beach, the gay-friendly spot is between Posto 8 and 9. For sleeps, Casa Cool Beans (p275) is gay-owned and operated.

Le Boy (Map p276; ☎2513-4993; www.leboy.com.br; Raul Pompéia 102, Copacabana; cover R$10-30; ⏲closed Mon) One of Rio's best (and largest) gay clubs. DJs spin house and house tribal. Drag shows are tossed into the mix. The ladies gather next door at La Girl.

Tô Nem Aí (Map p278; ☎2247-8403; cnr Farme de Amoedo & Visconde de Piraja, Ipanema; ⏲noon-3am) Slang for 'I couldn't care less,' this is the relaxed hangout of choice for devotees of Rio's laid-back Gay, Lesbian and Sympathetics (GLS) scene.

TV Bar (Map p276; www.bartvbar.com.br; Av NS de Copacabana, 1417, Shopping Cassino Atlântico , Copacabana; cover R$10-40) The hip and trendy new boy in town, with DJ spinning amid an audiovisual assault in the space of a former TV station.

Week (Map p268; ☎2253-1020; www.theweek.com.br; Rua Sacadura Cabral 154, Centro) The 2007 importation of this massive São Paulo institution inside a historical *carioca* (Rio local) mansion near the port was a smash hit from the get-go. Saturdays are the biggest, with international DJs and the lot.

Glória (Map p268; www.marinadagloria.com.br; Av Infante Dom Henrique s/n, Glória), internet radio station Rádio Rua puts on a free hip-hop/soul concert. Cover charges around town typically range from R$10 to R$30 (females pay less).

Bip Bip LIVE MUSIC
(Map p276; ☎2267-9696; Almirante Gonçalves 50, Copacabana; admission free; ⏲6pm-midnight Sun-Fri) One of the hidden gems among those in the know, Bip Bip is a simple storefront with great informal music. It's famous for its quality of musicians, and crowds usually spill into the sidewalk. Beer is self-serve, in case you're wondering.

Carioca da Gema SAMBA
(Map p268; www.barcariocadagema.com.br; Av Mem de Sá 79, Lapa; cover R$21-25; ⏲7pm-1:30am Mon-Thu, 9pm-3:30am Fri-Sun) One of Lapa's best samba clubs, Carioca da Gema is a small, warmly lit setting for catching some of the city's best samba bands.

TribOz JAZZ
(Map p268; ☎2210-0366; www.triboz-rio.com; Conde de Lages 19, Lapa; cover R$20-30; ⏲6-8pm & 9pm-1am Thu-Sat) This avant-garde jazz house run by an Australian ethnomusicologist is unique in Rio for its very serious approach to performances. It sits in a signless mansion in old Lapa that transforms into a beautiful showcase space for Brazil's most cutting-edge artists. Reservations are essential two days in advance by phone only.

Rio Scenarium SAMBA
(Map p268; www.rioscenarium.com.br; Rua do Lavradio 20, Lapa; cover R$20-40; ⏲Tue-Sat 7pm-4am) Río Scenarium pioneered Lapa's samba renaissance. There are three floors, each lavishly decorated with more than 10,000 antiques and movie-set props. It's the most touristy, but that doesn't mean the mile-long line to get in doesn't feature its fair share of *cariocas*.

Nightclubs

Cover charges range from R$40 to R$100, and women generally pay less than men. Often a portion of the charge covers *consumação* (drinks).

Fosfobox CLUB
(Map p276; ☎2548-7498; www.fosfobox.com.br; Siqueira Campos 143, Copacabana; admission R$15-30; ⏲11pm-4am Thu-Sat) This edgy, subterranean den is hidden under a shopping center near the metro station. Good DJs spin everything from funk to glam rock, and the crowd here is one of Rio's more eclectic.

00 LOUNGE, CLUB
(Map p278; http://00riodejaneiro.com.br/riodejaneiro.html; Av Padre Leonel Franca 240, Gávea; ⏲8pm-late) Housed in Gávea's planetarium, 00 is a restaurant by day and swanky, design-forward lounge by night.

Casa Rosa LIVE MUSIC, CLUB
(Map p272; ☎2557-2562; www.casarosa.com.br; Alice 550, Laranjeiras; cover R$25-40; ⏲11pm-5am

DON'T LEAVE HOME WITHOUT IT

If you're heading out to dance the night away in Lapa's atmospheric samba clubs, don't forget plenty of cash – banks are as scarce as sober folks in this lively neighborhood – then guard it (along with your phone) very carefully; pickpockets are magicians here.

Fri & Sat, 5pm-1am Sun) This wildly pink former brothel straddles the fence between dance club and samba club when its cavernous rooms get packed with sweat-soaked *cariocas*. There are DJs and live samba, *sambarock* and *forró*. The Sunday samba *feijoada* for R$35 is a steal.

Casa da Matriz CLUB
(Map p272; ☎2266-1014; www.casadamatriz.com.br; Henrique de Novaes 107, Botafogo; admission R$15-30; ⊙from 11pm, closed Tue & Sun) This avant-garde space in an old two-story Botafogo mansion attracts a younger, alternative crowd, who pack its various little rooms.

Dance

Starting in September, the big Carnaval schools open their rehearsals to the public. These are lively but informal affairs where you can dance, drink and join the party. The schools are in dodgy neighborhoods, so don't go alone, but by all means go. Most hostels organize outings if you want to hook up with a group.

Mangueira SAMBA
(☎2567-4637; www.mangueira.com.br; Visconde de Niterói 1072, Mangueira; ⊙10pm Sat)

Salgueiro SAMBA
(☎2238-0389; www.salgueiro.com.br; Silva Teles 104, Andaraí; ⊙10pm Sat)

Sports

Maracanã Football Stadium STADIUM
(☎8871-3950; www.suderj.rj.gov.br/maracana.asp; Av Maracanã, São Cristóvão; admission R$15-100; ⊙9am-7pm; underground rail Maracanã) Undergoing a US$480-million renovation to bring it up to standard for the 2014 FIFA World Cup, Maracanã is where the championship and the 2016 Olympic Games will be held. When it re-opens in 2013, capacity will be 85,000. Rio's big clubs are **Flamengo** (www.flamengo.com.br), **Fluminense FC** (www.fluminense.com.br), **Vasco da Gama** (www.vasco.com.br) and **Botafogo** (www.botafogo.com.br).

To get to the stadium take the metro to Maracanã station then walk along Osvaldo Aranha. The safest seats are on the lower-level *cadeira,* where the overhead covering protects you from descending objects like dead chickens and urine-filled bottles (no joke!). The ticket price is R$30 to R$80 for most games. Visits on nongame days or to check out the renovations are R$20.

Shopping

Hippie Fair MARKET
(Map p278; Praça General Osório; ⊙9am-6pm Sun) An Ipanema mainstay for good souvenirs and Bahian food.

Feira do Nordestino MARKET
(Nova Feira de São Cristóvão; www.feiradesaocristovao.org.br; Pavilhão de São Cristóvão near the Quinta da Boa Vista; admission Fri-Sun after 6pm R$3; ⊙10am-6pm Tue-Thu, to 9pm Fri-Sun) The Northeastern character of this food, drink and live-music fair is shrinking, but it's still well worth a weekend visit.

Brasil & Cia HANDICRAFTS
(Map p278; ☎2267-4603; www.brasilecia.com.br; Maria Quitéria 27) Quality Brazilian handicrafts.

Information

Dangers & Annoyances

In preparation for Rio's upcoming showcase events, the city is making great strides in cleaning up its none-too-stellar criminal record. Much of the city's headline-grabbing ferocity traditionally rose from an ongoing urban war between police and drug traffickers, who historically controlled many *favelas* around the city, but the continuing implementation of the *Unidade de Polícia Pacificadoras* (UPP's; Police Pacification Units) has dramatically reduced the areas in which traffickers freely operate. There is a visibly heavier police presence around high-traffic tourism areas in the *Zona Sul* which, together with installations of more CCTV cameras clustered around hotels in Copacabana, has contributed to less tourist crime. Street miscreants are also now being picked up daily by social services, reducing the amount of dodgy folks in the streets. There is a palpable improved sense of security.

Buses are well-known targets for thieves. Avoid taking them after dark, and keep an eye out while aboard. Take taxis at night to avoid walking along empty streets and beaches. That holds especially true for Centro, which you should avoid on weekends when it's deserted and dangerous.

The beaches are also targets for thieves. Don't take anything valuable to the beach, and always stay alert – especially during holidays (such as Carnaval), when the sands get fearfully crowded.

Maracanã stadium is worth a visit, but take only spending money for the day and avoid the crowded sections.

Despite the UPPs, it's still probably a bad idea to wander into the *favelas* unless going with a knowledgeable guide.

If you have the misfortune of being robbed, hand over the goods. Thieves are only too willing to use their weapons if given provocation. It's sensible to carry a fat wad of singles to hand over in case of a robbery.

Emergency

Tourist Police (☎2332-4924; cnr Afrânio de Melo Franco & Humberto de Campos, Leblon; ⊙24hr) Provides robbery reports for insurance companies.

Medical Services

Hospital Copa D'or (www.copador.com.br; Figueiredo de Magalhães 875; ⊙24hr) Rio's best hospital.

Money

ATMs for most card networks are widely available but often fussy. The best option is HSBC as it works with all cards and doesn't charge an exorbitant R$12 fee (except for some standalone HSBC ATMs on the Banco24Horas network in metro and bus stations), but new limits imposed as of early 2013 have left many travelers unable to pull more than R$300 per day anywhere other than Bradesco. Like HSBC, Bradesco and Banco do Brasil don't charge fees, but there will be a relatively frustrating trial-and-error period finding the best fit for your foreign ATM card. Don't even waste your time (or sanity) with Itaú, Unibanco or Caixa – they are Brazilian-only. The international airport has Banco do Brasil machines on the 3rd floor and currency-exchange booths on the arrivals floor (6am to 11pm). ATMs

GETTING INTO TOWN

Premium Auto Ônibus (www.premiumautoonibus.com.br; R$12) operates safe air-con buses from the international airport to Novo Rio bus station, Rio Branco (Centro), Santos Dumont Airport, southward through Glória, Flamengo and Botafogo and along the beaches of Copacabana, Ipanema and Leblon to Barra da Tijuca (and vice versa) every 20 minutes from 5:40am to 10:30pm and will stop wherever you ask. The same company runs buses between the international and domestic airports (R$10) as well as from the domestic airport to stops in Ipanema, Copacabana and Leblon (R$8.50 to R$12).

Heading to the airports, you can catch the Real bus from in front of the major hotels along the main beaches, but you have to look alive and flag them down.

From Galeão, radio taxis charge a set fare of RS$80 (cash)/R$105 (credit card) to Ipanema. Less-secure yellow-and-blue *comum* (common) taxis should cost around R$55. From the domestic airport, a radio taxi runs R$51 to Copacabana and R$63 to Ipanema, and *comums* are around R$25 and R$30.

If you arrive in Rio by bus, it's a good idea to take a taxi to your hotel or area you want to stay in. Rodoviária Novo Rio, the bus station, is in a seedy area. A small booth across from Riotur on the 1st floor organizes the yellow-and-blue *comums*. Sample fares (with one bag) are R$38 to R$45 to the international airport, R$30 to R$36 to Copacabana, R$30 to R$35 to Ipanema and R$28 to R$33 to Santa Teresa. Additional bags will increase the price.

Local buses to most destinations leave from an adjacent terminal – exit the bus station across from Riotur booth, look right, and you will see it. You can take buses from here (126, 127 and 136 to Copacabana; 136, 170 and 172 to Botafogo) but traveling on them with all your belongings is a little risky. It's much safer and more pleasant to catch the Premium Auto Ônibus (R$10 to R$12) just beyond the green fence on the street across from the Riotur booth; or, catch bus 133 to either Metrô Praça Onze or, if you miss it, Metrô Estácio shortly thereafter. Ask the bus driver for a metro/bus combination ticket (Integração Expressa; R$4.15) and transfer seamlessly to the subway for *Zona Sul*. To go back to the bus station, head to metro Estácio and follow the Integração signs to Rodoviária (Bus 209 – ignore the numbers for 406A). The bus stop is just out of the station to the left (not the first one you see just to the right). You must buy this combination at the metro station ticket window before embarking – otherwise you'll pay for both rides seperately (still only comes to R$5.95).

cluster on the 1st floor near the main entrance of Rio's Novo Rio bus station.

Banco do Brasil Centro (Senador Dantas 105); Copacabana (Av NS de Copacabana 1292); Galeão international airport (1st fl, Terminal 1)

Citibank Centro (Rua da Assembléia 100); Ipanema (Visconde de Pirajá 459A); Leblon (Visconde de Pirajá 1260A)

HSBC Centro (Av Rio Branco 108); Copacabana (Av NS de Copacabana 583); Ipanema (Vinícius de Moraes 71); Leblon (Cupertino Durão 219)

Post

Correios (post offices) are prevalent around Rio.

Central Post Office (Primeiro de Março 64, Centro)

Post Office Botafogo (Praia de Botafogo 324); Copacabana (Av NS de Copacabana 540A); Ipanema (Av Ataulfo de Paiva 822, Leblon)

Tourist Information

Central 1746 (☎2271-7048, 1746; www.1746.rio.gov.br; ⊙24hr) Rio's new City Hall Directory Assistance. Press 8 for tourist info; then 1 for English.

CIAT (☎2542-8080; ⊙9am-6pm Mon-Fri) English-speaking assistance.

Riotur (www.rioofficialguide.com) Bus station (☎2263-4857; Rodoviária Novo Rio; ⊙7am-11pm); Centro (☎2541-7522; Praça Pio X 119; ⊙9am-6pm Mon-Fri, Sun noon-9pm); Copacabana (☎2541-7522; Av Princesa Isabel 183; ⊙9am-6pm Mon-Fri); Copacabana kiosk (☎2447-4421; Av Atlântica at Hilário de Gouveia); international airport (☎3398-4077; Terminal 1 & 2; ⊙6am-11pm) Very useful city tourism bureau.

Getting There & Away

Air

Most flights depart from Aeroporto Galeão (GIG; also called Aeroporto Antônio Carlos Jobim), 15km north of the center on Ilha do Governador. Shuttle flights (*Ponte Aérea*) to/from São Paulo, and some flights for other nearby cities, use Aeroporto Santos Dumont (SDU) in the city center, 1km east of Cinelândia metro station.

Bus

Buses leave from the hugely improved **Rodoviária Novo Rio** (☎3213-1800; Av Francisco Bicalho 1), 2km northwest of Centro, which is fresh off a US$10-million face-lift that ramped up security and turned the entire 2nd floor into a pleasant area with a respectable food court. Several buses depart daily to most major destinations, but it's a good idea to buy tickets in advance.

Following are sample travel times and *executivo* fares (where applicable) from Rio:

DESTINATION	COST (R$)	DURATION (HR)
Arraial do Cabo	42	3
Angra dos Reis	41	3½
Belém	512	52
Belo Horizonte	105	6
Buenos Aires (Argentina)	240	42
Búzios	44	3
Campo Grande	270	22
Florianópolis	229	18
Foz do Iguaçu	252	22
Ouro Preto	122	7
Mangaratiba	40	2
Paraty	62	4½
Petrópolis	20	1½
Porto Alegre	269	26
Porto Velho	418	62
Recife	367	38
Salvador	269	27
Santiago (Chile)	394	60
São Paulo	91	6-7
Teresópolis	25.30	1½

Getting Around

Bike

Bike Rio (☎4063-3111; www.mobilicidade.com.br/bikerio.asp) allows you to peddle yourself around the city on bright-orange bikes found at some 60 stations throughout Rio. After registering on the site, you can buy a monthly pass (R$10) or a day pass (R$5). Instructions are in English at the stations and the bikes are released via mobile phone or app. Foreigners must register with a passport number instead of a Brazilian Cadastro de Pessoas Físicas (CPF; identity number).

Bus

Rio's new Bus Rapid System (BRS) bus scheme got an Olympic size efficiency makeover in 2011, with a new streamlined system that now includes dedicated public-transport corridors in Copacabana, Ipanema, Leblon and Centro. By the 2016 Olympics, four dedicated Bus Rapid Transit (BRT) lines linking surburban Barra de Tijuca, home to the Olympic village, with main neighborhoods in the city, will also be implemented. Buses are frequent and cheap, and because Rio is long and narrow it's easy to get the right bus and usually no big deal if you're on the wrong one. Nine out of 10 buses going south from the center will go to Copacabana, and vice versa. Fares on most buses are R$3.05.

WORTH A TRIP

PARQUE NACIONAL DA SERRA DOS ÓRGÃOS

The lush-capped peaks of **Parque Nacional da Serra dos Órgãos** (☎2642-1070; Hwy BR-116; admission day/camping R$3/6; ⊙8am-5pm), Rio state's best park, beckons travelers from the sands to the *serra* some 96km north of Rio near the town of **Teresópolis**. Famed for the strangely shaped peaks of Pedra de Sino (2263m), Pedra do Açu (2230m), Agulha do Diabo (2020m), Nariz do Frade (1919m), Dedo de Deus (1651m), Pedra da Ermitage (1485m) and Dedo de Nossa Senhora (1320m), the 118-sq-km park is Brazil's premier trekking, mountain- and rock-climbing region (with a little bird-watching thrown in for good measure).

The best walking trail is the Trilha Pedra do Sino, which takes about eight hours in a round trip. Most trails are unmarked but it's easy and inexpensive to hire a guide at the national park visitors center.

Buses run between Rio and Teresópolis every half hour from 6am to midnight (R$25.30, 1½ hours). From Teresópolis, there are seven daily buses to Petrópolis (R$14.22, 1½ hours). To get to the national park's main entrance from central Teresópolis, take the hourly 'Soberbo' bus (R$2.50), or the more frequent 'Alto' bus to the Praçinha do Alto, then walk a short way south to the entrance.

Metro

Lines 1 and 2 of Rio's subway system, **Metrô Rio** (www.metrorio.com.br; ⊙5am-midnight Mon-Sat, 7am-11pm Sun), connect Copacabana and Ipanema with Botafogo, Flamengo, Catete, Glória and Centro; while the planned Linha 4 expansion, due for completion by 2016, will finally connect the upper-class surburban district of Barra da Tijuca in *Zona Oeste* to Ipanema and Leblon. A single ride costs R$3.20.

Taxi

Rio's taxis are useful late at night and when you're carrying valuables. The flat rate is R$4.50, plus around R$1.60 per kilometer; slightly more at night and on Sunday.

THE SOUTHEAST

Those who manage to tear themselves away from Rio's charming clutches will find some of Brazil's most endearing attractions right in its backyard. Coastal highlights include the Costa do Sol (Sun Coast) north of Rio, home to the upscale beach resort of Búzios – a weekend city escape for hot-to-trot *cariocas* – and the spectacular Costa Verde (Green Coast) stretching south from Rio to São Paulo, boasting rainforest-smothered islands (Ilha Grande), perfectly preserved colonial villages (Paraty) and postcard-perfect beaches (the whole stretch). Head inland to the convivial state of Minas Gerais, famous throughout Brazil for its hearty cuisine and friendly population. Here time has frozen colonial-era gold-mining towns like Ouro Preto or sleepy villages like Tiradentes, where magical historical delights beckon around every corner. It all culminates in South America's intimidating cultural capital, São Paulo, where you'll find some of the best museums, nightclubs and restaurants in South America.

ℹ Getting There & Around

Rio de Janeiro is the major gateway to the coastal regions, though if coming from the south or west you can reach the Costa Verde via São Paulo. Belo Horizonte, Brazil's third-largest city, is the gateway to the old gold-mining towns in Minas Gerais.

Numerous flights connect the three major cities of the Southeast (Belo Horizonte, Rio and São Paulo) with plenty of bus links covering Southeastern destinations. Ilha Grande is reached by ferry from Angra dos Reis, Mangaratiba or Conceição de Jacare.

Búzios

☎0XX22 / POP 27,000

Before Búzios was to Rio de Janeiro what the Hamptons are to New York City – a summer playground for the blessed and beautiful – it was a simple fishing village and sun-soaked hideaway for French starlet Brigitte Bardot, who frollicked among the town's 17 fabled beaches way back in the '60s, when nobody cared but the fishermen. Located 167km east of Rio, today wonderful and wild Búzios is playfully referred to as Búzios Aires due to the increasing numbers of Argentines that

The Southeast

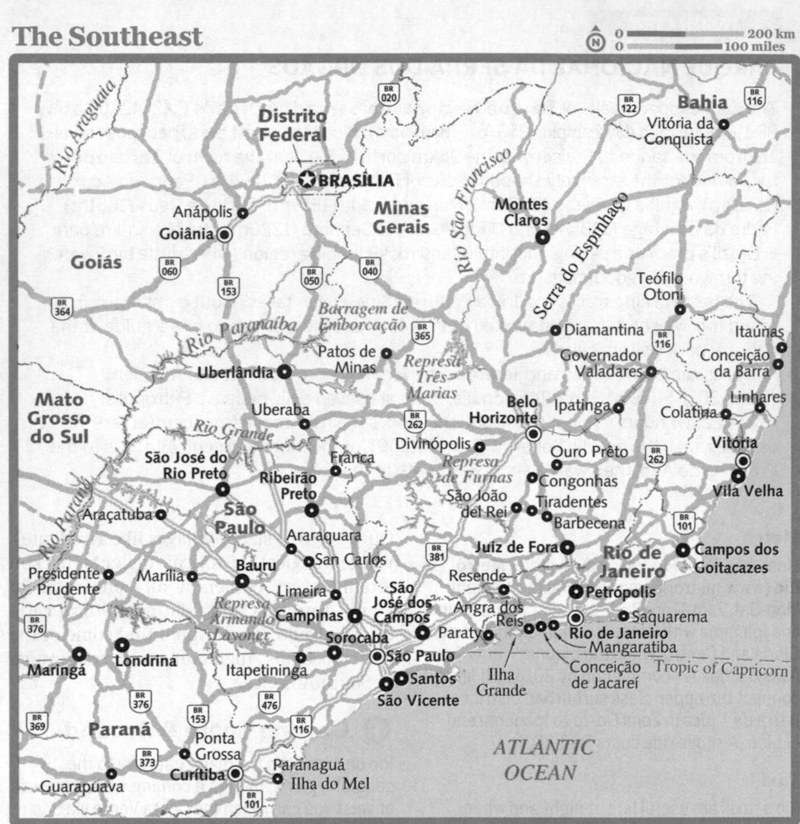

live and vacation here (payback for Brasiloche, we reckon). During the day, caramel-hued hard bodies beach-hop via water taxis from one sugary stretch of sand to another, eating just-grilled fresh fish on the beach, chased by perfect *caipirinhas*. At night, the rich, famous and foreign descend on pedestrianized Rua das Pedras/Orla Bardot, Búzios' rowdy strip of upscale restaurants, swanky clubs and rambunctious bars, where some of Brazil's trendiest infrastructure outside São Paulo weathers the swells of the bold and beautiful that roll in and out like every summer on a high tide of temptation.

Sights & Activities

You can dive, windsurf, sail or snorkel in Búzios, but the main activity is beach-hopping. Water taxis run R$5 to R$10 depending on distance. In general, the southern beaches are trickier to get to, but are prettier and have better surf. Geribá and Ferradurinha (Little Horseshoe), south of Manguinhos, are beautiful beaches with good waves, but the Búzios Beach Club has built condos here. Next on the coast is Ferradura, large enough for windsurfing. Praia Olho de Boi (Bull's Eye Beach), at the eastern tip of the peninsula, is a pocket-sized beach reached by a little trail from the long, clean Praia Brava. It attracts nudists. Near the northern tip of the promontory, João Fernandinho, João Fernandes (full of people and beach restaurants) and the topless Azedinha and Azeda are all good for snorkeling. Praia da Tartaruga is idyllic and home to numerous bars.

Tour Shop Búzios BUS TOUR
(☎2623-4733; www.tourshop.com.br; Orla Bardot 550; tours from R$50) Organizes four daily trips by schooner out to Ilha Feia, and to Tartaruga and João Fernandinho beaches.

Sleeping

Budget lodging is thankfully on the rise in Búzios, but still scarce during summer.

Nomad Búzios HOSTEL $$
(2620-8085; www.nomadbuzios.com.br; Rua das Pedras 25; dm R$60-90, tw R$180, d R$220-250;) Right on Rua das Pedras, Nomad can't be beaten for location – the sea slams right into the sundeck here. There are 30 dorms beds now and a slew of subtly decorated privates with sea views. It was expanding next door in 2013, turning this seaside motor court into a full-on budget resort.

Che Lagarto HOSTEL $$
(2623-1173; www.chelagarto.com; Rua da Paz 7; dm from R$62.35, d R$202;) This Argentine hostel chain snagged a lush villa in Búzios, just 50m from the 1001 bus stop. It's in tip-top shape, with nicely tiled flooring, marble tables, a small pool deck and functional, well-maintained dorms and privates. R$5 for wi-fi, though, is a bit chintzy and the music blares until midnight.

Zen-do Suites INN $$
(2623-1542; zendobuzios@mar.com.br; João Fernandes 60; r R$200-240; closed Aug;) This charming inn in Ossos is run by a sweetheart of a lady who puts her heart and soul into the three rooms on offer. It's not the João Fernandes 60 on the hill, but rather the *other* João Fernandes 60 down the hill to the left.

El Misti Yellow HOSTEL $
(2623-3174; www.elmistihostelbuzios.com; Rua da Mandrágora 13; dm R$40-62, s & d R$110-130;) This well-maintained hostel offers segregated and mixed dorms in four- to 15-bed configurations in an old renovated house. Private rooms are only available in low season (April to December 14). There's a lovely pool too. It's 15 minutes on foot from Rua das Pedras in Portal de Ferradura.

Eating & Drinking

TOP CHOICE **Deck** ITALIAN $$
(www.casasbrancas.com.br; Orla Bardot s/n; pizzas R$35-42; from 5pm) Búzios' best Italian eatery has a triumphant seaside position with soothing views. The Argentine-German owners do magical work with the excellent gourmet pizzas (try the parma!) and the place itself is romantically lit with tables and chairs facing the sea, Paris-bistro-style.

Restaurante do David SEAFOOD $$
(Manoel Turíbio de Farias 260; mains R$19-72) David's has been packed, for its high-quality seafood at little wooden tables with checkered tablecloths, since 1972. Excellent *bobó de camarão* (shrimp in *yuca* sauce).

Chez Michou CREPERIE $
(www.chezmichou.com.br; Rua das Pedras 141; crepes R$11-20;) Legendary open-air *creperia* in the heart of the action.

Bananaland BUFFET $$
(www.restaurantebananaland.com.br; Manoel Turíbio de Farias 50; per kg R$67.50; 11:30am-11pm) The best and most charming of several deluxe self-serve eateries on this street.

Information

ATMs bookend Rua das Pedras – they're in Praça Santos Dumont on the east end and inside Shopping N1 on the west end. There's a Banco do Brasil on Manoel de Carvalho. **Tourist information** (2623-2099; www.visitebuzios.com; Travessia dos Pescadores 151, Armação; 8am-9pm Sun-Thu, to 10pm Fri & Sat) sits just off the northeast corner of Praça Santos Dumont.

Getting There & Away

There is no bus station. Only **1001** (2623-2050; www.autoviacao1001.com.br; Estrada Velha da Usina 444, Loja 13) serves Búzios; eight daily buses run from Rio (R$44, three hours). Salineira runs municipal buses between Búzios and Cabo Frio (R$3.80), a 50-minute, 20km trip. Buses depart every 15 minutes or so along stops on Estrada Velha da Usina. From there you can reach Arraial do Cabo.

Getting Around

Búzios' two main streets, Rua das Pedras and Manoel Turíbio de Farias, are tiny and easily navigable on foot. To explore further afield, Coopergeribá minivans (R$2) ply the main thoroughfare and can get you within a five- to 20-minute walk of all the main beaches.

Ilha Grande

0XX24 / POP 3600

Located 150km southwest of Rio de Janeiro, Ilha Grande was once a tranquil hideaway that saw more bait and tackle than paparazzi, but these days it's a full-blown party. Most of the international partiers stay on private yachts and islands around Baía de Angra, while backpackers, middle-class Brazilians and international nomads collect in and around Vila do Abraão, Ilha Grande's main settlement.

The increase in popularity of Brazil's third-largest island is a no brainer: gorgeous beaches flank hillsides covered in lush forests, important remnants of the rapidly disappearing Mata Atlântica ecosystem. Sixty percent of the island is devoted to the 12,052-hectare Parque Estadual da Ilha Grande, Brazil's largest island park.

There are no banks or private cars on Ilha Grande, so get cash before you relax. **TurisAngra** (☎3367-7826; www.turisangra.com.br; Rua da Praia; ⊙7am-7pm) provides the municipality's offical tourist information at the new dock.

Sights & Activities

From Abraão, you can hike to other beaches around the island. It's a 2½-hour walk to stunning **Lopes Mendes** beach, and a two-hour hike to Dois Rios, which also has a lovely beach just beyond the ruins of the old prison. There's also Bico do Papagaio (Parrot's Beak), the highest point on the island at 982m (reached in three hours, guide recommended). As elsewhere, be smart: don't hike alone and be mindful of poisonous snakes in the forests. Several agencies in Abraão can arrange excursions, as can Jungle Lodge; mask and snorkel kits are available along Rua da Praia for R$10 per day.

Sleeping & Eating

Camping around the island runs R$10 to R$15 per person. At night, Rua da Praia becomes your atmospheric dining destination, with numerous restaurants setting up candlelit tables on the sand.

TOP CHOICE O Pescador INN $$$

(☎3361-5114; www.opescador.org; Rua da Praia 647; s/d with balcony R$210/230, without balcony from R$200/210; ❄@📶) Cozily furnished rooms and friendly Sicilian service are the appeal of this lovely midrange beach-facing guesthouse, but the island's best restaurant (mains for two people R$58 to R$98) round out the irresistible combination.

Jungle Lodge GUESTHOUSE $$

(☎9977-2405; www.ilhagrandeexpeditions.com; Caminho de Palmas 4; r per person R$70-90; @) Tucked away above town in the rainforest, this rustic guesthouse is run by Ronaldinho's doppelgänger, a wild-haired *pantaneiro* Tarzan who will seduce you with his tropical garden and good-soul hospitality. It's an entirely different experience than sleeping in Abraão, a 1.5km hike away.

Aquário HOSTEL $$

(☎3361-5405; www.aquariohostel.com; Praia da Julia; dm/s/d R$45/100/140; ❄@📶) The spacious sundeck overlooking the ocean and lively evening barbecues make this oceanfront hostel a backpacker favorite. To get here, head 1km east along the beach from the ferry dock.

El Misti HOSTEL $$

(☎3361-5835; www.elmistihostelilhagrande.com; Alice Kury da Silva 8; dm R$66-77, r R$215; ❄@📶) Ilha Grande's newest hostel offers mostly nine-bed dorms and artistically inclined privates with air-con and minibar. It's one block from the beach and in expectedly better shape than most others.

Lua y Mar BRAZILIAN $$

(Rua da Praia s/n; mains for 2 R$55-92; ⊙closed Wed) Excellent seafood risottos, *moquecas* (seafood stews) and fresh fish, right on Praia do Canto's sands.

Biergarten BUFFET, VEGETARIAN $$

(☎9839-9912; www.biergartenhostel.com; Getúlio Vargas 161; per kg R$48; ⊙noon-10pm Wed-Mon) The island's best *por kilo* restaurant and low-key, well-maintained hostel.

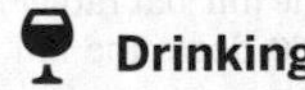

Drinking

Café do Mar CAFE, BAR

(Rua da Praia s/n) Candlelit beach lounge perfect for sundown cocktails.

Getting There & Away

BOAT There is now a head-spinning amount of boat options to Abraão from Mangaratiba, Angra dos Reis and Conceição de Jacareí on the mainland; the latter, tucked between Mangaratiba and Angra dos Reis, is the main and quickest departure point. Times vary by season, demand and which way the wind blows, so check ahead before setting out. From Conceição de Jacareí, speedboats depart daily at 10:30am, 12:30pm, 3pm and 5pm (R$25 to R$30, 25 minutes); schooners depart at 9:30am, 11am, 11:30am, 4pm and 6:15pm (R$15, 1½ hours), with an extra departure on Friday at 9pm. From Abraão, speedboats return to Conceição de Jacareí at 9:30am, 11:30am, 2pm, 4pm and 6:30pm; schooners depart at 7:30am, 9am, 10am, 12:30pm, 1pm, 3pm and 5pm.

From Angra, catamarans depart daily from Estacão Santa Luzia at 8am, 11am and 4pm

(R$20, 50 minutes), returning at 9am, 12:30pm and 5pm. From Angra's Cais de Lapa, schooners depart for Abraão Monday to Friday at 1:20pm and 2:30pm (R$15, 1½ hours), but there is only one return at 7:30am.

The cheapest way to go is the **CCR Barcas** (☎0800-721-1012; www.barcas-sa.com.br) ferry, which leaves Mangaratiba at 8am and returns at 5:30pm (R$4.50, 1½ hours), with an extra Friday-evening departure to the island at 10pm. From Angra dos Reis, Barcas departs Cais de Lapa at 3:30pm Monday to Friday and 1:30pm Saturday to Sunday (R$4.50, 1½ hours). From Abraão to Angra, it departs at 10am daily. There are also private door-to-door options from Rio (R$75).

BUS Costa Verde buses depart Rio hourly for Angra (R$41, 3½ hours) from 4am to 9pm and can drop you in Conceição de Jacareí 30 minutes before Angra *if* you tell the driver. Four daily buses from Rio go to Mangaratiba (R$30, 2 hours). Eight daily buses connect Angra with Paraty (R$9.50, two hours).

Paraty

☎0XX24 / POP 37,533

You know a place is authentic when the cobblestones are so uneven, it's actually painful to walk the streets. That's Paraty. One of Brazil's most cinematic destinations, this staunchly preserved colonial village can be overly touristy at times, but a sleepy dream of cobblestones and whitewash at others, only upset by the kaleidoscopic hues that pepper its historic walls. On summer weekends Paraty's plazas, sidewalk cafes and open-air restaurants come to life with live music. Paraty is crowded from Christmas to Carnaval and most weekends, but at other times is delightfully quiet and a perfect stopover between Rio and São Paulo.

Sights

Beaches BEACH

Paraty's biggest draw is its astounding assortment of 55 islands and 100 beaches nearby. The town's beach is **Praia do Pontal**, but it won't make the postcard cut. **Praia do Jabaquara**, 2km past Praia do Pontal, is a spacious beach with great views, several restaurants and a good campground. About an hour northeast from Paraty by boat are the **Vermelha** and **Lula** beaches. Small and idyllic; most of these beaches have *barracas* (bar stalls) serving beer and fish and, at most, a handful of beachgoers. **Praia de Parati-Mirim**, 27km east of Paraty, is hard to beat for accessibility, cost and beauty, and it has one *barraca* for sustenance. You can get there by municipal bus (R$3, 40 minutes) from Paraty bus station with 11 daily buses. Further east is **Saco do Mamanguá**, a stunning tropical fjord accessible only by boat from Parati-Mirim (R$150) or Paraty (R$350 to R$400), or guided trail. The village of **Trinidade**, 25km south, is a popular day trip from Paraty with several great beaches, but hosts enough infrastructure to support longer stays. Catch a frequent Colitur bus from Paraty (R$3, 40 minutes).

To visit the less accessible beaches, many tourists take one of the schooners from the docks. Tickets cost around R$30. The boats usually call at Praia da Lula, Praia Vermelho, **Ilha Comprida** and **Lagoa Azul** but daily routes and locations vary. An alternative is to hire one of the many small motorboats at the port. For R$50 to R$60 per hour, the skipper will take you where you want to go.

Colonial Churches CHURCH

Paraty's 18th-century prosperity is reflected in its beautiful old homes and churches. Three main churches served separate races. The 1725 **Igreja NS do Rosário e São Benedito dos Homens Pretos** (cnr Samuel Costa & Rua do Comércio; admission R$3; ⏲9am-noon & 2-5pm Tue-Sat) was built by and for slaves. The 1722 **Igreja de Santa Rita dos Pardos Libertos** (Praça Santa Rita; ⏲9am-noon & 2-5pm Wed-Sun) was the church for freed *mulatos* (people of mixed African-European ancestry), now housing the **Museu de Arte Sacra** (⏲9am-noon & 2-4pm Wed-Sun), though the African-Brazilian draped in chains posing with tourists as a slave here is odd, if not offensive. The 1800 **Capela de NS das Dores** (cnr Dr Pereira & Fresca; ⏲closed, art gallery 1:30-5pm) was the church of the colonial white elite.

Casa da Cultura CULTURAL CENTER

(☎3371 2325; www.casadaculturaparaty.org.br; Dona Geralda 177; adult/student R$6/4; ⏲10am-6:30pm Wed-Mon) A fascinating permanent exhibition that includes interviews with and stories from local residents (audio and video) in both English and Portuguese; also has excellent revolving exhibitions.

Activities

Rio-based Rio Hiking (p270) leads an unforgettable three-day **hiking** adventure from Laranjeiras to Praia Grande, taking in remote beaches and fishing villages like Praia do Sono and Martine de Sá along the way.

Paraty Explorer KAYAKING
(9952-4496; www.paratyexplorer.com) Excellent day- and multiday sea-kayaking trips around Paraty Bay. Paddy, the owner, has also opened Casa do SUP, a beachfront Stand Up Paddle–themed hostel in Jabaquara.

Paraty Tours BOAT TOURS
(3371-1327; www.paratytours.com.br; Roberto Silveira 11) The go-to agency for booking schooner trips to outlying beaches. Daily departures are 10am, 10:30am and 11am and trips last around five hours. Fresh fruit and coffee are served free after the (paid/optional) lunch. Additional costs: cover charge for on-board live music (R$5) and mask/snorkel rental (R$10).

Sleeping

Book ahead if you're coming from December to February. Once you hit the cobblestones, prices rise substantially.

TOP CHOICE **Hotel Solar dos Gerânios** INN $$
(3371-1550; www.paraty.com.br/geranio; Praça da Matriz; s/d/tr R$100/150/200;) This excellent-value colonial *pousada* overlooking the Praça da Matriz offers thick stone flooring, rustic antiques and several dogs and cats. Ramshackle rooms ooze history. Family-run since the 1960s.

Flor do Mar INN $$
(3371-1674; www.pousadaflordomar.com.br; Fresca 257; r R$220;) Another charmer in the old part of town, this secluded guesthouse is a little den of tranquility with cheery rooms and a bright, airy courtyard.

Che Lagarto HOSTEL $
(3361-9669; www.chelagarto.com; Benina Toledo do Prado 22; dm R$50, r from R$120;) These new digs in Paraty, just five minutes from the historic center, offer a social oasis, with a welcoming bar, BBQ and small pool area, so solitude seekers should ask for a room in the newly annexed second building, which faces away from the commotion.

Historic Centre Hostel HOSTEL $
(3371-2236; www.historiccentrehostel.com; Dona Geralda 211; dm/s/d/tr/q R$35/90/150/180/240;) A casual choice with basic but comfortable private rooms surrounding a stone courtyard, and a 10-bed dorm with small individual lockers. Bonus: R$5 *caipirinhas*.

Casa da Colônia INN $$
(3371-2343; www.casadacoloniapousada.com; Marechal Deodoro 502; s/d with aircon R$100/190, without aircon R$80/150;) Although it's 100m outside of the old town, this 18th-century guesthouse offers abundant colonial charm without the high price tag.

Eating & Drinking

Don't miss the sweet carts rolling around town as well as the *caipirinhas* – Paraty is second only to Minas Gerais in *cachaça* fame.

Casa do Fogo BISTRO $$
(3371-3163; www.casadofogo.com.br; Rua da Ferraria 390; mains R$30-64; 6pm-1am Thu-Tue) This lipstick-red bistro specializes in dishes flambéed in local *cachaça* – including one of Brazil's most unique, Gabriela (infused with cinnamon and clove) – makes excellent *moquecas* and is one of the few respecting sustainable fishing laws.

Istanbul TURKISH $
(Manoel Torres, Shopping Colonial; items R$4.50-10; closed Sun;) One block from the bus station, a cool Turkish chef named Kaan runs this bohemian cafe, serving coastal rarities like falafel; *dönar*, *köfte* and *sebze* kebabs; freshly made hummus and baba ganoush; and real Turkish coffee.

Thai Brasil THAI, BRAZILIAN $$$
(www.thaibrasil.com.br; Rua do Comércio 308A; mains R$34-58; dinner) It's worth the splurge to sample the limited but distinct Thai-Brazilian menu served up by the German chef/owner, who has returned to the old town after a multiyear absence.

Punto Divino ITALIAN $$
(www.puntodivino.com; Marechal Deodoro 129; pizzas R$23-42; noon-midnight) This cozy Italian restaurant has wonderful thin-crust pizzas and pastas.

Farandole FRENCH $
(Santa Rita 190; crepes R$13.90-23.90; dinner, closed Tuesday) A French couple from Brittany and Paris run this cute, colorful *creperia* tucked away on a quiet side street.

Sabor da Terra BUFFET $
(www.paraty.com.br/sabordaterra; Av Roberto Silveira 180; per kg R$36.80; 11:30am-10pm) Control your own price destiny at this long-standing *por kilo* restaurant.

Casa Coupe BAR
(Praça da Matriz s/n) A top bar; nice burger menu.

☆ Entertainment

Places to enjoy cocktails and bossa nova/Música Popular Brasileira (MPB) are **Sarau** (Marechal Deodoro 241) and **Paraty 33** (www.paraty33.com.br; Maria Jácome de Mello 357). For samba, head to **Armazem Paraty** (Dr Samuel Costa 18) on Saturday evenings from 8pm. Casa do Fogo is transformed into a *forró* funhouse after midnight on Thursday.

Expect cover charges around R$8 to R$20 when live music is present.

Information

Banco24Horas (Manoel Torres s/n, Supermercado Carlão; ⊙7am-10:30pm Mon-Sat, 4-9pm Sun) The closest ATM to the historic center is in this supermarket one block from the bus station. Bradesco and Banco do Brasil are nearby on Roberta da Silveira.

CIT (☎3371-6553; Roberto da Silveira s/n; ⊙8am-8pm) The municipal tourism office has moved to the entrance of town, a healthy hike from the old town.

Getting There & Away

The bus station is on Jango Pádua, 500m west of the old town. Around 10 daily buses connect Paraty with Rio (R$55, 4½ hours) and at least four with São Paulo (R$46, six hours). Buses leave nearly hourly to Angra dos Reis (R$9.50, two hours).

São Paulo

☎0XX11 / POP 11.3 MILLION

São Paulo is a monster. The gastronomic, fashion, finance and culture capital of Latin America is a true megalopolis in every sense of the word, home to 19 million people (metropolitan area) and more skyscrapers than could ever possibly be counted. Calling it the New York of South America wouldn't be inaccurate. The numbers are dizzying: first-rate museums and cultural centers (150), world-class restaurants (12,500 covering 52 types of cuisine), experimental theaters and cinemas (420). Sampa's nightclubs and bars are among the best on the continent (15,000 bars makes for one hell of a pub crawl) and the restaurants among the best in the world. Trendsetting *paulistanos* (inhabitants of the city) believe in working hard and playing harder, and despite constantly complaining about street violence, clogged roads and pollution, most wouldn't dare consider moving from the largest city in the southern hemisphere.

The city lacks the natural beauty of Rio. Instead, the charms of far more cosmopolitan Sampa (as locals affectionately call it) lie in its manageable districts – from the wealthy upscale neighborhoods of Jardim Paulista (home to Oscar Freire, Brazil's Rodeo Drive) to the artsy bohemian quarter of Vila Madalena, to the Japanese neighborhood of Liberdade – and its nook-and-cranny surprises: a startling architectural gem here, an unforgettable meal there, a sizzling avant-garde air about the place everywhere.

Sights & Activities

The atmospheric old center of São Paulo lies between Praça da Sé, Luz metro station and Praça da República. Cleverly titled Centro Velho, it's a pedestrianized maze offering a fascinating cornucopia of architectural styles (always look above the ground floor, which have all lost their charm to everyday shops). Other interesting neighborhood strolls are found in Liberdade, Sampa's Japan town (and home to other Asian communities); and Vila Madalena, the artistic quarter. Both host lively weekend street markets, the former at Praçada Liberdade, the latter at Praça Benedito Calixto (Saturday only).

TOP CHOICE **Mercado Municipal** MARKET
(Map p294; www.mercadomunicipal.com.br; Rua da Cantareira 306, Centro; ⊙7am-6pm Mon-Sat, to 4pm Sun) A foodie's dream, the awesome Mercado is one of South America's best urban markets, inside a neoclassical building dating back to 1928.

Pinacoteca do Estado MUSEUM
(Map p294; www.pinacoteca.org.br; Praça da Luz 2, Centro; adult/student R$6/3, Sat free; ⊙10am-6pm Tue-Sun) This contemporary art-filled museum is Sampa's oldest and its most striking.

Theatro Municipal ARCHITECTURE
(Map p294; ☎3397-0300; www.teatromunicipal.sp.gov.br; Praça Ramos de Azevedo, Centro) The city's pride is the baroque/art-nouveau Teatro Municipal just west of Viaduto do Chá on Praça Ramos de Azevedo. Call ahead for free tour info.

Museu do Futebol MUSEUM
(www.museudofutebol.org.br; Praça Charles Miller s/n, Pacaembu; adult/student R$6/3, Thu free;

Central São Paulo

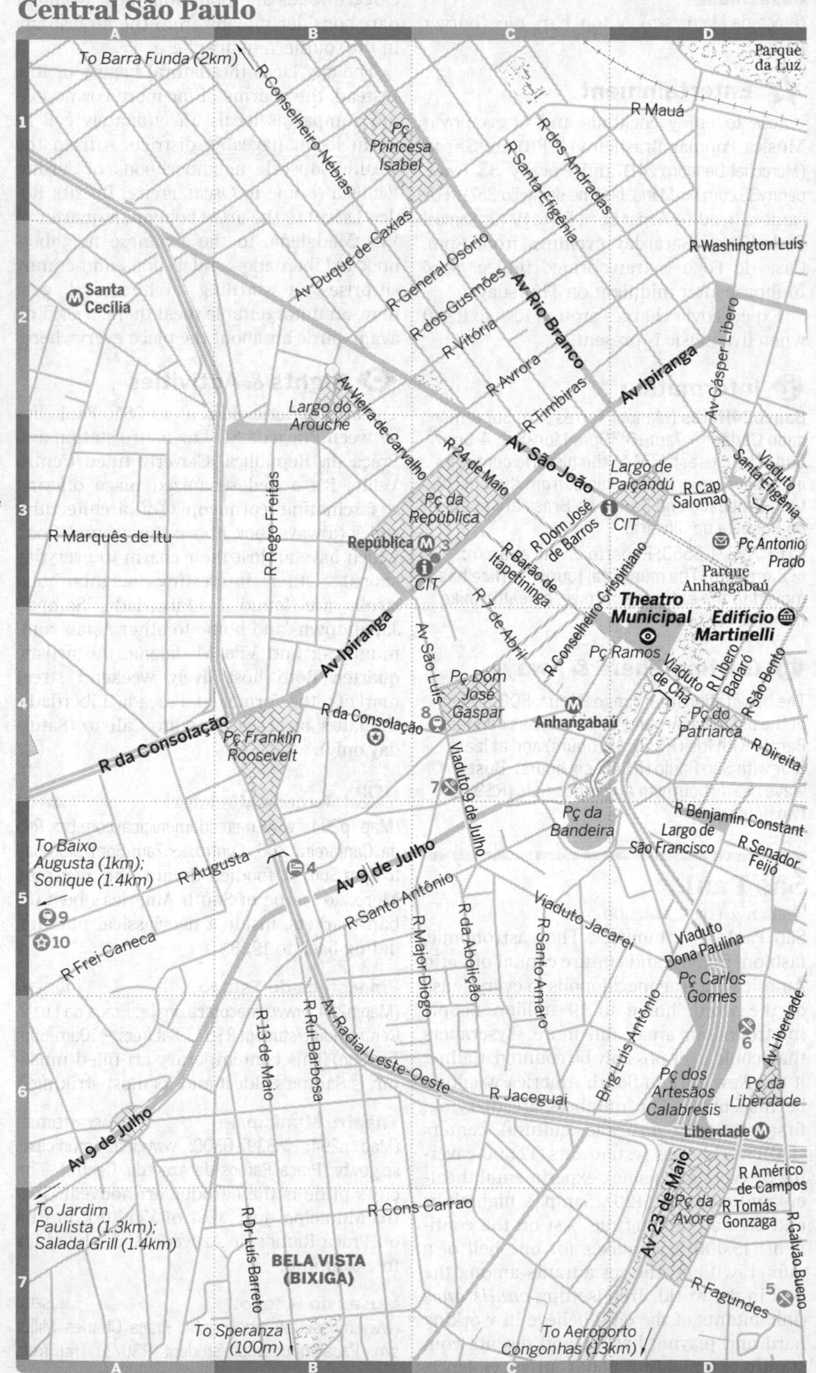

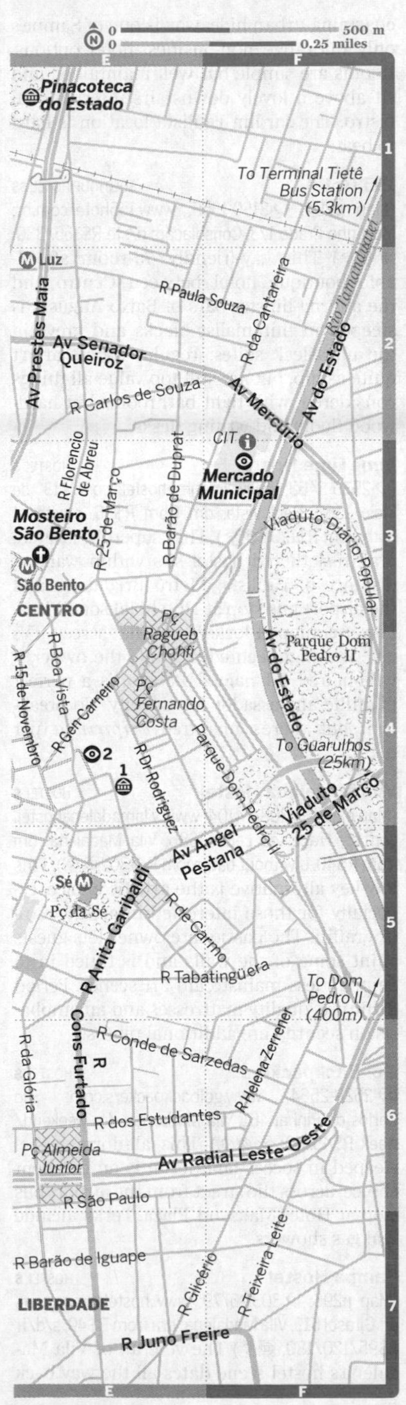

Central São Paulo

Top Sights

Edifício Martinelli	D4
Mercado Municipal	F3
Mosteiro São Bento	E3
Pinacoteca do Estado	E1
Theatro Municipal	D4

Sights

1 Casa da Imagem	E4
2 Páteo do Colégio	E4

Activities, Courses & Tours

3 SP Free Walking Tour	C3

Sleeping

4 155 Hotel	B5

Eating

5 Aska	D7
6 Chi Fu	D6
7 Estadão	C4

Drinking

8 Alberta #3	C4
9 Caos	A5

Entertainment

10 Beco 203	A5
Studio SP	(see 10)

⌚9am-5pm Tue-Sun) This R$32.5-million congratulatory 'slap on the ass' to Brazilian football is housed under the bleachers of Estádio do Pacaembu. The *torcida* (cheering section) exhibit is the next best thing to attending a match and perhaps the best use in history of space underneath a stadium. Catch bus 917M-31 'Morro Grande' on Av Dr Arnaldo at Cardoso de Almeida outside Metrô Clínicas and get off in front of Pão de Açúcar grocery store on Av Pacaembu.

Museu de Arte de São Paulo MUSEUM
(MASP; www.masp.art.br; Av Paulista 1578, Bela Vista; adult/student R$15/7, Thu free; ⌚10am-6pm Tue & Thu-Sun, to 8pm Wed) Has Latin America's best collection of Western art, with more than 8000 pieces.

Parque do Ibirapuera PARK
(www.parqueibirapuera.org) The massive Parque do Ibirapuera, 4km from Centro, contains several museums, monuments and attractions. Take bus 5154 'Term. Sto. Amaro' from Estacão da Luz.

Vila Madalena

0 200 m
0 0.1 miles

Vila Madalena

Sleeping

1 Casa Club Hostel A3
2 Sampa Hostel A2
3 Vila Madalena Hostel B3

Eating

4 Bacio di Latte A2
5 Feijoada da Lana A2
6 Mercearia São Pedro A1

Drinking

7 São Cristóvão A2

Sleeping

Sleeps are booming in São Paulo – over 30 hostels have opened since 2009. The best spot for travelers include the bohemian *bairro* of Vila Madalena, 6km west of Praça da Sé, which now boasts a bona fide hip hostel scene in addition to being the city's longstanding cradle of artsy boutiques, cutting-edge galleries and boisterous nightlife; and the leafy, upscale district of Jardim Paulista, 5km southwest of Centro.

Pousada Dona Ziláh INN $$
(☎3062-1444; www.zilah.com; Alameda Franca 1621, Jardins; s/d R$148/184; P❄@📶) This charming urban hideaway is one of Sampa's only midrange non-business-hotel options. Rooms are simple but well maintained and sit above a lovely downstairs international bistro. The Jardim Paulista location is hard to beat.

155 Hotel BOUTIQUE HOTEL $$
(Map p294; ☎3150-1555; www.155hotel.com.br; Martinho Prado 173, Consolacão; d/ste R$165/330; ❄@📶) This gay-friendly, 76-room affordable boutique hotel between Centro and the alterna-hipster bars of Baixo Augusta is steeped in minimalist blacks and greys in the ultrasleek suites; regular rooms aren't quite as hip, but are still top value all things considered, with tight bathrooms but hardwood floors and writing desks.

LimeTime Hostel HOSTEL $
(☎2935-5463; www.limetimehostels.com; 13 de Maio 1552, Bela Vista; dm from R$35, r without bathroom R$120; @📶) This superbly located, grafitti-slathered hostel sits within walking distance of Paulista, Metrô Brigadeiro and the airport bus stop at Hotel Maksoud Plaza. Power-equipped lockers and flat-screen TVs give it a high-tech edge, while the owner, a wild-haired DJ named Bebeto, is a perfect nightlife ambassador for the city. No breakfast, but there's one free *caipirinha* per night.

Vila Madalena Hostel HOSTEL $
(Map p296; ☎3034-4104; www.vilamadalenahostel.com.br; Francisco Leitão 686, Vila Madalena; dm from R$40, d without bathroom R$130; ❄@) This low-key alternative is the artistic choice, especially for those interested in architecture or graffiti. The passionate owner lets guests paint some of the walls and is tuned in to Sampa's less mainstream art scenes. Period furniture, quality mattresses and an emphasis on security are additional pluses.

Gol Backpackers HOSTEL $
(☎2528-2564; www.golbackpackers.com; São Carlos de Pinhal 461, Vila Madalena; dm weekend/week R$45/40; ❄@📶) This all-dorm hostel steeped in soccer fanaticism is an excellent choice, across the street from the airport bus stop at Hotel Maksoud Plaza. Perks include real gas showers.

Sampa Hostel HOSTEL $
(Map p296; ☎3031-6779; www.hostelsampa.com.br; Girasol 519, Vila Madalena; dm from R$40, s/d/tr R$95/120/180; @📶) The veteran of Vila Madalena's hostel scene dates all the way back

to 2008. There's four-, six- and eight-bed dorms, good-value private rooms, a tucked-away TV room and kitchen facilities.

Casa Club Hostel HOSTEL $
(Map p296; ☎3798 0051; www.casaclub.com.br; Mourato Coelho 973, Vila Madalena; dm from R$35, d R$110; @) Part hostel, part bar on one of Vila Madalena's best nightlife streets.

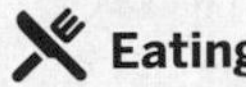

Eating

Eating is Sampa's godsend, boasting quality unrivaled in South America.

Bacio di Latte ICE CREAM $
(☎3662-2573; www.baciodilatte.com.br; Oscar Freire 136, Cerqueira César; scoops from R$8; ⏲noon-11pm Mon-Sat, to 10pm Sun;) A Scotsman and two Italians finally did what nobody outside Buenos Aires could previously do: produce foodgasmic Italian gelato in South America. Voted the city's best every year since its 2011 opening, it's Brazil's best as well. Travel-friendly outlets include this one at Cerqueira César and one at **Vila Madalena** (Map p296; www.baciodilatte.com.br; Harmonia 337, Vila Madalena; scoops from R$8; ⏲noon-11pm Mon-Sat, to 10pm Sun;).

Brasil a Gosto BRAZILIAN $$$
(☎3086-3565; www.brasilagosto.com.br; Azevedo do Amaral 70, Jardins; mains R$52-98; ⏲noon-3pm & 7pm-midnight Tue-Thu, noon-5pm & 7pm-1am Fri-Sat, noon-5pm Sun;) Practically everyone's favorite gourmet Brazilian restaurant, both for its tasteful modern decor and Chef Ana Luiza Trajano's precision-perfect mix of countrywide influences in her splurge-worthy cuisine. Reservations recommended.

Mercearia São Pedro BRAZILIAN $
(Map p296; Rodésia 34, Vila Madalena; appetizers for 2 R$18-37; ⏲9am-1am Mon-Fri, from 10am Sat, 11am-6pm Sun) This independently minded *boteco* five minutes' walk from Vila Madalena metro has been at it since 1968. It's crazy busy at night, when packs of sexy bohemians swill properly chilled bottled beer, fresh *pastels* (stuffed, fried pastries; R$4.50) and excellent, down-to-earth fare like *picanha* with sautéed onions. You will have a great time here without – as the Brazilians say – leaving your pants.

FREE SP!

There's no sugarcoating it: Brazil is expensive and São Paulo is the beast of the bunch. But that doesn't mean you can't have fun on a shoestring budget. Our favorite freebies:

Museu Afro-Brasil (www.museuafrobrasil.com.br; Parque do Ibirapuera, Moema; ⏲10am-5pm Tue-Sun) This hugely important Parque do Ibirapuera museum features a permanent 3rd-floor collection chronicling five centuries of African immigration (and a nod to the 10 million African lives lost in the construction of Brazil) while hosting a rotating array of contemporary Afro-centric exhibitions on its bottom two floors.

Edifício Martinelli (Map p294; www.prediomartinelli.com.br; São Bento 405, Centro; ⏲tours half-hourly 9:30-11:30am & 2:30-4:30pm Mon-Fri, 9am-1pm Sat) São Paulo's first skyscraper, in a gorgeous 1929 Beaux Arts building, features a mansion built on top of its 26th-floor viewing terrace. The terrace and its incredible views are now open for free visits (you must arrive on the half hour to gain entrance).

Casa da Imagem (Map p294; ☎3106-5122; www.casadaimagem.sp.gov.br; Roberto Simonsen 136B, Centro; ⏲9am-5pm Tue-Sun) Beautifully curated (and English-signed!) from some 710,000 historical photographs, this newly inaugurated museum inside a restored colonial downtown mansion is a must for those interested in São Paulo lore.

Mosteiro São Bento (Map p294; www.mosteiro.org.br; Largo de São Bento, s/n; ⏲6am-6pm Mon-Wed & Fri, 6-8am & 11:30am-6pm Thu, 6am-noon & 4-6pm Sat-Sun) This is the city's oldest and most important church, dating to 1598, though its neo-gothic facade is no older than the early 20th century. Inside, there's stunning stained glass and often Gregorian chants during mass.

SP Free Walking Tour (Map p294; www.spfreewalkingtour.com; ⏲tours 11:30am Sat) Culls over 450 years of Sampa history into a long but fascinating 3½-walk every Saturday at 11:30am. The tour meets next to the CIT at Praça da República and ends at Metrô Liberdade.

DON'T MISS

PIZZA PAULISTANA

Forget New York, Chicago (or even Naples, for that matter): one of the world's best-kept secrets is São Paulo's excellent *pizza paulistana*. Locals say the city's pizza is so good, even the Italians are jealous! It shouldn't be a surprise, though, as swarms of Italian immigrants settled here in the late 19th century, giving the city one of the largest Italian populations in the world outside Italy. Today, nearly 6000 or so pizzerias pepper the sprawling cityscape, with over one million pies engulfed per day. Do not depart without trying one of the following:

Bráz (www.casabraz.com.br; Vupabussu 271, Pinheiros; pizzas R$42-63.50; ⏲6:30pm-12:30am Sun-Thu, to 1:30am Fri & Sat; 📶) Start to finish, the experience here will leave you forgetting pizza ever originated in Italy. Do as Brazilians do and order a Brahma *chope* (draft beer) followed by an appetizer of warm *pão de calabresa* (sausage bread) dipped in spiced olive oil, then let the feast commence. *Fosca* (smoked ham, *catipury* cheese, mozzarella and tomato sauce) is a current favorite. You can duplicate this unforgettable experience in Rio (p281) if São Paulo is not in your itinerary; and at additional Sampa locations in Moema and Higienópolis.

Speranza (www.pizzaria.com.br; Treze de Maio 1004, Bixiga; pizzas R$33.50-61; ⏲6pm-1am Mon-Sat, to midnight Sun) One of São Paulo's oldest and most traditional pizzerias in the Italian neighborhood of Bixiga, where the Famiglia Tarallo has been serving serious pizza since 1958. Perfect meal: the life-changing bruschetta appetizer followed by an excellent, fiercely traditional pizza margherita. It's an easy walk from Paulista/Brigadeiro Metrô.

Maremonti (www.maremonti.com.br; Padre João Manuel 1160, Jardins; pizzas R$33-89; ⏲lunch & dinner) This high-end pizza newcomer hails from the coast of São Paulo, but opened its first city location in Jardins in 2011. It's a little fancy but extraordinarily notable for its four pizzas certified by the Associazione Pizzaiuoli Napoletani (based in Naples) – the margherita will send you into a gastro-fit of indescribable satisfaction.

St. Louis BURGERS $
(www.stlouisburger.com.br; cnr Batataes & Joaquim Eugênio de Lima, Jardins; burgers R$21-30; ⏲noon-3pm Tue-Sat & 6:30-10:30pm daily) Sampa is serious about burgers. This unpretentious burger joint is one of the city's best, and the American-born owner has perfected the char. Our favorite is the Pepper Crust (R$30). It's six blocks southwest of Paulista.

Estadão FAST FOOD $
(Map p294; www.estadaolanches.com.br; Viaduto 9 de Julho 193, Centro; sandwiches R$10-22; ⏲24hr) This classic, Centro *lanchonete* (snack bar) serves workers' meals at all hours, but its signature *pernil* (pork loin) sandwich, smothered in the cheese of your choice (provolone!) and sautéed onions, is one of Sampa's gastronomic musts.

Feijoada da Lana BRAZILIAN $$
(Map p296; Aspicuelta 421, Vila Madalena; feijoada weekday/weekend R$30/55; ⏲noon-3:30pm Tue-Fri, 12:30-5pm Sat & Sun) Lana, a journalist by trade, offers her hugely popular version of *feijoada*, Brazil's national dish, inside a smallish Vila Madalena house. Production here isn't as elaborate as more expensive options, but it's long on smiling service, hearty goodness and (on weekends!) *batidinhas de limão*, a sort of strained *caipirinha*.

Chi Fu CHINESE $$
(Map p294; Praça Carlos Gomes, Liberdade; mains R$18-50; ⏲11am-4pm & 6-10pm Mon-Fri, 11am-5pm Sat-Sun) The seriously authentic Cantonese cuisine near the Liberdade metro station appears pricey until the portions arrive, which easily serve three. The decor, the circular tables, the family-style seating and the staff – who barely have a grasp on Portuguese – are straight from the motherland.

Aska JAPANESE $
(Map p294; Galvão Bueno 466, Liberdade; mains R$12-16; ⏲11am-2pm & 6-9:40pm Tue-Sun) Steaming-hot bowls of pork ramen draw in legions at this Liberdade noodle restaurant that's entirely too cheap. It's practically Japan.

Drinking

Traditional bar neighborhoods are Vila Madalena (witness the corner of Aspicuelta and

Mourato Coelho on weekends!), along Mario Ferraz in Itaim Bibi; and Baixo Augusta, where the GLS scene (Portuguese slang for Gay, Lesbian and Sympathetics) mingles with artsy, alterna-hipsters in the city's coolest nightlife district. Paulista is also very lively at happy hour along the sidewalk bars near Joaquim Eugênio de Lima.

Cafes & Juice Bars

TOP CHOICE Santo Grão CAFE
(☎3062-9294; www.santograo.com.br; Oscar Freire 413, Jardins; coffee R$4.80-11.50; ⏰10am-1pm Mon, 9am-1am Tue-Sat, to midnight Sun; 📶) São Paulo's most serious coffee haunt is a stylish indoor-outdoor cafe popular for cappuccinos, wine, eclectic bistro fare (mains R$19 to R$60) and people-watching (that *includes* the staff).

Suco Begaço JUICE BAR
(www.sucobagaco.com.br; Haddock Lobo 1483, Jardins; juice R$5.90-12.50; ⏰8am-6pm, from noon Sun; 👪) The city's best juice spot – this trendy cafe burns through 600 glasses daily, mixed with either water, orange juice, tea or coconut water (two for one available before 11:30am).

Bars

TOP CHOICE Veloso BAR
(www.velosobar.com.br; Conceição Veloso 56, Vila Mariana; ⏰5:30am-12:30am Tue-Fri, from 12:45pm Sat, 4-11pm Sun) This tiny, outstanding *boteco*, a quick walk from Metrô Vila Mariana, serves the city's best and most exotic *caipirinhas* (R$15-19), shockingly good *coxinhas* (battered and fried shredded chicken, *catupury* cheese and spices; R$20) and the best house-made hot sauce we've found in the country.

Alberta #3 BAR
(Map p294; www.alberta3.com.br; Av São Luís 272, Centro; cover R$15-35; ⏰closed Sun & Mon) This three-story hipster hideout off Praça da República draws inspiration from '50s-era hotel bars and lobbies, and rides a soundtrack steeped mostly in classic rock, jazz and soul (DJ's often spin vinyl). No cover from 7pm to 10pm.

Empório Alto de Pinheiros BAR
(www.altodospinheiros.com.br; Vupabussu 305, Alto de Pinheiros; mains R$18-41; ⏰noon-midnight Sun-Thu, to 1am Fri & Sat) This neighborhood secret hosts beer geeks fretting nervously over which of the 400 bottled and 10 draft choices to try next, including rarer Brazilian microbrews. Draft Guinness sometimes goes for an unheard of R$7.50.

Caos BAR
(Map p294; www.caos584.com.br; Augusta 584, Baixo Augusta; ⏰8pm-late Tue-Fri, from 9pm Sat) This Baixo Augusta hangout is a microcosm of all that's great about the neighborhood: among the junkyard aesthetic (all for sale), you'll get beer fiends downing Brazilian microbrews, hot-rod gearheads arguing pinstipe width and wide-eyed gringos.

São Cristóvão BAR
(Map p296; Aspicuelta 533, Vila Madalena; mains R$36-74) This wildy atmospheric *boteco* is overspilling with soccer memorabilia from the owner's collection.

☆ Entertainment

Clubbing here rivals the excitement of New York and prices of Moscow. The hottest districts are Vila Olímpia (flashy, expensive, electronica) and Barra Funda/Baixo Augusta (rock, alternative, down-to-earth). Some clubs offer a choice between a cover charge averaging R$10 to R$40 (unless otherwise noted) or a pricier *consumação* option, recoupable in drinks. Most clubs offer a discount for emailing or calling ahead to be on the list.

São Paulo's three biggest soccer teams are **São Paulo FC** (www.saopaulofc.net), who play at the 67,428-capacity Estádio do Morumbi (also a 2016 Olympic Games venue); **Palmeiras** (www.palmeiras.com.br), moving to their new 60,000-capacity Nova Arena Palestra Itália, near Barra Funda, in 2013; and **Corinthians** (www.corinthians.com.br), who played at 40,199-capacity Estádio do Pacaembu at the time of writing, but were moving to the new R$820 million Arena de Itaquera, 24km east of Centro, by late 2013. This new stadium, reachable from Metrô Corinthians-Itaquera, will host six 2014 FIFA World Cup matches.

D-Edge CLUB
(☎3665-9500; www.d-edge.com.br; Auro Soares de Moura Andrade 141, Barra Funda; cover R$20-70; ⏰11pm-late Mon & Wed-Sat) With one of the city's most remarkable sound systems and a roster of world-famous DJs, this mixed gay-straight club is a must for electronica fans.

Studio SP LIVE MUSIC
(Map p294; www.studiosp.org; Augusta 591, Baixo Augusta; ⏰11pm-late Tue-Sat) This large, alt-

bent cultural space is Sampa's hottest spot for live local music. Early sessions are free.

Beco 203 CLUB
(Map p294; www.beco203.com.br; Augusta 609, Baixo Augusta; cover R$15-30; ⏰from 11pm Tue-Sat) This straightforward Porto Alegre transplant is chock-full of teenage anarchists and pop fans on Tuesdays, when it commandeers see-and-be-seen honors for the under-30 set. Other nights focus on indie rock.

Sonique CLUB
(www.soniquebar.com.br; Bela Cintra 461, Baixo Augusta; ⏰closed Mon-Tue) GLS-friendly and all dressed up in concrete and art deco lighting, this happening *pre-balada* (preparty) ultralounge hosts DJs nightly and staffs a clubbing concierge to direct everyone to the hot spots afterwards.

 Information

You are never far from an ATM – every bank imaginable lines Paulista (though they are pretty scarce in Vila Madalena).

Dangers & Annoyances

Crime is an issue in São Paulo, though tourists aren't often targeted unless you're an unlucky victim of an *arrastão*, when armed *banditos* rob an entire restaurant of patrons in the blink of an eye (a disturbing trend in the city of late). Be especially careful in the center at night and on weekends (when fewer people are about). You should watch out for pickpockets on buses and at Praça da Sé.

Emergency

Deatur Tourist Police (☎3257 4475; Rua da Consolação 247)

Medical Services

Einstein Hospital (☎2151-1233; www.einstein.com.br; Albert Einstein 627, Morumbi) One of Latin America's best hospitals.

Money

Bradesco (Wisard 308, Vila Madalena) Best international-friendly ATM in Vila Madalena.

HSBC Bela Vista (Paulista 949A); Centro (Antônio de Godói 53); Vila Madalena/Pinheiros (Pedroso de Moraes 1525)

Post

Post Office (Praça do Correios s/n, Centro) The main branch on Parque Anhangabaú.

Tourist Information

CIT (www.cidadedesaopaulo.com) Airport (Terminals 1 & 2; ⏰6am-10pm); Centro (☎3331-7786; Praça da República); Mercado Municipal (Rua da Cantareira 306, Rua E, Portão 4; ⏰9am-6pm Mon-Sat, 7am-4pm Sun); Olida (São João 473); Paulista (Av Paulista 1853; ⏰7am-6pm); Tietê bus station (Rodoviário Tietê, Santana; ⏰6am-10pm) The most helpful branches of the tourist information center for non-Portuguese speakers are in Olida and at Mercado Municipal.

 Getting There & Away

Air

São Paulo is the Brazilian hub for many international airlines and thus the first stop for many travelers. Before buying a domestic ticket, check which of the city's airports the flight departs

GETTING INTO TOWN

Passaro Marroon (www.passaromarron.com.br) operates two airport buses. The **Airport Bus Service** (www.airportbusservice.com.br; R$35) is the most efficient way to/from Guarulhos international airport, making stops at Aeroporto Congonhas, Barra Funda, Tiête, Praça da República and various hotels around Paulista and Augusta. The *cheapest* way is to catch suburban **Airport Service** (www.emtu.sp.gov.br; $4.30) lines 257 or 299 to/from Metrô Tatuapé (30 to 45 minutes; easily confused with the flashier aforementioned Airport Bus Service – they depart right next to each other outside Terminal 2), which depart every 15 minutes between 5am and midnight. To get to the airport, exit Tatuapé to the left towards Shopping Metrô Boulevard Tatuapé and the buses are on the street below to the left as you cross the pedestrian bridge. **Guarucoop** (www.guarucoop.com.br) is the only taxi service allowed to operate from the international airport and charges vacation-spoiling prices to the city (R$116 to Paulista, R$124.80 to Vila Madalena).

For Congonhas, catch bus 875A-10 'Perdizes-Aeroporto' from Metrô São Judas.

Both Terminal Tietê and Barra Funda, the two main bus stations, are connected to metro stations of the same name, which can whisk you off to Vila Madalena (Metrô Vila Madalena), Jardim Paulista/Baixo Augusta (Metrô Consolação or Trianon-Masp) or Centro (Metrô Sé) for R$3.

from as the international airport also serves many domestic flights.

Guarulhos (GRU), the international airport, is 25km east of the center. Most domestic and all international flights depart from Terminals 1 and 2 in the main building, but Azul, Trip and Webjet operate out of the new Terminal 4, 2km to the southwest. A free shuttle runs every four minutes, connecting the terminals 24 hours a day. At time of writing, plans were in place for additional domestic airlines to move to this terminal, so check ahead. A new and glamorous Terminal 3 was under construction at time of writing for a 2014 opening.

The domestic-only airport, Congonhas (CGH), 14km south of the center, services many domestic destinations, including the majority of flights to Rio (Santos Dumont Airport), which depart every half hour (or less).

Bus

South America's largest bus terminal, Terminal Tietê, 4.5km north of Centro, offers buses to destinations throughout the continent. Avoid bus arrivals during early morning or late afternoon – traffic jams are enormous.

Buses to the Pantanal leave from Terminal Barra Funda, 5.3km northwest of Centro.

DESTINATION	COST (R$)	DURATION (HR)
Angra dos Reis	62	7½
Asunción	159	20
Belo Horizonte	97	8
Brasília	105	15
Buenos Aires	324.50	36
Curitiba	94	6
Florianópolis	112	11
Foz do Iguaçu	165	15
Montevideo	310	32
Paraty	48	6
Pantanal (Cuiabá)	224	26
Pantanal (Campo Grande)	177	13½
Recife	388	45
Rio de Janeiro	99	6
Salvador	291	32
Santiago	355.50	54

Getting Around

São Paulo's immense public transport system is the world's most complex, boasting 15,000 buses and 1333 lines. Buses (R$3) are crowded during rush hours and confusingly thorough. You can reach many places on the excellent **Metrô São Paulo** (www.metro.sp.gov.br), the city's subway system. The metro is cheap, safe, fast and runs from 4:40am to midnight. A single ride costs R$3.

Belo Horizonte

☎0XX31 / POP 2.5 MILLION

Though Belo Horizonte, Brazil's third-largest city and the sprawling capital of Minas Gerais, hides a wealth of cultural attractions and architectural jewels peppered amid a concrete jungle, it is most famous as a place to eat, drink and be merry. Fueling the city's backbone as a rapidly growing industrial giant are hundreds of *botecos*, each with its own distinct personality and character. Its plethora of drinking dens has earned Beagá (the city's nickname, named for the pronunciation of its initials, BH) the title of the Bar Capital of Brazil.

Sights

Praça da Liberdade, Beagá's main square, has been transformed from government seat to cultural and museum epicenter. Flanked by historical buildings once housing government ministries (which have been moved 20km out of the city to the futuristic Oscar Niemeyer-designed Cidade Administrativa), the work in progress now hosts a wealth of new museums, cafes and cultural attractions.

TOP CHOICE Memorial Minas Gerais – Vale MUSEUM

(www.memorialvale.com.br; Praca da Liberdade s/n; admission free; ⏲10am-6pm Tue-Wed & Fri-Sat, to 10pm Thu, to 4pm Sun) The best of Praça da Liberdade's makeover, this contemporary museum chronicles Minas culture from the 17th to 21st centuries via three floors of cutting-edge interactive galleries and audiovisual installations. It's supremely cool.

Mercado Central MARKET

(www.mercadocentral.com.br; Augusto de Lima 744; ⏲7am-6pm Mon-Sat, 8am-1pm Sun) One of Brazil's best urban markets, full of artisan cheese, *cachaça,* sweets and all kinds of gourmet and practical goods.

Sleeping

Belo Horizonte lacks a centralized traveler neighborhood – most budget accomodations are scattered about residential areas.

WORTH A TRIP

INSTITUTO DE ARTE CONTEMPORÂNEA INHOTIM

A museum like no other, **Inhotim** (☎0xx31-3254-5440; www.inhotim.org.br; Rua B, 20, Inhotim, Brumadinho; adult/student Wed & Thu R$20/10, Sat & Sun R$28/14; ⏲9:30am-4:30pm Tue-Fri, to 5:30pm Sat & Sun), located 60km from Belo Horizonte in Brumadinho, is the must-see in the area. Though it houses 350 works from over 80 artists, Inhotim is as much about the space itself as its inventory of contemporary art. Formed by a nonlinear sequence of pavilions in the midst of a botanical garden, Inhotim's galleries pepper a lush and mesmerizing landscape that is a museum in itself.

Around every corner of the 3.5-hectare environmental park, there are works of art built into the landscape or housed in one of nine galleries. That means a line of multi-hued Volkswagen Beetles along the lake or a sailing boat hanging upside down in the Burle Marx gardens. Inhotim was the private collection of *mineiro* (Minas Gerais resident) entrepreneur Bernardo Paz until 2004, when he turned his private playground and farm into the Instituto Cultural Inhotim, a not-for-profit institution dedicated to the conservation, exhibition and production of contemporary artworks and environmental preservation. Today, it's the most astonishing museum you've never heard of.

Saritur (☎3419-1800; www.saritur.com.br) runs a direct bus from Belo's bus station at 9:15am, returning at 6:30pm Tuesday to Friday and 6pm on weekends (R$14.05, two hours).

TOP CHOICE La Em Casa HOSTEL $

(☎3653-9566; www.laemcasahostel.com; Eurita 30, Santa Tereza; dm R$32-40, d R$125, s/d without bathroom R$70/100; @📶) Owner Marília (sweeter than *doce de leite*) and her French husband (four languages between them) are consummate hosts. This is a spacious, airy historic house with parquet wood floors and good kitchen access. As the name implies, staying here feels like visiting a friend's (big) home.

Chalé Mineiro HOSTEL $

(☎3467-1576; www.chalemineirohostel.com.br; Santa Luzia 288; dm from R$28, s/d R$85/100, without bathroom R$65/800; @📶🏊) This hostel veteren offers decent rooms in a well-maintained home. Take bus 9801 from near the bus station. The central pool is a nice touch in an otherwise no-frills experience.

Hotel Rio Jordão HOTEL $$

(☎3214-2911; www.hotelriojordao.com.br; Rio de Janeiro 147; s/d/tr R$131/162/230) Solid mid-range downtown hotel, a few blocks north of Mercado Central. Basic rooms, location and friendly staff all get high ranks from travelers, though could be dicey walking around here at night.

Pousadinha Mineira HOSTEL $

(☎3423-4105; www.pousadinhamineira.com.br; Espirito Santo 604; dm R$25; 📶) Distinctly characterless and bare-bones, this institutional dorm-only hostel is as cheap as it gets. Tack on R$5 for breakfast and/or linens.

Eating & Drinking

The neighborhood of Savassi has many top restaurants, including the lion's share of *botecos* that Beagá is famous for. On Sundays, Alfonso Pena is closed down along Parque Municipal for a wonderful street fair with loads of food stalls.

Casa Cheira BRAZILIAN $$

(Augusto de Lima 744, Mercado Central; mains R$19-23; ⏲lunch) Inside Beagá's mesmerizing Mercado Central, this popular restaurant, as the name implies, is always full. Daily lunch specials feature down-home *mineiro* dishes (from the Minas Gerais state) on the cheap.

San Ro ASIAN, VEGETARIAN $

(Moraes 651; per kg weekday/weekend R$36.90/R$39.90; ⏲11:30am-3pm; 🌱) This Taiwanese-run Asian-vegetarian *por kilo* is a godsend. Vegetarian or not, you'll be beelining for it after a few plates of *comida mineira!*

Establecimento BRAZILIAN $$

(www.barestabelecimento.com; Monte Alegre 160; mains R$17-45) A good spot to dive into award-winning *comida di boteco* (*boteco* food), this unsigned Serra hot spot 3km from the center makes festive use of a residential driveway. It's noisy and standing-room only for all but first arrivals, but the food is a unique experience.

Café com Letras CAFE $$
(www.cafecomletras.com.br; Antônio Albuquerque 785; mains R$18-40;) Bookstore-café deeply rooted in Belo's music and arts scene.

Mambo LIVE MUSIC
(www.mambodrinkeria.wordpress.com; Antônio Albuquerque 71; closed Sun & Mon) This chic, two-story Savassi bar bucks the traditional *boteco* trend for Latin American nostalgia: there's live Latin jazz Thursday to Saturday and fantastic tapas (R$25 to R$35) with radical flavor marriages (tangerine-mustard curry drumsticks, spicy jelly bruschetta with bacon and basil). Don't skip the decadent dessert.

Archangelo BAR
(Rua da Bahia 1148, Ed Maleta, 2nd fl; closed Sun & Mon) The best bar of many inside the indie-intellectual Maleta building in Centro, with great views from its consistently packed 2nd-floor open-air patio. Voted Beagá's best happy hour.

Entertainment

Three soccer teams call Belo Horizonte home: **América** (www.americamineiro.combr), **Atlético Mineiro** (www.atletico.com.br) and **Cruzeiro** (www.cruzeiro.com.br). Important matches are held at the newly renovated, 70,000-seat Mineirão, 10km north of Centro, Brazil's second-largest soccer stadium and a 2014 FIFA World Cup and 2016 Olympic Games venue.

Information

PIT (Belotur; www.belohorizonte.mg.gov.br) Aeroporto Pampulha (3246-8015; Praça Bagatelle 204); bus station (3277-6907; Praça Rio Branco, Terminal Rodoviário; 8am-4:20pm Tue-Sun); Mercado Central (3277-4691; Augusto de Lima 744) Extraordinarily helpful municipal tourist organization; publishes excellent monthly guide in English. There's also a branch at Aeroperto Confins.

Getting There & Away

Belo's main airport is Aeroporto Confins (CNF), 40km north of the city, but some regional airlines use Aeroporto da Pampulha (PLU), 7km north of the center. **Expresso Unir** (3663-8000; www.conexaoaeroporto.com.br) runs frequent Conexão Aeroporto buses between downtown and Belo's two airports. The conventional bus (R$8.70) heads to/from Belo's bus station. The executive option (R$19.25) heads to/from **Terminal Alvares Cabral** (Alvares Cabral 387). Departures are every 15 to 30 minutes. Travel times are 30 minutes to Pampulha and 50 minutes to Confins.

The **bus station** (Praça Rio Branco 100) is in the north of the city center, near the north end of Afonso Pena. There is one departure weekly on Friday at 5pm to Tiradentes. Other times, catch a bus to São João del Rei and switch there.

Sample travel times and *executivo* fares (where applicable) from Belo Horizonte:

DESTINATION	COST (R$)	DURATION (HR)
Brasília	116	12
Curitiba	165	15
Foz do Iguaçu	261	27
Ouro Preto	24	2¾
Rio de Janeiro	99	7
Salvador	214	23
São João del Rei	44	3½
São Paulo	95	9½
Tiradentes	54	4½.

Ouro Preto

0XX31 / POP 70,280

Nestled among gorgeous mountain scenery 114km southeast of Belo Horizonte, Ouro Preto rises from the lush landscape like a bygone living museum, unyielding in its grip on the 18th century. Here the Unesco World Heritage–recognized historical center features numerous stunning baroque churches perched high on surrounding hillsides, standing sentinel over picturesque plazas and winding cobbled streets that were once the gilded paths of the crown jewel of the Minas Gerais gold-mining towns.

Sights & Activities

Avoid visiting on Mondays when most sites are closed.

Matriz NS do Pilar CHURCH
(Castilho Barbosa s/n, Praça Monsenhor João Castilho Barbosa; admission R$8; 9-10:45am & noon-4:45pm Tue-Sun) Further southwest from Igreja NS do Carmo, Matriz de NS do Pilar boasts 434kg of gold and silver in its ornamentation and is one of Brazil's finest showcases of artwork.

Igreja de São Francisco de Assis CHURCH
(Largo de Coimbra s/n; 8:30-11:50am & 1:30-5pm Tue-Sun) The most important piece of Brazilian colonial art after the *Prophets* in

Ouro Preto

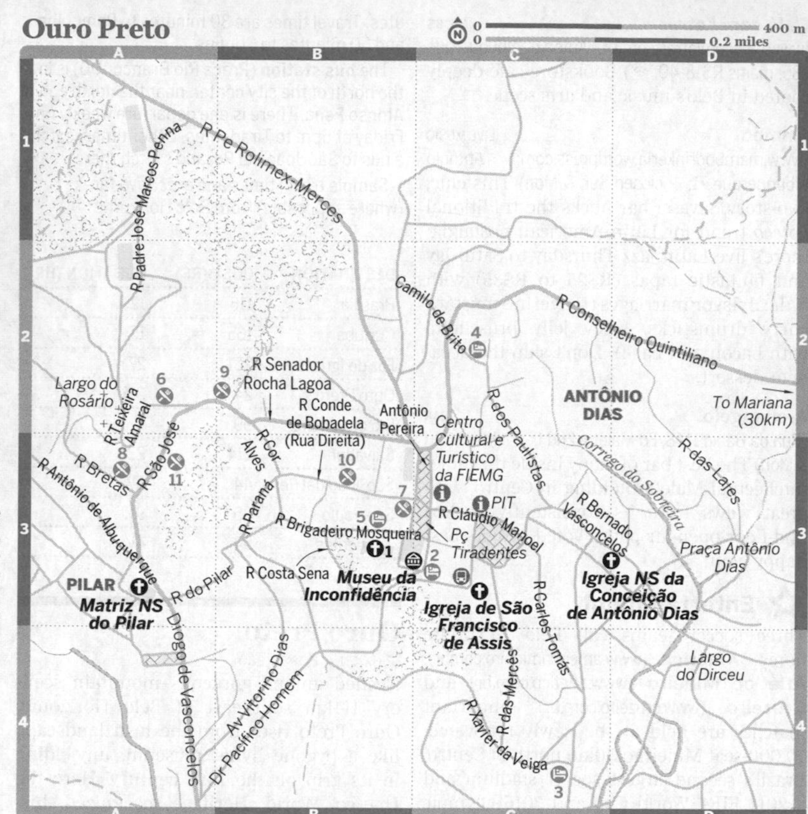

Congonhas. Aleijadinho carved its entire exterior and his long-term partner, Manuel da Costa Ataíde, painted the inside.

Museu da Inconfidência MUSEUM
(Praça Tiradentes; admission R$8; ⏲noon-5:30pm Tue-Sun) Houses documents of the Inconfidência Mineira, a memorial to Tiradentes, torture instruments and important works by Ataíde and Aleijadinho.

Igreja NS da Conceição de Antônio Dias CHURCH
(Rua da Conceição s/n; admission R$8; ⏲8:30am-noon & 1:30-5:30pm Tue-Sat, noon-5pm Sun) Designed by Aleijadinho's father, Manuel Francisco Lisboa, and built between 1727 and 1770, this church is where Aleijadinho is buried, near the altar of Boa Morte. An homage to his life, the attached **Museu Aleijadinho** is full of intricate crucifixes, elaborate oratories (niches with saints' images to ward off evil spirits) and a collection of religious figurines.

Igreja de Santa Efigênia dos Pretos CHURCH
(Santa Efigênia 396; ⏲8:30am-4:30pm Tue-Sun) Built between 1742 and 1749 by, and for, the black slave community. This is Ouro Preto's poorest church in terms of gold and its richest in artwork.

Capela do Padre Faria CHURCH
(Rua da Padre Faria s/n; admission R$3; ⏲8:30am-4:30pm Tue-Sun) One of Ouro Preto's oldest chapels (1701–04) and among the richest in gold and artwork.

Igreja NS do Carmo CHURCH
(Brigadeiro Mosqueira; admission R$2; ⏲8:40-11:15am & 1-4:45pm Mon-Sat, 10am-3pm Sun) Built as a group effort by the most important artists of the area between 1766 and 1772, its facade and two side altars are by Aleijadinho.

Ouro Preto

Museu do Oratório MUSEUM
(www.museudooratorio.org.br; Adro da Igreja do Carmo 28; admission R$2; 9:30am-5:30pm) Home to a fabulous, well-displayed collection of oratories.

Sleeping

TOP CHOICE **Pouso do Chico Rei** INN $$
(3551-1274; www.pousodochicorei.com.br; Brigadeiro Musqueira 90; s/d from R$190/220, without bathroom R$90/160;) Occupies a beautifully preserved 18th-century mansion in the heart of town – each room is unique, and most have antique furniture and fabulous views. Owners speak French and some English. It's not the deal it once was, but it's still our favorite.

Pousada Nello Nuno INN $
(3551-3375; www.pousadanellonuno.com.br; Camilo de Brito 59; s/d/tr R$110/140/175) In a quiet location just northeast of Praça Tiradentes, this family-run pousada has clean and airy *apartamentos* with lots of artwork around a cute flagstoned courtyard. French and English spoken.

Brumas Hostel HOSTEL $
(3551-2944; www.brumashostel.com.br; Antônio Pereira 43; dm/s/d from R$35/90/130;) In upgraded new digs directly behind the Museu da Inconfidência, this hostel mainstay offers well-maintained dorms and private rooms, most of which come with TVs. There is now a small outdoor kitchen and lounge, which catches some breezes off the surrounding hillsides.

Hospedaria Antiga INN $
(3551-2203; www.antiga.com.br; Xavier da Veiga 1; s/d/tr R$80/130/140;) Warped colonial floors, a small garden and a stunning medieval-style breakfast room are among the pluses at this friendly (price-negotiable) 18th-century guesthouse.

Eating

Typical Minas dishes include *tutu,* a pureed black-bean side dish; and *feijão tropeiro,* a mix of brown beans, kale, onions, eggs, manioc flour and sometimes bacon.

Por kilo options include **Adega** (Rua Teixeira Amaral 24; all-you-can-eat pizza R$20, per kg R$30; lunch & dinner), a buffet by day, pizzeria by night (nothing special, but cheap); and **Quinto do Ouro** (Direita 76; per kg R$42; 11am-3pm), which offers exceptional *mineira* cuisine.

TOP CHOICE **Restaurante Cháfariz** BUFFET $$
(São José 167; all-you-can-eat buffet R$31; lunch) Journey through *comida mineira* at this atmospheric all-you-can-eat buffet, the town's favorite. *Cachaça* included!

O Passo ITALIAN $$
(São José 56; pizzas R$24-54; noon-midnight) In a lovely 18th-century building, this restaurant has intimate candlelit rooms and a relaxed terrace overlooking the Casa de Contos. The pizzas are excellent, as are the interesting pasta dishes like the rich spaghetti with *carne de sol* and pumpkin sauce.

Chocolates Ouro Preto CAFE $
(www.chocolatesouropreto.com.br; Getúlio Vargas 72; soups/sandwiches R$8.80/12; lunch & dinner) This quaint cafe and dessert shop serves tortes with chicken or hearts of palm, as well as artisan chocolate treats. There's a new branch at **Praça Tiradentes** (3551-7330; Praça Tiradentes 111; snacks R$4-13; 9am-7pm).

Information

Unfortunately, the town can be a bit seedy at night, particularly around the bus station.

Centro Cultural e Turístico da FIEMG (3559-3637; www5.fiemg.com.br; Praça

WORTH A TRIP

ALEIJADINHO'S PROPHETS OF CONGONHAS

The otherwise unremarkable small town of Congonhas, 72km south of Belo Horizonte, would attract few visitors if not for the **Basílica do Bom Jesus de Matosinhos** (Praça da Basílica; ⌚8am-6pm Tue-Sun) and, more importantly, its magnificently carved sculptures by the Brazilian Michelangelo, Aleijadinho. Son of a Portuguese architect and an African slave, Aleijadinho lost the use of his hands and legs at the age of 30 but, with a hammer and chisel strapped to his arms, advanced art in Brazil from the excesses of baroque to a finer, more graceful rococo.

His masterworks and one of Brazil's finest Unesco offerings, the 12 Old Testament Prophets were sculpted from soapstone between 1800 and 1805. Aleijadinho was also responsible for the six chapels here and their wooden statues representing the Passion of Christ, which together are just as impressive as the prophets.

Frequent daily buses run from Belo Horizonte to Congonhas (R$21.20, 1½ hours) as well as Congonhas to São João del Rei (R$24.10, two hours). From Ouro Preto you must first catch a bus to Ouro Branco (R$9.55, 50 minutes), and then connect on to Congonhas (R$5.20, 30 minutes) on frequently departing daily buses. Local Profetta buses run between Congonhas bus station and the Basílica (R$2.10, 15 minutes), 1.5km away.

Tiradentes 4; ⌚9am-7pm) Offers information in English, Spanish and French, including a leaflet listing museum and church hours and a rough town map. English guided tours start at R$135 for four hours.

HSBC (São José 201) ATM.

PIT (☎3559-3287; www.ouropreto.org.br; Cláudio Manoel 61; ⌚8am-6pm Mon-Sat) Office of the Secretary of Tourism.

Getting There & Away

The bus station is 500m northwest of Praça Tiradentes (catch a 'Rodoviária' bus to/from a small stop next to Igreja São Francisco de Assis for R$1.90). Numerous daily buses run between Belo Horizonte and Ouro Preto (R$23.35, two hours). From Ouro Preto there are two daily buses to Rio (from R$73, seven hours), two daily buses to São Paulo (R$113.50, 11 hours) and one direct bus to Brasilia (7:30pm, R$128, 11½ hours).

Tiradentes

☎0XX32 / POP 6900

Sleepy Tiradentes is full of camera-ready charm, from its colorful, cobbled streets to its mountain vistas, with a wandering river trickling through town. Gastronomy and shopping rule here – Tiradentes is home to the highest concentration per capita of starred restaurants in the country and is famous throughout Brazil for its artisan furniture and high-quality homewares, arts and crafts. But there is plenty of wonderful countryside hiking on offer to turn back the caloric onslaught.

For tourist info, head to **CAT** (☎3355-1212; www.tiradentes.mg.gov.br; Resende Costa 71; ⌚9am-6pm Sun-Thu, to 8pm Fri & Sat) on the main square.

Sights

Igreja Matriz de Santo Antônio CHURCH
(Padre Toledo s/n; admission R$5; ⌚9am-5pm) The town's colonial buildings run up a hillside, where they culminate in this beautiful 1710 church with a facade by Aleijadinho and an all-gold interior rich in Old Testament symbolism.

Igreja Nossa Senhora Rosário dos Pretos CHURCH
(Direita s/n; admission R$2; ⌚11am-5pm Tue-Sun) Built by slaves, the 1708 church is Tiradentes' oldest; it contains several images of black saints.

Museu Liturgia MUSEUM
(www.museudaliturgia.com.br; Jogo de Bola 15; adult/child R$10/5; ⌚10am-5pm Tue-Sun) This museum houses a new and surprisingly modern collection of over 420 religious items spanning three centuries.

Museu do Padre Toledo MUSEUM
(Padre Toledo 190; admission R$10; ⌚10am-5pm Tue-Sun) The former mansion of a hero of the Inconfidência, but was undergoing extensive restorations at the time of writing.

Sleeping & Eating

Pousada da Bia GUESTHOUSE $
(☎3355-1173; www.pousadadabia.com.br; Ozanan 330; s/d midweek R$110/140, weekend R$110/160;) A longtime favorite, with rooms set around a grassy courtyard and swimming pool. Breakfast is divine.

Pousada Tiradentes INN $$
(☎3355-1232; www.pousadatiradentesmg.com.br; São Francisco de Paula 41; d/tr R$180/220;) Next to the bus station, offering well-maintained rooms decked out in modish white with blue trim.

Pousada da Sirlei INN $$
(☎3355-1440; www.pousadadasirlei.com.br; Antonio de Carvalho 113; s/d R$90/180;) Five minutes' walk from the cobblestones and bus station but kitty-corner to a pleasant plaza, this quaint inn is long on mismatched flooring and doting grandmotherly charm.

CasAzul MEXICAN, BRAZILIAN $$
(Rua da Cadeira s/n; mains R$21.80-45; dinner Wed, lunch & dinner Thu-Sat, lunch Sun) For a change of pace, this adorable Latin bistro does Brazilianized Mexican food which is much better than it sounds.

Divino Sabor SELF-SERVE $
(Gabriel Passos 300; per kg R$32.90; lunch Tue-Sun) A cozy *por kilo* on the main strip through the old town. Very popular.

Bar do Celso BRAZILIAN $$
(Largo das Forras 80A; mains R$18-28; 11:30am-9pm Wed-Mon) On Largo das Forras, this locally run *mineiro* restaurant offers hearty local dishes at reasonable prices.

Getting There & Around

The best approach to Tiradentes is the wonderful train trip from São João del Rei. The **Maria Fumaça** (☎3371-8485; São João station; 1-way/round-trip R$25/40) is pulled by 19th-century steam locomotives and chugs along a picturesque 13km track from São João. It departs on Friday and Saturday from São João at 10am and 3pm (returning at 1pm and 5pm) and Sunday at 10am and 1pm (returning at 11am and 2pm). Numerous buses connect Tiradentes with São João daily (R$2.55, 30 minutes).

THE SOUTH

Spectacular white-sand beaches, pristine subtropical islands and the thunderous roar of Iguaçu Falls are a few of the attractions of Brazil's affluent South. While often given short shrift by first-time visitors, the states of Paraná, Santa Catarina and Rio Grande do Sul offer a radically different version of what it means to be Brazilian. Here *gaúchos* (cowboys) still cling to the cowboy lifestyle on the wide plains bordering Argentina and Uruguay, while old-world architecture, European-style beer, blond hair and blue eyes reveal the influence of millions of German, Italian, Swiss and Eastern European immigrants.

Getting There & Away

The major air gateways in the region are Curitiba, Florianópolis, Porto Alegre and Foz do Iguaçu, which borders both Argentina and Paraguay. All of these cities have good bus connections to São Paulo.

DON'T MISS

ESTRELLAS DO SABOR

It would be a crying shame to come to Tiradentes and not shell out for one of its five-starred culinary offerings. Pinch *centavos* elsewhere, go big here. Three of the most affordable include: **Pau de Angu** (Estrada para Bichinho Km 3; mains for 2/4 people from R$68.90/115.70), which features select *mineira* specialties (pork, chicken or beef), served with all the traditional fixings on a farm 3km out of town; **Estralgem da Sabor** (☎3355-1144; Ministro Gabriel Passos 280; mains per person R$26-45; noon-4pm & 7-9:30pm Mon-Fri, 11am-10pm Sat, to 4pm Sun), which offers simple but excellently prepared *mineira* classics; and **Tragaluz** (☎3355-1424; www.tragaluztiredentes.com; Direita 52; mains R$40-65; 7pm-late Wed-Mon), which entices diners with a 40-page, pocket-sized contemporary menu that's laid out comic-book-style and features all sorts of cute tales about the history of the town and current staff. Don't miss dessert: dried guava fruit rolled in cashew nuts and fried, served over a bed of Brazilian cream cheese with guava ice cream. *Delícia!*

The South

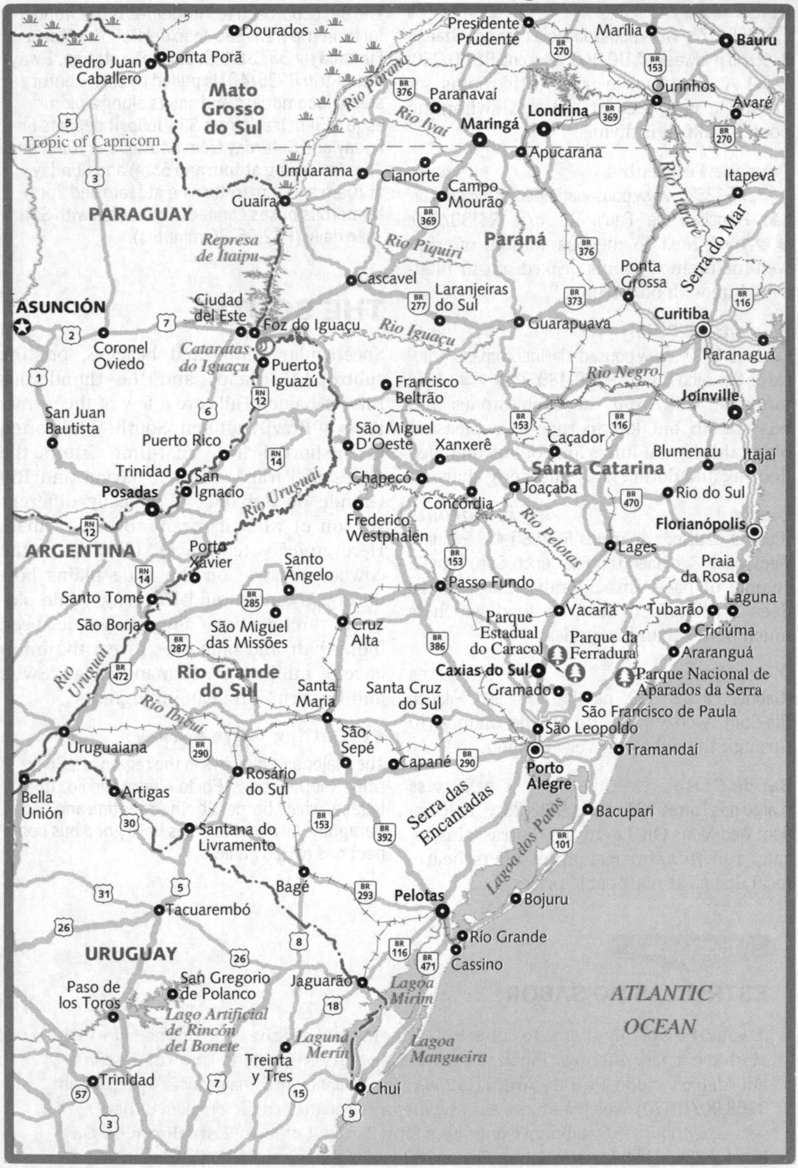

Getting Around

Short flights and longer bus journeys connect the four major cities of the South. If you're heading to Ilha do Mel, don't miss the scenic train ride from Curitiba through the Serra do Mar to Paranaguá, where you can hop a ferry to the island.

Curitiba

0XX41 / POP 1.7 MILLION

Known as Brazil's eco-evolved capital and famous for its efficient urban planning, Curitiba is one of Brazil's metropolitan success stories, with pleasant parks, well-preserved historic buildings, little traffic congestion and a large university population. It makes for a good pitstop.

Sights & Activities

The cobbled historic quarter around **Largo da Ordem** has beautifully restored buildings, art galleries, bars and restaurants, with live music after dark. Nearby, the pretty pedestrianized **Rua das Flores** (Brazil's first pedestrianized street, a section of 15 de Novembro) is lined with shops, restaurants and colorful flowers. For more greenery, visit the **Passeio Público** (Presidente Carlos Cavalcanti; ⌚6am-8pm Tue-Sun), a park with shady walks and a lake. Curitiba's attractions outside the center – including botanical gardens and the excellent Oscar Niemeyer art museum – are accessible via the **Linha Turismo Bus**.

Sleeping

Motter Home HOSTEL **$**
(☎3209-5649; www.motterhome.com.br; Desembargador Motta 3574; dm R$38-40, r without bathroom R$100, r/q R$120/200; @📶) In leafy Mercês (15 minutes' walk from Largo da Orderm) this newcomer makes artistic use of a striking canary-yellow turret-style mansion from the '50s. Gorgeous art, retro-sophisticated common areas and funky door handles reek of style, but petty charges for towels (even in expensive private rooms) and lack of single accommodation sours much of the fun.

Curitiba Casa HOSTEL **$**
(☎3044-7313; www.curitibacasahostel.com; Brasílio Itiberê 73; dm R$38-44, r R$110; @📶) Despite its odd location 15 minutes east of the *rodoferroviária* (bus and train station), this new hostel apparently has more fans than *futebol*. Clean, colorful and classy.

Roma Hostel HOSTEL **$**
(☎3224-2117; www.hostelroma.com.br; Barão do Rio Branco 805; dm/s/d R$47/70/120, s without bathroom R$47; @📶) This conveniently located HI-affiliated hostel is freshly made over, with chic, hardwood-floored privates and spacious 12-bed (men) and six-bed (women) dorms.

Palace Hotel HOTEL **$**
(☎3222-2554; www.palacehotelpr.com.br; Barão do Rio Branco 62; s/d R$67/95; 📶) Funky aged relic with acceptable rooms.

Eating & Drinking

Mercado Municipal, opposite the bus station, includes Brazil's first organic food court; Rua 24 Horas, near Praça General Osório, is a pleasant street-turned-enclosed-food-court (*not* open 24 hours!). Local chain Spich does 10-dish buffets for R$4.95.

TOP CHOICE **Madero** BURGERS **$$**
(www.restaurantemadero.com.br; Kellers 63; burger & fries R$16.80-29.90; ⌚11:45am-2:30pm & 6:15-11:30pm Mon-Thu, 6:15pm-midnight Fri, 11:45am-midnight Sat, to 11:30pm Sun; 📶) Chef of the Year, Restaurant of the Year... No, it's not a three-star Michelin eatery, it's a gorgeous, award-winning burger joint, even cheaper during the Monday to Thursday happy hour from 6:15 to 7:45pm.

Yü ASIAN **$$**
(www.yurestaurante.com.br; Praça Osório 485; per kg R$58.90; ⌚11:30am-3pm Mon-Fri, noon-3:30pm Sat-Sun) Reflecting Curitiba's significant Asian immigration, this pricier *por kilo* does high-quality Korean, Chinese and Japanese dishes, including sushi, sashimi and fantastic *lula apimentada* (spicy squid salad).

🍃 **Bouquet Garni** BUFFET **$**
(www.restaurantebouquetgarni.com; Carvalho 271; buffet weekday/weekend R$19/25; ⌚11am-3pm; 📶🖉) Most of the ingredients at this organic restaurant come from the owners' farm.

Entertainment

Curitiba's **Arena da Baixada** (☎2105-5630; Buenos Aires 1260; tours R$7; ⌚Tours 10am, 11am, noon, 2pm, 3pm and 4pm) is undergoing a R$138-million renovation in preparation for the 2014 FIFA World Cup. There are six tours daily, open to the public. It is the home stadium of **Atlético Paranaense** (www.atleticoparanaense.com).

Information

HSBC (15 de Novembro) One of many pedestrian-zone ATMs.

Post Office (15 de Novembro 700) Postal services.

PIT (☎3352-8000; www.turismo.curitiba.pr.gov.br) Airport (Arrivals Hall; ⌚7am-11pm); Praça Garibaldi (Praça Garibaldi 7; ⌚9am-6pm Mon-Sat, 9am-4pm Sun); train station (Rodoferroviária; ⌚8am-6pm) Curitiba's helpful tourist kiosks are full of colorful brochures and limited English. There's also a branch on Rua 24 Horas.

Getting There & Away

Air

There are direct flights from Afonso Pena International Airport (CWB), 18km southeast of Centro, to cities throughout Brazil.

Bus

Curitiba's *rodoferroviária* sits 2km southeast of downtown and was getting an R$34 million World Cup–ready face-lift at the time of writing.

Sample travel times and *executivo* fares:

DESTINATION	COST (R$)	DURATION (HR)
Asunción (Paraguay)	R$115	14
Buenos Aires (Argentina)	R$321	34
Florianópolis	R$65	4
Foz do Iguaçu	R$116	10
Paranaguá	R$22	1½
Porto Alegre	R$112	12
Rio de Janeiro	R$150	13
Santiago (Chile)	R$383	54
São Paulo	R$94	6

Train

The **Serra Verde Express** (☎3888-3488; www.serraverdeexpress.com.br; Estação Ferroviária) railway from Curitiba to Paranaguá is the most exciting in Brazil, with sublime panoramas.

The train leaves Curitiba at 8:15am daily, descending 900m through the lush Serra do Mar to the historic town of Morretes, arriving at 11:15am and returning at 3pm Monday to Saturday, 4pm on Sunday. For Paranaguá, the train departs on weekends only at 7:30am and returns at 2pm. One-way economy/tourist-class tickets to either Morretes or Paranaguá cost R$57/74. Sit on the left side for the best views.

Getting Around

An Aeroporto–Centro bus leaves every 30 minutes (R$2.60, 30 minutes) from 7 de Setembro. The classier **Aeroporto Executivo** (☎3381-1326; www.aeroportoexecutivo.com.br; R$10) goes direct every 15 to 20 minutes from 9am to 5:30pm to select Centro stops (bus station, Teatro Guaíra and Receita Federal are most convenient for tourists).

The double-decker **Linha Turismo** (www.turismo.curitiba.pr.gov.br; R$27; ⏲half-hourly from 9am to 5:50pm Tuesday to Sunday Mar-Oct, every 15 mins from 8:45am-6pm Nov-Carnival) bus is a great way to see the sights outside Curitiba's downtown. It leaves Praça Tiradentes half-hourly from 8am to 6pm Tuesday to Sunday. You can get off at any four of the 23 attractions and hop on the next bus.

Paranaguá

Paranaguá is both the terminus of the scenic train ride from Curitiba and the embarkation point for ferries to idyllic Ilha do Mel. Colorful but now faded buildings along the colonial waterfront create a feeling of languid tropical decadence.

Hostel Continente (☎3423-3224; www.hostelcontinente.com.br; Carneiro 300; dm R$38, s with/without air-con R$70/60, d with/without air-con R$95/80; ❄@🛜) has clean if cramped dorms and doubles in an enviable location across from the ferry dock.

Frequent buses to Curitiba (R$22, 1½ hours) and Morretes (R$4.20, 50 minutes) leave from the terminal just inland from the waterfront. The Sunday train service to/from Curitiba can differ from other days, so be sure to double-check departure times.

Ilha do Mel

☎0XX41 / POP 1200

Ilha do Mel (Honey Island) is Paraná state's most enchanting getaway. This oddly shaped island at the mouth of the Baía da Paranaguá offers mostly wild beaches, good surfing waves and scenic coastal walks. There are no cars, so traffic jams throughout the island's scenic sandy lanes consist of surfboard-toting Brazilians on bicycles and bedazzled foreigners in their new Havaianas.

Tourist information booths sit at arrival docks in both **Nova Brasília** (☎3254-1516; www.turismo.pr.gov.br; Arrival Dock, Nova Brasília; ⏲9am-7pm) and **Encantadas** (Encantadas; ⏲8am-6pm).

Sights & Activities

Ilha do Mel consists of two parts joined by the beach at Nova Brasília. The larger, northern part is mostly an ecological station, little visited except for Praia da Fortaleza, where a well-preserved 18th-century **fort** still stands.

For fine views, visit **Farol das Conchas** (Conchas Lighthouse), east of Nova Brasília. The best **beaches** are east-facing Praia Grande, Praia do Miguel and Praia de Fora. It's a 1½-hour walk along the coast from Nova Brasília to Encantadas or an R$8 boat ride.

Sleeping & Eating

Rooms book up fast in peak season, but you can always pitch a tent or sling a hammock in Nova Brasília (R$20 per person).

The biggest concentrations of *pousadas* are along the track heading east from Nova Brasília to Praia do Farol (better for couples, more charming) and at smaller Encantadas (better for singles, more social), near the island's southwest corner.

O Recanto do Francês II INN $$
(3426-9105; www.recantodofrances.com.br; s/d R$140/150;) With an adorable garden setting, friendly French owners (and their crepes) and Whisky, a blind Yorkshire terrier with deft soccer skills, this *pousada*, just steps from Mar do Fora beach, wins the charm-for-value race.

Marimar Farol HOSTEL $$
(3426-8032; www.hostelmarimar.com.br; dm R$60, r with fan/air-con R$175/210;) The first hostel you'll come to from the Nova Brasília dock, this places offers pleasant, rustic clapboard private rooms and four-bed dorms, but the real coup is the expansive deck overlooking a beautiful thatch of vegetation and the sea on the horizon.

Pousadinha Ilha do Mel INN $$
(3426-8026; www.pousadinha.com.br; r R$90-260, without bathroom R$80-120;) An island favorite offering something for all budgets, from small, shared-bathroom cells to new hardwood-chic rooms in a neighboring annex.

Marimar Encantadas HOSTEL $$
(3426-9052; www.hostelmarimar.com.br; Encantadas; dm/s/d/tr R$60/150/175/245;) This popular hostel facing Encantadas beach offers comfy common areas, a communal kitchen and a beachfront deck.

Hostel Encantadas Ecologic HOSTEL $
(9142-8087; hostel_ecologic@hotmail.com; Encantadas; dm R$30, camping with tent R$50, d with/without bathroom R$90/70;) The island cheapie is a colorful, sustainable choice.

TOP CHOICE **Mar e Sol** BRAZILIAN, SEAFOOD $
(Praça Felipe Valentim; meals R$14-22; 11am-10pm) En route to the lighthouse, Mar e Sol serves delicious fish, shrimp or crab *moquecas*, seafood risottos and cheaper daily specials. Junior, the local pet parrot, offers recommendations.

Ilha do Mel Cafe CAFE $
(Praça Felipe Valentim; mains R$7-20; 9am-10pm;) This charming blue house between Nova Brasília and Farol das Conchas offers upscale crepes courtesy of a freewheelin' Portuguese chef who learned from his French ex-wife. Has the island's best espresso as well.

ILHA DO CARTÃO

Bring plenty of cash and plastic to Ilha do Mel – there are no banks or cash machines on the island.

Praça de Alimentação SEAFOOD $
(Mar da Fora; mains R$15-40; 11am-6pm) This beachside restaurant complex south of Encantadas serves seafood, along with live music on Saturday nights.

Grajagan Surf Resort SEAFOOD $$
(www.grajagan.com.br; Praia Grande; mains for 2 R$68-98, pizzas R$38-44;) On Praia Grande, this whimsical surfer's bar and upscale restaurant is awash in intricately detailed carved wood and mosaics. Go for a tipple, whole-wheat pizzas or more sophisticated mains.

Getting There & Away

Abaline (Pontal do Sul 3455-2616; www.abaline.com.br; Paranaguá Ferry Dock) runs boats (R$32 return) at 9:30am and 3:30pm (more frequently in summer) from the jetty opposite Paranaguá's tourist office, stopping first in Nova Brasília (1½ hours), and afterwards in Encantadas (two hours). Back to the mainland, boats depart for Paranaguá at 8am and 5pm from Nova Brasília, a half hour earlier from Encantadas.

Alternatively, **Graciosa** (3213-5351; www.viacaograciosa.com.br) runs five daily buses from Curitiba to Pontal do Sul (R$28, 2½ hours), on the mainland opposite Encantadas, where you can embark for the 30-minute crossing to Nova Brasília or Encantadas (R$27 return). In high season boats leave every half hour from 8am to 8pm in both directions.

Ilha de Santa Catarina

0XX48

For years, gorgeous Ilha de Santa Catarina has been luring surfers and sun worshippers from all over Brazil, Argentina and Uruguay. Recently, visitors from other countries have begun to catch on. The island's varied landscape includes tranquil pine forests, dunes large enough to surf down and mountains covered by Mata Atlântica. There are two pretty lagoons: tranquil Lagoa do Peri and the more urbanized Lagoa da Conceição.

Ilha de Santa Catarina

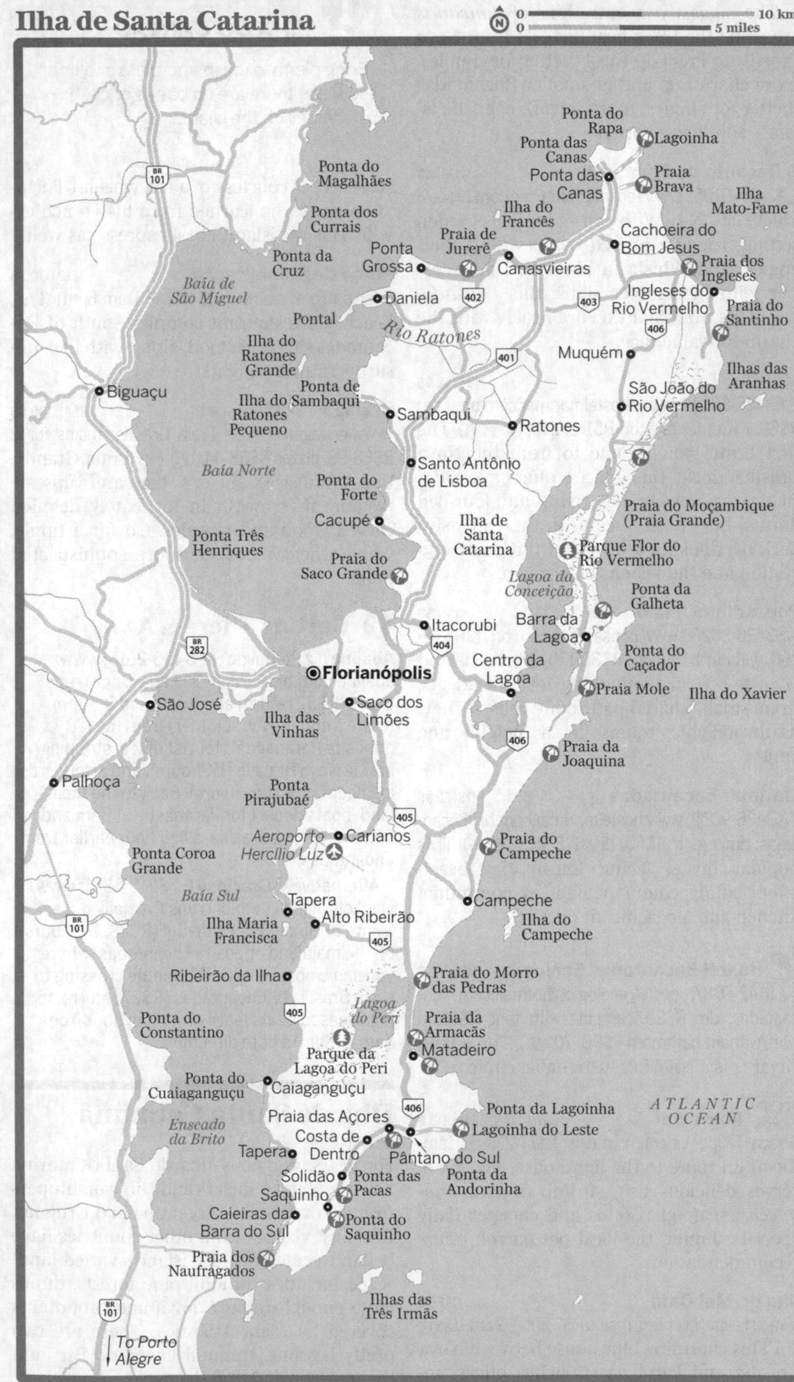

BRAZIL ILHA DE SANTA CATARINA

Beaches remain the island's main attraction, however, from long sweeps of unbroken sand to secluded little coves tucked into the wild, verdant shoreline.

Activities

Surfing, kitesurfing and diving outfits line the beach at Barra da Lagoa, on the island's eastern shore. A few kilometers south, try your hand at sandboarding (R$40 per day) on the dunes at Praia da Joaquina or stand-up paddling at Lagoa da Conceição (R$50 per lesson).

The island's southern tip offers excellent hiking, including the one-hour trek through lush forest from Pântano do Sul to pristine Lagoinha do Leste beach.

For excursions on Lagoa da Conceição, catch a water taxi (R$10 return) beside the bridge in Centro da Lagoa town.

Sleeping & Eating

Following are our favorites around the rowdy and social Lagoa da Conceição and the more tranquil south island, but the island has many more nooks and crannies of surf and sand spread throughout its 42 beaches. Prices drop between 15% and 40% outside high season.

Tucano House HOSTEL $$
(3207-8287; www.tucanohouse.com; Rua das Araras 229; dm R$50, r with/without bathroom R$180/160;) Brother-sister team Lila and Caio are your consummate hosts at this fabulous, eco-forward hostel in the heart of the Lagoa action. Their childhood home now features solar-heated showers and a recycled rainwater cistern, while amenities include free use of bikes and surfboards, island adventures in their decked-out VW van and frequent party barbeques.

TOP CHOICE **Pousada Sítio dos Tucanos** INN $$
(3237-5084; www.pousadasitiodostucanos.com; Ferreira 2776; d from R$230;) Tucked away high up in isolated and peaceful farm country, this German-run *pousada* boasts rustic but elegant rooms, most with balconies; common areas are flooded with light from tall French doors. If coming by bus 563, call ahead for pickup at the bus stop 800m away.

Backpackers Share House HOSTEL $
(3232-7606; www.backpackersfloripa.com; Servidão da Prainha 29; dm/d/tr R$50/140/195;) Across the pedestrian bridge from Barra da Lagoa beach in carless Prianha, this fortress with the souped-up motorcycle on the roof attracts an international party crowd with amenities including free use of surfboards and other beach toys, excursions and evening BBQs.

> **DON'T MISS**
>
> **FREE WHALIN'**
>
> From to June to November, southern right whales *(Baleia Francas)* depart chilly Antarctic waters for warmer seas off the Santa Catarina coast, where they give birth and nurse their young. The jaw-dropping show can be seen for free from a viewpoint on the island's south end called Morro das Pedras between Campeche and Armação beaches. These majestic sea beasts hang out as close as 100m from shore – an astonishing sight.

Backpackers Sunset HOSTEL $
(3232-0141; www.sunsetbackpackers.com; Rodovia Menezes 631; dm from R$45, d without bathroom R$140;) This resort-like hostel is perched on a rocky midisland hilltop above Lagoa. Private rooms are cramped but the dorms are roomy and view-licious.

Albergue do Pirata HOSTEL $
(3389-2727; www.alberguedopirata.com.br; Ferreira s/n; camping per person R$20, dm R$35, r without bathroom R$50;) A spartan hostel with rooms downstairs plus a couple of doubles upstairs, all 400m from Costa de Dentro beach, one of the south's prettiest.

Pousada do Pescador BUNGALOW $$
(3237-7122; www.pousadadopescador.com.br; Vidal 257; 1-/2-/4-/6-person chalet R$150/160/220/280;) In the old fishing village of Pântano do Sul, this family-run *pousada* has nice chalets with kitchens, patios and outdoor grills in a jungly bamboo garden setting one block from the beach.

TOP CHOICE **Bar do Arante** SEAFOOD $$
(www.bardoarante.com.br; mains for 2 R$58-110) A Pântano do Sul institution, Arante serves borderline socially irresponsible portions and is draped floor to ceiling with thousands of notes penned by former patrons. The island's must.

EIN BIER, POR FAVOR! (VALE EUROPEU BEER DETOUR)

Brazil's mainstream brews – Skol, Brahma and Antarctica – are fine for staving off the tropical heat, but let's face it: taste is not their strong suit. Luckily, the German immigrants of Blumenau (Santa Catarina state) are here to help. There is a true beer culture here dating back to the mid-1800s, with *real* beer like pale ale, bock, wheat and pilsen.

Cervejaria Bierland (3323-6588; www.bierland.com.br; Gustavo Zimmermann 5361, Blumenau; 4:30pm-midnight Tue-Fri, 10am-midnight Sat), **Cervejaria Das Bier** (3397-8600; www.dasbier.com.br; Bonifácio Haendchen 5311, Gaspar; 5pm-midnight Wed-Fri, 3pm-midnight Sat, 11am-7pm Sun), **Cervejaria Eisenbahn** (3488-7307; www.eisenbahn.com.br; Bahia 5181, Blumenau; 4pm-midnight Mon-Sat, 10am-1am Sat) and **Cervejaria Schornstein** (www.schornstein.com.br; Hermann Weege 60, Pomerode; 6-11pm Wed-Sun) breweries are the region's best, and all have fantastic tasting rooms in and around Blumenau. With a car and a designated driver, you can visit them all in a day. Even better, raise a stein with the locals at Blumenau's annual **Oktoberfest** (www.oktoberfestblumenau.com.br), Brazil's second biggest party after Carnaval.

Frequent buses connect Blumenau with Curitiba (R$31, four hours) and Florianópolis (R$29, three hours).

Café Cultura CAFE $$
(www.cafeculturafloripa.com.br; Severino de Oliveira 669; items R$6.50-36.90; 9am-12:30am;) Brunch all day (R$9.50 to R$14.50), waffles, salads, paninis – there is something for everyone at Floripa's best cafe, brought to you in Centro da Lagoa town by a Californian ex-Starbucks barista and his Brazilian coffee-heiress wife.

Florianópolis

0XX48 / POP 421,000

Ilha de Santa Catarina's metropolitan hub, beautifully sited Florianópolis sits on the island's western edge, surrounded by bay and mountain vistas. Although the town has pretty features that invite exploration, many travelers simply pass through en route to the outlying beaches.

Sleeping & Eating

The liveliest drinking spots are along the bay-facing Beira-Mar Norte.

TOP CHOICE **Cecomtur Executive** HOTEL $$
(2107-8800; www.cecomturhotel.com.br; Arcipreste Paiva 107; s/d R$164/194;) Centrally located, with abundant perks for weary travelers, business-oriented Cecomtur offers professional service and amenities for prices that easily drop 30% to 40% off posted rack rates.

Floripa Hostel – Centro HOSTEL $
(3225-3781; www.floripahostel.com.br; Duarte Schutel 227; dm/d R$50/115;) This basic HI hostel is a 10-minute walk from the bus station.

O Padeira de Sevilha BAKERY $
(3025-3402; www.opadeirodesevilha.com.br; Esteves Júnior 2144; items R$2.50-10; 6:50am-8:30pm Mon-Fri, 7am-2pm Sat;) Considered one of the top 30 bakeries in Brazil, this social hot spot features an 11m-long communal table flanked by a self-serve cornucopia of fresh-baked artisanal breads and sweets selected from some 200 recipes.

Central BUFFET $
(Vidal Ramos 174; per kg weekday/weekend R$39.90/45.90; 11am-3pm Mon-Fri;) This outstanding, award-winning *por kilo* buffet concentrates on a more subtle selection of daily dishes, each and all focused on high-quality, home-cooked goodness. Lines out the door not uncommon.

Information

CAT (3228-1095; www.visiteflori pa.com.br; Rodoviária; 8am-5:30pm Mon-Fri, 9am-6pm Sat-Sun) Provides city and island information.

HSBC (Schmidt 376) ATM.

Getting There & Away

Daily flights from Florianópolis-Hercílio Luz International Airport (FLN), 12km south of Florianópolis, serve Buenos Aires, Brasília, Campinas, Porto Alegre, Rio de Janeiro and São Paulo, among others. The bus station lies a few blocks west of the Praça XV de Novembro.

Sample travel times and *executivo* fares (where applicable):

DESTINATION	COST (R$)	DURATION (HR)
Asunción	167	20
Buenos Aires	283	25
Curitiba	65	5
Foz do Iguaçu	138	14
Montevideo	209	18, Sat & Tue only
Porto Alegre	82	6
Rio de Janeiro	178	17
Santiago	371	45, Tue only
São Paulo	123	12

Getting Around

Local buses leave from the TICEN terminal, one block east of Florianópolis' long-distance bus station.

Connections to the island's beaches are made via three outlying terminals: TIRIO (Rio Tavares Terminal), TILAG (Lagoa Terminal) and TICAN (Canasvieiras Terminal).

For southern beaches, including Armação, Pântano do Sul and Costa de Dentro, catch bus 410 'Rio Tavares' then transfer at TIRIO to bus 563.

For eastern beaches, catch bus 330 'Lagoa da Conceição', then transfer at TILAG for a second bus to your final destination, for example bus 360 to Barra da Lagoa.

For Canasvieiras and northern beaches, catch bus 210 from TICEN to TICAN.

To reach the airport, bus 183 'Corredor Sudoeste' (35 minutes) and 186 'Corredor Sudoeste Semi-Direto' (25 minutes) leave from TICEN terminal frequently between 5:20am and 12:30am. Taxis cost R$28 to R$32.

A single fare of R$2.90 (paid at the TICEN ticket booth) covers your initial ride plus one transfer. All of the above-mentioned buses leave from Platform B.

Porto Alegre

0XX51 / POP 1.4 MILLION

Porto Alegre is a good introduction to progressive Rio Grande do Sul. Built on the banks of the Rio Guaíba, this lively, modern port has a well-preserved neoclassical downtown, with handsome plazas, good museums and a vibrant arts and music scene.

Sights & Activities

Porto Alegre's **Linha Turismo** (www.portoalegre.travel; Travessa do Carmo 84; R$15; 9am-5:30pm Tue-Sun) tour is a convenient way to take in the sights of the historic center.

FREE **Museu de Arte do Rio Grande do Sul** MUSEUM
(www.margs.rs.gov.br; Praça da Alfândega; 10am-7pm Tue-Sun) Has a good collection of *gaúcho* art and a kitschy art deco cafe.

FREE **Museu Histórico Júlo de Castilhos** MUSEUM
(www.museujuliodecastilhos.blogspot.com; Duque de Caxias 1205; 10am-5pm Tue-Sat) This museum houses objects related to Rio Grande do Sul's history.

Sleeping

Most travelers now stay in Cidade Baixa, the first neighborhood southeast of the historic

WORTH A TRIP

JESUIT MISSIONS

In the early 17th century Jesuit missionaries established a series of Indian missions in a region straddling northeast Argentina, southeast Paraguay and neighboring parts of Brazil. Between 1631 and 1638, after devastating attacks by Paulista slaving expeditions and hostile indigenous people, activity was concentrated in 30 more easily defensible missions. These places became centers of culture as well as religion – in effect a nation within the colonies, considered by some scholars an island of utopian progress and socialism, which at its height in the 1720s had over 150,000 Guaran indigenous inhabitants.

Seven of the now-ruined missions lie in the northwest of Brazil's Rio Grande do Sul state, eight are in Paraguay and 15 in Argentina.

The town of **Santo Ângelo** is the main jumping-off point for the Brazilian missions; the most interesting and intact site is **São Miguel das Missões** (3381-1294; www.saomiguel.rs.gov.br; admission R$5; evening sound-&-light show R$5; 9am-noon & 2-6pm), 53km southwest of Santo Ângelo. Several buses daily run from Porto Alegre to Sânto Angelo (R$117.45, eight hours), where you can make onward connections to São Miguel das Missões (R$9.85, one hour, 11 daily).

Porto Alegre

Porto Alegre

Top Sights

Museu de Arte do Rio Grande do Sul A3

Sights

1 Museu Histórico Júlo de Castilhos B4

Sleeping

2 Hotel Ritz C4
3 Lido Hotel B3

Eating

4 Atelier das Massas C3
5 Mercado Público B2
6 Sabor Natural A3

Drinking

7 Chalé da Praça XV B2

center. In addition to being Porto Alegre's nightlife enclave, a healthy hostel scene has popped up.

TOP CHOICE **Porto Alegre Eco Hostel** HOSTEL $
(☎3019-2449; www.portoalegreecohostel.com.br; Luiz Afonso 276; dm from R$37, d from R$120, s/d without bathroom R$70/100; @📶🏊) Down a quiet residential street in the heart of Cidade Baixa, this excellent hostel, chock-full of demolition wood furniture and eco-awareness, offers a lovely backyard garden and fluent English infrastructure in a pristine '30s-era home.

Rock'n'Hostel HOSTEL $
(☎3557-3523; www.rocknhostel.com; Alberto Bins 954; dm R$24-30; @📶) Friendly, all-dorm hostel three blocks from the bus station and a five-minute walk to Mercado Público. Big, clean bathrooms highlight the family atmosphere inside a made-over apartment.

Lido Hotel HOTEL $
(☎3228-9111; www.lidohotel.com.br; Neves 150; r weekday/weekend R$146/104; ❄📶) A slick lobby gives way to basic but spacious rooms at this comfortable Centro hotel. Breakfast is R$10 extra.

Hotel Ritz GUESTHOUSE $
(☎3225-0693; www.hotelritz-portoalegre.com; André da Rocha 225; s/d/tr R$50/80/150; 📶) Ritz's tiny, clean rooms surround a sweet courtyard – a good, cheap long-stay option. No breakfast.

Eating & Drinking

TOP CHOICE **Atelier das Massas** ITALIAN $$
(Riachuelo 1482; mains R$22-42; ⏰11am-2pm & 7-11:30pm Mon-Fri, 11am-3pm & 7-11:30pm Sat; 📶) Crammed as much with atmosphere as with artisanal pastas, this dive-like pasta bar should be on your immediate to-do list.

Mercado Público MARKET $$
(www2.portoalegre.rs.gov.br/mercadopublico; ⏰7:30am-7:30pm Mon-Fri, to 6:30pm Sat) The 1869 food-focused Mercado Público (Public Market) and the adjacent Praça 15 de Novembro constitute the city's heart. Shops in the market sell the gaúchos' characteristic *cuia* (gourd) and *bomba* (silver straw), used in drinking maté tea. Recommended options include Banco 40, home of the incomparable *bomba royal* (a showy ice cream and fruit salad concoction; R$8.90); Gambrinus, an old-world Portuguese seafood restaurant (mains from R$19); and Café Do Mercado, one of the city's best cafes.

Boteco Natalicio BAR $$
(www.botaconatalicio.com.br; Genuíno 217; mains R$19-30; ⏰from 5pm Mon-Fri, from noon Sat; 📶) The walls of this lively, bilevel *boteco* straddling Centro and Cidade Baixa is covered in 200 Brazilian musings and packs a wild punch of *chopp*-starved locals, here to preempt the beer with regional delicacies like honey-smoked pork ribs and crunchy shrimp sandwiches with *catupiry* cheese.

Sabor Natural BUFFET $
(Campos 890; buffet R$15; ⏰11am-3pm Mon-Fri; 🥬) Absolutely excellent, vegetarian-friendly buffet.

TOP CHOICE **Dirty Old Man** BAR
(www.dirtyoldman.com.br; Lima e Silva 956; cocktails R$8-10; ⏰from 6pm Tue-Sun) The alt-leaning, awesomely named Cidade Baixa bar is a must for those interested in *very* regional microbrews: Baldhead is on tap, served in real pints and the crowd swilling it down is as eclectic and rare as the beer. A must.

Chalé da Praça XV BEER GARDEN
(www.chaledapracaxv.com.br; Praça 15 de Novembro) This ornate place, built in 1885, is a traditional favorite with *alegrenses* (residents of Porto Alegre) for late-afternoon beers.

Entertainment

Grêmio (www.gremio.net) and **Internacional** (www.internacional.com.br) are the city's high-profile rivals, the latter of which calls Porto Alegre's 2014 FIFA World Cup venue home. The renovated Beira-Rio Stadium, 4km south of the historic center, will hold 52,000

WORTH A TRIP

PARQUE NACIONAL DE APARADOS DA SERRA

This magnificent **national park** (☎3251-1227; admission R$6; ⏰8am-5pm Tue-Sun) is 18km from the town of Cambará do Sul, approximately 200km northeast of Porto Alegre. The most famous attraction is the **Cânion do Itaimbezinho**, a fantastic narrow canyon with dramatic waterfalls and sheer escarpments of 600m to 720m.

Two easy self-guided trails, **Trilha do Vértice** (2km return) and **Trilha Cotovelo** (6km return), lead from the park's visitors center to waterfalls and canyon vistas; the more challenging **Trilha do Rio do Boi** follows the base of the canyon for 7km, requires a guide and is closed during the rainy season. For guided trips, try the excellent eco-agency **Cânion Turismo** (☎3251-1027; www.canyonturismo.com.br; Getúlio Vargas 1098; ⏰8am-noon & 1-6pm).

Citral (☎0800-979-1441; www.citral.tur.br) offers one bus from Porto Alegre for Cambará do Sul (R$32.50, 5½ hours) at 6am Monday to Saturday. Returning to Porto Alegre, you must catch a 6:30am or 1:30pm bus to São Francisco de Paula and switch there. A taxi to the national park costs R$60 round trip.

rabid fans. The expansion of Metrô Linha 2 will reach the stadium.

Information

Money

Citibank (7 de Setembro 722) ATM.

HSBC (General Câmara 250) ATM.

Post

Post Office (Campos 1100)

Tourist Information

CIT (☎0800-51-7686; www.portoalegre.travel) Airport (Arrivals Hall, Terminal 1; ⏰8am-10pm); Baixa/Linha Turismo (Travessa do Carmo 84); bus station (Rodoviária; ⏰8am-5:30pm); Cidade city center (Praça 15 de Novembro; ⏰9am-6pm Mon-Sat) Useful tourist information booths are located in several spots around town.

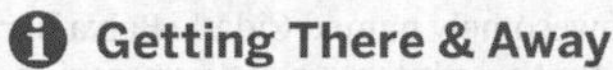

Getting There & Away

Terminals 1 and 2 of Salgado Filho International Airport (POA) are connected by a free shuttle. The majority of airlines operate out of Terminal 1, but Webjet and Azul depart from Terminal 2. International destinations include Buenos Aires, Lisbon, Montevideo and Panama City.

The busy bus station is just east of downtown. Sample travel times and *executivo* fares (where applicable):

DESTINATION	COST (R$)	DURATION (HR)
Cambará do Sul	32.50	5½
Curitiba	91	12
Florianópolis	82	6
Foz do Iguaçu	112	19
Montevideo	162	12
Rio de Janeiro	268	24
Sânto Angelo	117.45	8
São Francisco de Paula	20.30	3
São Paulo	154	18

Getting Around

Porto Alegre's metro, **Trensurb** (www.trensurb.gov.br; R$1.70; ⏰5am-11:20pm), has convenient stations located at Estação Mercado (by the port), Estação Rodoviária (the next stop) and the airport (three stops beyond). For Cidade Baixa, catch bus T5 from the airport or 282, 2821 or 255 from the bus station (R$2.85). Both the metro and the bus stop sit between Terminals 1 and 2 (closer to 2).

Foz do Iguaçu

☎0XX45 / POP 251,000

The stupendous roar of 275 waterfalls crashing 80m into the Rio Iguaçu seems to create a low-level buzz of excitement throughout the city of Foz, even though the famed Cataratas (falls) are 20km southeast of town. Apart from the waterfalls, you can dip into the forests of Paraguay or check out Itaipu Dam, one of the world's largest hydroelectric power plants.

Sights & Activities

To see the falls properly, you must visit both sides. Brazil gives the grand overview and Argentina the closer look. Most hostels offer full day trips to the Argentine side (p83) of the falls for R$100 to R$120. You'll save R$30 and a few hours if you opt to go independently.

Parque Nacional do Iguaçu WATERFALL
(☎3521-4400; www.cataratasdoiguacu.com.br; foreigners/Mercosul/Brazilians R$41.10/32.85/24.60; ⏰8:30am-5pm) The single not-to-be-missed experience on the Brazilian side of the falls is the **Trilha das Cataratas**, a scenic 1km trail leading to Garganta do Diabo (Devil's Throat), where the broad Rio Iguaçu makes its single most dramatic plunge, splitting into dozens of waterfalls. A regular shuttle bus loops around from park headquarters to the trailhead (stop number three).

TOP CHOICE **Itaipu Dam** DAM
(☎0800-645-4645; www.turismoitaipu.com.br; Tancredo Neves 6702; Panoramic/Special Tour R$22/56; ⏰hourly tours 8am-4pm) Itaipu Dam is another jaw-dropping attraction, especially when learning how much was destroyed to create it (indigenous villages, 700 sq km of forest and waterfalls to rival Iguaçu's). You can catch bus 101 or 102 (R$2.90, 30 minutes) which leave every 15 minutes from the Urban Bus Terminal (TTU).

Parque das Aves PARK
(Bird Park; www.parquedasaves.com.br; Av das Cataratas, Km 17.1; admission R$28; ⏰8:30am-5:30pm) Five minutes' walk from Iguaçu park headquarters is the worthwhile Parque das Aves. Its 5m-tall netted cages permit an up-close-and-personal look at 800 different bird species.

Foz do Iguaçu

Macuco Safari RAFTING, HIKING
(☎3574-4244; www.macucosafari.com.br; R$70-140; ⏰9am-5:20pm) Offers kayaking, hiking and rafting trips under the falls (R$70 to R$140). Park-approved guides also lead four- to five-hour outings (R$135) along the Trilha Poço Preto, a 9km trail leading to a small lagoon where you can observe monkeys, *jacaré* (caiman) and birdlife.

Foz do Iguaçu

Sleeping

1	Hostel Bambu	D4
2	Hotel Del Rey	B1

Eating

3	Oficina do Sorvete	B4
4	Tempero da Bahia	C3
5	Tropicana	B3
6	Vó Bertila	C2

Sleeping

TOP CHOICE **Hostel Natura** HOSTEL $
(☎3529-6949; www.hostelnatura.com; Av das Cataratas Km 12.5; camping/dm per person R$28/40, d without bathroom R$105, tr with/without bathroom R$150/110; ❄📶🏊) This hostel is set on a gorgeous piece of countryside that could easily pass for the American Midwest. Perks include pleasant and tidy rooms, ample outdoor lounge space, a fun bar, lakeside hammocks and, most obviously, tranquility. Reports of service slips notwithstanding, it's hard to deny this as one of Brazil's best hostels. Take bus 120 from TTU to the Remanso Grande stop and catch the free 'Alimentador' bus to the hostel, 12km from town on the way to the falls.

Favela Chic HOSTEL $
(☎3027-5060; www.favelachichosteliguassu.com; Raul de Mattos 78; camping per person R$18,

dm from R$35, s/d R$90/110, without bathroom R$50/80; ❄@📶) Warm-hearted Brit expat Nick is the heart and soul of this artsy hostel, which boasts a social bar, full English fry-ups for breakfast and a downright cozy converted van in the backyard that sleeps two. Seriously. A pool was being dug at time of writing.

Hostel Bambu HOSTEL $
(☎3523-3646; www.hostelbambu.com; Edmundo de Barros 621; dm R$45, s R$95, d/tr without bathroom R$120/150; ❄@📶) This laid-back hostel has ample lounge space, a bar, a guest kitchen and a patio with a small pool.

Hotel Del Rey HOTEL $$
(☎2105-7500; www.hoteldelreyfoz.com.br; Tarobá 1020; s/d from R$255/290; ❄@📶) A modern three-star hotel with spacious, comfy rooms and a good buffet breakfast.

Eating & Drinking

TOP CHOICE **Vó Bertila** PIZZERIA $$
(www.vobertilla.com.br; Bartolomeu de Gusmão 1116; pizzas R$17-57, pasta for 2 R$39-68; ⏰6pm-midnight) This informal, family-run cantina churns out wood-fired pizza and authentic pastas in heaped portions. All homey and hardwoods, it's the kind of down-home Italian spot Brazil does so very well. Expect it to be packed.

Tropicana CHURRASCARIA $
(www.pizzariareopicana.com.br; Kubitscheck 228; buffet R$22; ⏰11am-4pm & 7-11pm) This all-you-can-eat shoestring savior offers serious taste-for-money.

Tempero da Bahia BRAZILIAN $$
(www.restaurantetemporadabahia.com; Deodoro 1228; mains for 2 R$28-78; ⏰from 6pm Mon-Sat; 📶) Serves excellent Bahian fare (including a veggie *moqueca*), with live music Saturday nights (R$3 cover).

Oficina do Sorvete CAFE $
(www.oficinadosorvete.com.br; Av Jorge Schimmelpfeng 244; per kg sandwiches/ice cream R$37.50/39.50; ⏰1pm-1:30am; 📶) Glide on up to the bar and build your own baguette sandwich or salad; or take a dive into the long line of colorful ice cream on hand.

TOP CHOICE **Zeppelin Old Bar** BAR
(www.zeppelinoldbar.com; Raul Mattos 222; cover R$4-20; ⏰9pm-late Tue-Sat; 📶) Outstanding bar serving up excellent cockails and live music. The beautiful people congregate on Thursdays and Saturdays.

IGUAZÚ/IGUAÇU TOURIST CORRIDOR

Mercosul nationals can enter Argentina in the area around Iguazú Falls for less than 72 hours without a visa. Although citizens from most Western European countries do not need a visa, citizens of the United States, Australia and Canada must pay a reciprocity tax in advance (see boxed text, opposite). If you need a visa for Brazil you will need it to visit the falls from Argentina, even on an organized day trip.

Information

Along Av Brasil there are many banks and exchange houses.

Correios (www.correios.com.br; Praça Getúlio Vargas 72; ⏰9am-5pm Mon-Fri)

PIT (☎0800-45-1516; www.iguassu.tur.br) Airport (Aeroporto Internacional de Foz do Iguaçu/Cataratas; ⏰8am-10pm); local bus station (Kubitschek 1310; ⏰7:30am-6pm); long-distance bus station (Av Costa e Silva 1601; ⏰7am-6pm); Vila Yolanda (Av das Cataratas 2330; ⏰7am-11pm) Provides maps and detailed info about the area. The main office is south of town, reachable by bus 120.

Polícia Federal (☎3576-5500; Av Paraná 3471)

Getting There & Away

Daily flights link Foz's Cataratas International Airport (IGU), under renovation at the time of writing, to Lima, Rio, Salvador, São Paulo, Campinas, Curitiba and Porto Alegre. Sit on the left-hand side of the plane for good views of the falls.

DESTINATION	COST (R$)	DURATION (HR)
Asunción (Paraguay)	40	5
Buenos Aires (Argentina)	210	18
Campo Grande	124	15
Curitiba	115	10
Florianópolis	140	12
Rio de Janeiro	230	23
São Paulo	165	14

GETTING TO ARGENTINA & PARAGUAY

Many nationalities can enter Argentina without a visa, but double-check before you arrive or at the **Argentine consulate** (☎3574-2969; www.mrecic.gov.ar; Travessia Bianchi 26; ⊙10am-3pm Mon-Fri) in Foz. Citizens of the United States ($160 for 10 years), Australia ($100 single entry) and Canada ($75/$150 single entry/five years) must pay a reciprocity tax in advance through Provincia Pagos via www.migraciones.gov.ar (click on 'Pay Your Reciprocity Tax,' follow the steps and print out your receipt to take with you). For Paraguay, Americans ($100), Australians ($75) and Canadians ($65) need a visa (though not if you are only traveling to Ciudad del Este). Get this in advance at home or the **Paraguayan consulate** (☎3523-2898; Deodoro 901; ⊙8:30am-12:30pm & 1:30-4pm Mon-Fri) in Foz.

From Foz do Iguaçu, Brazil, to Puerto Iguazú, Argentina: if traveling by bus, at Brazilian immigration in either direction, most bus drivers won't wait around while you finish formalities. You must get a pass from the driver, get your passport stamped, then wait and board the next bus. It's important you pay attention as drivers ask if anyone needs to stop at immigration on the Brazilian side – but in Portuguese (or Spanish), if at all. Many travelers miss it and end up with serious immigration hassles later (ie hefty fines). At Argentine immigration, the bus always stops and waits for everyone to be processed. Both borders are open 24 hours but bus service ends around 7pm. You must catch the second-to-last bus back to Brazil. If you don't, there will be no bus coming after yours to scoop you up after you finish with border formalities.

To Ciudad del Este, Paraguay, take a bus from Kubitschek across from the Urban Bus Terminal (TTU; R$3.60, 30 minutes) or taxi to the border, get your passport stamped, then catch the next bus or a taxi to Ciudad del Este or walk across the Ponte da Amizade (Friendship Bridge). From Ponta Porã, Brazil to Pedro Juan Caballero, Paraguay, day visitors can simply walk across the border. If traveling further into Paraguay, you'll need to complete formalities with Brazil's Polícia Federal and the Paraguayan immigration authorities at the consulate.

Getting Around

Local bus fare runs R$2.90. City buses 105 and 115 cover the 6km between the long-distance bus station and the local terminal downtown (from TTU, you should catch it at Ala 3 for the correct direction). A taxi costs R$15. Bus 120 'Centro/TTU' goes from the airport (exit to far left end and look for blue 'Ônibus' sign) to Centro.

Bus 120 'Aeroporto/Parque Nacional' runs to the airport (30 minutes) and the Brazilian side of the waterfalls (40 minutes) every 22 minutes from 5:25am to midnight. Catch it at the local bus terminal or any stop along Juscelino Kubitschek south of Barbosa. A taxi from town to the airport costs around R$45.

For the Argentine side of the falls, catch a Puerto Iguazú bus (R$4, one hour) across from the local bus terminal. They pass every 15 minutes (30 minutes on Sunday) from 7:15am to 7pm (from 8am Sunday). At Puerto Iguazú bus station, transfer to a bus to the falls (A$50 return, 30 minutes).

Buses run every 10 minutes (25 minutes on Sunday) to Ciudad del Este, Paraguay (R$3.50, 30 minutes) from 6am to 7pm (from 7am Sunday) from the army base opposite Foz's local bus terminal.

THE CENTRAL WEST

A land of breathtaking panoramas and exceptional wildlife, Brazil's Central West is a must-see for nature lovers and outdoor enthusiasts. The Pantanal, one of the planet's most important wetland systems, is the region's star attraction. Its meandering rivers, savannas and forests harbor one of the densest concentrations of plant and animal life in the New World. Other regional attractions include dramatic *chapadas* (tablelands), which rise like brilliant red giants from the dark-green *cerrado* (savanna), punctuated by spectacular waterfalls and picturesque swimming holes; Bonito, where crystal-clear rivers teeming with fish highlight one of the world's most unique natural destinations; and Brazil's surreal, master-planned capital, Brasília.

Brasília

☎0XX61 / POP 2.6 MILLION

Well into middle age, Brazil's once futuristic capital remains an impressive monument to national initiative. Built from nothing in

The Central West

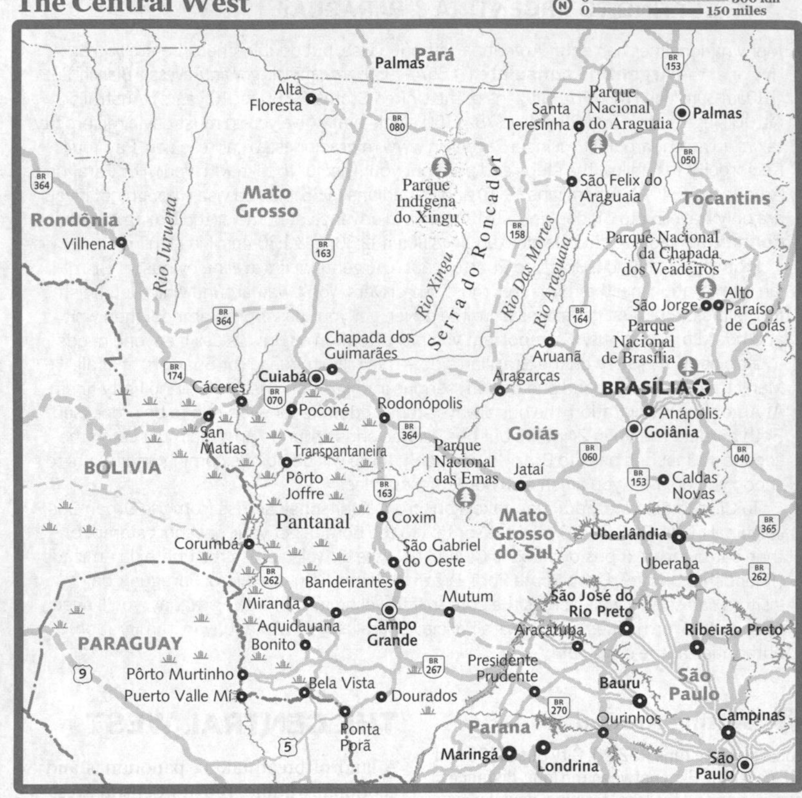

about three years, Brasília replaced Rio de Janeiro as Brazil's center of government in 1960 under the visionary leadership of President Juscelino Kubitschek, architect Oscar Niemeyer, urban planner Lucio Costa and landscape architect Burle Marx.

Sights & Activities

Brasília's major edifices are spread along a 5km stretch of the Eixo Monumental and are listed in northwest–southeast order here. Further south, in the 'cockpit' of the airplane ground plan, are the most interesting government buildings: **Palácio do Itamaraty** (Palace of Arches; ☎3411-8051; www.itamaraty.gov.br; admission free; ⏰2-4pm Mon-Fri, 10am-3pm Sat & Sun), **Palácio da Justiça** (☎2025-3216; Praça dos Trés Poderes; ⏰2-4pm Mon-Fri, 10am-3pm Sat & Sun) and **Congresso Nacional** (☎3216-1771; Parliament; admission free; ⏰9:30am-5pm). To visit them, combine buses 104 and 108 with long walks or, most conveniently, take a city tour. Only **Brasília City Tour** (☎3201-1222; www.catedralturismo.com.br; day ticket R$25) and **AeroVan Turismo** (☎3340-9251; www.aerovan.com.br) are licensed to give guided city tours (R$40 to R$55).

Memorial JK MUSEUM
(☎3226-7860; www.memorialjk.com.br; Praça do Cruzeiro; adult/child R$12/6; ⏰9am-6pm) Houses the tomb of President Juscelino Kubitschek underneath eerily beautiful stained glass by French artist Marianne Peretti, as well as exhibits on Brasília's construction.

TOP CHOICE **TV Tower** TOWER
(Eixo Monumental; ⏰8am-8pm) Take the elevator to the 75m-high observation deck of the TV Tower for a bird's-eye view of Brasília.

TOP CHOICE **Santuário Dom Bosco** CHURCH
(☎3223-6542; www.santuariodombosco.org.br; W3 Sul, Quadra 702; admission free; ⏰7am-7pm

This gorgeous church features 80 concrete columns that support 7500 pieces of illuminated Murano glass symbolizing a starry sky, and which cast a blue submarine glow over the pews.

TOP CHOICE **Museu Nacional** MUSEUM
(☎3325-5220; Esplanada dos Ministérios; admission free; ⏱9am-6:30pm) This spherical half-dome by architect Oscar Niemeyer hosts rotating exhibits.

TOP CHOICE **Catedral Metropolitana** CHURCH
(☎3224-4073; www.catedral.org.br; Esplanada dos Ministérios; admission free; ⏱8am-6pm) With its 16 curved columns, stained glass and haunting statues of the four evangelists, this is one of Brasília's architectural gems.

Sleeping

Brasília suffers from a severe dearth of budget accommodations, though many downtown hotels slash prices on weekends. Unlicensed budget *pousades* still operate along Via W3 Sul despite a 2008 government shutdown due to zoning laws. In Brasília, the fewer stories a hotel has, the cheaper it is.

Econotel HOTEL **$$**
(☎3204-7337; www.hoteleconotel.com.br; SHS Quadra 3, Bloco B; s/d/tr from R$159/189/219; P❄📶) The cheapest hotel in the SHS. Rooms are newer and better equipped than the majority of the other stagnant options in a higher range and staff are friendly.

Hotel Diplomat HOTEL **$**
(☎3204-2010; SHN, Quadra 2, Bloco L; cabin/s/d from R$99/139/159; ❄📶) Near the TV Tower and recently made over, the Diplomat offers train-compartment-sized *cabinas* for solo travelers; and good cheapish rooms otherwise.

Albergue da Juventude Brasília HOSTEL **$**
(☎3343-0531; www.brasiliahostel.com.br; Camping de Brasília; s/d R$57/105; @) Brasília's only dependable option under R$100, desolately situated 6km from the center – take bus 143 from section E02 inside Rodoviária Plano Piloto (the local bus station).

Eating & Drinking

You'll find cuisine from dozens of countries in cosmopolitan Asa Sul. Prime venues for restaurant-, bar- and club-hopping include the neighborhood commercial districts SCLS-209 and SCLS-403, both near metro stops. For walkable cheap eats from SHS and SHN, you're stuck with food courts in the air-conditioned downtown malls: **Shopping Brasília** (www.brasiliashopping.com.br; Quadra 5, Asa Norte SCN), **Pátio Brasil** (www.patiobrasil.com.br; SCS s/n, Quadra 7) and **Conjunto Nacional** (www.conjuntonacional.com.br; SDN CNB, Conjunto A); or try your luck at the simple subsidized restaurants in some ministeries, which are open to the public (Ministério da Agricultura is purportedly the best).

Students congregate over cheap suds at **Quadrado de Cerveja** (SCLN 408 Norte).

TOP CHOICE **Nossa Cozinha Bistrô** FUSION **$$**
(☎3326-5207; www.nossacozinhabsb.blogspot.com.br; SCLN 402, Bloco C; mains R$27.50-38; ⏱11.30am-3pm & 7.30pm-midnight, closed Sun; 📶) At this outstanding, near-makeshift bistro tucked away on Bloco C's backside, superb value awaits. The US-trained chef excels at gourmet treats like the signature pork ribs (Velvety! Chocolaty! Tasty!). For Brazil, the check is a pleasant shock.

Genaro Jazz Burger Café BURGERS **$$**
(www.genarojazzcafe.com.br; SCLN 114, Bloco A; burgers R$19-30; 🍸) Serious cocktails and gourmet burgers, and open-air live-jazz soundtrack to boot.

Engenho BUFFET **$**
(SCLS 408, Bloco A; per kg weekday/weekend R$35.90/39.90; ⏱lunch, closed Sun; 📶🍸) Excellent *por kilo* restaurant with organic emphasis.

BRASÍLIA BEARINGS

Brasília's central area is shaped like an airplane. Government buildings and monuments are concentrated in the fuselage (a long strip called Eixo Monumental). Hotels, banks and shopping centers are immediately adjacent, in sectors known by their abbreviations: SHN/SHS (hotel sectors north and south), SBN/SBS (banking sectors) and SCN/SCS (commercial sectors). Residential neighborhoods, each with its own SC (commercial sector) lie further out along the airplane's wings: Asa Norte (North Wing) and Asa Sul (South Wing).

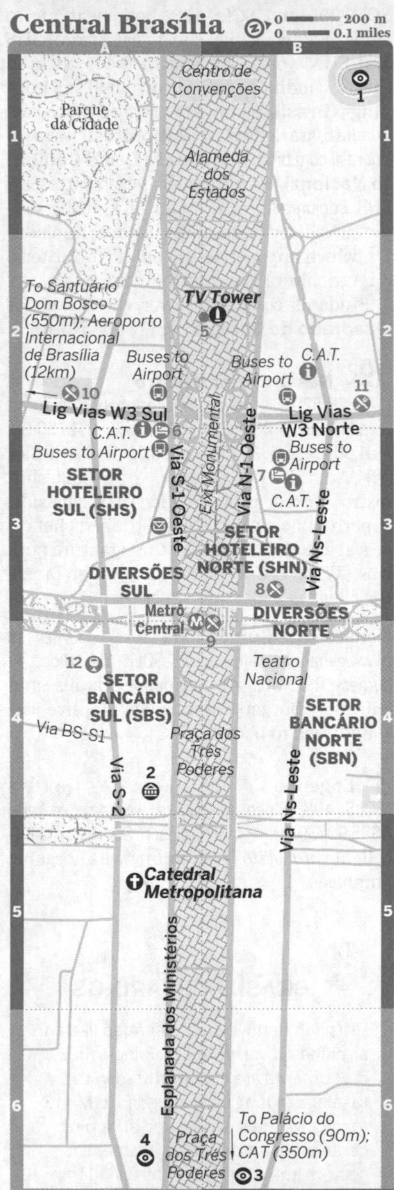

Central Brasília

Top Sights

Catedral Metropolitana ... A5
TV Tower ... B2

Sights

1 Estádio Nacional de Brasília ... B1
2 Museu Nacional ... A4
3 Palácio da Justiça ... B6
4 Palácio do Itamaraty ... A6

Activities, Courses & Tours

5 Brasília City Tour ... B2

Sleeping

6 Econotel ... A3
7 Hotel Diplomat ... B3

Eating

8 Conjunto Nacional ... B3
9 Pastelaria Viçosa ... B4
10 Pátio Brasil ... A2
11 Shopping Brasília ... B2

Drinking

12 Bar do Calaf ... A4

Pastelaria Viçosa FAST FOOD $
(www.pastelariavicosa.com.br; Rodoviária Plano Piloto; pastries R$1-3) Wildly popular Rodoviária Plano Piloto institution for *pastel* (stuffed, fried pastries) and *caldo de cana* (sugar-cane juice), two classic Brazilian street treats.

Bar Beirute BAR
(☎3244-1717; 109 Sul, Bloco A; light meals R$5-32) This lively *boteco* with outdoor seating is a Brasília institution (read: a jovial zoo). The **Asa Norte** (SCLN 107, Bloco D) location is more in favor these days.

☆ Entertainment

Brasília's rebuilt, centrally located Estádio Nacional de Brasília will hold 71,000 for the 2014 FIFA World Cup and 2016 Olympic Games. Brasília's two teams, **Brasiliense Futebol Clube** (www.brasiliensefc.net) and **Sociedade Esportiva do Gama** (www.segama.com.br), play in Brazil's lower divisions.

For live music, go to **Bar do Calaf** (☎3325-7408; www.calaf.com.br; SBS Quadra 2, Bloco S, Edificio Empire Center; cover R$10-25; ⊙closed Sun). Though technically a Spanish restaurant, the food is an afterthought to the wildly mixed crowd, all of whom rate the excellent live samba, *pagode* (popular samba) and *choro* (improvised samba) over the paella.

Information

Banks are spread about various sectors, but ATMs are most easily accessed in the shopping malls and transport stations and along Via W3.

CAT (www.vemviverbrasilia.com.br) Airport (☎3364-9102; Presidente Juscelino Kubitschek International Airport; 7am-10pm); Rodoviária (Nova Rodoviária Interestadual; 7am-10pm); SHS (SHS Quadra 3, Bloco B); SHN Alta (SHN, Quadra 5, Bloco G; 8am-6pm); SHN Baixa (SHN, Quadra 2, Bloco H) Brasília's well-organized offical tourism kiosks. By 2014, two mobile units are expected.

Main Post Office (SHS Quadra 2, Bloco B; 9am-5pm Mon-Fri)

Getting There & Away

Brasília's Presidente Juscelino Kubitschek International Airport (BSB), 12km south of the center, has flights throughout Brazil plus to Atlanta, Lima, Lisbon, Miami and Panama City. The easiest way to or from the airport is Ônibus Executivo Aeroporto (take bus 113), which does a loop from the airport to the Rodoviária Plano Piloto, the entire Esplanada dos Ministérios, and SHS (45 minutes) and SHN (30 minutes) every 30 minutes from 6:30am to 11pm. It departs outside the arrivals hall to the far right. Taxis to the airport cost R$38 and local bus 102 is R$2 (40 minutes).

From the new long-distance bus station **Nova Rodoviária Interestadual** (SMAS, Trecho 4, Conjunto 5/6), 3km southwest off the edge of Asa Sul, buses go almost everywhere.

DESTINATION	COST (R$)	DURATION (HR)
Alto Paraíso	36	3½
Belém	319	36
Belo Horizonte	118.50	11
Cuiabá	169	18
Foz do Iguaçu	275	22
Pirenópolis	23.50	3
Rio de Janeiro	229	17
Salvador	200	23
São Jorge	39.50	6
São Paulo	161	14

Getting Around

Bus

Brasília's Rodoviária Plano Piloto and Metrô Estação Central share space right in the heart of town. Buses depart for the airport, long-distance bus station, and Asa Sul and Asa Norte regularly. Brasília's Nova Rodoviária Interestadual and Rodoviária Plano Piloto are connected by subway (R$2 to R$3, 15 minutes) and bus 108.8 (R$2, 20 minutes).

Brasília's **Metrô-DF** (www.metro.df.gov.br; weekends/weekdays R$2/3; 6am-11:30pm Mon-Fri, 7am-7pm Sat & Sun) currently runs south from the Rodoviária Plano Piloto to the suburbs, stopping at time of writing at Galeria, 102 Sul, 108 Sul, 112 Sul, 114 Sul, Asa Sul, Shopping and on into the suburbs.

Bus departures from Rodoviária Plano Piloto include the following:

BUS	DESTINATION	PLATFORM	BOX
102	Airport	A	01
107	Via WS Sul/L2 Sul	E	10
108	Praça dos Três Poderes	A	04
108.8	Nova Rodoviária Interestadual	A	01
116	Via W3/L2 North	E	12

Taxi

Always carry a taxi phone number with you in Brasília. They are as scarce as snow in the Superquadras. With **Unitaxi** (3325-3030) or **Rádio Táxi Alvorada** (3321-3030; www.radiotaxi33213030.com.br), you are entitled to a 15% to 20% discount off the meter (not always announced to foreigners). Remind them: *'Com o desconto, por favor.'*

BRASÍLIA ON A BUDGET

For budget travelers, Brasília presents numerous challenges. Its sprawling ground plan was built for cars, so getting around on foot feels like a real-life game of *Frogger* meets *Super Mario Bros*. Accommodation is expensive, and the city's best restaurants and nightlife are concentrated far from the downtown hotel districts – posing the impractical dilemma of paying a R$30 round-trip taxi fare to eat a R$14 kebab. Once the subway extends to Asa Norte (2015), and the on-again, off-again R$1.5-billion **Metrô Leve de Brasília** (VLT; www.vlt.df.gov.br) light-rail project arrives, they will be game changers, but until then, you'll need to recalibrate your budget. But skipping Brasília because it's pricey and difficult would be a shame: the city packs serious wow in its acronym-rich hyper-plan; its retro-futuristic vibe and utopian prototype are unlike anything you have ever seen before. Public transport is intuitive and with a little determination and patience, it can be done cheaply, using buses to comb Asa Sul and Asa Norte (see table above), where it is relatively easy to walk around width-wise once you disembark.

WORTH A TRIP

PARQUE NACIONAL DA CHAPADA DOS VEADEIROS

This spectacular park 220km north of Brasília showcases the high-altitude *cerrado*, a sublime landscape where maned wolves, giant anteaters and 2.1m-tall rheas roam amid big skies, canyons, waterfalls and oasis-like stands of wine palms. The closest towns to the park are the new-agey Alto Paraíso de Goias (40km east) and tranquil São Jorge (2km south), both offering an abundance of comfy and charming accomodations. Outside the national park, **Vale da Lua** (Moon Valley; admission R$10; ⏲7am-5:30pm) is named for the pockmarked rocks lining its riverbed, though the surrounding hills' exuberant greenery makes it feel anything but lunar. The trailhead for the self-guided 600m walking loop, passing lovely natural pools, is 10km southeast of São Jorge.

Visitors to the national park must go with an accredited guide; book one at the park entrance or go with the excellent **Travessia** (☎3446-1595; www.travessia.tur.br; Av Valadão Filho 979, Alto Paraíso), which offers a full-day hike from R$100 for groups up to six. Main attractions include the canyons (Cânion I and Cânion II) along the **Rio Preto**, the waterfalls (**Salto do Rio Preto I & II**; 80m and 120m, respectively) and **Morro da Baleia**, a humpback hill with a 2.5km trail to the top.

From Brasília's local bus station (Rodoviária Plano Piloto), **Santo Antônio** (☎3328-0834; www.grupoamaral.com.br) runs a daily bus to São Jorge (R$39.50, 12:30pm, six hours) via Alto Paraíso. Buses from Brasília's long-distance Nova Rodoviária Interestadual only go as far as Alto Paraíso (R$34, 3½ hours).

Pirenópolis

☎0XX62 / POP 23,000

A Brazilian National Heritage site backed by lovely mountains, Pirenópolis attracts weekend escapees from Brasília (165km east) for some of the country's most picturesque 18th-century architecture and abundant waterfalls.

Pirenópolis' **CAT** (☎3331-2633; www.pirenopolis.tur.br; Rua da Bomfim 14; ⏲8am-6pm), near central Praça da Matriz, arranges guides to local nature reserves (from R$80 a day). Both **Banco do Brasil** (☎3331-1182; Rua Sizenando Jayme 1; ⏲11am-4pm Mon-Fri) and **Bradesco** (Rua do Imperador 268) ATMs are nearby on Sizenando Jayme.

Within about 20km of town, **Parque Estadual da Serra dos Pireneus** and **Reserva Ecológica Vargem Grande** (☎3331-3071; www.vargemgrande.pirenopolis.tur.br; admission R$20; ⏲9am-5pm) both have beautiful waterfalls and swimming holes; while **Santuário de Vida Silvestre Vagafogo** (☎3335-8515; www.vagafogo.com.br; ⏲9am-5pm) offers a self-guided forest walk (R$16) and a delicious weekend brunch (R$35).

The family-run **Rex Hotel** (☎3331-1121; Praça da Matriz 15; s/d R$45/90) is on the main square. West of the bus station, **Pousada Arvoredo** (☎3331-3479; www.arvoredo.tur.br; Av Abercio Ramos Qd 17 Lt 15; s/d weekend R$250/280, weekday R$120/140; ❄📶🏊) offers midweek deals on comfy rooms surrounding a pool and garden. On weekends, when restaurants and bars line Rua do Rosario with tables on the cobblestones, the atmosphere is electric. Elsewhere, **Pireneus Cafe** (☎3331-3047; www.pireneuscafe.com.br; Rua dos Pireneus 41; sandwiches R$18-25) is a great choice for killer foccacia sandwiches; and Rua Direita hosts a few spots for cheap Goiânian empanadas.

From the bus station, 500m west of the center, four daily buses run to Brasília (R$21.50, three hours) and one to Goiânia (R$12.50, two hours).

The Pantanal

This vast natural paradise is Brazil's major ecological attraction and offers a density of exotic wildlife found nowhere else in South America. During the rainy season (December to April), the Rio Paraguai and lesser rivers of the Pantanal inundate much of this low-lying region, creating *cordilheiras* (patches of dry land where animals cluster). The waters here in the world's largest freshwater wetlands rise as much as 3m above low-water levels around March in the northern Pantanal and as late as June further south. This seasonal flooding, while severely limiting human occupation of the area, provides an enormously rich feeding ground f wildlife. The waters teem with fish; birds in flocks of thousands and gather in e

The Pantanal

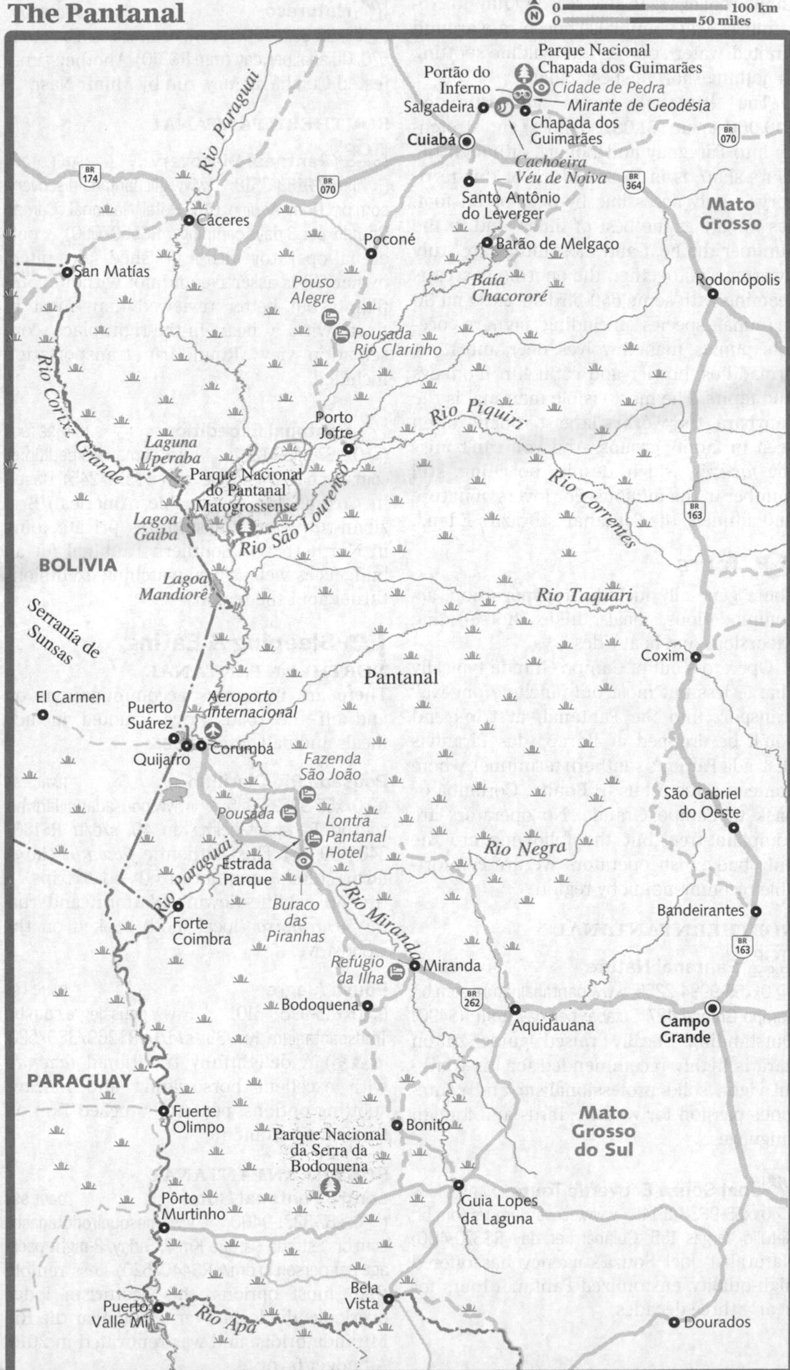

mous rookeries. In dry season (July to November), when animals concentrate around limited water sources, the wildlife-spotting is nothing short of spectacular.

The Pantanal covers an estimated 210,000 sq km (81,081 sq miles) and stretches into Paraguay and Bolivia, although the lion's share is in Brazil. Much of this territory is only accessible by boat or on foot. It's muggy at the best of times, and in the summer the heat and mosquitoes are truly awesome. Altogether, the enormous area is teeming with some 650 bird species and 80 mammal species, including jaguars, ocelots, pumas, maned wolves, deer, anteaters, armadillos, howler and capuchin monkeys and tapirs. The most visible mammal is the capybara, the world's largest rodent, often seen in family groups. And you can't miss the *jacarés,* which, despite poaching, still number in the millions. For lovers of nature and animals, the Pantanal is Brazil's Eden.

Tours

Tours generally include transportation, accommodations, meals, hikes, horse-riding excursions and boat rides.

Operators out of Campo Grande typically charge less but most only include one-way transport into the Pantanal; at trip's end you'll be dropped at Buraco das Piranhas (Estrada Parque's southern terminus), where you can catch a bus to Bonito, Corumbá or back to Campo Grande. No operators are complaint-free, but the following are the only budget-ish operators we are comfortable recommending by region.

NORTHERN PANTANAL

TOP CHOICE Pantanal Nature NATURE TOUR
(0xx65-9994-2265; www.pantanalnature.com.br; Campo Grande 487, Cuiabá; per day from R$490) Outstanding, locally raised guide Ailton Lara is highly recommended for his youthful vigor, solid professionalism and contagious passion for wildlife, birds and foreign languages.

Joel Souza Ecoverde Tours NATURE TOUR
(0xx65-9638-1614; www.ecoverdetours.com.br; Getúlio Vargas 155, Cuiabá; per day R$370-400) Naturalist Joel Souza's agency has offered high-quality, customized Pantanal tours for nearly three decades.

Natureco NATURE TOUR
(0xx65-3321-1001; www.natureco.com.br; Leite 570, Cuiabá; per day from R$310) Another time-tested Cuiabá agency, run by Munir Nasr.

SOUTHERN PANTANAL

TOP CHOICE Pantanal Discovery NATURE TOUR
(0xx67-9163-3518; www.gilspantanaldiscovery.com.br; Dom Aquino 610, Hotel Nacional, Campo Grande; per 3 days camping/r R$550/650) A perennial operator with a polished sales pitch, owner Gil is assertive and not without complaints but better reviewed than most in town with a heart-in-the-right-place conservation view. Round-trip transportation included.

Pantanal Expeditions NATURE TOUR
(0xx67-8469-1207; www.pantanalexpeditions.com; per day 2/4 people from R$310/245) Based in Coxim, this sustainable, American/Brazilian-run agency customizes private tours in Northern and Southern Pantanal for all budgets as well as bird-watching excursions throughout the region.

Sleeping & Eating

NORTHERN PANTANAL

There are numerous accommodations on and off the road. Prices quoted include meals and daily excursions.

Pousada Rio Clarinho RANCH $$
(0xx65-9959-2985; www.pousadarioclarinho.com.br; Transpantaneira, Km 40; s/d/tr R$180/340/450;) This authentic *fazenda* (large farm) offers nonmotorized boat trips, a treetop wildlife-viewing platform and rustic *pantaneira* (local food) cooked on the woodstove.

Pouso Alegre RANCH $$
(0xx65-9968-6101; www.pousalegre.com.br; Transpantaneira Km 33; s/d/tr R$260/380/520; @) A delightfully traditional *fazenda* with excellent horse-riding and macaw-spotting options, peacefully tucked 7km off the Transpantaneira.

SOUTHERN PANTANAL

Lontra Pantanal Hotel LODGE $$$
(0xx67-3231-9400; www.pesqueirodotadashi.com.br; Estrada Parque Km 7; 3-day, 2-night package per person in dm/r R$440/520) Less remote than most options, this ecoturism lodge overlooks the local river traffic near the Rio Miranda bridge and was renovated in 2010. A budget favorite.

CHOOSING A TOUR OPERATOR

Bringing tourists into the Pantanal is big business, and the two main cities that serve as jumping-off points to the region are flooded with operators – some of dubious repute. Whether you arrive in Campo Grande or Corumbá, you're likely to be approached by a guide fairly rapidly, though the Campo Grande bus station is easily Brazil's worst for aggressive touts. You have the lot: greedy opportunists, shady businessmen, and a few honest and hard-working good guys committed to ecotourism and sustainability. Distinguishing who's who is a challenge – the mudslinging among operators is thicker than the swamp itself. Go with your gut and consider the following:

» Resist making a snap decision off an overnight bus (or otherwise) and resist entertaining any aggressive tactics by touts in Campo Grande's bus station.

» Talk to other travelers who have just returned from a Pantanal trip – they're often your best source of up-to-the-minute information.

» Go to the local tourism office. They generally can't give independent advice because they're government funded but many keep complaints books that you're free to peruse.

» Remember that the owner or salesperson is not always your guide and it's the guide you're going to be with in the wilderness for several days. Ask to meet your guide if possible.

» Get things in writing and don't hand over your cash to any go-betweens.

» Compare your options. Many operators work out of the local bus station or airport so it's easy to shop around.

» Avoid operators that grab animals for photo ops and otherwise disrupt the Pantanal's fragile ecosystem by altering flora and fauna behavior.

» Obviously, the further away you are, the more you will pay for your tour. There have even been reports of fradulent Pantanal tours being sold at Foz do Iguaçu's bus station.

There's no obligation to go with a tour operator. You can drive or hitchhike along the Transpantaneira, a 145km-long road originating in Poconé, south of Cuiabá (Mato Grosso state), or the Estrada Parque that loops around the south (Mato Grosso do Sul). You'll see wildlife even without a guide.

Refúgio da Ilha LODGE **$$$**
(☎0xx67-3306-3415; www.refugiodailha.com.br; per person per night from R$514; wi-fi) Rave reviews follow this smart, biologist-run lodge on a 40-sq-km river-delta island, offering organic cuisine and excellent wildlife opportunities.

Cuiabá

☎0XX65 / POP 530,300

Mato Grosso's state capital is a sprawling frontier boomtown near the edge of three distinct ecosystems: the northern Pantanal, the *cerrado* of nearby Chapada dos Guimarães and the southern Amazon.

Sleeping

Pousada Ecoverde INN **$**
(☎9638-1614; www.ecoverdetours.com.br; Celtino 391; s/d without bathroom R$40/60) In a charmingly rustic historic home strewn with antique radios and Pantanal info, amiable and eccentric tour operator Joel Souza gives this classic *pousada* character in spades.

Hotel Panorama HOTEL **$**
(☎3322-0072; www.hotelpanorama.com.br; Ferreira Mendes 286; s/d/tr with fan R$50/78/96, with air-con R$72/100/114) This aged relic is nothing special, but windows and space in every room give it an advantage in this price range.

Hotel Mato Grosso HOTEL **$**
(☎3614-7777; www.hotelmatogrosso.com.br; Costa 643; s/d/tr without air-con from R$69/89/99, with air R$94/119/159; air-con, wi-fi) This contemporary, centrally located hotel offers cramped rooms but modern facilities.

Eating & Drinking

TOP CHOICE **Choppão** BOTECO **$$**
(www.choppao.com.br; Getulio Vargas s/n; mains for 2 R$50-80) This animated classic features old-school waiters serving obscenely large plates of meat or fish and freezing *chope* in

PANTANAL VS AMAZON?

Travelers often ask, 'Pantanal or Amazon?' Long story short: go to the Pantanal if you want to see animals, go to the Amazon if you want to see jungle. Of course, experiences vary, but generally speaking, animals are much harder to see hidden in the dense canopy of the Amazon; the Pantanal is a lowland swamp, where there are far fewer hiding places in dry season. But really, why choose? Go to both!

iced tankards. So popular, even bus placards advertise it as a stop!

Kinutre BUFFET **$**
(Getulio Vargas 714; per kg R$28.90; 11am-2pm Sun-Fri;) Excellent vegetarian oasis in a carnivore's desert.

Natura Sabores ICE CREAM, CAFE **$**
(Praça Alencastro; ice cream R$3-6; 6:30am-7pm Mon-Sat, to 12:30pm Sun) Owner Edson churns out nonindustrialized ice cream in exotic flavors like pumpkin with coconut and guava with cheese.

Mistura Cuiabana BUFFET **$**
(cnr Celestino & Mariano; per kg R$20; lunch Mon-Fri) A decent downtown *por kilo*.

Restaurante Popular de Cuiabá BRAZILIAN **$**
(Barão de Melgaço 3161; meals R$1.50; lunch Mon-Fri) Has government-subsidized R$1.50 lunches for devout shoestringers.

☆ Entertainment

Praça da Mandioca, near Pousada Ecoverde, is an authentic local nightlife square filled with drinking revelers. Head there for free samba and bossa nova on Thursday and Friday evenings.

Cuiabá's new multiuse Arena Pantanal, 3km west of Centro, will hold 42,500. Scheduled for a 2013 debut at the time of writing, it was being constructed for the 2014 FIFA World Cup. The city's three teams, Mixto, Dom Bosco and Cuiabá, play in lower divisions.

Information

CAT (Praça Rachid Jaudy; 8am-6pm Mon-Fri) Abandoned when we came through, with supposed plans to reopen.

HSBC (Av Getúlio Vargas 346) Has ATMs.

Sedtur (3613-9300; www.sedtur.mt.gov.br; Voluntários da Pátria 118; 1-7pm Mon-Fri) Provides information about attractions throughout Mato Grosso (but lacks an English speaker).

Getting There & Away

Multiple airlines connect Cuiabá's Marechal Rondon International Airport (CGB) with cities throughout Brazil. The bus station is 3km north of the center. Sample travel times and *executivo* fares (where applicable):

DESTINATION	COST (R$)	DURATION (HR)
Brasília	169	18
Campo Grande	102	11
Chapada dos Guimarães	11.60	1¼
Poconé	18	2
Porto Velho	155	23
Rio de Janeiro	237	32
São Paulo	227	27

Car-rental agencies outside the airport tend to be cheaper than those inside. The best vehicles for the Transpantaneira are a VW Golf or Fiat Uno; beware treacherous road conditions in wet weather, especially south of the Rio Pixaím bridge at Km 65.

Getting Around

The airport is in Varzea Grande, 7km south of Cuiabá. Buses for the center (24 or 55) and bus station (07; *rodoviária*) leave from opposite the Las Velas Hotel on Filinto Muller (exit airport 100m to the left). Buses from the center to the airport depart from Praça Ipiranga; and to the bus station from the 200 block of Getúlio Vargas near Praça Alencastro. Frequent local buses run from the bus station into town, dropping you along Isaac Póvoas. Local buses cost R$2.60. A taxi is R$13.

Around Cuiabá

PARQUE NACIONAL DA CHAPADA DOS GUIMARÃES

This high plateau 60km northeast of Cuiabá is a beautiful region reminiscent of the American Southwest. Its three exceptional sights are the 60m falls **Cachoeira Véu de Noiva**, the **Mirante de Geodésia** lookout (South America's geographical cente[r]) and the colorful rocky outcrops known [as] **Cidade de Pedra** (Stone City), though [the] latter is closed indefinitely due to lack o[f] frastructure. Véu de Noiva is the only part of the park you can visit independently. Otherwise, a certified guide is required. Access is split among three day-trip circuits: **Circuito das Cachoeiras** (Waterfall Circuit; from R$110 per person – does *not* include Véu de Noiva); **Circuito Vale do Rio Claro** (Claro River Valley Circuit; from R$130 per person), which does include Véu de Noiva; and the **Roteiro da Caverna Aroe Jari e Lagoa Azul** (Aroe Jari Cave Circuit; from R$130 per person plus R$20 cave admission), which includes Mirante de Geodésia and Brazil's largest sandstone cave. All trips begin by 9am and return by 6pm and should be reserved in advance, especially in July, August and September.

Chapada Explorer (☎3301-1290; www.chapadaexplorer.com.br; Praça Dom Wunibaldo 57; ⊙8-11:30am & 1:30-6:30pm Mon-Fri, 8-11:30am Sat & Sun), on the main plaza, is a great agency to get you into the park.

On the plaza, **Pousada Bom Jardim** (☎3301-2668; www.pousadabomjardim.com.br; Praça Dom Wunibaldo; s/d without air-con from R$75/100, d/tr with air-con from R$95/170; ❄📶) is good comfort and location for the money. Just off the plaza, the upgraded **Hotel São José** (☎3301-3013; pousadasaojose@uol.com.br; Souza 50; s/d with air-con R$100/140, with fan R$70/90; ❄📶) offers clean, well-maintained rooms. **Pomodori** (Caldas 60; mains R$22-32; ⊙from 4pm Mon-Fri, from noon Sat & Sun) is surely the cutest restaurant in the center, serving less than a handful of select Italian plates nightly and good *empadas* (stuffed pastries).

For town maps, visit **CAT** (☎3301-2045; cnr Perimetral & Gomes; ⊙7am-6pm Mon-Sat, 8am-noon & 2-5pm Sun).

Buses leave Cuiabá nearly hourly for the laid-back town of Chapada dos Guimarães (R$11.60, 1¼ hours), just outside the park. If you are only visiting Véu de Noiva, ask the driver to drop you at the park entrance, 10km west of town. Chapada's bus station is two blocks from the main plaza (Praça Dom Wunibaldo).

POCONÉ

Poconé, 100km southwest of Cuiabá, is the gateway to the Transpantaneira. From here, the 'highway' becomes little more than a pockmarked dirt track as it heads 145km south into the Pantanal, terminating at Porto Jofre. A friendly **CAT** (☎3345-1575; Praça do Menino Jesus s/n; ⊙7am-3pm Mon-Sat) has *pousada* information and a Transpantaneira map.

Skala Hotel (☎3345-1407; www.skalahotel.com.br; Praça Rondon; s/d/tr R$50/90/120; ❄@📶) on Poconé's main square is the best option in town, with its own restaurant and clean, modern digs.

Six daily buses run from Cuiabá to Poconé (R$18, two hours).

Campo Grande

☎0XX67 / POP 766,500

Mato Grosso do Sul's lively capital is the most sophisticated city in the region and a major jumping-off point for the Pantanal. Look out for the city's new star attraction, Aquário do Pantanal, purported to be the world's largest freshwater aquarium, by 2014.

Sleeping & Eating

Inexpensive hotels surround the old bus station, at the western end of Alfonso Pena. Nightlife is concentrated further east along the same avenue.

Pousada Dom Aquino INN $

(☎3384-3303; www.pousadadomaquino.com.br; Aquino 1806; s/d/tr R$75/105/126; ❄📶) A relaxed oasis in the city center just northwest of Praça da Repúblic, with international cable TV and a temperamental dog.

Turis Hotel HOTEL $

(☎3382-2461; www.turishotel.com.br; Kardec 200; s/d/tr R$83/128/169; ❄@📶) One of several modern hotels near the old bus station, Turis offers modern facilities but be weary of the street at night.

Hotel Nacional HOTEL $

(☎3383-2461; www.hotelnacionalpantanal.com.br; Dom Aquino 610; s/d $50/90, without bathroom R$40/60, without air-con R$50/70; ❄@📶) Spiffed up backpacker-level digs under new ownership. It's bright, clean and offers Pantanal tourism infrastructure.

TOP CHOICE **Cantina Romana** ITALIAN $

(www.cantinaromana.com.br; Rua da Paz 237; mains for 2 R$30-48) Shock-value old-school Italian cantina and pizzeria. Try the *tagliarini alla cacciatora* for two (R$35).

Comitiva Pantaneira BUFFET $$

(www.comitivapantaneira.com.br; Dom Aquino 2221; per kg weekday/weekend R$34.90/39.90;

lunch) A massive *por kilo* swarming with locals digging into seriously good Pantaneira cowboy cuisine.

Feira Central MARKET $
(cnr 14 de Julho & Calógeras; mains R$7.90-14; dinner Wed-Sun) Join the locals for soba and *yakisoba* (Japanese noodles) at the countless food booths in this lively indoor market.

Information

CAT (www.turismo.ms.gov.br) Bus station (3314-4448; Rodoviária; 6am-9:30pm); city center (3314-9968; cnr Afonso Pena & Noroeste; 8am-6pm Mon-Sat, 9am-noon Sun); Feira Central (3314-3872; Feira Central; 6-10pm Wed-Sun); international airport (3363-3116; arrivals hall; 6:15am-midnight) Campo Grande's main tourist office is five blocks west of Praça da República.

HSBC (Dom Aquino 1663) ATM.

Getting There & Away

Campo Grande International Airport (CGR), with flights to São Paulo, Campinas, Cuiabá, Curitiba, Manaus, Rio and Brasília, is 7km west of the center.

Campo Grande's bus station is 5km south of Centro on Costa e Silva. Sample travel times and *executivo* fares (where applicable):

DESTINATION	COST (R$)	DURATION (HR)
Bonito	60	5
Buraco das Piranhas	60	4
Corumbá	97	6
Cuiabá	91	10
Foz do Iguaçu	117	14-18
Ponta Porã	50	4½
São Paulo	149	13

The fastest way to Bonito is Vanzella (p334), a door-to-door van service, departing daily at 1pm and 2:30pm from the airport (R$70, four hours).

Getting Around

Buses 061 or 087 run south on 13 de Maio in Centro for the bus station (R$2.85), but Campo Grande buses no longer accept money. You must purchase an **Assetur** (0800-647-0060; www.assetur.com.br; Visconde de Taunay 345) *passe de ônibus* (bus pass) from select newstands, pharmacies or bus-stop kiosks, which come as *unitario* (one-time use) or *recarregável* (rechargeable).

A taxi from the airport or bus station to the center is R$25 to R$30.

Bonito

0XX67 / POP 19,500

Amid spectacular natural wonders, Bonito is both the model and epicenter of Brazil's eco-tourism boom, luring visitors with unique crystal-clear rivers and opportunities for rappelling, rafting, horse riding and bird-watching. It's no backpacker haven, but everything is top quality and truly unforgettable.

Sights & Activities

Most local attractions require a guide arranged through one of the authorized travel agencies along Bonito's main street. Prices are controlled, so shop around no further than the nearest agency. Trip prices generally include wetsuits, snorkel gear and sometimes an optional lunch, but not transport. Prices are for the December to February high season. No sunscreen or repellent is allowed in water activities. The following pack a whole lotta wow.

TOP CHOICE **Abismo de Anhumas** RAPPELLING, SNORKELING
(www.abismoanhumas.com.br; full-day excursion incl snorkeling/diving R$465/$650) Rapelling down this 72m abyss culminating in an underground lake full of incredible stalactite formations is like a journey to Middle Earth. Once at the bottom, choose snorkeling in the lake (visibility is 30m) or diving if you have a basic certificate (16 people per day only, four of whom can be divers). The rappelling training center is in town and you must successfully complete your training before 6pm on the day before your visit.

Rio da Prata SNORKELING
(www.riodaprata.com.br; 5hr trip incl lunch R$165) This marvelous river excursion includes a short trek through rainforest and a 3km snorkel downstream along the Rio Olha d'Agua, amazingly crystal clear and full of 55 species of fish; and Rio da Prata, a little foggier but still fantastic for viewing massive pacu and big, scary dourado fish. The farm serves an excellent organic lunch and is teeming with parrots.

Buraco das Araras BIRD-WATCHING
(www.buracodasararas.com.br; admission R$38) South America's largest sinkhole is home to an estimated 246 coupled scarlet macaws (among other birds) gawking and running flybys to your photographic heart's content.

Lagoa Mysteriosa SNORKELING, DIVING
(www.lagoamisteriosa.com.br; snorkeling/diving R$120/260) Reopened in 2011 after six years, this 220m-deep phreatic cave is Brazil's deepest. Choose between snorkeling or diving; either way, you're swimming in a translucent Photoshop-blue heaven.

Balneário Municipal SNORKELING
(admission R$15) Bonito's most affordable choice is the natural swimming pool on the Rio Formoso with clear water and lots of fish, 7km southeast of town.

Sleeping & Eating

Camping is available around town from around R$15 per person.

TOP CHOICE **Pousada Muito Bonito** INN $$
(3255 1645; www.hotelmuitobonito.com.br; Rebuá 1444; s/d/tr R$50/90/105;) This lovely family-run *pousada* is Bonito's best value, with comfortable en-suite rooms, an inviting courtyard and a helpful multilingual owner with an exhaustive knowledge of the local area.

Pousada São Jorge INN $$
(3255 4046; www.pousadasaojorge.com.br; Rebuá 1605; s/d/tr R$70/120/180;) Friendly, English-speaking and cheap, São Jorge is one of the best budget options in town. Also rents bikes.

A Casa do João SEAFOOD $$
(www.casadojoao.com.br; Nelson Felicio 664A; mains for 2 R$32-53; closed Tue) Especially famous for its *traíra* (a predatory fish), this popular fish house is one of Bonito's best (there's a load of meat and gourmet *jacaré*, too). All the furniture here is made from recycled wood from fallen trees.

Pastel Bonito FAST FOOD $
(www.pastelbonito.blogspot.com; Rebuá 1975; snacks R$3.50-9.50; from 3pm Mon-Sat) *Pastel*, a quintessential Brazilian street snack of stuffed, fried dough, is done well here, filled with regional delights like *pintado* (catfish), *jacaré* and the usual suspects.

O Casarão BUFFET $$
(Rebuá 1835; buffet R$22.90, rodizio de peixe R$44.90) Popular for its all-you-can-eat buffet or *rodizio de peixe,* where multiple local fish specialties swim past your table on waiter's trays.

Drinking

Taboa Bar BAR
(www.taboa.com.br; Rebuá 1837; 5pm-late) This lively bar-restaurant is famous for its trademark *taboa* (R$4), a shot of *cachaça* mixed with honey, cinnamon and *guaraná* (better in a *caipirinha* than as a shot).

Information

Bonito is tiny. Everything you need is along its freshly renovated main drag, Pilad Rebuá.

Bradesco (Rebuá 1942) ATM.

CAT (3255-1850; www.bonito-ms.com.br; Rodovia Bonito - Guia Lopes, Km 1) A bit of a haul on the town's outskirts.

Getting There & Away

AIR Trip (www.voetrip.com.br) flies from Campo Grande to Bonito's regional airport (BYO), 13km south of town on highway MS-178, on Thursday and Sunday but it's usually prohibitively expensive. There is also a Corumbá flight on the same days.

BONITO TRANSPORT

Bonito is beautiful...and expensive. One major cost-driver in town is the fact that none of the area's far-flung attractions include transportation. Unless you have your own ride, costs soar. The first rule of thumb is to make quick friends with locals or fellow travelers. Your round-trip options include the following:

Mototaxi A solo traveler option only, ranging from R$16 (Balneário Municipal) to R$70 (Rio da Prata).

Taxi Better for groups of two or more, ranging from R$40 (Parque Ecológico Rio Formoso) to R$160 (Boca da Onça).

Shared vans The best option, ranging from R$25 to R$45 round-trip, but **EK Turismo** (3255-3757; www.eklocadora.com.br) and **TransBonito** (9103-0441; www.ocompartil ado.com.br) only go to certain excursions on certain days, so your schedule must gel ith theirs.

BUS Five daily buses run from Bonito to Campo Grande (R$59.80, five hours) but require a quick switch in Guia Lopes. **Vanzella** (3255-3005; www.vanzellatransportes.com.br), a popular door-to-door van service (R$70, four hours), departs for Campo Grande's airport at 7:30am and 10:30am.

For Corumbá, **Cruzeiro do Sul** (3255-1606; www.cruzeirodosulms.com.br) runs one lowly bus at noon (R$63.60, six hours) daily except Sunday but most travelers use the direct 8am van service from **Catarino Transportes** (9615-4165; catarinotranssp@yahoo.com.br; 24 de Fevereiro 1640), which is timed for a seamless transfer to a Corumbá-bound bus from Campo Grande in Buraco das Piranhas (R$70, six hours). It returns to Bonito at 3:30pm.

Corumbá

Last stop in Brazil is the crumbling historic port town of Corumbá which, despite its geographic position as the gateway to the Pantanal and Bolivia, offers little to travelers other than astonishing sunsets over the Rio Paraguai. You can take a tour from here but tourism is in decline and most travelers choose instead to organize their Pantanal trips from Campo Grande or Cuiabá.

If you do get stuck sleeping here, try the simple and central **Hotel Santa Rita** (3231-5453; www.santaritahotel.com; Rua Dom Aquino 860; s/d/tr R$70/130/180;) or the bus-station-adjacent **Hotel El Dorado** (3231-6677; hotel_eldorado@top.com.br; Rua Porto Carreiro 554; s/d/tr R$100/126/160;). The best eats are found on the 400 and 500 blocks of Frei Mariano.

Corumbá International Airport (CMG) is served by Trip Airlines from Campo Grande and Bonito. There are numerous buses from Campo Grande to Corumbá (R$94.20, 6½ hours) and a direct van service from Bonito (R$70, six hours) to Buraco das Piranhas, where you can catch a passing bus from Campo Grande as well. Cruzeiro do Sul departs for Bonito (R$63.60, six hours) at 7am daily except Sunday.

THE NORTHEAST

Year-round warm climate, physical beauty and sensual culture rich in folkloric traditions all make Brazil's Northeast a true tropical paradise. More than 2000km of fertile coastline is studded with idyllic white-sand beaches, pockets of lush rainforest, sand dunes and coral reefs. A spectrum of natural environments creates the perfect backdrop for a wide variety of outdoor activities.

These parts of the country also breathe colonial history. The picturesque urban centers of Salvador, Olinda and São Luís are packed with beautifully restored and satisfyingly decaying architecture. Add to this the lively festivals, myriad music and dance styles and exotic cuisine loaded with seafood, and you will find Brazil's most culturally diverse region.

Salvador

0XX71 / POP 2.7 MILLION

Salvador da Bahia is among Brazil's brightest gems. It's the African soul of the country, where the descendants of slaves preserved their African culture more than anywhere else in the New World, creating thriving culinary, religious, musical, dance and martial-

GETTING TO BOLIVIA

The Fronteira bus (R$2.50, 15 minutes) goes from Corumbá's Praça Independência to the Bolivian border every 25 minutes from 6am to 7pm. From Corumbá's bus station, a taxi is around R$40 but groups of two or less traveling light are better off using a mototaxi (R$15).

All Brazilian exit formalities must be completed with the **Polícia Federal** (3234-7822; www.dpf.gov.br; 8-11am & 2-5pm Mon-Fri, 9am-1pm Sat & Sun) at the border. Both countries work limited matching office hours, so be prepared to overnight in Corumbá if you are crossing outside of them. To enter Bolivia, most countries do not need a visa, but citizens of the United States must obtain a visa (US$135) from abroad or at the **Bolivian consulate** (3231-5605; Porto Carrero 1650; 8am-12:30pm & 2-4:30pm Mon-Fri) in Corumbá. See Bolivia's US Embassy (www.bolivia-usa.org) for more information.

The Bolivian border town of Quijarro is little more than a collection of shacks. *Colectivos* (minibuses; B$3) and taxis (B$10) run the 3km between the border and Quijarro train station. Onward travel, from Quijarro to Santa Cruz, should be planned in advance.

The Northeast

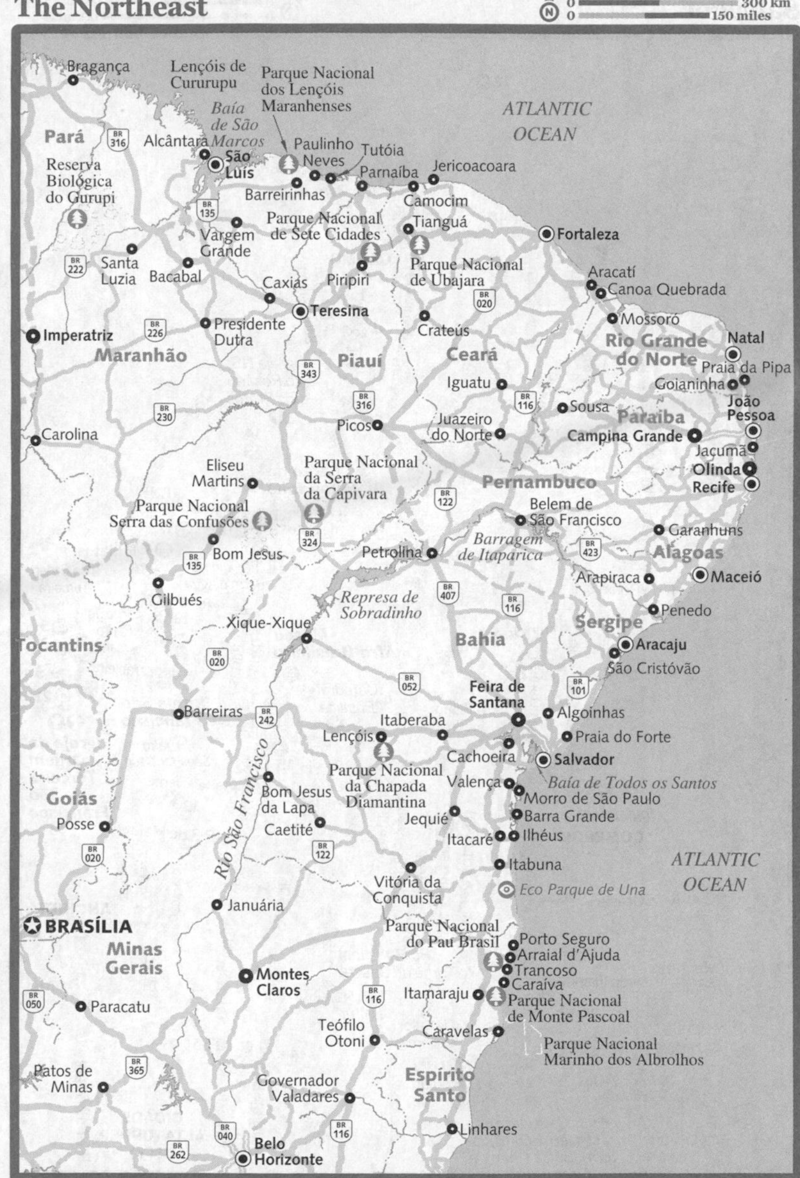

arts traditions. Underlying much of Salvador's culture is the Afro-Brazilian religion Candomblé, in which Catholic and animistic traditions blend to form rituals that involve direct communication with the spirit world.

Salvador's vibrant historic center, the Pelourinho, is a treat for the senses with its *dendê* oil aromas, thundering percussion and renovated colonial architecture. It has an anarchic quality that makes its party nights memorable. Don't be fooled into

Salvador

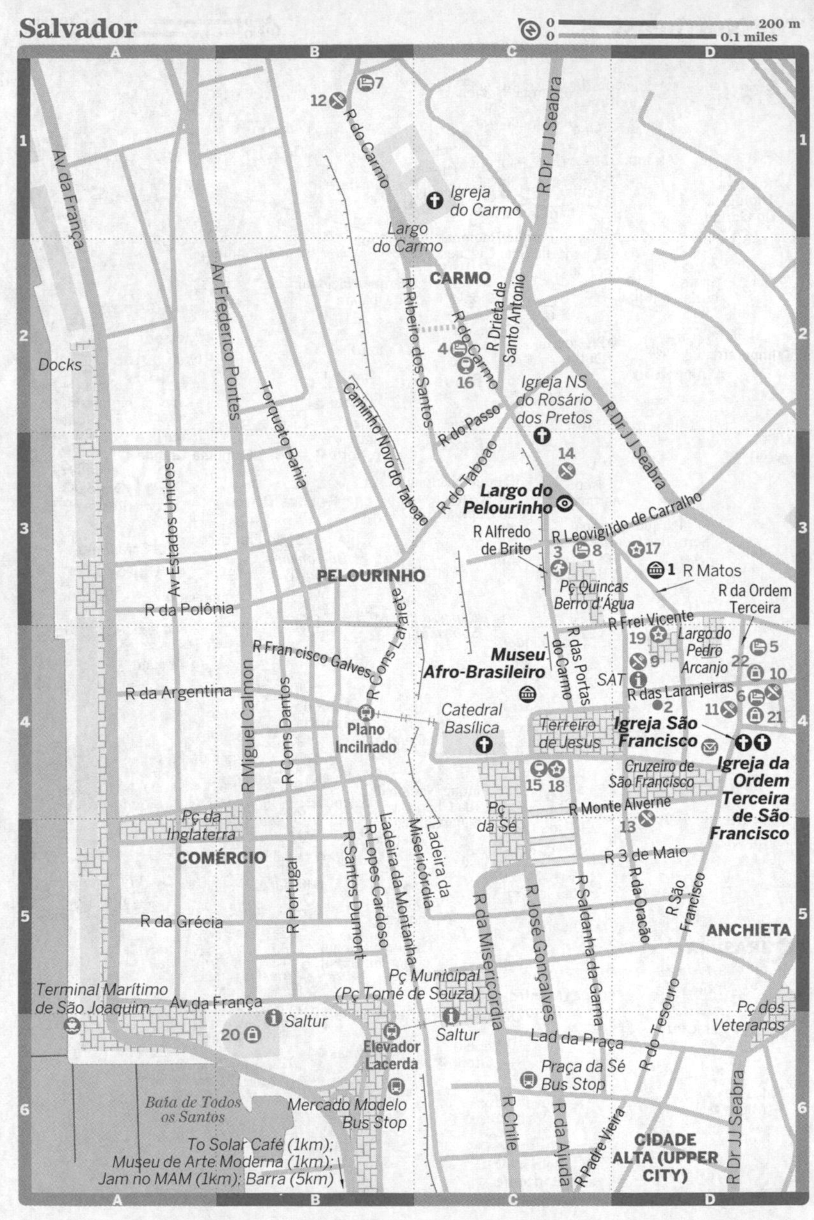

thinking the Pelô is nothing more than a tourist ghetto. Many of the studios here are at the cutting edge of contemporary Brazilian movement, dance, music and art. The surrounding area, however, is desperately poor.

Salvador sits on a peninsula on the Baía de Todos os Santos. The center is bayside and divided by a steep bluff into two parts: the Cidade Baixa (Lower City), containing the commercial center and port, and Cidade Alta (Upper City), containing the Pelou

Salvador

Top Sights

rinho. The Pelô is the center of Salvador's history, tourism and nightlife. Cidade Baixa and the stretch between Praça da Sé and Praça Campo Grande are noisy by day and deserted by night. South, at the tip of the peninsula, is affluent beachside Barra. Residential neighborhoods stretch northeast along the Atlantic coast, with Rio Vermelho and Itapuã the most interesting.

Sights

PELOURINHO

The Pelô has numerous churches, galleries, workshops and museums to browse as you wander its cobbled streets.

Museu Afro-Brasileiro MUSEUM
(www.mafro.ceao.ufba.br; Terreiro de Jesus; admission R$6; 9am-5pm Mon-Fri) Historic photos of Candomblé priests and gorgeous carved wood panels of the *orixás* (Afro-Brazilian deities) by Argentine-Brazilian artist Carybé are among the treasures displayed in this unique museum.

Igreja São Francisco CHURCH
(Cruzeiro de São Francisco; admission R$5; 9am-5:30pm Mon-Sat) One of Brazil's most magnificent churches, this baroque beauty is crammed with displays of wealth, including ornate wood carvings smothered in gold leaf and a convent courtyard paneled with hand-painted *azulejos* (Portuguese tiles).

Igreja da Ordem Terceira de São Francisco CHURCH
(São Francisco; admission R$3; 8am-4pm) This stunning baroque church features a majestic carved sandstone facade (the only one of its kind in Brazil) and marvelous panels of Portuguese tiles depicting Lisbon landmarks.

Largo do Pelourinho SQUARE
In this steep square, slaves were auctioned and likely publicly beaten on a *pelourinho* (whipping post).

FREE **Centro Cultural Solar Ferrão** MUSEUM
(Matos 45; 10am-6pm Tue-Fri, 1-5pm Sat & Sun) This attractively restored building holds permanent exhibitions of African art, Bahian folk art and religious art, along with temporary displays.

CIDADE BAIXA & BARRA

On the Barra waterfront, view the sunset at Bahia's oldest fort, **Santo Antônio** (1598).

FREE **Museu de Arte Moderna** MUSEUM
(MAM; www.mam.ba.gov.br; Av Contorno; 1-7pm Tue-Fri, 2-7pm Sat & Sun) Housed in an 18th-century mansion, this lovely modern-art museum has a bayside sculpture garden, waterfront cafe and good temporary exhibits. It's a short walk from Mercado Modelo; cab it after dark.

ITAPAGIPE PENINSULA

Igreja NS do Bonfim CHURCH
(Praça Senhor do Bonfim; ⌚8:30-11am & 1-6pm Tue-Sun) Candomblé's key church, built in 1745, houses a Christ renowned throughout Bahia for effecting miraculous cures; witness the vast and moving collection of photos, ex-voto limbs, offerings and tokens of thanks left by devotees. *Fitas* (ribbons) from Bonfim are a popular memento. Take the 'Bonfim' or 'Ribeira' bus from the base of Elevador Lacerda.

Activities

Much Bahian life revolves around the Afro-Brazilian religion Candomblé. A visit to a *terreiro* (the house of an Afro-Brazilian religious group) promises hours of ritual and possession, and will deepen your understanding of Bahian culture. Wear clean, light-colored clothes (no shorts) and go well-fed. **FENACAB** (fenacabbrasil.com.br; Brito 39; ⌚9am-noon & 2-5pm Mon-Fri) can provide addresses and schedules.

Praia do Porto in Barra is a small, usually packed beach with calm waters. For less crowded beaches and cleaner water, head out to **Piatã** (25km), **Itapuã** (27km) or beyond.

Courses

Associacão de Capoeira Mestre Bimba MARTIAL ARTS
(☎3322-0639; www.capoeiramestrebimba.com.br; Laranjeiras 1, Pelourinho) Runs classes in *capoeira* (martial art/dance), *maculelê* (stick fighting) and percussion. It also puts on shows.

Festivals & Events

Carnaval CULTURE
Salvador's Carnaval is the second largest in Brazil and, for many, the best. It's characterized by parades of *axé* and *pagode* bands atop creeping *trios elétricos* (long trucks of huge speakers). A *trio* or drum corps, together with its followers grouped in a roped-off area around it, form a *bloco*. People pay hundreds of reais for the *abadá* (shirt required for entry to the *bloco*) for a top band, mostly for prestige and the safety of those ropes. Choosing to *fazer pipoca* (be popcorn) in the street is still a fine way to spend Carnaval.

There are three main areas: the beachside Barra to Rio Vermelho circuit (most touristy), the narrow Campo Grande to Praça Castro Alves circuit, and the Pelourinho (no *trios* here, mostly concerts and drum corps). Check www.carnaval.salvador.ba.gov.br.

Lavagem do Bonfim RELIGION
Salvador's largest festival outside of Carnaval begins on the second Thursday in January with Bahian women in ritual dress washing the steps at Igreja NS do Bonfim, followed by a rowdy street party featuring percussion and *trios elétricos*.

Festa de Iemanjá RELIGION
Candomblé's most important festival, on February 2, brings crowds of devotees of Iemanjá, goddess of the sea and fertility, to Praia Rio Vermelho, where offerings of flowers, cakes, effigies, beer and perfume are blessed. The ensuing street festival involves some of Salvador's best bands and lasts late into the night.

Sleeping

Staying in the Pelô (packed with hostels) means being in the heart of the action, but it can be noisy and draining. Mellower, beachside Barra has easy transport to the Pelô and the conveniences of a residential neighborhood. Reservations are essential for Carnaval.

PELOURINHO

TOP CHOICE **Hostel Galeria 13** HOSTEL $
(☎3266-5609; www.hostelgaleria13.com; Ordem Terceira/Accioli 23; dm/d R$35/140; ❄@📶) Prime middle-of-the-Pelourinho location is just the start at this hostel much loved by international travelers. The endless list of perks includes breakfast till noon, on-site bar with free happy-hour *caipirinhas*, sociable dogs and a teeny pool patio for chilling out. Multilingual owner Paulo shares his in-depth knowledge and love of Salvador through a self-published guide available to all guests.

Hostel Cobreu HOSTEL $
(☎3117-1401; www.hostelcobreu.com; Ladeira do Carmo 22; dm R$26-35, d R$70; @📶) Colorful and cool, Cobreu offers tidy three- to 10-bed dorms, bargain-priced private rooms, a DVD theater, balconies overlooking the picturesque Ladeira do Carmo, and interiors done by a well-known local graffiti artist. The bar downstairs is another plus.

Laranjeiras Hostel HOSTEL
(☎3321-1366; www.laranjeirashostel.com.br; Ordem Terceira/Accioli 13; dm R$41, d with/without bathroom R$140/116; ❄@📶) Extremely

placed in the heart of the Pelourinho, this HI-affiliated hostel offers high-ceilinged dorms, doubles and triples, some with air-con and en-suite bathrooms, others with fans and shared bathrooms. There's an attractive cafe-creperie downstairs.

Nega Maluca GUESTHOUSE **$**
(☎3242-9249; www.negamaluca.com; Marchantes 15, Santo Antônio; dm with fan/air-con R$27/30, d with/without bathroom R$85/75;) A five-minute climb from the Pelô's noisy zone, this laid-back, traveler-run hostel offers dorms, doubles and one room with its own kitchen and fridge. Homey amenities include a guest kitchen, DVD library and honor bar.

Pousada Terra Nossa INN **$**
(☎3321-5267; www.pousadaterranossa.com; Leovigildo de Carvalho 3; dm/s/d R$35/80/100;) Warm atmosphere and a central location are the top draws at this *pousada*. Fan-cooled, high-ceilinged front rooms get ample natural light but suffer from street noise; air-conditioned back rooms are windowless but quieter, with exposed-brick walls.

CIDADE BAIXA & BARRA

TOP CHOICE **Open House Barra** INN **$**
(☎3264-0337; www.openhousebarra.com; Catarino 137, Barra; dm/s/d R$39/72/115, d without bathroom R$90;) This exuberantly colorful, high-ceilinged place is hosted by professional artists with ties to the local music, dance and film communities. Perks include periodic onsite concerts and *capoeira* demonstrations; Carnaval here is a memorable party experience. Dorms are for women only, private rooms are open to all.

Âmbar Pousada INN **$**
(☎3264-6956; www.ambarpousada.com.br; Celso 485; dm/s/d R$48/120/140;) Rooms aren't huge but the hangout space, multilingual reception and cheerful ambience make this the best of a string of *pousadas* two blocks back from the beach.

Albergue do Porto HOSTEL **$**
(☎3264-6600; www.alberguedoporto.com.br; Barão de Sergy 197; dm R$35-44, d R$130;) Just a block inland from Barra's best beach, this HI hostel with kindergarten-esque decor has airy, high-ceilinged dorm rooms of various sizes, a guest kitchen and great staff.

Pousada La Villa Française INN **$**
(☎3245-6008; www.lavilafrancaise.com; Recife 2, Jardim Brasil; dm/s/d R$40/80/120;) By a little nest of bars and restaurants near Barra Shopping a few blocks back from the beach, this French-run spot has cute, spotless rooms, use of a kitchen and a relaxing, cordial atmosphere.

Pousada Acácia INN **$**
(☎3264-4113; www.pousadaacacia.com.br; Oliveira 46/210; s/d R$100/140;) A motherly welcome and an abundant breakfast await at this peaceful Brazilian-run *pousada*. Rooms in the spacious 1950s main house are far preferable to the cramped units out back.

Eating

Salvador is well known for its African-influenced Bahian cuisine. A street-food staple is *acarajé* (Bahian fritters made of brown beans and dried shrimp). For cheap seafood snacks, join the locals at the stalls on Mercado Modelo's ground floor.

PELOURINHO

Senac BUFFET **$$**
(Largo do Pelourinho 13; per kg R$29, all you can eat R$40; ⏲per-kilo lunch Mon-Fri, buffet lunch daily) Salvador's restaurant school hosts a downstairs per-kilo lunch spot, plus a much more elaborate upstairs buffet where you can sample a vast array of helpfully labeled Bahian main dishes and desserts.

Cafélier CAFE **$**
(Carmo 50; snacks & light meals R$5-20; ⏲2:30-9:30pm Thu-Tue) This hideaway cafe serves sandwiches, soup, salads, omelets and light meals, accompanied by strong coffee and rich desserts. Grab a table at the back for spectacular sunset views over the bay.

Café Conosco VEGETARIAN **$**
(Ordem Terceira 4; snacks from R$6.20; ⏲10am-7pm Mon-Sat) For over a decade, Dona Nilza has been delighting visitors with sweet and savory treats, from homemade apple, passion fruit and coconut tarts to quiches laden with veggies.

Bar Zulu INTERNATIONAL **$$**
(Laranjeiras 15; sandwiches & salads R$11-22, mains R$18-35) This corner bar-restaurant affiliated with Hostel Galeria 13 serves a wide-ranging mix of Spanish tapas, veggie curries, Bahian and international dishes, along with juices and fruit-infused cocktails.

Ramma BUFFET, VEGETARIAN **$$**
(Cruzeiro de São Francisco 7; per kg R$40; ⏲lunch Mon-Sat;) High-quality vegetarian and

organic food at this upstairs restaurant. There's another branch in **Barra** (☎3264 0044; Lord Cochrane 76, Barra; per kg R$22; ⏰lunch Sun-Fri).

Axego BRAZILIAN **$$**
(João de Deus 1; dishes for 2 people R$40-70, moqueca half-portions from R$24; ⏰lunch & dinner) Expect warm service and fair prices at this attractive upstairs restaurant. Delicious *moquecas* are the highlight, and half-portions are available.

CIDADE BAIXA & BARRA

Barra and Rio Vermelho are full of restaurants, particularly the two parallel streets back from the Praia do Farol beach in Barra, and Rua Feira de Santana in Rio Vermelho.

Solar Café INTERNATIONAL **$$**
(Av Contorno s/n; mains R$26-48; ⏰closed Mon; wi-fi) Terrific sunset views, free wi-fi and a bayside setting in a 17th-century former sugar estate make this restaurant a winner even before you open the menu. International offerings include Asian salads, chicken quesadillas and other treats you won't find elsewhere. It's adjacent to Salvador's MAM art museum.

Acarajé da Dinha BRAZILIAN **$**
(Largo de Santana, Rio Vermelho; acarajé R$6; ⏰4:30am-11pm Mon-Sat) This street stall sells Salvador's most renowned *acarajé*.

Cabana da Cely SEAFOOD **$$**
(Av Marques de Leão 183; mains R$18-44) Locals flock in for cold beer, fresh fish, piping-hot *lambreta* (clams) and piles of fresh garlic shrimp at this casual eatery near Barra's lighthouse. Check the menu for good-value *pratos executivos* (lunch specials) and two-for-one specials.

Maria de São Pedro BRAZILIAN **$$**
(Mercado Modelo; moquecas R$30-60; ⏰11am-7pm Mon-Sat, to 4pm Sun) On the top floor of the market, this touristy restaurant with spectacular harbor views specializes in traditional Bahian food. The outdoor terrace is a classic sundowner spot.

Drinking

PELOURINHO

Plazas and cobbled streets fill with revelers sharing beer at plastic tables or dancing behind roaming bands of drummers. Tuesday is the big night. There's free live music in the *largos* (inner courtyards) of the Pelô and on the Terreiro de Jesus.

Bar Cravinho BAR
(Terreiro de Jesus; ⏰noon-11pm) Decorated with barrels and usually packed with a lively mix of locals and tourists, this neighborhood bar specializes in flavored shots of *cachaça*, including its trademark clove-infused variety.

Café Alquimia BAR
(Ladeira do Carmo 22) On the cobblestoned hillside leading up to Largo do Carmo, this bluesy cafe-bar draws young travelers, musicians and artistic types with its menu of finger foods, inexpensive cocktails and cold beer.

CIDADE BAIXA & BARRA

Barra's nightlife centers in Jardim Brasil, with cool open-air bars attracting a hip, mostly affluent crowd. Largo de Santana and Largo da Mariquita in bohemian Rio Vermelho pack with people drinking beer and eating *acarajé*. Hip bars surround these squares.

Barravento BAR
(Av Oceânica) This is Barra's only waterfront bar and restaurant, and a choice spot for a sundowner.

☆ Entertainment

Salvador is home to many world-class performers. Singers, bands and Carnaval groups hold weekly *ensaios* (rehearsals), essentially concerts, in the months leading up to Carnaval. The brotherhood Filhos de Gandhy is an *afoxé* (group tied to Candomblé traditions) that has come to represent Salvador itself. Excellent *blocos afros* (Afro-Brazilian groups with powerful drum corps) are Ilê Aiyê, Male Debalê and Dida; more poppy but still with strong percussion sections are Olodum (an institution), Araketu and Timbalada (brainchild of Carlinhos Brown).

For listings, see www.agendacultural.ba.gov.br, www.aldeianago.com.br and www.pelourinho.ba.gov.br.

Salvador's main soccer clubs are **Vitória** (www.ecvitoria.com.br) and the venerable **Bahia** (www.esporteclubebahia.com.br). The city's brand-new, 56,000-seat **Arena Fonte Nova** (www.arenafontenova.com.br), built on the site of the decades-old previous stadium of the same name, will host six World Cup 2014 matches, including one round-of-16 match and one quarter-final match. It's 1km southeast of the Pelourinho.

Balé Folclórico da Bahia DANCE, MUSIC
(www.balefolcloricodabahia.com.br; Matos 49, Teatro Miguel Santana; admission R$35; ⌚shows 8pm Mon & Wed-Sat) Shows include displays of *afro* (Afro-Brazilian dance), *samba de roda* (flirtatious samba performed in a circle), and dances of the *orixás*, *maculelê* and *capoeira*, all to live percussion and vocals.

Teatro Castro Alves LIVE MUSIC
(www.tca.ba.gov.br; Praça 2 de Julho, Campo Grande) Salvador's finest venue for quality performances. Its Concha Acústica (amphitheater) holds fun weekly shows.

Jam no MAM LIVE MUSIC
(www.jamnomam.com.br; Av Contorno) Popular outdoor jazz concerts (R$6) at the Museu de Arte Moderna from 6pm to 9pm on Saturday evenings.

Sankofa LIVE MUSIC
(☎3321-7236; www.sankofabrasil.com; Frei Vicente 7) This centrally located bar in the Pelourinho hosts live salsa and samba, as well as DJs who mix everything from reggae to Congolese rumba.

Fundo do Cravinho LIVE MUSIC
(Terreiro de Jesus) Live samba nightly (R$5) from about 8pm, down an alley behind the eponymous bar.

Borracharia CLUB
(Conselheiro Pedro Luís 101A, Rio Vermelho; ⌚11:30pm-5am Fri & Sat) Housed in a Rio Vermelho auto-repair shop, this popular club blasts everything from rock to reggae and pop to surf music on weekend nights.

Madrre CLUB
(www.madrre.com; Av Mangabeira 2471, Pituba) Dance club featuring a diversity of styles: pop, rock, *axé*, funk, *pagode*, *sertanejo* (Brazilian country music) and electronic music.

San Sebastian GAY
(www.sansebastiansalvador.com.br; Paciência 88, Rio Vermelho; ⌚midnight-late Fri & Sat, 8pm-midnight Sun) Popular gay-friendly nightclub, featuring Saturday-night electronica, Sunday *samba de roda* and a rotating Friday-night lineup that includes once-monthly lesbian nights.

Off Club GAY
(www.offclub.com.br; Dias D'Ávila 33, Barra; ⌚10pm-6am Thu-Sun) This is Salvador's oldest gay club.

Shopping

Mercado Modelo HANDICRAFTS
(Praça Visconde de Cayru; ⌚9am-7pm Mon-Sat, to 2pm Sun) The two-story, enclosed tourist market has dozens of stalls selling local handicrafts. Arriving slaves were once kept in the watery depths of this 19th-century building.

Midialouca BOOKS, MUSIC
(cnr Laranjeiras & Terceira Ordem; ⌚closed Tue) Brazilian music CDs and photo books about Salvador and Bahia.

Mestre Lua MUSIC
(Ordem Terceira 3; ⌚noon-7pm Mon-Sat) Run by a dreadlocked *capoeira* master, this musical workshop is a wonderful place to learn about Afro-Brazilian music and purchase handmade Bahian percussion instruments.

Information

If you're going to be pickpocketed or mugged in Brazil, Salvador is likely to be the place. This shouldn't prevent you from visiting but play it safe, especially at night. Avoid empty areas, and watch your pockets when moving through densely packed crowds. Travelers report 'feeling like a protected species' in the Pelô, but wandering off the beaten path there has proven to be unsafe. The stretch from the Largo do Pelourinho north to Santo Antônio has a reputation for nighttime muggings – take a taxi.

ATMs exist throughout the center as well as at the bus station, airport and shopping centers. Internet cafes and call centers cluster in the Pelô and Barra.

Banco do Brasil (Cruzeiro de São Francisco 11, Pelourinho)

Deltur (☎3116-6817; Cruzeiro de São Francisco 14, Pelourinho) Main tourist police office.

Hospital Espanhol (Sete de Setembro 4161, Barra)

Post Office (Cruzeiro de São Francisco; ⌚9am-5pm Mon-Fri, 9am-1pm Sat) Centrally located in Pelourinho.

Saltur (www.saltur.salvador.ba.gov.br) Elevador Lacerda (☎3321-3127; ⌚9am-8pm Mon-Fri, 9am-6pm Sat, 9am-1pm Sun); Mercado Modelo (☎3241-0242; ⌚8am-5:30pm Mon-Sat, 8am-2pm Sun) Municipal tourist office; less helpful than the state-run offices.

SAT (www.setur.ba.gov.br) Airport (☎3204-1244; ⌚7am-11pm); bus station (☎3450-3871; Rodoviária; ⌚8am-5pm); Pelourinho (☎3321-2133; cnr Laranjeiras & João de Deus; ⌚8:30am-9pm) Multilingual offices run by Bahia's state government.

CARNAVAL SAFETY TIPS

Crowds clearing to escape a fight pose the greatest threat, so be aware of your surroundings. Police are a noticeable presence. Hands will be all over you, searching your pockets and groping your person. Costumes aren't common – shorts and tennis shoes are usual. A few tips:

» Form small groups and avoid deserted areas.

» Women shouldn't walk alone or wear skirts.

» Carry little money, stashed in your shoe.

» Leave *all* jewelry, watches and nice-looking sunglasses behind.

» Don't challenge pickpockets – the ensuing fight isn't worthwhile.

» Carry a photocopy of your passport.

Getting There & Away

Air

Several domestic and international airlines serve Salvador's Luis Eduardo Magalhães International Airport (SSA). TAP and American Airlines fly directly to Europe and the USA respectively.

Bus

Long-distance buses from the south must take a lengthy, circuitous trip around the bay to reach Salvador's *rodoviária*. A faster, less expensive route into Salvador involves getting off at Valença on the main highway, then taking a bus (R$14, 1½ hours) to Bom Despacho on Ilha Itaparica, from where you can catch a ferry (R$4, 45 minutes) to Salvador's Terminal de São Joaquim. Coming this way saves up to two hours and R$60.

Sample travel times and fares from Salvador are as follows:

DESTINATION	COST (R$)	DURATION (HR)
Belo Horizonte	213	23
Brasília	223	22
Ilhéus	80-140	7-8
Natal	177-203	20
Porto Seguro	151	12
Recife	103-159	12-16
Rio	200-275	24-29
São Paulo	307	32

Getting Around

For Barra and Cidade Alta, cross the footbridge from the bus station (8km from the center) to Shopping Iguatemí and catch the Praça da Sé minibus (R$3, 30 to 45 minutes). Catch the same bus (R$3, one to 1½ hours) from the airport (30km from the center). For a slightly cheaper but more crowded ride (R$2.80), there are city bus terminals in front of both the bus station and the airport. Regular city buses ($2.80, 20 to 30 minutes) connect Praça da Sé and Barra.

Linking the lower and upper cities in the center are the fabulous art deco **Elevador Lacerda** (3322-7049; R$0.15; 24hr), and the exciting **Plano Inclinado** (R$0.15; 7am-7pm Mon-Fri, to 1pm Sat) funicular railway.

Lençóis

0XX75 / POP 10,000

Lençóis is the prettiest of the old diamond-mining towns in the Chapada Diamantina, a mountainous wooded oasis in the dusty *sertão* (dry interior). The surrounding area – bursting with caves, waterfalls and plateaus promising panoramic views – is a hiking hot spot and a nature lover's dream.

Sights & Activities

Walking & Swimming

Two walks near town are easily taken without a guide. The first heads southwest past the bus stop and follows the Rio Lençois 3km upstream into Parque Municipal da Muritiba. You'll pass a series of rapids known as **Cachoeira Serrano**, the **Salão de Areias Coloridas** (Room of Colored Sands, where artisans gather material for bottled sand paintings), the **Poço Halley** swimming hole and the **Cachoeirinha** and **Cachoeira da Primavera** waterfalls. The second walk follows Rua São Benedito 4km southeast out of town to **Ribeirão do Meio**, a series of swimming holes with a natural waterslide.

Hiking

Southwest of Lençóis, **Parque Nacional da Chapada Diamantina** comprises 1520 sq km of breathtaking scenery, waterfalls rivers, monkeys and striking geology. Th park has little infrastructure (trails are unmarked) and bus services are infrequent, making it difficult to penetrate without a guide. Make sure you only use certified guides; the **ACVL** (☎3334-1425; 10 de Novembro) guide association, local agencies or your *pousada* can hook you up with one. Ultra-knowledgeable English-speaking guides are **Roy Funch** (☎3334-1305; funchroy@yahoo.com) and **Olivia Taylor** (☎3334-1229; www.h2otraveladventures.com) at Pousada dos Duendes.

Multiday hikes usually involve a combination of camping or staying in local homes and *pousadas*. Prices, including food and accommodation, start around R$120 per day.

Climbing

Fora da Trilha Escalada ROCK CLIMBING
(☎3334-1326; www.foradatrilha.com.br; Pedras 202) An adventure operator specializing in rock climbing and abseiling.

Tours

Lençóis agencies (there's one on every corner) organize half- and full-day car trips (R$55 to R$150 per person depending on group size and destination) and guided hikes from a couple of hours to a week or longer. Various admission fees apply in the area; these are usually included in the tour price. There's a rotating schedule of trips. Agencies pool customers and rent out necessary gear.

Standout sights include **Poço Encantado**, a cave filled with stunningly beautiful blue water, **Lapa Doce**, another cave with impressive formations, and **Cachoeira da Fumaça**, Brazil's highest waterfall (420m). Near Lençóis, **Morro do Pai Inácio** is a mesa-style peak affording an awesome view over a plateau-filled valley.

Sleeping

Reserve for major holidays, particularly for São João, the town's major festival in late June.

TOP CHOICE **Alcino Estalagem & Atelier** INN $$
(☎3334-1171; www.alcinoestalagem.com; Tomba Surrão 139; s/d R$210/280, without bathroom R$140/190; ❄📶) For a memorable splurge, consider this lovely yellow mansion, decorated top to bottom with local artist Alcino's ceramic work. Mornings feature one of Brazil's most sumptuous breakfast spreads, with an ever-changing menu of more than a dozen sweet and savory homemade treats.

Pousada dos Duendes INN $
(☎3334-1229; www.pousadadosduendes.com; Pires; dm R$35, s/d R$80/115, without bathroom R$55/85; @📶) This brilliantly relaxed place offers cute rooms, very friendly atmosphere, a kitchen and internet. Upstairs rooms with their own balcony and hammock cost R$10 more. The English-speaking owner runs good excursions and can also advise on local guides.

Camping Lumiar CAMPGROUND $
(☎3334-1241; lumiar.camping@gmail.com; Praça do Rosário 70; campsite/r per person R$25/40, chalet R$150; 📶) Grassy campsites and chalets shaded by flowering trees in a gorgeous garden behind a church, plus rooms sleeping two to six in a grand historic home. Bar, restaurant and guest-use kitchen.

Pousada Casa de Hélia INN $
(☎3334-1143; www.casadehelia.com.br; Muritiba; dm/s/d R$40/50/90; ❄@📶🏊) Straggling across a hillside two minutes above the bus station, this tranquil retreat has an airy breakfast terrace and 22 spacious rooms, most with verandas, good views and ample natural light. Some rooms have air-con, and dorms feature twin beds rather than bunks.

Hostel Chapada HOSTEL $
(☎3334-1497; www.hostelchapada.com.br; Duarte 121; dm R$37-45, d R$90-100; 📶) Uncrowded dorms and simple doubles surround a back patio at this centrally located, HI-affiliated 140-year-old house. Women's dorms all have en-suite bathrooms. Kitchen, barbecue and laundry facilities are available, along with minisafes, backpack storage and hiking tours.

Eating & Drinking

O Bode BUFFET $
(Beco do Rio; per kg R$24; ⏰lunch) Just off the main square, this sweet riverside spot does the best-value lunch in town.

Cozinha Aberta ASIAN $$
(Barbosa 42; dishes R$28-44; ⏰noon-10:30pm) Treat yourself at this gourmet bistro following slow-food principles (everything is as fresh, organic and local as possible), with an emphasis on Thai and Indian curries.

El Jamiro ARGENTINE **$$**
(Baderna 60; mains R$15-36) Candlelit tables, friendly service and grilled meat are the big draws at this Argentine-run eatery. Daily specials (R$25) include tall *caipirinhas*, meat, rice, salad and delicious homemade potato chips.

Os Artistas da Massa ITALIAN **$$**
(Baderna 49; dishes R$19-25) This sweet spot serves excellent fresh pasta dishes accompanied by quality jazz tunes you pick off the menu.

Fazendinha & Tal BAR
(Pedras 125; cachaças R$2) In the heart of candlelit Rua das Pedras, this handsome bar offers dozens of *cachaça* infusions ranging from cinnamon to pineapple.

Information

The tourist office is in the market building next to the bridge. Internet places charge around R$3 per hour. Banco do Brasil has ATMs on the main square.

Getting There & Away

Air

Lençóis' Horacio de Mattos Airport (LEC), 22km east of town, has twice-weekly service to Salvador on Trip Airlines. A taxi from the airport to the center costs R$60.

Bus

Real Expresso runs four daily buses from Salvador (R$59.45, six to seven hours, at 7am, 1pm, 4:30pm and 11pm), returning from Lençois at 7:30am, 1:15pm, 3pm and 11:30pm.

Morro de São Paulo

☎0XX75

Trendy, isolated Morro, across the bay from Salvador and reached by boat, is known for never-say-die nightlife but still has a tranquil charm along its pedestrianized main street running between three jungle-topped hills.

Sights & Activities

The beaches, with their shallow, warm water, disappear with the tides, liberating you for a hike to the waterfall, a round-the-island boat trip (R$65), a visit to the quieter neighboring island of **Boipeba** or sunset-watching from the fort.

A short climb from the boat dock brings you to Morro's main square, where you'll find the town church. Follow Caminho da Praia down to the beaches, which are named in numerical order; most of the action is around Segunda (Second) and Terceira (Third) Praias, a 10- to 15-minute walk from the Praça.

Sleeping

Reservations are required for holiday periods, especially Carnaval and *ressaca* (five days of post-Carnaval hangover). The prices listed here are for January; they drop considerably off-season.

Che Lagarto Hostel HOSTEL **$**
(☎3652-1018; www.chelagarto.com; Fonte Grande; dm/d R$50/185; 📶) Close to the ferry dock and main square, this newish hostel has a youthful party vibe and a 'middle of the jungle' feel thanks to its forest-shrouded wooden sundeck.

Pousada Kanzuá do Marujo HOSTEL, INN **$**
(☎3652-1152; kanzua@hotmail.com; Terceira Praia; dm/s/d R$40/100/140; ❄@📶) A superbright two-story complex of modern rooms just back from the ocean at 'Third Beach.' Deep discounts outside of high season.

Pousada Ninho da Águia INN **$**
(☎3652-1201; pousadaninhodaaguia@hotmail.com; Caminho do Farol 8; r per person downstairs/upstairs R$60/65) On the hill above the dock, the tranquil Ninho da Águia is perched at eagle's-nest heights. It's a friendly, family-run affair with tidy, simple rooms (upstairs rooms have great views).

Pousada Passarte INN **$**
(☎3652-1030; www.pousadapassarte.com.br; s/d R$75/150; ❄📶) These small, simple rooms are conveniently located at the edge of the main square.

Eating & Drinking

There's a wide choice. Numerous places offer all-you-can-eat pizza *(rodízio)* for R$25. The party scene is around Segunda Praia.

Sabor da Terra SEAFOOD **$$**
(Caminho da Praia; daily specials R$18-22) For two decades this place has been preparing some of the island's best fish *moqueca* and *casquinha de siri* (shredded crab meat). *Pratos do dia* (daily specials) offer good value.

Tchê Kebab MIDDLE EASTERN **$**
(Caminho da Praia; sandwiches from R$6; ⏰4-11pm) Gaucho-style grilled meats are incor-

porated into delicious, reasonably priced Middle Eastern sandwiches at this new main-street eatery.

Alecrim BUFFET **$$**
(Caminho da Praia; per kg R$39) You'll find everything from shrimp *moqueca* and fried fish to chicken stewed in beer at this popular per-kilo place on the main pedestrian street.

Information

The **CIT Tur** (3652-1083; www.morrosp.com.br; Praça Principal; 8am-10pm) tourist office is on Morro's main square. There are a few ATMs and heaps of internet places (R$3 per hour).

Getting There & Away

Various boats (R$75, two hours, first 8am, last 2pm) cross to Morro six times daily from Salvador's Terminal Marítimo Turístico. It can be rough, so come with a fairly empty stomach. The first return from Morro is 8am, the last is 3pm. From the south, or for a cheaper option from Salvador, go to Valença from where regular launches (R$7, 1½ hours, hourly) and fast boats (R$15, 45 minutes) head to Morro. Morro agencies offer boat transfers to Itacaré (R$70, 3½ hours) and door-to-door boat-plus-bus transfers to Salvador's airport and hotels (R$80, three hours).

Itacaré

0XX73 / POP 24,000

Itacaré offers postcard-pretty surf beaches backed by wide stretches of Biosphere Reserve Atlantic rainforest. The laid-back surfer vibe makes it a great place to kick back, especially outside of peak season. Itacaré has grown considerably from its humble origins as a river-mouth fishing town; recently improved road access now brings in a steady influx of weekend vacationers from Salvador.

Activities

Surf lessons and rental are widely available. The pretty town beaches are river-mouth **Praia de Concha** and four tiny surf beaches sitting like manicured fingernails in a row along the ocean. A trail from the last of these leads to the thumb, idyllic **Prainha**, but don't walk it alone. Remoter paradises lie beyond; head out to **Engenhoca**, **Havaizinho** and **Itacarezinho**, 12km south of town, or cross on the ferry to explore the Península de Maraú, which includes stunning **Praia Taipús de Fora**, with excellent snorkeling and swimming. Local agencies arrange trips here; stay overnight to really enjoy it.

Brazil Trip Tour ECOTOUR
(8137-3367, 9950-9577; www.braziltriptour.com; Pedro Longo 245) One of several reliable agencies offering excursions, this multilingual outfit specializes in English-speaking surf lessons and ecological tours.

Sleeping

Numerous budget *pousadas* line the main drag; midrange ones back Praia da Concha. Prices reflect Christmas to Carnaval season (book ahead); they halve the rest of the year.

Bananas Hostel HOSTEL **$**
(9910-1416; www.bananashostel.com; Pedro Longo 169; campsite/dm/d R$18/40/120;) The inviting backyard kitchen and hammock area and the relaxed atmosphere make this hostel – right on the main street within stumbling distance of Itacaré's late-night bars – a prime chill-out spot by day and a party animal's dream by night.

Albergue O Pharol HOSTEL, INN **$**
(3251-2527; www.alberguoeopharol.com.br; Praça Santos Dummont 7; dm R$44, d with fan/air-con R$120/160; @) This versatile hostel-*pousada* is clean, friendly and centrally located. Dorms, doubles and a self-catering upstairs apartment come with verandas and hammocks. Common spaces include a guest kitchen, central patio and comfy living room with multiple internet stations.

Itacaré Hostel HOSTEL **$**
(3251-2510; www.itacarehostel.com; Barbosa 19; dm/d with fan R$38/110, with air-con R$45/130; @) A warm welcome is guaranteed at this family-run HI hostel in a brightly painted historical home. Free internet, kitchen and DVDs are all on hand.

Che Lagarto HOSTEL **$$**
(3251-3019; www.chelagarto.com; Pedro Longo 58; dm/d R$44/165;) Superbly positioned on the main street, this multistory hostel features its own Irish pub, lots of hammock space, air-conditioned dorms and pricey doubles.

Eating

Pizza do Turco PIZZERIA **$$**
(Praça Santos Dumont; pizzas R$18-27; Tue-Sun) Locals rave about the thin-crusted wonders that emerge from the wood-fired oven at this centrally located pizzeria.

Zé Senzala BUFFET $
(Av Castro Alves 360; per kg R$25; ⊙noon-10pm) Best 'kilo food' in town, with outdoor seating opposite Itacaré's riverfront beach.

Flor de Cacau SEAFOOD $
(Longo s/n; meals per person R$10-25) For copious portions of Bahian-style seafood that won't break the bank, try this simple eatery at the beach end of the main drag. Daily specials go for R$15.

Naturalmente VEGETARIAN $
(Almeida 37; sandwiches from R$6, dishes R$12-20; ⊙Mon-Sat;) Sandwiches, soy burgers, *pratos do dia* (R$12) and nightly pasta specials are excellent value at this little vegetarian and whole-food place.

Drinking & Entertainment

Favela BAR
(Longo s/n; ⊙5pm-late) Chatty buzz, good music and tasty *caipirinhas* made with smooth Minas Gerais *cachaça*. Two other bars (Jungle and Espaço Aberto) are next door, making this the heart of Itacaré's nightlife zone.

Mar e Mel LIVE MUSIC
(www.maremel.com.br; Praia da Concha; ⊙7pm-12:30am) The place to hear (and dance to) live *forró* four nights a week. There's a spacious wooden deck in front and abundant seafood and drink choices.

Information

There are ATMs, several internet cafes (R$3 per hour) and a **Setur** (3251-2940; sec.turismo@itacare.ba.gov.br; Gomes 179; ⊙8am-5pm) tourist office near the bus station.

Getting There & Around

Buses run hourly to Ilheús (R$12, 1½ hours) and once daily to Porto Seguro (R$57, eight hours). If traveling north, catch one of the eight daily buses to Bom Despacho (R$37, 4½ hours), from where ferries (R$4, 45 minutes) continue across to Salvador.

A minibus circuits local beaches; Ilheús-bound buses provide access to beaches south of town.

Ilhéus

0XX73 / POP 184,000

Bright turn-of-the-century architecture and oddly angled streets make Ilhéus' compact center a satisfying wander. The city's fame derives from cocoa and from being the hometown of novelist Jorge Amado.

Sights

Casa de Jorge Amado MUSEUM
(Amado 21; admission R$2; ⊙9am-noon & 2-6pm) A must-see for all Jorge Amado fans, the lovely wood-floored home where the author was raised houses a small collection of memorabilia.

Praia dos Milionários BEACH
Ilhéus' best beach is 7km south of town.

Igreja de São Jorge CHURCH
(Praça Rui Barbosa; admission by donation; ⊙Tue-Sun) Built in 1534, this is among Brazil's oldest churches.

Sleeping

Ilhéus Hotel HOTEL $
(3634-4242; www.ilheushotel.com.br; Bastos 144; s/d with fan R$78/96, with air-con R$135/150;) This centrally located, multistoried 1930s hotel has a fading grandeur and a vintage elevator that was hand-cranked until electrified in 1950. Some rooms have bay views.

Eating & Drinking

Bataclan BRAZILIAN, BUFFET $$
(3634-0088; Av 2 de Julho; all-you-can-eat lunch R$30, mains R$26-69) Once a cabaret frequented by cocoa tycoons (and a setting for Amado's *Gabriela*), this restored colonial beauty now houses a restaurant, lounge and cultural center staging concerts and art exhibitions. Linger over the lunchtime buffet, evening cocktails or Bahian dinners.

Sabor do Sul BUFFET $
(Paiva 53; per kg R$30; ⊙lunch Mon-Sat) Ilhéus' best per-kilo place, around the corner from the cathedral.

Vesúvio BAR
(Praça Dom Eduardo) Nothing beats *chope* on the terrace of this bar featured in Amado's work; the man himself sits larger-than-life at one of the tables, appreciating the great cathedral views.

Information

ATMs and internet places abound in the center. A tourist information kiosk lies between the cathedral and the water.

Getting There & Away

From the *rodoviária*, 4km from the center (local buses connect the two), buses run to Itacaré (R$12, 1½ hours, roughly hourly), Salvador

(R$80 to R$140, seven to eight hours, three daily) and Porto Seguro (R$47 to R$62, six hours, four daily).

Porto Seguro

0XX73 / POP 127,000

Porto Seguro is a popular Brazilian vacation destination with picturesque beaches and an active nightlife. It's also a gateway to the smaller seaside hideaways of Arraial and Trancoso. Porto is famous as the official first Portuguese landfall in Brazil, and for the *lambada* dance, so sensual it was once forbidden.

Sights & Activities

Cidade Histórica HISTORIC SITE

Stairs lead to the picturesque heights of the Cidade Histórica (among Brazil's earliest European settlements). Rewards include a sweeping view, colorful old buildings, venerable churches and *capoeira* demonstrations.

Beaches BEACHES

North of town, the beach is one long bay of calm water lined with *barracas* and clubs. Take a 'Taperapuã' or 'Rio Doce' bus (R$2.25) to the beach, a 'Campinho' or 'Cabralia' to return.

Festivals & Events

Carnaporto CULTURE

Porto Seguro's Carnaval (a smaller and safer version of Salvador's) lasts an additional three or four days, until the Friday or Saturday after Ash Wednesday.

Sleeping

There are plenty of budget and midrange *pousadas* just north of the port, but Arraial d'Ajuda (across the water) is a nicer base.

Camping Mundaí Praia CAMPGROUND $

(3679-2287; www.campingmundai.com.br; Av Beira Mar; campsite per person New Year's Carnaval/rest of year R$35/20;) Opposite the beach, 4km north of town. Plenty of shade and excellent facilities.

Pousada Solar da Praça GUESTHOUSE $

(3288-2585; www.pousadasolardapraca.com.br; Chateaubriand 75; s/d R$45/90;) This friendly guesthouse near the port has a range of small, tidy rooms; the best have balconies with partial sea views. Noisy at night.

Eating & Drinking

Barracas and beach clubs provide eating options along the length of the beach. The listings here are all near the port.

Tia Nenzinha BRAZILIAN $$

(Passarela 170; mains for 2 R$35-70) An excellent choice for succulent *picanha* and quality seafood dishes. Miles better than the competition on this touristy stretch.

Portinha BUFFET $$

(Marinho 33; per kg R$39; 11am-9pm) Some of Brazil's best per-kilo eating, with fire-warmed main courses, succulent salads and desserts to tempt the sourest heart.

A Torre BAKERY $

(Chateaubriand 45; snacks from R$2.50; 11am-11pm Tue-Sun) Perfect for a preferry snack, this authentic Portuguese bakery cranks out tasty codfish fritters, mini-pizzas, custard tarts and sandwiches on homemade *ciabata*.

Passarela do Álcool STREET STALLS

(Alcohol Walkway; nightly) Stands sell drinks, fruit cocktails and crafts. There's usually live music and often *capoeira*. Vendors here sell tickets for the nightly parties.

Information

Banks with ATM access include **HSBC** (Av Getúlio Vargas). For internet access, try **Gigabyte** (Periquitos 10; per hr R$2).

PORTO PARTYING

Porto Seguro is famous for nightly parties (increasingly popular with Brazilian teenagers newly freed from the parental leash) featuring *lambada, capoeira,* live *axé, forró* and samba. Parties are hosted by local beach clubs, including **Tôa-Tôa** (3679 1555; www.portaltoatoa.com.br; Av Beira Mar, Km 5, Praia de Taperapuã), **Barramares** (3679-2980; www.barramares.com.br; Av Beira Mar, Km 6, Praia de Taperapuã), **Bombordo** (Av 22 de Abril) and **Ilha dos Aquários** (3268 2828; www.ilhadosaquarios.com.br; Ilha Pacuio). Admission ranges from R$15 to R$40 (cheaper from vendors around town beforehand). Things start at about 10pm.

Getting There & Around

Porto Seguro's airport (BPS), served by several domestic carriers, is 1.5km west of the bus station and 3km northwest of the port.

From the bus station, 500m west of the Cidade Histórica, frequent buses hit Ilhéus (R$47 to R$62, six hours, four daily), Valença (R$82, nine hours, nightly), Salvador (R$160, 12 hours, nightly) and beyond. To save nearly R$60 going to Salvador, jump off at Valença, catch the early-morning bus to Bom Despacho (R$14, 1¾ hours) and cross the bay to Salvador by ferry (R$4, 45 minutes).

Arraial d'Ajuda

☎0XX73 / POP 13,000

Perched on a bluff above long sandy beaches, Arraial has a curious blend of upmarket tourism and chilled backpackerdom. Squat buildings painted bright colors surround a traditional plaza; roads lined with *pousadas,* bars and restaurants slope down to the beaches. Arraial caters to both party animals and those looking to unwind in the tropics.

Sights & Activities

The closest town beach is crowded **Praia Mucugê**, but a short walk south brings you to dreamy **Praia de Pitinga** and other gorgeous beaches beyond. **Arraial Ecoparque** (www.arraialecoparque.com.br; Praia d'Ajuda; adult/child R$75/40; ⏲Jul-Apr) has water slides, a wave pool and hosts big-name concerts. Friendly **Capoeira Sul da Bahia** (www.capoeirasuldabahia.com.br; Capoeira 57) offers Afro-Brazilian dance and *capoeira.*

Sleeping & Eating

Prices halve outside of high summer. There are cheap eats on central Praça São Bras and Praia Mucugê.

Arraial d'Ajuda Hostel HOSTEL **$**
(☎3575-1192; www.arraialdajudahostel.com.br; Campo 94; dm R$36-43, s R$65-130, d R$91-156; ❄@🛜🏊) Hostelling hits the luxury class at this super spot, with friendly, helpful staff, upbeat orange decor and an inviting central pool area.

Pousada Alto Mar HOSTEL **$**
(☎3575-1935; www.pousadaaltomar.net; Bela Vista 114; dm/d with fan from R$25/50; @) Human warmth makes up for the simple structure at this funky, well-shaded cheapie with guest kitchen on a dead-end street behind Arraial's church.

Mox Hostel HOSTEL **$**
(☎3575-1175; www.moxhostel.com.br; Mucugê 144; dm/d R$30/90; ❄🛜) Clean but sterile, with a paltry breakfast, this new hostel's main appeal is its prime location in Arraial's nightlife hub.

Paulo Pescador BRAZILIAN **$$**
(Praça São Bras; dishes R$23; ⏲noon-10pm) This well-loved eatery attracts a loyal following with superfriendly, multlingual service and ample *pratos feitos* (main dishes served with rice, beans and salad).

Miloca BURGERS, CREPES **$**
(Mucugê; burgers R$11-24, crepes R$13-22; ⏲10am-10pm) Stop in for burgers or sweet and savory crepes at this terrace eatery with occasional live music en route to the beach.

Manguti ITALIAN **$$**
(Mucugê 99; mains for 1 R$18-31, for 2 R$33-60; ⏲dinner) This well-established eatery with pleasant outdoor-deck seating specializes in hearty homemade gnocchi and filets of beef.

Drinking & Entertainment

Downtown Arraial's nightlife scene centers around Rua Mucugê and the adjacent Beco das Cores, a passageway with multiple drinking spots and live music on weekends. Waterfront clubs like **Sol Beach** (www.facebook.com/solbeachbrasil) also host seasonal beach parties.

Cineteatro Fellini LIVE MUSIC, CINEMA
(Beco das Cores) Doubles as a live-music venue, cinema and wine bar; perfect for an easygoing nightcap.

Morocha Club CLUB
(Mucugê; ⏲Mon-Sat) Relaxed and lounge-like earlier in the evening, busy with concerts, dancing and theme parties late at night.

Gonguê LIVE MUSIC
(Parracho) Locals' bar just off the main square, with a pool table on the front veranda and live *forró* every Thursday night.

Information

Several ATMs and internet places cluster around the center.

Getting There & Away

Passenger and car ferries run frequently between Porto Seguro and Arraial (R$3 to Arraial, free return, five minutes) during the day, and hourly on the hour after midnight. From Arraial's dock, jump on a bus or *combi* (small bus or minibus) to the center (R$2, 10 minutes).

Trancoso

0XX73 / POP 10,000

Perched atop a tall bluff overlooking the ocean, this small tropical paradise centers around the utterly picturesque **Quadrado**, a long grassy expanse with a white church flanked by low colorful houses, rooted in the town's history as a Jesuit mission. At night everyone turns out to lounge at outdoor restaurants surrounding the twinkling square. The beaches south of Trancoso are gorgeous, especially Praia do Espelho (20km south), off the road to Caraíva.

Sleeping & Eating

Most accommodations are pricey. Reserve ahead during holidays.

Café Esmeralda Albergue GUESTHOUSE $
(3668-1527; www.trancosonatural.com; Quadrado; r with/without bathroom R$100/80;) Fronting the beautiful grassy plaza, this friendly Argentine-Canadian place has a row of simple rooms, a cocoa tree and hammock chill-out space. No breakfast.

Pousada Quarto Crescente INN $$
(3668-1014; www.quartocrescente.net; Principal; r R$190-260;) This sweet, tree-shaded spot with spacious gardens, a well-stocked library, comfortable rooms and superb breakfasts is run by a globe-trotting Dutch-Brazilian family. Rates drop dramatically between Carnaval and Christmas, making this a worthwhile off-season splurge.

Pousada Cuba INN, CAMPGROUND $
(9122-7141; www.trancosobahia.com.br/pousadasdetrancoso/campingacuba.htm; Cuba; campsite/s/d R$30/50/80) Dirt paths connect simple cabins and campsites on a hillside around a communal kitchen, between the Quadrado and the new town square.

TOP CHOICE **A Portinha** BUFFET $
(Quadrado; per kg R$36; noon-9pm) This local classic woos diners with a sumptuous *por kilo* buffet and atmospheric seating at tree-shaded turquoise picnic tables with fabulous views of the Quadrado.

Maluco Beleza PIZZERIA $
(Itabela 136; pizzas R$12-28; dinner Tue-Sun) ...ana and Adenilson fire up some of Trancoso's best pizza on a spacious interior courtyard shaded by a giant jackfruit tree.

Lanchonete Nalva Sales BRAZILIAN $
(Neves; meals R$15) Ample *pratos do dia* featuring home-cooked meat, rice, beans and salad are served at plastic tables at this unpretentious local hangout adjoining Trancoso's market.

Information

ATMs and internet cafes are readily available.

Getting There & Away

The 13km walk along the beach from Arraial at low tide is beautiful. Hourly buses connect Trancoso with Arraial's dock (R$6.50, one hour) and center (R$5.20, 50 minutes).

Caraíva

0XX73 / POP 6400

For end-of-the-road isolation, head for remote, magical Caraíva, a sandy hamlet tucked between a mangrove-lined river and a long churning surf beach, made all the more tranquil by the absence of cars. In the low season, Caraíva all but shuts down. There are no ATMs – bring cash.

Boat journeys upriver, horse rides or walks to a Pataxó community can easily be organized. A 14km walk north (or you can hop on a bus) brings you to celebrated **Praia do Espelho**.

To fully appreciate Caraíva's magic, stay overnight. Accommodations range from simple campsites at **Camping Caraíva** (9992-6324; www.campingcaraiva.com.br; camping per person R$20) to beachfront *pousadas* like **Pousada da Praia** (3274-6833; www.pousadapraiacaraiva.com.br; s/d R$100/150;). Mosquito nets are essential. Bargain-priced eateries include **Canto da Duca** (daily specials R$15; 8am-5pm;), for excellent vegetarian *pratos feitos,* and **Culinaria Central** (meals from R$20), which serves a filling *refeição individual* (classic meal of fish, rice and beans). For more upscale *moquecas* with dreamy river views, try **Boteco do Pará** (moquecas for 2 R$62-97).

Two to three daily buses run north from Caraíva to Trancoso (R$11, two hours), central Arraial (R$13, three hours) and Arraial's port (R$13.50, 3¼ hours). From Caraíva's bus stop, rowboats (day/night R$4/5, five minutes) ferry you into town. For longer-distance connections north or south, head for Itabela (R$12, two hours, two daily).

Penedo

0XX82 / POP 59,000

This colonial town near the mouth of the Rio São Francisco is worth a stop for its rich collection of beautiful 17th- and 18th-century churches. Especially noteworthy are the **Igreja de NS da Corrente** (Praça 12 de Abril; 8am-6pm Tue-Sun), decorated with Portuguese *azulejos* in green, purple and gold, and the **Convento de São Francisco** (Praça Rui Barbosa; admission R$2; 8-11am & 2-5pm Tue-Fri, 8-11am Sat & Sun), widely recognized as the finest church in Alagoas state.

For comfortable budget lodging, try **Pousada Estylos** (3551-2429; Dâmaso do Monte 86; s/d with fan R$50/75, with air-con R$70/90;), just uphill from NS da Corrente. Closer to the water, **Pousada Colonial** (3551-2355; www.pousadacolonialdepenedo.com.br; Praça 12 de Abril 21; r with fan/air-con R$100/120;) is a coolly elegant restored colonial house with stained-wood floors, antique furniture and river views.

Pleasantly perched along the waterfront, **Oratório** (Av Beira Rio 301; lunch specials R$13-22, meals for 2 R$40-58; 9am-midnight) does tasty *petiscos* (bar food) and seafood, including *pitú* (giant river shrimp).

You'll find ATMs on Av Duque de Caxias, just off the main riverfront square. The **tourist office** (3551-3907; sectur.penedo@hotmail.com; Dâmaso do Monte 141; 8am-1:30pm Mon-Fri) gives out maps.

From Penedo's riverside bus station, *topiques* (vans; R$17, three hours) and Real Alagoas buses (R$15.45, three to five hours) travel to/from Maceió. From Salvador, catch Bonfim's daily bus at 8:45am (R$70, 10 hours); the return trip leaves Penedo at 6am.

Maceió

0XX82 / POP 933,000

Maceió, capital of Alagoas state, offers reef-sheltered swimming in vivid blue-green sea along its lengthy waterfront. The city beaches' swaying palms are seductive, but the real beach jewels are out of town, just an hour away.

Sights & Activities

Picturesque *jangadas* (traditional sailboats; R$20 per two hours) sail 2km out from Praia de Pajuçara, offering opportunities to snorkel in natural pools formed by the reef. **Praia de Ponta Verde** and **Jatiúca** are good city beaches with calm water. Pretty **Praia do Francês** (24km), lined with beach bars, is Maceió's major weekend destination and has lots of *pousadas*. Further south, **Praia do Gunga** sits across a river from Barra de São Miguel (34km). Pretty, less crowded beaches north of town include **Garça Torta** (12km), **Riacho Doce** (14km) and **Ipioca** (23km). Another worthwhile excursion is to **Pontal da Barra** (8km south of Maceió), a popular spot to purchase traditional Alagoan *filé* (crochetwork) and embark on scenic four-hour lagoon cruises (R$30).

Museu Théo Brandão MUSEUM
(Av da Paz 1490; admission R$2; 9am-5pm Tue-Fri, 2-5pm Sat) This museum displays Alagoan folk art, including festival headpieces weighing up to 35kg.

Mercado do Artesanato MARKET
(Levada; 7am-6pm Mon-Sat, to noon Sun) Browse local handicrafts at this market just north of the center.

Pedala Maceió BICYCLE RENTAL
(9183-9882; Otacílio s/n; bike rental per hr R$12; 6am-11pm) Explore Maceió's 20km-long waterfront bike path on a bicycle or three-wheeler; pick up and drop off at any of four rental locations between Pajuçara and Jatiúca beaches.

Sleeping

Accommodation is pricey in Maceió. The beachside *bairros* of Pajuçara and Ponta Verde are much more pleasant than the center.

Maceió Hostel Ponta Verde HOSTEL $
(3313-5056; www.maceiohostel.com.br; Av Sampaio Luz 169; dm with fan/air-con R$45/55, d R$100; @) Maceió's most welcoming budget option is hidden in a residential neighborhood several blocks from the beach. Four small dorms and three doubles share a nice guest kitchen and a spacious outdoor barbecue area with hammock space.

Maceió Hostel e Pousada INN $
(3231-7762; www.maceiohostel.com.br; Almirante Mascarenhas 85, Pajuçara; dm/d/tr R$35/90/120;) Efficiently managed but rather bland, this odd *pousada*-hostel hybrid two blocks from Pajuçara beach has rooms sleeping up to four, many with bunk beds. Despite t

hostel name, they emphasize the *pousada* role, preferring to receive individuals, couples or small groups.

Hotel Ibis HOTEL **$$**
(2121-6699; www.accorhotels.com.br; Av Gouveia 277, Pajuçara; s/d without breakfast R$125/155;) This clean, generic high-rise hotel offers decent rates for its beachfront location. Breakfast isn't worth the extra R$14.

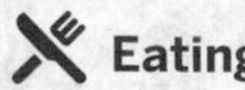

Eating

Barracas are dotted along the beachfronts. Favorite cheap treats include R$3 to R$10 *tapiocas recheadas* (tapioca pancakes with savory or sweet fillings) and the R$5 *caldo de polvo* (octopus stew) at Bar do Tatu in Ipioca.

Sarah's Esfihas MIDDLE EASTERN **$**
(Azevedo 59; esfihas R$3-5, other dishes R$10-20; 3-10pm) This popular Middle Eastern diner makes *esfihas* (fluffy breads topped or filled), in addition to passable hummus, tabouleh, and vine-leaf and cabbage rolls.

Divina Gula BRAZILIAN **$$**
(Paulo Nogueira 85, Jatiúca; mains R$29-58; closed Mon) Specializing in Minas Gerais and Northeastern dishes, this venerable eatery also boasts over 50 different kinds of *cachaça*.

Stella Maris CHURRASCARIA **$$**
(Paulo Nogueira 290, Jatiúca; all you can eat R$23.90) Feast on excellent all-you-can-eat meat at this well-loved *churrascaria*.

Entertainment

Lopana LIVE MUSIC
(www.lopana.com.br; Av Viana 27) This beachfront bar is always buzzing, with good food, weekend DJs and live music nightly.

Lampião LIVE MUSIC
(Av Álvaro Otacílio, Jatiúca) Touristy beachfront bar playing *forró*.

Information

Banco do Brasil (cnr Av Otacílio & Luz) On Ponta Verde waterfront.

Tourist Police (Av Otacílio; 24hr) On the waterfront.

Getting There & Away

Maceió's Zumbi dos Palmares International Airport (MCZ), 25km north of the center, has domestic connections. The long-distance bus station is 5km north of the center. Buses head to Recife (R$30 to R$60, four hours, 12 daily) and Salvador (R$93 to R$140, nine hours, four daily).

City buses (R$2.10) run to all northern and southern beaches.

Recife

0XX81 / POP 1.54 MILLION

Recife, one of the Northeast's major ports and cities, is renowned throughout Brazil for its dance and musical heritage. The bustling, somewhat gritty commerical center, with water on all sides, is busy during the day but deserted at night and on Sunday. Quieter Recife Antigo, on Ilha do Recife, has picturesque colonial buildings. Most travelers stay in Boa Viagem – an affluent suburb south of the center backing a long golden beach – or in Recife's more peaceful sister city, Olinda.

Sights & Activities

The old city has many restored noble buildings with explanatory panels in English. Strolling through Recife Antigo, you can admire the colorful houses and historic synagogue on **Rua Bom Jesus** and the customs-building-turned-shopping-mall **Paço Alfândega** (Rua da Alfândega 35). Across in Centro, **Pátio de São Pedro** is a pretty cobbled square lined with characterful buildings under the gaze of a handsome baroque church.

Oficina Cerâmica Francisco Brennand MUSEUM
(www.brennand.com.br; Várzea; admission R$10; 8am-5pm Mon-Thu, to 4pm Fri) Serpents stare, buttocks bulge and jaws gape at this seemingly exhaustive exhibition of the artist's peculiar sculptures. The extensive grounds make a nice picnic site. Take the UR7-Várzea bus from downtown along Av Guararapes to the end of the line (35 minutes). From there, catch a taxi (R$10) as the long walk is unsafe.

Museu do Homem do Nordeste MUSEUM
(www.fundaj.gov.br; Av 17 de Agosto 2187; admission R$4; 8:30am-5pm Tue-Fri, 1-5pm Sat & Sun) This worthwhile anthropological museum features historical and cultural exhibits covering everything from slavery to Carnaval. From Av Guararapes in downtown Recife, take bus 522 or 523 (Dois Irmãos) about 6km west. From Olinda, take bus 930 (Rio Doce/Dois Irmãos).

Recife

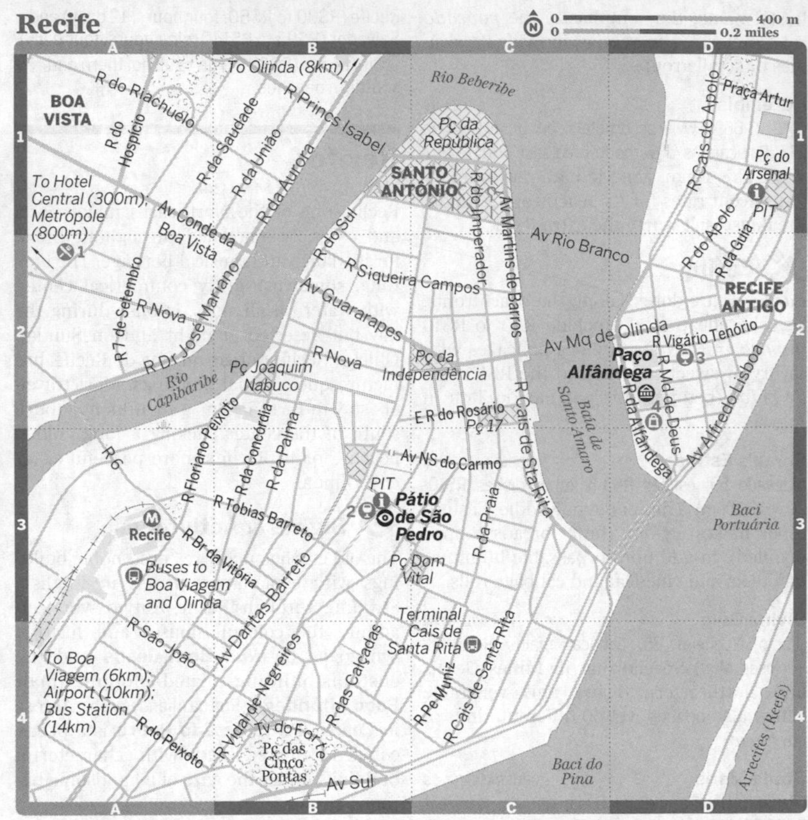

Praia Boa Viagem BEACH
This long, sandy beach is great for sun and strolling, but shark warnings deter plenty of locals from more than a paddle. Other worthwhile beaches further south include **Praia Pedra do Xaréu** (20km) and **Praia Calhetas** (23km).

Festivals & Events

Carnaval CARNAVAL
(www.carnavaldorecife.com.br) Recife is the location for one of Brazil's most colorful and folkloric Carnavals. Groups and spectators deck themselves out in elaborate costumes such as *maracatu* (headpieced warrior), harlequin, bull and *frevo* (crop tops with ruffled sleeves for both genders and a tiny umbrella) and shimmy for days to frenetic *frevo* and African-influenced *maracatu* beats.

PE Folia CULTURE
Formerly known as Recifolia, this out-of-season, Salvador-style Carnaval is held in late October or early November.

Sleeping

Boa Viagem is a better area than the Centro. Decent budget hotels are in short supply, but thankfully a new crop of hostels has moved in to fill the void.

Cosmopolitan Hostel HOSTEL $
(☎3204-0321; www.cosmopolitanhostel.com; Paulo Setúbal 53, Boa Viagem; dm/s/d R$45/130/140; ❄@📶) Doubles and six-bed dorms surround a courtyard with mango and acerola trees at this recently converted family home on a residential backstreet. Homey features include pet bunnies, a guest kitchen and a game room. Bilingual owner Filipe is a fount of local information.

Albergue Piratas da Praia HOSTEL $
(☎3326-1281; www.piratasdapraia.com; Av Conselheiro Aguiar 2034, Boa Viagem; dm with/without air-con R$50/40, r with/without air-con R$150/140; ❄@📶) Hidden away on the 3rd floor of Edificio Barão de Camaçari, this welcoming and colorful hostel feels a bit like staying in a friend's apartment. Private rooms are cutely appointed but overpriced.

Pousada Casuarinas GUESTHOUSE $$
(☎3325-4708; www.pousadacasuarinas.com.br; Antônio Pedro Figueiredo 151, Boa Viagem; s/d R$150/195, with verandah R$160/205; ❄@📶🏊) Folk art spices up the modern architecture at this friendly, quiet and immaculate *pousada* shaded by mango trees. Note that rooms with veranda and hammock cost R$10 more.

Arrecifes Hostel HOSTEL $
(☎3462-5867; www.arrecifeshostel.com.br; João Cardoso Ayres 560, Boa Viagem; dm/d R$52/120; ❄@📶) Recife's newest HI hostel occupies the ground floor of a small high-rise between the airport and Boa Viagem's southern beachfront. Its somewhat institutional feel is offset by friendly staff and modern facilities. Air-con costs R$5 extra.

Boa Viagem Hostel HOSTEL $
(☎3326-9572; www.hostelboaviagem.com.br; Lins 455, Boa Viagem; dm/d R$50/140; ❄📶🏊) On a quiet street a couple of blocks back from the avenue, this HI hostel's darkish, overpriced dorms are redeemed by a relaxing garden and pool area.

Hotel Central HOTEL $
(☎3222-4001; hotelcentralrecife@hotmail.com; Borba 209, Centro; s/d from R$80/130, s/tw without bathroom R$60/100; ❄) Bright rooms with high ceilings and faded art deco character make this 1930s jewel the best budget option downtown. The cheapest rooms feature twin beds and a sink, with bathroom facilities down the hall.

Eating

Parraxaxá BUFFET $$
(www.parraxaxa.com.br; Av Fernando Simões Barbosa 1200, Boa Viagem; per kg R$44.90; ⏲11:30am-11pm; 📶) Cowboy-costumed wait staff spice up your meal at this folklore-themed restaurant with festive decor. The per-kilo food is pricey but delicious, with lots of typical Pernambuco dishes.

La Vague CREPERIE $
(☎3465-1654; Rui Batista 120, Boa Viagem; crepes R$12.50-22; ⏲dinner; 🖉) This trendy place serves up great-value savory and sweet crepes and fab salads in a near-bar atmosphere. It has good vegetarian options.

Salada Mista BUFFET $
(Rua do Hospício 59, Boa Vista; per kg R$25; ⏲10:30am-8pm Mon-Fri, to 4pm Sat) One of Recife's better downtown per-kilo buffets.

Companhia do Chopp BUFFET $$
(João Cícero s/n, Boa Viagem; mains R$20-70, lunch per kg R$39.90) A quality sidewalk restaurant with a good-value, self-service lunch, satisfying meat dishes and top *chope.*

Drinking

In the Centro, the Patio de São Pedro is a popular hangout, especially on Terça Negra (Black Tuesday), a night of Afro-Brazilian rhythms. Recife Antigo has a few bars with outdoor tables along Bom Jesus that are active in the early evenings. Watch for *clones* (two-for-one specials), which are common throughout Recife.

Banguê BAR
(Pátio de São Pedro 20, Centro) The best of several bars on this beautiful square, unsigned Banguê stars in the great travel book *A Death in Brazil.* It serves good-value portions (R$14 to R$40) and a range of tasty *petiscos* (plates of bar food for sharing) like *charque* (dried beef).

Guaiamum Gigante BAR
(Av Boa Viagem, 2A Jardim, Boa Viagem; ⏲11:30am-1am Mon-Sat, to 11pm Sun) Locals flock to the breezy outdoor patio at this *boteco* opposite the Boa Viagem waterfront for happy-hour specials and good seafood.

✩ Entertainment

The port area in Recife's old town has a cluster of music bars. Nearby, the **Livraria Cultura** (Rua da Alfândega; ⏲10am-10pm Mon-Sat, noon-9pm Sun) bookstore occasionally hosts free live shows. Boa Viagem attracts affluent youth, with spread-out options the length of the main avenue.

Recife's three biggest soccer teams are **Nautico** (www.nautico-pe.com.br), **Santa Cruz** (www.coralnet.com.br) and **Sport** (www.sportrecife.com.br). Nautico will begin playing in the new, purpose-built 46,000-seat Arena Pernambuco, 20km west of Recife in the suburb of São Lourenço da Mata. In 2014 this same arena will host five World Cup matches, including one round-of-16 match (64 years after Recife hosted its first World Cup match in 1950).

Burburinho LIVE MUSIC
(www.facebook.com/barburburinho; Tomazina 106, Recife Antigo; ⏲5pm-late Mon-Sat) Visited by musicians, artists and journos, this bar has live blues on Friday and rock on Saturday.

Iguana Café CLUB
(www.iguanacafe.com.br; Av Conselheiro Aguiar 479, Boa Viagem; ⏲10pm-5am Wed-Sat) Latin-themed bar and nightspot featuring electronica and *música latina*, accompanied by Mexican food, margaritas and *caipiquilas* (tequila-infused *caipirinhas*).

Dona Carolina LIVE MUSIC
(www.bardonacarolina.com.br; Av Boa Viagem 123, Boa Viagem; ⏲8pm-5am Thu-Sat) Sleek, modern bar and restaurant hosting a dynamic mix of live music, from samba rock to *sertanejo* to MPB.

UK Pub LIVE MUSIC, DJ
(www.ukpub.com.br; Francisco da Cunha 165, Boa Viagem; ⏲8pm-late Tue-Sat, from 7pm Sun) This sophisticated lounge draws a sexy Anglophile crowd for live pop, rock, samba rock and DJs, and proper pints (Guinness, Erdinger, Newcastle and 1664).

Sala de Reboco LIVE MUSIC
(www.saladereboco.com.br; Gregório Junior 264, Cordeiro; ⏲9pm-4am Thu-Sat) It's worth the taxi trip (R$25 to R$30 from Boa Viagem) to this friendly, down-to-earth place, with a 'real Brazil' feel and cheerful live *forró*.

Metrópole GAY
(clubemetropole.com.br; Rua das Nínfas 125, Boa Vista; ⏲10pm-6am Fri & Sat) Recife's best gay (and GLS) club has drag shows, go-go boys, Saturday theme parties and a bar with live music.

ℹ Information

HSBC (Av Ferreira 2589, Boa Viagem) ATMs.

PIT Airport (☎3355-0128; ⏲24hr); Boa Viagem (☎3182-8297; Praça de Boa Viagem; ⏲8am-8pm); bus station (☎3182-8298; Rodoviária; ⏲7am-7pm), downtown (☎3355-3310; Patio de São Pedro, Santo Antônio; ⏲9am-5pm Mon-Fri); Recife Antigo (☎3355-3402; Praça do Arsenal; ⏲8:30am-9pm) Excellent tourist office with convenient locations.

Tourist Police (☎3322-4867; ground fl, airport; ⏲24hr)

ℹ Getting There & Away

Air

Several domestic airlines serve Recife's Guararapes International Airport (REC), 10km south of the center. TAP and American Airlines offer international nonstop service to Lisbon and Miami, respectively, with onward European and North American connections.

Bus

Recife's bus station is located 14km southwest of the center, connected by metro to the central Recife stop (R$1.60, 25 minutes). Destinations include João Pessoa (R$24, two hours, half-hourly), Natal (R$66, 4½ hours, nine daily), Maceió (R$34 to R$61, four hours, 10 daily) and Salvador (R$141 to R$159, 11 to 16 hours, three daily). Long-distance bus tickets can be purchased from Disk Rodoviária, a ticket delivery service.

ℹ Getting Around

To/From the Airport

From the airport, the 042 Aeroporto bus (R$2.15, R$2.65 with air-con) goes to Boa Viagem (20 minutes) and the center (45 minutes); there's a signposted stop outside the arrivals hall. A faster, cheaper option for downtown Recife is the metro (R$1.60, 15 minutes), but you'll have to brave the treacherous crossing of the busy road in front of the airport (no crosswalk at the time of writing, though a pedestrian overpass is scheduled for 2014).

Fixed-rate taxis advertised inside the terminal (R$17 to Boa Viagem, R$42 to central Recife, R$67 to Olinda) are worthwhile only at rush hour; otherwise save money by catching a metered *taxi comum* just outside the terminal building.

Bus

To get to Boa Viagem from the central metro station, catch the 'Setubal (Príncipe)' bus. For Olinda, catch the 983 'Rio Doce-Princesa Isabel'

WORTH A TRIP

PARQUE NACIONAL MARINHO DE FERNANDO DE NORONHA

An hour's flight from Recife or Natal is Brazil's greenest destination, **Parque Nacional Marinho de Fernando de Noronha** (www.icmbio.gov.br), on the idyllic island of the same name. Only 700 people per day can visit this tiny, pristine place, home to Brazil's most postcard-perfect beaches and staunchly protected marine life. Noronha's not only a sea-turtle sanctuary, but also the world's best place to see spinner dolphins. Throw in Brazil's best surfing and diving and you're rewarded with an unforgettable paradise.

Noronha only opened for tourism in 1988 (it was formerly a military installation and prison). Since then, no new construction has been allowed on its beaches, giving floury patches of sand like Baía de Sancho and Praia do Leão a dreamlike quality. There are restrictions on vehicles, boats and people as well – Brazilians aren't even allowed to live here unless they were born here (all others get hard-to-secure temporary residence permits). No condos, no chain hotels, no beach vendors, no *people*. In short, it's an environmental success story and true treat to visit.

But paradise comes at a price. Round-trip flights from Recife/Natal (with Trip or GOL) start around R$1000, and all visitors must pay a daily island tax of R$43.20 plus a one-time national-park entrance fee of R$130/65 for foreigners/Brazilians. Contact **Your Way** (☎81-9949-1087; www.yourway.com.br) for English assistance with accommodation and activities on the island.

or 992 'Pau Amarelo' bus. From the center to Boa Viagem, take any bus marked 'Aeroporto,' 'Shopping Center,' 'Candeias' or 'Piedade' from Av NS do Carmo. To return, take any bus marked 'Dantas Barreto.'

Olinda

☎0XX81 / POP 378,000

If Recife feels like a blue-collar worker scrabbling hard to make ends meet, Olinda is the sibling who dropped out of the rat race to get in touch with its inner artist. This picturesque, bohemian colonial town is packed with painters' studios, impromptu musical events and *cachaça*-fueled parties. Its gorgeous pastel-colored houses flank a stunning ensemble of baroque churches on the historic center's hillside overlooking the sea.

Sights & Activities

The historic center is easy to navigate and delightful to wander. Climb to **Alto da Sé**, the cathedral square at the top of town, for great views of Olinda's churches backed by the ocean and Recife's distant skyscrapers. The hilltop also hosts a lively street-food scene and **Sítio das Artes** (Bispo Coutinho 780; ⏲9am-10pm), a smartly converted historic building housing antique furniture, a wide range of embroidery and art for sale, a [illegible] and an upstairs restaurant.

Worthwhile churches include the newly restored **Igreja NS do Carmo** (Praça do Carmo) in the town center; baroque **Mosteiro de São Bento** (⏲8-11:30am & 2:15-5:30pm Mon-Sat, 8-9:30am & 2:30-5pm Sun), with an elaborate gilt altarpiece and a 14th-century Italian painting of Saint Sebastian; and **Convento de São Francisco** (Rua de São Francisco 280; admission R$3; ⏲8am-noon & 2-5pm Mon-Fri, 8am-noon Sat), with a memorable tiled cloister.

Museu de Arte Contemporânea MUSEUM
(Rua 13 de Maio 149; admission R$5; ⏲9am-5pm Tue-Sun) This former prison houses temporary exhibitions of contemporary art alongside a permanent collection of mostly 1930s works.

Angola Mãe COURSE
(acamolinda@gmail.com; Cunha 243) The *capoeira* school welcomes visitors for classes or to watch a *roda* (circle) at 6pm on Sunday.

Festivals & Events

You can get a taste of Carnaval on weekends (especially Sunday night) in the months leading up to it, when *blocos* rehearse in the streets.

Carnaval CARNAVAL
Olinda's Carnaval is traditional, colorful and has an intimacy and security not found in big-city Carnavals. Fast and frenetic *frevo*

Olinda

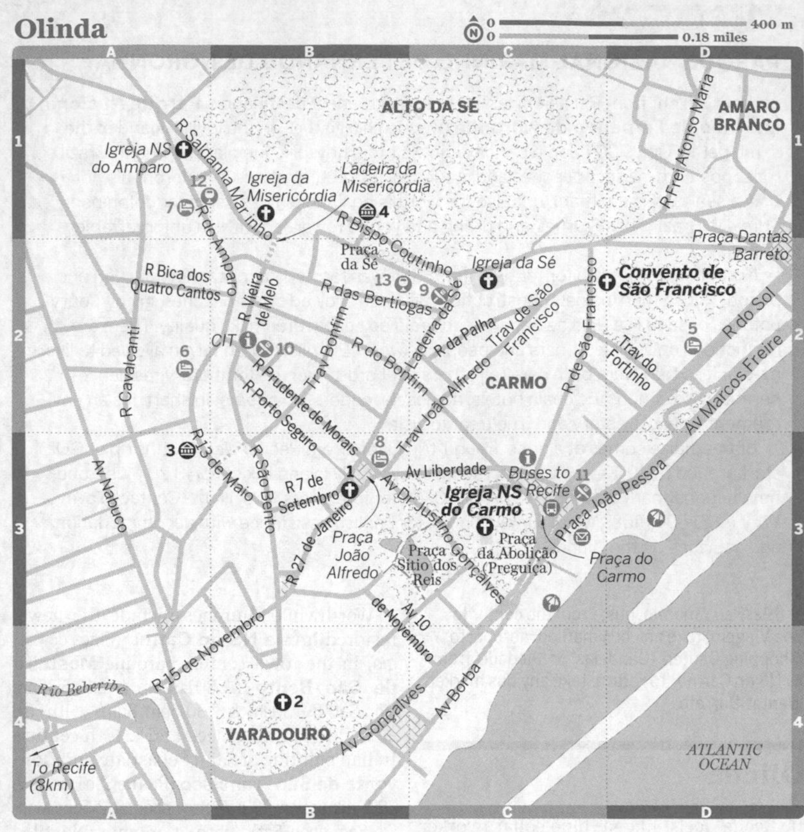

Olinda

Top Sights

- Convento de São Francisco D2
- Igreja NS do Carmo C3

Sights

1. Igreja São Pedro B3
2. Mosteiro de São Bento B4
3. Museu de Arte Contemporânea A3
4. Sítio das Artes B1

Sleeping

5. Albergue de Olinda D2
6. Pousada Alto Astral A2
7. Pousada Bela Vista A1
8. Pousada d'Olinda B3

Eating

9. Cantinho da Sé C2
   Creperia ..... (see 8)
10. Estação Café B2
11. Estação Maxambomba C3

Drinking

12. Bodega do Véio A1
13. Gres Preto Velho B2

music sets the pace, balanced by the heavy drumbeats of *maracatu*. Giant *bonecos* (6m-tall puppets), costumed *blocos* and spectators dance through the streets in this highly inclusive, playful and lewd festival.

Sleeping

You should book well ahead for Carnava[l]; it can sometimes be cheaper to rent a roo[m] or house.

Albergue de Olinda HOSTEL $
(☎3429-1592; www.alberguedeolinda.com.br; Rua do Sol 233; dm/s/d R$38/75/100;) Modern rooms in a historical building surround a nice garden with hammocks, pool and an outdoor kitchen. Downsides: you're not in the old part of town and there's noise from the busy road.

Pousada Alto Astral INN $
(☎3439-3453; www.pousadaaltoastral.com; Rua 13 de Maio 305; dm R$35, s/d R$100/130, without bathroom R$50/80;) This colorfully decorated *pousada* was undergoing major renovation at the time of writing, adding new suites, dorm space and a breakfast deck overlooking the recently expanded pool and garden area. Bright, spacious upstairs rooms are much better value than interior units with shared bathroom.

Pousada d'Olinda INN $
(☎3493-6011; www.pousadadolinda.com.br; Praça João Alfredo 178; dm/s/d R$35/80/100, s/d with air-con R$100/115;) The cavernous lone dorm can get noisy, and the private rooms are nothing special, but the friendly management, middle-of-town location and reasonable rates make this well-established *pousada* worth a look.

Pousada Bela Vista INN $$
(☎3429-3930; www.hotelbelavista.tur.br; Amparo 215; s R$90-100, d R$130-180;) Rooms here range from claustrophobic cells with windows opening onto corridors to more spacious units with views. The shared living room, terraces and backyard pool are all pleasant, as is the location on Rua Amparo.

Eating

For a no-frills snack, hit Alto da Sé, where stalls serve *tapioca* pancakes with various fillings, along with ice-cold coconuts and mixed drinks.

Creperia CREPERIE $$
(Praça João Alfredo 168; crepes R$6-32, pizza R$20-30) Enjoy a sweet or savory crepe or tasty salad in the palm-shaded patio or dining room hung with decorative plates at this charming restaurant.

Cantinho da Sé BRAZILIAN $
(Ladeira da Sé; mains for 2 people R$20-32) Typical Brazilian meat and fish dishes are complemented by a view over Recife at this unassuming spot below the cathedral. A fine spot to sip R$3.50 *caipirinhas* at sundown.

Estação Café CAFE $
(Prudente de Morais 440; items R$9-30; ⏲10am-10:30pm Tue-Sun) Tucked onto a tranquil back patio with fountain, this is a great pit stop for lighter bites such as quiche, salads and sandwiches.

Estação Maxambomba BUFFET $
(Praça João Pessoa 19; per kg R$24.90; ⏲lunch Mon-Sat, dinner Tue-Sun) Near the bus stop at the foot of town, Olinda's high-ceilinged former railway station makes an atmospheric spot for a reasonably priced per-kilo lunch.

Drinking & Entertainment

There are parties organized nearly every night somewhere or other; just ask for the *festa*. On Friday nights check out the live *forró* at Sítio das Artes (p355), and the *serenata*, a weekly procession in which strolling musicians make a circuit through town, joined in song by onlookers from the sidewalks; it leaves from **Igreja São Pedro** (Praça João Alfredo) at 10pm.

Bodega de Véio BAR
(Rua do Amparo 212; ⏲9am-11pm Mon-Sat) Grocery store sells beer. People drinking beer impede customers. Owner solves problem by installing tables and sound system. The three-sentence history of Olinda's most popular bar. The street out front becomes a party scene many evenings, with displays of fire-breathing, tightrope-walking and live music.

GRES Preto Velho SAMBA
(Praça da Sé) Has regular live *afoxé, axé,* samba and reggae sessions.

Information

Crime does exist in Olinda. Don't walk alone along deserted streets or carry valuables at night.

There are no international ATMs in the old town. Bring cash from Recife or take the 10-minute bus ride northeast from Praça do Carmo to Av Getúlio Vargas, where you'll find HSBC and other major banks. Avoid the ATM at the BP service station on Olinda's southern outskirts; it's a serious clone risk.

CIT (☎3305-1060; www.olinda.pe.gov.br; Prudente de Morais 472; ⏲8am-6pm Mon-Fri, 9am-6pm Sat & Sun) Municipal tourist office, uphill from the main square.

Empetur (☎3429-0244; www.empetur.com.br; Praça do Carmo; ⏲8am-6pm) Centrally located, air-conditioned state tourist office with lovely, English-speaking staff.

Tourist Police (3439-9696; Av Justino Gonçalves; 24hr)

Getting There & Around

Any 'Rio Doce,' 'Casa Caiada' or 'Jardim Atlantico' bus (R$3.25) connects central Recife to Olinda; from Recife's central metro station, take bus 983 'Rio Doce-Princesa Isabel' or 992 'Pau Amarelo.' Between Olinda and Boa Viagem, take bus 910 'Rio Doce/Piedade' or any 'Barra de Jangada/Casa Caiada' bus. A cab from central Recife costs around R$30.

Praia da Pipa

0XX84 / POP 3000

Pristine sands backed by handsome cliffs, with dolphins frisking close to shore, make Pipa one of Brazil's premier beach destinations. While the once-peaceful main street has long since become heavily commercialized, Pipa remains a tranquil place outside high season, and the quality of accommodation and food make it easy to lose a week here.

The long main drag has traveler-friendly installations like internet, ATMs, laundries, bars and restaurants. Local businesses distribute a useful free Pipa map-guide.

Sights & Activities

Guiana dolphins rest and frolic in the bay at **Praia dos Golfinhos**, accessible via the main beach at low tide only. Let them choose whether to approach you or not; don't chase or feed them.

Several other worthwhile beaches are easily accessed by walking or van, including surfer favorite **Praia do Amor** just south of town; rental boards and lessons are readily available. Another popular destination is **Lagoa de Guarairas**, 8km north of town; three-hour kayak excursions around the lagoon cost R$30, and the dockside **Creperia Marinas** (crepes R$8-20; 11am-8pm) is a brilliant sunset-viewing spot.

Santuário Ecológico de Pipa NATURE RESERVE
(www.ecopipa.com.br; admission R$10; 8am-5pm) Above the beach about 2km outside of town, this small flora and fauna reserve and turtle station is worth visiting for its easy hiking trails and spectacular views.

Sleeping

Competition keeps accommodation prices reasonable in Pipa. Reservations are recommended for all major holidays. There are campsites at both ends of town.

TOP CHOICE **Pousada Xamã** INN $
(3246-2267; www.pousadaxama.com.br; Cajueiros 12; s/d R$70/100;) Hidden up a side street at Pipa's southern edge is one of Brazil's best budget *pousadas*. Ultrahospitable owner Neuza presides over faultless rooms with minibar and air-con; the best open onto a leafy, flower-fringed pool and garden area, with hammocks, wi-fi and hummingbirds. Good breakfast.

Pousada Aconchego BUNGALOW $
(3246-2439; www.pousada-aconchego.com; Céu 100; s/d R$70/100;) Five simply constructed bungalows with hammocks surround a pretty garden, well-equipped guest kitchen and welcoming patio up a dead-end street in the heart of town. Mulilingual owner Marilia helps long-term guests discover off-the-beaten-track treasures outside Pipa.

Media Veronica Hostel HOSTEL $
(9997-7606; www.mediaveronicahostel.com.br; Albacora 555; dm/d without breakfast R$25/70;) Two friendly Argentine brothers run this new hostel with super-reasonable prices and an emphasis on cleanliness, comfort and energy-efficiency. Dorms are the cheapest in town; even better value are the three doubles out back, each with its own hammock and veranda. Optional breakfast (R$6 to R$15) is served down the street.

Sugar Cane Hostel HOSTEL $
(3246-2723; www.sugarcanehostel.com.br; Arara 19; dm/r R$40/90;) Superhospitable staff and central location make this one of Pipa's top hostels. Hammocks, solid tunes and a 2nd-floor patio/bar area foster an ambience of traveler camaraderie. Four- and six-bed dorms are complemented by doubles (one wheelchair accessible) and a guest kitchen.

Pipa Hostel HOSTEL $
(3246-2151; www.pipahostel.com.br; Arara 105; dm/d R$40/120;) The friendly welcome and grassy pool area out back compensate for slightly higher prices at Pipa's HI hostel. Spacious dorms and private rooms all come with air-con (nighttime only in the dorms). Kitchen and barbecue facilities abut a pleasant open-air dining area.

Pousada Vera My House GUESTHOUSE $
(☎3246-2295; veramyhouse@uol.com.br; Mata; r per person with/without breakfast R$25/20) One of several bare-bones, old-school budget *pousadas* on this street, Vera's simple rooms with marine-colored sheets and dolphin murals surround a narrow courtyard.

Eating & Drinking

There's a wide choice of cuisine in Pipa, much of it pricey. Nightlife is focused along the main drag and at a couple of beachside *barracas*.

TOP CHOICE Pane Vino ITALIAN $$
(Albacora; mains R$12-35; ⏲closed Mon) Growing his own basil with seeds smuggled from Italy and frequently driving 150km to get just the right ingredients, Roman-born chef Michele is passionate about authentic Italian food. His ever-changing menu includes fresh-baked bread, homemade tagliatelle and gnocchi, lamb with rosemary, roast suckling pig and Messina-style fish with capers and olives.

Oba JAPANESE $$
(Bem-Te-Vis 32; mains R$16-26; ⏲dinner) Genuine São Paulo–style Japazilian yakisoba is served with delectably gingery veggies, shrimp, chicken or steak. Lychee *sakerinhas* (using sake instead of *cachaça*) add to the fun.

Garagem SEAFOOD $$
(Ladeira do Cruzeiro; mains R$8-35; ⏲10:30am-sunset Mar-Nov, to midnight Dec-Feb) 'Holy shit' views of Pipa's cliffs, dunes and bobbing boats are reason enough to stop here for a drink, but this waterfront bar also serves Argentine *picanha* sandwiches, seafood skewers and full meals featuring fresh fish.

Dona Branca CHURRASCARIA, BUFFET $
(Av Baia dos Golfinhos; meals R$8) Places this affordable are a dying breed in touristy Brazilian beach towns. Choose any two meat items from the grill, then fill your plate with rice, beans and salads from the buffet – all for under R$10. Juices cost R$2 extra, and coffee is free.

Pipa Beach Club INTERNATIONAL $$
(Rua Praia Amor; mains R$12-29) Chill out under the palms enjoying two-for-one mid-afternoon *caipirinhas* and front-row views of surfers trundling along the beachfront boardwalk from Praia do Amor. The eclectic international menu features Thai and Indian curries, Asian wok dishes and baguette sandwiches.

Getting There & Away

Frequent buses run between Natal and Pipa (R$10.50, 1½ to two hours, hourly Monday to Saturday, nine on Sunday). Larger ones (three of which also stop at Natal's airport) terminate at

WORTH A TRIP

RED CLIFFS & NUDE SURFING: THE PARAÍBA COAST

Just north of the Pernambuco–Paraíba border, laid-back **Jacumã** is a humble village surrounded by stunning beaches with tall, arid red cliffs, palms and green water.

The best beaches are **Praia de Tabatinga** (4km south of Jacumã), **Praia do Coqueirinho** (8km) and **Praia de Tambaba** (14km); the latter is a regulated (man needs woman to enter) nudist beach that also hosts the one-of-a-kind **Open de Surf Naturista** (Nude Surfer's Festival) in September. You can walk the coast at low tide; otherwise mototaxis and infrequent buses are the only transport.

There are plenty of *pousadas* (small, family-run guesthouses) along this stretch of coast. In Jacumã, 30m from the beachfront, **Pousada do Inglês** (☎3290-1168; www.pousadadoingles.com.br; Ribero 100; dm from R$35, s/d with fan R$80/110, with air-con R$100/150; ❄📶🏊) offers dorms and veranda-and-hammock-equipped doubles surrounding a pool. At Tabatinga, 100m inland from the beach, friendly **Pousada dos Mundos** (☎3290-1356; www.pousadadosmundos.com.br; Praia de Tabatinga; s/d R$130/160; ❄📶🏊) invites lazy relaxation with hammocks overlooking the river, camping facilities, free kayaks, a swimming pool and an on-site restaurant (mains R$12 to R$24).

Buses and shared taxis for Jacumã (one hour, both R$5) leave from João Pessoa, capital of Paraíba state. The Jacumã bus stop is just outside João Pessoa's long-distance bus station on Rua Cicero Meireles. João Pessoa is accessible by regular buses from Natal (three hours, R$37) and Recife (two hours, R$24).

Pipa's *rodoviaria* 500m north of the center; three smaller ones continue to the south end of town.

Coming from Recife, João Pessoa and points south, get off at Goianinha and catch a *combi* to Pipa (R$3, one hour) from behind the blue church, 200m off the main highway.

Natal

☎0XX84 / POP 804,000

Sun and sand draw people to Natal, the relaxed capital of Rio Grande do Norte state, near Brazil's northeast corner. Occupying a long sandy peninsula, Natal's kilometers of beaches and dunes are regularly kissed by sunshine; the tourist board talks the town up as 'Sun City' thanks to 10 months' tanning time per year. Fourteen kilometers south of the center, the beach suburb of Ponta Negra is the most rewarding traveler hangout, with numerous places to stay and eat.

Sights & Activities

Centro de Turismo HISTORIC BUILDING
(Figueiredo 980; ⏲8am-7pm Mon-Sat, to 6pm Sun) In the center, this beautifully restored historic prison holds a gallery, craft shops and a restaurant with great views.

Forte dos Reis Magos FORT
(admission R$3; ⏲8am-4:30pm) Views are fantastic from this 16th-century Portuguese fort at Natal's northeastern tip.

Parque das Dunas PARK
(www.parquedasdunas.rn.gov.br; Av Alencar, Tirol; admission R$1, trail fee R$1; ⏲8am-6pm Tue-Sun) Between the center and Ponta Negra, this enormous city park has picnic areas and three marked trails through the dunes and vegetation.

Praia Ponta Negra BEACH
The nicest of Natal's city beaches, Ponta Negra (14km south of the center) basks in the shadow of towering **Morro de Careca** – a steep, monstrous dune that drops into the sea. Bus 56 runs from here to other city beaches.

Dunas de Genipabu ADVENTURE TOUR
Dune-buggy excursions to beautiful Genipabu are offered by would-be Ayrton Sennas. Trips *com emoção* (with excitement) include thrills like the Wall of Death. A six-hour trip costs about R$300 (for up to four) and can be arranged through *pousadas* or agencies. Be aware that these trips can damage the fragile dune ecosystem.

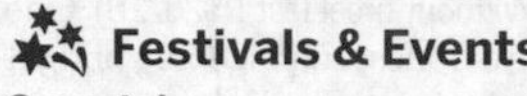

Festivals & Events

Carnatal PARADE, MUSIC
(www.carnatal.com.br) Natal's Salvador-style, out-of-season answer to Carnaval comes in the first week of December.

Sleeping

All listings below are in Ponta Negra, which is more welcoming than downtown.

Albergue da Costa HOSTEL $
(☎3219-0095; www.alberguedacosta.com.br; Av Praia de Ponta Negra 8932; dm/d R$50/120; ❄@🛜🏊) This superfriendly hostel has comfortable dorms, a tiny pool, good breakfasts and laid-back management. Other attractions include guest kitchen, free use of bikes and skateboards, surfboard rental and regular group activities (dance lessons, barbecues, movie nights etc).

Republika Hostel HOSTEL $
(☎3236-2782; www.republikahostel.com.br; Rua Porto das Oficinas 8944; dm/d R$40/100; ❄@🛜) Housed in a converted family home, Ponta Negra's newest hostel is run by youthful cousins Sofia and Anderson. Its low-lit bar and comfy hammock spaces create a cozy atmosphere for mingling with fellow travelers. Dorms and doubles are well priced if unexceptional.

Lua Cheia Hostel HOSTEL $
(☎3236-3696; www.luacheia.com.br; Araújo 500; dm R$49-59, d R$130-150; @🛜) Harry Potter fans will appreciate this peculiar castlelike, HI-affiliated hostel, complete with drawbridge, turrets, Gothic doorways, replica Renaissance paintings, Hogwarts-style dining table and lockers numbered in Latin. Don't expect privacy or peace and quiet – rooms have open chinks in the brick walls, and there's a nightclub on-site.

Pousada Recanto das Flores INN $
(☎3219-4065; www.pousadarecantodasflores.com.br; Av Freire 3161; s/tw/d R$70/90/130; ❄🛜🏊) Dowdy air-conditioned rooms with minibar surround a pool at this bland but cheap *pousada* two blocks above Ponta Negra's beach. Rooms 1 and 2 have dune views, as does the breakfast room.

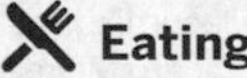

Eating

The following listings are all in Ponta Negra.

Cipó Brasil PIZZERIA **$$**
(Porpino Filho 3111; pizzas R$23-65; ⏰6pm-midnight) A unanimous favorite with a jungle theme, this place serves superb sesame-crusted pizza alongside savory and sweet crepes.

Casa de Taipa BRAZILIAN **$**
(Araújo 130A; dishes R$7-28; ⏰5pm-midnight) Imaginative couscous and tapioca creations, colorful tables and a corner location make this a favorite launchpad for a night out in Ponta Negra.

Tranquilo BUFFET **$**
(Erivan França 94; all you can eat R$12.90; ⏰11:30am-4pm & 6-10pm) Excellent all-you-can-eat value on Ponta Negra's beachfront. Load your plate with rice, beans and salads, then flag down a waiter for main courses like fried fish and garlic shrimp.

Tempero Mineiro BRAZILIAN **$**
(cnr Praia de Tibáu & Av Praia de Ponta Negra; daily specials from R$15) At the northern end of Ponta Negra, this family place with open-air tables offers good-value daily specials, solid fish and meat plates, and, at weekends, tasty *feijoada* (R$19.90 per person).

☆ Entertainment

Ponta Negra is Natal's nightlife center. There are a few dance clubs and a compact zone of cool, charismatic bars around Araújo. Hit **Rastapé** (rastapecasadeforro.com.br; Porpino 2198) for *forró*, **Meu Preto** (cnr Araújo & Oliveira) and **Sancho Music Bar** (www.sanchomusic.com.br; Porpino Filho 3163) for samba, or **Pepper's Hall** (peppershall.com.br; Av Freire 3071) for an eclectic mix of live music and DJs. For entertainment listings, see soltonacidade.com.br.

Local soccer teams include **Alecrim** (www.alecrimfc.com), **América** (www.americadenatal.com.br) and **ABC Futebol Clube** (www.abcfc.com.br). The traditional stadium for the former two teams, Machadão – 6km south of the center – is being demolished to make way for the brand-new Estádio das Dunas, which will host four World Cup 2014 matches.

Forró com Turista LIVE MUSIC
(www.forrocomturista.com.br; Figueiredo 980, Centro de Turismo; ⏰10pm-late Thu) This Thursday-evening tradition brings locals and tourists together for live *forró* in a historical courtyard downtown.

ℹ Information

ATMs line Ponta Negra's beachfront.

Emprotur (☎3232-2500) Airport (☎3087-1342; arrivals hall; ⏰8-11am & 1:30am-4:30pm); bus station (☎3232-7219; Av Gouveia 1237; ⏰7am-6pm); Centro de Turismo (☎3211-6149; Figueiredo 980; ⏰7am-6pm) Information kiosks run by Rio Grande do Norte's state secretary of tourism.

ℹ Getting There & Away

Air

Natal's Augusto Severo International Airport (NAT), 15km south of the center, is served by all major domestic carriers and direct TAP flights to Portugal.

Bus

Long-distance buses leave the Rodoviária Nova, 6km south of the center, for Fortaleza (R$75 to R$80, eight hours, five daily), Recife (R$62, five hours, eight daily), João Pessoa (R$35, three hours, eight daily) and Salvador (R$177 to R$202, 20 hours, two daily).

ℹ Getting Around

Coming from the south and heading for Ponta Negra, get off at Via Direta Shopping, cross the pedestrian overpass and catch bus 46 or 54 (R$2.20) to Ponta Negra.

From the airport, take Bus 'A' (R$2.60) to Via Direta Shopping and transfer as described above. A taxi from the airport to Ponta Negra costs $43.

From the Rodoviária Nova to Ponta Negra, take bus 66. Buses 48 and 54 run between Ponta Negra and the center, while 56 runs along all the city beaches. Bus fare is R$2.20.

Canoa Quebrada

☎0XX88 / POP 2800

Easily reached from Fortaleza, this fishing village turned hippie hangout has moved upmarket these days, but still represents a relaxing seaside spot for a few days' downtime or a bout of kitesurfing. Hard-packed beaches backed by rust-colored cliffs are pleasant and beach-buggy tours to the surrounding dunes (R$120 for up to four people) or **Ponta Grossa** (R$200) can be spectacular. The **kitesurfing** season is from July to December; lessons are available, as are **tandem paragliding** jaunts (R$70).

Canoa's cheapest accommodations are at **Pousada Europa** (☎3421-7004; www.portalcanoaquebrada.com.br; cnr Pereira & Caminho do Mar; s/d R$35/50; ❄@📶🏊), a tired-looking place with ocean-view rooms reached by rickety wooden staircases. Numerous midrange *pousadas* (very affordable off-season) offer considerably more comfort, such as the excellent British-Dutch **Pousada California** (☎3421-7039; www.californiacanoa.com; Nascer do Sol 136; d from R$150; ❄📶🏊), one block towards the beach from Canoa's main street.

On the beach, a long string of *barracas* offers excellent seafood at lunchtime (R$20 to R$40). Back in town, Italian-run **Bar Evolução** (Eliziário 1060; pizzas R$12-26; ⏰dinner) serves delicious wood-fired pizzas on a spacious outdoor patio. Nightlife is focused along the main street; there are also weekend beach parties in high season.

There are ATMs near the bus stop and internet cafes (R$3 per hour) along the main street.

São Benedito runs five buses (R$16.30, 3½ hours) daily between Canoa and Fortaleza. Faster door-to-door service (R$40, 2½ hours) is also available from hotels on Fortaleza's Meireles strip. From Natal, catch a bus to Aracatí (R$53 to R$63, six hours, six to seven daily) and then a bus or *combi* (R$3) the remaining 13km to Canoa.

In August 2012 a new airport was inaugurated in Aracati, with plans to start receiving regular commercial flights sometime in 2013.

Fortaleza

☎0XX85 / POP 2.45 MILLION

The sprawling capital city of Ceará state is a popular beach destination but offers little to the backpacker besides a couple of days on the sand and facilities to get you sorted before setting out again. Glitzy, gritty or tacky depending on where you find yourself, Fortaleza is best appreciated in its coastal neighborhoods, which have impressive nightlife and numerous restaurants.

Sights & Activities

FREE Centro Cultural Dragão do Mar de Arte e Cultura CULTURAL CENTER
(www.dragaodomar.org.br; Dragão do Mar 81, Iracema) Fortaleza's number-one cultural hot spot and evening hangout is this brilliant complex of restored buildings spanning three blocks and including a planetarium, cinema, theater, galleries, numerous restaurants and bars, and the worthwhile **Museu de Arte Contemporânea** (⏰9am-7pm Tue-Thu, 2-9pm Fri-Sun).

Beaches BEACHES
Praia do Meireles has an attractive waterfront promenade with homey beer *barracas* on the sand side and smart air-con restaurants alternating with hotels across the street. The fish market and evening craft fair are other draws. Further east, **Praia do Futuro** is the cleanest and most popular of the city beaches. Just northwest, tranquil **Praia do Cumbuco** has dunes and *jangada* trips. Enjoyable van (per person R$40) and beach-buggy (per vehicle R$400) excursions to the dramatic cliffs and dunes of **Morro Branco** are sold along Meireles's promenade.

Festivals & Events

Fortal (www.fortal.com.br) is a Salvador-style, out-of-season Carnaval in the second half of July.

Sleeping

The coastal neighborhood of Iracema has most of the budget options, but gets seedier the further west you go. A few backstreet Meireles options have worthwhile off-season prices. Both are preferable to the center.

At Home Hostel & Pub HOSTEL $
(☎3077-2233; www.athomehostel.com.br; Canuto de Aguiar 1424; dm/d R$45/100; ❄📶) A few blocks from Meireles beach in a middle-class neighborhood, this party-friendly hostel boasts comfy beds and an on-site British-style pub with frequent live music ranging from jazz to rock.

Hotel Casa de Praia HOTEL $
(☎3219-1022; www.hotelcasadepraia.com.br; Alves 169; s R$99-120, d R$110-140; ❄📶🏊) For its modest price, this hotel comes with plenty of advantages: rooms with partial ocean views, a shallow rooftop pool, a good breakfast and an easy two-block walk to Iracema beach.

Backpackers Ceará HOSTEL $
(☎3091-8997; http://backpackersce.com.br; Av Dom Manoel 89; dm/r without bathroom R$20/40; 📶) This well-established cheapie is in a semi-sketchy neighborhood only steps from the Centro Dragão. Bare-bones rooms surround a safe, enclosed patio, with a guest kitchen compensating for the lack of breakfast.

Hotel La Maison HOTEL **$**
(☎3242-6836; www.hotellamaison.com.br; Av Desembargador Moreira 201, Meireles; r R$110-140; ❄📶) Three blocks from Meireles beach, this midrange option offers bright, spotless rooms, buggy and 4WD trips and free airport/bus station pickups for guests staying three or more days.

Eating

Budget eateries abound in Iracema, while smarter restaurants line the Meireles strip. Centro Cultural Dragão do Mar is also good for dinner.

Santa Clara Café Orgânico CAFE **$**
(Dragão do Mar 81; items from R$10; ⏰3-10pm Tue-Sun) This wonderful cafe serves sandwiches, wraps, waffles, cheesecake and a variety of excellent coffee drinks. Don't miss the filled *tapiocas* – the one with *carne de sol* (salted sun-dried beef) and crunchy *coalho* cheese is a local classic.

Picanha Iracema CHURRASCARIA **$$**
(Alves 89; meat per kg R$22-67) The best of several meat-meat-meat restaurants on this quiet Iracema backstreet; order by weight for the best value.

Mercado de Peixe SEAFOOD **$$**
(Fish Market; Praia de Mucuripe) Buy fish, shrimp or lobster by the kilo at one stall and have it prepared in garlic and oil (around R$5) at another.

BomD+ BUFFET **$**
(Av Moreira 469; per kg R$28.80-31.80; ⏰lunch Mon-Sat) The buffet is excellent at this jolly open-air spot; R$3 extra per kilogram gets you great grilled meats.

Drinking

Students, artists and an alternative local crowd flock to the bars surrounding **Mercado dos Pinhões** (Praça Visconde de Pelotas), a French-built wrought-iron market that hosts live samba, *chorinho* (a samba variation), Afro-Brazilian and *forró* accompanied by cheap beer Tuesday to Sunday evenings.

Bixiga BAR
(Centro Dragão do Mar) Sidewalk tables, live music and *chopp de vinho* (draft wine) draw crowds at this traditional favorite.

Pirata Bar BAR
(Tabajaras 325; ⏰8pm-late) Decked out like a pirate ship, this touristy bar is famous for its 'happy Mondays,' when there's a great live show.

Entertainment

Iracema's legendary nightlife revolves around the bars and clubs surrounding Centro Cultural Dragão do Mar.

Fortaleza's three leading soccer teams are **Fortaleza** (www.fortalezaec.net), **Ceará** (www.cearasc.com) and **Ferroviário** (www.ferrao.com.br). The city's Castelão stadium, completely renovated to seat over 64,000 spectators, will host six World Cup 2014 matches (including one round-of-16 and one quarter-final match). It's located 6km southeast of Fortaleza's airport.

Órbita CLUB
(Dragão do Mar 207; ⏰9pm-late Thu-Sun) Great drinks, multiple pool tables and music ranging from samba-rock to reggae. Sundays are especially lively.

Mucuripe Club CLUB
(Travessa Maranguape 108; ⏰10pm-late Fri & Sat) Pricey and stylish, Ceará's biggest club draws a youthful, well-heeled crowd with multiple dance floors and a wide-ranging mix of rock, funk, *axé, eletrônica, sertanejo* and more.

Shopping

Ceará state has a strong craft tradition (Brazil's best hammocks!).

Centro de Turismo HANDICRAFTS
(Senador Pompeu 350; ⏰8am-5pm Mon-Sat, to noon Sun) Once a prison, the cells of the Centro de Turismo now house fabric and craft shops.

Mercado Central MARKET
(Av Nepomuceno 199; ⏰8am-5pm Mon-Sat, to noon Sun) Fortaleza's central market features several dozen vendors selling food, clothing, hammocks and regional handicrafts.

Information

Things have gotten less sleazy but you'll still encounter prostitution in Iracema and petty theft on beaches and buses.

Internet is widely available. There are ATMs at the airport, bus station, Mercado Central and along the Meireles strip, particularly around Av Abolição and the Club Náutico.

HSBC (Tabosa 1200)

Setfor (www.fortaleza.ce.gov.br/turismo) Airport (☎3392-1200; ⏰6am-midnight); bus station (☎3230-1111; Rodoviária; ⏰6am-8pm);

Fortaleza

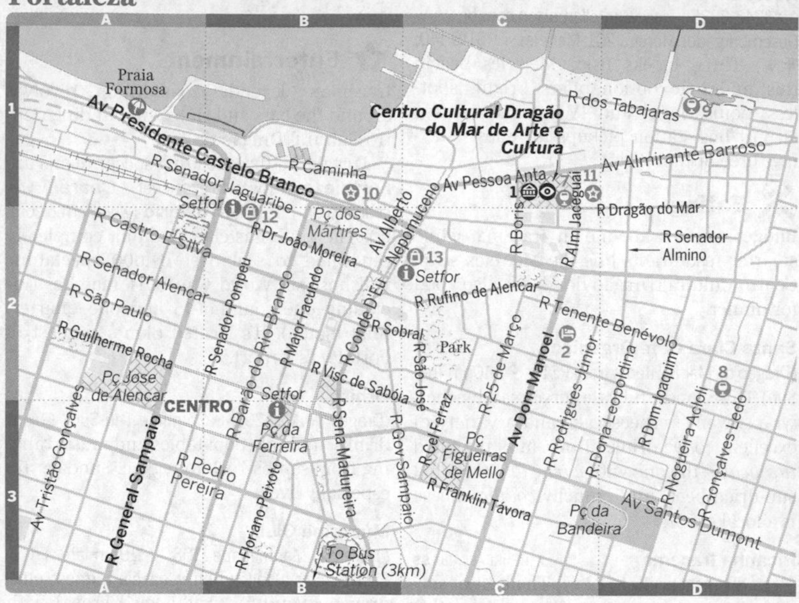

Fortaleza

Top Sights
- Centro Cultural Dragão do Mar de Arte e Cultura C1
- Praia do Meireles G2

Sights
- 1 Museu de Arte Contemporânea C1

Sleeping
- 2 Backpackers Ceará C2
- 3 Hotel Casa de Praia E2
- 4 Hotel La Maison H3

Eating
- 5 BomD+ H3
- 6 Picanha Iracema E2
- Santa Clara Café Orgânico .... (see 1)

Drinking
- 7 Bixiga C1
- 8 Mercado dos Pinhões D2
- 9 Pirata Bar D1

Entertainment
- 10 Mucuripe Club B1
- 11 Órbita C1

Shopping
- 12 Centro de Turismo B2
- 13 Mercado Central C2

Meireles beach (☎3105-2670; Av Beira Mar, Mucuripe; ⏰9am-9pm); Mercado Central (☎3105-1475; ⏰9am-5pm Mon-Fri); Praça da Ferreira (☎3105-1444; ⏰8am-5pm Mon-Sat) Good English map-guides. The main tourist office is on Meireles beach.

Tourist Police (☎3101-2488; Av Barroso 805)

Getting There & Around

Several airlines operate domestically from Fortaleza's Pinto Martins International Airport (FOR), and TAP flies nonstop to Lisbon, Portugal.

Long-distance buses include Nordeste's service to Natal (R$80, eight hours, eight daily), and Guanabara's service to São Luís (R$161, 19 hours, three daily).

Local buses cost R$2. Route 078 'Siqueira/Mucuripe' connects the bus station to the beaches at Iracema and Meireles. Route 404 'Aeroporto' connects the airport with downtown Fortaleza.

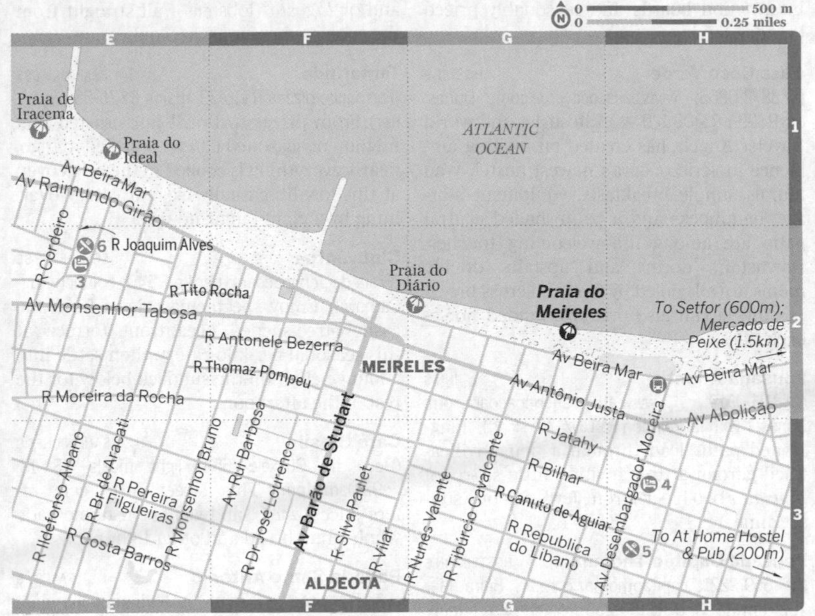

Jericoacoara

☎0XX88 / POP 2000

A truly special place, Jericoacoara (pronounced 'je-ri-kwah-*kwah*-ra,' or just Jeri) offers nightlife, endless beaches and an idyllically remote setting. The sand-street village faces a broad gray beach, shouldered by a huge yellow sand dune and rolling green hills. The relaxed vibe keeps hip Brazilians and travelers staying longer than planned. It's one of South America's best destinations for wind sports and there's a long-boarding wave great for learning to surf.

Jeri consists of six parallel *ruas* running down to the beach. From the big sand dune, heading east, they are: Nova Jeri, Dunas, São Francisco, Principal, Forró and Igreja.

Despite steady growth, Jeri has retained much of its dreamy 'end-of-the-road' feeling. That all may change in coming years if plans to build an international airport in Cruz, 20km away, come to fruition; at the time of writing, construction had been temporarily halted but a 2014 opening date (in time for the World Cup) was still anticipated.

Sights & Activities

The 3km walk to the rock arch **Pedra Furada** is beautiful and buggy trips (from R$40) to surrounding dunes and lakes, like **Lagoa do Paraíso**, are highly recommended. Several outfits, including **Jeri Kite School** (www.jerikiteschool.net), **Blu** (www.blukitesurfing.com) and **Kite Club Preá** (☎3669-2359; www.kiteclubprea.com), offer wind-sport lessons and rental gear. Don't miss the nightly pilgrimage to watch the sunset atop Duna Por do Sol at Jeri's western edge, or the traditional twilight *capoeira* circle on Jeri's main beach.

Sleeping

We gave up counting after reaching a hundred *pousadas* – you won't be short of a bed. During the wet season (March to June) prices drop dramatically and midrange places are a real bargain.

TOP CHOICE **Pousada Tirol/ Jericoacoara Hostel** HOSTEL $
(☎3669-2006; www.jericoacoarahostel.com.br; São Francisco; dm/d with fan R$40/90, with air-con R$50/120; ❄📶) Despite its rather basic dorms, this hostel two blocks from the bus stop wins huge points for its welcoming atmosphere. The large patio and hammock space with well-stocked 'honor fridge' promote easy socializing, and trilingual manager Gaúcho is constantly assisting guests with travel advice, well-organized

information boards and reasonably priced laundry service.

Casa Côco Verde HOSTEL **$**
(☎8872-0865; www.casacocoverde.com; Dunas; dm R$35, r R$100-120; 📶) Kitesurfer and world traveler Angela has created an inviting ambience in Jericoacoara's newest hostel. Wall murals, ample breakfasts, equipment storage, hammocks and a palm-shaded central patio are among the welcoming touches. Downstairs dorms and upstairs double rooms are all cooled by fans and cross breezes. Angela can also organize guided horseback rides.

Pousada Atlantis INN **$**
(☎8111-0819; www.atlantis-jericoacoara.com; Dunas; r with fan/air-con R$110/130; ❄📶) Flagstoned paths lead through a bouganvillea-filled garden at this inviting little six-room *pousada* two blocks from Jeri's famous sunset dune.

Pousada Capitão Thomaz HOSTEL, INN **$**
(☎3669-2221; capitaothomaz.com.br; Beira Mar 202; dm R$50, d R$150-250; ❄@📶🏊) Nicely situated on Jeri's beachfront, this *pousada* recently adapted two rooms into hostel-style dorms. The air-conditioned eight- to 10-bed units are a bit cramped, but hostel guests are free to enjoy the pool, ocean-view terrace, on-site pizzeria and bar. Doubles here aren't worth the extra cash.

Hostel Jeri Brasil HOSTEL **$**
(☎3669-2263; www.jeribrasil.com.br; Matriz 305; dm R$34-44, r R$80-95; ❄📶) Less appealing than most Brazilian HI affiliates, this hostel has clean, air-conditioned dorms and doubles and a small guest kitchen, but it's short on homey touches and suffers from poor layout (hammocks strung along narrow corridors with no room for others to pass or linger for conversation).

Eating

Several simple places around town offer *pratos feitos* for less than R$10.

Peixaria Peixe Brasileiro SEAFOOD **$$**
(Beco do Guaxeló; fish/shrimp/lobster per kg R$30/70/100; ⏲dinner) Some local fishermen had a bright idea: run a *peixaria* (fish shop) by day, throw some tables in the sand by night and grill whole fresh fish for tourists. Pick your dinner – *garoupa* (grouper), *pargo* (red snapper), *robalo* (sea bass), shrimp and/or *lagosta* (lobster) – all straight from the cooler, where it arrived only hours ago.

Tamarindo BRAZILIAN **$$$**
(Farmacia; pizzas R$16-39, mains R$26-58; ⏲dinner) From pizzas to Brazil nut–crusted filet mignon or seasoned fish with grilled mango, nearly everything is cooked in the brick oven at this low-lit, casually elegant eatery overhung by a giant tamarind tree.

Clubventos SELF-SERVE **$$**
(Praia de Jericoacoara; per kg R$40; ⏲lunch Aug-Carnaval) Enjoy spectacular views from the cashew-tree-shaded oceanfront terrace at this seasonal per-kilo eatery, then settle into a lounge chair on the sundeck below for the rest of the afternoon.

Café Brasil SANDWICHES **$**
(Beco do Guaxêlo 65A; light meals R$4-18; ⏲9:30am-11pm) This sweet little cafe offers juices, *açaí*, sandwiches on homemade whole-grain bread and other light meals.

Padaria Santo Antônio BAKERY **$**
(São Francisco; ⏲2-7am) A Jericoacoara classic, this bakery opens in the wee hours of the morning to provide coffee and fresh baked goods to party-goers on their way home.

Drinking & Entertainment

Beachfront carts at the foot of Rua Principal sell inexpensive *caipirinhas* and other mixed drinks to crowds of revelers day and night. Jeri has loads of nightspots with live music, including the legendary *forró* nights at **Dona Amelia** (Forró; ⏲midnight-5am Wed & Sat) and Friday-night samba at **Maloca** (Igreja). New venues pop up regularly.

Zchopp BAR
(Principal) Cold microbrewed beer and frequent live music are the draws at this laid-back spot opposite Jeri's main square.

Planeta Jeri BAR
(Principal; ⏲8pm-late) Just in from the waterfront, this place with a casual sand 'n' surf vibe is a reliable starting point from about 10pm and also a popular spot to reconvene in the wee hours.

Information

Avoid *bichos de pé* (burrowing foot parasites) by not walking barefoot. There are heaps of internet places (from R$2 per hour) and laundries (from R$8 per kilogram) but no banks: the closest ATM is an hour away at Jijoca. Many places accept credit cards.

WORTH A TRIP

FROM JERICOACOARA TO THE LENÇÓIS MARANHENSES

The adventurous ride from Jericoacoara to Parque Nacional dos Lençóis Maranhenses (p370) involves rattling on a wooden bench over a track between sand dunes, past isolated communities and gorgeous scenery. The low-budget, 24-hour version of this trip includes an overnight stay in the tiny town of Paulino Neves at the national park's eastern edge.

From Jericoacoara, hop on the early-morning 4WD truck to Camocim (around 7am Monday to Saturday, two hours), connecting Monday to Friday with a minibus (10:30am, three hours) to Parnaíba. Combined tickets for this initial leg of the journey (R$75) can be purchased direct from various hostels and *pousadas* around Jeri.

From Parnaíba, Viação Coimbra runs a daily 2pm bus to Paulino Neves (R$21, 3½ hours), where you can stay overnight in **Pousada Oásis dos Lençóis** (98-3487-1012; São Francisco 50; s/d with fan R$40/60, with air-con R$50/80) or **Pousada Rota dos Lençóis** (98-3487-1307; suz.reis@hotmail.com; Av Rio Novo 35; s/d with fan R$40/60, with air-con R$50/80) before continuing via 4WD truck the next morning to Barreirinhas (R$20, two to three hours), the main gateway to the national park. If you miss the Parnaíba to Paulino Neves bus, later buses run from Parnaíba to Tutoía (R$16, 2½ hours), where you can make connections to Paulino Neves (R$10, one hour).

The final stretch through the dunes west of Paulino Neves is rough but scenic; in the wet season expect to wade through muddy puddles and/or push your vehicle out of them. There are usually three trucks from Paulino Neves between 4:30am and noon – the earliest one reaches Barreirinhas early enough to link up with day trips into the national park.

If this all sounds too complicated, or if you're traveling west to east (public transport connections are less efficient in this direction), consider a direct transfer, offered by agencies in both Barreirinhas and Jericoacoara. Cost is R$800 to R$1200 for a vehicle holding up to four passengers; the trip takes eight to 10 hours.

Getting There & Away

Fretcar (www.fretcar.com.br) runs two to three daily buses from Fortaleza's bus station (R$60, seven hours, 8am and 7pm, with extra high-season service at 4pm), picking up passengers at Fortaleza's airport and Hotel Praiano on the Meireles beachfront before proceeding four hours west to Jijoca. Included in the ticket price is a one- to two-hour transfer in a 4WD truck from Jijoca to Jeri. Returning from Jeri to Fortaleza, departures are at 8am and 10:30pm (also at 3pm in high season) from **Global Connection Travel** (9900-2109; Forró), where tickets are sold. Numerous companies, such as **Girafatur** (www.girafatur.com.br), also offer direct door-to-door transfers from Fortaleza hotels to Jeri by van (R$60, six hours) or 4WD (R$450 up to four people, four hours).

To save a little money, buy your bus ticket from Fortaleza to Jijoca only (R$26 to R$35, 4½ to six hours), then hop one of the hourly transports that run between Jijoca and Jeri (R$10).

If arriving from the west, go via Parnaíba in Piauí state. **Guanabara** (www.expressoguanabara.com.br) runs overnight buses from São Luis to Parnaíba (R$74, eight hours), roughly connecting with a daily 7:15am bus from Parnaíba to Camocim (R$18, 2¼ hours). In Camocim you can catch 4WD transports to Jericoacoara Monday through Saturday (R$35, 1½ to three hours, usually 11am to noon, depending on tides). On Sundays or if you miss the 4WD, there's a lot of buggy traffic between Camocim and Jeri (an exciting ride); buggies seat four and cost around R$200.

São Luís

0XX98 / POP 1.1 MILLION

With its gorgeous colonial center offering just the right blend of crumbling elegance and unobtrusive renovation, São Luís is a real jewel in the Northeast's crown. The cobbled streets are lined with colorfully painted and appealingly tiled mansions, which have also earned a spot on Unesco's World Heritage List. São Luís has a rich folkloric tradition embodied by its colorful festivals and has become Brazil's reggae capital.

São Luís is divided into two peninsulas by the Rio Anil. On the southernmost, the Centro sits on a hill above the historic core of Praia Grande. On the northern peninsula lie affluent suburbs (São Francisco) and city beaches (Calhau).

São Luís

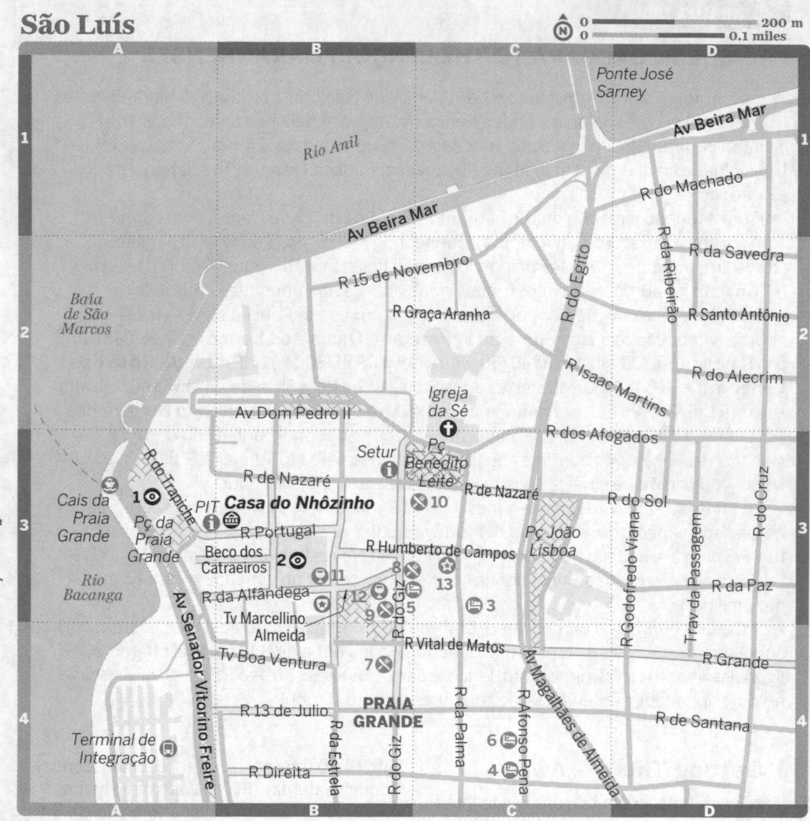

São Luís

Top Sights

Casa do Nhôzinho B3

Sights

1 Casa do Maranhão A3
2 Old Market B3

Sleeping

3 Albergue de Juventude Solar das Pedras C3
4 Pousada Colonial C4
5 Pousada Portas da Amazônia B3
6 Pousada Vitória C4

Eating

7 Crioula B4
8 La Pizzeria B3
9 Padaria de Valery B3
10 SENAC C3

Drinking

11 Antigamente B3
12 Bar da Faustina B3

Entertainment

13 Roots Bar C3

Sights & Activities

Projeto Reviver has restored life to the historic center, which now juxtaposes government offices, handicraft shops, galleries, cultural centers, *pousadas,* restaurants and bars.

Local beaches are broad and flat; some disappear at high tide. Locals pack windswept **Praia do Calhau** on weekends.

FREE **Casa do Nhôzinho** MUSEUM
(Portugal 185; 9am-7pm Tue-Sun) This blue-and-white-tiled three-story beauty features an impressive collection of Maranhão cultural artifacts, including delicate wooden fish traps, indigenous pottery and sculptures of Bumba Meu Boi figures by acclaimed Maranhense artist Nhozinho.

Casa do Maranhão MARKET
(Trapiche; 9am-7pm Tue-Sun) Downstairs, this historic waterfront building houses a handicrafts market; its upper floor, traditionally dedicated to Bumba Meu Boi festival costumes, was closed indefinitely for renovation at the time of writing.

Old Market MARKET
(Portugal) Stalls at this market in the heart of historic São Luís sell dried shrimp, beans, souvenirs and potent local liquors.

Festivals & Events

Carnaval CULTURE
A big event in São Luís (held in February or March).

São João & Bumba Meu Boi FOLKLORE
These June festivals are the focal point of São Luís' cultural calendar. The latter celebrates the legend about a bull whose death and resurrection are marked with music, dance and theater. Year-round rehearsals offer an enticing taste; you can ask the tourist office for locations.

Sleeping

Albergue de Juventude Solar das Pedras HOSTEL $
(3232-6694; www.ajsolardaspedras.com.br; Palma 127; dm/d/q R$30/75/120;) This hostel has good facilities and spacious dorms with lockers. Best: the restored colonial house, with exposed rock walls; worst: the subdued atmosphere created by the undermotivated staff.

Pousada Portas da Amazônia INN $$
(3222-9937; www.portasdaamazonia.com.br; Giz 129; s/d from R$139/189;) This Italian-run restored mansion has the Centro Histórico's most charming rooms, gleaming with polished wood floors and furniture. Two patio-gardens and an attached pizzeria enhance the appeal.

Pousada Colonial INN $
(3232-2834; www.hotelpousadacolonial.com.br; Pena 112; s/d R$115/141; @) Noble corridors and quiet elegance characterize this refurbished old-town mansion. Although the rooms don't quite live up to the ambience, they have crisp sheets and, in some cases, great views over the old town.

Pousada Vitória INN $
(3231-2816; Pena 98; r per person with fan & without bathroom R$30, d with fan/air-con R$85/100;) The perky little dogs running to greet you at the door and the family atmosphere, while somewhat dour, compensate for the less-than-stellar accommodations at this simple *pousada* surrounding an interior courtyard.

Eating

SENAC BUFFET $$
(Nazaré 242; all-you-can-eat lunch buffet R$30-35, dinner mains for 2 R$61-119; lunch Mon-Sat, dinner Thu & Fri) Showpiece for the São Luís branch of Brazil's best-known cooking school, this air-conditioned, high-ceilinged eatery gets packed at lunchtime, thanks to its high-quality all-you-can-eat buffet (R$5 more expensive on Fridays, when it features seafood).

La Pizzeria PIZZERIA $$
(Giz 129; pizza R$20-37; dinner) Popular and attractive old-town pizza joint in a high-ceilinged historic building.

Padaria de Valery FRENCH $
(Giz 164; quiches & light meals R$10-20; closed Sun) Formerly a bakery, this French-owned place recently transitioned into a bar serving quiches, salads and other light meals accompanied by live music ranging from piano-bar classics to acoustic blues.

Crioula BUFFET $
(cnr Giz & Vital de Matos; per kg R$27; closed Sun) This popular corner spot has high warehouse ceilings and a wall enlivened by a cheerful mural. Dish of the day is R$10; the buffet includes good traditional stews.

Drinking & Entertainment

From sunset into the wee hours, plastic tables fill the sidewalks on Travessa Marcelino Almeida and adjacent Praça do Comêrcio. **Bar da Faustina** (Tv Marcelino Almeida) is a classic here; around the corner, **Roots Bar** (Palma 86; 6pm-2am Wed-Fri) pumps out loud reggae on weekends. Other renowned reggae venues outside the historic center include **Bar do Nelson** (Av Litorânea 135, Calhau; 8am-6pm Mon-Fri, 10pm-late Sat) on Saturday nights and **Chama Maré** (Av São Marcos 8, Ponta d'Areia) on Sundays.

Antigamente BAR
(Estrela 220; ⏲11am-1am Mon-Sat) Locals and tourists alike congregate at this sidewalk bar in the heart of historic São Luís. Ice cold beers, *caipirinhas*, snacks and meals are accompanied by live music six nights a week (MPB, *chorinho*, jazz, blues, rock and bossa nova).

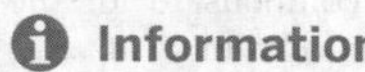

Information

Banco do Brasil (Travessa Boa Ventura) ATM.

PIT (www.turismo.ma.gov.br) Airport (☎3244-4500; ⏲24hr); bus station (☎3249-4500; ⏲8am-7pm); Centro (☎3231-4696; Portugal 165; ⏲8am-6:30pm Mon-Sat, to 1:30pm Sun) Maranhão state tourism office.

Setu (☎3212-6211; Praça Benedito Leite; ⏲8am-7pm Mon-Fri, to 1pm Sat & Sun) Municipal tourist office near the cathedral.

Tourist Police (☎190; cnr Estrela & Alfândega; ⏲24hr)

Getting There & Around

São Luís's Marechal Cunha Machado International Airport (SLZ), 15km southeast of town, is served by all major domestic airlines. A taxi from town costs R$35.

São Luís's long-distance bus station, 8km southeast of the center, is reachable by taxi (R$25) or bus 903 (R$2.10). Buses run to Belém (R$120 to R$277, 12 hours, four daily) and Fortaleza (R$157, 18 to 22 hours, three daily).

Robberies are frequently reported on night buses between São Luís and Belém; consider flying as an alternative.

São Luís has that rarest of Brazilian beasts, a working train station. **Vale** (☎3218-5114; www.vale.com.br) runs trains to Marabá (economy/executive class R$45/92, 13½ hours) Monday, Thursday and Saturday at 8am, returning the following day. Buses continue from Marabá to Belém or Santarém.

Alcântara

☎0XX98 / POP 22,000

This picturesque colonial treasure, slipping regally into decay, lies across the Baía de São Marcos from São Luís and makes for a memorable day trip. Built in the early 17th century, Alcântara was the hub of the region's sugar and cotton economy and home to Maranhão's rich landowners. Today the seat of Brazil's space program lies outside of town.

The streets around the village's highest point contain the finest architecture. On the Praça de Matriz, by a picturesque ruined church, is a grisly reminder of the days of slavery, a **pelourinho** (whipping post). On the same square is the **Museu Histórico** (admission R$2; ⏲9am-2pm), displaying personal effects from the 18th and 19th centuries.

Fish dishes dominate Alcântara's menus. For a sweet treat, stop by Rua das Mercés 401 to try *doce de especie,* the local specialty made from coconut and the juice of orange-tree leaves.

There are banks with ATMs, but take cash in case. It's well worth buying the excellent map-guide of the town, easily purchased in Alcântara or São Luís (R$6).

Launches and catamarans to Alcântara (R$24 return, 1¼ hours) depart twice each morning and once in the afternoon from the Cais da Praia Grande *hidroviária* (boat terminal), returning to São Luis once in the morning and twice in the afternoon. Departure times vary with the tides; check at the dock the day before. Keep an eye out for scarlet ibis.

Parque Nacional dos Lençóis Maranhenses

Fifteen hundred square kilometers of rolling white dunes make up this spectacular national park, which is best visited from March to September, when rainwater forms crystal-clear lakes between the sandy hills. The main access point is the town of Barreirinhas, prettily set on a bend in the Rio Preguiça. From here, numerous agencies – including the highly recommended **São Paulo Ecoturismo** (☎3349-0079; saopaulo ecoturismo.com.br; Rua Antônio Dias 3) – organize four- to five-hour trips by jeep (R$50, 9:30am and 2pm daily) to the edge of the park; motorized vehicles are not permitted to enter it. From here you walk a short way into the dunes; wear beach gear, as it's basically a sand-and-swim experience. If you want to venture further into the park, you can organize memorable two- or three-day hikes, or a spectacular half-hour flyover (R$250 per person). Try to check up on the local weather before you go, though – in 2012 two years of drought left all lakes dry except Lagoa de Peixe.

Other worthwhile outings from Barreirinhas include a 7½-hour boat excursion (R$60, at 8:30am daily) to the mouth of the

Rio Preguiça, stopping to hike the dunes at Vassouras, climb the lighthouse at Mandacaru and eat at the day-trippers' beach of Caburé. For end-of-the-line tranquility, you can also hop on a truck (R$20) from Barreirinhas to the remote river-mouth village of Atins, sandwiched between dunes, river and ocean, offering peaceful *pousada* accommodations.

There are many *pousadas* in and around town, including **Pousada do Porto** (☎0xx98-3349-0654; Anacleto de Carvalho 20; s/d R$50/80, with air-con R$60/100; ❄), just downriver from the bus station; best value are its fan- and breeze-cooled upstairs units with river views. For grilled fish, wood-fired pizza and live music nightly, head for the French-owned **A Canoa** (Beira Rio 300; pizzas from R$20). Other good fish restaurants line the river.

Banco do Brasil (Av Joaquim Soeiro de Carvalho; ⏲9am-2pm Mon-Fri, ATMs 6am-10pm daily) has ATMs, and there's internet a few doors down at **Net Point** (Av Carvalho 693; per hr R$2; ⏲8am-10pm Mon-Sat, 6-10pm Sun).

Cisne Branco (www.cisnebrancoturismo.com.br) runs four buses daily between São Luís and Barreirinhas (R$22 to 28, four hours). Vans and collective taxis (R$40) also travel this route, providing more efficient door-to-door service. Barreirinhas can be a jumping-off point for Jericoacoara (see p367).

THE NORTH

The Amazon conjures a romantic, near-mythical image in our minds, but nowadays also an urgently real one. The future of this immense expanse of rivers and jungle, a vital lung for the world, is of huge importance.

The numbers alone are mind-boggling: the Amazon Basin contains 6 million sq km of river and jungle, and just over half is in Brazil. It contains 17% of the world's fresh water and the main river-flow at its mouth is 12 billion liters per minute.

While you can still have amazing wildlife experiences in the vastnesses of the forest here, it's important to realize that pouncing jaguars and bulging anacondas are rare sightings. Nevertheless, a trip into the jungle ecosystem is deeply rewarding, both for the wildlife-watching and the chance to appreciate how local communities have adapted to this water world. Manaus is a popular base for river trips, but there are other good possibilities. The main city, Belém, is an appealing launchpad to the region, while the tranquil white sands of Alter do Chão make a peaceful stopover on your way upriver.

Getting There & Around

Bus travel is limited to a few routes in the North, so rivers serve as highways. Competing airlines occasionally offer fares cheaper than hammock-boat prices; check for specials.

Belém

☎0XX91 / POP 1.4 MILLION

Prosperous Belém has a cultural sophistication unexpected from a city so isolated. Its wealth comes from its position at the gateway to the Amazon; everything from timber to soybeans passes through here before going to market. Belém has recently invested in tourism, with impressive results. If you take some time to wander the mango tree-lined boulevards, indulge in its parks and museums, and savor its prime perspective on the Amazon River, this attractive city will reward like few others in Brazil.

The compact Comércio business district, roughly between Av Presidente Vargas and Av Portugal, is noisy by day and deserted by night. The quieter Cidade Velha (Old City) contains Belém's historical buildings. East of the center, prosperous Nazaré has some chic shops and restaurants.

Sights & Activities

The Cidade Velha centers around Praça Brandão, dominated by the city's **cathedral** (Praça Frei Brandão; ⏲7am-noon & 2-7:30pm). Most sights close on Mondays.

Forte do Presépio FORTRESS
(admission R$2; ⏲10am-6pm Tue-Fri, to 2pm Sat & Sun) With cannons covering the river, this 17th-century fortress was built by the Portuguese after they kicked out the Dutch and French. Its excellent archaeological museum includes fine indigenous ceramics, artistically displayed.

Museu de Arte Sacra MUSEUM
(Praça Frei Brandão; admission R$4; ⏲10am-6pm Tue-Fri, to 2pm Sat & Sun) Housed in a former Jesuit college, this museum houses a respectable religious art collection, but the real highlight is the beautifully illuminated array of bas-reliefs and carved wooden altars in the Igreja de São Francisco Xavier next door (included in ticket price).

The North

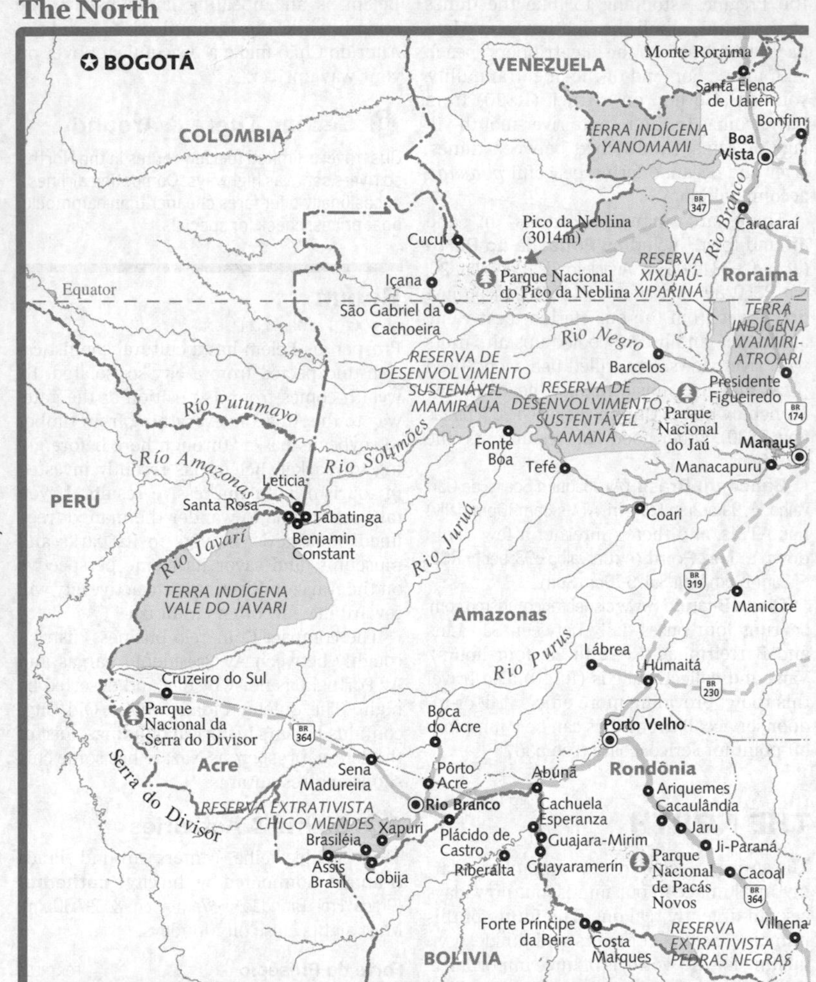

Mercado Ver-o-Peso MARKET

(Blvd Castilhos França; ⏲7:30am-6pm Mon-Sat, to 1pm Sun) At Belem's riverfront market, smells of Amazonian herbal remedies and dried shrimp mingle, and vendors trade tropical fruits and river fish. One of the two historic buildings holds a small, free exhibition on indigenous culture.

Teatro da Paz HISTORIC BUILDING

(Praça da República; admission R$4, Wed free; ⏲guided visits every hr 9am-noon & 2-5pm inclusive Tue-Fri, 9am-noon inclusive Sat &Sun) One of Belém's finest rubber-boom buildings, this elegant theater is resplendent with Italian marble and Brazilian tropical woods. If you can't catch a show, take the guided tour round the lavish interior.

Casa das Onze Janelas MUSEUM

(Praça Frei Brandão; admission R$1; ⏲10am-6pm Tue-Fri, to 2pm Sat & Sun) Various exhibitions of contemporary Brazilian artwork grace the walls of this attractive yellow mansion.

Basílica de NS de Nazaré CHURCH

(Praça da Basílica, Nazaré; ⏲6am-8pm) The vast, ornate marble interior of this 1909 basilica

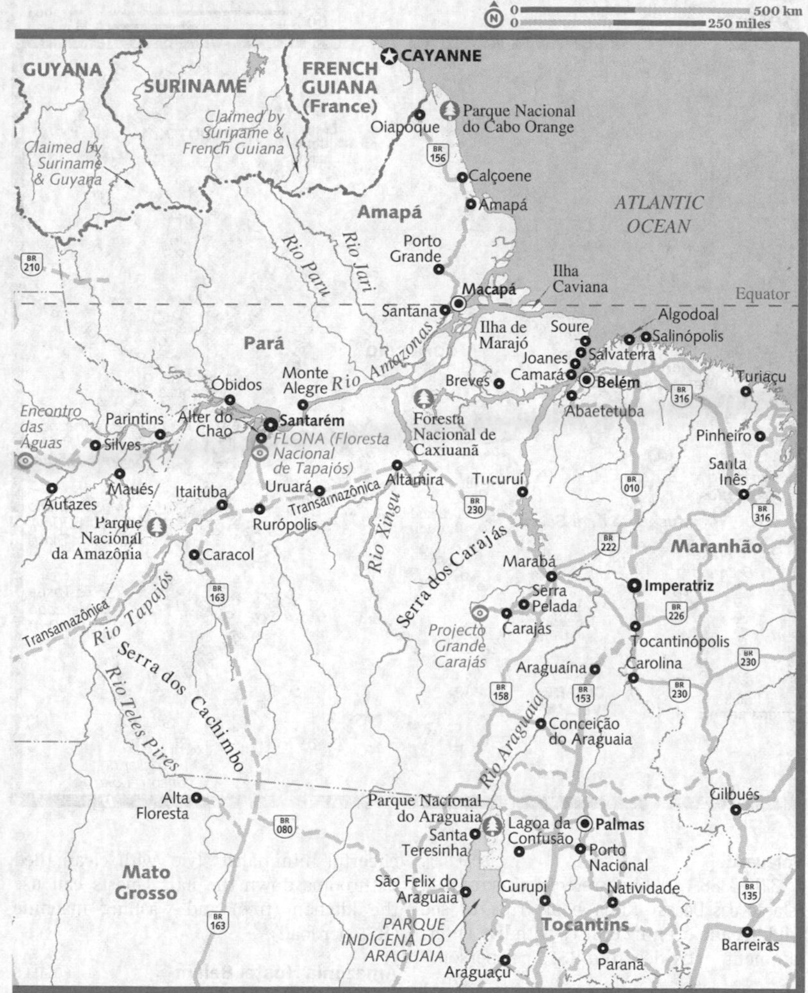

houses a miraculous statue of the Virgin of Nazaré, believed to have been sculpted in Nazareth.

Mangal das Garças PARK

(Praça do Arsenal; sights each R$2, for all 4 R$6; ⌚9am-6pm Tue-Sun) This small riverfront park features plenty of birds including the scarlet ibis, a butterfly house, an observation tower, a naval museum, restaurant and gift shop.

Bosque Municipal Rodrigues Alves PARK

(Av Barroso; R$2; ⌚8:30am-5pm Tue-Sun) In grand old botanical-garden style, this dense 15-hectare piece of rainforest has macaws, coatis, monkeys and the world's largest water lilies.

Museu Emílio Goeldi MUSEUM

(Av Barata; admission R$2; ⌚9am-5pm Tue-Sun) Amazonia's oldest research institution sits within a beautiful piece of rainforest in the middle of downtown Belém, with snakes, big cats, manatees, crocodiles and other Amazonian species. The on-site aquarium and indigenous culture museum were both undergoing renovation at the time of writing.

Belém

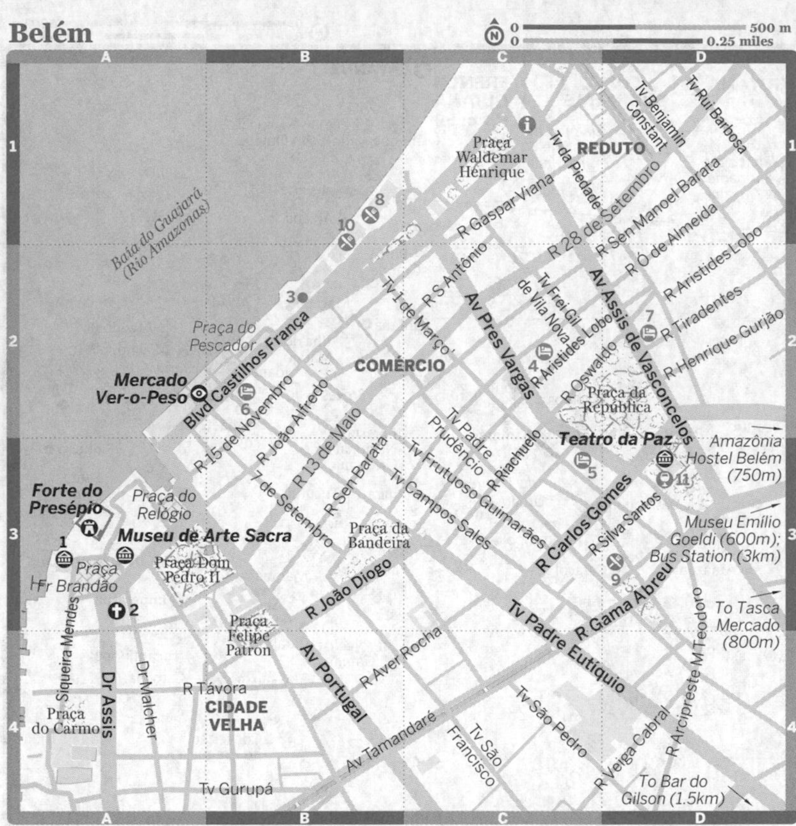

Valeverde BOAT TOUR
(☎3213-3388; www.valeverdeturismo.com.br; Estação das Docas) Runs boat trips to see wildlife, and evening cruises with live entertainment. Activities from R$25 per person.

Festivals & Events

Círio de Nazaré RELIGION
On the second Sunday in October, over a million devotees accompany the image of the Virgin of Nazaré from the cathedral to the Basílica de NS de Nazaré. Two weeks of serious partying follow.

Sleeping

TOP CHOICE **Residência B&B** GUESTHOUSE $
(☎3087-0330; www.residenciabeb.com; Tiradentes 23; dm/s/tw/d without bathroom R$30/50/80/90; ❄📶) An oasis of calm in Belém's bustling center, this sweet Japanese-and-Brazilian-run guesthouse has five rooms decorated in cheerful minimalist style, with clean tiled bathrooms down the hall. Guests can use the kitchen (free) and washing machine (R$5 per load).

Amazônia Hostel Belém HOSTEL $
(☎4008-4800; www.amazoniahostel.com.br; Av Governador José Malcher 592; dm R$58, s/d R$85/115, without bathroom R$65/105; ❄@📶) A lovely renovated historic building holds this bright hostel in a safe neighborhood convenient to the center. Segregated dorms include sheets and air-con. Private triples cost the same as doubles. There's a R$10 discount with HI card.

Hotel Grão Pará HOTEL $
(☎3221-2121; www.hotelgraopara.com.br; Av Presidente Vargas 718; s/d R$100/120; ❄📶) With 150 rooms, this great-value option sits directly opposite Praça da República. Request an upper-floor room for less street noise and better views of the square.

Belém

Hotel Amazônia HOSTEL, HOTEL $

(☎3222-8456; www.hotelamazoniabelem.com.br; Ó de Almeida 548; dm R$20, r with fan/air-con R$50/60; ❄@📶) This central option is geared to budget travelers and offers basic rooms with thin walls in varying configurations. A well-equipped guest kitchen compensates for the lack of breakfast.

Hotel Ver-o-Peso HOTEL $

(☎3241-2022; www.hotelveropeso.com.br; Blvd Castilhos França 208; s/d from R$70/85; ❄) This faded hotel's main claim to fame is its prime location opposite the bustling Ver-O-Peso market. Rooms with waterfront views cost double the price of those in back. Take a taxi late at night.

Eating

Belém is known for *pato no tucupi* (duck in manioc juice and tongue-tingling *jambu*-leaf sauce), *tacacá* (a gummy soup made from manioc root, dried shrimp and *jambu* leaves) and *maniçoba* (black beans, pork and manioc leaves). Classic budget eateries include the R$7 *tacacá* stands near Basílica de NS de Nazaré, and the vendors selling cheap juices, *salgados* and *pratos feitos* in Mercado Ver-o-Peso.

TOP CHOICE **Estação das Docas** RESTAURANTS $$

(www.estacaodasdocas.com.br; Blvd Castilhos França; ⊙10am-midnight daily, to 3am Thu-Sat) This long row of converted waterside warehouses contains multiple eateries offering lunch buffets and pricey à la carte dinners, with riverside seating and live music in the evenings.

TOP CHOICE **Tasca Mercado** SANDWICHES $

(Bocaiúva 1696; sandwiches & salads R$4-20) Tasty sandwiches come on fresh-baked baguettes and focaccia at this high-ceilinged, trendy cafe, from humble *misto quente* (ham and cheese) to more refined options with garlic eggplant, roasted peppers or smoked salmon. Salads, quiches and pizzas round out the menu.

Boteco das Onze BRAZILIAN $$

(Praça Frei Brandão; mains R$21-63) Splurge on a full meal in the art-filled dining room, or enjoy a sandwich or *caldinho* (soup) with fabulous Amazon views on the breezy back patio of this classy joint behind Casa das Onze Janelas. There's live music virtually every night (cover R$6 to R$10).

Cozinha de Bistrô FRENCH $$

(Travessa Ferreira Cantão 278; dishes R$14-28; ⊙lunch Mon-Sat) This enchanting, discreet backstreet spot with daily blackboard specials has a dark, romantic feel, a jazz theme and excellent French-influenced bistro plates such as coq au vin.

Cairu ICE CREAM $

(Estação das Docas; single cone R$4.50; ⊙10am-midnight) This multibranch Belém institution offers ice creams galore, including a vast rainbow of Amazon fruit flavors.

Drinking & Entertainment

Amazon Cervejaria BREWERY

(www.amazonbeer.com.br; Estação das Docas; ⊙from 5pm Mon-Fri, from 11am Sat & Sun) Deservedly the Estacão's most popular spot, with a convivial riverfront terrace, this microbrewery produces five tasty draft beers, accompanied by good but pricey food.

Bar do Parque BAR

(Praça da República; ⊙24hr) This curious beer kiosk and its mosaic-floored open terrace

RIVER TRAVEL

Riverboat travel is a unique Amazonian experience. Be warned that boats are always slow and crowded, often wet and smelly, sometimes dull and never comfortable. Do you like *forró* music? You won't after this trip! Luckily, Brazilians are friendly and river culture is interesting. Some tips:

» Downstream travel is considerably faster than upstream, but boats heading upriver travel closer to the shore, which is more scenic.

» Boats often moor in port a few days before departing – check boat quality before committing.

» Fares vary little between boats. Tickets are best bought onboard or at official booths inside port buildings. Street vendors may offer cheaper prices but you run the risk of being cheated.

» *Camarotes* (cabins) are usually available and afford additional privacy and security. Ensure that yours has a fan or air-con. *Camarotes* are usually the same price as flying.

» Put up your hammock (available at any market from R$20; don't forget rope!) several hours before departure. There are usually two decks for hammocks; try for a spot on the upper one (the engine's below), away from the smelly toilets. Others are likely to sling their hammocks above and/or below yours. Porters may offer to help you tie yours for a small tip: well worth it if knots aren't the ace in your pack.

» Bring a rain jacket or poncho, sheet or light blanket, toilet paper and diarrhea medication.

» Meals (included) are mainly rice, beans and meat, with water or juice to drink. It's advisable to bring a few liters of bottled water, fruit and snacks. There's usually a snack bar on the top deck.

» Watch your gear carefully, especially just before docking and while at port. Lock zippers and wrap your backpack in a plastic bag. Keep valuables with you. Get friendly with people around you, as they can keep an eye on your stuff.

is a Belém classic. In the evenings everyone from students to businessfolk to sex workers can be found at its tables, served by bow-tied waiters.

A Pororoca LIVE MUSIC
(www.apororoca.com.br; Av Senador Lemos 3316, Sacramenta; ⌚8pm-late Thu-Sun) A simple but superpopular dance club playing various styles like *pagode*, reggae and *brega* (a fast and free couples dance of Pará), usually with live bands.

Bar do Gilson LIVE MUSIC
(Travessa Padre Eutíquio 3172, Condor; ⌚8pm-3am Fri, noon-3am Sat, 8pm-midnight Sun) Under a tin roof and fueled by cheap beer, *chorinho* rules the house at one of Belém's most celebrated live-music spots.

 Information

Comércio has a reputation for muggings when fairly empty (at night and on Sunday). Take a taxi at night. Pickpocketing is common at Mercado Ver-o-Peso.

Hospital Adventista de Belém (☎3084-8686; www.hab.org.br; Av Barroso 1758)

HSBC (Av Presidente Vargas 670; ⌚10am-5pm Mon-Sat) ATMs opposite Praça da República.

Paratur (☎3212-0575; www.paraturismo.pa.gov.br; Praça Waldemar Henrique; ⌚8am-2pm Mon-Fri) Pará's state tourist office, with a branch in the airport (open 8:30am to 10pm).

Tourist Police (Estação das Docas)

 Getting There & Away

Air

Abundant domestic connections as well as flights north to Suriname leave from Belém's Val de Caeo International Airport (BEL), 8km north of the center. Buses 634 'Marex-Arsenal' and 'Pratinha–P Vargas' run between the traffic circle outside the airport and downtown Belém (R$2.20, 45 minutes). Taxis cost R$35 to R$45.

Boat

Boats use Belém's Terminal Hidroviária. Tickets are sold at booths inside. Boats to Santarém (hammock/cabin R$180/350, 2½ days) and Manaus (hammock/cabin R$250/600, five days) depart on Wednesday and Friday. Boats to Macapá (hammock/cabin R$130/250, 23 hours) depart Monday through Saturday.

Bus

The bus station is on Av Almirante Barroso, 3km east of the center. To get downtown, catch any 'Aero Club' or 'P Vargas' bus from across the road. Going to the bus station, take an 'Aeroclube' or 'Pratinha–P Vargas' bus from Av Presidente Vargas. Taxis to points along Av Presidente Vargas cost between R$12 and R$17.

Sample travel times and fares from Belém are as follows:

DESTINATION	COST (R$)	DURATION (HR)
Brasília	320	34
Fortaleza	233	25
Marabá	59	12
Rio de Janeiro	423-493	50-55
Salvador	314	36
São Luís	120-276	12

Algodoal

☎0XX91

Accessible only by boat, Algodoal is a simple village in an idyllic situation. Its sand streets, lack of cars, cheap accommodation and white beaches make it a relaxing place to kick back.

The village consists of three long parallel streets. At the far end cross a small river (wade at low tide, canoe at high) to lovely Praia do Farol, which turns a corner and becomes 8km-long Praia da Princesa. There are other small hamlets on this island, cut by channels into three main parts. Make your way around on foot, horsecart or canoe.

Every second home is nominally a *pousada,* most of which offer very basic rooms, hammocks and maybe a place to camp; bring a mosquito net. Competition keeps prices low. More upmarket choices include **Estrela Sol Hotel** (☎3854-1107; www.estrelasol.algodoal.com; d with fan R$60, with air-con from R$70; ❄🏊), which has a pretty pool, and **Jardim do Éden** (☎9997-0467; http://algodoal.chez.com; Praia do Farol; hammock space R$50, r R$125), right on Praia do Farol, with hammock space, comfortable rooms, brick cabins and good meals using local produce.

Most accommodations offer food, typically tasty fresh-fish dishes. Some hotels accept credit cards but there are no banks – bring cash.

Access is via mainland Marudá. Buses (R$19.50, four hours, five to seven daily) leave Belém's bus station for Marudá; quicker minibuses (R$23) leave from just behind it. Either will drop you at Marudá's port, where boats for Algodoal (R$6, 40 minutes) leave six to seven times daily. Horsecarts (R$7 to R$10) await the boats to take you to the village, only a 10-minute stroll away anyway. Returning to Belém, buses and minibuses leave Marudá's port until about 5pm.

Ilha de Marajó

☎0XX91 / POP 250,000

Lying at the mouth of the Amazon, this verdant island is larger than 70 of the world's countries but much of its interior is swampy and inaccessible. Though the main settlement, Breves, is in the island's southwest, three southeastern villages – Soure, Salvaterra and Joanes – are easily reached from Belém and make for a relaxing visit. The island is notable for its hospitable people and *carimbo,* a colorful folkloric dance. Buffalo are another trademark and their meat appears on most restaurant menus. Do as the locals do and hire a bike to get around.

JOANES

Closest to Camará, where the boat comes in, Joanes is a tiny hamlet with the fragments of an old Jesuit church and a good sandy beach. Livestock wander grassy streets lined with a few shops and sandwich stands. Attractive **Pousada Ventania do Rio-Mar** (☎3646-2067; www.pousadaventania.com; Quarta Rua; s/d R$85/105) sits atop a breezy headland overlooking the beach. The owners rent bikes, kayaks and canoes, offer meals (including some vegetarian options) and can organize excursions with local fisherfolk and other activities.

SALVATERRA

About 18km north of Joanes, slow-paced Salvaterra has more of a town feel and a decent beach, Praia Grande. A tourist information kiosk is on the plaza near the river.

Warmly welcoming **Pousada Bosque dos Aruãs** (☎3765-1115; Segunda Rua; s/d R$75/85; ❄📶) has good, simple wooden cabins on stilts in an attractive natural yard looking out over the water. It's a top spot to relax. Bicycles are available for rent (R$2/12 per hour/day). Walking up from the jetty, take your second left.

SOURE

Soure, the biggest town on this side of the island, has a spread-out grid of streets that peter out into buffalo paths.

In town, visit **Mbara-yo** (Travessa 20 btwn Ruas 3 & 4), the workshop of award-winning ceramicist Carlos Amaral, whose work combines Aruã and Marajoara ceramic traditions. A 3km bike ride north of Soure leads to **Praia Barra Velha**, where shacks sell drinks and seafood. Beyond lies **Praia de Araruna**, a long, starkly beautiful and practically deserted beach. There's an intervening river, which requires a boat at high tide. Alternatively, follow Rua 4 inland to **Praia do Pesqueiro** (11km), another popular weekend beach.

Pousada Asa Branca (☎3741-1414; Rua 4 btwn Travessas 11 & 12; s/d R$60/90; ❄) offers basic but clean rooms flanking a small backyard; for spiffier acommodations with wi-fi, try **Pousada O Canto do Francês** (☎3741-1298; http://ocantodofrances.blogspot.com.br; cnr Rua 6 & Travessa 8; s/d/tr R$110/130/160; ❄📶). **Paraíso Verde** (Travessa 17 btwn Ruas 9 & 10; mains for 2 people R$30-50), along the road to the northern beaches, serves typical buffalo and fish dishes in a peaceful, gorgeous and shady garden.

Banco do Brasil (Rua 3 btwn Travessas 17 & 18) and **Bradesco** (Rua 2 btwn Travessas 15 & 16) have ATMs. **Bimba** (Rua 4 btwn Travessas 18 & 19; per hour/day R$2/10) rents bicycles. There are a few cybercafes.

Getting There & Around

Boats leave Belém's Terminal Hidroviário for Camará (deck/air-con VIP lounge R$16/25.50, three hours) Monday through Saturday at 6:30am and 2:30pm, and Sunday at 10am, returning at 6:30am and 3pm (Sunday at 3pm only). Waiting buses (R$5) and air-con minibuses (R$6 to R$12) whisk passengers from Camará's dock to Joanes, Salvaterra and Soure.

The centers of Salvaterra and Soure are linked by a boat (R$3, 20 minutes) that leaves whenever it fills up (this can take a while). A few kilometers west of Salvaterra, an hourly vehicle ferry (free, five minutes) and frequent motorboats (R$1.75, five minutes) cross a much narrower channel to Soure. Mototaxis, taxis and infrequent vans move people around the island.

Santarém

☎0XX93 / POP 295,000

Most travelers rush between Belém and Manaus, skipping over the very thing they are desperate to see: the Amazon. A stop in riverfront Santarém not only breaks up a long boat trip, but also provides a chance to investigate the jungle and communities seen from your hammock. Santarém itself is rather bland, but the lovely river beaches and beautiful rainforest preserves nearby will entice you to prolong your stay.

GETTING TO FRENCH GUIANA

Right on the equator on the north side of the mouth of the Amazon, **Macapá** can be reached by boat or plane from Belém. The capital of Amapá state offers little in the way of sights except the 18th-century Fortaleza (fortress), but the riverfront is pleasant and you can have your equatorial moment at the monument 5km southwest of the center. The city has all services. **Hotel América Novo Mundo** (☎3223-2819; Av Coaracy Nunes 333; s/d R$60/80, without bathroom R$30/50; ❄) is a cheap spot to lay your head – get a breezy front room. **Peixaria Amazonas** (Beira Rio 218; 2-person mains from R$32; ⊙lunch & dinner Mon-Sat, lunch Sun) has river views and good fish.

From Macapá's bus station, 3km north of town, head north to **Oiapoque** (R$90, 12 to 15 hours). This rough-and-ready town is across the river from nicer but pricier St Georges in French Guiana. Before crossing the border, get your passport stamped at the **Polícia Federal** (☎3521-1380; ⊙8am-8pm) on the main street, 500m from the market where the bus stops. An international bridge across the river was completed in 2011, but remained closed indefinitely at the time of writing pending intergovernmental negotiations. If the bridge still hasn't opened by the time you read this, cross over by boat (R$15, 20 minutes).

Sights & Activities

Santarém's waterfront provides a nice perspective on the meeting of the waters between the tea-colored Rio Tapajós and the café-au-lait Rio Amazonas. The two flow side by side for a few kilometers without mingling.

Museu Dica Frazão MUSEUM
(Peixoto 281; admission by donation) Run by eccentric 90-something Dona Dica herself, this house displays and sells the beautiful clothing and tapestries she makes from Amazonian root fibers.

Sleeping & Eating

Central Hotel HOTEL
(3522-4920; Tapajós 258; s/d R$70/90;) Yes, this place is faded, and the interior rooms are claustrophobic, but the air-con works and the location at the heart of Santarém's waterfront can't be beat.

Mirante Hotel HOTEL $$
(3067-7100; www.mirantehotel.com; Corrêa 115; s/d weekend R$78/93, midweek R$140/165;) This modern business-oriented hotel with clean white linens and tiled bathrooms is worth a look on weekends, when prices get slashed almost in half.

Sabor Caseiro BUFFET $
(Peixoto 521; per kg R$26.90; lunch) With comfy black padded booths, air-con and plenty of juices, this is a terrific lunch spot. The above-average buffet includes regional specialties and hearty stews like *feijoada* at weekends.

Information

HSBC (Av Rui Barbosa) One of several banks with ATMs on this street.

Semtur (3523-2434; amigosdoturismo.blogspot.com.br; Praça do Pescador; 9am-9pm) On the waterfront. Eager to help but not especially useful.

Getting There & Around

Air

Domestic flights operate from Santarém's Eduardo Gomes Airport (STM), 15km west of the center. Special airfares to Manaus and Belém are sometimes cheaper than the boat. A taxi into town costs R$45. The 'Aeroporto' bus (R$1.90, 35 minutes) runs irregularly from early morning until about 6pm. Be careful not to catch the 'Aeroporto V' bus, which goes to where the airport used to be.

Boat

Boats to Manaus (hammock/double cabin R$120/500, two days, Monday to Saturday) and Belém (hammock/double cabin R$160/600, two days, Friday to Sunday) use the Docas do Pará, 2.5km west of the center. Booths outside the entrance sell tickets. Boats to Macapá (hammock/double cabin R$140/600, 36 hours, daily) depart from both here and Praça Tiradentes, 1km west of the center.

The 'Orla Fluvial' minibus (R$1.50) connects the downtown waterfront with both ports every 20 minutes until 7pm. The 'Circular Esperança' bus (R$1.90) runs directly from the center to the Docas do Pará but deviates on the return. A taxi costs around R$15 to Docas do Pará.

Bus

Buses to Alter do Chão (R$2.50, 50 minutes, roughly hourly) or the airport can be caught along Av Rui Barbosa.

Long-distance buses leave Santarém's bus station (5km west of town) for Cuiabá (R$304, 36 hours) and Marabá (R$220, from 30 hours) when road conditions permit, but travel times are significantly prolonged or runs canceled during the rainy season.

Around Santarém

FLORESTA NACIONAL (FLONA) DO TAPAJÓS

This 6500-sq-km primary rainforest reserve on the Rio Tapajós is notable for giant trees, including behemoth *sumauná* (a type of ceiba tree). Its *igarapés* (channels connecting rivers) and, in the rainy season, *igapós* (flooded forests) promise wildlife-viewing; sloths, monkeys, river dolphins and birds are relatively common. Much of the charm of a visit is experiencing life in the forest's indigenous communities. Guided visits can be arranged with agencies in Santarém or Alter do Chão. Otherwise, take the bus from Santarém or hire a boat in Alter do Chão.

Four small communities within FLONA have ecotourism schemes and welcome visitors for homestays and tours with local guides. The two most commonly visited are Maguary and Jamaraquá. Basic accommodation (around R$15 per night) is provided within each community, ranging from family homes to rustic (think hammocks on a screened porch) *pousadas*. Simple meals of fish, chicken, rice and beans are available from the towns' host families (R$5 for breakfast, R$10 for lunch or dinner). Bring bottled water, toilet paper, a flashlight and any additional food; there are no shops.

To visit, authorization (per day R$5.50) from **ICMBio** (☎3523-2964; flonatapajos.pa@icmbio.gov.br; Av Tapajós 2267, Santarém; ⏰7am-noon & 2-7pm Mon-Fri) is required; the fee can be paid at the reserve entrance. Guides are obligatory in the park. Fees for hikes and canoe trips (around R$40 per group) are accompanied by a community charge (per person R$5 to R$8).

Buses for Maguary and Jamaraquá (R$8, three to four hours) leave Santarém at 11am Monday to Saturday from Av São Sebastião near the Telemar building.

ALTER DO CHÃO

☎0XX93 / POP 7000

Bank on spending longer than you planned at this wonderfully relaxed riverside haven. With its white-sand river beaches and tropical ambience, Alter do Chão is one of Amazonia's most beautiful places to unwind. Beaches are largest from June to December but Alter is worth a visit at any time of year.

Opposite the town square, the **Ilha do Amor** is an idyllic sand island in the Rio Tapajós featured on numerous postcards. Nearby, the large **Lago Verde** lagoon is great to explore by boat or canoe. Surrounding attractions include the FLONA do Tapajós rainforest and the **Rio Arapiunes**, with blindingly white beaches and clear waters.

Activities

Paddle across to the Ilha do Amor (watch for stingrays), or, when the water's higher, take a boat (R$6 return). Kayak rentals (R$5 per hour) are available on the island.

Mãe Natureza ECOTOUR
(☎3527-1264; www.maenaturezaecoturismo.com.br; Praça Sete de Setembro) Offers kayak excursions on Lago Verde, riverboat trips to the primary forest at FLONA do Tapajós, and other tours led by multilingual indigenous guides.

Festivals & Events

Festa do Çairé FOLKLORE
Alter do Chão fills during this lively folkloric festival with dancing and processions held in the second week of September.

Sleeping & Eating

There are many low-key, backpacker-friendly *pousadas*.

TOP CHOICE **Pousada do Tapajós Hostel** HOSTEL, INN $
(☎9210-2166; www.pousadadotapajos.com.br; Sodré 100; hammock space/dm/s/d R$25/35/80/100; ❄📶) Five blocks west of the square, this newcomer impresses with friendly staff, ultraclean rooms, spacious kitchen and common areas, big grassy backyard, hammock space and well-organized information boards.

Belas Praias Pousada INN $
(☎3527-1365; belaspraias@gmail.com; cnr Rua da Praia & Praça 7 de Setembro; s/d R$70/120; ❄📶) Well-placed near the waterfront, this *pousada* has superb views of Ilha do Amor from the upstairs rooms, and picks up the *praça*'s free, fast wi-fi signal. It can get noisy at night.

Pousada Lago Verde INN $
(☎3527-1272; www.pousadalagoverde.blogspot.com.br; Sodré 62; s/d without breakfast R$40/75; ❄) Dona Rosa rents out four simple, immaculate tile-floored rooms with air-con and refrigerator in her humble pink-and-blue abode two blocks east of the plaza. Discounts for longer stays.

Pousada Tupaiulândia INN $
(☎3527-1157; pousadatupaiulandia@hotmail.com; Teixeira 300; s/d $80/100; ❄) Between the bus station and the square, this welcoming *pousada*'s circular buildings house spacious rooms with well-stocked fridges. Good breakfast.

Albergue da Floresta HOSTEL, INN $
(☎9132-7910; www.alberguedafloresta-alterdochao.blogspot.com.br; Travessa Antônio Pedrosa; hammock space R$20-30, s/d R$80/100, without bathroom R$60/80) About 500m east of the *praça*, this laid-back retreat offers open-air thatched-roof hammock space and tree-house-like rooms.

Mutunuy BRAZILIAN $
(Praça Principal; meals per person R$13-23; ⏰closed Sun night & Mon) Tasty local river fish grilled over the coals and front-row views of the town square are the star attractions at this open-air terrace restaurant.

Shopping

TOP CHOICE **Arariba** HANDICRAFTS
(www.araribah.com.br; Travessa Antônio Lobato; ⏰9am-1pm & 3:30-8:30pm) This excellent indigenous art store displays the artwork of eight different Amazonian tribes.

Information

On the square there's free wi-fi and a Banco do Brasil ATM at Minicenter Mingote; some businesses accept credit cards.

Getting There & Away

The bus station is three blocks uphill from the main square and waterfront. Hourly buses run to Santarém (R$2.50, 50 minutes). From Santarém's airport take the hourly bus to the Alter do Chão intersection and wait there for the Santarém–Alter do Chão bus. A taxi from the airport costs R$50 to R$70.

Manaus

☎0XX92 / POP 1.8 MILLION

The mystique of Manaus, the city in the heart of the Amazon jungle and a major port 1500km from the sea, wears off fairly fast – it's a sprawling, largely unromantic spot that doesn't make the most of its riverside position. But this is changing little by little, with restoration of noble buildings from the rubber-boom days. It is a friendly place, the transport hub of the Amazon region and the most popular place to organize a jungle trip. Once you're back from a few days in the wild, things like air-conditioning will make you feel friendlier toward the place.

Teatro Amazonas is the heart of downtown. Adjacent Praça São Sebastião has colorful restored buildings, terrace cafes and live music or cultural displays most nights from 7pm. The U-shaped area defined by Av Epaminondas, Av Floriano Peixoto and Av Getúlio Vargas is a busy, noisy commercial district by day, but gets deserted nights and Sundays. The Praça da Matriz and Zona Franca are also seedy at night.

Sights

Teatro Amazonas ARCHITECTURE
(☎3232 1768; Praça São Sebastião; guided tour R$10; 9am-5pm) Strikingly domed Teatro Amazonas is the city's emblematic rubber-boom building. A short but worthwhile English-language guided tour takes you into the opulent interior. There are frequent shows; check www.culturamazonas.am.gov.br for details.

FREE **Palacete Provincial** MUSEUM
(Praça Heliodóro Balbi; 9am-5pm Tue & Wed, 9am-7pm Thu-Sat, 4-8pm Sun) Beautifully restored, this 19th-century government palace houses multiple collections, including an art gallery, replicas of famous sculptures and coins, archaeology exhibits and a sound-and-film archive. There's also a good cafe.

Museu do Índio MUSEUM
(Duque de Caxias 296; admission R$5; 8:30-11:30am, 1-4:30pm Mon-Fri, 8:30-11:30am Sat) Set in a former convent hospital, this museum has an excellent collection of indigenous artifacts, though it's let down by a lack of information. Take bus 401 or 606 from Praça da Matriz or Av Sete de Setembro. On the way there look for Palácio Rio Negro, an ostentatious rubber baron's mansion now used for cultural events.

Bosque da Ciência PARK
(Forest of Science; http://bosque.inpa.gov.br/principal.htm; Av Cabral; admission R$5; 9am-noon & 2-5pm Tue-Fri, 9am-4pm Sat & Sun) Some 130 sq km of tranquil rainforest shelters giant otters, manatees, caimans and free-roaming turtles, monkeys, sloths and other creatures. Take bus 519 from the Praça da Matriz.

Boi-Bumbá DANCE
(Avenida Pedro Teixeira, 2565, Flores) Festival rehearsals for Boi-Bumbá (a legend about the death and resurrection of a bull, celebrated with music, dance and theater) are held at the *sambódromo* on Saturday at 9pm from September to June. Admission costs R$10 to R$20; catch bus 10, 201, or 214 to get there.

Activities

Encontro das Águas BOAT TOUR
Near Manaus, the dark Rio Negro and the coffee-colored Rio Solimões flow side by side for several kilometers without mingling (differences in speed, density and temperature), before merging to form the Amazon. Multiday jungle trips (see p385) often include this 'Meeting of the Waters' for free; the 'Encontro das Águas' day tours advertised around town are generally overpriced and best avoided.

Amazon Tree Climbing ECOTOUR
(☎8195-8585; www.amazontreeclimbing.com; per person from R$220) This smartly run outfit offers one-of-a-kind tours to massive *angelín* or *samaúma* trees – an amazing Amazonian experience. Day trips include just one ascent, but it can take an hour to reach the top, with mid-dangle discussions of canopy ecology, and plenty of time to soak up the view, a dozen-plus stories above the ground.

Sleeping

Location-wise, the area around Teatro Amazonas is ideal, though penny-pinchers can find plenty of cheap *pousadas* near the port.

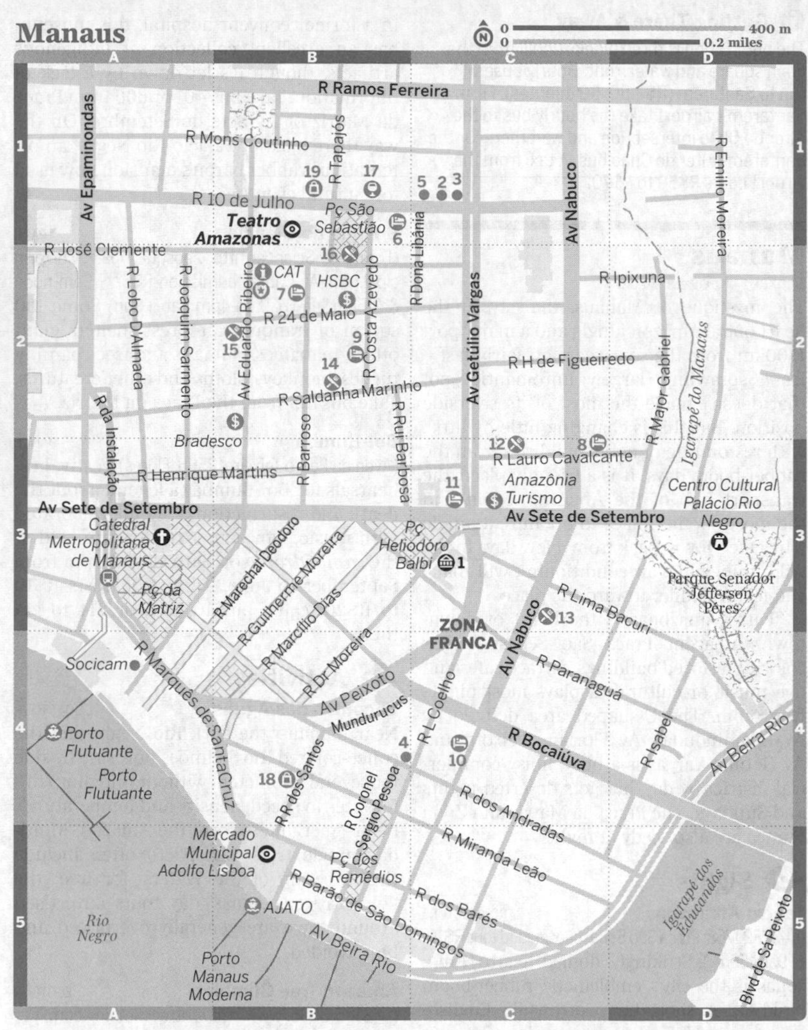

TOP CHOICE **Hostel Manaus** HOSTEL **$**
(☎3233-4545; www.hostelmanaus.com; Cavalcante 231; dm with fan/air-con R$27/30, s/d with fan R$60/66, with air-con R$70/76; ❄@📶) Not Manaus' newest hostel, but still its best, this HI affiliate impresses with friendly staff and pleasant open-air terraces, which make it ideal for hanging out and meeting other travelers. It's a 10-minute walk from Teatro Amazonas.

Gol Backpackers Manaus HOSTEL **$**
(☎3304-5805; www.golbackpackers.com; Barroso 365; dm R$25-30, r R$70; ❄🏊) The location half a block from Teatro Amazonas is mighty appealing at this new five-room hostel, but the backyard pool is small, the rooms only so-so and the common spaces rather uninviting. Still, you'll find nothing cheaper this close to the action.

Boutique Hotel Casa Teatro HOTEL **$$**
(☎3633-8381; www.casateatro.com.br; 10 de Julho 632; s/d standard R$120/140, superior R$160/180) Spent too many nights slapping mosquitoes in a threadbare hammock? This ultra-central hotel's superior rooms, gleaming with new wood and plush pillows, may be

Manaus

the perfect antidote; standard *apartamentos*, with glorified bunk beds, aren't worth the money.

Manaus Hostel 'Trip Tour' HOSTEL $
(☎3231-2139; www.manaushostel.com.br; Costa Azevedo 63; dm with fan/air-con R$20/30, r R$65;) Atmosphere doesn't live up to location at this hostel near Teatro Amazonas. Claustrophobic dorms and sterile private rooms adjoin a slightly nicer downstairs patio and kitchen area. Other downsides include fees for wi-fi (R$5 daily) and guest computer use ($2 per hour).

Pensão Sulista GUESTHOUSE $
(☎3234-5814; Av Joaquim Nabuco 347; s/d with air-con R$60/80, s/d without bathroom R$30/50;) Located near the port, this basic choice has high ceilings and colonial character. Rooms with fan share OK bathroom facilities.

Sombra Palace Hotel HOTEL $
(☎3234-8777; www.hotelsombra.com.br; Av Sete de Setembro 1325; s/d R$76/90) Better than the average downtown budget hotel, with recently remodeled rooms, tiled bathrooms and a breakfast terrace with distant river views. Back rooms are quieter, front rooms get noise and light from the busy street.

Eating

Av Getúlio Vargas and Praça São Sebastião are good places to find food at night.

TOP CHOICE **Tacacá da Gisela** BRAZILIAN $
(Praça São Sebastião; tacacá R$12; dinner) This iconic kiosk in the shadow of Teatro Amazonas specializes in delicious, steaming bowls of *tacacá*.

Budega 101 BUFFET $
(Cavalcante 101; per kg R$28.90; lunch Mon-Fri) Workers queue down the stairs at midday at this reliable buffet lunch spot. After 1pm there's a better chance of grabbing a table on the long covered patio or the air-conditioned room upstairs.

Churrascaria Búfalo CHURRASCARIA $$
(Av Joaquim Nabuco 628; weekday/weekend per kg R$46.90/50.90, all you can eat R$34.90/39.90; lunch) Manaus' classic *rodízio* restaurant is pricey but offers tasty cuts of meat, with all-you-can-eat, *por kilo* and takeaway options.

Gruta do Peixe BUFFET $
(Marinho 609; per kg R$23.90; lunch Mon-Sat) Housed in a pleasant stone-faced basement, this friendly family business serves a per-kilo lunch buffet including fish and chargrilled meats. After 2pm or so, when offerings get sparser, it's all you can eat for only R$7.

Drinking

The area surrounding Teatro Amazonas is the center's best place to hang out.

Bar do Armando BAR
(10 de Julho 593; ⏲5pm-1am) A big Brazilian thumbs-up for this old-fashioned bar, where a down-to-earth local crowd and travelers converge around streetside plastic tables in the evening. A Manaus classic.

Skina dos Sucos JUICE BAR
(cnr Av Eduardo Ribeiro & 24 de Maio; juices R$4-6, snacks R$4-10; ⏲7am-8pm Mon-Sat) Indulge all your Amazonian fruit-juice fantasies at this busy blue-tiled corner spot. Try super antioxidant *açaí* with caffeine-kick *guaraná* if you had a late one last night.

☆ Entertainment

Ponta Negra (13km from the center) is the main nightlife zone, with a river beach, promenade, bars and restaurants. Popular nightspots sit on the Estrada de Ponta Negra just before this area.

Manaus' most famous team, and the oldest in Amazonas state, is **Nacional** (www.nacionalfc.com.br). The city's brand-new 47,000-seat Arena Amazônia, constructed on the site of the former Vivaldão stadium, is halfway between the airport and downtown and will host four World Cup 2014 matches.

Porão do Alemão LIVE MUSIC
(www.poraodoalemao.com.br; Estrada da Ponta Negra 1986; ⏲9pm-late Wed-Sat) Live rock is a regular feature at this spot popular with a university-student crowd.

Shopping

Casa das Redes HAMMOCKS
(cnr Rocha dos Santos & Miranda Leão) One of several hammock shops for your boat-trip needs. Prices range from R$20 upwards. Haggle and remember to buy rope.

Ecoshop HANDICRAFTS
(www.ecoshop.com.br; 10 de Julho 509A) Handicrafts from a variety of indigenous artisans.

ℹ Information

At the airport, avoid the vultures touting jungle trips or city accommodations. After 11pm steer clear of the port area and the Praça da Matriz. If arriving late by boat, take a taxi to a hotel – muggings are common.

There are numerous free, government-sponsored wi-fi hot spots throughout the city.

Amazônia Turismo (Av Sete de Setembro 1251; ⏲9am-5pm Mon-Fri, to noon Sat) Changes euros, US dollars and traveler's checks.

Bradesco (Av Eduardo Ribeiro 475) International card ATMs.

CAT Airport (☎3182-9850; ⏲24h); city center (☎3182-6250; www.visitamazonas.am.gov.br; Av Eduardo Ribeiro 666; ⏲8am-5pm Mon-Fri, to noon Sat & Sun) Helpful main branch is located directly opposite Teatro Amazonas.

HSBC (24 de Maio 429) ATMs.

Tourist Police (☎3231-1998; Av Eduardo Ribeiro) Same building as the tourist office.

Fundação de Medicina Tropical (Tropical Medicine Foundation; ☎2127-3555; Av Pedro Teixeira 25) Specializes in tropical diseases.

ℹ Getting There & Away

Air

Several airlines operate domestic flights from Manaus' Eduardo Gomes International Airport (MAO). Internationally, American Airlines and TAM fly nonstop to Miami, and Copa has direct service to Panama City. Smaller airlines use Terminal 2 (Eduardinho), about 600m east of Terminal 1.

Boat

Large passenger boats use the Porto Flutuante (Floating Dock), aka Estação Hidroviária, a tranquil modern terminal with a cybercafe, ATMs, eateries and a good outdoor bar. From an office out front, **Socicam** (☎3233-7061; www.socicam.com.br) sells tickets on behalf of most boats, the majority of which dock further east, near the market. Hawkers may sell cheaper tickets, but if something goes wrong you'll be on your own.

Ajato (☎3622-6047; ajatonavegacao@r7.com; Porto Manaus Moderna; ⏲8am-5pm Mon-Fri, to noon Sat) runs fast boats upriver to Tefé (R$220, 14 hours) and Tabatinga (R$500, 36 hours) from a pier east of the port, which is also where tickets are sold. Fast boat services to Santarém were suspended at the time of writing.

DESTINATION	COST (R$) HAMMOCK/ CABIN	DURATION
Belém	220/1200	3½ days
Porto Velho	180/500	4 days
Santarém	120/590	30-36hr
Tabatinga	307/1290	6½ days

Bus

Eucatur (☎3301-5800; www.eucatur.com.br) runs five daily buses to Boa Vista (R$96, 10 to 12 hours). For onward service to Puerto La Cruz, Venezuela (R$225, 32 hours), take the 6pm departure from Manaus and change in Boa Vista.

GETTING TO VENEZUELA & GUYANA

The capital of Roraima state, **Boa Vista** is a spot without great traveler thrills, but it's a useful gateway to both Venezuela and Guyana. It's linked with Manaus by five daily buses (R$96, 12 hours). If you find yourself overnighting here, **Hotel Ideal** (☎3224-6342; Araújo Filho 481; s/d R$50/60; ❄) makes a good base, with tidy rooms and friendly service.

From Boa Vista, there are four daily buses to little Bonfim (R$18.50, 1½ hours) on the Guyanese border, and five to Pacaraima (R$22, three hours) on the Venezuelan border. One daily bus (7:30am) continues via Santa Elena to Puerto La Cruz, Venezuela (R$130, 20 hours), where you can make connections for Caracas.

Before boarding a bus to Venezuela, verify with the consulate in Manaus or Boa Vista whether you require a Venezuelan tourist card. Buses stop at a Brazilian Polícia Federal border post for exit stamps before entering Venezuela.

Get cash in Brazil before crossing into Venezuela; this will save you from getting hit with the (unfavorable) official exchange rate at Venezuelan ATMs.

For Guyana, get an exit stamp from the Polícia Federal near the river, which forms the international border. Some of the Boa Vista–Bonfim buses stop here and then continue to the riverfront. If yours doesn't, catch a taxi from Bonfim's bus station to the Polícia Federal (R$10) and walk the short remaining distance to the river. Motorized canoes (R$3) cross to the Guyana side. Lethem is 5km beyond the river crossing and has better accommodation options than Bonfim. Avoid arriving after dark.

Connections for Caracas can be made in Puerto La Cruz.

 Getting Around

The airport is 13km north of the center. Bus 306 (R$2.75, 30 minutes) and air-conditioned bus 813 (R$4.25) run roughly every half hour until 11pm. Taxis are set at R$58 but you can bargain a cheaper rate from town. Only get official taxis from the airport.

The bus station, 6km north of the center, is passed by several bus lines including 205, 209 and 315. From the station cross the footbridge out front, walk with traffic to the closest bus stop and take one of the buses listed under 'Centro' on the stop's sign.

Buses (R$2.75) to the center pass the Praça da Matriz, loop up on Av Floriano Peixoto and either head right on Av Sete de Setembro or straight on Av Getúlio Vargas.

For Ponta Negra, get bus 120 from Praça da Matriz. Take a cab late at night.

Amazon Jungle

Many visitors to Amazonia expect to stare down a growling jaguar or trade beads with spear-toting indigenous people just outside Manaus. This isn't going to happen. Manaus is a big city and the numbers of tourists are high. Even so, on a typical trip you are likely to glimpse pink and gray river dolphins, caymans, monkeys, tarantulas and plenty of birds. Sloths are relatively common. Manatees, anacondas, tapirs and jaguars are extremely hard to spot. The more remote, unpopulated and pristine the area, the better the chances of spotting wildlife will be.

Planning a Jungle Trip

While anything's possible, the typical jungle trip is two to four days. Most agencies offer a similar program, which usually includes piranha fishing, nighttime caiman-spotting, a jungle walk focusing on traditional medicinal and food plants, one night forest camping, a visit to a local home and a sunrise boat trip to see macaws or dolphins. Canoeing through *igarapés* and *igapós* – which have more flora and fauna than channels and rivers – is a priority. This is one reason the high-water period (roughly March to July) is the best time to visit.

'White' rivers, like the Lago Mamorí region, tend to have a higher density of wildlife than 'black' ones, like the Rio Negro. But they also have more mosquitoes and somewhat thicker vegetation, which inhibits wildlife-viewing.

You'll need sturdy shoes or boots, long pants, a long-sleeved shirt, a raincoat, insect repellent, a flashlight and a water bottle. High-power binoculars really improve the experience. Ask how much water is on-site and how much you'll need. Bring your passport.

TRIPLE FRONTIER

On the Amazon's northeast bank – about 1100km west of Manaus – **Tabatinga** (Brazil) and Leticia (Colombia) are separated by an invisible international border. The opposite bank of the river and the islands in the middle of it are part of Peru. Santa Rosa, Peru's border settlement, is on an island. This 'triple frontier' has travel routes linking all three countries and is a good base for jungle trips. In Leticia, the Novo Hotel (p609) is a good place to spend the night. Leticia is the largest and most pleasant of the three border towns and has the best services.

Tabatinga is linked by air with Manaus. Regular riverboats leave Tabatinga on Wednesday and Saturday for Manaus (hammock/cabin from R$150/800, 3½ to four days). Faster boats operated by Ajato cover the same distance in less than half the time (R$500, 36 hours), departing Tabatinga on Tuesday and Friday.

Dangers & Annoyances

You name it, it's happened on a jungle trip outside Manaus. Consider that you are placing your personal safety in another's hands in an unknown, isolated natural environment. It's best to use agencies or guides registered with the Amazonas state tourist office (don't believe the certificates; check online at www.visitamazonas.am.gov.br). Using a registered agency or guide means a better chance of being refunded should something go wrong. Women should consider being part of a group of three or more to avoid being alone in a remote location with a guide.

Manaus is full of scammers. Never pay for a tour anywhere other than the registered office of a tour agency. As the industry has become more competitive, scammers have gone so far as to create false IDs and receipts, fake confirmation phone calls to agencies, and falsely represent or impersonate guides and agencies listed in guidebooks. These scammers are most often found at the airport but also work on the street and at hotel receptions. The battle is also waged online, where reputable agencies are criticized on travel websites by 'dissatisfied tourists' who are actually rival agencies.

Tours

Manaus has scores of agencies. Those listed are recommended budget options offering a reasonably genuine and adventurous experience. Some agencies have a minimum-group-size requirement to set out, while others maintain a constant flow of clients in and out of a set spot. Yet other agencies pool their clients. Agencies can set up almost anything but most have expertise in a certain geographical area. Fees are generally all-inclusive (lodging, meals, drinking water, transfers, activities and guides). Unless the agency is very well established, insist on paying a portion of the fee up front and the rest upon return. Prices vary slightly according to numbers, but the general price range for operators listed here is R$150 to R$200 per person per day.

Take time to research the options. Many travelers have left Manaus disappointed with their once-in-a-lifetime Amazon experience because they rushed into booking the trip. Things to consider include: the guide's proficiency in your common language and level of experience within the trip's ecosystem, group size, ratio of travel time to time spent at the destination, availability of life jackets, how ecofriendly the company is really going to be (plenty of 'ecotourism' guides pull sloths out of trees for photo opportunities), and what the focus of the trip is – 'jungle experiences' or serious wildlife-viewing?

Amazon Gero Tours ECOTOUR
(☎9983-6273; www.amazongero.com; 10 de Julho 695) This friendly agency is run by English-speaking guides and piloted by helpful Gero himself. The typical trip is to the Lago Juma area, where a comfortable lodge offers hammock, dorm or room accommodations and decent bathrooms.

Amazon Green Tours ECOTOUR
(☎9106-5650; www.amazongreentour.com; cnr Av Getúlio Vargas & 10 de Julho) This newer agency offers a wide range of tours on the Rio Negro and Lagos Mamori, Juma and Tucuma. Options range from standard three- or four-day boat- or lodge-based trips to adventurous

survival tours involving longer hikes and multiple overnights in the jungle.

Amazon Antônio Jungle Tours/ Jungle Experience ECOTOUR
(☎3234-1294, 9961-8314; www.antonio-jungle tours.com; Cavalcante 231) Based at Hostel Manaus, this agency doesn't want for customers and sends out tours on a near-daily basis. Its lodge, in the Rio Urubú area, is reached via public bus and is basic but good, with an observation tower and activities.

Amazonas Indian Turismo ECOTOUR
(☎9198-3575; amazonasindian@hotmail.com; Andradas 311) This welcoming and nontrendy English-speaking indigenous outfit is recommended for off-the-beaten track experiences; you'll spend much more time in the jungle than hanging around the lodge. You travel by public bus then boat to a rustic camp on the Rio Urubú. Trips range from two to nine days.

Iguana Turismo ECOTOUR
(☎3633-6507; www.amazonbrasil.com.br; 10 de Julho 679) Iguana's typical trip goes to Lago Juma, where comfortable hammock or cabin accommodations with flush toilets are located next to Guyanese owner Gerry Hardy's riverfront home. His wife and her family are from the area and staff the lodge. Flexible itineraries.

Sleeping

Within reach of Manaus are many jungle lodges ranging from rustic (hammocks) to luxurious (suites). These are two of the best.

Malocas Jungle Lodge LODGE $$
(☎3648-0119; www.malocas.com; 3-night packages with hammock/private room accommodation R$695/750) Peace and quiet prevail at this French-Brazilian, solar-powered jungle lodge, located 80km down the winding Rio Preto da Eva. Three large circular structures hold guestrooms with thin beds and walls, hammock space and a dining/relaxation area. Activities include hiking, canoeing, fishing, sleeping in the forest and swimming in the area's many small waterfalls.

Uakari Lodge LODGE $$$
(☎0xx97-3343-4160; www.uakarilodge.com.br; 3-night packages per person from R$1440) This excellent, comfortable and beautiful ecotourist setup is located near Tefé, halfway between Manaus and the Triple Frontier. Part of the Mamirauá reserve, its 1.24 million hectares of protected forest combine nature conservation and scientific research, leading to improved opportunities for the communities within the reserve.

GETTING TO BOLIVIA & PERU

West of Xapuri, the town of **Brasiléia** sits across the Río Acre from considerably more hectic Cobija, Bolivia. You can cross the bridge between the two freely, but if you're heading further into Bolivia, get an exit stamp from the **Polícia Federal** (☎3546-3204; ⏲8am-7pm) in Brasiléia's neighboring town, Epitáciolândia. Buses from Rio Branco or Xapuri will drop you there.

For Bolivia, take a taxi (around R$15) or *mototaxi* (R$5) from the Polícia Federal over either Epitáciolândia's or Brasiléia's international bridge. The fare includes stopping at Bolivian immigration plus onward travel to a hotel or bus station. Cobija has places to stay, an airport and arduous bus connections.

Brasiléia has ATMs, money changers and a Bolivian consulate. **Pousada Las Palmeras** (☎3546-3284; Pratagi; s/d R$50/70; ❄) is an appealing sleeping option with an excellent breakfast. Buses run to Rio Branco (R$30, four hours, five daily) and Xapuri (R$9, 1½ hours, two daily). Collective taxis do the same trips for double the money and half the time.

For Peru, get an exit stamp in Epitáciolândia, catch a bus to Assis (R$13, two hours, three daily) and cross the Río Acre to Iñapari (Peru). Assis has better accommodations than Iñapari if you need to spend the night. Buses from Rio Branco to Assis theoretically stop at the Polícia Federal en route – check beforehand. There's a Peruvian consulate in Rio Branco.

Porto Velho

☎0XX69 / POP 429,000

Baking on the banks of the wide Rio Madeira, Porto Velho is Rondônia's capital but doesn't have a great deal to offer the traveler. Its status as a river port and conduit for Mato Grosso's soybean output has brought a certain prosperity. You won't linger long, however, before jumping on a riverboat to Manaus or a bus to more inviting Rio Branco.

Well-positioned sleeping options include **Vitória Palace Hotel** (☎3221-9232; Duque de Caxias 745; s/d R$50/60; ❄), with tidy rooms, high ceilings and hot water near the Pinheiro Machado nightlife zone, and friendly, family-run **Hotel Tereza Raquel** (☎3223-9234; Aranha 2125; s/d R$70/90; ❄📶), just off the main shopping street.

Down by the river, alongside the sheds of the old train station, a string of food kiosks blends into one shady beer-and-meal terrace, which is particularly happy and rowdy on Saturday and Sunday. Three blocks north, Praça Aloisio Ferreira becomes a sort of fairground at weekends and has a string of cheap but decent eateries offering typical dishes and snacks.

For awesome river views in late afternoon and live music on weekend nights, hit the terrace at the **Mirante II** (Barbosa 269; dishes for 2 R$28-45; ⏲lunch & dinner Wed-Mon) restaurant. Alternatively, head to Av Pinheiro Machado, the epicenter of Porto Velho's nightlife scene, where you'll find a cluster of boisterous bars.

Domestic flights leave from Porto Velho's Jorge Teixeira de Oliveira International Airport (PVH), 6km from the center. A taxi costs R$33 or take bus 201 (R$2.60) from Av Sete de Setembro near Praça Rondón.

Boats to Manaus (hammock R$150 to R$200, cabin R$400 to R$600, 2½ to three days) leave twice weekly from the river port in the town center. Agencies line the road down to the water; **Agência Amazonas** (☎3223-9743; ⏲7am-7pm Mon-Sat, to 11am Sun) is a reliable operator.

Buses (R$51, 4½ to six hours, six daily) and collective taxis (R$60, 3½ hours) run to Guajará-Mirim. Buses also serve Rio Branco (R$65, eight hours, three daily) and Cuiabá (R$134 to R$162, 22 to 26 hours, nine daily). From the bus station to the center (3km), take bus 201 (R$2.60) or a cab (R$15).

GETTING TO PERU & COLOMBIA

Before leaving Brazil, get an exit stamp from the **Polícia Federal** (☎3412-2180; Av da Amizade 26; ⏲8am-6pm) in Tabatinga.

For Peru, boats depart from the Porto da Feira to Santa Rosa (R$2, five minutes), from where you can travel onwards to Iquitos.

For Colombia, it's a short walk, a R$10 taxi ride or R$3 on a mototaxi to Leticia, or you can take one of the frequent *combis*.

Guajará-Mirim

☎0XX69 / POP 42,000

In this pleasant town just opposite Guayaramerín (Bolivia), bushy trees shade sidewalks, stained red by the earth, from the relentless sun. It's a backwater, but a pleasant one, and a useful border crossing.

There are several places to stay. On the main street between the bus station and the port, the family-run **Hotel Mine-Estrela** (☎3541-1206; 15 de Novembro 460; s/d R$40/60; ❄📶) is a sound bet with ageing but adequate rooms. Nearby restaurants include **Oásis** (15 de Novembro 460; per kg R$29), with a worthwhile lunch buffet featuring freshly grilled meats.

Bradesco (Av Costa Marques 430) has ATMs. Change currencies with the money changers at the port in Guayaramerín.

Buses run from the bus station, 2km east of the port, to Porto Velho (R$51, 4½ to six hours, six daily) and Rio Branco (R$61, eight hours, daily). Collective taxis also leave from here for Porto Velho (R$60, 3½ hours). A taxi between the station and the center is around R$15.

Rio Branco

☎0XX68 / POP 336,000

Remote Acre state is famous as one of the key battlegrounds fought over by the Brazilian environmental and logging lobbies. For travelers, it's a zone for off-the-beaten-track Amazon exploration and a gateway to the jungly north of Bolivia, which it once belonged to. Rio Branco, the state's very laid-back riverfront capital, makes a great stop for a day or two.

Beige-green **Palacio Rio Branco** (Praça Povos da Floresta; ⏲8am-6pm Tue-Fri, 4-8pm Sat) is a restored art deco masterpiece holding a historical exhibition.

In a restored noble mansion, the **Museu da Borracha** (Rubber Museum; Av Ceará 1441; ⏲8am-6pm Tue-Fri, 4-8pm Sat) has three small rooms with exhibits on the history of rubber-tapping and the life and work of Chico Mendes.

The most atmospheric place to stay is in the center, where tranquil **Hotel AFA** (☎3224-1396; www.afabistro.com.br; Ribeiro 109; s/d R$92/138; ❄📶) has spacious, recently renovated rooms and a welcoming attitude. Nearby, **Hotel do Papai** (☎3223-2044; Peixoto 849; s/d R$80/120; ❄📶) compensates for daytime road noise with cool, spotless, fridge-equipped rooms.

The riverbank, with picturesque bridges and cutely colorful houses, is the town's nicest part. Here, the beautifully renovated **Mercado Velho** (Praça Bandeira) – a historic port building – houses craft stalls, a food court with reasonably priced *pratos feitos* and the **Café do Mercado** (⏲3-11pm Tue-Sun), whose riverside terrace is perfect for evening beers. Hotel AFA's restaurant, **Bistrô d'Amazônia** (per kg weekday/weekend R$38.50/48; ⏲lunch; 🌶) ain't the cheapest lunch buffet but it's brilliant, with Lebanese-inspired salads, gourmet vegetarian dishes, succulent roast meats and weekend seafood.

Just below the Palacio Rio Branco, the **Setul** (⏲8am-6pm Mon-Sat, 4-9pm Sun) tourist office is willing but largely useless. Banks with ATMs are alongside.

Rio Branco's Plácido de Castro International Airport (RBR) is 20km northwest of the center. Buses (R$2.40, 40 minutes) run roughly hourly to the center of town.

The brand new **Rodoviária Internacional de Rio Branco** (☎3221-3693; www.rodoviariainternacional.com) is 5km south of the center. Buses run to Porto Velho (R$65, eight hours, four daily), Guajará-Mirim (R$61, eight hours, one daily), Xapurí (R$26, 3½ hours, 6am and 1:45pm) and Brasiléia (R$30, four hours, five daily). From the bus terminal to the center, catch a 'Norte-Sul' bus (R$2.40).

Xapuri

☎0XX68 / POP 16,000

Xapuri, whose sweet houses, thriving trees and red-dirt roads make it a charming stop, was home to rubber-tapper and famous environmental martyr Chico Mendes, murdered in 1988 after years of successful campaigning against the destruction of forests by loggers and ranchers. The **Fundação Chico Mendes** (www.chicomendes.org.br; Batista de Moraes 495; ⏲8am-6pm), a block from the bus station, displays touching Mendes photos and memorabilia, including blood-stained clothing and international awards. Staff guide you through Mendes' rustic house opposite, where he was gunned down. The activist's death sparked outrage that has led to extensive forest protection in the state.

Several fine budget *pousadas* rent comfortable rooms. A park near the plaza on Branão has laid-back spots to sit outdoors with a pizza or beer.

Buses run to Rio Branco (R$26, 3½ hours, two daily) and Brasiléia (R$9, 1½ hours, two daily). Collective taxis to Brasiléia (R$18, 45 minutes) leave from a kiosk on Branão.

GETTING TO BOLIVIA

Passenger launches (R$5, five minutes) to Guayaramerín depart 24 hours a day from the port at the end of the main street 15 de Novembro in Guayará-Mirim. Get your Brazilian exit stamp at the **Policía Federal** (☎3541-0200; cnr Dutra & Bocaiúva; ⏲8am-9pm); from the port, it's straight ahead two blocks and three to the left. There's a Bolivian consulate on the riverfront.

UNDERSTAND BRAZIL

Brazil Today

Brazil has always been touted as 'The Country of the Future,' based on the long-standing belief that with its vast resources and wealth, the country would eventually work out. The time-honored punchline among the population, however, always went: 'But the future never arrives.' Well, the times they have *a-changed.*

The country weathered 2008's ongoing global recession better than nearly everyone, and widespread economic growth has fattened the pockets for a blossoming middle class. Brazil overtook the UK as the 6th-largest economy in the world in 2012 and the economic polices of Dilma Rousseff, the country's first female president in its near 200-year history, have maintained Brazil's good fortune – much to the surprise of many of her detractors.

Brazil has made some headway against its biggest nemesis, the economic disparity between rich and poor (some 20% of the population has jumped classes during the much-ballyhooed Brazil Boom), but major challenges remain (poor education, violent crime). Rousseff has taken a hard line on another of the country's black sheep: corruption. Since taking office in 2011, several members of her cabinet have 'resigned' due to her government's clampdown on corruption. And then there's the *Mensalão* scandal, dating to 2005 and the administration of Rousseff's predecessor, Luíz Inácio da Silva ('Lula'). One of the largest corruption scandals in the country's history and the first to be prosecuted at this magnitude, 40 former or current federal deputies (and Lula allies) were indicted by Brazil's Supreme Court Tribunal. The sensational trial was captivating Brazilians in 2012 almost as much as *Avenida Brasil,* the most popular *telenovela* the country had seen since the '90s.

Politics aside, the excitement (and tension!) are building as the world spotlight now turns its critical eye on Brazil as host of the 2014 FIFA World Cup; and Rio de Janeiro as the host of the 2016 Olympic Games. Funnily enough, though, neither of these events are the biggest draws on the horizon. That honor goes to Pope Benedict XVI's 2013 visit during World Youth Day – over two million faithful are expected in Rio de Janeiro.

It all begs the question: If the future is now, is Brazil ready for it?

History

The Tribal Peoples

Little is known of Brazil's first inhabitants, but from the few fragments left behind (mostly pottery, trash mounds and skeletons), archaeologists estimate that the first humans may have arrived 50,000 years ago, predating any other estimates in the whole American continent.

The population at the time of the Portuguese landing in 1500 is also a mystery, and estimates range from two to six million. There were likely over 1000 tribes living as nomadic hunter-gatherers or in more settled, agricultural societies. Life was punctuated by frequent tribal warfare and at times, captured enemies were ceremonially killed and eaten after battle.

When the Portuguese first arrived, they had little interest in the natives, who were viewed as a Stone Age people; and the heavily forested land offered nothing for the European market. All that changed when Portuguese merchants expressed interest in the red dye from brazilwood (which later gave the colony its name), and slowly colonists arrived to harvest the land.

The natural choice for the work, of course, was the indigenous people. Initially the natives welcomed the strange, smelly foreigners and offered them their labor, their food and their women in exchange for the awe-inspiring metal tools and the fascinating Portuguese liquor. But soon the newcomers abused their customs, took their best land and ultimately enslaved them.

When colonists discovered that sugarcane grew well in the colony, the natives' labor was more valuable than ever and soon the sale of local slaves became Brazil's second-largest commercial enterprise. It was an industry dominated by *bandeirantes,* brutal men who hunted the indigenous people in the interior and captured or killed them. Their exploits, more than any treaty, secured the huge interior of South America for Portuguese Brazil.

Jesuit priests went to great lengths to protect the indigenous community. But they lacked the resources to stymie the attacks (and the Jesuits were later expelled from Brazil in 1759). Natives who didn't die at the hands of the colonists often died from introduced European diseases.

The Africans

During the 17th century African slaves replaced indigenous prisoners on the plantations. From 1550 until 1888 about 3.5 million slaves were shipped to Brazil – almost 40% of the total that came to the New World. The Africans were considered better workers and were less vulnerable to European diseases, but they resisted slavery strongly. *Quilombos,* communities of runaway slaves, formed throughout the colonial period. They ranged from *mocambos,* small groups hidden in the forests, to the great republic of Palmares, which survived much of the 17th century. Led by the African king Zumbí, it's thought Palmares had between 11,000 and

20,000 residents at its height (scholars debate the population).

According to Comissão Pró-Índio in São Paulo, an estimated 2000 to 3000 villages that formed as *quilombos* remain in Brazil today, their growth only stopped by abolition itself (1888).

Survivors on the plantations sought solace in their African religion and culture through song and dance. The slaves were given perfunctory instruction in Catholicism and a syncretic religion rapidly emerged. Spiritual elements from many African tribes, such as the Yorubá, were preserved and made palatable to slave masters by adopting a facade of Catholic saints. Such were the roots of modern Candomblé (Afro-Brazilian religion of Bahia) and Macumba (religon of African origin), prohibited by law until recently.

Life on the plantations was miserable, but an even worse fate awaited many slaves. In the 1690s gold was discovered in present-day Minas Gerais, and soon the rush was on. Wild boomtowns like Vila Rica de Ouro Preto (Rich Town of Black Gold) sprang up in the mountain valleys. Immigrants flooded the territory, and countless slaves were brought from Africa to dig and die in Minas.

The Portuguese

For years, the ruling powers of Portugal viewed the colony of Brazil as little more than a moneymaking enterprise. That attitude changed, however, when Napoleon marched on Lisbon in 1807. The prince regent (later known as Dom João VI) immediately transferred his court to Brazil. He stayed on even after Napoleon's Waterloo in 1815, and when he became king in 1816 he declared Rio de Janeiro the capital of a united kingdom of Brazil and Portugal, making Brazil the only New World colony to serve as the seat of a European monarch. In 1821 Dom João finally returned to Portugal, leaving his son Pedro in Brazil as regent.

The following year the Portuguese parliament attempted to return Brazil to colonial status. According to legend Pedro responded by pulling out his sword and shouting out '*Independência ou morte!*' (Independence or death!), crowning himself Emperor Dom Pedro I. Portugal was too weak to fight its favorite colony, so Brazil won independence without bloodshed.

Dom Pedro I ruled for nine years. He scandalized the country by siring a string of illegitimate children, and was finally forced to abdicate in favor of his five-year-old son, Dom Pedro II. Until the future emperor reached adolescence, Brazil suffered a period of civil war. In 1840 Dom Pedro II ascended the throne with overwhelming public support. During his 50-year reign he nurtured an increasingly powerful parliamentary system, went to war with Paraguay, meddled in Argentine and Uruguayan affairs, encouraged mass immigration, abolished slavery and ultimately forged a state that would do away with the monarchy forever.

The Brazilians

During the 19th century coffee replaced sugar as Brazil's primary export, at one time supplying three-quarters of world demand. With mechanization and the building of Brazil's first railroads, profits soared and the coffee barons gained enormous influence.

In 1889 a coffee-backed military coup toppled the antiquated empire, sending the emperor into exile. The new Brazilian Republic adopted a constitution modeled on the USA's, and for nearly 40 years Brazil was governed by a series of military and civilian presidents through which the armed forces effectively ruled the country.

Coffee remained king until the market collapsed during the global economic crisis of 1929. The weakened planters of São Paulo, who controlled the government, formed an opposition alliance with the support of nationalist military officers. When their presidential candidate, Getúlio Vargas, lost the 1930 elections, the military seized power and handed him the reins.

Vargas proved a gifted maneuverer, and dominated the political scene for 20 years. At times his regime was inspired by the Italian and Portuguese fascist states of Mussolini and Salazar: he banned political parties, imprisoned opponents and censored the press. He remained in and out of the political scene until 1954, when the military called for him to step down. Vargas responded by writing a letter to the people of Brazil, then shooting himself in the heart.

Juscelino Kubitschek, the first of Brazil's big spenders, was elected president in 1956. His motto was '50 years' progress in five.' His critics responded with '40 years of inflation in four.' The critics were closer to the mark, owing to the huge debt Kubitschek incurred during the construction of Brasília. By the early 1960s, inflation gripped the Brazilian economy, and Castro's victory in Cuba had spread fears of communism. Brazil's fragile democracy was crushed in 1964 when the military overthrew the government.

Brazil stayed under the repressive military regime for almost 20 years. Throughout much of this time the economy grew substantially, at times borrowing heavily from international banks. But it exacted a heavy toll on the country. Ignored social problems grew dire. Millions came to the cities, and *favelas* (shantytowns) spread at exponential rates.

Recent Decades

The last 20 years have been very good to Brazil. After Fernando Collor de Mello, its first democratically elected president in 30 years, was removed from office on charges of corruption in 1992, widespread economic growth has stabilized and blessed the South American workhorse.

Collor's replacement, Itamar Franco, introduced Brazil's present currency, the real, which sparked an economic boom that continues to this day, though it was his successor, former finance minister Fernando Henrique Cardoso, who presided through the mid-1990s over a growing economy and record foreign investment. He is most credited with laying the groundwork that put Brazil's hyperinflation to bed, though often at the neglect of social problems.

In 2002 socialist Luíz Inácio da Silva ('Lula') won the presidency under a promise of social reform. From a humble working-class background, Lula rose to become a trade unionist and a strike leader in the early 1980s. He later founded the Workers Party (PT), a magnet for his many followers seeking social reform. Lula ran one of the most financially prudent two-term administrations in years while still addressing Brazil's egregious social problems. Unfortunately, Lula's administration had some setbacks, most notably the wide-reaching *Mensalão* corruption scandal that broke in 2005, causing a number of his PT party members to resign in disgrace, and ended in 2012 in a sensational Supreme Court trial that captivated the country.

Lula's successor and fellow party member, Dilma Rousseff, was elected Brazil's first ever female president in 2011. A former Marxist guerilla who was allegedly tortured by the former military regime (who also imprisoned her for several years), her past radicalism has proved an appropriate resume for her administration's hard line on corruption. Brazil's eyebrow-lifting economic growth appears to be stabilizing under Rousseff's watch, though the rising cost of living continues to spark public-sector strikes (university teachers, federal police, tax officials and custom officials were all on strike in 2012, prompting a government worker walkout totaling nearly half the government workforce).

Though by 2020, São Paulo is expected to be the 13th-richest city in the world, the politics of economics versus social woes is sure to dominate Brazilian headlines as Roussef eyes re-election in 2014.

Culture

Brazilian culture has been shaped by the Portuguese, who gave the country its language and religion, and also by the indigenous population, immigrants and Africans. The influence of the latter is particularly strong, especially in the Northeast where African religion, music and cuisine have all profoundly influenced Brazilian identity.

Population

In Brazil the diversity of the landscape matches that of the people inhabiting it. Of the respondents in IBGE's 2010 census, 47.5% of the population are white, 43.4% mixed, 7.5% black, 1.1% Asian and 0.43% indigenous, but the numbers little represent the many shades and types of Brazil's rich melting pot. Indigenous people, Portuguese, Africans (brought to Brazil as slaves) and their mixed-blood offspring made up the population until the late 19th century. Since then there have been waves of immigration by Italians, Spaniards, Germans, Japanese, Russians, Lebanese and others.

Lifestyle

Although Brazil has the world's sixth-largest economy, with abundant resources and developed infrastructure, the living standard varies wildly. Brazil has one of the world's widest income gaps between rich and poor.

Since the mass urban migration in the mid-19th century, the poorest have lived in *favelas* that surround every city. Many dwellings consist of little more than a few boards pounded together, and access to clean water, sewage and healthcare are luxuries few *favelas* enjoy. Drug lords rule the streets and crime is rampant.

The rich often live just a stone's throw away, sometimes separated by nothing more than a highway. Many live in modern fortresses, with security walls and armed guards, enjoying a lifestyle similar to upper classes in Europe and America.

But the beauty of Brazil is when these crowds come together – at a samba club, a soccer match, a Carnaval parade or on the beach – and meld together seamlessly in celebration. Brazilians love a party, and revelries commence year-round. But it isn't all samba and *sakerinhas* in the land of the tropics. Brazilians suffer from *saudade*, a nostalgic, often deeply melancholic longing for something. The idea appears in many works by Jobim, Moraes and other great songwriters, and it manifests itself in many forms – from the dull ache of homesickness to the deep regret over past mistakes.

When Brazilians aren't dancing the samba or drowning in sorrow, they're often helping each other out. Kindness is both commonplace and expected, and even a casual introduction can lead to deeper friendships. This altruism comes in handy in a country noted for its bureaucracy and long lines. There's the official way of doing things, then there's the *jeitinho*, or the little way around it, and a little kindness – and a few friends – can go a long way.

Religion

Brazil is the world's largest Catholic country, but it embraces diversity and syncretism. Without much difficulty you can find churchgoing Catholics who attend spiritualist gatherings or appeal for help at a *terreiro* (the house of an Afro-Brazilian religious group).

Brazil's principal religious roots comprise the animism of the indigenous people, Catholicism and African religions introduced by slaves. The latest arrival is evangelical Christianity, which is spreading all over Brazil, especially in poorer areas.

The Afro-Brazilian religions emerged when the colonists prohibited slaves from practicing their native religions. Not so easily deterred, the slaves simply gave Catholic names to their African gods and continued to worship them. The most orthodox of the religions is Candomblé. Rituals take place in the Yoruba language in a *casa de santo* or *terreiro,* directed by a *pai de santo* or *mãe de santo* (literally, 'a saint's father or mother' – the Candomblé priests).

Candomblé gods are known as *orixás* and each person is believed to be protected by one of them. In Bahia and Rio, followers of Afro-Brazilian cults turn out in huge numbers to attend festivals at the year's end – especially those held during the night of 31 December and on New Year's Day. Millions of Brazilians go to the beach at this time to pay homage to Iemanjá, the sea goddess, whose alter ego is the Virgin Mary.

Arts

Architecture

Brazil's most impressive colonial architecture dazzles visitors in cities like Salvador, Olinda, São Luís, Ouro Preto and Tiradentes. Over the centuries, the names of two architects stand out: Aleijadinho, the genius of 18th-century baroque in Minas Gerais mining towns; and the late Oscar Niemeyer, the 20th-century modernist-functionalist who was chief architect for the new capital, Brasília, in the 1950s and designed many other striking buildings around the country. Niemeyer passed away in 2012 at the age of 104.

Cinema

Brazil's large film industry has produced a number of good films over the years. One of the most recent hits is 2007's *Tropa do Elite* (Elite Troop), a gritty look at Rio's crime and corruption from the viewpoint of its most elite police force, BOPE (Special Police Operations Battalion).

The same director, José Padilha, initially garnered Brazilian cinema attention with 2002's *Ônibus 174* (Bus 174), a shocking look at both the ineptness of the Brazilian police and the brutal reality of the country's socioeconomic disparities. It tells the story of a lone gunman who hijacked a Rio bus in 2000 and held passengers hostage for hours live on national TV. A dramatic version of the events, *Última Parada 174* (Last Stop 174), surfaced in 2008.

One of Brazil's top directors, Fernando Meirelles, earned his credibility and an Oscar nomination with 2002's *Cidade de Deus* (City of God), which showed the brutality of a Rio *favela.* Meirelles followed the success of *Cidade de Deus* with three Hollywood films, the most critically acclaimed of which is *The Constant Gardener* (2004), an intriguing conspiracy film shot in Africa that won the Oscar for Best Supporting Actor for Rachel Weisz.

Walter Salles, one of Brazil's best-known directors, won much acclaim (as well as an Oscar) for *Central do Brasil* (Central Station; 1998), the story of a lonely woman accompanying a young homeless boy in search of his father.

For a taste of the dictatorship days see Bruno Barreto's *O Que É Isso Companheiro* (released as *Four Days in September* in the US, 1998), based on the 1969 kidnapping of the US ambassador to Brazil by leftist guerrillas.

Another milestone in Brazilian cinema is the visceral film *Pixote* (1981), which shows life through the eyes of a street kid in Rio. When it was released, it became a damning inditement of Brazilian society.

Literature

Joaquim Maria Machado de Assis (1839–1908), the son of a freed slave, is one of Brazil's early great writers. Assis had a great sense of humor and an insightful – though cynical – take on human affairs. His major novels were *Quincas Borba, The Posthumous Memoirs of Bras Cubas* and *Dom Casmurro*.

Jorge Amado (1912–2001), Brazil's most celebrated contemporary writer, wrote clever portraits of the people and places of Bahia, notably *Gabriela, Clove and Cinnamon* and *Dona Flor and her Two Husbands*.

Paulo Coelho is Latin America's second-most-read novelist (after Gabriel García Márquez). His new-age fables *The Alchemist* and *The Pilgrimage* launched his career in the mid-1990s.

Music

Samba, a Brazilian institution, has strong African influences and is intimately linked to Carnaval. The most popular form of samba today is *pagode*, a relaxed, informal genre whose leading exponents include singers Beth Carvalho, Jorge Aragão and Zeca Pagodinho.

Bossanova, another Brazilian trademark, arose in the 1950s, and gained the world's attention in the classic song 'The Girl from Ipanema,' composed by Antônio Carlos Jobim and Vinícius de Moraes. Bossa nova's founding father, guitarist João Gilberto, still performs, as does his daughter Bebel Gilberto, who has sparked renewed interest in the genre, combining smooth bossa sounds with electronic grooves.

Tropicalismo, which burst onto the scene in the late 1960s, mixed varied Brazilian musical styles with North American rock and pop. Leading figures such as Gilberto Gil and Caetano Veloso are still very much around. Gil, in fact, was Brazil's Minister of Culture from 2003 to 2008.

The list of emerging talents gets longer each day, topped by actor/musician Seu Jorge, who starred in *Cidade de Deus*. Jorge earned accolades for the release of 2005's *Cru*, an inventive hip-hop album with politically charged beats, as well as its more stripped-down follow-up, 2007's *América Brasil*. His latest, 2010's *Seu Jorge & Almaz*, is a critically acclaimed soul, samba and rock collaboration with drummer Pupillo and guitarist Lucio Maia, both members of the legendary rock/hip-hop hybrid Nação Zumbi; with award-winning film-score composer Antonio Pinto (*Centrao do Brasil, Cidade de Deus*) on bass. Jorge performed at the 2012 Summer Olympics closing ceremony in London.

Brazilian rock (pronounced 'hock-ey') is also popular. Groups and artists such as Zeca Baleiro, Kid Abelha, Jota Quest, Ed Motta and the punk-driven Legião Urbana are worth a listen.

Wherever you go in Brazil you'll also hear regional musical styles. The most widely known is *forró* (foh-hoh), a lively, syncopated Northeastern music, which mixes *zabumba* (an African drum) beats with accordion sounds. *Axé* is a label for the samba-pop-rock-reggae-funk-Caribbean fusion music that emerged from Salvador in the 1990s, popularized especially by the flamboyant Daniela Mercury and now worshipped stadiums over by the sexy Ivete Sangalo. In the Amazon, you'll encounter the rhythms of *carimbo*, and the sensual dance that accompanies it.

Sertanejo, Brazilian country music, catapulted to international fame in 2011 when Michel Teló unleashed the inexplicable phenomenon that was 'Ai Se Eu Te Pego' – perhaps the most famous Brazilian song since 'The Girl from Ipanema.'

Cuisine

Brazilian restaurants serve huge portions, and many plates are designed for two – single travelers get hosed in these cases, as the bill can run 60% to 70% of the price for two when a portion for one is ordered (though often portions for two can feed three – you beat Brazil at its own illogical math game). The basic Brazilian diet revolves around *arroz* (white rice), *feijão* (black beans) and *farofa/farinha* (flour from the root of manioc or corn). The typical Brazilian meal, called *prato feito* (set meal, often abbreviated 'pf') or *refeição*, consists of these ingredients plus either meat, chicken or fish and costs R$8 to R$14 in most eateries.

Another good option are *por kilo* (per kilogram) lunch buffets. Here, you pay by the weight of what you serve yourself: typically between R$30 and R$40 per kilogram, with a big plateful weighing around half a kilo. Per-kilo places are good for vegetarians too. The fixed-price *rodízio* is another deal, and most *churrascarias* (meat BBQ restaurants) offer *rodízio* dining, where they bring endless skewers of different meat to your table. Overcharging and shortchanging are almost standard procedure. Check over your bill carefully.

Regional variations include *comida baiana* from Bahia's northeastern coast, which has a distinct African flavor, using peppers, spices and the potent oil of the *dendê* palm tree. Both the Pantanal and the Amazon region have some tasty varieties of fish. Rio Grande do Sul's *comida gaúcha* is meat-focused. Minas Gerais is legendary for its hearty, vein-clogging fare, often involving chicken and pork (Brazilians also say any dish in Brazil tastes better in Minas); while São Paulo, home to large populations of Italians, Japanese and Arab immigrants, is Brazil's food mecca.

The incredible variety of Brazilian fruits makes for some divine *sucos* (juices). Every town has plenty of juice bars, offering 30 or 40 different varieties at around R$5 to R$10 for a good-sized glass.

Cafezinho puro (coffee), as typically drunk in Brazil, is strong, hot and often sickly presweetened in rural or less sophiticated locales, usually served without milk (*leite*). *Refrigerantes* (soft drinks) are found everywhere. *Guaraná*, made from the fruit of an Amazonian plant, is as popular as Coke.

The two key alcoholic drinks in Brazil are *cachaça* (also called *pinga*), a high-proof sugarcane spirit, and *cerveja* (beer). *Cachaça* ranges from excrementally raw to exquisite and smooth, and is the basis of that celebrated Brazilian cocktail, the *caipirinha*. Of the common beer brands, Bohemia and Original are generally the best, but regional microbrews are finally catching on. Eisenbahn (from Santa Catarina) and Colorado (from São Paulo) are two of the best and easiest to find.

Key phrase: *Mais um chope!* (Another beer!).

BRAZILIAN BREWHAHA!

Chope (pronounced 'shoh-pee') is draft beer and stands pretty much at the pinnacle of Brazilian civilization. The head can take up half the glass – it's believed to be an indicator of quality. You can order it without *(sim colarinho)* but some bars refuse to serve a smaller head than the width of two fingers.

Sports

Brazil may be the world's largest Catholic country, but *futebol* (soccer) is its religion. And Brazilians are such a devout bunch for good reason. Most people acknowledge that Brazilians play the world's most creative, artistic and thrilling style of soccer (Brazil is the only country to have won five World Cups – 1958, 1962, 1970, 1994 and 2002), but the national team has bailed out on the early side of recent World Cups and Olympic Games. A massive national-team reshuffling, led by new coach Mano Menezes, saw a changing of the guards after the 2010 FIFA World Cup – superstars like Ronaldo, Ronaldinho and Kaká became mere memories on the backs of jerseys, with up-and-coming superstars like Neymar stepping into the spotlight as the face of the New World Order. After a dismal showing (by Brazilian standards) at the 2011 Copa América, Ronaldinho was invited back, and then Kaká, but the national team's woes couldn't yet be beat. Menez was fired in 2012, replaced by Luiz Felipe Scolari, who had been fired by São Paulo club Palmeiras earlier in the year (but had previously led Brazil to World Cup glory in 2002). By the end of the year, the national team had dropped to 18th in the FIFA rankings – their worst ranking ever.

Things had better change. And quick. Brazil is the host nation for both the 2013 FIFA Confederations Cup and the 2014 FIFA World Cup, which will only ratchet up pressure on the *Seleção* (selection) to

FIFA 2014 WORLD CUP

The FIFA World Cup is returning to what many people believe (the locals, at least!) to be football's most sacred land for the first time since 1950, from June 12 to July 13, 2014. The country is throwing all its spare *reais* at the project: an estimated R$1.9 billion in construction and remodeling of stadiums, R$5.3 billion in airport renovations and upgrades and another R$3 billion in transportation and general infrastructure. Games will be evenly distributed throughout the country (unlike 1950, when the South and Southeast hosted everything) and will include the first ever World Cup matches to be played in the Amazon. See FIFA's official website for ticket information. Brazil's official website for the cup is www.copa2014.gov.br.

The following cities and stadiums host action: Belo Horizonte (Mineirão); Brasília (Estádio Nacional de Brasília); Cuiabá (Arena Pantanal); Curitiba (Arena da Baixada); Fortaleza (Castelão); Manaus (Arena Amazônia); Natal (Arena das Dunas); Porto Alegre (Estádio Beira-Rio); Recife (Arena Pernambuco); Rio de Janeiro (Maracanã); Salvador (Arena Fonte Nova); and São Paulo (Arena de Itaquera).

stratospheric levels. In 1950, the last time Brazil hosted the cup, the national team lost in heartbreaking fashion to Uruguay at Maracanã in Rio – something many Brazilians to this day have not forgotten.

Environment

The Land

The world's fifth-largest country after Russia, Canada, China and the USA, Brazil borders every other South American country except Chile and Ecuador. Its 8.5-million-sq km area covers almost half the continent.

Brazil has four primary geographic regions: the coastal band, the Planalto Brasileiro, the Amazon Basin and the Paraná-Paraguai Basin.

The narrow, 7400km-long coastal band lies between the Atlantic Ocean and the coastal mountain ranges. From the border with Uruguay to Bahia state, steep mountains often extend all the way down to the coast. North of Bahia, the coastal lands are flatter.

The Planalto Brasileiro (Brazilian Plateau) extends over most of Brazil's interior south of the Amazon Basin. It's sliced by several large rivers and punctuated by mountain ranges reaching no more than 3000m.

The thinly populated Amazon Basin, composing 42% of Brazil, is fed by waters from the Planalto Brasileiro to its south, the Andes to the west and the Guyana shield to the north. In the west the basin is 1300km wide; in the east, between the Guyana shield and the *planalto* (plateau), it narrows to 100km. More than half the 6275km of the Amazon lies not in Brazil but in Peru, where the river's source is also found. The Amazon and its 1100 tributaries contain an estimated 20% of the world's freshwater. Pico da Neblina (3014m) on the Venezuelan border is the highest peak in Brazil.

The Paraná-Paraguai Basin, in the south of Brazil, extends into neighboring Paraguay and Argentina and includes the large wetland area known as the Pantanal.

Wildlife

Brazil is the most biodiverse country on Earth. It has more known species of plants (56,215), freshwater fish (3000) and mammals (578) than any other country in the world; and isn't far behind in birds (1721) and reptiles (651). Many species live in the Amazon rainforest, which occupies 3.6 million sq km in Brazil and 2.4 million sq km in neighboring countries. It's the world's largest tropical forest and most biologically diverse ecosystem, with 20% of the world's bird and plant species and 10% of its mammals.

Other Brazilian species are widely distributed around the country. For example the biggest Brazilian cat, the jaguar, is found in Amazon and Atlantic rainforests, the *cerrado* (savanna) and the Pantanal.

Many other Brazilian mammals are found over a broad range of habitats, including five other big cats (puma, ocelot, margay, oncilla and jaguarundi); the giant anteater; 77 primate species, including several types of howler and capuchin monkey, the squirrel monkey (Amazonia's most common primate) and around 20 small species of marmosets and tamarin; the furry, long-nosed coati (a type of raccoon); the giant river otter; the maned wolf; the tapir; peccaries (like wild boar); marsh and pampas deer; the capybara (the world's largest rodent at 1m in length); the pink dolphin, often glimpsed in the Amazon and its tributaries; and the Amazon manatee, an even larger river dweller.

Birds form a major proportion of the wildlife you'll see. The biggest is the flightless, 1.4m-high rhea, found in the *cerrado* and Pantanal. The brilliantly colored parrots, macaws, toucans and trogons come in dozens of species. In Amazonia or the Pantanal you may well see scarlet macaws and, if you're lucky, blue-and-yellow ones.

In Amazonia or the Pantanal you can't miss the alligators. One of Brazil's five species, the black caiman, grows up to 6m long. Other aquatic life in the Amazon includes the *pirarucú*, which grows 3m long. Its red and silvery brown scale patterns are reminiscent of Chinese paintings. The infamous piranha comes in about 50 species, found in the river basins of Amazon, Orinoco, Paraguai, and São Francisco, and rivers of the Guianas.

National Parks

Brazil is home to 67 national parks and 310 areas of conservation, managed by **ICMBio** (www.icmbio.gov.br). Some favorites:

Parque Nacional da Chapada Diamantina (p342) Rivers, waterfalls, caves and swimming holes make for excellent trekking in this mountainous region in the Northeast.

Parque Nacional da Chapada dos Guimarães (p330) On a rocky plateau northeast of Cuiabá, this canyon park features breathtaking views and impressive rock formations.

Parque Nacional da Chapada dos Veadeiros (p326) About 200km north of Brasília, among waterfalls and natural swimming holes, this hilly national park features an array of rare flora and fauna.

Parque Nacional da Serra dos Órgãos (p287) Set in the mountainous terrain of the Southeast, this park is a mecca for rock climbers and mountaineers.

Parque Nacional de Aparados da Serra (p317) Famous for its narrow canyon with 700m escarpments, this park in the Southeast features hiking trails with excellent overlooks.

Parque Nacional dos Lençóis Maranhenses (p370) Spectacular beaches, mangroves, dunes and lagoons comprise the landscape of this park in the Northeast.

Parque Nacional Marinho de Fernando de Noronha (p355) Pristine beaches, cerulean waters, world-class diving and snorkeling and one of the world's best spots to view spinner dolphins highlight Brazil's island Eden.

Environmental Issues

At last count more than one-fifth of the Brazilian Amazon rainforest had been completely destroyed, though deforestation has tapered off somewhat in recent years. The government continues development projects in the Amazon, although the protests have become more vocal in recent years. The most current and controversial is the hydroelectric Belo Monte Dam on the Xingu river in Pará (the world's third largest behind China's Three Gorges and Brazil-Paraguay's Itaipu). Construction on the US$16-billion project was given the green light in 2011, but a Brazilian Federal Court judge blocked the license citing environmental concerns in the country's largest public hearing in history. It was later overturned, halted, and overturned again, and by late 2012 the Brazilian Supreme Court ruled construction could continue. The project will flood 400 sq km of Amazon forest and displace some 20,000 indigenous people, though its license was granted under the premise some US$1.9 billion be earmarked to address social and environmental problems.

CUSTO BRASIL!

There is a phrase used to explain the high cost of doing business in Brazil – *custo Brasil*, which means 'Brazilian cost.' Travelers are sure to get a stiff dose of the *custo Brasil* themselves as everyone looks to rake in seriously hiked profits surrounding the 2014 FIFA World Cup and 2016 Summer Olympic Games. If you're joining in on the celebration, expect sticker-shock prices for everything from a hostel dorm bed to a coconut water on the beach.

SURVIVAL GUIDE

Directory A–Z

Accommodations

Brazilian accommodations are simple yet usually clean and reasonably safe, and nearly all come with some form of *café da manhã* (breakfast).

Youth hostels are traditionally called *albergues da juventude*, but carry a somewhat negative connotation in Portuguese. A true hostel scene using the more internationally recognized word is now emerging in Brazil with many excellent choices. A dormitory bed costs between R$25 and R$75 per person, depending on location, with most hovering around the R$35 to R$50 range.

Brazil's hotels are among South America's priciest, but you can still find good deals. At the low end, R$30/60 for very basic singles/doubles is possible in nonurban guesthouses. Better rooms with private bathrooms start at about R$50/90 for singles/doubles and cost substantially more in major cities like Rio. Prices typically rise by 40% during high season. Hotels in business-oriented cities such as Brasília, São Paulo and Curitiba readily give discounts on weekends.

A *pousada* usually means a small family-owned inn, though some hotels call themselves *pousadas* to improve their charm quotient.

Activities

Popular activities for adrenaline-fueled adventure include canyoning, paragliding, kitesurfing, wakeboarding, rafting, surfing, trekking, diving and mountain climbing.

Hiking and climbing activities are best during the cooler months, from April to October. Outstanding hiking areas include the national parks of Chapada Diamantina in Bahia, Serra dos Órgãos in Rio de Janeiro state, Chapada dos Veadeiros in Goiás and the Serra de São José near Tiradentes in Minas Gerais.

The best surfing is in Fernando de Noronha between December and March. Also good are the beaches in the South and Southeast: Saquarema, Ilha de Santa Catarina, São Francisco do Sul, Ilha do Mel, Búzios and Rio de Janeiro. In the Northeast, head to Itacaré and Praia da Pipa. The waves are best in the Brazilian winter (June to August).

Búzios in Rio state has good windsurfing and kitesurfing conditions, and access to rental equipment. But Brazil's hard-core windsurfing mecca is the Ceará coast northwest of Fortaleza, from July to December. Here, Jericoacoara and Canoa Quebrada are the most popular spots.

Business Hours

Reviews don't list business hours unless they differ from these standards.

Banks 10am to 4pm

Bars 7pm to 2am, and until 4am on weekends

Restaurants 8am to 10:30am (breakfast), 11am to 3pm (lunch), and 7pm to 11pm (dinner)

Shops and government services (including post offices) 9am to 5pm Monday to Friday, and 9am to 1pm Saturday

Electricity

Electrical current is not standardized in Brazil and can be almost anywhere between 110V and 220V. Carry a converter and use a surge protector with nondual electrical equipment.

SOCKET TO ME

In 2010 Brazil finally decided to enforce the standardization of its electrical outlets. The new three-prong plug (thus far unique to Brazil and South Africa though eventually expected to be adopted across Europe), is required for all new electrical appliances. The transition will take years, and the old two-prong/US-style hybrid is still the most common, but if you happen to sleep in a newly constructed hotel or one that has upgraded, you will need to purchase an adapter (R$4).

Embassies & Consulates

In addition to this list, nearly all countries of note have embassies in Brasília.

Argentinian Consulate (☎0xx21-2553-1646; consar.rio@openlink.com.br; Praia de Botafogo 228, Sobreloja/1st fl 201, Botafogo, Rio de Janeiro)

Australian Consulate (☎0xx21-3824-4624; www.dfat.gov.au/missions/countries/brri.html; Presidente Wilson 231, 23rd fl, Rio de Janeiro)

Bolivian Consulate Brasiléia (☎0xx68-3546-5760; Meireles 236); Guajará-Mirim (☎0xx69-3541-8620; Beira Rio 50); Rio de Janeiro

(☎0xx21-2552-5490; www.consuladodeboliviaenrio.org.br; Av Rui Barbosa 664 No 101)

Canadian Consulate (☎0xx21-2543-3004; www.brasil.gc.ca; 5th fl, Av Atlântica 1130, Copacabana, Rio de Janeiro)

Chilean Consulate (☎0xx21-3579-9658; www.chileabroad.gov.cl/rio-de-janeiro; Praia do Flamengo 344, 7th fl, Rio de Janeiro)

Colombian Consulate Manaus (☎0xx92-3234-6777; Rua 20 651A); São Paulo (☎0xx11-3078-0322; www.consuladoensaopaulo-br.gov.co; Tenente Negrao 140, 9th fl); Tabatinga (☎0xx97-3412-2104; Sampaio 623)

Ecuadorian Consulate (☎0xx21-3563-0380; www.embequador.org.br; Pintor Oswaldo Teixeira 465, Rio de Janeiro)

German Consulate (☎0xx21-2554-0004; www.rio-de-janeiro.diplo.de; Carlos de Campos 417, Rio de Janeiro)

Irish Consulate (☎0xx11-3147-7788; www.embassyofireland.org.br; Joaquim Eugênio de Lima 447, Bela Vista, São Paulo)

Israeli Embassy (☎0xx61-2105-0500; www.brasilia.mfa.gov.il; Av das Nações, SES, Q 809, Lote 38, Brasília)

Netherlands Consulate (☎0xx21-2157 5400; www.riodejaneiro.nlconsulaat.org; Praia de Botafogo 242, 10th fl, Rio de Janeiro)

Paraguayan Consulate (☎0xx21-2553-2294; Praia de Botafogo 24, 2nd fl, Rio de Janeiro)

Peruvian Consulate Manaus (☎0xx92-3236-9607; Constelação 16A, Bairro Aleixo); Rio Branco (☎0xx68-3224-2727; Pernambuco 1040); Rio de Janeiro (www.rree.gob.pe; Rui Barbosa 314, 2nd fl)

UK Consulate Recife (☎0xx81-2127-0200; Agamenon Magalhães 4775, Ilha do Leite); Rio de Janeiro (☎0xx21-2555-9600; www.reinounido.org.br; 2nd fl, Praia do Flamengo 284, Flamengo)

Uruguayan Consulate (☎0xx21-2553-6030; www.emburuguai.org.br; Praia de Botafogo 242, 6th fl, Rio de Janeiro)

US Consulate Recife (☎0xx81-3416-3050; Maia 163, Boa Vista); Rio de Janeiro (☎0xx21-3823-2000; www.embaixadaamericana.org.br; Av Presidente Wilson 147, Centro)

Gay & Lesbian Travelers

Machismo dominates in Brazil and being out is still a challenge. Rio, São Paulo and Florianópolis have the best gay scenes, though you'll find good gay bars in Salvador and elsewhere. These are all-welcome affairs attended by GLS *(Gays, Lesbians e Simpatizantes)* crowds of straights and gays. An excellent gay travel and excursions agency is **Rio G** (☎0xx21-3813-0003; www.riog.com.br; Prudente de Morais 167 C, Ipanema). Useful websites for gay and lesbian travelers are www.riogayguide.com and www.pridelinks.com/Regional/Brazil.

SLEEPING PRICE RANGES

The following price indicators apply (for high-season double with bathroom):

$ less than R$150

$$ R$150 to R$350

$$$ more than R$350

Health

Malaria is a concern in certain areas of the Amazon and Northwest Brazil. Travelers should weigh the risks of an appropriate malaria preventative (Chloroquine is not effective here), and cover up as much as possible to prevent mosquito bites. Brazil has become the epicenter of mosquito-borne dengue fever in Latin America, especially in and around Rio and in Bahía. If you are in an area where mosquitoes are biting during the day, you are at risk and should consider repellent.

Tap water is safe but not very tasty in most urban areas. In remote areas, filter your own or stick to bottled water.

The sun is powerful here and travelers should be mindful of heatstroke, dehydration and sunburn. Drink plenty of water, wear a strong sunscreen and allow your body time to acclimatize to high temperatures before attempting strenuous activities. A good drink when dehydrated is *agua de coco* (coconut water), which contains electrolytes.

A yellow fever immunization certificate is no longer compulsory to enter Brazil, but it's still highly recommended. At most Brazilian borders and major airports there are vaccination posts where you can have the jab (it's free for foreigners) and get the certificate immediately. But it's wise to do this in advance.

Internet Access

Wi-fi is widespread throughout Brazil and generally free at most lodgings.

FOOD PRICE RANGES

The following price indicators refer to a standard main course (including tax but excluding 10% service charge):

$ less than R$20

$$ R$20 to R$40

$$$ more than R$40

Language

Portuguese is generally considered the world's sixth most spoken language. Brazilian Portuguese has many differences from European Portuguese, but speakers can understand one another in most cases. This is not the case with Spanish – if you can speak Spanish, you'll be able to read some Portuguese but comprehending others is difficult. Some Brazilians also find it a tad offensive when foreigners arrive speaking Spanish and expect to be understood. Pick up a copy of Lonely Planet's *Brazilian Portuguese* phrasebook to get you talking.

It's exceedingly popular to arrange Portuguese classes in Brazil. Try **IBEU** (Instituto Brasil Estados Unidos; www.ibeu.org.br) in Rio or **Polyglot** (www.polyglot.com.br) or **Universidade Presbiteriana Mackenzie** (www.mackenzie.br) in São Paulo. Nationally, try **Wizard** (www.wizard.com.br). **Celpe-Bras** (http://portal.inep.gov.br/celpebras) offers the only certificate of proficiency in Portuguese as a Second Language recognized by the Brazilian Ministry of Education.

Legal Matters

Be wary but respectful of Brazilian police – you can be arrested in Brazil for shouting, cursing or otherwise losing your temper while interacting with any person of authority or public official.

Stiff penalties are in force for use and possession of drugs; the police don't share most Brazilians' tolerant attitude toward marijuana. Police checkpoints along the highways stop cars at random. Don't even think about drinking and driving – Brazil introduced a zero-tolerance law in 2008 and roadblocks (called '*blitz*') are common in major cities, especially Rio and São Paulo.

A large amount of cocaine is smuggled out of Bolivia and Peru through Brazil. If you're entering Brazil from one of the Andean countries and have been chewing coca leaves, be careful to clean out your pack first.

Maps

The best maps in Brazil are the *Quatro Rodas* series. These good regional maps (Norte, Nordeste etc) and state maps sell for around R$8; they also publish the *Atlas Rodoviário* road atlas (R$24.99), useful if you're driving, as well as excellent street atlases for the main cities.

Good topographical maps are published by the IBGE, the government geographical service, and the DSG, the army geographical service. Availability is erratic, but IBGE offices in most state capitals sell IBGE maps. Office locations can be found on the IBGE website (www.ibge.gov.br).

Money

Brazil's currency is the real (pronounced '*hay-ow*,' often written R$); the plural is *reais* ('*hay-ice*'). One real is made up of 100 centavos. Newly designed banknotes come in denominations of two, five, 10, 20, 50 and 100.

ATMS

ATMs are widely available, but are often finicky with foreign cards. Do yourself a favor and bring a few options, then find a bank that works with one of your cards and stick with it. Four-digit PINs are standard. In general, Citibank, HSBC, Banco de Brasil, Bradesco and Banco24Horas (a conglomeration of Brazilian banks) are the best ATMs to try. Only non-Banco24Horas HSBC ATMs, Banco do Brasil and Bradesco are feeless, but new daily limits imposed in early 2013 on foreign ATM transactions mean many travelers cannot withdraw more than R$300 per day anywhere other than Bradesco.

CREDIT CARDS

You can use credit cards to pay for many purchases in Brazil and to make cash withdrawals from ATMs. The most commonly accepted card is Visa, followed by MasterCard. American Express and Diners Club are far less accepted outside major metropolitan areas.

MONEY CHANGERS

Cash and traveler's checks, in US dollars, can be exchanged in *casas de cambio* (exchange offices) or some banks, which give better exchange rates but are much slower.

Post

The government-run Brazilian postal service is decked out in can't-miss yellow and blue and is called **Correios** (www.correios.com.br). Branches are ubiquitous.

Public Holidays

Ano Novo (New Year's Day) January 1

Carnaval (Friday to Tuesday preceding Ash Wednesday) February/March. Carnaval celebrations usually start well before the official holiday.

Paixão/Páscoa (Good Friday/Easter Sunday) March or April

Tiradentes (Tiradentes Day) April 21

Dia do Trabalho (May Day/Labor Day) May 1

Corpus Christi (60 days after Easter) Sunday May/June

Dia da Independência (Independence Day) September 7

Dia da Nossa Senhora de Aparecida (Day of Our Lady of Aparecida) October 12

Finados (All Souls' Day) November 2

Proclamação da República (Proclamation of the Republic Day) November 15

Natal (Christmas Day) December 25

Responsible Travel

We all have an obligation to protect Brazil's fragile environment. You can do your bit by using environmentally friendly tourism services wherever possible and avoiding those that aren't proactively taking steps to avoid ecological damage (this includes Pantanal operators that encourage touching of animals).

Using the services of local community groups will ensure that your money goes directly to those who are helping you, as does buying crafts and other products directly from the artisans or from their trusted representatives.

Safe Travel

Brazil receives a lot of bad press about its violence and high crime rate. Use common sense and take general precautions applicable throughout South America:

» Carry only the minimum cash needed plus a fat-looking wad of singles to hand over to would-be thieves.

» Dress down, leave the jewelry at home and don't walk around flashing iPhones, iPads and other expensive electronics.

» Be alert and walk purposefully. Criminals hone in on dopey, hesitant, disoriented-looking individuals.

» Use ATMs inside buildings. Before doing so, be very aware of your surroundings. Thieves case ATMs and exchange houses.

» Check windows and doors of your room for security, and don't leave anything valuable lying around.

» Don't take anything unnecessary to city beaches (bathing suit, towel, small amount of cash – nothing else!).

» After dark, don't ever walk along empty streets, deserted parks or urban beaches.

» Don't wander into *favelas* unaccompanied.

Telephone

DOMESTIC CALLS

You can make domestic calls from normal card-pay telephones on the street (called *orelhãos*). The cards are sold in units from 20 to 100 and range in price between R$4 and R$15 from vendors, newsstands and any other places advertising *cartões telefônicos*.

To make a local collect call, dial ☎9090, then the number. For calls to other cities, dial 0, then the code of your selected long-distance carrier, then the two digits representing the city, followed by the local number. You need to choose a long-distance carrier that covers both the place you are calling from and the place you're calling to. Carriers advertise their codes in areas where they're prominent, but you can usually use Embratel (code ☎21) or Telemar (code ☎31) nationwide.

COUVERT CAPER

You'll notice in decent Brazilian restaurants a little appetizer plate – sometimes breads and spreads, sometimes something far more elaborate – miraculously appears on your table as you peruse the menu. It's called a *couvert* and, despite appearances, it's not free. Waiters used to plop it down and walk away, but these days they are required by law to ask if you would like it or not. It's completely acceptable to politely send it away, so don't be shy if you aren't feeling the foodie favor.

FRAUD WARNING!

Credit-card and ATM fraud is widespread in Brazil, especially in the Northeast. Card-cloning (*Clonagem* in Portuguese) is the preferred method – an entrepreneurial opportunist sticks a false card reader into an ATM that copies your card and steals the PIN when you come along and withdraw money. Shazam! A few hours later, $1500 disappears from your account in Recife while you and your card are safe and sound sipping *caipirinhas* on the beach in Natal!

To combat fraud, restaurants will bring the credit-card machine to your table or ask you to accompany them to the cashier to run a credit-card transaction. Never let someone walk off with your card. Other tips:

» Use high-traffic ATMs inside banks during banking hours only.

» Always cover the ATM keypad when entering personal codes.

» Avoid self-standing ATMs whenever possible and never use an ATM that looks tampered with.

To make an intercity collect call, dial 9 before the 0xx. A recorded message in Portuguese will ask you to say your name and where you're calling from, after the tone.

INTERNATIONAL CALLS

Brazil's country code is ☎55. When calling internationally to Brazil, omit the initial 0xx of the area code.

International landline-to-landline calls from Brazil using Embratel start from 66¢ a minute to the USA, R$1.42 to Europe and R$1.42 to Australia.

Orelhãos are of little use for international calls unless you have an international calling card or are calling collect. Most pay telephones are restricted to domestic calls, and even if they aren't, a 30-unit Brazilian phone card may last less than a minute internationally.

Without an international calling card, your best option is Skype.

For international *a cobrar* (collect) calls, secure a Brazilian international operator by dialing ☎0800-703-2111 (Embratel).

CELL PHONES

Brazil uses the GSM 850/900/1800/1900 network, which is compatible with North America, Europe and Australia, but the country's 4G LTE network runs on 2500/2690 (for now), which is not compatible with many North American and European smartphones, including initial releases of the iPhone 5 (though the phone will work, it's just relegated to 3G). *Celular* (cell) phones have eight-digit numbers (nine in São Paulo) starting with a 6, 7, 8 or 9. Calls to mobiles are more expensive than calls to landlines. Mobiles have city codes like landlines, and if you're calling from another city, you have to use them.

Tim (www.tim.com.br), **Claro** (www.claro.com.br), **Oi** (www.oi.com.br) and **Vivo** (www.vivo.com.br) are the major operators. As of late 2012, foreigners can purchase a local SIM with a passport instead of needing a Brazilian CPF (tax ID number), a major bureaucratic roadblock dismantled.

Toilets

Public toilets are available at every bus station and airport; there's usually a small entrance fee of R$1 or so, depending on what you need to do!

Tourist Information

Tourist offices in Brazil are nearly all run by individual states or municipalities and are usually given the acronyms CIT (Centro de Informações Turísticas), CAT (Centro de Atendimento ao Turista) or PIT (Pontos de Informação Turística). Also common are Setur (Secretaria de Turismo), Semtur (Secretaria Municipal de Turismo) and Sedtur (Secretaria de Estado de Desenvolvimento do Turismo).

Visas

Citizens of the US, Australia and Canada need a visa; citizens from the UK, France, Germany and New Zealand do not.

Tourist visas are valid for arrival in Brazil within 90 days of issue and then for a 90-day stay. The fee and length depends on your nationality; it's usually between US$20 and US$65, though US citizens are hit with a whopping US$160 reciprocal bill. Processing times vary from five to 10 business days, sometimes less depending on nationality and consulate efficiency. Brazilian consulates will never entertain expedited visa services under any circumstance, so plan ahead. You'll generally need to present one passport photograph, proof of onward travel and a valid passport.

People under 18 years of age who wish to travel to Brazil without a parent or legal guardian must present a notarized Visa Consent Form from the nontraveling parent/guardian or from a court. Check with a Brazilian consulate well in advance about this.

For up-to-date information on visas check lonelyplanet.com and its links.

ENTRY/EXIT CARD

On entering Brazil, all tourists must fill out a *cartão de entrada/saida* (entry/exit card); immigration officials keep half, you keep the other. Don't lose this card! When you leave Brazil, the second half of the entry/exit card will be taken by immigration officials. If it's lost, Brazilian law levies a lofty fine (R$165) that you'll have to pay if you return to the country (though many travelers have reported being waived on through with little hassle – best to report the loss to the Policía Federal immediately).

Most visitors can stay for 90 days, but if for some reason you receive fewer days, this will be written in the stamp in your passport.

VISA EXTENSIONS

Brazil's Polícia Federal, which has offices in the state capitals and border towns, handles visa extensions. You must apply no less than five days before your entry/exit card or visa lapses. The convoluted process is as follows:

» Fill out and print the form 'Requerimento de Prorrogação de Prazo,' found in the 'Estrangeiros' section under the subheading 'Prorrogar Prazo de Estada de Turista e Viajante a Negócios (Temporário II)' from the Polícia Federal website (www.dpf.gov.br).

» Generate a government tax collection form called a 'GRU (Guia de Recolhimento da União),' found by clicking through from the same heading to 'GRU – FUNAPOL,' then 'Pessoas e Entidades Estrangeiras.' In that form, fill out your personal info; enter code '140090,' under 'Código da Receita STN;' choose the Polícia Federal office nearest you under the drop-down menu 'Unidade Arrecadadora;' and enter R$67 under 'Valor Total R$.' Then click 'Gerar Guia' to generate the bar-coded form.

» Take it to any bank, post office or lottery point and pay the R$67 fee; then head to the nearest Polícia Federal office with all in hand as well as your passport and original entry card. When you go, dress nicely! Some Fed stations don't take kindly to people in shorts. The extension is at the discretion of the officer and you may be asked to provide a ticket out of the country and proof of sufficient funds. If you get the maximum 90-day extension and then leave the country before the end of that period, you cannot return until the full 90 days have elapsed.

Volunteering

Rio-based **Iko Poran** (☎0xx21-2205-1365; www.ikoporan.org) links the diverse talents of volunteers with needy organizations. Previous volunteers in Brazil have worked as dance, music, art and language instructors among other things. Iko Poran also provides housing for volunteers. The UK-based **Task Brasil** (www.taskbrasil.org.uk) is another laudable organization that places volunteers in Rio.

Women Travelers

In the cities of the Southeast and South, foreign women without traveling companions will scarcely be given a sideways glance. In the more traditional rural areas of the Northeast, blonde-haired and light-skinned women, especially those without male escorts, will certainly arouse curiosity.

Machismo is less overt in Brazil than in Spanish-speaking Latin America. Flirtation is a common form of communication, but it's generally regarded as innocent banter; no sense of insult, exploitation or serious intent should be assumed.

It's advisable to adapt what you wear to local norms. The brevity of Rio beach attire generally is not suitable for the streets of interior cities, for instance.

In the event of unwanted pregnancy or the risk thereof, most pharmacies in Brazil stock the morning-after pill *(a pílula do dia seguinte)*, which costs about R$20. Tampons and other sanitary items are widely available in most pharmacies.

Work

Brazil has high unemployment and tourists are not supposed to take jobs. However, it's not unusual for foreigners to find language-teaching work in the bigger cities, either in language schools or through private tutoring. The pay is not great but if you can work for three or four days a week you can just about not starve on it.

Getting There & Away

Brazil has several gateway airports and shares a border with every country in South America except Chile and Ecuador.

Air

The busiest international airports are Aeroporto Galeão (formally known as Aeroporto Internacional António Carlos Jobim) in Rio de Janeiro and São Paulo's Aeroporto Guarulhos.

ARGENTINA

Round-trip flights from Buenos Aires are available on Aerolíneas Argentinas, GOL, LAN and TAM to São Paulo and, along with Emirates, to Rio de Janeiro as well. Other flights from Buenos Aires go to Porto Alegre, Curitiba, Florianópolis and Puerto Iguazú in Argentina, a short cross-border hop from Foz do Iguaçu.

BOLIVIA

GOL flies from Santa Cruz to Campo Grande and São Paulo. Inside Bolivia, Aerocon flies from other Bolivian cities to Cobija and Guayaramerin, across the border from the Brazilian towns of Brasiléia and Guajará-Mirim, respectively. Boliviana de Aviación also flies to Cobija and connects Santa Cruz with São Paulo three times a week.

CHILE

TAM and LAN (merged as Latam but operating independently) fly from Santiago to Rio and São Paulo. GOL flies from Santiago to Porto Alegre.

COLOMBIA

Copa and LAN fly from Bogotá to Leticia, from where you can walk, taxi or take a *combi* (minibus) across the border into Tabatinga, Brazil, and catch an onward flight there on Trip or TAM. Avianca and LAN fly direct from Bogotá to São Paulo.

ECUADOR

There are no direct flights between Quito or Guayaquil and Brazil. Taca and LAN tend to run the best deals to Rio or São Paulo, usually via Lima.

THE GUIANAS

Surinam Airways flies from Belém to both Paramaribo (Suriname) and Cayenne (French Guiana) two days per week. From Paramaribo, you can catch onward flights to Georgetown (Guyana).

PARAGUAY

TAM and GOL fly direct between Asunción and São Paulo. GOL also flies from Asunción to Curitiba. Alternatively, you can fly from Asunción to Ciudad del Este, a short cross-border hop from Foz do Iguaçu, Brazil.

PERU

TAM and Taca fly direct from Lima to São Paulo. Taca also flies direct to Rio.

URUGUAY

GOL flies direct from Montevideo to Porto Alegre. TAM flies direct between Montevideo and São Paulo.

VENEZUELA

TAM and GOL fly direct between Caracas and São Paulo.

Boat

From Peru fast passenger boats make the 400km trip along the Amazon between Iquitos (Peru) and Tabatinga (Brazil) in eight to 10 hours. From Tabatinga you can continue to Manaus and Belém. For Bolivia, boats (R$5, five minutes) depart to Guayaramerín (Bolivia) from Guajará-Mirim (Brazil) 24 hours a day.

Bus

ARGENTINA

The main border crossing used by travelers is Puerto Iguazú–Foz do Iguaçu, a 20-hour bus ride from Buenos Aires. Further south, you can cross between Uruguaiana (Brazil) and Paso de los Libres (Argentina), which is also served by buses from Buenos Aires. Other crossings are at San Javier–Porto Xavier and Santo Tomé–São Borja on the Río Uruguai.

Direct buses run between Buenos Aires and Porto Alegre (R$195, 18 hours) and Rio de Janeiro (R$240, 42 hours). Other destinations include Florianópolis (R$283, 14 hours), Curitiba (R$321.50, 30 hours) and São Paulo (R$324.50, 36 hours).

BOLIVIA

Brazil's longest border runs through remote wetlands and forests, and is much used by smugglers.

The busiest crossing is between Quijarro (Bolivia) and Corumbá (Brazil). Quijarro has a daily train link with Santa Cruz, Bolivia. Corumbá has bus connections with Bonito, Campo Grande, São Paulo, Rio de Janeiro and southern Brazil.

Cáceres, in Mato Grosso (Brazil) has two daily bus links with Santa Cruz (Bolivia) via the Bolivian border town of San Matías (one on Sunday).

Guajará-Mirim (Brazil) is a short river crossing from Guayaramerín (Bolivia). Both towns have bus links into their respective countries, but from late December to late February rains can make the northern Bolivian roads very difficult.

Brasiléia (Brazil), a 4½-hour bus ride from Rio Branco, stands opposite Cobija (Bolivia), which has bus connections into Bolivia. This route is less direct than the Guayaramerín–Guajará-Mirim option, and Bolivian buses confront the same wet-season difficulties.

CHILE

Although there is no border with Chile, direct buses run between Santiago and Brazilian cities, such as Porto Alegre (R$367, 26 hours), Curitiba (R$372.50, 54 hours), São Paulo (R$355.50, 54 hours) and Rio de Janeiro (R$388, 60 hours).

COLOMBIA

Leticia, on the Amazon in far southeast Colombia, is contiguous with Tabatinga (Brazil). You can cross the border on foot, by *combi* or taxi, but river and air are the only ways out of either town.

FRENCH GUIANA

The Brazilian town of Oiapoque, a rugged 560km bus ride from Macapá (R$90, 12 to 15 hours), stands across the Río Oiapoque from St Georges (French Guiana). A road connects St Georges to the French Guiana capital, Cayenne, with minibuses shuttling between the two. (Get there early in the morning to catch one.)

GUYANA

From Boa Vista, there are daily buses to Bonfim, Roraima (R$18.50, 1½ hours) on the Guyanese border, a short motorized canoe ride from Lethem (R$3; southwest Guyana).

PARAGUAY

The two major border crossings are Ciudad del Este–Foz do Iguaçu and Pedro Juan Caballero–Ponta Porã. Direct buses run between Asunción and Brazilian cities such as Florianópolis (R$167, 20 hours), Curitiba (R$129, 14 hours), São Paulo (R$159, 20 hours) and Foz do Iguaçu (R$40, five hours).

PERU

There is at least one daily bus connecting Rio Branco (Brazil) to Puerto Maldonado (Peru) via the border at Assis–Iñapari on the new US$2.75 billion Interoceanic Hwy. You can also reach Assis on daily buses from Epitáciolândia (R$13, two hours) and cross the Río Acre to Iñapari.

SURINAME

Overland travel between Suriname and Brazil involves first passing through either French Guiana or Guyana.

URUGUAY

The crossing most used by travelers is at Chuy (Uruguay)–Chuí (Brazil). Others are Río Branco–Jaguarão, Isidoro Noblia–Aceguá, Rivera–Santana do Livramento, Artigas–Quaraí and Bella Unión–Barra do Quaraí. Buses run between Montevideo and Brazilian cities such as Porto Alegre (R$162, 12 hours), Florianópolis (R$209, 18 hours) and São Paulo (R$310, 32 hours).

VENEZUELA

From Manaus, five daily buses run to Boa Vista (R$96, 12 hours) from where you can connect on to Puerto La Cruz, Venezuela (R$130, 20 hours), for access to Caracas or Isla Margarita.

Getting Around

Air

DOMESTIC AIR SERVICES

Brazil's biggest domestic carriers are GOL and TAM, along with Avianca, Trip, Webjet (part of GOL) and Azul, the latter operating out of Campinas, 100km northwest of São Paulo. A free shuttle to Campinas' Viracopas airport runs from Aeroporto Congonhas, Barra Funda metro station and Shopping El Dorado in São Paulo.

AIRLINE	WEBSITE	TELEPHONE
Avianca	www.avianca.com.br	0300-789-8160
Azul	www.voeazul.com.br	0800-887-1118
GOL	www.voegol.com.br	0300-115-2121
TAM	www.tam.com.br	0800-570-5700
Trip	www.voetrip.com.br	0300-789-8747
Webjet	www.webjet.com.br	0300-21-01234

HITCHHIKING

Hitchhiking in Brazil, with the possible exceptions of the Pantanal and Fernando de Noronha, is difficult and likely unsafe. The Portuguese for 'lift' is *carona*.

Major domestic airlines now accept major foreign credit cards through their websites, though it often doesn't work – you'll have to pay at an airline office or travel agent if your card is declined.

AIR PASSES

If you're combining travels in Brazil with other countries in South America, it's worth looking into the TAM South America Airpass, which allows for travel of up to 8200 miles between Argentina, Bolivia, Brazil, Chile, Paraguay, Peru, Uruguay and Venezuela. High-season prices start at US$402 and vary depending on distance.

For flights solely within Brazil, TAM (from US$532), Trip (US$479) and GOL (from US$582) all offer domestic passes, the latter offering a Northeast-only version as well (from US$440). These can be an excellent investment, but shop around as Brazil's low-cost carriers often offer unbelievably low fares during seasonal blowout sales.

Airpasses must be purchased abroad. Consult respective websites for additional rules and regulations.

Boat

The Ríos Negro, Solomões and Madeira are the highways of Amazonia, and you can travel thousands of kilometers along these waterways (which combine to form the mighty Amazon), exploring the vast Amazon Basin traveling to or from Peru or Bolivia.

Bus

Bus ticket prices in Brazil are among the highest in South America. **Itapemirim** (www.itapemirim.com.br) and **Cometa** (www.viacaocometa.com.br) are two of the best and biggest companies. The easiest resource to search national bus routes is **Busca Ônibus** (www.buscaonibus.com.br).

There are three main classes of long-distance buses. The cheapest, *convencional,* is fairly comfortable with reclining seats and usually a toilet and sometimes air-con. The *executivo* provides roomier seats, costs about 25% more and makes fewer stops. The more luxurious *leitos* can cost twice as much as *convencional* and have spacious, fully reclining seats with pillows, air-conditioning and sometimes an attendant serving sandwiches and drinks. Overnight buses, regardless of the class, often make fewer stops.

Most cities have one central bus terminal (*rodoviária,* pronounced 'hoe-doe-vee-ah-rhee-ya'). It's wise to book ahead on weekends and holidays (particularly December to February).

Car

Brazilian roads can be dangerous, especially busy highways such as the Rio to São Paulo corridor. There are tens of thousands of motor-vehicle fatalities every year. Driving at night is particularly hazardous because other drivers are more likely to be drunk and road hazards are less visible.

That said, driving can be a convenient (if expensive) way to get around Brazil. A small four-seat rental car costs around R$100 to R$120 a day with unlimited kilometers (R$140 to R$160 with air-con) and basic insurance. Ordinary gasoline costs around R$2.40 to R$2.90 a liter. Ethanol (known as *álcool* and produced from sugarcane) is about 50% less but goes around 30% quicker (most cars take both, known as Flex).

DRIVER'S LICENSE

The legal driving age in Brazil is 18. Most foreign licenses are legally valid in Brazil but we recommend obtaining an International Driving Permit, as the police you are likely to encounter as a foreign driver don't always know the law.

Local Transportation

BUS

Local bus services are frequent and cheap, covering extensive routes. Many buses list their destinations in bold letters on the front, making it easier to identify the one you need. Drivers don't usually stop unless someone flags them.

Typically, you enter the bus at the front and exit from the rear. The price is displayed near the money collector, who sits at a turnstile and provides change for the fare (usually between R$2.60 and R$3). Avoid riding the bus after 11pm and at peak (read packed) times: noon to 2pm and 4pm to 6pm in most areas.

TAXI

City taxis aren't cheap. In São Paulo, meters start at R$4.10 and rise by R$2.50 per kilometer (prices increase at night and on Sunday); other cities go down from there. Make sure the driver turns on the meter when you get in. In some small towns, prices are fixed and meters nonexistent. The handy **Tarifa de Taxi** (www.tarifadetaxi.com) plots point-to-point fares in major Brazilian cities.

Tours

Both the Amazon and the Pantanal are the two most popular areas for organized tours in Brazil. You will certainly enrich your experience with the services of a trained guide as well as gain the transport upper hand for reaching difficult-to-access spots for the best wildlife-viewing. In many of Brazil's national parks, such as Lençóis Maranhenses, Chapada dos Guimarães and Chapada Diamantina, guides are a necessity, if not required by regulation.

Train

There are very few passenger trains in service. One remaining line well worth riding runs from Curitiba to Paranaguá, descending the coastal mountain range.

Chile

Includes »

Why Go?

Spindly Chile stretches 4300km – over half the continent – from the driest desert in the world to massive glacial fields. In between the Andes and the Pacific, the landscape is dotted with volcanoes, geysers, beaches, lakes, rivers, steppe and countless islands. What's on offer? Everything: sweeping desert solitude, craggy Andean summits, the lush forests of the fjords, first-class wine regions, up-and-coming surfing hot spots, even the exotic getaway of Rapa Nui (Easter Island). Of course, Chile is more than its striking geography: its far-flung location has fired the imagination of literary heavyweights and has been known to make poets out of bartenders and dreamers out of presidents. The current president certainly has a specific dream – at the time of writing, Sebastián Piñera announced that he's aiming for a 'First World Chile' by 2020. If the country's well-developed tourist infrastructure is any indication, Chile is well on its way.

Best Places to Eat

» El Tercer Ojito (p459)
» Chaski (p444)
» Hostalomera (p494)
» La Marmita (p504)
» Liguria (p419)

Best Places to Stay

» El Tesoro de Elqui (p445)
» Casa Azul (p487)
» Domo Bahia Inglesa (p447)
» Hostal Luna Sonrisa (p433)
» Palafito 1326 (p494)

When to Go

Santiago

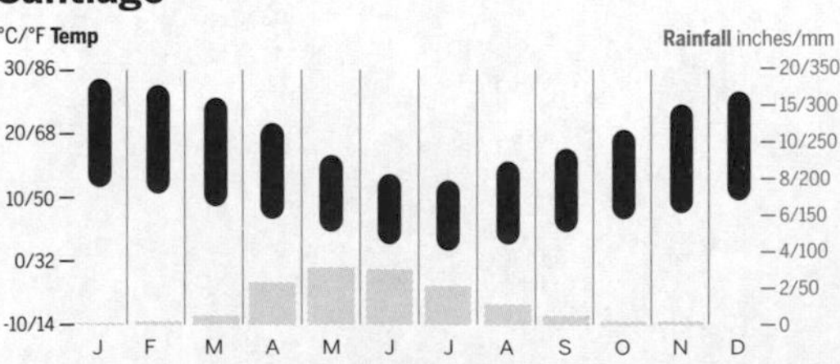

Nov–Feb Patagonia is best (and most expensive) but beaches are often crowded.

Mar–May, Sep & Oct Grape harvests in wine regions; pleasant Santiago temperatures.

Jun–Aug Fine weather in the north; Chileans go on winter vacation in July.

Connections

Chile's northern border touches Peru and Bolivia, while its vast eastern boundary hugs Argentina. Of the numerous border crossings with Argentina, only a few are served by public transportation.

Most international buses depart from the Terminal de Buses in Santiago. Unless you're crossing from Chile's extreme south, there's no way to avoid the Andes. Note that many passes close in winter.

Popular crossings include Santiago to Mendoza and Buenos Aires, Calama to Jujuy and Salta, La Serena to San Juan, Temuco to San Martin de los Andes, and the bus-ferry combination between Puerto Varas and Bariloche. Other international crossings include Arica to Tacna, Peru – served by train and *colectivo* (fixed-route taxi) as well as by buses – and Iquique to Colchane, Bolivia.

ITINERARIES

One Week

Spend a day exploring the museums and cafes of Santiago, then escape to the picturesque port of Valparaíso. From central Chile, you'll have to decide whether to venture north – to San Pedro de Atacama and its mystical desertscapes, adventure sports and starry skies – or to the glaciers and trekking paradise of Torres del Paine and Patagonia in the south.

Two Weeks

In the second week, choose your own adventure: taste wine in the Colchagua Valley, go skiing or hiking in the Andes at a resort such as Portillo, seek out a surf break in Pichilemu, venture to the end of the earth in Tierra del Fuego, or tour the *pisco* (grape brandy) distilleries of charming Pisco Elqui, a short trip from La Serena.

Essential Food & Drink

» **Pisco** The grape brandy is mixed with fresh lemon juice and sugar to make the famous *pisco sour* cocktail

» **Seafood** Chile's long coastline means a bounty of fabulously fresh *pescados* (fish) and *mariscos* (shellfish) used in soups, stews and *ceviche* (marinated raw seafood)

» **Pasteles** Find these hearty baked casseroles, a traditional specialty made with *choclo* (corn), *carne* (meat), *jaiva* (crab) or *papas* (potatoes), in small towns and at family tables

» **Wine** Chile's wine regions are rightfully world-famous; one varietal to try is Carmenere, a rich red that originated in Bordeaux but is now produced only here

AT A GLANCE

» **Currency** Chilean peso (CH$)

» **Language** Spanish

» **Money** ATMs widespread; credit cards widely accepted

» **Visas** Generally not required for stays of up to 90 days

» **Time** GMT minus four hours

Fast Facts

» **Area** 748,800 sq km

» **Population** 17.3 million

» **Capital** Santiago

» **Emergency** ☎133

» **Country code** ☎56

Exchange Rates

Australia	A$1	CH$489
Canada	C$1	CH$477
Euro zone	€1	CH$616
New Zealand	NZ$1	CH$386
UK	UK£1	CH$758
USA	US$1	CH$473

Set Your Budget

» **Hostel bed** CH$8000-12,000

» **Evening meal** CH$4000-10,000

» **Bus ticket from Santiago to Valparaíso** CH$5000

Resources

» **Go Chile** (www.gochile.cl)

» **Sernatur** (www.sernatur.cl)

Chile Highlights

1. Hike to the rugged spires of Chile's finest national park, **Torres del Paine** (p508)
2. Swirl, sniff and sip your way through Chile's best **vineyards** (p466) in the Central Valley
3. Wander steep passageways lined with urban art in the hills of bohemian **Valparaíso** (p429)
4. Drink in the wild starscape above the **Atacama Desert** (p451), the driest desert in the world
5. Encounter penguins, misty seascapes and mythical lore on the otherworldly archipelago of **Chiloé** (p491)
6. Go trekking, camping, kayaking and horse riding in **Patagonia** (p496), a wildly beautiful landscape
7. Gaze up at **Easter Island's** (p513) enigmatic *moai* (statues)
8. Catch a wave in the surf capitals of **Iquique** (p456) and **Arica** (p461)
9. Escape to **Tierra del Fuego** (p512), the quiet end of the earth

SANTIAGO

☎02 / POP 5,883,000

The Chilean capital has always had its measured charms – fine dining, perfectly landscaped gardens, a famous seafood market, the stunning backdrop of the Andes – but in the past few years, Santiago has undergone a cultural metamorphosis. In celebration of Chile's bicentennial, the city poured millions of pesos into the construction of sleek new cultural centers, museums and parks. Though Santiago may never be as glamorous as Rio or as dynamic as Buenos Aires, the understated but up-and-coming city has become more than a stop-off on the way to Chilean Patagonia or the Atacama – it's become a destination in its own right.

History

Founded by Pedro de Valdivia in 1541, Santiago's site was chosen for its moderate climate and strategic location for defense. It remained a small town until the nitrate boom in the 1880s; Gustave Eiffel designed its central station. In 1985 an earthquake shook down some of downtown's classic architecture; thanks to smart architecture and strict building codes, the February 2010 quake caused comparatively minimal damage in Chile's capital city.

Sights

'El Centro' is a compact, triangular area bounded by the Río Mapocho and Parque Forestal in the north, the Vía Norte Sur in the west, and Av General O'Higgins (the Alameda) in the south. Key public buildings cluster near the Plaza de Armas, which branches out into a busy graph of shopping arcades and pedestrian streets. North and east of the center is Barrio Bellavista, with Cerro San Cristóbal (Parque Metropolitano). To the west is Barrio Brasil, the bohemian enclave of the city. At the tip of this triangle and extending east are the wealthy *comunas* (sectors) of Providencia and Las Condes, accessed via the Alameda. Nuñoa is a residential neighborhood south of Providencia.

CENTRO

Architecturally, Santiago's downtown is exuberant rather than elegant: haphazardly maintained 19th-century buildings sit alongside the odd glittering high-rise, and its crowded pedestrian walkways are lined with inexpensive clothing stores and fast-food joints. Government offices, the presidential palace and the banking district are here; most tourists come to make the rounds to a handful of standout sights.

Plaza de Armas PLAZA

(Map p420; cnr Monjitas & 21 de Mayo; MPlaza de Armas) Since the city's founding in 1541, the Plaza de Armas has been its symbolic heart. In colonial times a gallows was the square's grisly centerpiece; today it's a fountain celebrating *libertador* (liberator) Simón Bolívar, shaded by more than a hundred Chilean palm trees.

Catedral Metropolitana CHURCH

(Map p420; Plaza de Armas; 9am-7pm Mon-Sat, 9am-noon Sun; MPlaza de Armas) Overlooking the Plaza de Armas is the neoclassical Catedral Metropolitana, built between 1748 and 1800. Bishops celebrating mass on the lavish main altar may feel uneasy: beneath them is the crypt where their predecessors are buried.

Barrio París-Londres NEIGHBORHOOD

(Map p420; cnr París & Londres; MUniversidad de Chile) This pocket-sized neighborhood, made up of two intersecting cobbled streets, París and Londres, is lined by graceful European-style town houses built in the 1920s. Look for the memorial at **Londres 38**, a building that served as a torture center during Pinochet's government.

Estación Mapocho CULTURAL CENTER

(Mapocho Station; Map p420; www.estacionmapocho.cl; Plaza de la Cultura s/n; event times vary, check website; MPuente Cal y Canto) Rail services north once left from Estación Mapocho. Earthquake damage and the decay of the rail system led to its closure, but it's been reincarnated as a cultural center that hosts art exhibitions and concerts. The soaring cast-iron structure of the main hall was built in France, then assembled in Santiago behind its golden beaux arts–style stone facade.

FREE **Palacio de la Moneda** HISTORIC BUILDING

(Map p420; Morandé 130; 10am-6pm Mon-Fri; MLa Moneda) Chile's presidential offices are inside this ornate neoclassical building, designed by Italian architect Joaquín Toesca in the late 18th century, and was originally the official mint – its name means 'palace of the coin.'

Centro Cultural Palacio La Moneda ARTS CENTER

(Map p420; www.ccplm.cl; Plaza de la Ciudadanía 26; exhibitions adult/child CH$2000/1000, free 9am-noon Mon-Fri; 9am-9pm, exhibitions to 7:30pm; MLa Moneda) Underground art takes on a new meaning in one of Santiago's newer cultural spaces beneath Plaza de la Ciudadanía. A glass-slab roof floods the vault-like space with natural light; features include a state-run art-house movie theater, two large temporary exhibition spaces, a fair-trade crafts shop, a few cafes and a gallery celebrating Chilean folk singer, artist and activist Violeta Parra.

Museo Chileno de Arte Precolombino MUSEUM

(Chilean Museum of Pre-Columbian Art; Map p420; www.precolombino.cl; Bandera 361; adult/child

SANTIAGO IN...

Two Days

Start at the bustling **Plaza de Armas**. Peer into the old train-station-turned-cultural-center **Estación Mapocho**, or have a coffee and check out contemporary art and fair-trade crafts at the **Centro Cultural Palacio La Moneda**. Have a seafood lunch at the **Mercado Central**, then hike up **Cerro Santa Lucía** to see the city from above. Head to Bellavista for a classic Chilean dinner at **Galindo**. On your second day, tour Pablo Neruda's house, **La Chascona**, then ride the funicular to the top of **Cerro San Cristóbal**. After a *ceviche* lunch at **Azul Profundo**, check out the cultural calendar and bookstore at **Centro Gabriela Mistral**. Later, have a *pisco sour* at the W Hotel's **Red2One** cocktail bar.

Four Days

On your third day, go hiking in the **Cajón del Maipo** or taste local varietals at a winery. Spend your fourth day admiring street art in **Barrio Brasil**, stopping for lunch at antique **El Café**. Toast your stay in Santiago with dinner and drinks at Providencia's **Liguria**.

Santiago

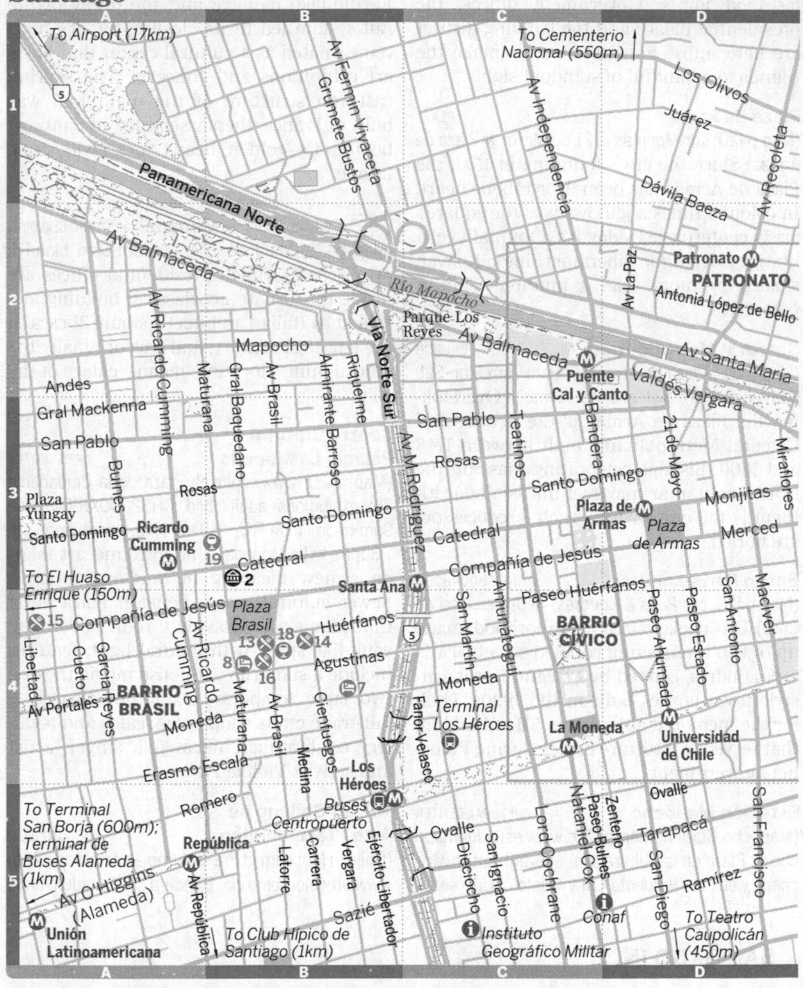

CH$3000/free; ⌚10am-6pm Tue-Sat, to 2pm Sun; ⓂPlaza de Armas) Chronicles a whopping 4500 years of pre-Columbian civilization throughout the Americas with breathtaking ceramics, gorgeous textiles and Chinchorro mummies. At the time of writing, the museum was closed while it was undergoing a major expansion; it is set to reopen in 2013.

BARRIOS LASTARRIA & BELLAS ARTES

Home to three of the city's best museums and the center of Santiago's cafe culture, these postcard-pretty neighborhoods are the city's twin hubs of hip.

Cerro Santa Lucía PARK

(Map p420; entrances cnr Alameda & Santa Lucía, cnr Santa Lucía & Subercaseaux; ⌚9am-7pm Mar-Sep, to 8pm Oct-Feb; ⓂSanta Lucía) This towering hill – once a hermitage, then a convent, then a military bastion – has offered respite from city chaos since 1875. At the southwest corner is the Terraza Neptuno, with fountains and curving staircases that lead to the summit.

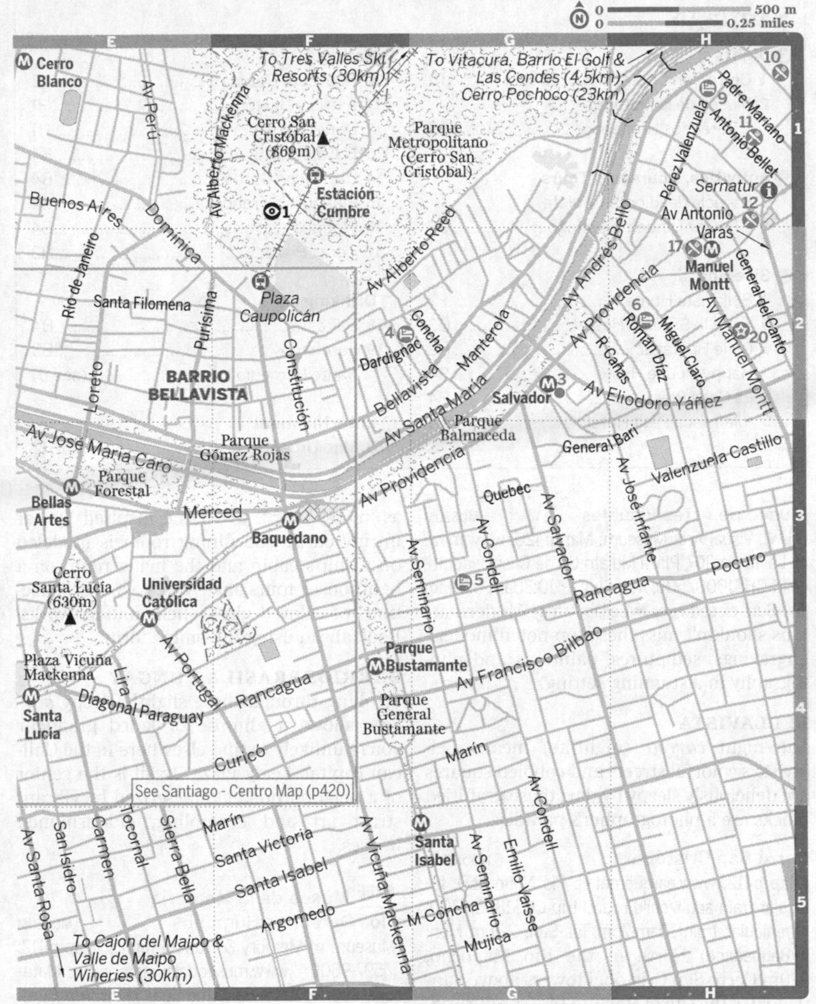

Palacio de Bellas Artes MUSEUM
(Map p420; www.mnba.cl; Parque Forestal s/n; adult/child CH$600/400; ⊙MNBA 10am-6:50pm Tue-Sun, MAC 11am-7pm Tue-Sat, 11am-6pm Sun; MBellas Artes) Modeled on the Petit Palais in Paris, Santiago's early-20th-century fine-arts museum houses two sights: **Museo Nacional de Bellas Artes (MNBA)**, with permanent collections of Chilean and European art, and the **Museo de Arte Contemporáneo (MAC)**, hosting modern photography, design, sculpture and web-art displays. You'll need a separate ticket for each *museo*.

TOP CHOICE **Centro Gabriela Mistral** ARTS CENTER
(GAM; Map p420; www.gam.cl; Av O'Higgins 227; admission free; ⊙plazas 8am-midnight, exhibition spaces 10am-8pm Tue-Sat, from 11am Sun; MUniversidad Católica) This striking cultural center – named for Chilean poet Gabriela Mistral, the first Latin American woman to win the Nobel Prize in Literature – is an exciting new addition to Santiago's art scene. Along with two large exhibition spaces and airy outdoor plazas, super-contemporary GAM comprises a delightful bookstore, a cool cafe and a small outdoor antiques fair.

Santiago

Sights
1 Cerro San Cristóbal F1
2 Museo de la Memoria y los Derechos Humanos B3

Activities, Courses & Tours
3 Escuela de Idiomas Violeta Parra/Tandem Santiago G2

Sleeping
4 Bellavista Home F2
5 Castillo Surfista Hostel G3
6 Chile Hostales H2
7 Happy House Hostel B4
8 La Casa Roja B4
9 Vilafranca Petit Hotel H1

Eating
10 Aquí Está Coco H1
11 Astrid y Gastón H1
12 Doner House H1
13 El Café B4
14 Las Vacas Gordas B4
15 Peluquería Francesa A4
16 Platipus B4
17 Voraz Pizza H2

Drinking
18 Baires B4
19 Eurohappy B3
Santo Remedio .... (see 6)

Entertainment
20 Mito Urbano H2

Museo de Artes Visuales MUSEUM
(MAVI, Visual Arts Museum; Map p420; www.mavi.cl; Lastarria 307, Plaza Mulato Gil de Castro; adult/child CH$1000/500, free Sun; ⏲10:30am-6:30pm Tue-Sun, closed Feb; Ⓜ Bellas Artes) Modern-art fans shouldn't miss these top-notch modern engravings, sculptures, paintings and photography in a stunning setting.

BELLAVISTA

Late-night *carrete* (nightlife) means Bellavista's colorful streets and cobbled squares are deliciously sleepy by day: these graffitied blocks are a photographer's paradise.

Cerro San Cristóbal MOUNTAIN
(Map p412; www.parquemet.cl; Pío Nono 450; funicular train adult/child round-trip CH$1800/1100; ⏲funicular train 10am-7pm Tue-Sun, 2-7pm Mon; Ⓜ Baquedano) North of the Río Mapocho, 870m Cerro San Cristóbal towers above Santiago; it's the site of **Parque Metropolitano**, the capital's largest park, with two swimming pools, a botanical garden and a zoo. Beam up to the summit via the **funicular train**, which departs from Plaza Caupolicán at the north end of Pío Nono in Bellavista.

TOP CHOICE **La Chascona** HISTORIC BUILDING
(Map p420; www.fundacionneruda.org; Fernando Márquez de La Plata 0192; admission by tour only, in Spanish/English CH$2500/3500, students CH$1500; ⏲10am-7pm Tue-Sun Jan & Feb, to 6pm Tue-Sun Mar-Dec; Ⓜ Baquedano) When poet Pablo Neruda needed a secret hideaway to spend time with his mistress Matilde Urrutia, he built La Chascona (loosely translated as 'messy hair'), the name inspired by her unruly curls. The dining room is modeled on a ship's cabin and the living room on a lighthouse; tours take you past his collections of colored glass, shells and artworks. Book ahead using the online form.

BARRIOS BRASIL & YUNGAY

Strolling through these slightly sleepy *barrios* allows a glimpse of faded grandeur you're unlikely to find elsewhere in the Chilean capital. Leafy Plaza Brasil is the center of a neighborhood characterized by vibrant street art and crumbling, old-fashioned houses.

FREE **Museo de la Memoria y los Derechos Humanos** MUSEUM
(Museum of Memory & Human Rights; Map p412; ☎597-9600; www.museodelamemoria.cl; Matucana 501; ⏲10am-6pm Tue-Sun; Ⓜ Ricardo Cumming) Opened in 2010, this museum isn't for the faint of heart: the exhibits expose the terrifying human rights violations and large-scale 'disappearances' that took place under Chile's military government between the years of 1973 and 1990. Learning about the 40,000 victims subjected to torture and execution is positively chilling – but a visit helps to contextualize Chile's tumultuous history.

LAS CONDES, BARRIO EL GOLF & VITACURA

Glittering skyscrapers, security-heavy apartment blocks, American chain restaurants and spanking-new malls: these neighborhoods are determined to be the international face of Chile's phenomenal economic growth.

TOP CHOICE **Museo de la Moda** MUSEUM

(Museum of Fashion; www.museodelamoda.cl; Av Vitacura 4562; adult/student CH$3500/2000, CH$1800 for all visitors on Wed & Sun; 10am-6pm Tue-Fri, 11am-7pm Sat & Sun; M Escuela Militar) Star attractions of this slick fashion museum include the 'cone bra' Jean Paul Gaultier designed for Madonna and an evening gown donned by Lady Diana in 1981. From Escuela Militar metro station, grab a taxi or take bus 305 from the west side of Américo Vespucio (you need a Bip! card) and get off at the intersection with Av Vitacura.

Costanera Center BUILDING

(www.costaneracenter.cl; Andrés Bello 2461; M Tobalaba) Financial woes have halted construction several times on this ambitious ongoing project; the four skyscrapers that make up the Costanera Center include **Gran Torre Santiago** (300m), the tallest building in South America. The towers contain luxury apartments, a pair of high-end hotels, a shopping mall and a food court with panoramic views.

BARRIO RECOLETA

Bustling Korean eateries, a happening marketplace overflowing with ripe fruit, a colorful jumble of street vendors – this burgeoning *barrio* is just a slight detour off the beaten path.

Cementerio General CEMETERY

(www.cementeriogeneral.cl; Av Profesor Alberto Zañartu 951; 8:30am-6pm; M Cementerios) A city of tombs where the names above the crypts read like a who's who of Chilean history: look for Salvador Allende's tomb and the Memorial del Detenido Desaparecido y del Ejecutado Político, a memorial to the 'disappeared' of Pinochet's dictatorship.

Patronato NEIGHBORHOOD

(Map p420; bordered by Recoleta, Loreto, Bellavista & Dominica; M Patronato) This *barrio* within a *barrio* is the beating heart of Santiago's Korean, Chinese and Arab immigrant populations. The colorful, run-down blocks are lined with antique buildings and illuminated by neon signs; poke around the bare-bones ethnic supermarkets, feast on street food or wander through the brash clothing market to watch the locals haggling over Chinese slippers.

La Vega Central MARKET

(Map p420; www.lavega.cl; cnr Nueva Rengifo & López de Bello; 6am-6pm Mon-Sat, 6am-3pm Sun; M Patronato) Raspberries, quinces, figs, peaches, persimmons, custard apples…if it grows in Chile, you'll find it at this market. Go early to see the hollering vendors in full swing. It's also a great spot for lunch.

Activities

Outdoor access is Santiago's strong suit. For a quick hiking fix, hoof it up Cerro San Cristóbal. For a more substantial day hike, try the locals' favorite: the 1800m **Cerro Pochoco**. The moderate hike, which will take you a few hours along a well-marked trail, is a great introduction to the Andes. To arrive at the trailhead, ask a taxi driver to take you to Pochoco Observatory; you can also walk to the observatory from Plaza San Enrique off Av Las Condes.

Santiago is flat and compact with a small network of *ciclovias* (bike lanes). Rent bikes and helmets from tour operator La Bicicleta Verde (p416). Check out the interactive map of bike paths and cyclist-friendly facilties at

PARQUE POR LA PAZ

During Chile's last dictatorship, some 4500 political prisoners were tortured and 266 were executed at Villa Grimaldi by the now-disbanded DINA (National Intelligence Directorate). The compound was razed to conceal evidence in the last days of Pinochet's dictatorship, but since the return of democracy it has been turned into a powerful memorial park known as **Parque por la Paz** (www.villagrimaldi.cl; Av Jose Arrieta 8401, Peñalolén; 10am-6pm). Each element of the park symbolizes one aspect of the atrocities that went on there and visits here are fascinating but harrowing – be sensitive about taking pictures as other visitors may be former detainees or family members. Check the website ahead of time to arrange a guided tour. Take Transantiago bus D09 or 513 (you need a Bip! card) from right outside the Av Vespucio exit of Plaza Egaña metro station; it drops you opposite the park entrance.

Recicleta (www.recicleta.cl/mapa-de-santiago-en-bicicleta), a group that promotes urban biking.

Excellent skiing is just a stone's throw from Santiago – the closest resort is **Farellones & El Colorado** (☎398-8080; www.elcolorado.cl; Apoquindo 4900, Oficina 48, Santiago). **Rafting** enthusiasts head to Cascada de las Animas (p429) from October to March for Class III descents of the Río Maipo. It also organizes hiking and horse-trekking trips at reasonable rates.

Courses

Reputable Spanish-language schools include the following.

Escuela de Idiomas Violeta Parra/Tandem Santiago LANGUAGE COURSE
(Map p412; ☎236-4241; www.tandemsantiago.cl; Triana 863, Providencia; enrollment fee US$55, intensive weeklong course with accommodations from US$390; Ⓜ Salvador) Combines an outstanding academic record with a friendly vibe and cultural activities.

Natalislang LANGUAGE COURSE
(Map p420; ☎222-8685; www.natalislang.com; Arturo Bürhle 047, Providencia; intensive 3-day traveler crash course from CH$135,000; Ⓜ Baquedano) Great for quick, intense courses.

Tours

TOP CHOICE **La Bicicleta Verde** GUIDED TOUR
(Map p420; ☎570-9338; www.labicicletaverde.cl; Loreto 6; bike tours CH$30,000, rentals half-day CH$5000-9000, per day CH$9000-15,000; Ⓜ Bellas Artes) Two-wheel town tours with a cultural bent: options include 'Bike at Night,' 'Parks and Politics' and 'Bike & Wine.' Bike rentals also available.

Free Tour Santiago WALKING TOUR
(Map p420; www.freetoursantiago.cl; ⊙tours begin at 10am & 3pm; Ⓜ Plaza de Armas) A free four-hour walking tour of downtown Santiago: guides work for tips only, so be prepared to offer gratuity. No booking necessary, just look for the guides wearing red shirts in front of Catedral Metropolitana.

Turistik BUS TOUR
(Map p420; ☎220-1000; www.turistik.cl; day pass from CH$17,100; ⊙9:30am-6pm; Ⓜ Plaza de Armas) Hop-on, hop-off double-decker bus tours run to 13 stops between the Centro district and Parque Arauco mall. Check the online map. One convenient place to 'hop on' is at Monjitas 821, just off Plaza de Armas.

Festivals & Events

Santiago a Mil THEATER
(www.stgoamil.cl) This major theater festival draws experimental companies from around the world to Santiago's stages in January.

Fiesta del Vino WINE
(www.fiestadelvinodepirque.cl) This wine festival in Pirque, one of many taking place around Santiago during harvest time (April), also features traditional cuisine and folkloric music.

Lollapalooza Chile MUSIC
(www.lollapaloozacl.com) The famous music festival now has a Chilean edition; national and international acts roll into Santiago at the end of March or early April.

Santiago Festival Internacional de Cine FILM
(SANFIC; www.sanfic.cl) Each August, Santiago's weeklong film festival showcases choice independent cinema throughout several movie theaters.

Sleeping

CENTRO

TOP CHOICE **CasAltura Boutique Hostel** HOSTEL $$
(Map p420; ☎633-5076; www.casaltura.com; San Antonio 811; dm/d incl breakfast CH$9975/33,725, s/d without bathroom CH$18,000/27,550; @; Ⓜ Cal y Canto) This sophisticated 'boutique hostel' is a traveler favorite thanks to kitchen access, high-end linens, a terrace overlooking Parque Forestal and the location near Mercado Central.

Hostel Plaza de Armas HOSTEL $
(Map p420; ☎671-4436; www.plazadearmashostel.com; Compañía de Jesus 960, Apt 607, Plaza de Armas; dm incl breakfast CH$7000-8550, d CH$28,500, s/d without bathroom CH$19,000/26,125; @; Ⓜ Plaza de Armas) You'll think you're in the wrong place when you show up at this busy apartment building. Take the elevator to the 6th floor to reach this cheery hostel with tiny dorms, a communal kitchen and great balconies overlooking Plaza de Armas.

Paris Londres – Hostel Boutique GUESTHOUSE $$
(Map p420; ☎638-2215; www.londres.cl; Londres 54; s/d/tr incl breakfast CH$30,000/36,000/45,000, s/d/tr without bathroom or breakfast

CH$15,000/24,000/30,000; @; MUniversidad de Chile) If you want to coax a little romance out of Santiago, you can't beat the cobbled streets of Barrio París. Under new ownership, Paris Londres still has great rates and pared-down, faded grandeur.

BARRIOS LASTARRIA & BELLAS ARTES

Hostal 168 Santa Lucía HOSTEL $
(Map p420; ☎664-8478; www.hostalsantalucia.cl; Santa Lucía 168; dm incl breakfast CH$8000, s/d CH$25,000/30,000, without bathroom CH$15,000/22,000; @☞; MSanta Lucia) A well-managed hostel that's intimate, stylish and central. Firm beds, white brocade covers and cozy shared spaces throughout, plus easy access to the metro, Cerro Santa Lucia, supermarkets and downtown.

Andes Hostel HOSTEL $
(Map p420; ☎633-1976; www.andeshostel.com; Monjitas 506; dm CH$8500, d with/without bathroom CH$30,800/23,715, apt for 1-4 people CH$35,575-65,300; @☞≋; MBellas Artes) Pistachio-colored walls, a zebra-print rug, mismatched retro sofas and a mosaic-tiled bar are some of the pop-art charms of this centrally located hostel. Unfortunately, dorms are rather airless on hot nights. It's worth splashing out more for an Andes apartment on the next block, especially as you'll get swimming pool access.

Hostal Forestal HOSTEL $
(Map p420; ☎638-1347; www.hostalforestal.cl; Coronel Santiago Bueras 120; dm incl breakfast CH$6500-8000, s without bathroom $18,000, d with/without bathroom CH$27,000/22,000; @☞; MBaquedano) Recent renovations and colorful new wall-sized murals have added some visual appeal to this lively hostel. Dorms with bunkbeds are functional and bathrooms basic; the private singles and doubles offer slightly more charm. Also on the menu are Chilean cooking classes, live music, bike rentals and weekly *asados* (barbecues).

BELLAVISTA

H Rado Hostel HOSTEL $$
(Map p420; ☎429-4420; www.radohostel.com; Pío Nono 5; dm incl breakfast CH$10,000, d with/without bathroom CH$32,000/23,715; @☞; MBaquedano) Conveniently located just next door to Patio Bellavista, this sleek four-story hostel features thoughtful details: dorm beds come equipped with reading lights while smart-looking private rooms have LCD televisions. The rooftop terrace, facing Cerro San Cristóbal, is lovely at sunset.

La Chimba HOSTEL $
(Map p420; ☎735-8978; www.lachimba.com; Ernesto Pinto Lagarrigue 262; dm incl breakfast CH$8000, d without bathroom CH$23,700; @☞; MBaquedano) Extra-wide bunks with well-sprung mattresses and feather quilts practically guarantee sweet dreams at this small hostel (though the beats from nearby clubs always filter in on weekends). The red-painted living room is cozy and the kitchen small but well-equipped. If only they'd put the same effort into the broken door handles and leaking showers.

Hostal Caracol HOSTEL $
(Map p420; ☎732-4644; www.caracolsantiago.cl; General Ekdhal 151; dm CH$8000, d/q from CH$28,000/CH$44,000; @☞; MPatronato) At this well-located new hostel, beds and bathrooms feel like they've hardly been used. Sleeping quarters can be tight, but you won't care if you've scored one of the en-suite doubles with a lovely private balcony. A grassy yard, spacious terrace and a sparkling-clean open kitchen round out the offerings.

Bellavista Home B&B $$
(Map p412; ☎735-9259; www.bellavistahome.cl; Capellán Abarzúa 143; s/d incl breakfast CH$35,000/45,000, s/d/tr without bathroom CH$25,000/40,000/55,000; @☞≋; MBaquedano) This four-room B&B is a tranquil and family-friendly respite from the *carrete* and crowds of Bellavista. Breezy rooms are outfitted with pristine white linens, colorful throw rugs and brightly painted wooden doors. All guests have kitchen access; round-the-clock coffee and tea can be enjoyed on the pretty garden patio.

BARRIOS BRASIL & YUNGAY

La Casa Roja HOSTEL $
(Map p412; ☎696-4241; www.lacasaroja.cl; Agustinas 2113; dm CH$7125, d incl breakfast with/without bathroom CH$22,325/19,000; @☞≋; MRicardo Cumming) With its airy patios, outdoor bar, garden and well-designed kitchen, it's easy to see why this Aussie-owned outfit is backpacker central – even if travelers complain about the grumpy staff. The lovingly restored 19th-century mansion has great-value doubles with stylish retro furniture.

Happy House Hostel HOSTEL $$
(Map p412; ☎688-4849; www.happyhousehostel.cl; Moneda 1829; dm CH$10,000, s/d/tr incl breakfast

34,000/37,000/45,000, s/d/tr without bathroom CH$22,000/25,000/33,000; @; MLos Héroes) Happy news indeed: this popular hostel has moved into new digs. Welcome features of this restored town house include open terraces, spacious doubles, a swimming pool and luggage storage services.

PROVIDENCIA

Castillo Surfista Hostel HOSTEL $
(Map p412; 893-3350; www.castillosurfista.com; Maria Luisa Santander 0329; dm CH$9000, d without bathroom CH$20,000-24,000; @; MBaquedano) Off the beaten path and run by a Californian surfer, this renovated house features homey dorms and doubles, tidy communal areas and laid-back hosts who can help you access the surf scene – the owner even runs daylong surf trips to lesser-known breaks and arranges camper rentals if you want to venture to the beaches alone.

Chile Hostales HOSTEL $$
(Map p412; 474-8489; www.chilehostales.com; Román Díaz 140; dm incl breakfast CH$9000-12,000, s/d CH$25,000/35,000, s/d without bathroom CH$22,000/30,000; @; MSalvador) Just off Av Providencia, this well-run hostel has a great book exchange, a leafy courtyard, basic but comfortable dorms and doubles, and a recently remodeled communal kitchen.

Vilafranca Petit Hotel B&B $$
(Map p412; 235-1413; www.vilafranca.cl; Pérez Valenzuela 1650; s CH$41,000, d CH$49,000-53,000; @; MPedro de Valdivia) Studiedly Martha Stewart, this lovely B&B has a trellised stone patio and eight rooms with big wooden trunks, firm beds in floral patterns and modern bathrooms. Breakfast includes fresh fruit such as blackberries or watermelon.

Eating

Cheap lunches abound in the city center; *barrios* Bellavista, Lastarria and Providencia are better suited for dinner. Restaurants usually close after lunch and reopen around 8pm.

CENTRO

Along the southern arcade of the Plaza de Armas, vendors serve *completos* (hot dogs) and empanadas.

TOP CHOICE **Mercado Central** CHILEAN, SEAFOOD $
(Central Market; Map p420; cnr 21 de Mayo & General MacKenna; food stands & restaurants 9am-5pm Mon-Fri, 7am-3:30pm Sat & Sun; MPuente Cal y Canto) Santiago's wrought-iron fish market is a classic for seafood lunches (and hangover-curing fish stews such as the tomato-and-potato-based *caldillo de congrio*, Pablo Neruda's favorite). Skip the touristy restaurants in the middle and head for one of the tiny, low-key stalls around the market's periphery.

TOP CHOICE **Bar Nacional** CHILEAN $
(Map p420; Bandera 317; mains CH$3400-5500; MPlaza de Armas) From the chrome counter to the waitstaff of old-timers, this *fuente de soda* (soda fountain) is as vintage as they come. It's been churning out Chilean specialties such as *lomo a lo pobre* (steak and fries topped with fried egg) for years. To save a buck (or a few hundred pesos) ask for the sandwich menu. There's a second branch around the corner on Huérfanos.

Empanadas Zunino BAKERY $
(Map p420; Puente 801; empanadas CH$850-1600; MPuente Cal y Canto) Founded in the 1930s, this classic bakery makes fantastic empanadas. In 2011, Chilean food journalists awarded it second place in a contest for the best empanadas in Santiago.

El Naturista VEGETARIAN $
(Map p420; Huérfanos 1046; mains CH$2800-4200; 9am-8pm Mon-Fri, 10am-3pm Sat; MUniversidad de Chile) A downtown vegetarian classic, El Naturista does simple but filling soups, sandwiches, salads, tarts and fresh-squeezed juices, plus light breakfasts and fruit-infused ice cream. There's another location nearby at Moneda 846.

BARRIOS LASTARRIA & BELLAS ARTES

Café Bistro de la Barra CAFE $
(Map p420; JM de la Barra 455; sandwiches CH$3500-7000; 9am-9:30pm Mon-Fri, 10am-9:30pm Sat & Sun; MBellas Artes) A teacup-sized cafe with some of the best brunches and *onces* (afternoon tea) in town, serving croissants and coffee, salmon-filled croissants, Parma ham and arugula on flaky green olive bread, and berry-drenched cheesecake.

Tambo PERUVIAN $$
(Map p420; Lastarria 65; mains CH$4000-7500; MUniversidad Católica) Occupying a prime spot along one of Lastarria's most scenic passages, this contemporary Peruvian eatery offers spicy twists on dishes and drinks that Chileans have since adopted – taste-test the

fantastic *ceviche* and delicious *maracuyá* (passion fruit)-spiked *pisco sours*.

Sur Patagónico CHILEAN **$$**
(Map p420; Lastarria 92; mains CH$3800-7500; Ⓜ Universidad Católica) Service is notoriously slow here, but the sidewalk tables on this well-traveled corner offer fantastic people-watching – enjoy the view with a cold Chilean microbrew in hand. The steamed mussels are ideal for sharing; more substantial Patagonian-inspired options range from mushroom risotto to steak and lamb seared on the *parrilla* (grill).

Emporio La Rosa ICE CREAM **$**
(Map p420; Merced 291; ice cream CH$900-1800, salads & sandwiches CH$2500-3900; ; Ⓜ Bellas Artes) Creamy, homemade ice cream with wild but oh-so-good flavors: Ulmo honey, chocolate basil and rose petal, to name a few.

BELLAVISTA

TOP CHOICE **Galindo** CHILEAN **$**
(Map p420; Dardignac 098; mains CH$2800-5800; Ⓜ Baquedano) This long-running local favorite is usually packed with noisy but appreciative crowds. It's easy to see why: unlike the precious restaurants around it, Galindo's all about hearty Chilean staples such as *chorrillana* (french fries topped with grilled onions and meat) washed down with freshly pulled pints or carafes of house wine.

Azul Profundo CHILEAN **$$**
(Map p420; Constitución 111; mains CH$7500-13,000; Ⓜ Baquedano) Step into this deep blue eatery – the telescope collection, maritime decor and vintage wooden bar no doubt inspired by Pablo Neruda's aesthetic – for fabulously fresh and inventive seafood. If you're up for sharing, order the delicious *ceviche* sampler.

El Caramaño CHILEAN **$$**
(Map p420; Purísima 257; mains CH$3200-7500; Ⓜ Baquedano) An extensive menu of well-prepared Chilean classics such as *machas a la parmesana* (razor clams au gratin), *merluza a la trauca* (hake baked in chorizo and tomato sauce) and *oreganato* (melted oregano-dusted goat cheese) keeps local families coming back here year after year.

BARRIO BRASIL

TOP CHOICE **El Café** CHILEAN **$**
(Map p412; cnr Av Brasil & Huérfanos; set lunch CH$3200-3500; Ⓜ Ricardo Cumming) Nearly as visually striking as this decorative pink-and-white corner building is the quaint interior with old-fashioned wooden tables and vintage tiled floors. Both the indoor and sidewalk tables are inviting for morning coffee, budget-friendly lunch specials or an afternoon beer overlooking Barrio Brasil's leafy central square.

TOP CHOICE **Peluquería Francesa** FRENCH **$$**
(Map p412; 682-5243; Compañía de Jesús 2789; mains CH$3300-7000; Ⓜ Ricardo Cumming) Although its official name is Boulevard Lavaud, locals call this restaurant 'Peluquería Francesa,' or 'French barbershop,' and that's exactly what this elegant corner building, dating from 1868, was originally used for. Decorated with quirky antiques (all available for purchase), the building still has turn-of-the-century charm; it gets crowded on weekend evenings with hip *santiaguinos* (locals) who come for the excellent French-inflected seafood dishes and funky atmosphere.

Platipus ASIAN **$**
(Map p412; Agustinas 2099; sushi CH$2900-5900; dinner Mon-Sat; ; Ⓜ Ricardo Cumming) Candles cast a warm glow on the exposed brick walls of this laid-back sushi spot. Don't come here in a hurry, but both the sushi and the *tablas* (boards of finger food) are worth the wait.

Las Vacas Gordas STEAKHOUSE **$$**
(Map p412; Cienfuegos 280; mains CH$4000-7000; Ⓜ Ricardo Cumming) Steak, pork, chicken and vegetables sizzle on the giant grill at the front of the clattering main dining area, then dead-pan old-school waiters cart it over to your table. This popular steakhouse is often packed, so come early.

PROVIDENCIA

TOP CHOICE **Liguria** MEDITERRANEAN **$$**
(334-4346; Av Pedro de Valdivia 47; mains CH$5200-8500; Ⓜ Pedro de Valdivia) A legend on the Santiago restaurant circuit, Liguria mixes equal measures of bar and bistro perfectly. Stewed rabbit or silverside in batter are chalked up on a blackboard, then dapper old-school waiters place them on the red-checked tablecloths with aplomb. The hugely popular **Bar: Liguria** (to 3am) is a drinking destination in itself. There's another branch in **Las Condes** (Luis Thayer Ojeda 019; Ⓜ Tobalaba).

Santiago - Centro

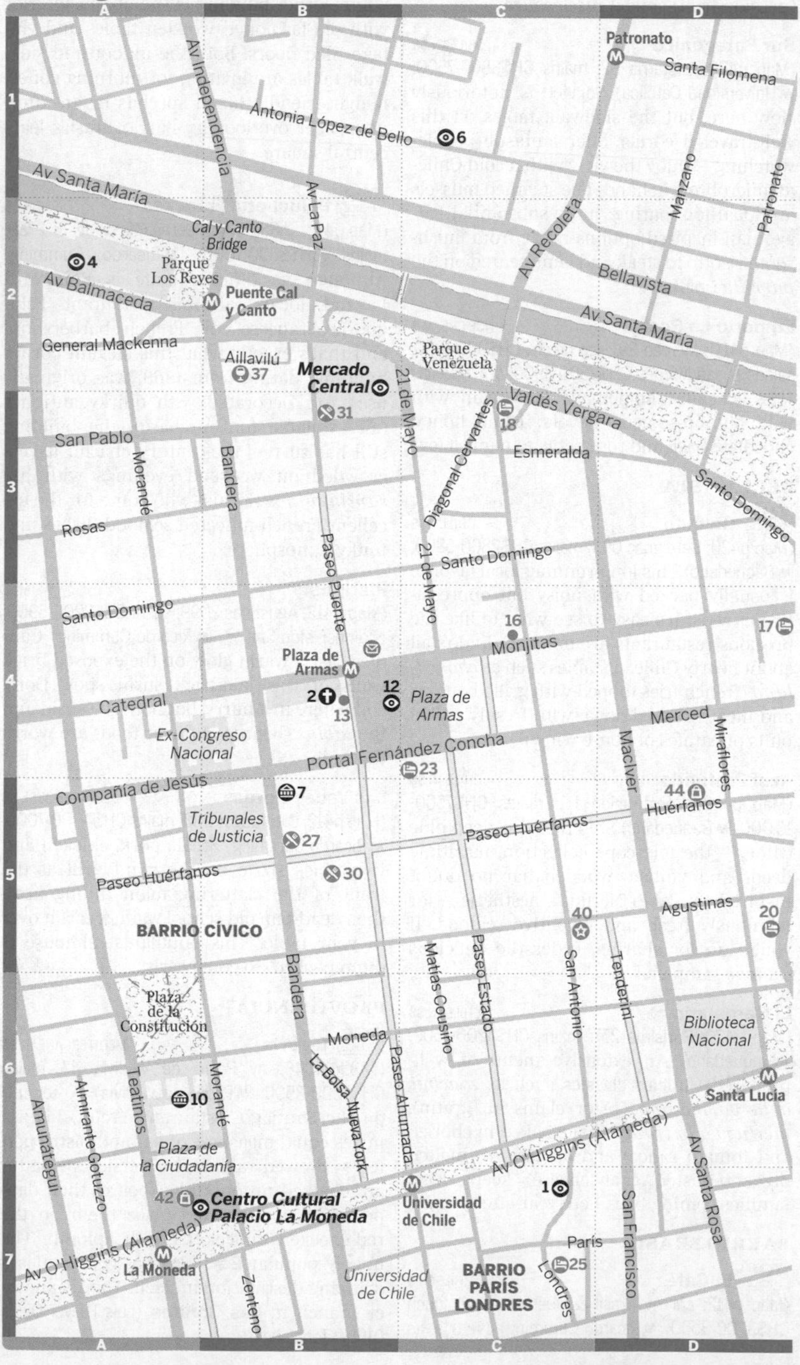

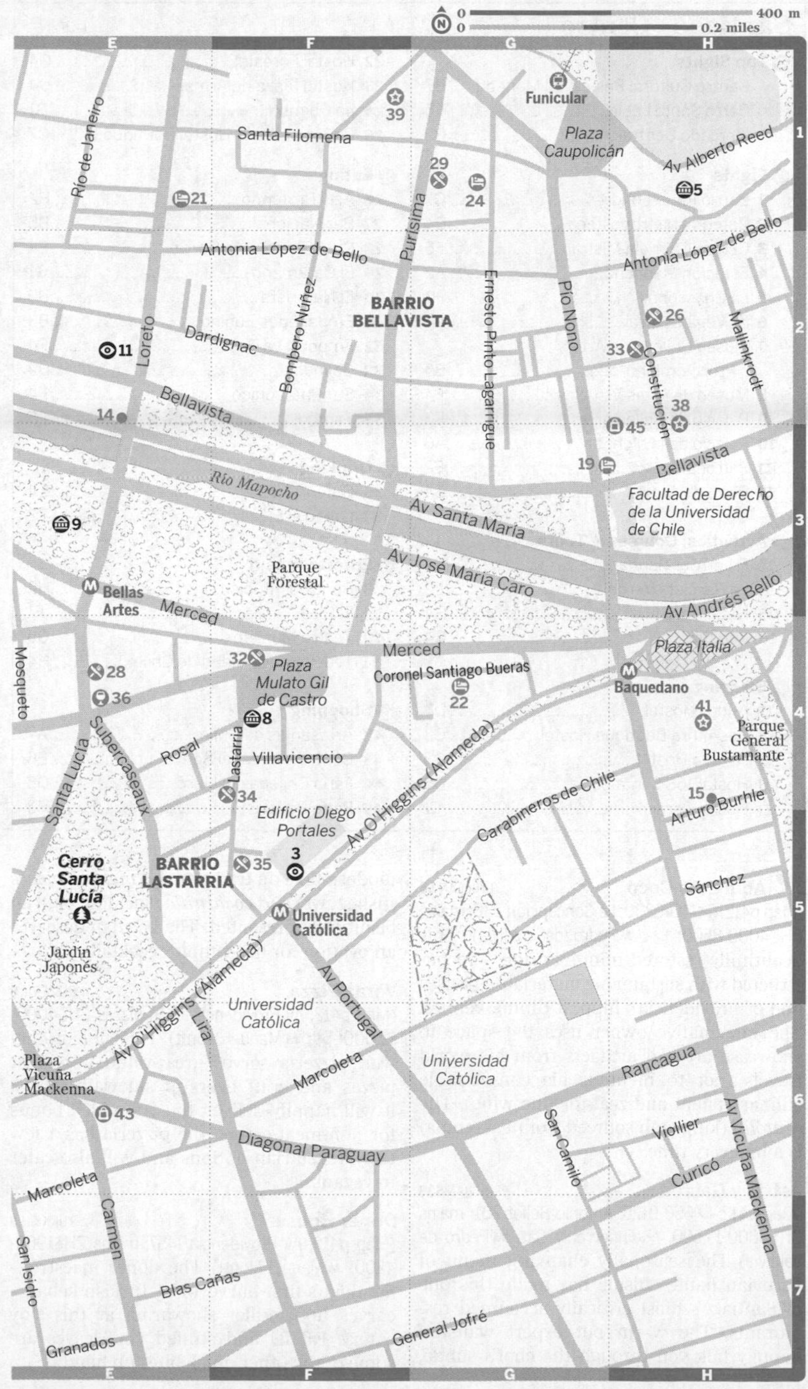
0 400 m
0 0.2 miles
E
F
G
H
Funicular
39
Santa Filomena
Plaza Caupolicán
Av Alberto Reed
Río de Janeiro
29
24
5
21
Purísima
Antonia López de Bello
Antonia López de Bello
BARRIO BELLAVISTA
Ernesto Pinto Lagarrigue
Pío Nono
26
Bombero Núñez
Malinkrodt
Dardignac
11
Loreto
33
Constitución
Bellavista
38
14
45
19
Bellavista
Río Mapocho
Facultad de Derecho de la Universidad de Chile
9
Av Santa María
Parque Forestal
Av José María Caro
Bellas Artes
Merced
Av Andrés Bello
Mosqueto
Merced
Plaza Italia
32
Plaza Mulato Gil de Castro
Coronel Santiago Bueras
28
Baquedano
36
22
8
41
Parque General Bustamante
Subercaseaux
Rosal
Lastarria
Villavicencio
Av O'Higgins (Alameda)
Santa Lucía
34
Carabineros de Chile
15
Arturo Burhle
Edificio Diego Portales
3
Cerro Santa Lucía
BARRIO LASTARRIA
35
Sánchez
Universidad Católica
Jardín Japonés
Av Portugal
Universidad Católica
Av O'Higgins (Alameda)
Lira
Plaza Vicuña Mackenna
Marcoleta
Universidad Católica
Rancagua
43
San Camilo
Viollier
Diagonal Paraguay
Curicó
Marcoleta
Av Vicuña Mackenna
Carmen
San Isidro
Blas Cañas
General Jofré
Granados
1
2
3
4
5
6
7

Santiago - Centro

Top Sights
Centro Cultural Palacio La Moneda B7
Cerro Santa Lucía E5
Mercado Central B2

Sights
1 Barrio París-Londres C7
2 Catedral Metropolitana B4
3 Centro Gabriela Mistral F5
4 Estación Mapocho A2
5 La Chascona H1
6 La Vega Central C1
7 Museo Chileno de Arte Precolombino B5
8 Museo de Artes Visuales F4
9 Palacio de Bellas Artes E3
10 Palacio de la Moneda A6
11 Patronato E2
12 Plaza de Armas B4

Activities, Courses & Tours
13 Free Tour Santiago B4
14 La Bicicleta Verde E2
15 Natalislang H4
16 Turistik C4

Sleeping
17 Andes Hostel D4
18 CasAltura Boutique Hostel C3
19 H Rado Hostel G3
20 Hostal 168 Santa Lucía D5
21 Hostal Caracol E1
22 Hostal Forestal G4
23 Hostel Plaza de Armas C4
24 La Chimba G1
25 Paris Londres - Hostel Boutique C7

Eating
26 Azul Profundo H2
27 Bar Nacional B5
28 Café Bistro de la Barra E4
29 El Caramaño G1
30 El Naturista B5
31 Empanadas Zunino B3
32 Emporio La Rosa F4
33 Galindo H2
34 Sur Patagónico F4
35 Tambo F5

Drinking
36 Catedral E4
37 La Piojera B2

Entertainment
38 Bar Constitución H2
39 El Clan F1
40 Teatro Municipal C5
41 Teatro Universidad de Chile H4

Shopping
42 Artesanías de Chile A7
43 Centro Artesanal Santa Lucía E6
44 Feria Chilena del Libro D5
45 Patio Bellavista H3

Aquí Está Coco CHILEAN **$$**
(Map p412; ☎410-6200; La Concepción 236; mains CH$4000-8500; ; Ⓜ Pedro de Valdivia) This beautifully restored mini-mansion – reconstructed with sustainable materials – houses one of Providencia's hippest dining venues. The imaginative owner uses the space to showcase art and artifacts from his world travels (not to mention his considerable culinary talent and zeal for fine wine). The *centolla* (king crab sourced from Patagonia) is a hit every time.

Astrid y Gastón PERUVIAN **$$$**
(Map p412; ☎650-9125; Antonio Bellet 201; mains CH$8000-13,500; ⊙dinner only Sat; Ⓜ Pedro de Valdivia) The seasonally changing menu of Peruvian haute cuisine has made this one of Santiago's most critically acclaimed restaurants. The warm but expert waitstaff happily talk you through the chef's subtle, modern take on traditional *ceviches*, *chupes* (fish stews) and *cochinillo* (suckling pig), all beautifully presented. The barman deserves an ovation for his complex cocktails.

Voraz Pizza PIZZERIA **$**
(Map p412; Av Providencia 1321; pizzas CH$4000-12,000; ; Ⓜ Manuel Montt) This hole-in-the-wall pizzeria serves great-value thin-crust pizzas and craft beers at sidewalk tables; it will happily deliver, too. An added bonus for non-meat-eaters: the pizzeria has a few tasty vegetarian options and will also cater to vegans.

Doner House TURKISH **$**
(Map p412; Av Providencia 1457; mains CH$1900-4200; Ⓜ Manuel Montt) The doner maestro – Santiago's first purveyor of Turkish kebab – carves up a killer shawarma at this tiny eatery. Falafel and stuffed vine leaves are some of the other quick bites on hand.

LAS CONDES, BARRIO EL GOLF & VITACURA

Tiramisú PIZZERIA $$

(Isidora Goyenechea 3141, Las Condes; pizzas CH$3500-7800; ; MTobalaba) Bright murals, rough-hewn tables and cheerful red-checked cloths set the tone at this busy pizzeria that's perennially popular with locals. You'll spend more time choosing one of the myriad thin-crust pizzas than wolfing it down.

Café Melba CAFE $

(Don Carlos 2898; sandwiches CH$2900, mains CH$4000-7500; ; MTobalaba) Eggs and bacon, muffins, bagels and gigantic cups of coffee are some of the all-day breakfast offerings at this cozy cafe run by a New Zealand expat. Well-stuffed sandwiches and heartier dishes such as green fish curry or pork medallions are popular with lunching local finance workers, but the specialty here is leisurely brunch.

Drinking

Catedral COCKTAIL BAR

(Map p420; JM de la Barra & Merced, Barrio Lastarria; MBellas Artes) Classy Catedral has a menu that goes way beyond bar snacks – anyone for a glass of champagne with violet crème brûlée? The minimal two-tone couches, smooth wood paneling and mellow music here are particularly popular with 20- and 30-somethings. It's just one of the stylish offerings of the restaurateurs behind the Opera restaurant; both are located in the same gorgeously restored corner building.

La Piojera BAR

(Map p420; Aillavilú 1030, Centro; MPuente Cal y Canto) Saved from developers by protests from its loyal clientele – including presidents and poets – this bare-bones drinking den is the real deal. Noisy regulars pack the sticky tables, which are crammed with glass tumblers of the two house specialties: *chicha* (sweet Chilean cider) and the earth-moving (or gut-wrenching) *terremoto*, a potent mix of wine and ice cream.

Red2One COCKTAIL BAR

(Isidora Goyenechea 3000, Las Condes; ; MEl Golf) Look past the awkward name: the swanky rooftop bar at the W Hotel is one of the city's most exclusive watering holes and worth the trip. The cool minimalist design and beautiful people are almost enough to distract you from the jaw-dropping view of the snow-capped Andes in the distance. Be here at sunset – if you can squeeze in.

Santo Remedio COCKTAIL BAR

(Map p412; Román Díaz 152, Providencia; MManuel Montt) Strictly speaking, this low-lit, high-ceilinged old house is a restaurant, and a romantic one at that. But it's the bar action people really come for: powerful, well-mixed cocktails and regular live DJs keep the 20- and 30-something crowds happy.

Eurohappy BAR

(Map p412; Maturana 516, Barrio Brasil; MRicardo Cumming) Over 400 types of beer – including local artisanal and microbrewed options – are expertly poured by Santiago's only beer sommelier.

Baires BAR

(Map p412; Brasil 255, Barrio Brasil; MRicardo Cumming) Technically, it's a 'sushi club,' but the nightlife at Baires is what brings in the crowds. The terrace tables fill up quickly, even on weeknights; there's an encyclopedia-sized drink list, and DJs get going upstairs on weekends.

Entertainment

Note that Santiago's excellent cultural centers – especially GAM (p413), Centro Cultural Palacio La Moneda (p411) and Estación Mapocho (p411) – are some of the city's best venues to catch live music, performing arts and entertainment. Admission to cultural events is often free: check the centers' websites or www.estoy.cl for listings.

Live Music

TOP CHOICE **El Huaso Enrique** TRADITIONAL MUSIC

(www.elhuasoenrique.cl; Maipú 462, Barrio Yungay; MQuinta Normal) On weekend nights, watch proud Chileans hit the dance floor at this traditional *cueca* venue, where they perform the national dance – a playful, handkerchief-wielding ritual that imitates the courtship of a rooster and hen – to the sounds of traditional live music.

Bar Constitución LIVE MUSIC

(Map p420; www.barconstitucion.cl; Constitución 62, Bellavista; MBaquedano) Bellavista's coolest nightspot hosts live bands and DJs nightly – the bar's eclectic (but infallible) tastes include electroclash, garage, nu-folk, house and more, so check the website for upcoming shows.

Teatro Caupolicán LIVE MUSIC

(www.teatrocaupolican.cl; San Diego 850; MParque O'Higgins) Latin American rockers who have played this stage include far-out Mexicans Café Tacuba, Argentinian electro-tango band Bajofondo and Oscar-winning Uruguayan Jorge Drexler. International acts such as Garbage and Snow Patrol also play concert dates here.

La Batuta LIVE MUSIC
(www.batuta.cl; Jorge Washington 52, Nuñoa; MPlaza Egaña) Enthusiastic crowds jump to ska, *patchanka* (think Manu Chao), *cumbia chilombiana*, rockabilly and surf – at La Batuta, anything alternative goes.

Nightclubs

Don't even think of showing up to any of these places before midnight. Note that many close their doors in summer and follow the crowds to the beach.

El Clan CLUB
(Map p420; www.elclan.cl; Bombero Núñez 363, Bellavista; from 11pm Tue-Sat; MBaquedano) The name's short for 'El Clandestino,' a throwback from this small club's undercover days. A small crew of resident DJs keep the 20-something crowds going – expect anything from '80s to house, R&B, funk or techno.

Mito Urbano CLUB
(Map p412; www.mitourbano.cl; Manuel Montt 350, Providencia; MManuel Montt) At this fun-loving nightclub, disco balls cast light on the good-looking crowds dancing to vintage hits and Chilean pop. Check the schedule for salsa classes, karaoke, live jazz, and other promotions that aim to bring people in before midnight.

Performing Arts

Teatro Municipal THEATER
(Map p420; 463-1000; www.municipal.cl; Agustinas 794, Centro; box office 10am-7pm Mon-Fri, 10am-2pm Sat & Sun; MSanta Lucía) This exquisite neoclassical building is the most prestigious performing-arts venue in the city. It's home to the Ballet de Santiago and also hosts world-class opera, tango and classical music performances.

Teatro Universidad de Chile THEATER
(Map p420; 634-5295; http://teatro.uchile.cl; Providencia 043, Centro; MBaquedano) The Orquesta Sinfónica de Chile and Ballet Nacional de Chile are two high-profile companies based at this excellent theater.

Sports

Estadio Nacional SOCCER
(National Stadium; 238-8102; Av Grecia 2001, Nuñoa; MIrarrázaval) Chileans are a pretty calm lot – until they step into a soccer stadium. The most dramatic matches are against rivals such as Peru or Argentina, when 'Chi-Chi-Chi-Lay-Lay-Lay' reverberates through the Estadio Nacional. Equally impassioned are the *hinchas* (fans) of Santiago's first-division soccer teams such as Colo Colo, Universidad de Chile and Universidad Católica.

Club Hípico de Santiago HORSE RACING
(www.clubhipico.cl; Av Blanco Encalada 2540; MParque O'Higgins) Horse racing happens at the grand Club Hípico de Santiago, where views of the Andes compete for your attention with the action on the track.

Shopping

Your best bet for a unique Chilean souvenir is a traditional artisan-made craft (look for alpaca shawls, lapis lazuli, silver jewelry, copper goods and fine leatherwork) or an accessory or garment created by a young designer. For clothes, shoes and department store goods, hit downtown's pedestrian streets such as Ahumada; for even cheaper goods, cross the river to Patronato. Shop for secondhand ski gear and used books at the shops around Providencia's Manuel Montt metro station.

Santiago's posh super-malls, a long haul from the center and often more popular with locals than visitors, include **Portal La Dehesa** (Av La Dehesa 1445, La Barnechea), **Parque Arauco** (Av Kennedy 5413; MManquehue) and **Alto Las Condes** (Av Kennedy 9001, Las Condes).

TOP CHOICE **Artesanías de Chile** ARTS & CRAFTS
(Map p420; Plaza de la Ciudadanía 26; 10am-6pm Mon-Sat; MLa Moneda) Not only do this foundation's jewelry, carvings, ceramics and woolen goods sell at reasonable prices, most of what you pay goes to the artisan who made them. This branch is located inside the Centro Cultural Palacio La Moneda (p411); look for more locations in Santiago and throughout Chile.

Galería Drugstore FASHION
(Av Providencia 2124, Providencia; 10:30am-8pm Mon-Sat; MLos Leones) Head to this cool four-story independent shopping center for clothes no one back home will have – it's home to the boutiques of several tiny, up-

CHILENISMOS 101

Chilean Spanish fell off the wagon: it is slurred, sing-song and peppered with expressions unintelligible to the rest of the Spanish-speaking world. *¿Cachay?* (You get it?) often punctuates a sentence, as does the ubiquitous *pues*, said as *'po.' Sípo*, all clattered together, actually means, 'well, yes.' Country lingo is firmly seeded in this former agrarian society, which refers to guys as *cabros* (goats), complains *'es un cacho'* ('it's a horn,' meaning a sticking point) and goes to the *carrete* to *carretear* ('wagon,' meaning party/to party). Lovers of lingo should check out John Brennan's *How to Survive in the Chilean Jungle*, available in Santiago's English-language bookstores. *¿Cachay?*

and-coming designers, arty bookstores and cafes.

Patio Bellavista SHOPPING CENTER
(Map p420; Pío Nono 73, Bellavista; ⏲11am-10pm; Ⓜ Baquedano) Posh contemporary crafts, plus leather goods, weavings and jewelry, sell at premium prices at this courtyard shopping center.

Centro Artesanal Santa Lucía ARTS & CRAFTS
(Map p420; cnr Carmen & Diagonal Paraguay, Centro; Ⓜ Santa Lucía) This artisan market sells lapis lazuli jewelry, hand-woven sweaters, shiny copperware and good-looking pottery.

Persa Bío Bío MARKET
(Franklin Market; cnr Bío Bío & Isidro; ⏲9am-7pm Sat & Sun; Ⓜ Franklin) Antiques, collectibles and fascinating old junk fill the cluttered stalls at this market between Bío Bío and Franklin. The origins of some items – such as secondhand bikes – may be a little sketchy, but sifting through it all is loads of fun.

El Mundo del Vino WINE
(Isidora Goyenechea 3000, Las Condes; Ⓜ Tobalaba) This revamped location of the high-end wine chain features 6000 bottles from around the world – or from just a short drive away in the Colchagua Valley – at the hip W Hotel.

Feria Chilena del Libro BOOKS
(Map p420; Paseo Huérfanos 623, Lastarria; Ⓜ Bellas Artes) Santiago's best-stocked bookstore, with some English paperbacks. Look for several more bookstores on the same block.

ℹ Information

Dangers & Annoyances

Santiago is relatively safe, but petty crime exists. Be on your guard around the Plaza de Armas, Mercado Central and Cerro San Cristóbal in particular. Organized groups of pickpockets sometimes target drinkers along Pío Nono in Bellavista, and Barrio Brasil's smaller streets can be dodgy after dark.

Emergency

Ambulance (☎131)
Fire Department (☎132)
Police (☎133)

Internet Access

Internet cafes are everywhere; expect to pay CH$400 to CH$1000 per hour. Many are located inside *centros de llamados* (call centers), where you can also make local and long-distance phone calls. You'll also find wi-fi in lots of hostels, hotels, cafes and restaurants.

Medical Services

Clínica Alemana (☎210-1111; www.alemana.cl; Av Vitacura 5951, Vitacura; Ⓜ Escuela Militar) One of the best – and most expensive – private hospitals in town.
Hospital de Urgencia Asistencia Pública (☎568-1100; www.huap.cl; Av Portugal 125; ⏲24hr; Ⓜ Universidad Católica) Santiago's main emergency room.

Money

ATMs *(redbanc)* are found throughout the city.
Cambios Afex (www.afex.cl; Agustinas 1050, Centro; ⏲9am-6pm Mon-Fri, 10am-2pm Sat; Ⓜ Universidad de Chile) Reliable exchange office.

Post

Post Office (Catedral 987; ⏲8am-10pm Mon-Fri, to 6pm Sat; Ⓜ Plaza de Armas)

Tourist Information

Conaf (Corporación Nacional Forestal; ☎663-0000; www.conaf.cl; Bulnes 285, Centro; ⏲9:30am-5:30pm Mon-Thu, 9:30am-4:30pm Fri; Ⓜ Toesca) Information on all of the parks and reserves, with some topographic maps to photocopy.
Sernatur (☎731-8310; www.chile.travel; Av Providencia 1550; ⏲9am-8pm Mon-Fri, 9am-2pm Sat; wi-fi; Ⓜ Manuel Montt) Santiago's high-tech tourist information office gives out maps, brochures and advice, reserves winery visits,

lists cultural events, and offers free wi-fi and interactive kiosks where you can learn about Chile's regions.

Getting There & Away

Air

Aeropuerto Internacional Arturo Merino Benítez (☎601-9001) is in Pudahuel, 20km northwest of downtown Santiago. Domestic carrier offices are **LAN** (☎600-526-2000; www.lan.com) and **Sky** (☎353-3100; Huérfanos 815, Centro; Ⓜ Plaza de Armas). Airfares can vary widely; you'll usually find better deals through the latter.

Sertur Student Flight Center (☎577-1200; www.sertur.cl; Hernando de Aguirre 201, Oficina 401, Providencia; Ⓜ Tobalaba) has bargains on air tickets.

Bus

A bewildering number of bus companies connect Santiago to the rest of Chile, Argentina and Peru. Services leave from several different terminals; make sure you know where you're going.

Santiago has four main bus terminals, from which buses leave for northern, central and southern destinations. The largest and most reputable bus companies are Tur Bus and Pullman Bus.

Terminal San Borja (☎776-0645; Alameda 3250; Ⓜ Estación Central) At the end of the shopping mall alongside the main railway station. The ticket booths are divided by region, with destinations prominently displayed. Destinations are from Arica down to the *cordillera* (mountain range) around Santiago.

Terminal de Buses Alameda (☎776-2424; cnr Alameda & Jotabeche; Ⓜ Universidad de Santiago) Home to **Tur Bus** (☎600-660-6600; www.turbus.cl) and **Pullman Bus** (☎600-320-3200; www.pullman.cl), both going to a wide variety of destinations north, south and on the coast.

Terminal de Buses Sur (☎376-1750; Alameda 3850; Ⓜ Universidad de Santiago) Has the most services to the central coast, international and southern destinations (the Lakes District and Chiloé).

PLAN AHEAD

No, you won't arrive in Santiago by sea – but **Navimag's** (☎442-3120; www.navimag.cl; Av El Bosque Norte 0440, Piso 11; ⏲9am-6:30pm Mon-Fri; Ⓜ Tobalaba) Santiago office is useful when you need to book ahead for ferry tickets in Chilean Patagonia.

Terminal Los Héroes (Tucapel Jiménez; Ⓜ Los Héroes) Near the Alameda in the Centro, this one is much more convenient and less chaotic. Buses mainly head north along the Carretera Panamericana (Pan-American Hwy), but a few go to Argentina and south to Temuco.

Fares between important destinations are listed, with approximate journey times and one-way fares for 'semi-cama' (comfortable, partly reclining seats) listed in the bus-fares table. Note that fares vary dramatically and spike during holidays; if you're not traveling at a peak time, you may pay significantly less than the fares published here. You'll pay more for fully reclining 'cama' seats on longer trips.

DESTINATION	COST (CH$)	DURATION (HR)
Antofagasta	39,000	19
Arica	49,000	30
Buenos Aires (Argentina)	50,000	22
Chillán	13,000	5
Concepción	15,000	6½
Copiapó	28,500	12
Iquique	48,500	25
La Serena	16,000	7
Mendoza (Argentina)	15,000	8
Osorno	29,000	12
Pucón	14,700	11
Puerto Montt	33,000	12
San Pedro de Atacama	47,200	23
Talca	6000	3½
Temuco	29,000	9½
Valdivia	25,500	10-11
Valparaíso	5000	2
Viña del Mar	5000	2¼

Train

Chile's slick intercity train system, **Empresa de Ferrocarriles del Estado** (☎600-585-5000; www.efe.cl), operates TerraSur trains out of **Estación Central** (Alameda 3170; Ⓜ Estación Central). Train travel is generally slightly slower and more expensive than going by bus, but wagons are well maintained and services are generally punctual.

The TerraSur rail service connects Santiago three to five times daily with San Fernando (CH$5400, 1½ hours), Curicó (CH$5600, 2¼ hours), Talca (CH$5600, three hours) and Chillán (CH$10,800, 5½ hours). Prices vary slightly according to availability.

GETTING INTO TOWN

Two cheap, efficient bus services connect the airport with the city center: **TurBus Aeropuerto** (www.turbus.cl; one way CH$1700) runs every 15 minutes between 6am to midnight, stopping at the Universidad de Santiago metro station. **Buses Centropuerto** (www.centro puerto.cl; one way CH$1400; ⏲6am-11:30pm, every 10-15min) provides a similar service to and from the Los Héroes and Estación Central metro stations. Both buses leave from right outside the arrivals hall; both also stop at the Pajaritos metro station. The trip takes about 40 minutes.

Use caution with taxis: although the ride to the city center should cost CH$16,000, drivers are famous for ripping tourists off. A safer bet for door-to-door transfers is minibus shuttle **Transvip** (www.transvip.cl; one way CH$5500-7000); you can pay with cash or a credit card at the airport desk inside the arrivals hall.

ℹ Getting Around

Bus

Transantiago (www.transantiago.cl) buses are a cheap and convenient way of getting around town, especially when the metro shuts down at night. Green-and-white buses operate in central Santiago or connect two separate areas of town. Each suburb has color-coded local buses and an identifying letter that precedes route numbers (for example, routes in Las Condes and Vitacura start with a C and are serviced by orange vehicles).

Buses generally follow major roads and stops are spaced far apart, often coinciding with metro stations. You can only pay for bus rides using a Bip! (a contact-free card you wave over sensors) – the card costs CH$1350 and one-way fares range from CH$560 to CH$670, depending on what time of day you're traveling. Bip! cards are available for purchase in almost all metro stations, but cannot be purchased on buses. A full list of locations selling Bip! cards is on the Transantiago website.

On Sundays and holidays, take advantage of the new **Circuito Cultural Santiago** (⏲10am-6:30pm Sun & holidays), a bus loop tour that passes by the city's main attractions (museums, cultural centers) starting at Estación Central. You use your Bip! card to pay for one regular bus fare, and the driver will give you a bracelet that allows you to board the circuit's buses as many times as you like. The buses are clearly marked 'Circuito Cultural.'

Car

Renting a car to drive around Santiago is stressful – if you must have your own set of wheels, the major agencies have offices at the airport. For more detailed information on driving and parking in Santiago, check out the helpful English-language section at **Car Rental in Chile** (www.mietwagen-in-chile.de); it will also rent you a vehicle.

Metro

The city's ever-expanding **metro** (www.metro santiago.cl; ⏲6am-11pm Mon-Fri, 6:30am-10:30pm Sat, 8am-10:30pm Sun) is an efficient way to get around. The **Transantiago website** (www.transantiago.cl) has downloadable route maps and a point-to-point journey planner. You'll need the same Bip! card that you use for the bus. You pay a nonrefundable CH$1350 for the card, and then charge it with as much money as you want; each one-way fare ranges from CH$560 to CH$670 and allows you two hours in the system, including multiple transfers.

Taxi

Santiago has abundant metered taxis, all black with yellow roofs. Flag-fall costs CH$250, then it's CH$100 per 200m (or per minute of waiting time). It's generally safe to hail cabs in the street.

AROUND SANTIAGO

National parks, sleepy villages, snowy slopes (in winter) and high-altitude hiking trails (in summer) all make easy escapes from the city.

Valle de Maipo

Just south of the center of Santiago lies Valle de Maipo, a major wine region specializing in big-bodied reds. You can go it alone: the wineries listed here are within 1½ hours of the city center on public transport. But if you'd rather hit the wine circuit with a knowledgeable guide, try the specialized tours at **Uncorked Wine Tours** (☎981-6242; www.uncorked.cl; half-/full-day tour US$135/195) – an English-speaking guide will take you to three wineries, and a lovely lunch is included. Also recommended is the winery bike tour with La Bicicleta Verde (p416), in which

SKI RESORTS AROUND SANTIAGO

Chilean ski and snowboard resorts are open from June to October, with lower rates early and late in the season. Most ski areas are above 3300m and treeless; the runs are long, the season is long and the snow is deep and dry. Three major resorts are barely an hour from the capital, while the fourth is about two hours away on the Argentine border.

Santiago's four most popular ski centers – El Colorado, Farellones, La Parva and Valle Nevado – are clustered in three valleys in the Mapocho river canyon, hence their collective name, **Tres Valles**. Although they're only 30km to 40km northeast of Santiago, the traffic-clogged road up can be slow going. All prices given here are for weekends and high season (usually early July to mid-August). Outside that time, there are hefty mid-week discounts on both ski passes and hotels. The predominance of drag lifts means that lines get long during the winter holidays, but otherwise crowds here are bearable. Ask about combination tickets if you're planning on skiing at multiple resorts.

El Colorado and **Farellones**, located approximately 40km east of the capital, are close enough together to be considered one destination, with 18 lifts and 22 runs from 2430m to 3330m in elevation. The eating and after-ski scenes are scanty here, so locals tend just to come up for the day. **Centro de Ski El Colorado** (☎355-7722; www.elcolorado.cl) has the latest information on snow and slope conditions.

Only 4km from the Farellones ski resort, exclusive **La Parva** is oriented toward posh Chilean families and features 30 runs from 2662m to 3630m. For the latest information, contact **Centro de Ski La Parva** (☎964-2100; www.laparva.cl).

Another 14km beyond Farellones, the vast **Valle Nevado** (☎477-7700; www.vallenevado.com) boasts almost 7000 acres of skiable domain – the largest in South America. It's also the best maintained of Santiago's resorts and has the most challenging runs, ranging from 2805m to 3670m, and some up to 3km in length.

In a class of its own, the ultrasteep **Portillo**, 145km northeast of the capital on the Argentine border, is one of Chile's favorite ski resorts. The US, Austrian and Italian national teams use it as a base for summer training and the 200km/h speed barrier was first broken here. Portillo has 14 lifts and 35 runs, from 2590m to 3310m; the longest run measures 2.4km. The on-site **Inca Lodge** (☎361-7000; www.skiportillo.com; dm per week full board from US$990) accommodates young travelers in dorms. Tickets are included in the price and low season offers some good deals. Contact **Centro de Ski Portillo** (☎263-0606; www.skiportillo.com) for the latest details.

Shuttles to the resorts abound. **KL Adventure** (☎217-9101; www.kladventure.com; round trip to Tres Valles CH$15,000, with hotel pick-up CH$25,000) goes to Tres Valles at 8am and returns at 5pm. It also rents equipment and runs transportation to Portillo (CH$25,000). **SkiTotal** (☎246-0156; www.skitotal.cl) rents equipment and arranges cheaper transportation (round trip CH$10,000 to CH$13,000 to Tres Valles, CH$20,000 to Portillo) to the resorts, with 8am departures and 5pm returns.

you'll be pedaling around the countryside to wineries within 10km of Santiago.

Worthwhile wineries include **Viña Cousiño Macul** (☎351-4100; www.cousinomacul.com; Av Quilín 7100, Peñalolen; incl 1 varietal & 1 reserva CH$8000; ⏲tours in English 11am, noon, 3pm & 4pm Mon-Fri, 11am & noon Sat), where tours take in the production process as well as the underground *bodega* (a storage area for wine), which was built in 1872. It is a 2¼km walk or a quick taxi ride from the metro.

Set at the foot of the Andes is the lovely **Viña Aquitania** (☎791-4500; www.aquitania.cl; Av Consistorial 5090; standard tour & tasting CH$7000; ⏲by appointment only 9am-5pm Mon-Fri). From Grecia metro station (Line 4), take bus D07 south from bus stop 6 and get off at the intersection of Av Los Presidentes and Consistorial (you need a Bip! card). Aquitania is 150m south.

At the boutique vineyard of **Viña Almaviva** (☎470-0225; www.almavivawinery.com; Av Santa Rosa 821, Paradero 45, Puente Alto; tours incl 1 pour US$80; ⏲by appointment only 9am-5pm Mon-Fri), high-end tastings are available by reservation only. Bus 207 from Estación Mapocho runs past the entrance, about 1km from the winery building. It's the more sophisticated sister of **Viña Concha y Toro** (☎476-5269; www.conchaytoro.com; Virginia Subercaseaux 210,

Pirque; standard tour & tasting CH$8000; ⏰10am-5pm) in Pirque, where you can see winemaking on a vast scale on one of the winery's mass-market tours. To get to Pirque, take the Santiago metro to Plaza de Puente Alto, the end of line 4. Then catch a blue minibus (labeled 'Pirque' in the window) and tell the driver you want to go to Plaza Pirque or Concha y Toro.

Other Maipo wineries include **Viña Santa Rita** (☎362-2594; www.santarita.com; Camino Padre Hurtado 0695, Alto Jahuel), **Viña de Martino** (☎819-2959; www.demartino.cl; Manuel Rodríguez 229, Isla de Maipo) and **Viña Undurraga** (☎372-2850; www.undurraga.cl; Camino a Melipilla, Km 34, Talagante).

Cajón del Maipo

Rich greenery lines the steep, rocky walls of this stunning gorge, which the Río Maipo flows through. Starting only 25km southeast of Santiago, it's popular on weekends with *santiaguinos*. November through March is rafting season, ski bums and bunnies flock here June through September, and horse riding is popular year-round.

The river itself is made up of a series of mostly Class III rapids with very few calm areas – indeed, rafters are often tossed into the water. Try a **rafting trip** (CH$21,000, 2-3hr) from the private nature reserve and working horse ranch **Cascada de las Animas** (☎861-1303; www.cascada.net; Camino al Volcan 31087, Casilla 57, San Alfonso). Led by experienced guides, and including helmets, wetsuits and life jackets, the adventure takes in some lovely gorges before ending up in San Jose de Maipo. Promotions and packages often include lunch and use of the inviting swimming pool; you can also use the shaded picnic facilities or have a meal at the treehouse-like restaurant perched high on a bluff over the river. You can arrange any number of hiking, riding and rafting options here, too.

Many opt to spend the night at Cascada de las Animas – choose between **wood cabins** (for 3/6/8 people CH$60,000/95,000/120,000) with log fires and well-equipped kitchens, or smaller **guest rooms** (d with/without bathroom CH$40,000/25,000). Alternatively, pitch your tent in the shady **campsite** (per person CH$10,000).

Only 93km from Santiago, 3000-hectare **Monumento Natural El Morado** (www.conaf.cl; adult/child CH$2000/1000; ⏰8:30am-2:30pm Oct-Apr) rewards hikers with views of 4490m Cerro El Morado at Laguna El Morado, a two-hour hike from the humble hot springs of Baños Morales. There are free campsites around the lake.

Refugio Lo Valdés (☎099-220-8525; www.refugiolovaldes.com; Refugio Alemán, Ruta G-25 Km 77; dm CH$15,000, d incl breakfast CH$48,000), a mountain chalet with simple, wood-clad rooms and a stunning view over the Cajón, is a popular weekend destination. The on-site restaurant is renowned for its hearty meals and *onces*. Eleven kilometers from here is **Baños Colina** (☎02-2985-2609; www.termasvalledecolina.cl; entrance per person incl campsite CH$8000, hostel d CH$30,000), where terraced hot springs overlook the valley.

To get to San Alfonso from Santiago, take metro line 4 to the Las Mercedes terminal, then hop onto bus 72 (CH$550) – or any bus that says 'San Alfonso' on the window. Some lines continue to Baños Morales from January to March. If you're going to Cascada de las Animas, the ride takes about ½ hours – ask the driver to drop you off at the entrance to the reserve. Cascada de las Animas also runs private van transportation to and from Santiago (one to two people round-trip CH$70,000).

Valparaíso

☎032 / POP 282,500

Pablo Neruda said it best: 'Valparaíso, how absurd you are… you haven't combed your hair, you've never had time to get dressed, life has always surprised you.' But Neruda wasn't the only artist to fall for Valparaíso's unexpected charms. Poets, painters and would-be philosophers have long been drawn to the frenetic port city. Along with the ever-shifting population of sailors, dockworkers and prostitutes, they've endowed gritty and gloriously spontaneous Valparaíso with an edgy air of 'anything goes.' Adding to the charm is the spectacular faded beauty of its chaotic *cerros* (hills), a maze of steep, sinuous streets, alleys and *escaleras* (stairways) piled high with crumbling mansions.

History

The leading merchant port along the Cape Horn and Pacific Ocean routes, Valparaíso was the stopover for foreign vessels, including whalers, and the export point of Chilean wheat destined for the California gold rush. Foreign merchants and capital made it Chile's financial powerhouse. Its decline began with the 1906 earthquake and the

Valparaíso

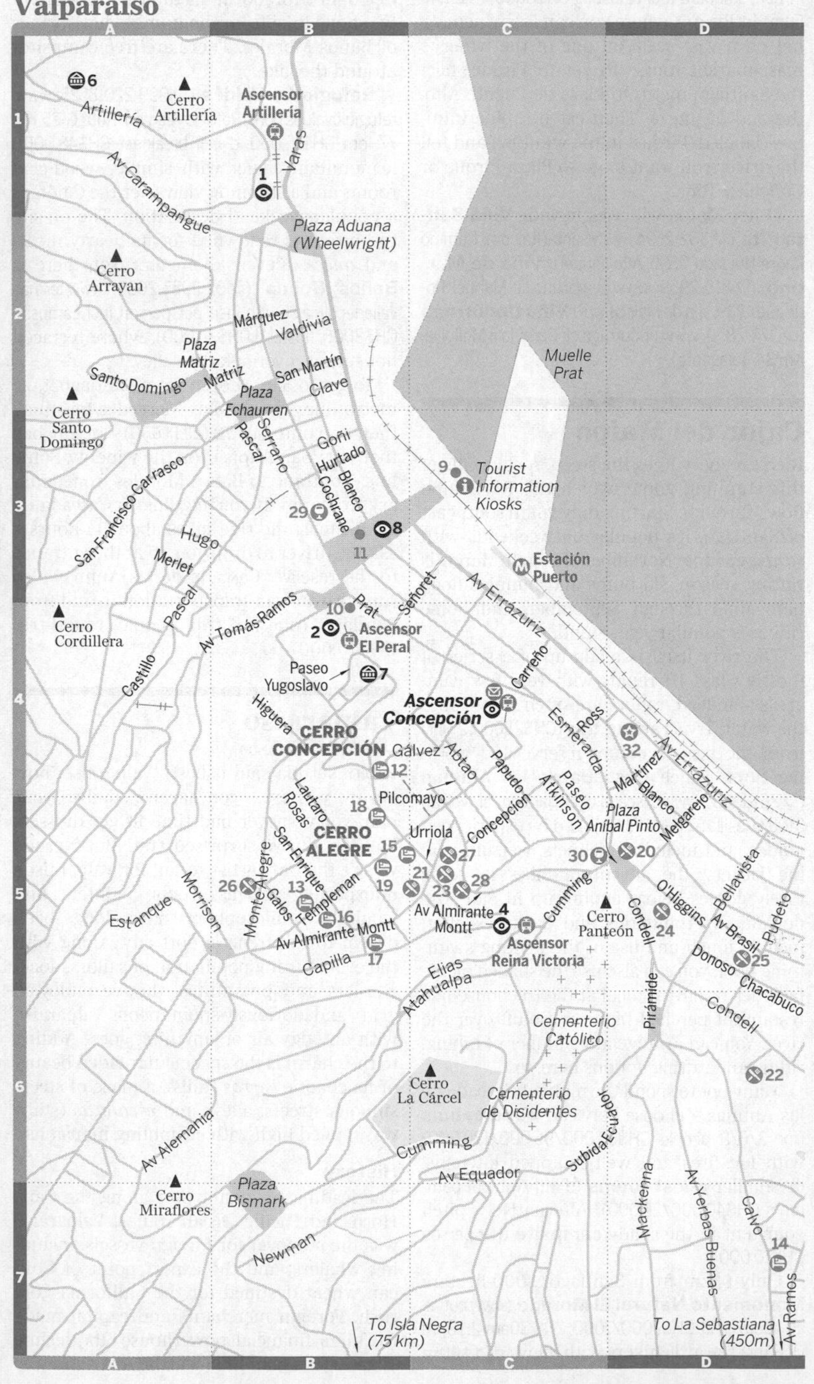

CHILE VALPARAÍSO

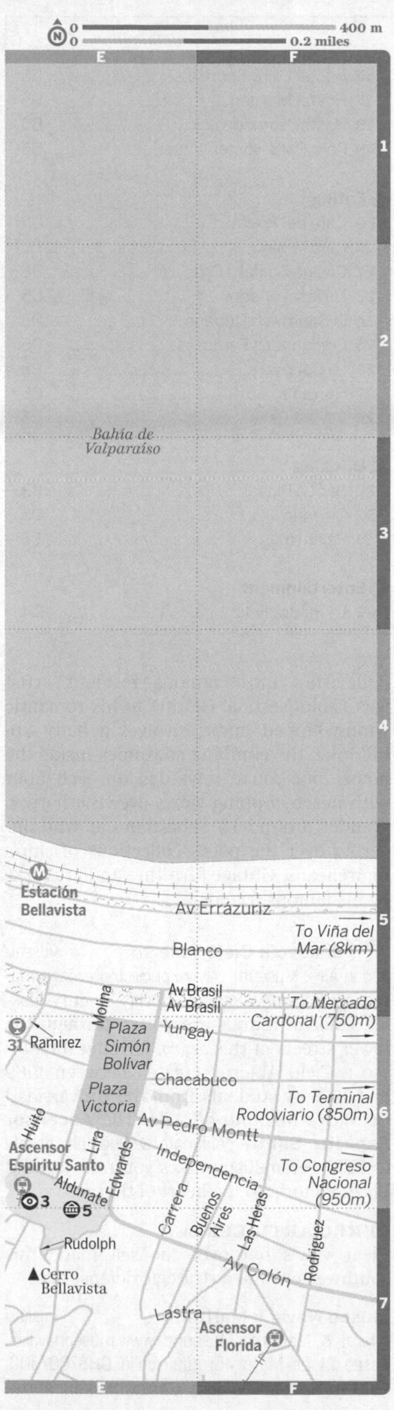

opening of the Panama Canal in 1914. Today 'Valpo' is back on the nautical charts as a cruise-ship stop-off, and Chile's growing fruit exports have also boosted the port. More significantly, the city has been Chile's legislative capital since 1990 and was voted the cultural capital in 2003. Unesco sealed the deal by giving it World Heritage status, prompting tourism to soar.

Sights & Activities

Don't take it from us, take it from Unesco: the whole of Valparaíso is a sight worth seeing. The best thing to do here is just walk the city streets and ride some of the 15 rattling *ascensores* (funiculars) built between 1883 and 1916; they crank you up into the hills and meandering back alleys. Wherever you wander, have your camera at the ready: Valpo brings out the photographer in most people.

EL PLAN & EL PUERTO

Valparaíso's flat commercial zone, El Plan, isn't as atmospheric as the hills that rise above it, but it contains a few monuments. In the port neighborhood, crumbling stone facades hint of times gone by. Start your wanderings at Muelle Prat, at the foot of Plaza Sotomayor, where you can hop on a quick **harbor tour** (Muelle Prat; 20min tour per person CH$1500-2000, 1hr tour on private boat CH$12,000; 9:30am-6:30pm).

Plaza Sotomayor PLAZA

The naval heart of the city is dominated by the palatial, blue **Edificio de la Comandancia Naval** (Naval Command Building). In the middle of the square lies the **Monumento a los Héroes de Iquique**, a subterranean mausoleum paying tribute to Chile's naval martyrs.

Congreso Nacional HISTORIC BUILDING

(cnr Av Pedro Montt & Rawson) One of Valpo's only modern landmarks is the controversial Congreso Nacional. Its roots lie in Pinochet's presidency both literally and legislatively: it was built on one of his boyhood homes and mandated by his 1980 constitution (which moved the legislature away from Santiago).

CERROS CONCEPCIÓN & ALEGRE

Sighing on every corner quickly becomes a habit on these two hills, whose steep cobbled streets are lined by traditional 19th-century houses with painted corrugated-iron facades that form a vivid patchwork of colors.

Valparaíso

Top Sights

Ascensor Concepción C4

Sights

1 Ascensor Artillería B1
2 Ascensor El Peral B4
3 Ascensor Espíritu Santo E6
4 Ascensor Reina Victoria C5
5 Museo a Cielo Abierto E7
6 Museo Naval y Marítimo A1
7 Palacio Baburizza B4
8 Plaza Sotomayor B3

Activities, Courses & Tours

9 Harbor Boat Tours C3
10 Natalis Language Center B4
11 Tours 4 Tips B3

Sleeping

12 Casa Aventura B4
13 Hostal Acuarela B5
14 Hostal Caracol D7
15 Hostal Jacaranda B5
16 Hostal Luna Sonrisa B5
17 Hostal Morgan B5
18 Hostal Nomades B5
19 Pata Pata Hostel B5

Eating

20 Café del Poeta D5
21 Café Vinilo C5
22 Casino Social J Cruz D6
23 El Desayunador C5
24 El Sandwich Cubano D5
25 Empanadas Famosas D5
26 La Cocó B5
27 Norma's C5
28 Viá Viá Café C5

Drinking

29 Bar La Playa B3
30 Cinzano C5
31 Pajarito E6

Entertainment

32 La Piedra Feliz D4

Note that a quick way up to the eastern side of Cerro Alegre is the **Ascensor Reina Victoria** (tickets CH$250; ⏲7am-11pm), which connects Av Elias to Paseo Dimalow.

Ascensor Concepción HISTORIC SITE
(Prat (El Plan) & Paseo Gervasoni (Cerro Concepción); tickets CH$250; ⏲7am-10pm) The city's oldest elevator, Ascensor Concepción takes you to Paseo Gervasoni, at the lower end of Cerro Concepción. Built in 1883, it originally ran on steam power.

Palacio Baburizza HISTORIC BUILDING
(Paseo Yugoslavo 166) This rambling art nouveau building dates from 1916; it houses the **Museo de Bellas Artes** (Fine Arts Museum), which was temporarily closed at the time of writing. From El Plan, arrive here on **Ascensor El Peral** (tickets CH$100; ⏲6am-11pm).

CERRO BELLAVISTA

Artists and writers have long favored this quiet residential hill; today a steady stream of hotels and eateries are opening here.

TOP CHOICE **La Sebastiana** HISTORIC BUILDING
(www.fundacionneruda.org; Ferrari 692; adult/child CH$3000/1500; ⏲10:30am-6:50pm Tue-Sun Jan & Feb, 10:10am-6pm Tue-Sun Mar-Dec) Bellavista's most famous resident artist was Pablo Neruda. Getting to his romantic wind-whipped home involves a hefty uphill hike; the climbing continues inside the house, but you're rewarded on each floor with heart-stopping views over the harbor. Wander around La Sebastiana at will, lingering over the poet's collections of ship's figureheads, vintage furniture and artworks by his famous friends.

FREE **Museo a Cielo Abierto** MUSEUM
(Open-Air Museum; www.pucv.cl/site/pags/museo; cnr Rudolph y Ramos; ⏲24hr) Twenty classic, colorful murals are dotted through the lower streets of this *cerro,* forming the Museo a Cielo Abierto, created between 1969 and 1973 by students from the Universidad Católica's Instituto de Arte. The **Ascensor Espíritu Santo** (Aldunate & Rudolph; tickets CH$250; ⏲7am-10pm) takes you from behind Plaza Victoria to the heart of this art.

CERRO ARTILLERIA

Clear views out over the sea made this southwestern hill a strategic defense spot.

Museo Naval y Marítimo MUSEUM
(Naval & Maritime Museum; www.museonaval.cl; Paseo 21 de Mayo 45; adult/child CH$700/300; ⏲10am-5:30pm Tue-Sun) Cannons still stand

ready outside this naval museum, where significant space is devoted to Chile's victory in the 19th-century War of the Pacific. Other exhibits include historical paintings, uniforms, ship's furniture, swords, navigating instruments and medals, all neatly displayed in exhibition rooms along one side of a large courtyard. Rattling **Ascensor Artillería** (tickets CH$250; ⊙7am-10pm) brings you here from Plaza Aduana.

Courses

Chilean Cuisine COOKING COURSE

(☎096-621-4626; www.cookingclasseschile.cl; course per person from CH$37,000) An energetic chef takes you to shop for ingredients at the local market, then teaches you to make *pisco sours*, taste local wines, and cook (and eat) a menu of Chilean classics. Check the online sample menus to get an idea: we like the seafood lesson, but great vegetarian options are also available. The meeting place is arranged with the reservation.

Natalis Language Center LANGUAGE COURSE

(☎246-9936; www.natalislang.com; Plaza Justicia 45, 6th fl, Oficina 602, El Plan; courses per week from CH$90,000, 3-day crash courses CH$135,000) Has a good reputation for quick results.

Tours

TOP CHOICE **Tours 4 Tips** WALKING TOUR

(www.tours4tips.bligoo.cl; Plaza Sotomayor 120, El Plan; ⊙10am & 3pm) Pay-as-you-wish walking tours every morning and afternoon, no booking required. Show up at Plaza Sotomayor for a friendly introduction to the city.

Festivals & Events

Año Nuevo NEW YEAR

A major event, thanks to spectacular fireworks that bring hundreds of thousands of spectators to the city.

Sleeping

Note that breakfast is included at the following places.

TOP CHOICE **Hostal Luna Sonrisa** HOSTEL $

(☎273-4117; www.lunasonrisa.cl; Templeman 833, Cerro Alegre; d CH$28,500, dm/s/d without bathroom CH$8500/12,000/22,000;) Small, quiet and close to Cerro Alegre's restaurants and bars, this welcoming hostel is run by a guidebook writer, who's happy to help you plan your adventures in the city, and his wife, who runs an excellent bakery nearby. For extra privacy, ask about the independent **apartment** (www.elnidito.cl) on the top floor of the building.

Hostal Nomades B&B $$

(☎327-0374; www.hostalnomades.cl; Urriola 562, Cerro Alegre; d CH$30,400, d/tr without bathroom CH$26,600/40,000;) The owner of this friendly B&B is also a talented painter; his large-scale works brighten the walls of an antique house that already has charm enough in its rustic wood beams and Spanish-style tiles. Although the place functions as a B&B, the communal amenities are hostel-style: guests have access to the kitchen, a TV room, luggage storage as well as a book exchange.

Pata Pata Hostel HOSTEL $

(☎317-3153; www.patapatahostel.com; Templeman 657, Cerro Alegre; d CH$30,000, dm/d without bathroom CH$9000/25,000;) 'Pata Pata' means 'stairs' in Quechua – you'll understand the name when you see this hostel's location off an incredibly picturesque staircase between Cerro Alegre and the sea. The place has bright, ultra-simple dorms, cozy doubles and a quiet atmosphere with an appealing communal patio.

TOP FIVE VALPO VIEWS

» Paseo 21 de Mayo on Cerro Artilleria to survey the cranes and containers of the port.

» Plaza Bismark on Cerro Carcel for a panoramic take of the bay.

» Mirador Diego Portales on Cerro Baron for a sweeping perspective of Valpo's colorful house-cluttered central views.

» The viewpoint at the end of Calle Merlet on Cerro Cordillera to see the rusting roofs of Barrio El Puerto and the civic buildings of Plaza Sotomayor from above.

» Paseo Atkinson on Cerro Concepción for views of typical Valpo houses during the day, and a twinkling sea of lights on the hills at night.

DON'T MISS

VALPARAÍSO'S MURALS

Wandering up and down the winding hills of Valparaíso, you'll see colorful public art everywhere, from dream-like wall paintings of glamorous women to political graffiti-style murals splashed across garage doors. Setting a fresh precedent for the city's outdoor artwork and causing another stir in the street-art scene is Chilean artist Inti, whose first solo show was a hit in Paris. His large-scale mural, painted across the surface of several neighboring buildings and visible from Cerro Concepción, was unveiled in early 2012. The vibrant sideways image shows a mysterious, partially fragmented figure draped with exotic jewelry. The highlight is the awkwardly beautiful pair of feet – you'll have to see it for yourself.

Hostal Jacaranda HOSTEL **$**
(☎327-7567; www.hostaljacaranda.blogspot.com; Urriola 636, Cerro Alegre; dm/d from CH$6800/24,200; 📶) Small but very welcoming – and perfectly located in a lively section of Cerro Alegre filled with small museums and cafes – this cheerful, sustainably run hostel (note the recycling efforts) features a terrace that's romantically illuminated at night. The owners are a wealth of knowledge; if you ask, they might even show you how to make Chilean specialties like *pisco sours* and empanadas.

Casa Aventura HOSTEL **$**
(☎275-5963; www.casaventura.cl; Pasaje Gálvez 11, Cerro Concepción; dm/s/d without bathroom CH$8000/16,000/20,000; 📶) This centrally located old house has airy, pastel-painted dorms, while doubles feature sky-high ceilings and original wooden floors. Though first-floor rooms can be noisy, travelers rave about the open kitchen and the breakfast of fresh fruit and eggs.

Hostal Morgan B&B **$$**
(☎211-4931; www.hostalmorgan.cl; Capilla 784, Cerro Alegre; d with/without bathroom CH$54,000/48,000; @📶) Sophisticated and hushed, Hostal Morgan is conspicuously aimed at travelers whose rucksack days are over. It's perfect for couples and those intent on extra zzz's.

Hostal Caracol HOSTEL **$**
(☎239-5817; www.caracolvalparaiso.cl; Calvo 371, Cerro Bellavista; dm/d CH$8000/28,000; @📶) Slightly off the beaten path, this refurbished colonial building has good communal spaces and beds topped with feather comforters.

Hostal Acuarela HOSTEL **$**
(☎318-0456; www.hostalacuarela.blogspot.com; Templeman 862, Cerro Alegre; dm/d without bathroom CH$8000/20,000; @) Location, location, location – Acuarela also has ample dorms, a remodeled kitchen, a cool spiral iron staircase and a small terrace.

Eating

Empanadas Famosas CHILEAN **$**
(Donoso 1379, El Plan; empanadas CH$800-2000; ⌚lunch) Celebrating its 50-year anniversary in 2012, this classic empanada joint has hardly changed since its early days. This is the locals' pick for baked *empanadas de pino* (beef) and *mariscos* (shellfish), plus deep-fried varieties from simple *queso* (cheese) to *camarones* (shrimp), all washed down with icy beer.

Viá Viá Café INTERNATIONAL **$**
(☎319-2134; Almirante Montt 217, Cerro Alegre; set lunch CH$6900-7900, mains CH$3900-5500; ⌚noon-5pm, dinner by reservation only, closed in winter; 📝) Viá Viá occupies a gorgeous old art deco house, employs eco-friendly practices (note the solar-powered kitchen), offers quiet outdoor tables under the shade of leafy trees and runs economical lunch specials on weekdays featuring rotating dishes such as portobello risotto and Belgian-style mussels. Don't miss the chocolate-topped waffles for dessert.

Norma's CHILEAN **$$**
(Almirante Montt 391, Cerro Alegre; set lunch $4900-6900; ⌚closed Mon) Climb the tall stairway into this cheerful restaurant for a surprisingly well-prepared set lunch that's friendlier on your wallet than most others in the area. The restored house still has polished wood and charming antique window frames from the original structure. Come for tangy *pisco sours*, Chilean dishes and delicious homemade flan.

La Cocó SANDWICHES **$**
(Monte Alegre 546, Cerro Alegre; sandwiches CH$3800-5000; ⌚closed Mon & Tue, lunch only Sun; 📝) This *sanguchería artesanal* (artisan sandwich-maker) is truly a delight. Gourmet

sandwiches come piled high with fresh seafood or vegetarian-friendly toppings (try the Simona, which features goat cheese, arugula, pesto, olives and sun-dried tomatoes). Beer, wine, coffee, salads and pastries round out the creative menu; look for live music in the evening.

Mercado Cardonal CHILEAN $
(cnr Yungay & Rawson, El Plan; set menus CH$3500-5000) Get your goat cheese and olives on this block of crisp and colorful produce; it's around the corner from the bus terminal. On the 2nd floor, casual seafood eateries such as El Rincon de Pancho offer set menus featuring fried fish, seafood stews and grilled meats.

El Desayunador BREAKFAST $
(Almirante Montt 399, Cerro Alegre; breakfasts CH$2500-4800; 8:15am-8:45pm Tue-Sat, 8:30am-8pm Sun;) This charming old-school cafe – housed in an old stone building complete with vintage tile floors and rustic wooden tables – does breakfasts all day, plus sandwiches, salads, desserts, coffee and fresh-squeezed juices.

Café Vinilo CHILEAN $$
(Almirante Montt 448, Cerro Alegre; mains CH$5200-8500) From bakers to butchers to effortlessly hip resto-bar: the mismatched-tile floor tells the story of the many incarnations of this Cerro Alegre institution. Sandwiches and chocolate-and-raspberry cake seduce during the day. Later, quirky Chilean fare takes center stage, the namesake vinyl gets turned up and things slip into bar mode.

Café del Poeta CAFE $
(Plaza Aníbal Pinto 1181, El Plan; mains CH$3500-7800; 8:30am-midnight Mon-Fri, from 11am Sat & Sun;) This sweet cafe and eatery brings some sophistication to a busy central plaza in El Plan. On the menu are savory crepes, pasta and seafood; there's also sidewalk seating, a relaxing afternoon tea and wines by the glass.

Casino Social J Cruz CHILEAN $
(Condell 1466, El Plan; mains CH$4500-6000) Graffiti covers the tabletops and windows at this no-frills eatery, tucked away down a narrow passageway in El Plan. Forget about menus, there's one essential dish to try: everybody orders *chorrillana* (a mountain of french fries under a blanket of fried pork, onions and egg).

El Sandwich Cubano SANDWICHES $
(O'Higgins 1224, Local 16, El Plan; sandwiches CH$1100-1600; noon-10pm Mon-Sat) Authentic, fresh, over-stuffed sandwiches. Try the *ropa vieja* (literally 'old clothes'; shredded beef).

Drinking & Entertainment

TOP CHOICE **Cinzano** BAR
(Plaza Aníbal Pinto 1182, El Plan; closed Sun) Drinkers, sailors and crooners have been propping themselves up on the cluttered bar here since 1896. It's now a favorite with tourists, too, who come to see tuneful old-timers knocking out tangos and boleros like there's no tomorrow.

Pajarito BAR
(Donoso 1433, El Plan; closed Sun) Artsy *porteños* (residents of Valparaíso) in their twenties and thirties cram the Formica tables at this laid-back, old-school bar.

Bar La Playa BAR
(Serrano 567, El Puerto) It might be over 80 years old, but this traditional wood-paneled bar shows no signs of slowing down. On weekend nights, cheap pitchers of beer, powerful *pisco* and a friendly but rowdy atmosphere draw crowds of local students and young bohemian types.

La Piedra Feliz BAR, CLUB
(www.lapiedrafeliz.cl; Av Errázuriz 1054, El Plan; from 9pm Tue-Sun) Jazz, blues, tango, son, salsa, rock, drinking, dining, cinema: is there anything this massive house along the waterfront doesn't do? In the basement, DJs spin till 4am at the nightclub La Sala.

Information

Dangers & Annoyances

The area around the Mercado Central and La Iglesia Matriz has a reputation for petty street crime and muggings. If you go, go early, avoid alleyways and leave valuables at the hostel. At night stick to familiar areas and avoid sketchy *escaleras* (stair passageways).

Internet Access

Call centers and internet cafes are widespread along Condell in El Plan.

Media

Valparaíso Times (www.valparaisotimes.cl) Online English-language newspaper.

Medical Services

Hospital Carlos Van Buren (☎220-4000; Av Colón 2454, El Plan)

Post

Post Office (Prat 856, El Plan; ⏰9am-6pm Mon-Fri, 10am-1pm Sat)

Tourist Information

Tourist Information Kiosks (☎293-9262; www.ciudaddevalparaiso.cl; Muelle Prat, El Plan; ⏰10am-2pm & 3-6pm Mon-Sat) Pick up a free map here.

Websites

Ascensores de Valparaíso (www.ascensoresvalparaiso.org) An interactive map of the city's old elevators.

Ciudad de Valparaíso (www.ciudaddevalparaiso.cl) Helpful, comprehensive listings of services in the city.

Valparaíso Map (www.valparaisomap.cl) The best map of a notoriously hard-to-navigate city.

Getting There & Away

All major intercity services arrive and depart from the **Terminal Rodoviario** (☎293-9695; Av Pedro Montt 2800, El Plan), across from the Congreso Nacional, about 20 blocks east of the town center. Be aware, especially if you're arriving at night, that taxis often aren't waiting around the terminal; if you need a ride to your hotel or hostel, you might have to call one or arrange a pick-up ahead of time. If you're walking between the bus station and the center, play it safe by sticking to a major thoroughfare such as Pedro Montt.

Tur Bus (☎221-2028; www.turbus.cl) runs frequently between Santiago and Valparaíso every day (CH$1900 to CH$5000, two hours); from Santiago, it's easy to connect to Chilean destinations north, south and east.

You can reach Mendoza (CH$15,000, eight hours) in Argentina with Tur Bus or **Cata Internacional** (☎225-7587; www.catainternacional.com).

The city transport network, **Transporte Metropolitano Valparaíso** (TMV; www.tmv.cl), has services to Viña del Mar and the northern beach towns. For Reñaca, take the orange 607, 601 or 605; the latter continues to Concón. All run along Condell then Yungay. You'll see other bus lines to the same destinations running along Av Errázuriz.

Getting Around

Walking is the best way to get about central Valparaíso and explore its *cerros* – you can cheat on the way up by taking an *ascensor* or a taxi *colectivo* (CH$500). *Micros* (minibuses; CH$400 to CH$600) run to and from Viña and all over the city. Avoid the traffic by hopping on **Metro Regional de Valparaíso** (Merval; www.merval.cl), a commuter train that leaves from **Estación Puerto** (cnr Errázuriz & Urriola) and **Estación Bellavista** (cnr Errázuriz & Bellavista) to Viña del Mar.

Viña del Mar

☎032 / POP 320,000

Clean, orderly Viña del Mar is a sharp contrast to the charming jumble of neighboring Valparaíso. Manicured boulevards lined with palm trees and beautiful expansive parks have earned it the nickname of Ciudad Jardin (the Garden City). Viña remains a popular weekend and summer destination for well-to-do *santiaguinos*, despite the fact that its beaches get seriously packed and the Humboldt Current means that waters are chilly enough to put off most would-be swimmers.

Sights

Museo de Arqueología e Historia Francisco Fonck MUSEUM

(www.museofonck.cl; 4 Norte 784; adult/child CH$2000/300; ⏰10am-6pm Mon-Sat, 10am-2pm Sun) Specializing in Rapa Nui (Easter Island) archaeology and Chilean natural history, this small museum features an original *moai* (enormous stone sculpture from Easter Island), Mapuche silverwork and Peruvian ceramics.

Parque Quinta Vergara PARK

(Errázuriz 563; ⏰7am-6pm) Viña's nickname (the Garden City) proves just at this magnificently landscaped public park, featuring plants from all over the world. On-site is the Venetian-style **Palacio Vergara** (1908), which contains the **Museo de Bellas Artes**. Unfortunately, the museum was badly damaged in the 2010 earthquake and was closed at the time of writing.

Sleeping

All accommodations include breakfast unless otherwise indicated.

Little Castle GUESTHOUSE $

(☎262-7906; Vista Hermosa 166; d CH$24,000) Four blocks from the beach, this friendly guesthouse features seven clean doubles with shared bathrooms, a living room with a cozy fireplace, a communal kitchen and a terrace with views over the ocean.

DON'T MISS

ISLA NEGRA

The spectacular setting on a windswept ocean headland makes it easy to understand why **Isla Negra** (☎035-461-284; www.fundacionneruda.org; Poeta Neruda s/n; admission by guided tour only in English/Spanish CH$3500/3000; ⏰10am-6pm Tue-Sun, to 8pm Sat & Sun Jan-Feb) was Pablo Neruda's favorite house. Built by the poet when he became rich in the 1950s, it was stormed by soldiers just days after the 1973 military coup when Neruda was dying of cancer. The house includes extraordinary collections of bowsprits, ships in bottles, nautical instruments and wood carvings. Neruda's tomb is also here, alongside that of his third wife, Matilde. Reservations are essential in high season. (Note that despite the name, Isla Negra is not an island.)

Isla Negra is an easy half-day trip from Valparaíso: **Pullman Bus Lago Peñuelas** (☎032-222-4025) leaves from Valparaíso's bus terminal (CH$3200, 1½ hours, half-hourly). From Santiago, **Pullman Bus** (www.pullman.cl) comes here direct from Terminal de Buses Alameda (CH$7500, 1½ hours, half-hourly).

Kalagen Hostel HOSTEL $$$
(☎299-1669; www.kalagenhostel.com; Av Valparaíso 618; dm CH$10,000-12,000, d with/without bathroom CH$75,000/69,000; 📶) This cheery, recently renovated hostel contains stylish dorms and doubles with colorful linens, hardwood floors and Asian-style paper lanterns. These are pricey hostel accommodations, even for the area, but the central location is great and the communal kitchen is inviting. Breakfast is not included.

Che Lagarto Hostel HOSTEL $
(☎262-5759; www.chelagarto.com; Portales 131; dm CH$5700-6500, d with/without bathroom CH$22,800/21,000; @📶) The huge garden in front of Viña's first hostel means you don't have to limit your open-air lounging to the beach. The right-on vibe stops at the door: clean but simple dorms make the place feel like a university residence.

Residencia Offenbacher-hof B&B $$
(☎262-1483; www.offenbacher-hof.cl; Balmaceda 102; s/d CH$38,000/44,600; 📶) There are fabulous views over the sea and city from this commanding clapboard house atop quiet Cerro Castillo. Sea views, newly renovated bathrooms and antique furnishings make the spacious superior rooms worth the extra cash.

Hotel Cap Ducal HISTORIC HOTEL $$
(☎262-6655; www.capducal.cl; Av Marina 51; r CH$57,000; ❄@) Waves batter the foundations of this iconic art deco building, built to resemble a ship. Spiral staircases and narrow corridors lead to irregular-shaped rooms with cruiseliner-worthy sea views. The furnishings are starting to look a bit dated, but it works with the faded grandeur theme. The seafood restaurant here is a Viña classic.

Eating & Drinking

The pedestrian area around Av Valparaíso offers a string of beer-and-sandwich joints and other cheap dining options. Paseo Cousiño is home to convivial pubs, some featuring live music.

Entremasas CHILEAN $
(5 Norte 377; empanadas CH$800-1200; 🖉) Creative empanadas – prawn and mushroom in a cheese-cilantro sauce, ground beef and chorizo with goat's cheese – make a quick and classic Viña lunch or late-afternoon snack. You'll see a few other locations in the area, including at 6 Poniente 235.

La Flor de Chile CHILEAN $
(8 Norte 601; mains CH$3000-6500) For nearly a century, *viñamarinos* young and old have downed their *schops* and dined on Chilean comfort food over the closely packed tables of this gloriously old-school bar.

Enjoy del Mar CHILEAN $$
(Av Perú s/n; set lunch $7900; 📶) A sunset drink here should be on everyone's Viña to-do list – there are panoramic views of the Pacific from its terrace above the mouth of the Rio Marga Marga. The set lunch is a much better deal than the pricey à la carte menu at night.

Samoiedo SANDWICHES $
(Valparaíso 637; sandwiches CH$2500-4500) For half a century, the old boys have been meeting at this traditional *confitería* (tearoom) for lunchtime feasts of steak and fries or well-stuffed sandwiches. The outdoor seating is greatly preferable to the interior, which opens to a busy shopping mall.

Divino Pecado ITALIAN **$$**
(Av San Martín 180; mains CH$6500-9900) The short but surprising menu at this intimate, candlelit Italian restaurant includes scallops au gratin, tuna carpaccio and fantastic fettuccini with lamb ragu.

Chez Gerald SPANISH **$$**
(Av Perú 496; mains CH$7900-10,900) An old-fashioned Viña classic just across from the beach, this place has been serving up stiff drinks, hearty lasagna, seafood pasta and Spanish-influenced dishes for over 50 years.

Entertainment

Café Journal CLUB
(www.cafejournal.cl; cnr Santa Agua & Alvares; 10pm-late Wed-Sat) Electronic music is mixed at this boomingly popular club with three heaving dance floors, beers on tap and walls plastered in yesterday's news.

Casino Municipal CASINO
(www.enjoy.cl/casino; Av San Martín 199) Overlooking the beach, this elegant local landmark is the place to squander your savings on slot machines, bingo, roulette and card games.

Information

Several banks have ATMs on Plaza Vergara, the main square.

Hospital Gustavo Fricke (265-2200; Alvares 1532)

Municipal Tourist Office (226-9330; www.visitevinadelmar.cl; Av Arlegui 715, Plaza Vergara; 9am-2pm & 3-7pm Mon-Fri, 10am-2pm & 3-7pm Sat & Sun) Provides city maps and events calendars. There's another branch at the bus station (275-2000; Av Valparaíso 1055; 9am-6pm).

Post Office (Plaza Latorre 32; 9am-7pm Mon-Fri, 10am-1pm Sat)

Getting There & Away

All long-distance services operate from the **Rodoviario Viña del Mar** (275-2000; www.rodoviario.cl; Valparaíso 1055), four long blocks east of Plaza Vergara. Nearly all long-distance buses to and from Valparaíso stop here.

Local buses go to Reñaca, Concón, and other northern beach towns. To catch one, go to Plaza Vergara and the area around Viña's metro station; expect to pay between CH$1200 and CH$2200 one-way, depending on your final destination.

Budget (268-3420; www.budget.cl; 7 Norte 1023) is your best bet for car rental.

Getting Around

Micros (minibuses; CH$400 to CH$600) go around the city and to Valparaíso; a commuter train run by **Metro Regional de Valparaíso** (Merval; www.merval.cl) also connects the two cities.

Around Viña del Mar

North of Viña del Mar, a beautiful road snakes along the coast, passing through a string of beach towns that hum with holidaying Chileans December through February. Towering condos overlook some, while others are scattered with rustic cottages and the huge summer houses of Chile's rich and famous.

Come to **Reñaca**, just north of Viña, for a sunset hike with incredible views on **Roca Oceanica**, a rocky hill looking out over the Pacific. Continue to **Concón**, 15km from Viña, for its unpretentious seafood restaurants. **Las Deliciosas** (Av Borgoño 25370; empanadas CH$900) does exquisite empanadas; the classic is cheese and crab.

Further north, **Horcón** was Chile's first hippie haven. Brightly painted, ramshackle buildings clutter the steep main road down to its small, rocky beach where fishing boats come and go. These days there's still a hint of peace, love and communal living – note the happy-go-lucky folks gathering on the beach at sunset with dogs, guitars, and bottles of liquor in paper bags.

About 21km north of Horcón, the long, sandy beaches of **Maitencillo** stretch for several kilometers along the coast. **Escuela de Surf Maitencillo** (www.escueladesurfmaitencillo.cl; Av del Mar 1250; group class per person CH$15,000) is a relaxed place to learn how to surf. A favorite restaurant and bar is **La Canasta** (Av del Mar 592; mains CH$5900-8800) for wood-baked pizzas and – of course – fresh fish.

The small, laid-back town of **Cachagua**, 13km north of Maitencillo, sits on the northern tip of a long crescent beach. Just across the water is a rocky outcrop that's home to more than 2000 Humboldt penguins, as well as a colony of sea lions.

Continue north 35km to reach **Zapallar**, the most exclusive of Chile's coastal resorts, with still-unspoiled beaches flanked by densely wooded hillsides. Superb seafood is yours at **El Chiringuito** (Caleta de Pescadores; mains CH$8200-12,400), with crushed shells underfoot and a wall of windows that peers to the sea.

Several bus companies visit Zapallar direct from Santiago, including Tur Bus (p426) and Pullman (p426). **Sol del Pacífico** (☎275-2030; www.soldelpacifico.cl) comes up the coast from Viña.

NORTHERN CHILE

Traveling inland, the balmy coast of sunbathers and surfers shifts to cactus scrub plains and dry mountains streaked in reddish tones. Mines scar these ore-rich mammoths whose primary reserve, copper, is high-octane fuel to Chile's economic engine. But there's life here as well, in the fertile valleys producing *pisco* grapes, papayas and avocados. Clear skies mean exceptional celestial observation opportunities – it's no wonder many international telescopic, optical and radio projects are based here. The driest desert in the world, the Atacama is a refuge of flamingos on salt lagoons, sculpted moonscapes and geysers ringed by snow-tipped volcanoes. In short, these places are an orgy for the senses and ripe for adventure and exploration.

Chile's 2000km northern stretch takes in Norte Chico, otherwise known as 'region of 10,000 mines,' a semiarid transition zone from the Valle Central to the Atacama. The stamp of ancient South American cultures is evident in enormous geoglyphs on barren hillsides. Aymara peoples still farm the *precordillera* (the foothills of the Andes) and pasture llamas and alpacas in the highlands. You can diverge from the desert scenery to explore the working mine of Chuquimaquata or brave the frisky surf of arid coastal cities.

Take precautions against altitude sickness in the mountains and avoid drinking tap water in the desert reaches.

Ovalle

☎053 / POP 104,000

Ovalle offers a glimpse of city life in the provinces and is the best base for Parque Nacional Fray Jorge. In the grand old train station, **Museo del Limarí** (cnr Covarrubias & Antofagasta; admission CH$600; ⏲9am-6pm Tue-Fri, 10am-1pm Sat & Sun) displays some gorgeous ceramics that indicate the existence of trans-Andean links between the Diaguita peoples of coastal Chile and northwestern Argentina.

Sleeping & Eating

Jamie Crazy House HOSTEL $
(☎098-591-8686; www.jaimecrazyhouse.com; Tocopilla 92; dm CH$6500; @) This relatively new hostel isn't what the name implies: there are basic, spacious dorms, but it's more like a family home than party central.

Club Social Árabe MEDITERRANEAN $
(Arauco 255; mains CH$4000) This lofty atrium serves superb stuffed grape leaves, summer squash or red peppers and baklava, in addition to Chilean specialties.

Drinking

Café Real CAFE
(Vicuña MacKenna 419; ⏲9am-2:30am Mon-Sat) Cheery and cosmopolitan, with young things knocking back espressos and cold Cristal.

Getting There & Away

From the **bus terminal** (cnr Maestranza & Balmaceda) plenty of buses go to Santiago (CH$7000, 5½ hours), La Serena (CH$3000, 1¾ hours) and more northerly points.

Around Ovalle

Petroglyphs, pictographs and ancient mortars blanket **Monumento Arqueológico Valle del Encanto** (adult/child CH$500/300; ⏲8:15am-8:30pm summer, to 7pm winter), a canyon 19km west of Ovalle in a rocky tributary of the Río Limarí. These dancing stick-men and alien-like forms are remnants of the El Molle culture (AD 200–700). To get here, take any westbound bus out of Ovalle and disembark at the highway marker; Valle del Encanto is an easy 5km walk along a gravel road, but with luck someone will offer you a lift.

An ecological island of lush Valdivian cloud forest in semidesert surroundings, **Parque Nacional Fray Jorge** (adult/child CH$2500/1000; ⏲9am-6pm) is 82km west of Ovalle. This Unesco World Biosphere Reserve protects 400 hectares of truly unique vegetation nourished by moist fog. There's no public transport, but agencies in La Serena and Ovalle offer tours.

La Serena

☎051 / POP 160,000

Blessed with neocolonial architecture, shady streets and golden shores, peaceful La Serena turns trendy beach resort come summer. Founded in 1544, Chile's second-oldest city is

Northern Chile (Norte Chico)

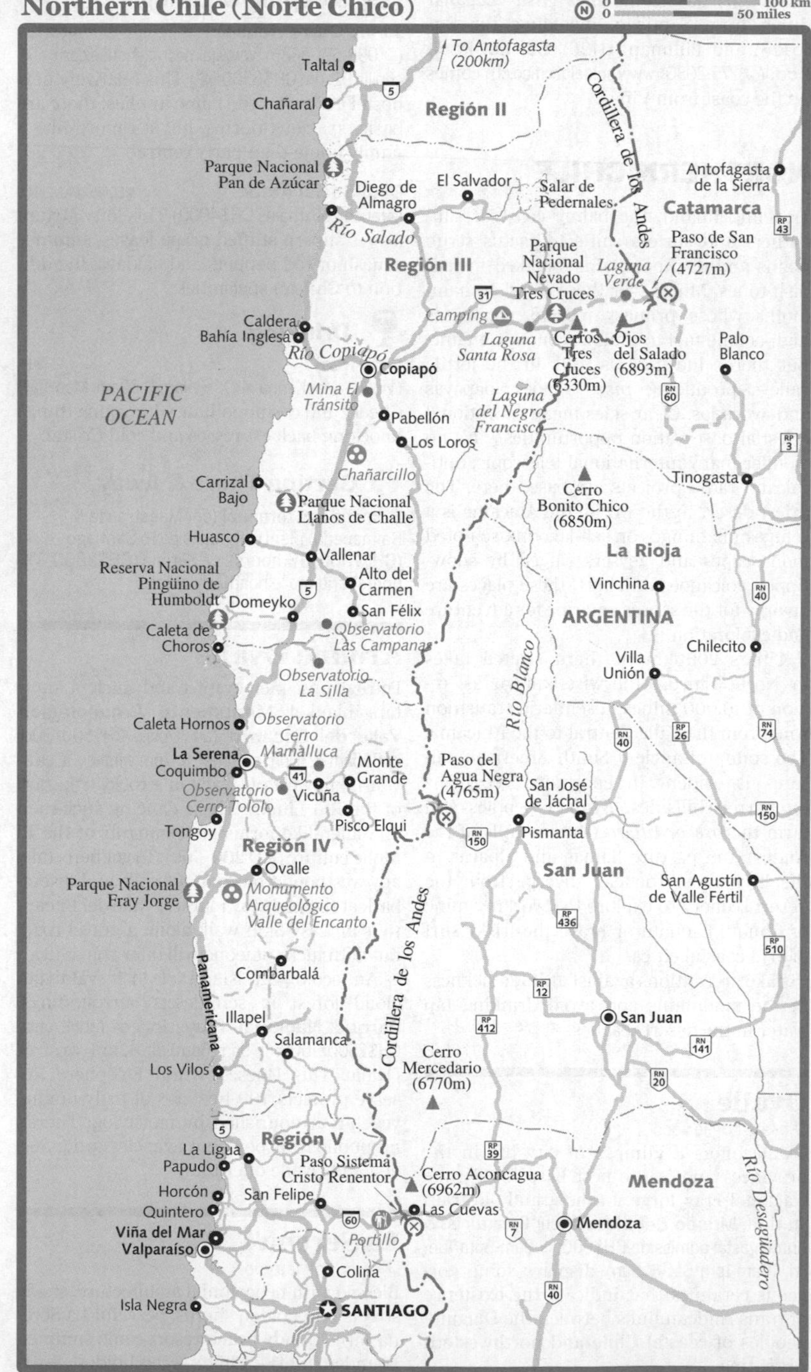

a short jaunt from character-laden villages, sun-soaked *pisco* vineyards and international observatories for stargazing. Nearby **Coquimbo** is more rough-and-tumble, but lives and breathes a hearty nightlife.

Sights & Activities

Excursions in the region range from visits to national parks to nighttime astronomical trips and *pisco*-tasting tours. Agencies in town offer full-day trips through the Valle del Elqui, Parque Nacional Fray Jorge and Parque Nacional Pingüino de Humboldt; try **Elqui Valley Tour** (☎214-846; www.goelqui.com; Matta 367).

La Serena has a whopping 29 churches: on the Plaza de Armas is the 1844 **Iglesia Catedral** (Plaza de Armas; ⏲10am-1pm & 4-8pm), and two blocks west is the mid-18th-century **Iglesia Santo Domingo** (cnr Cordovez & Munoz). The stone colonial-era **Iglesia San Francisco** (Balmaceda 640) dates from the early 1600s.

Museo Histórico Casa Gabriel González Videla MUSEUM
(Matta 495; adult/child CH$600/300; ⏲10am-6pm Mon-Fri, to 1pm Sat) Museo Histórico Casa Gabriel González Videla is named after La Serena's native son and Chile's president from 1946 to 1952, who took over the Communist Party, then outlawed it, driving Pablo Neruda out of the senate and into exile.

Museo Arqueológico MUSEUM
(cnr Cordovez & Cienfuegos; adult/child CH$600/300, Sun free; ⏲9:30am-5:50pm Tue-Fri, 10am-1pm & 4-7pm Sat, 10am-1pm Sun) Highlights of this museum are an Atacameña mummy, a hefty 2.5m-high *moai* (statue) from Easter Island and interesting Diaguita artifacts that include a dinghy made from sea-lion hide.

Mercado La Recova MARKET
(cnr Cantournet & Cienfuegos; ⏲9am-9pm Mon-Sat) Mercado La Recova offers a jumble of dried fruits and artisan jewelry.

Parque Japones Kokoro No Niwa PARK
(Parque Pedro de Valdivia; adult/child 5-12yr CH$1000/300; ⏲10am-8pm summer, to 6pm rest of year) Retreat into the ambience of trickling brooks, skating swans and rock gardens at Kokoro No Niwa, a well-maintained Japanese garden.

Beaches BEACH
Wide sandy beaches stretch from La Serena's nonfunctional lighthouse to Coquimbo. Avoid strong rip currents by choosing the beaches marked 'Playa Apta' south of Cuatro Esquinas and around Coquimbo. A **bike path** runs about 4km by the beach. Local **body-boarders** hit Playa El Faro, while Playa Totoralillo, south of Coquimbo, is rated highly for its surf breaks and **windsurfing**.

Sleeping

Hostal El Hibisco HOSTEL $
(☎211-407; hostalelhibisco@hotmail.com; Juan de Dios Pení 636; r per person CH$7000; wi-fi) A familial atmosphere prevails at this cheerful guesthouse. It offers a dozen clean rooms with hardwood floors, shared facilities, free laundry and breakfast with homemade jams. There's bike rental and a communal kitchen.

Hostal El Punto HOSTEL $
(☎228-474; www.hostalelpunto.cl; Bello 979; s CH$24,000-26,000, d CH$26,000-30,000, dm/s/d without bathroom CH$8500/17,000/18,000; @wi-fi) A gorgeous German guesthouse with a wide range of rooms, sunny terraces, bright mosaics, flower gardens and tree-trunk tables. The staff provide travel tips, yoga classes, tours, bike rental, laundry, book exchange… you name it. It's so popular that you'll want to book well ahead, especially in high season. Breakfast included.

Maria's Casa GUESTHOUSE $
(☎229-282; www.hostalmariacasa.cl; Las Rojas 18; dm CH$9000, s/d without bathroom 15,000/18,000; wi-fi) The cottage-style rooms at this family-run spot are simple and cozy. Backpacker-friendly amenities include well-scrubbed shared bathrooms, a quaint country kitchen, laundry service and bike rental.

Eating

Mercado La Recova (cnr Cantournet & Cienfuegos; ⏲9am-6pm) has cheap food stalls, while big supermarkets such as **Santa Isabel** (Cienfuegos 545; ⏲9am-10pm Mon-Sat, to 9pm Sun) offer good options to make your own picnic lunch. Trendy eateries line the beach toward Peñuelas.

Daniela II CHILEAN $
(Av Francisco de Aguirre 335; mains CH$2500-7500; ⏲closed dinner Sat) Cheerful local favorite serving hearty portions of Chilean comfort food. It gets packed at lunchtime, when set menus start at CH$1500.

La Serena

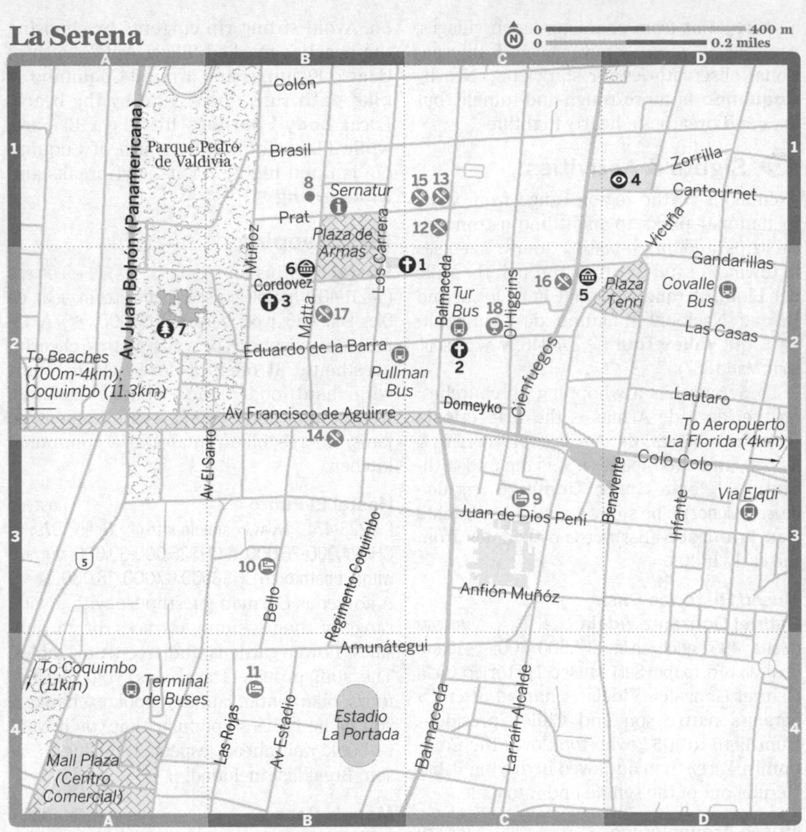

La Serena

Sights

- 1 Iglesia Catedral C2
- 2 Iglesia San Francisco C2
- 3 Iglesia Santo Domingo B2
- 4 Mercado La Recova D1
- 5 Museo Arqueológico C2
- 6 Museo Histórico Casa Gabriel González Videla B2
- 7 Parque Japones Kokoro No Niwa A2

Activities, Courses & Tours

- 8 Elqui Valley Tour B1

Sleeping

- 9 Hostal El Hibisco C3
- 10 Hostal El Punto B3
- 11 Maria's Casa B4

Eating

- 12 Café Colonial C1
- 13 Coffee Express C1
- 14 Daniela II B2
- Mercado La Recova .... (see 4)
- 15 Rapsodia C1
- 16 Supermercado Santa Isabel C2
- 17 Trento Caffe B2

Drinking

- 18 Takuba C2

Café Colonial INTERNATIONAL $
(Balmaceda 475; mains CH$3000-7000) This buzzy, tourist-friendly restaurant serves up anything from breakfasts and burgers to pizzas and pancakes. It's used to accommodating kids, vegetarians and non-Spanish speakers.

Trento Caffe CAFE $

(Matta 520; sandwiches CH$1800-2100) This modern coffee shop near the main square serves inexpensive gourmet panini.

Rapsodia INTERNATIONAL $$

(Prat 470; mains CH$5800-8900; ⊙closed dinner Sat & all day Sun) With several side rooms looking onto the inner courtyard with a giant palm tree, this old *casona* (house) serves up a variety of well-prepared snacks and dishes.

Drinking & Entertainment

Look for lively student bars around the intersection of O'Higgins and Av Francisco de Aguirre. Nightclubs lining the seafront to Coquimbo go full-on in the summer season.

Takuba BAR

(Eduardo de la Barra 589) University students rub shoulders to rock and pop sounds in this dimly lit little tavern. Cheap drinks are the house specialty – try a papaya sour or Serena libre.

Coffee Express CAFE

(Prat 492) This busy cafe serves pastries and some of La Serena's best java.

Information

Banks with 24-hour ATMs line the plaza. There are numerous internet cafes around town, most charging CH$600 per hour.

Hospital Juan de Diós (☎333-424; Balmaceda 916; ⊙24hr)

Sernatur (☎225-199; www.turismoregiondecoquimbo.cl; Matta 461; ⊙9am-8pm summer, 9am-6pm Mon-Fri, 10am-2pm Sat winter) Exceptionally attentive.

Getting There & Away

Air

La Serena's **Aeropuerto La Florida** (☎271-870) is 5km east of downtown. **LAN** (☎600-526-2000; Balmaceda 406) flies daily to Santiago (CH$112,000, 50 minutes) and Antofagasta (CH$133,000, 1¼ hours).

Bus

La Serena's **Terminal de Buses** (☎224-573; cnr Amunátegui & Av El Santo) has dozens of carriers plying the Carretera Panamericana from Santiago north to Arica, including **Tur Bus** (☎219-828; www.turbus.cl; Balmaceda 437) and **Pullman Bus** (☎218-879; www.pullman.cl; Eduardo de la Barra 435).

To get to Vicuña (CH$2000, 1½ hours), Ovalle (CH$2500, two hours), Monte Grande (CH$3500, two hours) or Pisco Elqui (CH$3500, 2½ hours), try Via Elqui at the main bus terminal.

For Argentine destinations, **Covalle Bus** (☎213-127; Infante 538) goes to Mendoza (CH$30,000, 14 hours) and San Juan (CH$30,000, 18 hours).

DESTINATION	COST (CH$)	DURATION (HR)
Antofagasta	23,000	13
Arica	34,000	23
Calama	26,000	16
Copiapó	12,000	5
Iquique	30,000	19
Santiago	16,000	7

Getting Around

For car hire, try **Avis** (☎271-509; airport) or **Econorent** (☎220-113; Av Francisco de Aguirre 0135).

Valle del Elqui

The heart of Chilean *pisco* production, the Elqui Valley is famous for its futuristic observatories, seekers of cosmic energies, frequent UFO sightings, poet Gabriela Mistral and quaint villages. This is a truly enchanting – and enchanted – area, and one of the must-visit places in Norte Chico.

VICUÑA

☎051 / POP 24,000

The spirit of Gabriela Mistral's somnambulist poetry seeps from every pore of snoozy little Vicuña. Just 62km east of La Serena, the town, with its low-key plaza, lyrical air and compact dwellings, is worth a visit for a day or two before you head out into the countryside to indulge in fresh avocados and papayas – not to mention the famous grapes that are distilled into *pisco*.

Sights & Activities

Observatorio Cerro Mamalluca OBSERVATORY

(www.mamalluca.org; Av Gabriela Mistral 260; tours CH$3500; ⊙evenings) A highlight of the region is ogling the galaxies through this observatory's 30cm telescope. Reserve online for bilingual tours and shuttle service; for visits from September to April, book well ahead.

Museo Gabriela Mistral MUSEUM

(Av Gabriela Mistral 759; adult/child CH$600/300; ⊙10:30am-6pm Mon-Sat, 10am-1pm Sun)

A tangible eulogy to one of Chile's most famous literary figures. Gabriela Mistral was born Lucila Godoy Alcayaga in 1889 in Vicuña. The museum charts her life (in Spanish only), from a replica of her adobe birthplace to her Nobel Prize.

Planta Pisco Capel PISQUERIA
(www.centroturisticocapel.cl; admission CH$1500; ⏲10am-7pm Jan & Feb, to 5pm Mar-Dec) Capel distills *pisco* and has its only bottling plant here, with 36 million bottles per year shipped to imbibers across the world Take a 45-minute bilingual tour of the facilities and the on-site museum before trying a few small samples. It's a (walkable) few kilometers from town; get here by heading southeast of town and across the bridge, then turning left.

Cerro de la Virgen HILL
Sweeping panoramas of the Elqui Valley make the hot, dusty hike up Cerro de la Virgen worthwhile. Just north of town, the summit is less than an hour's walk from the Plaza de Armas.

Inti Runa OBSERVATORY
(☎099-968-8577; www.observatorios.cl; Chacabuco 240; tours CH$6000; ⏲closed Jun-Aug) The German owner of this sun observatory claims he has two of the world's biggest solar telescopes. He keeps them in his lovely *casona* and offers one-hour tours. He also offers on-site nighttime observation, which includes a 90-minute video.

Elki Magic ADVENTURE SPORTS
(☎097-459-8357; www.elkimagic.com; Av Gabriela Mistral 472) Offers guided downhill bike jaunts (from CH$10,000), horse riding (CH$6000 per hour) and one-day van tours to valley highlights (from CH$30,000, with lunch). It also rents bikes (CH$6500 per day) and can supply you with a map of the 16km trail around the surrounding villages.

Sleeping

TOP CHOICE **Hostal Valle Hermoso** GUESTHOUSE $
(☎411-206; www.hostalvallehermoso.com; Av Gabriela Mistral 706; s/d/tr CH$14,000/25,000/33,000; wifi) Great lodging choice with eight airy and immaculately clean rooms around a sun-drenched patio inside an old adobe *casona*. Staff, managed by the adorable Señora Lucia, are warm and friendly, as if you were staying with old friends. Breakfast included.

Hostal Donde Rita B&B $
(☎419-611; www.hostaldonderita.com; Condell 443; s/d without bathroom CH$15,000/26,000; wifi pool) A motherly hostess who speaks German presides over this private home with a pool and four cozy rooms. There's breakfast with homemade jam and fresh coffee, a shared kitchen and a small wooden *quincho* (barbecue house).

Hostal Aldea del Elqui HOSTEL $$
(☎543-069; www.hostalaldeadelelqui.cl; Av Gabriela Mistral 197; s/d CH$22,000/38,000; wifi pool) Another of the *casonas* converted into accommodations, this friendly hostel has well-kept rooms with good beds and TVs, some on the 2nd floor of a newer adjacent building.

Eating

TOP CHOICE **Chaski** CHILEAN $$
(O'Higgins 159; mains CH$6500-7500; ⏲closed Tue) This tiny outdoor restaurant offers up Elqui Valley's most innovative dining. Local ingredients, such as quinoa, goat and amaranth, are prepared with a twist and doused in fragrant Andean herbs. Drinks include great *pisco* cocktails, a local artisanal beer and organic wines.

Halley CHILEAN $$
(Av Gabriela Mistral 404; mains CH$3000-7900; ⏲lunch & dinner) A spacious colonial-style restaurant on the square. This locals' favorite is recommended for typical Chilean food, including roast *cabrito* (goat) and plentiful salads.

Club Social de Elqui CHILEAN $$
(Av Gabriela Mistral 445; mains CH$4800-9800) Enthusiastic waiters usher passing travelers into this upmarket courtyard restaurant; come for a big breakfast.

Information

Tourist services huddle around the Plaza de Armas, including the **Oficina de Información Turística** (☎670-307; San Martín 275; ⏲8:30am-8pm Jan & Feb, 8:30am-5:30pm Mon-Fri, 9am-6pm Sat, 9am-2pm Sun Mar-Dec), post office, internet cafes and call centers. On Chacabuco, Banco Estado has an ATM and changes money.

Getting There & Around

A block south of the plaza, the **bus terminal** (cnr Prat & O'Higgins) has frequent buses to La Serena (CH$2000, one hour), Pisco Elqui (CH$1800, 50 minutes) and Monte Grande (CH$1800, 40

WORTH A TRIP

EXPLORING THE ELQUI VALLEY

Rent a bicycle from Turismo Migrantes or take your rental car to explore the charming villages around Pisco Elqui. Highlights include a stop at artisanal *pisqueria* **Los Nichos**, established in 1868. Located 3km south of Pisco Elqui, Los Nichos still produces *pisco* the old-fashioned way; stop by between 11am and 7pm for a free tasting, or you can join a **guided tour** (CH$1000; 12:30pm, 1:30pm, 4:30pm & 5:30pm daily in summer), in Spanish only.

Drive on from here and you'll reach **Horcón artisanal market** (noon-8:30pm) in the valley of its namesake village, worth a browse for its wealth of gorgeous handmade arts and crafts, and local natural food and cosmetic products, all sold out of bamboo stalls.

Fans of Nobel Prize–winning poet Gabriela Mistral shouldn't miss a quick visit to **Monte Grande**, her one-time home, and the **Casa de la Cultura Gabriela Mistral** (www.montegabriela.cl; admission free, guided tour CH$1000; 9am-1pm & 2-7pm Mon-Fri), a cultural center and women's cooperative that conducts textile and art workshops with underemployed women from the area. Buses between Vicuña and Pisco Elqui stop here.

minutes). Expresso Norte has a twice-daily service to Santiago (CH$10,000 to CH$12,000, seven hours). There's a wider choice of destinations in La Serena.

PISCO ELQUI

Renamed to publicize the area's most famous product, the former village of La Unión is a laid-back hideaway.

Sights & Activities

Distileria Pisco Mistral PISQUERIA
(www.piscomistral.cl; Plaza Pisco Elqui; tours CH$6000; noon-7:30pm Jan & Feb, 10:30am-6pm Tue-Sun Mar-Dec) The star attraction in town, the Distileria Pisco Mistral produces the premium Mistral brand of pisco. The hour-long 'museum' tour gives you glimpses of the distillation process and includes a free tasting of two *piscos* and a drink at the adjacent restaurant, which hosts occasional live music.

Turismo Migrantes OUTDOORS
(451-917; www.turismomigrantes.cl; O'Higgins s/n; 10am-2pm & 3-7pm) This energetic outfitter can organize horse riding (from CH$6000), trekking (CH$10,000), bike rentals and full-day excursions (CH$30,000) into the valley.

Sleeping

TOP CHOICE **El Tesoro de Elqui** HOTEL $$
(451-069; www.tesoro-elqui.cl; Prat s/n; dm CH$11,000, d CH$32,000-42,000, tr CH$39,000-52,000;) Up the hill from the center plaza, this tranquil oasis dotted with lemon trees, lush gardens and flowering vines has 10 wooden bungalows with terraces; features include hammocks and skylights. The dorm is small, so you should reserve well ahead.

Refugio del Angel CAMPGROUND $
(451-292; refugiodelangel@gmail.com; campsites per person CH$5000, day-use CH$2500) An idyllic riverside campground with swimming holes, bathrooms and a little shop. The turn-off is 200m south of the plaza on Manuel Rodriguez.

Ecohostal San Pedro HOSTEL $
(451-061; http://hostalsanpedro.blogspot.com.ar; Prat s/n; r without bathroom per person CH$10,000; @) This small and simple hostel's star feature is definitely the gaping valley view.

Eating & Drinking

Ranchito de Don Rene CHILEAN $
(Calle Centenario s/n; mains CH$3500-5500) This rustic local favorite specializes in Chilean comfort food.

Los Jugos CAFE
(Plaza s/n) Come to this airy cafe for the views of the plaza, and to enjoy delicious natural juices, strong coffee and fresh *pisco* cocktails at night.

Getting There & Away

Via Elqui (312-422; cnr Juan de Dios Pení & Esmeralda) buses run between Pisco Elqui and Vicuña (CH$1800, 50 minutes) throughout the day; catch one at the plaza.

WORTH A TRIP

PARQUE NACIONAL NEVADO TRES CRUCES

Hard-to-reach **Parque Nacional Nevado Tres Cruces** (adult/child CH$4000/1500) has all the rugged beauty and a fraction of the tourists of more famous high-altitude parks further north. Quite apart from pristine peaks and first-rate climbing challenges, the park shields some wonderful wildlife: flamingos spend the summer season here; large herds of *vicuñas* and *guanacos* roam the slopes; the lakes are home to giant and horned coots, Andean geese and gulls; and even the occasional condor and puma is spotted. Located just outside the park boundaries, 6893m **Ojos del Salado** is Chile's highest peak, a mere 69m short of Aconcagua, and the world's highest active volcano.

It's easy to get lost on your way to the national park, and there is no public transportation; consider taking a tour from Copiapó. English-speaking guide Ercio Mettifogo Rendic of **Puna de Atacama** (☎099-051-3202; www.punadeatacama.com; O'Higgins 21) comes recommended for tailored 4WD trips in the region. For rustic overnight accommodations at **Refugio Laguna del Negro Francisico** (per person per night CH$10,000), check with Conaf in Copiapó.

Copiapó

☎052 / POP 129,000

Welcoming Copiapó has little to hold travelers, but it does offer a handy base for the remote mountains bordering Argentina, especially the breathtaking Parque Nacional Nevado Tres Cruces, Laguna Verde and Ojos del Salado, the highest active volcano in the world. The discovery of silver at nearby Chañarcillo in 1832 provided Copiapó with several firsts: South America's first railroad and Chile's first telegraph and telephone lines.

Sights

The remains of Copiapó's mining heyday mark its center. Shaded by pepper trees, Plaza Prat showcases the early mining era with the elegant three-towered **Iglesia Catedral**, while the **Museo Mineralogico** (cnr Colipí & Rodríguez; adult/child CH$500/200; ⏲10am-1pm & 3:30am-7pm Mon-Fri, 10am-1pm Sat) is a loving tribute to the raw materials to which the city owes its existence.

Sleeping & Eating

Hotel La Casona HOTEL **$$**
(☎217-277; www.lacasonahotel.cl; O'Higgins 150; s/d from CH$43,000/49,000; @📶) This wonderfully homey 12-room hotel is a 10-minute walk west of Plaza Prat. It has a series of leafy patios, bilingual owners and rooms with hardwood floors and cable TVs.

Hotel Montecatini HOTEL **$**
(☎211-363; www.hotelmontecatini.cl; Infante 766; s/d standard CH$22,000/30,000, superior CH$30,000/37,000; 📶🏊) Staff aren't overly friendly, some rooms are outdated and the pool may or may not have water, but there's some charm to this olive-facade adobe with a leafy central courtyard.

Café Colombia CAFE **$**
(Colipí 484; snacks CH$1500) For a leisurely caffeine fix, this busy cafe turns out frothy cappuccinos and serves delectable sweets and sandwiches.

Tololo Pampa CHILEAN **$$**
(Atacama 291; 2-person tabla CH$8000; ⏲8pm-late Tue-Sat) A happening boho joint with an open-air back patio, rough-hewn furniture and an outdoor fireplace. Come for drinks and late-night snacks.

Don Elias CHILEAN **$**
(☎364-146; Los Carrera 421; mains CH$2800-7700; ⏲closed dinner Sun) A down-market diner serving good-value *almuerzos* (set lunches) and specialty seafood.

Information

Numerous ATMs are located at banks around the plaza. Internet cafes are found throughout the center and charge around CH$500 per hour.

Conaf (☎213-404; Juan Martínez 55; ⏲8:30am-5:30pm Mon-Thu, to 4:30pm Fri) Has information on regional parks.

Sernatur (☎212-838; www.chile.travel/en.html; Los Carrera 691; ⏲9am-8pm daily summer, 9am-7pm Mon-Fri, 9am-3pm Sat rest of the year) The well-run tourist office on the main plaza gives out a wealth of material and information in English.

Getting There & Away

Aeropuerto Desierto de Atacama is 40km northwest of Copiapó. **LAN** (☎600-526-2000; Colipí 484, Mall Plaza Real, Local A-102) flies daily to Santiago (CH$166,000, 1½ hours). **Sky** (☎214-640; www.skyairline.cl; Colipí 526) and **PAL Airlines** (☎524-603; www.palair.cl; O'Higgins 106, Local F, Edificio Plaza Real) offer cheaper fares to Antofagasta and Santiago.

Bus company **Pullman Bus** (☎212-977; Colipí 109) has a large terminal and a central **ticket office** (cnr Chacabuco & Chañarcillo). **Tur Bus** (☎213-724; Chañarcillo 650) also has a terminal and a **ticket office** (Colipí 510) downtown (tip: save time waiting in line by getting your bus tickets here). Other companies include **Expreso Norte** (☎231-176; Chañarcillo 655), **Buses Libac** (☎212-237; Chañarcillo 655) and **Flota Barrios** (☎213-645; Chañarcillo 631), all located in a common terminal.

Many buses to northern desert destinations leave at night. Sample fares include Antofagasta (CH$24,000, eight hours), Arica (CH$30,000, 18 hours), Calama (CH$28,000, 10 hours), Iquique (CH$30,000, 13 hours), La Serena (CH$13,000, five hours) and Santiago (CH$28,000, 12 hours).

If you're headed to Caldera/Bahía Inglesa, go to the bus ticketing offices clustered around the intersection of Chacabuco and Buena Esperanza.

Parque Nacional Pan de Azúcar

The cold Humboldt Current flows up the desert coastline, bringing with it its peppy namesake penguin and abundant marine life. The worthwhile 44,000-hectare **Pan de Azúcar** (www.conaf.cl; admission CH$4000) includes white-sand beaches, sheltered coves, stony headlands and cacti-covered hills.

Hired launches leave for a cruise around **Isla Pan de Azúcar**, home to about 2000 Humboldt penguins, as well as cormorants, gulls, otters and sea lions. Expect to pay from CH$5000 per person (with a 10-person minimum); in the low season, you could end up forking out as much as CH$50,000. Round trips take 1½ hours, and run from 10am to 6pm in summer, and to 4pm in winter.

There are five hiking trails in the park. The most popular is the 2.5km **El Mirador**;

WORTH A TRIP

BAHÍA INGLESA

With rocky outcrops jutting out of turquoise waters and a long white-sand beach, the sweet seaside resort of Bahía Inglesa is the place to come for a spot of beachside frolicking. The place takes its name from the British pirates who took refuge here in the 17th century. Today, it's become one of the north's most popular vacation spots, hectic in summer and mellow (and much cheaper) in the off-season. There's a cool Mediterranean feel and a beachfront promenade peppered with shops, restaurants and ice-cream shops. Locally harvested scallops, oysters and seaweed sweeten the culinary offerings.

Set sail on a windy jaunt down the coastline with **Nautica La Rada** (☎099-684-64032; antonioabelli@hotmail.com), or paddle out into crystal waters on a kayak with **Morro Ballena** (www.morroballena.cl). Sleep in an airy 'dome' and dine on *ceviche* (marinated raw seafood) in the similarly dome-shaped restaurant at cool **Domo Bahia Inglesa** (www.domobahiainglesa.cl; Av El Morro 610; s/d/tr CH$35,000/42,000/52,000, restaurant mains CH$5400-9900; ⏲restaurant closed Mon; 📶), or go for Thai curry, beachfront views and a funky bohemian vibe at trendy **El Plateao** (Av El Morro 756; mains CH$6000-8500). Outside of town, overlooking Bahía Inglesa, **Camping Playa Las Machas** (☎315-424; Playa Las Machas; campsites up to 6 people CH$18,700, cabañas CH$25,420-43,320) offers a sandy spot to pitch your tent. Stick around another day – you can take a day trip to virgin beaches, Pan de Azúcar or the San José mine near Copiapó with **Caldera Tour Atacama** (www.calderatouratacama.cl; Av El Morro 610b).

To get to Bahía Inglesa from Copiapó, you'll need to pass through the bus station in nearby Caldera. Several bus lines run hourly services from Copiapó to Caldera (CH$3500, one hour) – in Copiapó, locate the ticket offices around the intersection of Buena Esperanza and Chacabuco and hop on any line with 'Caldera' in the title (including Buses Caldera and Buses Expreso Caldera). From Caldera's bus terminal and main square, fast *colectivos* (fixed-route taxis) run to Bahía Inglesa (CH$900, 10 minutes).

LOS 33

For 121 years, the San José mine 45km north of Copiapó went about its business of digging for gold and copper deep in the Atacama Desert. Then, in the afternoon of August 5, 2010, a major cave-in trapped 33 of its workers 700m underground. Suddenly, San José was in the spotlight and 'Los 33,' as the buried miners became known, became unlikely superstars of one of the most televised rescue efforts in human history.

Under immense pressure, the government took over the rescue from the mine owners. The venture, at an estimated cost of US$20 million, involved international drilling rig teams as well as experts from NASA. On October 13, 2010, in a televised finale that lasted nearly 24 hours and drew an estimated viewing audience of one billion people from around the world, the last of the 33 men was hoisted up to freedom through a narrow shaft.

While they were trapped, the ordeal of Los 33 became a round-the-clock soap opera. At one point, a buried man had a wife and a lover waiting for him above. After 69 days in the pitch-dark depths of the earth, the 33 men resurfaced to find themselves in the spotlight. Afterwards, they found themselves cheered on by soccer fans at Wembley Stadium, jetted off to all-expenses-paid trips to Disneyland, showered with gifts and money, and flown to New York to be interviewed by David Letterman.

In summer 2011, it was announced that Los 33 had gone Hollywood by selling the film rights to their story to producer Michael Medavoy of *Black Swan* fame. The miners' story, a symbol of survival against all odds, has inspired many. For a definitive account of the rescue, read Jonathan Franklin's best-selling book *33 Men*.

en route you will see sea cacti, *guanaco* and chilla fox. Next up is **Las Lomitas**, an easy 4km trail with minimal slope.

Camping (per person from CH$1000) is available at Playas Piqueros and Soldado, with toilets, water, cold showers and tables. Lovely adobe cabins at **Pan de Azúcar Lodge** (www.pandeazucarlodge.cl; campsite per person CH$5000, cabins for 2/6 people CH$45,000/80,000) are fully equipped.

Pan de Azúcar is 30km north of Chañaral by a well-maintained paved road. Most people reach it by tour or transfer from Caldera/Bahía Inglesa or Copiapó.

Antofagasta

☎055 / POP 296,900

Chile's second-largest city, a rough-and-ready jumble of one-way streets, modern mall culture and work-wearied urbanites, is low on travelers' lists. Founded in 1870, the city earned its importance by offering the easiest route to the interior.

Sights

Nitrate-mining heydays left their mark with Victorian and Georgian buildings in the **Barrio Histórico** between the plaza and old port. The British-influenced **Plaza Colón** features Big Ben replica **Torre Reloj**. Sea lions circle Antofagasta's busy fish market **Terminal Pesquero**.

The oft-photographed national icon **La Portada** is a gorgeous natural arch located offshore, 20km north of Antofagasta.

Sleeping & Eating

Sleeping options are few and reduced by the numbers of traveling miners occupying hotels.

Hotel Paola HOTEL **$$**
(☎268-989; www.hotelpaola.cl; Matta 2469; s/d CH$35,700/50,000; wifi) By far the most stylish choice in the center, Hotel Paolo features an inner patio on the 3rd floor and five floors of rooms with hardwood floors, flat-screen TVs and fridges.

Camping Rucamóvil CAMPGROUND **$**
(☎262-358; Km 11; campsite per person CH$4000) A fairly well-equipped site south of town. Take micro 102 from Mercado Central and ask to be dropped off at Cruce Roca Roja.

Cafe del Sol CHILEAN **$$**
(Esmeralda 2013; set lunch CH$3000, mains CH$7000-8000; closed Sun) This ramshackle corner resto-bar serves a range of Chilean dishes in a cozy wooden interior.

El Arriero PARRILLA $$
(Condell 2644; mains CH$3800-12,000; ⏲closed dinner Sun) Generous portions of meat are the specialty at this rustic *parrilla* (steakhouse), full of old-fashioned charm.

Information

Hospital Regional (☎656-551; Av Argentina 1964)

Sernatur (☎451-818; Arturo Prat 384; ⏲8:30am-7pm Mon-Fri, 8:30am-2pm Sat Jan-Mar, 8:30am-5:30pm Mon-Fri Apr-Dec) The city tourist office, conveniently located by the plaza.

Getting There & Away

Air

Antofagasta's Aeropuerto Cerro Moreno is located 25km north of town. **LAN** (☎600-526-2000; www.lanchile.com; Arturo Prat 445) and **Sky** (☎600-600-2828; www.skyairline.cl; General Velasquez 890, Local 3) have daily nonstop flights to Santiago (CH$220,000, two hours) and Iquique (CH$48,000, 45 minutes).

Bus

The new **Terminal de Buses Cardenal Carlos Oviedo** (Av Pedro Aguirre Cerda 5750) serves most intercity destinations. Companies include **Flota Barrios** (Condell 2764), **Géminis** (Latorre 3055), **Pullman Bus** (☎224-976; www.pullman.cl; Latorre 2805) and **Tur Bus** (☎220-240; www.turbus.cl; Latorre 2751), with services to San Pedro de Atacama (CH$4900, four to five hours) several times daily. Other frequent services go to Copiapó (CH24,000, seven hours), La Serena (CH$26,000, 12 hours), Arica (CH$18,000, 10 hours) and Santiago (CH$34,500, 19 hours).

Calama

☎055 / POP 138,400

Copper statues, copper wall etchings, copper reliefs and a copper-plated cathedral spire are reminders of Calama's raison d'être – its existence is inextricably tied to the colossal Chuquicamata mine. For travelers, though, this murky city makes a quick stopover before San Pedro de Atacama. With inflated service prices and *schops con piernas* (like *cafés con piernas,* but with beer) it clearly caters to miners.

Sleeping & Eating

Hotel L&S HOTEL $$
(☎361-113; www.lyshotel.cl; Vicuña Mackenna 1819; s/d incl breakfast CH$39,000/49,000; @📶) Calama's best-value choice is this sleek 'business-lite' hotel with a fresh modern look, light-filled interiors, and sparkling-clean rooms.

Club Croata CHILEAN $$
(Abaroa 1869; mains CH$5000-8500, set lunch CH$3000-5500) Unexpectedly great for Chilean favorites such as *pastel de choclo* (maize casserole), this restaurant on the plaza is one of Calama's best traditional eateries.

Mercado Central MARKET $
(Latorre; set meals CH$2200-2500) Cheap and filling, the market *cocinerías* serve lunch to a workers' crowd between Ramírez and Vargas.

Information

Hospital Carlos Cisterna (☎655-700; Av Granaderos 2253)

Oficina Municipal de Información Turística (☎096-679-7253; http://calamacultural.cl; Latorre 1689; ⏲8am-1pm & 2-6pm Mon-Fri) Helpful and organizes tours.

Getting There & Away

Air

LAN (☎600-526-2000; www.lanchile.com; Latorre 1726) flies daily to Santiago (CH$225,000) from Aeropuerto El Loa; **Sky** (☎600-600-2828; www.skyairline.cl; Latorre 1499) often has cheaper fares.

Bus

In high season, purchase long-distance tickets as far as possible in advance. For frequent buses to Antofagasta (CH$4000, three hours) or overnights to Iquique (CH$14,000, 6½ hours), Arica (CH$15,000, seven to 10 hours) or Santiago (CH$30,000, 22 hours), try **Condor Bus/Flota Barrios** (☎345-883; www.condorbus.cl; Av Balmaceda 1852) or **Tur Bus** (☎688-812; www.turbus.cl; Ramírez 1852) – note that the Tur Bus terminal is a short taxi ride (CH$3000) outside of the center.

For San Pedro de Atacama (CH$3000, one hour) head to **Buses Frontera** (☎824-269; Antofagasta 2046), **Buses Atacama 2000** (☎316-664; Abaroa 2106) or Tur Bus.

International buses are invariably full, so reserve as far in advance as possible. To get to Uyuni, Bolivia (CH$16,000, nine hours), ask at Frontera and Buses Atacama 2000; buses only go a few times per week. Service to Salta and Jujuy, Argentina, is provided by **Pullman Bus** (☎341-282; www.pullmanbus.cl; Balmaceda 4155) and **Géminis** (☎892-050; www.geminis.cl; Antofagasta 2239) on Tuesday, Friday and Sunday mornings. Note that days and departure times are subject to change; confirm ahead with the bus companies.

Northern Chile (Norte Grande)

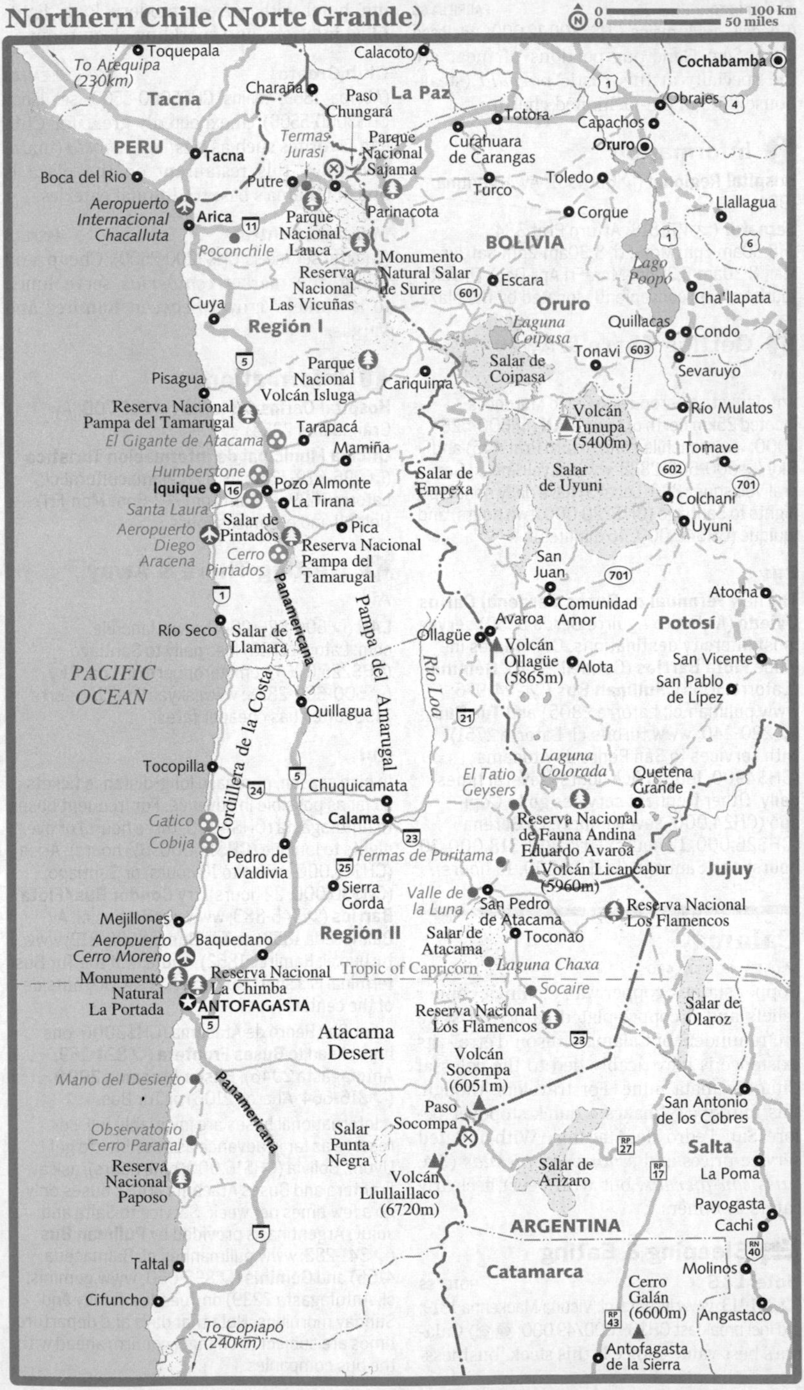

0 100 km
0 50 miles

Toquepala
To Arequipa (230km)
Calacoto
Cochabamba
Charaña
Paso Chungará
La Paz
Tacna
Obrajes
Totora
Capachos
Termas Jurasi
Parque Nacional Sajama
Curahuara de Carangas
Oruro
PERU
Tacna
Boca del Rio
Putre
Toledo
Turco
Aeropuerto Internacional Chacalluta
Arica
Parque Nacional Lauca
Parinacota
Corque
Llallagua
Poconchile
BOLIVIA
Monumento Natural Salar de Surire
Reserva Nacional Las Vicuñas
Escara
Lago Poopó
Cuya
Oruro
Cha'llapata
Región I
Laguna Coipasa
Quillacas
Condo
Tonavi
Parque Nacional Volcán Isluga
Salar de Coipasa
Sevaruyo
Pisagua
Cariquima
Reserva Nacional Pampa del Tamarugal
Volcán Tunupa (5400m)
Río Mulatos
El Gigante de Atacama
Tarapacá
Mamiña
Tomave
Humberstone
Salar de Empexa
Salar de Uyuni
Iquique
Pozo Almonte
Santa Laura
La Tirana
Colchani
Aeropuerto Diego Aracena
Salar de Pintados
Pica
Uyuni
Cerro Pintados
Reserva Nacional Pampa del Tamarugal
San Juan
Panamericana
Pampa del Tamarugal
Atocha
Comunidad Amor
Avaroa
Potosí
Río Seco
Salar de Llamara
Ollagüe
Volcán Ollagüe (5865m)
Alota
San Vicente
PACIFIC OCEAN
Río Loa
San Pablo de Lípez
Quillagua
Cordillera de la Costa
Laguna Colorada
Tocopilla
El Tatio Geysers
Quetena Grande
Chuquicamata
Gatico
Calama
Reserva Nacional de Fauna Andina Eduardo Avaroa
Cobija
Pedro de Valdivia
Termas de Puritama
Volcán Licancabur (5960m)
Jujuy
Sierra Gorda
Valle de la Luna
San Pedro de Atacama
Reserva Nacional Los Flamencos
Mejillones
Región II
Salar de Atacama
Toconao
Aeropuerto Cerro Moreno
Baquedano
Laguna Chaxa
Tropic of Capricorn
Monumento Natural La Portada
Reserva Nacional La Chimba
Socaire
ANTOFAGASTA
Reserva Nacional Los Flamencos
Salar de Olaroz
Atacama Desert
Volcán Socompa (6051m)
Mano del Desierto
Panamericana
San Antonio de los Cobres
Paso Socompa
Observatorio Cerro Paranal
Salar Punta Negra
Salta
Reserva Nacional Paposo
Volcán Llullaillaco (6720m)
Salar de Arizaro
La Poma
Payogasta
Cachi
ARGENTINA
Catamarca
Molinos
Taltal
Cerro Galán (6600m)
Cifuncho
Angastaco
To Copiapó (240km)
Antofagasta de la Sierra

Chuquicamata

Slag heaps as big as mountains, a chasm deeper than the deepest lake in the USA, and trucks the size of houses: these are some of the mind-boggling dimensions that bring visitors to gawk into the mine of Chuquicamata (or 'Chuqui'). This awesome abyss, gouged from the desert earth 16km north of Calama, is one of the world's largest open-pit copper mines.

First run by the US Anaconda Copper Mining Company, starting back in 1915, Chuqui is now operated by state-owned Corporación del Cobre de Chile. Chuquicamata was once integrated with a well-ordered company town, but environmental problems and copper reserves beneath the town forced the entire population out by 2004. Until quite recently, Chuqui was the world's largest single supplier of copper, producing a startling 630,000 tonnes annually.

The mine, which employs 20,000 workers, spews up a perpetual plume of dust visible for many miles in the cloudless desert. The elliptical pit measures an incredible 8 million sq meters and has a depth of up to 1250m. Most of the 'tour' offered by **Codelco** (☎322-122; visitas@codelco.cl; cnr Avs Granaderos & Central Sur, Calama; tour by donation; ⏲bookings 9am-5pm Mon-Fri) is spent simply gazing into its depths and clambering around an enormous mining truck with tires more than 3m high. Arrange visits by phone or email. Tours run from Monday to Friday, in both English and Spanish. Report to the Oficina on the corner of Avs Granaderos and Central Sur; bring identification and make a voluntary donation. Demand is high in January and February, so book at least a week ahead.

San Pedro de Atacama

☎055 / POP 4970

They say the high quantities of quartz and copper in the region give the people here positive energy – and the good vibes of northern Chile's number-one tourist draw, San Pedro de Atacama (elevation 2438m), are positively sky-high. The popularity of this adobe *precordillera* oasis stems from its position in the heart of some of northern Chile's most spectacular scenery. A short drive away lie the country's largest salt flat, its edges crinkled by volcanoes (symmetrical Licancábur, at 5916m, looms closest to the village); fields of steaming geysers; and a host of otherworldly rock formations and cool layercake landscapes.

San Pedro itself, 106km southeast of Calama, seems hardly big enough to absorb the hordes of travelers who arrive; it's little more than a handful of picturesque adobe streets clustering around a pretty tree-lined plaza and postcard-perfect church. But the last decade has seen a proliferation of guesthouses, eateries, internet cafes and tour agencies wedging their way into its dusty streets, molding it into a kind of adobe Disneyland. There are all the cons of fast development – steep prices, lackadaisical tour operators – and yet there is incredible quiet, an addictively relaxed atmosphere, psychedelic landscapes, courtyard bonfires under star-scattered heavens and hammock-strewn hostels. If you can manage to set your hours contrary to the rest of the sightseers, this is a magical destination.

Sights

Iglesia San Pedro CHURCH

(Plaza de Armas) Stop in the 17th-century Iglesia San Pedro, a delightful little colonial church built with indigenous materials – chunky adobe walls, a ceiling made from

CHUQUI THROUGH THE EYES OF CHE

Chuqui was already a mine of monstrous proportions when visited by a youthful Ernesto 'Che' Guevara more than 50 years ago. The future revolutionary and his traveling buddy Alberto Granado were midway through their iconic trip across South America, immortalized in Che's *Motorcycle Diaries*. An encounter with a communist during his journey to Chuqui is generally acknowledged as a turning point in Che's emergent politics, so it's especially interesting to read his memories of the mine itself (then in gringo hands). The wandering medical student wrote of such mines: '...spiced as they would be with the inevitable human lives – the lives of the poor, unsung heroes of this battle, who die miserably in one of the thousand traps set by nature to defend its treasures, when all they want is to earn their daily bread.'

San Pedro de Atacama

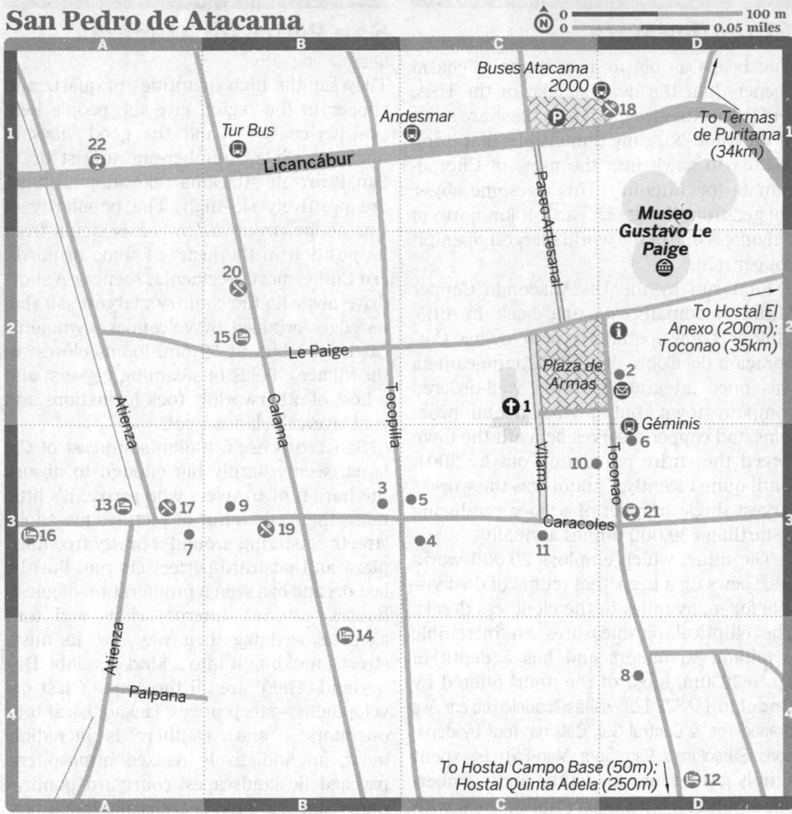

San Pedro de Atacama

Top Sights
Museo Gustavo Le Paige D2

Sights
1 Iglesia San Pedro C2

Activities, Courses & Tours
2 Atacama Inca Tour D2
3 Cordillera Traveler B3
4 CosmoAndino Expediciones C3
5 Desert Adventure C3
6 Grado 10 .... D3
7 Nomade A3
8 Rancho Cactus D4
9 San Pedro de Atacama Celestial Explorations B3
10 Terra Extreme C3
11 Vulcano Expediciones C3

Sleeping
12 Hostal La Ruca D4
13 Hostal Lickana A3
14 Hostal Rural B4
15 Hostal Sonchek B2
16 Takha Takha Hotel & Camping A3

Eating
17 Cafe Esquina A3
18 Food Stalls D1
19 La Casona B3
20 Las Delicias de Carmen B2

Drinking
21 Café Export D3
22 Quitor A1

cardón (cactus wood), floorboards that creak and sigh, and, in lieu of nails, hefty leather straps.

Museo Gustavo Le Paige MUSEUM
(Le Paige 380; adult/student CH$2500/1000; ⏲9am-6pm Mon-Fri, 10am-6pm Sat & Sun) Even if museums aren't your thing, make an exception: fascinating malformed skulls and mummy replicas will glue you to the glass here. There's also an extraordinary collection of shamanic paraphernalia for preparing, ingesting and smoking hallucinogenic plants.

Activities

A bewildering array of tours and activities are on offer. They can be as leisurely or challenging as you please: from nodding off in hot volcanic springs to bombing down steep trails on mountain bikes, from musing over the remains of ancient civilizations to sweating up active volcanoes, and from surfing down giant sand dunes to stargazing in the cloudless desert nights. Quality varies – some operators cancel abruptly or run unsafe vehicles – so stick to these recommended agencies or ask around with other travelers before booking a tour.

Hiking

Around San Pedro rise immense volcanoes, a few of them active. The excellent trekking agency **Nomade** (☎851-158; www.nomadeexpediciones.cl; Caracoles 163) runs treks to volcanoes and mountains, including day climbs (CH$60,000 to CH$90,000) to Sairecabur (5971m), Lascar (5592m) and Toco (5604m). Longer climbs take in Licancábur and Llullaillaco and involve an overnight stay in a *refugio* (rustic shelter).

Biking

Bikes are available for rent at several agencies and hotels for CH$6000 to CH$8000 per day; short trips from town include Pukara de Quitor (p456), Quebrada del Diablo and Catarpe. **Vulcano Expediciones** (☎851-023; www.vulcanochile.com; Caracoles 317) also runs downhill bike rides (from CH$35,000 for two hours).

Horse Riding

Sightseeing from the saddle is a rare treat in San Pedro. Tours vary from two-hour jaunts through the oasis to epic 10-day treks with camping. One outfitter to try is **Rancho Cactus** (☎851-506; www.rancho-cactus.cl; Toconao 568; trips of 2/3/5 hours CH$15,000/20,000/30,000).

Sandboarding

Jumping on a sandboard and sliding down enormous dunes is the most popular of the adrenaline-pumping activities around San Pedro. This happens in Valle de la Muerte, where 150m-high dunes make perfect terrain. **Atacama Inca Tour** (☎851-034; www.sandboardsanpedro.com; Toconao 421-A) is the top pick for pro boards and experienced instructors. Standard trips, for CH$10,000, depart either at 9am and return at noon or leave at 4pm, returning at 7pm. The latest offering is the night sandboard party (10:30pm till 1am), with spotlights for the dune, massive speakers and a DJ.

Tours

Dozens of agencies operate tours. The most reputable include **CosmoAndino Expediciones** (☎851-069; www.cosmoandino.cl; Caracoles 259), **Desert Adventure** (☎851-067; www.desertadventure.cl; cnr Caracoles & Tocopilla) and **Terra Extreme** (☎851-274; www.terraextreme.cl; Toconao s/n). A few agencies offer extra novelties for an extra cost, like **Grado 10** (☎560-600; www.turismogrado10.com; Toconao 435) – staff prepare a gourmet pancake breakfast in front of the geysers and transport passengers inside a huge all-terrain vehicle with picture windows. The most popular tours include the following destinations.

El Tatio Geysers GUIDED TOUR
(tours CH$18,000-20,000, entrance fee CH$5000) This hugely popular tour takes in the surreal sight of the geysers at sunrise. Leaves San Pedro between 4am and 6am and returns between noon and 1pm. Most tours include thermal baths and breakfast.

Valle de la Luna GUIDED TOUR
(tours CH$8000-10,000, entrance fee CH$3000) Leaves San Pedro mid-afternoon to catch the sunset over the valley, returning early evening. Often includes visits to Valle de la Muerte and Tres Marías.

Tulor and Pukará de Quitor GUIDED TOUR
(tours around CH$15,000, entrance fees CH$8000) Half-day archaeological tours take in this pair of pre-Columbian ruins (departures between 8am and 9am, returning between 1pm and 3pm).

Altiplano lakes GUIDED TOUR
(tours CH$10,000-25,000, entrance fees CH$5000-8000) Leaves San Pedro between 7am and 8am to see flamingos at Laguna Chaxa in the Salar de Atacama, then moves on to the town of Socaire, Lagunas Miñiques and Miscanti, Toconao and the Quebrada de Jere, returning between 4pm and 7pm.

Sleeping

Water is scarce (and not potable) in San Pedro, so buy your own drinking water and limit your shower time. Note that prices are high here, even outside high season.

Hostal Sonchek HOSTEL **$$**
(851-112; www.hostalsonchek.cl; cnr Paige & Calama; s without bathroom CH$11,000, d with/without bathroom CH$34,000/18,000;) Thatched roofs and adobe walls characterize the carpeted rooms at this lovely hostel. It's centered on a small courtyard, and there's a shared kitchen, luggage storage and a small garden out back with a few hammocks. The common bathrooms with solar-heated showers are some of the cleanest in town.

Hostal Campo Base HOSTEL **$$**
(851-472; www.hostalcampobase.cl; Toconao 535; dm/d incl breakfast CH$13,300/47,000, d without bathroom CH$36,000;) Backpackers rave about the thoughtful staff, ample breakfast and spotless public spaces of this centrally located hostel. There's hot water round-the-clock, a small patio and a communal kitchen.

Hostal Quinta Adela B&B **$$**
(851-272;www.quintaadela.wix.com/quinta-adela; Toconao 624; d incl breakfast CH$43,000-52,000; @) This friendly family-run place is a five-minute walk south of town – ideal if you're looking to escape the tourist crush and get a quiet night's sleep. The tidy, character-filled rooms and shady terrace are peaceful, and the guesthouse is situated alongside a sprawling orchard where you can take a siesta in a hammock.

Takha Takha Hotel & Camping HOTEL, CAMPGROUND **$$**
(851-038; www.takhatakha.cl; Caracoles 101-A; campsite per person CH$10,500, d incl breakfast CH$50,500-65,000, without bathroom CH$35,500;) A popular catch-all outfit with decent campsites, plain budget rooms and spotless midrange accommodations set around a sprawling flowery garden with a swimming pool.

Hostal Lickana GUESTHOUSE **$$**
(851-940; www.lickanahostal.cl; Caracoles 140; d/tr incl breakfast CH$47,000/57,600;) Just off the main drag, this hostel has super-clean rooms with big closets, colorful bedspreads and straw-covered front patios; what it lacks is the common-area ambience of other hostels.

WORTH A TRIP

4WD TO UYUNI, BOLIVIA

Colorful *altiplano* lakes, weird rock playgrounds worthy of Salvador Dalí, flamingos, volcanoes and, most famously of all, the blindingly white salt flat of Uyuni: these are some of the rewards for taking an excursion into Bolivia, northeast of San Pedro de Atacama. However, be warned that this is no cozy ride through the countryside, and for every five travelers who gush about Uyuni being the highlight of their trip, there is another declaring it a waking nightmare.

The standard trips take three days, crossing the Bolivian border at Hito Cajón, passing Laguna Colorada and continuing to the Salar de Uyuni before ending in the town of Uyuni. The going rate of CH$81,000 includes transportation in crowded 4WDs, basic and often teeth-chatteringly cold accommodations, plus food; an extra CH$15,000 to CH$23,000 will get you back to San Pedro on the fourth day (some tour operators drive through the third night).

Bring drinks and snacks, warm clothes and a sleeping bag. Travelers clear Chilean immigration at San Pedro and Bolivian immigration on arrival at Uyuni. Note that entrance fees to Bolivian parks are usually not included in trip package prices for most operators. These amount to approximately CH$16,000.

None of the agencies offering this trip get consistently glowing reports. **Cordillera Traveller** (851-291; www.cordilleratraveller.com; Toconao 447-B & Tocopilla 429-B) gets the best feedback from travelers.

Hostal Rural HOSTEL $
(☎560-337; www.hostalrural.cl; Calama 257; dm CH$10,000; 📶) This small but lively backpacker stop is a rare bargain in San Pedro. Convivial group barbecues are a treat, but note that you'll pay extra for towels and you'll have to find your own breakfast.

Hostal Sumaj Jallpa GUESTHOUSE $$
(☎851-416; www.hostalsumaj.cl; El Tatio 703, Sector Licancábur; s/d CH$28,000/37,000, d without bathroom CH$31,000; @) Pristine Swiss-Chilean guesthouse located 1km outside town; rent a bike or enjoy the stroll. A nice breakfast costs CH$2900 extra.

Hostal El Anexo GUESTHOUSE $$
(☎77-653-751; elanexo@sanpedroatacama.com; Le Paige 527-B; d CH$35,000, d without bathroom CH$20,000-25,000) Ideally located on the outskirts of town, this mellow adobe guesthouse has clean, colorful guest rooms and a pleasantly rustic setting on a small ranch with fruit trees and horses.

Hostal La Ruca HOSTEL $$
(☎851-568; www.larucahostal.cl; Toconao 513; d incl breakfast CH$45,000; @📶) This friendly budget spot has doubles spruced up with down comforters and sturdy furniture.

Eating & Drinking

Establishments only selling alcohol are outlawed, so nightlife centers on restaurants' open-air bonfires, open until 1am.

La Casona CHILEAN $$
(Caracoles 195; set lunch CH$6000-7000, mains CH$6000-8900) In a high-ceilinged dining room with dark wood paneling and an adobe fireplace in the middle, La Casona serves up sizzling *parrilladas* (mixed grills) and has a long list of Chilean wines.

Las Delicias de Carmen CHILEAN $
(Calama 370; mains CH$3000-8000; 🖋) Delicious cakes, empanadas and hearty Chilean dishes are on offer at this light-flooded restaurant with leafy views. Try a regional specialty, *pataska* (a stew made with corn, chopped vegetables and meat) for lunch.

Food Stalls CHILEAN $
(set lunches from CH$2000) The cheapest eats in town are served in rustic shacks in a parking lot behind the taxi rank on the northern edge of town. Expect simple set lunches of *cazuela* (stews), mains and dessert, and all-day empanadas for snacking.

ATACAMA DESERT ADVENTURES

A few off-the-beaten-track tours around Atacama are becoming increasingly popular, such as jaunts to **Laguna Cejar** and **Ojos de Salar** (you can swim in both, and in Cejar you can float just like in the Dead Sea), **Valle del Arcoiris** with its rainbowlike multicolored rock formations, and **Salar de Tara**. The last is one of the most spectacular, if back-breaking. Trips from San Pedro, involving a round-trip journey of 200km, reach an altitude of 4300m.

Cafe Esquina CAFE $
(Caracoles 160; mains CH$3000-4500) This laid-back little corner cafe serves natural juices, empanadas, sandwiches, pizzas and quesadillas. It tends to be quieter and has lower prices than other spots on the strip. Grab one of the tree-shaded streetside tables.

Quitor BAR
(Licancábur 154) Locals and Chilean tourists fill this laid-back eatery and bar at night; grab a seat next to the central fireplace and try the delicious *rica rica sour,* a twist on the *pisco sour* made with an aromatic herb indigenous to the region.

Café Export BAR
(cnr Toconao & Caracoles) Funky and candlelit, half the village squeezes in here come nightfall. Strengths include strong coffee and homemade pasta, though the ambience is superior to the food.

Information

It's wise to bring plenty of pesos to San Pedro de Atacama, as the two ATMs here often run out of money on weekends. Currency exchanges (don't expect good rates) and internet cafes (CH$800 to CH$1000 per hour) dot Caracoles; there's also free wi-fi in the main plaza. For useful visitor information, see www.sanpedrodeatacama.net.

ATM (cnr Caracoles & Vilama; ⏲9am-10pm) Visa only.

ATM (Le Paige s/n; ⏲9am-10pm) MasterCard only.

Oficina de Información Turística (☎851-420; cnr Toconao & Le Paige; ⏲9am-9pm)

Post Office (Toconao s/n)

Posta Médica (☎851-010; Toconao s/n) Health clinic east of the plaza.

Getting There & Away

Buses Atacama 2000 (Licancábur s/n) has regular departures to Calama (CH$2500), where you can connect to its Uyuni bus. **Buses Frontera del Norte** (Licancábur s/n) goes to Calama as well as Arica (CH$17,150) and Iquique (CH$14,000). **Tur Bus** (851-549; Licancábur 294) has hourly buses to Calama (CH$2900), from where you can connect to all major destinations in Chile, such as Santiago (CH$33,000, 22 hours), Arica (CH$14,000, nine hours) and Iquique (CH$11,000, six hours). **Andesmar** (www.andesmar.com; Licancábur s/n) serves Salta and Jujuy, Argentina, several times a week (CH$32,000, 16 hours with border time). **Géminis** (892-049; Toconao 428) also goes to Salta.

Several agencies in town offer transfer services to Calama airport; expect to pay around CH$16,000 per person.

Buses stop right near the plaza and the whole town can be explored on foot.

Around San Pedro de Atacama

There's more to see around San Pedro de Atacama than can be summarized here: it's worth your while to take a stroll past the tour agencies to see what's available and where exactly each trip will stop. Ask other travelers about what they've done, too – you'll probably hear rave reviews of tours you hadn't heard of before.

The crumbly 12th-century ruins of fortress **Pukará de Quitor** (admission CH$3000; 9am-7:30pm Jun-Aug, 9am-6pm Sep-May), 3km northwest of San Pedro de Atacama and accessible by rental bike, afford great views of the town and the oasis expanse. Another 3km on the right, **Quebrada del Diablo** (Devil's Gorge) offers a serpentine single track that mountain bikers dream of.

At 4300m above sea level, the famous **El Tatio** (95km north of San Pedro de Atacama; admission CH$5000) is the world's highest geyser field. Visiting the geysers at dawn is like walking through a gigantic steam bath, ringed by volcanoes and fed by 64 gurgling geysers and a hundred gassy fumaroles striking against the azure clarity of the *altiplano*. Swirling columns of steam envelop onlookers in a Dantesque vision, and the soundtrack of bubbling, spurting and hissing sounds like a field of merrily boiling kettles. As dawn wears on, shafts of sunlight crown the surrounding volcanoes and illuminate the writhing steam. You should dress in layers: keep in mind that it's toe-numbingly cold at dawn.

On the flipside, watching the sun set from the exquisite **Valle de la Luna** (admission adult/child CH$3000/2000; daylight hr) is an unforgettable experience. As you sit atop a giant sand dune, panting from the exertion of climbing it, drinking in spectacular views and watching the sun slip below the horizon, a beautiful transformation occurs: the distant ring of volcanoes, rippling Cordillera de la Sal and surreal lunar landscapes of the valley are suddenly suffused with intense purples, pinks and golds. The 'Valley of the Moon' is named after its lunar-like landforms eroded by eons of flood and wind. It's located 15km west of San Pedro de Atacama at the northern end of the Cordillera de la Sal.

The jagged crust of the **Salar de Atacama** looks for all the world like God went crazy with a stippling brush. But in the midst of these rough lifeless crystals is an oasis of activity: the pungent **Laguna Chaxa** (admission CH$5000), 67km south of town and home to three species of flamingo (James, Chilean and Andean), as well as plovers, coots and ducks.

The volcanic hot springs of **Termas de Puritama** (admission CH$12,000, on weekdays 2:30-6pm CH$7000), 30km north of San Pedro de Atacama, are accessible by taxi or tour. The temperature of the springs is about 33°C, and there are several falls and pools. Note that the hot springs were closed for repairs at the time of writing.

Iquique

057 / POP 216,400

Jutting into the sea and backed by the tawny coastal range, Iquique sits like a stage. And, in fact, the city is no stranger to drama. It first lived off guano reserves, grew lavish with 19th-century nitrate riches, since lost momentum, and now stakes its future on commerce and tourism, manifested in the duty-free mega-zone, the sparkly glitz of the casino and ubiquitous beach resort development. The real gems of this coastal city are the remainders of lovely Georgian-style architecture, Baquedano's fanciful wooden sidewalks, thermal winds and a ripping good surf.

DESERT STARGAZING

The flats of Chajnantor plateau, 5000m high and 40km east of San Pedro de Atacama, host the most ambitious radio telescope that the world has ever seen. The **Atacama Large Millimeter/Submillimeter Array** (ALMA; meaning 'soul' in Spanish) consists of 66 enormous antennae, most with a diameter of around 12m. Once finished in 2013, this field of interstellar 'ears' will simulate a telescope an astonishing 16km in diameter and make it possible to pick up objects in space as much as 100 times fainter than those currently detected. It is also slated to open a visitor center in 2013; for up-to-the-minute info, see www.almaobservatory.org.

ALMA is just the latest of northern Chile's cutting-edge astronomical facilities. Climatic conditions in the Atacama Desert make it an ideal location for stargazing. This is not only thanks to cloudless desert nights, but also the predictable winds that blow steadily in from the Pacific Ocean, causing minimal turbulence – a crucial requirement for observatories to achieve optimal image quality.

Consider taking a tour of the night sky from San Pedro. The standard choice is **San Pedro de Atacama Celestial Explorations** (SPACE; ☎851-935; www.spaceobs.com; Caracoles 166; star tours CH$18,000); French astronomer Alain Maury ferries travelers into the desert, far from intrusive light contamination, where they can enjoy the stars in all their glory. He owns several chunky telescopes through which visitors can gawk at galaxies, nebulae, planets and more. Shooting stars are guaranteed. Reserve in person or through the website; tours in Spanish, English and French leave nightly.

For a more intimate stargazing experience, try **Lodge Altitud Expeditions** (☎7-998-6745; www.lodgealtitud.cl; Av Pukara 9, Ayllu Quitor; tours CH$15,000), which offers a smaller group, several high-tech telescopes, and more one-on-one time with astronomy buffs. The friendly staff serve Chilean wine during the stargazing to stave off the night chill. You can even stay the night at the lovely lodge itself (singles/doubles CH$43,000/52,000), located within walking distance of town. Inquire online.

Sights & Activities

Plaza Prat PLAZA

The main plaza showcases the city's 19th-century architecture, with the 1877 **Torre Reloj** (Clock Tower) and the neoclassical **Teatro Municipal**, dating from 1890. At the northeastern corner, the Moorish 1904 **Casino Español** has elaborate interior tile work and *Don Quixote*–themed paintings. A handsomely restored **tram** occasionally jerks its way down Av Baquedano in the tourist high season, passing an impressive array of Georgian-style buildings.

Museo Corbeta Esmeralda MUSEUM

(www.museoesmeralda.cl; Paseo Almirante Lynch; admission CH$3000; ⌚10am-1pm & 2-6pm Tue-Sun) This replica of sunken *Esmeralda*, a plucky little Chilean corvette that challenged ironclad Peruvian warships in the War of the Pacific, is Iquique's new pride and glory. Guided tours take you inside the staff quarters, past the orange-lit engine and onto the ship's deck.

FREE **Centro Cultural Palacio Astoreca** HISTORIC BUILDING

(O'Higgins 350; ⌚10am-1pm & 4-7pm Mon-Fri, 11am-2pm Sat) Originally built for a nitrate tycoon, this 1904 Georgian-style mansion is now a cultural center, which exhibits contemporary work produced by local artists. It has a fantastic interior of opulent rooms with elaborate woodwork and high ceilings, massive chandeliers, a gigantic billiard table and balconies.

Beaches BEACH

Iquique's most popular beach, **Playa Cavancha** is worth visiting for swimming and bodysurfing. Further south, rip currents and crashing waves make the scenic **Playa Brava** better for sunbathing; take a *colectivo* from downtown or walk. **Playa Huaiquique**, on the southern outskirts of town, is also an exhilarating choice. **Vertical** (www.verticalst.cl; Av Arturo Prat 580) is surfer central – you can rent boards and wetsuits, and have lunch at the sushi bar.

Iquique

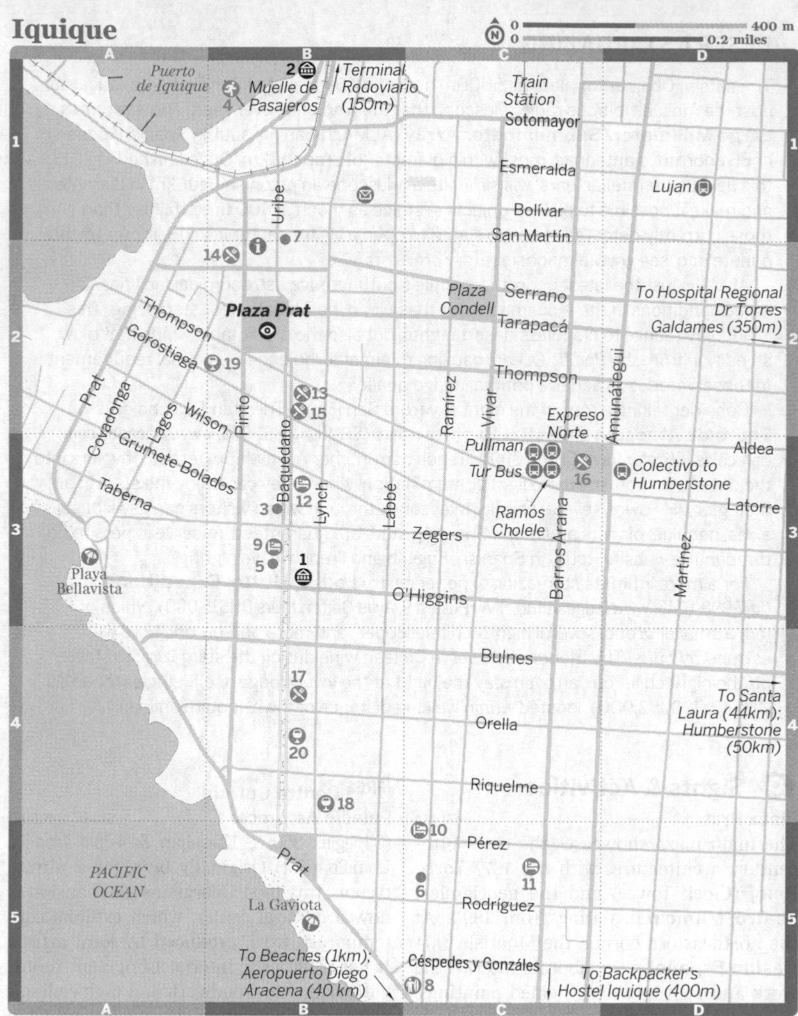

Boat Rides BOATING

(adult/child CH$3000/2000, minimum 11 passengers) Hour-long boat tours, departing from Iquique's 1901 passenger pier, pass by the commemorative buoy marking the spot where the *Esmeralda* sank.

Altazor ADVENTURE SPORTS

(☎380-110; www.altazor.cl; Vía 6, Manzana A, Sitio 3, Flight Park, Bajo Molle) Iquique's steep coastal escarpment, rising air currents and soft, extensive dunes are paradise for paragliders, ranking among the continent's top spots. Altazor offers paragliding courses (CH$40,000 per day, including equipment and transportation). An introductory tandem flight starts at CH$35,000.

Tours

Public transportation to many surrounding attractions is tricky, so tours are worth considering. In summer, agencies set up streetside tables on Prat and along Baquedano, hawking their most popular offerings. Among these is a day trip to the oasis towns of **Pica**, **La Tirana** and **Matilla**, taking in the nitrate ruins at **Humberstone** and **Santa Laura** en route (CH$20,000 to CH$28,000).

Iquique

Another fun excursion takes you for a dip in the thermal waters of **Mamiña** (CH$27,000). The most popular agencies include **Avitours** (☎527-692; www.avitours.cl; Av General Baquedano 997) and **OC Travel** (☎573-260; www.octravel.cl; Luis Uribe 445, Oficina 2H). With an environmental bent and a focus on responsible tourism, **Mistico Outdoors** (☎414-513; www.nomadesert.cl; Ramírez 1535; ⏲9am-3pm Mon-Fri) organizes inspiring day hikes, cycling outings and trips to indigenous villages, while **Magical Tour Chile** (☎217-290; www.magicaltour.tk; Baquedano 1035) runs creepy nocturnal tours of the ghost towns, departing at 8pm and getting you back into town around 2am.

Sleeping

Taxi drivers earn commission from some hotels; be firm or consider walking. Wild camping is free on the beaches north of Iquique near Pisagua and Cuya.

La Casona 1920 HOSTEL $
(☎413-000; www.casonahostel.com; Barros Arana 1585; dm CH$6000-8000, s/d without bathroom CH$13,000/21,000; @ wi-fi) Iquique's place to be, this cool and colorful hostel inside an old *casona* has dorms and a few doubles, some with balconies over the street. There's a shared kitchen, a pool table, weekly sushi parties with live DJs, poker nights, salsa classes and movie nights. Breakfast is included.

Backpacker's Hostel Iquique HOSTEL $
(☎320-223; www.hosteliquique.cl; Amunátegui 2075; dm/s/d CH$6500/10,000/19,000; @ wi-fi) Iquique's best hostel for beach bunnies, sitting steps from Cavancha and with a sociable 'surfer dude' vibe. There's a lounge, shared kitchen, hammocks, laundry, weekly barbecues, surf classes and sandboarding.

Hotel Pacifico Norte HOTEL $$
(☎429-396; hotelpacificonorte@chileagenda.cl; cnr Ramírez & Pérez; d incl breakfast CH$35,500; wi-fi) Located close to the southern end of Baquedano and the beach, this spotless hotel features bright doubles with polished hardwood floors, as well as mini fridges and cable TV.

Hotel de La Plaza HOTEL $$
(☎417-172; Baquedano 1025; s/d CH$19,000/32,000; wi-fi) One of the best deals in its category, this Georgian-style building is located right on the Baquedano pedestrian strip. There is a welcoming lobby with a big skylight; rooms with cable TVs come arranged around a patio.

YMCA HOSTEL $
(☎415-951; reservas@ymcaiquique.com; Baquedano 964; r per person CH$10,000; wi-fi) They took an elegant *casona* and wedged the works of a YMCA inside it. Rooms have bunk beds and clean bathrooms but can get noisy.

Eating

For a fast fresh-squeezed juice or a cheap seafood lunch, head to **Mercado Centenario** (Barros Arana s/n; set lunch CH$2500-4000); self-caterers, look for the large **Santa Isabel supermarket** on the corner of Labbé and Tarapacá. Note that many restaurants close on Sundays.

TOP CHOICE **El Tercer Ojito** INTERNATIONAL $$
(Lynch 1420; set weekday lunch CH$3900, mains CH$5200-8900; ⏲closed all day Mon & dinner Sun; vegetarian) Dine on sushi, Thai curry or Peruvian

ceviche in a candlelit courtyard filled with ferns and Buddha statues. Meals have excellent presentation and the atmosphere is utterly mellow.

Nomadesert CAFE $
(Ramírez 1535; sandwiches CH$1200-2500;) This tiny cafe, hip and eco-friendly, is locally famous for its rich coffee and gourmet quinoa burger. It's also the headquarters of the eco travel agency Mistico Outdoors and triples as a small boutique selling the wares of local artisans and designers. Come for a stylish breakfast, free wi-fi and inspiration to plan your adventures.

Ruta del Gigante CHILEAN $$
(Baquedano 1288; mains CH$6500-13,500) Savor Andean fusion cuisine, featuring dishes like llama stroganoff and charqui-stuffed eggplant, in this *altiplano*-themed restaurant with Andean tablecloths and bagpipes. Coca bread is served for free.

El Viejo Clipper INTERNATIONAL $$
(Baquedano 796; set lunch CH$3500, mains CH$3200-12,000) This Baquedano favorite packs 'em in for its delicious brick-oven pizzas and a wide range of international mainstays, from *tablas* and tapas to Thai chicken. Try the good-value set lunch at a sidewalk table.

Cioccolata CAFE $
(Pinto 487; snacks CH$1500-4500; closed Sun) This upscale coffee shop offers a wide selection of fresh, gooey cakes and coffee.

Boulevard INTERNATIONAL $
(Baquedano 790; mains CH$3000-8000; lunch & dinner) This streetside cafe does goat-cheese pizza and fish *papillot* (foil-wrapped); options are plenty but service is lethargic.

Drinking

Iquique has a fun-filled nightlife, with a few laid-back resto-bars in the center and clubs and pubs lining the seafront south of town.

Lobby Resto Bar BAR
(Gorostiaga 142; closed Sun) Sweet resto-bar with a boho vibe, Lobby has four small rooms and a loungy back patio. Come for great cocktails (try the raspirinha, with raspberry vodka and berries), the sushi bar, DJ-spun tunes on weekends, shared *tablas* and a nightly happy hour.

El Tercer Ojito BAR
(Lynch 1420) With tart two-for-one passion-fruit sours during happy hour, suddenly you find that new age doesn't mean 'good for you.'

Mi Otra Casa BAR
(Baquedano 1334; closed Sun) Laid-back artsy bar at the far end of Baquedano, with an interior full of mismatched objects and a range of different events, from poetry readings to live music.

Information

There are many ATMs downtown; several *cambios* exchange foreign currency and traveler's checks. Iquique's city center is jam-packed with internet cafes charging around CH$500 per hour.

Hospital Regional Dr Torres Galdames (395-555; Av Héroes de la Concepción 502) Ten blocks east of Plaza Condell.

Post Office (Bolívar 458)

Sernatur (419-241; www.sernatur.cl; Pinto 436; 9am-6pm Mon-Fri, to 2pm Sat) Offers free city maps and provides information.

Getting There & Away

Air

The local airport, **Aeropuerto Diego Aracena** (410-787), is 41km south of downtown via Ruta 1.

LAN (600-526-2000; www.lan.cl; Pinto 699; 9am-1:30pm & 4-8pm Mon-Fri, 9:30am-1pm Sat) has daily flights to Arica (CH$32,000, 50 minutes), Antofagasta (CH$47,000, 50 minutes) and Santiago (CH$120,500 to CH$200,000, 2½ hours). **Sky** (600-600-2828; www.skyairline.cl; Tarapacá 530), with slightly cheaper fares, also serves Arica, Antofagasta and Santiago as well as further south in Chile.

Bus

Most buses leave from the **Terminal Rodoviario** (427-100; Lynch); most companies also have ticket offices along the west and north sides of the Mercado Centenario. Several bus companies, including **Expreso Norte** (573-693; www.expresonorte.cl; Barros Arana 881), **Pullman** (www.pullman.cl; Barros Arana 825), **Ramos Cholele** (471-628; www.ramoscholele.cl; Barros Arana 851) and **Tur Bus** (Barros Arana 869), travel north to Arica (CH$7000, 4½ hours) and south to La Serena (CH$29,000, 18 hours), Antofagasta (CH$12,000, six hours), Copiapó (CH$24,000, 14 hours) and Santiago (CH$46,000, 24 hours).

To get to La Paz, Bolivia (CH$8000, 12 to 17 hours), try **Lujan** (326-955; Esmeralda 999). At the time of writing, the company offered two daily departures on weekdays. The easiest way to get to Peru is by going first to Arica (CH$7000), then hooking up with an international bus there.

East of Iquique

Ghost towns punctuate the desert as you travel inland from Iquique; they're eerie remnants of once-flourishing mining colonies that gathered the Atacama's white gold – nitrate. Along the way you will also pass pre-Hispanic geoglyphs, recalling the presence of humans centuries before. Further inland the barren landscape yields up several picturesque hot-spring villages.

If you only see one attraction outside Iquique, make it **Humberstone** (www.museodelsalitre.cl; adult/child CH$2000/500; ⏲9am-7pm), 45km northeast of the city. With the spark of the nitrate boom long gone cold, the ghost town remains a creepy shell. Built in 1872, the town's opulence reached its height in the 1940s: the theater drew Santiago-based performers, workers lounged about the massive cast-iron pool molded from a scavenged shipwreck, and amenities still foreign to most small towns abounded. The development of synthetic nitrates forced the closure of the *oficina* by 1960. Today some buildings are restored, but others are unstable; explore them carefully. A Unesco World Heritage Site, it makes the list of endangered sites for the fragility of the existing constructions. The skeletal remains of **Oficina Santa Laura** are a half-hour walk southwest. To get to Humberstone, catch a **colectivo** (Amunategui btw Aldea & Latorre; CH$2000) from the eastern side of Iquique's Mercado Centenario (p459). To return, stand at the bus stop outside the entrance of Humberstone and flag down any bus marked 'Iquique' (CH$1500).

The whopping pre-Columbian geoglyph **El Gigante de Atacama** (Giant of the Atacama), 14km east of Huara on the slopes of Cerro Unita is, at 86m, the world's largest archaeological representation of a human figure. Representing a powerful shaman, its blocky head emanates rays and its thin limbs clutch an arrow and medicine bag. Experts estimate it dates to around AD 900. The best views are from several hundred meters back at the base of the hill. To visit, go in a taxi or on a tour.

Amid Atacama's desolate pampas you'll find straggly groves of resilient tamarugo *(Prosopis tamarugo)* lining the Panamericana south of Pozo Almonte. The forest once covered thousands of square kilometers until clear-cutting for the mines nearly destroyed it. The trees are protected within the **Reserva Nacional Pampa del Tamarugal**, where you can also find 420 restored geoglyphs of humans, llamas and geometric shapes blanketing the hillside at **Pintados** (adult/child CH$2000/free; ⏲10am-4pm). A derelict nitrate railyard of ruined buildings and rusting rolling stock, the site lies 4.5km west of the Panamericana via a gravel road, nearly opposite the eastward turnoff to Pica.

The oasis of **Pica** is a chartreuse patch on a dusty canvas, 113km southeast of Iquique. Its fame hails from its pica limes, the key ingredient of the tart and tasty *pisco sour*. Day-trippers can enjoy splashing around the freshwater pool, **Cocha Resbaladero** (admission CH$2000; ⏲8am-8:30pm), fresh fruit drink in hand.

Mamiña, 125km east of Iquique (not on the same road to Pica) is a quizzical terraced town with thermal baths, a 17th-century church and a pre-Columbian fortress, **Pukará del Cerro Inca**. The village huddles into upper and lower sectors, the former clustered around the rocky outcrop where the 1632 **Iglesia de San Marcos** stands, while the latter lies low in the valley, where the hot springs are.

Arica

☎058 / POP 185,300

Summery days of ripping big surf and warm sea currents bless this otherwise drab city, flush against Peru. Arica is an urban beach resort, with long swaths of sand reaching the knobby headland of El Morro. You'll find Aymara people peddling their crafts at stalls, Eiffel's iron church and a few other architectural gems.

Sights & Activities

A pedestrian mall is on 21 de Mayo. South of town, along Av Comandante San Martín, the best beaches for swimming and lounging around are Playa El Laucho, just past the Club de Yates, followed by the comely, sheltered Playa La Lisera, with changing rooms and showers. Arica's treacherous tubes host high-profile surf championships. July sees the biggest breaks. The beaches north of downtown are rougher but cleaner. Playa Chinchorro, 2km away, features pricey eateries and jet-ski rentals. Playa Las Machas, a few kilometers north, is a surfers' haunt. Take bus 12 or 14 from 18 de Septiembre; get off on the corner of Av Antarctica and Av España.

TOP CHOICE **Museo de Sitio Colón 10** MUSEUM
(Colón 10; adult/child CH$2000/1000; ⊙10am-7pm Tue-Sun Jan-Feb, 10am-6pm Tue-Sun Mar-Dec) See the 32 excavated Chinchorro mummies in situ at this tiny museum below El Morro. You can gape at the glass-protected bodies as they were found, complete with their funerary bundles, skins and feathers of marine fowl. There are a few infants, with red-painted mud masks.

Museo Arqueológico San Miguel de Azapa MUSEUM
(☎205-551; Camino Azapa Km 12; adult/child CH$2000/1000; ⊙9am-8pm Jan & Feb, 10am-6pm Mar-Dec) This museum, 12km east of Arica, is home to some of the world's oldest mummies. There are superb local archaeological and cultural heritage displays and well-written guide booklets in English.

El Morro de Arica HILL
The imposing tawny hunk of rock looming 110m over the city, El Morro de Arica is reached by the footpath from the south end of Colón.

Iglesia San Marcos CHURCH
(Plaza Colón; ⊙mass 8:30am Mon-Fri, 8pm Sat, 10am-noon & 8pm Sun) Alexandre Gustave Eiffel designed the Gothic-style 1875 Iglesia San Marcos. Eiffel also designed **Aduana de Arica** (admission free; ⊙8:30am-8pm daily Jan & Feb, 8:30am-5:30pm Mon-Thu & 8:30am-4:30pm Fri Mar-Dec), the former customs house at Parque General Baquedano (before landfill, it fronted the harbor).

Tours

A variety of tour agencies, offering excursions into the surrounding regions and into Peru, line the pedestrian streets downtown.

Raíces Andinas GUIDED TOUR
(☎233-305; www.raicesandinas.com; Héroes del Morro 632) A well-run outfit recommended for encouraging better understanding of the local people. It specializes in trips of two or more days and offers expeditions to Sajama in Bolivia via Lauca, as well as adventures into Salar de Uyuni.

Sleeping

Free camping is possible in the north sector of Playa Las Machas.

Arica Surfhouse HOSTEL $
(☎312-213; www.aricasurfhouse.cl; O'Higgins 661; dm CH$10,000, d with/without bathroom CH$27,000/23,000; @☜) Doubling as Arica's surfer central, this is one of Arica's top hostels, with a variety of clean rooms, complimentary breakfast with real coffee, a great open-air communal area, 24-hour hot water and laundry service. There's a shuttle service to the beaches in winter months and the staff will hook you up with surf classes and equipment rental.

El Buey Hostal HOSTEL $$
(☎325-530; www.elbueyhostal.com; Punta del Este 605, La Lisera; s/d/ste CH$20,000/40,000/50,000; @☜) The coolest beachside option, this whitewashed Med-style house sits on the residential hillside above La Lisera beach. It's for surfers with style, with hardwood floors, gorgeous terraces, sparkling kitchens, ocean views, a communal rooftop terrace with hammocks, surf equipment rental and classes, and bike rental.

Sunny Days HOSTEL $
(☎241-038; www.sunny-days-arica.cl; Aravena 161; dm incl breakfast CH$9000, d with/without bathroom CH$24,000/20,000; @☜) A hop and a skip from the bus terminals in an alleyway behind Chinchorro beach, this supremely welcoming hostel is lovingly run by a helpful Kiwi-Chilean couple who live on site. Laundry, storage, bike rental, use of two communal kitchens and loads of info are all available.

Eating

Look for traditional seafood lunches on **Muelle Pesquero**, the fishing jetty. Tap water here is chemical-laden; buy your own bottles. Several supermarkets downtown provide picnic fixings for surfers and self-caterers. Many of the hippest bars and discos are strung along Playa Chinchorro.

Mercado Colón CHILEAN $
(cnr Colón & Maipú; set menus CH$1500-3500; ⊙breakfast & lunch) Small-time restaurants offer cheap fish lunches and flavorful soups in this bustling covered market.

El Arriero CHILEAN $$
(21 de Mayo 385; mains CH$4000-9100; ⊙closed Sun) This old-school eatery is perfect for red-blooded carnivores who don't mind waiting

for an old-fashioned *parrillada* (a mixture of grilled meats).

Boulevard Vereda Bolognesi INTERNATIONAL $
(Bolognesi 340; ⊙closed Sun) Hip little shopping mall with a clutch of cool cafes, restaurants and bars. Choose between a salad bar, a Peruvian joint, an Italian trattoria or a sushi bar, and eat on the central patio. There's real espresso, too.

Maracuyá SEAFOOD $$
(Av Comandante San Martín 0321; mains CH$6000-11,000) To treat yourself to a superb seafood meal complete with bow-tie service and sea views, head to this villa-style restaurant next to Playa El Laucho.

 Information

Internet cafes and call centers line 21 de Mayo and Bolognesi. There are numerous 24 hour ATMs and *cambios* along the pedestrian mall (21 de Mayo).

Conaf (☎201-200; tarapaca@conaf.cl; Av Vicuña Mackenna 820; ⊙8:30am-5:35pm Mon-Fri) This outlet carries some useful information about Región I (Tarapacá) national parks.

Hospital Dr Juan Noé (☎232-242; 18 de Septiembre 1000)

Post Office (Prat 305)

Sernatur (☎252-054; infoarica@sernatur.cl; San Marcos 101; ⊙9am-8pm Mon-Fri, 10am-2pm Sat Jan-Feb, 9am-6pm Mar-Dec) Helpful locale with brochures on Tarapacá and other Chilean regions.

Dangers & Annoyances

While Arica is a very safe city, it has a reputation for pickpockets. Be especially cautious at bus terminals and beaches.

 Getting There & Away

Air

LAN (☎600-526-2000; www.lan.com; Arturo Prat 391) has several daily flights to Santiago (CH$210,000, 2½ hours). **Sky** (☎600-600-2828; www.skyairline.cl; 21 de Mayo 356) has cheaper and less frequent domestic flights. Chacalluta Airport is 18km north of the city.

Bus

Arica has two main bus terminals. **Terminal Rodoviario de Arica** (Terminal de Buses; ☎241-390; Diego Portales 948) houses most companies traveling south to destinations in Chile. Next door, **Terminal Internacional de Buses** (☎248-709; Diego Portales 1002) handles international and some regional destinations. To reach the terminals, take *colectivo 8* from Maipú or San Marcos; a taxi costs between CH$1500 and CH$2500.

More than a dozen companies have offices in Terminal Rodoviario de Arica, and ply destinations toward the south, from Iquique to Santiago. Some major ones are **Buses Pullman Santa Rosa** (☎241-029), **Flota Barrios** (☎223-587), **Pullman Carmelita** (☎241-591), **Ramos Cholele** (☎221-029) and **Tur Bus** (☎222-217).

For Putre, **La Paloma** (☎222-710; Riesco 2071) has a direct bus at 7am (CH$3500, 1½ hours). To get to Tacna, Peru (CH$2000), **Adsubliata** (☎226-2495) buses leave the international terminal every half hour. To get to La Paz, Bolivia (around CH$8500, nine hours), the comfiest and fastest service is with **Chile Bus** (☎260-505), but cheaper buses are available with **Trans Salvador** (☎246-064) in the international bus terminal. Buses on this route will drop passengers in Parque Nacional Lauca, but expect to pay full fare to La Paz. **Buses Géminis** (☎351-465), in the main terminal, goes to Salta and Jujuy in Argentina (CH$43,000) a few times a week.

GETTING TO PERU & BOLIVIA

Travelers cross from Arica, Chile into Tacna, Peru by train, bus or *colectivo*. The border crossing at Tacna is open daily from 8am to 12am and 24 hours from Friday to Sunday. Buses with international routes simply cross; long-distance routes are best booked in Tacna, where you'll find lower prices. Train passengers will go through immigration and customs in the train stations. Have your passport and tourist card on hand and eat any stowaway fruits or vegetables before crossing. From October to February, Peruvian time is two hours behind Chilean time. The rest of the year it is one hour behind Chilean time.

The most popular route to cross into Bolivia is via Parque Nacional Lauca, crossing from the Chilean town of Chungara to Tambo Quemado. Most international buses have morning departures. Immigration is open from 8am to 9pm. You can also reach the border of Chungara via taxi from Putre: cross the border on foot and find local transportation in Tambo Quemado.

WORTH A TRIP

RUTA DE LOS MISIONES

In the isolated Andean foothills, a series of rough gravel roads connect traditional *precordillera* hamlets that time forgot. Over centuries, earthquakes have damaged the villages' pretty colonial churches, ancient agricultural terraces and *pukarás* (pre-Hispanic fortifications). But an Arica-based foundation, **Fundación Altiplano** (☎253-616; www.fundacionaltiplano.cl; Andres Bello 1515), is rebuilding the old churches and promoting sustainable development of these nearly forgotten Andean communities. The new heritage tourism circuit is called **Ruta de los Misiones**, or 'the mission route.' Adventurous travelers interested in architecture and archaeology will delight in the stunning restoration achievements in villages such as Belén and Socoroma. Log onto the foundation's website or stop by its office in Arica for a detailed guidebook explaining its projects.

For those with vehicles (note that a 4WD is highly recommended, if not imperative), this spectacular route is a great way to get from Codpa to Putre, or vice versa. Make sure you get a good road map, and don't attempt this journey during the rainy season (December through March), since rivers run amok due to heavy rains and often wash the roads away.

The fertile oasis of the Codpa valley is home to the area's best place to overnight, **Codpa Valley Lodge** (www.codpavalleylodge.cl; d incl breakfast CH$60,000; 🏊). This solar energy–powered hideaway has cozy rooms with private patios set around a swimming pool, a good restaurant and a variety of tours. For a homestay-style cultural experience in Belén, consider having a traditional Andean meal in the rustic kitchen of locally famous cook **Nila Santos** (☎8850-5008, in Arica 212-791; 21 de Mayo 79, Belén). Call her ahead of time and she'll prepare a feast featuring local produce; with advance notice she'll even make *la guatia* (a traditional northern dish of meat, vegetables and spices cooked in an underground 'oven'). She'll also accommodate overnight guests (dorm beds CH$5000).

La Paloma (☎222-710; Germán Riesco 2071) in Arica goes to Codpa (8:30am Monday, Wednesday and Friday, CH$2500) and Belén (7am Tuesday and Friday, CH$3500); Transportes Gonzalo Catalan has additional departures. It's not possible, however, to make a loop through all of the villages on public transportation.

DESTINATION	COST (CH$)	DURATION (HR)
Antofagasta	16,000	10
Calama	16,000	9
Copiapó	22,000	18
Iquique	7000	4
La Paz, Bolivia	8000	9
La Serena	27,000	23
Santiago	32,000	27

Train

Trains to Tacna (CH$1900, 1½ hours) depart from **Estación Ferrocarril Arica-Tacna** (☎097-633-2896; Av Máximo Lira 791) on weekday mornings.

Ruta 11 & Putre

The barren slopes of the Lluta Valley host hillside geoglyphs, **Poconchile** and its quake-ridden 17th-century church, candelabra cacti (consider yourself blessed if you see it in bloom, which happens one 24-hour period per year), and the chasmside ruins of the 12th-century fortress **Pukará de Copaquilla**.

Detour in Poconchile to **Eco-Truly** (☎096-875-0732; www.ecotrulyarica.cl; Sector Linderos, Km 29; campsites per person CH$4000, r incl breakfast CH$8000), a slightly surreal Hare Krishna 'ecotown' and yoga school, for an abundant vegetarian sampler lunch (CH$2500).

Aymara village **Putre** (population 1980; altitude 3530m) is 150km northeast of Arica and an appealing stop for visitors to acclimatize. There's a post office and call center in town, but only one bank – bring cash from Arica. Baquedano is the main strip.

Take advantage of the excellent hikes among ancient stone-faced terraces of alfalfa and oregano and tranquil village ambience. Colonial architecture includes the restored adobe **Iglesia de Putre** (1670). During the frivolously fun **Carnaval** in February, exploding flour balloons and live music rule the day.

An Alaskan biologist offers excellent birdwatching, wildflower and natural-history excursions through **Alto Andino Nature Tours** (☎099-890-7291; www.birdingaltoandino.com; Baquedano 299). Flavio of **Terrace Lodge & Tours** (☎584-275; www.terracelodge.com; Circunvalación 25) runs a range of wonderful guided tours to some hidden spots, both in the immediate area around Putre as well as further up north. The stylish and eco-friendly **Terrace Lodge** (☎584-275; www.terracelodge.com; Circunvalación 25; s CH$24,000-27,000, d CH$31,000; @ 📶) is a lovely place to spend a few nights as well.

Other recommended accommodations in Putre include **Chakana** (☎099-745-9519; www.la-chakana.com; dm/s/d CH$8000/21,000/28,000; @), a cozy delight that boasts the best views and breakfast in town. It's off an unmarked dirt road 750m from the plaza, but you can arrange for a free pickup with reservations. More centrally located, **Hostal Cali** (☎318-456; contacto@calitours.com; Baquedano s/n; s/d CH$15,000/24,000, d without bathroom CH$18,000; @ 📶), a family-run spot with 12 rooms, is a good bet for budget-busters.

On the main plaza, **Cantaverdi** (Plaza s/n; mains CH$1800-4500; 📶) is a casual eatery featuring *humitas* (corn dumplings) and home cooking, a roaring fireplace and wi-fi. **Kuchu Marka** (Baquedano 351; set lunch CH$3500, set dinner CH$5500; ⏲lunch & dinner) offers upscale *altiplano* cuisine (think quinoa and alpaca steaks) and good coffee.

Note that things seriously wind down in Putre from mid-December through February, the rainy season.

Buses La Paloma (☎222-710; Germán Riesco 2071) serves Putre daily; buses depart Arica at 7am and return at 2pm (CH$3500). Note that some international buses between Arica and La Paz, Bolivia, stop near Putre; to make the connection into Bolivia, you'll have to coordinate with the ticketing offices in Arica's bus terminal.

Parque Nacional Lauca

At woozy heights with snow-dusted volcanoes, remote hot springs and glimmering lakes, Lauca, 160km northeast of Arica, is an absolute treasure. Herds of *vicuña,* viscachas and bird species including flamingos, giant coots and Andean gulls inhabit the park (138,000 hectares; altitude 3000m to 6300m) alongside impressive cultural and archaeological landmarks.

Tours to the park cover the following highlights.

Lauca's crown jewel, the glittering **Lago Chungará** (4517m above sea level), is a shallow body of water formed by lava flows damming the snowmelt stream from **Volcán Parinacota** (6350m), a beautiful snowcapped cone that rises immediately to the north. **Laguna Cotacotani** has been partially drained by the national electricity company but you will still see diverse birdlife along its shores and scattered groves of *queñoa,* one of the world's highest-elevation trees. Wander around beautiful **Parinacota**, a tiny Aymara village of whitewashed adobe and stone streets. If you're lucky, the guide will procure the key for the town's undisputed gem, its 17th-century colonial church, reconstructed in 1789.

At the park's western entrance, **Las Cuevas** has a viewing point marked by a sculpture resembling *zampoña* (panpipes) balanced on a garish staircase. Some tours include a quick dip in **Termas Jurasi** (adult/child CH$2000/1000), a pretty cluster of thermal and mud baths huddled amid rocky scenery, 11km northeast of Putre.

Many tour agencies offer one-day blitzes from sea-level Arica – a surefire method to get *soroche* (altitude sickness). These tours cost from CH$20,000 (including a late lunch in Putre) and leave around 7:30am, returning about 8:30pm. Verify whether the operator carries oxygen on the bus, as many people become very sick at high altitudes. Avoid overeating, smoking and alcohol consumption the day before and while you are on your tour. Tours that include at least a night in Putre are a wiser option, allowing more time to acclimatize. If you are renting a car, or have your own, carry extra fuel and antifreeze, and contact **Conaf** (☎058-201-225; www.conaf.cl) for the latest conditions.

MIDDLE CHILE

Chile's heartland, covered with orchards and vineyards, is oft skipped by travelers scrambling further afield. But if this region existed anywhere else in the world, it would be getting some serious attention. The abundant harvests of the fertile central valley fill grocer's bins from Anchorage to Tokyo. Come for wine-tasting, great skiing, respectable surfing and unspoiled national parks.

Keep in mind that the region was at the epicenter of the February 2010 earthquake.

Middle Chile

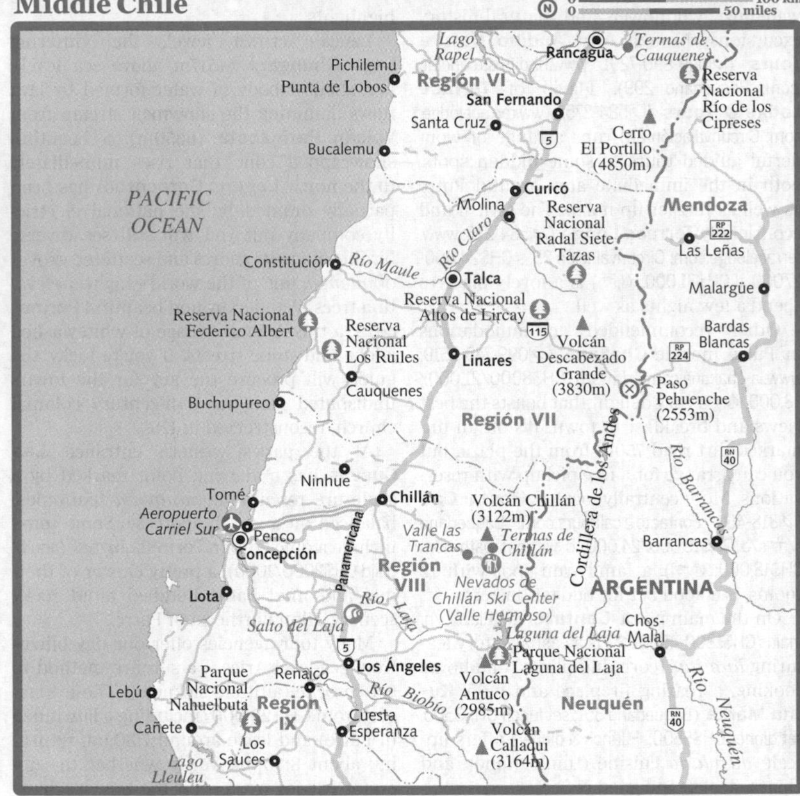

Towns and cities such as Concepción, Talca and Curicó were the hardest hit. The region has mostly bounced back, though you'll still come across crumbled churches and roped-off plazas.

Colchagua Valley

With around 20 wineries open to the public, the Colchagua Valley is Chile's biggest and best-established wine region. Its deep loamy soils, abundant water, dry air, bright sunshine and cool nights have given rise to some of the country's best reds: Cabernet Sauvignon, Merlot and Carmenere make up most of the grapes, but top-notch Malbecs are also appearing. Many travelers who come here to taste wine book hotel rooms in Santa Cruz.

SANTA CRUZ

072

Ground zero of Chile's winemaking and wine-touring scene is a fairly sleepy place with a picturesque main square. The place perks up during the lively **Fiesta de la Vendimia**, the grape-harvest festival held in the plaza at the beginning of March.

While in town, check out the vast **Museo de Colchagua** (821-050; www.museocolchagua.cl; Errázuriz 145; adult/child CH$5000/2000; 10am-7pm); the collection features pre-Columbian anthropomorphic ceramics from all over Latin America, weapons, religious artifacts, Mapuche silver, and *huasos* (cowboy) gear. Of particular interest is the exhibit *El Gran Rescate* (The Great Rescue), showing objects, photos and films related to the October 2010 rescue of the 33 miners trapped 700m underground in San José.

An extremely helpful resource on the main square is **Ruta del Vino** (823-199; www.rutadelvino.cl; Plaza de Armas 298; 9am-6pm Mon-Fri, 10am-6pm Sat & Sun). In addition to providing information about the region's wineries, it offers tasting tours (CH$10,000 to CH$22,000; reservations required 48 hours before tour). However, transportation to the wineries isn't included in the basic price (for a full tour with lunch and transportation, you'll be paying upwards of CH$128,500). If you're fine sticking with the wineries closer to town, you can pay for taxi rides. Car rental isn't available in Santa Cruz; one option is renting a car in Santiago and driving yourself around the wine country, even if you plan on joining a guided tour.

The **bus terminal** (Casanova 478) is four blocks west of the plaza. Twice every hour, **Buses Nilahué** (825-582; www.busesnilahue.cl) goes to Pichilemu (CH$4500, 3½ hours) and Santiago (CH$8000, four hours).

COLCHAGUA VALLEY WINERIES

Top wineries include the following; visit on a guided tour with Ruta del Vino or make reservations with the wineries ahead of time.

Viu Manent WINERY
(072-858-751; www.viumanent.cl; Carretera del Vino, Km 37; tasting CH$10,000; tours 10:30am, noon, 3pm & 4:30pm) Close to Santa Cruz; tours involve a carriage ride through 80-year-old vineyards.

Emiliana WINERY
(099-9225-5679; www.emiliana.cl; Camino Lo Moscoso s/n, Placilla; biodynamic tours incl 4 pours CH$10,000; tours 10:30am, 11:30am, 12:30pm, 2:30pm & 4:30pm) Biodynamic growing techniques are explained at this eco-friendly vineyard.

Lapostolle/Clos Apalta Winery WINERY
(072-321-803; www.lapostolle.com; tour incl 2 pours CH$20,000; 10:30am-5:30pm) The most exclusive setup in Colchagua produces a single premium wine from hand-picked, hand-separated grapes. Reserve online.

Pichilemu

072 / POP 12,500

Wave gods and goddesses brave the icy waters of Chile's unofficial surf capital year round, while mere beach-going mortals fill its long black sands December through March. Pichilemu's laid-back vibe and great waves make it easy to see why it's so popular with visiting board-riders.

The westernmost part of 'Pichi' juts out into the sea, forming **La Puntilla**, the closest surfing spot to town. **Escuela de Surf Manzana 54** (099-574-5984; www.manzana54.cl; Av Costanera s/n; full-day board & gear hire CH$7000-8000, 2hr classes CH$10,000) offers surf rentals and classes here. Fronting the town center to the northeast is calm Playa Principal (main beach), while south is the longer and rougher **Infiernillo**, known for its more dangerous waves and fast tow. The best surfing in the area is at **Punta de Lobos**, 6km south of Pichi proper, which you need to drive or hitchhike to.

If you're only here to surf, you'll be better off staying on the beaches, while other travelers will prefer being closer to the cafes, shopping, restaurants and services of Pichilemu itself. In town, **Hotel Chile España** (841-270; www.chileespana.cl; Av Ortúzar 255; s/d/tr incl breakfast CH$30,000/40,000/60,000;) is a pretty budget hotel that now caters largely to older travelers. Across the street is the rambling clifftop **Cabañas Guzmán Lyon** (841-068; www.cabanasguzmanlyon.cl; San Antonio 48; 2-person cabins incl breakfast CH$30,000-45,500;), where cute cottages offer private patios with beautiful views over the ocean and lake. *Residenciales* (budget accommodations) pop up around town in summertime, too. Down by the surf breaks, several hostels compete for business, including **Pichilemu Surf Hostal** (842-350; www.pichilemusurfhostal.com; Eugenio Diaz Lira 167; dm/s/d CH$12,000/30,000/36,000), also home to the famous eatery **El Puente Holandés** (mains CH$3500-6900; 9am-11pm). Come for seafood ravioli and grilled sea bass – the terrace is spot-on for a beer.

Back in town, **La Casa de las Empanadas** (Aníbal Pinto 268; empanadas CH$1200-1900) is a cheerful takeaway counter serving up huge gourmet empanadas such as *machas y queso* (razor clams and cheese). The low-key **Restaurante Pinpón** (Av Ross 9; mains CH$3000-5500) offers seafood stews and other Chilean staples; several similar options are nearby.

From the **Terminal de Buses** (841-709; cnr Av Millaco & Los Alerces) on Pichilemu's outskirts, buses run frequently to Santiago (CH$6000, four hours), Santa Cruz (CH$3000, three hours) and San Fernando (CH$3500, 3½ hours) where there are connections north and south.

Curicó

075 / POP 158,000

Drawing visitors interested in local vineyards and the exquisite Reserva Nacional Radal Siete Tazas, Curicó is a laid-back city, best known for its postcard-perfect **Plaza de Armas**, complete with palms and monkey- puzzle trees, a striking early-20th-century wrought-iron bandstand, and a wooden statue of the Mapuche chief Toqui Lautaro. Sadly, according to BBC reports, up to 90% of the older buildings in Curicó's historic center were destroyed in the February 2010 earthquake. Despite the recent hardship, Curicó still bursts into life for the **Festival de la Vendimia** (Wine Harvest Festival) in early fall.

Vineyard **Miguel Torres** (242-9360; www.migueltorres.cl; Panamericana Sur, Km 195; mains CH$8100-13,400), located 5km south of town, conducts daily tours and serves lunch at its stylish restaurant. Take *colectivos* going to Molina and ask to be dropped off, or take a taxi.

Rambling **Hotel Prat** (311-069; Peña 427; s/d incl breakfast CH$25,000/35,000;) is an economical sleeping option near the square. To upgrade, you can try the wine-themed **Hostal Viñedos** (326-785; www.hostalvinedos.cl; Chacabuco 645; s/d/tr incl breakfast CH$25,000/30,000/35,000;) with bright rooms and bouncy beds; it's in the countryside outside of town.

You'll find plenty of quick food options, from empanadas to fresh fruit, at the stands surrounding the bus station.

The **Terminal de Buses** (cnr Prat & Maipú) and the **Estación de Ferrocarril** (600-585-5000; Maipú 657) are four blocks west of the Plaza de Armas. There are seven trains a day to Santiago (CH$4000 to CH$8000, 2¼ hours) and Chillán (CH$8000, 2½ hours). **Talmocur** goes frequently to Talca (CH$1700). Buses to Santiago (CH$2500 to CH$3500, 2½ hours) leave about every half-hour; try **Bus Pullman Sur** (Henríquez), three blocks north of the plaza, or **Tur Bus** (312-115; www.turbus.cl; Av Manso de Velasco 0106).

To get to Reserva Nacional Radal Siete Tazas, catch a bus to Molina (CH$500, 35 minutes, every five minutes) with **Buses Aquelarre** (314-307) from the Terminal de Buses Rurales, opposite the main bus terminal. From Molina there are frequent services to the park in January and February.

Maule Valley

The Maule Valley, a hugely significant wine-producing region for Chile, is responsible for much of the country's export wine; the specialty here is full-bodied Cabernet Sauvignon. The area was at the epicenter of the February 2010 earthquake – one winery reported losing its 80,000-bottle collection, countless vineyard workers were left homeless and the nearby city of Talca lost its historic marketplace, hospital and museum.

Happily, the wine industry has largely recovered, thanks in part to some inspired community efforts. Apart from wine, many visitors use Talca as a base for exploring the wineries and the nearby Reserva Nacional Altos de Lircay.

TALCA

071 / POP 199,000

Founded in 1690, Talca was once considered one of the country's principal cities; Chile's 1818 declaration of independence was signed here. These days, it's mainly known as a convenient base for exploring the gorgeous Reserva Nacional Altos de Lircay and the Maule Valley wine country. You'll find a decent range of traveler's services, including dining and lodging options, plus lovely views of the Andes when you're strolling down the sunbaked pedestrian thoroughfare at midday.

Four blocks from the Plaza de Armas, **Cabañas Stella Bordestero** (235-545; www.turismostella.cl; 4 Poniente 1 Norte 1183; s/d/tr/q CH$20,000/30,000/36,000/42,000;) offers cozy, well-equipped clapboard cabins in a leafy garden. Accommodations are available at **Hostal Maea** (210-910; www.hostalmaea.cl; 1 Sur 1080; d with/without bathroom from CH$16,000/12,000;), just off Talca's pedestrian promenade. In the countryside outside of town, the lovely **Hostal Casa Chueca** (197-0096; www.trekkingchile.com/casachueca; Viña Andrea s/n, Sector Alto Lircay; dm CH$10,000-12,500, d CH$41,000;) is a destination in its own right; the knowledgeable owners can help you plan trekking and horse riding in Reserva Nacional Altos de Lircay. Contact the hostel ahead of time for pick-up information.

Centrally located **La Buena Carne** (cnr 6 Oriente & 1 Norte; mains CH$3000-5500) is a contemporary steakhouse with friendly service, wines by the glass and classic Chilean platters. **Cafeteria La Papa** (1 Sur 1271; snacks CH$800) does strong espresso and homemade cakes, while nearby **Centro Aleman** (1 Sur 1330, Local 21-26; sandwiches CH$1800-4200) offers delicious pork sandwiches and sidewalk seating. Head to **Pirandello** (5 Oriente 1186; pizzas CH$5000) for inexpensive pizzas and *pisco sours*; the new **Diagonal Cero** (cnr 1 Norte & Isidoro del Solar) is a top choice for cocktails on the leafy terrace.

There are plenty of ATMs and internet cafes in town. Don't miss a stop at the extremely helpful **Sernatur office** (233-669; www.chile.travel/en.html; 1 Oriente 1150; 8:30am-5:30pm Mon-Fri) on the main square.

North–south buses stop at Talca's main **bus station** (243-366; 2 Sur 1920, cnr 12 Oriente) or the nearby **Tur Bus** (265-715; www.turbus.cl; 3 Sur 1960) terminal. It's a hike from the center; hop in a *colectivo* marked 'plaza' (CH$450) to reach downtown. Destinations include Chillán (CH$4200, two hours), Puerto Montt (CH$15,000, 11 hours) and Santiago (CH$5000, three hours). To connect to Pichilemu, take the bus to Curicó (CH$1800). **Buses Vilches** (235-327) has several daily services to Vilches Alto, the gateway to the Reserva Nacional Altos de Lircay. From the **EFE train station** (226-254; 11 Oriente 1000), there are eight trains a day north to Santiago (CH$4000 to CH$8000, 2¾ hours) and south to Chillán (CH$9500, two hours).

MAULE VALLEY WINERIES

You can visit many of the vineyards independently or through one of the tours run by **Ruta del Vino** (08-157-9951; www.valledelmaule.cl; Av Circunvalación Oriente 1055, Casino Talca Hotel Lobby, Talca; 9am-6:30pm Mon-Fri).

Viña Balduzzi WINERY
(073-322-138; www.balduzziwines.cl; Av Balmaceda 1189, San Javier; tour incl 4 pours CH$5000; 9am-6pm Mon-Sat) A visitor-friendly fourth-generation winery surrounded by spacious gardens and well-kept colonial buildings. Unlike at many other wineries, no booking is required and it's easy to reach by public transportation. From the bus terminal in Talca, look for a bus labeled 'San Javier Directo,' which drops you off near the winery.

Via Wines WINERY
(071-415-511; www.viawines.com; Fundo Las Chilcas s/n; tour incl 3 pours CH$10,000; 9am-5pm Mon-Sat, by reservation) One of Chile's first certifiably sustainable wineries, Via Wines turns out delicious Sauvignon Blanc and Syrah.

Viña Gillmore WINERY
(073-197-5539; www.gillmore.cl; Camino Constitución, Km 20; tour incl 2 pours CH$5000; 9am-5pm Mon-Sat) This winery turns out a fabulous Cabernet Franc and features beautiful hiking trails and a spa offering various wine-based therapies.

Chillán

042 / POP 180,200

Earthquakes have battered Chillán throughout its turbulent history; the 2010 earthquake was yet another hit. While this perpetually rebuilding city isn't especially interesting, it is a gateway to some of the loveliest landscapes in middle Chile.

In response to the devastation that the 1939 quake caused, the Mexican government donated the **Escuela México** (Av O'Higgins 250; donations welcome; 10am-1:30pm & 2-6pm Mon-Fri, 10am-6pm Sat & Sun) to the city. At Pablo Neruda's request, Mexican muralists David Alfaro Siqueiros and Xavier Guerrero painted spectacular tributes to indigenous and post-Columbian figures in history; today it's a working school, and visitors' donations are encouraged.

A tumbling sprawl of produce and crafts (leather, basketry and weaving), the **Feria de Chillán** (Plaza de la Merced) is one of Chile's best markets. It's part of the **Mercado de Chillán** (set lunches CH$1500-3200; 9am-6pm), also an excellent locale for a budget lunch – *longaniza* (pork sausage) is a local staple.

Sleeping & Eating

Hotel Bavaria GUESTHOUSE $
(217-235; www.hotelbavaria.cl; 18 de Septiembre 648; d incl breakfast CH$20,000-30,000;) This cozy house, which now operates as a small hotel, has tidy doubles with twin beds, TVs and private bathrooms. The downside is a smoky lobby.

Hostal Canadá GUESTHOUSE $
(234-515; Av Libertad 269; s/d CH$8000/16,000) Spending a night in this no-nonsense mother-and-daughter setup is like staying in their apartment – fraying floral sheets, worn carpets, lumpy pillows and all.

Arcoiris Vegetariano VEGETARIAN $
(El Roble 525; set lunches CH$2000-4900; 9am-6:30pm Mon-Sat;) This colorful vegetarian restaurant is good for breakfast and economical lunches.

WORTH A TRIP

SIETE TAZAS & ALTOS DE LIRCAY

Clear water ladles into seven basalt pools in the lush **Reserva Nacional Radal Siete Tazas** (www.conaf.cl; adult/child CH$4000/600; ⏲8:30am-8pm Dec-Feb, to 5:30pm Mar-Nov) with the spectacle ending at a 50m waterfall. Two well-marked hiking trails loop from **Camping Los Robles** (☎075-228-029; 6-person campsites CH$8000): the 1km **Sendero el Coigüe** and 7km **Sendero Los Chiquillanes**, which has great views of the Valle del Indio (plan on about four hours in total). Conaf runs two cold-water **campsites** (☎075-228-029; campsite per person CH$1500) at Parque Inglés. The park is 65km from Curicó. During January and February **Buses Hernández** goes frequently from Molina to Parque Inglés (CH$1800, 2½ hours).

In the Andean foothills, 65km east of Talca, **Reserva Nacional Altos de Lircay** (www.altosdelircay.cl; adult/child CH$3500/600; ⏲8:30am-5:30pm) offers fabulous trekking under a chattery flutter of *tricahues* and other native parrots. A helpful team of Conaf rangers who run the park give detailed advice about hiking and camping within it. Arguably the best hike in the whole of middle Chile, the full-day **Sendero Enladrillado** takes you to the top of a unique 2300m basaltic plateau with stunning views. Alternatively, the shorter **Sendero Laguna** leads uphill to the gorgeous Laguna del Alto, a mountain-ringed lake at 2000m above sea level. Hostal Casa Chueca (p468) outside Talca offers excellent guided day hikes.

Conaf runs the excellent **Camping Antahuara** (campsites per person CH$2500 & one-off site fee CH$8000) about 500m beyond the *administración* (headquarters), next to Río Lircay. From Talca, Buses Vilches goes several times daily to Vilches Alto (CH$1500, two hours), 5km from the *administración*. It takes about 1½ hours to drive to the reserve from Talca.

ℹ Information

Internet cafes, ATMs and call centers abound. There's free wi-fi on the pedestrian walkways downtown.

Hospital Herminda Martín (☎208-221; Francisco Ramírez 10)

Sernatur (☎223-272; www.chile.travel/en.html; 18 de Septiembre 455; ⏲8:30am-1:30pm & 3-6pm Mon-Fri)

ℹ Getting There & Away

Most long-distance buses use **Terminal María Teresa** (☎272-149; O'Higgins 010), just north of Av Ecuador. *Colectivo* 22 (CH$450) runs back and forth from the center. **Tur Bus** (☎248-327; www.turbus.cl) goes to Talca (CH$4200, two hours), **Pullman Bus** (☎272-178; www.pullmanbus.cl) runs to destinations in northern Chile, and **Sol Pacifico** (☎272-177) serves Viña del Mar and Valparaíso (CH$9500, eight hours). **Condor** (☎270-264) goes to Temuco (CH$3800, five hours).

The other terminal is the old **Terminal de Buses Inter-Regional** (☎221-014; Constitución 01), five blocks west of Plaza de Armas, from where you can catch Tur Bus and **Línea Azul** (☎211-192; www.buseslineaazul.cl), with the fastest service to Concepción (CH$2200, 1½ hours).

Local and regional buses use **Terminal de Buses Rurales** (☎423-814; Maipón 890), south of Maipó.

Nevados de Chillán & Valle Las Trancas

The southern slopes of the 3122m Volcán Chillán are the stunning setting of the **Nevados de Chillán ski center** (www.nevadosdechillan.com; day ski pass adult/child CH$35,000/23,000). There are 32 runs (up to 2500m long), maxing out at 1100m of vertical. Hikers come out on summer weekends, but it's quiet on a weekday in the off-season – bring your own picnic and don't count on hotels being open. You should bring cash from Chillán.

Soak in the thermal springs at **Valle Hermoso** (www.nevadosdechillan.com; adult/child CH$4500/2500; ⏲thermal springs 9am-5pm), where you'll find a **campground** (per campsite CH$21,000) and mini-market. **Riding Chile Hostal & Restaurant** (☎07-779-197; www.ridingchile.com; Ruta 55, Camino Termas de Chillán, Km 73; dm/d without bathroom CH$10,000/20,000; 📶✖), at the foot of the mountains, is a wooden lodge offering simple rooms and an appealing cafe on the wooden terrace. Another budget option is **Chil'in Hosteria** (☎042-247-075; www.chil-in.com; Ruta 55, Camino Termas de Chillán, Km 72; dm/d without bathroom CH$10,000/25,000; @📶), a ski lodge–style hostel and pizzeria. The après-ski scene is happening at **Snow Pub** (Camino Termas de Chillán, Ruta 55, Km 71; ⊙1pm-late).

From Chillán's Terminal de Buses Rurales, **Rembus** (☎229-377) has buses to Valle Las Trancas (CH$2000, 1¼ hours) five to seven times a day, with some services continuing to Valle Hermoso (CH$3200, 1½ hours).

Concepción

☎041 / POP 221,100

'Conce' was yet another city terribly damaged in the February 2010 earthquake; it was also ravaged by looting and lawlessness during the aftershocks. Despite its slightly shabby appearance, Concepción is very important to Chile's economy – the city is on the northern bank of the Río Biobío, Chile's only significant navigable waterway, and is home to port facilities and a major manufacturing industry. Chileans consider Concepción a socialist hotbed, mainly because of the intellectual influences of its universities.

Sights

Plaza Independencia PLAZA

On January 1, 1818, Bernardo O'Higgins proclaimed Chile's independence at the city's Plaza Independencia. On the grounds of the Barrio Universitario, the **Casa del Arte** (cnr Chacabuco & Paicaví; ⊙10am-6pm Tue-Fri, 10am-5pm Sat, 10am-2pm Sun) houses the massive mural by Mexican Jorge González Camarena, *La Presencia de América Latina* (1965).

Sleeping & Eating

Catering more to businesses than backpackers, accommodations here can be slim pickings.

Hotel San Sebastián HOTEL $

(☎295-6719; www.hotelsansebastian.cl; Rengo 463; s/d/tr CH$18,000/25,000/30,000, without bathroom CH$15,000/18,000/26,000) Spruced up optimistically with plastic flowers and lilac walls, the b side of this budget hotel is sagging beds and old carpets. Downstairs doubles are cleaner and brighter.

TOP CHOICE Don Quijote CHILEAN $

(Barros Arana 673; mains $3500-7000; ⊙closed Sun) This spacious, upscale cafe-eatery is your best bet in Concepción at any time of the day. Locals come in for coffee and cake, gigantic ice-cream sundaes, sandwiches and *pisco sours*; the large menu also features *ceviche,* fajitas and other well-prepared dishes. It's located on the main square.

Chela's DINER $

(Barros Arana 405; mains CH$2000-3500) Spike your cholesterol alongside other happy diners with hearty portions of *chorrillana* and steaks.

Information

ATMs and cyber cafes abound downtown.

Conaf (☎262-4000; www.conaf.cl; Barros Arana 215; ⊙8:30am-1pm & 2:30-5:30pm Mon-Fri) Information on parks and reserves.

Hospital Regional (☎220-8500; cnr San Martín & Av Roosevelt)

Sernatur (☎02-741-4145; www.chile.travel/en.html; Pinto 460; ⊙8:30am-8pm Jan & Feb, 8:30am-1pm & 3-6pm Mon-Fri Mar-Dec) Provides brochures.

Getting There & Away

Bus

Long-distance buses go to **Terminal de Buses Collao** (☎274-9000; Tegualda 860) – take a taxi into town or catch a *colectivo* (CH$500) on nearby Av Collao – and **Terminal Chillancito** (☎231-5036; Camilo Henríquez 2565).

There are dozens of daily services to Santiago (CH$8500) with companies including **Eme Bus** (☎232-0094), **Pullman Bus** (☎232-0309; www.pullmanbus.cl) and **Tur Bus** (☎231-5555; www.turbus.cl; Tucapel 530), which also goes to Valparaíso and south to Temuco (CH$6500), Valdivia (CH$8000) and Puerto Montt (CH$12,500). **Línea Azul** (☎286-1179; www.buseslineaazul.cl) runs frequently to Chillán (CH$2200).

Los Ángeles

☎043 / POP 170,000

A useful base for visiting Parque Nacional Laguna del Laja, Los Ángeles is an otherwise unprepossessing agricultural and industrial service center 110km south of Chillán. Visit **Sernatur** (☎317-107; www.chile.travel/en.html; Caupolicán 450, 3rd fl, Oficina 6; ⊙9am-5:30pm Mon-Fri) for the latest park information.

A string of *residenciales* (budget accommodations) line Caupolicán west of

WORTH A TRIP

LAGUNA DEL LAJA & NAHUELBUTA

The sparkling centerpiece of **Parque Nacional Laguna del Laja** (www.conaf.cl; adult/child CH$1200/600; ⌚8:30am-8pm Dec-Apr, to 6:30pm May-Nov) is the towering snowcone of Volcán Antuco (2985m). A fantastic trek, **Sendero Sierra Velluda**, circles its skirt, taking three days, or you can go for a day hike to get a taste of the action. Stay at a campsite or cabin at **Lagunillas** (☎043-321-086; campsites CH$10,000, 6-person cabins CH$30,000) and eat at the small restaurant at **Club de Esqui de los Ángeles** (☎043-322-651; www.skiantuco.cl; mains CH$3000-4500). Departing from Los Ángeles' Terminal de Buses Rurales, local buses (CH$1700, 1½ hours, seven daily) go to the village of El Abanico, 11km from the park entrance. The last bus back to Los Ángeles leaves Abanico at 5:30pm (Monday to Saturday) and at 7:15pm on Sunday.

Pehuéns, or monkey-puzzle trees, grow up to 50m tall and 2m in diameter on the green slopes of **Parque Nacional Nahuelbuta** (www.parquenahuelbuta.cl; adult/child CH$4500/2000; ⌚8:30am-8pm), a fine destination for hiking and mountain biking. You can pitch your tent at **Camping Pehuenco** (6-person campsites CH$12,000). From Angol, 35km to the east, the Terminal de Buses Rurales has buses to Vegas Blancas (CH$1700, 1½ hours). Some lines go on Monday, Wednesday and Friday, others on alternate days. Buses generally return from Vegas Blancas at 6pm – confirm these times so you don't get stranded.

the Plaza de Armas. Despite appearances, they're not particularly cheap and mostly function as men's boarding houses, so women travelers might not feel comfortable there. Recently renovated **Hotel del Centro** (☎236-961; www.hoteldelcentro.cl; Lautaro 539; s/d incl breakfast CH$31,500/40,000) is a better option.

You'll see plenty of casual cafes and teahouses serving inexpensive sandwiches and cakes around the busy *centro*. The bright corner bar-restaurant **Solcito** (cnr Villagrán & Lautaro; mains CH$2800-4500; ⌚9am-midnight Mon-Sat, noon-7pm Sun; 📶) serves coffee and sandwiches during the day and, at night, grilled steaks, fish and icy beer.

Long-distance buses leave from the **Terminal Santa María** (Villagrán 501), on the northeast outskirts of town. The **Tur Bus** (www.turbus.cl) terminal is nearby. For service to the village of El Abanico, 11km from the entrance of Parque Nacional Laguna del Laja, go to the **Terminal de Buses Rurales** (Terminal Santa Rita; ☎313-232; Villagrán 501).

THE LAKES DISTRICT

The further south you go, the greener it gets, until you find snow-clad volcanoes rising over verdant hills and lakes. This bucolic region makes a great escape to a slower pace. The Araucanía, named for the monkey-puzzle tree, is the geographical center of Mapuche culture. Colonized by Germans in the 1850s, the area further south is a provincial enclave of stocking-clad grannies, fruit pies and lace curtains. So perfectly laid-back, you'll start to feel a little sleepy. Don't. Outside your shingled dwelling, tons of adventures wait: from rafting to climbing, from hiking to hot-springs hopping, from taking *onces* in colonial towns to sipping maté with the local *huasos*. Hospitality is the strong suit of *sureños* (southerners); take time to enjoy it.

Though they love the malls, rural roots still mark most city dwellers (about half the population), who split wood and make homemade jam as part of their daily routine. Seek out the green spaces bursting beyond the city limits. The isolated interior (from Todos los Santos to Río Puelo), settled in the early 1900s, maintains pioneer culture thanks to its isolation, but road building signals inevitable changes.

Temuco

☎045 / POP 259,100

With its leafy, palm-filled plaza, pleasant Mercado Municipal and intrinsic link to Mapuche culture, Temuco is the most palatable of all Sur Chico's blue-collar cities to visit. It's also the regional transit hub, with steady transportation to Santiago and connections to everywhere in Sur Chico and beyond.

Sights

Museo Regional de la Araucanía MUSEUM
(Av Alemania 084; adult/child CH$600/300; ⌚9:30am-5:30pm Tue-Fri, 11am-5pm Sat, 11am-2pm Sun) Museo Regional de la Araucanía recounts the sweeping history of the Araucanian peoples. Buses 1, 9 and 7 run along Av Alemania, but the route is also a reasonable walking distance from the *centro*.

Monumento Natural Cerro Ñielol HISTORIC SITE
(Calle Prat; adult/child CH$1200/600; ⌚8am-7pm) Cerro Ñielol is a hill that sits among some 90 hectares of native forest – an oasis of green in the city. It was here in 1881, at the tree-shaded site known as La Patagua, that Mapuche leaders ceded land to the colonists to found Temuco.

Sleeping & Eating

Cheap digs around the train station and Feria Pinto can be sketchy, especially for women; the neighborhood between the plaza and university is preferable.

Hospedaje Tribu Piren GUESTHOUSE $
(☎985-711; www.tribupiren.cl; Prat 69; r per person after/before 6pm CH$10,000/12,000; @ 📶) A great choice for foreigners: everything is clean and polished, and rooms, some of which open out onto a small terrace, offer cable TV and central heating.

Hospedaje Klickmann GUESTHOUSE $
(☎748-292; claudiz_7@hotmail.com; Claro Solar 647; r per person with/without bathroom CH$14,500/11,800; @ 📶) This clean and friendly *hospedaje* (basic hotel) is a stone's throw from several bus companies. Breakfast included.

TOP CHOICE **Tradiciones Zuny** CHILEAN $
(☎792-2295; Tucapel 1374; meals CH$1700-3300; ⌚breakfast & lunch Mon-Sat) Temuco's best-kept secret is an underground local's haunt specializing in the fresh, simple food of the countryside: a typical menu might include salad, beef *cazuela* (stew) with pumpkin, and bread with a smoky hot sauce. It's hard to find, but the cheap, Chilean-Mapuche fusion is worth it.

Feria Pinto CHILEAN $
(Av Barros Arana; mains CH$2000; ⌚8am-5pm) The cheapest eats can be had at this dynamic market; vendors churn out *cazuelas*, *sopapillas con queso* (traditional fried dough with cheese), empanadas and seafood stews.

Information

Internet centers are cheap (CH$400 per hour) and ubiquitous, as are ATMs.

Hospital Hernán Henríquez Aravena (☎212-525; Manuel Montt 115; ⌚24hr) Six blocks west and one block north of the plaza.

Post Office (cnr Diego Portales & Prat)

Sernatur (☎312-857; Thiers 539; ⌚8:30am-8pm Mon-Fri, 10am-2pm Sat)

Tourist Kiosk (☎973-628; Mercado Municipal; ⌚8am-8pm Mon-Sat, 9am-4pm Sun) Has city maps and lodgings lists.

Getting There & Away

Air

Airport Maquehue is 6km south of town. **LAN** (☎600-526-2000; www.lan.com; Bulnes 687; ⌚9am-1:30pm & 3-6:30pm) flies to Santiago (from CH$155,000); **Sky** (☎777-300; www.skyairline.cl; Bulnes 677; ⌚9am-2pm & 3-7:30pm Mon-Fri, 9:30am-1:30pm Sat) has better rates.

Bus

Terminal Rodoviario (☎225-005; Pérez Rosales 1609) is at the northern approach to town; many bus companies also have ticket offices downtown. **Terminal de Buses Rurales** (☎210-494; Av Aníbal Pinto 32) serves local and regional destinations. **Nar-Bus** (☎407-777; Balmaceda 995) goes to Melipeuco (CH$1800, two hours) seven times daily as well as having one daily direct departure to Parque Nacional Conguillío itself (CH$3200, three hours, Monday to Saturday 10:30am). **Buses Jac** (☎465-465; cnr Av Balmaceda & Aldunate) offers the most frequent service to Villarrica and Pucón, plus service to Lican Ray and Coñaripe. **Buses Biobío** (☎465-351; www.busesbiobio.cl; Lautaro 854) runs frequent services to Angol, Los Ángeles, Concepción, Curacautín and Lonquimay.

DESTINATION	COST (CH$)	DURATION (HR)
Chillán	6500	4
Concepción	8000	4½
Curacautín	3500	2
Osorno	8000	4
Pucón	3600	2
Puerto Montt	8000	5
Santiago	22,000	9
Valdivia	3200	3
Zapala & Neuquén, Argentina	25,000	10

The Lakes District

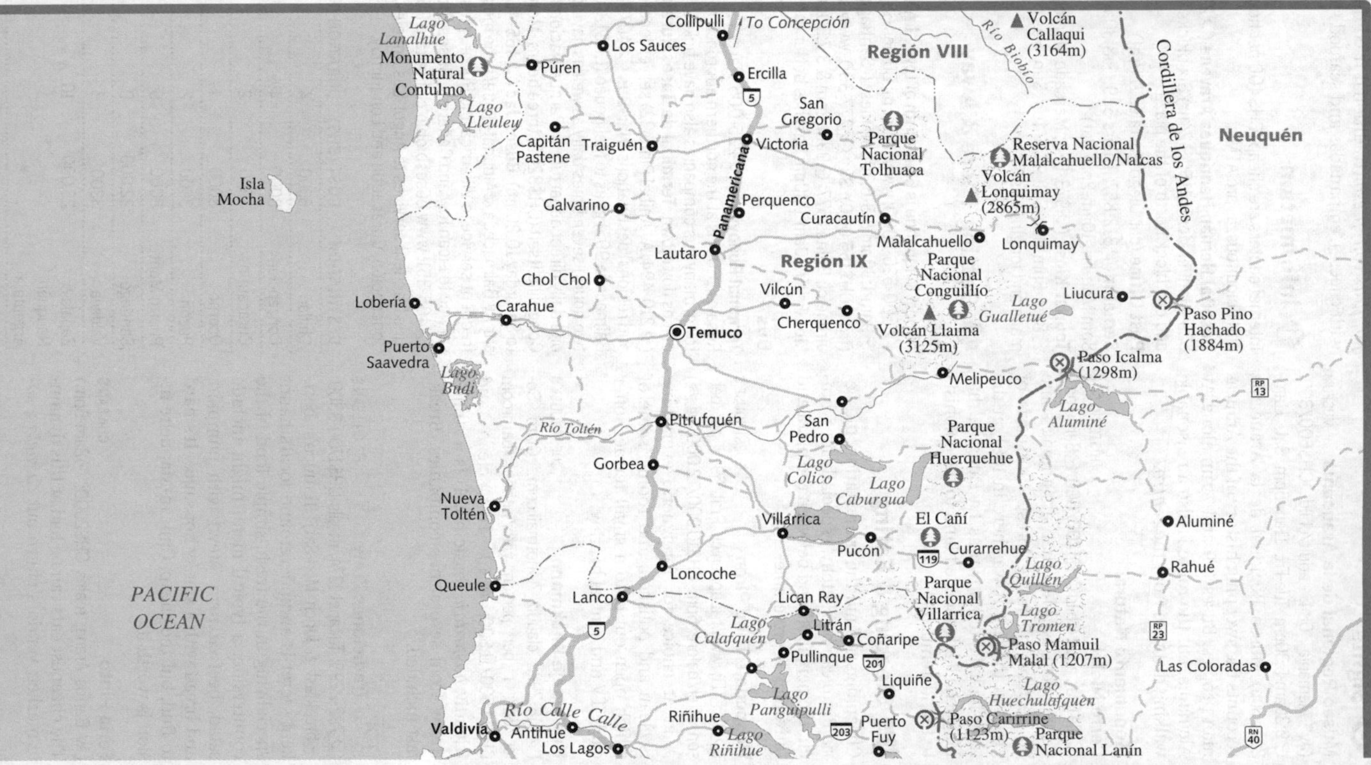

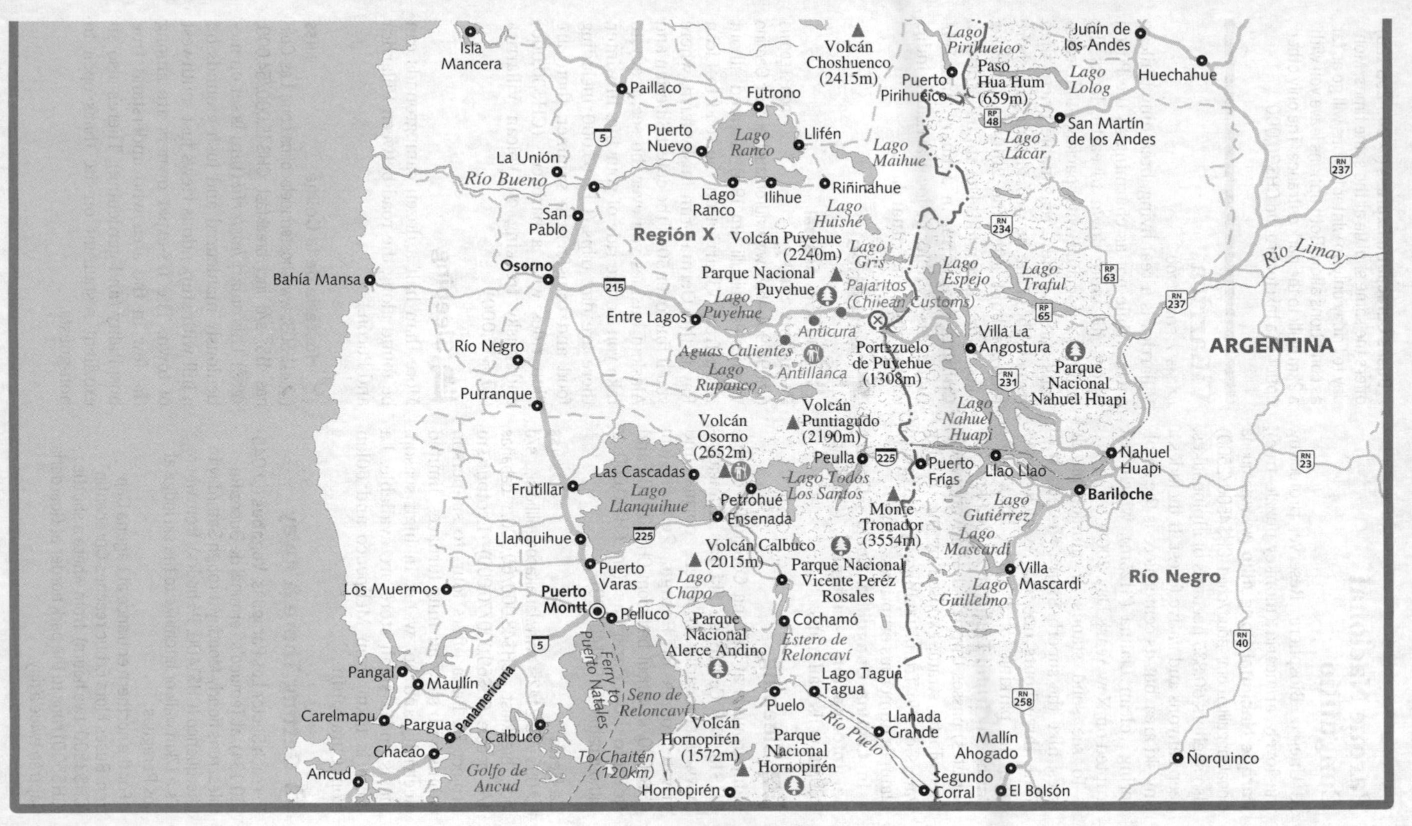
Isla Mancera
Paillaco
Futrono
Volcán Choshuenco (2415m)
Lago Pirihueico
Puerto Pirihueico
Paso Hua Hum (659m)
Junín de los Andes
Lago Lolog
Huechahue
San Martín de los Andes
Lago Lácar
Puerto Nuevo
Lago Ranco
Llifén
Lago Maihue
La Unión
Río Bueno
Lago Ranco
Ilihue
Riñinahue
Lago Huishé
San Pablo
Región X
Volcán Puyehue (2240m)
Lago Gris
Lago Espejo
Lago Traful
Río Limay
Osorno
Bahía Mansa
Parque Nacional Puyehue
Pajaritos (Chilean Customs)
Lago Puyehue
Entre Lagos
Anticura
Villa La Angostura
Parque Nacional Nahuel Huapi
ARGENTINA
Río Negro
Aguas Calientes
Lago Rupanco
Antillanca
Portezuelo de Puyehue (1308m)
Purranque
Volcán Osorno (2652m)
Volcán Puntiagudo (2190m)
Lago Nahuel Huapi
Peulla
Puerto Frías
Llao Llao
Nahuel Huapi
Las Cascadas
Frutillar
Lago Llanquihue
Petrohué
Lago Todos Los Santos
Monte Tronador (3554m)
Bariloche
Lago Gutiérrez
Ensenada
Llanquihue
Volcán Calbuco (2015m)
Lago Mascardi
Villa Mascardi
Puerto Varas
Parque Nacional Vicente Peréz Rosales
Río Negro
Los Muermos
Lago Chapo
Lago Guillelmo
Puerto Montt
Pelluco
Parque Nacional Alerce Andino
Cochamó
Estero de Reloncaví
Ferry to Puerto Natales
Pangal
Maullín
Seno de Reloncaví
Lago Tagua Tagua
Puelo
Carelmapu
Pargua
Panamericana
Calbuco
Volcán Hornopirén (1572m)
Río Puelo
Llanada Grande
Mallín Ahogado
Ñorquinco
Chacao
Parque Nacional Hornopirén
Ancud
Golfo de Ancud
To Chaitén (120km)
Hornopirén
Segundo Corral
El Bolsón
5
215
225
RP 48
RN 234
RP 63
RP 65
RN 231
RN 237
RN 23
RN 40
RN 258

Parque Nacional Conguillío

A Unesco Biosphere Reserve protecting the lovely araucaria (monkey-puzzle tree), **Parque Nacional Conguillío** (www.parquenacionalconguillio.com; adult/child CH$4500/2500) also shelters 60,835 hectares of alpine lakes, deep canyons and native forest. It includes a tiny ski area, but its centerpiece is the smoldering Volcán Llaima (3125m), which last erupted on New Year's Day, 2008.

To see solid stands of monkey-puzzle trees, hike the superb **Sierra Nevada trail** (7km, three hours one-way), which leaves from the parking lot at Playa Linda. The **Cañadon Truful-Truful trail** (0.8km, 30 minutes) passes through the canyon, where the colorful strata, exposed by the rushing waters of Río Truful-Truful, are a record of Llaima's numerous eruptions.

In **Laguna Conguillío**, Conaf's **Centro de Información Ambiental** (8:30am-9:30pm) sells trail maps.

Sleeping

Campgrounds at Laguna Conguillío charge CH$18,000. Centro de Ski Las Araucarias (www.skiaraucarias.cl) offers dorms and private rooms in **Refugio Pehuén** (dm CH$8000, d without bathroom CH$20,000) and **Refugio Los Paraguas** (dm CH$10,000, tr without bathroom CH$40,000).

La Baita CABIN **$$**
(099-733-2442; www.labaitaconguillio.cl; s/d incl breakfast CH$48,000/60,000, cabañas 4/6 people CH$60,000/70,000) Ecotourism project La Baita offers four- to six-person cabins with slow-burning furnaces, limited electricity and hot water. In high season, meals and a small store are available. La Baita is 15km from Melipeuco and 60km from Curacautín.

Getting There & Away

To reach Sector Los Paraguas, **Vogabus** (045-910-134), at Temuco's Terminal de Buses Rurales, runs hourly Monday through Saturday to Cherquenco (CH$1400, 1½ hours), from where it's a 17km walk or hitchhike to the ski lodge at Los Paraguas.

For the northern entrance at Laguna Captrén, Buses Flota Erbuc reaches Curacautín (CH$3500, two hours), from where a shuttle (CH$500) runs to the park border at Guardería Captrén twice a day.

Buses Curacautín Express (045-258-125) offers the same shuttle at the same times, Monday to Friday only. In winter the bus will go as far as conditions allow. Both options leave you with a 2km walk to the park entrance. The only other option is a taxi for around CH$30,000.

Villarrica

045 / POP 39,700

Villarrica is a real living, breathing Chilean town. While not as charming as the Pucón resort, it's more down to earth, lacks the bedlam associated with package-tour caravans and has more reasonable prices than its neighbor. The new *costanera* (lakeshore road), rebuilt after the 2010 earthquake, makes for a nice walk. The annual **Muestra Cultural Mapuche**, in January and February, has exhibits of local artisans, indigenous music and ritual dance.

Activities

TOP CHOICE **Aurora Austral Patagonia Husky** DOG SLEDDING
(098-901-4518; www.auroraaustral.com; Camino Villarrica-Panguipulli Km 19.5) Located about 19km from Villarrica on the road to Lican Ray is this German-run husky farm, where you'll find over 50 of the cutest Siberian and Alaskan huskies you ever did see, ready to take you on the ride of your life. In winter, there are day trips (CH$65,000 including food and transfer); in summer, there are 6km rides with a barbecue (CH$30,000) and husky trekking on Volcán Villarrica (CH$45,000).

Sleeping

More than half a dozen campgrounds can be found along the road between Villarrica and Pucón.

Hostería de la Colina INN **$$**
(411-503; www.hosteriadelacolina.com; Las Colinas 115; s/d incl breakfast CH$45,000/54,000; @) This smart *hostería* (inn) is set on meticulously manicured and lush grounds on a hill with stupendous views just southwest of town. The US-expat owners are among the few in the area who understand true hospitality (and gardening). There's also an excellent restaurant on-site that's open to non-guests.

La Torre Suiza HOSTEL $
(☎411-213; www.torresuiza.com; Bilbao 969; dm CH$8500, s/d from CH$16,000/22,000; @📶) This charming wooden chalet and traveler staple offers a fully equipped kitchen, laundry, multilingual book exchange, mountain-bike rental, lots of area information and all the traveler camaraderie you're seeking.

Hostal Don Juan INN $
(☎411-833; www.hostaldonjuan.cl; General Körner 770; d/tr incl breakfast CH$24,000/30,000; @📶) Don Juan wins travelers over with its numerous distractions: a game room, a large *fogón* (outdoor oven) and a multi-use room that includes a kitchen.

Eating & Drinking

TOP CHOICE **The Travellers** INTERNATIONAL $
(Valentin Letelier 753; mains CH$3950-8500; ⏲breakfast-late dinner; 📶) Chinese, Mexican, Thai, Indian, Italian – it's a passport for your palette at this resto-bar that is ground zero for foreigners. Come for the expansive terrace, traveler advice and lengthy happy hours with awesome cocktails and *enchuladas* (draft beer, Tabasco, lime and salt).

Huerto Azul DESSERTS $
(Camilo Henríquez 341; items CH$690-1900; ⏲10am-9pm) Highlights of this fabulous gourmet store/ice-cream parlor include artisanal marmalades and chutneys, homemade Belgian chocolate bars and Italian-style gelato, also made on the premises.

El Sabio PIZZERIA $
(Zegers 393; pizzas CH$3900-8900; ⏲lunch & dinner, closed Mon Mar-Dec; 📶) Featuring fantastic oblong pizzas served on small cutting boards.

Café Bar 2001 CAFE $
(Camilo Henríquez 379; mains CH$2750-5600; ⏲breakfast, lunch & dinner) The economical breakfast specials here include *küchen* (German-style cake), toast, juice and coffee; there's also a decent selection of rarer microbrews and an extensive coffee menu.

Information

Internet cafes and banks with ATMs are plentiful.

Hospital Villarrica (San Martín 460; ⏲24hr)

Oficina de Turismo (☎206-619; www.visitvillarrica.cl; Av Pedro de Valdivia 1070; ⏲8am-11pm Jan-Feb, 9am-1pm & 2:30-6pm Mar-Dec) Has helpful staff and a list of lodgings.

Getting There & Away

Villarrica has a main **bus terminal** (Av Pedro de Valdivia 621), though a few companies have separate offices nearby.

Buses JAC (☎467-775; Bilbao 610) goes to Pucón (CH$900, 45 minutes) and Temuco (CH$1800, one hour) every 20 minutes, and Lican Ray (CH$700, 40 minutes) and Coñaripe (CH$1100) every 30 minutes. Several other lines make the journeys from the main terminal.

For Argentine destinations, **Igi Llaima** (☎412-733; www.igillaima.cl), in the main terminal, leaves every morning for San Martín de los Andes (CH$12,000, five hours), where you can make connections north or south.

Pucón

☎045 / POP 16,970

A shimmering lake under the huffing cone of 2847m Volcán Villarrica feeds the mystique of village-turned-megaresort Pucón. Summertime draws a giddy mix of families, adventurers, package tourists and new-age gurus to this mecca. Where else in Chile can you party and play slots till dawn, leave in time to hike the volcano (alongside 300 other enthusiasts), go to the beach or hot springs, drink a caramel latte, buy a gem-encrusted handbag, run into half of Santiago, get a massage and sleep in a teepee? Something does exist for everyone here and, snootiness aside, the mix of international wanderers, the zippy social scene and backyard of natural wonders is often a blast.

The town is walkable, with most tour operators and services on the commercial main strip of Av O'Higgins. Restaurants and shops dot Fresia, which leads to the plaza. Slightly beyond the plaza is the beach.

Activities

Hiking & Climbing

The masses come to hike the smoking, lava-spitting crater of **Volcán Villarrica**. The full-day excursion (CH$50,000) leaves Pucón around 7:30am. For serious rock hounds, challenging climbing routes range from 5.8 to 5.12d.

Horse Riding

Rides take in various environments and may include stopovers so riders can meet with local *huasos* (cowboys) or Mapuche communities. Half- and full-day rides hover around CH$18,000 to CH$42,000.

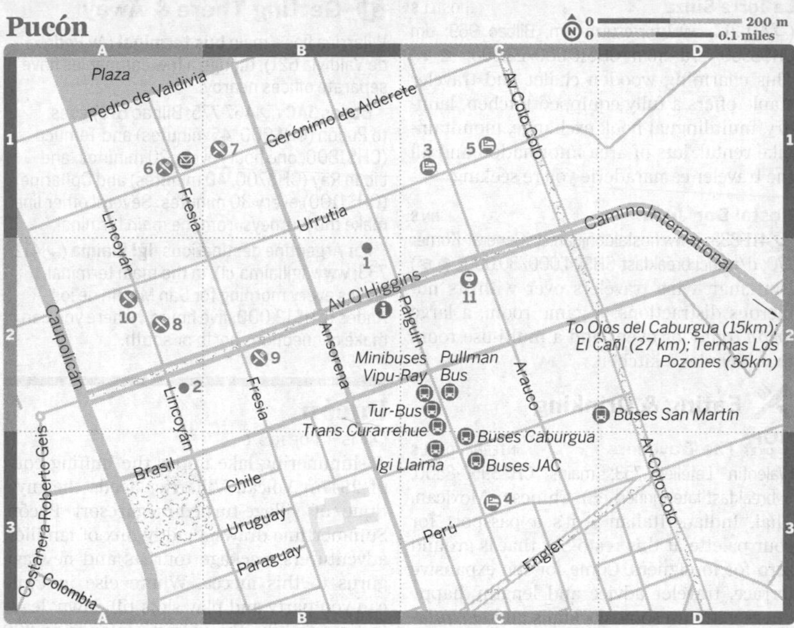

Pucón

Activities, Courses & Tours
- 1 Aguaventura B2
- 2 Kayak Pucón A2

Sleeping
- 3 iécole! C1
- 4 Hospedaje Victor C3
- 5 The Tree House C1

Eating
- 6 La Maga A1
- 7 Latitude 39° B1
- 8 Pizza Cala A2
- 9 Trawen B2
- 10 Viva Perú A2

Drinking
- 11 Mama's & Tapas C2

Mountain Biking

Mountain bikes can be rented all over town for CH$5000 to CH$7500. The most popular route is the **Ojos de Caburgua Loop**. Take the turnoff to the airfield, about 4km east of town and across Río Trancura.

Rafting & Kayaking

Pucón is known for both its river sports and the quality of the rafting and kayaking infrastructure. The rivers near Pucón and their corresponding rapids classifications are: Lower Trancura (III), Upper Trancura (IV), Liucura (II-III), the Puesco Run (V) and Maichín (IV-V).

Tours

The wealth of adventure operators lining Av O'Higgins, and the bounty of activities on offer in and around Pucón, can easily overwhelm. Reputable outfitters include the following.

TOP CHOICE Aguaventura OUTDOORS
(☎444-246; www.aguaventura.com; Palguín 336) French-owned agency on the cutting edge of rafting, kayaking, rappelling, canyoning and snow sports. One-stop shop for all excursions.

Kayak Pucón KAYAKING
(☎099-716-2347; www.kayakpucon.net; Av O'Higgins 211) This well-regarded kayak operator offers courses and introductory tours on Class III rapids.

Huepilmalal Centro Ecuestre HORSE RIDING
(☎099-643-2673; www.huepilmalal.cl; Km 28 Camino Pucón-Huife) This reputable equestrian center does half-day to multiday treks in the Cañi *cordillera*.

Sleeping

¡école! HOSTEL $
(☎441-675; www.ecole.cl; Urrutia 592; dm with/without bedding CH$10,000/7000, d/tr CH$30,000/38,000, d/tr without bathroom CH$20,000/25,000; @📶) The artsy, ecoconscious ¡école! is Pucón's most interesting place to stay: the owners were preaching sustainability decades before it was trendy. Rooms are small, clean and comfortable, and the excellent vegetarian restaurant (mains CH$3900 to CH$4800) is as much an attraction as the lodging.

Bambu Lodge R&B $$
(☎096-802-9145; www.bambulodge.com; Camino a Volcán Km 4.2; s/d incl breakfast CH$40,000/50,000; @) This discerning four-room B&B in a woodsy spot on the road to the volcano is a wonderful find. The French owner has imported much of his decor from Morocco; a taxi from town is CH$5000.

Tree House HOSTEL $
(☎444-679; www.treehousechile.cl; Urrutia 660; dm from CH$12,000, d with/without bathroom CH$30,000/24,000; 📶) This spotless hostel is welcoming, with pleasant shared spaces and garden hammocks. Most of the shared dormitories have no more than four beds.

Hospedaje Victor GUESTHOUSE $
(☎443-525; www.pucon.com/victor; Palguín 705; dm CH$10,000, r CH$25,000; @📶) Victor stands out for cleanliness and a warm atmosphere, ensured by several wood-burning stoves. It offers kitchen access, big TVs and two kitchens for guest use.

Eating

Trawen CHILEAN, FUSION $
(Av O'Higgins 311; mains CH$3900-8900; ⏰breakfast, lunch & dinner; 📶🍷) This time-honored favorite does some of Pucón's best gastronomic work for the price, boasting innovative flavor combinations and fresh-baked everything. Highlights include home-style breakfasts, Antarctic-krill empanadas and seafood risotto.

Viva Perú PERUVIAN $$
(Lincoyán 372; mains CH$5900-8900; ⏰lunch & dinner Tue-Sun; 📶) This intimate Peruvian restaurant does all the classics: *ceviche, chicharónes* (deep-fried pork rinds) – even Peru's famous Chinese fusion *chifa* dishes.

La Maga STEAKHOUSE $$
(Gerónimo de Alderete 276; steak CH$8900-10,900; ⏰lunch & dinner Tue-Sun) This Uruguayan steakhouse, while not the cheapest in town, stands out for its *bife de chorizo* (steak) and house-cut fries.

Pizza Cala PIZZERIA $$
(Lincoyán 361; pizzas CH$3200-12,000; ⏰lunch & dinner; 📶) The best pizza in town comes from a massive 1300-brick oven by an Argentine-American pizza maker who grows his own basil.

Latitude 39° NORTH AMERICAN $
(Gerónimo de Alderete 324-2; mains CH$3400-4900; ⏰breakfast, lunch & dinner) California-transplant owners filling a gringo niche – juicy American-style burgers, fat breakfast burritos, veggie tacos, BLTs, chili – but consistency has been an issue.

Drinking

Mama's & Tapas BAR, CLUB
(Av O'Higgins 597; ⏰6pm-late) Known simply as 'Mama's,' this is the most popular place to go out in Pucón. Recent renovations have expanded the outdoor patio, trendied up the inside and added a club in the back on weekends. The resident DJ spins everything from indie rock to old-school hip-hop; the CH$5000 admission charge includes one drink.

Information

There are several banks with ATMs along Av O'Higgins. Note that petty theft is on the rise in Pucón, especially in the areas surrounding the beach.

Chile Pucón (www.chile-pucon.com) Useful internet resource.

Hospital San Francisco (www.hospsanfrancisco.cl; Uruguay 325; ⏰24hr)

Oficina de Turismo (☎293-002; www.municipalidadpucon.cl; cnr Av O'Higgins & Palguín; ⏰9am-5pm Mon-Fri, 110am-2pm Sat & Sun) With brochures and usually an English speaker on staff.

Post Office (Fresia 183)

Getting There & Away

Frequent buses go to/from Santiago (CH$10,000 to CH$44,000, 9½ hours) – **Tur Bus** (☎443-934; Av O'Higgins 910), east of town, and **Pullman Bus** (☎443-331; www.pullman.cl; Palguín 555), in the center, are your best bets.

Buses JAC (☎990-885; www.jac.cl; cnr Uruguay & Palguín) goes to Puerto Montt (CH$10,000, five hours), Valdivia (CH$3500, three hours), and every 20 minutes to Temuco (CH$2500, one hour). From the same station, **Minibuses Vipu-Ray** (☎096-835-5798; Palguín 550) and **Trans Curarrehue** (☎089-528-4958; Palguín 550) have continuous services to Villarrica (CH$800, 30 minutes). Buses JAC and **Buses Caburgua** (☎098-038-9047; Palguín 555) go to Parque Nacional Huerquehue (CH$1900, 45 minutes). For San Martín de los Andes, Argentina (CH$12,000, five hours), **Buses San Martín** (☎443-595; Av Colo Colo 612) departs twice weekly, stopping in Junín. **Igi Llaima** (☎444-762; cnr Palguín & Uruguay) also makes the trip.

Getting Around

Pucón is very walkable. A number of travel agencies rent cars and prices can be competitive.

Around Pucón

RÍO LIUCURA VALLEY

East of Pucón, the Camino Pucón–Huife cuts through a lush valley hosting a myriad of hot springs. The best value is at the end of the road: **Termas Los Pozones** (Km 37; day use adult/child CH$4000/2000, night use CH$5000/3000), with six natural stone pools open nearly 24 hours. It gets crowded, so come during nighttime hours (8pm to 6am) to soak under the stars. Arrange a transfer with a travel agency; it's also reachable on public transportation from Pucón.

Formed by citizens to nip logging interests in this spectacular swath of native forest, the nature sanctuary **El Cañi** (www.santuariocani.cl; Km 21; admission with/without guide CH$10,000/3000) protects some 400 hectares of ancient araucaria forest. A three-hour, 9km hiking trail ascends a steep trail to gorgeous views. Camping is also now available (CH$3000); email ahead (through the website) for details. You can also make arrangements to visit El Cañi at ¡école! in Pucón – the standard day trip costs CH$15,000 per person.

CURARREHUE

Heading toward the Argentine border at Mamuil Malal, this route provides off-piste pleasures. Immerse yourself in Mapuche culture in quiet and colorful **Curarrehue**. The **tourist office** (☎197-1587; Plaza; ⊙9:30am-8:30pm Dec 15-Mar 15) opens in summer only. Before town, the Mapuche family farm **Kila Leufu** (☎87-911-455; www.kilaleufu.cl; Palguin Bajo Km 23; dm/d incl breakfast CH$10,000/25,000) welcomes guests warmly. The small but interesting museum **Aldea Intercultural Trawupeyüm** (☎451-971-574; Héroes de la Concepción 21; adult/child CH$1000/500; ⊙10am-8pm Dec-Mar, to 6pm Apr-Nov) explores Mapuche culture. Curarrehue's real attraction is **Cocina Mapuche Mapu Lyagl** (☎098-788-7188; Camino al Curarrehue; tasting menu CH$4800; ⊙lunch & dinner; 🌿), where a Mapuche chef turns seasonal ingredients into adventurous vegetarian tasting menus. Indigenous delicacies include *mullokiñ* (bean puree rolled in quinoa).

Parque Nacional Huerquehue

Rushing rivers, waterfalls, monkey-puzzle trees and alpine lakes adorn the 12,500-hectare **Parque Nacional Huerquehue** (adult/child CH$4500/2500), only 35km from Pucón. Stop at Conaf's **Centro de Informaciones Ambientales** (☎096-157-4809; ⊙10:30am-2:30pm & 4:30-7:30pm) for maps and information at the entrance.

The **Los Lagos trail** (7km, four hours round-trip) switchbacks through dense *lenga* forests to monkey-puzzle trees surrounding a cluster of pristine lakes. At Laguna Huerquehue, the trail **Los Huerquenes** (two days) continues north then east to cross the park and access **Termas de San Sebastián** (☎02-196-8546; www.termassansebastian.cl; Río Blanco; day access CH$4000, campsites per person CH$5000, cabins for 2/5 CH$35,000/50,000), just east of the park boundary.

Camp at Conaf's Lago Tinquilco or Renahue (CH$15,000 per person). The excellent **Refugio Tinquilco** (☎09-539-2728; www.tinquilco.cl; dm incl breakfast with/without bedding CH$13,000/11,500, d with/without bathroom CH$34,900/27,900; ⊙closed Jun-Aug) is a luxurious lodge with amenities such as French press coffee and a forest sauna. It's at the base of the Lago Verde trailhead. Meals are available (CH$6500), or you can cook for yourself.

Buses Caburgua (☎098-038-9047; Uruguay 540, Pucón) serves Pucón three times daily (CH$2000, one hour). Many agencies offer organized excursions, too.

Parque Nacional Villarrica

This is one of the most popular parks in the country because of its glorious mix of volcanoes and lakes. The highlights of the 630-sq-km park are the three volcanoes: 2847m Villarrica, 2360m Quetrupillán and, along the Argentine border, a section of 3747m Lanín.

South of Pucón, **Rucapillán** takes in the most popular hikes. The **Challupen Chinay trail** (23km, 12 hours) rounds varied terrain on the volcano's southern side to the entrance to the **Quetrupillán** sector.

Ski Pucón (www.skipucon.cl; Clemente Holzapfel 190, Pucón office at Enjoy Tour at Gran Hotel Pucón; full-day lift ticket adult/child CH$25,000/19,000; ⏲Jul-Sep) is best for beginners but experienced skiers have good out-of-bounds options. Windy or covered conditions shut this active volcano down; check conditions before going. Agencies and hotels provide minivans (CH$7000 to CH$9500) to the base lodge.

Lago Calafquén

Black-sand beaches and gardens draw tourists to this island-studded lake, to fashionable **Lican Ray** (30km south of Villarrica) and the more down-to-earth **Coñaripe** (22km east of Lican Ray). Out of season, it's dead. Lican Ray is tiny and organized around its only paved street, Av General Urrutia, which has most of the cabins, restaurants, cafes and artisan markets. In Coñaripe, look for a friendly tourist kiosk on the main square. The road heading north of Coñaripe leads to a number of rustic hot springs.

Sleeping & Eating

Within 5km on either side of Lican Ray are lakeside campgrounds.

Hotel Elizabeth HOTEL $$
(☎063-317-279; www.hotelelizabeth.cl; Beck de Ramberga 496, Coñaripe; s/d CH$30,000/44,000; @📶) The nicest digs in town, with balconies and a well-regarded restaurant.

Hostal Chumay GUESTHOUSE $
(☎099-744-8835; www.lagocalafquen.com; Las Tepas 201, Coñaripe; d incl breakfast CH$20,000-30,000; @📶) A good choice for simple rooms, central heating, a renovated restaurant and convenience to the in-house adventure outfitter.

Los Ñaños CHILEAN $
(☎045-431-026; Urrutia 105, Lican Ray; mains CH$3000-6300) Excellent for empanadas, seafood, *cazuela* and pasta on an outdoor patio.

Getting There & Away

Buses JAC (☎063-317-241) has several buses daily from Villarrica to Coñaripe (CH$1100, one hour) via Lican Ray (CH$600, 30 minutes).

Valdivia

☎063 / POP 139,500

Valdivia was crowned the capital of Chile's newest Región XIV (Los Ríos) in 2007 after years of defection talk surrounding its inclusion in the Lakes District despite its various geographical, historical and cultural differences. It's also the most important university town in southern Chile and, as such, offers a strong emphasis on the arts, student prices at many hostels, restaurants and bars, as well as a refreshing dose of youthful energy.

Sights & Activities

Av Costanera Arturo Prat is a major focus of activity, but the most important public buildings are on Plaza de la República.

TOP CHOICE **Cervecería Kunstmann** BREWERY
(www.lacerveceria.cl; Ruta T-350 950; ⏲noon-midnight) Valdivia is the seat of German culture in Chile and a tour to the best large-scale brewery in the south certainly informs: this is real beer, some of South America's best. Tours leave hourly every afternoon (CH$5000) and include a takeaway glass mug and a sampling of the Torobayo unfiltered, straight from the tank. There's a menu of hearty German fare, too. Take a taxi from the center.

Museo Histórico y Antropológico MUSEUM
(☎212-872; Los Laureles 47; admission CH$1300; ⏲10am-8pm Dec 15-Mar 15, to 6pm Mar 16-Dec 14) Housed in a fine riverfront mansion on Isla Teja, this museum includes Mapuche

Valdivia

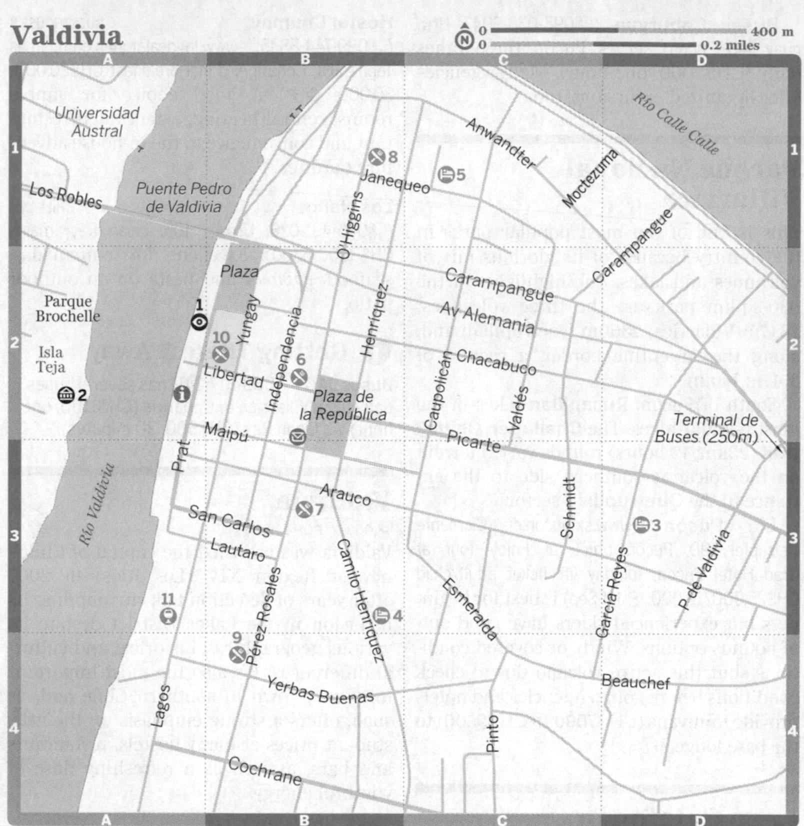

Valdivia

Sights

1 Feria Fluvial A2
2 Museo Histórico y Antropológico A2

Sleeping

3 Airesbuenos Hostel D3
4 Hostal BordeRío B3
5 Hostel Bosque Nativo C1

Eating

6 Café Moro B2
7 Entrelagos B3
8 La Calesa B1
9 La Última Frontera B4
10 Mercado Municipal B2

Drinking

11 Santo Pecado A3

indigenous artifacts and household items from early German settlements.

Feria Fluvial MARKET
(Av Prat s/n; ⏲7am-3:30pm) The lively riverside market south of the Valdivia bridge, where vendors sell fresh fish, meat and produce.

Boat Cruises BOAT TOUR
(6½hr cruises CH$18,000-20,000) Valdivia's traditional tourist attraction, boats ply the rivers to visit nearby forts. Most take the same route, stopping at Corral and Isla Mancera; all include lunch and *onces*. Tours depart from Puerto Fluvial at the base of Arauco.

Festivals & Events

Bierfest/Oktoberfest BEER
Kunstmann-organized suds festival every January; newly inaugurated Oktoberfest in Parque Saval.

Sleeping

During the school year the university crowd monopolizes the cheap sleeps; summer has better options.

Airesbuenos Hostel HOSTEL $
(☎222-202; www.airesbuenos.cl; Garcia Reyes 550; dm incl breakfast CH$9000, s/d CH$16,000/25,000; @) This long-standing traveler's mainstay has had a sustainable makeover: besides the new recycling and composting programs, you'll find comfy, colorful dorm rooms and simple private rooms, plus plenty of backpacker amenities.

Hostel Bosque Nativo HOSTEL $
(☎433-782; www.hostelnativo.cl; Pasaje Fresia 290; dm CH$9500, s/d CH$18,000/25,000, without bathroom CH$16,000/20,000; @) This excellent and cozy hostel, run by a sustainable forestry management NGO, is a wooden den of comfort hidden away down a gravel lane. It's in a residential neighborhood a short walk from the bus station.

Hostal BordeRío GUESTHOUSE $$
(☎214-069; www.borderiovaldivia.cl; Camilo Henríquez 746; s/d CH$30,000/35,000; @) Well-equipped with a sunny breakfast nook, large bathrooms, colorful bedspreads and even loveseats in most of the rooms.

Eating & Drinking

Isla Teja, across the river from the city, is the latest ubertrendy neighborhood for restaurants. The main concentration of nightlife is on Esmeralda – take your pick.

TOP CHOICE **La Última Frontera** CAFE $
(Pérez Rosales 787; sandwiches CH$2600-3900; lunch & dinner Mon-Sat;) Hidden away in a restored mansion, this bohemian cafe offers creative sandwiches, fresh juices and a substantial artisanal draft-beer list day and night, courtesy of the town's hip artistic front.

Entrelagos CAFE $
(Pérez Rosales 640; sandwiches CH$2570-5300; lunch & dinner) This classic *salón de té* (tea house) with Parisian-style seating is where Valdivians go for delicious coffee, cakes and crepes. Hearty set menus and toasted sandwiches draw those looking for something more filling.

Café Moro CHILEAN $
(Paseo Libertad 174; sandwiches CH$1400-3500; breakfast, lunch & dinner Mon-Sat;) On a pedestrianized alley leading to the water, this is an excellent (though smoker-friendly) spot for an economical set-menu lunch.

La Calesa PERUVIAN $$
(O'Higgins 160; mains CH$6400-7900; lunch & dinner Tue-Sat, lunch Sun) This place serves Peruvian staples, such as garlic-roasted chicken and *lomo saltado* (stir-fried beef with spices, onions, tomatoes and potatoes).

Mercado Municipal CHILEAN $
(Prat s/n; mains CH$2500-4000; lunch) Fat plates of fish and chips or *choritos al ajillo* (mussels in garlic and chilies) are served in three floors of restaurants with river views.

Santo Pecado BAR
(Yungay 745;) Funky lounge chairs and banquettes keep this red-hued restaurant-bar ubertrendy. There's gourmet food, too, and unstoppable river views from its waterfront back patio.

Information

Downtown ATMs are abundant, as are internet cafes. There's a tourist kiosk at the Terminal de Buses.

Clínica Alemana (www.alemanavaldivia.cl; Beauchef 765; 24hr) Better, faster and closer than the public hospital.

Post Office (O'Higgins 575)

Sernatur (☎239-060; Prat s/n; 9am-6pm Mon-Fri, to 3pm Sat) Offers traveler advice on the riverfront.

Getting There & Away

Air

LAN (☎246-494; www.lan.com; Maipú 271) flies daily to Santiago (CH$105,000, 2¼ hours); **Sky** (☎216-280; www.skyairline.cl; Schmidt 303) has cheaper fares and regular departures in summer.

Bus

Valdivia's **Terminal de Buses** (Anfión Muñoz 360) has frequent services to destinations between Puerto Montt and Santiago. **Tur Bus** (☎212-430) and Pullman are just a few of the bus companies to choose from. **Buses JAC** (☎212-925) accesses Villarrica (CH$4000, 2½ hours), Pucón and Temuco. **Andesmar** (☎224-665) travels to Bariloche, Argentina.

DESTINATION	COST (CH$)	DURATION (HR)
Bariloche, Argentina	13,000	7
Castro	8500	7
Neuquén, Argentina	22,500	12
Osorno	3600	1¾
Panguipulli	2900	2¼
Pucón	4300	3
Puerto Montt	6400	3½
San Martín de los Andes, Argentina	12,500	8
Santiago	from 23,000	11
Temuco	6200	2½

Osorno

064 / POP 149,400

Osorno is a bustling place and the commercial engine for the surrounding agricultural zone. Though it's an important transportation hub, most visitors spend little time here.

Sleeping & Eating

You'll find plenty to eat along the main drag, Juan McKenna, and in the blocks east and west of Plaza de Armas; the **Mercado Municipal** (cnr Prat & Errázuriz) is also a safe bet for a budget lunch.

Hostal Vermont HOSTEL $
(247-030; www.hostalvermont.cl; Toribio Medina 2020; dm CH$9000, s/d without bathroom CH$13,000/23,000; @) Aside from the creaky old floors, this is everything you want in a hostel: it's friendly, clean and well-equipped. From the bus station, walk two blocks south to Juan McKenna, five blocks east to Buenos Aires and one-and-a-half blocks south to Toribio Medina.

Hostal Rayenco GUESTHOUSE $
(236-285; www.hostalrayenco.cl; Freire 309; d incl breakfast CH$25,000; @) For a few extra pesos over the budget options, you'll be extra comfortable at this family-run guesthouse, with a nice living room and breakfast area.

Getting There & Away

Long-distance and Argentine-bound buses use the main **bus terminal** (Av Errázuriz 1400), five blocks from Plaza de Armas. Companies are **Pullman Bus** (310-529; www.pullman.cl), **Tas-Choapa** (233-933; www.taschoapa.cl) and **Tur-Bus** (201-526; www.turbus.cl), among many others. Most services going north on the Panamericana start in Puerto Montt, departing hourly, with mainly overnight services to Santiago.

Try **Queilen Bus** (233-633; www.queilenbus.cl) for Coyhaique, and Pullman Bus for Punta Arenas. **Igi Llaima** (234-371; www.igillaima.cl) goes to Zapala and Neuquén on weekdays via Temuco, while **Cruz del Sur** (232-777; www.busescruzdelsur.cl), Tas-Choapa and **Via Bariloche** (253-633; www.viabariloche.com.ar) have daily services to Bariloche.

Other local and regional buses use the **Terminal Mercado Municipal** (cnr Errázuriz & Arturo Prat), two blocks west of the main terminal. **Buses Barria** (201-306; www.busesbarria.cl) goes to Entre Lagos (CH$1400, 45 minutes), while **Expreso Lago Puyehue** (243-919) goes to Termas Puyehue/Aguas Calientes.

Around Osorno

The indigenous Huilliche communities of Osorno's gorgeous coast are sitting on an *etnoturismo* gold mine – these off-the-beaten-path communities are just beginning to embrace visitors. You can immerse yourself in their way of life over multiday trips that involve some of Chile's most stunning beaches, Valdivian forest treks and sleeping in rural homes around **San Juan de la Costa** and **Territorío Mapu Lahual** (www.mapulahual.cl), an indigenous protected zone that stretches south into Río Negro province.

In San Juan de la Costa, a series of five magnificent *caletas* (bays) are accessible by car and could be visited as day trips from around Osorno for those short on time. **Bahía Mansa, Pucatrihue** and **Maicolpué** are villages where dolphins and sea lions practically swim to shore and women scramble about wild and rugged beaches collecting *luga* and *cochayuyo*, two types of seaweed that help fuel the local economy. On either side are the two best *caletas*, **Manzano**, 20km north of Bahía Mansa, and **Tril-Tril**, 7km south of Bahía Mansa.

Parque Nacional Puyehue

Volcán Puyehue (2240m) blew its top the day after the 1960 earthquake, turning its dense humid evergreen forest into a stark landscape of sand dunes and lava rivers. Today, **Parque Nacional Puyehue** (www.parquepuyehue.cl) protects 107,000 hectares of this cool contrasting environment. **Aguas Calientes** (www.termasaguascalientes.cl; day use incl lunch CH$17,000-21,000) is an unpretentious hot-springs resort. You can access the free Pocitos Termas 80m across the Colgante bridge from the Conaf parking lot.

Small ski resort **Centro de Esqui Antillanca** (064-612-070; www.skiantillanca.cl; office at O'Higgins 1073, Osorno) is 18km beyond Aguas Calientes on the flanks of 1990m-high Volcán Casablanca. In summer a trail leads to a crater outlook with views of the mountain range. At the base is **Hotel Antillanca** (064-612-070; s/d in refugio CH$35,280/50,400, in hotel CH$78,750/110,250; @), with rustic and more mainstream options.

Trails abound at **Anticura**, 17km northwest of the Aguas Calientes turn-off. Pleasant, short walks take you to a lookout and waterfall. Two kilometers west of Anticura, the private **El Caulle** is the southern entrance for the trek across the base of Volcán Puyehue. The **Puyehue Traverse** (three to four days) and the **Ruta de los Americanos** (six to eight days) are the most popular routes.

Frutillar

065 / POP 14,550

The mystique of Frutillar is its Germanness, a 19th-century immigrant heritage that the village preserved. To come here is to savor this idea of simpler times, float in the lake, eat home-baked pies and sleep in rooms shaded by lace curtains. For many it is simply too still to linger; for others, it remains a serene alternative to staying in more chaotic Puerto Varas.

The town has two sectors: Frutillar Alto is a no-frills working town, Bajo fronts the lakes and has all of the tourist attractions. **Museo Colonial Alemán** (www.museosaustral.cl; cnr Pérez Rosales & Prat; adult/child CH$2000/500; 9am-7:30pm Jan-Feb, to 5:30pm Mar-Dec) features reconstructions of a mill, smithy and mansion set among manicured gardens.

Many visit as a day trip from Puerto Varas; budget options are scarce. The inviting **Hotel Ayacara** (421-550; www.hotelayacara.cl; Av Philippi 1215; s/d CH$75,000/94,000; @) is a remodeled 1910 house turned eight-room boutique hotel. On a lavender farm just outside town, **Lavanda Casa de Te** (www.lavandacasadete.cl; Km 1.5 a Quebrada Honda; menu CH$10,500; lunch) is a lakeside favorite for tea, gourmet lavender products and farm-fresh lunches. Worth a taxi outing, **Se Cocina** (08-972-8195; www.secocinachile.com; Km 2 a Quebrada Honda; mains CH$9500; lunch & dinner Tue-Sat, lunch only Sun), housed in a beautiful 1850s farmstead 2km from Frutillar, remains the lake's only surefire foodie destination; come for the organic greens, innovative cuisine and homemade beer. Reservations essential.

Minibuses to Puerto Varas (CH$900, 30 minutes), Puerto Montt (CH$1400, one hour) and Osorno (CH$800, 40 minutes) leave from a small parking lot on Pedro Montt near Av Philippi. Everything else leaves from Frutillar Alto, including **Tur Bus** (421-810; Christiana y Misonera) and **Cruz del Sur** (451-552; Alessandri 52) buses to Osorno (CH$1000), Valdivia (CH$3700) and Santiago (CH$25,000).

Puerto Varas

065 / POP 32,200

Two menacing, snowcapped volcanoes stand sentinel over picturesque Puerto Varas like soldiers of adventure. Just 23km from Puerto Montt but worlds apart in charm, scenery and options for the traveler, Puerto Varas has been touted as the 'next Pucón.' There's great access to water sports here – kayaking and canyoning in particular – as well as climbing, fishing, hiking and even skiing, making it a top choice for an extended stay. Note that while it gets packed in summer, it shuts down in winter.

Sights & Activities

Visitors can stroll around town to take in the 19th-century German architecture, punctuated by the 1915 **Iglesia del Sagrado Corazón** (cnr San Francisco & Verbo Divino), based on the Marienkirche of the Black Forest, Germany. Grab a city map at the tourist information office, which highlights the **Paseo Patrimonial**, a suggested walking tour of 10 different houses classified as national monuments.

Nearby lakes, mountains, rivers and fjords provide a variety of activities. On warm summer days, brave the frigid Lago Llanquihue; the best beaches are east of the center in Puerto Chico. Adventurous travelers can try **canyoning** or **rafting** Río Petrohué's ice-green waters. Rafting trips run around CH$32,000; all-day kayaking on Lago Todos Los Santos costs about CH$65,000. Secret

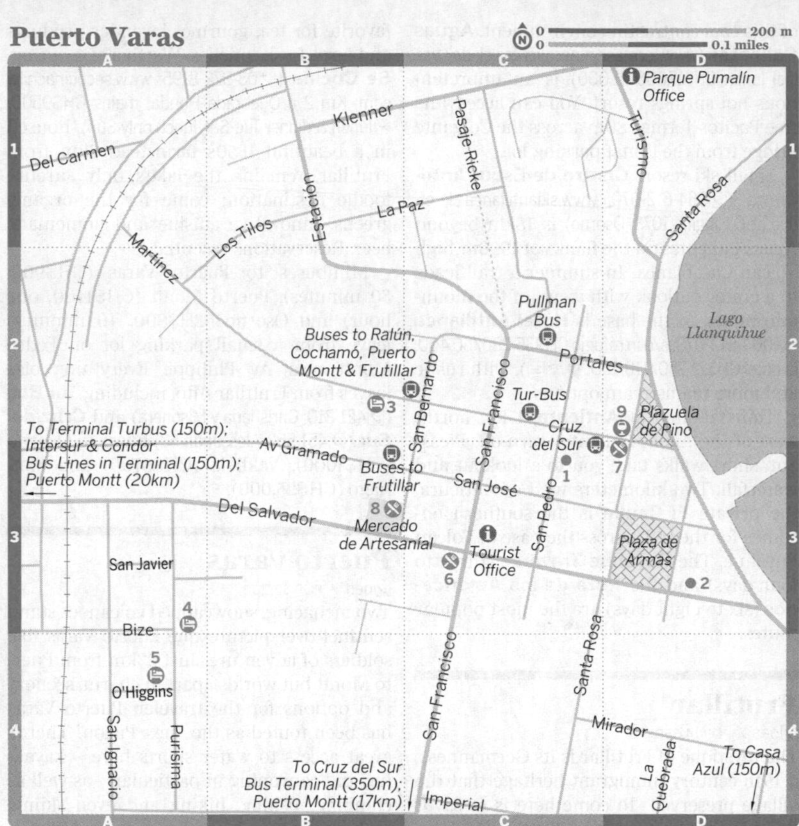

Puerto Varas

Activities, Courses & Tours

1 Secret Patagonia C3
2 TurisTour D3

Sleeping

3 Hostel Melmac Patagonia B2
4 Margouya 2 Patagonia A3
5 The Guest House A4

Eating

6 Café Dane's C3
7 Caffé El Barrista D3
8 Donde El Gordito B3

Drinking

9 Garage D2

spots to cast a line abound: these waters are a good place to try **fly-fishing**. The best spot for a **horse trek** is the Río Cochamó Valley.

Tours

Secret Patagonia OUTDOORS

(☎232-921; www.secretpatagonia.com; San Pedro 311) This eco-sensitive collective specializes in custom-tailored adventure trips to less explored areas of the Río Puelo Valley, Cochamó Valley and beyond. Highlights include hiking in the Cochamó Valley, extensive mountain-bike trips, remote French retreats on Isla Las Bandurrias in Lago Las Rocas, and multiday horse-riding/cultural farmstay trips between Argentina and Chile.

TurisTour OUTDOORS, GUIDED TOUR

(☎228-440; www.turistour.cl; Del Salvador 72) This agency runs the Cruce Andino crossing to/from Argentina (CH$134,680) as well as excursions through the region.

Sleeping

Book ahead in January and February. For camping, go around the lake or to Ensenada.

TOP CHOICE **Casa Azul** HOSTEL $$
(☎232-904; www.casaazul.net; Manzanal 66; dm incl breakfast CH$9000, d CH$31,000, s/d without bathroom CH$17,000/23,000; @📶) This impeccably kept German-Chilean operation in a quieter residential neighborhood has spacious rooms, an expansive guest kitchen and common area with cool furniture fashioned from tree branches. There is central heating throughout.

The Guest House GUESTHOUSE $$
(☎231-521; www.theguesthouse.cl; O'Higgins 608; dm incl breakfast CH$15,000, s/d CH$39,000/43,000; @📶) This art nouveau-era home caters to baby boomers with backpacks: it's simply but tastefully decorated with antiques, snug beds and beautifully restored doors made out of *alerce* (coniferous-tree wood). Breakfast here is legendary.

Margouya 2 Patagonia HOSTEL $
(☎237-695; www.margouya2.com; Purisima 681; dm CH$8000, d CH$25,000, s/d without bathroom CH$14,000/19,000; @📶) This spacious and historic 1932 home is the nicest hostel in town, offering quieter and much larger rooms and bathrooms for the same price as the more central Casa Margouya; there's also cheap bike rental.

Hostel Melmac Patagonia HOSTEL $
(☎230-863; www.melmacpatagonia.com; Martínez 561; dm CH$8000-9000, s/d CH$25,000/29,000, without bathroom CH$15,000/20,000; @📶) The only hostel we've ever stumbled across that will prep a relaxing bath for you after a day of hiking.

Eating

Caffé El Barrista CAFE $
(Martínez 211; mains CH$2700-4200; ⏲breakfast, lunch & dinner) Everyone meets up at this popular coffeehouse serving rich Italian roast, fresh pies and sandwiches; later on, come for microbrews and mojitos.

Café Dane's CAFE $
(Del Salvador 441; mains CH$1350-6300; ⏲breakfast, lunch & dinner) This local favorite serves *küchen* (cake), oven-baked empanadas, *apfelstrudel* (apple strudel) and *pastel de choclo* (maize casserole).

Donde El Gordito CHILEAN, SEAFOOD $
(San Bernardo 560; mains CH$5000-7500; ⏲lunch & dinner, closed Jun) This down-to-earth local's favorite is a great seafood spot in the Mercado Municipal.

Drinking

Garage BAR
(Martínez 220) Attached to the Copec gas station, Garage caters mainly to an artsy, alternative crowd, staying up later than it should and hosting everything from impromptu jazz sessions to Colombian *cumbia* shakedowns.

Bravo Cabrera BAR
(Vicente Pérez Rosales 1071; ⏲closed Sun) Along the *costanera*, this fashionable resto-bar is where you'll find upper-class locals sipping on trendy cocktails mixed by real bartenders. A late-night taxi back to *centro* costs CH$1500.

Information

There are numerous ATMs and internet cafes downtown.

Chile on Board (☎237-206; www.chileonboard.com; Santa Rose 632) Booking for Navimag and Naveira Austral in Puerto Varas.

Clínica Alemana (Otto Bader 810; ⏲24hr)

Parque Pumalín Office (☎250-079; www.pumalinpark.org; Klenner 299; ⏲closed Sat & Sun)

Tourist Office (☎361-194; www.puertovaras-chile.cl; Del Salvador 320) Helpful, with brochures and free maps of the area.

Getting There & Away

Most long-distance buses originate in Puerto Montt. Find ticket offices in town and terminals on the perimeter of town. The **Terminal Turbus** (☎234-163; terminal Del Salvador 1093, office San Pedro 210) houses Turbus, JAC, Intersur and Condor bus lines. **Cruz del Sur** (☎236-969; Martínez 230) has the most departures (from the terminal at San Francisco 1317), including to Chiloé (CH$6300) and Punta Arenas (CH$45,000). For Santiago, **Tur Bus** (☎234-163; San Pedro 210) and **Pullman Bus** (☎234-626; Portales 18) have the most departures.

For Bariloche, Argentina, Cruz del Sur leaves daily (CH$14,000). For information on the popular bus-boat combination to Bariloche, see boxed text, p488.

Minibuses to and from Ensenada (CH$1200, one hour), Petrohué (CH$2200, 1½ hours), Puerto Montt (CH$800, 15 minutes), Cochamó (CH$2000, three hours) and Río Puelo (CH$2500, 1½ hours) all leave from a small stop near the corner of Walker Martínez and San Bernardo. For Frutillar (CH$900, 30 minutes), buses depart from a small stop on Av Gramado near San Bernardo.

DON'T MISS

THROUGH THE ANDES

Once braved by Che Guevara (as told in *Motorcycle Diaries*), **Cruce de Lagos** is a popular 12-hour trip (approximately CH$140,000) between Petrohué, Chile, and Bariloche, Argentina. The trip is a series of buses and boats from one breathtaking view to the next, including the Saltos del Petrohué (waterfalls), Lago Todos Los Santos and Volcán Osorno.

Cruce Andino (www.crucedelagos.cl) runs the trip and can be contacted via its agency arm, TurisTour (p486), at its office in Puerto Varas or Puerto Montt. Check for seasonal discounts and pricing for students and seniors; note that prices increase an astounding US$50 every two years.

Ensenada

Rustic Ensenada, 45km along a picturesque shore-hugging road from Puerto Varas, is really nothing more than a few restaurants, *hospedajes* and adventure outfitters, but for those looking for more outdoors and fewer hardwood floors, it's a nice natural setting in full view of three majestic beasts: Volcán Osorno, Volcán Calbuco and Volcán Puntiagudo. To completely get away, stay at the French-run, rural **Casa Ko** (☎097-703-6477; www.casako.com; Camino a Ensenada Km 37; dm incl breakfast CH$12,000, d CH$38,000, s/d without bathroom CH$18,000/32,000; @), a sweet old farmhouse with homemade dinners (CH$9500), and walks out the back door. Call ahead to arrange transportation. If you plan to climb or ski Osorno, you can save an hour of sleep by overnighting here.

Parque Nacional Vicente Peréz Rosales

In this park of celestial lakes and soaring volcanoes, Lago Todos Los Santos and Volcán Osorno may be the standouts, but they're actually just part of a crowd. One lake leads to the next and volcanoes dominate the skyline on all sides of this storied pass through the Andes range.

Parque Nacional Vicente Peréz Rosales (admission CH$1500) protects 251,000 hectares, including snow-tipped volcanoes Osorno, Puntiagudo (2190m) and Monte Tronador (3554m). Ruta 225 ends in Petrohué, 50km east of Puerto Varas, where there's park access. Minibuses from Puerto Varas are frequent in summer, but limited to twice daily the rest of the year.

Waterfalls boom over basalt rock at **Saltos del Petrohué** (admission CH$1500), 6km before the village. **Petrohué** has beaches, trailheads and the dock for *Cruce de Lagos* departures to Peulla. Try the woodsy **Conaf campground** (www.conaf.cl; campsites 1-5 persons CH$7000). From there, a dirt track leads to **Playa Larga**, a long black-sand beach, from where **Sendero Los Alerces** heads west to meet up with **Sendero La Picada**. The sandy track climbs to Volcán Osorno's Paso Desolación, with scintillating panoramas of the lake, Volcán Puntiagudo and Monte Tronador. There is no road around the lake, making the interior trails only accessible by boat.

Expediciones Petrohué (☎065-212-025; www.petrohue.com; ⏲9am-6:30pm Sep-Jun) runs climbing, rafting and canyoning excursions and offers kayaks right on the lake for CH$3500 per hour.

Access to climb or ski Volcán Osorno is near Ensenada. Ski area **Volcán Osorno** (☎065-233-445; www.volcanosorno.com) has two lifts for skiing and sightseeing. It has ski and snowboard rentals; in summer, ride the ski lift (CH$9000 to CH$12,000) up for impossibly scenic views, or try ziplining or mountain biking.

Downhill from the ski slopes, the rustic **Refugio Teski** (☎065-566-622; www.teski.cl; dm incl breakfast CH$15,000, d CH$45,000; ⏲year-round) offers unparalleled access to the mountain; you can have the outstanding views of Lago Llanquihue all to yourself once the tourist buses depart in the late afternoon. Rent out a mountainside hot tub (CH$40,000 for three hours, including a *pisco sour*), take advantage of two-for-one happy-hour drinks at sunset and make a night of it. You'll need your own sleeping bag for the dorm beds.

To get to the ski area and the *refugio*, take the Ensenada–Puerto Octay road to a signpost about 3km from Ensenada and continue driving 10km up the lateral. It's well worth your money renting a car and driving up the paved road, taking in spectacular views. There are no transportation services to or from the slopes for anyone except for package-tour buyers.

Puerto Montt

☎065 / POP 168,200

If you choose to visit southern Chile's ominous volcanoes, its celestial glacial lakes and its mountainous national parks, you will most likely be visiting the capital of the Lakes District and the region's commercial and transportation hub. Puerto Montt's most redeeming quality is that of its plethora of exit points: be it by plane, ferry, bus or rental car, you can make a quick and virtually painless getaway to a near-endless inventory of memorable locales. Otherwise, travelers have occasionally become endeared of the unpolished working-class Chilean atmosphere here.

Sights

Puerto Montt's downtown stretches along the sea. Streetside stalls line busy and exhaust-ridden Av Angelmó; their prices go up every time a cruise ship docks at port. At the end of the strip are *palafitos* (buildings terraced over the water), an excellent fish market and more crafts in the picturesque fishing port of Angelmó, 3km west.

FREE Casa del Arte Diego Rivera GALLERY

(Quillota 116; 9am-1pm & 3-6:30pm Mon-Fri) A joint Mexican-Chilean project finished in 1964, specializing in works by local artists, sculptors and photographers. Also houses a small cafe and an excellent boutique.

Iglesia Catedral CHURCH

(Urmeneta s/n) The town's oldest building is the 1856 cathedral on the Plaza de Armas.

Sleeping

Puerto Montt is a business town and port rather than a destination in itself. Most travelers spend little more than one night here.

Casa Perla GUESTHOUSE $

(☎262-104; www.casaperla.com; Trigal 312; dm CH$8000-9000, d without bathroom CH$20,000; @☎) This welcoming family home's matriarch, Perla, will have you feeling like a sibling. All bathrooms are shared and guests can use the kitchen. It's hard to find without a map, so consider a taxi from the bus station (CH$2000).

Hospedaje Vista al Mar GUESTHOUSE $

(☎255-625; www.hospedajevistaalmar.unlugar.com; Vivar 1337; d CH$30,000, s/d without bathroom CH$13,000/24,000; @☎) Another family-run favorite with travelers, this is the nicest of the residential guesthouses at this end of town, decked out in great-condition hardwoods with spick-and-span bathrooms, rooms with cable TV and wonderful bay views.

House Rocco Backpacker GUESTHOUSE $

(☎272-897; www.hospedajerocco.cl; Pudeto 233; dm/s/d CH$12,000/20,000/25,000; @☎) This Chilean-American traveler's mainstay five blocks from the Navimag has a large sunny kitchen, warm wooden walls and floors and feather duvets. Home-cooked breakfasts of sweet crepes and real coffee are pluses.

Hostal Vista Hermosa GUESTHOUSE $

(☎319-600; www.hostalvistahermosa.cl; Miramar 1486; d without bathroom CH$18,000; @☎) Vista

WORTH A TRIP

COCHAMÓ & RÍO PUELO VALLEYS

Emerald rivers and deep, pristine valleys are just some of the wonders of this stunning remote region, now threatened by several dam proposals. But something this good should be shared and preserved. Rugged and rustic, these valleys get few visitors.

Puerto Varas' excellent **Campo Aventura** (☎099-289-4318; www.campoaventura.cl) leads popular horse-riding excursions, traversing the valley from its riverside lodge, Campo Aventura Adventure Lodge, with as much emphasis on a cultural experience as nature. In the hamlet of Río Puelo, **Domo Camp** (☎099-138-2310; www.andespatagonia.cl; Puelo Alto; d/tr/q CH$40,000/50,000/60,000; @☎) offers a unique sleep in cool domes, connected by planks through native forest and outfitted with fireplaces and sleeping bags. The attached restaurant, open to the public, offers an excellent set lunch (CH$5800). Small-outfitter collective Secret Patagonia (p486) brings adventurers to both the Cochamó and Puelo Valleys via kayak, mountain bike and hiking trails.

There are four daily bus departures to and from Puerto Montt (CH$3800, four hours), stopping in Puerto Varas, Ensenada and Cochamó.

Puerto Montt

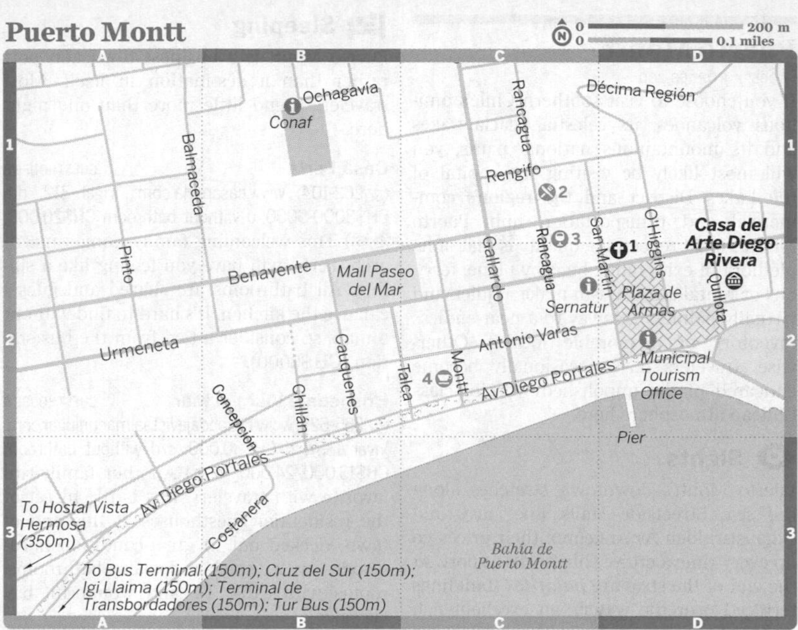

Puerto Montt

Top Sights

Sights

Eating

Drinking

Hermosa has comfortable budget rooms with cable TV. To get here, exit the bus station north on Calle Lillo and turn left on Calle Miramar, across the street from Santa Isabel supermarket, and ascend to the end.

Eating & Drinking

There are several low-rent spots for a drink around the plaza. Busy, diesel-fume-laden Av Angelmó is a dizzying mix of streetside stalls and touristy seafood restaurants; enjoy the frenzy, but keep on going. The best-quality food is found at the end of the road, at Angelmó, easily reached by frequent local buses and *colectivos*.

TOP CHOICE **Fogón del Leñador** STEAKHOUSE $$
(Rancagua 246; mains CH$6000-9500; lunch & dinner) The best *parrilla* in Sur Chico. *Sopapillas* are served with four housemade sauces, all of which are just as tasty on the superior fillet; solo carnivores appreciate the single-serving, fair-trade bottles of red wine.

Sanito CHILEAN $
(www.sanito.cl; Copiapó 66; menu CH$2500-5000; 9am-9pm Mon-Fri) Healthy and homey food, served up fresh in an artistic atmosphere. There's a daily set menu as well as à la carte salads and sandwiches.

Boule Bar BAR
(Benavente 435; closed Sun) Old *Rolling Stone* covers and other musical paraphernalia dot this multiroomed bar lit with candles and featuring several tables and a bar rack made from tree bark.

Sherlock CAFE, BAR
(Antonio Varas 452; lunch & dinner) This cafe/bar has a touch more style than the cookie-cutter competition and has live music most nights of the week.

Information

Internet cafes and ATMs abound. At night the area around the bus terminal harbors petty crime; take precautions and don't walk alone here or along the waterfront.

Conaf (☎486-118; Ochagaviá 458) Can provide details on nearby national parks.

Hospital Regional (Seminario s/n; ⊙24hr) Near the intersection with Décima Región.

Municipal Tourism Office (☎223-027; Antonio Varas 415; ⊙8:15am-9pm) More eager to help than Sernatur, with plenty of national park info. It's on the plaza.

Sernatur (☎258-087; San Martín 80; ⊙8:30am-1pm & 2:30-5pm Mon-Fri, 9am-2pm Sat)

Getting There & Away

Air

LAN (☎600-526-2000; O'Higgins 167, Local 1-B) flies several times daily to Punta Arenas (from CH$145,000, 2¼ hours), Balmaceda/Coyhaique (from CH$112,000, one hour) and many times daily to Santiago (from CH$185,000, 1½ hours). **Sky Airlines** (☎437-555; www.skyairline.cl; cnr San Martín & Benavente) flies to Punta Arenas and Santiago with slightly cheaper fares.

Boat

Puerto Montt is the main departure port for Patagonia. At the **Terminal de Transbordadores** (Av Angelmó 2187), you can find ticket offices and waiting lounges for Navimag, housed inside the same building. The most popular trip is on Navimag's ferry *Evangelistas,* which sails on Friday from Puerto Montt to Puerto Natales and back on Friday (boarding Thursday evening). It's a popular three-night journey through Chile's fjords; book passage at Navimag offices in Santiago, Puerto Montt, Puerto Natales or via the website.

High season is from November to March and low season is April to October. Prices for the trip include full board (vegetarian meals can be requested). Per-person fares vary according to the view and whether it is a private or shared bathroom; in high season, single berths start at around CH$680,000, doubles from CH$359,000 per person. Cars are extra. Bicycles and motorcycles can also be carried along for an additional cost. The southern route includes passage by the glacier Pio XI, the largest in South America (it's as big as Santiago), and there are more beautiful and photogenic glaciers along the route.

Bus

Puerto Montt's renovated waterfront **bus terminal** (☎283-000; cnr Av Diego Portales & Lillo) is the main transportation hub. Summer trips to Punta Arenas and Bariloche sell out, so book ahead.

Minibuses go to Puerto Varas (CH$900, 25 minutes) and Frutillar (CH$1300, one hour). Buses also go to Cochamó (CH$2200, 2½ hours) four times daily, and all carry on to Río Puelo (CH$3500).

Cruz del Sur (☎483-127; www.busescruzdelsur.cl) has frequent buses to Chiloé. **Tur Bus** (☎253-329) has daily buses to Valparaíso/Viña del Mar. Both of these, plus **Igi Llaima** (☎254-519; www.igillaima.cl) and **Pullman Bus** (☎254-399; www.pullman.cl), go to Santiago, stopping at various cities along the way.

For Bariloche (Argentina), Cruz del Sur, **Via Bariloche** (☎253-841; www.viabariloche.com.ar) and **Andesmar** (☎280-999; www.andesmar.com) go daily.

DESTINATION	COST (CH$)	DURATION (HR)
Ancud	4000	2½
Bariloche, Argentina	14,000	6
Castro	5300	4
Concepción	16,000	10
Coyhaique	25,000	24
Osorno	1500	1½
Pucón	9100	5½
Punta Arenas	45,000	30
Quellón	7200	6
Santiago	22,000	12-14
Temuco	7000	5
Valdivia	4800	3½
Valparaíso/ Viña del Mar	32,800	15

Getting Around

ETM (☎256-253; www.busesetm.cl; Genesis 128) shuttles go to **Aeropuerto El Tepual** (☎252-019), 16km west of town, from the bus terminal (CH$2000). Catch the bus 1½ hours before your flight's departure. Car-rental agencies such as **Europcar** (☎286-277; Antonia Varas 162) can help get the permission certificate to take rental vehicles into Argentina with two days' notice.

CHILOÉ

When the early-morning fog shrouds misty-eyed Chiloé, it's immediately apparent something different this way comes. Isla Grande de Chiloé is the continent's second-largest island and is home to a fiercely independent, seafaring people who developed culturally and historically in defiance of Santiago.

On the surface you will see changes in architecture and cuisine: *tejuelas*, the famous Chilote wood shingles; *palafitos* (houses mounted on stilts along the water's edge); more than 150 iconic wooden churches (14 of which are Unesco World Heritage Sites); and the renowned meat, potato and seafood stew, *curanto*. A closer look reveals a rich spiritual culture that is based on a distinctive mythology of witchcraft, ghost ships and forest gnomes.

All of the above are weaved among landscapes that are windswept and lush, with undulating hills, wild and remote national parks, and dense forests, giving Chiloé a distinct flavor unique in South America. In an archipelago of more than 40 minor islands, the main island is a lush quilt of pastureland of rolling hills, 180km long but just 50km wide. Towns and farms tilt toward the eastern side; the western shores are a nearly roadless network of thick forests lapping the wild Pacific.

Chiloé

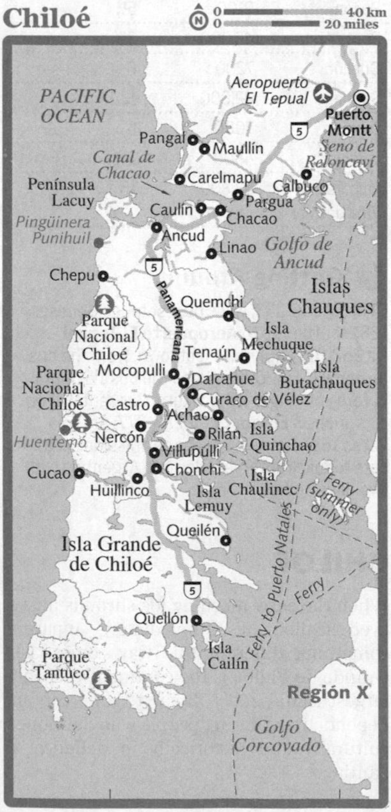

Ancud

☎065 / POP 49,550

Bustling and weathered, urban Ancud offers an earthy base to explore the penguin colonies and walk or sea kayak the blustery, dazzling north coast.

Sights

TOP CHOICE Centro de Visitantes Inmaculada Concepción MUSEUM

(Errázuriz 227; ⌚9:30am-7pm) This excellent museum, housed in an 1875 convent, has two wooden scale models of each of Chiloé's Unesco churches. You'll also find an interesting museum shop, artisan shop and cafe.

Museo Regional de Ancud MUSEUM

(Museo Chilote; Libertad 370; adult/child CH$600/300; ⌚10am-7:30pm Jan-Feb, 10am-5:30pm Tue-Fri, 10am-2pm Sat & Sun Mar-Dec) Has a full-sized replica of the *Ancud* (which sailed the treacherous fjords of the Strait of Magellan to claim Chile's southernmost territories) and a massive blue whale skeleton.

FREE Fuerte San Antonio FORTRESS

(cnr Lord Cochrane & Baquedano; ⌚8:30am-9pm Mon-Fri, 9am-8pm Sat & Sun) During the wars of independence, Fuerte San Antonio was Spain's last Chilean outpost. From the early-19th-century remains of the fortress, the views and historical significance are impressive.

Tours

Many agencies around town run minibus tours to see the penguins at Monumento Natural Islotes de Puñihuil for around CH$13,000 to CH$15,000.

Austral Adventures OUTDOORS

(☎625-977; www.austral-adventures.com; Av Costanera 904) This is the go-to agency for various English-speaking tours, including extended nature-centric jaunts to see the penguins and whales, kayaking on the bay and birdwatching.

Sleeping

Hostal Mundo Nuevo HOSTEL $$

(☎628-383; www.newworld.cl; Costanera 748; dm incl breakfast CH$12,000, s/d CH$29,000/39,000, s/d without bathroom CH$22,000/31,000; @☎) This hostel boasts postcard-perfect sunset views over the Bay of Ancud from a big, comfortable bench on its naturally lit front porch. Rooms and dorms frame the sea; new feather pillows and duvets ensure a good night's rest.

The Tower GUESTHOUSE **$$**
(☎625-977; www.austral-adventures.com; Playa Lechagua; r CH$30,000, apt CH$40,000, cabaña for 2-7 people CH$50,000-70,000) For those with extra pesos and a penchant for solitude. The owners built three lodgings on their property on an isolated beach 6km south of Ancud: two stylish apartments with kitchenettes and a huge beachfront *cabaña* (cabin) called 'La Casita.'

13 Lunas Hostel HOSTEL **$**
(☎622-106; www.13lunas.cl; Los Carrera 855; dm incl breakfast from CH$8500, d with/without bathroom CH$25,000/22,000; @📶) This lovely hostel oozes coziness with bright hardwood floors, beacons of natural light, hotel-level bathrooms and a wonderful terrace with views.

Camping Arena Gruesa CAMPGROUND **$**
(☎623-428; www.arenagruesa.cl; Av Costanera Norte 290; campsites per person CH$4500, s/d CH$18,500/29,000; @📶) Located atop a bluff on the north side of town, city campsites don't get much better views than this. Semi-grassy and decently maintained with electricity and hot water.

Eating & Drinking

Tucked away next to the **Mercado Municipal** (Prat) is the **Mercado Gastronómico**, serving *cazuela* (meat and vegetable stew) and set lunch menus for around CH$2500.

Kuranton CHILEAN, SEAFOOD **$**
(Prat 94; mains CH$5000-7200; ⊙lunch & dinner) This institution specializes in *curanto*, Chiloé's gastronomic bombshell. This hearty stew of mussels, clams, chicken, pork and three types of potatoes is really a meal fit for hibernation.

Retro's Pub BURGERS, MEXICAN **$**
(Ramírez 317; mains CH$3000-7500; ⊙lunch & dinner Mon-Sat; 📶) The best bar in Ancud spreads itself among several rooms; the menu features Tex-Mex, killer burgers, stone-cooked pizza, sandwiches and pasta, all made from scratch.

La Botica de Café CAFE **$**
(Pudeto 277; desserts CH$800-2100; ⊙breakfast, lunch & dinner) A modern coffeehouse serving gourmet espresso and a ridiculously tempting selection of international desserts.

Information

Banco de Chile (Libertad 621) ATM.

BancoEstado (Ramírez 229) ATM.

Conaf (☎627-520; Errázuriz 317; ⊙9am-12:15pm & 2:15-5:30pm Mon & Wed, 9am-12:15pm & 2:15-4:30pm Fri) National park info.

Hospital de Ancud (Almirante Latorre 301; ⊙24hr) At the corner of Pedro Montt.

Sernatur (☎622-665; Libertad 665; ⊙8:30am-7pm Mon-Fri, 9:30am-7pm Sat & Sun) Helpful staff, brochures, town map and list of accommodations.

Getting There & Away

Cruz del Sur (☎622-265; www.busescruzdelsur.cl) owns and operates the main **Terminal de Buses** (cnr Los Carreras & Cavada), which offers nearly hourly departures to Chiloé's more southerly towns, and to cities on the Panamericana to the north, including three daily departures to Santiago (CH$32,000, 17 hours). It's a five-minute walk from the waterfront and downtown.

Chiloé's more rural destinations to the east are serviced by buses that leave from the small inter-rural bus station on Colo Colo above the Bigger supermarket (buy tickets on the bus).

Castro

☎065 / POP 34,500

Castro is the attractive, idiosyncratic capital of Chiloé. With the last decade's salmon boom, this working-class town transformed its ever-casual island offerings with modern supermarkets and boutique hotels. At times loud and boisterous, the capital of the archipelago somehow retains its local Chilote character side by side with a comfortable tourism infrastructure. Located in the dead center of the island, Castro is a perfect base for exploring attractions further afield.

Sights

Don't miss the distinctive *palafitos* houses, which testify to Castro's heritage with humble beginnings in 1567. From the street, they resemble any other house in town, but the backsides jut over the water and, at high tide, serve as piers with boats tethered to the stilts. They're mostly along Costanera Pedro Montt, north of town.

TOP CHOICE **Iglesia San Francisco de Castro** CHURCH
(San Martín) This is one of Chiloé's Unesco gems, colored a faded marigold with eggplant

trim, and with a stunning varnished-wood interior and rows of stained-glass windows.

FREE **Museo Regional de Castro** MUSEUM
(Esmeralda 255; 9:30am-5pm Mon-Fri, 9:30am-6:30pm Sat, 10:30am-1pm Sun Jan-Feb, 9:30am-1pm & 3-6:30pm Mon-Fri, 9:30am-1pm Sun Mar-Dec) Houses a well-organized collection of Huilliche relics, musical instruments, traditional farm implements and Chilote wooden boat models.

Tours

TOP CHOICE **Chiloétnico** CULTURAL, ADVENTURE TOURS
(630-951; www.chiloetnico.cl; Ernesto Riquelme 1228) This highly recommended agency does great mountain-biking and hiking trips to Parque Nacional Chiloé, Parque Tantauco and nearby islands.

Sleeping

Palafito Hostel HOSTEL $$
(531-008; www.palafitohostel.com; Ernesto Riquelme 1210; dm incl breakfast CH$13,000, s/d CH$35,000/45,000, s without bathroom CH$25,000;) This upmarket hostel was the catalyst for turning Riquelme into Castro's coolest street. You will pay more for a dorm here, but the quality outweighs the difference, with great breakfasts, dreamy views and a cabin-cool feel throughout.

TOP CHOICE **Palafito 1326** BOUTIQUE HOTEL $$
(530-053; www.palafito1326.cl; Ernesto Riquelme 1326; s/d incl breakfast from CH$41,500/47,500;) Following a Chilote design aesthetic carved entirely from tepú and cypress woods, this *palafito* design hotel has 12 smallish rooms with high-style touches like wool throws from Dalcahue.

Palafito Sur Hostel HOSTEL $
(536-472; www.palafitosur.com; dm incl breakfast CH$12,000, d/tr CH$24,000/36,000;) This design-forward hostel is a short walk along the *costanera* from the port. It sits over the water; at high tide you can take its kayaks right from the terrace.

Hostal Cordillera GUESTHOUSE $
(532-247; www.hostalcordillera.cl; Barros Arana 175; s/d without bathroom CH$12,000/24,000;) At this traveler's hub, you'll get sea views, large bathrooms, comfy beds and cable TV. Breakfast included.

Eating & Drinking

TOP CHOICE **Hostalomera** CHILEAN $
(Latorre 120; menu CH$2000; lunch & dinner Mon-Sat;) You can't eat this well in this cool kind of atmosphere for this price anywhere. How it can be done without bleeding money is an extraordinary question, but this art-fueled lunch hot spot offers three exceptional home-cooked choices per day, including an appetizer, juice and organic fig or barley coffee, for a shocking CH$2000.

Mar y Canela CHILEAN $
(Ernesto Riquelme 1212; mains CH$3600-8900; lunch & dinner Mon-Sat, lunch only Sun;) Features delicacies such as hazelnut-crusted brie, a small selection of fresh seafood, sandwiches and burgers, and an intimate atmosphere.

Café del Puente CAFE, BREAKFAST $
(Ernesto Riquelme 1180b; mains CH$1200-4200; breakfast, lunch & dinner;) This atmospheric cafe-teahouse does eggs, bacon, French toast, and muesli...and does it well.

Brújula del Cuerpo DINER $
(O'Higgins 308; mains CH$1310-5990; breakfast, lunch & dinner;) A Chilote-style diner offering pizza, fajitas, American-style breakfast and other *comida rapida* (fast food).

Patrimonial BAR
(Balmaceda 291) The bohemian bar of choice, warmed by a wood-burning stove. It's a good spot to try Chiloé's own craftbrew, Vertus (porter and golden ale).

Information

ATMs and cyber cafes are found around the plaza.

Conaf (547-706; Gamboa 424; 8:45am-1pm & 2-5:45pm Mon-Fri) Limited information on Parque Nacional Chiloé.

Hospital de Castro (www.hospitalcastro.gov.cl; Freire 852)

Post Office (O'Higgins 388; 9am-1:30pm & 3-6pm Mon-Fri, 10am-12:30pm Sat)

Tourist Kiosk (547-706; Plaza de Armas)

Getting There & Away

Air

LAN and Sky will soon connect Chiloé with the rest of the country via the brand new Aerodrómo Mocopulli, located 20km north of town and in the finishing stages at the time of writing.

Boat

Summer ferries to/from Chaitén are operated by **Naviera Austral** (☎65-270-430; www.navieraustral.cl; Angelmó 2187, Puerto Montt), which departs Saturday at midnight in January and February. Fares range from CH$16,000 (seat) to CH$25,700 (berth with window). Vehicles cost CH$82,000.

Bus

Centrally located Castro is the major hub for bus traffic on Chiloé. **Terminal de Buses Municipal** (San Martín) has the most services to smaller destinations around the island and some long-distance services. Buses to Mocopulli (CH$500), Dalcahue (CH$700), Chonchi (CH$800), Isla Quinchao (CH$1500 to CH$1700) and Tenaún (CH$1500) all leave from here. The **Cruz del Sur terminal** (☎635-152; www.busescruzdelsur.cl; San Martín 486) focuses on transportation to Quellón and Ancud, and has more long-distance services. Sample fares include Ancud (CH$2000, 1½ hours), Puerto Montt (CH$5500, four hours), Temuco (CH$10,500, 10 hours) and Santiago (CH$25,000, 16 hours).

Dalcahue & Isla Quinchao

Dalcahue, 20km northeast of Castro, has a 19th-century Unesco church, **Nuestra Señora de Los Dolores**, and a famous Sunday **crafts fair** (⏲9:30am-8pm Sun Jan-Feb, 10am-5:30pm Sun Mar-Dec) where you can buy the island's most authentic arts and crafts – sweaters, socks and hats woven from *oveja* (wool) and dyed with natural pigments made from roots, leaves and iron-rich mud.

Midway between Dalcahue and Achao, **Curaco de Vélez** dates from 1660 and has a treasure of Chilote architecture, plus an outstanding **open-air oyster bar** at the beach. Buses between Achao and Dalcahue stop in Curaco.

Isla Quinchao, southeast of Dalcahue, is one of the most accessible islands, and worth a day trip. Isla Quinchao's largest town, **Achao**, features Chiloé's oldest church. Wooden pegs, instead of nails, hold together **Iglesia Santa María de Loreto**.

Good lodging options include **Hospedaje Sol y Lluvias** (☎661-383; hospedaje.solylluvias1@gmail.com; Ricardo Jara 9; r CH$24,000, s without bathroom CH$10,000; @📶), in a wonderful rust-orange house, and **Hostal Plaza** (☎661-283; Amunátegui 20; s/d CH$8000/15,000, without bathroom CH$7000/12,000), a friendly family home. Overlooking the pier, **Mar y Velas** (Serrano 2; mains CH$3900-7800; ⏲lunch & dinner) serves up mussels, clams and cold beer.

The **bus terminal** (cnr Miraflores & Zañartu) is a block south of the church. Buses run daily to Dalcahue (CH$1200) and Castro (CH$1600) every 15 to 30 minutes.

Parque Nacional Chiloé

Gorgeous, evergreen forests meet taupe stretches of sand and the boundless, thrashing Pacific in this 43,000-hectare **national park** (adult/child CH$1500/free), 54km west of Castro. The park protects diverse birds, Chilote fox and the reclusive *pudú* (the world's smallest deer). Visitors are at the mercy of Pacific storms, so expect lots of rain.

Access the park through Cucao, a minute village with growing amenities, and park sector Chanquín, where Conaf runs a **visitor center** (⏲9am-7:30pm Jan-Feb, to 6pm Mar-Dec) with information. **Sendero Interpretivo El Tepual** winds 1km along fallen tree trunks through thick forest. The 2km **Sendero Dunas de Cucao** leads to a series of dunes behind a long, white-sand beach. The most popular route is the 25km **Sendero Chanquín–Cole Cole**, which follows the coast past Lago Huelde to Río Cole Cole. The hike continues 8km north to Río Anay, passing through groves of red myrtles.

Sleeping & Eating

Most accommodations and restaurants are past the bridge from Cucao.

TOP CHOICE **Parador Darwin** GUESTHOUSE $
(☎099-799-9923; Sector Chanquín; s/d CH$20,000/25,000; ⏲closed Apr-Oct; @📶) Full of character and charm, this colorful German-owned wooden house is a fantastic sleeping choice. Or just come for the restaurant, featuring *nueva Chilota* cuisine, including hot smoked salmon you won't soon forget, Hungarian goulash, great pizzas and *pisco sours*.

Camping del Parque CAMPGROUND $
(☎971-027; www.parquechiloe.cl; campsites per person CH$4000, cabins up to 6 people CH$48,000) This Conaf-maintained camping and cabin complex lies about 200m beyond the visitor center – sites have running water, firewood, hot showers and toilets.

Hospedaje El Paraíso GUESTHOUSE $
(☎099-296-5465; Laura Vera, Cucao; campsites per person CH$3000, r without bathroom CH$9000)

The basic budget option in Cucao; has a fantastic river view.

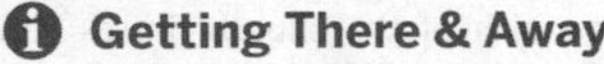

Getting There & Away

There is regular bus transportation between Castro and Cucao. Schedules vary, but there are usually numerous buses daily (CH$1500, one hour).

Quellón

065 / POP 23,100

Those imagining a pot of gold and rainbows at the end of the Carretera Panamericana will be surprised by this dumpy port – most travelers only head this way to make ferry connections to Chaitén. Waterfront lodging **Hotel El Chico Leo** (681-567; ligorina@hotmail.com; Costanera Pedro Montt 325; d CH$22,000, r per person without bathroom CH$8000;) offers the best value, with clean, bright rooms, attentive staff and quality beds. Its popular restaurant (mains CH$2600 to CH$6500) is known for seafood.

Cruz del Sur and Transchiloé buses leave frequently from the **bus terminal** (cnr Pedro Aguirre Cerda & Miramar) for Castro (CH$1200, two hours). **Naviera Austral** (682-506; www.navieraustral.cl; Pedro Montt 457) sails to Chaitén (CH$16,000 to CH$26,000) on Thursday at midnight throughout the year.

NORTHERN PATAGONIA

A web of rivers, peaks and sprawling glaciers long ago provided a natural boundary between northern Patagonia and the rest of the world. Pinochet's **Carretera Austral** (Hwy 7) was the first road to effectively link these remote regions in the 1980s. Isolation has kept the local character fiercely self-sufficient and tied to nature's clock. *'Quien se apura en la Patagonia pierde el tiempo,'* locals say ('Those who hurry in Patagonia lose time'). Weather decides all in this nowhere land beyond the Lakes District. So don't rush. Missed flights, delayed ferries and floods are routine to existence; take the wait as locals would – another opportunity to heat the kettle and strike up a slow talk over maté.

Starting south of Puerto Montt, the Carretera Austral links widely separated towns and hamlets all the way to Villa O'Higgins, a total of just over 1200km. High season (from mid-December through February) offers considerably more travel options and availability. Combination bus and ferry circuits afford visitors a panoramic vision of the region. As well as Parque Pumalín to Lago General Carrera, there's plenty more to see in this region. Don't hesitate to tread off the beaten track: the little villages along the road and its furthest hamlets of Cochrane, Caleta Tortel and Villa O'Higgins are fully worth exploring.

Parque Pumalín

Verdant and pristine, this 2889-sq-km park encompasses vast extensions of temperate rainforest, clear rivers, seascapes and farmland. A remarkable forest-conservation effort, **Parque Pumalín** (www.parquepumalin.cl; admission free) attracts international visitors keen to explore these tracts of forest stretching from near Hornopirén to Chaitén. Owned by American Doug Tompkins, it is Chile's largest private park and one of the largest private parks in the world. Visit the excellent website for more information.

The 2008 eruption of Volcán Chaitén kept the park closed for several years; it reopened in 2011. Popular treks include **Sendero Cascadas** (three hours round-trip), an undulating climb through dense forest that ends at a large waterfall, and the hike to **Volcán Chaitén Crater**. Given the volcano's activity in recent history, it's very important to check with rangers before heading out, and preferably go with a guide. **Austral Adventures** (065-625-977; www.austral-adventures.com; Av Costanera 904, Ancud, Chiloé) does sailing trips around Chiloé's islands and through Pumalín's fjords. Information centers and the park website have details on available campgrounds, including **Camping Rio Gonzalo** (Caleta Gonzalo; campsites with fire pit CH$5000) on the shores of Reñihué Fjord.

Information

Centros de Visitantes (www.parquepumalin.cl; Caleta Gonzalo & El Amarillo; 9am-7pm Mon-Sat, 10am-4pm Sun) Has park brochures; the website has updated information.

Getting There & Away

Naviera Austral (065-270-431) ferries sail daily from Caleta Gonzalo to Hornopirén (five to six hours) daily in high season. Bus-boat combos from Puerto Montt can drop visitors in the park on the way to Chaitén. Log on to the park website for details.

Carretera Austral

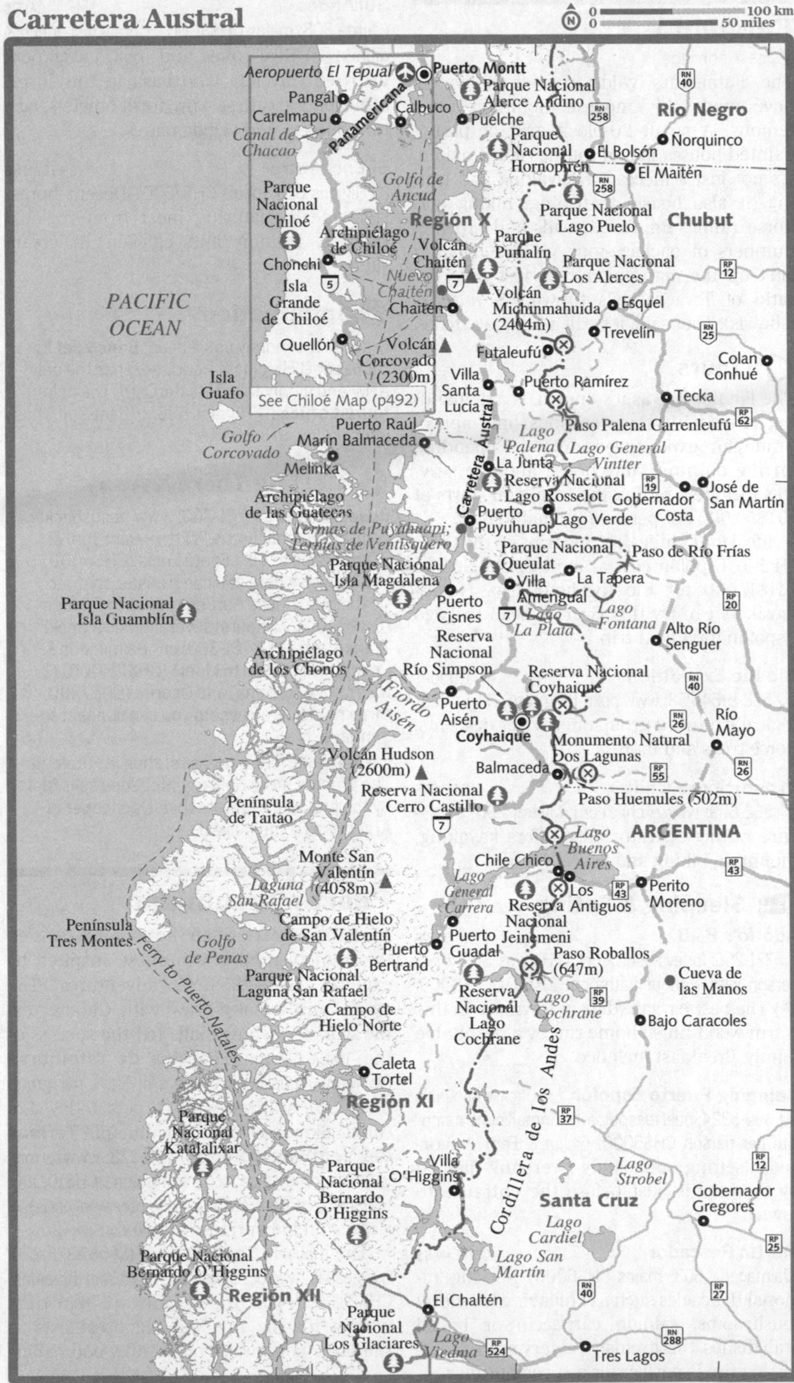

Futaleufú

065 / POP 1800

The Futaleufú's wild, frosty-mint waters have made this modest mountain town famous. A small 20-block grid of pastel-painted houses 155km southeast of Chaitén, it's not just a mecca for kayaking and rafting, it also boasts fly-fishing, hiking and horse riding. Improved roads and growing numbers of package-tour visitors mean it isn't off the map anymore – just note the ratio of Teva sandals to woolen *mantas* (shawls). That said, it's still a fun place to be.

Tours

The Futa or 'Fu,' as it's known, is a demanding river, with some sections only appropriate for experienced rafters. Depending on the outfitter you choose and the services included, rafting the Futaleufú starts at CH$50,000 per person for a half-day.

Ideal for families, rafting trips on the Class III Río Espolón cost around CH$15,000 to CH$17,000 for the five-hour trip. Novice kayakers can try this river or head to Lago Espolón for a float trip.

Bio Bio Expeditions OUTDOORS
(562-1964-258; www.bbxrafting.com) This ecologically minded group offers river descents, horse treks and more.

Expediciones Chile OUTDOORS
(562-639; www.exchile.com; Mistral 296) A secure rafting operator; also offers kayaking, mountain biking and horse riding.

Sleeping & Eating

Adolfo's B&B B&B $
(721-256; lodeva@surnet.cl; O'Higgins 302; r per person with/without bathroom CH$10,000/8000; @) The best bargain digs in town are in this warm wood-finish home run by a hospitable family. Breakfast included.

Camping Puerto Espolón CAMPGROUND $
(696-5324; puertoespolon@latinmail.com; campsite per person CH$5000; Jan & Feb) A gorgeous setting on a sandy riverbank flanked by mountains, just before the entrance to town.

Martín Pescador CHILEAN $$
(Balmaceda 603; mains CH$6000) Serving regional delicacies such as chicken with morel mushrooms, salmon carpaccio or baked crab dishes, this exclusive eatery with a roaring log fire is perfect for a special dinner.

SurAndes CAFE $
(Cerda 308; mains CH$4000; breakfast, lunch & dinner;) Real coffee and fresh juices perk up tired travelers who bask in this lovely atmospheric cafe serving fresh omelets, custom burgers and veggie plates.

El Encuentro CHILEAN $$
(O'Higgins 653; meals CH$7000) Decent homestyle meals featuring meat from regional ranches, salmon and chicken in cream sauce.

Information

Bring all the money you'll need; **Banco del Estado** (cnr O'Higgins & Rodríguez) has the only ATM, and it only takes MasterCard. The helpful **tourist office** (O'Higgins 536; 9am-9pm) has information on local treks.

Getting There & Away

Buses Becker (721-360; www.busesbecker.com; cnr Balmaceda & Pratt; 9am-1pm & 3-7pm) goes to Villa Santa Lucía (CH$6000, two hours), where you can transfer south to Coyhaique. Buses Cardenas goes to Chaitén (CH$8000, 3½ hours) several times a week. **TransAustral** (721-360; cnr Balmaceda & Pratt) goes to Puerto Montt (CH$25,000, 12 hours via Argentina) and Osorno (CH$7200, three hours), from where you can connect to Santiago.

Note that there is no gas station in Futaleufú. The grocery store on Sargento Aldea sells fuel by the jug; also be aware that it's cheaper in Argentina (if you make it).

Puerto Puyuhuapi

In 1935 four German immigrants settled this remote rainforest outpost, inspired by explorer Hans Steffen's adventures. The agricultural colony grew with Chilote textile workers, whose skills fed the success of the 1947 German **Fábrica de Alfombras** (www.puyuhuapi.com; Aysen s/n; tours per group CH$5000), still weaving carpets today. Located 6km south of Puyuhuapi, **Termas del Ventisquero** (067-325-228; www.termasventisqueropuyuhuapi.cl; admission CH$10,000; 9am-11pm Dec-Feb & some winter weekends) is a peaceful hot springs complex.

The historic **Casa Ludwig** (067-325-220; www.casaludwig.cl; Uebel 202; s/d incl breakfast CH$23,000/44,000) is elegant – a real treat with a roaring fire and big breakfasts at the large communal table. All-wood cabins

VOLCÁN CHAITÉN WAKES UP

No one even considered it a volcano, but that changed quickly. On May 2, 2008, Volcán Chaitén, 10km northeast of its namesake town, began a month-long eruption with a 20km-high column of ash. During the first week, successive explosions emitted more than a cubic kilometer of rhyolitic ash. The rampage caused flooding and severe damage to homes, roads and bridges, decimated thousands of livestock and spewed ash as far as Buenos Aires. Chaitén's 4000 inhabitants were evacuated.

The government sanctioned relocating the town slightly northwest to the village of Santa Barbara (Nuevo Chaitén), but recent improvements in the old town infrastructure has locals returning to recover their homes in Chaitén.

Located in Parque Pumalín, the volcano is easily viewed from sections of the main park road. It's also possible to view forests on the volcano's northeastern flank calcified by pyroclastic flows. The crater has yawned open to 3km in diameter, hosting within it a new complex of quickly formed rhyolitic domes. You can hike to the crater with a local guide, though great care should be taken.

The park reopened in 2011, thanks to park rangers who have worked tirelessly in its recovery, and remains under constant monitoring by the government agency of geology and mining. For updates, contact Parque Pumalín (p496) or local tourism offices.

have paraffin stoves, snug white bedding and small balconies at **Cabañas Aonikenk** (325-208; www.aonikenkpuyuhuapi.cl; Hamburgo 16; s/d incl breakfast from CH$30,000/32,000, cabin for 4/5 people CH$50,000/60,000;); the attached cafe offers whole-wheat sandwiches, cakes and salads. **El Muelle** (Otto Ubel s/n; mains CH$5000-8000; lunch & dinner) does big lunches of fresh seafood.

Buses that run between Coyhaique and Chaitén will drop passengers in Puyuhuapi. Buy your return ticket as far ahead as possible. Buses stop at restaurant El Muelle, where tickets are also sold. **Buses Becker** (232-167) goes to Chaitén and Futaleufú a few days a week.

Parque Nacional Queulat

The 1540-sq-km **Parque Nacional Queulat** (admission CH$4000) is a wild realm of rivers winding through forests thick with ferns and southern beech. Its steep-sided fjords are flanked by creeping glaciers. From Conaf's **Centro de Información Ambiental** (9am-6pm) there is a 3km hike to a lookout with views of **Ventisquero Colgante**, a chalk-blue hanging glacier.

Just north of the southern entrance at Pudú (Km 170), a damp trail climbs the valley of the **Río de las Cascadas** through a dense forest to a granite bowl where half a dozen waterfalls spring from hanging glaciers.

Coyhaique

067 / POP 44,900

The cow town that kept growing, Coyhaique is the regional hub of rural Aisén, urbane enough to house the latest techie trends, mall fashions and discos. All this is plopped in the middle of an undulating mountain range, with rocky humpback peaks and snowy summits in the backdrop. For the visitor, it's the launch pad for far-flung adventures, be it fly-fishing, trekking the ice cap or rambling the Carretera Austral to its end. For those fresh from the rainforest wilderness of northern Aisén, it can be a jarring relapse into the world of semi trucks and subdivisions. Industry is braced to pounce here, with a number of regional hydroelectric projects in the works.

Sights & Activities

Mirador Río Simpson LOOKOUT

For prime river vistas, walk west on JM Carrera to this viewpoint.

Museo Regional de la Patagonia MUSEUM

(cnr Av General Baquedano & Lillo; admission CH$500; 9am-6pm Dec-Feb, limited hr rest of year) This museum catalogues pioneer artifacts and Jesuit regalia; it also houses a fine collection of photographs on regional history.

Lago Elizalde LAKE

One of many serene mountain lakes great for trout fishing, kayaking or beach time. It's

33km from Coyhaique; buses depart from the bus terminal.

Reserva Nacional Coyhaique HIKING
(admission CH$2000) These hiking trails are only 5km from town. Take Baquedano north across the bridge and go right at the gravel road; from the entrance it's 3km to Laguna Verde.

Tours

Casa del Turismo Rural CULTURAL TOUR
(☎214-031; www.casaturismorural.cl; Dussen 357-B) Sets up rural homestays and local guide services for a grassroots approach to trekking, fishing and horse riding.

GeoSur Expediciones-Patagonia Learning Adventures ADVENTURE TOUR
(☎099-264-8671; www.patagonialearning.com; Símon Bolívar 521) Combines local cultural experiences with trekking, kayaking, fly-fishing or a day in the country at its adventure center.

Sleeping

TOP CHOICE **Patagonia Hostel** HOSTEL $
(☎096-240-6974; www.patagonia-hostel.com; Lautaro 667; dm/d CH$10,000/30,000; @) A welcoming German-run hostel; rooms are stylish and minimal, but splurge with 2m-long beds and huge pillows. Check out its tour services, which include nearby mountain treks. Breakfast included.

Albergue Las Salamandras GUESTHOUSE $
(☎211-865; www.salamandras.cl; Km 1.5; dm/s/d without bathroom CH$8500/16,000/20,000, s/d CH$20,000/28,000, 2-6 person cabins CH$30,000-60,000, campsite per person CH$6000; @) On a wooded bank of Río Simpson, this rustic guesthouse offers ample common spaces, two kitchens and dorm beds weighted in blankets. It's 2km south of town.

Hostal Español GUESTHOUSE $$
(☎242-580; www.hostalcoyhaique.cl; Aldea 343; s/d CH$25,000/35,000; @) Tasteful and modern, this ample wooden house has 10 rooms with fresh quilted bedding. Put your feet up by the living room's crackling fire.

Kooch Hostel HOSTEL $
(☎527-186; www.koochhostel.com; Camino Piedra del Indio 2; dm/s/d CH$10,000/15,000/24,000; @) This big, cozy home has a communal kitchen and patio. All beds feature down duvets and bright colors. It's 10 blocks from the plaza.

Camping La Alborada CAMPGROUND $
(☎238-868; Km 1 Coyhaique - Puerto Aysén; campsite per person CH$2500) Exceptionally clean and sheltered sites (with roofs), lots of bathrooms and individual sinks, hot showers, fire pits and electricity.

Eating

TOP CHOICE **Mamma Gaucha** PIZZERIA $$
(Paseo Horn 47; mains CH$4500-8000; ⊙breakfast, lunch & dinner, closed Sun) A down-home setting for fresh-mint lemonade, organic wine or a pint of La Tropera, locally brewed upstairs. The mainstays are clay-oven pizzas, homemade pastas and salad bowls filled with local produce.

Carnes Queulat PARRILLA $$
(Ramón Freire 327; mains CH$4000-7000; ⊙lunch & dinner, closed Sun) Serves the best steaks in the region. *Carne a las brasas* – meat attentively grilled over wood fire – is the worthy house specialty.

TOP CHOICE **Café Confluencia** INTERNATIONAL $
(21 de Mayo 544; mains CH$3000-5000; ⊙closed Sun) This chic eatery serves heaping bowls of greens and has themed dinner nights that bring fresh tacos way south. It's a crowded nightspot, too.

La Ovejita CAFE $
(cnr Lillo & Moraleda; sandwiches CH$3000; ⊙breakfast, lunch & dinner;) An ideal nook to settle down with a pot of tea, raspberry mousse that's lighter than air and creative sandwiches.

Casino de Bomberos CHILEAN $
(Parra 365; fixed-price lunch CH$3500; ⊙lunch) This classic but windowless eatery packs with locals downing seafood plates or steak and eggs.

Café Holzer CAFE $
(Dussen 317; cakes CH$2000; ⊙9:30am-9pm Tue-Fri, 10am-9pm Sat & Sun;) Sumptuous cakes and tarts are flown here from a reputable Santiago bakery; real coffee is also served.

Information

Banks with ATMs and internet cafes line Condell. Get cash here; it is one of the few stops on the Carretera Austral with Visa ATM access.

Conaf (☎212-109; Av Ogana 1060; ⏲9am-8pm Mon-Sat, 10am-6pm Sun) Park information.

Hospital Regional (☎219-100; Ibar 68; ⏲24hr)

Post Office (Lord Cochrane 202)

Sernatur (☎233-949; Bulnes 35; ⏲8:30am-8pm Mon-Fri, 10am-6pm Sat & Sun summer) Excellent information on the region.

Getting There & Away

Air

The region's main airport is in Balmaceda, 50km southeast of Coyhaique. **LAN** (☎600-526-2000; Parra 402) has daily flights to Puerto Montt (CH$96,500 one hour) and Santiago (CH$205,000, 2½ hours). Another choice is **Sky** (☎240-827; www.skyairline.cl; Arturo Prat 203). There are several shuttle services to and from the airport, including **Transfer Velasquez** (☎250-413).

Bus

Buses operate from the **bus terminal** (☎258-203; cnr Lautaro & Magallanes) and separate offices. Schedules change continuously; check with Sernatur for the latest information. The following leave from the terminal.

For northern destinations, companies include **Buses Becker** (☎232-167; www.busesbecker.com; General Parra 335), **Queilen Bus** (☎240-760) and **Transaustral** (☎232-067). For southern destinations, try **Buses Don Carlos** (☎231-981; Cruz 63). Sample fares include Chaitén (CH$25,000, nine to 11 hours), Puyuhuapi (CH$8200, six hours) and Puerto Montt (CH$30,000, 23 hours).

Lago General Carrera

Shared with Argentina (where it's called Lago Buenos Aires), this massive 224,000-hectare lake is a wind-stirred green-blue sea in the middle of sculpted Patagonian steppe. Its rough and twisty roads dwarf the traveler: you'll feel like you're crawling through the landscape. An excellent journey follows the Carretera Austral south from Coyhaique, around the lake's western border.

Just before reaching Balmaceda from Coyhaique, a right-hand turn-off (the sign points to Cochrane) heads toward **Reserva Nacional Cerro Castillo**. The spires of glacier-bound Cerro Castillo tower over some 180,000 hectares of southern beech forest.

Along the western shore, **Puerto Río Tranquilo** is the launch point for more budget-minded tours to the stunning Glaciar San Rafael. Boat tours visit the gorgeous caves of **Capilla de Mármol** (Marble Chapel) when the water's calm. North of town an (unfinished) glacier-lined road to **Parque Nacional Laguna San Rafael** bumps toward the coast. Adventure base camp **El Puesto** (☎02-196-4555; www.elpuesto.cl; Pedro Lagos 258; s/d incl breakfast CH$50,000/62,000; 📶) is a lovely B&B owned by a professional guide whose ice-trekking trips come recommended.

About 13km east of Cruce El Maitén, **Puerto Guadal** has petrol and provisions. With rave reviews, ecocamp and hostel **Un Destino No Turistico** (☎098-756-7545; www.destino-noturistico.com; Camino Laguna La Manga, Km 1; campsites per person CH$5500, dm/d CH$10,000/25,000) provides a lovely countryside getaway.

Chile Chico

☎067 / POP 4000

Gold and silver mines dot the roller-coaster road from Puerto Guadal, ending in Chile Chico, a sunny oasis of wind-pummeled poplars and orchards. From here, buses connect to Los Antiguos and Ruta 40 leading to southern Argentine Patagonia. **Reserva Nacional Jeinemeni** (admission CH$1000), 60km away, is a treasure of flamingos and turquoise mountain lagoons. Aside from a few tours, there's little transportation; try **Expeditions Patagonia** (☎098-464-1067; www.expeditionspatagonia.com; O'Higgins 333, Galeria Municipal; ⏲9am-1pm & 2:30-8pm).

There is a helpful **Oficina de Informacion Turistica** (☎411-338; www.chilechico.cl; cnr O'Higgins & Blest Ghana; ⏲9am-9pm Mon-Fri, 10am-9pm Sat & Sun) and a **BancoEstado** (González 112; ⏲9am-2pm Mon-Fri) for money exchange; the ATM only takes MasterCard.

Stay at the ultrafriendly **Kon Aiken** (☎411-598; Burgos 6; r per person without bathroom CH$9000, 6-person cabaña CH$35,000) or a 'farmstay' such as **Hostería de la Patagonia** (☎411-337; hdelapatagonia@gmail.com; Camino Internacional s/n; dm incl breakfast CH$15,000, s/d CH$25,000/40,000), with charming rooms among the gardens. The quirky **Café Elizabeth y Loly** (☎411-451; González 25; mains CH$2500-5000; ⏲lunch & dinner) serves strong coffee and authentic baklava.

Getting There & Away

Ferry Chelenco goes back and forth to Puerto Ibáñez (CH$1500, 2½ hours) a few times a week.

A number of shuttle buses leave from O'Higgins 420 and cross the border to Los Antiguos,

Argentina (CH$3000, 20 minutes), just 9km east. Los Antiguos has connections to El Chaltén.

Seguel (☎245-237, 067-431-224; O'Higgins 394) goes to Puerto Guadal (CH$6000, three hours) on Monday to Thursday afternoons.

Villa O'Higgins

The Carretera Austral doesn't end at Lago General Carrera; in fact, it rumbles nearly 300km further south to the remote village of Villa O'Higgins. Only the massive glacial barrier of the Southern Ice Field kept it from going any further, but that doesn't stop hardy adventurers from tackling the ferry-trek-ferry combination to El Chaltén, Argentina. In Villa O'Higgins, **El Mosco** (☎67-431-819; www.patagoniaelmosco.com; camping/dm per person CH$5000/9000, d with/without bathroom CH$45,000/30,000) offers friendly lodgings and the lowdown on local hikes. Guided horse riding, trekking trips and bike rental are available with advance booking through **Villa O'Higgins Expediciones** (☎431-821/2; www.villaohiggins.com).

SOUTHERN PATAGONIA

The wind is whipping, the mountains are jagged and waters trickle clear. This desolate area first attracted missionaries and fortune seekers from Scotland, England and Croatia. Writer Francisco Coloane described these early adventurers as 'courageous men whose hearts were no more than another closed fist.' The formation of *estancias* (extensive grazing establishments, either for cattle or sheep, with a dominant owner or manager and dependent resident labor force), and the wool boom that followed created reverberating effects: great wealth for a few gained at the cost of native populations, who were nearly exterminated by disease and warfare. Later the region struggled as wool values plummeted and the Panama Canal diverted shipping routes.

Patagonia's worth may have been hard-won and nearly lost but it is now under reconsideration. While wealth once meant minerals and livestock, now it is in the very landscape. For visitors, the thrill lies in Patagonia's isolated, spectral beauty. Parque Nacional Torres del Paine is the region's star attraction. Among the finest parks on the continent, it attracts hundreds of thousands of visitors every year.

Punta Arenas

☎061 / POP 130,130

If these streets could talk: this wind-wracked former penitentiary has hosted tattered sailors, miners, seal hunters, starving pioneers and wealthy dandies of the wool boom. Exploitation of one of the world's largest reserves of hydrocarbon started in the 1980s and has developed into a thriving petro-chemical industry. Today's Punta Arenas is a confluence of the ruddy and the grand, geared toward tourism and industry.

Sights

Plaza Muñoz Gamero PLAZA

A central plaza of magnificent conifers surrounded by opulent mansions. There's a **monument** commemorating the 400th anniversary of Magellan's voyage. Just east is the former **Sociedad Menéndez Behety**, which now houses Turismo Comapa. The **cathedral** sits west.

Museo Regional Braun-Menéndez MUSEUM

(Magallanes 949; admission CH$1500, free Sun; 10:30am-5pm Mon-Sat, 10:30am-2pm Sun in summer, to 2pm daily in winter) This mansion testifies to the wealth and power of pioneer sheep farmers in the late 19th century. The well-maintained interior houses a regional historical museum and original French-nouveau family furnishings.

FREE **Cementerio Municipal** CEMETERY

(main entrance at Av Bulnes 949; 7:30am-8pm) This is among South America's most fascinating cemeteries, with both humble immigrant graves and flashy tombs, like that of wool baron José Menéndez (a scale replica of Rome's Vittorio Emanuele monument). It's an easy 15-minute stroll northeast of the plaza, or catch any taxi *colectivo* in front of the Museo Regional Braun-Menéndez on Magallanes.

Museo Naval y Marítimo MUSEUM

(Pedro Montt 981; adult/child CH$1200/600; 9:30am-12:30pm & 2-5pm Tue-Sat) A naval and maritime museum with historical exhibits, which include a fine account of the Chilean mission that rescued Sir Ernest Shackleton's crew from Antarctica. The most imaginative display is a replica ship complete with bridge, maps, charts and radio room.

Punta Arenas

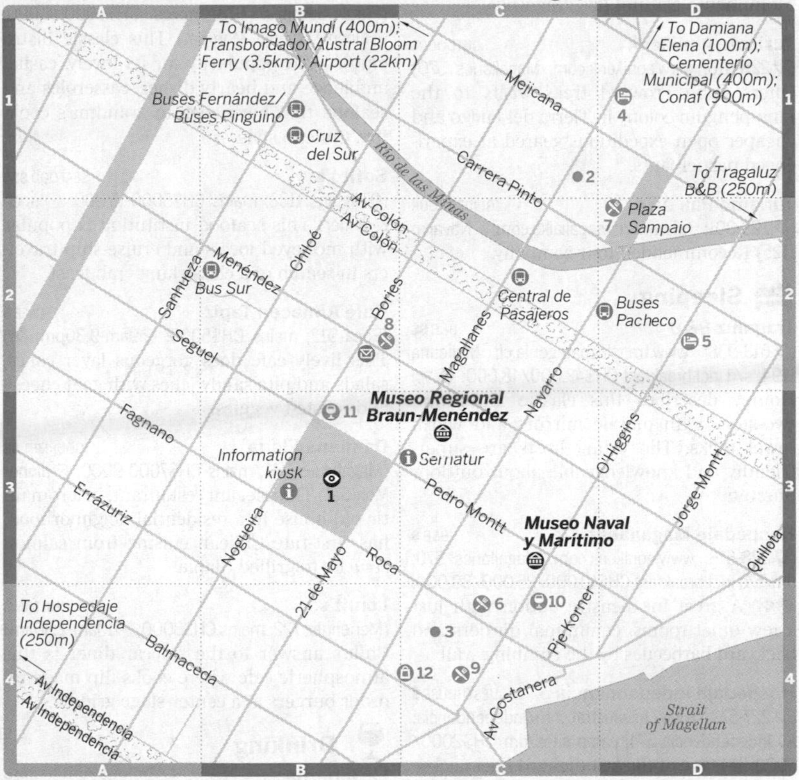

To Imago Mundi (400m); Transbordador Austral Bloom Ferry (3.5km); Airport (22km)
To Damiana Elena (100m); Cementerio Municipal (400m); Conaf (900m)
To Tragaluz B&B (250m)
To Hospedaje Independencia (250m)
Buses Fernández/ Buses Pingüino
Cruz del Sur
Bus Sur
Central de Pasajeros
Buses Pacheco
Plaza Sampaio
Museo Regional Braun-Menéndez
Information kiosk
Sernatur
Museo Naval y Marítimo
Strait of Magellan

Punta Arenas

Top Sights

- Museo Naval y Marítimo C3
- Museo Regional Braun-Menéndez C3

Sights

- 1 Plaza Muñoz Gamero B3

Activities, Courses & Tours

- 2 Turismo Aonikenk C1
- 3 Turismo Pali Aike C4

Sleeping

- 4 Hospedaje Magallanes D1
- 5 Hostal La Estancia D2

Eating

- 6 Café Almacen Tapiz C4
- 7 La Marmita D2
- 8 Lomit's B2
- 9 Sotito's C4

Drinking

- 10 Jekus C4
- 11 La Taberna B3

Shopping

- 12 The Art Corner C4

 Tours

Worthwhile day trips include tours to the Seno Otway *pingüinera* (penguin colony), 48km to the north, and visits to the town's first settlements at Fuerte Bulnes and Puerto Hambre. If you have the time, a more atmospheric alternative to Seno Otway is the thriving Magellanic-penguin colonies of Monumento Natural Los Pingüinos.

Turismo Aonikenk OUTDOORS
(☎228-616; www.aonikenk.com; Magallanes 570) Offers Cabo Froward treks, visits to the king-penguin colony in Tierra del Fuego and cheaper open expeditions geared at experienced participants.

Turismo Pali Aike GUIDED TOUR
(☎223-301; www.turismopaliaike.com; Navarro 1125) Recommended tour company.

Sleeping

Tragaluz B&B B&B **$$**
(☎613-938; www.tragaluzpatagonia.cl; Mejicana 1194; s/d incl breakfast CH$42,000/48,000; @) Homey describes this classic aluminum two-story with mosaic mirrors and warm towel racks. The young hosts are super-friendly and knowledgeable about outdoor pursuits.

Hospedaje Magallanes B&B **$**
(☎228-616; www.aonikenk.com; Magellanes 570; dm/s/d incl breakfast CH$10,000/25,000/30,000; @) A great inexpensive option with just a few quiet rooms, communal dinners and backyard barbecues by the climbing wall.

Hospedaje Independencia GUESTHOUSE **$**
(☎227-572; www.chileaustral.com/independencia; Av Independencia 374; camp sites/dm CH$2000/5000; @) One of the last diehard backpacker haunts with cheap prices, reasonably clean rooms, kitchen privileges, camping and bike rentals.

Imago Mundi HOSTEL **$**
(☎613-115; www.imagomundipatagonia.cl; Mejicana 252; dm incl breakfast CH$12,000; @) Infused with wanderlust, this rambling house has snug bunks in electric colors and cozy spaces; at night it doubles as a cultural space featuring arthouse cinema and live jazz.

Hostal La Estancia GUESTHOUSE **$**
(☎249-130; www.estancia.cl; O'Higgins 765; d CH$30,000, dm/s/d without bathroom CH$12,000/20,000/25,000; @) An old downtown house with big rooms, vaulted ceilings and tidy shared bathrooms.

Eating

Local seafood is an exquisite treat: go for *centolla* (king crab) or *erizos* (sea urchins). The inexpensive **Mercado Municipal** (21 de Mayo 1465) is a good place to try them.

TOP CHOICE **La Marmita** CHILEAN **$$**
(Plaza Sampaio 678; mains CH$6000-10,000; lunch & dinner Mon-Sat) This classic bistro enjoys wild popularity for its lovely, casual ambience and hearty dishes, casseroles and seafood that hark back to grandma's cooking, Chilean style.

Sotito's SEAFOOD **$$$**
(O'Higgins 1138; mains CH$5000-15,000; lunch & dinner) This seafood institution is popular with moneyed locals and cruise-ship travelers in search of a classy king-crab feast.

Café Almacen Tapiz CAFE **$**
(Roca 912; mains CH$5000; 9am-9:30pm) This lively cafe does gorgeous layer cakes, salads and pita sandwiches with goat cheese and roasted veggies.

Damiana Elena GOURMET **$$**
(Magallanes 341; mains CH$7000-9000; dinner Mon-Sat) This elegant restaurant, in a romantic old house in a residential neighborhood, has first-rate Chilean cuisine from salmon *ceviche* to grilled tilapia.

Lomit's CHILEAN **$**
(Menéndez 722; mains CH$3000; 10am-2:30am) Chile's answer to the sidecar diner is this atmospheric cafe where cooks flip made-to-order burgers at a center-stage griddle.

Drinking

La Taberna BAR
(Sara Braun Mansion, Plaza Muñoz Gamero; 7pm-2am, to 3am weekends) This dark and elegant subterranean bar, with polished wood fixtures and cozy nooks reminiscent of an old-fashioned ship, is a classic old-boys' club.

Jekus PUB
(O'Higgins 1021; 6pm-3am) A restaurant that serves as a popular meeting spot for drinks, with happy hours, karaoke and soccer on the tube.

Shopping

Art Corner ARTS & CRAFTS
(Errázuriz 910, 2nd fl) A great place for innovative handmade gifts, with gorgeous woolens and crafts.

Zona Franca DUTY FREE
(Zofri; Km 3.5 Norte Zona Franca Punta Arenas; Mon-Sat) The duty-free zone offers heaps of electronics, outdoor gear, camera and film equipment. *Colectivos* shuttle back

and forth from downtown along Av Bulnes throughout the day.

Information

Internet access is widely available and ATMs are common.

Conaf (230-681; Bulnes 0309; 9am-5pm Mon-Fri) Has details on the nearby parks.

Hospital Regional (205-000; cnr Arauco & Angamos)

Information Kiosk (200-610; Plaza Muñoz Gamero; 8am-7pm Mon-Sat, 9am-7pm Sun) South side of the plaza.

Post Office (Bories 911) Located one block north of the plaza.

Sernatur (241-330; www.sernatur.cl; Navarro 999; 8:15am-8pm Mon-Fri Dec-Feb) This place has friendly, well-informed, multilingual staff and provides lists of accommodations and transportation.

Getting There & Away

The tourist offices distribute a useful brochure that details all forms of transport available.

Air

Aeropuerto Presidente Carlos Ibáñez del Campo is 20km north of town. **LAN** (241-100; www.lan.com; Bories 884) flies several times daily to Santiago (CH$212,000) with a stop in Puerto Montt (CH$125,000). **Sky** (710-645; www.skyairline.cl; Roca 935) flies daily between Santiago and Punta Arenas, with a stop either in Puerto Montt or Concepción. **Aerolineas Argentina** (0810-222-86527; www.aerolineas.com.ar) goes to various cities in Argentina. **Aerovias DAP** (616-100; www.aeroviasdap.cl; O'Higgins 891) flies to Puerto Williams and Porvenir in summer.

Boat

Transbordador Austral Broom (580-089; www.tabsa.cl) operates ferries to Tierra del Fuego. The car/passenger ferry *Crux Australis* to/from Porvenir (CH$5500/34,900 per person/vehicle, 2½ to four hours) usually leaves in the morning but has some afternoon departures; check the online schedule.

Broom sets sail for Isla Navarino's Puerto Williams (reclining seat/berth CH$88,000/122,000 including meals, 34 hours) three or four times per month on Wednesday only, returning Saturday. Confirm schedules online.

Bus

Buses depart from company offices, most within a block or two of Av Colón. Buy tickets several hours (if not days) in advance. The **Central de Pasajeros** (245-811; cnr Magallanes & Av Colón) is the closest thing to a central booking office.

Bus Sur (614-221; www.bus-sur.cl; José Menéndez 552) El Calafate, Puerto Natales, Río Gallegos, Ushuaia and Puerto Montt.

Buses Fernández/Buses Pingüino (221-429; www.busesfernandez.com; Armando Sanhueza 745) Puerto Natales, Torres del Paine and Río Gallegos.

Buses Pacheco (242-174; www.busespacheco.com; Av Colón 900) Puerto Natales, Río Gallegos and Ushuaia.

Cruz del Sur (227-970; www.busescruzdelsur.cl; Armando Sanhueza 745) Puerto Montt, Osorno and Chiloé.

DESTINATION	COST (CH$)	DURATION (HR)
Puerto Montt	45,000	32
Puerto Natales	4000	3
Río Gallegos	10,000	5-8
Río Grande	20,000	7
Ushuaia	30,000	10

Getting Around

Buses depart directly from the airport to Puerto Natales. Punta Arenas has Chilean Patagonia's most economical car rental rates; try **Adel Rent a Car/Localiza** (235-472; www.adelrentacar.cl; Pedro Montt 962). Cars are a good option for exploring Torres del Paine, but renting one in Chile to cross the border into Argentina gets expensive due to international insurance requirements.

Puerto Natales

061 / POP 18,000

A pastel wash of corrugated-tin houses shoulder to shoulder, this once dull fishing port on Seno Última Esperanza has become the hub of Gore Tex–clad travelers headed to the continent's number-one national park. While not a destination in itself, the village is pleasant, the austral lights are divine and visitor services are getting ever more savvy.

Sights & Activities

FREE **Museo Histórico** MUSEUM
(411-263; Bulnes 28; 8:30am-12:30pm & 2:30-6pm Tue-Sun) For a crash course in local history, check out these archaeological artifacts, a Yaghan canoe, Tehuelche bolas and historical photographs of Puerto Natales' development.

Puerto Natales

Puerto Consuelo ESTANCIA
(Eberhard Ranch; ☎412-262; www.fiordoeberhard.com; Km 23 Norte) Surrounded by tranquil fjords and looming mountains, this *estancia* is impossibly scenic and gives a taste of the area. Here you can see *gauchos* (cowboys) at work, including the slaughter of sheep – so it's not for the faint of heart. To arrange a visit contact Estancia Travel.

Mirador Dorotea LOOKOUT
For a little warm-up hike, head to this large rocky outcrop; the hike takes you through a *lenga* forest and up to a splendid view back over Puerto Natales, the glacial valley and the surrounding mountains.

Tours

Antares Patagonia TOUR
(☎414-611; www.antarespatagonia.com; Montt 161) Specializes in trekking in El Calafate, El Chaltén and Torres del Paine.

Baqueano Zamora HORSE RIDING
(☎613-530; www.baqueanozamora.cl; Baquedano 534) Runs horse-riding trips in Torres del Paine.

Erratic Rock OUTDOORS
(☎410-355; www.erraticrock.com; Baquedano 719) Offers a free Torres del Paine introduction talk for trekkers (daily at 3pm) and rents gear; guides specialize in treks to Cabo Froward and Isla Navarino.

Estancia Travel HORSE RIDING
(☎412-221; www.estanciatravel.com; Bories 13-B, Puerto Bories) Facilitates horse-riding trips in and out of Torres del Paine.

Sleeping

Note that hostels often rent equipment and help arrange transportation to Torres del Paine.

Puerto Natales

Kau B&B $$
(415-978; www.kaulodge.com; Pedro Montt 161; d incl breakfast CH$55,000;) Thick woolen throws, picnic-table breakfast seating and well-worn, recycled wood lend casual intimacy to this cozy hotel. Rooms boast fjord views; the **Coffee Maker** espresso bar boasts killer lattes.

Amerindia B&B $$
(411-945; www.hostelamerindia.com; Barros Arana 135; d with/without bathroom CH$40,000/30,000, 6-person apt CH$75,000; closed Jul; @) An earthy retreat with a woodstove, beautiful weavings and raw wood beams. Guests wake up to cake, eggs and oatmeal in a cafe open to the public.

Singing Lamb HOSTEL $
(410-958; www.thesinginglamb.com; Arauco 779; dm incl breakfast CH$10,000) Sparkling clean and green (with compost, recycling, rainwater collection and linen shopping bags), this fresh hostel has dorms that feel a little institutional, but thoughtful touches compensate, like central heating and a tasty breakfast.

Lili Patagonico's Hostal HOSTEL $
(414-063; www.lilipatagonicos.com; Prat 479; dm incl breakfast CH$8000, d with/without bathroom CH$27,000/20,000; @) A sprawling house with a climbing wall, a variety of dorms and colorful doubles with brand-new bathrooms and down comforters.

Hospedaje Nancy GUESTHOUSE $
(410-022; www.nataleslodge.cl; Ramirez 540; d with/without bathroom CH$24,000/16,000; @) This two-story home offers lived-in rooms with kitchen privileges and internet access. Breakfast included.

4Elementos GUESTHOUSE $$
(415-751; www.4elementos.cl; Esmeralda 811; dm incl breakfast CH$8000, s without bathroom CH$12,000, d with/without bathroom CH$40,000/30,000) A pioneer of Patagonian recycling, this guesthouse has Scandinavian breakfasts and offers park bookings.

Erratic Rock II B&B $$
(414-317; www.erraticrock2.com; Benjamin Zamora 732; d incl breakfast CH$38,000, tr without bathroom CH$39,000; @) Billed as a 'hostel alternative for couples,' this cozy home offers spacious doubles with throw pillows and tidy bathrooms.

Yaganhouse HOSTEL $$
(414-137; O'Higgins 584; dm incl breakfast CH$9000, d with/without bathroom CH$32,000/25,000;) Typical local house-turned-hostel, with funky additions; there are homey shared spaces with colorful throws and rugs, laundry service and equipment rental.

Hostel Natales HOSTEL $$
(414-731; www.hostelnatales.cl; Ladrilleros 209; dm/s/d incl breakfast CH$12,000/24,000/32,000; @) Tranquil and toasty, this hostel doesn't have the energy of others, but dorms are good value.

Eating & Drinking

TOP CHOICE **Afrigonia** FUSION $$
(Eberhard 343; mains CH$8000; lunch & dinner) Outstanding and original, this romantic gem was dreamed up by a hardworking

Zambian/Chilean couple. Fragrant rice, fresh *ceviche* and mint roasted lamb are prepared with succulent precision.

La Mesita Grande PIZZERIA $
(Prat 196; pizza CH$5500; ⌚lunch & dinner) Happy diners share a long, worn table for outstanding thin-crust pizza, quality pasta and organic salads.

Cangrejo Rojo CAFE $
(Santiago Bueras 782; mains CH$2000-4000; ⌚9am-1:30pm & 3-10:30pm, closed Mon) Unfathomably friendly and cheap, this cute corrugated-tin cafe serves pies, ice cream, sandwiches and hot clay-pot dishes such as seafood casserole.

El Living CAFE $
(Prat 156; mains CH$2600-4200; ⌚11am-11pm Nov–mid April; ☑) This chill London-style cafe has proper vegetarian fare and a stream of eclectic tunes.

La Aldea MEDITERRANEAN $$
(Barros Arana 132; mains CH$7000; ⌚8pm-midnight) At this eight-table restaurant, the focus is fresh and Mediterranean: grilled clams, lamb tagine and quinoa dishes.

Patagonia Dulce CAFE $
(Barros Arana 233; ⌚9am-8pm) This coffee and chocolate shop serves fresh baked goods, homemade ice creams and velvety hot chocolate.

Baguales BREWERY
(Bories 430; ⌚7pm-2am daily, weekends only in winter; ☎) This microbrewery makes gringo-style burgers and generous veggie tacos. Get here early to grab a booth, supplied with its own metered tap.

Shopping

La Maddera OUTDOOR EQUIPMENT
(☎413-318, 24hr-service 099-418-4100; Prat 297; ⌚8am-11:30pm) You'll find camping gear galore at this friendly shop; also fixes damaged gear and does after-hours business for trekkers with early departures.

Information

Most banks in town are equipped with ATMs. The best bilingual portal for the region is www.torresdelpaine.cl.

Conaf (☎411-438; Baquedano 847) National parks service administrative office.

Municipal Tourist Office (☎614-808; Plaza de Armas; ⌚8:30am-12:30pm & 2:30-6pm Tue-Sun) In the Museo Histórico, with attentive staff and region-wide lodgings listings.

Post Office (Eberhard 429)

Sernatur (☎412-125; infonatales@sernatur.cl; Pedro Montt 19; ⌚9am-7pm Mon-Fri, 9:30am-6pm Sat-Sun) There's a second location with the municipal tourist office on the plaza.

Getting There & Away

Boat

For many travelers, a journey through Chile's spectacular fjords aboard the **Navimag Ferry** (☎56-2-442-3114; www.navimag.com) becomes a highlight of their trip. This four-day voyage has become so popular it should be booked well in advance. You can also try your luck; contact **Turismo Comapa** (☎414-300; www.comapa.com; Bulnes 541; ⌚9am-1pm & 3-7pm Mon-Fri, 10am-2pm Sat) a couple of days before your estimated arrival date.

Bus

Puerto Natales has no central bus terminal. Book ahead in high season. Service is limited off-season.

To Torres del Paine, bus lines including **Buses Gomez** (☎415-700; www.busesgomez.com; Prat 234), **Buses Pacheco** (☎414-800; www.busespacheco.com; Ramírez 224) and **Buses JB** (☎410-242; Prat 258) leave daily at around 7:30am, passing Laguna Amarga at 9:45am, Pudeto at 10:45am and Administración just before noon. To catch the same bus back to Puerto Natales, wait at Administración at 1pm for an arrival back in the city around 5:30pm. Buses run the same route leaving from Puerto Natales at 2:30pm.

Bus Sur (☎614-220; www.bus-sur.cl; Baquedano 668) and Buses Pacheco go to Punta Arenas (CH$4800, three hours); the latter also goes to Ushuaia (CH$30,000, 13 hours). Bus Sur, **Turismo Zaahj** (☎412-260; www.turismozaahj.co.cl; Prat 236/270) and **Cootra** (☎412-785; Baquedano 244) serve El Calafate (CH$12,000, five hours).

Getting Around

Many hostels rent bikes. Car rental is expensive and availability is limited; you'll get better rates in Punta Arenas or Argentina.

Parque Nacional Torres del Paine

Soaring almost vertically more than 2000m above the Patagonian steppe, the granite pillars of Torres del Paine (Towers of Paine) dominate the landscape of what may be South America's finest national park. A

Unesco Biosphere Reserve since 1978, the park has 181,000 hectares. Most come for the park's greatest hit but, once here, realize that other (less crowded) attractions offer equal wow power: azure lakes, trails that meander through emerald forests, roaring rivers you'll cross on rickety bridges and one big, radiant blue glacier.

The park is home to flocks of ostrich-like rhea (known locally as the *ñandú*), Andean condor, flamingo and many other bird species. Its star success in conservation is undoubtedly the *guanaco*, which grazes the open steppes where pumas cannot approach undetected. After more than a decade of effective protection from poachers, these large and growing herds don't even flinch when humans or vehicles approach.

When the weather is clear, panoramas are everywhere. However, unpredictable weather systems can sheath the peaks in clouds for hours or days. Some say you get four seasons in a day here, with sudden rainstorms and knock-down gusts part of the hearty initiation. Bring high-quality foul-weather gear, a synthetic sleeping bag and, if you're camping, a good tent. If you want to sleep in hotels or *refugios* (rustic shelters), you must make reservations in advance. Plan a minimum of three to seven days to enjoy the hiking and other activities.

At the end of 2011, a raging fire burned over 40,000 acres, destroyed old forest, killed animals and burned several park structures. An international visitor was charged with accidentally setting the fire while trying to start an illegal campfire. The affected area, mostly between Pehoé and Refugio Grey, is essentially the western leg of the 'W' trek. Visitors should be prepared for a landscape that is charred and ashen. The panoramic views remain, but it may take centuries for the forest to recover. Be conscientious and tread lightly – you are among hundreds of thousands of yearly guests.

Activities

Hiking

Torres del Paine's 2800m granite peaks inspire a mass pilgrimage of hikers from around the world. Most go for the Paine Circuit or the 'W' to soak in these classic panoramas, leaving other incredible routes deserted. The Paine Circuit (the 'W' plus the backside of the peaks) requires seven to nine days, while the 'W' (named for the rough approximation to the letter that it traces out on the map) takes four to five. Add another day or two for transportation connections.

Tour operators in Puerto Natales offer guided treks, which include all meals and accommodations at *refugios* or hotels. If you're just looking for a day hike, walk from Guardería Pudeto, on the main park highway, to **Salto Grande**, a powerful waterfall between Lago Nordenskjöld and Lago Pehoé. Another easy hour's walk leads to **Mirador Nordenskjöld**, an overlook with superb views of the lake and mountains.

The 'W' — HIKING

Most people trek the 'W' from right to left (east to west), starting at Laguna Amarga – accessible by a twice-daily 2½-hour bus ride from Puerto Natales. But hiking west to east – especially between **Lago Pehoé** and **Valle Francés** – provides superior views of the black sedimentary peaks known as **Los Cuernos**. To start the W from the west, catch the catamaran across Lago Pehoé, then head north along Lago Grey or Campamento Italiano, from which point excellent (and pack-free) day hikes are possible. Trekking alone, especially on the backside of the circuit, is inadvisable.

The moderate hike (four hours one-way) between Refugio Las Torres and **Mirador Las Torres** offers the closest view of the towers. Hikers should keep to the lower trail on the hike from the *refugio* to Los Cuernos (seven hours one-way). Valle Francés is not to be missed – budget time to reach the **lookout** at Campamento Británico. Mountain Lodge Paine Grande to Refugio Lago Grey (four hours one-way from Lago Pehoé) is a relatively easy trail with access to the glacier lookout, camping and *refugios*.

The Circuit — HIKING

For solitude, stellar views and bragging rights over your compadres doing the 'W,' this longer trek is the way to go. This loop takes in the 'W,' plus the backside between Refugio Lago Grey and Refugio Las Torres. There's one *refugio* at Los Perros, the rest is rustic camping.

Kayaking

A great way to get up close to glaciers. **Indomita Big Foot** (☎414-525; www.indomitapatagonia.com; Bories 206, Puerto Natales) leads three-hour tours of the iceberg-strewn Lago Grey in summer.

Parque Nacional Torres del Paine

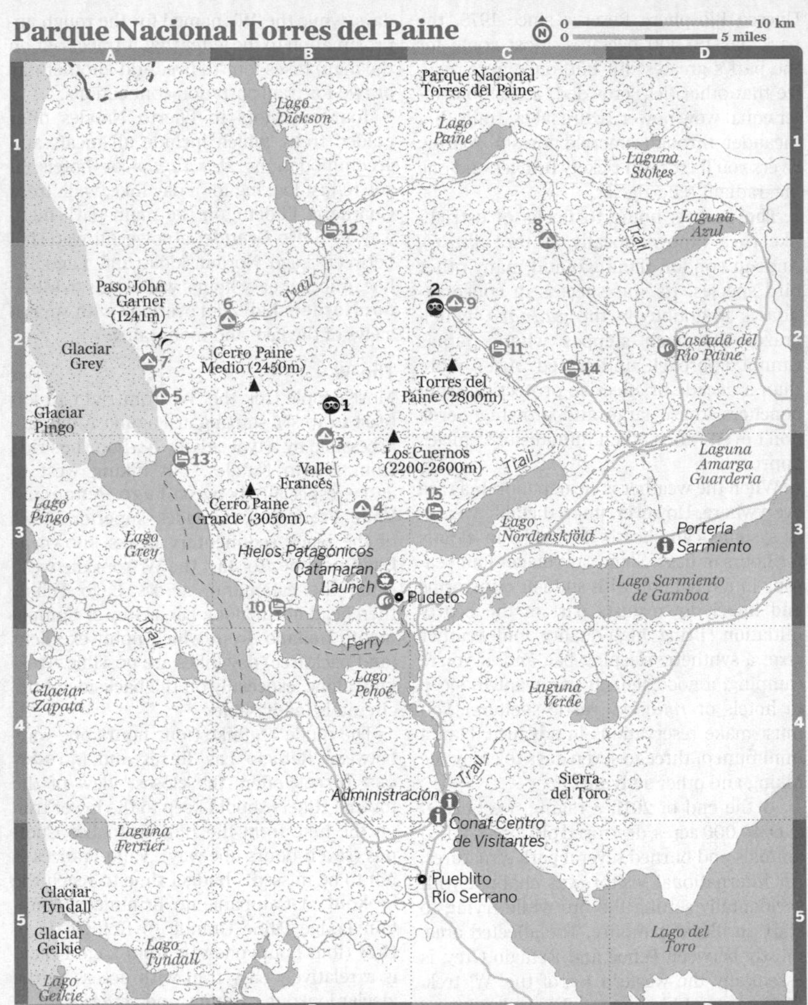

Parque Nacional Torres del Paine

Sights
1 Lookout ... B2
2 Mirador Las Torres ... C2

Sleeping
3 Campamento Británico ... B3
4 Campamento Italiano ... B3
5 Campamento Los Guardas ... A2
6 Campamento Los Perros ... B2
7 Campamento Paso ... A2
8 Campamento Serón ... C1
9 Campamento Torres ... C2
10 Mountain Lodge Paine Grande ... B3
11 Refugio Chileno ... C2
12 Refugio Lago Dickson ... B1
13 Refugio Lago Grey ... A3
14 Refugio Las Torres ... C2
15 Refugio Los Cuernos ... C3

Horse Riding

Due to property divisions, horses cannot cross between the western and privately-owned eastern sectors. Baqueano Zamora (p507) runs excursions to Lagos Pingo, Paine and Azul, and Laguna Amarga (half-day CH$25,000).

Sleeping

The park has both fee camping and free camping. Camping at the *refugios* costs CH$4000 to CH$8000 per person. *Refugios* rent tents (CH$6500 per night) and sleeping bags (CH$4000), but potential shortages in high season make it prudent to pack your own gear. Small kiosks sell expensive pasta, soup packets and butane gas. Campgrounds generally operate from mid-October to mid-March. Many campers have reported wildlife (in rodent form) lurking around campsites, so don't leave food in packs or in tents – hang it from a tree instead.

Refugio rooms have four to eight bunk beds each, kitchen privileges (during specific hours only), hot showers and meals. A bed costs CH$22,500 to CH$35,000, plus sleeping-bag rental and meals (CH$5500 to CH$11,000). Should a *refugio* be overbooked, staff provide all necessary camping equipment. Most *refugios* close by the end of April.

It's important to make reservations. Arriving without them, especially in the high season, enslaves you to bringing your own camping gear. Reserve directly through the concessions: **Vertice Patagonia** (412-742; www.verticepatagonia.com; Ladrilleros 209) manages **Mountain Lodge Paine Grande** (in Puerto Natales 061-412-742; dm CH$24,900, incl full board CH$44,500; year-round; @), *refugios* Lago Grey and **Lago Dickson** (dm CH$15,000, incl full board CH$35,500; Nov-Mar) and Campamento Los Perros. **Fantástico Sur** (061-710-050; www.fantasticosur.com; Esmeralda 661, Puerto Natales; 9am-1pm & 3-6pm Mon-Fri) owns *refugios* **Las Torres** (dm CH$21,500, incl full board CH$44,500; Sep-Apr; @), **Chileno** (dm CH$19,500, incl full board CH$42,500; Oct-Mar) and **Los Cuernos** (dm CH$19,500, incl full board CH$42,500; Sep-Apr), and Serón and their associated campgrounds.

Campsites on the trekking routes administered by Conaf are free but very basic. They do not rent equipment or offer showers. These accommodations include Campamento Británico, Campamento Italiano, Campamento Paso, Campamento Serón, Campamento Torres and Campamento Los Guardas.

Bring your passport or a copy for check-in. Staff can radio ahead to confirm your next reservation. Given the huge volume of trekkers, snags are inevitable, so practice your Zen composure. Rates listed are basic – if you want bed linens (versus your own sleeping bag), it's extra.

Information

The main entrance where fees are collected is **Portería Sarmiento** (www.pntp.cl; admission high/low season CH$18,000/10,000). **Conaf Centro de Visitantes** (9am-8pm in summer), located 37km from Portería Sarmiento, has good information on park ecology and trail status. The website **Torres del Paine** (www.torresdelpaine.com) has useful information; **Erratic Rock** (61-410-355; www.erraticrock.com; Baquedano 719, Puerto Natales) features a good backpacker equipment list.

Getting There & Away

Shuttles (CH$2500) drop off and pick up passengers at Laguna Amarga, at the **Hielos Patagónicos catamaran launch** (411-438) at Pudeto, and at Administración.

The catamaran leaves Pudeto for Mountain Lodge Paine Grande (one way/round-trip per

WORTH A TRIP

PARQUE NACIONAL BERNARDO O'HIGGINS

Virtually inaccessible, O'Higgins remains an elusive cache of glaciers. As it can be entered only by boat, full-day excursions with **Turismo 21 de Mayo** (061-411-978; www.turismo21demayo.cl; Eberhard 560, Puerto Natales) are organized to the base of Glaciar Serrano. Passengers stop for lunch at Estancia Balmaceda and continue up Río Serrano, arriving at the southern border of the park by 5pm. The cost is from about CH$95,000, which includes lunch but not the park entrance fee (CH$1500).

person CH$12,000/22,000) at 9am, 12:30pm and 6pm December to mid-March, at noon and 6pm in late March and November, and at noon only in September, October and April.

There is a bus service from Puerto Natales to the park (CH$15,000 round-trip).

TIERRA DEL FUEGO

Foggy, windy and wet, Chile's slice of Tierra del Fuego includes half of the main island of Isla Grande, the far-flung Isla Navarino, and a group of smaller islands, many of them uninhabited. Only home to 7000 people, this is the least populated region in Chile. Porvenir is considered the main city, though even that status could be considered an overstatement. These parts can't help but exude a rough and rugged charm, and those willing to venture this far can relish its end-of-the-world emptiness.

Isla Navarino

Forget Ushuaia – the end of the world starts where colts roam Main St and yachts rounding Cape Horn take refuge. With more than 150km of trails, Isla Navarino is a rugged backpackers' paradise, with remote slate-colored lakes, mossy *lenga* forests and the ragged spires of the **Dientes de Navarino**. Some 40,000 beavers introduced from Canada in the 1940s now plague the island; they're even on the menu. The only town, **Puerto Williams** (population 2500), is a naval settlement and the official port of entry for vessels en route to Cape Horn and Antarctica.

Sights & Activities

The island has fabulous trekking. Day hike to **Cerro Bandera** for expansive views of the Beagle Channel. The trail starts at the Navarino trailhead, ascending steeply through *lenga* to blustery stone-littered hilltops. Self-supported backpackers continue on for the five-day, 53.5km **Circuito Dientes de Navarino**, with raw and windswept vistas under Navarino's toothy spires. A multilingual trekking guide is available through **Fuegia & Co** (☎621-251; fuegia@usa.net; Ortiz 049), while **Turismo SIM** (☎621-062; www.simltd.com; Margaño 168) offers sailing trips on the Beagle Channel and to Cape Horn.

Museo Martín Gusinde MUSEUM
(cnr Araguay & Gusinde; donation requested; ⏲9am-1pm & 3-6pm Mon-Fri, limited hrs in off-season) An attractive museum honoring the German priest and ethnographer who worked among the Yahgans from 1918 to 1923.

Sleeping & Eating

Lodgings often offer meals and can arrange tours of the island or airport transfers; expensive provisions are available at a few supermarkets in town.

Residencial Pusaki GUESTHOUSE $
(☎621-116; pattypusaki@yahoo.es; Piloto Pardo 242; s/d CH$11,500/26,000) Run by a fun matriarch, this small home is well cared for. Fresh seafood dinners are also available to nonguests (mains CH$6000 to CH$10,000).

Refugio El Padrino HOSTEL $
(☎621-136; Costanera 276; dm incl breakfast CH$10,000) Friendly and conducive to meeting others, this clean, self-service hostel offers small dorm rooms.

La Picada del Castor SANDWICHES $
(Plaza de Ancla; mains CH$3500-5000; ⏲10am-10pm Mon-Sat) The most likely to be open, serving huge sandwiches and platters of fries at low-lit booths.

La Trattoria de Mateo ITALIAN $$
(Plaza de Ancla; mains CH$4500-7000; ⏲noon-3:30pm & 6-10pm Tue-Sat, 12:30-4pm Sun) An Argentine-run cafe featuring homemade pasta with seafood options and pizzas.

Getting There & Away

Puerto Williams is accessible by plane or boat. **Aerovias DAP** (☎621-051; www.aeroviasdap.cl; Plaza de Ancla s/n) flies from Punta Arenas (CH$65,000, 1¼ hours) at 11:30am Monday to Saturday from November to March, with fewer flights in winter.

Transbordador Austral Broom (www.tabsa.cl) sails from the Tres Puentes sector of Punta Arenas to Puerto Williams three or four times a month on Wednesdays, with departures from Puerto Williams back to Punta Arenas on Saturdays (reclining seat/bunk CH$88,000/122,000 including meals, 38 hours).

Porvenir

For a slice of home-baked Fuegian life, this is it. Spending a night in this rusted village of metal-clad Victorians affords you an opportunity to explore the nearby bays and countryside and absorb the laid-back local life. **Far South Expeditions** (www.fsexpeditions.com; 4-passenger tours CH$60,000) offers transportation to the king-penguin colony, naturalist-run tours, and wonderful overnight accommodations in a historic Magellanic home, **Hosteria Yendegaia** (☎581-919; www.hosteriayendegaia.com; Croacia 702; s/d incl breakfast CH$25,000/40,000; 📶). Expect an abundant breakfast, views of the strait and spacious rooms with thick down duvets.

RAPA NUI (EASTER ISLAND)

Far from continents, this isolated world is a treasure trove of archaeology whose mysteries resist easy explanation. The enigmatic *moai* (huge statues) overshadow the island's subtler assets such as crystalline surf, wild horses and grass-sculpted landscapes. Known as Te Pito o Te Henua (the Navel of the World) by its inhabitants, tiny Polynesian Rapa Nui (117 sq km) is a distant but worthwhile leap for travelers in South America.

Dutch admiral Roddeveen landed here on Easter Sunday, 1722, creating the name. The island became Chilean territory in 1888, though it was run as a sheep *estancia*, confining indigenous Rapa Nui to Hanga Roa until 1953. Finally, in the 1960s they regained access. Today's islanders speak Rapa Nui, an eastern Polynesian dialect related to Cook Islands' Maori, and Spanish. Essential expressions include *iorana* (hello), *mauruuru* (thank you), *pehe koe* (how are you?) and *riva riva* (fine, good).

Each February island culture is celebrated through the elaborate and colorful **Tapati Rapa Nui festival**. Peak tourist season coincides with the hottest months from January to March; off-season is comparatively quiet. Allow at least three days to see the major sites. Note that Rapa Nui is two hours behind mainland Chile, six hours behind GMT (five in summer).

ℹ Getting There & Away

LAN (☎210-0920; Av Atamu Tekena s/n; ⏲9am-4:30pm Mon-Fri, to 12:30pm Sat), near Av Pont, is the only airline serving Rapa Nui. There are almost daily flights to and from Santiago (US$600 to US$1000) and twice weekly to and from Papeete (Tahiti).

ℹ Getting Around

Rent a Car Insular (☎210-0480; www.rentainsular.cl; Av Atamu Tekena s/n) rents out scooters and motorcycles (per day from CH$20,000).

Rapa Nui (Easter Island)

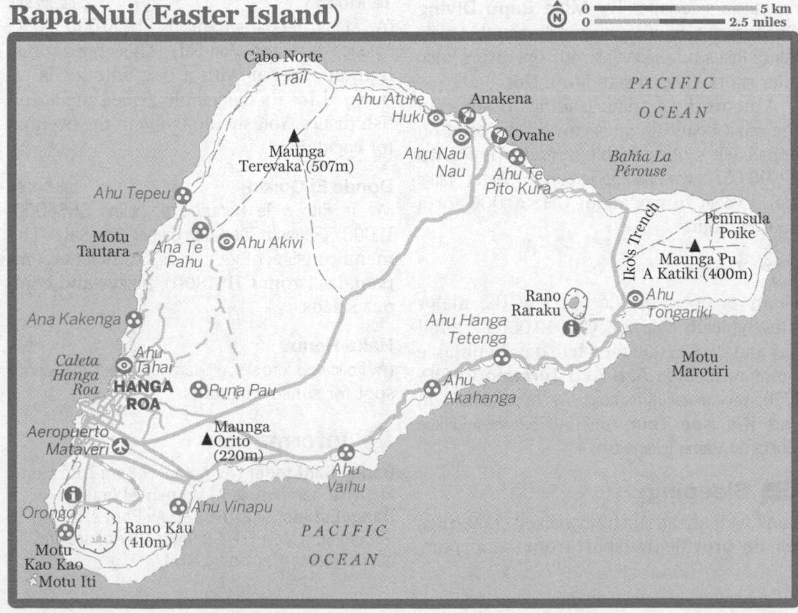

Hanga Roa

☎032 / POP 6700

Hanga Roa is the island's sole town, home to nearly all the island's hotels, restaurants, shops and services.

Sights

TOP CHOICE **Museo Antropológico Sebastián Englert** MUSEUM
(www.museorapanui.cl; admission CH$1000; ⏲9:30am-5:30pm Tue-Fri, to 12.30pm Sat & Sun) Explains the island's history and culture; displays basalt fishhooks, obsidian spearheads and other weapons, and a *moai* head with reconstructed fragments of its eyes, among other items.

Caleta Hanga Roa & Ahu Tautira ARCHAEOLOGICAL SITE
Your first encounter with the *moai* will probably take place at Ahu Tautira, which overlooks Caleta Hanga Roa, the fishing port in Hanga Roa at the foot of Av Te Pito o Te Henua. Here you'll find a platform with two superb *moai*.

Activities

Opportunities abound for hiking, sailing and cycling. There's also excellent diving on Easter Island, with gin-clear visibility and a dramatic seascape. Try **Mike Rapu Diving Center** (☎255-1055; www.mikerapu.cl; Caleta Hanga Roa s/n; ⏲Mon-Sat); all operators also offer snorkeling trips to Motu Nui.

A network of trails leading to some of the most beautiful sites can be explored on horseback – one reliable operator is **Pantu** (☎210-0577; www.pantupikerauri.cl; Sector Tahai s/n). Expect to pay about CH$30,000 for a half-day tour.

Tours

Plenty of operators do tours of the major sites, typically charging CH$42,000 for a full day and CH$25,000 for a half day. Reputable agenices include **Aku Aku Turismo** (☎210-0770; www.akuakuturismo.cl; Av Tu'u Koihu s/n) and **Kia Koe Tour** (☎210-0852; www.kiakoetour.cl; Av Atamu Tekena s/n).

Sleeping

Book well ahead for high season. Lodgings usually provide transport from the airport.

Te Ora CABIN **$$**
(☎255-1038; www.rapanuiteora.com; Av Apina s/n; r CH$40,000-65,000; 📶) Fine value lodgings with kitchen access. If she's around, the Canadian owner will give you the lowdown on all that's worth seeing on the island.

Cabañas Mana Ora BUNGALOW **$$$**
(☎210-0769; www.manaora.cl; Sector Tahai; d CH$80,000) An adorable nest with two attractively decorated cottages perched on a slope overlooking the ocean. They come equipped with a handy kitchenette and a terrace with sea views. You'll want a bike to get here.

Hare Swiss BUNGALOW **$$$**
(☎255-2221; www.hareswiss.com; Sector Tahai; s/d incl breakfast CH$40,000/63,000; 📶) A solid option, with three immaculate bungalows, great sea views and a communal kitchen.

Eating & Drinking

For self-caterers, there are a couple of supermarkets on Av Atamu Tekena.

Mikafé CAFETERIA, SANDWICHES **$**
(Caleta Hanga Roa s/n; ice cream CH$1500-2500, sandwiches & cakes CH$2500-4500; ⏲9am-8pm) Luxuriant homemade ice cream, addictive cakes and delicious sandwiches.

Te Moana CHILEAN **$$$**
(Av Atamu Tekena s/n; mains CH$10,000-17,000; ⏲lunch & dinner Mon-Sat) This buzzy restaurant and bar with a cozy interior is renowned for its delectable grilled meat and fish dishes. You should come in the evening for cocktails.

Donde El Gordo CHILEAN **$$**
(Av Te Pito o Te Henua s/n; mains CH$6000-11,000; ⏲lunch Tue-Sun, dinner Tue-Sat) The menu consists of generous sandwiches, empanadas (from CH$1800), pizzas and copious salads.

Haka Honu BAR
(Av Policarpo Toro s/n; ⏲11am-late Tue-Sun) A cool spot for sunset cocktails.

Information

Banco Santander (Av Apina; ⏲8am-1pm Mon-Fri) Visa-compatible ATM open 24 hours.

BancoEstado (☎210-0221; Av Pont s/n; ⏲8am-1pm Mon-Fri) Changes US dollars and euros. MasterCard-only ATM.

Hospital Hanga Roa (☎210-0215; Av Simon Paoa s/n)

Post Office (Av Te Pito o Te Henua s/n; ⏰9am-1pm & 2.30-6pm Mon-Fri, 9am-12:30pm Sat)

Sernatur (☎210-0255; www.chile.travel/en.html; Tu'u Maheke s/n; ⏰9am-6pm Mon-Fri, 10am-5pm Sat) Distributes maps of the island.

Parque Nacional Rapa Nui

Teeming with caves, *ahu* (stone platforms), fallen *moai* and petroglyphs, this **national park** (www.conaf.cl; admission CH$30,000) encompasses much of Rapa Nui and all the archaeological sites. The admission fee is charged in Orongo and Rano Raraku. Respect the sites: walking on the *ahu* and removing or relocating rocks of archaeological structures are strictly taboo. Handle the land gently and the *moai* will smile upon you.

Near Hanga Roa, **Ahu Tahai** is a short hike north of town, lovely at sunset, with three restored *ahu*. Four kilometers north of Tahai, **Ahu Tepeu** has several fallen *moai* and a village site. On the nearby coast, **Ana Kakenga** has two windows open to the ocean. **Ahu Akivi** is the site of seven *moai*, unique because they face the sea, though like all *moai* they overlook the site of a village. At the equinoxes their gaze meets the setting sun.

With white sands, clear water and leggy palms, Anakena beach is a stunning destination that abuts two major archaeological sites: **Ahu Nau Nau** and **Ahu Ature Huki**, the latter re-erected by Thor Heyerdahl and a dozen islanders.

Dazzling in scale, **Ahu Tongariki** has 15 *moai* along the largest *ahu* built against the crashing surf. A 1960 tsunami demolished several *moai* and scattered topknots, but the Japanese company Tadano re-erected *moai* in the early 1990s.

An ethereal setting of half-carved and buried *moai*, **Rano Raraku** is known as 'the nursery,' where *moai* were quarried from the slopes of this extinct volcano. It's worth a wander through the rocky jigsaw patterns of unfinished *moai*. There are 600, with the largest 21m tall. The crater holds a reedy lake under an amphitheater of handsome heads.

Visitors shouldn't miss **Rano Kau** and its crater lake, a cauldron of *tortora* reeds. Along a sea cliff 400m above, the fragile **Orongo Ceremonial Village** (admission CH$30,000; ⏰9am-5pm) is where bird-cult rituals were performed. A cluster of boulders with petroglyphs depict Tangata Manu (the birdman) and Make Make (their god). Walking (7km) or biking is possible; take water.

UNDERSTAND CHILE

Chile Today

Too bad there is no award for the most dogged country, because Chile would be a serious candidate. After an 8.8-magnitude earthquake hit off the central coast in February 2010, Chile dug in. The earthquake carried the power of 10,000 Hiroshima bombs: with the ensuing tsunami it was responsible for hundreds of deaths and US$30 billion dollars in damage. Yet two months later, students returned to school and the affected roads, ports and airports were up. The recovery depended in large part on citizens who helped each other with no formal emergency response in place. Chile is no stranger to natural disaster (it was witness to the 2011 eruptions of Cordon Caulle, which also buried parts of Argentina under ash) – and the past years have once again proved the nation's staying power.

Mind the Gap

In 2010 Chile became the first South American country to earn membership in the Organization for Economic Co-operation and Development (OECD). Chile is now ranked as the world's 40th most developed country; health care has improved and life expectancy is up. In October 2012, president Sebastián Piñera announced his goal to make Chile a 'first world' nation by the year 2020.

Still, of all OECD members, Chile has the greatest levels of inequality. The number of millionaires in Chile doubled in the early 2000s, but the number of those living in extreme poverty is over 600,000. Although poverty has declined in the past decade by nearly a third, critics argue that the national poverty line is just too low for an accurate picture.

Behind the problem, many say, is education. There is little assistance for middle- or lower-class children to attend college. Tired of this, students in 2011 took to the streets. When the Piñera government turned a deaf ear, protesters broke out into Michael Jackson's *Thriller* and paraded as zombies outside the presidential palace. The 'Chilean Winter' became the largest public protest in decades. They were led by Camila Vallejo, a 23-year-old University of Chile student activist. First cast as upstarts, the students eventually gained access to La Moneda for negotiations. But the fairy tale stops there. Negotiations hit a stalemate, though Chilean public opinion swayed in the students' favor. Internationally, *Time*, *Newsweek* and the *Guardian* all paid homage to Vallejo.

In spite of domestic woes, in the first decade of the millennium Chile rose as an economic star – boosted by record prices for its key export, copper. When the world economic crisis hit, Chile remained in good standing. Chile was the first South American state to go free trade with the US, though China is now the country's number-one trading partner, boosting the price of copper thanks to its rapid industrialization. As hard as Chile tries to diversify, copper still accounts for a whopping 55% of exports.

In recent years, Chile has been widely praised for its efforts to attract foreign entrepreneurs, earning the nickname 'Chilecon Valley.' At the end of 2012, the government announced that the economy had grown 4.7% in the calendar year – faster than forecasted – adding that there was a further drop in unemployment, with the jobless rate dipping to 6.1%, the lowest figure in years. Despite this, the president's approval rating is dismal: Piñera hasn't eradicated extreme poverty, as he promised early in his presidency, and while the middle class is earning more than ever before, it has less economic and social security.

History

Early History

The discovery of a single 12,500-year-old footprint in Monte Verde, near Puerto Montt, marks Chile's earliest tangible roots. In the north, Aymara and Atacameño farmers and herders predated the Inca. Other early peoples include the El Molle and the Tiwanaku, who left their mark with geoglyphs; Chango fisherfolk on the northern coast; and Diaguita who inhabited inland river valleys.

Shifting cultivators from the southern forests, the Mapuche, were the only indigenous group to successfully hold off Inca domination. Meanwhile, the Cunco fished and farmed Chiloé and the mainland. In the south, groups such as Selk'nam and Yaghan long avoided contact with Europeans, who would eventually bring them to the brink of extinction.

Colonial Times

Conquistador Pedro de Valdivia and his men crossed the harsh Atacama Desert to found Santiago in the fertile Mapocho Valley in 1541. They set up the famous *encomiendas:* forced labor systems exploiting the north's relatively large, sedentary population. In the south there was no such assimilation – the Mapuche fought European colonization for over three centuries. When the *encomiendas* lost value, agricultural haciendas or *fundos* (farms), run by South American–born Spanish took their place. These *latifundios* (estates) became the dominant force in Chilean society, with many remaining intact into the 1960s.

Revolutionary Wars & the Early Republic

Spain's trade control over the Viceroy of Peru provoked discontent among the colonies. Independence movements swept South America, with Argentine José de San Martín liberating Santiago in 1818. Under San Martín's tutelage, Chilean Bernardo O'Higgins, the illegitimate son of an Irishman, became 'supreme director' of the Chilean republic.

O'Higgins dominated politics for five years after independence, decreeing political, social, religious and educational reforms, but landowners' objections to these egalitarian measures forced his resignation. Businessman Diego Portales, spokesman for the landowners, became de facto dictator until his execution in 1837. His custom-drawn constitution centralized power in Santiago and established Catholicism as the state religion.

Expansion & Development

Chile's expansion began with its triumph over Peru and Bolivia in the War of the Pacific (1879–83), which added the nitrate-rich Atacama Desert, and treaties with the Mapuche, which added the southern Lakes District. In 1888 Chile annexed remote Rapa Nui (Easter Island).

British, North American and German capital turned the Atacama into a bonanza; nitrate prosperity also funded the government. The nitrate ports of Antofagasta and Iquique boomed until the Panama Canal (1914) reduced traffic around Cape Horn and the development of petroleum-based fertilizers made mineral nitrates obsolete.

Mining also created a new working class and nouveau riche, both of whom challenged the landowners. Elected in 1886, President José Manuel Balmaceda tackled the dilemma of unequally distributed wealth and power, igniting congressional rebellion in 1890 and a civil war that resulted in 10,000 deaths, including his own suicide.

The Struggle to Form & Reform

As late as the 1920s, up to 75% of Chile's rural population still depended on haciendas, which controlled 80% of prime agricultural land. As industry expanded and public works advanced, urban workers' welfare improved, but that of rural workers declined, forcing day laborers to the cities. The period from 1930 to 1970 saw a multifaceted struggle for agrarian reform.

During this period, the copper mines, a future cornerstone of Chile's economy, were North American–run. Elected in 1964, reformist president Eduardo Frei advocated the 'Chileanization' of the industry, giving the government 50% ownership of US-controlled mines.

Too reformist for the right and too conservative for the left, Frei's Christian Democratic administration faced many challenges, including from violent groups such as the MIR (the Leftist Revolutionary Movement), which found support among coal miners and urban laborers. Activism also caught on with peasants who agitated for land reform. As the 1970 election grew near, the Christian Democratic Party, unable to satisfy society's expectations for reform, grew weaker.

Allende Comes to Power

Socialist candidate Salvador Allende's Unidad Popular (Popular Unity or UP) coalition offered a radical program advocating the nationalization of industry and the expropriation of *latifundios*. Elected in 1970 by a small margin, Allende instituted state control of many private enterprises, creating massive income redistribution. Frustrated with slow reforms, peasants seized land and the country became increasingly unstable. Declining harvests, nationalization and the courting of Cuba provoked US hostility and meddling. By 1972 Chile was paralyzed by the strikes supported by the Christian Democrats and the National Party.

After a failed military coup in June 1973, the opposition gathered force and a *golpe de estado* by relative unknown General Augusto Pinochet took place on September 11, 1973. The coup resulted in the death of Allende (an apparent suicide) and thousands of his supporters. Thousands of leftists, suspected leftists and sympathizers were apprehended. In Santiago's National Stadium, many detainees suffered beatings, torture and execution. Hundreds of thousands went into exile.

The Pinochet Dictatorship

From 1973 to 1989, General Pinochet headed a durable junta that dissolved congress, prohibited nearly all political activity and ruled by decree. In 1980, voters supported a new constitution that ratified Pinochet's presidency until 1989. Progress came in the form of a stabilized and prosperous economy. Nonetheless, voters rejected Pinochet's 1988 bid to extend his presidency until 1997. In 1989, 17 parties formed the coalition Concertación para la Democracia (Consensus for Democracy), whose candidate Patricio Aylwin easily won. Aylwin's presidency suffered the constraints of the new constitution, but it did see the publication of the Rettig report, which documented thousands of deaths and disappearances during the Pinochet dictatorship.

In September 1998 General Pinochet was put under house arrest in London following investigation of the deaths and disappearances of Spanish citizens in the 1973 coup aftermath. Despite international uproar, both the Court of Appeals (in 2000) and the Supreme Court (2002) ruled him unfit to stand trial. Pinochet returned to Chile, where he died in 2006. His legacy remains extremely controversial among Chileans.

Resetting the Compass

The 21st-century governments across South America became increasingly left-leaning. In Chile the trend resulted in the 2000 election of moderate leftist Ricardo Lagos, followed by his 2005 successor, Michelle Bachelet. A watershed event, it marked Chile's first woman president, a single mother who had been detained and tortured under the Pinochet regime. Suddenly, conservative Chile looked a lot more progressive.

The Bachelet presidency was plagued by divisions within her coalition (La Concertación Democrática), which made pushing through reforms difficult. Emerging crises such as the chaotic institution of a new transportation system in Santiago, corruption scandals and massive student protests made her tenure a difficult one.

A Seismic Shift

In the early hours of February 27, 2010, one of the largest quakes ever recorded in history hit off the coast of central Chile. The 8.8-magnitude earthquake caused massive destruction, triggering tsunamis on the coast and Archipiélago Juan Fernández and claiming 525 lives. Many homes and highways were destroyed and insurance companies estimated billions of dollars worth of damages. After some initial looting in affected areas, order returned quickly. Chile's Teletón, a yearly charity fundraising event, raised an unprecedented US$39 million for the cause. Overall, the government was praised for its swift action in initial reparations, and the outpouring of solidarity demonstrated by the Chilean people was a boost to national pride.

Bachelet's tenure was nearly over at the time of the earthquake. After 20 years of rule by the liberal Concertacíon, Chile elected conservative billionaire businessman Sebastián Piñera from the center-right Alianza por Chile. While Piñera took his oath of office, a 6.9-magnitude aftershock rocked Santiago. Liberal commentators, including novelist Isabel Allende, seized the metaphor, but around the globe observers were curious what the first right-wing government since Pinochet would herald.

Though Piñera enjoyed early popularity for his successful handling of the operation to remove 33 trapped miners from 700m underground near Copiapó, Chile, his approval rating dipped sharply after the student-led educational protests (the 'Chilean Winter') in 2011. At one point, the rating dropped to 26%, the lowest of any postdictatorship administration.

Culture

Centuries with little exposure to the outside world, accompanied by an especially influential Roman Catholic Church, fostered a high degree of cultural conformity and conservatism in Chile. If anything, this isolation was compounded during the Pinochet years of repression and censorship. Perhaps for this reason, outsiders often comment on how Chileans appear more restrained than other Latin American nationalities: they seem less verbal, more heads-down and hard-working. But the national psyche is now at its most fluid, as Chile undergoes radical social change. Nowhere is this trend more evident than with the urban youth. In the past, Chileans were known for compliance and passive political attitudes, but read today's news and unrest simmers. Internet, malls and Direct TV have contributed to the recalibration of tastes and social norms in even the most rural outposts of this once super-conservative society.

Population

While the vast majority of the population is of Spanish ancestry mixed with indigenous groups, several moderate waves of immigrants have also settled here – particularly British, Irish, French, Italians, Croatians

69 DAYS UNDERGROUND

The world was watching on October 13, 2010, when 33 Chilean miners who had been trapped for 69 days in the San José Mine were hauled up one by one from 700m down in the earth. They emerged stumbling, blind as moles in the desert glare, into the bosoms of waiting wives and lovers (some even attending the same man). The universe sighed in collective relief.

Their survival was only possible because of a borehole that had penetrated their chamber 17 days into their ordeal. After the hole came a tube and what the Chileans called *palomas* – messenger doves. In these capsules, videos and love letters went up, baked pies and medication went down. It was the line that connected the surface to the depths, life to a world devoid of it, and billions of viewers to 33 anxious souls. Above ground, the line was no longer necessary but had instead become symbolic. Chile, no stranger to struggle, had something else. Solidarity.

and Palestinians. Germans also began immigrating in 1848 and left their stamp on the Lakes District. The northern Andes is home to around 69,000 indigenous Aymara and Atacameño peoples. Almost 10 times that amount (around 620,000 people) are Mapuche. About 3800 Rapa Nui, of Polynesian ancestry, live on Easter Island. Over a third of the country's estimated 17 million people reside in the capital and its suburbs.

Lifestyle

Travelers crossing over from Peru or Bolivia may wonder where the stereotypical 'South America' went. Chilean lifestyle superficially resembles its European counterparts. A yawning gulf separates the highest and lowest incomes in Chile, resulting in a dramatic gap of living standards and an exaggerated class consciousness. Lifestyles are lavish for Santiago's *cuicos* (upper class), with swish apartment blocks and house service, while at the other end of the scale people live in precarious homes without running water.

Chileans have a strong work ethic, but are always eager for a good *carrete* (party). Young people usually remain dependent on their parents through university years and live at home through their twenties.

Generally, the famous Latin American *machismo* (masculine pride) is subtle in Chile and there's a great deal of respect for women. For gays and lesbians, Chile is still quite a conservative culture with little public support for alternative lifestyles.

Religion

About 70% of Chileans are Catholic, with Evangelical Protestantism gaining ground with 15% of the population, and 8% is without any religious affiliation.

Arts

Literature

This land of poets earned its repute with Nobel Prize–winners Gabriela Mistral (1889–1957) and Pablo Neruda (1904–73). Vicente Huidobro (1893–1948) is considered one of the founders of modern Spanish-language poetry and Nicanor Parra (1914–) continues the tradition.

Chile's best known export, contemporary writer Isabel Allende (1942–), bases much of her fiction in her native country. Other key literary figures include José Donoso (1924–96), whose novel *Curfew* narrates life under dictatorship through the eyes of a returned exile, and Antonio Skármeta (1940–), who wrote the novel *Burning Patience,* upon which the award-winning Italian film *Il Postino* (The Postman) is based. Luis Sepúlveda (1949–) has made outstanding contributions such as *Patagonia Express* and *The Old Man Who Read Love Stories.*

Marcela Serrano (1951–) is praised as the best of current Latina authors. Pedro Lemebel (1955–) writes of homosexuality, transgender issues and other controversial subjects with top-notch shock value. Worldwide, Roberto Bolaño (1953–2003) is acclaimed as one of Latin America's best. The posthumous publication of his encyclopedic *2666* sealed his cult-hero status.

Cinema

Chilean cinema has proved dynamic and diverse in recent years. Addressing class stratification, Sebastián Silva's *La nana* (The Maid) won two Sundance awards in 2009. Twenty-something director Nicolás López used dark humor and comic-book culture to the delight of youth audiences with *Promedio rojo* (2005). *Mi mejor enemigo* (My Best Enemy, 2004) tells of not-so-distant enemies in a 1978 territorial dispute with Argentina in Tierra del Fuego. Andrés Wood's hit *Machuca* (2004) chronicles coming-of-age during class-conscious and volatile 1973. Acclaimed documentarian Patricio Guzmán explores the social impact of the dictatorship; his credits include the fascinating *Obstinate Memory* (1997).

In 2012, two Chilean films took home notable awards at the Sundance Film Festival: *Violeta se fue a los Cielos*, another Andres Wood film about the life of folk artist Violeta Parra, and *Joven y Alocada*, a provocative coming-of-age story that was the cinematic debut of director Marialy Rivas.

Next up, look for the story of 'Los 33' – the trapped Chilean miners – on the silver screen, courtesy of producer Michael Medavoy of *Black Swan* fame.

Cuisine

Food

Chilean cuisine is built around fantastic raw materials: in the markets you can get anything from goat cheese to avocados, fresh herbs and a fantastic variety of seafood.

Though breakfast is meager – instant coffee or tea, rolls and jam – food and drink options get more appealing as the day progresses. At lunch, fuel up with a hearty *menú del día* (inexpensive set meal) with soup and a main dish of fish or meat with rice or vegetables. Central markets are an ideal place for these cheap and traditional meals; even the most basic eateries offer plenty of fresh lemon wedges and spicy sauces you can use to doctor up your plate.

Favorite sandwiches include the prolific *completo* (hot dog with mayo, avocado and tomato) and *churrasco* (steak sandwich with avocado and tomato). Empanadas are available everywhere, from the classic *pino* (beef) to the gourmet seafood-stuffed varieties found in coastal towns. Indeed, some of Chile's most delicious specialties are found at the beach, from *machas a la parmesana* (razor clams baked in Parmesan cheese and white wine) to aromatic seafood stews such as *paila marina* and *caldillo de congrio* – the latter was famously Pablo Neruda's favorite. *Chupe de mariscos* is shellfish baked in a medley of butter, bread crumbs and cheese.

Everywhere in Chile, you'll find hearty classics like *lomo a lo pobre* (steak topped with fried eggs and french fries), *pastel de choclo* (baked corn casserole) and the heart-stopping *chorrillana* (a mountain-high platter featuring fries topped with onions, fried eggs and beef).

Drinks

Chile and Peru both claim authorship of *pisco*, a potent grape brandy, and the famous *pisco sour* cocktail, in which *pisco* is mixed with fresh lemon juice and sugar. Many Chileans indulge in the citrusy aperitif at the start of a leisurely lunch or dinner. Young Chilenos drink *piscolas* (pisco and Coca-Cola) at parties.

With ample sunshine and moderate temperatures, Chile also boasts the ideal terrain for growing and producing wine. While Cabernet Sauvignon still reigns supreme, many foreigners actually fall in love with another red: Carmenere, originally produced in France and now unique to Chile. You can log onto www.winesofchile.org to learn more about Chilean wine regions and labels.

Kunstmann and Cólonos are Chile's best beers. A draft beer is called *schop*. *Bebidas* (soft drinks) are universally adored. Street vendors sell *mote con huesillo*, a refreshing peach nectar made with barley and peaches – it's a unique liquid snack you should try at least once.

Instant Nescafé is a national plague: while some cafes sell *cafe en grano* ('real' coffee), you shouldn't count on it. Bring your own equipment if you need a caffeine fix every day; you can buy ground coffee in supermarkets.

Sports

Fútbol (soccer) is the most rabidly popular spectator sport – the Chilean national team made a respectable effort at the 2010 World Cup – but tennis has gained ground, thanks to Nicolás Massú and Fernando Gonzáles being awarded Olympic gold medals in 2004, and Massú's silver medal in 2008. Most young Chileans who can afford it go big on individual sports such as surfing, skiing and windsurfing. Chilean rodeos proliferate in the summer, when flamboyantly dressed *huasos* (cowboys) compete in half-moon stadiums.

Environment

The Land

Continental Chile stretches 4300km from Peru to the Strait of Magellan. Less than 200km wide on average, the land rises from sea level to above 6000m in some areas, pocked with volcanoes and with a narrow depression running through the middle.

Mainland Chile, dry-topped and glacial heavy, has distinct temperate and geographic zones, with the length of the Andes running alongside. Norte Grande runs from the Peruvian border to Chañaral, dominated by the Atacama Desert and the *altiplano* (Andean high plain). Norte Chico stretches from Chañaral to Río Aconcagua, with scrubland and denser forest enjoying increased rainfall. Here, mining gives way to agriculture in the major river valleys.

Middle Chile's wide river valleys span from Río Aconcagua to Concepción and the Río Biobío. This is the main agricultural and wine-growing region. The Araucania and Lakes District go south of the Biobío to Palena, featuring extensive native forests and lakes. Chiloé is the country's largest island, with dense forests and a patchwork of pasturelands. Patagonia has indeterminate borders: for some it begins with the Carretera Austral, for others it starts in rugged Aisén, running south to the Campos de Hielo (the continental ice fields) and ending in Magallanes and Tierra del Fuego.

Wildlife

Bounded by ocean, desert and mountain, Chile is home to a unique environment that developed much on its own, creating a number of endemic species.

In the desert north, candelabra cacti grow by absorbing water from the fog *(camanchaca)*. Animals include *guanaco* (a large camelid), *vicuña* (found at high altitudes) and their domestic relatives llama and alpaca. The gangly ostrich-like rhea (called *ñandú* in Spanish) and the plump, scraggly-tailed viscacha (a wild relative of the chinchilla) are other unusual creatures. Birdlife is diverse, from Andean gulls and giant coots to three species of flamingo.

Southern forests are famed for the monkey-puzzle tree *(pehuén)* and *alerce,* the world's second-oldest tree. Abundant plant life in Valdivian temperate rainforest includes the *nalca,* the world's largest herbaceous plant. Puma roam the Andes, along with a dwindling population of *huemul* (Andean deer) in the south. The diminutive *pudú* deer inhabits thick forests, *bandurrias* (buff-necked ibis) frequent southern pastures and *chucao* tweet trailside. A colony of Humboldt and Magellanic penguins seasonally inhabit the northwestern coast of Chiloé.

From the Lakes District to Magallanes, you'll find verdant upland forests of the widespread genus *Nothofagus* (southern beech). Decreased rainfall on the eastern plains of Magallanes and Tierra del Fuego creates extensive grasslands. Protected *guanaco* have made a comeback within Torres del Paine, and Punta Arenas hosts colonies of Magellanic penguins and cormorants. Chile's long coastline features diverse marine mammals, including sea lions, otters, fur seals and whales.

National Parks

Parklands comprise 19% of Chile, a nice number until you realize that some of these 'protected' areas allow logging and dams. Though tenuous and fragile, these wild places are some of the most stunning and diverse landscapes on the continent. In terms of visitors, Chilean parks are considerably underutilized, with the notable exception of Torres del Paine. Parks and reserves are administered by the underfunded Corporación Nacional Forestal, with an emphasis on forestry and land management, not tourism. Visit Conaf (p425) in Santiago for inexpensive maps and brochures.

Chile has around 133 private reserves, covering almost 4000 sq km. Highlights include Parque Pumalín in northern Patagonia and El Cañi (the country's first), near Pucón. Big projects in the works include Parque Tantauco on Chiloé and Valle Chacabuco – the future Patagonia National Park, near Cochrane.

Below are some popular and accessible national parks and reserves:

Alerce Andino Preserves stands of *alerce* trees near Puerto Montt.

Altos del Lircay A reserve with views of the Andean divide and a loop trek to Radal Siete Tazas.

Chiloé Features broad sandy beaches, lagoons and myth-bound forests.

Conguillío Mixed forests of araucaria, cypress and southern beech surrounding the active, snowcapped Volcán Llaima.

Huerquehue Near Pucón, hiking trails through araucaria forests, with outstanding views of Volcán Villarrica.

Lauca East of Arica, with active and dormant volcanoes, clear blue lakes, abundant birdlife, *altiplano* villages and extensive steppes.

Los Flamencos Covering the area in and around San Pedro de Atacama, this reserve protects salt lakes and high-altitude lagoons, flamingos, eerie desert landforms and hot springs.

Nahuelbuta In the high coastal range, preserves the area's largest remaining araucaria forests.

Nevado Tres Cruces East of Copiapó, with a 6330m-high namesake peak and 6893m-high Ojos del Salado.

Puyehue Near Osorno, with fancy hot springs and a family ski resort. Has a popular hike through volcanic desert, up the crater, to thermals and geyser fields.

Queulat Wild evergreen forest, mountains and glaciers stretch across 70km of the Carretera Austral.

Torres del Paine Chile's showpiece near Puerto Natales, with an excellent trail network around the country's most revered vistas.

Vicente Peréz Rosales Chile's second-oldest national park includes spectacular Lago Todos Los Santos and Volcán Osorno.

Villarrica Volcán Villarrica's smoking symmetrical cone attracts trekkers, snowboarders and skiers.

Environmental Issues

With so much recent growth in industry, Chile is facing a spate of environmental issues. Along with Mexico City and São Paulo, Santiago is one of the Americas' most polluted cities. Further afield, Chile's forests continue to lose ground to plantations of fast-growing exotics, such as eucalyptus and Monterey pine. Caught in a tug-of-war between their economic and ecological value, native tree species have also declined precipitously due to logging. In the south of Chile, an area considered ideal for dams due to its many rivers and heavy rains, there's an ongoing battle between construction companies and environmental groups, with the government in the middle. The continued expansion of southern Chile's salmon farms is polluting water, devastating underwater ecology and depleting other fish stocks. In Torres del Paine, the notorious 2011 fire (allegedly ignited accidentally by an illegal camper) brought to public attention the lack of funding for professional firefighting.

SURVIVAL GUIDE

Directory A–Z

Accommodations

In tourist destinations, prices may double during high season (late December to mid-March), and extra-high rates are charged at Christmas, New Year, Easter week and in mid-September around Chile's Independence Day. If there is any question as to whether the 19% IVA (value-added tax) is included in the rates, clarify before paying.

Apart from hotels, Chile has a range of lodging options for the budget-minded traveler. Stylish hostels, most located in urban or touristy areas, offer dorm-style lodgings and usually set aside a few more expensive doubles for couples who want a social atmosphere but greater creature comforts. Look for pamphlets for **Backpackers Chile** (www.backpackerschile.com), which has many European-run listings and a good standard of quality.

Excellent value for small groups or families, *cabañas* (cabins) are common in resort towns and national-park areas. Both *hospedajes* and *residenciales* (budget accommodations) offer homey, simple accommodations, usually with foam-mattress beds, hard pillows, clean sheets and blankets.

Chile's campgrounds are family-oriented with large sites, full bathrooms and laundry, fire pits and a restaurant or snack bar. Santiago's **Sernatur** (www.sernatur.cl) has a free pamphlet listing campsites throughout Chile. Within some national parks, Conaf maintains *refugios* (rustic shelters) for hikers and trekkers.

Activities

Climbers intending to scale border peaks such as the Pallachatas or Ojos del Salado must have permission from Chile's **Dirección de Fronteras y Límites** (Difrol; ☎02-671-4110; www.difrol.cl; Bandera 52, 4th fl, Santiago). It's possible to request permission prior to arriving in Chile on the agency's website.

Business Hours

Shop hours run roughly from 10am to 8pm, often closing for lunch between 1pm to 3:30pm. Government offices and businesses open weekdays from 9am to 6pm. Banks are open 9am to 2pm weekdays. Tourist offices keep long hours daily in summer. Museums are often closed Monday. Restaurant hours vary widely, but most open from noon till 11pm and close on Sundays.

Electricity

Chile operates on 220 volts at 50 cycles. Two and three rounded prongs are used.

Embassies & Consulates

Argentinian Embassy Santiago (☎02-582-2606; www.embargentina.cl; Vicuña Mackenna 41); Antofagasta (☎055-220-440; Blanco Encalada 1933); Puerto Montt (☎065-253-996; Pedro Montt 160, 6th fl; ⊙9am-1pm Mon-Fri); Punta Arenas (☎061-261-912; 21 de Mayo 1878)

Australian Embassy (☎02-500-3500; consular.santiago@dfat.gov.au; Goyenechea 3621, 12th fl, Las Condes, Santiago)

Bolivian Consulate Santiago (☎02-232-8180; cgbolivia@manquehue.net; Av Santa María 2796); Antofagasta (☎055-259-008; Washington 2675); Arica (☎058-231-030; www.rree.gov.bo; Lynch 298); Calama (☎055-341-976; Latorre 1395); Iquique (☎057-421-777; Gorostiaga 215, Dept E)

Brazilian Embassy (☎02-698-2486; www.embajadadebrasil.cl; Ovalle 1665, Santiago)

Canadian Embassy (☎02-362-9660; enqserv@dfait-maeci.gc.ca; Tajamar 481, 12th fl, Santiago)

Dutch Embassy Santiago (☎02-756-9200; www.holanda-paisesbajos.cl; Las Violetas 2368, Providencia); Punta Arenas (☎061-248-100; Sarmiento 780)

French Embassy (☎02-470-8000; www.france.cl; Av Condell 65, Santiago)

German Consulate (☎02-463-2500; www.embajadadealemania.cl; Las Hualtatas 5677, Vitacura, Santiago)

Irish Embassy (☎02-245-6616; Goyenechea 3162, Oficina 801, Las Condes, Santiago)

Israeli Embassy (☎02-750-0500; San Sebastián 2812, 5th fl, Las Condes, Santiago)

New Zealand Embassy (☎02-290-9802; embajada@nzembassy.cl; El Golf 99, Oficina 703, Las Condes, Santiago)

Peruvian Embassy Santiago (☎02-235-4600; conpersantiago@adsl.tie.cl; Padre Mariano 10, Oficina 309, Providencia); Arica (☎058-231-020; 18 de Septiembre 1554); Iquique (☎057-411-466; Zegers 570, 2nd fl)

UK Embassy Santiago (☎02-370-4100; consular.santiago@fco.gov.uk; Av El Bosque Norte 0125, 3rd fl, Las Condes); Punta Arenas (☎061-244-727; Cataratas del Niagara 01325); Valparaíso (☎032-221-3063; Blanco 1199, 5th fl; ⊙10:30am-1pm)

USA Embassy (☎02-232-2600; santiago.usembassy.gov; Av Andrés Bello 2800, Las Condes, Santiago)

Gay & Lesbian Travelers

Chile is still a conservative, Catholic-minded country, yet recent strides in tolerance have been made, particularly in urban areas. Santiago has an active gay scene, with most gay bars and clubs found in Barrio Bellavista.

Chilean males are often more physically demonstrative than their counterparts in Europe or North America, so behaviors such as a vigorous embrace will seem innocuous.

Gay Chile (www.gaychile.com) has the lowdown on all things gay, including current events, Santiago nightlife, lodging recommendations, legal and medical advice and personals.

Health

Public hospitals in Chile are reasonable but private *clínicas* are your best option. Outside of the Atacama Desert, tap water is safe to drink. Altitude sickness and dehydration are the most common concerns in the north, and sunburn in the ozone-depleted south – apply sunscreen and wear sunglasses. Chile does not require vaccinations, but Rapa Nui may have restrictions or documentation requirements; check first.

Insurance

Signing up for a travel-insurance policy is a good idea. For Chile, a basic theft/loss and medical policy is recommended – note that some companies exclude adventure sports from coverage.

Worldwide travel insurance is available at www.lonelyplanet.com/travel_services. You can buy, extend and claim online anytime – even if you're already on the road.

Internet Access

Most regions have excellent internet connections, wi-fi access and reasonable prices. Rates range from CH$400 to CH$2000 per hour.

Legal Matters

Chile's *carabineros* (police) have a reputation for being professional and polite. Don't *ever* make the error of attempting to bribe the police, whose reputation for institutional integrity is high. Penalties for common offenses are similar to those given in much

SLEEPING PRICE RANGES

Reviews are listed in order of preference. In this chapter, the following price indicators apply for a double room in high season. Prices include bathrooms unless otherwise indicated.

$ less than CH$30,000

$$ CH$30,000 to CH$60,000

$$$ more than CH$60,000

of Europe and North America. However, the possession, use or trafficking of drugs – including soft drugs such as cannabis – is treated very seriously and results in severe fines and imprisonment. Police can demand identification at any time, so carry your passport. Throughout the country, the toll-free emergency telephone number for the police is ☎133.

Maps

In Santiago, the **Instituto Geográfico Militar** (☎02-460-6800; www.igm.cl; Dieciocho 369, Centro; ⏰9am-5:30pm Mon-Fri) near Toesca metro station sells 1:50,000 regional topo maps; you can also buy them online. These are the best maps for hikers, though some are outdated. Conaf in Santiago allows photocopying of national-park maps. JLM Mapas publishes regional and trekking maps at scales ranging from 1:50,000 to 1:500,000. While helpful, they don't claim 100% accuracy.

Santiago maps are available at **Map City** (www.mapcity.cl). Some local government websites have interactive maps with search capabilities. If driving, pick up a Copec driving guide with detailed highway maps and excellent plans of Chilean cities, towns and many villages.

Money

The Chilean unit of currency is the peso (CH$). Bank notes come in denominations of 500, 1000, 2000, 5000, 10,000 and 20,000 pesos. It can be difficult to change bills larger than CH$5000 in rural areas. Solicit change with an apologetic face and the words '*¿Tiene suelto?*' (Do you have change?).

Santiago has the best exchange rates and a ready market for European currencies. Chile's currency has been stable in recent years, with the value of the dollar lower during peak tourist season. It's best to pay all transactions in pesos.

ATMS

Chile's many ATM machines, known as *redbanc,* are the easiest and most convenient way to access funds. Your bank will likely charge a small fee for each transaction. Most ATMs have instructions in Spanish and English: choose 'foreign card' *(tarjeta extranjera)* when starting the transaction. You *cannot* rely on ATMs in San Pedro de Atacama, Pisco Elqui, Bahia Inglesa or in small Patagonian towns.

CASH

A few banks will exchange cash (usually US dollars only); *casas de cambio* (exchange houses) in Santiago and more tourist-oriented destinations will also exchange cash.

CREDIT CARDS

Most established businesses welcome credit cards, although it's best not to depend on it. Consumers may be charged the 6% surcharge businesses must pay. Credit cards can also be useful to show 'sufficient funds' before entering another country.

TIPPING

It's customary to tip 10% of the bill in restaurants. Taxi drivers do not require tips, although you may round off the fare for convenience.

Post

Correos de Chile (☎800-267-736; www.correos.cl), Chile's national postal service, has reasonably dependable but sometimes rather slow postal services. Sending parcels is straightforward, although a customs official may have to inspect your package before a postal clerk will accept it. Vendors in or near the post office will wrap parcels upon request. International courier services are readily available in Santiago, less so outside the capital.

Public Holidays

National holidays, when government offices and businesses are closed, are listed below.

Año Nuevo (New Year) January 1

Semana Santa (Easter Week) March or April

Día del Trabajo (Labor Day) May 1

Glorias Navales Commemorating the naval Battle of Iquique; May 21

Corpus Christi May/June; dates vary

FOOD PRICE RANGES

The following price ranges refer to a standard main course.

$ less than CH$6000

$$ CH$6000 to CH$12,000

$$$ more than CH$12,000

Día de San Pedro y San Pablo (St Peter and St Paul's Day) June 29

Asunción de la Virgen (Assumption) August 15

Día de Unidad Nacional (Day of National Unity) First Monday of September

Día de la Independencia Nacional (National Independence Day) September 18

Día del Ejército (Armed Forces Day) September 19

Día de la Raza (Columbus Day) October 12

Todo los Santos (All Saints' Day) November 1

Inmaculada Concepción (Immaculate Conception) December 8

Navidad (Christmas Day) December 25

Safe Travel

Compared with other South American countries, Chile is remarkably safe. Still, watch out for petty thievery in larger cities and bus terminals (*custodias* are generally a secure place to leave bags). Thefts are high in beach resorts and the port area of Valparaíso. Photographing military installations is strictly prohibited. Natural dangers include earthquakes and strong offshore currents. When swimming, look for signs '*apta para bañar*' (swimming OK) and '*no apta para bañar*' (no swimming).

Telephone

Throughout Chile there are call centers with private cabins and reasonable international rates, although these are rapidly being replaced by internet cafes with Skype.

Chile's country code is ☎56; most landline numbers include six or seven digits. Remote tour operators and lodges have satellite phones with a Santiago prefix.

Cell-phone numbers have eight digits, plus the two-digit prefix ☎09. The prefix must be used when calling from a landline or Skype-type calling service. Throughout this book, cell numbers are listed with their prefix. Drop the prefix when calling cell-to-cell. If calling cell-to-landline, add the landline's area code. Cell phones sell for as little as CH$12,000 and can be charged up by prepaid phone cards.

Do your homework if you want to bring your own cell phone: you'll need a SIM unlocked GSM-compatible phone that operates on a frequency of 850MHz or 1900MHz (commonly used in the US). If you have such a phone you can buy a new SIM card from a Chilean operator such as Entel or Movistar, then purchase phone credit in kiosks.

Time

For most of the year, Chile is four hours behind GMT, but from mid-December to late March, because of daylight-saving time, the difference is three hours.

Toilets

Public toilets rarely provide toilet paper, so carry your own wherever you go.

Tourist Information

The national tourist service, **Sernatur** (www.sernatur.cl) has offices in Santiago and most cities. Many towns have municipal tourist offices, usually on the main plaza or at the bus terminal.

Visas

Nationals of the US, Canada, Australia and the EU do not need a visa to visit Chile. Passports are obligatory and are essential for cashing traveler's checks and checking into hotels.

The Chilean government collects a US$160/132/95 'reciprocity fee' from arriving US/Canadian/Australian citizens in response to these governments imposing a similar fee on Chilean citizens applying for visas. The payment applies only to tourists arriving by air in Santiago and is valid for the life of the passport.

On arrival, you'll be handed a 90-day tourist card. Don't lose it! You will be asked for it upon leaving the country.

Volunteering

Experiment Chile (www.experiment.cl) organizes 14-week language-learning and volunteer programs. Language schools can often place students in volunteer work as well. The nonprofit organization **Un Techo Para Chile** (www.untechoparachile.cl) builds homes for low-income families throughout the country. The annual *Directorio de Organizaciones Miembros* published by **Renace** (Red Nacional de Acción Ecológica; www.renace.cl) lists environmental organizations, some of which may accept volunteers.

Women Travelers

Compared to their hot-blooded neighbors, Chilean men are often shy and downright circumspect. In north-central Chile, guys may be quick with *piropos* (come-ons), but these hormonal outbursts evaporate upon utterance – don't dwell on them. The biggest bother is being constantly asked how old you are and if you're married.

Getting There & Away

Entering the Country

Most short-term travelers touch down in Santiago, while those on a South American odyssey come via bus from Peru, bus or boat from Argentina, or 4WD trip from Bolivia. Entry is generally straightforward as long as your passport is valid for at least six months beyond your arrival date.

Chile's northern border touches Peru and Bolivia, while its vast eastern boundary hugs Argentina. Of the many border crossings with Argentina, only a few are served by public transportation. Most international buses depart from Terminal de Buses in Santiago.

Crossing the border into Argentina is the easiest option. Buses with international routes simply cross – no changing, no fees. Border outposts are open daylight hours, although a few long-haul buses cross at night.

Air

Chile has direct connections with North America, the UK, Europe, Australia and New Zealand, in addition to neighboring countries. International flights within South America tend to be fairly expensive, but there are bargain round-trip fares between Santiago and Buenos Aires and Lima.

Santiago's **Aeropuerto Internacional Arturo Merino Benítez** (☎02-690-1752; www.aeropuertosantiago.cl) is the main port of entry. Some regional airports have international service to neighboring countries. Only LAN flies to Rapa Nui (Easter Island). DAP Airlines flies between major destinations in southern Patagonia.

Bus

ARGENTINA

There are 19 crossings between Chile and Argentina. Popular crossings:

- Calama to Jujuy and Salta
- La Serena to San Juan
- Santiago or Valparaíso to Mendoza and Buenos Aires
- Temuco to San Martín de los Andes
- Osorno to Bariloche via Paso Cardenal Samoré
- Puerto Ramírez to Esquel
- Puerto Natales to Río Turbio and El Calafate

Major lines include the following: **Andesmar** (☎02-779-6839; www.andesmar.com) and **Cata** (www.catainternacional.com) go to Mendoza. **Buses Ahumada** (www.busesahumada.cl) goes to Buenos Aires. **Crucero del Norte** (☎02-776-2416; www.crucerodelnorte.com.ar) goes to Brazil and Paraguay. **El Rápido** (www.elrapidoint.com.ar) goes to Uruguay. **Via Bariloche** (www.viabariloche.com.ar) goes to Bariloche from the Chilean Lakes District.

BOLIVIA

Road connections between Bolivia and Chile have improved, with a paved highway running from Arica to La Paz. The route from Iquique to Colchane is also paved – although the road beyond to Oruro is not. There are buses on both routes, but more on the former.

BRAZIL

Lines include **Chilebus International** (☎02-776-5557) and **Pluma** (☎02-779-6054; www.pluma.com.br); the São Paulo–Santiago trip lasts a punishing 55 hours.

PERU

Tacna to Arica is the only overland crossing, with a choice of bus, *colectivo*, taxi or train.

Car & Motorcycle

In order to drive into Argentina, special insurance is required (try any insurance agency; the cost is about CH$15,000 for seven days). There can be additional charges and confusing paperwork if you're taking a rental car out of Chile; ask the rental agency to talk you through it.

Getting Around

Air

Time-saving flights have become more affordable in Chile and are sometimes cheaper than a comfortable long-distance bus. **LAN** (☎600-526-2000; www.lan.com) and **Sky** (☎600-600-2828; www.skyairline.cl) are the two principal domestic carriers; the latter often offers cheaper fares.

Bicycle

To pedal your way through Chile, a *todo terreno* (mountain bike) is essential – find them for rental in more touristy towns and cities. For cyclists, the climate can be a real challenge. Chilean motorists are usually courteous, but on narrow two-lane highways without shoulders passing cars can be a hazard. Most towns outside the Carretera Austral have bike repair shops.

Boat

Passenger/car ferries and catamarans connect Puerto Montt with points along the Carretera Austral, including Caleta Gonzalo (Chaitén) and Coyhaique. Ferries and catamarans also connect Quellón and Castro, Chiloé to Chaitén.

A highlight is the trip from Puerto Montt to Puerto Natales on board Navimag's *Evangelistas*. Book with **Navimag** (☎02-442-3120; www.navimag.com; Av El Bosque Norte 0440, Piso 11, Santiago) far in advance. This is a cargo vessel outfitted for tourism, not a cruise ship. The cheapest beds (recliner chairs) share few bathrooms and are vulnerable to tossing waves.

Known as the Cruce de Lagos, a 12-hour scenic boat/bus combination travels between Petrohué, Chile, and Bariloche, Argentina.

Bus

The Chilean bus system is fabulous. Tons of companies vie for customers with *ofertas* (seasonal promotions), discounts and added luxuries such as movies. Long-distance buses are comfortable, fast and punctual, and have safe luggage holds and toilets.

Chile's biggest bus company is the punctual **Tur Bus** (☎600-660-6600; www.turbus.cl), with an all-embracing network of services around the country. Its primary competitor is **Pullman Bus** (☎600-320-3200; www.pullman.cl), with extensive services around the country.

Specifically aimed at backpackers, **Pachamama by Bus** (☎02-688-8018; www.pachamamabybus.com; Agustinas 2113, Barrio Brasil, Santiago) is a hop-on, hop-off service with two long routes exploring the north and south, respectively. It's not cheap, but it takes you straight to many out-of-the-way national parks and other attractions not accessible by public transport.

Car & Motorcycle

Having wheels gets you to remote national parks and most places off the beaten track. This is especially true in the Atacama Desert, Carretera Austral and Rapa Nui (Easter Island). Security problems are minor, but always lock your vehicle and remove valuables.

DRIVER'S LICENSE

Bring along an International Driving Permit (IDP) as well as the license from your home country. Some rental-car agencies don't require an IDP.

Local Transportation

Towns and cities have taxis, which are metered or have set fees for destinations. *Colectivos* are taxis with fixed routes marked on signs. Rates are about CH$400 per ride. *Micros* are city buses, clearly numbered and marked with their destination. Santiago's quick and easy-to-use metro system connects the most visited neighborhoods.

Tours

Adventure-tour operators have mushroomed throughout Chile; most have offices in Santiago and seasonal offices in the location of their trips. **Chilean Travel Service** (☎02-251-0400; www.ctsturismo.cl; Antonio Bellet 77, Providencia, Santiago) has well-informed multilingual staff and can organize accommodations and tours all over Chile through your local travel agency.

Train

Empresa de Ferrocarriles del Estado (www.efe.cl) runs a southbound passenger service from Santiago to Chillán, with many intermediate stops. Check the website for updates and information.

Colombia

Includes »

Best Adventures

- » Trek to Ciudad Perdida (p562)
- » Journey to Punta Gallinas (p564)
- » Mountain-biking Chicamocha (p552)
- » Hiking in El Cocuy (p548)
- » Rafting Río Suárez (p549)

Best Festivals

- » Carnaval de Barranquilla (p564)
- » Festival de Música del Pacífico Petronio Álvarez (p592)
- » Carnaval de Negros y Blancos (p605)
- » Desfile de Yipao (p588)
- » Feria de las Flores (p579)

Why Go?

Colombia is an exhilarating cocktail of condensed South America with a shot of Caribbean thrown in. The country's striking landscapes and colorful people will leave you impressed with its variety: in one day it's possible to travel from glacier-covered Andean peaks to crystalline Caribbean beaches, or move from immense sand dunes to lush tropical rainforest.

Colombia is also a fascinating mix of the old and new, with impressive pre-Columbian ruins and enchanting colonial towns vying for your attention alongside progressive cities with chic dining and vibrant nightlife. Add a mix of indigenous, Afro-descendant and European cultures and you'll discover that Colombia is so much more than the old clichés of kidnapping, narcotics and plastic surgery.

Check your preconceptions at the door and uncover more than a few surprises in this accessible and utterly thrilling destination.

When to Go

Bogotá

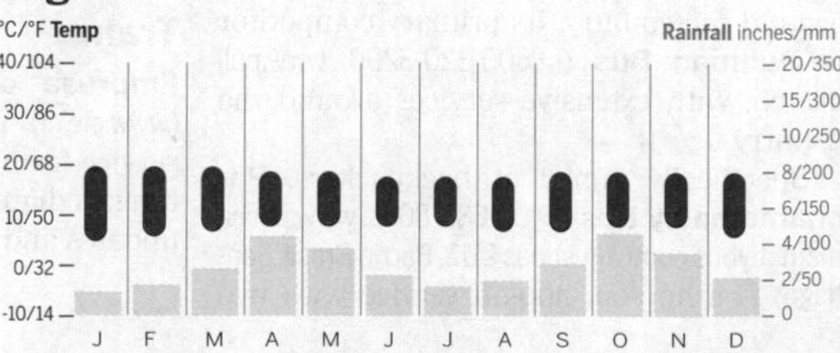

Feb Sunny skies in the Andean and Caribbean regions are perfect for outdoor activities.

Aug & Sep The cultural scene blossoms. Major festivals include Medellín's Feria de las Flores.

Oct & Nov Heavy rains send the crowds packing and prices drop; best trekking in the Amazon.

Connections

Sitting proudly at the top of the continent, Colombia is a strategic gateway between South and Central America. While there is no land crossing with Panama, it is possible to cross via private yacht from Cartagena or by small boat from the idyllic Caribbean town of Capurganá.

Major land crossings include the borders with Venezuela at Maicao, in the arid Guajira, and Cúcuta, on the far side of the soaring peaks of the Cordillera Oriental. The main crossing point to Ecuador is at Ipiales in the southern mountainous region of Nariño.

Heading further south, there are adventurous river crossings into Brazil and Peru from Leticia in the Amazon.

ITINERARIES

One Week

Begin your whirlwind Colombian tour by walking the romantic streets of colonial Cartagena before heading along the Caribbean coast to cool off beneath the majestic Sierra Nevada at the jungle-clad beaches of Parque Nacional Natural Tayrona. Then head south for a day of high-adrenaline outdoor adventure in San Gil. Finish your trip in Bogotá, visiting the capital's fascinating museums and atmospheric nightspots.

Two Weeks

After completing the one-week itinerary, head south to San Agustín for horse riding among the impressive pre-Columbian statues scattered around rolling green hills. Continue to Salento to take a stroll through coffee plantations and learn to prepare the perfect cup. Crane your neck to admire the towering wax palms in nearby Valle de Cocora before continuing onto Medellín to party with the *paisas*, Colombia's most outgoing residents.

Essential Food & Drink

» **Bandeja paisa** Artery-clogging tray of sausage, beans, ground beef, pork rind, avocado, egg, plantains and rice

» **Ajiaco** Andean chicken soup with corn, many kinds of potatoes and a local herb known as *guasca*

» **Aguardiente** Alcoholic spirit flavored with anise that produces wild nights and shocking hangovers

» **Tamale** Chopped pork with rice and vegetables folded in a maize dough, steamed in banana leaves with many different regional varieties

» **Chocolate santafereño** A cup of hot chocolate served with a chunk of cheese and bread

» **Lulada** Refreshing iced drink from Valle de Cauca made from crushed *lulo* fruit and lemons

» **Hormigas culonas** Large fried ants, unique to Santander

AT A GLANCE

» **Currency** Peso (COP$)

» **Language** Spanish

» **Money** ATMs in most towns; credit cards widely accepted

» **Visas** Not required for most Western countries

» **Time** GMT minus five hours

Fast Facts

» **Area** 1.14 million sq km

» **Population** 45 million

» **Capital** Bogotá

» **Emergency** ☎123

» **Country code** ☎57

Exchange Rates

Australia	A$1	COP$1844
Canada	C$1	COP$1837
Euro zone	€1	COP$2325
New Zealand	NZ$1	COP$1469
UK	UK£1	COP$2882
USA	US$1	COP$1797

Set Your Budget

» **Dorm bed** COP$21,000

» **Set lunch** COP$8000

» **Beer in a bar** COP$3000-5000

» **Local bus** COP$1800

Resources

» **ProExport** (www.colombia.travel)

» **El Tiempo** (www.eltiempo.com)

» **Colombia Reports** (www.colombiareports.com)

» **Parques Nacionales** (www.parquesnacionales.gov.co)

Colombia Highlights

1. Wander the enchanting, perfectly preserved streets of colonial **Cartagena** (p565)
2. Visit **Bogotá's** (p532) excellent museums, cozy bars and vibrant discos
3. Soak up the sun on **Parque Nacional Natural Tayrona's** (p560) spectacular jungle-lined beaches
4. Hike through the dense jungle of the Sierra Nevada to the mysterious ruins of **Ciudad Perdida** (p562)
5. Try your hand picking fresh coffee beans on a working farm in the **Zona Cafetera** (p577)
6. Gallop around **San Agustín's** (p601) glorious countryside peppered with

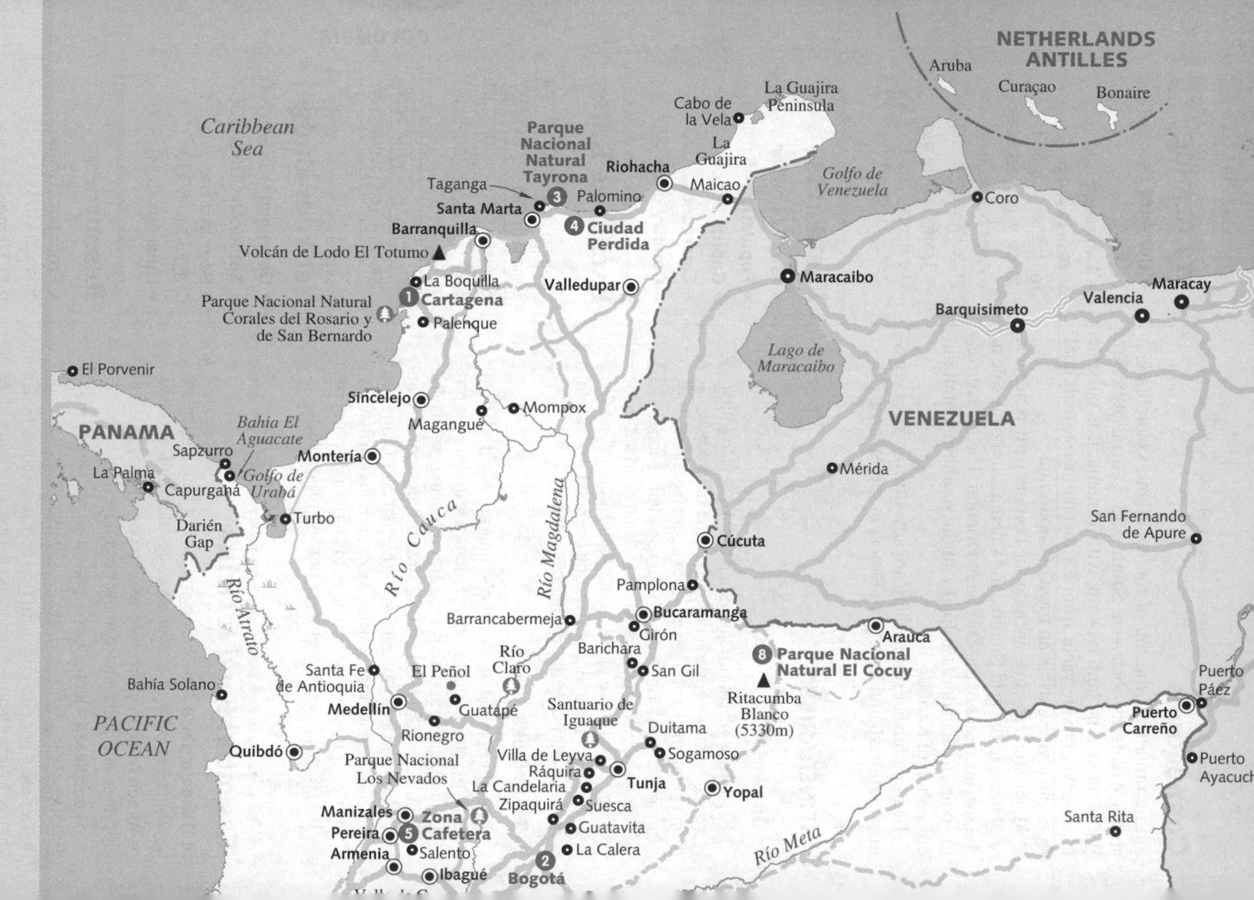

ancient sites and statues

7 Paddle through flooded forests and spot pink dolphins in **the Amazon** (p605)

8 Trek among the glaciers of **Parque Nacional Natural El Cocuy** (p548)

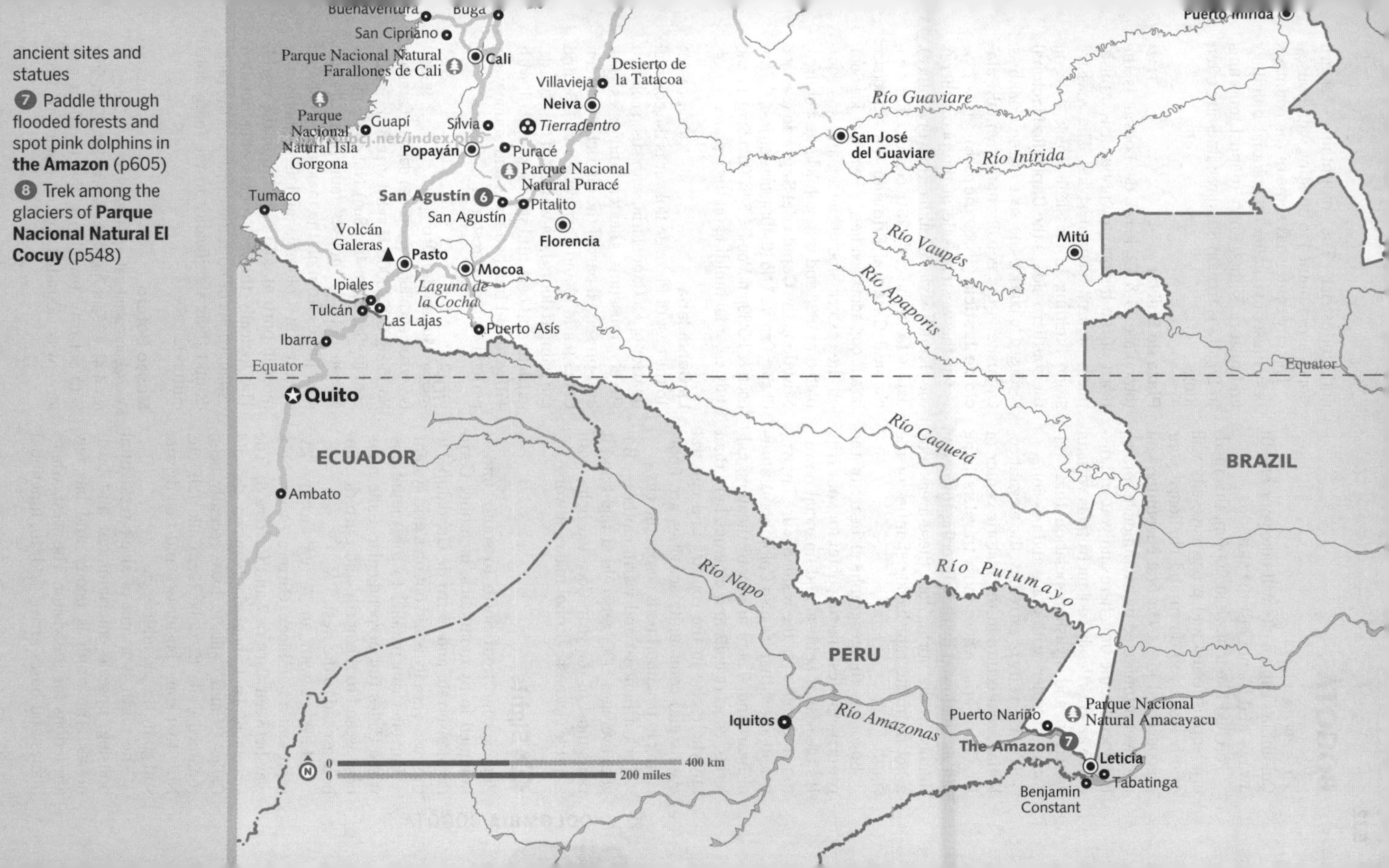

BOGOTÁ

☎1 / POP 7.4 MILLION

Colombia's capital city will take your breath away – and it's not just the altitude.

Perched like a hawk at 2600m, this modern, sophisticated and progressive city will calmly stare you down and challenge your preconceived ideas. On first encounter, you may feel intimidated by its immense sprawl, but spend some time here and you will discover an effortlessly cool metropolis with an educated and stylish population that welcomes outsiders with grace and passion.

It's also a city of extremes: the elegant colonial architecture in the historic center of La Candelaria, where most travelers hang out, is shadowed by the glittering towers of finance in the north. Both these areas look away from the ramshackle shanties of the south.

Bogotá is the geographical heart of the country, an ideal starting point for your trip. It's the seat of political and financial power, too, and *rollos* (as the residents are known) would argue that it's also Colombia's cultural heartland. There are more theaters, galleries, concert halls and cinemas here than anywhere else in the country and cultural events and community activities are flourishing in neighborhoods across the city.

Pack a raincoat and warm clothes – Bogotá averages 14°C, gets cold at night and it rains most of the year. Coca tea helps with altitude sickness; alcohol makes it worse.

Sights

Bogotá runs from north to south, and is hemmed in by mountains, including Cerro de Monserrate and Cerro de Guadalupe, to the east. The city is laid out on a grid system.

Carreras run parallel to the mountains, while Calles run perpendicular. Calle numbers ascend to the north, and Carrera numbers ascend to the west.

Addresses with an 'A' (eg Carrera 7A) represent a half-block (Carrera 7A is a halfway between Carrera 7 and Carrera 8). The streets of La Candelaria between the old Calles 12 and Calle 16 have recently been renamed Calle 12, Calle 12a, Calle 12b, etc. Note that some businesses and taxi drivers still go by the old addresses.

The north is a mix of sleek residential housing, upscale entertainment and businesses. The south is poorer and has few attractions for the visitor. The west, where planes and buses arrive, is drab, functional and industrial. The mountains' eastern slopes are crammed to bursting with houses.

The city center has some of the country's best museums, galleries, colonial buildings and historic sights. Entry to most museums in Bogotá is free on Sundays; lines are often long.

Plaza de Bolívar PLAZA

(btwn Calle 10 & 11) Plaza de Bolívar is the heart of the historic town, but it is a mishmash of architectural styles. The massive stone building in classical Greek style on the southern side is the **Capitolio Nacional** (closed to public), the seat of the Congress. Opposite is the equally monumental **Palacio de Justicia** (closed to public).

On the western side of the plaza there's the French-style Alcaldía (mayor's office), dating from the early 20th century. The neoclassical **Catedral Primada** (www.catedraldebogota.org; admission free; 9am-5pm Tue-Sun), on the eastern side of the square, was completed in 1823 and is Bogotá's largest church. Next door, the **Capilla del Sagrario** (Sagrario Chapel; Carrera 7 No 10-40; admission free; 7am-noon & 1-5:30pm Mon-Fri, 3-5:30pm Sun) is the only colonial building on the square.

La Candelaria NEIGHBORHOOD

To the east of Plaza de Bolívar is the colonial quarter of La Candelaria, with steep cobbled streets, museums, theaters and cafes. The best-preserved part of the district is between Calles 9 and 13 and Carreras 2 and 5. Behind the painted doors lie a warren of courtyards, gardens and beautiful spaces, some still with 470-year-old bamboo roofs and adobe walls perfectly intact or restored.

TOP CHOICE **Museo del Oro** MUSEUM

(www.banrepcultural.org/museo-del-oro; Carrera 6 No 15-88; COP$3000 Mon-Sat, free Sun; 9am-6pm Tue-Sat, 10am-4pm Sun) Not-to-be-missed Museo del Oro houses more than 34,000 gold pieces from all the major pre-Hispanic cultures in Colombia and is arguably the most important gold museum in the world. The logically themed rooms offer detailed explanations of both the artistry of the pieces and their significance to the indigenous cultures.

Museo Botero MUSEUM

(www.banrepcultural.org/museobotero; Calle 11 No 4-41; 9am-7pm Mon & Wed-Sat, 10am-5pm Sun) Set over two floors, this excellent gallery was founded by a donation from

Colombia's most famous artist and evangelist of all things chubby, Fernando Botero. The 208-piece collection contains 123 of Botero's own works, including his paintings, drawings and sculptures, plus 85 works by artists such as Picasso, Chagall, Miró, Dali, Renoir, Matisse and Monet.

FREE **Museo Nacional** MUSEUM
(National Museum; www.museonacional.gov.co; Carrera 7 No 28-66; ⏲10am-6pm Tue-Sat, to 5pm Sun) The Museo Nacional, in an old prison, gives an insight into Colombian history – from the first indigenous inhabitants to modern times – through a wealth of exhibits that include historic objects, photos, maps, artifacts, paintings, documents and weapons.

Iglesia de Santa Clara CHURCH
(www.museoiglesiasantaclara.gov.co; Carrera 8 No 8-91; adult/child COP$3000/500; ⏲9am-5pm Tue-Fri, 10am-4pm Sat & Sun) Iglesia de Santa Clara, now only open as a museum, has one of Colombia's most ornate church interiors, with more than 100 paintings and statues of saints from the 17th and 18th centuries.

Quinta de Bolívar MUSEUM
(www.quintadebolivar.gov.co; Calle 20 No 2-91 Este; adult/child COP$3000/1000; ⏲9am-5pm Tue-Fri, 11am-4pm Sat & Sun) About 250m downhill to the west from Monserrate station, this lovely historic home once belonging to Simón Bolívar is set in a garden at the foot of the Cerro de Monserrate. Its rooms are filled with period pieces, including Bolívar's sword.

FREE **Casa de Moneda** MUSEUM
(Mint; www.banrepcultural.org; Calle 11 No 4-93; ⏲9am-7pm Mon-Sat, 10am-5pm Sun) This interesting museum is dedicated to the history of currency. Exhibits here include a fascinating look into pre-Columbian exchanges of pots and displays of misshapen coins from the early colonial period. Behind the coins are the 10 halls of the **Colección de Arte**, which features works by modern Colombian painters.

Museo de Arte Colonial MUSEUM
(Museum of Colonial Art; ☎341-6017; www.museocolonial.gov.co; Carrera 6 No 9-77; adult/student COP$3000/2000; ⏲9am-5pm Tue-Fri, 10am-4pm Sat & Sun) Museo de Arte Colonial has a fine display of paintings and drawings by Gregorio Vásquez de Arce y Ceballos (1638–1711), the most important painter of the colonial era.

FREE **Museo Histórico Policía** MUSEUM
(Museum of Police History; Calle 9 No 9-27; ⏲8am-5pm Tue-Sun) Straddling the macabre and the unintentionally comic is Museo Histórico Policía. Pablo Escobar's gold-adorned Harley, the jacket he was wearing when police killed him in a rooftop shootout in 1993 in Medellín, and a blood-stained roof tile are the standout pieces. Unconvincing dummies of the drug lord prompt stifled giggles.

Mirador Torre Colpatria VIEWPOINT
(Carrera 7 No 24-89; admission COP$3500; ⏲6-9pm Fri, 11am-5pm Sat, Sun & hols) Mirador Torre Colpatria offers 360-degree views from the 48th story of this 180m skyscraper, Bogotá's highest.

DON'T MISS

CERRO DE MONSERRATE

Towering over the historic center of Bogotá, the 3200m-high Cerro de Monserrate is more than a mountain, it's a symbol of pride for the capital's residents.

The top has gorgeous views of the 1700-sq-km capital sprawl. On a clear day you can even spot the symmetrical cone of Nevado del Tolima, part of Los Nevados volcanic range. The church on the summit, with a statue of the Señor Caído (Fallen Christ), is an important destination for pilgrims.

It's possible to climb the 1500 steps to the top – a tough 60-to-90-minute walk. The best time to go is on the weekend, when hordes of locals make the trip. During the week it's quiet and robberies have been reported. Otherwise take the sketchy-looking funicular, which makes a gravity-defying crawl up the mountainside, or *teleférico* (cable car), which alternate schedules up the mountain from **Monserrate station** (www.cerromonserrate.com; round trip from COP$15,400 Mon-Sat, COP$9000 Sun; ⏲7:45am-midnight Mon-Sat, 6:30am-6:30pm Sun). Generally the funicular goes before noon (3pm on Saturday), and the cable car after.

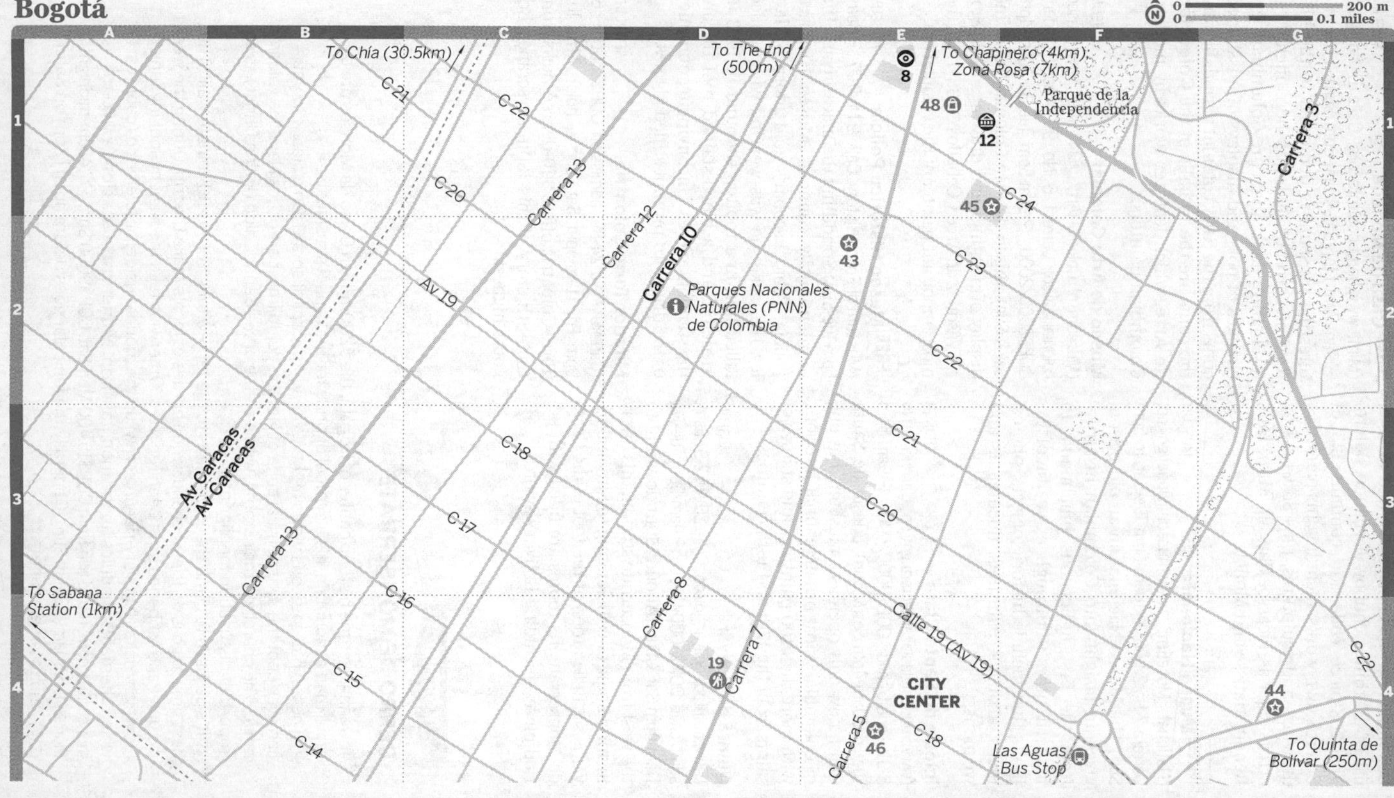
Bogotá
200 m
0.1 miles
To Chía (30.5km)
To The End (500m)
To Chapinero (4km); Zona Rosa (7km)
Parque de la Independencia
Carrera 3
8
48
12
45
43
Parques Nacionales Naturales (PNN) de Colombia
Carrera 13
Carrera 12
Carrera 10
Av 19
C-21
C-22
C-20
C-24
C-23
C-22
C-21
C-20
C-18
C-17
C-16
C-15
C-14
Av Caracas
Av Caracas
Carrera 13
Carrera 8
Carrera 7
19
To Sabana Station (1km)
Calle 19 (Av 19)
CITY CENTER
Carrera 5
46
C-18
Las Aguas Bus Stop
44
C-22
To Quinta de Bolívar (250m)

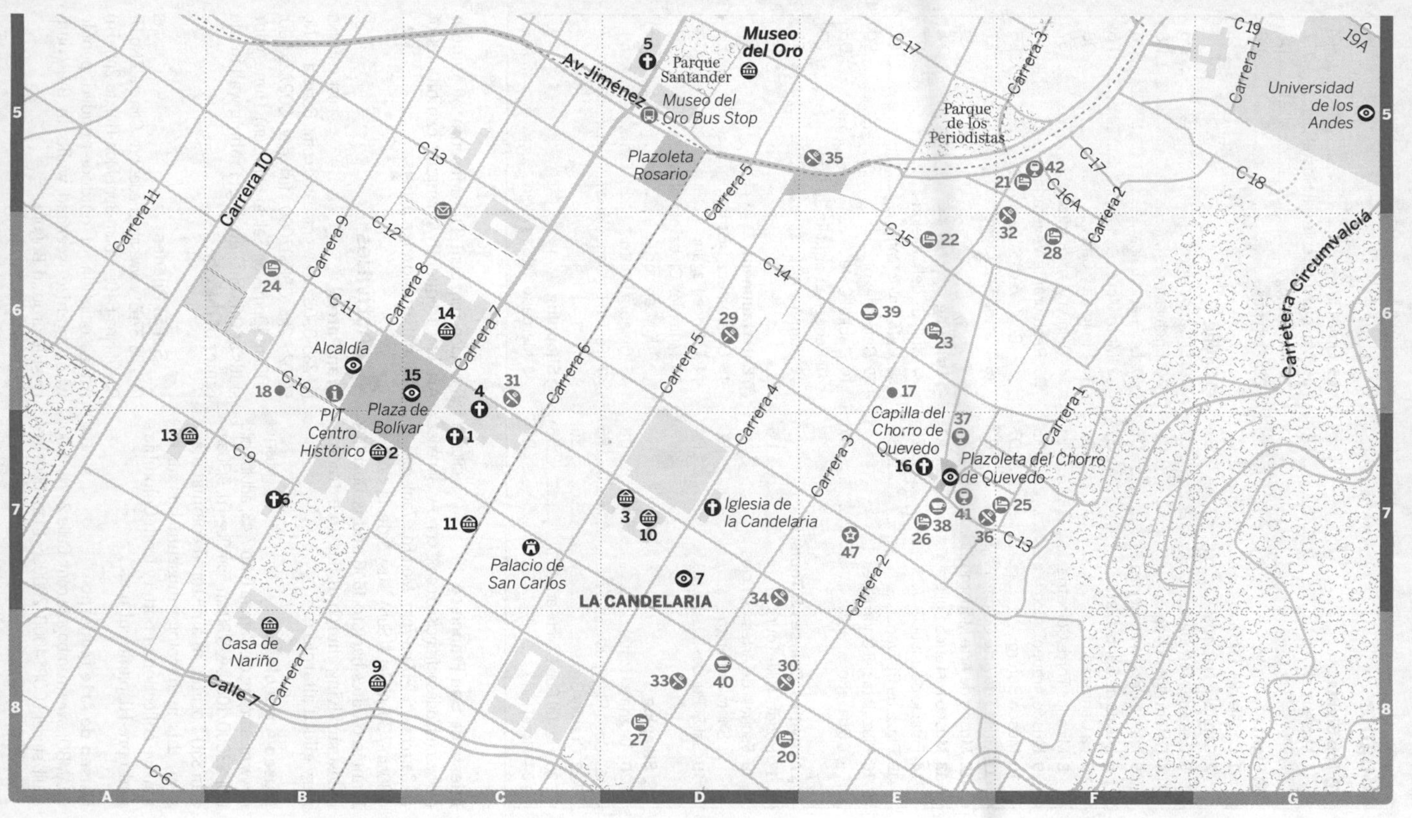
Museo del Oro
Parque Santander
Av Jiménez
Museo del Oro Bus Stop
Plazoleta Rosario
Parque de los Periodistas
Universidad de los Andes
Carretera Circumvalciá
Carrera 11
Carrera 10
Carrera 9
Carrera 8
Carrera 7
Carrera 6
Carrera 5
Carrera 4
Carrera 3
Carrera 2
Carrera 1
C 19
C 19A
C 18
C 17
C 16A
C 15
C 14
C 13
C 12
C 11
C 10
C 9
C 6
Alcaldía
Plaza de Bolívar
PIT Centro Histórico
Capilla del Chorro de Quevedo
Plazoleta del Chorro de Quevedo
Iglesia de la Candelaria
Palacio de San Carlos
LA CANDELARIA
Casa de Nariño
Calle 7

Bogotá

Top Sights
Museo del Oro ... D5

Sights
1 Capilla del Sagrario ... C7
2 Capitolio Nacional ... B7
3 Casa de Moneda ... D7
4 Catedral Primada ... C6
5 Iglesia de San Francisco ... D5
6 Iglesia de Santa Clara ... B7
7 La Candelaria ... D7
8 Mirador Torre Colpatria ... E1
9 Museo Arqueológico ... B8
10 Museo Botero ... D7
11 Museo de Arte Colonial ... C7
12 Museo de Arte Moderno ... E1
13 Museo Histórico Policía ... A7
14 Palacio de Justicia ... C6
15 Plaza de Bolívar ... C6
16 Plazoleta del Chorro de Quevedo ... E7

Activities, Courses & Tours
17 Bogotá Bike Tours ... E6
18 Escuela de Artes y Oficios Santo Domingo ... B6
19 Sal Si Puedes ... D4

Sleeping
20 Alegria's Hostal ... D8
21 Casa Platypus ... F5
22 Cranky Croc ... E6
23 Hostal Sue Candelaria ... E6
24 Hotel Lido ... B6
25 Lima Limon ... F7
26 Masaya Intercultural Hostel ... E7
27 Musicology ... D8
28 Platypus ... F6

Eating
29 El Candelario ... D6
30 Enchiladas ... D8
31 La Puerta Falsa ... C6
32 Mora Mora ... F6
33 Pimienta y Café ... D8
34 Quinua y Amaranto ... D7
35 Restaurante Vegetariano Boulevard Sésamo ... E5
36 Trattoria Nuraghe ... E7

Drinking
37 Bullitas del Callejon ... E7
38 Café Color Café ... E7
39 Café del Sol ... E6
40 Capital Cafe ... D8
41 Pequeña Santa Fe ... E7
42 Yumi Yumi ... F5

Entertainment
43 Cinemateca Distrital ... E2
44 El Goce Pagano ... G4
45 Multiplex Cine Colombia: Embajador ... E1
46 Quiebra Canto ... E4
47 Teatro La Candelaria ... E7

Shopping
48 Mercado de San Alejo ... E1

Iglesia de San Francisco CHURCH
(www.templodesanfrancisco.com; cnr Av Jiménez & Carrera 7; 7am-7pm Mon-Fri, 7am-2pm & 4:30am-7:30pm Sat & Sun) Busy Iglesia de San Francisco dates back to 1556 and is Bogotá's oldest surviving church. It has an extraordinary gilded altarpiece.

Museo Arqueológico MUSEUM
(www.musarq.org.co; Carrera 6 No 7-43; adult/child COP$3000/1000; 8:30am-5pm Tue-Fri, 9:30am-5pm Sat) Located in a restored colonial mansion, this archaeology museum has an extensive collection of pottery from Colombia's main pre-Hispanic cultures.

Museo de Arte Moderno MUSEUM
(MAMBO; www.mambogota.com; Calle 24 No 6-00; adult/student COP$4000/2000; 10am-6pm Tue-Sat, noon-5pm Sun) The Museum of Modern Art has frequently changing exhibitions of national and foreign artists.

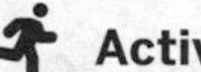

Activities

Gran Pared ROCK CLIMBING
(285-0903; www.granpared.com; Carrera 7 No 50-02; 2hr COP$17,000, full day COP$25,000; 10am-10pm Mon-Sat, to 6pm Sun) Hone your skills at this challenging climbing wall in the center of the city.

Sal Si Puedes HIKING
(283-3765; www.salsipuedes.org; Carrera 7 No 17-01, Oficina 640; 8am-3pm Mon-Thu, to 2pm Fri) An association of outdoor-minded people who organize weekend walks in the countryside around Bogotá.

Courses

Universidad Nacional LANGUAGE
(☎316-5335; www.unal.edu.co; cnr Carrera 30 & Calle 45) Offers best-value Spanish-language courses.

Punta y Taco DANCE
(☎300-218-7199; www.puntaytaco.com; Calle 85 No 19A-25; private classes COP$50,000) Offers classes in salsa and other Latin rhythms. On Friday evenings there are free group classes.

Escuela de Artes y Oficios Santo Domingo CRAFTS
(☎282-0534; www.eaosd.org; Calle 10 No 8-65; courses from COP$150,000) This donation-sustained organization offers one- and two-month (and beyond) courses in woodworking, leather, silver and embroidery in a gorgeous restored building in La Candelaria.

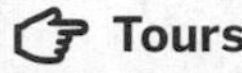

Tours

The central tourism office (p542) runs free daily walking tours around the city center.

TOP CHOICE **Bogotá Bike Tours** CYCLING
(☎281-9924; www.bogotabiketours.com; Carrera 3 No 12-72; tour COP$30,000, rentals half-/full day COP$15,000/30,000) A fascinating way to see Bogotá, especially the neighborhoods that would otherwise be a no-go for anyone other than crazies. Tours leave daily at 10:30am and 1:30pm from the La Candelaria office. Also rents bikes.

Festivals & Events

Festival Iberoamericano de Teatro THEATER
(⊙Mar & Apr) Theater festival featuring groups from Latin America and beyond takes place in March/April of every even-numbered year.

Festival de Cine de Bogotá CINEMA
(⊙Oct) Bogotá's film festival in October usually attracts a strong selection of Latin American films.

Rock al Parque MUSIC
(www.rockalparque.gov.co; ⊙Oct & Nov) Three days of (mostly South American) rock/metal/pop/funk/reggae bands at Parque Simón Bolívar. It's free and swarming with fans.

Expoartesanías ARTS & CRAFTS
(⊙Dec) This crafts fair in December gathers together artisans along with their crafts from all around the country.

Sleeping

Most budget accommodations are in La Candelaria, a short walk from Bogotá's historic sights. A couple of pioneering hostels have opened their doors in Chapinero, a hip part of town with a more local flavor.

Masaya Intercultural Hostel HOSTEL $$
(☎747-1848; www.masaya-experience.com; Carrera 2 No 12-48; dm COP$25,000 r with/without bathroom from COP$100,000/70,000; @☎) Taking flashpacker luxury to a new level, this large new hostel has the best dorms in Bogotá, with individual privacy curtains, bean bags,

BOGOTÁ: A CYCLIST'S PARADISE

One of the best ways to get around Bogotá and avoid its gnarly traffic is on two wheels. Bogotá has around 350km of dedicated cycle lanes, making it one of the most bike-friendly cities in South America.

Not being a city to rest on its infrastructure laurels, there is also the **Ciclovía** (www.idrd.gov.co): from 7am to 2pm every Sunday, 120km of Bogotá's main highways are closed to traffic and cyclists rule the roads. It's another example of how this progressive city puts many of its first-world counterparts to shame.

For slightly more subversive two-wheeled fun, check out the **Ciclopaseo** (Calle 96 No 10-57; ⊙7pm every 2nd Wed), a social-media-fueled nocturnal cruise through the city accompanied by throngs of like-minded strangers. It's all about safety in numbers, there's no need to close roads when there is a sweaty mass of 200 cyclists all pedaling in one direction. The Ciclopaseo takes a new route every week and visits interesting parts of the city that few visitors ever see. It takes place every other Wednesday, with riders meeting in the north of the city.

To join the action, either rent a bike from your hostel or hire a deluxe model from Bogotá Bike Tours.

and fluffy pillows and duvets. You'll also find plush private rooms, great common areas, piping-hot showers and regular cultural activities, including concerts and language exchanges.

Alegria's Hostal HOSTEL $
(☎286-8047; www.alegriashostel.com; Carrera 2 No 9-46; dm COP$18,000-25,000, s/d COP$50,000/60,000; @📶) Relaxed and peaceful spot away from the melee in two elegant colonial houses. Basic dorms are more spacious than at many of the competitors and the affable young owner likes to personally accompany guests to the hippest bars around town. Couples should shoot for the romantic top room in the main house which has a glorious view. Breakfast included.

Cranky Croc HOSTEL $$
(☎342-2438; www.crankycroc.com; Calle 12D No 3-46; dm COP$22,000, s/d/tr COP$56,000/70,000/105,000, without bathroom COP$46,000/60,000/90,000; @📶) This is a neat and tidy hostel with good firm beds, a cool communal vibe and great staff. Dorms have individual lockers and reading lamps, while the small restaurant offers a varied menu of budget meals, including some vegetarian options.

La Pinta HOSTEL $$
(☎211-9526; www.lapinta.com.co; Calle 65 No 5-67; dm COP$24,000-26,000, s/d from COP$66,000/86,000; @📶) In an unmarked residential home in a great Chapinero location just steps from La Septima, this spotless little secret has hardwood-floored rooms that approach boutique-hotel levels. A great choice if you don't dig La Candelaria. Breakfast included.

Lima Limon HOSTEL $
(☎281-1260; www.limalimonhostel.com.co; Carrera 1 No 12B-15; dm COP$20,000-22,000, r COP$50,000; @📶) Set around a colorful internal courtyard, this cozy hostel has tons of character. Its small size and chilled, artistic vibe make it feel more like a house share than a big city hostel. There is an excellent kitchen for preparing communal meals.

Casa Platypus GUESTHOUSE $$$
(☎281-1801; www.casaplatypus.com; Carrera 3 No 12F-28; dmCOP$40,000, s/d/tr COP$130,000/150,000/170,000; @📶) Set in a gracefully restored colonial house, this newer 'boutique' branch to the Platypus hostel has elegant rooms, modern bathrooms, charming communal spaces and a lovely kitchen. Breakfast included.

Hostal Sue Candelaria HOSTEL $
(☎344-2647; www.suecandelaria.com; Carrera 3 No 12C-18; dm COP$22,000-24,000, s/d without bathroom COP$40,000/55,000; @📶) The friendly and bright Sue Candelaria, the newer of the two Sues in La Candelaria, has a fine string of rooms in a smaller, colonial-style layout. The bar at this location gives it a leg up over the original location a couple of blocks away. Breakfast included.

Musicology HOSTEL $
(☎286-9093; www.musicologyhostel.com; Calle 9 No 3-15; dm COP$18,000-26,000; @📶) This all-dorm hostel has a pleasant garden and is a top choice for those on a really tight budget. Prices include both breakfast and dinner, which while not gourmet, are tasty enough and filling.

Hotel Lido HOTEL $$
(☎341-2582; www.hotellidoplaza.com; Calle 11 No 9-45; s/d/tr COP$70,000/94,000/147,000; @📶) On a block of tailors, a block-and-a-half south of the main plaza, this neat 20-room job has compact carpeted rooms, with TV, telephone and private bathrooms. Super friendly.

Platypus HOSTEL $
(☎352-0127; www.platypusbogota.com; Calle 12F No 2-43; dm COP$22,000, s/d COP$55,000/60,000, without bathroom COP$40,000/48,000; @📶) This unpretentious hostel fills a couple of neighboring homes with simple, clean rooms and offers deals for longer term visitors. Breakfast included.

Eating

You can fill yourself to bursting with an *almuerzo corriente* (set lunch) at one of a thousand spots around Bogotá.

El Candelario COLOMBIAN $
(Calle 12B No 4-94; meals COP$9000-10,500) It looks expensive but don't be fooled by the massive chandeliers, exposed brickwork and chic polished concrete floors. This popular restaurant in a converted mansion serves some of the best-value lunches in town. Choose from a variety of hearty Colombian classics that will arm you against the Bogotá chill. At night it morphs into a happening club.

Quinua y Amaranto VEGETARIAN $
(Calle 11 No 2-95; set lunch COP$12,000; ⏲lunch Mon, lunch & dinner Tue-Sat; ☑) This sweet vegetarian spot, run by a team of ladies in an open-front kitchen, prepares tasty set lunches and empanadas, salads and coffee. A small section of baked goods and tempting chunks of artisanal cheese round out the homey offerings.

Davril COLOMBIAN $
(☎249-6304; www.davril.co; Carrera 6 No 58-43; set meals COP$12,000, mains COP$15,000) Like the table you're eating at? Buy it! Everything is for sale, from the glasses to the paintings on the wall, at this atmospheric restaurant-bazaar in Chapinero. The tasty modern Colombian food is great value. Ring the bell if the gate is closed.

Central Cevichería SEAFOOD $$
(www.centralcevicheria.com; Carrera 13 No 85-14; ceviche COP$14,800-16,800) This good-time, high-concept *cevichería* is the real deal: Bogotá's high and mighty ogle over each other as well as the superb *ceviche* (marinated raw seafood), split into spicy and non-spicy categories, of which there are a dozen inventive offerings.

Restaurante Vegetariano Boulevard Sésamo COLOMBIAN $
(Av Jiménez 4-64; set menus COP$7700-10,500; ⏲8am-4pm Mon & Tue, to 8pm Wed-Sat, to 3pm Sun; ☑) Cleanse your palate of fried chicken with a healthy set lunch including soup, fresh fruit juice and a plate of mixed vegetable dishes. Prepares vegan and vegetarian versions of many typical Colombian dishes.

La Puerta Falsa FAST FOOD $
(Calle 11 No 6-50; candies COP$1500, snacks COP$3500-5000) This Bogotá institution, founded in 1816, serves sensational and filling tamales, *chocolate santafereño* (hot chocolate with cheese and bread) and lurid, dentist-worrying confections. Drop your cheese in the chocolate – it's what locals do and it's actually pretty good.

Trattoria Nuraghe ITALIAN $$
(Calle 12B No 1-26; mains COP$9000-16,000) Choose from a variety of home-style Italian dishes at this cozy restaurant run by friendly Sardinians. The bargain lunch special (COP$15,000) includes both a pasta and meat main.

Pimienta y Café COLOMBIAN $$
(Carrera 3 No 9-27; set menus COP$8000-14,000, mains COP$18,000; ⏲noon-4pm Mon-Fri, noon-5pm Sat & Sun) Great-value hearty Colombian food including an excellent *ajiaco* (Bogotá's classic rib-sticking potato soup with corn, chicken, capers, avocado and sour cream).

Mora Mora SANDWICHES $
(Carrera 3A No 15-98; sandwiches from COP$4400, smoothies COP$4200; ⏲9am-6pm Mon-Fri, 9:30am-3pm Sat) Smartly decked out, this place is popular with university students snacking on great Swiss-cheese sandwiches or a Mexican baguette.

Enchiladas MEXICAN $$
(Calle 10 No 2-12; meals COP$14,000-28,000; ⏲noon-5pm Sun-Mon, to 10pm Tue-Sat) Authentic burritos, fajitas and tacos with clean, fresh flavors, excellent decor and a warm fireplace. Great Mexican jukebox.

Drinking

Bogotá's most atmospheric cafes and drinking holes are around La Candelaria, where drinks are served in old colonial houses with fireplaces. Begin your evening with a spot of street drinking among the bohemian crowd in the weed-scented **Plazoleta del Chorro de Quevedo** (cnr Carrera 2 & Calle 12B). It's perfectly safe – there's usually a pair of bemused cops hanging around.

Café Color Café CAFE
(Carrera 2 No 12B-06; ⏲noon-11pm) You can sit on mismatched sofas or cushions on the floor in one of the many small rooms in this cozy cafe. The chilled music facilitates conversation.

Mi Tierra BAR
(Calle 63 No 11-47; ⏲4:30pm-3am) Find a space among the busted typewriters, sombreros, moose heads, musical instruments and televisions at this friendly Chapinero bar that resembles a flea market. It attracts a chilled crowd, so you don't need to be overly concerned about the collection of old machetes.

Bullitas del Callejon BAR
(Carrera 2 No 13A-42) Awesome hole-in-the-wall bar offering a crowd-pleasing mix of hard rock, cheap beer (COP$2000) and *chicha* (corn beer). Wear black.

DON'T MISS

PARTY IN A PIÑATA

Andrés Carne de Res (☎863-7880; www.andrescarnederes.com; Calle 3 No 11A-56, Chía; mains COP$16,202-65,405, cover Fri & Sat COP$15,000; ⏲11am-3am Thu-Sat, to midnight Sun) could make a vegetarian capitulate. It's a sprawling, gloriously theatrical complex that's a cross between a Cirque du Soleil show, the best steakhouse you ever visited and a liquor-drenched Colombian knees-up. More than 250,000 people eat 10 tons of meat a year here, before partying till 5am in a series of interlinked rooms and dance floors bedecked with magic-realist bric-a-brac. By midnight it's a total madhouse, with hundreds of crazed-but-friendly locals dancing on the tables to *vallenato* (Colombian accordion music), disco or cumbia and pouring rum into any passing mouth. It's in Chía – a COP$60,000 cab ride away. Many Bogotá hostels run a party bus here on weekends. It costs around COP$50,000 and includes round-trip transport, entry and booze on the bus.

Taller de Té TEAHOUSE
(www.tallerdete.com; Calle 60A No 3A-38; ⏲closed Sun; 📶) Sip organic tea with a great indie soundtrack in the small garden of this fantastic teahouse in Chapinero. There's a small library of travel books on Colombia and the gregarious owner is extremely knowledgeable about off-the-beaten track destinations.

Pequeña Santa Fe BAR
(Carrera 2 No 12B-14) A cozy, historic two-story home with a fireplace by the bar and soft-lit loft upstairs. A great spot to sample a hot mug of *canelazo* Santa Fe (a yerba-buena tea with aguardiente).

Café del Sol CAFE
(Calle 12C No 3-60; ⏲8am-8:30pm) Good coffee, snacks, sandwiches and breakfast.

Capital Cafe CAFE
(Calle 10 No 2-99) Homey little hangout serving great coffee.

Yumi Yumi COCKTAILS
(Carrera 3 No 12F-40; ⏲closed Sun) Great experimental cocktails made with fresh local fruits.

Kea BAR
(Carrera 14A No 83-37; ⏲8am-3am Tue-Sat) Young, relaxed Asian-themed lounge bar in Zona Rosa with occasional live bands.

☆ Entertainment

The Zona Rosa is Bogotá's main party zone. It's the northern sector of the city, between Carreras 11 and 15, and Calles 81 and 84. Dress up or you'll feel out of place. La Candelaria and Chapinero are cheaper and more low-key.

To find out what's going on around town, check out the listings in local paper *El Tiempo* or visit **Plan B** (www.planb.com.co) and **Vive.In** (www.bogota.vive.in).

Nightclubs

El Goce Pagano CLUB
(www.elgocepagano.co; Carrera 1 No 20-04; ⏲7pm-3am Fri & Sat) In an interesting colonial house that was once a brothel, this salsa/reggae bar near Los Andes University fills up with sweat-soaked bodies from all over Colombia moving to ethnic rhythms.

Titicó BAR
(Calle 64 No 13-35) Inspired by the classic *salsotecas* (salsa clubs) in the south of the country, this hidden salsa bar in Chapinero is like a piece of Cali in the capital, with plush red booths and a big octagonal dance floor. There are often live orchestras keeping the crowd moving.

Invitro CLUB
(Calle 59 No 6-38, 2nd fl) This gritty Chapinero Tuesday-night staple got its start showing independent films (still going at 8pm Tuesday) but morphed into a streetwise urban club. Funk, house, *electrocumbia* and drum 'n' bass rule the decks.

Asilo CLUB
(cnr Av Caracas & Calle 40) Rubbish dancer? Head to this great retro pop/rock club where awkward is cool and indie shoegazers rule the dance floor. Rotating DJs play an eclectic mix of punk, rock and synth-pop classics. All you need is big hair and funky trousers.

Boogaloop CLUB
(Calle 58 No 13-88) This graffiti-covered disco space hosts energetic live performances by talented local musicians.

Armando Records CLUB
(www.armandorecords.org; Calle 85 No 14-46, 4th fl; ⏲to 3am Wed-Sat) This ultra-hip place in the Zona Rosa has an open terrace to beat the smoking ban, minimalist Euro decor and the city's most eclectic, open-minded music policy.

Quiebra Canto CLUB
(www.quiebracanto.com; Carrera 5 No 17-76; ⏲6:30pm-2:30am Thu-Sat) Dependable double-level disco which is popular with both Colombians and foreigners, playing salsa and crossover.

Theatron CLUB
(☎235-6879; www.theatrondepelicula.com; Calle 58 No 10-32; ⏲9pm-late Thu-Sat) This massive gay club in Chapinero packs huge crowds into eight different environments in a converted film house.

The End CLUB
(☎341-7903; Carrera 10 No 27-51, 30th fl; ⏲8pm-late Fri & Sat) After Bogotá shuts down, a kaleidoscopic cross-section of *bogotano* life turns up at this 30th-floor hot spot to party past sunrise.

Cinemas

Bogotá has dozens of mainstream cinemas. Go before 3pm for cheaper tickets. For something more thought-provoking, check the programs of the *cinematecas* (art-house cinemas).

Cinemateca Distrital CINEMA
(www.cinematecadistrital.gov.co; Carrera 7 No 22-79) Art-house cinema that hosts frequent film festivals.

Multiplex Cine Colombia: Embajador CINEMA
(☎404-2463; Calle 24 No 6-01) Multiplex in the city center.

Theater

Teatro La Candelaria THEATER
(www.teatrolacandelaria.org.co; Calle 12 No 2-59; tickets adult/student COP$20,000/10,000) Alternative theater.

Teatro Nacional THEATER
(☎217-4577; www.teatronacional.com.co; Calle 71 No 10-25; tickets from COP$30,000) Traditional theater.

Sports

Big local soccer rivals are **Millonarios** (www.millonarios.com.co) (blue and white) and **Santa Fe** (www.independientesantafe.co) (red and white). For international matches, buy tickets in advance at **Federación Colombiana de Fútbol** (www.fcf.com.co).

Estadio El Campín STADIUM
(☎315-8726; Carrera 30 No 57-60) Matches are on Wednesday nights and Saturday evenings. Tickets can be bought at the stadium before matches (from COP$14,000).

Shopping

Authors BOOKSTORE
(Calle 70 No 5-23) Books in English.

Mercado de San Alejo FLEA MARKET
(Carrera 7 btwn Calles 24 & 26; ⏲9am-5:30pm Sun) This city-center classic fills a parking lot with a host of yesteryear items (posters, books, knickknacks) that are fun to sift through. Consider combining your visit with a trip on the Ciclovía (p537).

Information

Dangers & Annoyances

Like any major urban center, Bogotá requires common sense and moderate vigilance. In the center of town, policing has improved greatly and crime has dropped significantly, but keep your wits about you, especially at night. Taxis are cheap, secure, metered and plentiful – use them if you're nervous.

There have been reports of muggings around Monserrate, both on the mountainside and on the short walk between the entrance and La Candelaria. At the time of research the area was considered safe, but check before you head out.

Emergency

Ambulance, Fire & Police (☎123)

Tourist Police (☎280-9900)

Internet Access

La Candelaria is full of cheap internet cafes charging from COP$1500 to COP$2000 per hour.

Medical Services

Clínica de Marly (www.marly.com.co; Calle 50 No 9-67) A recommended clinic with doctors covering most specialties; sometimes handles vaccinations.

Hospital San Ignacio (☎594-6161; www.husi.org.co; Carrera 7 No 40-62) University hospital in Chapinero with professional service.

Money

BBVA (Av Jiménez No 4-16) Reliable ATM.

Citibank (cnr Carrera 12A & Av 82) ATM.

Edificio Emerald Trade Center (Av Jiménez No 5-43) There are several exchange offices here.

Titán Intercontinental (www.titan.com.co; Carrera 7 No 18-42) A *casa de cambio;* can also receive money from overseas.

Western Union (Calle 28 No 13-22)

Post

4-72 (Carrera 8 No 12A-03)

Tourist Information

The **Instituto Distrital de Turismo** (www.bogotaturismo.gov.co) runs Puntos de Información Turística (PITs) throughout the city, at the bus terminal and at the airport.

Parques Nacionales Naturales (PNN) de Colombia (☎353-2400 ext 138; www.parquesnacionales.gov.co; Carrera 10 No 20-34) Provides information and permits for visits to Colombia's national parks.

PIT Centro Histórico (☎283-7115; cnr Carrera 8 & Calle 10) Facing Plaza de Bolívar, this helpful government tourism office has English-speaking employees and offers free walking tours in English at 2pm Tuesday and Thursday.

Travel Agencies

Aventure Colombia (☎702-7069; www.aventurecolombia.com; Av Jiménez No 4-49, Oficina 204) Specializes in trips to off-the-beaten-path destinations nationwide.

Visa Information

Migración Colombia (☎595-3525; www.migracioncolombia.gov.co; Calle 100 No 11B-27; ⏲7:30am-4:30pm Mon-Fri) For visa extensions.

Getting There & Away

Air

Bogotá's airport, Aeropuerto El Dorado, is 13km northwest of the city center and handles all domestic and international flights. It was undergoing a major facelift at the time of research and the new facility is set to open its doors in 2014. Until then, there are two terminals: the main terminal, **El Dorado** (☎425-1000; Av El Dorado), is 1km west of the **Puente Aéreo** (☎413-9511; Av El Dorado), which is used for some **Avianca** (www.avianca.com) flights.

In El Dorado, you will find several money-exchange services at the arrivals gate, and there are plenty of ATMs on the upper level.

Bus

Bogotá's main bus terminal, **La Terminal** (La Terminal; ☎423-3600; www.terminaldetransporte.gov.co; Diagonal 23 No 69-60, off Av de La Constitución), is around 5km west of the city center in the neighborhood of La Salitre. It's large, functional and extremely well organized. It has a tourist office, restaurants, cafeterias, showers and left-luggage rooms. The website has a full schedule of departures.

Buses travel around the clock to the following destinations:

DESTINATION	COST (COP$)	DURATION (HR)
Bucaramanga	70,000	8
Cali	55,000	9
Cartagena	140,000	20
Cúcuta	95,000	15
Ipiales	85,000	23
Medellín	60,000	9
Popayán	70,000	12
San Agustín	52,000	12
Santa Marta	120,000	16

Getting Around

Bus & Buseta

TransMilenio (www.transmilenio.gov.co) has revolutionized Bogotá's public transportation. Huge buses charge through the main thoroughfares on their own dedicated roads. The service is cheap (COP$1700 peak, COP$1400 off-peak), frequent and fast, and runs from 5am to 11pm. Tickets are bought at the station. Buses get very crowded at rush hour. Watch your pockets.

The main TransMilenio route is Av Caracas, which links the center to both southern and northern suburbs. There are also lines on Carrera 30, Av de Las Américas, Calle 26, Calle 80 and a short spur on Av Jiménez up to Carrera 3. The closest stops to La Candelaria are Las Aguas and Museo del Oro. The northern terminus, Portal del Norte, is an important transport hub.

Some buses visit every stop while others run express through the city. It takes some practice to work out how the system works. Plan your journey online at www.surumbo.com.

Aside from TransMilenio, Bogotá's public transportation is operated by buses and *busetas* (small buses) that travel all over the city at full speed. There are few bus stops – you just wave down the vehicle. The flat fare (around COP$1400, depending on the class of the vehicle) is posted by the door or on the windscreen.

Taxi

Bogotá's efficient, bright-yellow taxis are metered; the meter registers 'units' which are then converted to a price at the end of the trip. When you get in, the meter should read '25'. The minimum fare is 50 units, or COP$3400. There is normally a price chart hanging from the back of the passenger seat.

AROUND BOGOTÁ

Zipaquirá

☎1 / POP 101,000

One of Colombia's most fascinating attractions is the hauntingly beautiful underground **salt cathedral** (www.catedraldesal.gov.co; adult/child COP$20,000/14,000) near the pretty town of Zipaquirá, 50km north of Bogotá.

The cathedral was born from an old salt mine, dug straight into a mountain outside the town. The mines date back to the Muisca period and have been intensively exploited, but they still contain vast reserves that will last another 500 years.

Opened to the public in 1995, the cathedral is 75m long and 18m high and can accommodate 8400 people.

From the northern terminus of TransMilenio (known as Portal del Norte), buses from Bogotá to Zipaquirá (COP$3600, one hour) run every 10 minutes. TransMilenio from Bogotá's center will take you to Portal del Norte in 40 minutes. The mines are about a 15-minute walk uphill from Zipaquirá's center.

The alternative is to take the **Turistren** (www.turistren.com.co), a steam locomotive, which runs from Bogotá to Zipaquirá on weekends and holidays. The train (return COP$42,000) departs **Sabana station** (☎375-0557; Calle 13 No 18-24) at 8:30am, stops briefly at **Usaquen station** (Calle 100 & Carrera 9A) at 9:20am and reaches Zipaquirá at 11:30am. The return leg leaves from Cajica, 15km south, at 3:15pm. While you are on the train, buy a combined ticket for the cathedral and transport to Cajica for the return leg (COP$26,000). From Cajica, you'll reach Sabana at 5:40pm.

Suesca

☎1 / POP 14,000

Suesca is an adventure-sports center near Bogotá, with rock climbing, mountain biking and whitewater rafting. Visit at weekends, when local outfitters are open.

To get to Suesca, take the TransMilenio to its northern terminus at Portal del Norte, and catch a frequent direct bus (COP$4500, one hour) to Suesca.

Hugo Rocha (☎315-826-2051; contacto@dealturas.com), an English-speaking guide and instructor, has 15 years' experience in the area and offers day/overnight rock-climbing trips and lessons, including all equipment. A day climb costs COP$120,000 and a five-day course costs COP$500,000. Hugo organizes accommodation in private rooms for COP$25,000 per night.

On a local farm, **El Vivac Hostal** (☎311-480-5034; www.elvivachostal.com; tent/dm/r COP$20,000/25,000/65,000) is run by a local ecologist and a climbing pioneer. They arrange climbs (from COP$40,000 per person), horse-riding trips and bike rental.

NORTH OF BOGOTÁ

This is Colombia's heartland. The region of deep gorges, fast-flowing rivers and soaring peaks was the first to be settled by the conquistadors, and a number of their colonial towns stand today. It's also the revolutionary heart of the country: it was here that Simón Bolívar took on Spain in the decisive fight for Colombia's independence.

The departments of Boyacá, Santander and Norte de Santander are tourist-friendly: they're within easy reach of Bogotá on a good network of roads with bus services, and there's loads to see and do, including

GETTING INTO TOWN

Both El Dorado Airport and the Puente Aéreo are connected with the TransMilenio system via a shuttle bus to the nearby Portal El Dorado. A planned extension will soon see the TransMilenio running all the way to the airport doors.

Taxis from either facility to the city center cost COP$21,000 including the airport surcharge (COP$3300). There are taxi booths at both terminals where you will be given a slip of paper showing the destination and price which you pass to the first available driver.

If arriving at the bus terminal, *buseta* Ruta C-23 stops outside the tourist information booth and will take you along Carrera 4 through the heart of La Candelaria. The trip may take up to an hour. There is a taxi booth inside *módulo* 5 where you will be given a receipt for travel in an authorized vehicle. A taxi to La Candelaria will cost around COP$11,000.

WORTH A TRIP

GUATAVITA

Also called Guatavita Nueva, this town was built from scratch in the late 1960s when the old colonial Guatavita was flooded by the waters of a reservoir. The town is an interesting architectural blend of old and new, and is a popular weekend destination for people from Bogotá.

About 18km from town is the famous **Laguna de Guatavita** (admission COP$13,200; ⏲9am-4pm Tue-Sun), the sacred lake and ritual center of the Muisca indigenous people, and the birthplace of the El Dorado myth. The emerald-green lake was an important place of worship where gold, emeralds and food were offered by the Muiscas to their gods.

Bogotá's Museo del Oro's (p532) most intricate and startling exhibit, the tiny Muisca Raft, portrays the scenes once played out here, although the piece was not found anywhere nearby. It's an intriguing experience to gaze at the waters and imagine shamans in jaguar masks accompanying a naked chieftain daubed in gold dust as he floated out to perform a ritual that we cannot hope to comprehend.

Dozens of greedy dreamers have tried a variety of schemes to steal riches supposedly submerged in the lake's calm depths. Few have ever managed it.

From Bogotá, take a bus to the town of Guatavita (COP$7000) from Portal del Norte and get off 11km before reaching the town (6km past Sesquilé), where there is a sign directing you to the lake, then walk 7km uphill along a dirt road. On Sundays there are usually *colectivos* (shared taxis) from Guatavita to the lake.

450-year-old colonial towns, craft markets, heart-pumping adventure sports and spectacular national parks.

Tunja

☎8 / POP 171,000

Tunja, the chilly capital of Boyacá, sits at 2820m and has fine colonial architecture and elegant mansions adorned with some of South America's most unique artwork. Many travelers rush through on their way to Villa de Leyva, but fans of colonial history and ornate churches will enjoy a day or two here.

The city was founded by Gonzalo Suárez Rendón in 1539 on the site of Hunza, the pre-Hispanic Muisca settlement. Almost nothing is left of the indigenous legacy, but much colonial architecture remains.

Sights

Tunja's churches are noted for their *mudéjar* art, an Islamic-influenced style that developed in Christian Spain between the 12th and 16th centuries. It is particularly visible in the ornamented, coffered vaults.

Founded in 1571, the **Iglesia y Convento de Santa Clara La Real** (Carrera 7 No 19-58; admission COP$3000; ⏲8am-noon & 2-6pm) is thought to be the first convent in Nueva Granada. It has been converted into a museum. The single-naved church interior shelters a wealth of colonial artwork on its walls.

Other churches worth a visit include **Iglesia de Santo Domingo** (Carrera 11 No 19-55) – look out for the exuberant Capilla del Rosario, to the left as you enter the church – and **Iglesia de San Francisco** (Carrera 10 No 22-23).

The old colonial mansions **Casa del Fundador Suárez Rendón** (Carrera 9 No 19-68; admission COP$2000; ⏲8am-noon & 2-6pm) and **Casa de Don Juan de Vargas** (Calle 20 No 8-52; admission COP$2000; ⏲9am-noon & 2-5pm Tue-Fri, 10am-4pm Sat & Sun) are worth a look for their ceilings, which are covered with paintings featuring human figures, animals and mythological scenes.

Sleeping

Hotel Casa Real HOTEL **$$**
(☎743-1764; www.hotelcasarealtunja.com; Calle 19 No 7-65; s/d COP$55,000/67,000; @📶) Uncluttered, elegant rooms with wooden floors and stylish bathrooms set around a flower-filled courtyard. Excellent value.

Hotel Conquistador de América HOTEL **$**
(☎742-3534; Calle 20 No 8-92; s/d/tr COP$25,000/40,000/60,000; 📶) At the corner of Plaza de Bolívar, this colonial building has 20 clean rooms with tiny hot-water bathrooms and small TVs.

Hostería San Carlos GUESTHOUSE **$**
(☎742-3716; Carrera 11 No 20-12; s/d/tr COP$35,000/60,000/75,000; 📶) A downtown budget option located in a rambling colonial home.

Eating & Drinking

Plenty of restaurants in Tunja serve cheap set lunches for around COP$6000.

El Salon de Onces El Hojaldre CAFE, DESSERTS **$**
(Carrera 11 No 19-96; items COP$900-3700; ⏲closed Sun) Break sweet bread among nuns, desperate housewives, movers and shakers and politicians at this classic coffee- and snack-stop. The pastries are absolutely delicious: try the chicken and mushroom curry version, and the cookies aren't too shabby either.

Santo Domingo de Guzmán COLOMBIAN **$$**
(Carrera 11 No 19-66; set meals COP$7200, mains COP$15,000-20,000) One of downtown Tunja's most popular eateries, this family-run restaurant serves traditional dishes in a homey atmosphere.

Pussini CAFE, BAR
(Carrera 10 No 19-53) Friendly little drinking hole right on the plaza.

Information

Banco BBVA (Carrera 11 No 18-41) ATM.

Bancolombia (Carrera 10 No 22-43) Changes traveler's checks and US dollars.

Secretaría de Educación, Cultura y Turismo (☎742-3272; Carrera 9 No 19-68; ⏲8am-noon & 2-6pm) Ground floor of the Casa del Fundador Suárez Rendón; helpful staff.

Getting There & Away

The bus terminal is on Av Oriental, a short walk southeast of Plaza de Bolívar. Buses to Bogotá (COP$18,000, three hours) depart every 10 to 15 minutes. Buses to Bucaramanga (COP$35,000, seven hours) run hourly and pass through San Gil (COP$25,000, 4½ hours). Minibuses to Villa de Leyva (COP$6000, 45 minutes) depart regularly until around 6:30pm.

Villa de Leyva

☎8 / POP 9600

Enchanting Villa de Leyva, declared a national monument in 1954, is a beautiful colonial settlement that has been preserved in its entirety; virtually no modern architecture exists here. If you are only going to visit one colonial town on your trip, this is your place.

The town, founded in 1572, is much more than just a walk-through museum. It enjoys a healthy, dry and mild climate, far warmer than Tunja (a mere 39km away) and is close to some wonderful landscapes. There are great bird-watching opportunities, ancient stone circles, impressive waterfalls, good food and excellent hiking; nature-lovers could easily spend a week here.

Villa de Leyva is a place to relax and escape the chilly heights of Bogotá, and as such, it's a popular getaway for *bogotanos*, who fill the town's many hotels, craft shops and tourist-oriented restaurants at weekends. Come early in the week for better-value hotel deals.

Sights

The splendid, **Plaza Mayor**, is one of the largest town squares in the Americas. It is paved with large cobblestones and surrounded by magnificent whitewashed colonial houses and a charming **parish church**.

Check out **Casa de Juan de Castellanos** (Carrera 9 No 13-15), **Casa Quintero** (cnr Carrera 9 & Calle 12) and **Casona La Guaca** (Carrera 9 No 13-57), three meticulously restored colonial mansions on Carrera 9 (just off the plaza) that now house cafes, craft shops and restaurants.

There's a colorful **market** held on Saturday on the square three blocks southeast of Plaza Mayor – it's best and busiest early in the morning.

TOP CHOICE **Casa Museo de Luis Alberto Acuña** MUSEUM
(Plaza Mayor; admission COP$4000; ⏲9am-6pm) Casa Museo de Luis Alberto Acuña features works by this painter, sculptor, writer and historian who was inspired by influences ranging from Muisca mythology to contemporary art.

Museo Paleontológico MUSEUM
(Vía Arcabuco; admission COP$3000; ⏲9am-noon & 2-5pm Tue-Sun) The Paleontological Museum, about 1km northeast of town, has local fossils from the period when the area was a seabed (100 to 150 million years ago).

Museo del Carmen MUSEUM
(Plazuela del Carmen; admission COP$2500; ⏲10am-1pm & 2-5pm Sat & Sun) Next to Iglesia del Carmen is Museo del Carmen, a museum of religious art with valuable paintings,

Villa de Leyva

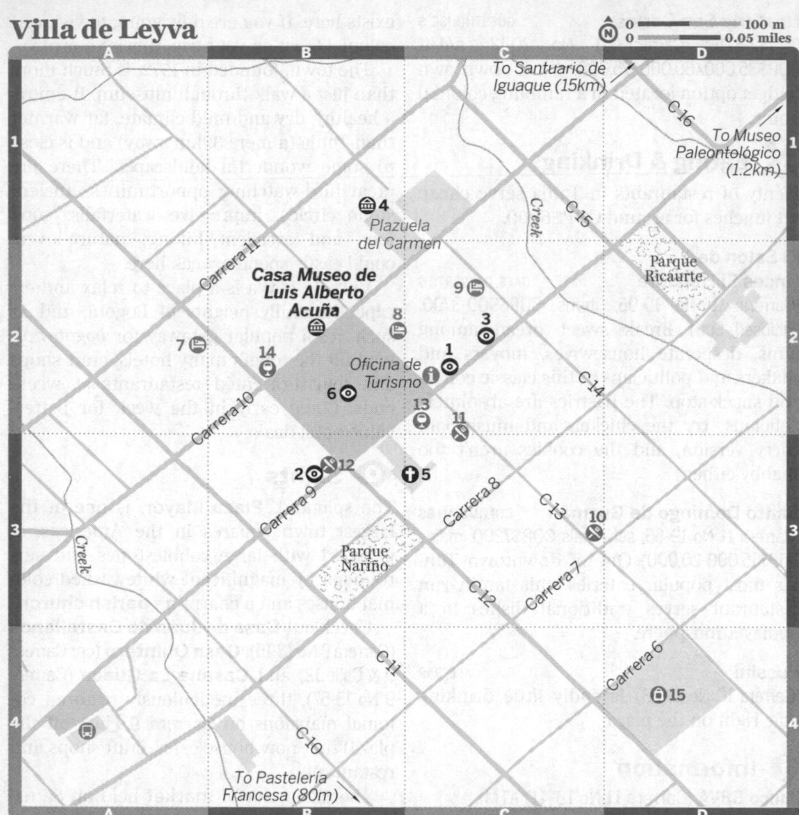

carvings, altarpieces and other religious objects dating from the 16th century.

Activities

The area surrounding Villa de Leyva is pleasant for hiking. There are several routes taking in some of the many attractions around the town or climb the path beside Renacer Guesthouse to reach a natural lookout point with great views.

Other ways to explore the area include cycling and horse riding organized through tour agencies in town or at Colombian Highlands. Bikes cost around COP$4000/16,000 per hour/half-day; horses are COP$40,000 for three hours.

Tours

Villa de Leyva's small fleet of taxis offer trips to the attractions surrounding the town. The classic route takes in El Fósil, the Estación Astronómica Muisca and Convento del Santo Ecce Homo and costs around COP$60,000 for up to four passengers.

Colombian Highlands ADVENTURE SPORTS
(☎310-769-6561, 732-1201; www.colombianhighlands.com; Av Carrera 10 No 21) Run by biologist and Renacer Guesthouse owner Oscar Gilède, this agency has a variety of off-beat tours including ecotours, nocturnal hikes, bird-watching, rappelling/abseiling, canyoning, caving and hiking. English spoken. Located inside the Renacer Guesthouse, 1km out of town.

Sleeping

Prices in town rocket and rooms become scarce during holidays and long weekends. We've listed weekday rates here.

TOP CHOICE **Renacer Guesthouse** HOSTEL $
(☎310-769-6561, 732-1201; www.colombianhighlands.com; Finca Renacer, Av Carrera 10 No 21;

Villa de Leyva

campsite per person with/without tent rental COP$18,000/9000, dm COP$18,000-22,000, s/d from COP$55,000/60,000; @ wi-fi) This charming 'boutique hostel' has fantastic facilities, including hammocks surrounding an immaculate garden, a communal, open-air kitchen with brick oven, snug lounge with fireplace and very comfortable dorms and rooms. There is also a small cafe serving healthy meals. It's a 1.2km walk uphill from the plaza but they will credit guests' first taxi ride on arrival.

Casa Viena HOSTEL $
(☎732-0711; www.casaviena.com; Carrera 10 No 19-114; dm COP$15,000, r COP$45,000, s/d without bathroom COP$24,000/35,000; @ wi-fi) This family-run hostel offers three simple rooms with good mattresses and warm bedspreads. The best of the lot is the room with a private bathroom, which also boasts a nice terrace.

Hospedería La Roca GUESTHOUSE $
(☎316-465-8602; larocahospederia@gmail.com; Plaza Mayor; r per person COP$60,000; wi-fi) Located directly on Plaza Mayor, this great-value place has a variety of pleasant rooms with new flat-screen TVs, high ceilings and modern bathrooms surrounding a plant-filled courtyard.

Posada San Martín GUESTHOUSE $
(☎732-0428; Calle 14 No 9-43; s/d/tr COP$30,000/60,000/90,000) Hidden behind a high wall, this quiet and welcoming guesthouse in a brightly-painted old home has fine rooms with nice tile floors and firm beds. Offers discounts for long term stays. Breakfast included.

Hospedería Colonial GUESTHOUSE $$
(☎312-448-9928; Calle 12 No 10-81; s/d COP$35,000/70,000) Just a block off the plaza, Hospedería Colonial has nice rooms with exposed wooden beams and saggy beds.

Eating & Drinking

Not all restaurants are open on weekdays.

Restaurante Estar de la Villa COLOMBIAN $
(Calle 13 No 8-85; set meals COP$8000; ⌚8:30am-5pm Sun-Fri, to 7pm Sat) Honest to goodness, clean-cut cheapie serving up delicious wholesome dishes. Go for the set meal which includes a small self-serve salad bar. Also offers around a dozen tasty breakfast options.

Pastelería Francesa BAKERY, FRENCH $
(cnr Calle 10 & Carrera 6; ⌚8am-7pm Thu-Mon) Who doesn't love a French patisserie? Great apple tart and hot chocolate.

Restaurante Casa Blanca COLOMBIAN $$
(Calle 13 No 7-16; set meals COP$9000, mains COP$15,000-22,000; ⌚8am-9pm) Excellent-value *comida corriente* (basic set meal), mains are equally good, with trout, chicken and beef all cooked beautifully.

Restaurante Savia VEGETARIAN, ORGANIC $$
(Casa Quintero, cnr Carrera 9 & Calle 12; mains COP$12,000-28,000; ⌚4-10pm Fri, 10am-10pm Sat & Sun; ✎) Good selection of creative vegan and vegetarian dishes, alongside interesting chicken and seafood options. No red meat.

Dortkneipe BAR
(Carrera 9 No 12-88) On Plaza Mayor, folks spill out of this small, unpronounceable bar that draws hordes for its draft beer selection served in COP$5000 1L portions.

La Cava de Don Fernando BAR
(Carrera 10 No 12-03) Soft-lit bar on the plaza with loud music.

Information

Banco Popular (Calle 12 No 9-43) Reliable ATM.

Oficina de Turismo (☎732-0232; cnr Carrera 9 & Calle 13; ⌚8am-12:30pm & 2-6pm) Free maps.

Getting There & Away

The bus terminal is located three blocks southwest of Plaza Mayor, on the road to Tunja. Minibuses run between Tunja and Villa de Leyva every 15 minutes from 5am to 6:30pm (COP$6000, 45 minutes). There are direct buses to Bogotá (COP$20,000, four hours) at 4:30am, 5am, noon, 12:30pm, 1pm, 2pm, 4pm and 5pm.

Around Villa de Leyva

Here you'll find archaeological relics, colonial monuments, petroglyphs, caves, lakes, waterfalls and fossils. You can walk to some of the nearest sights, or go by bicycle or on horseback.

El Fósil (www.museoelfosil.com; admission COP$4000; ⌚7am-6pm) is an impressive 120-million-year-old baby kronosaurus fossil. It's the world's most complete specimen of this prehistoric marine reptile. The fossil is 7m long; the creature was about 12m in size but the tail did not survive. It is located off the road to Santa Sofía, 6km west of Villa de Leyva. It's a little more than an hour walking, or you can take the Santa Sofía bus, which will drop you off 80m from the fossil.

The **Estación Astronómica Muisca** (El Infiernito; admission COP$4000; ⌚9am-noon & 2-5pm Tue-Sun) dates from the early centuries AD and was used by indigenous people to determine the seasons. It was named 'Little Hell' by Catholics who wanted to put the fear of (a Christian) God into the locals, and encourage them to associate it with the devil. It is made up of large, cylindrical stone monoliths sunk into the ground in two parallel lines. By measuring the length of shadows, the *indígenas* (indigenous people) were able to identify the planting seasons. You can walk here from El Fósil in about 25 minutes.

Around 16km out of town, but well worth the journey, is **Convento del Santo Ecce Homo** (admission COP$4000; ⌚9am-5pm), a large stone-and-adobe convent founded in 1620 that features a lovely courtyard.

Parque Nacional Santuario de Iguaque

Covering the mist-covered upper slopes of an imposing mountain range to the northeast of Villa de Leyva, Iguaque is a 67.5-sq-km **national park** (admission COP$36,500) in an area of pristine wilderness held sacred by the indigenous Muiscas.

There are eight small mountain lakes in the northern part of the reserve, surrounded by *páramo* (high-altitude grassland) at an altitude of between 3550m and 3700m, including **Laguna de Iguaque**, the most important site in Muisca legend.

The **visitors center** (naturariguaque@yahoo.es; dm per person high/low season COP$35,000/28,000, campsite per person COP$8000) is at an altitude of 2950m, 3km off the Villa de Leyva–Arcabuco road. Take warm clothing. It offers meals, dorm beds, and collects the entrance fee. If you plan on sleeping at the center, check in advance at Bogotá's national park office.

From Villa de Leyva take a bus to Arcabuco (COP$3000), get off after 12km at Casa de Peidra (also known as Los Naranjos) and walk to the visitors center (3km). The walk from the visitors center uphill to the Laguna de Iguaque takes two to three hours.

Parque Nacional Natural El Cocuy

With snowcapped peaks, scintillating alpine lakes and glorious green valleys, Parque Nacional Natural (PNN) El Cocuy ranks as one of Colombia's most spectacular protected areas. Located in the highest part of the Cordillera Oriental, it tops out at Ritacumba Blanco, a 5330m peak.

The mountain chain is relatively compact and not difficult to reach – the gateway towns are Güicán and El Cocuy in northern Boyacá. It's an ideal place for trekking, although the routes are more suited to experienced walkers. There are no facilities in the park so you'll need to bring all your food and equipment including sleeping bags, warm clothing and a tent. If you don't have gear, the only way to explore the mountains is in a series of day hikes.

All visitors to the park must report to Parques Nacionales offices based in either **Güicán** (☎310-230-3302; Carrera 4 No 3-30; Colombians/foreigners COP$13,500/36,500; ⌚8am-noon & 1-5pm Mon-Sat) or **El Cocuy** (☎789-0359; cocuy@parquesnacionales.gov.co; Calle 8 No 4-74; Colombians/foreigners COP$13,500/36,500; ⏰8am-noon & 1-5:45pm), in order to register their itineraries and pay the admission fee.

Note that guides are not mandatory, but they are highly recommended. You can hire guides at any of the *cabañas* (cabins) near the park boundary or at **Ecoturismo Comunitario Sisuma** (☎314-348-9718; www.elcocuyboyaca.com) in El Cocuy. Expect to pay about COP$45,000 a day for a *campesino* (peasant farmer, who can merely show you the way) for up to eight people; or COP$80,000 for an actual accredited trekking guide for up to six people. Horses and horse handlers will each cost about COP$35,000 per day. Veteran climber **Rodrigo Arias** (☎320-339-3839; www.colombiatrek.com) from Coopserguías is an experienced, highly recommended guide and he is the only English speaker in the mountains.

San Gil

☎7 / POP 44,600

There are few small cities that are able to demand as many days on your itinerary as San Gil, the beating heart of Colombia's burgeoning adventure sports industries. And with the mighty Río Suárez boasting some of the best Grade 4+ rapids in South America, your heart might just stop beating.

San Gil is a center for rafting, rappelling, *torrentismo* (rappelling down a waterfall), horse riding, paragliding, hydrospeeding, caving and mountain biking, but there are also enough calmer activities to please nature-lovers who want the view without the adrenaline. There are fantastic swimming holes, waterfalls, beautiful rivers and easy, wonderful hikes within 30 minutes of the town.

However, San Gil is more than just top natural attractions; it's also a pleasant and authentic small Colombian city, an unpretentious place that goes about its business quietly, where tourism is important but not all consuming. It's where locals like to meet for evening drinks under the huge old ceiba trees in the main square and the local market is full of wonderful fresh fruit and vegetables, not souvenirs. It all pulls together into a highly-entertaining destination that many travelers wish they had discovered earlier.

Sights

IN TOWN

Parque El Gallineral PARK

(☎724-4372; cnr Malecón & Calle 6; admission COP$6000; ⏰8:15am-5:15pm) The town's best spot to relax is Parque El Gallineral. It's a beautiful, ethereal riverside park, where the trees are covered with *barbas de viejo* – long silvery fronds of *tillandsia* (a fronded, drooping plant that grows hanging off trees). It's one of Colombia's most beautiful public spaces.

OUT OF TOWN

Cascadas de Juan Curi WATERFALL

(entrance COP$5000) This magnificent 180m-high waterfall is made up of three separate 60m torrents with a natural pool at the base that is great for a refreshing dip. Maniacs are welcome to abseil down. The falls are 22km from San Gil on the road to Charalá. There are two buses an hour to Charalá (COP$3500) from the local bus station. Ask the driver to let you out at the *cascadas* (waterfalls), and walk about 20 minutes up a trail to the falls.

Quebrada Curití RIVER

This river, 12km northeast of San Gil, has crystalline swimming pools and natural slides. Take a bus to the village of Curití, from where it's a 40-minute walk.

Activities

There are 18 adventure tour agencies in San Gil. The most popular activity is whitewater rafting trips. A standard 10km run on Río Fonce (Grades 1 to 3) costs COP$30,000 per person and takes 1½ hours. The perilous and thrilling Río Suárez is a world-class run that even experienced rafters say still scares them. It's a full day's trip, and costs COP$120,000.

There are several great caves to explore around San Gil, the best of which is the water-filled Cueva Vaca. Most operators also offer horse riding, paragliding, rappelling, rock climbing and ecological walks. Many firms act as intermediaries between the few companies that have the right to operate in each location.

TOP CHOICE **Colombian Bike Junkies** MOUNTAIN BIKING

(☎316-327-6101; www.colombianbikejunkies.com; Calle 12 No 8-35) Based out of Gringo Mike's, this extreme mountain-bike company offers cross-country and high-adrenaline downhill adventures on quality bikes, including a 50km downhill trip through the Chicamocha Canyon. When they say full day, they mean it – don't expect to be back before dark!

Colombia Rafting Expeditions RAFTING
(☎311-283-8647; www.colombiarafting.com; Carrera 10 No 7-83) This is the best-equipped rafting outfit in town, with experienced, often English-speaking guides. It also offers kayaking courses.

Macondo Adventures ADVENTURE SPORTS
(☎724-8001; www.macondohostel.com; Carrera 8 No 10-35) Save time by going direct to this efficient booking office run by the knowledgeable staff inside Macondo Guesthouse. They have videos of most activities to check out before you sign up.

Pozo Azul SWIMMING
A lovely freshwater pool just 1km north of the center of town. It's popular with Colombians at weekends; during the week it's quiet.

Courses

Connect4 LANGUAGE
(☎726-2660; www.idiomassangil.com; Carrera 8 No 12-25, Local 201) Offers a 12-hour Spanish-language express course (COP$264,000) and private lessons (from COP$22,000 per hour).

Sleeping

Macondo Guesthouse HOSTEL $
(☎724-8001; www.macondohostel.com; Carrera 8 No 10-35; dm COP$18,000, s/d COP$55,000/65,000, without bathroom COP$35,000/45,000; @) Dressed up in new digs, this San Gil classic remains a laid-back hostel that's a bit like crashing at a friend's place. The new space offers a wonderful leafy courtyard with a 10-person Jacuzzi, and there's a variety of dorm and private room options. The professional staff are highly knowledgeable about local adventure sports.

Sam's VIP HOSTEL $$
(☎724-2746; www.samshostel.com; Carrera 10 No 12-33; dm COP$17,000, s/d COP$50,000/70,000, without bathroom COP$35,000/50,000; @) A discerning choice with elegant furnishings, spotless rooms and an expansive terrace overlooking the plaza. There is also a small pool with wonderful mountain views and a superb, straight-out-of-suburban-America kitchen for guests.

Santander Alemán HOSTEL $
(☎724-2535; www.hostelsantanderaleman.com; Calle 12 No 7-63; dm from COP$18,000, s/d COP$25,000/40,000; @) Peaceful, homely hostel with bright spacious dorms featuring big windows onto the street and a tastefully decorated private room. The charming owners also run a more upmarket venture with mostly private rooms near the local bus terminal.

Hotel Abril HOTEL $
(☎724-8795; cnr Calle 8 & Carrera 10; s/d/tr COP$30,000/50,000/70,000) The best-value private rooms in town, with minibar, TV, great beds and linen, and pleasant rooms set away from the road. It's cool, fresh, clean and well managed.

El Dorado HOSTEL $
(☎723-7588; www.eldoradohostel.com; Calle 12 No 8-55; dm COP$17,000-18,000, s/d without bathroom COP$35,000/45,000) This small, welcoming hostel has a great location a few doors from the plaza and young, adventure-loving owners who run their own caving and abseiling activities.

Eating

TOP CHOICE **El Maná** COLOMBIAN $
(Calle 10 No 9-42; set meals COP$10,000; ⏲11am-2:30pm & 6-8:30pm Mon-Sat, 11am-2:30pm Sun) Easily the best Colombian restaurant in town, serving huge set meals featuring traditional dishes like chicken in plum sauce, *carne asada* (barbecued meat) and grilled mountain trout. The bummer is it closes early if you're out all day.

Gringo Mike's AMERICAN, BURGERS $
(www.gringomikes.net; Calle 12 No 8-35; sandwiches and burgers COP$9500-14,000; ⏲8am-noon & 5-11pm;) Hugely popular with locals, this great-value place in a colonial courtyard serves up the best gringo food in Colombia. From juicy half-pound burgers to tasty gourmet sandwiches and real quesadillas, it's all here. The huge breakfasts will set you up for a full day of extreme sports.

Donde Pablito COLOMBIAN $
(Carrera 10 No 9-88; mains COP$11,000; ⏲2pm-10pm) Bring your post-rafting/rappelling/biking appetite to this unpretentious diner and enjoy massive thin steaks with plantain, potato and *arepa* (savoury corn bread) served in a fluorescent-lit corridor with a

blaring TV and clashing paint job. Thankfully they also do takeout.

Plaza de Mercado MARKET $

(Carrera 11; ⏲6am-3pm Mon-Wed, to 2pm Thu & Sun, to 4pm Fri & Sat) Between Calles 13 and 14, this covered market sells dirt-cheap breakfasts, *comida corriente,* juices and tamales.

Drinking

Most of the action in the early evening revolves around beers in the central plaza.

La Habana BAR

(Carrera 9 No 11-68, Local 212; ⏲6pm-midnight Sun-Thu, 6pm-2am Fri & Sat) Hidden away on the 2nd floor of the Camino Real shopping mall is this cool nightspot with *son,* salsa, rock and reggae. Best choice on weekdays when everywhere else is dead.

La Isla BARS

(Vía San Gil-Bogotá, Km 1) This large gas station on the way out of town is (inexplicably) the hottest after-hours ticket in San Gil. Choose from a loud bar, karaoke lounge and a disco. There is also a food court for late munchies. Most locals just sit around drinking outside.

Information

The official tourism website for San Gil is www.sangil.com.co. There are several ATMs around the plaza.

4-72 (Carrera 10 No 10-50) Post office; next to Cajasan Supermercado.

Ares (☎724-5463; Calle 12 No 8-74) Changes dollars and will buy your excess bolívars.

Banco Popular (Carrera 9 No 11-75) ATM.

Getting There & Away

The main intercity bus terminal is 3km west of the town center on the road to Bogotá. Urban buses shuttle regularly between the terminal and the center, or you can take a taxi (COP$3400). Frequent buses from here run to Bogotá (COP$35,000, eight hours), Bucaramanga (COP$15,000, three hours), Santa Marta (COP$60,000, 14 hours) and Medellín (COP$65,000, 11 hours). Buses to Bucaramanga (COP$15,000, two hours) leave every 20 minutes from the **Cotrasangil bus office** (Carrera 11 No 8-10) until 7:30pm. Buses to Barichara (COP$3300, 40 minutes) leave every 30 minutes from 5am to 6:30pm from the **local bus terminal** (cnr Calle 15 & Carrera 10) in the center. Buses to Guane, Charalá and Curití also leave from here.

Barichara

☎7 / POP 7400

Tiny Barichara is like a film set, boasting immaculately renovated 300-year-old whitewashed buildings and atmospheric stone streets. Visit on the weekend and you'll have hordes of visitors from Bogotá for company; during the week you'll have the place to yourself, although many bars and restaurants may be closed.

The 18th-century sandstone **Catedral de la Inmaculada Concepción**, on the main plaza, is the largest and most elaborate building in town. The **Casa de la Cultura** (☎726-7002; Calle 5 No 6-29; admission COP$1000; ⏲9am-noon & 2-5:30pm Mon-Sat, 9am-1pm Sun) features a small fossil collection and pottery by the local Guane indigenous people.

The nearby village of **Guane**, located 10km to the northwest, is the land that time forgot. It has a fine rural church and a museum with a collection of fossils and Guane artifacts.

Sleeping & Eating

Los Tiestecitos GUESTHOUSE $

(☎726-7224; Carrera 5 No 7-62; r per person COP$12,000) Walk past the handmade pottery through the vibrant plant nursery to reach these three rustic rooms with modern private bathrooms in the home of a hardworking local woman. The paint is peeling and the plaster is cracking, but this is the real, non-boutique Barichara and the price is unbeatable.

HORMIGAS CULONAS: A SULTRY SNACK

While travelling in Santander, make sure to keep a look-out for the peculiar local delicacy, the *hormiga culona,* or big-assed ant. The giant dark-brown leafcutter ants are fried or roasted and eaten whole in a tradition inherited from the indigenous Guane. Only the voluptuous fertile princess ants are eaten – the humble workers simply don't have the curves. They are sold at small shops throughout the region, especially in Bucaramanga, San Gil and Barichara.

La Casa de Heraclia GUESTHOUSE **$$**
(☎300-223-9349; lacasadeheraclia@hotmail.com; Calle 3 No 5-33; dm COP$25,000, s/d COP$45,000/80,000; @📶) There are beanbags on a terrace as you enter and a large, open dining area in front of the quiet, modest and lovely rooms.

Tinto Hostel HOSTEL **$**
(☎726-7725; tinto-hostel@hotmail.com; Calle 6 No 2-61; dm COP$17,000, s/d/tr COP$40,000/50,000/60,000; @📶) This new hostel has private rooms with mountain views, small dorms and a friendly owner who is always around to give advice.

Hotel Corató HISTORIC HOTEL **$$**
(☎726-7110; hotelcorata@hotmail.com; Carrera 7 No 4-08; s/d/tr COP$70,000/80,000/120,000, s without bathroom COP$40,000; @📶) Historical hotel in a 280-year-old building decorated with antiques and wooden furnishings.

TOP CHOICE **Color de Hormiga** COLOMBIAN **$$**
(☎315-297-1621; www.colordehormiga.com; Calle 6 No 5-35; mains COP$16,000-25,000) The signature dish at Barichara's famous ant-inspired restaurant is filet mignon with ant sauce, but there are also fantastic arthropod-free dishes and delectable homemade fruit ice cream here. Out the back, the magnificent colonial house has been converted into a boutique hostel (dorms/rooms COP$20,000/60,000) with meticulously renovated private rooms and grapevines giving shade to the wide courtyard. Alternatively, arrange a stay on the owner's charming farm where many of the ants are sourced.

Restaurante La Casona COLOMBIAN **$**
(Calle 6 No 5-68; set meals COP$8000, mains COP$9000-16,000) This friendly family restaurant serves cheap lunches and typical regional dishes in an artistic courtyard.

Nuestro Café CAFE
(☎311-422-1870; Carrera 5 No 2-87) Head to this cute little cafe with just two tables to try organic Barichara coffee and buy bags of whole beans to take home. Also prepares light meals.

ℹ Getting There & Away

Buses shuttle between Barichara and San Gil every 45 minutes (COP$4000, 40 minutes). They depart from the **Cotrasangil bus office** (Carrera 6 No 5-74) on the plaza.

Buses to Guane (COP$1700, 15 minutes) depart at 6am, 9:30am, 11:30am, 2:30pm and 5:30pm. You can also hike there on the ancient, fossil-encrusted Camino Real, which starts at the north end of Calle 4. It's not strenuous, but take a hat and water.

Parque Nacional del Chicamocha

This so-called **national park** (www.parquenacionaldelchicamocha.com; Km 54, Via Bucaramanga-San Gil; adult/child COP$13,000/7000; ⏲9am-6pm Wed-Thu, to 7pm Fri-Sun) is not really a park at all (in Colombia real national parks are called Parque Nacional Natural), but rather a glorified rest stop in a spectacular location overlooking the Cañon del Chicamocha. Nicknamed 'Panachi', it is on the main highway between San Gil and Bucaramanga, a scenic mountain-hugging road that winds through glorious barren landscapes.

Most of the tourist activities here are a waste of both time and money; the real reason to come here is the **canyon**. There is a 360-degree lookout point, though some of the best shots are obstructed by the park's 'attractions'. For the best views, take a ride in the **teleférico** (return cable-car ticket incl park entrance COP$38,000; ⏲9am-11am & 1-5:30pm Wed-Thu, 9am-4:30pm Fri-Sun), which first swoops you down into the depths and then raises you back up on the other side of the canyon. If you want more action, there are also a couple of zip lines (COP$14,000 to COP$19,000).

Any bus between San Gil and Bucaramanga will drop you here. Book your return ticket at the small Cotransangil ticket office inside the main entrance. It is also possible to travel by bus from Bucaramanga to less developed Mesa de Los Santos on the other side of the canyon and buy a one-way ticket across on the teleférico.

Bucaramanga

☎7 / POP 524,000

The capital of Santander is a modern, busy commercial and industrial center with a mild climate. Dubbed 'The City of Parks', there are indeed several lovely green spaces here, however in general the city is not particularly attractive. Most travelers only stop here to break up an overland journey to the coast, although Buca's friendly locals and throbbing nightlife means those that like to party may end up staying a little longer than planned.

Sights

Museo Casa de Bolívar MUSEUM
(Calle 37 No 12-15; admission COP$2000; ⏲8am-noon & 2-6pm Mon-Fri, 8am-noon Sat) Museo Casa de Bolívar contains ethnographic and historic collections, including artifacts of the Guane people, who inhabited the area before the Spanish arrived.

Catedral de la Sagrada Familia CHURCH
(Calle 36 No 19-56) Facing Parque Santander, this massive, eclectic edifice has fine stained-glass windows and a ceramic cupola brought from Mexico.

Activities

With spectacular surrounding countryside and consistent thermal winds, Bucaramanga has become a popular paragliding destination.

Colombia Paragliding PARAGLIDING
(☎432-6266; www.colombiaparagliding.com; Ruitoque) Based atop the Ruitoque mesa, Colombia Paragliding offers 15-minute tandem rides for COP$50,000. Owner/instructor Richi speaks English and also runs a hostel near the launch site.

Bolo Club Puerto del Sol TRADITIONAL SPORTS
(☎647-8588; Carrera 27 No 58-56; ⏲2pm-3am Mon-Sat, 3pm-midnight Sun) The traditional sport known as *tejo* is big in these parts. Come and throw rocks at gunpowder and see what all the fuss is about.

Sleeping

Kasa Guane Bucaramanga HOSTEL $
(☎312-432-6266, 657-6960; www.kasaguane.com; Calle 49 No 28-21; dm COP$20,000-25,000, s/d without bathroom COP$40,000/60,000; @📶) Located in one of the nicest neighborhoods in town, this friendly hostel offers dorms and private rooms, kitchen and laundry facilities, and a pleasant bar area with a pool table on the terrace. It has a nice social vibe but could do with some more bathrooms.

Hotel Principe HOTEL $$
(☎630-4317; www.hotel-principe.net; Carrera 17 No 37-69; s/d with air-con COP$77,000/98,000, with fan COP$66,000/88,000; ❄📶) This moderately priced hotel in the heart of downtown has large rooms with cable TV.

Eating & Drinking

TOP CHOICE **Mercagán** STEAKHOUSE $$
(Carrera 33 No 42-12; steaks COP$15,900-36,400) Touted by locals as the best steak in Colombia, this traditional *parrilla* (grillhouse) is worth the hype: perfect cuts of meat from the owners' farm come in 200g, 300g or 400g (good luck!) sizes, served on sizzling iron plates with cassava and an *arepa*. It's hugely popular, so come early to get a table.

SazonArt COLOMBIAN $
(cnr Calle 48 & Carrera 27A; set meals COP$7000, mains COP$14,000; ⏲7am-1pm Tue-Sat, 8am-3pm Sun-Mon) A very clean corner restaurant serving a changing menu of tasty traditional dishes.

Café Con-Verso CAFE
(Calle 44 No 28-63; ⏲from 5pm Mon-Sat) Beautiful chill-out lounge with great music and drinks.

Information

There are many ATMs near Parque Santander and in Sotomayor on Carrera 29.

Bancolombia (Carrera 18 No 35-02)

Tourism Police (☎634-5507; www.imct.gov.co; Parque de Los Niños) Tourist Information office at the Biblioteca Pública Gabriel Turbay. There are also PITs at the airport and bus terminal.

Getting There & Away

Bucaramanga's bus terminal is southwest of the center, midway to Girón; frequent city buses marked 'Terminal' go there from Carreras 15 and 33. Taxis are COP$6000. Buses depart from here regularly for Bogotá (COP$70,000, 10 hours), Cartagena (COP$80,000, 12 hours), Cúcuta (COP$40,000, six hours) and Santa Marta (COP$60,000, nine hours).

Girón

☎7 / POP 136,000

The calm, cobbled streets of San Juan de Girón are just 9km from the bustle of Bucaramanga but feel a world away.

The town center, founded in 1631, has been largely restored and is the main attraction here, with its old whitewashed houses. The **Catedral del Señor de los Milagros** on the main plaza is worth poking your head into, while **Plazuela Peralta** and **Plazuela de las Nieves** are both pleasant plazas.

GETTING TO VENEZUELA

If you are heading to Venezuela from the interior you will need to cross the border at Cucutá, a true champion amongst crap frontier towns. It is a hot, dirty and dangerous place: get in and out as fast as possible.

To reach San Antonio del Táchira in Venezuela take one of the frequent buses or *colectivos* (shared taxis; COP$2500) from Cucutá's bus terminal, on the corner of Av Diagonal Santander and Calle 8, in the center of town. Changing transportation at the border is not necessary. Don't forget to get off just before the bridge to have your passport stamped at Migracíon Colombia. This border is open 24 hours a day, seven days a week.

Move your watch forward 30 minutes when crossing from Colombia into Venezuela. Consider stocking up on Colombian pesos in Cucutá and changing them to bolívares at the border to avoid poor rates from ATMs inside Venezuela. Once in Venezuela, pick up a tourist card – it's issued directly by the **SAIME office** (in Venezuela 0276-771-2282; Carrera 9, btwn Calles 6 & 7; 24hr) in San Antonio del Táchira. From San Antonio there are seven departures a day to Caracas (BsF220, 14 hours), all departing in the late afternoon or early evening for an overnight trip.

The road from Bucaramanga to Cucutá passes through some spectacular mountain scenery but is in very poor condition and gets cold, so bring warm clothes. If you want to break up the journey, check out Pamplona, a delightful town of old churches and narrow streets set in the spectacular Valle del Espíritu Santo, 71km before Cucutá. It has a refreshingly cool climate and several fine museums. **Hotel El Álamo** (568-2137; Calle 5 No 6-68; s/d/tr COP$30,000/40,000/50,000) is a reliable budget choice.

Hotel Las Nieves (646-8968; Calle 30 No 25-71; s/d COP$44,000/77,000), on the main plaza, has comfortable rooms, some with private balconies, and a decent budget restaurant. For cheap, typical food head to the *malecón*, where half-a-dozen stalls offer deep-fried sausages, ribs and other fatty animal products served over greasy chips, without a vegetable in sight. You could bust an artery just looking at it, so consider yourself warned! More upmarket meals are served at **Restaurante La Casona** (Calle 28 No 28-09; mains COP$15,000-34,000; to 8pm).

There are two ATMs on the eastern side of the Parque Principal. Frequent city buses (COP$1550) from Carreras 15 and 33 in Bucaramanga will drop you at Girón in 30 minutes, or you can take a taxi (COP$12,000).

THE CARIBBEAN COAST

Colombia's Caribbean coast is a sun- and rum-drenched playground, which stretches 1760km from the jungles of the Darién in the west to the striking barren landscapes of La Guajira in the wild, wild east.

With the lures of pristine beaches, coral reefs and virgin rainforest in Parque Nacional Natural Tayrona, or the renowned jungle trek to the ancient Ciudad Perdida (Lost City), your main problem will be packing it all in. The hippy-magnet diving resort of Taganga and the intoxicating colonial city of Cartagena – one of the continent's most beautiful and historically important destinations – suck many travelers in for months.

For more low-key times, check out Mompox, a living museum that's straight out of a Gabriel García Márquez novel, or laid-back Sapzurro and Capurganá, where time gently vanishes into the sunset of each day. Then snap out of your hammock-swinging reverie with Colombia's most giddying party, the Carnaval of Barranquilla, a week-long Mardi Gras riot of dancing, booze and music.

The Caribbean coast region also happens to be Colombia's main tourist destination for the locals, which means that most people you meet will be in holiday mode and ready to rumba, or to just kick back and idle the time away.

Santa Marta

5 / POP 426,000

Santa Marta is where Colombians go when they want sun on their backs, sand under their feet and rum in their glasses. It has a famous colonial past as one of the continent's oldest cities, and is where Simón Bolívar died after a heroic attempt to make Latin America one united republic.

Its grace as a colonial city has faded somewhat because of newer concrete buildings, but it's still a pleasant enough seaside town and ongoing restoration work is bringing back some of the downtown area's lost charm.

Most travelers whiz through and base themselves in Taganga, or head directly to Parque Nacional Natural Tayrona, leaving downtown Santa Marta with a local, untouristy feel. Spend some time here and you'll find fine restaurants, pleasant plazas and good nightlife. It's also the place to organize a trip to Ciudad Perdida, the great pre-Hispanic city of the Tayrona.

Sights

Quinta de San Pedro Alejandrino MUSEUM
(☎433-1021; www.museobolivariano.org.co; Av Libertador; adult/child COP$12,000/10,000; ⌚9:30am-4:30pm) This is the hacienda where Simón Bolívar, spent his last days and died. The impressive main house has been meticulously preserved, with many of the original furnishings. The lush grounds are full of lazy iguanas and are themselves a worthy attraction. Take a bus towards Mamatoco from the waterfront to get there (COP$1200, 20 minutes).

Catedral CHURCH
(cnr Carrera 4 & Calle 17) The massive whitewashed cathedral claims to be Colombia's oldest church, but work was not actually completed until the end of the 18th century. It holds the ashes of the town's founder, Rodrigo de Bastidas.

FREE **Museo del Oro** MUSEUM
(Calle 14 No 1-37; ⌚8:30am-6pm Mon-Fri, 9am-1pm Sat) This museum has an interesting collection of Tayrona objects, mainly pottery and gold.

Sleeping

La Brisa Loca HOSTEL $$
(☎431-6121; www.labrisaloca.com; Calle 14 No 3-58; dm with/without air-con from COP$28,000/20,000, r with air-con from COP$70,000; ❄@📶🏊) Professionally run, entertaining hostel with fantastic facilities, including a great pool, riotous bar and kick-ass rooftop terrace with cathedral views. It seems like a recipe for unmitigated mayhem, but the friendly owners run a tight ship and keep everything (just about) in order. Staying here makes backpacking fun.

Aluna HOSTEL $$
(☎432-4916; www.alunahotel.com; Calle 21 No 5-72; dm COP$20,000, s/d COP$60,000/80,000, without air-con COP$40,000/55,000; ❄) A comfortable and quiet choice, this lovely hostel has nicely proportioned dorms, neat private rooms and spacious, breezy communal areas. The well-equipped kitchen has lockers. The best book exchange on the coast speaks of an intelligent, widely read crowd.

Casa Familiar GUESTHOUSE $
(☎421-1697; www.hospederiacasafamiliar.freeservers.com; Calle 10C No 2-14; dm COP$15,000, s/d COP$22,000/35,000; 📶) A popular backpacker hangout, with private rooms and dorms. There's a nice rooftop terrace for lounging. Some of the single rooms are boxy.

Hotel Miramar HOTEL $
(☎423-3276; elmiramar_santamarta@yahoo.com; Calle 10C No 1C-59; dm with/without air-con COP$15,000/10,000, s/d COP$15,000/25,000, without bathroom COP$12,000/20,000; @📶) If you long for the golden age of no-frills independent travel, rest your head at Santa Marta's original backpacker hostel and re-

GETTING TO VENEZUELA

Half-hourly buses depart Santa Marta for Maicao (COP$34,000, four hours), where you change for a *colectivo* (shared taxi) to Maracaibo in Venezuela. *Colectivos* depart regularly from about 5am to 3pm (BsF120, three hours) and go as far as Maracaibo's bus terminal. Maicao is an edgy, gritty town, so be alert.

Venezuelan entry formalities are done in Paraguachón, on the Venezuelan side of the border. Make sure your driver is prepared to wait while you get your stamp, as locals don't need to go through the same process. Wind your watch 30 minutes forward when crossing from Colombia into Venezuela.

There are also two buses daily from Santa Marta direct to Venezuela, operated by **Expresos Amerlujo** (☎430-4144) and **Expreso Brasilia** (☎430-6244). They come through from Cartagena, go to Maracaibo (COP$95,000, nine hours) and continue to Caracas (COP$185,000, 20 hours).

Santa Marta

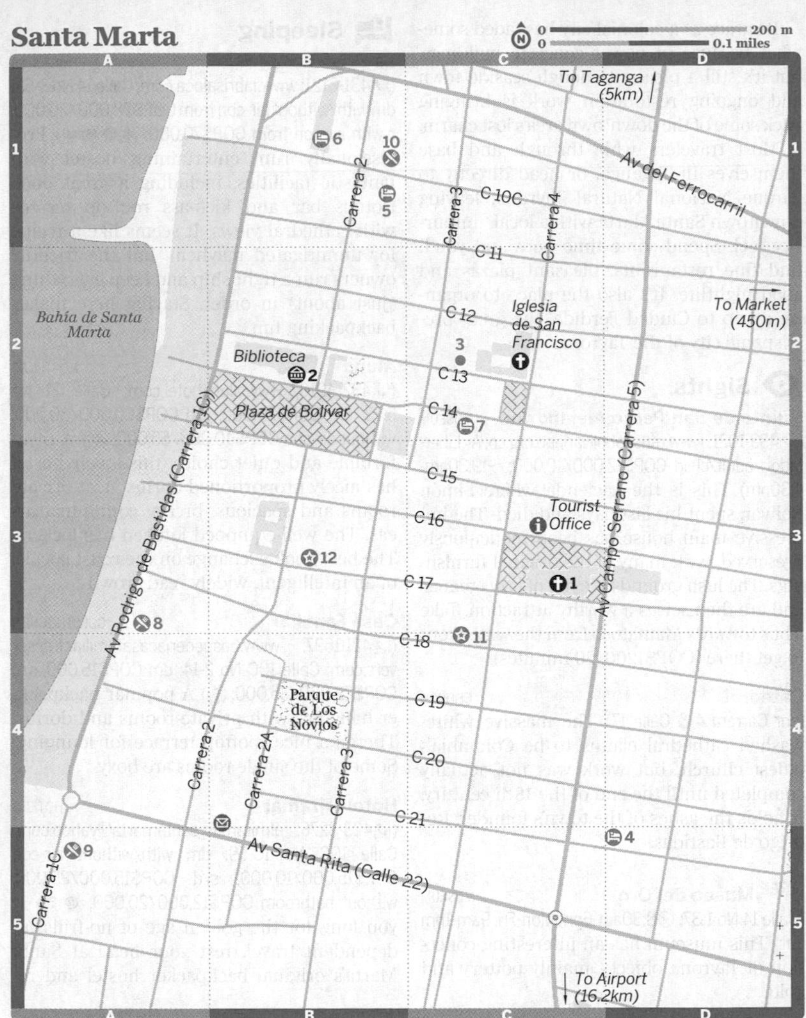

live the magic. Sure it's dark, the beds are either soft or rock-hard and there are no toilet seats, but it's cheap, friendly and has plenty of atmosphere.

Eating

There are a lot of cheap restaurants around the budget hotels, particularly on Calles 11 and 12 near the waterfront, where you can get lunch for around COP$6000.

Cocteleria Juancho KIOSK $
(Carrera 1; ceviche COP$5000-13,000; breakfast, lunch & dinner) Squeeze in among the locals on the wooden benches at this street-side *ceviche* stall and order a *ceviche mixto,* a medley of fresh shrimp, octopus, fish and conch. It's always full so you know it's fresh. Find it between Calles 22 and 23.

Restaurante Welcome SEAFOOD $$
(Calle 10C No 2-11; mains COP$14,000-19,000;) It doesn't look like much, but this humble diner packs a crowd for its great-value seafood. You won't find a better *cazuela de mariscos* (mixed seafood pot) at any of the flashier restaurants around town. It also serves breakfast and vegetarian dishes.

Santa Marta

Sights
1 Catedral....C3
2 Museo del Oro....B2

Activities, Courses & Tours
3 Turcol....C2

Sleeping
4 Aluna....D5
5 Casa Familiar....B1
6 Hotel Miramar....B1
7 La Brisa Loca....C2

Eating
Agave Azul....(see 7)
8 Ben & Josep's....A3
9 Cocteleria Juancho....A5
10 Restaurante Welcome....B1

Entertainment
11 Crabs....C4
12 La Puerta....B3

Agave Azul MEXICAN $$
(☎431-6121; Calle 14 No 3-58; mains COP$18,000-25,000; ⊙dinner Mon-Sat) Fantastic Mexican food, including great burritos and quesadillas, prepared in an open kitchen and served in a fresh, cool atmosphere.

Ben & Josep's STEAKHOUSE $$$
(☎317-280-5039; Carrera 1 No 18-53; mains COP$24,000-39,000; ⊙dinner Mon-Sat) The best of the waterfront eateries. Its got a mixed menu, but the beef dishes are the best.

Entertainment

Begin your evening in the freshly remodeled Parque de los Novios, either at one of the many small bars or in the plaza itself.

La Puerta CLUB
(Calle 17 No 2-29; ⊙6pm-1am Tue & Wed, to 3am Thu-Sat) A nightclub in the finest tradition: a dance floor heaving to salsa, reggaeton, hip-hop and a side of funk, with ice-cold margaritas fueling the outrageous flirtation and dancing. It's free to get in and weekends are best.

Crabs BAR
(Calle 18 No 3-69; ⊙8pm-3am Wed-Sat) A great bar with a pool table and video screens that pay homage to some of the more obscure monsters of rock. The only place in Colombia to watch classic Captain Beefheart concerts.

Information

Some *casas de cambio* are on Calle 14 between Carreras 3 and 5.

4-72 (☎421-0180; Calle 22 No 2-08; ⊙8am-noon & 2-6pm Mon-Fri, to noon Sat)

Banco de Bogotá (Plaza de Bolívar) ATM.

Tayrona Money Exchange (Calle 14 No 4-45) Private money changer.

Tourist Office (☎421-1833; Calle 16 No 4-15; ⊙8am-noon & 2pm-6pm)

Getting There & Away

Air

The airport is 16km south of the city on the Bogotá road. Taxis here cost around COP$23,000. City buses marked 'El Rodadero Aeropuerto' will take you there in 45 minutes from Carrera 1C (COP$1500).

Bus

The bus terminal is on the southeastern outskirts of the city. Local buses (COP$1200, 45 minutes) run into town, but it's far faster in a taxi (COP$5000).

Half-a-dozen buses run daily to Bogotá (COP$110,000, 20 hours) and approximately the same number travel to Bucaramanga (COP$87,000, nine hours). Buses to Barranquilla (COP$12,000, 1¾ hours) depart every 15 to 30 minutes. Some of them go direct to Cartagena (COP$31,000, five hours), but if not, there are immediate connections in Barranquilla.

Taganga

☎5 / POP 5000

Taganga is a tiny fishing village that doesn't quite know what's hit it. Set around an iridescently turquoise horseshoe-shaped bay near Santa Marta, with beautiful coral reefs nearby, its beauty and pace of life have attracted backpackers in their thousands. It has a reputation for cheap scuba diving and lodging, easy camaraderie and a youthful, hedonistic atmosphere. It's a popular base from which to explore nearby Parque Nacional Natural Tayrona or Ciudad Perdida.

However, popularity brings pitfalls, and Taganga has its share. The town's infrastructure is not built for the massive influx of visitors and litter is a serious problem. Many still-impoverished locals feel crowded out by the foreign newcomers. Add to this a small but aggravating local petty crime spree (especially on beaches and from hotel rooms) and you have to question the impact of unregulated development on small communities.

Taganga's beach is dirty, overcrowded and not particularly attractive. Better, but still far from top class, is **Playa Grande**, a 20-minute walk or five-minute boat ride away.

Activities

Taganga is one of the world's cheapest places to get PADI (Professional Association of Diving Instructors) or NAUI (National Association of Underwater Instructors) certified. A four-day open-water course including six dives costs around COP$630,000. A two-tank dive for trained divers with lunch and all gear costs around COP$130,000. It's often possible to find even cheaper deals on offer around town, but don't be lured by low prices alone. Be sure to choose a good-quality and safe dive school.

TOP CHOICE Aquantis DIVING
(☎310-288-3099; www.aquantisdivecenter.com; Calle 18 No 1-39) The friendly, professional, and eco-aware Aquantis is the town's best, with very high standards of training and the newest equipment. Add to that great customer service (divers don't have to carry, clean or hang their gear, and it even serves proper English tea) and it wins by a country mile.

Centro de Buceo Poseidon DIVING
(☎421-9224; www.poseidondivecenter.com; Calle 18 No 1-69) Well run and equipped with a training pool, but feels like a PADI-cert assembly line.

Elemento ADVENTURE SPORTS
(☎421-0870; www.elementooutdoor.com; Calle 18 No 3-31) Offers downhill mountain biking in the Sierra Nevada and other activities.

Sleeping

Casa de Felipe HOSTEL $$
(☎316-318-9158, 421-9120; www.lacasadefelipe.com; Carrera 5A No 19-13; dm COP$16,000-25,000, s/d COP$45,000/65,000, apt COP$80,000/90,000; @☜) The original and still the best backpacker hostel in town, with lovely shady common areas, plenty of hammocks and a great lookout. The high quality rooms are spotless, with real mattresses and big windows to let in the breeze. It's a bit of a trek from the beach but worth it.

Casa D'mer HOTEL $$
(☎421-9438; www.casadmer.com; Calle 9 No 1-33; s/d COP$60,000/85,000; ☜≋) A stone's throw from the beach, this tidy small hotel has fan-cooled rooms with spacious sparkling bathrooms and a small dipping pool in the back courtyard. There are great views of the bay and surrounding mountains from its rooftop lounge.

La Tortuga HOSTEL $$
(☎421-9048; www.tortugahostel.com; Calle 9 No 3-116; dm from COP$22,000, r COP$80,000; ☜) Bright new hostel with beautiful bamboo construction, a great kitchen and fresh sea breezes high up on the sunset-facing terrace bar.

CHOOSING A DIVE SCHOOL

When choosing a dive school, consider the following factors:

- Is the dive center authorized by PADI or NAUI?
- Does the dive center look organized and professional?
- Is the dive equipment well maintained?
- Is all paperwork in order?
- Will you have a certified instructor with you underwater?
- Will this same instructor sign your scuba diving forms and certification?
- Does the price include a study book and a certification for every course you take?
- When was the last hydrostatic test carried out on the tanks (should be every five years)?
- Ask to test the tank's air. It should be smell- and taste-free.
- What is the instructor-to-student ratio?
- How is the theory component of your course taught?
- Do the firm's boats have two engines?
- Is there oxygen on board?
- Are the staff certified oxygen providers?
- Do boats have adequate and sufficient lifejackets and a radio?

WORTH A TRIP

MINCA

If you need to escape the heat of the coast, head to this small village with great coffee and good bird-watching opportunities 600m up into the Sierra Nevada above Santa Marta. It's very quiet and slow-paced: country walks alongside the Río Gaira, healthy food and early nights are the order of the day.

There is a tourist kiosk at the entrance to the village that arranges a variety of walks, birdwatching tours and adventure activities.

A steep climb behind the main church, **Casa Loma** (☎313-808-6134; hammock COP$12,000, s/d without bathroom COP$30,000/50,000, treehouse COP$60,000) is a fine new budget lodge with fantastic views and a relaxed vibe. A 15-minute walk from town, **Sans Souci** (☎310-590-9213; sanssouciminca@yahoo.com; campsite per person COP$10,000, dm COP$15,000, s/d COP$40,000/50,000, without bathrom COP$25,000/35,000; 🏊) has lovely grounds but some of the rooms are pretty drab.

Minca is reached by *colectivo* (shared taxi; COP$6000, 45 minutes) from the 'estación Minca' on the corner of Calle 11 and Carrera 12 in Santa Marta. The battered old vehicles leave when full, so if you're in a hurry pay for all four seats.

Mora Mar HOSTEL **$**
(☎421-9202; www.hostalmoramar.com; Carrera 4 No 17B-83; dm COP$15,000, s/d COP$25,000/50,000; @📶) Friendly Colombian-run hostel with a family atmosphere and a decent communal kitchen, though it's a tad run-down and the rooms can feel a little airless.

Oso Perezoso HOSTEL **$**
(☎421-8041; Calle 17 No 2-36; hammock COP$15,000, r per person from COP$22,000; 📶) Rooms are small but neat, though the stairs to them are perilous, and there's a breezy rooftop bar where you can string your own hammock. Prices include breakfast.

Eating

Taganga has new restaurants opening every week, only to close a few months later. Fishermen sell small tuna, jackfish, barracuda and snapper at decent prices at the far end of the beach.

TOP CHOICE **Babaganoush** INTERNATIONAL **$$**
(Carrera 1 No 18-22; mains from COP$15,000, full meal COP$23,500; 📶) Splash out and enjoy the best food in Taganga, served in a magnificent thatched dining area with spectacular views over the bay. Everything here is top-notch, from the authentic Thai curries to the tender filet mignon and mouthwatering desserts. Get there early to nab a table right by the railing and sip sunset cocktails.

Bitácora ITALIAN **$$**
(☎421-9121; Carrera 1 No 17-13; mains COP$14,000-24,000; ⏰breakfast, lunch & dinner) Semi-stylish spot serving everything from filet mignon in bacon-and-mushroom sauce to veggie lasagna. At night, it's good for a pre-clubbing drink and to watch the street scenes.

Los Baguettes de Maria SANDWICHES **$**
(Calle 18 No 3-47; sandwiches COP$5000-10,000; ⏰lunch & dinner Sun-Fri, dinner Sat) A genius formula: massive baguettes filled to bursting with delicious, healthy ingredients fed to starving peso-pinchers in a quiet garden.

Cafe Bonsai BAKERY **$$**
(Calle 13 No 1-07; sandwiches COP$10,000-12,000, mains COP$14,000-18,000; ⏰breakfast, lunch & dinner; ❄📶) A little slice of paradise for homesick travelers, this cute cafe has real lattes made with organic coffee from the Sierra Nevada and gourmet sandwiches on homemade sourdough bread.

Entertainment

At the time of research, Taganga's once-rocking nightlife had been seriously curtailed by a new 1am curfew on bars and discos. However, enterprising locals regularly set up poorly hidden 'private' after-parties: ask around to find out where the rumba is going to be.

El Mirador CLUB
(Carrera 1B No 18-117; ⏰8:30pm-late Wed-Sat) Here they are in their ragged tropi-cool finery; shaking and thumping, boozing and bumping – it's your 100% uncut backpacker disco paradiso. The rum flows, the speakers throb with mainstream pop, and the bayview dance floor burns with promise and passion (or maybe that's just your sunburn).

If you like discos, drinking and flirting, you'll love it here.

Information

The path to Playa Grande is a hot spot for robberies. Don't take anything you can't afford to lose.

Taganga's sole Bancolombia ATM refuses to accept many foreign cards, so bring plenty of cash from Santa Marta. Even so, sooner or later you are probably going to have to make a bank run.

Policía Nacional (Carrera 2 No 17A-38)

Getting There & Away

Taxis between Santa Marta and Taganga cost COP$7000 during the day and up to COP$10,000 at night. Buses (COP$1200, 20 minutes) run every 10 minutes. Pick them up anywhere along Carrera 5 in Santa Marta.

There is a boat service from Taganga to Cabo San Juan de Guía en Parque Tayrona (COP$40,000, one hour) at 10am daily. Park officials will meet your boat on arrival to charge the entrance fee.

Parque Nacional Natural Tayrona

One of Colombia's most popular national parks, **Tayrona** (admission Colombians/foreigners COP$13,500/36,500) is set in a supernaturally beautiful region. Its palm-fringed beaches are scattered with huge boulders that were once worshipped by the local indigenous people, after whom the park is named. It has become an essential stopoff for travelers and has plenty of places to stay and eat. Beware: many of the beaches here are tormented by treacherous currents that have killed hundreds of foolhardy daredevils.

The region was once the territory of the Tayrona indigenous people and some remnants have been found in the park, the most important being the ruins of the pre-Hispanic town of Pueblito.

The park's main entrance is in El Zaíno, on the Santa Marta–Riohacha coastal road, where you pay the entrance fee. From El Zaíno, a paved road runs for 6km to Cañaveral, on the seaside. Here you'll find the park's administrative center, a campground, ludicrously overpriced so-called 'ecohabs' (in reality these are just thatched cottages) and a restaurant.

Food inside the park is expensive and pretty poor, so self-catering is essential for longer visits. Leave all your bulky items in a garbage bag at your hostel and fill your backpack with food and bags of water. It is prohibited to bring alcohol into the park; rangers will search your bags on arrival.

Sights & Activities

The park is covered in dense jungle full of birds, squirrels and monkeys, and is perfect for exploring on foot. Set out early, before it gets too hot, and take plenty of water.

From Cañaveral, most visitors take about a 45-minute walk west to Arrecifes, where there are budget lodging and eating facilities and the coast is spectacular, dotted with massive boulders. If you have plenty of gear, consider hiring a horse (COP$16,000).

From Arrecifes, a 20-minute walk northwest along the beach will bring you to La

Parque Nacional Natural Tayrona

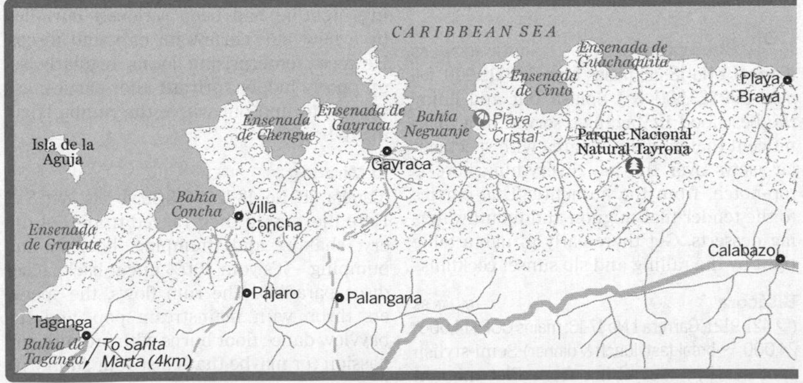

Aranilla, a sandy beach surrounded by huge boulders in a tiny bay, where the water dances with light and is flecked with sparkling golden mineral flakes. Snacks are available here. Next along is La Piscina, a deep bay partly cut off from the open sea by an underground rocky chain. Another 20-minute walk will take you to Cabo San Juan de la Guía, a beautiful cape with fantastic beaches and views. From the Cabo, a scenic path goes inland uphill to Pueblito, a 1½-hour walk away, providing some splendid tropical forest scenery. Take a flashlight, spare batteries, and watch out for snakes after dark.

Sleeping & Eating

The best budget accommodations are in the area around Arrecifes. While the beach here is not apt for swimming, you are a short walk away from several calm bays. The other option is at Cabo San Juan de la Guía, which has fantastic beaches, but is noisy and overcrowded.

Camping Don Pedro CAMPGROUND **$$**
(☎317-253-3021, 315-320-8001; campingdonpedro@hotmail.com; hammocks COP$12,000, campsite per person with/without tent hire COP$15,000/10,000, cabañas COP$80,000) A short walk back from the beach at Arrecifes, this friendly, peaceful place is hands-down the best backpacker choice in the park. In a lovely yard full of fruit trees, it serves hearty food to carnivores and vegetarians, and has a basic wood-fired kitchen for self-caterers. There is a small shop and bakery selling hot bread every morning.

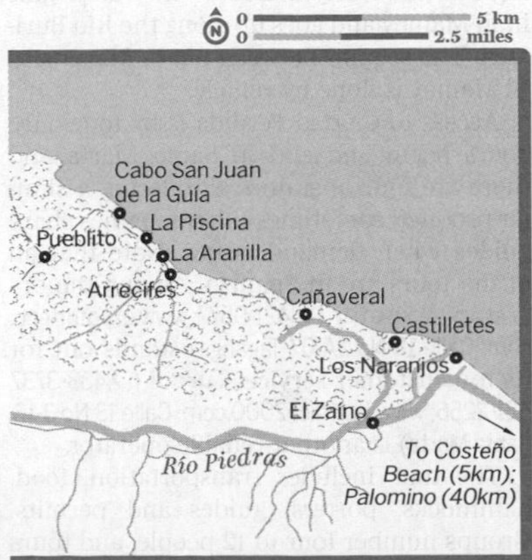

Camping Cabo San Juan de la Guía CAMPGROUND **$$**
(☎312-604-2941; www.cecabosanjuandelguia.com.co; campsite COP$15,000, hammocks with/without view COP$25,000/20,000, r COP$100,000) A fantastic location by two of Colombia's most spectacular beaches, but facilities are pathetic: four bathrooms for 300 people and hammock sheds resembling chicken factories? Instead shoot for the two private rooms and the breezy hammock area in the *mirador* (lookout) up on the rocks; there are several flights of stairs to use the bathroom, but views are phenomenal.

Bukaru CAMPGROUND **$$**
(☎321-686-1022, 316-414-6846; paraisobukaru@hotmail.com; hammocks COP$14,000, campsite per person with/without tent hire COP$20,000/10,000, r COP$120,000; 📶) A laid-back budget option behind a lagoon right on the beach at Arrecifes, where your evenings are accompanied by the sound of the crashing waves. Serves basic meals.

Panadería Vere BAKERY **$**
(Arrecifes; pastries COP$3000) Serves huge, oven-fresh chocolate loaves (calling them *pan au chocolate* doesn't do them justice) that will fill you up all day.

Getting There & Away

You can get to El Zaíno (COP$5000, one hour) by Palomino buses that depart regularly from Santa Marta's **market** (El Mercado; cnr Carrera 11 & Calle 11). From El Zaíno, catch the jeep that shuttles between the entrance and Cañaveral (COP$2000, 10 minutes) or walk for 45 minutes.

Palomino

☎5 / POP 4000

While technically in La Guajira department, this lovely Caribbean beach, a short bus ride east of Parque Nacional Natural Tayrona, is geographically and culturally tied to the Sierra Nevada. It's framed by two majestic rivers and accessed from the nondescript town of Palomino, which is little more than a truck stop on the highway.

If the beaches of Taganga seem scruffy and rowdy, and Parque Nacional Natural Tayrona feels like a ganja-scented social club, a trip here will reinvigorate your faith in the simple pleasures of swimming and wandering along an empty beach, buying a fish from a local, cooking it on a fire and eating it as the sun sets.

DON'T MISS

SURF'S UP: COSTEÑO BEACH

A short distance beyond Parque Nacional Natural (PNN) Tayrona, the new eco-friendly **lodge** (☎310-368-1191; www.costenosurf.com; hammocks COP$15,000, dm COP$25,000, huts COP$40,000, r COP$80,000) and surf camp at Costeño Beach has already established itself as an off-the-beaten-track hangout for travelers looking for a little downtime. Hardcore surfers might be a bit disappointed (this *is* the Caribbean), but it's a great place to scratch the itch if you haven't been in the water for a while. It offers classes for beginners, with knowledgeable and patient instructors. There are a variety of accommodation options, including hammocks, dorms, small thatched huts and rooms, all constructed right on the beach among coconut palms. The kitchen serves up cheap and delicious collective meals.

To get here, take a Palomino-bound bus from Santa Marta or Tayrona and ask to be let off at the entrance, which is 1km past Río Mendihuaca. From here it's a 30-40 minute walk down to the beach. It's an isolated spot, so reservations are essential.

The budget choice by the beach, **La Casa de Rosa** (☎315-445-9531; campsite with/without tent hire COP$8000/6000, hammocks COP$8000) is a refreshingly simple affair with bucket showers and a couple of hammocks slung around the yard.

Further along the beach, you'll find **Finca Escondida** (☎320-560-8280; www.chillandsurfcolombia.com; hammocks COP$20,000, dm COP$30,000, r COP$100,000), with spacious dorms and a decent restaurant. It has lovely grounds and elegant rooms, though some of the 'privates' are not particularly private, with walls that reach nowhere near the roof.

Next door is **La Sirena** (☎312-861-4850; www.ecosirena.com; rooms from COP$55,000 per person, cabañas from COP$70,000 per person), a slow-paced retreat with a variety of accommodations, including great new private huts with thatched roofs and open-air bathrooms. The restaurant serves excellent food and juices.

Buses to Palomino (COP$7000, 2½ hours) leave regularly from the market in Santa Marta. Jump off at the gas station and walk for 20 minutes down to the beach or take a *mototaxi* (motorbike rickshaw; COP$2000). Watch out for falling coconuts – about your only concern here.

Ciudad Perdida

Ciudad Perdida (literally, 'Lost City') is one of the largest pre-Columbian towns discovered in the Americas. It was built between the 11th and 14th centuries on the northern slopes of the Sierra Nevada de Santa Marta and was most probably the Tayronas' biggest urban center. During their conquest, the Spaniards wiped out the Tayronas, and their settlements disappeared under the lush tropical vegetation, as did Ciudad Perdida for four centuries, until its discovery in 1975 by *guaqueros* (robbers of pre-Columbian tombs).

Ciudad Perdida sits at an altitude of between 950m and 1300m, about 40km southeast of Santa Marta. The central part of the city is set on a ridge, from which various stone paths descend. There are about 150 stone terraces that once served as foundations for the houses. Originally the urban center was completely cleared of trees, before being reclaimed by the jungle.

While the ruins are a fascinating place, this trip is really all about the journey and the breathtaking scenery along the way. The return trip is a stiff five-day hike, challenging but not overly difficult. The trail begins in El Mamey and goes up along the Río Buritaca. The section between Santa Marta and El Mamey is done by vehicle.

Access to Ciudad Perdida is by tour only. Tours begin and end in Santa Marta and there are four operators all offering a similar product; sometimes the companies share guides when demand is low. Note that all of the tours are in Spanish. Among the operators, **Expotur** (☎421-9577; www.expotur-eco.com; Calle 18 No 2A-07, Taganga) stands out for its top customer service. **Turcol** (☎433-3737, 421-2256; www.buritaca2000.com; Calle 13 No 3-13, Santa Marta) is another reliable operator.

The tour includes transportation, food, hammocks, porters, guides and permits. Groups number four to 12 people, and tours depart year-round as soon as a group is assembled. Expect departures every day during high season. You carry your own personal belongings. Take a flashlight, a water container, diarrhea medicine, plus masses of insect repellent (this cannot be stressed strongly enough). Some travelers have returned with hundreds of bites.

The trip takes 2½ days uphill to Ciudad Perdida, half a day at the site and two days back down. The hike may be tiring due to the heat, and if it's wet (as it is most of the year) the paths are muddy. The driest period is from late December to February or early March. There are several creeks to cross, sometimes waist-deep, on the way.

La Guajira Peninsula

Say 'La Guajira' to Colombians and most people's expressions will sharpen. This remote peninsula is seen as the wild, wild east, a place beyond the back of beyond, but it rewards the intrepid with solitude and landscapes unlike any others on the continent: scenes of epic, inhospitable beauty softened by the glow of the brilliant Caribbean sea.

Riohacha (pop 170,000), the capital of La Guajira, is 175km northeast of Santa Marta and was traditionally the furthest east most travelers reached, unless they were heading for the Venezuelan border. However, there isn't much here for travelers and these days most pass right through on their way to the surreal landscapes of the Alta Guajira around Cabo de La Vela and Punta Gallinas.

The local indigenous people of the peninsula, the Wayuu, have a fierce reputation going back to the revolutionary days of Simón Bolívar, when they supported 'El Libertador' and were the only indigenous people in Colombia who knew how to ride horses and use firearms. They have never been ruled by the Spanish, and 20,000 of them fought the colonists with arms smuggled by the Dutch and English, contributing to Colombia's independence.

That said, today the Wayuu are not running off visitors but rather welcoming them into their homes, as tourism on the peninsula, still in its infancy, begins to take hold. There's still a fierce pride here, a sense of otherness and resistance that pervades all interaction. The landscape is harsh, with blistering sun, dust and diesel fumes, and goats may seem like your only friends. But as the sun dips below the horizon and you tuck into bargain lobster after a day on a deserted, pristine beach, adventurous travelers will relish the isolation of this forgotten corner of Colombia.

CABO DE LA VELA

☎5 / POP 1500

Cabo de la Vela isn't for everybody. Really. Getting here by public transportation involves a bone-shaking ride in the back of a truck, possibly driven at lunatic speed by a man with no apparent fear of death or injury. He may spend much of the journey draining beer cans in a single slug. With luck, his assistant will be reasonably sober and will manage not to fall out of the truck. Fingers crossed.

The landscape is brutal scrub, and the local dish is *viche,* goat cooked in its own fat and served with its innards. Thankfully, lobster is cheap, fresh, plentiful and exquisite, and softening the harsh landscape is the brilliantly blue Caribbean Sea that hugs a coastline of small cliffs and deserted sandy beaches, plus a fantastic sunset viewed from the lighthouse.

Sights

If you're not into kitesurfing, there's absolutely nothing to do in Cabo, except swim in the sea and take a walk to El Faro (the lighthouse) to watch the sunset.

Ojo de Agua BEACH

A short walk beyond the lighthouse, this crescent-shaped beach gets its name from a tiny freshwater pool hidden away nearby. It's less popular than Playa de Pilón, and has no facilities. It's wild, remote-feeling and craggily beautiful, with iguanas roving the clifftops.

Playa del Pilón BEACH

The most spectacular beach in the area has safe and surprisingly cool waters that lap at vivid orange-sand backed by low, rocky cliffs glowing a spectacular shade of greenish-blue. Pilón de Azucar, a high hillside, looms over the beach and provides fantastic panoramic views of the Alta Guajira.

Sleeping & Eating

You can stay with almost any Wayuu family in Cabo, under the government's *posadas turísticas* scheme (www.posadasturisticas decolombia.com). You will be sleeping in simple rooms, hammocks or more comfortable *chinchorros* (locally made woolen hammocks). Nearly all the *posadas* also have restaurants serving pretty much the same thing: fish or goat for around COP$10,000 to COP$15,000 and lobster at market price.

Posada Pujuru GUESTHOUSE **$**
(☎313-580-4205, 310-659-4189; posadapujuru@hotmail.com; hammocks COP$10,000, chinchorros COP$15,000, s/d COP$25,000/50,000) Run by an attentive Wayuu woman named Nena, this *posada* offers well-constructed rooms with private bathrooms and big lockers for those in hammocks. The restaurant serves up a tasty *pargo rojo* (red snapper) and there is a kitesurfing school attached.

Tienda Mana GUESTHOUSE **$**
(☎311-677-0538; hammock COP$10,000, chinchorro COP$18,000, r per person COP$25,000) The simple huts and hammocks next to this small shop are a good deal and you don't have to go far to stock up on supplies. Showers are via the trusty bucket method.

Getting There & Away

From Riohacha, catch a *colectivo* at **Cootrauri** (☎728-0976; Calle 15 No 5-39) to Uribia (COP$12,000, one hour); it departs when full daily from 5am to 6pm. Leave Riohacha before 1pm in order to make the Uribia–Cabo connection. The driver will know you are going to Cabo and will bundle you from the bus onto an ongoing 4WD service to Cabo (COP$12,000 to COP$15,000, two hours). You may have to wait while your vehicle is packed to bursting point with other passengers, boxes and goats.

PUNTA GALLINAS

Literally the end of the road for travelers, Punta Gallinas is the northernmost point in South America and, fittingly, is surrounded by some of the most spectacular landscapes on the continent. Immense sand dunes roll down to the Caribbean sea, while impossible iridescent bays lined with green mangroves contrast against the brilliant yellow and red sands.

Punta Gallinas is also one of the harshest environments in Colombia and not an easy place for budget travelers. It's home to just eight Wayuu families, three of which run simple guesthouses a fair way from each other. The best is **Hospedaje Luzmilla** (☎312-647-9881; luzmilita10@gmail.com; chinchorro COP$15,000, r per person COP$30,000), which has running water, a variety of accommodations and serves great meals.

To really get a feel for immense variety of landscapes you have to get out and explore either on foot, by bicycle or on a tour. Don't miss **Playa Taroa**, a magical beach accessed by sliding down a giant sand dune all the way to the water. The sense of isolation here is entrancing.

The only transport to Punta Gallinas is run by the guesthouses themselves, which means that by taking a particular boat you are locked into staying at the owner's place. Transport from Cabo de la Vela (COP$70,000 one way) involves a car to Puerto Bolívar followed by a two-hour boat trip across the open ocean. It's sometimes possible to arrange transport by road direct from Uribia (COP$80,000), a spectacular trip through the heart of the Alta Guajira.

If you are on a tight schedule, **Kai Ecotravel** (☎311-436-2830; www.kaiecotravel.com) organizes all inclusive trips with private transport, including visits to many sites along the way.

Barranquilla

☎5 / POP 1,186,600

Barranquilla seems like one long, intensely hot traffic jam hemmed in by heavy industry and Caribbean swamps. Colombia's fourth-biggest city is focused on trade and shipping, and other than its four-day Carnaval there's little to detain the traveler here.

The city's pre-Lenten Mardi Gras Carnaval is a one-way trip into bedlam, with revelers from all over the country descending on the town to drink it dry, while flinging flour and water bombs at each other – you'd be mad to miss it if you're nearby. Watch for pickpockets in the crowd, buy a disposable camera and don't dress to impress.

If you are looking for a cheap bed, **The Meeting Point** (☎368-6461; themepoho@gmail.com; Carrera 61 No 68-100; dm COP$25,000; r per person with/without bathroom COP$35,000/30,000, with air-con COP$40,000) is a friendly hostel with a family atmosphere and air-con dorms, or check out the **Hotel Colonial Inn** (☎379-0241; Calle 42 No 43-131; s/d with air-con COP$50,000/65,000, with fan COP$40,000/50,000; ❄📶). Hell-bent sightseers could kill an hour checking out the stained-glass windows at the **Catedral Metropolitana** (cnr Calle 53 & Carrera 46).

The bus terminal is 7km from the city center. It can take an hour to get there by local bus. Taxis are a better bet (COP$12,000, 20 minutes).

Cartagena

5 / POP 945,000

A fairy-tale city of romance, legends and sheer beauty, Cartagena de Indias is the most beautiful city in Colombia, with cobbled alleys, enormous balconies shrouded in bougainvillea and massive churches casting their shadows across leafy plazas.

Founded in 1533, Cartagena swiftly blossomed into the main Spanish port on the Caribbean coast and the gateway to the north of the continent. Treasures plundered from the indigenous people was stored here until the galleons were able to ship it back to Spain. It attracted pirates and in the 16th century alone suffered five sieges, the best known of which was led by Francis Drake in 1586.

In response, the Spaniards made Cartagena an impregnable port and constructed elaborate walls encircling the town, and a chain of forts. These fortifications helped save Cartagena from subsequent sieges.

Cartagena continued to flourish and during the colonial period the city was the key outpost of the Spanish empire, influencing much of Colombia's history.

Today, Cartagena has expanded dramatically and is surrounded by vast suburbs. It is Colombia's largest port and an important industrial center. Nevertheless, the old walled town has changed very little.

Cartagena has also become a fashionable seaside resort. A modern tourist district has sprung up on Bocagrande and El Laguito, south of the old town. Most backpackers, however, stay in the historic part of town.

Cartagena's climate is hot but a fresh breeze blows in each evening, making this a pleasant time to stroll around the city. Theoretically, the driest period is from December to April, while October and November are the wettest months.

Sights

Cartagena's old town is its principal attraction, particularly the inner walled town consisting of the historical districts of El Centro and San Diego, with many beautiful squares and flower-bedecked balconies. Almost every street is a postcard-worthy scene of 16th- and 17th-century architecture.

Getsemaní, the outer walled town, is not so well preserved but there is more street life here, a few good drinking holes and one lovely square, **Plaza Trinidad**.

The old town is surrounded by **Las Murallas**, the thick walls built to protect it. Construction was begun toward the end of the 16th century after the attack by pirate Francis Drake; until that time Cartagena was almost completely unprotected. The project took two centuries to complete, due to repeated storm damage and pirate attacks.

Most churches have entrance fees, but if you are on a tight budget, it is possible to visit for free during mass; there are usually services around 5-6pm. Many museums are free on the last Sunday of the month.

Castillo de San Felipe de Barajas FORTRESS
(Av Arévalo; adult/child COP$17,000/8500; 8am-6pm) Imposing Castillo de San Felipe de Barajas is the greatest fortress constructed by the Spanish in any of their colonies. Work begun in 1639 but was not completed until some 150 years later; it proved to be truly unassailable and was never taken. Don't miss the impressive walk through the complex system of tunnels.

Palacio de la Inquisición MUSEUM
(Plaza de Bolívar; adult/child COP$14,000/10,000; 9am-6pm Mon-Sat, 10am-4pm Sun) The haunting Palace of the Inquisition is one of the finest buildings in town, an excellent example of late-colonial architecture. Heretics were denounced here and about 800 folk were condemned to death and executed. The palace is today a museum, displaying the Inquisitors' instruments of torture and a collection of pre-Columbian pottery.

Convento & Iglesia de San Pedro Claver MUSEUM
(664-4991; Plaza de San Pedro Claver; adult/child COP$8000/5000; 8am-6pm Mon-Fri, to 5pm Sat & Sun) This convent is named in honor of Spanish-born monk Pedro Claver (1580–1654), who lived here ministering to the slaves brought from Africa. It's a monumental three-story building surrounding a tree-filled courtyard and part of it is open to visitors as a museum. The adjacent church has an imposing stone facade and the remains of Claver are contained in a glass coffin in the high altar.

Plaza de Bolívar PLAZA
A leafy plaza in a particularly beautiful area of the old town. Its fountains keep it cool and fresh, and local dance bands practice here in the evenings. It's a great place to spend a few hours, but bring repellent at dusk.

Cartagena – Old Town

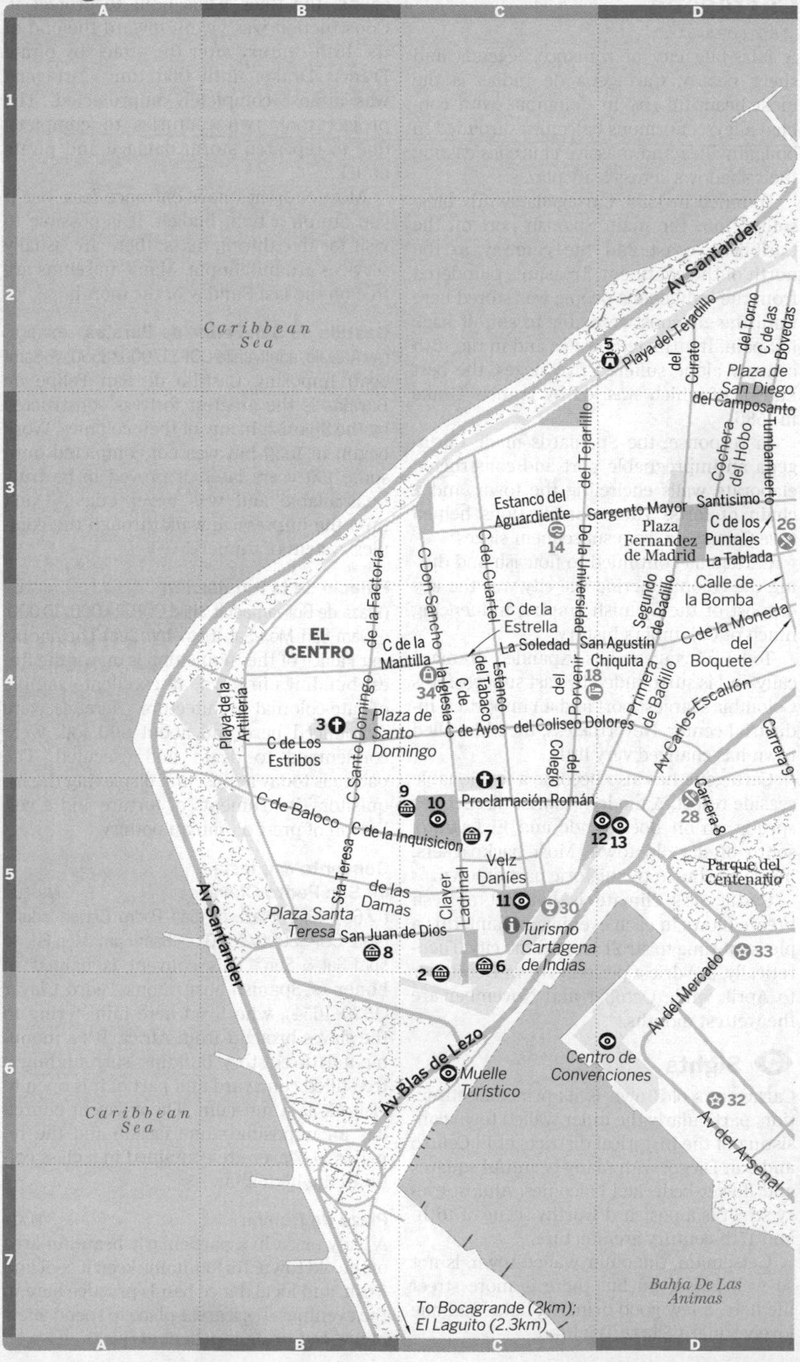

Convento de la Popa CHURCH
(adult/child COP$8000/6000; ⏲8am-6pm) This convent, perched on top of a 150m hill beyond the San Felipe fortress, was founded by the Augustinians in 1607. It has a nice chapel and a lovely flower-filled patio, and offers panoramic views of the city. Take a taxi – there's no public transportation and there have been robberies. Pay around COP$20,000 round trip.

Iglesia de Santo Domingo CHURCH
(Plaza de Santo Domingo; adult/child COP$12,000/8000; ⏲9am-7pm Tue-Sat, noon-8pm Sun) The city's oldest church has a spacious and lofty interior. Entry includes a 20-minute self-guided audio tour, offered in a variety of languages.

Puerta del Reloj GATE
The main gateway to the inner town was what is now the Puerta del Reloj (the clock tower was added in the 19th century). Just behind it is the **Plaza de los Coches**, a square once used as a slave market, where there's a monument to Pedro de Heredia, the founder of the city. On the other side of the plaza is **El Portal de los Dulces**, an arcaded walkway where you can buy dozens of local sweets.

Catedral CHURCH
(adult/child COP$8000 incl audio tour; ⏲10:30am-7pm) The cathedral was begun in 1575 but was partially destroyed by Francis Drake in 1586, and not completed until 1612. The dome on the tower was added early in the 20th century.

Plaza de la Aduana PLAZA
The oldest and largest square in the old town. It was used as a parade ground and all government buildings were gathered around it.

Museo del Oro Zenú MUSEUM
(☎660-0778; www.banrepcultural.org/cartagena; Plaza de Bolívar; ⏲10am-1pm & 3-7pm Tue-Fri, 10am-1pm & 2-5pm Sat, 11am-4pm Sun) On Plaza de Bolívar, the Museo del Oro Zenú has a good collection of gold and pottery from the Zenú culture. Its air-conditioning is set to stun, making it an oasis.

Museo de Arte Moderno MUSEUM
(Plaza de San Pedro Claver; adult/child COP$5000/2000; ⏲9am-noon & 3-6pm Mon-Thu, 9am-noon & 3-7pm Fri, 10am-1pm Sat, 5pm-9pm Sun) The Museum of Modern Art is housed in the 17th-century former Royal Customs House.

Cartagena – Old Town

Sights

1	Catedral	C5
2	Convento & Iglesia de San Pedro Claver	C6
3	Iglesia de Santo Domingo	B4
4	Las Bóvedas	E1
5	Las Murallas	D2
6	Museo de Arte Moderno	C5
7	Museo del Oro Zenú	C5
8	Museo Naval del Caribe	B5
9	Palacio de la Inquisición	C5
10	Plaza de Bolívar	C5
11	Plaza de la Aduana	C5
12	Plaza de los Coches	D5
13	Puerta del Reloj	D5

Activities, Courses & Tours

14	Diving Planet	C3

Sleeping

15	Casa Viena	E5
16	Casa Villa Colonial	F5
17	El Viajero Cartagena	E3
18	Hotel El Viajero	C4
19	Hotel Familiar	E5
20	Mama Waldy	E6
21	Media Luna Hostel	E5

Eating

22	Café de la Trinidad	E6
23	Donde Magola	E3
24	Gato Negro	E5
25	Getsemaní Café Bar	E5
26	Girasoles	D3
27	I Balconi	E5
28	Ostrería del Mar Rojo	D5
29	Restaurante Coroncoro	E5

Drinking

30	Donde Fidel	C5

Entertainment

	Café Havana	(see 27)
31	Ciudad Movil	F5
32	Mister Babilla	D6
33	Quiebra-Canto	D5

Shopping

34	Ábaco	C4

It presents temporary exhibitions from its own collection, including works by Alejandro Obregón, one of Colombia's most remarkable painters.

Museo Naval del Caribe MUSEUM
(Calle San Juan de Dios No 3-62; adult/child COP$8000/4000; 10am-5:30pm) Located in a reputedly haunted former hospital, this museum traces the naval history of Cartagena and the Caribbean.

Las Bóvedas HISTORIC BUILDING
At the northern tip of the old town are Las Bóvedas, 23 dungeons built in the defensive walls at the end of the 18th century. This was the last construction done in colonial times, and was destined for military purposes. Today the dungeons are tourist shops.

Activities

Cartagena has grown into an important scuba-diving center. However, prices are far lower in Taganga.

Diving Planet DIVING
(664-2171; www.divingplanet.org; Calle Estanco del Aguardiente No 5-94) Two-tank dives including transportation, lunch and certified instructors cost COP$240,000. Also offers PADI-certification courses (COP$963,000).

Courses

Crazy Salsa DANCE
(660-1809; www.crazysalsa.net; Calle Tumbamuertos, Local 2, San Diego; private instruction COP$70,000, group classes COP$20,000-25,000) Latin dance classes mainly in salsa and merengue.

Festivals & Events

Hay Festival ARTS
(www.hayfestival.com) The Latin American version of the acclaimed literature and arts festival is a must-attend event for culture vultures in January.

Festival Internacional de Cine CINEMA
(www.ficcifestival.com) Held shortly before Semana Santa, usually in March, this is Latin America's oldest film festival.

Concurso Nacional de Belleza BEAUTY PAGEANT
(www.srtacolombia.org) National beauty pageant held on November 11 to celebrate Cartagena's independence day. The event, also known as the Carnaval de Cartagena or Fiestas del 11 de Noviembre, is the city's

most important annual bash. The parallel fringe beauty contests held around town are much more fun than the silicon-inspired main event.

Sleeping

Most backpackers stay in Getsemaní. Once a red light district, things have changed dramatically with the influx of travelers. Hostels, hip bars and restaurants now far outnumber flophouses and brothels and the streets, while still a little edgy, are for the most part safe to explore. There are also a number of new budget accommodations in the inner walled town.

Media Luna Hostel HOSTEL **$$**
(664-3423; Calle de la Media Luna 10-46, Getsemaní, dm COP$25,000, s/d COP$50,000/90,000;) Set in a lovely renovated colonial mansion, this megahostel is popular with the party crowd, attracted by the rocking bar, rooftop lounge and small but refreshing pool.

Casa Viena HOSTEL **$**
(664-6242; www.casaviena.com; Calle San Andrés 30-53, Getsemaní; dm COP$20,000, s/d COP$45,000/48,000, without bathroom COP$28,000/44,000;) Traditional backpacker hangout with the most comprehensive and trustworthy tourist info in town. The rooms are smallish and a little dark but are good value, and the dorm is kept cool by efficient air-conditioning.

Mama Waldy HOSTEL **$**
(645-6805; Calle la Sierpe 29-03; dm with/without air-con COP$20,000/17,000;) A refreshing antidote to the corporate hostel blues, this intimate new hostel is run by a pair of young brothers in their former family home. It's a little makeshift at times but it's cheap, laid-back and the enthusiastic owners will lend you a bike to get around.

Hotel Familiar HOSTEL **$**
(664-2464; Calle del Guerrero 29-66, Getsemaní; s/d COP$23,000/40,000;) No-frills locally run option that offers a little more peace and quiet than other budget spots. Avoid the airless boxes upstairs – the rooms around the rear courtyard are the nicest. Don't expect shower curtains or toilet seats.

El Viajero Cartagena HOSTEL **$$**
(660-2598; www.hostelcartagena.com; Calle 7 Infantes 9-45, Cartagena de Indias; dm from COP$26,000, s/d without bathroom COP$55,000/110,000;) Not to be confused with the nearby hotel of the same name, this large centrally located hostel is a good choice for its air-conditioned dorms set around a sunny courtyard. The bathroom-less private rooms are overpriced. Breakfast included.

Hotel El Viajero HOTEL **$$**
(664-3289; www.hotelelviajero.com; Calle del Porvenir 35-68; s/d with air-con COP$70,000/90,000, with fan COP$60,000/80,000;) This neat 14-room hotel has a fine San Diego location, a kitchen for guests and a bright, spacious common area.

Casa Villa Colonial HOTEL **$$**
(664-5421; www.casavillacolonial.com; Calle de la Media Luna 10-89, Getsemaní; s/d COP$90,000/140,000,) Fantastically friendly service, comfortable beds and air-con in this wonderfully restored family-owned hotel.

Eating

Cartagena is a good place to eat, especially at the top end, but cheap places are also plentiful.

Very characteristic of Cartagena are *butifarras* (small smoked meatballs), only sold on the street by *butifarreros,* who walk along with big pots, striking them with a knife to get your attention.

Dozens of spots in the old town serve *almuerzos* for COP$6000 to COP$8000. Among the best are **Restaurante Coroncoro** (664-2648; Calle Tripita y Media 31-28, Getsemaní; breakfast, lunch & dinner) and **Café de la Trinidad** (Plaza Trinidad, Getsemaní; set meals COP$7000). For veggie meals, try **Girasoles** (664-5239; Calle de los Puntales 37-01; set meals COP$5000; breakfast & lunch;). Small stalls in Plaza Trinidad serve up cheap and tasty street food in the evenings.

Donde Magola FAST FOOD **$**
(Calle Portobelo 10-94; snacks COP$1500-3500) Head to this humble diner for some excellent hangover-busting *fritos* (fried food). This is fast food *costeño*-style – everything is cheap, greasy and delicious, and comes accompanied by six varieties of sauce. The *arepa de huevo* with shrimp is phenomenal.

I Balconi PIZZERIA **$$**
(660-9880; Calle del Guerrero 29-146, 2nd fl; pastas COP$9000-12,000, pizzas COP$10,000-20,000; lunch & dinner) Stylishly perched on the 2nd floor of an imposing Getsemaní mansion, this Italian-owned place serves up the best pizza in Cartagena, if not Colombia.

The many balconies let in plenty of breeze and there's cool art on the walls.

Gato Negro CAFE $
(660-0958; Calle San Andrés 30-39, Getsemaní; mains COP$7000-8000; breakfast & lunch;) A peaceful breakfast spot with great omelets and intensely welcome muesli, with free wi-fi while you wait. Maintains a current list of sailing boat departures to Panama.

Ostrería del Mar Rojo SEAFOOD $$
(cnr Av Venezuela & Carrera 8; Ceviche COP$5000-22,000) The best of many *coctelerías* on Av Venezuela, this unpretentious local institution serves up fresh seafood delights in polystyrene cups. Look for the giant sombrero.

Getsemaní Café Bar COLOMBIAN $
(317-781-5694; Calle San Andrés 30-34, Getsemaní; mains COP$8000-15,000; breakfast, lunch & dinner) Set in an old arched building, GCB serves piping-hot à-la-carte dishes and filling Colombian snacks. Also prepares a quality set lunch. Cheap and delicious.

Kiosco El Bony SEAFOOD $$$
(Av 1 Bocagrande; mains COP$15,000-30,000; 10am-10pm Mon-Sun) Right on the beach at Bocagrande and owned by ex-Olympic boxer Bonifacio Avila, El Bony is famous for its vast fish lunches. It's thronged with Colombians on weekends.

Drinking & Entertainment

Donde Fidel BAR
(664-3127; El Portal de los Dulces 32-09, Centro; 11am-2am) The best sound system in Cartagena belting out classic salsa. Chairs in the square are a great, breezy spot to start the night.

Café Havana CLUB
(664-7568; cnr Calles del Guerrero & de la Media Luna, Getsemaní; 8pm-4am Thu-Sat, 5pm-2am Sun) Live salsa and the best mojitos in Colombia, with a mixed, friendly crowd of locals and tourists. Pricey but worth a splurge.

Safari CLUB
(Av Pedro de Heredia No 39-246, Sector Iglesia Maria Auxiliadora) 'Salsa is an orgasm' reads the sign above the entrance and by the looks of some of those dancing here it's true. In a working class neighborhood, this unpretentious open-air club is where ordinary cartageneros let loose and dance. It's a COP$8000 taxi ride from the center but free entrance and cheap drinks make it worth the trip.

Quiebra-Canto CLUB
(664-1372; Camellon de los Martines, Edificio Puente del Sol, Getsemaní; 7pm-4am Tue-Sat) Popular salsa place that gets packed to the rafters with serious dancers. The best place in the center to show off your moves.

Mister Babilla CLUB
(664-7005; Av del Arsenal 8B-137, Getsemaní; 9pm-4am) A fun place to get drunk, dance and flirt.

Ciudad Movil CULTURAL CENTER
(311-652-0842; movil.ciudad@gmail.com; Calle del Espirito Santo 29-140) Hip cultural center with regular concerts. During the day they host workshops including yoga, zumba and dance.

Shopping

Ábaco BOOKSTORE
(664-8338; cnr Calles de la Iglesia & de la Mantilla; 9am-8:30pm Mon-Sat, 4-8:30pm Sun) English-language choices, coffee, air-conditioning and free wi-fi.

Information

Money

Citibank (Av Venezuela, Edificio Citibank, 1st fl)

BBVA (Plaza de la Aduana) Reliable ATM.

Giros & Finanzas (Av Venezuela 8A-87) Agent for Western Union.

Post

4-72 (Calle 8B, Edificio Villa Anamaria, Local 1; 8am-5pm Mon-Fri, to noon Sat)

Tourist Information

Turismo Cartagena de Indias (660-1583; www.turismocartagenadeindias.com; Plaza de la Aduana; 9am-1pm & 3-7pm Mon-Sat, 9am-5pm Sun) Main tourist office. English speaking staff are very efficient.

This is Cartagena (www.ticartagena.com) Comprehensive website covering events and attractions.

Getting There & Away

Air

All major Colombian carriers operate flights to and from Cartagena. The airport is in the suburb of Crespo, 3km northeast of the old city, and is serviced by frequent local buses that depart from various points, including India Catalina and Av Santander. *Colectivos* to Crespo (COP$1500) depart from India Catalina. A private cab is COP$11,000.

Boat

At the time of research, the on-again-off-again plans for a new ferry service between Cartagena and Colón in Panama seemed to have been shelved indefinitely. This leaves travelers with the traditional way of getting to Panama by sailboat. There are various yachts that take travelers from Cartagena to Colón via the Kuna Yala (San Blas) Archipelago (Panama) and vice versa. The trip takes four to six days and normally includes a couple of days at San Blas for snorkeling and spear fishing. It costs about US$550. Your experience will be influenced greatly by your choice of captain and boat, so take some time to choose and get references from other travelers. Both Casa Viena and Gato Negro maintain departure schedules.

Bus

The bus terminal is on the eastern outskirts of the city; it can take up to an hour to get there from the old town. Large green-and-red-signed air-conditioned Metrocar buses make the trip every 15 to 30 minutes (COP$2000, 40 minutes). In the center you can catch them on Av Santander. A taxi will run around COP$15,000.

Half-a-dozen buses go daily to Bogotá (COP$130,000, 20 hours) and another half-a-dozen to Medellín (COP$85,000, 13 hours). Buses to Barranquilla run every 15 minutes or so (COP$10,000, two hours), and some continue on to Santa Marta (COP$20,000, four hours); if not, just change in Barranquilla. Unitransco has one bus to Mompox at 7:30am (COP$51,000, eight hours). For Turbo, take one of the frequent departures to Montería (COP$55,000, 4½ hours) and change.

Expreso Brasilia (☎663-2119; www.expresobrasilia.com) and **Expresos Amerlujo** (☎653-0907) operate daily buses to Caracas (COP$220,000, 20 hours), and Venezuela via Maracaibo (COP$135,000, 12 hours).

Around Cartagena

ISLAS DEL ROSARIO

This archipelago, about 35km southwest of Cartagena, consists of 27 small coral islands, including some tiny islets only big enough for a single house. The whole area has been protected as **Parque Nacional Corales del Rosario y de San Bernardo**.

Cruises through the islands are well established. Tours depart year-round from the Muelle Turístico (Turismo Cartagena de Indias) in Cartagena. Boats leave between 8am and 9am daily and visit a number of islands and Playa Blanca, before returning around 4pm to 6pm. The cruise office at the muelle sells tours in big boats for around COP$40,000. Avoid the freelance salesmen who will try to sell you the same tour for double the price. It's easier to arrange the tour through one of the budget hostels in Cartagena. Tours normally include lunch, but not the entrance fee to the park (COP$6000), the aquarium (COP$20,000) on one of the islands or the port tax (COP$12,000).

PLAYA BLANCA

☎5

This is one of the most beautiful beaches around Cartagena. It's about 20km southwest of the city, on Isla de Barú, and is a usual stop for the boat tours to the Islas del Rosario. The place is also good for snorkeling, as a coral reef begins just off the beach. You can hire snorkeling gear for around COP$3000.

The beach has some rustic places to stay and eat but when it's dry there is no fresh water, so don't plan on showering while here. The best option is **Los Corales** (☎318-385-0378; anlydete@yahoo.com; hammocks COP$7000-10,000, r COP$50,000), which has hammocks with nets, big lockers and elevated rustic huts. It also serves tasty meals.

Direct boat services (COP$25,000, one hour) from the Bazurto to Playa Blanca depart every morning (except Sunday) between 8am and 9:30am. Coming back, it's usually possible to jump on one of the Isla del Rosario tour boats for around COP$10,000.

The cheapest way to reach the beach is to take a bus from Mercado Bazurto to Pasocaballos (COP$1500), take a boat across the river (COP$1000) and hire a *colectivo* or *mototaxi* to Playa Blanca (COP$10,000). Plan about three hours for the trip.

VOLCÁN DE LODO EL TOTUMO

About 50km northeast of Cartagena, on the bank of the shallow Ciénaga del Totumo, is a 15m mound that looks like a miniature volcano, but instead of lava it spews mud forced out by the pressure of gases emitted by decaying organic matter underground.

You can climb to the top by specially built stairs, then go down into the crater and have a lukewarm mud bath (entry COP$5000). The mud contains minerals acclaimed for their therapeutic properties. Once you've finished your session, go down and wash the mud off in the *ciénaga* (lagoon).

To go there independently take a bus from Cartagena's city center to its bus terminal (COP$2000). From there take the hourly bus to Galerazamba and get off at Loma de Arena (COP$7000). From there it's a 45-minute walk, or take a *mototaxi* (COP$2000). The whole one-way trip takes about 2½ hours. The last bus back from Loma de Arena leaves around 3pm. Leave Cartagena before 10am – otherwise you'll miss it.

Mompox

5 / POP 42,600

Stranded on an island in the eastern backwaters of the muddy Río Magdalena, Mompox is a town lost in space and time. Founded in 1537, 230km southeast of Cartagena, Mompox became an important port – all merchandise from Cartagena passed to the interior of the colony through here, and several imposing churches and many luxurious mansions were built.

Toward the end of the 19th century shipping was diverted to the other branch of the Magdalena as the river silted up, ending the town's prosperity. Mompox has been left in isolation and little has changed since. It's now a Unesco World Heritage Site.

In the evenings, the residents sit on the narrow streets and creak back and forth in rocking chairs (the town is famous for its furniture) and hundreds of bats flit about in a surreal gothic-tropical scene.

Sights

Mompox is a place to take a wander. Most of the central streets are lined with fine whitewashed colonial houses with characteristic metal-grill windows, imposing doorways and lovely hidden patios. Six colonial churches complete the scene; all are interesting, though rarely open. Don't miss the **Iglesia de Santa Bárbara** (cnr Calle 14 & Carrera 1), with its Moorish-style tower, unique in Colombian religious architecture.

Museo Cultural MUSEUM
(Carrera 2 No 17-20; admission COP$3000; 8am-noon & 2-4pm Mon-Fri, 9am-noon Sat) A collection of religious art in a house once occupied by Simón Bolívar.

Jardín Botánico GARDEN
(Calle 14; entry by donation; 8am-5pm) A small botanical garden with lots of hummingbirds and butterflies. Knock on the gate and the eccentric owner will let you in.

Festivals & Events

Semana Santa RELIGIOUS
(Holy Week) Celebrations are very elaborate in Mompox. The solemn processions circle the streets for several hours on Maundy Thursday and Good Friday nights.

Sleeping

Residencias Villa de Mompox GUESTHOUSE $
(685-5208; Real del Medio 14-108; s/d/tr with air-con COP$30,000/50,000/70,000, with fan COP$20,000/35,000/50,000;) Low-priced air-con rooms set around a small garden. The polystyrene ceilings detract from the colonial charm but it's clean, friendly and centrally located. A great budget choice.

La Casa Amarilla HOSTEL $$
(685-6326, 301-362-7065; www.lacasaamarillamompos.com; Carrera 1 No 13-59; dm COP$18,000, s/d COP$95,000/140,000, ste COP$250,000;) Excellent, renovated riverside home with friendly, professional service. Dorms have just four beds in each while the private rooms are spacious with air-con and include breakfast. Rents bikes and organizes tours of the wetlands.

Eating & Drinking

Plaza Santa Domingo has passable street food for a few thousand pesos a plate.

TOP CHOICE **Comedor Costeño** COLOMBIAN $
(685-5263; Calle de la Albarrada 18-45; meals COP$7000-14,000; 7am-5pm) Fantastic riverfront restaurant serving up big portions of delicious local specialties at outdoor tables. *Bocachica* fish is a specialty. Also serves hearty breakfasts.

Bar Luna de Mompós BAR
(Calle de la Albarrada; 6pm-1am Mon-Thu, to 3am Fri-Sun) Atmospheric riverside boozing joint in an elegantly decaying colonial house with old musical instruments hanging on the walls. Go early to grab an outside table.

Information

BBVA (Plaza de Bolívar) Reliable ATM.

Getting There & Away

Mompox is well off the main routes, but can be reached by road and river from the coast or by road from Bogotá. Cartagena is the usual departure point. Unitransco has one direct bus leaving Cartagena at 6:30am daily (COP$51,000, eight hours). It's faster to take one of the regular buses to Magangué (COP$35,000, four hours), change for a boat to Bodega (COP$7000, 20 minutes, frequent departures until about 3pm) and continue by *colectivo* to Mompox (COP$12,000, 40 minutes).

Departing from Bogotá, take an overnight bus to El Banco, Magdalena (COP$90,000, 12 hours) and continue to Mompox by jeep (COP$30,000, two hours).

Note that El Banco bus terminal has dozens of incredibly hectic, pestering touts who want you on 'their' bus. They will surround you and bellow at you. Stay cool, lower your shades, and make your own choice.

DON'T MISS

WHAT AN ASS!

Colombia has plenty of entertaining festivals, but few are as bizarre as the **Festival del Burro** (Donkey Festival), a colorful five-day event in the small town of San Antero, Córdoba. Held during Semana Santa (Holy Week), the festival includes concerts, dance, and traditional foods, but the undeniable highlights are the *desfile de burros disfrazados*, where donkeys are dressed as celebrities and paraded through town, and the coronation of the king and queen donkeys. Keep your eyes peeled for the equine Shakira or you may even spot Burrock Obama! Charge your batteries, you're guaranteed to get some classic 'only-in-Colombia' shots.

Golfo de Urabá

The pristine Golfo de Urabá is home to charming small towns nestled between the dense jungle-covered mountains of the Darién and brilliant Caribbean sea. Most of the region is undeveloped, with the exception of the ultra-chilled getaway spots of Capurganá and Sapzurro right by the Panamanian border. The gateway to the area is the scruffy port of Turbo.

TURBO

☎4 / POP 139,000

Turbo is a gritty port town and maritime gateway to Capurganá and Sapzurro. Unless you are coming on the night bus from Medellín, you will have to spend the night here before taking the morning boat.

Sleeping & Eating

Hotel Carnaval HOTEL $

(☎313-704-3319, 827-2312; cnr Av 14 & Calle 104; r COP$20,000) A 10-minute walk from the dock, in front of the municipal water tank, this great-value hotel has spotless rooms with comfortable mattresses and cable TV (which you'll need in Turbo).

Residencias Florida HOTEL $

(☎311-327-2569, 827-3531; Carrera 13 No 99A-56; s/d with fan COP$20,000/30,000) This shabby but friendly hotel right by the dock is an OK option if you arrive late.

Panadería Diana BAKERY $

(Carrera 14 No 101-67; meals COP$5000) Cheap, filling meals and baked products.

Information

Banco de Bogotá (Calle 101 No 12-131) ATM.

Getting There & Away

From Cartagena, take a bus to Montería (COP$55,000, 4½ hours) and change for Turbo (COP$41,000, four hours). Leave Cartagena before 11am to make it to Turbo the same day. **Cootransuroccidente** (www.cootransuroccidente.com; Carrera 14 No 99A-49) runs to and from Medellín almost hourly from 5am to 10pm (COP$62,000, eight hours).

Boats to Capurganá (COP$55,000, 2½ hours) leave daily from the port at 8:30am. Boats fill up quickly, so arrive one hour early to buy your ticket or, if possible, buy it the day before. The tickets are numbered and the first arrivals get to choose the best seats. It can be a horrifically bumpy journey. Sit near the back of the boat and buy a trash bag at the dock (COP$1000) to keep your luggage dry. You'll laugh about this journey one day – if you don't bite your tongue off and smash all your teeth en route.

CAPURGANÁ

☎4 / POP 2000

Capurganá is everything Taganga once was: a Caribbean backwater where you drop your gear the second you arrive. With its painted wooden houses, lack of cars, and extremely laid-back atmosphere, it has a distinct island vibe. Children fish from the pier in the afternoon, the taxi service is a horse and cart, and locals are in no rush to do anything.

Tourism here is dominated by all-inclusive hotels for wealthy Colombians, though this is changing, and there are a number of backpacker-friendly accommodations.

There are fantastic nature-watching opportunities nearby, and you can spot hundreds of varieties of bird and howler monkey troops. Fishing in the bay is said to be excellent, with huge fish landed often.

Electricity is intermittent and usually only runs until 2am, so be sure to pack plenty of

GETTING TO PANAMA

It's now possible to get to Panama from Colombia without flying or taking a sailboat trip. The basic route is Turbo–Capurganá by boat, Capurganá–Puerto Obaldia (Panama) by boat, and Puerto Obaldia–Panama City by plane. It's slow, but it's safe and it's the cheapest way to pass from South to Central America.

» Ensure your yellow fever vaccination is up to date. Panama demands it.

» Get your Colombian exit stamp at the **Migración Colombia** (☎311-746-6234; ⏲8am-5pm Mon-Fri, 9am-4pm Sat) office in Capurganá the day before heading to Puerto Obaldia. Spend the night in Capurganá; it's lovely.

» Catch a motorboat from Capurganá's harbor to the first town in Panama, Puerto Obaldia (COP$25,000, 45 minutes). These leave at 7am Tuesday, Thursday and Sunday, and connect with onward flights from Puerto Obaldia to Panama City.

» Get a Panama entry stamp at Panamanian immigration when you arrive. From here, you can fly onward to Panama City (US$92) with **Air Panama** (☎507-316-9000; www.flyairpanama.com) on Tuesday, Thursday and Sunday. Puerto Obaldia is a particularly unpleasant place – make sure you have a confirmed flight reservation before leaving Colombia or you'll be scurrying back. Panama's currency is the US dollar.

It is also possible to travel on tour boats from Capurganá to Cartí in Panama, spending a couple of days in the idyllic San Blas islands. The trip takes three days and costs around US$350. **The Darién Gapster** (www.thedariengapster.com) has regular departures.

repellent and a mosquito net for when the fans whir down. Note that no addresses are given, because none exist. The town is *tiny*.

Activities

The diving here beats Taganga on a few important points: you can dive without a wetsuit and the coral is better preserved and closer to land. Though prices are higher, groups are smaller, and attention is more personalized. If groups of eight can be formed, you can dive the waters of the nearby Kuna Yala indigenous reserve, some of the most pristine and unfished coral in the Caribbean.

Dive and Green DIVING
(☎316-781-6255; www.diveandgreen.com; r per person COP$25,000; ⏲8:30am-12:30pm & 2-5:30pm) Located directly left from the dock. Offers two-tank dives costing COP$190,000. PADI certification costs COP$820,000 and snorkel gear is COP$20,000 per day. Also rents simple but comfortable wooden rooms with sea views.

WALKING

Sapzurro is a short and fairly easy hike through the teeming jungle just outside Capurganá. It's well signposted and you don't need a guide. **El Cielo** is another popular jungle route, with natural *piscinas* (swimming pools) to cool down in. **Aguacate** is also a pleasant one-hour walk. Wear walking shoes or trainers for all of these, as it gets muddy.

Sleeping

Cabañas Darius HOTEL $
(☎310-397-7768, 314-6225-638; www.cdarius.blogspot.com; r per person COP$35,000) Tucked away in a peaceful wooded area, this cozy Capurganá cabin has neat and tidy rooms and bathrooms with freshly tiled floors and a large outdoor kitchen for guests. A 'taxi' here is COP$10,000.

Posada del Gecko GUESTHOUSE $
(☎314-221-7154; www.posadadelgecko.com; r per person with/without bathroom COP$20,000/15,000, with air-con COP$25,000) Friendly guesthouse with simple wooden rooms and nicer options with air-con and private bathrooms. Attached bar-restaurant serves authentic pizza and pastas and is a fine place for a drink.

Luz de Oriente HOTEL $
(☎310-371-4902; s/d COP$30,000/60,000; 📶) Chilled little hotel-restaurant offering comfortable rooms with small balconies overlooking the dock.

Hostal Los Delfines HOTEL $
(☎310-421-5703; dm COP$12,000, r per person COP$15,000-20,000; ❄) This is a great spot for the price – rooms include TVs, private

bathrooms, and patio hammocks and air-conditioning (when the generator's going).

Luna Verde Hostel HOSTEL $
(☎313-812-7172; www.capurgana-sanblas.com; dm COP$10,000, r per person without bathroom COP$14,000) Very rustic rooms in a colorful wooden house. Kitchen access is COP$2000. The Italian owner organizes budget trips to the San Blas with connections to Panama City.

Hostal Capurganá HOSTEL $
(☎316-482-3665; Calle de Comercio; dm COP$14,000, r per person COP$22,000) Professionally run place on the main drag with fresh, fan-cooled rooms. Accepts credit-card payments.

Eating & Drinking

There is decent street food to be found around town, including fantastic fish empanadas (COP$1000) in front of the clinic. There are a couple of noisy bars around the park and one disco on Playa Blanca, which gets packed with visiting *paisas* (residents of Antioquia).

TOP CHOICE **Josefina's** SEAFOOD $$
(☎310-627-1578; mains COP$18,000-35,000; ⊙lunch & dinner) Josefina serves vast portions of fresh seafood cooked with elegant simplicity. Her *pulpo al ajillo* (garlic octopus) is breathtaking. By the time you read this, she should be installed in her new restaurant on Playa Blanca, so ask around.

Capurgarepa COLOMBIAN $
(arepas COP$3000-7000, meals COP$8000-12,000; ✎) Right by the park, this hole-in-the-wall prepares delicious grilled *arepas* with all kinds of savory fillings and cheap meals. With advance notice they also make tasty vegetarian dishes.

Information

Bring enough funds with you, as the closest ATM is in Turbo.

Capurganá Tours (☎824-3173; ⊙8am-noon & 2-6pm Mon-Sat) Friendly travel agency on the town's only commercial street. Agent for Western Union and sells tickets for buses from Turbo.

Migración Colombia (☎311-746-6234; ⊙8am-5pm Mon-Fri, 9am-4pm Sat) Immigration services. Near the church, three minutes' walk from the boat harbor.

Getting There & Away

There are only two ways to reach Capurganá and Sapzurro. Cheapest is to catch a boat from Turbo.

ADA (☎1-800-051-4232; www.ada-aero.com) operates flights from Medellín on Monday, Tuesday, Thursday, Friday and Saturday at noon in low season. It's not cheap at around COP$300,000 each way. Sometimes there are online deals available.

SAPZURRO

☎4 / POP 1000

Sapzurro is an archetypal small Caribbean town, with children strolling the narrow streets carrying fresh fish, elderly ladies with hair curlers in selling coconut ice cream, men wandering about at a snail's pace. The beaches are pristine and the surrounding forest is a riot of wildlife. There are no cars and it's blissful. Beware: it's often plagued by mosquitoes and sandflies once night falls.

La Miel is one of the area's loveliest beaches, and lies over the hill from Sapzurro, just inside Panama. Bring your passport for the checkpoint. You don't need to get entry or exit stamps.

Sleeping & Eating

There is a lack of budget restaurants in Sapzurro, although some hotels offer plans with meals. If you're on a tight budget, bring food to cook or eat fresh *patacones* (fried green plantains) smothered with cheese by the dock.

Camping El Chileno CAMPGROUND, HOTEL $
(☎313-685-9862; hammock COP$10,000, campsite per person with/without tent hire COP$15,000/10,000, dm COP$15,000, r per person COP$35,000) Simple camping and hammock accommodations on the nicest end of Sapzurro's beach. Guests have access to the kitchen. Ask anyone in town for 'El Chileno' (the nickname of the owner) and they'll point you in the right direction. Or you may spot his smile at 100m.

Campamento Wittenberg HOTEL $
(☎311-436-6215; hammocks COP$10,000, r per person COP$18,000) A friendly French-owned joint right on the border of Panama, where you can find a basic room, plenty of hammocks, cheap and healthy breakfasts, fishing trips and sailing courses.

Zingara GUESTHOUSE $$
(☎320-687-4678; www.hospedajesapzurrozingara.com; r per person COP$35,000-40,000) Owner Clemencia will make you feel instantly welcome in this wooden guesthouse that is also her home. Rooms are simple, clean and airy, and some have ocean views.

SAN ANDRÉS & PROVIDENCIA

The islands of San Andrés and Providencia offer a tranquil and idyllic taste of Caribbean island life, with gorgeous beaches lapped by turquoise seas rammed with pristine coral – the second-largest barrier reef in the northern hemisphere is here. For reggae, rum, sun and sand, a splurge here is well worth considering.

These Colombian territories lie 220km off Nicaragua's Miskito Coast, and 800km northwest of Colombia. Both islands have a strong British influence, in food, language and architecture, and are popular snorkeling and scuba centers. The rainy season is September to December and average temperatures are 26°C to 29°C, with high humidity.

The islands were originally claimed by the Spanish but were pretty much ignored until the British invaded in 1631. The new colonizers immediately began to bring in African slaves to work on the plantations. The descendants of these slaves would go on to be known as the Raizal, the Afro-Caribbean indigenous inhabitants of the islands.

The Spanish tried to take over in 1635 but failed, and legendary pirate Henry Morgan operated here from 1670 onwards. Colombia won independence in 1819 and claimed the islands, despite Nicaraguan protestations. The International Court of Justice reaffirmed Colombia's sovereignty in 2007.

Getting There & Away

Buy a tourist card (COP$46,000) on the mainland before checking in for your San Andrés-bound flight. The airport is in San Andrés Town, a 10-minute walk northwest of the center or COP$10,000/5000 by taxi/*mototaxi*. **Avianca** (www.avianca.com), **Copa** (www.copaair.com), and **LAN** (www.lan.com) have flights to San Andrés from most major Colombian cities.

Satena (☎512-3139; www.satena.com) fly between San Andrés and Providencia (return from COP$360,000). A cheaper option is to cross the sea by boat (return COP$240,000, 2½ hours) on the **Sensation** (☎512-3358; www.catamaranelsensation.com). It generally operates Monday, Wednesday, Friday and Sunday leaving San Andrés at 7:30am and returning from Providencia at 3:45pm. If you get seasick pay for the flight, as the boat is often rough.

San Andrés

☎8 / POP 68,000

The larger of the two islands, at 12.5km long and 3km wide, San Andrés has the most developed tourist infrastructure. Its isolated beaches are postcard-perfect, though the island's commercial center is far from pretty. All the amenities are in San Andrés Town: there's a **tourist office** (Secretaría de Turismo; ☎512-5058; www.sanandres.gov.co; Av Newball; ⊙8am-noon & 2-6pm Mon-Fri) and several ATMs. **Cafe Internet Platinium** (Av 20 de Julio; per hr COP$2500; ⊙8am-10pm) provides internet.

The other two small towns, La Loma in the central hills and San Luis on the eastern coast, are far less tourist-oriented and boast some fine English-Caribbean wooden architecture. The **Johnny Cay Natural Regional Park** is a protected coral islet 1.5km north of San Andrés Town, covered with coconut groves and surrounded by a lovely, white-sand beach.

Due to the beautiful coral reefs all around, San Andrés has become an important diving center, with more than 35 dive spots. **Banda Dive Shop** (☎513-1080; www.bandadiveshop.com; Hotel Lord Pierre, Av Colombia; ⊙8am-noon & 2-6pm Mon-Sat) is a friendly dive center offering two-tank dives for COP$150,000 and PADI open-water certification for COP$750,000.

Lodge with Raizal locals at **Cli's Place** (☎512-6957; luciamhj@hotmail.com; Av 20 de Julio; r per person from COP$50,000; 📶) or stay in one of nine simple, cozy rooms two blocks from the beach at **Hotel Mary May Inn** (☎512-5669; jfgallardo@gmail.com; Av 20 de Julio 3-74; s/d COP$60,000/90,000; ❄). If you're looking for a dorm bed, check out **El Viajero** (☎512-7497; Av 20 de Julio 3A-12; dm COP$35,000, s/d COP$90,000/134,000; ❄📶). In San Luis, **Posada Nativa Green Sea** (☎317-751-4314, 512-6313; Harmony Hall Hill; r per person COP$30,000; ❄) has peaceful simple cottages with kitchens.

The open-air **Fisherman Place** (☎512-2774; Av Colombia; mains COP$13,000-45,000; ⊙noon-4pm) has great lobster. Across from the Club Nautico is **Miss Celia O'Neill Taste** (☎513-1062; Av Colombia; mains COP$20,000-35,000; ⊙lunch & dinner), with local specialties such as *rondon* (steamed seafood with starchy vegetables in coconut sauce), stewed crab and fish. For nightspots in San Andrés Town, head along the eastern end of Av Colombia.

Providencia

☎8 / POP 5000

Lying 90km north of San Andrés, Providencia is 7km long and 4km wide, and is less commercialized than the larger island, with dozens of small villages of multicolored wooden houses. Santa Isabel is the main town and is where you'll find the **tourist office** (☎514-8054), an ATM at **Banco de Bogotá** (⊙8-11:30am & 2-4pm Mon-Thu, 8-11:30am & 2-4:30pm Fri) and internet at **Communication Center** (☎514-8871; per hr COP$2500; ⊙9am-12:30pm & 4-9pm Mon-Sat, 2:30-9pm Sun).

Diving trips and courses can be arranged with **Felipe Diving Shop** (☎514-8775; www.felipediving.com) run by a native Raizal. Don't miss **El Pico Natural Regional Park** for outstanding 360-degree views of the Caribbean. The most popular trail begins in Casabaja, where you can find a guide, or seek directions. Take water and sunscreen.

For accommodations, **Mr Mac** (☎514-8283; r per person COP$50,000) is a fine option with large rooms right by the water in the Aguadulce area. In Santa Isabel **Hotel Flaming Trees** (☎514-8049; s/d COP$600,000/100,000; ❄) has spacious rooms with fridge, TV and local art.

Pizza's Place (☎514-8224; sandwiches COP$6000, pizzas COP$13,000; ⊙dinner) serves sandwiches, pizza and island staples, while **Caribbean Place** (☎514-8698; mains COP$18,000-53,000; ⊙lunch & dinner) is worth a splurge with specialties including mountainous black crab, unique to the archipelago. **Roland Roots Bar** (☎514-8417; Bahía Manzanillo) is an atmospheric, archetypal bamboo beach bar with booming reggae and strong booze.

NORTHWEST COLOMBIA

The northwest of Colombia is mountainous with a mild climate, fertile volcanic soil that blooms with millions of flowers, verdant coffee farms, ethereal cloud forests and small, busy university towns full of hard-working *paisas,* as locals are known here.

The department of Antioquia is the biggest, richest and most populous in the region, with Medellín, a gleamingly modern and forward-looking metropolis in its center. Its inhabitants are renowned nationally for their independent and entrepreneurial spirit.

To the south of Antioquia, spread over parts of the Cordillera Occidental and the Cordillera Central mountain ranges is the Zona Cafetera, Colombia's major coffee-growing area and the exporter of many sleepless nights. Coffee is the world's second-most traded commodity after oil, and Colombia is the world's third-biggest exporter.

The Zona Cafetera is a mountainous area comprised of three main cities: Manizales, a major university town (with good nightlife) and important economic engine of national trade; Pereira, a manically busy commercial center that lies near some stunning thermal springs; and Armenia, an unremarkable small city best known as the gateway to Salento, a laid-back colonial mountain hideaway set in glorious countryside and close to the not-to-missed Valle de Cocora.

Medellín

☎4 / POP 3 MILLION

Medellín, the city of Colombia's proudest residents, the *paisas,* is back with a vengeance. Once the world's most murderous city, you'd never know it today. With a perfect, perpetual spring-like climate, chic shopping malls, world-class restaurants and vibrant nightlife, the city seduces the senses and will make you feel instantly at home.

Medellín has always dwelt in the shadows of Cartagena and Bogotá, but many visitors find this city, which also has pleasant green spaces and striking public art, more relaxing than the former and more welcoming than the latter. It's got culture, class and the friendliest locals in Colombia; no wonder tourism is flourishing.

In the 1990s Medellín was the center of the worldwide cocaine trade, with motorbike-riding *sicarios* (hitmen) carrying out gangland hits for the city's most notorious son, drug lord Pablo Escobar (who remains popular here with some for his generosity to the poor). Escobar was so rich he once offered to pay off Colombia's foreign debt, and paid his hitmen US$1000 for every cop they killed. The city was a no-go zone for foreigners until the kingpin was gunned down on a Medellín rooftop by security forces in 1993.

The economic engines of the city today are cut flowers, coffee and textiles, and *paisas* are known for their industriousness and shrewd business acumen. This has been coupled in recent years with intelligent planning

Medellín

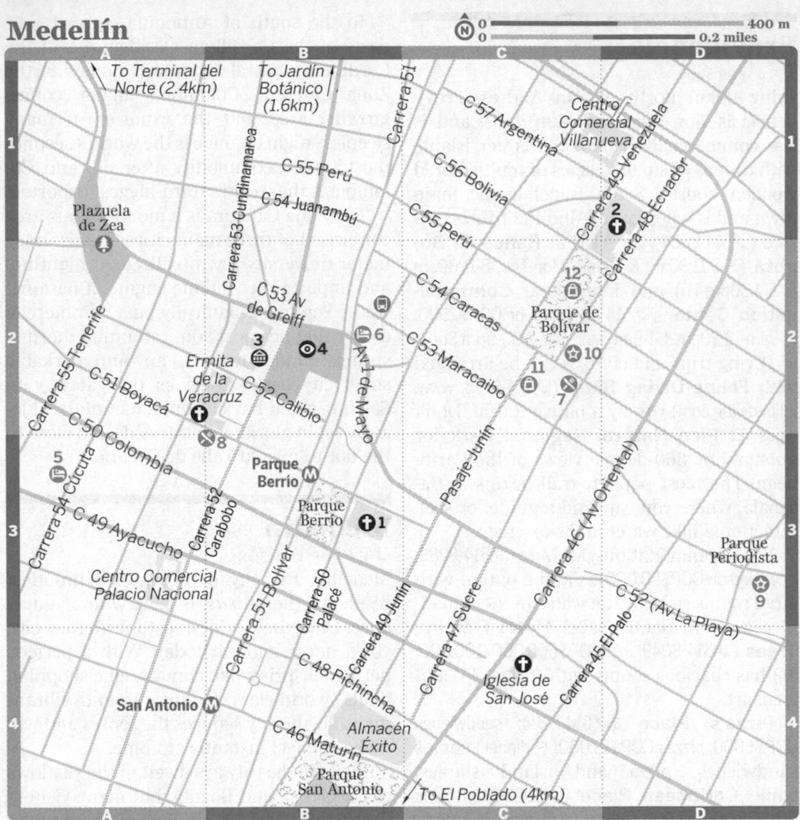

and investment in innovative urban infrastructure. The result is a sleek, modern city that boasts Colombia's only metro system – a clean, graffiti-free, safe and affordable public transportation system that shuttles you around comfortably and quickly. The cable cars that swoop over some of the poorer barrios have fostered peace, and are well worth the ride.

Medellín's character of proud self-reliance stems from its history: the town was founded in 1616 by European immigrants who worked hard, farming the land themselves to achieve their successes. The city is surrounded by lush, mountainous terrain and spills north and south down a narrow valley, with soaring buildings blooming like geometric sunflowers.

But beware: they play as hard as they work here – if you're heading for a night out with a gang of *paisas* you likely won't get home before dawn.

Sights

Apart from a few old churches, the city's colonial architecture has virtually disappeared.

For a spectacular bird's-eye look at the city, ride one of the two Metrocable lines running up the mountainsides. The San Javier line offers the most spectacular views, but complete a full loop and don't hop out on route, as it passes over some of Medellín's roughest barrios.

Museo de Antioquia MUSEUM

(Map p578; 251-3636; www.museodeantioquia.org.co; Carrera 52 No 52-43; adult/student COP$10,000/5000; 10am-5:30pm Mon-Sat, to 4pm Sun) The Museo de Antioquia features pre-Hispanic, colonial, independence and modern art collections, spanning Antioquia's 400-year-long history, plus Fernando Botero's donation of 92 of his own works and 22 works by international artists. His 23 large bronze sculptures have been placed

Medellín

Sights

Sleeping

Eating

Entertainment

Shopping

in front of the museum, in **Plazoleta de las Esculturas** (Map p578).

FREE **Casa Museo Pedro Nel Gómez** MUSEUM
(☎233-2633; Carrera 51B No 85-24; ⏲9am-5pm Mon-Sat, 10am-4pm Sun) The Casa Museo Pedro Nel Gómez, set in the house where the prolific artist lived and worked, houses nearly 2000 of his works including watercolors, oil paintings, drawings, sculptures and murals.

Cerro Nutibara LOOKOUT
For panoramic views of the city, go to the Cerro Nutibara, a hill 2km southwest of the city center. A replica of a typical Antioquian village, **Pueblito Paisa**, has been built on the summit.

Parque Arví PARK
(www.parquearvi.org; Veredas Mazo & Piedras Blancas) This big chunk of mountain wilderness in Santa Elena makes a great escape from the city. Inside the boundaries of the 17.61-sq-km park are hiking trails, free bike hire and several private reserves. It's accessible by Metrocable (Linea L) from the Santo Domingo interchange (COP$3500 one way, 15 minutes). The cable car is closed for maintenance on Mondays.

Museo de Arte Moderno de Medellín GALLERY
(☎444-2622; www.elmamm.org; Carrera 44 No 19A-100; admission COP$7000; ⏲9am-5:30pm Mon-Fri, 10am-5pm Sat & Sun) Another important city museum, the Museo of Modern Art stages changing exhibitions of contemporary art.

FREE **Jardín Botánico** GARDEN
(www.botanicomedellin.org; Calle 73 No 51D-14; ⏲9am-5pm) Medellín's fabulous botanic gardens cover 14 hectares and showcases 600 species of trees and plants, a lake, herbarium, auditorium and a butterfly enclosure.

Basílica de la Candelaria CHURCH
(Map p578; cnr Carrera 50 & Calle 51) The most interesting of the historic churches is the Basílica de la Candelaria, built in the 1770s and functioning as the city's cathedral until 1931.

Catedral Metropolitana CHURCH
(Map p578; Carrera 48) The gigantic neo-Romanesque Catedral Metropolitana was completed in 1931.

Activities

Zona de Vuelo PARAGLIDING
(☎312-832-5891, 388-1556; www.zonadevuelopara-pentemedellin.com; Km 5.6, Vía San Pedro de los Milagro) Offers tandem paragliding flights over the city (COP$80,000 to COP$100,000). It's professional, accredited and trusted.

Courses

Universidad EAFIT LANGUAGE
(☎261-9399; www.eafit.edu.co; Carrera 49 No 7 Sur-50) Private university offering intensive Spanish study in a group setting.

Tours

Paisa Road GUIDED TOURS
(☎317-489-2629; www.paisaroad.com) Urban tourism company run by energetic young *paisas* that offers a variety of interesting tours including Medellín's best Pablo Escobar tour (COP$30,000).

Festivals & Events

Feria de las Flores CULTURAL
(www.feriadelasfloresmedellin.gov.co; ⏲Aug) Held for a week in early August, this is Medellín's biggest event. Its highlight is the Desfile de Silleteros, when hundreds of *campesinos* (peasant farmers) come down from the mountains and parade along the streets

carrying *silletas* (huge baskets) full of flowers on their backs.

Alumbrado Navideño RELIGIOUS

(⏲Dec & Jan) Each year at Christmas time the city ignites the riverfront with a spectacular lightshow. It lasts from December 7 until the second week in January.

Sleeping

The El Poblado *barrio*, with its shopping malls, office blocks and Zona Rosa filled with neon-lit bars, clubs and restaurants has hoovered up most of the new gringos, and its environs are now considered a new central district. The area around 'La 70' and Laureles is another popular upmarket area, while the rough-and-tumble center is fun if you want to experience a bustling Colombian city.

Casa Kiwi HOSTEL $$

(Map p581; ☎268-2668; www.casakiwi.net; Carrera 36 No 7-10; dm COP$20,000, s/d COP$60,000/70,000, without bathroom COP$40,000/50,000; @📶) El Poblado's original hostel has undergone a major transformation and now boasts bright rooms, a small dipping pool on the rooftop and a great deck overlooking the street downstairs. Its excellent location in the heart of the Zona Rosa (nightlife zone) makes it the destination for those who like to party.

Black Sheep HOSTEL $$

(Map p581; ☎317-518-1369, 311-1589; www.blacksheepmedellin.com; Transversal 5A No 45-133; dm COP$20,000-22,000, s/d COP$60,000/75,000, without bathroom COP$45,000/60,000; @📶) Well-managed hostel with every conceivable amenity, including on-site Spanish classes, and comfortable rooms with big beds and piping hot showers. It has a relaxed, social vibe and on Sundays the owner prepares a fantastic filling barbecue (COP$13,000).

Wandering Paisa HOSTEL $$

(☎436-6759; www.wanderingpaisahostel.com; Calle 44A No 68A-76; dm COP$20,000-23,000, s/d COP$55,000/70,000; @📶) Conveniently located near the bars and restaurants of La 70, this comfortable new hostel has enthusiastic management that are constantly arranging social events and group outings.

61 Prado GUESTHOUSE $$

(☎254-9743; www.61prado.com; Calle 61 No 50A-60; s/d/ste COP$45,000/70,000/80,000; @📶) This fine guesthouse in the historic Prado neighborhood has elegant rooms with high ceilings and touches of art throughout. There is no sign – look for the black gate.

Hotel Conquistadores HOTEL $

(Map p578; ☎512-3232; hotelconquistadores@gmail.com; Carrera 54 No 49-31; s/d COP$28,000/34,000; 📶) On a noisy, unattractive street downtown, this clean family-owned hotel offers plenty for the price. All rooms have private bath, hot water and cable TV. It's not the best area to walk around after dark.

Palm Tree Hostal HOSTEL $

(☎260-2805; www.palmtreemedellin.com; Carrera 67 48D-63; dm $18,000, s/d without bathroom COP$28,000/40,000; @📶) Close to the metro and plenty of cheap eateries, this hostel offers added value, with free basic breakfasts, internet access and barbecues.

Eating

The center is flooded with affordable restaurants. Restaurants in El Poblado are pricier. If you're after a supermarket, **Exito** (Map p581; Calle 10 No 43E-135) has a wide selection and low prices while **Carulla** (⏲24hr) is more gourmet.

Verdeo VEGETARIAN $

(Map p581; www.ricoverdeo.com; Carrera 35 No 8A-3; mains COP$12,000-16,000; ⏲closed Mon; 🖉) You don't have to be a vegetarian to enjoy the creative dishes on offer at this groovy Poblado co-operative. Take your pick from delicious vegetarian shawarma, burgers, ravioli and salads. The attached grocers sells organic veggies.

El Taxista COLOMBIAN $

(Map p581; Carrera 43B No 10-22; meals COP$5000-6,000) Tradesmen sit shoulder to shoulder with sharp-suited businessmen at this busy hole-in-the-wall diner near Parque Poblado, which serves delicious *paisa* favorites from a tiny kitchen full of women frantically frying. You won't find better value anywhere in Medellín.

Bahía Mar SEAFOOD $$$

(Map p581; ☎352-0938; Calle 9 No 43B-127; mains COP$20,000-40,000; ⏲lunch & dinner Mon-Sat, lunch Sun) This top-notch seafood place offers *mariscos* (seafood) in an unpretentious Caribbean setting. The signature dish is *langostino Providencia* (Providencia-style king prawns) but it also does enormous shrimp cocktails and light platters of seafood crepes.

El Poblado

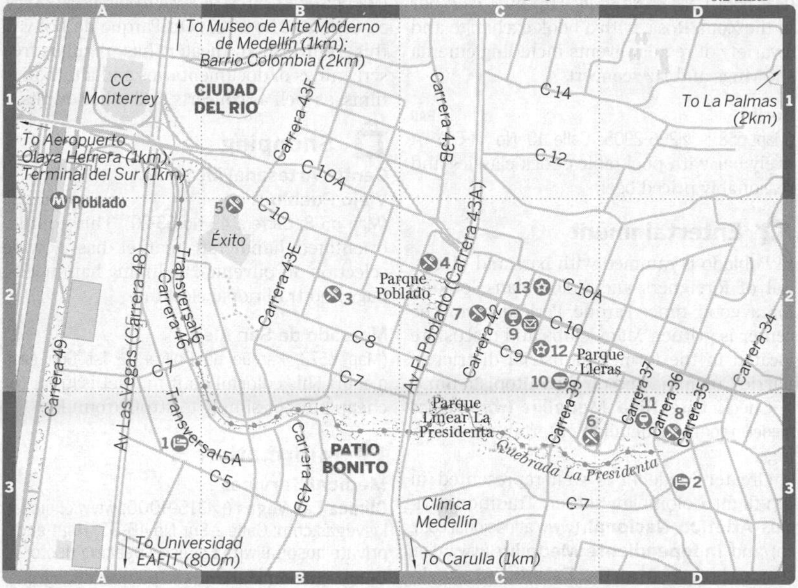

Il Forno ITALIAN **$**
(Map p581; Carrera 37A No 8-9; mains COP$7000-18,000) Excellent pizza and lasagna, with a few passable salads.

La Casa de Beto COLOMBIAN **$**
(Map p581; Carrera 42 No 9-53; mains COP$8000-11,000) More than a little out of place in chic Poblado, Beto's is a no-nonsense diner that serves up hearty plates of simple *paisa* food at budget prices.

Los Toldos COLOMBIAN **$$**
(Map p578; Calle 54 No 47-11; mains COP$15,000-18,000; ⏲lunch & dinner) Elderly waiters wear traditional costumes and old-style Colombian folk music plays on the stereo at this typical *paisa* place. Go for the daily special.

Restaurante Vegetariano Govinda's VEGETARIAN **$**
(Map p578; Calle 51 No 52-17; meals COP$7000; ⏲9am-2:30pm Mon-Sat; 🖉) Large buffet is good value for vegetarians, with soup, salad, main meal, juice and dessert.

Drinking

Café Le Bon CAFE
(Map p581; Calle 9 No 39-09; ⏲9am-1am Mon-Sat, to 11pm Sun) One of Medellín's few real coffee shops, Le Bon would not be out of place in a funky arts neighborhood in any North American city. In the evening the stereo stays leashed, making it a quiet spot for a cocktail or a beer.

El Poblado

Sleeping

1	Black Sheep	A3
2	Casa Kiwi	D3

Eating

3	Bahía Mar	B2
4	El Taxista	C2
5	Exito	B2
6	Il Forno	C3
7	La Casa de Beto	C2
8	Verdeo	D3

Drinking

9	Berlín	C2
10	Café Le Bon	C2
11	Tinto Tintero	D3

Entertainment

12	Babylon	C2
13	Sampues	C2

Tinto Tintero BAR, CAFE

(Map p581; Calle 8A No 36-14) Hip little cafe-bar in the Zona Rosa, with a book exchange and a variety of regular events including cinema showings and jazz concerts.

Berlín BAR

(Map p581; ☎266-2905; Calle 10 No 41-65) A lively bar with pool tables, rock classics and reasonably priced beer.

☆ Entertainment

El Poblado is rammed with bars and discos, full of foreigners and Colombians looking for a good time. Parque Periodista in the center is grittier. Many clubs and discos are located in the former industrial district of Barrio Colombia and on the Autopista Sur.

Check **Que Rico Medellín** (www.quericomedellin.com) for detailed entertainment listings.

Greater Medellín is well represented in top-flight Colombian soccer. Traditional rivals **Atlético Nacional** (www.atlnacional.com.co) and **Independiente Medellín** (www.dim.com.co) both play at the **Estadio Atanasio Giradot**, while **Envigado Fútbol Club** (www.envigadofutbolclub.net) play in the southern municipality of Envigado and neighbouring Itagui is home to the **Aguilas Doradas** (www.aguilasdoradasitagui.com).

El Tibiri CLUB

(cnr Carrera 70 & Calle 44B; ⊙8pm-2am Thu-Sat) Hidden in an unsigned sweaty basement on La 70, this intimate salsa club is one of the best places in town to perfect your moves. There is no cover and the cheap drinks will get even non-dancers onto the floor.

Babylon CLUB

(Map p581; Carrera 41 No 9-22) A couple of blocks from Parque Lleras, Babylon is popular with an energetic young crowd that comes to dance on tables to reggaeton. On Thursdays there is an open bar.

Eslabon Prendido CLUB

(Papayera; Map p578; Calle 53 No 42-55) This diminutive salsa bar packs a crowd on Tuesdays for its live-band performances. The vibe is very sociable; you don't need to bring a dance partner.

Sampues CLUB

(Map p581; Calle 10A No 40-37) This popular Poblado disco attracts an unpretentious, friendly crowd that dances non-stop to Colombian crossover.

Teatro Lido CINEMA, THEATER

(Map p578; ☎251-5334; www.medellincultura.gov.co; Carrera 48 No 54-20) On Parque de Bolívar, this refurbished theater has regular free screenings of documentaries and alternative films, as well as concerts and other events.

Shopping

Centro Artesanal Mi Viejo Pueblo HANDICRAFTS

(Map p578; Carrera 49 No 53-20) This tourist-orientated handicraft market has a wide selection of souvenirs, including hammocks, bags and traditional clothing.

Mercado de San Alejo MARKET

(Map p578; Parque de Bolívar; ⊙1st Sun each month) This colorful craft market is great for cheap buys or simply to stroll around.

ⓘ Information

Medical Services

Clínica Las Vegas (☎315-9000; www.clinicalasvegas.com; Calle 2 Sur No 46-55) High-end private hospital with English-speaking doctors.

Congregación Mariana (http://www.congregacionmariana.org.co; Calle 52 No 40-146) Non-profit clinic with low prices.

Money

Banco de Bogotá (Calle 50 No 51-37) ATM in the center.

CC Oviedo (Carrera 43A No 6 Sur-15) There are lots of money changers, ATMs and bank branches in Centro Comercial (CC) Oviedo.

Citibank (Carrera 43A No 1A Sur-49) Poblado ATM.

Giros & Finanzas (Centro Comercial Villanueva, Calle 57 No 49-44, Local 241) Currency exchange and Western Union agent.

Post

4-72 (Calle 10 No 41-25)

Tourist Information

The local government has Puntos de Información Turísticas (PITs) in strategic points around the city, including at both bus terminals and airports.

PIT Plaza Mayor (☎232-1624; www.medellin.gov.co; Hall Principal, Plaza Mayor; ⊙8am-6pm) Main tourist information kiosk. Friendly and professional.

Visa Information

Migración Colombia (☎238-9252; www.migracioncolombia.gov.co; Calle 19 No 80A-40, Barrio Belén; ⊙7-11am & 2-4pm Mon-Fri) For visa extensions. From El Poblado take the

Circular Sur 302 bus heading south along Av Las Vegas, or take a taxi (COP$10,000).

Getting There & Away

Air

Medellín's main airport, Aeropuerto Internacional José María Córdoba (MDE), 35km southeast of the city, takes all international and most domestic flights. Frequent minibuses (COP$7500, one hour) shuttle between the city center and the airport, leaving from behind **Hotel Nutibara** (Map p578; ☎511-5111; www.hotelnutibara.com; Calle 52A No 50-46). Alternatively, take a *colectivo* (COP$11,000, 45 minutes) from the Terminal Sur. Regular taxis charge COP$57,000, but **Rápido Medellín Rionegro** (☎361-1187) runs the trip for COP$48,000.

Some regional flights use the Aeropuerto Olaya Herrera (EOH) adjacent to the Terminal Sur, a short taxi ride from El Poblado.

Bus

Medellín has two bus terminals. The Terminal del Norte, 2km north of the city center, handles buses to the north, east and southeast, including Santa Fe de Antioquia (COP$10,000, two hours), Bogotá (COP$60,000, nine hours), Cartagena (COP$85,000, 13 hours) and Santa Marta (COP$94,000, 16 hours). It's easily accessed by metro (alight at Estación Caribe).

The Terminal del Sur, 4km southwest of the center, handles all traffic to the west and south including Manizales (COP$32,000, five hours), Armenia (COP$36,000, six hours), Pereira (COP$34,000, five hours) and Cali (COP$45,000, nine hours). From El Poblado, take a cab (COP$5000).

Getting Around

Medellín's metro consists of a 26km north–south line and a 6km western leg, with 27 stations. Three Metrocable cable car systems connect the service to low-income barrios in the hills and up to Parque Arví in Santa Elena.

Apart from the metro, urban transportation is serviced by buses and *busetas*. The majority of routes originate on Av Oriental and Parque Berrío, from where you can get to almost anywhere within the metropolitan area.

Santa Fe de Antioquia

☎4 / POP 23,700

Santa Fe de Antioquia is a wonderfully preserved colonial town that makes a great day trip from Medellín. Founded in 1541, it is the oldest town in the region. It was a prosperous center during Spanish rule and the capital of Antioquia until 1826. When the capital moved to Medellín, it lost commercial importance and as a result escaped the wrecking ball of progress, leaving its narrow cobblestone streets, lovely plazas and whitewashed houses intact. These days, its warm climate makes it a popular getaway for Medellín urbanites.

Sights

The town is famous for its carved wooden doorways and flower-filled patios.

Puente de Occidente BRIDGE

This unusual 291m bridge over the Río Cauca is 5km east of town. When completed in 1895, it was one of the first suspension bridges in the Americas. It's an exceedingly boring and hot 45-minute walk downhill, so a *mototaxi* (round trip COP$12,000) is money well spent. Be sure to climb the dirt path behind the entrance for complete aerial photos of the bridge.

Iglesia de Santa Bárbara CHURCH

(cnr Calle 11 & Carrera 8; ⌚5-6:30pm & Sun morning mass) The 18th-century Iglesia de Santa Bárbara is noted for its fine wide baroque stone facade.

Museo Juan del Corral MUSEUM

(☎853-4605; museojuandelcorral@mincultura.gov.co; Calle 11 No 9-77; admission COP$1000; ⌚10am-5pm, closed Wed) Interesting regional museum set in a meticulously restored colonial mansion.

Festivals & Events

Fiesta de los Diablitos CULTURAL

(⌚Dec) Celebrated with music, dancing, a craft fair, bullfights and a beauty contest held December 27–31.

Sleeping & Eating

Prices increase by 25% at weekends.

TOP CHOICE **Hostal Plaza Mayor** HOSTEL $

(☎853-3448; r per person COP$20,000; ❄📶🏊) Set in an old colonial building on the main square, this backpacker-oriented place is superb value. It has neat renovated rooms inside the house and bamboo huts by the pool.

Hospedaje Franco GUESTHOUSE $

(☎853-1654; Carrera 10 No 8A-14; r COP$40,000; @📶) This basic place has acceptable rooms with cable TV around a tidy courtyard.

Piel Roja COLOMBIAN $
(cnr Carrera 9 & Calle 10; meals COP$7000) Cheap diner on the main plaza serving huge portions of *comida corriente*.

Getting There & Away

There are buses (COP$10,000, 1½ hours) every half-hour between Santa Fe and Medellín's Terminal del Norte.

Río Claro

Three hours east of Medellín lies the **Reserva Natural Cañón de Río Claro** (265-8855; www.rioclaroelrefugio.com; Km 132, Autopista Medellín-Bogotá; admission COP$5000; campsite per person COP$10,000, r per person incl 3 meals COP$80,000-100,000), a tranquil river with a marble bed running through a spectacular jungle-lined canyon. Here you can visit a wonderful cave, go whitewater rafting, canopying, or swim and hike along its banks, which have great bird-watching. Maniacs leap into the water from the 15m-high banks of the canyon – emulate them at your peril.

Make sure to visit the **Caverna de los Guácharos** (COP$12,000), an impressive cave complex filled with guacharos, a missing link in bat-bird evolution. You'll be given a life vest and expected to swim part of the way.

There are a number of accommodation options available within the reserve, with open walls facing the jungle. The best places to stay are the cabins set on a hillside a 15-minute walk upstream from the reception area, where the jungle thrum will wake you with a start and lull you to sleep. You can arrive unannounced midweek, but the owners advise early reservations, especially at weekends and holidays.

If you are on a tight budget, consider visiting the reserve as a day trip and basing yourself in the nearby town of Doradal, which has several cheap hotels.

Getting There & Away

From Medellín's Terminal del Norte take any one of dozens of Bogotá buses (COP$20,000, three hours), which will drop you at the entrance.

Guatapé

4 / POP 4200

The tiny town of Guatapé is a popular weekend getaway for *paisas* who want to wander its pretty streets and take trips out onto the artificial lake, **El Embalse del Peñol**. Looming over the lake is La Piedra del Peñol, a vast granite monolith you can climb. You can do both as a day trip or spend the night in Guatapé.

Part of Guatapé was flooded in 1970 in order to create the lake that now generates much of the region's power. Today, it is noted for its cute streets; many houses are decorated with *zocalos* (colorful concrete bas-relief scenes). They were originally designed to prevent chickens pecking at the walls, and to stop children chipping away at the buildings with ball games. Visit during the week for low prices and peace, or at weekends for a hard-drinking *paisa* jamboree.

Sights

La Piedra del Peñol MONOLITH
(El Peñon; per climb COP$10,000; 8am-6:30pm) La Piedra del Peñol or El Peñon is a 200m-high granite monolith that soars above the banks of El Embalse del Peñol. You can climb the rock's 659 steps to hover above the eagles and grab a magnificent view of the region. As you stand gasping at the snack bar at the top, spare a thought for the workers who dragged the cement and water to craft the staircase you just climbed.

Buses and *chivas* (basic rural buses) from Guatapé (COP$2000) will drop you at the gas pump on the highway, from where it's a stiff 1km hike up to the entrance to the rock. A *mototaxi* direct to the entrance costs COP$10,000.

Calle de Recuerdos STREET
A steep street decorated with many *zocalos,* and home to the **Museo Turístico** (entry by donation; 10am-6pm Sat & Sun), which, though it gets full marks for effort, is more like an antiques shop than a museum, as it has no coherent theme.

Iglesia del Calma CHURCH
Iglesia del Calma, on the main square, has an unusual wooden roof and columns.

La Casa Familiar García HISTORIC BUILDING
Just behind the church, this is a large, old house that the owners usually leave open so tourists can snoop around inside.

Activities

Boat trips out to the islands in the center of the lake are the main activity here. The large boats (per person COP$10,000) are slow but have a bar and dance floor; they are a great chance to get to know the phenomenon that is partying *paisas*. The smaller boats (up to seven passengers, COP$90,000) are more flexible if you want to visit specific destinations.

Sleeping & Eating

TOP CHOICE El Encuentro HOSTEL $$
(☎861-1374; www.hostelelencuentro.com; Vereda Quebrada Arriba; dm COP$22,000, s/d 65,000/75,000, without bathroom 45,000/55,000;) Combining a peaceful ambience, spectacular views and gardens sloping down to a private swimming area, this place feels more like an expensive retreat than a hostel. It is a 15-minute walk from town – take a *mototaxi* if you have bags.

El Descanso del Arriero GUESTHOUSE $
(☎861-0878; Calle 30 No 28-82; s/d COP$25,000/50,000) Rooms are pokey, but clean and comfortable. The bar downstairs plays mellow music and serves cheap meals.

La Fogata COLOMBIAN $$
(mains COP$15,000-18,000) Right opposite the lake with a view of the water, this place does great *paisa* food. Go for the *trucha* (trout).

Getting There & Away

Buses to and from Medellín run on the hour all day (COP$12,000, two hours) from the northern bus terminal.

Manizales

☎6 / POP 388,500

This is a wealthy town that is home to six universities, and though the town is not classically pretty (your camera will hardly leave your bag), its modern houses and steep, tidy streets offer a curious contrast to all other Colombian cities. It has a fresh, chilly climate and an air of scholarly seriousness that gives way as the sun drops and the students kick back. It was founded in 1849 but was later leveled by earthquakes. From here, you can visit coffee farms and gaze in awe at the glacier-covered peak of the active volcano, **Nevado del Ruiz**, one of Colombia's most majestic mountains.

Sights

The tribute to El Libertador (Simón Bolívar) in **Plaza de Bolívar** is curious: Rodrigo Arenas Betancur has cast his subject here as a condor atop a horse.

Catedral de Manizales CHURCH
(tower climb COP$7000; ⊙tower 9am-noon & 2-6pm Thu-Mon) The Plaza de Bolívar's south side is dominated by the odd but impressive cathedral. Begun in 1929 and built of reinforced concrete, it is among the first churches of its kind in Latin America, and its main tower is 106m high, making it the highest church tower in the country. You can climb to the top for great views of the city.

Monumento a Los Colonizadores MONUMENT
(Av 12 de Octubre, Chipre) Located atop a hill in the neighborhood of Chipre, this massive monument to the city's founders was crafted from 50 tonnes of bronze, but the real attraction here is the spectacular view over town and to PNN Los Nevados.

FREE Los Yarumos PARK
(☎875-5621; Calle 61B No 15A-01; ⊙9am-7pm Tue-Sun) Under new management, this 53-hectare municipal park offers forest trails, canopy lines and other adventure activities. It's a great place to come on a clear afternoon, when you can see the peaks of PNN Los Nevados. A cable car (COP$1400) links the park directly with Cable Plaza, but runs sporadically; or it's about a 40-minute walk.

Tours

Kumanday Adventures ADVENTURE TOUR
(☎887-2682, 315-590-7294; www.kumanday.com; Calle 66 No 23B-40) This full-service adventure-tour company, inside the hostel of the same name, offers mountaineering and mountain-biking tours nationwide. Also rents and sells tents, sleeping bags and mountaineering equipment.

Festivals & Events

Feria de Manizales BULLFIGHTING
(⊙Jan) Bullfights, parades and tiara-clad girls with cartoon smiles take over the town in January and prices double.

Festival Internacional de Teatro THEATRE
(⊙Sep & Oct) Major theatrical festival.

Sleeping

The best places to stay are near the Zona Rosa, off Cable Plaza. Check out the old cable-car tower, which used to haul goods across the ridgetops.

Mountain Hostels Manizales HOSTEL $
(☎887-4736, 887-0871; www.mountainhousemanizales.com; Calle 66 No 23B-91; dm

COP$20,000-22,000, r with/without bathroom COP$60,000/50,000; @) Now filling two houses on the same street, the original Manizales hostel is still the best budget choice in town. The newer wing houses the reception and bright private rooms, while the original house is exclusively dorms. It's one of the few hostels where Colombian travelers and backpackers mix, and the obliging staff offer advice on excursions in the area.

Hostal Palogrande HOSTEL $
(886-3984; www.hostalpalogrande.com; Calle 62 No 23-36; dm COP$25,000, s/d COP$30,000/60,000;) This locally owned hostel right in the Zona Rosa is cheap and super clean, with big bathrooms and a nice lounge area. The drawbacks – thin mattresses and the paper-thin walls make it feel as though you're in bed with your neighbors.

Kumanday Adventures HOSTEL $$
(315-590-7294, 887-2682; www.kumanday.com; Calle 66 No 23B-40; dm COP$35,000, s/d COP$45,000/70,000;) Run by a pioneering local adventure-tour company, this new hostel near the Zona Rosa has spacious-enough rooms but the lack of decoration and fluorescent lighting gives it a bit of a hospital feel. Breakfast included.

Eating

It's far from a gourmet's paradise, but dining in Manizales is cheap and the portions are usually huge. There are plenty of cheap fast-food outlets on Carrera 23 in the Zona Rosa.

Los Geranios COLOMBIAN $$
(886-8738; Carrera 23 No 71-67, Milan; mains COP$16,000-18,500) Famous for its large portions of traditional Colombian food, the menu here includes *bandeja paisa* (an artery busting platter that includes meat, sausage, beans, egg and pork rinds), five kinds of *sancocho* (clear soup), *ajiaco* (creamy chicken soup), steak, chicken and a few fish dishes. Meals come with five different kinds of sauce.

Kibbes & Felafel MIDDLE EASTERN $
(Calle 66 No 22A-56; mains COP$5000-10,000; 11am-2am daily) Just around the corner from Mountain Hostels, this unimpressive-looking drive-through-style restaurant has cheap and fantastic felafel with real tahini.

La Suiza BAKERY $
(Carrera 23B No 26-57; mains COP$12,000-15,000; 9am-8:30pm Mon-Sat, 10am-7:30pm Sun;) A great spot for breakfast, with veggie options such as mushroom crepes.

Don Juaco COLOMBIAN $
(Calle 65 No 23A-44; mains COP$7000-14,000) Juicy burgers and a great-value set lunch (COP$14,000), which includes a main course, dessert and excellent local coffee.

Drinking & Entertainment

Manizales bars change hands more times than a fake banknote, so don't be surprised if any of these spots have changed names. Avenida Santander is the main street leading away from Cable Plaza, head down there and see where's busy.

Valentino's Gourmet CAFE
(Carrera 23 No 63-128; 10am-10pm) Great coffee, hot chocolate and pastries.

Bar La Plaza CAFE, BAR
(Carrera 23B No 64-80; 11am-11pm Mon-Wed, to 2am Thu-Sat) This is the place to start your evening. A delicatessen by day, at night it fills up fast and by 9pm you'll have to wait for a table. The music isn't too loud, so you can converse. There is an extensive cocktail menu and gourmet sandwiches.

Prenderia BAR
(Carrera 23 No 58-42; 8pm-2am Thu-Sat) Wonderfully relaxed bar with talented local musicians playing to an older laid-back crowd. Try the lethal *carajillo* – strong espresso spiked with rum – and try not to slide off the bar stools.

Bar C CLUB
(Vía Acueducto Niza; Thu-Sat) The city's shiny end-up spot, open late with mainstream house, reggaeton and salsa rocking the well-dressed crowd.

Information

BBVA (Casa Luker) Reliable ATM in the Zona Rosa, next door to Cable Plaza.

Tourist Office (873-2901; www.ctm.gov.co; cnr Carrera 22 & Calle 31; 7am-7pm) City-run tourist office with enthusiastic staff and plenty of maps and brochures.

Getting There & Away

AIR **Aeropuerto La Nubia** (874-5451) is 8km southeast of the city center, off the Bogotá road. Take a city bus to La Enea, from where it's a five-minute walk to the terminal, or take a taxi (COP$10,000). The airport is often closed because of the weather, so don't book tight connections from here.

BUS Manizales' bright and modern **bus terminal** (☎878-7858; www.terminaldemanizales.com; Carrera 43 No 65-100) is connected to the center of town by a cable car (COP$1400), which offers panoramic views over the city. If you are staying near the Zona Rosa it is cheaper and faster to take a taxi (COP$6000) direct to your accommodations.

Buses depart regularly to Bogotá (COP$50,000, eight hours), Medellín (COP$35,000, six hours) and Cali (COP$30,000, five hours). There are many minibuses every hour to Pereira (COP$11,000, 1¼ hours) and Armenia (COP$17,000, 2¼ hours).

Around Manizales

Sights & Activities

Recinto del Pensamiento NATURE RESERVE
(☎874-4157; www.recintodelpensamiento.com; Km 11, Vía al Magdalena; admission COP$11,000-15,000; ⏲9am-4pm Tue-Sun) Set in the cloud forest 11km from Manizales, this nature reserve boasts a fine *mariposario* (butterfly enclosure), several short walks through an impressive orchid-populated forest, a medicinal herb garden and a mature bonsai garden, plus there is good bird-watching in the morning. You'll also see big plantations of *guadua* and *chusqué* (two kinds of Colombian bamboo). Take a bus headed to Sera Maltería from Cable Plaza in Manizales (COP$1400, 30 minutes, every 15 minutes), or take a taxi (COP$8000).

Hacienda Venecia FARM
(☎320-636-5719; www.haciendavenecia.com; Vereda el Rosario, San Peregrino; budget r per person with/without bathroom COP$40,000/30,000, s/d COP$220,000/300,000, without bathroom COP$180,000/220,000; coffee tour COP$20,000) Set around a charming old *paisa* farmhouse, the *hacienda* has won numerous awards for its coffee and offers a tour in English that includes an informative presentation about Colombian coffee, an introduction to coffee cupping, a class in coffee preparation and a walking tour through the plantation. A somewhat meager lunch is available for COP$10,000 and they will pick you up and drop you off at your hotel in Manizales for an additional COP$10,000 (round trip). If you want to hang around longer, there are budget rooms available in a new building across the river from the main house.

Hacienda Guayabal FARM
(☎850-7831; www.haciendaguayabal.com; Km 3, Vía Peaje Tarapacá, Chinchiná; r per person incl breakfast, lunch & dinner COP$85,000) A working coffee farm near Chinchiná, Guayabal runs coffee tours (COP$25,000/20,000 in English/Spanish) that follow the coffee process from the plant to the cup. Make sure to stay for lunch (COP$20,000), as the traditional farm-style food is absolutely delicious. Accommodations are available in simple rooms in the modern farmhouse set up on a hill with great views over the surrounding plantations.

To get here, take any bus from Manizales to Chinchiná (COP$2300, 30 minutes), then from the main plaza in Chinchiná take the bus marked 'Guayabal Peaje' (COP$1000, 10 minutes, every 15 to 30 minutes). Ask the driver to let you off before the toll booth at the small village of Guayabal; from here it's a 2km walk up the small road between the houses.

Termales Tierra Viva THERMAL BATHS
(☎874-3089; www.termalestierraviva.com; Km 2, Vía Enea-Gallinazo; admission COP$12,000-14,000; ⏲9am-10pm Mon-Thu, to 11pm Fri-Sun) These small thermal baths are located on the edge of Río Chinchiná just outside town. There are three baths set among a pretty garden that attracts hummingbirds and butterflies. There is also an excellent elevated restaurant overlooking the river. It's quiet during the week, but on the weekends it can feel a little overcrowded. To get here take the Enea–Gallinazo bus (COP$1500) from downtown Manizales. By taxi it is around COP$10,000.

RETRO RIDES: COLOMBIA'S CHIVAS

Part-truck, part-bus, with a custom-built wooden body and bright paintwork, *chivas* are more than a means of transport – they are part of Colombia's cultural identity. Fast to load and unload, these open-sided workhorses with rows of hard bench seats were once the principal means of road transport around the country. These days, their work in cities is mainly restricted to *chivas rumberas* (a kind of party bus) but they are still in dignified employment in some rural regions, particularly in mountainous areas.

Parque Nacional Natural Los Nevados

This snow-capped **range** of volcanic peaks offers some of the most stunning vistas in the Colombian Andes. Following an extended period of increased activity, **Nevado del Ruiz** (5325m), the largest and the highest volcano of the chain, burst to life in 2012, throwing plumes off ash high into the air. At the time of research the park was completely closed to visitors. Even when it re-opens, it is likely that restrictions on visitor movements will remain in place. Check the latest situation with Mountain Hostels (p585) or Kumanday Adventures (p585) – both in Manizales – before making plans.

Pereira

☎6 / POP 457,100

You don't come to Pereira for the architecture, the food, or to hang out. Neither do Colombians – they come to make money and do business in this city, the largest of the coffee region. The streets are hectic with commercial activity, and there is really nowhere to escape the bedlam.

The curious centerpiece of the town, **Bolívar Desnudo** (Plaza Bolívar), is a huge bronze sculpture of El Libertador riding his horse Nevado bareback – and fully naked. He seems to be flying furiously toward the town's grand cathedral across the plaza.

If you plan to spend the night, **Hostel Sweet Home** (☎345-4453; www.sweethomehostel.com; Carrera 11 No 44-30; dm COP$20,000, s/d COP$35,000/55,000; @📶) is located a little way out of the center, but is easily the best budget option and breakfast is included. **Grajales Autoservicios** (Carrera 8 No 21-60; mains COP$8000-15,000; ⊙24hr) is a self-service restaurant that has basic fodder and good breakfast choices.

Aeropuerto Matecaña (☎326-0021) is 5km west of the city center, 20 minutes by urban bus, or COP$10,000 by taxi. The **bus terminal** (☎321-5834; Calle 17 No 23-157) is about 1.5km south of the city center.

Armenia

☎6 / POP 272,500

Like Manizales and Pereira, this departmental capital offers few sights for the visitor but is the gateway to a number of interesting attractions and some enchanting small towns in Quindío department.

If you need to kill time, check out the **Museo del Oro Quimbaya** (☎749-8433; museoquimbaya@banrep.gov.co; Av Bolívar 40N-80; admission free; ⊙10am-5pm Tue-Sun), a small but interesting gold museum located 5km northeast of the center, on the road to Pereira. And if you are lucky enough to be around in October, don't miss the **Desfile de Yipao** (⊙Oct), when the department's classic Willys jeeps are driven down from the mountains and paraded fully loaded through the city's streets – on two wheels!

For internet, try **Facilcom Comunicaciones** (Calle 21 No 15-53; per hr COP$1500; ⊙8am-9pm Mon-Sat, to 7pm Sun), and there are reliable ATMs at **Banco de Bogotá** (Calle 21 No 16-30).

Casa Quimbaya (☎732-3086; www.casaquimbaya.com; Calle 16N No 14-92; dm COP$20,000, s/d COP$45,000/60,000; 📶) is a comfortable hostel run by friendly young locals. The **bus terminal** (☎747-3355; Calle 35 No 20-68) is around 1.5km southwest of the center. **Aeropuerto Internacional El Edén** (☎747-9400) is 18km southwest of Armenia, near the town of La Tebaida.

Parque Nacional del Café

This **amusement park** (☎741-7417; www.parquenacionaldelcafe.com; Km 6, Vía Montenegro; admission COP$18,000-50,000; ⊙9am-4pm Wed-Sun) is basically a funfair with a shot of espresso tacked on as an afterthought: what a waterslide and a rollercoaster have to do with the production of coffee is anyone's guess. However, it does have a few fun rides (alas, no dodgems in the shape of giant coffee beans, or a whirling waltzer in the form of spinning espresso cups) and definitely beats spending the day in Armenia. It's about 15km west of town. Four buses an hour (COP$1400, 30 minutes, until 7pm) run the route.

Salento

☎6 / POP 7200

After the jarring concrete horrors of Manizales, Pereira and Armenia, Salento comes as a relief to the senses. Despite being a very popular destination, for Colombian and international visitors alike, Salento still retains much of its small-town charm. The gentle rolling hills are carpeted in thick

DON'T MISS

HOT SPRINGS OF RISARALDA

Termales de Santa Rosa (☎363-4959; www.termales.com.co; admission COP$35,000; ⏲9am-10pm) are 9km east of Santa Rosa de Cabal, a town on the Pereira–Manizales road. A tourist complex including thermal pools, a hotel, restaurant and bar has been built near the springs at the foot of a 170m-high waterfall. You can stay on-site, but it's overpriced.

Around 800m down the hill, and under the same management, are the more low-key **Balneario de Santa Rosa** (☎314-701-9361; www.termales.com.co; admission COP$30,000; ⏲9am-midnight) thermal pools, which are surrounded by fantastic gardens and constructed under a splendid waterfall that divides into half-a-dozen different streams.

If you want to stay nearby, try **Cabaña El Portal** (☎320-623-5315; r per person COP$20,000), a couple of blocks further down hill from the baths. From Santa Rosa de Cabal catch a *chiva* (basic rural bus) from the market at 7am, 10am, noon, 3pm and 5pm (COP$2500, 45 minutes). Upon arrival, the *chivas* return immediately. Jeeps (COP$20,000) also do the run; ask around in the main plaza.

Set in a spectacular misty valley at the foot of Parque Nacional Natural (PNN) Los Nevados, 18km from Santa Rosa de Cabal, **Termales San Vicente** (www.sanvicente.com.co; admission COP$25,000; r per person COP$80,000-180,000, campsite per person COP$55,000; ⏲8am-midnight) are the most relaxing option for all water babies. Here you will find several concrete pools, natural saunas and a canopy line, but the clear highlights are the *pozos de amor* – natural pools formed in a fast-flowing river surrounded by lush vegetation. You can stay here in a variety of pricey-but-worth-it accommodations or sign up at the **booking office** (☎333-6157; Av Circunvalar No 15-62; ⏲8am-5pm Mon-Fri, to 3pm Sat) in Pereira for the excellent value day trip (COP$55,000), which includes round-trip transportation, admission, lunch and a refreshment.

forest that embrace the undulations of the land like a mother with her newborn, while the town's architecture is a chocolate-box colonial fantasy. The peaceful streets are lined with many shops selling handicrafts and there are plenty of relaxing bars, cafes and billiard halls.

Its proximity to the fabulously beautiful Valle de Cocora makes Salento a required stop on any Colombian itinerary, however tight. During the week it's serene, but on weekends hordes of day-trippers descend on the town and the main square is full of families laughing, singing and dancing.

Sights & Activities

Charismatic coffee grower Don Elías offers tours in Spanish of his **organic farm** (Spanish only; COP$5000). The farm is about a 45-minute walk from town – from the central park walk north for a block, then west across the yellow bridge. Keep going straight, it is about 200m after the turnoff to El Ocaso.

Plantation House offers tours of their coffee farm in English every morning. If you want to learn more about what to do with the end product, head to La Eliana (p590) for coffee-making classes.

Several places around town rent horses and offer guided excursions through the spectacular surrounding countryside. A recommended guide is **Álvaro Gomez** (☎311-375-8293, 759-3343), who has a great deal of experience and keeps his horses in fine condition. Book in advance and he will meet you at your hostel.

Sleeping

La Serrana HOSTEL $
(☎296-1890; www.laserrana.com.co; Km 1.5, Via Palestina ; dm COP$20,000, s/d COP$55,000/65,000, without bathroom COP$45,000/55,000; @📶) On a peaceful hilltop dairy farm with stunning views across the valley, this hostel has top-notch facilities and a fantastic atmosphere. The restaurant prepares excellent budget meals and there is a lovely yard in which to pitch a tent. Well worth the solid 20-minute walk from town. If you have heavy bags, hire a jeep (COP$6000).

Plantation House HOSTEL $
(☎316-285-2603; www.theplantationhousesalento.com; Calle 7 No 1-04; dm COP$19,000-22,000,

s/d/tr COP$48,000/53,000-66,000, without bathroom COP$38,000/43,000/57,000; tours guests/visitors COP$10,000/20,000; @) The original Salento hostel is an old-school backpacker experience. While it is not luxurious, it has amazing views and a bright new kitchen/social area with an open fireplace. It is possible to stay on the owner's nearby coffee farm and there are quality mountain bikes for rent.

Tralala HOSTEL **$**
(314-850-5543; www.hosteltralalasalento.com; Carrera 7 No 6-45; dm COP$18,000, s/d COP$45,000/60,000, without bathroom COP$35,000/45,000;) In a brightly renovated colonial house only half a block from the town's central park, this small, well-run hostel is set around a lush garden with a peaceful elevated terrace.

Hotel Las Palmas GUESTHOUSE **$**
(759-3065; Calle 6 No 3-02; dm COP$23,000, s/d COP$30,000/50,000;) Hospitable locally run place that is a fine choice for those who prefer to be around Colombians rather than travelers. The wood-lined rooms are neat and tidy but have low ceilings.

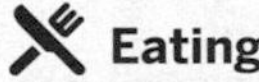

Eating

In the main plaza many stands and kiosks sell excellent-value local dishes, including cracker-thin *patacones* loaded with tasty *hogao* (warm tomato chutney), shredded chicken and guacamole, and delicious local trout.

Rincón del Lucy COLOMBIAN **$**
(Carrera 6 No 4-02; meals COP$6000) Simple, generous portions of food served fast in the town's busiest and best place for *comida corriente*. The beans are marvelous, and even the cheapest cuts of meat are prepared with finesse.

La Eliana INTERNATIONAL **$**
(Carrera 2 No 6-65; mains COP$5000-12,000; coffee-making classes COP$10,000; 8am-1pm & 4-9pm) Prepares quality breakfasts as well as gourmet pizzas, sandwiches, and, if you're in the mood for something different, real Indian curries. The portions are generous and prices are very reasonable for the quality.

Drinking

The main plaza is lined with bars that kick out the jams at the weekends. Take your pick – they're all great.

TOP CHOICE **Billar Danubio Hall** BAR
(Carrera 6 No 4-30; 8am-midnight Mon-Fri, to 2am Sat & Sun) Your every Latin small-town fantasy rolled into one: old men in non-ironic ponchos and cowboy hats sip *aguardiente* (cane alcohol) while playing dominos and breaking into ragged harmony whenever an anthem of heartbreaking personal relevance is played. It's a bastion of unreconstructed male behavior, so women may be treated as a curiosity at best. You're safe though – they're total gentlemen.

Donde Mi Apá BAR
(Carrera 6 No 5-24) Brilliantly snug bar with leglessly drunk clientele who have been carrying heavy objects up steep hills all day. A classic of its kind. Note the hundreds of envy-inspiring vinyl LPs (which they won't bloody sell you) behind the bar.

Speakeasy BAR
(Calle 6 No 0-48; 6pm-midnight) Sip cheap mojitos at candlelit tables in the backyard of this groovy bar at the entrance to town.

Café Jesús Martín CAFE
(www.cafejesusmartin.com; Carrera 6A No 6-14; 8am-9pm) Great local coffee, an OK wine list and a relaxed, smart atmosphere.

Getting There & Away

Buses to Salento from Armenia (COP$3400, 50 minutes) run every 20 to 30 minutes until 9pm. There are half a dozen buses a day between Pereira and Salento (COP$5500, 1¼ hours), otherwise take any Armenia bound bus to Los Flores, cross the road and flag down an Armenia–Salento service.

Valle de Cocora

East of Salento, the stunning Valle de Cocora is like a lush, tropical version of Switzerland, with a broad, green valley floor framed by rugged peaks. However, you'll remember you're a few degrees from the equator when, a short walk past Cocora, you suddenly encounter hills covered with the *palma de cera* (wax palm). The trees tower above the cloud forests in which they thrive. It is an almost hallucinatorily beautiful sight.

The most spectacular part of the valley is east of Cocora. Take the rough road heading downhill to the bridge over the Río Quindío (a five-minute walk from the restaurants) and you will see the strange 60m-high palms. After an hour or more of walking you'll come to a signpost, with **Reserva Natural Acaime** (admission COP$3000 incl refreshment) to the right. Here you'll find a wonderful hummingbird reserve, at least six varieties are always present, with dozens of birds zipping past at once. Admission includes a piping hot cup of coffee or *agua panela*. You can also stay at on-site **accommodations** (dm COP$15,000).

Head back to the signpost, and either double back the way you came or take the harder road uphill towards La Montaña for some of Colombia's most mind-blowing landscapes.

Six jeeps (COP$3000, 35 minutes, 6:10am, 7:30am, 9:30am, 11:30am, 3pm and 4pm) depart daily from Salento's plaza to Cocora. Arrive 15 minutes before the departure time to ensure you get a spot.

SOUTHWEST COLOMBIA

Southwest Colombia will spin your head with its blend of ancient and modern culture. Cali, its largest city, throbs with tropical energy and attitude; the remarkable archaeological sites of San Agustín and Tierradentro, nestled deep in majestic mountain landscapes, are benign and fascinating, while the Desierto de la Tatacoa is an arid anomaly.

The colonial city of Popayán, the other major tourist draw, is a living museum of Spanish rule, with many ornate churches, fascinating museums and a smart, relaxed atmosphere.

Approaching the border with Ecuador at Ipiales, the landscape gets vertiginous and the scene gets Andean; here you'll feel more like you're in Ecuador than Colombia. The beautiful Laguna de la Cocha, in Pasto, and the Santuario de las Lajas, a neo-Gothic church in Ipiales that spans a wide gorge, are the major attractions here.

Desierto de la Tatacoa

The 330-sq-km Tatacoa Desert is a curiosity, as it's surrounded on all sides by greenery. The mountain peaks around Nevado de Huila grab most of the incoming precipitation, leaving Tatacoa a parched spot where temperatures reach up to 50°C. It features a variety of landscapes ranging from eroded grey-sand ridges to other-planet-like labyrinths carved out of bright red rock and is made up of several distinct ecosystems, where skipping goats, inquisitive foxes and scampering armadillos dodge between the cacti.

Apart from the magnificent panoramas, the main attraction here is the **Observatorio Astronómico de la Tatacoa** (879-7584; www.tatacoa-astronomia.com; Cuzco; viewings COP$10,000; visitors center 10am-9pm). The lack of light pollution and thin air facilitate spectacular stargazing. Between 7pm-9pm, local astronomer **Javier Fernando Rua Restrepo** (310-465-6765) shows visitors around the sky using two tripod telescopes. Call ahead to check on conditions. The visitors center here rents bicycles and arranges guided hikes and tours on horseback.

Despite being conveniently located midway between Bogotá and San Agustín, Tatacoa remains off the gringo trail and has little in the way of tourist facilities. It's accessed by the sleepy town of Villavieja, where the locals have a fantastic, sing-song way of speaking. There are a number of small hotels in the town, the best of which is **Villa Paraiso** (879-7727; hotelvillaparaisovillavieja@yahoo.es; Calle 4 No 7-69; s/d COP$20,000/50,000).

For the full Tatacoa experience, stay at one of the many simple *posadas* (guesthouses) in the desert with local residents. About 400m past the observatory, **Estadero Doña Lilia** (313-311-8828; r per person with/without bathroom COP$25,000/20,000) has comfortable rooms with impressive views and serves delicious meals. Behind the observatory is a large **campground** (Cuzco; campsite per person COP$5000) with room for 40 tents. You can also rent a hammock for COP$10,000 and string it up outside on the Greek pillars on the front porch.

There are a handful of *mototaxis* in Villavieja that charge COP$15,000 to COP$20,000 to take up to three passengers to the observatory. They also offer guided tours of the area (COP$80,000, two to three hours).

Getting There & Away

Vans hop the 37km between Neiva and Villavieja (COP$5000, one hour) from 5am to 7:30pm. There are regular buses from Neiva to Bogotá (COP$35,000, five hours) and San Agustín (COP$23,000, four hours).

Cali

2 / POP 2.5 MILLION

Cali is Colombia right in your face. The attitude, the heat, the traffic, the music and the food all combine in a delightful, dizzying haze. Compared with Popayán's genteel politeness, Medellín's confident strut and Bogotá's refined reserve, Cali is all front – but just behind that front is a passionate, rebellious Colombian city that will love you if you love it.

It's not a city without attractions: the arty colonial neighborhood of San Antonio, with its bohemian park, is a great place for a wander and there are several classy dining districts. But without a doubt Cali's biggest attribute is its proud residents, a multiethnic mix rich in Afro-Colombian heritage, for whom there is no greater blessing than being born *caleño*.

If salsa is the soul music of Latin America then it's no surprise that Cali, a tough, working town that has seen its fair share of trouble, is obsessed with it. Salsa is not entertainment here, it's a way of life. If you've never heard the explosive, insurrectionary power of a salsa orchestra live, this is your chance – don't miss it.

Cali doesn't cater to tourists with the same eagerness as other destinations, but this somehow contributes to its charm. Cali needs you less than you need it. It's a busy, tough, and at times grimy and unsafe town, but when night falls and the temperature drops on the streets, the locals seize the night with the ferocity of people who've worked hard and who want, no, *need* to party. You're welcome along for the ride.

Sights & Activities

Museo Arqueológico la Merced MUSEUM
(Carrera 4 No 6-59; admission COP$4000; 9am-1pm & 2-6pm Mon-Sat) Housed in a former colonial-era convent, the Museo Arqueológico la Merced features an interesting collection of pre-Columbian pottery.

FREE **Museo del Oro** MUSEUM
(Calle 7 No 4-69; 10am-5pm Mon-Sat) A small but well-selected collection of gold and pottery pieces of the Calima culture.

Iglesia de la Merced CHURCH
(cnr Carrera 4 & Calle 7; 6:30am-10am & 4-7pm) The lovely mid-16th-century Iglesia de la Merced is Cali's oldest church.

Cerro de las Tres Cruces VIEWPOINT
No trip to Cali is complete without a visit to the three crosses that tower over the city. It's a hefty three-hour hike from the Santa Monica neighborhood. Go in a group or go on the weekend, when there are plenty of locals on the path. Alternatively, take a taxi (COP$40,000 round trip).

Museo de Arte Moderno La Tertulia GALLERY
(www.museolatertulia.com; Av Colombia 5 Oeste-105; admission COP$4000; 10am-6pm, closed Mon) The Museo de Arte Moderno La Tertulia presents temporary exhibitions of contemporary painting, sculpture and photography.

Zoológico de Cali ZOO
(892-7474; www.zoologicodecali.com.co; cnr Carrera 2A Oeste & Calle 14 Oeste; admission COP$11,000; 9am-5pm) Colombia's best zoo covers 10 hectares and is home to about 1200 animals (belonging to about 180 species), both native and foreign.

Courses

Manicero DANCE
(513-0231; faimball@hotmail.com; Carrera 39 No 9-56) Best dance academy for group salsa classes.

Festivals & Events

TOP CHOICE **Festival de Música del Pacífico Petronio Álvarez** MUSIC
(www.festivalpetronioalvarez.com; Aug) A festival of Pacific music, heavily influenced by the African rhythms brought by the many slaves that originally populated the Pacific coast.

Festival Mundial de Salsa SALSA
(www.mundialdesalsa.com; Sep) Top salsa dancers take to the stage.

Feria de Cali CULTURE
(www.feriadecali.com; Dec) This is the main event, from December 25 extending to the end of the year with parades, salsa concerts, bullfights and a beauty pageant.

Sleeping

For a chilled Cali experience, choose San Antonio; if you are after nightlife, go for Granada.

Guest House Iguana HOSTEL $
(660-8937; www.iguana.com.co; Av 9N No 22N-46; dm COP$17,000-19,000, s/d COP$45,000/55,000,

without bathroom COP$35,000/45,000; @) Laid-back hostel with a variety of comfortable accommodations spread over two adjoining houses. There is a pleasant garden area and free salsa classes several times a week.

Pelican Larry HOSTEL **$**
(396-8659; www.pelicanlarry.com; Calle 20N No 6AN-44; dm COP$18,000, r COP$60,000, s/d without bathroom COP$30,000/50,000) With a great central location and a lively ambience, this social hostel is a great base from which to explore the city's nightlife. It has fresh dorms and big spacious rooms with solid beds.

Café Tostaky HOSTEL **$$**
(893-0651; www.cafetostaky.blogspot.com; Carrera 10 No 1-76; dm COP$17,000, s/d without bathroom COP$25,000/40,000, apt COP$50,000-80,000; @) Right by Parque San Antonio, this French-owned hostel is a popular choice among more mellow travelers. The rooms are basic but spacious and all share bathrooms. Downstairs there is a chilled bar-cafe that serves crepes and good coffee.

Jardín Azul GUESTHOUSE **$$**
(556-8380; www.jardinazul.com; Carrera 24A No 2A-59; r COP$100,000-120,000;) Spotless small guesthouse offering huge, bright rooms with big beds and imported cotton sheets. There is a small pool set in an appealing garden that attracts plenty of birds.

Jovita's Hostel HOSTEL **$**
(893-8342; www.jovitashostel.com; Carrera 5 No 4-56; dm COP$20,000, s/d without bathroom COP$35,000/40,000; @) In a freshly renovated colonial house in San Antonio, Jovita's is a hostel, salsa school and yoga center rolled into one. Many of the rooms don't have windows but the high roof keeps them cool. The dorms have towering triple bunks. Offers free daily dance classes.

Calidad House HOSTEL **$**
(661-2338; www.calidadhouse.com; Calle 17N No 9AN-39; dm COP$15,000, s/d without bathroom COP$30,000/40,000; @) Clean, neat and tidy hostel with low prices and a fine location. Has one of the better guest kitchens in town.

La Casa Café HOSTEL **$**
(893-7011; www.lacasacafecali.blogspot.com; Carrera 6 No 2-13; dm COP$18,000, s/d without bathroom COP$25,000/30,000; @) This groovy cafe-bar in San Antonio rents great-value dorm beds and private rooms on the 2nd floor of its colonial building.

Bamboo GUESTHOUSE **$**
(314-890-5966, 668-4572; Av 9N No 26N-16; dm COP$20,000, s/d COP$35,000/40,000) In a quiet residential street, this friendly guesthouse is great value with clean, bright rooms with cable TV and kitchen access. Rooms with bathroom are the same price as those without.

Eating

TOP CHOICE **Lulodka** FUSION **$$**
(Calle 2 No 6-17; set meals COP$7500, mains COP$15,000-30,000) You won't find better value for your peso than at this groovy fusion restaurant in a lovely colonial house. The gourmet set lunches include soup, salad, main course, fresh juice and dessert. Everything is cooked to perfection, with delicately

DON'T MISS

SAN CIPRIANO

Surrounded by thick jungle, San Cipriano is a tiny Afro-Colombian town that is a fantastic budget destination for nature lovers. A crystal-clear river flows through the center of the community. Walk upstream and float back down on an inner tube or cool off in one of the many swimming holes.

The town is as famous for its mode of arrival as for its natural wonders. Situated on the little-used Cali–Buenaventura railroad and 15km from the nearest road, residents have come up with ingenious homemade rail trolleys powered by motorcycles that fly through the jungle at breakneck speed. Hold on tight and wear shoes so you can jump off in an emergency.

It's possible to visit on a day trip from Cali but why rush? There are a number of extremely basic budget hotels here all charging COP$10,000 to COP$15,000 per person.

From Cali, any Buenaventura-bound bus will drop you at Córdoba (COP$18,000, three hours), from where it's a 15-minute ride by mototrolley (COP$8000 return).

Cali

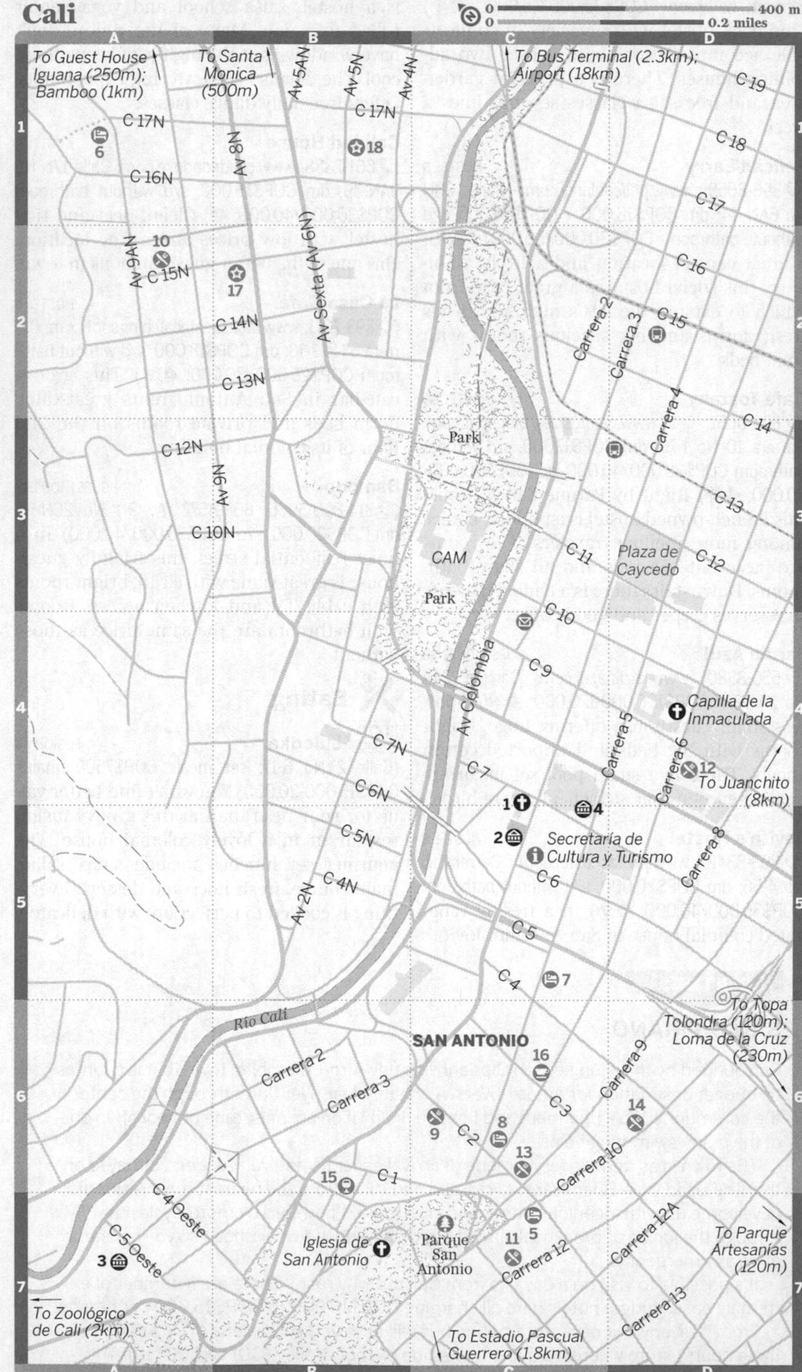

To Guest House Iguana (250m); Bamboo (1km)
To Santa Monica (500m)
To Bus Terminal (2.3km); Airport (18km)
Park
CAM
Park
Plaza de Caycedo
Capilla de la Inmaculada
To Juanchito (8km)
Secretaría de Cultura y Turismo
Río Cali
SAN ANTONIO
To Topa Tolondra (120m); Loma de la Cruz (230m)
Iglesia de San Antonio
Parque San Antonio
To Parque Artesanías (120m)
To Zoológico de Cali (2km)
To Estadio Pascual Guerrero (1.8km)
Av Sexta (Av 6N)
Av Colombia
Carrera 2
Carrera 3
Carrera 4
Carrera 5
Carrera 6
Carrera 8
Carrera 9
Carrera 10
Carrera 12
Carrera 12A
Carrera 13
C 4 Oeste
C 5 Oeste
COLOMBIA CALI

Cali

Sights

Sleeping

Eating

Drinking

Entertainment

balanced flavors and textures and the experience is enhanced by great music and decor.

Dona Francia ICE CREAM $
(Carrera 27 No 3-100; snacks COP$5000) Sit on benches outside this Cali institution and enjoy sensational juices, sorbets and possibly the best fruit salad in all of Colombia. It's one block east of Parque del Perro.

Bahareque COLOMBIAN $$
(Calle 2 No 4-52; set lunch COP$7000, mains COP$15,000-20,000; ⌚lunch daily, dinner Fri-Sat) You might have to fight for a table at this popular San Antonio restaurant, which serves a great set meal. Sample amazing salads garnished with tropical fruit, plus good steaks and chicken for carnivores.

Zahavi BAKERY $
(Carrera 10 No 3-81; pastries COP$2000-6000, sandwiches COP$12,000) This posh bakery in San Antonio serves excellent coffee, rich gooey brownies and delicious gourmet sandwiches.

Govindas VEGETARIAN $
(Carrera 6 No 8-48; set meals COP$6000; ⌚11am-3pm; 🖉) Cheap vegetarian restaurant in the center with tasty set meals and meat-free *papas rellenas* (filled potato balls deep-fried in batter) for a rare veggie street snack.

El Zaguán de San Antonio COLOMBIAN $$
(Carrera 12 No 1-29; mains COP$20,000-24,000) This San Antonio favorite serves huge portions of traditional *vallecaucana* food, which means plenty of meat, and sensational fresh juices. Sit upstairs for great views.

El Solar ITALIAN $$$
(Calle 15N No 9-62; mains COP$18,000-34,000) Serves consistently excellent Italian food in a large covered courtyard. On the menu are fresh homemade pastas, risottos, gourmet pizzas and salads.

Drinking

Most *caleños* don't really go out to drink, they go out to dance. Grassy Parque San Antonio offers great views of the city lights and is a popular place for some early evening beers. There are dozens of small bars in the area around Parque del Perro.

La Colina BAR
(Calle 2 Oeste No 4-83) Friendly neighborhood shop-bar hybrid in San Antonio. Cheap beer and classic salsa and boleros.

Macondo Café CAFE
(Carrera 6 No 3-03; ⌚noon-midnight Mon-Sat, 4:30pm-midnight Sun) Relaxed San Antonio spot with delicious coffee, snacks and original tropical cocktails.

Entertainment

El País newspaper has a good listing section.

Cali's dance floors are not for the faint-hearted or stiff-hipped – the salsa style here is faster and more complex than elsewhere, with fancier footwork. The most exclusive clubs are in the north. Calle 5 south of the river is less dressy.

Clubs in Cali are only permitted to open until 3am, however venues on the outskirts stay open later, including the flash discos of Menga and the famous *salsotecas* (salsa clubs) of Juanchito, a suburb on the other side of the Río Cauca.

Cali has two soccer teams. **Deportivo Cali** (www.deportivocali.com.co) play in the Estadio Deportivo Cali near the airport in Palmira. **América de Cali** (www.america.com.co), who at the time of research were languishing in the second division, play in the city at **Estadio Pascual Guerrero** (cnr Calle 5 & Carrera 34). Any Palmira-bound bus can take you to the former; to the latter, take the Mio.

Zaperoco SALSA CLUB
(www.zaperocobar.com; Av 5N No 16-46; ⊙Tue, Fri & Sat) Fun *salsoteca* with exuberant sounds and a torrid, tropical atmosphere. The sound-system is set to 'ear-splitting'.

Tin Tin Deo SALSA CLUB
(www.tintindeocali.com; Calle 5 No 38-71; cover COP$5000-10,000; ⊙7pm-2am Thu, to 3am Fri & Sat) This iconic, unpretentious 2nd-floor salsa joint in San Fernando sometimes feels like a gringo circus (especially on Thursdays) but is a great place for novice dancers to get on the floor.

Topa Tolondra BAR
(Calle 5 No 13-27) Humble small salsa bar with a fun ambience near Loma de la Cruz. The tables are all pushed right up against the walls leaving the concrete floor free for you to get your boogie on.

Changó SALSA CLUB
(www.chango.com.co; Vía Cavasa) The most famous *salsoteca* in Juanchito has lost a bit of its energy but is still worth checking out. It's huge, with plush booths and a big, smoking-hot dance floor. There's no cover charge, but it's a COP$15,000, 20-minute taxi ride from town.

Kukaramakara CLUB
(www.kukaramakara.com; Calle 28N No 2bis-97) Live bands. Gets full early.

Cinemateca La Tertulia CINEMA
(☎893-2939; www.museolatertulia.com; Av Colombia No 5 Oeste-105; admission COP$5000) Cali's best art-house cinema has screenings at 7pm and 9:15pm daily.

FREE **Lugar a Dudas** CULTURAL CENTER
(☎668-2335; www.lugaradudas.org; Calle 15N No 8N-41; ⊙11am-8pm Tue-Fri, 4:30am-8pm Sat) Attracts large crowds for its weekend film screenings. Serves coffee and snacks.

Shopping

Parque Artesanías MARKET
(⊙10am-8pm) On Loma de la Cruz, this is one of Colombia's best *artesanía* (handicrafts) markets. You'll find authentic, handmade goods from the Amazon, Pacific Coast, southern Andes and even Los Llanos.

Information

Cali has an edge, especially south of the river: avoid walking alone east of Calle 5. Taxis are the safest way to travel.

4-72 (Carrera 3 No 10-49)

Banco de Occidente (Av Colombia 2-72) Closest ATM to San Antonio.

Citibank (Av 5N No 23AN-49, Parque Versalles) ATM.

Giros & Finanzas (Carrera 4 No 10-12) Changes cash and is a Western Union agent.

Migración Colombia (☎397-3510; www.migracioncolombia.gov.co; Av 3N 50N-20, La Flora) For visa extensions.

Secretaría de Cultura y Turismo (www.cali.gov.co/cultura; cnr Calle 6 & Carrera 4; ⊙9am-noon & 2pm-5pm)

Getting There & Away

Air

The Palmaseca Airport is 16km northeast of the city. Minibuses between the airport and the bus terminal run every 10 minutes until about 8pm (COP$4000, 30 minutes), or take a taxi (COP$50,000).

Bus

The bus terminal, **La Terminal** (www.terminalcali.com; Calle 30N No 2AN-29), is 2km north of the center. It's a sweaty walk in Cali's heat; take the Mio or a taxi (COP$6000).

Buses run regularly to Bogotá (COP$60,000, 10 hours), Medellín (COP$46,000, nine hours) and Pasto (COP$40,000, nine hours). Pasto buses will drop you off in Popayán (COP$12,000, three hours) or you can take the hourly minibuses (COP$14,000, 2½ hours). There are also regular departures to Armenia (COP$20,000, four hours), Pereira (COP$22,000, four hours) and Manizales (COP$35,000, five hours).

Getting Around

You can cover the new and old centers on foot. Taxis in Cali are all metered; make sure the driver turns it on when you hop in. The meter records 'units', which represent distance covered. The minimum fare is COP$4000.

Cali's air-conditioned integrated bus system, the **Mio** (www.mio.com.co), is similar to the TransMilenio in Bogotá. The most useful route for visitors runs from north of the bus terminal along the river, through the center, and down the length of Av 5 to the Universidad del Valle. Single journeys cost COP$1600.

Popayán

☎2 / POP 266,000

Popayán is an enigma. It's a delightful, elegantly preserved town, second only to Cartagena as Colombia's most impressive colonial settlement, with excellent cheap eats and a lively young population. It should be a booming budget travel hot spot but receives surprisingly few visitors.

However, Popayán's lack of tourist game is a windfall for those who make the effort to know it. It's an immaculate example of Spanish-colonial architecture, with chalk-white houses, magnificent museums set in old mansions, splendid churches and a central plaza where locals fan themselves against the midday heat in the shade of palm trees and tropical conifers. The town also boasts one of Colombia's best universities and is famed for its flavorful culinary traditions.

Founded in 1537, Popayán quickly became an important political, cultural and religious center, and was a key stopping point on the route between Quito and Cartagena as the Spanish plunderers looted the continent of much of its gold. The town's mild climate attracted wealthy Spanish settlers from the sugarcane farms near Cali. Several imposing churches and monasteries were built in the 17th and 18th centuries, when the city was flourishing.

In just 18 seconds, all this was unceremoniously torn down when a powerful earthquake ripped through the town on March 1, 1983, before the Maundy Thursday religious procession. The rebuilding work took more than 20 years, but all of its churches have now been restored.

Today, the town is best known for its eerie Easter Week celebrations, when huge, neo-kitsch floats depicting the Passion of Christ are carried through town by bearers in medieval costume amid a fog of incense.

Sights

Popayán has some of Colombia's finest museums, most of which are set in old colonial mansions.

Walk north up Carrera 6 to the river to see two unusual old bridges. The small one, **Puente de la Custodia**, was constructed in 1713 to allow the priests to cross the river to bring the holy orders to the sick of the poor northern suburb. About 160 years later the 178m-long 12-arch **Puente del Humilladero** was built alongside the old bridge and is still in use.

Iglesia de San Francisco CHURCH
(cnr Carrera 9 & Calle 4; guided tour COP$2000; ⏲8am-noon & 4-6pm) The city's largest colonial church and arguably the best, with its fine high altar and a collection of seven amazing side altarpieces. Other colonial churches famed for their rich original furnishings include **Iglesia de Santo Domingo** (cnr Carrera

WORTH A TRIP

PACIFIC COAST

Colombia's Pacific Coast hasn't traditionally offered much love to the budget traveler. The infrastructure is poor, and traveling is improvised and expensive – mainly by ship, speedboat and light plane, since only one road links it with the interior of the country (the Cali–Buenaventura road).

However, things are changing. Security has improved dramatically and now the only stretches that remain off-limits are the departments of Cauca and Nariño south of Buenaventura and the extreme northern Chocó near the border with Panama. And while most accommodations in these parts are still targeted at wealthy domestic tourists, the first backpacker hostel in the region has opened near **El Valle**, and several places around **Ladrilleros** in Valle de Cauca now offer budget whalewatching tours.

Community-based tourism is taking off too. In villages throughout the Chocó there are co-operatives of guides that take visitors on cheap trips in the jungle, along rivers or in the mangroves, while to the south of El Valle volunteers are able to contribute to an important turtle conservation program.

If you do choose to visit the Pacific Coast, a copy of Lonely Planet's *Colombia* is highly recommended.

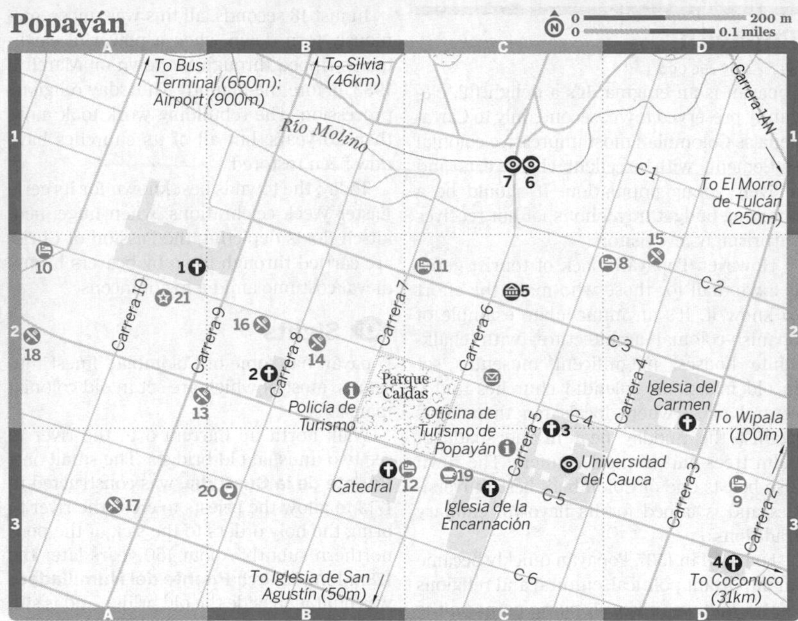

5 & Calle 4), **Iglesia de San José** (cnr Calle 5 & Carrera 8) and **Iglesia de San Agustín** (cnr Calle 7 & Carrera 6).

El Morro de Tulcán HILL

Behind the university, this hill is said to be the sight of a pre-Columbian pyramid and offers great views over the city. Come in a group and don't bring any valuables, as robberies have been reported on the path.

FREE **Museo Guillermo Valencia** MUSEUM

(Carrera 6 No 2-69; ⏲10am-noon & 2-5pm, closed Mon) This late-18th-century building is full of period furniture that once belonged to the Popayán-born poet who lived here. It has been left more or less as it was when Guillermo Valencia died in one of the upstairs bedrooms.

Museo de Historia Natural MUSEUM

(museo.unicauca.edu.co; Carrera 2 No 1A-25; admission COP$3000; ⏲9am-noon & 2-5pm) Has extensive collections of insects, butterflies and stuffed birds.

Iglesia La Ermita CHURCH

(cnr Calle 5 & Carrera 2) Popayán's oldest church (1546) is worth seeing for the fragments of old frescoes, which were discovered after the earthquake.

Festivals & Events

Semana Santa RELIGIOUS

(Holy Week) Head here during Holy Week and you will see the night-time processions that are organized on Maundy Thursday and Good Friday. The **festival of religious music** is held at the same time, inadvertently proving that the devil does in fact have all the best tunes.

Congreso Nacional Gastronómico FOOD

(www.gastronomicopopayan.org; ⏲Sep) Top chefs are invited to come and cook up a storm at this gourmet food festival in the first week of September. Admission to all of the week's events costs COP$300,000, but there are many free activities.

Sleeping

Prices in many places increase dramatically during Semana Santa.

Hosteltrail Guesthouse HOSTEL $

(☎831-7871; www.hosteltrrail.com; Carrera 11 No 4-16; dm COP$18,000, s/d COP$40,000/55,000, without bathroom COP$30,000/45,000; @) Welcoming backpacker hostel with all you need: dorms, kitchen, wi-fi and lockers. Friendly, informed owners.

Popayán

Sights

Sleeping

Eating

Drinking

Entertainment

Parklife Hostel HOSTEL $
(☎300-249-6240; www.parklifehostel.com; Calle 5 No 6-19; dm COP$17,000, s/d COP$40,000/50,000, without bathroom COP$35,000/45,000; @📶) Stylish hostel with a great location next to the cathedral. The front rooms have superb views over Parque Caldas.

Casa Familiar Turística HOSTEL $
(☎824-4853; Carrera 5 No 2-07; dm COP$14,000, s/d COP$20,000/30,000; 📶) Popayán's original budget accommodations are a great option for those looking to immerse themselves in local culture, as you're basically sharing the colonial house with the friendly Colombian owners.

Hostel Caracol HOSTEL $
(☎820-7335; www.hostelcaracol.com; Calle 4 No 2-21; dm COP$19,000, s/d without bathroom COP$32,000/50,000; @📶) This chilled hostel in a renovated colonial house is popular with slightly older independent travelers.

Hotel Los Balcones HOTEL $$
(☎824-2030; www.hotellosbalconespopayan.com; Carrera 7 No 2-75; s/d/apt COP$61,600/115,000/170,100; @📶) Climb 200-year-old stone stairs to your room in this regal 18th-century abode. Rooms are spacious and have TV.

Eating

Plenty of places in the center offer set lunches for as little as COP$4000.

Lonchería La Viña COLOMBIAN $$
(Calle 4 No 7-79; mains COP$14,000-24,000; ⏰24hr) Popular grill restaurant that prepares bargain steaks on a large barbecue in the middle of the dining room. The *bife de chorizo* cut is a winner. At lunch it offers a fine set meal for COP$8000.

Mora Castilla CAFE $
(Calle 2 No 4-44; snacks COP$2500-4000; ⏰10am-7pm) This tiny cafe prepares excellent juices and traditional snacks including tamales and *carantantas* (a kind of toasted corn chip).

Sabores del Mar SEAFOOD $
(Calle 5 No 10-97; lunch COP$6000) Run by an energetic family from Guapi, this tiny nautical-themed place serves a great-value seafood lunch. Try the fillets of *toyo* (a kind of shark).

La Fresa CAFETERIA $
(Calle 5 No 8-89; snacks COP$400-2000; ⏰8am-8pm) A grimy corner store with a couple of plastic tables, La Fresa is famed throughout Popayán for its outrageously delicious *empanadas de pipián* (fried potato pastries).

Restaurante Vegetariano Maná VEGETARIAN $
(Calle 7 No 9-56; meals COP$4000; 🥬) The best of several cheap vegetarian diners in Popayán, Maná has a set meal with plenty of options to choose from and serves a tasty hot breakfast.

Restaurante Italiano ITALIAN $$
(Calle 4 No 8-83; mains COP$15,000-26,000) Swing open the saloon doors of this Swiss-owned Italian joint and you'll find great pizza and pasta. The set lunch (COP$8500) is top-notch.

Drinking & Entertainment

Wipala BAR
(Carrera 2 No 2-38; ⏰2pm-1am Mon-Sat, 3-10pm Sun; 📶) Groovy cafe-bar with a small garden

that serves organic local coffee, *hervidos* (fruit infusions) and their own energy drink made with coca tea, ginger and ginseng. They also make an awesome veggie burger. Come for the great live entertainment, which could be anything from belly dancing to rock.

Capriccio Café CAFE
(Calle 5 No 5-63; ⊙8:30am-12:30pm & 2-8:30pm Mon-Sat) Local cafe favored by serious coffee drinkers. Roasts its own organic beans.

El Sotareño BAR
(Calle 6 No 8-05) Popayán institution, playing *bolero, ranchero* and *milonga* off original vinyl. Try not to drool in envy at the collection.

Bar La Iguana BAR
(Calle 4 No 9-67) The dance floor gets packed at this lively bar playing mostly salsa.

Information

4-72 (Calle 4 No 5-74)

Banco de Bogotá (Parque Caldas) ATM on Parque Caldas.

Banco de Occidente (Parque Caldas) Has a reliable ATM.

Migración Colombia (☎823-1027; Calle 4N No 10B-66) Visa extensions.

Oficina de Turismo de Popayán (☎824-2251; Carrera 5 No 4-68; ⊙8am-noon & 2-6pm Mon-Fri, 9am-1pm Sat & Sun)

Policía de Turismo (☎822-0916; Carrera 7 No 4-36) Tourist Police. More helpful than the regular tourist office.

Getting There & Away

Air

The airport is just behind the bus terminal, a 15-minute walk north of the city center. **Avianca** (☎824-4505; Carrera 5 No 3-85; ⊙8am-5pm Mon-Sat) has three flights daily to and from Bogotá.

Bus

The bus terminal is a short walk north of the city center. Plenty of buses run to Cali (COP$15,000, three hours) and there are also express minivans (COP$17,000, 2½ hours). There are several daily buses direct to Armenia (COP$40,000, seven hours). Buses to Medellín (COP$60,000, 11 hours) depart at 7pm, 8pm and 1am.

Buses to Pasto (COP$25,000, six hours) leave every hour and there are six buses daily to San Agustín (COP$30,000, six hours). Avoid night buses on these routes, as security is still an issue on both highways.

Around Popayán

SILVIA

☎2 / POP 31,500

Of Colombia's 68 indigenous groups, the Guambino are the most immediately recognizable, and have survived colonialism, repression and modernization with their language, dress and customs intact. On Tuesday, they descend from their *resguardo* (reserve), which lies an hour further east, and hit Silvia for market day, to sell their produce, to buy tools and clothes, and to hang out in the main square of this small and otherwise unremarkable town.

The men and women dress in flowing, shin-length blue woolen skirts, edged with pink or turquoise, with a thin, dark woolen poncho laid over the shoulders – this is 2800m above sea level, and their reserve lies higher still. Scarves are ubiquitous, and both men and women wear a kind of felt bowler hat, some choosing to fold in the top of it so it resembles a trilby. It's a rakish look however it's worn.

Most of the older women wear many strings of small beads clustered about their necks, and carry a wooden needle which they use to spin yarn from a ball of sheep fleece that they store in their net sacks.

You should keep your camera in your pocket unless you enjoy needless aggravation. True, it can be frustrating not to record such a colorful and 'foreign' scene, but you'll quickly make yourself a spectacle and cause offense, period.

The main square, and the market southwest of it, are where the action's at. Don't expect some kind of theme park show for your entertainment, though. This is a working town, and people are here to do business. There are few arts and crafts on sale, and you're more likely to see an indigenous elder haggling over the price of boots and saucepans (or chatting on his cell phone) than offering wisdom for coins.

The best entertainment is provided by traveling performers, snake-oil salesmen, bogus telepathists and assorted magicians and mentalists who perform in the square on market day. Stand and watch some tricksters putting on a show as the raucous church bell clangs through the cool mountain air, surrounded by the smiling, impossibly ancient faces of the Guambino and dozens of laughing Colombians, and divisions soon dissolve.

There are hourly buses to Silvia from Popayán's terminal (COP$6000, 1½ hours). Leave around 8am to catch the market in full swing.

PARQUE NACIONAL PURACÉ

This mountainous **national park** (☎823-1223; admission Colombian/foreigner COP$8500/19,500) 45km east of Popayán offers good trekking through fascinating landscapes gurgling with geysers and a couple of dramatically set waterfalls. It's also the only place in Colombia to spot condors in the wild.

The **visitors center** (campsite per person COP$8000, r per person COP$33,000) rents unheated cabins and serves budget meals; there's no hot water, but some cabins have fireplaces. This is the starting point for the hike to the crater of **Volcán Puracé** (4650m), the highest of the seven volcanoes in the Coconuco range. It's about five hours up and three hours down along a well-signposted trail, although because of the difficulty of the climb a guide is recommended. Set out early – the mist soon descends and you'll see nothing from the top.

To reach the park, take any La Plata-bound bus from Popayán to **Cruce de la Mina** (COP$10,000, 1¼ hours), from where it's a 2.5km walk uphill to the visitors center. On the way you may be asked to pay a small fee in the indigenous settlement of Puracé to enter the community lands. If you're coming for the day, it's best to take the first bus at 4:30am.

A further 8km along the highway from Cruce de la Mina is the entry point for the **Termales de San Juan**, some natural springs in an utterly otherworldly setting, swathed in mosses and lichens, with hot water bursting through the rock and gushing around in every direction. Beware of the toxic clouds of sulfur and don't bathe – you'll upset the ecosystem's delicate balance.

The last bus back to Popayán passes Cruce de la Mina around 5pm. Bring food, water and a copy of your passport for the military checkpoint in Puracé.

San Agustín

☎8 / POP 11,000

Long before Europeans came to the Americas, the rolling hills around San Agustín were ruled by a mysterious group of people who buried their dead and honored them with magnificent statues carved from volcanic rock. The legacy that they left behind is now one of the continent's most important archaeological sites. Hundreds of freestanding monumental statues were left next

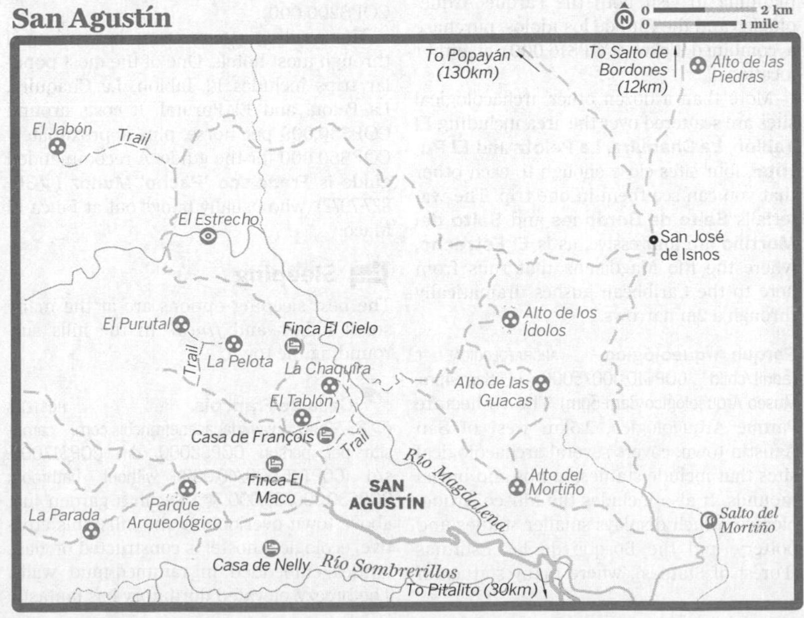

to the tombs of tribal elders of a now disappeared tribe. Pottery and gold objects were also left behind, although much of it was stolen over the centuries.

San Agustín culture flourished between the 6th and 14th centuries AD. The best statuary was made only in the last phase of the development, and the culture had presumably vanished before the Spaniards came. The statues were not discovered until the middle of the 18th century.

So far more than 500 statues have been found and excavated. A great many are anthropomorphic figures – resembling masked monsters. Others are zoomorphic, depicting sacred animals including the eagle, the jaguar and the frog. The statues vary both in size, from about 20cm to 7m, and in their degree of detail.

Today, San Agustín captivates travelers thanks to its history and tranquility, along with the significantly reduced security risks for foreigners in the area. The countryside is beautiful, prices are low and the air and light is crystalline. It's a perfect place to decompress.

Sights & Activities

The statues and tombs are scattered over a wide area on both sides of the gorge formed by the upper Río Magdalena. If you are planning to visit both the Parque Arqueológico and the Alto de los Ídolos, purchase a combined ticket (COP$16,000) at either location.

More than a dozen other archaeological sites are scattered over the area including **El Tablón**, **La Chaquira**, **La Pelota** and **El Purutal**, four sites close enough to each other that you can see them in one trip. The waterfalls **Salto de Bordones** and **Salto del Mortiño** are impressive, as is **El Estrecho**, where the Río Magdalena that runs from here to the Caribbean gushes dramatically through a 2m narrows.

Parque Arqueológico ARCHAEOLOGICAL SITE
(adult/child COP$10,000/5000; 8am-4pm, Museo Arqueológico 8am-5pm) The 78-hectare Parque Arqueológico, 2.5km west of San Agustín town, covers several archaeological sites that include statues, tombs and burial mounds. It also includes the Museo Arqueológico, which displays smaller statues and pottery, and the Bosque de las Estatuas (Forest of Statues), where many statues of different origins are placed along a forest footpath.

Alto de los Ídolos ARCHAEOLOGICAL SITE
(admission COP$10,000; 8am-4pm) This is another archaeological park, noted for burial mounds and large stone tombs. The largest statue, 7m tall, but with 4m visible and 3m underground, is here. The park is a few kilometers southwest of San José de Isnos, on the other side of the Río Magdalena from San Agustín town. It's a two-hour walk from San Agustín, or you can take a *colectivo* (COP$3000).

Magdalena Rafting RAFTING
(311-271-5333; www.magdalenarafting.com; Calle 5 No 16-04) This is an experienced whitewater rafting operator that offers half-day trips (COP$45,000 per person) on the Río Magdalena.

Tours

The usual way of visiting San Agustín's sights (apart from the Parque Arqueológico) is by jeep tour and horse-riding excursion. The standard jeep tour includes El Estrecho, Alto de los Ídolos, Alto de las Piedras, Salto de Bordones and Salto de Mortiño. It takes seven to eight hours and costs COP$30,000 per person. Alternatively, get a group together and hire a vehicle (COP$150,000 to COP$200,000).

Horse-riding tours can be arranged through most hotels. One of the most popular trips includes El Tablón, La Chaquira, La Pelota and El Purutal. It costs around COP$30,000 per horse, plus approximately COP$60,000 for the guide. A recommended guide is **Francisco 'Pacho' Muñoz** (311-827-7972), who usually hangs out at Finca El Maco.

Sleeping

The best sleeping options are at the many small lodges and *fincas* in the hills surrounding the town.

Casa de François HOSTEL $
(837-3847; www.lacasadefrancois.com; campsite per person COP$8000, dm COP$17,000, s/d COP$45,000/40,000, without bathroom COP$30,000/35,000; @) Set in a garden just above town overlooking the hills, this creative, ecological hostel is constructed of glass bottles embedded in rammed-mud walls. The breezy, elevated dormitory has fantastic

views and the spacious shared kitchen is one of the best around.

Finca El Maco HOSTEL $
(☎311-271-802, 837-3437; www.elmaco.ch; campsite per person COP$8000, dm COP$17,000, s/d from COP$33,000/48,000; @) Popular hostel with a variety of rooms and cabins set amid a lush garden. The restaurant serves homemade organic yogurt and an excellent Thai curry. It's out of town off the road to the Parque Arqueológico. Take a taxi (COP$7000) if you have luggage.

Casa de Nelly HOSTEL $$
(☎310-215-9067; www.hotelcasadenelly.co; Vereda La Estrella; dm COP$18,000, s/d COP$35,000/70,000, without bathroom COP$25,000/50,000) The original San Agustín hostel has a spacious social area with an open fireplace and a range of comfortable accommodations set around what has to be the prettiest garden in town.

Hospedaje El Jardín GUESTHOUSE $
(☎837-3455; Carrera 11 No 4-10; r with/without bathroom COP$20,000/15,000) Basic but neat option in town near the bus offices.

Finca El Cielo HOTEL $$
(☎313-493-7446; www.fincaelcielo.com; Via al Estrecho; r per person COP$40,000 incl breakfast) Elegant *posada* constructed from *guadua* that offers tremendous views out over the surrounding, misty green hills. Breakfast included.

Eating

TOP CHOICE **Tomate** VEGETARIAN $
(Calle 5 No 16-04; meals COP$7000; ⏲8am-3pm; ✎) Some of the best vegetarian food you'll find in Colombia made from fresh ingredients and bursting with flavor. Also sells wholegrain breads.

Donde Richard COLOMBIAN $$
(☎312-432-6399; Vía al Parque Arqueológico; mains COP$15,000-22,000; ⏲noon-7pm, closed Wed) This popular grill is a great choice if you have the cash and a very empty belly. Gorge on smoked leg of pork for dinner and you won't need breakfast the next day.

Mercado de San Agustín MARKET $
(cnr Carrera 11 & Calle 2; mains COP$3000-5000) Local market with great cheap lunches and fresh basic provisions if you're doing your own cooking.

Information

Banco Agrario de Colombia (cnr Carrera 13 & Calle 4) ATM; often has long lines.

Banco de Bogotá (Calle 3 No 10-61) Reliable ATM.

Oficina de Turismo (☎837-3007; Carrera 11 No 3-61) There are fake 'tourist offices' around town, but the real deal is located inside the Casa de la Cultura.

Getting There & Away

San Agustín's brand new bus terminal on the highway out of town should be open by the time you read this. If not, buses are probably still departing from Calle 3 near the corner of Carrera 11.

Five buses a day go to Popayán (COP$16,000, six to eight hours, at 7am, 9am, 11:30am, 2pm and 4pm) via a rough but spectacular road through Isnos. Do not travel at night, as robberies are not uncommon.

There are around a dozen daily departures to Bogotá (COP$55,000 to COP$60,000, 10 hours). For Tierradentro, go to Pitalito (COP$5000, 45 minutes) and change for La Plata (COP$20,000, four hours), from where buses leave for San Andrés de Pisimbalá (COP$10,000, 2½ hours).

Getting Around

Taxis have set prices depending on the zone with a full list posted inside the vehicle. Buses run every 15 minutes between town and the Parque Arqueológico (COP$1200).

Tierradentro

☎2 / POP 600

Travelers who brave the rough ride along the pitted dirt roads that lead through mountains and cliffs to Tierradentro will find tranquility, friendly locals, and one of the continent's most important and awe-inspiring archaeological sites.

Buried under the lush green fields above the tiny pueblo of San Andrés de Pisimbalá are dozens of intricately designed and decorated sacred burial sites hewn out of the volcanic rock, left behind by a disappeared tribe of indigenous Colombians, who archaeologists say lived around the 7th and 9th centuries AD. The Páez people who live here today say they are not connected to the tomb-diggers, and so the sites' origins remain uncertain.

The elaborate circular tombs once contained the ashes and remains of a people highly skilled in engineering, with a harmonious aesthetic sense revealed by the mysterious geometric designs etched, painted and chiseled into the walls of dozens of chambers. Around 100 tombs have been excavated so far and several dozen statues similar to those found at San Agustín are also found here.

Tierradentro used to have a bad reputation (not entirely deserved) as a guerrilla stronghold, but today that is no longer the case. Thanks to the negative publicity, if you visit the sites soon you'll likely be alone, staring at the tombs with unanswered questions in your head and ripe guavas in your pocket, taken from the trees that line the paths.

Apart from the tombs, the area has cheap lodging and farm-fresh food for a few dollars a plate. True, there's no internet, few restaurants and zero entertainment, but the nearby village of San Andrés de Pisimbalá is a calming place to hang out for a few days. The landscapes here will make your soul gently soar, and the only sounds at night are cicadas and the distant rush of the Río San Andrés.

Sights

The **Parque Arqueológico** (Archaeological Park; ☎313-829-3066; adult/child or senior COP$10,000/5000; ⌚8am-4pm) is made up of four main archelogical sites and two museums. Tickets are valid for two consecutive days.

It's worth visiting the museums before heading out to the tombs. The **Museo Arqueológico** contains pottery urns that were found in the tombs; the **Museo Etnográfico** has utensils and artifacts of the Páez.

You'll need at least half a day to see a good selection of tombs here, so plan to arrive before midday. Some of the tombs have electric lights, but it's also worth bringing a flashlight.

A 20-minute walk up the hill north of the museums will bring you to **Segovia**, the most important burial site. There are 28 tombs here, some with well-preserved decoration.

Other burial sites include **El Duende** (four tombs without preserved decoration) and **Alto de San Andrés** (six tombs, two of which have their original paintings). **El Aguacate** is high on a mountain ridge, a spectacular and strenuous two-hour one-way walk from the museum. There are a few dozen tombs there, but most have been destroyed by *guaqueros* (grave robbers). Statues have been gathered together at El Tablón.

The tiny village of **San Andrés de Pisimbalá**, about a 25-minute walk west of Tierradentro, has a beautiful 400-year-old thatched church with reeling swallows darting around the ancient rafters.

Sleeping & Eating

Whether it's the result of walking all day or the crystalline mountain air, every single thing you eat and drink here tastes delicious. There are several cheap *hospedajes* clustered around the entrance to the museums. They are fine for those on a short visit, but if you plan to stick around longer, better choices are available in San Andrés de Pisimbalá.

TOP CHOICE **La Portada** GUESTHOUSE $
(☎311-601-7884; San Andrés de Pisimbalá; s/d COP$20,000/30,000) Right where the bus drops you in San Andrés, this elegant wooden lodge has large, clean rooms with private hot-water bathrooms and the best food in town. Try the homemade ice cream. The friendly owners will give you a map and plenty of advice on visiting the tombs and onward transport. They can also organize horse rental.

Hospedaje Pisimbalá GUESTHOUSE $
(☎311-605-4835; Tierradentro; r per person COP$12,000) Smallish rooms with hot water near the museums. It serves excellent cheap meals including vegetarian options.

Viajero GUESTHOUSE $
(☎312-746-5991; Calle 6 No 4-09, San Andrés de Pisimbalá; r per person COP$10,000) Cheap basic option in the village with cold showers.

Residencias Lucerna GUESTHOUSE $
(Tierradentro; r per person COP$10,000) This simple place next to the museums has a kitchen for guests.

Getting There & Away

Buses to Tierradentro (COP$18,000, five hours) leave Popayán at 5am, 8am, 10:30am, 1pm and 3pm. Only the 10:30am service goes all the way to San Andrés de Pisimbalá, passing the museums on the way. The others will drop you off at El Cruce de San Andrés, from where it's a tough 4km walk uphill to the village. Grab a *mototaxi* (COP$3000) if there are any around.

Heading back to Popayán, one bus leaves San Andrés each morning at around 6am and passes in front of the museums. If you miss that, walk to El Cruce and flag down a bus passing at around 9am, 11am, 1pm and 4pm.

Buses leave San Andrés at 6:30am, 8am, 12pm and 4pm for La Plata (COP$10,000, two hours), where you can pick up connections to Bogotá, San Agustín and Neiva for the Desierto de la Tatacoa.

AMAZON BASIN

Colombia's Amazon makes up a third of the national territory, as large as California but with hardly a trace of infrastructure. It's mostly rainforest, woven loosely together by rivers and sparsely populated by isolated indigenous communities, many of whom shun the modern world.

Nothing can prepare visitors for their first glimpse of the Amazon rainforest: neither a guidebook, nor a film. Its total size is staggering beyond any conception; 5.5 million sq km. Looking at its infinite forests from an airplane window is like visiting a new planet; it seems to mock human attempts to comprehend its size. Paddling through it in a canoe is exhilarating and life-affirming.

This region is the most biodiverse location on earth, hosting 10% of all living species, but it is fragile and damaged and therefore it is very important to minimize the impact that your presence inevitably makes here. Use small boats where possible, travel in groups, travel by public transportation, and use operators that support indigenous communities.

GETTING TO ECUADOR

The road to Ecuador takes in Pasto and Ipiales, neither of which will detain travelers much. Pasto is really only worth a stay during the crazy festival, **Carnaval de Negros y Blancos** (Black and White Festival), held on January 4 and 5, when the entire city throws paint, flour, soot and chalk at each other in commemoration of a colonial-era festival, when slaves and owners switched face color for a day.

The only must-see is nearby **Laguna de la Cocha**, one of Colombia's most beautiful lakes. It's surrounded by ramshackle wooden houses painted in bright colors, many of them budget hotels and restaurants serving fresh trout. You can rent a motorboat (per hour COP$25,000), seating up to eight people, and buzz across the lake to visit **Isla Corota** (admission COP$1000) in its center. *Colectivos* (minibuses or shared taxis; COP$3800, 30 minutes, 25km) to the lake depart regularly on weekdays from the Iglesia de San Sebastián in central Pasto, and on weekends from the back of the **Hospital Departamental** (cnr Calle 22 & Carrera 7).

Pasto's only backpacker hostel is the **Koala Inn** (☎722-1101; Calle 18 No 22-37; s/d COP$20,000/30,000, without bathroom COP$14,000/25,000); it could do with a makeover but it's cheap, central and has laundry service. **Hotel San Sebastian** (☎721-8851; Carrera 22 No 15-78; s/d/tr COP$33,000/53,000/73,000; wi-fi) is as characterless as a shop dummy, but has very clean rooms with hot water, wi-fi and cable TV.

An hour and a half further down the Panamericana is Ipiales, a major crossing point to Ecuador. It's a functional border town saved by its famous neo-Gothic **El Santuario de las Lajas**. You don't need to stay overnight to visit the church. Drop your bags in the bus terminal's left luggage and take a *colectivo* (COP$2500, 20 minutes) to see the church, which spans a gorge and contains the cliff face where a local man says he saw an image of the Virgin appear in 1754. Pilgrims nationwide flock here and attribute thousands of miracles to the Virgin.

If you need to stay the night in Ipiales, try the **Hotel Belmont** (☎773-2771; Carrera 4 No 12-111; s/d COP$12,000/19,000), with simple rooms.

Ipiales has a large bus terminal about 1km northeast of the center. It's linked to the center by buses (COP$900) and taxis (COP$3000). There are regular buses to Bogotá (COP$100,000, 22 hours) and Cali (COP$45,000, 11 hours). All these will drop you in Popayán in eight hours. Avoid night travel between the border and Popayán.

Regular *colectivos* travel the 2.5km to the border at Rumichaca (COP$1500), leaving from the bus terminal and the market area near the corner of Calle 14 and Carrera 10. After crossing the border on foot, take another *colectivo* to Tulcán (6km). On both routes, Colombian and Ecuadorian currency is accepted.

Much of the Amazon territory is held by guerrilla groups and coca producers and is not somewhere that fosters independent travel. However, the town of Leticia, which boasts easy access to Peru and Brazil, and the surrounding border region along the Amazon River, is safe and relatively easy to explore.

Leticia

☎8 / POP 39,700

Leticia could be considered the end of the road in Colombia, that is if it wasn't located more than 800km from the nearest national highway. Lying in splendid isolation in the far south of the country, it's an outpost of cold beer and grilled fish, paved roads and internet cafes, tooting mopeds, ATMs, nightclubs, comfortable beds and air-con. But just a few hours away from this curious city lie thrilling rainforest excursions, fascinating indigenous communities, and flora and fauna in abundance.

Many travelers use Leticia as a transit point for onward travel – there are boat connections to Iquitos (Peru) and Manaus (Brazil), but a trip here in its own right is definitely worth making.

Leticia lies right on the Colombia–Brazil border. Just south across the frontier is Tabatinga, a Brazilian town of similar size. The towns are virtually merging together, and there are no border checkpoints between the two. On the island in the Amazon opposite Leticia–Tabatinga is Santa Rosa, a Peruvian village.

July and August are the only relatively dry months. The wettest period is from February to April. The Amazon River's highest level is from May to June, while the lowest is from August to October. The difference between low and high water can be as great as 15m.

Sights & Activities

Have a look around the **market** and stroll along the waterfront. Visit the **Parque Santander** before sunset for an impressive spectacle, when thousands of screeching parrots (locally called *pericos*) arrive for their nightly rest in the park's trees.

Mundo Amazónico GARDEN

(☎592-6087; www.mundoamazonico.com; Km 7.7, Via Tarapacá; tours COP$20,000; ⏲7am-2pm Mon-Sat) This interesting 29-hectare reserve outside town was designed to preserve endangered flora and fauna of the Amazon. The extensive botanical gardens boast some 700 species of flora divided into five sections. English spoken.

Río Tacana RIVER

(Km 11, Via Leticia-Tarapacá) This tree-lined river in the multiethnic community of Tacana is a popular bathing spot and is also a fine place to take a low-budget walk in the jungle. From the turnoff at Km 11, walk for 3km or take a *mototaxi* (COP$3000) to reach the river.

Museo del Hombre Amazónico MUSEUM

(☎592-7729; Carrera 11 No 9-43; ⏲8-11:30am & 1:30am-5pm Mon-Fri, 9am-1pm Sat) The small Museo del Hombre Amazónico features artifacts and household implements of indigenous groups living in the region. It was undergoing renovations at the time of research but should be open again by the time you read this.

Omagua NATURE RESERVE

(☎310-337-9233; www.amazonasomagua.com; Km 10, Via Tarapacá; ⏲8am-2:30pm) Great for active types, this private reserve offers a day package (COP$50,000) that includes a hike, tree climbing, zipline, and canopy walk on a hanging bridge. Accommodation in huts surrounded by jungle cost COP$60,000 per person, including a night walk.

Reserva Tanimboca NATURE RESERVE

(☎310-791-7570; www.tanimboca.com; Km 11, Via Tarapacá; zip-lining COP$60,000, kayaking COP$35,000; hammock/bed per person COP$20,000/25,000; ⏲8am-4pm) Slide along zip lines through the beautiful forest canopy or go kayaking at this private nature reserve. Stay in budget accommodations or splash out for a spectacular tree-house (per person including breakfast and nocturnal hike COP$99,000).

Tours

Authentic jungle experiences are generally not found along the Amazon proper but rather upstream in its many tributaries. The deeper you go, the better the chances of seeing wildlife in pristine habitats. This doesn't come cheap.

For a real low-cost jungle fix, take short trips with the locals from Puerto Nariño (p611). Bring plenty of sunscreen and mosquito repellent.

Leticia

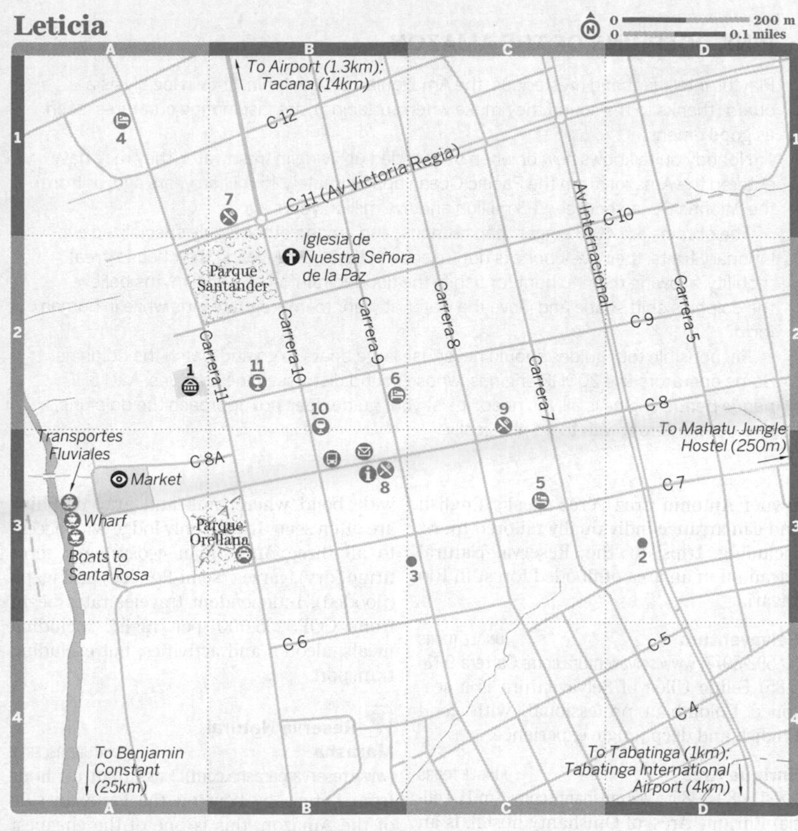

Jungle Guides

Travel here is not geared towards independent travel, as there is little public transportation and remote accommodations are not prepared for drop-in visitors.

The closest thing to an independent experience is hiring a guide and creating your own trip. The following recommended guides and companies can tailor excursions by land or river. Expect to pay around COP$400,000 per day for individual tours deep in the jungle, including crocodile-spotting, piranha-fishing, dolphin-watching, jungle walks and river trips, with transportation, food and accommodation included. Prices drop dramatically for groups.

Amazon Jungle Trips JUNGLE TOURS
(☎592-7377; www.amazonjungletrips.com.co; Av Internacional No 6-25) One of the oldest and most reliable tour companies in Leticia.

Leticia

Sights
1 Museo del Hombre Amazónico A2

Activities, Courses & Tours
2 Amazon Jungle Trips D3
3 Selvaventura C3

Sleeping
4 Hospedaje Los Delfines A1
5 Hotel de la Selva C3
6 La Jangada B2

Eating
7 La Casa del Pan B1
8 Restaurante El Sabor B3
9 Tierras Amazónicas C2

Drinking
10 Barbacoas B2
11 Titicó B2

PINK DOLPHINS OF THE AMAZON

Playful, intelligent and mysterious, the Amazonian pink dolphin, known locally as a *bufeo* (thanks to the sound they make when surfacing), are fascinating creatures, seen as good omens.

Nobody quite knows how or when they ended up living in freshwater, they may have entered the Amazon from the Pacific Ocean approximately 15 million years ago, or from the Atlantic Ocean between 1.8 million and five million years ago.

Their brains are 40% bigger than humans', and among other highly specialized evolutionary traits, their neck bone is not fused with their spine, giving their heads great mobility, allowing them to hunt for fish in the flooded rainforest. Local myths believe the dolphins shift shape and leave the water at night to impregnate girls while in human form.

Responsible tour guides should never use large boats to go and watch the dolphins. Some operators use 200HP engines, whose sound distresses the dolphins. A 10.5HP *peque peque* engine is all you need. Insist your guide does not approach the dolphins, and never interact with them physically.

Owner Antonio Cruz Pérez speaks English and can arrange individually tailored tours, including trips to the Reserva Natural Zacambú in an area of flooded forest in Río Yavarí.

Selvaventura JUNGLE TOURS
(☎592-3977; www.selvaventura.com; Carrera 9 No 6-85) Felipe Ulloa of Selvaventura is a seasoned Colombian professional, with good English and deep jungle experience.

Enrique Arés JUNGLE TOURS
(☎311-489-8985; www.omshanty.com; Km 11, Leticia) Enrique Arés, of Omshanty hostel, is an ice-cool, English speaking Basque biologist. He organizes trips deep into the jungle and also more budget-orientated trips closer to Leticia.

Jungle Lodges

Another way to get into the wilderness is to book accommodation directly at one of the lodges in the jungle surrounding Leticia. All lodges offer packages that include meals, accommodations and activities.

Legally you should have a Brazilian or Peruvian visa to stay in the reserves over the borders, although in reality this is rarely enforced. Check the situation with the lodge before you leave.

TOP CHOICE **Reserva Natural Palmarí** NATURE RESERVE
(☎in Bogotá 610-3154; www.palmari.org) About 90km by river from Leticia, on Río Yavarí, this rambling lodge sits on the high south (Brazilian) bank of the river overlooking a wide bend where pink and gray dolphins are often seen. It's the only lodge with access to all three Amazonian ecosystems: terra firme (dry), várzea (semi-flooded) and igapó (flooded). Independent traveler rates begin from COP$235,000 per night, including meals, alcohol and activities, but excluding transport.

Reserva Natural Marasha NATURE RESERVE
(www.reservamarasha.com) Less than an hour from Leticia by boat on the Peruvian side of the Amazon, this is one of the cheapest private jungle reserves. The lodge is located next to a lake, about a 90-minute walk through the jungle from the dock (make sure to hire rubber boots). An overnight trip including meals and a boat ride around the lake costs around COP$225,000 per person. Book at the **office** (☎592-7195; www.reservamarasha.com; Carrera 10 No 7-55) in Leticia.

Sleeping

LETICIA

Mahatu Jungle Hostel HOSTEL $
(☎311-539-1265; www.mahatu.org; Calle 7A No 1-40; dm COP$20,000-25,000, s/d COP$50,000/60,000; @🛜≋) An urban jungle four blocks from downtown Leticia, this hostel sits on five hectares, complete with duck-filled ponds, turtles and loads of exotic fruit trees. The simple rooms are tidy and facilities include a refreshing pool, kitchen for guests and even a soccer field.

La Jangada GUESTHOUSE $$
(☎312-361-6506; lajangadaamazonas.com; Carrera 9 No 8-106; dm COP$25,000, s/d COP$50,000/70,000, without bathroom COP$35,000/50,000; @📶) An excellent downtown guesthouse with a warm welcome. There's a spacious five-bed dorm with a breezy balcony and hammock and a few private rooms with fan.

Omshanty HOSTEL $
(☎311-489-8985; www.omshanty.com; Km 11, Leticia; hammock COP$10,000, dm COP$15,000, s/d/tr COP$35,000/55,000/75,000) Located 11 kilometers from town, this backpacker lodge is a great option if your budget won't run to a trip, as it's surrounded by nature. It has simple, spacious cabins with small kitchens and good beds. If you bring your own hammock you can stay for just COP$5000. Bring food, as you'll eventually tire of the cheap restaurant across the road.

Hotel de la Selva HOTEL $$
(☎314-803-4661; hoteldelaselvaleticia@hotmail.com; Calle 7 No 7-28; s/d COP$60,000/100,000, without air-con COP$45,000/80,000; ❄📶) Pass through the plant-filled entrance corridor and common areas to reach the 14 peaceful rooms with private bathrooms in this small friendly hotel.

Hospedaje Los Delfines GUESTHOUSE $$
(☎592-7488; losdelfinesleticia@hotmail.com; Carrera 11 No 12-81; s/d COP$40,000/70,000; 📶) Small family-run place offering eight neat rooms with fan and fridge, arranged around a leafy patio. Could do with some new mattresses and toilet seats, but it's pretty good value.

TABATINGA

Novo Hotel HOTEL $
(novohoteltbt@hotmail.com; Rue Pedro Texeira 9; s/d/tr COP$50,000/60,000/70,000) Conveniently located just three blocks from Porta da Feira, this friendly, clean option is perfect if you're catching an early boat.

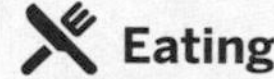

Eating

Local fish *gamitana* and *pirarúcu* – which can grow to 300kg – are delicious. The best cheap eats in town are at the barbecue stands that set up on the corner of Av Internacional and Calle 7 in the evenings.

Tierras Amazónicas SEAFOOD $$
(Calle 8 No 7-50; mains COP$10,000-18,000; ⏲closed Mon) The cheesy Amazonia knickknacks on the wall make it look like a tourist trap, but this lively restaurant serves up fantastic meals. Go for fresh local fish. There's a full bar and occasional live music.

Restaurante El Sabor COLOMBIAN $
(Calle 8 No 9-25; set meals COP$7000, mains COP$15,000; ⏲6am-11pm Mon-Sat) Leticia's best budget eatery, with excellent-value set meals and massive mains. Great *pirarúcu*.

La Casa del Pan BAKERY $
(Calle 11 No 10-20; breakfast COP$4500) You're in the middle of nowhere, and there's a decent bakery that does breakfast. What more could you ask for?

GETTING TO BRAZIL & PERU

Leticia may be in the middle of nowhere, but it's a popular route to Brazil and Peru. The quickest way out is by air from Tabatinga to Manaus in Brazil. Although slower, the more enjoyable route is by boat to Manaus or Iquitos in Peru. Iquitos is as isolated as Leticia, if not more so.

To Manaus, two boats a week leave from Porto Fluvial de Tabatinga, at 2pm on Wednesday and Saturday and stop by Benjamin Constant. The trip to Manaus takes three days and four nights and costs R$170 in your own hammock, or R$800 to R$1000 for two passengers in a double cabin. Food is included. Bring snacks and bottled water and watch your bags. **Rápida Puma** (☎in Brazil +97-9154-2597) runs a fast boat service (R$450, 30 hours) that leaves from Porto Bras in Tabatinga at 8am Friday.

Golfinho (☎in Brazil +97-3412-3186) and **Transtur** (☎in Brazil +97-3412-2945; www.transtursa.com; Marechal Mallet 248, Tabatinga) run modern, high-speed passenger boats between Santa Rosa and Iquitos. There are departures at 4am daily except Monday. The trip costs US$70 (or COP$140,000) and takes around 12 hours. Buy your tickets in Santa Rosa or at the agencies in Tabatinga and complete your immigration formalities in Santa Rosa the day before the trip. From Iquitos into Peru, you have to fly or continue by river to Pucallpa (five to seven days), from where you can go overland to Lima and elsewhere.

Drinking

Barbacoas BAR, POOL HALL

(Carrera 10 No 8-28) This pool hall has a fine sidewalk cafe to people-watch over a beer or Leticia's best *tinto* (black coffee).

Titicó BAR

(Calle 9 No 10-40; ⌚Wed-Sat) Adjoining Discoteca Kahlua, this nice chill-out bar is much more inviting than its neighbor, with a terrace overlooking the city.

Information

Emergency

Police (☎592-5060; Carrera 11 No 12-32)

Money

Change all the money of the country you're leaving in Leticia–Tabatinga. There are *casas de cambio* on Calle 8 between Carrera 11 and the market.

Banco BBVA (cnr Carrera 10 & Calle 7) Has an ATM.

Banco de Bogotá (cnr Carrera 10 & Calle 7) Also has an ATM.

Post

4-72 (Calle 8 No 9-56)

Tourist Information

Secretaría de Turismo y Fronteras (☎592-7569; Calle 8 No 9-75; ⌚8am-noon & 2-5pm Mon-Fri) Tourist Information. Also has a branch at the airport.

Visa Information

Locals and foreigners are allowed to come and go between Leticia, Tabatinga and Benjamin Constant in Brazil, and Santa Rosa in Peru without visas or passport control. If you plan on traveling further, get your exit stamp at the **Migración Colombia** (www.migracioncolombia.gov.co; Leticia Airport; ⌚7am-6pm Mon-Fri, 7am-4pm & 7pm-10pm Sat & Sun) office at Leticia's airport.

Complete your entry formalities in Brazil at **Policía Federal** (☎in Brazil 97-3412-2180; Av da Amizade 650, Tatabinga; ⌚8am-noon & 2-6pm), near the hospital in Tabatinga. If you're heading to Peru, get your stamp at the immigration office in Santa Rosa.

Citizens of many countries need a visa to enter Brazil. It is highly recommended to obtain it before traveling to the Amazon, but if you must, bring your passport and yellow fever certificate to the **Brazilian Consulate** (☎592-7530; Calle 10 No 9-104; ⌚8am-2pm). It can take up to three days.

If you need a Colombian visa extension, there is no need to pay an extension fee. Simply stamp out and head to Brazil or Peru for one day and return for a fresh entrance stamp up to the permitted limit.

Getting There & Away

Air

Tourists arriving at Leticia's airport are charged a compulsory COP$19,000 tax.

Copa (www.copaairlines.com) and **LAN** (www.lan.com) fly from Leticia to Bogotá daily. **Trip** (www.voetrip.com.br) and **TAM** (www.tam.com.br) fly from Tabatinga International Airport to Manaus.

Boat

Leticia connects downstream to Manaus (Brazil) or upriver to Iquitos (Peru).

To get to Puerto Nariño and Parque Nacional Amacayacu, buy tickets for the fast boat from Transportes Fluviales near the market in Leticia. Boats leave at 8am, 10am and 2pm, take 2½ hours and cost COP$29,000.

Getting Around

The *mototaxi* is king in Leticia; a short ride in the center costs COP$1000 or COP$2000 at night. Flag down any of the dudes riding round with a spare helmet in their hands. There is also a small fleet of tuk tuks that charge roughly double the motorbike price. Regular taxis here are more expensive than elsewhere in Colombia, the short trip from the airport to town costs COP$7000.

There is a regular bus service (COP$2400) during daylight hours from Parque Orellana to the Km 11 mark on Leticia's only highway, the Via Tarapacá.

Minibuses (COP$2000) run between Leticia–Tabatinga departing from morning until early evening. Boat taxis to Santa Rosa (COP$3000, 10 minutes) congregate near the market.

Parque Nacional Amacayacu

Parque Nacional Amacayacu takes in 2935 sq km of jungle on the northern side of the Amazon, about 55km upstream from Leticia.

A luxury hotel chain has been given the concession to run the facilities and now offers a sanitized version of the rainforest experience at sky-high prices to visitors who don't want to get their shoes dirty. The combined cost of the park entry fee (COP$36,500) and accommodations (simple dorm beds cost up to COP$195,000 depending on the season) rule this out for most budget travelers.

Boats from Leticia to Puerto Nariño will drop you off at the park's visitors center.

Getting back to Leticia is trickier, and you can get stranded for hours if the fast boats from Puerto Nariño fill up before they pass.

Puerto Nariño

☎8 / POP 2000

Puerto Nariño, a charming small town 60km up the Amazon from Leticia, is an appealing oddity. It's the second biggest settlement in the Colombian Amazon but there are no motor vehicles, and all rainwater is recycled – as is all garbage. Its narrow 'streets' are kept incredibly clean, thanks to daily sweeping patrols by proud women and girls, known as *escobitas*.

Sights & Activities

On a hill in the center of town, the shaky **Mirador Naipata** (Lookout; admission foreigner/Colombian COP$7000/5000; ⏲6am-6pm) affords spectacular views over the town and surrounding forest. On the riverfront, the **Centro de Interpretación Natütama** (www.natutama.org; admission COP$5000; ⏲8am-12:30pm & 2pm-5pm Wed-Mon) has a fascinating museum with nearly 100 life-sized wood carvings of Amazonian flora and fauna.

About 10km west of Puerto Nariño is **Lago Tarapoto**, a tranquil lake accessible only by river, where you can see pink dolphins playing. A half-day trip to the lake in a small boat can be informally organized with locals from Puerto Nariño (per boat for up to four people around COP$50,000).

Sleeping & Eating

TOP CHOICE **Alto del Águila** GUESTHOUSE **$**
(☎311-502-8592; altodelaguila@hotmail.com; r per person COP$20,000) A 20-minute walk from town, this magical hilltop retreat with basic rooms is run by a genial and eccentric holy man. As the friar welcomes you into his lodge he calls his pets and before you know it several monkeys gather around you and a pair of macaws swoop down from the canopy. It's possible to arrange cheap excursions into the jungle and nearby communities. Call (or ask around at the dock) when you arrive and they'll pick you up in a boat.

Malokas Napü GUESTHOUSE **$**
(☎310-488-0998; olgabeco@yahoo.com; Calle 4 No 5-72; r per person with/without balcony COP$30,000/25,000; @) The friendly owners offer good cheap rooms with fans, and a pleasant garden. The best rooms are at the back.

Las Margaritas COLOMBIAN, AMAZONIAN **$$**
(Calle 6 No 6-80; set meals COP$15,000) Excellent home-cooked meals are served buffet-style from traditional clay cookware under a huge *palapa* (thatchedf-roof shelter with open sides).

Delicias Amazónicas COLOMBIAN **$**
(meals COP$10,000) Cheap and tasty typical Colombian meals.

Information

There are no banks or ATMs in Puerto Nariño, so bring enough cash from Leticia.

Tourist Office (☎313-235-3687; cnr Carrera 7 & Calle 5; ⏲closed Sun) Located inside the *alcaldía* (municipal town hall building).

Getting There & Away

Fast boats leave Puerto Nariño for Leticia (COP$29,000, 2½ hours) at 7am, 11am and 4pm. Buy your ticket in advance at the office by the dock.

UNDERSTAND COLOMBIA

Colombia Today

It's hard to avoid the sensation upon visiting Colombia that this is a country on the verge of great things. The economy is booming, security has improved dramatically and the government is sitting down to talk peace with the Fuerzas Armadas Revolutionarias de Colombia (FARC), the country's largest rebel group, after nearly half a century of conflict.

Having been hand-picked as his successor by former president Álvaro Uribe, Harvard-educated former journalist, President Juan Manuel Santos, wasted no time in showing he is his own man. While continuing his predecessor's firm military crackdown on guerrillas, he also actively pursued negotiations with FARC behind the scenes, leading to the formal peace talks that got underway in November 2012 in Havana, the first official negotiations in more than a decade.

At the time of research, the talks had been running for three months without any declared progress. Some see the fact that discussions have not broken down as positive in itself, but violent clashes have continued throughout the country. The Santos government has refused the FARC's proposal for a total ceasefire (claiming that the group would use such an event to regather its forces) and set a time limit for concluding negotiations by November 2013.

Santos has shown himself to be a pragmatic leader: his economic policies are firmly neo-liberal and in May 2012 he oversaw the introduction of the long-delayed free trade agreement with the United States. However, he also forged closer ties with the late Venezuelan leader Hugo Chávez, much to the distaste of his former boss Uribe.

President Santos has publicly called for a major rethink on the drug war, arguing that as long as demand remains high in the USA and Europe, production and supply will remain profitable. Despite costly US-funded drives to eradicate crops and take out cartels, Colombia is still the world's top producer of cocaine. While several drug kingpins have been killed or arrested under Santos, the trafficking organizations remain powerful in many parts of the country. The influence of cartels in Colombian society was highlighted in August 2012 by the prosecution in the US of Uribe's former chief of security, General Mauricio Santoyo on charges of aiding the trafficking organizations. Facing calls for an investigation, Uribe has denied any knowledge of the general's illicit activities.

History

Pre-Columbian Times

Colombia's original inhabitants have left behind three main prehistoric sites: San Agustín, Tierradentro and Ciudad Perdida, along with the continent's finest gold work. They were highly skilled goldworkers and metalsmiths. Their work can be seen throughout Colombia in *museos del oro* (gold museums). Bogotá's is the best.

Scattered throughout the Andean region and along the Pacific and Caribbean coasts, the pre-Columbian cultures of Colombia developed independently. The most notable were the Calima, Muisca, Nariño, Quimbaya, San Agustín, Sinú, Tayrona, Tierradentro, Tolima and Tumaco.

The Conquistadors Arrive

In 1499 Alonso de Ojeda was the first conquistador to set foot on Colombian soil and to see its people using gold objects. Several short-lived settlements were founded, but it was not until 1525 that Rodrigo de Bastidas laid the first stones of Santa Marta, the earliest surviving town. In 1533 Pedro de Heredia founded Cartagena, which soon became the principal center of trade.

In 1536 a general advance toward the interior began independently from both the north and south. Jiménez de Quesada set off from Santa Marta and founded Santa Fe de Bogotá two years later. On the way he conquered the Muisca, a blow that would foretell the ultimate ruin of civilizations throughout the New World.

Meanwhile, Sebastián de Benalcázar deserted from Francisco Pizarro's army, which was conquering the Inca empire, and mounted an expedition from Ecuador. He subdued the southern part of Colombia, founding Popayán and Cali along the way, before reaching Bogotá in 1539.

With the growth of the Spanish empire in the New World a new territorial division was created in 1717, and Bogotá became the capital of its own viceroyalty, the Virreinato de la Nueva Granada. It comprised the territories of what are today Colombia, Panama, Ecuador and Venezuela.

Independence Wars

As the 18th century closed, disillusionment with Spanish domination matured into open protests and rebellions. When Napoleon Bonaparte invaded Spain and placed his own brother on the throne in 1808, the colonies refused to recognize the new monarch. One by one Colombian towns declared their independence.

In 1812 Simón Bolívar, who was to become the hero of the independence struggle, arrived in Cartagena to attack the Spanish. In a brilliant campaign to seize Venezuela, he won six battles, but was unable to hold Caracas and had to withdraw to Cartagena. By then Napoleon had been defeated at Waterloo, and Spain set about reconquering its colonies. Colonial rule was reestablished in 1817.

Bolívar doggedly took up arms again. After assembling an army of horsemen from the Venezuelan Llanos, strengthened by a British legion, he marched over the Andes into Colombia. Independence was won at Boyacá on August 7, 1819.

Independence & Civil War

Two years after declaring independence, revolutionaries sat down in Villa del Rosario (near Cúcuta) to hash out a plan for their new country. It was there that the two opposing tendencies, centralist and federalist, came to the fore. Bolívar, who supported a centralized republic, succeeded in imposing his will. The Gran Colombia (which included modern-day Ecuador, Colombia, Venezuela and Panama) came into being and Bolívar was elected president.

From its inception, the state started to disintegrate. It soon became apparent that a central regime was incapable of governing such a vast and diverse territory. The Gran Colombia split into three separate countries in 1830.

The centralist and federalist political currents were both formalized in 1849 when two political parties were established: the Conservatives (with centralist tendencies) and the Liberals (with federalist leanings). Colombia became the scene of fierce rivalries between the two forces; chaos ensued. During the 19th century the country experienced no less than eight civil wars. Between 1863 and 1885 there were more than 50 antigovernment insurrections.

In 1899 a Liberal revolt turned into a full-blown civil war – the so-called War of a Thousand Days. That carnage resulted in a Conservative victory and left 100,000 dead.

In 1903 the US took advantage of the country's internal strife and fomented a secessionist movement in Panama (at that time a Colombian province). By creating a new republic, the US was able to build a canal across the Central American isthmus.

La Violencia

After a period of relative peace, the struggle between Liberals and Conservatives broke out again in 1948 with La Violencia, the most destructive of Colombia's many civil wars, which left a death toll of some 300,000. Urban riots broke out on April 9, 1948 in Bogotá following the assassination of Jorge Eliécer Gaitán, a charismatic populist Liberal leader. Liberals soon took up arms throughout the country.

By 1953 some groups of Liberal supporters had begun to demonstrate a dangerous degree of independence. As it became evident that the partisan conflict was taking on revolutionary overtones, the leaders of both the Liberal and Conservative parties decided to support a military coup as the best means of retaining power and pacifying the countryside. The 1953 coup of General Gustavo Rojas Pinilla was the only military intervention the country experienced in the 20th century.

The dictatorship of General Rojas was not to last. In 1957 the leaders of the two parties signed a pact to share power. The party leaders, however, repressed all political activity that remained outside the scope of their parties, thus sowing the seeds for the appearance of guerrilla groups.

Birth of FARC & the Paramilitaries

During the late 1950s and early 1960s Colombia witnessed the founding of many guerrilla groups, each with its own ideology and its own political and military strategies. The most significant – and deadly – movements included FARC, Ejército de Liberación Nacional (ELN; National Liberation Army) and Movimiento 19 de Abril (M-19; April 19 Movement).

Until 1982 the guerrillas were treated as a problem of public order and persecuted by the army. President Belisario Betancur (r 1982–86) was the first to open direct negotiations with the guerrillas in a bid to reincorporate them into the nation's political life. Yet the talks ended in failure, and the M-19 guerrillas stormed the capital's Palacio de Justicia in November 1985, leaving more than 100 dead.

The Liberal government of President Virgilio Barco (r 1986–90), succeeded in getting M-19 to lay down their arms and incorporated them into the political process.

Another group emerging in the 1980s was the Autodefensas Unidas de Colombia (AUC; United Self-Defense Forces of Colombia). The AUC, paramilitary groups formed by rich Colombians looking to protect their lands, was responsible for dozens of massacres. This group supposedly disbanded in Uribe's second term, but many observers, including Human Rights Watch, say the disarmament was a sham.

All sides have committed and continue to commit atrocities, and the UN High Commissioner for Refugees (UNHCR) says Colombia has more than 4 million internally displaced people (almost 10% of the population), with the rural poor caught in the crossfire between the guerrillas, the still-active paramilitaries and the army.

White Gold

The cocaine mafia started in a small way in the early 1970s but, within a short time, the drug trade developed into a powerful industry with its own plantations, laboratories, transportation services and protection.

The boom years began in the early 1980s. The Medellín Cartel, led by Pablo Escobar, became the main mafia and its bosses lived in freedom and luxury. They founded their own political party and two newspapers, and in 1982 Escobar was elected to congress.

In 1983 the government launched a campaign against the drug trade, which gradually turned into an all-out war. The war became even bloodier in August 1989 when Luis Carlos Galán, the leading Liberal contender for the 1990 presidential election, was assassinated.

The election of the Liberal President César Gaviria (r 1990–94) brought a brief period of hope. Following lengthy negotiations, which included a constitutional amendment to ban extradition of Colombians, Escobar and the remaining cartel bosses surrendered and the narcoterrorism subsided. However, Escobar escaped from his palatial prison following the government's bumbling attempts to move him to a more secure site. An elite 1500-man special unit hunted Escobar for 499 days, until it tracked him down in Medellín and killed him in December 1993.

Despite this, the drug trade continued unaffected. The Cali Cartel, led by the Rodríguez Orejuela brothers, swiftly moved into the shattered Medellín Cartel's markets and became Colombia's largest trafficker. Although the cartel's top bosses were captured in 1995, the drug trade continued to flourish, with other regional drug cartels, paramilitaries and the guerrillas filling the gap left by the two original mafias.

In 1999 then-President Andrés Pastrana launched Plan Colombia with US backing. The plan called for the total eradication of the coca plant from Colombia by spraying fields with herbicide. While the program has achieved some success on paper (cultivated land has been cut by around half), it has also generated dire environmental effects, as impoverished growers moved their crops into national parks, where the spraying is banned.

The job of eradicating cocaine from Colombia appears Sisyphean. Despite US aid of around US$6 billion, latest figures show that production has stabilized and Colombia is still the world's largest producer.

President Álvaro Uribe

Right-wing hard-liner Álvaro Uribe was elected president in 2002. He inherited a country on the brink of collapse, a pariah state plagued by security problems, with many highways in the country roadblocked and controlled by the rebels. Uribe promised decisive military action against the guerrillas and he delivered. Suddenly, the country's roads were open, swamped with military, and safe.

Hugely popular, Uribe took a second term in 2006 after a constitutional amendment allowed him to run for power again. He forged on with further assaults on the guerrillas. His soldiers took the fight to the leftist rebels and pushed them back into remote jungles, where they remain today, weakened and isolated.

Uribe was viewed as a national hero but his presidency was ultimately tainted by scandal. By 2008, 60 congressmen had been arrested or questioned for alleged 'parapolitics' (links with paramilitaries).

The biggest scandal broke in October 2008, when journalists discovered that the army was killing civilians, dressing them in rebel uniforms and claiming them as combat kills in order to gain promotions or days off. It is estimated that during Uribe's presidency the Colombian army killed 3000 young, uneducated, so-called 'false positive' *campesinos* (peasant farmers) in a strategy described by UN Special Rapporteur on extrajudicial, summary or arbitrary executions, Philip Alston, as 'systemic.' When the scandal hit, Uribe launched a purge of the army, but prosecutions remain rare.

Yet more embarrassment for the Uribe regime came in early 2009, when the magazine *Semana* reported that the country's secret police, the Departamento Administrativo de Seguridad (DAS), had been tapping the phones of judges, opposition politicians, journalists and human-rights workers.

FARC on the Defensive

The last decade has been a disastrous period for FARC. The armed group has lost as many as half of its fighters and several key leaders through a combination of combat deaths and demobilizations.

In 2008 the rebels' chief bargaining pawn, French-Colombian presidential candidate Ingrid Betancourt, kidnapped six years earlier, was snatched in an audacious and legally questionable jungle raid by army forces.

But the biggest blow to the organization was delivered in November 2011 when army troops shot dead FARC leader and chief ideologist Alfonso Cano in rural Cauca. Within days of the death of Cano, new leader Rodrigo Londoño Echeverri, alias Timochenko, took control of the organization, announcing that FARC would continue to battle on all fronts, but behind the scenes the seriously weakened FARC entered preliminary talks with the government and within a year were sitting at the table in formal peace negotiations.

Culture

Everyone you meet who comes to Colombia with an open mind says the same: the people are genuinely friendly and helpful.

Colombia is the third-most populous country in Latin America. Its diverse population is an amalgam of three main groups – indigenous, Spanish and African. While 58% of the country claims *mestizo* (mixed indigenous and Spanish) heritage, other ethnicities include: 20% white, 14% mixed white and black, 4% black, 3% mixed black and indigenous, and 1% indigenous. Colombia's indigenous population speaks about 65 languages and nearly 300 dialects belonging to several linguistic families.

The divide between rich and poor in Colombia remains enormous. The wealthiest 10% of the country controls 45% of the country's wealth, while the poorest 10% control less than 1%, making Colombia one of the most unequal countries on the continent. While the nation's rapidly growing economy has seen some reduction in poverty, around one in three urban residents and almost half of rural Colombians still live below the poverty line.

In their hearts urban Colombians are all cowboys and they romanticize rural life, dreaming of a *finca* (country house with land), while many rural Colombians struggle to survive and dream of life in the big cities.

Colombian families are tight-knit and supportive and, in common with most Latin Americans, children are adored. Most couples that live together are married, though this is beginning to change.

The majority of Colombians are Roman Catholic. However, over the past decade there has been a proliferation of various Protestant congregations, which have succeeded in converting millions of Colombians, especially in rural areas.

Arts

Literature

During the independence period and up to WWII, Colombia produced few internationally acclaimed writers other than José Asunción Silva (1865–96), perhaps the country's best poet, and considered the precursor of modernism in Latin America.

A postwar literary boom thrust many great Latin American authors into the international sphere, including Colombian Gabriel García Márquez (b 1928). Gabo's novel *Cien años de soledad* (One Hundred Years of Solitude), published in 1967, immediately became a worldwide best seller. It mixed myths, dreams and reality, and amazed readers with a new form of expression that critics dubbed *realismo mágico* (magic realism). In 1982 García Márquez won the Nobel Prize in Literature.

There are several contemporaries who deserve recognition, including poet, novelist and painter Héctor Rojas Herazo, and Álvaro Mutis, a close friend of Gabo.

Music

Colombians love music and it is ever present in any journey through the country. From first thing in the morning, sound systems are turned up to full, playing a variety of music as diverse as the country itself.

The Caribbean Coast is the birthplace of *vallenato,* based (some might say excessively) on the European accordion. This is the most popular Colombian musical genre today and is played nonstop at earsplitting volume on long distance buses. The region also vibrates with African-inspired rhythms including cumbia, Colombia's most famous musical export, *mapalé* and *champeta,* an afro-electronic fusion with reggae influences.

The music of the Pacific Coast, such as *currulao,* is even more influenced by African elements and features a strong drum pulse with melody supplied by the *marimba de chonta,* also known as the 'piano of the jungle.'

Salsa is adored by everyone here, and nowhere is it more popular than in Cali, which has adopted the genre as its own and produced more than its share of great *salseros.*

Colombian Andean music has been strongly influenced by Spanish rhythms and instruments, and differs notably from its Peruvian and Bolivian counterparts.

Visual Arts

The colonial period in Colombia was dominated by Spanish religious art. The most renowned colonial artist was Bogotá-born Gregorio Vásquez de Arce y Ceballos, who painted more than 500 works that are now distributed among churches and museums across the country.

With the arrival of independence, visual arts departed from strictly religious themes, but it was not until the revolution in European painting at the turn of the 19th century that Colombian artists began to create truly original work.

Among the most distinguished modern painters and sculptors are Pedro Nel Gómez (known for his murals, oils and sculptures), Luis Alberto Acuña (a painter and sculptor who used motifs from pre-Columbian art), Alejandro Obregón (a painter tending to abstract forms), Rodrigo Arenas Betancur (Colombia's most famous monument creator) and Fernando Botero (the most internationally renowned Colombian artist). Spot a fat statue or portrait in Colombia and it's likely the latter's.

Contemporary artists worth your attention include Bernardo Salcedo (conceptual sculpture and photography) and Miguel Ángel Rojas (painting and installations).

Cuisine

While you probably didn't come to Colombia for the food, it's fairly easy to eat well, especially if you seek out some of the varied regional specialties.

Variety does not, unfortunately, apply to the *comida corriente* (basic set meal), which is the principal diet of most Colombians eating out. It is a two-course meal with *sopa* (soup) and *bandeja* (main plate). A *seco* (literally 'dry') is just the main course without soup. At lunchtime (from noon to 2pm) it is called *almuerzo*; at dinnertime (after 6pm) it becomes *comida,* but it is identical to lunch. The *almuerzos* and *comidas* are the cheapest way to fill yourself up, usually costing between COP$6000 and COP$8000. Breakfasts are dull and repetitive, normally *arepa* (grilled cornmeal patty) and eggs.

Typical food along the Caribbean Coast tends to involve fish, plantains and rice with coconut, while in the interior, meat, potatoes and beans are the norm.

Colombian food generally offers little variety when it comes to vegetables. However, many towns have dedicated vegetarian restaurants and local markets are full of great fresh produce, including amazing fruits, some of which you won't find anywhere else. Try feijoa, *guanábana* (soursop), *lulo, curuba, zapote, mamoncillo* (Spanish lime), *uchuva, granadilla, maracuyá* (passionfruit), *tomate de árbol, borojó* (tamarillo), *mamey* and *tamarindo* (tamarind).

Coffee is the number one drink – though the quality in most establishments will not impress aficionados. *Tinto,* a small cup of (weak) black coffee, is served everywhere. Other coffee drinks are *perico* or *pintado,* a small milk coffee, and *café con leche,* which is larger and uses more milk.

Traditional tea is not very popular, however there are several other excellent hot beverages. In mountainous areas, *té de coca* (coca tea) is widely available and will relieve symptoms of altitude sickness. *Aromáticas* – herbal teas made with various plants such as *cidrón* (lemon balm) and *yerbabuena* (mint) – are cheap and good. *Agua de panela* (unrefined sugar melted in hot water) is tasty with lemon.

Beer is popular, cheap and generally not bad. Colombian wine is vile. In rural areas, try homemade *chicha* and *guarapo* (alcoholic fermented maize or sugarcane drinks).

Sports

Soccer and cycling are Colombia's most popular spectator sports. Colombia regularly takes part in international events in these two fields, such as the World Cup and the Tour de France, and has recorded some successes. The national soccer league has matches most of the year. Baseball is limited to the Caribbean Coast.

Tejo is a truly Colombian sport that involves throwing large metal discs at paper bags filled with gun powder that let off a loud bang when you hit the target. It is usually accompanied by copious amounts of beer drinking.

Environment

Colombia covers about the same size as France, Spain and Portugal combined. It occupies the northwestern part of the continent and is the only South American country with coasts on both the Pacific (1448km long) and the Caribbean (1760km). Colombia is bordered by Panama, Venezuela, Brazil, Peru and Ecuador.

The physical geography of Colombia is extremely diverse. Most of the population live in the western part, which is mountainous with three Andean chains – the Cordillera Occidental, Cordillera Central and Cordillera Oriental – running roughly parallel north–south. More than half of the territory lies east of the Andes and is a vast lowland, which is divided into two regions: the savanna-like Los Llanos in the north and the rainforest-covered Amazon in the south.

Colombia has several small islands. The major ones are the archipelago of San Andrés and Providencia (in the Caribbean Sea, 750km northwest of mainland Colombia), the Islas del Rosario (near the Caribbean Coast) and Isla Gorgona (in the Pacific Ocean).

There are more plant and animal species per unit area in Colombia than in any other country in the world. This abundance reflects Colombia's numerous climatic zones and microclimates, which have created many different habitats and biological islands in which wildlife has evolved independently.

Colombia is home to the jaguar, ocelot, peccary, tapir, deer, armadillo, spectacled bear and numerous species of monkey, to mention just a few of the 350-odd species of mammals. There are more than 1920 recorded species of birds (nearly a quarter of the world's total), ranging from the huge Andean condor to the tiny hummingbird. Colombia's flora is equally impressive and includes some 3000 species of orchid alone. The national herbariums have classified more than 130,000 plants.

The best place to spot wildlife is in the country's excellent network of 56 national parks, sanctuaries and reserves. Only a handful of parks provide accommodations and food for visitors. The rest have no tourist amenities at all and some, especially those in remote regions, are virtually inaccessible. Some very isolated parks can be unsafe for tourists because of guerrilla presence.

Colombia's most popular parks are situated along the country's pristine beaches. Parque Nacional Natural (PNN) Tayrona (p560) is by far Colombia's biggest natural attraction, followed by Parque Nacional Corales del Rosario y de San Bernardo (p571). Trekkers will want to head inland to PNN El Cocuy (p548), PNN Los Nevados (p588) or PNN Puracé (p601) for adventurous trails through spectacular mountain scenery.

Many parks have admission fees that are collected on site. Accommodation in all parks can be organized through the Parques Nacionales Naturales office (p542) in Bogotá, while regional offices around the country are able to make reservations for parks in the local area.

SURVIVAL GUIDE

Directory A–Z

Accommodations

Colombia's backpacker market is growing daily, and with it comes the huge growth in facilities familiar to the continent. Even smaller, less-visited cities now have hostels with dormitories, internet, wi-fi, laundry services and travel advice. See www.colombianhostels.com for some of the most popular hostels in each city.

While dormitories are usually the cheapest option for budget travelers, private rooms in hostels in Colombia are often fancier and more expensive than local-oriented budget options. It's usually possible to find cheaper rooms, albeit with less facilities at your disposal, at local *hospedajes, residencias* and *posadas.*

A hotel generally suggests a place of a higher standard, and almost always has a private bathroom, while *residencias, hospedajes* and *posadas* often have shared facilities. You may want to bring a cotton or silk sleeping-bag liner for hygiene if you're staying in ultra-low-budget spots.

Motels rent rooms by the hour. They're found on the outskirts of the city and usually have garish signs. Many Colombians live at home until marriage, so couples check in here for a few hours of passion and privacy.

Camping is gaining in popularity as the country's safety improves. Note that army-style kit is forbidden for private use.

SLEEPING PRICE RANGES

The following price ranges refer to a double room with bathroom.

$ less than COP$65,000

$$ COP$65,000 to COP$160,000

$$$ more than COP$160,000

Activities

Hikers planning to visit remote national parks, including PNN El Cocuy, need to register their itineraries with the local Parques Nacionales (www.parquesnacionales.gov.co) office beforehand.

Business Hours

The working day is usually eight hours long, from 8am to noon and 2pm to 6pm Monday to Friday. Many offices in bigger cities have adopted the *jornada continua*, a working day without a lunch break, which finishes two hours earlier.

In this chapter, specific opening hours are only listed when they differ from the following:

Banks 9am to 4pm Monday to Friday and 9am to noon on Saturday

Bars From 6pm until around 3am; fiscos usually open around 10pm from Thursday to Saturday

Museums Generally closed on Monday but are open on Sunday

Restaurants Open until 10pm or later in larger cities; in smaller towns they usually close by 9pm or earlier

Shops 9am to 5pm Monday to Saturday (some close for lunch, others stay open); large stores and supermarkets usually stay open until 8pm or 9pm or later

Electricity

Colombia uses two-pronged US-type plugs that run at 110V, 60Hz.

Embassies & Consulates

Brazilian Embassy (1-218-0800; www.bogota.itamaraty.gov.br; Calle 93 No 14-20, Piso 8, Bogotá) Leticia (592-7530; Calle 10 No 9-104; 8am-2pm); Medellín (4-372-022; Carrera 42 No 54A-155)

Canadian Embassy (657-9912; www.colombia.gc.ca; Carrera 7 No 114-33, Bogotá)

Ecuadorian Consulate (1-317-5329; cecubogota@mmrree.gob.ec; Calle 67 No 7-35, Oficina 11-02, Piso 11, Bogotá) Ipiales (2-773-2292; Carrera 7 No 14-10); Medellín (4-250-8656; Calle 47 No 80-27); Cali (2-661-2264; Calle 19N No 2-29, Oficina 23-02)

French Embassy (1-645-9393; www.ambafrance-co.org; Carrera 11 No 93-12, Bogotá)

German Embassy (1-423-2600; www.bogota.diplo.de; Carrera 69 No 25B-44, 7th fl, Bogotá)

Panamanian Embassy (1-257-5067; www.empacol.org; Calle 92 No 7A-40, Bogotá) Cartagena (5-655-1055; Carrera 1 No 10-10, Bocagrande; 8am-noon Mon-Sat); Capurganá (314-846-8515; 8am-noon & 1-4pm Mon-Fri)

Peruvian Embassy (1-257-0505; Calle 80A No 6-50, Bogotá) Leticia (8-592-7755; Calle 11 No 5-32)

UK Embassy (1-326-8300; www.ukincolombia.fco.gov.uk; Carrera 9 No 76-49, 9th fl, Bogotá)

USA Embassy (1-275-4900; http://bogota.usembassy.gov; Calle 24Bis No 48-50, Bogotá)

Venezuelan Consulate (1-636-4011; Av 13 No 103-16, Bogotá) Cartagena (5-665-0382; Edificio Centro Executivo, Carrera 3 No 8-129, Piso 14; 9-11:30am & 1:30am-4pm Mon-Fri); Cúcuta (7-579-1956; Av Camilo Daza); Medellín (4-351-1614; www.consulvenemedellin.org; Calle 32B No 69-59)

Gay & Lesbian Travelers

Compared to other Latin American nations, homosexuality is well tolerated in Colombia. Bogotá has the largest gay and lesbian community and the most open gay life; head to the Chapinero district for bars and clubs. Visit www.gaycolombia.com, which lists bars, discos, events, activities, publications and other related matters.

Health

Colombia has some of the best medical facilities in South America, but they are not cheap. Many private clinics will not begin treatment (other than emergency stabilization) until your insurance has cleared or a deposit is made. Keep your travel insurance details handy. Public hospitals are generally overcrowded and should be considered only as a last resort.

Tap water in the large cities is safe to drink, but in rural areas water should be boiled or disinfected with tablets.

Yellow fever vaccinations are required for those visiting several national parks and may be required by your next destination after a visit to Colombia.

Internet Access

Except for La Guajira, every place we have reviewed has public net access, and nearly every backpacker hostel has wi-fi. Internet connections are fastest in the major urban centers, while they can be pretty slow in some remote places. Access normally costs around COP$1500 to COP$2000 per hour. Many public spaces, including all town plazas in Antioquia, have free wi-fi.

Language

Colombia can be a good place to study Spanish. The Spanish spoken in Colombia is clear and easy to understand and there are language schools in the big cities.

The most intense option is to enroll in one of the specialist language courses at one of Colombia's major universities. They are able to organize long-term visas. Private language centers are often more costly but require less of a commitment.

Legal Matters

If you get arrested, you have the right to an attorney. If you don't have one, an attorney will be appointed to you (and paid for by the government). There is a presumption of innocence.

The most common situation that most travelers find themselves in involves drugs. It is illegal to buy or sell drugs in any quantity. The possession of small quantities of marijuana (22g) and cocaine (1g) for personalized use has been decriminalized by the Santos government and police are no longer authorized to detain civilians in these situations. However, some officials may still attempt to shake down naive visitors.

If you do have to deal with the police, maintain a respectful attitude and ask to speak with a member of the Tourist Police, who are usually far less uptight than their bullet-dodging colleagues.

Maps

The widest selection of maps of Colombia is produced and sold by the **Instituto Geográfico Agustín Codazzi** (IGAC; ☎1-368-3443; www.igac.gov.co; Carrera 30 No 48-51, Bogotá), the government mapping body. Folded national road maps are sold at the entrance of toll roads. They're really useful for off-the-beaten-track journey planning.

Money

Colombia's official currency is the peso. There are 50-, 100-, 200-, 500- and 1000-peso coins, and paper notes of 1000, 2000, 5000, 10,000, 20,000 and 50,000 pesos. No one ever has change, so try to avoid the latter. Forged 50,000-peso notes are easy to spot for a local, not so for a visitor. The peso is fairly stable and is generally the only currency accepted throughout the country. While it's possible to change dollars, euros and other currencies in all cities, most travelers find it easy to rely on Colombia's extensive ATM network. Consider bringing a small stash of foreign currency (either US dollars or euros) for an emergency.

Bargaining is limited to informal trade and services such as markets, street stalls, unmetered taxis and long-distance buses.

ATMS

ATMs are the easiest way to manage your cash in Colombia. Most towns have ATMs linked to Cirrus (Mastercard) and Plus (Visa) but they don't always work with all foreign cards. ATH machines are the most reliable.

Advances are in Colombian pesos. Davivienda and Citibank have larger withdrawal limits (up to COP$720,000), meaning you save on repeated bank charges.

CREDIT CARDS

Credit cards are widely accepted in urban areas, and most banks offer peso advances. Visa is the best card for Colombia, followed by MasterCard.

MONEY CHANGERS

Most major banks change cash and traveler's checks (principally Amex), though these are uncommon. The most useful banks include Bancolombia and Banco Santander. Currencies other than US dollars are best changed in major cities. Always take your passport original – not a copy.

You can also change cash at *casas de cambio* (authorized money-exchange offices), found in virtually all major cities and border towns. They are secure, efficient and offer similar rates to banks.

The only street money markets worth considering are those at border crossings, where there may be simply no alternative.

FOOD PRICE RANGES

The following price ranges refer to a standard main course.

$ less than COP$15,000

$$ COP$15,000 to COP$25,000

$$$ more than COP$25,000

Post

The official Colombian postal service is operated by **4-72** (www.4-72.com.co). Postal charges in Colombia are exorbitant – a letter to the US costs around COP$10,000. Identification is required to ship packages or letters from Colombia, so head to the post office with your passport.

Public Holidays

The following holidays and special events are observed as public holidays in Colombia. When the dates marked with an asterisk do not fall on a Monday, the holiday is moved to the following Monday to make a three-day-long weekend, referred to as a *puente* (bridge).

There are three local high seasons, when Colombians rush to travel: late December to mid-January, the Easter Week, and mid-June to mid-July, when buses and planes get more crowded, fares rise and hotels fill up faster.

Año Nuevo (New Year's Day) January 1

Los Reyes Magos (Epiphany) January 6*

San José (St Joseph) March 19

Jueves Santo (Maundy Thursday) March/April, date varies

Viernes Santo (Good Friday) March/April, date varies

Día del Trabajador (Labor Day) May 1

La Ascensión del Señor (Ascension) May, date varies

Corpus Cristi (Corpus Christi) May/June*, date varies

Sagrado Corazón de Jesús (Sacred Heart) June*

San Pedro y San Pablo (St Peter & St Paul) June 29*

Día de la Independencia (Independence Day) July 20

Batalla de Boyacá (Battle of Boyacá) August 7

La Asunción de Nuestra Señora (Assumption) August 15*

Día de la Raza (Discovery of America) October 12*

Todos los Santos (All Saints' Day) November 1*

Independencia de Cartagena (Independence of Cartagena) November 11*

Inmaculada Concepción (Immaculate Conception) December 8

Navidad (Christmas Day) December 25

Responsible Travel

When visiting national parks, hire guides from the closest local community, not only are you creating jobs, you'll learn a whole lot more about the area than with a tour from the city.

Respect indigenous culture and beliefs – you should ask permission before taking pictures and only enter communities if you have been explicitly invited. Support local artisans by purchasing crafts direct at the source but avoid those made from coral, turtles or fossils.

Colombians rarely talk politics with anyone but friends and you should follow their lead. The country is polarized by the conflict and many Colombians have first-hand experience of the violence. You never really know who you are talking to, or who is listening to your conversation, and it can be quite easy to offend someone if you start ranting about the government or guerrillas.

Safe Travel

If you use common sense, you'll find that Colombia is far safer for travelers than Venezuela, Ecuador and Brazil. Kidnapping of foreigners is almost unheard of these days, and urban attacks by FARC have been cut back to irrelevance.

DRUGS

Consuming illegal drugs in Colombia directly funds the armed conflict that has killed hundreds of thousands of Colombians and displaced millions more around the country. Cocaine is widely available and you will likely be offered it at some point on your journey. If you do decide to take it, beware that it is far stronger than in the US and UK. Paranoid delusions, tachycardia, stroke or overdose can and do occur. If somebody you are with overdoses, call an ambulance immediately, and tell the paramedics exactly what happened.

Burundanga is a legitimate concern. The usual method of administration is a spiked drink or cigarette. It is tasteless and odorless and renders victims senseless, only to wake up with no recollection of the previous few hours, minus their wallets and valuables. The drug is obtained from a nightshade species widespread in Colombia. Don't accept a drink, snack or cigarette from a stranger, especially when traveling alone, and especially on buses.

GUERRILLAS

The threat of guerrilla activity to travelers has decreased to such a point that traveling in the most visited areas of Colombia no longer requires any special planning.

Throughout the country cases of kidnapping for ransom have decreased significantly and, in 2012, shortly before the announcement of peace talks with the government, FARC publicly declared an end to the kidnapping of civilians. The smaller ELN guerrilla group has yet to sign up.

At the time of research, the principal areas of conflict were in rural Cauca, Chocó, Putumayo, Southwest Nariño, Meta, the jungle region east of the Andes (excluding Leticia) and areas bordering Venezuela in Norte de Santander and Arauca.

Telephone

Landline numbers are seven digits long. Area codes are single digits. If you are calling a landline from a cell phone you need to add '03' before the area code. Cell phone numbers are 10 digits and have no area codes.

Cell phone networks are operated by Movistar, Claro and Tigo. Claro leads the pack for network coverage. You can buy a SIM card for around COP$5000.

Public telephones exist in cities and large towns but, except for the centers of the largest cities, they are few and far between, and many are out of order.

If you need to make a call within Colombia, look for the fluorescent signs advertising '*minutos*' in small shops or the roaming vendors with a variety of cell phones chained to their shirts. Calls cost from COP$150 to COP$300 per minute.

Colombia's country code is ☎57. Many internet places have a couple of booths for cheap international calls.

Toilets

Public toilets are rare in Colombia and where they do exist, you'll almost always pay a fee to use them. The attendant will give you a miserly amount of toilet paper (it always pays to carry a spare roll). Most big shopping centers and museums have free toilets.

Tourist Information

Municipal tourist information offices in departmental capitals and other popular destinations administer tourist information. In some locations, the tourist police also run an office. Colombia's main tourist information portal is the excellent www.colombia.travel.

Visas

Nationals of many countries, including most of Western Europe, the Americas, Japan, Australia and New Zealand, don't need a visa to enter Colombia; otherwise, the fee is between US$23 and US$50. It's a good idea for you to check this before your planned trip, because visa regulations change frequently.

All visitors get an entry stamp in their passport from Migración Colombia upon arrival at any international airport or land border crossing. Make sure your passport is stamped immediately. The stamp indicates how many days you can stay in the country; 90 days is most common. An onward ticket is legally required and you may be asked to show one. Upon departure, immigration officials will put an exit stamp in your passport. Again, check it to avoid any future problems.

VISA EXTENSIONS

Visitors are entitled to extend their stay into Colombia in 30-day increments up to a total of 6 months in a year by visiting Migración Colombia in any departmental capital.

FLYING FOR LESS

Airlines in Colombia offer regular promotions that slash the price of flights, sometimes to less than the bus fare.

» Book well in advance. Cheap seats go fast.

» Shop around. An airline that costs more on one route is often much cheaper on another.

» Travel off-peak. Prices are usually much lower late at night.

» Many online promotions are not available with foreign credit cards. Find your flight online and visit an agent where, for a small fee, you are usually able to pay for the same ticket in cash.

DEPARTURE TAX

The airport tax on international flights out of Colombia is US$35. It's usually included in your ticket, but check with your airline. A further charge of US$35 is made if you have been in the country longer than two months. Both are payable at the airport in US dollars or pesos.

To apply for an extension, known as a 'Prórroga de Permanencia,' you'll be asked to submit your passport, two photocopies of your passport (picture page and arrival stamp) and two passport-sized photos. You may also be asked for an air ticket out of the country.

The fee of COP$72,350 must be deposited into the government bank account, which was Davivienda at the time of writing but often changes. Go to the Migración Colombia office to fill out the forms and they'll direct you to a nearby bank to pay the fee. Expect the process to take an entire morning or afternoon.

Volunteering

Foreign volunteering is in its infancy in Colombia, but there are a number of worthwhile organizations that accept travelers.

Misíon Gaia (www.misiongaia.org) An environmental education project in the Sierra Nevada that is often looking for volunteers.

Techo para mi País (www.techo.org) Accepts volunteers to work on its housing and social development projects in impoverished urban communities around Cali and Medellín.

Tiempo de Juego (www.tiempodejuego.org) Welcomes volunteers to take part in sports-based programs for underprivileged children around Colombia.

Women Travelers

Women traveling in Colombia's cities and rural areas are unlikely to get major hassle. Culturally, you'll have to deal with a little more machismo than at home: you'll definitely receive more overtly flirtatious attention from males simply for being foreign.

If you want to fend off unwelcome advances, dress conservatively. A cheap wedding band is also worth a shot.

Work

It's illegal to work in Colombia on a tourist visa and you are potentially at risk of deportation, although in practice this is unlikely.

You may be able to find some informal work teaching English, but your pay will probably barely cover your costs. Professionally run language institutes will arrange working visas for their teachers.

Some hostel and bar owners offer work to backpackers, however, think twice about accepting such an offer as it takes jobs away from a sector of Colombian society where they are desperately needed.

Getting There & Away

Air

Sitting on the northwestern edge of the continent, Colombia is a convenient and reasonably cheap gateway to South America from the US and even from Europe. Despite their proximity, flights between Central America and Colombia are fairly expensive.

Bogotá has Colombia's major international airport, but some other cities including Cartagena, Medellín and Cali also handle international flights.

The country is serviced by many major international airlines, including Air Canada, Air France, Iberia, United and American Airlines, and several regional carriers. Budget carriers Spirit and JetBlue fly to Colombia from the United States.

Boat

Regular riverboat services connect Leticia in the Colombian Amazon with Iquitos, Peru and Manaus, Brazil.

There are private sailboats running between Colón in Panama and Cartagena in Colombia.

It's also possible to cross from Colombia to the San Blas region in Panama via small boat from Capurganá/Sapzurro.

Bus, Car & Motorcycle

Almost all travelers crossing between Ecuador and Colombia use the Carretera Panamericana border crossing through Ipiales and Tulcán.

There are several border crossings between Colombia and Venezuela. The most popular with travelers is the route via Cúcuta and San Antonio del Táchira, on the main

Bogotá–Caracas road. Another major border crossing is at Paraguachón, on the Maicao-Maracaibo road. There are shared taxis between Maicao and Maracaibo, and direct buses between Cartagena and Caracas.

There is no overland route between Colombia and Panama, but it is possible to deliver a car between the two countries on a cargo ship. The pick-up and drop-off points are Colón and Cartagena.

Getting Around

Air

Colombia has a well-developed airline system and a solid network of domestic flights. The most commonly used passenger airlines include **Avianca** (www.avianca.com), **Copa** (www.copaair.com) and **LAN** (www.lan.com), all of which also have international flights. **Satena** (☎1-800-091-2034; www.satena.com) services more remote domestic destinations.

A new budget airline, **Viva Colombia** (www.vivacolombia.co), was just getting off the ground at the time of research. It offers cheap flights to a few domestic destinations. However, like with most budget airlines, the fees and charges add up.

Boat

With more than 3000km of Pacific and Atlantic coastline, there is a considerable amount of shipping traffic, consisting mostly of irregular cargo boats that may also take passengers.

Scheduled passenger boats are the cheapest way to get to Capurganá and between San Andrés and Providencia.

Rivers are the only transportation routes in much of Chocó and the Amazon.

Bus

Buses are the main means of getting around Colombia. The bus system is well developed and extensive, reaching even the smallest villages. Buses range from ordinary bangers to modern-day luxury liners.

The best buses *(climatizado)* have plenty of leg room, reclining seats, large luggage compartments and toilets. Carry warm clothes, as drivers usually set the air-con to full blast.

On the main routes buses run frequently, so there is little point in booking a seat in advance. In some places off the main routes, where there are only a few buses daily, it's better to buy a ticket some time before departure. The only time you really need to book is during the Christmas and Easter periods, when hordes of Colombians are on holiday.

Colectivos are a cross between a bus and a taxi. They are usually large cars (sometimes jeeps or minibuses) that cover fixed routes, mainly over short and medium distances. They leave when full, not according to a schedule, and are a reasonable option if there is a long wait for the next bus or if you are in a hurry.

Bus travel is reasonably cheap in Colombia. As a rule of a thumb, the *climatizado* bus costs roughly COP$6000 for every hour of travel. Always haggle – discounts of up to 33% are not uncommon. In holiday periods, you have no chance of a discount.

Car & Motorcycle

Getting around with your own vehicle is getting easier in Colombia. There are still security concerns in some remote parts of the country, but your main danger nowadays is haphazard Colombian drivers and the shocking condition of some of the highways.

Hiring vehicles is expensive in Colombia and with cheap taxis in the cities and comfortable intercity buses it makes little sense.

DRIVER'S LICENSE

If you plan on driving in Colombia your foreign driving license is technically sufficient, but avoid debates with traffic cops by obtaining an International Driving Permit.

Tours

It it necessary to join a group tour if you want to trek to the Ciudad Perdida. The only destinations where tours are really worth the expense are in the Guajira and Amazonas, where independent travel is often time-consuming and costly.

Ecuador

Includes »

Best Adventures

- » Climbing Cotopaxi (p657)
- » Whitewater rafting near Tena (p683)
- » Mountain biking down Chimborazo (p670)
- » Trekking to Ingapirca (p676)

Best Places to Stay

- » Secret Garden Cotopaxi (p658)
- » Rose Cottage (p654)
- » Pululahua Hostal (p650)
- » Caskaffesu (p652)

Why Go?

Amazonian rainforest, snow-covered mountains, premontane cloud forests and the Galápagos Islands set the stage for incredible adventures in this small Andean nation. You can spend one day whitewater rafting and the next gazing up to the summit of a 6000m-high volcano. You can take dramatic treks through the *páramo* (high-altitude grassland), surf excellent breaks off the west coast, and hike, mountain bike or simply unwind amid dramatic scenery.

Wildlife-watching is another way to enjoy Ecuador's riches, with dozens of animal and plant species found nowhere else on earth. Even on a short Ecuadorian adventure, it's possible to photograph monkeys from jungle canopy towers, swim with sea lions in the Pacific and admire some of Ecuador's 1600 bird species in misty forests.

Ecuador harbors a rich cultural heritage, from gorgeous Spanish colonial centers to traditional highland towns, where buzzing Quichua markets and baroque 16th-century churches are all part of the dramatically varied landscape.

When to Go

Quito

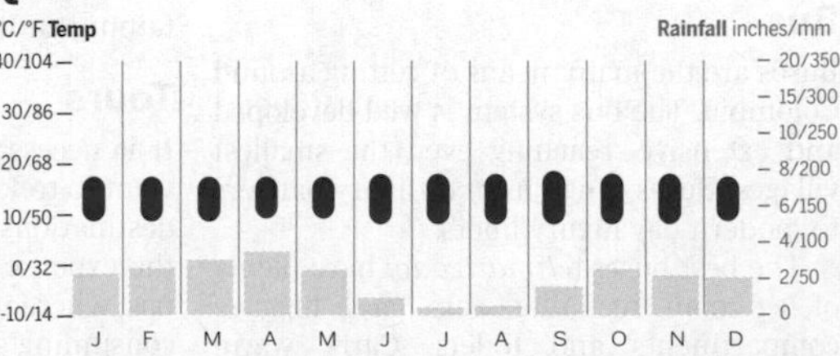

Jun–Sep Best weather for visiting the highlands with less rain and warmer, clearer days.

Oct & Nov Best time to visit the Amazon (Oriente): rivers are passable, and it's not too wet.

Dec–May Rainy season on the coast, but sunny and lush between downpours – good beach days.

Connections

Major border crossings into Peru are at busy Tumbes/Aguas Verdes (near the coast), Macará and La Balsa (a few hours south of Vilcabamba); hardy travelers with heaps of time can also go by river via Nuevo Rocafuerte. To Colombia, the safest crossing (and the only one we recommend) is at Tulcán–Ipiales, a few hours northwest of Ibarra.

ITINERARIES

Three Weeks

Begin your trip in Quito. Spend two days soaking up the architectural gems of the Old Town, then head northwest to the lush cloud forests of Mindo, continuing east to Otavalo for its famous Saturday markets and hikes around alpine lakes. Next go to Coca, gateway to the Amazon. Spend a few nights at a jungle lodge on the lower Río Napo. On your way back to Quito, stop in Tena, for a whitewater rafting trip, and Baños, for thermal baths, waterfalls and great scenery. End the tour amid spectacular Andean scenery near Cotopaxi or Quilotoa.

Six Weeks

From Quito head west, spending a week exploring the coast: beach days in Canoa, whale-watching in Puerto Lopez and surf culture in Montañita. Continue onto Guayaquil and fly out to the Galápagos Islands for a week of wildlife-watching and island-hopping. Back in Guayaquil, head east to lovely Cuenca. Visit nearby Parque Nacional Cajas, and the Inca ruins of Ingapirca. Continue south to Loja and the stunning cloud forests of Parque Nacional Podocarpus, and then onto peaceful Vilcabamba, a scenic base for outdoor adventures.

Essential Food & Drink

» **Llapingachos** Fried potato-and-cheese pancakes

» **Seco de chivo** Goat stew

» **Locro de papa** Potato soup served with avocado and cheese

» **Pollo a la brasa** Roast chicken, often served with fries

» **Churrasco** Fried beef, eggs and potatoes, a few veggies, slices of avocado and tomato, and rice

» **Arroz con pollo** Rice with small bits of chicken mixed in

» **Cuy** Roasted guinea pig

» **Hornado** Whole roasted pig

» **Ceviche** Marinated raw seafood

» **Encocado** Shrimp or fish cooked in a rich coconut sauce

» **Maito** Fish or chicken grilled in palm leaves

» **Encebollado** A brothy seafood and onion soup poured over *yuca* and served with fried banana chips and popcorn

» **Sopa marinera** Soup loaded with fish, shellfish and shrimp

AT A GLANCE

» **Currency** US dollar (US$)

» **Language** Spanish

» **Money** ATMs in cities and larger towns; credit cards accepted only at high-end places

» **Visas** Not required for most nationalities

» **Time** GMT minus five hours

Fast Facts

» **Area** 283,560 sq km

» **Population** 14.7 million

» **Capital** Quito

» **Emergency** ☎131

» **Country code** ☎593

Exchange Rates

Australia	A$1	US$1.06
Canada	C$1	US$1
Euro zone	€1	US$1.32
New Zealand	NZ$1	US$0.83
UK	£1	US$1.57

Set Your Budget

» **Hostel bed** US$7-10

» **Two-course evening meal** US$10

» **Fixed-price set lunch** US$2.75

» **Six-hour bus ride** US$6

» **One-hour private Spanish lesson** US$7-10

Resources

» **Hip Ecuador** (www.hipecuador.com)

» **Ministry of Tourism Ecuador** (http://ecuador.travel)

Ecuador Highlights

❶ Delve into Quito's picturesque **Old Town** (p628), its cobblestone streets crisscrossing one of Latin America's finest colonial centers

❷ Experience the **Amazon** (p685) by staying in a jungle lodge, taking wildlife-watching excursions and visiting indigenous villages

❸ Snorkel with sea lions, spot penguins, and come face to face with gigantic tortoises on the spectacular **Galápagos Islands** (p704)

❹ Haggle over handmade treasures in **Otavalo** (p652), home to one of South America's biggest open-air markets

❺ Hike in cloud forests, frolic in waterfalls and go zip-lining over the canopy in pretty **Mindo** (p651)

❻ Hike past topaz lakes and peaceful villages high up in the Andes on the **Quilotoa Loop** (p659)

❼ Chill out on the beach in the surf-loving town of **Montañita** (p696)

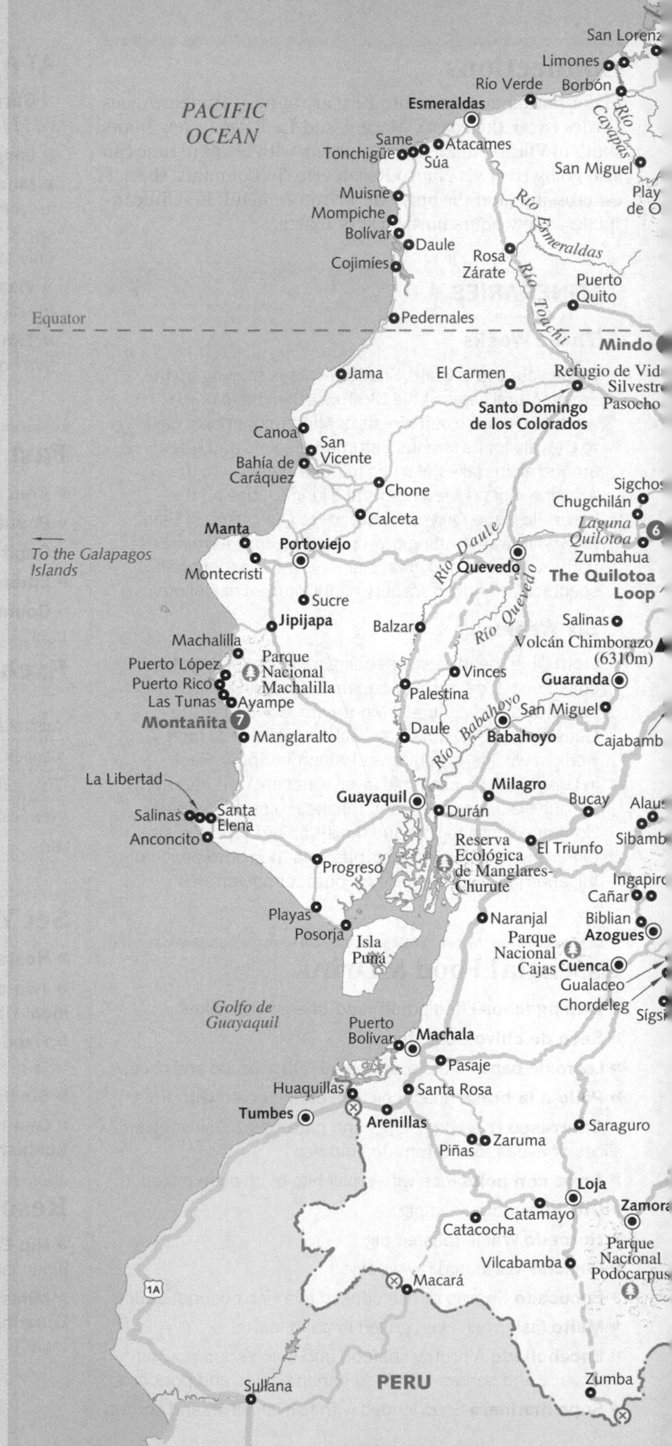

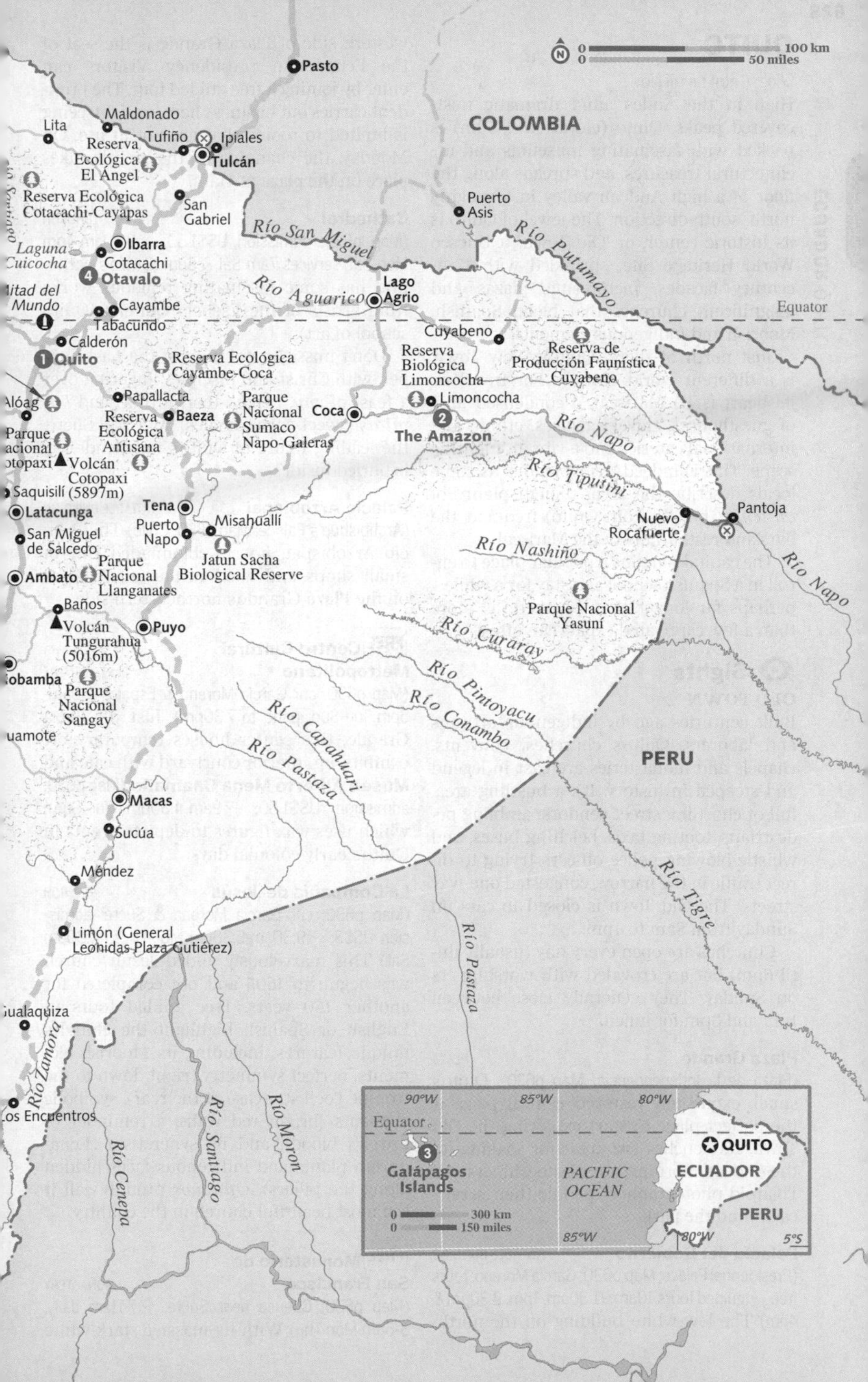

0 100 km
0 50 miles
COLOMBIA
Pasto
Maldonado
Lita
Tufiño
Ipiales
Reserva Ecológica El Ángel
Tulcán
Reserva Ecológica Cotacachi-Cayapas
San Gabriel
Puerto Asis
Río San Miguel
Río Putumayo
Laguna Cuicocha
Ibarra
Cotacachi
Otavalo
Río Aguarico
Lago Agrio
Mitad del Mundo
Cayambe
Tabacundo
Equator
Calderón
Cuyabeno
Quito
Reserva Ecológica Cayambe-Coca
Reserva Biológica Limoncocha
Reserva de Producción Faunística Cuyabeno
Papallacta
Parque Nacional Sumaco Napo-Galeras
Coca
Limoncocha
Alóag
Reserva Ecológica Antisana
Baeza
The Amazon
Río Napo
Parque Nacional Cotopaxi
Volcán Cotopaxi
Río Tiputini
Saquisilí (5897m)
Latacunga
Tena
Nuevo Rocafuerte
Pantoja
Puerto Napo
Misahuallí
San Miguel de Salcedo
Río Nashiño
Ambato
Parque Nacional Llanganates
Jatun Sacha Biological Reserve
Río Napo
Baños
Parque Nacional Yasuní
Volcán Tungurahua (5016m)
Puyo
Río Curaray
Riobamba
Río Pintoyacu
Parque Nacional Sangay
Río Conambo
Guamote
Río Capahuari
PERU
Río Pastaza
Macas
Sucúa
Méndez
Río Tigre
Limón (General Leonidas Plaza Gutiérez)
Río Pastaza
Gualaquiza
Río Zamora
Los Encuentros
Río Santiago
Río Moron
Río Cenepa
90°W
85°W
80°W
Equator
QUITO
Galápagos Islands
PACIFIC OCEAN
ECUADOR
PERU
0 300 km
0 150 miles
85°W
80°W
5°S

QUITO

☎02 / POP 1.8 MILLION

High in the Andes amid dramatic mist-covered peaks, Quito (elevation 2850m) is packed with fascinating museums and architectural treasures, and spreads along the floor of a high Andean valley in a roughly north–south direction. The jewel of Quito is its historic center, or 'Old Town,' a Unesco World Heritage Site, sprinkled with 17th-century facades, picturesque plazas and magnificent churches that blend Spanish, Moorish and indigenous elements.

Just north of there, Quito's 'New Town' is a different world entirely. For travelers, its heart is La Mariscal, a condensed area of guesthouses, travel agencies, ethnic and international eateries and a vibrant nightlife scene. This is indeed 'gringolandia' as some locals describe the area, though plenty of *quiteños* (people from Quito) frequent the bars and restaurants of the Mariscal.

The capital remains a popular place to enroll in a Spanish school and stay for a while – perhaps far longer than planned, as more than a few captivated expats can attest.

Sights

OLD TOWN

Built centuries ago by indigenous artisans and laborers, Quito's churches, convents, chapels and monasteries are cast in legend and steeped in history. It's a bustling area, full of chortling street vendors, ambling pedestrians, tooting taxis, belching buses, and whistle-blowing police officers trying to direct traffic in the narrow, congested one-way streets. The Old Town is closed to cars on Sunday from 8am to 4pm.

Churches are open every day (usually until 6pm) but are crowded with worshippers on Sunday. They generally close between 1pm and 3pm for lunch.

Plaza Grande PLAZA
(Plaza de la Independencia; Map p630) Quito's small, exquisitely restored central plaza is the perfect place to start exploring the Old Town. Its benches are great for soaking up the Andean morning sun as shoeshiners and Polaroid photographers peddle their services around the park.

Palacio del Gobierno NOTABLE BUILDING
(Presidential Palace; Map p630; García Moreno; tours free; ⊙guided tours 10am, 11:30am, 1pm, 2:30pm & 4pm) The low white building on the northwestern side of Plaza Grande is the seat of the Ecuadorian presidency. Visitors can enter by joining a free guided tour. The president carries out business here, so sightseeing is limited to rooms that are not in use. On Monday, the changing of the guards takes place on the plaza at 11am.

Cathedral CHURCH
(Map p630; admission US$1.50; ⊙9:30am-4pm Mon-Sat, services 7am Sat & Sun) Quito's cathedral has some fascinating religious works from artists of the Escuela Quiteña (Quito school of art).

Don't miss the painting of the Last Supper, with Christ and disciples lingering over a feast of *cuy*, *chicha* (corn drink) and *humitas* (sweet-corn tamales). Mariscal Sucre, the leading figure of Quito's independence, is buried inside.

Palacio Arzobispal NOTABLE BUILDING
(Archbishop's Palace; Map p630; Chile) The Palacio Arzobispal, now a colonnaded row of small shops and good restaurants, stands on the Plaza Grande's northeastern side.

FREE **Centro Cultural Metropolitano** ARTS CENTRE
(Map p630; cnr García Moreno & Espejo; ⊙9am-5pm Tue-Sun, patio to 7:30pm) Just off Plaza Grande, this center houses temporary art exhibits, an interior courtyard with cafe and **Museo Alberto Mena Caamaño** (Map p630; admission US$1.50; ⊙9am-4:30pm Tue-Sun), which uses wax figures to depicts events in Quito's early colonial days.

La Compañía de Jesús CHURCH
(Map p630; cnr García Morena & Sucre; admission US$3; ⊙9:30am-5:30pm Mon-Fri, to 4:30pm Sat) This marvelously gilded Jesuit church was begun in 1605 and not completed for another 160 years. Free guided tours in English or Spanish highlight the church's unique features, including its Moorish elements, perfect symmetry (right down to the trompe l'oeil staircase at the rear), symbolic elements (bright red walls, a reminder of Christ's blood), and its syncretism (Ecuadorian plants and indigenous faces hidden along the pillars). *Quiteños* proudly call it the most beautiful church in the country.

FREE **Monasterio de San Francisco** MONASTERY
(Map p630; Cuenca near Sucre; ⊙7-11am daily, 3-6pm Mon-Thu) With its massive stark-white

Greater Quito

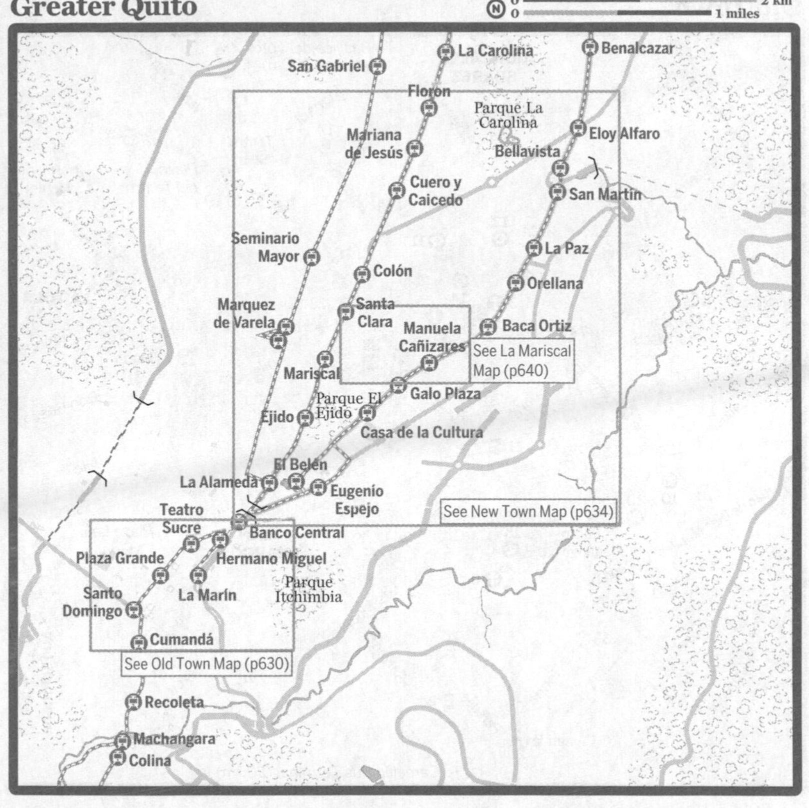

towers and a mountainous backdrop of Volcán Pichincha, this monastery is one of Quito's most marvelous sights – both inside and out. It's the city's largest colonial structure and its oldest church (built from 1534 to 1604). Much of the church has been rebuilt because of earthquake damage. The **Capilla del Señor Jesús del Gran Poder**, to the right of the main altar, has original tilework, and the **main altar** itself is a spectacular example of baroque carving.

Museo Franciscano MUSEUM

(Map p630; Cuenca near Sucre; admission US$2; ⌚9am-5:30pm Mon-Sat, to 12:30pm Sun) To the right of Monasterio de San Francisco's main entrance is the Museo Franciscano, which contains some of the church's finest artwork. The admission fee includes a guided tour, available in English or Spanish. Good guides will point out *mudéjar* (an architectural style that developed in Spain beginning in the 12th century) representations of the eight planets revolving around the sun on the ceiling, an example of indigenous influence on Christian architecture.

Casa del Alabado MUSEUM

(Map p630; Cuenca 335; admission US$3; ⌚9am-5pm Tue-Sat, to 12:30pm Sun) This thoughtfully designed museum displays an exquisite collection of pre-Columbian artworks. Dramatic lighting and fine works in stone, metal and ceramic (with some English signage) explore ancient indigenous beliefs about life and death, the spirit world, the role and power of the shaman, and ancestors. To get more out of your visit, pay the extra US$2 for an audio guide (available in English).

Museo de la Ciudad MUSEUM

(Map p630; García Moreno near Rocafuerte; admission US$3; ⌚9:30am-5:30pm Tue-Sun) Just past the 18th-century **Arco de la Reina**, this first-rate museum depicts Quito's daily life

Old Town

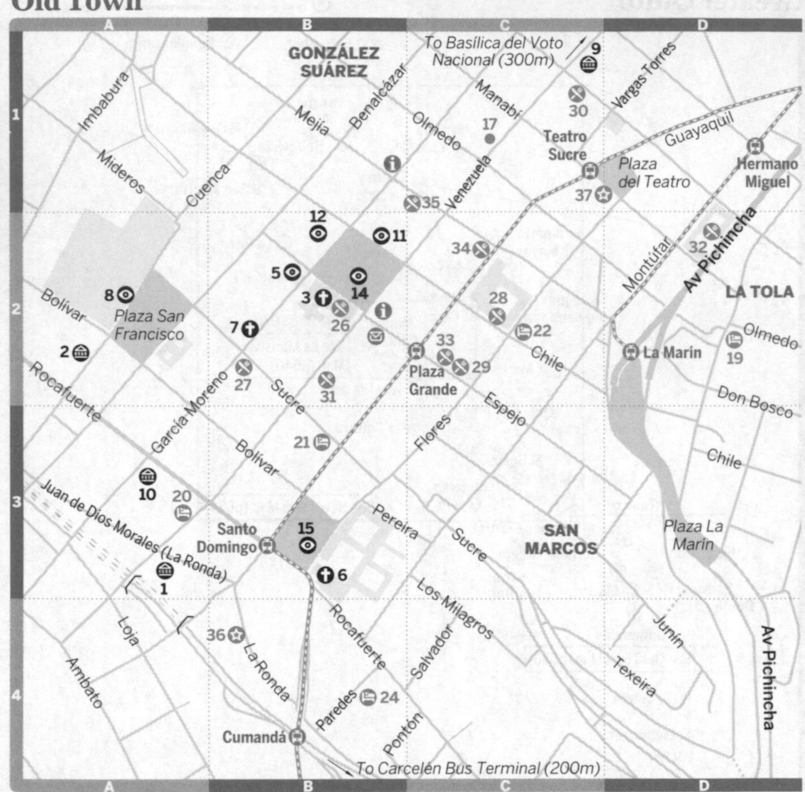

through the centuries, with displays including dioramas, model indigenous homes and colonial kitchens. The 1563 building itself (a former hospital) is a work of art. Admission includes free guided tour in Spanish. Guides also available in English and French (an extra US$4).

Plaza Santo Domingo PLAZA

(Map p630) This plaza is a regular haunt for street performers. Crowds of neighborhood *quiteños* fill the plaza to watch pouting clowns and half-cocked magicians do their stuff. The plaza is beautiful in the evening, when the domes of the 17th-century **Iglesia de Santo Domingo** (Map p630; cnr Flores & Rocafuerte; admission free; ⏲7am-1pm & 5-7pm), on the southeast side of the plaza, are floodlit. Next door to the church, a **museum** (admission US$2; ⏲9am-5pm Mon-Fri, to 2pm Sat) has a pretty garden cloister and a fine assortment of colonial religious art.

FREE **Museo Camilo Egas** MUSEUM

(Map p630; Venezuela 1302 at Esmeraldas; ⏲9am-1pm Tue-Fri) Museo Camilo Egas contains a small but iconic collection of works by the late Camilo Egas, one of the country's foremost indigenous painters.

Basílica del Voto Nacional CHURCH

(cnr Venezuela & Carchi; admission church/tower US$1/2; ⏲9am-4:30pm) High on a hill in the northeast part of the Old Town stands the Gothic Basílica del Voto Nacional, built over several decades beginning in 1926. The highlight is the basilica's towers, which you can climb to the top of if you have the nerve; the ascent requires crossing a rickety wooden plank inside the main roof and climbing steep stairs and ladders to the top.

El Panecillo HILL

The small hill to the south of the Old Town is called El Panecillo (Little Bread Loaf) and is a major Quito landmark. It is topped by a

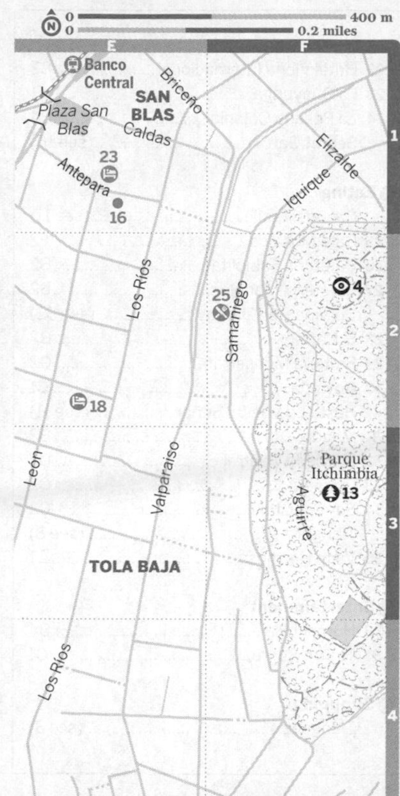

huge statue of **La Virgen de Quito** (Virgin of Quito), with marvelous views of the sprawling city and the surrounding volcanoes. Go early morning, before the clouds roll in. Definitely don't climb the stairs at the end of Calle García Moreno on the way to the statue – they're unsafe due to muggings. A taxi from the Old Town costs about US$4, and you can hail one at the top for the trip back to town.

Parque Itchimbia PARK
(Map p630) High on a hill east of the Old Town, this grassy park boasts magnificent views of the city. The park's centerpiece is the **Centro Cultural Itchimbia** (Map p630; admission free; ⏲vary), a large glass-and-iron building modeled after the city's original Mercado Santa Clara. It hosts regular art exhibitions and cultural events. The park is a popular destination for runners.

Buses signed 'Pintado' go here from the Old Town, or you can walk up (east) Elizalde, from where signed stairways lead to the park.

TelefériQo VIEWPOINT
(Av Occidental near Av La Gasca; admission US$9; ⏲8am-8pm) For spectacular views over Quito's mountainous landscape, hop aboard the TelefériQo, a sky tram that takes passengers on a 2.5km ride up the flanks of Volcán Pichincha to the top of Cruz Loma. Once you're at the top (a mere 4100m), you can hike to the summit of Rucu Pichincha (4680m), approximately a three-hour hike for fit walkers. Don't attempt the hike to Rucu Pichincha until you've acclimatized to the altitude in Quito. The views here are best in the morning; the clouds usually roll in by noon. A taxi costs about US$4 from the Mariscal.

NEW TOWN

FREE **Museo Nacional** MUSEUM
(Map p634; cnr Av Patria & Av 12 de Octubre; ⏲9am-5pm Tue-Fri, 10am-4pm Sat & Sun) Across from Parque El Ejido, this rather unappealing circular glass building houses one of the country's most important museums. Here you'll find a showcase of fine works of pre-Columbian and colonial religious art.

Highlights include figures showing skull deformation practiced by the Machalilla culture, wild Asian-looking serpent bowls from the Jama-Coaque, ceramic representations of *tzantzas* (shrunken heads), 'coin axes' from the Milagro-Quevedo culture and the famous ceremonial stone chairs of the Manteños.

Quito Observatory MUSEUM
(Map p634; Parque la Alameda; admission US$2; ⏲10am-5pm Tue-Sun) In the center of the small Parque la Alameda, this four-sided observatory is the oldest on the continent. It houses a museum of 19th-century pendulums, sextants, chronometers and other historic instruments, and opens for stargazing on Thursday and Friday nights (with sessions at 6pm and 7:30pm, admission US$3) – only go if the sky is clear.

Parque El Ejido PARK
(Map p634) Northeast of La Alameda, the pleasant, tree-filled Parque El Ejido is the biggest park in downtown Quito. On weekends, open-air **art shows** are held along Av Patria, and artisans and crafts vendors set up stalls all over the northern side of the park, turning it into Quito's largest **handicrafts market**

Old Town

Sights

1 Casa de las Artes A3
2 Casa del Alabado A2
3 Cathedral B2
4 Centro Cultural Itchimbia F2
5 Centro Cultural Metropolitano B2
6 Iglesia de Santo Domingo B3
7 La Compañía de Jesús B2
8 Monasterio de San Francisco A2
Museo Alberto Mena Caamaño .... (see 5)
9 Museo Camilo Egas C1
10 Museo de la Ciudad A3
Museo Franciscano .... (see 8)
11 Palacio Arzobispal B2
12 Palacio del Gobierno B2
13 Parque Itchimbia F3
14 Plaza Grande B2
15 Plaza Santo Domingo B3

Activities, Courses & Tours

16 CarpeDM Adventures E1
17 Quito Antiguo Spanish School C1

Sleeping

18 Colonial House E2
19 Community Hostel D2
20 Hostal Ecuador A3
Hostal San Blas .... (see 23)
21 Hotel San Francisco de Quito B3
22 Hotel Viena Internacional C2
23 La Guayunga E1
24 La Posada Colonial B4
Secret Garden .... (see 16)

Eating

Café del Fraile .... (see 11)
25 Café Mosaico F2
26 Cafetería Fabiolita B2
27 Cafetería Modelo B2
Corvina Don 'Jimmy' .... (see 32)
28 El Cafeto C2
29 Frutería Monserrate C2
30 Govindas C1
Hasta La Vuelta, Señor .... (see 11)
31 Magda B2
32 Mercado Central D2
33 Pizza SA C2
34 San Agustín C2
Tianguez .... (see 8)
35 Vista Hermosa C1

Entertainment

36 Humanizarte B4
37 Teatro Sucre C1

Shopping

Tianguez .... (see 8)

A solitary stone archway at the northern end of Parque El Ejido marks the beginning of modern Quito's showpiece street, Av Amazonas. North of the park, it's the main artery of the Mariscal neighborhood.

FREE Centro de Arte Contemporáneo MUSEUM
(www.centrodeartecontemporaneo.gob.ec; Calles Luis Dávila & Venezuela; ⏲9am-5:30pm Tue-Sun) Inside a beautifully restored former military hospital, a short stroll north of the Basilica del Voto Nacional, this excellent new museum showcases cutting-edge multimedia exhibits as well as top modern-art shows that travel to the city (a Picasso show was a big hit in 2012). There's a cafe on-site.

Parque La Carolina PARK
(Map p634) North of the Mariscal lies the giant Parque La Carolina. On weekends, it fills with families who come out for paddleboats, soccer and volleyball games, and exercise along the bike paths. A few unusual attractions include an old Douglas DC-3 that kids can check out, horse rides and several museums, including a **Vivarium** (Map p634; www.vivarium.org.ec; adult/child US$3/2; ⏲9:30am-5:30pm Tue-Sun), where you can glimpse (and even handle a few) reptiles and amphibians. Nearby is the snoozy **Museo de Ciencias Naturales** (Map p634; adult/child US$2/0.60; ⏲8am-1pm & 1:45-4:30pm Mon-Fri, 9am-1pm Sat), full of dead insects and stuffed creatures (condor, tapir, harpy eagle and, uh, Bengal tiger, among others).

Jardín Botánico GARDENS
(Map p634; www.jardinbotanicoquito.com; adult/child US$3.50/2; ⏲9am-5pm) Parque La Carolina's most popular attraction is this small botanical garden with native habitats covering *páramo*, cloud forest and wetlands, plus an orchid greenhouse, ethnobotanical garden (exploring the plants used by indigenous groups) and Amazonian greenhouse.

Museo Guayasamín MUSEUM
(www.guayasamin.org; Bosmediano 543; admission US$4; ⏲10am-5pm Mon-Fri) In the former home of the world-famous indigenous painter Oswaldo Guayasamín (1919–99), the Museo Guayasamín houses the largest collection of his works. Guayasamín was also an avid collector, and the museum displays his outstanding collection of over 4500 pre-Columbian ceramic, bone and metal pieces from throughout Ecuador.

Capilla del Hombre CHURCH
(Chapel of Man; www.guayasamin.org; Mariano Calvache at Lorenzo Chávez; admission US$4, with purchase of entry to Museo Guayasamín US$2; ⏲10am-5pm Mon-Fri) The fruit of Guayasamín's greatest vision, this giant monument-cum-museum is a tribute to humankind, to the suffering of Latin America's indigenous poor, and to the undying hope for a better world. It's a moving place, and the tours (available in English, French and Spanish and included in the admission price) are highly recommended.

Museo Guayasamín and chapel are located in the neighborhood of Bellavista, northeast of downtown. You can walk uphill, or take a bus along Av 6 de Diciembre to Av Eloy Alfaro and then a Bellavista bus up the hill. A taxi costs about US$2.

Mindalae – Museo Etnográfico de Artesanía de Ecuador MUSEUM
(Map p634; www.sinchisacha.org; Reina Victoria N26-166 & La Niña; admission US$3; ⏲9am-5:30pm Mon-Sat) Just north of the Mariscal, this small but worthwhile ethnographic museum exhibits the artwork, clothing and utensils of Ecuador's indigenous people, with special emphasis on the peoples of the Oriente.

Santuario de Guápulo CHURCH
(⏲9am-6pm, sometimes closed for lunch) In a green valley northeast of the Mariscal, the 17th-century Santuario de Guápulo has a picturesque location. It has an excellent collection of Escuela Quiteña art and sculpture. Don't miss the stunning 18th-century pulpit carved by master woodcarver Juan Bautista Menacho.

To get here, follow Av 12 de Octubre up the hill from the Mariscal and turn right after passing the Hotel Quito. As you descend toward El Guápulo, you'll also pass the **Statue of Francisco de Orellana** (Map p634; Calle Larrea). In addition to fine views, the spot commemorates Orellana's epic journey from Quito to the Atlantic – the first descent of the Amazon by a European.

Activities

Quito is one of the best places in the country to hire guides and organize both single- and multiday excursions.

Cycling

Every other Sunday, the entire length of Av Amazonas and most of the Old Town are closed to cars, and loads of peddlers take to the street for the bimonthly **ciclopaseo** (bicycle ride). Visit www.ciclopolis.ec (in Spanish) for more info.

Local mountain-biking companies rent bikes and offer excellent single- and two-day guided off-road rides in Andean settings you'd otherwise never see. Day trips cost about US$50 per person, not including park entrance fees. Two companies with good bikes and solid reputations are **Biking Dutchman** (Map p640; ☎256-8323; www.bikingdutchman.com; Foch E4-283 near Amazonas; 1-day tours from US$49) and **Arie's Bike Company** (☎238-0802; www.ariesbikecompany.com).

Climbing

Rocódromo ROCK CLIMBING
(Map p634; Queseras del Medio s/n; admission US$2; ⏲8am-8pm Mon-Fri, to 6pm Sat & Sun) Climbers can get a serious fix at the Rocódromo, a 25m-high climbing facility located just outside the Estadio Rumiñahui (a stadium) and within walking distance from the Mariscal. There are more than a dozen climbing routes, and all gear is available to rent. Bring a partner to belay.

Compañía de Guías de Montaña ROCK CLIMBING
(Map p634; ☎290-1551; www.companiadeguias.com; cnr Av 6 de Diciembre N20-50 & Washington) A top-notch mountain-climbing operator with guides who are all licensed instructors and speak several languages. Two-day trips up Cotopaxi or Chimborazo cost US$180 per person.

Alta Montaña ROCK CLIMBING
(Map p634; ☎252-4422; Washington 8-20 near Av 6 de Diciembre) Owner Ivan Rojas has been on the Ecuadorian mountain scene for years and is an invaluable resource for expeditionists. Courses, guide recommendations and equipment rental are available.

New Town

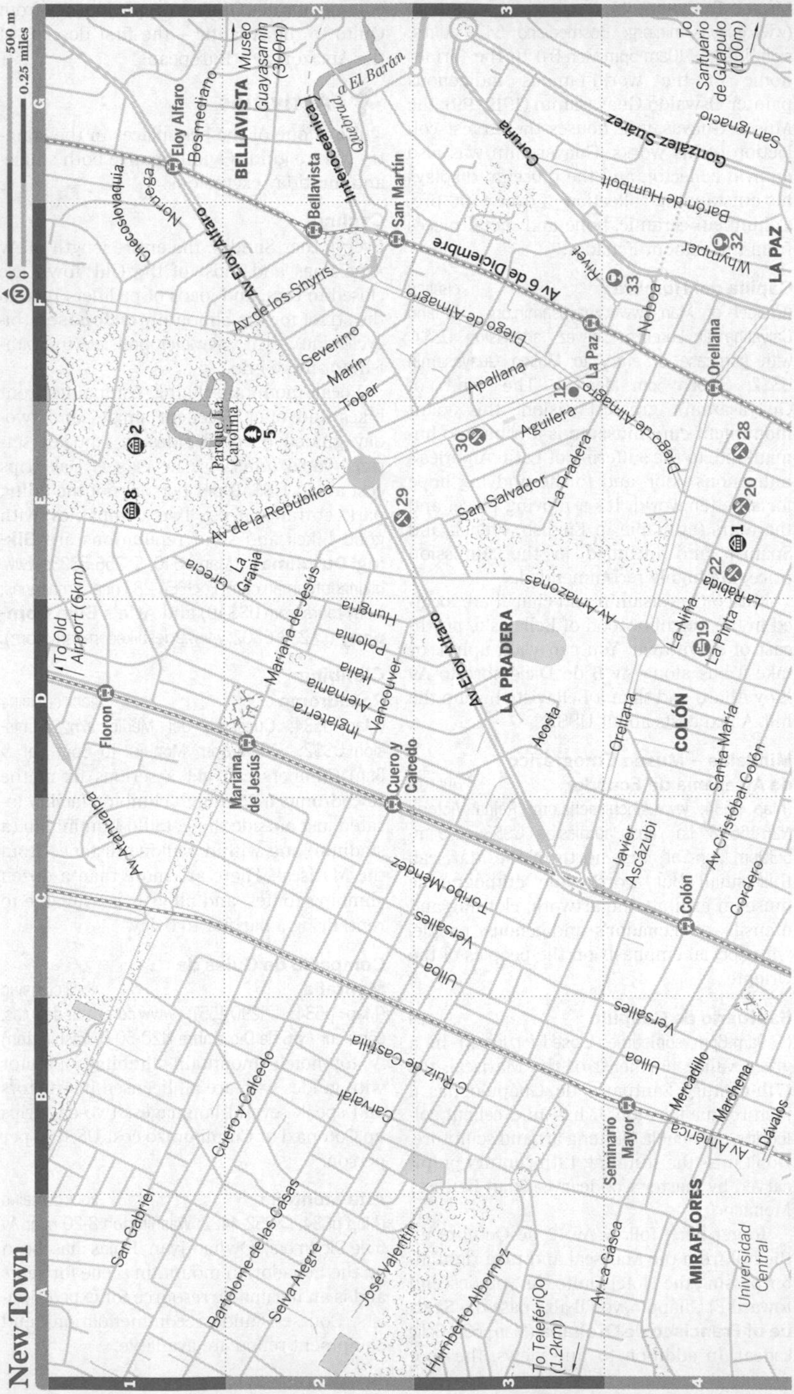

0 500 m
0 0.25 miles

A B C D E F G
1 2 3 4

To Old Airport (6km)
Floron
Av Atahualpa
San Gabriel
8
2
Checoslovaquia
Noruega
Eloy Alfaro
Bosmediano
Parque La Carolina
5
BELLAVISTA
Museo Guayasamín (300m)
Bartolome de las Casas
Cuero y Calcedo
Mariana de Jesús
Grecia
La Granja
Av de la República
Av Eloy Alfaro
Av de los Shyris
Selva Alegre
Mariana de Jesús
Bellavista
Interoceánica
Quebrada El Barán
José Valentín
Carvajal
C Ruiz de Castilla
Inglaterra
Alemania
Italia
Polonia
Hungria
Vancouver
Severino
Marín
Tobar
San Martín
Cuero y Caicedo
29
Ulloa
Versalles
Toribo Méndez
Av Eloy Alfaro
Humberto Albornoz
30
San Salvador
Apallana
Diego de Almagro
Av 6 de Diciembre
LA PRADERA
Aguilera
12
Coruña
To TeleféríQo (1.2km)
Acosta
Av Amazonas
La Pradera
La Paz
Rivet
Av La Gasca
Seminario Mayor
Ulloa
Versalles
Javier Ascázubi
Orellana
Diego de Almagro
33
Noboa
Baron de Humbolt
González Suárez
MIRAFLORES
Av América
Mercadillo
Colón
COLÓN
La Niña
19
La Pinta
La Rábida
22
1
20
28
Orellana
Whymper
32
San Ignacio
To Santuario de Guápulo (100m)
Universidad Central
Marchena
Dávalos
Av Cristóbal Colón
Santa María
Cordero
LA PAZ

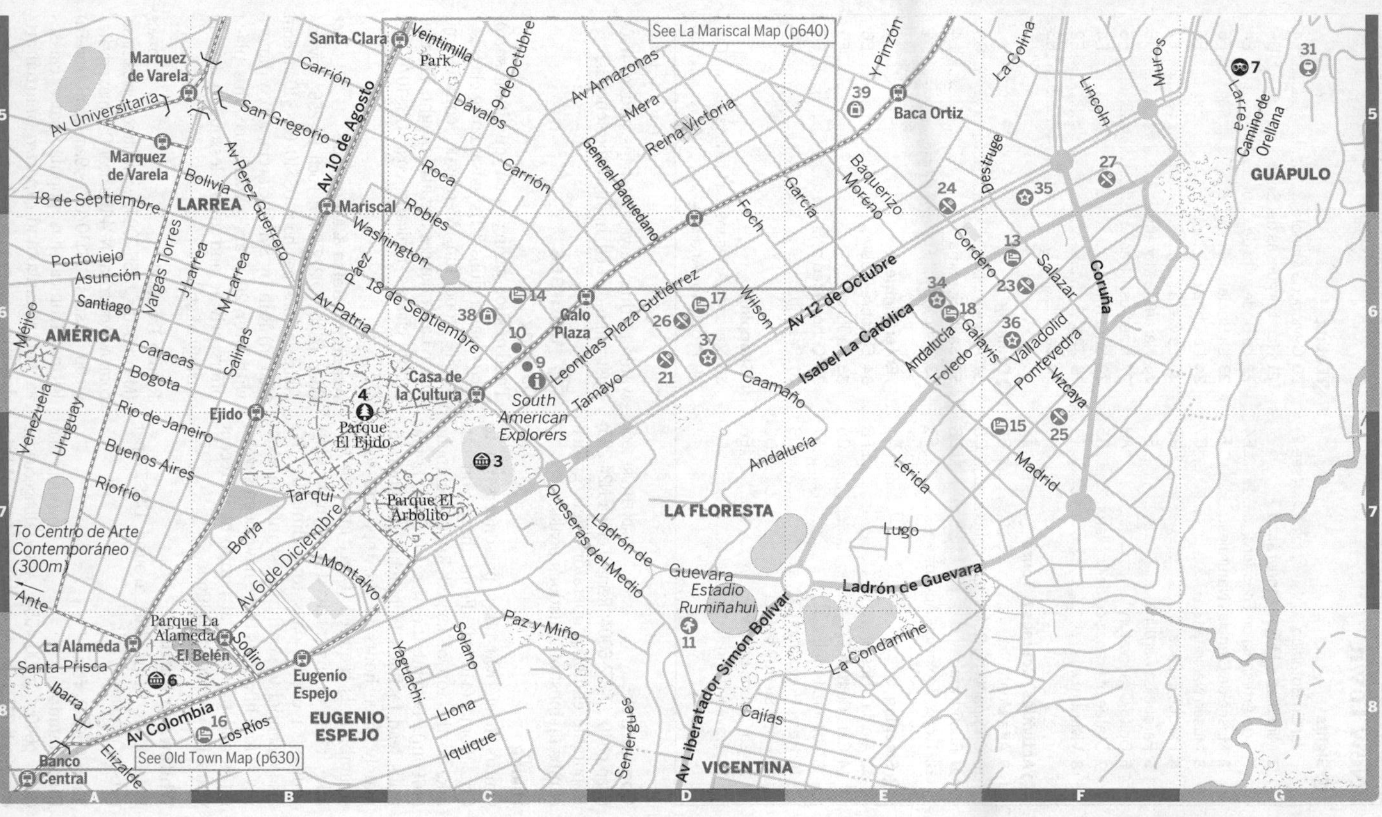
See La Mariscal Map (p640)
Santa Clara
Veintimilla
Park
Marquez de Varela
Carrión
9 de Octubre
Av Amazonas
Mera
Reina Victoria
Y Pinzón
39
Baca Ortiz
La Colina
Lincoln
Muros
7
Larrea
Camino de Orellana
31
GUÁPULO
Av Universitaria
San Gregorio
Av 10 de Agosto
Dávalos
Marquez de Varela
Bolivia
Av Perez Guerrero
Roca
Carrión
General Baquedano
Baquerizo Moreno
García
Foch
Destruge
24
35
27
18 de Septiembre
LARREA
Mariscal
Robles
Washington
Cordero
13
Salazar
Coruña
Portoviejo
Asunción
Santiago
Vargas Torres
J Larrea
M Larrea
Páez
18 de Septiembre
14
Leonidas Plaza Gutiérrez
17
Wilson
Av 12 de Octubre
34
18
23
Méjico
AMÉRICA
Caracas
Bogota
Salinas
Av Patria
38
Galo Plaza
10
9
26
37
Isabel La Católica
Andalucía
Galavis
36
Valladolid
Pontevedra
Vizcaya
Venezuela
Uruguay
Rio de Janeiro
Ejido
4
Parque El Ejido
Casa de la Cultura
South American Explorers
Tamayo
21
Caamaño
Toledo
15
25
Buenos Aires
Riofrío
3
Andalucía
Lérida
Madrid
Tarqui
Parque El Arbolito
Queseras del Medio
LA FLORESTA
Lugo
To Centro de Arte Contemporáneo (300m)
Borja
Av 6 de Diciembre
J Montalvo
Ladrón de Guevara
Estadio Rumiñahui
Ladrón de Guevara
Ante
Parque La Alameda
La Alameda
El Belén
Sodiro
Paz y Miño
11
Av Libertador Simón Bolívar
La Condamine
Santa Prisca
6
Eugenio Espejo
Yaguachi
Solano
Ibarra
Av Colombia
16
Los Ríos
EUGENIO ESPEJO
Llona
Iquique
Senierges
Cajías
VICENTINA
Banco Central
Elizalde
See Old Town Map (p630)

New Town

Sights

- Jardín Botánico .... (see 2)
- 1 Mindalae – Museo Etnográfico de Artesanía de Ecuador E4
- 2 Museo de Ciencias Naturales E1
- 3 Museo Nacional C7
- 4 Parque El Ejido B6
- 5 Parque La Carolina E2
- 6 Quito Observatory A8
- 7 Statue of Francisco de Orellana G5
- 8 Vivarium E1

Activities, Courses & Tours

- 9 Alta Montaña C6
- 10 Compañía de Guías de Montaña C6
- 11 Rocódromo D8
- 12 Tropic Ecological Adventures F3

Sleeping

- 13 Aleida's Hostal F6
- 14 Café Cultura C6
- 15 Folklore Hotel F7
- 16 Hostel Revolution B8
- 17 Hotel Sierra Madre D6
- 18 La Casona de Mario E6
- 19 Travellers Inn D4

Eating

- 20 Cevichería Manolo E4
- 21 Hamburguesas del Sesé D6
- 22 La Bodeguita de Cuba E4
- 23 La Briciola F6
- 24 La Choza E5
- 25 La Cleta F7
- 26 Naranjilla Mecánica D6
- 27 Noe Sushi Bar F5
- 28 Supermaxi E4
- 29 Zao E2
- 30 Zazu E3

Drinking

- 31 Ananké G5
- 32 Santa Espuma F4
- 33 Z(inc) F4

Entertainment

- 34 El Pobre Diablo E6
- 35 La Juliana F5
- 36 Ocho y Medio F6
- 37 Seseribó D6

Shopping

- 38 Mercado Artesanal La Mariscal C6
- 39 Productos Andinos E5

Condor Trek ADVENTURE TOUR
(Map p640; ☎222-6004; Reina Victoria N24-295) Reputable climbing operator offers guided climbs up most of Ecuador's peaks.

Hiking

Quito's TelefériQo takes passengers up to Cruz Loma (4100m). From there you can hike to the top of jagged Rucu Pichincha (4680m). Beyond the rise of Cruz Loma, trails lead to Rucu Pichincha. It's approximately three hours to the top, and some scrambling is required. Don't attempt this hike if you've just arrived in Quito; allow yourself a couple days to acclimatize. It's also essential to get the latest info on security before hiking as there have been several rapes and robberies at gunpoint in recent years. It's unwise to go alone.

Whitewater Rafting

Rafting day trips start around US$75 per person per day.

Yacu Amu Rafting/ Ríos Ecuador ADVENTURE TOUR
(Map p640; ☎290-4054; www.raftingecuador.com; Foch 746 btwn Amazonas & Mera) Whitewater rafting, kayaking trips and courses. Australian-owned, highly experienced.

Courses

Dancing

Tired of shoe-gazing when you hit the *salsotecas* (salsa clubs)? Try salsa dance classes – they're good fun. Merengue, cumbia and other Latin dances are also taught. Private/group classes typically cost US$10/6 per hour.

Academia Salsa & Merengue DANCE
(Map p640; ☎222-0427; Foch E4-256; private/group lessons per hour US$10/6; ⏲10am-8pm Mon-Fri) Run by Sylvia Garcia, a pro dancer with over 20 years' experience, this place offers private and group lessons in a wide variety of styles.

Ritmo Tropical DANCE
(Map p640; ☎255-7094; www.ritmotropicalsalsa.com; Av Amazonas N24-155 near Calama; private/group lessons US$10/6; ⏲9am-8pm Mon-Fri) Ritmo Tropical has popular salsa classes as well as tango and *capoeira* (martial art/dance).

Ritmo Salvaje DANCE
(Map p640; ☎222-4603; García E5-45; private lessons US$10; ⊙10am-8pm Mon-Fri) Offers a free introductory lesson on Thursday nights at 8pm. Friday and Saturday nights it becomes a popular salsa spot (admission US$3; free if you take lessons).

Language

Quito is one of the top places in South America to learn Spanish. Most schools offer group or one-on-one instruction and can arrange homestays with families. Rates for private lessons vary between US$7 and US$10 per hour. Some schools charge an inscription fee (usually around US$20).

Ecole Idiomas LANGUAGE COURSE
(Map p640; ☎601-4757; www.ecoleidiomas.com; García E6-15 near Mera) This well-run, Dutch-owned school offers private and group classes from a lovely location in the Mariscal. Volunteer opportunities available.

Quito Antiguo Spanish School LANGUAGE COURSE
(Map p630; ☎228-8454; www.quitoantiguospanish.com; Venezuela N7-31) The Old Town's only language school with many study options.

Yanapuma Language School LANGUAGE COURSE
(Map p640; ☎254-6709; www.yanapuma.org; Veintimilla E8-125, 2nd fl) Excellent foundation-run school with opportunities to study while traveling or volunteering, both in Quito and in remote communities.

Vida Verde LANGUAGE COURSE
(Map p640; ☎222-6635; www.vidaverde.com; Leonidas Plaza Gutiérrez near Wilson) A recommended, Ecuadorian-owned school.

Tours

Quito is one of the easiest places in Ecuador to arrange a guided tour, be it a Galápagos cruise, climbing trip or jungle tour. For mountain-biking, rafting and climbing tours near Quito, see also p633. Be sure to stop by on weekdays; many offices close on weekends.

CarpeDM Adventures GUIDED TOUR
(Map p630; ☎295-4713; www.carpedm.ca; Antepara E4-70) Canadian-owned CarpeDM earns high marks for its excellent prices and wide range of tours, though it's the excellent service (and follow-up) that makes this agency run by the kind-hearted Paul Parreno stand out from many others.

Eos Ecuador ECOTOUR
(Map p640; ☎601-3560; www.eosecuador.travel; Av Amazonas N24-66 at Pinto) Eos offers a wide range of conventional and off-the-beaten-path tours, including jungle tours and adventure treks.

Gulliver OUTDOORS
(Map p640; ☎252-9297; www.gulliver.com.ec; cnr Mera & Calama; ⊙8am-8pm) Trekking, climbing, mountain-biking and horse-riding trips in the Andes.

Happy Gringo GUIDED TOUR
(Map p640; ☎222-0031; www.happygringo.com; Foch near Reina Victoria) A well-respected operator that has a full range of trips and tours. One of the best places in town to plan a Galápagos trip.

Rainforestur ADVENTURE TOUR
(Map p640; ☎223-9822; www.rainforestur.com; Av Amazonas N21-108 near Robles) Offers well-received rafting trips on the Río Pastaza near Baños, and trips to Cuyabeno, Yasuní and elsewhere. Also offers hiking trips (Cotopaxi) and Quito city tours.

Safari Tours GUIDED TOUR
(Map p640; ☎255-2505; www.safari.com.ec; Reina Victoria N25-33, 11th fl, near Av Colon) Excellent reputation and long in the business. Offers a range of tours and trips, from volcano climbs and jungle trips to local jeep tours and personalized off-the-beaten-track expeditions.

Sierra Nevada Expeditions ADVENTURE TOUR
(Map p640; ☎255-3658; www.sierranevadatrek.com; Pinto near Cordero) Sierra Nevada offers climbing and river-rafting trips. Owner Freddy Ramirez is well established and a very reputable mountain guide.

Tropic Ecological Adventures GUIDED TOUR
(Map p634; ☎222-5907; www.tropiceco.com; Pasaje Sanchez Melo near Av Galo Plaza Laso) Long-standing agency offering numerous three- to six-day tours to the Oriente, Andes and cloud forest. Good rates. Located near the airport.

Festivals & Events

The city's biggest party celebrates the founding of Quito in the first week of December, when bullfights are held daily at Plaza de Toros. On New Year's Eve, life-size puppets (often of politicians) are burned in the streets at midnight. **Carnaval** is celebrated with intense water fights – no one is spared.

Colorful religious processions are held during Easter week.

Semana Santa RELIGIOUS
(Holy Week) Colorful religious processions held the week before Easter throughout Ecuador, but particularly popular in Quito.

Fundación de Quito CARNIVAL
(Founding of Quito) Celebrated the first week of December with bullfights, parades and dancing.

Sleeping

Most travelers stay in the Mariscal neighborhood so they can be near the many bars, cafes and restaurants. Unfortunately, the Mariscal has an untamed crime problem. Plaza Foch, which has a police presence, remains safe; two or three blocks away, however, muggings still occur. Take a taxi after dark.

Street noise can be an issue at many places but is especially bad in the Mariscal. Light sleepers should bring heavy-duty earplugs if planning to get any rest on a weekend night.

While lacking in Thai restaurants and expat bars, the Old Town has much better colonial ambience, and you won't feel like you're bunking in gringolandia.

Adjacent to the Mariscal, the hip La Floresta neighborhood has a few inviting places to stay.

OLD TOWN

Colonial House GUESTHOUSE $
(Map p630; ☎316-3350; www.colonialhousequito.com; Olmedo 432 near Los Ríos; dm US$10, r with/without bathroom US$25/20; @ 📶) True to name, this guesthouse is set in a sprawling colonial house with 16 colorfully decorated guestrooms, various lounges and common areas, and a rustic back garden sprinkled with fruit trees. The vibe is friendly, bohemian and easygoing and there's a laundry and guest kitchens.

Hostel Revolution GUESTHOUSE $
(Map p634; ☎254-6458; www.hostelrevolutionquito.com; Los Ríos N13-11; dm/s/d/tr US$9/16/25/30; @ 📶) For an escape from the Mariscal circus, this Australian-Ecuadorian-owned colonial house is an excellent, laid-back option with comfy rooms, shared kitchen, terrace with views and colorful bar-lounge where you can meet other travelers.

Community Hostel HOSTEL $
(Map p630; ☎228-5108; www.communityhostel.com; Pedro Fermín Cevallos N6-78 near Olmedo; dm US$10-12.50, d US$30) Community Hostel creates a warm, homelike ambience, and the family-style meals are a great time to meet other travelers. Excellent beds and clean facilities overall.

Hostal San Blas GUESTHOUSE $
(Map p630; ☎228-9480; www.hostalsanblas.com.ec; Caldas E1-38, Plaza San Blas; s/d US$15/24, without bathroom US$13/20) This friendly, family-run hotel on the attractive Plaza San Blas is a good deal if you don't mind small rooms. Rooms are dark (windows open onto a small interior patio) but clean.

Secret Garden HOSTEL $
(Map p630; ☎295-6704; www.secretgardenquito.com; Antepara E4-60; dm US$11, d with/without bathroom US$39/32; @ 📶) This popular hostel, owned by an Ecuadorian-Australian couple, has a party vibe and attracts a mix of young backpackers. The rooms are cramped, but the small 5th-floor terrace with superb views is an excellent place to meet other travelers.

La Guayunga HOSTEL $
(Map p630; ☎228-8544; www.laguayungaquito.com; Antepara E4-27; dm US$10, d with/without bathroom US$28/35; P @ 📶) La Guayunga is an easygoing, family-run guesthouse with simple, wood-floored rooms, an open-sided terrace with views and decent amenities (laundry, guest kitchen, parking).

La Posada Colonial GUESTHOUSE $
(Map p630; ☎228-2859; www.laposadacolonial.com; Paredes S1-49 near Rocafuerte; r per person US$6-12; 📶) This wood-floor guesthouse is still one of the best value places in the Old Town. Beds are saggy, but it's well kept and secure. It's near the lively restaurants of La Ronda.

Hotel San Francisco de Quito HOTEL $$
(Map p630; ☎228-7758; www.sanfranciscodequito.com.ec; Sucre Oe3-17; s/d US$32/51) This historic converted house boasts spotless rooms with telephone, TV and constant hot water. Because it's a colonial building, most rooms lack windows, but double doors open onto a balcony over an interior courtyard. It's popular so reserve well ahead.

Hotel Viena Internacional HOTEL $$
(Map p630; ☎295-9611; www.hotelvienaint.com; Flores N5-04; s/d US$24/44; 📶) Though the '70s-style wallpaper may make your eyes

water, the spotless rooms, top-notch service and cheerful interior patio make this fine value. Rooms have hardwood floors, TVs, hot water and good showers.

Hostal Ecuador GUESTHOUSE $$
(Map p630; ☎295-2629; www.hostalecuadorquito.com; Venezuela S-128 near Rocafuerte; s/d US$23/40) The rooms are small but clean and comfortable, with shiny wood floors; they open onto an interior courtyard.

LA MARISCAL

Hostal El Arupo GUESTHOUSE $
(Map p640; ☎255-7543; www.hostalelarupo.com; Rodríguez E7-22; s/d/tw incl breakfast US$30/45/48; @ wi-fi) One of several good guesthouses on the quietest street in the Mariscal, El Arupo is a spotless and homey converted house with a lovely front patio. Some rooms are small and a little dark, but all are spotless, with dark-wood floors and firm beds. There's an immaculate communal kitchen.

Vibes HOSTEL $
(Map p640; ☎255-5154; www.vibesquito.com; Pinto near Av 6 de Diciembre; dm US$7-9, d US$25; wi-fi) Set in a converted colonial house, this seven-room hostel attracts a laid-back crowd, and it's a good spot to meet other travelers for nights out in the Mariscal. There's a bar with a pool table for starting off the evening. Santiago, the friendly owner, is a good source of local info.

Blue House GUESTHOUSE $
(Map p640; ☎222-3480; www.bluehousequito.com; Pinto E8-24; dm US$8, d with/without bathroom US$30/24; @ wi-fi) This friendly guesthouse has eight pleasant rooms with wood floors in a converted house on a quiet street. There's a grassy yard in front for barbecues, a comfy lounge with fireplace and a kitchen for guests.

Posada del Maple GUESTHOUSE $
(Map p640; ☎254-4507; www.posadadelmaple.com; Rodriguez E8-49; dm US$10, s/d US$25/41, without bathroom US$23/30; @ wi-fi) Maple is a friendly place with clean but dated rooms, comfy lounge areas and outdoor space. It's well liked by many travelers.

Hostal Nassau GUESTHOUSE $
(Map p640; ☎256-5724; www.nassauhostal.com; Pinto E4-342; s/d US$15/25, without bathroom US$10/20; wi-fi) Nassau is a clean and well-run place, with friendly hosts, tidy rooms and a small shared kitchen. Upstairs rooms have wood floors and are brighter than the downstairs quarters.

Travellers Inn GUESTHOUSE $$
(Map p634; ☎255-6985; www.travellersecuador.com; La Pinta E4-435 near Av Amazonas; s/d incl breakfast US$33/45, without bathroom US$17/27; @ wi-fi) The family-owned Travellers Inn has small but clean rooms, and the breakfast is substantial. It's in a good location near the Mariscal, but far enough away from the bars so you can get decent sleep.

Magic Bean GUESTHOUSE $$
(Map p640; ☎256-6181; www.magicbeanquito.com; Foch E5-08; dm/s/d US$14/28/36; wi-fi) Better known for its lively restaurant, the Magic Bean has just four rooms – all very tidy and nicely designed. Light sleepers beware: it gets awfully noisy on the weekends.

Casa Kanela GUESTHOUSE $$
(Map p640; ☎254-6162; www.casakanela.mamey.org; Rodríguez E8-46; s/d US$25/38, without bathroom US$16/31; @ wi-fi) An excellent new addition to the Mariscal, Kanela offers minimalist but stylish rooms in a pleasant converted house on pretty Rodríguez. It's a friendly, welcoming place.

Casa Helbling GUESTHOUSE $
(Map p640; ☎222-6013; www.casahelbling.de; Veintimilla 531; s/d US$30/40, without bathroom US$19/28; @ wi-fi) In a homey, colonial-style house in the Mariscal, Casa Helbling is clean, relaxed and friendly. It has a guest kitchen, laundry facilities and plenty of common areas for chilling out.

Hotel Sierra Madre GUESTHOUSE $$
(Map p634; ☎250-5687; www.hotelsierramadre.com; Veintimilla 464; s/d US$61/75; @ wi-fi) In a handsomely restored colonial building, the Sierra Madre has rooms of varying size, but most have wood floors, excellent beds and a warm color scheme; the best have vaulted ceilings and verandas. There's a reasonable restaurant below.

Café Cultura GUESTHOUSE $$$
(Map p634; ☎222-4271; www.cafecultura.com; Robles 513; s/d US$100/122; @ wi-fi) This atmospheric boutique hotel is set in a converted mansion with a garden, crackling fireplaces and handsome mural-filled bedrooms, all adding to the considerable charm. Reservations are recommended.

Galápagos Natural Life GUESTHOUSE $
(Map p640; ☎252-0575; galapagos_natural_life@hotmail.com; Pinto near Av 6 de Diciembre; r per person with/without US$12.50/8; @ wi-fi) This good-value, family-run place has bright, sizable

La Mariscal

rooms that are well maintained. Good breakfasts; hot water is sometimes lacking.

LA FLORESTA & AROUND

La Casona de Mario GUESTHOUSE $

(Map p634; ☎254-4036; www.casonademario.com; Andalucía N24-115; r per person US$12; 📶) Situated in a converted old house, La Casona de Mario offers homey rooms, shared bathrooms, a garden, a TV lounge and a guest kitchen.

Aleida's Hostal GUESTHOUSE $$

(Map p634; ☎223-4570; www.aleidashostal.com.ec; Andalucía 559; s/d US$28/45, without bathroom US$19/34; @📶) This friendly three-story guesthouse in La Floresta is family-run and has a very spacious feel with lots of light, huge rooms, high wooden ceilings and hardwood floors.

Folklore Hotel GUESTHOUSE $$

(Map p634; ☎255-4621; www.folklorehotel.com; Madrid E13-93 near Pontevedra; s/d/ste incl breakfast US$29/39/49) This delightfully converted house in La Floresta has spacious, colorful rooms with blue-and-yellow checkered bedspreads that match the house paint job. It has a small garden and a welcoming family feel.

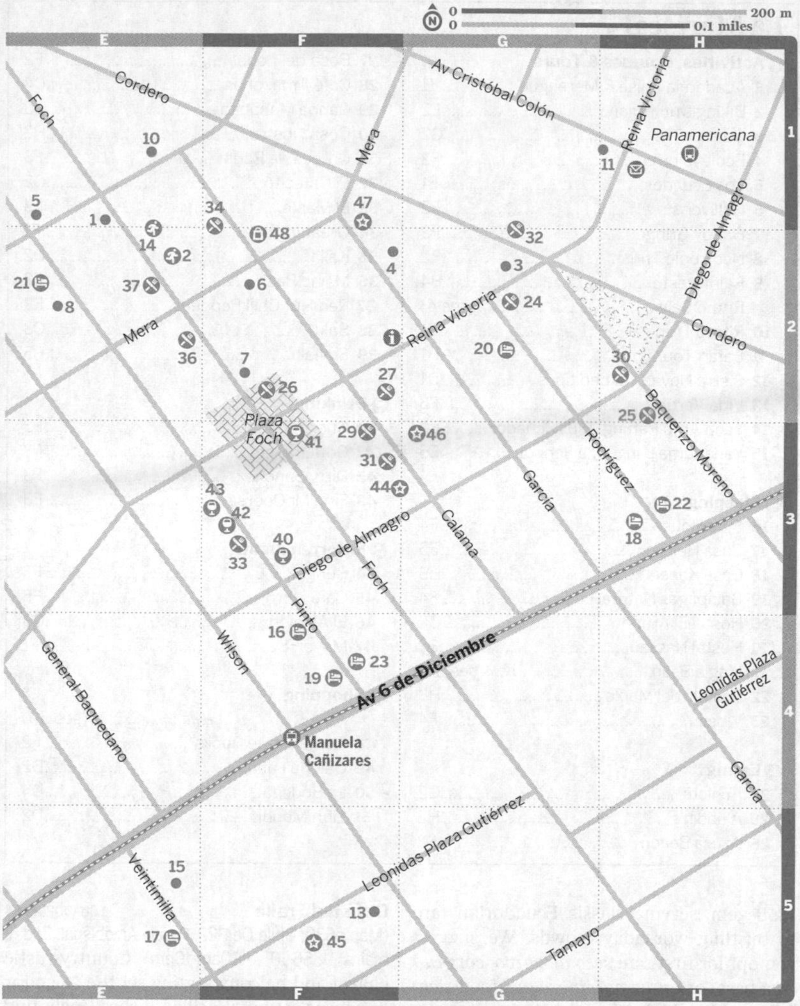

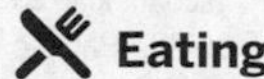

Eating

Quito has a rich and varied restaurant scene, with a fine mix of traditional Ecuadorian fare along with dozens of ethnic and international eateries. All budgets and tastes are catered for, and you'll find everything from streamlined sushi counters to old-fashioned dining rooms serving up Andean classics.

The Mariscal has the densest concentration of restaurants, including local and international eateries. For more high-end dining, look to La Floresta, La Pradera and neighboring areas: these are home to the city's best restaurants.

If you're low on funds, stick to good-value *almuerzos* or *meriendas* (fixed-price set lunches and dinners). Many restaurants close on Sunday.

OLD TOWN

TOP CHOICE **San Agustín** ECUADORIAN **$$**

(Map p630; Guayaquil N5-59; mains US$6-9; 9:30am-6pm Mon-Fri, 10:30am-4pm Sat & Sun) Decorated with oil paintings and elegant light fixtures, San Agustín is a two-story

La Mariscal

Activities, Courses & Tours
1 Academia Salsa & Merengue E1
2 Biking Dutchman E2
3 Condor Trek G2
4 Ecole Idiomas F2
5 Eos Ecuador E1
6 Gulliver F2
7 Happy Gringo F2
8 Neotropic Turis E2
9 Rainforestur B4
Ritmo Salvaje .... (see 4)
10 Ritmo Tropical E1
11 Safari Tours H1
12 Sierra Nevada Expeditions D1
13 Vida Verde F5
14 Yacu Amu Rafting/Ríos Ecuador E2
15 Yanapuma Language School E5

Sleeping
16 Blue House F4
17 Casa Helbling E5
18 Casa Kanela H3
19 Galápagos Natural Life F4
20 Hostal El Arupo G2
21 Hostal Nassau E2
Magic Bean .... (see 36)
22 Posada del Maple H3
23 Vibes F4

Eating
24 Achiote G2
25 Aladdin's H2
26 Azuca Beach F2
27 Boca del Lobo F2
28 Café Amazonas C4
29 Canoa Manabita F3
30 Cosa Nostra H2
31 Crêpes de Paris F3
32 El Cafecito G2
33 El Maple F3
34 Great India F1
35 Kallari D2
36 Magic Bean E2
37 Red Hot Chili Peppers E2
38 Sakti C3
39 Suvlaki B5

Drinking
40 Cherusker F3
41 Coffee Tree F3
42 Dirty Sanchez F3
43 Finn McCool's F3

Entertainment
44 Bungalow 6 .... F3
45 Café Libro F5
46 El Aguijón G3
47 Mayo 68 .... F1

Shopping
Ag .... (see 50)
48 Confederate Books F2
49 Galería Latina D2
50 La Bodega D4
51 Libri Mundi D2

1858 gem, serving classic Ecuadorian fare to bustling workaday crowds. We suggest you opt for first-rate *seco de chivo, corvina* (sea bass) or *arroz marinero* (seafood rice) followed by old-fashioned *helados de paila* (ice cream handmade and served in big copper bowls).

Vista Hermosa INTERNATIONAL **$$**
(Map p630; ☎295-1401; Mejía 453, 5th fl; mains US$10-13; ⊙1pm-midnight Mon-Sat, to 9pm Sun) A much-loved spot in El Centro, Vista Hermosa (Beautiful View) delivers the goods with a magnificent 360-degree panorama over the Old Town from its open rooftop terrace. Live music on Thursday to Saturday (from 8pm onwards) adds to the magic. Arrive early to beat the crowds.

Café del Fraile ECUADORIAN **$$**
(Map p630; Chile Oe4-22, Pasaje Arzobispal, 2nd fl; mains US$6-10; ⊙10am-10pm) Country-rustic charm and balcony seating set the stage for a tasty selection of grilled dishes (including trout and *corvina*), sandwiches and cocktails.

Hasta La Vuelta, Señor ECUADORIAN **$$**
(Map p630; ☎258-0887; Chile Oe4-22, Palacio Arzobispal, 3rd fl; mains US$7-12; ⊙10am-10pm Mon-Sat, to 9pm Sun) Ecuadorian cuisine is prepared with panache at this excellent restaurant with balcony seating. Reliable favorites include *ceviche, seco de chivo,* tilapia and sea bass.

Café Mosaico CAFE **$$**
(Map p630; ☎254-2871; Samaniego N8-95; mains US$10-12; ⊙11am-11pm) Serving up a mix of Ecuadorian and Greek fare near Parque

Itchimbia, vine-covered Mosaico is famed for its magnificent views. The open-sided terrace is great for a sundowner.

El Cafeto CAFE $

(Map p630; Chile 930 near Flores; mains US$4-6; ⏲8am-7:30pm Mon-Sat) This quaint little Ecuadorian-owned coffee shop serves excellent coffee made from 100% organic Ecuadorian beans. Omelets, sandwiches, salads and desserts (cheesecake) are available.

Cafetería Fabiolita ECUADORIAN $

(El Buen Sanduche; Map p630; Espejo Oe4-17; sandwiches US$2; ⏲9am-6pm) For more than 40 years this tiny eatery has served up Quito's favorite *seco de chivo*, one of Ecuador's most traditional dishes. Arrive early, before they run out (9am to 11am only). *Sanduiches de pernil* (ham sandwiches) are also quite satisfying.

Cafetería Modelo CAFE $

(Map p630; cnr Sucre & García Moreno; snacks US$1-2.50; ⏲8am-7:30pm) Opened in 1950, Modelo is one of the city's oldest cafes, and a great spot to try traditional snacks like *empanadas de verde* (plantain empanadas filled with cheese), *quimbolitos* (a sweet cake steamed in a leaf), tamales and *humitas*.

Tianguez ECUADORIAN $

(Map p630; Plaza San Francisco; mains US$4-9; ⏲9:30am-6pm Sun-Wed, to 7pm Thu, to 8:30pm Fri & Sat) Tucked into the stone arches beneath the Monasterio de San Francisco, this bohemian-style cafe prepares tasty appetizers (tamales, soups) as well as heartier mains.

Govindas VEGETARIAN $

(Map p630; ☎296-6844; Esmeraldas 853; mains US$1.50; ⏲9am-3pm Mon-Sat; ✓) Proudly serving 100% vegetarian cuisine, the Hare Krishnas whip up tasty fresh lunch plates from a changing menu, plus yogurt and granola, juices and sweets.

Frutería Monserrate ECUADORIAN $

(Map p630; ☎258-3408; Espejo Oe2-12; mains US$4; ⏲8:30am-8pm Mon-Fri, 9am-6pm Sat & Sun) A mix of travelers and locals stop in for the filling breakfasts and giant fruit salads. Empanadas and *ceviche* (raw marinated seafood) are also among the offerings.

Pizza SA PIZZERIA $$

(Map p630; Espejo Oe2-46; pizzas US$8-16; ⏲noon-9pm Mon-Sat, to 8pm Sun) Located on a restaurant-filled lane facing the Teatro Bolívar, this casual spot bakes up delicious, individually sized thin-crust pizzas. You can also enjoy sandwiches, salads and calzones. Sidewalk seating.

Mercado Central MARKET $

(Map p630; Av Pichincha; meals US$1-3; ⏲8am-4pm Mon-Sat, to 3pm Sun) For stall after stall of some of Quito's most traditional (and cheapest) foods, head straight to the Mercado Central, where you'll find everything from *locro de papa* (potato soup with cheese and avocado) and seafood to *yaguarlocro* (potato soup with chunks of fried blood sausage). Fruits and veggies too.

Corvina Don 'Jimmy' SEAFOOD $

(Map p630; Mercado Central, Av Pichincha; mains US$4-6; ⏲8am-4pm Mon-Sat, to 3pm Sun) Open since 1953, this is the Mercado Central's most famous stall, serving huge portions of *corvina*. Ask for it with rice if you don't want it over a big bowl of *ceviche*.

Magda SUPERMARKET

(Map p630; Venezuela N3-62; ⏲8:30am-7pm Mon-Sat, 9am-5pm Sun) A conveniently located and well-stocked supermarket.

LA MARISCAL

Achiote ECUADORIAN $$

(Map p640; cnr Rodriguez & Reina Victoria; mains US$9-15; ⏲noon-10pm) A colorful new addition to the Mariscal, Achiote prepares Ecuadorian dishes with a twist in a warmly lit contemporary setting. Empanadas, *ceviche*, rich seafood stews and *llapingachos* are all first-rate. Live music Thursday to Sunday nights (from 7pm).

Boca del Lobo INTERNATIONAL $$

(Map p640; Calama 284; mains US$8-14; ⏲5pm-1am) The ambience at this hip restaurant is pure kitsch, with colored glass globes, empty birdcages and psychedelic paintings. The menu features raclette, crepes, open-faced sandwiches, baked desserts and sugary-sweet cocktails.

Azuca Beach SEAFOOD $$

(Map p640; Foch near Reina Victoria; mains US$10-14; ⏲closed Sun; ᯤ) Overlooking buzzing Plaza Foch, Azuca Beach brings a touch of the coast to landlocked Quito. *Encocado de camarones* (shrimp and coconut stew), *sopa marinera* (seafood soup) and various *ceviche* are among the hits. Tropical cocktails, a bamboo-trimmed bar and potted palms add to the loungelike space, which becomes a popular drinking spot at night.

Cosa Nostra ITALIAN $$
(Map p640; cnr Baquerizo Moreno & Diego de Almagro; mains US$9-13; ⏲12:30-3pm & 6:30-10:30pm Tue-Sun) Italian-owned Cosa Nostra has a pleasant front patio, cozy dining room and excellent pizzas piled with generous toppings and fired up in a brick oven. Tiramisu and good espresso for dessert.

El Cafecito INTERNATIONAL $
(Map p640; Cordero 1124; mains US$6-10; ⏲8am-11pm;) This lovely cafe and restaurant with colonial color scheme serves up salads, pastas, desserts and cocktails. The prices are high and the service slow, but the ambience (candlelit by night) is first-rate. Great breakfasts too.

La Bodeguita de Cuba CUBAN $$
(Map p634; Reina Victoria 1721; mains US$8; ⏲noon-11pm Mon & Tue, to 1am Wed & Thu, to 2am Fri & Sat) With its wooden tables and graffiti-covered walls, this is a great place for Cuban food and fun. Live bands perform from time to time, and there's outdoor seating.

El Maple VEGETARIAN $
(Map p640; Pinto E7-68 near Diego de Almagro; mains US$5-8; ⏲noon-9pm Mon & Tue, to 10:30pm Wed-Sat, to 6pm Sun;) This well-loved restaurant serves good vegetarian food with global influences (Tex-Mex-style burritos, Asian noodle dishes, creamy pastas). The four-course set lunches are good value, and the juices are tops.

Great India INDIAN $
(Map p640; Calama E4-54; mains US$4-6; ⏲11am-midnight) Amid photos of the Taj Mahal, Indian film stars and Bollywood films, this ever-popular outpost serves filling lamb or chicken masala, veggie curries, lassis and chicken shawarmas and falafel sandwiches. The food is good but lacks heat.

Aladdin's MIDDLE EASTERN $
(Map p640; cnr Diego de Almagro & Baquerizo Moreno; mains US$3-7; ⏲11am-11pm Mon-Thu, to 1am Fri & Sat, to 4:30pm Sun) Aladdin's is a souk-themed restaurant with covered front patio serving satisfying falafel and shawarma sandwiches, as well as heartier main courses. This is also a fine place to indulge in a bit of hookah action.

Kallari CAFE $
(Map p640; www.kallari.com; Wilson E4-266; breakfasts US$3.50, lunches US$4.30; ⏲9am-7pm Mon-Sat) This Quichua coop serves up satisfying breakfasts and lunches, and stocks its famous chocolate bars.

Magic Bean INTERNATIONAL $$
(Map p640; Foch E5-08; mains US$6-12; ⏲7am-11pm;) Longtime epicenter of the Mariscal, the Magic Bean serves well-prepared breakfasts, lunches, juices and snacks for the ever-present crowd of hungry travelers.

Cevichería Manolo ECUADORIAN $
(Map p634; cnr Diego de Almagro & La Niña; mains US$4-6; ⏲8am-5pm or 6pm) Join the locals at this excellent and affordable seafood restaurant, with several types of Ecuadorian and Peruvian *ceviche* on the menu, plus great seafood dishes.

Canoa Manabita ECUADORIAN $
(Map p640; Calama 247; mains US$4-7; ⏲11am-2:30pm Tue-Sun) This casual and unassuming place is extremely popular with locals for its mouthwatering servings of *ceviche* and seafood plates.

Red Hot Chili Peppers MEXICAN $
(Map p640; Foch E4-314; mains US$4-6; ⏲noon-10:30pm Mon-Sat) Think fajitas – the rest of the menu is good, but doesn't quite measure up to that sizzling plate of chicken or beef. Wash it down with smooth piña coladas.

Naranjilla Mecánica INTERNATIONAL $$
(Map p634; Tamayo N22-43; mains US$6-12; ⏲noon-2am Mon-Fri, 6pm-2am Sat) This art-loving restaurant and bar serves inventive salads, pastas and sandwiches. The menu comes in comic-book form (the images may kill your appetite), and the decor is bohemian chic. There's an art gallery upstairs.

Suvlaki GREEK $
(Map p640; Av Amazonas N21-108; mains US$4; ⏲8:30am-7pm Mon-Fri, to 4pm Sat) The go-to spot for skewers of tasty grilled meat (the eponymous souvlaki), this casual spot has a growing following for its speedy service, cheery interior (complete with photos of Greek icons) and outdoor seating.

Sakti VEGETARIAN $
(Map p640; 252-0466; www.sakti-quito.com; Carrión E4-144; mains US$3-5;) This simple vegetarian restaurant serves up tasty lasagnas, soups and salads; it also runs an inexpensive guesthouse behind the restaurant.

Café Amazonas ECUADORIAN $$
(Map p640; cnr Av Amazonas & Roca; mains US$5-9; ⏲7am-9pm Mon-Sat, to 7pm Sun) A Quito clas-

sic, with outdoor tables and prime people-watching.

Crêpes de Paris FRENCH $
(Map p640; Calama E7-62; mains US$3-5; ⏲12:30-9:30pm Tue, to 11pm Wed-Sat) Amid oversize posters of the Eiffel Tower, Montmartre and Saint Michel, this small eatery serves up a satisfying selection of sweet and savory crepes – a good pit stop while pub-crawling along bar-lined Calama.

Hamburguesas del Sesé BURGERS $
(Map p634; cnr Tamayo & Carrión; mains US$3; ⏲11am-9pm Mon-Wed, to midnight Thu, to 2am Fri & Sat) One of many student hangouts in the area, Sesé serves some of Quito's best burgers (veggie burgers too). Chow down inside or on the rooftop patio.

Supermaxi SUPERMARKET
(Map p634; cnr La Niña & Pinzón; ⏲daily) The biggest and best supermarket located near the Mariscal.

La Floresta & Around

La Choza ECUADORIAN $$
(Map p634; ☎223-0839; Av 12 de Octubre N24-551; mains US$7-12; ⏲noon-4pm & 6:30-10pm Mon-Sat, noon-4pm Sun) One of Quito's best restaurants for traditional Ecuadorian cuisine, La Choza serves up hearty plates of *llapingachos*, grilled *corvina* and steak with all the fixings in an airy setting with colorfully woven tablecloths and Andean music.

Noe Sushi Bar JAPANESE $$$
(Map p634; ☎322-7378; Isabel La Católica N24-827; 2-person dinner US$50-80; ⏲12.30-4pm & 6.30-10pm) This stylish, minimalist restaurant offers tender, fresh sushi and sashimi, teppanyaki, Kobe beef and a range of other Japanese delicacies.

La Briciola ITALIAN $$
(Map p634; ☎254-5157; Toledo 1255; mains US$10-13; ⏲12:30-3pm & 7:30-11pm Mon-Sat) This longtime favorite has an outstanding and varied menu. The portions are large, and the wine is fairly priced. Reservations recommended.

La Cleta CAFE $$
(Map p634; Lugo N24-250; pizzas US$4-12; ⏲3-11pm Mon-Sat; 📶) Bicycle lovers shouldn't miss this small, cleverly designed cafe-restaurant, where you can enjoy tasty pizzas and lasagnas, along with coffee, wine and other drinks.

LA PRADERA & LA CAROLINA

TOP CHOICE **Zazu** FUSION $$$
(Map p634; ☎254-3559; Mariano Aguilera 331 near La Pradera; mains US$18-33; ⏲12:30pm-midnight Mon-Fri, 7pm-midnight Sat) One of Quito's best restaurants, Zazu serves beautifully prepared seafood dishes, grilled meats and *ceviche* in a stylish setting. The Peruvian chef seamlessly blends East with West, with dishes like pistachio-crusted tuna and Wagyu tartare with gorgonzola mousse.

Zao ASIAN $$
(Map p634; ☎252-3496; Av Alfaro N10-16 near San Salvador; mains US$8-10; ⏲12:30-3:30pm daily, 7-11:30pm Mon-Sat) Adorned with carved wooden screens and glowing paper lanterns, Zao is a buzzing spot serving up samosas, rich noodle dishes, vegetable stir-fries, sushi and other flavors from Asia.

Drinking

Much of the *farra* (nightlife) in Quito is concentrated in and around the Mariscal, where things get raucous most nights (and very crowded on weekends). At night, remember to always take a cab home – even if it's just a few blocks.

Cherusker BAR
(Map p640; cnr Pinto & Diego de Almagro; ⏲1pm-1am Mon-Thu, to 3am Fri & Sat) In a red, two-story colonial house, Cherusker has earned a loyal following for its tasty microbrews, warm bohemian ambience and buzzing front patio. Occasional live bands play on weekends.

Finn McCool's IRISH PUB
(Map p640; Diego de Almagro near Pinto; ⏲5pm-2am) This Irish-owned bar is the current favorite among expats, for its welcoming vibe, pub quiz nights (Tuesday at time of writing) and pool, darts and table football. The classic wood-lined bar also serves fish and chips, shepherd's pie, burgers and other pub grub.

Dirty Sanchez LOUNGE
(Map p640; Pinto E7-38 near Reina Victoria) The cheekily named Dirty Sanchez is a small art-filled lounge with a bohemian vibe. Decent cocktails (and coffee), better music and a more laid-back crowd make this expat-owned place a standout.

Coffee Tree BAR
(Map p640; cnr Reina Victoria & Foch; ⏲24hr) A good place to start the night off is this outdoor bar anchoring lively Reina Victoria.

DON'T MISS

LA RONDA

One of the biggest Old Town success stories of recent years is the restoration of 'La Ronda.' This narrow lane is lined with colorful colonial buildings, with placards along the walls describing (in Spanish) some of the street's history and the artists, writers and political figures who once resided here. Today, it is home to a jumble of restaurants, cafes, shops and galleries, such as the excellent **Casa de las Artes** (Map p630; Casa 989, La Ronda; admission free; ⌚10am-7pm Tue-Thu, to 10pm Fri & Sat, 11am-3pm Sun), though La Ronda remains a delightfully local and unpretentious affair. The street is at its liveliest on Friday and Saturday nights, when *canelazo* (*aguardiente* – sugarcane alcohol – with hot cider and cinnamon) vendors keep everyone warm and cozy and live music spills out of restaurant windows.

There's great people-watching from the plaza tables, and numerous other eating and drinking spots nearby.

Ananké LOUNGE
(Map p634; Orellana 781, Guápulo) This cozy little bar-pizzeria sits perched on the hillside in Guápulo. It has a small terrace (complete with fireplace) and several good nooks perfect for secreting away with a cocktail and a friend.

Santa Espuma BREWERY
(Map p634; Whymper N29-02) Santa Espuma (which means Holy Foam) has a dark-wood interior, meaty pub grub and specialty beers brewed on-site. Go early to get a front table with views over the city.

Z(inc) LOUNGE
(Map p634; Rivet near Coruña; mains US$10-16; ⌚noon-4pm & 7pm-midnight Mon-Sat) A creative addition to Quito's night spots, Z(inc) is equal parts restaurant and bar, with a multilevel industrial-chic interior and a front patio. Excellent (but pricey) cocktails.

☆ Entertainment

Hitting the dance floor of one of Quito's *salsotecas* is a must. If you don't know how to salsa, try a few classes first (see p636).

TOP CHOICE **El Pobre Diablo** LIVE MUSIC
(Map p634; ☎223-5194; www.elpobrediablo.com; Isabel La Católica E12-06; ⌚noon-3pm & 7pm-2am Mon-Sat) Locals and expats rate El Pobre Diablo as one of Quito's best places to hear live music. It's a friendly, laid-back place with live jazz, blues, world music and experimental sounds most nights. It's also a great place to dine, with fusion fare and a solid cocktail menu.

Bungalow 6 CLUB
(Map p640; cnr Calama & Diego de Almagro; ⌚7pm-3am Wed-Sat) Bungalow 6 plays a good mix of beats, with a small but lively dance floor and a warren of colorfully decorated rooms (with table football, pool table and small outdoor terrace) upstairs. Weekends are almost as packed as ladies' night on Wednesday (gals drink for free from 8pm to 10pm). Arrive early to beat the long line.

El Aguijón CLUB
(Map p640; Calama E7-35; admission US$5-10; ⌚9pm-3am Tue-Sat) Attracting a mix of locals and foreigners, El Aguijón is an open, somewhat industrial, space. DJs spin a little of everything on weekends with live bands on Thursday and popular salsa nights on Wednesday.

Seseribó CLUB
(Map p634; Edificio Girón, Veintimilla & Av 12 de Octubre; admission US$5-10; ⌚9pm-2am Thu-Sat) Quito's best *salsoteca* is a must-stop for salsa fans. The music is tops, the atmosphere is superb and the dancing is first-rate.

La Juliana LIVE MUSIC
(Map p634; Av 12 de Octubre near Coruña; admission US$10-20; ⌚10pm-2am Thu-Sat) In an old converted house, La Juliana is a colorfully decorated space with a good mix of bands (rock, salsa, merengue) lighting up the dance floor most weekend nights.

Café Libro LIVE MUSIC
(Map p640; ☎223-4265; www.cafelibro.com; Leonidas Plaza Gutiérrez N23-56; admission US$3-20; ⌚noon-2pm Mon-Fri, 5pm-midnight Tue-Thu, 6pm-2am Fri & Sat) Live music, poetry readings, contemporary dance, tango, jazz and other performances draw an arts-loving crowd to this long-running venue.

Mayo 68 CLUB

(Map p640; García 662) This popular salsa club is small and conveniently located in the Mariscal; it has a local following.

Teatro Sucre PERFORMING ARTS

(Map p630; ☎228-2136; www.teatrosucre.org; Manabí N8-131; admission US$5-50) Overlooking the Plaza del Teatro, this historical theater has a wide-ranging repetorie: classical and rock concerts, musicals, opera and film screenings. Some events are free.

Humanizarte DANCE

(Map p630; www.humanizarte.org.ec; Casa 707, La Ronda; admission US$5; ⏲9pm Fri & Sat) Presents both contemporary and Andean dance.

Ocho y Medio CINEMA

(Map p634; www.ochoymedio.net; Valladolid N24-353 & Vizcaya; ⏲cafe 11am-10:30pm) This Floresta film house shows great art films (often in English) and has occasional dance, theater and live music. There's a cafe attached.

Cinemark CINEMA

(www.cinemark.com.ec; Naciones Unidas & Av América) The most recent Hollywood blockbusters are shown here.

Shopping

Stores in the Mariscal sell traditional indigenous crafts. Quality is often high, but so are the prices.

On Saturday and Sunday, the northern end of Parque El Ejido turns into Quito's biggest crafts market and sidewalk art show. Two blocks north, **Mercado Artesanal La Mariscal** (Map p634; Washington btwn Mera & Reina Victoria; ⏲9am-7pm daily) is an entire block filled with craft stalls.

The best deals can be found at these markets, where indigenous, mostly *otavaleño* (people from Otavalo), vendors sell their goods.

Apart from Tianguez, which is in the Old Town, all listings are in the New Town.

TOP CHOICE Galería Latina HANDICRAFTS

(Map p640; Mera N23-69) Spread among many rooms of this well-stocked handicrafts shop is an excellent selection of high-quality items.

Tianguez HANDICRAFTS

(Map p630; Plaza San Francisco) Attached to the eponymous cafe, Tianguez is a member of the Fair Trade Organization and sells some outstanding crafts collected from throughout Ecuador.

La Bodega HANDICRAFTS

(Map p640; Mera N22-24) High-quality crafts, old and new.

Ag HANDICRAFTS

(Map p640; Mera N22-24) Ag's selection of rare, handmade silver jewelry from across South America is outstanding.

Productos Andinos HANDICRAFTS

(Map p634; Urbina 111) This two-floor artisan's cooperative is crammed with reasonably priced crafts.

Confederate Books BOOKS

(Map p640; cnr Calama & Mera) Secondhand books in English and other languages.

Libri Mundi BOOKS

(Map p640; Mera 851) Quito's best bookstore; excellent selection of books in Spanish, English, German and French.

Information

Dangers & Annoyances

Quito has a bad reputation for robberies and petty crime, and you should take precautions to avoid becoming a target. Despite the animated streets of the Mariscal area, it remains a dangerous neighborhood after dark; a police presence keeps Plaza Foch safe, but a few dark streets away, muggings still occur. Take a taxi after dark – even if you have only a few blocks to walk. Sundays, when no one else is around, is a dodgy time to wander around.

With the restoration of the Old Town and increased police presence there, the historic center is safe until 10pm or so. Don't climb up El Panecillo hill; take a taxi instead (there are plenty up top for the return trip). The buses are prime hunting ground for thieves; keep a close watch on your belongings – backpacks and handbags are routinely and adroitly slashed and pilfered without the owner even realizing it. If you are robbed, obtain a police report within 48 hours from the police station on the corner of Reina Victoria and Roca, New Town, or the corner of Mideros and Cuenca, Old Town.

If you are arriving from sea level, Quito's 2850m elevation might make you somewhat breathless and give you headaches or cotton mouth. These symptoms of *soroche* (altitude sickness) usually disappear after a day or two. To minimize symptoms, take it easy upon arrival, drink plenty of water and lay off the smokes and alcohol.

Emergency

Fire (☎102)

Emergency (☎911)

Police (☎101)

Red Cross Ambulance (☎131, 258-0598)

Internet Access

Internet cafes are a dying breed in Quito, although you will find a few in the Mariscal area. Prices are around US$1 per hour. Many guesthouses and a growing number of cafes and restaurants offer free wi-fi.

Medical Services

Clínica Pichincha (☎256-2296, 256-2408; cnr Veintimilla 1259 & Páez) Located in the New Town; does lab analysis for parasites, dysentery etc.

Hospital Metropolitano (☎399-8000; Mariana de Jesús & Av Occidental) Best hospital in town.

Hospital Voz Andes (☎226-2142; cnr Villalengua Oe2-37 & Av 10 de Agosto) American-run hospital with outpatient and emergency rooms.

Money

There are several banks and *casas de cambio* (currency exchange bureaus) in the New Town along Av Amazonas between Av Patria and Orellana, and dozens of banks throughout town. Banks listed here have ATMs.

Banco de Guayaquil Av Amazonas (Av Amazonas N22-147 at Veintimilla); Colón (Colón at Reina Victoria)

Banco del Pacífico New Town (cnr 12 de Octubre & Cordero); Old Town (cnr Guayaquil & Chile)

Banco del Pichincha (Guayaquil btwn Olmedo & Manabí)

Producambios (Av Amazonas 350, La Mariscal)

Western Union Av de la República (Av de la República); Colón (Av Cristóbal Colón 1333)

Post

Central post office (Espejo 935, Old Town)

La Mariscal post office (cnr Av Cristóbal Colón & Reina Victoria)

Tourist Information

South American Explorers (SAE; ☎222-5228; www.saexplorers.org; Washington 311 & Plaza Gutiérrez) This is an excellent travelers' organization.

Tourist offices (Corporación Metropolitana de Turismo; www.quito.com.ec) La Mariscal (☎255-8440; Reina Victoria N24-263; ⏰10am-8pm Tue-Sun); Old Town (☎257-2445; cnr Venezuela & Espejo, Plaza Grande; ⏰9am-6pm Mon-Fri, to 5pm Sat); Airport (☎330-0163)

Websites

Corporación Metropolitana de Turismo (www.quito.com.ec)

Gay Guide to Quito (http://quito.queercity.info)

ℹ Getting There & Away

Air

Opened in 2013, Quito's new airport is located in Tababela, some 37km east of the city. It goes by the name **Aeropuerto Mariscal Sucre** (☎02-294-4900; www.quitoairport.com; Av Amazonas at Av de la Prensa, UIO) – the same name as the old airport, which is no longer in operation. The new airport boasts a longer runway at a lower elevation, which now allows for long-haul flights to North America and Europe. The downside is the longer travel time between the city and the airport – 60 to 90 minutes by taxi depending on traffic.

There are regular flights connecting Quito with Coca, Cuenca, Esmeraldas, the Galápagos, Guayaquil, Lago Agrio, Loja, Macas, Machala, Manta and Tulcán. All mainland flights last under one hour and cost around US$70 to US$100 one way. Galápagos flights cost significantly more (US$480 to US$530 round trip) and take 3¼ hours from Quito (including a layover in Guayaquil) and 1½ hours from Guayaquil.

Bus

Quito has two new bus terminals and they are both a long way from the center (allow at least an hour by public transit, 25 minutes or more by taxi).

Terminal Quitumbe (☎398-8200), southwest of Old Town, handles the central and southern Andes, the coast, and the Oriente (ie Baños, Cuenca, Guayaquil, Coca and – aside from Otavalo – most destinations of interest to travelers). It can be reached by Trole bus (C4); get off at the last stop. A taxi to/from here costs about US$10.

Carcelén Bus Terminal (☎396-1600), in the north, services Otavalo, Ibarra, Santo Domingo, Tulcán and other northern destinations. To get here, you can take the Trole bus north to La Y Terminal and transfer to a 'Carapungo'-bound bus; tell the driver where you're headed as this bus passes about a block from the terminal, where you can continue on foot. A taxi runs about US$10.

Approximate one-way fares and journey times are shown in the following table. More expensive luxury services are available for long trips.

For comfortable buses to Guayaquil from the New Town, travel with **Panamericana** (☎255-7134; Av Cristóbal Colón btwn Reina Victoria & Diego de Almagro) or **Transportes Ecuador** (☎222-5315; Mera N21-44). Panamericana also has long-distance buses to other towns, including Machala, Loja, Cuenca, Manta and Esmeraldas.

A few buses leave from other places for some destinations in the Pichincha province. **Cooperativa Flor de Valle/Cayambe** (www.flordelvalle.com.ec) goes daily to Mindo (US$2.50, 2½ hours) from Quito's northern Ofelia station, reachable by taking the Metrobus line to the last stop.

DESTINATION	COST (US$)	DURATION (HR)
Ambato	2	2½
Atacames	9	7
Bahía de Caráquez	10	8
Baños	3.50	3
Coca	10	9 (via Loreto)
Cuenca	10-12	10-12
Esmeraldas	9	5-6
Guayaquil	7-10	8
Huaquillas	10	12
Ibarra	3	2½
Lago Agrio	8	7-8
Latacunga	1.50	2
Loja	14-17	14-15
Machala	10	10
Manta	10	8-9
Otavalo	2	2¼
Portoviejo	9	9
Puerto López	12	12
Puyo	6	5½
Riobamba	4	4
San Lorenzo	7	6½
Santo Domingo	3	3
Tena	6	5-6
Tulcán	5	5

Train

A tourist **train** (www.trenecuador.com; return US$20) leaves Quito at 8.15am Thursday to Sunday and chugs 2½ hours south to the Area Nacional de Recreación El Boliche, adjoining Parque Nacional Cotopaxi. It returns the same day, arriving back at Quito at 5pm.

The **train station** (Estación Eloy Alfaro, Chimbacalle; ☎1800-873-637; www.trenecuador.com; Sincholagua & Maldonado) is located about 2km south of the Old Town. You can purchase tickets in the tourist office facing Plaza Grande, on the corner of Venezuela and Espejo.

Getting Around

Bus

The local buses (25¢) are fairly convenient, but pickpocketing is a serious problem so keep a close watch on your belongings. Buses have destination placards in their windows (not route numbers), and drivers will usually tell you which bus to take if you flag the wrong one.

Taxi

Cabs are yellow and have taxi-number stickers in the window. Drivers may or may not use *taxímetros* (meters); to be safe, it's best to agree on a price before entering a taxi. The going rate between the Mariscal and Old Town is about US$2, though you'll have to pay more at night and on Sundays.

Trole, Ecovía & Metrobus

Quito has three electrically powered bus routes: the Trole, the Ecovía and the Metrobus. Each runs north–south along one of Quito's three main thoroughfares. Each line has designated stations and car-free lanes, making them speedy and efficient; however, as the fastest form of public transportation, they are usually crowded and notorious for pickpockets. They run about every 10 minutes from 6am to 12:30am (more often in rush hours), and the fare is 25¢.

GETTING INTO TOWN

Quito's new airport, which opened in 2013 (and has the same name as the old airport), is located 37km east of the city. Public buses (US$2) connect the airport with Rio Coca bus station (in Quito's north) and Quitumbe terminal (in the south).

There are also express shuttle buses operated by **Aeroservicios** (http://aeroservicios.com.ec; US$8), departing every 30 minutes, which connect the new airport with the old airport (8km north of La Mariscal). From there, you can take a taxi to La Mariscal (US$8) or the old town ($10). Eventually, a metro service will connect the old airport (slated to become a convention center) with other parts of town. Taxis from the new airport to La Mariscal or the Old Town will cost US$20 to US$26, and major hotels will likely run private shuttles. For the latest updates, visit www.quito.com.ec. For information on Quito's bus terminals, see opposite.

The Trole runs along Maldonado and Av 10 de Agosto. In the Old Town, southbound trolleys take the west route (along Guayaquil), while northbound trolleys take the east route (along Montúfar and Pichincha). The Ecovía runs along Av 6 de Diciembre, and the Metrobus runs along Av América.

AROUND QUITO

Mitad del Mundo & Around

02

Ecuador's biggest claim to fame is its location on the equator. **Mitad del Mundo** (Middle of the World City; www.mitaddelmundo.com; admission US$2, monument admission US$3; 9am-6pm Mon-Fri, to 7pm Sat & Sun), 22km north of Quito, is the place where Charles-Marie de la Condamine made the measurements in 1736, proving that this was the equatorial line. Although the monument constructed there isn't actually on the equator (GPS readings indicate true 0°00' latitude lies about 300m north), it remains a popular, if touristy, destination. On Sunday afternoons live salsa bands play in the central plaza area. The ethnographic museum (and its viewing platform up top), a scale model of Quito's Old Town and other attractions cost extra. **Calima Tours** (239-4796; www.mitaddelmundotour.com; tour per person US$3-8), located inside the complex, offers trips to Pululahua hourly. The 10am trip includes a hike around the rim. At 3pm Calima runs a tour to Rumicucho, which includes a visit to a shaman's house.

A few hundred meters north is **Museo Solar Inti Ñan** (adult/child US$4/2; 9:30am-5pm), offering a fun-house atmosphere of water and energy demonstrations. You'll have to decide for yourself if the 'scientific' experiments are hoaxes.

Rumicucho (admission US$1; 9am-3pm Mon-Fri, 8am-4pm Sat & Sun) is a small pre-Inca site under excavation, 3.5km north of Mitad del Mundo. On the way to Calacalí, about 5km north of Mitad del Mundo, is the ancient volcanic crater and geobotanical reserve of **Pululahua**. The views (in the morning) are great from the rim, or you can hike down to the tiny village on the crater floor. Near the rim of Pululahua is the castlelike **Templo del Sol** (admission US$3; 10am-5pm Tue-Sun), a re-creation of an Inca temple, complete with pre-Columbian relics and stone carvings. The guided tour (in Spanish) is a bit gimmicky, led by a heavily decorated 'Inca prince' who touches on presumed ancient beliefs and rituals. You can overnight inside the crater at **Pululahua Hostal** (09-946-6636; www.pululahuahostal.com; cabana s/d from US$30/40, without bathroom US$20/30), an ecologically friendly guesthouse with simple, comfortable rooms. Tasty meals (mains US$2 to $4) feature ingredients from the organic farm. Guests can hire bikes (US$3 per hour) or horses (US$8 per hour).

To get to Mitad del Mundo from Quito, take the Metrobus (US25¢) north to the last stop, Ofelia station. From there, transfer to the Mitad del Mundo bus (an additional US15¢); the entire trip takes one hour to 1½ hours. The bus drops you off right in front of the entrance.

Buses continue past the complex and will drop you off at the entrance road to Pululahua – ask for the Mirador de Ventanillas (the lookout point where the trail into the crater begins).

Termas de Papallacta

02

Home to Ecuador's most luxurious and most scenic thermal baths, the Termas de Papallacta are pure medicine for long days of travel. **Balneario** (admission US$7.50; 6am-11pm, last entry 9pm) boasts more than 25 blue pools of varying temperatures surrounded by plush grass and red-orange blossoms. Towels and lockers are available. There's little reason to spend the extra US$11 to visit the spa pools.

About 67km (two hours) from Quito, the complex, part of the posh Hotel Termas de Papallacta, makes for an excellent jaunt from Quito. Cheaper hotels are available outside the complex in the village of Papallacta itself, although it's easy enough to head back to Quito. It's best to go during the week to avoid the huge weekend crowds.

Any of the buses from Quito heading toward Baeza, Tena or Lago Agrio can drop you off in Papallacta. To visit the Termas de Papallacta complex, ask the driver to let you off on the road to the baths, 1.5km before the village. Then catch an awaiting *camioneta* (small truck) for the US$2 ride up the bumpy road.

NORTHERN HIGHLANDS

The steep green hills, dust-blown villages, bustling provincial capitals and cultural riches of the northern highlands lie a few hours' drive northeast of Quito. Those traveling to or from Colombia are bound to pass through the region, and there's plenty worth stopping for: the famous Otavalo market, which dates back to pre-Inca times, is the largest crafts market in South America, and several small towns are known for their handicrafts, including wood carvings and leatherwork.

Northwest of Quito lie the misty cloud forests hugging the western slopes of the Andes. The big draw here is Mindo, a tranquil village transformed into an ecotourist hot spot, with bird watching, hiking and river tubing the orders of the day.

Mindo

☎02

With its breathtaking setting surrounded on all sides by steep mountainsides of cloud forest, tiny Mindo has become something of a backpacker buzzword in Ecuador and now lives and breathes tourism. Helpfully located just off the main road from Quito to Esmeraldas, Mindo is entered by a dramatically steep and curvy hillside descent that takes you down past dozens of hotels and lodges to a sleepy town center. Bird-watchers, hikers and weekenders from Quito and beyond all flock here and friendly locals have created an impressive infrastructure for actively enjoying the cloud forest, including butterfly farms, zip-lines over the treetops, mountain biking, tubing and orchid collections.

Sights & Activities

Mariposas de Mindo BUTTERFLY FARM
(☎224-2712; www.mariposasdemindo.com; admission US$5; ⏲9am-4pm) Mindo has several butterfly farms, but this is the best of them. Visit in the warmest part of the day, around 11am, when butterflies are most active. To get there, take Mindo's main road east past the main plaza and turn right. At the fork veer left.

Tarabita CABLE CAR
(road to Cascada de Nambillo; admission US$5; ⏲8:30am-4pm Tue-Sun) This unique open-air *tarabita* (cable car) takes you 152m above a lush river basin over thick cloud forest to the Bosque Protector Mindo-Nambillo, where there's a number of waterfalls you can hike to along well-signposted trails. Admission includes a primitive map with routes shown on it. The *tarabita* is a 4km taxi ride (US$2) from town.

Concierto de las Ranas WALKING TOUR
(☎217-0201; www.mindolago.com.ec; admission US$3.50; ⏲6:30pm daily except Tue & Sun) At the 'concert of the frogs' you'll take a fascinating nighttime walk around lush property spotting various species of frogs and other nocturnal creatures. It's held at the Mindo Lago *hostería*, located on the main road heading toward the highway, about 2km uphill from town.

El Quetzal TOUR
(www.elquetzaldemindo.com; Calle 9 de Octubre; tour per person US$5; ⏲tour 4pm daily) This artisanal chocolate maker gives tours in English that reveal the stages of production from cacao pods to richly baked perfection. Free samples too! Coming into town on the main street, turn left at the Parque Central and you'll see it 300m down on the left.

Tubing

Tour operators along Av Quito offer low-tech thrill rides (per person US$6 with four-person minimum) along the churning Río Mindo. You and a goup of three others will jostle down white water on a raft of thick inner tubes lashed together. The price should include transportation, a helmet, life vest and a guide, as tubing the rapids on the Río Mindo can be dangerous.

Zip-Lining

Halfway up the road to the *tarabita*, two dueling zip-line companies compete for adrenaline seekers. Fly over the canopy in a harness attached to a cable strung above the trees, an activity that gets faster in the rain. **Mindo Canopy Adventure** (☎09-453-0624; www.mindocanopy.com; 2½hr circuit per person US$15), the original company, has 13 different cables ranging from 20m to 400m in length. **Mindo Ropes & Canopy** (☎09-172-5874; www.mindoropescanopy.com; 2½hr circuit per person US$15) offers a similar experience on 12 cables.

Bird-Watching

With more than 400 species of birds recorded, Mindo has become a major center for bird-watchers. The going rate for a competent, professional guide runs from US$80 to US$220 per day. Recommended English-speaking guides include **Irman Arias** (☎217-0168, 09-170-8720; www.mindobirdguide.com), **Danny Jumbo** (☎09-328-0769) and **Julia Patiño** (☎08-616-2816, 390-0419; juliaguideofbird@yahoo.com).

Sleeping & Eating

TOP CHOICE Caskaffesu GUESTHOUSE **$**
(☎09-386-7154, 217-0100; www.caskaffesu.com; Sixto Duran Ballen near Av Quito; r per person US$16;) This chilled-out and friendly spot has two storys of brightly painted brick rooms. Downstairs you'll find a popular restaurant (mains US$5 to $9) and a charming garden courtyard. To get there, take the second right after crossing the bridge into town.

La Casa de Cecilia HOSTEL **$**
(☎09-334-5393, 217-0243; lacasadececiliamindo@hotmail.com; Calle 9 de Octubre; r per person US$7-10;) Just past El Quetzal, Cecilia's is a rustic spot with all-wood rooms and an open-sided deck on the edge of the river. Excellent value.

Jardin de los Pájaros GUESTHOUSE **$**
(☎390-0459, 09-422-7624; Barrío El Progreso; r per person incl breakfast US$13-15;) Take the first right after you cross the bridge to find this family-run guesthouse. The rooms are large and comfortable and the large, shaded deck makes for a pleasant place to relax, as does the heated swimming pool.

Arco Iris GUESTHOUSE **$**
(☎217-0105; www.arcoirismindo.com; Calle 9 de Octubre; r per person US$10) This good-value budget option overlooking the Parque Central has clean rooms with wood floors and small hot-water bathrooms.

El Quetzal ECUADORIAN **$**
(www.elquetzaldemindo.com; Calle 9 de Octubre; mains US$4-8; 8am-11pm;) This laid-back cafe has good coffee, breakfasts and sandwiches, and a daily changing Ecuadorian main course. The chocolate produced onsite is fantastic. Don't miss the famous (and enormous) brownie or the chocolate shakes.

El Chef STEAKHOUSE **$**
(Av Quito; mains US$3-8; 9am-7pm) A popular spot for set meals, this basic steakhouse also serves up the sizzling *lomo a la piedra* (steak cooked on a 'stone') or a hearty burger.

Restaurant Pizzeria El Tigrillo PIZZERIA **$$**
(Av Quito; mains US$8-10) On Mindo's main street, El Trigrillo whips up piping-hot, brick-oven pizzas as well as inexpensive *almuerzos* (from US$2.75).

Information

There's an ATM near Parque Central, but it doesn't always work, so get cash before arriving.

Centro Municipal de Información Turistica (Av Quito & Plaza Grande) Helpful tourist office that gives out maps and advice on hiking, tours and lodging.

Getting There & Away

There are several daily buses to Quito (US$2.50, 2½ hours) and seven daily buses to Santo Domingo (US$3, three hours), which has onward connections to the coast. Other buses to Quito or the coast can be picked up at the top of the hill, where the road to Mindo intersects the main highway.

Otavalo

☎06 / POP 40,000

The friendly and prosperous town of Otavalo (elevation 2550m) is famous for its giant Saturday market, where traditionally dressed indigenous people sell handicrafts to hordes of foreigners who pour in every Saturday to get in on the deals. Despite the market's popularity, the *otavaleños* themselves remain self-determined and culturally uncompromised. The setting is fabulous, and the entire experience remains enchanting.

Sights

Crafts Market MARKET
(Plaza de Ponchos) Every day vendors hawk an astounding array of goods at the Plaza de Ponchos, the nucleus of the crafts market. But the real action happens on Saturday, official market day, when the market swells into adjacent roads. There is an astounding array of traditional crafts including tapestries, blankets, ponchos, sweaters, hammocks, carvings, beads, original paintings and more.

Animal Market MARKET
(Carretera Panamericana; 6am-1pm Sat) The animal market, on the western edge of town, offers an interesting break from the hustle of the crafts market. Beneath the volcanic backdrop of Cotacachi and Imbabura, indigenous men and women mill around with pigs, cows, goats and chickens and inspect, haggle and chat in the crisp morning air.

Parque Cóndor BIRD SANCTUARY
(www.parquecondor.org; admission US$3.75; ⌚9:30am-5pm Tue-Sun) This Dutch-owned foundation rehabilitates raptors, vultures and other birds of prey. Don't miss free flight demonstrations at 11:30am and 4:30pm. The center is perched on the steep hillside of Pucara Alto, 4km east of town between Otavalo and the Lago de San Pablo.

Activities

There's great hiking around Otavalo, especially in the Lagunas de Mojanda area.

Runa Tupari Native Travel CULTURAL TOUR
(☎292-2320; www.runatupari.com; cnr Sucre & Quiroga, 3rd fl) Partners with local indigenous communities, offering hiking, horse-riding and mountain-biking trips. Day trips include a 2000m mountain-bike descent into tropical cloud forest and a round-trip 10-hour hike up Cotacachi (4939m).

Ecomontes Tour ADVENTURE TOUR
(☎292-6244; www.ecomontestour.com; cnr Sucre & Morales) This Quito-based agency has an office in Otavalo and offers day trips, including biking, climbing, horse-riding, canyoning and rafting tours. Homestays with indigenous families are also offered.

Courses

Otavalo is a good place to learn Spanish. Recommended language schools, with homestay and volunteer options, include **Mundo Andino** (☎292-1864; www.mandinospanishschool.com; Salinas 4-04 near Bolívar; individual/group lessons per hour US$6/4.50), **Instituto Superior de Español** (☎299-2424; www.instituto-superior.net; Sucre near Morales; courses per week from US$94) and **Otavalo Spanish Language Academy** (☎292-1404; www.otavalospanish.com; cnr 31 de Octubre & Salinas; lessons per hour US$7).

Festivals & Events

Inti Raymi RELIGIOUS
Millennia-old indigenous celebration of summer equinox celebrated throughout northern highlands, especially in Otavalo, where it's also combined with feasts of St John the Baptist (June 24) and Sts Peter and Paul (June 29). Held from June 21 to 29.

Fiesta del Yamor HARVEST FESTIVAL
Held in late August and early September, Yamor features processions, music and dancing in the plazas, and fireworks.

Sleeping

Guesthouses fill on Friday, so arrive early for the best choice of accommodations.

Rincón del Viajero GUESTHOUSE $
(☎292-1741; www.hostalrincondelviajero.com; Roca 11-07; r per person incl breakfast with/without bathroom US$14/12; 📶) Warm hospitality, colorful murals and homey, snug rooms make this place a great deal. It has a TV lounge, a fireplace, hot water and a rooftop terrace strung with hammocks.

Hostal Valle del Amanecer GUESTHOUSE $
(☎292-0990; www.hostalvalledelamanecer.com; cnr Roca & Quiroga; r per person incl breakfast with/without bathroom US$15/12; 📶) Rooms are small and dark, but the pebbled courtyard strewn with hammocks still draws plenty of budget travelers. On-site restaurant and bike rental for US$8 per day.

Hotel Riviera-Sucre GUESTHOUSE $
(☎292-0241; www.rivierasucre.com; cnr García Moreno 380 & Roca; s/d US$15/28; @📶) This Belgian-owned hotel in a large, old home has high-ceilinged rooms, endless nooks, a garden, fireplaces, courtyard hammocks and a small cafe.

Hostal Doña Esther GUESTHOUSE $$
(☎292-0739; www.otavalohotel.com; Montalvo 4-44; s/d/tr US$34/49/61; 📶) This small, Dutch-owned colonial-style hotel is cozy, with attractive rooms surrounding a courtyard ornamented with ceramics and ferns. Good restaurant.

Hotel Santa Fe HOTEL $
(☎292-3640; www.hotelsantafeotavalo.com; Roca btwn García Moreno & Montalvo; r per person US$13; P📶) Lovers of wooden interiors will find this southwestern-style place very much to their liking, even if the kitschy rooms are rather on the small side and those not on the street are a little dark.

Acoma HOTEL $$
(☎292-6570; www.hotelacoma.com; Salinas 7-57; s/d incl breakfast US$30/41; P@📶) The rooms at Acoma have lovely cedar floors, mosaic tiles and skylights. There's an attractive bar and restaurant.

Cabañas El Rocío GUESTHOUSE $
(☎292-4606; rocioe@hotmail.com; Barrio San Juan; r per person US$11.20; P) Despite the roadside location on the Panamericana highway, this place is great vaue for its

Otavalo

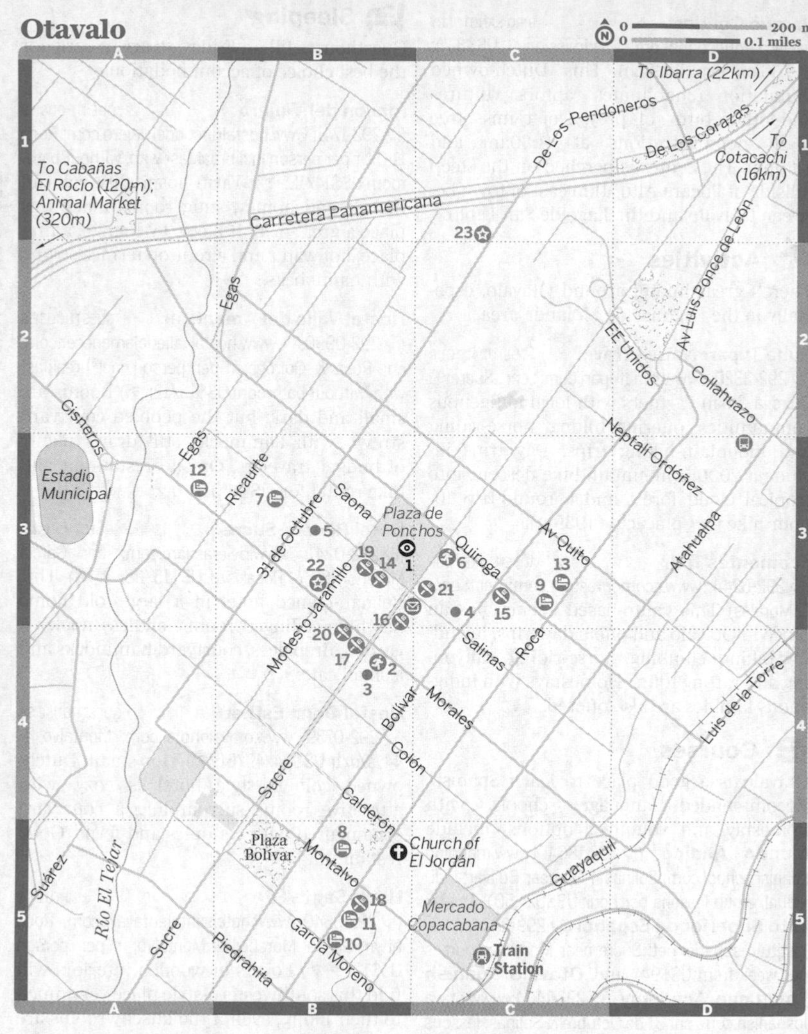

vaguely alpine rooms and cabins just a short walk from the center of Otavalo.

Rose Cottage GUESTHOUSE $
(☎09-772-8115; www.rosecottageecuador.com; dm US$10, r with/without bathroom from US$28/15) Outside of Otavalo, Rose Cottage has great ambience. You'll also find picturesque views, a spacious lounge/library, a tennis court and nearby hiking trails. Communal dinners are a good place to meet other travelers. To get there, from the highway take the turn-off to Lagos de Mojanda and an immediate left, and follow the steep cobbled road another 3km. A taxi costs US$3.

La Luna GUESTHOUSE $
(☎09-829-4913, 09-315-6082; www.lalunaecuador.com; campsites US$8, dm US$12, s/d US$26/42, without bathroom US$20/32; 📶) La Luna has pretty views, a fireplace, dining room and kitchen. From the highway take the turnoff to Lagos de Mojanda and an immediate left, and follow the steep cobbled road another 4km. A taxi costs US$4.

Otavalo

Sights
1 Crafts Market ... B3

Activities, Courses & Tours
2 Ecomontes Tour ... B4
3 Instituto Superíor de Español ... B4
4 Mundo Andino ... C3
5 Otavalo Spanish Institute ... B3
6 Runa Tupari Native Travel ... C3

Sleeping
7 Acoma ... B3
8 Hostal Doña Esther ... B5
9 Hostal Valle del Amanecer ... C3
10 Hotel Riviera-Sucre ... B5
11 Hotel Santa Fe ... B5
12 Residencial El Rocío ... A3
13 Rincón del Viajero ... C3

Eating
14 Buenavista ... B3
15 Deli ... C3
16 Green Coffee Shop & Dinner ... B3
17 Mi Otavalito ... B4
Oraibi ... (see 17)
18 Quino ... B5
19 Shenandoah Pie Shop ... B3
20 Siciliano ... B4
21 Tabasco's ... C3

Entertainment
22 Amauta ... B3
23 Peña La Jampa ... C1

Residencial El Rocío HOSTEL $
(☎292-4606; Morales 11-70; r per person with/without bathroom US$7/6) Friendly, clean accommodations found on the quieter side of downtown – this is the best of the ultra-cheapies.

Eating

Quino SEAFOOD $$
(Roca near Montalvo; mains US$5-9; ⏲noon-11pm Tue-Sun) This popular eatery offers up the town's best seafood. All main courses are cooked from scratch, so it's not the best choice if you're in a hurry.

Buenavista INTERNATIONAL $
(Plaza de Ponchos; mains US$3-6; ⏲10am-10pm Wed-Mon; 🖉) On a fine location above the Plaza de Ponchos, Buenavista whips up grilled trout, burgers and bistro fare to a mostly foreign crowd. It's a good spot for a drink as well.

Deli INTERNATIONAL $$
(cnr Quiroga & Bolívar; mains US$5-10) An inviting bamboo and wood-filled dining room that serves mostly Tex-Mex: burritos, fajitas, enchiladas and the like – plus pizza and spaghetti for good measure. A fire flickers on chilly nights.

Tabasco's MEXICAN $
(cnr Sucre & Salinas, 2nd fl; mains US$5-7) The rooftop patio overlooking Plaza de Ponchos serves tasty enchiladas, burritos, tacos and tropical cocktails.

Green Coffee Shop & Dinner ORGANIC $
(Sucre near Salinas; mains US$4-7; ⏲10am-9pm Mon-Fri, from 8am Sat; 🖉) Located in an eclectic, disheveled courtyard, this spot serves up 100% organic salads, grills, pasta dishes, sandwiches and breakfasts.

Oraibi VEGETARIAN $
(cnr Sucre & Colón; mains US$3-10; ⏲11am-7pm Wed-Sat; 🖉) You can enjoy nicely prepared vegetarian fare in the courtyard garden inside an old hacienda.

Mi Otavalito ECUADORIAN $$
(Sucre 11-19; mains US$6.50-8; ⏲11:30am-9pm) This well-loved local place with rustic farmhouse decor serves classic Ecuadorian dishes.

Siciliano ITALIAN
(Morales near Sucre) Burlap sacks and oversized paintings of fruit adorn this cosy wood-beamed place, which serves Otavalo's best pizzas.

Shenandoah Pie Shop BAKERY $
(Plaza de Ponchos; pie slices US$2; ⏲10am-9pm; 🖉) Serves up delicious deep-dish pies à la mode.

Entertainment

Otavalo slumbers midweek but draws revelers – mostly very young *otaveleños* – on the weekends.

Amauta LIVE MUSIC
(Morales 5-11 & Modesto Jaramillo; ⏲8pm-4am Fri & Sat) A classic Otavalo *peña* (a club that hosts

informal folk-music gatherings), Amauta is the best place to hear Andean music.

Peña La Jampa LIVE MUSIC
(cnr 31 de Octubre & Carretera Panamericana; ⌚7pm-3am Fri & Sat) Offers a mix of live salsa, merengue, *rock en español* (Spanish rock) and *música folklórica* (traditional Andean music).

Information

Banco del Pacífico (cnr Bolívar & García Moreno) Bank with ATM.
Post office (cnr Sucre & Salinas, 2nd fl)

Getting There & Around

The **bus terminal** (cnr Atahualpa & Collahuazo) is two blocks north of Av Quito. Transportes Otavalo/Los Lagos is the only company from Quito (US$2, 2½ hours) that enters the terminal. Expresso Baños runs two buses a day direct to Baños (US$5.50, 5½ hours). Other companies drop passengers on the Panamericana (a 10-minute walk from town) on their way north or south. Frequent buses depart the terminal for Ibarra (US50¢, 35 minutes).

Around Otavalo

☎06

The quality of light, the sense that time has stopped, and the endless Andean vistas give the countryside around Otavalo an enchanting character. Scattered with lakes, hiking trails and traditional indigenous villages, it's an area well worth exploring. Tour agencies in Otavalo can provide information or organize hikes, or you can explore on your own.

The beautiful **Lagunas de Mojanda**, in the high *páramo* some 17km south of Otavalo, make for unforgettable hiking. Taxis from Otavalo charge about US$20 each way. You could also organize a trip through Rose Cottage (p654). Runa Tupari (p653) offers guided hikes that include transportation.

Strung along the eastern side of the Panamericana, a few kilometers north of Otavalo, are the mostly indigenous villages of **Peguche**, **Ilumán** and **Agato**. You can walk or take local buses to all three. In Peguche, **Hostal Aya Huma** (☎269-0333; www.ayahuma.com; s/d US$18/30) is a beautifully set, mellow *hostal* that serves good, cheap homemade meals (veggie options too). You can also hike to a pretty **waterfall** 2km south of Peguche.

Laguna San Pablo can be reached on foot from Otavalo by heading roughly 3km southeast on any of the paths heading over the hill behind the railway station. You can then walk the paved road that goes all the way around the lake.

The village of **Cotacachi**, some 15km north of Otavalo, is famous for its leatherwork, which is sold in stores all along the main street. There are hourly buses from Otavalo and a few hotels in Cotacachi.

About 12km west of Cotacachi, the spectacular crater lake **Laguna Cuicocha** lies within an extinct, eroded volcano. The lake is part of the **Reserva Ecológica Cotacachi-Cayapas**, which was established to protect the large area of western Andean forest that extends from **Volcán Cotacachi** (4939m) to the Río Cayapas in the coastal lowlands. A walk around the lake should take about six hours. You can also take a short boat trip on the lake (US$15 per 25-minute trip split by up to six people). There are two places to stay and eat by the lake including **El Mirador** (☎301-7221; s/d US$15/24). To get there, take a taxi (about US$6, one way) from Cotacachi.

Ibarra

☎06 / POP 134,000

Though growth has diminished the former small-town allure of Ibarra's colonial architecture, leafy plazas and cobbled streets make it a handsome city (elevation 2225m) – at least on weekends when the streets aren't so choked with traffic. Ibarra's unique blend of students, *mestizos* (people of mixed Spanish and indigenous descent), indigenous highlanders and Afro-Ecuadorians give it an interesting multicultural edge. For a look at archaeological relics as well as masks and costumes from local festivals, visit **Centro Cultural** (cnr Sucre & Oviedo; admission free; ⌚9am-5pm Mon-Sat).

Ibarra's old architecture and shady plazas sit north of the center. The latest tourist attraction is Ibarra's restored rail line, which departs Ibarra **train station** (☎295-0390; Espejo) at 10:30am Wednesday to Sunday and makes a 90-minute journey to Salinas (returning at 4:30pm). Buy tickets (US$15 return) at least one week ahead.

Sleeping

Hostal El Dorado HOSTEL $
(☎295-8700; cnr Oviedo 5-41 & Sucre; r per person US$10; 📶) The best among the budget options, El Dorado offers clean, tidy rooms; some have balconies.

GETTING TO COLOMBIA

The Rumichaca border crossing, 6.5km north of **Tulcán**, is the principal gateway to Colombia and currently the only recommended crossing. Formalities are straightforward at the border, which is open 24 hours every day. Crossing is free. Minibuses (US80¢) and taxis (US$3.50) run regularly between the border and Tulcán's Parque Isidro Ayora, about five blocks north of the central plaza. The buses accept Colombian pesos or US dollars. Be absolutely certain that you have your papers in order and be ready for drugs and weapons searches on both sides. Once across the border, there is frequent taxi transportation to Ipiales (US$1), the first town in Colombia, 2km away.

If you need to break your journey at Tulcán, there are many basic (but generally shabby) guesthouses. Better picks include **Hotel San Francisco** (☎06-298-0760; Bolívar near Atahualpa; r per person US$7) and **Hotel Azteca Inernacional** (☎06-298-0481; cnr Bolívar & Atahualpa; r per person US$7). Direct buses from Tulcán go to Ibarra (US$2.50, 2½ hours), Quito (US$5, five hours), Guayaquil (US$13, 13 hours) and Cuenca (US$17, 17 hours). The **bus terminal** (cnr Bolívar & Arellano) is 2.5km southwest of the town center, reachable by city bus (US20¢) or taxi (about US$1).

Hostal El Ejecutivo HOTEL $
(☎295-6575; Bolívar 9-69; s/d US$9/17) The rooms at this misnamed place are spacious and comfortable. Those on the street side have balconies.

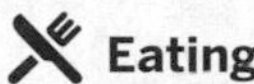

Eating

La Hacienda CAFE $
(cnr Oviedo & Sucre; mains around US$4; ⏲8:15am-11pm Mon-Sat) Pull up a hay-stuffed bench at this friendly, barn-themed eatery. Baguette sandwiches are the specialty, but it also offers coffees and desserts and a full breakfast menu.

Café Arte DELI $
(Salinas 5-43; mains US$5-8; ⏲5pm-midnight Mon-Sat) A funky and relaxed artist-owned gathering spot, this is a good place to socialize and check out local bands. Food leans toward Mexican.

Heladería Rosalía Suárez ICE CREAM $
(Oviedo 7-82; cone/cup US90¢/$1.30; ⏲8am-6pm) Ecuador's most famous ice-cream shop has been whipping up refreshing *helados de paila* for over a century.

Information

Banco del Pacífico (cnr Olmedo & Moncayo) Has an ATM.

Tourist office (iTur; ☎260-8489; cnr Oviedo & Sucre; ⏲8:30am-1pm & 2-5pm Mon-Fri) Two blocks south of Parque Pedro Moncayo.

Getting There & Away

Ibarra's new bus terminal is located at the end of Av Teodoro Gómez de la Torre. You can grab a taxi to or from the center for US$1. There are regular departures to Quito (US$3, 2½ hours), Guayaquil (US$10, 10 hours), Esmeraldas (US$9, nine hours), Tulcán (US$3, 2½ hours), Otavalo (US50¢, 35 minutes) and numerous other destinations.

CENTRAL HIGHLANDS

South of Quito the Panamericana winds past eight of the country's 10 highest peaks, including the picture-perfect snowcapped cone of Volcán Cotopaxi and the glaciated behemoth Volcán Chimborazo. For trekkers and climbers, the central highlands are a paradise, and even inexperienced climbers can have a go at summiting some of the country's highest peaks. You can also hike between remote Andean villages near the Quilotoa Loop, gorge yourself on homemade cheeses and chocolate in Guaranda and Salinas, barrel downhill to the Oriente on a rented mountain bike from Baños, hike or trek in spectacular national parks or ride the scenic train down the famous Nariz del Diablo. The central highlands are home to scores of tiny indigenous villages and many of the country's most traditional markets.

Parque Nacional Cotopaxi

☎03

The centerpiece of Ecuador's most popular **national park** (☎Mon-Fri 593-2-2041520, Sat & Sun 593-9-94980121; admission US$10) is the snowcapped and downright astonishing **Volcán Cotopaxi** (5897m), Ecuador's second-highest peak. The park is almost deserted midweek, when nature freaks can have the breathtaking (literally) scenery nearly to themselves.

The park has a small museum, an information center, a *refugio* (climbers' refuge) and some camping and picnicking areas. The gate is open from 7am to 3pm (longer on weekends), but hikers can come through any time. Note that you aren't technically allowed to enter the park without a guide, and you certainly shouldn't even consider climbing the mountain without a competent guide.

The park's main entrance is via a turnoff from the Panamericana, roughly 30km north of Latacunga. From the turnoff, it's 6km to **Control Caspi**, the entrance station. Any Quito–Latacunga bus will let you off at the turnoff. Follow the main unpaved roads (also signed) to the entrance. It's another 9km or so to the museum. About 4km beyond the museum is **Laguna de Limpiopungo**, a shallow Andean lake 3830m above sea level; a trail circles the lake and takes about half an hour to walk. The *refugio* is about 12km past (and 1000m above) the lake.

Continuing beyond the *refugio* requires snow- and ice-climbing gear and expertise. Outfitters in Quito and Latacunga offer guided summit trips and downhill mountain-biking tours of Cotopaxi. A two-day summit trip costs about US$200 per person from Quito, or US$170 from Latacunga.

It's also possible to reach the park through the northern entrance, known as **Control Norte**, via Machachi, but you'll need to hire a pickup or rent a car (the cobbled road is badly rutted; a 4WD is recommended). The 21km route is well signed.

One of the best-value accommodations in the area is the **Secret Garden Cotopaxi** (☎09-357-2714; www.secretgardencotopaxi.com; camping per person incl 3 meals US$22, dm/d incl 3 meals from US$37/65,). This lovely but rustic property on the way to the northern entrance has superb views (when the clouds clear) and loads of activities: hiking, horse riding, mountain biking or simply relaxing in a hammock, sitting fireside or soaking in the Jacuzzi. Transfers from Quito are available through the sister hostel Secret Garden (p638).

Near the main entrance to the park, about 2km west (and across the Panamericana), **Albergue Cuello de Luna** (☎271-8068, 09-970-0330; www.cuellodeluna.com; dm/s/d incl breakfast from US$18/40/50) is a friendly and popular guesthouse that serves good meals. For a splurge, consider staying at the lovely 300-year-old **Hostería La Ciénaga** (☎271-9182; www.hosterialacienega.com; s/d/tr incl breakfast US$74/89/107;), located 1km south of the village of Lasso and 2km west of the Panamericana.

At the base to the summit, climbers also bunk in the refuge; there are cooking facilities, or you can order meals in the restaurant.

Latacunga

☎03 / POP 88,000

Many travelers end up passing through Latacunga, either to access the Quilotoa Loop, the Thursday-morning market in Saquisilí, or Parque Nacional Cotopaxi. But for those who stick around, Latacunga also offers a quiet and congenial historic center that's famous for its Mamá Negra festival. You'd never know that such a charming city lies behind the loud and polluted section that greets visitors on the Panamericana.

Activities

Several tour operators offer day trips and two- to three-day climbing trips to Cotopaxi. Day trips run about US$50 per person, depending on the size of your group. Two-day climbing trips to Cotopaxi cost about US$170 per person – make sure your guide is qualified and motivated if you're attempting the summit.

Tovar Expeditions ADVENTURE TOUR
(☎281-1333; www.tovarexpeditions.com; Vivero 1-31) Based out of the Hostal Tiana.

Neiges HIKING
(☎281-1199; neigestours@hotmail.om; Guayaquil 6-25 near Quito) Offers well-organized climbing tours of Cotopaxi.

Grievag HIKING
(Guayaquil near Orellana) Runs a range of climbing tours, including multiday Cotopaxi ascents.

Festivals & Events

Fiesta de la Mamá Negra RELIGIOUS
Latacunga's major annual fiesta (September 23 and 24) honors La Virgen de las Mercedes. More popularly known as the Fiesta de la Mamá Negra, the event features processions, costumes, fireworks, street dancing and Andean music.

Sleeping

Hotels fill up fast on Wednesday afternoon for the Thursday-morning indigenous market at Saquisilí.

Hostal Tiana HOSTEL $
(281-0147; www.hostaltiana.com; Vivero 1-31; dm US$10, d inc breakfast with/without bathroom US$31/24;) Latacunga's best budget option is situated in a century-old house with a pretty courtyard cafe. This good-vibes place has everything a good hostel should: kitchen, free internet, book exchange, free luggage storage and free breakfast.

Hotel Central HOTEL $
(280-2912; hotelcentralatacunga@hotmail.com; Orellana near Salcedo; r per person US$10-12;) Giving travelers a warm welcome, the family-run Central has comfortable rooms with kitschy finishing touches.

Hotel Rosim HOTEL $
(280-0853; www.hotelrosim.com; Quito 16-49; r per person US$15;) This good-value hotel in a 90-year-old building has high ceilings and firm beds.

Eating

Latacunga's traditional dish is the *chugchucara,* a tasty plate of *fritada* (pieces of fried pork meat), *mote* (hominy) and various sides.

Chugchucaras La Mamá Negra ECUADORIAN $
(Quijano y Ordoñez 1-67; chugchucaras US$5.90; 10am-7pm Tue-Sun) One of the best places for *chugchucara.*

Guadalajara MEXICAN $
(Quijano & Ordoñez; mains US$5-9; Mon-Sat) A clean, friendly place that serves excellent *almuerzos* for US$2.20, and satisfying Mexican dishes (fajitas, enchiladas, burritos) by night.

Chifa Dragón II CHINESE $
(2 de Mayo & Salcedo; mains US$4-6; 10am-9pm;) Enter the dragon for mean stir-fries and other Chinese classics.

Pollos Jimmy's LATIN AMERICAN $
(Quevedo 8-85 near Valencia; mains US$3.50-6.50; 10am-10pm) Always packed, Jimmy's serves tasty rotisserie chicken served with rice, potatoes and soup.

Nice Cream ICE CREAM $
(cnr Guayaquil & Orellana; single/double scoop US$1.10/1.80) Serves excellent ice cream.

Information

Banco de Guayaquil (Maldonado 7-20) Bank with ATM.

Getting There & Away

Buses from Quito (US$1.50, two hours) will drop you off at the **bus terminal** (Panamericana) if Latacunga is their final destination. If you're taking a bus that's continuing to Ambato or Riobamba, it will drop you off at the corner of 5 de Junio and Cotopaxi, about five blocks west of the Panamericana.

Buses to Ambato (US$1, 45 minutes) and Quito leave from the bus terminal. If you're heading south to Riobamba, it's easiest to catch a passing bus from the corner of 5 de Junio and Cotopaxi.

From the terminal, Transportes Cotopaxi departs hourly for the rough but spectacular descent to Quevedo (US$4, 5½ hours) via Zumbahua (US$2, two hours). There are other transportation options to other destinations on the Quilotoa Loop.

The Quilotoa Loop

03

Bumping along the spectacular dirt roads of the Quilotoa Loop and hiking between the area's Andean villages is one of Ecuador's most exhilarating adventures. Transportation is tricky but the rewards are abundant: highland markets, the breathtaking crater lake of Laguna Quilotoa, splendid hikes, and traditional highland villages. Allow yourself *at least* three days for the loop and bring warm clothes (it gets painfully cold up here), water and snacks. If you're planning a multiday hike through the area, do yourself a favor and leave your heavy backpack in a guesthouse in Latacunga (carrying only the essentials).

LATACUNGA TO ZUMBAHUA

Ten kilometers west of Latacunga, **Pujilí** has a Sunday market and interesting Corpus Christi and All Souls' Day celebrations. The road winds into the upper reaches of the *páramo,* passing the specklike village of **Tigua** about 45km after Pujilí. Tigua is known for the bright paintings of Andean life made on sheepskin canvases. Cozy lodging is available at **Posada de Tigua** (281-4870, 09-161-2391; posadadetigua@yahoo.com; Via Latacunga–Zumbahua Km 49; dm/r per person incl breakfast & dinner US$25/35), a working dairy ranch. Horse riding is also available.

TIGUA PAINTINGS

One of Ecuador's homegrown art forms (and a worthy collector's item) is a style of painting called Tigua that originated near the shores of Laguna Quilotoa. The name comes from the small community of Tigua, where indigenous people had decorated drum skins for many generations. During the 1970s, Julio Toaquiza, a young indigenous man from the area, got the idea to turn those skins into canvases and paint colorful scenes from Quichua legends. The artist, who spent his days growing potatoes and tending llamas, depicted these legends against the beautiful Andean scenery where he lived. He painted the condor wooing a young girl and flying over the mountains in a red poncho, the 'bottomless' Quilotoa lake with spirits hovering over its waters, and Volcán Cotopaxi, a sacred place that highland indigenous people called 'Taita' (Father).

Originally working with enamel paints and chicken-feather brushes, Toaquiza taught all of his children and neighbors how to paint. They began to incorporate new themes, such as Catholic processions, interiors of indigenous homes and even important political events. Today they use acrylic and oil paints.

Toaquiza's art has brought fame to Tigua, and today more than 300 painters are at work in the highlands with about 20 studios in Tigua itself. The pieces are exhibited at the community galleries in Tigua, in selected galleries in Quito and in exhibitions around the world.

Some 15km west of Tigua, the tiny village of **Zumbahua** has a small but fascinating Saturday market and is surrounded by green patchwork peaks, a setting that makes for spectacular walking.

Accommodations and food in Zumbahua are basic. The town's three lodgings fill up fast on Friday, so get there early; the best of them is **Cóndor Matzi** (☎281-4611; r per person US$8), on the square.

ZUMBAHUA TO SAQUISILÍ

From Zumbahua buses and hired trucks trundle up the 14km of unpaved road leading north to one of Ecuador's most staggering sights – **Laguna Quilotoa**, a stunning volcanic crater lake. Near the crater rim are several extremely basic, inexpensive accommodations owned by friendly indigenous folks. Bring a warm sleeping bag. If you want to stay near the lake, **Hostería Alpaca Quilotoa** (☎09-212-5962; r per person incl dinner & breakfast US$25; @) is the best option.

About 14km north of the lake is the wee village of **Chugchilán**, which is an excellent base for hiking and has several traveler-friendly hotels. **Hostal Mama Hilda** (☎270-8005; www.mamahilda.com; s/d incl breakfast & dinner from US$25/43; wi-fi) is friendly and popular with backpackers. Delightful **Hostal Cloud Forest** (☎270-8181; josecloudforest@gmail.com; s/d incl breakfast & dinner US$15/24; @ wi-fi) is the cheapest and simplest. A pricier, but highly rated option is the ecofriendly **Black Sheep Inn** (☎270-8077; www.blacksheepinn.com; r per person incl 3 meals US$35-100).

Some 14km northeast of Chugchilán and just off the Quilotoa Loop, the beautiful village of **Isinliví** makes a good hike from either Chugchilán or Sigchos. A woodworking and cabinetry shop makes high-end furniture, and locals can direct you to nearby *pucarás* (pre-Inca hill fortresses). **Llullu Llama** (Little Llama; ☎281-4790; www.llullullama.com; dm/r per person incl breakfast & dinner from US$18/21) is an enchanting old farmhouse with comfortable rooms and a wood-burning stove. A delicious dinner and breakfast is included.

About 23km north of Chugchilán is the village of **Sigchos**, which has a couple of basic lodgings. From here, it's about 52km east to **Saquisilí**, home of one of the most important indigenous markets in the country. Each Thursday morning inhabitants of remote indigenous villages, most of whom are recognized by their felt porkpie hats and red ponchos, descend upon the market in a cacophony of sound and color. Accommodations are available in several cold-water cheapies.

Getting There & Around

No buses go all the way around the loop. From Latacunga they only travel as far as Chugchilán (US$4, four hours), and they either go clockwise (via Zumbahua and Quilotoa) or counter-clockwise (via Saquisilí and Sigchos). The bus via Zumbahua departs Latacunga's bus terminal daily at noon, passing Zumbahua at around 1:30pm, Laguna Quilotoa at around 2pm, arriving in Chugchilán at about 4pm. The bus via Sigchos departs daily at 11:30am, passing Saquisilí just before noon and Sigchos at around 2pm, arriving in Chugchilán at around 3:30pm; the Saturday bus via Sigchos leaves at 10:30am.

From Chugchilán, buses returning to Latacunga via Zumbahua leave Chugchilán Monday through Friday at 4am (good morning!), passing Quilotoa at around 6am, Zumbahua at around 6:30am, arriving in Latacunga at around 8am. On Saturday this bus leaves Chugchilán at 3am, and on Sunday at 6am and 10am. Buses via Sigchos leave Monday through Friday at 3am, passing Sigchos at around 4am, Saquisilí at around 7am, arriving in Latacunga at around 8am. On Saturday this bus departs at 7am. On Sunday you must switch buses in Sigchos.

A morning milk truck (US$1) leaves Chugchilán for Sigchos around 8:30am and will take passengers, allowing you to skip the predawn wake-up. In Zumbahua, trucks can be hired to Laguna Quilotoa or anywhere on the loop.

You should confirm bus departure times at your guesthouse.

Ambato

☎03 / POP 220,000

Compared to nearby Baños, Ambato offers little for the traveler, except the chance to experience a nontouristy Ecuadorian city. Ambato's claims to fame are its chaotic **Monday market**; its flower festival, **Fiesta de Frutas y Flores** (Fruit & Flower Festival), held in the second half of February; and its *quintas* (historic country homes) outside the center. Above town, there are picturesque views of the puffing Volcán Tungurahua.

The bus terminal is 2km from downtown. City buses marked 'Centro' go to Parque Cevallos (US25¢), the central plaza.

Sleeping & Eating

Gran Hotel HOTEL $

(☎282-4235; cnr Rocafuerte & Lalama; s/d US$12/24;) The Gran may lack grandeur but the carpeted rooms have hot showers and TVs, and the staff is pleasant.

Delicias del Paso BAKERY $

(cnr Sucre & Quito; baked items US$2; ⏰10am-6pm) This cafeteria serves tasty quiches and cakes, and you can order them to go right from the street.

Mercado Central MARKET $

(12 de Noviembre; mains US$1.50; ⏰7am-7pm) The 2nd floor of Ambato's indoor market has particularly good *lapingachos* (fried mashed-potato-and-cheese pancakes).

Information

Banco del Pacífico (cnr Lalama & Cevallos) Bank with an ATM.

Tourist office (☎282-1800; www.turismo.gob.ec; Guayaquil & Rocafuerte; ⏰8am-5pm Mon-Fri)

Getting There & Away

From the bus terminal (2km north of the center; taxi US$1.50), regular services go to Baños (US$1, one hour), Riobamba (US$1.25, one hour), Quito (US$2.50, 2½ hours) and Guayaquil (US$7, six hours). Less-frequent, daily buses travel to Guaranda (US$2, two hours), Cuenca (US$8, seven hours) and Tena (US$5, five hours).

Baños

☎03 / POP 15,000

Hemmed in by luxuriant green peaks, blessed with steaming thermal baths and adorned by a beautiful waterfall, Baños is one of Ecuador's most enticing and popular tourist destinations. Ecuadorians and foreigners alike flock here to hike, soak in the baths, ride mountain bikes, zip around on rented quad-runners, volcano-watch, party, and break their molars on the town's famous *melcocha* (taffy). Touristy as it is, it's a wonderful place to hang out for a few days.

Baños (elevation 1800m) is also the gateway town into the jungle via Puyo. East of Baños, the road drops spectacularly toward the upper Amazon Basin and the views are best taken in over the handlebars of a mountain bike, which you can rent in town.

Baños' annual fiesta is held on December 16 and preceding days.

Activities

A small town in a fabulous setting, Baños offers an excellent range of outdoor adventures, plus hot baths for a refreshing soak when the day is done.

Thermal Baths

A soak in a thermal bath is an essential Baños experience. Go on weekdays to beat the crowds. Towels are generally available for rent, though sometimes they run out.

Baños

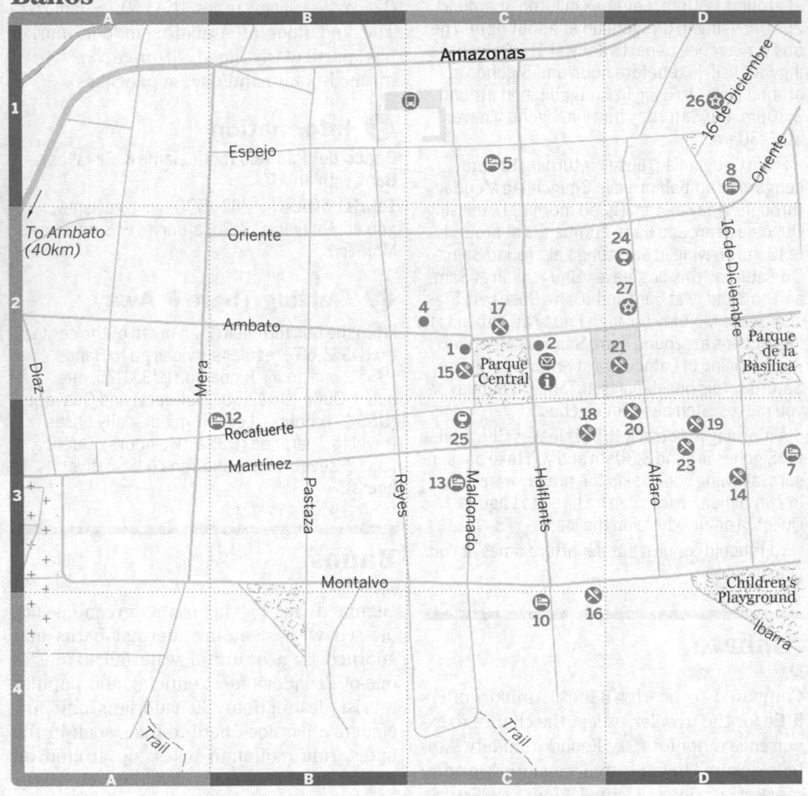

Baños

Activities, Courses & Tours

1 Expediciones Amazónicas C2
2 GeoTours C2
3 Piscina de la Virgen F3
4 Rainforestur C2

Sleeping

5 D'Mathias C1
6 Hostal Chimenea F3
7 Hostal Plantas y Blanco D3
8 Hostal Transilvania D1
9 Hostel Backpackers Los Pinos F1
10 La Floresta Hotel C4
11 Posada del Arte F4
12 Residencia Princesa María B3
13 Timara Hostal C3

Eating

14 Café Good D3
15 Café Hood C2
16 Café Mariane C4
17 Cafe Ricooo Pan C2
18 Casa Hood C3
19 La Bella Italia D3
20 Mega Bodega Supermarket D3
21 Mercado Central D2
22 Quilombo E3
23 Swiss Bistro D3

Drinking

24 Jack Rock D2
25 Stray Dog C3

Entertainment

26 Peña Ananitay D1
27 Peña Bar Mocambo D2

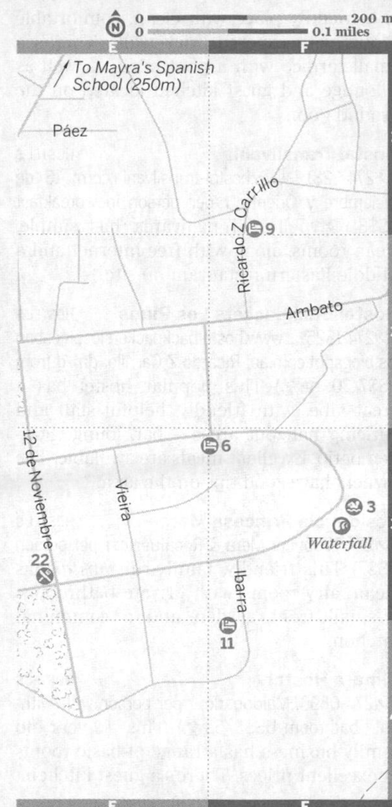

In the town proper are the baths of **Piscina de la Virgen** (admission day/night US$2/3; ⏲4:30am-4:30pm & 6-9:30pm). Slightly more scenic are **Piscina El Salado** (admission day/night US$3/4; ⏲5am-5pm & 6-10pm), 2km from the center. To get there, follow Rua Martinez west past the cemetery, and take the first narrow lane down (on your right) across the river. Turn left when you reach the road at the top of the riverbank.

Hiking

Baños has some great hiking. The tourist office (p665) provides a crude but useful map showing some of the trails around town.

From the bus terminal, a short trail leads to Puente San Francisco (San Francisco Bridge), across Río Pastaza. Continue up the other side as far as you want.

At the southern end of Maldonado a footpath leads to **Bellavista** (the white-cross lookout high over Baños) and then to the settlement of Runtún, about 1km away. South on Mera, a footpath leads to the **Mirador de la Virgen del Agua Santa** and onto Runtún.

Mountain Biking

Numerous companies rent bikes for US$6 to US$10 per day. You can find several outfitters along the streets south of Parque de la Basílica. Check the equipment carefully. The best paved ride is the dramatic descent to Puyo, about 60km away by road. Be sure to stop at the spectacular **Pailón del Diablo** (admission US$1.50), a waterfall about 18km from Baños. There is a passport control near the town of Shell so carry your documents. From Puyo (or anywhere along the way) take a bus back to Baños with the bike on the roof.

Climbing & Trekking

Climbs of Cotopaxi and Chimborazo can be arranged. Reputable climbing outfitters are **Expediciones Amazónicas** (☎274-0506; Maldonado) and Rainforestur (p663). The going rate for climbs with an overnight stay in the refuge is around US$150 per person.

At the time of writing, Volcán Tungurahua (5016m), part of **Parque Nacional Sangay** (admission US$10), was off-limits owing to recent eruptions.

Rafting & Canyoning

GeoTours ADVENTURE TOUR
(☎274-1344; www.geotoursbanios.com; cnr Ambato & Halflants) This reputable operator offers half-day trips on the Río Patate for US$30 and full-day trips on the Río Pastaza (class IV–V) for US$100. The full-day trip is 10 hours, with four hours on the river. Prices include food, transportation, guides and equipment. Other offerings include canyoning, rock climbing, trekking and paragliding.

Rainforestur ADVENTURE TOUR
(☎08-446-9884; www.rainforestur.com; Ambato 800) Leads a wide range of adventure tours, including rafting, climbing and canyoning.

Chiva Tours

A number of tour operators around town offer three-hour *chiva* (open-sided bus) tours; these visit various waterfalls and scenic overlooks, and you'll have the opportunity to try '*puenting*' (akin to bungee jumping), riding on a cable car over a valley and zip-lining. The *chiva* tour costs US$6 per person; activities are charged separately. By night, *chiva* tours run a different circuit. These take in views over Baños and with luck the glow of Tungurahua (US$3, two hours).

Jungle Trips

Loads of jungle trips are advertised from Baños, but not all guides are experienced. Those listed here have received good reports. Three- to seven-day jungle tours cost about US$50 to US$75 per person per day, depending on the destination. It's difficult to see animals in the forests closer to Baños; if you want primary rainforest, make sure you're going as deep as the lower Río Napo area.

Recommended operators are Rainforestur (p663) and Expediciones Amazónicas (p663). They both lead culture and nature tours near Puyo and Lago Agrio.

Courses

One-on-one language classes start around US$7 per hour (slightly less for small-group instruction). Schools offerings homestays include **Baños Spanish Center** (☎098-704-5072; www.spanishcenterschool.com; Oriente & Cañar), **Mayra's Spanish School** (☎274-3019; www.mayraspanishschool.com; Eduardo Tapia 112 near Oriente) and **Raíces Spanish School** (☎274-1921; www.spanishlessons.org; 16 de Diciembre & Pablo Suarez). To get to the latter, take 16 de Diciembre 200m northeast of the center.

Sleeping

There are scores of hotels in Baños, and competition is stiff, so prices are low. Rates are highest on Friday evenings and holiday weekends when every hotel in town can fill up.

Hostal Chimenea HOSTEL $
(☎274-2725; www.hostalchimenea.com; Martínez near Vieira; dm/s/d from US$7.50/10/17; @≋) This popular budget choice near the baths has clean, comfortable rooms with wood floors. There's a small dip pool, a hot tub and a sauna, and the upstairs terrace has great views.

Hostal Plantas y Blanco HOSTEL $
(☎274-0044; www.plantasyblanco.com; Martínez & 12 de Noviembre; dm US$6.50, d with/without bathroom US$22/19; @) Attractively decorated and eternally popular, 'Plants & White' scores big points with travelers for its rooftop terrace, filling breakfasts, on-site steam bath and overall value.

D'Mathias GUESTHOUSE $
(☎274-3203; www.hostaldmathias.com; Espejo near Halflants; r per person US$6;) One of the best value places in town, D'Mathias is a friendly place with clean, comfortable rooms with exposed brick walls. There's a small terrace with a pool table, as well as a lounge and guest kitchen located on the ground floor.

Hostal Transilvania HOSTEL $
(☎274-2281; www.hostal-transilvania.com; 16 de Diciembre y Oriente; r per person incl breakfast US$8; @) The Transilvania has simple, clean rooms, along with free internet and a Middle Eastern restaurant on-site.

Hostel Backpackers Los Pinos HOSTEL $
(☎274-1825; www.hostelbackpackerslospinosbanios.blogspot.com.au; Ricardo Z Carrillo; dm/d from US$7/20; @) This popular hostel has a great vibe, with friendly, helpful staff and enticing hangout areas – bar, lounge, garden patio. Excellent meals are available. The owners have good tips on the area.

Residencia Princesa María HOSTEL $
(☎274-1035; cnr Mera & Rocafuerte; r per person US$7) This friendly, family-run *hostal* has clean, airy rooms with private bathrooms, a small front garden and a communal kitchen.

Timara Hostal HOSTEL $
(☎274-0599; Maldonado; r per person with/without bathroom US$8/5;) This 40-year-old family business has a range of basic rooms at excellent prices. There's a guest kitchen.

Posada del Arte BOUTIQUE HOTEL $$
(☎274-0083; www.posadadelarte.com; Ibarra; s/d incl breakfast from US$36/68;) This handsome little guesthouse has colorful, comfortable rooms, wood floors, a rooftop terrace, gigantic breakfasts and art all around. Great restaurant with fireplace on-site (mains US$4 to US$8).

La Floresta Hotel HOTEL $$
(☎274-1824; www.laflorestahotel.com; cnr Montalvo & Haflants; s/d/tr incl breakfast US$35/55/75; @) This comfortable inn situated around a pretty interior garden has friendly staff and spacious rooms with big windows and comfortable beds.

Eating

Baños is famous for its *melcocha*; makers pull it from wooden pegs in doorways around town. For a pick-me-up try a glass of *jugo de caña* (sugarcane juice), sold at stalls behind the bus station.

Mercado Central MARKET $
(Alfaro & Rocafuerte; lunch US$2-3; 7am-6pm) For fresh fruit and vegetables and cheap, cheap *almuerzos,* visit the town's central market.

Casa Hood INTERNATIONAL $
(Martínez near Halflants; mains US$4-7; 8am-10:15pm) Named for owner Ray Hood, a longstanding gringo-in-residence, this excellent cafe has nourishing breakfasts, a cheap *almuerzo* and a menu of Thai, Mexican and Middle Eastern dishes. The Casa is a welcoming place to eat, exchange books, meet with friends, chill *solito* (alone), watch free films and even take yoga classes.

Swiss Bistro EUROPEAN $$
(Martínez near Alfaro; mains US$7-12; noon-11pm) This charming spot offers tasty European and Swiss specialties, which include fondue, steaks, fresh salads, soups and a Swiss potato dish called Röesti.

Café Hood INTERNATIONAL $
(Maldonado; mains US$3-6; 10am-9pm Thu-Tue;) A welcoming spot that serves a wide mix of international dishes from Mexican to Greek to Indian. Lots of veggie options.

Café Good INTERNATIONAL $
(16 de Diciembre; mains US$4-7; 8am-10pm) Café Good serves satisfying veggies dishes with wholesome brown rice, as well as some chicken and fish.

Cafe Ricooo Pan ECUADORIAN $
(Ambato near Maldonado; mains US$4; 7am-7pm) Best bread in town and filling breakfasts.

La Bella Italia ITALIAN $
(Martínez; mains US$5-6; noon-11pm) This elegant little Italian bistro serves pasta and pizzas in a quiet atmosphere.

Café Mariane FRENCH $$
(Montalvo; mains US$7-11; 11am-11pm) Mariane's French-Mediterranean cuisine features excellent fondues and beautifully prepared pasta and meat dishes.

Quilombo ARGENTINE $$
(cnr Montalvo & 12 de Noviembre; mains US$4-8; noon-11pm Wed-Sun) *Quilombo* means 'mess' or 'insanity' in Argentine slang – come see why it's a fitting name for this excellent Argentine grillhouse.

Mega Bodega Supermarket SUPERMARKET
(cnr Alfaro & Rocafuerte) Stock up here.

Drinking & Entertainment

Nightlife in Baños means dancing in local *peñas* and hanging out in bars. The best place to bar-hop is the two-block strip along Alfaro, north of Ambato.

Stray Dog BREWERY
(cnr Rocafuerte & Maldonado; 3-11pm Tue-Sun) The only brew pub in Baños features surprisingly good artisanal offerings like light Llamas' Breath Belgian and bold Stray Dog Stout. Also serves good pub grub (pulled pork sandwiches, steak burgers and the like).

Jack Rock THEME BAR
(Alfaro 5-41; 8pm-2am) Jack Rock boasts a rock-and-roll theme and the best pub atmosphere in town. It plays classic rock during the week and salsa, merengue and reggaeton on weekends.

Peña Bar Mocambo LIVE MUSIC
(Alfaro; 10am-2am Mon-Sat) This place is always a popular option thanks to its sidewalk bar, party atmosphere and upstairs billiards room.

Peña Ananitay LIVE MUSIC
(16 de Diciembre; 9pm-3am Fri & Sat) This is the best place in town to catch live *música folklórica.* It can get packed, but that's part of the fun.

Information

Banco del Pichincha (cnr Ambato & Halflants) Bank with ATM.

Post office (274-0901; Halflants near Ambato)

Tourist office (274-0483; mun_banos@andinanet.net; Halflants near Rocafuerte; 8am-12:30pm & 2-5:30pm Mon-Fri) There is also an office at the bus terminal.

Getting There & Away

From many towns it may be quicker to change buses in Ambato, where there are frequent buses to Baños (US$1, one hour).

From the **terminal** (Amazonas) in Baños many buses leave for Quito (US$3.50, 3½ hours), Puyo (US$2.50, 1½ hours), Tena (US$4, four hours) and Coca (US$10, 10 hours). Expresso Baños runs two direct buses daily to Otavalo (US$5.50, 5½ hours). The road to Riobamba (US$2, two hours) via Penipe was closed at the time of writing, meaning you'll have to backtrack through Ambato.

Guaranda

03 / POP 31,000

Half the fun of Guaranda is getting there. The 99km 'highway' from Ambato reaches an altitude of over 4000m and passes within 5km of the glacier on Volcán Chimborazo (6310m). The road slices through windswept *páramo* and past little troops of *vicuña* (a wild relative of the llama) before suddenly plunging toward Guaranda.

The capital of Bolívar province, Guaranda is small and uneventful, though it is famous for its Carnaval celebrations. It's also the departure point for the delightful village of Salinas.

Sleeping & Eating

Hotel Bolívar HOTEL **$**
(298-0547; Sucre 7-04; r per person US$18;) Bolívar is one of Guaranda's best-value options with clean and welcoming rooms and a pleasant courtyard. The attached restaurant has good *almuerzos* (US$2 to US$3).

Los 7 Santos CAFE **$**
(Convención de 1884; mains US$1-3; 10am-11pm Mon-Sat) Thoroughly out of place in Guaranda, Los 7 Santos is an artsy cafe with great atmosphere along with breakfast, small sandwiches and *bocaditos* (snacks) all day.

La Bohemia ECUADORIAN **$**
(Convención de 1884 & 10 de Agosto; mains US$2-4; 8am-9pm Mon-Sat) Close to Parque Bolívar, La Bohemia serves *almuerzos* (US$2) in a laid-back but attentive atmosphere. Chase your meal down with one of the giant *batidos* (fruit shakes).

Information

Banco del Pichincha (Azuay near 7 de Mayo) Bank with an ATM.

Clínica Bolívar (298-1278; near Plaza Roja) One of several clinics and pharmacies near Plaza Roja, south of the hospital.

Hospital (Cisneros s/n)

Getting There & Away

The bus terminal is 500m east of downtown, just off Av de Carvajal. Buses run to Ambato (US$2, two hours), Quito (US$5, five hours), Riobamba (US$2, two hours) and Guayaquil (US$4, five hours). To Salinas, buses (US25¢, one hour) and white pickup collective taxis (US$1) depart from Plaza Roja.

Salinas

03 / POP 1000

Set in wild, beautiful countryside and famous for its excellent cheeses, salamis, divine chocolate and rough-spun sweaters, the tiny mountain village of Salinas, 35km north of Guaranda, makes for an interesting jaunt off the beaten track. The elevation is a whopping 3550m. Facing the main plaza, the **tourist office** (239-0022; www.salinerito.com) will organize visits to Salinas' unique cooperatives.

Two blocks above the plaza, **El Refugio** (221-0044; turismosalinas@salinerito.com; r per person with/without bathroom US$14/8) is a nice traveler's lodge with wood details, views of town, and a roaring fireplace in the lobby. It is owned and operated by the community of Salinas. It's best to call (or email) ahead.

Facing the main plaza, **La Minga Café** (El Salinerito at Guayamas; mains US$1.50-3; 7:30am-10pm) has good set meals and serves tourists and locals throughout the day.

Buses to Salinas (25¢, one hour) leave Plaza Roja in Guaranda at 6am and 7am daily and hourly from 10am to 4pm Monday through Friday. Buses for Guaranda (25¢, one hour) depart at 11am, 1pm and 3pm daily. Collective taxis also run frequently ($1, 45 minutes).

Riobamba

03 / POP 184,000

Deemed 'the Sultan of the Andes,' Riobamba (elevation 2750m) is an old-fashioned, traditional city that both bores and delights travelers. It's sedate yet handsome, with wide avenues and random mismatched shops tucked into imposing 18th- and 19th-century stone buildings. The city is both the starting point for the spectacular train ride down the Nariz del Diablo, and one of the best places in the country to hire mountain guides.

Sights

Mercado MARKET
Saturday is market day and this is when Riobamba's streets become a hive of activity, especially along the streets northeast of Parque de la Concepción.

RIDING THE ANDEAN RAILS

Ecuador's train service was receiving a massive makeover at the time of writing, and more lines should be operational by 2014. Currently two different tourist trains depart from Riobamba's handsomely restored **train station** (www.trenecuador.com; 10 de Agosto near Carabobo).

The **Tren del Hielo** (return US$11) goes from Riobamba to Urbina and back, departing at 8am on Thursdays to Sundays. On clear days, you'll have fine views of Chimborazo. In Urbina, you can visit a small museum exploring the history of the *hieleros* (men who harvested ice from the glaciers). Visitors arrive back in Riobamba around noon.

The **Sendero de los Ancestros** train (return US$15) goes 25km from Riobamba to Colta, where you can take a scenic boat ride on Lago Colta and visit the 16th-century Balbanera church. The train departs Riobamba at noon Thursdays to Sundays and returns around 4:15pm.

For information about the train ride down the Nariz del Diablo, see p670.

Museo de Arte Religioso MUSEUM
(Argentinos; admission US$2; ⏲9am-noon & 3-6pm Tue-Sat) The beautifully restored 16th-century convent of the Conceptas nuns contains a fascinating collection of religious art. Its signature piece is a priceless, 360kg gold monstrance inlaid with more than 1500 precious stones.

Activities

Thanks to the proximity of Volcán Chimborazo, Riobamba is one of Ecuador's most important climbing towns. Two-day summit trips cost around US$185 per person for Chimborazo and include guides, climbing gear, transportation and meals.

Mountain biking is also popular, and one-day trips cost US$35 to US$55 per person depending on the route. Downhill descents from the refuge on Chimborazo are an exhilarating way to take in the views.

Julio Verne Tour Operator ADVENTURE TOUR
(☎296-3436; www.julioverne-travel.com; Espectador 22-25) Dutch-Ecuadorian owned agency offering climbing, trekking (including the Camino Inca to Ingapirca), mountain biking and more. Ask about the extraordinary Hidden Valleys bike ride.

Ecuador Eco Adventure ADVENTURE TOUR
(☎296-8412; www.ecuadorecoadventure.com; Av Borja near Uruguay) Recommended operator that leads a wide range of outdoors adventures (climbing, trekking, horseriding), especially for those who like to be challenged. Also runs tours to the Amazon and other areas, and provides excellent volunteer opportunities.

Pro Bici ADVENTURE TOUR
(☎295-1759; Primera Constituycnte & Larrea) Recommended mountain-bike trips and rentals. English spoken.

Veloz Coronado Mountain Guides ADVENTURE TOUR
(☎296-0916; www.velozexpeditions.com; Chile 33-21 & Francia) Highly experienced climbing operator.

Courses

Riobamba is a good place to learn Spanish.

Chimborazo School LANGUAGE COURSE
(☎296-3645; chimborazoschool@yahoo.com; Veloz 30-45 near Montalvo) The German-Ecuadorian-run Chimborazo School offers private and group classes in Spanish, German and French. On-site lodging and homestays are also available.

Sleeping

Mansion Santa Isabella BOUTIQUE HOTEL $$$
(☎296-2947; www.mansionsantaisabella.com; Veloz near Carabobo; s/d/tr/ste incl breakfast US$55/80/100/120; @📶) In a beautifully restored mansion, Santa Isabella has elegantly designed rooms with lovely wood floors, antique furnishings, oversized windows and lux bathrooms (some with separate shower and tub). High-end products add to the appeal as do the first-rate restaurant and cozy wine cellar-bar.

Hostal Oasis HOSTEL $
(☎296-1210; www.oasishostelriobamba.com; Veloz 15-32; s/d US$12/24; @📶) When it comes to friendliness, value and down-home cutesiness, it's hard to beat Oasis. Simple

Riobamba

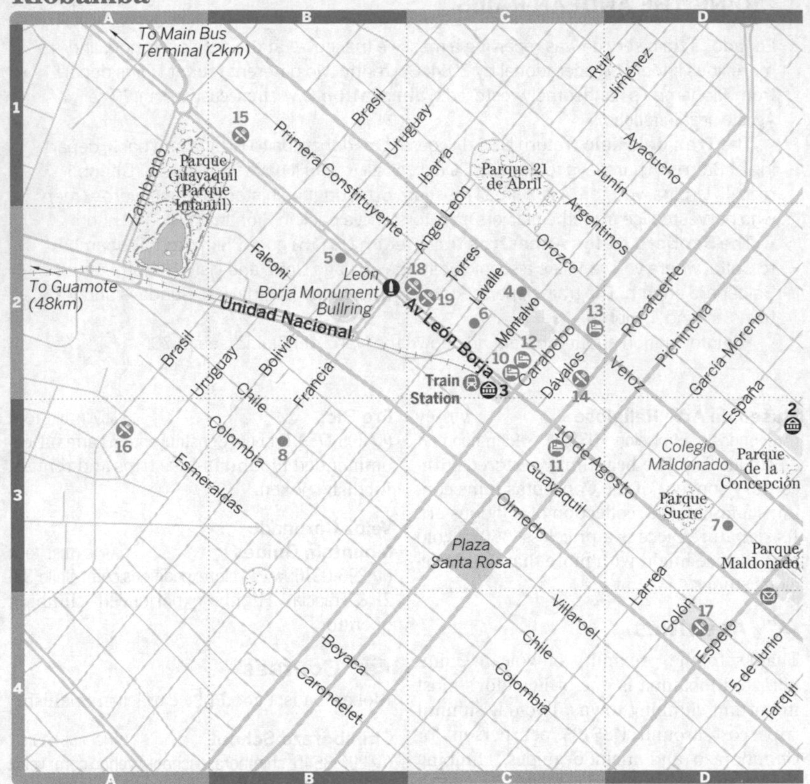

rooms are set around a garden with squawking parrots. A few blocks away, the recently opened Oasis II also offers lovely accommodation – check in at the main hostel.

Hotel Los Shyris HOTEL $

(☎296-0323; www.hotellosshyris.com; cnr Rocafuerte & 10 de Agosto; s/d incl breakfast US$12/18, without bathroom US$7/14; @) The best of the cheapies, Shyris is set in an unappealing modern building, but the rooms are clean and sunny with tile floors and big windows.

Hotel Tren Dorado HOTEL $

(☎296-4890; www.hoteltrendorado.com; Carabobo 22-35; r per person US$15; P 📶) Conveniently close to the train station, the friendly Tren Dorado has clean, comfortable rooms in pastel color schemes.

Hotel El Libertador HOTEL $

(☎294-7393; www.hotelellibertador.com; Av Borja & Carabobo; s/d US$15/25; @ 📶) This basic hotel housed in a renovated building with wooden floors sits conveniently across the street from the train station. There's a busy restaurant-grill downstairs that opens early and closes late.

Eating & Drinking

La Abuela Rosa ECUADORIAN $

(cnr Brasil & Esmeraldas; mains US$1-3; ⏲4-9pm Mon-Sat) One of Riobamba's most charming spots, La Abuela Rosa has a series of small antique-filled dining rooms fronting a garden courtyard. Come for hot chocolate, sandwiches, smoked meat plates and traditional snacks (*quimbolitos,* tamales and *humitas*).

Mercado La Merced MARKET $

(Mercado M Borja; Guayaquil btwn Espejo & Colón; mains US$3; ⏲7am-6pm) A great spot to try Ecuador's classic *hornado* (whole roast pig). Best on Saturday.

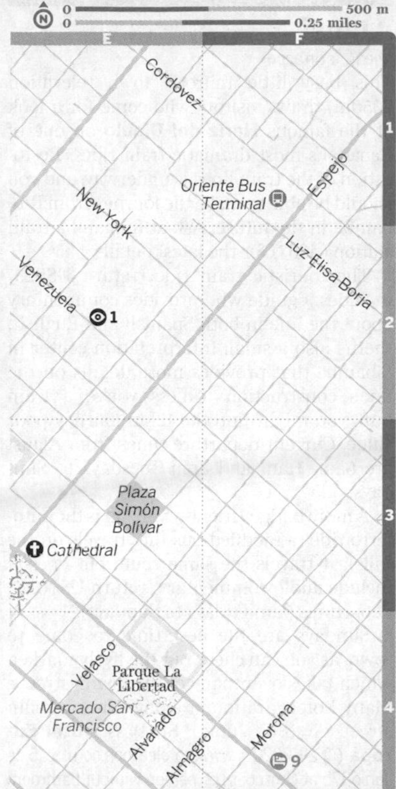

Riobamba

Sights
1 Mercado ... E2
2 Museo de Arte Religioso ... D3
3 Train Station ... C2

Activities, Courses & Tours
4 Chimborazo School ... C2
5 Ecuador Eco Adventure ... B2
6 Julio Verne Tour Operator ... C2
7 Pro Bici ... D3
8 Veloz Coronado Mountain Guides ... B3

Sleeping
9 Hostal Oasis ... F4
10 Hotel El Libertador ... C2
11 Hotel Los Shyris ... C3
12 Hotel Tren Dorado ... C2
13 Mansion Santa Isabella ... C2

Eating
14 Café El Delirio ... C2
15 El Rey del Burrito ... B1
16 La Abuela Rosa ... A3
17 Mercado La Merced ... D4
18 Pizzería D'Baggios ... C2
19 Pizzería San Valentin ... C2

El Rey del Burrito MEXICAN $
(Av Borja 38-36; mains US$4-6;) Large burritos, tacos and enchiladas come nicely prepared at this friendly restaurant decorated with colorful murals.

Pizzería D'Baggios ITALIAN $$
(cnr Av Borja & Angel León; pizzas US$3-8; noon-10pm Mon-Sat) This corner pizzeria is a popular gathering for locals and travelers alike, with a menu including dozens of satisfying medium-thick-crust pizzas, out of Baggio's wood oven.

Café El Delirio ECUADORIAN $$
(Primera Constituyente 28-16; mains US$7-10; noon-10pm Tue-Sun) Named for a poem by the great liberator, Simón Bolívar, this historic monument-turned-restaurant serves *comida típica* (traditional Ecuadorian food) in a dimly lit, antique atmosphere. Service is slow.

Pizzería San Valentin INETERNATIONAL $$
(cnr Av Borja & Torres; mains US$5-10; 6pm-midnight Mon-Thu, to 2am Fri & Sat) The cornerstone of Riobamba's nightlife, San Valentin is a lively place, great for both eating and socializing. A mix of expats and locals come for game nights and filling pub fare – pizza, hamburgers and Tex-Mex.

Information

Banco de Guayaquil (Primera Constituyente) Bank with ATM.

Parque Nacional Sangay Office (295-3041; parquesangay@andinanet.net; Av 9 de Octubre; 8am-1pm & 2-5pm Mon-Fri) West of downtown, near Duchicela; get information and pay entry fees to Parque Nacional Sangay here.

Post office (cnr Espejo & 10 de Agosto)

Getting There & Away

The **main bus terminal** (Av León Borja at Av de la Prensa) is 2km northwest of the center. Buses run frequently to Quito (US$4, four hours), Guayaquil (US$5, five hours) and Alausí (US$2, two hours), and less frequently to Cuenca (US$6, six hours). There's at least one morning bus to Machala (US$6.40, seven hours). Local buses run along Av León Borja, connecting the terminal with downtown.

Buses to Baños (US$2, two hours) and the Oriente leave from the **Oriente bus terminal** (cnr Espejo & Luz Elisa Borja) just northeast of the center.

Volcán Chimborazo

Not only is the extinct Volcán Chimborazo the highest mountain in Ecuador, but its peak (6310m), due to the earth's equatorial bulge, is also the furthest point from the center of the earth – tell that to your K2-climbing buddies. The mountain is part of **Reserva de Producción de Fauna Chimborazo**, which also encompasses **Volcán Carihuairazo** (5020m). Incidentally, it is called a 'fauna-production reserve' because it is home to hundreds of *vicuña*. You're sure to see them if you explore the park.

Two small lodges on the lower slopes of Chimborazo are interesting places to see the countryside and learn a bit about local culture. **La Casa del Cóndor** (357-1379; r per person US$5), in the small indigenous community of **Pulinguí San Pablo** (3900m) on the Riobamba–Guaranda road, offers simple accommodations; locals provide basic guiding services, mountain bikes are available, and there are fascinating interpretation trails in the area.

The two high **climbers' refuges** (beds US$10), at 4800m and 5000m, on the other hand, are pretty much a place to eat some grub and catch a few winks before heading out on an all-night climb. The refuges have mattresses, water and cooking facilities; bring warm sleeping bags.

Climbing beyond the refuge requires snow- and ice-climbing gear and mountaineering experience, as does the ascent of Carihuairazo. Contact one of the recommended guide outfits listed under Riobamba or Quito. Avoid inexperienced guides; a climb at this altitude is not to be taken lightly.

There are also excellent trekking opportunities between the two mountains. Topographical maps of the region are available at the Instituto Geográfico Militar in Quito. June through September is the dry season in this region, and the nights are very cold year-round.

If you're up for an 8km walk (not easy at this altitude), you can take a Guaranda-bound bus from Riobamba and ask the driver to drop you off at the park entrance road.

Alausí

03 / POP 8200

This busy little railroad town (elevation 2350m) draws visitors who come for a look at the famous **Nariz del Diablo** on one of Ecuador's most dramatic train rides. Restoration of the train lines is underway, and you should be able to make the journey from Riobamba in the future. Ask at Riobamba train station (p667) for the latest details.

The touristic train ride (return US$25) includes a guide who provides commentary about the line in both Spanish and English; there's also a small interpretation center in Sibambe that provides more details on the line's construction. Unless you're a train buff, you might find the 12km journey poor value. Current departure times from Alausí are 8am, 11am and 3pm Tuesdays to Sundays.

A more budget-friendly version is the autoferro ride (a modfied bus that travels on the rails); it travels the same route but doesn't include audio commentary (return US$6.50, departures 9am Fridays to Sundays).

Sundays are the best time to come to town, as you can check out the lively market, which takes over many of the town's streets. Many hotels are found along Alausí's main street (Av 5 de Junio). Spotless **Hotel Europa** (293-0200; www.hoteleuropa.com.ec; 5 de Junio 175 at Orozco; r per person without bathroom US$10/18;) is one of the best options. Other decent options include **Hotel Panamericano** (293-0278; 5 de Junio & 9 de Octubre; s/d US$15/25, s/d with/without US$10/16) and **Hotel Gampala** (293-0138; www.hotelgampala.com; 5 de Junio 122; s/d/tr/ste incl breakfast US$22/44/60/60;).

Buses run hourly to and from Riobamba (US$2, two hours) and several buses a day also go to Cuenca (US$5, four hours).

SOUTHERN HIGHLANDS

As you roll down the Panamericana into the southern highlands, the giant snowcapped peaks of the central highlands fade from view. The climate gets a bit warmer, distances between towns become greater, and the decades clunk down by the wayside. Cuenca – arguably Ecuador's most beautiful city – and handsome little Loja are the region's only sizable towns.

Even though you won't be out scaling glaciers in the southern highlands, a variety of outdoor activities abounds. The lake-studded Parque Nacional Cajas offers excellent hiking and camping, while in Parque Nacional Podocarpus you can explore cloud forest, tropical humid forest and *páramo* within the same park. From the laid-back gringo hangout of Vilcabamba, you can spend days walking or horse riding through captivating mountain country, returning each evening to massages, hot tubs and delicious food.

Cuenca

07 / POP 506,000

Comparing the colonial beauty of Cuenca and Quito is a favorite pastime around here. In grandeur, Quito wins hands down. But Cuenca – that tidy jewel of the south – takes the cake when it comes to charm. Its narrow cobblestone streets and whitewashed red-tiled buildings, its handsome plazas and domed churches, and its setting above the grassy banks of the Río Tomebamba, all create a city that's supremely impressive. Though firmly anchored in its colonial past, Ecuador's third-largest city (elevation 2530m) also has a modern edge, with international restaurants, art galleries, cool cafes and welcoming bars tucked into its magnificent architecture.

Sights

For a scenic stroll, head down to 3 de Noviembre, a lane lined with colonial buildings, which follows the northern bank of the **Río Tomebamba**.

Clustered around the Plazoleta de la Cruz del Vado you'll find a few interesting sites, including the **Prohibido Museo de Arte Extremo** (La Condamine 12-102; admission 50¢; noon-late), a goth-lovers' gallery, bar and cafe, and **Laura's Antiguidades y Curiosidades** (La Condamine 12-112; 9am-1pm & 3-6pm Mon-Fri), which showcases a hodgepodge of curios and objets d'art in a 19th-century house.

FREE **Museo del Banco Central 'Pumapungo'** MUSEUM
(www.pumapungo.org; Larga btwn Arriaga & Huayna Capac; 8am-5:30pm Mon-Fri, 9am-1pm Sat) Cuenca's most important museum has an entire floor of colorfully animated dioramas displaying traditional costumes of Ecuador's diverse indigenous cultures. There's also an eerie display of *tsantsas* (shrunken heads). Out back is an Archaeological Park, where you can walk through the extensive ruins of buildings believed to be part of the old Incan city of Tomebamba.

FREE **Museo Manuel Agustín Landivar** MUSEUM
(cnr Larga 2-23 & Vega; 9am-1pm & 3-6pm Mon-Fri) At the east end of Larga, this museum has archaeological exhibits and tours of the **Ruinas de Todos Santos**, which reveal Cañari, Inca and Spanish ruins, layered one over the other. You can also see them from below on Av de Todos Santos.

Parque Calderón PLAZA
The main plaza is dominated by the handsome **new cathedral** (c 1885) with its huge blue domes. On the opposite side of the park stands the diminutive **old cathedral** (Parque Calderón; 9am-1pm & 2-6pm Mon-Fri, 10am-1pm Sat & Sun) (construction began in 1557), known as El Sagrario.

Museo de Arte Moderno MUSEUM
(cnr Mariscal Sucre & Talbot; admission by donation; 9am-6.30pm Mon-Fri, to 1pm Sat) In a former home for the insane, this museum houses a vibrant collection of Ecuadorian and Latin American art.

Museo de las Culturas Aborígenes MUSEUM
(museoarq@etapaonline.net.ec; Larga 5-24; admission US$2; 9am-6pm Mon-Fri, to 1pm Sat) Houses an excellent collection of more than 5000 archaeological pieces representative of about 20 pre-Columbian cultures from present-day Ecuador.

Museo del Sombrero de Paja Toquilla MUSEUM
(Larga 10-41) This small museum and hat seller reveals how panama hats have been made over the years. There's also a cafe with river views.

Activities

Cuenca is an ideal base for exploring nearby attractions such as Parque Nacional Cajas, the Inca ruins of Ingapirca and indigenous villages. Day trips cost approximately US$45 per person. You can also arrange horse riding, biking, canyoning and other outdoors adventures.

Cuenca

Expediciones Apullacta ADVENTURE TOUR
(☎283-7815; www.apullacta.com; Gran Colombia 11-02, 2nd fl) Runs popular outings to Cajas, village tours, canyoning adventures, rock-climbing and many other options.

Mamá Kinua Cultural Center CULTURAL TOUR
(☎099-747-6337; Torres 7-45) A community tourism project offering tours and home-stays in the nearby indigenous community of Parcoloma. One-day tours cost US$35; and

two-day tours (with an overnight in the community) cost US$75. No English is spoken.

Terra Diversa Travel Center TOUR
(☎09-920-4832; www.terradiversa.com; Larga near Cordero) Biking, horse-riding, hiking, Inga-pirca trips, village tours and old-town walking tours.

Courses

Cuenca is an excellent setting to study Spanish. One-on-one classes cost US$7 to US$10 per hour. Some recommended schools:

Simón Bolívar Spanish School LANGUAGE COURSE
(☎284-4555; www.bolivar2.com; Luís Cordero 10-25) Offers homestays and excursions.

Amauta LANGUAGE COURSE
(☎284-6206; www.amauta.edu.ec; Hermano Miguel 7-48) Small, charming school run by a nonprofit organization.

Spanish Institute LANGUAGE COURSE
(☎282-4736; www.spanish-institute-cuenca.com; Calle Larga 2-92) A recommended school with ties to school in the US (Boulder, Colorado); emphasizes homestays with local families.

Centers for Interamerican Studies LANGUAGE COURSE
(CEDEI; ☎283-4353; www.cedei.org; Gran Colombia 11-02) Professionally run outfit; good for long-term studies.

Festivals & Events

Cuenca's independence as a city is celebrated on November 3 with a major fiesta. Christmas Eve parades are very colorful. The founding of Cuenca (April 10 to 13) and Corpus Christi are also busy holidays. Carnaval is celebrated with boisterous water fights.

Sleeping

Cuenca has a great selection of hotels, but prices are a bit higher than elsewhere.

Casa Ordonez GUESTHOUSE $$
(☎282-3297; www.casa-ordonez.com; Mariscal Lamar 859; s/d incl breakfast US$55/65) In the same family since 1906, this warmly welcoming guesthouse has attractive rooms and common areas that are set with antique furnishings and original details.

Hostal Posada del Angel B&B $$
(☎284-0695; www.hostalposadadelangel.com; Bolívar 14-11; s/d/tr incl breakfast US$48/67/83; @) Color, character, history – the Posada del Angel has handsomely designed rooms overlooking an interior courtyard.

Hostal Macondo HOTEL $
(☎284-0697; www.hostalmacondo.com; Tarqui 11-64; s/d incl breakfast US$27/38, without bath-

Cuenca

Sights
1 Laura's Antiguidades y Curiosidades B3
2 Museo de Arte Moderno A2
3 Museo de las Culturas Aborígenes D5
4 Museo del Banco Central 'Pumapungo' F6
5 Museo del Sombrero de Paja Toquilla B4
6 Museo Manuel Agustín Landivar E6
7 New Cathedral C3
8 Old Cathedral D3
9 Parque Calderón C3
10 Prohibido Museo de Arte Extremo B3

Activities, Courses & Tours
11 Amauta D3
Centers for Interamerican Studies .... (see 12)
12 Expediciones Apullacta B2
13 Mamá Kinua Cultural Center B3
14 Simón Bolívar Spanish School D2
15 Spanish Institute E5
16 Terra Diversa Travel Center C4

Sleeping
17 Casa del Río B4
18 Casa Ordonez D2
19 El Cafecito D4
20 Hogar Cuencano D4
21 Hostal Cofradía del Monje B3
22 Hostal Macondo B1
23 Hostal Posada del Angel A2
24 La Cigale D4
25 Posada del Río D5

Eating
26 Akelarre Tapas Españolas C2
27 Bapu Shawarma C4
28 Café Austria C4
29 El Cafetal del Loja C2
30 Fabiano's E3
31 Govinda's D4
32 Guajibamba D1
33 Inca Lounge & Bistro C4
34 Maria's Alemania D3
35 Moliendo Café D4
36 Raymipampa C2
37 Sakura Sushi D5
38 Tiestos D4

Drinking
39 Café Eucalyptus C2
40 La Compañía D4
41 Wunderbar D5

Shopping
42 Cemuart B3

room US$21/3; 🛜) The colonial-style Hostal Macondo has palatial rooms in the front, older section, and small but cozy rooms situated around a big, sunny garden out back.

Hostal Cofradía del Monje GUESTHOUSE $
(☎283-1251; www.hostalcofradiadelmonje.com; Presidente Córdova 10-33; s/d incl breakfast US$29/48; 🛜) In a refurbished century-old home, the 'brotherhood of the monks' has high timbered ceilings, polished wood floors and expansive views of the plaza and market below.

La Cigale HOSTEL $
(☎283-5308; lacigalecuencana@yahoo.fr; Vasquez 7-80; dm/s/d incl breakfast US$9/17/24) La Cigale has clean rooms with wood floors and good showers, though the best feature is the attractive courtyard restaurant with great ambience that draws backpackers and a more stylish local crowd.

El Cafecito HOSTEL $
(☎283-2337; www.cafecito.net; Vásquez 7-36; dm US$7, r with/without bathroom US$25/15; 🛜) A longtime backpacker favorite, El Cafecito has a lively courtyard cafe that's an ideal spot for meeting other travelers. The rooms themselves are worn and noisy – with late-night chatter right outside your door.

Posada del Río HOSTEL $
(☎282-3111; posadadelriocuenca@yahoo.com; Hermano Miguel 4-18; dm/s/d US$7/$15/22; @🛜) This simple and tasteful inn near the river has a rooftop terrace with views and a communal kitchen. Bright colors and woodwork adorn throughout, and the shared bathrooms are clean.

Casa del Río GUESTHOUSE $
(☎282-9659; hostalcasadelrio@hotmail.com; Bajada del Padrón 4-07; r per person with/without bathroom from US$15/10; @) Above the river, this small guesthouse with terrace has a

range of rooms, from small dusty quarters to tidy numbers with pretty views.

Hogar Cuencano HOSTEL $
(☎283-4941; hostelhogarcuencano@hotmail.com; Hermano Miguel 4-36; dm US$7, r per person with/without US$11/9) This friendly place has clean, simple rooms and a good location in the old town. There are no common areas, so it's not great for meeting other travelers.

Hostal Alternative HOSTEL $
(☎408-4101; anhostels@gmail.com; cnr Huayna Capac & Cacique Duma; dm US$9, d without bathroom US$20; 📶) Although removed from the action, this sparkly hostel has good facilities with shared kitchen, TV room and excellent terrace. To get there, take Calle Larga east; it's a five-minute walk past the Museu del Banco Central 'Pumapungo'.

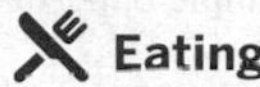

Eating

Most restaurants close on Sunday.

Tiestos ECUADORIAN $$$
(☎283-5310; Juan Jaramillo 7-34; mains US$13-17; ⏰12.30-3pm Tue-Sun & 6-10pm Tue-Sat) A bit touristy, but still one of Cuenca's best restaurants, the artwork-filled Tiestos specializes in decadent roast meat and fish dishes, best shared among groups of two to four. Reserve ahead.

Akelarre Tapas Españolas SPANISH $$
(Torres 8-40; tapas/mains from US$3/7; ⏰11am-10pm Mon-Fri, 3-5pm Sat) Akelarre serves traditional tapas like *patatas bravas* (spicy fried potatoes), *camarones al ajillo* (garlic prawns) and *jamon serrano* (cured Spanish ham). There's excellent paella on Sundays.

Guajibamba ECUADORIAN $$
(☎283-1016; Luís Cordero 12-32; mains US$7-10; ⏰noon-3pm & 6-11pm Mon-Sat) This atmospheric restaurant serves traditional *seco de chivo* and gourmet *fritada*. It's also one of the best places to try *cuy* (call an hour before you go for prep time).

Café Austria EUROPEAN $$
(Benigno Malo 5-95; mains US$6-9; ⏰9am-10.30pm; 📶) Austrian-style cakes, coffee and sandwiches.

Moliendo Café COLOMBIAN $
(Vásquez 6-24; mains US$3-6; ⏰noon-9pm Mon-Sat) Moliendo Café serves satisfying Colombian *arepas* (a corn and cheese pancake), topped with anything from beans and cheese to slow-cooked pork. Good set lunches (US$2.50).

Raymipampa ECUADORIAN $
(Benigno Malo 8-59; mains US$4-8; ⏰8:30am-10:30pm Mon-Fri, from 9.30am Sat & Sun) This Cuenca institution serves *ceviche*, soups, crepes (sweet and savory), and many other selections in a comfortable ambience.

Govinda's INTERNATIONAL $
(Jaramillo 7-27; set lunches US$2.50, mains US$4; ⏰8:30am-3pm Mon-Sat, plus 6-10pm Wed-Sat; 🌿) Enjoy pizzas, lentil burgers and filling vegetarian lunches amid Indian tapestries and Eastern-influenced electronica.

Sakura Sushi JAPANESE $$
(cnr Paseo 3 de Noviembre & Escalinata; sushi combo for 1/2 US$9/20; ⏰lunch & dinner Tue-Sat) Sakura prepares fresh, authentic sushi (the coast is only three hours away), plus good-value lunch specials.

Inca Lounge & Bistro BURGERS $
(Paseo 3 de Noviembre; mains US$5-7; ⏰Tue-Sat) This multistory restaurant and bar facing the river serves Cuenca's best burgers, plus other pub grub. Televised sports draw the expats on game days.

Fabiano's ITALIAN $
(☎282-4517; Presidente Córdova 4-84; mains US$3-6) Popular with expats, this friendly, locally owned spot serves up filling pizzas, calzones, pastas and stromboli sandwiches. Good value.

Maria's Alemania BAKERY $
(Hermano Miguel near Mariscal Sucre; snacks US$2; ⏰7:30am-6:30pm Mon-Fri) Cuenca's best bakery serves filling empanadas (try the chicken curry) as well as doughnuts, fruit-filled Danishes and other pastries.

El Cafetal del Loja CAFE $
(Mariscal Sucre 10-20; snacks US$1; ⏰9am-1pm & 3-7pm Mon-Fri) Follow the scent of freshly roasted coffee at this small cafe with a courtyard in back.

Bapu Shawarma MIDDLE EASTERN
(cnr Larga & Benigno Malo; mains US$3) Piping hot shawarma sandwiches served in a hurry.

Drinking & Entertainment

Outside of Thursday to Saturday nights, Cuenca is pretty sedate. You'll find the densest collection of bars along Calle Larga and nearby Vásquez and Hermano Miguel.

La Compañía BREWERY
(cnr Borrero & Vásquez) Cuenca's first microbrewery caters to a young rocker crowd and offers up decent hand-crafted stouts, Irish reds and golden brews.

Wunderbar BAR
(Escalinata 3-43; ⏲11am-1am Mon-Fri, 3pm-1am Sat) This Austrian-owned place above the river has classic publike ambience, a sizable menu and outdoor seating in warm weather.

Café Eucalyptus BAR
(Gran Colombia 9-41; small plates US$3-6; ⏲5pm-midnight Mon-Sat) Better for drinks than food, this spacious, atmospheric pub has live music some nights.

Shopping

Cemuart HANDICRAFTS
(Centro Municipal Artesanal; Torres) The best place for browsing for handicrafts is Cemuart, which houses dozens of crafts stalls.

Information

Banco de Guayaquil (Mariscal Sucre near Borrero) Bank with ATM.

Banco del Pichincha (cnr Solano & 12 de Abril) Bank with ATM.

Clínica Santa Inés (☎281-7888; Daniel Córdova 2-113) Some English-speaking staff on hand.

Post office (cnr Gran Colombia & Borrero)

Tourist office (iTur; ☎282-1035; Mariscal Sucre at Luís Cordero; ⏲8am-8pm Mon-Fri, 8:30am-1:30pm Sat) Helpful; English spoken.

Getting There & Away

Air

Cuenca's **Aeropuerto Mariscal Lamar** (Av España) is 2km from downtown. **TAME** (☎288-9581, 288-9097; www.tame.com.ec; Astudillo 2-22, Downtown; ⏲8:30am-1pm & 2-6:30pm Mon-Fri, 9:30am-12:30pm Sat) and **Aerogal** (☎410-3104; www.aerogal.com.ec; Aguilar near Solano; ⏲8:30am-1pm & 2-6:30pm Mon-Fri, 9:30am-12:30pm Sat) fly daily to Quito (US$115) and Guayaquil (US$110).

Bus

Cuenca has two major bus stations. The majority of buses leave from **Terminal Terrestre** (Av España), 1.5km northeast of the center. Buses to Guayaquil (US$8) go either via Parque Nacional Cajas (3½ hours) or Cañar (5½ hours). There are regular departures to Quito (US$10, 10 to 12 hours). Several buses go to Machala (US$5.50, four hours); a few continue on to Huaquillas (US$7, seven hours). Buses go regularly to Alausí (US$5, four hours). Several buses a day head to Loja (US$7.50, 5½ hours), Macas (US$8.50, eight hours via Guarumales, 10 hours via Limón) and other Oriente towns. Buses for Gualaceo (80¢, one hour) leave every 30 minutes.

Some buses (including those to Parque Nacional Cajas) leave from Terminal Sur, 2.5km west of the center.

Getting Around

Cuenca is very walkable. A taxi to or from the bus terminal or airport costs about US$2. Buses depart regularly to downtown (25¢) from the front of the Terminal Terrestre bus station.

Around Cuenca

☎07

From small indigenous villages to hot springs and hiking, there's ample opportunity for excursions from Cuenca.

INGAPIRCA

The most important Inca site in Ecuador, Ingapirca was built toward the end of the 15th century during the Inca expansion into present-day Ecuador. The **site** (admission with guided tour US$6; ⏲8am-6pm), 50km north of Cuenca, was built with the same mortarless, polished-stone technique used by the Inca in Peru. Although less impressive than sites in Peru, it's definitely worth a visit. A guided tour (English available) explains the design and significance of the various ruins.

For an economical visit, catch a direct Transportes Cañar bus (US$2.50, two hours) from Cuenca's bus terminal at 9am and 12:20pm. Buses return to Cuenca at 1pm and 3:45pm. More frequent buses from Cuenca depart half-hourly to El Tambo, where you can catch an onward bus or taxi (US$5) to Ingapirca, 8km further.

GUALACEO, CHORDELEG & SÍGSIG

Seeing these three villages (famous for their Sunday markets) together makes a great day trip from Cuenca. If you start early, you can be back in Cuenca by the afternoon. Gualaceo has the biggest market, with fruit and vegetables, animals and various household goods. Chordeleg's market, 5km away, is smaller and more touristy. Sígsig's market is 25km from Gualaceo and is an excellent place to see the art of panama hat-making.

From Cuenca's bus terminal, buses leave every 30 minutes to Gualaceo (US80¢, one hour), Chordeleg (US$1, one hour) and Sígsig (US$1.25, 1½ hours). You can walk the

DON'T MISS

THE INCA TRAIL TO INGAPIRCA

Though it sees only a fraction of the traffic that the Inca Trail to Machu Picchu gets, the three-day hike to Ingapirca is a memorable trek. Parts of the approximately 40km hike follow the original royal road that linked Cuzco with Quito and Tomebamba (at present-day Cuenca).

The starting point for the hike is the village of **Achupallas**, 23km southeast of Alausí. The route is faint in places and sometimes even nonexistent, so travel with a compass and three 1:50,000 topographical maps – Alausí, Juncal and Cañar – available at Instituto Geográfico Militar in Quito.

To get to Achupallas, take one of the daily trucks from Alausí or, more reliably, hire a taxi-pickup for about US$10 to US$15 one way. Alternatively, south-bound Panamericana buses from Alausí can drop you off at La Moya (also known as Guasuntos), where you can wait for passing trucks headed to Achupallas, 12km up a slim mountain road. You can hire guides in Achupallas for about US$30 per day. Among other operators, Julio Verne (p667) in Riobamba runs trips for about US$250 per person. If you want to go on your own, check out a hiking guide, such as *Ecuador: Climbing and Hiking Guide* by Rob Rachowiecki and Mark Thurber.

5km from Gualaceo to Chordeleg if you don't want to wait for the bus.

PARQUE NACIONAL CAJAS

The stunning, chilly, moorlike *páramo* of Parque Nacional Cajas is famous for its many lakes, great trout fishing and rugged camping and hiking. It's a good day trip from Cuenca (only 30km away). **Camping** (per person US$4) is allowed, and a small *refugio* has eight cots and a kitchen; the latter fills up fast. Hiking solo in Cajas can be dangerous – the abundance of lakes and fog is disorienting. It's best to be finished by 4pm when the fog gets thick. Shorter trails are well marked. Glossy, topographical trail maps are free with admission.

Transporte Occidental buses (US$1.25, one hour) leave from Terminal Sur in Cuenca (2.5km west of the historic center) at 6:15am, 7am, 8am, 10am, noon and in the afternoon. To return to Cuenca, you can flag any passing Cuenca-bound bus. Cuenca tour agencies run day trips for about US$45 per person.

Saraguro

☎07

South of Cuenca the road winds through eerie *páramo* until, after 165km, it reaches Saraguro, which means 'land of corn' in Quichua. Quaint little Saraguro is home to the indigenous Saraguro, the most prosperous indigenous group in the southern highlands. The group originally lived in the Lake Titicaca region of Peru but were forcibly relocated through the Inca empire's system of colonization, known as *mitimaes*.

Today, the Saraguro are readily identifiable by their traditional dress. Both men and women (but especially the women) wear striking flat white felt hats with wide brims that are often spotted on the underside.

The best day to be in Saraguro is Sunday, when the local market draws Saraguros from the surrounding countryside. Sleep at the pretty **Hostal Achik Wasi** (☎220-0058; Intiñan, Barrio La Luz; r per person incl breakfast US$15), 10 minutes out of town, or the central but extremely basic **Residencial Saraguro** (☎220-0286; cnr Loja & Antonio Castro; r per person with/without bathroom US$6/5). For memorable homestays in nearby villages, contact **Operadora de Turismo Comunitario Saraurku** (☎220-0331; www.turismosaraguro.com; 18 de Noviembre & Loja). You'll find tasty meals at indigenous-run **Mamá Cuchara** (Parque Central; mains US$3; ⏰7am-10pm Sun-Fri).

Any Loja-bound bus from Cuenca (US$5, 3½ hours) will drop you off a block from the main plaza. Buses to Loja (US$2, 1½ hours) leave hourly during the day.

Loja

☎07 / POP 185,000

Thanks to its proximity to the Oriente, Loja (elevation 2100m) is blessed with a delightfully temperate climate. The city is famous for its musicians (a result of Loja's important conservatory) and its parks. The town itself is noisy and busling, though its historic center makes for a fine day of exploring. Loja is a good base for visiting nearby Parque Nacional Podocarpus and is the main stop before heading south to Vilcabamba and Peru.

Good views can be had from the **Virgen de Loja Statue** (La Salle). The annual **Fiesta of the Virgen del Cisne** (August 20) is celebrated with huge parades and a produce fair.

Sleeping

Hotel Londres HOSTEL $
(☎256-1936; Sucre 07-51; r without bathroom per person US$6) With creaky wooden floors, big white walls and saggy beds, Hotel Londres is as basic as they come, but it's a tried-and-true traveler favorite.

Hotel Metropolitan HOTEL $
(☎257-0007; 18 de Noviembre 6-41; r per person US$12-15; 📶) The Metropolitan is friendly and comfortable, with hardwood floors, decent beds and cable TV. It's dark, though, so try to score a room with a window.

Eating & Drinking

El Tamal Lojano ECUADORIAN $
(18 de Noviembre 05-12; light items US$1, set lunches US$2; ⏰9am-2pm & 4-8pm Mon-Sat) People flock here for the excellent *quimbolitos, humitas* and *tamales lojanos* (all delicious variations on corn dumplings) as well as *empanadas de verde*.

Casa Sol CAFE $
(24 de Mayo 07-04; snacks US$0.80-1.50; ⏰9am-11pm) Casa Sol serves drinks and traditional snacks at balcony tables overlooking a little park. It's best in the evening.

GETTING TO PERU

Most people buy tickets direct to Piura, Peru, from Loja aboard **Loja International** (☎257-0505, 257-9014). Several buses depart daily from Loja, stop at the border for passengers to take care of exits and entries, and then continue on to Piura. The entire ride takes nine hours and costs US$10. Try to buy your tickets at least a day before you travel. If you want to break the journey from Loja, do so at Catacocha. The Loja–
Piura bus stops in Catacocha and Macará, so you can get on in either town as well.

A lo Mero Mero MEXICAN $
(Sucre 06-22; mains US$4, set lunches US$2; ⏰9:30am-9pm Mon-Sat; 🖉) The Mexican menu here has bulging burritos and hearty enchiladas served in a friendly and colorful dining room.

Casa Tinku BAR
(Lourdes btwn Bolivar & Sucre) Casa Tinku is a spirited little bar with a great vibe. There's usually live music on weekends.

Information

Banco de Guayaquil (Eguiguren near Valdivieso) Bank with ATM.

Clínica San Agustín (☎257-0314; cnr 18 de Noviembre & Azuay) Clinic with a good reputation.

Ministerio del Medio Ambiente (☎258-5927; Sucre 4-35, 3rd fl) Provides information on Parque Nacional Podocarpus.

Post office (cnr Colón & Sucre)

Tourist office (iTur; ☎258-1251; cnr Bolívar & Eguiguren; ⏰8am-1pm & 3-6pm Mon-Fri, 9am-1pm Sat) In the Town Hall.

Getting There & Away

Loja is served by La Toma airport in Catamayo, 30km west of town. **TAME** (☎257-0248; www.tame.com.ec; Av Ortega near 24 de Mayo; ⏰8:30am-1pm & 2:30-6pm Mon-Fri, 9am-1pm Sat) flies to Quito (US$82) daily and to Guayaquil (US$73) on Tuesday, Thursday and Saturday.

Loja's bus terminal is 2km north of town. Several buses a day run to Quito (US$15 to $17, 15 hours), Macará (US$6, six hours), Guayaquil (US$10, nine hours), Machala (US$6, five hours), Zamora (US$2.50, two hours) and Cuenca (US$7, five hours), as well as other destinations.

Vilcabambaturis has fast minibuses to Vilcabamba (US$1.30, one hour). There are also speedier *taxis colectivos* (shared taxis; US$2, 45 minutes), which leave from the **Ruta 11 de Mayo taxi stop** (Av Universitaria), 10 blocks south of Alonso de Mercadillo; ask a local taxi driver to take you.

Zamora

☎07 / POP 15,200

Perspiring peacefully on the tropical banks of the Río Zamora, this easy going jungle town is the best launching pad for exploring the verdant lowlands of Parque Nacional Podocarpus. Although it's geographically part of the Oriente, Zamora (elevation 970m) is closer to Loja by bus (two hours) than to other jungle towns, most of which are quite a long way north. Decent budget hotels in town include **Hotel Chonta Dorada** (☎260-6384; Jaramillo near Amazonas; r per person US$9; P📶) and **Hotel Betania** (☎260-7030; Francisco de Orellana; r per person US$12; 📶). Outside town, bird-watchers should book a cabin in the lovely private reserve of **Copalinga** (☎09-347-7013; www.copalinga.com; Vía al Podocarpus Km 3; cabins per person incl breakfast US$24-55). Meals are also available.

Continuing north through the Oriente by bus, you will find a few basic hotels in the small towns of Gualaquiza (five hours), Limón (about nine hours), Méndez and Sucúa. Macas is approximately 13 to 15 hours away.

Parque Nacional Podocarpus

One of the most biologically rich areas in the country and a wonderful park to explore, Parque Nacional Podocarpus protects habitats at altitudes ranging from 3600m in the *páramo* near Loja to 1000m in the steamy rainforests near Zamora. The topography is wonderfully rugged and complex, and the park is simply bursting with plant and animal life. Parque Nacional Podocarpus' namesake, *Podocarpus*, is Ecuador's only native conifer.

The main entrance to the highland sector of the park is **Cajanuma**, about 10km south of Loja. From here, a track leads 8.5km up to the ranger station and trailheads. The best bet for a day trip is to ride all the way up in a taxi from Loja (about US$10), hike for several hours and walk the 8.5km back to the main road where you can flag a passing bus.

To visit the tropical, lowland sector, head to Zamora and get a taxi (US$4 one way) or walk the 6km dirt road to the **Bombuscaro entrance**, where there is a ranger station, trails, swimming, waterfalls, a **camping area** (admission free) and a small **refugio** (cabins per person US$3) without mattresses. Access from Vilcabamba is possible by horseback.

Vilcabamba

☎07 / POP 4200

Deemed the valley of longevity, Vilcabamba (elevation 1500m) is famous for its long-lived inhabitants. Although few residents celebrate a 100th birthday anymore, most agree that their simple, stress-free lives amid lovely Andean scenery and fresh air are conducive to a long life. Backpackers stop here to get in on the mellowness and to hike, ride horses, enjoy the food, get massages and chill out in Vilcabamba's inexpensive guesthouses. It's also the perfect stopping point en route to or from Peru via Zumba.

Activities

There's great hiking in the area. The most popular hike is up Cerro Mandango (but there have been robberies, so enquire about safety and leave behind valuables before setting out). Most naturalists and horse guides charge about US$35 per day.

Rumi Wilco Nature Preserve HIKING
(admission US$2) For a taste of the region's biodiversity, the scenic 30-hectare Rumi Wilco Nature Preserve has short hiking trails, where over 100 bird species have been sighted.

Caballos Gavilán HORSE RIDING
(☎089-133-2806; gavilanhorse@yahoo.com; Sucre 10-30) Offers affordable, highly recommended horse-riding trips, which can last from four hours to three days.

El Chino BICYCLE RENTAL
(cnr Sucre & Agua de Hierro) Rents mountain bikes for US$2 per hour or US$10 per day.

Sleeping

Hostería y Restaurante Izhcayluma RESORT **$$**
(☎302-5162; www.izhcayluma.com; dm US$10, s/d/tr US$25/35/45, s/d without bathroom US$10/20/28, cabins s/d US$30/45, all incl breakfast; 📶🏊) With sweeping views over the valley, a swimming pool, a flower-filled garden, an excellent restaurant (mains US$5 to $7) and attractive rooms, the Hostería y Restaurante Izhcayluma is a popular destination. Located 2km south of town. Book well ahead.

Rendez-Vous Hostal Guesthouse HOTEL **$**
(☎099-219-1180; www.rendezvousecuador.com; Diego Vaca de la Vega 06-43; dm/s/d/tr US$12/18/28/36; @📶) French-owned Rendez-Vous is a lovely place near the river with immaculate rooms (each has a hammock) that open onto a beautiful garden. Breakfast includes homemade bread.

GETTING TO PERU

About 125km south of Vilcabamba lies the wonderfully remote border crossing known as La Balsa, near the outpost of Zumba. From Vilcabamba (or Loja), it's an all-day journey to San Ignacio, Peru, the best place to spend the night before continuing the journey. **Transportes Nambija** (US$7.50, six hours) and Sur Oriente buses depart several times daily from Loja for Zumba, all stopping in Vilcabamba.

From Zumba, several daily *rancheras* (open-sided trucks) go to the border at La Balsa (US$2, 1½ hours to 2½ hours), where you get your exit stamp. Enquire about conditions on the road between Zumba and La Balsa before setting out. Heavy rains can lead to road closure altogether.

On the other side of the 'international bridge' in Peru there are *taxis colectivos* (shared taxis) to San Ignacio (US$3, 1½ hours), where you can spend the night before heading to Jaén (three hours), on to Bagua Grande (another hour) and then to Chachapoyas (three more hours), the first sizable town. From Jaén you can also travel to Chiclayo, on the Peruvian coast.

At the time of writing new service run by Transportes Nambija was slated to get underway, with buses running direct from Loja to Jaén, Peru. Check at the bus station for the latest update.

Hostal Jardín Escondido HOSTEL $
(☎264-0281; jardinescondido@yahoo.com; Sucre & Agua de Hierro; dm/r per person incl breakfast US$10/15;) Built around a tranquil interior garden with songbirds, all rooms have high ceilings and big bathrooms, and breakfast comes with homemade bread and good coffee.

Rumi-Wilco Ecolodge LODGE $
(www.rumiwilco.com; dm US$7, campsite per person US$3.50, s/d without bathroom from US$12/18) About a 12-minute walk from town, Rumi Wilco has a series of cabins and dorm rooms set within a 30-hectare nature reserve. The setting is lovely though maintenance and cleanliness are sometimes lacking.

Eating & Drinking

Jardín Escondido MEXICAN $$
(Sucre & Agua de Hierro; mains US$5-7; ⌚8am-8:30pm) This little Mexican-owned cafe serves delicious dishes with *mole* (a chocolate-based spicy sauce), rich traditional soups and filling burritos.

Charlito's INTERNATIONAL $$
(Diego Vaca de la Vega; mains US$3-7; ⌚11am-9pm Tue-Sun) The friendliest restaurant in town serves up simple food like burritos, pizza and pasta with a smile. The ingredients are the freshest around.

Terraza Center Restaurant INTERNATIONAL $$
(cnr Diego Vaca de la Vega & Bolívar; mains US$4-8; ⌚9am-9:30pm) Grab a table outside for some serious people-watching at this laid-back eatery on the Central Plaza. Popular dishes include burritos, sandwiches and Asian noodle combos.

Shanta's Bar PIZZERIA $$
(Diego Vaca de la Vega; mains US$6-8; ⌚1:15-9pm) On the road to Río Yambala, Shanta's serves big plates of trout, pizza and frogs' legs in an open-air, rustic setting.

Restaurant Katerine ECUADORIAN $
(Sucre, at Jaramillo; mains US$2.50-4) Head here for cheap and wholesome set lunches (US$2.50).

Getting There & Away

Transportes Loja runs buses every 90 minutes to Loja (US$1, 1½ hours). Shared taxis leave from the bus terminal and take five passengers to Loja (US$2, 45 minutes). Buses leave daily to Zumba (US$6.50, five hours), near the Peruvian border.

THE ORIENTE

Ecuador's slice of the Amazon Basin – aka El Oriente – is one of the country's most thrilling travel destinations. Here you can paddle canoes up to caimans lurking in blackwater lagoons, spot two-toed sloths and howler monkeys, fish for piranhas and hike through some of the wildest plantlife you'll ever lay eyes upon. At night, after quelling your fear of the things outside, you'll be lulled to sleep by a psychedelic symphony of insects and frogs.

This section describes the Oriente from north to south (Zamora and the region's southernmost towns). The northern Oriente sees more travelers, while the region south of Río Pastaza has a real sense of remoteness. Buses from Quito frequently go to Puyo, Tena, Coca and Lago Agrio. Buses from Cuenca go through Limón to Macas. Buses from the southern highlands town of Loja go via Zamora to Limón and on to Macas. From Macas, a road leads to Puyo and the northern Oriente. It's possible, although arduous, to travel down the Río Napo to Peru and the Amazon.

Lago Agrio

☎06 / POP 49,000

Unless you like edgy frontier towns, Lago's main tourist draw is its status as the jumping-off point for the nearby Cuyabeno wildlife reserve. The Sunday morning **market** is visited by the indigenous Cofan people and might be worth a peak. Booking a tour to Cuyabeno from Lago can be difficult: most people arrive from Quito with a tour already booked, guides show up, and everyone's gone the next morning.

If stuck in town, try **Hotel Selva Real** (☎283-3867; Av Quito 261 near Colombia; s/d with fan US$10/20, with air-con US$15/40; ❄📶) or **Hotel D'Mario** (☎283-0172; www.hoteldmario.com; Av Quito 263; s/d from US$15/22; ❄📶🏊). Both are on the main drag, where you'll find just about everything else. The latter has a popular pizzeria.

Nearby activity of Colombian guerrillas, antirebel paramilitaries and drug smugglers make Lago Agrio an unsafe place. Bars can be sketchy and side streets unsafe, so stick to the main drag. Take a taxi at night.

Getting There & Away

The airport is 5km east of town; taxi fare is US$3. **TAME** (☎283-0113; Orellana near 9 de Octubre) has daily flights to Quito (US$54 to US$63); it's best to book in advance.

The bus terminal is about 2km northwest of the center. Buses head to Quito regularly (US$8, eight hours). There are one or two daily departures, mainly overnight, to Tena (US$7, eight hours), Cuenca, Guayaquil (US$14, 14 hours) and Machala. Buses to Coca aren't usually found in the bus terminal; flag a *ranchera* (open-sided truck; US$3, 2½ hours) on Av Quito in the center – ask locally for where to wait.

Reserva de Producción Faunística Cuyabeno

This beautiful, 6034-sq-km **reserve** (www.reservacuyabeno.org) protects the rainforest home of the Siona, Secoya, Cofan, Quichua and Shuar people. It also conserves the Río Cuyabeno watershed, where rainforest lakes and swamps harbor fascinating aquatic species such as freshwater dolphins, manatees, caiman and anaconda. Monkeys abound, and tapirs, peccaries, agoutis and several cat species have been recorded. The birdlife is abundant. Though there have been numerous oil spills, huge parts of the reserve remain pristine and worth a visit. Most visitors to the reserve arrive via one of the following lodges. The nearest town is Lago Agrio.

Sleeping

Cuyabeno Lodge LODGE **$$$**

(☎02-252-1212; www.cuyabenolodge.com; per person 3 nights US$220-395, 4 nights US$275-475) This recommended place is run by Quito-based **Neotropic Turis** (Map p640; ☎252-1212; www.neotropicturis.com; Pinto E4-360), in close cooperation with the local Siona people. Thatched huts spread out over a hillside offer a bit of privacy, although the cheapest rooms are four-berth dorms with shared facilities. Bilingual naturalist guides get top reviews from guests. Canoes and kayaks are available to paddle around the lake; many guests jump in for a swim.

Nicky Amazon Lodge LODGE **$$**

(☎02-254-6590; www.amazondracaena.com; cabins per person 4/5 nights US$200/240) Run by the Quito-based Dracaena Amazon Rainforest Explorations, Nicky Amazon Lodge offers seven stilted cabins with private bathrooms. Daily expeditions include piranha fishing, wildlife-spotting and a trip to a local community. A canopy tower enhances birdwatching opportunities.

Coca

☎06 / POP 31,000

If you're one of those folks who dig sitting around in tropical heat guzzling beer and watching small-town street life, you'll probably find Coca oddly appealing. Otherwise, it's just a dusty, sweltering oil town and little more than a final stop before boarding an outboard canoe and heading down the mighty Río Napo. It's also a good place to hire a guide for visits to Pañacocha, Cuyabeno and Parque Nacional Yasuní. For organized tours in the Amazon and stays at jungle lodges, see boxed text, p685.

Sleeping

Hotel El Auca HOTEL $$
(☎288-0166; tatiana.wall@yahoo.com; Napo; s/d/ste incl breakfast from US$34/54/90; ❄📶) This fancy establishment on one side of Coca's new city park is the smartest place in town. The good on-site restaurant, Dayuma, can be overrun with tour groups in the evenings.

Hotel San Fermin HOTEL $
(☎288-0802; robertvaca@amazonwildlife.ec; cnr Quito & Bolívar; s/d/ste US$15/25/32, s/d without bathroom US$8/16; ❄@📶) This friendly and well-run place is an excellent deal, with spacious, wood-trimmed rooms. The rooms up top are best.

Hostería La Misión HOTEL $$
(☎288-0260; hlamision@hotmail.com; Camilo de Torrano; s/d US$28/41; ❄📶🏊) This longtime Coca standard has small rooms overlooking the Río Napo. Several pools and a riverside restaurant enhance the value.

Hotel Santa María HOTEL $
(☎288-0097; Rocafuerte; r per person US$8, s/d with air-con US$15/20; ❄) The cheapest acceptable bed in town, but don't expect much.

Eating

La Casa del Maito SEAFOOD $
(Espejo; mains US$4-6; ⊙7am-6pm) Squeeze between the noisy locals for the heavenly house specialty, *maito* (fish cooked in leaves).

WARNING: CUYABENO ROBBERIES

In recent years, there have been several major incidents targeting tourists en route to the Cuyabeno reserve. In 2011 a boatload of some 20 tourists was robbed, while in 2012 five foreign visitors were assaulted and two were kidnapped before their subsequent rescue. Check the latest situation before visiting; until security in the area improves, we don't recommend visiting Cuyabeno.

Matambre STEAKHOUSE $$
(cnr Quito & Espejo; mains US$6-10; ⊙noon-10pm) This open-sided restaurant serves up melt-in-the-mouth cuts of beef in many different styles and is always full of family groups at lunch and dinner.

Cevichería Colorado SEAFOOD $
(Napo; mains US$5-7; ⊙8am-8pm) Head toward the riverside for a bowl of tangy *ceviche* and a cold beer.

Information

Banco del Pinchincha (cnr Bolívar & 9 de Octubre) Bank with ATM.

Tourist information office (☎288-0532; Transportes Fluviales Orellana Bldg, Chimborazo; ⊙8am-noon & 2-6pm Mon-Sat) Helpful office with free internet access.

Getting There & Away

Air

The airport is 2km north of town. **TAME** (☎288-3340, 288-1078; cnr Napo & Roca-fuerte) and **Aerogal** (☎288-1742; www.aerogal.com.ec; Coca airport terminal) fly daily to Quito (US$75).

Boat

Around 7:30am on Sunday, Tuesday, Thursday and Friday, **Coop de Transportes Fluviales Orellana** (☎288-0231, 288-0087; Chimborazo at docks) offers passenger service to Nuevo Rocafuerte (US$15, 10 hours) on the Peruvian border. Another boat returns upriver to Coca (12 to 14 hours) on the same days, departing Nuevo Rocafuerte at 5am. Although there's usually a stop for lunch, you should bring some food and water for the trip. Travelers arriving and departing by river must register their passport at the *capitanía* (harbormaster's office) by the landing dock. If you're on an organized tour, your guide will usually take care of this.

Bus

There are bus offices in town and at the bus terminal, north of town. Several buses a day go to Quito (US$10, nine hours via Loreto, 13 hours via Lago Agrio), Tena (US$7, six hours) and Lago Agrio (US$3, two hours), as well as other jungle towns. Open-sided trucks called *rancheras* or *chivas* leave from the terminal for various destinations between Coca and Lago Agrio, and to Río Tiputini to the south.

Nuevo Rocafuerte

☎06

A distant dot on the map for most, Nuevo Rocafuerte lies five hours downstream from Pañacocha (eight to 10 hours from Coca),

GETTING TO PERU

Exit and entry formalities in Ecuador are handled in Nuevo Rocafuerte; in Peru, try your best to settle them in Pantoja, with Iquitos as backup. The official border crossing is at Pantoja, a short ride from Nuevo Rocafuerte. Boats from Nuevo Rocafuerte charge US$50 to US$80 per boat to Pantoja. Timing is the key, which is really just a matter of luck: about three cargo boats a month travel from Pantoja to Iquitos (a four- to six-day trip); they depart when they have enough cargo to justify the trip. A hammock and plenty of water (plus water-purification tablets), in addition to food, are recommended; food on the boats can be awful. Be warned that conditions can be rough: there may only be one bathroom, absurdly crowded conditions and lots of livestock on board.

completing a seriously arduous journey to the Peruvian border. There are several lodging options, the best of which is **Hotel Chimborazo** (233-2109; r per person US$5) with clean, wood-paneled rooms.

If you are continuing to Peru, you'll need patience and a high tolerance for squalor while traveling by cargo boat. Bring adequate supplies of water-purification tablets, insect repellent and food. For less hassle, some operators in Coca offer jungle tours which end in Iquitos, Peru. See below for more information on getting to Peru.

Parque Nacional Yasuní

Ecuador's largest mainland **park** (admission US$2, parrot clay lick US$20) is a massive 9620-sq-km swath of wetlands, marshes, swamps, lakes, rivers and tropical rainforest. It contains a variety of rainforest habitats, wildlife and a few Huaorani communities. Unfortunately, poaching and (increasingly) oil exploration are damaging the park.

Visiting the park independently is difficult, but operators in Coca and Quito offer tours. Recommended independent guides include Jarol Fernando Vaca (p685), a Quito-based naturalist and butterfly specialist. Bataburo Lodge (p685) and Napo Wildlife Center (p685) are also located in the park.

Tena

06 / POP 28,000

Ecuador's de facto whitewater-rafting capital (elevation 518m) sits at the confluence of two lovely rivers, Río Tena and Río Pano, and draws paddlers from all over the world. It's an attractive, relaxed town where kayaks lie around hotel-room entrances and boaters hang out in pizza joints, rapping about their day on the rapids. Rafting tours, which offers an adrenaline rush amid stunning jungle and cloud-forest scenery, are easily arranged. Depending on difficulty, day trips run US$50 to US$75 per person. Several operators offer interesting jungle trips.

Sights & Activities

Parque Amazónico ZOO

(btwn Ríos Pano & Tena; admission US$2; 8am-5pm) Stroll over a small bridge to Parque Amazónico, a 27-hectare island with a self-guided trail passing labeled local plants and animal enclosures.

River People RAFTING

(288-8384; www.riverpeoplerafting.com; cnr Calles 15 de Noviembre & 9 de Octubre) British-operated River People is a top-notch outfitter that consistently receives positive reviews for its professionalism and attention to safety. Popular runs include a trip along the class IV Misahaullli (US$75 per person) and the class III Rio Napo (US$55 per person).

Ríos Ecuador RAFTING

(288-6727; www.riosecuador.com; Tarqui) Long in the business, Ríos offers rafting trips for all tastes. Its most popular is a US$65 day trip down a 25km stretch of the upper Napo (class III).

AguaXtreme RAFTING

(288-8746; www.axtours.com; Orellana) This operator, based on the riverfront in Tena, offers rafting trips as well as horse-riding, caving, kayaking and biking trips.

Tours

Ricancie TOUR

(Indigenous Network of Upper Napo Communities for Cultural Coexistence & Ecotourism; 284-6262; www.ricancie.nativeweb.org; Av Chofer near Pullurcu; 8am-6pm) Nine

EXPERIENCING THE AMAZON

Organized tours and jungle lodges help you get close to an incredible array of wildlife. Some outfits are also run by the indigenous, and include visits to local communities.

Quito is generally the best place to arrange a jungle trip. Unless otherwise mentioned, these sites are all accessible from Coca.

Tours

Otobo's Amazon Safari (www.rainforestcamping.com) Native Huaorani Otobo and his family operate Otobo's Amazon Safari, a remote site on the Río Cononaco with platform tents and a thatched-roof lodge. Visitors can hike around the Parque Nacional Yasuni with a native English-speaking guide, visit lagoons and a local village. The site can be reached by small plane from Puyo or two-day bus/motorized canoe journey from Coca.

Jarol Fernando Vaca (☎02-227-1094; shiripuno2004@yahoo.com) A Quito-based naturalist and butterfly specialist who can take visitors into the Shiripuno area and is authorized by Huaorani to guide in their territory. He also runs the **Shiripuno Lodge** (www.shiripunolodge.com), located 75km south of Coca.

Luis Duarte (☎288-2285; cocaselva@hotmail.com) Organizes customized tours, including river passage to Peru or stays with Huaorani families. Find him at La Casa del Maito (p682).

Zábalo This small Cofán community on Rio Aguarico is a seven-hour canoe ride from Lago Agrio. Tours can be arranged through **Randy Borman** (☎02-247-0946; randy@cofan.org), an English-speaking guide who's one of the leaders of the Cofán Federation.

Sleeping

Bataburo Lodge (☎02-250-5600; www.kempery.com) Located on the edge of Huaorani territory, about nine hours from Coca by boat and bus. Canoes motor into the remote Ríos Tiguino and Cononaco and tours combine wildlife-viewing with cultural visits.

Quichua communities have joined to improve life for their 200 families through ecotourism. They organize adventure tours, bird- and animal-watching, demonstrations of healing plants, handicrafts and cooking for US$45 per day.

Agency Limoncocha TOUR
(☎284-6303; limoncocha.tripod.com; Sangay 533) Run from **Hostal Limoncocha** (☎284-6303; limoncocha@andinanet.net; Av De Chofer; r per person US$8; @☎), this agency offers tours to nearby jungle and indigenous villages for US$40 to US$55 per day, as well as rafting trips.

Gareno Lodge TOUR
(☎09-9859-2388, 09-9561-2225; www.garenolodgehuao.com; Rueda) Arranges visits to Huaorani territory in rainforest 77km east of Tena. Wildlife-watching, visits to Huaroni communities and overnights in the jungle can all be arranged. Prices per person including lodging, food and guides start at about US$55 per day.

Sleeping

Brisa del Río GUESTHOUSE **$$**
(☎288-6444; Orellana; r per person US$15, without bathroom US$9; ❄☎) Friendly owners and spacious rooms with fans have made this riverfront *hostal* a popular choice. Shared bathrooms are clean. The thatch-roof outdoor kitchen/eating area is a nice feature.

Hostal La Posada GUESTHOUSE **$**
(☎288-7897; Rueda 280; s/d US$12/20; ☎) This great-value family-run place offers an array of simple fan-cooled rooms right on the riverside. Four rooms have river views, and a pool is in the works.

Hostal Austria GUESTHOUSE **$**
(☎288-7205; Tarqui; s/d US$12/20; ❄☎) This large gated house has clipped shrubbery and Adirondack chairs. Recommended for its bright, high-ceilinged rooms.

Hostal Los Yutzos HOTEL **$$**
(☎288-6717; www.uchutican.com/yutzos; Rueda 190; s/d incl breakfast US$24/40, with air-con US$37/49; ❄☎) A riverside gem with spa-

La Selva Jungle Lodge (☎02-255-0995, 02-254-5425; www.laselvajunglelodge.com; cabins per person full board 3/4 nights US$948/729) With more than 500 bird species, La Selva is a major attraction for bird-watching. A 43m-high canopy platform affords even better viewing. Cabins are set near the shores of Laguna Garzacocha. Swimming and canoeing are also both possible on the lake. Tours are most easily arranged through the organization's headquarters in Quito.

Napo Wildlife Center (NWC; ☎02-600-5893; www.napowildlifecenter.com; s/d full board 3 nights US$1230/1640, 4 nights US$1523/2030; @) As the only lodge within the boundaries of Parque Nacional Yasuní, the highly rated Napo Wildlife Center offers a pristine yet luxurious setting with unparalleled access to wildlife. This ecotourism project is 100% owned by Añangu's Quichua community, which makes up almost the entire lodge staff.

Yarina Lodge (☎02-250-3225, 02-250-4037; www.yarinalodge.com; cabins per person full board 2/3/4 nights US$270/360/450) Roughly an hour downstream from Coca, Yarina has 26 bamboo, thatched-roofed *cabañas* (cabins). Yarina is geared toward budget travelers and doesn't feel as remote as those camps further downstream, but it provides good services and has enthusiastic and professional guides.

Sani Lodge (☎02-323-7139; www.sanilodge.com; per person full board 3 nights s/d/tent US$924/627/396, 4 nights US$1166/814/506;) Owned by the local Sani community, Sani Lodge is one of the lower-priced options available, but unlike other economy lodges it's located very deep in the rainforest and enjoys one of the most beautiful locations of any lodge in Ecuador.

Sacha Lodge (☎02-256-6090; www.sachalodge.com; s/d full board 3 nights US$1185/1580, 4 nights US$1485/1980; @) Enjoying a truly spectacular setting on an inland lake a short hike and canoe ride from the Río Napo, Sacha Lodge is one of Ecuador's best jungle lodges. The lodge's showpiece is a massive metal canopy that stretches between three platforms, 60m off the ground.

cious and attractive rooms, a relaxing balcony with wooden loungers and a lush garden.

Eating & Drinking

For the adventurous, grills by the pedestrian bridge cook up sausages, chicken and *guanta* (a jungle rodent). There's also cold beer and riverside seating.

Café Tortuga INTERNATIONAL **$**
(Orellana; snacks US$1.50-5; ⏲7:30am-9pm Tue-Sat, to 12.30pm Sun & Mon;) The Swiss-run cafe on the riverfront is a traveler favorite, serving sandwiches, fresh juices, crepes, coffees, breakfast and more.

Bella Selva PIZZA **$**
(Orellana; small/medium/large pizza from US$5/8/11; ⏲11am-11pm) Open-sided riverfront pizza parlor with decent cheese-laden pizzas.

Chuquitos ECUADORIAN
(main plaza; mains US$5-8) An old favorite for its waterside terrace and varied menu, including fish.

Marquis Grille STEAKHOUSE **$$$**
(☎288-6513; Amazonas 251 near Olmedo; mains US$9-12; ⏲noon-10pm Mon-Sat) This is the most formal restaurant for miles, with a menu of Chilean wines, steamed tilapia and grilled steaks.

Information

Tourism office (☎288-8046; Rueda; ⏲7am-5pm Mon-Fri) Stop here to find out about the wealth of indigenous-run *turismo comunitario* lodging options available in the area – think simple rustic cabins set amid rainforest. Some staff members speak basic English.

Banco del Austro (15 de Noviembre) Traveler's checks; ATM.

Police station (☎288-6101; main plaza)

Getting There & Away

The bus terminal is less than 1km south of the main plaza. Several buses a day head for Quito (US$6, five hours), Lago Agrio (US$7, eight hours), Coca (US$7, six hours), Baños (US$4, five hours) and other places. Buses for Misahuallí (US$1, one hour) depart hourly from in front of the terminal.

Misahuallí

06

One of the Oriente's sleepiest jungle towns, Misahuallí sits swathed in greenery at the junction of two major rivers. The town has popular sandy beaches and a famous cadre of monkeys adept at swiping sunglasses and cameras from visitors. While wildlife-watching isn't the draw here, there are lovely walks to be had, and a variety of jungle birds, tropical flowers, army ants, dazzling butterflies and other insects can be seen.

There's no bank; get cash before arriving.

Activities

The dirt roads around Misahuallí make for relaxing walks to outlying villages. You can also visit the nearby **Las Latas waterfall** for swimming and picnics. To get there, take a Misahuallí–Puerto Napo bus and ask the driver to drop you off at Río Latas, about 20 minutes from Misahuallí; ask for *el camino a las cascadas* (the trail to the falls). Follow the river upstream to the falls, about 30 minutes' walk up the river.

Tours

If you're hoping to see any of the wildlife, make sure you're venturing well away from Misahuallí, and be sure to hire an experienced and licensed guide (not the touts in the main plaza). Tours range from one day to 10 days and prices usually include the guide, food, water, accommodations (which range from jungle camping to rustic cabins) and rubber boots. Rates run from US$35 to US$60 per person per day.

The following operators, all found near the main square, are recommended:

Teorumi ECOTOUR
(289-0313; www.teorumi.com; tours per day US$60) Working with local indigenous communities, Teorumi is a good choice for anyone interested in native culture as well as wildlife. Tours can be tailored to fit your interests, though most feature bird-watching, fishing, medicinal plant demonstrations and jungle hikes.

Selva Verde ECOTOUR
(289-0165; www.selvaverde-misahualli.com; tours per day US$40-60) Luís Zapata, an English-speaking guide with years of experience in the region, specializes in river trips and visits to indigenous villages.

Runawa Tours ECOTOUR
(289-0031; www.misahualliamazon.com; tours per day from US$35) Offers nocturnal jungle tours, tubing and rafting trips, bird-watching and river tours.

Sleeping & Eating

Don't miss *maitos* (whole tilapia or chicken wrapped in a leaf and char-grilled), which are fired up by the plaza around lunchtime from Friday to Sunday.

France-Amazonia GUESTHOUSE $$
(289-0009; www.france-amazonia.com; Av Principal; r per person incl breakfast US$18-30;) On the road into town (400m from the plaza), you'll find shady thatched huts surrounding a sparkling pool, an enticing bar (for guests) and sandy fire pit. French-owned.

Hostal Shaw HOSTEL $
(289-0163; r per person US$8) This *hostal* has simple rooms with fans and private bathrooms with hot water. There's a cafe downstairs. On the main plaza.

Yana Watsaru HOSTEL $
(289-0158; Calle Napo; r per person US$8) A short stroll from the plaza, Yana Watsaru has small, all-wooden rooms with fans and tiny bathrooms. There's an open-sided deck and guests can use the kitchen.

Hotel El Paisano GUESTHOUSE $$
(289-0027; hotelelpaisano@yahoo.com; Rivadeneyra; s/d/tr incl breakfast US$19/28/42; P@) Off the plaza, this backpacker haunt has cement rooms, tiny bathrooms, hot water, fans and mosquito nets. Vegetarian dishes at the open-air restaurant.

Comunidad de Shiripuno CABINA $
(http://shiripuno.free.fr; cabins per person US$10) Run by an indigenous women's association, Shiripuno consists of simple thatch-roof cabins, some with views overlooking jungle and river. Meals available. It's just outside of Misahuallí, reachable by motorized canoe (US$2) from the public dock or taxi (US$1.50) and a 500m walk. You can reserve through Teorumi.

Doña Carmita ECUADORIAN $
(mains US$2.75-7) On the main square, this local spot serves up filling set lunches (*almuerzos*) and dinners (*meriendas*) for under US$3.

Getting There & Away

Buses to Tena (US$1, one hour) leave hourly from the plaza.

Jatun Sacha Biological Reserve

On the southern bank of the Río Napo, about 7km east of Misahuallí, **Jatun Sacha Biological Reserve** (02-331-8156, 09-9490-8265; admission US$6) is a biological station and rainforest reserve with hiking trails and a narrow 30m tower affording views over the rainforest. Lodging is mostly for volunteers, though if space is available, you can stay in one of the rustic **cabins** (per person per day incl 3 meals US$30).

To get there, take an Ahuano or Santa Rosa bus from Tena and ask the driver to drop you off at the entrance. It's about 27km east of Tena.

Puyo

03 / POP 36,000

A lazy river slinks through this concrete outpost, which is part mellow jungle town and part commercial, government hub. The streets are filled with missionaries, vendors pushing street carts and indigenous people from far-flung corners of the Amazon. Dense green jungle flourishes around the town's edges while jagged snowcapped mountains rise in the distance. It makes a good starting point for reaching indigenous villages.

Marín and Atahualpa are the principal downtown streets with the most services.

Sights & Activities

Parque Omaere PARK
(www.fundacionomaere.org; admission US$3; 9am-5pm Tue-Sun) North of downtown, a bridge crossing the Río Puyo leads to this ethnobotanical park, where you can learn about rainforest plants and indigenous traditions on guided one- or two-hour tours. A pleasant **trail** (called the *paseo turístico*) continues past Omaere for 1.7km along the river to the Puyo–Tena road, where you can flag a bus back to town every 20 minutes or return along the trail.

Jardín Botáncio las Orquídeas GARDENS
(288-4855; admission US$5; 8am-6pm) Visitors rave about the Jardín Botánico Las Orquídeas, located 15 minutes south from Puyo on the road to Macas. Enthusiastic owner Omar Taeyu guides visitors through hills of lush foliage and fishponds to see gorgeous plants and countless rare orchids. Call ahead.

Tours

Papangu Tours TOUR
(288-7684; www.papangutours.org; cnr Calle 27 de Febrero & Sucre; tours per day from US$42) The recommended Papangu Tours is a unique Quichua-run tour operator specializing in community tourism. Most popular are the three-day trips to Sarayaku or Hola Vida (Quichua communities) or Cueva de los Tayos (Shuar).

Selvavida TOUR
(288-9729; www.selvavidatravel.com; Marin near Villamil) Offers a wide range of multi-day tours to indigenous communities (including trips to visit remote Huaorani communities in Parque Nacional Yasuní). Also **offers** adventure activities – rafting, canyoning, zip-lining.

Sleeping

El Jardín GUESTHOUSE $$
(288-7770; Paseo Turístico, Barrio Obrero; r per person incl breakfast US$38; P @) Puyo's most charming accommodation is just across the footbridge by the entrance to the Parque Omaere, some way from the center of town. It has attractive, wood-panelled rooms set around a verdant garden.

Hostal del Río GUESTHOUSE $
(288-6090; cnr Loja & Cañar; r per person incl breakfast US$13) On the way out of the town center (heading toward El Jardín), this slightly upscale place has clean, comfortable rooms. The best are upstairs with balconies and access to a roof terrace.

Hostal Mexico HOTEL $
(288-5668; btwn Ortiz & Calle 24 de Mayo; r per person US$12;) A good-value central option. Only some rooms have private bathroom.

Hotel Libertad HOTEL $
(288-3282; cnr Orellana & Manzano; r per person US$7) This tranquil spot has a range of clean, green-hued rooms, some with big windows.

Eating

TOP CHOICE **El Jardín** ECUADORIAN $$
(288-7770; Paseo Turístico, Barrio Obrero; mains US$8-15; noon-4pm & 6-10pm Mon-Sat;) This

recommended spot by the river serves some of the Oriente's best cooking.

El Fariseo INTERNATIONAL $
(Atahualpa; mains US$4-7; ⏲7am-10pm Mon-Fri, 8am-10pm Sat; 📶) Sit streetside for a frothy cappuccino and slice of cake. *Platos fuertes* (mains) include burritos, burgers and steaks.

Pizzeria Buon Giorno PIZZERIA $
(☎288-3841; Orellana near 27 de Febrero; mains US$6-11; ⏲3-11pm) In the town center, this simple place offers freshly made pizzas, lasagna and salads. It also delivers.

Information

Banco del Austro (Atahualpa) Bank with ATM.
Cámara de Turismo (☎288-3681; Marín, Centro Commercial Zuñiga; ⏲8:30am-12:30pm & 3-6pm Mon-Fri) Regional maps and info.

Getting There & Away

The bus terminal is 3km out of town (a taxi should cost US$1). Buses run regularly to Baños (US$2.50, 1½ hours), Quito (US$5, 5½ hours), Macas (US$5, four hours) and Tena (US$2.50, 2½ hours). Services to other towns are also available.

Macas

☎07 / POP 17,000

Macas' slow and steady pace and approachable locals make it a welcoming stop. It's also an excellent launch pad for adventures further afield. Macas is situated above the banks of the wild Río Upano, and there are great views of the river and the Río Upano valley from behind the town's cathedral. On a clear day you can glimpse the often-smoking Volcán Sangay, located some 40km northwest.

Tours

Be aware that the Shuar don't want unguided visitors in their villages. Multiday trips cost US$40 to $75 per day.

Planeta Tours TOUR
(☎270-1328; www.planetaselva.travel; cnr Comín & Soasti; multiday trips per day US$45-75) Offers cultural tours in Shuar territory, waterfall hikes, fishing, whitewater rafting on the Río Upano and canoeing.

Tsuirim Viajes TOUR
(☎270-1681; leosalgado18@hotmail.com; cnr Don Bosco & Sucre; tours per person per day US$30-60) Offering a range of jungle tours, including community visits to the Shuar, shamanic rituals, canyoning, tubing and jungle-trekking.

Sleeping & Eating

The *comedores* (basic cafeterias) on Comín near Soasti sell tasty *ayampacos*, a jungle specialty of meat, chicken or fish grilled in *bijao* leaves.

Hotel La Orquidea GUESTHOUSE $
(☎270-0970; cnr Calle 9 de Octubre & Sucre; r per person with/without hot water US$11/10; 📶) A pleasant, old-fashioned *pensión* (short-term budget accommodations) that's run by a friendly family.

Guayusa Bar La Maravilla ECUADORIAN $
(Soasti near Sucre; mains US$3-6; ⏲4pm-midnight Mon-Sat) This atmospheric eatery serves creative fare and delicious cocktails.

Getting There & Away

TAME (☎270-1162) and **Saereo** (☎270-2764; www.saereo.com) fly several times a week to Quito (US$53 to $79). The bus terminal has several daily departures for Cuenca (US$8.50, eight hours), Guayaquil (US$10, 10 hours) and Riobamba (US$5, five hours). Buses to Puyo (US$7, five hours) leave 10 times daily; some continue to Tena.

PACIFIC COAST & LOWLANDS

Ecuador, land of lively Andean markets, Amazon adventures and… palm-fringed beaches? While not high priority for most travelers, Ecuador's coast offers a mix of surf towns, sleepy fishing villages, whale-watching in the south, and Afro-Ecuadorian culture in the north. Keep in mind the weather: December to May is the rainy season, but also the sunniest; the sun blazes both before and after the afternoon downpour. June through November has mild days (and chilly nights) but it's often overcast.

Getting There & Away

Most places along the coast can be reached from Quito in a day's travel. Key gateways are Esmeraldas in the north (six hours from Quito) and Puerto Lopez (10 hours from Quito or 4½ hours from Guayaqui) in the south. Once on the coast, it's fairly easy to make your way in either direction. For speedier access, catch a flight to Manta.

Esmeraldas

☎06 / POP 154,000

Lively, noisy and notoriously dodgy, Esmeraldas is an important port and home to a major oil refinery. For travelers, it's little more than a necessary stop to make bus connections. If you need to spend the night, **Hotel Central** (☎272-2502; Sucre 9-03; r per person US$17; ❄) on the plaza is a decent option.

The airport is 25km up the road to San Lorenzo; taxi fare is around US$7. **TAME** (☎272-6863; cnr Bolívar & 9 de Octubre), near the plaza, has daily flights to Quito (US$65) and less-frequent services to Guayaquil (US$105).

Buses leave from a new terminal 4km from the city center in the direction of Atacames. Regular departures go to Atacames (US$1, one hour), Quito (US$7.25, six hours), Mompiche (US$3.15, 2½ hours), Bahía de Caráquez (US$9, eight hours) and Guayaquil (US$9.20, nine hours).

Atacames

☎06 / POP 16,000

The raucous beach town of Atacames inspires pure excitement or dread, depending on how you like your beach getaways. For some *serranos* (highlanders), Atacames equals nonstop party, with a wide packed beach, bustling guesthouses and a jumble of thatched-roof bars blaring salsa and reggaeton at all hours of the day.

The beach is unsafe at night, when assaults and rapes have been reported. Robberies have also occurred on isolated sections of the beach between Atacames and Súa.

Buses drop passengers off in the center of town, on the main road from Esmeraldas (get off at the motorized-tricycle stand). The center is on the inland side of the highway, and the beach is reached by a small footbridge over the Río Atacames or by tricycle 'eco-taxi' (US$1). Most of the hotels and bars are along the *malecón* (waterfront promenade).

Sleeping & Eating

Hotel Jennifer HOTEL $

(☎273-1055; near Malecón; s/d without hot water US$10/18, with hot water US$12/25) This simple, straightforward place has clean, Spartan rooms that get a decent amount of light.

Cabañas Los Bohíos CABINS $

(☎272-7478; Los Ostiones; s/d US$10/20) Near the fetid Río Atacames, Los Bohíos offers a mix of clean rooms and small bamboo cabins.

Punto y Como SEAFOOD $

(Malecón; mains US$4-9; ⏲11am-10pm) Crowds pack into this cozy seafood restaurant.

Pizzería da Giulio PIZZERIA $$

(Malecón; mains US$7-10; ⏲5:30pm-midnight Tue-Fri, 10:30am-midnight Sat & Sun) Run by a Sicilian, this restaurant with balcony seating serves tasty thin-crust pizzas.

Getting There & Away

There are regular buses to Esmeraldas (US$1, one hour), as well as south to Súa (30¢, 10 minutes), Same (30¢, 15 minutes) and Muisne (US$1.50, 1½ hours). Transportes Occidentales and Aerotaxi, whose offices are near the highway, both go to Quito daily (US$8, seven hours).

Súa

☎06

This friendly fishing village, 6km west of Atacames, is far more tranquil than its party-town neighbor. The mellow bay is a fine spot for a swim, although early in the morning it's busy with trawlers.

There are fewer lodgings here than in Atacames, but they're also quieter and often better value if you aren't looking for nightlife. All have cold-water bathrooms. **Hotel Chagra Ramos** (☎247-3106; Malecón; r per person US$11) is a friendly, wind-battered classic. **Sol de Súa** (☎247-3121; Malecón; cabins per person US$5) consists of small cabins scattered around a sandy yard.

Same & Tonchigüe

☎06

Same ('*sah*-may') boasts the prettiest beach in the area, a striking 3km-long stretch of palm-fringed coast only lightly touched by development. The village itself, which lies 7km southwest of Súa, is small with only a sprinkling of (pricier) guesthouses and restaurants. Located at the turnoff where Same's main 'street' leaves the coastal road, **Azuca** (☎08-882-9581; azuca2@hotmail.com; Same; r per person US$5) offers good-value wooden rooms and has a decent restaurant (mains US$4 to $6). About 1km south of Same, **El Acantilado** (☎273-3466; www.hosteria

elacantilado.com; s/d/q US$25/50/75;) provides lovely sea views from its clifftop cabins.

About 3km past Same, Tonchigüe is a tiny fishing village whose beach is a continuation of the Same beach. **Playa Escondida** (09-973-3368, 273-3122; www.playaescondida.com.ec; per person low season US$10-15, r high season US$20-36) is 3km west of Tonchigüe and 10km down the road to Punta Galeras. It's an isolated, beautiful spot, run by a Canadian expat. It has a restaurant and a scenic beach cove.

In town, don't miss a seafood feast at **Seaflower Lateneus** (247-0369; Same; mains US$10-25; 8am-midnight), probably the best restaurant on Ecuador's Pacific Coast.

Mompiche

05

Mompiche is a tiny fishing village with a pretty beach, where wide, hard-packed sands stretches for 7km. The surfing here can be excellent. The town itself is just a few sandy lanes, dotted with simple guesthouses and laid-back eateries that cater to a mostly surf and backpacker crowd. A high-end resort (the Decameron) was completed in 2012 and more construction dots the village, but for the moment, Mompiche retains its peaceful, end-of-the-road vibe.

The most popular place to bunk for the night is the seafront **Hostería Gabeal** (09-969-6543; mompiche_gabeal@hotmail.com; camping/r per person US$3/15; @), which is a large complex of bamboo rooms with cold-water bathrooms. You can also camp on the lawn. Decent meals and a beachside bar add to the appeal. About 10 minutes' north of here, up the beach, small German-run **Casa Yarumo** (08-867-2924; www.casayarumo mompiche.com; per person US$15) is a pleasant getaway with several large, nicely designed cabin-style rooms. If you really want to escape the crowds, head to **Cabañas del Mar** (09-998-7072; dm/cabin US$10/30), which has small, seafront thatch-roof cabins with private bathrooms in a palm-shaded setting. It's 2.3km north on the beach.

Good places for a bite include beach-facing **Milicho's** (Malecón; mains US$6-11; 8am-10pm), where you can enjoy a hearty breakfast or filling plates of seafood; the *encocado mixto* (mixed seafood in coconut milk) is a favorite. One street back from the beach, **La Facha** (mains US$5-8; noon-10pm) serves up mouthwatering burgers (including veggie burgers), crispy-crust pizzas, salads and seafood plates. It also rents simple rooms for US$10 per person.

Buses go to and from Esmeraldas several times per day (US$4, 3½ hours), passing Same and Atacames on the way.

Canoa

05 / POP 6200

Surfers, fishermen and sunseekers share this attractive strip of beach – and the village continues to grow. In addition to surfing and beach walks, you can arrange boat trips, go biking in the countryside and visit the **Río Muchacho Organic Farm** (09-147-9849; www.riomuchacho.com; r per person US$30), which offers sustainable-farming classes and accepts volunteers. Surfboard rental is available at many guesthouses as well as along the beach (about US$10 for the day).

Sleeping

Hotel Bambu HOTEL

(261-6370; www.ecuadorexplorer.com/bambu; dm US$10, s/d/cabaña US$15/30/45;) This longtime traveler favorite rents cottagelike rooms on the beach. The grounds are scattered with hammocks, the restaurant is excellent, and the peaceful location (being the last spot on the beach) is ideal for a sunset drink.

Coco Loco GUESTHOUSE $

(09-245-6308; hotalcocoloco@yahoo.com; dm/d US$8/30, without bathroom US$6/20;) The beachfront Coco Loco draws a good mix of a backpackers, with a sand- and palm-filled yard that hosts a lively happy hour and barbecue nights.

Casa Shangri-La GUESTHOUSE $

(09-146-8470; per person US$8;) A few hundred meters north of the center, Shangri-La is a chilled-out surfer spot with nice rooms set around a garden and pool.

La Posada de Daniel GUESTHOUSE $

(09-750-8825; posadadaniel83@hotmail.com; camping per tent incl breakfast US$8, r per person incl breakfast US$17;) A few blocks inland, Daniel's has comfortable, recently renovated rooms overlooking a pool and thatch-roof bar.

La Vista GUESTHOUSE $
(☎09-228-8995; Malecón; s/d US$18/26; 📶) On the beach, La Vista is a slightly more upscale four-story guesthouse with comfortable rooms with hammock-strung balconies.

Eating

Surf Shack INTERNATIONAL $
(Malecón; mains US$5-10; ⊙8am-midnight) The popular seafront bar-restaurant Surf Shack serves up pizzas, burgers and plenty of rum cocktails for a festive, foreign crowd.

Amalur SPANISH $
(mains US$4-8; ⊙noon-9pm) Two blocks inland, the minimalist Basque-owned Amalur offers grilled pork with red peppers, calamari in ink, and tapas plates as well as Ecuadorian seafood favorites (like *encocado*).

Getting There & Away

Buses between Bahía de Caráquez and Esmeraldas will all stop in Canoa.

Bahía de Caráquez

Chalk-colored high-rises, red tile roofs, manicured yards and swept sidewalks give this self-proclaimed 'eco-city' a tidy impression. Today, the town market recycles its waste, organic shrimp farms flourish, and reforestation projects dot the hillside. There are several interesting eco and cultural tours worth checking out, as well as a small beach. Bird-watchers shouldn't miss a visit to **Isla Corazon** (☎302-9316; www.islacorazon.com; admission incl 2-hr guided tour from US$5), where you can take guided tours through mangroves in search of frigate birds, herons, egrets and other species. It's located 7km east of San Vicente, reachable by a bus (US50¢) or taxi (US$5).

Banco de Guayaquil (cnr Bolívar & Riofrío) has an ATM.

Tours

Tours in Bahía are unique. The following operators devote themselves to ecotourism and will show you local environmental projects. Both companies offer day trips to Islas Fragatas in the Chone estuary.

Guacamayo Tours ECOTOUR
(☎269-1412; www.guacamayotours.com; cnr Bolívar & Arenas) Excellent outfit that shows off Bahia's ecotourism projects; also arranges stays at Río Muchacho Organic Farm.

Bahía Dolphin Tours TOUR
(☎269-0257; www.bahiadolphintours.com; Virgílio Ratti 606, Casa Grande Oceanfront Boutique Hotel) Offers visits to its nearby archaeological site.

Sleeping

Coco Bongo HOSTEL
(☎08-544-0978; www.cocobongohostal.com; cnr Intriago & Arenas; dm/d from US$6/25) Overlooking the park, this cheery, yellow Aussie-owned guesthouse makes an excellent base for exploring Bahía and the surrounding area. The rooms are simple but clean and the atmospheric cafe-lounge area on the ground floor is a good spot to meet other travelers.

Centro Vacacional Life CABINS $
(☎269-0496; cnr Octavio Vitteri & Muñoz Dávila; r per person US$15; ❄📶) Six small cabins sit on this gated grassy lot with a playground. Each has cable TV and a kitchenette, and some have hot water.

Hotel La Herradura HOTEL $$
(☎269-0446; Bolívar 202; s/d/ste from US$50/60/100, s/d without air-con or hot water US$25/40; ❄📶) An old Spanish home with antiques and artwork brimming from its nooks.

Eating

Muelle Uno ECUADORIAN $
(Malecón; mains US$4-10) Next to the public dock, this friendly local favorite grills up sizzling plates of meat and seafood.

Arena Bar PIZZERIA $
(Marañón; mains US$4-8; ⊙5pm-midnight) Chow down on pizzas, inventive salads and tasty sandwiches at this easygoing spot.

Puerto Amistad INTERNATIONAL $$
(Malecón Santos; mains US$6-12; ⊙noon-11pm Mon-Sat) An expat favorite, upscale Puerto Amistad serves salads, savory crepes, quesadillas and grilled dishes in an airy waterside setting.

Getting There & Away

A new bridge from San Vicente across the Río Chone links Bahía with the north coast, making it an easy stop when coming from Canoa. The bus terminal is 4km east of the centre. From there, you'll find regular services to Manta (US$3, three hours, three daily), Quito (US$7 to $10, eight hours, four daily), Guayaquil (US$7, six hours, seven daily) and Canoa (US$1, 45 minutes).

If you're heading to Canoa, you can also take the ferry from the main dock across to San Vicente, then catch a blue-and-white local bus direct to Canoa (50¢, every 30 minutes). Alternatively, a taxi to Canoa from Bahía costs around US$8.

Montecristi

05

Montecristi is known throughout the world for producing the finest straw hat on the planet – the mistakenly labeled **panama hat**. In Ecuador they're called *sombreros de paja toquilla* (*toquilla* straw is a fine fibrous straw endemic to the region). Countless places in town sell hats, but for a proper *super-fino* (the finest, most tightly woven hat of all), you'll need to visit the shop and home of **José Chávez Franco** (Rocafuerte 386; 7am-7pm), behind the church. You can pick up a beauty for less than US$100, cheaper than just about anywhere else in the world. Montecristi is 30 minutes by bus from Manta (50¢). Cuenca is another great place to buy these hats.

Manta

05 / POP 218,000

The largest city in the province, Manta is a bustling and prosperous port town, graced with high-rises and a few urban beaches that draw mostly national tourists. As an important center for the fishing and tuna industries, Manta is not a huge draw for foreign travelers. It does have a lively nightlife scene, and you may pass through if you're visiting the handicraft town of Montecristi.

A fetid inlet divides the town into Manta (west side) and Tarqui (east side); the two sides are joined by a vehicle bridge. Manta has the main offices, shopping areas and bus terminal, while Tarqui has cheaper hotels.

Sights

Playa Murciélago BEACH
A couple of kilometers northwest of downtown, Playa Murciélago is the town's most popular beach, backed by snack bars and restaurants and umbrella rental spots.

Playa Tarqui BEACH
This beach is interesting in the early morning when fisherfolk haul their catches ashore in front of the boat-building area.

Museo del Banco Central MUSEUM
(Malecón de Manta near Calle 20; admission US$1; 9am-5pm Tue-Sat, 11am-3pm Sun) Here you'll find a showcase of artifacts from pre-Columbian Manta culture, as well as quirky fishing memorabilia.

Sleeping

The best eating and nightlife options are out near Playa Murciélago. Avoid staying in Tarqui, which is not very safe.

Manakin GUESTHOUSE $$
(262-0413; Calle 17 & Av 21; s/d/tr incl breakfast US$40/50/65;) Near the heart of all the nightlife, Manakin is a converted one-story house with a pleasant laid-back vibe. Narrow, well-ordered rooms are nicely furnished, and the house offers fine places to unwind, including the front patio.

Antares Hostal HOSTEL $$
(262-6493; www.hostal-antares.com; cnr Calle 29 & Av Flavio Reyes; s/d US$40/65;) Located in a peaceful residential neighborhood above Playa Murciélago, Antares offers trim and cheerfully painted rooms with wood details.

Leo Hotel HOTEL $
(262-3159; Av 24 de Mayo; s/d US$15/25;) Across from the bus station, Leo offers small, clean rooms, some of which lack windows.

Eating & Drinking

The epicenter of Manta's nightlife is the intersection of Av Flavio Reyes and Calle 20, uphill from Playa Murciélago.

Trosky Burguer BURGERS $
(cnr Av 18 & Flavio Reyes; mains US$3-7; 6pm-3am Tue-Sun) This popular surfer-run snack spot serves juicy burgers amid rock and reef sounds. Friendly English-speaking owner.

Beachcomber STEAKHOUSE $
(cnr Calle 20 & Flavio Reyes; mains US$4-10; 6pm-midnight) Popular Beachcomber is a favorite for its grilled meats. Dine in the lush backyard garden or on the open-sided front porch.

Trovador Café CAFE $
(Av 3 & Calle 10; mains US$2-5; 8am-8pm Mon-Sat) On a pleasant pedestrian lane set back just a short distance from the Malecón, this place offers frothy cappuccinos, sandwiches and inexpensive lunch plates. There's outdoor seating.

Information

Banco del Pacífico ATM (cnr Av 107 & Calle 103, Tarqui)

Banco del Pichincha (cnr Av 2 & Calle 11, Manta) Has an ATM.

Municipal tourist office (☎262-2944; Av 3 N10-34; ⏲8am-12:30pm & 2:30-5pm Mon-Fri) Friendly office.

Post Office (Calle 8)

Getting There & Away

The **airport** (☎262-1580) is some 3km east of Tarqui; a taxi costs about US$2. **TAME** (☎262-2006; Malecón de Manta) flies daily to Quito (US$70).

Frequent buses depart from the **terminal**, conveniently in Manta, one block off the *malecón*, to Montecristi (50¢, 15 minutes), Guayaquil (US$5, four hours), Quito (US$10, nine hours) and Bahía de Caráquez (US$3, 2½ hours); and to Puerto López (US$3, 2½ hours) and Montañita (US$5.50, 3½ hours). Coactur goes to Canoa regularly (US$4, four hours).

Parque Nacional Machalilla

☎05

Preserving isolated beaches, coral formations, two offshore islands, tropical dry forest, coastal cloud forest, archaeological sites and 20,000 hectares of ocean, Ecuador's only coastal national park is a marvelous and unique destination. The tropical dry forest seen here used to stretch along much of the Pacific Coast of both Central and South America, but sadly it has been whacked nearly into extinction. Plants in the park include cacti, various figs and the giant kapok tree. Howler monkeys, anteaters and an estimated 200 bird species inhabit the forest interior, while the coastal edges are home to frigate birds, pelicans and boobies, some of which nest in colonies on the offshore islands.

The turnoff to the lovely beach of **Los Frailes** is about 10km north of Puerto López, just before the town of Machalilla. Framed by dramatic headlands, the picturesque beach is one of Ecuador's loveliest. Buses stop near the ranger station, from where a 3km road and a 4km trail lead to the beach. Seabirds are plentiful and camping is allowed.

The barren, sun-charred **Isla de la Plata**, an island 40km northwest of Puerto López, is a highlight of the park, especially from mid-June to September when humpback whales mate offshore and sightings from tour boats (arranged in Puerto López) are practically guaranteed. The island itself hosts nesting seabird colonies, and a guided hike is usually included in the tour. Fast boats make the trip in about an hour.

From the mainland park entrance, 6km north of Puerto López, a dirt road goes 5km to **Agua Blanca** (admission US$5), a small indigenous village. Admission includes a visit to the small intriguing **archaeological museum** (⏲8am-6pm), followed by a walk through the community to a sulfur pool where you can take a dip and cover yourself with therapeutic mud if so inclined. You can also arrange longer hiking and horse treks, including overnight trips.

Puerto López

☎05 / POP 14,000

Chipped blue fishing boats bob on a beautiful fishhook bay, and cheerful hotels, a smattering of expats, slow smiles, happy cafes and a dirt-road pace of life make it tough to leave. With its unbeatable location near Parque Nacional Machalilla, Puerto López makes for an obligatory stop on any coastal jaunt.

There are internet cafes around town, and **Banco de Pichincha** (Malecón) also has an ATM.

Tours

Numerous outfits offer trips to Isla de la Plata and/or tours of the mainland area of the park. Most agencies charge US$40 to US$45 per person (plus a US$1 municipal entrance fee) for a trip to the island and seasonal whale-watching. Licensed companies have better boats and more equipment (such as life jackets, radio and backup) than the unlicensed guides who offer the trip for nearly half the price.

Tour companies with good reputations include **Machalilla Tours** (☎230-0234; www.machalillatours.org; Malecón Julio Izurieta), which can organize island tours, horse-riding trips, kayaking, hang-gliding and guided rainforest hikes.

For diving, try **Exploramar Diving** (☎230-0123; www.exploradiving.com; Malecón Julio Izurieta). Surfing and diving packages are offered by **Hostal Yemayá** (☎08-864-6118; www.hostalyemaya.com; Gral Córdova; per person US$10; 📶).

Manta

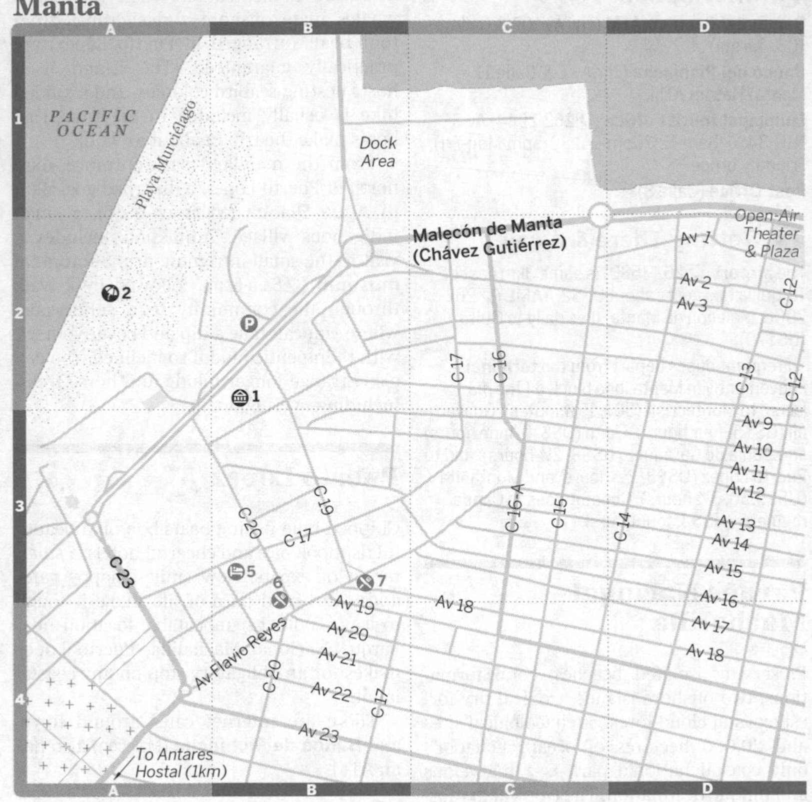

Manta	
Sights	
1 Museo del Banco Central	B2
2 Playa Murciélago	A2
3 Playa Tarqui	G1
Sleeping	
4 Leo Hotel	F3
5 Manakin	B3
Eating	
6 Beachcomber	B3
7 Trosky Burguer	B3
8 Trovador Café	E2

Sleeping

TOP CHOICE **Hostería Mandála** CABINS $$
(☎230-0181;www.hosteriamandala.info;s/dUS$31/44; @☎) At the northern end of the beachfront, this beautiful place has a handful of ecologically minded cabins set in a labyrinthine garden. The lodge has a bar and restaurant that serves good breakfasts, Italian fare and local seafood.

Hostal Sol Inn HOSTEL $
(☎230-0248; www.hostalsolinn.com; Juan Montalvo near Eloy Alfaro; camping per person US$5, dm US$8, r per person with/without bathroom US$14/10; ❄☎) This mellow backpacker retreat has compact wood-and-bamboo rooms, each with front-porch hammocks; there's an outdoor kitchen and living area.

Hostería Itapoá HOSTEL $
(☎255-1569; itapoa_25@hotmail.com; Malecón Julio Izurieta; cabins per person incl breakfast US$13) This hospitable place is an affordable retreat of thatched-roof *cabañas* set around a blooming garden bordered by hammocks. There are mountain bikes for hire (and bike tours), and an English-speaking biologist runs tours out of here.

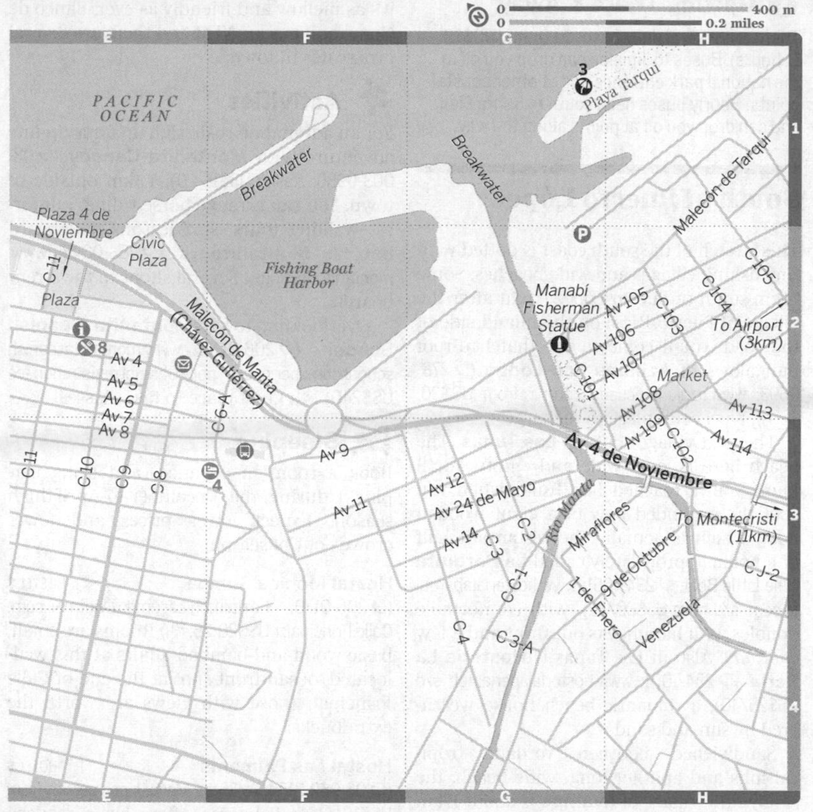

Hostal Monte Libano GUESTHOUSE $
(☎230-0231; hostalmontelibano@yahoo.com; r per person with/without bathroom from US$15/8) At the south end of the beach, Monte Libano has simple, clean rooms and a friendly, familial ambience. There's a guest kitchen and lounge, and a relaxing deck on the upper floor. One much-requested room has a treehouselike design.

Eating

Along the *malecón* you'll find traditional seafood restaurants with patio dining. **Restaurant Carmita** (Malecón; mains US$6-12) is among the most popular.

Patacon Pisa'o COLOMBIAN $
(Gral Córdova; mains US$5-8; 📶) This tiny outdoor spot serves delicious Colombian specialties including its namesake: large, thin, crisply fried plantains, served with your choice of topping (pork, beef, beans or six other options).

Casa Vecchia ITALIAN
(mains US$8-10; ⏲4-10pm Tue-Sun) Toward the north end of the beachfront, Casa Vecchia whips up satisfying thin-crust pizzas. Dine inside or in the small front garden.

Bellitalia ITALIAN
(Malecón; mains US$8-12; ⏲6-10pm Mon-Sat) In an elegant new space on the Malecón, Bellitalia prepares excellent Italian food, best enjoyed in the lush garden.

Etnias Café CAFE $
(Gral Córdova; mains US$3; ⏲8am-3pm; 📶) Just down the block from Patacon Pisa'o, this French-owned spot does good crepes, desserts and frozen coffee drinks. Etnias also runs an indigenous-made crafts shop next door.

Getting There & Away

There are several daily buses to Quito (US$12, 11 hours). Buses to Jipijapa can drop you off at the national park entrance and at other coastal points. Hourly buses head south to Santa Elena and can drop you off at points along the way.

South of Puerto López

04

This stretch of the south coast is dotted with tiny fishing villages and wide beaches. Some 14km south of Puerto López (right after the village of Puerto Rico) on the inland side of the road, you'll come to the thatched-roof bungalows of **Azuluna Eco-Lodge** (278-0693; www.azuluna-ecuador.com; r from US$20;), a peaceful place to recharge.

The next village south is **Las Tunas**. The beach here is long, wide and empty. You'll know you've reached Las Tunas when you spot the grounded bow of a giant wooden boat, which is actually the restaurant half of a hotel, appropriately called **La Barquita** (The Little Boat; 234-7051; www.hosterialabarquita.com; s/d from US$20/32), with comfortable doubles with hammocks out front and a few *cabañas*. Also in Las Tunas is **Hostería La Perla** (234-7001; www.hosterialaperla.net; s/d US$25/40), a romantic beach house weathered by sun and sand.

Sandwiched between verdant tropical hills and another long, wide beach, the sandy little village of **Ayampe** is about 17km south of Puerto López, right on the Guayas–Manabí provincial line. For village charm, Ayampe is the pick of the bunch. For surf lessons, yoga classes or Spanish instruction, contact **Otra Ola** (08-884-3278; www.otraola.com; 90min surf lesson US$15), which also runs a laid-back cafe. Among the handful of tranquil guesthouses here is the lovely **Finca Punta Ayampe** (02-222-3206; www.fincapuntaayampe.com; r/cabañas per person from US$16/21). On the beach, **Cabañas La Tortuga** (05-258-9363; www.latortuga.com.ec; cabañas US$20-30;) has worn thatched-roof cabins, plus a camping annex nearby.

Montañita

04

Blessed with the country's best surf – and more budget hotels than you can shake your board at – Montañita means bare feet, baggy shorts, surf and scene. Some dig it, others despise it. Despite its rapid growth, it's as mellow and friendly as ever. Banco de Guayaquil has an ATM and there are several cybercafes in town.

Activities

For an adrenaline rush, sign up for a zip-line adventure with **Montañita Canopy** (08-003-0950; zipline US$15-20), 1.5km outside of town. You can arrange horse riding, rainforest walking tours, surf lessons and board hire at **Montañitours** (206-0043; www.montanitours.com). Several shops in town rent boards.

Overlooking town, **Montañita Spanish School** (206-0116; www.montanitaspanishschool.com; per person per 20hr incl registration fee US$240) is a great place to take classes.

Sleeping

Book a room in advance (and bring earplugs) during the December-to-April high season. Expect lower prices and fewer crowds out of season.

Hostal Mohica Sumpa HOSTEL **$**
(206-0170; hostalmohicasumpa@hotmail.com; Calle Principal; r US$20-25;) Rooms are small, basic wood-and-bamboo affairs at this well-located, ocean-front spot at the end of Calle Principal; those with views are worth the extra bucks.

Hostal Las Palmeras HOTEL **$**
(06-969-2134; Av 15 de Mayo; r per person from US$10) Las Palmeras offers basic modern rooms (the best with ocean views) and there are hammocks in the courtyard.

Tiki Limbo HOSTEL **$**
(09-954-0607; www.tikilimbo.com; dm/d from US$10/30;) This longtime budget favorite on the main strip has worn, pastel-colored rooms with bamboo details, an open-sided 2nd-floor lounge and an excellent (but pricey) restaurant. Like other guesthouses on this street, it's noisy at night.

Hostal Kundalini HOSTEL **$**
(05-950-5007; www.hostalkundalini.com.ec; r US$25-30;) Just across the creek that marks the northern border of town, Kundalini offers a peaceful beachfront setting amid thatched-roof *cabañas* with bamboo walls and individual hammocks.

Nativa Bambu CABINA **$**
(206-0095; www.nativabambu.com; cabins from US$20) These peacefully set all-wood *cabañas* with thatched-roofs, private bath-

rooms and small front decks have lovely views overlooking Montañita and the ocean beyond. Look for the signed entrance off the highway near Calle Principal.

Paradise South HOSTEL $
(☎09-787-8925; r US$14-30; ❄) Down near the beach and great for those seeking silence, these adobe-walled cottages have ceramic tiled floors and modern bathrooms.

Charo's Hostal HOSTEL $
(☎206-0044; www.charoshostal.com; r from US$30; ❄📶🏊) Charo's has bright, clean, straightforward hotel rooms, along with a beachfront location and a courtyard pool and Jacuzzi.

Iguana Backpackers HOSTEL $
(☎09-499-6098; dm/d from US$6/16; 📶) Pass the river and turn right to reach this brick-and-bamboo building with a handful of simple rooms: the cheapest option is an open-sided loft (with mosquito nets over each bed). Shared kitchen and welcoming ambience.

Eating & Drinking

Carts near the beach whip up inexpensive fruit-filled cocktails. Fronting the beach, the two-story Nativa Bambu has live music and DJs. Hola Ola is another big bar with live music and dancing.

Marea PIZZERIA $
(mains US$6-8; ⏲7-11pm) Down a side street toward the beach, Marea serves good thin-crust, brick-oven pizza.

Wipeout INTERNATIONAL
(mains US$4-12) Just past the church, this Peruvian-run spot serves tasty, good-value lunches as well as top-notch grilled tuna steaks and other high-end fare by night.

Getting There & Away

Three CLP buses pass Montañita each day on their way south to Guayaquil (US$5.50, 3½ hours). Buses south to Santa Elena (US$1.50, two hours) and La Libertad, or north to Puerto López (US$2.50, one hour) pass every 15 minutes.

Guayaquil

☎04 / POP 2.2 MILLION

Although it's hot, noisy and chaotic, Guayaquil has come a long way from its dismal days as the crime-ridden port of yesteryear. The transformed *malecón* overlooking the Río Guayas has helped redefine the city. The historical neighborhood of Las Peñas, as well as Guayaquil's principal downtown thoroughfare, 9 de Octubre, have also been restored. There's much to explore in these areas, although if you're not enamored of big cities, you probably won't like this one either.

Most travelers stay in the center of town, which is organized in a gridlike fashion on the west bank of Río Guayas. The main east–west street is 9 de Octubre. The riverfront Malecón 2000 stretches along the bank of the Río Guayas, from the Mercado Sur at its southern tip, to Barrio Las Peñas and the hill of Cerro Santa Ana to the north. The suburb of Urdesa, which is frequently visited for its restaurants and nightlife, is about 4km northwest and 1.5km west of the airport.

All flights to the Galápagos either stop or originate in Guayaquil. Subsequently, it's the next best place (after Quito) to set up a trip to the islands.

Sights

MALECÓN 2000

If you've just arrived, head down to the **waterfront promenade** (⏲7am-midnight) and take a stroll beside the Río Guayas. Known as Malecón 2000, the waterfront is Guayaquil's flagship redevelopment project, stretching 2.5km along the river, with playgrounds, tropical gardens, restaurants and an IMAX movie theater. The area is well policed and generally safe, even at night.

Bustling 9 de Octubre is Guayaquil's main commercial street; at the point where it intersects the Malecón you'll find the impressive **La Rotonda** monument.

Museo Antropológico y de Arte Contemporáneo MUSEUM
(MAAC; ☎230-9383; cnr Malecón Simón Bolívar & Loja; ⏲10am-5:30pm Tue-Sat, 11am-3:30pm Sun) Near the northern end of Malecón, the MAAC houses a fine collection of archaeological treasures as well as contemporary Ecuadorian art. MAAC also has a theater (for plays, concerts and film), an open-air stage and a food court.

LAS PEÑAS & CERRO SANTA ANA

At the northern end of the Malecón, these two historic neighborhoods have been refurbished into an idealized version of a quaint South American hillside village, with

Guayaquil – City Centre

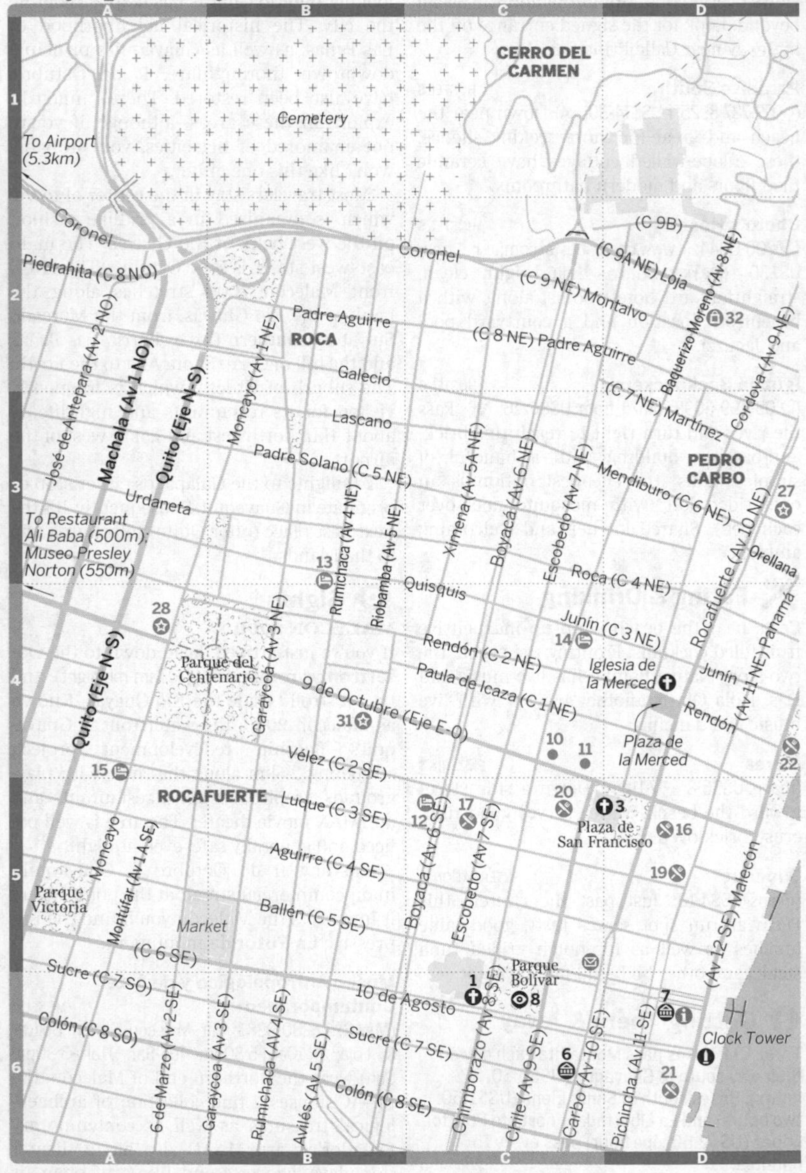

brightly painted homes, cobblestone alleyways and all. The stairway winding up Cerro Santa Ana past the brightly painted buildings is lined with informal restaurants and neighborhood bars. The views from the hilltop fort, called **Fortín del Cerro**, and the **lighthouse** (admission free; ⏲10am-10pm) are spectacular.

To the right of the stairs, the historic cobbled street of **Numa Pompillo Llona** winds past elegantly decaying wooden colonial houses, some of which house art galleries.

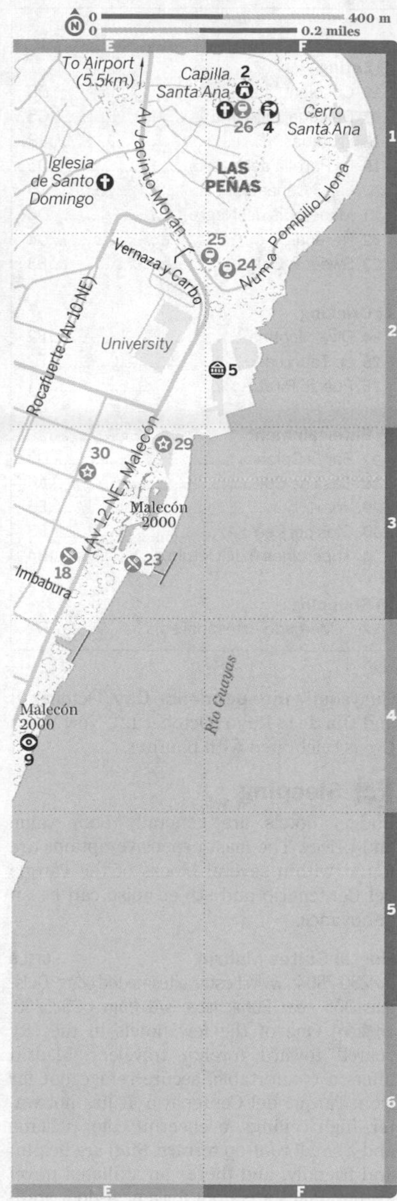

DOWNTOWN AREA

The main thoroughfare, 9 de Octubre, is definitely worth a stroll to experience Guayaquil's commercial vibrancy.

Parque Bolívar PLAZA
(Parque Seminario, cnr Chile & Ballén) Prehistoric-looking iguanas roam the handsome, tree-filled Parque Bolívar and stare down children for their snacks. They're an odd sight. The modern **cathedral** is on the plaza's western side.

FREE **Museo Municipal** MUSEUM
(252-4100; Sucre; 9am-5:30pm Tue-Sat) A block south of Parque Bolívar, you'll find an assortment of artifacts and objects from pre-Colombian and colonial times. Standouts include a large stone used for human sacrifices, various models of the early city and dramatic paintings depicting Guayaquil's devastating 1896 fire.

FREE **Museo Nahim Isaias** MUSEUM
(232-4182; www.museonahimisaias.com; cnr Pichincha & Ballén; 9am-5pm Tue-Fri, from 10am Sat) In the Plaza de Administración building, Nahim Isaias exhibits an excellent collection of sculptures, paintings and artifacts from the colonial period.

Iglesia de San Francisco CHURCH
(9 de Octubre near Chile) The city's most impressive church is the Iglesia de San Francisco, which has been reconstructed and restored since the devastating 1896 fire.

MALECÓN EL SALADO & AROUND

Smaller than the more famous development on the Río Guayas, the Malecón El Salado is a waterfront promenade dotted with eateries and cafes. **Rowboats** (per 30min US$3.50) are available for a short paddle along the mangrove-lined estuary.

FREE **Museo Presley Norton** MUSEUM
(229-3423; Av 9 de Octubre; 9am-5pm Tue-Fri, 10am-5pm Sat & Sun) A few blocks southeast of Maleconí El Salado, this small, beautifully restored mansion houses an impressive collection of archaeological artifacts – more akin to works of art – including pottery and figurines made by Ecuador's earliest peoples.

Tours

The following recommended companies can organize tours both to the Galápagos and within the local area.

Centro Viajero TOUR
(230-1283; centrovi@telconet.net; cnr Baquerizo Moreno 1119 & 9 de Octubre, Office 805, 8th fl) Spanish, English and French spoken.

Guayaquil – City Centre

Sights
1 Cathedral C6
2 Fortín del Cerro F1
3 Iglesia de San Francisco D5
4 Lighthouse F1
5 Museo Antropológico y de Arte Contemporáneo F2
6 Museo Municipal C6
7 Museo Nahim Isaias D6
8 Parque Bolívar C6
9 Waterfront Promenade E4

Activities, Courses & Tours
10 Centro Viajero C4
11 Galasam Tours C4
Travel Galapagos .... (see 13)

Sleeping
12 Casa de Romero C5
13 Hostal Suites Madrid B3
14 Hotel Andaluz C4
15 Hotel Sander A4

Eating
16 Cocolon D5
17 Dulcería La Palma C5
18 Frutabar E3
19 La Parrilla del Nato D5
20 Las 3 Canastas C5
21 Menestras del Negro D6
22 Resaca D4
23 Sweet & Coffee E3

Drinking
24 Diva Nicotina F2
25 La Taberna F2
26 Puerto Pirata F1

Entertainment
27 Bar El Colonial D3
28 Casa de Cultura A4
29 Imax E3
30 Ojos del Perro Azul E3
31 Supercines 9 de Octubre B4

Shopping
32 El Mercado Artesanal Loja D2

Dreamkapture Travel TOUR
(☎224-2909; www.dreamkapture.com; cnr Benjamín Carrión & Av Francisco de Orellana) French-Canadian owned, at the Dreamkapture Hostal.

Galasam Tours TOUR
(☎230-4488; www.galapagos-islands.com; 9 de Octubre 424, Office 9A) Great deals, but bargain hard. Some complaints.

Tangara Tours TOUR
(☎228-2828; www.tangara-ecuador.com; Manuela Sáenz & O'Leary, Ciudadela Bolivariana, Block F, Casa 1; s/d US$37/49) Run out of the guest-house of the same name. Good for local day tours and ecotourism.

Travel Galapagos TOUR
(☎233-1335; www.travelgalapagos.ec; Quísquis 305 near Rumichaca) Recommended agency run out of Hostal Suites Madrid. Good last-minute deals to Galápagos.

Festivals & Events

The whole city parties during the last week of July, celebrating **Simón Bolívar's birthday** (July 24) and **Guayaquil Foundation Day** (July 25). Hotels fill up and services are disrupted. Celebrations are huge during Guayaquil's **Independence Day** (October 9) and **Día de la Raza** (October 12). New Year's Eve is celebrated with bonfires.

Sleeping

Budget hotels are generally poor value and pricey. The least expensive options are found within several blocks of the Parque del Centenario and street noise can be an annoyance.

Hostal Suites Madrid HOTEL $
(☎230-7804; www.hostalsuitesmadrid.com; Quísquis 305 near Rumichaca; s/d from US$25/30; ❄@🛜) One of the few hotels in the city geared toward foreign travelers, Madrid offers a comfortable, secure refuge not far from Parque del Centenario. It has hot water, high ceilings, a cheerful color scheme and a small rooftop terrace. Staff are helpful and friendly; and there's an affiliated travel agency. Plans are afoot for a next-door addition, including a pool and bar.

Hotel Sander HOTEL $
(☎232-0030; www.sanderguayaquil.com; Luque 1101; d with fan/air-con US$18/20; ❄) Despite the bare-bones rooms and large bunker-like appearance, the 24-hour security, friendly ser-

vice and a working elevator make the Sander one of the better cheapies.

Dreamkapture Hostal HOSTEL $

(224-2909; www.dreamkapture.com; Bernal near Av Carrion; s/d incl breakfast from US$17/25;) In the northern suburb of Alborada, this friendly Canadian-Ecuadorian-owned *hostal* boasts spotless rooms and a small garden. There's lots of travel info, and a small pool for cooling off. The *hostal* is hard to find; call or email ahead for directions, and look for the fantasy paintings.

Iguanazú Hostal HOSTEL $$

(220-1143; www.iguanazuhostel.com; Ciudadela La Cogra manzana 1, villa 2, Km 3.5, Av Carlos Julio Arosemena; dm/s/d incl breakfast from US$17/50/60;) Iguanazú is an oasis of tranquility located about 5km northwest of downtown. Besides charming rooms, there's a terrace with hammocks and wonderful views, a lawn, pool and living room/restaurant area.

Hotel Andaluz HOSTEL $$

(230-5796; www.hotelandaluz-ec.com; Baquerizo Moreno 840 & Junín; s/d/tw US$25/34/40;) There's something mildly charming about the Andaluz, with a colonial-esque facade, and bright rooms with artwork on the walls. The open-side, plant-filled lounge upstairs is a fine spot for a bit of fresh air.

Casa de Romero B&B $$

(488-6116; www.casaderomero.es.tl; cnr Vélez 501 & Boyacá, 7th fl; s/d incl breakfast US$25/40;) For a taste of downtown *guayaquileño* living, try this friendly place with nine pleasant rooms (most with small balconies), located in a high-rise residential building.

Eating

Downtown Guayaquil has an abundance of inexpensive restuarants including informal *parrillas* (grill restaurants) near Parque del Centenario and fast-food restaurants along the Malecón 2000. For high-end dining, head to the northwestern suburb of Urdesa.

Resaca INTERNATIONAL $$

(info 242 3390; Malecón at Rendon; lunch US$3.50) This two-story spot on the Malecón serves filling lunch plates and a wide range of Ecuadorian classics; it also has all-you-can-eat crab (most nights from 8pm; US$17, including limitless pilsners). The rooftop deck makes a fine spot for an evening drink.

Cocolon ECUADORIAN $$

(Av Carbo; mains US$8-10) In a streamlined modern setting, Cocolon serves Ecuadorian favorites like *llapingachos* and *seco de chivo* as well as burgers and sandwiches.

Menestras del Negro ECUADORIAN $

(cnr Malecón & Sucre; mains from US$3) This Ecuadorian fast-food chain serves grilled meat, fish and chicken dishes along with large servings of beans.

Restaurant Ali Baba MIDDLE EASTERN $

(Av 9 de Octubre; mains US$3-4) You should head to Ali Baba for Middle Eastern staples like hummus, falafel and juicy shawarmas.

Las 3 Canastas CAFE $

(cnr Vélez & Chile; snacks US$2-4) A downtown spot for fruit shakes, fruit juices and ice cream. Outdoor tables too.

Dulcería La Palma BAKERY $

(Escobedo btwn Vélez & Luque; snacks US$1-3; 7:30am-7:15pm) The old-school Dulcería La Palma is perhaps the most atmospheric place downtown. Tasty *cachitos* (mini-croissants) and other bakery items.

Frutabar CAFE $

(Malecón; sandwiches US$4-5) A surfer-themed place that serves up fruit shakes, sandwiches and light meals.

La Parrilla del Nato ECUADORIAN $$

(cnr Luque & Pichincha; mains US$10) This two-story Guayaquil institution (there's another branch in Urdesa) is always crowded. La Parrilla specializes in personalized grills – meat or seafood – fired up at your table.

Sweet & Coffee CAFE

(cnr Carbo & Luque;) A popular Starbucks imitator with excellent cakes; there's also a

SAFETY IN GUAYAQUIL

The downtown area is fine during the day, but sketchy after dark. Watch your belongings in the bus terminal. There is a persistent problem with post-ATM-withdrawal robberies, so be extra aware for at least a few blocks after leaving the bank. Be careful when selecting a taxi as 'express kidnappings' and robberies have occurred. It's safest to have your guesthouse call you one.

branch near Oro de Verde on Avenida 9 de Octubre.

 Drinking & Entertainment

The *farra* (nightlife) in Guayaquil is spread around town, but some of the most atmospheric bars are found in Las Peñas.

Diva Nicotina BAR
(Cerro Santa Ana; 7pm-midnight Mon-Thu, to 2am Fri & Sat) At the foot of the hill, this place draws a young crowd and is one of the more happening spots when there's live music.

Puerto Pirata BAR
(Escalón 384; 5pm-midnight) After summiting Cerro Santa Ana, stop in for a breather at this faux pirate ship below the lighthouse. It has drinks and food, and live music on weekends.

La Taberna BAR
(Cerro Santa Ana) Join the young neighborhood crowd at this nostalgic space decorated with football paraphernalia.

Bar El Colonial BAR
(Rocafuerte 623; 4pm-midnight Mon-Thu, to 2am Fri & Sat) One of the Zona Rosa's oldest hot spots with live music on weekends.

Ojos del Perro Azul CLUB
(cnr Panamá 213 & Aguirre; 8pm-midnight Wed & Thu, to 2am Fri & Sat) One of the Zona Rosa clubs with live cover bands; also has billiards and a voluminous whiskey selection.

Imax CINEMA
(www.imaxmalecon2000.com; Malecón 2000; admission US$4) Near Museo Antropológico y de Arte Contemporáneo.

Casa de Cultura CINEMA
(cnr 9 de Octubre & Moncayo) Foreign films and art flicks.

Supercines 9 de Octubre CINEMA
(www.supercines.com; cnr 9 de Octubre 823 & Avilés; admission US$2) Modern multiplex.

 Shopping

El Mercado Artesanal Loja MARKET
(Baquerizo Moreno; 9am-7pm Mon-Sat, 10am-5pm Sun) A large artisans' market with a huge variety of crafts from all over Ecuador.

 Information

Emergency

Police (101)
Cruz Roja (Red Cross; 131)

Medical Services

Clínica Kennedy (238-9666; Av del Periodista) Guayaquil's best hospital. Located in the suburb of Kennedy, 3.5km northwest of downtown.

Dr Serrano Saenz (230-1373; cnr Boyacá 821 & Junín) Takes drop-ins; speaks English.

Money

There are ATMs all over downtown, especially around Plaza de la Merced.
Banco de Guayaquil (cnr Rendón & Panamá) Changes traveler's checks and has an ATM.

Post

Post Office (cnr Carbo & Ballén; 8am-7pm Mon-Fri, to noon Sat)

Tourist Information

Dirección Municipal de Turismo (232-4182; www.visitaguayaquil.com; cnr Pichincha & Ballén; 9am-5pm Tue-Sat) Inside the city hall building.

Getting There & Away

Air

TAME (256-0728; www.tame.com.ec; Av 9 de Octubre 424, Gran Pasaje) and **LAN** (www.lan.com) have daily flights to Quito (US$70, one hour). TAME also flies to Cuenca (US$80, 30 minutes) and Loja (US$87, 45 minutes). LAN, TAME and **Aerogal** (268-7566; www.aerogal.com.ec; Junín 440) fly to Isla Baltra and San Cristóbal in the Galápagos (US$450 to $500 round trip, 1½ hours).

Bus

The bus terminal is 2km beyond the airport. There are services to most major towns in the country. Many buses go daily to Quito (US$10, seven to 10 hours), Manta (US$7.50, four hours) and Cuenca (US$9, 3½ hours).

Several companies at the terminal go to Machala (US$5, three hours) and Huaquillas (US$6, four hours) on the Peruvian border. The easiest way to Peru, however, is with one of the international lines. Most highly recommended is **Cruz del Sur** (www.cruzdelsur.com.pe), which charges US$75 all the way to Lima (26 hours, 2pm Sun, Tue & Fri). Next is **Expreso Internacional Ormeño** (214-0847; www.grupo-ormeno.com.pe), and finally **Rutas de America** (223-8673; www.rutasenbus.com; Los Rios 3012 near Letamendi). **Ormeño** (213-0379; www.cifainternacional.com) has daily departures for Lima (US$80, 11:30am). Its office and terminal is on Avenida de las Americas, just north of the main bus terminal.

These services are convenient because you don't have to get off the bus to take care of border formalities.

Getting Around

To/From the Airport

The airport is about 5km north of the center on Av de las Américas. The bus terminal is 2km north of the airport. A taxi to the center should cost about US$5 from either location. If you cross the street in front of the airport, you can take a bus downtown. From the center, the best bus to take to the airport is the No 2 Especial (25¢), which takes under an hour. It runs along the Malecón but is sometimes full, so allow plenty of time.

Buses from the center to the bus terminal leave from Parque Victoria, near 10 de Agosto and Moncayo. Several buses leave from the terminal for downtown including the No 71. You can also take faster Metrovía buses, which head downtown from the Terminal Río Daule, opposite the bus station.

Local Transport

Walking is the easiest way of getting around downtown. City buses are cheap (25¢) but routes are complicated. A taxi within downtown shouldn't cost more than US$1.50. To Urdesa, count on US$3 to US$4. Agree on fares before entering a taxi.

Machala

☎07 / POP 230,000

The self-proclaimed 'banana capital of the world,' Machala is a chaotic, workaday city. Most travelers going to and from Peru will only pass through here, but few decide to stay more than a night. Páez is a pedestrian-only zone between Rocafuerte and 9 de Octubre.

Sleeping & Eating

There are several cheap *parrilla* restaurants serving inexpensive grilled chicken and steaks on Sucre near Tarqui.

Hostal Saloah HOTEL $
(☎293-4344; Colón 1818; s/d incl breakfast US$22/30; ❄@🛜) On a bustling block near several bus companies, the Saloah has well-kept rooms with tiny windows. There's a rooftop patio with views.

Hotel Bolívar Internacional HOTEL $
(☎293-0727; falvarado@hotmail.com; cnr Bolívar & Colón; s/d US$18/26; ❄@🛜) This clean and friendly hotel is only a short walk from the busy center.

Information

The **tourist office** (cnr 9 de Mayo & 9 de Octubre) distributes city and area maps. A few major banks with ATMs are located around the central plaza.

Getting There & Away

The airport is 1km southwest of town; a taxi costs about US$1. **Saereo** (☎292-2630; www.saereo.com) flies once or twice daily to both Guayaquil and Quito.

There is no central bus terminal. Buses with **CIFA** (cnr Guayas & Bolívar) run regularly to Huaquillas (US$1.50, 1½ hours) at the Peruvian border, and to Guayaquil (US$5, three hours) from 9 de Octubre near Tarqui. **Rutas Orenses** (Rocafuerte near Tarqui) and **Ecuatoriana Pullman** (Av 25th de Junio near Colón) also serve Guayaquil; the latter has air-conditioned buses.

Panamericana (Colón near Bolívar) offers several buses a day to Quito (US$10, 10 hours).

GETTING TO PERU

This busy border crossing is notorious for rip-offs. Keep your wits about you, and don't believe any stories about border closings, the necessity to take a private car, bribe officials or other scams. To avoid getting ripped off, consider taking an international cross-border bus from Guayaquil. Try to change some dollars into soles before arriving to avoid getting ripped off.

The Ecuadorian **immigration office** (⏰24hr) is 4km outside Huaquillas and 3km north of the border. Entrance and exit formalities are carried out here; there are no fees. The bus doesn't wait, but if you save your ticket, you can board another passing bus for free. There are also taxis.

When leaving Ecuador, you'll get an exit stamp from the Ecuadorian immigration office. After showing your passport to the international bridge guard, take a mototaxi (S3) to the Peruvian immigration building, about 2km south of the border. From here, *colectivos* (shared taxis) go to Tumbes (S3.50; beware of overcharging).

Transportes Cooperativa Loja (Tarqui near Bolívar) goes to Loja (US$4.50, five hours).

Huaquillas

07 / POP 30,000

Called Aguas Verdes on the Peruvian side, Huaquillas is the main border town with Peru and lies 80km south of Machala. There's little reason to stop. Almost everything happens on the long main street. Ecuadorian banks don't change money (though they have ATMs). The briefcase-toting money changers do change money, but numerous rip-offs have been reported.

If you need to spend the night, **Hotel Vanessa** (299-6263; www.hotelvanessa-ec.com; Calle 1 de Mayo & Hualtaco; s/d US$18/24;) is a safe bet.

CIFA buses run frequently to Machala (US$1.50, 1½ hours) and five times daily to Guayaquil (US$5, four hours) from the main street, two blocks from the border. Panamericana goes daily to Quito (US$10, 12 hours). Pullman Sucre and Azuay Internacional, both on Teniente Cordovez, have four departures daily to Cuenca (US$7, five hours).

GALÁPAGOS ISLANDS

05 / POP 30,000

Inspiration to Charles Darwin (who came here in 1535), the Galápagos Islands may make you think differently about the world. A trip to this extraordinary region is like visiting an alternate universe, some strange utopian colony organized by sea lions – the golden retrievers of the Galápagos – and arranged on principles of mutual cooperation. What's so extraordinary for visitors is the fearlessness of the islands' famous inhabitants. Blue-footed boobies, sea lions, prehistoric land iguanas – all act as if humans are nothing more than slightly annoying paparazzi. Nowhere else can you engage in a staring contest with wild animals and lose!

Visiting the islands is expensive, however, and the only way to truly experience their marvels is by taking a cruise. It's possible to visit four of the islands independently, but you will not see the wildlife or the many smaller islands that you will aboard a cruise.

The most important island is Isla Santa Cruz. On the southern side of the island is Puerto Ayora, the largest town in the Galápagos and where most of the budget tours are based. It has many hotels and restaurants. North of Santa Cruz, separated by a narrow strait, is Isla Baltra, home of the islands' main airport. A public bus and a ferry connect the Baltra airport with Puerto Ayora.

Isla San Cristóbal, the most easterly island, is home to the provincial capital, Puerto Baquerizo Moreno, which also has hotels and an airport. The other inhabited islands are Isla Isabela and Isla Santa María. Note that most of the islands have two or even three names.

Environment

The Galápagos Islands were declared a national park in 1959. Organized tourism began in the 1960s and by the 1990s some 60,000 people visited annually. Today, around 150,000 people visit each year, which continues to place added stress on the islands' delicate ecology.

Other problems facing the Galápagos include oil spills, the poaching of sea lions for bait, overfishing, illegal fishing for shark, lobster and other marine life, and the introduction of nonnative animals. Despite conservation efforts by organizations like the **Galapagos Conservancy** (www.galapagos.org), the future of the islands remains unclear. Since 2007, Unesco has treated the World Heritage–listed islands as being 'in danger.'

Practicalities

Fees Before boarding a flight to the islands, foreign visitors must pay US$10 at the airport in either Guayquail or Quito. Upon arrival in the Galapagos, visitors must pay another US$100 (cash only) to the national park.

High season The high season is from December to January, around Easter, and from June to August; during these periods, budget tours may be difficult to arrange.

Time Galápagos time is one hour behind mainland Ecuador.

Goings-on For the latest news on the islands, check out the **Charles Darwin Foundation** (www.darwinfoundation.org) news site.

Costs

Plan on spending more money than you want to. The least expensive boat tours

Galápagos Islands

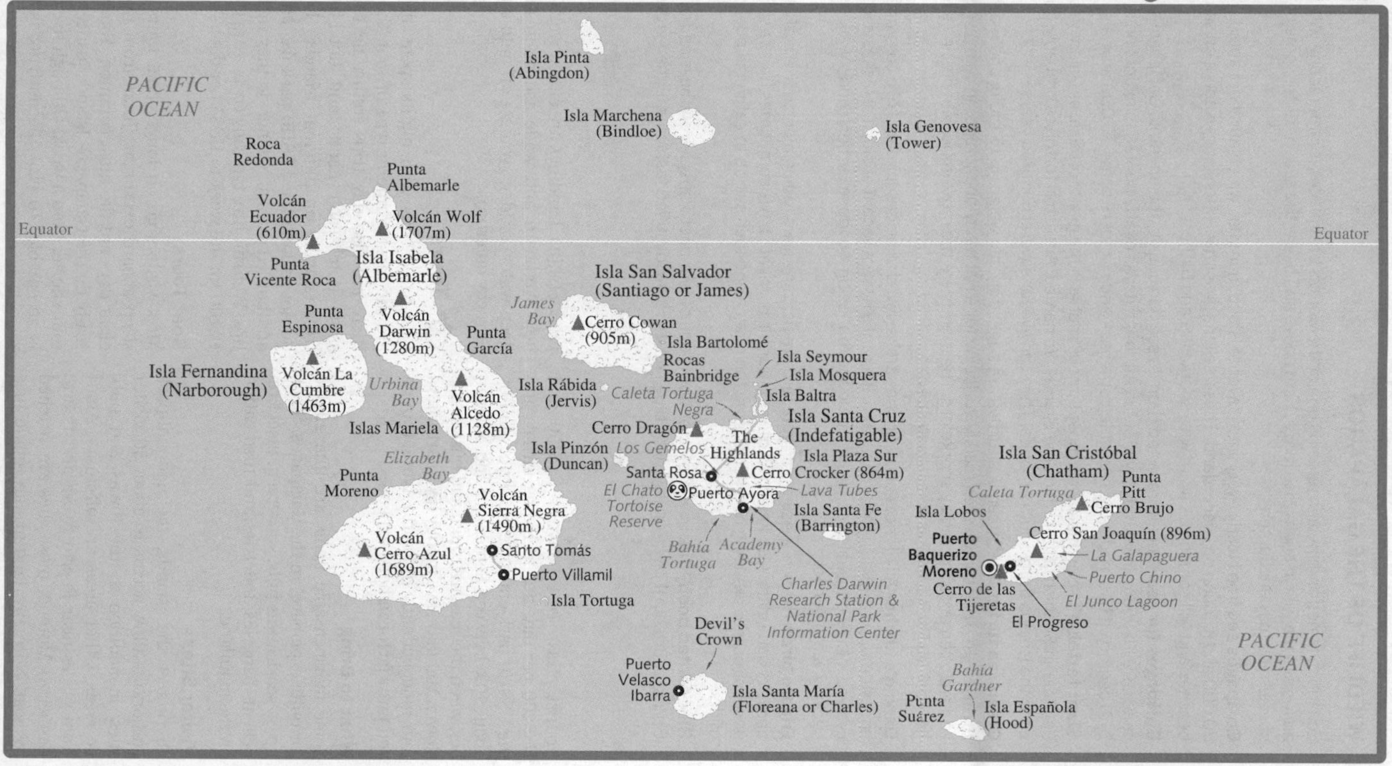

0 50 km
0 25 miles
PACIFIC OCEAN
Isla Pinta (Abingdon)
Isla Marchena (Bindloe)
Isla Genovesa (Tower)
Roca Redonda
Punta Albemarle
Volcán Ecuador (610m)
Volcán Wolf (1707m)
Equator
Punta Vicente Roca
Isla Isabela (Albemarle)
Isla San Salvador (Santiago or James)
James Bay
Cerro Cowan (905m)
Punta Espinosa
Volcán Darwin (1280m)
Punta García
Isla Bartolomé
Rocas Bainbridge
Isla Seymour
Isla Mosquera
Isla Fernandina (Narborough)
Volcán La Cumbre (1463m)
Urbina Bay
Volcán Alcedo (1128m)
Isla Rábida (Jervis)
Caleta Tortuga Negra
Isla Baltra
Isla Santa Cruz (Indefatigable)
Islas Mariela
Cerro Dragón
The Highlands
Isla Pinzón (Duncan)
Los Gemelos
Isla Plaza Sur
Elizabeth Bay
Santa Rosa
Cerro Crocker (864m)
Isla San Cristóbal (Chatham)
Punta Moreno
El Chato Tortoise Reserve
Puerto Ayora
Lava Tubes
Punta Pitt
Caleta Tortuga
Volcán Sierra Negra (1490m)
Isla Santa Fe (Barrington)
Isla Lobos
Cerro Brujo
Cerro San Joaquín (896m)
Volcán Cerro Azul (1689m)
Santo Tomás
Bahía Tortuga
Academy Bay
Puerto Baquerizo Moreno
La Galapaguera
Puerto Villamil
Puerto Chino
Isla Tortuga
Charles Darwin Research Station & National Park Information Center
Cerro de las Tijeretas
El Junco Lagoon
El Progreso
Devil's Crown
PACIFIC OCEAN
Puerto Velasco Ibarra
Isla Santa María (Floreana or Charles)
Bahía Gardner
Punta Suárez
Isla Española (Hood)

WILDLIFE OF THE GALÁPAGOS

Ecuador's famed archipelago remains one of the world's best places for interacting with animals in the wild at such close range, both above and below the sea. Here are some of the species you may encounter:

Galápagos sea lion Nearly everyone's favorite island mammal, which numbers about 50,000 and is found on every island. These delightful animals often lounge about on sandy beaches and will sometimes swim with snorkelers and bathers.

Galápagos fur seal More introverted than its sea-lion cousin, the endemic Galápagos fur seal has a luxuriant, insulating layer of fur. Although it was nearly hunted to extinction in the 19th century, it has made a remarkable comeback and numbers some 30,000 animals.

Giant tortoise The archipelago's most famous reptile is the giant tortoise, or Galápagos ('saddle' in Spanish), after which the islands are named. Ancestral tortoises probably drifted to the islands from South America. They can live for several hundred years.

Green sea turtle Adult green sea turtles are huge: they can weigh up to 150kg and reach 1m in length. They can be seen readily surfacing for air at many anchorages in calm water and are often encountered by snorkelers. The islands are the most important nesting site in the eastern Pacific for this threatened species.

Darwin's finches All of the islands' finches are believed to be descendants of a common ancestor. Upon arrival in the archipelago, it found a host of vacant ecological niches and evolved into 13 unusual species, including the tool-using woodpecker finch and the blood-sucking vampire finch.

Frigate birds The two species of frigate bird are dazzling fliers, riding high on thermals above coastal cliffs. Also known as man-o'-war birds, frigate birds sometimes harass smaller seabirds into dropping or regurgitating their catch and then swoop to catch the booty in midair.

Blue-footed booby The blue-footed booby is one of four booby species on the islands. During courtship it picks up its bright-blue feet in a slow, dignified fashion and then grows

(tourist class), cost between US$150 and US$200 per day, not including airfare and the US$110 park-entrance fee. Prices fall by about 20% between September and November, when the seas are rough and business is slower. You may save money if you arrange a tour independently in Puerto Ayora, though you must factor in hotel expenses.

What to Bring

Some indispensable items are unavailable (or quite expensive) in the Galápagos. Stock up on seasickness pills, sunscreen, insect repellent, batteries, toiletries and medication on the mainland.

Visitor Sites

To protect the islands, the national-park authorities allow access to about 50 visitor sites, in addition to the towns and public areas. Other areas are off-limits. Apart from places near Puerto Ayora and Puerto Baquerizo Moreno, most sites are reached by boat. Normally, landings are made in a *panga* (skiff). Landings are either 'wet' (you hop overboard and wade ashore in knee-deep water) or 'dry' (you get off onto a pier or rocky outcrop).

 Tours

Boat-based trips with nights spent aboard are the most common type of tour, though there are also day trips (returning to the same hotel each night) and hotel-based trips (staying on different islands). Prices do not include the US$110 park fee, airfare and bottled drinks. Neither do they include tips. Wet-suit hire typically costs extra (from US$10 for the week to US$5 per day).

Boat Tours

Most visitors go on longer boat tours and sleep aboard overnight. Tours from five to eight days are the most common. You can't really do the Galápagos Islands justice on a tour shorter than a week, although five days is acceptable. To visit the outlying islands more animated, bowing, wing-spreading and sky-pointing in an enchanting, if rather clownish, display. They are also magnificent fishers, diving like arrows into the sea.

Flightless cormorant Apart from penguins, the flightless cormorant is the only flightless seabird in the world, and it is endemic to the Galápagos. When an ancestral population colonized this predator-free archipelago the birds eventually lost the need for flight. About 700 pairs remain.

Galápagos penguin Long ago, a population of penguins followed the cool Humboldt Current up from Antarctica and settled in the Galápagos. Today, it is the most northerly penguin in the world and the only species that lives in the tropics.

Waved albatross The waved albatross is helpless in calm weather, relying utterly on southeast trade winds to transport it to feeding areas. The archipelago's largest bird (weighing 5kg, with a 2.4m wingspan) is the only albatross species that breeds at the equator.

Galápagos flamingo Pretty in pink, these striking and unmistakable birds are part of the largest of the world's five species.

Marine iguana The remarkable marine iguana is the world's only seagoing lizard, and is common on the rocky shores of all the Galápagos Islands. Its size and coloration vary between islands, with the largest specimens growing up to 1.5m.

Galápagos land iguana Despite their large size and fearsome appearance, land iguanas are harmless vegetarians that thrive on succulent opuntias (pear cactuses). Mature males weigh up to 13kg and grow to 1m; they are territorial, engaging in head-butting contests to defend their terrain.

Lava lizards Tortoises and iguanas may be more famous, but the most commonly seen reptiles on the islands are the various species of lava lizard, which are frequently seen scurrying across rocks or even perched on the backs of iguanas.

Sally Lightfoot crab This abundant marine animal is blessed with spectacular coloration. Sally Lightfoot crabs (named by English seafarers) adorn the rocks on every island and are extremely agile.

of Isabela and Fernandina, a cruise of eight days or more is recommended. On the first day of a prearranged tour, you arrive from the mainland by air at about noon, so this leaves only half a day in the Galápagos; on the last day, you have to be at the airport in the morning. Thus a 'five-day' tour gives only three full days in the islands.

Tour boats range from small yachts to large cruise ships. The most common type of boat is a motor sailer carrying up to 20 passengers. The four categories and price per day are roughly as follows: economy class (up to US$200), tourist class (US$200 to $300), first class (US$300 to $400) and luxury (from US$400).

Seven-night/eight-day economy tours are generally aboard small boats with six to 12 bunks in double, triple and quad cabins. Bedding is provided and the accommodations are clean, but damp and cramped, with little privacy. Plenty of simple but fresh food and juice is served at all meals, and a guide accompanies the boat (few guides on economy tours speak English).

There are toilets and fresh water is available for drinking. Bathroom facilities may be saltwater deck hoses or freshwater showers on some boats. The preset itineraries allow you to visit most of the central islands and give enough time to see the wildlife.

DANGERS & ANNOYANCES

There are some common pitfalls with Galápagos boat tours. It's sometimes the case that the cheaper the trip, the more likely you are to experience problems. That's not to say that costlier boasts are glitch-free, but the companies are often more attentive and quick to respond to complaints.

Occasionally, things go wrong, and when they do, a refund is difficult to obtain. Recurring complaints include last-minute changes of boat (which the contractual small print allows), poor crew, a lack of bottled drinks, changes to the agreed itinerary, mechanical breakdowns, poor-quality snorkeling gear, bad smells, bug infestations and overbooking. Passengers have to share cabins and are not guaranteed that their cabin mates will be of the same gender; if you are uncomfortable sharing a cabin with a stranger of the opposite sex, make sure you are guaranteed in writing that you won't have to do this. Generally speaking, the cheaper the tour, the less comfortable the boat and the less knowledgeable the guide.

Arranging Tours in Advance

Most travelers arrange tours in Quito (p637) or Guayaquil (p699). Check various agencies to compare prices and get a departure date that works for you. Sometimes you can get on a great boat for a budget price, particularly when business is slow – agencies will drop their prices at the last minute rather than leave berths empty.

Recommended tour operators include the following:

Columbus Travel BOAT TOUR
(☎02-254-7587, in the US 877-436-7512; www.columbusecuador.com) Excellent customer service; can book a range of boats depending on budget and dates of travel.

Ecoventura BOAT TOUR
(☎02-290-7396, in the US 800-633-7932; www.ecoventura.com) One of the pioneers in conservation and sustainable tourism. All of its four boats, including its diving live-aboards are highly recommended.

Ecuador Adventure BOAT TOUR
(☎02-604-6800, in the US 800-217-9414; www.ecuadoradventure.ec) Specializes in hotel-based and multisport tours including mountain biking and kayaking.

Ecuador Travel BOAT TOUR
(www.ecuador-travel.net/galapagos.htm) Dependable and honest broker for a wide range of boats, from economic to luxury.

Happy Gringo Travel BOAT TOUR
(☎02-290-6077; www.happygringo.com) Highly recommended for offering good prices for a wide range of boats. Also has last-minute deals.

Sangay Touring BOAT TOUR
(☎02-222-1336; www.sangay.com) An experienced outfit that books over 60 boats.

Independent Travel

Most people get around the islands by organized boat tour, but it's easy to visit some of the islands independently. Santa Cruz, San Cristóbal, Isabela and Santa María (Floreana) all have accommodations and are reachable by affordable interisland boat rides or more expensive flights. Keep in mind, however, that you'll only scratch the surface of the archipelago's natural wonders if traveling independently.

Getting There & Away

Flights from the mainland arrive at two airports: Isla Baltra, just north of Santa Cruz, and Isla San Cristóbal. The airlines flying to the Galápagos Islands are **TAME** (www.tame.com.ec), **Aerogal** (www.aerogal.com.ec) and **LAN** (www.lan.com). They operate morning flights daily from Quito via Guayaquil to the Isla Baltra airport (just over an hour away from Puerto Ayora by public transportation) as well as several flights weekly to San Cristóbal airport. All return flights are in the early afternoon of the same day.

Flights from Guayaquil cost US$480/440 (high/low season) round trip and take 1½ hours. From Quito, flights cost US$530/480 round trip and take 3½ hours, due to the layover in Guayaquil. It's also possible to fly from Quito and return to Guayaquil or vice versa; it's often more convenient to fly into Baltra and out of San Cristóbal or vice versa. A transit control fee of US$10 must be paid at the Instituto Nacional Galápagos (Ingala) office next to the ticket counter at either Quito or Guayaquil airport; the charge may be included in some prearranged boat tours.

Flights to the Galápagos are sometimes booked solid, so make sure you arrange your trip well in advance.

Getting Around

AIR The small airline **Emetebe** (www.emetebe.com.ec), with offices located in **Guayaquil** (☎229-2492), **Puerto Ayora** (☎252-6177; Av Charles Darwin, Proinsular Supermarket, 2nd fl), **Puerto Villamil** (☎252-9255) and **San Cristóbal** (☎252-0615), flies small passenger aircraft between Baltra and Puerto Villamil (Isla Isabela), between Baltra and Puerto Baquerizo Moreno (Isla San Cristóbal), and between Puerto Baquerizo Moreno and Puerto Villamil. **Saereo** (www.saereo.com), which began operations in 2012, runs a similar service. Fares range from US$110 to US$180 one way, and there is a 9kg baggage limit per person.

BOAT Private speedboats known as *lanchas* or fibras (short for 'fiberglass boats') offer daily passenger-ferry services between Santa Cruz and San Cristóbal and Isabela (there are no direct trips between San Cristóbal and Isabela). Fares are US$25 on any passage and are purchased either on the day before or the day of departure. Ask around in Puerto Ayora, Puerto Baquerizo Moreno and Puerto Villamil.

Isla Santa Cruz

Most visitors only pass through Isla Santa Cruz (Indefatigable), the archipelago's most populous island, on their way from Isla Baltra to Puerto Ayora. But Santa Cruz is a destination in and of itself, with easily accessible beaches and remote highlands that offer adventurous activities far from the tourist trail.

Puerto Ayora

Clean, prosperous Puerto Ayora is the Galápagos' main population center and the heart of the tourist industry. It's a friendly place to linger for a few days and the best place in the islands to set up a cruise.

Sights

Aside from Tortuga Bay, the following sites are popular with visiting groups, but you can easily go on your own. Arrive early in the day to beat the crowds.

Charles Darwin Research Station WILDLIFE RESERVE
(252-6146; www.darwinfoundation.org; 6am-6pm) A 20-minute walk northeast of town, this conservation site is a good place to observe giant tortoises and land iguanas. Signage in Spanish and English describe efforts to restore their populations on islands where they've been pushed to the brink of extinction. A path leads through arid-zone vegetation such as salt bush, mangroves and prickly pear cacti.

Just after the entrance to the site is a sign for **Playa Estación**, a small patch of sand fronted by large rocks.

Las Grietas LAKE
This dramatic water-filled crevice in the rocks makes a refreshing spot for a swim. Fearless locals climb the nearly vertical walls to plunge into the water below. Take a water taxi (per person 60¢) to the dock for the Angermeyer Point restaurant, then walk another 700m further, following a rocky, well-signed path.

Tortuga Bay BEACH
This lovely white-sand beach sits at the end of a 2.5km paved trail southwest of Puerto Ayora. There's good surfing, but with dangerous currents, it's not recommended for swimming. The beach is backed by mangroves, and you may spot harmless sharks (worry not), pelicans and even flamingos. Marine iguanas abound. Beware of strong currents on the exposed side of the spit. To get there, take Charles Binford west.

Rancho Primicias WILDLIFE RESERVE
(admission US$3; 8am-5pm) About 18km north of Puerto Ayora, this private reserve is home to dozens of giant tortoises, and you can wander around at will. The turnoff is about 1km beyond Santa Rosa; a dirt road leads 4km further to the site. A taxi there costs about US$12. You can also try to catch one of the infrequent buses that depart from the Citteg bus station, 2km north of the harbor. Enquire at the tourist office about the current schedule.

Lava Tunnels UNDERGROUND TUNNELS
(8am-5pm) Around 700m before Rancho Primicias, you'll pass these large underground tunnels, which were formed when the outside skin of a molten-lava flow solidified. One side of the tunnels is lit with florescent lights; for the other side, you'll need a torch and proper gear (including a rope) to explore.

Activities

The best dive centers in town are **Scuba Iguana** (252-6497; www.scubaiguana.com; Av Charles Darwin), near the cemetery, and **Galápagos Sub-Aqua** (230-5514; www.galapagos-sub-aqua.com; Av Charles Darwin). Both are excellent and offer a variety of tours that include gear, boat and guide. The standard rate for two boat dives at either is about US$200. Full PADI-certification courses are available.

Lonesome George Travel Agency WATER SPORTS
(252-6245; www.lonesomegeorge.com.ec; Baltra near Enrique Fuentes) Rents snorkeling equipment (US$8 per day), kayaks (US$30 per half-day), bicycles (US$2 per hour), surfboards (US$20 per half-day) and wet suits (US$8 per day).

Tours

If you're setting up a cruise from Puerto Ayora, visit the following agencies to compare prices and tours. They all offer last-minute deals (when they exist).

Iguana Travel TOUR
(Av Charles Darwin) Arranges day tours and books last-minute overnight yachts on the lower end of the pay scale.

Joybe Tours TOUR
(☎252-4385; Islas Plaza & Opuntia) Last-minute overnight boat deals and day tours.

Moonrise Travel TOUR
(☎252-6348; Av Charles Darwin) Reputable agency long in the business; can arrange camping at its private ranch in the highlands, plus boat tours.

Sleeping

Most hotels are within a few blocks of Av Charles Darwin (the meandering main road closest to the waterfront).

Hotel Lirio del Mar HOTEL $
(☎252-6212; Islas Plaza; r per person US$17; ❄) Three floors of colorful concrete rooms are basic but clean, and a shared terrace catches the breeze.

Hotel Salinas HOTEL $$
(☎252-6072; Islas Plaza; s/d from US$21/34; 📶) Two-story hotel with plain rooms, hot water, TV and fans. Try for a room on the 2nd floor.

Hotel Gardner HOTEL $$
(☎252-6979; Tomás de Berlanga; s/d incl breakfast from US$25/35; ❄📶) The Gardner has a covered rooftop patio with lounge chairs and hammocks and simple rooms.

Hotel Sir Francis Drake HOTEL $$
(☎252-6221; www.sirfrancisdrakegalapagos.com; Av Baltra; s/d from US$25/30; ❄📶) The bright ground-floor rooms all the way in the back have big windows and are great value at this friendly hotel.

Hostal Los Amigos HOSTEL $
(☎252-6265; hostal.losamigos@gmail.com; Av Charles Darwin; s/d without bathroom US$15/25; 📶) The best-value cheapie in town. There's no hot water, but the rooms are clean (and small) with wood floors. A kitchen and lounge with TV is available for guests.

Eating

A handful of popular kiosks whip up *encocado,* lobster and grilled meat along Charles Binford, just east of Av Padre Julio Herrera. There's a festive atmosphere at the outdoor tables on the street.

Restaurant Tintorera ECUADORIAN $$
(Av Charles Darwin; mains US$6-16; ⏲closed Mon; 📶) This spot near the turtle statue has an outdoor patio and becomes atmospheric at night. There's a wide selection of fare, from burgers and lasagna to Cajun blackened fish and lobster. Excellent *almuerzos* (US$4.50).

Galápagos Deli DELI, PIZZERIA $
(Tomás de Berlanga; pizzas US$5-8; ⏲10:30am-10:30pm Tue-Sun; 📶) Head to this sleek and modern place for brick-oven pizza and high-quality deli sandwiches, as well as brewed coffee and gelato (US$2).

Descanso del Guia ECUADORIAN $
(Av Charles Darwin near Los Colonos; mains US$8-11) Next to the passenger pier, this open-sided cafeteria is always bustling during lunchtime when it serves filling *almuerzos* (US$4.50).

Information

Banco del Pacífico (Av Charles Darwin; ⏲8am-3:30pm Mon-Fri, 9:30am-12:30pm Sat) The town's only bank has a MasterCard/Cirrus ATM and changes traveler's checks.

Cámara de Turismo (Tourist Information Office; www.galapagostour.org; Charles Binford near 12 de Febrero) Distributes a free useful guide to the Galápagos.

Getting There & Away

It is recommended that you reconfirm your flight departures with **Aerogal** (☎252-6798; cnr Av San Cristobál & Lara), **LAN** (☎269-2850; Av Charles Darwin; ⏲8am-6pm Mon-Sat, 10am-1pm Sun) or **TAME** (☎252-6527; cnr Av Charles Darwin & Av 12 de Febrero; ⏲8am-noon & 2-5pm Mon-Fri, 9am-noon Sat) offices.

If you are traveling independently, take the public bus signed 'Muelle' from the airport to the dock (a free 10-minute ride) for the ferry to Isla Santa Cruz. A 10-minute ferry ride (US80¢) will take you across to Santa Cruz, where you will be met by a Citteg bus to take you to Puerto Ayora, about 45 minutes away (US$1.80).

Arriving air passengers on prebooked tours will be met by a boat representative for the bus-boat-bus journey to Puerto Ayora.

Private speedboats head daily to Isabela and San Cristóbal at 2pm (US$25 to $30, two hours). Buy tickets from travel agencies or the small kiosk near the water-taxi pier.

Around Puerto Ayora

In addition to sites mentioned in the Puerto Ayora section, the following sites require a guide. You can arrange day trips with tour operators in Puerto Ayora.

A footpath north from Bellavista leads toward the highlands, including **Cerro Crocker** and other hills and extinct volcanoes. This is a good chance to see local vegetation and birds. It is about 6km from Bellavista to the crescent-shaped hill of Media Luna and another 3km to the base of Cerro Crocker.

The twin craters called **Los Gemelos** are 5km beyond Santa Rosa. They are sinkholes, rather than volcanic craters, and are surrounded by Scalesia forest. Vermilion flycatchers are often seen and short-eared owls are spotted on occasion. Although less than 100m from the road, the craters are hidden by vegetation, so go with a guide.

Near Santa Rosa, **El Chato Tortoise Reserve** (admission US$3; ⏲8am-5pm) protects giant tortoises roaming in the wild. You can also visit this area by horseback.

Isla San Cristóbal

Locals call San Cristóbal the capital of paradise, and since Puerto Baquerizo Moreno is the capital of Galápagos province, it technically is. The island has several easily accessible visitor sites, incredible surf and the lovely, laid-back capital itself.

PUERTO BAQUERIZO MORENO

Often just called Cristóbal, Puerto Baquerizo Moreno is a relaxed little town, busy with tourists during the high season and sleepy the rest of the year. It's possible to arrange tours here, though it's a great spot just to unwind. Three world-class surf breaks are nearby.

Air passengers arriving in Puerto Baquerizo Moreno can walk into town in minutes.

Sights & Activities

The intriguing exhibits at the modern **Interpretation Center** (☎252-0358, ext 102; admission free; ⏲8am-5pm) on the north side of the bay explains the history and significance of the Galápagos better than anywhere else in the islands.

La Lobería BEACH

Just after the school, and before the airport, a road leads several kilometers (about a 30-minute walk) to La Lobería, a rocky beach with a lazy sea-lion colony. It's good for year-round surfing, and there are lots of land iguanas along the trail leading past the beach.

Sharksky Tours SNORKELING, DIVING

(☎252-1188; www.sharksky.com; Av Charles Darwin) This company has snorkeling day trips (US$50), overnight hotel-based tours, and scuba diving (two boat dives US$145) and is probably the best resource for surfing information and board and bike rentals (US$15).

Sleeping & Eating

Casa Blanca HOTEL $$

(☎252-0392; www.casablancagalapagos.com; Av Charles Darwin; s/d/tr/q US$50/70/90/100; ❄) In town, this whitewashed adobe building has charmingly decorated rooms, some with sea-facing balconies. It sits on the *malecón* directly across from the passenger pier.

Casa de Laura Hostal HOSTEL $

(☎252-0173; hostalcasadelaura@hotmail.com; Av de la Armada; r per person US$15; ❄) This friendly, family-owned hideaway is one of the best-value places in town, with a nicely landscaped courtyard, and hammocks in the tiny cacti garden in front. It's across from the basketball court at the western end of Av Charles Darwin.

Cabañas Don Jorge CABINA $$

(☎252-0208; www.cabanasdonjorge.com; Av Alsacio Northia; s/d US$25/40; 📶) Looking very much like a survivalist camp, these aging, rustic cabins are a good option for self-catering. Look for Don Jorge on your right on the way to Playa Mann.

Inexpensive restaurants abound and *almuerzos* are good value. Be sure to have a *batido* at **Cabaña Mi Grande** (José de Villamil; drinks US$1.50).

AROUND PUERTO BAQUERIZO MORENO

You can visit the following sites without a guide. About 1.7km northeast of Puerto Baquerizo Moreno, **Cerro de las Tijeretas** (Frigate-Bird Hill) provides good views and can be reached on a trail without a guide. You'll pass a national park information office en route, and there's excellent snorkeling on the ocean side.

For about US$20 round trip, taxis in Puerto Baquerizo Moreno will go to the farming center of **El Progreso**, about 8km east at the base of the Cerro San Joaquín (896m), the highest point on San Cristóbal. From El Progreso, you can catch one of the occasional buses (or hire a jeep, hitchhike or walk the 10km) to **El Junco Lagoon**, a freshwater lake about 700m above sea level with superb views. The road continues beyond the lagoon and branches to the isolated beach of **Puerto Chino**, where you can camp with permission from the Galápagos **national park office** (☎252-0138; www.galapagospark.org) in Puerto Baquerizo Moreno. The other branch goes to **La Galapaguera**, where giant tortoises can be seen.

About an hour north of Puerto Baquerizo Moreno by boat is tiny, rocky **Isla Lobos**, the main sea-lion and blue-footed booby colony open to visitors (a guide is required) to Isla San Cristóbal. The island has a 300m trail and you can see lava lizards here.

Isla Isabela

Isabela is the largest island in the archipelago and boasts dramatic landscapes sprinkled with active volcanoes.

Puerto Villamil is the main town on seldom visited Isla Isabela. Backed by a lagoon where flamingos and marine iguanas live and situated on a beautiful white-sand beach, it's a sleepy little village of sandy roads and small homes. All of the town's and island's fresh water is shipped by boat from Santa Cruz.

Behind and to the west of the village is the **Villamil Lagoon** (⏲trail 6am-6pm), which is known for its marine iguanas and migrant birds, especially waders – more than 20 species have been reported here. A 1km-long trail begins just past the Iguana Crossing Hotel as a wooden boardwalk over the lagoon passing through mangroves and dense vegetation, eventually ending in the **Centro de Crianza de Tortugas** (Giant Tortoise Breeding Center). Volunteers here can explain the work being done to help restore the population of this species on Isabela.

About 4km west of town is the **Muro de las Lágrimas** (Wall of Tears), a 100m-long wall of lava rocks built by convicts under harsh and abusive conditions. The penal colony closed in 1959 but the wall stands as a monument to an infamous chapter in the island's history. Accommodations on the island run a wide range of tours on and around the island.

With its beachfront bar, hammocks, bonfires, live music and sea-facing deck, **Caleta Iguana Hotel & Surf Camp** (☎252-9405; www.caletaiguana.com; Casa Rosada; r per person without bathroom from US$15, s/d from US$35/60) is the place to go for a lively, laid-back social scene. It's on the beach at the western edge of town. One of the best-value budget options in town is the family-run **La Posada del Caminante** (☎252-9407; www.posadadelcaminante.com; r per person US$10-15; 📶). It's a few blocks behind Poza Salinas and west of the intersection of Avenidas 16 de Marzo and Cormorant.

There are a half-dozen restaurants located on the central square on Av Antonio Gill, between Las Fragatas and 16 de Marzo.

Isla Santa María

Also known as Floreana, this island has fewer than 100 inhabitants, most spread near **Puerto Velasco Ibarra**, the island's only settlement. There you will find **Hostal Wittmer** (☎252-9506; s/d/tr US$30/50/70), which also doubles as the best eatery and information and guide center. Most of the beachfront rooms are in a small, white two-story building and have private balconies; meals can be provided. It's run by the family of the late Margaret Wittmer, who is famous for being one of the islands' first settlers.

UNDERSTAND ECUADOR

Ecuador Today

Until recently, Ecuador was an economic basket case, a prototypical 'banana republic,' plagued by widespread poverty, economic inequality and political turmoil – with more than 80 changes of government since the republic's founding in 1830. Yet over the last decade, Ecuador has seen momentous development, with huge investments in education, health care and infrastructure. For many Ecuadorians, it's one of the most hopeful and empowering times in the nation's history.

Much of the credit for this dramatic turn of events is given to Rafael Correa, Ecuador's popular young president, who ushered in a serious of bold changes following his election. A new constitution in 2008, approved by popular referendum, laid the groundwork for a new social archetype: one that increased spending on health care and the poor, gave more rights to indigenous groups, accorded new protections to the environment and even allowed civil unions for gay couples.

Ecuador has doubled social spending since 2006, investing some $8.5 billion in education and over $5 billion in health care. Over 5500km of roads and highways have been built or repaired. A new program for the disabled has helped 300,000 people, while the poorest off now receive a monthly stipend. The poverty rate has fallen significantly, declining by 9% between 2006 and 2011. Middle-class Ecuadorians have also benefitted under programs such as a $5000 grant for first-time homebuyers.

What's fueling this growth in public spending? (Hint, it's not bananas.) It's the thirst for oil – and those high crude prices on the world market. Ecuador is particularly well endowed when it comes to petroleum, home to the third-largest oil reserves in South America after Venezuela and Brazil. Oil accounts for over 30% of government revenues and half of all export earnings.

Until Correa, however, much of the wealth from Ecuador's reserves flowed out of the country. A new law in 2010 changed the terms of contracts with multinational corporations and increased the government's share of gross oil revenues from 13% to 87%, boosting state revenues by $870 million in 2011.

Oil is a hot topic in Ecuador – particularly following the landmark $18-billion judgment in 2011 against Chevron for allegedly dumping toxic wastes in the Ecuadorian jungle. The Yasuni Reserve, a pristine area of the Amazon (and home to uncontacted tribes) holds huge oil reserves, which the government has offered to leave untapped if enough money can be raised on the world market.

Despite widespread popularity, Correa is not without his critics. His often-combative approach has earned him many enemies, particularly among right-wing elites who feel targeted by Correa's reformist agenda. In 2010 the nation briefly erupted in chaos when Correa was taken hostage by a group of mutinous police (an event he later described as a coup), which ended following a shoot-out with loyal military troops when they rescued him.

Some also worry about Correa's warm relations with Venezuela, and his periodic anti-American rhetoric – the expelling of the US ambassador in 2010 and the welcoming of Iran's Ahmadinejad in 2012 over trade negotiations didn't add to the good cheer in Washington. (The US, however, remains Ecuador's largest trading partner.) More worrying is Ecuador's poorly diversified economy: if oil prices fall significantly, the effect on Ecuador's ambitious social programs could be devastating.

History

The land of fire and ice has certainly had a tumultuous history. Since becoming an independent nation in 1830, Ecuador has gone through countless changes in government and 20 constitutions – the most recent drafted in 2008. Fueling the Andean nation's volatility are rivalries both internal (conservative, church-backed Quito versus liberal, secular Guayaquil) and external (border disputes with Peru and Colombia).

Early Cultures

The oldest tools found in Ecuador date back to 9000 BC, meaning that humans were mucking about in the region in the Stone Age. The most important early societies developed along the coast, which was obviously a more habitable landscape than the frigid highlands. Ecuador's first permanent sedentary culture was the Valdivia, which emerged along the Santa Elena Peninsula nearly 6000 years ago.

By the 11th century AD, Ecuador had two dominant cultures: the expansionist Cara along the coast and the peaceful Quitu in the highlands. These cultures merged and became known as the Quitu-Caras, or the Shyris. They were the dominant force in the highlands until the 1300s, when the Puruhá of the central highlands became increasingly powerful. The third important group was the Cañari, further south. These were the cultures the Inca encountered when they began their expansion north from present-day Peru.

Land of the Four Quarters

Until the early 15th century, the Inca empire was concentrated around Cuzco, Peru. That changed dramatically during the rule of Inca Pachacutec, whose expansionist policies set into motion the creation of the vast Inca empire, Tahuantinsuyo, meaning 'Land of the Four Quarters' in Quichua (called Quechua elsewhere in South America). By the time the Inca reached Ecuador they were under the rule of Túpac Yupanqui, Pachacutec's successor, and they met with fierce resistance, both from the Cañari and the Quitu-Caras. In one battle the Inca massacred thousands of Caras and dumped them in a lake near Otavalo, which supposedly turned the waters red and gave the lake its name, Laguna Yaguarcocha (Lake of Blood).

The subjugation of the north took many years, during which the Inca Túpac fathered a son with a Cañari princess. The son, Huayna Capác, grew up in present-day Ecuador and succeeded his father to the Inca throne. Huayna Capác had two sons: Atahualpa, who grew up in Quito, and Huáscar, who was raised in Cuzco.

When Huayna Capác died in 1527, he left his empire not to one son, as was traditional, but to two. Rivalry developed between the sons, which eventually boiled into civil war. After several years of fighting, Atahualpa defeated Huáscar near Ambato in central Ecuador. Atahualpa was thus ruling a weakened and still divided Inca empire when Francisco Pizarro landed in Peru in 1532.

The Spanish Power Play

Pizarro's advance was rapid and dramatic. He successfully exploited divisions within the Inca empire and enlisted many non-Inca ethnic groups that had been recently and reluctantly subjugated by the Inca. Most importantly, Inca warriors on foot were no match for the fully armored conquistadors on horseback who slaughtered them by the thousands. Within three years, and after betraying Inca rulers on several occasions, the Spanish controlled the former Inca empire.

Settling In

From 1535 onward, the colonial era proceeded with no major uprisings by indigenous Ecuadorians. Francisco Pizarro made his brother Gonzalo the governor of Quito in 1540. Hoping to find more gold, Gonzalo sent his lieutenant, Francisco de Orellana, to explore the Amazon. The lieutenant and his force ended up floating all the way to the Atlantic, becoming the first party to descend the Amazon and cross the continent. This feat took almost a year and is still commemorated in Ecuador.

During the first centuries of colonial rule, Lima (Peru) was the seat of Ecuador's political administration. In 1563 Ecuador, originally a *gobernación* (province), became known as the Audiencia de Quito, a more important political division. In 1739 the Audiencia de Quito was transferred from the viceroyalty of Peru, of which it was a part, to the viceroyalty of Colombia (then known as Nueva Grenada).

Ecuador remained a peaceful colony during these centuries, and agriculture and the arts flourished. Churches and monasteries were constructed atop every sacred indigenous site and were decorated with unique carvings and paintings, the result of a blend of Spanish and indigenous artistic influences. This so-called Escuela Quiteña (Quito school of art), still admired by visitors today, has left an indelible stamp on both the colonial buildings of the time and Ecuador's unique art history.

Life was comfortable for the ruling colonialists, but the indigenous people – and later, the *mestizos* (people of mixed Spanish and indigenous descent) – were treated abysmally under their rule. A system of forced labor was not only tolerated but encouraged, and by the 18th century there were several indigenous uprisings against the Spanish ruling classes. Social unrest, as well as the introduction of cocoa and sugar plantations in the northwest, prompted land-owners to import African slave laborers. Much of the rich Afro-Ecuadorian culture found in Esmeraldas province today is a legacy of this period.

Adiós, España

The first serious attempt at independence from Spain was made on August 10, 1809, by a partisan group led by Juan Pío Montúfar. The group took Quito and installed a government, but royalist troops regained control in only 24 days.

A decade later, Simón Bolívar, the Venezuelan liberator, freed Colombia in his march southward from Caracas. Bolívar then supported the people of Guayaquil when they claimed independence on October 9, 1820. It took another two years for Ecuador to be entirely liberated from Spanish rule. The decisive battle was fought on May 24, 1822, when Mariscal (Field Marshall) Sucre, one of Bolívar's best generals, defeated the royalists at Pichincha and took Quito.

Bolívar's dream was to form a united South America. He began by amalgamating Venezuela, Colombia and Ecuador into the independent state of Gran Colombia. This lasted eight years, with Ecuador becoming fully independent in 1830. That same year a treaty was signed with Peru, establishing a boundary between the two nations.

Liberals Versus Conservatives

Following independence from Spain, Ecuador's history unfolded with the typically Latin American political warfare between liberals and conservatives. Quito emerged as the main center for the church-backed conservatives, while Guayaquil has traditionally been considered liberal and socialist. The rivalry between these groups has frequently escalated to extreme violence: conservative President García Moreno was shot and killed in 1875, and liberal President Eloy Alfaro was killed and burned by a mob in Quito in 1912. The rivalry between the two cities continues on a social level today. Over time, the military began assuming control, and the 20th century saw more periods of military than civilian rule.

War with Peru

In 1941 war broke out with Peru over border disputes. The boundary was redrawn by a conference of foreign-government ministers in the 1942 Protocol of Rio de Janeiro. Ecuador never recognized this border, and minor skirmishes with Peru have occurred because of it – the most serious was the short war in early 1995, when several dozen soldiers on both sides were killed. Finally, after more fighting in 1998, Peru and Ecuador negotiated a settlement in which Peru retained a majority of the land in question.

Recent Political Developments

Ecuador's most recent period of democracy began in 1979, when President Jaime Roldos Aguilera was elected. Over the next two decades, control flip-flopped democratically between liberals and conservatives.

In the 1998 elections Jamil Mahuad, former mayor of Quito, emerged victorious and was immediately put to the test. The devastating effects of El Niño and the sagging oil market of 1997–98 sent the economy into a tailspin in 1999. The sucre, Ecuador's former currency, depreciated from about 7000 per US dollar to about 25,000 by January 2000.

When Mahuad declared his plan to dump the national currency in exchange for the US dollar, the country erupted in protest. On January 21, 2000, marches shut down the capital and protesters took over the Ecuadorian congress building, forcing Mahuad to resign. The protesters were led by Antonio Vargas, Coronel Lucio Gutiérrez and former supreme court president Carlos Solórzano, who immediately turned the presidency over to former vice president Gustavo Noboa. Noboa went ahead with 'dollarization,' and in September 2000, the US dollar became Ecuador's official currency.

Presidential Comings & Goings

President Noboa was succeeded in 2002 by former coup leader Lucio Gutiérrez, whose populist agenda led to his election. But shortly after taking office, Gutiérrez began backing down on his promises of radical reform and implemented IMF-encouraged austerity measures to finance the country's massive debt. In 2004 he also tossed out most of the supreme court, which allowed him to expel his rivals from the court and change the constitution in order to drop corruption charges against his former ally, the popularly despised ex-president Antonio Bucaram. As a consequence, protests erupted in the capital, and in April 2005 the congress finally voted Gutiérrez out, replacing him with vice president Alfredo Palacios. Ousted and exiled, Gutiérrez made a surprise return to Ecuador in 2005, claiming he was the country's rightful leader. He was immediately jailed, but upon his release began campaigning for the presidency once again. However, his political days were over, and in 2006 Rafael Correa, a US-educated economist and former finance minister (under Palacios) was elected president.

Culture

Population

Ecuador has the highest population density of any South American country – about 53 people per square kilometer. Despite this, the country still feels incredibly wild, mainly because over 30% of the population is crammed into the cities of Quito and Guayaquil, and another 30% resides in Ecuador's other urban areas. Nearly half of the country's people live on the coast (including the Galápagos), while about 45% live in the highlands. The remainder live in the

Oriente, where colonization is slowly increasing.

About 65% of the Ecuadorian people are *mestizos,* 25% are indigenous, 7% are Spanish and 3% are black. Other ethnicities account for less than 1%. The majority of the indigenous people speak Quichua and live in the highlands. A few small groups live in the lowlands.

Lifestyle

How an Ecuadorian lives is a matter of geography, ethnicity and class. A poor *campesino* (peasant) family that cultivates the thin volcanic soil of a steep highland plot lives very differently from a coastal fishing family residing in the mangroves of Esmeraldas province, or a family staying in the slums of Guayaquil. An indigenous Saraguro family that tends communally owned cattle in the southern highlands has a dramatically different life to that of an upper-class *quiteño* (people from Quito) family, which might have several maids, all the latest electronic gadgets and an expensive car in the garage.

An estimated 40% of Ecuadorians live below the poverty line, and paying for cooking fuel and putting food in the belly is a constant concern for most people. But, as most first-time visitors are astounded to experience, even the poorest Ecuadorians exude an openness, generosity and happiness all too rare in developed countries. Fiestas are celebrated with fervor by everyone, and you'll sometimes roll around in bed, kept awake until dawn by the noise of a nearby birthday bash.

Religion

The predominant religion (over 80% of the population) is Roman Catholicism, with a small minority of other churches. Indigenous people tend to blend Catholicism with their own traditional beliefs.

Arts

Music

Música folklórica (traditional Andean music) has a distinctive, haunting sound that has been popularized in Western culture by songs such as Paul Simon's version of 'El cóndor pasa' ('If I Could'). Its otherworldly quality results from the use of a pentatonic (five-note) scale and pre-Colombian wind and percussion instruments that conjure the windswept quality of *páramo* (high-altitude grassland) life. It is best heard at a *peña* (folk-music club or performance).

Northwest Ecuador, particularly Esmeraldas province, is famous for its marimba music, historically the sound of Afro-Ecuadorian population. Today, it's becoming increasingly difficult to hear live because many Afro-Ecuadorians have swapped it for salsa and other musical forms.

If there's one music you won't escape, it's cumbia, with a rhythm resembling that of a trotting three-legged horse. Originally from Colombia, Ecuadorian cumbia has a more raw (almost amateur), melancholic sound and is dominated by the electronic keyboard. Bus drivers love the stuff, perhaps because it so strangely complements those back-road journeys through the Andes.

Although most people associate Ecuador with *folklórica,* the country's most popular national music is the *pasillo,* which is rooted in the waltz. The origins of *pasillo* date back to the 19th century when Ecuador was part of Gran Colombia. These poignant songs with their melancholic melodies often touch on themes of disillusionment, lost love and unquenchable longing for the past. Pasillo's most famous voice was that of Julio Jaramillo (1935–78), who popularized the genre throughout Latin America.

When it comes to youth culture, reggaeton (Caribbean-born blend of Puerto Rican *bomba,* dance hall and hip-hop) is the anthem among urban club-goers. Ecuador also has its share of Latin pop artists, with singers like teen-idol Fausto Miño filling the airwaves.

Architecture

Many of Quito's churches were built during the colonial period, and the architects were influenced by the Escuela Quiteña (Quito school of art). In addition, churches often show Moorish influences, particularly in the decorative details of interiors. Known as *mudéjar,* this reflects an architectural style that developed in Spain beginning in the 12th century. The overall architecture of colonial churches is overpoweringly ornamental and almost cloyingly rich – in short, baroque.

Many colonial houses have two storys, with the upper floors bearing ornate balconies. The walls are whitewashed and the roofs are red tile. Quito's Old Town and Cuenca are Unesco World Heritage Sites and both abound with beautifully preserved colonial architecture.

Visual Arts

The colonial religious art found in many churches and museums – especially in Quito – was produced by indigenous artists trained by the Spanish conquistadors. The artists portrayed Spanish religious concepts, yet infused their own indigenous beliefs, giving birth to a unique religious art known as the Escuela Quiteña. The Quito school died out with independence.

The 19th century is referred to as the Republican period, and its art is characterized by formalism. Favorite subjects included heroes of the revolution, important members of the new republic's high society, and florid landscapes.

The 20th century saw the rise of the indigenist school, whose unifying theme is the oppression of Ecuador's indigenous inhabitants. Important *indigenista* artists include Camilo Egas (1889–1962), Oswaldo Guayasamín (1919–99), Eduardo Kingman (1913–97) and Gonzalo Endara Crow (1936–96). You can (and should!) see the works of these artists in Quito's galleries and museums. The former home of Guayasamín, also in Quito, houses a stunning showcase of his work.

Cuisine

Ecuadorian Dining 101

Lunch is the main meal of the day for many Ecuadorians. A cheap restaurant will serve a decent *almuerzo* (lunch of the day) for as little as US$2.50. An *almuerzo* consists of a *sopa* (soup) and a *segundo* (second dish), which is usually a stew with plenty of rice. Sometimes the *segundo* is *pescado* (fish), *lentejas* (lentils) or *menestras* (generally, bean stew). Some places serve salad, juice and *postre* (dessert), as well as the two main courses.

The *merienda* (evening meal) is a set meal, usually similar to lunch. If you don't want the *almuerzo* or *merienda,* you can choose from the menu, but this is always more expensive.

Parrillas (or *parrilladas*) are grillhouses. Steaks, pork chops, chicken breasts, blood sausage, liver and tripe are all served (together or individually, depending on the establishment).

Chifas (Chinese restaurants) are generally inexpensive. Among other standards, they serve *chaulafan* (rice dishes) and *tallarines* (noodle dishes). Vegetarians will find that *chifas* are reliable spots for a meatless dish.

Seafood can be delicious, particularly in Esmeraldas and Manabí provinces. The most common types of fish are *corvina* (technically white sea bass, but usually just a white fish) and *trucha* (trout). Popular throughout Ecuador, *ceviche* is uncooked seafood marinated in lemon and served with popcorn and sliced onions. *Ceviche* comes as *pescado* (fish), *camarones* (shrimp), *concha* (shellfish) or *mixto* (mixed). Unfortunately, improperly prepared *ceviche* is a source of cholera, so avoid it if in any doubt.

It's impossible to consider food from the highlands without discussing the once highly revered crop, *maìz* (corn). In its numerous varieties, corn has been the staple of the Andean diet for a millennium, and today it forms the basis of countless highland specialties. Kernels are toasted into *tostada* (toasted corn), popped into *cangil* (popcorn), boiled and treated to make *mote* (hominy) and milled into cornmeal.

Potatoes, of course, originated in the Andes, and are another essential food.

Drinking

Purify all tap water or buy bottled water. Some pharmacies, cafes and a growing number of guesthouses allow travelers to refill their water bottles from their purified source – a good option for those concerned about all the empty bottles that end up in landfills. *Agua con gas* is carbonated; *agua sin gas* is not carbonated.

Bottled drinks are cheap and all the usual soft drinks are available. The local ones have endearing names such as Bimbo or Lulu. Ask for your drink *helada* if you want it out of the refrigerator, *al clima* if you don't. Remember to say *sin hielo* (without ice) unless you really trust the water supply.

Jugos (juices) are available everywhere. Make sure you get *jugo puro* (pure) and not *con agua* (with water). The most common kinds are *mora* (blackberry), *tomate de árbol* (a strangely addictive local fruit), *naranja* (orange), *toronja* (grapefruit), *maracuyá* (passion fruit), *piña* (pineapple), *sandía* (watermelon), *naranjilla* (a local fruit that tastes like bitter orange) and papaya.

Coffee is widely available but often disappointing. Instant coffee, served *en leche* (with milk) or *en agua* (with water), is the most common. Espresso is found in better restaurants.

Té (tea) is served black with lemon and sugar. *Té de hierbas* (herb tea) and hot chocolate are also popular.

For alcoholic drinks, local *cervezas* (beers) are palatable and inexpensive. Pilsener is available in 650mL bottles, while Club comes in 330mL bottles. Imports are tough to find.

Ron (rum) is cheap and can be decent. The local firewater, *aguardiente,* is sugarcane alcohol, and is an acquired taste. A favorite Quito drink is *canelazo,* which is similar to a hot spiced rum. It's made with *aguardiente,* cinnamon and citrus juice, and is the perfect antidote to chilly highland nights.

Environment

Land

Despite its diminutive size, Ecuador has some of the world's most varied geography. The country can be divided into three regions: the Andes form the backbone of Ecuador; the coastal lowlands lie west of the mountains; and the Oriente, to the east, comprises the jungles of the upper Amazon Basin. In only 200km as the condor flies, you can climb from the coast to snowcaps, over 6km above sea level, and then descend to the jungle on the country's eastern side. The Galápagos Islands lie on the equator, 1000km west of Ecuador's coast, and constitute one of the country's 21 provinces.

Wildlife

Ecuador is one of the most species-rich countries on the globe, deemed a 'megadiversity hot spot' by ecologists. The country has more than 20,000 plant species, with new ones discovered every year. In comparison, there are only 17,000 plant species on the entire North American continent. The tropics, in general, harbor many more species than temperate regions do, but another reason for Ecuador's biodiversity is simply that the country holds a great number of habitat types. Obviously, the Andes will support very different species than the tropical rainforests, and when intermediate biomes and the coastal areas are included, the result is a wealth of different ecosystems, a riot of life that draws nature lovers from the world over.

Bird-watchers flock to Ecuador for the great number of bird species recorded here – some 1600, or about twice the number found in any one of the continents of North America, Europe or Australia. But Ecuador isn't just for the birds: some 300 mammal species have been recorded, from monkeys in the Amazon to the rare Andean spectacled bears in the highlands.

National Parks

Ecuador has over 30 government-protected parks and reserves (of which nine carry the title of 'national park'), as well as numerous privately administered nature reserves. Eighteen percent of the country lies within protected areas. Ecuador's first *parque nacional* (national park) was the Galápagos, formed in 1959. Scattered across mainland Ecuador are eight other national parks. The following are the most visited (from north to south):

Parque Nacional Cotopaxi (p657) The towering ice-capped cone of Volcán Cotopaxi makes for spectacular year-round hiking and mountaineering.

Parque Nacional Yasuní (p683) Amazon rainforest, big rivers and caiman-filled lagoons, plus monkeys, birds, sloths and more, mean year-round forest fun.

Parque Nacional Machalilla (p693) Coastal dry forest, beaches and islands are home to whales, seabirds, monkeys and reptiles. Hiking opportunities and beaches are superb.

Parque Nacional Sangay (p669) Volcanoes, *páramo* and cloud forest harbor spectacled bears, tapirs, pumas and ocelots, and offer hiking, climbing and wildlife-watching year-round.

Parque Nacional Cajas (p677) Shimmering lakes and moorlike *parámo* make this highland park an excellent adventure from Cuenca.

Parque Nacional Podocarpus (p679) From cloud forest to rainforest, this epic southern park is best explored from Loja, Zamora or Vilcabamba.

Many parks are inhabited by native peoples who were living in the area long before it achieved park status. In the case of the Oriente parks, indigenous hunting practices (which have a greater impact as outside interests diminish their original territories and resources) have met with concern from those seeking to protect the park. The issue of how to best protect these areas from interests such as oil, timber and mining industries, while recognizing the rights of indigenous people, continues to be extremely complicated.

As of 2012, all national parks – apart from the Galápagos (which costs $110 to enter) – are now free. This may change in coming years.

Environmental Issues

Ecuador has one of South America's highest deforestation rates. In the highlands, almost all of the natural forest cover has disappeared, and only a few pockets remain, mainly in privately administered nature reserves. Along the coast, once plentiful mangrove forests have all but vanished to make way for artificial shrimp ponds.

About 95% of the forests of the western slopes and lowlands have become agricultural land, mostly banana plantations. Although much of the rainforest in the Ecuadorian Amazon remains standing, it is being seriously threatened by fragmentation. Since the discovery of oil, roads have been laid, colonists have followed and the destruction of the forest has increased exponentially. The main drives behind the destruction are logging, cattle ranching, and oil and mineral extraction.

The rainforest's indigenous inhabitants – who depend on the rivers for drinking water and food – are also dramatically affected. Oil residues, oil treatment chemicals, erosion and fertilizers all contaminate the rivers, killing fish and rendering formerly potable water toxic. The documentary *Crude*, which premiered in 2009, provides a disturbing portrait of the heavy toll exacted on local inhabitants.

SURVIVAL GUIDE

Directory A–Z

Accommodations

There is no shortage of places to stay in Ecuador, but during major fiestas or the night before market day, accommodations can be tight, so plan ahead. Most hotels have single-room rates, although during high season some beach towns charge for the number of beds in the room, regardless of the number of people checking in. In popular resort areas, high-season prices (running from June to August and mid-December to January) are about 30% higher than the rest of the year.

Ecuador has a growing number of youth hostels, as well as inexpensive *pensiones* (short-term budget accommodations in a family home). Staying with families is an option in remote villages.

Activities

Where to begin? There are so many exciting activities in Ecuador that any list will certainly miss something. For climbers, the volcanic, snowcapped peaks of Ecuador's central highlands – including Chimborazo (a doozy at 6310m) and Cotopaxi (5897m) – attract mountaineers from around the world. Quito, Riobamba, Baños and Latacunga are the best towns to hire guides and gear.

How about hiking? The moorlike landscape of Parque Nacional Cajas; the cloud forests of Parque Nacional Podocarpus or Mindo; the windswept *páramo* of Lagunas de Mojanda near Otavalo; the spectacular high-Andean Quilotoa Loop area; and the coastal dry forests of Parque Nacional Machalilla are just a few of Ecuador's hiking possibilities.

Ecuador is also one of the world's top bird-watching destinations, with over 1600 species on record. Mindo, the lower Río Napo region of the Amazon and the Galápagos are extraordinary places for bird-watching.

Tena in the Oriente is Ecuador's kayaking and river-rafting capital, where it's easy to set up day runs down the nearby Río Napo (class III) or Río Misahuallí (class IV+).

The surfing is excellent at Montañita and on Isla San Cristóbal in the Galápagos. Playas has some decent nearby breaks, but you'll have to make friends with the locals (try the Playas Club Surf) to find them. The

SLEEPING PRICE RANGES

The following price ranges refer to a double room in high season. Room prices include bathroom. Exceptions are noted in specific listings.

$ less than US$30

$$ US$30 to US$80

$$$ more than US$80

Galápagos are also famous for scuba diving and snorkeling (think hammerhead sharks and giant manta rays).

Mountain biking is growing in popularity, with a handful of outfitters in Quito and Riobamba offering memorable trips over challenging terrain (like Volcán Chimborazo). You can also head off on your own on trips like the dramatic descent from Baños to Puyo. You can rent bikes for about US$7 to US$10 per day in places such as Baños, Vilcabamba and Riobamba, or go for the extreme downhill day trips offered by outfitters in those towns, as well as in Quito and Cuenca.

Books

Lonely Planet's *Ecuador & the Galápagos Islands* has more detailed travel information on the country.

If there's one book that nails Ecuadorian culture on the head, it's the eloquent and humorous *Living Poor,* written by Moritz Thomsen. Joe Kane's *Savages* illustrates the oil industry's impacts on the Ecuadorian Amazon.

The Panama Hat Trail, by Tom Miller, is a fascinating book about the author's search for that most quintessential and misnamed of Ecuadorian products, the panama hat. For a more literary (and surreal) impression of Ecuador, read Henri Michaux' *Ecuador: A Travel Journal,* or Kurt Vonnegut's absurd *Galápagos,* which takes place in a futuristic Guayaquil as well as on the islands.

Business Hours

Reviews found throughout this book provide opening hours when they differ from the following standard hours.

Banks 8am to 2pm or 8am to 4pm Monday to Friday

Bars 6pm to midnight Monday to Thursday, to 2am Friday & Saturday

EATING PRICE RANGES

The following price ranges refer to a main course. Unless otherwise stated service charges and taxes are included in the price.

$ less than US$7

$$ US$7 to US$14

$$$ more than US$14

Post offices 8am to 6pm Monday to Friday, 8am to 1pm Saturday

Restaurants 10:30am to 11pm Monday to Saturday

Shops 9am to 7pm Monday to Friday, 9am to noon Saturday

Electricity

Ecuador uses 110V, 60 cycles, AC (the same as in North America). Plugs have two flat prongs, as in North America.

Embassies & Consulates

Embassies and consulates are best visited in the morning. New Zealand has no consular representation in Ecuador.

Australian Embassy (☎04-601-7529; ausconsulate@unidas.com.ec; Rocafuerte 520, 2nd fl, Quito)

Canadian Embassy Quito (☎02-245-5499; www.canadainternational.gc.ca/ecuador-equateur; Av Amazonas 4153 & Unión de Periodistas); Guayaquil (☎04-215-8333; cnr Avs Joaquin Orranita & Juan Tanca Marengo)

Colombian Embassy Quito (☎02-222-2486; Av Colón 1133 & Amazonas, 7th fl); Guayaquil (☎04-263-0674/5; www.ccolombiaguayaquil.com; Francisco de Orellana, World Trade Center, Tower B, 11th fl); Lago Agrio (☎06-283-0084; Av Quito 1-52); Tulcán (☎06-298-0559; Av Manabi 58-087)

Dutch Embassy (☎02-222-9229; www.embajadadeholanda.com; cnr Av 12 de Octubre 1942 & Cordero, World Trade Center, Tower 1, 1st fl, Quito)

French Embassy Quito (☎02-294-3800; cnr Leonidas Plaza 127 & Av Patria); Guayaquil (☎04-232-8442; cnr José Mascote 909 & Hurtado)

German Embassy Quito (☎02-297-0820; Naciones Unidas E10-44 at República de El Salvador, Edificio Citiplaza, 12th fl); Guayaquil (☎04-220-6867/8; cnr Avs Las Monjas 10 & CJ Arosemena, Km 2.5, Edificio Berlín)

Irish Embassy (☎02-357-0156; cnr Yanacocha N72-64 & Juan Procel, Quito)

Peruvian Embassy Quito (☎02-246-8410; www.embajadadelperu.org.ec; cnr República de El Salvador N34-361 & Irlanda); Guayaquil (☎04-228-0114; www.consuladoperuguayaquil.com; Av Francisco de Orellana 501); Loja (☎07-257-9068; Sucre 10-56); Machala (☎07-293-0680; cnr Bolívar & Colón)

UK Embassy Quito (☎297-0800; http://ukinecuador.fco.gov.uk/en; cnr Naciones Unidas

& República de El Salvador, Edificio Citiplaza, 14th fl); Guayaquil (☎04-256-0400; cnr Córdova 623 & Padre Solano)

USA Embassy Quito (☎398-5000; http://ecuador.usembassy.gov; cnr Av Avigiras E12-170 & Eloy Alfaro); Guayaquil (☎04-232-3570; http://guayaquil.usconsulate.gov; cnr 9 de Octubre & García Moreno)

Gay & Lesbian Travelers

Ecuador is probably not the best place to be outwardly affectionate with a partner of the same sex. Homosexuality was illegal until 1997. Quito and Guayaquil have underground social scenes, but outside the occasional dance club, they're hard to find. Check out the somewhat useful **Gay Guide to Quito** (http://quito.queercity.info) or **Gayecuador** (www.gayecuador.com).

Health

Medical care is available in major cities, but may be difficult to find in rural areas. Most doctors and hospitals will expect payment in cash, regardless of whether you have travel health insurance. Pharmacies in Ecuador are known as *farmacias*.

The main health hazards to be aware of are altitude sickness, malaria, typhoid and yellow fever. See the Health chapter (p1066) for more information.

Internet Access

All but the smallest of towns have internet cafes. Prices hover around US$1 per hour, though they get higher in small towns and on the Galápagos.

Language

Ecuador is one of the best places to study Spanish on the entire continent. Quito and Cuenca, and to a lesser extent Otavalo and Baños, all have schools where you can have one-on-one classes and stay with a local host family. Private classes (one-on-one) range from US$7 to US$10 per hour; group classes are marginally cheaper (about US$5 to US$6 per hour).

Legal Matters

Drug penalties in Ecuador for possession of even small amounts of illegal drugs (which include marijuana and cocaine) are severe. Defendants often spend months in jail before they are brought to trial, and if convicted (as is usually the case), they can expect several years in jail.

Treat plainclothes 'policemen' with suspicion. If you're asked for ID by a uniformed official in broad daylight, show your passport.

In the event of a car accident, unless extremely minor, the vehicles should stay where they are until the police arrive and make a report. If you hit a pedestrian, you are legally responsible for the pedestrian's injuries and can be jailed unless you pay, even if the accident was not your fault. Drive defensively.

Maps

Ecuadorian bookstores carry a limited selection of Ecuadorian maps. The best selection is available from the **Instituto Geográfico Militar** (www.igm.gob.ec) in Quito.

Money

Ecuador's currency was the sucre until it was switched to the US dollar in 2000, a process called 'dollarization.'

ATMS

ATMs are the easiest way of getting cash. They're found in most cities and even in smaller towns, although note that they can sometimes be out of order. Make sure you have a four-digit PIN. Banco del Pacífico and Banco del Pichincha have Mastercard/Cirrus ATMs. Banco de Guayaquil has Visa/Plus ATMs.

BARGAINING

Bargaining is expected at food and crafts markets. Sometimes you can bargain on hotels during low season.

CASH

Bills are the same as those used in the US. Coins are identical in shape, size and material to their US counterparts, but instead of US presidents, they feature the faces and symbols of Ecuador. US coins are also used interchangeably.

Change is often quite difficult to come by. Trying to purchase inexpensive items with a US$20 bill (or even a US$10 bill) generally results in either you or the proprietor running from shop to shop until someone produces some change. If no one does, you're out of luck. Change bills whenever you can. To ask for change, make a deeply worried face and ask '*¿Tiene suelto?*' (Do you have change?).

CREDIT CARDS

Credit cards are a fine backup, but not widely accepted. Merchants accepting credit cards will often add from 4% to 10% to the bill. Paying cash is often better value. Visa and Mastercard are the most widely accepted cards.

MONEY CHANGERS

Foreign currencies can be exchanged into US dollars easily in Quito, Guayaquil and Cuenca, where rates are also the best. You can also change money at most of the major border crossings. In some places, however, notably the Oriente, it is quite difficult to exchange money. Exchange houses, called *casas de cambio,* are normally the best places; banks will also exchange money but are usually much slower. Generally, exchange rates are within 2% of one another in any given city.

TRAVELER'S CHECKS

Very few banks, hotels or retailers will cash traveler's checks, making them a poor option for visitors to Ecuador. Those that do change them typically tack on a rate of 2% to 4%. It's much more useful to have a supply of US cash and an ATM card (plus a backup ATM card just in case).

Public Holidays

On major holidays, banks, offices and other services are closed and public transportation is often very crowded; you should book ahead if possible. The following are Ecuador's major national holidays; they may be celebrated for several days around the actual date:

New Year's Day January 1

Epiphany January 6

Semana Santa (Easter Week) March/April

Labor Day May 1

Battle of Pichincha May 24. This day honors the decisive battle of independence from Spain in 1822.

Simón Bolívar's Birthday July 24

Quito Independence Day August 10

Guayaquil Independence Day October 9. This combines with the October 12 national holiday and is an important festival in Guayaquil.

Columbus Day/Día de la Raza October 12

All Saints' Day November 1

Day of the Dead (All Souls' Day) November 2. Celebrated by flower-laying ceremonies in cemeteries, it's especially colorful in rural areas, where entire indigenous families show up at cemeteries to eat, drink and leave offerings in memory of the departed.

Cuenca Independence Day November 3. Combines with the national holidays of November 1 and 2 to give Cuenca its most important fiesta of the year.

Christmas Day December 25

Safe Travel

Ecuador has a growing crime problem, and you'll need to travel smart to avoid becoming a victim. Armed robbery targeting tourists occurs in Quito and Guayaquil. Despite a police presence, Quito's Mariscal neighborhood is particularly bad. Always take a taxi after dark in Quito, even if your guesthouse is only a few blocks away.

Buses – both local and long-distance – are prime targets for thieves. Keeping your bag under your seat or on your back is a bad idea, as adroit thieves can slash-and-steal before you even realize anything is amiss. Every year or so, a few long-distance night buses are robbed on the way to/from the coast. Avoid taking night buses through the provinces of Guayas or Manabí unless you have to.

Taxis aren't always a safe bet. 'Express' kidnappings occur: holding people hostage while their ATM accounts are drained. Most of these incidents have been reported in Guayaquil; to avoid the risk, have someone call you a taxi rather than hailing one on the street.

Bandits have begun targeting tourists heading to jungle lodges in the Oriente, and there are also occasional flare-ups of guerrilla activity in some areas near the Colombian border. Before you go to this area, do some basic research.

As elsewhere in South America, take the normal precautions: ie, pickpocketing occurs in crowded places, such as markets and terminals. If you are robbed, get a *denuncia* (police report) from the local police station within 48 hours – they won't process a report after that.

Telephone

Travelers who aren't sporting cell phones can find a *centro de llamada* (telephone call center) in larger towns, though it's cheaper to make international calls through internet cafes, most of which have terminals equipped with Skype.

Public street phones are also common. Some use phone cards, which are sold in convenient places such as newsagents. Others only accept coins. All but the most basic hotels will allow you to make local city calls.

Hotels that provide international phone connections very often surcharge extremely heavily.

All telephone numbers in Ecuador have seven digits, and the first digit – except for cellular phone numbers – is always a '2.' If someone gives you a six-digit number (which sometimes happens), simply put a '2' in front of it.

From a private phone within Ecuador, dial ☎116 for an international operator.

Two-digit area codes (indicated after town headings) change by province. Drop the area code if you're calling within a province. If calling from abroad, drop the 0 from the code. Ecuador's country code is ☎593. All fixed-line telephone numbers in Ecuador have seven digits.

CELL PHONES

» Cellular telephone numbers in Ecuador are always preceded by ☎09.

» If bringing your own phone, GSM cell phones operating at 850MHz (GSM 850) will work on Claro and Movistar networks. Alegro uses the 1900MHz (GSM 1900).

» The cheapest way of staying connected is to purchase a SIM card (called a 'chip,' and costing around US$5 to US$7) from one of the above networks. Add credit by purchasing a *tarjeta pregago* (phone card) with your chosen carrier, which are available at many convenience stores, supermarkets and pharmacies.

Toilets

Ecuadorian plumbing has very low pressure. Putting toilet paper into the bowl may clog the system, so use the waste basket. This may seem unsanitary, but it's much better than clogged bowls and water overflowing onto the floor. Expensive hotels have adequate plumbing.

Public toilets are limited mainly to bus terminals, airports and restaurants. Toilets are called *servicios higiénicos* and are usually marked 'SS.HH.' People needing to use the toilet often ask to use the *baño* in a restaurant; toilet paper is rarely available – carry a personal supply.

Tourist Information

The government-run **Ministerio de Turismo** (http://ecuador.travel) is responsible for tourist information at the national level. It is slowly opening tourist information offices – known as **iTur** offices – in important towns throughout Ecuador.

South American Explorers (SAE; ☎222-5228; www.saexplorers.org; Washington 311 & Plaza Gutiérrez) has a clubhouse in Quito.

Travelers with Disabilities

Unfortunately, Ecuador's infrastructure for travelers with disabilities is virtually nonexistent.

Visas

Most travelers entering Ecuador as tourists, including citizens of Australasian countries, Japan, the EU, Canada and the USA, do not require visas. Upon entry, they will be issued a T-3 tourist card which is valid for up to 90 days. Sixty-day stamps are rarely given, but double-check if you're going to be in the country for a while. Residents of most Central American and some Asian countries require visas.

All travelers entering as diplomats, refugees, students, laborers, religious workers, businesspeople, volunteers and cultural-exchange visitors require nonimmigrant visas. Various immigrant visas are also available. Visas must be obtained from an Ecuadorian embassy and cannot be arranged within Ecuador.

Officially, to enter the country you must have a ticket out of Ecuador and sufficient funds for your stay, but border authorities rarely ask for proof of this. International vaccination certificates are not required by law, but some vaccinations, particularly against yellow fever, are advisable.

See also lonelyplanet.com and its links for up-to-date visa information.

VISA EXTENSIONS

New regulations mean it's a real headache getting visa extensions. Unless you're from an Andean pact country, tourist visas are not extendable. If you wish to stay longer than 90 days, you'll need to apply for a 12-IX Visa; you can also do this in the country, though it's more time-consuming. Pick up the necessary paperwork for the 12-IX Visa, and pay the

US$230 fee at the **Ministerio de Relaciones Exteriores** (02-299-3200; www.mmrree.gob.ec; Carrión E1-76 & Av 10 de Agosto, Quito) in Quito.

No matter what, don't wait until your visa has expired to sort out your paperwork, as the fine for overstaying can be hefty – US$200 to US$2000.

Volunteering

Numerous organizations look for the services of volunteers; however, many require at least a minimal grasp of Spanish, a minimum commitment of several weeks or months, as well as fees (anywhere from US$300 to US$600 per month) to cover the costs of room and board. Volunteers can work in conservation programs, help street kids, teach, build nature trails, construct websites, do medical or agricultural work – the possibilities are endless. Many jungle lodges also accept volunteers for long-term stays. To keep your volunteer costs down, your best bet is to look for a position when you get to Ecuador. Plenty of places need volunteers who only have their hard work to offer.

South American Explorers (SAE; 222-5228; www.saexplorers.org; Washington 311 & Plaza Gutiérrez) in Quito has a volunteer section where current offerings are posted. The classifieds section of the **Ecuador Explorer** (www.ecuadorexplorer.com) website has a list of organizations seeking volunteers.

Andean Bear Conservation Project (www.andeanbear.org) Trains volunteers as bear trackers.

AmaZOOnico (www.amazoonico.org) Work in the animal rehabilitation sector.

Bosque Nublado Santa Lucia (www.santaluciaecuador.com) Involved in reforestation, trail maintenance, construction, teaching English.

Ecole Idiomas (601-4757; www.ecoleidiomas.com; García E6-15 near Mera, Quito) A respected Quito language school and tour agency that offers a range of volunteer opportunities.

FEVI (Fund for Intercultural Education & Community Volunteer Service; www.fevi.org) FEVI works with children, the elderly, women's groups and indigenous communities.

Fundación Natura (www.fnatura.org) Ecuadorian nongovernment organization that needs volunteers for research and reforestation.

Junto con los Niños (www.juconi.org.ec) Work with street kids in the slum areas of Guayaquil.

Merazonia (www.merazonia.org) A refuge for injured animals.

New Era Galápagos Foundation (www.neweragalapagos.org) Sustainable tourism in the Galápagos. Volunteers live and work on Isla San Cristóbal.

Rainforest Concern (www.rainforestconcern.org) British nonprofit.

Reserva Biológica Los Cedros (www.reservaloscedros.org) In the cloud forests of the western Andean slopes.

Río Muchacho Organic Farm (www.riomuchacho.com) Volunteer opportunities in organic agriculture.

Yanapuma Foundation (02-290-7643; www.yanapuma.org; Veintimilla E8-125, 2nd fl, near Av 6 de Diciembre, Quito) Teaching English, reforestation, building houses, coastal clean-ups.

Women Travelers

Women travelers will generally find Ecuador safe and pleasant, although machismo is alive and well. Ecuadorian men often make flirtatious comments and whistle at single women. Women who firmly ignore unwanted verbal advances are often treated with respect.

On the coast, you'll find that come-ons are more predatory, and solo female travelers should take precautions such as staying away from bars and discos where they will likely get hit on, opting for taxis over walking etc. Racy conversation with a guy, while it may be ironic or humorous, is not common here, and a man will probably assume you're after one thing.

We have received warnings from women who were molested while on organized tours. If you're traveling solo, it's essential to do some investigating before committing to a tour: find out who's leading the tour, what other tourists will be on the outing and so on. Women-only travel groups or guides are available in a few situations.

Work

Officially, you need a work visa to get a job in Ecuador. English-teaching positions occasionally pop up in Quito or Cuenca. The pay is low but enough to live on. Tourist services (jungle lodges, tour operators etc) are good places to look for work.

Getting There & Away

Entering the Country

Entering the country is pretty straightforward, and border officials, especially at the airports, will efficiently whisk you through. At land borders, officers may take a little more time examining your passport, if only to kill a little time. Officially, you need proof of onward travel and evidence of sufficient funds for your stay, but in reality this is rarely requested. Proof of US$20 per day or a credit card is usually evidence of sufficient funds. However, international airlines flying to Quito may require a round-trip or onward ticket or a residence visa before they let you on the plane; you should be prepared for this possibility, although it's unlikely. Finally, though it's not legally required, you may be asked to show proof of vaccination against yellow fever if you are entering Ecuador from an infected area.

Air

AIRPORTS & AIRLINES

About 20km east of Quito, a new international airport was scheduled to open in late 2013. Check www.quiport.com for the latest details.

Currently, two international airports serve Ecuador: Quito's **Aeropuerto Mariscal Sucre** (www.quitoairport.com) and Guayaquil's **Aeropuerto José Joaquin de Olmedo** (GYE; ☎04-216-9000; www.tagsa.aero; Av de las Américas s/n).

TAME (☎02-396-6300; www.tame.com.ec) and **Aerogal** (☎1800-237-6425; www.aerogal.com.ec) are Ecuador's main airlines, but offer limited international flights. Aerogal has an impressive safety record; TAME less so, though it's been in the process of upgrading its fleet in recent years.

TICKETS

Ticket prices are highest during tourist high seasons: mid-June through early September, and December through mid-January. Working with a travel agent that deals specifically in Latin American travel is always an advantage.

Departure tax is now included in ticket prices rather than payable at the airport.

Bus

International bus tickets sold in Quito often require a change of bus at the border. It's usually cheaper and just as convenient to buy a ticket to the border and another ticket in the next country. The exceptions are the international buses going from Loja to Piura, Peru (via Macará), and from Guayaquil to Peru (via Huaquillas); on these, you don't have to change buses, and the immigration officials usually board the bus to take care of your paperwork. These are the primary routes between Ecuador and Peru. Zumba, south of Vilcabamba, is an alternative route to/from Peru in a scenic and less used location. The main bus route between Colombia and Ecuador is via Tulcán. Other border crossings between Colombia and Ecuador are not recommended for travelers owing to safety concerns.

River

For information on boat travel between Nuevo Rocafuerte (Ecuador) and Iquitos (Peru), see p683.

Getting Around

You can usually get anywhere quickly and easily. Bus is the most common mode of transportation, followed by plane. Buses can take you from the Colombian border to Peru's border in 18 hours. Boats are used in the northern coastal mangroves and in the Oriente.

Whatever form of transportation you choose, always carry your passport with you, both to board planes and to proffer during document checks on the road. People without documents may be arrested. If your passport is in order, these procedures are cursory. If you're traveling anywhere near the borders or in the Oriente, expect more frequent passport checks.

Air

With the exception of flying to the Galápagos, most internal flights are relatively cheap. One-way flights average US$70 to US$100. Almost all flights originate or terminate in Quito or Guayaquil. Some domestic flights have marvelous views of the snowcapped Andes – when flying from Quito to Guayaquil, sit on the left. Return flights to the Galápagos, incidentally, cost around US$530 from Quito and US$480 from Guayaquil.

Ecuador's domestic carriers include the following:

Aerogal (www.aerogal.com.ec) Serves Quito, Guayaquil, Cuenca, Isla Baltra (Galápagos), Isla San Cristóbal (Galápagos), Manta, plus Bogotá (Colombia), Medellín (Colombia), and Miami (USA).

Emetebe (☎09-932-2907; www.emetebe.com) Galápagos-based airline that flies between Isla Baltra, Isla San Cristóbal and Isla Isabela. Also flies from Quito via Guayaquil to Baltra and Isla San Cristóbal.

LAN (☎02-330-1484; www.lan.com) Flies from Quito to Cuenca, Guayaquil and the Galápagos (San Cristóbal and Isla Baltra, both via Guayaquil).

Saero (☎02-330-1152; www.saereo.com) Serves southern destinations (including Macas and Santa Rosa, near Machala) from Quito and/or Guayaquil.

TAME (www.tame.com.ec) Serves Coca, Cuenca, Esmeraldas, Isla Baltra (Galápagos), Isla San Cristóbal (Galápagos), Guayaquil, Lago Agrio, Loja, Macas, Manta, Portoviejo, Quito, Tulcán, plus Cali (Colombia) and Manaos (Brazil).

If you can't get a ticket for a particular flight (especially out of small towns), go to the airport early and get on the waiting list in the hope of a cancellation.

Boat

Motorized dugout canoes are the only transportation available in some roadless areas. Regularly scheduled boats are affordable, although not as cheap as a bus for a similar distance. Hiring your own boat and skipper is possible but extremely expensive. The lower Río Napo from Coca to Peru are the places you'll most likely travel to by boat (if you get out that far).

Bus

Buses are the lifeblood of Ecuador and the easiest way to get around. Most towns have a *terminal terrestre* (central bus terminal) for long-distance buses, although in some towns buses leave from various places. To get your choice of seat, buy tickets in advance from the terminal. During holiday weekends, buses can be booked up for several days in advance.

If you're traveling lightly, keep your luggage with you inside the bus. Otherwise, heave it onto the roof or stuff it into the luggage compartment and try to keep an eye on it.

Long-distance buses rarely have toilets, but they usually stop for 20-minute meal and bladder-relief breaks at fairly appropriate times. If not, drivers will stop to let you fertilize the roadside.

Local buses are usually slow and crowded, but cheap. You can get around most towns for about US25¢. Local buses also often go out to nearby villages (a great way to explore an area).

Car & Motorcycle

Few people rent cars in Ecuador, mainly because public transportation makes getting around so easy. Ecuador's automobile association is **Aneta** (☎1800-556-677; www.aneta.org.ec), which offers 24-hour roadside assistance to its members. It offers some services to members of foreign automobile clubs, including Canadian and US AAA members.

Hitchhiking

Hitchhiking is possible, but not very practical in Ecuador. Public transportation is relatively cheap and trucks are used as public transportation in remote areas, so trying to hitch a free ride isn't easy. If the driver is stopping to drop off and pick up other passengers, assume that payment will be expected. If you're the only passenger, the driver may have picked you up just to talk to a foreigner.

Taxi

Taxis are relatively cheap. Bargain the fare beforehand though, or you're likely to be overcharged. A long ride in a large city (Quito or Guayaquil) shouldn't go over US$5, and short hops in small towns usually cost about US$1 to US$2. Meters are sometimes used during the day in Quito (where the minimal fare is US$1) but rarely seen elsewhere. On weekends and at night, fares are always about 25% to 50% higher. A full-day taxi hire should cost around $50.

Tours

Much of the Galápagos archipelago is accessible to visitors only by guided tour (ie a cruise). Many travelers also opt to visit the Amazon on organized tours, as these are efficient, educational and often the only way to get deep into the rainforest.

Train

Ecuador's rail system is finally being restored, but for the moment, only a few stretches of the old lines are in operation. The most famous is the dramatic descent from Alausí along Nariz del Diablo, a spectacular section of train track that was one of the world's greatest feats of railroad engineering.

Another line is the train excursion between Quito and the Area Nacional de Recreación El Boliche, near Cotopaxi. You can also continue all the way down to Latacunga on this line.

Plans are underway to continue restoring the tracks, and in coming years it may be possible to travel between Quito and Guayaquil by rail (as it once was in the last century). For the latest info, visit www.trenecuador.com.

Truck

In remote areas, *camiones* (trucks) and *camionetas* (pickup trucks) often double as buses. If the weather is OK, you get fabulous views; if not, you have to crouch underneath a dark tarpaulin and suck dust. Pickups can be hired to get to remote places such as climbers' refuges.

French Guiana

Includes »

Best Places to Eat

- » Central Market, Cayenne (p731)
- » Les Palmistes (p733)
- » Cacao's Sunday market (p736)
- » Chez Félicia (p741)
- » Auberge des Îles de Salut (p739)

Best Walks

- » Iles du Salut (p739)
- » Downtown Cayenne (p731)
- » Sentier Molokoï de Cacao (p736)
- » Grand Matoury Nature Reserve (p736)
- » Trésor (p736)

Why Go?

French Guiana is a tiny country of cleaned-up colonial architecture, eerie prison-camp history and some of the world's most diverse plant and animal life. It's a strange mix of French law and rainforest humidity where only a few destinations along the coast are easily accessed and travel can be frustratingly difficult as well as expensive. As a department of France, it's one of South America's wealthiest corners, with funds pouring in to ensure a stable base for the satellite launcher. But not even a European superpower can tame this vast, pristine jungle – you'll find potholes in newly paved roads, and ferns sprouting between bricks while Amerindians, Maroons and Hmong refugees live traditional lifestyles so far from *la vie Metropole* that it's hard to believe they're connected at all.

When to Go

Cayenne

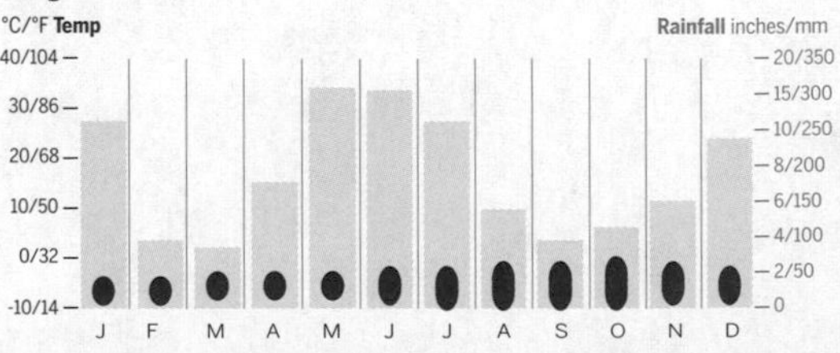

Jan–Jun Expect sogginess during these months, with the heaviest rains in May.

Late Jan–Mar You can always expect Cayenne to throw a wild and exciting Carnival.

Jul–Sep It rains less during the dry season although it's hot and humid year round.

Connections

French Guiana has a border crossing at St George, where the Oyapock River marks the frontier with Brazil, and at St Laurent, where the Maroni River is the border with Suriname. Both border crossings are made by boat although a bridge has been built to Brazil and will probably open in the lifetime of this book. South from these borders you'll find Amerindian and Maroon villages that eventually give way to dense jungle and dodgy gold mining camps.

ITINERARIES

One Week

Start in Cayenne, making sure to visit the market, stroll the steets and to eat out often. Drive to Cacao on Sunday for the Laotian market. On Wednesday or Thursday afternoon, make sure to visit Chou-Aï, the sloth protection center where you can cuddle a sloth. If there's a shuttle launch in Kourou, call or email the Centre Spatial Guyanaise to secure an invite to see it, then try to work in an overnight visit to the Îles du Salut that won't conflict with the launch (the islands close before and after launches).

Two Weeks

Follow the above itinerary, extending your stay to two or more nights on the Îles du Salut. Take an overnight tour of Kaw, where you'll stay on a floating lodge, and look for scarlet ibis, black caiman and a huge array of bird species. Spend your last few days in St Laurent du Maroni, checking out creepy, old prison camps and exploring Amerindian and Maroon cultures on trips down the Fleuve de Maroni.

Essential Food & Drink

» **Pho** Vietnamese soup made with beef broth, rice noodles, many fragrant herbs and meat

» **Mie/nasi goreng** Javanese style fried rice/noodles

» **Gibier** Bush meat like capybara, wild boar and agouti is legally hunted and found widely on restaurant menus

» **Pizza** Find delicious thin crust, French-style wood-fired pizzas in most main towns

» **Jamais goûté** A delicate freshwater fish that's best steamed in banana leaves

» **Croissant** Flaky pastries as well as simple baguettes are a big part of the French Guianan diet, particularly at breakfast

» **Ti'punch** Literally a 'small punch' made with local rum, lime juice and sugar cane syrup – a Caribbean favorite

» **Fricassee** Rice, beans and sauteed meat stewed in gravy – unlike French fricassee, the Caribbean style has a brown or red sauce with a kick of Cayenne pepper

AT A GLANCE

» **Currency** Euro (€)

» **Languages** French, Creole

» **Money** ATMs in bigger towns, the only cambio is in Cayenne, credit cards widely accepted

» **Visas** Not needed for 90 days for most nationalities

Fast Facts

» **Area** 91,000 sq km

» **Population** 221,500

» **Capital** Cayenne

» **Emergency** ☎17

» **Country code** ☎594

Exchange Rates

Australia	A$1	€0.80
Canada	C$1	€0.76
New Zealand	NZ$1	€0.65
UK	UK£1	€1.18
USA	US$1	€0.77

Set Your Budget

» **Hammock space in a *carbet* (open-air hut)** €10

» **Pho at the Cayene Central Market** €5

» **Daily car rental** €45

» **Tour of the Camp de la Transportation** €5

Resources

» **French Guiana Tourism Commity** (www.tourisme-guyane.com)

» **Guiana Shield Media Project** (www.gsmp.org)

» **Reseau France Outre Mer** (www.guyane.rfo.fr)

0 50 km
0 25 miles
ATLANTIC OCEAN
Galibi Nature Reserve
Plage les Hattes
4 Awala-Yalimopo
Mana
Moengo
Javouhey
Organabo
RN 1
Iracoubo
Albina
6 St Laurent du Maroni
St Jean
Pripri Yiyi Trail Head
Sinnamary
1 Îles du Salut
Centre Spatial Guyanais 2
Kourou
Apatou
Camp Voltaire
Cascades Voltaire
Langatabbetje
Barrage de Petit Saut
Tonate (Macouria)
Cayenne 5
Montjoly
Rémire
Montsinéry
Félix Eboué International Airport
Matoury
St Élie
Roura
Trésor & Kaw Nature Reserves
Mont Favard (200m)
Cacao 3
7 Kaw
RN 2
Les Nouragues Nature Reserve
Baie de L'Oyapock
Régina
Fleuve Maroni (Marowijne River)
Fleuve Mana
Fleuve Sinnamary
Fleuve Approuague
Grand Santi
Ouanary
St Georges de l'Oyapock
Oiapoque
Mont Machoulou (782m)
Maripasoula
Saül
SURINAME
Rivière Grand Inini
Rivière Waki
Pic Coudreau (711m)
Fleuve Oyapock
Rio Uaçá
Camopi
Rivière Tampok
Rivière Camopi
Litani River
Claimed by Suriname & French Guiana
Caçiporé
Tumac - Humac Mountains
Mont St Marcel (635m)
BRAZIL

French Guiana Highlights

1. Cast away to **Îles du Salut** (p739) for sand, palms and a creepy, defunct penal colony
2. See one of the world's busiest satellite launchers at the **Centre Spatial Guyanais** (p737) and, with luck, watch a launch
3. Gorge on Laotian treats and admire ornate embroidery in the Hmong community of **Cacao** (p736)
4. Watch the peaceful ritual of dinosaur-like leatherback turtles laying their eggs in the moonlit sand of **Awala-Yalimopo** (p742)
5. Sip a cold beer and people watch at Cayenne's quintessential cafe, **Les Palmistes** (p733)
6. Get an eerie tour of the **Camp de la Transportation** (p740) in prisoner-haunted St Laurent du Maroni
7. Spend the night in a floating lodge surrounded by jungle and flourishing bird life at **Kaw** (p736)

Cayenne

POP 63,000

A crossroads of the Caribbean, South America and Europe, Cayenne is a city of myriad cultures surrounded by all the colors of the Caribbean. The streets are lined with colonial wrought-iron balconies with louvered shutters painted in tropical pinks, yellows and turquoise. The vibrant markets and excellent Brazilian, Creole, French and Chinese restaurants make this town as pleasing to the belly as it is to the eye; you won't want to be skipping any meals here. Outside the city center, highways and urban sprawl reminds you that you're still in the 21st century.

Sights

Cayenne is easy to see on foot in one day. The center of the action is the Place des Palmistes, lined with cafes and palm trees, in the northwest corner. To its west, Place Léopold Héder (aka Place Grenoble) is the oldest part of the city. After siesta, cruise Av du Général de Gaulle, the main commercial street, to experience Cayenne at its bustling peak. La Place Des Amandiers near the coast is the place to go to relax with *pétanque* and dominos.

TOP CHOICE Central Market MARKET

(cnr Brassé & Ste Rose; 4:30am-1pm Wed, Fri & Sat) Inside Cayenne's main market, eager shoppers will find a vibrant jumble of Amerindian basketry, African-style paintings and carvings, piles of exotic spices at great prices, and soup stalls that serve up the best Vietnamese *pho* (€5) in the Guianas. Endless aisles of fruit and vegetable stands – overflowing with daikon, bok choy and bean sprouts – make this look more like Southeast Asia than South America.

Fort Cépérou RUINS

(cnr Rue Louis Blanc & Claudon Chandon) Off the gardened Place Léopold Héder are the remains of Fort Cépérou, perched on land bought in 1643 from the Galibi people by the first French colonists. Most of the site is now a restricted military zone, but you can still stroll around for good views of Cayenne and the river.

Musée Départemental MUSEUM

(1 Rue de Rémire; adult/child & student €3/free; 10am-2pm & 3-6pm Mon, 8am-2pm & 3-6pm Wed-Fri, 9am-1:30pm Sat) The centrally located Musée Départemental features a frighteningly large stuffed black caiman, as well as other preserved local critters, an ethnobotanical display and an air-conditioned 'butterfly room.' The upstairs area recaptures life in the old penal colony and displays some Amerindian handicrafts.

Botanical Gardens GARDENS

(Blvd de la République) The sizable Botanical Gardens, built in 1879 and renovated in 2009, today flourish with tropical Guianese flora.

Musée des Cultures Guyanaises MUSEUM

(31-4172; 78 Payé; 8am-12:45pm & 3-5:45pm Mon, Tue, Thu & Fri, 8-11:45am Sat) The smaller Musée des Cultures Guyanaises is devoted to Guiana's early history, from its geologic formation through precolonial, Amerindian times. It houses a relaxing, air-conditioned library (upstairs) that has publications in French, English and other languages.

Tours

French Guiana's pristine jungles are impenetrable and dangerous without a knowledgeable guide. Licensed Cayenne-based agencies run tours, often hiring out guides throughout the country (and taking a commission on their services). Using an agency will ensure that you have permission to enter Amerindian communities. A cheaper alternative is to go directly to local guides, usually found at lodgings throughout French Guiana, and make your own arrangements. The better tour companies include these ones:

JAL Voyages TOUR

(31-6820; www.jal-voyages.com; 26 Av du Général de Gaulle) Has a popular overnight jaunt on a floating *carbet* in Kaw (from €180).

Takari Tour TOUR

(31-1960; www.takaritour.com; 8 Rue du Cap Bernard) The oldest and most respected operator.

Couleurs Amazone TOUR

(28-7000; www.couleursamazone.fr; 21 Blvd Jubelin) Offers one-day and multiday trips on every major river in French Guiana (from €550 for five days).

Festivals & Events

Carnaval REGIONAL

(January to February or March; dates vary) Carnaval is a gigantic, colorful occasion, with festivities from Epiphany to several solid days of partying before Ash Wednesday.

Cayenne

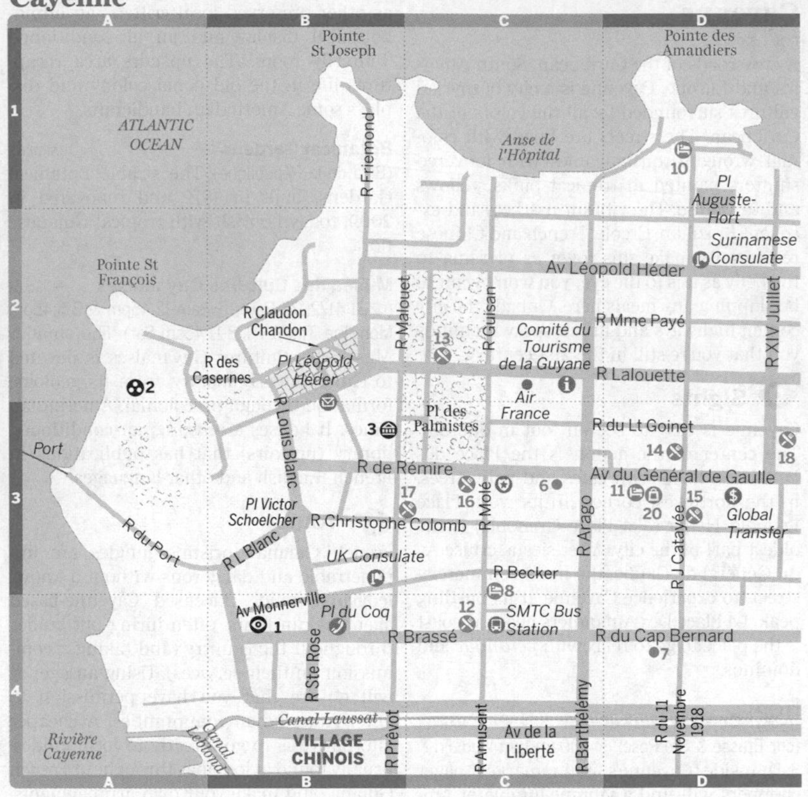

Cayenne

Sights

1 Central Market B4
2 Fort Cépérou A2
3 Musée Départemental B3
4 Musée des Cultures Guyanaises E2

Activities, Courses & Tours

5 Couleurs Amazone F2
6 JAL Voyages C3
7 Takari Tour D4

Sleeping

8 Central Hôtel C3
9 Hotel Ket Tai E4
10 Hotel Les Amandiers D1
11 Le Dronmi D3

Eating

12 Denis C4
13 Food Stalls C2
14 Le Café Crème D3
15 L'Entracte D3
16 Les Palmistes C3
17 Les Pyramides C3
18 Porta Verde D3

Drinking

Le Bistro .... (see 11)
19 Le Cosmopolitan E3

Shopping

20 Galerie des 3 Fontaines D3

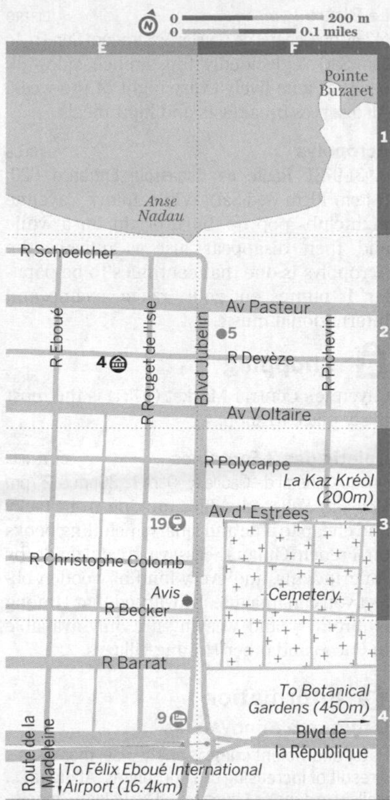

Sleeping

In Cayenne, one person usually has to pay the full price of a double room. Skip the hotels' expensive breakfasts and hit the cafes and markets for your morning meal.

Central Hôtel HOTEL $$
(☎25-6565; www.centralhotel-cayenne.fr; cnr Molé & Rue du Lieutenant Becker; s/d €70/78; ❄📶) The newly refurbished Central isn't interesting in any particular way but the big, comfortable, clean rooms, tip-top location and great service make it the best deal in town.

Oyasamaïd PENSION $
(☎31-5684; www.oyasamaid.com; studio/d incl breakfast from €55/60; ❄📶🏊) A French family pension *à la Guianese,* this four-room place is friendly, bright and impeccably clean. All the spacious rooms have Jacuzzi bathtubs, and a swimming pool seals the deal. It's a short drive from the town center so you'll need a car to stay here. You'll see signs for it on the Route de la Madeleine, near the roundabout and Geant supermarket.

Le Dronmi BOUTIQUE HOTEL $$
(☎21-5995; www.ledronmi.com; 42 Av du Général de Gaulle; d from €115; ❄📶) Easily the hippest place in Cayenne, the new rooms and studios here are built with hardwoods and decorated with modern/mid-century flair; the central location couldn't be better. We haven't tried sleeping here, but noise from the popular downstairs bar could be a problem.

Hotel Les Amandiers HOTEL $
(☎31-3875; amandiers@hotmail.com; Place Auguste-Hort; d/ste €58/75; ❄📶) Run by an elderly couple and with plenty of character, the fading, Faulty Towers-esque Amandiers overlooks the languorous Place Des Amandiers next to the sea. Request a room with a view.

Hotel Ket Tai HOTEL $
(☎28-9777; 72 Blvd Jubelin; s/d/t €45/55/63; ❄📶) Rooms are bland, small and institutional feeling, but the Ket Tai is friendly and relatively well located.

Eating

For the best bang for your buck, you can slurp noodles at Cayenne's daytime market or browse the nighttime **food stalls** (Place des Palmistes) at the Place de Palmistes for burgers (about €3). Small Chinese takeout joints and grocery shops make self-catering a breeze. The sit-down options in Cayenne can be outstanding.

TOP CHOICE **Les Palmistes** FRENCH $
(12 Av du Général de Gaulle; pizzas from €10, mains around €18; ⏲6:30-1am Mon-Sat, 10am-11pm Sun; 📶) The best place to people-watch on the palm tree–lined Place des Palmistes also serves up perfect Caribbean-French ambience. Sit on the wooden terrace with its wrought-iron balustrade to dine on fantastic salads, crêpes, pizzas and full meals while sipping a cold beer. Bliss.

La Kaz Kréòl CREOLE $
(☎39-0697; 35 Av d'Estrées; mains €14-20; ⏲12-2pm & 6:30am-10:30pm Tue-Sun) The best sit-down Creole restaurant in Cayenne serves outstanding stuffed cassava, meat stews and seafood in a homey setting. Try the Creole breakfasts on Saturdays and Sundays.

GETTING INTO TOWN

Félix Eboué International Airport is 16km southwest of Cayenne. From the airport, consider sharing a taxi (€35, 20 minutes). To the airport, it's cheaper to take a *taxi colectif* (minibus) to Matoury (€2, 15 minutes, 10km), then a taxi for the remaining 6km.

Porta Verde BRAZILIAN $
(☎29-19-03; 60 Rue du Lieutenant Goinet; meals €15-28 per kilo; ⏲12-2:30pm Mon-Sat) A Brazilian locals' favorite, get a buffet lunch priced by the kilo.

Le Café Crème CAFE $
(44 Catayée; sandwiches from €4; ⏲6:15am-4:30pm Mon-Fri, to 3:30pm Sat) Get Parisian-style coffee, sizable sandwiches and delicate pastries at this sidewalk cafe *à la française*. Your best bet for coffee before 7am.

Les Pyramides MIDDLE EASTERN $
(cnr Colomb & Malouet; mains €16; ⏲noon-3pm & 7-11pm Tue-Sun) This superb Middle Eastern restaurant makes hearty, heaped platters of couscous to rave reviews.

L'Entracte ITALIAN $
(☎30-0137; 65 Catayée; pizzas from €9; ⏲noon-2:30pm & 6:30am-10:30pm) Eat the cheapest (but tasty!) pizza in town while admiring the movie posters that cover the walls.

Denis CHINESE $
(Brassé; mains around €5; ⏲11:30am-10:30pm) One of the best of a slew of affordable Chinese restaurants. This friendly place has plenty of vegetarian options and a wide variety of meat and seafood dishes.

Drinking & Entertainment

Live music, wine and rum punch flow freely in bars and clubs throughout Cayenne and there are many, many more than those we've listed below – ask around.

Reggae music rocks small clubs in Village Chinois and a few Brazilian and Dominican bars dot Av de la Liberté.

Le Cosmopolitan BAR
(☎35-8566; 118 Av du Général de Gaulle; ⏲5pm-2am) Trendy nightspot with a young, mixed clientele getting down to electronica and Caribbean music.

Le Bistro BISTRO
(42 Av du Général de Gaulle; ⏲8am-1am Sun-Fri, to 2am Sat) A decidedly hip, French sidewalk bar that gets lively every night of the week. Also serves breakfasts and light meals.

Acropolys CLUB
(☎31-9781; Route de Cabassou; Entrance €20; ⏲from 10pm Wed-Sat) While many Cayenne nightclubs pop up, burn bright for a while and then disappear just as quickly, the Acropolys is one that continues to be popular. It pumps out zouk, ragga, techno and international music.

Shopping

Cayenne's Central Market (p731) is the most lively place to shop.

Galerie des 3 Fontaines SOUVENIRS
(Av du Général de Gaulle; ⏲9am-12:30pm & 2-7pm Mon-Sat) Sells souvenirs ranging from tacky and cheap to chic and smart, including books on French Guiana, cassava treats made by Amerindians, and every kind of wooden object you can imagine. Be warned that Hmong embroidery and weaving are only available in Cacao and other Hmong villages.

Information

Dangers & Annoyances

Petty and violent crime is on the rise, mostly as a result of increasing drug problems. At night, walk in groups or take a taxi. The Village Chinois (aka Chicago) area, south of the market, should be reached by taxi.

Emergency

Fire (☎18)
Police (☎17)

Internet Access

Most hotels and many French-oriented cafes and restaurants have free wi-fi.

Medical Services

Centre Hospitalier Cayenne (☎39-5050; 3 Av Flamboyants)

Money

Banks and ATMs are all over the city, but traveler's checks and foreign currency can only be cashed at *cambios* (currency-exchange offices).

Global Transfer (64 Av du Général de Gaulle; ⏲7:30am-11am & 3-6pm Mon-Fri, 7:30am-11am Sat) Central location.

Post

Post Agence de Ceperou (Place Léopold Héder; ⏲7:30am-1:30pm Mon-Fri, to 11:45am

Sat) This conveniently located post office gets swamped the first two weeks of every month when it distributes unemployment checks.

Telephone

Digicel has SIM cards for €20 which includes €5 of talk credit. The most convenient place to buy one in Cayenne is **Alpha Connexion** (☎25-0212; 2 Place de Coq). Top ups are available at shops and restaurants all around town.

Tourist Information

Comité du Tourisme de la Guyane (☎29-6500; www.tourisme-guyane.com; 12 Lalouette; 8am-1pm & 3-6pm Mon-Fri, 8am-noon Sat) Filled with pamphlets, maps and information, the office is always staffed with someone to answer questions. An information desk at the airport stays open late for arriving flights.

Getting There & Away

All international and domestic flights leave from **Félix Eboué International Airport** (Rochambeau; ☎29-9700).

Airfares change frequently so check around but at the time of research round-trip fares to Fort-de-France (Martinique; 2 hours) were €532 and to Paris (France, 8½ hours) were €841.

Getting Around

At the time of writing there were no public buses serving destinations within the Cayenne area.

To/From the Airport

Félix Eboué International Airport is 16km southwest of Cayenne. The only way to/from the airport is by taxi (€35, 20 minutes).

Car

Renting a car can be cheaper than public transport if two or more persons are traveling together. Most companies have offices in Kourou, St Laurent du Maroni and at the airport (some have airport-pickup surcharges of up to €20). Expect to pay from €45 per day for a compact with unlimited mileage. Cars are not allowed over the border.

Avis (☎30-2522; www.avis.fr; 58 Blvd Jubelin, Airport)

Budget (☎35-1020; www.budget-guyane.com; Zone Galmot, Airport)

Taxi

Taxis charge a hiring fee of €1.75, plus €0.75 per kilometer; the per-kilometer charge increases to €1 from 7pm to 6am and on Sundays and holidays. There's a taxi stand on the southeast corner of Place des Palmistes.

Rémire-Montjoly

POP 19,500

Though technically two separate towns, Rémire-Montjoly, only 8km from Cayenne, functions as a single village. Its sweeping beaches cover some of the country's best waterfront. Despite the persistence of mosquitoes and biting sand flies (make sure you bring repellent), locals flock here in droves. Topless sunbathing is de rigueur at the best beach, **Plage Montjoly**, reachable by taxi or bus from Cayenne. The renovated historical ruins at **Fort Diamant** (☎35-4110; admission with/without guided tour €5/3), an old coastal battery dating from the early 19th century, are along the main beach road. The easy 2.5km **Salines Trail** at the end of Rue St Domenica, or the 4km **Rorota Trail** to the top of Montagne du Mahury, both offer excellent views of the coastal marshland and the ocean. On the RN2 heading toward the

BUSES FROM CAYENNE

Buses to the following destinations leave from the **SMTC bus station** (for schedule ☎25-4929; cnr Rue du Cap Bernard & Molé) Monday to Friday with less services on Saturday and none on Sunday. For up-to-date information go to www.cg973.fr/Lignes-de-transport-prevues. For other destinations you will have to transfer buses; connections usually link up.

DESTINATION	COST (€)	DURATION (HR)	FREQUENCY (DAILY)
Kaw	11.50	2	2
Kourou	10	1¼	8
Macouria	6.50	0.5	8
Regina	19	1½	4
Roura	5	1	4
St Laurent	40	4	5

DON'T MISS

CHOU-AÏ SLOTH PROTECTION CENTER

Ever wanted to cuddle a three-toed sloth? Here's your chance. **Chou-Aï** (www.chouai.free.fr; Near the Pointe Liberte Bridge, Macouria; €5 donation; ⌚1:45am-4pm Wed & Thu) sloth protection center opens its gates to the public every Wednesday and Thursday from 1:45 to 4pm. Hang out in an enclosure where a few of the center's 20 or so sloths move around freely (but *very* slowly). Two sloths, Juju and Cyclone, were raised in captivity, are used to people and won't ever have the skills to survive in the wild, and thus they are passed from arm to arm between adoring visitors. If one of the sloths feels particularly comfortable with you, he or she may fall asleep in your arms. Nothing can compare to this experience.

Most of the sloths are taken into the center when their trees have been felled during logging or building projects. Once they are deemed fully healthy they are re-released into other forested areas. There are also several two-toed sloths but these potentially more aggressive critters are in enclosures at the back of the center and are hard to see.

airport, the 5km hike into the **Grand Matoury Nature Reserve** is the best jungle jaunt in striking distance of Cayenne and is good for bird-watching and wildlife in the early mornings and afternoons.

Motel du Lac (☎38-0800; moteldulac@orange.fr; Chemin Poupon, Rte de Montjoly; d €70; ❄📶🏊) is a well-run place with a great pool, near Montjoly beach and a lakeside ecological reserve. Otherwise try **Motel Beauregard 'Cric-Crac'** (☎35-4100; www.le-cric-crac.com; PK9, 2 Rte de Rémire; d from €70; ❄📶🏊), which has a bowling alley, tennis courts and a gym as well as a pool; it's endearingly kitsch and only 10km from Cayenne.

Cacao

POP 950

A tidy slice of Laos in the hills of Guiana, Cacao, about 75km southwest of Cayenne, is a village of sparkling clear rivers, vegetable plantations and no-nonsense wooden houses on stilts. The Hmong refugees, who left Laos in the 1970s, keep their town a safe, peaceful haven, and it's now a favorite weekend day trip among locals from Cayenne. Sunday, market day, is the best time for a visit if you want to shop for Hmong embroidery and weaving, and feast on a smorgasbord of Laotian treats. Don't miss **Le Planeur Bleu** (☎27-0034; cleplaneurbleu@wanadoo.fr; admission adults/children under 12 €4/free; ⌚9am-1pm & 2-4pm Sun, other times by appointment) to see butterflies and arachnids, both dead and alive, or hold live tarantulas. Just up the hill from Le Planeur Bleu, **Le Potier** (⌚Sun mornings), can be found demonstrating how he makes ceramic wears from the local clay and offering pieces for sale.

For a wildlife- and insect-spotting adventure, embark on the 18km hike along the **Sentier Molokoï de Cacao** (Cacao Molokoï Nature Trail), one of the few deep-forest jaunts that can be accomplished independently. The track links the rustic-chic **Auberge des Orpailleurs** (☎27-0622; www.aubergedesorpailleurs.com; PK62, RN 2; r from €40, hammock spaces per person €7), on the road to St Georges, with the more basic, activity-oriented **Quimbe Kio** (☎27-0122; www.quimbekio.com; Le Bourg de Cacao; d €40, hammock spaces €15, with hammock €20) in Cacao. These two *gîtes* (guesthouses) are also great places to arrange other eco-tourism excursions within this region – both also have good restaurants. Bring plenty of water, insect repellent and rain gear. A small refuge hut midway is the best place to overnight (€5 per person). Make reservations and get maps and advice at either *gîte*.

At the time of research there was no public bus to Cacao.

Trésor & Kaw Nature Reserves

The Trésor Nature Reserve is one of French Guiana's most accessible primary rainforests, and the bordering swamps of the Kaw Nature Reserve are excellent for observing caimans (best at night) and spectacular waterfowl like the scarlet ibis. Getting to Trésor is easy enough if you have a car: Drive 17km from Roura on the D6 to Trésor's 1.75km **botanical trail** with rich diversity, plenty of deep forest atmosphere and protected wildlife.

However, Kaw, which is partially reached by another 18km along the D6 from Trésor, is nearly impossible to get to unless you're on a tour. Reaching the village requires boat transport. JAL Voyages (p731) is a good tour choice.

Between Trésor and Kaw, 28km from Roura, the friendly **Auberge de Camp Caïman** (☎30-7277; d €35, hammock spaces €16, meals €14-20) is the best place to stay in the area, offering a restaurant and all-inclusive, two-day catamaran excursions of Kaw from €135. Reserve in advance because it's not always open.

Saül

POP 150

The defunct gold-mining village of Saül – the geographic center of French Guiana – is an untamed paradise explored mostly by professional biologists. The Big Tree path – with the largest tree ever recorded in French Guiana – is just one of hundreds of kilometers of trails built by French and American research institutes in the area. The best place to stay is the new-ish and well-run **Auberge A Ke Nou** (www.gite-restaurantakenou-saul.com; s/d €35/50, 2-night packages incl meals & activities from €260 per person) in town.

Get to Saül with Air Guyane (p745) who have two flights per week to/from Cayenne (round-trip €130, 40 minutes). You can also organize an eight-day river-jungle-village adventure to Saül through tour agencies in Cayenne.

Kourou

POP 21,000

On a small peninsula overlooking the Atlantic Ocean and Kourou River, this small city of modern apartment blocks once existed solely to serve the mainland and offshore penal colonies. Now it seems to exist solely to serve the **Centre Spatial Guyanais** (Guyanese Space Center), a satellite construction facility and launch pad that employs thousands of people. A few beaches suitable for sunbathing line the easternmost part of town, but Kourou is mostly a way station for visiting the Space Center and catching a boat to the Îles du Salut. If you must hang out, head to Le Vieux Bourg (Old Town), a great strip for eating, drinking and wondering why the rest of the town isn't this hip.

Sights

Centre Spatial Guyanais SPACE CENTER
(CSG; ☎32-6123; www.cnes-csg.fr; Tour incl museum €7; ⏲tours 7:45am & 12:45pm Mon-Thu & 7:45am Fri) In 1964 Kourou was chosen to be the site of the Centre Spatial Guyanais because it's close to the equator, is away from tropical storm tracks and earthquake zones, and has a low population density. The center is run by CNES (Centre National d'Études Spatiales; www.cnes.fr) in collaboration with the ESA (European Space Agency; www.esa.com) and Arianespace (www.arianespace.com).

Ariane 5, a heavy lift launcher, was the first rocket to take off from the center, but two more launchers, Vega (a light-lift rocket) and Soyuz (a Russian-owned medium-lift launcher), are also now in service, increasing the number of liftoffs to nearly a dozen per year. This frequency makes it much easier to coordinate your visit with a launch, during which rockets blast off at speeds approaching 8km per second after a thrilling countdown of exploding booster fire.

The launch site is the only one in the world this close to the equator (within five degrees), where the earth's spin is significantly faster than further north or south; this means that the site benefits from the 'slingshot effect,' which boosts propulsion and makes launches up to 17% more energy-efficient than those at sites further away from the equator. Since 1980 two-thirds of the world's commercial satellites have been launched from French Guiana.

Visit the ESA website to find out the launch schedule and reserve a space at one of several observation points within the space center. Email csg-accueil@cnes.fr well ahead of time, providing your full name, address, phone number and age. It's free, but children under 16 are not permitted at sites within 6km of the launch pad and those under eight are not permitted within 12km. You can watch it, reservation-free, with locals at Kourou's beaches or at the Carapa Observation Site, 15km west of the city center.

Space junkies will love the free three-hour tours at the Space Center, which include a visit to the massive launch pad; phone ahead for reservations and bring your passport. Tour guides sometimes speak English or German; ask when you book.

GETTING TO BRAZIL

Getting to the Border

It's best to avoid picking up hitchhikers or driving at night along the sketchy road connecting Régina (population 300), a near ghost town, and St Georges de l'Oyapock (population 2750), a sleepy outpost on the Brazilian border.

Minibuses leave when full (early mornings are best) to/from the town center to Cayenne (€35, two hours). Buses to/from Cayenne require a transfer in Regina and take a bit longer. St Georges to Regina buses leave four times per day and cost €12 – onward to Cayenne to/from Regina is another €19.

St Georges de l'Oyapock

St Georges serves as a departure point for visits to Amerindian villages and the ruins of Silver Mountain Penal Colony on the Oyapock River, but not much else. Accessing the villages requires permission from local authorities and an experienced guide, so it's best to contact a Cayenne-based tour company. If you get stuck in St Georges for a night (and many travelers do), try the popular **Chez Modestine** (37-0013; modestine@wanadoo.fr; Place du village, Rue Elie-Elfort; r from €39;) or the quieter **Caz-Calé** (37-0054; Rue Elie-Elfort; r from €39;).

At the Border

Stamp out at the **Douane** (8am-12pm & 2-6pm) on the riverside in St Georges. A gigantic, very out-of-place looking bridge is slated to open in spring of 2013 after years of delay but if that's still not an option, dugouts make the crossing to Oiapoque for €4 (15 minutes). Once in Oiapoque, it's a 10-minute walk away from the river to the Police Federal, where you stamp into Brazil. Daily buses (morning and afternoon, R$90, 10 hours) and planes leave Oiapoque for Macapá.

Musée de l'Espace MUSEUM
(Space Museum; adult/child €5/3, with tour €7/4; 8am-6pm Mon-Fri, 2-6pm Sat) Don't miss the excellent Musée de l'Espace, with informative displays in English and French. Note that the Space Center is closed on days after a launch.

Sleeping

Kourou has pitifully few inexpensive options. Both of the budget places have reception hours from noon to 2pm and 6pm to 8pm every day.

Hotel Ballahou GUESTHOUSE $
(22-0022; http://pagesperso-orange.fr/ballahou; 1-3 Martial; d/apt €45/55;) The best beds are at the welcoming Hotel Ballahou, within short walking distance of the beaches. It can be tricky to find, but they'll pick you up in town. Reserve well in advance.

Le Gros Bec GUESTHOUSE $
(32-9191; hotel-legrosbec@wanadoo.fr; 56 Rue du De Floch; s/d/tr €55.50/63.50/69.50;) Right next to Le Vieux Bourg, has spacious split-level studios with kitchenettes.

Eating & Drinking

Potholed, colorful Le Vieux Bourg, centralized along Av Général de Gaulle, is by far the most eclectic area of Kourou and the best place for cheap and delicious Indian, Creole, Chinese, Moroccan, French cuisine and more. There are also some hopping bars with live music – cruise the street and take your pick.

Outside of Le Vieux Bourg, **Le Glacier des 2 Lacs** (68 Av des Deux Lacs; 8am-11:30pm Wed-Sun) has sinful ice cream, perfect for Kourou's sunny afternoons, and **La Pizzeria** (38 King; pizzas from €6; noon-10:30pm) does Italian dishes and pizzas.

Self-catering is easy thanks to the produce **market** (Place de la Condamine; Tue & Fri) as well as ubiquitous grocery stores.

Information

Point Information Tourisme (32-9833; Av Victor Hugo; 7:30am-1:30pm Mon-Fri) Tucked away in a complex across the street from Église Notre Dame.

Getting There & Away

Buses run eight times per day between Kourou and Cayenne (€10, 1 hour 15 minutes) and five times to St Laurent (€28, 3 hours). Two rental companies that service both Cayenne and Kourou, **Avis** (☎32-5299; 4 Av de France) and **Budget** (☎32-4861; ZI Paracaibo), enable one-way jaunts but these include a hefty fee.

Îles du Salut

Known in English as the Salvation Islands, these were anything but that for prisoners sent here from the French mainland by Emperor Napoleon III and subsequent French governments. The three tiny islands, 15km north of Kourou over choppy, shark-infested waters, were considered escape-proof and particularly appropriate for political prisoners, including Alfred Dreyfus. From 1852 to 1947, some 80,000 prisoners died from disease, inhumane conditions and the guillotine on these sad isles.

Since then, the islands have become a lackadaisical delight – a place to escape *to*. Île Royale, once the administrative headquarters of the penal settlement, has several restored prison buildings, including a restaurant-auberge, while the smaller Île St Joseph, with its eerie solitary-confinement cells and guards' cemetery, has overgrown with coconut palms.

The old **director's house** (⌚2-4pm Tue-Sun) has an interesting English-language history display; two-hour free guided tours of Île Royale (usually in French) begin here. Surprisingly abundant wildlife includes green-winged Ara macaws, agoutis, capuchin monkeys and sea turtles. Carry a swimsuit and towel to take advantage of the white-sand beach and shallow swimming holes on St Joseph. The Centre Spatial Guyanais has a huge infrared camera on Île Royale, and the islands are evacuated when there's an eastward launch from the space center.

Sleeping & Eating

It's possible to camp for free along some of the paradisiacal areas along the shore of Île Royale (but bring mosquito repellent, nets and rain gear).

TOP CHOICE **Auberge des Îles du Salut** AUBERGE $$
(☎32-1100; www.ilesdusalut.com; hammock spaces €10, 'guard rooms' from €60, s/d incl full board €166/235) The welcome hasn't improved much since the days of arriving convicts, but the rooms, in the artfully renovated director's house, are something out of a breezy Bogart film. If you want a more Papillon-like experience, you can stay in simpler rooms in old guards' quarters (some with terraces) or sling a hammock in the cleaned-up prison dormitories.

Don't leave without having at least one meal (set menu €26) at the restaurant, which serves the best fish soup (€10) this side of Provence. There are no cooking facilities, but bringing picnic supplies (and plenty of water – it's not potable on the islands) can keep your costs to a minimum.

PAPILLON: ESCAPE ARTIST OR CON MAN?

Of all the prisoners who did hard time on Devil's Island, only Alfred Dreyfus, the Frenchman wrongly convicted of treason in 1894, achieved anything near the fame of Henry Charrière, who became known – or notorious – for his epic tale of nine remarkable escapes from French Guiana's infamous prison camps. Nicknamed Papillon (Butterfly) for a tattoo on his chest, Charrière claims in his autobiography that after being wrongly convicted of murder he escaped from Îles du Salut by floating toward the mainland on a sack full of coconuts and braved harsh malarial jungles to flee eastward. Fashioning himself into an international man of mystery living among native villagers, he eventually became a Venezuelan citizen and was portrayed by Steve McQueen in a Hollywood version of his life.

Although Papillon always claimed his innocence, research has suggested otherwise. Paris police reports reveal that 'Papillon' was almost certainly guilty of the murder that incarcerated him, and firsthand accounts from prison guards describe Charrière as a well-behaved convict who worked contentedly on latrine duty. His published story is widely believed to be a compilation of his own adventures and stories he heard about other convicts' escapades while he was in prison.

Getting There & Away

Comfortable, fume-free catamarans and sailboats take about 1½ to two hours to reach the islands. Most boats to the islands depart around 8am from Kourou's *ponton des pêcheurs* (fishermen's dock, at the end of Av Général de Gaulle) and return between 4pm and 6pm. Call to reserve 48 to 72 hours in advance, or book with tour operators in Cayenne or Kourou. Boat taxis to Île St Joseph are an additional €5 per person round trip unless stated otherwise. Seafaring options include the following:

Îles du Salut (☎32-3381; €48) Owned by the auberge, this catamaran ferries up to 100 passengers to Île Royal.

Royal Ti'Punch (☎32-0995; www.royalti punch.pageperso-orange.fr; €48) This is the auberge's smaller, 28-passenger catamaran.

Tropic Alizés (☎25-1010; www.ilesdesalute -guyane.com; €48) This boat leaves from the Nautical Club of Kourou; price includes a sunset cocktail but goes up to €60 if you chose to stay overnight. Best choice for day trips from Cayenne.

St Laurent du Maroni

POP 34,336

St Laurent is an intriguing place with some of the country's finest colonial architecture and, even 60 years after the penitentiary's closure, it's dominated by penal buildings and the ghosts of its prisoners. Along the banks of the Fleuve Maroni (Marowijne River), bordering Suriname, St Laurent is also the place to take a river trip to Maroon and Amerindian settlements. It's set up better for tourism than any other town in the country, including Cayenne, and if you've been getting frustrated by French Guiana's lack of travel-ease, you'll find it refreshingly easy to organize activities here.

Sights & Activities

Stop by the tourist office for excellent free maps for self-guided walking tours, as well as information on the full range of activities available in the area.

You can get combination tickets at the tourist office for the following two prison camps for €8. For €5 (or €12 with the two camp tours) you can take a guided spin around the town's heritage area, known as 'Le Petit Paris,' on a white and blue children's park-style car train. The train also winds through the lowest income part of town where the local kids laugh at you and the adults glare.

TOP CHOICE Camp de la Transportation HISTORIC SITE

(tours €5 per person; ⌚tours 8am, 9:30am, 11am, 3pm & 4:30pm Mon-Sat, 9:30am & 11am Sun) The eerily quiet Camp de la Transportation, where prisoners arrived for processing, was the largest prison in French Guiana. Convicts arrived by boatfuls of 500 to 600 men, who had taken 20 days to cross the Atlantic. The Tourism Office offers 1½-hour tours although most guides speak minimal English. Otherwise, ask for a brochure with a map that points out the tiny cells, leg shackles, dorm-style toilets (known to prisoners as the 'love room') and public execution areas. One cell has Papillon's name engraved near the bed, but whether this was really his cell is up for debate.

Fleuve de Maroni RIVER

(half-day tours around €40) Explore the Amerindian and Maroon cultures that inhabit the shores of this great river. You'll usually also visit the island of an old leper colony (mentioned in Papillion) and take a jungle stroll. The tourist office will know which of the several local river tour companies have scheduled trips, and can direct to guides who speak English. Agami (p741) is a great choice.

Longer multi-jaunts usually involve more exploration, a night or more in a hammock in a traditional Amerindian hut and a taste of the local cuisine.

Le Camp de la Relégation HISTORIC SITE

(St Jean; €5 per person; ⌚tours 3:30pm Tue-Sun) St Jean, another abandoned prison camp 17 kilometers from St Laurent, is accessed via two-hour tours by the tourist office. These buildings once were home to 'the claws' – light offenders who were given a good deal of freedom. As such, the atmosphere here isn't as creepy as French Guiana's other prison-day relics.

Today the old prison is surrounded by a French military camp.

Sleeping & Eating

St Laurent has very few hotels; two are in town, and there is cheaper hammock space available further out.

Several small grocery stores and a midsize market provide self-catering options. Stalls at the lovely Wednesday and Saturday food and craft market (5am to 1pm) offer filling *bami goreng* (fried noodles), *pho* (noodle soup) and French-style quiche, all for around €4.

St Laurent du Maroni

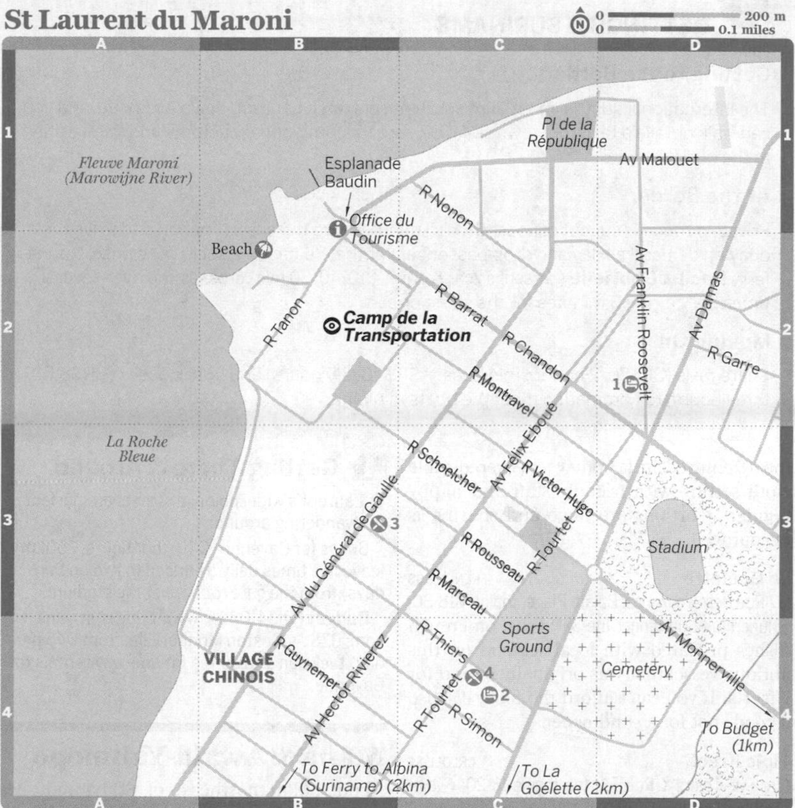

TOP CHOICE Hôtel La Tentiaire HOTEL $
(☎34-2600; tentiaire@wanadoo.fr; 12 Av Franklin Roosevelt; r from €55; P❄📶≋) The best in the center, Tentaire has classy rooms with wood accents in a renovated administrative penitentiary building. Some rooms have balconies looking over the little adjacent park, and two levels that comfortably sleep a family of four.

Agami HAMMOCK $
(☎34-7403; PK 10; hammock spaces with/without hammock €15/10) Dominican Carmen and her husband have traditional Amerindian huts for hammocks in their gardens of grapefruits and bananas. The restaurant serves the best set meal (€20) of traditional Amerindian food found in the Guianas. Reasonably priced, low-key and very non-touristy feeling canoe tours are also available. Agami is on the road to St Jean.

St Laurent du Maroni

Top Sights

Camp de la Transportation ... B2

Sleeping

1 Hôtel La Tentiaire ... D2
2 Hôtel Star ... C4

Eating

3 Chez Félicia ... B3
4 Tipic Kreol ... C4

Hôtel Star HOTEL $
(☎34-1084; 26 Thiers; r from €55; ❄📶≋) With its public-high-school decor and mildewy rooms, this is a place to stay only if the Tentiaire is full.

Chez Félicia CREOLE $
(23 Av du Général de Gaulle; mains €11-14; ⌚lunch & dinner, closed Sun nights) This local favorite has tasty Creole cuisine (including bush

GETTING TO SURINAME

Getting to the Border

The international quay is about 2km south of central St Laurent, down Av Eboué, and you can walk or take a taxi from town (€4). Be sure to stamp out at customs and immigration at the quay.

At the Border

Private *pirogues* (dugout canoes; €10, 10 minutes) are the easiest option and leave the quay on demand all day and drop passengers at the Albina ferry dock. Otherwise, the car ferry **Bac La Gabrielle** (passenger/car & driver €10/40; 30 min) crosses the river several times per day in 30 minutes for the same price.

Moving On

Share taxis (SR$70, 2 hours), minibuses (SR$30, 2½ hours) and public buses (SR$8.50, three hours) to Paramaribo meet the boats in Albina.

meat) enjoyed in a homey, checkered-tablecloth setting with friendly staff and happy regulars. Portions are huge and sharing is encouraged.

La Goélette FRENCH **$$$**
(17 Rue des Amazones, Balate Plage; mains €18-30; ⏰lunch Tue-Sun, dinner Tue-Sat) Feast on French dishes prepared with local seafood on this antique vessel that was originally bound for Nigeria. If you can't afford the food, it's also a good spot for a sundowner.

Tipic Kreol CREOLE **$$**
(cnr Rue Thiers & Rue Tourtet; mains 13-20; ⏰dinner Mon-Sat, lunch Tue-Sun) Busy and central with a choice of sidewalk seating for people watching or more intimate inside tables in a plant-filled, polished wood restaurant area. The food, including bush meat, fish, steaks and salads, is copious and tasty.

Information

Internet Access

Wi-fi is widely available.

Money

Banks and ATMs are scattered throughout town but none exchange foreign currency or traveler's checks. You'll have to wait to get to Cayenne if you need to exchange money.

Tourist Information

Office du Tourisme (☎34-2398; www.97320.com; Esplanade Baudin; ⏰7:30am-6pm Mon-Fri, 7:45am-12:45pm & 2:45am-5:45pm Sat, 9am-1pm Sun, only Sat hr in Jul & Aug) Everything there is to do and see in St Laurent can be arranged from here. Plus the staff speak English and give out free maps.

Getting There & Around

St Laurent's wide, colonial streets are perfect for wandering around.

Buses for Cayenne (€40, four hours, 250km) leave five times daily (reduced to two on Sundays) from the *gare routière* at the stadium.

Budget (☎34-0294; www.budget-guyane.com; 328 Av Gaston Monnerville; from €45 per day) tacks on a €100 fee for one-way rentals to Cayenne.

Mana & Awala-Yalimopo

About 50km northeast of St Laurent lies the rustic village of Mana (population 600), which boasts a particularly scenic waterfront on the Mana River, considered one of the loveliest and least spoiled rivers in northern South America.

There's an ATM at the **post office** (Rue Bastille) in Mana, and the last gas station heading east is at the roundabout at the Mana entrance. There's no other way to get to this area than by car.

Amerindian settlements populate Awala-Yalimopo (population 1200) and **Plage Les Hattes**. The latter is one of the world's most spectacular nesting sites for giant leatherback turtles, which can grow up to 600kg; nesting occurs from April to July, and their eggs hatch between July and September. The number of turtles that come ashore is so high that one biologist has likened the scene to a tank battle.

Maison de la Reserve Natural l'Amana (☎34-8404; adult/child €2/free; ⏰8am-noon & 2-6pm Mon, Wed & Fri & Sat 2-6pm Tue & Thu) has a little museum, information about turtle biology and two nature trails leading from its premises.

In Mana, stay at the excellent value, riverside **Le Samana Hotel** (☎27-8667; hotel samana@orange.fr; 18 Rue Bruno Aubert; d/studio €60/70; P❄📶) – which is near the roundabout when you drive into town – and don't miss a chance to dine on French cuisine with a Guianaise twist at **Le Buffalo** (☎34-4280; 36 Rue AM Javouhey; mains €7-21; ⏰lunch & dinner Tue-Sun). Awala-Yalimopo lodging (reserve in advance) includes the Amerindian-style *carbets* just 50m from Les Hattes beach at **Chez Judith & Denis** (☎34-2438; hammock shelter for two people incl breakfast €32, hammock rental €9), and the similar but larger **L'Auberge de Jeunesse Simili** (☎34-1625; dorm bed €20, hammock spaces with/without hammock €15/7). Places at both fill quickly during turtle-viewing periods. Try to reserve a French-Amerindian lunch or dinner at **Yalimalé** (☎34-3432; meals €23; ⏰closed Sun dinner & Mon) although it's rarely open outside of turtle season.

UNDERSTAND FRENCH GUIANA

French Guiana Today

Developments at the Centre Spatial Guyanais (Guianese Space Center) in Kourou dominate the news in French Guiana. Russians are moving in to French Guiana in greater numbers, adding to the cultural mix, ever since their country's Soyuz medium-load launcher made it's maiden voyage in 2009. Meanwhile, more and more countries are using Korou as their spaceport; Azerbaijan launched its first satellite from there in February 2013. With gold prices increasing, gold mining has also become more prevalent around the country, particularly along the eastern Brazilian border. In 2010 the population voted against increased autonomy from France, so it seems the country will remain a overseas department with European funds flooding in for some time.

History

The earliest French settlement was in Cayenne in 1643, but tropical diseases and hostile local Amerindians limited plantation development. After various conflicts with the Dutch and British and an eight-year occupation by Brazil and Portugal, the French resumed control, only to see slavery abolished (1848), and the few plantations almost collapsed.

About the same time, France decided that penal settlements in Guiana would reduce the cost of French prisons and contribute to colony development. Napoleon III sent the first convicts in 1852; those who survived their sentences had to remain there as exiles for an equal period of time. With 90% of them dying of malaria or yellow fever, this policy did little to increase the population or develop the colony. French Guiana became notorious for the brutality and corruption of its penal system, which lasted until 1953.

Guyane became an overseas department of France in 1946, and in 1964 work began on the Centre Spatial Guyanais, which has brought an influx of scientists, engineers, technicians and service people from Europe and elsewhere, turning the city of Kourou into a sizable, modern town responsible for 15% of all economic activity. The first Hmong refugees from Laos arrived in 1975 and settled primarily in the towns of Cacao and Javouhey. They now make up about 1.5% of the population and have become vital agricultural producers, growing about 80% of the department's produce.

Successive French governments have provided state employment and billions of euros in subsidies, resulting in a near-European standard of living in urban areas. Rural villages are much poorer, and in the hinterland many Amerindians and Maroons still lead a subsistence lifestyle.

Culture

French Guiana is a tantalizing mélange of visible history, fabulous cuisine and the sultry French language with the vastness and ethnic diversity of Amazonia. Though Cayenne and Kourou enjoy somewhat continental economies, the majority of the populace struggles financially and lives a modest lifestyle.

The Guianese take pride in their multicultural universe borne of multiregional influences. French Guiana has about 220,000 permanent inhabitants, with temporary and migrant workers from Haiti and Brazil making up the 60,000-and-growing balance. Around 38% of the

SLEEPING PRICE RANGES

The following price ranges refer to a double room with bathroom outside of Carnaval (which runs from January to February or March). Unless otherwise stated, all taxes are included.

$ less than €75

$$ €75 to €150

$$$ more than €150

population claims a mixed African (or Creole) heritage, 8% are French, 8% Haitian, 6% Surinamese, 5% are from the French Antilles, 5% are Chinese and 5% are Brazilian. The remainder of the population is a smattering of Amerindian, Hmong and other South American ethnicities.

The country is predominantly Catholic, but Maroons and Amerindians follow their own religious traditions. The Hmong also tend to be Roman Catholic due to the influence of Sister Anne-Marie Javouhey, who brought them to French Guiana.

Environment

French Guiana borders Brazil to the east and south, while the Maroni and Litani Rivers form the border with Suriname.

The majority of Guianese people live in the Atlantic coastal zone, which has most of French Guiana's limited road network. The coast is mostly mangrove swamp with only a few sandy beaches. The densely forested interior, where the terrain rises gradually toward the Tumac-Humac Mountains on the Brazilian frontier, is largely unpopulated.

SURVIVAL GUIDE

Directory A–Z

Accommodations

Hotels in French Guiana are generally charmless but comfortable. Most hotels have some English-speaking staff.

The most economical options include long-stay *gîtes* (inquire at tourist offices) in Cayenne, Kourou and St Laurent, and rustic *carbets* for hammocks.

Activities

Bird-watching, hiking and canoeing are popular in French Guiana. Water sports – windsurfing, kitesurfing and sailing – are a major pastime on beaches at Montjoly and Kourou, but renting gear is practically impossible. Sport fishing is gaining popularity, especially around Kourou; stop by **Guyanespace Voyages** (☎tel, info 22-3101; 39 Av Hector-Berlioz).

Business Hours

Many businesses close up shop in the heat of the day; generally hours are 8am to noon and 2pm to 5pm, while restaurants tend to serve from noon to 2pm and again from 7pm to 10pm or later. The country stops on Sunday and sometimes Monday, especially in St Laurent. Nightclubs and bars open at around 10pm.

Electricity

Plugs are three pronged European. Currents are 220/127V, 50 Hz.

Embassies & Consulates

Brazilian Embassy (☎29-6010; 444 Chemin St Antoine, Cayenne) Off Rue de Baduel.

Dutch Embassy (☎34-0504; ZI Dégrad des Cannes, Rémire-Montjoly) Off the main highway towards the airport.

Surinamese Consulate (☎594-28-2160; cg.sme.cay@wanadoo.fr; 3 Av Léopold Héder, Cayenne; ⏲8:30am-5:30pm Mon-Fri) Often busy, but if you're lucky you can get a tourist card issued within a few minutes.

UK Consulate (☎31-1034; 16 Av Monnerville, Cayenne)

Health

Chloroquine-resistant malaria is present in the interior, and French Guiana is considered a yellow fever–infected area. If you need a vaccination while here, contact the **Centre de Prévention et de Vaccination** (☎30-2585; Rue des Pommes Rosas, Cayenne; ⏲8:30am-noon Mon & Thu). Excellent medical care is available, but few doctors speak English. Water is fine in bigger towns; drink bottled or boiled water elsewhere.

Language

The official language is French and most people speak it fluently. Creole is spoken casually by the Creole population, while French

Guianese is a mixture of Creole and other languages. Otherwise, the Hmong population speak Hmong, there are several Amerindian dialects spoken by the native population, and along the Suriname border many Maroons speak Sranan Tongo (the language of Suriname).

Money

French Guiana is one of the most expensive regions in South America, in part because it uses the euro and imports many goods from France. The only *cambios* for currency exchange are in Cayenne but ATMS are found in most mid-sized to large towns.

Credit cards are widely accepted, and you can get Visa or MasterCard cash advances at *guichets automatiques* (ATMs), which are on the Plus and Cirrus networks. Eurocard and Carte Bleu are also widely accepted.

Post

The postal service is very reliable, although all mail is routed through France. To receive mail in French Guiana, it's best to have the letters addressed to France but using the French Guianese postal code.

Public Holidays

New Year's Day January 1

Ash Wednesday February/March

Good Friday/Easter Monday March/April

Labor Day May 1

Bastille Day July 14

All Saints' Day November 1

All Souls' Day November 2

Armistice (Veterans' Day) November 11

Christmas Day December 25

Safe Travel

Larger towns warrant caution at night. Crime and drug trafficking has increased throughout the country in recent years, and you'll often find customs roadblocks on coastal routes. Both locals and foreigners may be searched.

Locals hitchhike around Cayenne and west toward St Laurent, but it's riskier for travelers, who may be seen as money-laden targets. Never hitch at night or on the road between Régina and St Georges, which is more dangerous and remote.

FOOD PRICE RANGES

The following price ranges refer to a standard main course, including service.

$ less than €12

$$ €12 to €20

$$$ more than €20

Telephone

Digicel SIM cards are available in Cayenne, Kourou and St Laurent for €20 including €5 of credit. There are no area codes in French Guiana.

Visas

Passports are obligatory for all visitors, except those from France. Visitors should also have a yellow-fever vaccination certificate. Australian, New Zealand, Japanese, EU and US nationals, among others, do not need a visa for stays up to 90 days.

Those who need visas should apply with two passport photos at a French embassy and be prepared to show an onward or return ticket. Officially, all visitors, even French citizens, should have either onward or return tickets.

Getting There & Away

Air

All international passengers must fly through Cayenne's **Félix Eboué International Airport** (Rochambeau; ☎29-9700).

Air Caraïbes (☎29-3636; www.aircaraibes.com; Centre de Katoury, Rte Rocade) Services several Caribbean destinations including Port-au-Prince and Santo Domingo.

Air France (☎29-8700; www.airfrance.gf; 17 Lalouette) Flies to Paris, Fort-de-France and Pointe-a-Pitre. Also has an airport office.

Air Guyane (☎29-3630; www.airguyane.com; Félix Eboué International Airport) Flies to Saül

DEPARTURE TAX

For flights to any international destination (besides Paris, which is considered a domestic flight), the departure tax (US$20) is included in the ticket price.

and other destinations within French Guiana.

TRIP Lineas Aereas (www.voetrip.com.br; Félix Eboué International Airport) Service to Belem scheduled to start in 2013.

Boat

From St Laurent du Maroni (in the west) boats and a car ferry head to Suriname and there's a bridge from St Georges de l'Oyapock (in the east) to Brazil.

Getting Around

Getting around French Guiana without your own wheels is much more difficult and costly than in mainland France, where public transport and hitchhiking are more common. Even though renting a car might blow your budget, it's probably the most cost-efficient way to cruise the country.

Air

From Cayenne, small planes operated by Air Guyane fly to Saül.

Boat

Tours often use river transport, but individuals can try to catch a boat at Kaw and St Laurent. Catamarans sail to the Îles du Salut.

Car

Although most roads are in exceptional condition, some secondary and tertiary roads can be bad in the rainy season – have a spare tire, spare gas and spare time. If you are traveling in a group, renting a car (from €45 per day) may actually save money. An International Driving Permit is recommended but not legally required. You must be at least 21 years old to rent.

Guyana

Includes »

Best Adventures

» Dadanawa (p759)
» Kaieteur Falls (p756)
» Jordan Falls (p759)
» Bushmasters (p751)

Best Wildlife Encounters

» Caiman House (p758)
» Karanambu (p758)
» Shell Beach turtles (p756)
» Rewa Eco-Lodge (p758)

Why Go?

Few places on the planet offer raw adventure as authentic as densely forested Guyana. Although the country has a troubled history of political instability and interethnic tension, underneath the headlines of corruption and economic mismanagement is a joyful and motivated mix of people who are turning the country into one of the continent's premier ecotourism destinations.

Georgetown, the country's crumbling colonial capital, is distinctly Caribbean with a rocking nightlife, great places to eat and an edgy market. The interior of the country is more Amazonian with its Amerindian communities and unparalleled wildlife-viewing opportunities tucked quietly away from the capital's hoopla. From sea-turtle nesting grounds along the country's north coast to riding with *vaqueros* at a ranch in the south, Guyana is well worth the mud, bumps and sweat.

When to Go

Georgetown

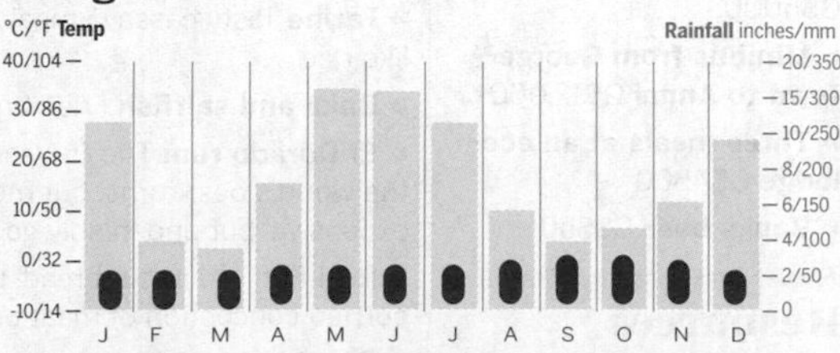

Mid-Nov–Mid-Jan Coastal rainy season and the height of tourism for expats returning for Christmas.

May–Aug Interior and second coastal rainy season. Road travel becomes difficult.

Late Dec 'Cashew rains' in the interior – light showers provide a welcome temperature drop.

AT A GLANCE

» **Currency** Guyanese dollar (G$), US dollars (US$) widely accepted

» **Language** English

» **Money** Not all ATMs accept foreign cards; credit cards rarely accepted

» **Visas** 90 days on arrival for most visitors

» **Time** GMT minus four hours

Fast Facts

» **Area** 215,000 sq km

» **Population** 765,000

» **Capital** Georgetown

» **Emergency** ☎911

» **Country code** ☎592

Exchange Rates

Australia	A$1	G$223
Canada	C$1	G$211
Euro zone	€1	G$276
New Zealand	NZ$1	G$179
UK	UK£1	G$325
USA	US$1	G$213

Set Your Budget

» **Budget hotel room** G$5000

» **Minibus from Georgetown to Annai** G$12,000

» **Three meals at an eco-lodge** G$4500

» **Banks beer** G$350

Resources

» **Guyana Tourism** (www.guyana-tourism.com)

» **Starbroek News** (www.starbroeknews.com)

» **Explore Guyana** (www.exploreguyana.org)

Connections

Guyana's only legal border crossings are at Nieuw Nickerie (Suriname) and Bonfim (Brazil), which can both be reached via minibus. Yes Venezuela shares much of the country's west coast, but crossing anywhere is technically illegal and not recommended. The only legal route from Venezuela to Guyana is to first go to Bonfim, Brazil, and then into Guyana via Lethem. Flights from Georgetown, Guyana go to/from Paramaribo (Suriname), Bridgetown (Barbados), Port of Spain (Trinidad and Tobago), Miami and New York.

ITINERARIES

One Week

Stay in Georgetown for a night or two and take a day trip by plane to outrageous Kaieteur Falls. Next, fly or travel overland into the interior to stay in the Amerindian village of Surama for two nights. From here take road and river to either Caiman House to help with Caiman research or Karanambu to help with giant river otter protection.

Two Weeks

Follow the above itinerary but begin your adventure with a night at Iwokrama's Canopy Walkway before going to Surama. After Caiman House or Karanambu spend your last nights at either Rewa Eco-Lodge to search for arapima (the world's largest scaled fish) or put on your cowboy hat to live with the *vaqueros* at Dadanawa Ranch, near the wildlife-filled Kanuku Mountains.

Essential Food & Drink

» **Pepper pot** A savory Amerindian game-and-cassava stew

» **Cook-up rice** Beans and rice mixed with whatever else happens to be on hand

» **Farine** Tasty cassava meal served as an accompaniment like rice

» **Bake and saltfish** Fried bread and salted cod

» **El Dorado rum** The 15-year-old drop is considered one of the world's best rums, but most people settle with the less expensive, but undeniably good five-year-old variety

» **Roti** Soft Indian flatbread, usually wrapped around a curried concoction of meat or vegetables

» **Cow heel soup** A very popular savory Caribbean soup made with split peas, vegetables, dumplings and cow heels

» **Banks beer** Brewed in Georgetown, comes in both regular and premium versions, both of which are delicious

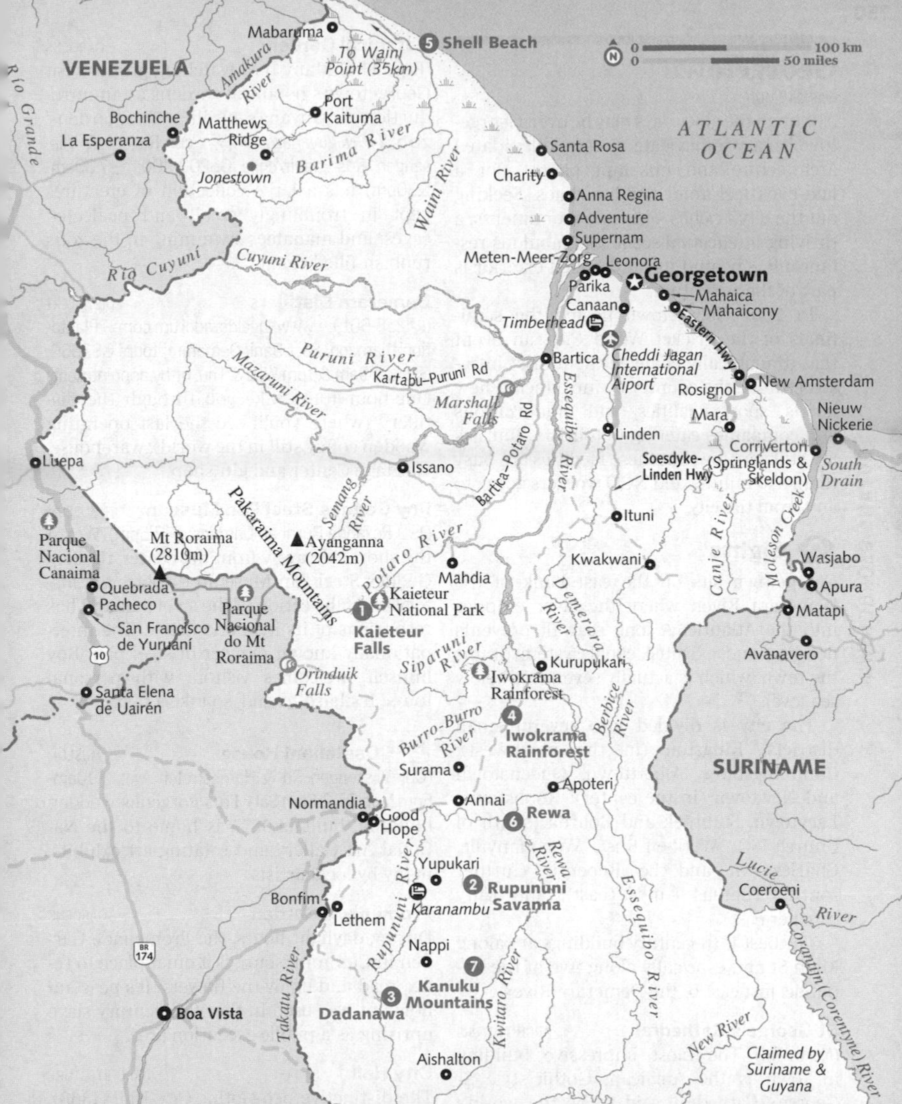

Guyana Highlights

1 Stand on the ledge of the world's highest single-drop fall, **Kaieteur Falls** (p756)

2 Paddle though thriving populations of giant river otters and black caimans in the **Rupununi Savanna** (p758)

3 Go on a cattle drive with local *vaqueros* (cowboys) at **Dadanawa Ranch** (p759)

4 Eco-tour the deep forests of **Iwokrama** (p757)

5 Pass through rice-farming villages and cross rivers teeming with wildlife en route to **Shell Beach** (p756)

6 Catch a glimpse of Nessie-sized arapaima, the planet's biggest fresh water scaled fish, near **Rewa Eco-Lodge** (p758)

7 Camp at the top of **Jordan Falls** (p759) deep in the pristine Kanuku Mountains

Georgetown

POP 240,000

Although the glory days may be over, Georgetown's easy-to-navigate streets, dilapidated architecture and unkempt parks offer a laid-back feel amid real-life chaos. Seeking out the city's riches – historic monuments, a thriving intellectual scene and fabulous restaurants – behind its hard-boiled exterior is part of the adventure.

In 2007 Georgetown hosted the semi-finals of the Cricket World Cup, an event that dramatically changed the tourist infrastructure of the country by introducing new hotels, sport facilities, and organizations and companies catering to tourists. Tourists are still very few, but these facilities are busy thanks to mining and NGO workers going to and from the city.

Sights

Georgetown sits on the east bank of the Demerara River, where the river empties into the Atlantic. A long seawall prevents flooding and a Dutch canal system drains the town, which is actually seven feet below sea level.

The city is divided into several small districts: Kingston (in the northwest); Cummingsburg, Alberttown, Queenstown and Newtown (in the center); Robbstown, Lacytown, Stabroek and Bourda (south of Church St); Werk-en-Rust, Wortmanville, Charlestown and Le Repentir (further south); Thomas Lands (east); and Kitty (further east).

The best 19th-century buildings are along Main St and especially along Ave of the Republic, just east of the Demerara River.

St George's Cathedral ARCHITECTURE
(North Rd) The most impressive building in town is the Anglican, Gothic-style St George's Cathedral, said to be the world's tallest wooden building. It was completed in 1892 and was built with a native hardwood called greenheart.

Stabroek Market MARKET
(Water St) One of the city's most prominent landmarks is Stabroek Market, a cast-iron building with a corrugated-iron clock tower. The market dates back to the late 1700s, although the current structure was built in 1880. A visit to this frenetic and colorful place is a must but don't bring any valuables and keep a grip on your bag.

Botanical Gardens GARDENS
(Regent Rd) Many bird-watching groups visit Georgetown's botanical gardens as an introduction to Guyana's birdlife. The gardens' **zoo** (www.guyanazoo.org.gy; cnr Regent & Vlissengen Rds; adult/child G$200/100; 7:30am-5:30pm) has a large collection of creatures kept in troublingly small and neglected cages, and manatees swimming in the zoo's rubbish-filled canal.

Demerara Distillers DISTILLERY
(256-5019; www.theeldoradorum.com; Plantation Diamaon, East Bank Demerara; tours G$3000; tours 9am & 1pm Wed & Thu, or by appointment) One-hour tours take you through the distillery (where you'll see the last operating wooden coffey still in the world), warehouse, Heritage Center and gift shop.

Roy Geddes Steel Pan Museum MUSEUM
(190 Roxanne Burnhan Gardens; 2-5pm) Worth the short ride away from the center, the Roy Geddes Steel Pan Museum displays the history and fabrication of the steel pan and has recordings of its hypnotic music. The internationally known pioneer of steel pan, Roy himself, welcomes visitors with personal tours. It's hard to find, so take a taxi.

FREE **Castellani House** MUSEUM
(Cnr Vlissengen Rd & Homestretch Ave; 10am-5pm Mon Fri, 2-6pm Sat) This gorgeous wooden building, built in 1877, is home to the National Art Gallery and rotating art exhibits, many by local artists.

Promenade Garden GARDENS
During daylight hours, the Promenade Garden in Cummingsburg is a quiet place to relax, read and enjoy the flowers. It's peaceful now but was used in the 19th century slave uprising as a public execution area.

City Hall ARCHITECTURE
The distinctive neo-Gothic City Hall (1868), has a 23m tower from which colonial-period wives apparently watched for their husbands' ships to come into port, and is one of Georgetown's more striking buildings.

National Library LIBRARY
(cnr Ave of the Republic & Church St) Andrew Carnegie built the National Library in 1909. Go inside to find a collection of old books.

National Museum MUSEUM
(Museum of Guyana; cnr North Rd & Hincks St; 9am-5pm Mon-Fri, till noon Sat) This old-fashioned institution documents the nation's

cultural, social and political history via some odd artifacts and very old stuffed critters.

Walter Roth Museum of Anthropology MUSEUM
(61 Main St; ⏲8am-4:30pm Mon-Fri) A small museum in a breezy old building with lots of Amerindian items from Guyana's nine tribes.

Tours

Guyana is one to watch on the South American ecotourism scene, thanks to increased investment by the government to promote sustainable travel. Although it's possible (and adventurous) to visit the interior of Guyana independently, most visitors go with a tour. Tours can make your life a lot easier and save you lots of time but they will also cost much more money.

Wilderness Explorers ADVENTURE TOUR
(☎227-7698; www.wilderness-explorers.com; Cara Suites, 176 Middle St) A long-running, reliable company with tons of itinerary choices all around the country, including specialty tours such as fishing and remote trekking.

Bushmasters ADVENTURE TOUR
(☎682-4175; www.bushmasters.co.uk/guyana; Lethem) One- and two-week jungle survival courses, and cowboy holidays, horseback tours and safaris mostly through the Rupununi. Plans are in the works for river scuba diving and rappelling down Kaituer Falls.

Evergreen Adventures ADVENTURE TOUR
(☎226-0605; www.evergreen-adventures.com; 159 Charlotte St) Puts together superb customized trips, and is run by the same company that owns Trans Guyana Airways – so a reliable choice for booking flights with lodges all around the country.

Rainforest Tours ADVENTURE TOUR
(☎227-2011; www.rftours.com; Hotel Tower, 74 Main St) Frank Singh's Rainforest Tours arranges an adventurous five-day overland journey to Kaieteur Falls (US$850).

Wonderland Tours ADVENTURE TOUR
(☎225-3122; www.wonderlandtoursgy.com; 85 Quamina St) Offers bargain day trips to the Essequibo River, including Santa Mission (G$16,000).

Sleeping

Unless otherwise noted, all the following charge a 5% service fee when accepting credit cards.

Rima Guest House GUESTHOUSE $
(☎225-7401; rima@networksgy.com; 92 Middle St; s/d/tr G$5500/6500/9000; 📶) This backpackers' favorite is a family-run place with giant rooms and shared bathrooms in a large colonial house. The owners are friendly and helpful. Cash only.

Sleepin International HOTEL $$
(☎227-3446; www.sleepininternationalhotel.com; 24 Brickdam St; r G$8000-20,000; ❄📶🏊) There are two locations of Sleepin: the Sleepin International and the **Guesthouse** (☎231-7667; www.sleepinguesthouse.com; 151 Church St; r G$7000-13,000). Both are centrally located and have clean, modern, great-value rooms with hot water and TVs. Sleepin International is the flashier choice with a pool and big restaurant but the guesthouse's budget rooms have air-con, which you will be thankful for.

Hotel Ariantze HOTEL $$
(☎226-5363; www.ariantzesidewalk.com; 176 Middle St; s/d incl breakfast from G$10,000/13,000; ❄📶) This boutique-style hotel has colonial architecture, big, bright windows and helpful staff (although only the guards are onsite after around 5pm). Nice restaurant and jazz cafe downstairs.

Cara Lodge HOTEL $$$
(☎225-5301; www.carahotels.com; 294 Quamina St; d from G$27,000; ❄@📶) Something about the gingerbread details and art-adorned corridors make this feel like a hideaway for glamorous film stars. There's an old-fashioned ballroom, a patio bar around a 100-year-old mango tree and a classy, rich-and-famous-worthy restaurant downstairs. Ask for a standard room, which are actually nicer than the higher-priced rooms.

YWCA HOSTEL $
(☎226-5610; 106 Brickdam St; dm G$2000) The cheapest option in town has 50 dorm beds for both men and women. You don't get much more than you pay for, but it's in the heart of Georgetown and secure. No credit cards.

Eating

Some of the best food in the Guianas can be had for a few coins in Georgetown. *Snackettes* are small eateries that serve inexpensive small meals (you usually order at the counter and the food is brought to your table). Grocery stores and markets all over town offer self-catering options.

Georgetown

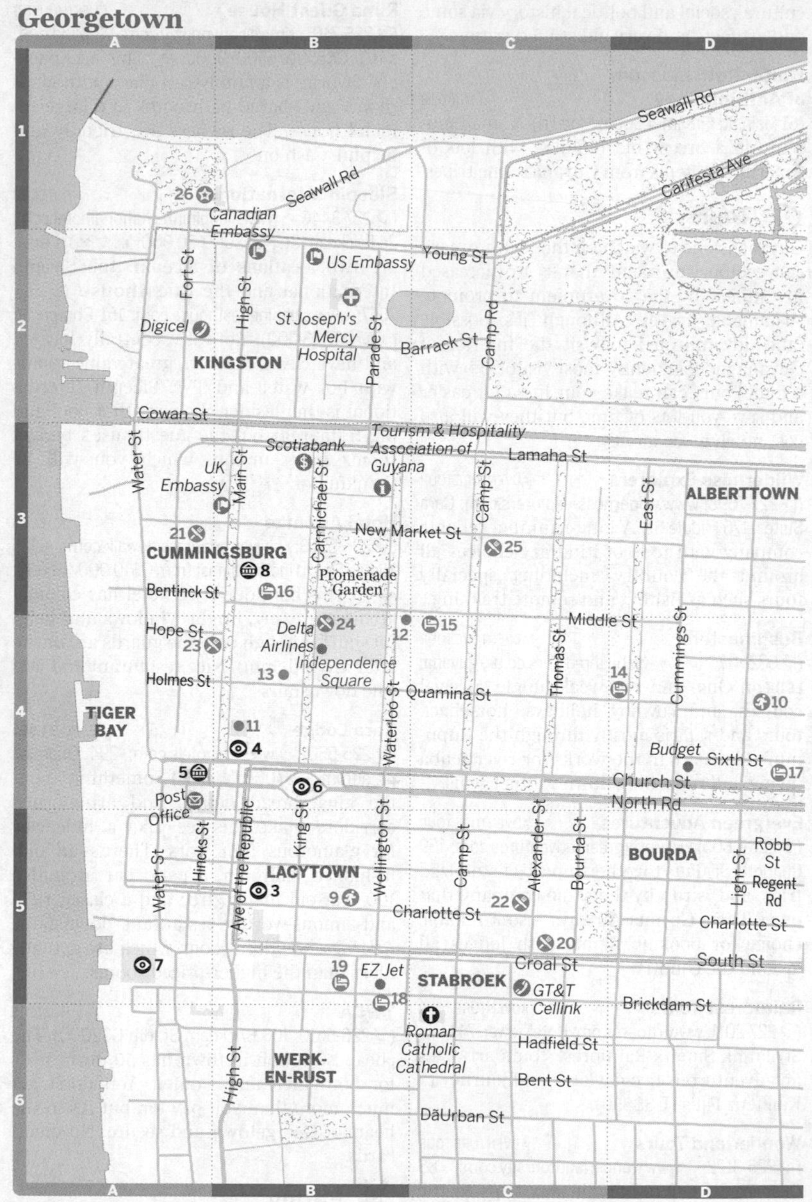

TOP CHOICE Shanta's INDIAN $
(225 Camp St; light meals from G$450; ⏲8am-6pm) For more than a half century, Shanta's has been filling Georgetown's bellies with the best roti, curries and *chokas* (roasted vegetables) this side of India. It's unbelievably inexpensive considering how delicious the food is. Try everything.

House of Flavors CARIBBEAN $
(177 Charlotte St; light meals from G$200; ⏲6am-9pm Mon-Sat, to 4pm Sun) Serving only one

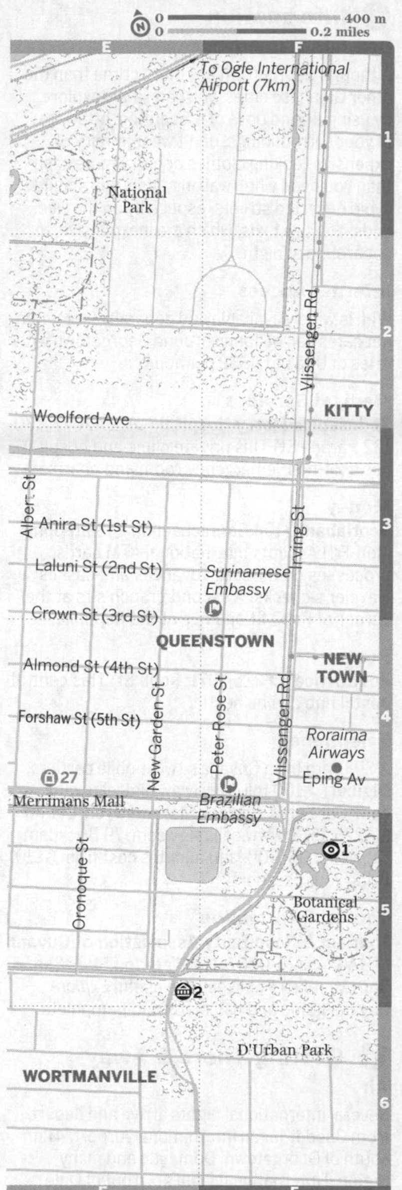

Georgetown

Sights

1 Botanical Gardens' Zoo F5
2 Castellani House E5
3 City Hall B5
4 National Library B4
5 National Museum A4
6 St George's Cathedral B4
7 Stabroek Market A5
8 Walter Roth Museum of Anthropology B3

Activities, Courses & Tours

9 Evergreen Adventures B5
10 Fly Brasil Travel Agency D4
11 Rainforest Tours B4
12 Wilderness Explorers B4
13 Wonderland Tours D4

Sleeping

14 Cara Lodge D4
15 Hotel Ariantze C4
16 Rima Guest House B3
17 Sleepin - Guesthouse D4
18 Sleepin - International B5
19 YWCA B5

Eating

20 Brasil Churrascaria & Pizzaria C5
21 German's A3
22 House of Flavors C5
23 New Thriving A4
24 Oasis Café B4
25 Shanta's C3

Entertainment

26 Club Latino A1
Sidewalk Café and Jazz Club .... (see 15)

Shopping

27 Austin's Book Services E4

dish – home-cooked rice, beans, veggies, and mango *achar* (spicy pickled condiment) – in a calabash, this Rastafarian (and vegetarian) restaurant doubles as a music store and caters to long lines of diners, many with impressive dreadlocks.

Brasil Churrascaria & Pizzaria BRAZILIAN $$$
(208 Alexander St; G$4000 per kilo or G$3500 all you can eat; ⌚11am-9pm Mon-Sat) If you're a big meat eater, head here. Start with the salad and buffet bar, then tuck in as servers carve perfectly grilled meats on your plate as they come off the grill. Great pizzas too.

Oasis Café WESTERN $
(www.oasiscafegy.com; 125 Carmichael St; snacks & sandwiches G$400-1000; ⌚7:30am-6:30pm Mon-Thu, 7:30am-8:30pm Fri, 9am-9:30pm Sat, 10am-6pm Sun; 📶) With real coffee, a lunchtime salad/entree bar (G$2100), rich desserts and

GETTING INTO TOWN

The Timeri bus (G$500, one hour) services Cheddi Jagan International Airport to/from the Timeri Bus Park behind the Parliament Building in central Georgetown; the bus is safe enough, but at night a taxi (G$5000) is a much wiser choice. For early morning flights from Cheddi Jagan International Airport, make taxi arrangements the day before.

wi-fi, this place really is an oasis. Try the 'bake and saltfish' (fried bread with salted cod) for breakfast.

German's GUYANESE $
(8 New Market St; meals from G$400) Stop in for lunch to dine on local specialties like pepper pot and ox heel soup. It's in a relatively dodgy area so take a taxi.

New Thriving CHINESE $$
(cnr Main & Hope Sts; mains G$1100-2500; ⌚10:30am-9:30pm) Extremely popular, central and with more upscale decor than most Georgetown favorites, we found the mediocre Chinese food here overpriced but locals never cease to recommend it.

Drinking & Entertainment

East of Newtown, Sheriff St is a raucous parade of bars, discos and nightclubs with an equally raucous clientele plying the streets; it might be the action you're looking for, but it's not Georgetown's safest strip. The party gets rolling about 10pm and goes until dawn.

Club Latino CLUB
(Seawall Rd) The DJ at the tame Club Latino, in the faded Le Meriden Pegasus Hotel, spins Latin beats. Thursday is the best night to go – some say the only night to go.

Sidewalk Café and Jazz Club CAFE, JAZZ
(176 Middle St) At the Hotel Ariantze this is an ambient place for a drink any night, or live jazz Thursday nights.

Shopping

You can find local handicrafts at the kiosks in **Hibiscus Craft Plaza**, in front of the post office. **Austin's Book Service** (190 Church St; ⌚8am-4pm Mon-Fri, to 1pm Sat) has the widest selection of books.

Information

Dangers & Annoyances

Although Georgetown has more crime than the other Guianese cities, you can safely explore by using a good dose of precaution: be aware of your surroundings, don't wear jewelry or expensive-looking clothes or carry more cash than you need when walking. Also, you should avoid deserted streets, especially on the weekends, and use taxis, which are inexpensive, to get around at night.

Internet Access

Wi-fi is widely available and generally free. Internet cafes can be found around Georgetown with rates of US$1 to US$2 per hour.

Medical Services

St Joseph's Mercy Hospital (☎227-2072; 130-132 Parade St) This private clinic and hospital has a 24-hour emergency room and pharmacy.

Money

Scotiabank (104 Carmichael St; ⌚8am-6pm Mon-Fri) Accepts international ATM cards, processes credit-card advances and cashes traveler's checks. A second branch sits at the corner of Robb St and Ave of the Republic.

Post

Post Office (☎225-7071; Robb St) This central postal hub can be hectic.

Telephone

A SIM card from Guyana's two mobile carriers, **Digicel** (☎100 toll-free; www.digicelguyana.com; Cnr Fort & Barrack Sts) and **GT&T Cellink** (☎225-1513; www.cellinkgy.com; 79 Brickdam St), costs G$1000, and minutes cost from G$10. Bring your passport.

Tourist Information

Tourism & Hospitality Association of Guyana (THAG; ☎225-0807; 157 Waterloo St; ⌚8am-5pm Mon-Fri) Publishes the useful *Explore Guyana* guide and has maps and pamphlets.

Getting There & Away

Air

Several international flights arrive and depart from Cheddi Jagan International Airport, 41km south of Georgetown. Domestic and many regional international flights run out of Ogle International Airport, closer to town.

Air Guyana/Wings Aviation (☎222-6513; www.airguyana.net; Ogle Aerodrome) Regular flights to Lethem (US$120) plus charters to many destinations including Trinidad and Tobago, and French Guiana.

Air Services Limited (☎222-4357; www.aslgy.com; Ogle Aerodrome) Regular flights to

Lethem (US$115), Kaieteur (US$115) and other destinations in the interior.

Delta Airlines (☎225-7800; www.delta.com; 126 Carmichael St) Flies nonstop to New York (US$650, 6½ hours, four times weekly).

EZ Jet (☎225-7585; www.ezjetair.com; 23 Brickdam Rd) Six weekly direct flights to/from New York (from US$400) and one weekly flight to Toronto (from US$650).

Roraima Airways (☎225-9648; www.roraima airways.com; R8 Eping Ave, Bel Air Park) Charter flights mainly to the interior.

Trans Guyana Airways (TGA; ☎222-2525; www.transguyana.com; Ogle Aerodome) Services the most flights to the most destinations within the country (around 35) as well as daily code-share flights with Gum Air to Paramaribo in Suriname (US$225; one hour). Has the best safety reputation.

Bus & Minibus

Economical, cramped minibuses to destinations along the coast depart from Stabroek Market, have no fixed schedules and leave when full. Fares around Georgetown are G$80 to G$200.

ℹ Getting Around

Car

Budget (☎225-5595; 75 Church St) rents cars (G$7000 per day, three-day minimum), but with bad roads full of farm animals and crazy driving, you may as well leave the driving to others.

Taxi

For simplicity and safety, taxis are *the* way to get around central Georgetown; trips around the center are around G$300 even at night. Have your hotel call a reliable cab company. If you need to flag down a taxi, use only registered ones painted yellow (all registered taxi license plates start with an 'H') and try to find ones with a company logo on the side.

Berbice

The Eastern Hwy follows the coastal plain from Georgetown to the Suriname border. The road travels through town after unremarkable town, passing potholes, suicidal dogs, unfenced livestock and the resultant roadkill. At **Rosignol**, about two hours' drive from Georgetown, you cross the Berbice River to **New Amsterdam** via a floating bridge.

The whole coastal region stretching from Rosignal to Corriverton is collectively known as Berbice, and Corriverton is actually an amalgamation of the two small towns of **Springlands** and **Skeldon**, on the west bank of the Corentyne River, bordering Suriname.

Corriverton's main street, Public Rd, is a lively strip with mosques, churches, a Hindu temple, cheap hotels, eateries and bars. Brahman cattle roam round the market like the sacred cows of India. If you need to stay the night, try **The Ritz** (☎335-3605; 171 Springlands; G$4500-7500; ❄📶), which is clean and easy to find.

Although most travelers speed through Berbice, the little towns have hidden (though run-down) colonial buildings. The quintessential Berbice activity, however, is taking a ride in a Tapir, the only car ever to be manufactured in Guyana. Named after one of the most awkward and lethargic animals in the

GETTING TO SURINAME

Getting to the Border

For direct minibus service to Paramaribo from Georgetown, leaving around 5am, call **Champ** (☎629-6735).

At the Border

The Canawaima ferry to Suriname (G$2000, 25 minutes, 10am & noon daily) leaves from Moleson Creek and crosses the Corentyne River to the Suriname border at South Drain, 45 minutes south of Nieuw Nickerie. Get to the ferry no later than one hour before departure to stamp passports and go through customs control.

Moving On

Minibuses to Nieuw Nickerie and Paramaribo meet the ferry on the Suriname side. It's best to change your Guyanese currency before leaving Guyana in case no one's buying across the river. Make sure you know your rates before you make the exchange.

Suriname is an hour ahead of Guyana; remember to set your watch *ahead* one hour.

wild, these boxy cars are proudly decorated by their owners and used as taxis to ferry passengers through and between the towns.

Buses and Tapirs run from Public Rd in Corriverton to New Amsterdam and, the other way, to the Suriname ferry at Moleson Creek (G$800, 20 minutes). Be sure to depart Corriverton before 10am to reach the ferry.

Northwest Coast

About 20km west of Georgetown, the coastal highway passes Meten-Meer-Zorg, where you'll find the **Guyana Heritage Museum and Toucan Inn** (275-0028; 17 Meeten-Meer-Zorg; admission G$100; 7:30am-5:30pm). Owner Gary Serrao and his eclectic collection of historical artifacts and maps dating to the 17th century make for a fascinating dip into Guyanese history. Also on site is an inn (rooms G$6000 to G$12,000); take a dip in the pool and enjoy the rooftop views of the Essequibo rushing into the Atlantic.

Further west along the coastal highway, boats travel from **Parika** southward to the lively mining town of **Bartica** (population 11,100). Near Bartica, the Essequibo meets the Mazaruni River and Marshall Falls, a series of rapids and a jungle waterfall reached by a short hike. **Arrowpoint Nature Resort** (225-9650; www.roraimaairways.com; per person incl full board & activities from US$200;) is pricey but has tons of activities and is in a gorgeous location; from here you can easily access the Amerindian village of **Santa Mission**, a favorite destination for Guyanese who want to appreciate Carib and Arawak customs, such as making cassava bread. Tour operators offer day trips to all of the above places from Georgetown.

The west bank of the Essequibo River can be reached by boat (G$1000, 45 minutes, leaving when full from dawn to dusk) from Parika to **Supernam**. Heading west from the Essequibo, a coastal road passes quaint rice-mill and farming villages to the town of **Charity**, about 50km away. From here you'll need a boat to go further – through bird-filled rivers, mangrove swamps and savannas – to **Shell Beach**, which extends for about 140km along the coast toward the Venezuelan border and is a nesting site for four of Guyana's eight sea turtle species. This is one of the least developed areas of the entire South American coastline; the only human alterations are in the form of temporary fishing huts and small Amerindian settlements. **Waini Point** near the beautiful town of **Mabaruma** (population 700) is the most spectacular sighting area for the scarlet ibis. Georgetown agencies can help you set up a tour through the area or arrange a flight or boat directly to Mabaruma.

Kaieteur National Park

This area is home to one of the world's most impressive waterfalls, a tiny population of Amerindians and the endless biodiversity of the Guiana Shield, a massive geological formation covered in rainforest and savanna. It has, however, been subject to the strategies of government and mining interests to limit its boundaries since it first became a park in 1929; after several expansions and contractions, it now encompasses 62,700 hectares and is actively protected by the government – largely because the park's tourism potential depends on it being intact.

KAIETEUR FALLS

You may have been to Salto Ángel or Iguazú Falls, seen Niagara or not even be particularly interested in waterfalls, it doesn't matter – go to **Kaieteur Falls** (www.kaieteurpark.gov.gy). Watching 30,000 gallons of water shooting over a 250m cliff (allegedly making this the world's highest single-drop falls) in the middle of a misty, ancient jungle without another tourist in sight is a once-in-a-lifetime experience. The brave can actually stand at the top of the falls and gaze over the precipice. Depending on the season, the falls are from 76m to 122m wide. Swifts nest under behind the falls, and dart in and out of the waters around sunset each night. The trail approaching the falls is home to scarlet red Guiana cock-of-the-rock birds, and miniscule golden frogs that produce a poison that is the same type of alkaloid as (but 160,000 times more potent than) cocaine – if the toxins get into the blood they can be fatal.

Several Georgetown tour operators offer day trips with small planes; make early inquiries and be flexible, since the flights go only when a full load of five to eight passengers can be arranged (usually on weekends). Tours with a guide are available from Wonderland Tours (p751) and several other tour companies from around US$250; you can also choose to add in Orinduik Falls (with massive falls cascading over several levels where you can bathe) or a stop at Baganara Resort (on an island with white-sand beaches on the Essequibo River), for an additional US$30. The cheapest flight option we found was to Kaietuer only, without a guide (but on the same flight as folks who did hire a guide) through **Fly Brasil Travel Agency** (☎225-8002; rose084@hotmail.com; 107 Bourda St) for US$125 return.

More adventurous options include a five-day overland journey to Kaieteur (from US$850) through Rainforest Tours (p751), or hook up with Bushmasters (p751) who are planning on adding a rappelling Kaieteur option to their tour programs that would allow climbers of all levels to get a spectacular, vertiginous view of the falls.

It's possible to stay in a rustic **lodge** (per person G$3600) at Kaieteur Falls, bookable through the **National Parks Commission** (☎226-7974, 226-8082). You'll have to bring your own food and may have to pay extra freight charges on your flight if you're carrying over 10kg total.

Iwokrama Rainforest

The **Iwokrama Centre for Rainforest Conservation and Development**, established in 1996, is a unique living laboratory for tropical forest management and socioeconomic development for Amerindians. Amid 371,000 hectares of virgin rainforest, this exceptional region is home to the world's highest recorded number of fish and bat species, South America's largest

RUPUNUNI: DO-IT-YOURSELF TRANSPORTATION

Getting There

Most people fly from Georgetown to either Annai, Lethem or Karanambu. Air Guyana, Air Services Limited and TGA each fly once or twice a day from Georgetown to Lethem and Annai – the TGA flight will stop at Karanambu on the morning flight only on demand. One-way to any destination is G$25,000.

You can also reach the Rupununi's main ports of call on Georgetown–Lethem–Georgetown minibuses (G$12,000, daily, may be cancelled during the wet season), which leave Georgetown (on Church St between Cummings and Light Sts) and Lethem at 6pm and take around 16 hours. Note that you'll still need to arrange pickup from the main road to all the lodges except Rock View Lodge (p759). The long voyage involves a ferry crossing, stopping to sleep at a hammock camp for up to six hours (hammock rental available for G$500) and several police checkpoints; bring warm clothes, your passport and some patience.

The big Intraserve bus had stopped running at the time of research but it's possible that another big bus will start serving the Georgetown–Lethem route again during the life of this book.

Getting Around

If you book your trip on a tour, or even directly through lodges, they will shuttle you around in their high-cost overland 4WDs and boats, and will probably not offer you other options unless you ask. The lodges themselves aren't trying to pillage you – it's the cost of fuel in the Rupununi that make these options so expensive and yet most people choose to travel this way for convenience. Sample one-way fares for a jeep for four people are: Annai to Lethem (G$56,000), Annai to Karanambu (G$90,000) and Lethem to Dadanawa (G$50,000) – travel times are highly variable, depending on the season. Traveling in groups can ease the sticker shock.

If you're not in a group, getting around by motorbike is a much cheaper option. This entails finding a local willing to take you (lodges will help with this), having small enough luggage to strap on the back of a motorbike or wear on your back, and having a very sturdy rear end (expect VERY bumpy rides). Sample costs per person are: Lethem to Dadanawa (G$12,000) and Caiman House to Nappi (G$12,000).

You can also try and hop on the Lethem–Georgetown–Lethem minibuses to get along stretches of the main road, although this can be problematic since these travel at night and you'll have to book in advance to ensure a seat.

If you have much more time than money, try to hitch a ride with lodges when they make their supply runs.

cat (jaguar), the world's largest freshwater fish (arapaima), and the world's largest otters, river turtles, anteaters, snakes, rodents, eagles and caimans.

Unlike a national park, Iwokrama is not funded by the government and must therefore take a realistic approach to economic survival without overexploiting its resources. The community practices selective tree felling while studying sustainable logging techniques; the profits from the timber are used to help finance ecotourism work and biological research. Amerindian peoples inhabit parts of the forest and are encouraged to work with ecotourism projects and create cottage industries.

Iwokrama's Georgetown **office** (☎225-1504; www.iwokrama.org; 77 High St) arranges transportation and accommodations; stay in riverside, eco-chic cabins or a more economical hammock camp at the **field station** (Iwokrama base camp; cabins s/d G$14,000/24,400, hammocks G$4070). Full-board is an additional G$7950 per person per day. Mix-and-match tours can include visits to Amerindian villages, forest walks and nighttime caiman-spotting, with each activity costing from G$3460 to G$11,200.

Only 60km south of the of the field station, Iwokrama's **Canopy Walkway** (www.iwokramacanopywalkway.com; day pass G$3600), a series of suspension bridges hoisted 30m above the forest floor, offers bird's-eye views of native greenheart trees, high-dwelling red howler monkeys and lots of birds. To be ready for the early morning canopy action, sleep at **Atta Rainforest Camp** (www.iwokramacanopywalkway.com; hammock/s/d G$18,330/30,550/26,500 per person incl guide & full-board), which offers comfortable brick cabins and a hammock camp about 500m from the canopy walkway.

North Rupununi

The Rupununi savannas are Africa-like plains scattered with Amerindian villages, small 'islands' of jungle and an exceptional diversity of wildlife. Rivers full of huge caimans and the world's largest water lilies *(Victoria amazonica)* cut through plains of golden grasses and termite mounds, and a mind-boggling array of birds fly across the sky. On a human level, the Rupununi feels like a tight-knit, small town spread over 104,400 sq km, and you'd be hard-pressed to find a safer place in South America.

The heart of the north Rupununi is at **Annai** (population 300), a crossroads of Amerindian peoples with a police station and an airstrip at Rock View Lodge.

Sleeping

At the time of research a phone tower was planned in Annai but by early 2013 there was still no phone reception. There is internet and wi-fi, however, so reservations at the following places (all community-run) can be made through their websites.

Karanambu Ranch RANCH **$$$**
(www.karanambutrustandlodge.com; bungalow incl meals & activities G$40,700 per person; wi-fi) About 60km south by road and boat from Annai, is this real-life Jane Goodall–like experience, where octogenarian Diane McTurk has devoted her life to saving the giant river otter. On occasion, a few otter orphans animate the ranch, as does Diane, who is just as interesting. Accommodations are in ranch-meets-Amerindian-style huts and activities range from bird-watching to giant anteater tracking.

Surama LODGE **$$**
(www.suramaecolodge.com; huts with full board & activities per person from G$25,600; @ wi-fi) The Amerindian village of Surama will impress you with its dignified approach to tourism. Local guides lead visitors through the village to learn about daily life, including cassava processing and medicinal plant usage. There are lots of hiking and dugout canoe trips on offer too. Digs are in a simple, yet beautiful lodge about a kilometer from the village.

Rewa Eco-Lodge LODGE **$**
(www.rewaguyana.com; r per person incl full board G$8150; wi-fi) Deep in the jungle, about 50 miles up the Rupununi River, far from any other civilization, this lovely lodge sits on a river bank a short walk from the beautiful, tiny thatched village of Rewa. The specialty here is catch-and-release fishing and arapaima (world's largest fresh water fish) spotting, but there are also hikes and cultural village visits.

Caiman House LODGE **$$**
(www.rupununilearners.com; r per person incl full board US$17,300; wi-fi) This artistically designed lodge is in the heart of the lively, hilltop Amerindian village of Yupikari. Accommo-

GETTING TO BRAZIL

Crossing the Border

A Brazilian-built bridge – with a cool lane-crossing system that switches from Guyana's left-hand driving to Brazil's right-hand driving – straddles the Takutu River from Lethem on Guyana's side to Bonfim, Brazil, on the other. Stamp out of customs and immigration at the bridge on the Guyana side and stamp into the corresponding office on the Brazil end. Note that American, Canadian and Australian nationals need visas (available in Georgetown – count on a week for processing), and all need to present their yellow fever certificate, as well. Money changers abound – you can't miss 'em.

Moving On

There are five buses to Boa Vista (R$15, one hour 15 minutes) between 6:30am and 4pm daily. The 'Federales' custom officials on the Brazilian side of the bridge are very friendly and can update you on the schedule. From Boa Vista, planes and buses connect to further destinations.

dations are spacious, ranch-style rooms in a big wooden two-story house. The lodge was started as a caiman research centre and now tourism is the key to financing the ongoing study. Take part in nighttime (dry season only) 'caimaning' where you help catch (sometimes huge) caimans to tag. Walks and river trips are also available.

Rock View Lodge LODGE $$
(☎226-5412; www.rockviewlodge.com; s/d with full board G$28,000/44,000; @ 📶 ≋) Hummingbirds may flit through the windows of your room at this elegant hacienda-style retreat at the scenic Annai airstrip. Find cheaper, equally plush bungalows, basic hammock spaces (G$2040) and cheap meals (G$700 to G$1200) at nearby Oasis under the same management, but the roadside setting isn't nearly as nice. Both arrange walks, village visits and horseback riding.

South Rupununi

The biggest settlement in the Rupununi is much further south at **Lethem**, a dusty *vaquero* town on the Brazilian border that's experiencing an economic boom from Brazilian shoppers coming over the bridge for grocery and supply bargains. Other than deal hounds, the region attracts gold miners and a collection of eccentric characters fanatical about wildlife, conservation and living life to the fullest. Every Easter, the Rupununi Rodeo in Lethem attracts hundreds of visitors to see the rodeo spectacles with a distinctly Rupununi/Amerindian touch. Local waterfalls, several ranches and a cooperative cashew-processing plant are interesting year-round attractions.

At Lethem's airstrip, **New Kanuku Bar** (☎772-2085; ⊙8am-11pm) – previously named Don & Shirley's – is the best place to get information about the local attractions, guides and other points of interest in the area. They are also very efficient at booking lodges around the Rupununi.

At the time of writing the nearest ATM that accepted foreign cards was in Bonfim, Brazil.

Sleeping & Eating

The lodges far from Lethem get poor phone reception and no internet, so it can take a while to hear back if you want to make a booking. Plan ahead.

Lethem has a few basic eating options. Your best hunting grounds are around the airstrip.

Dadanawa Ranch RANCH $$
(www.dadanawaranchguyana.com; cabins per person incl full board G$24,000) Duane and Sandy's remote ranch at the base of the Kanukus, is straight out of *National Geographic*. Extreme treks – tracking harpy eagles, jaguars and the recently rediscovered red siskin finch – complement days partaking in ranch work or even riding on a cattle drive to Lethem. Rooms in the guesthouses are basic with mosquito nets but have an undeniable cowboy charm to them.

Maipaima Lodge LODGE $$$
(guybalatacraft@gmail.com; r per person incl full board & activities $G24,500) This rustic choice

gets you into the pristine Kanuku Mountains. The lodge is about 10km from the photogenic Amerindian village of Nappi, from where you're accompanied by a guide and cook. The signature activity here is to hike (a challenging 13km) to 275m-high Jordan Falls and camp in hammocks overnight at the top. Plenty of other hikes are available too. Rooms are in a row, on stilts about a meter off the jungle floor, and have aging wood plank floors, simple mosquito-netted beds and tiny attached bathrooms.

Takutu Hotel HOTEL **$**
(☎772-2094; www.takutuhotel.com; Takutu Dr, Lethem; d from G$5000; ❄@📶) Best all-arounder in Lethem, popular with traveling Rupununi locals, offering everything from cheap and clean air-conditioned doubles to fancier suites and a *benab* (palm-thatched hut) to sling hammocks for G$1000. There's on onsite restaurant and a bar, which gets loud especially on Wednesday karaoke nights.

UNDERSTAND GUYANA

Guyana Today

Guyana is a part of CARICOM (Caribbean Community) and has strong relations with Caribbean nations, particularly Trinidad and Tobago and Barbados. Long-running land disputes with Suriname over maritime space with oil potential has been cleared in recent years, with most of the territory being awarded to Guyana. Disputes with Venezuela over a maritime area near the border between the two countries is ongoing, however, so relations between the two countries are strained and there's no official border crossing.

Donald Ramotar of the People's Progressive Party was elected president in 2011. The party has been in power since 1992, when Cheddi Jagan won the presidency.

Logging and gold and bauxite mining have greatly benefited the top tier of Guyana residents in recent years, although the wealth hasn't trickled down to the masses. Roads are still waiting to be paved and areas of extreme poverty are put in greater perspective by massive housing developments for the nouveau riche. Guyana has been feeling pressures from overseas investors, particularly China, to 'develop resources' – this is often at odds with the country's long-standing dedication to preserving its forests.

History

Both Carib and Arawak tribes inhabited the land that is now Guyana before the Dutch arrived in the late 16th century. Running a plantation economy dependent on African slaves, the Dutch faced a widespread rebellion, known as the Berbice Slave Revolt, in 1763. The rebel leader, Kofi, remains a national hero despite the ultimate failure of the slaves to gain their freedom.

The British took control in 1796, and in 1831 the three colonial settlements of Essequibo, Demerara and Berbice merged to become British Guiana. After the abolition of slavery in 1834, Africans refused to work on the plantations for wages, and many established their own villages in the bush and became known as Maroons. Plantations closed or consolidated because of the labor shortage, but the sugar industry was resurrected with the help of imported, indentured labor from Portugal, India, China and other countries, drastically transforming the nation's demographic.

British Guiana was run very much as a colony until 1953, when a new constitution provided for home rule and an elected government. In 1966 the country became an independent member of the British Commonwealth with the new name, Guyana, and in 1970 it became a republic with an elected president.

Only a few years later, in 1978, Guyana attracted the world's attention with the mass suicide-murder of more than 900 members of American Jim Jones' expatriate religious community of Jonestown.

For decades after independence, most of the important posts had been occupied by Afro-Guyanese, but more recently Indo-Guyanese have been appointed to influential positions, fueling racial tensions between groups of African and East Indian descent. Cheddi Jagan, Guyana's first elected president, died in office in 1997 and was replaced by his US-born wife Janet, resulting in continued political tension. In 1999 Janet Jagan retired from the presidency on health grounds and named Bharrat Jagdeo her successor.

Elections scheduled for January 2001 were delayed until March 2001 because of election irregularities. This move antagonized voters in an already racially charged campaign, and entire blocks of Georgetown were set ablaze by opposition supporters as the ruling PPP/Civic (led by an Indo-

Guyanese majority) was declared victor and claimed a third consecutive term. Police and protestors clashed in the capital for weeks. Fortunately, violence on this scale has not returned to Georgetown since 2001, but racial tensions continue to be a part of Guyanese politics. However, new efforts at tolerance education have made a positive impact on Guyanese youth, and many people acknowledge that more cooperation to end racial conflict is needed.

Guyana's economy relies on commodities exports, especially bauxite but also gold, sugar, rice, timber and shrimp. The Indo-Guyanese control most of the small business, while the Afro-Guyanese have dominated the government sector until the late '90s.

Culture

Guyana's culture is a reflection of its colonialist plantation past. African slaves lived under severe conditions that destroyed much – but not all – of their culture. East Indian laborers arrived under better circumstances and managed to keep much of their heritage intact. The main groups of Amerindians, who reside in scattered interior settlements – Arawak, Carib, Makushi and Wapishana – still live significantly off the land. Ethnic tension and distrust rack contemporary Guyanese society, which is also increasingly distrustful of Brazilians, who are perceived to want access to Guyana's natural resources. Today, about 44% of the population is East Indian, 30% African, 17% mixed heritage and 9% Amerindian

Guyana's population is 765,000, but some 500,000 Guyanese also live abroad, mostly in Canada, the UK, USA, and Trinidad and Tobago. This leads many people to believe that more Guyanese live outside of the country than inside, but the numbers don't bear this out; still, Guyana is concerned, and probably justifiably so, about 'brain drain,' as they lose skilled workers overseas.

Most Afro-Guyanese are Christian, usually Anglican, but a handful are Muslim. The Indo-Guyanese population is mostly Hindu, with a sizable Muslim minority, but Hindu-Muslim friction is uncommon. Since independence, efforts have been made to recognize all relevant religions in national holidays.

Environment

Guyana is swarming with rivers, including its three principal waterways (listed east to west): the Berbice, Demerara and Essequibo. The narrow strip of coastal lowland (with almost no sandy beaches) is 460km long and comprises 4% of the total land area but is home to 90% of the population. The Dutch, using a system of drainage canals and seawalls, reclaimed much of the marshy coastal land from the Atlantic and made it available for agriculture.

TRAGEDY AT JONESTOWN

On November 18, 1978, 913 people (including more than 270 children) were killed in a mass suicide-murder in a remote corner of Guyana's northwestern rainforest. Since then, Guyana has been sadly associated with this horrific event that became known as the Jonestown Massacre.

In the 1950s, Jim Jones, a charismatic American leader, started a religious congregation in Indiana called the Peoples Temple. With utopian ideas of an egalitarian agricultural community, Jones attracted hundreds of followers, but by the 1960s, after moving his church to San Francisco, he became increasingly paranoid and the Peoples Temple started to resemble a cult. Jones' next move took the congregation to the Guyanese bush, and by 1977 word leaked from escaped members that Jones was running the settlement more like a French Guiana prison camp. California congressperson Leo Ryan, along with journalists and worried family members, visited Jonestown, where they encountered several frightened Temple members who wanted to leave. Not realizing how dangerous Jones really was, Ryan tried to take several residents with him, only to meet gunfire from Jones' followers on the Jonestown airstrip. Ryan and four others were killed. That night Jones ordered his followers to drink cyanide-laced punch; while many 'drank the Kool-Aid,' others were found shot or with slit throats. Jones either shot himself or ordered someone to do it.

Director Stanley Nelson provides a modern perspective on this mysterious tragedy in his excellent 2006 documentary *Jonestown: The Life and Death of Peoples Temple*.

Tropical rainforest covers most of the interior, though southwestern Guyana features extensive savannas between the Rupununi River and the Brazil border.

Guyana is home to more than 2000 animal species and the likelihood of seeing some of the bigger and more famous ones – such as the black caiman, giant anteater, howler monkey, paccary, capybara, giant river otter and tapir – are high. You'll probably get to see a slew of monkeys and, if you're lucky, you might even spot a jaguar or harpy eagle.

SURVIVAL GUIDE

Directory A–Z

Accommodations

In Georgetown, the cheapest hotels often double as 'love inns,' which locals use by the hour – so be careful of questionably low rates. There are a few good, clean guesthouses around town, however, with rooms that include shared bathrooms from around US$30. Rainforest lodges and savanna ranches often seem expensive but note that food and activities are often included – although this still doesn't make them cheap. In the interior, the most budget-friendly accommodation is in a hammock (space in a hut costs around US$5 to US$10 per night); either your own or one provided by your hosts (for an extra US$5).

Activities

The interior and coastal areas offer countless outdoors adventure possibilities, from river rafting, trekking and bird-watching to wildlife-viewing and fishing. Community tourism is growing, particularly in the Rupununi. Most folks arrange adventures through Georgetown's tour agencies, but independent travel is also possible.

SLEEPING PRICE RANGES

The following price ranges refer to a double room and include a private bathroom unless otherwise indicated:

$ less than G$12,000

$$ G$12,000 to G$30,000

$$$ more than G$30,000

Books

Tracing the country's history with a modern-day voyage, *The Wild Coast* by John Gimlette is a must for any visitor to the region. It also includes shorter chapters on Suriname and French Guiana.

Ninety-Two Days by Evelyn Waugh describes a rugged trip from Georgetown across the Rupununi Savanna.

Journey to Nowhere: A New World Tragedy by Shiva Naipaul is a moving account of the Jonestown tragedy, published in the UK as *Black and White*.

Business Hours

Commerce awakens around 8:30am and tends to last until 4pm or so. Saturdays are half days, if shops open at all, and Georgetown becomes a ghost town on Sundays. Restaurants generally serve lunch from about 11:30am to 3pm and dinner from around 6:30pm to 10pm.

Electricity

Guyana uses American two-square pronged plugs. Currents are 127V, 60Hz.

Embassies & Consulates

The following embassies and consulates are in Georgetown.

Brazilian Embassy (☎225-7970; bragetown@solutions2000.net; 308-309 Church St) Visa processing takes three to seven days.

Canadian Embassy (☎227-2081; www.canadainternational.gc.ca/guyana; cnr High & Young Sts)

Surinamese Embassy (☎226-7844; surnmemb@gol.net.gy; 171 Crown St) Visa services open 9am to 11:30am Monday, Wednesday and Friday only. Visa processing takes one to five days depending on nationality (US passports take the longest).

UK Embassy (☎226-5881; http://ukinguyana.fco.gov.uk/en; 44 Main St)

US Embassy (☎225-4902; http://georgetown.usembassy.gov; 100 Young St)

Health

Adequate medical care is available in Georgetown, at least at private hospitals, but facilities are few elsewhere. Chloroquine-resistant malaria is endemic, and dengue fever is also a danger, particularly in the interior and even in Georgetown – protect yourself against mosquitoes and take a malaria prophylaxis. Typhoid, hepatitis A, diphtheria/tetanus and polio inoculations are recommended. Guyana is regarded as a yellow-fever-infected area, and your next destination may require a vaccination certificate, as does Guyana when you arrive. Tap water is suspect, especially in Georgetown. Cholera outbreaks have occurred in areas with unsanitary conditions, but precautions are recommended everywhere.

Internet Access

Georgetown's internet cafes charge about G$600 per hour and free wi-fi is widely available.

Language

English is the official language, but it's distinctly Guyanese, with plenty of musical lilts and colorful idioms that can make it nearly impossible to understand at first. Creole is a language spoken by most of the African community, mixing several languages, but can be relatively easy to understand once you develop an ear for it. More difficult are the many Amerindian dialects and the East Indian languages of Hindi and Urdu.

Money

The Guyanese dollar (G$) is stable and pegged to the US dollar, which is widely accepted. You also may be able to spend your euros or even British pounds. Credit cards are accepted at Georgetown's better hotels and restaurants (usually for a 5% service charge), although not at gas stations or most anywhere else. Scotiabank is the easiest place to get cash advances (up to US$200), and their ATMs are the only ones that accept foreign cards.

Cash can be exchanged at banks, but *cambios* (foreign-exchange offices) offer better rates and less red tape. Sometimes hotels change cash for a small commission.

Post

Postal services are iffy. For important shipments, try these international shippers with offices in Georgetown businesses: **UPS** (Mercury Couriers; ☎227-1853; 210 Camp St) and **DHL** (USA Global Export; ☎225-7772; 50 E 5th St, Queenstown)

Public Holidays

Republic Day celebrations in February are the most important national cultural events of the year, though Hindu and Muslim religious festivals are also significant. Amerindian Heritage Month (September) features cultural events, such as handicraft exhibits and traditional dances. An annual Rupununi Rodeo at Easter is held in Lethem.

New Year's Day January 1

Republic Day (Marking the slave rebellion of 1763) February 23

Phagwah/Holi (Hindu New Year) March/April

Good Friday/Easter Monday March/April

Labor Day May 1

Emancipation Day August 1

Diwali (Hindu Festival of Lights) October/November

Christmas Day December 25

Boxing Day December 26

Eid-ul-Fitr (Lebaran or Bodo in Indonesian) End of Ramadan; dates vary.

Telephone

You can get SIM cards with local mobile companies. Hotels and restaurants generally allow free local phone calls. There are

FOOD PRICE RANGES

The following price ranges refer to a standard main course:

$ less than G$1200

$$ G$1200 to G$2000

$$$ more than G$2000

USING US DOLLARS

If you aren't planning on traveling far off the tourist trail, you can get by using US dollars at most hotels, rainforest lodges, restaurants and taxis to the airports. The going user rate is G$200 for US$1 which is the same as the bank rate, and only seven cents difference (in their favor) compared to the *cambio* rate. Using US dollars can save you from dodgy trips to *cambios* as well as carrying around a huge stack of bills (the largest bill in Guyana is G$1000, worth about US5). Do plan on having a small stash of G$, however, for short taxi rides and snacks.

> **DEPARTURE TAX**
>
> Outbound passengers pay a departure tax of US$20 (payable in US dollars).

no area codes in Guyana. See p754 for more details.

Visas

Travelers from the USA, Canada, EU countries, Australia, New Zealand, Japan, the UK and most Caribbean countries do not need a visa; confirm with the nearest embassy or consulate. A 90-day stay is granted on arrival in Guyana with an onward ticket. If you do need a visa, file your application at least six weeks before you leave your home country.

As well as a passport, carry an international yellow-fever vaccination certificate with you (although you probably won't be asked for this), and keep other immunizations up to date.

To stay longer than 90 days, appeal to the **Ministry of Home Affairs** (☎226-2445; 6 Brickdam Rd, Georgetown; ⊙8-11:30am & 1-3pm Mon-Fri).

Visas are required for nationals of many countries entering Brazil and Suriname.

Women Travelers

Guyana's not-so-safe reputation should put women travelers on particular alert. Never go out alone at night and stick to well-peopled areas if walking alone during the day in Georgetown. In the interior, traveling alone should pose few problems.

Getting There & Away

Travelers flying to Guyana arrive at Cheddi Jagan International Airport, south of the capital, or Ogle International Airport closer to town that services smaller regional flights. See p754 for more details.

In the far south of Guyana, via Lethem, a bridge connects Guyana with Boa Vista in Brazil. In the northeast, a ferry connects Corriverton (Springlands) via Moleson Creek to Suriname. The only crossing between Venezuela and Guyana is the remote, difficult and dangerous road between Bochinche and Mabaruma but there are no immigration officials; you're better off going through Brazil.

Getting Around

Air

Charter air services to interior destinations such as Annai, Kaieteur and Iwokrama, are available from the Ogle International Airport in Georgetown.

Boat

Regular ferry services cross the Essequibo River between Charity and Bartica, with a stop at Parika (reached by paved highway from Georgetown). More frequent speedboats (river taxis) carry passengers from Parika to Bartica.

Car

Rental cars are available in Georgetown, though not from the airport at the time of writing. A driving permit (available for free at the Cheddi Jagan International Airport arrivals terminal) is required for car rental (an international driving permit won't suffice).

Minibus

Cheap local buses speed between points all over Georgetown. Minibuses from Georgetown to destinations along the coast cost up to G$1100. From Georgetown to Lethem one way is G$12,000.

Taxi

Many taxi companies travel between Georgetown and coastal destinations, although they cost significantly more than buses and minibuses. They can be a good value for a group. A taxi from Georgetown to the Cheddi Jagan International Airport costs US$25.

Paraguay

Includes »

Best Places to Eat

» Paulista Grill (p772)

» Parador Pirahú (p784)

» Benndo (p777)

» Hiroshima (p779)

» Mehin (p788)

Best Wildlife-Watching

» The Chaco (p786)

» Parque Nacional San Rafael (p780)

» Reserva Natural Laguna Blanca (p783)

» Mbaracayú Biosphere Reserve (p783)

» Paraguayan Pantanal (p785)

Why Go?

Little-visited, little-known Paraguay is a country much misunderstood. Despite its location at the heart of the continent, it is all too often passed over by travelers who wrongly assume that a lack of 'mega-attractions' means there's nothing to see. But it's ideal for those keen to get off the gringo trail for a truly authentic South American experience.

Paraguay is a country of remarkable contrasts: it's rustic and sophisticated; it's extremely poor and obscenely wealthy; it boasts exotic natural reserves and massive human-made dams; it is a place where horses and carts pull up by Mercedes Benz cars, artisans' workshops abut glitzy shopping centers, and Jesuit ruins in rural villages lie just a few kilometers from sophisticated colonial towns. The steamy subtropical Atlantic Forest of the east is a stark contrast to the dry, spiny wilderness of the Chaco; location of the isolated Mennonite colonies.

When to Go

Asunción

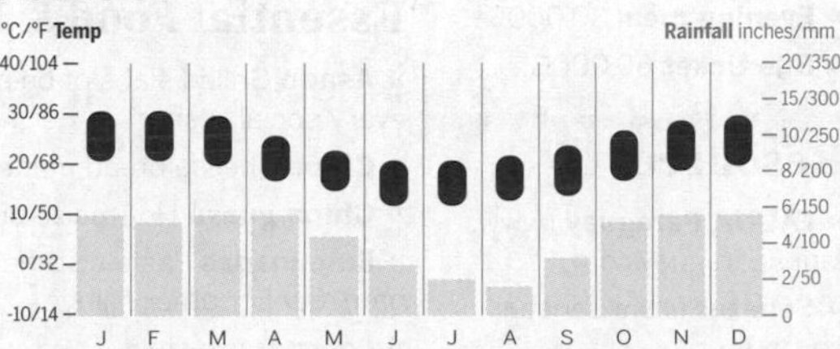

Feb Let loose during Carnaval season in Encarnación.

Jul–Aug Pleasant winter climate makes it the best time to visit the Chaco.

Dec Follow the pilgrims to the Caacupé basilica on the Día de la Virgen.

AT A GLANCE

» **Currency** Guaraní (G)

» **Languages** Spanish and Guaraní (official), German

» **Money** ATMs widespread, plastic rarely used

» **Visas** Not available at the border

» **Time** GMT minus four hours

Fast Facts

» **Area** 406,752 sq km

» **Population** 6.5 million

» **Capital** Asunción

» **Emergency** ☎911

» **Country code** ☎595

Exchange Rates

Australia	A$1	4230G
Canada	C$1	4014G
Euro zone	€1	5259G
New Zealand	NZ$1	3421G
UK	UK£1	6195G
USA	US$1	4069G

Set Your Budget

» **Hostel bed** 70,000G

» **Evening meal** 30,000G

» **Bus ticket** 60,000G

Resources

» **FAUNA Paraguay** (www.faunaparaguay.com)

» **Senatur** (www.senatur.gov.py)

» **Discovering Paraguay** (http://discoveringparaguay.com)

Connections

Despite its location at the heart of the continent, Paraguay is often circumvented by travelers. A country almost surrounded by major rivers, many of its land border points involve a bridge crossing with customs offices at either end. The main border crossings are Foz do Iguaçu (Brazil) to Ciudad del Este; Posadas (Argentina) to Encarnación; or via the Ruta Trans-Chaco from Bolivia. As a member of Mercosur, a trade bloc of southern states, Paraguayans don't need to complete customs formalities to cross to Brazil and Argentina. Foreigners do.

ITINERARIES

Two Weeks

Start with a historic tour of Asunción, take the tourist train to Areguá and visit Caacupé and San Bernardino along the way. From here head east to Laguna Blanca, where you could volunteer with Para la Tierra Biological Station, before moving on to Ciudad del Este to visit the awe-inspiring Itaipú Dam. A night in the forest at Hotel Tirol will prepare you for a few days' bird-watching in the real wilderness at Parque Nacional San Rafael. Return to civilization at Encarnación, a great base for visiting Jesuit Missions before crossing the international bridge to Posadas, Argentina.

Three Weeks

Complete the two week itinerary but return to Asunción and head north to colonial Concepción. Take a boat up the Río Paraguay Bahía Negra and visit the Paraguayan Pantanal, before experiencing the landscape contrast in the dry Chaco at the Mennonite colonies of Loma Plata and Filadelfia. Visit one of the Chaco national parks before continuing along the Ruta Trans-Chaco and crossing into Bolivia.

Essential Food & Drink

» **Asado** Grilled slabs of beef and pork are the focal point of every social event

» **Chipa** Cheese bread made with manioc flour

» **Chipa guasú** Hot maize pudding with cheese and onion

» **Empanadas** Pasties stuffed with chicken, cheese and ham, beef or other fillings

» **Locro** Maize stew

» **Mbeyú** A grilled cheese and manioc pancake

» **Sooyo** Thick soup of ground meat, often with a floating poached egg

» **Sopa paraguaya** Cornbread with cheese and onion

» **Terere** Iced yerba mate tea drank ubiquitously

» **Vori-Vori** Chicken soup with cornmeal balls

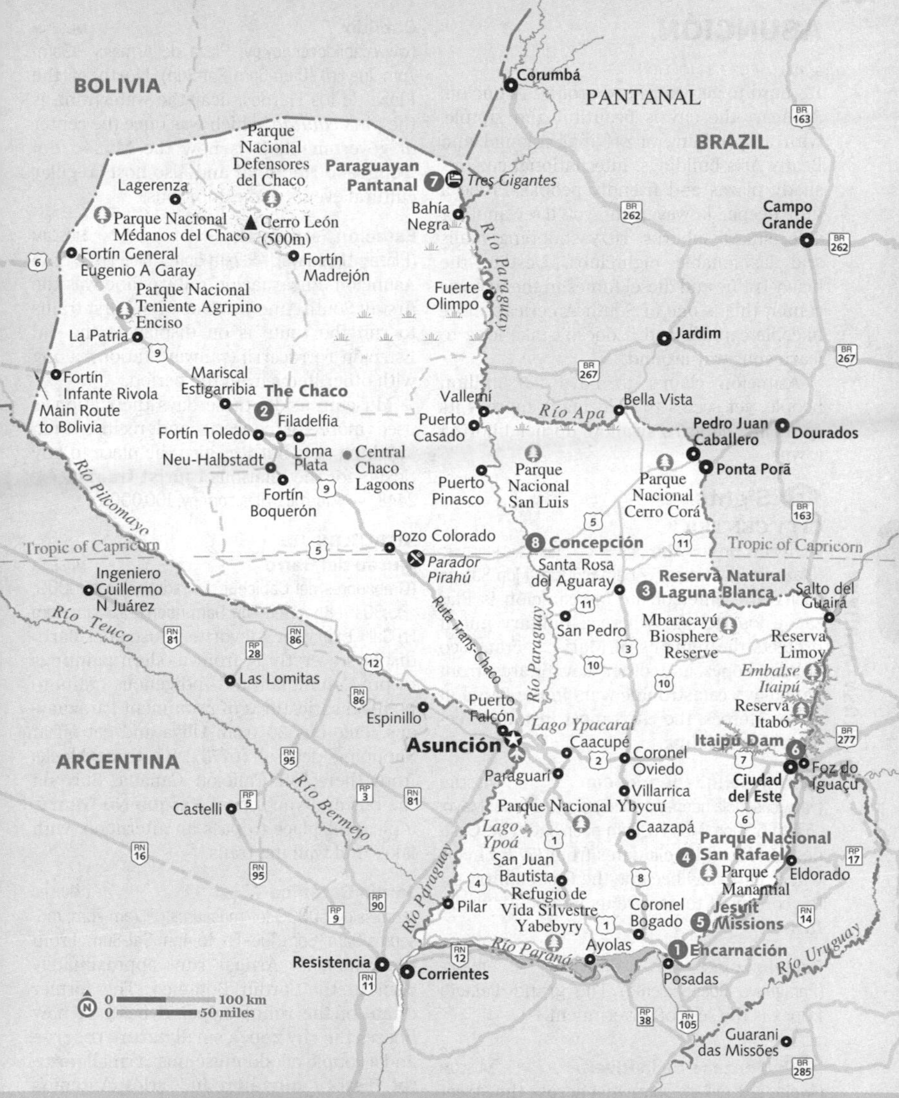

Paraguay Highlights

1. Party til well after dawn during Encarnación's original take on **Carnaval** (p779)
2. Spot a jaguar, sleep under the stars and experience the absence of humanity in the **Chaco** (p786)
3. Forget the rest of the world exists on the beach at tranquil **Laguna Blanca** (p783)
4. Wild out in the endangered Atlantic Forest in **Parque Nacional San Rafael** (p780), Paraguay's most biodiverse reserve
5. Explore the picturesque remnants of the **Jesuit Missions** (p780), one of the world's least-visited Unesco sites
6. Gaze in awe at **Itaipú Dam** (p782), now only the second biggest in the world, but still damned big
7. Ogle the animals in Paraguay's part of the **Pantanal** (p785)
8. Stroll the dusty streets of colonial **Concepción** (p784)

ASUNCIÓN

☎021 / POP 2.33 MILLION

It's hard to get your head around Asunción. At heart the city is beautiful and simple, with a sprinkling of original colonial and Beaux Arts buildings, international cuisine, shady plazas and friendly people. Probe a little deeper, however, and you'll see another side: smart suburbs, ritzy shopping malls and fashionable nightclubs. Despite the heavy traffic and diesel fumes in the historic center, this is one of South America's more likeable capitals and it doesn't take long to learn your way around.

Asunción claims to have 2.3 million people, yet seems to hold many more – its sprawling suburbs swallow up neighboring towns.

Sights

CITY CENTER

Panteón de los Héroes HISTORIC BUILDING

(Plaza de los Héroes; 6am-6:30pm Mon-Sat, to noon Sun) Center of life in Asunción is Plaza de los Héroes, where a military guard protects the remains of Mariscal Francisco Solano López and other key figures from Paraguay's catastrophic wars in the Panteón de los Héroes, the city's most instantly recognizable building.

Casa de la Independencia MUSEUM

(www.casadelaindependencia.org.py; 14 de Mayo; 7am-6:30pm Mon-Fri, 8am-noon Sat) The Casa de la Independencia dates from 1772. This is where Paraguay became the first country on the continent to declare its independence in 1811.

Palacio López PALACE

(Paraguayo Independiente) The grand Palacio López is the seat of government.

FREE **Manzana de la Rivera** MUSEUM

(Ayolas 129; 7am-9pm) Just across the street from Palacio López is the Manzana de la Rivera, a complex of nine colorful and restored houses. The oldest is **Casa Viola** (1750), where the **Museo Memoria de la Ciudad** houses a history of Asunción's urban development.

FREE **Museo Naval Humaitá** MUSEUM

(8-11am & 2-5pm Mon-Fri) Docked on the river behind the Palacio López, this naval museum is aboard a battle cruiser that saw action during the Chaco War (1932–5).

Cabildo MUSEUM

(www.cabildoccr.gov.py; Plaza de Armas; 9am-7pm Tue-Fri, 10am-5pm Sat-Sun) North of the Plaza de los Héroes, near the waterfront, is the pink *cabildo,* which was once the center of government. It is now the **Museo del Congreso Nacional** and also hosts regular cultural events and exhibitions.

Estación Ferrocarril MUSEUM

(Plaza Uruguaya; 7am-5pm Mon-Fri) The Asunción–Encarnación railway line was the first in South America. One of the first trains to run the route is on display at the old Estación Ferrocarril (railway station), along with other items from the period.

Museum aside, these days the station is used more for concerts and recitals than anything else, but it is also the place to buy tickets for the hilarious **tourist train** (☎44-2448; www.ferrocarriles.com.py; 100,000G).

SUBURBS

Museo del Barro MUSEUM

(Grabadores del Cabichui s/n; admission 15,000G; 3:30am-8pm Wed-Thu, 9am-noon & 3:30am-8pm Fri-Sat) Everyone's favorite, Museo del Barro displays everything from modern paintings to pre-Columbian and indigenous crafts to political caricatures of prominent Paraguayans. Take bus 30 from Oliva and get off at Shopping del Sol (p773). It's three blocks from there, off Callejón Cañada. Stay on the bus and you'll pass **Parque Ñu Guazú**, a pleasant place to pass an afternoon, with lakes and walking trails.

Jardín Botánico GARDENS

(admission 5000G for museums; 7am-7pm; museums 9am–6pm Tue–Fri, to 4pm Sat-Sun) From the center, Av Artigas runs approximately 6km to the Jardín Botánico. The former estate of the ruling López dynasty, it now houses the city **zoo**, a small **nature reserve** and a couple of odd museums: a small **natural history museum** in Carlos Antonio's humble colonial house and the **Museo Indigenista** in his son Francisco's former mansion. Take bus 24 or 35 from Cerro Corá.

Supermercado Ykua Bolaños MEMORIAL

(Av Artigas) En route to the Jardín Botánico, you'll pass the charred remains of the Supermercado Ykua Bolaños, which hit the world headlines in 2006. Almost 1000 people burnt to death inside when the owner elected to 'lock-down' after a small fire broke out in the kitchen. A moving **shrine** to the deceased is worth a look.

Cementerio de la Recoleta CEMETERY

The Cementerio de la Recoleta, 3km east of the center along Av Mariscal López, is a maze of incredible mausoleums as Asunción's wealthy try to do outdo each other in the grandeur of their resting places. Eliza Lynch, hated mistress of Mariscal López, is buried here.

Sleeping

Accommodation is more expensive in Asunción than in the rest of the country, but it's unlikely to bust your budget.

CITY CENTRE

Palmas del Sol HOTEL $$

(☎44-9485; Av España 202; s/d 170,000/231,000G; ❄@☎≋) Despite its location on a noisy central road, this place is a real oasis with a quiet courtyard and tastefully functional rooms. The breakfast (included) is a treat. Relaxing on a poolside sun lounger, you'll feel a million miles away from the traffic fumes outside.

El Viajero Hostel & Suites HOSTEL $$

(☎44-4563; www.elviajerohostels.com; Juan Alberdi 73; dm 70,000G, d 200,000G incl breakfast; ❄@☎≋) Backpacker hostels have finally arrived in Paraguay! This is part of a successful chain of South American hostels with air-conditioned dorms, a spacious garden and a refreshing splash pool in an old colonial mansion.

Gran Hotel del Paraguay HOTEL $$$

(☎20-0051; www.granhoteldelparaguay.com.py; cnr De la Residenta & Padre Pucheu; s/d 350,000/430,000G; ❄@☎≋) Dripping with the kind of colonial-era luxury that you'll probably either love or hate, this historic hotel is said to be the place where Paraguay's national anthem was heard for the first time in July 1860.

Hotel Preciado HOTEL $$

(☎44-7661; Azara 840; s/d 160,000/190,000G; ❄☎≋) This modern number is a decent bet, located a couple of blocks from the center's best nightlife, but you should choose your rooms carefully as some are better than others.

Hotel Miami HOTEL $

(☎44-4950; México 449; s/d 90,000/120,000G; ❄) A very bland hospital-type hallway, but it's clean, central and is an acceptable budget option.

> **POMBERO**
>
> Guaraní folklore includes many colorful mythological figures, but none is so widely believed to be true as Pombero. A mischievous little imp, said to be short, muscular and hairy, he emerges at night when he should only be referred to as Karai Pyhare (Lord of the Night). His presence is commonly used to explain pretty much anything from strange sounds and missing items to unfortunate minor accidents. Pombero's penchant for young women – accompanied or otherwise – can only be overcome by diverting his attentions with a glass of *caña* (rum) or cigarettes, which are left as a gift. Apparently you should place them on the roadside and high-tail out of there!

SUBURBS

TOP CHOICE **Portal del Sol** HOTEL $$

(☎60-9395; www.portaldelsol.com; Roa 1455; s/d 210,000/265,000G; ❄@☎≋) Beautiful rooms, mammoth breakfast, a pleasant splash pool, good restaurant and airport pick-up. Out by the Shopping del Sol in a plush residential area, this is one of the most popular hotels with tour groups, so book ahead.

La Misión Hotel BOUTIQUE HOTEL $$$

(☎62-1800; www.lamision.com.py; Eulogio Estigarribia 4990, Villa Morra; r 835,000G; ❄@☎≋) A charismatic Jesuit-style boutique hotel close to the Shopping Mariscal López. Individually decorated rooms range from minimalist to classy and cozy, and extend to the oddly floral octagon rooms.

Posada del Cielo HOTEL $$

(☎66-4882; www.hotelposadasdelcielo.com.py; Del Maestro 1446, Villa Morra; s/d 220,000/275,000G; ❄@☎≋) Colorful Posada del Cielo makes you feel like you are staying in somebody's house, while packing in a number of individually decorated rooms into the illusion. Some rooms are a little pokey though, so ask to see a selection.

Eating

Asunción's eating options reflect its cultural diversity: sophisticated local, Asian and international foods abound and vegetarians

Asunción

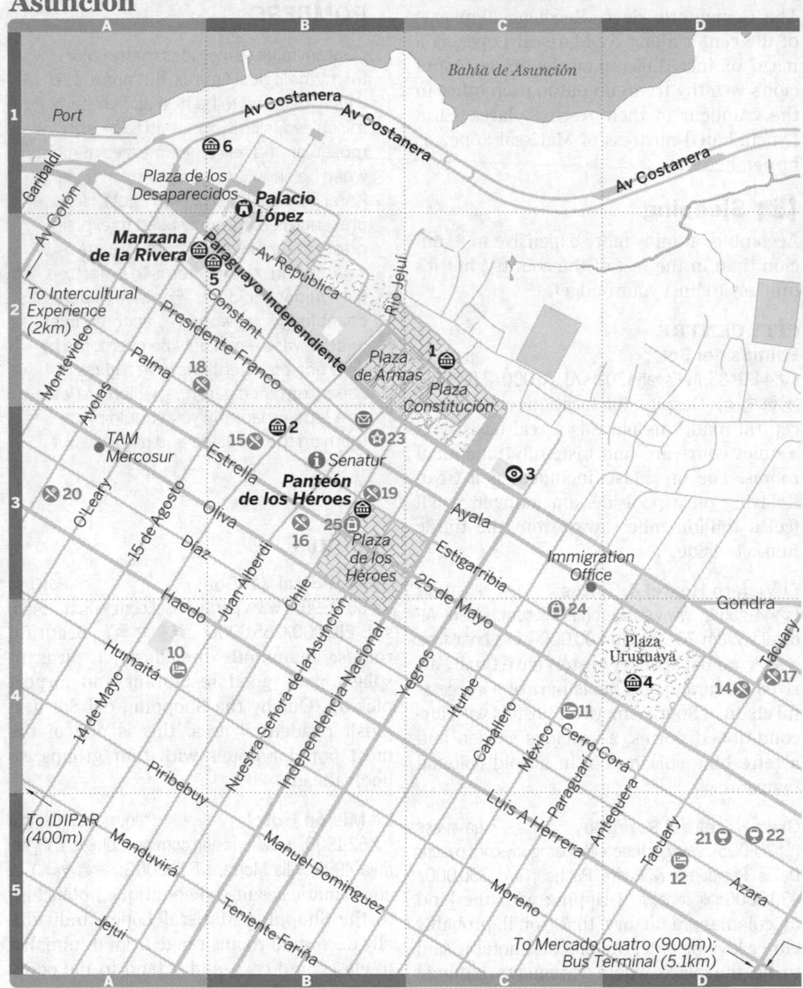

are also catered for. Non-vegetarians, however, will find the ubiquitous all-you-can-eat grill restaurants hard to resist. Although there are some good pit-stops in the center, Asunción's most refined restaurants are located in the eastern suburbs, especially Villa Morra.

CITY CENTER

For typical Paraguayan food, try out the million and one options south of the center along Av Figueroa, known locally as La Quinta Avenida, or sample the *asadito* (mini-meat kebabs with mandioca) stands (2000G) on street corners.

Bellini ITALIAN **$$**
(cnr Palma & 15 de Agosto; 24,000G) Join the queue to pick your ingredients and watch while the chefs simmer up a delicious plate of fresh pasta before your eyes. Hugely popular and deservedly so.

Taberna Española SPANISH **$$$**
(☎44-1743; Ayolas 631; mains 33,000-195,000G) A slice of Spain in Paraguay. The energetic ambience of this 'food museum', with dangling bottles, cooking implements and bells,

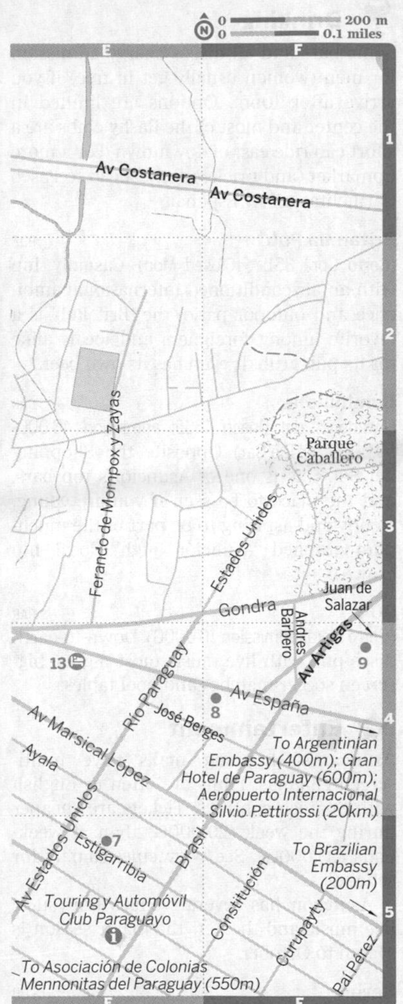

Asunción

Top Sights

Manzana de la Rivera	A2
Palacio López	B1
Panteón de los Héroes	B3

Sights

1 Cabildo	C2
2 Casa de la Independencia	B3
3 Catedral Metropolitana	C3
4 Estación Ferrocarril	D4
5 Museo Memoria de la Ciudad	B2
6 Museo Naval Humaitá	B1

Activities, Courses & Tours

7 Alianza Francesa	E5
8 Centro Cultural Paraguayo-Americano	F4
9 Instituto Cultural Paraguayo Alemán	F4

Sleeping

10 El Viajero Hostel & Suites	A4
11 Hotel Miami	C4
12 Hotel Preciado	D5
13 Palmas del Sol	E4

Eating

14 Bar San Roque	D4
15 Bellini	B3
16 Confitería Bolsi	B3
17 La Flor de la Canela	D4
18 La Vida Verde	A2
19 Lido Bar	B3
20 Taberna Española	A3

Drinking

21 904	D5
22 Britannia Pub	D5

Entertainment

23 Teatro Municipal	B3

Shopping

24 Folklore	C4
25 Open-Air Market	B3

is only the backdrop for good-value tapas and paella.

Bar San Roque INTERNATIONAL **$$**

(cnr Tacuary & Eligio Ayala; mains 15,000-45,000G)
This place is an Asunción landmark, offering a warm turn-of-the-20th-century atmosphere. The counter displays fresh goods which come directly from the family farm, and the wine list is just as impressive as the menu consisting of fish and meat dishes. As many locals will attest, it's a culinary 'must', and there is service to match.

La Flor de la Canela PERUVIAN **$$$**

(☎49-8928; Tacuary 167; mains 30,000-80,000G)
The Peruvian food is more genuine than this smart place's faux Inca statues. The menu is dominated by fish and *mariscos* (seafood), and the *ceviche* (marinated raw seafood) is fantastic.

Confitería Bolsi INTERNATIONAL **$$**
(www.bolsi.com.py; Estrella 399; mains 15,000-50,000G) More than a *confitería* (cafe/snack bar), this traditional place (its been going since 1960) serves everything from sandwiches to curried rabbit and garlic pizza. Try the *surubí casa nostra* (a superb selection of different pasta types and flavors on one dish).

Lido Bar DELI **$**
(cnr Chile & Palma; mains 7000-25,000G) Asunción's historic diner is famous for its sidewalk tables opposite the Panteón de los Héroes, making it the city's most popular meeting place. Though it serves a variety of Paraguayan specialties in generous portions, the location is better than the food.

La Vida Verde VEGETARIAN **$$**
(Palma & 15 de Agosto; per kg 35,000G;) Assess your mood by one of the 32 quirkily sculptured emotional 'faces' on the wall – 'satisfied' is how you'll feel after this eating experience. A delicious daily buffet of Chinese vegetarian delights (although they bend the rules a bit!).

SUBURBS

On Sundays it's best to head to one of the large shopping centers such as Mariscal López (p773) or Shopping del Sol (p773), which both have large food courts.

TOP CHOICE **Paulista Grill** RODIZZIO **$$$**
(cnr San Martín & Mariscal López, Villa Morra; buffet 65,000G) One of the city's most famous all-you-can-eat restaurants. There are more than 15 different cuts of juicy meat, salad, pasta and sushi bars to peruse, as well as exotic desserts. Attentive table service.

Hacienda Las Palomas MEXICAN **$$$**
(Guido Spano 1481, Villa Morra; mains 55,000-80,000G) Las Palomas manages to capture the vibrant colors of Mexico in the decor as much as it captures the vibrant flavors of Mexican food on the plate. With friendly waitstaff and generous portions, it is a refined yet relaxed dining experience.

Ciervo Blanco RODIZZIO **$$$**
(cnr Flores & Radio Operadores del Chaco, Barrio Pinozá; meals 45,000-65,000G) If you're looking for a traditional Paraguayan experience, this place just southeast of the center has it. Juicy *asado*, traditional music and bottle dancers will keep you entertained.

Drinking

Some bars and all discos charge admission for men (women usually get in free) if you arrive after 10pm. Options are limited in the center and most of the flashy clubs are a short cab ride east of downtown. For a more upmarket (and pricier) scene, head to Paseo Carmelitas off Av España.

Britannia Pub PUB
(Cerro Corá 851; Closed Mon) Casually hip with an air-conditioned international ambience and outdoor patio, the 'Brit Pub' is a favorite among foreigners and locals alike for its pub grub. It even has its own beer.

Bambuddha BAR
(Aviadores del Chaco 1655; admission 40,000-50,000G; Tue-Sat) Opposite the Shopping del Sol, this is one of Asunción's top bars, and the place to be seen if you are young, trendy and aspiring to be part of the much-photographed 'Asunción high' (local hip crowd).

904 BAR
(Cerro Corá; admission 10,000G) Down-to-earth disco-pub with live music most nights, big-screen soccer matches and pool tables.

Entertainment

Asunción's shopping malls have multi-screen cinemas. Films are often in English with Spanish subtitles. Tickets are cheaper during the week (20,000G) than at weekends (25,000G). See www.cines.com.py for schedules.

Asunción has several venues that stage live music and theater; the major season is March to October.

Seven CLUB
(cnr República Argentina 222 & Marsical López; admission 20,000G) The disco-bar of the moment, where the young and the restless wild-out to techno and house tunes until the sun comes up.

Coyote CLUB
(Sucre 1655; admission 40,000-80,000G) Starts late, ends late – this bouncing disco is for young, wealthy, beautiful people who like to dance till they drop.

Teatro Municipal PERFORMING ARTS
(cnr Alberdi & Presidente Franco) Check the listing outside for show times at the Teatro Municipal.

Shopping

Asunción offers Paraguay's best souvenir shopping. The typical Paraguayan souvenir is a *matero, bombilla* and *termos* (cup, straw and flask) for *tereré* consumption, and these are ubiquitous – though quality varies. The ground floor of the Senatur office (p773) has examples of local *artesanías* (craft work) from around the country, ranging from intricate Luque silver to fine *ñandutí* (lace).

Folklore ARTS & CRAFTS
(cnr Caballero & Estigarribia) A good bet for quality Paraguayan handicrafts, though not cheap.

Open-Air Market MARKET
(Plaza de los Héroes) Stocked with *ao po'i* or *lienzo* (loose-weave cotton) garments and other indigenous crafts, it expands considerably on weekends.

Mercado Cuatro MARKET
Mercado Cuatro is a lively trading lot occupying the wedge formed by the intersection of Avs Francia and Pettirossi, and stretching over several blocks.

Shopping del Sol MALL
(cnr Aviadores del Chaco & González) This is Asunción's biggest and glittziest mall.

Shopping Mariscal López MALL
(cnr Quesada & Charles de Gaulle) Shopping Mariscal López is a trendy mall, and also a city landmark.

Information

Dangers & Annoyances

Asunción is a comparatively safe city but, as with anywhere else, keep your eye on your belongings, particularly at the bus station. Plaza Uruguaya and the streets around Palma are frequented by prostitutes after dark – don't be surprised if you are solicited. On Sunday the city center is a ghost town.

Emergency

Fire department (☎71-1132)
Medical emergency (☎20-4800)
Police (☎911)

Internet Access

Numerous *locutorios* (small telephone offices) generally also offer decent internet access for around 4000G per hour.

Medical Services

Hospital Bautista (☎60-0171; Av República Argentina) Recommended private hospital.

Money

All the major banks have ATMs, though most have a daily withdrawal limit of 1,500,000G, and some charge a usage fee of 25,000G. Along Palma and its side streets it is hardly possible to walk a block without money changers shouting *'cambio'* at you, but rates are better in the numerous *casas de cambio* (foreign currency exchange houses) and banks that line this road. There are ATMs and money changers at the bus station and airport.

Post & Telephone

Locutorios are widespread.

Directory Inquiries (☎112)
Main Post Office (cnr Alberdi & Paraguayo Independiente; ⏲7am-7pm Mon-Fri) Send your mail *certificado* (registered) if you want it to have a hope of arriving.

Tourist Information

For online city information, see www.quickguide.com.py. It also periodically publishes an excellent magazine packed with maps and current events.

Senatur (☎49-4110; www.senatur.gov.py; Palma 468; ⏲7am-7pm)

Getting There & Away

Air

Aeropuerto Internacional Silvio Pettirossi (☎64-5600) is in the suburb of Luque, 20km east of Asunción. For flight information, see p796.

Bus

Asunción's **bus terminal** (☎55-1740; www.mca.gov.py/toa.htm; Av República Argentina) is several kilometers southeast of downtown – its website provides full details of schedules and costs. City buses 8 and 31 run along Oliva to the terminal, while buses 14, 18.2 and 38 run along Haedo.

GETTING TO ARGENTINA

The San Ignacio de Ayolas bridge links Puerto Falcón with Clorinda in Argentina and customs offices are found at either end. International buses take this route, and a local bus marked Falcón leaves hourly from Mercado Cuatro (p773) and passes the stop at Av República Argentina outside the Asunción bus terminal (p773). The ferry crossing to Clorinda is not recommended for tourists.

BUS FARES FROM ASUNCIÓN

DESTINATION	COST (G)	DURATION (HR)
Buenos Aires (Argentina)	180,000-290,000	18-21
Ciudad del Este	40,000-75,000	4½-6
Concepción	60,000	4½-6
Encarnación	50,000-80,000	5-6
Filadelfia	70,000	8
Pedro Juan Caballero	60,000-100,000	6-7½
Rio de Janeiro (Brazil)	450,000	30
Santa Cruz (Bolivia)	250,000	20-24
São Paulo (Brazil)	250,000	18-20

Purchase long-distance tickets at the company offices on the 2nd floor of the bus terminal. Don't be put off by the touts shouting destinations at you – take your time to choose the company you want.

Getting Around

TO/FROM THE AIRPORT Buses displaying '*Aeropuerto*' signs head out along Av Aviadores del Chaco between the airport and the center. Airport taxis are expensive (100,000G), but if you flag one down on the road outside it's half the price.

BUS Noisy, bone-rattling kamikaze-like city buses (3000G) go almost everywhere, but few run after 10pm. Nearly all city buses start their route at the western end of Oliva and post their destinations in the front window.

TAXI Taxis are metered and reasonable but tack on a surcharge late at night and on Sunday. A taxi from the center to the bus terminal costs about 40,000G.

TRAIN A tourist train (p768), akin to a mobile theater, departs the Jardín Botánico on Sundays at 10am for Areguá, returning at 5pm. Buy tickets from Estación Ferrocarril (p768).

AROUND ASUNCIÓN

Prepare yourself for a taste of rural and historical Paraguay. Humble communities dominated by colonial buildings observe long siestas, disturbed only by occasional ox- or horse-drawn carts clacking up cobbled streets. The tourist industry plugs the area as the Circuito Central, and all towns are accessible on frequent local buses that leave from the *subsuelo* (lower floor) of the Asunción bus terminal (platforms 30 and 35; 5000G to 7000G).

Itauguá & Areguá

These two small towns are known for their artesanal cottage industries. Itauguá's women are famous for their unique weaving of multicolored spiderweb *ñandutí* (lace – *nandu* means spider in Guaraní). These exquisite pieces range in size from doilies to bedspreads. Smaller ones cost only a few dollars but larger ones are upward of 250,000G. In July the town celebrates its annual **Festival de Ñandutí**.

Areguá is renowned for its ceramics, displayed en masse along the main street. The historic cobbled lanes are lined with exquisite colonial homes, and the village atmosphere is completed with a church perched on the hill and an enviable position overlooking **Lago Yparacaí**.

Buses to Itauguá and Areguá depart from Av República Argentina just outside the Asunción bus terminal. **La Itaugueña** buses leave approximately hourly for Itauguá and for Areguá **La Aregueña** runs every half hour. A ferry from San Bernadino operates to Areguá in the high season, but by far the most atmospheric way to get there is on the Sunday tourist train (p768) from Asunción.

San Bernardino

☎0512

Renowned as the elite escape for the privileged of Asunción, tranquil 'San Ber' is a trendy place to relax or party – pubs, discos, upmarket hotels and restaurants line the shady cobbled streets of Lago Ypacaraí's eastern shore. Despite its reputation, there's plenty for budget travelers as well. In high season a pleasure boat takes passengers for short cruises on the lake (15,000G). Don't swim in the lake though – it's filthy.

Sleeping

Hotel del Lago HOTEL **$$**
(☎23-2201; Teniente Weiler 411; s/d 240,000/260,000G; ❄@🛜🏊) On the lakeside of the plaza, this hotel is worn and romantically Victorian, full of antique furniture. Each room is different.

Hostal Brisas del Mediterraneo HOSTEL **$$**
(☎23-2459; Ruta Kennedy; camping 45,000G, dm 90,000G, d 250,000G incl breakfast; ❄🏊) Travelers rave about this place perched on the edge of the lake, offering excellent facilities with prices that include breakfast. Follow the cobbled Ruta Kennedy for 2km around the lake from outside the Copaco office.

Getting There & Away

From Asunción **Cordillera de los Altos** buses run hourly from platform 35 (1½ hours).

Caacupé

☎0511

Paraguay's answer to the Vatican City, the enormous **Basilica de Caacupé** looks quite out of place in this otherwise quiet provincial town. Caacupé really comes alive on El Día de la Virgen (8 December) when crowds of worshippers undertake pilgrimages from all corners of the country to worship and ask the Virgin for favors. As many as 300,000 of the faithful may crowd onto the plaza during the festival and participate in a spectacular candlelit procession.

If you want to stay the night, **Hotel Katy Maria** (☎24-2860; Pino; s/d 150,000/200,000G; ❄@🛜) is a decent choice in sight of the basilica, but needless to say you should book well in advance during the festival when prices rise exponentially.

Caacupé is 54km east of Asunción and Empresa Villa Serrana departs every 10 minutes from platform 35.

Yaguarón

Yaguarón, 48km southeast of Asunción, has an 18th-century Franciscan church that is a landmark of colonial architecture. The nearby **Museo del Doctor Francia** (⏲7:30am-noon & 2-6pm Mon-Fri) was the first dictator's house and is interesting for its period portraiture and statues. San Buenaventura has hourly departures to Yaguarón from platform 30.

Piribebuy

Piribebuy, located 75km from Asunción, is a small rural town that was briefly nominated the capital of the nation during the War of the Triple Alliance (1865–70). With Asunción captured, it became the site of a famous siege in 1869, when an army of children led by the local schoolteacher bravely held off the invading Brazilian forces. The remarkable events are recounted in the small **museum** (⏲7:30am-noon & 2-6pm Mon-Fri). Empresa Piribebuy runs every 45 minutes from platform 35 in Asunción; the trip takes two hours.

SOUTHERN PARAGUAY

Paraguay's southernmost region, east of the Río Paraguay, is home to some of the country's most important historical sites. The Jesuit ruins, national parks and the *locura* (madness) of Carnaval make it an eclectic and fascinating area to visit.

On the way from Asunción to Encarnación you'll pass through the town of **Coronel Bogado**. Known as the 'Capital de Chipa' – *chipa* is a bread made of manioc flour, eggs and cheese – Coronel Bogado is the best place to sample this national obsession. There's no need to get off the bus – the vendors will come to you and it's as cheap as *chipa* (2000G).

WORTH A TRIP

PILAR

Squirreled away in the far southwest corner of Paraguay, in the tongue-twister department of Ñeembucú (Nyeembookoo), the dusty streets of Pilar give a charming insight into traditional Paraguay. Though the town is the textile capital of Paraguay and its threads are much sought-after nationwide, visitors may be more interested in the statues of native animals located around the town (pick up a guidebook and do the statue tour) and the small butterfly house at the university.

Southern & Eastern Paraguay

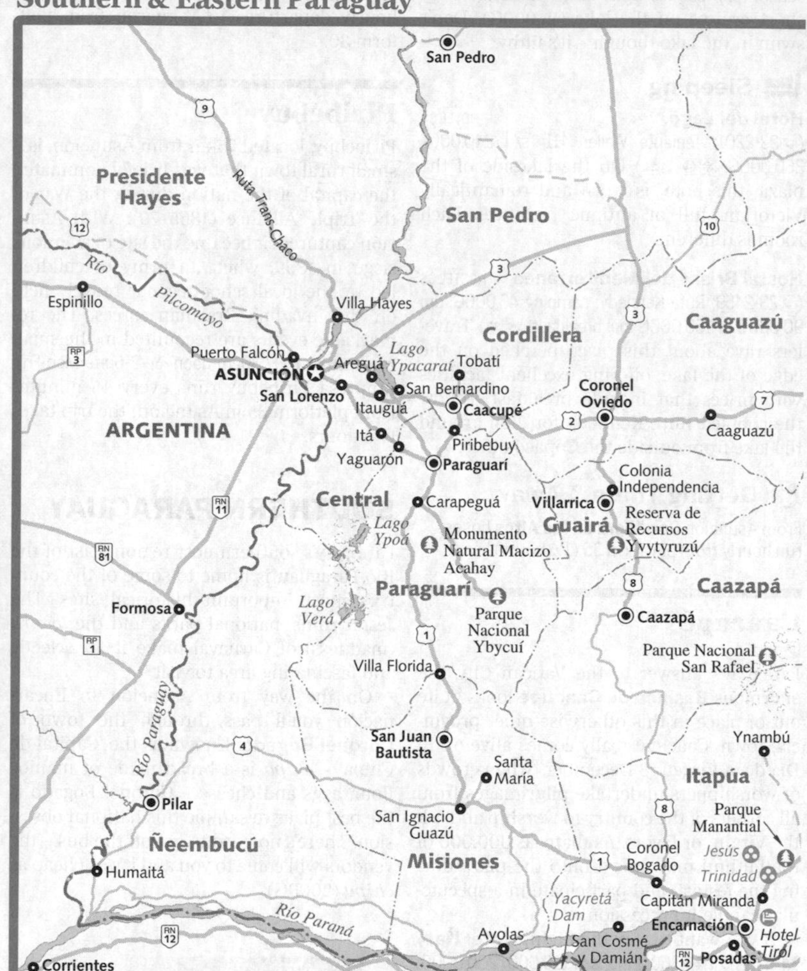

Encarnación

071 / POP 120,000

Encarnación, 'La Perla del Sur', is Paraguay's most attractive city. It's also known as the 'Capital de Carnaval' and, following the completion of the new *costanera* (riverside promenade) with its fabulous river beach, is referred to rather ambitiously by some locals as the new Rio de Janeiro.

It is rather less proud to be the birthplace of dictator Alfredo Stroessner. His **former house** (Memmel & Carlos Antonio Lopez) is now a private university just behind the bus terminal.

The town is the best base for visiting the Jesuit *reducciónes* (settlements) of Trinidad and Jesús.

Sights & Activities

The city center is a pleasant enough place for a stroll, but there isn't much in the way of sights, so you might as well head for the river.

Costanera & Beach BEACH

(Av Costanera) Slap on your flip-flops and jostle for a place on Encarnación's new river beach, located on the flash new coastal promenade, a hive of activity during the summer months.

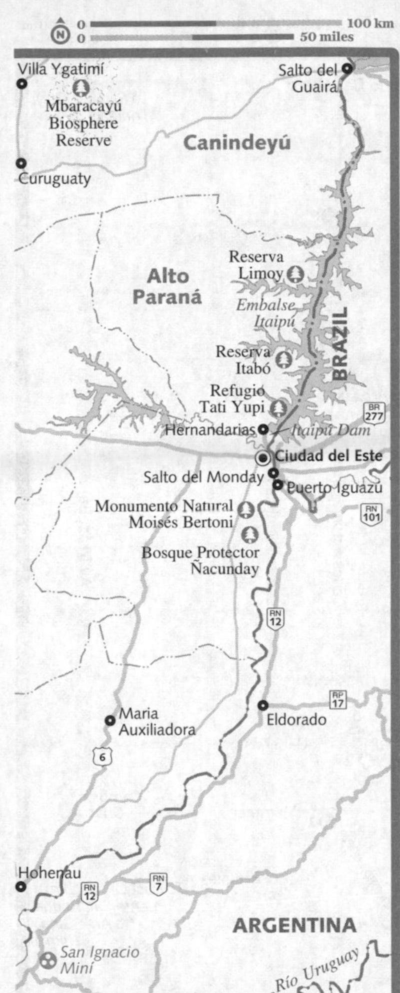

Karumbés TOUR

(Cabañas; per person 10,000G) Look out for *karumbés,* yellow horse-drawn carriages that once served as taxis. Rides are free on weekends. Pick one up at the bus terminal.

Sleeping

There are lots of clean, reasonably priced places to choose from in Encarnación. Most of the cheaper places also have rooms with air-conditioning for about twice the price. You won't regret splashing out. Book ahead for Carnaval when prices rise considerably.

TOP CHOICE **Hotel de la Costa** HOTEL **$$$**

(☎20-0590; cnr Av Gaspar R de Francia & Cerro Corá; s/d 178,000/312,000G, ste 534,000G; ❄@📶🏊) Arguably the city's best hotel, with excellent service, a welcoming pool in the attractive garden and a plum location near the beach with river views of Argentina. The suite, with Jacuzzi and champagne breakfast, is good value.

Casa de la Y Bed & Breakfast B&B **$**

(☎20-3981; casadelay@gmail.com; Carmen de Lara Castro 422; per person 70,000G; ❄@) A tiny homestay *hostal* with a warm welcome from hostess Doña Yolanda and a menu of *comida tipica*. There are two spacious five-bed dorms with gigantic private bathrooms, so it is perfect for small groups. The wonderfully floral garden is a cute place to sip *terere* in the sunshine. Reservation required by email only.

Hotel Domingo Savio HOTEL **$**

(☎20-5800; 29 de Septiembre; s/d 150,000/240,000G incl breakfast; ❄@🏊) A decent midrange choice with nice, if unspectacular, rooms, and an outdoor pool.

Hotel Germano HOTEL **$**

(☎20-3346; Cabañas; s/d 80,000/120,000G, without bathroom 50,000/70,000G) Across from the bus terminal, Hotel Germano couldn't be better located for late arrivals. Its the best-value budget spot in the center, with spotless rooms and helpful staff.

Eating

Encarnación has some of the best eats in Paraguay outside of Asunción, as well as an astounding number of junk-food joints. You can stock up with goodies at **Super 6** (Av Irrazábal), a supermarket that also has a great-value pay-by-weight restaurant, and you shouldn't leave without trying a *lomito Arabe* – a Paraguayan-style kebab invented by the ex-pat Arab community.

TOP CHOICE **Benndo** MEXICAN, PIZZERIA **$$**

(cnr 25 de Mayo & Tte González; pizza 40,000-60,000G) When a restaurant makes the claim that you eat free if you don't like the food, you can be pretty sure it's going to be good. Benndo offers a mixed menu of Mexican dishes, crazily good pizzas and gigantic sandwiches, all served in a friendly, no-fuss ambience that will have you counting the hours before you can come back.

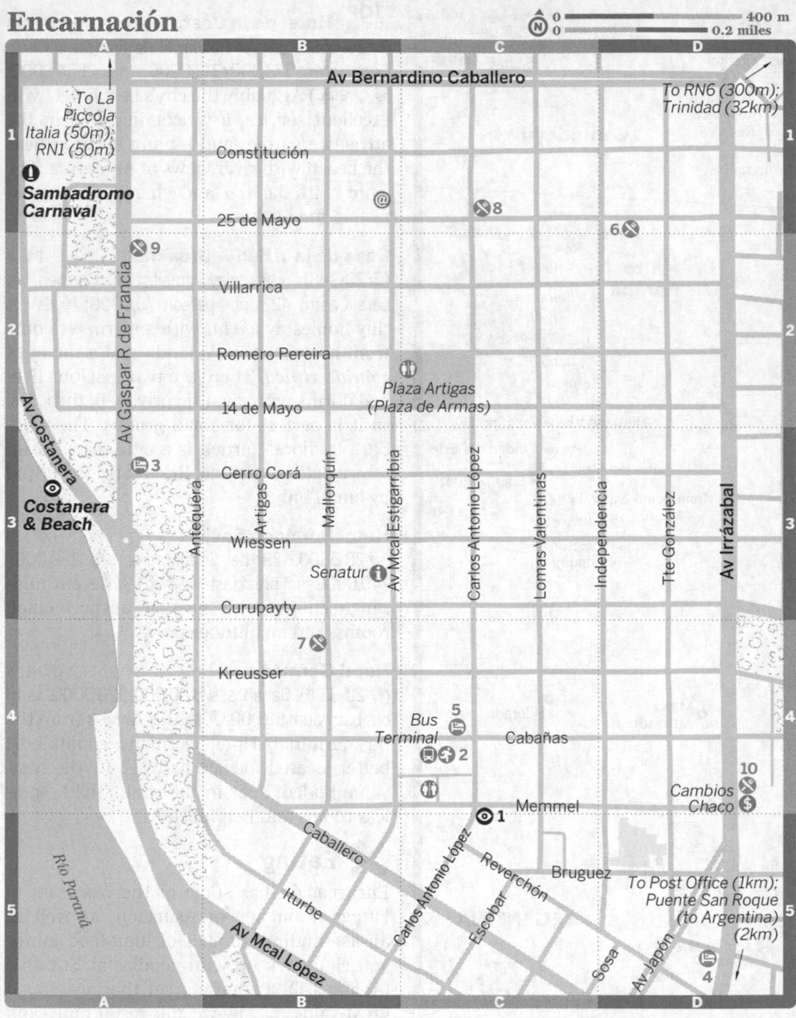

Encarnación

Top Sights
Costanera & Beach A3
Sambadromo Carnaval A1

Sights
1 Former House of Stroessner C5

Activities, Courses & Tours
2 Karumbés C4

Sleeping
3 Hotel de la Costa A3
4 Hotel Domingo Savio D5
5 Hotel Germano C4

Eating
6 Benndo D1
7 Habib´s B4
8 Hiroshima C1
9 Milord A2
10 Super 6 .... D4

CARNAVAL!

Carnaval Paraguayan-style might not be on the same scale or as famous as Rio's, but if you are young and looking for a wild party, then you may find it more fun. More bare flesh, louder music and obligatory crowd involvement all make for a mad night out. Don't forget your *lanzanieves* (spray snow) and a pair of sunglasses (you don't want that stuff in your eyes), pick your place in the rickety stands and get ready to party hard with the locals – it's surprisingly infectious.

Carnaval now spans every weekend in late January and February, from Saturday to Sunday night. The **Sambadromo Carnaval** (parade ground; Av Costanera) is along Av Costanera, behind Av Francia, which is Encarnación's main strip for nightlife. Tickets (from 50,000G) can be bought in advance around the city or from touts on the night at a slightly higher price. Gates open around 9pm, but the action starts around 10pm. It's all over by 2am, when everybody piles into the local discos.

TOP CHOICE **Hiroshima** JAPANESE $$
(cnr 25 de Mayo & Lomas Valentinas; mains 20,000-80,000G) This place has top-notch Japanese food and is a deserved local favorite with unbelievable udon, super sushi and tempting tofu dishes. Food fit for a Japanese Crown Prince.

Brasilianl Grill & Pasta RODIZZIO $$
(☎071 20-2181; www.brasiliani.com.py; Ruta Internacional at customs point; buffet 40,000G) The best of a series of Brazilian-style all-you-can-eat places, offering a unique twist on the traditional meat feast by also bringing gourmet pizza and pasta to your table. It's new in town, but already has the locals drooling.

Milord EUROPEAN $$
(www.milord.com.py; cnr Av Gaspar R de Francia & 25 de Mayo; mains 30,000-60,000G) With a chef who studied in Paris, formal waiters and a more refined atmosphere than other city restaurants, Milord is widely regarded as the place to be seen by fine diners. The menu is varied and inventive and, despite the slight ly more elevated price tag, you won't feel that you've overspent.

La Piccola Italia ITALIAN $$
(cnr Ruta 1 & Av Gaspar R de Francia; mains 12,000-40,000G) Great value pizza and pasta in huge portions served in distinctly Mediterranean surroundings. This is probably your best bet if you want to eat well on a tight budget.

Heladería Mako ICE CREAM $
(cnr Av Bernardino Caballero & Lomas Valentinas; ice cream per kg 40,000G) Delicious pastry delights, artesanal ice cream, great coffee and magazines make this well worth the trek.

Habib´s FAST FOOD $
(cnr Mallorquín & Curupayty; lomito Arabe 12,000G) Habib's is the best bet for local specialty *lomito Arabe*.

ℹ Information

Internet Access

Ciberkfe (cnr Mcal Estigarribia & Constitución; per hr 4,000G)

Money

Most banks are on or near the plaza and all have ATMs. Money changers congregate around the bus station and at the border, but check rates before handing over any money. A more reliable option for exchanging money is **Cambios Chaco** (Av Irrazábal), next to Super 6 supermarket.

Telephone

Telephone cabins are scattered around town, especially in the area around the bus terminal.

Tourist Information

Senatur (☎20-5021; Mcal Estigarribia & Curupayty; ⏲8am-6pm Mon-Fri, to noon Sat-Sun)

ℹ Getting There & Away

The **bus terminal** (☎20-2412; Cabañas) is a few blocks north of the *costanera*. Frequent buses run from Encarnación to Asunción (50,000 to 80,000G, 5½ hours) with **La Encarnacena** and **Nuestra Señora de la Asunción** providing the best service. The latter also runs an executive minibus service for the same cost. Buses run east almost hourly to Ciudad del Este (60,000 to 70,000G, six hours), though they stop frequently and the route is painfully slow.

GETTING TO ARGENTINA

International buses (5000G) cross to Posadas in Argentina via the Puente San Roque leaving from outside Encarnación's bus terminal (p779). You must get off the bus at the immigration offices at both ends of the international bridge for exit and entry stamps. Buses don't always wait – take your luggage and keep your ticket to catch the next one. If you are in a group, a taxi to the Paraguayan customs post is around 30,000G, but the price rises to take it across the bridge.

Picturesque ferries (5000G) also cross the Río Paraná from the eastern end of the *costanera* in Encarnación to/from the *costanera* of Posadas.

The Jesuit Missions

Set atop a lush green hill 28km northeast of Encarnación, **Trinidad** is Paraguay's best-preserved Jesuit *reducción*. You can hire a Spanish-speaking guide near the gate (5000G) or hang around until dark for the atmospheric light show, which projects a history of the site onto the walls of the ruins.

Jesús, 12km north, is a nearly complete reconstruction of the Jesuit mission that was interrupted by the Jesuits' expulsion in 1767.

More difficult to access but worth the effort is **San Cosme y Damián**, 27km south of the main road to Asunción at Km 308 (about 57km west of Encarnacion), which was the location of the astronomical observatory.

Getting There & Away

From Encarnación, frequent buses go to Trinidad (5000G) between 6am and 7pm, but any bus headed east along Ruta 6 to Ciudad del Este or Hohenau will drop you off nearby – get off when you see the power station on your right.

Getting to Jesús from Encarnación without your own transport is difficult, but there are sometimes taxis hanging around (8000G per person). Alternatively, walk 100m along the *ruta* to the crossroads – you'll see the sign to Jesús – and wait for the Jesús–Obligado bus, which supposedly passes hourly (3000G).

La Sancosmeña buses run to San Cosme from Encarnación at 9:15am and 2:30pm.

FAUNA Paraguay (p797) run day tours from Encarnación that include brief visits to all three ruins. The entry ticket to any one *reducción* (25,000G) includes entry to all the others.

Around Encarnación

PARQUE MANANTIAL

On Ruta 6, 35km outside of Encarnación near the town of Hohenau, lies **Parque Manantial** (☎0755-23-2250; entry 10,000G, camping 20,000G, pool per day 15,000G; P ❄ ≈), a forested oasis for travelers who like to get away from it all. There is a pleasant new hotel here (s/d 160,000/250,000G), but for much of the year you'll likely have the 200 hectares with swimming pools and walking trails to yourself. Horse riding (35,000G per hour) is available, as well as a zipline, and if you prefer things *au naturelle,* a river for paddling.

HOTEL TIROL

A favorite with the King of Spain, the timeless red-stone **Hotel Tirol** (☎071-20-2388; www.hoteltirol.com.py; s/d 200,000/250,000G) is set in 20 hectares of humid forest and makes for a great day-trip from Encarnación. Almost 200 species of bird have been recorded here and four inviting swimming pools (10,000G for nonguests) are a great way to cool off after walking the *senderos* (trails). Should you wish to stay, you should book ahead in the high season (October to December), though it's often empty at other times of year.

To get here, take local bus 1y2 (marked Capitán Miranda) from along Av Artigas in Encarnación. The end of the line is the entrance to the hotel. Any bus headed for Trinidad or Ciudad del Este also passes in front.

Parque Nacional San Rafael

Southern Paraguay's last great tract of Atlantic Forest, gorgeous San Rafael is a lush wilderness and a bird-watcher's paradise with more than 420 species recorded. Comfortable accommodation in wooden cabins is available on the southern tip of the reserve at **Procosara** (☎0768-29-5046; r per person with meals 125,000G, without meals 50,000G; 📶) and the surroundings are beautiful with 7km of forest trails and a tantalising lake to cool off in.

To get deeper into the park, you'll need your own 4WD or a guide. The grasslands at **Guyra Reta** (☎021-22-9097; www.guyra.org.py; r per person 90,000G, incl meals 145,000G) lodge are the only other place to stay, but you must contact Guyra Paraguay (p795) in Asunción well in advance to arrange your visit, especially if you want to be fed.

Ricketty **Pastoreo** buses run from Encarnación to Ynambú, 12km outside the reserve, every morning at 8am and 11:30am (20,000G, three hours), but if you are not part of a tour you will have to arrange a pick up from there in advance. FAUNA Paraguay (p797) runs recommended all-inclusive three- to four-day bird-watching trips to the park from Encarnación, which include visits to both Procosara and Guyra Reta.

EASTERN PARAGUAY

Corresponding to the region known as Alto Paraná, this area was once the domain of ancient impenetrable forests teeming with wildlife. The building of the second-largest dam in the world changed all that, flooding huge areas of pristine forest and swallowing up a set of waterfalls comparable to those at Iguazú. The dam brought development to this primeval region, leading to the founding of a city once named after a hated dictator and an influx of farmers bent on turning what was left of the ancient forests into soy fields.

Ciudad del Este

061 / POP 356,000

Originally named Puerto Presidente Stroessner after the former dictator, the 'City of the East' is a renowned center for contraband goods, earning it the nickname 'the Supermarket of South America'. The part near the busy Brazilian border is chaotic, but you'll find the rest of the city is surprisingly pleasant, with some interesting attractions nearby. Of course, if you're here to shop, then you will be in your element.

Sleeping

Most accommodation in Ciudad del Este is aimed at business travelers using expense accounts. Midrange places, however, are definitely worth the extra couple of bucks, especially once you sample the megavalue breakfast buffets, which are included in the price.

Hotel Austria HOTEL **$$**
(50-0883; www.hotelrestauranteaustria.com; Fernández 165; s/d 180,000/200,000G;) Superclean European number with spacious rooms, big baths and even bigger breakfasts. Great restaurant, too, with German/Austrian specialties.

Hotel Munich HOTEL **$$**
(50-0347; Fernández 71; s/d 160,000/200,000G;) Solid midrange bet a stone's throw from the border, with comfortable and spacious rooms including cable TV.

Hotel Tía Nancy HOTEL **$**
(50-2974; cnr Garcete & Cruz del Chaco; r 80,000G, with air-con 100,000G;) Near the bus terminal, this friendly place has dark rooms but is perfectly adequate for a tranquil transit stop. It's better value if you are a couple, as the prices are per room.

Eating

The cheapest options are the stalls along Capitán Miranda and Av Monseñor Rodriguez, while Av del Lago is lined with Brazilian-style *rodizzio* restaurants where slabs of meat are brought to your table and you eat until you (almost) explode.

Faraone INTERNATIONAL **$$**
(Av Rogelio Benítez; mains 30,000-55,000G) Top-notch à la carte meals at affordable rates. Finish off with some of the tempting cakes at the delicious *confitería* next door.

Patussi Grill RODIZZIO **$$$**
(Pampliega; buffet 85,000G) You'll feel the Brazilian influence here with this all-you-can-eat meat-fest. Don't forget to make full use of the salad bar!

WORTH A TRIP

VILLARRICA

Colonial Villarrica is a tranquil old-fashioned town in the heart of eastern Paraguay that is rarely visited by travelers. With its colorful period architecture and slow-pace of life, the lively Carnaval that takes place here in February comes as something of a surprise. Though there isn't much to do in town except chill and stroll the avenues, Villarrica makes a good base for visiting some eccentric nearby villages such as **Colonia Independencia** as well as the **Yvytyruzú Reserve**. Check it out and let us know what you think.

GETTING TO BRAZIL OR ARGENTINA

The border with Brazil (Foz do Iguaçu) is at the Puente de la Amistad (Friendship Bridge). Immigration is at both ends of the bridge. Walking over the bridge is not safe, so catch a bus from the local bus terminal in Foz do Iguaçu (R$3, every 10 minutes) from 6am to 7:30pm to get to Ciudad del Este. Buses to Foz do Iguaçu (6000G) pass by immigration (until 8pm), as do nonstop buses to Puerto Iguazú, Argentina (you have to go via Brazil to reach Puerto Iguazú – no Brazilian visa necessary; 6000G). It's probably more convenient to walk or take a taxi to immigration and catch the bus from there. If you catch a bus to immigration, make sure you disembark to obtain all necessary exit stamps – locals don't need to stop.

Information

Money

Street money changers lounge around the Pioneros de Este rotunda. Banks line Av Adrián Jara and all have ATMs.

Post

Post Office (cnr Alejo Garcia & Centro Democrático; 8am-5pm Mon-Fri, to noon Sat)

Tourist Information

Senatur Office (50-8810; cnr Av Adrián Jara & Mcal Estigarribia; 7am-7pm daily)

Getting There & Away

Air

The Aeropuerto Guaraní is 30km west of town on Ruta 2. **TAM Mercosur** (50-6030; Boquerón 310) flights pass through here several times a day en route to and from Brazil.

Bus

The **bus terminal** (51-0421; Chaco Boreal) is about 2km south of the center. City buses (3000G) shuttle frequently between here and the center, continuing on to the border. There are frequent buses to Asunción (40,000-75,000G, 4½ to 6 hours) and Encarnación (60,000-70,000G, 5½ hours). Daily buses with Pluma and Sol del Paraguay run to São Paulo, Brazil (220,000G, 17 hours).

Taxi

Taxis are fairly expensive – around 30,000G to downtown.

Itaipú Dam

Paraguay's publicity machine is awash with facts and figures about the Itaipú hydroelectric project – the world's second-largest dam (China's new Three Gorges Dam is bigger). Itaipú's generators supply nearly 80% of Paraguay's electricity and 25% of Brazil's entire demand.

While project propaganda gushes about this human accomplishment, it omits the US$25 billion price tag and avoids mention of environmental consequences. The 1350-sq-km, 220m-deep reservoir drowned Sete Quedas, a set of waterfalls that was more impressive than Iguazú.

Free tours leave from the **visitors center** (061-599-8040; www.itaipu.gov.py; tours 8am-4pm daily), north of Ciudad del Este, near the town of Hernandarias; passports are required. Any bus marked 'Hernandarias' (3000G, every 15 minutes) passes in front of the dam and **Flora and Fauna Itaipú Binacional**. A taxi will charge 40,000G one way or 60,000G return, including waiting time.

Salto del Monday

This impressive 80m-high **waterfall** (admission 3000G; 8am-7pm) 10km outside of Ciudad del Este suffers from its close proximity to Iguazú Falls on the other side of the border. If you have time on your hands, it's well worth the visit, especially as dusk falls and tens of thousands of swifts gather in the air like a cloud before zipping in one after the other like miniature torpedoes to their precarious roosts on the slippery rocks behind the cascades. And in case you are wondering, it is pronounced Mon-Da-OO! A return taxi ride will cost around 60,000G, including waiting time.

Itaipú Ecological Reserves

As a result of the catastrophic flood damage caused by Itaipú, the dam company was obliged to set up a series of eight private reserves that now protect the last remnants of the Alto Paraná Atlantic Forest. Three of the most interesting are Refugio Tati Yupi, Reserva Itabó and Limoy.

Refugio Tati Yupi, 26km north of Ciudad del Este, is the easiest to visit. A popular weekend spot, the reserve is best visited during the week if you hope to see animals. Serious animal-watchers will prefer **Reserva Itabó**, 100km north of the city. The forest here is undisturbed and teeming with wildlife, including friendly armadillos and endangered Vinaceous Amazon parrots. There are good accommodations, too, though occasionally they're occupied by school groups. The largest reserve is **Limoy**, another 65km further on, but the facilities are basic and access is difficult without a 4WD.

Unless your visit is part of a tour, you'll need your own vehicle and prior permission from **Flora and Fauna Itaipú Binacional** (☎061-599-8652; Hernandarias Supercarretera), 18km from the center of Ciudad del Este on the road to the dam. It has a good zoo of rescued animals and museums on indigenous culture and natural history to make it worth the trip.

Basic accommodation is available free of charge at some reserves, but you will have to bring your own bedclothes and food, and prepare your own meals. For short guided day trips (in Spanish only), contact Nelson Pérez of the **Itaipú company** (☎0981-54-2415).

Mbaracayú Biosphere Reserve

Singled out by the WWF as one of the 100 most important sites for biodiversity on the planet, the 70,000 hectare Mbaracayú Biosphere Reserve is one of Paraguay's natural treasures. Consisting of pristine Atlantic Forest and *cerrado* (savanna) in approximately equal quantities, it is home to more than 400 bird species and a swathe of large mammals. Bird-watchers will be in search of the bare-throated bellbird (Paraguay's national bird), the rare helmeted woodpecker and the endangered black-fronted piping-guan.

There is also a resident Aché indigenous tribe here who are allowed to hunt using traditional methods. Look out for some of the tribe in full dress at sunrise at the **Jejui-Mi Hotel** (☎0347-20147; Mbaracayú Biosphere Reserve; reserve admission 10,000G, s/d 150,000/250,000G, meals 35,000G).

This model reserve is run by the **Fundación Moisés Bertoni** (☎021-60-8740; www.mbertoni.org.py; Argüello 208, Villa Morra, Asunción). You'll need a 4WD if you want to drive here yourself, or else take the 2pm bus from Asunción to Villa Ygatimi (50,000G, 8 hours) and arrange pick up from there.

DON'T MISS

RESERVA NATURAL LAGUNA BLANCA

A pristine, crystal-clear lake, Laguna Blanca is named for its breathaking sandy beach and lake bed – it looks pure white when viewed from the air. The surrounding *cerrado* habitat is home to rare birds and mammals such as the maned wolf and the endangered white-winged nightjar, this being one of only three places in the world where the latter species breeds.

If lounging around on the beach isn't your cup of tea, there are volunteering opportunities with scientific research, outreach and environmental education projects at the **Para La Tierra Biological Station** (☎0985-26-0074; www.paralatierra.org; Reserva Natural Laguna Blanca; 125,000G incl meals, reductions for longer stays), which also offers accommodation. Alternatively, camp or stay at the basic accommodation with shared bathrooms for nonvolunteers, which are booked in advance through owner **Malvina Duarte** (☎021-424760; www.lagunablanca.com.py; per person 150,000G, excl meals).

To get to Laguna Blanca, take any one of the frequent buses from Asunción to San Pedro or Concepción and get off at Santa Rosa del Aguaray (50,000G, six hours) where volunteers will be met. If you are not volunteering, infrequent local buses to Santa Barbara pass the entrance to the property, from where it is a 3km walk to the accommodation. Santa Barbara buses leave at 10am, 2:30pm and occasionally 5pm (10,000G, two hours), so you'll need to leave Asunción before 8am to avoid getting stranded in Santa Rosa. If you do get stuck, **Hotel Cristal** (☎0451-23-5442; Ruta 3, Santa Rosa del Aguaray; s/d 125,000/200,000G) on the main road is good value and has an excellent grill restaurant.

NORTHERN PARAGUAY

Northern Paraguay is off the radar for most travelers, but the colonial city of Concepción is the best place to catch a boat heading north along the Río Paraguay. Natural wonders abound in this remote area, and the road east from Pozo Colorado to Concepción is famed for its abundance of wildlife. En route to Pozo Colorado along the Ruta Trans-Chaco, be sure to stop at the famous **Parador Pirahú** (Ruta Trans-Chaco Km 249; empanadas 4000-8000G) at Km 249 – it serves the best empanadas in Paraguay.

Concepción

☎0331 / POP 70,000

'La Perla del Norte' is an easygoing city on the Río Paraguay with poetic early-20th-century buildings and a laid-back ambience. 'Action' around here means a trotting horse hauling a cart of watermelons or a boatload of people and their cargo arriving at the port. Indeed, river cruises are the main reason travelers come to Concepción, whether it's for an adventurous odyssey north to Brazil or just a short weekend jaunt upriver with the locals to nearby sandy beaches.

Sights & Activities

Several stunning **mansions**, now municipal buildings, stand out along Estigarribia.

Maria Auxiliadora MONUMENT

(Agustín Pinedo) The city's most eye-catching monument is the enormous statue of Maria Auxiliadora (Virgin Mary), which towers over the northern end of the main avenue.

Museo del Cuartel de la Villa Real MUSEUM

(cnr Marie López & Cerro Cordillera; ⏲7am-noon Mon-Sat) If you don't catch the town's sleepy syndrome, the Museo del Cuartel de la Villa Real in the beautifully restored barracks exhibits historical and war paraphernalia.

Museo de Arqueología Industrial MUSEUM

(Agustín Pinedo) If machines rev you up, this open-air museum features an assortment of antique industrial and agricultural mechanisms.

Sleeping

It's not cheap to stay in Concepción and you may be a little disappointed at what you get for your money.

TOP CHOICE **Concepción Palace** LUXURY HOTEL $$$

(☎24-1858; www.concepcionpalace.com.py; Mcal López 399; s/d 330,000/440,000G; ❄@🛜≋) Far and away the most upmarket hotel in the city, with a price to boot, the stylish wood and leather rooms have pretensions that look beyond the dusty streets outside. An impressive pool and the best restaurant in town complete the effect.

Hotel Frances HOTEL $

(☎24-2383; cnr Franco & CA López; s/d 100,000/150,000G; ❄@≋) Whet your appetite in every respect at this pleasant place, which has lovely gardens, buffet breakfast (and restaurant) and unique handmade lamps in very room.

Hotel Flamingo HOTEL $

(☎24-1211; Ruta 5, Km 1.5; s/d 100,000/150,000G; ❄) A little removed from the center with not a flamingo in sight, but decent value for bland, air-conditioned rooms. Service can be a bit hit and miss, but friendly enough.

Hotel Center HOTEL $

(☎24-2360; cnr Franco & Yegros; s/d 50,000/100,000G; ❄) An outdated and rather dingy dive, but the air-conditioned rooms will be welcome if you are on a budget.

Eating

There is not much to write home about in terms of gastronomy, unless you happen to be addicted to rotisserie chicken – in which case Franco is lined with places ready to sell you a fix.

Restaurante Toninho y Jandiri RODIZZIO $$

(cnr Mcal Estigarribia & Iturbe; mains 50,000G) This place is worth the pressure on both stomach and purse. Come to this Brazilian grill for plentiful portions of meats and fish served on sizzle plates.

Ysapy FAST FOOD $

(cnr Yegros & Mcal Estigarribia; mains 7000-30,000G) Packed with local youths who enjoy decent pizzas, burgers and energy drinks.

Getting There & Away

Boat

The most traditional (but not the most comfortable) way to get to/from Concepción is by riverboat. Typically these are cargo boats that lack basic services (including a toilet) and youll need to take your own food and drink. Boats heading upriver to Vallemí (65,000G, 30 hours) or as far as Bahía Negra (120,000G, 2½ to three days) include the *Aquidabán* (departs Tuesday at 11am, returns on Friday) and the erratic *Guaraní*, which leaves fortnightly on Monday afternoon, but goes only as far as Fuerte Olimpo via Vallemí, and returns on Thursday. Check **schedules** (☎24-2435) and boats in advance; they change frequently.

Bus

The **bus terminal** (☎24-2744; Profesor Andres Koff cnr Asunción) is eight blocks north of the center.

For Asunción (60,000G, 4½ to six hours), **La Santaniana** and **La Concepciónera** offer the best service. Several services head to Pedro Juan Caballero (35,000G, four hours) and Filadelfia (80,000G, six hours). There's a daily departure with **Empresa García** at 12:15pm to Ciudad del Este (90,000G, nine hours).

Taxi

Car or motorcycle taxis cost about 20,000G; *karumbés* are twice as much fun (15,000G) but confirm your price before you are 'taken for a ride'.

Vallemí

Vallemí might be most famous nationally for its cement plant, but it's beginning to make a name for itself among visitors as an ecotour center for trips along the spectacular Río Apa. There's plenty to see, with *cerros* (hills) and caves in the area giving boundless opportunities for adventure tourism. There is even a tour of the cement plant.

Tourism is highly controlled, with visits to local attractions organized through the municipality-sponsored **Vallemí Tour** (☎0985-17-0952; Río Apa cnr 13 de Junio), whose staff can also assist with hotel bookings and transport arrangements.

Parque Nacional Cerro Corá

This national park protects an area of dry tropical forest and *cerrado* in a landscape of steep, isolated hills. Cultural and historical features include pre-Columbian caves, petroglyphs and the site of Mariscal López' death, which, in 1870, ended the War of the Triple Alliance; it's marked with a monument at the end of a long line of busts of war heroes.

There's a camping area and you could ask about using the cabin here. Otherwise, the nearest accommodation is in Pedro Juan Caballero (pricey). Try the retro **Eiruzú** (☎0336-27-2435; Mariscal López; s/d 165,000G/330,000G; ❄@📶🏊).

Buses running between Concepción and Pedro Juan Caballero pass the park entrance (three hours from Concepción; one hour from PJC) and it's a 1km walk to the visitors center.

Bahía Negra & the Paraguayan Pantanal

The Paraguayan Pantanal (Pantanal Paraguayo) is remote and little visited, but if you are willing to make the effort, and to spend more than you would do in Brazil to see the Pantanal, then it is a fantastic, off-the-beaten track destination for those with an interest in wildlife.

UP THE RÍO PARAGUAY TO THE PANTANAL

North of Concepción, Río Paraguay wends its way slowly to the Paraguayan Pantanal. Unlike in the Brazilian Pantanal, you are unlikely to see another tourist here, and except for your boat mates your main companions will be the wildlife. Bring a hammock and a mosquito net for the boat trip, prepare yourself for unusual bedfellows and claim your territory early – it gets crowded with locals. Some boats have basic cabins (around 30,000G per night) but they need to be booked well in advance. You should bring your own food.

Typical routes leave Concepción for Vallemí, then Fuerte Olimpo (last place to obtain an exit stamp, though it's safer to get one before leaving Asunción) with some continuing on to tiny Bahía Negra, near the frontiers with Bolivia and Brazil. The exit stamp is only required if you're considering carrying on north into Brazil or Bolivia; if staying in Paraguay it's not needed.

For details of boat departures, see opposite.

The main access town is Bahía Negra, and while there isn't much there except a military base, a visit is a necessary evil to organize your river trips along the Río Negro. Wildlife abounds in this area, with raptors and waterbirds flushing from the riverside, marsh deer grazing in reed beds and caiman and capybara sunning themselves on exposed banks.

Access to the best areas is by motorboat only, but options are limited and expensive, as fuel costs in this remote area are high. **Don Alicci** (☎0982-46-9942; day-trip 500,000G) has the most reliable motor and knows the best spots for wildlife. He also runs the rustic **Hospedaje la Victoria** (Bahía Negra; per person 25,000G) on the main street in town.

The only place to stay in the Pantanal itself is **Tres Gigantes** (☎021-22-9097; per person 130,000G, excl meals), but you should be sure to reserve your visit in advance with Guyra Paraguay (p795) in Asunción if you want food to be provided. It's a good idea to bring petrol for the generator.

Getting There & Away

From Asunción, **Estel Turismo** runs an uncomfortable weekly bus to Bahía Negra (200,000G, 18 hours) leaving at 7pm on Tuesdays and returning at 7pm on Thursdays. Basic food is available on board, but if you want to vary your diet consider taking snacks with you.

If you have time on your hands and prefer river travel, the dawdling *Aquidabán* departs from Concepción on Tuesdays at 11am for Bahía Negra (120,000G, 2½ to three days) and returns on Fridays.

THE CHACO

Reports of large-scale deforestation in the Gran Chaco have hit the international headlines in recent times and although the situation continues, for the time being the Chaco remains a good place to experience raw wilderness. This vast plain – roughly divided into the flooded palm savannas of the Humid Chaco (the first 350km west of Asunción) and the spiny forests of the Dry Chaco (the rest) – encompasses the entire western half of Paraguay and stretches into Argentina and Bolivia.

Bisected by the **Ruta Trans-Chaco**, it's a paradise for wildlife, with flocks of waterbirds and birds of prey abounding, easily spotted along the roadside. Although the Chaco accounts for more than 60% of Paraguayan territory, less than 3% of the population actually lives here. Historically it was a refuge for indigenous hunter-gatherers; today the most obvious settlements are the Mennonite communities of the Central Chaco.

Each September sees the **Rally Trans-Chaco**, a three-day world motor-sport competition, said to be one of the toughest on the planet. Book accommodation in advance if visiting at this time.

Tours

Thomas & Sabine Vinke TOUR
(☎0981-10-2143; www.chaco-wildlife.org; per car load incl lunch 450,000-950,000G) Organizes recommended nature-watching tours in the Central Chaco area with professional, English-speaking naturalists.

GETTING TO BOLIVIA

The Ruta Trans-Chaco is now fully paved on the Paraguayan side and several companies run the route from Asunción to Santa Cruz, Bolivia, daily, though frustratingly all leave in the early evening. The journey supposedly takes 24 hours (250,000G) but often takes longer depending on road conditions on the Bolivian side of the border.

All buses stop at the customs building in Mariscal Estagarribia in the wee hours of the morning, where you must get your exit stamp, before crossing a few hours later into Bolivia at Fortín Infante Rivola (this is a border post only – no stamps). The asphalt ends here and it's another 60km to Ibibobo for Bolivian formalities. Quality of service provided by Bolivia-bound bus companies varies considerably. Unfortunately they operate a passenger share policy, so the company you buy your ticket with isn't necessarily the one that you travel on.

Bolivia-bound buses do not pass through the Mennonite colonies (though you can buy tickets there) and you will need to head to Mariscal Estigarribia on the morning NASA bus from Filadelfia and hang around until the early hours of the following morning to make your connection. Alternatively plan your trip so that heading back to Asunción is not too much of a hassle.

MENNONITE COMMUNITIES IN THE CHACO

Some 15,000 Mennonites inhabit the Chaco. According to their history, Canadian Mennonites were invited to Paraguay to settle what they believed to be lush, productive territory in return for their rights – religious freedom, pacifism, independent administration of their communities, permission to speak German and practice their religious beliefs. The reality of the harsh, arid Chaco came as a shock, and a large percentage of the original settlers succumbed to disease, hunger and thirst as they struggled to gain a foothold.

There are other Mennonite communities elsewhere in Paraguay, but those in the Chaco are renowned for both their perseverance in the 'Green Hell,' and subsequent commercial success; their cooperatives provide much of the country's dairy products, among other things.

Today there are three main colonies in the Chaco. The oldest colony, **Menno**, was founded by the original settlers in 1927, and is centered around Loma Plata. **Fernheim** (capital Filadelfia), was founded in 1930 by refugees from the Soviet Union, followed by **Neuland** (capital Neu-Halbstadt), founded by Ukrainian Germans in 1947.

Walter Ratzlaff TOUR
(☎0492-25-2301) Cultural tours in the Mennonite colonies and surroundings can be arranged through this friendly, knowledgeable German- and English-speaking guide.

The Mennonite Colonies

Of the three Mennonite Colonies in the Central Chaco, only two are easily accessible on public transport – **Filadelfia** and **Loma Plata**. Many people are surprised by just how small these towns are. Although there's not much to do here except take in the unique atmosphere, they make for an interesting short break and are good bases for exploring the surrounding area.

Getting There & Away

Bus companies have offices along and near Av Hindenburg in Filadelfia. NASA has a daily service to Asunción (70,000G, eight hours), and a daily bus runs to Concepción (80,000G, eight hours). Buses to/from Filadelfia pass through Loma Plata en route.

As most locals have their own transport, getting between the colonies by bus is tricky. Local transport is infrequent, usually leaving in the early morning and late evening.

FILADELFIA

☎0491 / POP 7000 (COLONY)

This neat Mennonite community, administrative center of Fernheim colony, resembles a suburb of Munich plonked in the middle of a sandy desert. Though dusty Av Hindenburg is the main street, the town lacks a real center; its soul is the giant dairy cooperative.

Sights

Jakob Unger Museum MUSEUM
(Av Hindenburg; ⏲7-11:30am Mon-Fri) The flash new natural history museum, named after the famous Mennonite naturalist, is stuffed with stuffed animals.

FREE **Colonists Museum** MUSEUM
(Av Hindenburg; ⏲7-11:30am Mon-Fri) The creaky wooden building that houses the museum is the original colony headquarters. It's filled with a bit of everything, from information about Mennonite history to handmade flame throwers for combating locusts and colorful Nivaclé headdresses.

Sleeping & Eating

Hotel Florida HOTEL **$$**
(☎43-2151; Hindenburg 984; dm 30,000G, s/d 145,000/190,000G; ❄) As orderly as a German train schedule and by far Filadelfia's nicest accommodation, including the cheaper rooms.

Girasol RODIZZIO **$$**
(Unruh; buffet 53,000G) In addition to Hotel Florida's restaurant, Girasol is a good option that serves delicious all-you-can-eat Brazilian *asados*.

Shopping

Cooperativa Mennonita SUPERMARKET
(cnr Unruh & Hindenburg) It's worth a trip to the gigantic, well-stocked Cooperativa Mennonita supermarket. It's amazing how much you can fit under one roof, but you may find yourself the only person paying; the Mennonites deal in credit more than hard currencies.

Information

Tourist Information (Av Hindenburg, Filadelfia; 7-11:30am Mon-Fri) Information in English, German and Spanish.

LOMA PLATA

0492 / POP 8800 (COLONY)

The Menno colony's administrative center is the oldest and most traditional of the Mennonite settlements. The rambling Co-Operativa Supermarket is worth a visit for an insight into Mennonite life.

Sights

FREE **Museum of Mennonite History** MUSEUM
(Loma Plata; 8am-noon Mon-Fri) An excellent little museum, in a complex of pioneer houses, with a remarkable display of original photographs and documents chronicling the colony's history.

Sleeping & Eating

TOP CHOICE **Loma Plata Inn** HOTEL $$
(25-3235; s 130,000-150,000, d 180,000-200,000G, buffet 65,000G; P) Comfortable and professionally run. It's the best place to stay in town and has a pricey but excellent *rodizzio* restaurant, Chaco Grill.

Hotel Mora HOTEL $
(25-2255; Sandstrasse 803; s/d 90,000G/140,000G;) Appealing, spotless rooms around a grassy setting.

TOP CHOICE **Mehin** CHINESE $$
(Loma Plata; mains 25,000-40,000G) A real treat, and a bit of a surprise considering the location (out near the airstrip). It serves probably the best Chinese food in the country.

Fortín Boquerón & Fortín Toledo

Fortín Boquerón is the site of one of the decisive battles of the Chaco War (1932–35). There is an excellent **museum** (admission 5000G; 8am-6pm Tue-Sat) as well as a graveyard of the fallen and a gigantic monument constructed from the original defenses and trenches. Look for the hollowed-out *palo borracho* tree used as a sniper's nest. From the front it looks like a woodpecker hole but, despite being gutted more than 70 years ago, the tree is still alive.

Fortín Toledo also preserves Chaco War trenches but is perhaps more interesting for the **Proyecto Taguá** (www.cccipy.com.py; donations accepted) Chaco peccary breeding project. This pig-like creature was known only from fossil remains until its remarkable rediscovery in the 1970s. The project, initiated by San Diego Zoo, acts as a reintroduction program for this painfully shy and critically endangered species. Herds of friendly collared and frankly nasty white-lipped peccaries are also kept here, giving you a unique opportunity to compare all three species and their differing characters. Look out for the rare black-bodied woodpecker in the surroundings, too.

Fortín Boquerón is 65km south of a turnoff at Cruce Los Pioneros on the Ruta Trans-Chaco. Fortín Toledo is accessed via a turnoff at Km 475. Follow the peccary signs for 5km or so. There is **self-catering accommodation** (0972-10-7200; per person 80,000G) in a spic-and-span house here, but you'll need to call project coordinator Juan Campos in advance to book it.

Central Chaco Lagoons

A series of ephemeral saline lakes that form in the area to the east of Loma Plata have been declared an 'Important Bird Area' because of their importance for migrating birds. Though individual lagoons may be dry for several years before filling after a good rainstorm, the birds somehow find them. They are best from May to September when flocks of exotic ducks and flamingos obscure the water. From October to December and March to April they are used by waders on passage.

One accessible place to visit is Laguna Capitán. The lagoons are often dry here but the surroundings teem with wildlife. For waterbirds and particularly flamingos, head to **Campo Maria** (admission 10,000G), which usually has water and is a great place to see mammals such as tapirs and peccaries.

Northwestern National Parks

Once the realm of nomadic Ayoreo foragers, **Parque Nacional Defensores del Chaco** is a wooded alluvial plain; isolated **Cerro León** (500m) is its greatest landmark. The dense thorn forest harbors large cats such as jaguars and pumas, as well as tapirs and herds of peccary. The free accommodation is a bit rough, and you'll need to bring all your own food, drink and fuel for the generator. 'Defensores' is a long 830km from Asunción, over roads impassable to ordinary vehicles, and there's no regular public transport. It's not a good idea to attempt to visit without a guide, and don't bother if you don't have a 4WD vehicle.

A more accessible option is **Parque Nacional Teniente Agripino Enciso**, which boasts a sophisticated infrastructure including an interpretation center and a visitors house with kitchen and some air-conditioned rooms. Again, bring all your own food and water.

A short hop further north is **Parque Nacional Médanos del Chaco**. There are no accommodations here and it should not be attempted without a guide. The habitat is more open than at Enciso and bird-watchers should keep their eyes peeled for local species such as the quebracho crested-tinamou and spot-winged falconet.

NASA runs a single weekly minibus on Tuesdays at 7am from Mariscal Estigarribia to Nueva Asunción (60,000G, four hours) that passes in front of the visitors centre at Enciso and returns at 3pm from the park the same afternoon. Your best bet for coordinating with it is to take one of the Santa Cruz bound buses from Asunción on Monday evening and get off at Mariscal (70,000G, eight hours) when everybody else does their customs formalities. There is nowhere recommendable to stay in Mariscal Estigarribia so be prepared to sit around for a few hours before the sun comes up.

UNDERSTAND PARAGUAY

Paraguay Today

Paraguay is currently somewhat of a pariah in South America, following a series of events in 2012 that led to the impeachment of the elected president Fernando Lugo. Vice-president Federico Franco took the reins following a political struggle in which Lugo was tried and found guilty of failing to perform his presidential duties by the senate, with regards to his handling of land-rights disputes. The brevity of the trial process, which was completed in less than 24 hours, raised eyebrows internationally and resulted in accusations of an anti-democratic abuse of process from neighboring countries.

The events were officially declared a coup d'état by the trade bloc Mercosur, of which Paraguay is a member, and Argentina, Brazil and Uruguay all refused to recognize the legitimacy of the Franco government. Mercosur suspended Paraguay from the bloc until free elections are held in April 2013, and this position was later followed unanimously by Unasur (Union de Naciones Suramericanas), of which every country in South America is a member. Following the suspension of Paraguay from Mercosur, Venezuela was admitted as a full member. Paraguay had previously vetoed Venezuela's inclusion.

Defenders of the process claim that Paraguay was exercising its democratic and sovereign rights to govern as permitted in the national constitution, and called the disapproval of its neighbors a modern-day attack by the Triple Alliance.

At the time of writing, President Franco continues to work to convince trade partners of his legitimacy and to battle unpopularity on the domestic front. He has sought to forge closer ties with the US but his relationship with other South American governments remains tense. With Franco unable to stand in the April 2013 elections, ordinary Paraguayans await the opportunity to make their opinions heard at the ballot box.

History

Pedro de Mendoza's expedition founded Asunción in 1537, and the city became the most significant Spanish settlement east of the Andes for nearly 50 years until Buenos Aires was fully established. It declined in importance once it became clear that the hostile Chaco impeded the passage towards the fabled 'City of Gold' in modern-day Peru.

In the early 17th century, Jesuit missionaries created *reducciónes* (settlements) where the indigenous Guaraní were introduced to European high culture, new crafts, new crops and new methods of cultivation. By the time of their expulsion in 1767 (because of Madrid's concern that their power had become too great), the Jesuit influence had spread to what is today Bolivia, Brazil and Argentina.

The bloodless revolution of May 1811 gave Paraguay the distinction of being the first South American country to declare its independence from Spain. However, since independence Paraguayan history has been dominated by a cast of dictators who have influenced the direction of the country.

Dr José Gaspar Rodríguez de Francia was the first leader of independent Paraguay. Chosen as the strongest member of the Próceres de Mayo (founding fathers), the 'El Supremo' was initially reluctant to take charge, insisting he would accept the role only until somebody better-equipped was found. That somebody never was found, and he ruled until his death in 1840. Francia sealed the country's borders to promote self-sufficiency, expropriated the properties of landholders, merchants and even the church, and established the state as the only political and economic power. Though he was controversial, under his rule Paraguay became the continent's dominant power.

By the early 1860s, Francia's successor, Carlos Antonio López, had ended Paraguay's isolation by building railroads, a telegraph system, a shipyard and a formidable army. Paraguay was in a strong position at the time of his death, when power passed to his son, Francisco Solano López. Seduced by his European education, Mariscal López longed to be seen as the Napolean of the Americas. At his side was the Irish courtesan Eliza Lynch, who had her own fantasies about French high society. Her dream of making Asunción the 'Paris of the Americas' turned her into an unpopular Marie Antoinette figure, and the country rapidly deteriorated under their combined rule.

When Brazil invaded Uruguay in 1865, López jumped at the opportunity to prove his military genius and save the smaller nation from its fate. In order to send his army to the rescue, permission was required to cross Argentine territory. Argentina's refusal, led him to declare war on them, too. With Uruguay quickly overwhelmed by the Brazilians, Paraguay suddenly found itself at war with three of its neighbors simultaneously. The disastrous War of the Triple Alliance had begun and the course of Paraguayan history would be changed forever. Allied forces outnumbered Paraguayans 10 to one, and by the end of the campaign boys as young as 12 years old were fighting on the front lines armed only with farm implements. By the end Paraguay had lost half of its prewar population and 26% of its national territory.

The next war wasn't too far away. In the early 1900s and with Paraguay in political turmoil, the Bolivians began to slowly advance into the Chaco, resulting in the irruption of full-scale hostilities in 1932. The exact reasons for the Chaco War are debated, but Bolivia's desire for a sea port (via the Río Paraguay) and rumors of petroleum deposits in the area are often cited as factors.

In the punishingly hot, arid Chaco, access to water was key to military success and the war hinged around the capture and protection of freshwater sources. Paraguay further benefited from a British-built railway line, which allowed them to bring supplies to troops from Asunción. The British had earlier warned the Bolivians not to touch their railway line or risk adding another more formidable enemy to their list. As a result the Paraguayan troops were able to overcome Bolivia's numerically stronger forces and even advance as far as the southern Bolivian town of Villamontes. With the futility of the war becoming ever more obvious, a 1935 cease-fire left no clear victor but more than 80,000 dead.

Paraguay subsequently entered into a decade of disorder before a brief civil war brought the Colorado party to power in 1949. A 1954 coup installed General Alfredo Stroessner as president. His brutal 35-year, military-dominated rule was characterized by repression and terror and is the longest dictatorship in South American history. Perceived political opponents were persecuted, tortured and 'disappeared,' elections were fraudulent and corruption became a national industry. By the time Stroessner was overthrown in yet another coup, 75% of Paraguayans had known no other leader.

Stroessner was eventually driven into exile on 3 February 1989 and Paraguay's first democratic elections were held the same year. They were won by the Colorado candidate Andrés Rodríguez, who had masterminded the coup. The Colorados then went on to win every successive election until their grip was finally broken during the historic events of April 2008, which saw Archbishop Fernando Lugo, a man with no prior political experience, elected president of the republic. Campaigning on social reform, an end to corruption and equal opportunities for all, Lugo's power base stemmed from the numerically superior lower classes – his campaign slogan 'Paraguay Para Todos' (Paraguay for everybody) struck the right note with voters. With the Colorado Party in turmoil, there was at last a sense that corruption and social injustice really could be consigned to the dustbin of history.

President Lugo's government viewed social and economic progress as one and the same and actively sought closer trade links with neighboring countries. His relationship with Evo Morales and the late Hugo Chávez brought criticism from his opponents, but marked improvements at the domestic level kept his critics at bay. By 2010 the Paraguayan economy was the third fastest growing in the world, a positive renegotiation of the greatly unfavorable Itaipú Dam contracts had been completed, ensuring that Brazil would pay Paraguay a fair rate for its electricity usage, and at last the country was beginning to move away from the bottom of the international corruption tables.

There were obstacles, however, and Lugo's election had come at a price. In order to form a government he was required to broker an uneasy alliance with several political parties, the largest of which, the Liberals, provided his vice-president Federico Franco. From the outset the relationship with the Liberals and Franco in particular was a tense one, as they demanded ever increasing influence in government. To complicate matters the Colorado Party retained a majority in the senate (which must approve new government policy) and used this power to pressure for their own demands.

Following a breakdown in relations in 2012, the Liberal party withdrew its support for Lugo and joined forces with its traditional rivals the Colorados to impeach the president. The official reasons given included a breakdown of security and a failure to address the problems associated with land rights. Over 80% of the land in Paraguay is owned by just 1% of the population, and Lugo had promised to address the decades-long social imbalance by providing land for landless *campesinos*. This had infuriated the land-owning classes, who accused him of failing to protect their interests, while a lack of progress had also led to the mobilisation of the *campesino* groups, pressurising for their own rights to be respected.

With his future in the hands of a senate dominated by the same parties that sought to oust him, Lugo was declared guilty on 22 June 2012 after a shotgun trial. Vice-president Franco was sworn in the same day.

Culture

Some 95% of Paraguayans are considered *mestizos* (of mixed indigenous and Spanish descent). Spanish is the language of business and most prevalent in the cities, while in the *campaña* (countryside) Guaraní is more common. *Jopará* (a mixture of the two) is used in some parts of the media. The remaining 5% of the population are descendants of European immigrants (mainly Ukrainians and Germans), Mennonite farmers and indigenous tribes. Small but notable Asian, Arab and Brazilian communities are found, particularly in the south and east of the country.

More than 95% of the population lives in eastern Paraguay, only half in urban areas. Unicef reports a literacy rate of 99%, an infant mortality rate of 2.5% and an average life expectancy of 72 years. The annual population growth rate is 2.3%.

Statistically Paraguay is the second-poorest South American country (after Bolivia), though walking around the country's cities you might find it hard to believe. Lines of souped-up Mercedes Benz' whizz around, classy restaurants are full to bursting and there are houses the size of palaces. Contrast this with the lives of the rural poor, where landless *campesinos* (peasant farmers) live hand to mouth and are exploited by wealthy landowners. This group continues to represent the country's biggest social problem.

Paraguayan towns are frequently nicknamed 'Capital of...' after their most notable features or products. Encarnación, for example, is 'Capital de Carnaval', Coronel Bogado 'Capital de Chipa' and Itauguá 'Capital de Ñandutí'.

Paraguayans are famously laid-back and rightly renowned for their warmth and hospitality. Sipping *tereré* in the 40°C shade while shooting the breeze takes the better part of a day. *Siesta* is obligatory and in some communities extends from noon to sunset, making the early morning and dusk the busiest times of day.

Though things have improved, corruption remains a part of daily life. For visitors corruption is most likely to manifest itself in the form of police soliciting bribes or higher prices for gringos.

Ninety percent of the population claims to be Roman Catholic, but folk variants are common and evangelical Christianity is on the rise. Most indigenous peoples have retained their religious beliefs, or modified them only slightly, despite nominal allegiance to Catholicism or evangelical Protestantism.

Arts

As many intellectuals and artists will tell you, the Government gives little funding to the arts. Many artists, musicians and painters have left the country to perform or work elsewhere. Nevertheless, the country boasts some well-known figures.

Paraguay's major literary figures are poet-critic and writer Josefina Plá and poet-novelist Augusto Roa Bastos, winner of the 1990 Cervantes Prize (he died in 2005 aged 87). Despite many years in exile, Bastos focused on Paraguayan themes and history, drawing from personal experience. Contemporary writers include Nila López, poet Jacobo A Rauskin, Luis María Martínez, Ramón Silva Ruque Vallejos, Delfina Acosta and Susy Delgado.

Paraguayan music is entirely European in origin. The most popular instruments are the guitar and the harp, while traditional dances include the lively *polkas galopadas* and the *danza de la botella*, where dancers balance bottles on their heads.

Cuisine

Beef is succulent, abundant and easily rivals that of Argentina. The best cuts are *tapa de cuadril* (rump steak) and *corte americano* (T-bone), though the most common (and cheapest) are fatty *vacio* (flank) and chewy *costillas* (ribs).

Grains, particularly maize, are common ingredients in traditional foods, while *mandioca* (manioc) is the standard accompaniment for every meal. *Chipa* (a type of bread made with manioc flour, eggs and cheese) is sold everywhere but is best in the southern town of Coronel Bogado. Empanadas are great wherever you buy them.

Paraguayans consume massive quantities of yerba mate (a type of tea), most commonly as refreshing ice-cold *tereré* (iced mate) and generously spiked with *yuyos* (medicinal herbs). Roadside stands offer *mosto* (sugarcane juice), while *caña* (cane alcohol) is the fiery alcoholic alternative. Local beers, especially Baviera and Pilsen, are excellent.

Sports

Paraguayans are *fútbol*-mad. It's not uncommon to see large groups of men in bars supping Pilsen and watching the Copa Libertadores on a communal TV. The most popular soccer teams, Olímpia and Cerro Porteño, have a fierce rivalry and the national team defied all the odds to reach the quarter finals of the 2010 World Cup and finish runner-up in the 2011 Copa America. The headquarters of **Conmebol** (☎021-65-0993; www.conmebol.com; Av Sudamericana Km 12), the South American football confederation, is in Luque, on the road to the airport. It houses an impressive museum depicting the history of the sport on the continent. Tennis, basketball, volleyball, hunting and fishing are also popular.

Environment

The country is divided into two distinct regions, east and west of the Río Paraguay. Eastern Paraguay historically was a mosaic of Atlantic Forest and *cerrado* savanna, with the unique Mesopotamian flooded grasslands in the extreme south of the country. Much of the original habitat has now been converted to agriculture, especially in Departamentos Itapúa and Alto Paraná, but substantial tracts of these pristine but globally endangered habitats still remain. To the west is the Gran Chaco, a lush palm savanna in its lower reaches (Humid Chaco), and a dense, arid, thorny forest (Dry Chaco) further north and west. The northeastern Chaco represents the southern extent of the great Pantanal wetland.

Wildlife

Wildlife is diverse, but the expanding rural population is putting increasing pressure on eastern Paraguay's fauna. Mammals are most abundant and easy to see in the largely unpopulated Chaco. Anteaters, armadillos, maned wolves, giant otters, lowland tapirs, jaguars, pumas, peccaries and brocket deer are all still relatively numerous here. In the mid-1970s the Chaco peccary, a species previously known only from fossilized remains, was found alive and well in the Paraguayan Chaco, where it had evaded discovery for centuries.

Birdlife is abundant, and Paraguay is home to more than 700 bird species. The national bird is the bare-throated bellbird, named for its remarkable call, but serious bird-watchers will be in search of endangered, limited-range species, such as the white-winged nightjar, saffron-cowled blackbird, lesser nothura, helmeted woodpecker and black-fronted piping-guan. Reptiles, including caiman and anaconda, are also widespread. The amphibian that will most likely catch your eye is the enormous rococo toad, which is attracted to lights, even in urban areas.

National Parks

Paraguay's national parks are largely remote and typically inadequately protected. Most have no visitor facilities, but those covered in this book have some kind of infrastructure set up for visitors. There is also a series of excellent and well-run private reserves across the country.

The body responsible for the maintenance of national parks is **SEAM** (☎021-61-5805; www.seam.gov.py; Av Madame Lynch 3500, Asunción; ⏰7am-1pm Mon-Fri) and the tourist secretariat is Senatur (p773). The impressive private Mbaracayú Biosphere Reserve comes under the auspices of the Fundación Moisés Bertoni (p783), while the Itaipú Ecologica Reserves in eastern Paraguay are managed by **Itaipú Binacional** (☎061-599-8989; www.itaipu.gov.py; Rodríguez 150, Ciudad del Este).

Environmental Issues

The disappearance of the eastern Atlantic Forest has been alarming; much of the rainforest has been logged for cropping, especially soy bean and wheat crops, and mostly to the benefit of large-scale, wealthy farmers. The construction of the Itaipú hydroelectric plant was not without controversy, and a second dam at Yacyretá, near Ayolas, has permanently altered the southern coastline of the country.

The country's most pressing environmental worry, however, now concerns the rapid deforestation of the previously pristine Chaco. With the Paraguayan economy healthy and new technological advances making it easier than ever to raise cattle in this harsh environment, wealthy ranchers are taking advantage of the low land prices in the western region to establish new *estancias* (ranches). The resulting deforestation has been rapid and has hit the world headlines.

SURVIVAL GUIDE

Directory A–Z

Accommodations

City hotels are good value with air-conditioning, private bathrooms and usually wi-fi access. *Residenciales* (guesthouses), though worn and of a distant era, are usually clean. Camping facilities are rare. Most land is privately owned, so you can't pitch a tent without permission. In the Chaco, outside of the main towns, you will need your own food, drink and bed sheets.

Activities

Biodiversity makes Paraguay a notable destination for ecotourism, in particular bird-watching.

Books

» For travel accounts, grab a copy of *At the Tomb of the Inflatable Pig* by John Gimlette.

» For more about Paraguay's notorious wars, read Harris Gaylord Warren's *Rebirth of the Paraguayan Republic* or Augusto Roa Bastos' novel *Son of Man*.

» For a look at Paraguay's heinous dictators, try Bastos' book *I the Supreme* about Francia, and Carlos Miranda's *The Stroessner Era*.

» For fiction, read *The News from Paraguay* by Lily Tuck, about Mariscal López and his relationship with Eliza Lynch, and Mark Jacobs' *The Liberation of Little Heaven and Other Stories*, a collection of fictional Paraguayan shorts.

» For an anthropological slant, see Pierre Clastres' *Chronicle of the Guayaki Indians* or Matthew Pallamary's novel *Land Without Evil*.

» For history, buffs should look for Andrew Nickson's *Historical Dictionary of Paraguay*.

SLEEPING PRICE RANGES

The following price ranges refer to a double room with bathroom in high season. Unless otherwise stated, breakfast is included in the price.

$ less than 150,000G

$$ 150,000G to 300,000G

$$$ more than 300,000G

Business Hours

Banks 8am to 1pm Monday to Saturday – *casas de cambio* (exchange houses) keep longer hours

Government offices 7am to 1pm or 2pm Monday to Friday

Restaurants noon to 3pm & 6pm to 11pm; many close on Mondays

Shops 8am to noon & 2pm to 7pm Monday to Friday and Saturday mornings

Electricity

Use plugs with two round or flat pins and no grounding pin – 220V, 50Hz.

Embassies & Consulates

A full, updated list of diplomatic offices in Paraguay is available at www.mre.gov.py. All of the embassies below are in Asunción.

Argentinian Embassy (021-21-2320; cnr España & Perú, Asunción)

Bolivian Embassy (021-62-1426; Campos Cevera 6421)

Brazilian Embazzy (021-24-8400; Irrazábal & Eligio Ayala, Asunción; 7am-noon Mon-Fri) Consulate in Ciudad del Este (061-50-0984; Pampliega 205, Ciudad del Este; 7am-noon Mon-Fri).

French Embassy (021-21-3840; Av España 893)

German Embassy (021-21-4009; Av Venezuela 241)

UK Embassy (021-21-0405; Eulógio Estigarribia 4846)

USA Embassy (021-21-3715; Mariscal López 1776)

Gay & Lesbian Travelers

Paraguay is an old-fashioned country, with conservative views. Public displays of affection between same-sex couples are unknown. Gay bars are appearing in Asunción, but on the whole homosexuality is not widely accepted.

FOOD PRICE RANGES

The following price ranges refer to a standard main course.

$ less than 15,000G

$$ 15,000G to 55,000G

$$$ more than 55,000G

Health

Paraguay presents relatively few health problems for travelers. Private hospitals are better than public hospitals, and those in Asunción, Ciudad del Este and Encarnación are the best.

- There are occasional minor outbreaks of dengue fever, but no malaria.
- Water is drinkable in the cities, but avoid it in the countryside. In the Chaco it is positively salty.
- Carry sunscreen, a hat and plenty of bottled water to avoid becoming dehydrated.
- Avoid cheap brands of condom.

Internet Access

Internet is widely available in cities, but limited in smaller towns. An hour of use costs around 3000G to 6000G.

Language

Following are some recommended institutions offering Spanish language classes:

Alianza Francesa (21-0382; Estigarribia 1039, Asunción)

Centro Cultural Paraguayo-Americano (22-4831; Av España 352, Asunción)

IDIPAR (021-44-7896; www.idipar.edu.py; Manduvirá 963, Asunción) Spanish and Guaraní courses with homestay options.

Instituto Cultural Paraguayo Alemán (22-6242; Juan de Salazar 310, Asunción)

Intercultural Experience (021-48-2890; www.ie.com.py; cnr Av Colón & La Habana, Asunción) Offers language immersion placements with local families. Ask at the cultural centers for private language classes.

Maps

The **Touring y Automóvil Club Paraguayo** (021-21-0550; www.tacpy.com.py; cnr 25 de Mayo & Brasil) produces a series of road and town maps for tourists. For more detailed maps of the interior, the **Instituto Geográfico Militar** (021-20-6344; Artigas 920, Asunción; 7am-5:30pm Mon-Fri) sells topographical maps that cover most of the country.

Money

Paraguay survived the economic crisis as the world's third fastest growing economy. Though prices haven't changed much over the last few years, the guaraní currency is stronger than it has ever been and the cost of living in dollars has risen exponentially.

Banknote values are 2000G, 5000G, 10,000G, 20,000G, 50,000G and 100,000G; increasingly useless coins come in denominations of 50G, 100G, 500G and 1000G. Keep plenty of change and small notes as you go along – it comes in handy.

ATMS & CREDIT CARDS

» ATMs in major cities and towns are connected to Visa, MasterCard and Cirrus networks.

» Outside of the Mennonite Colonies there are no ATMs in the Chaco.

» Plastic is rarely accepted outside the major cities, and sometimes comes with a surcharge.

EXCHANGING MONEY

» *Casas de cambio* are abundant in major cities, but shop around for rates.

» Street money changers give slightly lower rates for cash only, but can be lifesavers at weekends.

Post

The Paraguayan *correo* claims to be the best on the continent, but in reality things are regularly lost en route. Essential mail should be sent *certificado* (registered) for a small additional fee (4000G).

Public Holidays

Government offices and businesses in Paraguay are closed for the official holidays in the following list:

Año Nuevo (New Year's Day) 1 January

Cerro Corá (Heroes Day) 1 March

Semana Santa (Easter) March/April – dates vary

Día de los Trabajadores (Labor Day) 1 May

Independencia Patria (Independence Day) 15 May

Paz del Chaco (End of Chaco War) 12 June

Fundación de Asunción (Founding of Asunción) 15 August

Victoria de Boquerón (Battle of Boquerón) 29 September

Día de la Virgen (Immaculate Conception Day) 8 December

Navidad (Christmas Day) 25 December

Responsible Travel

» Avoid buying crafts made from native woods (such as *lapacho* and *palo santo*) or wild animals.

» Visitors interested in natural history and conservation should contact **Para la Tierra** (☎0985-26-0074; www.paralatierra.org; Reserva Natural Laguna Blanca; 125,000G incl meals, reductions for longer stays), the **Fundación Moisés Bertoni** (☎021-60-8740; www.mbertoni.org.py; Argüello 208, Villa Morra, Asunción) or **Guyra Paraguay** (☎22-9097; Gaetano Martino 215).

Safe Travel

Despite what you may hear from people who have never been, Paraguay is one of the continent's safest countries. With the exception of Ciudad del Este and certain parts of Asunción, cities are quite safe to walk around, even at night. The Chaco environment is hostile and desolate with limited infrastructure – it is highly recommended that you go with a guide. Beware of strong currents when swimming in rivers.

Telephone

» Private *locutorios* (phone offices) have sprung up everywhere, often with internet service as well.

» International calls cost more than US$1 per minute, even with lower nighttime rates.

» Local cell phone rates are low and some companies offer free SIM cards, or SIM cards with *saldo* (credit) already charged to them for a small fee.

» The best cell phone companies are Tigo and Claro; their *tarjetas* (cards) for charging credit to your phone are sold at every newsagent.

» Claro SIM cards can be formatted to work in both Brazil and Argentina.

» International operator: ☎0010

» International direct dial: ☎002

Toilets

You're likely to see more jaguars than public toilets – they're rare! Most bus terminals have one – for 1000G you get a smelly loo and an (often insufficient) wad of paper. Go when you can in restaurants or hotels. Carry your own toilet paper and don't throw it down the pipes. Most buses have an onboard toilet but cheaper services and those in more remote areas do not.

Tourist Information

The government-run **Senatur** (☎49-4110; www.senatur.gov.py; Palma 468; ⏰7am-7pm) has picked up its game in the last few years and there are good tourist offices in Asunción and the other major cities. The **Asociación de Colonias Mennonitas del Paraguay** (☎021-22-6059; www.acomepa.org; Colombia cnr Estados Unidos, Asunción) has brochures about Mennonite communities and runs informative offices in Loma Plata and Filadelfia.

Visas

Visitors from Canada, New Zealand and the US need visas that must be solicited in the Paraguayan embassy of the respective countries prior to travel, or in a Paraguayan consulate in a bordering country. It is not possible to get visas at the border.

Others nationalities need only a valid passport for entry. Visas may be requested and obtained on the same day at most consulates but requirements and cost depend where you are soliciting. Typically you will need two passport photos and two copies of each of the following: your passport, proof of onward travel and proof of sufficient funds.

Get your passport stamped on entering the country or face a fine upon leaving.

Visa requirements change frequently. Check lonelyplanet.com for the latest information or visit the **Immigration Office** (☎021-44-6673; Ayala cnr Caballero; ⏰7am-1pm Mon-Fri) in Asunción.

Volunteering

Para la Tierra (☎0985-26-0074; www.paralatierra.org; Reserva Natural Laguna Blanca; 125,000G incl meals, reductions for longer stays) based at Laguna Blanca offers an award-winning volunteer and intern program for eco-minded visitors. A variety of volunteer opportunities are offered by **Intercultural Experience** (☎021-48-2890; www.ie.com.py; cnr Av Colón & La Habana, Asunción), including language immersion placements with local families. **Apatur** (☎021-49-7028; www.turismorural.org.py), a rural tourism association, can help make placements on *estancias* (extensive grazing establishments).

DEPARTURE TAX

There is a US$41 airport tax on all departing flights, payable at the desk adjacent to the entrance to the departure lounge. You will receive a sticker on your ticket in return for your payment.

Women Travelers

Paraguay is a reasonably safe country for women but solo travelers should take care. Young unaccompanied women are likely to be hit on by Paraguayan men, especially if they are drinking alcohol. Generally it is harmless; be firm but polite and not rude. Modest dress is important.

Getting There & Away

Air

Paraguay's **Silvio Pettirossi International Airport** (☎021-64-5600) is in Luque, a satellite town of Asunción. The airport in Ciudad del Este connects Asunción and major Brazilian destinations.

AIRLINES

Gol (☎021-62-1121; www.voegol.com.br; Paseo Carmelitas , Asunción) Flies to Brazilian destinations via Ciudad del Este.

LAN Chile (☎021-23-3487; www.lan.com; cnr Juan de Salazar 791 & Washington, Asunción) Flies to Santiago.

TAM Mercosur (☎021-49-1040; www.tam.com.py; Oliva 761, Asunción) Has the most daily flights from/to Buenos Aires (Argentina), São Paulo (Brazil), Santa Cruz (Bolivia) and Santiago (Chile), as well as to Ciudad del Este.

Land

Negotiating Paraguayan borders can be harrowing; on the bus, off the bus, on the bus... Pay special attention when crossing from Brazil or Argentina. Ask the driver to stop at immigration (locals don't always need to) and be sure your papers are in order.

River

Ferries cross into Ciudad del Este and Encarnación from Argentina. With patience and stamina, unofficial river travel from Concepción to Isla Margarita on the Brazilian border is possible.

Getting Around

Buses dominate transportation, and offer cheap fares and reasonably efficient service. Journeys between Paraguayan cities typically take less than eight hours, depending on the start and end destinations. Boats are the easiest way to get between Concepción and cities higher up Río Paraguay.

Air

Flights save time but cost more than buses, with the only scheduled flight linking Asunción with Ciudad del Este en route to/from Brazilian destinations. A new Encarnación airport does not yet receive charter flights.

Pilot **Juan Carlos Zavala** (☎0971-20-1540) runs an *aerotaxi* service to the Pantanal region and the Chaco. Three passengers fit in the smallest plane and flights cost from US$440 per hour. Note that you will be charged for the return flight whether you use it or not. Bank on two hours to Fuerte Olimpo and three to Bahía Negra from Asunción.

Boat

You can travel by boat up Río Paraguay. See the boxed text, p785.

Bus

Bus quality varies from luxury services with TV, air-conditioning and comfortable reclining seats to bumpy sardine cans with windows that don't open and aisles crammed with people picked up along the way. Typically you get what you pay for.

Larger towns have central terminals. Elsewhere, companies are within easy walking distance of each other. Recommended companies for major routes are noted in the destination text.

Car & Motorcycle

It is not cheap to rent a car in Paraguay, but can be worth it if there's a few of you. Flexibility is your main advantage, although buses go most places accessible to an ordinary car. Anywhere away from the main *rutas* and you'll need a 4WD. Companies often charge extra mileage for distances above 100km. Better deals are available for longer rentals.

DRIVER'S LICENSE

Most rental agencies accept a home driver's license, but it's wise to back it up with an International Driver's License – the lack of one is a favorite scam for soliciting bribes.

Taxi

In Asunción taxi fares are metered; don't get in the taxi if it's not. In other cities they often are not, but no trip within city limits should cost more than 30,000G in Ciudad del Este and 20,000G elsewhere (usually less). Drivers in Asunción legally levy a 30% *recargo* (surcharge) between 10pm and 5am, and on Sundays and holidays.

Tours

DTP (☎22-1816; www.dtp.com.py; Gral Brúguez 353) Organizes a smorgasbord of day trips.

FAUNA Paraguay (☎0985-74-6866; www.faunaparaguay.com) Best for ecotourism and animal-watching excursions. Reservations by email.

Peru

Includes »

Best Places to Eat

» Central (p810)

» Taita (p883)

» Picantería restaurants, Arequipa (p831)

» La Quinta Eulalia (p848)

» Frio y Fuego (p899)

Best Places to Stay

» Hacienda Concepción (p893)

» Loki del Mar (p877)

» Pachamama (p835)

» Ecopackers (p847)

» Backpacker's Family House (p807)

Why Go?

Welcome to a land of extreme and intrigue. Peru's terrain ranges from glaciated Andean peaks and sprawling coastal deserts, to the steamy rainforests of the Amazon Basin. Excavate the past – with temples entangled in jungle vines, windswept desert tombs and shamanic rituals still used today – to find your own lost-world adventure.

You can take the standard route chasing perfect waves off a sunny Pacific beach and ending at the cloud-topping Inca citadel of Machu Picchu. Or step off the beaten path and groove to Afro-Peruvian beats, explore remote ruins in the north or ride a slow boat down the Amazon. Wildlife, from soaring Andean condor to tapir marauding through the tropical forest, provides one more connection to the elemental.

Wherever your journey takes you, you'll find Peruvians' complex culture holds a deep lust for life. Small wonder, then, that the land of the Incas is one of the continent's top picks for adventurous travelers.

When to Go

Lima

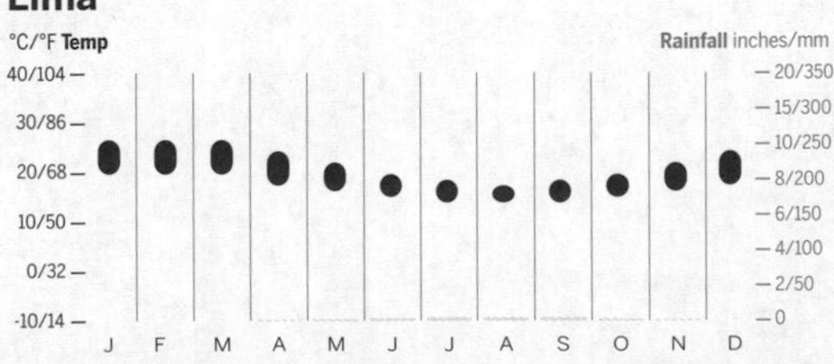

Dec–Mar The hottest, blue-sky months ideal for surf and sun on the coast.

Jun–Aug Dry season ideal for hiking the Andean highlands and eastern rainforest.

Sep–Nov & Mar–May Decent travel weather and fewer tourists.

Connections

Border crossings include Arica (Chile) via Tacna; Huaquillas, Guayaquil and Macará (Ecuador), reached from the northern coast and highlands; Kasani and Desaguadero (Bolivia) along Lake Titicaca; and multiple Brazilian and Bolivian towns and river ports in the Amazon.

ITINERARIES

Two Weeks

Start by exploring Lima's great food scene, nightlife and museums. Journey south by boat to the wildlife-rich Islas Ballestas. Then it's on to the sandboarding oasis of Huacachina. Fly over the mysterious Nazca Lines, then turn inland to Arequipa to trek the incredible Cañón del Colca or Cañón del Cotahuasi. Climb to Puno. From here you can boat to Lake Titicaca's traditional islands. Go on to Cuzco, with history, ruins and the colorful markets of the Sacred Valley. Finish by trekking to Machu Picchu via an adventurous alternative route.

Four Weeks

Follow the two-week itinerary. From Cuzco, brave the 10-hour bus ride to Puerto Maldonado to kick back at a riverside Amazon Basin wildlife lodge. Alternatively, overland tours from Cuzco visit the Manu area; with animals from the kinkajou to caiman, it's one of the planet's most biodiverse regions. Back in Lima, head to Huaraz and trek around the Cordillera Blanca's precipitous peaks. Then bus up the coast to historic Trujillo and hit the ruins of the largest pre-Columbian city in the Americas, Chan Chan, and Huacas del Sol y de la Luna. Wrap up with a seaside break at the bustling surf town of Máncora.

Essential Food & Drink

» **Aji de gallina** Shredded-chicken and walnut stew

» **Anticuchos** Beef-heart skewers, usually grilled as a snack

» **Buttifara** Ham sandwiches served on French bread

» **Causa** Mashed-potato terrines stuffed with seafood, vegetables or chicken

» **Criollo cooking** A blend of Spanish, Andean, Chinese and African influences

» **Cuy al horno** Roasted guinea pig

» **Lomo saltado** Steak stir-fried with onions, tomatoes and potatoes, served with rice

» **Novoandina** Haute cuisine devised with traditional Andean ingredients

» **Rocoto relleno** Whole pepper stuffed with ground meat

» **Pisco sour** Peru's national drink is a tart grape brandy mixed with lime, sugar, egg white and bitters

AT A GLANCE

» **Currency** Nuevo sol (S)

» **Languages** Spanish, Quechua, Aymara

» **Money** ATMs widely available, except in small villages

» **Visas** Generally not needed for tourism (see p913)

» **Time** GMT minus five hours

Fast Facts

» **Area** 1,285,220 sq km

» **Population** 29.5 million

» **Capital** Lima

» **Emergency** ☎105

» **Country code** ☎51

Exchange Rates

Australia	A$1	S2.57
Canada	C$1	S2.72
Euro zone	€1	S4.27
New Zealand	NZ$1	S2.13
UK	UK£1	S4.64
USA	US$1	S2.90

Set Your Budget

» **Budget hotel room** S85

» **Set lunch** S9

» **Pisco sour** S8

» **Eight-hour bus ride** S34-98

Resources

» **Peru Official Tourism Website** (www.peru.info)

» **Living In Peru** (www.livinginperu.com)

» **Peru Links** (www.perulinks.com)

» **South American Explorers** (www.saexplorers.org)

Peru Highlights

1 Trek a breathless rite of passage to awe-inspiring ancient Inca ruins hidden in cloud forest at **Machu Picchu** (p857)

2 Pound colonial Andean cobblestone streets of **Cuzco** (p841), take in historical museums and trek humbling Inca hillsides

3 Explore the historical city of **Arequipa** (p826), surrounded by imposing volcanoes and sunken canyons

4 Tackle **Huaraz** and the **Cordilleras Blanca and Huayhuash** (p879), one of South America's most spectacular mountain ranges

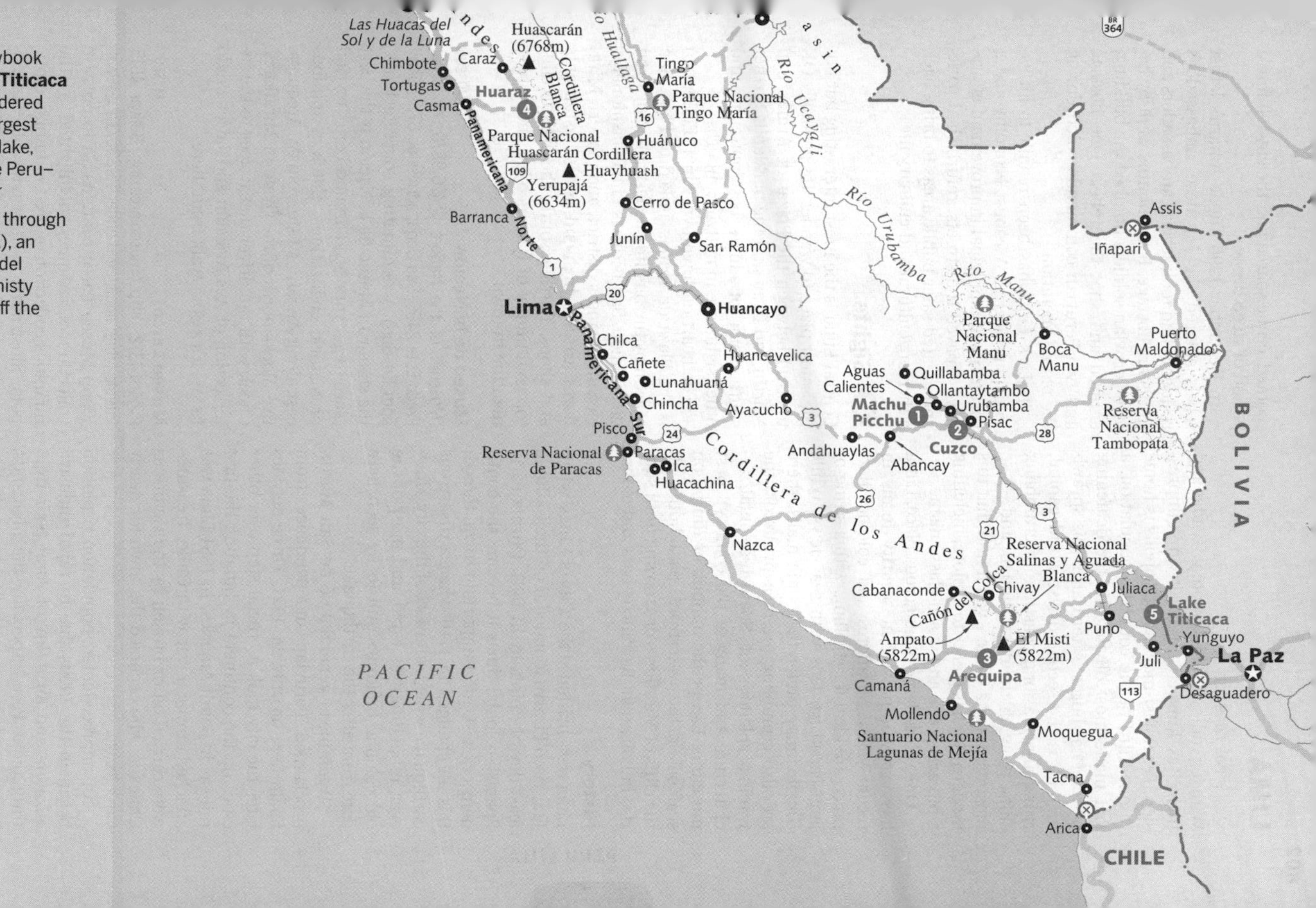

5 Visit storybook isles on **Lake Titicaca** (p835), considered the world's largest high-altitude lake, straddling the Peru–Bolivia border

6 Scramble through **Kuélap** (p891), an immense citadel shrouded in misty cloud forest off the beaten track

LIMA

☎01 / POP 7,606,000

With fog rolling over its colonial facades and high rises, Lima creates a gritty first impression. Peru's fast-moving metropolis is home to one-third of the country's population, a fact made most obvious by the deafening blare of car horns. After Cairo, this sprawling city is the second-driest world capital, rising above a long coastline of crumbling cliffs. Blow off the dust, though, and – like most who stay a while – you'll find that this modern city has plenty to explore, including a hip arts scene and world-class cuisine.

Once considered a dangerous place, Lima has vastly improved in security terms in recent years. Miraflores and colonial Barranco are ideal for strolling, with a string of landscaped gardens with sea views. While *limeños* may prefer their chic malls, there are also crumbling pre-Inca pyramids, the waning splendor of Spanish-colonial architecture and many of the country's best museums. Escape the hubbub by dining on seafood on the waterfront, paragliding off the cliffs of Miraflores or grooving until sunrise in bohemian Barranco's bars and clubs.

History

Lima was christened the 'City of Kings' when Francisco Pizarro founded it on the Catholic feast day of Epiphany in 1535. During early Spanish-colonial times it became the continent's richest, most important town, though this all changed in 1746 when a disastrous earthquake wiped out most of the city. However, rebuilding was rapid, and most of the old colonial buildings still to be seen here date from after the earthquake.

Argentinean general José de San Martín proclaimed Peruvian independence from Spain here on July 28, 1821. Three decades later the city took a crucial step over other cities on the continent by building the first railway in South America. In 1881 Lima was attacked during a war with Chile. Treasures were carried off or broken by the victorious Chileans, who occupied the town for nearly three years.

An unprecedented population explosion began in the 1920s due to rapid industrialization and an influx of rural poor from throughout Peru, especially the highlands. The migration was particularly intense during the 1980s, when armed conflicts in the Andes displaced many. Shantytowns mushroomed, crime soared and the city fell into a period of steep decay.

In December 1996 Túpac Amaru's leftist rebels entered the Japanese ambassador's residence and took several ambassadors and ministers hostage. Four months went by before Peruvian soldiers bombed the building, entered and shot the rebels. One hostage and two Peruvian commandos died during the rescue operation.

Today's Lima has been rebuilt to an astonishing degree. A robust economy and a vast array of municipal improvement efforts have repaved the streets, refurbished parks and created safer public areas to bring back a thriving cultural and culinary life.

Sights

Central Lima is the most interesting but not the safest place to wander. It's generally OK to stroll between the Plazas de Armas, San Martín and Grau and the parklands further south. Some of Lima's best museums and other sights are in outlying suburbs.

The heart of downtown Lima (El Centro) is the Plaza de Armas, linked to Plaza San Martín by the bustling pedestrian mall Jirón de la Unión. San Isidro is Lima's fashionably elegant business district, and modern Miraflores features high-end hotels, restaurants and shops. Further south, the artistic clifftop community of Barranco has the hottest nightlife in town.

Museo de la Nación MUSEUM

(Museum of the Nation; ☎476-9878; Av Javier Prado Este 2466, San Borja; admission S7; ⏱9am-6pm Tue-Sun) A dominating concrete block, the state-run Museo de la Nación is the best place to get your head around Peru's myriad prehistoric civilizations. Catch a minibus east along Angamos Este from Av Arequipa, five blocks north of the Óvalo in Miraflores. Check with the driver that it goes to the intersection of Avs Aviación and Javier Prado Este – it's a 50m walk from there.

Museo Larco MUSEUM

(☎461-1312; http://museolarco.org; Bolívar 1515, Pueblo Libre; adult/child under 15 S30/15; ⏱9am-10pm) Museo Larco contains an impressive collection of ceramics, highlighted by the infamous collection of pre-Columbian erotic pots, illustrating with remarkable explicitness the sexual practices of ancient Peruvian men, women, animals and skeletons in all combinations of the above. Catch a minibus

Metropolitan Lima

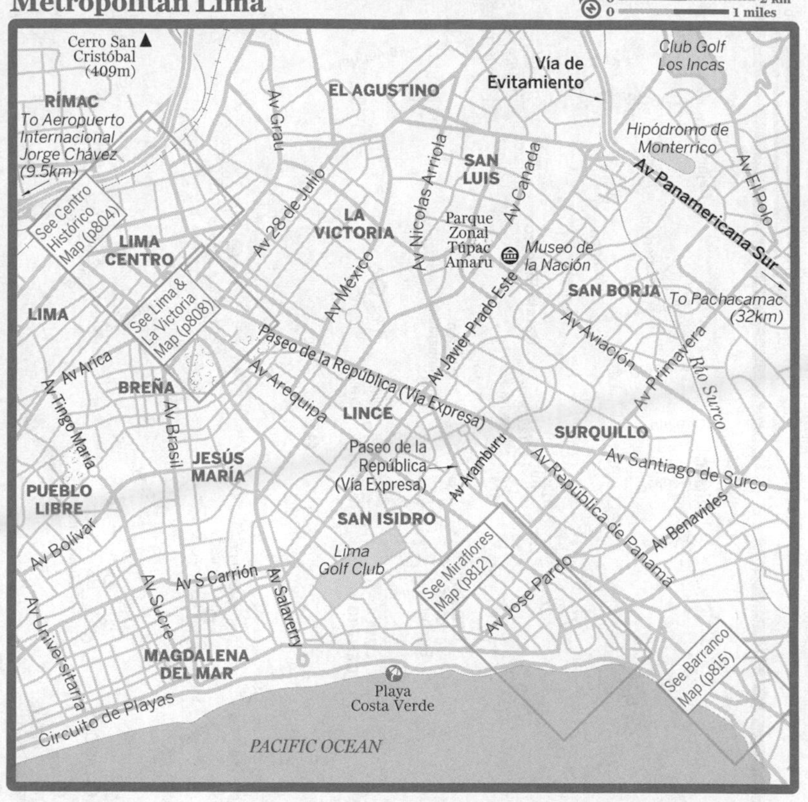

marked 'Todo Bolívar' from Av Arequipa in Miraflores to the 15th block of Av Bolívar.

Museo de Arte de Lima MUSEUM
(Map p808; ☎204-0000; www.mali.pe; Paseo Colón 125; adult/child S12/4; ⏲10am-5pm, closed Wed) Known locally as MALI, Lima's principal fine-art museum is housed in a striking beaux arts building that was recently renovated. Subjects span from pre-Columbian to contemporary art; there are also guided visits to special exhibits. On Sunday, entry is just S1.

Museo de la Cultura Peruana MUSEUM
(Museum of Peruvian Culture; Map p804; ☎423-5892; http://museodelacultura.perucultural.org.pe; Alfonso Ugarte 650; admission S3.60; ⏲10am-5pm Tue-Fri, to 2pm Sat) About half a dozen blocks west of the Plaza San Martín, on a traffic-choked thoroughfare, resides the Museo de la Cultura Peruana, a repository of Peruvian folk art.

FREE **Museo de la Inquisición** MUSEUM
(Map p804; ☎311-7777, ext 5160; www.congreso.gob.pe/museo.htm; Jirón Junín 548; ⏲9am-5pm) In the building used by the Spanish Inquisition from 1570 to 1820, with free multilingual tours. Visitors can explore the basement where prisoners were tortured, and there's a ghoulish waxwork exhibit of life-size unfortunates on the rack or having their feet roasted.

La Catedral de Lima CHURCH
(Map p804; ☎427-9647; museum admission S10; ⏲9am-5pm Mon-Fri, 10am-1pm Sat) Originally built in 1555, the church has been destroyed by earthquakes and reconstructed several times, most recently in 1746. Look for the coffin of Francisco Pizarro in the mosaic-covered chapel to the right of the main door. A debate over the authenticity of his remains raged for years after a mysterious body with multiple stab wounds and a severed head were unearthed in the crypt in the

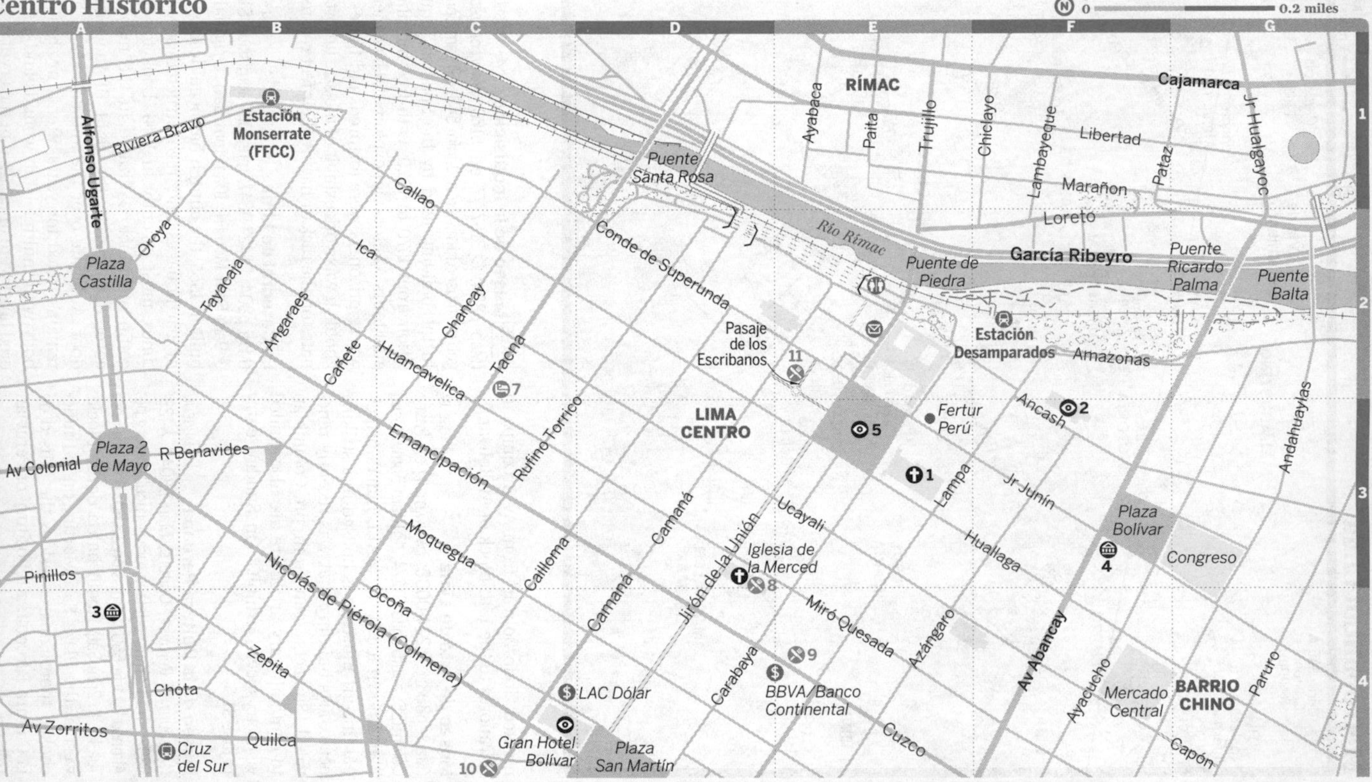
Centro Histórico
0
400 m
0
0.2 miles
N
A
B
C
D
E
F
G
1
2
3
4
RÍMAC
LIMA CENTRO
BARRIO CHINO
Río Rímac
Cajamarca
Jr Hualgayoc
Ayabaca
Paita
Trujillo
Chiclayo
Lambayeque
Libertad
Pataz
Marañon
Loreto
García Ribeyro
Puente Santa Rosa
Puente de Piedra
Puente Ricardo Palma
Puente Balta
Estación Monserrate (FFCC)
Riviera Bravo
Alfonso Ugarte
Plaza Castilla
Oroya
Tayacaja
Angaraes
Cañete
Callao
Ica
Chancay
Huancavelica
Tacna
Conde de Superunda
Pasaje de los Escribanos
Estación Desamparados
Amazonas
Andahuaylas
Ancash
Fertur Perú
Lampa
Jr Junín
Huallaga
Plaza Bolívar
Congreso
Plaza 2 de Mayo
R Benavides
Av Colonial
Emancipación
Rufino Torrico
Moquegua
Cailloma
Camaná
Ucayali
Jirón de la Unión
Iglesia de la Merced
Pinillos
Ocoña
Nicolás de Piérola (Colmena)
Miró Quesada
Azángaro
Av Abancay
Ayacucho
Mercado Central
Paruro
Zepita
Chota
Carabaya
BBVA/Banco Continental
LAC Dólar
Gran Hotel Bolívar
Plaza San Martín
Cuzco
Capón
Av Zorritos
Quilca
Cruz del Sur
1
2
3
4
5
7
8
9
10
11

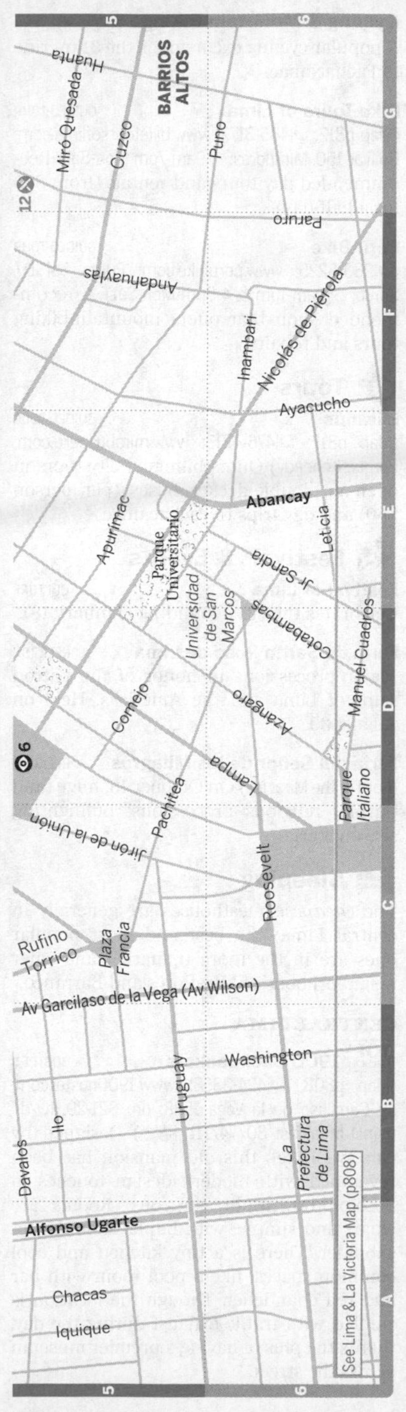

Centro Histórico

Sights

1 La Catedral de Lima E3
2 Monasterio de San Francisco F3
3 Museo de la Cultura Peruana A4
4 Museo de la Inquisición F3
5 Plaza de Armas E3
6 Plaza San Martín D5

Sleeping

7 Pensión Ibarra C2

Eating

8 La Merced D3
9 Metro E4
10 Queirolo C4
11 Tanta E2
12 Wa Lok G5

late 1970s. After a battery of tests, scientists concluded that the remains previously on display were of an unknown church official, and that the body from the crypt was indeed Pizarro's.

Monasterio de San Francisco MONASTERY
(Map p804; ☎426-7377; www.museocatacumbas.com; cnr Lampa & Ancash; adult/child under 15 S7/1; ⏲9:30am-5:30pm) The monastery is famous for its catacombs and remarkable library with thousands of antique texts, some dating back to the Spanish Conquest. The church is one of the best preserved of Lima's early colonial churches, largely restored to its original baroque style with Moorish influence. The underground catacombs are the site of an estimated 70,000 burials, with unnerving bone-filled crypts.

Huaca Huallamarca RUINS
(☎222-4124; Nicolás de Rivera 201, San Isidro; adult/child S5.50/1; ⏲9am-5pm Tue-Sun) Walking up to the ceremonial platform of Huaca Huallamarca, a highly restored Maranga adobe pyramid built c AD 500, gives you a novel perspective over contemporary Lima. Take a taxi from Miraflores (S8).

Huaca Pucllana RUINS
(Map p812; ☎617-7138; cnr Borgoño & Tarapacá, Miraflores; admission S7; ⏲9am-4:30pm) More easily accessible is Huaca Pucllana, an adobe pyramid of the Lima culture from AD 400. A guided tour is included with admission. There's a tiny museum and an upscale restaurant with spectacularly romantic nighttime views over the ruins.

Plaza de Armas PLAZA

(Map p804) The oldest part of the Plaza de Armas (Plaza Mayor) is its central bronze fountain, erected in 1650. To the left of the cathedral, the exquisitely balconied **Archbishop's Palace** dates from around 1924. On the cathedral's northeastern flank, the **Palacio de Gobierno** is the home of Peru's president; the changing of the guard outside takes place at noon.

Plaza San Martín PLAZA

(Map p804) The early-20th-century Plaza San Martín is presided over by the aged **Gran Hotel Bolívar**. It's well worth a stop in the hotel's yesteryear bar for a sip or two of its famous *pisco sour* (cocktail made from grape brandy). Also on the plaza you can see a bronze statue of liberator General José de San Martín. But get closer and you'll spy the overlooked **statue of Madre Patria**. It was commissioned in Spain under instruction to give the good lady a crown of flames, but nobody thought to iron out the double meaning of the Spanish word for 'flame' *(llama),* and the hapless craftsmen duly placed a delightful little llama on her head.

Activities

Paragliding

Peru Fly PARAGLIDING

(Map p812; ☎993-086-795; www.perufly.com) Tandem flights (S150) take off from the beachfront cliffs in Miraflores between noon and 6pm. Make a reservation in advance, since there's no office.

Swimming & Surfing

Limeños hit the beaches in droves during the coastal summer months of January to March, despite publicized warnings of pollution. Don't leave anything unattended for a second.

The nearby surfing hot spots **Punta Hermosa** and **San Bartolo** have hostels near the beach. **Punta Rocas** is for experienced surfers, and has one basic hostel for crashing. You'll have to buy or rent boards in Lima, though, and hire a taxi to transport them.

To get to the southern beaches, take a 'San Bartolo' bus from the Puente Primavera (taxi to bridge from Miraflores S6). Get off where you want and hike down to the beaches, which are mostly 1km or 2km from the Carr Panamericana.

Cycling & Mountain Biking

A popular cycling excursion is the 31km ride to Pachacamac.

Bike Tours of Lima GUIDED TOUR

(Map p812; ☎445-3172; www.biketoursoflima.com; Bolívar 150, Miraflores; ⊙9am-7pm Mon-Sat) Recommended day tours and rentals (from S30 for a half-day).

Perú Bike GUIDED TOUR

(☎260-8225; www.perubike.com; Punta Sal D7, Surco; ⊙9am-1pm & 4-8pm Mon-Sat) A recommended shop that offers mountain-biking tours and repairs.

Tours

Mirabús GUIDED TOUR

(Map p812; ☎476-4213; www.mirabusperu.com; Parque Kennedy) Offers bilingual city tours in open-air double-decker buses (per person S60) and day trips to Pachacamac.

Festivals & Events

Festival of Lima CULTURE

Celebrates the city's founding (January 18).

Feria de Santa Rosa de Lima RELIGION

Major processions in honor of the patron saint of Lima and the Americas. Held on August 30.

Feria del Señor de los Milagros RELIGION

(Lord of the Miracles) On October 18, huge (and purple) religious processions; bullfighting season starts.

Sleeping

The *cheapest* guesthouses are generally in central Lima; the best and most popular ones are in the more upmarket and safer neighborhoods of Miraflores and Barranco.

CENTRAL LIMA

TOP CHOICE **1900 Backpackers** HOSTEL $

(Map p808; ☎424-3358; www.1900hostel.com; Av Garcilaso de la Vega 1588; dm S21-29, tw/d/tr incl breakfast 80/74/111; @🛜) Designed by Gustave Eiffel, this old mansion has been revamped with modern design touches to become downright gorgeous. Rooms are smart and simple, with bunks shoulder-to-shoulder. There is a tiny kitchen and cool common spaces, like a pool room with bar and red chandelier. Though the location is riddled with traffic exhaust during the day, there's the plus of having a premier museum across the street.

Pensión Ibarra GUESTHOUSE $

(Map p804; ☎427-8603; pension ibarra@gmail.com; No 152, Tacna 359, 14th fl; s/d without bathroom from S25/35) Inside a scruffy concrete apartment block, the helpful Ibarra sisters keep seven basic guest rooms that are clean and stocked with firm beds. There is a shared kitchen and laundry service.

Hostal Iquique HOTEL $

(Map p808; ☎433-4724; www.hostaliquique.com; Iquique 758; s/d without bathroom S38/63, s/d/tr incl breakfast S55/70/82; @) A little out-of-the-way budget gem that's clean, safe, friendly and easy on the eyes with its lovely tiled archways. There is a rooftop terrace, kitchen facilities and cable TV.

La Posada del Parque HOTEL $$

(Map p808; ☎99-945-4260, 433-2412; www.incacountry.com; Parque Hernán Velarde 60; s/d/tr incl breakfast S96/127/164; @ wi-fi) A graceful Spanish colonial building on a gorgeous residential street convenient to both Centro and Miraflores. It's run by the very chatty Mónica and her daughter. All rooms have cable TV, and luggage storage is available.

MIRAFLORES

The area around Parque Kennedy is gringo ground zero.

TOP CHOICE **Backpacker's Family House** HOSTEL $

(Map p812; ☎447-4572; www.backpackersfamilyhouse.com; Juan Moore 304; dm/d incl breakfast S27/81; @ wi-fi) This refreshingly designed hostel is in a small brick home with parquet floors and graffiti murals. It's vibrant, super-clean and uncluttered, with games like foosball and ping-pong and an attentive owner.

Hostal El Patio GUESTHOUSE $$

(Map p812; ☎444-2107; www.hostalelpatio.net; Ernesto Diez Canseco 341A; s/d incl breakfast S126/156, s/d superior S156/186; @ wi-fi) This quaint inn is an urban oasis boasting a cheery English-speaking owner who takes her role as guesthouse hostess seriously. The sunny courtyard, fountain and trailing plants transcend solitude, and there are several terraces for chillin'. Check the website for special offers.

Inka Frog HOTEL $$

(Map p812; ☎445-8979; www.inkafrog.com; Iglesias 271; s/d incl breakfast S103/127; @ wi-fi) As budget

WORTH A TRIP

PACHACAMAC

Although it was an important Inca site and a major city when the Spanish arrived, **Pachacamac** (☎430-0168; http://pachacamac.perucultural.org.pe; admission S6; ⏰9am-5pm Mon-Fri) had been a ceremonial center for 1000 years before the expansion of the Inca empire. This sprawling archaeological complex is about 30km southeast of the city center.

The name Pachacamac, translated as 'he who animated the world' or 'he who created land and time,' comes from the powerful Wari god, whose wooden two-faced image can be seen in the on-site museum. The main temple at the site was dedicated to this deity and held a famous oracle. Pilgrims traveled to the center from great distances, and its cemetery was considered sacrosanct.

Most of the buildings are now little more than piles of rubble that dot the desert landscape, but some of the main temples have been excavated and their ramps and stepped sides revealed. In 2012 an untouched 80-person burial chamber was discovered, to much excitement. Hidden under newer burials, a 60ft oval chamber contained mummies wrapped in textiles and buried with valuables, offerings, and even dogs and guinea pigs. Investigators think the tomb may contain pilgrims who were drawn to the site to seek cures for serious illnesses.

Guided tours from Lima run around S115 per person. Minibuses signed 'Pachacamac' leave from the corner of Ayacucho and Grau in central Lima (S2, 45 minutes). From Miraflores, take a taxi to the intersection of Angamos and the Panamericana, also known as the Puente Primavera, then take the bus signed 'Pachacamac/Lurín' (S1 to S2, 30 minutes). Tell the driver to let you off near the *ruinas* or you'll end up at Pachacamac village, 1km beyond the entrance.

Lima & La Victoria

See Centro Histórico Map (p804)

Lima & La Victoria

Sights
1 Museo de Arte de Lima C2

Sleeping
2 1900 Backpackers B2
3 Hostal Iquique A1
4 La Posada del Parque C3

Eating
5 Cevichería la Choza Nautica A1

Entertainment
6 Circuito Mágico del Agua D4
7 Estadio Nacional C3
8 Las Brisas del Titicaca A2

Transport
Civa .... (see 11)
9 Móvil Tours D3
10 Ormeño D1
11 Rutas de América C2
12 Soyuz/PerúBus D1

lodgings go, this is one of Lima's best. Subdued and friendly, it features ample and spotless modern rooms with fans and flat-screen TVs, some on a cute roof patio. Enjoy the complimentary coffee hour on plush sofas. Staff is helpful and the street is refreshingly quiet.

Ekeko Hostel HOSTEL $
(Map p812; ☎635-5031; Garcia Calderon 274; dm/s/d incl breakfast S27/42/85; @📶) Tucked into a comfortable middle-class neighborhood, this well-run hostel is a find. A spacious home with a huge kitchen and oversized breakfast table, it also features nonstandard

amenities like hairdryers and a Japanese-speaking host. Guests will enjoy the nice backyard and impeccable service.

Hitchhikers HOSTEL $
(Map p812; ☎242-3008; www.hhikersperu.com; Bolognesi 400; dm/s/d without bathroom S28/64/70, s/d incl breakfast S70/84; @📶) Occupying an enormous century-old *casona* (mansion), this longtime hostel has a wide array of rooms. Secure and sleeper-friendly, it includes a lounge with cable TV and a DVD library, while a (bare) outdoor patio has barbecue facilities and a ping-pong table. Overall, a good choice.

Flying Dog HOSTEL $
(Map p812; ☎444-5753; www.flyingdogperu.com; Lima 457; dm S30, d with/without bathroom S90/66; @📶) Of Flying Dog's four Lima hostels, this is the newest and the best, featuring a lovely outdoor garden bar and 3rd-floor hang room with expansive views over Parque Kennedy. Two kitchens make for a shorter line to fry up your burgers and the included breakfast is taken at the terrace restaurants across the park.

BARRANCO

TOP CHOICE **3B Barranco B&B** B&B $$
(☎247-6915; www.3bhostal.com; Centenario 130; s/d incl breakfast S146/175; @📶) Cool, clean and modern, this new service-oriented boutique hotel is poised to be a traveler favorite. A common area charged with Warholesque pastiche art leads to 16 minimalist rooms with plush burlap-colored bed covers, polished-concrete vanities and windows opening on lightboxes of tended gremenery. For the price it's a great value.

Backpackers Inn HOSTEL $
(☎247-1326; www.barrancobackpackersinn.com; Mariscal Castilla 260; dm/tw incl breakfast S$27/92) A standout option, this British-run backpacker hangout is housed in a renovated mansion on a quiet street with 24-hour security. Dorms are ample; some have ocean views. There's a kitchen, help with trips and tours, a TV lounge and a trail leading to the beach.

Aquisito B&B GUESTHOUSE $$
(☎247-0712; www.aquisito.com.pe; Centenario 114; s incl breakfast 65-80, d incl breakfast 95-110; @📶) In a convenient location, this well-appointed guesthouse offers single travelers a hotel-quality room without being shaken down for the price of a double.

Point Lodge HOSTEL $
(Map p814; ☎247-7997; www.thepointhostels.com; Malecón Junín 300; dm S27-35, d with shared bathroom S70; @📶) Reminiscent of a well-worn fraternity house, this party villa has ultra-basic rooms but with all the toys backpackers crave: cable TV, DVDs, and ping-pong and pool tables. There's a kitchen and a hammock-strewn garden.

Eating

Lima's dining scene is among the best on the continent. Miraflores houses most of the gourmand haunts. *Ceviche* (raw seafood marinated in lime juice, onions and spices) is sublime here.

CENTRAL LIMA

Cheap lunch *menús* (set meals) are offered in local restaurants. Barrio Chino (Chinatown), southeast of the Plaza de Armas, is blessed with Asian eateries.

For self-catering, there's **Metro** (Map p804; Cuzco 255; ⏲9am-10pm).

Cevichería la Choza Nautica CEVICHE $$
(Map p808; ☎423-8087; www.lachozanautica.com.pe; Breña 204; ceviches S20-36, mains S19-39; ⏲8am-11pm Mon-Sat, 8am-9pm Sun) The bright spot in a dingy area, this popular *cevichería*, tended by bow-tied waiters, offers more than a dozen types of delicious *ceviches* and *tiraditos* (Japanese-style *ceviche*, without onions). A second space is across the street.

Wa Lok CHINESE $$
(Map p804; ☎427-2750, 447-1329; Paruro 878; mains S10-80; ⏲9am-11pm Mon-Sat, to 10pm Sun) Amongst Chinatown's best, serving light and savory seafood fried rice and sizzling meats that come on steaming platters. Dishes can serve two.

La Merced PERUVIAN $
(Map p804; ☎428-2431; Miró Quesada 158; menú S10-18; ⏲9am-8pm Mon-Sat) A madhouse at lunch, with traditional dishes and an intricately carved wooden ceiling.

Queirolo PERUVIAN $
(Map p804; ☎425-0421; Camaná 900; mains S10-33; ⏲9:30am-1am Mon-Sat) Lined with wine bottles, Queirolo kills with cheap *menús* (S9) featuring staples such as *papa rellena* (stuffed potatoes). Also popular for mellow evening gatherings.

Tanta CAFE $$
(Map p804; ☎428-3115; Pasaje de los Escribanos 142, Central Lima; mains S21-46; ⏲9am-10pm

Mon-Sat, to 6pm Sun) Chef Gastón Acurio's shady sidewalk cafe is a casual spot for fat empanadas, tasty sandwiches and one of Lima's best breakfasts, *huevos de Gastón* (eggs scrambled with sausage and *yuca* (manioc tuber).

MIRAFLORES

By far the most varied neighborhood for eating, with open-air cafes and pizzerias around Parque Kennedy. For self-caterers, there's **Vivanda** (Map p812; Benavides 487; ⏲24hr). Another branch is located on Av José Pardo.

El Punto Azul CEVICHE $$
(Map p812; ☎445-8078; San Martín 595; mains S22-30; ⏲noon-5pm) An excellent value, this pleasant family eatery dishes up super-fresh *ceviches* and *tiraditos,* as well gargantuan rice dishes. On weekends show up before 1pm if you want a table.

El Enano SANDWICHES $
(Map p812; Chiclayo 699; sandwiches S7-10; ⏲6am-3am) Patrons grab open-air stools for tasty roasted chicken, ham and *chicharrón* (fried pork rib) sandwiches on French-bread with marinated onions and chillies. Fresh juices come in oversized glass jars.

El Rincón del Bigote CEVICHE $$
(Map p812; José Galvez 529; S21-28; ⏲noon-4pm Tue-Sun) Bare bones and wildly popular. Pair *almejas in su concha* (marinated clams) with a side of crisp *yuca* fries and a bottle of cold pilsner and you're in heaven.

DON'T MISS

CENTRAL

The toast of Lima, **Central** (Map p812; ☎242-8515; centralrestaurante.com.pe; Santa Isabel 376; mains S52-88; ⏲1-3:30pm & 8-11:30pm Mon-Fri, 8-11:30pm Sat) awes many a critic with its seductive creations. Chef Virgilio Martinez spent a decade in the top kitchens of Europe and Asia, but coming home meant reinventing local traditions. Seafood (such as the charred-octopus starter) is a star, but Peruvian classics like suckling pig dazzle, reinvented with pears, mustard and *tomate de árbol*. A menu featuring sustainable fish and the produce of a rooftop herb garden enhances the ultra-fresh appeal.

El Pan de la Chola CAFE $
(Av La Mar 918; mains S8-15; ⏲8am-8pm Tue-Sat, 9am-1pm Sun) Bakes real wholegrain bread, served with organic coffee from the Peruvian Amazon, Greek yogurt and sweets.

Quattro D ICE CREAM $
(Map p812; ☎445-4228; Av Angamos Oeste 408; mains S16-32, ice cream from S7; ⏲6:30am-11:45pm Mon-Thu, 6:30am-12:30am Fri & Sat, 7-11am Sun) This is where you will find the city's best gelato.

La Pascana de Madre Natura CAFE $
(Map p812; Chiclayo 815; mains S5-16; 🖉) Herbivore Eden, serving up salads, pizza and other treats in a Zen courtyard. Veggie burgers are world-class, with the carrot cake a close second.

Restaurant Huaca Pucllana PERUVIAN $$
(Map p812; ☎445-4042; www.resthuacapucllana.com; Gral Borgoño cuadra 8; mains S18-60; ⏲12:30pm-midnight Mon-Sat, to 4pm Sun) Overlooking the illuminated ruins at Huaca Pucllana, this sophisticated restaurant serves contemporary Peruvian dishes from grilled *cuy* (guinea pig) to seafood chowders, along with a smattering of Italian-fusion specialties. Portions are large.

Rincón Chami PERUVIAN $
(Map p812; ☎444-4511; Esperanza 154; mains S6-27; ⏲8am-8:30pm Mon-Sat, noon-5pm Sun) A classic 40-year-old dining hall renowned for skillfully prepared dishes such as *pastel de choclo* (maize casserole) as well as *milanesa* (breaded steaks) as big as a platter.

BARRANCO

A charming little district for a bite to eat, especially along the passageway below the Puente de los Suspiros.

TOP CHOICE **Burrito Bar** MEXICAN $
(Map p814; ☎987-352-120; Grau 113; mains S12-15; ⏲noon-11pm Tue-Sat, to 5pm Sun) Try the Baja-style fish tacos served with fresh salsa in homemade flour tortillas. The fresh mint limeade may be the best in the city, but you'll probably want one of the Sierra Andina microbrews. For dessert, the chocolate tamale (chocolate in corn dough, wrapped in jungle leaves) is a no-brainer.

Cafe Bisetti CAFE $
(☎713-9565; Av Pedro de Osma 116; coffee S8-16; ⏲8am-9pm Mon-Fri, 10am-11pm Sat, 3-9pm Sun) A roasting house with the finest lattes in town,

well matched with fresh pastries or bitter chocolate pie.

La Canta Rana CEVICHE $$
(Map p814; ☎247-7274; Génova 101; mains S25-38; ⏰8am-11pm Tue-Sat) A great *cevichería,* serving all manner of seafood. The tables are as packed as the walls.

Drinking

Lima overflows with bars, from San Isidro's pricey havens for the urbane elite to Barranco's cheap and cheerful watering holes. Plaza de Armas downtown and Miraflores have several streetfront cafes. The latter is also home to the low-rent pedestrianized San Ramón (aka Calle Pizza), where touristy pizzerias and Latin-themed clubs fight for real estate – your best bet for a cheap pub crawl (trendier options abound around the corner on Francisco de Paula Camino). In Barranco you can bounce among the tight-knit nightclubs near Parque Municipal and the pedestrianized Calle Carrión all night long.

In Central Lima drop in at the Gran Hotel Bolívar to quaff Peru's national cocktail, the pisco sour, in a traditional setting. Barranco is thronged with revelers on Friday and Saturday nights.

TOP CHOICE **Ayahuasca** COCKTAIL BAR
(Map p814; ☎247-6751; www.ayahuascabar.com; San Martín 130, Barranco; ⏰8pm-close, closed Sun) This trendsetting bar is one of Lima's most atmospheric, with hyperreal decor and sexy *limenõs* lounging around. There's a long list of contemporary pisco cocktails, like the tasty Ayahuasca sour made with jungle fruit and coca leaves.

Santos LOUNGE
(Map p814; ☎247-4609; Jirón Zapita 203, Barranco; ⏰5pm-1am Mon-Thu, 5pm-3am Fri-Sat; 📶) In a creaky old mansion, this funky and congenial bar has multiple rooms and a balcony with sea views (also perfect for people watching). Start here with tapas and a daily two-for-one that goes until 9pm.

El Dragón BAR
(Map p814; ☎477-5420; www.eldragon.com.pe; Nicolas de Pierola 168, Barranco; cover up to S20; ⏰Thu-Sat) Small but dark and sexy, this lounge boasts a hip ethos that maneuvers between resident DJs spinning a Latin cocktail of salsa and electronica to live jazz and surf guitar.

Wahio's BAR
(Map p814; ☎477-4110; Plaza Espinosa, Barranco; ⏰Thu-Sat) A large and lively bar with a fair share of dreadlocks and a classic soundtrack of reggae, ska and dub.

Bar Piselli BAR
(Map p814; ☎252-6750; Av 28 de Julio 297, Barranco; ⏰10am-11pm Mon-Thu, to 3am Fri & Sat) This neighborhood bar, reminiscent of old Buenos Aires, beats all for ambience. There's live music on Thursdays, provoking boisterous sing-alongs of Peruvian classics.

Entertainment

Many top-end hotels downtown and in San Isidro and Miraflores have slot-machine casinos.

Circuito Mágico del Agua SHOW
(Map p808; Parque de la Reserva; admission S4; ⏰3-1:30pm Wed-Sun) This Bellagio-style fountain and laser show is Lima's best entertainment bang for the buck.

La Noche LIVE MUSIC
(Map p814; ☎247-1012; www.lanoche.com.pe; Av Bolognesi 307, Barranco) Get ready to groove! This well-known tri-level bar is *the* spot to see rock, punk and Latin music acts in Lima.

Gótica CLUB
(Map p812; ☎628-3033; www.gotica.com.pe; Malecón de la Reserva 610, LarcoMar, Miraflores; admission S40) A fashionable, high-energy dance spot with a churchy interior and a mix of DJs playing electronica, hip-hop and pop. It sometimes serves as a venue for live Latin dance bands.

Cocodrilo Verde LIVE MUSIC
(Map p812; ☎242-7583; Francisco de Paola 226; minimum tab S20; ⏰6:30pm-close Mon-Sat) With great bands that range from popular music to jazz and bossa nova, this hip lounge is good for a night out.

Sargento Pimienta CLUB
(Map p814; ☎247-3265; www.sargentopimienta.com; Bolognesi 755, Barranco; admission S20) A reliable night out, the barn-like 'Sergeant Pepper' hosts various theme nights and occasional live bands.

Las Brisas del Titicaca TRADITIONAL MUSIC
(Map p808; ☎715-6960; www.brisasdeltiticaca.com; Wakuski 168, Central Lima; admission from S25) The best *folklórica* show in Lima is at this *peña* (club with folk music) near Plaza Bolognesi downtown.

Miraflores

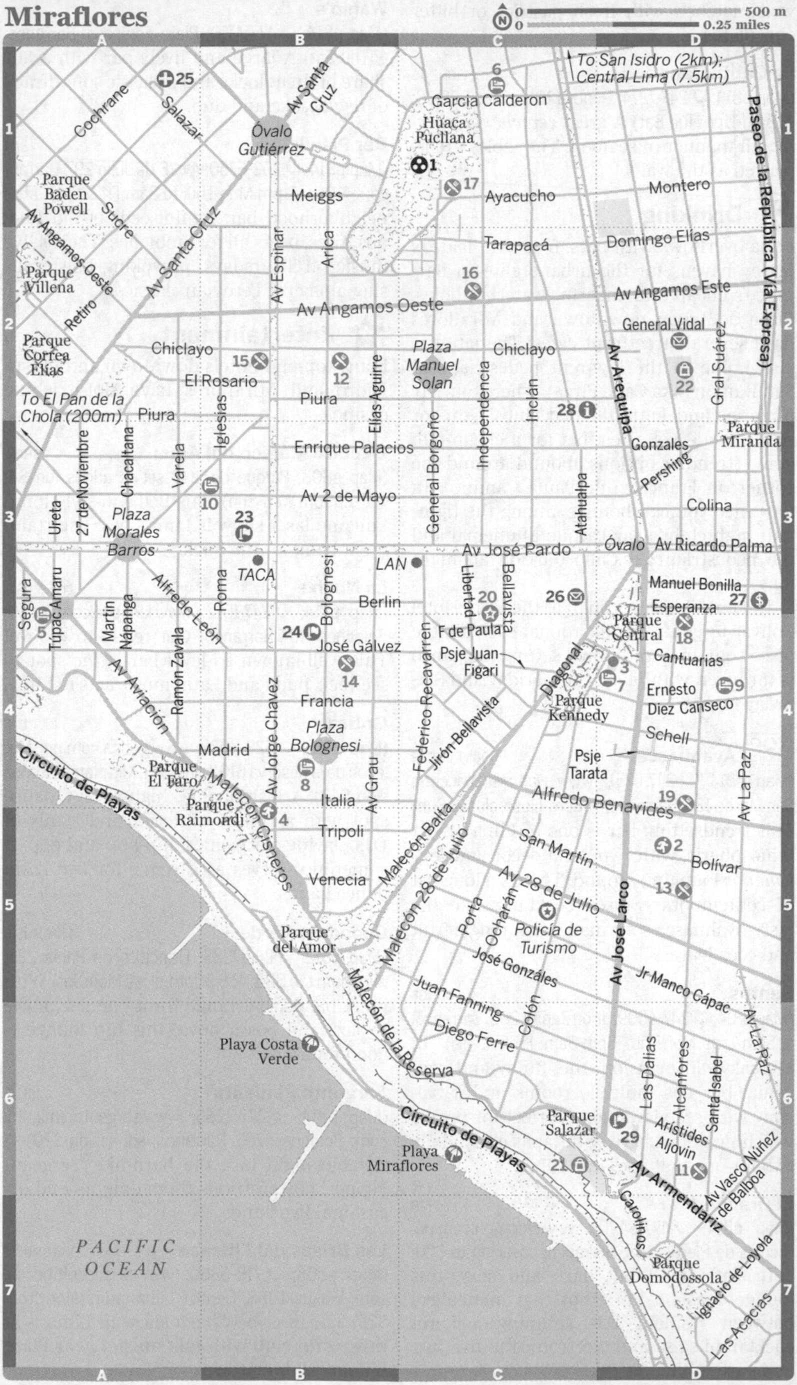

0 500 m
0 0.25 miles

To San Isidro (2km); Central Lima (7.5km)
Garcia Calderon
Huaca Pucllana
Cochrane
Salazar
Av Santa Cruz
Óvalo Gutiérrez
Parque Baden Powell
Sucre
Meiggs
Ayacucho
Montero
Paseo de la República (Vía Expresa)
Av Angamos Oeste
Parque Villena
Retiro
Av Espinar
Arica
Tarapacá
Domingo Elías
Av Angamos Este
General Vidal
Gral Suárez
Parque Correa Elías
Chiclayo
El Rosario
Plaza Manuel Solan
Av Arequipa
To El Pan de la Chola (200m)
Piura
Iglesias
Elías Aguirre
Independencia
Inclán
Parque Miranda
Gonzales
Pershing
27 de Noviembre
Chacaltana
Varela
Enrique Palacios
General Borgoño
Atahualpa
Colina
Ureta
Plaza Morales Barros
Av 2 de Mayo
Av José Pardo
Óvalo
Av Ricardo Palma
TACA
LAN
Manuel Bonilla
Segura
Túpac Amaru
Alfredo León
Martin Napanga
Roma
Bolognesi
Berlin
Libertad
Bellavista
Esperanza
Parque Central
Ramón Zavala
José Gálvez
F de Paula
Psje Juan Figari
Diagonal
Cantuarias
Av Aviación
Federico Recavarren
Parque Kennedy
Ernesto Diez Canseco
Francia
Jirón Bellavista
Schell
Av Jorge Chavez
Plaza Bolognesi
Madrid
Psje Tarata
Circuito de Playas
Parque El Faro
Malecón Cisneros
Av Grau
Italia
Alfredo Benavides
Av La Paz
Parque Raimondi
Tripoli
Malecón Balta
San Martín
Malecón 28 de Julio
Av 28 de Julio
Bolívar
Venecia
Porta
Ocharán
Policía de Turismo
Av José Larco
Parque del Amor
José Gonzáles
Jr Manco Cápac
Juan Fanning
Colón
Diego Ferre
Malecón de la Reserva
Playa Costa Verde
Las Dalias
Alcanfores
Santa Isabel
Parque Salazar
Arístides Aljovin
Playa Miraflores
Av Armendariz
Av Vasco Núñez de Balboa
Carolinos
PACIFIC OCEAN
Parque Domodossola
Ignacio de Loyola
Las Acacias

Miraflores

Sights
1 Huaca Pucllana C1

Activities, Courses & Tours
2 Bike Tours of Lima D5
3 Mirabús D4
4 Peru Fly B5

Sleeping
5 Backpacker's Family House A4
6 Ekeko Hostel C1
7 Flying Dog D4
8 Hitchhikers B4
9 Hostal El Patio D4
10 Inka Frog B3

Eating
11 Central D6
12 El Enano B2
13 El Punto Azul D5
14 El Rincón del Bigote B4
15 La Pascana de Madre Natura B2
16 Quattro D C2
17 Restaurant Huaca Pucllana C1
18 Rincón Chami D4
19 Vivanda D4

Entertainment
20 Cocodrilo Verde C3
Gótica .... (see 21)

Shopping
21 LarcoMar C6
22 Mercado Indio D2

Information
23 Brazilian Embassy B3
24 Canadian Embassy B4
25 Clínica Anglo-Americana A1
26 Federal Express C3
iPerú .... (see 21)
27 LAC Dólar D3
PeruRail .... (see 21)
28 South American Explorers C2
29 UK Embassy D6

Estadio Nacional STADIUM
(Map p808; Central Lima) *Fútbol* is the national obsession, and Peru's Estadio Nacional, off *cuadras* 7 to 9 of Paseo de la República, is the venue for the most important matches and other events. Teleticket (www.teleticket.com.pe) has listings and sales.

Shopping

Shopping malls include the underground **LarcoMar** (Map p812; Malecón de la Reserva 610), with a spectacular location built right into the oceanfront cliffs, selling high-end artisan crafts, electronics, photographic supplies, outdoor gear, books and music.

Mercado Indio MARKET
(Map p812; Av Petit Thouars 5245, Miraflores) The best place to find everything from pre-Columbian-style clay pottery to alpaca rugs to knock-offs of Cuzco School canvases. Prices vary; shop around.

Feria Artesanal MARKET
(Av de la Marina, Pueblo Libre) Crafts market.

Information

Dangers & Annoyances

Like any large Latin American city, Lima is a land of haves and have-nots, something that has made stories about crime here the stuff of legend. To some degree, the city's dangers have been overblown. The most common offense is theft and readers have reported regular muggings. You are unlikely to be physically hurt, but it is nonetheless best to keep a streetwise attitude.

Take extra care on the beaches, where violent attacks have happened. Bus terminals are in disadvantaged neighborhoods and notorious for theft, so buy your tickets in advance and take a taxi. It's also best to take a taxi from the airport.

Emergency

Ambulance (☎117)

Fire (☎116)

Police (☎105) Emergencies only.

Police Headquarters (☎460-1060; Moore 268, Magdalena del Mar; ⏲24hr)

Policía de Turismo (Poltur; ☎460-0844; Colón 246; ⏲24hr) Provides reports for insurance claims or traveler's check refunds; some English spoken.

Medical Services

The following clinics offer emergency services and some have English-speaking staff:

Clínica Anglo-Americana (Map p812; ☎616-8900; Salazar 350, San Isidro) Stocks yellow-fever and tetanus vaccines.

Clínica San Borja (☎475-4000; www.clinicasanborja.com.pe; Av Guardia Civil 337, San Borja) Another reputable clinic, with cardiology services.

Barranco

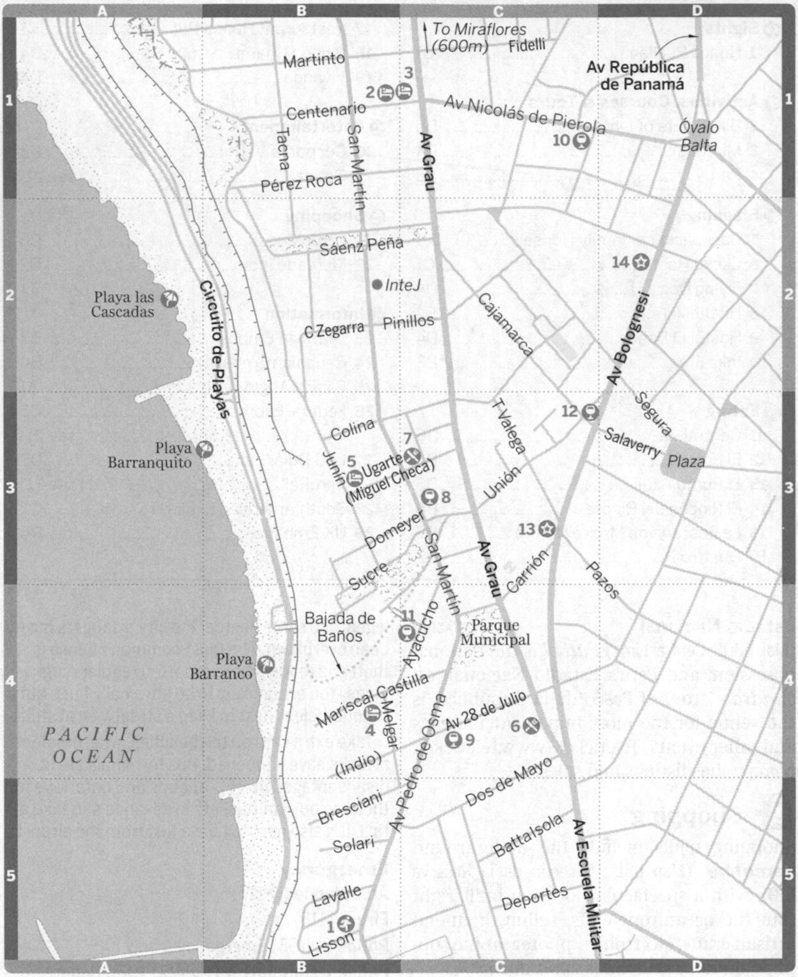

Barranco

Activities, Courses & Tours
1 Perú Bike B5

Sleeping
2 3B Barranco B&B B1
3 Aquisito B&B C1
4 Backpackers Inn B4
5 Point Lodge B3

Eating
6 Burrito Bar C4
7 La Canta Rana C3

Drinking
8 Ayahuasca C3
9 Bar Piselli C4
10 El Dragón C1
11 Santos C4
12 Wahio's C3

Entertainment
13 La Noche C3
14 Sargento Pimienta D2

Money

You'll find 24-hour ATMs throughout Lima. Other *casas de cambio* (foreign-exchange offices) are scattered about Camaná in central Lima and along Larco in Miraflores. Green-jacketed official money changers *(cambistas)* are all over Lima and safe to use, but get their official stamp on your bills to protect yourself against counterfeits.

BBVA/Banco Continental Central Lima (Cuzco 290); Miraflores (cnr Av José Larco & Tarata) Visa representative; with international ATMs.

Banco de Crédito del Perú (BCP; www.viabcp.com; ⌚9am-6:30pm Mon-Fri, 9:30am-1pm Sat)

LAC Dólar (⌚9:30am-6pm Mon-Fri, 9am-2pm Sat) Central Lima (☎428-8127; Camaná 779); Miraflores (Map p812; ☎242-4069; Av La Paz 211) A reliable exchange house; can deliver cash to your hotel in exchange for traveler's checks.

Post

Federal Express (FedEx; Map p812; ☎242-2280; www.fedex.com.pe; Pasaje Olaya 260, BSC Miraflores, Miraflores; ⌚9am-7pm Mon-Fri, 10am-3pm Sat)

Main Post Office (Pasaje Piura, central Lima; ⌚8am-9pm Mon-Sat) Poste restante mail can be collected here, though it's not 100% reliable. Bring ID.

Serpost (Av Petit Thouars 5201; ⌚8am-8:45pm Mon-Sat, 9am-1:30pm Sat, 9am-2pm Sun)

Tourist Information

iPerú Airport (☎574-8000; Aeropuerto Internacional Jorge Chávez); Miraflores (Map p812; ☎445-9400; LarcoMar; ⌚11am-1pm & 2-8pm); San Isidro (☎421-1627; Jorge Basadre 610; ⌚8:30am-5pm Mon-Fri) The main office dispenses maps and offers the services of the tourist-protection agency (Indecopi). In Miraflores, you'll find helpful booths on Parque Kennedy, LarcoMar and Huaca Pucllana, among others. Inside LarcoMar is the main office, handy on weekends.

PeruRail (Map p812; ☎241-5068; www.perurail.com; LarcoMar; ⌚11am-9:30pm) Get information and make bookings for Cuzco–Machu Picchu and Cuzco–Puno trains.

South American Explorers (SAE; Map p812; ☎445-3306; www.saexplorers.org; Piura 135, Miraflores; ⌚9:30am-5pm Mon, Tue, Thu & Fri, to 8pm Wed, to 1pm Sat) SAE is a member-supported, nonprofit organization that functions as an invaluable information center for travelers.

Getting There & Away

Air

Lima's Aeropuerto Internacional Jorge Chávez (p914) is in Callao. International airport taxes (payable in US dollars or nuevos soles, cash only) are US$31 but are now usually included in ticket prices; domestic flight taxes are always included.

Student airfares can be booked through the official ISIC office **InteJ** (☎247-3230; www.intej.org; San Martín 240, Barranco; ⌚9:30am-12:45pm & 2-5:45pm Mon-Fri, 9:30am-12:45pm Sat) or **Fertur Perú** (☎427-2426; www.ferturtravel.com; Jirón Junín 211, central Lima; ⌚9am-7pm Mon-Fri, to 2pm Sat), with a second office at Shell 485 in Miraflores.

Many international airlines have offices in Lima. Airlines offering domestic flights include the following:

LAN (☎213-8200; www.lan.com; Av José Pardo 513, Miraflores)

LC Peru (☎204-1313; www.lcperu.pe; Av Pablo Carriquirry 857, San Isidro)

Star Perú (☎705-9000; www.starperu.com; Espinar 331, Miraflores)

TACA (☎511-8222; Av José Pardo 811, Miraflores)

Bus

Lima has no central bus terminal. Each company runs its own office and station, many of which cluster around Av Javier Prado Este in La Victoria. Others are found in central Lima several blocks east of Plaza Grau, just north of Av Grau and south of Av 28 de Julio, on both sides of Paseo de la República. Make sure you verify which station your bus departs from when buying tickets. There are countless companies, so examine the quality of the buses before deciding.

Major companies include the following:

Cruz del Sur (www.cruzdelsur.com.pe) Central Lima (☎424-1003; www.cruzdelsur.com.pe; Quilca 531); La Victoria (☎225-3748; www.

GETTING INTO TOWN

From **Aeropuerto Internacional Jorge Chávez** (☎517-3100; www.lap.com.pe) take a taxi – S45, 30 minutes to one hour (rush hour) to Miraflores, Barranco or San Isidro, faster for downtown Lima. Many flights arrive in the wee hours, so be sure to have a hotel booked ahead. Or a *combi* (minibus) **'La S'** (per person S2-3) – with a giant 'S' pasted to the windshield – runs various routes to Miraflores and beyond. From the airport, these can be found heading south along Av Elmer Faucett. For the return trip, La S *combis* can be found traveling north along Av Petit Thouars and east along Av Angamos in Miraflores.

cruzdelsur.com.pe; Av Javier Prado Este 1109) The nicest and most reliable. The Central Lima branch is is a none-too-pleasant area; La Victoria is preferable.

Ormeño (www.grupo-ormeno.com.pe) Central Lima (Map p808; ☎472-5000; www.grupo-ormeno.com.pe; Carlos Zavala Loayza 177); La Victoria (☎472-1710; www.grupo-ormeno.com.pe; Av Javier Prado Este 1059) Quality of service varies wildly. Has extensive international service. The Central Lima branch is is a none-too-pleasant area; La Victoria is preferable.

Rutas de América (Map p808; ☎534-3195; www.rutasenbus.com; Av 28 de Julio 1145) Connects Lima with most continental capitals, including Bogotá, Buenos Aires, Caracas, La Paz, Quito, Rio de Janeiro and Santiago.

Civa (Map p808; ☎418-1111; www.civa.com.pe; Av 28 de Julio 1145) Also shares a ticket office with Cruz del Sur and Soyuz at Carlos Zavala Loayza and Montevideo.

Móvil Tours (Map p808; ☎716-8000; www.moviltours.com.pe; Paseo de la República 749) For Chachapoyas, Chiclayo, Huancayo, Huaraz and Tarapoto.

Soyuz/PerúBus (Map p808; ☎266-1515; www.perubus.com.pe; Carlos Zavala Loayza 221) Frequent buses to Cañete, Chincha, Ica and Nazca.

Tepsa (☎470-6666; www.tepsa.com.pe; Av Javier Prado Este 1091) Comfortable buses to Arequipa, Cajamarca, Chiclayo, Cuzco, Ica, Lambayeque, Máncora, Nazca, Piura, Tacna, Trujillo and Tumbes.

APPROXIMATE FARES

This table indicates approximate fares and durations for one-way travel from Lima with the top companies.

DESTINATION	COST* (S)	DURATION (HR)
Arequipa	101-143	15
Ayacucho	50-95	10
Cajamarca	80-130	16
Chiclayo	40-125	12-14
Cuzco	130-175	21
Huancayo	57-175	7
Huaraz	35-100	8
Ica	22-76	4½
Nazca	50-86	8
Piura	59-144	12-16
Puno	140-170	18-21
Tacna	50-144	18-22
Trujillo	25-100	8-9
Tumbes	132-165	19

** Prices are general estimates for normal/luxury buses.*

Train

Highland rail services to Huancayo leave from Lima's **Estación Desamparados** (☎263-1515; Ancash 203).

Getting Around

To/From the Airport

The airport (p914) is in the port city of Callao, 12km west of downtown.

Official taxis directly outside the terminal exit charge from S40 to S50 to the city center and Miraflores. Taxis in the lot charge S10 or so less, but it's notably less secure. Most hostels also offer airport pickup for slightly less. Alternatively, turn left outside the terminal, walk 100m to the pedestrian gate, turn right and walk 100m to the road outside the airport, where you can get an unofficial taxi for less, or a *combi* to Miraflores. Look for the 'Callao-Ate' minibus (spy the red 'S' or ask for it by its nickname, 'La S,' pronounced 'la e-se') for S2 to S3 (more for bulky luggage).

A safe and secure option is **Taxi Green** (☎484-4001; www.taxigreen.com.pe). Maddening traffic and road construction often lead to lengthy delays, so allow at least an hour for the ride to/from the airport.

Unfortunately, there is no central bus terminal in Lima. Each bus company runs its own offices and terminals, mostly in shady neighborhoods east of the city center – take a taxi.

Bus

El Metropolitano (www.metropolitano.com.pe), a new trans-Lima electric express bus system, is the fastest and most efficient way to get into the city center. Routes are few, though there are intentions to expand coverage to the northern part of the city. Ruta Troncal (S1.50) goes through Barranco, Miraflores and San Isidro to Plaza Grau in the center of Lima. Users must purchase a *tarjeta intelligente* card (S4.50), which can be credited for use.

Otherwise, minivans are organized by destination placards taped to the windshield. *Combis* (minibuses) are generally slow and crowded, but they're startlingly cheap: fares run from S1 to S3, depending on the length of your journey.

The most useful routes link central Lima with Miraflores along Av Arequipa or Paseo de la República. Minibuses along Garcilaso de la Vega (also called Av Wilson) and Av Arequipa are labeled 'Todo Arequipa' or 'Larco/Schell/Miraflores' when heading to Miraflores and, likewise, 'Todo Arequipa' and 'Wilson/Tacna' when leaving Miraflores for central Lima. Catch these buses along Av José Larco or Av Arequipa in Miraflores.

To get to Barranco, look for buses along Av Arequipa labeled 'Chorrillos/Huaylas/Metro' (some will also have signs that say 'Barranco'). You can also find these on the Diagonal, just west of Parque Kennedy, in Miraflores.

Taxi

Taxis don't have meters, so make sure you negotiate a price before getting in. As a (very) rough guide, a trip within Miraflores costs around S5 to S8. From Miraflores to central Lima is S10 to S15, to Barranco from S5 to S10, and to San Isidro from S6 to S12. You can haggle fares, though it's harder during rush hour. If there are two or more passengers, ask whether the fare is per person or for the car.

SOUTH COAST

Inspect the barren, foggy, bone-dry desert of Peru's southern coastline for the first time and you will inevitably wonder: how does anyone live here? Yet people don't just live here, they positively thrive – check out Ica's wine industry or Chincha's Afro-Peruvian culture if you want proof. What's more, they've been thriving for millennia. The perplexing Nazca Lines, a weird collection of giant geoglyphs etched into the desert, date from 400 to 650 AD, while intricate cloths unearthed on the Paracas peninsula were woven 1000 years before Pachacuti led the Incas out of Cuzco. Though Machu Picchu hogs most of the limelight in southern Peru, the south coast is pierced by a lesser 'gringo trail' whose obligatory stops include adventure nexus Lunahuaná, wildlife-obsessed Paracas, Nazca and the desert oasis of Huacachina.

Lunahuaná

☎056 / POP 3600

Almost 15km past the surfers' beach of Cerro Azul – Carr Panamericana (Pan-American Hwy) at Km 131 – the dusty market town of San Vincente de Cañete is the gateway to the sweet wine country of Lunahuaná. It's packed for the **harvest festival** in the second week of March, but on weekends throughout the year and daily in summer, *bodegas* (wineries) and artisanal *pisco* producers set up booths and the plaza fills with revelers getting sauced at outdoor cafe tables.

The town is also a major adventure hub. Whitewater rafting (river running) on the Río Cañete runs December to April, and rapids can reach Class IV. The town is packed with outfitters, but the safest and most experienced one is just by the river west of town: **Río Cañete Expediciones** (☎284-1271; www.riocanete.com) also runs **Camping San Jerónimo** (☎284-1271; Carretera Cañete–Lunahuaná, Km 33; sites per person S15).

Basic but dependable, **Hostal Los Andes** (☎284-1041; Los Andes; s/d/tr S40/50/70) is a three-storied yellow block with some 2nd-floor rooms offering peek-a-boo river views. There's hot water and cable TV, but no wi-fi. At several nearby seafood restaurants, the local specialty is crawfish.

From Cañete, where coastal buses stop on the Panamericana, catch a *combi* to Imperial (S1, 10 minutes), then another *combi* to Lunahuaná (S3.50 to S4, 45 minutes), nearly 40km away. Rent mountain and quad bikes near Lunahuaná's main plaza.

Pisco

☎056 / POP 54,000

Crushed by a 2007 earthquake that destroyed its infrastructure but not its spirit, Pisco is a town on the rebound. Irrespective of the substantial damage, the town remains open for business, promoting itself along with nearby beach resort El Chaco (Paracas) as a base for forays to the Paracas Reserve and Islas Ballestas.

Located 235km south of Lima, Pisco is generally the base from which to see the abundant wildlife of the Islas Ballestas and Península de Paracas, but the area is also of historical and archaeological interest, having hosted one of the most highly developed pre-Inca civilizations – the Paracas culture – from 900 BC until AD 200.

Sights & Activities

Post-earthquake, Pisco's main **Plaza de Armas** is a mishmash of the vanquished and the saved. The equestrian **statue of José de San Martín**, sword raised in defiance, falls into the latter category. The **cemetery** has a few hidden secrets: buried here is suspected 19th-century English vampire Sarah Ellen Roberts, who claimed that she would arise again after 100 years. In 1993, much to everyone's disappointment, she didn't. The cemetery is now a memorial to the more than 500 victims of the 2007 earthquake.

ISLAS BALLESTAS

Nicknamed 'the poor man's Galápagos,' these offshore islands make for a worthwhile laid-back excursion. The outward boat journey takes about 1½ hours. En route

WORTH A TRIP

EL CARMEN

A doppelganger for parts of Cuba, rustic El Carmen is famous for the rhythm-heavy Afro-Peruvian music heard in its *peñas* (bars and clubs featuring live folkloric music) about 15km outside town. The best times to visit are during the cultural festivals: **Verano Negro** (late Feb-early Mar), **Fiestas Patrias** (late Jul) and **Fiesta de Virgen del Carmen** (Dec 27).

Festival or no festival, the **Ballumbrosio Estate** (San José 325), the house of El Carmen's most famous dancing family, often has weekend music. Stay in the town's only hotel, the **Parador Turístico** (27-4060; Plaza de Armas; s/d S25/40). Or splurge at the recently restored, 300-year-old **Hacienda San José** (31-3332; www.casahaciendasanjose.com; r S210-250;), with heady colonial-era opulence. African slaves worked this former sugar and honey plantation until a dramatic 1879 rebellion. Guided Spanish-language tours go into the ghoulish catacombs.

El Carmen is just outside Chincha, at Km 202 along the Carr Panamericana. Soyuz/PerúBus visits Chincha from Lima (S20 to S23, 2½ hours). *Combis* (minibuses) to El Carmen (S2, 30 minutes) leave from Chincha's central market, a few blocks from the main plaza. It's a short taxi ride from the Panamericana.

you'll see the famous three-pronged **Candelabra**, a giant figure etched into the sandy hills. An hour is spent cruising around the island's arches and caves, watching noisy sea lions sprawl on the rocks. You may also spot Humboldt penguins, Chilean flamingos and dolphins. The most common guano-producing birds are cormorants, boobies and pelicans, present in thousands-strong colonies.

RESERVA NACIONAL DE PARACAS

Beyond the village of Paracas is the entrance to this desert-filled **national reserve** (admission S5). Next to the visitors center, which has kid-friendly exhibits on conservation and ecology, the **Museo JC Tello** (9am-5pm) (which opened in July 2012) has upped the ante significantly. It houses a limited collection of weavings, trophy heads and trepanned skulls (showing a medical technique used by ancient cultures whereby a slice of the skull is removed, relieving pressure on the brain resulting from injuries).

Tours

Boat tours to the Islas Ballestas leave daily at 7am (S45 plus S1 dock tax). Minibuses go from Pisco to the port at Paracas, where there is a nice seafront full of sidewalk restaurants and vendors (look out for Viviana's *chocotejas,* addictive pecans doused in caramel and covered in chocolate, a specialty of Ica). There are no cabins on the boats, so dress for wind, spray and sun. Wear a hat, as it's not unusual to receive direct guano hits. You can continue on a less interesting afternoon tour of the Península de Paracas (S25 with Islas Ballestas), which briefly stops at the visitors center and museum (entry fees not included) and whizzes by coastal geological formations.

Aprotur TOURS
(50-7156; www.aproturpisco.webs.com; San Francisco 112) Organizes trips to all the local sights including the Islas Ballestas (S45), the Paracas peninsula (S25) and Tambo Colorado (S20). Guides speak six languages, including Hebrew.

Sleeping

Many hotels will pick you up from the San Clemente turnoff on Carr Panamericana Sur.

Posada Hispana Hotel HOTEL $
(53-6363; www.posadahispana.com; Bolognesi 236; s/d/tr incl breakfast S39/65/91; @) With legions of fans, this friendly hotel has attractive bamboo and wooden fittings, a full-service restaurant, and a roof terrace for kicking back. Some of the well-worn rooms are musty, though all have fans and cable TV.

Hotel Residencial San Jorge HOTEL $$
(53-2885; www.hotelsanjorgeresidencial.com; Barrio Nuevo 133; s/d/tr incl breakfast S85/110/130; @) This building withstood the quake but has been recently added to. The breezy, modern entryway sets the tone, and there's also a bright cafe, and a back garden with lounge chairs and tables for picnicking around the pool. Rooms in the new wing have a splash of tropical color; those in the old wing can be dark and cramped.

Hostal Villa Manuelita HOTEL **$$**
(☎53-5218; www.villamanuelitahostal.com; San Francisco 227; s/d/tr incl breakfast S70/95/125; @) Heavily renovated post-earthquake, this hotel still achieves the grandeur of its colonial foundations. It's conveniently located half a block from the plaza.

Hostal La Casona HOTEL **$**
(☎53-2703; www.hostallacasona.com; San Juan de Dios 252; s/d S55/80; 📶) A huge wooden door serves as a slightly deceiving portal to this hotel half a block from the main square which, though clean, isn't as grand as its entryway suggests. There's a small cafeteria.

Eating & Drinking

TOP CHOICE **As de Oro's** PERUVIAN **$$**
(www.asdeoros.com.pe; San Martín 472; mains S30-50; ⊙noon-midnight Tue-Sun) The plush 'Golden Ass' serves up spicy mashed potato with octopus, plaice with butter and capers, and grilled prawns with fried *yuca* overlooking a small swimming pool, as the rest of the town struggles back to its feet.

La Concha de Tus Mares PERUVIAN **$**
(Calle Muelle 992; mains S15-25) Pictures of Pisco pre-2007 quake adorn the walls of this nostalgic place next to the Colegio Alexander Von Humboldt 1km south of the center. The huge fish plates are lauded by the locals.

El Dorado BREAKFAST, INTERNATIONAL **$**
(☎53-4367; Progreso 171; mains S10-20; ⊙6:30am-11pm) Pretension-free, El Dorado serves instant Nescafé, compensated for by excellent *tres leche* cakes and simple but effective breakfasts on the main square.

Taberna de Don Jaime BAR
(☎53-5023; San Martín 203; ⊙4pm-2am) This clamorous tavern is a favorite with locals and tourists alike. It is also a showcase for artisanal wines and *piscos*. On weekends the crowds dance to live Latin and rock tunes.

Information

Internet cafes and banks with 24-hour ATMs surround the main plaza.

Dangers & Annoyances

On its knees post-earthquake, Pisco acquired a reputation for crime, but the curtain is lifting. The commerce-packed streets are fine during the daytime (there's a notable police presence in the city center). Nonetheless, it is best to take a taxi after dark, particularly around the bus station and market areas. If you arrive late, get the ticket agent at your bus-company office to hail you a reputable cab.

Getting There & Around

Pisco is 6km west of Carr Panamericana Sur, and only buses with Pisco as the final destination actually go there. **Ormeño** (☎53-2764; San Francisco), **Flores** (☎79-6643; San Martín) and **Soyuz** (www.soyuz.com.pe; Av Ernesto R Diez Canseco 4) offer daily departures north to Lima and south to Ica, Nazca and Arequipa. If you're not on a direct bus, ask to be left at the San Clemente turnoff, where fast and frequent *colectivos* (minibuses or shared taxis) wait to shuttle passengers to central Pisco's Plaza de Armas (S3, 10 minutes) or Paracas (S10, 20 minutes).

Transportation from Pisco to Paracas is possible via *combi* (S1.50, 30 minutes), or *colectivo* (S2.50, 20 minutes), which leave frequently from near Pisco's central market.

DESTINATION	COST (S)	DURATION (HR)
Arequipa	60-144	12-15
Ica	4-15	1½-2
Lima	28-76	4½
Nazca	17-35	4

Ica

☎056 / POP 220,000

There are worse places to be stuck than Ica, the capital of the department of the same name. The bustling city boasts a thriving wine and *pisco* industry, raucous festivals and an excellent museum. The leafy plaza ain't bad either. Still, most travelers opt to bed down in nearby Huacachina. Remnants of damaged buildings from the 2007 earthquake remain, but Ica is more or less business as usual.

Sights

Peruvian wines and *piscos* can be sampled at **bodegas** outside town. Dozens of smaller, family-owned artisanal wineries lie further afield.

Museo Regional de Ica MUSEUM
(Ayabaca cuadra 8; admission S10; ⊙8am-7pm Mon-Fri, 9am-6pm Sat & Sun) The museum houses an unmatched collection of artifacts from the Paracas, Nazca and Inca cultures, including superb Paracas weavings, well-preserved mummies, trepanned skulls and shrunken trophy heads. Out back is a scale model of the Nazca Lines. Three textiles were stolen in 2004, but one has since been recovered. The

museum is 1.5km southwest of the center. Take a taxi from the Plaza de Armas (S3).

FREE **Bodega Tacama** WINE TASTING
(☎58-1030; www.tacama.com; Camino Real s/n, Tinguiña; ⏲9am-4pm Mon-Sat, to noon Sun) Possibly the most professional and lauded of Ica's wineries, Tacama offers free tours and tastings of its rather good malbecs and chardonnays. It's 11km northeast of Ica; take a taxi (S15).

Bodega Vista Alegre WINE TASTING
(Camino a La Tinguina, Km 2.5; admission S5; ⏲8am-noon & 1:45pm-4:45pm Mon-Fri, 7am-1pm Sat) Three kilometers northeast of Ica in the La Tinguiña district, this is the easiest of the large commercial wineries to visit (a one-way taxi ride is S5). It's best to go in the morning, as the winery occasionally closes in the afternoon.

Festivals & Events

Fiesta de la Vendimia HARVEST
With beauty contests and horse shows, music and dancing, and of course, free-flowing *pisco* and wine, the harvest festival is held in early to mid-March. Note that the festival also features cockfights.

El Señor de Luren RELIGION
The religious pilgrimage of El Señor de Luren culminates in fireworks and an all-night procession in late October.

Tourist Week MUSIC, FOOD
Events in mid-September.

Sleeping

Most travelers stay in nearby Huacachina, where there are more popular backpacker crash pads. If you end up in Ica overnight, dozens of depressing budget hotels line the streets east of the bus terminals and north of the plaza, especially along Tacna.

Hotel Sol de Ica HOTEL $$
(☎23-6168; www.hotelsoldeica.com; Lima 265; s/d/tr incl buffet breakfast S110/140/190; @≋) This dazzlingly white, three-story central hotel is hidden down a long, dark passage behind reception that delivers more than it initially promises. Remarkably small rooms have unusual wood paneling, TVs and phones. There are two swimming pools and a sauna.

Hotel Colón Plaza HOTEL $
(☎21-6487; Av Grau 120; s/d/ste S50/80/100; @📶) Worthwhile mostly for the corner suites, which are radically superior to the rest of the rooms, with cinema-sized flat-screen TVs, antique furniture, king-size beds, power showers and plaza views.

Eating

Several shops east of the main plaza sell *tejas* (caramel-wrapped candies flavored with fruit and nuts).

Anita BAKERY $$
(Libertad 135; menús from S12, mains S15-36; ⏲8am-midnight) Anita does a mean stuffed avocado and the bakery counter knocks out some hard-to-resist cakes. This is the best restaurant in the main square by far.

El Otro Peñoncito PERUVIAN, INTERNATIONAL $$
(Bolívar 225; mains S9-26; ⏲8am-midnight Mon-Fri; 🖉) Ica's most historic and characterful restaurant serves a varied menu of Peruvian and international fare that includes plenty of options for vegetarians. The formal bartenders here shake a mean *pisco sour,* too.

Plaza 125 PERUVIAN $
(Lima 125; mains S10-16) Your quick stop on the main square backs up homespun *lomo saltado* (stir-fried steak) with more internationally flavored spaghetti bolognese and chicken fillets. It's riotously popular with locals in a hurry.

Information

Around the plaza, internet cafes stay open until late.

BCP (Plaza de Armas) Changes traveler's checks and cash, and has a Visa ATM.

Hospital (☎23-4798; Cutervo 104; ⏲24hr) For emergencies.

Police (☎23-5421; JJ Elias, 5th block; ⏲24hr) At the city center's edge.

Serpost (San Martín 521) Postal services.

Dangers & Annoyances

Take the normal precautions against petty theft, particularly around the bus terminals and market areas.

Getting There & Away

Bus companies cluster on Lambayeque at the west end of Salaverry and along Manzanilla west of Lambayeque. For Lima, **Soyuz/PerúBus** (☎23-3312; Manzanilla 130) and **Flores** (☎21-2266) have departures every 10 to 15 minutes, while less-frequent luxury services, **Cruz del Sur** (☎22-3333; Lambayeque 140) and **Ormeño** (☎21-5600; Lambayeque s/n) go to Pisco; Ormeño has direct buses, while other bus companies drop passengers at the San Clemente turnoff on the Panamericana. Most companies have direct daytime buses to Nazca. Services to Arequipa and Cuzco are mostly overnight. Tacna (S80, 15 hours), near the Chilean border, is serviced by Ormeño.

DESTINATION	COST (S)	DURATION (HR)
Arequipa	50-144	12
Chincha	7-10	2
Lima	22-76	4½
Nazca	7-35	2½
Pisco	4-15	1½-2

Huacachina

☎056 / POP 200

Surrounded by mountainous sand dunes that roll into town over the picturesque lagoon featured on the back of Peru's S50 note, there's no denying Huacachina's majestic setting. Just 5km west of Ica, this tranquil oasis boasts graceful palm trees, exotic flowers and attractive antique buildings – all testament to the bygone glamour of this resort town built for the Peruvian elite. These days, it's a sandy gringo playground where backpackers tend to lose themselves for days.

Activities

You can rent sandboards for S5 an hour to slide, surf and somersault your way down the irresistible dunes. Thrilling rollercoaster-esque dune-buggy/sandboarding tours cost S45 (plus S3.60 'sand tax'). Go at sunset, when the scenery is at its most miraculous, rather than in the morning. All the *hostales* organize tours.

Sleeping & Eating

Camping is possible in the dunes around the lagoon – just bring a sleeping bag. For entertainment, follow the music.

TOP CHOICE El Huacachinero Hotel HOTEL $$

(☎21-7435; www.elhuacachinero.com; Perotti; s/d/tr incl breakfast S100/110/140;) Recently upgraded, the Huacachinero logs the finest restaurant in the oasis by a stretch. There's a relaxing pool area (no blaring music), and immediate dune access via the back gate if you're up for a 45-degree, one-step-forward-two-steps-back climb to the sunset of your dreams. Agreeably rustic rooms have super-comfortable beds but no TVs – then again, who needs them?

Desert Nights HOSTEL $

(☎22-8458; Blvd de Huacachina; dm from S15;) The menu might have been ripped off from Koh Samui or anywhere else on the banana-pancake trail, but this international hostel with a decent and very popular cafe out front is somewhere you're guaranteed to meet other travelers. The excellent shade-grown Peruvian coffee is backed up by peanut butter-and-jam sandwiches, burgers, pizza and brownies. The shared dorms are basic, and the owners are friendly.

Hostería Suiza HOTEL $$

(☎23-8762; www.hosteriasuiza.com.pe; Balneario de Huacachina; d S172-215;) The oasis's top-end hotel has a Swiss air of cleanliness about it, making it popular with families and older travelers. Positioned strategically at the far end of the lagoon, it remains out of earshot of Huacachina's rowdiest bars – a blessing for some.

Casa de Arena HOTEL $

(☎23-7398, 21-5274; www.casa-de-arena.com; Balneario de Huacachina; r per person with/without bathroom S50/40;) With a rowdy reputation, the Arena has well-worn rooms that come with or without baths, allowing scrimpers to scrimp. The boisterous Friday-night disco gets the thumbs down from nearby operators who feel their tranquility is being violated. If you want peace, go elsewhere. If you want to party, hello!

Hostal Curasi HOTEL $$

(☎21-6989; www.huacachinacurasi.com; Balneario de Huacachina; s/d S80/110;) Strangely, Huacachina's newest hotel doesn't look as spiffy as some of the older stalwarts, though it has the obligatory pool and restaurant and basic rooms, and the price is right.

Information

There's a global ATM at El Huacanicero.

Dangers & Annoyances

Though safer than Ica, Huacachina is not a place to be lax about your personal safety or to forget to look after your property. Some guesthouses have reputations for ripping off travelers and also harassing young women with sexual advances. Check out all of your options carefully before accepting a room.

Getting There & Away

A taxi between Ica and Huacachina costs S5 to S7.

Nazca

☎056 / POP 22,000

Bone dry and baking hot, Nazca was a desert-scorched dead town until a flyby by American scientist Paul Kosok revealed one of Peru's most enigmatic and mysterious achievements – the world-famous Nazca Lines. In 1939 a routine ancient-irrigation research flight across the barren region unearthed the puzzling scratches in the sand, engraved on the desert floor like the graffiti of giants armed with sticks the size of redwoods. Now a Unesco World Heritage site, the lines draw floods of travelers to this otherwise unremarkable small town.

Sights

Nazca Lines RUINS

Spread across 500 sq km of arid, rock-strewn plain, the Nazca Lines form a striking network of more than 800 lines, 300 geometric figures (geoglyphs), and some 70 animal and plant drawings (biomorphs). The most elaborate designs include a monkey with an extraordinarily curvaceous tail, a spider and an intriguing figure popularly called the astronaut, though some think it's a priest with an owl's head. Overflights of the lines are unforgettable, but they're not cheap.

You'll get only a sketchy idea of the lines at the **mirador** (admission S1), on the Panamericana 20km north of Nazca, which has an oblique view of three figures: the lizard, the tree and the hands (or frog, depending on your point of view). Signs warning of land mines are a reminder that walking on the lines is strictly forbidden. To get to the observation tower, catch a northbound bus (S1.50, 30 minutes) and ask the driver to let you off at the tower. To return, you'll need to flag down a southbound bus.

Another 5km north is the small **Maria Reiche Museum** (admission S5; ⏲9am-6pm). Though it's disappointingly scant on information, you can see where the mathematician lived, amid the clutter of her tools and obsessive sketches, and pay your respects at her tomb. For more information see boxed text, p824. To return to Nazca, flag down any passing bus.

Scripted but interesting multilingual lectures on the lines are given every evening at Nazca's small **planetarium** (☎52-2293; Nazca Lines Hotel, Bolognesi 147; admission S20; ⏲in French 6pm, in English 7pm, in Spanish 8:15pm).

Museo Didáctico Antonini MUSEUM

(☎52-3444; Av de la Cultura 600; admission/cameras S20/5; ⏲9am-7pm) On the east side of town, this archaeological museum boasts an original pre-Columbian aqueduct running through the back garden, plus reproductions of burial tombs and a scale model of the lines. You can get an overview of the Nazca culture and a glimpse of Nazca's outlying sites here.

Outlying Sites

It's safest to visit the outlying archaeological sites with an organized tour and guide, as robberies and assaults on tourists have been reported. At the **Cantallo aqueducts** (admission S10), just outside town, you can descend into the ancient stonework by means of spiraling *ventanas* (windows) – a wet, claustrophobic experience. The popular **Cemetery of Chauchilla** (admission S7.50), 30km south of Nazca, will satisfy any maca-

Nazca

bre urges you have to see bones, skulls and mummies. A dirt road travels 25km west to **Cahuachi**, an important Nazca center still being excavated.

Activities

Cerro Blanco ADVENTURE TOUR

An off-the-beaten-track expedition is to Cerro Blanco, the world's highest known sand dune (2078m). It's a real challenge for budding sandboarders fresh from Huacachina. Sandboarding tours start at S90.

Tours

Overflights of the Nazca Lines are tinged with controversy. In 2010 two small aircraft carrying tourists on *sobrevuelos* (overflights) crashed within eight months of each other, resulting in a total of 13 fatalities. The crashes followed a 2008 accident that killed five French tourists, and a 2009 incident when a plane was forced to make an emergency landing on the Carr Panamericana Sur.

In reaction to these incidents some changes have been made: all planes now fly with two pilots, and prices have gone up to ensure that companies don't cut corners with poorly maintained aircraft or overfilled flights.

Nonetheless, it pays to put safety before price when choosing your overflight company. Avoid anyone who offers less than US$80 for the standard 30-minute excursion and don't be afraid to probe companies on their safety records and flight policies. **Aeroparacas** (www.aeroparacas.com) is one of the better companies. Other long-standing operators include **Aerodiana** (☎444-3057; www.aerodiana.com.pe) and **Alas Peruanas** (☎52-2497; www.alasperuanas.com). Some countries, including the UK and USA, still place warnings about overflights on their foreign-office websites.

Because the small aircraft bank left and right, it can be a stomach-churning experience, so motion-sickness sufferers should consider taking medication. Looking at the horizon may help mild nausea.

Most airline companies use **María Reiche Neuman Airport**, 4km southwest of Nazca, although you can also depart from Pisco and Lima. On top of the tour fee, the aerodrome normally charges a departure tax of S20.

Alegría Tours GUIDED TOUR

(☎52-3775; www.alegriatoursperu.com; Lima 168, Hotel Alegría) A reputable agency.

Sleeping

Kunan Wasi Hotel HOTEL $

(☎52-4069; www.kunanwasihotel.com; Arica 419; s/d/tr S40/50/60; @ 📶) Very clean and bright (each room has a different color scheme), Kunan Wasi has nailed the budget end of the market with facilities that more than justify the asking price. Welcome to a perfectly packaged Nazca bargain, run by English-speaking Yesenia, who has lived in LA.

Hotel La Encantada HOTEL $$

(☎52-2930; www.hotellaencantada.com.pe; Callao 592; s/d/tr S95/115/140; @ 📶) A good, clean, new hotel, this place has made the opposition look over its shoulder with bright, freshly painted rooms and a pleasant terrace out front.

Nazca

Sights

1 Nazca Planetarium C2

Activities, Courses & Tours

Alas Peruanas .... (see 3)
Alegría Tours .... (see 3)

Sleeping

2 Hospedaje Yemayá D1
3 Hotel Alegría C2
4 Hotel La Encantada D1
5 Hotel Sol del Sur B2
6 Kunan Wasi Hotel E1

Eating

7 La Taberna D2
8 Rico Pollo C2
9 Via La Encantada D2

MYSTERIES IN THE SAND

The awesome, ancient Nazca Lines were made by removing sun-darkened stones from the desert surface to expose the lighter soil below. But who constructed the gigantic lines and for what reason? And why bother when they can only be properly appreciated from the air? Maria Reiche, a German mathematician and longtime researcher of the lines, theorized that they were made by the Paracas and Nazca cultures from 900 BC to AD 600, with additions by the Wari in the 7th century. She believed the lines were an astronomical calendar mapped out by sophisticated mathematics (and a long rope). Others theorize that the lines were ritual walkways connected to a water or fertility cult, giant running tracks, extraterrestrial landing sites or representations of shamans' dreams brought on by hallucinogenic drugs. Take your pick – no one really knows!

Hotel Alegría HOTEL **$$**
(52-2702; www.hotel-alegria.com; Lima 168; s/d incl breakfast S100/130;) This is a classic travelers' haunt with a restaurant, manicured grounds and a pool. It has narrow, carpeted rooms with TVs and fans, and its own tour company. Rates include a free half-hour of internet access and a pickup from the bus station, where you should ignore touts from the Hotel Alegría II.

Hospedaje Yemayá HOTEL **$**
(52-3146; www.hospedajeyemaya.com; Callao 578; s/d incl breakfast S55, tr S75;) An indefatigably hospitable family deftly deals with all of the backpackers that stream through the doorway. On offer are a few floors of small but well-cared-for rooms with hot showers and cable TV. There's a sociable terrace with a handy washing machine and dryer.

Hotel Sol del Sur HOTEL **$$**
(52-3716; www.hotelsoldelsur.com; Av Guardia Civil 120; s/d S70/100;) A cut above your standard bus-station dive (though it's right next to it), with a downstairs restaurant, clean rooms, and windows thick enough to keep out the sound of screeching 10-ton buses.

Hotel Nasca HOTEL **$**
(52-2085; marionasca13@hotmail.com; Lima 438; s/d/tr S35/45/65) A rock-bottom, bargain-basement place with friendly elderly owners. Army barracks–style rooms offer bare-bones facilities; some have private bathrooms.

Eating & Drinking

West of the Plaza de Armas, Bolognesi is lined with backpacker pizzerias, restaurants and bars.

TOP CHOICE **Via La Encantada** EUROPEAN, PERUVIAN **$$**
(www.hotellaencantada.com.pe; Bolognesi 282; mains S20-40) La Encantada sparkles in Nazca's dusty center with well-placed wine displays, great coffee and courteous and friendly wait staff. The extensive menu mixes Europhile food (pasta and the like) with Peruvian favorites.

Rico Pollo PARRILLA **$**
(Lima 190; mains from S12) A local lunchtime phenomenon, this very cheap, very crowded grill offers some of the best barbecued meat cuts on the south coast. Cakes and salads (S10) provide an excellent supporting act.

La Taberna PERUVIAN **$**
(52-3803; Lima 321; menús S6, mains from S15; lunch & dinner;) Scribbles covering every inch of wall are testament to this spot's hole-in-the-wall popularity. Try the spicy fish, challengingly named *'Pescado a lo Macho'* ('macho fish') or choose from a list of vegetarian options.

Information

BCP (Lima 495) Has a Visa/Mastercard ATM; changes traveler's checks.

DIRCETUR (Parque Bolognesi, 3rd fl) Government-sponsored tourist-information office; can recommend local tour operators. There's an information booth in the park itself.

Getting There & Around

Bus companies cluster at the western end of Calle Lima, near the *óvalo*. Buses to Arequipa generally originate in Lima; to get a seat you have to pay the Lima fare.

Most long-distance services start in the late afternoon. Located on Av Los Incas, **Cruz del Sur** (52-3713) and **Ormeño** (52-2058) have luxury buses daily to Lima. Intermediate points like Ica and Pisco are faster served by smaller, *económico* (cheap) bus companies, such as Flores and **Soyuz** (☎52-1464), which run buses to Ica every half-hour from Av Los Incas.

To Cuzco, several companies take the paved road east via Abancay. This high-altitude route gets very cold, so bring warm clothes and your sleeping bag (if you have one) on board. There are also direct buses to Cuzco via Arequipa.

For Ica, fast *colectivos* (S15, two hours) and slower minibuses leave when full from near the gas station on the *óvalo*.

A taxi from central Nazca to the aerodrome, 4km away, costs about S4.

DESTINATION	COST (S)	DURATION (HR)
Arequipa	40-144	10-12
Cuzco	120-180	14
Ica	7-35	2½
Lima	50-86	8
Pisco	5-15	1½-2
Tacna	70-120	15

Tacna

☎052 / POP 242,500

It's a long and dusty trail to Tacna, Peru's most heroic city, sitting staunchly at the tail end of the Carr Panamericana, nearly 1300km southeast of Lima. In fact, this well-developed border outpost was occupied by Chile after the War of the Pacific in 1880, but townsfolk staged a border-shuffle coup in 1929 and voted to return to Peru's welcoming arms. You'll also find that there is added civility in this part of the country. For travelers, it's mostly a transit stop on the way to Chile.

The countryside around Tacna is known for its olive groves, orchards and *bodegas*. Catch a bus or *micro* (minibus) along Bolognesi (S0.50, 10 minutes) to visit the *bodegas* and restaurants in suburban Pocollay.

Sleeping

Hotel rooms are overpriced and fill up very fast, especially on weekends.

Dorado Hotel HOTEL $$
(☎42-1111, 41-5741; www.doradohoteltacna.com; Av Arias Aragüez 145; s/d/tr incl breakfast S100/130/165; @ 📶) Posing as Tacna's grandest hotel, the Dorado is the sort of place where the curtains are heavy, the lobby sports shiny balustrades, and a bellboy will carry your bags.

Maximo's Hotel HOTEL $$
(☎24-2604; Av Arias Aragüez 281; s/d/tr incl breakfast S90/115/130; 📶) Quirky Maximo's has a lobby that's overladen with plants, balconies and candelabras. There's also a snack bar, a sauna (S8 for guests), and good, clean rooms with fans.

Universo Hostal HOTEL $
(☎41-5441; Zela 724; s/d/tr S30/40/60) This broken-in hotel is a secure option with accommodating staff, hot showers and cable TV, though rooms are on the small side.

Eating & Drinking

Pocollay is popular for its rural restaurants, which often have live music on weekends. The small pedestrian streets of Libertad and Vigil are ground zero for Tacna's limited nightlife.

TOP CHOICE **Café Da Vinci** EUROPEAN $$
(Calle Arias Aragüez 122; mains S23-40; ⏲11am-11pm) A wood-paneled domain where well-dressed wait staff give out Mona Lisa smiles. Menus highlight fabulous baguettes, pizzas, generous glasses of dry red wine, and decent Peruvian staples. Pride of place goes to the real Italian espresso machine.

WORTH A TRIP

SANTUARIO NACIONAL LAGUNAS DE MEJÍA

About 6km southeast of Mejía along an unbroken line of beaches, this 690-hectare **sanctuary** (Carretera Mollendo, Km 32; admission S5; ⏲dawn-dusk) protects coastal lagoons that are the largest permanent lakes in 1500km of desert coastline. They attract more than 200 species of coastal and migratory birds, best seen in the very early morning. The visitors center has maps of hiking trails leading through the dunes to *miradors* (lookouts). From Mollendo, *colectivos* (shared taxis or minibuses) pass by the visitors center (S3, 30 minutes) frequently during the daytime. Ask the staff to help you flag down onward transportation, which peters out by the late afternoon.

GETTING TO CHILE

Border-crossing formalities are relatively straightforward. There are three main transport options: train, public bus or *colectivo* (shared taxi or minibus), with the latter proving to be the most efficient. The five-passenger taxis are run by professional companies with desks inside Tacna's International bus terminal. They charge approximately S18 to take you the 65km to Arica in Chile with stops at both border posts. It's fast and efficient – most of the paperwork is done before you get in the car. The public bus is cheaper (S10), but slower, as you have to wait for all the passengers to disembark and clear customs.

The Chilean border post is open 8am to midnight from Sunday to Thursday, and 24 hours on Friday and Saturday. Note that Chile is an hour ahead of Peru (two hours during daylight-saving time from the last Sunday in October to the first Sunday in April). From Arica you can continue south (by air or bus) into Chile or northeast into Bolivia.

Uros Restaurante FUSION **$$**
(www.restauranteuros.com; Av San Martín 608; mains S22-35) Tacna's stab at *novoandina* cuisine avoids too many pretensions, if you can get past the (admittedly photogenic) photos of the food on the menu. There's another branch on the town's periphery.

La Mia Mama ITALIAN **$**
(☎24-2022; Av Arias Aragüez 204; mains S10-18; ⏰6-11pm Mon-Sat) A great place to sip a glass of *vino de chacra* (local table wine) over one of the menu's classic pizzas or pastas. Tables fill up quickly.

Information

Chilean pesos, nuevos soles and US dollars can be easily exchanged.

BCP (San Martín 574) Has a Visa/MasterCard ATM, gives Visa cash advances and changes traveler's checks.

iPerú (☎42-5514; San Martín 491; ⏰8:30am-7:30pm Mon-Fri, to 2:30pm Sat) Helpful travel info on the northeast end of the plaza.

Getting There & Around

Air

Tacna's **airport** (TCQ; ☎31-4503) is 5km west of town. **LAN** (☎42-8346; Apurímac 101; ⏰8:30am-7pm Mon-Fri, 9am-2pm Sat) and **Peruvian Airlines** (www.peruvian.pe; Av Bolognesi 670) both offer daily passenger services to Lima, and some seasonal services to Arequipa and Cuzco.

Bus

Most long-distance departures are from the Terminal Terrestre (departure tax S1), a taxi ride from the center (S4). Most Lima-bound buses will drop you off at other coastal towns, including Nazca and Ica. Comfortable overnight buses with **Julsa** (☎24-7132) reach Puno via Desaguadero. For Cuzco, switch in Arequipa or Puno.

Frequent buses (S10) to Arica, Chile, leave between 6am and 10pm from the international terminal opposite the Terminal Terrestre.

DESTINATION	COST (S)	DURATION (HR)
Arequipa	15-35	7
Cuzco	60-125	17
Lima	50-144	18-22
Puno	25-45	10

Train

Trains between Tacna's **train station** (☎42-4981; Av 2 de Mayo) and Arica, Chile (S10/CH$2000, 1½ hours) are the cheapest and most charming but also the slowest way to cross the border. An entry stamp is made upon arrival. Service can be erratic and inconveniently timed: visit the station for up-to-date schedules.

AREQUIPA & CANYON COUNTRY

Colonial Arequipa, with its sophisticated museums, architecture and nightlife, is surrounded by some of the wildest terrain in Peru. This is a land of active volcanoes, thermal springs, high-altitude deserts and the world's deepest canyons. Traveling overland, it's a must-stop en route to Lake Titicaca and Cuzco.

Arequipa

☎054 / POP 905,000

Bombarded by volcanic eruptions and earthquakes nearly every century since the Spanish arrived in 1540, Arequipa doesn't lack for drama. The perfect cone-shaped volcano of El Misti (5822m) rises behind the cathedral on the Plaza de Armas, flanked to the left by ragged Chachani (6075m) and to the right by Pichu Pichu (5571m). Set against this majestic backdrop are Arequipa's grand colonial buildings, whitewashed in volcanic stone called *sillar* that dazzles in the sun and on camera. Yes, you're still in the Andes, but with the cosmopolitan flair of cobblestones, gourmet restaurants and raucous nightlife – after all, this is Peru's second-largest city.

Sights

Arequipa is known as 'the white city' for the distinctive stonework that graces the stately Plaza de Armas and its enormous *sillar* **cathedral**, as well as many other exquisite colonial churches, convents and mansions. Don't miss **La Casa de Moral** and **Casa Ricketts**, which are well-preserved examples of the latter.

Monasterio de Santa Catalina MONASTERY
(☎22-9798; www.santacatalina.org.pe; Santa Catalina 301; admission S35; ⏲9am-5pm, last entry 4pm, plus 7-9pm Tue & Thu) Occupying a whole block and guarded by imposing walls, this monastery is practically a citadel within the city. A wealthy widow who chose her nuns from the richest Spanish families founded it in 1580, but her new nuns kept living it up in the style to which they were accustomed. After almost three centuries of these hedonistic goings-on, a strict Dominican nun arrived to straighten things out. The complex remained shrouded in mystery until it was forced open to the public in 1970. Today it's a meditatively mazelike place that lets you enter a forgotten world of narrow, twisting streets, tiny fruit-filled plazas, hidden staircases, beautiful courtyards and ascetic living quarters. Visit at night on Tuesday and Thursday for a completely different aesthetic.

Museo Santuarios Andinos MUSEUM
(☎20-0345; www.ucsm.edu.pe/santury; La Merced 110; admission S20; ⏲9am-6pm Mon-Sat, to 3pm Sun) Taking top billing is 'Juanita, the Ice Princess' – the frozen Inca maiden who was sacrificed on the summit of Ampato (6310m) over 500 years ago. This university museum examines the Incan perception of mountains as violent deities who could only be appeased by sacrifices. Multilingual tours every 20 minutes feature a video followed by a look at burial artifacts, then a viewing of the chilled mummy itself. Although Juanita is not on display from January through April, you can get your child-sacrifice fix with one of 12 other mummies. Guides here are students working for tips.

Iglesia de La Compañía CHURCH
(⏲9am-12:30pm & 3-6pm Mon-Fri, 11:30am-12:30pm & 3-6pm Sat, 9am-noon & 5-6pm Sun) One of Arequipa's oldest churches, this Jesuit church is noted for its ornate main facade. The **San Ignacio chapel** (admission S4) inside has a polychrome cupola with lush murals featuring mingling warriors and angels.

Monasterio de la Recoleta MONASTERY
(La Recoleta 117; admission S5; ⏲9am-noon & 3-5pm Mon-Sat) On the west side of the Río Chili, this musty 17th-century Franciscan monastery has a fascinating library with over 20,000 historic tomes, maps and a museum of Amazonia collected by missionaries. The neighborhood is dicey, so take a taxi.

Activities

Santa Catalina and Jerusalén have dozens of fly-by-night travel agencies offering disappointingly rushed tours of the Cañón del Colca and also trekking, mountaineering and rafting trips. There are many folks muscling in on the action, so shop carefully.

Carlos Zárate Adventures ADVENTURE SPORTS
(☎20-2461; www.zarateadventures.com; Santa Catalina 204, Oficina 3) The granddaddy of *arequipeño* climbing agencies also runs trekking and mountain-biking tours. Rents climbing gear, but – as with all operators in South America – inspect it carefully.

Colca Trek ADVENTURE SPORTS
(☎20-6217; www.colcatrek.com.pe; Jerusalén 401B) Eco-conscious adventure-tour agency run by English-speaking Vlado Soto. Buys, sells and rents equipment, including campstove fuel, mountain bikes, climbing gear and topography maps; it also spearheads an annual Cañón cleanup. Vlado organizes a spectacular four-day trek into Cañón del Cotahuasi, Peru's deepest canyon.

Naturaleza Activa ADVENTURE SPORTS
(☎22-2257; www.peruexploration.com; Santa Catalina 211) A favorite of those seeking adventure tours, with mountain-biking, trekking and climbing tours.

Mountaineering

Superb mountains surround Arequipa. Though many area climbs aren't technically difficult, they should never be undertaken

Arequipa's Canyon Country & Lake Titicaca

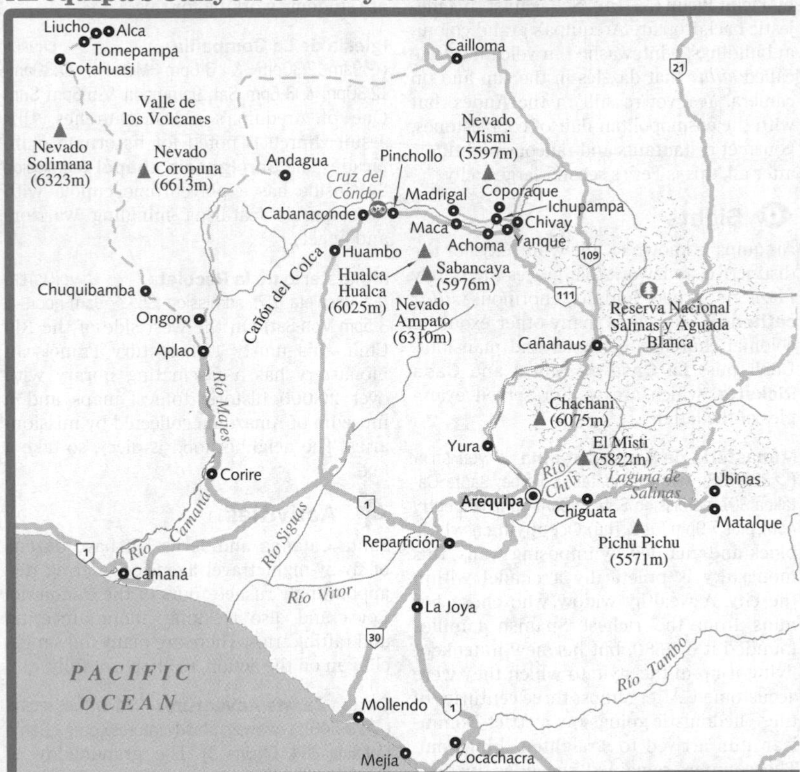

lightly. Hazards include extreme weather, altitude and lack of water (carry 4L per person per day). The Association of Mountain Guides of Peru warns that many guides are uncertified and untrained, so climbers are advised to go well informed about medical and wilderness-survival issues and carry first aid.

Looming above Arequipa, **El Misti** (5822m) is the most popular local climb. It can be tackled solo, but going with a guide helps protect against robberies, which have happened on the Apurímac route. One popular route is from Chiguata, an eight-hour hard uphill slog on rough trails to base camp (4500m). From there to the summit and back takes eight hours. The return from base camp to Chiguata takes three hours or less. **Chachani** (6075m) is one of the easiest 6000m peaks in the world, but you'll still need crampons, an ice ax and a good guide to hike it.

Trekking

Agencies offer off-the-beaten-track tours in Arequipa's canyon country, but it's better to DIY if you're just visiting the Cañón del Colca. Register at **High Mountain Rescue** (☎53-1165; Siglo XX, Chivay) before setting out. Optimal hiking season is from May to November. Cañón del Colca has a smattering of **campgrounds** (sites per person S10-15), but it's forbidden to camp by Cruz del Cóndor. For indispensable trekking maps and excellent guided trips into Cañón del Cotahuasi, contact Colca Trek.

Rafting

The **Río Chili** is the most frequently run local river, with a half-day beginners' trip leaving daily from March to November. Further afield, the **Río Majes** passes grade II and III rapids.

Casa de Mauro (☎959-336-684; www.lacasademaurotoursperu.com; Ongoro, Km 5; sites per person S15, dm S30) is a convenient base for raft-

ing the Majes. Take a Transportes del Carpio bus from Arequipa's Terminal Terrestre to Aplao (S10, three hours, hourly) and then a *combi* (S1.50) or a taxi (S12) to the village of Ongoro, 190km by road west of Arequipa.

Courses

Many schools offer Spanish classes (about S14 to S30 per hour).

CEPESMA LANGUAGE
(☎959-961-638; www.cepesmaidiomasceci.com; Av Puente Grau 108) Spanish with supplemental activities.

Juanjo LANGUAGE
(www.spanishlanguageperu.com; 2nd epata C-4, Urb Magisterial, Yanahuara) Spanish; recommended by travelers.

ROCIO LANGUAGE
(☎22-4568; www.spanish-peru.com; Ayacucho 208) Individual and group Spanish classes.

Festivals & Events

Arequipeños are a proud people, and their fiery celebration of the city's founding on August 15 renews their sense of difference from coastal Lima.

Sleeping

Many more budget guesthouses lie along Puente Grau, west of Jerusalén.

TOP CHOICE **Hostal Casona Solar** HOTEL $$
(☎22-8991; www.casonasolar.com; Consuelo 116; r from S104; wi-fi) Arequipa's best bargain is this 'secret garden' of gorgeousness near the main square. Grand 18th-century rooms are crafted from huge *sillar* stones, some with mezzanine bedrooms. Service is equally dazzling.

Casablanca Hostal HOTEL $$
(☎22-1327; www.casablancahostal.com; Puente Bolognesi 104; s/d/tr incl breakfast S80/120/160; @) Bank on prime corner-of-main-plaza location, beautiful exposed-*sillar* brickwork, and rooms large enough to keep a horse (or two) in. Service is discreet and breakfast is taken in a lovely sun-filled cafe.

La Casa Blanca HOTEL $
(☎28-2218; Jerusalén 412; r without/with bathroom S35/70; @ wi-fi) A reasonably priced find with a fantastic coffee bar in the courtyard out front. Rooms are quite basic, but the staff is friendly and eager to please.

La Casa de Sillar HOTEL $
(☎28-4249; www.thecasadesillar.com; Rivero 504; without/with bathroom s S35/45, d S60/70; @ wi-fi) Another colonial mansion, this one doesn't pretend to be boutique, but it does offer a fine bargain, especially if you're prepared to share a bathroom.

Wild Rover Hostel HOSTEL $
(☎21-2830; www.wildroverhostels.com; Calle Ugarte 111; dm from S25; @ wi-fi pool) If halfway through your Peruvian sojourn you get a sudden compulsion to consume bangers and mash with Swedish backpackers in the familiar confines of an Irish pub, then the Wild Rover awaits you with open arms.

Le Foyer HOSTEL $
(☎28-6473; www.hlefoyer.com; Ugarte 114; s/d/tr S50/65/90, dm/s/d without bathroom S25/35/55; @ wi-fi) A cheap hostel-type hotel with a wraparound upstairs verandah where you can enjoy a standard bread-and-jam breakfast

Arequipa

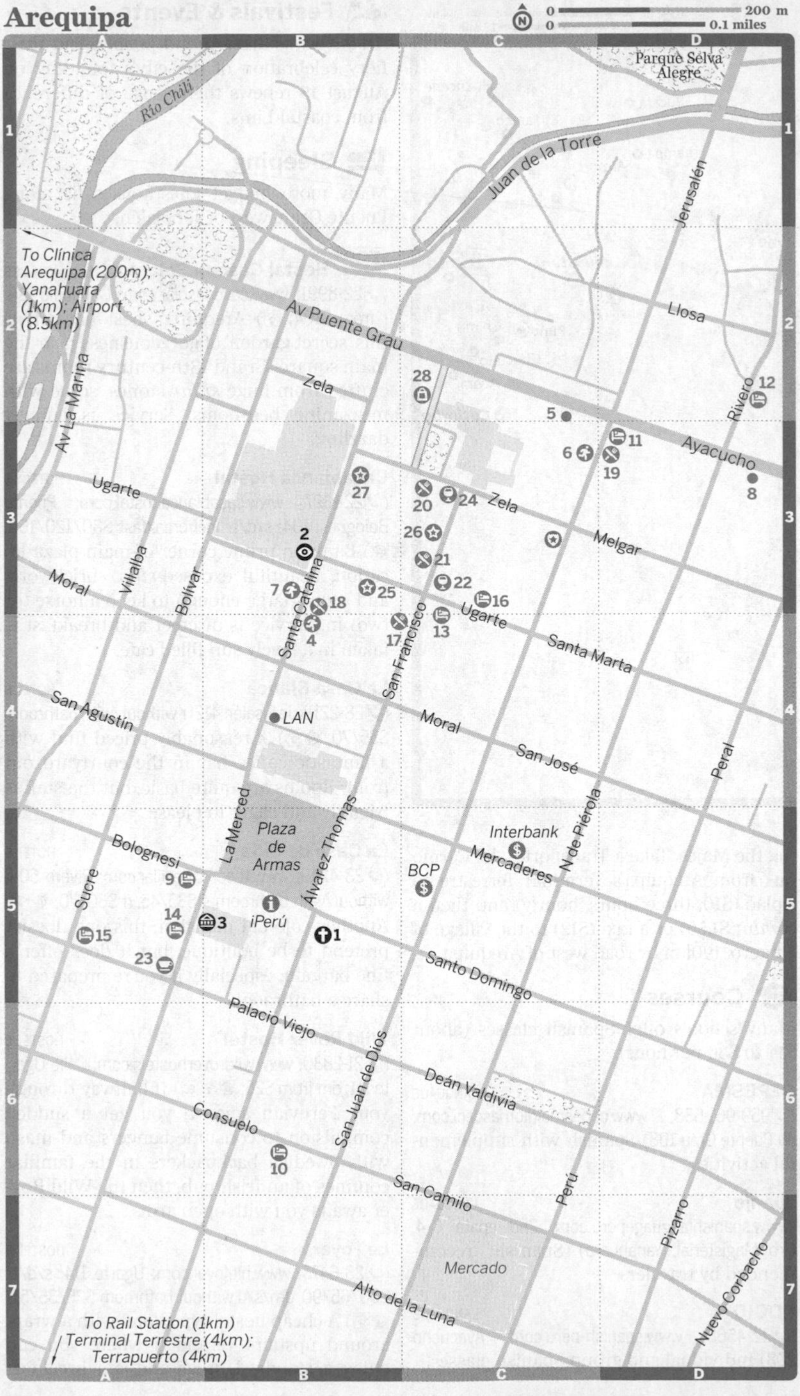

0 — 200 m
0 — 0.1 miles

A B C D

1 2 3 4 5 6 7

Parque Selva Alegre
Río Chili
Juan de la Torre
Jerusalén
To Clínica Arequipa (200m); Yanahuara (1km); Airport (8.5km)
Av Puente Grau
Llosa
Zela
Av La Marina
Rivero
Ayacucho
Ugarte
Zela
Melgar
Villalba
Bolívar
Moral
Santa Catalina
Ugarte
Santa Marta
San Francisco
San Agustín
LAN
Moral
San José
Peral
N de Piérola
Interbank
Mercaderes
Plaza de Armas
La Merced
Álvarez Thomas
Bolognesi
BCP
Sucre
iPerú
Santo Domingo
Palacio Viejo
San Juan de Dios
Deán Valdivia
Consuelo
San Camilo
Perú
Pizarro
Nuevo Corbacho
Mercado
Alto de la Luna
To Rail Station (1km) Terminal Terrestre (4km); Terrapuerto (4km)

1 2 3 4 5 6 7 8 9 10 11 12 13 14 15 16 17 18 19 20 21 22 23 24 25 26 27 28

Arequipa

Sights

Activities, Courses & Tours

Sleeping

Eating

Drinking

Entertainment

Shopping

overlooking busy Jerusalén. Rooms are nothing to brag about, but the location is prime.

Los Andes Bed & Breakfast HOTEL, B&B $
(☎33-0015; www.losandesarequipa.com; La Merced 123; s/d S48/72, without bathroom S31/50; @☎) With giant, sterile rooms and an ample communal kitchen popular with climbing groups and long-term stays. A font of information for the surrounding 'outdoors'.

Point Hostel HOSTEL $
(☎28-6920; www.thepointhostels.com; Palacio Viejo 325; dm incl breakfast S19-24; @☎) Two blocks from the main square, this chain hostel features popular billiards/pool tables and bar; definitely a place for people who like to socialize and don't necessarily need to be tucked up in bed quietly by 10pm.

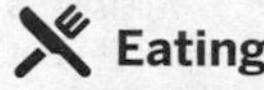

Eating

Trendy upscale restaurants are on San Francisco, while a few outdoor cafes line Pasaje Catedral.

TOP CHOICE **Zingaro** PERUVIAN $$
(www.zingaro-restaurante.com; San Francisco 309; mains S25-45; ⊙noon-11pm Mon-Sat) In an old *sillar* building with wooden balconies, stained glass and a resident pianist, culinary legends are made. The stunning *nouveau* renditions of Peruvian standards include alpaca ribs, *ceviche*, or perhaps your first *cuy* (guinea pig).

Zig Zag PERUVIAN $$
(☎20-6020; www.zigzagrestaurant.com; Zela 210; mains S33-40; ⊙6pm-midnight) Upscale but not ridiculously pricey, this concept restaurant inhabits a two-story colonial house with an iron stairway designed by Gustave Eiffel. The menu classic is a meat selection served on a unique volcano-stone grill with various sauces. The fondues are also good.

Crepisimo CAFE, CREPERIE $
(www.crepisimo.com; Alianza Francesa, Santa Catalina 208; mains S6-16; ⊙8am-11pm Mon-Sat, noon-11pm Sun; ☎) This is a truly great cafe with blockbusting food, service and ambience. Crepes are offered with 100 different types of filling, from Chilean smoked trout to exotic South American fruits.

Café Fez-Istanbul MIDDLE EASTERN $
(San Francisco 229; mains S6-11; ⊙7:30am-11pm) Falafels are the main draw – in a crepe or in a sandwich – served in a rather trendy resto-bar with a people-watching mezzanine floor. Other favorites are hummus, fresh-cut fries and various sandwiches. Portions are snack fodder, but served in a cool environment.

La Nueva Palomino PERUVIAN $$
(Leoncio Prado 122; mains S14-29; ⊙lunch) Definitely the local favorite, this informal *picantería* can turn boisterous, serving local specialties and *chicha de jora* (corn beer).

Café Casa Verde CAFE, SANDWICHES $
(Jerusalén 406; snacks S2-6; 8am-6pm) This nonprofit courtyard cafe staffed by underprivileged kids dishes up yummy German-style pastries and sandwiches, though service can be slow. Attached is a local nonprofit handicraft store.

Lakshmivan VEGETARIAN $
(Jerusalén 400; menús S4-6; 9am-9pm;) Set in a colorful old building with a tiny outdoor courtyard, this place has various *menús* and an extensive à la carte selection, all with a South Asian flair.

Drinking

A slew of great bars and clubs are concentrated just north of the plaza at the corner of San Francisco and Ugarte.

Cusco Coffee Company CAFE
(La Merced 135; drinks S5-11; 8am-10pm Mon-Sat, noon-7pm Sun;) Come here only if you're missing chocolate-chip muffins, bucket-sized lattes and sofas full of non-communicative wi-fi nerds.

Déjà Vu COCKTAIL BAR
(San Francisco 319B; 9am-late) With a rooftop terrace overlooking the church of San Francisco, this eternally popular haunt has a long list of crazy cocktails and a lethal happy hour every evening. After dark, decent DJs keep the scene alive on weekdays and weekends alike.

Brujas Bar BAR
(San Francisco 300; 5pm-late) Nordic-style pub with Union Jack flags, happy-hour cocktails and plenty of local and expat chinwaggers.

Entertainment

Café Art Montréal LIVE MUSIC
(Ugarte 210; 5pm-1am) This smoky, intimate little bar with live bands playing on a stage at the back could pass for a bohemian student hangout on Paris's Left Bank.

Las Quenas TRADITIONAL MUSIC
(Santa Catalina 302; closed Sun) An exception to the rule, this traditional *peña* features performances almost nightly, starting around 9pm. The music varies, although *música folklórica* predominates. It also serves decent *arequipeño* food starting at 8pm.

Casona Forum CLUB
(www.casonaforum.com; San Francisco 317) A five-in-one excuse for a good night out in a *sillar* building incorporating a pub, a pool club, a sofa bar, a nightclub and a restaurant.

Shopping

Artisan and antique shops abound, especially around Monasterio Santa Catalina.

Fundo El Fierro CRAFT MARKET
(San Francisco 200; 9am-8pm Mon-Sat, to 2pm Sun) Buy direct from the source at this *artesanía* (handicrafts) foundation's many stalls.

Information

Dangers & Annoyances

Petty theft is often reported in Arequipa, so travelers are urged to hide their valuables. Be wary of wandering outside of touristy zones at night. Take great care in Parque Selva Alegre, north of the city center, as muggings have been reported. Instead of hailing a cab on the street, ask your hostel or tour operator to call you an official one; it's worth it for the added safety.

WORTH A TRIP

YANAHUARA

The peaceful neighborhood of Yanahuara makes for an excursion from downtown Arequipa. It's within walking distance: go west on Av Puente Grau over the Puente Grau (Grau Bridge) and continue on Av Ejército for half a dozen blocks. Turn right on Av Lima and walk five blocks to a small plaza with **Iglesia San Juan Batista**, dating from 1750. At the side of the plaza, a *mirador* (lookout) has excellent views of Arequipa and El Misti.

Head back along Av Jerusalén, parallel to Av Lima. Just before reaching Av Ejército you'll see the well-known restaurant **Sol de Mayo** (25-4148; Jerusalén 207; mains S16-39), where you can stop for a tasty lunch of typical *arequipeño* food. The walk is two hours round-trip. Otherwise, *combis* (minibuses) to Yanahuara leave from along Av Puente Grau (and returning from Yanahuara's plaza to the city) every few minutes (S1, 10 minutes).

Emergency

Policía de Turismo (Tourist Police; ☎20-1258; Jerusalén 315-317; ⏲24hr)

Medical Services

Clínica Arequipa (☎25-3416, 25-3424; Bolognesi near Puente Grau; ⏲8am-8pm Mon-Fri, to 12:30pm Sat)

Paz Holandesa Policlinic (☎43-2281; www.pazholandesa.com; Av Jorge Chávez 527; ⏲8am-8pm Mon-Sat) Appointment-only travel clinic that provides vaccinations.

Money

Money changers are found east of the Plaza de Armas. There are also global ATMs inside Casona Santa Catalina and the Terminal Terrestre.

BCP (San Juan de Dios 125) Has a Visa ATM and changes US dollars.

Interbank (Mercaderes 217) Has a global ATM.

Post

Serpost (Moral 118; ⏲8am-8pm Mon-Sat, 9am-1pm Sun)

Tourist Information

iPerú (☎22-3265; iperuarequipa@promperu.gob.pe; Portal de la Municipalidad 110, Plaza de Armas; ⏲8:30am-7:30pm) Government-supported source for objective information on local and regional attractions. Also has a branch at the airport (☎44-4564; 1st fl, Main Hall, Aeropuerto Rodríguez Ballón; ⏲10am-7:30pm).

 Getting There & Away

Air

The **airport** (AQP; ☎44-3464) is 8km northwest of the center. **LAN** (☎20-1100; Santa Catalina 118C) serves Lima and Cuzco daily. A taxi to Centro runs S15.

Bus

Most companies leave from the Terminal Terrestre or the smaller Terrapuerto bus station next door. Both are 3km south of the center (departure tax S2).

For Lima, **Cruz del Sur** (☎42-7375), **Ormeño** (☎42-3855) and other companies operate several daily buses, mostly with afternoon departures. Many buses stop en route at Nazca and Ica. Many companies also have overnight buses to Cuzco.

Buses to Puno leave frequently; since this route is notorious for accidents, day buses are best. Ormeño continues on to Desaguadero on the Bolivian border and La Paz (Bolivia). Cruz del Sur has the most comfortable buses to Tacna via Moquegua.

For Cañón del Colca, there are a few daily buses for Chivay (S12, three hours), continuing to Cabanaconde (S15, six hours). Recommended companies include **Andalucía** (☎44-5089) or **Señor de los Milagros** (☎28-8090).

DESTINATION	COST (S)	DURATION (HR)
Cabanaconde	17	6
Chivay	15	3
Cuzco	25-126	9-11
Ica	40-114	13-15
Lima	50-144	14-16
Moquegua	18	4
Nazca	40-144	10-12
Pisco	40-144	15
Puno	15-72	6
Tacna	20-57	6

 Getting Around

Combis and minibuses go south along Bolívar to the Terminal Terrestre (S2, 20 minutes), next door to the Terrapuerto bus terminal, but it's a slow trip via the market area. Always use officially licensed taxi companies such as **Tourismo Arequipa** (☎45-8888) and **Taxitel** (☎45-2020).

Cañón del Colca

One of the world's deepest canyons at 3191m, Colca ranks second only to neighboring Cañón del Cotahuasi, which is 163m deeper. Trekking is by far the best way to experience village life, although the roads are dusty. As you pass through the villages, look out for the local women's traditional embroidered clothing and hats. On an environmental note, do not dispose of trash at the bins in the canyon as they overflow and locals simply dump them in the river. Take your own trash out.

The road from Arequipa climbs north through the **Reserva Nacional Salinas y Aguada Blanca**, where *vicuñas* – the endangered wild cousins of llamas and alpacas – are often sighted. The road continues through bleak *altiplano* (high Andean plateau) over the highest point of 4800m, before dropping spectacularly into Chivay.

CHIVAY

☎054 / POP 4600

The provincial capital at the head of the canyon is a small, dusty transit hub. Bring plenty of Peruvian cash, as only a few stores exchange US dollars or euros.

Sights & Activities

Astronomical Observatory OBSERVATORY
(Huayna Cápac; admission S25) No light pollution equals excellent Milky Way vistas. The Casa Andina hotel has a tiny observatory that holds nightly sky shows in Spanish and English. Entry includes a 30-minute talk and the chance to peer into the telescope. Clear skies are rare between December and April.

La Calera Hot Springs THERMAL BATHS
(admission S15; 4:30am-7pm) A good way to acclimatize is to stroll 3km to Calera Hot Springs and examine the canyon's slopes (surprisingly shallow at this end) al fresco while lying in the famous pools. This isn't your average shopping-mall spa (forget the pampering), but the water's warm, the setting's idyllic and you'll be entertained by the whoops of zip-liners sailing overhead. *Colectivos* from Chivay cost S1 to S2.

Sleeping

Though it's a tiny town, Chivay has plenty of *hostales* to choose from.

Hotel Pozo del Cielo HOTEL $$
(34-6547; www.pozodelcielo.com.pe; Huascar; d/ste S88/135;) One half expects the seven dwarves to come marching out of the low doors or along the winding paths. But, surrealism aside, this place works: it's a functional yet comfortable abode with individually crafted rooms and a fine *mirador* restaurant.

Hostal La Pascana HOTEL $
(53-1001; Siglo XX 106; s/d/tr incl breakfast S55/70/87;) This good old-fashioned crash pad will seem like a luxury after hiking the canyon. Simple rooms have blankets (thank heavens!), the staff is gracious and there's a small but decent restaurant.

Casa Andina BOUTIQUE HOTEL $$$
(53-1022, 53-1020; www.casa-andina.com; Huayna Cápac; s/d incl breakfast from S250;) Rustic rooms inhabit thatched-roof cottages in sculpted grounds, but the star features are the unusual extras, which include an observatory, oxygen and nightly culture shows.

Hostal Estrella de David HOTEL $
(53-1233; Siglo XX 209; s/d/tr S20/20/40) A simple, clean *hospedaje*; some rooms have cable TV. It's a few blocks from the plaza toward the bus terminal.

Hostal Anita HOSTEL $
(53-1114; Plaza de Armas 607; s/d/tr S20/40/50) With a pretty interior courtyard, this friendly hostel smack on the main plaza has hot showers and affable owners. Breakfast available upon request.

BOLETO TURÍSTICO

To access the sites in the Colca canyon you need to purchase a *boleto turístico* (tourist ticket; S70) from a booth on the Arequipa road just outside Chivay. If you are taking an organized tour, the cost of the tour usually does not include this fee. If you are traveling alone, tickets can be purchased on most public buses entering or leaving Chivay, or in the town of Cabanaconde. Half of the proceeds from this ticket go to Arequipa for general maintenance and conservation of local tourist attractions, while the other half goes to the national agency of tourism.

Eating

Innkas Café PERUVIAN $
(Plaza de Armas 705; mains S12-20; 7am-11pm) An old building with cozy window nooks warmed by modern gas heaters (and boy do you need 'em). With damn good *lomo saltado*, sweet service and even sweeter cakes and coffee.

Aromas Caffee CAFE $
(www.aromascaffeecolca.com; cnr Plaza de Armas & Av Salaverry) The tiny cappuccino machine works overtime, but your Peruvian coffee, when it emerges, is worth the wait.

Cusi Alina PERUVIAN $$
(Plaza de Armas 201; buffet S25;) One of a couple of restaurants in Chivay with an all-you-can-eat lunchtime buffet. The food represents a good Peruvian smorgasbord with plenty of vegetarian options. It's popular with tour buses, so get in before 1pm to enjoy more elbow room.

Getting There & Away

The bus terminal is a 15-minute walk from the plaza. There are 11 buses daily to Arequipa (S15, three hours) and six to Cabanaconde (S5, 2½ hours) via Cruz del Cóndor.

CHIVAY TO CABANACONDE

The main road follows the south bank of the upper Cañón del Colca and leads past several picturesque villages and some of the most extensive pre-Inca terracing in Peru.

One of these villages, the more culturally intact **Yanque**, has an attractive 18th-century church and an excellent, small **cultural museum** (admission S5; ⏲9am-5pm Mon-Sat) at the plaza. A 30-minute walk to the river leads to some hot springs (admission S3). There are simple guesthouses and hotels scattered around town.

Eventually the road reaches **Cruz del Cóndor** (entry with *boleto turístico*). Andean condors that nest by the rocky outcrop can occasionally be seen gliding on thermal air currents. Early morning or late afternoon are the best viewing times, but you'll need luck.

If traveling independently with plans to stop in Cruz del Cóndor before continuing on to Cabanaconde, it's best to leave Arequipa on the unfortunately timed 1am bus. You will be in Cruz del Cóndor at daybreak with enough time to enjoy it and still catch a bus on to Cabanaconde from Arequipa. Later in the afternoon, those buses are few and far between, and you could be stuck in Cruz del Cóndor for several hours.

CABANACONDE

☎054 / POP 1300

Cabanaconde is an excellent base for some spectacular hikes into the canyon, including the popular two-hour trek down to Sangalle (The Oasis) at the bottom, where there are natural pools for swimming (S5), simple bungalows and campsites. The return trek is thirsty work; allow three to four hours.

Local guides can also be hired by consulting with your hostel or the *municipalidad* in Cabanaconde. The going rate for guides is S30 to S60 per day. They can also suggest a wealth of other treks, to waterfalls, geysers, remote villages and archaeological sites.

Pachamama (☎25-3879, 959-316-322; www.pachamamahome.com; San Pedro 209; incl breakfast dm S15, d without bathroom S35, r with bathroom S50; @) is an ubercozy place offering simple dorms and rooms as a complement to the canyon's best hangout spot: a candlelit pizzeria and bar run by a hip, guitar-wielding brother team from Ayacucho, who provide the singalong soundtrack to cavorting travelers. You can rent bikes, chill in the hammocks or just soak up the global vibe. This is travel.

The basic **La Posada del Conde** (☎83-0033, 40-0408; www.posadadelconde.com; San Pedro s/n; s/d incl breakfast S35/50; 📶) has well-cared-for doubles.

Several daily buses bound for Chivay (S5, 2½ hours) and Arequipa (S17, six hours) via Cruz del Cóndor leave from the plaza.

LAKE TITICACA

Covering 8400 sq km and sitting at 3808m, Lake Titicaca is considered the world's largest high-altitude lake. At this altitude the air is crisp and sunlight suffuses the *altiplano* and sparkles on the deep waters. Horizons encompass banner-blue skies, marked with ancient funerary towers and crumbling colonial churches. The port of Puno is a good base for visiting the far-flung islands dotted across Lake Titicaca – from artificial ones constructed of reeds to remote, rural isles where villagers live much as they have for centuries.

Juliaca

☎051 / POP 220,000

This is a brash, unfinished eyesore on an otherwise beautiful big-sky landscape. Principally a market town, it has the department's only commercial airport, though most tourists hightail it out of baggage claim for its more attractive lakeside neighbor, Puno. The city bustles with the commerce (and contraband) due to its handy location near the border. Daytime muggings and drunks on the street are not uncommon.

If you are in a pinch, the towering **Royal Inn Hotel** (☎32-1561; www.royalinnhoteles.com; San Román 158; s/d/tr S100/130/150) boasts newly revamped modern rooms with hot showers, heating and cable TV, plus one of Juliaca's best restaurants (mains from S18).

The **airport** (JUL; ☎32-4248) is 2km west of town. **LAN** (☎32-2228; San Roman 125) has daily flights to/from Lima, Arequipa and Cuzco. To the airport, take a taxi (S10). Direct minibuses to Puno (S15, 45 minutes) usually await incoming flights. Cheaper minibuses depart from the intersection of Piérola and 8 de Noviembre, northeast of the plaza (S3.50, 45 minutes).

Puno

☎051 / POP 118,000

With a regal plaza, concrete-block buildings and crumbling bricks that blend into the hills, Puno has its share of both grit and cheer. Few colonial buildings remain, and local women garbed in multilayered dresses and bowler hats bustle on the streets. You'll want to multilayer too – Puno nights are bitterly cold, especially in winter, when temperatures reel below freezing.

Sights & Activities

Yavari HISTORICAL SITE
(☎36-9329; www.yavari.org; admission by donation; ⏰8am-1pm & 3-5:30pm) The oldest boat on Lake Titicaca, the iron-hulled *Yavari* was built in England and shipped in 2766 pieces around Cape Horn to Arica, then transported to Tacna by train and hauled by mule over the Andes to Puno (taking a mere six years), where it was reassembled and launched in 1870. Due to a coal shortage, the engines were often powered by dried llama dung. The Peruvian navy eventually decommissioned the ship. Now moored by the Sonesta Posada Hotel del Inca (take a *mototaxi*, S3), the ship is open for tours and now operates as a very cool novelty lodging option (per person including breakfast S99).

Museo Carlos Dreyer MUSEUM
(Conde de Lemos 289; admission with English-speaking guide S15; ⏰9:30am-7pm Mon-Sat) Houses a beautiful collection of archaeological artifacts and art.

Coca Museum MUSEUM
(☎36-5087; Deza 301; admission S5; ⏰9am-1pm & 3-8pm) Chronicles the history of coca (in English).

Tours

Some travelers find the island-hopping tours disappointing, even exploitative; others report great fun. Ask around at your guesthouse for a local guide, preferably someone with ties to the islands, then go to the docks in the early morning and get on the next boat; or choose your tour company wisely.

All Ways Travel GUIDED TOUR, CULTURAL TOUR
(☎35-3979; www.titicacaperu.com; Deustua 576, 2nd fl) Offers both classic and 'non-touristy' tours.

Edgar Adventures GUIDED TOUR, CULTURAL TOUR
(☎35-3444; www.edgaradventures.com; Lima 328) Longtime agency with positive community involvement.

Nayra Travel GUIDED TOUR, CULTURAL TOUR
(☎975-1818, 36-4774; www.nayratravel.com; Lima 419, Oficina 105) Local package-tour operator.

Festivals & Events

La Virgen de la Candelaria RELIGION
(Candlemas) The region's most spectacular festival spreads out for several days around the actual date (February 2), depending upon which day of the week Candlemas falls. If it falls between Sunday and Tuesday, things get under way the previous Saturday; if Candlemas occurs between Wednesday and Friday, celebrations get going the following Saturday.

Puno Week CULTURE
A huge celebration marking the legendary birth of Manco Cápac, the first Inca. Events are held the first week of November, centered on Puno Day (November 5).

Epiphany RELIGION
Held on January 6.

Sleeping

TOP CHOICE **Casa Panq'arani** B&B **$$**
(☎951-677-005, 36-4892; www.casapanqarani.com; Jirón Arequipa 1086; s/tw/d incl breakfast S70/120/130; 📶) A delightful find, with a flower-filled courtyard and inviting rooms with crocheted bedspreads, lining a 2nd-floor balcony. Sincere hospitality, sunny spots for lounging and Consuelo's gourmet *altiplano* cooking (meals S30 with advance request) make it highly recommended.

Hotel Italia HOTEL **$$**
(☎36-7706; www.hotelitaliaperu.com; Valcárcel 122; s/d/tr S110/150/190; @📶) Snug rooms have parquet floors, cable TV, hot showers and heating but vary in quality at this large, well-established spot. The long-serving staff is efficient, and the delicious buffet breakfast includes salty black olives and Puno's triangular anise bread. Credit cards accepted.

Inka's Rest HOSTEL **$**
(☎36-8720; www.inkasresthostel.com; Pasaje San Carlos 158; dm/d incl breakfast S24/60; @📶) Tucked into a small alley, this hostel earns high marks for service. Very clean, it features bunks with down duvets, attractive old tiles and parquet floors.

Duque Inn HOTEL **$**
(☎20-5014; Ayaviri 152; r per person without/with bathroom S15/20) A steal for budget travelers/serious trekkers. If you're not up for splurging on taxis, consider the long haul up an endless hill to get here. Cordial but kooky, this budget lodging is spruced up with satin

Puno

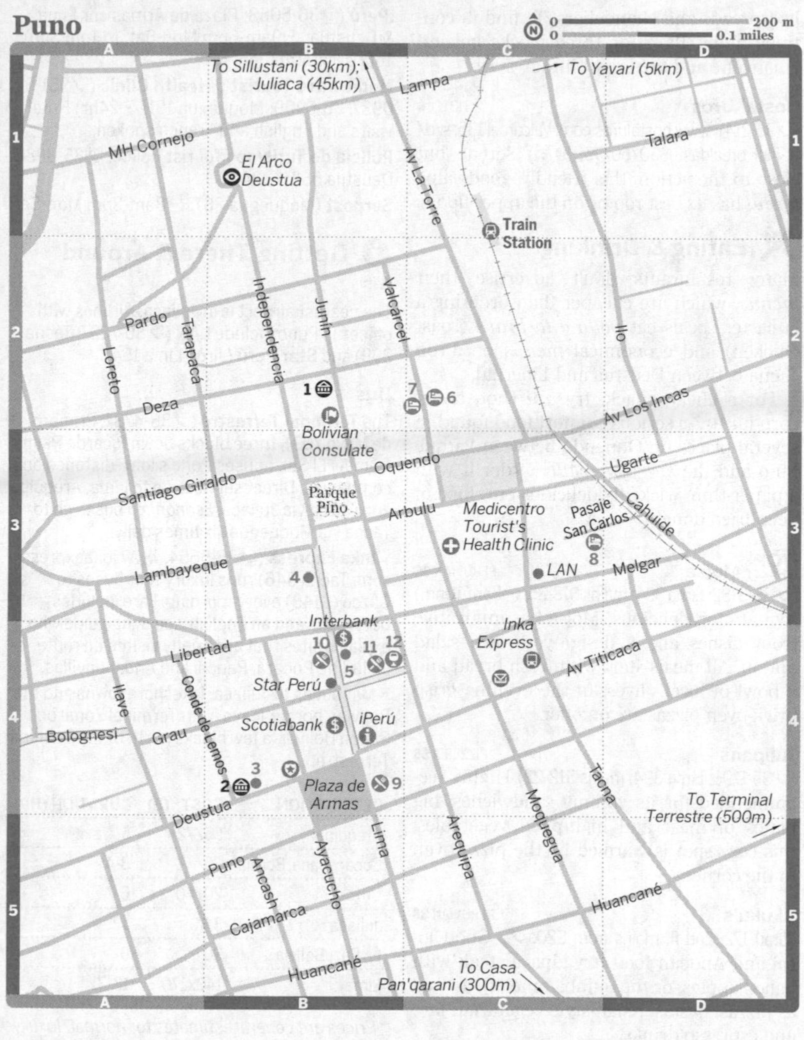

Puno

Sights

1 Coca Museum ... B2
2 Museo Carlos Dreyer ... B4

Activities, Courses & Tours

3 All Ways Travel ... B4
4 Edgar Adventures ... B3
5 Nayra Travel ... B4

Sleeping

6 Hostal Uros ... C2
7 Hotel Italia ... C2
8 Inka's Rest ... C3

Eating

9 Mojsa ... B4
10 Tulipans ... B4
11 Ukuku's ... B4

Drinking

12 Kamizaraky Rock Pub ... B4

bedspreads and chandeliers. To find it, continue along Ilave for three blocks beyond Huancané and turn right into Ayaviri.

Hostal Uros HOTEL **$**
(☎35-2141; www.hostaluros.com; Valcárcel 135; s/d/tr incl breakfast S30/50/75; @📶) Serene but close to the action, this friendly, good-value *hostal* has its best rooms on the upper floors.

Eating & Drinking

Many restaurants don't advertise their *menús*, which are cheaper than ordering à la carte. Locals eat *pollo a la brasa* (roast chicken) and economical *menús* on Jirón Tacna between Deustua and Libertad.

For a cheap snack, try *api* (hot, sweet corn juice) – a serious comfort food found in several places on Oquendo between Parque Pino and the *supermercado*. Order it with a paper-thin, wickedly delicious envelope of deep-fried dough.

TOP CHOICE **Mojsa** PERUVIAN **$$**
(☎36-3182; Lima 394; mains S18-35; ⏰8am-10pm) Aymara for 'delicious,' Mojsa has innovative trout dishes and a design-your-own salad option. All meals start with fresh bread and a bowl of local olives. In the evening crisp brick-oven pizzas are on offer.

Tulipans PIZZERIA **$$**
(☎35-1796; Lima 394; mains S12-22) Highly recommended for its yummy sandwiches, big plates of meat and high-piled vegetables, this cozy spot is warmed by the pizza oven in the corner.

Ukuku's PERUVIAN **$$**
(Grau 172, 2nd fl; mains from S20; 🥕) Good local and Andean food (try alpaca steak with baked apples, or the quinoa omelet), as well as pizzas, pastas, Asian-style vegetarian fare and espresso drinks.

Kamizaraky Rock Pub PUB
(Grau 158) With a classic-rock soundtrack, unbelievably cool bartenders and liquor-infused coffee drinks essential for staying warm during Puno's bone-chilling nights, it may be a hard place to leave.

Information

Money can be exchanged in town or at the border.

Scotiabank (Jirón Lima 458) ATM.

Interbank (Lima 444) Global ATM; changes traveler's checks.

iPerú (☎36-5088; Plaza de Armas cnr Lima & Deustua; ⏰9am-6pm Mon-Sat, to 1pm Sun) Tourist information.

Medicentro Tourist's Health Clinic (☎951-62-0937, 36-5909; Moquegua 191; ⏰24hr) Hotel visits and English and French spoken.

Policía de Turismo (Tourist Police; ☎35-3988; Deustua 558; ⏰24hr)

Serpost (Moquegua 267; ⏰8am-8pm Mon-Sat)

Getting There & Around

Air

The nearest airport is in Juliaca. Airlines with offices in Puno include **LAN** (☎36-7227; Tacna 299) and **Star Perú** (Jirón Lima 154).

Bus

The **Terminal Terrestre** (☎36-4737; Primero de Mayo 703), three blocks down Ricardo Palma from Av El Sol, houses Puno's long-distance bus companies. Direct services go to Lima, Arequipa and Cuzco via Juliaca. *Económico* buses go to Tacna via Moquegua six times daily.

Inka Express (☎36-5654; www.inkaexpress.com; Tacna 346) runs luxury tour buses to Cuzco (S143) every morning. Fare includes beverages and an English-speaking guide who explains sites that are briefly visited en route, including Pucará, Raqchi and Andahuayillas.

Minibuses to Juliaca, lakeshore towns and the Bolivian border leave from Terminal Zonal on Simón Bolívar, a few blocks north of the Terminal Terrestre.

DESTINATION	COST* (S)	DURATION (HR)
Arequipa	56/72	5
Copacabana, Bolivia	25	3-4
Cuzco	20/40	6-7
Juliaca	3.50	1
La Paz, Bolivia	30	6
Lima	140/170	18-21

** Prices are general estimates for normal/luxury buses.*

Taxi

A short taxi ride around town costs S4. *Mototaxis* are cheaper, but make sure the negotiated fare is per ride, not per person.

Train

Cuzco-bound trains depart from Puno's **train station** (☎36-9179; www.perurail.com; Av La Torre 224; US$150; ⏰7am-noon & 3-6pm Mon-Fri, 7am-3pm Sat) at 8am, arriving at 6pm. Services run on Monday, Wednesday and Saturday from November to March, with an extra departure on Friday from April to October. Tickets can be purchased online.

Around Puno

SILLUSTANI

Sitting on rolling hills in the Lago Umayo peninsula, these ruined **towers** (admission S10) stand out for miles against the unforgiving landscape. The ancient Colla people were a warlike, Aymara-speaking tribe that buried their nobility in these impressive *chullpas* (funerary towers), made from massive coursed blocks and reaching heights of up to 12m. There are also 20 or so local *altiplano* homes in the area that welcome visitors.

Puno travel agencies run 3½-hour tours (S35 including entrance fee) that leave around 2:30pm daily. To DIY, catch any bus to Juliaca and get off where the road splits to Sillustani. From there, occasional *combis* (S2, 20 minutes) go to the ruins.

CUTIMBO

Almost 20km from Puno, this dramatic windswept **site** (admission S6) has an extraordinary position atop a table-topped volcanic hill surrounded by a sprawling plain. Its modest number of exceptionally well-preserved *chullpas*, built by the Colla, Lupaca and Inca cultures, come in both square and cylindrical shapes. Look closely and you'll find several monkeys, pumas and snakes carved into the structures.

Combis leave the cemetery by Parque Amistad, 1km from Puno's town center, every half-hour (S3, one hour). You can't miss the site, a steep climb up from the right-hand (east) side of the road.

Titicaca Islands

The only way to see Lake Titicaca is to spend a few days visiting its fairy-tale islands. That said, negative impacts from tourism are being felt in many communities. You could also hop over the Bolivian border to visit the more chilled Isla del Sol from Copacabana.

ISLAS UROS

The unique **floating islands** (admission S5) of the Uros people – around 50 reed islands in all – have become quite commercial, though there is still nothing quite like them anywhere else. The islands are built using layers of the buoyant *totora* reeds that grow abundantly in the shallows of Lake Titicaca. It's like a reed Disneyland.

GETTING TO BOLIVIA

There are two overland routes from Puno to La Paz, Bolivia. The Yunguyo route, which is safer and easier, allows you to take a break at the lakeshore resort of Copacabana. The Desaguadero route, which is slightly faster and cheaper, can be combined with a visit to the ruins at Tiwanaku. Beware of immigration officials trying to charge an illegal 'entry tax' or search your belongings for 'fake dollars' to confiscate. US citizens require a visa to enter Bolivia (US$135 at border posts).

Via Yunguyo

The most convenient way to reach Bolivia is with a cross-border company like **Tour Peru** (☎20-6088; www.tourperu.com.pe; Tacna 285); purchase tickets a day ahead. Buses depart at 7:30am, stopping at Peruvian and Bolivian border posts, then Copacabana (S25, three to four hours), where you board another bus to La Paz (S30, 3½ hours). Officials in Copacabana will make you pay just to enter town (S1).

Alternatively, frequent minibuses depart Puno's Terminal Zonal for Yunguyo (S6.50, 2½ hours), where you can grab a taxi for the final leg to the border (S3). In Bolivia, which is an hour ahead of Peru, the border post is open from 8:30am to 7pm daily. From the border, it's another 10km to Copacabana (*combis* B$3).

Via Desaguadero

Combis leave Puno's Terminal Zonal for Desaguadero (S8, 2½ hours) throughout the day. Avoid spending the night here. Border hours are 8:30am to 8:30pm, but because Bolivia is an hour ahead of Peru, plan to cross before 7pm Peruvian time. Many buses go from Desaguadero to La Paz (B$30, three hours) during daylights hours, passing the turnoff for Tiwanaku. There are no ATMs in Desaguadero, so bring cash from Puno if your nationality requires a tourist visa.

Intermarriage with Aymara-speaking indigenous peoples has seen the demise of the pure-blooded Uros. Always a small tribe, they began their floating existence centuries ago in an effort to isolate themselves from the aggressive Collas and the Incas. Today several hundred people still live on the islands.

Indeed, the lives of the Uros are completely interwoven with the reeds, which are used to make their homes, boats and crafts. The islands' reeds are constantly replenished from the top as they rot away, so the ground is always soft and springy – mind your step!

Those seeking homestays on Isla Khantati meet with boundless personality **Cristina Suaña** (☎951-47-2355, 951-69-5121; uroskhantati@hotmail.com; per person full board S165), an Uros native whose entrepreneurship has earned her international accolades.

Ferries leave from the port for Uros (return trip S12) at least once an hour from 6am to 4pm. The community-owned ferry service visits two islands, on a rotation basis. Ferries to Taquile and Amantaní can also drop you off in the Uros.

ISLA TAQUILE

Inhabited for many thousands of years, this 7-sq-km **island** (admission S5) often feels like its own little world. The Quechua-speaking islanders maintain lives minimally changed by mainland modernities and have a long tradition of weaving. Look for the menfolk's tightly woven woolen hats, resembling floppy nightcaps, which denote social status. Women wear multilayered skirts and delicately embroidered blouses.

Several hills have pre-Inca terracing and small ruins set against the backdrop of Bolivia's snowcapped Cordillera Real. Visitors are free to wander around, but you can't do that on a day trip without missing lunch or the boat back, so stay overnight if you can. Travelers will be met by islanders next to the arch atop the steep stairway up from the dock. Homestays can be arranged here (per person S20), though tourism has altered the landscape here somewhat and travelers looking for a less tainted experience should sleep on nearby Amantaní, which is still in its tourism infancy and offers a more authentic sleepover. If you do sleep on Taquile, beds are basic but clean, and facilities are minimal. You'll be given blankets, but bring a sleeping bag and flashlight.

Most island shops and restaurants close by midafternoon, when all the tour groups leave, so arrange dinner with your host family in advance. Gifts of fresh fruit from Puno's markets are appreciated. You can buy bottled drinks at the shops, though it's worth bringing purifying tablets or a water filter. Also bring small bills (change is limited) and extra money for souvenirs.

Boats leave Puno's dock for the incredibly slow 34km trip to Taquile daily at 6:45am (S20 round-trip, three hours); some stop at Islas Uros. The return boat leaves in the early afternoon, arriving in Puno around nightfall. Remember to bring sunscreen and mosquito repellent.

Puno travel agencies organize two-day guided tours for S50 and up (some with much faster boats charge upwards of S180).

ISLA AMANTANÍ

This less frequently visited **island** (admission S5) is a few kilometers northeast of Taquile. Ruins of the Tiwanaku culture top several hills. **Amantani Community Lodging** (☎36-9714), essentially made up of the island's families, allocates accommodation according to a rotating system. Expect limited facilities but a unique and welcoming experience. Boats to Amantaní leave Puno between 7:30am and 8:30am most mornings; pay the captain directly (S30 return, 3½ hours). Unpredictable boat connections usually make it easiest to travel from Puno to Amantaní and on to Taquile, rather than in reverse. Puno travel agencies charge S75 to S90 for a two-day tour to Amantaní, with a quick visit to Taquile and the floating islands. This is by far the most authentic choice for overnight stays.

It's important to keep in mind that Titicaca's island families will benefit more if you visit independently – there are some agencies that consistently exploit them, undercutting the agreed fee they are supposed to receive for each tourist. Go it alone, or choose your tour operator wisely.

CUZCO & THE SACRED VALLEY

As the heart of the once mighty Inca empire, the magnetic city of Cuzco heads the list of many traveler itineraries. Each year it draws hundreds of thousands of visitors to its lofty elevations, lured by the colonial splendor built on hefty stone foundations of the Incas. And lying within easy hopping distance of the city is the country's biggest drawcard:

the 'lost' city of the Incas, Machu Picchu, perched high on a remote mountaintop. The department of Cuzco also has superb trekking routes and a long list of flamboyant fiestas and carnivals in which Peru's pagan past colorfully collides with Catholic rituals and modern Latin American mayhem.

Cuzco

084 / POP 349,000

The high-flying city of Cuzco (Qosq'o in the Quechua language) sits at a 3300m crossroads of centuries-old Andean tradition and modern Peruvian life. As the continent's oldest continuously inhabited city, it was once the Inca empire's foremost stronghold, and is now both the undisputed archaeological capital of the Americas as well as one of the continent's most staunchly preserved colonial living museums. Massive Inca-built walls line steep, narrow cobblestone streets and plazas thronged with the descendants of the mighty Incas and Spanish conquistadors – who hobble about in colorful traditional wares among the hustle and bustle of contemporary *cuzqueños* making a living from the town's present-day lifeblood: tourism. And lots of it.

Though Cuzco is at the tipping point of being completely overrun with international tourism, its historical charms and breathtaking setting cannot be denied.

History

Cuzco is so steeped in history, tradition and myth that it can be difficult to know where fact ends and story begins. Legends tell that in the 12th century the first Inca, Manco Capác, was charged by the ancestral sun god Inti to find the *qosq'o* (the navel of the earth). When at last Manco discovered such a point, he founded the city there.

The ninth Inca Pachacutec wasn't only a warmonger; he also proved himself to be a sophisticated urban developer, devising Cuzco's famous puma shape and diverting rivers to cross the city. Pachacutec also built the famous Qorikancha temple and the palace fronting what is now the Plaza de Armas.

After murdering the 12th Inca Atahualpa, the Spanish conquistador Francisco Pizarro marched on Cuzco in 1533 and appointed Manco Inca as puppet ruler of the Incas. After a few years, Manco rebelled and laid siege to Spanish-occupied Cuzco. Only a desperate battle at Saqsaywamán saved the Spanish from annihilation. Manco was forced to retreat to Ollantaytambo and eventually into the jungle at Vilcabamba. Once the city had been safely recaptured, looted and settled, the seafaring Spaniards turned their attentions to coastal Lima, making Cuzco just another quiet colonial backwater.

Earthquakes rocked Cuzco in 1650 and 1950, and a failed indigenous uprising was led by Túpac Amaru II in 1780. But the rediscovery of Machu Picchu in 1911 has affected the city more than any event since the arrival of the Spanish.

Sights

Students usually pay half-price admission. To visit most sites, you will need Cuzco's official **boleto turístico** (tourist ticket; adult/student under 26 with ISIC card S130/70), valid for 10 days. Among the 17 sites included are: Saqsaywamán, Q'enqo, Pukapukara, Tambomachay, Pisac, Ollantaytambo, Chinchero and Moray, as well as an evening performance of Andean dances and live music at the Centro Qosqo de Arte Nativo. While some inclusions are duds, you can't visit any of them without the ticket. It's also possible to buy partial one-day *boletos* costing S70. A similar scheme for religious sites, the Circuito Religioso, costs S50 and is valid for a month. Purchase *boletos turísticos* from **DIRCETUR/Cosituc** (261-465; www.boletoturistico.com; Av El Sol 103, La Municipalidad, Oficina 102; 8am-6pm Mon-Fri) or at participating sites outside the city.

The city centers on the Plaza de Armas, while traffic-choked Av El Sol is the main business thoroughfare. The alley off the northwest side of the plaza is Procuradores (Tax Collectors), nicknamed 'Gringo Alley'. Beside the cathedral, Triunfo climbs to San Blas, Cuzco's artistic *barrio* (neighborhood).

Plaza de Armas PLAZA

Colonial arcades surround the plaza, which was the heart of the ancient Inca capital.

Taking almost 100 years to build, Cuzco's **cathedral** (admission S25 or with boleto religioso; 10am-5:45pm) sits on the site of Inca Viracocha's palace and was erected using blocks from Saqsaywamán. It's one of the city's greatest repositories of colonial art. Look for *The Last Supper* by Marcos Zapata, with a plump roast *cuy* (guinea pig) stealing the show. Opposite the silver altar is a magnificently carved 17th-century choir. The cathedral is joined with the church of **Jesus María** (1733) and **El Triunfo** (1536),

Cuzco

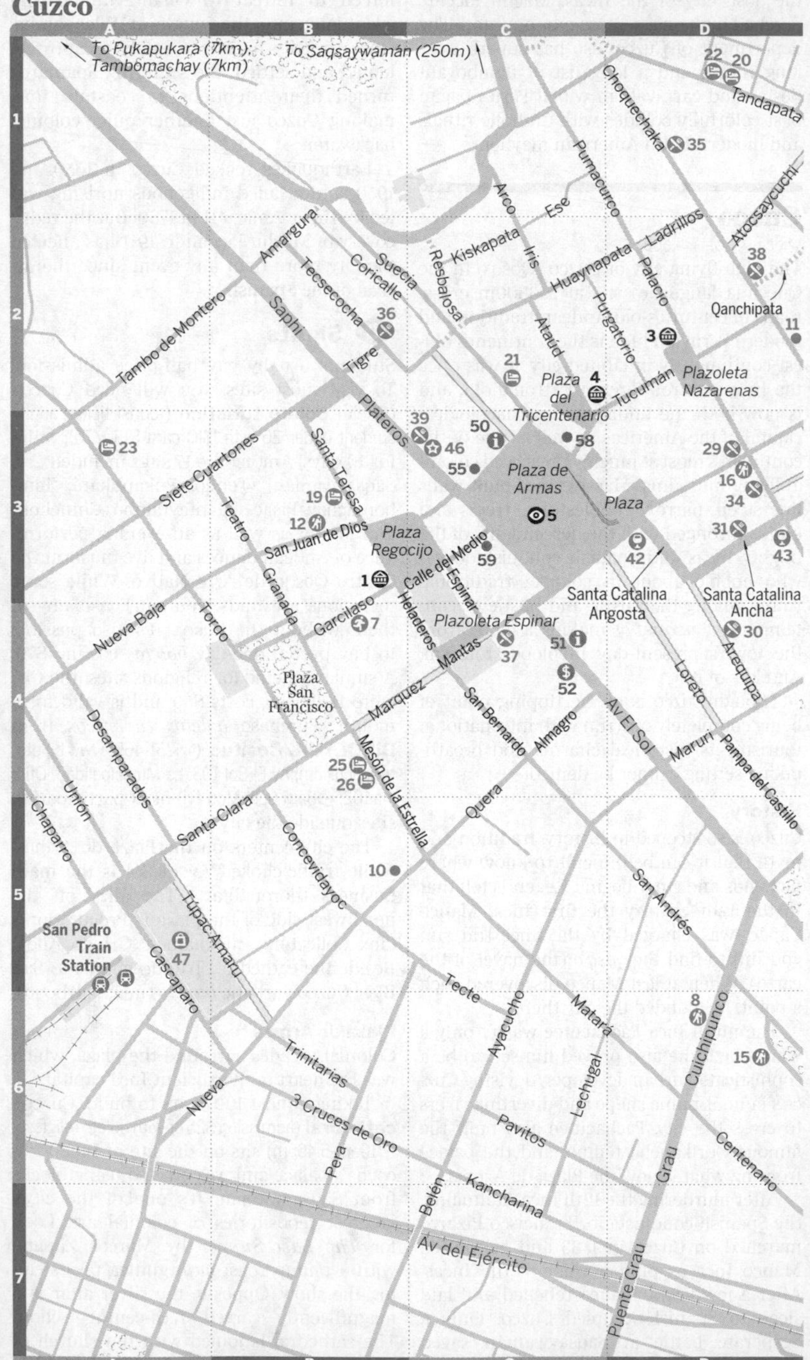
A
B
C
D
1
2
3
4
5
6
7
To Pukapukara (7km);
Tambomachay (7km)
To Saqsaywamán (250m)
Choquechaka
Tandapata
Pumacurco
Arco
Ese
Kiskapata
Iris
Huaynapata
Ladrillos
Atocsaycuchi
Palacio
Purgatorio
Ataud
Resbalosa
Suecia
Coricalle
Amargura
Tecsecocha
Saphi
Tambo de Montero
Tigre
Plateros
Qanchipata
Plaza del Tricentenario
Tucumán
Plazoleta Nazarenas
Plaza de Armas
Plaza
Siete Cuartones
Santa Teresa
Teatro
San Juan de Dios
Plaza Regocijo
Calle del Medio
Espinar
Santa Catalina Angosta
Santa Catalina Ancha
Nueva Baja
Tordo
Granada
Garcilaso
Heladeros
Plazoleta Espinar
Mantas
Plaza San Francisco
Marquez
San Bernardo
Almagro
Av El Sol
Loreto
Arequipa
Maruri
Pampa del Castillo
Desamparados
Unión
Chaparro
Mesón de la Estrella
Santa Clara
Quera
Concevidayoc
San Andrés
San Pedro Train Station
Túpac Amaru
Cascaparo
Tecte
Ayacucho
Matará
Lechugal
Cuichipunco
Trinitarias
Nueva
3 Cruces de Oro
Pera
Pavitos
Centenario
Grau
Belén
Kancharina
Puente Grau
Av del Ejército
1
3
4
5
7
8
10
11
12
15
16
19
20
21
22
23
25
26
29
30
31
34
35
36
37
38
39
42
43
46
47
50
51
52
55
58
59

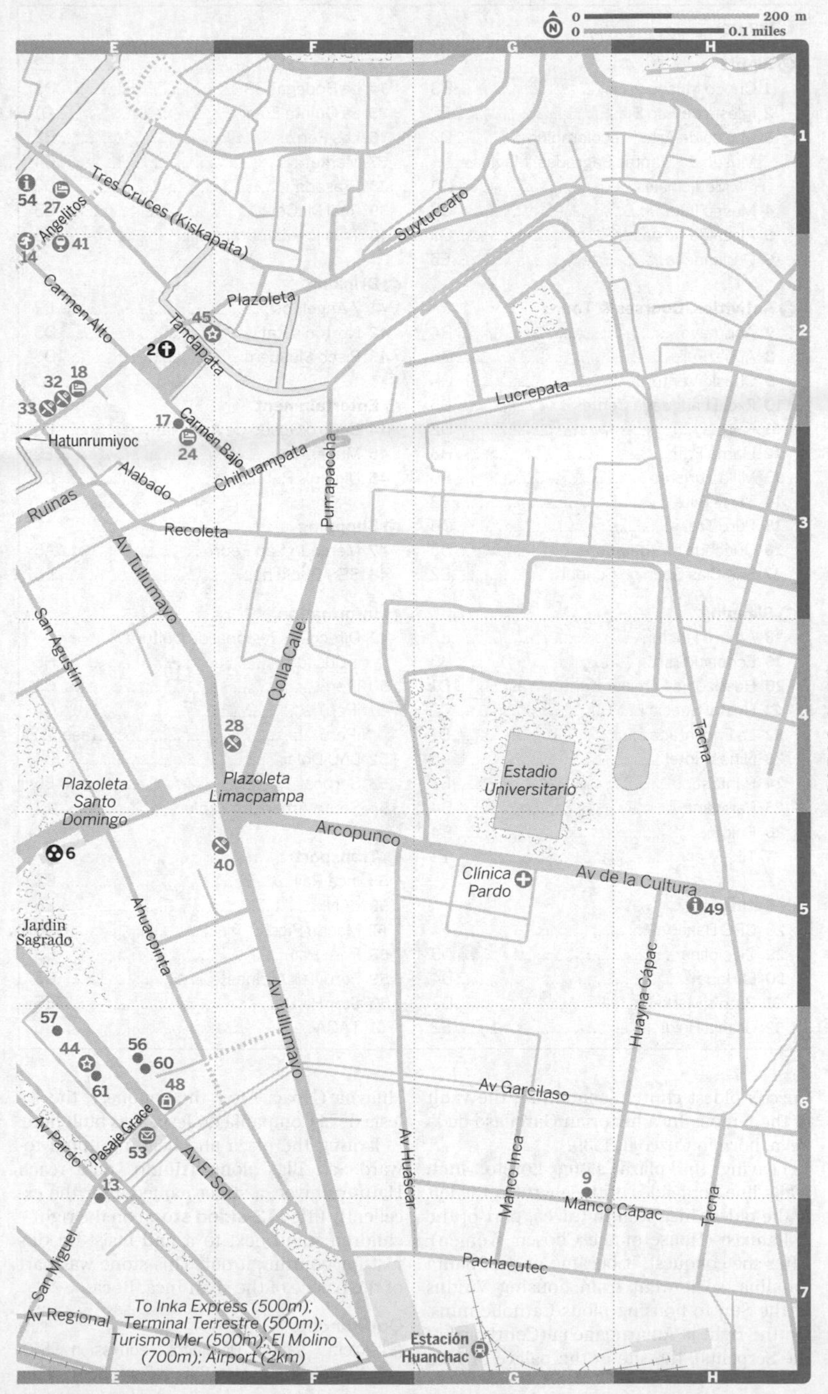
0 200 m
0 0.1 miles
Tres Cruces (Kiskapata)
Angelitos
Carmen Alto
Suytuccato
Plazoleta
Tandapata
Lucrepata
Hatunrumiyoc
Carmen Bajo
Chihuampata
Alabado
Ruinas
Recoleta
Purrapaccha
Av Tullumayo
San Agustin
Qolla Calle
Plazoleta Santo Domingo
Plazoleta Limacpampa
Arcopunco
Estadio Universitario
Clínica Pardo
Av de la Cultura
Tacna
Jardin Sagrado
Ahuacpinta
Huayna Cápac
Av Garcilaso
Av Huáscar
Manco Inca
Manco Cápac
Pachacutec
Av Pardo
Pasaje Grace
Av El Sol
San Miguel
Av Regional
To Inka Express (500m); Terminal Terrestre (500m); Turismo Mer (500m); El Molino (700m); Airport (2km)
Estación Huanchac

Cuzco

Sights

1 Choco Museo ... B3
2 Iglesia de San Blas ... E2
3 Museo de Arte Precolombino ... D2
Museo de Plantas Sagradas, Mágicas y Medicinales ... (see 19)
4 Museo Inka ... C2
5 Plaza de Armas ... C3
6 Qorikancha ... E5

Activities, Courses & Tours

7 Apumayo ... B4
8 Apu's Peru ... D6
9 Chaski Ventura ... G6
10 Excel Language Center ... B5
11 Fairplay ... D2
12 Llama Path ... B3
13 Milla Turismo ... E6
14 Party Bike ... E2
15 Peru Treks ... D6
16 Quechua's Expeditions ... D3
17 San Blas Spanish School ... E2

Sleeping

18 Amaru Hostal ... E2
19 Ecopackers ... B3
20 Hospedaje Familiar Kuntur Wasi ... D1
21 Hostal Suecia I ... C2
22 La Encantada ... D1
23 Niños Hotel ... A3
24 Pantastico ... E3
25 Pariwana ... B4
26 Point ... B4
27 Tika Wasi ... E1

Eating

28 CBC Bakery ... F4
29 Cicciolina ... D3
30 El Hada ... D4
31 Gato's Market ... D3
32 Granja Heidi ... E2
33 Jack's Café ... E2
34 La Bodega 138 ... D3
35 La Quinta Eulalia ... D1
36 Los Perros ... B2
37 Market ... C4
38 Prasada ... D2
39 Real McCoy ... C3
40 Trujillo Restaurant ... F5

Drinking

41 7 Angelitos ... E2
42 Norton's Rat ... D3
43 Pisco Musuem ... D3

Entertainment

44 Centro Qosqo de Arte Nativo ... E6
45 Muse, Too ... E2
46 Ukuku's Pub ... C3

Shopping

47 Mercado San Pedro ... A5
48 SBS Bookshop ... E6

Information

49 Dirección Regional de Cultura Cusco ... H5
50 iPerú ... C3
51 iPerú ... C4
iPerú ... (see 51)
52 LAC Dolar ... C4
53 Serpost ... E6
54 South American Explorers ... E1

Transport

55 Inca Rail ... C3
56 LAN ... E6
57 Machu Picchu Train ... E6
58 Peru Rail ... C3
59 Peruvian Airlines ... C3
60 Star Perú ... E6
61 TACA ... E6

Cuzco's oldest church, containing the vault of the famous Inca historian Garcilaso de la Vega, born in Cuzco in 1539.

Leaving the plaza along Loreto, **Inca walls** line both sides of the alley. On the left is the oldest Inca wall in Cuzco, part of the Acllahuasi (House of the Chosen Women). After the conquest, it became part of Santa Catalina, so it went from housing Virgins of the Sun to housing pious Catholic nuns. On the right is Amaruqancha (Courtyard of the Serpents), the site of the palace of Inca Huayna Capác. After the conquest, the Iglesia de la Compañía de Jesús was built here.

Exiting the plaza and heading uphill toward San Blas along Triunfo you'll reach Hatunrumiyoc, a street named after the excellently fitted **12-sided stone** on the right – children stand next to it and insist on tips just for pointing it out. This stone was part of the palace of the sixth Inca, Roca.

Qorikancha RUIN

(Plazoleta Santo Domingo; admission S10; ⌚8:30am-5:30pm Mon-Sat, 2-5pm Sun) This

Inca site forms the base of the colonial church of **Iglesia de Santo Domingo**. Compare the colonial building with the Inca walls, most of which survived Cuzco's historic earthquakes with hardly a hairline crack. There's a modern protective roof of glass and metal.

In Inca times, Qorikancha (Quechua for 'golden courtyard') was literally covered with gold. Not only used for religious rites, it was also an observatory from which priests monitored major celestial activities. Today all that remains of the Inca empire's richest temple is its masterly stonework – Spanish conquistadors looted the rest. But it's fascinating to visit nonetheless, with excellent interpretive signs for self-guided tours.

Museo de Arte Precolombino MUSEUM
(☎23-3210; map.perucultural.org.pe; Plazoleta Nazarenas 231; admission S22; ⏰9am-10pm) Inside a Spanish-colonial mansion with an Inca ceremonial courtyard, this dramatically curated museum showcases a stunningly varied collection of priceless archaeological pieces previously buried in the vast storerooms of Lima's Museo Larco. Labels are in Spanish, English and French. It ranks right up there with the continent's best.

Museo Inka MUSEUM
(☎23-7380; Tucumán near Ataúd; admission S10; ⏰8am-6pm Mon-Fri, 9am-4pm Sat) The modest Museo Inka inhabits one of the city's finest colonial buildings. It's jam-packed with metal- and goldwork, pottery, textiles, *queros* (wooden Inca drinking vessels), mummies and more. In the courtyard, highland weavers sell their traditional textiles to the public.

Choco Museo MUSEUM
(☎24-4765; www.chocomuseo.com; Garcilaso 210; admission S2; ⏰10:30am-6:30pm) The wafting aromas of bubbling chocolate will mesmerize you from the start. While the museum is frankly lite, the best part of this French-owned enterprise are the organic chocolate-making workshops (S70 per person). You can also come for fondue or a fresh cup of fair-trade hot cocoa. It also organizes chocolate farm tours close to Santa María (northwest of Cuzco). It's multilingual and children-friendly.

Museo de Plantas Sagradas, Mágicas y Medicinales MUSEUM
(☎22-2214; Santa Teresa 351; admission S15; ⏰10am-7pm Mon-Sat, noon-6pm Sun) This fascinating new museum leaves no leaf unturned, exploring the history and workings of Peruvian medicinal plants, sacred plants and hallucinogenics. It's worthwhile to contract an English-speaking guide (S4 per person).

Iglesia de San Blas CHURCH
(Plaza San Blas; admission S15 or with boleto religioso; ⏰10am-6pm Mon-Sat, 2-6pm Sun) This adobe church has a pulpit which some call the finest example of colonial woodcarving in the Americas. It's the creator's skull that, according to legend, is nestled in the topmost part.

Activities

Scores of outdoor outfitters in Cuzco offer trekking, rafting and mountain-biking adventures, as well as mountaineering, horseriding and paragliding trips. Be wary of outfitters lining Plateros and Santa Ana – most are just looking to cash in on the tourism bonanza.

Trekking

The Inca Trail is on most hikers' minds, but a dizzying array of other treks surround Cuzco. Many agencies organize trips to remote Inca ruins, such as Choquequirau and Vilcabamba and around Ausangate. Prices are *not* fixed. Shop around and ask questions (eg how many people per tent, how many porters are coming, what are the arrangements for special diets). Inspect all rental gear carefully. South American Explorers sells topo maps and is an excellent source of independent info.

Travelers usually flock to the following agencies:

Apu's Peru HIKING
(☎23-3691; www.apus-peru.com; Cuichipunco 366) A recommended outfitter.

Llama Path HIKING
(☎24-0822; www.llamapath.com; San Juan de Dios 250) A popular Inca Trail outfitter, though not as personable as the others.

Peru Treks HIKING
(☎25-2721; www.perutreks.com; Av Pardo 540) Locally co-owned, eco-conscious and with ethical treatment of porters.

Quechua's Expeditions HIKING
(☎23-7994; www.quechuasexpeditions.com; Suecia 344) Another recommended outfitter.

THINK AHEAD: MACHU PICCHU TICKETS

Since Machu Picchu tickets can no longer be purchased online, get this business done early with an authorized agent listed at www.machupicchu.gob.pe or in person at Cuzco's Dirección Regional de Cultura. To add entry to the coveted Huayna Picchu hike, purchase even earlier.

River Running & Mountain Biking

Popular whitewater-rafting trips visit **Río Urubamba**. It's not very wild but offers some spectacular scenery and a chance to visit some of the best Inca ruins near Cuzco. Rivers here are unregulated. For more remote rivers, book with a top-quality outfit using experienced rafting guides who know first aid, because you will be days away from help in the event of illness or accident. The same goes for mountain-biking trips.

The **Río Apurímac** has challenging rapids through deep gorges and protected rainforest but can only be run from May to November. A wilder trip is the technically demanding **Río Tambopata**, run from June to October. Trips start north of Lake Titicaca and reach Reserva Nacional Tambopata in the Amazon.

If you're experienced, there are awesome mountain-biking possibilities around the Sacred Valley and downhill trips from Cuzco to the Amazon jungle. Always inspect rental bikes carefully. Make sure you get a helmet, puncture-repair kit, pump and tool kit.

Some reputable companies for rafting and biking trips include the following:

Amazonas Explorer ADVENTURE TOUR
(☎25-2846; www.amazonas-explorer.com; Av Collasuyu 910, Miravalle) This professional international operator with top-quality equipment and guides offers rafting on the Ríos Apurímac and Tambopata, and mountain biking.

Apumayo RAFTING
(☎24-6018; www.apumayo.com; Jirón Ricardo Palma Ñ-11, Urb Santa Monica) Another professional outfitter.

Party Bike ADVENTURE TOUR
(☎24-0399; www.partybiketravel.com; Carmen Alto 246) Traveler-recommended, with downhills and tours to the valley and in Cuzco.

Courses

Excel Language Center LANGUAGE
(☎23-5298; www.excel-spanishlanguageprograms-peru.org; Cruz Verde 336) Highly recommended for its professionalism.

Fairplay LANGUAGE
(☎984-78-9252; www.fairplay-peru.org; Choquechaca 188) Individual classes.

San Blas Spanish School LANGUAGE
(☎24-7898; www.spanishschoolperu.com; Carmen Bajo 224) Offers Spanish classes.

Tours

There are hundreds of registered travel agencies in Cuzco, but none can ever be 100% recommended. Ask around. Cuzco is an excellent place to organize trips to the jungle, especially to Parque Nacional Manu. None are cheap, though. Try the following:

Chaski Ventura CULTURAL TOUR
(☎23-3952; www.chaskiventura.com; Manco Cápac 517) Pioneer of alternative and community tourism. French, English and Spanish are spoken.

Manu Expeditions ADVENTURE TOUR
(☎22-4235, 22-5990; www.manuexpeditions.com; Clorinda Matto de Turner 330, Urb Magisterial) Destinations include Parque Nacional Manu and horseback riding around the Sacred Valley.

Milla Turismo TOUR
(☎23-1710; www.millaturismo.com; Av Pardo 800) Reputable conventional tour operator with travel-agency services.

Festivals & Events

El Señor de los Temblores CULTURE
(The Lord of the Earthquakes) This procession on the Monday before Easter dates to the earthquake of 1650.

Q'oyoriti CULTURE
Lesser known are these traditional Andean rites, held the Sunday before Corpus Christi near Ausangate.

Corpus Christi RELIGION
Held on the ninth Thursday after Easter, Corpus Christi usually occurs in early June. Features fantastic religious processions.

Inti Raymi CULTURE
(Festival of the Sun) Held on June 24, Cuzco's most important festival attracts thousands

of visitors and culminates in a re-enactment of Inca winter-solstice ceremonies at Saqsaywamán.

Sleeping

Side streets northwest of the Plaza de Armas (especially Tigre, Tecsecocha and Suecia) are bursting with dime-a-dozen *hostales*. Budget guesthouses also surround the Plaza San Blas, though you'll have to huff and puff to get up there.

TOP CHOICE **Ecopackers** HOSTEL $$
(☎23-1800; www.ecopackersperu.com; Santa Teresa 375; dm S25-41, d/ste S120/135; @ 📶) Thought has been put into this big backpacker haven. One of the all-inclusives (with bar, pool room and sunbathing), it ups the ante by being clean, friendly and service-minded. There are lovely wicker lounges in the courtyard and the sturdy beds are extra-long. There's also 24-hour security.

La Encantada BOUTIQUE HOTEL $$$
(☎24-2206; www.encantadaperu.com; Tandapata 354; s/d incl breakfast S212/265; @ 📶) A worthwhile splurge for couples, this modern boutique hotel features terraced gardens and immense views from iron-rail balconies. A circular staircase leads to small, tasteful rooms with soft linens and king-size beds. The on-site spa helps hikers work out the aches and kinks. Be aware that the checkout is at 9am.

Niños Hotel HOTEL $$
(☎25-4611, 23-1424; www.ninoshotel.com; Meloc 442; s/d without bathroom S63/126, d/tr incl breakfast S137/200; @ 📶) These beloved hotels (there are two) are run by a Dutch nonprofit serving underprivileged children in Cuzco. Both are in rambling colonials with sunny courtyards. Refurbished rooms with bright trim feature plaid throws and portable heaters. The public cafeteria features homemade cakes and breads as well as box lunches. The other branch is at Fierro 476.

Pariwana HOSTEL $$
(☎23-3751; www.pariwana-hostel.com; Av Mesón de la Estrella 136; dm S24-36, d without/with bathroom S85/98; @ 📶) Resembling spring break, this notably clean, newer hostel is filled with uni types lounging on poufs and playing ping-pong in the courtyard of a huge colonial.

Tika Wasi HOTEL $$
(☎23-1609; www.tikawasi.com; Tandapata 491; s/d/tr incl breakfast S89/122/155, superior s/d/tr S89/166/199; 📶) Behind a tall wall, this modern inn offers a personable option. Rooms are bright and airy, overlooking small, sunny decks to hang out on.

Amaru Hostal HOTEL $$
(☎22-5933; www.cusco.net/amaru; Cuesta San Blas 541; s/d/tr incl breakfast S105/135/189; @ 📶) Brightly lit courtyards – one with open-air views over Cuzco – characterize this charming midrange option. Space heaters are provided; internet is extra.

Pantastico GUESTHOUSE $$
(☎95-4387; www.hotelpantastico.com; Carmen Bajo 226; dm/s/d with shared bathroom S30/45/70/90, s/d S65/90; @ 📶) With good water pressure and a hardcore hippie groove: if you want to shop for San Pedro experiences or make organic pizza, it's your spot.

Hospedaje Familiar Kuntur Wasi HOTEL $
(☎22-7570; Tandapata 352A; r per person without/with bathroom S35/60) Quiet and economical, a monastic hotel with ship-shape rooms and free buffet breakfast.

Hospedaje Turismo Caith GUESTHOUSE $
(☎23-3595; www.caith.org; Pasaje Sto Toribio N4, Urb Ucchullo Alto; r per person incl breakfast S70; 📶) This rambling farmhouse-style place also runs an on-site girls foundation. Huge windows, balconies and patios look toward the Plaza de Armas, a 20-minute walk or a five-minute taxi ride away.

Point HOSTEL $
(☎25-2266; www.thepointhostels.com; Mesón de la Estrella 172; dm S22-30, s/d with shared bathroom S50/80; @ 📶) An industrial-size party palace, with daily events, on-site bar The Horny Llama, foosball and a grassy backyard with hammocks.

Hostal Suecia I HOTEL $$
(☎23-3282; www.hostalsuecia1.com; Suecia 332; s/d incl breakfast S60/90; 📶) Most rooms are very basic, but location and staff are fabulous and there's a sociable, stony, indoor courtyard.

OVER THE RAINBOW

A common sight in Cuzco's Plaza de Armas is the city's much-loved flag representing the *arco iris* (rainbow) sacred to the Incas. Don't take it for the international gay-pride banner, though it's remarkably similar!

Eating

Budget eateries abound on Plateros and Gringo Alley, where you can walk away with full stomach for under S10. For *chicharrón* (fried pork ribs), head to 'pork street,' Pampa del Castillo.

Grocery shops include **Gato's Market** (Santa Catalina Ancha 377; ⏲9am-11pm) and the original **market** (Mantas 119; ⏲8am-11pm).

TOP CHOICE Cicciolina INTERNATIONAL **$$$**
(☎23-9510; Triunfo 393, 2nd fl; mains S30-55; ⏲8am-late) On the 2nd floor of a lofty colonial courtyard mansion, Cuzco's best restaurant serves eclectic, sophisticated food. It's divine, starting with house-marinated olives, continuing with crisp polenta squares with rabbit carpaccio, huge green salads, charred octopus and satisfying mains like squid-ink pasta and tender lamb. The service is impeccable and the arty atmosphere cozy. Highly recommended.

TOP CHOICE La Bodega 138 PIZZERIA **$$**
(☎26-0272; Herrajes 138; mains S18-35; ⏲6:30am-11pm Mon-Sat) A fantastic laid-back enterprise run by a family in their former home. Thin-crust pizzas are fired up in the adobe oven, organic salads are fresh and abundant and the prices are reasonable. A true find.

El Hada ICE CREAM **$**
(Arequipa 167; ice cream from S6; ⏲11am-8pm Mon-Sat) Served in fresh-made cones with a hint of vanilla or lemon peel, these exotic ice creams are ecstasy.

DON'T MISS

MUSEO DEL PISCO

Pisco 101, the new **pisco museum** (☎26-2709; museodelpisco.org; Santa Catalina Ancha 398; ⏲11am-1am), extols the wonders of the national drink. Opened recently by an enthusiastic expat, this museum-bar is combined with a tapas and sushi lounge. Ambitions go far beyond the standard *pisco sour*, although those do border on perfection. Tapas like delicious alpaca miniburgers on sesame buns and *tiradito* (Japanese-style *ceviche*) marinated in cumin-chili sate your hunger. Look for special tastings and master-distiller classes announced on the Facebook page.

Trujillo Restaurant PERUVIAN **$$**
(☎23-3465; Av Tullumayo 542, near Plaza Limacpampa; mains S15-28; ⏲8am-8pm Mon-Sat, noon-6pm Sun) This simple dining hall nails northern classics. Their *aji de gallina* (creamy chicken stew) is the best in all of Cuzco.

Jack's Café CAFE **$**
(☎25-4606; Choquechaka 509; mains S12-20; ⏲7:30am-11:30pm; 🌿) For long-haulers on the road, this homesickness remedy serves excellent, comforting international fare, including veggie options, at decent prices. A favorite.

Granja Heidi CAFE **$$**
(☎23-8383; Cuesta San Blas 525, 2nd fl; mains S18-38; ⏲11:30am-9:30pm Mon-Sat) This alpine cafe does a wide range of breakfasts, crepes and comfort food, all chemical-free and wholesomely prepared.

Prasada VEGETARIAN **$**
(☎25-3644; Qanchipata 269; mains S6; ⏲8am-6pm; 🌿) The best bang for your sol, serving tacos, tortilla soup and lentil burgers with fresh toppings and generous servings.

La Quinta Eulalia PERUVIAN **$$**
(☎22-4951; Choquechaca 384; mains S25-50) The chalkboard menu features the tenderest roast lamb, alpaca and traditional sides like the phenomenal *rocoto relleno* (spicy peppers stuffed with beef, peas and carrots and topped with dribbling cheese). It is one of the best places to order *cuy*.

Real McCoy PUB **$**
(☎26-1111; Plateros 326, 2nd fl; mains from S14; ⏲7:30am-late; 📶) You think fish and chips at 3300m is easy? It's not. The friendly, Brit-expat owners pull it off shockingly well, along with a wealth of other comforting pub grub.

Los Perros FUSION **$**
(Tecsecocha 436; mains S17-24) Australian-run godsend, serving exotic, Asian- and Indian-slanted bar food at stunning prices in an intimate 'couch bar.' The burger is insane.

CBC Bakery BAKERY **$**
(☎23-4035; qosqomaki.org/tallerpanaderia; Av Tullumayo 465; pastries S3; ⏲7:30am-8pm Mon-Sat) The best chocolate croissants in town, plus other scrumptious baked goods, are made at this charitable foundation that trains local at-risk youths as bakers.

Drinking

In popular backpacker bars, especially those around the Plaza de Armas, both sexes should beware of drinks being spiked – don't let go of your glass, and think twice about using free-drink coupons. Happy hour kicks off as early as 1pm.

Norton's Rat PUB
(Santa Catalina Angosta 116; ⌚7am-late) Down-to-earth pub with wooden tables overlooking the plaza, and TVs, darts and billiards, plus the best sloppy burgers in town. Breakfast all day.

7 Angelitos BAR
(7 Angelitos 638) The way townsfolk rave about the *mojitos* here, you'd think Fidel Castro was behind the bar. They're OK, but it's more about the nightly live music and the divey atmosphere.

Entertainment

Several restaurants have evening *folklórica* music and dance shows; expect to pay S50 to S60 including buffet. Most live-music venues don't charge admission.

TOP CHOICE **Ukuku's Pub** LIVE MUSIC
(Plateros 316; ⌚8pm-late) Usually full to bursting, Ukuku's plays a winning combination of Latin pop, reggae, alternative, salsa, ska, soul, jazz and more, and hosts live local bands nightly.

Centro Qosqo de Arte Nativo PERFORMING ARTS
(☎22-7901; Av El Sol 604; admission with boleto turístico) Nightly *folklórica* shows.

Muse, Too LIVE MUSIC
(☎984-76-2602; Tandapata 710; ⌚8am-late) A good option for live entertainment, it's the laid-back San Blas version of the center's iconic cafe-bar at Triunfo 338.

Shopping

Cuzco offers a cornucopia of artisan workshops and stores selling knitted woolens, woven textiles, colorful ceramics, silver jewelry and more, and there are contemporary art galleries as well. Book exchanges abound.

Mercado San Pedro MARKET
(Plazoleta San Pedro) Cuzco's central market is a must-see. Pig heads for *caldo* (soup), frogs (to enhance sexual performance), vats of fruit juice, roast *lechón* (suckling pig) and tamales are just a few of the foods on offer. Around the edges are typical clothes, spells, incense and other random products to keep you entertained for hours.

Center for Traditional Textiles of Cuzco HANDICRAFTS
(Av El Sol 603A) This nonprofit organization promotes the survival of traditional Andean weaving techniques, and has shop-floor demonstrations of finger-twisting complexity. Beautiful wares!

SBS Bookshop BOOKS
(Av El Sol 781A; ⌚8:30am-1:30pm & 3:30pm-7:30pm Mon-Sat, 8:30am-1pm Sat) This is a fantastic bookstore with regional maps and books in English on nature, culture and travel.

Information

Dangers & Annoyances

Train stations, festivals and markets are prime areas for pickpockets. Use only official taxis (look for the company's telephone number on the roof), lock your doors and never allow additional passengers. Late-night revelers returning from bars or trekkers setting off before sunrise are most vulnerable to 'choke and grab' muggings. Drug dealers and police are known to work together, especially on Procuradores, where locals warn you can make a drug deal and get busted, all within a couple of minutes.

Beware of altitude sickness if you're flying in from sea level – it's no joke.

Emergency

Policía de Turismo (☎23-5123; Plaza Túpac Amaru s/n; ⌚24hr) Offers official theft reports for insurance claims.

Medical Services

Medical facilities are limited: go to Lima for serious procedures.

Clínica Pardo (☎24-0997; Av de la Cultura 710; ⌚24hr)

Traveler's Clinic Cusco (☎22-1213; Puputi 148; ⌚24hr)

Money

Many banks on Av El Sol and shops around the Plaza de Armas have ATMs. The main bus terminal has a global ATM.

LAC Dolar (Av El Sol 150; ⌚9:30am-1pm & 2-7pm Mon-Sat) Reliable *casa de cambio* (exchange office).

Post

Serpost (Av El Sol 800; ⌚8am-8pm Mon-Sat)

Tourist Information

Dircetur (☎22-3702; www.dirceturcusco.gob.pe; Plaza Túpac Amaru) Cuzco's regional tourism board.

Dirección Regional de Cultura Cusco (☎58-2030; www.drc-cusco.gob.pe; Av de La Cultura 238; ⌚7:15am-6:30pm Mon-Sat) The place in Cuzco to purchase Machu Picchu entry tickets; closed on holidays.

iPerú (☎25-2974; Portal de Harinas 177, Plaza de Armas; ⌚8:30am-7:30pm) Efficient and helpful, with another branch located at the airport (☎23-7364; Main Hall, Airport; ⌚6am-5pm).

South American Explorers (SAE; ☎24-5484; www.saexplorers.org; Atocsaykuchi 670; ⌚9:30am-5pm Mon-Fri, to 1pm Sat) Immeasurable traveler information and maps sold. Cultural events and some volunteering info for nonmembers as well as rooms for rent by the week (singles/doubles S224/324).

Getting There & Away

Air

Most flights from Cuzco's **airport** (CUZ; ☎22-2611), 2km southeast of the center, are in the morning.

LAN (☎25-5555; www.lan.com; Av El Sol 627B; ⌚8:30am-7pm Mon-Sat, to 1pm Sun)

Peruvian Airlines (☎25-4890; www.peruvianairlines.pe; Calle del Medio 117; ⌚9am-7pm Mon-Sat, to noon Sun)

Star Perú (☎01-705-9000; www.starperu.com; Av El Sol 679; ⌚9am-1pm & 3-6:30pm Mon-Sat, 9am-12:30pm Sun)

TACA (☎0800-18-2222; www.taca.com; Av El Sol 602)

Bus

INTERNATIONAL

All international services depart from the **Terminal Terrestre** (☎22-4471; Vía de Evitamiento 429), about 2km out of town towards the airport. Take a taxi (S3).

For Bolivia, catch a **Trans Salvador** (☎23-3680), **Littoral** (☎24-8989), **Real Turismo** (☎24-3540) or **San Luis** (☎22-3647) service to La Paz via Copacabana; all depart at 10pm. **Tour Peru** (☎24-9977; www.tourperu.com.pe) offers the best-value service to Copacabana, departing at 8am daily. **CIAL** (☎in Lima 01-330-4225) departs at 10:30pm for La Paz via Desaguadero (S70, 12 hours). This is the quickest way to La Paz.

Ormeño (☎26-1704; www.grupo-ormeno.com.pe) travels to most South American capitals.

DESTINATION	COST* (S)	DURATION (HR)
Arequipa	25/126	9-11
Ayacucho	65/95	14-16
Copacabana, Bolivia	50/70	15
Ica	90/176	14-15
Juliaca	20-35	5-6
La Paz, Bolivia	60/80	12
Lima	90/176	18-22
Nazca	90/180	14
Puerto Maldonado	50/70	11
Puno	20-40	6-7
Tacna	60/125	17

** Prices are general estimates for normal/luxury buses.*

LONG DISTANCE

Buses to major cities leave from the Terminal Terrestre. Buses for more unusual destinations leave from elsewhere, so check carefully in advance.

Ormeño and **Cruz del Sur** (☎24-3621; www.cruzdelsur.com.pe) have the safest and most comfortable buses across the board. Of the cheaper companies, **Wari** (☎22-2694) and Tour Peru have good buses.

There are hourly departures to Juliaca and Puno. Cheap, slow options include **Power** (☎22-7777) and **Libertad** (☎950-018-836); use them to access towns along the route. Midrange-priced **Littoral** (☎23-1155) and **CIAL** (☎965-401-414) are faster and more comfortable.

The most enjoyable way to get to Puno is via **Inka Express** (☎24-7887; www.inkaexpress.com; El Óvalo, Av La Paz C32) or **Turismo Mer** (☎24-5171; www.turismomer.com; El Óvalo, Av La Paz A3), which run luxury buses every morning.

Departures to Arequipa cluster around 6am to 7am and 7pm to 9:30pm. Ormeño offers a deluxe service at 9am.

Cruz del Sur, **CIVA** (☎24-9961; www.civa.com.pe) and **Celtur** (☎23-6075) offer relatively painless services to Lima. Wari is the best of the cheaper options. Most buses to Lima stop in Nazca (12 hours) and Ica (14 hours). These buses go via Abancay and can suffer holdups in rainy season. Between January and April, it may be worth going via Arequipa (25 to 27 hours) instead.

If you're going to Ayacucho by bus, wear all of your warm clothes; if you have a sleeping bag, bring it on board.

San Martín (☎984-61-2520) and **Expreso Sagitário** (☎22-9757) offer direct buses to

Tacna (S70, 17 hours). Expreso Sagitário also goes to Arequipa, Lima and Puno.

Various companies depart for Puerto Maldonado between 3pm and 4:30pm; CIVA is probably the best option.

Buses to Quillabamba via Santa María (change here for Santa Teresa) leave from the Santiago terminal, a brisk 20-minute walk from the center. Departures leave at 8am, 10am, 1pm and 8pm.

Transportes Gallito de las Rocas (☎22-6895; Diagonal Angamos) buses depart to Pilcopata (S20, 10 to 12 hours) Monday, Wednesday and Friday at 5am. The office is on the first block off Av de la Cultura.

Train

Cuzco has two train stations. **Estación Huanchac** (☎58-1414; ⏲7am-5pm Mon-Fri, to midnight Sat & Sun), near the end of Av El Sol, serves Puno. Estación Poroy, east of town, serves Ollantaytambo and Machu Picchu.

You can take a taxi to Poroy (S30) or the station in Ollantaytambo (S80) from Cuzco. Return trips are slightly more expensive.

TO OLLANTAYTAMBO & MACHU PICCHU

The only way to reach Aguas Calientes (and access Machu Picchu) is via train. It takes about three hours. Three companies currently offer the service, the latter two only from Ollantaytambo:

Peru Rail (www.perurail.com; Estación Huanchac; ⏲7am-5pm Mon-Fri, to noon Sat) Formerly the only service to Aguas Calientes, with multiple departures daily from Estación Poroy, 20 minutes outside of Cuzco. There are three levels of service: Expedition (from US$144 round-trip), Vistadome (from US$160 round-trip) and the luxurious Hiriam Bingham (from US$700 round-trip). The Hiram Bingham includes brunch, afternoon tea, entrance to Machu Picchu and a guided tour. It runs daily except Sunday.

Inca Rail (☎23-3030; www.incarail.com; ticket office Portal de Panes 105, Plaza de Armas, Cuzco) New company with environmentally sustainable business practices. Has three departures daily from Ollantaytambo and four levels of service (round-trip US$82 to US$180). Children get a significant discount.

Machu Picchu Train (☎22-1199; www.machupicchutrain.com; ticket office Av El Sol 576, Cuzco; ⏲7am-5pm Mon-Fri, to noon Sat) New service of panoramic-view trains; travels only from Ollantaytambo to Aguas Calientes (round-trip adult/child from US$100/70) three times daily in high season. Breakfast or snacks may be served.

Fares may vary according to departure hours: more desirable times are usually more expensive. It's common for trains to sell out, especially at peak hours, so buy your ticket as far ahead as possible.

The quickest 'cheaper' way to get from Cuzco to Aguas Calientes is to take a *combi* to Ollantaytambo and catch the train from there.

TO PUNO

Peru Rail The Andean Explorer (tickets US$150) is a luxury train with a glass-walled observation car. Trains depart from Estación Huanchac at 8am, arriving at Puno around 6pm, on Monday, Wednesday and Saturday from November to March, with an extra departure on Friday from April to October. Lunch is included.

Getting Around

To/From the Airport

Frequent *colectivos* run along Ayacucho to just outside the airport (S0.70). An official taxi to/from the city center costs S14. Be wary of rogue taxis working outside the terminal building – robberies are not uncommon. Many guesthouses offer free airport pickups.

Bus & Colectivo

In 2014 the government will restrict the use of old *colectivos*: some of these services may be cut or reduced.

Minibuses to Pisac (S2.50, one hour) leave frequently both from the terminal at Av Tullumayo 207 and the terminal in Puputi, just north of Av de la Cultura.

Minibuses to Urubamba (S6, 1½ hours) and Ollantaytambo (S12, two hours) via Chinchero (S4, one hour) leave from near the Puente Grau. Just around the corner in Pavitos, faster *colectivos* leave when full for Urubamba (S7, one hour) and Ollantaytambo (S10 to S15, 1½ hours) via Chinchero.

Taxi

Trips around town cost S5. Official taxis are much safer than 'pirate' taxis. A reliable company is **AloCusco** (☎22-2222).

Around Cuzco

The archaeological ruins closest to Cuzco are **Saqsaywamán**, **Q'enqo**, **Pukapukara** and **Tambomachay** (⏲7am-6pm) – admission is with a *boleto turístico* (p834). Take a Pisac-bound bus and get off at Tambomachay, the ruin furthest away from Cuzco (and, at 3700m, the highest). It's an 8km walk back to Cuzco. Be aware that violent attacks against tourists have occurred along this route, even during daylight hours. Go in a group, and return before nightfall.

SAQSAYWAMÁN

The name means 'satisfied falcon,' though most travelers remember it by the mnemonic 'sexy woman.' The sprawling site is 2km from Cuzco. Climb steep Resbalosa, turn right past the Iglesia de San Cristóbal and continue to a hairpin bend in the road. On the left is a stone staircase, an Inca stone road leading to the top.

Although Saqsaywamán seems huge, what today's visitor sees is only about 20% of the original structure. Soon after the conquest, the Spaniards tore down walls and used the blocks to build their own houses in Cuzco.

In 1536 the fort saw one of the fiercest battles between the Spanish and Manco Inca, who used Saqsaywamán to lay siege to the conquistadors. Thousands of dead littered the site after the Inca defeat, which attracted swarms of Andean condors. The tragedy was memorialized by the inclusion of eight condors in Cuzco's coat of arms.

Most striking are the magnificent three-tiered fortifications. Inca Pachachutec envisioned Cuzco in the shape of a puma, with Saqsaywamán as the head, and these 22 zigzag walls form the teeth. The parade ground is used for Inti Raymi celebrations.

Admission is through the *boleto turístico*.

Q'ENQO

The name of this fascinating small ruin means 'zigzag.' It's a large limestone rock riddled with niches, steps and extraordinary symbolic carvings, including channels that may have been used for ritual sacrifices of *chicha* (corn beer), or perhaps blood. Scrambling up to the top of the boulder you'll find a flat surface used for ceremonies and laboriously etched representations of animals. Back below, explore the mysterious subterranean cave with altars hewn into the rock.

The site is 2km from Saqsaywamán, on the left as you descend from Tambomachay.

TAMBOMACHAY & PUKAPUKARA

About 300m from the main road, **Tambomachay** is a beautifully wrought ceremonial bath, still channeling clear spring water that earns it the title El Baño del Inca (Inca Bath). On the opposite side of the road is the commanding ruin of **Pukapukara**. Its name means 'red fort,' though it was more likely a hunting lodge, guard post or stopping point for travelers. The upper esplanade has panoramic views.

The Sacred Valley

The Valle Sagrado (Sacred Valley) of the Río Urubamba is about 15km north of Cuzco as the condor flies. Its star attractions are the lofty Inca citadels of Pisac and Ollantaytambo, but the valley is also packed with more peaceful Inca sites, as well as frenzied markets and high-altitude Andean villages. Investigate the idyllic countryside with Peter Frost's in-depth book *Exploring Cusco*.

PISAC

☎084 / POP 2000

It's not hard to succumb to the charms of sunny Pisac (elevation 2715m), a bustling colonial village just 33km northeast of Cuzco at the base of a spectacular Inca fortress perched on a mountain spur. Its pull is universal; recent years have seen an influx of expats and new age followers in search of an Andean Shangri-La.

Sights & Activities

Pisac Ruins RUINS

(admission with boleto turístico; ⏲dawn-dusk) This Inca citadel lies high above the village on a plateau with a plunging gorge on either side. Take the steep 4km footpath starting along the left side of the church (or take a taxi for S20). It's a spectacular climb up through terraces, sweeping around mountainous flanks and along cliff-hugging footpaths defended by massive stone doorways, vertigo-inducing staircases and a short tunnel carved out of the rock.

Topping the terraces is the ceremonial center, with an Intihuatana (Hitching Post of the Sun), several working water channels and some neat masonry inside well-preserved temples. A path leads up the hillside to a series of ceremonial baths and around to the military area. A cliff behind the site is honeycombed with hundreds of Inca tombs plundered by *guaqueros* (grave robbers).

Sleeping

TOP CHOICE **Hotel Pisac Inca** GUESTHOUSE $

(☎43-6921; www.hotelpisacinca.com; Vigil 242; s/d 35/70, s/d/tr with shared bathroom S25/50/75; @☜) Sisters Tatiana and Claudia run this small, cheerful lodging with a handful of colorful rooms around a tiny courtyard. Kitchen use is extra, but it's a steal.

Hospedaje Beho GUESTHOUSE $

(☎20-3001; artesaniasbeho@yahoo.es; Intihuatana 113; s/d/tr S35/70/105, s/d with shared bathroom

S20/40) On the path to the ruins, this family-run handicrafts shop offers no-frills lodging with warm showers.

Hospedaje Kinsa Ccocha HOTEL $
(☎20-3101; Arequipa 307A; s/d S50/70, s/d with shared bathroom S25/50) A comfortable budget option, down a quieter secondary street parallel to the plaza.

Pisac Inn INN $$
(☎20-3062; www.pisacinn.com; Plaza Constitución; d incl breakfast from S146; @ 📶) One of the most colorful spots to stay in the valley, this adobe-style abode is full of Andean-chic indigenous touches and has lovely staff (though its high-season prices are up there). Massages and entry to the sauna are extra amenities. The restaurant offers some organic cuisine and focuses on local products. Some small beds mean it's not for tall folks.

La Casa del Conde GUESTHOUSE $$
(☎78 7818; www.cuzcovalle.com; s/d S50/70, s/d/tr incl breakfast S119/159/212; 📶) Guests rave about this lovely country house nestled into the foothills. There's no car access. It's a 10-minute walk uphill from the plaza, but a *mototaxi* can leave you at the chapel, a five-minute walk away.

Eating

Massive clay-oven bakeries on Mariscal Castilla vend piping-hot flatbreads and empanadas.

Ulrike's Café CAFE $
(☎20-3195; Plaza Constitución; vegetarian/meat menús S17/20, mains from S11; ⏲9am-9pm; 📶 ✍) This sunny cafe serves up a great vegetarian *menú,* plus homemade pastas and melt-in-the-mouth cheesecake and brownies.

Mullu FUSION $$
(☎20-3073; www.mullu.pe; Mariscal Castilla 375, 2nd fl; mains S14-44; ⏲9am-9pm) Above an art gallery, this alt-cultural cafe commands a prime position over the plaza. There's a deliciously long list of juices and exotic fusion fare like ostrich stir-fry, stuffed alpaca ravioli and pumpkin stew; and Peru's best T-shirts.

Prasada VEGETARIAN $
(Arequipa 306; mains S7-12; ⏲11am-5pm Tue-Sun; ✍) With its main outlets in Cuzco, this humble cafe serves quick, healthy bites like tacos and oversized lentil burgers – a good bang for the buck.

Shopping

The Sunday market kicks into life in the early morning. Around 10am the tour buses deposit their hordes into an already chaotic scene, thronged with buyers and overrun with crafts stalls. Although the market retains a traditional side, prices are comparable to those in Cuzco's shops. There are smaller markets on Tuesday and Thursday and an excellent daily artisan market in the plaza.

Getting There & Away

Buses to Urubamba (S2.50, one hour) and Cuzco (S3.50, one hour) leave from near the bridge at Plazoleta Leguiz and Av Amazonas.

URUBAMBA

☎084 / POP 10,800

There is precious little to see in Urubamba (elevation 2870m), at the junction of the valley thoroughfare with the road back to Cuzco via Chinchero, but for those traipsing through the Sacred Valley, it's a necessary transit hub. There's a global ATM at the *grifo* (gas station) on the main road, about 1km east of the bus terminal.

Sights & Activities

Many outdoor activities that are organized from Cuzco take place at Urubamba, including horse riding, mountain biking, paragliding and hot-air balloon trips. Trips also often take in the nearby amphitheater-like terraces of **Moray** (admission S10) and **Salinas** (admission S5), where thousands of salt pans have been harvested since Inca times.

Sleeping & Eating

Los Jardines HOTEL $
(☎20-1331; www.los-jardines-urubamba.com; Jr Convención 459; s/d S56/80) This family hotel, recommended by readers, occupies a large adobe home surrounded by flower gardens. Rooms are basic but clean; some feature large picture windows. The buffet breakfast served in the garden is extra. It's within walking distance of the plaza.

Hostal los Perales GUESTHOUSE $
(☎20-1151; ecolodgeurubamba.com; Pasaje Arenales 102; r per person S25) Tucked down a hidden lane, this welcoming family-run guesthouse offers good-value, simple rooms. Its elderly owners are sweet, serving banana pancakes for breakfast. It's easy to get lost, so take a *mototaxi* (S1) from the terminal.

Around Cuzco

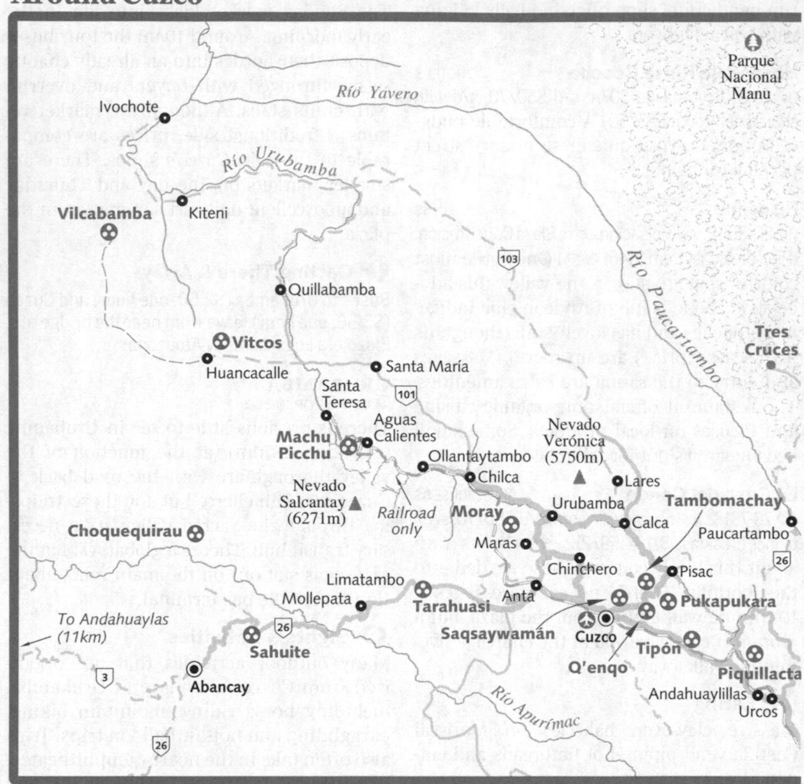

TOP CHOICE Huacatay PERUVIAN $$

(☎20-1790; Arica 620; mains S28-42; ⊙1-9:30pm Mon-Sat) In a little house tucked down a narrow side street, Huacatay is worth hunting down. The tender alpaca steak, with creamy quinotto topped with a spiral potato chip, is the very stuff memories are made of.

Getting There & Away

Buses going to Cuzco (S4, two hours) via Pisac (S2.50, one hour) or Chinchero (S3, 50 minutes) and *colectivos* to Ollantaytambo (S2.50, 30 minutes) all leave frequently from the bus terminal.

OLLANTAYTAMBO

☎084 / POP 2000

Tiny Ollantaytambo (elevation 2800m) is the best surviving example of Inca city planning and the most atmospheric of Sacred Valley destinations – its massive fortress stands sentinel over the cobblestoned village like a guardian against the heavens. Apart from the advent of the internet, nothing much has changed here in 700 years.

Sights

Ollantaytambo Ruins RUINS

(admission with boleto turístico; ⊙7am-5pm) The spectacular, steep terraces guarding the Inca complex mark one of the few places where the conquistadors lost a major battle, when Manco Inca threw missiles and flooded the plain below. But Ollantaytambo was as much a temple as a fort to the Incas. A finely worked ceremonial area sits on top of the terracing. In a stupendous feat of construction, the stone was quarried from the mountainside high above the Río Urubamba and transported in huge blocks.

Sleeping

Casa de Wow HOSTEL $$

(☎20-4010; www.casadewow.com; Patacalle s/n; dm/s/d with shared bathroom S40/55/90, d S110; @📶) A cozy little home away from home.

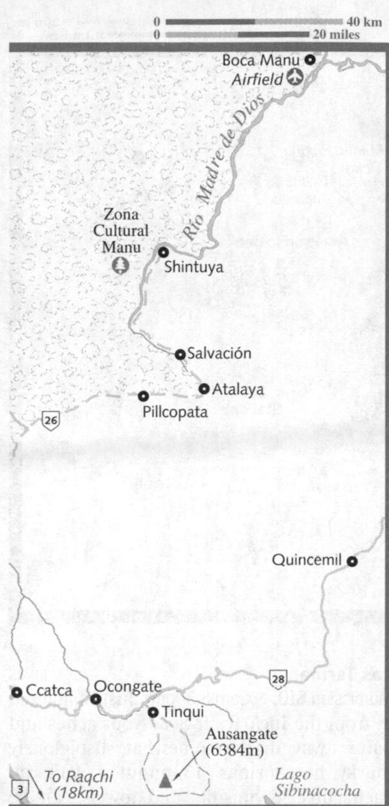

Bunks are snug and couples have a shot at the fantastic handmade Inca royalty bed (though, unlike in the original set-up, these raw beams are held together with rope, not llama innards).

KB Tambo Hostal GUESTHOUSE $
(20-4091; www.kbperu.com; Ventiderio s/n; per person regular/superior incl breakfast S58/77;) With comfortable doubles, this homey American-owned guesthouse is friendly and generous with local tips. KB also runs mountain-biking trips featuring the best-quality bikes in Ollantaytambo.

Chaska Wasi HOSTEL $
(20-4045; www.hostalchaskawasi.com; Plaza de Armas s/n; d without/with bathroom S40/50;) Cheerful basic rooms with electric showers are excellent value, shared spaces are chilled out and perfect for meeting people, and there are bicycles for rent and a DVD library.

Hospedaje las Portadas GUESTHOUSE $
(20-4008; Principal s/n; dm/s/d/tr S15/30/50/75) This tranquil family-run place has a flowery courtyard, a grassy lawn and a rooftop terrace made for stargazing. Camping is allowed for S10 per person.

Eating & Drinking

Puka Rumi CAFE $$
(20-4091; Ventiderio s/n; mains S5-32; 7:30am-10pm) A tiny place where locals rave about the steaks, travelers melt over the breakfasts, and everyone enjoys the fresh but non-traditional burritos.

Hearts Café CAFE $
(20-4078; cnr Ventiderio & Av Ferrocarrill; 7am-9pm;) Serving healthy and hearty food, beer and wine and fabulous coffee, Hearts is a longtime local favorite, with some organic produce and box lunches for excursions.

Ganso BAR
(984-30-8499; Waqta s/n; 2pm-late) Treehouse meets circus meets *Batman!* The hallucinatory decor in tiny, friendly Ganso is enough to drive anyone to drink.

Getting There & Away

Frequent *colectivos* for Urubamba's bus terminal (S1.50, 30 minutes) depart just southeast of the plaza next to the market from 5am to 8pm. *Colectivos* (S12) and taxis (S100) for Cuzco mill about the train station only when trains arrive. Alternatively, head to Urubamba and transfer there.

Trains to Aguas Calientes are much cheaper from here than from Cuzco.

Aguas Calientes

084 / POP 2000

Also known as Machu Picchu Pueblo, this town lies in a deep gorge below the ruins. A virtual island, it's cut off from all roads and enclosed by stone cliffs, towering cloud forest and two rushing rivers. Despite its gorgeous location, Aguas Calientes has always been a bit of a no-man's land, with a large itinerant population, slack services that count on one-time customers and an architectural tradition of rebar and unfinished cement. With merchants pushing the hard sell, it's difficult not to feel overwhelmed. Your best bet is to go without expectations.

Yet spending the night offers one distinct advantage: early access to Machu Picchu, which turns out to be a pretty good reason to stay.

Aguas Calientes

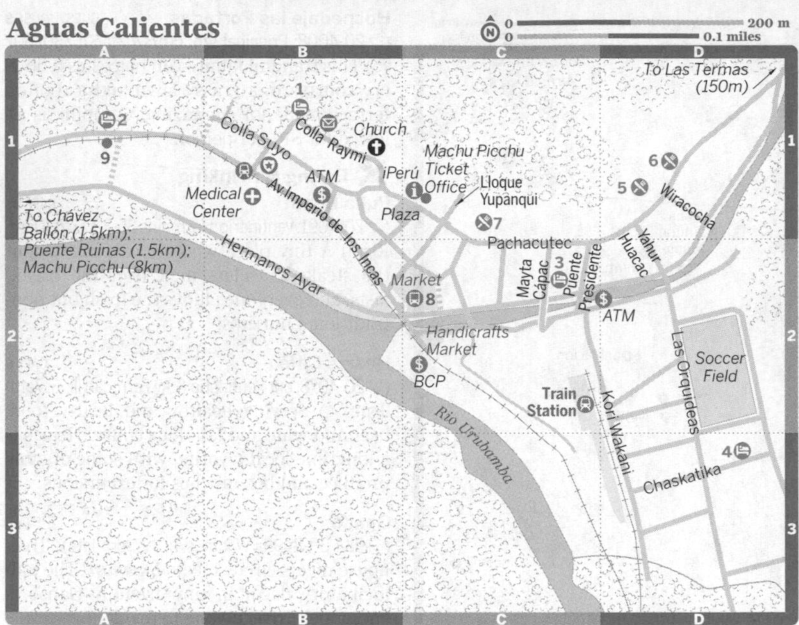

Aguas Calientes

Sleeping

1 Gringo Bill's B1
2 Hospedaje los Caminantes A1
3 Hostal John C2
4 Supertramp Hostel D3

Eating

5 Café de Paris D1
6 Govinda D1
7 Indio Feliz C1

Transport

8 Machu Picchu Bus Tickets & Bus Stop C2
9 Trains to Hydroelectric Station (Transport to Santa Teresa) A1

Sights & Activities

Museo de Sitio Manuel Chávez Ballón MUSEUM

(admission S22; 9am-5pm) By Puente Ruinas at the base of the footpath to Machu Picchu, this museum has superb multimedia displays on excavations of Machu Picchu and the ancient Incas' building methods, cosmology and culture.

Las Termas HOT SPRINGS

(admission S10; 5am-8:30pm) Just staggered in from the Inca Trail? Soak your aches and pains away in the somewhat suspiciously murky hot springs, 10 minutes' walk up Pachacutec. Swimsuits and towels can be rented cheaply outside the entrance.

Sleeping

Everything is grossly overpriced, but the off season offers discounts. Early checkout times are the norm.

Gringo Bill's HOTEL $$$

(21-1046; www.gringobills.com; Colla Raymi 104; d/tr/ste incl breakfast S199/278/358; @) One of the original Aguas Calientes lodgings, friendly Bill's features well-heeled rooms in a multitiered building. Rooms are smart, with beds covered in thick cotton quilts and large bathrooms. Suites feature TVs and massage-jet tubs. The mini pool has space for just two. Larger suites easily accommodate families.

Hospedaje los Caminantes GUESTHOUSE $

(21-1007; los-caminantes@hotmail.com; Av Imperio de los Incas 140; per person without/with bathroom S20/35;) The best bargain digs are in this big, multistory guesthouse. Dated but clean rooms with laminate floors feature reliable hot water and a few balconies. The train whistling directly outside your window at 7am is an unmistakable wake-up call. Breakfast isn't included but is available for S8 to S10 below at the strangely upscale in-house cafe.

Supertramp Hostel HOSTEL **$**
(79-1224; supertramphostel@hotmail.com; Chaskatika s/n; dm incl breakfast from S26;) Pancakes at 5am will brighten anyone's day, so it matters less that the hot water is on-and-off and rooms are a little cramped. It's the only real hostel in town, with good staff, kitchen access and a small store with provisions nearby. Train-station pick-up is available.

Hostal John HOTEL **$**
(21-1022; jtrujillo3@hotmail.com; Mayta Cápac 105; per person S20) Uphill from the plaza, this friendly spot offers bare, cell-like rooms that might mean incarceration elsewhere but offer unbeatable value in Aguas Calientes. The related Hotel Joe across the street is similar but less appealing.

Municipal Campground CAMPGROUND **$**
(sites per tent S15) With toilets, showers and kitchen facilities for rent. It's a 20-minute walk downhill from the center of town on the road to Machu Picchu, before the bridge.

Eating & Drinking

Tourist restaurants (all practically identical) cluster alongside the railway tracks and Pachacutec toward the hot springs. You'll find backpacker bars with extra-long happy hours up Pachacutec, but you don't need to hear it from us – every one of them will try to lure you in.

TOP CHOICE **Indio Feliz** FRENCH **$$$**
(21-1090; Lloque Yupanqui 4; menú S55, mains from S38; 11am-10pm) It's hard to overstate the pleasure that can be derived from this multi-award-winning Franco-Peruvian bistro. It's miles away from anything in the vicinity in quality, experience and atmosphere. The three-course set menu is superb and portions are substantial. Think hearty soups, grilled trout with crisp garlic-laced potatoes and apple *tartine*. You have one night in town: eat here. A bar is in the works.

Café de Paris BAKERY **$**
(Plaza Wiyawaina s/n; pastries S1-4; 7am-9pm) Real *pain au chocolat*, fresh croissants and desserts.

Govinda VEGETARIAN **$$**
(Pachacutec s/n; menús S15-30; 10:30am-9pm;) A trusty Hare Krishna vegetarian standby serving chapati bread and non-meat interpretations of Peruvian classics.

Information

There's a helpful branch of **iPerú** (21-1104; cuadra 1, Pachacutec; 9am-1pm & 2-6pm) near the **Machu Picchu ticket office** (5:20am-8:45pm). If the ATM at **BCP** (Av Imperio de los Incas s/n) runs out of money, there are four others, including one on Av Imperio de los Incas. Currency and traveler's checks can be exchanged in various places at highly unfavorable rates. Pay phones and cybercafes are scattered around the town, and there's a small **post office** (Colla Raymi s/n). There's a **medical center** (21-1005; Av Imperio de los Incas s/n; emergencies 24hr) by the train tracks.

Getting There & Around

Aguas Calientes is the final train stop for Machu Picchu.

To Santa Teresa (45 minutes), Peru Rail travels at 6:44am, 12:35pm and 1:30pm daily. Tickets (US$18) can only be bought from Aguas Calientes train station on the day of departure, but trains actually leave from the west end of town, outside the police station. You can also do this route as a guided multisport tour.

Machu Picchu

For many visitors to Peru and even South America, a visit to the Inca city of **Machu Picchu** (adult S128, with Huiana Picchu S152; Aguas Calientes ticket office 5am-10pm; from Aguas Calientes, then bus or walk) is the long-anticipated high point of their trip. In a spectacular location, it's the best-known archaeological site on the continent. This awe-inspiring ancient city was never revealed to the conquering Spaniards and was virtually forgotten until the early part of the 20th century.

The site is most heavily visited between 10am and 2pm. In the high season, from late May until early September, 2500 people arrive daily.

History

The actual purpose and function of Machu Picchu is still a matter of speculation and educated guesswork. The citadel was never mentioned in the chronicles kept by the colonizing Spaniards, which served as a written archive of thitherto unrecorded Inca history.

Machu Picchu

0 — 200 m
0 — 0.1 miles

To Wayna Picchu & Temple of the Moon
Registration Booth
Sacred Rock
Three Doorways
Residential Sector
Industrial Sector
Intihuatana
Mortars
Sacristy
Principal Temple
Prison Group
Temple of the Three Windows
Temple of the Condor
Sacred Plaza
House of the High Priest
Royal Palace
Ceremonial Baths
Main Entrance
Temple of the Sun & Royal Tomb
Agricultural Terraces
Hut of the Caretaker of the Funerary Rock
Ticket Gate
Inca Trail
To Museo de Sitio Manuel Chávez Ballón (2km); Aguas Calientes (3.5km)
Machu Picchu Sanctuary Lodge
To Train Station (8km); Aguas Calientes (8km)
To Inca Drawbridge
Inca Trail to Intipunku & Wiñay Wayna

Apart from the indigenous Quechuas, nobody knew of Machu Picchu's existence until American historian Hiram Bingham came upon the thickly overgrown ruins in 1911 while being guided by a local boy. Bingham's search was actually for the lost city of Vilcabamba, the last stronghold of the Incas, and he thought he had found it at Machu Picchu. His book *Inca Land: Explorations in the Highlands of Peru* was first published in 1922. It's downloadable for free from Project Gutenberg (www.gutenberg.org).

Despite more recent studies of the 'lost' city of the Incas, knowledge of Machu Picchu remains sketchy. Some believe the citadel was founded in the waning years of the last Incas as an attempt to preserve Inca culture or rekindle Inca predominance, while others think it may have already become a forgotten city at the time of the conquest. Another theory suggests that the site was a royal retreat abandoned upon the Spanish invasion.

Whatever the case, the exceptionally high quality of the stonework and ornamentation tell that Machu Picchu must once have been vitally important as a ceremonial center. Indeed, to some extent, it still is: Alejandro Toledo, the country's first native Quechua-speaking president, staged his colorful inauguration here in 2001.

Sights

You aren't allowed to bring large backpacks, walking sticks, food or water bottles into the ruins. There's a storage room just before the main entrance.

Proceed from the ticket gate along a narrow path to the mazelike main entrance to Machu Picchu, where the ruins now reveal themselves and stretch out before you. To get a visual fix of the whole site and snap the classic postcard shot, climb the zigzagging staircase to the **Hut of the Caretaker of the Funerary Rock**, which is one of the few buildings that has been restored with a thatched roof, making it a good rain shelter. The Inca Trail enters the site just below this hut.

From here, take the steps down and to the left of the plazas into the ruined sections containing the **Temple of the Sun**, a curved, tapering tower with some of Machu Picchu's finest stonework. The temple is cordoned off to visitors, but you can see into it from above. Below is an almost-hidden natural rock cave that has been carefully carved with a steplike altar and sacred niches by the Inca's stonemasons, known as the **Royal Tomb**, though no mummies were ever found here.

Climbing the stairs above the 16 nearby **ceremonial baths** that cascade down the ruins brings you to the **Sacred Plaza**, from which there is a spectacular view of the Río Urubamba valley and across to the snow-capped Cordillera Vilcabamba in the distance. The **Temple of the Three Windows** overlooks the plaza.

Behind the **Sacristy** – known for the two rocks flanking its entrance, each of which is said to contain 32 angles – a staircase climbs to the major shrine, **Intihuatana** (Hitching Post of the Sun), which lies atop a small hill. The carved rock at the summit is often called a sundial, though it was connected to the passing of the seasons rather than the time of day. Years ago it was chipped by a clumsy crane, in an attempt to make a beer commercial. Otherwise, Spaniards smashed most such shrines trying to wipe out the pagan blasphemy of sun worship.

At the back of Intihuatana is another staircase that descends to the **Central Plaza**, which divides the ceremonial sector of Machu Picchu from the more mundane **residential** and **industrial** sectors. At the lower end of this area is the **Prison Group**, a labyrinthine complex of cells, niches and passageways. The centerpiece of the group is a carving of the **head of a condor**, the natural rocks behind it resembling the bird's outstretched wings.

Activities

Behind the ruins is the steep-sided mountain of **Wayna Picchu**. It takes 40 to 90 minutes to scramble up the steep path, but for all the huffing and puffing it takes to get there, you'll be rewarded with spectacular views. Only 400 people are permitted to climb per day. These spots sell out a week in advance in low season and sooner in high season, so plan accordingly. Take care in wet weather as the steps get dangerously slippery.

Part of the way up Wayna Picchu, another path plunges down to your left via ladders and an overhanging cave to the small **Temple of the Moon**, from where you can climb steeply to Wayna Picchu – a circuitous route taking about two hours.

Another option is to walk to a viewpoint of the **Inca drawbridge**. It's a flatter walk from the Hut of the Caretaker of the Funerary Rock that hugs a narrow cliff-clinging trail (under 30 minutes each way) with sheer vertical drops into the valley.

Information

The ruins are typically open from dawn till dusk, but are most heavily visited between 10am and 2pm. One-day tickets cost S122/61 per adult/student with ISIC card. Spots to hike Wayna Picchu go fast; purchase this extra ticket (S24) with admission well in advance. Purchase tickets through a tour operator, Cuzco's Dirección Regional de Cultura (p850) or at the INC office in Aguas Calientes – they are not sold at the site itself.

Getting There & Away

From Aguas Calientes, frequent buses for Machu Picchu (S50 round-trip, 25 minutes) depart from a ticket office along the main road from 5:30am to 2:30pm. Buses return from the ruins when full, with the last departure at 5:45pm.

From Santa Teresa, daily trains (one way/return US$18/30) leave from the hydroelectric station, about 8km out of town, at 7:54am, 3pm and 4:35pm.

Otherwise, it's a steep walk (8km, 1½ hours) up a tightly winding mountain road from Aguas Calientes. It's also possible to walk the train tracks from Santa Teresa.

The Inca Trail

The most famous trek in South America, this four-day trail to Machu Picchu is walked by thousands of backpackers every year. Although the total distance is only 43km, the ancient trail laid by the Incas winds its way up, down and around the mountains, snaking over three high passes en route. The views of snowy peaks and cloud forest can be stupendous, and walking from one cliff-hugging ruin to the next is a mystical and unforgettable experience.

You cannot hike the Inca Trail independently. All trekkers must go with a guide in an organized group. You must also carry your passport (not a photocopy) and ISIC card to present at checkpoints. Don't litter or defecate in the ruins or pick plants in the national park. It is illegal to graffiti any trees or stones en route.

All trekking gear can be rented from outfitters in Cuzco. The trail gets extremely cold at night, so make sure sleeping bags are warm enough. Also remember sturdy shoes, rain gear, insect repellent, sunscreen, a flashlight (with fresh batteries), water- purification tablets, high-calorie snacks and a basic first-aid kit. Take a stash of small Peruvian currency for buying bottled water and snacks along the way, as well as for tipping the guide, cook and porters (around S100, S30 more if your hire a personal porter). You will not regret picking up a walking stick from vendors in Ollantaytambo on the first morning, either.

Tours

Guided tours depart year-round, except during February when the trail is closed for maintenance. However, in the wettest months (December to March), trails can be slippery, camp sites muddy and views obscured behind a thick bank of clouds. The dry season from June to August is the most popular and crowded time to go. To skip the crowds, consider going before and after the rainy season: from April to May (best vegetation, orchids and bird life) or September to November.

Tour prices range from US$480 to US$600 and above, plus tips for porters and cooks. Only 500 people each day (including guides and porters) are allowed to start the trail. Permits are issued to operators on a first-come, first-served basis. Take some time to research your options – you won't regret it. It's best to screen agencies for a good fit before committing. Also make sure you have international travel insurance that covers adventure activities.

If price is your bottom line, keep in mind that cheapest agencies may cut corners by paying their guides and porters lower wages. Other issues are substandard gear (ie leaky tents) and dull or lackadaisical guiding. Yet paying more may not mean getting more, especially since international operators take their cut and hire local Peruvian agencies. Talk with a few agencies to get a sense of their quality of service. You might ask if the guide speaks English (fluently or just a little), request a list of what is included, and inquire about group size and the kind of transport used. Ensure that your tour includes a tent, food, a cook, one-day admission to the ruins and the return train fare.

It is important to book your trip at least six months in advance for dates between May and August. Outside these months, you may get a permit with a few weeks' notice, but it's very hard to predict.

THE HIKE

This is not an easy trek. Altitude and seemingly endless climbs, especially on day two,

THE INCA TRAIL: THE GOOD, THE BAD & THE UGLY

The Inca Trail is a rite of passage for many (some say too many), but what's it really like? Here's the lowdown:

The good: Besides the spectacular scenery – jaw-dropping mountain vistas, Inca ruins bathed in eerie morning mists, moss-draped cloud forests and lush lower jungle – there are some unexpected treats along the way. The food is shockingly good considering the circumstances – there are trout, lamb, beef, pork and plenty of veggie options, to name just a few of the borderline gourmet meals served en route. Kudos to the chefs. The camping equipment is in good condition and not of the cheap variety. There is even 'tent service' on some days, where the guides deliver your morning pick-me-up of choice (coca tea, coffee) along with your wake-up call. And let us not forget the porters, who are clearly not of this earth! Hiring one will incalculably enhance your enjoyment of this adventure; not hiring one could easily ruin it.

The bad: Regardless of season, you are almost guaranteed cold weather at night, bone-chillingly so on some nights, even in summer. With bathrooms almost always a considerable hike away, this makes for some excruciating nights battling the dilemma: to go or not to go? Despite the very nice tents and sleeping bags, the mats are a little skimpy, and you won't forget that you're sleeping on the ground. Although there are well-built bathroom facilities along the way, showers are not part of the equation before the third day. Bring deodorant.

The ugly: It's difficult to find fault with this trek in all aspects except one: the bathrooms. Though much nicer than expected from a facility standpoint, their daily maintenance is atrocious. The experience hovers somewhere between European rock festival, day two, and Bangkok nightclub, 5am. A bucket of cleaner and a hose could go a long way here.

combine to make for a very challenging walk in the mountains. Though altitude sickness does not discriminate between the fit and the unfit, the long, steep climbs, generally thin air and knee-seizing steps along the way do pose a challenge for those in less than stellar physical condition. By all means go, but don't expect a breezy Sunday stroll.

Most agencies run minibuses to the start of the trail past the village of Chilca at Piscakucho (Km 82). After you cross the Río Urubamba (and take care of trail fees and registration formalities), you'll follow the gently sloping trail alongside the river to the first archaeological site of **Llactapata** before heading south down a side valley of the Río Cusichaca. The trail south leads 7km to the hamlet of **Wayllabamba** (3100m), where you can take a breather to appreciate the views of snowy **Nevado Verónica** (5750m).

You'll cross the Río Llullucha, then climb steeply up along the river. This area is known as **Tres Piedras** (Three Stones), and from here it is a long, very steep 3km climb. The trail eventually emerges on the high, bare mountainside of **Llulluchupampa**, where the flats are dotted with camp sites.

From Llulluchupampa, a good path up the left-hand side of the valley climbs for the two-hour ascent to **Warmiwañusca** (4198m), colorfully known as 'Dead Woman's Pass.' This is the highest and most difficult point of the trek, which leaves many a trekker gasping. From Warmiwañusca, the trail continues down a long, knee-jarringly steep descent to the river, where there are large camp sites at **Paq'amayo** (3500m). The trail crosses the river over a small footbridge and climbs right toward **Runkurakay**, a round ruin with superb views about an hour's walk above the river.

Above Runkurakay, the trail climbs to a false summit before continuing past two small lakes to the top of the second pass at 3950m, which has views of the snowcapped Cordillera Vilcabamba. The trail descends to the ruin of **Sayaqmarka**, a tightly constructed complex perched on a small mountain spur with incredible views, then continues downward, crossing a tributary of the Río Aobamba.

The trail leads on across an Inca causeway and up again through cloud forest and an **Inca tunnel** carved into the rock to the third pass at 3670m. Soon afterward, you'll reach

Inca Trail

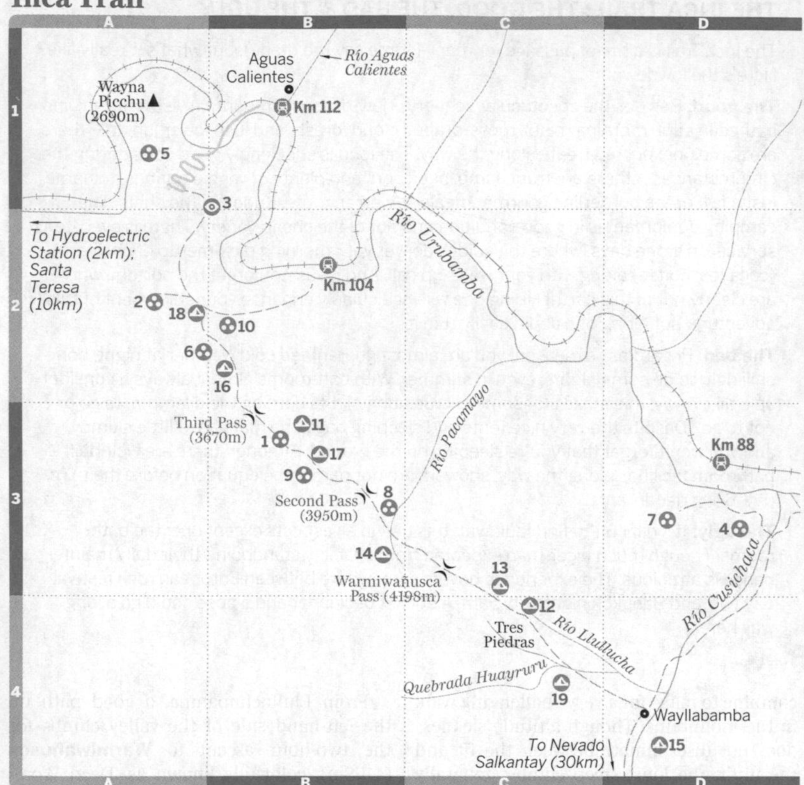

the beautiful, well-restored ruin of **Phuyupatamarka** (3600m above sea level). The site contains a beautiful series of ceremonial baths with water running through them.

From Phuyupatamarka, the trail takes a dizzying dive into the cloud forest below, following an incredibly well-engineered flight of many hundreds of Inca steps, affectionately known as the Gringo Killer. After passing through a tunnel, the trail eventually zigzags its way down to **Wiñay Wayna**.

From the **Wiñay Wayna guard post**, the trail contours around through cliff-hanging cloud forest for about 1½ hours to reach **Intipunku** (unofficial reduced-charge admission fee to Inca Trail around US$3.00; ⏲checkpoint closes around 3pm) (Sun Gate) – where you may get lucky enough to catch your first glimpse of majestic Machu Picchu as you wait for the sun to rise over the mountaintops.

The final triumphant descent takes about 30 minutes. Backpacks are not allowed into the ruins, and guards will pounce upon you to check your pack and to stamp your trail permit. Trekkers generally arrive before the morning trainloads of tourists, so you can enjoy the exhilarated exhaustion of reaching your goal without having to push through as many crushing crowds.

CENTRAL HIGHLANDS

Far off the gringo trail, the central Peruvian Andes are ripe for exploration. Traditions linger longer here, with delightful colonial towns among the least spoiled in the entire Andean chain. A combination of geographical isolation, harsh mountain terrain and terrorist unrest (Maoist group the Sendero Luminoso was born in Ayacucho) made travel difficult for decades. Over the past decade a more stable political situation and improved transportation infrastructure

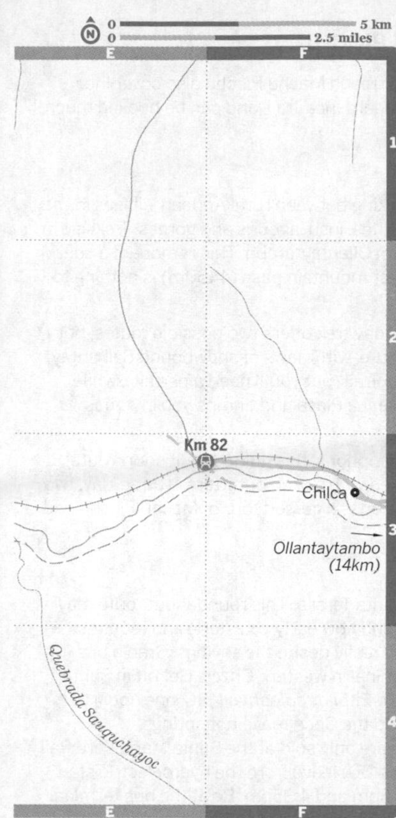

have made travelers' lives easier. But visiting the region is still challenging enough, with ear-popping passes and wearisome bus journeys.

Inca Trail

Sights

1 Inca Tunnel ... B3
2 Intipata ... A2
3 Intipunku ... B1
4 Llactapata ... D3
5 Machu Picchu ... A1
6 Phuyupatamarka ... A2
7 Q'ente ... D3
8 Runkurakay ... B3
9 Sayaqmarka ... B3
10 Wiñay Wayna ... B2

Sleeping

11 Chaquicocha Campground ... B3
12 Corralpunku Campground ... C4
13 Llulluchupampa Campground ... C3
14 Paq'amayo Campground ... B3
15 Paucarcancha ... D4
16 Phuyupatamarka Campground ... B2
17 Sayaqmarka Campground ... B3
18 Wiñay Wayna Campground ... A2
19 Yuncahimpa (Tres Piedras) Campground ... C4

Ayacucho

066 / POP 151,000

As the epicenter of Peru's once horrendous battle with domestic terrorism, the fascinating colonial city of Ayacucho (elevation 2750m) was off-limits to travelers for the better part of the '80s and '90s – and that's part of its allure now. This modern city tucked away in the Central Andes clings fiercely to its traditional past – its Semana Santa celebrations are the country's most dazzling and famous. In town, colonial quirks abound, from hidden interior courtyards to an array of ornate 16th-, 17th- and 18th-century churches (33 in all).

Sights

The town center has a 17th-century **cathedral**, along with a dozen other elaborate **churches** from the past 300 years, and several old **mansions** near the main plaza.

Templo de Santo Domingo CHURCH

(9 de Diciembre, cuadra 2) Be sure to check out this striking temple, with its triple-arched belfry on the left side of the facade, where heretics were said to be punished during the Inquisition.

FREE **Museo de Arte Popular** MUSEUM

(Portal Independencia 72; 8am-1pm & 1:30-3:15pm Mon-Fri) Showcases Ayacucho's folkcraft specialties.

Museo de la Memoria MUSEUM

(Prolongación Libertad 1229; admission S2; 9am-1pm & 3-5pm) In an unlikely location 1.5km northwest of the center is Ayacucho's most haunting museum, remembering the impact of the Sendero Luminoso.

Wari Ruins RUINS

(Huari; admission S3; 8am-5:30pm) Sprawling for several kilometers along a cactus-forested roadside are the extensive ruins of Wari, the capital of the Wari empire, which predated the Incas by five centuries. Beyond

ALTERNATIVE ROUTES TO MACHU PICCHU

Gaining in popularity, these alternative routes to reach Machu Picchu also cover Inca ground. Tours are usually cheaper than the standard Inca Trail, and can be booked much closer to your departure date.

By Trekking

Valle Lares Trek Spend three days or more walking between rural Andean villages in the Sacred Valley, past hot springs, archaeological sites, lush lagoons and gorges. Trekkers finish by taking the train to Aguas Calientes from Ollantaytambo. This is more of a cultural trek, not a technical one, though the highest mountain pass (4450m) is nothing to sneeze at. The average price is US$460.

Salkantay Trek This demanding four- to seven-day trek offers two possible routes, both around 55km. The Mollepata–Huayllabamba route, with views of snowbound Salkantay, tops out at 4880m and can link up with the Inca Trail (but you'll need a permit), while the Mollepata–Santa Teresa route heads through La Playa and dumps you in Aguas Calientes. The average price is US$400.

Inca Jungle Trail With hiking, biking and rafting options, this guided multisport route stages to Machu Picchu via Santa Teresa. Booked with Cuzco outfitters, a three-day, two-night trip costs around US$379, and usually includes a guided tour of Machu Picchu and a return train ticket to Ollantaytambo.

By Bus/Train from Santa Teresa

Lots of people are going to Machu Picchu via Santa Teresa. This roundabout route may take two days (depending on ticket availability and how early you start) and requires some harrowing driving, so think carefully if you really desire the savings. Grab a bus headed for Quillabamba from the Santiago terminal in western Cuzco. Get off in Santa María (S25 to S35, 4½ hours) and catch a local *combi* or *colectivo* (S10, one hour) to Santa Teresa, where there are basic lodgings and the Cocalmayo hot springs.

For Machu Picchu, train tickets on this route are only sold at the Santa Maria Peru Rail ticket office. Daily trains (one way/return US$18/30) leave from the hydroelectric station, about 8km from Santa Teresa, at 7:54am, 3pm and 4:35pm. Be at the bus terminal an hour prior to your train to catch a *combi* (S3, 25 minutes). The 13km train ride to Aguas Calientes takes 45 minutes. Some choose to walk by the railway tracks instead, an outstandingly cheap way to get to Machu Picchu; it takes around four very dusty and sweaty hours.

lies the interesting village of **Quinua**, where a huge monument and small museum mark the site of the Battle of Ayacucho (1824). This small *pueblo* (town) is famous for its unique ceramic handicrafts and makes for nice, picturesque strolling. Wari is 20km and Quinua is 34km northeast of Ayacucho. *Colectivos* and *combis* go to Quinua (S3.50, one hour) via the ruins from Paradero Magdalena at the traffic circle at the east end of Cáceres in Ayacucho. Travel agencies in town offer Spanish-language tours (S60).

Festivals & Events

Semana Santa RELIGION

Held the week before Easter, Peru's finest religious festival begins the Friday before Palm Sunday and continues at fever pitch for 10 days until Easter Sunday. The Friday before Palm Sunday is marked by a procession in honor of La Virgen de los Dolores (Our Lady of Sorrows), during which it's customary to inflict 'sorrows' on bystanders by firing pebbles with slingshots. Every day sees another solemn yet colorful procession, culminating in an all-night party before Easter Sunday, with a dawn fireworks display.

Sleeping

Prices skyrocket during Semana Santa.

TOP CHOICE **Via Via** HOTEL $$

(☎31-2834; www.viaviacafe.com; Portal Constitución 4; s/d/ste S90/120/130; Wi-Fi) The most imaginative sleeping option is this new kid on the block, with an enviable plaza location and cool, vibrantly decorated rooms themed around different continents. A veritable oasis, it has a sun roof and hammock room, all centered on a plant-filled courtyard. English and Dutch are spoken. Has a great recommended restaurant with organic fusion cuisine.

Hotel Sevilla HOTEL **$$**

(☎31-4388; www.hotelsevillaperu.com; Jirón Libertad 635; s/d incl breakfast S60/95; 📶) One of the nicest, brightest, best-value hotels in Ayacucho. Cozy rooms get desks, minifridges and microwaves! Accommodation is set back across a courtyard from the street. Crucially, the owners know how to take care of their guests. A restaurant is under construction.

Hostal Tres Máscaras GUESTHOUSE **$**

(☎31-2921; Tres Máscaras 194; s/d S40/50, without bathroom S18/30) The pleasing walled garden and friendly staff make this an enjoyable place to stay. Hot water is on in the morning and later on request. TV and breakfast are extra.

Hostal El Marqués de Valdelirios GUESTHOUSE **$**

(☎31-7040; Bolognesi 720; s/d S50/70) This lovely, unsignposted colonial building is about 700m from the center, a walk that's noticeably unlit at night. Food is served in a grassy garden. Rooms vary, but all have beautiful furniture, cable TV and hot showers.

Hostal Florida GUESTHOUSE **$**

(☎31-2565; fax 31-6029; Cuzco 310; s/d S35/50) This traveler-friendly *hostal* has a relaxing courtyard garden and clean rooms (those on the upper level are better) with bathroom and TV; there's hot water in the morning and later upon request. There is a basic cafeteria, too.

Hotel La Crillonesa HOTEL **$**

(☎31-2350; Nazareno 165; s/d S30/40) Popular and helpful, offering a rooftop terrace with views, a TV room, tour information and 24-hour hot water. Small, clean rooms have comfy beds and generally functioning cable TV. The best rooms are right at the top.

Eating

Regional specialties include *puca picante* (a curry-like potato stew in peppery peanut sauce, served with rice and a side of *chicharrones*). The colonial courtyard inside Centro Turístico Cultural San Cristóbal is full of travel-friendly bars and cafes. Further down, Plaza Moré offers eateries that are positively gourmet.

Via Via INTERNATIONAL **$$**

(☎31-2834; Portal Constitución 4; mains S14-24; ⏲10am-10pm Mon-Thu, to midnight Fri & Sat) With its upstairs plaza-facing balcony, Via Via has the best views (and steepest prices). Food is ethically sourced and organic – the spicy *albondigas* (meatballs) are tempting – but there's also quinotto, a risotto with quinoa, or *salteado de Alpaca* and some South American wine (from S30) to wash it down.

Mamma Mia ITALIAN **$$**

(Jirón 28 de Julio 262; pizzas S18-25; ⏲4pm-midnight) The only pizza place worth coming to. You can laze away the late afternoon with real coffee and great cakes, or come later for delicious pizza and pasta.

Café Miel CAFE **$**

(Portal Constitución 4; snacks from S2; ⏲10am-10pm) With chirpy atmosphere and checkered tablecloths, Café Miel has recommended breakfasts: we're talking great fruit salads and some of Ayacucho's best (freshly brewed) coffee. It serves hearty lunches and terrific chocolate cake.

El Niño PARRILLA **$**

(Jirón 9 de Diciembre 205; mains S10-20; ⏲11am-2pm & 5-11pm) In a colonial mansion with a sheltered patio containing tables overlooking a garden, El Niño specializes in grills yet dishes up a variety of Peruvian food in generous portions. It's among Ayacucho's best restaurants.

La Casona PERUVIAN **$**

(Bellido 463; mains S12-22; ⏲7am-10:30pm) An ambient courtyard restaurant recommended by several travelers for its big portions. It focuses on Peruvian food, such as the excellent *lomo saltado*, and often has regional specialties.

Wallpa Sua FAST FOOD **$**

(Calle de la Vega 240; mains S8-20; ⏲6-11pm Mon-Sat) This is an upscale, locally popular and ever-busy chicken restaurant, with a quarter-chicken and fries starting at S8.

Drinking

Taberna Magía Negra BAR

(Jirón 9 de Diciembre 293; ⏲4pm-midnight Mon-Sat) This bar-gallery has local art, beer, pizza and great music.

TOP CHOICE Rock DISCO
(Cáceres 1035; ⊙to 2am Wed-Sat) The liveliest local disco.

Shopping

Ayacucho is famous for folk crafts. The **craft market** (Independencia & Quinua; ⊙10am-8:30pm) is a good place to start.

Information

BCP (Portal Unión 28) Has a Visa/Mastercard ATM.
Clínica de La Esperanza (☎31-7436; Independencia 355; ⊙8am-8pm) English is spoken.
iPerú (☎31-8305; Portal Municipal 45; ⊙9am-6pm Mon-Sat, to 1pm Sun) Good tourist information.
Policía de Turismo (☎31-7846; 2 de Mayo 100)
Serpost (Asamblea 293) Postal services.
Wari Tours (☎31-1415; Lima 138)

Getting There & Away

The **airport** (☎31-2088) is 4km from the town center (taxis cost S10). Daily flights to Lima are with **Star Perú** (☎31-3660; Jirón 9 de Diciembre 127) at 6:50am and with **LC Peru** (☎31-6012; Jirón 9 de Diciembre 160) at 5pm.

Most buses (to long-distance north- and southbound destinations) arrive and depart from the snazzy new Terminal Terrestre to the north of the city center. For Lima (S30 to S90, nine hours), there are **Empresa Molina** (☎31-9989; 9 de Diciembre 473) and **Cruz del Sur** (☎31-2813) buses, the latter with its own terminal.

For Huancayo (S30 to S40, nine to 12 hours), Empresa Molina is preferred, though if you want to continue from there to Pucallpa (S75, 30 hours), you're better off on **Turismo Central** (☎31-7873; Copac 499). Take note: this is a tough 250km trip, not for the faint of heart.

For Cuzco (S65, 14 to 16 hours), **Celtur** (☎31-3194; Pasaje Cáceres 174) has the most modern fleet and the recommended day departure time of 7am. It's a long and rough trip, but the journey can be broken at Andahuaylas (S35, six to seven hours).

Huancayo

☎064 / POP 323,000

At first glance, there's nothing much to Huancayo, the largest city in the central highlands, its frenzied and crowded streets not seemingly dissimilar from those of any other workhorse Peruvian town. But despite its chaotic nature, Huancayo has its charms, and travelers often hang around longer than they planned. There are Spanish classes to take, some 400 fiestas per year to immerse yourself in, and loads of trekking, mountain biking and cultural tours to experience in the surrounding highlands.

Sights & Activities

Museo Salesiano MUSEUM
(☎24-7763; Arequipa 105; admission S5; ⊙8am-noon & 2-6pm Mon-Fri) Has Amazonian fauna, pottery and archaeological exhibits.

Cerro de la Libertad VIEWPOINT
(cnr Giráldez & Torre Tagle; ⊙dawn-dusk) About 2km from the town center, a popular recreational and dining locale with city views, artwork stalls and a playground.

Parque de la Identidad Huanca PARK
This fanciful park is about 5km from the center in the San Antonio neighborhood.

Tours

Incas del Perú ADVENTURE TOUR
(☎22-3303; www.incasdelperu.org; Giráldez 652) Offers multiday mountain-biking tours and Andean mountain-trekking expeditions to the lake and glacier of Huaytapallana for up to three days; the cost for trekking per one/two people is around S1000/1700 for three-day excursions. The same company arranges Spanish and Quechua lessons with homestays.

Festivals & Events

There are hundreds of fiestas in Huancayo and surrounding villages – supposedly one almost every day somewhere in the Río Mantaro valley! Huancayo's **Semana Santa** processions leading up to Easter are famous.

Sleeping

TOP CHOICE La Casa de la Abuela HOSTEL $
(☎22-3303; www.incasdelperu.com; Giráldez 691; dm/s/d with shared bathroom incl breakfast S30/40/70; @) A wonderfully charismatic hostel full of well-worn Andean furniture, antique radios and one of the cutest families you ever did see. A garden, talking parrot, hot water, laundry, and multilingual book exchange round out the fun. The hospitable owner, Lucio Hurtado, is almost singlehandedly responsible for putting Huancayo on the tourism map. Camping is S15.

Peru Andino GUESTHOUSE $
(☎22-3956; www.peruandino.com; Psje San Antonio 113; s/d incl breakfast S40/90, without bath-

room S35/80) Though you might find all English on the website and emails, not a lick is spoken upon arrival. Still, it's been run by a talkative older couple since 1978 with all the comforts of home, though it's a bit northeast of the center.

Hotel los Balcones HOTEL $
(☎21-1041; Puno 282; s/d/tr S/45/55/75; @☜) A spacious new-style hotel with plenty of balconies. Tastefully furnished rooms come with cable TV, phone, alarm clock and reading lights. There's a busy in-house restaurant as well.

Casa de la Abuela VIP GUESTHOUSE $$
(☎23-4383; www.incasdelperu.com; Huancas 381; s/d S80/120; ☜) Incas del Peru's latest venture is a step up from backpacker accommodation with private bathrooms and even a suite (S150) alongside a delicious breakfast that includes real coffee.

Eating & Drinking

The blocks of Real south of the plaza abound in cake shops and snack stalls selling strips of grilled *pollo* (chicken) and *lomo* (beef), often in kebab format.

TOP CHOICE **Café Coqui** BAKERY $
(Puno 298; snacks from S3; ⊙7am-10.30pm) Perhaps the best breakfast stop in the Central Andes, serving tasty sandwiches, pastries, empanadas, real espresso and other coffees. Evenings there's pizza and other more substantial fare. What more could you want? Prompt service? Forget it.

Huancahuasi PERUVIAN $$
(☎24-4826; Mariscal Castilla 222; mains S16.50-29.50; ⊙8am-7pm Sun-Thu, to 2am Fri & Sat) The local eatery-of-choice is this classy establishment with well-presented regional goodies like *pachamanca, papas a la huancaína* and *ceviche de trucha* (river-trout *ceviche*). A taxi ride from the center is S3.

Sofa Café Paris CAFE $
(Puno 254; snacks from S3, meals S12; ⊙4-11pm) With a wrap-around mezzanine, this trendy cafe favors Nirvana over pan pipes. Elaborate coffees (made with what must be Huancayo's second coffee machine) and cakes are served alongside other more ample Peruvian fare.

Chicharronería Cuzco LATIN AMERICAN $
(Cuzco 173; mains S5-10) Traditional plates of *chicharrones* (deep-fried pork chunks) at this carnivore-dedicated hole-in-the-wall are about S7.

Detrás de la Catedral PERUVIAN $
(Ancash 335; mains S15-22; ⊙11am-11pm) Cozy spot serving excellent trout *tiradito*, extra-charred burgers, and a long list of other Peruvian specialties, all identified by helpful colorful photos on the menu.

La Cabaña INTERNATIONAL $
(Giráldez 652; mains around S15; ⊙5-11pm) The house *calientito* (a warm street brew made with herbs and vodka or *pisco*), fantastic pizza, al dente pasta and juicy grills fuel a party crowd of locals and travelers alike. *Folklórico* bands perform Thursday to Saturday nights.

Information

Internet cafes are along Giráldez. BCP, Interbank and other ATMs are on Real.

Clínica Ortega (☎23-2921; Carrión 1124; ⊙24hr) For emergencies.

Policía de Turismo (☎21-9851; Ferrocarril 580)

Serpost (Plaza Huamamarca 350) Postal services.

Getting There & Away

Bus

Services vary depending on the season and demand. Some smaller long-distance buses may use the Terminal Los Andes, 500m north of Ayacucho.

Lima (S30 to S80, six to seven hours) is most frequently and comfortably serviced by **Etucsa** (☎23-6524; Puno 220) and **Cruz del Sur** (☎22-3367; Ayacucho 281). For the rough road to Ayacucho (S30, eight to nine hours), **Empresa Molina** (☎21-4902; Angaraes 334) has morning and overnight departures.

Turismo Central (☎22-3128; Ayacucho 274) has buses north to Huánuco (S36, seven hours).

If you are in a hurry, **Comité 12** (Loreto 421) has speedy *colectivo* taxis to Lima (S50, five hours).

Train

Train-buff favorite **Ferrocarril Central Andino** (☎01-226-6363; www.ferroviasperu.com.pe) reaches a head-spinning elevation of 4829m. A special tourist train, it runs fortnightly up from Lima between mid-April and October for S120/195 one way/round-trip (S85/130 for children). There are more expensive *turístico* services that include accommodation in Huancayo. The 12-hour trip leaves Lima at 7am Friday and departs Huancayo for the return trip at the

Huancayo

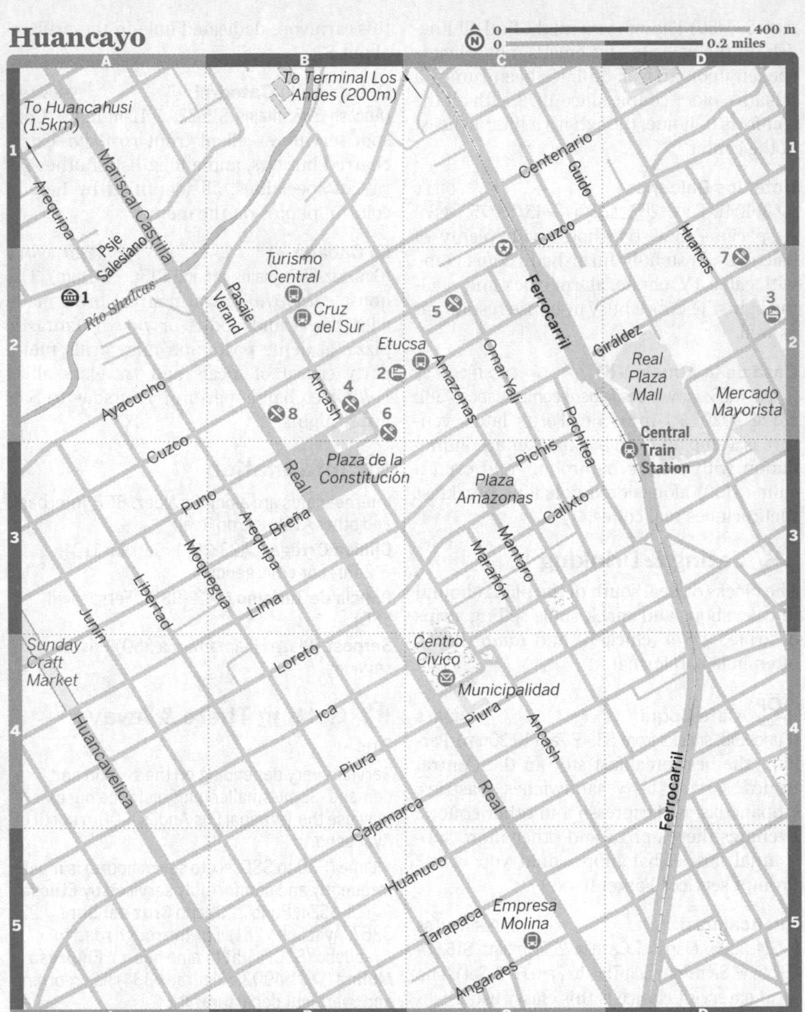

rather inconvenient time of 6pm Sunday. For this return night leg bring along warm clothes and perhaps a blanket.

NORTH COAST

The unruly northern coast is a haven of sun and surf, but in its distant past it was a thriving center of pre-Inca peoples, going back to the continent's oldest civilization. Come north to explore its animated colonial towns, laze away days at seaside resorts and watch world-class surfers take on the gnarled breaks. If you're heading to Ecuador, the further north you go, the better the weather gets.

Trujillo

044 / POP 682,800

Francisco Pizarro's Trujillo marks a notable change from other northern Peruvian cities. Here colonization *has* left an indelible mark, from the immense and beautiful Plaza de Armas to the little architectural hallmarks that pepper many of the city's colorful colonial constructions. Founded by

Huancayo

Sights
1 Museo Salesiano A2

Activities, Courses & Tours
Incas del Perú .... (see 7)

Sleeping
2 Hotel los Balcones B2
3 La Casa de la Abuela D2

Eating
4 Café Coqui B2
5 Chicharronería Cuzco C2
6 Detrás de la Catedral B2
7 La Cabaña D2
8 Sofa Café Paris B2

Pizarro in 1534 and named after his hometown in Spain, Trujillo quickly grew into northern Peru's biggest city, though it had been ground zero for several civilizations prior to the Spanish. Nearby, 1500-year-old Moche pyramids, Las Huacas del Sol y de la Luna, and the ancient Chimú adobe metropolis of Chan Chan loom over the desertscape as testament to once great empires turned to sand and mud.

If you want to take in the ancient culture but not the bustling city, base yourself in the nearby surfing hamlet of Huanchaco, once a tranquil fishing village, now a full-on sea-and-sun affair.

Sights

An 18th-century **cathedral** with a famous basilica fronts the Plaza de Armas.

Many other elegant colonial churches and mansions have wrought-iron grillwork and pastel coloring that typify Trujillo. **Casa de la Emancipación** (Pizarro 610), **Palacio Iturregui** (Pizarro 688) and **Casa Ganoza Chopitea** (Independencia 630), with its art gallery and two lions standing guard out front, all deserve a look.

Museo Cassinelli MUSEUM
(N de Piérola 607; 9am-1pm & 3-6pm Mon-Sat) An excellent archaeological collection in the same building as a Repsol gas station!

Museo de Arqueología MUSEUM
(Junín 682; adult/child S5/1; 9am-5pm Mon-Sat, to 1pm Sun) This well-curated museum features a rundown of Peruvian history from 12,000 BC to the present day.

Tours

Chan Chan Tours CULTURAL TOUR
(24-3016; chanchantourstrujillo@hotmail.com; Independencia 431; 8am-1pm & 3-8pm) Right on the square, offering trips to Chan Chan and Las Huacas del Sol y de la Luna for S15 to S20 per person (two-person minimum).

Festivals & Events

The *marinera* (traditional Peruvian dance) and *caballos de paso* (horseback dressage displays) are highlights of many festivals.

La Fiesta de la Marinera DANCE
The biggest of its kind, held in late January.

La Fiesta de la Primavera CULTURE
Held during the last week of September, with Peru's most famous parade and much dancing and entertainment.

Sleeping

Many travelers prefer the beach vibe in Huanchaco.

TOP CHOICE **Hostal Colonial** HISTORIC HOTEL $$
(25-8261; www.hostalcolonial.com.pe; Independencia 618; s/d/tr S60/90/120;) With a great location near the Plaza de Armas, this tastefully renovated colonial mansion has a pleasant courtyard, garden and restaurant with great breakfast sandwiches. Cozy rooms have hot showers (though cramped bathrooms), some with balcony views.

Residencial Munay Wasi GUESTHOUSE $
(23-1462; www.munaywasihostel.com; Colón 250; dm S30, s/d/tr incl breakfast S45/70/100; @) You are sleeping in someone's home – and your experience follows suit. Perks include a nice courtyard, hot water, a guest kitchen and a wholly different atmosphere than in most spots in Trujillo.

Hospedaje el Conde de Arce GUESTHOUSE $
(29-5117; elcondedearce@hotmail.com; Independencia 577; dm S20, s/d S45/60;) Overseen by a friendly and English-speaking host, this weathered, courtyard-style budget inn is right in the center.

Hostal el Ensueño GUESTHOUSE $
(24-2583; Junín 336; s S20-40, d S40-50;) Cramped quarters with mismatched door sizes are at first off-putting, but nice rooms with large bathrooms, hot water and cable TV keep this a decent budget contender.

Trujillo

Trujillo

Sights

1 Casa de la Emancipación C3
2 Casa Ganoza Chopitea C3
3 Museo de Arqueología D4
4 Palacio Iturregui C3

Activities, Courses & Tours

5 Chan Chan Tours A4

Sleeping

6 Hospedaje el Conde de Arce B3
7 Hostal Colonial B3
8 Hostal el Ensueño B2
9 Residencial Munay Wasi B1

Eating

10 Café Bar Museo C2
11 Casona Deza C3
12 El Sol Restaurante Vegetariano B2
13 Jugería San Augustín C4
14 Oviedo C3

Drinking

15 El Celler de Cler B3
16 Picasso Lounge C3

Eating

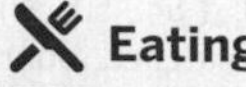 **Mar Picante** PERUVIAN/SEAFOOD $$
(www.marpicante.com; Húsares de Junín 412; mains S18-30; ⊙10am-5pm) True to its name ('Spicy Sea'), if you come to Trujillo without subjecting yourself to this bamboo-lined seafood palace's *ceviche mixto* ordered with a side of spicy, you haven't lived life on the edge. Service is swift and friendly as well – no

small feat considering it's always packed. Take a taxi (S3.50) or leg it southwest on Larco from centro; 200m south of España, Húsares de Junín splits off to the southeast.

Casona Deza CAFE $
(Independencia 630; mains S10-25;) In a 1735 mansion, this atmospheric cafe offers excellent espresso, house-made desserts and tasty pizzas and sandwiches, often sourced organically. It all goes down brilliantly in the airy courtyard or antique-lined rooms.

Jugería San Augustín JUICE, SNACKS $
(Bolívar 526; juice S2-5; 8:30am-1pm & 4-8pm Mon-Sat, 9am-1pm Sun) You will salivate at the thought of your sandwich experience at this frantically popular juice bar for years to come. A real treat.

Café Bar Museo CAFE $
(cnr Junín & Independencia; mains S6-15, cocktails S18-22; closed Sun) This locals' favorite with wood-paneled walls and classic marble-top bar feels like a cross between an English pub and a Parisian Left Bank cafe.

Oviedo BREAKFAST, CAFE $
(Pizarro 758; breakfast & sandwiches S6-14; 8am-midnight) Breakfasts range from a simple Continental to a hearty *criollo* that comes with a pork chop.

El Sol Restaurante Vegetariano VEGETARIAN $
(Zepita 704; mains S3-8; 8:30am-6pm Mon-Sat, to 4pm Sun;) Lots of nonvegetarians eat here, attesting to its hearty, delicious offerings, and it has macrobiotic options to boot.

Drinking

TOP CHOICE **El Celler de Cler** BAR
(cnr Gamarra & Independencia; mains S12-24, cocktails S12-18; 6pm-1am) The classic *chilcano* (*pisco*, ginger ale, lime juice) is souped up here with any number of twists (*rocoto*, *ají limo*, *maracuya* etc) and served on a stunning colonial balcony.

Picasso Lounge CAFE, BAR
(www.picassocafelounge.com; Bolívar 762) This shotgun-style cafe and bar approaches Trujillo's trendiness tipping point and is great forr checking out some modern local art.

Information

BCP (Gamarra 562)

Clínica Americano-Peruano (24-5181; Mansiche 802) The best clinic.

iPerú (29-4561; Almagro 420; 9am-6pm Mon-Sat, to 2pm Sun) Tourist information.

Policía de Turismo (29-1770; Independencia 572) Tourist police.

Getting There & Away

Air

The **airport** (TRU; 46-4013) is 10km northwest of town. Take a taxi (S15 to S18) or a bus bound for Huanchaco and walk 1km. **LAN** (22-1469; Pizarro 340) and **Taca** (0-800-1-8222; www.taca.com; Real Plaza, César Vallejo Oeste 1345) have daily flights to/from Lima.

Bus

Buses are often full, so purchase seats in advance and double-check from where your bus leaves.

DESTINATION	COST (S)	DURATION (HR)
Cajamarca	16-135	6-7
Chachapoyas	60-75	15
Guayaquil (Ecuador)	137.50-201	18
Huaraz	35-60	5-9
Lima	25-100	8-9
Máncora	27-70	8-9
Piura	25-45	6
Tarapoto	85-105	18
Tumbes	27-80	9-12

Cruz del Sur (26-1801; www.cruzdelsur.com.pe; Amazonas 437) To Lima.

El Dorado (29-1778; Nicolás de Piérola 1070) El Dorado has rudimentary buses to Máncora and Tumbes.

Linea booking office (24-5181; www.linea.pe; cnr San Martín & Obregoso; 8am-9pm Mon-Sat); terminal (29-9666; Panamerica Sur 2855) Goes to Piura, Cajamarca and Chiclayo. Buses for Lima and Huaraz are mostly overnight.

Móvil Tours (28-6538; Panamerica Sur 3955) Comfy overnight buses to Lima, Huaraz, Chachapoyas and Tarapoto.

Ormeño (25-9782; www.moviltours.com.pe; Ejército 233) Overnight buses to Lima and Tumbes, as well as direct international services to Ecuador, Colombia and Venezuela.

Getting Around

White-yellow-and-orange B *combis* to La Huaca Esmeralda, Chan Chan and Huanchaco run along España past the corners of Ejército and Industrial every few minutes. Buses for La Esperanza go northwest along the Panamericana to La Huaca Arco Iris. Fares run S1.50 to S2.

A taxi to the airport from the city center should cost S15.

Around Trujillo

The Moche and the Chimú are the two cultures that have left the greatest mark on the Trujillo area, but they are by no means the only ones – more new sites are being excavated each year.

A **combined ticket** (adult/student S11/6), valid for two days, can be purchased for Chan Chan and **Huaca Esmeralda** and **Huaca Arco Iris**, two smaller temples in the area. All are open 9am to 4pm daily.

CHAN CHAN

Built around AD 1300, Chan Chan is the largest pre-Columbian city in the Americas, and the largest adobe city in the world. As you approach along the Panamericana, it's impossible not to be impressed by the vast area of crumbling mud walls stretching away into the distance.

At the height of the Chimú empire, Chan Chan housed an estimated 60,000 inhabitants in thousands of structures, from royal palaces lined with precious metals to huge burial mounds. Although the Incas conquered the Chimú around 1460, the city was not looted until the gold-hungry Spanish arrived, and *guaqueros* finished their work.

The Chimú capital contained nine subcities, or royal compounds. The restored **Tschudi complex** is near the entrance area by the **site museum** on the main road about 500m before the Chan Chan turn-off. Tschudi's walls once stood over 10m high with impressive friezes of fish, waves and sea life. A king was once buried in the mausoleum with a treasure trove of ceremonial objects for the afterlife – and plenty of sacrificial companions.

Combis to Chan Chan leave Trujillo every few minutes, passing the corners of España and Ejército, and España and Industrial. A taxi from Trujillo runs S10.

LAS HUACAS DEL SOL Y DE LA LUNA

These **Moche temples** (www.huacasdemoche.pe; admission & guided tour adult/student S11/6; ⌚9am-4pm), 10km southeast of Trujillo, are 700 years older than Chan Chan, and are attributed to the Moche period.

The **Huaca del Sol** is Peru's largest pre-Columbian structure; 140 million adobe bricks were used to build it. Originally the pyramid had several levels, connected by steep stairs, huge ramps and walls sloping at 77 degrees to the horizon. Now it resembles a giant sand pile, but its sheer size makes it an awesome sight nonetheless.

The smaller **Huaca de la Luna** is riddled with rooms containing ceramics, precious metals and the beautiful polychrome friezes for which the Moche were famous. Their custom of 'burying' old temples under new ones has facilitated preservation, and archaeologists are still peeling away the layers. A new museum is under construction here.

Keep an eye out for Peruvian hairless dogs that hang out here. The body temperature of these dogs is higher than that of normal dogs, and they've traditionally been used as body-warmers for people with arthritis!

Combis for the Huacas del Sol y de la Luna pass Ovalo Grau in Trujillo every 15 minutes or so. You can also take a taxi (S15).

WORTH A TRIP

SOUTH AMERICA'S OLDEST RUINS

Between Lima and Trujillo along Peru's northern coast, two amazing archaeological ruins are worth seeing, though neither sits near any remarkable towns to visit. About 25km inland from Barranca lie the monumental ruins of **Caral** (adult/student S11.20/3.60; ⌚9am-5pm), part of South America's oldest civilization, arising simultaneously with Egypt, India and China. **Proyecto Especial Arqueológico Caral** (☎01-495-1515; www.caralperu.gob.pe) has information and runs full-day tours from Lima (S160). Most coastal buses can drop you off at Km 187 north of Lima, from where *colectivos* (shared taxis or minibuses) to Caral (S3.50) depart from the Mercado de Supe.

Shrouded in mystery, the well-preserved ruins at **Sechín** (adult/student S6/4; ⌚8am-6pm), 5km outside Casma, date from 1600 BC. The walls of the main temple are covered with gruesomely realistic bas-relief carvings of warriors and captives being vividly eviscerated. Take a *mototaxi* (motorized rickshaw; S3) from Casma, served by **Tepsa** (☎01-98-901-5381; Huarmey 356) from Lima and **Yungay Express** (☎94-360-6837; Ormeño 139) from Huaraz.

Huanchaco

☎044 / POP 18,000

Once upon a time, the quaint fishing village of Huanchaco, 12km northwest of Trujillo, must have been quite a scene, what with all those high-ended, cigar-shaped *totora* boats called *caballitos* (little horses) on which fishermen paddled beyond the breakers and all. Today, a few remain, but surfers and other bohemians have taken over Huanchaco and turned it into a less nocturnally oriented Máncora.

For those seeking more sun and sand between their archaeological visits in the Trujillo area, Huanchaco offers a laid-back vibe that's only disrupted by armies of bleached-blond surfers (December to April) and packs of wild Peruvian holidaymakers (weekends).

Activities

You can rent surfing gear (S15 to S30 per day for a wetsuit and surfboard) from several places along the main drag.

Muchik SURFING

(☎63-4503; www.escueladetablamuchik.com; Larco 650) The town's longest-running surf school and said to be the most reliable. Two-hour lessons run S45 and board/wetsuit rental is S15 per day each.

Sleeping

You'll find budget lodgings all over town. If there's a particular restaurant or hangout whose vibe you're digging, chances are it has rooms, too.

TOP CHOICE **Naylamp** GUESTHOUSE $

(☎46-1022; www.hostalnaylamp.com; Larco 1420; campsites without/with tent S10/13, s/d/tr S35/50/80; @📶) Top of the pops in the budget stakes, great rooms share a spacious sea-view patio, and the lush campground has perfect sunset views. Kitchen and laundry service, and a cafe are all thrown in. The only thing missing is the water in the pool.

Hospedaje Oceano GUESTHOUSE $

(☎46-1653; www.hospedajeoceano.com; Los Cerezes 105; r/tr from S40/60; @📶) This superbly welcoming family-run spot features nice Mediterranean-tilted rooms. Even better are the addictive homemade *cremoladas* (Italian ices; S2).

> **WARNING!**
>
> It is dangerous to walk along Buenos Aires beach between Chan Chan and Huanchaco. Travelers have also been attacked while visiting archaeological sites. Go in a group, stay on the main paths and don't visit late in the day.

Hostal Caballito de Totora BOUTIQUE HOTEL $$

(☎46-1154; www.hotelcaballitodetotora.com.pe; La Rivera 348; incl breakfast s S35, d from S90, ste from S360; ❄@📶≋) If you want to splurge, the trendy suites offer perfect sea views; there are wide circular tubs and private patios to boot. A cozy bar adds to the ambience.

La Casa Suiza GUESTHOUSE $

(☎46-1285; www.casasuiza.com; Los Pinos 308; dm S20, S25, d without/with bathroom S40/65; @📶) The Swiss House's spacious rooms have Peru-themed, airbrushed murals. The little cafe downstairs prepares crunchy-crust pizzas, and the patio upstairs hosts a nice view and the occasional barbecue. Good-quality bikes are also available for rent (per half-day S15).

Surf Hostal Meri HOSTEL $

(☎46-2264; hostel.meri@gmail.com; La Rivera 720; dm S20, s/d without bathroom S30/50, tr S75; @📶) Full of tattered antique furniture, this rustic spot across the street from the beach is vaguely hippie-esque with a good communal hostel vibe.

Eating

Huanchaco has oodles of seafood restaurants on the beach – the weak-stomached should be wary.

Otra Cosa VEGETARIAN $

(Larco 921; mains S6-13; ⏰from 8am; 📶🖉) This Dutch-Peruvian beachside pad serves up yummy falafel, crepes, Spanish tortillas, Dutch apple pie and tasty curry-laced burritos (one of which is *almost* a breakfast burrito!). Coffee is organic as well. Half of the tips are donated to charity.

Restaurante Mococho PERUVIAN, SEAFOOD $$

(Bolognesi 535; 3-course meals S45; ⏰1-3pm, closed Mon) Wen, the only Chinese-Peruvian restaurante owner in town, serves up just two dishes with the day's catch: a *ceviche* appetizer and a steamed whole fish (filets for solo diners) in a sharply colored, wildly flavorful *criollo* sauce. It's not cheap, but it's fresh and delicious.

El Caribe PERUVIAN, SEAFOOD **$$**
(Athualpa 150; mains S20-25; ⏲10am-5pm) A local favorite for reasonably priced seafood and *comida criolla*. *Ceviche* here is half the price of the expensive options, double the price of the cheapies, but do you really want to eat raw fish on the cheap?

Getting There & Away

Combis will take you from España (near Industrial) in Trujillo to Huanchaco's beachfront (S1.50). A taxi costs S12.

Chiclayo

☎074 / POP 738,000

Lively Chiclayo saw its share of Spanish missionaries in the 16th century, though never its share of conquistadors, but what it lacks in colonial beauty it more than makes up for in thrilling archaeological sites. The Moche, the Sícan and the Chimú all thrived in the area, making this well-rounded city an excellent base for exploring their ancient pyramids, tombs and artifacts.

Sights & Activities

During summer the coastal beaches of Pimentel and Santa Rosa are popular for **surfing**, especially at El Faro.

Mercado de Brujos MARKET
(Arica, btwn Balta & Cugilevan; ⏲7am-8pm Mon-Sat, to 2pm Sun) Next to the sprawling Mercado Modelo, this fascinating market houses a superstore of shamanistic herbs, elixirs and sagely curiosities. Need a love potion or a cure for warts? Herbalist and *brujo* (witch doctor) stalls sell dried herbs, bones, claws, hooves and other weird and wonderful healing charms.

Tours

Moche Tours SIGHTSEEING TOURS
(☎23-4637; www.mochetourschiclayo.com.pe; Calle 7 de Enero 638; ⏲8am-8pm Mon-Sat, to noon Sun) Recommended daily tours in English and Spanish.

Sleeping

TOP CHOICE **Hotel Embajador** HOTEL **$$**
(☎20-4729; www.hotelembajadorchiclayo.com; 7 de Enero 1368; s/d/tr incl breakfast S80/120/140; @) A fun and festive choice that's toploaded with value and personality: a minimalist cafe, suite Jacuzzi tubs, included airport transfers and a lovely front-desk staff. Everything is clean, freshly painted and cheery. Hop aboard the citrus spectacular!

Hotel Paraíso HOTEL **$$**
(☎22-8161; www.hotelesparaiso.com.pe; Ruiz 1064; s/d incl breakfast S80/100; @) Bright and pleasant, this good-value hotel boasts all the mod cons of far fancier hotels for a fraction of the price. Spotless and modern tiled rooms have decent furniture, hot showers and cable TV. Breakfast is available in the 24-hour cafe.

Hostal Sicán HOTEL **$**
(☎20-8741; hsican@hotmail.com; Izaga 356; s/d/tr incl breakfast S40/55/75; @) Polished wood and wrought iron create an effective illusion of grandeur at this great choice on one of Chiclayo's most charming brick-lined streets. Rooms are small, comfortable and cool.

Hospedaje San Lucas GUESTHOUSE **$**
(☎99-328-4301; pamelacalambrogio@hotmail.com; Aguirre 412; s/d S20/35; @) Elementary, but kept trim and tidy, this shoestringer has a nice city view from the top floor and electric hot showers.

Eating & Drinking

El Pescador SEAFOOD, PERUVIAN **$**
(San José 1236; mains S10-20; ⏲11am-6pm) This little local's secret packs in the droves for outstanding seafood and regional dishes. The *ceviches* (S10 to S12) are every bit as good as at places charging double or even triple the price; and weekend specials like *cabrito con frijoles* (goat with beans; Saturday) and *arroz con pato* (duck with rice; Sunday) are steals for under S14. Owner Oscar and his brother (the chef) work their tails off to make sure you're happy.

Restaurant Romana PERUVIAN **$$**
(Balta 512; mains S13-25; ⏲7am-1am;) Start with tasty *humitas* (corn dumplings) at this popular spot. For bigger appetites, there are pastas, steaks, seafood, chicken or pork *chicharrones* (breaded and fried) with *yuca* – you name it.

Chez Maggy PIZZERIA **$**
(Balta 413; pizzas S12-31; ⏲6-11pm) The wood-fired pizzas here have a pretty darn good crispy crust and fresh toppings. Personal pizzas are convenient for solo diners.

Mi Tia BURGERS $
(Aguirre 662; burgers S1-6) Lines run deep at this no-frills burger joint where plates come loaded with fries. A long list of country staples are served by smiling staff.

Tribal Lounge BAR
(Lapoint 682; cocktails S12-22; closed Mon) A rock-themed bar run by a local who returned from San Francisco after a decade. Good cocktails as well as live music (acoustic to rock) at midnight.

Information

Internet cafes abound. Several banks are on the 600 block of Balta.

BCP (Balta 630) Has a 24-hour Visa and MasterCard ATM.

Clínica del Pacífico (23-6378; Ortiz 420) For medical attention.

iPerú (20-5703; 7 de Enero 579; 9-6pm Mon-Sat, to 1pm Sun) The best spot for tourist info in town; with another booth at the airport.

Policía de Turismo (49 0892; Saenz Peña 830) Tourist police.

Getting There & Around

Air

The **airport** (CIX; 20-4934) is 2km southeast of town (taxi S5). **LAN** (27-4875; Izaga 770) and **Taca** (0-800-1-8222; www.taca.com; Cáceres 222, C.C. Real Plaza) offer daily flights to Lima.

Bus & Colectivo

Many bus companies are along Bolognesi, including **Cruz del Sur** (23-7965; Bolognesi 888), **Línea** (23-2951; Bolognesi 638) and **Móvil Tours** (27-1940; Bolognesi 199). A sample of long-distance destinations:

DESTINATION	COST (S)	DURATION (HR)
Cajamarca	16-40	6
Chachapoyas	30-50	10
Jaén	20-25	6
Lima	40-125	12-14
Máncora	30-35	6
Piura	12-14	3
Tarapoto	45-120	14
Tumbes	25-50	8

The minibus terminal at the intersection of San José and Lora y Lora has regular *combis* to Lambayeque (S1.50, 20 minutes). Buses for Ferreñafe (S2, 30 minutes) and Sipán (S3, 45 minutes) leave from the **Terminal de Microbuses Epsel** (Nicolás de Píerola, at Oriente). *Colectivos* depart from Prado near Sáenz Peña. For Túcume, buses leave from the 13th block of Leguia near Óvalo del Pescador (S2.50, one hour).

Around Chiclayo

Tours cost between S50 and S130, depending on whether entrance fees to museums are included.

LAMBAYEQUE

The pride of northern Peru, the impressive **Museo Tumbas Reales de Sipán** (www.amigosmuseosipan.com; admission S10; 9am-5pm Tue-Sun) is a world-class facility (save the Spanish-only signage) showcasing the dazzling finds of the Royal Tombs of Sipán, including that of the Lord of Sipán himself. Also in Lambayeque is the older **Bruning Museum** (admission S8; 9am-5pm), which houses artifacts from the Chimú, Moche, Chavín and Vicus cultures.

SIPÁN

The story of this **site** (80-0048; Huaca Rayada; admission S8; 9am-5pm), 30km southeast of Chiclayo, is an exciting one of buried treasure, *guaqueros,* the black market, police, archaeologists and at least one murder. Hundreds of exquisite and priceless artifacts have been recovered, and a gold-smothered royal Moche burial site – of the Lord of Sipán – was discovered in 1987. A small but well-done museum opened here in 2009 showcasing the latest finds from the 2007 opening of the chamber of the warrior priest.

FERREÑAFE

About 18km northeast of Chiclayo, the excellent **Museo Nacional Sicán** (www.sicanperu cultural.org.pe; adult S8; 9am-5pm Tue-Sun) displays replicas of some of the largest tombs ever found in South America. Interestingly, the Lord of Sicán was buried upside down, in a fetal position with his head chopped off, along with a sophisticated security system to ward off *guaqueros* – a red dust that's toxic when inhaled.

TÚCUME

This little-known **site** (adult/student S8/3; 8am-4:30pm Tue-Sun) can be seen from a spectacular clifftop *mirador* about 30km north of Lambayeque on the Panamericana. It's worth the climb to see the vast complex of crumbling walls, plazas and more than two dozen pyramids.

Piura

☎073 / POP 377,500

Sun-scorched Piura presents itself out of the dusty tumbleweeds of the Desierto de Sechura as a mere regional transportation hub. There's little to do here, but it works just fine as a speed bump in your journey north or south – some cobblestone streets boasting character-filled houses and northern Peru's best crafts market in nearby Catacaos add to the appeal.

Sights & Activities

Crafts Market MARKET
(⏲10am-6pm) About 12km southwest of Piura, the dusty village of Catacaos claims northern Peru's best crafts market, which sprawls for several blocks near the plaza.

Sleeping & Eating

Hotel Vicus HOTEL $
(☎34-3201; www.hotelvicus.com; Guardia Civil B-3; s/d/tr S60/80/105; ❄@🛜≋) Rooms are spaced out with a lush communal patio and have everything you might crave. It's a nice location just across the bridge from centro, comparatively quiet and the best nightlife is a block away.

Hospedaje Aruba GUESTHOUSE $
(☎30-3067; Junín 851; s/d 30/50, without bathroom S25/35) All white and bright, the small, spartan rooms here fulfill the basic crash-pad role.

TOP CHOICE **Capuccino** CAFE $$
(www.capuccino-piura.com; Tacna 786; mains S22-45; ⏲closed Sun; 🛜) This excellent modern cafe offers gourmet sandwiches and salads (S14 to S22) and more sophisticated fare for a fine night out with a bottle of wine at dinner. Desserts (Toblerone cheesecake, pecan pie) are astonishing.

Chifa Canton CHINESE $$
(cnr Sánchez Cerro & Tacna; mains S22-32) Fresh and flavorful, it's the perfect antidote when you tire of *ceviche*.

Snack Bar Romano BREAKFAST, PERUVIAN $
(Ayacucho 580; menús S6-22, mains S7.50-15; ⏲closed Sun) Double thumbs-up for *ceviches*, *sudados* and local specialties.

Information

The post office and banks with ATMs are on the Plaza de Armas.

Clínica San Miguel (www.csmpiura.com; Los Cocos 111-153; ⏲24hr) Medical care.

iPerú (☎32-0249; Ayacucho 377; ⏲9am-6pm Mon-Sat, to 1pm Sun) Tourist information.

Getting There & Away

Air

The **airport** (PIU; ☎34-4503) is 2km southeast of the city center. **LAN** (☎30-2145; Grau 140), **Taca** (☎0-800-1-8222; www.taca.com; Sánchez Cerro 234, CC Real Plaza) and **Peruvian Airlines** (☎32-4206; www.peruvianairlines.pe; Libertad 777) have daily flights to/from Lima.

Bus

Buses go to Lima (S59 to S135, 12 to 16 hours) with **Cruz del Sur** (☎33-7094; cnr Bolognesi & Lima), **Tepsa** (☎30-6345; Loreto 1198), Linea, Ittsa and Transportes Chiclayo. For other destinations try the companies listed below.

For Cajamarca and the northern Andes, it's best to connect in Chiclayo.

Combis for Catacaos (S1.50 to S2, 25 minutes) leave east of the San Miguel pedestrian bridge. Buses to Huancabamba depart from Terminal El Castillo 1km east of town.

El Dorado (☎32-5875; Cerro 1119) To Máncora (S16 to S25, three hours), Tumbes (S16 to S25, five hours) and Trujillo (S25 to S35, six hours).

El Sol Peruano (☎41-8143; Cerro 1112) Daily to Tarapoto (S60, 18 hours).

Ittsa (☎33-3982; Cerro 1142) To Trujillo and by *bus-cama* ('bed-bus', with fully reclining seats) to Lima.

Línea (☎30-3894; Cerro 1215) Hourly to Chiclayo (S15, three hours).

Transportes Chiclayo (☎30-8455; Cerro 1121) Hourly to Chiclayo, daily to Tumbes and by *bus-cama* to Lima.

Máncora

☎073 / POP 10,000

Despite being Peru's principal beach resort and home to one of northwestern South America's best beaches, Máncora itself is little more than a glorified surfing village of shockingly rustic proportions (the fancy stuff combs its outskirts). Year-round sunshine and waves pushing 3m draw in swaths of surfers, who rub sunburnt shoulders with the Peruvian *Caras* crowd on weekends year-round. From December to March the scene (and price) gets deliriously rowdy.

Activities

You can go **surfing** year-round, but the best waves hit from November to February. Rent

GETTING TO ECUADOR VIA LA TINA

The border post of La Tina lacks hotels, but the Ecuadorian town of Macará (3km from the border) has adequate facilities. La Tina is reached by *colectivo* (shared taxi or minibus; S12, 2½ hours) leaving from Sullana, 40km north of Piura, throughout the day. A better option is **Transportes Loja** (☎073-30-5446; www.cooperativaloja.com; Sánchez Cerro, Km 1, Piura), with three daily buses from Piura (9:30am, 1pm and 9pm) that conveniently go straight through here and on to Loja (S28, eight hours).

The border is the international bridge over the Río Calvas and is open 24 hours. Formalities are relaxed as long as your documents are in order. There are no banks; you'll find money changers at the border or in Macará. By the time you read this, a new bridge and completely revamped immigration facilities will be in place with both Peruvian and Ecuadorian immigration offices sharing the same building on the bridge.

Travelers entering Ecuador will find taxis (US$1) and *colectivos* (US$0.50) to take them to Macará. Most nationalities are simply given a T3 tourist card, which must be surrendered when leaving, and granted 90 days' stay in Ecuador. There is a Peruvian **consulate** (☎07-269-4030; www.consuladoperumacara.com; Bolívar 134) in Macará. See Lonely Planet's *Ecuador & the Galápagos Islands* for more on Ecuador.

surfboards at the beach's southern end. The best breaks in the area are on **Máncora Beach** in town and **Lobitos**, a 64km trek south. Haggle a taxi (S20 to S50).

Winds can reach 30 knots during kitesurfing season (from April to November).

Laguna Camp SURFING
(☎41-1587; www.vivamancora.com/lagunacamp) Surf lessons for S50 for 90 minutes of instruction (including board rental).

Del Wawa ADVENTURE SPORTS
(☎25-8427; www.delwawa.com) Kitesurfing lessons (per six hours S624). Keep in mind it generally takes six hours for beginners to get riding.

Iguana's ADVENTURE TOUR
(☎63-2762; www.iguanastrips.com; Piura 245) Full-day trips to the Los Pilares dry forest, which include wading through sparkling waterfalls, swimming, horseback riding, a soak in the mud baths and lunch for S180 per person. Sea-kayaking trips, ideal for bird spotting, cost S140 per person for the day.

Sleeping

Cheap sleeps are mostly found in the center and at the beach's southern end.

TOP CHOICE **Loki del Mar** HOSTEL $
(☎25-8484; www.lokihostel.com; incl breakfast dm S28-36, r S86; ❄@📶🏊) Elevating the hostel to entirely new levels, Loki has outdone itself (and others) with this hostel-resort complete with a swimming pool, an upscale cocktail menu and grub by an actual chef. Wake up to the sound of crashing waves (if you can fall asleep with the obnoxiously loud bar the night before).

Claro de Luna HOTEL $$
(☎25-8080; www.clarodelunamancora.com; Antigua Panamericana, Km 1216; s/d incl breakfast S130/220; @📶🏊) Cozy, downhome atmosphere. Tasteful rooms, two pools, a movie-projection room, kayaks for use and a lovely oceanside patio-lounge (ideal for sipping Argentine wine) ensure there's something for everyone.

Del Wawa HOTEL $$
(☎25-8427; www.delwawa.com; 8 de Octubre s/n; s/d S50/100; ❄📶) This surfer's mecca has its share of chipped paint and dangerously rusty hot-water heaters but it has the most idyllic common area on the town beach. There are umbrella-shaded beach lounges, surfboard rental, kitesurfing instruction and daily yoga. If you get the right room, you win.

Laguna Surf Camp BUNGALOW $
(☎99-401-5628; www.vivamancora.com/laguna camp; Veraniego s/n; r per person S40; 📶🏊) Laid-back Laguna has rustic Indonesian-style bamboo bungalows and kitchen facilities on the quieter side of the beach.

Kokopelli HOSTEL $$
(☎25-8091; www.hostelkokopelli.com; Piura 209; incl breakfast dm S30, r S95; ❄@📶) This Dutch-Peruvian effort is the most intimate hostel in town, with a small pool, a cool bar area, colorful dorm rooms boasting loads of

GETTING TO ECUADOR

Shady practices at the border crossing between Ecuador and Peru at Aguas Verdes have earned it the dubious title of 'the worst border crossing in South America.' We can't prove it, but it pays to be wary. If you need to change money, avoid doing so at the border as scams and counterfeit bills are rampant here.

The Peruvian border town of Aguas Verdes is linked by an international bridge across the Río Zarumilla with the Ecuadorian border town of Huaquillas.

The last major hub north on the Peru side is **Tumbes** – not a bad spot to shack up for a night and explore the surrounding mangroves and ecological reserves. **Preference Tours** (52-5518; turismomundial@hotmail.com; Grau 427; 9am-7:30pm Mon-Sat, to 11am Sun) can get you out and about. On the plaza, **SíSeñor** (Bolívar 115; mains S15-35) has the usual array of cheap Peruvian staples, and **Hotel Roma** (52-4137; Bolognesi 425; s/d/tr S45/70/95;) offers wi-fi, cable TV, high-powered fans and hot showers. Beware of vicious mosquitoes in the area, and book ahead – the rooms go quickly.

To avoid scams, it is smart to take a direct bus across the border with a major bus company from Tumbes like Cruz del Sur, Civa, Ormeño or **Cifa** (52-5026; www.cifainternacional.com; Tumbes 958); options include to Machala (S12, three hours) or Guayaquil (S25 to S118, six hours) in Ecuador, departing every two hours. From Tumbes to the border, the cheap way is a *colectivo* (shared taxi; S3.50, 25 minutes) and minibuses (S2, 40 minutes) leaving from various spots, including from the corner of Puell and Tumbes or Castilla and Feijoo, the latter near the market.

The **immigration office** (56-1178; El Complejo; 24hr) in Aguas Verdes is 3km from the border. On public transportation, make sure you stop there for border formalities. *Mototaxis* (motorized rickshaws) will then whisk you to the border (S3).

About 3km to the north of the bridge, Ecuadorian immigration is also open 24 hours. There are no entry fees into Ecuador, so be polite but insistent with any border guards trying their luck. Take a taxi from the bridge (US$2.50). There are basic hotels in Huaquillas, but most people catch an onward bus to Machala.

From Tumbes, **Cruz del Sur** (52-6200; Tumbes 319) offers the most comfortable services to Lima (S50 to S165). For Máncora, *combis*/air-con vans (S7/25) go every 30 minutes from the corner of Tumbes and Piura in Tumbes.

exposed brick and three private rooms with in-room safes.

Eating

Seafood rules here, but the gringo onslaught has inspired everything from breakfast burritos to Greek salads. Breakfast is well spoken for, but forget about lunch before 1pm.

La Sirena d'Juan SEAFOOD, PERUVIAN **$$**
(25-8173; Piura 316; mains S30-35; closed Tue;) Local boy done good Juan has turned his intimate little main-drag seafooder into northern Peru's best restaurant, with showstopper fish served as *tiradito* or grilled with mango chutney. Service is personalized and on point.

Tao THAI, CHINESE **$$**
(Piura 240; mains S12-35; closed Mon) Travelers flock here for the taste-bud flip: red, yellow, green and Panang curries and fusion stir-fry and noodles; a worthy culinary upgrade.

Angela's Place BREAKFAST, VEGETARIAN **$**
(Piura 396; breakfasts S6.50-14, mains S5-12; from 8am;) Creative and substantial vegetarian (and vegan!) dishes, energizing breakfast combos and sweet pastries.

Green Eggs & Ham BREAKFAST **$**
(Grau 503; mains S15-18; 7:30am-4:30pm) A little beachfront shack good for scrumptious breakfasts.

Beef Grill BURGERS, STEAKHOUSE **$$**
(Piura 253; burgers S18-23; from 5pm) Monstrous burgers are an ideal antidote to the seafood blues, but there are more serious slabs of meat coming out of the kitchen, too.

Information

Av Piura is lined with internet cafes, ATMs and *lavanderías* (laundry services). Exchange US dollars at **Banco de la Nación** (Piura 625). Tread wearily on the beach at night, as thieves pose as joggers. The website www.vivamancora.com has useful tourist information.

Getting There & Away

Most southbound coastal buses headed for Lima originate in Tumbes. Frequent *combis* for Tumbes (S10, two hours) drive along Máncora's main drag. **El Dorado** (☎25-8161; Grau 213) offers the most frequent services to more southerly towns of interest, like Piura (S15 to S30), Chiclayo (S26 to S50) and Trujillo (S27 to S60).

HUARAZ & THE CORDILLERAS

All around Huaraz, the mountainous region of the Cordilleras Blanca and Huayhuash boasts calm topaz lakes huddled below peaks teetering on avalanche – some 22 ostentatious summits over 6000m make this the highest mountain range in the world outside the Himalayas.

Both Peru's highest point, the 6768m Huascarán, and the picture-perfect 5999m Artesonraju (rumored to be the mountain in Paramount Pictures' live-action logo), loom here over Andean villages as well as the pleasant city of Huaraz, the nerve center of one of South America's premier trekking, mountain-biking and climbing areas. Superlatives crash and burn in a brazen attempt to capture the awesome natural beauty of it all.

Huaraz

☎043 / POP 90,000

The restless Andean adventure capital of Huaraz came into its own based on a blessed location amidst some of the prettiest mountains in the world. Though nearly wiped out by the earthquake of 1970, Huaraz rebounded to become Peru's high-adrenaline showpiece, with trekking and mountaineering leading the heart-thumping charge. It buzzes with adventure seekers of all ilks in high season (May to September) and slows to little more than a crawl the rest of the year, when many folks shut up shop and head for the beaches.

Sights

Museo Regional de Ancash MUSEUM
(Plaza de Armas; adult/child S5/1; ⌚8:30am-5:15pm Tue-Sat, 9am-2pm Sun) Small but interesting archaeology exhibits.

Monumento Nacional Wilkahuaín RUIN
(adult/student S5/2; ⌚9am-5pm) This small but well-preserved Wari site, 7km northeast of town, has a three-story temple. The two-hour walk sees robberies often; take a taxi (S10) or look for *combis* by the Río Quilcay.

Activities

Trekking & Mountaineering

The best treks are in the **Cordillera Blanca** inside Parque Nacional Huascarán and in the Cordillera Huayhuash. All the equipment and help you need can be hired or bought, including trail maps, guidebooks, pack animals, *arrieros* (drivers) and local guides. Expect to pay around S120 to S150 per person per day for an all-inclusive trek or climbing expedition. Always inspect rental gear carefully.

Check certified guides and register before heading out at Casa de Guías (p883).

Skyline Adventures TREKKING, MOUNTAINEERING
(☎42-7097; www.skyline-adventures.com; Pasaje Industrial 137) Based just outside of Huaraz and comes highly recommended. Provides guides for treks and mountain climbs and leads six- and 10-day mountaineering courses.

Active Peru TREKKING
(☎99-648-3655; www.activeperu.com; Gamarra 699) A well-regarded, Belgian-run agency that also rents gear.

MountClimb TREKKING, MOUNTAINEERING
(☎42-4322; www.mountclimb.com.pe) Reputable trekking guide and mountaineering school; rents top-end gear.

Huascarán TREKKING
(☎42-2523; www.huascarin-peru.com; Campos 711) Gets repeatedly good reviews; also does tours.

Rock Climbing

You'll find great bolted sports climbs in the Cordillera Blanca, particularly at Chancos (near Marcará), Monterrey and Recuay. For big-wall action to keep you chalked up for days, head to the famous Torre de Parón (aka the Sphinx) at Laguna Parón, 32km east of Caraz. Many trekking agencies offer rock-climbing trips and rent gear. Galaxia Expeditions has an indoor climbing wall, too.

Mountain Biking

Mountain Bike Adventures MOUNTAIN BIKING
(☎42-4259; www.chakinaniperu.com; Lúcar y Torre 530, 2nd fl; ⌚9am-1pm & 3-8pm) Has been in business for over a decade. It has a good safety record and selection of bikes. The

Huaraz

English-speaking owner is a lifelong resident of Huaraz and he knows the region's single track better than anyone. Rates start at S100 per day for guided tours. Ask about more challenging 12-day circuits of the Cordillera Blanca.

 Tours

One bus tour visits the ruins at Chavín de Huántar; another goes through Yungay to the beautiful Lagunas Llanganuco, where there are spectacular views of Huascarán; a third takes you through Caraz to scenic

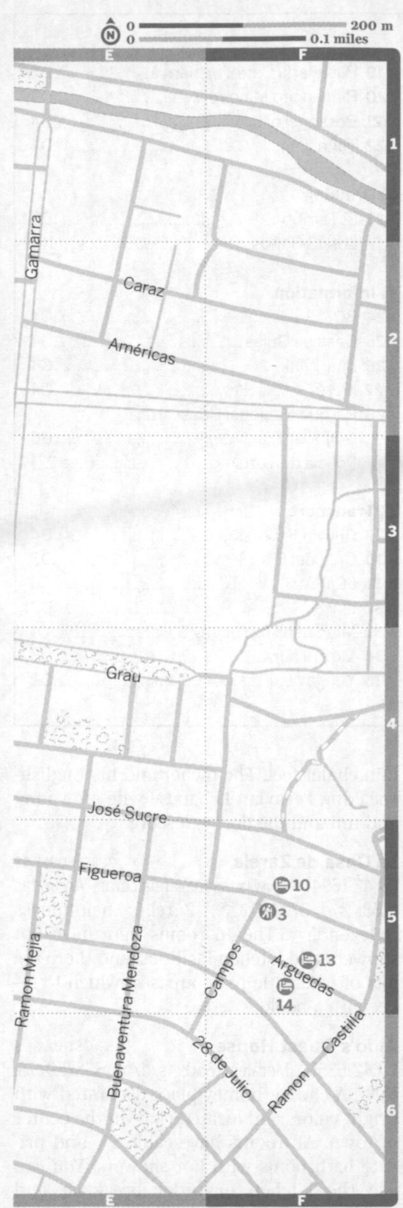

Laguna Parón; and a fourth goes to see the extraordinary giant *Puya raimondii* plant (which can take 100 years to grow to its full height – often 10m!) and the glacier at Nevado Pastoruri. Full-day tours cost S30 to S45, excluding entry fees. Services are geared towards Peruvians – do not count on English.

Out of the throng of agencies in Huaraz, **Pablo Tours** (☎42-1145; www.pablotours.com; Luzuriaga 501) and **Sechín Tours** (☎42-1419; www.sechintours.com; Morales 602) are popular with travelers.

Festivals & Events

Semana Santa RELIGION
(Holy Week) In March-April, tongue-in-cheek funeral processions for *Ño Carnavalón* (King of Carnaval) are on Ash Wednesday.

El Señor de la Soledad CULTURE
Huaraz pays homage to its patron saint during this festival, with fireworks, music, dancing, costume parades and lots of drinking, in early May.

Semana de Andinismo MOUNTAINEERING
International mountaineering exhibitions and competitions in June.

Sleeping

Locals meet buses to offer rooms in their houses, and *hostales* do the same. Don't pay until you've seen the room.

TOP CHOICE **Albergue Churup** BOUTIQUE HOSTEL $$
(☎42-4200; www.churup.com; Figueroa 1257; dm S28, s/d incl breakfast S69/99; @☎) A top choice with immaculate and comfortable rooms. The fireplace-warmed top-floor lounge has magnificent 180-degree mountain views. The Quirós family are consummate hosts and offer a cafe and bar, a communal kitchen and a travel office that rents out trekking gear and arranges Spanish lessons. A new, equally homey annex, Churup II, has opened a block over on Arguedas. Reservations essential.

Olaza's Bed & Breakfast GUESTHOUSE $$
(☎42-2529; www.olazas.com; Arguedas 1242; s/d/tr incl breakfast S80/100/140; @☎) This smart little guesthouse has a boutique feel, spacious bathrooms and comfortable beds, but the best part is the big lounge area upstairs and massive panoramic terrace. The owner can point you in the right direction no matter where you want to go (when he is around). Bus-station pickup is included.

Familia Meza Lodging GUESTHOUSE $
(☎94-369-5908; Lúcar y Torre 538; r per person S20) In the same building as Café Andino (whose wi-fi you can use) and Mountain

Huaraz

Sights

1 Museo Regional de Ancash ... C5

Activities, Courses & Tours

2 Active Peru ... D4
3 Huascarán ... F5
4 Mountain Bike Adventures ... C3
5 MountClimb ... C6
6 Pablo Tours ... C3
7 Sechín Tours ... C3
8 Skyline Adventures ... C3

Sleeping

9 Albergue Benkawasi ... A6
10 Albergue Churup ... F5
11 Aldo's Guest House ... C4
12 Cayesh Guesthouse ... D4
Familia Meza Lodging ... (see 4)
13 La Casa de Zarela ... F5
14 Olaza's Bed & Breakfast ... F5

Eating

Café Andino ... (see 4)
15 California Café ... B5
16 Chili Heaven ... D4
17 El Horno ... C4
18 La Brasa Roja ... C6
19 Pastelería Café Turmanyé ... D4
20 Rinconcito Mineiro ... D3
21 Rossonero ... C4
22 Taita ... D4

Drinking

23 El Tambo ... D3
Los 13 Buhos ... (see 16)

Information

24 BCP ... C4
25 Casa de Guías ... D4
26 Interbank ... C4
27 iPerú ... C4
28 Parque Nacional Huascarán Office ... B6
Policía de Turismo ... (see 27)

Transport

29 Chavín Express ... B4
30 Cruz del Sur ... D3
31 LC Perú ... C6
32 Línea ... D3
33 Minibuses to Yungay & Caraz ... C1
34 Móvil Tours ... D3
35 Yungay Express ... D2

Bike Adventures, this charming family guesthouse has cheery rooms and is decorated throughout with homey, frilly touches.

Jo's Place GUESTHOUSE $
(☎42-5505; josplacehuaraz@hotmail.com; Villazón 278; campsites per person S10, dm S15, s/d without bathroom S25/35, s/d with bathroom S30/45; @ 🛜) The slightly chaotic nature of English expat Jo and his modest guesthouse should suit wandering souls with its grassy camping and basic rooms, some with bathrooms and hot water. There's a full English breakfast.

Cayesh Guesthouse GUESTHOUSE $
(☎42-8821; www.cayesh.net; Morales 867; dm S20, s/d S30/50, without bathroom S25/40; 🛜) These hosts take backpackers' delights seriously, offering an extensive DVD library, free kitchen use and luggage storage. Rooms are simple but have comfortable beds with views of magnificent peaks. Fluent English is spoken.

Albergue Benkawasi GUESTHOUSE $
(☎43-3150; www.huarazbenkawasi.com; Parque Santa Rosa 928; dm S15, s/d/tr S35/60/90; @ 🛜) The brick building has a kind of '70s mountain chalet feel. The owner and his English-speaking Peruvian-Lebanese wife are young and fun and the dorm's a score.

La Casa de Zarela GUESTHOUSE $$
(☎42-1694; www.lacasadezarela.com; Arguedas 1263; s/d S70/90; 🛜) Zarela's helpfulness is legendary. The 16 rooms here have hot showers and kitchen facilities, and there are lots of neat little patio areas in which to relax with a book.

Aldo's Guest House GUESTHOUSE $
(☎42-5355; Morales 650; s/d/tr S35/50/75; @ 🛜) A cheery, homey place decorated with bright colors and located right in the center of town. All rooms have cable TV and private bathrooms with hot showers. You can use the kitchen or order breakfast and lunches.

Eating

TOP CHOICE **Café Andino** CAFE $
(www.cafeandino.com; Lúcar y Torre 530, 3rd fl; breakfast S8.50-20, mains S7-25; 🛜 ✍) A serious java joint (they roast their own coffee beans)

and Huaraz' ultimate hangout, with great mountain vistas, organic coffee roasted on-site and a well-stocked lender library in memoriam of a mountaineer. Breakfast is served all day (think *huevos rancheros*) and interesting mains like quinoa curries highlight the menu.

Chili Heaven INDIAN, THAI **$$**
(Parque Ginebra; mains S18-35) The fiery curries at this English-run hot spot will seize your taste buds upon arrival, plus they bottle their own hot sauces.

Taita PERUVIAN **$**
(Larrea y Laredo 633, 2nd fl; mains S4.50-15; 10am-3pm) Superior and popular, this place is covered head-to-toe in historical photos of beauty queens, sports teams and school classes. Try *chocho*, it's made with *lupine* (an Andean legume). They also do *ceviche*, *leche de tigre* (*ceviche* juice) and *chicharrones*.

Rinconcito Mineiro PERUVIAN **$**
(Morales 757; menús S7-12;) The daily blackboard of 10 or so options includes an excellent *lomo saltado* as well as grilled trout, *tacu-tacu* (an Afro-Peruvian fusion dish of rice, beans and a protein) and the like. It's all served up in a welcoming and clean space tastefully decorated with Andean textiles.

California Café BREAKFAST, CAFE **$**
(www.huaylas.com; Calle 28 de Julio 562; breakfast S10-22; 7:30am-6:30pm, to 2pm Sun;) This hip traveler magnet does breakfasts at any time, plus light lunches and salads – it's a funky, chilled space with books and music to while away many hours.

La Brasa Roja PERUVIAN **$**
(Luzuriaga 915; mains S10-26) This upscale *pollería* (restaurant specializing in roast chicken) is the ultimate budget refueling stop. Not only is the chicken perfect, but you get five sauces – count 'em, five! – instead of the usual three (black olive and mustard make a surprise appearance) as well as a live violinist. No lie.

El Horno PIZZERIA **$**
(www.elhornopizzeria.com; Parque el Periodista; pizzas S9.50-23.50, mains S12-26; closed Sun) The different varieties of meat skewers and delicious thin-crust pizzas are the best picks here. The place often fills up with trekking groups, so arrive early.

Pastelería Café Turmanyé BREAKFAST, CAFE **$**
(www.arcoiristurmanye.com; Morales 828; sandwiches S3.50-9, pastries S1.50-5; from 7am, closed Sun) It's slow as dial-up, but excellent paella, sandwiches and rich Spanish-style pastries and cakes are a hit at this little eatery that also benefits a children's foundation.

Rossonero DESSERTS **$**
(Luzuriaga 645, 2nd fl; desserts S3.50-7.50;) A modern den of decadence doling out cheesecakes, chocolate cake and artisanal housemade ice creams.

Drinking

TOP CHOICE **Sierra Andina** BREWERY
(www.sierraandina.com; Centenario 1690, Cascapampa; pint/pitcher S7/30; 3-10pm) The S5 taxi ride to Cascapampa is a small price to pay for the wares afforded at this genuine microbrewery pioneered by Colorado beer enthusiasts.

Los 13 Buhos BAR
(Parque Ginebra; 5pm-late) Located above Makondo's, this hip and snug bar draws the cool folks, mainly for its new, coca-infused home brew or the Long Andean Iced Tea (made with coca-infused liquors).

El Tambo BAR, CLUB
(José de la Mar 776; to 4am) A cool club where the soundtrack runs from techno-cumbia to pop to reggaeton, the crowd from young and restless to town cougars.

Information

Dangers & Annoyances

Huaraz is a safe city that sees little crime; unfortunately, robberies of trekkers and tourists do happen, especially in the area of the Mirador de Retaqeñua and the Wilkahuaín (sometimes also spelled Wilcawain) ruins, and to groggy backpackers arriving early in the morning on overnight buses. In these cases, stay alert and walk with a group or hire a taxi to avoid problems.

Emergency

Casa de Guías (42-1811; www.casadeguias.com.pe; Parque Ginebra 28G; 9am-1pm & 4-8pm Mon-Sat) Offers safety and rescue courses and will save your life – if you're trekking or climbing with one of its guides certified by the Mountain Guide Association (AGM). Ask for a list of guides or see the website. Register here before heading out on a trek or climb.

Policía de Turismo (94-310-8929; Luzuriaga 724)

Money

BCP (Luzuriaga 691) Visa ATM and no commission on traveler's checks.

Interbank (José Sucre 687) Global ATM.

Post

Serpost (Luzuriaga 702) Postal services.

Tourist Information

The new English newspaper, **The Huaraz Telegraph** (www.huaraztelegraph.com), is also a good source of information.

iPerú (☎42-8812; Pasaje Atusparia, Oficina 1, Plaza de Armas; ⏰9am-6pm Mon-Sat, to 1pm Sun) Has general tourist information but little in the way of trekking info.

Parque Nacional Huascarán Office (☎42-2086; www.sernanp.gob.pe; Sal y Rosas 555; ⏰8:30am-1pm & 2:30-6pm Mon-Fri, to noon Sat) Staff have limited information about visiting the park.

Getting There & Away

The Huaraz **airport** (ATA) is actually at Anta, 23km north of town. A taxi will cost about S20. **LC Perú** (☎42-4734; www.lcperu.pe; Luzuriaga 904) operates daily flights from Lima.

Expect midmorning or late-evening departures for Lima. **Cruz del Sur** (☎42-8726; Bolívar 491) has nonstop luxury services. **Móvil Tours** (☎42-2555; www.moviltours.com.pe; Confraternidad Internacional Oeste 451) is also comfortable and has a **ticket office** (Bolívar 452) in town.

Línea (☎42-6666; Bolívar 450) and Móvil Tours go direct to Chimbote, continuing to Trujillo. Spectacular though rough rides via the amazing Cañón del Pato (that will have you scavenging for Xanax) or 4225m-high Punta Callán to Chimbote are worth seeing with **Yungay Express** (☎42-4377; Raimondi 930).

Chavín Express (☎42-8069; Cáceres 330) goes to Chavín de Huántar, continuing to Huari.

Daytime minibuses for Caraz and Yungay depart frequently from near the Quilcay bridge on Fitzcarrald.

Sample travel times and costs from Huaraz are as follows (prices fluctuate with the quality of the bus/classes):

DESTINATION	COST (S)	DURATION (HR)
Caraz	6	1½
Chavín	12	2½
Chimbote	20-60	5-9
Huari	15	5
Lima	35-100	8
Trujillo	35-60	7
Yungay	5	1

Parque Nacional Huascarán

Encompassing almost the entire area of the Cordillera Blanca above 4000m, this 3400-sq-km **national park** (per day/week S5/65) is bursting with picturesque emerald lakes, brightly colored alpine wildflowers and red *quenua* trees.

The most popular backpacking circuit, the **Santa Cruz** trek, takes four days and rises to the Punta Unión pass (4760m), which arguably has the best Andean views in Peru. The trail, which passes by icy waterfalls and lakes, mossy meadows and verdant valleys, is well marked. *Colectivo* taxis frequently leave from Caraz for the main trailhead at Cashapampa (S10, 1½ hours).

Trails range from day hikes to ambitious two-week treks. The scenery is just as jaw-dropping, minus the crowds. Many routes aren't clearly marked, however, so go with a guide or take along top-notch topographic maps. If you are short on cash or time, the day-long trek to **Laguna 69** is stunning, dripping with marvelous mountain and waterfall views, and culminating in the blue lake that gives the trek its name – a perfect peek into the awesome scenery in this area.

In Huaraz, the **Mountain Institute** (☎42-3446; www.mountain.org; Ricardo Palma 100) works closely with sustainable-tourism initiatives along the Inca Naani trail between Huari and Huanuco. Check with local agencies for more information.

Register with your passport at the national park office (p884) in Huaraz and pay the park entrance fee. You can also register and pay at control stations, but operating hours vary. Don't dodge or begrudge paying the fee: the Cordillera Blanca is one of the most amazing places on the planet. Some trailhead communities, such as Cashapampa, charge a fee (around S10 per person).

Though arbitrarily enforced, law requires a licensed guide to accompany all trekkers, unless you are a card-carrying member of a UIAA-approved mountaineering club. This is especially enforced for mountaineering.

North of Huaraz

As the Río Santa slices its way north through El Callejón de Huaylas, a paved road passes several subdued towns to Caraz, and on to the menacingly impressive **Cañón del Pato**.

Huaraz & the Cordilleras

0 50 km
0 25 miles
Río Santa
Champará (5850m)
Punta Unión Pass (4760m)
Alpamayo (5947m)
Pomabamba
Piscobamba
Huallanca
Cañón del Pato
Colcabamba
Yanama
Vaquería
Cashapampa
Laguna Parón
Caraz
Lagunas Llanganuco
Huascarán (6768m)
San Luis
Río Marañón
Llamellín
104
Chacas
Yungay
3
Parque Nacional Huascarán
103
Cordillera Negra
Shilla
105
Monzón
Carhuaz
Marcará
Cordillera Blanca
Huari
Anta
Tantamayo
Casma
Monterrey
105
Sechín
Huaraz
106
San Marcos
Chavín de Huántar
Chavín
Olleros
Recuay
Lago Querococha
Catac
La Unión
Nevado Pastoruri (5240m)
Huallanca
3
Huarmey
Chiquián
Lago Conococha
Cordillera Huayhuash
Yerupajá (6634m)
1
109
PACIFIC OCEAN
102
Cajatambo

Many hiking trailheads are accessible from towns along this route, and two unsealed roads valiantly cross the Cordillera, one via Chacas and another via Yungay.

LAGUNAS LLANGANUCO

A dirt road climbs through the valley to two stunning **lakes**, **Laguna Chinancocha** and **Laguna Orconcocha**, 28km east of Yungay. Nestled in a glacial valley below the snow line, the pristine lagoons glow with bright turquoise and emerald hues. A 1½-hour nature trail hugs Chinacocha, passing rare *polylepis* trees. National-park entry costs S5. *Colectivos* leave from Yungay (round-trip S20) in high season (June to August). Trips during other months depend on demand. You can also take a tour from Huaraz.

CARAZ

043 / POP 12,000

A more traditional backdrop for your Cordillera base camp than Huaraz, the little colonial village of Caraz sees trekking and hiking trails meander in all directions from its location 67km north of Huaraz. There is far less to do in town here, but far more Andean color as well. You'll likely end up here if you tackle the Santa Cruz trek, as this is its traditional end point.

Bring cash with you, as there are no ATMs. **Pony Expeditions** (39-1642; www.ponyexpeditions.com; José Sucre 1266) rents all manner of gear, mountain bikes and arranges trekking, fishing and climbing excursions. It also sells ready-made meals (even veggie) for the mountains. The popular **Los Pinos Lodge** (39-1130; www.lospinoslodge.com; Parque San Martín 103; dm S30, s/d without bath S35/60, s/d S120/140, all incl breakfast; @) has outstanding rooms for all budgets, plus information and a restaurant. Budget favorite **Hostal La Casona** (39-1334; Raymondi 319; r per person S15, without bathroom S10; @) has dark rooms at a nice price.

Start with good coffee and pancakes at **Café La Terraza** (José Sucre 1107; mains S12-20; ⌚closed Mon), also serving pizzas and pastas. **Café de Rat** (meals S4-10) is an atmospheric, wood-beamed restaurant doing salads (rare), pizza and other staples, as well as box lunches in high season.

Minibuses to Yungay (S2, 15 minutes) and Huaraz (S6, 1½ hours) leave from the Terminal Terrestre on the Carr Central. *Colectivos* for Cashapampa (S8, 1½ hours) leave from Ramón Castilla at Santa Cruz. Long-distance buses to Lima (S30 to S75, eight hours) go with **Móvil Tours** (☎39-1184; Pasaje Santa Teresita 334) and other companies.

CHAVÍN DE HUÁNTAR

☎043 / POP 2900

Located near this small village are the ruins of **Chavín** (adult/student S11/6; ⌚9am-5pm Tue-Sun), built between 1200 and 800 BC by one of the continent's oldest civilizations. The site contains highly stylized cultist carvings of a jaguar or puma, Chavín's principal deity, and of condors, snakes and humans undergoing mystical (often hallucinogenic) transformations. The site's snaking underground tunnels are an exceptional feat of 3000-year-old engineering, comprising a maze of alleys, ducts and chambers – it's worth hiring a guide. Look out for the exquisitely carved, dagger-like rock known as the Lanzón de Chavín.

Don't miss the small but excellent **Museo Nacional Chavín** (☎45-4011; 17 de Enero s/n; ⌚9am-5pm Tue-Sun), funded by the Japanese and inaugurated in 2008, which houses many of the site's important artifacts, including 19 *pututos* (shell trumpets) and 16 of the stone heads that once graced the outer walls of the complex. Here you will also find the original **Tello Obelisk**, one of the most important pieces of Chavín art ever discovered in the Andes.

There are a few decent hotels and restaurants in town, though most folks opt for a long day trip from Huaraz.

Transportes Sandoval buses go to Huaraz (S12, two hours).

Cordillera Huayhuash

Often playing second fiddle to the Cordillera Blanca, the Huayhuash nevertheless has an equally impressive medley of glaciers, summits and lakes all packed into an area only 30km across. Increasing numbers of travelers are discovering this rugged and remote territory, where strenuously high passes over 4500m throw down the gauntlet to the hardiest of trekkers. The feeling of utter wilderness, particularly along the unspoiled eastern edge, is a big draw. You are more likely to spot an Andean condor here than another tour group.

Several communities along the classic 10-day trekking circuit charge fees of S15 to S40 (at the time of research, the entire trek fees totaled S165). These fees go toward improving security for hikers and continuing conservation work. Support local preservation efforts by paying your fees, carrying plenty of small bills and always asking for official receipts. Always check that the dates of your camping permits are correct.

At the trailhead, Llamac has basic *hospedajes* and campsites. **Turismo Nazario** (☎82-4431; Grau s/n) departs Huaraz for Llamac (S25, 4½ hours) via Chiquián (S15, two hours) at 5am daily, returning from Llamac at 11:30am.

NORTHERN HIGHLANDS

Vast tracts of unexplored jungle and mountain ranges shrouded in mist guard the secrets of Peru's northern highlands, where Andean peaks and cloud forests stretch all the way from the coast to the deepest Amazon jungle. These outposts are interspersed with the relics of ancient warriors and Inca kings, their connections by better routes just emerging.

Cajamarca

☎076 / POP 162,000

The cobblestone colonial streets of Cajamarca mark the last stand for the powerful Inca empire – Atahualpa, the last Inca, was defeated here by Francisco Pizarro and later executed in the main square. Only the striking baroque, Gothic and Renaissance architecture of numerous churches remains, with the lone exception of Cuarto del Rescate, where Atahualpa was held prisoner – the last Inca ruin in the city. Now fertile farmland carpets the valley, which turns even lusher during the rainy season.

Sights & Activities

The following central sights are officially open from 9am to 1pm and 3pm to 6pm Tuesday to Saturday and from 3pm to 6pm Sunday. They don't have addresses. For admission, you must buy an all-encompassing ticket from the **Instituto Nacional de Cultura** (El Complejo de Belén; admission S4.50; ⏱9am-1pm & 3-6pm Tue-Sun).

El Cuarto del Rescate RUIN
(adult/student S5/2; ⏱9am-1pm & 3-6pm Tue-Sat, 9am-1pm Sun) The only remaining Inca building here is El Cuarto del Rescate (Ransom Chamber). Despite the name, this is actually where Francisco Pizarro kept Inca Atahualpa prisoner before killing him off, not where the ransom was stored. Tickets include same-day admission to **El Complejo de Belén**, a sprawling 17th-century colonial complex with a small archaeology museum, and the **Museo de Etnografía**, which has exhibits on traditional highland life.

Museo deArqueológico & Etnografía MUSEUM
(⏱9am-1pm & 3-6pm Tue-Sat, 9am-1pm Sun) Displays artifacts from pre-Inca Cajamarca culture.

Iglesia de San Francisco CHURCH, MUSEUM
(admission S3; ⏱9am-noon & 4-6pm Mon-Fri) Facing the Plaza de Armas, Iglesia de San Francisco has catacombs and a religious-art museum.

Cerro Santa Apolonia LOOKOUT
(admission S1; ⏱7am-6pm) These hilltop gardens with pre-Columbian carvings have impressive city views. Huff and puff your way up the 100m of stairs at the end of 2 de Mayo.

Cumbe Mayo RUIN
An astounding yet mysterious feat of pre-Inca engineering, the aqueducts at Cumbe Mayo, 19km outside Cajamarca, run for several kilometers across the bleak mountaintops. The site can be reached on foot from Cerro Santa Apolonia via a signposted road. It's about a four-hour walk, if you take shortcuts and ask locals for directions. Tours from Cajamarca cost S25.

Also nearby are the pre-Inca necropolises known as **Ventanillas de Otuzco**, built into a hillside 8km from Cajamarca. You can walk to Otuzco from Cajamarca or Los Baños del Inca or take a combo tour with the *baños* (S25). Buses from Cajamarca leave from north of the main plaza (S1, 20 minutes). Better-preserved *ventanillas* (windows) at Combayo, 30km from Cajamarca, are most easily visited on a tour.

Los Baños del Inca HOT SPRINGS
(admission S3, private baths per hr S4-6, sauna or massage S10-20; ⏱5am-8pm) Atahualpa was camped by Los Baños del Inca, the impressive hot springs 6km east of Cajamarca, before his fateful run-in with Pizarro. Show up before 7am to avoid the rush, especially on weekends. *Colectivos* for Los Baños del Inca leave frequently from along Sabogal, near 2 de Mayo (S1, 20 minutes). Bring your own towel or buy one from vendors. You can also sleep here.

Tours

Travel agents include **Mega Tours** (☎34-1876; www.megatours.org; Puga 691) and **Clarín Tours** (☎36-6829; www.clarintours.com; Del Batán 161).

Festivals & Events

Carnaval FESTIVAL
The Cajamarca version of the Carnaval involves nine days of dancing, eating, singing, partying, costumes, parades and rowdy mayhem. Water fights can get pretty wild. Hotels raise their rates and fill up weeks beforehand, so hundreds of visitors end up sleeping in the plaza. It's held in February or March, depending on the year.

Sleeping

TOP CHOICE **Hotel Los Jazmines** HISTORIC HOTEL **$**
(☎36-1812; www.hospedajelosjazmines.com.pe; Amazonas 775; s/d S50/80, without bathroom S40/60; @ 📶) In a land of ubiquitous colonial courtyards, this German-run inn is a value standout for its lush version with even more extensive back gardens and a public espresso bar. Comfy rooms offer hot water and cable TV, some with exposed brick walls.

Hostal Plaza HISTORIC HOTEL **$**
(☎36-2058; Puga 669; s/d/tr without bathroom S15/30/40, with bathroom S30/50/70; 📶) This top budget choice is a rambling colonial mansion with courtyards. The 10 good-value private rooms are colorfully decorated with kitschy objects and the occasional stuffed animal, have cable TV and offer 24-hour hot water, whereas the flow is only steamy in the communal bathrooms in the mornings and evenings.

Casa Mirita HOMESTAY **$**
(☎36-9361; www.casa-mirita.blogspot.com; Cáceres 1337; s without bathroom S15, r S25; @) To get

to this simple homestay, take a S2 *mototaxi* ride to a residential neighborhood southeast of the town center. It's an interesting choice for long-stayers or those looking to be completely off the gringo grid. Two sisters run the show. Rooms are rustic and there's a kitchen for guests' use, or you can get meals for S5.

Hostal Jusovi HOTEL $
(☎36-2920; hostaljosuvicajamarca@hotmail.com; Amazonas 637; s/d/tr S40/50/60; 📶) A clean, decent budget option with a rooftop terrace. Wi-fi in lobby only.

Eating

There are a lot of cows around Cajamarca – what to do with the brains? Eat them! The local specialty is known as *sesos*. Sweet tooths will not suffer – regal bakeries abound all over Centro.

TOP CHOICE **Magredana** FUSION $$
(Sara Macdougal 140-144; mains S29-40; ⏰closed Mon & dinner Sun) The most creative menu in the Peruvian Andes comes courtesy of an Irish chef who has cooked in 11 countries, not to mention toured the world with Van Morrison for nearly a decade. The menu reflects this itinerary, with influences from India, Spain, Thailand and his native Ireland creeping into the eclectic range of sophisticated choices. The house chicken – stuffed with pork, pistachios and herbs, rolled in bacon and finished with a red wine and tarragon sauce – is a doozy. The ambience is a bit haphazard, but the food immediately erases those quirks on arrival. Shaun, the chef, has a three-year plan, so get there before 2014.

Heladería Holanda DESSERTS $
(www.heladosholanda.com.pe; Puga 657; ice creams S2-4) Northern Peru's best ice cream with a

Cajamarca

Top Sights
- El Cuarto del Rescate C3
- Iglesia de San Francisco C3

Sights
- 1 Museo de Arqueológico & Etnografía .. B4

Activities, Courses & Tours
- 2 Clarín Tours B2
- 3 Mega Tours C2

Sleeping
- 4 Hostal Jusovi C2
- 5 Hostal Plaza C2
- 6 Hotel Los Jazmines C2

Eating
- 7 El Marengo B3
- 8 Heladería Holanda B2
- 9 Sanguchon.com B3

Drinking
- 10 Gruta 100 .... C4

Information
- Dirección de Turismo .... (see 11)
- 11 Instituto Nacional de Cultura C3

Transport
- 12 LAN B3

fair-trade philosophy, and they're not stingy with samples. Try regional fruit flavors like *capuli, sauco* or *poro poro*.

Sanguchon.com FAST FOOD, BAR **$**
(www.sanguchon.com.pe; Junín 1137; sandwiches from S5.90-13.50; 6pm-midnight;) A popular hipster hamburger and sandwich joint and a rowdy bar as well.

El Marengo PIZZERIA **$**
(Junín 1201; pizzas S11.50-25.50; 7-11pm) The wood-fired brick oven heats the entirety of this tiny pizzeria and the best pie in town comes out. Squeeze in, get a pitcher of sangria and call it a night.

Drinking & Entertainment

The best bars congregate around the corner of Puga and Gálvez.

TOP CHOICE **Usha-Usha** DIVE BAR
(Puga 142; admission S5; closed Sun & Mon) A graffiti-decked hole-in-the-wall, where owner Jaime Valera sings his heart out with musician friends, gifting patrons with an unforgettable travel memory.

Gruta 100 BAR
(cnr Santisteban & Belén; 8pm-late Thu-Sat) This is a sophisticated drinking den with an attached DIY fire pit and backyard amphitheater.

Information

Scotiabank (Amazonas 750) Changes traveler's checks and has an ATM accepting Visa and MasterCard.

Clínica Limatambo (36-4241; Puno 265)

Dirección de Turismo (36-2997; El Complejo de Belén; 7:30am-1pm & 2:30-5pm Mon-Fri) Also operates a small info booth (8:30am-12:30pm & 3:30-5:30pm Mon-Fri) next to Iglesia de San Francisco.

Policía de Turismo (Tourist Police; Jirón del Comercio 1013, Poltur; 7:45am-1pm & 5-8pm)

Getting There & Away

Air

The airport is 4km north of town. Local buses for Otuzco, leaving from several blocks north of the plaza, pass the airport (S1); taxis are faster (S8), rickshaw-like *mototaxis* are cheaper (S3). **LAN** (36-7441; www.lan.com; Jirón del Comercio 832) and **LC Perú** (36-3115; www.lcperu.pe; Jirón del Comercio 1024) serve Lima daily.

Bus

Most terminals are between the 2nd and 3rd blocks of Atahualpa, 1.5km southeast of town on the road to Los Baños del Inca.

Many companies have buses to Chiclayo (S20 to S45, six hours), Trujillo (S20 to S40, six hours) and Lima (S80 to S130, 16 hours). **Línea** (36-6100; Atahualpa 316) and **Tepsa** (36-3306; Sucre 442) have comfortable Lima-bound buses. Luxury *bus-camas* to Lima go with **Cruz del Sur** (36-2024; Atahualpa 884).

Línea also has buses to Piura (S45, nine hours) via Chiclayo, where you can continue on to Ecuador.

A few companies go to Celendín (S10, 3½ hours). It's easier to reach Chachapoyas from Chiclayo.

Chachapoyas

041 / POP 23,000

Colonial Chachapoyas seems wildly out of place, both as the unlikely capital of the Amazonas department, and in its location: surrounded by more mountainous terrain than jungle. But 'Chacas' is a bustling market town and an ideal place from which to explore Kuélap – the awesome ruins left behind by the fierce cloud forest–dwelling civilization that ruled here from AD 800 until the Incas came in the 1470s – and the surrounding waterfalls and trekking routes.

Activities

The dry season (May to September) is best for hiking, including the five-day **Gran Vilaya** trek to the Valle de Belén or a three-day trip to **Laguna de los Cóndores** on foot and horseback.

Tours

Day tours from Chacas focus on Kuélap. Travel agencies hover around the plaza.

Chachapoyas Tours GUIDED TOUR
(94-196-3327; www.kuelapperu.com; Santo Domingo 432) With rave reviews for day tours; also organizes multiday treks and has some English-speaking guides.

Sleeping

TOP CHOICE **Hostal Las Orquídeas** GUESTHOUSE $$
(47-8271; www.hostallasorquideas.com; Ayacucho 1231; s/d incl breakfast S60/100; @) Long on friendliness and value, this upscale guesthouse has bright rooms with designer granite-slab bathrooms. The staff will help you book travel and arrange excursions, and prices include transfer from the bus station.

Hotel Revash GUESTHOUSE $$
(47-7391; www.chachapoyaskuelap.com.pe; Grau 517; s S35-60, d S70-150; @) The courtyard in this classic mansion is a little more overgrown than endearing, but sleeping here still offers exceptional value and scorching showers. Rooms are colorful and old-fashioned in a sweet way.

Hostal Belén GUESTHOUSE $
(47-7830; www.hostalbelen.com; Ortiz Arrieta 540; s/d S45/55; @) Also on the plaza in a well-maintained building, with small but tidy rooms, each with one brightly painted wall to cheer up the relative darkness.

Hostal Johumaji GUESTHOUSE $
(47-7819; hostaljohumajieirl@hotmail.com; Ayacucho 711; s/d/tr from S20/30/45; @) The better of the town's super-cheap hotels, with small, spartan rooms prone to street noise. Regardless, it's a tidy, friendly choice. Tack on S5 for cable TV.

Eating & Drinking

Look for *juanes* (*bijao* leaf-steamed fish, beef or chicken with olives), made locally with *yuca* instead of rice.

TOP CHOICE **El Tejado** PERUVIAN $$
(Santo Domingo 426; mains S15-25) With a charming courtyard, this great lunch spot has a S7 weekday *menú*. Its specialty is *tacu-tacu*, served here in nine varieties. *Lomo saltado* is conversation-stopping good, especially doused in the house chili sauce.

Café Fusiones CAFE, BREAKFAST $$
(Chincha Alta 445; breakfast S6-9, mains S20-60; from 7am, closed Sun;) The traveler congregation gathers at this artsy cafe serving organic coffee and espresso, great breakfast (including regional choices like *juanes*), muffins doused in *manjar blanco* (milk caramel), lentil burgers and the like.

Terra Mia Café BREAKFAST, PERUVIAN $
(www.terramiacafe.com; Chincha Alta 557; breakfast S8-13.50; from 7am;) This sophisticated cafe boasts a wonderful menu of both regional and international breakfasts (ahem… waffles!), espresso and great sandwiches on perfectly soft-crunchy French bread.

Dulcería Santa Elena DESSERTS $
(Amazonas 800-804; desserts S1-5) The crotchety old man here serves the town's best pastries and cakes; if he likes you, though, he might throw something in for free.

La Reina BAR
(Ayacucho 520) An artsy spot to get drunk very cheaply on exotic fruit and Amazonian liquors. Try the *maracuyá*.

Information

Most of the following are on the Plaza de Armas, plus internet cafes and several shops changing dollars.

BCP (Plaza de Armas) Changes US dollars and traveler's checks, and has a Visa/MasterCard ATM.

Serpost (Ortiz Arrieta 632) Postal services; just south of the plaza.

iPerú (47-7292; Arrieta 582; 8am-7pm) Excellent maps, transportation information and recommendations.

Getting There & Away

Buses to Chiclayo (S30 to S55, nine hours) and on to Lima (S80 to S135, 22 hours) take a route that is paved beyond Pedro Ruíz. Companies include **Civa** (47-8048; Salamanca 956) and comfortable **Móvil Tours** (47-8545; Libertad 464).

Getting directly to Kuélap independently is a bit of a pain and requires an early rise. **Transportes Roller** (94-174-6658; Grau 300) has one 4am bus that goes to Tingo Viejo, María and on to La Marca, where you'll find the ticket booth and parking lot for Kuélep, returning at 6am. It's a 15-minute walk along a stone sidewalk to the ruins from there. Otherwise, frequent minibuses and *colectivos* for Tingo Viejo and María depart from the 300 block of Grau, from where you'll need to leg an additional two hours (from María) or five to six hours (from Tingo Viejo).

There are frequent *colectivos* for Tingo Viejo (S8, 45 minutes), which may continue to María (S15, 2½ hours). *Colectivos* also go to Pedro Ruíz (S5, 45 minutes), where eastbound buses to Tarapoto stop.

A taxi for the day to Kuélap or to sites around Chachapoyas and Leimebamba costs S150.

Kuélap

Matched in grandeur only by the more famous ruins of Machu Picchu, the fabulous ruins of this pre-Inca **citadel** (adult/student/child S15/8/2; 8am-5pm), constructed between AD 900 and 1100, are perched in the mountains southeast of Chachapoyas. The site (elevation 3000m) receives remarkably few visitors, though those who make it get to see one of the most significant and impressive pre-Columbian ruins in South America.

Though most travelers visit Kuélap on a day tour from Chachapoyas, below the ruins **Hospedaje El Bebedero** (98-978-3432; r per person S15) and **Hospedaje El Imperio** (94-173-5833; r per person S10-15) have bare-bones rooms without electricity; Imperio has running water – bring a sleeping bag and water-purification equipment. *Hospedajes* also abound in **María**, the nearest hamlet to the ruins. **Hospedaje el Torreón** (94-170-8040; Av Kuélep s/n; s/d S20/30) is your best bet.

Tarapoto

042 / POP 117,000

A muggy and lethargic rainforest metropolis, Tarapoto balances precariously between the tropical Amazon Basin and weathered Andean foothills. If it weren't for the lengthy umbilical cord that is the long, paved road back to the rest of Peru, it would sit as isolated – and nearly as manic – as Iquitos. From here you can take the plunge deeper into the Amazon, or just enjoy the easily accessible jungle lite.

Tours

Martín Zamora Tours GUIDED TOURS
(52-5148; www.martinzamoratarapoto.com; Grau 233) Tarapoto's go-to operator for day tours and longer excursions to local lakes and waterfalls and cultural trips.

Sleeping

La Patarashca GUESTHOUSE **$$**
(52-7554, 52-3899; www.lapatarashca.com; Lamas 261; incl breakfast with/without air-con s S70/50, d S135/90, tr without air-con S120;) Tucked away on sprawling grounds flush with jungly fauna, the varied rooms are homey, all have hot-water electric showers, and cable TVs. A few ornery macaws drive home a sense of place, as does the best regional restaurant in town, attached by a small walkway.

El Mirador GUESTHOUSE **$**
(52-2177; www.elmiradorentarapoto.blogspot.com; San Pablo de la Cruz 517; s/d/tr incl breakfast S60/85/95;) A friendly choice, replete with grandmotherly love and excellent breakfasts on the terrace with jungle views. With fans, hot showers and cable TV; a new annex is in the works. Rates include airport transfers.

La Posada Inn GUESTHOUSE **$$**
(52-2234; laposada_inn@latinmail.com; San Martín 146; s/d incl breakfast S55/110, with air-con S70/120;) With beamed ceilings and an inviting wooden staircase, rooms are an eclectic mix. Though right in the center, the inn manages to remain quiet.

Eating & Drinking

TOP CHOICE La Patarashca PERUVIAN $$
(www.lapatarashca.com; San Pablo de la Cruz 362; mains S13-32;) Outstanding regional Amazon cuisine includes a salad made of *chonta*, a local heart of palm, and avocados doused in vinaigrette; or the namesake *patarashcas* – heaped platters of giant shrimp or fish served soaking in a warm bath of tomatoes, sweet peppers, onions, garlic and *sacha culantro* (a type of cilantro) wrapped in a *bijao* leaf. Avoid wild *paiche* from October to February; fishing of it is prohibited due to its commercial near-extinction.

Tío Sergio Fast Food Amazonico PERUVIAN $
(San Pablo de la Cruz 244; mains S7-20; 24hr;) Trendy but tasty burgers, house-made pastas and sandwiches (there's even a kids menu). The pleasant back patio never closes.

Café d' Mundo ITALIAN $$
(Calle de Morey 157; mains S8-32, pizzas S15-32; 6pm-midnight) This hip restaurant and bar has outdoor seating and snug indoor lounges. Good pizzas are the mainstay (try the caprese with avocado), but some interesting regional lasagnas and other pastas adorn the small menu.

TOP CHOICE La Alternativa BAR
(Grau 401; 9am-8pm) Like drinking in a medieval pharmacy or maybe a Tarantino film, a night out here harkens to a time when alcohol was literally medicine.

Stonewasi Taberna BAR
(Lamas 218; cocktails S6-18) Still the northern highlands' best bar, with recycled sewing tables street side, and a theme of international rock and house music.

Information

Internet cafes are everywhere.

BCP (Maynas 130) Cashes traveler's checks and has an ATM.

Clínica San Martín (San Martín 274; 24hr)

Tourist Information Office (52-6188; Hurtado s/n; 8:30am-8pm Mon-Sat, 9am-1pm Sun) Tourist info on the northwest side of the plaza.

Getting There & Around

The **airport** (TPP; 53-1165) is 3km southwest of the center. **LAN** (52-9318; Hurtado 183) has daily flights to/from Lima. **Star Perú** (52-8765; San Pablo de la Cruz 100) flies daily to Lima and Iquitos on Monday, Wednesday, Friday and Sunday.

All these companies can be found along the same block of Salaverry in the Morales district, a S2 *mototaxi* ride from the town center. If you're heading to Chachapoyas, you'll need to change in Pedro Ruíz.

A short *mototaxi* ride around town costs S2, to the bus terminal/airport S3/5.

DESTINATION	COST (S)	DURATION (HR)
Chiclayo	40-80	14
Lima	100-165	26-30
Pedro Ruíz	40-45	7
Piura	60	16-17
Pucallpa	100	16-18
Tingo María	80	13
Trujillo	65-150	15-18
Yurimaguas	15-20	2½

Civa (52-2269; www.civa.com.pe; Salaverry 840) Has a comfortable 2:45pm bus to Lima stopping at Chiclayo and Trujillo.

Móvil Tours (52-9193; www.moviltours.com.pe; Salaverry 880) Top-end express buses to Lima, Trujillo and Chiclayo.

Transmar Express (53-2392; Moraca 117) Departs to Pucallpa via Tingo María.

Transportes Gilmer (53-0749; Ugarte 1346) Plies the newly paved road to Yurimaguas every two hours from 5am to 7pm.

TSP (97-963-9716; Aviación 100) Has a direct Piura bus at noon.

AMAZON BASIN

Thick with primary and secondary jungle, Peru's Amazon Basin is dense and dizzying, an exotic and isolated frontier zone that spills out from all sides with exhilarating jungle-adventure opportunities. Iquitos, the area's largest city, is the gateway to once-in-a-lifetime excursions down the Amazon River but also holds interest for its solitary, end-of-the-road atmosphere (even though the road ended in Yurimaguas). Pucallpa and Yurimaguas offer slow boats that ply the waterways to Iquitos, accessible otherwise only by air. The country's largest reserve, the bigger-than-New-Jersey Reserva Nacional Pacaya-Samiria, is also here, home to pink dolphins and 449 bird species.

Further south, the Unesco-declared Parque Nacional Manu is considered one of the world's most pristinely preserved thatches of Tarzan terrain and one of South

America's best spots to see tropical wildlife. Around Puerto Maldonado, jungle lodges beckon along the Madre de Dios and Tambopata rivers (the latter is in the Reserva Nacional Tambopata) – two more of Peru's most unspoiled settings for wildlife and jungle adventure.

Puerto Maldonado

082 / POP 56,500

Diesel-fumed Puerto Maldonado, capital of the Madre de Dios region, is the ramshackle epicenter of Peru's southern Amazon. Were it not the gateway to one of South America's finest jungles, it might be forgotten (save a few great bars). The completion of the controversial Interoceánica Hwy, which now links the Atlantic and Pacific, reroutes massive commerce through here (and foretells the expedited extraction of natural resources). For most travelers, the city is a launching pad to a wild and exotic Amazon adventure.

Tours

If you haven't prearranged a river and jungle tour, there are several local guides, some quite reputable and experienced, others just interested in making quick money. Shop around, never pay for a tour beforehand and, when you agree on a price, make sure it includes the return trip! Officially licensed guides charge around S75 to S175 per person per day (excluding park fees), depending on the destination and number of people. Boat rides, which are usually needed to get out of Puerto Maldonado, are notoriously expensive.

Rainforest Expeditions TOURS
(57-2575; www.perunature.com; Av Aeropuerto, Km 6, CPM La Joya) Coordinates various area lodges and has reputable rainforest tours and budget-oriented Tambopata homestays (from US$24).

Sleeping

Watch out for overcharging. Outside town are some jungle lodges.

TOP CHOICE **Tambopata Hostel** HOSTEL $
(57-4201; www.tambopatahostel.com; 26 de Diciembre 234; dm S25, s/d S50/80, without bathroom S40/70;) A winner, this clean, relaxing hostel has a mix of dorm and private rooms abutting a garden courtyard with hammocks, and a huge breakfast is included in the price. There are secure lockers and the owner is one of the town's best jungle guides.

Anaconda Lodge LODGE $$
(79-2726; www.anacondajunglelodge.com; Av Aeropuerto, Km 6; bungalow s/d/tr S100/160/220, without bathroom s/d S50/80;) The pleasure

JUNGLE LODGES

There are dozens of jungle lodges along the Ríos Tambopata and Madre de Dios from Puerto Maldonado. Lodges and jungle tours are expensive but often offer life-changing experiences.

Down the Madre de Dios, **Hacienda Concepción** (in Cuzco 084-57-2823, in Lima 01-610-0400; www.inkaterra.com; 3 days & 2 nights s/d US$357/616, cabins s/d US$434/704;) offers some pretty astounding luxury accommodations on a private reserve on 12,000 hectares with a learning center and one of South America's largest canopy walks.

On Lago Sandoval, a haven for exotic wildlife, family-run **Señora Leny Mejía Lodge** (982-684-700; lenitokon@hotmail.com; r per person around US$25) has been offering basic backpacker accommodations and Spanish-language expeditions for nearly two decades.

Along the Río Tambopata, **Tambopata Research Center** (082-57-2575; www.perunature.com; 5 days & 4 nights s/d US$1015/1590) offers the opportunity to see scores of parrots and macaws. It's a seven-hour trip from Puerto Maldonado.

You will see the same species, but fewer birds, at **Posada Amazonas** (01-421-8347; www.perunature.com; 3 days & 2 nights s/d US$485/750), two hours from Puerto Maldonado along Río Tambopata.

To visit **Reserva Nacional Tambopata** (admission up to 4 nights S100), purchase an entrance permit at the **park office** (57-3278; Av 28 de Julio, block 8; 8am-1pm & 3-5pm Mon-Fri, 9am-noon Sat) before leaving Puerto Maldonado.

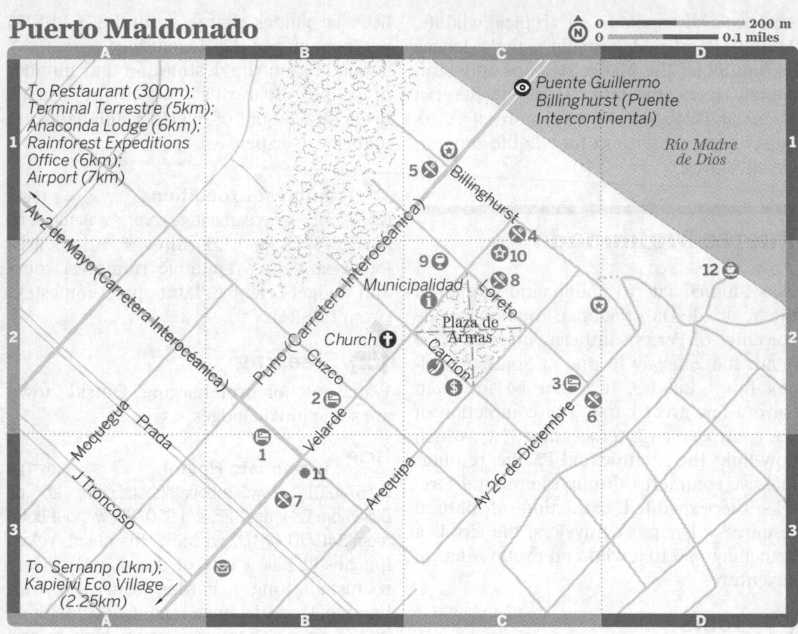

Puerto Maldonado

Sleeping
1 Hospedaje Royal Inn....B3
2 Señora Leny Mejia Lodge....B2
3 Tambopata Hostel....C2

Eating
4 Burgo's House....C1
5 Burgo's House....C1
6 El Catamaran....C2
7 La Casa Nostra....B3
8 Los Gustitos del Cura....C2

Drinking
9 Tsaica....C2

Entertainment
10 Discoteca Witite....C2

Transport
11 LAN....B3
12 Madre de Dios Ferry Crossing Dock....D2
Puerto Capitania (Madre de Dios Dock)....(see 12)
River-Boat Hire....(see 12)

of bunking at this Swiss- and Thai-run lodge (set amid a botanical garden next to the airport rather than in town) is immeasurable. Simple but well-done bungalows with mosquito nets, a crystal-clear pool and – drum roll, please – wonderful Thai food means there's no reason to leave before braving the jungle.

Kapieivi Eco Village LODGE **$$**
(☎79-5650; katherinapz@hotmail.com; Carr Tambopata, Km 1.5; 1-/2-person bungalows incl breakfast S100/125; 🏊) This rustic, reader-recommended retreat, 2km southwest of town, lets backpackers experience a taste of lodge life without the price tag, in several bungalows enclosed within a wild plot of jungle scrub. The laid-back owners offer vegetarian food, *ayahuasca* ceremonies and yoga classes. Food and drink is an additional S18 per person per day.

Hospedaje Royal Inn GUESTHOUSE **$**
(☎57-3464; 2 de Mayo 333; s/d S35/50; 📶) A good choice for travelers, sporting lots of large, clean rooms with fans and cable TV. Get a courtyard-facing room as street-facing rooms are noisy.

Eating

Regional specialties include *chilcano* (fish-chunk soup flavored with cilantro) and *parrillada de la selva* (marinated-meat BBQ in an *ají* (chili) and Brazil-nut sauce).

Restaurant PERUVIAN **$**
(cnr Av 2 de Mayo & Madre de Dios; mains S10-15; ⊙dinner) It may have no name, street number or phone number, but this place is far from unknown by the locals, who flock here for great fish with rice and *plátano*. Food is prepared on a grill outside and tables fill up fast.

La Casa Nostra CAFE **$**
(Av 2 de Mayo 287A; snacks S3-8; ⊙8am-1pm & 5-11pm) Though a tad complacent, La Casa offers worthwhile varied breakfasts, tamales, great juices, snacks and Puerto Maldonado's best coffee.

Los Gustitos del Cura DESSERTS **$**
(Loreto 258; snacks S3-8; ⊙11am-10pm) For a sweet treat or the best ice cream in town, drop in to this patisserie.

Burgo's House PERUVIAN **$$**
(Velarde 127; mains S15-23; ⊙11am-midnight; 🖉) A standout cooking Peruvian Amazon staples in innovative ways. Ample vegetarian options are offered alongside the seafood specialties. There's another **branch** (☎57-3653; Puno 106; mains S13-22; ⊙11am-midnight) one block east.

El Catamaran CEVICHE **$$**
(Jirón 26 de Diciembre 241; mains S18-30; ⊙7:30am-3pm) The place to feast on great freshwater *ceviche*, according to local dignitaries. There's deck service with river views.

Drinking & Entertainment

The best-known nightclub is **Discoteca Witite** (Velarde 151; ⊙Fri & Sat). **Tsaica** (Loreto 329) is a lively watering hole.

Information

BCP (Plaza de Armas) ATM.

Locutorio (Carrión cuadra 2; per hr S2) Internet cafe on the Plaza.

Dircetur airport (⊙10am-1pm Mon-Fri); city center (☎57-1164; San Martín s/n; ⊙7am-1pm & 2-4pm) Municipal tourist info.

Hospital Santa Rosa (☎57-1046, 57-1019; Cajamarca 171)

Serpost (Velarde 675) Postal services.

Sernanp (☎57-3278; www.sernanp.gob.pe/sernanp; Av 28 de Julio 875) The national park office gives information and collects entrance fees (in nearly all cases, guides sort this out); standard entrance to the Tambopata reserve zone is S30 but increases to S65 if you want to visit areas further away from the riverside lodges.

Tourist Booth (airport) Run by the Ministerio de Industria y Turismo; provides limited information on tours and jungle lodges.

Getting There & Around

Air

The **airport** (PEM) is 7km west of town; *mototaxis* cost S10. **Star Perú** (☎57-3564; Velarde 151) and **LAN** (☎57-3677; Velarde 503) have daily flights to Lima via Cuzco.

Boat

Boat hire at the Madre de Dios ferry dock for excursions or to travel down to the Bolivian border is expensive. Upriver boats toward Manu are difficult to find.

Bus

From the new **Terminal Terrestre** (cnr Avs Elmer Faucett & Aeropuerto) buses ply the new (and paved) Transoceanic Hwy (La Interocéanica) southwest to Cuzco and northeast to Río Branco, Brazil. Numerous companies leave either during the morning or in the evening (around 8pm) to Cuzco (S50, 10 hours). Options to Río Branco are more scant but include **Móvil Tours** (☎989-176-309; S100) departing Tuesday and Friday at 12:30pm. It's advisable to buy your ticket as much in advance of travel as possible.

Parque Nacional Manu

Covering almost 20,000 sq km, **Parque Nacional Manu** (entry S150) is widely regarded as the most pristine and best-preserved thatch of jungle in the world. This Unesco Natural Heritage Site is one of the best spots in South America to see tropical wildlife. Starting in the eastern slopes of the Andes, the park plunges down into the lowlands, covering a wide range of cloud-forest and rainforest habitats containing 1000 bird species, not to mention 13 species of primate, armadillos, kinkajous, ocelots, river turtles and caiman, and countless insects, reptiles and amphibians. More elusive species include jaguars, tapirs, giant anteaters, tamanduas, capybaras, peccaries, the near-extinct giant river otter, and, perhaps most amazingly, uncontacted communities of hunter-gatherer peoples!

GETTING TO BRAZIL & BOLIVIA

The paved Interoceánica goes from Puerto Maldonado to Iñapari on the Brazilian border. *Colectivos* to Iñapari (S30, three hours) leave with **Mi Nuevo Peru** (☎57-4325; cnr Piura & Ica) when they have four passengers. Iberia, 170km north of Puerto Maldonado, and Iñapari, 70km beyond Iberia, have a couple of basic hotels. At Iñapari, where Peruvian exit formalities are conducted, cross the bridge to Assis, Brazil, which has better hotels and a paved road via Brasiléia to Río Branco. US, Australian and Canadian citizens need to get a Brazilian visa in advance.

From Puerto Maldonado, boats can be hired for the half-day trip to the Bolivian border at Puerto Pardo for about US$100. Cheaper passages are available on infrequent cargo boats. Make sure to get exit stamps before leaving Peru at Puerto Maldonado's **immigration office** (☎57-1069; 28 de Julio 467; ⏲8am-1pm & 2:30-4pm Mon-Fri). From Puerto Heath, a few minutes away from Puerto Pardo by boat, it takes several days (even weeks) to arrange a boat (expensive) to Riberalta, which has road and air connections. Travel in a group to share costs, and avoid months when the water is too low. Another option is to go to Brasiléia, cross the Río Acre by ferry or bridge to Cobija, on the Bolivian side, where there are hotels and erratic flights. There's also a dry-season gravel road onward to Riberalta.

The best time to visit the park is after the rainy season (April to November). Manu is harder to access during the rainiest months (January to April), though most of the authorized companies still run (wet) tours.

It's illegal to enter the park without a licensed guide and a permit, which can be arranged at Cuzco travel agencies. Transportation, accommodations and meals are also part of the tour package. Beware: not all companies enter the park itself – there are only eight agencies authorized to do so. Others offer cheaper 'Manu tours' that cover areas outside the park, but these still boast good wildlife-watching.

Costs depend on whether you arrive and depart overland or by air, but they range from US$100 to US$300 per day for four- to nine-day itineraries, ranging from overland trips to all-inclusive with flights. Book well in advance, but be flexible with your travel plans, as tours can often return a day late. Camping is only permitted in the multiuse zone (not the reserve).

It is possible for independent travelers to reach the reserve's environs without taking a tour, but it is time consuming and somewhat dangerous. If you're determined to go solo, buses leave from Cuzco via Pilcopata to Shintuya (three hours past Pilcolpata). From Pilcolpata on, it's possible to switch to sporadic river transport. On the road, breakdowns, extreme overcrowding and delays are common, and during the rainy season (even during the dry) vehicles slide off the road. It's safer, more comfortable and more reliable to take the costlier tourist buses offered by Cuzco tour operators.

The boat journey down the Alto Madre de Dios to the Río Manu takes almost a day. A few minutes from the village of Boca Manu is an airstrip, often the starting or exit point for commercial trips into the park, where entry is paid.

Despite its preservation and world-class setting, the park sees few visitors per year, and is under a threefold threat from narcotraffickers, illegal timber exploitation and illegal gold panning.

Pucallpa

☎061 / POP 205,000

A trip to tumbledown Pucallpa, capital of the Ucayali department, is like a visit with the in-laws: it ain't fun, but you gotta do it. However, it is pleasant to land in the tropics after the long bus ride down from the chilly Andes, and the view of the torrential Río Ucayali tearing through town from the relatively nice *malecón* (waterfront) is an impressive sight. Travelers come here in search of the riverboats combing the first navigable Amazon tributary to Iquitos or to visit indigenous communities near Yarinacocha.

Sights & Activities

Most activities center around Yarinacocha.

Sleeping

TOP CHOICE Antonio's Hotel HOTEL $$
(☎57-3721; www.hotelantonios.com; Progreso 545; s/d S100/120; ❄📶🏊) With huge rooms, hot showers, comfortable mattresses and mini-fridges. One of Pucallpa's best swimming pools awaits in the garden.

Hospedaje Komby GUESTHOUSE $
(☎57-1562; hostalkomby@hotmail.com; Ucayali 360; s S50-70, d S65-95; ❄📶🏊) Accommodation overall is clean but basic, brightened by the small pool.

Hospedaje Barbtur GUESTHOUSE $
(☎57-2532; Raimondi 670; s/d S30/40, without bathroom S20/30) This family-run hotel has the best budget digs: small, friendly and well maintained, with cold showers.

Eating & Drinking

TOP CHOICE C'est Si Bon CAFE $
(Independencia 560; snacks S7-15) This bright plaza-abutting spot does Pucallpa's best coffee. Also head here for breakfasts, good ice cream, sandwiches and other snacks.

Restaurant Kitty PERUVIAN $
(Tarapaca 1062; menús S5-15; ⊙7am-11pm Mon-Sat, to 5pm Sun) The Kitty is clean and popular, and brings in local lunch crowds for a wide variety of Peruvian culinary classics. Join 'em!

Chez Maggy PIZZA $$
(Inmaculada 643; pizzas S21-23) Superb pizzas from a wood-burning oven. An unusual, tropical sangria goes down well with all dishes.

Restaurant El Golf SEAFOOD $$
(Huáscar 545; mains S20; ⊙10am-5pm Tue-Sun; ❄) This upscale fish restaurant has a variety of *ceviche* made with freshwater fish – try the local *doncella* rather than the endangered *paiche*.

Information

Several banks change money and traveler's checks and have ATMs; *casas de cambio* are along the 4th, 5th and 6th blocks of Raimondi.

Clínica Monte Horeb (☎57-1689; Inmaculada 529; ⊙24hr)

Viajes Laser (☎57-1120; www.laserviajes.pe; Raimondi 399) Western Union is here, at one of Pucallpa's better travel agencies.

Getting There & Away

Air

Pucallpa's **airport** (PCL; ☎57-7329; Federico Basadre) is 5km northwest of town. Taxis/*mototaxis* charge S15/7 for the trip. Currently scheduled flights are to Lima only with **LAN** (Tarapacá 805) and **Star Perú** (☎59-0586; 7 de Junio 865). The latter flies direct to Iquitos as well.

Boat

During high water (January to April), boats depart from next to Parque San Martín. As water levels drop, the port creeps northeast to several places along the banks, including **Puerto Henry** (Manco Capác s/n) and beyond, eventually ending up 3km northeast of centro.

Crowded boats to Iquitos (S100 to S400) take three to five days. Passengers can sleep aboard in hammocks, which are sold in the market on 9 de Diciembre, or in prison-like cabins, and basic meals are provided. In the past, travelers have used Tingo María as a breaking point in this journey, but think twice: it's well regarded around Peru as a jungle no-man's-land, and readers have reported armed robberies and even rape. Single travelers must spring for cabins to ensure the safety of their belongings. Bring a lock.

It's worth noting that this trip is easier and more organized from Iquitos to Pucallpa than the reverse.

Bus

Several companies go to Lima (S70 to S100, 18 to 20 hours) via Tingo María, Huánuco, Cerro de Pasco and Junín, though armed robberies have happened on this route. **León de Huánuco** (☎57-5049; Tacna 765) serves Lima at 8:30am, 1pm *(bus-cama)* and 5:30pm. Another good company is **Turismo Central** (☎59-1009; Raimondi 768), which has one morning departure and two afternoon departures.

Getting Around

Mototaxis to the airport or Yarinacocha are about S6; taxis are S10.

Yarinacocha

This lovely oxbow lake is 10km northwest of Pucallpa. You can go canoeing, watch wildlife, visit matriarchal Shipibo communities and visit local shamans.

Popular boat trips include the Shipibo villages of San Francisco and Santa Clara. You can hire guides for jungle walks and overnight treks. *Peki-peki* boats with drivers cost about S20 per hour. Overnight tours are S125 per person per day (two-person minimum). Recommended guides include

Gilber Reategui Sangama (☎messages 57-9018) with his boat *Mi Normita*. Another good outfit is reader-recommended father-and-son-operated **Ucayali Tours** (☎961-72-8108; http://ucayali-tour.blogspot.co.uk), which charges around S90 for guided tours of Yarinacocha and the more distant waterways of the Río Ucayali. It's easy to find their boats, which are all pulled up along the waterfront. (While you're looking, don't fall for the old, 'Oh, that boat sank. Why don't you take a tour with me?' tactic.)

With several rustic bungalows, **La Jungla** (☎57-1460; bungalows per person S70-80) is enthusiastically run on the far shore, northeast of the Puerto Callao dock.

There are also pricier lakeside lodges, such as the welcoming **Pandisho Amazon Ecolodge** (☎961-65-9596, 59-1597; www.amazon-ecolodge.com; 2 days & 1 night incl meals per person S310), which offers a full program of wildlife and community visits. It's 40 minutes from Puerto Callao.

Iquitos

☎065 / POP 371,000

Linked to the outside world by air and by river, Iquitos is the world's largest city that cannot be reached by road. It's a prosperous, vibrant place teeming with the usual, inexplicably addictive Amazonian anomalies. The city is well known for many things one might expect from a jungle metropolis, not least of which are its steamy humidity, sexy population and gaggle of expat characters with entertaining – if not questionable – back stories.

Iquitos is your launching pad for trips along the famed Amazon River, but don't discount a few days in town, taking in the vibe in this manic jungle Sodom.

Sights & Activities

Casa de Fierro HISTORIC BUILDING

(Iron House; cnr Putumayo & Raymondi) Designed by Gustave Eiffel, this building was made in Paris and imported piece by piece to Iquitos around 1890. It looks like what it is: a bunch of metal sheets bolted together. It's now a general store.

Belén NEIGHBOURHOOD

The floating shantytown of Belén houses thousands of people living on huts that rise and fall with the river, and canoes selling and trading jungle produce daily from around 7am. This is a poor area, but it's relatively safe in daylight. Take a cab to Los Chinos, walk to the port and rent a canoe to paddle you around during the November to May high-water season; it's difficult to navigate in other months. The **market**, on the west side of Belén, is one of the world's gnarliest – if it ever moved, it's for sale here, and someone is eating it: all manner of Amazonian spices, meat, fish, turtles, toucans, monkeys, caiman (there is no concern here for endangered species). There's an especially interesting section of shamanic herbs and liquors. Look for Chuchuhuasi tree bark that is soaked in rum for weeks, then used as a tonic (it's even served in local bars).

Pilpintuwasi Butterfly Farm WILDLIFE RESERVE

(☎23-2665; www.amazonanimalorphanage.org; Padre Cocha; admission S20; ⏰9am-4pm Tue-Sun) It's well worth visiting this conservatorium and breeding center for Amazonian butterflies, but it's the orphaned exotic animals – including a capuchin monkey, tapir, jaguar, giant anteater and manatee – that steal the show. A visit here is pure joy and not without unexpected excitement (watch your belongings: the ornery monkeys love a little petty theft). From Puerto Bellavista-Nanay port, 2.5km north of Iquitos, take a small boat to Padre Cocha (S3). The farm is a signposted 1km walk through the village.

Amazon Golf Club GOLF

(☎975-4976, 963-1333; Quistacocha; per day incl golf-club rental S60; ⏰6am-6pm) Built by nostalgic expats, the wacky, wonderful Amazon Golf Club is the only golf course in the Peruvian Amazon. To take a swing, enquire at **Mad Mick's Trading Post** (☎50-7525; Putumayo 163; ⏰9am-8pm), where you can buy, rent, sell or trade goods for a jungle expedition.

Tours

Dawn on the Amazon Tours & Cruises CRUISE

(☎965-93-9190, 22-3730; www.dawnontheamazon.com; Malecón Maldonado 185; per person day trips incl lunch US$74.75, multiday cruises per day US$199) Run by a likable ex-Indiana farmer, Dawn on the Amazon offers day and custom multiday Amazon cruises. It's the best of the affordable options and the food is excellent. The tri-river cruise is a favorite local trip: whilst on board, fishing and birdwatching are the most popular activities.

Sleeping

Mosquitoes are rarely a serious problem, so netting isn't provided. All rooms have fans unless otherwise noted.

TOP CHOICE **La Casa Fitzcarraldo** GUESTHOUSE $$
(☎60-1139, 60-1138; http://lacasafitzcarraldo.com; Av La Marina 2153; r S180-350; ❄📶🏊) It's a pricey midrange option, but movie buffs will want to sleep where the cast and crew of Werner Herzog's *Fitzcarraldo* were based during the filming of the 'most difficult movie ever made.' The jungly oasis has a fantastic pool and multilevel tree house. It's run by the executive producer, Walter Saxer.

Camiri HOSTEL $$
(☎965-982-854; marcelbendayan@hotmail.com; end of Pevas cuadra 1; dm/d S30/100) This floating hostel-bar is accessed by boardwalks over the river. Dorms sleep either six or 10. River views are exquisite and the owner is a mine of intriguing information. Be warned: the atmospheric bar can get pretty wild.

Flying Dog Hostel HOSTEL $
(☎in Lima 01-445-6745; http://flyingdogperu.com; Malecón Tarapaca, btwn Brasil & Ricardo Palma; dm/d S30/75) Part of the same hostel chain you'll find in Lima and Cuzco, with clean, bright rooms, hot water and kitchen facilities. Doubles are a tad pricey, but some have private bathrooms.

Posada del Cauchero GUESTHOUSE $$
(☎22-2914; ermivaya@yahoo.es; Raimondi 449; s/d/ste S100/120/180; ❄🏊) Massive, chalet-style rooms decorated with tribal-themed art. There is a pool and great river views.

La Casa Del Francés GUESTHOUSE $
(☎23-1447; info@lacasadelfrances.com; Raimondi 183; dm/s/d S20/40/45) A secure, hammock-strung courtyard leads back to this pleasant budget choice offering several large, simple, colonial-style rooms with spotless tiled bathrooms.

Mad Mick's Bunkhouse HOSTEL $
(☎965-754-976; michaelcollis@hotmail.com; Putumayo 163; dm S15) The city's cheapest accommodations option: a dark, eight-bed dorm (four bunks) with one bathroom (interesting graffiti) that attracts shoestringers in droves.

Eating

TOP CHOICE **Belén Mercado** MARKET $
(cnr Prospero & Jirón 9 de Diciembre; set menus S5) The set *menú* here, including *jugo especial* (jungle juice), is a sure bet. Or you could dare meaty Amazon worms, *ishpa* (simmered sabalo fish intestines and fat) and *sikisapa* (fried leafcutter ants; abdomens are supposedly tastiest). Meanwhile, watch your valuables.

Frio y Fuego FUSION $$
(☎965-607-474; Embarcadero Av La Marina 138; mains S15-35; ⏲noon-4pm & 7-11pm Tue-Sat, noon-5pm Sun) Take a boat out to this floating foodie paradise in the middle of the mouth of the Río Itaya. The emphasis is on river-fish dishes (with delectable *doncella*). The address given is the boat embarkation point.

Amazon Bistro INTERNATIONAL $$
(Malecón Tarapaca 268; breakfasts S12, mains S15-40; ⏲6am-midnight) Only in Iquitos: a Belgian owner offers an Amazonic take on a New York–style breakfast bar. Tasty crepes and pizzas, Argentine steaks and Belgian beers… oh, and the city's best coffee. It's also a good evening drinking spot.

WORTH A TRIP

OTORONGO LODGE

For a magical, personal encounter with the Amazonian wilderness, **Otorongo Lodge** (☎965-75-6131, 065-22-4192; www.otorongoexpeditions.com; Departamento 203, Putumayo 163, Iquitos; 5 days & 4 nights per person d US$761) is run by a falconer who can imitate an incredible number of bird sounds and get you up close and personal with a huge variety of wildlife. Travelers are raving about this relatively new, rustic-style lodge, 100km from Iquitos. Located down a tributary off the Amazon and surrounded by walkways, it's down to earth. There are 12 rooms with private bathrooms and a relaxing common area. The five-day option includes off-the-beaten-path visits to nearby communities, and camping trips deeper in the jungle. Ask about its 'extreme fishing' trips. Passersby en route to the Colombian border can score a daily rate of US$50.

Iquitos

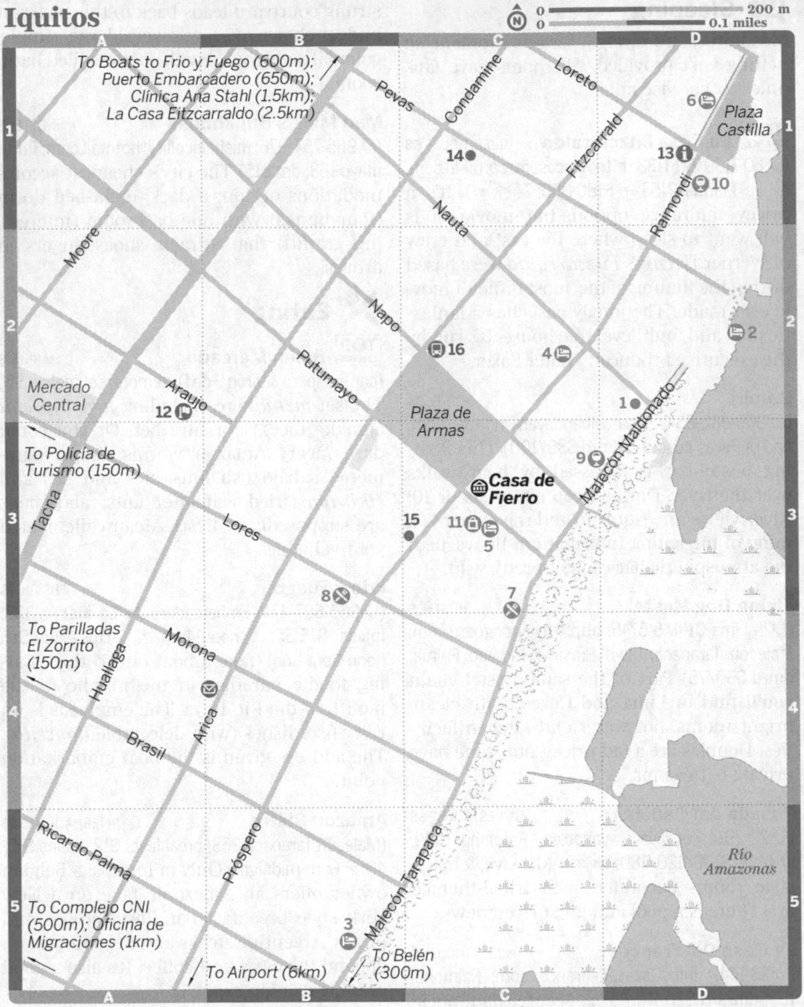

0 200 m
0 0.1 miles
To Boats to Frio y Fuego (600m); Puerto Embarcadero (650m); Clínica Ana Stahl (1.5km); La Casa Fitzcarraldo (2.5km)
Pevas
Condamine
Loreto
Fitzcarrald
Nauta
Raimondi
Plaza Castilla
Moore
Napo
Putumayo
Araujo
Mercado Central
Plaza de Armas
Casa de Fierro
Malecón Maldonado
To Policía de Turismo (150m)
Tacna
Lores
To Parilladas El Zorrito (150m)
Morona
Huallaga
Arica
Brasil
Ricardo Palma
Próspero
Malecón Tarapaca
To Complejo CNI (500m); Oficina de Migraciones (1km)
To Airport (6km)
To Belén (300m)
Río Amazonas

Dawn on the Amazon Café INTERNATIONAL $$
(Malecón Maldonado 185; mains S20; 7:30am-10pm) Serving North American, Peruvian, Spanish and (logically) Chinese dishes. Travel wherever your taste buds desire, but bear in mind that the steamed fish is very good. Ingredients are all non-MSG and those on *ayahuasca* (a hallucinogenic) diets are catered for.

Parilladas El Zorrito PARRILLA $
(Fanning 355; mains S5-10) Food is cooked outside on a grill at this lively, ambient, immensely popular local joint. *Juanes* and river fish are the thing to go for here. Portions are huge. With live music at weekends.

Ivalú PERUVIAN $
(Lores 215; snacks from S2; breakfast & lunch) Very popular for juice and cake, with a handy sideline in tamales. It normally opens at 8am; go early for a seat.

Drinking

Arandú Bar BAR
(Malecón Maldonado 113; till late) The liveliest of several thumping Malecón bars, great for

Iquitos

Top Sights
Casa de Fierro ... C3

Activities, Courses & Tours
1 Dawn on the Amazon Tours & Cruises ... D2

Sleeping
2 Camiri ... D2
3 Flying Dog Hostel ... B5
4 La Casa Del Francés ... C2
5 Mad Mick's Bunkhouse ... C3
Otorongo Lodge ... (see 5)
6 Posada del Cauchero ... D1

Eating
7 Amazon Bistro ... C3
Dawn on the Amazon Café ... (see 1)
8 Ivalú ... B3

Drinking
9 Arandú Bar ... C3
10 Musmuqui ... D1

Shopping
11 Mad Mick's Trading Post ... C3

Information
12 Colombian Consulate ... A2
13 iPerú ... D1
14 Reserva Nacional Pacaya-Samiria Office ... C1

Transport
15 LAN ... C3
16 Star Perú ... C2

people-watching and always churning out loud rock-and-roll classics.

Musmuqui BAR
(Raimondi 382; ⌚to midnight Sun-Thu, to 3am Fri & Sat) Popular lively bar with two floors and a range of aphrodisiac cocktails concocted from wondrous Amazon plants.

☆ Entertainment

Complejo CNI LIVE MUSIC
(Caceres cuadra 10; ⌚Thu-Sat) Iquitos' best disco, attracting hundreds of *iquiteños* on a weekend evening.

Information

Dangers & Annoyances

Aggressive street touts and many self-styled jungle guides are irritatingly insistent and dishonest. They are working for commissions, and usually for bog-standard establishments. There have been reports of these guides robbing tourists. It is best to make your own decisions by contacting hotels, lodges and tour companies directly. Exercise particular caution around Belén, which is very poor and where petty thieving is quite common. That said, violent crime is almost unknown in Iquitos.

Emergency

Clínica Ana Stahl (☎25-2535; La Marina 285; ⌚24hr)
Policía de Turismo (☎24-2081; Lores 834)

Money

Many banks change traveler's checks, give credit-card advances and have ATMs. Changing Brazilian or Colombian currency is best done at the border.
BCP (Próspero & Putamayo) ATM.

Post

Serpost (Arica 402; ⌚8am-6pm Mon-Fri, to 5pm Sat)

Tourist Information

iPerú (☎23-6144; Loreto 201; ⌚9am-6pm Mon-Sat, to 1pm Sun) Also has a branch at the airport (☎26-0251; Main Hall; ⌚6-7am & 3-9pm).
Iquitos Times (www.iquitostimes.com) Very helpful English-language tourist newspaper.
Reserva Nacional Pacaya-Samiria Office (☎60-7299; Pevas 339; ⌚7am-3pm Mon-Fri)

Getting There & Away

Air

Iquitos' **airport** (IQT; ☎22-8151; Abelardo Quiñones) is 6km south of town. Lima is served daily with **LAN** (☎23-2421; Próspero 232), and Lima and Pucallpa with **Star Perú** (☎23-6208; Napo 256). The latter also flies to Tarapoto. For Panama City, **Copa Airlines** (☎in Panama 1-800-359-2672; www.copaair.com) operates twice-weekly flights.

Boat

Most cargo boats leave from **Puerto Masusa** (Los Rosales), 2.5km north of the town center. Dry-erase boards at the office (look for 'Aquí Radio Masusa' on the left side of Los Rosales just before the port entrance) tell you which boats are leaving when (though departures often change overnight, and boats tend to leave hours or days late). Boats (hammock/cabin S100/S180) go to Yurimaguas (upriver, three to six days) and Pucallpa (upriver, four to seven days). Tickets are sold on the boats. Be sure to pop into the port and inspect the boats before committing. *Eduardo 1-6* are considered the most comfortable to Yurimaguas.

The Henry Boats ply the Iquitos–Pucallpa route and have their own more organized **port** (☎965-678-622; ⏰7am-7pm) on Av La Marina, closer to the center.

If you are traveling these waterways alone, a cabin is almost essential in order to secure your valuables. Without a companion to watch over them, they will be stolen. Bring a lock. Note that these boats are blatantly unfriendly to the fragile Amazon ecosystem: they dump their trash and waste straight into the river, even at port.

Getting Around

Taxis from the airport cost S15, *mototaxis* S8. Buses and trucks for nearby destinations, including the airport, leave from Arica at 9 de Diciembre. *Motocarro* (motorbike rickshaw) rides around town cost S1.50 to S2.

Reserva Nacional Pacaya-Samiria

Boats from Yurimaguas to Iquitos usually stop in the remote village of **Lagunas**, which has no money-changing facilities and limited food, but it's a launching pad for visiting the wildlife-rich **Reserva Nacional Pacaya-Samiria** (3-day admission S60), home to Amazon manatees, caimans, river dolphins, turtles, monkeys and abundant bird life. Avoid visiting during the February to May rainy season. Your experience will highly depend on your guide – try to meet this person beforehand. There are two guide associations: the highly regarded **Estypel** (☎40-1080; www.estypel.com.pe; Jr Padre Lucero 1345, Lagunas) and **ETASCEL** (☎40-1007; etascel@hotmail.com; Fiscarral 530, Lagunas). Tours cost approximately S120 to S150 per person per day, including accommodations, food and transportation, but not park entrance fees. Boats from Yurimaguas take 10 to 12 hours and arrive in Lagunas most days. Both towns have basic lodging options.

GETTING TO COLOMBIA & BRAZIL

Colombia, Brazil and Peru share a three-way border. Even in the middle of the Amazon, border formalities must be adhered to and officials will refuse passage if your passport, tourist card and visas are not in order. Regulations change, but the riverboat captains know where to go. You can travel between the three countries without formalities, as long as you stay in the tri-border area. However, if you're leaving Peru, get an exit stamp at the Peruvian immigration post in Santa Rosa, on the south side of the river, just before the border (boats stop for this – ask the captain).

From Iquitos, boats to the Peruvian border with Brazil and Colombia leave from Puerto Masusa (p901). A few weekly departures make the two-day journey (per person S50 to S80). Boats will stop at Pevas (hammock space S20, about 15 hours) and other ports en route. Boats may dock closer to the center if the water is very high (from May to July).

Speedboats to the tri-border leave from tiny Puerto Embarcadero, departing at 6am daily except Monday. Purchase your ticket in advance from speedboat offices on Raimondi near the Plaza Castilla. Standard fares are S170 to Pevas or S200 for the 10- to 12-hour trip to Santa Rosa, on the Peruvian side, including meals.

The biggest town is Leticia (Colombia), which has hotels, restaurants and a hospital. Get your passport stamped here for official entry into Colombia. Ferries from Santa Rosa (S8) reach Leticia in about 15 minutes. From Leticia there are daily flights to Bogotá. Otherwise, infrequent boats go to Puerto Asis on the Río Putumayo, a trip of up to 12 days. From Puerto Asis, buses go further into Colombia.

Leticia is linked with Tabatinga (Brazil) by road (a short walk or taxi ride). Get your official entry stamp for Brazil from Tabatinga's police station. Tabatinga has an airport with flights to Manaus, Brazil. Boats to Manaus, about four days away, leave from downriver twice weekly. Speedboats leave from Porto Brass, a three-day trip. North Americans, Australians and others must obtain visas to enter Brazil.

In Lagunas, make sure you double-check the departure times for your boat at the port and be on alert. If you depend on others to ensure that you're ready to go when the boat departs, you could very well be left behind.

UNDERSTAND PERU

Peru Today

Between the violence of the Conquest, the chaos of the early republic and the succession of dictatorships that swallowed up much of the 20th century, stability has been a rare commodity in Peru. But the first decade of the new millennium has offered uncharacteristic grace. Peru's economy has grown every year since 2003. Foreign investment is up and exports – in agriculture, mining and manufacturing – have been strong. Tourism is also big: the number of foreign travelers doubled between 2003 and 2010.

In 2011 former army officer Ollanta Humala was elected to the presidency. He is the son of a Quechua labor lawyer from Ayacucho, and social inclusion is a theme of his presidency. For starters, he made it a legal requirement for native peoples to be consulted on mining or other extractive activities in their territories.

The good times have resulted in a surge of cultural productivity – much of it revolving around food. Local celebrity chefs and gastronomic festivals highlight one of the most exciting cuisines on the planet. Inspiration has rippled to the arts, with music fusing folk with electronica and a booming contemporary arts scene.

Yet serious challenges remain. Though the poverty rate has plummeted a staggering 23% since 2002, rural poverty remains nearly double the national average.

In addition, Sendero Luminoso (Shining Path), the Maoist guerilla group that took the country to the brink of civil war in the 1980s, has seen a comeback with help from narcotrafficking, occasionally launching attacks on police and high-profile industrial projects in the central Andes.

In mid-2012 the city of Cajamarca was wracked by civil unrest over proposed gold mining in the region, with locals protesting its possible effect on the water supply. And, of course, there is the Amazon, now bisected by the Interoceanic Hwy connecting Peru and Brazil. There is concern about the impact this engineering marvel will have on one of the world's last great wilderness areas.

History

Early Cultures

The Inca civilization is merely the tip of Peru's archaeological iceberg.

The country's first inhabitants were loose-knit bands of nomadic hunters, fishers and gatherers, living in caves and killing fearsome (now extinct) animals like giant sloths, saber-toothed tigers and mastodons. Domestication of the llama, alpaca and guinea pig began between 7000 and 4000 BC. Various forms of the faithful potato (Peru boasts almost 4000 varieties!) were domesticated around 3000 BC.

Roughly from 1000 to 300 BC, the Early Horizon or Chavín Period evidenced at Chavín de Huántar near Huaraz saw widespread settled communities, plus the interchange of ideas, enhanced skills and cultural complexity, although the Chavín horizon inexplicably disappeared around 300 BC. The next 500 years saw the rise and fall of the Paracas culture south of Lima, which produced some of the most exquisite textiles in the Americas.

Between AD 100 and 700, pottery, metalwork and textiles reached new heights, and the Moche built their massive pyramids near Trujillo and at Sipán near Chiclayo. Around this time, the Nazca sculpted their enigmatic lines in the desert.

From about 600 to 1000 the first Andean expansionist empire emerged, and the influence of the Wari (Huari), from north of Ayacucho, can still be seen throughout most of Peru.

During the next four centuries several states thrived, including the Chimú, who built the city of Chan Chan near Trujillo, and the Chachapoyas, who erected the stone fortress of Kuélap. Several smaller, warlike highland groups lived near Lake Titicaca and left impressive circular funerary towers, including those at Sillustani and Cutimbo.

Inca Empire & Spanish Conquest

For all its glory, Inca pre-eminence only lasted around 100 years. The reign of the first eight Incas spanned the period from the

12th century to the early 15th century, but it was the ninth Inca, Pachacutec, who gave the empire its first bloody taste of conquest. A growing thirst for expansion had led the neighboring highland tribe, the Chankas, to Cuzco's doorstep around 1438, and Viracocha Inca fled in the belief that his small empire was lost. However, his son Pachacutec rallied the Inca army and, in a desperate battle, he famously routed the Chankas.

Buoyed by victory, Pachacutec embarked upon the first wave of Inca expansion, promptly bagging much of the central Andes. Over the next 25 years, the Inca empire grew until it stretched from the present-day border of Ecuador and Colombia to the deserts of northern Chile. During this time scores of fabulous mountaintop citadels were built, including Machu Picchu.

When Europeans came to the New World, epidemics including smallpox swept down from Central America and the Caribbean. In 1527 the 11th Inca, Huayna Capác, died in one such epidemic. He had divided his empire between his two sons – Atahualpa, born of a Quiteña mother, who took the north, and the pure-blooded native Cuzqueñan Huáscar, who took Cuzco and the south. Civil war eventually ensued, precipitating the slow downfall of the Inca empire.

By 1526 Francisco Pizarro had started heading south from Panama and soon discovered the rich coastal settlements of the Inca empire. After going back to Spain to court money and men for the conquest, he sailed to Ecuador and marched overland toward Peru and the heart of the Inca empire, reaching Cajamarca in 1532, by which time Atahualpa had defeated his half-brother Huáscar.

This meeting was to change the course of South American history. Atahualpa was ambushed by a few dozen armed conquistadors who killed thousands of unarmed indigenous tribespeople in his capture. For his freedom, the Inca offered a ransom of gold and silver from Cuzco, including that stripped from the walls of Qorikancha.

But after imprisoning Atahualpa for months and adding ransom requests, Pizarro had him killed anyway, and marched on Cuzco. Wearing armor and carrying steel swords, the Spanish cavalry was virtually unstoppable. Despite sporadic rebellions, the Inca empire was forced to retreat into the mountains and jungle, and never recovered its glorious prestige or extent.

Colonial Peru

In 1535 Pizarro founded the capital of Lima. Decades of turmoil ensued, with Peruvians resisting their conquerors, who were fighting among themselves for control of the rich colony. Pizarro was assassinated in 1541 by the son of conquistador Diego de Almagro, whom Pizarro had put to death in 1538. Manco Inca nearly regained control of the highlands in 1536 but by 1539 had retreated to his rainforest hideout at Vilcabamba, where he was killed in 1544. Inca Túpac Amaru also attempted to overthrow the Spaniards in 1572 but was defeated and executed.

For the next two centuries Lima was the major political, social and commercial center of Andean nations, while Cuzco became a backwater. The *encomienda* system, whereby settlers were granted land and native slaves, exploited natives. This system eventually spurred the 1780 uprising under the self-proclaimed ruler Inca Túpac Amaru II. The rebellion was crushed and its leaders cruelly executed.

Independence

By the early 1800s rebellion was stirring. Colonists resisted high taxes imposed by Spain, and hoped to take control of the country's rich mineral deposits, beginning with prime *guano* (seabird droppings) used for fertilizer.

Change came from two directions. After liberating Argentina and Chile from Spain, José de San Martín entered Lima and formally proclaimed Peru's independence in 1821. Meanwhile Simón Bolívar had freed Venezuela, Colombia and Ecuador. San Martín and Bolívar met in Ecuador and Bolívar continued into Peru. Two decisive battles were fought at Junín and Ayacucho in 1824, and the Spanish finally surrendered in 1826.

Peru also won a brief war with Spain in 1866 and lost a longer war with Chile (1879–83) over the nitrate-rich northern Atacama Desert. Chile annexed much of coastal southern Peru but returned some areas in 1929. A little over a decade later, Peru went to war with Ecuador over another border dispute. A 1942 treaty gave Peru the area north of the Río Marañón, but Ecuador disputed this and skirmishes occurred every few years. It wasn't until 1998 that a peace treaty finally put an end to the hostilities.

Modern Times

Despite periods of civilian rule, coups and military dictatorships characterized Peru's government during most of the 20th century.

In the late 1980s the country experienced severe social unrest. Demonstrations protesting the disastrous handling of the economy by President Alan García Pérez were an everyday occurrence – at one point, inflation reached 10,000%! His first term was shadowed by the disruptive activities of Maoist terrorist organization Sendero Luminoso, which waged a guerrilla war resulting in the death or disappearance of at least 40,000 people, mostly in the central Andes.

In 1990 Alberto Fujimori, the son of Japanese immigrants, was elected president. Strong, semidictatorial actions led to unprecedented improvements in the economy. Popular support propelled Fujimori to a second term in 1995 (after he amended the constitution expressly so he could run again), but that support was dwindling by 1998. In September 2000 a video was released showing Fujimori's head of intelligence bribing a congressman, causing Fujimori's 10-year presidency to spiral out of control. Amid the scandal and human-rights abuse accusations, Fujimori resigned during a state trip to Asia and hid in Japan, which refused Peru's repeated extradition requests. In 2005 he was arrested while on a trip to Chile, and extradited to Peru in 2007, when he was initially tried and convicted for ordering an illegal search and sentenced to six years in prison. In 2009 Fujimori was sentenced to an additional 25 years for crimes against humanity.

Despite the blemish on the family record, Fujimori's daughter Keiko was elected to the Peruvian Congress in a landslide in 2006 and ran for president in 2011, losing in a tight run-off election to former army officer Ollanta Humala.

Humala was initially thought to be a populist in the Hugo Chávez vein (the Lima stock exchange plunged when he was first elected). But his administration has been quite friendly to business. Though the economy has functioned well under his governance, civil unrest over a proposed gold mine in the north, as well as a botched raid on a Sendero Luminoso encampment in the highlands, combined to send his approval rating into a tailspin by the middle of 2012.

Culture

With a geography that encompasses desert, highland and jungle, Peru is relentlessly touted as a land of contrasts. This also applies to the lives of its people: the country is a mix of rich and poor, modern and ancient, agricultural and urban, indigenous and white. Day-to-day existence can be difficult – but it can also be profoundly rich. For centuries, this has been the story of life in Peru.

Population

Peru is essentially a bicultural society: the part that is indigenous, and the part that is European-influenced. Peruvians who speak Spanish and adhere to *criollo* tradition (Peru-born Spaniards during the colony) are a racial mix of those who are white (15% of the population) and those who are *mestizo*, people of mixed indigenous and European heritage (another 37%).

About 45% of Peru's population is pure *indígena* (people of indigenous descent), making it one of three countries in Latin America to have such high indigenous representation. A disproportionate share of *indígenas* inhabit rural areas in the Andes and work in agriculture. Most *indígenas* speak Quechua and live in the Andean highlands, while a smaller percentage speak Aymara and inhabit the Lake Titicaca region. In the vast Amazon, various indigenous ethnicities speak a plethora of other languages.

Approximately 3% of Peruvians are of African or Asian descent. Afro-Peruvians are descended from slaves brought by the Spanish conquistadors.

Lifestyle

Though the recent economic boom has been good to the country, there is still a yawning disparity between rich and poor. The minimum monthly wage stands at less than US$200. And, according to a UN report from 2010, almost a third of the population lives below the poverty line, while one in 10 survive on less than a US$1 a day. Though the official national unemployment rate is only 7.9%, underemployment is rampant, especially in cities. In Lima underemployment is estimated to affect 42.5% of the population.

In rural areas, the poor survive largely from subsistence agriculture, living in traditional adobe or tin houses that often lack electricity and indoor plumbing. In cities, the extreme poor live in shantytowns, while the lower and middle classes live in concrete, apartment-style housing or small stand-alone homes. More affluent urban homes consist of large stand-alone houses, often bordered by high walls.

Across the board, homes are generally shared by more than one generation.

Religion

More than 81% of Peruvians identify as Roman Catholics, and Catholicism is the official religion. However, while some *indígenas* are outwardly Catholic, they often combine elements of traditional beliefs into church festivals and sacred ceremonies. Evangelicals and other Protestants are now around 13% of the population.

Cuisine

Peru has long been a place where the concept of 'fusion' was a part of everyday cooking. Over the course of the last 400 years, Andean stews mingled with Asian stir-fry techniques, and Spanish rice dishes absorbed flavors from the Amazon, producing the country's famed *criollo* cooking (a blend of Spanish, Andean, Chinese and African). In the past decade, a generation of experimental young innovators has pushed this local fare to gastronomic heights. This *novoandina* approach interprets Peruvian cooking through the lens of haute cuisine.

Food tends toward the spicy, but *ají* (chili condiment) is served separately. Conventional eaters can find refuge in a *chifa* (Chinese restaurant) or *pollería* (rotisserie restaurant). Vegetarian options are expanding, and Peru's many innovative potato dishes are worth trying. Restaurants commonly offer a *menú del día* (set meal, usually lunch), consisting of soup, main course and possibly dessert for S8 to S22. Dried corn called *canchita* is a ubiquitous table snack.

WARNING

Avoid food prepared from once or currently endangered animals. Sometimes *chanco marino* (dolphin) may be served up or, in the jungle areas, *huevos de charapa* (tortoise eggs), *paiche* (the largest scaled freshwater fish), caiman, *motelo* (turtle) or even *mono* (monkey).

Incluye impuesto (IGV) means a service charge has been included in the price. Better restaurants add 18% in taxes and 10% in tips to the bill.

Drinks

ALCOHOLIC DRINKS

Beers come light or sweet and dark (called *malta* or *cerveza negra*). Cuzco and Arequipa are fiercely proud of their beers, Cuzqueña and Arequipeña.

Dating back to pre-Columbian times, traditional highland *chicha* (corn beer) is stored in earthenware pots and served in huge glasses in small Andean villages and markets, but is not usually commercially available. This home brew is an acquired taste – the fermentation process begins with someone chewing the corn.

Peruvian wines are decent but not up to the standard of Chilean or Argentine tipple. A white-grape brandy called *pisco* is the national drink, usually served in a *pisco sour,* a cocktail made from *pisco,* egg white, lemon juice, syrup, crushed ice and bitters. The firewater of choice in the jungle is *aguardiente* (sugarcane spirits flavored with anise).

NONALCOHOLIC DRINKS

Agua mineral (mineral water) is sold *con gas* (with carbonation) or *sin gas* (without carbonation). Don't leave without trying Peru's top-selling, fizzy-bubblegum-flavored Inca Kola at least once. *Jugos* (fruit juices) are widely available, and in reputable spots made with filtered water. You can also get yours with *leche* (milk). *Chicha morada* is a sweet, refreshing, noncarbonated drink made from purple corn. *Maté de coca* (coca-leaf tea) does wonders for warding off the effects of altitude. Though the country exports coffee to the world, many Peruvians drink it instant. In touristy areas cafes serving espresso and cappuccino have proliferated.

Sports

Fútbol (soccer) inspires fanaticism in Peru, even though its squad hasn't qualified for the World Cup since 1982. The big-boy teams mostly hail from Lima: the traditional *clásico* (classic match) pitches Alianza Lima against rivals Universitario (La U). The season is late March to November.

Bullfighting is also part of the national culture. Lima's Plaza de Acho attracts international talent. In remote Andean festivals, condors are tied to the back of the bull – representative of indigenous struggle against Spanish conquistadors.

Arts

The country that has been home to empires both indigenous and European has a wealth of cultural and artistic tradition. Perhaps the most outstanding achievements are in the areas of music (both indigenous and otherwise), painting and literature – the latter of which received plenty of attention in 2010 when Peruvian novelist Mario Vargas Llosa won the Nobel Prize for Literature.

Music

Like its people, Peru's music is an intercontinental fusion of elements. Pre-Columbian cultures contributed bamboo flutes, the Spaniards brought stringed instruments and the Africans gave it a backbone of fluid, percussive rhythm. By and large, music tends to be a regional affair: African-influenced *landós* with their thumbing bass beats are predominant on the coast; high-pitched indigenous *huaynos*, heavy on bamboo wind instruments, are heard in the Andes; and *criollo* waltzes are a must at any dance party on the coast.

Over the last several decades, the *huayno* has blended with surf guitars and Colombian *cumbia* (a type of Afro-Caribbean dance music) to produce *chicha* – a danceable sound closely identified with the Amazon region. (Well-known *chicha* bands include Los Shapis and Los Mirlos.) *Cumbia* is also popular. Grupo 5, which hails from Chiclayo, is currently a favorite in the genre.

On the coast, guitar-inflected *música criolla* (*criollo* music) has its roots in both Spain and Africa. The most famous *criollo* style is the *vals peruano* (Peruvian waltz), a three-quarter-time waltz that is fast moving and full of complex guitar melodies. The most legendary singers in this genre include singer and composer Chabuca Granda (1920–83), Lucha Reyes (1936–73), and Arturo 'Zambo' Cavero (1940–2009). Cavero in particular was revered for his gravelly vocals and soulful interpretations. *Landó* is closely connected to this style of music but features the added elements of call-and-response. Standout performers in this vein include singers Susana Baca (b 1944) and Eva Ayllón (b 1956).

Visual Arts

The country's most famous art movement dates to the 17th and 18th centuries, when the native and *mestizo* artists of the Cuzco School produced thousands of religious paintings, the vast majority of which remain unattributed. *Cuzqueña* canvases are proudly displayed in many highland churches.

Traditional Crafts

Peru has a long tradition of producing extraordinarily rendered crafts and folk art. Here's what to look for:

Textiles You'll see intricate weavings with elaborate anthropomorphic and geometric designs all over Peru. Some of the finest can be found around Cuzco.

Pottery The most stunning pieces of pottery are those made in the tradition of the pre-Columbian Moche people of the north coast. But also worthwhile is Chancay-style pottery: rotund figures made from sand-colored clay. Find these at craft markets in Lima.

Religious crafts These abound in all regions, but the *retablos* (three-dimensional dioramas) from Ayacucho are the most spectacular.

Literature

Peru's most famous novelist is the Nobel Prize–winning Mario Vargas Llosa (b 1936), who ran unsuccessfully for president in 1990. His complex novels, including *The Time of the Hero,* delve into Peruvian society, politics and culture.

Considered Peru's greatest poet, César Vallejo (1892–1938) wrote *Trilce,* a book of 77 avant-garde, existentialist poems. Vallejo was known for pushing the Spanish language to its limits, inventing words when real ones no longer served him.

Two writers noted for their portrayals of indigenous communities are José María Arguedas (1911–69) and Ciro Alegría (1909–67). Rising literary star Daniel Alarcón (b 1977) is a Peruvian-American whose 2007 debut novel *Lost City Radio* achieved wide acclaim.

Environment

Few countries have topographies as rugged, as forbidding and as wildly diverse as Peru. The third-largest country in South America, at 1,285,220 sq km, it is five times larger than the UK, almost twice the size of Texas and one-sixth the size of Australia. It lies in the tropics, south of the equator, straddling three strikingly different geographic zones: the arid Pacific Coast, the craggy Andes mountain range and a good portion of the Amazon Basin.

The Land

The coastal strip is mainly desert, punctuated by cities and rivers down from the Andes forming agricultural oases. The country's best road, the Carr Panamericana, slices through coastal Peru from border to border.

The Andes rise rapidly from the coast to spectacular heights over 6000m just 100km inland. Most mountains are between 3000m and 4000m, with jagged ranges separated by deep, vertiginous canyons. Huascarán (6768m) is Peru's highest peak.

The eastern Andes get more rainfall than the dry western slopes, and so they're covered in cloud forest, merging with the rainforest of the Amazon Basin.

Wildlife

With mammoth deserts, glaciated mountain ranges, tropical rainforests and almost every imaginable habitat in between, Peru hosts a menagerie of wildlife.

Bird and marine life is abundant along the coast, with colonies of sea lions, Humboldt penguins, Chilean flamingos, Peruvian pelicans, Inca terns and the brown booby endemic to the region. Remarkable highland birds include majestic Andean condors, puna ibis and a variety of hummingbirds. The highlands are also home to camelids such as llamas, alpacas, guanacos and *vicuñas,* while cloud forests are the haunts of jaguars, tapirs and endangered spectacled bears.

Swoop down toward the Amazon and with luck you'll spot all the iconic tropical birds – parrots, macaws, toucans and many more. The Amazon is home to over a dozen species of monkey, plus river dolphins, frogs, reptiles, fish and insects galore. Snakes? Don't panic. Many species live here, but they're mostly shy of humans.

National Parks

Peru's wealth of wildlife is protected by a system of national parks and reserves, with 60 areas covering almost 15% of the country. Yet these areas seriously lack infrastructure and are subject to illegal hunting, fishing, logging and mining. The government simply doesn't have the money to patrol the parks, though international agencies contribute resources to conservation projects.

Some highlights include Parque Nacional Huascarán, a prime spot for trekking in the Cordillera Blanca, and Parque Nacional Manu, among the world's most biodiverse rainforests, located northwest of Cuzco. Many reserves or *reservas nacionales* and protected areas – such as Cañón del Colca and Lake Titicaca – are just as worthy of a visit.

Environmental Issues

Peru faces major challenges in the stewardship of its natural resources, with problems compounded by a lack of law enforcement and its impenetrable geography. Deforestation and erosion are major issues, as is industrial pollution, urban sprawl and the continuing attempted eradication of coca plantations on some Andean slopes. In addition, the Interoceanic Hwy through the heart of the Amazon may imperil thousands of square kilometers of rainforest.

DEFORESTATION & WATER PROBLEMS

At the ground level, clear-cutting of the highlands for firewood, of the rainforests for valuable hardwoods, and of both to clear land for agriculture, oil drilling and mining has led to severe erosion. In the highlands, where deforestation and overgrazing of Andean woodlands and *puna* (highlands) grass is severe, soil quality is rapidly deteriorating. In the Amazon rainforest, deforestation has led to erosion and a decline in bellwether species such as frogs. Erosion has also led to decreased water quality in this area, where silt-laden water is unable to support micro-organisms at the base of the food chain.

Other water-related problems include pollution from mining in the highlands. Sewage contamination along the coast has led to many beaches around some coastal cities being declared unfit for swimming. In the south, pollution and overfishing have led to the continued decline of the Humboldt penguin (its numbers have declined by more than a third since the 1980s).

PROTECTIVE STEPS

In 1995 Peru's congress created a National Environmental Council (CONAM) to manage the country's national environmental

TOP WILDLIFE-WATCHING SPOTS

» Remote jungle in **Parque Nacional Manu** (p895); your best chance to see jaguars, tapirs and monkeys

» The coastal reserve of **Islas Ballestas** (p817) and **Reserva Nacional de Paracas** (p818), with penguins, flamingos and sea lions

» Canopy walkways, jungle lodges and river cruises in **Iquitos** (p898)

» Andean condors and *vicuñas* in **Parque Nacional Huascarán** (p884)

» Capybaras and macaws near **Puerto Maldonado** (p893)

» **Cañón del Colca** (p833) – the easiest place to spot Andean condors

» Oxbow lake **Yarinacocha** (p897), home to pink dolphins, huge iguanas and myriad bird species

» Pristine rainforest reserve **Reserva Nacional Pacaya-Samiria** (p902), explored by dugout canoe

» More than 400 species of rare and endemic birds around **Machu Picchu** (p857)

policy. Though there have been some success stories (such as flagrant polluters being fined for poor practices), enforcement remains weak.

Some positive measures are being taken to help protect the country's environment. For example, the Peruvian government and private interests within the tourism industry have come together to develop sustainable travel projects in the Amazon.

SURVIVAL GUIDE

Directory A–Z

Accommodations

Lima and the tourist mecca of Cuzco are the most expensive places to stay in Peru. During high season (June through August), major holidays and festivals, accommodations are likely to be full and rates can triple. At other times, the high-season rates we quote taper off. Foreign tourists normally aren't charged the 10% sales tax on accommodations. *Incluye impuesto* (IGV) means a service charge has been included in the price. At better hotels, taxes and service charges combined may total 28%. Budget hotels usually have hot (or, more likely, tepid) showers some of the time. Dormitory beds come with shared bathrooms, while single and double rooms (including those in *hostales*, which are guesthouses and not the same as backpacker hostels) have private bathrooms unless otherwise noted.

Activities

Most activities are available year-round, but certain times of year are better than others. Peak season for most outdoor activities is during the winter dry season (June to August). Trekking in the highlands is a muddy proposition during the wet season, especially December to March, when the heaviest rains fall. However, those hotter summer months are best for swimming and surfing along the Pacific Coast.

For your safety, avoid the cheapest, cutrate tour agencies and outdoor outfitters. For specialized activities, bring high-quality gear from home.

If birdwatching gets you in a flap, head for the Amazon Basin, Islas Ballestas and Cañón del Colca for starters.

When it comes to mountain climbing, Huascarán (6768m), Peru's highest mountain, is experts-only, but easier peaks abound near Huaraz and Arequipa. Rock and ice climbing are popular around Huaraz.

Horse rentals can be easily arranged. For a real splurge, take a ride on a graceful Peruvian *paso* horse near Urubamba.

Gearing up for some downhill adventures? Easy or demanding single-track trails await mountain bikers outside Huaraz, Cuzco and Arequipa.

Paragliding is especially popular in Lima.

Whitewater-rafting (river-running) agencies in Cuzco and Arequipa offer a multitude of day runs and longer hauls (grade III to IV+ rapids). Travelers have died on these rivers, so be especially cautious about which rafting company to trust with your life. The best place for beginners is Lunahuaná.

SLEEPING PRICE RANGES

The following price ranges refer to a double room with bathroom in high season, unless otherwise stated.

$ less than S85 (includes dorm rooms)

$$ S85 to S250

$$$ more than S250

Surfing has a big fan base in Peru. There are some radical waves up north, famously at Huanchaco, Máncora and just south of Lima. For something completely different, sandboard down humongous dunes in the coastal desert near Huacachina and Nazca.

Trekkers, pack your boots – the variety of trails in Peru is staggering. The Cordillera Blanca can't be beaten for peaks, while the nearby Cordillera Huayhuash is similarly stunning. But if you've heard of *any* trek in Peru, you'll have heard of the world-famous Inca Trail to Machu Picchu – and everyone else has, too, so consider taking an alternative route. The spectacular six-day Ausangate circuit and ancient ruins hidden in cloud forests outside Chachapoyas are a few more possibilities. Alternatively, get down into the world's deepest canyons – the Cañón del Cotahuasi and Cañón del Colca.

Business Hours

Shops open at 9am or 10am and close from 6pm to 8pm. A two-hour lunch break is common. Shops may stay open through lunch in big cities, and there are 24-hour supermarkets in Lima. Banks are generally open 9am to 6pm Monday to Friday, to 1pm Saturday. Post offices and *casas de cambio* (money-exchange offices) keep highly variable hours. Almost everything closes on Sunday.

Electricity

Peru runs on a 220V, 60Hz AC electricity supply. Even though two-pronged outlets accept both flat (North American) and round (European) plugs, electronics built for lower voltage and cycles (eg 110V to 120V North American appliances) will function poorly or not at all, and plugging them in without using a converter can damage them.

Embassies & Consulates

Australian Embassy (☎01-630-0500; www.embassy.gov.au/peru; Av Victor A Belaúnde 147, Suite 1301, Torre Real 3, San Isidro, Lima 27)

Argentinian Embassy (☎01-433-3381; Av 28 de Julio 828, Lima 1)

Bolivian Embassy (☎01-440-2095; Los Castaños 235, San Isidro, Lima 27) Puno (☎051-35-1251; fax 051-35-1251; Arequipa 136, 3rd fl); Tacna (☎052-25-5121; Bolognesi 1751)

Brazilian Embassy (Map p812; ☎01-512-0830; www.embajadabrasil.org.pe; Av José Pardo 850, Miraflores, Lima 18) Iquitos (☎065-23-5151; Lores 363)

Canadian Embassy (Map p812; ☎01-319-3200; www.canadainternational.gc.ca/peru-perou; Bolognesi 228, Miraflores, Lima 18)

Chilean Embassy (☎01-710-2211; chileabroad.gov.cl/peru; Javier Prado Oeste 790, San Isidro, Lima 27) Tacna (☎052-42-3063; Presbitero Andía s/n)

Colombian Embassy (☎01-441-0954; www.embajadacolombia.org.pe; Jorge Basadre 1580, San Isidro, Lima 27) Iquitos (☎065-23-1461; Calvo de Araujo 431)

Ecuadorian Embassy (☎01-212-4161, 01-212-4171; www.mecuadorperu.org.pe; Las Palmeras 356, San Isidro, Lima 27) Tumbes (☎072-52-5949; Bolívar 129, 3rd fl, Plaza de Armas)

French Embassy (☎01-215-8400; www.ambafrance-pe.org; Av Arequipa 3415, San Isidro)

German Embassy (☎01-203-5940; www.lima.diplo.de; Av Arequipa 4210, Miraflores, Lima 18)

UK Embassy (Map p812; ☎01-617-3000; www.ukinperu.fco.gov.uk; Av José Larco 1301, Edificio Parquemar, 22nd fl, Miraflores, Lima 18)

US Embassy (☎01-618-2000; http://lima.usembassy.gov; Av Encalada, 17th block, Monterrico, Lima)

Gay & Lesbian Travelers

Peru is a strongly conservative, Catholic country. Gays and lesbians tend to keep a low profile. Homosexual rights in a political or legal context don't even exist as an issue for most Peruvians. (Note that the rainbow flag seen around Cuzco is *not* a gay-pride flag – it's the flag of the Inca empire.) When the issue does arise in public, hostility is most often the official response.

Kissing on the mouth is rarely seen in public, by either heterosexual or homosexual couples. Peruvians are physically demonstrative with their friends, though, so kissing on the cheek in greeting or an *abrazo* (backslapping hug exchanged between men) are innocuous, everyday behaviors. When in doubt, do as locals do.

Lima is the most accepting of gay people, while Cuzco, Arequipa and Trujillo are more tolerant than the norm. **Movimiento Homosexual-Lesbiana** (☎01-332-2945; www.mhol.org.pe) is Peru's best-known gay political organization. Lima has Peru's most openly gay scene. **Deambiente** (www.deambiente.com) is a Spanish-language online magazine of politics and pop culture, plus nightlife listings. **Gayperu.com** (www.gayperu.com), another Spanish-language guide, lists bars to bathhouses. **Rainbow Peruvian Tours** (☎01-215-6000; www.perurainbow.com; Río de Janeiro 216, Miraflores, Lima) is a gay-owned tour agency with a multilingual website.

Internet Access

Internet cafes *(locutorios)* are found on every other street corner in Peru. Even small towns will have at least one *cabina* tucked away somewhere. Access is fast and inexpensive (around S1.50 per hour) in cities but pricier and painfully unreliable in rural areas. Often internet cafes have 'net-to-phone' and 'net-to-net' capabilities (such as Skype).

Language

Peru has language schools in Lima, Cuzco, Arequipa, Huaraz, Puerto Maldonado and Huancayo.

Legal Matters

There are *policía de turismo* (tourist police) stations in over a dozen major cities, and they usually have someone on hand who speaks at least a little English. Though bribery is illegal, some police officers (and tourist police) may be corrupt. As most travelers won't have to deal with traffic police, the most likely place you'll be expected to pay officials a little extra is at overland border crossings. This too is illegal, and if you have the time and fortitude to stick to your guns, you will eventually be allowed in.

Maps

The best road map of Peru, *Mapa Vial* (1:2,000,000), published by Lima 2000, is sold in bookstores. Topographic maps are easily available from outdoor outfitters in major cities and tourist destinations.

Money

The currency is the nuevo sol (S), divided into 100 *céntimos*. For exchange rates, see p799.

ATMS

Most cities and some small towns have 24-hour ATMs on the Plus (Visa) and Cirrus (Maestro/MasterCard) systems. American Express and other networks are less widespread. Bigger airports and bus stations, as well as Interbank and BCP branches, have global ATMs that accept almost all foreign cards. ATMs in Peru will only accept your debit, bank or traveler's-check card if you have a four-digit PIN. Both US dollars and Peruvian currency are dispensed.

CASH

The following bills are commonly in circulation: S10, S20, S50 and S100. When changing money, always ask for plenty of small bills. Coins of S0.5, S0.10, S0.20, S0.50, S1, S2 and S5 are also in use. US dollars are accepted at many tourist-oriented establishments, but you'll need nuevos soles to pay for transportation, cheap meals and guesthouses etc. Counterfeiting is a major problem in Peru.

CREDIT CARDS

Better hotels, restaurants and shops accept *tarjetas de crédito* (credit cards) but usually tack on a fee of 7% or more for paying with plastic. Your own credit card may add an international-use fee (around 3%).

EXCHANGING MONEY

Currencies other than US dollars can be exchanged only in major cities and at a high commission. Worn, torn or damaged bills are not accepted. *Casas de cambio* are open longer than banks and are much faster.

FOOD PRICE RANGES

Restaurant listings are organized according to author preference, considering value for cost. Midrange to high-end restaurants charge a 10% service fee and a 19% tax. The following price ranges refer to a main-course dish.

$ less than S20

$$ S20 to S45

$$$ more than S45

Official money changers *(cambistas)* are useful for exchange outside banking hours or at borders where there are no banks, but beware of 'fixed' calculators, counterfeit notes and short-changing.

Post

Serpost (www.serpost.com.pe) is the privatized postal system. It's relatively efficient, but expensive. Airmail postcards and letters cost about S5 to S6.50 each to most foreign destinations, arriving in about two weeks from Lima, longer from provincial cities.

Lista de correos (poste restante/general delivery) can be sent to any major post office. South American Explorers will hold mail and packages for members at its clubhouses in Lima and Cuzco.

Public Holidays

On major holidays, banks, offices and other services are closed, fully booked hotels double or triple their rates, and transportation becomes overcrowded. Fiestas Patrias is the biggest national holiday, when the entire nation seems to be on the move.

Año Nuevo (New Year's Day) January 1

Good Friday March/April

Día del Trabajador (Labor Day) May 1

Inti Raymi June 24

Fiestas de San Pedro y San Pablo (Feast of St Peter and St Paul) June 29

Fiestas Patrias (National Independence Days) July 28 and 29

Fiesta de Santa Rosa de Lima August 30

Battle of Angamos Day October 8

Todos Santos (All Saints Day) November 1

Fiesta de la Purísima Concepción (Feast of the Immaculate Conception) December 8

Navidad (Christmas Day) December 25

Responsible Travel

Archaeologists are fighting a losing battle with *guaqueros* (grave robbers), particularly along the coast. Refrain from buying original pre-Columbian artifacts, and do not contribute to wildlife destruction by eating endangered animals or purchasing souvenirs made from skins, feathers, horns or turtle shells. Some indigenous communities make their living from tourism. Visiting these communities may financially support their initiatives but also weaken traditional cultures. If you go on an organized tour, make sure the company is locally owned and ask if any of the proceeds benefit the places you'll be visiting.

Safe Travel

Peru has its fair share of traveler hassles, which may often be avoided by exercising common sense.

The most common problem is theft, either stealth or snatch – theft by violent mugging is rare, though it's not to be ruled out. Watch out for 'choke and grab' attacks, especially at archaeological sites. Robberies and fatal attacks have occurred even on popular trekking trails, notably around Huaraz.

Avoid unlicensed 'pirate' taxis, as some drivers have been known to be complicit in 'express' kidnappings. Take good-quality day buses instead of cheap, overnight services to lower the risk of having an accident or possibly being hijacked.

Do *not* get involved with drugs. Gringos who have done so are being repaid with long-term incarceration in harsh Peruvian prisons. Any suspect in a crime (which includes vehicle accidents, whether or not you're the driver at fault) is considered guilty until proven innocent.

While terrorism lingers in Peru, narcotrafficking is serious business. Areas to avoid are the Río Huallaga valley between Tingo María and Juanjui, and the Río Apurímac valley near Ayacucho, where the majority of Peru's illegal drug-growing takes place. Currently, it is unadvisable to visit Vilcabamba, Ivochote, Kiteni and beyond, but the situation is subject to change.

Not all unexploded ordinance (UXO) along the Ecuadorian border has been cleaned up. Use only official border crossings and don't stray off the beaten path in border zones.

Soroche (altitude sickness) can be fatal.

Telephone

Public payphones are available in even the tiniest towns. Most work with phone cards, and many with coins. Dial ☎109 for a Peruvian operator, ☎108 for an international operator and ☎103 for information. Internet cafes are often much cheaper for making local, long-distance and international phone calls than **Telefónica-Perú** (www.telefonica.com.pe) offices.

CELL PHONES

It's possible to use a tri-band GSM world phone in Peru (GSM 1900). Other systems in use are CDMA and TDMA. This is a fast-changing field, so check the current situation before you travel. In larger cities, you can buy cell phones in stands at the supermarket that use SIM cards for about S48, then pop in a SIM card that costs from S14. Claro has a popular pay-as-you-go plan. Cell-phone rentals may be available in major cities and tourist centers. Cell-phone reception may be poor in the mountains or jungle.

PHONE CARDS

Called *tarjetas telefónicas,* phone cards are widely available from street vendors or kiosks. Some have an electronic chip, but most make you dial a code to obtain access. Dial a 3-digit connection and enter the code on the back of your card; a message in Spanish conveys your balance, then you dial the number and your call connects. Ask around for which companies' cards offer the best deals.

PHONE CODES

Peru's country code is ☎51. To call a foreign country, dial ☎00, the country code, area code and local number.

Each region of Peru (called a department) has its own area code, which begins with 0 (☎01 in Lima, 0 plus two digits elsewhere). To call long distance within Peru, include the 0 in the area code. If calling from abroad, dial your international access code, the country code (☎51), the area code without the 0, then the local number.

Toilets

Peruvian plumbing leaves something to be desired. Even a small amount of toilet paper in the bowl can muck up the entire system – that's why a small plastic bin is routinely provided for disposing of it. Except at museums, restaurants, hotels and bus stations, public toilets are rare in Peru. Always carry toilet paper with you.

Tourist Information

PromPerú's official tourism website (www.peru.info) offers information in Spanish, Portuguese, English, French, German and Italian. PromPerú also runs **iPerú** (☎24hr hotline 01-574-8000) information offices in Lima, Arequipa, Ayacucho, Chiclayo, Cuzco, Huaraz, Iquitos, Piura, Puno, Tacna and Trujillo. Municipal tourist offices are found in other cities we cover. The South American Explorers clubhouses in Lima and Cuzco are good sources of information for travelers, but you'll get more help as a paying member.

Travelers with Disabilities

Peru offers few conveniences for travelers with disabilities. Peru's official tourism organization PromPerú has a link from the 'Special Interests' section of its website (www.peru.info) to Accessible Tourism, where you can find reports on wheelchair-accessible hotels, restaurants and attractions in Lima, Cuzco, Aguas Calientes, Iquitos and Trujillo.

Visas

With few exceptions (for citizens of a handful of Asian, African and communist countries), visas are not required for tourism. Passports should be valid for at least six months from your departure date. Travelers are permitted a 90-day initial stay, stamped into their passports and onto an Andean Immigration Card that you must keep and return when leaving Peru.

If you lose your card, visit an **oficina de migraciónes** (Immigration Office; www.digemin.gob.pe) for a replacement. Extensions can be obtained at immigration offices in Lima, Arequipa, Cuzco, Iquitos, Puerto Maldonado, Puno and Trujillo, as well as near the Chilean and Ecuadorian borders. Forms and information in English can be found online. For extensions, click on 'Foreigners and Extension of Stay.' The cost is S12.25 for a right of paperwork and an additional US$20 for the 30-day extension. Two extensions are allowed per year.

While traveling around Peru, carry your passport and immigration card with you at all times, as you can be arrested if you don't have proper ID.

See lonelyplanet.com and its links for up-to-date visa information.

Volunteering

Most volunteer programs charge you for program fees, room and board. Watch out for fake charities and illegitimate programs that are scams. Spanish-language schools usually know of casual volunteer opportunities. South American Explorers clubhouses have firsthand reports from foreign volunteers in Lima and Cuzco. **ProWorld Service**

Corps (ProPeru; ☎in UK 0-18-6559-6289, in USA 877-429-6753; www.myproworld.org) organizes two- to 26-week cultural, service and academic placements in the Sacred Valley and is affiliated with NGOs throughout Peru.

Women Travelers

Most women encounter no serious problems in Peru, though they should come mentally prepared for being a conspicuous center of attention. Machismo is alive and well in Peruvian towns and cities, where curious staring, whistling, hissing and *piropos* (cheeky, flirtatious or vulgar remarks) are an everyday occurrence. Ignoring provocation is generally the best response. Most men don't follow up their idle chatter with something more threatening unless they feel you've insulted their manhood.

If you appeal to locals for help, you'll find most Peruvians act protectively toward women traveling alone, expressing surprise and concern when you tell them you're traveling without your husband or family. If a stranger approaches you on the street to ask a question, *don't* stop walking, which would allow attackers to quickly surround you. Never go alone to a bar, and stay alert at archaeological sites, even during daylight hours. Take only authorized taxis and avoid overnight buses.

Abortions are illegal in Peru, except when they can save the life of the mother. Planned Parenthood–affiliated **Instituto Peruano de Paternidad Responsable** (Inppares; ☎01-583-9012; www.inppares.org.pe) runs a dozen sexual- and reproductive-health clinics for both sexes around the country.

Work

Officially you need a work visa in Peru, though language centers in Lima or Cuzco sometimes hire native speakers to teach English. This is illegal, and such jobs are increasingly difficult to get without a proper work visa.

Getting There & Away

Air

Lima's **Aeropuerto Internacional Jorge Chávez** (code LIM; ☎517-3100; www.lap.com.pe) is the main hub for flights to Andean countries and Latin America, North America and Europe.

Boat

Boats ply the Amazon from Iquitos to Leticia, Colombia, and Tabatinga, Brazil. It's difficult to reach Bolivia by river from Puerto Maldonado. It's possible, but time consuming, to travel along the Río Napo from Iquitos to Coca, Ecuador.

Bus, Car & Motorcycle

The major border crossings: Tacna to Chile; Tumbes, La Tina or Jaén to Ecuador; and Yunguyo or Desaguadero by Lake Titicaca to Bolivia. Brazil is reached (but not easily) via Iñapari.

Train

There are inexpensive, twice-daily trains between Tacna and Arica, Chile.

Getting Around

On the road keep your passport and Andean Immigration Card with you, not packed in your luggage, as overland transport goes through police checkpoints.

Air

Most airlines fly from Lima to regional capitals, but service between provincial cities is limited. The domestic airlines listed below are the most established and reliable.

Morning departures are most likely to be on time. Show up at least one hour early for all domestic flights (90 minutes in Lima, two hours in Cuzco). Flights are often fully booked during holidays.

LAN (www.lan.com) Peru's major domestic carrier flies to Arequipa, Chiclayo, Cuzco, Iquitos, Juliaca, Piura, Puerto Maldonado, Tacna, Tarapoto and Trujillo. Additionally, it offers link services between Arequipa and Cuzco, Arequipa and Juliaca, Arequipa and Tacna, Cuzco and Juliaca, and Cuzco and Puerto Maldonado.

Peruvian Airlines (www.peruvianairlines.pe) Flies to Lima, Arequipa, Cuzco, Piura, Iquitos and Tacna.

Star Perú (www.starperu.com) Domestic carrier, flying to Ayacucho, Cajamarca, Cuzco, Iquitos, Pucallpa, Puerto Maldonado, Talara and Tarapoto, with link service between Tarapoto and Iquitos.

TACA (www.taca.com) Central American airline with service between Lima and Cuzco.

Boat

Small, slow motorboats depart daily from Puno for Lake Titicaca's islands.

In Peru's eastern lowlands, *peki-pekis* (dugout canoes, usually powered by an outboard engine) act as water buses on the smaller rivers. Where the rivers widen, larger cargo boats are normally available. This is the classic way to travel down the Amazon – swinging in your hammock aboard a banana boat piloted by a grizzled old captain. You can travel from Pucallpa or Yurimaguas to Iquitos, and on into Brazil, Colombia or Ecuador this way. These boats aren't big, but they have two or more decks: the lower deck is for cargo, the upper for passengers and crew. Bring a hammock. Basic food is provided, but you may want to bring your own. To get aboard, just go down to the docks and ask for a boat to your destination. Arrange passage with the captain (nobody else). Departure time normally depends on filling up the hold. Sometimes you can sleep on the boat while awaiting departure to save costs.

Bus

Peru's notoriously dangerous buses are cheap and go just about everywhere.

Less traveled routes are served by ramshackle old chicken buses, but more popular destinations are served by fast luxury services (called *imperial* or something similar), charging up to 10 times more than *económico* (economy) buses. It's worth paying more for long-distance bus trips, if only for safety's sake. Some overnight routes offer *bus-camas* (bed-buses) with seats that fully recline. For safety, security and comfort, there is **Cruz del Sur** (www.cruzdelsur.com.pe) at the top and pretty much all goes downhill from there. Peruvians swear by **Oltursa** (www.oltursa.com.pe).

Many cities now have central bus terminals, while others have bus companies clustered around a few blocks or scattered all over town. Travel agencies are convenient for buying tickets but they will overcharge you. Instead, you should buy them directly from the bus company at least a day in advance. Note also that schedules and fares change frequently. Prices skyrocket around major holidays, when tickets may be sold out several days ahead of time. Coastal buses are packed all summer long, especially on Sunday.

AIRPORT TAX

International airport taxes are now almost always included in your ticket price. Lima's international tax is US$31, payable in US dollars or nuevos soles (cash only). Domestic airport taxes are included in ticket prices.

Buses rarely leave or arrive on time and can be greatly delayed during the rainy season due to landslides and treacherous road conditions. Try not to take overnight buses, which are more vulnerable to fatal accidents, hijackings and luggage theft. It can get freezing cold on highland buses, so dress warmly. Long-distance buses generally stop for meals, though toilets are highly unpredictable. Some companies have their own restaurants in the middle of nowhere, practically forcing you to eat there. But you can also buy snacks from onboard vendors or bring your own food and drinks.

Car & Motorcycle

With the exception of the Carr Panamericana and new roads leading inland from the coast, road conditions are generally poor, distances are great and renting a car is an expensive, often dangerous hassle. Keep in mind that road signage is deficient and most major roads are also toll roads. Renting a private taxi for long-distance trips costs little more than renting a car, and avoids most of these pitfalls. Motorcycle rental is an option mainly in jungle towns, and there are a few outfitters in Cuzco.

DRIVER'S LICENSE

A driver's license from your home country is sufficient for renting a car. An International Driving Permit (IDP) is only required if you'll be driving in Peru for more than 30 days.

Local Transportation

Taxis are unmetered, so ask locals about the going rate, then haggle; drivers often double or triple the standard rate for unsuspecting foreigners. A short run in most cities costs S3 to S5 (in Lima S5 to S8). Be aware that street hawkers sell florescent taxi stickers throughout Peru, and anybody can just stick one on their windscreen. Some drivers of these unlicensed 'pirate' taxis have been known to be complicit in violent crimes against passengers, especially in Arequipa. It's safer if more expensive to take officially regulated taxis, requested by telephone.

Mototaxis (motorized rickshaws) are common in some of the smaller towns. *Colectivos* (shared minivans, minibuses or taxis) and trucks (in the Amazon) run between local and not-so-local destinations.

Tours

Some protected areas such as the Inca Trail and Parque Nacional Manu can only be entered with a guided tour. Other outdoor activities, such as trekking in the Andes or wildlife watching in the Amazon, may be more rewarding with an experienced guide.

Train

Three rail companies link Cuzco and the Sacred Valley with Aguas Calientes, the town near Machu Picchu. **PeruRail** (www.perurail.com) offers a scenic thrice-weekly service that travels between Cuzco and Lake Titicaca.

Other railways connect Lima and the Andean highland towns of Huancayo and Huancavelica.

Suriname

Includes »

Best Places to Stay

- » Kabalebo (p927)
- » Zus & Zo (p921)
- » Awarradam (p926)
- » Kininipaati (p927)
- » Anaula (p927)

Best Tour Destinations

- » Palumeu & Awarradam (p926)
- » Raleighvallen (p927)
- » Brownsberg Nature Reserve (p926)
- » Commewijne Sunset & Dolphin (p925)

Why Go?

Suriname is a warm, dense convergence of rivers that thumps with the lively rhythm of ethnic diversity. From Paramaribo, the country's effervescent Dutch-colonial capital, to the fathomless jungles of the interior, you'll get a genuine welcome to this tiny country – whether from the descendants of escaped African slaves, Dutch and British colonialists, Indian, Indonesian and Chinese indentured laborers or indigenous Amerindians.

You get the best of both worlds here: a city that's chock-full of restaurants, shopping venues and night spots and an untamed jungle utterly away from modern development. It's not easy to get around this river-heavy, forest-dense country, and the mix of languages can make it hard to communicate, sometimes even for Dutch speakers. Don't forget that a meeting of culinary traditions means the food here is as spicy and rich as the country itself.

When to Go

Paramaribo

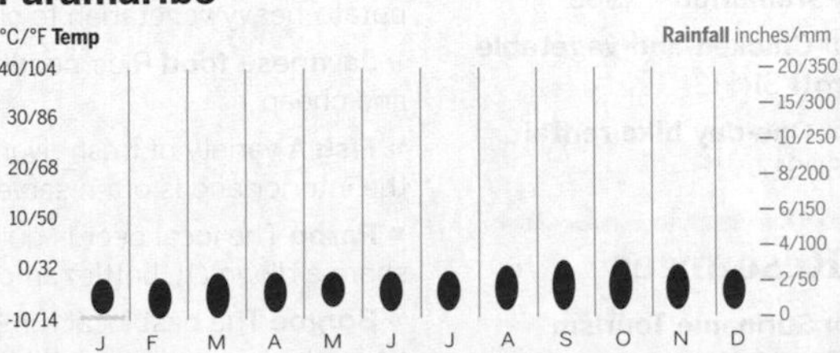

Feb–Apr The first dry season is slightly cooler than the second, and the best time to visit.

Aug–Nov The second dry season is a bit busier and hotter than the first.

Dec–Jan Paramaribo is known for its explosive New Year's Eve celebrations.

AT A GLANCE

» **Currency** Suriname dollar (SR$)

» **Languages** Dutch, Sranan Tongo

» **Money** RBC ATMs accept most foreign cards; credit cards rarely accepted

» **Visas** 90-day tourist cards prior to arrival

» **Time** GMT minus three hours

Fast Facts

» **Area** 163,800 sq km

» **Capital** Paramaribo

» **Population** 529,419

» **Emergency** ☎112

» **Country code** ☎597

Exchange Rates

Australia	A$1	SR$3.42
Canada	C$1	SR$3.23
Euro zone	€1	SR$4.28
New Zealand	NZ$1	SR$2.78
UK	UK£1	SR$5.02
USA	US$1	SR$3.29

Set Your Budget

» **Guesthouse in Paramaribo** SR$65

» **Chicken-and-vegetable roti** SR$12

» **One-day bike rental** SR$17

Resources

» **Suriname Tourism Foundation** (www.suriname-tourism.org)

» **Suriname Tourism Network** (www.surinametourism.net)

» **Surinam.net** (www.surinam.net)

Connections

Suriname's border crossings are at Corriverton (Guyana) and St Laurent du Maroni (French Guiana). Both of these crossings are made by boat across massive rivers that flow into the Caribbean. While Brazil borders the country to the south, there are no roads through the impenetrable jungle into Suriname and thus you can't cross the border here.

ITINERARIES

One Week

Spend three days exploring Paramaribo and the plantations of the Commewijne River by bike or on foot. On one afternoon be sure to take a sunset dolphin-viewing tour and, if you've still got energy, get out on the town for a night of dancing, Suriname style. Next, head to the interior – either Raleighvallen, the upper Suriname River or Brownsberg Nature Reserve – for your remaining days to look for Amazonian critters and meet the locals.

Two Weeks

Follow the above itinerary but take the trip further. You could make brief visits to Raleighvallen, the upper Suriname River and Brownsberg Nature Reserve or visit several places on the upper Suriname, 'island-hopping' along the river to different resorts. Taking the route south, you may be able to fly back to Paramaribo so you don't have to backtrack. If it's turtle season, consider substituting your time at either Raleighvallen or Brownsberg with a trip to the Galibi Nature Reserve.

Essential Food & Drink

» **Pom** Creole creation using grated *tayer* root, shredded chicken, onion and spices baked into a yummy casserole

» **Roti** Indian flat bread stuffed with all sorts of curries, from potato-heavy vegetarian to chunks of beef

» **Javanese food** Rice-noodle and soup dishes are tasty and cheap

» **Fish** A variety of fresh river fish is the staple in most of the interior and is often served fried or in soup

» **Parbo** The local beer is quite good; it's customary to share a *djogo* (1L bottle) among friends

» **Borgoe** The best local rum, with many types to chose from; the best-seller is lethal Mariënburg White (90% alcohol) that's flavorless in cocktails

» **Pastei** Creole-style chicken pot pie with peas and carrots

» **Moksi-alesi** Mixed boiled rice with salted meat or fish and vegetables – the best include coconut cream

» **Hagelslag** Dutch-style chocolate sprinkles to go on toast for breakfast

Suriname Highlights

1. Explore Maroon culture, swim in the jungle and relax along the **upper Suriname River** (p926)
2. Drive through jungle and savanna, then canoe past Maroon villages to **Raleighvallen** (p927)
3. Listen to unsurpassed jungle knowledge of Amerindian elders in tranquil **Palumeu** (p926)
4. Tread lightly on the beaches at **Galibi Nature Reserve** (p928) where giant leatherback turtles lay their eggs in the sand
5. Marvel at primate-filled forests surrounding an endless, eerie artificial lake at **Brownsberg and Brokopondo** (p926)
6. Stroll along **Paramaribo's** (p920) Unesco-listed historic waterfront lined with stately colonial architecture
7. Discover the **Commewijne River** (p925) via bicycle or boat tour, and possibly spot pink river dolphins

Paramaribo

POP 250,000

Amsterdam meets the Wild West in Paramaribo, the most vivacious and striking capital in the Guianas. Black-and-white colonial Dutch buildings line grassy squares, wafts of spices escape from Indian roti shops and mingle with car exhaust, while Maroon artists sell colorful paintings outside somber Dutch forts. Inhabitants of Paramaribo, locally known as 'Parbo,' are proud of their multiethnicity and the fact that they live in a city where mosques and synagogues play happy neighbors. In 2002 the historical inner city was listed as a Unesco World Heritage Site.

Sights & Activities

This capital of colonial architecture and lively main streets could fill two days with exploration. Southwest along Waterkant from Fort Zeelandia are some of the city's most impressive colonial buildings, mostly merchants' houses built after the fires of 1821 and 1832. The streets inland from here, particularly Lim-a-Postraat, have many old wooden buildings, some restored, others in picturesque decay. Especially interesting are **Mosque Keizerstraat**, the biggest mosque in the Caribbean, and the expansive **Neveh Shalom synagogue**, completed in 1723 – sitting harmoniously side by side on Keizerstraat.

Central Market MARKET

(Waterkant) Not for the fainthearted, the frenzied central market is divided into distinct areas: the meats, fish, fruits and vegetable section on the main floor (including an Asian and Indian sprawl) and a bazaar-feeling clothing area, on the second. But the most interesting part is the 'Witch's Market' (aka the Maroon Market) in a separate entrance just to the west on Waterkant, that sells all varieties of herbs, bones, shells and mysterious concoctions.

TWEETY FEST

On Sunday mornings, people – mostly men – engage in peaceful yet secretly cutthroat bird-song competitions on the Onafhankelijkheidsplein. Everyone brings their favorite *twatwa* (song bird), usually a seed finch purchased from Amerindian people in the interior. The *twatwa* that can best belt it out wins. Something of a national obsession, this competition is well worth observing, though its popularity is petering out.

Fort Zeelandia MUSEUM

(⌚9am-5pm Tue-Sun, museum 9am-2pm Tue-Sat, 10am-2pm Sun, tours in Dutch 11am & 12:30pm Sun) Inside well-restored Fort Zeelandia, a star-shaped 18th-century fort built on the site where the first colonists alighted, is the worthwhile **Stichting Surinaams Museum** (☎42-5871; admission SR$5), featuring colonial-era relics, period rooms and temporary exhibitions.

Het Surinaamsch Rumhuis DISTILLERY

(☎473-3344; www.rumhuis.com; 18 Cornelis Jongbawstraat; 1½-/2-hour tours SR$50/65 per person; ⌚Fri by appointment only) Tours here begin with a 'happy shot' then it's through the distillery, rum museum and tasting room where you will learn to sample each variety like a pro. Finish with cocktails on the patio. Shorter tours skip the distillery.

Zin Resort SWIMMING POOL

(☎47-2224; www.zinresort.sr; Van Rosevetkade 20; SR$15) Beat the heat at this party-vibe swimming pool next to a cocktail bar. Skip the rooms, but on weeknights there are excellent value three-course dinner specials for SR$20 that include the use of the pool.

Onafhankelijkheidsplein SQUARE

Surrounding the centrally located Onafhankelijkheidsplein (Independence Square) are the contrasting stately 18th-century **Presidential Palace** (open to the public November 25 only) and aging colonial government buildings. Behind the palace is the **Palmentuin**, a shady haven of tall royal palms.

Tours

Suriname's exemplary national parks, reserves and cultural offerings are most easily accessed via tours with Paramaribo-based operators. You should shop around, but not too much – prices are competitive, and most of the agencies work together to assemble the minimum number of participants for trips. All charge 5% extra for credit card payments.

METS ECOTOUR

(Movement for Eco-Tourism in Suriname; ☎47-7088; www.surinamevacations.com; JF Nassylaan 2) Organized and easily the most professional and eco-minded agency, METS donates proceeds to conservation and conducts a wide range of trips, including sightseeing tours of Paramaribo (SR$150, full day), nearby plantations (from SR$300) and jungle expeditions to the deep interior (from SR$3000, five days).

Orange Suriname TOURS
(☎42-6409; www.orangesuriname.com; Van Sommelsdijckstraat; ⏰9am-6pm) A comprehensive and professional company with extremely knowledgeable and helpful staff.

Waterproof Suriname BOAT TOUR, ECOTOUR
(☎96-2927; www.waterproofsuriname.com) Runs laid-back boat cruises (SR$120) to see river dolphins (sometimes combined with walks around the Commewijne River plantations) as well as day trips to watch sea turtles at Matapica Beach (SR$670). The company will pick you up; it doesn't have an office.

Cardy Adventures BIKING
(☎42-2518; www.cardyadventures.com; Cornelis Jongbawstraat 31; Bike rental per day SR$17-35; ⏰8am-7pm Mon-Sat) Has bike tours to the nearby Commewijne plantations as well as longer tours, of up to 10 days, to the interior.

Fietsen in Suriname BIKING
(☎52-0781; www.fietseninsuriname.com; Zus & Zo; Bike rental per day SR$65-110) A slick new bike tour and rental agency at Zus & Zo guesthouse. Self-guided bike maps are SR$15 and tours start at SR$215.

Stinasu TOURS
(Stichting Natuurbehoud Suriname; ☎47-6597; www.stinasu.sr; Cornelis Jongbawstraat 14) The Foundation for Nature Conservation in Suriname runs lodges (many in a bad state of repair) as well as guided trips to Brownsberg (from SR$290), the Galibi or Matapica turtle reserves (from SR$670), and Raleighvallen/Voltzberg/Foengoe Island (SRD$1715, four days).

Sleeping

Guesthouses in Paramaribo are roughly the equivalent of hostels in neighboring countries and are the most inexpensive lodging options in town. Some guesthouses only have cold showers, which is not a big problem in Parbo's hot climate.

TOP CHOICE **Zus & Zo** GUESTHOUSE $
(☎52-0905; www.zusenzosuriname.com; Grote Combéweg 13A; r from SR$65; ❄📶) A backpacker's hostel that can also please slightly more upscale travelers, the bright and inviting Zus & Zo (say it 10 times fast!) has rooms with a shared hot-water bathroom on the top floor of a classic Paramaribo colonial-style house. Use the kitchen to make your own meals or head to the ground-floor cafe.

It sometimes holds music and other artsy events and runs the city's best gift/souvenir shop. The staff can help you arrange almost any excursion in Suriname.

Guesthouse TwenTy4 GUESTHOUSE $
(☎42-0751; www.twenty4suriname.com; Jessurunstraat 24; r from SR$65; 📶) Owned by the Zus & Zo folks, the TwenTy4 has more period charm but is less equipped (no air-con). The homey house is on a central, quiet backstreet, and the whole place has a relaxed, welcoming vibe. You can get breakfast (SR$17) and beer and set up your activities with the help of the staff.

Eco-Resort HOTEL $$
(☎42-5522; www.ecoresortinn.com; Cornelis Jongbawstraat 16; r incl breakfast SR$280-380; ❄@📶🏊) What makes this modern and professional hotel 'eco' is not clear, but the price includes a buffet breakfast, free airport transfer with a two-night stay and use of the swanky facilities at the Hotel Torarica. The more expensive 'river view' rooms don't really have river views, but they are set closer to the water than the standards.

Un Pied A Terre GUESTHOUSE $
(☎47 0488, 0867 2551; www.un-pied-a-terre.org; Costerstraat 59; s/d from Euro20/25; ❄📶) A gorgeous classified World Heritage building with all the paint-chipped, louvered-widowed, creaky-wood floor charm that entails. Roel, who runs the place, is super-friendly and will cook meals on request. Only the lower level rooms are ensuite and have air-con but the prettiest choices are upstairs.

Guesthouse Albergo Alberga GUESTHOUSE $
(☎52-0050; www.guesthousealbergoalberga.com; Lim-a-Postraat 13; s/d SR$70/90, d with air-con SR$150; ❄📶🏊) This long-running favorite is situated on a quintessentially colonial Parbo street in an endearing World Heritage–listed building. Some rooms are quite spacious. The little pool out back is great for a dunk after a long day exploring Parbo.

Hotel Torarica HOTEL $$$
(☎47-1500; www.torarica.com; Rietbergplein 1; r from SR$525; ❄@📶🏊) Las Vegas meets

Paramaribo

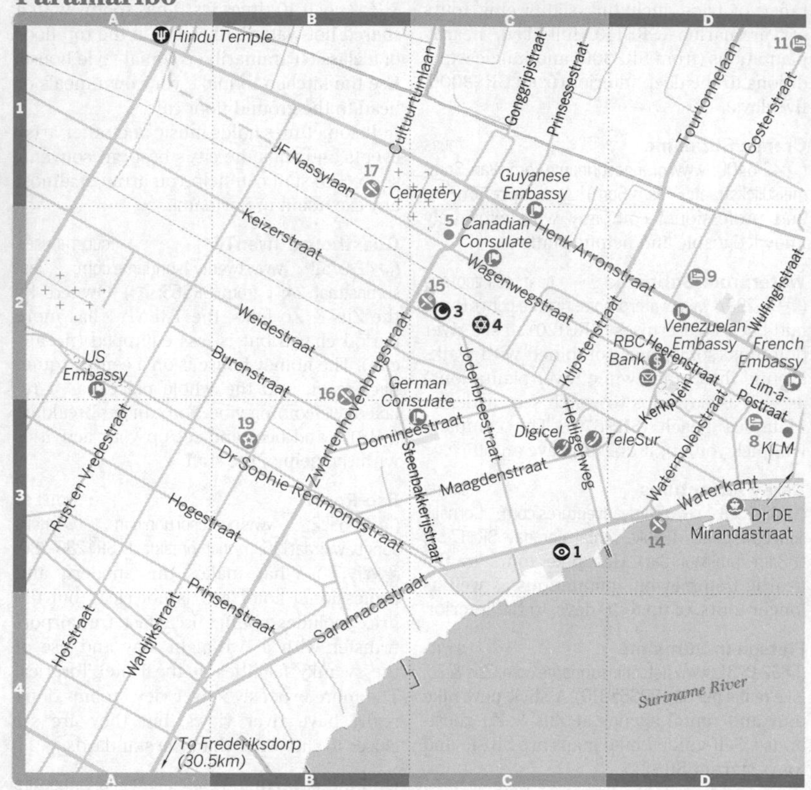

Suriname at the mirrored, chandeliered and recently remodeled Hotel Torarica. It's known for its casino, but the big round pool and waterfront gazebo are pleasant retreats from Parbo's hot and bustling streets.

Eating

Tourists frequent 'the strip' across from Hotel Torarica, which has restaurants to fit all budgets – take your pick of Dutch pancake shops, Indonesian, Creole and others. The cheapest city-center options are at the frenetic **central market** and Indonesian stalls along Waterkant. **Eating in Suriname** (www.eteninsuriname.com) is a useful website with information on restaurants in Paramaribo.

TOP CHOICE Blaugrond JAVANESE $
(Blaugrond; dishes SR$15-30; ⌚dinner) Family-run Javanese eateries line this laid-back residential street about 10 minutes by taxi from downtown Paramaribo. **Rena**, **Mirioso**, **Pawiro** and **Saoto** are some of the better known spots but any one will serve cheap and delicious noodle, rice and soup dishes. The ambiance alone is worth the trip.

Zus & Zo INTERNATIONAL $$
(Grote Combéweg 13A; meals from SR$30; ⌚9am-11pm; 📶) This guesthouse is actually more well-known for its restaurant and bar that serve up some of the best food and cocktails in town. Dishes range from Surinamese soups to French cheese pies, burgers and salads. Live music is held here on occasion.

Jiji's SURINAMESE $$
(Waterkant; mains around SR$50; ⌚6-11pm) Upstairs in a building next to De Waag, this is a casual spot to enjoy great food while overlooking the river. Try the pastas, meat and seafood dishes in creative sauces, some of which use local rum.

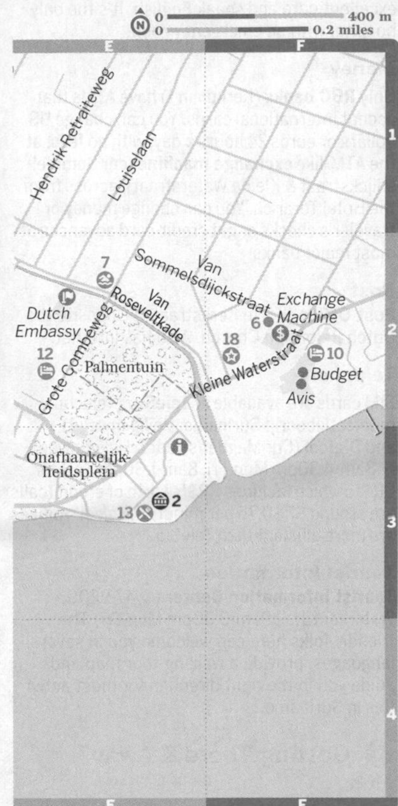

Paramaribo

Sights

1	Central Market	C3
2	Fort Zeelandia	E3
3	Mosque Keizerstraat	C2
4	Neveh Shalom Synagogue	C2
	Stichting Surinaams Museum	(see 2)

Activities, Courses & Tours

	Fietsen in Suriname	(see 12)
5	METS	C2
6	Orange Suriname	F2
7	Zin Resort	E2

Sleeping

8	Guesthouse Albergo Alberga	D3
9	Guesthouse TwenTy4	D2
10	Hotel Torarica	F2
11	Un Pied A Terre	D1
12	Zus & Zo	E2

Eating

13	De Gadri	E3
14	De Waag Restaurant	D3
	Jiji's	(see 14)
15	Joosje Rotishop	C2
16	Power Smoothie	B2
17	Restaurant Dumpling #1	B1
	Zus & Zo	(see 12)

Entertainment

18	Café-Bar 't Vat	F2
19	Club Touché	B3

Joosje Rotishop INDIAN $
(Zwartenhovenbrugstraat 9; roti from SR$10; ⏲8:30am-10pm Mon-Sat; ❄) Serving delicious roti since 1942, this is the locals' favorite for a sit-down, air-conditioned meal. There's also a convenient take-out counter.

De Gadri SURINAMESE $
(Zeelandiaweg 1; mains SR$13-26; ⏲Mon-Fri 8am-10pm, Sat 11am-10pm) This quiet, outdoor eatery overlooking the river has Paramaribo's best Creole food as well as exceptionally friendly service. We recommend you try the delicious peanut, cassava or banana soup, accompanied by roast chicken and *pom,* a kind a casserole.

Power Smoothie CAFE $
(☎47-7047; Zwartenhovenbrugstraat 62; smoothies from SR$10, sandwiches from SD$12; ⏲8am-9pm Mon-Sat) Fresh and nourishing juices, smoothies, sandwiches, wraps and salads make this little eat-in or take-away place a great pit stop any time of day. In true Suriname fashion you can add a shot of rum to your beverage along with the standard protein powders and other extras.

De Waag Restaurant ITALIAN $$$
(☎47-4514; Waterkant 5; lunch SR$15, dinner SR$35-70; ⏲9am-3pm & 6-11pm Mon-Sat) This chic restaurant located in an old, renovated weight house from Parbo's shipping heyday, serves stacked sandwiches and Italian specialties like lasagna and tortellini. While the food isn't anything that special, the setting is lovely.

Restaurant Dumpling #1 CHINESE $
(JF Nassylaan 12; mains SR$12-35; ⏲7am-2pm & 5-11pm Tue-Sun) The name says it all. Don't miss the succulent dumplings and other Chinese classics, like steamed spare ribs and tofu soup pot.

Drinking & Entertainment

Casinos are everywhere in Paramaribo and are extremely popular with locals and Dutch tourists. Tuck inside a few to see a different side of the city. This is also a town that loves to party, with hopping nightlife from Wednesday through Saturday. For cheap drinks with locals, head to the outdoor stalls near Platte Brug on Waterkant.

FREE **Havana Lounge** CLUB
(☎40-2258; Hogerhuystraat 13) The club of the moment is at its best on Thursday, when salsa plays till 1am, then switches from reggae to hip-hop. Expect a meat market.

Café-Bar 't Vat BAR, CAFE
(Kleine Waterstraat 1; ⏲8am-1am Mon-Thu, 8am-3am Fri, 9am-3am Sat, 9am-1am Sun) The night begins at Café-Bar 't Vat, an outdoor bar/cafe with occasional live music.

Club Touché CLUB
(cnr Waldijkstraat & Dr Sophie Redmondstraat; ⏲10pm-3am Wed-Sat) Dance the night away with techno downstairs and salsa upstairs. Wednesday is the biggest night.

Information

Dangers & Annoyances

Avoid quiet streets and secluded areas after dark; the Palmentuin and Watremolenstraat in particular are known for drug dealing and robberies at night. Watch for pickpockets around the market area, even in daylight hours.

Internet Access

All the hotels and guesthouses listed have free wi-fi, which is also available at many more upscale restaurants and cafes around town. There are a few internet cafes around Paramaribo, charging around SR$3 per hour.

Medical Services

Academisch Ziekenhuis (AZ; ☎44-2222; Flustraat; ⏲6-10pm Mon-Fri, 9am-10pm Sat & Sun) Has general practitioners who provide excellent care and speak English. It's the only hospital with an emergency room.

PAY WITH EUROS

Most Paramaribo businesses take euros, and most tours and guesthouses quote prices in euros only. Know your exchange rates and make sure you're not paying more than you would in SR$ or vice versa.

Money

Only **RBC banks** (Kerkplein 1) have ATMs that accept international cards. You can change US dollars or euros 24 hours a day, with no fees, at the ATM-like **exchange machine** (cnr Sommelsdijckstraat & Kleine Waterstraat), across from the Hotel Torarica. You can change money or traveler's checks or get credit-card advances at most major banks.

Post

Post Office (Korte Kerkstraat 1) Opposite the Dutch Reformed Church. Also has internet.

Telephone

SIM cards are available at **TeleSur** (Telecommunicatiebedrijf Suriname; Heiligenweg 1) and **Digicel** (Cnr Magdenstraat & Heligenweg; ⏲8am-4:30pm Mon-Fri, 8am-1:30pm Sat) for SR$15 which includes SR$5 worth of credit (calls are around SR$0.75 per minute). Digicel's offices are more efficient than TeleSur.

Tourist Information

Tourist Information Center (☎47-9200; Waterkant 1; ⏲9am-3:30pm Mon-Fri) The friendly folks here can welcome you in several languages, provide a walking-tour map and guide you in the right direction for most activities in Suriname.

Getting There & Away

Air

There are two airports in Paramaribo: nearby Zorg-en-Hoop (for domestic and Guyana flights) and the larger Johan Pengel International Airport (for all other international flights) – which is usually referred to as Zanderij – 45km south of Parbo.

Bus & Minibus

Minibuses to Brownsberg (SR$50, three hours) leave from the corner of Prinsenstraat and Saramacastraat. Public buses to Nieuw Nickerie (SR$15, four hours) and other western destinations leave throughout the day from the corner of Dr Sophie Redmondstraat and Hofstraat; for a private minibus (SR$50), ask your hotel for a list of companies that will pick you up. To Albina, public buses (SR$8.50, three hours, 140km) leave hourly and private buses (SR$30, 3½ hours) leave when full from Waterkant at the foot of Heiligenweg. There are connecting boats to Albina and Nieuw Nickerie.

Car

Both **Avis** (☎42-1567; www.avis.com) and **Budget** (☎42-4631; www.budgetsuriname.com) have offices at the Hotel Torarica and the airport. Compact cars rent from SR$90 per day, and 4WDs are available.

Taxi

Taxis are a fast and many work on a share system. Most share taxis are minivans that hold up to eight people and if you leave in the morning they fill quickly. Expect to pay SR$70 per person to Albina and SR$100 per person to Nieuw Nickerie. Ask at your hotel for a list of drivers and/or to call them for you.

Getting Around

Bicycle

In good Dutch fashion, many people see Parbo and its environs, including the old plantations across the Suriname River, on bicycles. Helmets are rarely worn and are hard to rent. Road and mountain bikes are available for rent from SR$17 per day.

Bus

Most of Parbo's buses leave from Heiligenweg. Ask at points of departure or at your guesthouse for departure times.

Taxi

Taxis are usually reasonably priced but unmetered and negotiable (a short trip will cost around SR$6).

Water Taxi

The Paramaribo–Meerzorg bridge has displaced ferry service, but fast and frequent **water taxis** (boats SR$25) still leave from **Platte Brug** on Waterkant just south of Keizerstraat.

GETTING INTO TOWN

From Johan Pengel International Airport (aka Zanderij), 45km south of Parbo, you can grab a taxi into town (SR$100, one hour). Airport shuttles organized through your hotel cost SR$65. Still cheaper, minibuses go to/from Zanderij (SR$6) and the Zorg-en-Hoop airfield (SR$4) from Heiligenweg in daytime hours only. A taxi from Zorg-en-Hoop is about SR$20.

Commewijne River

Opposite Paramaribo, the banks of the Commewijne River are lined with old plantation properties divided by canals and strewn with the remains of coffee, cacao and cane-processing buildings.

Many visitors rent bikes to spend a full day touring the well-defined routes past the plantations. The most popular route crosses the two rivers using water taxis to reach **Frederiksdorp** (☎45-3083; www.frederiksdorp.com; r per person incl full board SR$190), a plantation complex that has been lovingly restored and turned into a hotel and restaurant. **Fort Nieuw Amsterdam** is the place to go to see artifacts of the slave trade and an impressive Dutch-engineered system of locks holding back the river. Beautiful **Peperpot**, about 10km from Parbo, stands in eerie dilapidation across the Meerzorg bridge and is a favorite bird-watchers' locale. Cardy Adventures (p921), Fietsen In Suriname (p921) and the Tourist Information Center (p924) can provide maps and information about the routes.

Tours

Popular boat tours are available to the same sites you can get to by bike. These can save you from the heat, but they are expensive and – without the thrill of exploration – are much less exciting.

North of Fort Nieuw Amsterdam, Matapica is a tranquil and almost mosquito-free beach where sea turtles come ashore April to August. Tours generally reach it by boating through the plantation canals and a swamp rich in birdlife. Stinasu (p921) runs a small camp there.

Spotting friendly faced river dolphins along the Commewijne is also popular, especially at sunset, and most plantation boat tours will attempt to point them out to passengers when passing through the dolphins' feeding grounds. One-day boat excursions dedicated to dolphin-viewing are available year-round.

Cola Creek

It certainly doesn't advertise itself as such, but **Colakreek** (☎47-2621; www.surinamevacations.com; hammock lodge/tent SR$45/60, cabins SR$295) could uniquely be considered an Airport Jungle Lodge. Got an early flight out or late flight in? Instead of driving into Paramaribo, go straight into the jungle 6km to the south of the airport – then maybe even stay a few days.

Run by METS (p920), this beautiful 'recreation center' is on a sandy bank along Pepsi-colored Cola Creek and offers everything from inexpensive hammock space and tents to more luxurious cabins. Swimming and jungle walks are the main activities and it's also possible get a pass to stay just for the day (good for evening flight departures). Be warned that it can get very busy with locals on weekends and holidays.

Brownsberg Nature Reserve & Brokopondo

Brownsberg's park headquarters are located on a high plateau overlooking Brokopondo, about 100km from Paramaribo along a red-dirt highway. Monkeys seem to be everywhere, whether red howlers growling in the canopy or precious black-bearded sakis checking you out from a tree limb. Stinasu (p921) has rustic lodges (from SR$350) for groups, and camping (SR$42) and hammock sites (SR$30) at the headquarters.

Brokopondo is really a man-made reservoir, created in 1964 when the government dammed the Suriname River to produce hydroelectric power for processing bauxite. Views of storm clouds moving in over the 1500-sq-km lake are breathtaking, but a closer look reveals a rainforest graveyard, in which dead trees stick up over the water's surface from what was once the forest floor. The park has some interesting displays explaining how the dam project required relocating thousands of mostly Maroon and Amerindian people as well as hundreds of thousands of animals.

It's relatively easy to visit Brownsberg on your own: take an Atjoni-bound bus run from the Saramacastraat bus station near the central market in Paramaribo and ask to be let off at the village of Brownsberg (SR$60, three hours). From here, arrange in advance for Stinasu to pick you up and drive you to the park (SR$70, 30 minutes); several Parbo-based tour agencies also do Brownsberg as a (very) long day trip.

Upper Suriname River

This is Suriname's cultural grab bag, where you can stay in river lodges on stunning white sand beaches amid the jungle and get a glimpse into the neighboring Maroon or Amerindian villages. All locally run, the lodges hope to create a sustainable future for these remote communities that would otherwise rely on the logging and hunting industries.

Lodges range from luxurious (swimming pools, spacious restaurant/bars and fine linens) to basic (hammock hooks under a roof, a dorm full of mattresses and family-style dining), with nightly prices ranging from SR$60 or less for hammock space, to SR$300 or more for a bungalow.

Swimming and village visits are the main activities, and the more established places put on dance or live music performances at night. Don't miss a visit to the interesting and well-managed **Maroon Museum** (Marronmuseum Saamaka; Kumalu; entry SR$20; ⏲10am-3pm).

Awarradam can be reached on tours run by METS (p920). A tour for four days and

DIY UPPER SURINAME RIVER EXPLORATION

If you're up for a real Surinamese adventure without the massive price tag of a tour, grab your hammock, sunscreen and insect repellant, and head down the Upper Suriname River by boat. Eco-lodges run by the Maroon villages along this stretch are popping up everywhere, so there are plenty of places to stay.

From Paramaribo, take an early morning bus to Atjoni (SR$70, 4½ hours; buses leave when full) from the Saramacastraat bus station next to the market (note that Atjoni is often shown as Pokigron on maps). Everyone getting off the bus in Atjoni will be taking the boat to their villages (count on paying SD$50) so hop on with them and take your pick of where you want to stop (see above for more details). If you don't want to backtrack, several airstrips along the way offer regular connections to Paramaribo, and some tour-agency charters might be able to offer you a seat as well. With time you can potentially make it all the way to Awarradam. Bring plenty of cash as no one down here will take credit cards.

Stichting Lodeholders Boven Suriname (Association of Saramacaan Lodge Holders; www.upper-suriname.com), maintains an online map of villages and lodges, although it's not always up to date. Bryan the owner of Zus & Zo (p921) in Paramaribo is another great resource.

GETTING TO GUYANA

Getting to the Border

From Nieuw Nickerie it's about 45 minutes along a paved road to South Drain to catch the Canawaima ferry (SR$30, 25 minutes, 10am and noon daily) across the Corantijn River to Moleson Creek, Guyana. There are also direct minibuses to/from Paramaribo to South Drain (SR$60, 3½ hours) that link up with the ferry arrivals/departures. If the road between Nieuw Nickerie and South Drain is impassable because of rain, don't be tempted to follow the locals and 'do the backtrack' – this involves crossing the Corentyne on small motorboats to Springlands, Guyana, and is illegal. Cops tend to turn a blind eye to backtracking locals but will arrest foreigners who do it. Your hotel or your driver from Parbo will know the road situation and can help you make other arrangements if needed.

Moving On

After getting stamped in and passing a customs check in Guyana, you'll find several minibuses to Georgetown (G$2500, three hours).

Guyana is an hour behind Suriname; remember to set your watch back one hour.

An easy way to get directly to Georgetown from Paramaribo is by bus. The driver, Champ, leaves Paramaribo at between 4am and 5am to meet the ferry in South Drain; the journey takes nine to 12 hours, depending on the roads and total cost for the ride (not including the ferry) is SR$120 or G$7000.

three nights costs €535 including all meals and activities.

Some other better-known Maroon villages with lodges include **Kininipaati** (☎885 9255; www.kinini-island.com; per person SR$50), **Anaula** (3-day/2-night packages incl transport per person SR$1025) and **Danpaati** (☎47 1113; www.danpaati.net; 3-day/2-night packages incl transport per person SR$1430).

For Amerindian culture, see **Palumeu** (which can also be reached on tours run by METS) on the stunning banks of the Boven Tapanahoni River off the Upper Suriname.

Central Suriname Nature Reserve

Any map of Suriname reveals huge swaths of protected areas. One of the biggest, covering 12% of Suriname's land area, is this 1.6-million-hectare reserve, established in 1998 with a US$1 million donation from Conservation International. Around 40% of Central Suriname Nature Reserve's plants and animals are found only in the Guianas.

Raleighvallen (Raleigh Falls) is a low, long staircase of cascading water on the upper Coppename River, about two hours upriver from the nearest Maroon village. Resident wildlife include free-swinging spider monkeys, electric eels and Guiana cock-of-the-rock, a spectacular blood-orange bird. Stinasu (p921) has tourist lodges – accessible by a flight or a five-hour drive and two-hour boat ride (via tour only) – on Foengoe Island next to the falls. Voltzberg is a 240m granite dome accessible by a 2½-hour jungle trail and then a steep ascent – the 360-degree views of the jungle from the top are simply astounding.

Kabalebo River

Way out west near the Guyana border, remote **Kabalebo** (☎42-6532; www.kabalebo.com; all-incl 2-night standard packages per person SR$1862; 🏊) is in the middle of pristine jungle. Accommodation ranges from an economical 'jungle camp,' to some of the most private and luxurious retreats in the country. Tons of activities are on offer, from fishing to wildlife-spotting and hiking to kayaking.

Nieuw Nickerie

POP 13,100

This bustling border town of wide streets was once a major balata collecting center, although now it's mostly a banana and rice production hub with a large port. It's also the last stop before Guyana and the departure point for exploring **Bigi Pan**, a swampy reservoir known for caimans, scarlet ibis and more than 100 other birds.

GETTING TO FRENCH GUIANA

Destroyed during the Maroon rebellion of the 1980s and still recovering, Albina (population 4000) is the last stop before crossing the Marowijne River to St Laurent du Maroni, French Guiana. Some travelers pass through here on tours to the Galibi Reserve to see turtles, but the town is notorious for crime and there's little reason to stay.

Getting to the Border

Share taxis (SR$70, two hours), minibuses (SR$30, 2½ hours) and public buses (SR$8.50, three hours) to/from Paramaribo leave to/from central Albina.

At the Border

Motorboats leave on demand from the Albina ferry dock for the crossing (SR$50; 10 minutes) during daylight hours, and are the way most people without cars cross the river. The French **car ferry** (per passenger SR$50; 8am & 5pm Mon-Fri, 8:30am & 9:30am Sat, 3pm & 4pm Sun) crosses the Marowijne River from Albina to St Laurent du Maroni, French Guiana, in 30 minutes several times per day. From St Laurent du Maroni, there are usually taxis that can take you into town from where you can rent a car or catch a bus to Cayenne (if you arrive early enough in the day, otherwise plan on spending the night). Be sure to get your exit and entrance stamps at immigration at the ferry docks on both sides of the river.

Note there is no place to change money in St Laurent du Maroni but there is an ATM. There are plenty of moneychangers in Albina who will approach you before you cross – know your rates in advance.

To stay overnight, the **Concord Hotel** (23-2345; Wilhelmina- straat 3; d SR$105;) is a good, small and clean motel-style place.

All buses and minibuses arrive at and leave from the market. Government buses travel to Paramaribo (SR$14, four hours) at 6am and 1pm daily, and a private bus (SR$20) leaves when full after the first government bus leaves. Taxis to Paramaribo (SR$90 per person) take three to four hours. Minibuses to South Drain (SR$14) for the ferry to Guyana leave at 8am, and it's best to reserve with the driver the day before; your hotel can help with this.

Galibi & Coppename Nature Reserves

Galibi's turtle-nesting area hosts hordes of sea turtles, including the giant leatherback, during egg-laying season (April through August). You can get there from Albina with permission from members of the local Carib community and a hired canoe, or more easily from Paramaribo with the tour operator, Stinasu.

The Coppename Nature Reserve, at the mouth of the Coppename River, is home to the endangered manatee and is a haven for bird-watchers. Stinasu organizes trips by request.

UNDERSTAND SURINAME

Suriname Today

Suriname's president since 2010 is Desiré Bouterse, a former coup leader who in the 1980s civil war period was the country's military-backed dictator. In 2012 the Suriname parliament passed an amnesty law protecting Bouterse from the trial for 1982's 'December Murders' (see opposite). Despite this history, Suriname loves their multiethnic president, particularly the younger generations who weren't alive during the civil war.

The Netherlands ended their security aid to Suriname with the election of Bouterse, who was convicted in 1999 of smuggling over 1000lb of cocaine into the Netherlands. If he should alight on Dutch soil, he will be arrested.

Suriname relies on bauxite for 70% of its foreign exchange. Agriculture, particularly irrigated rice cultivation and bananas, is a major industry for the republic, and the fishing industry is growing. The country is also making a conscious effort to develop ecotourism in the interior.

History

Suriname was the last outpost of what was once a substantial Dutch presence in South America. During the 19th century, Indians and Indonesians (locally referred to as 'Javanese') arrived as indentured plantation workers.

Despite limited autonomy, Suriname remained a colony until 1954, when the area became a self-governing state; it gained independence in 1975. A coup in 1980, led by Sergeant Major (later Lieutenant Colonel) Desiré Bouterse, brought a military regime to power. Bouterse was later brought to trial for ordering the execution of 15 prominent opponents in Fort Zeelandia – an event now called the 'December Murders' – in 1982. In 1986 the government carried out a campaign to suppress Maroon rebellion, led by Ronnie Brunswijk and his Jungle Commando (the Maroon military). Many of those loyal to Brunswijk fled to French Guiana as their villages were destroyed.

In 1987 a civilian government was elected, but it was deposed by a bloodless coup in 1990. Another civilian government led by Ronald Venetiaan was elected in 1991 and it signed a peace treaty with the Jungle Commando and other armed bands in 1992.

Venetiaan was re-elected in May 2000 and held office until 2010. This period was marked by economic difficulty and unrest: in 2004, the Suriname dollar replaced the Dutch Guider; flooding in 2006 caused a national disaster and left up to 20,000 people homeless; and in 2009, government troops were sent to gold mining areas near Albina to quell anti-Chinese and anti-Brazilian protests.

Culture

Suriname is a cultural free-for-all of incredibly friendly and generous people. Paramaribo's level of acceptance and unity is primarily undisturbed by religious and racial tension, which is remarkable given the intimacy of so many groups living in such a small corner of the world; however, Maroons and Amerindians in the interior live with high poverty levels and fewer educational opportunities.

Many Surinamese live or have lived in the Netherlands, either to enjoy its greater economic opportunities or to escape military repression, and are consequently knowledgeable of European trends.

About 40% of Suriname's well-integrated population are nominally Christian, but some also adhere to traditional African beliefs. Hindus compose 26% of the population (most of the East Indian community), while 19% are Muslim (ethnic Indonesians plus a minority of East Indian origin). A small number are Buddhists, Jews and followers of Amerindian rcligions. In terms of ethnicities – 37% of the population are Indian, 31% are Creole, 15% are Javanese, 10% are Maroons, 2% are Amerindian, 2% are Chinese and 1% are Dutch (the remaining 2% percent are 'other').

Some cultural forms – such as gamelan music, often heard at special events – derive from the Indonesian immigrant populations. Other art forms that visitors enjoy include intricate Amerindian basketry and wood carvings by Maroons, who are widely regarded as the best carvers in tropical America.

Environment

Suriname is divided into a coastal region and dense tropical forest and savannas. To its west, the Corantijn (Corentyne in Guyana) River forms the border, disputed in its most southerly reaches with Guyana; the Marowijne (Maroni in French Guiana) and Litani Rivers form the border with French Guiana.

The majority of Surinamese inhabit the Atlantic coastal plain, where most of the country's few roads are located. The nearby Afobaka Dam created one of the world's largest (1550 sq km) reservoirs, Brokopondo, on the upper Suriname River.

Being mostly rainforest, Suriname has diverse wildlife, from the flashy jaguar and black caiman to humble agouti and squirrel monkeys. Birders flock to see a wide range of bird species including the red ibis and harpy eagle.

SURVIVAL GUIDE

Directory A–Z

Accommodations

Fairly affordable hotels and guesthouses are readily found in Paramaribo, starting at SR$60, while sleeping in the interior can involve more rustic accommodations through to luxurious eco-lodges.

Activities

Suriname's best activity is experiencing nature and culture in the interior. Birdwatching and other wildlife-spotting adventures are once-in-a-lifetime experiences, as many of the critters are endemic or more prolific in this big, healthy swathe of jungle, and boating and trekking opportunities are abundant. The accessible Maroon cultures are something unique to the country. People explore by bike, but only in areas around the coastal cities.

Books

The most popular book on Suriname is Mark Plotkin's *Tales of a Shaman's Apprentice*, which also includes information on Brazil, Venezuela and the other Guianas.

The Guide to Suriname by Els Schellekens and famous local photographer Roy Tjin is published in English and sometimes available at Vaco Press.

How Dear Was the Sugar? by Cynthia McLeod, perhaps Suriname's most important historical novelist, explores the sugarcane industry of the 18th century.

Business Hours

General business hours are 7:30am to 3pm weekdays, with perhaps a few hours on Saturday. Most restaurants serve lunch from around 11am to 2:30pm, and dinner from about 6pm to 10pm. A small number of places open for breakfast at 8am.

SLEEPING PRICE RANGES

The following price ranges refer to a double room with bathroom in high season.

$ less than SR$150

$$ SR$150 to SR$400

$$$ over SR$400

Opening hours are not listed in reviews unless they vary widely from these.

Electricity

Plugs are European standard two round prong. Currents are 110/220V, 60Hz.

Embassies & Consulates

The embassies and consulates listed below are all in Paramaribo.

Brazilian Embassy (☎40-0200; www.brazil-embassy.net/suriname-paramaribo.html; Maratakkastraat 2, Zorg-en-Hoop)

Canadian Consulate (☎47-1222; Wagenwegstraat 50)

Dutch Embassy (☎47-7211; http://suriname.nlambassade.org; Van Roseveltkade 5)

French Embassy (☎47-6455; www.ambafrance-sr.org; Henk Arronstraat 5-7, 2nd fl)

German Consulate (☎47-1150; www.german-embassy.com/suriname-paramaribo.html; Domineestraat 34-36)

Guyanese Embassy (☎477895; guyembassy@sr.net; Henk Arronstraat 82)

UK Embassy (☎40-2870; Van't Hogerhuysstraat 9-11, VSH United Bldg)

US Embassy (☎47-2900; http://suriname.usembassy.gov; Dr Sophie Redmondstraat 129) Also responsible for US citizens in French Guiana.

Venezuelan Embassy (☎47-5401; www.embajadavzla.org.sr; Henk Arronstraat 23-25)

Health

A yellow-fever vaccination certificate is technically required for travelers arriving from infected areas, although you probably won't be asked for one. Typhoid and chloroquine-resistant malaria are present in the interior. Tap water is safe to drink in Paramaribo but not elsewhere.

Internet Access

Parbo and Nieuw Nickerie have affordable internet cafes, charging SR$5 to SR$6 per hour. Most guesthouses, hotels and some cafes offer free wi-fi.

Language

Dutch is the official national language, but many people speak Sranan Tongo (similar to Creole), which can be understood fairly well by English speakers once you develop an ear for it. Other languages include Hindi, Urdu,

Javanese, Mandarin, Cantonese and several dialects of both Maroon and Amerindian languages. English is also widely spoken.

Money

Although the official unit of currency is the Surinamese dollar (SR$), some businesses quote prices in euros or US dollars. Most banks will accept major foreign currencies, but you may run into difficulty trying to change Guyanese dollars and Brazilian reales.

RBC ATMs are the most reliable at accepting foreign cards. You can exchange traveler's checks and get credit card advances at RBC banks and some hotels. Major hotels and travel agencies – but hardly anywhere else – accept credit cards (usually for a fee).

Locals are always changing money, and many get fair rates without a transaction fee at the ATM-like **exchange machine** (cnr Sommelsdijckstraat & Kleine Waterstraat) in Paramaribo.

Public Holidays

New Year's Day January 1; the biggest celebration of the year.

Day of the Revolution February 25

Holi Phagwah (Hindu New Year) March/April

Good Friday/Easter Monday March/April

Labor Day May 1

National Union Day/Abolition of Slavery Day July 1

Independence Day November 25

Christmas Day December 25

Boxing Day December 26

Eid-ul-Fitr (Lebaran or Bodo in Indonesian) End of Ramadan; dates vary.

Telephone

The national telephone company is **TeleSur** (Telecommunicatiebedrijf Suriname; Heiligenweg 1), which sells SIM cards, although service is considerably better at **Digicel** (Cnr Magdenstraat & Heligenweg; ⏲8am-4:30pm Mon-Fri, 8am-1:30pm Sat) and the cost is the same (SR$15). There are no area codes in Suriname.

Visas

Visitors from the US, UK, Australia, Canada, New Zealand and Western Europe need to apply for a tourist card (US$25) valid for 90 days and available at any Surinamese Embassy. Longer stays or multiple entries will require a visa – US passport holders must pay US$100 for a five-year multiple-entry visa, while all other nationalities requiring a visa have to pay from US$30 to US$175, depending on the length of stay and number of entries. For up-to-date info and embassy locations check www.surinameembassy.org.

Allow approximately four weeks for a postal visa or tourist card application. The Suriname Consulates in Georgetown (Guyana) and Cayenne (French Guiana) can issue tourist cards within a couple of hours, but visas can take up to five working days. Bring a passport-size photo and your ticket out of South America.

Visitors planning to stay in Suriname for more than 30 days should register at the **Vreemdelingenpolitie** (Immigration Service; ☎40-3609; Laachmonstraat; ⏲7am-2pm Mon-Fri) in Paramaribo within eight days of arrival.

FOOD PRICE RANGES

The following price ranges refer to a standard main course. Most restaurants charge 10% for service; if it's not on the bill, leave between 10% and 15%.

$ less than SR$25

$$ SR$25 to SR$50

$$$ over SR$50

Women Travelers

Female travelers, especially those traveling alone, may encounter harassment from local males, but they are rarely physically threatening. Constant 'hissing' and 'sucking' noises can be annoying, if not truly disconcerting – you will find that ignoring them usually helps.

Getting There & Away

Air

Long-haul international flights arrive at Suriname's outdated Johan Pengal International Airport (more often called Zanderij), while domestic and regional international flights arrive mostly and Zorg-en-Hoop.

The following airlines offer services from Paramaribo:

Blue Wings (☎43-0370; www.bluewingairlines.com; Zorg-en-Hoop) Scheduled and charter services to many domestic destinations.

Gum Air (☎49-8760; www.gumair.com; Kwattaweg 254) Charters dozens of domestic flights and has code shares with **Trans Guyana Airways** (TGA; ☎222-2525; www.transguyana.com; Ogle Aerodome) To/from Georgetown.

KLM (☎47-2421; www.klm.com; Dr DE Mirandastraat 9) Services Amsterdam.

Suriname Airlines (☎43-2700; www.slm.firm.sr; Dr Sophie Redmondstraat 219) One-way destination and fares as follows: Aruba (US$256, two weekly); Belém, Brazil (US$272, three weekly); Curaçao (US$250, three weekly); Georgetown, Guyana (US$159, twice weekly); Port of Spain, Trinidad (US$186, three weekly); Amsterdam (US$1265, up to five weekly) and Miami (US$381, five weekly).

Boat

From Albina (in the east of Suriname) and Nieuw Nickerie, via South Drain (in the west of Suriname), ferries traverse the river borders with French Guiana and Guyana, respectively.

Getting Around

Air

Small planes shuttle people between Paramaribo and remote destinations, including some nature reserves.

Boat

Rivers offer scenic routes to parts of the interior that are otherwise inaccessible. Scheduled services are few, and prices are negotiable. Ferries and launches cross some major rivers, such as the Suriname and the Coppename.

Bus & Minibus

In order from cheapest to priciest, you can choose from scheduled government buses, private minibuses that leave when full from designated points, and minibuses that pick you up from your hotel. Trips to the interior cost significantly more than those on coastal routes.

Car

Suriname's roads are limited and difficult to navigate. Passenger cars can handle the roads along the coast and to Brownsberg, but tracks into the interior are for 4WDs only. Driving is on the left. An international driving permit is required.

Taxi

Shared taxis cover routes along the coast. They can be several times more expensive than minibuses but are markedly faster. Local cab fares are negotiable and reasonable; set a price before getting in. A private taxi to Zanderij International Airport is SR60 and around town expect to pay SR5–10. A shared taxi to the French Guiana border is around SR70.

Uruguay

Includes »

Best Places to Eat

» Mercado del Puerto (p940)

» La Fonda del Pesca (p955)

» Lentas Maravillas (p945)

» Cero Stress (p958)

» Dueto (p940)

» Medio Mundo (p947)

Best Places to Stay

» El Viajero Hostel (p944)

» Red Hostel (p937)

» Tas D'Viaje Hostel (p955)

» El Diablo Tranquilo (p958)

Why Go?

Now more than ever, Uruguay is a country that moves to its own grooves. While nearby Argentina and Bolivia lurch from one crisis to the next, Uruguay as a nation moves forward much like its citizens – calm and self-assured. Social reforms are moving along nicely and, while there will always be complaints, much of the population seems pretty happy.

Traveling in Uruguay has never been easier. The excellent hostel scene, extensive bus network, good restaurants and abundant campsites make it a backpacker's dream. Even world-class destinations such as Colonia del Sacramento and Punta del Este offer abundant cheap sleeps in all but the absolute peak periods.

People come for the wild, surf-pounded beaches, for celeb-spotting at Punta and the history-soaked smugglers' port of Colonia. They stay for the people – warm, open and sincere folk who have constructed one of South America's most progressive societies. And when they leave, they almost always say they're coming back.

When to Go

Montevideo

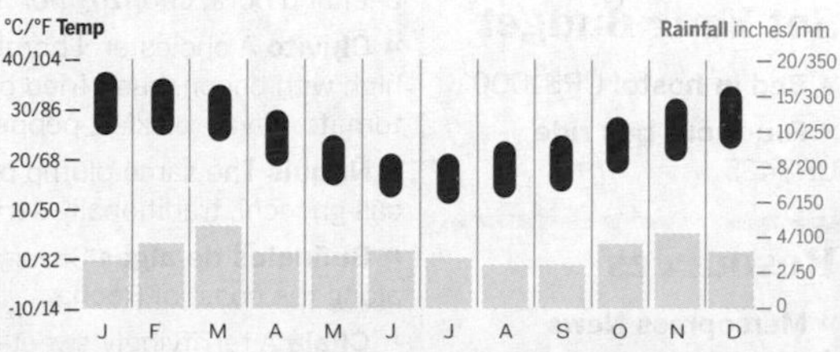

Dec–Mar As temperatures rise the beaches pack out and Uruguay comes into its own.

Feb–Apr The 40 days leading up to Easter see Montevideo's streets filled with *candombe* music.

Jun–Oct Chilly temperatures mean no crowds and discounted accommodations.

AT A GLANCE

» **Currency** Urguayan peso (UR$)

» **Language** Spanish

» **Money** ATMs and credit card facilities widespread

» **Visas** Not required for nationals of Western Europe, Australia, USA, Canada or New Zealand

» **Time** GMT minus three hours; daylight savings October to March

Fast Facts

» **Area** 176,215 sq km

» **Population** 3.5 million

» **Capital** Montevideo

» **Emergency** ☎911

» **Country code** ☎598

Exchange Rates

Australia	A$1	UR$21.8
Canada	C$1	UR$21.4
Euro zone	€1	UR$27.2
New Zealand	NZ$1	UR$17.2
UK	UK£1	UR$33.8
USA	US$1	UR$20.9

Set Your Budget

» **Bed in hostel** UR$1000

» **Four-hour bus ride** UR$425

Resources

» **Mercopress News Agency** (www.mercopress.com)

» **Uruguay Tourism Ministry** (www.turismo.gub.uy)

» **Uruguay surf info** (www.olasyvientos.com.uy)

Connections

Coming from Argentina, most people arrive by boat, departing either from Buenos Aires (for Montevideo and Colonia del Sacramento) or Tigre (for Carmelo). Land crossings are also possible (and much cheaper), leaving from the Argentine towns of Colón, Gualeguaychú and Concordia. There are various crossings from Brazil – the one most commonly used is Chuí/Chuy.

ITINERARIES

One Week

With a week up your sleeve you won't see it all, but if you keep on the move you can see some of the best of what Uruguay has to offer. Start in the easygoing, picturesque historical river port of Colonia and head for the urban attractions of Montevideo, both an easy ferry ride from Buenos Aires. From Montevideo, continue north along the Atlantic Coast and sample a few of Uruguay's best beaches: the 1930s-vintage resort of Piriápolis, glitzy Punta del Este, isolated Cabo Polonio, surfer-friendly La Paloma or the relaxed beach-party town of Punta del Diablo. Alternatively, follow the Río Uruguay upstream toward Iguazú Falls via the quirky industrial museum at Fray Bentos and the wonderful hot springs of Salto.

Two Weeks

Adding another week will allow you to do the above at a more leisurely pace, plus get out and explore Uruguay's scenic and little-visited interior, where the *gaucho* (cowboy) tradition lives on.

Essential Food & Drink

» **Asado** Uruguay's national gastronomic obsession, a mixed grill cooked over a wood fire, featuring various cuts of beef and pork, chorizo, *morcilla* (blood sausage) and more

» **Chivito** A cholesterol bomb of a steak sandwich piled high with bacon, ham, fried or boiled egg, cheese, lettuce, tomato, olives, pickles, peppers and mayonnaise

» **Ñoquis** The same plump potato dumplings the Italians call gnocchi, traditionally served on the 29th of the month

» **Buñuelos de algas** Savory seaweed fritters, a specialty along the coast of Rocha

» **Chajá** A terrifyingly sweet concoction of sponge cake, meringue, cream and fruit, invented in Paysandú

» **Medio y medio** A refreshing blend of half white wine, half sparkling wine, with ties to Montevideo's historic Café Roldós

» **Grappa con miel** Strong Italian-style grappa (grape brandy), sweetened and mellowed with honey

Uruguay Highlights

1 Get snap-happy on the cobbled streets of the former smugglers' port of **Colonia del Sacramento** (p943)

2 Hit the beach in style or in the wild along the country's beautiful stretch of **Atlantic Coast** (p951)

3 Get those hips moving to the *candombe* rhythm at Montevideo's **Carnaval** (p937) party

4 Soak those weary traveling bones in the **Termas de Daymán** (p949), the country's favorite hot springs

5 Mingle with sea lions, penguins and whales in the secluded hippie beach town of **Cabo Polonio** (p954)

6 Cross Uruguay's interior, from **Chuy to Tacuarembó** (p959), through beautiful countryside few travelers ever see

7 Kick back riverside in the country's super-mellow second city, **Paysandú** (p948)

MONTEVIDEO

POP 1.3 MILLION

Montevideo is a favorite for many travelers. Small enough to walk around, but big enough to have some great architecture and happening nightlife.

The young *montevideanos* (people from Montevideo) who don't escape across the water to Buenos Aires have a real pride in their city, and the arts and artisan scene is particularly strong.

Many of the grand 19th-century neoclassical buildings, legacies of the beef boom, are in various stages of crumbling, although vestiges of Montevideo's colonial past still exist in the Ciudad Vieja (Old Town), the picturesque historic center.

Sights

Most of Montevideo's interesting buildings and museums are in the **Ciudad Vieja**, west of Plaza Independencia.

TOP CHOICE Mercado del Puerto MARKET
(Pérez Castellano) The 1868 Mercado del Puerto is a wrought-iron superstructure sheltering a gaggle of restaurants. On Saturday artists and musicians frequent the area.

FREE Espacio de Arte Contemporáneo GALLERY
(2929-2066; www.eac.gub.uy; Arenal Grande 1929; 2-8pm Wed-Sat, 11am-5pm Sun) Between downtown and the Tres Cruces bus terminal, Montevideo's brand-new gallery makes thought-provoking use of the cells of a 19th-century prison, creating an avant-garde exhibit space for revolving exhibitions of contemporary art.

Museo Torres García MUSEUM
(2916-2663; Sarandí 683; admission UR$65; 9:30am-7:30pm Mon-Fri, 10am-6pm Sat) The Museo Torres García displays the works of Joaquín Torres García (1874–1949), the Uruguayan artist who spent much of his career in France producing abstract and Cubist work.

Museo del Carnaval MUSEUM
(2916-5493; www.museodelcarnaval.org; Rambla 25 de Agosto 218; admission UR$65, free Tues; 11am-5pm Tue-Sun) In the same building as the Mercado del Puerto, the Museo del Carnaval documents past and present traditions of Montevideo's Carnaval with plenty of photos, masks, costumes and a couple of floats on display.

Mausoleo Artigas MEMORIAL
(9am-5pm) On Plaza Independencia, a huge statue of the country's greatest hero tops the eerie underground Mausoleo Artigas, where fans of famous dead people can tick another one off the list.

Teatro Solís THEATER
(2-1950-1856; www.teatrosolis.org.uy; Buenos Aires 678) Just off the plaza, the recently renovated 1856 Teatro Solís is Montevideo's leading theater. Guided tours (UR$20/40 in Spanish/English, free tours in Spanish Wednesday) are available Tuesday to Sunday at 11am, midday and 4pm.

Casa Rivera HISTORIC BUILDING
(2915-1051; Rincón 437; 11am-5pm Mon-Fri, 10am-3pm Sat) The neoclassical 1802 Casa Rivera houses a fascinating collection of indigenous artifacts, colonial treasures and oil paintings, including a spectacular panoramic depiction of Montevideo at the end of the 18th century.

FREE Museo Romántico MUSEUM
(25 de Mayo 428; 11am-6pm Mon-Fri) The Museo Romántico is filled with the opulent furnishings of Montevideo's 19th-century elite. Check out the ladies' traveling vanity case, replete with brushes, combs, scissors, perfume bottles and fold-out candleholders; you can bet there were some arguments about whose backpack *that* monster was going in.

Activities

Pedalers can hire a bike from El Viajero Ciudad Vieja Hostel (UR$300 per day, also available to nonguests) and go cruising along the riverfront Rambla, a walking-jogging-cycling track that leads to the city's eastern beaches. After about 2km you'll get to **Playa Pocitos**, which is best for swimming and where you should be able to jump in on a game of beach volleyball.

Strong swimmers could also strike out from Playa Buceo for **Isla de las Gaviotas**, a sandy, palm-covered island about 700m offshore.

If all that seems a bit too energetic for you, bus 64 goes from Av 18 de Julio along the coast road – just jump off when you see a beach you like.

Courses

The following courses don't cater for the casual learner – you'd want to be staying at least a month to get your money's worth.

Academia Uruguay LANGUAGE COURSE
(☎2915-2496; www.academiauruguay.com; Juan Carlos Gómez 1408; group/individual classes per hr UR$220/500) Spanish tuition costs UR$500 per hour for one-on-one or UR$4750 for 20 hours of group classes. Can arrange homestays, private apartments and volunteer work.

Complejo Multicultural Afro Mundo DANCE COURSE
(☎2915-0247; www.afromundo.org; Ciudadela 1229, Mercado Central, 1st fl) Classes in African drumming, *capoeira* (martial art/dance performed to rhythms of an instrument called the *berimbau;* developed by Bahian slaves) and *candombe* (African-influenced musical style) dance.

Joventango TANGO COURSE
(☎2901-5561; www.joventango.org; Aquiles Lanza 1290) Tango classes for all levels, from gringo to expert.

Festivals & Events

Carnaval CARNIVAL
Takes place on the Monday and Tuesday before Ash Wednesday. Highlights include *candombe* dance troupes beating out African-influenced rhythms on large drums.

Semana Criolla RODEO
During Semana Santa, this is part rodeo, part arts fair, part outdoor concert – it's *gaucho*-rama. Festivities take place at Prado, easily reached by bus 552.

Festival Cinematográfico Internacional del Uruguay FILM
(www.cinemateca.org.uy/festivales.html) Every March this two-week festival showcases Uruguayan and international films.

Sleeping

TOP CHOICE **Red Hostel** HOSTEL $$
(☎2908-8514; www.redhostel.com; San José 1406; dm/s/d UR$400/1100/1300; @☎) Set in a classic old house downtown, with some good common areas, including a great rooftop bar. Book ahead online for cheaper rates.

Che Lagarto HOSTEL $$
(☎2903-0175; www.chelagarto.com; Plaza Independencia 713; dm UR$414-529, d with/without bathroom UR$1518/1242; @☎) A sweet little hostel set in an old house right on the main plaza. Private rooms are surprisingly large – an excellent deal.

Hotel Palacio HOTEL $
(☎2916-3612; www.hotelpalacio.com.uy; Bartolomé Mitre 1364; r without/with balcony UR$900/1000; ❄☎) Rooms aren't huge, but they have some classy touches such as antique tile work and wooden floorboards. Those at the front have balconies, but suffer from street noise. Room 67, with its wide balcony and cathedral views, is well worth the extra UR$100.

Hotel Ideal HOTEL $
(☎2901-6389; hotelideal@montevideo.com.uy; Colonia 914; s/d UR$650/850; ❄☎) A very tidy little budget hotel in a reasonably central location. If you're really pinching pesos, but want your own room, this is a good deal.

Posada al Sur B&B $$
(☎2916-5782; www.posadaalsur.com.uy; Castellano 1424; dm UR$320, s/d UR$1146/1251, without

WORTH A TRIP

ESTANCIA LIVING ON A BUDGET

What do you get when you cross a tourist *estancia* and a hostel? Find out at the unique **Hostel Estancia El Galope** (☎099-10-5985; www.elgalope.com.uy; Colonia Valdense; dm UR$500, d with/without bathroom UR$1800/1400) in the countryside 115km from Montevideo and 60km from Colonia. Experienced world travelers Mónica and Miguel offer guests a chance to settle into the relaxing rhythms of rural life, sharing stories by starlight late into the night. Optional activities include horse rides (UR$700) and cycling (rental bikes provided). There's a sauna and a teeny-weeny pool to cool off in. Breakfast is included; other meals, from fondue to full-fledged *asados* (barbecues) are available for UR$240. Pickup from the bus stop in nearby Colonia Valdense is available upon request.

Montevideo

A B C D

1 2 3 4 5 6 7

Bahía de Montevideo
Dársena 2
Muelle B
Puerto de Montevideo
Dársena 1
Rambla Franklin D Roosevelt
Muelle A
Ferry Terminal
Dársena Fluvial
National Tourism Ministry
Rambla 25 de Agosto de 1825
Florida
Ciudadela
Juncal
Bartolomé Mitre
Ituzaingó
Treinta y Tres
Piedras
Cerrito
Yacaré
Colón
Solís
Buquebus
3
22
Mercado del Puerto
7
11
17
10
33
13
5
2
4
1
Plaza Constitución (Plaza Matriz)
25
27
Bacacay
Iglesia Matriz
Maciel
Guaraní
25 de Mayo
14
Plaza Zabala
19
Misiones
Juan Carlos Gómez
6
Liniers
Ciudadela
Washington
Sarandí
Alzáibar
Zabala
Brecha
29
8
CIUDAD VIEJA
Cuestas
Pérez Castellano
Plaza España
26
Reconquista
Buenos Aires
Rambla Gran Bretaña
Rambla Francia

A B C D

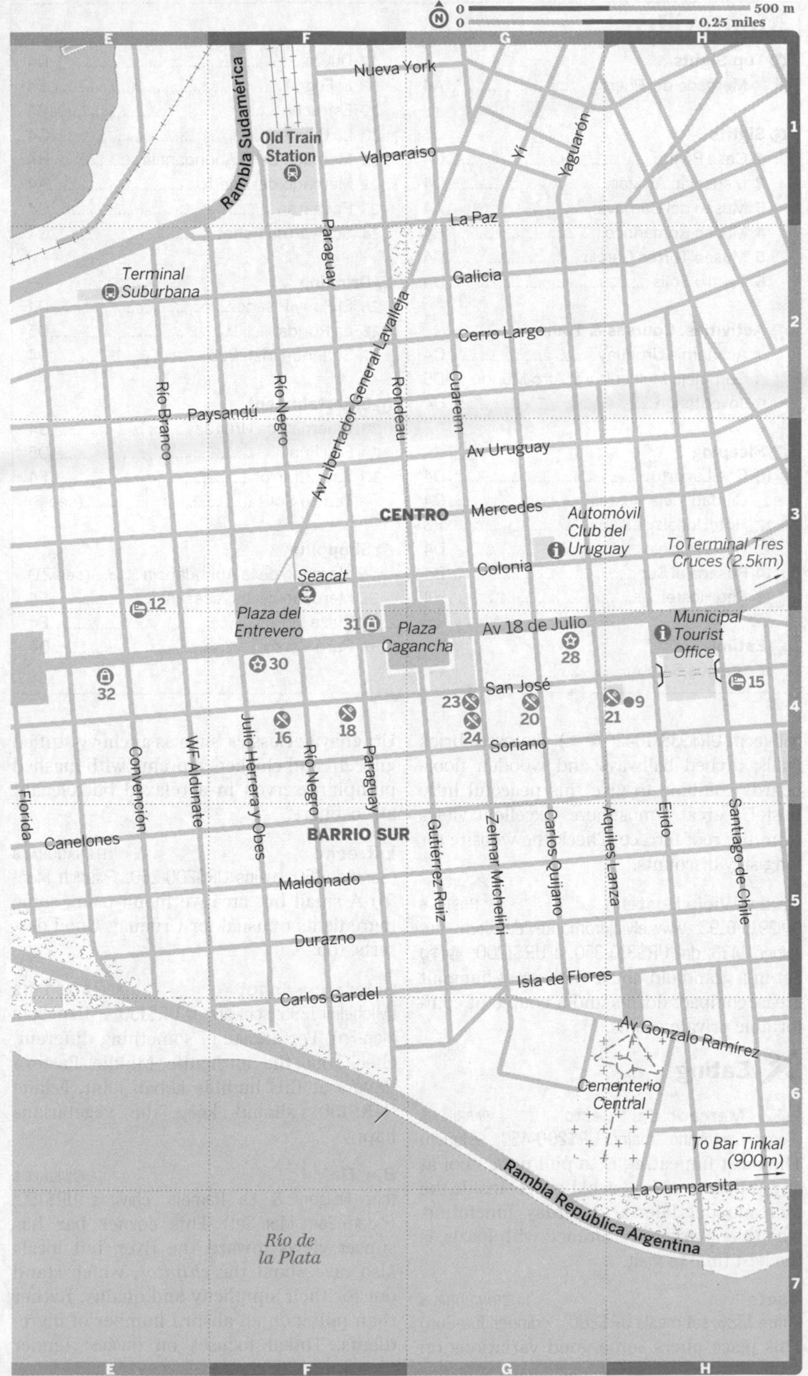
0 500 m
0 0.25 miles
Nueva York
Rambla Sudamérica
Old Train Station
Valparaiso
Yí
Yaguarón
La Paz
Paraguay
Galicia
Terminal Suburbana
Av Libertador General Lavalleja
Cerro Largo
Río Branco
Río Negro
Rondeau
Cuareim
Paysandú
Av Uruguay
CENTRO
Mercedes
Automóvil Club del Uruguay
ToTerminal Tres Cruces (2.5km)
Seacat
Colonia
12
Plaza del Entrevero
31
Plaza Cagancha
Av 18 de Julio
Municipal Tourist Office
28
30
32
San José
15
23
20
21
9
16
18
24
Soriano
Convención
WF Aldunate
Julio Herrera y Obes
Río Negro
Paraguay
Florida
Canelones
BARRIO SUR
Gutiérrez Ruiz
Zelmar Michelini
Carlos Quijano
Aquiles Lanza
Ejido
Santiago de Chile
Maldonado
Durazno
Isla de Flores
Carlos Gardel
Av Gonzalo Ramírez
Cementerio Central
To Bar Tinkal (900m)
La Cumparsita
Rambla República Argentina
Río de la Plata

Montevideo

Top Sights
Mercado del Puerto A4

Sights
1 Casa Rivera C4
2 Mausoleo Artigas D4
3 Museo del Carnaval A4
4 Museo Romántico B4
5 Museo Torres García D4
6 Teatro Solís D4

Activities, Courses & Tours
7 Academia Uruguay C4
8 Complejo Multicultural Afro Mundo D5
9 Joventango H4

Sleeping
10 Che Lagarto D4
11 Ciudad Vieja Hostel C4
12 Hotel Ideal E3
13 Hotel Palacio D4
14 Posada al Sur B4
15 Red Hostel H4

Eating
16 Bosque Bambú F4
17 Dueto D4
18 El Fogón F4
19 Estrecho C4
20 La Cibeles G4
21 Mercado de la Abundancia H4
22 Mercado del Puerto A4
23 Pacharán G4
24 Schwarma Ashot G4

Drinking
25 El Pony Pisador D4
26 La Ronda D5
27 Shannon Irish Pub D4

Entertainment
28 Cinemateca Uruguaya G4
29 Fun Fun D5
30 Sala Zitarrosa F4
Teatro Solís .... (see 6)

Shopping
Mercado de la Abundancia .... (see 21)
31 Mercado de los Artesanos F4
32 Plaza Libros E4
33 Puro Verso D4

bathroom UR$938/1042; @📶) Exposed brick walls, arched hallways and wooden floorboards combine to give this peaceful little hostel a great atmosphere. Excellent views from the roof terrace. Check the website for long-stay discounts.

Ciudad Vieja Hostel HOSTEL $
(☎2915-6192; www.elviajeromontevideo.com; Ituzaingó 1436; dm UR$310-350, d UR$1200; @📶) Set in a grand old house with great hangout areas, compact dorms and a couple of comfortable private rooms.

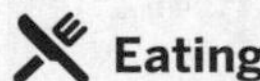

Eating

TOP CHOICE **Mercado del Puerto** PARRILLA $
(Pérez Castellano; mains UR$200-450; ⏲lunch) The most fun eating is to pull up a stool at any of the *parrillas* (steakhouses) inside the Mercado del Puerto. Saturday lunchtime, when the market is crammed with locals, is the best time to visit.

Dueto INTERNATIONAL $
(Mitre 1386; set meals UR$280; ⏲dinner Tue-Sun) This place offers some good variations on Uruguayan classics, such as anchovy-stuffed gnocchi and chicken supreme with mashed pumpkin, served in a relaxed but elegant atmosphere.

Estrecho INTERNATIONAL $
(Sarandí 460; mains UR$200-250; ⏲lunch Mon-Fri) A small but creative menu using some ingredients unusual for Uruguay. Good desserts, too.

Schwarma Ashot MIDDLE EASTERN $
(Michelini 1295; schwarmas UR$150; ⏲11am-5pm Mon-Fri) For a taste of something different, check out the authentic Middle Eastern flavors at this humble kebab joint. Felafel (UR$130) should keep the vegetarians happy.

Bar Tinkal SANDWICHES $
(cnr Frugoni & La Rambla; chivitos UR$150; ⏲8am-2am Mon-Sat) This corner bar has sunset views toward the river, but locals also rave about the *chivitos*, which stand out for their simplicity and quality. Rather than piling on an absurd number of ingredients, Tinkal focuses on basics: tender

meat, fresh lettuce and a good roll to hold everything together.

El Fogón PARRILLA $$
(San José 1080; mains UR$250-350; ⊙lunch & dinner) A long-running downtown *parrilla*, also offering plenty of pasta and seafood selections. A good UR$290 set lunch seals the deal.

Pacharán SEAFOOD $$
(San José 1168; ⊙lunch & dinner) An excellent selection of Basque and Spanish dishes are on offer here, in the somewhat-atmospheric dining room of the Basque cultural center.

Bosque Bambú VEGETARIAN $
(www.comidavegetarianabambu.com; San José 1060; all-you-can-eat UR$260; ⊙noon-3pm Mon-Sat; ✎) One of the few truly veggie options in this meat-crazed country, this popular healthfood store offers food by the kilo or an all-you-can-eat lunch buffet; drinks cost extra.

La Cibeles URUGUAYAN $
(San José 1242; empanadas 6 for UR$225, mains UR$230; ⊙11am-6pm Mon-Sat) Some of the yummiest empanadas in town, in a variety of flavors (including a beguiling *dulce de leche* – caramelized milk). Full meals available, too.

Mercado de la Abundancia URUGUAYAN $
(cnr San José & Aquiles Lanza; set meals UR$150-300; ⊙lunch & dinner) The downtown Mercado de la Abundancia is a popular and atmospheric spot for lunch or dinner and often has live music on weekend nights.

Drinking

The most happening bar precinct in town is along Mitre, between Buenos Aires and Sarandí in the old city. The best idea is to go for a wander and see where the crowd is, but the classics are the **Pony Pisador** (Bartolomé Mitre 1324; ⊙5pm-late Mon-Fri, 8pm-late Sat & Sun) and **Shannon Irish Pub** (www.theshannon.com.uy; Bartolomé Mitre 1318; ⊙7pm-late), which both have reasonably priced drinks, DJs and occasional live music.

La Ronda BAR
(Ciudadela 1182, Centro; ⊙noon-late Mon-Sat, 7pm-late Sun) If you're wondering where Montevideo's boho set hangs out, check out this little graffiti-covered bar, where the crowd spills out onto the sidewalk when things heat up.

☆ Entertainment

TOP CHOICE **Fun Fun** LIVE MUSIC
(☎2915-8005; www.barfunfun.com; Ciudadela 1229, Mercado Central, Ciudad Vieja; ⊙9pm-late Wed-Sat) Located in the Mercado Central, Fun Fun attracts tango enthusiasts, with live bands on weekends and a pleasant deck area out the front.

W Lounge CLUB
(cnr Rambla Wilson & Sarmiento, Parque Rodó; cover UR$50-150; ⊙midnight-7am Thu-Sat) For the megadisco experience, this club in the Parque Rodó, a couple of kilometers east along the waterfront from downtown, has been *the* place to shake your thang for years. Dress to impress, but don't be disappointed if you fail. A taxi from the center costs around UR$100.

Sala Zitarrosa PERFORMING ARTS
(☎2901-7303; www.salazitarrosa.com.uy; Av 18 de Julio 1012, Centro) Hosts rock bands and occasional live theater.

Cinemateca Uruguaya CINEMA
(☎2900-9056; www.cinemateca.org.uy; Av 18 de Julio 1280; membership per month UR$275, plus 1-time sign-up fee UR$130) For art-house flicks, this cinema is also a film club with a modest membership fee allowing unlimited viewing at its five cinemas.

Teatro Solís PERFORMING ARTS
(☎2-1950-1856; www.teatrosolis.org.uy; Buenos Aires 678, Ciudad Vieja; admission from UR$220) The most prestigious playhouse in town, but there are many others. Check the *Guía del Ocio* for listings for this and other theaters.

Shopping

Plaza Constitución hosts an enjoyable flea market on Saturday.

> **GETTING INTO TOWN**
>
> Airport buses (UR$33, 40 minutes) leave from **Terminal Suburbana** (☎1975; cnr Río Branco & Galicia). Buses CA1, 21, 61, 180, 187 and 188 go from Terminal Tres Cruces to Av 18 de Julio (UR$19). A taxi from the airport costs about UR$630. Local buses go everywhere for UR$19.

TOP CHOICE **Feria de Tristán Narvaja** MARKET
(Tristán Narvaja, Cordón) This is a bustling outdoor market that sprawls for seven blocks, running north from Av 18 de Julio, and selling pretty much everything from antique knickknacks and jewelry to artisan crafts and fried fish.

Mercado de los Artesanos HANDICRAFTS
(Plaza Cagancha; ⏲10am-9pm Mon-Sat) Sells excellent handicrafts at reasonable prices.

Mercado de la Abundancia HANDICRAFTS
(cnr San José & Yaguarón) You'll find most of the same stuff on sale at the Mercado de los Artesanos here.

Puro Verso BOOKS
(Sarandí 675) One of the city's many bookstores, with a good selection of Uruguayan writers and music CDs.

Plaza Libros BOOKS
(Av 18 de Julio 892) A good selection of books in English plus a decent range of Lonely Planet titles.

Information

Emergencies

Ambulance (☎105)
Fire (☎104)
Police (☎911)

Media

The *Guía del Ocio,* which lists cultural events, cinemas, theaters and restaurants, appears on Friday in newsstands.

Medical Services

Hospital Británico (☎2487-1020; www.hospitalbritanico.com.uy; Av Italia 2420) Private, highly recommended hospital with English-speaking doctors.

Hospital Maciel (☎2915-3000; cnr 25 de Mayo & Maciel, Ciudad Vieja) The city's public hospital.

Money

Most downtown banks have ATMs. Av 18 de Julio is lined with *casas de cambio* (exchange houses) that change traveler's checks and cash.

Post

Post Office (Misiones 1328) This is the main post office. The downtown branch is at the corner of Ejido and San José.

Tourist Information

National Tourism Ministry (☎1885, ext.111 or 155; Rambla 25 de Agosto & Yacaré, Port; ⏲9am-6pm Mon-Fri) Better equipped than the municipal offices.

Municipal Tourist Office (☎1950, ext. 2263; cnr Av 18 de Julio & Ejido, Centro; ⏲10am-4pm Mon-Fri) Small but well informed.

Oficina de Informes (☎1885, ext. 801; Tres Cruces bus terminal) Well equipped and handy for fresh arrivals.

Tourist Police (☎0800-8226; Uruguay 1667)

Getting There & Away

Air

Montevideo's **international airport** (Aeropuerto Carrasco; ☎2604-0272; www.aeropuertocarrasco.com.uy) is 20km east of downtown.

Boat

Seacat (☎2900-6617; www.seacatcolonia.com.uy; Río Negro 1400) does bus-ferry combinations to Buenos Aires, via Colonia del Sacramento (UR$1160, four hours). It also has a branch at **Terminal Tres Cruces** (☎2915-0202). **Buquebus** (☎130; www.buquebus.com.uy; cnr Colonia & Florida, Centro) runs high-speed ferries that cross directly to Buenos Aires from Montevideo (from UR$2020, three hours).

Cacciola (☎2401-9350; www.cacciolaviajes.com; Tres Cruces bus terminal) runs a bus-launch service to Buenos Aires (UR$929, eight hours) via Carmelo and the Argentine Delta suburb of Tigre.

GETTING TO ARGENTINA

Ferry crossings are the most popular way to cross this border – either direct from Montevideo to Buenos Aires (from UR$2020), via Colonia del Sacramento to Buenos Aires (from UR$1120) or via Carmelo to Tigre (from UR$929), a suburb of Buenos Aires. Immigration is carried out at the port, so try to arrive an hour ahead of your departure time. You can also get to Uruguay from Argentina by boat.

Local buses run across the Río Uruguay from Fray Bentos, Paysandú and Salto to their Argentine counterparts, Gualeguaychú, Colón and Concordia, and are by far the cheapest way to cross. Immigration procedures are often handled on the bus, but if you have to disembark, the bus will wait. Borders are open 24 hours.

Bus

Montevideo's **Terminal Tres Cruces** (☎2409-7399; www.trescruces.com.uy; cnr Artigas & Italia) has restaurants, clean toilets, a left-luggage facility, a *casa de cambio* (money exchange office) and ATMs.

There are daily departures to various destinations in Argentina (via Fray Bentos), including services to Buenos Aires (UR$930, nine hours), Rosario (UR$1524, 10 hours), Córdoba (UR$1901, 15 hours) and Mendoza (UR$2326, 24 hours).

EGA goes to Porto Alegre (UR$1878, 11 hours), Florianópolis (UR$2860, 18 hours) and Curitiba in Brazil (UR$3481, 24 hours).

DESTINATION	COST (UR$)	DURATION (HR)
Chuy	462	5
Colonia	235	2½
Fray Bentos	422	4½
La Paloma	324	4
Maldonado	194	2
Mercedes	383	4
Minas	163	2
Paysandú	514	5
Punta del Diablo	409	4½
Punta del Este	200	2½
Salto	672	6
Tacuarembó	527	5
Treinta y Tres	396	4

WESTERN URUGUAY

The land west of Montevideo is in many ways the 'real' Uruguay – little river towns separated by large expanses of pampas and wheat fields. It's far off the tourist trail, mostly, except for the region's superstar, Colonia del Sacramento, whose charms attract visitors from all over the world.

Colonia del Sacramento

POP 23,100

Take some winding, cobbled streets, add an intriguing history and put them on a gorgeous point overlooking the Río de la Plata. What do you get? A major tourist attraction.

But the snap-happy hordes can't kill the atmosphere of 'Colonia.' This place has got 'it', whatever that is, as well as enough restaurants, bars and nightlife to keep you happy for weeks.

The Portuguese founded Colonia in 1680 to smuggle goods across the Río de la Plata into Buenos Aires. The Spanish captured it in 1762 and held it until 1777, when tax reforms finally permitted foreign goods to proceed directly to Buenos Aires.

Sights

The Barrio Histórico begins at the restored **Puerta de Campo** (1745), on Manuel de Lobos, where a thick fortified wall runs to the river. At the southwest corner of the plaza are the **Casa de Lavalleja** (Calle de la Peña), formerly General Lavalleja's residence, ruins of the 17th-century **Convento de San Francisco** (Plaza Mayor 25 de Mayo) and the restored 19th-century **faro** (admission UR$20; 9am-6pm) which you can climb for great city views.

Colonia's museums are open 11:15am to 4:45pm and close one day per week on a rotating basis. The UR$50 entrance ticket (available from the Museo Municipal) covers all of the following.

Plaza de Armas PLAZA

Turning east along Calle de la Playa will take you to Vasconcellos and the Plaza de Armas, where you'll find the landmark 1680 **Iglesia Matriz** (formally known as the Basilica de Sacramento), Uruguay's oldest church. Nearly destroyed by fire in 1799, it was rebuilt by Spanish architect Tomás Toribio. The interior retains its simple aesthetic appeal.

Centro Cultural Bastión del Carmen GALLERY

(cnr Cevallos & Rivadavia; 11am-9pm Tue-Sun) One block east of the port, the Centro Cultural Bastión del Carmen incorporates part of the ancient fortifications and now showcases traditional and contemporary art by local and international artists. Occasional live performances take place in the attached theater.

Puerto Viejo HISTORIC SITE

(Old Port) At the north end of the street is the Old Port. Although it has long ceased to function as a port, it's a picturesque place to soak up some of the atmosphere of the old smuggling days.

Museo Portugués MUSEUM

(Calle de los Suspiros; closed Mon) A short distance west of Puerta de Campo, off Plaza Mayor 25 de Mayo, tile-and-stucco colonial houses line narrow, cobbled Calle de los

Colonia del Sacramento

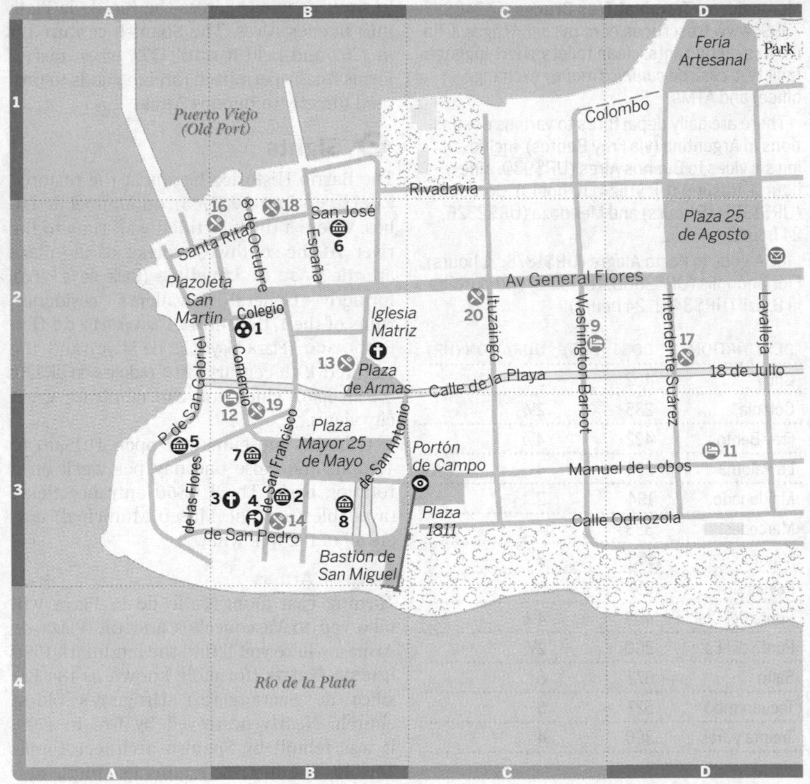

Suspiros; just beyond is the Museo Portugués, where you'll find some great old seafaring maps and a very fanciful depiction of the Lobo family tree.

Museo del Azulejo MUSEUM
(cnr Misiones de los Tapes & Paseo de San Gabriel; closed Tue) Located at the west end of Misiones de los Tapes, the tiny Museo del Azulejo is a 17th-century house showcasing colonial tile work.

Paseo de San Gabriel WATERFRONT
The riverfront Paseo de San Gabriel leads to Colegio, where a right turn onto Comercio heads to the ruined **Capilla Jesuítica** (Jesuit Chapel; cnr Colegio & Comercio).

Museo Español MUSEUM
(San José 164; closed Mon) Across Av Flores, the Museo Español exhibits replicas of colonial pottery, clothing and maps.

Museo Municipal MUSEUM
(Plaza Mayor 25 de Mayo 77; closed Tue) At the west end of the plaza, on Calle de San Francisco, the Museo Municipal has antique homewares and dinosaur remains.

Activities

Hostal Colonial organizes half-day horse treks down to the coast for UR$600/700 for guests/non-guests. Shorter and longer rides are also available. Bicycles can be rented from the hostels.

Sleeping

Colonia is very short on budget hotels, but some of the hostels offer decent-value private rooms.

TOP CHOICE **El Viajero Hostel** HOSTEL $$
(4522-2683; www.elviajerocolonia.com; Washington Barbot 164; dm UR$340-400, d UR$1200-1500;) Winner of the fancy-pants hostel

award, this one's all style, set in a great house with air-con dorms, a rooftop bar and a sweet lounge-hangout area.

Hostel el Español HOSTEL $
(☎4523-0759; www.hostelelespaniol.com; Manuel de Lobos 377; dm from UR$300, s/d UR$900/950, without bathroom UR$750/800; ❄@📶) Set in a charming old adobe house. Much more humble than Colonia's other hostels, and many love it for just that reason.

Hostal Colonial HOSTEL $
(☎4523-0347; hostelling_colonial@hotmail.com; Av Flores 440; dm UR$350, d without bathroom UR$800; @📶) Good courtyard rooms line this old building. Rates include breakfast and bike hire, making it a good deal.

Posada San Gabriel INN $$
(☎4522-3283; psangabriel@adinet.com.uy; Comercio 127; r downstairs/upstairs UR$1480/1600; ❄@📶) Situated in a lovely old house in the

Colonia del Sacramento

Sights
1 Capilla Jesuítica B2
2 Casa de Lavalleja B3
3 Convento de San Francisco B3
4 Faro B3
5 Museo del Azulejo A3
6 Museo Español B2
7 Museo Municipal B3
8 Museo Portugués B3

Sleeping
9 El Viajero Hostel C2
10 Hostal Colonial E2
11 Hostel el Español D3
12 Posada San Gabriel B3

Eating
13 El Drugstore B2
14 El Santo B3
15 Irene's E2
16 Lentas Maravillas B2
17 Nuevo San Cono D2
18 Patrimonio B2
19 Pulpería de los Faroles B3
20 Punta Piedra C2

Barrio Histórico, this little inn lays on the charm and atmosphere at a relatively low price.

Camping los Nogales CAMPGROUND $
(☎098-171-008; campingcolonia@hotmail.com; Severino Ortiz & Ruta 1; camp sites per person UR$150, per additional person UR$50) Three kilometers northeast of the Barrio Histórico, this is a well-equipped campground with shady lots and good bathroom facilities.

Eating & Drinking

TOP CHOICE **Lentas Maravillas** INTERNATIONAL $$
(Santa Rita 61; mains from UR$300; ⏲8am-7:30pm) The best breakfast/brunch/lunch spot in town is this hip little nook with a lovely grassy terrace running down to the water. The menu here is small but with innovative dishes.

Nuevo San Cono PARRILLA $
(☎28964; cnr Intendente Suárez & 18 de Julio; mains UR$150-300; ⏲noon-midnight) It's kind of nice to see a neighborhood bar 'n' grill hanging in there among Colonia's glitz and glam. Good value *parrilla* and a couple of worthwhile seafood dishes.

Punta Piedra INTERNATIONAL $
(cnr Flores & Ituzaingó; mains UR$150-300; breakfast, lunch & dinner) An atmospheric little main street eatery, set in a classic stone building. The menu's particularly wide, with a good range of seafood dishes and some cheaper set meals.

El Drugstore INTERNATIONAL $$
(Portugal 174; mains UR$230-460; noon-midnight) With the funkiest decor in town and a great plaza-side location, this place is rightly popular. A good, varied menu rounds out the picture. Live music on weekends.

Irene's VEGETARIAN $
(Flores 441; breakfast & lunch;) A good selection of vegetarian dishes and wholemeal pastas alongside your standard pizza, pasta and *parrilla* offerings.

El Santo INTERNATIONAL $
(cnr San Francisco & San Pedro; mains UR$250-400; lunch & dinner) In the heart of the historic district, this is a great place to take a breather, with river views from the deck out front. The menu's wide, but the flame-grilled stuffed fish dishes steal the show.

Pulpería de los Faroles SEAFOOD $
(www.pulperiadelosfarolesrestaurant.com; Misiones de los Tapes 101; dishes UR$200-400; noon-midnight) Specializing in seafood and pasta – choose from the artsy interior dining room or the sea of tables out on Plaza Mayor 25 de Mayo. Best cocktail list in town.

Patrimonio BAR $
(San José 111; dishes UR$190-270; noon-2am Thu-Tue) Offering excellent river views from the shady deck, this is a good place to grab a drink. There's some decent food on offer here, too.

Information

Antel (cnr Lavalleja & Rivadavia, Centro)
Banco Acac (cnr Av Flores & Barbot) Has an ATM.
Banco República (Puerto) Operates exchange facilities at the port.
Cambio Viaggio (cnr Av Roosevelt & Florida; closed Sun)
Post Office (Lavalleja 226)

Getting There & Away

Boat

Buquebus (130; www.buquebus.com.uy; Av Roosevelt) has daily ferries to Buenos Aires (UR$689 to UR$2040, three hours). **Colonia Express** (www.coloniaexpress.com) does the job much quicker (UR$700 to UR$997, one hour). There are huge discounts for booking up to 20 days in advance – see the website for details. Immigration is located at the port.

Bus

Colonia's **terminal** (cnr Manuel Lobo & Av Roosevelt) is near the port.

DESTINATION	COST (UR$)	DURATION (HR)
Carmelo	99	1
Mercedes	223	3
Montevideo	235	2½
Paysandú	409	6
Salto	557	8

Getting Around

Local buses leave from Av Flores to Camping los Nogales. Bicycles can be rented from the hostels. For motorized action, try **Viaggio Rent** (cnr Rivera & Odriozola; 8am-7pm).

Carmelo

POP 17,800

A super-mellow little town with a lush central square, Carmelo's streets slope down to its carefully restored waterfront. Ferries depart for the most interesting (and cheapest) of the Argentine river crossings – a two-hour ride through the delta to the Buenos Aires suburb of Tigre.

A large park on the other side of the arroyo offers camping, swimming and a monstrous casino.

The **main tourist office** (4542-2001; 19 de Abril 246; 7am-2pm), in the Casa de Cultura, has lots of information and a good city map. It also runs a kiosk in the main plaza. *Casas de cambio* are located near Plaza Independencia.

Sleeping & Eating

Hotel Urbano HOTEL $$
(4542-2224; www.hotelurbanocarmelo.com; Sarandí 308; s/d UR$900/1300;) A great lobby and impressive facade leads on to fairly plain rooms. Best of the midrange picks in town.

Hotel Bertolutti HOTEL $
(4542-2030; Uruguay 171; s/d UR$500/800) About as cheap as you want to go in this town, rooms here are basic and functional. It'll do for a night.

Camping Náutico Carmelo CAMPGROUND $
(☎4542-2058; dnhcarmelo@adinet.com.uy; Arroyo de las Vacas s/n; per tent UR$200) On the south side of Arroyo de las Vacas.

Fay Fay URUGUAYAN $
(18 de Julio 358; dishes UR$150-280) A fantastic little family-run restaurant on the plaza. The menu sticks closely to Uruguayan standards, but throws in a few surprises. Homemade desserts are wonderful.

Getting There & Away

Chadre/Sabelin (☎4542-2987) on Plaza Independencia goes to Montevideo (UR$308, four hours), Fray Bentos (UR$173, three hours) and Paysandú (UR$300, five hours). **Berruti** (☎4542-2504; Uruguay 337) is around the corner on Uruguay, with most departures for Colonia (UR$99, one hour).

Cacciola (☎4542-7551; www.cacciolaviajes.com; Wilson Ferreira 263; ⏲4:30-5:30am & 9am-7:30pm) has launches to the Buenos Aires suburb of Tigre (UR$629, two hours).

Fray Bentos

POP 25,050

Land must be cheap in Fray Bentos – the whole town is dotted with big, leafy plazas. This used to be the most popular land crossing between Argentina and Uruguay, and if the border ever opens, it will be again. If you've got a few hours to kill between buses, the town boasts a fascinating museum that's well worth checking out.

The helpful **tourist office** (☎4532-2233; 33 Orientales 3260) is just off Plaza Constitución.

Sights

Teatro Young NOTABLE BUILDING
(cnr 25 de Mayo & Zorrilla) The landmark 400-seat Teatro Young, bearing the name of the Anglo-Uruguayan *estanciero* (landowner) who sponsored its construction, hosts cultural events.

Museo de la Revolución Industrial MUSEUM
(☎4562-3690; admission UR$50; ⏲7am-2:30pm Mon, 8am-5pm Tue-Sun) Possibly the words 'tour an old meat extraction plant' don't appear on your list of must-dos for Uruguay, but Museo de la Revolución Industrial highlights a major part of the country's history, when the British beef barons moved in and started the Uruguayan beef industry in earnest.

Sleeping & Eating

There are plenty of *confiterías* (cafes that serve coffee, tea, desserts and simple food orders) and pizza joints scattered around the main plaza.

Hotel 25 de Mayo HOTEL $$
(☎4562-2586; cdelfant@adinet.com.uy; cnr 25 de Mayo & Lavalleja; s/d UR$800/1100; ❄📶) Impeccable, modern rooms a few blocks from the plaza.

Club Atlético Anglo CAMPGROUND $
(☎4562-2787; Rambla Costanera; per tent UR$80) This club maintains a campground with hot showers and beach access, picturesquely situated among shade trees on the waterfront between Plaza Constitución and the Museo de la Revolución Industrial.

TOP CHOICE **Medio Mundo** ITALIAN $
(25 de Mayo 331; mains UR$150-270; ⏲lunch & dinner) About the only restaurant with any real *onda* (vibe) in town, this one does excellent pasta and pizza alongside some innovative fish dishes.

Getting There & Away

The otherwise rundown **bus terminal** (☎4562-2737; 18 de Julio, btwn Varela & Blanes) features a grand piano. It's 10 blocks east of Plaza Constitución. CUT goes to Mercedes (UR$35, 45 minutes) and Montevideo (UR$384, four hours). Chadre goes to Salto (UR$272, four hours), Paysandú (UR$124, two hours) and Montevideo.

Mercedes

POP 44,800

The shady, cobblestone streets of Mercedes are enchanting (unless your taxi has no suspension, in which case they're total kidney-crunchers). The riverfront is largely undeveloped, but there are plenty of grassy spots for lazing around between dips.

Plaza Independencia, located in the center of downtown, is dominated by the imposing neoclassical **cathedral** (1860).

Sleeping & Eating

Hotel Mercedes HOTEL $
(☎4532-3204; Giménez 659; r with/without bathroom per person UR$300/200) An excellent deal right in the center of town, with a shady courtyard. Reservations are a good idea.

Mercedes Rambla Hotel HOTEL $$
(☎4533-0696; mercedesramblahotel.com.uy; Asencio 728; s/d from UR$925/1400; ❄📶) By far the best location in town, just across the road from the river. Rooms are spacious and plain and there's a good garden courtyard. Add about 10% if you want river views.

Camping Isla del Puerto CAMPGROUND $
(☎4532-2733; Isla del Puerto; sites per person/tent UR$20/40) On an island in the Río Negro, linked by a bridge to the mainland, with excellent facilities. Closes when the river floods.

Martín Fierro INTERNATIONAL $
(☎4532-0877; Rambla Costanera s/n; dishes UR$130-260; ⏲lunch & dinner Tue-Sun) The riverfront setting at the foot of 18 de Julio is complemented by a varied menu featuring homemade pasta, grilled meat and fish, and wild cards such as the warm salad of wok-sauteed vegetables.

Information

The **tourist office** (☎4532-2733; cnr Zorrilla de San Martín & 19 de Abril), in a new, inconvenient location down by the waterfront, has a good city map. *Casas de cambio* around the plaza change cash but not traveler's checks. The **post office** (cnr Rodó & 18 de Julio) is nearby.

Getting There & Away

The **bus terminal** (Plaza General Artigas) has departures to Colonia (UR$223, three hours), Montevideo (UR$347, four hours) and some interior destinations. The center is 10 blocks from the bus terminal. Either walk straight up Colón with Plaza Artigas on your right, catch any local bus or fork out UR$30 for a taxi.

Paysandú

POP 78,900

A big (at least in Uruguayan terms), serious city, Paysandú wakes up every Easter for its annual **beer festival**, with plenty of live music, open-air cinema and a ready supply of a certain carbonated alcoholic beverage. The rest of the year it's kinda sleepy, but spasms into life on weekends when everybody's out and about in the restaurants, bars and discos.

Most of the fun happens down on the riverbanks, with plenty of splashing around during the day and more serious partying at night.

Sights

FREE **Museo Histórico** MUSEUM
(☎4722-6220, ext 247; Av Zorrilla 874; ⏲8am-4:45pm Mon-Fri, 9am-1:45pm Sat) The Museo Histórico has a great selection of hand-drawn maps, household objects and war etchings. If you thought Vista was slow, check out the slide 'n' punch 'writing machine' – a one-way ticket to Carpal Tunnel Syndrome if you ever saw one.

Sleeping & Eating

Paysandú doesn't have that many hotels, and they can fill up quickly (particularly during vacation periods). The tourist office keeps a list of *casas de familia* (family homes) offering simple accommodations for around UR$250 per person. The town's lack of hotels is matched by a surprising scarcity of restaurants.

Hotel Rafaela HOTEL $
(☎4722-4216; 18 de Julio 1181; s/d with air-con & bathroom UR$700/950, s/d with fan & shared

BIRTH OF A LEGEND

There's little doubt that Carlos Gardel gave birth to tango, but – even 70 years after his death – there's still discussion over which country gave birth to Gardel.

Much like the Greek/Turkish controversy over who invented the souvlaki/doner kebab, there are three countries claiming Gardel as their own: Argentina, Uruguay and France.

The Uruguayan version goes like this: the maestro was born in Tacuarembó on December 11, 1887 (and to be fair, there are documents to prove it – signed by the Argentines before Gardel became famous – in the Museo Carlos Gardel).

The 'confusion' seems to have arisen because like pretty much every other Uruguayan musician, Gardel went to Buenos Aires to make it big, and then France to make it even bigger, with each country claiming him along the way.

We warmly anticipate readers' letters on the subject.

bathroom UR$480/650; ❄) Downstairs rooms have their own bathrooms, but lack ventilation. Upstairs, the cheaper rooms with shared bathroom are a better deal and you get a shared balcony, too.

La Casona HOTEL $
(☎4722-2998; lacasonadeldecntro@paysandu.com; San Martín 975; s/d UR$500/900, without bathroom UR$400/800; ❄📶) Spacious, plain rooms in a converted family house right on the plaza. Those with private patios are a good deal.

Pan Z URUGUAYAN $$
(☎4722-9551; cnr 18 de Julio & Setembrino Pereda; dishes UR$140-350; ⏲lunch & dinner) The most popular eating place in town – it serves pizza, pasta, *chivitos* and sangria in an informal dining room or on the breezy outdoor deck.

Va Bene PARRILLA $
(cnr 18 de Julio & Batlle Berres; mains around UR$230; ⏲lunch & dinner) A straight-up neighborhood *parrilla*, conveniently located on the main drag. The decor's not much, but the price list is a winner.

Drinking & Entertainment

Dance clubs are located around the river end of Av Brasil, the extension of 18 de Julio. Another option is to fill a bottle with something and cola and hang out with everybody else in Plaza Artigas.

Veinte XXII CLUB
(cnr Brasil & Ledesma; admission around UR$100; ⏲10pm-late Thu-Sat) This was the place to be, disco-wise, at time of research.

Patricia BAR
(Batllé y Ordonez s/n; admission UR$60-130; ⏲9pm-late Wed-Sat) A somewhat laid-back bar that heats up and has dancing later on in the evening.

Information

If you're coming from Argentina and need Uruguayan pesos fast, Copay at the bus terminal offers bank rates.

Banco Acac (Av 18 de Julio 1020) Has an ATM.

Cambio Fagalde (Av 18 de Julio 1002) Exchanges currency.

Tourist Office (☎4722-6220, ext 184; turismo@paysandu.gub.uy; 18 de Julio 1226; ⏲7am-8pm Mon-Fri, 10am-8pm Sat & Sun) Opposite Plaza Constitución.

Getting There & Away

Paysandú's **bus terminal** (☎4722-3225; cnr Artigas & Av Zorrilla) has a bus to Colón, Argentina (UR$90, 45 minutes). Domestic departures include Montevideo (UR$514, five hours) and Salto (UR$157, two hours). To get to the center from the bus terminal, walk seven blocks north on Av Zorrilla. A taxi costs around UR$70.

Salto

POP 108,200

People come to Salto for two reasons – to cross the border to Concordia, Argentina, and to visit the nearby **hot springs** at Daymán. Otherwise, the town's pretty enough, but unlikely to grab your attention for very long.

Sights & Activities

FREE **Museo del Hombre y la Tecnología** MUSEUM
(cnr Av Brasil & Zorrilla; ⏲2-7pm) In the former market; features displays on local history.

Termas de Daymán THERMAL BATHS
(www.termasdedayman.com; admission UR$80) Eight kilometers south of Salto, the Termas de Daymán is the largest and most developed of several thermal bath complexes in northwestern Uruguay and a popular destination for Uruguayan and Argentine tourists. Look for buses running along Av Brasil with the sign 'Termas' in the windshield (UR$14, 40 minutes).

Sleeping & Eating

Salto's accommodations tend toward the overpriced and underwhelming. Below are a couple of exceptions.

Salto Hostel HOSTEL $
(☎4733-7157; www.saltohostel.com; Uruguay 941; dm/s/d without bathroom UR$340/500/860; ⏲early-Mar–late Nov; @📶) In Salto's historic center, this comfortable hostel features spacious common areas, convenient computer facilities and helpful staff. Front dorms have tall windows overlooking the busy main street – great for light and air circulation, but it can get noisy at night.

Hostal del Jardín HOTEL $
(☎4733-2325; hostaldeljardin@hotmail.com; Colón 47; d UR$900; ❄📶) Set in a great spot between the river and downtown, the cheery

terracotta-tiled rooms here overlook a big, grassy garden.

La Caldera PARRILLA $
(Uruguay 221; dishes UR$100-240; ⌚lunch & dinner Tue-Sun) With fresh breezes blowing in off the river and sunny outdoor seating, this *parrilla* makes a great lunch stop; at dinnertime, the cozy interior dining room, with its view of the blazing fire, is equally atmospheric.

Trouville PIZZERIA $
(cnr Uruguay & Sarandí; mains UR$200-350) Nominally a pizzeria, though there are plenty of other options available at this bright and cheerful main street eatery.

Casa de Lamas URUGUAYAN $$
(☎4732-9376; Chiazzaro 20; dishes UR$120-345; ⌚lunch & dinner Thu-Mon, dinner Wed) The datenight favorite, with finely prepared food and a deck overlooking the river.

Information

The **tourist office** (☎4733-4096; Uruguay 1052; ⌚8am-8pm Mon-Sat) is vaguely useful and can supply information about visiting the local hot springs. There are *casas de cambio* downtown.

Getting There & Around

Bus 1 goes from the bus terminal to the center of town.

Chadre/Agencia Central goes to Concordia, Argentina (UR$81, one hour) Monday to Saturday. Immigration procedures are carried out on the bus.

Domestic buses go to Montevideo (UR$619, six hours) and Paysandú (UR$149, two hours).

From the port at the foot of Calle Brasil, **launches** (☎4733-2461) cross the river to Concordia (UR$100, 10 minutes) Monday to Saturday. Immigration is at the port.

Tacuarembó & Around

POP 55,000

This is *gaucho* country. Not your 'we pose for pesos' types, but your real-deal 'we tuck our baggy pants into our boots and slap on a beret just to go to the local store' crew. It's also the alleged birthplace of tango legend Carlos Gardel.

The mid-March **Fiesta de la Patria Gaucha** (Cowboy Festival; www.patriagaucha.com.uy) merits a visit from travelers in the area.

Tacuarembó's center is Plaza 19 de Abril. There's a **tourist office** (☎4632-7144; www.imtacuarembo.com; ⌚8am-7pm Mon-Fri, 9-11am Sat) in the bus terminal which keeps incredibly erratic hours. The **downtown office** (☎4362-7144; Suaréz 215; ⌚8am-7pm) is more regular. The terminal's *informes* (information) office has a town map. The bus terminal is 2km from the center: turn left on exiting, walk through the small plaza, veer right onto Herrera and walk four blocks to 18 de Julio. A taxi costs UR$35.

The **Museo del Indio y del Gaucho** (cnr Flores & Artigas; admission free; ⌚noon-6pm Tue-Sun) pays romantic tribute to Uruguay's original inhabitants and *gauchos*.

Valle Edén, a lush valley 24km southwest of Tacuarembó, is home to the **Museo Carlos Gardel** (☎4632-3520, ext 30; admission UR$20; ⌚9:30am-6:30pm), which documents various facets of the singer's life, including the birth certificate which Uruguayans hold as proof that Gardel was in fact born in Tacuarembó. Empresa Calibus runs infrequent buses from Tacuarembó to Valle Edén (UR$30, 20 minutes).

Sleeping & Eating

Hotel Plaza HOTEL $$
(☎4632-7988; hotelplaza@hotmail.com; 25 de Agosto 247; s/d UR$700/1150; ❄@📶) Several steps up in comfort from others in this price range, with sweet little rooms a block and a half from the square.

Hospedaje Beatriz HOTEL $
(☎4632-3324; Ituzaingo 211; s/d UR$480/700, without bathroom UR$350/500) A back-to-basics budget hotel. No frills, but it'll do for a night or if you're on a tight budget.

Balneario Municipal Iporá CAMPGROUND $
(☎4632-2612; per tent UR$30, plus UR$25 per person) Seven kilometers north of town, the campsites have clean toilets and good hot showers. Buses leave from near Plaza 19 de Abril.

La Rueda PARRILLA $
(W Beltrán 251; dishes UR$120-280; ⌚lunch & dinner Mon-Sat, lunch Sun) A friendly neighborhood *parrilla* with thatched roof and walls covered with *gaucho* paraphernalia.

La Rinconada URUGUAYAN $
(25 de Agosto 208; dishes UR$180-300) A dark and atmospheric local bar-restaurant serving up standard pizza and meat dishes.

WORTH A TRIP

VALLE DE LUNAREJO

This gorgeous valley, 95km north of Tacuarembó, is a place of marvelous peace and isolation, with birds and rushing water providing the only soundtrack.

Enchanting **Posada Lunarejo** (☎4650-6400; www.posadalunarejo.com; Ruta 30, Km 238; r per person incl breakfast UR$1200, with full board 1500-1800) occupies a restored 1880 building 2km off the main road, 3km from the river and a few steps from a *garza* (crane) colony. Further up the road, local guide **Mario Padern** (☎099-450653; Ruta 30, Km 230; walking tour UR$600-1000) leads hikes from the canyon's edge down to a series of natural pools near the river's headwaters.

CUT (www.cutcorporacion.com.uy) offers the most convenient schedule to Valle de Lunarejo on its daily Montevideo–Tacuarembó–Artigas bus (leaving Tacuarembó at 4:50pm, UR$105, 1½ hours). Posada Lunarejo can meet your bus if you call ahead.

Getting There & Away

The **bus terminal** (☎4632-4441; cnr Ruta 5 & Victorino Perera) is on the northeastern outskirts of town. Fares include Montevideo (UR$527, five hours) and Salto (UR$359, five hours). You can also go cross-country to Chuy – the first leg being via Melo (UR$275, three hours). See boxed text, p959.

EASTERN URUGUAY

This is Uruguay's playground (and, to an extent, Brazil's, Chile's, Argentina's, Spain's etc) – a long stretch of beaches all the way from Montevideo to the Brazilian border offering something for everyone – surfers, party animals, nature lovers and family groups.

Conflicts between Spain and Portugal, and then between Argentina and Brazil, left eastern Uruguay with historical monuments such as the fortresses of Santa Teresa and San Miguel. The interior's varied landscape with palm savannas and marshes is rich in birdlife.

In the peak of summer, prices skyrocket and these towns seriously pack out. During the rest of the year you might have them to yourself.

Piriápolis

POP 8600

In the 1930s entrepreneur Francisco Piria built the landmark Hotel Argentino and an eccentric residence known as 'Piria's castle,' and ferried tourists directly from Argentina. Nowadays it's a budget alternative to beach resorts further east, mostly attracting families from Montevideo on short breaks.

The problem with this town is obvious – a four-lane highway separates it from the beach. Still, if you don't mind doing the chicken run a couple of times a day, the water's clean and there are plenty of places to lay your towel.

Sights & Activities

SOS Rescate de Fauna Marina WILDLIFE RESERVE
(☎094-330795; sosfaunamarina@gmail.com; admission UR$50; ⏲by appointment) Runs a marine-fauna rescue operation about 10km south of town. If you want to tour the facilities, reservations are a must.

Chairlift VIEWPOINT
(tickets UR$120; ⏲9am-sunset) Goes to the top of Cerro San Antonio at the eastern part of town for spectacular views over the bay and surrounds. Don't fret – there's a *parrilla* up there.

Sleeping & Eating

Hotel Luján HOTEL $$
(☎4432-2216; www.lujanhotel.com; Sanabria 939; s/d UR$1000/1600;) Finely kept, spacious rooms half a block from the beach. Prices halve off-season.

Hostel Piriápolis HOSTEL $
(☎4432-0394; www.hostelpiriapolis.com; Simón del Pino 1136; dm/tw/d incl breakfast UR$330/780/850, nonmember surcharge per person UR$100;) This 240-bed hostel, one of South America's largest, has several four-bed dorms, dozens of doubles (the best-value budget rooms in town) and a guest kitchen. It's a desolate as an airplane hangar when empty, but full of life (and often booked solid) in January and February.

HOSTEL-HOPPING UP THE COAST

Summer Bus (☎598-4277-5781; www.summerbus.com) is a new hop-on, hop-off bus service allowing travelers flexibility in traveling between hostels up and down Uruguay's Atlantic Coast. With a single UR$1500 ticket, you can start your journey at the hostel of your choice and visit all 12 destinations, from Montevideo to Punta del Diablo.

Camping Piriápolis FC CAMPGROUND **$**
(☎4432-3275; cnr Misiones & Niza; campsites per person UR$130; ⏰mid-Dec–late Apr) Opposite the bus terminal, this place has plenty of sporting facilities.

La Goleta SEAFOOD **$$**
(cnr Rambla de los Argentinos & Sierra; mains UR$220-380; ⏰breakfast, lunch & dinner) One of the few waterfront restaurants to stay open year-round. There's a wide range of seafood on offer, alongside all the standards.

Information

The **tourist office** (☎4432-5055; www.turismopiriapolis.com; Rambla de los Argentinos; ⏰9am-midnight Dec-Mar, 10am-6pm Apr-Nov) has maps, brochures and current hotel prices. There's another office in the bus terminal that operates in summer. The chamber of tourism website www.piriapolistotal.com is packed with information.

There's an ATM at the corner of Piria and Buenos Aires. Change cash at **Hotel Argentino** (☎4432-2791; Rambla de los Argentinos s/n).

Getting There & Away

The **bus terminal** (☎4432-4526; cnr Misiones & Niza) is three blocks from the beach. Destinations include Montevideo (UR$131, 1½ hours), Punta del Este (UR$74, 45 minutes) and Minas (UR$86, 45 minutes).

Around Piriápolis

PAN DE AZÚCAR

Ten kilometers north of town, there's a trail to the top of **Cerro Pan de Azúcar** (493m), Uruguay's third-highest point, crowned by a 35m-high cross and a conspicuous TV aerial. At the nearby Parque Municipal is the small but well-kept **Reserva de Fauna Autóctona** (Ruta 37, Km 5), with native species such as capybaras and gray foxes. Across the highway is the **Castillo de Piria** (☎4432-3268; Ruta 37, Km 4; admission free; ⏰10am-5pm Tue-Sun), Francisco Piria's outlandishly opulent former residence. It's worth a wander if you're in the neighborhood.

MINAS

POP 39,000

This charming little hill town doesn't have a whole lot going for it apart from being a charming little hill town. Fans of Uruguay's bottled water Salus can check out its source, on the outskirts of town. There's a **post office** (Rodó 571) and an **Antel** (cnr Beltrán & Rodó). The **tourist office** (☎4442-9796) is handily located in the bus terminal.

Every April 19, up to 70,000 pilgrims visit the site of **Cerro y Virgen del Verdún**, 6km west of Minas. Among the eucalyptus groves in **Parque Salus**, 10km west of town, is the source of Uruguay's best-known mineral water. Buses for the complex (which includes a reasonable restaurant) leave from Minas' bus terminal every 15 minutes (UR$25).

Inexpensive camping is possible at the leafy **Municipal Campground** (☎4440-2503; campsites UR$50-90; 🏊), 10km north on the road to Polanco (public transportation is available). The three-star hotels around the plaza have rooms for around UR$1300. More humble, but totally adequate, is the **Posada Verdún** (☎4442-4563; www.hotelposadaverdun.com; Beltrán 715; s/d UR$550/1000), with good-sized rooms and leafy patios. There's plenty of *parrilla* action going on around the plaza. **Ombu** (cnr Treinta y Tres & Pérez; dishes UR$200-300) seems to be the local favorite. Make sure you stop in to **Confitería Irisarri** (Plaza Libertad; snacks UR$60-120), a local institution, and check out its subterranean dungeon-museum.

There are regular buses to Montevideo (UR$163, two hours) and Piriápolis (UR$86, 45 minutes).

VILLA SERRANA

Those seeking an off-the-beaten-track retreat will love the serenity of this little village nestled in hills above a small lake, 20km northeast of Minas. Nearby attractions include **Salto del Penitente**, a 60m waterfall.

Picturesquely perched above the valley, **La Calaguala** (☎4440-2955; www.lacalaguala.com; Ruta 8, Km 145; campsites per person/tent UR$180/320, r per person incl breakfast from UR$1000) is a friendly family-run *posada* (guesthouse) with attached restaurant; horseback riding, cycling and hiking excursions can be arranged. The slightly more expensive room with whirlpool tub and fireplace is extremely cozy on chilly nights. Full- and half-board options are available.

To get here, take a **COSU** (☎4442-2256) bus from Minas to Villa Serrana (UR$50, 30 minutes, 9am and 5:30pm Tuesday and Thursday). Alternatively, any bus traveling northbound from Minas along Ruta 8 can drop you at Km 145, from where it's a stiff 4km uphill walk into town.

Maldonado

POP 65,900

This used to be the place to stay if you wanted to avoid the outrageous prices in nearby Punta del Este, but then the Maldonado hoteliers cottoned on and jacked up all their prices. There are a couple of interesting museums and some good restaurants in town. If you're looking for a budget hotel, Maldonado's still your best bet. If you're into hostel living, Punta's the place to be.

Sights

Cuartel de Dragones y de Blandengues MUSEUM

(Rafael Peréz del Puerto s/n; ⏲10am-6pm) Built between 1771 and 1797, the Cuartel de Dragones y de Blandengues is a block of military fortifications along 18 de Julio and Rafael Pérez del Puerto. Its **Museo Didáctico Artiguista** (☎225378; 25 de Mayo s/n; admission free; ⏲10am-6pm) honors Uruguay's independence hero. Artigas was a busy guy – check out the maps of his battle campaigns, and don't miss the room with the bronze busts of the Liberators of the Americas.

Museo Regional de Maldonado MUSEUM

(Ituzaingó 789; ⏲10am-6pm) Maldonado's best museum is the Museo Regional de Maldonado, a jumble of old documents, knickknacks, household items, weapons, furniture, artwork and photographs, all set in a house built in 1782. There's a contemporary art gallery down the back of the garden.

Sleeping

Hotel Sancar HOTEL $$

(☎4222-3563; Edye 597; r UR$1100) A short walk north of the center, with reasonably spacious, fairly basic rooms. Some rooms have TV.

Hotel Le Petit HOTEL $$

(☎4222-3044; cnr Florida & Sarandí; s/d UR$1000/1200; ❄) Centrally located right on the plaza, rooms here are small but comfortable. Enter through the shopping arcade off the pedestrian walkway.

Camping San Rafael CAMPGROUND $

(☎4248-6715; www.campingsanrafael.com.uy; campsites from UR$500; ⏲Nov-Easter) On the eastern outskirts of town, with fine facilities on leafy grounds. Take bus 5 from downtown. See the website for price variations throughout the year.

Eating

Sumo CAFE $

(cnr Florida & Sarandí; sandwiches UR$90; ⏲breakfast, lunch & dinner) This plaza-side *confitería* is a great place for breakfast, coffee or a spot of people watching.

Mundo Natural VEGETARIAN $

(Guerra 918; set lunch UR$80; ⏲lunch Mon-Sat; ✎) Vegetarians: had enough of the salad bar yet? Stop in here for a range of meat-free delights, plus some yummy homemade desserts.

El Tronco PARRILLA $

(Santa Teresa 820; mains UR$120-250; ⏲dinner Tue-Sun) One of the coziest *parrillas* in town, with a wide menu that goes way beyond the usual suspects.

Information

The **tourist office** (☎4223-0050; Parada 24, Playa Mansa; ⏲8am-7pm) is inconveniently located. More convenient is the **Casa de la Cultura** (☎4236-1786; cnr Sarandí & Rafael Pérez del Puerto; ⏲8am-3pm), which has maps and general info.

Casas de cambio are clustered around Plaza San Fernando. The post office is at the corner of Ituzaingó and San Carlos.

Getting There & Away

Terminal Maldonado (☎4222-5701; cnr Roosevelt & Sarandí) is eight blocks south of Plaza San Fernando. Plenty of buses go to Montevideo (UR$173, two hours), La Paloma (UR$161, two hours) and Chuy (UR$272, three hours). Buses to La Pedrera leave from nearby San Carlos (UR$35, 15 minutes) at 8am and 8pm.

Local buses link Maldonado with Punta del Este and the beaches. They run through the center of town, saving you the trek out to the terminal – ask a local where the nearest *parada* (bus stop) is.

Punta Ballena

Casapueblo (☎4257-8041; admission UR$120; ⊙10am-sunset) is an unconventional Mediterranean villa and art gallery at scenic Punta Ballena, 10km west of Maldonado, built by famed Uruguayan artist Carlos Páez Viló without right angles and boasting stunning views. Nearby **Camping Internacional Punta Ballena** (☎4257-8902; www.campinginternacionalpuntaballena.com; Ruta 10, Km 120; campsites per person from UR$220, 4-person cabins UR$1650) provides the most economical accommodations in the area. Buses from Maldonado drop you at a junction 2km from the house.

Punta del Este

POP 6800

OK, here's the plan: tan it, wax it, buff it at the gym and then plonk it on the beach at 'Punta.' Once you're done there, go out and shake it at one of the town's famous clubs.

Punta's an international beach resort and if you like that kind of thing, you're going to love it here. If not, there are plenty of other beaches to choose from along this coast.

Activities

Twelve kilometers off Punta's east coast, **Isla de los Lobos** boasts large colonies of southern fur seals and sea lions.

Beach-hopping is common in Punta, depending on local conditions and the general level of action. The most popular (and fashionable) beaches, such as Bikini, are north along Playa Brava. Playa Olla gets good surf and tends to be less crowded.

During summer, parasailing, waterskiing and Jet Skiing are possible on Playa Mansa. Operators set up on the beach along Rambla Claudio Williman between Paradas 2 and 20.

Surf shops in town rent surfboards and wetsuits during summer. In the low season, they can be much harder to find – ask at Tas D'Viaje.

Dimar Tours BOAT TOUR
(☎4244-4750; www.isladelobos.com.uy; Puerto) Offers tours to Isla de los Lobos (UR$1012 per person) and Isla Gorrotti (UR$300 per person), leaving daily in the high season, and on weekends in the low season. Make reservations in advance. Other operators have offices along the same boardwalk – it's

URUGUAYAN BUDGET BEACH BREAKS

In summertime, all along the Uruguayan coast, towns fill up and hotel prices skyrocket. As well as hostels in Piriápolis, Punta del Este, La Paloma and Punta del Diablo, there are a few others dotted along the coastline that let you get your fill of sun, sand and surf without breaking the bank.

Manantiales Hostel (☎4277-4427; www.elviajeropuntadeleste.com; Ruta 10, Km 164; dm UR$290-700, d UR$900-2400; ⊙Nov-Easter; ❄@🛜🏊) At the eastern edge of La Barra de Maldonado, outside of Punta del Este, this hostel overlooks famed Playa Bikini (although it's a good 15-minute walk to the water). Rooms are comfy and stylish, there's a good kitchen and surfboard hire. Buses to La Barra depart hourly from Punta del Este (UR$30, 25 minutes).

El Viajero Pedrera (☎4479-2252; www.elviajerolapedrera.com; cnr Calles 3 & 11; dm UR$340-550, d UR$1200-2200; ⊙Nov-Easter; @🛜) A rustic and stylish hostel located 200m from the bus terminal in the little town of La Pedrera. It's a 10-minute walk to the wide sandy beach that attracts surfers from all over the world. Buses to La Pedrera leave from San Carlos, near Maldonado (UR$40, one hour) and La Paloma (UR$28, 20 minutes).

Cabo Polonio Hostel (☎099-445943; www.cabopoloniohostel.com; dm/d UR$600/1050) This wonderfully rustic beach shack–hostel is set in the tiny fishing village of Cabo Polonio, which is home to a gorgeous stretch of beach and a staggering amount of wildlife – there's sea lions and seals March to January, penguins in July and southern right whales in October and November. To get here, catch any La Paloma–Valizas bus, get off at the turnoff and pay UR$75 for the 30-minute 4WD trip across the dunes into town. Otherwise it's a long, hot 7km hike across the sand.

worth going for a wander to see who has the best prices on the day.

Golden Bikes BICYCLE RENTAL
(☎4244-7394; El Mesana s/n) Rents bikes for UR$450 per day.

Sleeping

Many of Punta's hotels close off-season. Prices listed here are for the high (but not absolute peak) season. If you're coming in late December to early January, add at least 30%. Off-season the prices may halve.

Punta has two separate grids. North of a constricted neck east of the harbor is the high-rise hotel zone; the southern area is largely residential. Streets bear both names and numbers. Av Juan Gorlero is the main commercial street.

TOP CHOICE **Tas D'Viaje Hostel** HOSTEL $$
(☎4244-8789; www.tasdviaje.com; Calle 24 btwn 28 & 29; dm UR$430-648, r with/without bathroom UR$1300/1100;) Just one block from Playa El Emir, this hostel has the best set-up in town with good indoor and outdoor areas, a variety of rooms and dorms and a fantastic location.

Trip Hostel HOSTEL $$
(☎4248-8181; www.thetriphostel.com; Sader btwn Artigas & Francia; dm UR$400-610, d UR$1220;) Nowhere near as snazzy as Punta's other hostels, this one makes up for it with plenty of *onda* (vibe), a cozy lounge, full on-site bar and a great rooftop terrace. You'll find it a couple of blocks north of the bus terminal.

Hotel Amsterdam HOTEL $$
(☎4244-4170; www.hotelamsterdampunta.com; El Foque 759; r from UR$1900;) Looking like a big white ship run aground out on the peninsula, this huge hotel has decent-sized, vaguely modern rooms. Pay an extra UR$240 for sweeping ocean views.

Eating

TOP CHOICE **La Fonda del Pesca** SEAFOOD $
(Calle 29, btwn Gorlero & Calle 24; mains UR$200-300; ⏲noon-11pm) An atmospheric hole-in-the-wall seafood joint, decorated with murals and very popular with the locals.

El Pobre Marinero SEAFOOD $
(cnr Virazón & Solís; mains UR$200-300; ⏲lunch & dinner) Still going strong after all these years, this is a no-frills eat-in/take-out joint with some of the best-value seafood in town.

HAND IN THE SAND

La mano en la arena (Hand in the Sand), sculpted in iron and cement by Chilean artist Mario Irarrázabal, won first prize in a monumental art contest in 1982 and has been a Punta del Este fixture ever since. The hand exerts a magnetic attraction over visitors to Punta, who climb and jump off its digits and pose for thousands of photos with it every year.

Up close, the hand is starting to show its age. There's graffiti scrawled all over it, and its ungraceful cement base often gets exposed by shifting sands. But watch out – the hand's still likely to reach out and grab you!

Drinking & Entertainment

Year-round, the most happening area at nighttime is the port area – try the hip, minimalist **Soho** (www.sohopuntadeleste.com; Calle 13, btwn Calles 10 & 12), **Moby Dick** (www.mobydick.com.uy; Calle 13, btwn Calles 10 & 12) for a more laid-back pub atmosphere or the **Mambo Club** (☎448956; cnr Calles 13 & 10) for Latin grooves. All stay open as long as there's a crowd and sometimes have live music on weekends.

Punta is famed for its club scene, and there are two pieces of irony operating here. One is that the club zone (La Barra) is about 10km out of town. The other is that these places only really stay open for the one-month superpeak period. **Ocean Club** (Rambla Batllé Parada 12; admission from UR$100; ⏲11pm-late Fri & Sat) is one of the best clubs operating year-round, and is the place to go for beachside dancing, where you can stomp the sand until the sun comes up. The name of this place changes frequently, but the party goes on regardless.

Information

The **tourist office** (☎4244-6510; cnr Baupres & Inzaurraga) also maintains an **Oficina de Informes** (☎4244-6519) on Plaza Artigas. Both places have reams of information and make hotel reservations.

Punta del Este

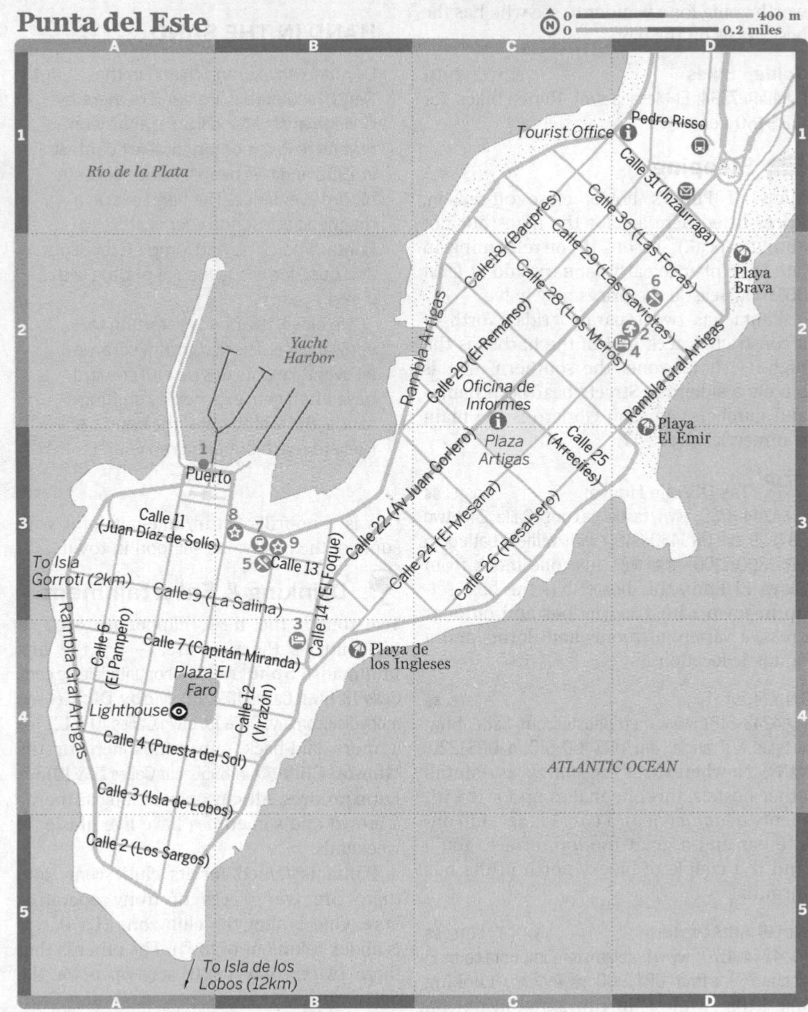

Nearly all banks and *casas de cambio* are along Av Juan Gorlero. The **post office** (Av Juan Gorlero 1035) is at Los Meros between Av Juan Gorlero and El Remanso.

Getting There & Away

Air

Aeropuerto Laguna del Sauce (☎4255-9777; www.puntadeleste.aero), west of Maldonado, can be reached by COT shuttle (UR$100).

Pluna (www.flypluna.com) has daily flights to Buenos Aires, plus summer schedules to São Paulo and other Brazilian destinations.

Bus

The **bus terminal** (☎4249-4042; cnr Calle 32 & Bulevar Artigas) has services that are an extension of those to Maldonado. International carriers include TTL to Porto Alegre, Brazil (UR$2230, 12 hours).

COT covers the Uruguayan coast from Montevideo to the Brazilian border. Copsa goes to Montevideo (UR$180, two hours).

Frequent buses from Rambla Artigas (there are stops every couple of blocks) connect Punta del Este with Maldonado (UR$20).

Punta del Este

Activities, Courses & Tours

1 Dimar Tours A3
2 Golden Bikes D2

Sleeping

3 Hotel Amsterdam B4
4 Tas D'Viaje Hostel D2

Eating

5 El Pobre Marinero B3
6 La Fonda del Pesca D2

Drinking

7 Moby Dick B3

Entertainment

8 Mambo Club B3
9 Soho B3

Sierra de Rocha

About halfway between Punta del Este and the Brazilian border, the Sierra de Rocha is a lovely landscape of grey rocky crags interspersed with rolling rangeland. **Caballos de Luz** (☎099-40-0446; www.caballosdeluz.com; r per person incl full board & horse rides UR$2000), run by the multilingual Austrian-Uruguayan couple Lucie and Santiago, has hill-country horse treks lasting from two hours to a week, complete with three delicious vegetarian meals daily and overnight accommodation in a pair of comfortable thatched guesthouses. They'll meet you at the bus station in Rocha, or you can drive there yourself (it's about 30 minutes off Hwy 9).

La Paloma

POP 3550

This town is a surfer's dream – it's out on a point, and if there's no swell on the left, it'll be coming in on the right. At weekends in summer, the town often hosts free concerts down on the beach, making accommodations bookings essential.

Peteco (Av Nicolás Solari s/n) rents surfboards from UR$400 per day.

Sleeping & Eating

Hostel Ibirapitá HOSTEL $$
(☎4479-9303; www.hostelibirapita.com; La Paloma s/n; dm/d UR$600/1220; @) A bit cramped, but closer to town than other area hostels, Ibirapitá has dorms and doubles, and rents bikes and surfboards.

Hotel La Tuna HOTEL $$
(☎4479-6083; hoteleslatunaycribe.com; cnr Neptuno & Juno; s/d/tr from UR$950/1400/1950; @) The owners have kept this place in mint condition since its last overhaul back in the '70s. Front rooms have great bay views.

Camping La Aguada CAMPGROUND $
(☎4479-9239; www.complejoaguada.com; Ruta 15, Km 2.5; campsites per person UR$200, cabins for 2 from UR$1200) At the northern approach to town, this campground has beach access, hot showers, a supermarket, a restaurant and electricity.

Bahía Restaurante SEAFOOD $$
(cnr Av del Navío & del Sol; dishes UR$300-450; lunch & dinner) Repeatedly recommended by locals as La Paloma's best restaurant, the Bahía specializes in seafood.

La Ballena CAFE $
(cnr Avs del Navío & Nicolás Solari; mains UR$200-400; breakfast, lunch & dinner) A cozy little main street eatery offering good-value seafood and pasta dishes.

Information

The **tourist office** (☎4479-6088; Av Nicolás Solari s/n) is in the Liga de Fomento building. There's another at the bus terminal that opens during summer. The post office and Antel are on Av Nicolás Solari.

Getting There & Around

Cynsa goes to Rocha (UR$40, 30 minutes) and Montevideo (UR$324, 3½ hours). Rutas del Sol goes to Montevideo and Punta del Diablo (UR$141, three hours), the turnoff for Cabo Polonia (UR$70, one hour) and La Pedrera (UR$35, 20 minutes).

Bikes can be rented from **Bicicletas El Topo** (Canopus; per day UR$500).

Punta del Diablo

POP 750

Fabulously remote, somewhat underdeveloped and stunningly picturesque, this little fishing-surfing village of wooden cabins and winding dirt streets is like an anti-Punta del Este. It attracts a corresponding crowd – more nature-oriented and far less glamorous. Of all the towns along this coast, this one shows the greatest contrast between high and low seasons – in the winter months, it's like a ghost town, but when summer rolls around the population can swell to nearly 25,000.

Parque Nacional Santa Teresa is within easy hiking distance. **Horse riding** can be arranged through the Diablo Tranquilo hostel.

Camping Punta del Diablo (☎4477-2060; www.portaldeldiablo.com.uy/camping; Ruta 9, Km 298; campsites per person around UR$400; ⊙Dec-Apr), 2km northwest of town, has excellent facilities, including a supermarket and a restaurant.

El Diablo Tranquilo (☎4477-2519; www.eldiablotranquilo.com; Av Central; dm from UR$800, d with/without bathroom UR$ 3250/2450; @☎) is one of the better hostels in the country, with roomy dorms, romantic doubles and great hangout areas. There's kitchen access and a **restaurant** (dishes from UR$200; ⊙lunch Mon-Thu, lunch & dinner Sat & Sun) a short walk away on the beachfront, serving Uruguayan classics, seafood and gringo comfort food. You can hire surfboards here, but they're free for longer-term guests. Staff can arrange kitesurfing in summer and horseback riding year-round.

La Casa de las Boyas (☎4477-2074; www.lacasadelasboyas.com; Playa del Rivero; dm UR$300-800, apt UR$2000-3200; @☎≋) is set in a cute little house perched on the hillside. Rooms are medium-sized and decorated with driftwood and other natural items. Prices drop in the low season.

There are a multitude of private *cabañas* (cabins) for rent in the village; ask in the pharmacy, supermarket and newsstand for availability or check online at www.portaldeldiablo.com.uy.

Locally caught seafood is a specialty. Turning right from the bus stop, you get to the town's *patio de comidas* (food court) – basically a bunch of restaurants clustered around a parking lot. On the main street, **Cero Stress** (Av de los Pescadores; mains UR$250-360; ⊙lunch & dinner; ☎✎) is charmingly ramshackle and serves up interesting meals accompanied by breathtaking views. Little bars open up along the seafront during summer, but the best parties happen on the beach, where locals and visitors gather around beach fires to play guitars, sing songs and just generally hang out.

Rutas del Sol has buses to La Paloma (UR$200, three hours), Chuy (UR$60, one hour) and Montevideo (UR$390, four hours).

GETTING TO BRAZIL

To get to Brazil from Chuy, walk north along Av Artigas for about 1km to get to the immigration offices. The main street (Av Brasil/Uruguay) forms the official border here. The border is theoretically open 24 hours, but it's best to cross during normal business hours.

Parque Nacional Santa Teresa

More a historical than a natural attraction, this coastal **park** (☎4477-2101; ⊙10am-7pm), 35km south of Chuy, contains the hilltop **Fortaleza de Santa Teresa** (admission UR$20; ⊙10am-7pm daily Dec-Mar, 10am-6pm Thu-Sun Apr-Nov), begun by the Portuguese but captured and finished by the Spaniards. Santa Teresa's a humble place, but visitors enjoy its uncrowded beaches and decentralized forest **camping** (☎4477-2101; campsites per person from UR$50) with basic facilities. **Cabañas** (☎4477-2103; UR$500-3400) are also available.

The park gets crowded during Carnaval, but otherwise absorbs visitors well. Services at park headquarters include a post office, supermarket and restaurant. Rutas del Sol travels from Punta del Diablo (UR$40, 25 minutes) at 9am directly to the park headquarters, returning at 4:35pm. Buses traveling east to Chuy can also drop you off at the park entrance on Ruta 9.

Chuy & Around

POP 11,300

Warning: if you're not on your way to or from Brazil – or to Tacuarembó via the back road – you're seriously lost, buddy. Turn around and go back.

But if you are here don't miss restored **Fuerte San Miguel** (admission UR$90; ⊙noon-5pm, but varies year-round), a pink-granite fortress built in 1734 during hostilities between Spain and Portugal and protected by a moat. It's 7km west of Chuy.

Ten kilometers south of Chuy, a coastal lateral heads to **Camping Chuy** (☎4474-9425; www.complejoturisticochuy.com; Ramal Ruta 9, Km 331, Barra del Chuy; campsites per person around UR$250); local buses go there.

THE BACK ROAD: CHUY TO TACUAREMBÓ

All over the country, you'll hear the same thing: there's no way of getting from Chuy to Tacuarembó. It's true, and it's not. There's definitely no direct bus running this line, and it's certainly much quicker to backtrack via Montevideo, but where's the fun in that?

The road passes through some of Uruguay's most beautiful, least seen countryside – rolling hills where *gauchos* (cowboys) go about their business on horseback, swampy wetlands filled with birdlife and impressive strands of eucalypt forest.

You need to make an early start from Chuy – Tureste has an 8:30am bus for Treinta y Tres (UR$198, three hours). In Treinta y Tres there's tourist info, budget hotels and restaurants on the plaza. The bus stations are all within a block of the plaza. **Nuñez** (☎4452-3703; cnr Lavalleja & Freire) has a 1:30pm departure for Melo (UR$125, two hours).

With any luck (and if it's not a Sunday), you'll get there with ample time to catch the 4:30pm bus to Tacuarembó (UR$275, three hours). Failing that, don't fret – there are much worse places to have to spend the night. Melo has good hotels, such as the **Principio de Asturias** (☎4462-2064; Herrera 668; r per person UR$550) and fine restaurants along the main street. Tourist info is available in the bus terminal.

The next day you can take your pick – buses leave for Tacuarembó (UR$204, three hours) at the early hour of 6:45am, or the more reasonable 2:30pm.

Connections are better going back the other way – provided you take the 6:30am bus out of Tacuarembó you can easily make it to Chuy in one day, arriving around 6pm, any day of the week.

Accommodations are available at **Hotel Internacional** (☎4474-2055; Brasil 679; r standard/deluxe UR$500/850; ❄@📶), with decent rooms in a good location. Deluxe here (TV and a recent paintjob) may not be worth the extra money. The **Etnico Hostel** (☎4474-2281; Laguna Negra 299; dm/d UR$260/800; @📶) is probably a better deal.

Sadly, there are no Brazilian flavors creeping over the border onto menus here. **Hotel Plaza** (cnr Artigas & Arachanes) has a good breakfast buffet (UR$150) and **Miravos** (Brasil 505; dishes UR$200-350; ⏲lunch & dinner) has the best menu, with pasta, *parrilla*, pizza and *minutas* (short-order snacks) in a vaguely hip environment.

COT and Cynsa buses for Montevideo (UR$421, five hours) and the coast leave from near the corner of Oliviera and Brasil. Tureste leaves from the **Agencia Mesones office** (cnr Brasil & Mauro Silva) for Treinta y Tres (UR$198, three hours).

UNDERSTAND URUGUAY

Uruguay Today

Recent years have seen a radical development in Uruguayan politics. After nearly two centuries of back-and-forth rule between the two traditional parties, Blancos and Colorados, Uruguayans elected the leftist Frente Amplio (Broad Front) to power in 2005 and again in 2009. Over that time, the Frente Amplio government has presided over numerous social changes, including the banning of smoking in public; the legalization of abortion, civil unions between same-sex partners, and the state-controlled sale of marijuana; and an ambitious program called Plan Ceibal that is in the process of distributing internet-ready laptops to every student in the country.

The current president, José Mujica, is noteworthy for having survived 13 years of imprisonment and torture during Uruguay's period of military rule (including two years imprisoned in the bottom of a well). Even so, in the same election that brought Mujica to power, Uruguayans voted down a referendum that would have opened the doors to prosecuting human rights abuses perpetrated during the 1973–1985 military dictatorship. The issue continues to divide the country, as evidenced by a May 2011 Congressional vote that nearly overturned the amnesty provisions (despite Mujica's own urgings to let sleeping dogs lie).

Mujica is well known for his grandfatherly style and humility. He famously donates over two-thirds of his salary to charities, refuses to live in the presidential palace, and for most of his political career he has eschewed suits and ties in favor of sweaters.

History

In the Beginning...

The Charrúa were here first, huntin' and fishin'. They had no gold and a nasty habit of killing European explorers, so the Spanish left them alone. Eventually they mellowed out, got some horses and cattle, and started trading. Once the big cattle farmers moved in, the Charrúa got pushed out and they now exist in isolated pockets around the Brazilian border.

Everybody Wants a Piece

The Jesuits were on the scene as early as 1624 and the Portuguese established present-day Colonia del Sacramento (commonly shortened to 'Colonia') in 1680 so they could smuggle goods into Buenos Aires. Spain responded by building its own citadel at Montevideo. For almost 200 years the Portuguese, Spanish and British fought to get a foothold.

From 1811 José Artigas repelled the Spanish invaders, but Brazil ended up controlling the region. Artigas was exiled to Paraguay where he died in 1850, after inspiring the 33 Orientales who, reinforced by Argentine troops, liberated the area in 1828, establishing Uruguay as a buffer between the emerging continental powers of Argentina and Brazil.

More Drama

Liberation didn't bring peace. There were internal rebellions, insurrections and coups. Argentina besieged Montevideo from 1838 to 1851 and Brazil was an ever-present threat. Uruguay's modern political parties, the Colorados and the Blancos, have their origins in this time – early party membership comprised large numbers of armed *gauchos*. By the mid-19th century the economy was largely dependent on beef and wool production. The rise of the *latifundios* (large landholdings) and commercialization of livestock led to the demise of the independent *gaucho*.

José Batllé, We Love You

In the early 20th century, visionary president José Batllé y Ordóñez introduced such innovations as pensions, farm credits, unemployment compensation and the eight-hour work day. State intervention led to the nationalization of many industries, and general prosperity. The invention of refrigerated processing and shipping facilities opened many overseas markets for Uruguayan beef. However, Batllé's reforms were largely financed through taxing the livestock sector, and when this sector faltered the welfare state crumbled.

The Wheels Fall Off

By the 1960s economic stagnation and massive inflation were reaching crisis points, and social unrest was increasing. President Oscar Gestido died in 1967 and was replaced by running mate Jorge Pacheco Areco.

Pacheco sprang into action, outlawing leftist parties and closing leftist newspapers, which he accused of supporting the guerrilla Movimiento de Liberación Nacional (commonly known as Tupamaros). The country slid into dictatorship. After Tupamaros executed suspected CIA agent Dan Mitrione (as dramatized in Costa Gavras' film *State of Siege*) and engineered a major prison escape, Pacheco put the military in charge of counterinsurgency. In 1971 Pacheco's chosen successor, Juan Bordaberry, handed control of the government over to the military.

Jobs for the Boys

The military occupied almost every position of importance in the 'national security state.' Arbitrary detention and torture became routine. The forces determined eligibility for public employment, subjected political offenses to military courts, censored libraries and even required prior approval for large family gatherings.

Voters rejected a military-drawn constitution in 1980. Four years passed before Colorado candidate Julio María Sanguinetti became president under the existing constitution. His presidency implied a return to democratic traditions, but he also supported a controversial amnesty, ratified by voters in 1989, for military human-rights abuses.

Later in 1989, the Blancos' Luis Lacalle succeeded Sanguinetti in a peaceful transition. Sanguinetti returned to office in the November 1994 elections and was succeeded by Jorge Battle Ibáñez, another Colorado candidate, in March 2000.

A Taste of Stability

The military were still lurking around, however – one of Ibáñez' first official duties was to dismiss the head of the army for suggesting that another coup might be in order. The

Frente Amplio – a coalition of leftist parties – became a serious political contender, winning popularity for its antiprivatization, prowelfare stance.

Bad Omens

When the spread of foot-and-mouth disease led to the banning of Uruguayan beef exports, it was bad news for the economy. When Argentine banks froze deposits and thousands of Argentines withdrew their cash from Uruguayan banks, it was *really* bad news. Argentine deposits made up 80% of foreign reserves in Uruguay's banks. Uruguayans watched in horror as their economy – previously one of the strongest in South America – crumbled, and inflation (3.6% in 2001) rocketed to 40% by the end of 2002. The peso plummeted in value, the economy minister resigned and the government declared a bank holiday to prevent a run on the banks.

Independence?

What followed then was a massive bailout. Ibáñez' emergency measures (cutting public spending and increasing sales tax) were rewarded by loans from the US, International Monetary Fund and World Bank, totaling US$1.5 billion. But despite that, Uruguay was still showing some pluck politically – condemning the sanctions against Cuba, the coup in Venezuela and the war in Iraq.

Swingin' to the Left

In March 2005 Tabaré Vázquez swept into power, heading Frente Amplio. Commentators saw Vázquez' election as part of a leftward swing throughout South American politics, encompassing Argentina, Bolivia, Brazil, Chile and Venezuela. Uruguayans collectively held their breath, waiting to see if the new government would live up to the rhetoric of the campaign trail, or if the country was in for more of the same.

Early signs were puzzling. Vázquez sought a free-trade deal with the US (surprising and alienating Uruguay's Mercosur trade partners) and granted leases to two foreign multinationals to build pulp mills on the Río Uruguay, which forms the border between Uruguay and Argentina (infuriating Argentines, environmentalists and hardcore lefties). The latter action gave rise to plenty of cross-border mud-slinging, court challenges and even an attempt at mediation by King Juan Carlos of Spain. One mill opened in late 2007, but bitterness over the issue remains.

The lead-up to the October 2009 presidential election was dominated by debates over security, the rising crime rate and Uruguay's faltering economy which, following the global trend, entered into recession in mid-2009. Problems were exacerbated by a severe drought that hit the country, sending beef exports plummeting and necessitating countrywide water-saving measures.

The election went pretty much as predicted, though – Vazquez's successor, senator and ex-Tupamaro guerilla José Mujica won after a second-round run-off and took office in early 2010.

Culture

The one thing that Uruguayans will tell you is that they're not anything like their *porteño* (people from Buenos Aires) cousins across the water. In many ways they're right. Where Argentines are brassy and sometimes arrogant, Uruguayans are relaxed and self-assured. Where the former have always been a regional superpower, the latter have always lived in the shadow of one. Those jokes about Punta del Este being a suburb of Buenos Aires don't go down so well on this side of the border. There are lots of similarities though – the near-universal appreciation for the arts and the Italian influence, with a love for pizza, pasta, wine and cheese. The *gaucho* thing plays a part, too, and the rugged individualism and disdain that many Uruguayans hold for *el neoliberalismo* (neoliberalism) can be traced directly back to those romantic cowboy figures.

The Uruguayan population is predominantly white (88%) with 8% *mestizo* (people with mixed Spanish and indigenous blood) and 4% black. Indigenous peoples are practically nonexistent. The population growth rate is 0.5%, one of the lowest in the world. Population density is 18.3 people per sq km. The population is well-educated, although public-school standards are slipping. The once-prominent middle class is disappearing as private universities become the main providers of quality education.

Forty-seven percent of Uruguayans are Roman Catholic. There's a small Jewish minority, estimated at 1% of the population. Unusually for a Latin American country, a little over 17% of Uruguayans identify themselves as atheist or agnostic and a further

23% 'believe in God but without religion.' Evangelical Protestantism is gaining ground and the Unification Church owns the afternoon daily *Últimas Noticias*.

Arts

Uruguay's small population produces a surprising number of talented artists and literary figures. While Juan Carlos Onetti is probably the most famous Uruguayan writer, most young Uruguayans have a big soft spot for journalist Eduardo Galeano, who has written many books and poems, including *Las venas abiertas de América Latina*, the English translation of which recently shot onto the best-seller list after the late Venezuelan President Hugo Chávez gave a copy to US President Barack Obama. Other major contemporary writers include author and journalist Hugo Burel, postmodernist Enrique Estrázulas, rising star Ignacio Alcuri and the late poet, essayist and novelist Mario Benedetti.

The Uruguayan film industry is developing nicely, and critics are noticing – *Whisky* (2004), a witty black comedy set in Montevideo and Piriápolis, won a couple of awards at Cannes. *Gigante* (2009), a beautifully shot art-house piece, scored three awards at the prestigious Berlin International Film Festival.

Tango is big in Montevideo – Uruguayans claim tango legend Carlos Gardel as a native son, although the Argentines and French have other ideas. During Carnaval, Montevideo's streets reverberate to the energetic drum beats of *candombe*, an African-derived rhythm brought to Uruguay by slaves from 1750 onwards.

Theater is popular and playwrights such as Mauricio Rosencof are prominent. The most renowned painters are Juan Manuel Blanes and Joaquín Torres García. Sculptors include José Belloni, whose life-size bronzes can be seen in Montevideo's parks.

DAY OF THE GNOCCHI

Most Uruguayan restaurants make a big deal out of serving gnocchi on the 29th of each month. At some places, this is the only day you can get it.

This tradition dates back to tough economic times when everybody was paid at the end of the month. By the time the 29th rolled around, the only thing people could afford to cook were these delicious potato dumplings.

So, in their ever-practical way, Uruguayans turned a hardship into a tradition and the 29th has been Gnocchi Day ever since.

Something to think about next time you're paying US$30 a plate at your favorite Italian restaurant back home.

Food & Drink

Food

Breakfast to a Uruguayan generally means *café con leche* (coffee with milk) and a *medialuna* (croissant) or two, followed by serious amounts of maté. Most restaurants will be able to offer some *tostados* (toasted sandwiches) or an omelet to those accustomed to eating something more substantial in the morning. Any later than, say 10am, huge slabs of beef are the norm, usually cooked over hot coals on a *parrilla* (grill or barbecue). The most popular cut is the *asado de tira* (ribs), but *pulpo* (fillet steak) is also good. Seafood is excellent on the coast.

The standard snack is *chivito* (a steak sandwich with cheese, lettuce, tomato, ham and condiments). If you order this *al plato* (on the plate) make sure you're hungry, and be prepared for a literal pile of food. Other typical items are *puchero* (a beef stew) and *olímpicos* (club sandwiches).

Vegetarians can usually find something on the menu, often along the lines of pizza and pasta. Most vegans end up very familiar with the Uruguayan supermarket scene.

Uruguayans are probably the best dessert-makers in all of Latin America and sometimes the dessert menu is just as long as the main menu. Regional goodies include *chajá* (a meringue and ice-cream delight), *flan casero* (crème caramel) and *masini* (a custard cream pastry topped with burnt sugar). Standards such as black forest cake, chocolate mousse and tiramisu rarely disappoint.

Drinks

ALCOHOLIC

Local beers, including Pilsen, Norteño and Patricia, are good. The 330mL bottles are rare outside tourist areas – generally *cerveza* (beer) means a 1L bottle and some glasses, which is a great way to meet people – pour your neighbor a beer and no doubt they'll return the favor.

Cleric is a mixture of white wine and fruit juice, while *Medio y medio* is a mixture of sparkling wine and white wine. A shot of *grappa con miel* (grappa with honey) is worth a try – you might just like it.

NONALCOHOLIC

Tap water's OK to drink in most places, but bottled water is cheap if you have your doubts.

Bottled drinks are inexpensive, and all the usual soft drinks are available. Try the *pomelo* (grapefruit) flavor – it's very refreshing and not too sweet.

Jugos (juices) are available everywhere. The most common options are *naranja* (orange), *piña* (pineapple) and papaya. *Licuados* are juices mixed with either milk or water.

Coffee is available everywhere and always good, coming mostly *de la máquina* (from the machine). Uruguayans consume even more maté (a strong green tea) than Argentines and Paraguayans. If you get the chance, try to acquire the taste – there's nothing like whiling away an afternoon passing the maté with a bunch of newfound friends. *Té* (tea) drinking is not that common, but most cafes and bars have some lying around somewhere.

Sports

In Uruguay, sport means football and football means soccer. Uruguay has won the World Cup twice, including the first tournament, played in Uruguay in 1930. The most notable teams are Montevideo-based Nacional and Peñarol. If you go to a match between these two, sit on the sidelines, not behind the goal, unless you're up for some serious passion-induced rowdiness.

The **Asociación Uruguaya de Fútbol** (☎2400-7101; www.auf.org.uy; Guayabos 1531) in Montevideo can provide information on matches and venues.

Environment

Uruguay's rolling northern hills extend from southern Brazil with two main ranges of interior hills, the Cuchilla de Haedo, west of Tacuarembó, and the Cuchilla Grande, south of Melo, neither of which exceeds 500m in height. West of Montevideo the terrain is more level. The Atlantic Coast has impressive beaches, dunes and headlands. Uruguay's grasslands and forests resemble those of Argentina's Pampas or of southern Brazil. Patches of palm savanna persist in the southeast, along the Brazilian border.

Uruguay isn't big on national parks. Parque Nacional Santa Teresa and Parque Nacional San Miguel are the country's only parks, but the purpose of both is to protect the colonial-era forts found within – they don't have a whole lot going on nature-wise.

SURVIVAL GUIDE

Directory A–Z

Accommodations

Uruguay has a substantial network of youth hostels and campgrounds, especially along the coast. An International Student Identity Card (ISIC) or membership of **Minihostels** (www.minihostels.com), **HoLa** (www.holahostels.com) or **Hostelling International** (www.hihostels.com) will help with discounts in hostels. In towns, *hospedajes, residenciales* and *pensiones* offer budget accommodations from about UR$700 per person.

Activities

Uruguay is making its mark on the world surf map. Punta del Diablo, Punta del Este and La Paloma get excellent waves and have stores that hire equipment. Check **Olas y Vientos** (www.olasyvientos.com.uy) for more details. Punta del Este is the place to head for upmarket beach activities, such as parasailing, waterskiing and Jet Skiing.

Bike riders can easily while away a day or two cycling around the atmospheric streets of Colonia del Sacramento and along the waterfront in Montevideo.

Books

Lonely Planet's *Argentina* has a dedicated Uruguay chapter that contains more information than what is presented here. For an account of Uruguay's Dirty War, see Lawrence Weschler's *A Miracle, a Universe: Settling Accounts with Torturers.* Onetti's novels *No Man's Land, The Shipyard, Body Snatcher* and *A Brief Life* are mostly available in Spanish and English. *The Tree of Red Stars,* Tessa Bridal's acclaimed novel set in Montevideo during the 1970s, provides one of the best descriptions of life in Uruguay available to English readers.

SLEEPING PRICE RANGES

The following price ranges refer to a double room with bathroom in high season.

$ less than UR$1000

$$ UR$1000 to UR$2000

$$$ more than UR$2000

Business Hours

Exceptions to the following hours are noted in the text.

Banks afternoons Monday to Friday in Montevideo; mornings elsewhere

Bars 9pm to late

Confiterías 8am to late

Government offices 7:30am to 1:30pm Monday to Friday mid-November to mid-March, noon to 7pm mid-March to mid-November

Restaurants lunch noon to 3pm, dinner after 9pm

Shops 8:30am to 12:30pm or 1pm, mid-afternoon to 7pm or 8pm Monday to Saturday

Electricity

Uruguay runs on 220V, 50Hz. There are various types of plugs in use, the most common being the two round pins with no earthing/grounding pin.

Embassies & Consulates

Argentinian Embassy Montevideo (2902-8166; cmdeo.mrecic.gov.ar; Cuareim 1470); Colonia del Sacramento (4522-2093; Av Flores 350); Paysandú (4722-2253; Gómez 1034); Salto (4733-2931; Artigas 1162)

Brazilian Embassy Montevideo (2901-2024; Convención 1343, 6th fl); Chuy (4474-2049; Fernández 147)

Canadian Embassy (2902-2030; www.canadainternational.gc.ca/uruguay; Plaza Independencia 749, Oficina 102, Montevideo)

French Embassy (2-1705-0000; www.ambafranceuruguay.org; Av Uruguay 853, Montevideo)

German Embassy (2902-5222; www.montevideo.diplo.de; La Cumparsita 1435, Montevideo)

Swiss Embassy (2711-5545; Federico Abadie 2936, 11th fl, Montevideo)

UK Embassy (2622-3630; ukinuruguay.fco.gov.uk; Marco Bruto 1073, Montevideo)

USA Embassy (2418-7777; uruguay.usembassy.gov; Lauro Muller 1776, Montevideo)

Gay & Lesbian Travelers

Uruguay has gotten more GLBT-friendly in recent years. In January 2008 it became the first Latin American country to recognize same-sex civil unions nationwide.

In Montevideo, look for the pocket-sized **Friendly Map** (www.friendlymap.com.uy) listing GLBT-friendly businesses throughout Uruguay.

Internet Access

There are internet cafes on just about every street in cities and on the main streets in every town; access costs around UR$15 an hour.

Language

Cafes in tourist areas (particularly Colonia) often have notice boards advertising private Spanish tuition and there are options for more organized classes in Montevideo.

Legal Matters

Drugs are freely available in Uruguay, and with the exception of personal-use quantities of marijuana, getting caught with them is as much fun as anywhere else in the world. Uruguayan police and officials are not renowned bribe-takers.

Maps

Uruguayan road maps are only a partial guide to the highways. Visit the **Automóvil Club del Uruguay** (1707; www.acu.com.uy; Libertador 1532, Montevideo), and Shell and Ancap stations, for the best ones. For more detailed maps, try the **Instituto Geográfico Militar** (2487-1810; www.sgm.gub.uy; 8 de Octubre 3255, Montevideo; 8am-1pm Mon-Fri).

Money

The unit of currency is the Uruguayan peso (UR$). Banknote values are 20, 50, 100, 200, 500, 1000 and 2000. There are coins of one, two, five, 10 and 50 pesos.

ATMS

For speed and convenience, nothing beats ATMs. They're found in most cities and smaller towns. Banco de la República Oriental del Uruguay seems to have the least temperamental machines. Be aware that for 'security reasons' you can only withdraw the equivalent of US$200 per transaction (with a seemingly unlimited amount of transactions possible). Check with your bank (and maybe shop around) to avoid hefty foreign transaction fees.

CREDIT CARDS

Credit cards are useful, particularly when buying cash from a bank. Most of the better hotels, restaurants and shops accept credit cards.

MONEY CHANGERS

There are lots of *casas de cambio* in Montevideo, Colonia and the Atlantic Coast beach resorts, but banks are the rule in the interior. *Casas de cambio* offer slightly lower rates and sometimes charge commissions. There's no black market for currency exchange.

Post

Postal rates are reasonable, though service can be slow. If something is truly important, send it by registered mail or private courier.

For poste restante, address mail to the main post office in Montevideo. It will hold mail for up to a month, or two months with authorization.

Public Holidays

Año Nuevo (New Year's Day) January 1

Epifanía (Epiphany) January 6

Viernes Santo/Pascua (Good Friday/ Easter) March or April

Desembarco de los 33 (Return of the 33 Exiles) April 19

Día del Trabajador (Labor Day) May 1

Batalla de Las Piedras (Battle of Las Piedras) May 18

Natalicio de Artigas (Artigas' Birthday) June 19

Jura de la Constitución (Constitution Day) July 18

Día de la Independencia (Independence Day) August 25

Día de la Raza (Columbus Day) October 12

Día de los Muertos (All Souls' Day) November 2

Navidad (Christmas Day) December 25

Responsible Travel

Responsible tourism in Uruguay is mostly a matter of common sense, and the hard and fast rules here are ones that apply all over the globe.

Bargaining isn't part of the culture here and serious red-in-the-face, veins-out-on-forehead haggling is completely out of phase with the Uruguayan psyche. Chances are you're paying exactly what the locals are, so ask yourself how important that 25 cents is before things get nasty.

Telephone

Antel is the state telephone company, but there are private *locutorios* (telephone offices) on nearly every block.

Prepaid phone cards are (finally!) starting to appear in Uruguay. Available from most newsstands, these cards invariably offer better rates for international calls than you will get at Antel offices.

Making credit-card or collect calls to the US and other overseas destinations is also often cheaper than paying locally.

Many internet cafes have headphone-microphone setups and Skype installed on their computers.

Rather than use expensive roaming plans, many travelers bring an unlocked cell phone (or buy a cheap one here) and simply insert a local SIM card. These are readily available at most kiosks, as are prepaid cards to recharge your credit. Cell-phone numbers begin with ☎09.

Toilets

You'll find that toilets in Uruguay are generally clean and of a similar design to what you're probably used to. Some older establishments offer the choice of a squat toilet – a hole in the floor with a foot-stand on either side. It doesn't take much imagination to figure out what to do. If there's a wastepaper basket next to the toilet, put used toilet paper in there.

FOOD PRICE RANGES

The following price indicators apply to the cost of a main course.

$ less than UR$300

$$ UR$300 to UR$500

$$$ more than UR$500

Tourist Information

Almost every municipality has a tourist office, usually on the plaza, at the bus terminal or both. Failing that, there should be an office at the *intendencia* (city hall). Hours vary widely, but they are generally open 10am to 6pm on weekdays, and 11am to 6pm on weekends. Maps are excellent, showing the town grid and surrounding attractions. The **Ministerio de Turismo** (☎1885, ext 111 or 155; Rambla 25 de Agosto & Yacaré, Port; ⌚9am-6pm Mon-Fri) in Montevideo answers general inquiries on the country and has a fact-filled website. Uruguayan embassies and consulates overseas can sometimes help with tourist inquiries.

Travelers with Disabilities

Uruguay is beginning to restructure for travelers with special needs, but still has a long way to go. As renovations take place (in Montevideo's Plaza Independencia and Teatro Solís, for example), ramps and dedicated bathrooms are being installed. Footpaths countrywide are level(ish) but easy-access buses are nonexistent, with one exception (the CA1, which runs between downtown and the bus terminal in Montevideo). Many budget hotels have at least one set of stairs and no elevator. On the bright side, taxis are cheap and plentiful, and locals are more than happy to help when they can.

Visas

Uruguay requires passports of all foreigners, except those from neighboring countries. Nationals of Western Europe, Australia, the USA, Canada and New Zealand automatically receive a 90-day tourist card, renewable for another 90 days. Other nationals may require visas. For extensions, visit the **immigration office** (☎2916-0471; Misiones 1513) in Montevideo or local offices in border towns.

Passports are necessary for many everyday transactions, such as cashing traveler's checks, buying bus tickets and checking into hotels.

DEPARTURE TAX

International passengers leaving from Carrasco pay US$17 departure tax if headed to Argentina, US$36 to other destinations. You can pay in pesos, US dollars or by credit card.

Check www.lonelyplanet.com and its links for up-to-date visa information.

Volunteering

All Uruguayan organizations that accept volunteers require a minimum commitment of one month, and many of them also expect at least basic Spanish proficiency. The following list includes some of the Montevideo-based NGOs.

Cruz Roja (Red Cross; ☎2707-0335; Massini 3125) The Red Cross helps people avoid, prepare for and cope with emergencies.

Karumbe (www.karumbe.org/) Sea turtle conservation.

Unicef (☎2403-0308; www.unicef.org/uruguay; Artigas 1659) The local branch of the UN Children's Fund.

Women Travelers

Uruguayans are no slouches when it comes to machismo, but their easygoing nature means that in all but the most out-of-the-way places, this will probably only manifest as the odd wolf-whistle or sleazy remark (or compliment, depending on your point of view).

Getting There & Away

Air

Most international flights to and from Montevideo's Aeropuerto Carrasco pass through Buenos Aires. Direct flights go to Porto Alegre, Florianópolis, Rio de Janeiro and São Paulo (Brazil), Asunción (Paraguay) and Santiago (Chile).

Boat

Most travelers cross from Montevideo to Argentina by ferry, sometimes with bus combinations to Colonia or Carmelo.

Bus

Direct buses run from Montevideo to Buenos Aires via Gualeguaychú, but are slower than land/river combinations across the Río de la Plata. There are other bridge crossings over the Río Uruguay from Paysandú to Colón and Salto to Concordia. There are multiple crossings to Brazil – the most popular one is Chuy to Chuí and Pelotas. Buses generally continue through the border and passport formalities are normally conducted on the bus.

Getting Around

Bus

Uruguayan buses and roads are well maintained. Montevideo is *the* transport hub. If you stay on the coast or river roads, you'll never be waiting long for a bus. Try something tricky like Chuy to Tacuarembó and you may experience otherwise. Due to its small size, Uruguay is perfect for bus travel – the longest ride you're likely to take is a measly six hours.

Most towns have a *terminal de ómnibus* (central bus terminal) for long-distance buses. To get your choice of seat, buy tickets in advance from the terminal. Local buses are slow and crowded, but cheap.

Car & Motorcycle

Due to the excellent bus network, few visitors use independent transportation to get around Uruguay. Cars and motorbikes can be hired in tourist centers such as Colonia and Punta del Este.

DRIVER'S LICENSE

Visitors to Uruguay staying less than 90 days need only a valid driver's license from their home country, although an international license may be required to hire a car.

Hitchhiking

Hitchhikers are rare in Uruguay – you might get picked up for novelty value. It's not a particularly dangerous country, but hitching is a gamble anywhere in the world. Take the usual precautions.

Taxi

Taxis are so cheap they're hard to resist. Meters work on segments and drivers consult a photocopied chart to calculate the fare. A long ride in Montevideo shouldn't go over UR$250; short hops in small towns usually cost around UR$45. On weekends and at night, fares are 25% to 50% higher.

Tours

Organized tours are starting to appear in Uruguay, but mostly aimed at family groups and not going anywhere that you couldn't go on your own, using a little common sense.

Venezuela

Includes »

Best Adventures

» Kitesurfing (p1015)

» Catatumbo lightning (p1003)

» Wildlife-watching (p1006)

» Sand surfing (p996)

» Warairarepano cable car (p990)

Places to Stay

» Posada Casa Sol (p1002)

» Casa Nova (p993)

» Posada El Gallo (p996)

» Posada La Casita (p1017)

» Le Petit Jardin (p1009)

Why Go?

Venezuela is a land of stunning variety. The country has Andean peaks, endless Caribbean coastline, idyllic offshore islands, grasslands teeming with wildlife, the steamy Amazon and rolling savanna punctuated by flat-topped mountains called *tepuis*. Those seeking adventure will find hiking, snorkeling, scuba diving, kitesurfing, windsurfing, paragliding and more. Even better, most of these attractions lie within a one-day bus trip of each other.

Venezuela receives considerably fewer visitors than other major South American countries. Tourism infrastructure exists, but it's primarily geared toward domestic travelers. That said, Venezuelans love to have a good time, and that spirit is infectious.

After the death of President Hugo Chávez in March 2013, the future of his socialist 'Bolivarian Revolution' is uncertain. Regardless of who takes power, Venezuela – and indeed all of South America – will be a different place without this controversial and iconic leader.

When to Go

Caracas

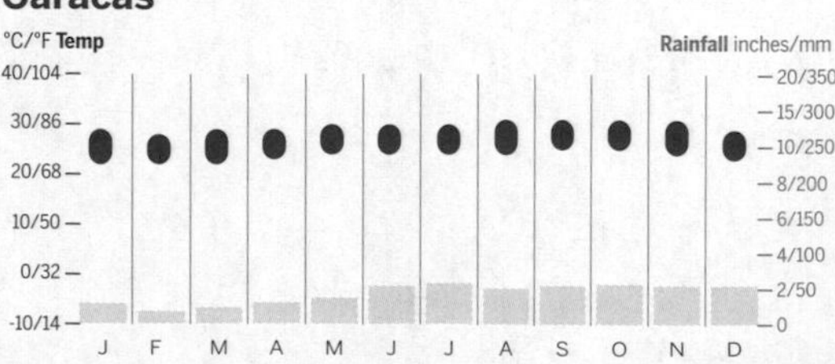

May–Oct Salto Ángel and the Gran Sabana waterfalls gush, swollen with rainy season flow.

Oct & Nov Low season brings the best prices before the Christmas and New Year holidays.

Feb & Mar The country vacations during Carnaval, with special festivals in some cities and towns.

Connections

Caracas is Venezuela's main transportation hub, with buses and flights radiating out to the entire country. There are four border crossings to Colombia, with the coastal Maracaibo to Maicao route being the most heavily used by foreign travelers, followed by the Andean route between San Antonio del Táchira and Cúcuta. Only one main road connects Brazil and Venezuela; it leads from Manaus through Boa Vista in Brazil, to the border crossing at Santa Elena de Uairén and continues to Ciudad Guayana. Brazil can also be accessed via remote southern Amazonas and onward to Manaus along the Río Negro. A weekly ferry connects Trinidad from Güiria on the Península de Paria, but no official crossings exist between Venezuela and Guyana.

ITINERARIES

One Week

One week will barely scratch the surface, but you can get a taste. Make your way to the colonial city of Ciudad Bolívar and explore the historical district along the mighty Río Orinoco. From there, fly to the lagoonside village of Canaima, skirting the iconic tabletop *tepui* mountains. Take a boat tour to the base of Salto Ángel (Angel Falls), and spend the night in the jungle. Then head to the Caribbean coast to clock in a few days of beach time in laid-back Puerto Colombia.

One Month

Now we're talking. Set sail for the Andes and learn to paraglide in Mérida, then make your way east across Los Llanos on a wildlife tour. Fly to Canaima and visit Salto Ángel from Ciudad Bolívar and follow up with an outdoor adventure to the Orinoco Delta or a week-long trek to Roraima. Then get some sand in your shoes as you sunbathe and snorkel in the islands of Parque Nacional Mochima.

Essential Food & Drink

» **Arepa** A grilled corn pancake stuffed with cheese, beef or other fillings – ubiquitous fast food, and often eaten for breakfast

» **Pabellón criollo** The Venezuelan national dish of shredded beef, black beans, rice and plantains

» **Polar beer** If there was a national beverage, it would be these icy mini-bottles of brew

» **Coffee** Aromatic espresso shots of homegrown liquid heaven, served in little plastic cups at the *panadería* (bakery)

» **Chocolate** Not widely exported, Venezuelan chocolate is some of the best in the world

AT A GLANCE

» **Currency** Bolívar fuerte (BsF)

» **Languages** Spanish; various indigenous

» **Money** Lots of ATMs; inflation can create difficulties (see p1041)

» **Visas** Not required for most nationalities

» **Time** GMT minus 4½ hours

Fast Facts

» **Area** 912,050 sq km

» **Population** 27.2 million

» **Capital** Caracas

» **Emergency** ☎171

» **Country code** ☎58

Exchange Rates

Australia	A$1	BsF6.47
Canada	C$1	BsF6.24
Euro zone	€1	BsF8.40
New Zealand	NZ$1	BsF5.78
UK	UK£1	BsF9.75
USA	US$1	BsF6.30

Set Your Budget

» **Budget lodging** BsF250

» **Dinner main** BsF50

» **Salto Ángel tour (Ciudad Bolívar)** from BsF2600

Resources

» **Venezuela** (www.venezuelaturismo.gob.ve)

» **Rumba Venezuela** (www.rumbavenezuela.com)

» **Politics and human rights** (www.venezuelablog.tumblr.com)

Venezuela Highlights

1. Stretch out on white-sand beaches or snorkel and scuba dive the day away at the tiny, undeveloped islands of **Archipiélago Los Roques** (p989)
2. Be on the lookout for capybaras, anacondas, caimans and other wildlife in **Los Llanos** (p1006), the grassy flatlands of Venezuela's cowboy country
3. Feel the adrenaline rush while playing outside in the adventure-sports capital of **Mérida** (p999)
4. Marvel at **Salto Ángel** (Angel Falls; p1021), the world's highest waterfall, dropping over 300 stories in Parque Nacional Canaima
5. Hike to the lost world of the **Roraima** (p1024) table mountain for moonscape scenery and unique plant life
6. Encounter dolphins, howler monkeys and parrots in the wildlife-rich **Orinoco Delta** (p1020)
7. Bird-watch, beach-hop and then kick back in lively **Puerto Colombia** (p993)
8. Spelunk through the cacophonous darkness of **Cueva del Guácharo** (p1011), Venezuela's longest cave

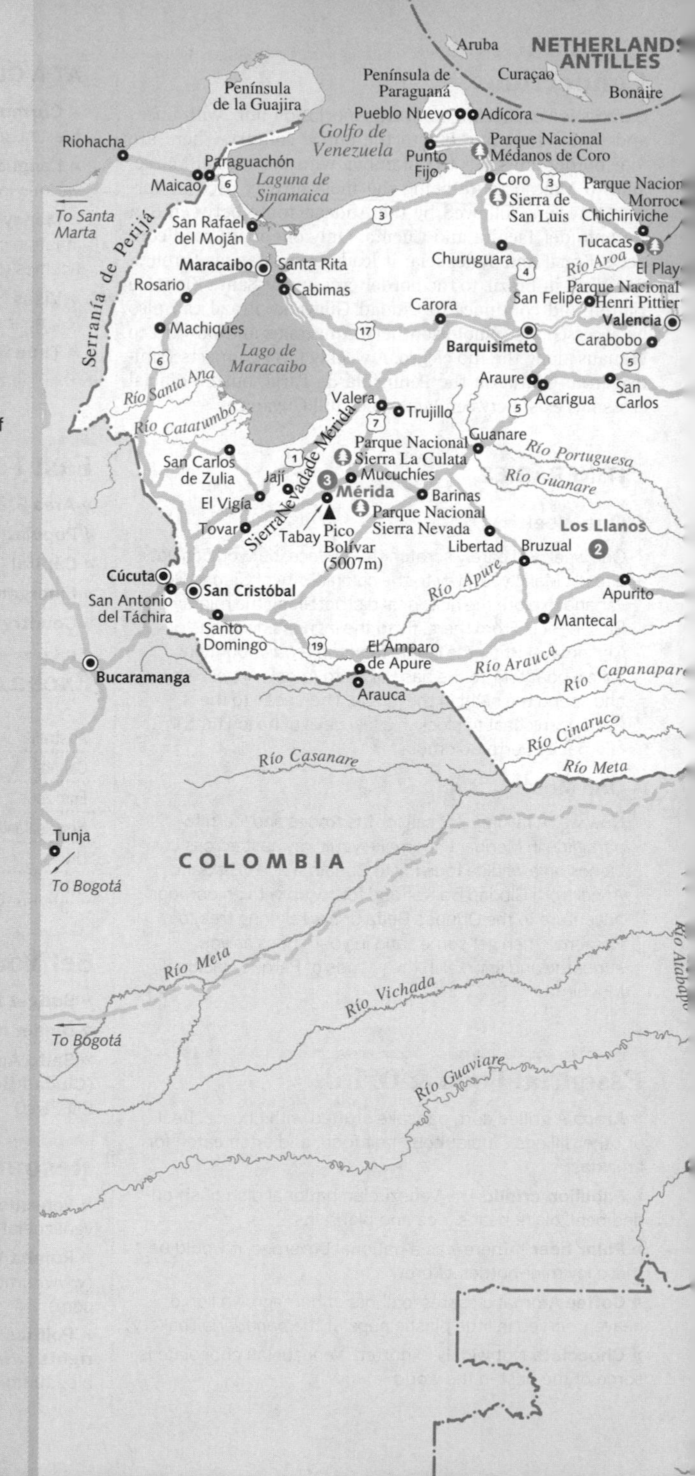

Caribbean Sea
Parque Nacional Archpiélago Los Roques
Archipiélago Los Roques
Isla La Orchila
Isla La Blanquilla
GRENADA
ST VINCENT & THE GRENADINES
200 km
100 miles
Isla La Tortuga
Isla de Margarita
La Asunción
Porlamar
Isla Cubagua
Península de Paria
Parque Nacional Península de Paria
Tobago
TRINIDAD & TOBAGO
Catia La Mar
Puerto Colombia
Chuao
Maiquetía
Parque Nacional El Ávila
CARACAS
Maracay
Cúa
El Guapo
Valle del Tuy
San Francisco de Yare
Cumaná
Puerto La Cruz
Barcelona
Píritu
Parque Nacional Mochima
Carúpano
Península de Araya
Río Caribe
Cueva del Guácharo
Caripe
Parque Nacional El Guácharo
Güiria
PORT OF SPAIN
Trinidad
Maturín
ATLANTIC OCEAN
El Sombrero
Anaco
Zaraza
Valle de la Pascua
Calabozo
El Tigre
Tucupita
Orinoco Delta
Barrancas
Piacoa
Ciudad Bolívar
Ciudad Guayana
Upata
Río Manapire
Río Orinoco
San Fernando de Apure
Caicara del Orinoco
Maripa
Ciudad Piar
Embalse de Guri
Bochinche
El Callao
Tumeremo
Río Caura
La Paragua
El Dorado
Puerto Páez
El Burro
Puerto Carreño
El Playón
Río Paragua
Canaima
Río Caroní
Salto Ángel (Angel Falls)
GUYANA
Sierra de Maigualida
Puerto Ayacucho
Samariapo
Morganito
Amazonas
Río Ventuari
Parque Nacional Canaima
Gran Sabana
Roraima (2810m)
Cerro Autana (1248m)
Santa Elena de Uairén
El Paují
Icabarú
Pacaraima
San Fernando de Atabapo
Río Orinoco
Río Uraricoera
Yavita
Boa Vista
Río Guainía
Maroa
San Carlos de Río Negro
Casiquiare
Brazo
BRAZIL
Caracaraí
San Simón de Cocuy
Parque Nacional Serranía la Neblina
Río Negro
Río Branco
To São Gabriel da Cachoeira (70km)
To Manaus

CARACAS

☎0212 / POP 3.5 MILLION

A sprawling metropolis choked with traffic, Caracas incites no instant love affairs. The political and cultural capital of Venezuela is densely overpopulated and hectic, with a solid dose of crime and pollution. Few sections of the city are pedestrian-friendly and almost no quality accommodations exist for budget travelers.

That said, there's no postapocalyptic bogeyman waiting to get you, and no need to barricade yourself in a hotel room. Nestled between verdant peaks at an altitude of about 900m, the city enjoys both a spectacular setting and an unbeatable climate. Evocative fog descends from lush mountains, keeping the city comfortable year-round, and chirping *sapitos* (little frogs) form a lovely evening chorus.

Pulsing nightlife, excellent restaurants and pleasant central plazas are easily explored via an efficient, inexpensive metro system and a legion of relatively inexpensive taxis. Devotees of Simón Bolívar, El Libertador (the Liberator) of South America, will find numerous places of worship, as will fashionistas.

Caracas isn't a primary destination for most travelers, but it has a side worth seeing.

Sights

Sprawling for 20km along a narrow coastal valley, Caracas is bordered to the north by the Parque Nacional El Ávila and to the south by a mix of modern suburbs and *barrios* (shantytowns) stacked along the steep hillsides. Downtown Caracas stretches for 8km or so west–east from the neighborhood of El Silencio to Chacao. Museums, theaters and cinemas are clustered around Parque Central on the eastern edge of the historic center.

THE CENTER & AROUND

The historic sector is the heart of the original Caracas. It still retains glimpses of its colonial past but is peppered with newer buildings and a lot of questionable architecture from the last century. It's a lively area and worth visiting for its historical sites, particularly those pertaining to Simón Bolívar.

Plaza Bolívar PLAZA

(Map p976; Ⓜ Capitolio, El Silencio) Like any Venezuelan population center with a heartbeat, Caracas' central plaza is dedicated to Bolívar. Its equestrian statue was cast in Europe and unveiled in 1874, after some delay when the ship carrying it foundered on Archipiélago Los Roques. The plaza is a place to hang out under jacarandas and African tulip trees, listen to soapbox politicians or browse the street stalls for religious trinkets, Chávez propaganda or souvenirs.

FREE **Simón Bolívar Mausoleum** MAUSOLEUM

(Map p976; Av Norte) Can't a Liberator just rest in peace? After a 2010 exhumation to confirm cause of death, Chávez built his hero this grand new mausoleum, which was due to open sometime in 2013. The US$140 million price tag and bold architecture – a gleaming white wave that mirrors the Ávila range or a gnarly 17-story skate ramp, depending on your opinion – set tongues wagging even before Chávez' death, with some cheeky pundits opining that he had plans to join Bolívar here in perpetuity.

FREE **Catedral** CHURCH

(Map p976; Plaza Bolívar; ⊙8-11:30am & 4-6pm Mon-Fri, 9am-noon & 4:30am-6pm Sat & Sun; Ⓜ Capitolio, El Silencio) On the eastern side of the Plaza Bolívar, the cathedral shouldn't be missed. Rebuilt from 1665 to 1713 after being flattened by an earthquake, it houses the Bolívar family chapel, where his wife and parents are buried. The chapel is in the middle of the right-hand aisle, marked by a mournful sculpture of El Liberator.

Museo Sacro de Caracas MUSEUM

(Map p976; Plaza Bolívar; adult/student BsF15/10; ⊙9am-4pm Mon-Sat; Ⓜ Capitolio, El Silencio) Accommodated in a meticulously restored colonial building that stands upon the site of the old cathedral cemetery, this museum displays a modest but carefully selected collection of religious art. Duck through the low doorway into the dark, old ecclesiastical prison, where remains of early church leaders still lie in sealed niches. There's a delightful cafe (mains BsF105 to BsF125) inside a former chapel of the adjacent cathedral.

FREE **Asamblea Nacional** HISTORIC BUILDING

(Capitolio Nacional; Map p976; off Plaza Bolívar; ⊙8am-noon Sat & Sun; Ⓜ Capitolio, El Silencio) The entire block just southwest of the plaza contains the Asamblea Nacional, the seat of congress built in the 1870s. In the central

Greater Caracas

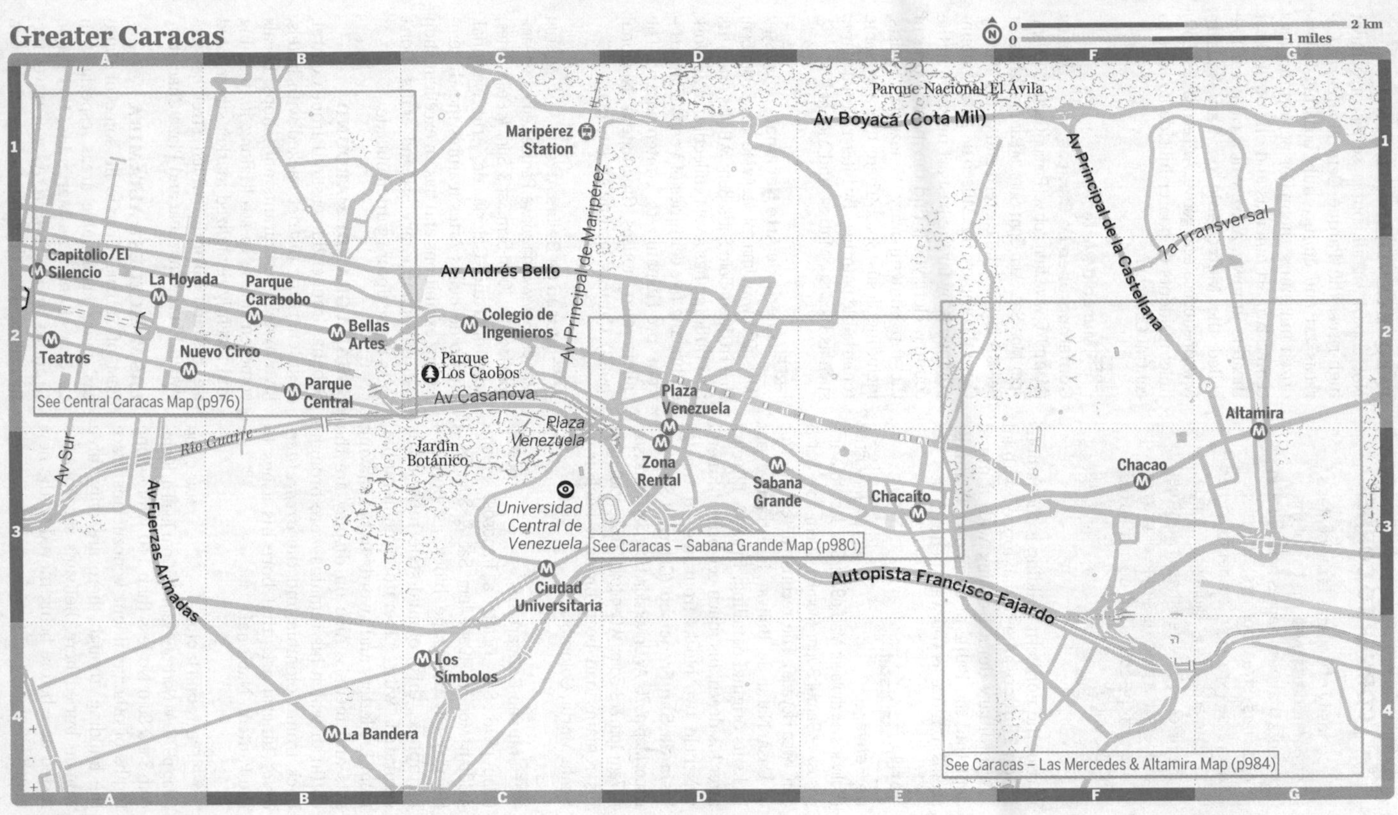

CORNER TO CORNER

A curiosity of Caracas is the center's street-address system. It's not the streets that bear names here, but the *esquinas* (street corners); therefore, addresses are given 'corner to corner.' So if an address is 'Piñango a Conde,' the place is between these two street corners. If a place is situated on a corner, just the corner will be named (eg Esq Conde).

part of the northern building is the famous **Salón Elíptico**, an oval hall topped with an extraordinary domed ceiling with a mural depicting the Battle of Carabobo. It almost seems to move as you walk beneath it.

FREE Casa Natal de Bolívar MONUMENT, MUSEUM

(Bolívar's birthplace; Map p976; San Jacinto a Traposos; ⏲9am-4:30pm Mon-Fri, 10am-4pm Sat & Sun; Ⓜ La Hoyada) The reconstructed interior of Casa Natal de Bolívar is attractive but lacks its original detailing. In 1842, 12 years after his death, his much-celebrated funeral was held two blocks from here at the **Iglesia de San Francisco** (Church of San Francisco; Map p976; Av Universidad, cnr San Francisco; ⏲7am-1pm & 3-6pm; Ⓜ Capitolio/El Silencio) after his remains had been brought back from Santa Marta, Colombia.

FREE Museo Bolivariano MUSEUM

(Map p976; San Jacinto a Traposos; ⏲9am-4:30pm Mon-Fri, 10am-4pm Sat & Sun; Ⓜ La Hoyada) On the same block as Bolívar's birthplace, this colonial-style museum is saturated with Liberator memorabilia, from his letters and swords to his shaving sets and medals. Also on display are the coffin in which his remains were brought back from Colombia and the *arca cineraria* (funeral ark) that bore his ashes to the Panteón Nacional.

FREE Panteón Nacional MAUSOLEUM

(Map p976; Av Norte; ⏲9am-4:30pm Tue-Fri, 10am-4pm Sat & Sun) No less than 140 white-stone tombs of other eminent Venezuelans grace the building, though there are only three women buried here. Bolívar's sarcophagus rested here before being moved to the new mausoleum.

PARQUE CENTRAL & AROUND

Not a park at all, but a series of cement high-rises, the Parque Central area is Caracas' art and culture hub, boasting half-a-dozen museums, the major performing arts center, two art cinemas and one of the best theaters in town. A jazzy new cable-car line called the **Metrocable de San Agustín** (www.metrodecaracas.gob.ve; Av Lecuna; BsF1.50) links residents of poorer hillside *barrios* to central Caracas.

FREE Museo de Arte Contemporáneo de Caracas MUSEUM

(Map p976; www.fmn.gob.ve; Parque Central; ⏲9am-7pm Mon-Sat, 9am-5pm Sun; Ⓜ Parque Central or Bellas Artes) On the eastern end of the Parque Central complex, the Museo de Arte Contemporáneo is by far the best art museum in the country. Here you'll find the major works of the top contemporary Venezuelan artists, including Jesús Soto. There are also some remarkable paintings by international giants such as Picasso, Matisse and Monet.

FREE Galería de Arte Nacional MUSEUM

(Map p976; www.fmn.gob.ve; Av México; ⏲9am-5pm Mon-Fri, 10am-5pm Sat & Sun; Ⓜ Bellas Artes) Its new building has a vast collection of artwork embracing five centuries of Venezuelan art – from pre-Hispanic to contemporary. The gallery also houses Cinemateca Nacional (p983), Caracas' leading art cinema.

FREE Museo de Bellas Artes MUSEUM

(Map p976; www.fmn.gob.ve; Parque Central; ⏲9am-4pm Mon-Fri, 10am-5pm Sat & Sun; Ⓜ Bellas Artes) Adjoining the Galería de Arte Nacional, Museo de Bellas Artes features mostly temporary exhibitions and has an excellent shop selling contemporary art and crafts. Don't miss the sculpture garden outside.

SABANA GRANDE & AROUND

Sabana Grande, 2km east of Parque Central, is an energetic district packed with hotels, love motels, restaurants and shops. Locals come en masse to stroll along its teeming and recently revitalized market street, **Blvd de Sabana Grande**, which stretches between Plaza Venezuela and Plaza Chacaíto.

LAS MERCEDES & ALTAMIRA

East of Sabana Grande lie some of Caracas' more fashionable areas, especially in **La Castellana**, **Las Mercedes**, **Los Palos Grandes** and **Altamira**. As you travel further east, you descend the social ladder, eventually reaching some of the city's most downtrodden *barrios*.

EL HATILLO

El Hatillo was once its own village, but has now been absorbed into Caracas. It's a popular getaway for folks who live in the more congested urban core, with narrow central streets and plaza stacked with brightly painted colonial buildings that house restaurants, art galleries and craft shops. Located 15km southeast of the city center, this area overflows with people on the weekend. There's always a tranquil atmosphere in the afternoon and early evening, when diners and cafe-goers can sit back and relax to the sounds of crickets and *sapitos*.

Metro bus 202 (BsF1.50) leaves from near the Altamira metro station on weekday mornings (until 10am) and afternoons (from 4pm).

Activities

The best place for **hiking** near Caracas is Parque Nacional El Ávila. Groups like the **Centro Excursionista Universitario** (CEU; www.ucv.ve/ceu) and **Centro Excursionista Caracas** (CEC; www.centroexcursionistacaracas.org.ve) organize local and regional outdoor excursions for activities such as hiking and rock climbing.

Tours

Leo Lameda Tours WALKING TOUR
(☎0412-998-1998; leo.lameda@gmail.com; full-day tour US$60) For a less conventional view of Caracas, Leo Lameda Tours leads walking tours, hitting some of the city's less-visited pockets, such as the central university and cemetery, while offering plenty of illuminating historical insights along the way.

Sociedad Conservacionista Audubón de Venezuela BIRD-WATCHING
(SCAV; Map p984; ☎272-8708; www.audubonvenezuela.org; Calle Arichuna, El Marqués, Edificio Sociedad Venezolana de Ciencias Naturales) Organizes bird-watching tours. Also guided walks in and around Caracas (BsF70), as well as Parque Nacional Henri Pittier (BsF150) and other national parks.

Festivals & Events

The biggest celebrations are Christmas, Carnaval and Easter. All offices close, as do most shops, and intercity bus transportation is frantic. Flights can be fully booked.

Semana Santa (Holy Week, culminating in Easter) is also a major celebration, with festivities focused in Chacao. Traditional outlying areas celebrate holy days with more vigor than do central districts. El Hatillo boasts local feasts on several occasions during the year (including May 3, July 16 and September 4).

The festival of Diablos Danzantes (see boxed text, p1034), which takes place in Francisco de Yare, is a day trip from Caracas.

Sleeping

There's little to like about accommodations in Caracas for budget travelers. Most inexpensive rooms can only be found in love motels, which tend to be in neighborhoods that are dangerous after dark. And in response to the destruction of housing stock by a few seasons of heavy rains, the government has nationalized some hotels for use as public housing, making it even more difficult for visitors to find rooms.

Business travelers saturate hotels during the weekdays, so always reserve in advance. It's worth considering staying in a midrange place in a safer neighborhood such as Altamira so you can walk around at night and breathe easier.

CENTRAL CARACAS

Central Caracas is bustling during the day, but the area mostly shuts down and empties by 8pm or 9pm, so you won't want to linger outside your lodging at night.

TOP CHOICE **Dal Bo Hostal** HOSTEL $
(Map p976; ☎0424-215-0799; Pajaritos a San Francisco; dm incl breakfast US$40 or €30; wi-fi; M Capitolio, El Silencio) These folks have more hospitality than any five-star Venezuelan hotel. A modest apartment near the Plaza Bolívar, this popular new hostel has two bunkrooms (a two-bed and a four-bed), a gleaming shared bathroom and a small kitchen. The attentive English-speaking owners equip all guests pre-programmed cell phones, and there's a staggering Blu-Ray movie collection. Reserve ahead.

Hotel Grand Galaxie HOTEL $$
(Map p976; ☎864-9011; www.hotelgrandgalaxie.com; Caja de Agua a Truco; r BsF290-350, ste BsF400-420; P air-con wi-fi; M Capitolio/El Silencio) Four blocks north of Plaza Bolívar, this modern eight-story tower has rather dreary standard rooms, whereas suites tend to be in better condition. All have TVs. There's wi-fi

Central Caracas

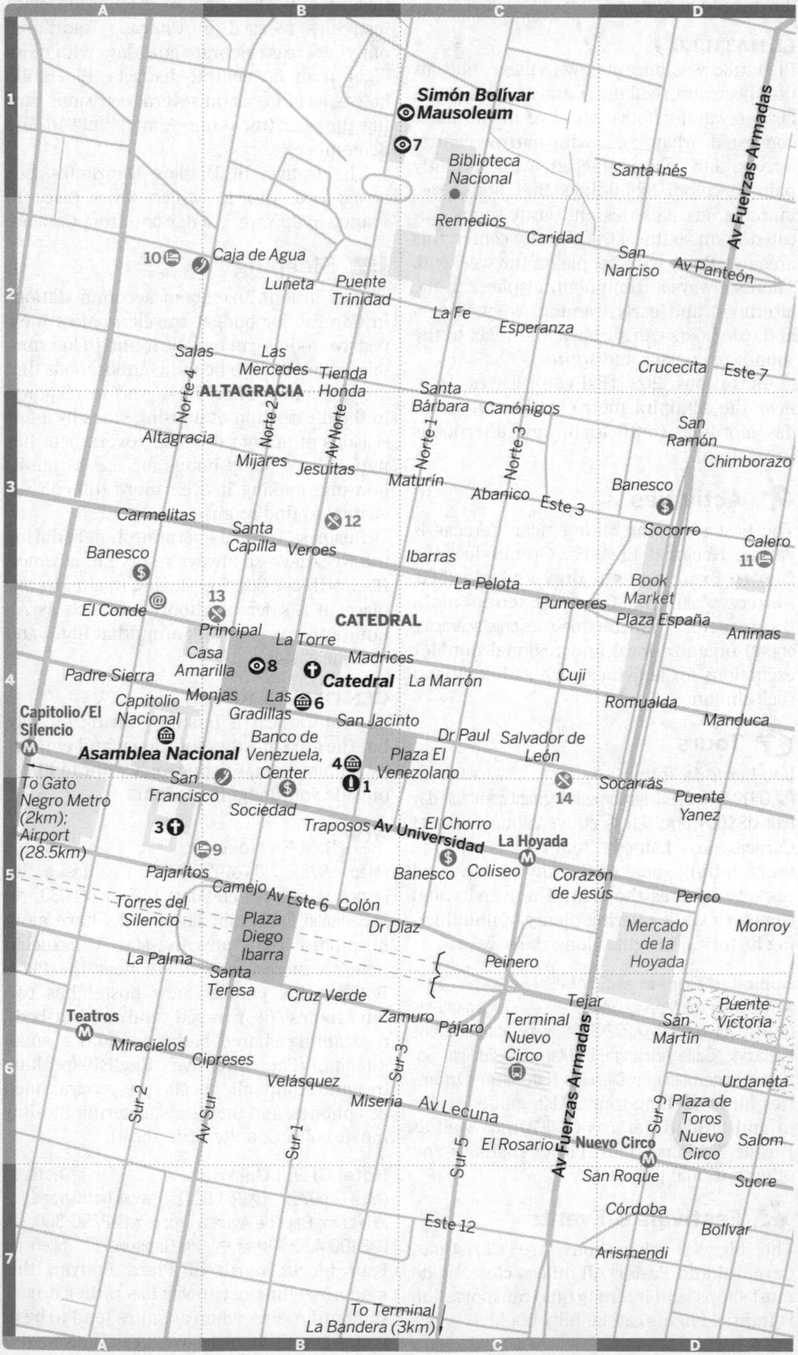

A B C D

1 2 3 4 5 6 7

Simón Bolívar Mausoleum
7
Biblioteca Nacional
Santa Inés
Av Fuerzas Armadas
Remedios
Caridad
10
Caja de Agua
San Narciso
Av Panteón
Luneta
Puente Trinidad
La Fe
Esperanza
Salas
Las Mercedes
Tienda Honda
Crucecita
Este 7
ALTAGRACIA
Santa Bárbara
Canónigos
Norte 4
Norte 2
Av Norte
Norte 1
Norte 3
Altagracia
San Ramón
Mijares
Jesuitas
Chimborazo
Maturín
Banesco
Abanico
Este 3
Carmelitas
12
Santa Capilla
Veroes
Socorro
Banesco
Ibarras
Calero
11
La Pelota
Book Market
13
El Conde
Punceres
Plaza España
CATEDRAL
Principal
La Torre
Animas
Casa Amarilla
8
Madrices
Catedral
Padre Sierra
La Marrón
Cuji
Monjas
Las Gradillas
6
Romualda
Capitolio/El Silencio
Capitolio Nacional
San Jacinto
Manduca
Banco de Venezuela
Dr Paul
Salvador de León
Asamblea Nacional
Plaza El Venezolano
4
San Francisco
Center
1
To Gato Negro Metro (2km); Airport (28.5km)
Socarrás
14
Puente Yanez
Sociedad
3
Traposos
Av Universidad
El Chorro
La Hoyada
9
Banesco
Coliseo
Pajaritos
Corazón de Jesús
Camejo
Av Este 6
Colón
Perico
Torres del Silencio
Plaza Diego Ibarra
Dr Díaz
Mercado de la Hoyada
Monroy
La Palma
Peinero
Santa Teresa
Cruz Verde
Tejar
Teatros
Zamuro
Pájaro
Terminal Nuevo Circo
San Martín
Puente Victoria
Miracielos
Cipreses
Sur 3
Velásquez
Urdaneta
Sur 2
Av Sur
Sur 1
Miseria
Av Lecuna
Sur 9
Plaza de Toros Nuevo Circo
Av Fuerzas Armadas
Sur 5
El Rosario
Nuevo Circo
Salom
San Roque
Sucre
Córdoba
Este 12
Bolívar
Arismendi
To Terminal La Bandera (3km)

VENEZUELA CARACAS

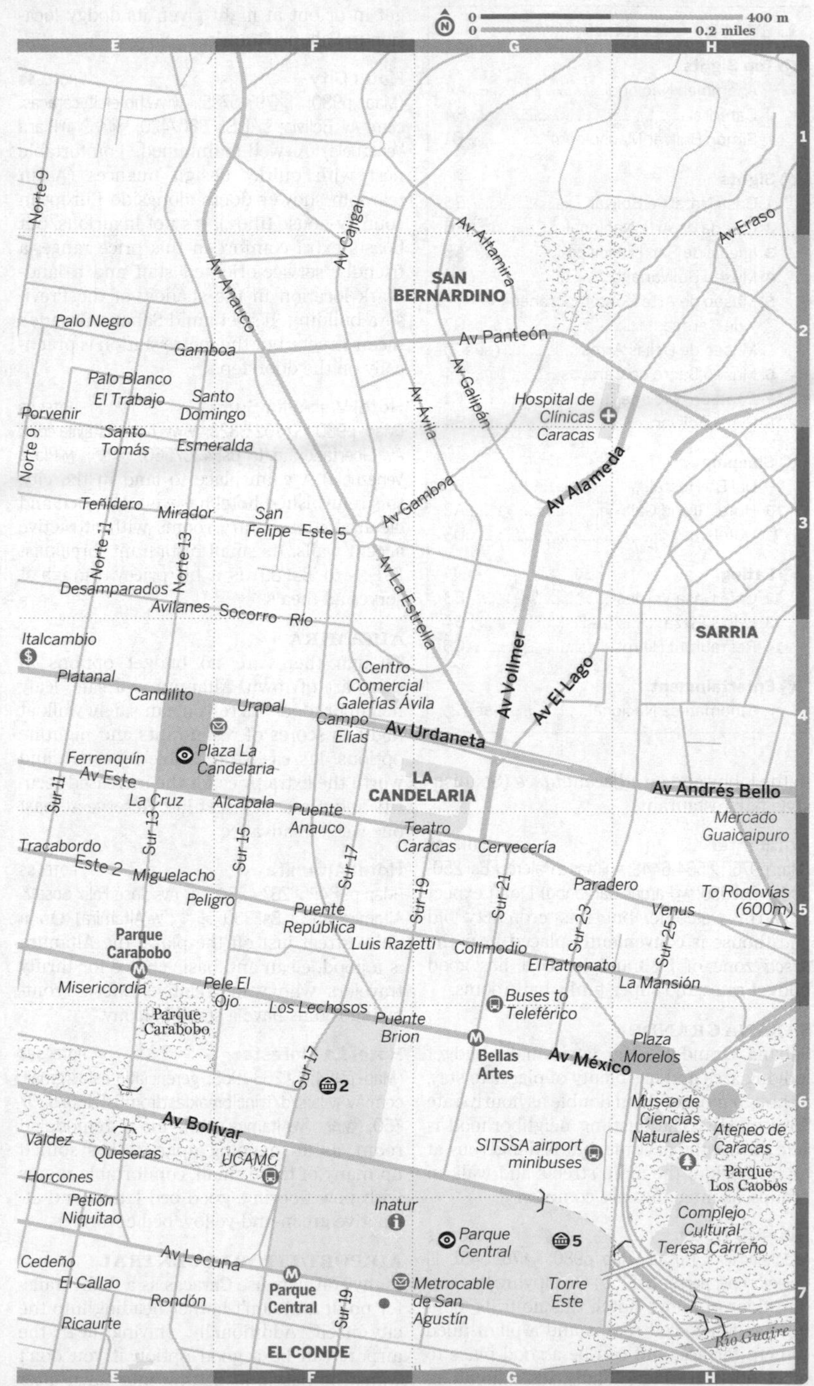
0 400 m
0 0.2 miles
SAN BERNARDINO
LA CANDELARIA
SARRIA
EL CONDE
Av Cajigal
Av Altamira
Av Eraso
Av Anauco
Av Panteón
Av Galipán
Av Ávila
Av Gamboa
Av La Estrella
Av Alameda
Av Vollmer
Av El Lago
Av Urdaneta
Av Andrés Bello
Av Este
Este 2
Este 5
Av México
Av Bolívar
Av Lecuna
Norte 9
Norte 11
Norte 13
Sur 11
Sur 13
Sur 15
Sur 17
Sur 19
Sur 21
Sur 23
Sur 25
Palo Negro
Gamboa
Palo Blanco
El Trabajo
Santo Domingo
Porvenir
Santo Tomás
Esmeralda
Teñidero
Mirador
San Felipe
Desamparados
Avilanes
Socorro
Río
Italcambio
Platanal
Candilito
Urapal
Centro Comercial Galerías Ávila
Campo Elías
Ferrenquín
Plaza La Candelaria
La Cruz
Alcabala
Puente Anauco
Teatro Caracas
Cervecería
Tracabordo
Miguelacho
Peligro
Puente República
Luis Razetti
Colimodio
Paradero
Venus
To Rodovías (600m)
El Patronato
La Mansión
Parque Carabobo
Misericordia
Pele El Ojo
Los Lechosos
Puente Brion
Buses to Teleférico
Bellas Artes
Plaza Morelos
Museo de Ciencias Naturales
Ateneo de Caracas
Parque Los Caobos
Hospital de Clínicas Caracas
Mercado Guaicaipuro
2
Valdez
Queseras
UCAMC
Horcones
Petión
Niquitao
SITSSA airport minibuses
Inatur
Parque Central
5
Complejo Cultural Teresa Carreño
Cedeño
El Callao
Rondón
Ricaurte
Metrocable de San Agustín
Torre Este
Río Guaire
E
F
G
H
1
2
3
4
5
6
7

Central Caracas

Top Sights

Asamblea Nacional A4
Catedral B4
Simón Bolívar Mausoleum C1

Sights

1 Casa Natal de Bolívar B5
2 Galería de Arte Nacional F6
3 Iglesia de San Francisco A5
4 Museo Bolivariano B4
5 Museo de Arte Contemporáneo de Caracas G7
Museo de Bellas Artes .... (see 2)
6 Museo Sacro de Caracas B4
7 Panteón Nacional C1
8 Plaza Bolívar B4

Sleeping

9 Dal Bo Hostal B5
10 Hotel Grand Galaxie A2
11 Hotel Inter D3

Eating

12 Café Casa Veroes B3
13 Evio's Pizza B4
14 Restaurant Beirut C5

Entertainment

Cinemateca Nacional .... (see 2)

in the lobby and an adjacent *tasca* (Spanish-style bar/restaurant).

Hotel Inter HOTEL **$$**

(Map p976; ☎564-6448; Animas a Calero; r BsF250-300, tr BsF350; Ⓜ Parque Carabobo) Don't expect a warm welcome, but this crotchety old guesthouse is conveniently placed near the *tasca* zone of La Candelaria. It has good budget rates and super-funky bathrooms.

SABANA GRANDE

Sabana Grande is the city's main budget lodging area and has plenty of places to stay, although most of them double as hourly-rate 'love motels.' The bustling neighborhood is safe during the daytime, but is dangerous at night. Stick to the main streets and walk in groups, as muggings are common.

Nuestro Hotel HOTEL **$**

(Backpacker's Hostel; Map p980; ☎761-5431; El Colegio; r per person BsF150) Occupying the second floor of a love hotel, this no-frills lodging has fan-cooled rooms and a plant-filled cement terrace, and can be a good place to meet other travelers. Sadly, it's difficult to get in or out at night given its dodgy location in Sabana Grande.

Hotel City HOTEL **$$**

(Map p980; ☎793-5785; www.hotelcitycaracas.com; Av Bolivia; s/d BsF380/420; ; Ⓜ Plaza Venezuela) A well-maintained, comfortable nest with quirky design nuances (Asian tearoom shower doors alongside European country-house tiling). It's not luxurious, but boasts extra comfort in this price range, a friendly, service-oriented staff and a landmark location in the shadow of the Previsora building. It's set amid Sabana Grande's mean streets, but the metro station is practically on the doorstep.

Hotel VistAvila Suites HOTEL **$$**

(Map p980; ☎762-3828; www.hotelvistavila.com; Av Libertador; d/tr BsF420/560; ; Ⓜ Plaza Venezuela) A calm place to land in the city, this refurbished hotel has well-designed and clean, contemporary rooms with attractive accent walls. Its small restaurant (breakfast BsF45 to BsF85) is a bit pricey, though it serves all meals.

ALTAMIRA

Though there are no budget options in this part of town, Altamira is a safe, leafy neighborhood where you can safely walk at night to scores of restaurants and nightlife options. It's easily accessible by metro and worth the extra price for the increased security and pleasant street life. Reserve at least one week in advance.

Hotel Altamira HOTEL **$$**

(Map p984; ☎267-4284; cnr Avs José Félix Sosa & Altamira Sur; r BsF330; ; Ⓜ Altamira) On a quiet street just off the plaza, the Altamira is a good, clean and basic choice for thrifty travelers who want relative safety. Front-facing rooms have a small balcony.

Hotel La Floresta HOTEL **$$$**

(Map p984; ☎263-1955; gerenciafloresta@gmail.com; Av Ávila; s/d/tr incl breakfast from BsF460/520/650; @; Ⓜ Altamira) Ask for a remodeled room, as an ongoing upgrade has spiffed up many of these small, comfortable rooms with new flooring, good bed lamps and attractive green-and-yellow bed coverings.

AIRPORT/LITORAL CENTRAL

Many travelers use Caracas as a flight transfer point and don't bother heading into the city itself. Additionally, staying near the airport can be a good option if you don't want the hassle of getting into town after dark. The coastal towns of Catia La Mar and Macuto are near Maiquetía and have a number of good, safe places to stay. All hotels can arrange airport transfers and many will change money at better rates than you'll find in the terminals. Daytime traffic along the coast can be fierce, but less hectic than making a morning flight from the city center. Since travelers are advised to check in three hours before international flights, you're crazy not to stay here for morning flights. Official airport taxis to Catia La Mar are BsF100 to BsF120, and BsF160 for Macuto.

Hotel Plazamar HOTEL $
(☎339-5242; www.hotelplazamarvenezuela.net; Calle Macuto, Plaza de las Palomas; d/tr/q from BsF 180/300/350; ❄@📶) Off a plaza dedicated to pigeon housing, family-run Plazamar has super-clean, well-kept rooms with cable TV and an ample lobby with a fridge and microwave. A friendly laid-back place with hanging plants, there's also a pleasant upstairs terrace overlooking the plaza and breezes blowing from the beach a block away. Airport transfers cost BsF140.

Hotel Catimar HOTEL $$$
(☎351-9097; www.hotelcatimar.com; Av Principal de Puerto Viejo, Catia La Mar; d BsF460-500, tr & q BsF550-600; ❄@📶) Right across the street from the beach, this professional operation has 75 comfortable rooms, an excellent ocean-view restaurant, good internet access and rates that include all airport transfers.

Hostal Tanausu HOTEL $$
(☎352-1704; www.hoteltanausu.com.ve; Av Atlántida, Catia La Mar; s/d/tr BsF300/390/460; ❄📶) This busy motel-style option has kitschy exterior decor – check out the whimsical patchwork tiling in the hallways – but firm new beds. Pass on the windowless rooms off the upstairs corridor. A *tasca* restaurant sprouting tree columns serves all meals, and airport transfers are BsF100 per carload.

Il Prezzano HOTEL $$
(☎351-2626; www.ilprezzano.com.ve; Av Principal de Playa Grande; s/d/tr/q BsF320/345/370/420; ❄@📶) A popular, safe lodging (across from a police station) with an attached restaurant and a bakery next door. It has clean, good-sized rooms and the upstairs ones have new beds and flat-screen TVs. No deposit required for reservations.

Hotel La Parada HOTEL $$$
(☎351-2148; www.hotelturisticolaparada.amawebs.com; Av Atlántida, Catia La Mar; s/d/tr/q BsF 480/572/670/780; ❄@📶) Kitschy nature murals enliven the hallways, and cheerful rooms have carved wooden headboards, pleasant bedspreads and interior windows, though the bathrooms show the years. Its restaurant serves lunch and dinner, and the front desk sells toiletry kits if your luggage never arrived. Rates include airport transfers, or otherwise are about BsF100 less without.

Eating

The center is packed with low- to mid-priced eateries, and sidewalk vendors sell *cachapas* (corn pancakes; BsF20) along Av Universidad near Parque El Calvario. The Sabana Grande neighborhood has lots of budget lunch spots. A fashionable dining district that becomes particularly lively in the evening, Las Mercedes mostly has restaurants that cater to an affluent clientele, but there are also some budget options.

CENTRAL CARACAS

TOP CHOICE Evio's Pizza PIZZERIA, VENEZUELAN $
(Map p976; Esq Principal, Plaza Bolívar; mains BsF36-62; ⏰noon-9:30pm Mon-Sat; 🌶; Ⓜ Capitolio/El

PERUVIAN MARKET

Looking for a cheap bite when most restaurants are closed? On Sundays from 8am until 4pm or 5pm, follow the *caraqueños* to the bustling Peruvian market for a heaping plate of Peruvian cuisine. For about BsF55, fill up at one of the table buffets serving dishes like *causa rellena* (potato dish stuffed with chicken, tuna or other fillings), chicken and rice, quinoa salad and ceviche, and don't skimp on the *cancha* (toasted corn kernels). Or you can shop for purple potatoes, get a bottle of homemade *chicha* (nonalcoholic corn drink) and watch the musical performances.

The weekly market is outside the Colegio de Ingenieros metro (between the Bellas Artes and Plaza Venezuela stops); exit at Av Libertador Sur/Blvr Santa Rosa and then turn right.

Caracas – Sabana Grande

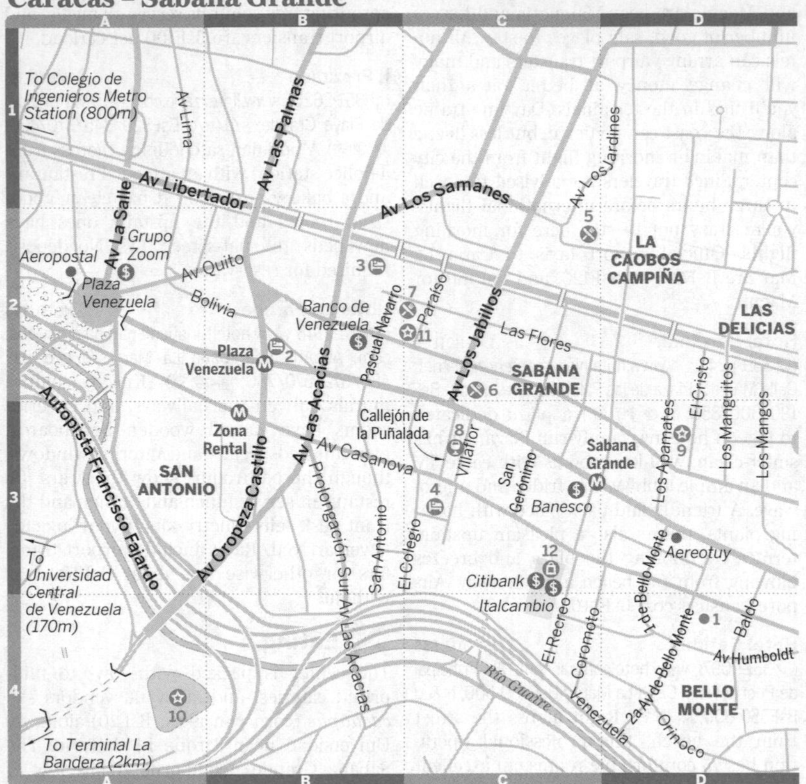

Silencio) There's pizza and then there's the city's best. When famous Venezuelan musician Evio di Marzo isn't performing, he makes gourmet pizza and a fusion menu he terms '*bol-che-vista*' (BOL-ivariano, CHE-guevarista and cha-VISTA). Locals idle over lunch at the shaded tables off the plaza and pack the place for the live salsa, jazz and fusion sets Thursday to Saturday from 7pm.

Restaurant Beirut LEBANESE **$**
(Map p976; Salvador de León a Socarrás; mains BsF43-85; ⌚cafe 7am-5:30pm Mon-Sat, restaurant lunch Mon-Sat; ; Ⓜ La Hoyada) Grab a coffee and baklava at the cafe downstairs or sit upstairs for tasty Lebanese food amid the turquoise walls and orange alcoves.

Café Casa Veroes CAFE, VENEZUELAN **$$$**
(Map p976; Jesuitas a Veroes; mains BsF99-193; ⌚9am-3:30pm Mon-Fri; Ⓜ Capitolio/El Silencio) For some of the city's best coffee, search out this hidden, open-air cafe tucked away in the leafy backyard of a home-turned-museum donated by the Polar beer family – it's a true local's secret. There's a rotating chalkboard menu of modern Venezuelan creations, and the terrace has wooden rocking chairs perfect for lingering over the newspapers-on-a-stick. Spotless bathrooms too!

SABANA GRANDE

El Vegetariano de la Florida VEGETARIAN **$**
(Map p980; Av Los Jardines, La Campiña, a block north of Av Libertador; menú BsF40; ⌚lunch Mon-Fri; ; Ⓜ Sabana Grande) After 50 years of successfully pulling in the customers, they must be doing something right. This is a venerated vegetarian spot, renowned for its filling quality *menú del día*. Look for a house under a magnificent mango tree, and buy your ticket before 1pm – the food runs out fast.

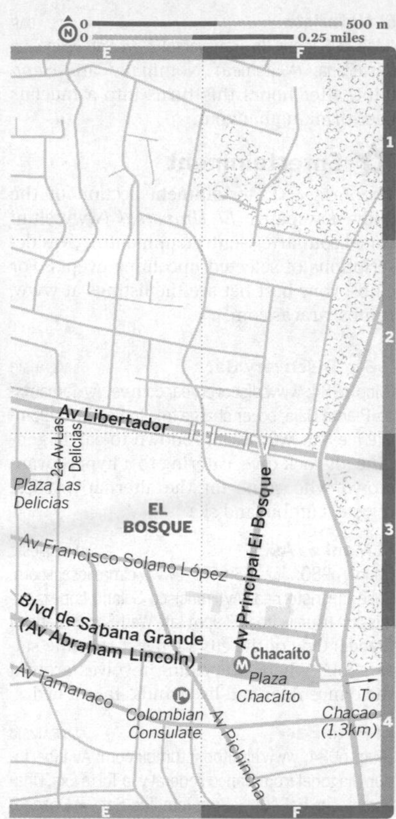

Caracas – Sabana Grande

Restaurant Vegetariano Sabas Nieves VEGETARIAN $
(Map p980; Navarro 12; menú BsF35; lunch Mon-Sat; ; Plaza Venezuela) A tranquil spot in a hectic neighborhood, its rotating fixed-price lunches can keep vegetarians entertained for the length of their stay.

K'Sualmania MIDDLE EASTERN $$
(Map p980; Av Los Jabillos, Edificio Argui; combo platters BsF50-65; lunch Mon-Sat; Sabana Grande) Run by a corps of kinetic young women, this spiffy little Middle Eastern joint has some of the finest falafels and *tabaquitos* (stuffed grape leaves) around.

ALTAMIRA

Café Il Botticello ITALIAN $$
(Map p984; 2a Transversal; pizzas BsF57-90, pasta BsF45-56; lunch & dinner Mon-Sat; ; Altamira) Ring the bell to enter this tiny dining room serving pastas and excellent pizzas.

Pollo en Brasas El Coyuco FAST FOOD $
(Map p984; 3a Av near 3a Transversal, Los Palos Grandes; half/full roast chicken BsF47/94; lunch & dinner; Miranda) This classic spot in a popular restaurant corridor is often packed with locals chowing down on lusciously seasoned roasted chicken and yucca within a rustic, log-cabin setting.

Restaurant Gran Horizonte VENEZUELAN $$
(Map p984; Av Blandín; arepas & cachapas BsF25-62; 24hr; Chacao) Tuck into your favorite *arepa* (stuffed corn pancake) combo, a perfect sweet-corn *cachapa* or a filling plateful of BBQ meats (BsF75 to BsF120) at this cow-themed all-hours *arepera* near the Centro Comercial San Ignacio.

Miga's CAFE $$
(Map p984; cnr 1a Transversal & Av Luis Roche; sandwiches & salads BsF53-85; breakfast, lunch & dinner; ; Altamira) An indoor-outdoor bakery/cafe, with an army of servers that guarantees superfast breakfasts (BsF49 to BsF60) and hefty sandwiches.

Arábica Coffee Bar CAFE $$
(Map p984; Av Andrés Bello, Los Palos Grandes; breakfast from BsF57; 7am-11pm Mon-Wed, to midnight Thu-Sun; ; Altamira) Caffeine junkies unite here over the house-roasted beans whose waft is discernable up and down the

block. The Moorish-accented interior and shady garden are a delightful place to sample made-to-order empanadas and nibble on excellent pastries over a cappuccino.

Las Mercedes

La Casa del Llano VENEZUELAN $$

(Map p984; Av Río de Janeiro, Las Mercedes; mains BsF70-120; ⊙24hr) A no-nonsense all-night diner, with *arepas*, *parrilla* (grilled meat) and other Venezuelan standards.

Drinking

Las Mercedes and La Castellana (particularly the Centro Comercial San Ignacio) hold most of the city's nightlife, but bars and discos dot other neighborhoods as well, including Sabana Grande, El Rosal and Altamira. Many nightclubs have basic dress codes. If a club has a cover charge, it often entitles you to your first drink or two.

Callejón de la Puñalada BAR

(Map p980; Pasaje Asunción, Sabana Grande; Ⓜ Plaza Venezuela, Sabana Grande) Students, punks and hippies socialize over beer and cigarettes outside the half-dozen bars along this muraled and well-lit pedestrian alley.

El León BEER HALL, PIZZERIA

(Map p984; Plaza La Castellana, La Castellana; Ⓜ Altamira) Sit on a lofty concrete terrace and knock back cheap beers and pizza in this well-known Caracas spot.

360° Roof Bar BAR

(Map p984; 1a Av btwn 1a & 2a Transversal, Hotel Altamira Suites, Los Palos Grandes; ⊙5pm-late; Ⓜ Altamira) This innovative open-air lounge atop the Altamira Suites attracts hip scene-makers, who come to chill out on hammocks and sofas in the 19th-floor restaurant and sip innovative cocktails over startling panoramic views of the city on the circular rooftop terrace. Access is through the hotel's rear entrance on 1a Av – and subject to a coolness size up. Go on a clear night.

Barra Bar LOUNGE

(Map p984; Centro Comercial Mata de Coco, Av San Marino, San Marino; cover BsF20-50; ⊙9pm-4am Wed-Sat; Ⓜ Chacao) If the decked out see-and-be-seen club extravaganza at Centro Comercial San Ignacio isn't your thing, try this intimate lounge nearby, tucked in a pedestrian alley next to the Seniat building. Locals throng here on Thursdays for the live salsa bands, and you'll hear electronica on weekends.

El Naturista BAR

(Map p984; cnr 2a Transversal & Av San Felipe, La Castellana; Ⓜ Altamira) Nominally an *arepa* joint, after hours this turns into a raucous beer-drinking hangout.

☆ Entertainment

The Arts & Entertainment section of the daily newspaper *El Universal* (www.eluniversal.com/arte-y-entretenimiento) gives descriptions of selected upcoming events. For clubs, your best bet are the listings at www.rumbacaracas.com.

Discovery Bar LIVE MUSIC

(Map p984; www.discoverybar.com.ve; Av Tamanaco, Planta Baja; cover charge free to BsF50; ⊙9pm-late Tue-Sat; Ⓜ Chacaíto) A down-to-earth, genuine alt-rock dive, catering to a hyper-aware crowd who come for the alternative rock, reggae, cumbia and ska.

El Maní es Así LIVE MUSIC

(Map p980; ☎763-6671; www.elmaniesasi.com; Calle El Cristo near Av Francisco Solano López; admission usually free; ⊙9pm-late Wed-Sat; Ⓜ Sabana Grande) One of the city's longest-running salsa spots, where everything revolves around the dance floor and live bands. Take a taxi.

El Puto Bar LIVE MUSIC

(Map p984; www.elputobar.tumblr.com; Av Libertador, diagonal from Banco Federal y la Torre Exa, Chacao; cover BsF40; ⊙8pm-late Tue-Sat; Ⓜ Chacao) Red velvet curtains and a text-plastered bar festoon this cave-like hipster venue, and DJs and live bands play salsa, rock, reggae and house. Try the house craft beer, *Los Miaos de Dios* (the Meows of God) and look for the guy with the crazy hair who acts like he owns the place. He does.

Centro Comercial San Ignacio CLUB, BAR

(Map p984; www.centrosanignacio.com; cnr Blandín & Arturo Uslar Pietri) With more than a dozen nightclubs and bars, this mall comes alive at night. Dress to impress.

Gay & Lesbian Venues

Caracas has by far the most open gay community in what is still a relatively conservative country. There are long-established gay and lesbian bars and clubs in Las Mercedes, Sabana Grande and La Castellana.

Tasca Pullman GAY

(Map p980; ☎761-1112; Av Francisco Solano López, Edificio Ovidio; ⊙from 5pm-late Tue-Sun; Ⓜ Plaza Venezuela) A friendly and unpretentious place, the Pullman is the most popular of a group of small gay taverns in Sabana Grande. Don't walk alone near here after dark.

Copa's Dancing Bar GAY, LESBIAN
(Map p984; ☎951-3947; Calle Guaicaipuro, Edificio Taeca; cover BsF120; ⏰10:30pm-6:30am Wed-Sat; Ⓜ Chacaíto) A mix of men and women pack the crisp-white high-energy dance space, though Thursday is reserved for women. Prepare to be sized up through the front-door peephole and show your passport.

Cultural Centers

Celarg CINEMA, THEATER
(Centro de Estudios Latinoamericanos Rómulo Gallegos; Map p984; ☎285-2990; www.celarg.org.ve; cnr Av Luis Roche & 3a Transversal; movie admission adult/student BsF3.50/1.80; 📶; Ⓜ Altamira) A pleasant place to soak up the arts, this state-subsidized venue shows a large selection of international films (with Spanish subtitles). It also hosts contemporary world cinema festivals and some free weekend screenings. Spanish-speakers should also check out its excellent live theater (tickets BsF100 to BsF140) schedule.

Cinemateca Nacional CINEMA
(Map p976; ☎576-1491; www.cinemateca.gob.ve/fcn; Galería de Arte Nacional, Bellas Artes, Plaza de Los Museos, Parque Los Caobos; admission up to BsF10; Ⓜ Bellas Artes) The main showplace of the country's national cinema program, the Cinemateca Nacional screens a wide range of domestic and international films (subtitled in Spanish).

FREE **Centro de Acción Social por la Música** CLASSICAL MUSIC
(Center for Social Action Through Music; ☎597-0511; www.fesnojiv.gob.ve; Blvd Amador Bendayán, Quebrada Honda; Ⓜ Colegio de Ingenieros) Hear top-notch classical recitals for free at the Sala Simón Bolívar, one of the venues for El Sistema, Venezuela's world-renowned youth orchestra program.

FREE **La Estancia** ARTS CENTER
(Map p984; ☎0800-743-6272; www.pdvsalaestancia.com; Av Francisco de Miranda; Ⓜ Altamira) Sponsored by the government oil company, this arts center hosts yoga and music classes, programs for kids and weekend concerts. Everything is free.

Teatro Trasnocho Cultural ARTS CENTER
(Map p984; ☎993-1910; www.trasnochocultural.com; Av Principal de las Mercedes, Las Mercedes, Centro Comercial Paseo Las Mercedes) This buzzing contemporary arts center buried in a mall sub-basement contains a theater, cinema, cafes, a yoga studio and a queer-friendly hipster bar.

Sports

Estadio Universitario BASEBALL
(University Stadium; Map p980; ☎0500-226-7366; tickets BsF30-225; Ⓜ Ciudad Universitaria) *Béisbol* (baseball) is the local sporting obsession. Professional-league games are played from October to February at this 18,500-seat stadium, home to the Leones de Caracas (Caracas Lions; www.leones.com), on the grounds of the Universidad Central de Venezuela. Tickets may be purchased up until game time, usually 7:30pm Tuesday to Friday nights, 6pm Saturday and 4:30pm Sunday; or in advance between 10am and 5pm Monday to Friday at Galerias El Recreo in Sabana Grande.

Shopping

Shopping is one of the city's greatest pastimes and malls are an important part of *caraqueño* life.

Centro Comercial Sambil MALL
(Map p984; www.sambilmall.com; Av Libertador; ⏰10am-9pm Mon-Sat, noon-8pm Sun; Ⓜ Chacao) Touted as South America's largest shopping mall.

Centro Comercial El Recreo MALL
(Map p980; www.elrecreo.com.ve; Av Casanova; ⏰10am-9pm Mon-Sat, noon-8pm Sun; Ⓜ Sabana Grande) The big mall in Sabana Grande.

Centro Comercial Paseo Las Mercedes MALL
(Map p984; Av Principal de las Mercedes) An upscale shopping destination with restaurants, a movie theater and an excellent cultural center. From the metro Chacaíto, take Metrobús 221.

Centro Comercial San Ignacio MALL
(Map p984; www.centrosanignacio.com; Av Blandín, La Castellana) Also one of the city's best centers for nightlife.

Bookstores

American Book Shop BOOKS
(Map p984; Centro Comercial Centro Plaza, Jardín level, Los Palos Grandes; Ⓜ Altamira) Offers a decent selection of English titles and used books.

Caracas - Las Mercedes & Altamira

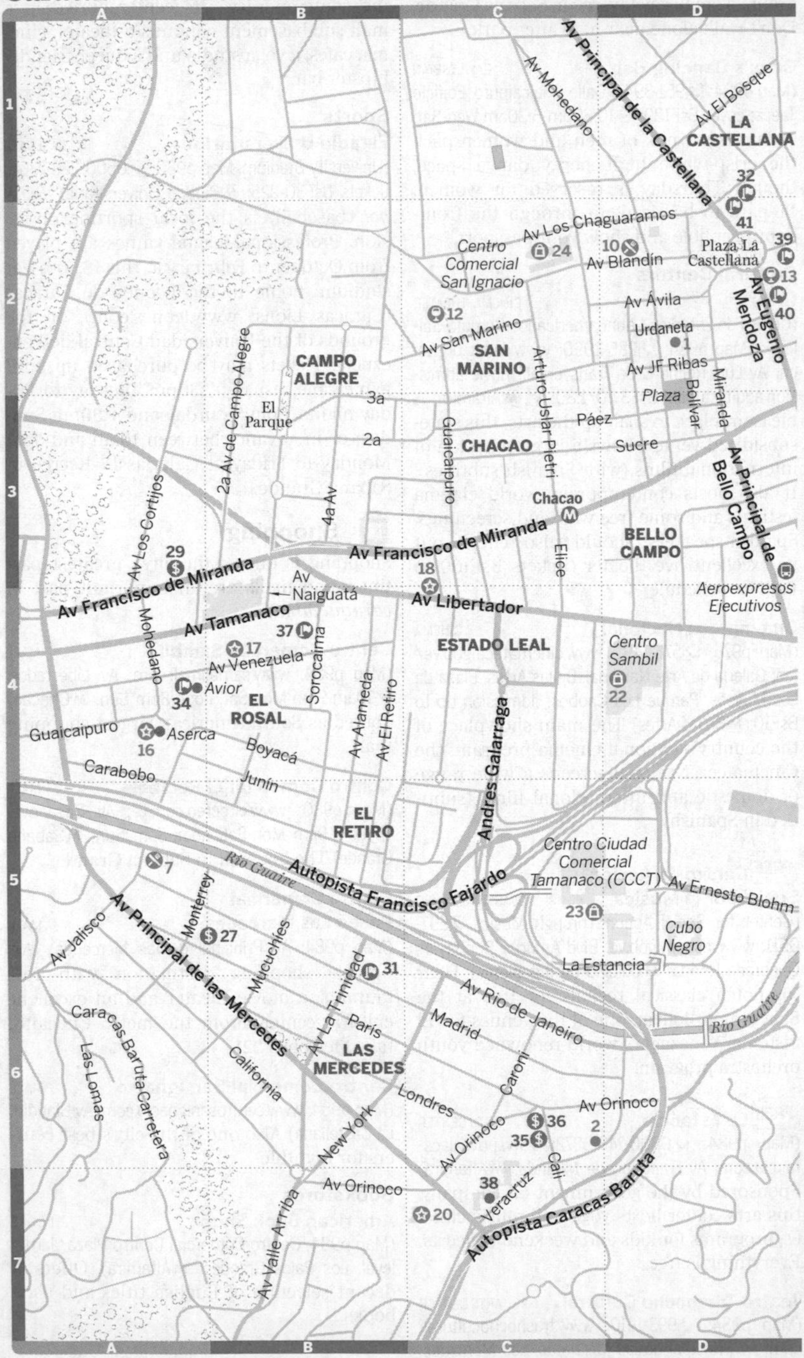

A B C D
1 2 3 4 5 6 7

Av Principal de la Castellana
Av Mohedano
Av El Bosque
LA CASTELLANA
32
41
Av Los Chaguaramos
Centro Comercial San Ignacio
24
10
Av Blandín
Plaza La Castellana
39
13
40
Av Eugenio Mendoza
Av Ávila
12
Urdaneta
1
Av San Marino
SAN MARINO
Arturo Uslar Pietri
Av JF Ribas
Miranda
Bolívar
Plaza
CAMPO ALEGRE
2a Av de Campo Alegre
3a
El Parque
2a
Guaicaipuro
Páez
CHACAO
Sucre
Av Principal de Bello Campo
4a Av
Av Los Cortijos
Chacao
BELLO CAMPO
Av Francisco de Miranda
Elice
29
18
Av Naiguatá
Av Libertador
Aeroexpresos Ejecutivos
Av Tamanaco
37
ESTADO LEAL
Centro Sambil
17
Av Venezuela
Mohedano
22
34
Avior
EL ROSAL
Sorocaima
Av Alameda
Av El Retiro
Andrés Galarraga
Guaicaipuro
16
Aserca
Boyacá
Carabobo
Junín
EL RETIRO
Centro Ciudad Comercial Tamanaco (CCCT)
Río Guaire
7
Autopista Francisco Fajardo
Av Ernesto Blohm
Av Principal de las Mercedes
Monterrey
23
Av Jalisco
27
Cubo Negro
Mucuchíes
La Estancia
31
Av La Trinidad
Av Río de Janeiro
Río Guaire
Caracas Baruta Carretera
París
Madrid
Las Lomas
California
LAS MERCEDES
Caroní
Londres
Av Orinoco
36
2
35
Av Orinoco
New York
Cali
Av Orinoco
38
Veracruz
Autopista Caracas Baruta
20
Av Valle Arriba

VENEZUELA CARACAS

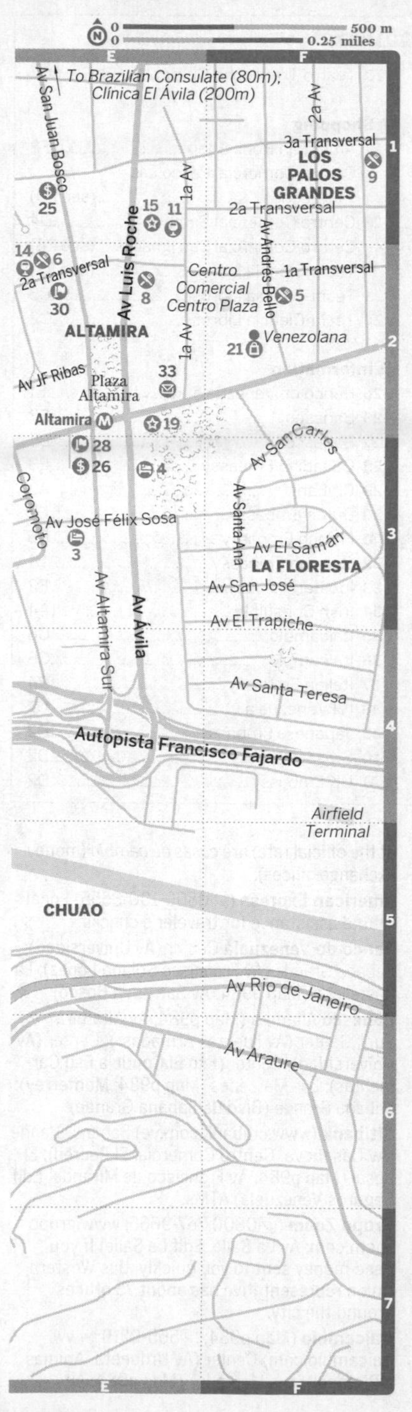

Tecni-Ciencia Libros BOOKS
(www.tecniciencia.com) Centro Ciudad Comercial Tamanaco (Map p984; Av Ernesto Blohm); Centro Sambil (Map p984; Nivel Acuario, Av Libertador; Ⓜ Chacao); Centro Comercial San Ignacio (Map p984; Nivel Chaguaramos; Ⓜ Chacao) Chain bookstore with a reliable collection of texts in English and Spanish, including some Lonely Planet guidebooks.

Information

Dangers & Annoyances

Caracas has a justifiably bad reputation for petty crime, robbery and armed assaults. Sabana Grande and the city center are the riskiest neighborhoods, although they are generally safe during the day (but watch for pickpockets in dense crowds). Altamira and Las Mercedes are considerably safer. Travelers should always stick to well-lit main streets or use taxis after dark. Be alert about your surroundings, but don't succumb to paranoia.

Perhaps more than street crime, traffic in Caracas is the greatest danger, particularly for pedestrians. Cars, but especially motorcycles, routinely ignore traffic signals and often speed up to show dominance over life forms with legs. Never assume you have right of way in any crossing, and try to cross with others.

The Caracas airport, especially the international arrivals area, is awash with official-looking touts trying to arrange your transportation or change your cash. In the past, travelers using unofficial airport transportation have been robbed or 'express kidnapped,' where they are held and forced to withdraw money from ATMs. If you haven't arranged an airport pickup, only use the official airport taxis (black Ford Explorers with yellow shields on the doors), or the airport buses (p989). Black-market money changers at the airport (and other locations) may rip you off if you aren't aware of the current exchange rate or appearance of the currency.

Always carry your passport, or a copy showing the entrance stamp, as police have been known to harass foreigners without documents.

Emergency

Emergency Center (☎Police, fire & ambulance 171; ⏲24hr) Operators rarely speak English.

Internet Access

Internet cafes are not difficult to come by, and rates run around BsF5 to BsF10 per hour. The modern shopping malls tend to have cybercafes with fast connections and the newest equipment, and most hotels have wi-fi. Also see Movistar (p987). Maiquetía's airport terminals have free wi-fi (post-security), and there's an internet cafe before security at the international terminal.

Caracas – Las Mercedes & Altamira

Activities, Courses & Tours
1 Akanan Travel & Adventure D2
2 Sociedad Conservacionista Audubón de Venezuela C6

Sleeping
3 Hotel Altamira E3
4 Hotel La Floresta E3

Eating
5 Arábica Coffee Bar F2
6 Café Il Botticello E2
7 La Casa del Llano A5
8 Miga's E2
9 Pollo en Brasas El Coyuco F1
10 Restaurant Gran Horizonte D2

Drinking
11 360° Roof Bar E1
12 Barra Bar C2
13 El León D2
14 El Naturista E2

Entertainment
15 Celarg E1
Centro Comercial San Ignacio .... (see 24)
16 Copa's Dancing Bar A4
17 Discovery Bar B4
18 El Puto Bar C3
19 La Estancia E2
20 Teatro Trasnocho Cultural C7

Shopping
21 American Book Shop F2
Centro Comercial Paseo Las Mercedes .... (see 20)
22 Centro Comercial Sambil D4
Centro Comercial San Ignacio ..... (see 24)
Tecni-Ciencia Libros .... (see 22)
23 Tecni-Ciencia Libros C5
24 Tecni-Ciencia Libros C2

Information
25 Banco de Venezuela E1
26 Banesco E3
27 Banesco B5
28 Canadian Embassy E3
29 Citibank A3
30 Dutch Embassy E2
31 French Embassy B5
32 German Embassy D1
33 Ipostel E2
34 Irish Consulate A4
35 Italcambio C6
36 Italcambio C6
37 Italian Embassy B4
38 IVI Venezuela C7
39 Japanese Embassy D2
40 Swiss Embassy D2
41 UK Embassy D2

Medical Services

Most minor health problems can be solved in a *farmacia* (pharmacy). There's always at least one open in every neighborhood and you can easily recognize them by the neon sign that says 'Turno.' Some dependable *farmacia* chains found throughout the city include Farmatodo and FarmAhorro.

These reputable medical facilities can help with more serious medical problems:

Clínica El Ávila (☎276-1111; www.clinicaelavila.com; cnr Av San Juan Bosco & 6a Transversal, Altamira; Ⓜ Altamira)

Hospital de Clínicas Caracas (☎508-6111; www.clinicaracas.com; cnr Avs Panteón & Alameda, San Bernardino)

Money

International banks and ATMs blanket the city and the airport terminals, but keep in mind that extracting cash will net you the official exchange rate, and you cannot change BsF back to dollars. The usual places to change foreign cash (also at the official rate) are *casas de cambio* (money exchange offices).

American Express (☎0800-100-3555) Local refund assistance for traveler's checks.

Banco de Venezuela Center (Av Universidad); Sabana Grande (Av Francisco Solano López); La Castellana (Map p984; Av San Juan Bosco)

Banesco Altamira (Map p984; Av Altamira Sur); Center (Av Fuerzas Armadasr); Center (Av Universidad); Center (Esq El Conde a Esq Carmelitas); Las Mercedes (Map p984; Monterrey); Sabana Grande (Blvd de Sabana Grande)

Citibank (www.citibank.com.ve) Sabana Grande (Av Casanova, Centro Comercial El Recreo); El Rosal (Map p984; Av Francisco de Miranda, Edif Seguros Venezuela) ATMs.

Grupo Zoom (☎0800-767-9666; www.grupozoom.com; Av La Salle, Edif La Salle) If you need money sent to you quickly, this Western Union representative has about 75 offices around the city.

Italcambio (Map p984; ☎565-0219; www.italcambio.com) Center (Av Urdaneta, Animas a Platanal); Las Mercedes (Map p984; Av

Orinoco); Maiquetía airport (international & national terminals); Sabana Grande (Av Casanova, Centro Comercial El Recreo) Currency exchange.

Post

FedEx (☎205-3333; www.fedex.com/ve)

Ipostel (www.ipostel.gob.ve) Altamira (Map p984; Av Francisco de Miranda); La Candelaria (Plaza La Candelaria); Parque Central (Av Lecuna, Edif Mohedano)

Telephone

Domestic calls can be made from card-operated public phones (cards are for sale at many small shops) or stands with cell phones for rent. International calls are best made from telephone centers such as the ones below, or in some malls.

Movistar Center (Av Universidad, Esq San Francisco; ⏰9am-6pm Mon-Sat); Center (Esq Caja de Agua; ⏰8am-7pm Mon-Fri, 8am-5pm Sat; 📶) Internet at Caja de Agua branch.

Tourist Information

Inatur (www.inatur.gob.ve) Maiquetía airport international terminal (☎355-1442, 355-2104; ⏰6am-10pm); Maiquetía airport domestic terminal (⏰7am-8pm) Have free city and country maps, and can arrange lodging. Sometimes have English or French speakers.

Travel Agencies

See Caracas tour companies (p975), which can also book flights.

IVI Venezuela (Map p984; ☎993-8365; www.ivivenezuela.com; Av Principal de las Mercedes, Residencia La Hacienda; ⏰8am-6pm Mon-Fri) Offers reasonable airfares and useful information to foreign students, teachers and people under 26.

Getting There & Away

Air

The **Aeropuerto Internacional 'Simón Bolívar'** (www.aeropuerto-maiquetia.com.ve; 📶) is in Maiquetía, near the port of La Guaira on the Caribbean coast, 26km from central Caracas. It's generally referred to as 'Maiquetía.' There are three terminals: the **international terminal** (☎303-1526), the **domestic terminal** (☎303-1408) and a small auxiliary terminal used by some smaller charter airlines. The two main terminals are separated by an easy walk of 400m, and it's about the same distance to the auxiliary terminal. There's no shuttle service between them.

The terminals have most conveniences, including tourist offices, car rental desks, *casas de cambio*, banks, ATMs, post and telephone offices, restaurants and a bunch of travel agencies, but no left-luggage office.

Arrive at least three hours before international flights, as security screenings can be lengthy. Departure tax is now included in all tickets.

Bus

Caracas has two modern intercity bus terminals and a central terminal for shorter regional journeys. The **Terminal La Bandera** (Av Nueva Granada; Ⓜ La Bandera), 3km south of the center, handles long-distance buses to anywhere in the country's west and southwest. It has good facilities, including computerized ticket booths, ATMs, telephones, a left-luggage office, an information desk and lots of food outlets. The terminal is 300m from La Bandera metro station; you can walk the distance during the day, but take precautions at night when the area becomes unsafe. From the metro, take the Granada/Zuloaga exit, cross the avenue and turn left.

The city's other main bus terminal, the **Terminal de Oriente** (☎243-3253; Autopista Caracas-Guarenas), is on the eastern outskirts of Caracas, on the highway to Barcelona, 5km beyond Petare (about 18km from the center). It's accessible by many local buses from the city center or via a 15-minute minibus ride from the Petare metro stop. It handles much of the traffic to the east and southeast of the country. It also houses government-run **SITSSA** (☎0800-748-7720; www.sitssa.gob.ve) buses serving the entire country, which cost about half as much but require queuing before the ticket windows open at 6am.

Bus companies **Aeroexpresos Ejecutivos** (☎266-2321; www.aeroexpresos.com.ve; Av Principal de Bello Campo; Ⓜ Altamira) and **Rodovías** (☎577-6622; www.rodovias.com.ve; Av Libertador; Ⓜ Colegio de Ingenieros) have less chaotic private terminals conveniently located in the downtown area, with (slightly higher) prices and schedules listed on their websites. They both service destinations including Ciudad Bolívar, Maracaibo, Ciudad Guayana and Puerto La Cruz.

See boxed text, p989, for details on Maiquetía airport buses.

INFOCENTRO

A government project to provide internet services to all, **Infocentro** (www.infocentro.gob.ve; ⏰variable Mon-Sat) aims to provide 30 minutes of free access available at dozens of libraries, schools and other sites. Expect a wait. The full location list is on its website; scroll down to 'Ubica tu Infocentro.'

BUS FARES FROM TERMINAL LA BANDERA

DESTINATION	COST (BSF)	DURATION (HR)
Barinas	121-148	8½
Coro	94-133	7
Maracaibo	137-180	10½
Maracay	35-44	1½
Mérida	161-212	13
Paraguachón	188-249	13
San Cristóbal	162-213	13
San Fernando de Apure	84-109	8
Valencia	44-48	2½

BUS FARES FROM TERMINAL DE ORIENTE

DESTINATION	COST (BSF)	DURATION (HR)
Cartagena, Colombia	760	23
Ciudad Bolívar	103-155	9
Ciudad Guayana	115-180	10
Cumaná	89-110	6½
Maturín	101-145	8
Puerto La Cruz	75-100	5
Santa Elena	216-300	20
Santa Marta, Colombia	620	18

Getting Around

Bus

An extensive bus network covers all suburbs within the metropolitan area, as well as major neighboring localities. Privately run *carritos* (small buses) are the main type of vehicle operating city routes, in addition to the city-run metrobus (p988) system. Buses run frequently but move only as fast as traffic allows. However, they go to many destinations inaccessible by metro, have the same price and run later at night.

Car & Motorcycle

Are you nuts? Driving in Caracas is only for people with lots of confidence, lots of nerves and a lot more insurance. It is easy to get lost and the traffic is usually gridlocked. If you still insist, pay for parking in a monitored lot.

Metro

A godsend to this chaotic city, the **metro** (www.metrodecaracas.com.ve; ⌚5:30am-11pm) is safe, fast, easy, well organized, clean and affordable – and it serves most major city attractions and tourist facilities. A single ticket for a ride of any distance is BsF1.50. A 10-trip *multiabono* costs BsF13.50 and is worth it to avoid the long ticket lines.

While the metro is generally safe, some opportunistic pickpockets exist.

Taxi

Identifiable by the 'Taxi' or 'Libre' sign, taxis are a fairly inexpensive means of getting around and sometimes the only option at night (when rates go up). None have meters, so always fix the fare before boarding – don't be afraid to bargain. It is recommended that you use only white cars with yellow plates and preferably those from taxi ranks, of which there are plenty, especially outside shopping malls. Alternatively, many hotels and restaurants will call a reliable driver upon request.

In-a-hurry locals swear by the omnipresent Road Warrior–style *mototaxis* (motorcycle taxis). Though after you see how insanely they drive (watch your back on the sidewalk), you may choose to cool your heels.

AROUND CARACAS

Want a break from the bustle of Caracas? There are a number of exciting places to visit nearby, including the Caribbean islands of Los Roques for which Caracas is the main jumping-off point.

Parque Nacional El Ávila

One of the great attractions of the Caracas area, this national park encompasses some 90km of the coastal mountain range north of the city. The highest peak in the range is Pico Naiguatá (2765m), while the most visited is Pico El Ávila (2105m), which is accessed by the *teleférico* (cable car). The southern slope of the range, overlooking Caracas, is uninhabited but crisscrossed with about 200km of walking trails. Most of the trails are well signposted and there are a number of campgrounds.

A dozen entrances lead into the park from Caracas; all originate from Av Boyacá, commonly known as Cota Mil (closed to traffic on Sunday between 6am and 1pm, it's a popular place for riding bikes and jogging) because it runs at an altitude of 1000m. Because of safety concerns, solo hiking is not recommended; check with park staff about camping.

There are plenty of options for a half- or full-day hike. One recommended way is to catch a bus from the east side of Plaza de

GETTING TO/FROM TOWN

Caracas' main airport is at Maiquetía, 26km northwest of the city center. It's linked to the city by a freeway that cuts through the coastal mountain range with a variety of tunnels and bridges. The journey takes approximately 45 minutes without traffic. Almost all hotels and travel outfitters can arrange for transfers from the airport. It's fine during daytime, but do not hang around outside the main airport terminals at night.

Bus

Comfortable government-run **SITSSA airport minibuses** (www.sitssa.gob.ve; Sur 25 near Av México, Hotel Alba Caracas; BsF10) run every half hour, departing from the domestic terminal to the Hotel Alba Caracas (next to Parque Central) from 7:30am to 8:30pm and from outside the hotel to the airport from 6am to 7pm. At the airport, buy tickets inside at its desk next to Inatur. In town, purchase tickets from the office inside the hotel's shopping arcade.

UCAMC (576-9851; Sur 17, btwn Mexico & Av Lecuna; BsF25) airport–city buses depart from the domestic terminal approximately every half hour between 7am to 10:30pm. In the city, buses depart between 5am to 5pm from beside Parque Central (at Sur 17, directly underneath Av Bolívar). With traffic, the fastest option from the airport is to take this bus to the Gato Negro metro station and hop on the metro, though this is not recommended after dark. Other city drop-off points include Plaza Miranda and Parque Central (the final stop). The Parque Central location is under a busy overpass, and rather noisy and dark.

Taxi

In both terminals, official airport taxi kiosks print out tickets listing the posted price of your destination (BsF220 to BsF250 to central Caracas, depending on area and time of day; cash only); pay the driver upon arrival. Taxis are black Ford Explorers with yellow placards on the side and spiffily attired drivers. Unregistered taxis are *not* recommended because of reports of robberies and kidnappings.

Francia in Altamira (by the Hotel Caracas Palace) to the Sabas Nieves entrance, from which it's a 300m hike up to the ranger post. From there, you can pick up an easy-to-handle nature trail along the southern slope that passes a series of streams, waterfalls and caves. Another trail from Sabas Nieves climbs the mountain, one of four main ascents to the park's highest points, Pico Oriental (2640m) and Pico Naiguatá. One of the most scenic routes is along the Fila Maestra, following the crest of the Ávila range from Pico de Ávila to Pico Naiguatá and rewarding hikers with splendid views toward both the valley of Caracas and the Caribbean Sea.

Archipiélago Los Roques

0237 / POP 1800

Island-hopping is the primary activity on Los Roques, a group of nearly 300 shimmering, sandy islands that lie in aquamarine waters some 160km due north of Caracas. It's pricier than the mainland because everything is imported, but for those who love undeveloped beaches, snorkeling and diving, the trip is worth every bolívar. There are no high-rise hotels and you can walk barefoot on Gran Roque's sand streets. The whole archipelago, complete with the surrounding waters (2211 sq km), was made a national park in 1972.

The great majority of the islands are uninhabited except for pelicans and can be visited by boats from Gran Roque. The surrounding waters are known for their sea life, particularly lobsters.

For sunset views at Gran Roque, climb the hill to the remains of Faro Holandés, an 1870s lighthouse.

Gran Roque has the only village – a grid of four or so sandy car-free streets, a plaza and dozens of quaint *posadas* (small, family-run guesthouses). Bring a flashlight in case of power outages. All visitors to Los Roques must pay a BsF180 national park entry fee upon arrival.

Activities

Snorkeling & Diving

Los Roques is one of Venezuela's top destinations for snorkeling. Among the best places

DON'T MISS

TELEFÉRICO WARAIRAREPANO

Rising high above Caracas to the peak of El Ávila (2105m), the **Teleférico Warairarepano** (Warairarepano cable car; ☎792-7050; www.ventel.gob.ve; adult/child BsF45/25; ⏲9:30am-8pm Tue-Thu, 9:30am-10pm Fri & Sat, to 8pm Sun, closed Mon Jul 22–Sep 15; noon-8pm Tue, 10:30am-8pm Wed-Sun Sep 16-Jul 21) runs 4km from Maripérez station (980m), next to Av Boyacá in Caracas, to Pico El Ávila. It's a phenomenal gondola ascent with some nail-biting heights, counting views of thick forest canopy, secret falls and the whole of Caracas.

The summit also offers breathtaking views of Caracas and the Valle del Tuy beyond; towards the north is a stunning panorama of the coastline and the Caribbean Sea stretching away to the horizon. The area around the *teleférico* station has been developed as a sort of fun park with a playground, 3D cinema and an ice-skating rink, as well as several restaurants and numerous stands along the main path selling coffee, hot chocolate and snacks.

Buses (Sur 21) to Maripérez station, labeled 'Sarria–Teleférico,' run from just north of Bellas Artes metro station (BsF3, 15 minutes); taxis charge BsF40 to BsF50 from the center or Altamira.

are Boca de Cote, Crasquí and Noronquises (here you can swim with the sea turtles), but there are other excellent reef sites closer to Gran Roque. The most popular spot is the so-called *piscina* (literally 'swimming pool') on Francisquí de Arriba.

You can get snorkeling gear at many shops and most *posadas*. Scuba diving is also fabulous here; a two-dive excursion including equipment costs US$95.

Dive companies:

Aquatics Diving Center DIVING
(☎0212-239-1882, 0424-138-1240; www.adclosroques.com; Plaza Bolívar)

Arrecife DIVING
(☎0412-249-5119; www.divevenezuela.com) Next to Inparques.

Ecobuzos DIVING
(☎0416-696-5775; www.ecobuzos.com)

Wind & Water Sports

Los Roques is also a top-notch spot for windsurfing and kitesurfing. Both of the following operators offer kitesurfing classes (about BsF3000 for a six-hour class) and rentals.

Play Los Roques WATER SPORTS
(☎0414-905-5557; www.playlosroques.com) Next to Inparques, with stand-up paddleboarding rentals (BsF500/700 for half/full day) and excursions.

Vela Windsurf Center WINDSURFING
(☎0414-012-6751; www.velawindsurf.com) On the island of Francisquí de Abajo, this place rents windsurfing equipment (per hour/half-day/day US$20/35/60) and has lessons (for two hours with equipment US$50).

Sleeping

See www.los-roques.com/posadas.htm for photos and more information about *posadas* and private campgrounds.

Camping

Free camping is permitted on all the islands within the recreation zone, including Gran Roque. After arrival, go to **Inparques** (☎0416-614-2297; ⏲8am-noon & 2-5pm Mon-Fri, longer hrs in high season) at the far end of the village for a free permit and information (note that fires and hanging hammocks are prohibited). They will often safeguard passports and valuables if asked. Oscar Shop (p991) rents tents and Roquelusa charges BsF40 per day bathroom usage for Gran Roque campers, though shower access is limited in high season.

Posadas

There are over 60 *posadas* providing some 500 beds on Gran Roque; almost all offer meals. Rates given here are low season per person; prices jump 30% to 70% in high season (Christmas, Carnaval, Semana Santa and August through mid-September). Weekdays during low season, you can show up and bargain, especially for longer stays. Inclusive flight and lodging package deals generally don't save money.

Conserve water – it's a very precious resource here.

El Botuto GUESTHOUSE $$
(☎0414-238-1589; www.posadaelbotuto.com; r per person incl breakfast/half board BsF385/525;) Known for its fantastic service and sociable dining area, beachside El Botuto has six colorful, airy rooms with small private patios and outdoor showers.

Ranchito Power GUESTHOUSE $$
(☎0414-141-3568; www.posadaranchitopower.com; r per person incl breakfast BsF400-450;) Tiny and simple, this is a great five-room, Italian-run budget option offering clean rooms with crotchety fans, along with a nice rooftop area.

Posada La Laguna GUESTHOUSE $$
(☎0424-262-7913; www.lalaguna.it; La Salina; r per person incl breakfast BsF500;) Blue cement floors and sparkling white walls give this homey Italian-run place a Mediterranean feel. Excellent multicourse dinners upon request.

Doña Carmen GUESTHOUSE $$
(☎0414-318-4926; richardlosroques@hotmail.com; Plaza Bolívar; r per person incl breakfast & dinner BsF500;) The longest-running *posada* on the island (30 years), its concrete rooms are nothing special, though a couple face the beach or have air-con, and there's an upstairs terrace surveying the sea.

Roquelusa GUESTHOUSE $$
(☎0414-113-4548; r per person with/without half-board BsF500/300;) A reliable if dingy option with small bathrooms, although all rooms have air conditioning.

Doña Magali GUESTHOUSE $$
(☎0414-120-4096; Plaza Bolívar; r per person incl breakfast & dinner BsF350;) As inexpensive as you're going to get, this bare-bones basic shelter has chilly air-conditioners and is sometimes used as housing for government oil workers.

Eating & Drinking

Most visitors eat at their *posadas*, but self-catering or eating out at a less expensive restaurant will cut costs. Don't expect *posadas* to permit kitchen use.

For self-caterers there's a small **grocery store** (7am-8pm Mon-Sat, 7am-1pm Sun) near the Inparques office; a **bakery** (7am-1pm & 3-9pm) by the school sells sandwich meats and fresh bread.

La Chuchera PIZZERIA, INTERNATIONAL $$
(Plaza Bolívar; mains BsF60-110; 10:30am-11pm Tue-Sun;) La Chuchera is the main budget restaurant in town (although it's not necessarily cheap), serving pizza (after 4pm), sandwiches and pasta dishes. It's a fun place to have beers.

Aquarena Cafe INTERNATIONAL $$
(mains BsF81-110; 9am-10pm Tue-Sun) Near Macanao Lodge, this beachside cafe amid billowing palms serves sushi, cooked fish, hamburgers, pizza and salads.

Las Guaras BARBECUE $$
(half/whole chicken BsF80/160, parilla BsF180; dinner Tue-Sat) On the beach behind the Guardia Nacional, this driftwood-signed eatery does two things and does them well.

Kiosko La Sirena FAST FOOD $
(empanadas BsF10, mains BsF60; 6-10am, noon-2pm & 6pm-midnight) If you're on a strict budget, settle in at this food shack by the lagoon. Breakfast is empanadas, and hamburgers and *comida criolla* (creole food) are available in the evening. There's another no-name empanada and *arepa* kiosk nearby, next to the bridge.

Information

A new medical clinic sits next to the school.

Banesco (☎221-1265; Plaza Bolívar; 8am-noon & 2-5pm Mon-Fri, 8am-1pm Sat) The only bank and ATM; arranges cash advances on Visa and MasterCard.

Enzosoft (8am-9pm Mon-Fri, 8am-noon & 3-9pm Sat & Sun) The only reliable internet connection is pricey (BsF20 per hour). International calls cost BsF3 per minute.

Oscar Shop (☎0414-291-9160; oscarshop@hotmail.com) This small shop and informal tourist office near the airport organizes boat transportation to the islands and full-day boat tours. Also rents snorkeling equipment, surfboards, beach chairs and tents (per night US$10).

Getting There & Away

Air

Maiquetía–Los Roques flights (approximately BsF2100 to BsF2600 roundtrip) take about 40 minutes. It is easiest to book flights through an agency, as smaller airlines come and go and may only have a desk at the airport. Normally only 10kg of free luggage is permitted on flights to Los Roques; every additional kilogram costs BsF5.

All of the following Caracas-based carriers fly to Los Roques:

Chapi Air (☎0212-355-1965; reservacioneschapiair@gmail.com; Maiquetía domestic terminal)

Albatros Airlines (☎0212-355-2643; www.albatrosair.com.ve; Maiquetía domestic terminal)

Boat

There are no passenger boats to Los Roques.

Getting Around

Oscar Shop (p991) or other boat operators in Gran Roque will take you to the island of your choice and pick you up at a prearranged time. Round-trip fares per person run from BsF120 to BsF200.

THE NORTHWEST

Easily reached from Caracas, the country's northwest is stocked with beaches, rainforests, deserts, caves, waterfalls, a dozen national parks and South America's largest lake. Parque Nacional Morrocoy attracts visitors with its colorful reefs, beaches and Sahara-like desert near the colonial town of Coro. Puerto Colombia is a favorite stop for backpackers and locals to hang out, soak up the sun and enjoy a few drinks or break out the binoculars and spot rare birds.

Maracay

☎0243 / POP 590,000

A few hours from Caracas, Maracay is a busy metropolis and the 300-year-old capital of Aragua state. From 1899 to 1935 it was home base for infamous *caudillo* (provincial strongman) Juan Vicente Gómez, who built up its infrastructure and shaped it into the nation's aviation and air force hub. The center of an important agricultural and industrial area, it's usually visited as a stopover on the way to Parque Nacional Henri Pittier and doesn't have many attractions to otherwise hold the traveler.

Sleeping & Eating

Make advance reservations for lodging, as hotels book up and most options are hourly love hotels. Staying near the bus station isn't recommended, and the neighborhood isn't safe after dark. Bakeries and other inexpensive eateries dot Av Bolívar.

TOP CHOICE Posada El Limón GUESTHOUSE $$

(☎283-4925; www.posadaellimon.com; El Piñal 64, El Limón; hammock BsF120, d/tr/q BsF350/440/550;) In the suburb of El Limón, this enchanting mosaic-covered *posada* has leafy patios and mountain views. Perks include a compact pool, a restaurant serving breakfast, wi-fi and a bar. Call the owners in advance to organize hammock space. From the bus terminal, take the local bus marked 'Circunvalación' (BsF4) or a cab (BsF40 to BsF50).

Hotel Mar del Plata HOTEL $

(☎246-4313; mardelplatahotel@gmail.com; Av Santos Michelena Este 23; r/tr/q BsF170/200/220;) Maracay's most pleasant and central budget option has 30 tidy, clean rooms with hot water and cable TV.

El Arepanito VENEZUELAN $

(cnr Av 19 de Abril & Junín; arepas BsF27-32; 7am-midnight Mon-Thu, to 4am Fri-Sun;) Open later than most places in town, this popular restaurant serves tasty *arepas*, pizza and fruit juices in a pleasant plant-filled patio or in the air-conditioned dining room.

Royal III BAKERY $

(☎247-1813; cnr Calle López Aveledo & 3a Transversal; sandwiches BsF40-60; breakfast, lunch & dinner) Open daily, this massive, well-heeled *panadería/pastelería* (bakery/pastry shop) does it all: 59 sandwiches, loads of stuffed croissants, pizza and a wealth of sweets and treats. Bonus sugar cookies accompany sit-down coffee drinks.

Mercado Principal MARKET $

(Av Santos Michelena; mains BsF35-45; breakfast & lunch) For a really inexpensive and filling meal, try one of the market food stalls.

Getting There & Away

Two side-by-side bus terminals are located on the southeastern outskirts of the city center on Av Constitución. 'Centro' city buses (BsF4) go into town and 'Terminal' buses will bring you back. A taxi across town costs around BsF25. At night, it's safest to take the official checkboard-painted taxis *(la línea de taxis)* near the terminal exit.

Regional buses depart from the Interurbano terminal (the eastern side), while most long-distance and air-conditioned buses depart from the Extraurbano terminal (the western side). There are departures approximately every 15 minutes to Caracas (BsF35, 1½ hours) and Valencia (BsF18, one hour), and frequent departures to Barquisimeto (BsF70, 3½ hours), Maracaibo (BsF144, eight hours) and San Fernando de Apure (BsF110, five hours). Less frequent buses service Mérida (BsF173, 11 hours).

Parque Nacional Henri Pittier

0243

Venezuela's oldest national park, Henri Pittier rolls over 1078 sq km of rugged coastal mountain-range and then plunges down to epic Caribbean beaches. There's something for everyone to love here: a glistening coastline, 600 species of birds, twisting hiking trails through verdant mountains, and quaint colonial towns with tasty food, comfortable *posadas* and even a bit of nightlife.

The national park is also home to various towns and villages, and the chaotic Maracay Interurbano bus terminal is the departure point for accessing them via the two paved roads crossing the park from north to south. One of the biggest and most popular towns is Puerto Colombia, at the end of the eastern road. It's the park's main tourist destination and offers the widest choice of services. El Playón, toward the end of the western road, is a bit rougher and less popular with foreign tourists. Expect crowds and traffic on holidays and weekends, and potential carsickness from the narrow winding curves.

PUERTO COLOMBIA

Puerto Colombia's beachside location makes it one of the major backpacker hangouts in Venezuela. In this attractive and laid-back colonial village packed with *posadas* and restaurants, most folks spend their days on the beach and evenings sipping *guarapita* (cane alcohol mixed with passion-fruit juice and lots of sugar) down on the waterfront, where drumming circles rev up on weekends. Note that Venezuelans refer collectively to the whole area, including Puerto Colombia, as Choroní.

The most popular beach is **Playa Grande**, a five- to 10-minute walk by road east of town. It's about half a kilometer long and shaded by coconut palms, but is busy and can be packed on weekends. There are several restaurants at the entrance to the beach. You can camp on the beach or sling your hammock between the palms, but don't leave your stuff unattended. Bathrooms and showers are available.

Other area beaches normally visited by boat include **Playa Aroa** (BsF25, 15 minutes), **Playa Uricao** (BsF30, 20 minutes – highly recommended), **Playa Aroa** (BsF25, 15 minutes), **Playa Valle Seco** (BsF20, 15 minutes – for good snorkeling), **Playa Chuao** (BsF25, 30 minutes) and **Playa Cepe** (BsF30, 45 minutes). Prices are per person each way.

Though there are ATMs in Puerto Colombia and Choroní (one in each), but only seem to accept Venezuelan cards. Bring cash with you or make arrangements to exchange money through your *posada*. There's an internet cafe (with phones) inside Hostal Colonial.

Sleeping

Casa Luna GUESTHOUSE $

(951-5318; www.jungletrip.de; Morillo 35; dm BsF70, d BsF120-150, tr BsF170; @) A friendly *posada* with a very helpful German owner, its five very clean rooms have shared cold-water bathrooms, and a four-person dorm. There's a sociable courtyard with hammocks, as well as a kitchen and a book exchange. Caracas airport transfers (BsF700 to BsF800 per vehicle) are available.

Casa Nova GUESTHOUSE $

(951-5318; www.jungletrip.de; Parcellamiento San Antonio 7a; d/tr with fan BsF230/270, d/q with air-con BsF300/350; @) Tucked away in a more tranquil location off the main drag, this new Casa Luna–affiliated guesthouse offers an upgrade in creature comforts in its eight rooms – all but one with private bathrooms and hammocks. Watch flocks of parrots cackle overhead as you shower in the upstairs rooms with screened-in bathroom ceilings. There's a spacious communal kitchen as well.

Posada Casa Riqui Riqui GUESTHOUSE $$

(991-1061; www.posadacasariquiriqui.com; Morillo 56; d/tr/q/apt from BsF253/280/330/407;) Near the Guardia Nacional post, this comfortable *posada* is set on lovely planted grounds with a bit of a hacienda feel. The tasteful new 2nd-floor rooms offer the most character and style, though at the sacrifice of space. Hammocks and a small pool offer relaxation, and there's a wonderful barbecue area. Breakfast available.

Posada Tucán GUESTHOUSE $

(264-4961; www.posadatucan.com; Morillo; s/d/tr with fan BsF90/180/225, d/tr/q with air-con from BsF225/270/300;) Run by a German-Peruvian couple, this casual place has 10 colorful, comfortable rooms. Area tours and airport transfers are available, and there's a wonderful kitchen area.

Hostal Colonial GUESTHOUSE $
(☎431-8757; www.choroni.net; Morillo 37; d BsF120-150, without bathroom BsF95; @🛜) The centrally located Colonial has a wide variety of rooms, plus hot-water bathrooms and ample breakfasts (BsF26 to BsF35) served on a pretty back courtyard. Phone reservations only.

IguanAcción CAMPGROUND, GUESTHOUSE $
(☎0424-741-6035; iguanaccion@hotmail.com; hammock & tent per person BsF30, r person BsF50) Along the river, camp in an artsy and ramshackle wonderworld of ziplines and mosaic-tiled archways. There's a basic kitchen and lockers (bring a lock), and reservations aren't necessary. A few rooms are available in the main building, but they're pretty dumpy and mostly used for luggage storage.

Eating & Drinking

For late-night cheap eats, look for the half dozen fast-food shacks across the road from the *malecón* (waterfront promenade). A small supermarket sits on Morillo right before the beach.

Oasis VENEZUELAN, SEAFOOD $$
(Trino Rangel; mains BsF40-80; ⏲lunch & dinner) Housed under a tin roof, this economical restaurant serves pastas, fresh fish and *pollo al gusto* (chicken made to order).

La Perla del Pirata MEDITERRANEAN, SEAFOOD $$$
(Morillo; mains BsF70-150; ⏲dinner Fri & Sat, plus Wed & Thu high season) Sip sophisticated cocktails on a romantic garden patio and delve into creative Italian dishes enhanced by sauces from local fruits. Save room for the cake concocted with Chuao chocolate.

Paco's Pizza PIZZERIA $$
(Trino Rangel; salads, pizzas & pastas BsF45-85; ⏲breakfast, lunch & dinner; 🌿) A new Italian eatery with tasty thin-crust pizzas and homemade pastas. Excellent ravioli.

Bar Restaurant Araguaneyes VENEZUELAN, SEAFOOD $$
(Los Cocos 8; mains BsF60-110, breakfasts BsF30-40; ⏲8am-10pm Mon-Thu, to 11pm Fri-Sun) Sit on the airy upstairs terrace and enjoy international and *criollo* fare, including a good selection of fresh fish.

Jalío Surf Bar LOUNGE
(Calle Concepcion; ⏲6pm-3:30am Thu-Sun) This imaginative lounge is way too hip for Henri: Moroccan-esque day beds, hippie-tinged decor, edgy music and an artsy crowd converge over exotic cocktails (BsF30 to BsF50), such as white-chocolate daiquiris and strawberry mojitos – a funky step forward from Polars on the *malecón*.

Getting There & Away

From Anden 5 of Maracay's Interurbano terminal, buses depart every one or two hours (BsF30, 2¼ hours). The last bus back to Maracay departs Puerto Colombia at around 6pm (later on weekends). *Por puestos* (shared taxis; BsF60 during the day, BsF75 at night and weekends, 1¾ hours) are faster and more frequent.

Parque Nacional Morrocoy

☎0259

One of the most spectacular coastal environments in Venezuela, Parque Nacional Morrocoy comprises a strip of park on the mainland, and extends offshore to scores of islands, islets and cays. Some islands are fringed by white-sand beaches and surrounded by coral reefs. The most popular of the islands is **Cayo Sombrero**, which has fine (though increasingly damaged) coral reefs and some of the best shaded beaches. Other snorkeling spots include **Cayo Borracho**, **Playuela** and **Playuelita**.

The park gets rather crowded on weekends, but is considerably less full during

CHOCOLATE COAST

The production of Venezuela's world-famous cocoa is most heavily concentrated around Chuao and along the coast of Parque Nacional Henri Pittier, home to the most rare and sought after variety, *criollo*. Chocolatiers the world over seek out its virtually bitter-free, delicate taste, and you'll find broad swaths of red-scorched cocoa drying in the sun at plantations in the area. Representing only 5% to 10% of the world's cocoa production, *criollo* is considered a delicacy among cocoa varieties, and you can seek it out on a day trip to Chuao, where locals peddle everything from hot chocolate to chocolate ice-cream to chocolate liqueurs – a real sweet treat.

In Puerto Colombia, seek out **Chuao Sabor a Cacao** (José Maitín; ⏲9am-1pm & 3-7pm), a small family-run shop selling milk chocolates (BsF15) wrapped in colorful recycled government pamphlets.

the week. Holidays are complete bumper-to-bumper madness.

Morrocoy lies between the towns of Tucacas and Chichiriviche, which are its main gateways.

Getting Around

Boats to the islands from both Tucacas and Chichiriviche take up to eight people and charge roundtrip by the boat, though you can also do combinations. Bargain hard if the boat's not full. See relevant sections for costs.

CHICHIRIVICHE

Chichiriviche is the northern gateway to Parque Nacional Morrocoy, providing access to half a dozen neighboring cays. Be prepared for frequent power outages.

Popular trips via boat include the close cays of Cayo Muerto (BsF200), Cayo Sal (BsF250), Cayo Veradero (BsF300) and Cayo Sombrero (BsF500). A worthwhile one-hour excursion (BsF400) visits Cueva del Indio, a limestone formation with petroglyphs, and Cueva de la Virgen, which houses over 1000 statues and a shipwreck with visible masts.

Sleeping & Eating

Camping is no longer permitted on the park's islands.

Villa Gregoria GUESTHOUSE $
(☎818-6359; www.posadavillagregoria.blogspot.com; Mariño; d/tr/q BsF250/300/350, apt with kitchen for 5/7 people BsF650/700; ❄) This Spanish-run and Spanish-themed place a short walk from the bus stop contains a small garden and comfortable rooms with cable TV. Prices drop outside of high season.

Morena's Place GUESTHOUSE $
(☎0412-489-2576; posadamorenas@hotmail.com; Sector Playa Norte; dm/d BsF50/120) One block from the beach, near the Lyceo Ramon Yanez, this cheerfully cluttered budget option has laundry service and kitchen usage; English and some French are spoken.

Restaurant El Rincón de Arturo VENEZUELAN $
(Av Zamora; breakfast BsF20-50, lunch menú BsF55; ⏰7:30am-6pm) Two blocks from the beach, this small and popular corner eatery has tasty and straightforward meals.

Information

Banco Bicentenario (cnr Plantél & Calvario)

Getting There & Away

Chichiriviche is about 22km off the main Morón–Coro Hwy and is serviced by half-hourly buses from Valencia (BsF45, 2½ hours). There's no direct bus service to Chichiriviche from Caracas or Coro. To get here from Caracas, take any of the frequent buses to Valencia (BsF44 to BsF48, 2½ hours) and change there for a Chichiriviche bus. From Coro, take any bus to Valencia, get off in Sanare (BsF70, 3¼ hours), at the turnoff for Chichiriviche, and then grab a bus to Chichiriviche.

TUCACAS

This ordinary, hot town on the Valencia–Coro road has nothing to keep you for long. It's worth a day trip to go to the islands or for scuba diving, but staying in 'ChiChi' is a much better and safer option.

Snorkeling gear can be rented from some boat operators and hotels, and many offer beach, snorkeling and bird-watching excursions. **Frogman Dive Center** (☎0414-340-1824; www.frogmandive.com; Centro Comercial Bolívar, Plaza Bolívar) has diving certification classes (BsF4700), two-tank dives including equipment (BsF840) and snorkeling trips (BsF400).

Popular destinations from Tucacas are Playa Paiclás, Playuela and Cayo Sombrero.

Tucacas sits on the Valencia–Coro road, so buses run frequently to both Valencia (BsF30, 1½ hours) and Coro (BsF60, 3½ hours). Buses from Valencia pass through regularly on their way to Chichiriviche (BsF15, 40 minutes).

Coro

☎0268 / POP 259,000

Caressed by pleasant sea breezes, Coro is one of the prettiest colonial cities in Venezuela and the entry point to the magnificent sand dunes of the Parque Nacional Médanos de Coro. The cobblestone **Zamora**, where most of the historic mansions are located, rivals any other colonial architecture in the country, and the city has been on Unesco's World Heritage list since 1993. An excellent base for exploring the region, especially the **Península de Paraguaná** and the mountainous **Sierra de San Luis**, it boasts a large student population and excellent budget accommodations.

Sights

Parque Nacional Médanos de Coro PARK
Mesmerizing zebra stripes of sand shimmer in the breeze at the Parque Nacional Médanos de Coro, a spectacular desert landscape with sand dunes of 30m in height.

DON'T MISS

SURFING THE SANDS OF CORO

The climb, calf-deep in sand, seems interminable. You reach the top of the dune, breathless. Wax the board, strap both feet in and zoom – you've zipped down 100m in seconds flat. Despite the difficulty – or maybe because of it – sandboarding the finger of land known as Los Médanos is both exhilarating and addictive.

Only the basics are required: a board, some sunblock and a little joie de vivre. It's hands-down the best way to see the sunset over Coro. A background in snowboarding is helpful but by no means required. Should you lose your balance, just lean back and let the bottomless *arena* (sand) cushion the blow.

Weeks after you return from Venezuela, you'll still find sand in your shoes – and your memory.

Late afternoon is the best time to visit, when the sun is not so fierce. To get there, take the Carabobo bus from Calle 35 Falcón and get off 300m past the large *Monumento a la Federación*. From here it's a 10-minute walk north along a wide avenue to another public sculpture, the *Monumento a la Madre*, and then the dunes begin.

La Vela de Coro BEACH

This colonial port town to the northeast has a sandy beach punctuated by orange rock columns and a view of a half-sunk shipwreck. It's easy to reach by public transit – *por puestos* (BsF5.50, 20 minutes) leave from the corner of Avs Manuare and Rómulo Gallegos.

Tours

Full-day tours (BsF300 to BsF360 for up to four persons) to the windy desert of Península de Paraguaná or the cooler pine forest, caves and evocative sinkholes of the Sierra de San Luis are organized by Araguato Expeditions (p997), and Posada El Gallo (p996) and La Casa de los Pájaros (p996) guesthouses.

They also offer boards and transportation for sandboarding (BsF150 to BsF200).

Sleeping

Coro has some of the best-value budget accommodations in the country. All have cooking facilities and include morning coffee.

Posada El Gallo GUESTHOUSE $

(252-9481; www.hosteltrail.com/posadaelgallo; Calle 66 Federación 26; hammock BsF60, dm/d/tr without bathroom 90/140/210, d/tr/q with bathroom BsF180/270/360;) Situated in a restored colonial building with bright colors, wood beams and a lovely terrace, this place is one of the best deals in town. It also has a laundry service, regional tours, a book exchange and an honor bar, and does excellent sandboarding tours on boards they custom-make.

La Casa de los Pájaros GUESTHOUSE $

(252-8215; www.casadelospajaros.com.ve; Monzón 74; dm with fan BsF90, d/tr/q with air-con BsF230/330/450;) Built by architect-owners, this gorgeous seven-room house dazzles with high ceilings, good lighting and artisan mosaic bathrooms.

La Casa del Mono GUESTHOUSE $

(251-1590; Calle 66 Federación 16; dm/s/d without bathroom BsF80/130/150, d with bathroom & air-con BsF220;) Crack open a beer from the honor bar and swing in a hammock in the garden courtyard of this colorful colonial house. Comfortable rooms have fan or air-con and groovy mosaic tiling.

Casa Tun Tun GUESTHOUSE $

(404-4260; casatuntun@hotmail.com; Calle 33 Zamora 92; s/d without bathroom BsF120/150, with bathroom BsF150/200;) This colonial enclave sports simple, clean rooms (all with air-con), a basic kitchen and a TV lounge. Reception is open from 7am to midnight.

Eating

For inexpensive lunches and dinners, try the Venezuelan fast-food places on Av Pinto Salinas between Av Independencia and Garcés, in the newer section of town, about 2.5 km east of the cathedral. Especially good are the *patacones* (sandwiches bookended by fried green plantains) at **Ciudad de Maracaibo** (Av Pinto Salinas btwn Av Maracaibo & Calle 41 Garcés; patacones BsF35-42; open until midnight) and the *cachapas* at the **Casa de la Gran Cachapa** (Av Pinto Salinas btwn Av Maracaibo & Calle 41 Garcés; cachapas from BsF25).

Panadería La Gran Costa Nova BAKERY $
(Av Manaure near Calle 33 Zamora; sandwiches BsF25, pizza BsF10; ⏲6am-9:30pm) This mammoth bakery packs them in at all times of the day, and no wonder – they crank out yummy breakfasts, lunches and snacks. Wholewheat bread available.

Pizzería La Barra del Jacal PIZZERIA $$
(Calle 29 Unión; meals BsF55-100; ⏲11:30am-2am Mon-Sat, to 11pm Sun; ✎) This attractive open-air restaurant offers more than just pizzas, and is a refreshing spot to sit with a beer, especially in the evening when a gentle breeze dissipates the heat of the day.

Restaurante Shangri La VEGETARIAN $
(Av Josefa Camejo; per portion BsF7; ⏲breakfast & lunch Mon-Sat; ✎) A few blocks east of the airport, Lee Tzu serves up veggie breakfasts and lunches in this small joint, as well as a variety of herbal teas to cure what ails you. The offerings change daily.

Supermercado Mundo Ofertas SUPERMARKET $
(Calle 68 Colón near Calle 41 Garcés; ⏲8am-6pm) Self-caterers can stock up at this supermarket southwest of the Plaza Bolívar. Market stalls two blocks north sell fruits and veggies until late afternoon.

Drinking

TOP CHOICE **Artesanía Curiana** BAR
(Paseo Alameda; ⏲variable) This is a tiny free-standing shop and craft distillery specializing in *cocuy* (alcohol distilled from the cocuy agave). Drink from the barrel stock infused with *semeruco* (Barbados cherry) or honey and cinnamon while snacking on *dulce de queso de cabra* (goat-cheese sweets).

Bar Garua BAR
(cnr Calles Monzon & 68 Colón; ⏲7pm-late Tue-Sat) This classic old-time bar has been here since 1943. Sit with a cold one and soak up the atmosphere, or chat with friendly locals.

☆ Entertainment

Teatro Armonía THEATER
(Calle 33 Zamora) Its **Sala Cinemateca Coro** (www.cinemateca.gob.ve) is a good bet for inexpensive arthouse movie screenings; the excellent orchestra holds free concerts on Thursdays. Shows international films with Spanish subtitles.

ℹ Information

Araguato Expeditions (☎0426-560-0924; www.araguato.org) This excellent agency can organize local and national tours and transportation. English, Italian and Slovenian spoken.

Banco Bicentenario (cnr Av Manaure & Zamora)

Movistar (Ampíes btwn Garcés & Buchivacoa; ⏲8am-noon & 2-6pm Mon-Fri)

ℹ Getting There & Away

Air

The **Aeropuerto Internacional José Leonardo Chirinos** (☎251-5290; Av Josefa Camejo) is just a five-minute walk north of the city center. Conviasa flies to and from Caracas three times weekly.

Bus

The **Terminal de Pasajeros** (Av Los Médanos) is 2km east of the city center and accessible by frequent city transport or a taxi (BsF20). Ordinary buses to Punto Fijo (BsF30, 1¼ hours), Maracaibo (BsF65, four hours) and Valencia (BsF70, five hours) run every half hour until about 6pm. Most of the direct buses to Caracas (BsF105 to BsF125, seven hours) depart in the evening, or take a bus to Valencia and change. One direct bus goes nightly to Mérida (BsF176, 13 hours) via Maracaibo, or you can go to Barquisimeto and change there.

You can make it to Santa Marta, Colombia in one (long) day by taking an early morning *por puesto* to Maracaibo (BsF100 to BsF120, three hours) and continuing from there; see boxed text, p999.

The government-subsidized SITSSA line, also in the terminal, has super-cheap departures to Maracay and Caracas, if you can score a ticket when they open at 7am.

Adícora

☎0269

On the eastern coast of the Península de Paraguaná, the small blustery town of Adícora is one of the country's **windsurfing** and **kitesurfing** capitals. Pros and beginners come from all over the world to ride the local winds. It is the most popular destination on the peninsula and offers a reasonable choice of accommodations and restaurants. Windsurfing lessons run BsF150 per hour, and an eight-hour (two-day) kitesurfing course costs BsF2000.

On Playa Sur (South Beach) at the entrance to town, a few local operators offer courses, equipment rental and accommodations with kitchen facilities. They include the newly relocated **Windsurf Adícora** (0416-769-6196; www.kitesurfingadicora.com; Santa Ana; tr BsF200, with kitchen BsF250;), with good rooms with or without kitchens, and the laissez-faire **Archie's Surf Posada** (988-8285; www.kitesurfing-venezuela.com; camping/hammock per person BsF20/50, dm/d BsF90/180, apt BsF350-450;), a German-run school awash with dogs and chickens, near the entrance to town. Right on Playa Norte beach and a step up, colonial **Posada La Casa Rosada** (988-8004; www.posadalacasarosada.com; Calle Malecón; d/tr/q BsF280/350/380;) has a garden courtyard and a good restaurant.

Adícora is linked to Coro (BsF17, one hour) by eight buses a day, the last departing at around 5pm. *Por puestos* charge double.

Maracaibo

0261 / POP 1.5 MILLION

Unless you're in the oil business, it's unlikely you'll do more than change buses in baking-hot Maracaibo, Venezuela's second-largest city and the oil industry's nerve center. Some two-thirds of the national oil output comes from beneath the Lago de Maracaibo.

A metropolis with vast suburbs, Maracaibo encompasses the dilapidated historic center to the south and a characterless new center of high-rises to the north. Getting between the two is easy and fast, so it doesn't really matter much where you stay. The new center offers more upscale hotels, restaurants and bars, and is safer at night, though most lodging options are pricey and unexciting. The historic center boasts more colonial sights, but the area is unsafe and ghost-town-deserted at night except in the Calle 94 nightlife district.

Sleeping

Posada O'Leary MOTEL $

(0416-085-3852, 723-2390; www.posadaoleary.com; Av Padilla, Historic Center; r/tr BsF200/300;) Popular with in-the-know business travelers, this new six-room lodging looks humdrum from the outside but the snug and ultra-modern white rooms sport phones, flat-screen TVs and strong wi-fi. There's a 24-hour night watchman to let you in if you want to go clubbing in the historic center.

Hotel Caribe HOTEL $

(722-5986; hotel_caribe@cantv.net; Av 7, No 93-51, Historic Center; s/d/tr BsF180/220/270;) Two blocks from the Plaza Bolívar, the 60-room Caribe has an older section with good basic rooms and a newer area with better beds. A grand art-deco staircase graces the lobby. Avoid the rooms backing onto the nightclub.

Nuevo Hotel Unión HOTEL $

(616-3137; Calle 84, No 4-60, New Center; s/d/tr/q BsF150/160/250/300;) This budget spot has 16 basic rooms with colonial tiled floors.

Eating & Drinking

Inexpensive lunch eateries abound in the historic center; in the new center, the Plaza República area has upscale and evening options, plus fast food. The happening new club district on colonial Calle 94 Carabobo has a half-dozen fun dinner and nightlife options, including a queer disco and a massive dance/beach club, plus helicopter parent-like private security keeping the area safe.

Wok ASIAN $

(Calle 94, Carabobo btwn Av 5 & 6; mains BsF45; dinner Tue-Sun) Throbbing music, muraled ceilings and a minimalist modular wood decor set the stage for tasty stir frys and sushi. Proceed to the adjoining rooftop bar after slurping your noodles.

TOP CHOICE **Ateneo Pop** BAR, PIZZERIA

(www.facebook.com/ateneopopmcbo; Calle 94, Carabobo btwn Av 5 & 6; admission BsF26 after 11pm Thu-Sun; 6pm-late Tue-Sun) With film projections on the wall, fabulous DJ sets and everyone downing pizzas (BsF42 to BsF90) and buckets of icy beer, this hip roof-terrace beer garden is a funky place to chill out. Two beers included when there's a cover.

Pastelería Jeffrey's BAKERY $$

(Calle 78, btwn Avs 3H & 3G, New Center; sandwiches & salads BsF40-70; 7am-9pm Mon-Sat, to 2pm Sun;) A popular upscale bakery-cafe near the Plaza República serving simple breakfasts, good coffee, attractive pastries, cakes, truffles and freshly made juices.

Information

Banco de Venezuela Historic Center (cnr Av 5 & Calle 97); New Center (cnr Av Bella Vista & Calle 74) Accepts foreign cards.

Banesco New Center (cnr Av Bella Vista & Calle 71); New Center (Av Bella Vista, btwn Calles 83 & 84) Accepts foreign cards.

Italcambio (793-2983; Av El Milagro, Centro Comercial Lago Mall, New Center) Also has a branch at the airport.

GETTING TO COLOMBIA

From Maracaibo, the cheapest and most convenient way to reach Colombia is by *por puesto* from the main bus terminal to the Colombian border town of Maicao (BsF120, three hours). *Por puestos* depart frequently from about 4am to 7pm and go as far as Maicao's bus station. From there, **Expreso Brasilia** (www.expresobrasilia.com) and **Copetran** (www.copetran.com.co) operate buses to Santa Marta (COP$34,000, four hours) and Cartagena (COP$40,000, eight hours); buses depart regularly until about 5pm.

Expresos Amerlujo (☎787-7872; www.expresosamerlujo.com; cnr Av Circunvalación 2 & Calle 98, Centro Comercial San Rafael) runs the only direct air-conditioned bus from Maracaibo to Colombia, with one daily departure at 5:30am from a private terminal about 5km southwest of the main bus terminal. Destinations include Santa Marta (BsF430, seven hours) and Cartagena (BsF590, 11 hours).

All passport formalities are done in Paraguachón, the Venezuelan border town. At the first stop you must pay a BsF90 *impuesto de salida* (departure tax), in cash bolívares; you take the receipt and line up for an exit stamp at a second stop. Colombian immigration is a few buildings beyond. Factor in an additional 30 minutes to an hour to go through immigration at the border, and much longer during high-season holidays. *Por puestos* and buses will wait for you, though it can be a mess trying to find where they've parked.

Keep in mind that you need to wind your watch back a half hour when crossing from Venezuela to Colombia.

For information on traveling to Venezuela from Santa Marta, Colombia, see p555.

Movistar (Av 3Y, Plaza República, New Center; ⌚8am-7pm Mon-Fri, 9am-1pm Sat) Phones.

Getting There & Away

La Chinita international airport is 12km southwest of the city center. It's not linked by public transportation so you'll need to take a taxi. Most flights go through Caracas.

The busy bus terminal is 1km southwest of the center, with left luggage and an internet cafe with late hours. Regular buses run to Coro (BsF65, four hours) and Caracas (BsF170 to BsF186, 10½ hours). Several night buses run to Mérida (BsF113, nine hours) and San Cristóbal (BsF108, eight hours).

Buses and battered *colectivo* taxis ply fixed routes on major streets and charge BsF3.50.

THE ANDES

Hot-blooded Venezuela is not usually associated with snow-encrusted mountains and windswept peaks. However, Venezuela is, in fact, home to the 400km-long northern end of the Andes range, crowned by the country's tallest mountain, Pico Bolívar (5007m). For those who aren't hardcore mountaineers, the region offers lush valleys of cloud forest, cascading creeks and waterfalls, and charming mountain villages accessible by narrow winding roads.

Mérida state is in the heart of the Venezuelan Andes and has the highest mountains and the best-developed facilities for travelers. The city of Mérida is one of the continent's top adventure-sports destinations, and is also the gateway to Los Llanos grasslands. The two other Andean states, Trujillo and Táchira, are less visited, but have many trekking opportunities for intrepid travelers.

Mérida

☎0274 / POP 244,000

The adventure-sports capital of Venezuela, Mérida (elevation 1600m) is an affluent Andean city with a youthful energy and a robust arts scene. It has an unhurried, friendly and cultured atmosphere derived from the massive university and outdoor-sports presence. Active visitors will be spoiled for choice, with myriad options for hiking, canyoning, rafting, mountain biking and paragliding. The city is also the major jumping-off point for wildlife-viewing trips to Los Llanos.

Affordable and safe, Mérida has a high standard of accommodations and numerous budget eateries. While not a place to indulge in colonial architecture, it has a vibrant and unpretentious nightlife, and is a major stop on backpacking circuits.

Mérida

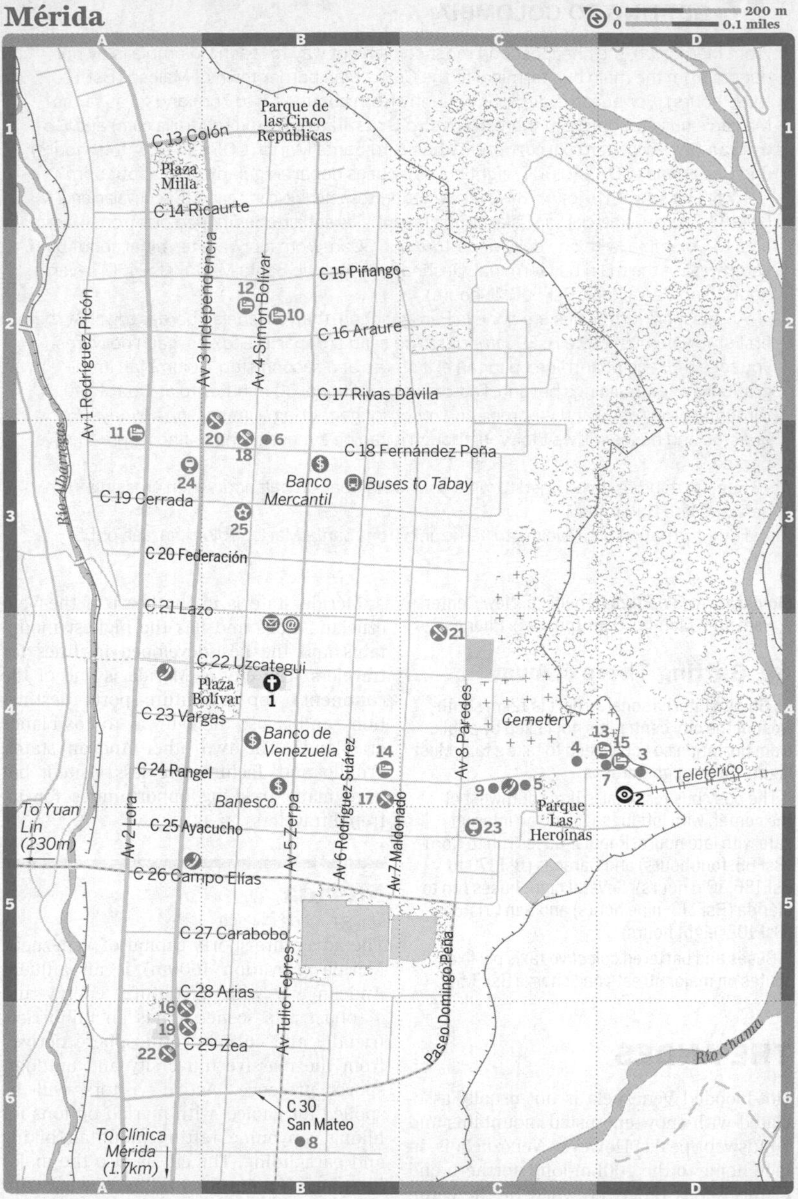

Sights

Teleférico CABLE CAR

(Parque Las Heroínas) At the end of 2012, Mérida's famed *teleférico*, the world's highest and longest cable-car system, was in the process of being rebuilt, with the government promising a seemingly optimistic 2013 reopening date. When in service, the *teleférico* runs 12.5km from the bottom station of Barinitas (1577m) in Mérida to the top of Pico Espejo (4765m), covering the ascent in four stages.

Mérida

Sights

1	Catedral de Mérida	B4
2	Teleférico	D4

Activities, Courses & Tours

3	Arassari Trek	D4
4	Guaguanco Tours	C4
5	Guamanchi Expeditions	C4
6	Iowa Institute	B3
7	Jakera	D4
8	Natoura Adventure Tours	B6
9	Xtreme Adventours	C4

Sleeping

10	La Casona de Margot	B2
11	Posada Alemania	A3
12	Posada Casa Sol	B2
	Posada Guamanchi	(see 5)
13	Posada Jama Chía	D4
14	Posada La Montaña	B4
15	Posada Patty	D4

Eating

16	La Sazón del Llano	A6
17	Buona Pizza	B4
18	El Vegetariano	B3
19	Heladería Coromoto	A6
20	La Abadía	B3
21	Supermercado Pequín	C4
22	Taperio Café	A6

Drinking

23	El Ático del Cine	C5
24	Gurten Café Poco Loco	A3

Entertainment

25	El Hoyo del Queque	B3

Catedral de Mérida CHURCH

(cnr Av 4 Simón Bolívar & Calle 22 Uzcategui) Work on this monumental cathedral began in 1800, based on the plans of the 17th-century cathedral of Toledo in Spain, but it wasn't completed until 1958, and probably only then because things were sped up to meet the 400th anniversary of the city's founding. Check out the gargoyle detailing visible from Calle 22.

Activities

Outdoorsy adventurers will love this region for the excellent range of sports, including rock climbing, ziplining, bird-watching, horse riding, hiking, mountaineering and rafting.

Paragliding

Paragliding *(parapente)* is Mérida's most iconic adventure sport. There are even pictures of paragliders on the side of the city's garbage trucks.

Most visitors fly on tandem gliders with a skilled pilot, meaning no previous experience is necessary. The usual starting point for flights is Las González, an hour-long jeep ride from Mérida, from where you glide for 20 to 30 minutes down 850 vertical meters. The cost (BsF480) includes jeep transportation.

You can also take a paragliding course (about BsF8000) that takes approximately a week, covering theory (available in English) and practice (including solo flights). Most Mérida tour agencies have their own pilots or will contract one for you.

For those who want to learn to experience the joy of solo, motorless flight, Xtreme Adventours (p1002) is the main paraglider operator, with expert instructors.

Rafting & Canyoning

Rafting is organized on some rivers at the southern slopes of the Andes. It can be included in a tour to Los Llanos or done as a two-day rafting tour (BsF1300 to BsF1800 per person) during the rainy season between May through November. The rapids range from grade two to four.

Canyoning (climbing, rappelling and hiking down a river canyon and its waterfalls) is another very popular activity. Full-day, all-inclusive canyoning tours go for around BsF480 to BsF600.

The gold standard of rafting and canyoning tours is Arassari Trek (p1002).

Mountain Biking

Several tour companies in Mérida organize bike trips. Shop around, as bicycle quality and rental prices (BsF150 to BsF200 per day) may differ substantially between the companies. One of the popular bike tours is the loop around the remote mountain villages south of Mérida known as Pueblos del Sur. For a more challenging ride, try a trip up and back to El Refugio in Parque Nacional Sierra la Culata. The downhill through the high grasslands really gets the adrenaline pumping.

Courses

There are plenty of students and tutors offering private language lessons – check *posada* bulletin boards. Some institutions and programs offering Spanish courses:

Iowa Institute LANGUAGE COURSE
(☎252-6404; www.iowainstitute.com; cnr Calle 18 Fernandez Pena & Av 4 Simón Bolívar; group/private classes per week US$120/160) Weekly homestays available for US$205.

TOP CHOICE **Jakera** LANGUAGE COURSE
(☎252-4732; www.jakera.com; Calle 24 Rangel 8-205; group classes per week incl lodging, breakfast & dinner USD$345) Its popular 'traveling classroom' program incorporates Spanish classes, volunteering and country-wide adventure travel. Homey *posada* with kitchen.

VEN-USA LANGUAGE COURSE
(☎263-7631; www.venusacollege.org; Av Urdaneta, Edificio Guilam) A study abroad school offering a large number of full-term classes for university credit. Subjects include Spanish language immersion and Latin American studies and culture; all students are placed in homestays. Prices vary significantly, so contact the school for more information.

Tours

There are plenty of agencies in town, many of which nestle near Parque Las Heroínas and along Calle 24. Shop around, talk to other travelers and check things thoroughly before deciding. Mountain trips are popular and include treks to Pico Bolívar, Pico Humboldt and Pico Pan de Azucar, costing about BsF600 per person.

An unmissable excursion out of Mérida is a wildlife safari to Los Llanos, and most companies offer this trip usually as a four-day tour for BsF1700 to BsF1800 (depending on the number of people and the quality of transportation, guide and accommodations). Two-day trips to see Relámpago de Catatumbo (Catatumbo Lightning) run around BsF1300. Remember that you usually get what you pay for. If you're pressed for time and cash, reserve in advance to ensure a spot in a group.

Most agencies can also book airline tickets. Recommended and reliable local tour companies:

TOP CHOICE **Andes Tropicales** TOUR
(☎263-8633; www.andestropicales.org; cnr Av 2 Lora & Calle 41) A non-profit foundation that helps organize hiking itineraries to rural mountain homes known as *mucuposadas* (see p1005).

Arassari Trek RAFTING
(☎0414-746-3569; www.arassari.com; Calle 24 Rangel) A heavyweight local operator with some of the most experienced guides; offers rafting, canyoning, trekking and horse-riding tours, plus Los Llanos tours and lightning trips to a camp deep in Catatumbo.

Cocolight TOUR
(☎0414-756-2575; www.cocolight.com) Respected naturalist Alan Highton specializes in Catatumbo tours, with a unique camp as well as projects helping the local community there.

Guaguanco Tours TOUR
(☎252-3709; www.guaguanco.com.ve; Calle 24 Rangel) An experienced operator with a large variety of tours, including Los Llanos, coffee plantations and hot springs.

Guamanchi Expeditions TOUR
(☎252-2080; www.guamanchi.com; Calle 24 Rangel) A long-running operator strong on mountain-related activities; also has Los Llanos trips, kayaking, bird-watching and bike tours. On-site *posada*.

Natoura Adventure Tours TOUR
(☎252-4216; www.natoura.com; Calle 31 Junín) A heavyweight local operator known for mountain trekking and climbing, it runs a full range of trips. Small group tours with quality camping and mountaineering equipment.

Xtreme Adventours EXTREME SPORTS
(☎252-7241; www.xatours.com.ve; Calle 24 Rangel) The main place in town for paragliding; young, adventurous Venezuelan-owned agency that has hiking, mountain biking, ATV and bungee jumping.

Sleeping

Perhaps because there's no need to pay for air-con, Mérida has some of the best-value accommodations in the country. Prices rise for traditional Venezuelan high seasons. All options listed have hot-water bathrooms.

TOP CHOICE **Posada Casa Sol** BOUTIQUE HOTEL **$$$**
(☎252-4164; www.posadacasasol.com; Av 4 Simón Bolívar; s/d/tr/ste incl breakfast BsF420/480/510/600; @📶) Adorned with contemporary art, this exquisite and luxurious boutique hotel inhabits a colonial mansion with paint-textured walls, rainforest shower heads and a lovely garden with a mature avocado tree.

Posada Guamanchi GUESTHOUSE $
(☎252-2080; www.guamanchi.com; Calle 24 Rangel; dm BsF80, r with/without bathroom BsF200/160, q with/without bathroom BsF380/320; 📶) Popular with its tour clients, this rambling *posada* has two kitchens and is a good place to meet like-minded travelers. Back rooms have killer mountain views.

Posada Alemania GUESTHOUSE $
(☎252-4067; www.posadaalemania.com; Av 2 Lora No 17-76; dm BsF70-80, s/d/tr without bathroom BsF150/180/240, d with bathroom BsF220; @📶) This Venezuelan-run *posada* is a popular one. Rooms surround a central garden courtyard, and there's a good kitchen guests can use. The owner runs a tour agency.

Posada La Montaña GUESTHOUSE $$
(☎252-5977; www.posadalamontana.com; Calle 24; s/d/tr/q BsF180/280/340/390; @📶) A gorgeous colonial house with comfortable rooms featuring decorative mosaic bedside tables, safety boxes and daily room cleaning. There's a restaurant downstairs serving all meals.

Casa Alemana-Suiza GUESTHOUSE $$
(☎263-6503; www.casa-alemana.com; cnr Av 2 & Calle 38; d BsF369-403, s/tr/q BsF336/436/481; @📶) A spacious and stylish building away from the more touristy center, with ample and quiet retro-style rooms, a mountain-view roof deck, a pool table and breakfast upon request (BsF70).

Posada Jama Chía GUESTHOUSE $
(☎252-5767; Calle 24 Rangel No 8-223; dm BsF70, d without bathroom BsF140; 📶) Comfy beds and colorful fabrics enliven this unsigned and good-value three-floor *posada*. Kitchen use, and mountain views out back.

La Casona de Margot GUESTHOUSE $$
(☎252-3312; www.lacasonademargot.com; Av 4 Simón Bolívar; r/tr/q BsF290/360/480, 6-/8-person r with full kitchen BsF540/700; 📶) Built around two cute courtyards, some of the updated rooms have tall loft ceilings and house up to eight.

Posada Patty GUESTHOUSE $
(☎251-1052; claferlis_diana_24@hotmail.com; Calle 24; dm BsF50, r without bathroom BsF100) A friendly and familiar basic backpacker place with a kitchen and shared meals. Inexpensive laundry (BsF30 per load) available.

Eating

Self-caterers can stock up at the mid-sized **Supermercado Pequín** (Calle 31 Lazo) and the larger **Yuan Lin** (cnr Av Las Américas & Calle 26 Campo Elías).

La Sazón del Llano VENEZUELAN, BAKERY $
(Av 3 Independencia; menú BsF30-35; ⏲cafeteria 7-11am & 11:30am-9pm Mon-Sat, bakery 6:30am-9pm daily) A side-by-side bakery and cafeteria always abuzz with happy diners. You could bust a gut polishing off the four-dish *criollo*

DON'T MISS

LIGHTNING WITHOUT THUNDER

Centered on the mouth of the Río Catatumbo at Lago de Maracaibo, this shocking phenomenon consists of frequent flashes of lightning with no accompanying thunder. The eerie, silent electrical storm can be so strong and constant that you will be able to read this book at night.

Referred to as Relámpago de Catatumbo (Catatumbo Lightning) or Faro de Maracaibo (Maracaibo Beacon), it can be observed at night all over the region, weather permitting, from as far away as Maracaibo and San Cristóbal. You'll get a glimpse of it traveling by night on the Maracaibo–San Cristóbal or San Cristóbal–Valera roads but, the closer you get, the more impressive the spectacle becomes. Tours organized from Mérida are the easiest way to see the Catatumbo lightning close up.

Various hypotheses have been put forth to explain the lightning, but so far none have been proven. The theory that stands out is based on the topography of the region, characterized by the proximity of 5000m-high mountains (the Andes) and a vast sea-level lake (Lago de Maracaibo) – a dramatic configuration found nowhere else in the world. The clash of the cold winds descending from the freezing highlands with the hot, humid air evaporating from the lake is thought to produce the ionization of air particles responsible for the lightning.

Sightings are best from September through November, when there can be 150 to 200 flashes per minute.

and international *menú*, and the bakery's a good bet when everything's closed tight on Sunday.

Heladería Coromoto ICE CREAM $

(Av 3 Independencía; ice cream BsF15; ⌚2:15am-9pm Tue-Sun) An ice-cream shop in the *Guinness World Records* for the largest number of flavors, it scoops out more than 900 types (not all at the same time!), including Polar beer, salmon and black bean.

Mercado Principal MARKET $

(Av Las Américas; breakfast BsF25-40, menús BsF35-65; ⌚7am-4pm; ✍) The 2nd floor of the main city market is home to some of the city's best traditional food.

Buona Pizza PIZZERIA $$

(Av 7 Maldonado; pizzas from BsF65; ⌚noon-11pm; ✍) Convenient, central and open late, this colorful pizza restaurant has tasty thick pies. An affordable choice popular with families.

El Vegetariano VEGETARIAN $

(cnr Av 4 Simón Bolívar & Calle 18 Fernández Peña; mains BsF36-55; ⌚8am-9pm Mon-Sat; ✍) Large-portioned vegetarian meals like baked eggplant and meat-free *pabellón* (the Venezuelan national dish, which usually has shredded beef, black beans, rice and plantains) presented in a lofty dining space and wholewheat empanadas available to go. A few other vegetarian spots inhabit this block.

Taperio Café CAFE $

(cnr Av 3 Independencia & Calle 29 Zea; menú BsF30-35; ⌚7am-11pm Mon-Sat) Choose from breakfasts, sandwiches, pizza and delicious herbal tea infusions at this hip, open-air cafe restaurant. It's a good place for a coffee by day or a beer by night.

La Abadía INTERNATIONAL $$$

(Av 3 Independencía; mains BsF70-150; ✍) This atmospheric colonial mansion serves quality salads, meats and pastas, and has a cocktail bar in a basement catacomb, plus several intimate indoor and alfresco dining nooks. Also has a cybercafe, with 30 minutes' complimentary internet after your meal.

Drinking & Entertainment

A number of throbbing discotheques and trendy bars can also be found in the *centros comerciales* (shopping centers) of Viaducto, Mamayeya, Las Tapias and Alto Prado.

TOP CHOICE **El Hoyo del Queque** CLUB

(cnr Av 4 Simón Bolívar & Calle 19 Cerrada; admission Thu-Sat BsF20; ⌚until 1am) This renowned and endlessly fun venue always fills up, and live bands and DJs get the party going with salsa, electronica, rock and reggae.

El Ático del Cine BAR

(Calle 25 Ayacucho; admission BsF20 Fri & Sat) College students and faculty tipple movie-themed cocktails in this hip loft bar and pizza restaurant (pizza from BsF45) plastered in Venezuelan film posters. It's owned by a university film professor and her husband.

Gurten Café Poco Loco SPORTS BAR

(Av 3 Independencia, btwn Calles 18 Fernández Peña & 19 Cerrada; admission BsF20 Fri & Sat) This Swiss-owned sports bar packs them in till late with a mixture of rock, reggae and salsa. The owner loves *fútbol* (soccer) and it's on every hour the bar is open.

Information

Internet Access

Internet cafes charge BsF5 to BsF8 per hour.

Medical Services

Clínica Mérida (☎263-6395, 263-0652; Av Urdaneta No 45-145)

Money

Banco de Venezuela (Av 4 Simón Bolívar) Has ATM.

Banco Mercantil (cnr Av 5 Zerpa & Calle 18 Fernández Peña) Has ATM.

Banesco (Calle 24 Rangel) Has ATM.

Italcambio (☎263-2977; Av Urdaneta, airport)

Post

Ipostel (Calle 21 Lazo)

Telephone

CANTV Calle 21 Lazo (cnr Calle 21 Lazo & Av 5 Zerpa; ⌚7:30am-5pm Mon-Fri, to noon Sat); Calle 24 Rangel (Calle 24 Rangel; ⌚9am-7pm Mon-Sat)

Movistar (Calle 22 Uzcategui; ⌚8:30am-6pm Mon-Sat)

Tourist Information

Cormetur (Corporación Merideña de Turismo; ☎0800-637-4300; cormeturpromocion@hotmail.com) Bus terminal (☎263-3952; Av Las Américas; ⌚7am-6pm); Main tourist office (☎263-1603; cnr Av Urdaneta & Calle 45; ⌚7am-7pm); Mercado Principal (☎263-1570; Av Las Américas; ⌚8am-3pm, to 1:30pm Tue & Sun) One of the most helpful tourism offices in the country; some English spoken at main office.

Inparques (☎262-1529; www.inparques.gob.ve; Sector Fondur, Parcelamiento Albarrega)

Getting There & Away

Air

The **airport** (Av Urdaneta) discontinued flights in 2008, but still has airline tickets offices. It's 2km southwest of Plaza Bolívar, next to the tourist office. The closest airport is an hour away in El Vigía, where there are direct flights from Caracas and Porlamar.

Transfers Mérida (☎0414-723-4680) runs air-conditioned vans (per person BsF90, BsF30 extra for pick-up) from Centro Comercial Glorias Patrias to El Vigía airport. There's a five-person minimum from El Vigía airport to Mérida. Reserve three days in advance. Official taxis charge BsF300.

Bus

The **bus terminal** is on Av Las Américas, 3km southwest of the city center; it's linked by frequent public buses (BsF3) that depart from the corner of Calle 25 Ayacucho and Av 2 Lora. Regional destinations, including El Vigía (BsF20), Apartaderos (BsF16) and Jají (BsF8.50), are serviced regularly throughout the day. For Ciudad Bolívar, it's fastest to take a *buseta* to Barinas and change there.

DESTINATION	COST (BSF)	DURATION (HR)
Barinas	62	4
Caracas	167-200	13
Coro	176	13
Maracaibo	119	9
Maracay	173	11
San Cristóbal	178	5

Around Mérida

The most popular high-mountain trekking area is the **Parque Nacional Sierra Nevada**, east of Mérida, which has all of Venezuela's highest peaks. **Pico Bolívar** (5007m), Venezuela's highest point and a mere 12km from Mérida, is one of the most popular peaks to climb. Without a guide you can hike along the trail leading up to Pico Bolívar. It roughly follows the cable-car line, but be careful walking from Loma Redonda to Pico Espejo – the trail is not clear and it's easy to get lost. Venezuela's second-highest summit, **Pico Humboldt** (4942m) is also popular with high-mountain trekkers.

An easier destination is **Los Nevados**, a charming mountain village nestled at about 2700m. Jeeps to Los Nevados (BsF80, four hours) leave from Mérida's Parque Las Heroínas between 7am and 8am, and at noon in high season. Simple accommodations and food are available here, or you can walk an hour to overnight in the *mucuposada* and working farm of **Hacienda El Carrizal** (☎0274-789-5723).

The **Parque Nacional Sierra La Culata**, to the north of Mérida, also offers some amazing hiking territory and is particularly noted for its desertlike highland landscapes. Take a *por puesto* to La Culata (departing from the corner of Calle 19 Cerrada and Av 2 Lora), from where it's a three- to four-hour hike uphill to a primitive shelter known as El Refugio, at about 3700m. Continue the next day for three to four hours to the top of **Pico Pan de Azúcar** (4660m). Consider staying another night to explore local hot springs and swimming holes. The last *por puesto* back to Mérida leaves around 4pm. Other great hikes include **Pico El Águila** (4118m), **Paso del Cóndor** (4007m) and **Pico Mucuñuque** (4672m).

To overnight in the parks independently, you need a permit from Inparques (p1005). Offices are located in Mérida, Tabay and Los Nevados, and caretakers stationed at park entry points issue on-the-spot permits.

WORTH A TRIP

HOT SPRINGS

Tabay Only 12km from Mérida, these *aguas termales* (hot springs) consist of a cement pool a half-hour's walk in and second natural one 30 minutes past it. Frequent *busetas* (small buses; BsF4) leave from from Av 6.

La Musui (www.aguastermaleslamusui.blogspot.com; admission BsF5) Take an early morning *buseta* to Mucuchíes (BsF16, 1¼ hours) and then a taxi (BsF30 per car, 20 minutes) up to the high elevation town of La Musui. From here, it's about an hour-long walk up to a stone-walled natural pool. Last transport back to Mérida departs around 4:30pm. Last transport back to Mérida from Mucuchíes departs around 4:30pm, though it's worth strolling the charming 400-year-old, 3000m-high Andean town, and lots of accommodations are available if you want to stay overnight.

For hikers, one of the most interesting (and super-safe) off-the-beaten-path experiences is the network of trails to indigenous mountain villages, where you can spend the night in accommodations called **mucuposadas** (*mucu* means 'place of' in the local dialect). Spaced a day's walk apart, you can traipse through cloud forest, pastureland and glacial landscapes from village to village and end the day with hot showers, cooked meals and a comfy bed. Prices are BsF190 per person per day for lodging and BsF120 for full board. Guides aren't necessary, but can be hired for about BsF150 per day. In Mérida, the EU-funded foundation Andes Tropicales (p1002), which helped develop the network, can organize *mucuposada*, walking, biking or jeep tours or consult with travelers (for free) on how to arrange independent trips; their new Pueblos del Sur network (www.destinopueblosdelsur.com), helps culturally curious travelers explore the spectacular Andean villages southwest of Mérida.

One very beautiful route that's easy to organize with public transportation includes stays at **Mucuposada Michicaba** (☎0426-702-9467, 0274-511-8701; Gavidia), **Mucuposada El Carrizal** (☎0273-511-6941; Carrizal), **Mucuposada San José** (☎0273-414-3502; San José) and **Mucuposada Los Samanes** (☎0273-400-1299; Santa María de Canaguá). From Mérida, take a bus 48km east to Mucuchíes (BsF20, 1½ hours), a 400-year-old town, and then a jeep to Gavidia (one hour). At the end of the route, Mucuposada Los Samanes can organize your transportation or you can hike 20km to the highway and take a *por puesto* to Barinas.

San Cristóbal

☎0276 / POP 286,000

Encircled by evocative green hills, San Cristóbal is a thriving commercial center fueled by its proximity to Colombia, just 40km away. This proximity has also raised safety concerns in recent years. You'll find yourself in San Cristóbal if you are traveling overland to or from anywhere in Colombia except the Caribbean Coast. Though the city is not a destination in itself, it is a modern and comfortable place with friendly inhabitants. It is worth staying a bit longer in January, when the city goes wild for two weeks celebrating its Feria de San Sebastián.

Sleeping & Eating

If you're coming by bus and just need a budget shelter for the night, check out one of several basic hotels on Calle 4, a short block south of the bus terminal. Alternatively, try one of the budget hotels in the city center (a 10-minute ride by local bus). Inexpensive Chinese restaurants dot Avs 5 and 7, staying open until 10pm or 11pm.

Suite Ejecutivo Dinastía HOTEL **$**

(☎343-9530; cnr Calle 13 & Av 7 Isaias Medina Angarita; r with fan/air-con BsF200/250, tr BsF270; ❄) An offspring of the more expensive Hotel Dinastía, one block to the north, this small place provides comfortable and quiet rooms (not suites as its name would suggest). Guests can use the glacial wi-fi at the bigger hotel.

Hotel Central Park HOTEL **$**

(☎341-9077; cnr Calle 7 & Carrera 4; r BsF200-230, tr BsF260; ❄) Festooned with brickface,

DON'T MISS

LOS LLANOS

One of Venezuela's best destinations is the wildlife-rich Los Llanos, an immense savanna plain south of the Andes that's also the home of Venezuela's cowboys and the twangy harp music of *joropo* (traditional music of Los Llanos). With Venezuela's greatest repository of wildlife found here, you'll be flat-out dazzled by caimans, capybaras, piranhas, anacondas and anteaters, plus an enormous variety of birds. In the rainy season, the land is half-flooded and animals are dispersed but still visible everywhere. The dry months (mid-November to April) are the high season, with a greater concentration of animals clustered near water sources.

Mérida's tour companies provide fascinating excursions for BsF1700 to BsF1800, usually as four-day all-inclusive packages; add BsF300 for rafting.

Keep in mind that wildlife-watching should not be stressful for the animals. Guides should *not* be encouraged to handle or harass animals, including anacondas.

GETTING TO COLOMBIA

San Antonio del Táchira is the busy Venezuelan border town across from Cúcuta, Colombia (12km). Wind your watch back 30 minutes when crossing from Venezuela to Colombia.

SAIME (p554), the government immigration department, will stamp you in or outside Venezuela. All tourists leaving Venezuela are charged a BsF90 *impuesto de salida* (departure tax). You must pay in cash and buy a stamp for this amount in a shop (open 24 hours) across the street. Unless you take a private taxi to Cúcuta (BsF250), transport from San Cristóbal drops passengers off two blocks from the SAIME office and won't wait for you.

From San Antonio, buses (BsF6) and *por puestos* (BsF12) run frequently to the Cúcuta bus terminal in Colombia (12km). You can catch both on Av Venezuela, or save yourself some time by walking across the bridge over the Río Táchira (the actual border), getting your Colombian entry stamp from the Migración Colombia office (on your right), and looking for a shared taxi on the other side. You can pay in Venezuelan bolívares or Colombian pesos.

From Cúcuta, there are frequent buses and flights to all major Colombian destinations. See p554 for information on traveling to Venezuela from Colombia.

this well-positioned 70-room hotel doubles as a residence for youthful Cuban doctors. There's an internet cafe right next door.

Hotel El Andino GUESTHOUSE $
(343-4906; Carrera 6, btwn Calles 9 & 10; d with fan BsF140, q with air-con BsF250;) Just half a block from the Plaza Bolívar, this cheapie is secure and family-run, although it has some *por rato* (by the hour) guests. Rooms vary considerably in size. A few other budget hotels are close by.

Tienda Naturista Gustico VEGETARIAN $
(Calle 7 btwn Av 7 Isaias Medina Angarita & Carrera 8; mains BsF25; 8am-6pm Mon-Sat;) This lunchtime vegetarian place cranks out homemade yogurt, wholemeal bread, wholemeal empanadas (BsF6) as well as other yummy snacks. It serves excellent fruit juices too.

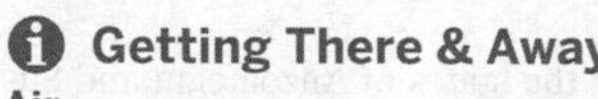

Getting There & Away

Air

The main regional **airport** (STD;) is about 1½ hours away in Santo Domingo, about 38km southeast of San Cristóbal, with no direct public transportation. Reserve a day ahead with driver **Señor Ovalles** (344-2604, 344-2804) to arrange door-to-door van service for BsF50. Taxis charge BsF150.

Bus

From the bus terminal, more than a dozen buses daily go to Caracas (BsF162 to BsF213, 13 hours). Most depart in the late afternoon or evening for an overnight trip via El Llano highway. Ordinary buses to Barinas (BsF65 to BsF80, five hours) run hourly between 5am and 6:30pm.

Expresos Unidos buses to Mérida (BsF78, five to six hours) go every 1½ hours from 5:30am to 7pm, but depart earlier if full (arrive by 6pm to make the last departure). Frequent buses depart nightly for Maracaibo (BsF108, eight hours); make sure the route takes the faster Panamerican Hwy.

Minibuses to San Antonio del Táchira (BsF15, 1¼ hours), on the Colombian border, run every 10 or 15 minutes; it's a spectacular but busy road. If you are in a rush, consider taking a *por puesto* (BsF50).

THE NORTHEAST

Venezuela's northeast is a mosaic of natural marvels, with Caribbean beaches, coral reefs and verdant mountains. It also boasts Isla de Margarita, one of the most famous island destinations in the Caribbean, and the Cueva del Guácharo, Venezuela's biggest and most impressive cave system. Parque Nacional Mochima and the remote stretches of sand beyond Río Caribe offer the opportunity for endless beach-hopping. The city of Cumaná was also the first Spanish settlement founded on the South American mainland. Once you've spent time in the northeast, you'll understand what prompted Columbus to whimsically declare the region 'paradise on earth.'

Puerto La Cruz

☎0281 / POP 454,000

A transit hub for Isla de Margarita and Parque Nacional Mochima, Puerto La Cruz is a bustling and rapidly expanding city. Not a particularly attractive place, its best feature is a lively waterfront boulevard, Paseo Colón, packed with hotels, bars and restaurants. This area comes to life in the late afternoon and evening as temperatures cool and street stalls open.

Beach seekers should continue further along the coastline to smaller Playa Colorada, Santa Fe or Mochima.

Sleeping & Eating

Lodging in Puerto La Cruz is overpriced for what you get. Browse the Paseo Colón for the biggest selection of inexpensive international and fast-food eateries facing the water; more cheap eats are near the bus station.

Hotel Neptuno HOTEL $
(☎ph/fax 265-3261; cnr Paseo Colón & Juncal; s/d/tr/q BsF180/220/250/280; ❄@📶) Sea breezes buffet this tired waterfront hotel with aging rooms and even older bathroom fixtures. Pluses include an internet cafe in the lobby and an open-sided rooftop restaurant with dynamite Caribbean views.

Hotel Europa HOTEL $
(☎268-8157; cnr Plaza Bolívar & Sucre; s/d/tr BsF225/240/260; ❄) High-ceilinged rooms are plain but spacious, and there's a small common area. Angle for a sea-view terrace.

Hotel Guayana HOTEL $
(☎265-2175; Plaza Bolívar; r/tr BsF130/150; ❄) A cheap stay with eight rooms, located on Plaza Bolívar. You won't be bowled over by the welcome, but at least the place is safe and central.

El Amir Palace MIDDLE EASTERN $$
(Paseo Colón 123; mains BsF40-120; ⏰11am-11pm Tue-Sun; 🍴) Crisply dressed waiters shuttle Middle Eastern specialties like shawarma and (so-so) falafel to your table, although its long menu also includes pasta, fish and salads.

Centro Naturalista La Colmena VEGETARIAN $$
(Paseo Colón 27; 3-course menú BsF80; ⏰11:45am-2pm Mon-Fri; 🍴) Hungry vegetarians will swoon for this tasty, lunch-only veggie cafe. A small covered terrace looks out across the boulevard to the sea.

Getting There & Away

Boat

Puerto La Cruz is the major departure point for Isla de Margarita, with services offered by **Conferry** (☎267-7847; www.conferry.com; Sector Los Cocos), **Naviarca/Gran Cacique** (☎267-7286; www.grancacique.com.ve; Sector Los Cocos) and **Navibus** (☎0295-500-6284; www.navibus.com.ve). Smaller excursion boats leave from the small piers in town. See the transport section for Isla de Margarita (p1013) for details.

The ferry terminals are accessible by *por puesto* from the center, or you can take a taxi (BsF30). It's best to go in the daytime – it's a spectacular journey out through the islands of Parque Nacional Mochima.

Bus

The bustling bus terminal is three blocks from Plaza Bolívar, with lots of connections. Going eastward (to Cumaná or further on), grab a seat on the left side of the bus, as there are some dreamy views over the islands of Parque Nacional Mochima. Minibuses frequently depart from near the terminal for Santa Fe (BsF12, 45 minutes) and Playa Colorada (BsF12, 30 minutes).

Por puestos also run to Caracas (BsF200, four hours), Maturín (BsF90, 2½ hours) and Cumaná (BsF70, 1¼ hours).

Aeroexpresos Ejecutivos (☎267-8855; www.aeroexpresos.com.ve) has a bus terminal next to Conferry, with three daily departures to Caracas (BsF84).

DESTINATION	COST (BSF)	DURATION (HR)
Caracas	85	5
Carúpano	55	4
Ciudad Bolívar	85	4
Cumaná	35	1½
Güiria	85	6½

Parque Nacional Mochima

☎0293

Straddling the states of Anzoátegui and Sucre, Parque Nacional Mochima comprises a low, dry mountain range that drops down to fine bays and beaches and continues offshore to a mesmerizing constellation of three-dozen arid islands. Dolphins are a common sight in the area's waters. The best beaches are on the islands and accessed by short boat trips from Santa Fe, Mochima or other coastal towns. Coral reefs surround a few of the islands and provide decent snorkeling and scuba diving. Tranquility seekers should visit midweek.

PLAYA COLORADA

A crescent of orange sand shaded by coconut groves, Playa Colorada draws weekend hordes of young Venezuelan party-goers and sun-seekers. But it's very quiet during the week and an easy day trip from both Santa Fe and Puerto La Cruz. A few small shops sell produce, bread and other foodstuffs, and scores of food shacks open on the beach for weekends. There are a few small *posadas*, though no banks or internet access.

An adventure-sports boot camp, Spanish language school and an excellent place to meet up with other energetic travelers, **Jakera Lodge** (☎995-5841; www.jakera.com; hammock/dm incl half board BsF175/200) offers dorm accommodations with communal meals and scores of scuba, canyoning and kayak outings. Its full-day boat tours to do bouldering at Isla de Mono (BsF245) are very popular. Look for its corrugated steel gate on the highway.

SANTA FE

A beachside town popular with international backpackers, Santa Fe comprises two separate worlds: the beach, a sedate haven of seaside *posadas* ringed with barbed-wire security fences; and the rest of the town, a rough-and-tumble fishing village. Be careful at night.

There's little reason to leave the intimate *posada*- and cafe-lined sandy strip other than to walk to the bus terminal or visit the town's rowdy nightclub. The beach is a chill spot to sit in the sand and sip beers and fruit juices. If you are looking for more remote and pristine beaches, small boats make day trips to the islands of Parque Nacional Mochima.

After stopping at the bus terminal just off the highway (1km to the beach *posadas*, but don't walk it at night), transportation from Puerto La Cruz and Cumaná will usually deposit you by the beach. The police station is across the street from here, and helpful officers may offer an escort to your *posada*.

Sleeping & Eating

Unless noted, the following are all along the beach.

TOP CHOICE **Le Petit Jardin** GUESTHOUSE $$
(☎231-0036; www.lepetitjardin-mochima.com; Cochima; s/d/tr incl breakfast BsF195/360/410; ❄📶🏊) You'll never want to leave beautiful Le Petit Jardin, where mango, banana and passion fruit blossom near the swimming pool. The five colorful rooms are contemporary and peaceful, with gorgeous bathroom tiling and an ample outdoor kitchen. It's a block from the beach, behind the Santa Fe Resort.

Posada Bahia del Mar GUESTHOUSE $
(☎231-0073; www.capvenezuela.fr; s/d/tr BsF150/200/250; ❄@📶) This newer French-run place has a mix of good brightly colored rooms; those without air-con are upstairs with mosquito nets and breezy ocean views. A pretty little garden and huge outdoor kitchen beckon out back near the beach.

Posada Café del Mar GUESTHOUSE $
(☎231-0009; La Marina, entering the beach; hammock BsF50, r with fan/air-con BsF100/150, tr with fan/air-con BsF130/180) A restaurant (mains from BsF45), bar and *posada*, with simple fan-cooled rooms with glass doors. Hang a hammock on the breezy rooftop terrace, but lock up your valuables.

La Sierra Inn GUESTHOUSE $
(☎231-0042; cooperativasantafedemisamores@hotmail.com; r/tr/q BsF160/240/320; ❄@) Under new management, La Sierra sports no-nonsense hot-water rooms and an ample shaded beach. There's a kitchen, laundry service, computer usage for guests and regional tours.

Las Molinas VENEZUELAN, SEAFOOD $
(breakfast BsF12-18, mains BsF38-100; ⏲8am-8pm) A tropical oasis, this welcoming little roofed kiosk serves pastas, soups (including a vegetarian lentil), *comida criolla* and tempting cocktails.

MOCHIMA

A tiny town where everyone seems to know everyone else since childhood, Mochima is a completely different experience from nearby Santa Fe. A quaint, attractive village on the edge of its namesake national park, it has no beach and is more popular with Venezuelan families than international backpackers. Frequent boats run from the waterfront to the numerous island beaches of the park. The town is nearly empty during the week.

At the central wharf, *lancheros* (boat drivers) wait on the shore for tourists. They can take you to destination beaches for about BsF150 to BsF200 or a tour of five to six islands for BsF500. These are round-trip fares per boatload, and you can be picked up whenever you want. To camp on the islands, you need to pick up a permit (BsF10

DON'T MISS

TABAQUERIA LA CUMANESA

Tabaqueria La Cumanesa (Carabobo 27 btwn Av Bermúdez & Sarmiento; ⏲6:30am-noon & 1:30-5pm Mon-Fri) Cumaná is renowned for its export-quality cigars, and at this company, founded in 1893, you can stroll the factory and watch the workers sort and hand-roll the 13 varieties. All save one are made from Venezuelan-grown tobacco; the *cabreras* are a milder smoke and the *tierra firme* have the strongest flavor. Packets of five cost BsF65 to BsF150, and boxes of 25 run from BsF90 to a cool BsF740 for the luxurious Presidentes. Look for the 'Cabrera' sign.

per person nightly) at the Inparques office across from the wharf, but heed to safety recommendations.

Both the **Aquatics Diving Center** (☎0426-581-0434; www.scubavenezuela.com) and **La Posada de los Buzos** (☎0212-961-2531, 416-0856; www.laposadadelosbuzos.com) organize diving courses, dives and excursions, and handle snorkel rental. The latter also runs rafting trips on the Río Neverí.

Mochima has a good choice of accommodations and food facilities. Locals rent out rooms and houses if there is demand.

In shades of aqua, yellow and orange, the five tropical sea-themed rooms at the **Posada Casa Cruz** (☎416-0810, 0414-773-5535; posadacasacruzmochima@hotmail.com; Calle Principal; d BsF200-300; ❄) all have TV and fridges, with a pleasant front porch out front. Enquire at the Restaurant Puerto Viejo.

Moored motorboats bobble alongside **Restaurant Puerto Viejo** (mains BsF60-100; ⏲11am-8pm Wed-Mon), a festively painted seafood place featuring pasta, chicken as well as calamari and very fresh fish. Displays of local art and shellacked tables adorned with aquatic scenes make it a great place to linger for a meal.

Busetas departing from Cumaná will bring you to the village's center (BsF8, 40 minutes), next to the wharf. To Puerto La Cruz or Santa Fe, take a bus to the *crucero* (highway crossroad), then flag down the proper bus.

Cumaná

☎0293 / POP 365,000

Founded by the Spanish in 1521, Cumaná has the distinction of being the oldest remaining Spanish settlement on the South American mainland. It boasts a pretty historical district, but it's primarily used as a stepping stone to Isla de Margarita, Península de Araya, Santa Fe, Mochima and the Cueva del Guácharo. Stock up on cash and other city conveniences here before visiting smaller nearby towns, and take care when walking at night.

For the best views of the city and coastline, hoof it up to the **Castillo de San Antonio de la Eminencia** (⏲7am-7pm), a colonial structure that has endured earthquakes and pirate attacks since it was built in 1659.

Sleeping & Eating

Hotel Astoria GUESTHOUSE $
(☎433-2708; hotelastoria_7@hotmail.com; Sucre 51; s/d/tr/q BsF145/185/225/275; ❄📶) A friendly cheapie featuring a small bar and pizzeria, the hotel's 18 windowless rooms have good lighting, cable TV and air-con, and often fill up.

Posada San Francisco GUESTHOUSE $
(☎431-3926; www.orienteweb.com/posadasanfrancisco; Sucre 16; s/d/tr BsF220/240/270; ❄📶) This two-building *posada* contains a beautiful renovated old *casona* (large house) with spacious rooms arranged around a tranquil, palm-filled patio with traditional-style tiles, plus an attractive bar, a pool table and a good restaurant. The rooms across the street are pretty humdrum.

Posada La Cazuela GUESTHOUSE $
(☎432-1401; narant@hotmail.com; Sucre 63; r/tr/q BsF190/220/230; ❄@📶) Artisan crafts decorate this clean and cheerful six-room family home *posada* with good mattresses, cable TV and bamboo ceilings. Some kitchen use is OK.

Sopas y Algo Más VENEZUELAN $
(Av Aristiguieta; mains BsF40-60; ⏲11am-3pm Tue-Sun) Just three soups, six main dishes and four desserts are available at this small but hopping restaurant set in a shady concrete patio. The menu is on the wall, the service is quick, and the food is cheap and delicious. Look for the green garage door.

Panadería Super Katty BAKERY $
(Plaza Blanco; pastries BsF15; ⊙6am-10pm) A bakery with good coffee, excellent pastries and fancy cakes.

Bar Restaurant Jardín Sport VENEZUELAN $
(Plaza Bolívar; mains BsF15-40; ⊙6am-9:30pm) From breakfast *arepas* to soups, sandwiches, burgers and *parrilla*, this courtyard restaurant and bar is a lively place to refuel. Come in the evening for cheap beer and a game of pool.

Information

Banesco (cnr Mariño & Carabobo) Has an ATM accepting international cards.

Getting There & Away

Air

The airport is 4km southeast of the city center. **Venezolana** (www.ravsa.com.ve) flies to Caracas.

Boat

All ferries and boats to Isla de Margarita depart from the docks next to the mouth of the Río Manzanares and go to Punta de Piedras on Isla de Margarita. The principal operator is **Naviarca/Gran Cacique** (☎432-0011; www.grancacique.com.ve).

The area around the ferry docks in Cumaná is not famous for its safety, so take a *por puesto* (BsF3) from just north of the bridge, or a taxi (BsF25).

Bus

The bus terminal is 1.5km northwest of the city center and linked by frequent urban buses along Av Humboldt. Discount SITSSA buses are in a small separate terminal alongside it, with hard-to-get departures at a third of the price.

Por puestos run to Puerto La Cruz (BsF70, 1¼ hours) and Carúpano (BsF80, four hours). For the Cueva del Guácharo, take a *por puesto* bound for Caripe (BsF70, 2½ hours). The cave is just before Caripe; ask to be let off at the entrance.

Busetas to Santa Fe (BsF8, 45 minutes) and Mochima (BsF8, 40 minutes) depart from near the Mercadito, one block off the Redoma El Indio.

DESTINATION	COST (BSF)	DURATION (HR)
Caracas	112-125	6½
Carúpano	70	2½
Ciudad Bolívar	130	6
Mérida	250	15
Puerto La Cruz	38-44	1½

Cueva del Guácharo

Venezuela's longest and most magnificent cave, **Guácharo Cave** (admission adult/child BsF20/5; ⊙8am-4pm Tue-Sun, last full tour at 2:30pm), 12km from Caripe toward the coast, has 10.2km of caverns. An impressive portal and cave system, it's inhabited by the shrieking *guácharo* (oilbird), which lives in total darkness and leaves the cave only at night in search of food. *Guácharos* have a radar-location system (similar to bats) and enormous whiskers that enable them to navigate in the dark. From August to December, the population in the cave is estimated at 10,000 and occasionally up to 15,000. Within its maze of stalactites and stalagmites, the cave also shelters crabs, fish and fast-moving rodents. Arrange a late taxi pickup after closing time or camp for a small fee across from the cave entrance and witness the birds pouring out of the cave mouth at around 6:30pm and returning at about 4am.

All visits to the cave are by guided group tours; full tours take about 1½ hours. The tour visits 1200m of the cave, but high water in August and/or September occasionally limits sightseeing to 500m. Across the road, it's a 20-minute hike to **Salto La Paila**, where you can swim in a chilly pool at the foot of a ribbon cascade.

From Maturín, buses (BsF30, 2½ hours) and faster *por puestos* go to Caripe. From Cumaná, ask Caripe-bound *por puestos* (BsF70, 2½ hours) to drop you off at the cave entrance. In Caripe, taxis charge BsF20 to the cave, and the **Hotel Samán** (☎0292-545-1183; www.hotelsaman.com; Av Chaumer 29; r/tr/q BsF260/280/390; 📶) is a good place to lay your head for the night.

Río Caribe

☎0294 / POP 14,000

The former splendor of the old port town of Río Caribe can be spotted along the wide, tree-shaded Av Bermúdez with its once-magnificent mansions. Once a major cacao exporter, the town now serves as a laid-back holiday destination and a springboard for incredible beaches further east. Don't miss the 18th-century church on Plaza Bolívar or the weekend activity at Plaza Sucre, along Av Bermúdez closer to the beach.

There's an ATM on Calle 14 de Febrero near the gas station.

Sleeping & Eating

TOP CHOICE **Posada Shalimar** GUESTHOUSE $$
(☎646-1135; www.posada-shalimar.com; Av Bermúdez; s/d/tr BsF270/300/350;) A lush Arabic-accented courtyard cradles a lap-worthy pool at the heavenly Posada Shalimar. This funky place can be addictive, even if you're not staying there, with surfboards for rent (per day BsF100), an excellent bar and restaurant (breakfast BsF55), a computer for hire and numerous local tours available.

Posada de Arlet GUESTHOUSE $
(☎646-1290; www.posadaarlet.com; Calle 24 de Julio 22; s/d/tr/q BsF150/200/280/350;) This immaculate Swiss-owned *posada* near the Plaza Bolívar has cheerful light-filled upstairs rooms – some with great hill views – along a breezy terrace.

Pensión Papagayos GUESTHOUSE $
(☎646-1868; cricas@web.de; cnr 14 de Febrero & Junin, near police station; r per person BsF80;) Rent out one of four good, well-kept rooms sharing two bathrooms in this small home (the owners live a block away) where you can use the kitchen. There's a tiny garden and pleasant common dining area.

Restaurant Manos Benditas VENEZUELAN $
(Av Gallegos; mains BsF30-80; lunch & dinner Mon-Sat) On the seafront a block from Bermúdez, the town's most popular restaurant bustles with local life throughout the day. Its menu is pure *comida criolla*, and includes a delicious *pollo a cacao* (chocolate chicken).

Da More ITALIAN $
(Av Bermúdez; pizza & pasta BsF45-58; lunch & dinner Tue-Sun;) This relaxed and airy place cooks up great pizzas and pastas. You can create your own topping combination or choose from the menu. No alcohol served.

Getting There & Away

From Plaza Bolívar, there are frequent *por puestos* (BsF12, 30 minutes) and buses (BsF7) to Carúpano. Two daily buses service Caracas (BsF150, 10 hours) via Puerto La Cruz (BsF90, five hours) Monday through Saturday.

Around Río Caribe

A bonanza of two dozen beaches on the 50km coastal stretch between Río Caribe and San Juan de Unare (the last seaside village accessible by road), the coast here has some of the most gorgeous and least-visited sandy spots in the country. Bring repellant if you stay overnight.

An easy jaunt from Río Caribe before hitting the beach, chocoholics shouldn't miss **Chocolates Paria** (☎0416-282-6027; www.chocolatesparia.com; tour BsF20; 9am-4pm), where you can tour the small-scale organic shade-grown cacao plantation and nibble on samples of varying concentration. Tours available in German, English and French. Take a *por puesto* (BsF8, 15 minutes) to Hacienda Bukare.

PLAYA MEDINA

Crescent-shaped Playa Medina is fringed by tall palms and has gentle surf perfect for swimming. There's no camping permitted, and the only beachside lodging is pricey, so it's better as a day trip.

PLAYA PUI PUY

Beautiful Playa Pui Puy has free camping plus an affordable *posada* and restaurant at the very far end of the Playa Pui Puy beach.

The charming **Posada Rincón de Pui Puy** (☎0414-492-3625; Playa Pui Puy; s/d/tr with fan BsF100/250/300, s/d/tr incl half board & aircon BsF250/500/700;) has panoramic bay views from its patio and 20 colorful rooms ranging from tiny to large; the cheapest have showers outside, the best have their own huge balconies.

PLAYA QUEREPARE

Playa Querepare is best known for the sea turtles that nest here from April to August; a conservation project collects the eggs in a beachside hatchery.

Campamento Querepare (☎reservations 0245-261-4419; www.naturaraid.com; Playa Querepare; r BsF180) has 13 basic *cabañas* and rooms with mosquito nets. Bring food (and pay to have them cook it) unless you come on a full-board package through Natura Raid. There's no electricity in turtle-nesting season.

SAN JUAN DE LAS GALDONAS

The seaside village of San Juan de las Galdonas has especially fine beaches.

The rustic **Posada Las Tres Carabelas** (☎0294-411-2265; lastrescarabelas3@gmail.com; San Juan de las Galdonas; r per person half board BsF200) sits spectacularly on top of a cliff high above the beach, providing gorgeous views over the sea and has 14 good fan-cooled rooms. There's also a restaurant here that serves up delicious dishes – try their sublime fish soup.

Getting There & Away

It's easiest to visit beaches by boat from Río Caribe; the road to Playa Medina is bad –and tortuous to Pui Puy. Return fares per boatload (up to 12 people) are BsF100 to Playa Medina (25 minutes) and BsF200 to Playa Pui Puy (40 minutes).

From the southeastern end of Río Caribe, opposite the gas station, infrequent *por puesto* pickup trucks run Monday to Saturday morning to the villages of Medina (BsF7), Pui Puy (BsF10) and San Juan de Las Galdonas (BsF40, 1½ hours). They don't get as far as the beaches of Medina and Pui Puy; you'll need to walk a half-hour to get the rest of the way, though locals sometimes run *mototaxis*. Río Caribe *posadas* can also arrange drivers or tours.

ISLA DE MARGARITA

☎0295 / POP 462,000

While Isla de Margarita itself certainly has some of the country's best beaches and enjoys a dramatic, mountainous interior to boot, its unchecked development, traffic-clogged roads and creeping urban sprawl has made something of a joke out of its tropical paradise reputation. That said, there are lots of reasons to come here (just ask any Venezuelan where they want to go on holiday), but if you come expecting a Caribbean idyll, you'll be disappointed.

The urban sprawl around the island's largest town, Porlamar, is the favored haunts of holidaying Venezuelans, and full of glitzy shops, huge hotels and beach bars. Independent travelers should avoid this corner of the island and escape the crowds. By far the best bits of the island are to be found elsewhere – the terrific beach towns of El Yaque and Juangriego, the inland mountains and the largely untouched Península de Macanao are the real highlights of any visit here.

Getting There & Away

Air

Many major national airlines fly into **Aeropuerto Internacional del Caribe General Santiago Mariño** (PMV; ☎400-5057; www.aeropuerto-margarita.gob.ve). Besides Caracas, destinations include Barcelona, Valencia, Maturín and Puerto Ordaz. Aereotuy flies to Los Roques (US$240) and both Aereotuy and Conviasa fly direct to Port of Spain, Trinidad.

There are no buses servicing the airport. An official taxi stand covers the entire island at fixed prices (see individual towns in this section).

Boat

Isla de Margarita has links with the mainland via Puerto La Cruz and Cumaná from the ferry terminal, Punta de Piedras (29km west of Porlamar). There are also small seasickness-inducing boats that depart approximately every 2½ hours (or when full) from 7am to 3pm to Chacopata (BsF30, 1½ hours) from Porlamar. On all ferries noted here, children aged two to seven and seniors over 60 pay half price. Check the websites for current schedules.

From side-by-side terminals in Puerto La Cruz, government-owned **Conferry** (☎0501-2663-3779; www.conferry.com; Av Llano Adentro) has two and **Gran Cacique/Navlarca** (☎0281-263-0935; www.grancacique.com.ve; Prolongación Paseo Colón; ⊙8am-noon & 2-6pm Mon-Fri, 8am-2pm Sat) runs two to three daily departures. Both charge BsF120 per passenger and BsF230 per car and take about 4½ hours. Check websites for exact dates and times.

From Cumaná, **Gran Cacique/Naviarca** (☎0293-432-0011; www.grancacique.com.ve; Vía Terminal de Ferrys; ⊙8am-noon & 2-6pm Mon-Fri, 8am-2pm Sat) has two to three departures daily (passenger/car BsF90/170, 3½ hours).

Faster **Navibus** (☎0295-500-6284; www.navibus.com.ve) has one to two daily departures from both Cumaná (passenger/car BsF99/BsF167, three hours) and Puerto La Cruz (BsF137/232, four hours).

Once daily, **Ferryven** (☎0295-2637446; www.ferryven.net) runs passenger-only service to/from Carúpano (BsF140, three hours).

Small buses regularly shuttle from Punta de Piedras to Porlamar (BsF7); taxis to El Yaque are BsF100 and BsF120 for Juangriego.

Porlamar

☎0295 / POP 101,500

Porlamar is Margarita's largest and busiest city, though more of a transit point and commercial center than a prime destination for independent travelers. Tree-shaded Plaza Bolívar is Porlamar's historic center, but the city has expanded eastward, merging with Los Robles and Pampatar to form an ugly scar across this section of the island. Take care after dark.

Isla de Margarita

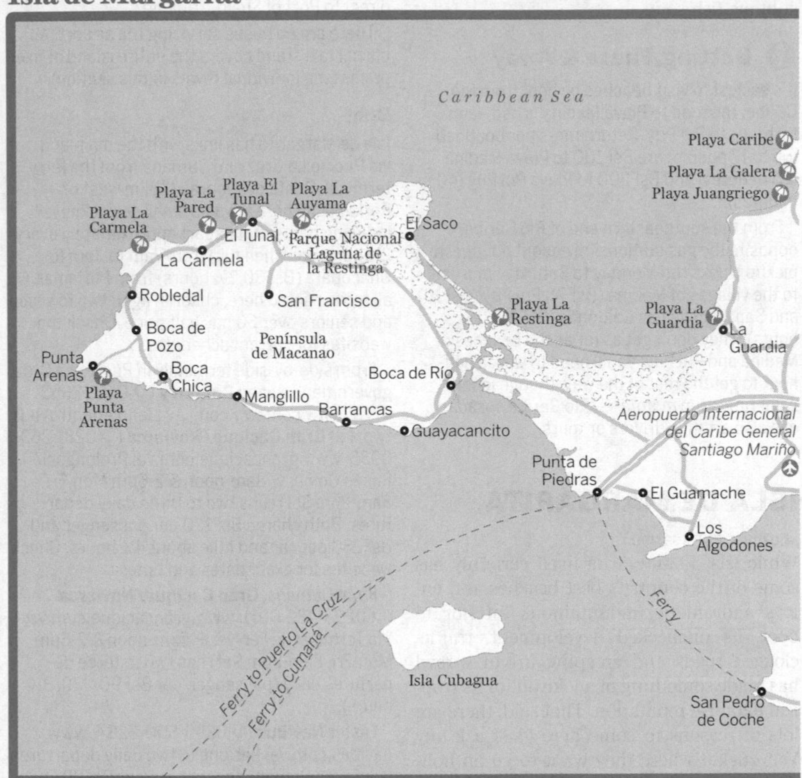

Sleeping

Casa Lutecia B&B $
(☎263-8526; Campos btwn Cedeño & Marcano; d/ste incl breakfast BsF230/280; ❄📶🏊) Your best bet in Porlamar, this Mediterranean-style *posada* has adobe-colored walls, a Spanish-tile roof and a courtyard of brilliant bougainvillea. Comfortable rooms are equipped with mosquito nets and some have ceiling fans for those who detest air-conditioning. The rooftop pool is heavenly. French is also spoken.

Hotel Jinama HOTEL $
(☎261-7186; Mariño btwn Maneiro & Zamora; r/tr/q BsF180/200/240; ❄) A simple and cheerful hotel, with in-room fridges and cable TV making up for thinnish mattresses. Also has a pleasant common area overlooking the street.

Eating

Budget eateries are plentiful across the city, particularly in the old town where food carts set up around the plaza. There's a small but lively restaurant row around the corner of Patiño and Malavé.

Vivaldi Panadería CAFE $
(cnr Patiño & Malavé; pastries from BsF7; ⏰7am-10pm Mon-Sat, 7:30am-2pm Sun; ❄) A tranquil spot for frothy cappuccinos, excellent pastries and a morning newspaper, Vivaldi's bakery has a pleasant little terrace or air-con interior from which to choose.

Restaurant Punto Criollo VENEZUELAN $$
(Igualdad 19, btwn Fraternidad & Fajardo; mains BsF40-80; ⏰10:30am-10:30pm; ❄) A large, no-nonsense Venezuelan restaurant with a lengthy bit-of-everything menu, smartly bow-tied waiters and a long drinks list.

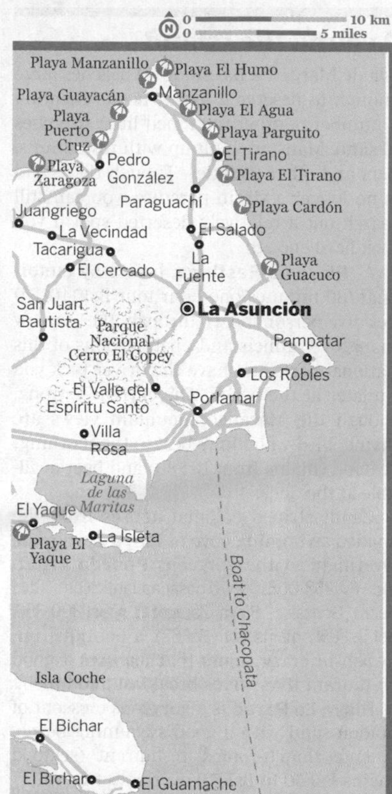

Casa Italia ITALIAN **$$**
(cnr Patiño & Malavé; pizza & pasta BsF60-120; ⏲lunch & dinner; 🖉) Choose from a long list of meat and chicken offerings, or one of its almost 20 delectable pasta dishes.

Information

Cambios Cussco (Velázquez, btwn Narváez & Av Santiago Mariño)
Corp Banca (cnr Velázquez & Fraternidad) ATM. Two blocks east of the plaza.

Getting Around

The **minibus station** (Velásquez, btwn Buenaventura & Meneses), four blocks west of the Plaza Bolívar serves western destinations El Yaque (BsF6, hourly until 6pm), Punta de Piedras (BsF7, frequent) and Macanao (BsF14.50, when full).

Minibuses for Pampatar, Juangriego and Playa El Agua depart from stops along the first and second blocks north of Plaza Bolívar; they cost BsF8 to BsF12.

El Yaque

☎0295 / POP 1500

Just south of the airport, with a guarded entrance, El Yaque is a hot spot for independent travelers drawn by its tranquil waters and steady winds that are perfect for **windsurfing** and **kitesurfing**. This safe beach town boasts an international reputation and is also a hangout for the Venezuelan and European windsurfing community (don't be surprised to see prices in euros).

Several professional outfits on the beachfront offer windsurf rental (per hour/day BsF100/700). Lessons (in a variety of languages) average BsF160 per hour, or BsF1200 for an advanced course of 10 hours. Kitesurfing lessons run about BsF800/2100/3900 for two/six/12 hours; gear rental without lessons costs BsF600/1000/1400 for one/two/three days.

There's an ATM in front of the Hotel El Yaque Paradise, though many places will accept euros or PayPal.

Taxis from the airport cost BsF90 or BsF100 from Punta de Piedras. Hourly minibuses run from Porlamar (BsF6). From Punta de Piedras, you can take a Porlamar-bound *por puesto* to the El Rayado turnoff (BsF5) and then change for an El Yaque *por puesto* (hourly) or hitch the rest of the way.

Sleeping & Eating

Pricier hotels, bars and restaurants are clustered along the beach at the east end of town. Kiosks sell BsF10 *arepas* and empenadas.

Posada La Iguana GUESTHOUSE **$$**
(☎0414-235-7106; www.posadalaiguana.com.ve; Calle Principal; s/d/tr incl breakfast BsF300/400/500; ❄📶) On the beachside lagoon beside the town entrance, these lovely rooms have wood-beamed ceilings and spacious tiled bathrooms with rainforest showerheads. The landscaped grounds include a thatched restaurant and bar by the water.

Surfhotel Jump'n Jibe GUESTHOUSE **$$$**
(☎263-8396; www.jumpnjibe.com; Calle Principal; s/d/tr incl breakfast BsF500/650/780; ❄📶) Of several midrange hotels fronting onto El Yaque beach, this cool, relaxed choice is one of the best. It has 17 sparkling rooms (including one apartment), a palm-filled garden and terrific sea views (even better if you can afford a private balcony). A small terrace overlooks the beach area.

Posada Margarita GUESTHOUSE **$$**
(☎0416-295-2453, 263-0624; www.posada-margarita.com; Las Flores 3; d BsF250-280, tr BsF360, apt BsF560; ❄📶) Bright textiles and painted wooden fish festoon these comfortable rooms and kitchenette apartments. Breakfast (BsF50) and good island tours are available.

Juangriego

☎0295 / POP 34,000

One of the nicest and most low-key beach towns on the island, Juangriego is famous for its burning sunsets. Set on the edge of a dramatic bay in the north of the island, it's a relaxing place to hang out on the beach, with rustic fishing boats, visiting yachts and pelicans. Nearby beach options are **Playa La Galera**, within easy walking distance and favored by locals, and the lovely **Playa Caribe**, 10 minutes away by taxi. When the sun sets over the peaks of Macanao far off on the horizon, the hillside **Fortín de la Galera** is the place to watch the blazing show.

Por puestos only arrive from Porlamar, so take a taxi from Punta de Piedras (BsF120) or the airport (BsF100).

Sleeping & Eating

Curiously, one of the best places to eat inexpensively is at the bus terminal (a 10-minute walk from the beach), which has a dozen food stalls. Numerous good seafood restaurants can be found along the beach behind Hotel Patrick, with set lunches for about BsF45.

Hotel Patrick GUESTHOUSE **$**
(☎253-6218; www.hotelpatrick.com; El Fuerte; s/d/tr BsF150/250/300; ❄@📶🏊) Not far from the beach, Hotel Patrick is a perennial favorite, run by a friendly and voluble Irishman and his Venezuelan wife. There are nine colorful and attractive rooms (those upstairs have fantastic views toward the sunset from outside on the balcony), plus a good hangout area with tables, sofas, hammocks, a pool table, a plunge pool and a popular bar.

El Caney GUESTHOUSE **$**
(☎253-5059; elcaney1@hotmail.com; Guevara 17; s/d/tr BsF180/200/230, q BsF250-300; ❄📶🏊) El Caney is a colorful *posada* run by a Peruvian-Canadian couple. It's equipped with a kitchen, and nice touches include a palm-thatched terrace out front and a plunge pool with waterfall.

Around the Island

Isla de Margarita has some 50 beaches large enough to deserve a name, not to mention a number of other unnamed little stretches of sand. Many are built up with restaurants, bars and other facilities. Though the island is no longer a virgin paradise, you can still search out a relatively deserted spot if you look hard enough.

At **Playa La Restinga**, breeze by motorboat (30 minutes/one-hour tour BsF140/170 per five-person boat) through the narrow mangrove tunnels and open lagoons of this national park, and have the driver pick you up later at the beach. The current's strong, though the Macanao mountain views are divine. Bird-watching's best in the morning; seafood (mains from BsF80) and beer available at the dock.

Candy-striped colonial houses front the shaded swimming cove of **Playa Zaragoza**. Overnight at the gorgeous **Posada Atlantic** (☎258-0061; www.posadaatlantic.com; Blvd Pedro González, Playa Zaragoza; r BsF300-350, apt BsF650, mains from BsF62), a boutique inn awash in crazy colors that features a good restaurant that serves breakfast and lunch.

Playa La Pared is a gorgeous crescent of golden sand with a good swimming beach. A cute thatch-roofed restaurant (seafood mains BsF50 to BsF70) overlooks the water.

Playa El Agua is Margarita's busiest stretch of sand, though its tall waves are better for surfing than swimming. During holidays, the beach gets crammed with visitors. It's generally an upmarket place, but there are some budget options in the back streets.

Other popular beaches include **Playa Guacuco** and **Playa Manzanillo**. Perhaps Margarita's finest beach is **Playa Puerto Cruz**, which arguably has the island's widest, whitest stretch of sand and still isn't overdeveloped. **Playa Parguito**, next to Playa El Agua, has strong waves good for surfing and rentals available. If you want to escape from people, head for **Península de Macanao**, the wildest part of the island.

GUAYANA

The southeastern region of Guayana (not to be confused with the country Guyana) showcases Venezuela at its exotic best. The area is home to the world's highest waterfall, Salto Ángel; the impossibly lush Parque

Nacional Canaima; the wildlife-rich Orinoco Delta (Delta del Orinoco) and Río Caura; the Venezuelan Amazon and La Gran Sabana (The Great Savanna) where flat-topped *tepui* mountains lord over rolling grasslands. Visitors often spend an entire trip in this area of the country.

The majority of the country's indigenous groups live in Guayana, including the Warao, Pemón and Yanomami, which constitute about 10% of the region's total population.

Ciudad Bolívar

☎0285

The proud capital of Venezuela's largest state, Ciudad Bolívar has an illustrious history as a center of the independence struggle, and wears its status proudly. The Casco Histórico (historic center) is one of the country's finest – a gorgeous ensemble of brightly painted colonial buildings, shady squares and the fine Paseo Orinoco - overlooking the country's greatest river. Travelers on their way through to Angel Falls and the Parque Nacional Canaima are usually glad to have made a stopover here.

Simón Bolívar came here in 1817, soon after the town had been liberated from Spanish control, and set up the base for the military operations that led to the final stage of the War of Independence. The town was made the provisional capital of the yet-to-be-liberated country. The Angostura Congress convened here in 1819 and gave birth to Gran Colombia, a unified republic comprising Venezuela, Colombia and Ecuador.

The historic center clears out after dark and everything is closed on Sundays. Walking alone at night is not recommended.

Sights

The colonial heart of the city is **Plaza Bolívar**. The lively waterfront, **Paseo Orinoco**, is lined with street vendors and old arcaded houses, some of which go back to the days of Simón Bolívar. From the Río Orinoco shoreline or viewpoints in the city, you can see the appropriately named island **Piedra del Medio** (Rock in the Middle).

Airplane of Jimmie Angel LANDMARK
Standing in front of the airport terminal is the restored airplane of gold-seeker Jimmie Angel, who landed atop what was eventually named Salto Ángel (Angel Falls).

Museo de Arte Moderno Jesús Soto MUSEUM
(☎632-0518; cnr Avs Germania & Briceño Iragorry; ⌚9:30am-5:30pm Tue-Fri, 10am-5pm Sat & Sun) Museo de Arte Moderno Jesús Soto has an extensive collection of kinetic works by this renowned artist.

Tours

Ciudad Bolívar is the main departure point for tours to Canaima (Salto Ángel), Río Caura and onward travel to Santa Elena de Uairén (Roraima). A three-day all-inclusive tour to Salto Ángel runs about BsF2600 to BsF3300. One-day tours to Canaima with a Salto Ángel overflight and tour of the lagoon run about BsF2600 (minimum four people).

Almost all operators broker Salto Ángel tours through either Excursiones Kavac or budget-oriented Tiuna Tours, both based in Canaima.

A few of the many operators:

Gekko Tours TOUR
(☎0414-854-5146, 632-3223; www.gekkotours-venezuela.de; airport terminal, Ciudad Bolívar) Run by Posada La Casita, Gecko Tours is a responsible full-service agency offering a wide range of tours and flights across the region and the country.

Sapito Tours TOUR
(☎0414-854-8234; www.sapitotours.com; airport terminal) Representative of Bernal Tours from Canaima.

Excursiones Salto Ángel TOUR
(☎632-1904; www.saltoangel.com.ve; Libertad 31) Offers the standard budget-range tours.

Sleeping

Ciudad Bolívar has a number of lovely *posadas* to choose from.

TOP CHOICE **Posada La Casita** GUESTHOUSE **$$**
(☎0414-856-2925, 617-0832; www.posada-lacasita.com; Urbanización 24 de Julio; camping per person BsF50, s/d/tr/q BsF190/300/390/470; ❄@≋) Lounge by the pool at this relaxing rural compound just outside the city. There's easy access (free 24-hour pickup from the airport or bus station, and a shuttle to town), a sociable atmosphere and excellent rooms. Snacks, drinks and inexpensive meals are available.

Posada Don Carlos GUESTHOUSE **$**
(☎632-6017; www.hosteltrail.com/hostels/posadadoncarlos; Boyacá 26; hammock or outdoor bed

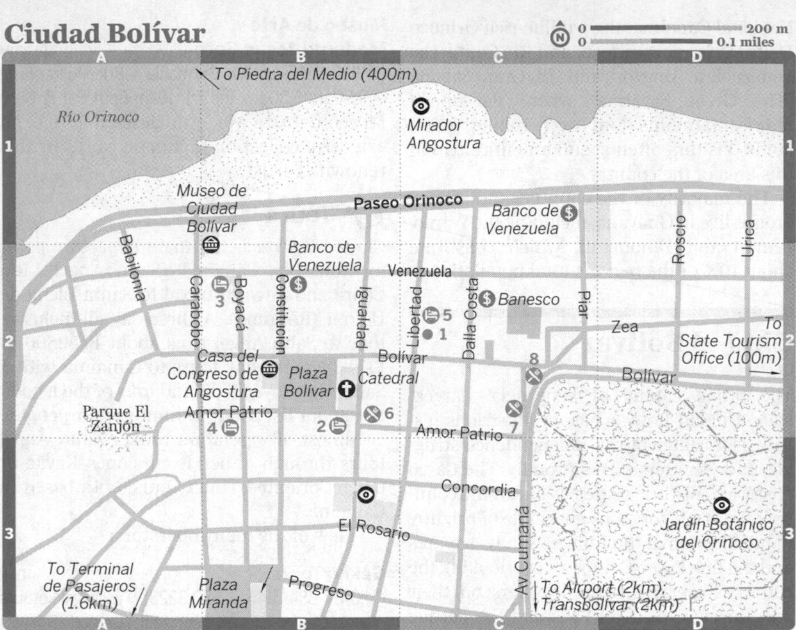

Ciudad Bolívar

Activities, Courses & Tours
1 Excursiones Salto Ángel C2

Sleeping
2 Posada Amor Patrio B2
3 Posada Casa Grande B2
4 Posada Don Carlos B2
5 Posada Doña Carol C2

Eating
6 Mini Lunch Arabian Food B2
7 Portales Gastronómico C2
8 Tostadas Juancito's C2

BsF80, s/d with fan BsF150/250, d/tr/q with air-con BsF300/350/400; ❄@📶) An atmospheric colonial mansion with two ample patios and an antique bar, this *posada* has neat, clean accommodations, a kitchen, and meals upon request. Air-con rooms have towering ceilings and enormous wood doors. Río Caura and Salto Ángel tours can be organized.

Posada Doña Carol GUESTHOUSE $$
(☎0426-999-5724, 634-0989; www.hosteltrail.com/posadadonacarol; Libertad 28; s/d with fan & shared bathroom BsF150/180, d/q with air-con BsF250/350; ❄@📶) This friendly establishment in the heart of town has five simple rooms and use of the kitchen, though Doña Carol's home-cooked meals are amazing (and inexpensive). Downstairs rooms have no exterior windows, but one of the large upstairs rooms has a breezy terrace.

Posada Amor Patrio GUESTHOUSE $
(☎0414-854-4925; www.posadaamorpatrioaventura.com; Amor Patrio 30; r/tr with shared bathroom BsF150/210; @📶) A historic 275-year-old house right behind the cathedral, with five playfully themed rooms, a rooftop hammock terrace, a kitchen and an airy salon celebrating Cuban jazz. Also does Río Caura tours.

Posada Casa Grande BOUTIQUE HOTEL $$$
(☎632-6706; www.cacaotravel.com; cnr Venezuela & Boyacá; s/d/tr/ste incl breakfast BsF603/856/1110/1290; ❄@📶🏊) A lovely (though overpriced) boutique hotel in a restored colonial building; rooftop views at sunset are spectacular.

Eating & Drinking

If you wish to pick up a few nibbles in the center, there's a small fruit and vegetable market behind Tostadas Juancito's that carries a bare minimum of pasta and other staples. For a late-night fast-food fix, get a taxi to the **Calle del Hambre** (Hungry Street; Estacionamiento del Estadio Heres), a block-long carnival of bright lights and a few dozen food stalls that buzz and sizzle until the wee hours of the morning.

Mini Lunch Arabian Food MIDDLE EASTERN **$$**
(cnr Amor Patrio & Igualdad; mains BsF40-80; 7am-5pm Mon-Fri, until noon Sat;) This small family-run cafe ramps up at lunchtime, with hearty vegetarian lentil soup chock-full of greens, and filling falafels; or try the tasty shawarma and kebabs.

Portales Gastronómico VENEZUELAN, VEGETARIAN **$**
(Av Cumaná; menú BsF40-50; breakfast & lunch Mon-Sat;) Though not exclusively vegetarian, this mother-daughter restaurant emphasizes healthy food and fresh vegetables. Try the soy croquettes or baked chicken, and housemade pastas on Saturdays.

Tostadas Juancito's VENEZUELAN **$**
(cnr Av Cumaná & Bolívar; arepas BsF20-30, menú BsF25-45; 7am-6pm Mon-Sat) Hang out with the locals at this popular *arepera* and snack bar that has occupied this busy street corner forever.

 Information

Medical Services

Hospital Ruiz y Páez (632-4146; Av Germania)

Money

Banco de Venezuela Paseo Orinoco (cnr Paseo Orinoco & Piar); Center (cnr Venezuela & Constitución)

Banesco (cnr Dalla Costa & Venezuela)

Tourist Information

State Tourism Office (0800-674-6626; www.turismobolivar.gob.ve; Bolívar; 8am-noon & 2-5:30pm) Just inside the Jardín Botánico; very helpful, with English, German and Italian spoken. Toll-free information line open 8am to 8pm Monday to Saturday.

 Getting There & Away

Air

The **airport** (632-4978; Av Jesús Soto) is 2km southeast of the riverfront and linked to the city center by local buses. **Rutaca** (0800-788-2221, 600-5300; www.rutaca.com.ve) flies to Caracas (BsF500), Santo Domingo and San Antonio daily, and to Santa Elena de Uairén (via Canaima; BsF1500) if there are five passengers. Most flights from here are charters to Canaima, which run BsF1300 roundtrip without a tour.

Destinos Car Rental (632-7566; destinoscarrental@gmail.com) and **Representaciones Turísticas Lozano** (0414-861-5335) rent cars here from around BsF650 per day.

Bus

The **Terminal de Pasajeros** (cnr Avs República & Sucre) is 2km south of the center. To get there, take the westbound *buseta* marked 'Terminal' from Paseo Orinoco. The Rodovías terminal is also here; its Caracas-bound buses arrive at a convenient downtown terminal instead of the Terminal de Oriente.

Frequent buses go to Caracas (BsF150, nine hours); most depart in the evening. Direct buses service Valencia (BsF175, 10½ hours) via the shorter Los Llanos route that bypasses Caracas. Take these to go to Venezuela's northwest or the Andes without connections in Caracas.

A few daily buses run to Puerto La Cruz (BsF85, four hours). Small buses depart regularly throughout the day to Puerto Ayacucho (BsF87 to BsF180, 10½ to 12 hours), but only some have air-con. To avoid the longer 12-hour journey, take a *directo* bus. To Puerto Ordaz (BsF20 to BsF50, 1½ hours), buses depart every 15 to 30 minutes, and a half dozen daily departures go to Santa Elena de Uairén (BsF175 to BsF200, 10 to 12 hours).

Transbolívar (Airport; 6am-8pm Mon-Sat, 1:30am-7:30pm Sun), the state bus company, has one evening departure from the airport to Santa Elena de Uairén (BsF150). It's not a *buscama* (bus with deeply reclining seats) but there's no loud TV.

Ciudad Guayana

0286 / POP 826,000

Officially 'founded' in 1961 to serve as an industrial center for the region, Ciudad Guayana sits on two rivers, the Río Orinoco and Río Caroní, and encompasses the unlikely twin cities of Puerto Ordaz and San Félix. The colonial town of San Félix, on the eastern side of the Caroní, is a working-class city with a historical center, but little tourist infrastructure and a reputation for being unsafe. Puerto Ordaz is a wealthy and modern prefab city, with a large middle-class population, and a smorgasbord of restaurant and entertainment options. Locals generally refer to 'San Félix' or 'Puerto Ordaz,' and tend to disregard the official title of 'Ciudad Guayana.' Don't bother to ask for Ciudad Guayana at a bus station or travel agency, because the place is little more than a name.

All listings below are in Puerto Ordaz.

Sights

Puerto Ordaz has three stunning parks along the Río Caroní. The 52-hectare **Parque Cachamay** (Av Guayana) has a spectacular view of the river's 200m-wide waterfalls. Pushy monkeys enliven the adjoining **Parque Loefling** (Av Guayana), which has roaming capybaras and tapirs and contains a small zoo of native wildlife. The 160-hectare **Parque La Llovizna** (Av Leopoldo Sucre Figarella) is on the other (eastern) side of the Río Caroní, with 26 wooded islands carved by thin water channels and linked by 36 footbridges. The 20m-high waterfall Salto La Llovizna kicks up the park's namesake *llovizna* (drizzle).

Sleeping

With its relative wealth and high number of business travelers, there aren't many good budget accommodations in Puerto Ordaz.

La Casa del Lobo GUESTHOUSE **$**
(0414-871-9339, 961-6286; www.lobo-tours.de; Zambia 2, Manzana 39, Villa Africana; r BsF150;) The only backpacker option in town, this messy German-owned house a few kilometers south of the center has five rooms, a kitchen, meals prepared on request and delta tours. There's also free pickup service from Puerto Ordaz bus terminal with advance notice; taxis cost BsF45 but can never find it.

Posada Turística Kaori GUESTHOUSE **$$**
(923-4038; www.posadakaori.com; Argentina, Campo B; r/tr/q BsF270/320/380;) With small, clean and contemporary rooms with cable TV and good mattresses, this *posada* is within walking distance of the center.

Posada San Miguel GUESTHOUSE **$**
(924-9385; Moitaco; r BsF180-200, tr BsF350) This largely subterranean *posada* may not win any awards for charm, but it's right in

TOURING THE ORINOCO DELTA

Roaring howler monkeys welcome the dawn. Piranhas clamp onto anything that bleeds. Screaming clouds of parrots gather at dusk, and weaving bats gobble insects under the blush of a million stars. For wildlife-viewing on the water's edge, it's hard to outshine the Orinoco Delta (Delta del Orinoco).

A deep-green labyrinth of islands, channels and mangrove swamps engulfing nearly 30,000 sq km – the size of Belgium – this is one of the world's great river deltas and a mesmerizing region to explore. Mixed forest blankets most of the land, which includes a variety of palms. Of these, the moriche palm is the most typical and important, as it is the traditional staple food for the delta's inhabitants, the Warao people, and provides material for their crafts, tools, wine and houses.

The best time to see the wildlife in the delta is in the dry season (January to May), when wide, orange, sandy beaches emerge along the shores of the channels. In the rainy months (August and September), when rivers are full, boat travel is easier, but the wildlife disperses and is more difficult to see.

All-inclusive three-day tours average BsF1800 to BsF2600. Some recommended companies with their own *campamentos* (camps):

Campamento Oridelta (0414-868-2121, 0286-961-5526; www.deltaorinoko.com.ve) Runs trips in the Río Grande area of the Delta del Orinoco, with a *campamento* in Piacoa. The owner, Roger Ruffenach, is an authority on the wildlife of the delta, speaks English, German and French, and personally guides all the trips, which never have more than 10 guests.

Orinoco Eco Camp (0414-091-4844; www.orinoco-eco-camp.com) Within the Reserva Nacional de Fauna Silvestre Gran Morichal; traveler recommended.

Cooperativa Osibu XIV (721-3840; campamentomaraisa@hotmail.com) This long-standing family-owned business conducts tours to San Francisco de Guayo, in the far eastern part of the delta. It's a four-hour boat ride to their *cabaña* camp with beds. Minimum six people.

Viajes & Excursiones Turísticas Delta (0287-721-0835, 0416-897-2285; www.aventuraturisticadelta.com) One of the least expensive agencies (almost half as much as the others), with a hammock-only *campamento* in Pedernales.

the center of town and is good value, offering 12 clean rooms all with private bathrooms and cable TV.

Eating

Mercado Municipal VENEZUELAN $
(Calle Guasipati; meals BsF35-50; breakfast & lunch) A line of a dozen food kiosks serving typical local fare on a shaded sidewalk.

RicArepa VENEZUELAN $
(Carrera Upata; arepas BsF28-38; 24hr) You can choose from almost two dozen types of fillings in this buzzing *arepera*.

La Cuarenta Platos de Alí Babá MIDDLE EASTERN $$
(Carrera Ciudad Piar; mains BsF42-88; 11:30am-7:30pm;) Feast on falafels and stuffed grape leaves, or ask for the *plato mini típico variado* and sample a little bit of everything.

Panadería y Exquisiteces La Pradera BAKERY $
(Torre Loreto II, Av Las Américas; pastries BsF12; 6:30am-9pm) Pastries and strong coffee in a gleaming bakery-cafe. A hearty lunch *menú* draws a midday crowd.

Information

Banco de Venezuela (cnr Avs Las Américas & Monseñor Zabaleta)
Movilnet (cnr Av Las Américas & Carrera Tumeremo) Phones.

Getting There & Away

Ciudad Guayana is a major transit hub for buses and flights.

Air

A busy regional air hub, the **Aeropuerto Puerto Ordaz** (Av Guayana) is at the western end of town on the road to Ciudad Bolívar and is served by local buses. Note that the airport appears in all schedules as 'Puerto Ordaz,' not 'Ciudad Guayana.'

Bus

Ciudad Guayana has two main bus terminals, one in Puerto Ordaz, on Av Guayana 1km east of the airport, and another in San Félix. The Puerto Ordaz terminal is smaller, cleaner, quieter and safer than the busier San Félix station, and most buses stop at both terminals.

From Puerto Ordaz, most buses to Caracas depart in the evening. Direct buses to Maracay and Valencia take the shorter Los Llanos route and bypass Caracas; they're handy for connections to the Andes and the northwest.

Buses to Ciudad Bolívar depart every half hour or so; faster *por puestos* cost BsF50. Night buses come through from Ciudad Bolívar daily on their way to Santa Elena de Uairén. Expresos Caribe has one daily night bus to Boa Vista, Brazil.

Across the street from the Puerto Ordaz terminal, the gleaming **Rodovías bus terminal** (951-9633; Av Guayana) has free spick-and-span bathrooms and six daily departures to its private terminal in central Caracas (BsF187, 10 hours).

BUS FARES FROM PUERTO ORDAZ (MAIN TERMINAL)

DESTINATION	COST (BSF)	DURATION (HR)
Boa Vista, Brazil	265	14
Caracas	115-169	10½
Caracas (SITSSA)	55	10½
Ciudad Bolívar	20	1½
Maracay	185-201	11
Santa Elena de Uairén	110-176	9-11
Valencia	205	12

Salto Ángel (Angel Falls)

Salto Ángel is the world's highest waterfall and Venezuela's number-one tourist attraction. Its total height is 979m, with an uninterrupted drop of 807m – about 16 times the height of Niagara Falls. The cascade pours off the towering Auyantepui, one of the largest of the *tepuis*. Salto Ángel is not named, as one might expect, for a divine creature, but for an American bush pilot Jimmie Angel, who landed his four-seater airplane atop Auyantepui in 1937 while in search of gold.

The waterfall is in a distant, lush wilderness with no road access. The village of Canaima, about 50km northwest, is the major gateway to the falls. Canaima doesn't have an overland link to the rest of the country either, but is accessed by numerous small planes from Ciudad Bolívar, Puerto Ordaz and Isla de Margarita.

A visit to Salto Ángel is normally undertaken in two stages, with Canaima as the stepping-stone. Most tourists fly into Canaima, where they take a light plane or boat to the falls. Most visitors who visit by boat opt to stay overnight in hammocks at one of the camps near the base of the falls. The trip upriver, the surrounding area and the experience of staying at the camp are as memorable as the waterfall itself.

Salto Ángel, Auyantepui, Canaima and the surrounding area lie within the boundaries of the 30,000-sq-km Parque Nacional Canaima. All visitors must pay a BsF150 national-park entrance fee at Canaima airport.

Canaima

☎0286 / POP 1500

The closest population center to Salto Ángel, Canaima is a remote indigenous village that hosts and dispatches a huge number of tourists. Although it's a base to reach Venezuela's number-one natural attraction, Canaima is truly gorgeous as well. The **Laguna de Canaima** sits at the heart of everything, a broad blue expanse framed by a palm-tree beach, a dramatic series of seven picture-postcard cascades and a backdrop of anvil-like *tepuis*. Most tours to Salto Ángel include a short boat trip and hike that allows you to walk behind some of the falls and get the backstage experience of the hammering curtains of water. Their color is a curious pink, caused by the high level of tannins from decomposed plants and trees.

The rambling Campamento Canaima is on the west of the lagoon, with the best beach for swimming and taking photos. When swimming, stay close to the main beach – a number of drownings have occurred close to the hydroelectric plant and the falls.

Tours

Almost everyone arrives in Canaima on an all-inclusive tour, as it's not really worth the hassle or negligible savings to do it independently. The following are the main operators, whose tours are sold by other agencies:

Excursiones Kavac TOUR
(☎0416-685-2209; exc.kavac@hotmail.com) A good agency managed by the indigenous Pemón community. Marginally cheaper than Bernal Tours, it also has a *campamento* in front of Salto Ángel. It offers Kamarata Valley tours too (see boxed text, p1024).

Bernal Tours TOUR
(☎0414-854-8234; www.bernaltours.com) Family-run company based on an island in Laguna de Canaima, where participants stay and eat before and after the tour. Bernal Tours has its *campamento* on Isla Ratoncito, opposite Salto Ángel.

Tiuna Tours TOUR
(☎962-4255, 0416-692-1536; tiunatours@hotmail.com) The cheapest local player, with a large *campamento* in Canaima and another up the Río Carrao at the Río Aonda.

> **RAIN OR SHINE?**
>
> The amount of water going over Salto Ángel depends on the season, and the contrast can be dramatic. In the dry months (January to May), it can be pretty faint – just a thin ribbon of water fading into mist before it reaches the bottom. Boat access is impossible in the driest months. In the rainy season, particularly in the wettest months (August and September), the waterfall is a spectacular cascade of plummeting water – but you run the risk of rain and of the view being obscured by clouds.

Sleeping

There are a dozen *campamentos* and *posadas* in Canaima. Most are managed by the main tour agencies, serve all meals and will meet you at the airport. Camping on the lagoon is no longer permitted.

Campamento Churúm GUESTHOUSE $$
(☎0289-540-2233, 0416-586-0648; exc.kavac@hotmail.com; r per person without/with full board BsF350/750) Located opposite the soccer pitch, Excursiones Kavac's clean, comfortable camp has almost two dozen rooms with fans.

Campamento Tiuna HOSTEL $
(☎0414-864-0033, 0426-296-0520; hammock/tent per person BsF120/200, dm per person with/without meals BsF600/300) In an open stone building at the northern part of the village, this basic *campamento* offers hammocks and small dormitory rooms. There's free hammock lodging if you eat all meals there. Breakfast is BsF60, lunch or dinner BsF120.

Posada Kusary GUESTHOUSE $$
(☎0414-884-0940; r per person BsF300; ❄) Run by the owners of Tienda Canaima, this well-maintained *posada* in the northern area of town has 13 rooms, a few with air-con. Breakfast is BsF60, lunch or dinner BsF120.

Posada Wey Tupü GUESTHOUSE $
(☎0416-997-9565, 0416-185-7231; r per person with/without meals BsF460/200) Opposite the old school in the south part of the village,

Parque Nacional Canaima

Wey Tupü has simple rooms with fans and provides some of the cheapest meals for guests.

Eating & Drinking

A *comedor* (basic cafeteria) next to the internet cafe sells roast chicken lunches (BsF120), and a thatched eatery across the street has breakfast *arepas* and empanadas for BsF10 to BsF20. Along the lagoon, the Posada Restaurant Morichal runs an incongruous full bar with a massive sound and light system.

Sakaikapa MARKET $
(⏲7am-9pm) This *bodegita* (little store) just past the soccer pitch sells BsF10 *quesadillas* (cheese rolls) and some foodstuffs.

Mentanai PUB $
(mains BsF20-45; ⏲6-11:30pm Fri-Sun, longer hours Aug-Sep) Next to Excursiones Kavac, this burger-and-sandwich grill has a pool table and a bar serving beer and Cuba Libres.

ℹ Information

Computers are available near the airport at Posada Restaurant Morichal (BsF20 per hour), and an internet cafe is due to open on the corner across from Mentanai.

Banco de Venezuela Near the airport, inside Campamento Canaima compound; BsF300 maximum daily withdrawal.

Tienda Canaima Near the airport, this expensive shop stocks the biggest inventory of groceries (including ice cream), toiletries, maps and souvenirs. It also changes US dollars, euros and British pounds at an intermediary rate and gives cash on ATM cards at the official rate. Pay phone available.

ℹ Getting There & Away

Several regional carriers fly between Canaima and Ciudad Bolívar on a semi-regular or charter basis (BsF1300); add BsF600 for a falls overflight. A few airlines, including Aereotuy and **Transmandu** (☎0285-632-1462; Ciudad Bolívar airport terminal) have services to and

WORTH A TRIP

KAMARATA VALLEY

The Kamarata Valley, on the other (southern) side of massive Auyantepui, is a wonderworld of massive waterfalls, traditional indigenous settlements and virgin rainforest only accessible by air taxi. Come here to explore the Parque Nacional Canaima without the crowds; it's even possible to hike to Salto Ángel from here.

Kamarata is the chief settlement on the eastern side of Auyantepui, an old Pemón village on the Río Akanán and a growing access point for Salto Ángel. There are a few simple places to stay and eat in town. Most travelers stay at the nearby tourist camp at Kavac, a two-hour walk from here, or a short drive on a dirt road by the town's service jeep.

Kavac consists of 20-odd *churuatas* (traditional circular palm-thatched huts) built in the traditional style, resembling a manicured Pemón settlement and sitting at the bottom of Auyantepui with some fabulous views toward the summit. The area's major attraction is the spectacular **Cueva de Kavac**, not a cave but a deep gorge with a waterfall plunging into it. There's a natural pool at the foot of the waterfall, which you reach by swimming upstream in the narrow canyon.

Uruyén is a newer community-owned *campamento* at the foot of gorgeous Auyantepui by a small river with a great swimming hole. Uruyén's stellar attraction is the easy hike to the **Cueva de Yurwan**, a breathtaking river gorge that culminates in a spectacular waterfall an hour's walk from the camp.

Angel-Eco Tours (☎0212-762-5975, in US 888-423-3864; www.angel-ecotours.com), Excursiones Kavac (in Canaima) and Gekko Tours (Ciudad Bolívar) can help with travel planning and tours of all lengths, including an 11-day trek over Auyantepui to Salto Ángel (from BsF5000).

from Porlamar. If there are enough passengers to schedule a flight, Rutaca's Cessna charter flights between Canaima and Santa Elena de Uairén (BsF1500) provide some of the best *tepui* views in the country. **Serami** (☎952-0424; www.serami.com.ve) has a direct service from Puerto Ordaz.

GRAN SABANA

A wide open grassland that seems suspended from endless sky, the Gran Sabana invites poetic description. Scores of waterfalls appear at every turn, and *tepuis,* the savanna's trademark table mountains, sweep across the horizon, their mesas both haunting and majestic. More than 100 of these plateaus dot the vast region from the Colombian border in the west to Guyana and Brazil in the east, but most are here in the Gran Sabana. One of the *tepuis,* Roraima, can be climbed; this trip is an extraordinary natural adventure.

The largest town is Santa Elena de Uairén, close to the Brazilian border. The rest of the sparsely populated region is inhabited mostly by the 30,000 indigenous Pemón people, who live in nearly 300 scattered villages.

ℹ Getting Around

The Ciudad Guayana–Santa Elena de Uairén Hwy provides access to this fascinating land, but public transportation on this road is infrequent, making individual sightseeing inconvenient and time consuming. Tours from Ciudad Bolívar or Santa Elena de Uairén are more convenient.

Passengers taking the bus from Santa Elena de Uairén to Ciudad Guayana and points beyond should note that there's a major security checkpoint along the highway near Upata, about an hour before Ciudad Guayana. Be prepared to claim your luggage for a full baggage search, plus the inconvenience of an extra hour added to your journey.

Roraima

A stately table mountain towering into churning clouds, Roraima (2810m) lures hikers and nature-lovers looking for Venezuela at its natural and rugged best. Unexplored until 1884, and studied extensively by botanists ever since, the stark landscape contains strange rock formations and graceful arches, ribbon waterfalls, glittering quartz deposits and carnivorous plants. The frequent mist only accentuates the otherworldly feel.

Although it's one of the easier *tepuis* to climb and no technical skills are required, the trek is long and demanding. However, anyone who's reasonably fit and determined can reach the top. Be prepared for wet weather, nasty *puri puris* (invisible biting insects) and frigid nights at the summit. And give yourself at least six days round-trip so you have sufficient time to explore the vast plateau of the *tepui*.

Climbing Roraima

Roraima lies approximately 47km east of the El Dorado–Santa Elena de Uairén Hwy, just east of the town of San Francisco de Yuruaní. Twenty-six kilometers east of San Francisco, the hamlet of Paraitepui is the usual starting point for the trip, and hikers must sign in at the Inparques office there before setting out. There's a BsF100 fee per group if you're not with an organized tour.

You can organize a compulsory Pemón guide in Santa Elena de Uairén, San Francisco de Yuruaní or Paraitepui. Most people opt to go on an organized tour from Santa Elena de Uairén, where agencies contract guides and porters and arrange for meals, transportation and equipment. Though it costs less to organize a trip from San Francisco de Yuruaní or Paraitepui, remember that in terms of quality, you generally get what you pay for; some travelers have complained about hiring guides there who were careless with safety, unknowledgeable or inebriated.

The trip to the top normally takes two to three days (total net walking time is about 12 hours up and 10 hours down). There are several campsites (with water) on the way. They are Río Tek (four hours from Paraitepui), Río Kukenán (30 minutes further on) and at the foot of Roraima at the so-called *campamento base* (base camp), three hours uphill from the Río Kukenán. The steep, tough, four-hour ascent from the base camp to the top is the most spectacular (yet demanding) part of the hike.

Once atop Roraima, you'll camp in one of the dozen or so *hoteles* – semisheltered camping spots under rock overhangs. The guides coordinate which group sleeps where.

The scenery is a moonscape sculpted by the wind and rain, with gorges, creeks, pink beaches, lookout points and gardens filled with unique flowering plants. An eerie, shifting fog often snakes across the mountaintop. While guides may have seemed superfluous on the clear trails below, they are helpful on the labyrinthine plateau. If you stay for two nights on the top you will have time to hike with your guide to some of the attractions, including **El Foso** (a crystalline pool in a massive sinkhole), the **Punto Triple** (the tri-border of Venezuela, Brazil and Guyana), **Bahia de Cristal** (a small valley brimming with quartz) and the stunning viewpoint of **La Ventana** (the Window).

The *tepui* is an ecologically delicate area. Visitors need to pack out all garbage, including human waste, and collecting quartz is strictly forbidden. Inparques searches bags at the end of the hike, and will fine you for collecting souvenirs.

Make sure to pack good rain gear, extra socks, warm clothes, insect repellant and an extra camera battery.

Santa Elena de Uairén

0289 / POP 30,000

A bustling low-key border town where dusty 4x4 drivers wave at their friends, Santa Elena is the primary transit point for treks to Roraima and the first stop in Venezuela for travelers entering by land from Brazil. This small yet happening town is also a good base for exploring the Gran Sabana.

Though the city is quite safe, it's also a brazen black market and smuggling hub. Gas prices in Brazil are almost 30 times higher than in Venezuela (where gas is cheaper than water), meaning there is serious money to be made. There's a thriving trade in gas sold from private homes, and sellers have acquired the unfortunate moniker of '*talibanes*.' Look for the huge *colas* (lines) at the town gas stations – they pale in comparison to the absolute feeding frenzy at the station along the border, where drivers sometimes camp out in their vehicles for days.

 Tours

All Santa Elena tour agencies run one-, two- or three-day jeep tours around the Gran Sabana, with visits to the most interesting sights, mostly waterfalls. Budget between BsF300 up to BsF800 per person per day, depending on group size and whether the tour includes just guide and transportation, or food and accommodations as well.

For most visitors, the main attraction is a Roraima tour, generally offered as an all-inclusive six-day package for BsF3200 to BsF3500 per person (you get what you pay for). If you have your own gear and food and don't need a porter, most agencies will organize a guide and transportation to Paraitepui, the starting point for the Roraima

Santa Elena de Uairén

Santa Elena de Uairén

Activities, Courses & Tours

- Backpacker Tours .... (see 5)
- 1 Mystic Tours B2
- 2 Nativa Tours Khasen C2
- 3 Ruta Salvaje C1

Sleeping

- 4 Hotel Lucrecia C2
- 5 Posada Backpacker Tours C2
- Posada Michelle .... (see 5)

Eating

- 6 Alfredo's Restaurant C2
- 7 ServeKilo Nova Opção C2
- 8 Tienda Naturalista Griselda Luna B3
- 9 Tumá Serö A2

trek, for BsF1800. Check on specifics, including group size, hiker-to-guide ratio and equipment quality before signing up for any Roraima tour.

Most agencies also sell Salto Ángel and Orinoco Delta tours. Recommended local tour companies:

Adrenaline Expeditions ADVENTURE TOUR
(☎0426-894-8143, 0414-886-7209; www.adrenalinexpeditions.com) Ricardo handles the Gran Sabana with great passion and knowledge, offering all manner of tours, with an emphasis on extreme sports.

Backpacker Tours TOUR
(☎995-1430; www.backpacker-tours.com; Urdaneta) The local powerhouse, it has the most organized, best-equipped and most expensive tours of Roraima and the region. Also rents mountain bikes.

Ruta Salvaje EXTREME SPORTS
(☎995-1134; www.rutasalvaje.com; Av Mariscal Sucre) The standard tours, plus rafting trips, paragliding (BsF500) and paramotoring (BsF700).

Mystic Tours TOUR
(☎414-5696; www.mystictours.com.ve; Urdaneta) Some of least expensive tours to Roraima, and local tours with a New Age bent.

Alvarez Trekking Expedition TOUR
(☎0414-385-2846; rstgransabana@hotmail.com; bus terminal) Personable and helpful, with regional tours and camping equipment rentals. Also has a budget *posada* (d BsF90) on the rural outskirts of town.

Nativa Tours Khasen BIRD-WATCHING
(☎995-1861; nativatours@hotmail.com; Av Perimetral 64) Family-run agency specializing in

bird-watching tours. Day tours to Boa Vista, Brazil.

Sleeping

Posada Michelle GUESTHOUSE $
(☎995-2017; hotelmichelle@cantv.net; Urdaneta; s/d/tr BsF80/120/180) A backpacker institution (leaf through the myriad travel journals in the lounge) with some of the best-value budget rooms in the country. Sweat-caked Roraima hikers can take advantage of half-day rest and shower (BsF80 per room) or shower only (BsF20) rates before taking the night bus out. Kitchen too.

Posada Backpacker Tours GUESTHOUSE $
(☎995-1415; www.backpacker-tours.com; Urdaneta; dm/s/d/tr BsF60/80/120/180; @ 📶) An outdoor restaurant (breakfast BsF40 to BsF50) and internet cafe make this simple 10-room lodging a popular evening hangout spot. Ask about its swank *posada* with pool.

Hotel Lucrecia GUESTHOUSE $$
(☎995-1105; www.hotellucrecia.com.ve; Av Perimetral; r/tr BsF250/300; ❄ @ 🏊) Slightly removed from the central hubbub, Lucrecia has 15 bright hot-water rooms arranged around a lush garden veranda. Breakfast and dinner are available upon request.

Eating

ServeKilo Nova Opção BRAZILIAN, BUFFET $
(Av Perimetral; buffet per kg BsF80; ⏰lunch; 🚭) For almost two decades, this Brazilian eatery has replenished famished hikers with its scrumptious buffet. Vegetarian options available.

Tumá Serö VENEZUELAN, INTERNATIONAL $
(off Calle Bolívar; menú BsF30-60; ⏰7am-8pm) For a cheap meal in a fun atmosphere head to this 'boulevard of food' with dozens of different outlets serving everything from *arepas* to noodles.

Alfredo's Restaurant ITALIAN $$
(Av Perimetral; mains BsF50-110; ⏰11am-3pm & 6-10pm Tue-Sun; 🚭) Perhaps the best restaurant in town, Alfredo's has an unusually long menu, with fantastic pasta, reasonable steaks and fine pizzas from its wood-burning oven.

Tienda Naturalista Griselda Luna VEGETARIAN, MARKET $
(Icabarú; empanadas & pastries BsF10; ⏰8am-noon & 3-6pm Mon-Sat; 🚭) Stock up on dried fruit and vegetarian protein for the Roraima trek. Awesome wholewheat fruit pastries and natural yogurt available.

Information

Money changers (for US dollars and euros) work the corner of Bolívar and Urdaneta, popularly known as Cuatro Esquinas. This is the safest place in the country to delve into the black market, with the best rates – though it's technically illegal.

Internet is BsF5 to BsF7 per hour.

Banco Caroní (Plaza Bolívar)

Banco Industrial de Venezuela (Calle Bolívar)

Hospital Rosario Vera Zurita (☎995-1155; Icabarú)

Ipostel (Urdaneta)

Getting There & Away

Air

The tiny airport is 7km southwest of town, off the road to the Brazilian border. There's no public transportation; take a taxi. With enough passengers, Rutaca flies five-seater Cessnas to Ciudad Bolívar via Canaima (BsF1500). The flight from Canaima offers spectacular *tepui* and winding river views.

LTA has infrequent weekly flights from Puerto Ordaz.

Bus & Jeep

The bus terminal is on the Ciudad Guayana Hwy, about 2km east of the town's center. There are no buses – catch a taxi or get a ride from a tour operator. Ten buses depart daily to Ciudad Bolívar (BsF115 to BsF172, 10 to 12 hours), all stopping at Ciudad Guayana. Some continue to Caracas (BsF280 to BsF311, 20 hours).

From Icabarú, two to three jeeps leave for the counterculture artisan community of El Paují (BsF50, two to three hours) in the morning.

GETTING CASH IN BRAZIL

If you've run out of money and don't want to take a hit by withdrawing money at the official exchange rate in Venezuela, there's a bank with an ATM across the Brazilian border before the bus station. You don't need to have your passport stamped if you're not going past the border town of Pacaraima, and you can then change Brazilian reals to Venezuelan bolívares in Santa Elena.

GETTING TO BRAZIL

Both Venezuelan and Brazilian passport formalities are done at the border itself, locally known as La Línea, 15km south of Santa Elena de Uairén. *Por puestos* from Icabarú travel to the bus station in the Brazilian border town of Pacaraima, but you have to commandeer the whole taxi (BsF60) or they won't wait for you while you have your passport stamped at the Venezuelan and Brazilian immigration offices at La Línea. There's no departure tax here.

From the tiny bus station, comfortable and frequent minivan **taxis** (Icabarú) go *por puesto* to Boa Vista (R$25, 2½ hours); **Eucatur** (www.eucatur.com.br) runs three buses (R$16.50) Monday through Friday and two on Saturday and Sunday.

You need a yellow-fever card to enter Brazil.

AMAZONAS

Venezuela's southernmost state, Amazonas, is predominantly Amazonian rainforest crisscrossed by rivers and sparsely populated by indigenous communities whose primary form of transportation is the dugout canoe called a *bongo*. It covers 180,000 sq km, or one-fifth of the national territory, yet it's home to less than 1% of the country's population. The current indigenous population, estimated at 76,000, comprises three main groups (the Piaroa, Yanomami and Guajibo/Jivi) and a number of smaller communities.

In contrast to the Brazilian Amazon, Venezuela's Amazonas state is topographically diverse, with *tepuis* as one of the most striking features. Although they are not as numerous as those in the Gran Sabana, the *tepuis* give the green carpet of rainforest a distinctive appearance. At the southernmost part of Amazonas, along the border with Brazil, lies the Serranía la Neblina, a scarcely explored mountain range containing the highest South American peaks east of the Andes.

The best time to explore the region is from October to December, when the river level is high enough to navigate but rains have started to ease.

Getting Around

The region has almost no roads, so most transportation has to be by river or air. Other than a few short hops from Puerto Ayacucho, however, there's no regular passenger service on the rivers, which makes independent travel difficult, if not impossible. Tour operators in Puerto Ayacucho can take you just about everywhere, at a price.

Puerto Ayacucho

0248 / POP 91,000

Walk on the shady side of the street or you'll wilt in the heat of this riverside city. The only significant urban center in Venezuela's Amazon, Puerto Ayacucho is a languid and often rainy place with a slow tempo, frequent power outages and few tourists. Set on a colorful section of the Río Orinoco, just down from the spectacular rapids of Raudales Atures, it's the starting point for adventurous trips into the roadless state of Amazonas.

Sights

For a true sense of the city and its river history, get a bird's-eye view from one of its hills. **Cerro Perico** is a good place to survey the Río Orinoco and the city, and Cerro El Zamoro, commonly known as **El Mirador**, overlooks Orinoco's feisty **Raudales Atures** rapids.

Museo Etnológico de Amazonas MUSEUM
(Av Río Negro; admission BsF4; 8:30am-11:30am & 2:30am-6pm Tue-Fri, 9am-noon & 3:30am-6pm Sat) A fascinating display of regional indigenous culture, the Museo Etnológico de Amazonas displays personal items and model-housing replicas from groups including the Piaroa, Guajibo, Ye'kwana and Yanomami.

Mercado Indígena MARKET
(Av Río Negro) Across from the museum, the market sells some indigenous crafts and lots of black velvet paintings. But the most interesting items are the bottles of *catara* sauce (hot sauce made from ants), and the medicinal barks and herbs for sale.

Puerto Ayacucho

☞ Tours

Among the popular shorter tours are a three-day trip up the Río Cuao and a three-day trip up the Ríos Sipapo and Autana to the foot of Cerro Autana (1248m). Expect to pay from BsF500 to BsF700 per person per day.

The far southeastern part of Amazonas beyond La Esmeralda, basically all of Parque Nacional Parima-Tapirapeco, where the Yanomami live, is a restricted area; you need special permits that are virtually impossible to get – some agents get around the ban by visiting Yanomami villages on the Río Siapa off Brazo Casiquiare.

Booking in advance is recommended. Puerto Ayacucho doesn't get a reliable stream of tourists, and most operators fashion individualized trips. Autana trips are more frequent, and one-day area tours can visit the pre-Columbian petroglyphs of Piedra Pintada, Piedra La Tortuga, an enormous boulder that looks like a giant turtle and the Parque Tobogan de la Selva, a natural waterslide.

Puerto Ayacucho

Sights
1 Mercado Indígena....C2
2 Museo Etnológico de Amazonas....C2

Sleeping
3 Hotel Cosmopolita....C3
4 Residencia Internacional....B2

Eating
5 Mercadito....D3
6 Panadería Las Tres Espigas....C1
7 Restaurant Cherazad....C2
8 Restaurant El Amir....C2

Entertainment
9 Sala Cinemateca Puerto Ayacucho....C1

Cooperativa Coyote Tour TOUR
(☎0414-486-2500, 521-3750; coyotexpedition@cantv.net; Av Aguerrevere) In business for almost 25 years, its main offerings are three-day Autana and Cuao tours, but also runs longer trips and can book flights.

Expediciones Selvadentro TOUR
(☎0414-487-3810, 414-7458; www.selvadentro.com; Vía Alto Carinagua) Long, adventurous trips to distant destinations aboard the *Iguana,* its 17m-long comfortable catamaran with toilet and kitchen.

Tadae TOUR
(☎521-4882, 0414-486-5923; www.tadaeaventura.wordpress.com) Apart from the staple Autana and Cuao tours, offers sport fishing plus rafting on Raudales Atures.

Sleeping

Residencia Internacional GUESTHOUSE $
(☎521-0242; Av Aguerrevere; r with fan/air-con BsF150/180; ❄) A long-time backpacker favorite, this friendly, family-operated place in a quiet residential area has a rooftop terrace and a rainbow palette of basic rooms with TVs set around a long patio. Kitchen use OK.

Hotel Apure HOTEL $
(☎521-4443; fax 521-0049; Av Orinoco 28; r BsF185-250, tr/q BsF290/380; ❄) Slightly sterile but spotlessly clean, the Apure has 17 good-sized rooms with air-con and cable TV. Comfy lounges and a dramatic wooden entryway add nice touches, and there's a convenient restaurant downstairs.

Hotel Cosmopolita HOTEL $$
(☎521-3037; Av Orinoco; r BsF250-290; ❄) A central if somewhat bland midrange option, it offers three floors of comfortable executive-style rooms with phones, TVs and fridges.

Eating

For cheap evening eats, try a *pepito cubano* (BsF32) from the street-food stands that set up outside the Hotel Cosmopolita from about 4pm until 6am. Big enough to satisfy two, these mega-sandwiches are crammed with eggs, ham, cheese, veggies and potato chips and drowned in sauce.

Panadería Las Tres Espigas BAKERY $
(Av Río Negro; pastries BsF5-10; ⏲6am-8pm Mon-Sat, to noon Sun; ❄) Four powerful air-conditioners will keep you cool while you recharge with strong coffee and morning pastries.

Restaurant El Amir MIDDLE EASTERN $
(Av Orinoco; sandwiches BsF40, mains BsF40-65; ⏲lunch & dinner Mon-Sat; 🖉) This family-run local favorite has decent falafels and tasty yogurt.

Restaurant Cherazad INTERNATIONAL $$
(cnr Avs Aguerrevere & Río Negro; mains BsF65-120; ⏲lunch & dinner Mon-Sat) One of the best restaurants in town, drape-shrouded Cherazad provides a sizable choice of pasta, steaks and fish, plus Middle Eastern dishes.

Mercadito MARKET $
(Av Orinoco) For an inexpensive meal or a quick empanada fix, duck into this maze of food stalls, or try one of the basic *criollo* eateries nearby on Av Amazonas.

Entertainment

Sala Cinemateca Puerto Ayacucho CINEMA
(www.cinemateca.gob.ve; Atabapo) Government-subsidized arthouse cinema. International films with Spanish subtitles.

Information

Banco de Venezuela (Av Orinoco)

Banesco (Av Orinoco)

CANTV Av Río Negro (⏲8am-noon & 2-6pm Mon-Fri) Av Orinoco (⏲8am-6pm Mon-Fri) Telephones and the best internet access (BsF6 per hour).

SAIME (Av Aguerrevere; ⏲8am-noon & 1-4pm Mon-Fri) Have your passport stamped here when leaving or entering Venezuela via Amazonas. No departure tax.

Getting There & Away

Air

At the airport, 6km southeast of town, Conviasa flies to Caracas (BsF530) three times per week. One small local carrier, **Wayumi** (☎521-0635; Evelio Roa), operates scheduled and charter flights within Amazonas to a few smaller destinations.

Boat

Transporte Fluvial La Roca (☎809-1595; Av Orinoco, Pasaje Orinoco, Centro Comercial Rapagna) has a daily service to San Fernando de Atabapo (BsF150, 2½ hours).

Bus

The small bus terminal is 6km east of the center, on the outskirts of town. City buses go there from Av 23 de Enero, but are so infrequent citywide that taxis (fixed at BsF10 to anywhere in town) are the standard form of transportation. *Busetas* to Ciudad Bolívar (BsF140, 10½ to 12 hours) depart regularly throughout the day. Until 3pm, eight buses depart daily to San Fernando de Apure (BsF110, seven hours), from where you can get buses to Caracas, Maracay, Valencia, Barinas and San Cristóbal. *Carritos* (BsF32, 1¼ hours) and minibuses (BsF20) to Samariapo depart from a corner *panadería* on Av Orinoco.

UNDERSTAND VENEZUELA

Venezuela Today

The death of President Hugo Chávez in March 2013 left his 'Bolivarian Revolution' in a state of uncertainty. A charismatic yet divisive leader for 14 years, Chávez was known for both his larger-than-life personality and his economic and social reforms. It's doubtful anyone can fill his beret. The lineup expected for the next election will pit Vice President and Chávez protégé Nicolás Maduro against Henrique Capriles Radonski, who captured the opposition's strongest showing (44% of the vote) against Chávez in 2012.

The 2012 election highlighted the intense political polarization of Venezuela. Opposition voters decried cronyism and a lack of progress by the president in dealing with issues of safety and inflation, while his supporters trumpeted the far-reaching social programs that provide subsidized food and free health care. Leading up to the election, Chávez revealed that he had been diagnosed with cancer, but never provided full details.

Following the 2012 reelection, Chávez spent two months in Cuba for an undisclosed surgical procedure. He missed his constitutionally mandated swearing-in and released no personal communications, feeding speculations that he was dying. Flown back to Venezuela in mid-February, he passed away on March 5, 2013. The country declared seven days of national mourning, and tens of thousands of grief-stricken Venezuelans flooded the streets to pay tribute.

Whoever becomes the next president will govern a divided nation with many problems. Decaying infrastructure and frequent power outages plague parts of the country, though the major issues on people's lips continue to be the high level of crime nationwide, referred to as *la inseguridad* (insecurity/safety), and a crippling inflation rate, which drives up the price of food.

History

Pre-Columbian Times

There is evidence of human habitation in northwest Venezuela going back more than 10,000 years. Steady agriculture was established around the first millennium, leading to the first year-round settlements. Formerly nomadic groups began to develop into larger cultures belonging to three main linguistic families: Carib, Arawak and Chibcha. By the time of the Spanish conquest at the end of the 15th century, some 300,000 to 400,000 indigenous people inhabited the region that is now Venezuela.

The Timote-Cuica tribes, of the Chibcha linguistic family, were the most technologically developed of Venezuela's pre-Hispanic societies. They lived in the Andes and developed complex agricultural techniques including irrigation and terracing. They were also skilled craftspeople, as we can judge by the artifacts they left behind – examples of their fine pottery are shown in museums across the country.

Spanish Conquest

Christopher Columbus was the first European to set foot on Venezuelan soil, which was also the only place where he landed on the South American mainland. On his third trip to the New World in 1498, he anchored at the eastern tip of the Península de Paria, just opposite Trinidad. He originally believed that he was on another island, but the voluminous mouth of the Río Orinoco hinted that he had stumbled into something slightly larger.

A year later Alonso de Ojeda, accompanied by the Italian Amerigo Vespucci, sailed up to the Península de la Guajira, on the western end of present-day Venezuela. On entering Lago de Maracaibo, the Spaniards saw indigenous people living in *palafitos* (thatched homes on stilts above the water). Perhaps as a bit of sarcasm, they called the waterside community 'Venezuela,' meaning 'Little Venice.' The first Spanish settlement on Venezuelan soil, Nueva Cádiz, was established around 1500 on the small island of Cubagua, just south of Isla de Margarita. The earliest Venezuelan town still in existence, Cumaná (on the mainland directly south of Isla Cubagua) dates from 1521.

Simón Bolívar & Independence

Venezuela lurked in the shadows of the Spanish empire through most of the colonial period. The country took a more primary role at the beginning of the 19th century, when Venezuela gave Latin America one of its greatest heroes, Simón Bolívar. A native of Caracas, Bolívar led the forces that put the nail in the coffin of Spanish rule over South America. He is viewed as being largely responsible for ending colonial rule all the way to the borders of Argentina.

Bolívar assumed leadership of the revolution, which had been kicked off in 1806. After unsuccessful initial attempts to defeat the Spaniards at home, he withdrew to Colombia and then to Jamaica to plot his final campaign. In 1817 Bolívar marched over the Andes with 5000 British mercenaries and an army of horsemen from Los Llanos, defeating the Spanish at the battle of Boyacá and bringing independence to Colombia. Four months later in Angostura (present-day Ciudad Bolívar), the Angostura Congress proclaimed Gran Colombia a new state, unifying Colombia (which included present-day Panama), Venezuela and Ecuador – though the last two were still under Spanish rule.

The liberation of Venezuela was completed with Bolívar's victory over Spanish forces at Carabobo in June 1821, though the royalists put up a rather pointless fight from Puerto Cabello for another two years. Gran Colombia existed for only a decade before splitting into three separate countries. Bolívar's dream of a unified republic fell apart before he died in 1830.

Caudillo Country

On his deathbed, Bolívar proclaimed: 'America is ungovernable. The man who serves a revolution plows the sea. This nation will fall inevitably into the hands of the unruly mob and then will pass into the hands of almost indistinguishable petty tyrants.' Unfortunately, he was not too far off the mark. Venezuela followed independence with nearly a century of rule by a series of strongmen known as *caudillos*. It wasn't until 1947 that the first democratic government was elected.

The first of the *caudillos*, General José Antonio Páez, controlled the country for 18 years (1830–48). Despite his tough rule, he established a certain political stability and strengthened the weak economy. The period that followed was an almost uninterrupted chain of civil wars that was only stopped by another long-lived dictator, General Antonio Guzmán Blanco (1870–88). He launched a broad program of reform, including a new constitution, and assured some temporary stability, yet his despotic rule triggered popular opposition, and when he stepped down the country fell back into civil war.

20th-Century Oil State

The first half of the 20th century was dominated by five successive military rulers from the Andean state of Táchira. The longest-lasting and most ruthless was General Juan Vicente Gómez, who seized power in 1908 and didn't relinquish it until his death in 1935. Gómez phased out the parliament and crushed the opposition on his path to monopolization of power.

The discovery of oil in the 1910s helped the Gómez regime to put the national economy on its feet. By the late 1920s, Venezuela was the world's largest exporter of oil, which not only contributed to economic recovery but also enabled the government to pay off the country's entire foreign debt.

As in most petrol states, almost none of the oil wealth made its way to the common citizen. The vast majority continued to live in poverty. Fast oil money also led to the neglect of agriculture and development of other types of production. It was easier to just import everything from abroad, which worked temporarily but proved unsustainable.

After a short flirtation with democracy and a new constitution in 1947, the inevitable coup took place and ushered in the era of Colonel Marcos Pérez Jiménez. Once in control, he smashed the opposition and plowed oil money into public works and modernizing Caracas – not making many friends in the process.

Coups & Corruption

Pérez Jiménez was overthrown in 1958 by a coalition of civilians and military officers. The country returned to democratic rule, and Rómulo Betancourt was elected president. He enjoyed popular support and was the first democratically elected president to complete his five-year term in office. There was a democratic transition of power though the country drifted to the right.

Oil money buoyed the following governments well into the 1970s. Not only did production of oil rise but, more importantly, the price quadrupled following the Arab–Israeli war in 1973. The nation went on a spending spree, building modern skyscrapers in Caracas and Maracaibo, and importing all sorts of luxury goods. But what goes up must come down and by the late 1970s the bust cycle was already in full swing, and the economy continued to fall apart throughout the 1980s.

In 1989 the government announced IMF-mandated austerity measures, and a subsequent protest over rising transportation costs sparked the *caracazo,* a series of nationwide riots put down by military force that killed hundreds – maybe thousands – of citizens. Lingering instability brought two attempted coups d'état in 1992. The first, in February, was led by a little-known paratrooper named Colonel Hugo Chávez Frías. The second attempt, in November, was led by junior air-force officers. The air battle over Caracas, with warplanes flying between skyscrapers, gave the coup a cinematic dimension. Both attempts resulted in many deaths.

Corruption, bank failures and loan defaults plagued the government in the mid 1990s. In 1995, Venezuela was forced to devalue the currency by more than 70%. By the end of 1998, two-thirds of Venezuela's 23 million inhabitants were living below the poverty line.

A Left Turn

Nothing is better in political theater than a dramatic comeback. The 1998 election put Hugo Chávez, the leader of the 1992 failed coup, into the presidency. After being pardoned in 1994, Chávez embarked on an aggressive populist campaign: comparing himself to Bolívar, promising help (and handouts) to the poorest masses and positioning himself in opposition to the US-influenced free-market economy. He vowed to produce a great, if vague, 'peaceful and democratic social revolution.'

Since then, however, Chávez's 'social revolution' has been anything but peaceful. Shortly after taking office, Chávez set about rewriting the constitution. The new document was approved in a referendum in December 1999, granting him new and sweeping powers. The introduction of a package of new decree laws in 2001 was met with angry protests and was followed by a massive and violent strike in April 2002. It culminated in a coup d'état run by military leaders sponsored by a business lobby, in which Chávez was forced to resign. He regained power two days later, but this only intensified the conflict.

While the popular tensions rose, in December 2002 the opposition called a general strike in an attempt to oust the president. The nationwide strike paralyzed the country, including its vital oil industry and a good part of the private sector. After 63 days, the opposition finally called off the strike, which had cost the country 7.6% of its GDP and further devastated the oil-based economy. Chávez again survived and claimed victory.

21st-Century Socialism

National politics continued to be shaky until Chávez survived a 2004 recall referendum and consolidated his power. He won reelection in 2006 by a comfortable margin. After an unsuccessful attempt in 2007 to eliminate presidential term limits, Chávez won a referendum to amend the constitution in 2009, positioning him to run for reelection indefinitely.

Chávez expanded his influence beyond the borders of Venezuela, reaching out to leftist leaders across the continent, oil-producing countries in the Middle East, and China, an increasingly important South American trade partner. He allied himself with Cuba's Fidel Castro and Bolivia's Evo Morales, and stoked a combustible relationship with the US. Bad blood exists between Venezuela and neighboring Colombia over accusations that Venezuela supports FARC guerillas (Colombia's main insurgent group, Fuerzas Armadas Revolucionarias de Colombia) and shelters them within its borders.

Supporters highlighted the country's programs for the poor. Chávez' government-sponsored projects called *misiones* (missions) provided adult literacy classes, free medical care and subsidized food. Large land holdings were broken up in land redistribution programs and given to subsistence farmers. Opponents criticized the centralization of power, intolerance of political dissent, a policy of nationalization that scares off international investment and the liberal use of government funds for partisan affairs.

His supporters hailed the 2009 referendum as a means for him to continue his social and economic programs to benefit ordinary Venezuelans and the poor, while his opponents viewed it as a power grab by an increasingly centralized and autocratic federal government.

Culture

Venezuela is an intensely patriotic nation that's proud of its national history. The War of Independence and the exploits of Simón Bolívar are still championed throughout the country. And it enjoys seeing itself on the world stage. Whether it's the crowning of its most recent Miss Universe or a major league baseball shutout, you can guarantee that the folks at home will be cheering.

However, unlike some neighboring South American nations, there are few defining factors of contemporary Venezuelan culture. Many attribute this to the fact that, as a petrol state, Venezuela has spent much of its existence consuming goods from abroad and not needing or bothering to produce much at home. But just like the oil pumped out of the country, Venezuela does produce raw materials and raw talent, including a prolific supply of beauty queens and baseball players.

Regardless of national ills and social tensions, Venezuelans are full of life and humor. People are open, willing to talk and not shy about striking up conversations with a stranger who becomes an instant *chamo* (pal or friend). Wherever you are, you're unlikely to be alone or feel isolated, especially if you can speak a little Spanish. There's always a rumba brewing somewhere.

Population

Venezuela has a young and mostly urban population, with half its population under 27 and 90% living in urban areas. Venezuela's population density is a low 32 people per sq km. However, the population is unevenly distributed: over one-fifth of the country's population lives in Caracas alone, while Los Llanos and Guayana are relatively empty.

About 70% of the population is a blend of European, indigenous and African ancestry, or any two of the three. The rest are full European (about 20%), African (8%) or indigenous (3%). Of that 3%, there are about 24 highly diverse indigenous groups comprising some 725,000 people, scattered throughout the country.

The literacy rate in Venezuela is 95%.

Lifestyle

The country's climate and the restricted space of Venezuelan homes create a more open, public life where many activities take place outside. Don't be surprised to see people getting together for a beer on the street, serenaded by a car stereo at full volume. That said, noise is a constant companion, and locals are undisturbed by blaring music, ear-splitting car horns and screeching street vendors. Cell phones are also ubiquitous, with full-throated conversations the norm.

Except when driving, Venezuelans seldom seem to be in a rush. People amble at a leisurely pace best suited for the tropics. This tempo also extends to business and consumer interactions, where you may need to wait while someone finishes gabbing with coworkers or watching TV before they acknowledge your presence.

DANCING WITH DEVILS

Drums pound while hundreds of dancers clad in red devil costumes and diabolical masks writhe through the streets. This is the festival of the **Diablos Danzantes** (Dancing Devils), a wild spectacle that takes place in Venezuela one day before Corpus Christi (the 60th day after Easter, a Thursday in May or June) and on the holy day itself.

Why devils on such a holy day in such a Catholic country? It is said that the festival demonstrates the struggle between good and evil. In the end, the costumed devils always submit to the church and demonstrate the eventual triumph of good.

The festival is a blend of Spanish and African traditions. The origins lie in Spain, where devils' images and masks were part of Corpus Christi feasts in medieval Andalusia. When the event was carried over to colonial Venezuela, it resonated with African slaves who had their own tradition of masked festivals. They also added African music and dance to the celebration. The celebrations in San Francisco de Yare and Chuao are best known throughout the country, as are their masks.

There is no direct transportation from Caracas to San Francisco de Yare. From the Nuevo Circo regional bus terminal (in central Caracas), take a frequent bus to either Ocumare del Tuy or Santa Teresa de Tuy and change for San Francisco de Yare.

There is a significant divide between rich and poor in Venezuela, with about 30% of the population living below the poverty line, though government programs have increased access to medical care and education for many people. Women make up about a third of Venezuela's workforce, and about half of the nation's workers earn their living within the untaxed informal economy.

Religion

Some 95% of Venezuelans are at least nominally Roman Catholic. Chávez has had words with the church in recent years and has been criticized by the Vatican. Many indigenous groups adopted Catholicism and only a few isolated tribes still practice their traditional beliefs. Evangelicals compete with Catholics for converts and are gaining ground across the country. There are small populations of Jews and Muslims, particularly in Caracas.

Arts

Literature

The classic work in Latin American colonial literature of the treatment of the indigenous populations by the Spanish – which happens to also document Venezuela's early years – is *Brevísima relación de la destrucción de las Indias Occidentales* (A Short Account of the Destruction of the West Indies), written by Fray Bartolomé de las Casas in 1542.

As for contemporary literature, a groundbreaking experimental novel from the middle of the century is *El falso cuaderno de Narciso Espejo* (The False Notebook of Narciso Espejo) by Guillermo Meneses (1911–78). Another influential work was Adriano González León's (1931–2008) powerful magical-realism novel *País portátil* (Portable Country), which contrasts rural Venezuela with the urban juggernaut of Caracas.

Ednodio Quintero is another contemporary writer to look for. His work *La danza del jaguar* (The Dance of the Jaguar; 1991) is one of several translated into other languages. Other writers worth tracking down include Teresa de la Parra, Antonia Palacios, Carlos Noguera and Orlando Chirinos.

Cinema

Venezuela's film industry is small, but has gained momentum in recent years.

The biggest smash in new Venezuelan cinema was 2005's *Secuestro Express* (Kidnap Express) by Jonathan Jakubowicz. The film, which was criticized by the government for its harsh portrayal of the city, takes a cold look at crime, poverty, violence, drugs and class relations in the capital. It broke all box-office records for a national production and was the first Venezuelan film to be distributed by a major Hollywood studio.

Those interested in learning more about Venezuelan film should track down a couple of films. *Oriana* (Fina Torres, 1985) recounts a pivotal childhood summer at a seaside family hacienda; *Huelepega* (Glue Sniffer; Elia Schneider, 1999) is a portrayal of Caracas street children using real street youth; *Amaneció de golpe* (A Coup at Daybreak; Carlos Azpúrua, 1999) is the story of how Chávez burst onto the political scene; and *Manuela Saenz* (Manuela Saenz; Diego Risquez, 2000) depicts the War of Independence through the eyes of Bolívar's mistress.

Also worth seeing is *The Revolution Will Not Be Televised,* a documentary shot by Irish filmmakers who were inside the presidential palace during the coup d'état of 2002.

NONVERBAL GESTURES

» A subtle and quick **nose wrinkling** (think rabbit) is the equivalent of 'huh?' or 'what?'

» When asking about price or indicating desired items to a salesperson, people will **pucker and point** their lips to what they're refering to.

Music

Music is omnipresent in Venezuela. Though the country hasn't traditionally produced a lot of its own music, by law at least 50% of radio programming must now be by Venezuelan artists, and, of that music, 50% must be 'traditional.' The result has been a boon for Venezuelan musicians. The most common types of popular music are salsa, merengue and reggaeton, *vallenato* from Colombia, and North American and European pop – everything from rock to hip-hop to house. The king of Venezuelan salsa is Oscar D'León (1943–).

The country's most popular folk rhythm is the *joropo,* also called *música llanera,* which developed in Los Llanos. The *joropo* is usually sung and accompanied by the harp, *cuatro* (a small, four-stringed guitar) and maracas.

Caracas is an exciting center of Latin pop and the *rock en español* movement, which harnesses the rhythm and energy of Latin beats and combines them with international rock and alternative-rock trends. The most famous product of this scene is the Grammy-winning Los Amigos Invisibles.

Begun in 1975, a nationwide orchestra program for low-income youth (nicknamed *El Sistema* – the System) has popularized classical music and trained thousands of new musicians. The top ensemble is the Simón Bolívar Youth Orchestra of Venezuela.

Visual Arts

Venezuela has a strong contemporary art movement. The streets and public buildings of Caracas are filled with modern art and the city houses some truly remarkable galleries.

Large-scale public art developed with the internal investment of the Guzmán Blanco regime in the late 19th century. The standout painter of that period – and one of the best in all of Venezuelan history – was Martín Tovar y Tovar (1827–1902). Some of his greatest works depicting historical events can be seen in Caracas' Asamblea Nacional.

There is a rich visual-arts scene among the current generation. Keep an eye out for the works of Carlos Zerpa (painting), the quirky ideas of José Antonio Hernández-Díez (photo, video, installations) and the emblematic paintings, collages and sculptures of Miguel von Dangel. And you'll see plenty more in the contemporary art museum of Caracas.

Jesús Soto (1923–2005) was Venezuela's number one internationally renowned contemporary artist. He was a leading representative of kinetic art (art, particularly sculpture, that contains moving parts). The largest collection of his work is in the museum dedicated to him in Ciudad Bolívar.

Cuisine

Food

On the whole, dining options in Venezuela are good and relatively inexpensive. Various local dishes, international cuisine and an array of snacks and fast foods are all available. Budget travelers should look for restaurants that offer a *menú del día* or *menú ejecutivo*, which is a set meal consisting of soup and a main course. It will cost roughly BsF35 to BsF60, which is cheaper than any à la carte dish. Another budget alternative can be roasted chicken, usually called *pollo en brasa*. Filling local choices also include *pabellón criollo, arepas, cachapas* and empanadas.

For breakfast, you can visit any of the ubiquitous *panaderías* (bakeries), which sell sandwiches, pastries and yogurt, plus delicious espresso.

Venezuela is very much a meat-eating country, though vegetarian restaurants now exist in most cities and even moderate-sized grocery stores sell dried *carne de soya* (textured vegetable protein) and other items for self-catering. However, good fresh vegetables can be hard to find. Meatless *arepas* are a reliable option, and Chinese, Middle Eastern and Italian eateries often have a veggie dish as well. For bus journeys with limited food stops, non-meat-eaters should pack sandwiches.

In almost every dining or drinking establishment, a 10% service charge will automatically be added to the bill. It's customary to leave a small tip at fancier places.

By law, all restaurants forbid smoking indoors.

The following are some typical Venezuelan dishes and a few international foods with different names in Spanish:

arepa – small, grilled corn pancake stuffed with a variety of fillings

cachapa – larger, flat corn pancake, served with cheese and/or ham

cachito – croissant filled with chopped ham and served hot

cambur – banana

caraota – black bean

casabe – huge, flat bread made from yucca; a staple in indigenous communities

empanada – deep-fried cornmeal turnover stuffed with various fillings

hallaca – maize dough with chopped meat and vegetables, wrapped in banana leaves and steamed; like a Mexican tamale

lechosa – papaya

pabellón criollo – shredded beef, rice, black beans, cheese and fried plantain; Venezuela's national dish

papelón – crude brown sugar; also drink flavoring

parchita – passion fruit

parrilla – mixed grill
patilla – watermelon
quesillo – caramel custard
teta – iced fruit juice in plastic wrap, consumed by sucking

Drinks

Venezuela has good, strong espresso coffee at every turn. Ask for *café negro* if you want it black; *café marrón* if you prefer half coffee, half milk; or *café con leche* if you like milkier coffee.

A staggering variety of fruit juices is available in restaurants, cafes and even in some fruit stores. Juices come as *batidos* (pure or cut with water) or as *merengadas* (made with milk).

The number-one alcoholic drink is *cerveza* (beer), particularly Polar and Solera (also owned by Polar). Beer is sold everywhere in cans or tiny bottles at close to freezing temperature. Among spirits, whiskey and then *ron* (rum) lead the pack in popularity.

Sports

Soccer? What soccer? In Venezuela, *béisbol* (baseball) rules supreme. The next most popular sports are *básquetbol* (basketball, also known as *básquet* or *balon-cesto*), followed by *fútbol* (soccer), which has a professional league that plays from August till May. That said, soccer is still the sport of choice among the country's indigenous population, and is increasing in popularity.

Environment

The Land

About twice the size of California, Venezuela claims a multiplicity of landscapes. The traveler can encounter all four primary South American landscapes – the Amazon, the Andes, savannas and beaches – all in a single country.

The country has two mountain ranges: the Cordillera de la Costa, which separates the valley of Caracas from the Caribbean Sea, and the northern extreme of the Andes range, with its highest peaks near Mérida.

The 2150km Río Orinoco is Venezuela's main river, its entire course lying within national boundaries. The land south of the Orinoco, known as Guayana, includes the Río Caura watershed, the largely impenetrable Amazon rainforest, vast areas of sun-baked savanna and hundreds of *tepuis*.

A 2813km-long stretch of coast features a 900,000 sq km Caribbean marine zone with numerous islands and cays. The largest and most popular of these is Isla de Margarita, followed by the less developed Archipiélago Los Roques.

Wildlife

Along with the variety of Venezuelan landscape, you will find an amazing diversity of wildlife. Visitors often seek out anacondas, capybaras, caimans and birds. There are 341 species of reptiles, 284 species of amphibians, 1791 species of fish, 351 species of mammals and many butterflies and other invertebrates. More than 1417 species of birds (approximately 20% of the world's known species) reside in the country, and 48 of these species are endemic. The country's geographical setting on a main migratory route makes it a bird-watcher's heaven.

National Parks

Venezuela's national parks offer a diverse landscape of evergreen mountains, beaches, tropical islands, coral reefs, high plateaus and rainforests. The national parks are the number-one destination for tourism within the country. Canaima, Los Roques, Mochima, Henri Pittier, El Ávila and Morrocoy are the most popular parks. Some parks, especially those in coastal and marine zones, are easily accessible and tend to be overcrowded by locals during holiday periods and weekends; others remain unvisited. A few of the parks offer tourism facilities, but these are generally not very extensive.

Some 50% of the country is protected under national law. Many of these areas are considered national parks and natural monuments, though some are designated as wildlife refuges, forests and biosphere reserves.

Environmental Issues

Far and away the most obvious environmental problem in Venezuela is waste management (or lack thereof). There is no recycling policy, and dumping of garbage in cities, along roads and natural areas is common practice. Untreated sewage is sometimes dumped in the sea and other water bodies. There's a general lack of clear environmental policy and little to no culture of environmental stewardship outside of the park areas.

Many of the waste and pollution issues are a direct result of overpopulation in urban areas and a lack of civil planning and funds to cope with the rampant development.

Other major environmental issues include the hunting and illegal trade of fauna and flora that takes place in many parts of the country – even in protected areas – and the inevitable pollution from oil refineries and mining. Food security is also a concern. Two-thirds of the country's food supply is imported, and it's rare to see agriculture land use besides cattle pasture.

SURVIVAL GUIDE

Directory A-Z

Accommodations

There are budget and midrange hotel options in most towns, though Caracas has few quality budget accommodations. Popular tourist areas are packed to the rafters in high season (July and August) and on major holidays (Christmas, Carnaval and Semana Santa), when beach towns will rarely have vacancies. Campgrounds are rare, though you can rough it in the countryside. Camping on the beach is popular, but be cautious and don't leave your tent unattended. Venezuela has almost no hostels. Be aware that during the day urban budget hotels often double as hourly-rates love motels, which are a common – though not necessarily sleazy – option in this privacy-starved country. However, even the cheapest places still provide towels and soap.

The most popular accommodations choice is the *posada,* a small, family-run guesthouse. They usually have more character than hotels and offer more personalized attention. Most are budget places but there are some midrange ones and a few top-end *posadas* as well.

> **SLEEPING PRICE RANGES**
>
> The following price ranges refer to a double room with bathroom in high season.
>
> **$** less than BsF250
>
> **$$** BsF251 to BsF450
>
> **$$$** more than BsF450

Another kind of countryside lodging is *campamentos* (literally 'camps'), which exist even in very remote areas. Not to be confused with campgrounds, this can be anything from a rustic shelter with a few hammocks to a posh country lodge with a swimming pool and its own airstrip. More commonly, it will be a collection of *cabañas* (cabins) plus a restaurant. *Campamentos* provide accommodation, food and usually tours, sometimes selling these services as all-inclusive packages.

As in most developing countries, prices are not set in stone and can change due to the day of the week or the mood of the person at the front desk. Never count on being able to use a credit card – even if they say that they accept plastic. Many *posadas,* especially those run by expatriates, will discreetly accept cash or online money transfers in dollars or euros.

While many accommodations list email addresses or websites, the reality is that management may not respond to queries or reservation requests in a timely manner (if at all). If possible, calling is always a better bet.

Books

Elizabeth Kline's bilingual and doorstopper-sized *Guide to Camps, Posadas and Cabins in Venezuela* details 1200 accommodations options and is updated yearly.

German geographer and botanist Alexander von Humboldt describes exploring various regions of Venezuela for Volume 2 of *Personal Narratives of Travels to the Equinoctial Regions of America During the Year 1799–1804* (also abridged into the slim *Jaguars and Electric Eels*). *The Search for El Dorado* by John Hemming offers a fascinating insight into the conquest of Venezuela. Sir Arthur Conan Doyle's *The Lost World* was inspired by the Roraima *tepui*. *Venezuela: A Century of Change* by Judith Ewell provides a comprehensive 20th-century history and H Micheal Tarver and Julia Frederick's *The History of Venezuela* skims the period from Columbus' first sighting up through the Chávez presidency.

There are dozens of books on Chávez and his 'Bolívarian Revolution,' though most sources take either a fervent pro- or anti-Chávez stance. Two more recent and even-handed explorations include *Dragon in the Tropics: Hugo Chavez and the Politi-*

cal Economy of Revolution in Venezuela by Javier Corrales and Michael Penfold, and *Venezuela Speaks!: Voices from the Grassroots* by Carlos Martinez, Michael Fox and JoJo Farrell.

Serious bird-watchers may want to get *A Guide to the Birds of Venezuela* by Rodolphe Meyer de Schauensee and William H Phelps, Steven Hilty's *Birds of Venezuela* or *Birding in Venezuela* by Mary Lou Goodwin.

For fun travel lit, check out Jamie Maslin's *Socialist Dreams and Beauty Queens: A Couchsurfer's Memoir of Venezuela*.

Business Hours

The working day is theoretically eight hours, from 8am to noon and 2pm to 6pm Monday to Friday, but in practice many businesses work shorter hours. Shops open Monday through Friday at 9am and close at 6pm or 7pm (though laundromats open at about 7am and internet cafes may stay open later); Saturdays are usually the same, but some shops close at 1pm. Banks are open 8:30am to 3:30pm Monday through Friday. Restaurants serve from noon to 9pm or 11pm Monday through Saturday. Almost everything is closed on Sundays (except *panaderías*).

The business hours are just a guideline – don't count on them too much.

Children

Venezuela's child protection law requires that children not traveling with two parents carry a copy of their birth certificate and a notarized permission letter from the non-traveling parent(s). Single, widowed and same-sex parents should check with their home country to ensure that they bring sufficient documentation.

Electricity

Venezuela operates on 110V at 60 Hz. The country uses US-type plugs.

Embassies & Consulates

The following embassies are in Caracas, unless otherwise noted. If you can't find your home embassy, check a Caracas phone directory, which will include a full list.

Brazilian Consulate (☎0212-261-5505; http://cgcaracas.itamaraty.gov.br; Av San Juan Bosco btwn 5a & 6a Transversal) Santa Elena de Uairén (☎995-1256; Edificio Galeno, Los Castanos, Urbanización Roraima del Casco Central; ⏲8am-2pm Mon-Fri); Puerto Ordaz (☎0286-961-2995; Carrera Tocoma, Edificio Eli-Alti, Alta Vista)

Canadian Embassy (Map p984; ☎0212-600-3000; www.canadainternational.gc.ca/venezuela; cnr Avs Francisco de Miranda & Sur Altamira, Altamira, Caracas; Ⓜ Altamira) Also has consular services for Israelis.

Colombian Consulate (☎0212-951-3631; www.consuladoencaracas-ve.gov.co; Guaicaipuro, El Rosal, Caracas; Ⓜ Chacaíto) Maracaibo (☎0261-751-1750; www.consuladoenmaracaibo-ve.gov.co; Av 17 Baralt at Calle 69A , Sector Paraíso); Puerto Ayacucho (☎521-0789; Calle Yacapana, Quinta Beatriz 5; ⏲8am-1pm Mon-Fri); Mérida (☎0274-245-9724; www.consuladoenmerida-ve.gov.co; Av de las Américas)

Dutch Embassy (Map p984; ☎0212-276-9300; http://venezuela.nlembajada.org; cnr 2a Transversal & Av San Juan Bosco, Edif San Juan, 9th fl, Altamira, Caracas; Ⓜ Altamira)

French Embassy (Map p984; ☎0212-909-6500; www.ambafrance-ve.org; cnr Madrid & Av La Trinidad, Edif Embajada de Francia, Las Mercedes, Caracas)

German Embassy (Map p984; ☎0212-219-2500; www.caracas.diplo.de; Av Principal de la Castellana, Torre La Castellana, La Castellana, Caracas; Ⓜ Altamira)

Guyanese Embassy (☎0212-267-7095; www.guyana.org/spanish/consular_venezuela.html; 2a Av btwn 9a y 10a Transversal, Quinta Los Tutis, Altamira, Caracas)

Irish Consulate (Map p984; ☎0212- 951-3645; irlconven@cantv.net; Av Venezuela, Torre Clement, 2nd fl, El Rosal, Caracas)

Italian Embassy (Map p984; ☎0212-952-7311; www.ambcaracas.esteri.it; Calle Sorocaima, Edificio Atrium, El Rosal, Caracas)

Japanese Embassy (Map p984; ☎0212-261-8333; www.ve.emb-japan.go.jp; Edif Bancaracas, 11th fl, Plaza La Castellana, La Castellana, Caracas; Ⓜ Altamira)

Spanish Embassy (☎0212-263-2855; www.maec.es/embajadas/caracas; Av Mohedano, Quinta Marmolejo, La Castellana, Caracas; Ⓜ Altamira)

Swiss Embassy (Map p984; ☎0212-267-9585; www.eda.admin.ch/caracas; Av Eugenio Mendoza near San Felipe, Centro Letonia, Torre Ing-Bank, La Castellana, Caracas; Ⓜ Altamira)

Trinidad & Tobago Embassy (☎0212-261-3748; embassytt@cantv.net; 3a Av btwn 6a & 7a Transversal, Quinta Poshika, Altamira, Caracas; Ⓜ Altamira)

FOOD PRICE RANGES

The following price ranges refer to a standard main course.

$ less than BsF50

$$ BsF51 to BsF100

$$$ more than BsF100

UK Embassy (Map p984; ☎0212-263-8411; www.ukinvenezuela.fco.gov.uk; Av Principal de la Castellana, Torre La Castellana, La Castellana, Caracas; Ⓜ Altamira)

USA Embassy (☎0212-975-6411; http://caracas.usembassy.gov; cnr Calles F & Suapure, Urbanización Colinas del Valle Arriba, Caracas) Maracaibo (☎0261-200-0600; Calle 77 (5 de Julio) at Av 3F, Sector Valle Frio)

Gay & Lesbian Travelers

Homosexuality isn't illegal in Venezuela, but it is suppressed and frowned upon by the overwhelmingly Catholic society. Homosexual men, in particular, should be very discreet in smaller towns and rural areas. At the same time, pockets of tolerance do exist. Caracas has the largest gay and lesbian community and the most open gay life, including an annual gay pride festival in June that draws tens of thousands.

When looking for gay-oriented venues, the phrase to watch out for is *en* (or *de*) *ambiente*. Some club listings can be found at www.rumbacaracas.com.

Health

Venezuela has a wide array of pharmacies, clinics and hospitals. Good medical care is available in Caracas, but may be difficult to find in rural areas. Public hospitals and clinics are free, but the quality of medical care is better in private facilities. If you need hospital treatment in Venezuela, by far the best facilities are in Caracas. Smaller issues can be dealt with directly in pharmacies, as they are allowed to give injections and administer a wide range of medicines.

Malaria and dengue fever are present in some tropical areas, and while other insect bites don't necessarily cause illness they can cause major discomfort. Overall, your biggest dangers are the standard risks of travel: sunburn, food-borne illness and traffic-related concerns.

Tap water is generally fine for brushing your teeth, but is not recommended for consumption.

Internet Access

All cities and most towns have cybercafes, and wi-fi has become common in *posadas* and larger hotels. An hour of internet access costs between BsF5 and BsF9. Some CANTV and Movistar outlets have fast, inexpensive computers. The government **Infocentro** (www.infocentro.gob.ve; ⏱variable Mon-Sat) program offers free 30-minute blocks at locations nationwide.

Most websites listed are in Spanish only; they are included for the benefit of Spanish speakers.

Language

Venezuela has language schools in most big cities. You can also find an independent teacher and arrange individual classes. Mérida is a popular place to study Spanish as it is an attractive, affordable city with a major university population.

Legal Matters

Venezuela police are to be treated with respect, but with a healthy dose of caution. Cases of police corruption, abuse of power and use of undue force are unfortunately common.

Penalties for trafficking, possessing and using illegal drugs are some of the heaviest in all of Latin America. Venezuelan jails are dangerous free-for-alls, and consular officials can do little besides visit you.

Maps

The best general map of Venezuela is published by **International Travel Maps** (www.itmb.com), but it's not generally available in the country. Within Venezuela, folded road maps of the country are produced by several local publishers and are available in bookstores, limited tourism offices and some hotels and tour agencies that cater to foreign visitors. You can usually score detailed city maps in the front of phone books.

Money

ATMS

Cajeros automáticos (ATMs) are the easiest way of getting cash. ATMs can be found at most major banks, including Banco de Venezuela, Banco Mercantil and Banesco. ATMs are normally open 24 hours. You should always have a backup though, as some machines will eat cards.

Many ATMs require a two-digit identification number in order to make a withdrawal. You can use any two numbers, but be consistent with them or your card may be flagged and subsequently denied at all ATMs throughout the country.

BLACK MARKET

An active black market (*mercado negro* or *dólar paralelo*) buys and sells the more stable dollars and euros, with rates boomeranging between BsF8 to BsF22 per dollar. Many Venezuelans will ask you to change currency in airports, bus stations or the center of towns. Websites such as www.dollar.nu list the current exchange rates. Though black-market exchange is illegal and has penalties of up to 10 years in jail, it is commonplace; the government mostly turns a blind eye except in the case of career currency traders. Beware of counterfeit bills, especially at Maiquetía airport.

Though they don't advertise it, most established *posadas* and tour operators will accept payment (or sometimes give you cash at the black-market rate) through online money transfers to international bank accounts.

CASH

In 2008 Venezuela lopped three zeros off its currency and issued new money called '*bolívares fuertes*,' abbreviated to BsF. There are coins of 1, 5, 10, 12½ and 50 *céntimos* and BsF1, and paper notes of 2, 5, 10, 20, 50 and 100. Be aware that some people cling to the old ways and will still quote prices in *miles* (thousands).

Unless you're near the border, it's impossible to get Venezuelan currency before you enter the country.

CREDIT CARDS

Visa and MasterCard are the most useful credit cards in Venezuela, though it's important to note that credit card transactions will always be more costly because they are calculated using the official exchange rate. Many lodgings and restaurants accept cards (though tour operators may charge 10% more for the service), but not across the board. They are also useful for taking cash advances from banks or ATMs. Make sure you know the number to call if you lose your credit card, and be quick to cancel it if it's lost or stolen, as credit card fraud is not uncommon.

MONEY CHANGERS

US dollars (especially) and euros are the most popular and accepted currencies in Venezuela. They can be exchanged in some banks, but very few banks handle foreign-exchange transactions.

The *casas de cambio* (authorized money-exchange offices) are more likely to exchange your money, but may pay less and charge higher commission. The best-known *casa de cambio* is Italcambio, which has offices in most major cities and exchanges both cash and traveler's checks. Note that *casas de cambio* don't buy back Venezuelan money. The ubiquitous black market has the best rates for exchanging currencies, but is still illegal.

TIPPING

Most restaurants include a 10% service charge and list it clearly on the bill. A small tip of 5% to 10% beyond the service charge is standard in a nicer restaurant, but not required. Taxi drivers are not usually tipped unless they help carry bags. Tipping of hotel employees, dive masters, guides and so on is left to your discretion; it is rarely required but always appreciated. Keep in mind that porters and other support workers on

PRICE WARNING!

Currency controls peg the bolívar fuerte to the US dollar at an artificially high rate, resulting in a two-tier market for changing money within Venezuela. As of 2013, the official exchange rate is fixed at BsF6.3 per dollar. When using credit cards or exchanging money at a bank or *casa de cambio*, you will always receive this rate.

Brazilian and Colombian currencies are not subject to controls; it's a good strategy to withdraw money from ATMs in those countries and change it at the border.

Venezuela has one of the highest rates of inflation in South America (averaging 20% to 30% per year) and prices are especially vulnerable to change. Prices quoted should be used as rough guidelines only.

guided tours get paid very little for what is often back-breaking work. The simple act of buying a drink for a boat driver or cook can go a long way.

Post

Ipostel (www.ipostel.gov.ve), the national postal service, has post offices throughout the country. Some are in combined government services offices called Puntos de Gestión Centralizada (Central Administration Offices). The usual opening hours are 8:30am to 11:30am and 1:30pm to 5pm Monday to Friday, with regional variations. Offices in the main cities may open longer hours and on Saturday.

Service is extremely unreliable and slow. Mail can take up to a month to arrive, if it arrives at all. If you are mailing something important or time-sensitive, use a reliable international express mail carrier.

Public Holidays

Given the strong Catholic character of Venezuela, many holidays follow the church calendar – Christmas, Carnaval, Easter and Corpus Christi are celebrated all over the country. Carnaval is particularly big in El Callao. The religious calendar is dotted with saints' days, and every village and town has its own patron saint and will hold a celebration on that day.

Most Venezuelans take vacations over Christmas, Carnaval (several days prior to Ash Wednesday), Semana Santa (the week before Easter Sunday) and during July and August. In these periods, it can be tricky to find a place to stay in more popular destinations, and prices shoot up. The upside is that they really come alive with holiday merrymakers.

Some official public holidays:

New Year's Day January 1

Carnaval Monday and Tuesday prior to Ash Wednesday, February/March

Easter Maundy Thursday and Good Friday, March/April

Declaration of Independence April 19

Labor Day May 1

Battle of Carabobo June 24

Independence Day July 5

Bolívar's Birthday July 24

Discovery of America October 12

Christmas Day December 25

Safe Travel

Contrary to popular belief, Venezuela is a reasonably safe place to travel. Still, theft, robbery and common crime have increased over the last decade. Theft is more serious in the larger cities and urban centers than in the countryside. Caracas is, far and away, the most dangerous place in the country, and you should take care while strolling around the streets, particularly at night.

Be aware of your surroundings when withdrawing cash from an ATM at any time of the day. In our experience, police are not necessarily trustworthy (though many are), so do not blindly accept the demands of these authority figures. Travelers have also reported theft by security personnel during airport sceenings and border crossings.

Venezuela is somewhat obsessed with identification, and *cédulas* (Venezuelan ID cards) or passport numbers are often required for the most banal transactions. Always carry your passport (or a copy with the entrance stamp), or you may end up explaining yourself in a police station.

The border with Colombia is considered generally risky because of cross-border drug-trafficking and the presence of FARC guerillas.

Telephone

Cell-phone saturation has edged out demand for the once-ubiquitous call centers *(centros de comunicaciones)* – the best option for international calls when you can find them – though Movistar and CANTV still run a few in larger cities. Some internet cafes also have phones.

During the day entrepreneurs set up small tables at street corners and bus terminals with a few cell phones, and they charge by the minute for calls. For domestic calls, this can be more convenient (but usually noisier), and you can also send text messages.

CANTV public phones are everywhere, though most don't work. Phone cards for these phones come in a few different values and can be purchased at many stores and kiosks.

Those who plan to stay longer in Venezuela may opt to purchase a cell phone or buy a local SIM card for their own handset. The malls all have numerous competing cellphone offices. Movilnet has the best coverage countrywide, followed by Movistar and Digitel. As with most transactions in the country, you'll need to show your passport to buy a SIM card. Venezuela has one of the highest cell-phone-per-capita ratios in Latin America, and phone time is inexpensive.

All phone numbers in the country are seven digits and area codes are 0 plus three digits. Area codes are listed under the destination headings throughout this guide. Note that all cell phones have an area code that begins with 04. The country code for Venezuela is 58. To call Venezuela from abroad, dial the international access code of the country you're calling from, Venezuela's code (58), the area code (drop the initial 0) and the local phone number. To call internationally from Venezuela, dial the international access code (00), then the country code, area code and local number.

Time

Venezuela has a unique time zone that's 4½ hours behind Greenwich Mean Time. There's no daylight saving time.

Toilets

Since there are no self-contained public toilets in Venezuela, use the toilets of establishments such as restaurants, hotels, museums, shopping malls and bus terminals. Don't rely on a public bathroom to have toilet paper or soap and remember to always throw the used paper into the wastebasket provided. Many public restrooms charge a small fee, which includes an allotment of paper.

Tourist Information

Inatur (Instituto Autónomo de Turismo de Aragua; www.inatur.gov.ve) is the Caracas-based government agency that promotes tourism and provides tourist information; it has offices at Maiquetía airport. Outside the capital, tourist information is handled by regional tourist bodies. Some are better than others, but on the whole they lack city maps and brochures, and the staff members rarely speak English. Tour and travel agencies are the best source of current information.

Visas

Nationals of the US, Canada, Australia, New Zealand, Japan, the UK and most of Western and Scandinavian Europe do not need a visa to enter Venezuela; a free tourist card *(tarjeta de ingreso)* is all that is required. The card is normally valid for 90 days and can be extended. Airlines flying into Venezuela provide these cards to passengers while on the plane. Overland visitors bearing passports of the countries listed above can obtain the card from the immigration official at the border crossing.

On entering Venezuela, your passport will be stamped (make sure this happens) by SAIME border officials. Keep the copy of the tourist card while traveling in Venezuela (you may be asked for it during passport controls) and return it to immigration officials when leaving the country – although not all are interested in collecting the cards. Immigration officials may not permit entry if a passport expires within six months.

Visa and tourist-card extensions are handled by the office of SAIME in Caracas.

Women Travelers

Like most of Latin America, Venezuela is very much a man's country. Women travelers will attract more curiosity, attention and advances from local men, who will quickly pick you out in a crowd and are not shy to show their admiration through whistles, endearments and flirtatious comments. The best way to deal with unwanted attention is simply to ignore it. Dressing modestly will make you less conspicuous. Although Venezuelan women wear revealing clothes, they're a lot more aware of the culture and the safety of their surroundings.

Women will constantly be asked about their marital status and whether they have children.

Getting There & Away

Air

Most international visitors arrive at Caracas' **Aeropuerto Internacional Simón Bolívar** (www.aeropuerto-maiquetia.com.ve) in Maiquetía, 26km from Caracas. Venezuela has several other airports servicing international flights, but these change frequently and unexpectedly.

Set at the northern edge of South America, Venezuela has one of the fastest journeys from North America, making it a convenient northern gateway to the continent. However, air traffic disputes between the US and the government have trimmed the number of flights to and from the US. Venezuela is also served by flights to Europe, the Caribbean and the major cities of South America.

The national carrier is Conviasa; it was banned from European Union airspace in 2012 because of safety concerns.

DEPARTURE TAX

Departure taxes are now included in all airfares to/from Aeropuerto Internacional Simón Bolívar (but only here), so you no longer need to pay at the airport. Other airports charge BsF54 for domestic flights.

Boat

Acosta Asociados (☎0294-982-1556; Calle Bolívar 31, Güiria; ⏰8am-noon & 2-5pm) operates the *Sea Prowler,* a comfortable and air-conditioned passenger boat that runs between Güiria (on the Península de Paria) and Chaguaramas, near Port of Spain, Trinidad. It arrives every Wednesday at around 2pm and departs back to Chaguaramas between 2:30pm and 3pm (taking 3½ hours). You should be there by 1:30pm. Fares are BsF1020/1950 one-way/round trip.

There are no longer ferries between Venezuela and the Netherlands Antilles.

Bus, Car & Motorcycle

Passengers must disembark for passport control along the borders. There's a BsF90 land departure tax, though it's not collected at the Brazilian border crossing at Santa Elena de Uairén (see boxed text, p1028).

Drivers in Venezuela will find some of the cheapest gasoline on the planet (BsF10 per liter), but huge lines to buy it near the border, where smugglers mark it up for sale in Colombia and Brazil. For more information on driving, see opposite.

For border crossings, see p999 and p1007.

Getting Around

Air

Venezuela has a number of airlines and a reasonable network of air routes. Maiquetía, where Caracas' airport is located, is the country's major aviation hub and handles flights to most airports around the country. Cities most frequently serviced from Caracas include Porlamar, Maracaibo and Puerto Ordaz (officially known as Ciudad Guayana). The most popular destinations with travelers are El Vigía, Ciudad Bolívar, Canaima, Porlamar and Los Roques. Except for Maiquetía, all airports have a separate departure tax.

A number of provincial carriers cover regional and remote routes on a regular or charter basis. Canaima and Los Roques have their own fleets of Cessnas and other smaller planes that fly for a number of smaller airlines. It is best to book these flights through an agent.

Though flights aren't very expensive, they can be unreliable, and delayed flights are unfortunately common. It's risky to to schedule a domestic flight to connect with a same-day international flight.

Some domestic airlines servicing Caracas:

Aeropostal (☎0212-708-6220, 0800-284-6637; www.aeropostal.com; Av Paseo Colón, Torre Polar Oeste, ground fl, Plaza Venezuela, Caracas; Ⓜ Plaza Venezuela) Services Maracaibo, Porlamar, Puerto Ordaz and Valencia.

Aereotuy (LTA; ☎0295-415-5778, 0212-212-3110; www.tuy.com; Blvd de Sabana Grande, Edif Sabana Grande, 5th fl, Caracas; Ⓜ Sabana Grande) Serves the tourism hot spots of Canaima, Los Roques and Porlamar.

Aserca (☎0212-905-5333; www.asercaairlines.com; Calle Guaicaipuro, Edif Taeca, ground fl, Caracas; Ⓜ Chacaíto) Flies to domestic airports including Barcelona, Maracaibo, Santo Domingo and Porlamar.

Avior (☎213-0600; www.avior.com.ve; Av Venezuela, Torre Clement, ground fl, El Rosal, Caracas; Ⓜ Chacaíto) Destinations include Aruba, Barcelona, Barinas, Curaçao, Maturín, Porlamar and Puerto Ordaz.

Conviasa (☎578-4767, 0500-266-8427; www.conviasa.aero; cnr Av Sur 25 & Av México, Hotel Alba Caracas, Caracas; Ⓜ Parque Central) State-owned airline with destinations including Barinas, El Vigía, Maracaibo, Maturín and Puerto Ayacucho, Puerto Ordaz and the Caribbean.

Laser (☎0212-202-0106; www.laser.com.ve; Av Francisco de Miranda, Torre Bazar Bolivar, Piso 8, Caracas; Ⓜ La California) Carrier with service between Caracas and Porlamar, El Vigía and Aruba.

Rutaca (☎0800-788-2221, 0212-237-9317; www.rutaca.com.ve; Av Francisco de Miranda, Centro Seguros La Paz, Caracas; Ⓜ Los Cortijos) Serves Canaima, Ciudad Bolívar, Porlamar, Puerto Ordaz, Santo Domingo, San Antonio del Táchira and Santa Elena de Uairén.

Venezolana (☎0212-208-8400; www.ravsa.com.ve; Centro Comercial Centro Plaza, Mezzanina, Los Palos Grandes, Caracas; Ⓜ Altamira) Flights to Cumaná, Santo Domingo, Porlamar, Maracaibo, Maturín and Caribbean destinations.

Boat

Venezuela has a number of islands, but only Isla de Margarita is serviced by regular scheduled boats and ferries; see Puerto La Cruz (p1008), Cumaná (p1011) and Isla de Margarita (p1013).

The Río Orinoco is the country's major inland waterway. The river is navigable from its mouth up to Puerto Ayacucho, with limited scheduled passenger service.

Bus

As there is no passenger-train service in Venezuela, almost all traveling is done by bus. Buses are generally fast and run regularly day and night between major population centers. Bus transportation is affordable and usually efficient.

Buses range from sputtering pieces of junk to the most recent models. All major companies offer *servicio ejecutivo* (executive class) in comfortable (but seriously icy) air-conditioned buses, which cover all of the major long-distance routes and are the dominant means of intercity transportation. A step up, *buscama* coaches have seats with a steeper recline.

Caracas is the most important transport hub, handling buses to just about every corner of the country. Except for the almost-free SITSSA buses, which sell out right after the ticket windows open, there's no need to buy tickets more than a couple of hours in advance for major routes, except around holidays.

Many short-distance regional routes are served by *por puestos* (literally 'by the seat'), which is a cross between a bus and a taxi. *Por puestos* are usually large old US-made cars (less frequently minibuses) that ply fixed routes and depart when all seats are filled. They cost about 40% to 80% more than buses, but they're faster and often leave more frequently.

Always travel with your passport handy, warm clothes for any bus with air-con and ear plugs for amped-up radio volume on smaller buses; as a security measure, some long-distance bus companies videotape passengers before departing. Most bus terminals require payment of a small departure tax (about BsF1). Get a receipt at the kiosk; the bus or *por puesto* driver will collect them.

Car & Motorcycle

You can use any type of driver's license to operate a car in Venezuela. However, you need a superhuman level of patience and Formula 1 driving skills to make your way around Caracas in a car. Outside of Caracas, traveling by car can be a comfortable way of getting around (especially on the highway to Santa Elena). The road network is extensive and mostly in acceptable shape. Gas stations are numerous and fuel is just about the cheapest in the world – you can fill up your tank for a dollar. This rosy picture is slightly obscured by Venezuelan traffic and local driving manners. Traffic lights are routinely ignored throughout the country, speed limits are a pipe dream and police are known to pull over motorists for nonexistent infractions in an attempt to collect bribes.

Bringing a car to Venezuela (or to South America in general) is time-consuming, expensive and involves plenty of paperwork, and few people do it. It's much more convenient and cheaper to rent a car locally, and major international rental companies are in all the large cities. Rental rates aren't necessarily budget-oriented, but gasoline isn't a major expense. If your lodging doesn't have parking, monitored lots are recommended.

Local Transport

BUS & METRO

All cities and many major towns have their own urban transportation systems, which in most places are small buses or minibuses. Depending on the region, these are called *busetas, carros, carritos, micros* or *camionetas,* and fares are usually no more than BsF4. In many larger cities you can also find urban *por puestos,* swinging faster than buses through the chaotic traffic. Caracas has a comprehensive subway system, and Valencia and Maracaibo have smaller offerings.

TAXI

Taxis are fairly inexpensive and worth considering, particularly for transportation between the bus terminal and city center when you are carrying all your bags. Taxis don't have meters, so always fix the fare with the driver before boarding the cab. It's a good idea to find out the correct fare beforehand from an independent source, such as someone who works in the bus station or a hotel reception desk.

Anyone can slap a neon sticker on their car windshield and declare it a taxi. Unlicensed taxis are known as *piratas*, and they're fine to take in most situations. But at night, it's best to have a hotel or restaurant call a trusted driver or to seek out a *línea* (officially licensed) taxi. These generally are newer vehicles, professionally painted with the company name, and you can find stands at bus terminals and shopping centers.

Tours

Independent travelers who have never taken an organized tour in their lives will find themselves signing up with a group in Venezuela. As vast areas of the country are virtually inaccessible by public transportation (eg the Orinoco Delta or Amazon Basin) or because a solitary visit to scattered sights in a large territory (eg the Gran Sabana) may be inconvenient, time-consuming and expensive, tours are a standard option in Venezuelan travel.

Although under some circumstances it makes sense to prebook tours (eg when stringing together various tours in a short period of time), it is most cost-effective to arrange a tour from the regional center closest to the area you are going to visit.

Companies can also help by coordinating various excursions or domestic flights for you and making reservations during busy tourism seasons.

Akanan Travel & Adventure (Map p984; ☎0212-264-2769; www.akanan.com; Calle Bolívar, Edif Grano de Oro, grnd fl; ⓂChacao) This major operator in Caracas doesn't have the most budget prices, but has reliable quality trips, including treks to Auyantepui and Roraima, and bicycle trips from La Paragua to Canaima.

Araguato Expeditions (☎0426-560-0924; www.araguato.org) Coro-based Araguato offers tours countrywide, including Los Llanos; excellent service.

Gekko Tours (☎0414-854-5146, 632-3223; www.gekkotours-venezuela.de; airport terminal, Ciudad Bolívar) In Ciudad Bolívar, with a wide range of good-quality tours, especially Salto Ángel. It also has its own planes.

Global Exchange (www.globalexchange.org/tours) A US-based social-justice organization, its 'reality tours' meet with community activists and cultural workers.

Osprey Expeditions (Map p980; ☎0212-762-5975, 0414-310-4491; www.ospreyexpeditions.com; Av Casanova at 2a Av de Bello Monte, Edificio La Paz, office 51, Sabana Grande, Caracas; ⓂSabana Grande) Small, personable, Venezuelan-owned Caracas agency attuned to a budget traveler's perspective (but with offerings ranging the gamut). It can organize tours throughout Venezuela but it's particularly strong on Los Roques, Canaima and the Orinoco Delta.

Survival Guide

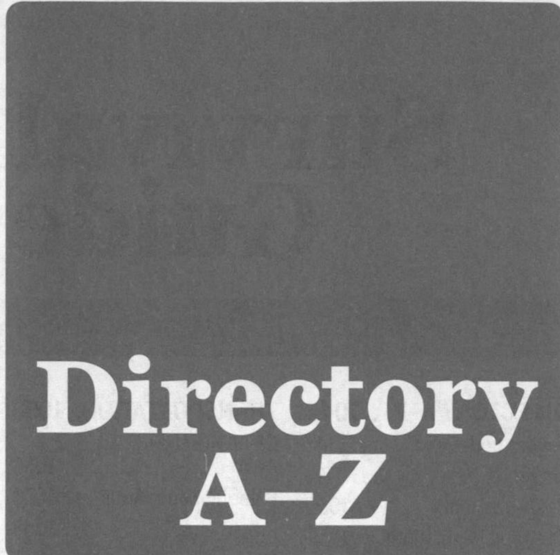

Accommodations

We list accommodations in order of preference. For those nights when you need a break from shared showers and thin mattresses, we've also included a few midrange options as well as a few splurges for a real break from the long-haul grind.

Accommodations costs vary from country to country, with Andean countries (especially Bolivia) being the cheapest (from around US$5 per night) and Brazil, Chile, Argentina and the Guianas the costliest (upwards of US$30).

Camping

Camping is an obvious choice in parks and reserves and a useful budget option in pricier countries such as Chile. In the Andean countries (Bolivia, Ecuador and Peru), there are few organized campgrounds. In Argentina, Chile, Uruguay and parts of Brazil, however, camping holidays have long been popular.

Bring all your own gear. While camping gear is available in large cities and in trekking and activities hubs, it's expensive and choices are usually minimal. Camping gear can be rented in areas with substantial camping and trekking action (eg the Lake District, Mendoza and Huaraz), but quality is sometimes dubious.

An alternative to tent camping is staying in *refugios* (simple structures within parks and reserves), where a basic bunk and kitchen access are usually provided. For climbers, most summit attempts involve staying in a *refugio*.

Hostels

Albergues (hostels) have become increasingly popular throughout South America and, as throughout the world, are great places to socialize with other travelers. You'll rarely find an official *albergue juvenil* (youth hostel); most hostels accept all ages and are not affiliated with Hostelling International (HI).

Hotels

When it comes to hotels, both terminology and criteria vary. The costliest in the genre are *hoteles* (hotels) proper. A step down in price are *hostales* (small hotels or guesthouses). The cheapest places are *hospedajes, casas de huéspedes, residenciales, alojamientos* and *pensiones*. A room in these places includes a bed with (hopefully) clean sheets and a blanket, maybe a table and chair and sometimes a fan. Showers and toilets are generally shared, and there may not be hot water. Cleanliness varies widely, but many places are remarkably tidy. In some areas, especially southern Chile, the cheapest places may be *casas familiares*, family houses whose hospitality makes them excellent value.

In Brazil, Argentina and some other places, prices often include breakfast, the quality of which is usually directly related to the room price.

Hot-water supplies are often erratic, or may be available only at certain hours of the day. It's something to ask about (and consider paying extra for), especially in the highlands and far south, where it gets cold.

When showering, beware the electric shower head, an innocent looking unit that heats cold water with an electric element. Don't touch the shower head or anything metal when the water is on, or you may get shocked – never strong enough to throw you across the room, but hardly pleasant.

Dormitory prices are for rooms with shared bathrooms, while room prices include private bathrooms, unless otherwise noted.

Activities

Whether you take to the jungle, the mountain or the ocean blue, opportunities for serious adventure are virtually boundless in South America.

Cycling

Pedaling in South America can prove an arduous undertaking, but the rewards are beyond anything the bus-bound can imagine. You can cycle the 'World's Most Dangerous Road,' scream down the flanks of an Ecuadorian volcano and battle the roaring winds of Patagonia. No matter where you end up riding, bring everything from home as equipment is hard to find outside major cities, and even then it can be painfully expensive.

If you're not bringing your bike, you'll find opportunities to rent for a day or join a mountain-biking tour. Online, check out **South American Bicycle Touring Links** (www.transamazon.de/links) for a long list of touring links. The **Warm Showers List** (www.warmshowers.org) is a list of cyclists around the world who offer long-haulers a free place to crash.

Diving

Major destinations for divers are the Caribbean coast of Colombia (particularly Taganga) and Venezuela, islands such as Providencia (a Colombian island that is actually nearer to Nicaragua), the Galápagos and Brazil's Fernando de Noronha.

Hiking & Trekking

South America is a brilliant hiking and trekking destination. Walking in the Andean countries is not limited to the national parks: because the network of dirt roads is so extensive, you can pretty much walk anywhere and, with the region's indigenous population often doing the same, you won't be alone.

The Andean countries are famous for their old Inca roads, which are ready-made for scenic excursions. The overtrodden, four-day tramp along the Inca Trail to Machu Picchu is, of course, the classic, but alternative routes are more highly recommended because they are cheaper, less touristed, more scenic and less destructive. There are other treks along Inca trails as well, including Ecuador's lesser-known Inca trail to Ingapirca, and numerous trails along ancient Inca routes through Bolivia's Cordilleras to the Yungas.

The national parks of southern South America, including Chile's Torres del Paine, those within the Argentine Lake District, and even Argentina's storm-pounded but spectacular Fitz Roy range, are superb and blessed with excellent trail infrastructure and accessibility. And for getting well off the beaten path, northern Patagonia in Chile has some excellent treks.

Lesser-known mountain ranges, such as Colombia's Sierra Nevada de Santa Marta (for the Ciudad Perdida) and Venezuela's Sierra Nevada de Mérida, also have great potential. The two- to three-day hike to the top of Venezuela's Roraima is one of the continent's most unforgettable experiences. Colombia's Parque Nacional El Cocuy is also a great site for non-technical trekking among glaciers.

When trekking in the Andes, especially the high parks and regions of Bolivia, Ecuador and Peru, altitude sickness is a very real danger. Elevations in the southern Andes are much lower. Most capital cities have an Instituto Geográfico Militar, which is usually the best place for official topographical maps.

For more details on Patagonian treks, check out Lonely Planet's *Trekking in the Patagonian Andes*.

Mountaineering

On a continent with one of the world's greatest mountain ranges, climbing opportunities are almost unlimited. Ecuador's volcanoes, the high peaks of Peru's Cordillera Blanca and Cordillera Huayhuash, Bolivia's Cordillera Real and Argentina's Aconcagua (the western hemisphere's highest peak) all offer outstanding mountaineering opportunities. Despite its relatively low elevation, Argentina's Fitz Roy range – home to Cerro Torre, one of the world's most challenging peaks – chalks in as a major climbing destination.

River Rafting

Chile churns with good white water: the Maipó, Trancura and Futaleufú rivers are all world class. River running is also possible on the scenic Río Urubamba and other rivers near Cuzco, the Río Cañete south of Lima, and in the canyon country around Arequipa, in Peru. In Argentina, several rivers around Bariloche and Mendoza are worth getting wet in. Baños and especially Tena in Ecuador are both rafting hubs. In Colombia, the Río Suárez near San Gil has decent runs.

Skiing & Snowboarding

South America's most important downhill ski areas are in Chile and Argentina. The season is roughly June to September.

Surfing

Brazil is South America's best-known surfing destination, with great breaks near Rio and in the southeast, and sprinkled all along the coast from Santa Catarina to São Luís. If you've got the cash, the surfing in Fernando de Noronha is spectacular. You'll find good waves in Mar del Plata (Argentina), on the northern coast of Peru (but you'll need a wetsuit), on

BOOK YOUR STAY ONLINE

For more accommodations reviews by Lonely Planet authors, check out http://hotels.lonelyplanet.com. You'll find independent reviews, as well as recommendations on the best places to stay. Best of all, you can book online.

Chile's central and northern coasts (especially surfing hot spot Pichilemu), Ecuador, Uruguay and Venezuela. For more far-flung possibilities there's the Galápagos Islands and Rapa Nui (Easter Island).

For detailed information, get a copy of the *Surf Report* from **Surfer Publications** (www.surfermag.com). It has individual reports on most parts of the South American coast. On the web, check out **Wannasurf** (www.wannasurf.com). For forecasts, subscribe to **Surfline** (www.surfline.com).

Wind Sports

Windsurfing and kitesurfing are becoming more popular. Adícora and Isla de Margarita in Venezuela, San Andrés and Cabo de la Vela in Colombia and numerous places along Brazil's northeast coast – especially Jericoacoara and Canoa Quebrada – are outstanding kitesurfing and windsurfing destinations. In Argentina, San Juan province's Cuesta del Viento reservoir (ask about it at the San Juan tourist office) is one of the best wind-sport destinations in the world.

Paragliding and hang-gliding also have their followers. Top destinations include Iquique (Chile), Mérida (Venezuela), and Medellín and Bucaramanga (Colombia). You can even fly from urban locations such as Miraflores in Lima and Pedra Bonita in Rio de Janeiro.

Business Hours

Generally, businesses are open from 8am or 9am to 8pm or 9pm Monday through Friday, with a two-hour lunch break around noon. Businesses are often open on Saturday, usually with shorter hours. Banks usually only change money Monday through Friday. On Sunday, nearly everything is closed. In the Andean countries, businesses tend to close earlier.

Customs Regulations

Customs vary slightly from country to country, but you can generally bring in personal belongings, camera gear, laptops, handheld devices and other travel-related gear. All countries prohibit the export (just as home countries prohibit the import) of archaeological items and goods made from rare or endangered animals (snake skins, cat pelts, jewelry made with teeth etc). Avoid carrying plants, seeds, fruits and fresh meat products across borders. If you're traveling overland to/from Colombia, expect thorough customs inspections on both sides of the border.

Discount Cards

A Hostelling International–American Youth Hostel (HI-USA) membership card can be useful in Brazil and Chile (and to a lesser extent in Argentina and Uruguay), where there are many hostels, and accommodations tend to be, or traditionally have been, costlier. Elsewhere on the continent, cheap hotels and *pensiones* typically cost less than affiliated hostels.

An International Student Identity Card (ISIC) can provide discounted admission to archaeological sites and museums. It may also entitle you to reductions on bus, train and air tickets. In less developed countries, student discounts are rare, although high-ticket items such as the entrance to Machu Picchu (discounted 50% for ISIC holders under 26) may be reduced. In some countries, such as Argentina, almost any form of university identification will suffice where discounts are offered.

Electricity

Electricity is not standard across South America. Voltage ranges from 100V to 240V, with the most common plug types being flat-pronged American style and rounded European style. See the individual country Directory sections for details.

Embassies & Consulates

For embassy and consulate addresses and phone numbers, see the Directory section of individual country chapters.

As a visitor in a South American country, it's important to realize what your own embassy – the embassy of the country of which you are a citizen – can and cannot do. Generally speaking, it won't be much help in emergencies where you're even remotely at fault. Remember that you are bound by the laws of the country you are in. Your embassy will not be sympathetic if you end up in jail after committing a crime locally, even if such actions are legal in your own country.

In genuine emergencies you may get some assistance, but only if other channels have been exhausted. For example, if you have all your money and documents stolen, it might assist in getting a new passport, but a loan for onward travel will generally be out of the question.

Gay & Lesbian Travelers

Buenos Aires, Rio de Janeiro and São Paulo are the most gay-friendly cities, though gay couples are openly out only in certain neighborhoods. Salvador (Brazil), Bogotá, and to a lesser extent Santiago, also have lively gay scenes. Elsewhere on the continent, where public displays of affection by same-sex couples may get negative reactions, do as the locals do – be discreet to avoid problems.

Despite a growing number of publications and websites devoted to gay travel, few have specific advice on South America. One exception is **Purple Roofs** (www.purpleroofs.com), an excellent guide to gay-friendly accommodations throughout South America.

Insurance

A travel insurance policy covering theft, loss, accidents and illness is highly recommended. Many policies include a card with toll-free numbers for 24-hour assistance, and it's good practice to carry it with you. Note that some policies compensate travelers for misrouted or lost luggage. Baggage insurance is worth its price in peace of mind. Also check that the coverage includes worst-case scenarios: ambulances, evacuations or an emergency flight home. Some policies specifically exclude 'dangerous activities,' such as scuba diving, motorcycling, or even trekking. If such activities are on your agenda, avoid this sort of policy.

There are a wide variety of policies available and your travel agent will be able to make recommendations. The policies handled by student-travel organizations usually offer good value. If a policy offers lower and higher medical-expense options, the low-expenses policy should be OK for South America – medical costs are not nearly as high here as elsewhere in the world.

If you have baggage insurance and need to make a claim, the insurance company may demand a receipt as proof that you bought the stuff in the first place. You must usually inform the insurance company by airmail and report the loss or theft to local police within 24 hours. Make a list of stolen items and their value. At the police station, you complete a *denuncia* (statement), a copy of which is given to you for your insurance claim.

Worldwide travel insurance is available at www.lonelyplanet.com/travel_services. You can buy, claim and extend online anytime – even if you're already on the road.

Internet Access

Internet access is widely available. Many hostels have a computer available for guests and wi-fi is increasingly common – not only at hostels, but also at higher-end cafes and restaurants. In the text we've indicated where wi-fi (📶) and/or a guest computer (@) are available.

In contrast, internet cafes aren't quite as prevalent as they once were. Rates generally hover around US$1 to US$2 per hour (upwards of US$6 per hour in Brazil, Argentina and Chile). Either 'Alt + 64' or 'Alt-Gr + 2' is the command to get the '@' symbol on almost any Spanish-language keyboard.

Language Courses

Spanish-language courses are available in many South American cities, with Cuzco and Arequipa (Peru), Quito and Cuenca (Ecuador) and Buenos Aires being some of the best. For Portuguese, Rio de Janeiro is a great place to spend some time studying. For Quechua and Aymara, try Cochabamba (Bolivia) or Cuzco.

Legal Matters

In city police stations, an English-speaking interpreter is a rarity. In most cases you'll either have to speak the local language or provide an interpreter. Some cities have a tourist police service, which can be more helpful.

If you are robbed, photocopies (even better, certified copies) of original passports, visas and air tickets, and careful records of credit card numbers and traveler's checks will prove invaluable during replacement procedures. Replacement passport applications are usually referred to the home country, so it helps to leave a copy of your passport details with someone back home.

Maps

International Travel Maps & Books (ITMB; www.itmb.com) produces a range of excellent maps of Central and South America. For the whole continent, it has a reliable three-sheet map at a 1:4,000,000 scale and a commemorative edition of its classic 1:500,000 map. The maps are huge for road use, but they're helpful for pre-trip planning. More detailed ITMB maps are available for the Amazon Basin, Ecuador, Bolivia and Venezuela. All are available on the ITMB website.

Maps of the South American continent as a whole are widely available; check any well-stocked map or travel bookstore. **South American Explorers** (www.saexplorers.org) has scores of reliable maps, including topographical, regional and city maps.

Money

Prices quoted are given in the locally used currency. Note that US dollars are used in Ecuador, and euros in French Guiana. For exchange rates, see www.xe.com.

Fraud

Unfortunately, ATM-card cloning is a big worry in Brazil, and your account can be drained of thousands of dollars before you even realize it. While fool-proof prevention is nearly impossible, there are a few tips that can help minimize the risk (see p402).

ATMs

ATMs are available in most cities and large towns, and are almost always the most convenient, reliable and economical way of getting cash. The rate of exchange is usually as good as any bank or legal money changer. Many ATMs are connected to the Cirrus or Plus network, but many countries prefer one over the other. If your ATM card gets swallowed by a machine, generally the only thing you can do is call your bank and cancel the card. Although such events are rare, it's well worth having an extra ATM card (to a different account), should something go wrong.

If possible, sign up with a bank that doesn't charge a fee for out-of-network ATM withdrawals. Also, find a bank that offers a low exchange-rate fee (1% to 2%). Before hitting the road, call your bank, informing them of your travel plans – that way the bank won't put a hold on foreign withdrawals while you're on the road.

Many ATMs will accept a personal identification number (PIN) of only four digits; find out whether this applies to the specific countries you're traveling to before heading off.

Bargaining

Bargaining is accepted and expected when contracting long-term accommodations and when shopping for craft goods in markets. Haggling is a near sport in the Andean countries, with patience, humor and respect serving as the ground rules of the game. Bargaining is much less common in the Cono Sur (Southern Cone; a collective term for Argentina, Chile, Uruguay and parts of Brazil and Paraguay). When you head into the bargaining trenches, remember that the point is to have fun while reaching a mutually satisfying end: the merchant should not try to fleece you, but you shouldn't try to get something for nothing either.

Black Market

Nowadays, official exchange rates are generally realistic in most South American countries, so the role of the black market is declining. Most people end up using the *mercado negro* (black market) when crossing isolated borders, where an official exchange facility might be hours away. Some travelers might still want to use street money changers if they need to exchange cash outside business hours, but with the convenience of ATM cards, this necessity is declining. The one notable exception to this is Venezuela, where ATM withdrawals and credit-card transactions cost about twice as much as exchanging cash on the black market.

Street money changers may be legal or not legal (but are often tolerated), and the practice of changing money on the street is prone to scams – one such trick consists of money changers handing their client the agreed amount less a few pesos; when the client complains, they will take it back adding the few pesos while making a few larger notes disappear. Money changers may also distract their customers during the transaction, alerting them to supposed alarms such as 'police' or any other 'danger,' or use fixed calculators that give an exchange rate favorable only to the money changer, or pass counterfeit, torn, smudged or tattered bills.

Cash

It's convenient to have a small wad of US cash tucked away (in US$20 denominations and less; US$100 bills are difficult to exchange). US currency is by far the easiest to exchange throughout South America. Of course, unlike traveler's checks, nobody will give you a refund for lost or stolen cash. When you're about to cross from one country to another, it's handy to change some cash. Trying to exchange worn notes can be a hassle, so procure crisp bills before setting out.

In some countries, especially in rural areas, *cambio* (change) can be particularly hard to come by. Businesses even occasionally refuse to sell you something if they can't or don't want to change your note. So break down those larger bills whenever you have the opportunity, such as at busy restaurants, banks and larger businesses.

Credit Cards

The big-name credit cards are accepted at most large stores, travel agencies and better hotels and restaurants. Credit card purchases sometimes attract an extra *recargo* (surcharge) on the price (from 2% to 10%), but they are usually billed to your account at favorable exchange rates. Some banks issue cash advances on major credit cards. The most widely accepted card is Visa, followed by MasterCard (those with UK Access should insist on its affiliation with MasterCard). American Express and Diners Club are also accepted in some places.

Money Changers

Traveler's checks and foreign cash can be changed at *casas de cambio* (currency-exchange offices) or banks. Rates are usually similar, but *casas de cambio* are quicker, less bureaucratic and open longer hours. Street money changers, who may or may not be legal, will only handle cash. Sometimes money can also be changed unofficially at hotels or in shops that sell imported goods (electronics dealers are an obvious choice).

It is preferable to bring money in US dollars, although banks and *casas de cambio* in capital cities will change euros, pounds sterling, Japanese yen and other major currencies. Changing these currencies in smaller towns and on the street is next to impossible.

Traveler's Checks

Traveler's checks are not nearly as convenient as ATM cards, and you may have difficulty cashing them – even at banks. High commissions (from 3% to upwards of 10%) also make them an unattractive option. If you do take traveler's checks, American Express is the most widely accepted brand, while Visa, Thomas Cook and Citibank are the next best options. To facilitate replacement in case of theft, keep a record of check numbers and the original bill of sale in a safe place. Even with proper records, replacement can be a tedious, time-intensive process.

Photography

Photographing People

Ask for permission before photographing individuals, particularly indigenous people. Paying folks for their portrait is a personal decision; in most cases, the subject will tell you right away the going rate for a photo.

Restrictions

Some tourist sites charge an additional fee for tourists with cameras. Don't take photos of military installations, military personnel or security-sensitive places such as police stations. Such activities may be illegal and could even endanger your life. In most churches, flash photography (and sometimes any photography) is not allowed.

Post

International postal rates can be quite expensive. Generally, important mail and parcels should be sent by registered or certified service, otherwise they may go missing. Sending parcels can be awkward: often an *aduana* (customs) officer must inspect the contents before a postal clerk can accept them, so wait to seal your package until after it has been checked. Most post offices have a parcels window, usually signed *encomiendas* (parcels). The place for posting overseas parcels is sometimes different from the main post office.

UPS, FedEx, DHL and other private postal services are available in some countries, but are prohibitively expensive.

Safe Travel

There are potential dangers to traveling in South America, but with sensible precautions, you are unlikely to encounter serious problems. Your greatest threats will likely be reckless drivers, pollution, fiesta fireworks and low-hanging objects (watch your head!).

Confidence Tricks & Scams

Keep your wits about you if nefarious substances (mustard, bird droppings, human excrement) are thrown upon you followed by the appearance of someone who lends a helping hand, while others steal your belongings. Other scams to be aware of involve a quantity of cash being 'found' on the street, whereby the do-gooder tries to return it to you; elaborate hard-luck stories from supposed travelers; and 'on-the-spot fines' by bogus police. Be especially wary if one or more 'plainclothes' cops demand to search your luggage or examine your documents, traveler's checks or cash. Insist that you will allow this only at an official police station or in the presence of a uniformed officer, and don't allow anyone to take you anywhere in a taxi or unmarked car. Thieves often work in pairs to distract you while lifting your wallet. Simply stay alert.

Kidnapping

Be careful when taking taxis. 'Express' kidnappings occur in some cities. These incidents involve whisking travelers to far-off neighborhoods and holding them there while their ATM accounts are emptied; sometimes assaults have also occurred. We've noted in individual country chapters the known places that pose this kind of risk to travelers. To be on the safe side, have your guesthouse call you a taxi rather than hailing one on the street, and use official taxis at airports rather than those outside the gates. And never ride in

GOVERNMENT TRAVEL ADVICE

The following government websites offer travel advisories and information on current hot spots.

» Australian Department of Foreign Affairs (www.smarttraveller.gov.au)

» British Foreign Office (www.fco.gov.uk/en/travel-and-living-abroad)

» Canadian Department of Foreign Affairs (www.dfait-maeci.gc.ca)

» US State Department (http://travel.state.gov)

a vehicle that already has a passenger in it.

Drugging

Lonely Planet has received letters from travelers who were unwittingly drugged and robbed after accepting food from a stranger.

Be very careful in bars – there are occasional reports of folks being drugged then raped or robbed. Always keep a close eye on your drink, and be cautious when meeting new friends.

Drugs

And now a word from your mother: marijuana and cocaine are big business in parts of South America, and are available in many places but illegal everywhere. Indulging can either land you in jail or worse. Unless you're willing to take these risks, avoid illegal drugs.

Beware that drugs are sometimes used to set up travelers for blackmail and bribery. Avoid any conversation with someone proffering drugs. If you're in an area where drug trafficking is prevalent, ignore it entirely, with conviction.

In Bolivia and Peru, chewing coca leaves or drinking *maté de coca* (coca leaf–infused tea) may help alleviate some of the effects of altitude. Keep in mind, though, that transporting coca leaves over international borders is illegal.

Natural Hazards

The Pacific Rim 'ring of fire' loops through eastern Asia, Alaska and all the way down through the Americas to Tierra del Fuego in a vast circle of earthquake and volcanic activity that includes the whole Pacific side of South America. Volcanoes usually give some notice before blowing and are therefore unlikely to pose any immediate threat to travelers. Earthquakes, however, are not uncommon, occur without warning and can be very serious. The last big one in the region was a 7.9-magnitude quake that hit the south coast of Peru (in Ica province, 265km south of Lima), killing more than 300 people. Recovery has come slowly, and parts of the region remain visibly devastated. Andean construction rarely meets seismic safety standards; adobe buildings are particularly vulnerable.

If you're in an earthquake, take shelter in a doorway or dive under a table; don't go outside.

Police & Military

In some places, you may encounter corrupt officials who are not beyond enforcing minor regulations in hopes of extracting a bribe.

If you are stopped by 'plainclothes policemen,' never get into a vehicle with them. Don't give them any documents or show them any money, and don't take them to your hotel. If the police appear to be the real thing, insist on going to a police station on foot.

The military often maintains considerable influence, even under civilian governments. Avoid approaching military installations, which may display warnings such as 'No stopping or photographs – the sentry will shoot.' In the event of a coup or other emergency, state-of-siege regulations suspend civil rights. Always carry identification and be sure someone knows your whereabouts. Contact your embassy or consulate for advice.

Theft

Theft can be a problem, but remember that fellow travelers can also be accomplished crooks, so where there's a backpacker scene, there may also be thievery. Here are some common-sense suggestions to limit your liability:

» A small padlock is useful for securing your pack zippers and hostel door, if necessary. Twist ties, paper clips or safety pins can be another effective deterrent when used to secure your pack zippers.

» Even if you're just running down the hall, never leave your hotel door unlocked.

» Always conceal your money belt and its contents, preferably beneath your clothing.

» Keep your spending money separate from the big stuff (credit cards, tickets etc).

» Be aware of the risk of bag slashing and the theft of your contents on buses. Keep close watch on your belongings – the bag isn't safe under your seat, above your head or between your legs (it's better on your lap). Be mindful in crowded markets or terminals where thefts are more likely to occur.

» When exploring cities, consider ditching the daypack and carrying what you need in a plastic bag to deter potential thieves.

Trouble Spots

Some countries and areas are more dangerous than others. The more dangerous places warrant extra care, but don't feel you should avoid them altogether. Colombia is much safer than it has been in years, but certain regions are still off-limits. The northern border region of Ecuador, specifically in the Oriente, can be dodgy due to guerrilla activity, and there have been attacks on travelers visiting jungle lodges there. Travelers have been assaulted at remote and even well-touristed archaeological sites, primarily in Peru; stay informed. La Paz (Bolivia), Caracas (Venezuela), Rio and São Paulo (Brazil) and Quito (Ecuador) are all notorious for assaults on tourists.

Tours

There are loads of great adrenaline activities on offer, from rafting to mountain biking, but do your research on an agency before joining a tour. Travelers have lost their lives owing to poorly maintained equipment and reckless, ill-prepared guides. It's never wise to choose an operator based on cost alone. In Bolivia, for instance, the mine tours in Potosí, bike trips outside La Paz and the 4WD excursions around Salar de Uyuni have become so hugely popular that some agencies are willing to forgo safety. Talk to other travelers, check out equipment and meet with guides before committing to anything.

Telephone

Internet cafes with net-to-phone service provide the cheapest way to make international calls, with rates varying between US10¢ and US50¢ per minute to the USA and Europe.

From traditional landlines, the most economical way of calling abroad is by phone cards. You can also try direct-dial lines, accessed via special numbers and billed to an account at home. There are different access numbers for each telephone company in each country – get a list from your phone company before you leave.

It is sometimes cheaper to make a collect (reverse-charge) or credit-card call overseas than to pay for the call at the source. Many towns and cities have a telephone office with a row of phone booths for local and international calls. Rates can be high.

Cell Phones

Cell-phone numbers in South America often have different area codes than fixed-line numbers, even if the cell-phone owner resides in the same city. Calling a cell-phone number is always more expensive (sometimes exorbitantly so) than calling a fixed line.

If you plan to carry your own cell phone, a GSM tri- or quad-band phone is your best bet. Another option is purchasing a prepaid SIM card (or cards) for the countries where you plan on traveling. You will need a compatible international GSM cell phone that is SIM-unlocked. Or you can simply purchase one when you arrive (a cheap phone costs about US$30).

If you plan to travel with an iPhone or other smartphone, you may want to purchase an international plan to minimize (what could be) enormous costs. On the other hand, it's possible to call internationally for free or very cheaply using Skype or other VoIP (Voice over Internet Protocol) systems.

Phone Cards

Aside from Skype, the cheapest way to make an international call is by using a phone card, the type you purchase at a kiosk or corner store. These allow you to call North America or Europe for as little as US5¢ per minute with a good card. The caveat is that you need a private phone line or a permissive telephone kiosk operator to use them.

Time

South America spans four time zones; see the opening pages of each country chapter for details. Chile and parts of Brazil observe daylight savings time from October to February or March.

Toilets

There are two toilet rules for South America: always carry your own toilet paper and don't ever throw anything into the toilet bowl. Except in the most developed places, South American sewer systems can't handle toilet paper, so all paper products must be discarded in the wastebasket. Another general rule is to use public bathrooms whenever you can, as you never know when your next opportunity will be. Folks posted outside bathrooms proffering swaths of paper require payment.

Tourist Information

Every country in South America has government-run tourist offices, but their quality and breadth of coverage vary. Local tourist offices are mentioned in this book wherever they exist.

South American Explorers (SAE; www.saexplorers.org) is one of the most helpful organizations for travelers to South America. Founded in 1977, SAE functions as an information center for travelers, adventurers and researchers. It supports scientific fieldwork, mountaineering and other expeditions, wilderness conservation and social development in Latin America. It has traveler clubhouses in Buenos Aires, Lima, Cuzco and Quito, as well as the **US office** (☎607-277-0488; 126 Indian Creek Rd, Ithaca, NY 14850), which publishes the quarterly magazine *South American Explorer*. The clubhouses have extensive libraries of books, maps and traveler's reports, plus a great atmosphere. The club itself sells maps, books and other items at its offices and by mail order.

Annual SAE membership is US$60/90 per individual/couple. Members can use services at any club, including internet access, libraries, storage facilities, mail service, trip reports and book exchange, and discounts at numerous hotels and travel services. Clubs also host workshops, Spanish conversation classes, excursions and other events.

Travelers with Disabilities

In general, South America is not well set up for travelers with disabilities, but the more modernized Southern Cone countries are slightly more accommodating – notably Chile, Argentina and the bigger cities of Brazil. Unfortunately, cheap local lodgings probably won't be well equipped to deal with physically challenged travelers; air travel will be more feasible than local buses (although this isn't impossible); and well-developed tourist attractions will be more accessible than off-the-beaten-track destinations. Start your research with the following websites:

Access-able Travel Source (www.access-able.com) Offers little information specifically on South America, but provides some good general travel advice.

Emerging Horizons (www.emerginghorizons.com) Features well-written articles and regular columns full of handy advice.

Mobility International (www.miusa.org) This US-based outfit advises travelers with disabilities and runs educational-exchange programs – a good way to visit South America.

Royal Association for Disability and Rehabilitation (www.radar.org.uk) Good resource for travelers from the UK.

Society for Accessible Travel & Hospitality (SATH; www.sath.org) Good, general travel information; based in the USA.

Visas & Arrival Fees

Some travelers – including those from the USA – may require visas to enter several countries. These are best arranged in advance. Some countries, such as Chile and Argentina, don't generally require visas but levy a huge fee for those arriving by air. If no visa is required, a tourist card is issued upon arrival. See the Directory section in the individual country chapters for more details.

Carry a handful of passport-sized photos for visa applications. Hold onto any entry-exit cards you are given. There can be serious fines and complications if you lose them!

If you need a visa for a country and arrive at a land border without one, be prepared to backtrack to the nearest town with a consulate to get one. Airlines won't normally let you board a plane for a country to which you don't have the necessary visa. Also, a visa in itself does not guarantee entry: you may still be turned back at the border if you don't have 'sufficient funds' or an onward or return ticket.

Onward or Return Tickets

Some countries require you to have a ticket out of their country before they will admit you at the border, grant you a visa or let you board their national airline. The onward- or return-ticket requirement can be a major nuisance for travelers who want to fly into one country and travel overland through others. Officially, Peru, Colombia, Ecuador, Venezuela, Bolivia, Brazil, Suriname and French Guiana demand onward tickets, but only sporadically enforce it. Still, if you arrive in one of the countries technically requiring an onward ticket or sufficient funds and a border guard is so inclined, he or she *can* enforce these rules (yet another reason to be courteous and neatly dressed at border crossings).

While proof of onward or return tickets is rarely asked for by South American border officials, airline officials, especially in the US, sometimes refuse boarding passengers with one-way tickets who cannot show proof of onward or return travel or proof of citizenship (or residency) in the destination country. One way around this is to purchase a cheap, fully refundable ticket out of the country and cash it in after your arrival. The downside is that the refund can take up to three months. Before purchasing the ticket, you should also ask specifically where you can get a refund, as some airlines will only refund tickets at the office of purchase or at their head office.

Any ticket out of South America plus sufficient funds are usually an adequate substitute for an onward ticket. Having a major credit card or two may help.

Sufficient Funds

Sufficient funds are often *technically* required but rarely asked for. Immigration officials may ask (verbally or on the application form) about your financial resources. If you lack 'sufficient funds' for your proposed visit, officials may limit the length of your stay, but once you are in the country, you can usually extend your visa by producing a credit card or two.

Volunteering

If you want to donate your hard work, there are plenty of local organizations that will take you on, though you'll have better luck looking once you're in the country. A good place to start is at a Spanish language school (Quito, Cuenca or Cuzco are top choices); many schools link volunteers with organizations in need.

If you prefer to set something up before you go, keep in mind that most international volunteer organizations require a weekly or monthly fee (sometimes up to US$1500 for two weeks, not including airfare), which can feel a bit harsh. This is usually to cover the costs of housing you, paying the organization's staff, rent, website fees and all that stuff.

Here are a few places to start the search:

Amerispan (www.amerispan.com/volunteer_intern) Volunteer and internship programs in Argentina, Bolivia, Brazil, Chile, Ecuador and Peru.

Cross Cultural Solutions (www.crossculturalsolutions.org) Volunteer programs with an emphasis on cultural and human interaction in Brazil and Peru.

Go Abroad (www.goabroad.com) Extensive listings of volunteer and study-abroad opportunities.

Idealist.org (www.idealist.org) Action Without Borders' searchable database of thousands of volunteer positions throughout the world. Excellent resource.

Rainforest Concern (www.rainforestconcern.org) British nonprofit offering affordable volunteer positions in forest environments in several South American countries. Volunteers pay a weekly fee.

Transitions Abroad (www.transitionsabroad.com) Useful portal for both paid and volunteer work.

UN Volunteers (www.unv.org) The lofty international organization offers volunteer opportunities for peace and development projects across the globe.

Volunteer Latin America (www.volunteerlatinamerica.com) Worth a peek for its interesting programs throughout Latin America.

Working Abroad (www.workingabroad.com) Online network of grassroots volunteer opportunities with trip reports from the field.

Women Travelers

At one time or another, solo women travelers will find themselves the object of curiosity – sometimes well intentioned, sometimes not. Avoidance is an easy, effective self-defense strategy. In the Andean region, particularly in smaller towns and rural areas, modest dress and conduct are the norm, while in Brazil and the more liberal Southern Cone, standards are more relaxed, especially in beach areas.

Machista (macho) attitudes, stressing masculine pride and virility, are fairly widespread among South American men (although less so in indigenous communities). They are often expressed by boasting and in exaggerated attention toward women. Snappy put-down lines or other caustic comebacks to unwanted advances may make the man feel threatened, and he may respond aggressively. Most women find it easier to invent a husband and leave the guy with his pride intact, especially in front of others.

There have been isolated cases of South American men raping women travelers. Women trekking or taking tours in remote or isolated areas should be especially cautious. Some cases have involved guides assaulting tour group members, so it's worth double-checking the identity and reputation of any guide or tour operator. Also be aware that women (and men) have been drugged, in bars and elsewhere, using drinks, cigarettes or pills. Police may not be very helpful in rape cases – if a local woman is raped, her family usually seeks revenge rather than calling the police. Tourist police may be more sympathetic, but it's possibly better to see a doctor and contact your embassy before reporting a rape to police.

Tampons are generally difficult to find in smaller towns, so stock up in cities or bring a supply from home. Birth-control pills are sometimes tricky to find outside metropolitan areas, so you're best off bringing your own supply from home. If you can't bring enough, carry the original package with you so a pharmacist can match a local pill to yours. Pills in most South American countries are inexpensive. 'Morning after' pills are readily available in some countries, notably Brazil.

International Planned Parenthood Federation (www.ippf.org) offers a wealth of information on member clinics (Family Planning Associations) throughout South America that provide contraception (and abortions, where legal).

Work

Aside from teaching or tutoring English, opportunities for employment are few, low-paying and usually illegal. Even tutoring, despite good hourly rates, is rarely remunerative because it takes time to build up a clientele. The best opportunities for teaching English are in the larger cities, and, although you won't save much, it will allow you to stick around longer. Other work opportunities may exist for skilled guides or in restaurants and bars catering to travelers. Many people find work at foreign-owned lodges and inns.

There are several excellent online resources, including the following:

Association of American Schools in South America (www.aassa.com) Places accredited teachers in many academic subjects in schools throughout South America.

Dave's ESL Café (www.eslcafe.com) Loads of message boards, job boards, teaching ideas, information, links and more.

EnglishClub.com (www.englishclub.com) Great resource for ESL teachers and students.

TEFL Net (www.tefl.net) This is another rich online resource for teachers, from the creators of EnglishClub.com.

Transportation

GETTING THERE & AWAY

Entering South America

Passport

Make sure your passport is valid for at least six months beyond the projected end of your trip and has plenty of blank pages for stamp-happy officials. Carrying a photocopy of your passport (so you can leave the original in your hotel) is sometimes enough if you're walking around a town, but *always* have the original if you travel anywhere (never get on a bus leaving town without it).

Air

Airports & Airlines

Every South American country has an international airport in its capital and often in major cities as well. Main gateways include Bogotá (Colombia); Buenos Aires (Argentina); Caracas (Venezuela); La Paz (Bolivia); Lima (Peru); Quito and Guayaquil (Ecuador); Rio de Janeiro and São Paulo (Brazil); and Santiago (Chile). Less frequently used international gateways include Asunción (Paraguay); Manaus, Recife and Salvador (Brazil); Montevideo (Uruguay); Río Gallegos (Argentina); and Santa Cruz (Bolivia).

Owing to massive changes in the airline industry, some countries no longer have a 'flag carrier.' New airlines appear, just as old ones go into bankruptcy. At press time, these were the biggest South American airlines:

Aerolíneas Argentinas/ Austral (www.aerolineas.com.ar; Argentina)

Avianca (www.avianca.com; Colombia)

Boliviana de Aviación (www.boa.bo; Bolivia)

Gol Airlines (www.voegol.com.br; Brazil)

LAN (www.lan.com; Argentina, Chile, Colombia, Ecuador & Peru)

TAM (www.tam.com.br; Brazil)

North American, European and Australian airlines offering regular South American connections include the following:

American Airlines (www.aa.com)

Air France (www.airfrance.com)

British Airways (www.britishairways.com)

Continental Airlines (www.continental.com)

Delta (www.delta.com)

Iberia (www.iberia.com)

KLM (www.klm.com)

Qantas (www.qantas.com.au)

Swiss (www.swiss.com)

Tickets

Airfares to South America depend on the usual criteria: point and date of departure, destination, your access to discount travel agencies and whether you can take advantage of advance-purchase fares and special offers. Airlines are the best source for finding information on routes, timetables and standard fares, but they rarely sell the cheapest tickets.

Flights from North America, Europe, Australia and New Zealand may permit a stopover in South America en route to your destination city. This gives you a free air connection within the region, so it's worth considering when comparing flights. International flights may also include an onward connection at a much lower cost than a separate fare. Be sure to investigate Air Passes (p1060) before you purchase your ticket. Some Air Passes require you to purchase your arrival ticket on a codeshare partner.

From Central America

Flights from Central America are usually subject to high tax, and discounted flights are almost unobtainable.

You must have an onward ticket to enter Colombia, and airlines in Panama and Costa Rica are unlikely to sell you a one-way ticket to Colombia unless you already have an onward ticket or are willing to buy a round-trip flight. Venezuela and Brazil also demand an onward ticket. If you have to purchase a round-trip ticket, check whether the airline will give you a refund for unused portions of the ticket.

The cheapest flights are generally between Panama City and points south – Bogotá and other Colombian cities or Quito. Some travelers prefer going by boat from Panama to Cartagena.

Land

From North America, you can journey overland only as far south as Panama. There is no road connection onward to Colombia: the Carretera Panamericana (Pan-American Hwy) ends in the vast wilderness of the Darién Province, in southeast Panama. This roadless area between Central and South America is called the Darién Gap. In the past it has been difficult, but possible, to trek across the gap with the help of local guides, but since around 1998 it has been prohibitively dangerous, especially on the Colombian side. The region is effectively controlled by guerrillas and is positively unsafe.

Border Crossings

There are ample border crossings in South America, so you generally never have to travel too far out of your way to get where you eventually want to go. This is particularly true in Argentina and Chile, where a shared 3500km-long frontier provides many opportunities (especially in Patagonia) to slide between countries. Most crossings are by road (or bridge), but there are a few that involve boat travel (such as across the Río de la Plata between Buenos Aires and Uruguay; several lake crossings between Argentina and Chile, and across Lake Titicaca between Bolivia and Peru).

With the influx of footloose foreigners in the region, border police are used to backpackers turning up at their often isolated corner of the globe. That said, crossing is always easier if you appear at least somewhat kempt, treat the guards with respect, and make an attempt at Spanish or Portuguese. If, on the off chance, you encounter an officer who tries to extract a little *dinero* from you before allowing you through (it does happen occasionally), maintain your composure. If the amount is small (and it generally is), it's probably not worth your trouble trying to fight it. Generally, border police are courteous and easy going.

Before heading to a border, be sure to get the latest information on visas – whether or not you need one – with a little on-the-ground research.

Bus

The cheapest but most time-consuming way to cross South American borders is to take a local bus to the border, handle immigration formalities and board another bus on the other side. To save a few hours, you might consider boarding an international bus that connects major towns in neighboring countries. See individual country chapters for more information.

Sea

One of the most popular modes of travel between South and Central America is by booking passage on one of the foreign sailboats that travel between Cartagena and the San Blás islands, with some boats continuing to Colón (Panama). The typical passage takes four to six days and costs upwards of US$550. A good source of information regarding schedules and available berths is at **Casa Viena** (☎05-664-6242; www.casaviena.com; Calle San Andrés 30-53, Getsemaní) in Cartagena and **Captain Jack's** (http://boatstocolombia.com; Hostel Portobelo, Calle Guinea, Portobelo, Colón) in Portobelo, Panama. Do some serious research before joining any tour; there are many unsavory operators out there, and a few boats have even sunk.

A less expensive way to reach Panama from Colombia is via small boat from Capurgana to Puerto Obaldia, from where you can take a domestic flight to Panama City or continue up through the San Blás islands. For more details see p574.

Officially, both Panama and Colombia require an onward or return ticket as a

CLIMATE CHANGE & TRAVEL

Every form of transport that relies on carbon-based fuel generates CO_2, the main cause of human-induced climate change. Modern travel is dependent on airplanes, which might use less fuel per kilometer per person than most cars but travel much greater distances. The altitude at which aircraft emit gases (including CO_2) and particles also contributes to their climate change impact. Many websites offer 'carbon calculators' that allow people to estimate the carbon emissions generated by their journey and, for those who wish to do so, to offset the impact of the greenhouse gases emitted with contributions to portfolios of climate-friendly initiatives throughout the world. Lonely Planet offsets the carbon footprint of all staff and author travel.

condition of entry. This may not be enforced in Colombia, but it's wise to get one anyway, or have lots of money and a plausible itinerary. Panama requires a visa or tourist card, an onward ticket and sufficient funds, and has been known to turn back arrivals who don't meet these requirements.

There are occasional reports of pirate attacks off the coast of South America, most of which occur in the Caribbean region.

GETTING AROUND

Whether aboard a rickety *chiva* (open-sided bus) on the Ecuadorian coast, a motorized canoe in the Amazon, or a small aircraft humming over the Andes, transport on this continent is a big part of the South American adventure.

Air

There is an extensive network of domestic flights, with refreshingly low price tags, especially in the Andean countries (Bolivia, Ecuador and Peru). After 18-hour bus rides across 350km of mountainous terrain on atrocious roads, you may decide, as many travelers do, to take the occasional flight.

There are drawbacks to flying, however. Airports are often far from city centers, and public buses don't run all the time, so you may end up spending a bit on taxis (it's usually easier to find a cheap taxi *to* an airport than *from* one). Airport taxes also add to the cost of air travel; they are usually higher for international departures. If safety concerns you, check out the 'Fatal Events by Airline' feature at www.airsafe.com.

In some areas, planes don't depart on time. Avoid scheduling a domestic flight with a close connection for an international flight or vice versa. Many a traveler has been stranded after setting too tight an itinerary that hinges on their international flight arriving on time and connecting with a domestic leg to a far-flung outpost. Reconfirm all flights 48 hours before departure and turn up at the airport at least an hour before flight time (two to three hours for international flights).

Flights from North America and Europe may permit stopovers on the way to the destination city. It's worth considering this when shopping for an international flight, as it can effectively give you a free air connection within South America. Onward connections in conjunction with an international flight can also be a cheap way to get to another South American city.

Air Passes

Air passes offer a number of flights within a country or region, for a specified period, at a fixed total price. Passes are an economical way to cover long distances in limited time, but they have shortcomings. Some are irritatingly inflexible: once you start using the pass, you're locked into a schedule and can't change it without paying a penalty. The validity period can be restrictive and some passes require that you enter the country on an international flight – you can't travel overland to the country and then start flying around with an air pass. Citizens of some countries are not eligible for certain air passes, etc. For an overview of the various passes and their minutiae, see Air Passes in the Flight pages (under Planning) of **Last Frontiers** (www.lastfrontiers.com).

MULTICOUNTRY AIR PASSES

A few South America air passes exist and can save you a bit of money, provided you can deal with a fixed itinerary. These mileage-based passes allow travelers to fly between cities in a limited set of countries. The restrictions vary, but flights must be completed within a period ranging from 30 days to 12 months. You'll pay higher rates (or be ineligible) if you arrive in South America on a carrier other than the one sponsoring the air pass.

Gol Mercosul Airpass (www.voegol.com.br) This pass includes Brazil, Argentina, Bolivia, Chile, Paraguay and Uruguay.

Lan South American Airpass (www.lan.com) Includes flights serving Argentina, Bolivia, southern Brazil, Chile, Colombia, Ecuador, Peru, Uruguay and Venezuela.

One World Alliance Visit South America Airpass (www.oneworld.com) Similar to the LAN pass, but also includes American Airlines and British Airways flights serving Argentina, Bolivia, southern Brazil, Chile, Colombia, Ecuador, Peru, Uruguay and Venezuela.

South American Pass (www.aerolineas.com.ar) Aerolíneas Argentinas offers this multicountry pass, which is valid for Argentina, Bolivia, southern Brazil, Chile, Colombia, Paraguay, Peru, Uruguay and Venezuela.

TAM South America Airpass (www.tam.com.br) Includes Argentina, Bolivia, Brazil, Chile, Paraguay, Peru, Uruguay and Venezuela.

SINGLE-COUNTRY AIR PASSES

Most air passes are only good within one country and are usually purchased in combination with a round-trip ticket to that country. In addition, most air passes must be purchased outside the destination country; check with a travel agent. Argentina, Brazil and Chile all offer domestic air passes.

Bicycle

Cycling South America is a challenging yet highly rewarding alternative to public transport. While better roads in Argentina and Chile make the Cono Sur (Southern Cone; a collective term for Argentina, Chile, Uruguay and parts of Brazil and Paraguay) countries especially attractive, the entire continent is manageable by bike, or – more precisely – by mountain bike. Touring bikes are suitable for paved roads, but only a *todo terreno* (mountain bike) allows you to tackle the spectacular back roads (and often main roads!) of the Andes.

There are no multicountry bike lanes or designated routes. Mountain bikers have cycled the length of the Andes, and a select few have made the transcontinental journey from North to South America. As for road rules, forget it – except for the logical rule of riding with traffic on the right-hand side of the road, there are none. Hunt down good maps that show side roads, as you'll have the enviable ability to get off the beaten track at will.

Bring your own bicycle since locally manufactured ones are less dependable and imported bikes are outrageously expensive. Bicycle mechanics are common even in small towns, but will almost invariably lack the parts you'll need. Before setting out, learn bicycle mechanics and purchase spares for the pieces most likely to fail. A basic road kit will include extra spokes and a spoke wrench, a tire patch kit, a chain punch, inner tubes, spare cables and a cycling-specific multitool. Some folks box up spare tires, leave them with a family member back home and have them shipped to South America when they need them.

Drawbacks to cycling include the weather (fierce rains, blasting winds), high altitude in the Andes, poor roads and reckless drivers – the biggest hazard for riders. Safety equipment such as reflectors, mirrors and a helmet are highly recommended. Security is another issue: always take your panniers with you, lock your bike (or pay someone to watch it) while you sightsee and bring your bike into your hotel room overnight.

Before you fly, remember to check your airline's baggage requirements; some allow bikes to fly free, while others don't. It's also essential that you box your bike up correctly to avoid damage during handling.

SAMPLE AIRFARES

Unless noted otherwise, the following chart shows sample mid-season, one-way airfares, quoted directly by airlines for purchase in South America. With some savvy research you may find better fares. Sometimes, purchasing an *ida y vuelta* (return-trip) ticket is cheaper than buying a one-way ticket; be sure to ask.

ORIGIN	DESTINATION	COST (US$)
Asunción	Buenos Aires	251
Bogotá	Quito	323
Buenos Aires	Santiago	340
Buenos Aires	Ushuaia	340
Guayaquil	Galápagos Islands	440-480 (round trip)
Guayaquil	Lima	540
Lima	La Paz	515
Punta Arenas	Falkland Islands	480-530 (round trip)
Punta Arenas	Santiago	415
Quito	Galápagos Islands	360-420 (round trip)
Rio de Janeiro	Manaus	200-500
Rio de Janeiro	Montevideo	375
Rio de Janeiro	Santa Cruz, Bolivia	480
Salvador	Rio de Janeiro	180
Santa Cruz, Bolivia	Florianópolis	560
Santiago	Rapa Nui (Easter Island)	740 -1182 (round trip)
Santiago	La Paz	475-780
Santiago	Lima	530-650

Boat

From cruises through the mystical fjords of Chilean Patagonia and riverboat chugs up the Amazon to outboard canoe travel in the coastal mangroves of Ecuador, South America offers ample opportunity to travel by boat. Safety is generally not an issue, especially for the established ferry and cruise operators in Chile and Argentina. There have been a couple of recent problems with tourist boats in the Galápagos (including a few that have sunk over the years), so we recommend you do some research before committing to a cruise.

Lake Crossings

There are outstanding (but expensive) lake excursions throughout southern Chile and Argentina, as well as on Lake Titicaca, in and between Bolivia and Peru. Some of the most popular routes:

» Copacabana (Bolivia) to the Lake Titicaca islands of Isla del Sol and Isla de la Luna

» Lago General Carrera (Chile) to Chile Chico and Puerto Ingeniero Ibáñez (Chile)

» Puerto Montt and Puerto Varas (Chile) to Bariloche (Argentina)

» Puno (Peru) to the Lake Titicaca islands

Riverboat

Long-distance travel on major rivers such as the Orinoco or Amazon is possible, but you'll have a more idyllic time on one of the smaller rivers such as the Mamoré or Beni, where boats hug the shore and you can see and hear the wildlife. On the Amazon, you rarely even see the shore. The river is also densely settled in its lower reaches, and its upper reaches have fewer passenger boats than in the past. Other river journeys include the Río Paraguay from Asunción (Paraguay) to Brazil, or the Río Napo from Coca (Ecuador) to Peru. River travel in Bolivia is less common than it once was, with more folks opting to take short flights between destinations.

Riverboats vary greatly in size and standards, so check the vessel before buying a ticket and shop around. When you pay the fare, get a ticket with all the details on it. Downriver travel is faster than upriver, but boats going upriver travel closer to the shore and offer more interesting scenery. The time taken between ports is unpredictable, so river travel is best for those with an open schedule.

Food is usually included in ticket prices and means lots of rice and beans and perhaps some meat, but bring bottled water, fruit and snacks as a supplement. The evening meal on the first night of a trip is not usually included. Drinks and extra food are generally sold on board, but at high prices. Bring some spare cash and insect repellent.

Unless you have cabin space, you'll need a hammock and rope to sling it. It can get windy and cool at night, so a sleeping bag is recommended. There are usually two classes of hammock space, with space on the upper deck costing slightly more; it's cooler there and worth the extra money. Be on the boat at least eight hours prior to departure to get a good hammock space away from engine noise and toilet odors.

Overcrowding and theft on boats are common complaints. Don't allow your baggage to be stored in an insecure locker; bring your own padlock. Don't entrust your bag to any boat officials unless you are quite certain about their status – bogus officials have been reported.

Sea Trips

The best-known sea trip, and a glorious one at that, is the **Navimag** (☎02-442-3120; www.navimag.com; Av El Bosque Norte 0440, Santiago) ferry ride down the Chilean coast, from Puerto Montt to Puerto Natales. Short boat rides in some countries take you to islands not far from the mainland, including Ilha Grande and Ilha de Santa Catarina in Brazil, Isla Grande de Chiloé in Chile and Isla Grande de Tierra del Fuego in Argentina. More distant islands are usually reached by air. In parts of coastal Ecuador, outboard canoes act as public transport through the mangroves.

Bus

If there's one form of transport in South America that's guaranteed to give you fodder for your travel tales, it's the bus. Whether you're barreling down a treacherous Andean road in a bus full of chickens in Ecuador, or relaxing in a reclining leather chair sipping sparkling wine with dinner on an Argentine long-hauler, you will rarely be short on entertainment. In general, bus transport is well developed throughout the continent. Note that road conditions, bus quality and driver professionalism, however, vary widely.

Highland Peru, Bolivia and Ecuador have some of the worst roads, and bad stretches are found in parts of Colombia and the Brazilian Amazon. Much depends on the season: vast deserts of red dust in the dry season become oceans of mud in the rainy season. In Argentina, Uruguay, coastal and southern Brazil, and most of Venezuela, roads are generally better. Chile and much of Argentina have some of the best-maintained roads and most comfortable and reliable bus services in South America.

Most major cities and towns have a *terminal de autobuses* or *terminal de ómnibus* (bus terminal); in Brazil, it's called a *rodoviária*, and in Ecuador it's a *terminal terrestre*. Often, terminals are on the outskirts of town, and you'll need a local bus or taxi to reach it. The biggest and best terminals have restaurants, shops, showers and other services, and the surrounding area is often a good (but frequently ugly) place to look for cheap sleeps and eats. Village 'terminals' in rural areas often amount to dirt lots flanked by dilapidated metal hulks called 'buses' and men hawking various destinations to passersby; listen for your town of choice.

Some cities have several terminals, each serving a different route. Sometimes each bus company has its own terminal, which is particularly inconvenient. This is most common in Colombia, Ecuador and Peru, especially in smaller towns.

Classes

Especially in the Andean countries, buses may be stripped nearly bare, tires are often treadless, and rock-hard suspension ensures a less-than-smooth ride, particularly for those at the back of the bus. After all seats are taken, the aisle is packed beyond capacity, and the roof is loaded with cargo to at least half the height of the bus, topped by the occasional goat or pig. You may have serious doubts about ever arriving at your destination, but the buses usually make it. Except for long-distance routes, different classes often don't exist: you ride what's available.

At the other extreme, you'll find luxurious coaches in Argentina, Brazil, Chile, Colombia, Uruguay, Venezuela and even Bolivia along main routes. The most expensive buses usually feature reclining seats, and meal, beverage and movie services. Different classes are called by a variety of names, depending on the country. In Argentina, Chile and Peru, the deluxe sleeper buses, called *coche-cama* or *bus-cama* (literally 'bus-bed') – or *leito* (sleeping berth) in Brazil – are available for most long-distance routes.

Costs

In the Andean countries, bus rides generally add up to about US$1 per hour of travel. When better services (such as 1st class or *coche-cama*) are offered, they can cost double the fare of a regular bus. Still, overnighters obviate the need for a hotel room, thereby saving you money.

Reservations

It's always wise to purchase your ticket in advance if you're traveling during peak holiday seasons (January through March in the Southern Cone; and around Easter week and during holiday weekends everywhere). At best, bus companies will have ticket offices at central terminals and information boards showing routes, departure times and fares. Seats will be numbered and booked in advance. In places where tickets are not sold in advance, showing up an hour or so before your departure will usually guarantee you a seat.

Safety

Anyone who has done their share of traveling in South America can tell you stories of horrifying bus rides at the mercy of crazed drivers. And there are occasionally accidents. But remember this: in countries where the vast majority of people travel by bus, there are bound to be more bus wrecks. Choosing more expensive buses is no guarantee against accidents; high-profile crashes sometimes involve well-established companies. Some roads, particularly those through the Andes, can be frightening to travel. A few well-placed flights can reduce bus anxiety.

Car & Motorcycle

Driving around South America can be mentally taxing and at times risky, but a car allows you to explore out-of-the-way places – especially parks – that are totally inaccessible by public transport. In places like Patagonia and other parts of Chile and Argentina, a short-term rental car can be well worth the expense. If you're driving your own car, so much the better.

There are some hurdles to driving. First off, it's a good idea to have an International Driving Permit to supplement your license from home. Vehicle security can be a problem anywhere in South America. Avoid leaving valuables in your car, and always lock it up. Parking is not always secure or even available; be mindful of where you leave your car, lest it be missing when you return.

Bring Your Own Vehicle

Shipping your own car or motorcycle to South America involves a lot of money and planning. Shipping arrangements should be made at least a month in advance. Stealing from vehicles being shipped is big business, so remove everything removable (hubcaps, wipers, mirrors), and take everything visible from the interior. Shipping your vehicle in a container is more secure, but more expensive. Shipping a motorcycle can be less costly.

If you're driving from North America, remember there is no road connecting Panama and Colombia, so you'll have to ship your vehicle around the Darién Gap.

Driver's License

If you're planning to drive anywhere, obtain an International Driving Permit or Inter-American Driving Permit (Uruguay theoretically recognizes only the latter). For about US$10 to US$15, any motoring organization will issue one, provided you have a current driver's license.

Insurance

Home auto insurance policies generally do not cover you while driving abroad. Throughout South America, if you are in an accident that injures or kills another person, you can be jailed until the case is settled, regardless of culpability. Fender benders are generally dealt with on the spot, without involving the police or insurance agents. When you rent, be certain your contract includes *seguro* (insurance).

Purchase

If you're spending several months in South America, purchasing a car is worth considering. It will be cheaper than hiring if you can resell it at the end of your stay. On the other hand, any used car can be a financial risk, especially on rugged roads, and the bureaucracy involved in purchasing a car can be horrendous.

The best countries in which to purchase cars are Argentina, Brazil and Chile, but, again, expect exasperating bureaucracies. Be certain of the title; as a foreigner, getting a notarized document authorizing your use of the car is a good idea, since the bureaucracy may take its time transferring the title. Taking a vehicle purchased in South America across international borders may present obstacles.

Officially, you need a *carnet de passage* or a *libreta de pasos por aduana* (customs permit) to cross most land borders in your own vehicle, but you'll probably never have to show these documents. The best source of advice is the national automobile club in the country where you buy the car.

Rental

Major international rental agencies such as Hertz, Avis and Budget have offices in South American capitals, major cities and at major airports. Local agencies, however, often have better rates. To rent a car, you must be at least 25 and have a valid driver's license from home and a credit card. Some agencies rent to those under 25 but charge an added fee. If your itinerary calls for crossing borders, know that some rental agencies restrict or forbid this; ask before renting.

Rates can fluctuate wildly (ranging from US$40 to US$80 per day). It's always worth getting a group together to defray costs. If the vehicle enables you to camp out, the saving in accommodations may offset much of the rental cost, especially in Southern Cone countries.

Road Rules

Except in Guyana and Suriname, South Americans drive on the right-hand side of the road. Road rules are frequently ignored and seldom enforced; conditions can be hazardous; and many drivers, especially in Argentina and Brazil, are reckless and even willfully dangerous. Driving at night is riskier than the day due to lower visibility and the preponderance of tired and/or intoxicated nighttime drivers sharing the road.

Road signs can be confusing, misleading or nonexistent – a good sense of humor and patience are key attributes. Honking your horn on blind curves is a simple, effective safety measure; the vehicle coming uphill on a one-way road usually has the right of way. If you're cruising along and see a tree branch or rock in the middle of the road, slow down: this means there's a breakdown, rock slide or some other trouble up ahead. Speed bumps can pop up anywhere, most often smack in the center of town, but sometimes inexplicably in the middle of a highway.

Hitchhiking

Hitchhiking is never entirely safe in any country. Travelers who decide to hitch should understand they are taking a potentially serious risk. Hitching is less dangerous if you travel in pairs and let someone know where you are planning to go.

Though it is possible to hitch all over South America, free lifts are the rule only in Argentina, Chile, Uruguay and parts of Brazil. Elsewhere, hitching is virtually a form of public transport (especially where buses are infrequent) and drivers expect payment. There are generally fixed fares over certain routes; ask the other passengers what they're paying. It's usually about equal to the bus fare, marginally less in some places. You get better views from the top of a truck, but if you're hitching on the *altiplano* (Andean high plain of Peru, Bolivia, Chile and Argentina) or *páramo* (humid, high-altitude grassland) take warm clothing. Once the sun goes down or is obscured by clouds, it gets very cold.

There's no need to wait at the roadside for a lift, unless it happens to be convenient. Almost every town has a central truck park, often around the market. Ask around for a truck going your way and how much it will cost; be there about 30 minutes before the departure time given by the driver. It is often worth soliciting a ride at *servicentros* (gas stations) on the outskirts of large cities, where drivers refuel their vehicles.

Online, check out the South America section of **digihitch** (www.digihitch.com).

Local Transportation

Local and city bus systems tend to be thorough and reliable throughout South America. Although in many countries you can flag a bus anywhere on its route, you're best off finding the official bus stop. Still, if you can't find the stop, don't hesitate to throw your arm up to stop a bus you know is going your direction. Never hesitate to ask a bus driver which is the right bus to take; most of them are very generous in directing you to the right bus.

As in major cities throughout the world, pickpockets are a problem on crowded buses and subways. If you're on a crowded bus or subway, always watch your back. Avoid crowded public transport when you're loaded down with luggage.

Taxis in most big cities (but definitely not all) have meters. When a taxi has a meter, make sure the driver uses it. When it doesn't, always agree on a fare *before* you get in the cab. In most cities, fares are higher on Sundays and after 9pm.

Train

Trains have slowly faded from the South American landscape, but several spectacular routes still operate. It's worth noting that Ecuador is heavily investing in rehabilitating its old lines. By 2014, you should be able to travel from Quito all the way to Guayaquil by train. Uruguay is also revitalizing its old lines, though it's still years from completion.

For great scenery with a touch of old-fashioned railway nostalgia, try the following routes:

Curitiba–Paranaguá (Brazil) Descending steeply to the coastal lowlands, Brazil's best rail journey offers unforgettable views.

Oruro–Uyuni–Tupiza–Villazón (Bolivia) The main line from Oruro continues south from Uyuni to Tupiza (another scenic rail trip through gorge country) and on to Villazón at the Argentine border.

Puno–Juliaca–Cuzco (Peru) From the shores of Lake Titicaca and across a 4600m pass, this train runs for group bookings in high season. Departures are unpredictable, but when it does run, it's open to non-group passengers.

Riobamba–Sibambe (Ecuador) One of a growing number of short tourist-train jaunts in the country, the Nariz del Diablo (Devil's Nose) is an exhilarating, steep descent via narrow switchbacks.

Salta–La Polvorilla (Argentina) The Tren a las Nubes (Train to the Clouds) negotiates switchbacks, tunnels, spirals and death-defying bridges during its ascent into the Andean *puna* (highlands). Unfortunately, schedules are extremely unreliable.

Uyuni (Bolivia)–Calama (Chile) On Monday at 3am a train trundles five hours west to Avaroa on the Chilean border, where you cross to Ollagüe and may have to wait a few hours to clear Chilean customs. From here, another train continues to Calama (six hours further). The whole trip can take up to 24 hours but it's a spectacular, if uncomfortable, journey.

There are several types of passenger trains in the Andean countries. The *ferrobus* is a relatively fast, diesel-powered single or double car that caters to passengers going from A to B but not to intermediate stations. Meals are often available on board. These are the most expensive trains and can be great value.

The *tren rápido* is more like an ordinary train, pulled by a diesel or steam engine. It is relatively fast, makes few stops and is generally cheaper than a *ferrobus*. Ordinary passenger trains, sometimes called *expresos*, are slower, cheaper and stop at most intermediate stations. There are generally two classes, with 2nd class being very crowded. Lastly, there are *mixtos*, mixed passenger and freight trains; these take everything and everyone, stop at every station and a lot of other places in between, take forever and are dirt cheap.

The few remaining passenger trains in Chile and Argentina are generally more modern, and the salon and Pullman classes are generally comfortable and still more affordable than flying. The *economía* or *turista* classes are slightly cheaper, while the *cama* (sleeper class) is even more comfortable.

Health

Prevention is the key to staying healthy while in South America. Travelers who receive the recommended vaccines and follow common-sense precautions usually go away with nothing more than a little diarrhea.

Before You Go

Bring medications in their original, clearly labeled containers. A signed and dated letter from your physician describing your medical conditions and medications, including generic names, is also a good idea. If carrying syringes or needles, be sure to have a physician's letter documenting their medical necessity.

Insurance

If your health insurance doesn't cover you for medical expenses abroad, consider getting extra insurance. Find out in advance if your insurance plan will make payments directly to providers or reimburse you later for overseas health expenditures. (In many countries doctors expect payment in cash.)

Recommended Vaccinations

Since most vaccines don't produce immunity until at least two weeks after they're given, you should visit a physician four to eight weeks before departure. Ask your doctor for an International Certificate of Vaccination (otherwise known as the yellow booklet), which will list all the vaccinations you've received. This is mandatory for countries that require proof of yellow-fever vaccination upon entry, but it's a good idea to carry it wherever you travel.

The only required vaccine is yellow fever, and that's only if you're arriving from a yellow fever–infected country in Africa or the Americas. (The exception is French Guiana, which requires yellow-fever vaccine for all travelers.) However, a number of vaccines are recommended (see opposite).

Medical Checklist

» Acetaminophen (Tylenol) or aspirin
» Acetazolamide (Diamox; for altitude sickness)
» Adhesive or paper tape
» Antibacterial ointment (eg Bactroban; for cuts and abrasions)
» Antibiotics for diarrhea (eg Norfloxacin, Ciprofloxacin or Azithromycin)
» Antihistamines (for hay fever and allergic reactions)
» Anti-inflammatory drugs (eg ibuprofen)
» Bandages, gauze, gauze rolls
» Diarrhea 'stopper' (eg loperamide)
» Insect repellent containing DEET for the skin
» Iodine tablets (for water purification)
» Oral rehydration salts
» Permethrin-containing insect spray for clothing, tents and bed nets
» Pocket knife
» Scissors, safety pins, tweezers
» Steroid cream or cortisone (for poison ivy and other allergic rashes)
» Sunblock
» Thermometer

Internet Resources

There is a wealth of travel health advice on the internet. The **World Health Organization** (www.who.int/ith) publishes a superb book called *International Travel and Health,* which is revised annually and available online (as a downloadable pdf) for $12. Another resource of general interest is **MD Travel Health** (www.mdtravelhealth.com), which provides complete travel health recommendations for every country in the world; information is updated daily.

It's usually a good idea to also consult your government's travel-health website before departure, if one is available. Here are the main ones:

Australia (www.smartraveller.gov.au)

Canada (www.travelhealth.gc.ca)

UK (www.fco.gov.uk)

USA (wwwnc.cdc.gov/travel)

In South America

Availability & Cost of Health Care

Good medical care may be more difficult to find in smaller cities and impossible to locate in rural areas. Many doctors and hospitals expect payment in cash, regardless of whether you have travel health insurance. If you develop a life-threatening medical problem, you'll probably want to be evacuated to a country with state-of-the-art medical care. Since this may cost tens of thousands of dollars, be sure you have insurance to cover this before you depart. You can find a list of medical evacuation and travel-insurance companies on the **US State Department website** (travel.state.gov/travel).

Infectious Diseases

DENGUE

Dengue fever is a viral infection found throughout South America. Dengue is transmitted by Aedes mosquitoes, which bite preferentially during the daytime and are usually found close to human habitations, often indoors. They breed primarily in artificial water containers, such as jars, barrels, cans, cisterns, metal drums, plastic containers and discarded tires. As a result, dengue is especially common in densely populated, urban environments.

Dengue usually causes flu-like symptoms, including fever, muscle aches, joint pains, headaches, nausea and vomiting, often followed by a rash. The body aches may be quite uncomfortable, but most cases resolve uneventfully in a few days.

There is no treatment for dengue fever except to take analgesics such as acetaminophen/paracetamol (Tylenol) and drink plenty of fluids. Severe cases may require hospitalization for intravenous fluids and supportive care. There is no vaccine. The cornerstone of prevention is protection against insects.

Keep an eye out for outbreaks in areas where you plan to visit. A good website on the latest information is the **CDC** (wwwnc.cdc.gov/travel).

MALARIA

Malaria occurs in every South American country except Chile, Uruguay and the Falkland Islands. It's transmitted by mosquito bites, usually between dusk and dawn. The main symptom is high spiking fevers, which may be accompanied by chills, sweats, headache, body aches, weakness, vomiting or diarrhea. Severe cases may involve the central nervous system and lead to seizures, confusion, coma and death.

There is a choice of three malaria pills, all of which work about equally well. Mefloquine (Lariam) is taken once weekly in a dosage of

RECOMMENDED VACCINATIONS

VACCINE	RECOMMENDED FOR	DOSAGE	SIDE EFFECTS
Chickenpox	Travelers who've never had chickenpox	Two doses one month apart	Fever; mild case of chickenpox
Hepatitis A	All travelers	One dose before trip; booster 6-12 months later	Soreness at injection site; headaches; body aches
Hepatitis B	Long-term travelers in close contact with the local population	Three doses over six-month period	Soreness at injection site; low-grade fever
Measles	Travelers born after 1956 who've had only one measles vaccination	One dose	Fever; rash; joint pains; allergic reactions
Rabies	Travelers who may have contact with animals and may not have access to medical care	Three doses over three- to four-week period	Soreness at injection site; headaches; body aches
Tetanus-diphtheria	Travelers who haven't had booster within 10 years	One dose lasts 10 years	Soreness at injection site
Typhoid	All travelers	Four oral capsules, one taken every other day	Abdominal pain; nausea; rash
Yellow fever	Travelers to jungle areas at altitudes above 2300m	One dose lasts 10 years	Headaches; body aches; severe reactions are rare

250mg, starting one to two weeks before arrival and continuing through the trip and for four weeks after your return. The problem is that a certain percentage of people (the number is disputed) develop neuropsychiatric side effects, which may range from mild to severe. Atovaquone/proguanil (Malarone) is a newly approved combination pill taken once daily with food starting two days before arrival and continuing through the trip and for seven days after departure. Side effects are typically mild. Doxycycline is a third alternative, but may cause an exaggerated sunburn reaction.

Protecting yourself against mosquito bites is just as important as taking malaria pills, since none of the pills are 100% effective.

If you do not have access to medical care while traveling, bring along additional pills for emergency self-treatment, which you should take if you can't reach a doctor and you develop symptoms that suggest malaria, such as high spiking fevers. One option is to take four tablets of Malarone once daily for three days. However, Malarone should not be used for treatment if you're already taking it for prevention. An alternative is to take 650mg of quinine three times daily and 100mg of doxycycline twice daily for one week. If you start self-medication, see a doctor at the earliest opportunity.

If you develop a fever after returning home, see a physician, as malaria symptoms may not occur for months.

RABIES

Rabies is a viral infection of the brain and spinal cord that is almost always fatal. The rabies virus is carried in the saliva of infected animals and is typically transmitted through an animal bite, though contamination of any break in the skin with infected saliva may result in rabies. Rabies occurs in all South American countries.

Rabies vaccine is safe, but a full series requires three injections and is quite expensive. Those at high risk for rabies, such as animal handlers and spelunkers (cave explorers), should certainly get the vaccine. The treatment for a possibly rabid bite consists of rabies vaccine with rabies-immune globulin. It's effective, but must be given promptly. Most travelers don't need rabies vaccine.

All animal bites and scratches must be promptly and thoroughly cleansed with large amounts of soap and water, and local health authorities should be contacted to determine whether further treatment is necessary.

TYPHOID

Typhoid fever is caused by ingestion of food or water contaminated by a species of salmonella known as *Salmonella typhi*. Fever occurs in virtually all cases. Other symptoms may include headache, malaise, muscle aches, dizziness, loss of appetite, nausea and abdominal pain. Either diarrhea or constipation may occur. Possible complications include intestinal perforation, intestinal bleeding, confusion, delirium or (rarely) coma.

Unless you expect to take all your meals in major hotels and restaurants, the typhoid vaccine is a good idea.

The drug of choice for typhoid fever is usually a quinolone antibiotic such as ciprofloxacin (Cipro) or levofloxacin (Levaquin), which many travelers carry for treatment of travelers' diarrhea. However, if you self-treat for typhoid fever, you may also need to self-treat for malaria, since the symptoms of the two diseases may be indistinguishable.

YELLOW FEVER

Yellow fever is a life-threatening viral infection transmitted by mosquitoes in forested areas. The illness begins with flu-like symptoms, which may include fever, chills, headache, muscle aches, backache, loss of appetite, nausea and vomiting. These symptoms usually subside in a few days, but one person in six enters a second, toxic phase characterized by recurrent fever, vomiting, listlessness, jaundice, kidney failure and hemorrhage, leading to death in up to half of the cases. There is no treatment except for supportive care.

Yellow-fever vaccine can be given only in approved yellow-fever vaccination centers, which provide validated International Certificates of Vaccination (yellow booklets). The vaccine should be given at least 10 days before any potential exposure to yellow fever and remains effective for approximately 10 years. Reactions to the vaccine are generally mild and may include headaches, muscle aches, low-grade fevers, or discomfort at the injection site. Severe, life-threatening reactions have been described but are extremely rare. In general, the risk of becoming ill from the vaccine is far less than the risk of becoming ill from yellow fever, and you're strongly encouraged to get the vaccine.

Taking measures to protect yourself from mosquito bites is an essential part of preventing yellow fever.

Other Infections

CHAGAS DISEASE

Chagas disease is a parasitic infection that is transmitted by triatomine insects (reduviid bugs), which inhabit crevices in the walls and roofs of substandard housing in South and Central America. Chagas disease is extremely rare in travelers. However, if you sleep in a poorly constructed house, especially one made of mud, adobe or thatch, be sure to protect yourself with a bed net and a good insecticide.

GNATHOSTOMIASIS

Gnathostomiasis is an intestinal parasite acquired by eating raw or undercooked freshwater fish, including *ceviche* (marinated, uncooked seafood).

LEISHMANIASIS

Leishmaniasis occurs in the mountains and jungles of all South American countries except for Chile, Uruguay and the Falkland Islands. The infection is transmitted by sand flies, which are about one-third the size of mosquitoes. Leishmaniasis may be limited to the skin, causing slow-growing ulcers over exposed parts of the body or (less commonly) disseminate to the bone marrow, liver and spleen. There is no vaccine. To protect yourself from sand flies, follow the same precautions as for mosquitoes, except that netting must be finer-mesh (at least 18 holes to the linear inch).

Environmental Hazards

ALTITUDE SICKNESS

Altitude sickness may develop in those who ascend rapidly to altitudes greater than 2500m. Being physically fit offers no protection. Those who have experienced altitude sickness in the past are prone to future episodes. The risk increases with faster ascents, higher altitudes and greater exertion. Symptoms may include headaches, nausea, vomiting, dizziness, malaise, insomnia and loss of appetite. Severe cases may be complicated by fluid in the lungs (high-altitude pulmonary edema) or swelling of the brain (high-altitude cerebral edema).

When traveling to high altitudes, it's also important to avoid overexertion, eat light meals and abstain from alcohol.

If your symptoms are more than mild or don't resolve promptly, see a doctor. Altitude sickness should be taken seriously; it can be life-threatening when severe.

ANIMAL BITES

Do not attempt to pet, handle or feed any animal, with the exception of domestic animals known to be free of any infectious disease.

Any bite or scratch by a mammal, including bats, should be promptly and thoroughly cleansed with large amounts of soap and water, followed by application of an antiseptic such as iodine or alcohol. The local health authorities should be contacted immediately for possible post-exposure rabies treatment, whether or not you've been immunized against rabies.

Snakes and leeches are a hazard in some areas of South America. In the event of a bite from a venomous snake, place the victim at rest, keep the bitten area immobilized, and move the victim immediately to the nearest medical facility. Avoid tourniquets, which are no longer recommended.

COLD EXPOSURE & HYPOTHERMIA

Cold exposure may be a significant problem in the Andes, particularly at night. Be sure to dress warmly, stay dry, keep active, consume plenty of food and water, get enough rest, and avoid alcohol, caffeine and tobacco. Watch out for the 'umbles' – stumbles, mumbles, fumbles and grumbles – which are important signs of impending hypothermia.

Hypothermia occurs when the body loses heat faster than it can produce it and the core temperature of the body falls. If you're trekking at high altitudes or simply taking a long bus trip over mountains, particularly at night, be prepared. In the Andes, you should always be prepared for cold, wet or windy conditions even if it's just for a few hours. It is best to dress in layers, and a hat is also important.

The symptoms of hypothermia include exhaustion, numbness, shivering, slurred speech, irrational or violent behavior, lethargy, stumbling, dizzy spells, muscle cramps and violent bursts of energy. To treat mild hypothermia, you should first get people out of the wind or rain, remove their clothing if it's wet and give them something warm and dry to wear. Make them drink hot liquids – not alcohol – and some high-calorie, easily digestible food. Do not rub victims – instead allow them to slowly warm themselves.

HEATSTROKE

To protect yourself from excessive sun exposure, you should stay out of the midday sun, wear sunglasses and a wide-brimmed sun hat, and apply sunscreen with SPF 15 or higher, with both UVA and UVB protection. Travelers should also drink plenty of fluids and avoid strenuous exercise when the temperature is high.

INSECT BITES & STINGS

To prevent mosquito bites, wear long sleeves, long pants, a hat and shoes (rather than sandals). Bring along a good insect repellent, preferably one containing DEET, which should be applied to exposed skin and clothing, but not to eyes, mouth, cuts, wounds or irritated skin. Products containing lower concentrations of DEET are as effective, but for shorter periods of time. In general, adults and children over 12 years should use preparations containing 25% to 35% DEET, which usually lasts about six hours. Children between two and 12 years of age should use preparations containing no more than 10% DEET, applied sparingly, which will usually last about three hours. DEET-containing compounds should not be used on children under the age of two.

Insect repellents containing certain botanical products, including oil of eucalyptus and soybean oil, are effective but last only 1½ to two hours. DEET-containing repellents are preferable for areas where there is a high risk of malaria or yellow fever. Products based on citronella are not effective.

For additional protection, you can apply permethrin to clothing, shoes, tents and bed nets. Permethrin treatments are safe and remain effective for at least two weeks, even when items are laundered. Permethrin should not be applied directly to skin.

PARASITES

Intestinal parasites occur throughout South America. Common pathogens include Cyclospora, amoebae and Isospora. A tapeworm called Taenia solium may lead to a chronic brain infection called cysticercosis. If you exercise discretion in your choice of food and beverages, you'll sharply reduce your chances of becoming infected. Choose restaurants or market stalls that are well attended. If there's a high turnover, it means food hasn't been sitting around that long.

A parasitic infection called schistosomiasis, which primarily affects the blood vessels in the liver, occurs in Brazil, Suriname and parts of north-central Venezuela. The disease is acquired by swimming, wading, bathing or washing in fresh water that contains infected snails. It's therefore best to stay out of bodies of fresh water, such as lakes, ponds, streams and rivers, in places where schistosomiasis might occur.

A liver parasite called Echinococcus (hydatid disease) is found in many countries, especially Peru and Uruguay. It typically affects those in close contact with sheep. A lung parasite called Paragonimus, which is ingested by eating raw infected crustaceans, has been reported from Ecuador, Peru and Venezuela.

TRAVELERS' DIARRHEA

To prevent diarrhea, avoid tap water unless it has been boiled, filtered or chemically disinfected (with iodine tablets); only eat fresh fruits or vegetables if cooked or peeled; be wary of dairy products that might contain unpasteurized milk; and be highly selective when eating food from markets and street vendors.

If you develop diarrhea, be sure to drink plenty of fluids, preferably an oral rehydration solution containing salt and sugar. Gastrolyte works well for this. A few loose stools don't require treatment but you may want to take antibiotics if you start having more than three watery bowel movements within 24 hours, and it's accompanied by at least one other symptom – fever, cramps, nausea, vomiting or generally feeling unwell. Effective antibiotics include Norfloxacin, Ciprofloxacin or Azithromycin – all will kill the bacteria quickly. Note that an antidiarrheal agent (such as loperamide) is just a 'stopper' and doesn't get to the cause of the problem. Don't take loperamide if you have a fever or blood in your stools. You should seek medical attention quickly if you don't respond to an appropriate antibiotic.

WATER

Tap water is generally not safe to drink. Vigorous boiling for one minute is the most effective means of water purification. At altitudes greater than 2000m, boil for three minutes.

Other methods of treating water include using a handheld ultraviolet light purifier (such as a SteriPEN), iodine and water filters.

WANT MORE?

For in-depth language information and handy phrases, check out Lonely Planet's *Brazilian Portuguese Phrasebook*, *Latin American Spanish Phrasebook* and *Quechua Phrasebook*. You'll find them at **shop.lonelyplanet.com**, or you can buy Lonely Planet's iPhone phrasebooks at the Apple App Store.

Latin American Spanish is the language of choice for travelers in all of South America except for Brazil (where Portuguese is the national tongue) and the Guianas (where French, Dutch or English are widely spoken).

PORTUGUESE

A characteristic feature of Brazilian Portuguese is the use of nasal vowels (pronounced as if you're trying to force the sound through the nose). In Portuguese, vowels followed by a nasal consonant (*m* or *n*) or those written with a tilde over them (eg *ã*) are nasal. In our pronunciation guides, the ng after a vowel indicates a nasal sound. The consonant sounds are very similar to those of English. Keep in mind that rr is strongly rolled, zh is pronounced as the 's' in 'pleasure', ly as the 'll' in 'million' and ny as in 'canyon'. If you read our colored pronunciation guides as if they were English, you'll be understood. The stressed syllables are in italics.

Where necessary, both masculine and feminine forms of words are included, separated by a slash and with the masculine form first, eg *obrigado/obrigada* (m/f).

Basics

Hello.	*Olá.*	o·*laa*
Goodbye.	*Tchau.*	tee·*show*
How are you?	*Como vai?*	*ko*·mo vai
Fine, and you?	*Bem, e você?*	beng e vo·*se*
Excuse me.	*Com licença.*	kong lee·*seng*·saa
Sorry.	*Desculpa.*	des·*kool*·paa
Please.	*Por favor.*	por faa·*vorr*
Thank you.	*Obrigado/Obrigada.* (m/f)	o·bree·*gaa*·do/o·bree·*gaa*·daa
You're welcome.	*De nada.*	de *naa*·daa
Yes./No.	*Sim./Não.*	seeng/nowng

What's your name?
Qual é o seu nome? — kwow e o *se*·oo *no*·me

My name is ...
Meu nome é ... — *me*·oo *no*·me e ...

Do you speak English?
Você fala inglês? — vo·*se* *faa*·laa eeng·*gles*

I don't understand.
Não entendo. — nowng eng·*teng*·do

Accommodations

Do you have a single/double room?
Tem um quarto de solteiro/casal? — teng oom *kwaarr*·to de sol·*tay*·ro/kaa·*zow*

How much is it per night/person?
Quanto custa por noite/pessoa? — *kwang*·to *koos*·taa porr *noy*·te/pe·*so*·aa

Does it include breakfast?
Inclui café da manhã? — eeng·*kloo*·ee kaa·*fe* daa ma·*nyang*

campsite	*local para acampamento*	lo·*kow* *paa*·raa aa·kang·paa·*meng*·to
guesthouse	*hospedaria*	os·pe·daa·*ree*·a
hotel	*hotel*	o·*tel*
youth hostel	*albergue juventude*	ow·*berr*·ge zhoo·veng·*too*·de

air-con	*ar condicionado*	aarr kong·dee·syo·*naa*·do
bathroom	*banheiro*	ba·*nyay*·ro
bed	*cama*	*ka*·maa
window	*janela*	zhaa·*ne*·laa

Directions

Where's ...?
Onde fica ...? — ong·de fee·kaa ...

What's the address?
Qual é o endereço? — kwow e o eng·de·*re*·so

Could you please write it down?
Você poderia escrever num papel, por favor? — vo·se po·de·*ree*·aa es·kre·*verr* noom paa·*pel* porr faa·*vorr*

Can you show me (on the map)?
Você poderia me mostrar (no mapa)? — vo·se po·de·*ree*·aa me mos·*traarr* (no *maa*·paa)

at the corner	*à esquina*	aa es·*kee*·naa
at the traffic lights	*no sinal de trânsito*	no see·*now* de *trang*·zee·to
behind ...	*atrás ...*	aa·*traaz* ...
in front of ...	*na frente de ...*	naa *freng*·te de ...
near ...	*perto ...*	*perr*·to ...
next to ...	*ao lado de ...*	ow *laa*·do de ...
opposite ...	*do lado oposto ...*	do *laa*·do o·*pos*·to ...
right	*à direita*	aa dee·*ray*·taa
straight ahead	*em frente*	eng *freng*·te

Eating & Drinking

I'd like the menu, please.
Eu queria o cardápio, por favor. — e·oo ke·*ree*·aa o kaar·*daa*·pyo porr faa·*vorr*

What would you recommend?
O que você recomenda? — o ke vo·se he·ko·*meng*·daa

Do you have vegetarian food?
Você tem comida vegetariana? — vo·se teng ko·*mee*·daa ve·zhe·taa·ree·*a*·naa

I don't eat (red meat).
Eu não como (carne vermelha). — e·oo nowng *ko*·mo (*kaar*·ne verr·*me*·lyaa)

That was delicious!
Estava delicioso! — es·*taa*·vaa de·lee·see·*o*·zo

Cheers!
Saúde! — sa·*oo*·de

Please bring the bill.
Por favor traga a conta. — porr faa·*vorr* *traa*·gaa aa *kong*·taa

KEY PATTERNS

To get by in Portuguese, mix and match these simple patterns with words of your choice:

When's (the next flight)?
Quando é (o próximo vôo)? — *kwaang*·do e (o *pro*·see·mo *vo*·o)

Where's the (tourist office)?
Onde fica (a secretaria de turismo)? — *ong*·de *fee*·kaa (aa se·kre·taa·*ree*·aa de too·*rees*·mo)

Where can I (buy a ticket)?
Onde posso (comprar passagem)? — *ong*·de *po*·so (kong·*praar* paa·*sa*·zheng)

Do you have (a map)?
Você tem (um mapa)? — vo·*se* teng (oom *maa*·paa)

Is there (a toilet)?
Tem (banheiro)? — teng (ba·*nyay*·ro)

I'd like (a coffee).
Eu gostaria de (um café). — e·oo gos·taa·*ree*·aa de (oom *kaa*·fe)

I'd like (to hire a car).
Eu gostaria de (alugar um carro). — e·oo gos·taa·*ree*·aa de (aa·loo·*gaarr* oom *kaa*·ho)

Can I (enter)?
Posso (entrar)? — *po*·so (eng·*traarr*)

Could you please (help me)?
Você poderia me (ajudar), por favor? — vo·*se* po·de·*ree*·aa me (aa·zhoo·*daarr*) por faa·*vorr*

Do I have to (get a visa)?
Necessito (obter visto)? — ne·se·*see*·to (o·bee·*terr* *vees*·to)

I'd like a table for ...	*Eu gostaria uma mesa para ...*	e·oo gos·taa·*ree*·aa oo·maa *me*·zaa *paa*·raa ...
(eight) o'clock	*(às oito) horas*	(aas *oy*·to) *aw*·raas
(two) people	*(duas) pessoas*	(*doo*·aas) pe·*so*·aas

Key Words

appetisers	*aperitivos*	aa·pe·ree·*tee*·vos
bottle	*garrafa*	gaa·*haa*·faa
bowl	*tigela*	tee·*zhe*·laa
breakfast	*café da manhã*	kaa·*fe* daa ma·*nyang*
children's menu	*cardápio de crianças*	kaar·*da*·pyo de kree·*ang*·saas
(too) cold	*(demais) frio*	(zhee·*mais*) *free*·o
dinner	*jantar*	zhang·*taarr*

food	*comida*	ko·*mee*·daa
fork	*garfo*	*gaar*·fo
glass	*copo*	*ko*·po
hot (warm)	*quente*	*keng*·te
knife	*faca*	*faa*·kaa
lunch	*almoço*	ow·*mo*·so
main courses	*pratos principais*	*praa*·tos preeng·see·*pais*
plate	*prato*	*praa*·to
restaurant	*restaurante*	hes·tow·*rang*·te
spoon	*colher*	ko·*lyer*
with	*com*	kong
without	*sem*	seng

Meat & Fish

beef	*bife*	*bee*·fe
chicken	*frango*	*frang*·go
duck	*pato*	*paa*·to
fish	*peixe*	*pay*·she
lamb	*ovelha*	o·*ve*·lyaa
lobster	*lagosta*	laa·*gos*·taa
pork	*porco*	*porr*·ko
prawn	*camarão*	kaa·maa·*rowng*
tuna	*atum*	aa·*toong*
turkey	*perú*	pe·*roo*
veal	*bezerro*	be·ze·ho

Fruit & Vegetables

apple	*maçã*	maa·*sang*
apricot	*damasco*	daa·*maas*·ko
asparagus	*aspargo*	aas·*paarr*·go
avocado	*abacate*	aa·baa·*kaa*·te
banana	*banana*	baa·*na*·naa
bean	*feijão*	fay·*zhowng*
beetroot	*beterraba*	be·te·*haa*·baa
cabbage	*repolho*	he·*po*·lyo
carrot	*cenoura*	se·*no*·raa
cauliflower	*couve flor*	*ko*·ve flor
cherry	*cereja*	se·*re*·zhaa
corn	*milho*	*mee*·lyo
cucumber	*pepino*	pe·*pee*·no
fruit	*frutas*	*froo*·taas
grapes	*uvas*	*oo*·vaas
lemon	*limão*	lee·*mowng*
lentil	*lentilha*	leng·*tee*·lyaa
lettuce	*alface*	ow·*faa*·se
mushroom	*cogumelo*	ko·goo·*me*·lo
nut	*noz*	noz
onion	*cebola*	se·*bo*·laa
orange	*laranja*	laa·*rang*·zhaa
peach	*pêssego*	*pe*·se·go
pea	*ervilha*	err·*vee*·lyaa
pepper (bell)	*pimentão*	pee·meng·*towng*
pineapple	*abacaxi*	aa·baa·kaa·*shee*
plum	*ameixa*	aa·*may*·shaa
potato	*batata*	baa·*taa*·taa
pumpkin	*abóbora*	aa·*bo*·bo·raa
spinach	*espinafre*	es·pee·*naa*·fre
strawberry	*morango*	mo·*rang*·go
tomato	*tomate*	to·*maa*·te
vegetables	*legumes*	le·*goo*·mes
watermelon	*melancia*	me·lang·*see*·aa

Other

bread	*pão*	powng
butter	*manteiga*	mang·*tay*·gaa
cheese	*queijo*	*kay*·zho
eggs	*ovos*	*o*·vos
honey	*mel*	mel
jam	*geléia*	zhe·*le*·yaa
oil	*óleo*	*o*·lyo
pasta	*massas*	*maa*·saas
pepper	*pimenta*	pee·*meng*·taa
rice	*arroz*	aa·*hos*
salt	*sal*	sow
sugar	*açúcar*	aa·*soo*·kaarr
vinegar	*vinagre*	vee·*naa*·gre

Drinks

beer	*cerveja*	serr·*ve*·zhaa
coffee	*café*	kaa·*fe*
(orange) juice	*suco de (laranja)*	*soo*·ko de (laa·*rang*·zhaa)
milk	*leite*	*lay*·te
red wine	*vinho tinto*	*vee*·nyo *teeng*·to
tea	*chá*	shaa
(mineral) water	*água (mineral)*	*aa*·gwaa (mee·ne·*row*)
white wine	*vinho branco*	*vee*·nyo *brang*·ko

Signs – Portuguese

Banheiro	Toilet
Entrada	Entrance
(Não) Tem Vaga	(No) Vacancy
Pronto Socorro	Emergency Department
Saída	Exit

Emergencies

Help! *Socorro!*	so·ko·ho
Leave me alone! *Me deixe em paz!*	me *day*·she eng paas
Call the police! *Chame a polícia!*	*sha*·me aa po·*lee*·syaa
Call a doctor! *Chame um médico!*	*sha*·me oom *me*·dee·ko
I'm lost. *Estou perdido/ perdida.* (m/f)	es·*to* perr·*dee*·do/ perr·*dee*·daa
I'm ill. *Estou doente.*	es·*to* do·*eng*·te
I'm allergic to (antibiotics). *Tenho alergia à (antibióticos).*	*te*·nyo aa·lerr·*zhee*·aa aa (ang·tee·bee·o·*tee*·kos)
Where are the toilets? *Onde tem um banheiro?*	*on*·de teng oom ba·*nyay*·ro

Shopping & Services

I'd like to buy ... *Gostaria de comprar ...*	gos·taa·*ree*·aa de kong·*praarr* ...
I'm just looking. *Estou só olhando.*	es·*to* so o·*lyang*·do
Can I look at it? *Posso ver?*	*po*·so verr
Do you have any others? *Você tem outros?*	vo·*se* teng *o*·tros
How much is it? *Quanto custa?*	*kwang*·to *koos*·taa
That's too expensive. *Está muito caro.*	es·*taa mweeng*·to *kaa*·ro
Can you lower the price? *Pode baixar o preço?*	*po*·de bai·*shaarr* o *pre*·so
There's a mistake in the bill. *Houve um erro na conta.*	*o*·ve oom *e*·ho naa *kong*·taa

ATM	*caixa automático*	*kai*·shaa ow·to·*maa*·tee·ko
market	*mercado*	merr·*kaa*·do
post office	*correio*	ko·*hay*·o
tourist office	*secretaria de turismo*	se·kre·taa·*ree*·aa de too·*rees*·mo

Question Words – Portuguese

How?	*Como?*	*ko*·mo
What?	*Que?*	ke
When?	*Quando?*	*kwang*·do
Where?	*Onde?*	*ong*·de
Who?	*Quem?*	keng
Why?	*Por que?*	porr ke

Time & Dates

What time is it? *Que horas são?*	ke *aw*·raas sowng
It's (10) o'clock. *São (dez) horas.*	sowng (des) *aw*·raas
Half past (10). *(Dez) e meia.*	(des) e *may*·aa

morning	*manhã*	ma·*nyang*
afternoon	*tarde*	*taar*·de
evening	*noite*	*noy*·te
yesterday	*ontem*	*ong*·teng
today	*hoje*	*o*·zhe
tomorrow	*amanhã*	aa·ma·*nyang*
Monday	*segunda-feira*	se·*goong*·daa·*fay*·raa
Tuesday	*terça-feira*	*terr*·saa·*fay*·raa
Wednesday	*quarta-feira*	*kwaarr*·taa·*fay*·raa
Thursday	*quinta-feira*	*keeng*·taa·*fay*·raa
Friday	*sexta-feira*	*ses*·taa·*fay*·raa
Saturday	*sábado*	*saa*·baa·doo
Sunday	*domingo*	do·*meeng*·go
January	*janeiro*	zha·*nay*·ro
February	*fevereiro*	fe·ve·*ray*·ro
March	*março*	*marr*·so
April	*abril*	aa·*bree*·oo
May	*maio*	*maa*·yo
June	*junho*	*zhoo*·nyo
July	*julho*	*zhoo*·lyo
August	*agosto*	aa·*gos*·to
September	*setembro*	se·*teng*·bro
October	*outubro*	o·*too*·bro
November	*novembro*	no·*veng*·bro
December	*dezembro*	de·*zeng*·bro

Transportation

Public Transportation

boat	*barco*	*baarr*·ko
bus	*ônibus*	*o*·nee·boos
plane	*avião*	aa·vee·*owng*
train	*trem*	treng

Numbers – Portuguese

1	*um*	oom
2	*dois*	doys
3	*três*	tres
4	*quatro*	*kwaa*·tro
5	*cinco*	*seeng*·ko
6	*seis*	says
7	*sete*	se·te
8	*oito*	oy·to
9	*nove*	naw·ve
10	*dez*	dez
20	*vinte*	*veeng*·te
30	*trinta*	*treeng*·taa
40	*quarenta*	kwaa·*reng*·taa
50	*cinquenta*	seen·*kweng*·taa
60	*sessenta*	se·*seng*·taa
70	*setenta*	se·*teng*·taa
80	*oitenta*	oy·*teng*·taa
90	*noventa*	no·*veng*·taa
100	*cem*	seng
1000	*mil*	*mee*·oo

first	*primeiro*	pree·*may*·ro
last	*último*	*ool*·tee·mo
next	*próximo*	*pro*·see·mo
airport	*aeroporto*	aa·e·ro·*porr*·to
aisle seat	*lugar no corredor*	loo·*gaarr* no ko·he·*dorr*
bus stop	*ponto de ônibus*	*pong*·to de *o*·nee·boos
cancelled	*cancelado*	kang·se·*laa*·do
delayed	*atrasado*	aa·traa·*zaa*·do
ticket office	*bilheteria*	bee·lye·te·*ree*·aa
timetable	*horário*	o·*raa*·ryo
train station	*estação de trem*	es·taa·*sowng* de treng
window seat	*lugar na janela*	loo·*gaarr* naa zhaa·*ne*·laa
a ... ticket	*uma passagem de ...*	*oo*·maa paa·*sa*·zheng de ...
1st-class	*primeira classe*	pree·*may*·raa *klaa*·se
2nd-class	*segunda classe*	se·*goom*·daa *klaa*·se
one-way	*ida*	*ee*·daa
return	*ida e volta*	ee·daa e *vol*·taa

Does it stop at ...?
Ele para em ...? — e·le *paa*·raa eng ...

What station is this?
Que estação é esta? — ke es·taa·*sowng* e *es*·taa

What time does it leave/arrive?
A que horas sai/chega? — aa ke *aw*·raas sai/*she*·gaa

Please tell me when we get to ...
Por favor me avise quando chegarmos à ... — porr faa·*vor* me aa·*vee*·ze *kwang*·do she·*gaarr*·mos aa ...

I'd like to get off here.
Gostaria de saltar aqui. — gos·taa·*ree*·aa de sow·*taarr* aa·*kee*

Driving & Cycling

I'd like to hire a/an ...	*Gostaria de alugar ...*	gos·taa·*ree*·aa de aa·loo·*gaarr* ...
4WD	*um carro quatro por quatro*	oom *kaa*·ho *kwaa*·tro porr *kwaa*·tro
bicycle	*uma bicicleta*	*oo*·ma bee·see·*kle*·taa
car	*um carro*	oom *kaa*·ho
motorcycle	*uma motocicleta*	*oo*·ma mo·to·see·*kle*·taa

child seat	*cadeira de criança*	kaa·*day*·raa de kree·*ang*·saa
diesel	*diesel*	*dee*·sel
helmet	*capacete*	kaa·paa·*se*·te
hitchhike	*pegar carona*	pe·*gaarr* kaa·*ro*·naa
mechanic	*mecânico*	me·*ka*·nee·ko
petrol/gas	*gasolina*	gaa·zo·*lee*·naa
service station	*posto de gasolina*	*pos*·to de gaa·zo·*lee*·naa
truck	*caminhão*	kaa·mee·*nyowng*

Is this the road to ...?
Esta é a estrada para ...? — es·*taa* e aa es·*traa*·daa *paa*·raa ...

Can I park here?
Posso estacionar aqui? — *po*·so es·taa·syo·*naarr* aa·*kee*

The car has broken down.
O carro quebrou. — o *kaa*·ho ke·*bro*

I had an accident.
Sofri um acidente. — so·*free* oom aa·see·*deng*·te

I've run out of petrol/gas.
Estou sem gasolina. — es·*to* seng gaa·zo·*lee*·naa

I have a flat tyre.
Meu pneu furou. — *me*·oo pee·*ne*·oo foo·*ro*

SPANISH

Latin American Spanish pronunciation is easy, as most sounds are also found in English. The stressed syllables are indicated with italics in our pronunciation guides.

Note that kh is a throaty sound (like the 'ch' in the Scottish *loch*), v and b are like a soft English 'v' (between a 'v' and a 'b'), and r is strongly rolled. There are some variations in spoken Spanish across Latin America, the most notable being the pronunciation of the letters *ll* and *y*. In our pronunciation guides they are represented with y because they are pronounced as the 'y' in 'yes' in most of Latin America. In some parts of the continent, though, they sound like the 'lli' in 'million', while in Argentina, Uruguay and highland Ecuador they are pronounced like the 's' in 'measure', or the 'sh' in 'shut'.

Where both polite and informal options are given in this section, they are indicated by the abbreviations 'pol' and 'inf'. The masciline and feminine forms are indicated with 'm' and 'f' respectively.

Basics

Hello.	*Hola.*	o·la
Goodbye.	*Adiós.*	a·*dyos*
How are you?	*¿Qué tal?*	ke tal
Fine, thanks.	*Bien, gracias.*	byen *gra*·syas
Excuse me.	*Perdón.*	per·*don*
Sorry.	*Lo siento.*	lo *syen*·to
Please.	*Por favor.*	por fa·*vor*
Thank you.	*Gracias.*	*gra*·syas
You are welcome.	*De nada.*	de *na*·da
Yes.	*Sí.*	see
No.	*No.*	no

My name is ...
Me llamo ... — me *ya*·mo ...

What's your name?
¿Cómo se llama Usted? — *ko*·mo se *ya*·ma oo·*ste* (pol)
¿Cómo te llamas? — *ko*·mo te *ya*·mas (inf)

Do you speak English?
¿Habla inglés? — *a*·bla een·*gles* (pol)
¿Hablas inglés? — *a*·blas een·*gles* (inf)

I don't understand.
Yo no entiendo. — yo no en·*tyen*·do

Accommodations

I'd like a single/double room.
Quisiera una habitación individual/doble. — kee·*sye*·ra *oo*·na a·bee·ta·*syon* een·dee·vee·*dwal*/*do*·ble

How much is it per night/person?
¿Cuánto cuesta por noche/persona? — *kwan*·to *kwes*·ta por *no*·che/per·*so*·na

Does it include breakfast?
¿Incluye el desayuno? — een·*kloo*·ye el de·sa·*yoo*·no

air-con	*aire acondicionado*	*ai*·re a·kon·dee·syo·*na*·do
bathroom	*baño*	*ba*·nyo
bed	*cama*	*ka*·ma
campsite	*terreno de cámping*	te·*re*·no de *kam*·peeng
guesthouse	*pensión*	pen·*syon*
hotel	*hotel*	o·*tel*
youth hostel	*albergue juvenil*	al·*ber*·ge khoo·ve·*neel*
window	*ventana*	ven·*ta*·na

Directions

Where's ...?
¿Dónde está ...? — *don*·de es·*ta* ...

What's the address?
¿Cuál es la dirección? — kwal es la dee·rek·*syon*

Could you please write it down?
¿Puede escribirlo, por favor? — *pwe*·de es·kree·*beer*·lo por fa·*vor*

Can you show me (on the map)?
¿Me lo puede indicar (en el mapa)? — me lo *pwe*·de een·dee·*kar* (en el *ma*·pa)

at the corner	*en la esquina*	en la es·*kee*·na
at the traffic lights	*en el semáforo*	en el se·*ma*·fo·ro
behind ...	*detrás de ...*	de·*tras* de ...
in front of ...	*enfrente de ...*	en·*fren*·te de ...
left	*izquierda*	ees·*kyer*·da
near	*cerca*	*ser*·ka
next to ...	*al lado de ...*	al *la*·do de ...
opposite ...	*frente a ...*	*fren*·te a ...
right	*derecha*	de·*re*·cha
straight ahead	*todo recto*	*to*·do *rek*·to

Signs – Spanish

Abierto	Open
Cerrado	Closed
Entrada	Entrance
Hombres/Varones	Men
Mujeres/Damas	Women
Prohibido	Prohibited
Salida	Exit
Servicios/Baños	Toilets

Eating & Drinking

Can I see the menu, please?
¿Puedo ver el menú, por favor? — pwe·do ver el me·*noo* por fa·*vor*

What would you recommend?
¿Qué recomienda? — ke re·ko·*myen*·da

Do you have vegetarian food?
¿Tienen comida vegetariana? — tye·nen ko·*mee*·da ve·khe·ta·*rya*·na

I don't eat (red meat).
No como (carne roja). — no *ko*·mo (*kar*·ne *ro*·kha)

That was delicious!
¡Estaba buenísimo! — es·*ta*·ba bwe·*nee*·see·mo

Cheers!
¡Salud! — sa·*loo*

The bill, please.
La cuenta, por favor. — la *kwen*·ta por fa·*vor*

I'd like a table for ...	*Quisiera una mesa para ...*	kee·*sye*·ra *oo*·na *me*·sa *pa*·ra ...
(eight) o'clock	*las (ocho)*	las (*o*·cho)
(two) people	*(dos) personas*	(dos) per·*so*·nas

Key Words

appetisers	*aperitivos*	a·pe·ree·*tee*·vos
bottle	*botella*	bo·*te*·ya
bowl	*bol*	bol
breakfast	*desayuno*	de·sa·*yoo*·no
children's menu	*menú infantil*	me·*noo* een·fan·*teel*
(too) cold	*(muy) frío*	(mooy) *free*·o
dinner	*cena*	*se*·na
food	*comida*	ko·*mee*·da
fork	*tenedor*	te·ne·*dor*
glass	*vaso*	*va*·so
hot (warm)	*caliente*	kal·*yen*·te
knife	*cuchillo*	koo·*chee*·yo
lunch	*comida*	ko·*mee*·da
main course	*segundo plato*	se·*goon*·do *pla*·to
plate	*plato*	*pla*·to
restaurant	*restaurante*	res·tow·*ran*·te
spoon	*cuchara*	koo·*cha*·ra
with	*con*	kon
without	*sin*	seen

Meat & Fish

beef	*carne de vaca*	*kar*·ne de *va*·ka
chicken	*pollo*	*po*·yo
duck	*pato*	*pa*·to
fish	*pescado*	pes·*ka*·do
lamb	*cordero*	kor·*de*·ro
lobster	*langosta*	lan·*gos*·ta
pork	*cerdo*	*ser*·do
shrimps	*camarones*	ka·ma·*ro*·nes
tuna	*atún*	a·*toon*
turkey	*pavo*	*pa*·vo
veal	*ternera*	ter·*ne*·ra

KEY PATTERNS

To get by in Spanish, mix and match these simple patterns with words of your choice:

When's (the next flight)?
¿Cuándo sale (el próximo vuelo)? — *kwan*·do *sa*·le (el *prok*·see·mo *vwe*·lo)

Where's (the station)?
¿Dónde está (la estación)? — *don*·de es·*ta* (la es·ta·*syon*)

Where can I (buy a ticket)?
¿Dónde puedo (comprar un billete)? — *don*·de *pwe*·do (kom·*prar* oon bee·*ye*·te)

Do you have (a map)?
¿Tiene (un mapa)? — *tye*·ne (oon *ma*·pa)

Is there (a toilet)?
¿Hay (servicios)? — ai (ser·*vee*·syos)

I'd like (a coffee).
Quisiera (un café). — kee·*sye*·ra (oon ka·*fe*)

I'd like (to hire a car).
Quisiera (alquilar un coche). — kee·*sye*·ra (al·kee·*lar* oon *ko*·che)

Can I (enter)?
¿Se puede (entrar)? — se *pwe*·de (en·*trar*)

Could you please (help me)?
¿Puede (ayudarme), por favor? — *pwe*·de (a·yoo·*dar*·me) por fa·*vor*

Do I have to (get a visa)?
¿Necesito (obtener un visado)? — ne·se·*see*·to (ob·te·*ner* oon vee·*sa*·do)

Fruit & Vegetables

apple	*manzana*	man·*sa*·na
apricot	*albaricoque*	al·ba·ree·*ko*·ke
artichoke	*alcachofa*	al·ka·*cho*·fa
asparagus	*espárragos*	es·*pa*·ra·gos
banana	*plátano*	*pla*·ta·no
beans	*judías*	khoo·*dee*·as
beetroot	*remolacha*	re·mo·*la*·cha
cabbage	*col*	kol

carrot	*zanahoria*	sa·na·o·rya
celery	*apio*	a·pyo
cherry	*cereza*	se·re·sa
corn	*maíz*	ma·ees
cucumber	*pepino*	pe·pee·no
fruit	*fruta*	froo·ta
grape	*uvas*	oo·vas
lemon	*limón*	lee·mon
lentils	*lentejas*	len·te·khas
lettuce	*lechuga*	le·choo·ga
mushroom	*champiñón*	cham·pee·nyon
nuts	*nueces*	nwe·ses
onion	*cebolla*	se·bo·ya
orange	*naranja*	na·ran·kha
peach	*melocotón*	me·lo·ko·ton
peas	*guisantes*	gee·san·tes
pepper (bell)	*pimiento*	pee·myen·to
pineapple	*piña*	pee·nya
plum	*ciruela*	seer·we·la
potato	*patata*	pa·ta·ta
pumpkin	*calabaza*	ka·la·ba·sa
spinach	*espinacas*	es·pee·na·kas
strawberry	*fresa*	fre·sa
tomato	*tomate*	to·ma·te
vegetable	*verdura*	ver·doo·ra
watermelon	*sandía*	san·dee·a

Other

bread	*pan*	pan
butter	*mantequilla*	man·te·kee·ya
cheese	*queso*	ke·so
egg	*huevo*	we·vo
honey	*miel*	myel
jam	*mermelada*	mer·me·la·da
oil	*aceite*	a·sey·te
pasta	*pasta*	pas·ta
pepper	*pimienta*	pee·myen·ta
rice	*arroz*	a·ros
salt	*sal*	sal
sugar	*azúcar*	a·soo·kar
vinegar	*vinagre*	vee·na·gre

Question Words – Spanish

How?	*¿Cómo?*	ko·mo
What?	*¿Qué?*	ke
When?	*¿Cuándo?*	kwan·do
Where?	*¿Dónde?*	don·de
Who?	*¿Quién?*	kyen
Why?	*¿Por qué?*	por ke

Drinks

beer	*cerveza*	ser·ve·sa
coffee	*café*	ka·fe
(orange) juice	*zumo (de naranja)*	soo·mo (de na·ran·kha)
milk	*leche*	le·che
red wine	*vino tinto*	vee·no teen·to
tea	*té*	te
(mineral) water	*agua (mineral)*	a·gwa (mee·ne·ral)
white wine	*vino blanco*	vee·no blan·ko

Emergencies

Help!	*¡Socorro!*	so·ko·ro
Go away!	*¡Vete!*	ve·te
Call ...!	*¡Llame a ...!*	ya·me a ...
a doctor	*un médico*	oon me·dee·ko
the police	*la policía*	la po·lee·see·a

I'm lost.
Estoy perdido/a. — es·toy per·dee·do/a (m/f)

I'm ill.
Estoy enfermo/a. — es·toy en·fer·mo/a (m/f)

I'm allergic to (antibiotics).
Soy alérgico/a a (los antibióticos). — soy a·ler·khee·ko/a a (los an·tee·byo·tee·kos) (m/f)

Where are the toilets?
¿Dónde están los baños? — don·de es·tan los ba·nyos?

Shopping & Services

I'd like to buy ...
Quisiera comprar ... — kee·sye·ra kom·prar ...

I'm just looking.
Sólo estoy mirando. — so·lo es·toy mee·ran·do

Can I look at it?
¿Puedo verlo? — pwe·do ver·lo

I don't like it.
No me gusta. — no me goos·ta

How much is it?
¿Cuánto cuesta? — kwan·to kwes·ta

That's too expensive.
Es muy caro. — es mooy ka·ro

Can you lower the price?
¿Podría bajar un poco el precio? — po·dree·a ba·khar oon po·ko el pre·syo

There's a mistake in the bill.
Hay un error en la cuenta. — ai oon e·ror en la kwen·ta

ATM	*cajero automático*	ka·*khe*·ro ow·to·*ma*·tee·ko
market	*mercado*	mer·*ka*·do
post office	*correos*	ko·*re*·os
tourist office	*oficina de turismo*	o·fee·*see*·na de too·*rees*·mo

Time & Dates

What time is it?
¿Qué hora es? ke o·ra es

It's (10) o'clock.
Son (las diez). son (las dyes)

It's half past (one).
Es (la una) y media. es (la *oo*·na) ee *me*·dya

morning	*mañana*	ma·*nya*·na
afternoon	*tarde*	*tar*·de
evening	*noche*	*no*·che
yesterday	*ayer*	a·*yer*
today	*hoy*	oy
tomorrow	*mañana*	ma·*nya*·na
Monday	*lunes*	*loo*·nes
Tuesday	*martes*	*mar*·tes
Wednesday	*miércoles*	*myer*·ko·les
Thursday	*jueves*	*khwe*·ves
Friday	*viernes*	*vyer*·nes
Saturday	*sábado*	*sa*·ba·do
Sunday	*domingo*	do·*meen*·go
January	*enero*	e·*ne*·ro
February	*febrero*	fe·*bre*·ro
March	*marzo*	*mar*·so
April	*abril*	a·*breel*
May	*mayo*	*ma*·yo
June	*junio*	*khoon*·yo
July	*julio*	*khool*·yo
August	*agosto*	a·*gos*·to
September	*septiembre*	sep·*tyem*·bre
October	*octubre*	ok·*too*·bre
November	*noviembre*	no·*vyem*·bre
December	*diciembre*	dee·*syem*·bre

Transportation

Public Transportation

boat	*barco*	*bar*·ko
bus	*autobús*	ow·to·*boos*
plane	*avión*	a·*vyon*
train	*tren*	tren

Numbers – Spanish

1	*uno*	*oo*·no
2	*dos*	dos
3	*tres*	tres
4	*cuatro*	*kwa*·tro
5	*cinco*	*seen*·ko
6	*seis*	seys
7	*siete*	*sye*·te
8	*ocho*	*o*·cho
9	*nueve*	*nwe*·ve
10	*diez*	dyes
20	*veinte*	*veyn*·te
30	*treinta*	*treyn*·ta
40	*cuarenta*	kwa·*ren*·ta
50	*cincuenta*	seen·*kwen*·ta
60	*sesenta*	se·*sen*·ta
70	*setenta*	se·*ten*·ta
80	*ochenta*	o·*chen*·ta
90	*noventa*	no·*ven*·ta
100	*cien*	syen
1000	*mil*	meel

first	*primero*	pree·*me*·ro
last	*último*	*ool*·tee·mo
next	*próximo*	*prok*·see·mo
airport	*aeropuerto*	a·e·ro·*pwer*·to
aisle seat	*asiento de pasillo*	a·*syen*·to de pa·*see*·yo
bus stop	*parada de autobuses*	pa·*ra*·da de ow·to·*boo*·ses
cancelled	*cancelado*	kan·se·*la*·do
delayed	*retrasado*	re·tra·*sa*·do
ticket office	*taquilla*	ta·*kee*·ya
timetable	*horario*	o·*ra*·ryo
train station	*estación de trenes*	es·ta·*syon* de *tre*·nes
window seat	*asiento junto a la ventana*	a·*syen*·to *khoon*·to a la ven·*ta*·na

A ... ticket, please.	*Un billete de ..., por favor.*	oon bee·*ye*·te de ... por fa·*vor*
1st-class	*primera clase*	pree·*me*·ra *kla*·se
2nd-class	*segunda clase*	se·*goon*·da *kla*·se
one-way	*ida*	*ee*·da
return	*ida y vuelta*	*ee*·da ee *vwel*·ta

Does it stop at ...?
¿Para en ...? pa·ra en ...

What stop is this?
¿Cuál es esta parada? kwal es es·ta pa·*ra*·da

What time does it arrive/leave?
¿A qué hora llega/sale? a ke o·ra *ye*·ga/*sa*·le

Please tell me when we get to ...
¿Puede avisarme cuando lleguemos a ...? pwe·de a·vee·*sar*·me *kwan*·do ye·*ge*·mos a ...

I want to get off here.
Quiero bajarme aquí. *kye*·ro ba·*khar*·me a·*kee*

Driving & Cycling

I'd like to hire a ...	*Quisiera alquilar ...*	kee·*sye*·ra al·kee·*lar* ...
4WD	*un todo-terreno*	oon to·do·te·*re*·no
bicycle	*una bicicleta*	*oo*·na bee·see·*kle*·ta
car	*un coche*	oon *ko*·che
motorcycle	*una moto*	*oo*·na *mo*·to
child seat	*asiento de seguridad para niños*	a·*syen*·to de se·goo·ree·*da* *pa*·ra *nee*·nyos
diesel	*petróleo*	pet·*ro*·le·o
helmet	*casco*	*kas*·ko
hitchhike	*hacer botella*	a·ser bo·*te*·ya
mechanic	*mecánico*	me·*ka*·nee·ko
petrol/gas	*gasolina*	ga·so·*lee*·na
service station	*gasolinera*	ga·so·lee·*ne*·ra
truck	*camion*	ka·*myon*

Is this the road to ...?
¿Se va a ... por esta carretera? se va a ... por es·ta ka·re·*te*·ra

Can I park here?
¿Puedo aparcar aquí? pwe·do a·par·*kar* a·*kee*

The car has broken down.
El coche se ha averiado. el *ko*·che se a a·ve·*rya*·do

I had an accident.
He tenido un accidente. e te·*nee*·do oon ak·see·*den*·te

I've run out of petrol/gas.
Me he quedado sin gasolina. me e ke·*da*·do seen ga·so·*lee*·na

I have a flat tyre.
Se me pinchó una rueda. se me peen·*cho* oo·na *rwe*·da

AYMARÁ & QUECHUA

The few Aymará and Quechua words and phrases included here will be useful for those traveling in the Andes. Aymará is spoken by the Aymará people, who inhabit the highland regions of Bolivia and Peru and smaller adjoining areas of Chile and Argentina. While the Quechua included here is from the Cuzco dialect, it should prove helpful wherever you travel in the Andes. The exception is Ecuador, where it is known as Quichua – the dialect that's most removed from the Cuzco variety.

In the following lists, Aymará is the second column, Quechua the third. The principles of pronunciation for both languages are similar to those found in Spanish. An apostrophe (') represents a glottal stop, which is the 'nonsound' that occurs in the middle of 'uh-oh.'

Hello.	*Kamisaraki.*	*Napaykullayki.*
Please.	*Mirá.*	*Allichu.*
Thank you.	*Yuspagara.*	*Yusulipayki.*
Yes.	*Jisa.*	*Ari.*
No.	*Janiwa.*	*Mana.*
How do you say ...?	*Cun saña-sauca'ha ...?*	*Imainata nincha chaita ...?*
It's called ...	*Ucan sutipa'h ...*	*Chaipa'g sutin'ha ...*
Please repeat.	*Uastata sita.*	*Ua'manta niway.*
How much?	*K'gauka?*	*Maik'ata'g?*
father	*auqui*	*tayta*
mother	*taica*	*mama*
food	*manka*	*mikíuy*
river	*jawira*	*mayu*
snowy peak	*kollu*	*riti-orko*
water	*uma*	*yacu*
1	*maya*	*u'*
2	*paya*	*iskai*
3	*quimsa*	*quinsa*
4	*pusi*	*tahua*
5	*pesca*	*phiska*
6	*zo'hta*	*so'gta*
7	*pakalko*	*khanchis*
8	*quimsakalko*	*pusa'g*
9	*yatunca*	*iskon*
10	*tunca*	*chunca*

GLOSSARY

Unless otherwise indicated, the terms listed in this glossary refer to Spanish-speaking South America in general, but regional variations in meaning are common. Portuguese phrases, which are only used in Brazil, are indicated with 'Bra.'

aduana – customs
aguardiente – sugarcane alcohol
ají – chili
albergue – hostel
alcaldía – town hall; virtually synonymous with *municipalidad*
almuerzo – fixed-price set lunch
alojamiento – rock-bottom accommodations with shared toilet and bathroom facilities
altiplano – Andean high plain of Peru, Bolivia, Chile and Argentina
apartamento – apartment or flat; in Brazil, a hotel room with private bathroom
artesanía – handicrafts; crafts shop
asado – roasted; in Argentina, a barbecue which is often a family outing
ascensor – elevator
audiencia – colonial administrative subdivision
ayahuasca – hallucinogenic brew made from jungle vines
Aymará – indigenous people of highland Bolivia, Peru and Chile (also called *Kolla*); also their language

balneario – bathing resort or beach
baños – baths
barrio – neighborhood, district or borough; in Venezuela, a shantytown; in Brazil, *bairro*
bloco (Bra) – group of musicians and dancers who perform in street parades during Brazil's Carnaval
bodega – winery or storage area for wine
bus-cama – literally 'bus-bed'; very comfortable bus with fully reclining seats; also called *coche-cama*

cabaña – cabin
cabildo – colonial town council
cachaça (Bra) – sugarcane rum, also called *pinga*; Brazil's national drink
cachoeira (Bra) – waterfall
caipirinha (Bra) – Brazil's national cocktail
calle – street
cambista – street money changer
camino – road, path, way
camión – open-bed truck; popular form of local transport in the Andean countries
camioneta – pickup or other small truck; form of local transport in the Andean countries
campamento – campsite
campesino/a – rural dweller who practices subsistence agriculture; peasant
caña – rum
Candomblé (Bra) – Afro-Brazilian religion of Bahia
capoeira (Bra) – martial art/dance developed by Bahian slaves
Carnaval – all over Latin America, pre-Lenten celebration
casa de cambio – authorized foreign-currency exchange house
casa de familia – modest family accommodations
casa de huésped – literally 'guesthouse'; form of economical lodging where guests may have access to the kitchen, garden and laundry facilities
casona – large house, usually a mansion; term often applied to colonial architecture in particular
catarata – waterfall
caudillo – in 19th-century South American politics, a provincial strongman
cazuela – hearty stew
cena – dinner; often an inexpensive set menu
cerro – hill; also refers to very high Andean peaks
certificado – registered (for mail)
cerveza – beer
ceviche – marinated raw seafood (it can be a source of both cholera and gnathostomiasis)
charango – Andean stringed instrument, traditionally made with an armadillo shell as a soundbox
chicha – in Andean countries, a popular beverage (often alcoholic) made from ingredients such as yucca, sweet potato or maize
chifa – Chinese restaurant (term most commonly used in Peru, Bolivia and Ecuador)
chiva – in Colombia, basic rural bus with wooden bench seats
churrasquería – restaurant featuring barbecued meat; in Brazil, *churrascaria*
cocalero – coca grower
coche-cama – see *bus-cama*
colectivo – depending on the country, either a bus, a minibus or a shared taxi
combi – small bus or minibus; also called *micro*
comedor – basic eatery or dining room in a hotel
comida corriente – in Colombia, basic set meal
confitería – cafe that serves coffee, tea, desserts and simple food orders
cordillera – mountain range
correo – post office; in Brazil, *correio*

costanera – in the Southern Cone, a seaside, riverside or lakeside road

costeño – inhabitant of the coast

criollo/a – Spaniard born in colonial South America; in modern times, a South American of European descent

cumbia – big on horns and percussion, a cousin to salsa, merengue and lambada

curanto – Chilean seafood stew

cuy – roasted guinea pig, a traditional Andean food

denuncia – affidavit or statement, usually in connection with theft or robbery

edificio – building

esquina – corner (abbreviated to 'esq')

estancia – extensive grazing establishment, either for cattle or sheep, with a dominant owner or manager *(estanciero)* and dependent resident labor force

FARC – Fuerzas Armadas Revolucionarias de Colombia (Revolutionary Armed Forces of Colombia); guerrilla movement

farmacia – pharmacy

favela (Bra) – slum or shantytown

fazenda (Bra) – large ranch or farm, similar to *hacienda*

ferrobus – type of passenger train

ferrocarril – railway, railroad

ferroviária (Bra) – railway station

flota – fleet; often a long-distance bus line

fútbol – soccer; in Brazil, *fútebol*

gaucho – in Argentina and Uruguay, a cowboy, herdsman; in Brazil, *gaúcho*

golpe de estado – coup d'état

gringo/a – a foreigner or person with light hair and complexion; not necessarily a derogatory term

guanaco – undomesticated relative of the llama

guaraná – Amazonian shrub with berries believed to have magical and medicinal powers; in Brazil, a popular soft drink

Guaraní – indigenous people of Argentina, Brazil, Bolivia and Paraguay; also their language

hacienda – large rural landholding with a dependent resident labor force under a dominant owner *(hacendado)*

hidroviária – boat terminal

hospedaje – budget accommodations with shared bathroom; usually a family home with an extra guest room

hostal – small hotel or guesthouse

huaso – cowboy

humita – a sweet-corn tamale or dumpling

iglesia – church; in Brazil, *igreja*

Inca – dominant indigenous civilization of the central Andes at the time of the Spanish Conquest; refers both to the people and, individually, to their leader

indígena – native American; indigenous person

isla – island; in Brazil, *ilha*

lago – lake

laguna – lagoon; shallow lake

lanchero – boat driver

latifundio – large landholding, such as a *hacienda* or cattle *estancia*

lavandería – laundry

leito (Bra) – luxury overnight express bus

licuado – fruit shake blended with milk or water

lista de correos – poste restante

locutorio – small telephone office

machismo – exaggerated masculine pride

malecón – shoreline promenade

Mapuche – indigenous people of northern Patagonia

marisquería – seafood restaurant

mate – see *yerba mate*

mate de coca – coca-leaf tea

menú del día – inexpensive set meal

mercado – market

mercado negro – black market

mestizo/a – a person of mixed indigenous and Spanish descent

micro – small bus or minibus; also called *combi*

migración – immigration office

minuta – short-order snack in Argentina, Paraguay and Uruguay

mirador – viewpoint or lookout, usually on a hill but often in a building

moai – enormous stone statues on Easter Island

mototaxi – in Peru, three-wheeled motorcycle rickshaw; also called *motocarro*

mudéjar – a Moorish-influenced architectural style that developed in Spain beginning in the 12th century

mulato/a – person of mixed African and European ancestry

municipalidad – city or town hall

museo – museum; in Brazil, *museu*

música criolla – creole music

música folklórica – traditional Andean music

nevado – snow-covered peak

oferta – promotional fare for plane or bus travel

oficina – office (abbreviated to 'of')

onces – morning or afternoon tea; snack

Pachamama – Mother Earth, deity of the indigenous Andean people

panadería – bakery

panama – traditional lightweight straw hat, actually of Ecuadorian origin

parada/paradero – bus stop

páramo – humid, high-altitude grassland of the northern Andean countries

parque nacional – national park

parrilla/parrillada – barbecued or grilled meat; also used to refer to a steakhouse restaurant or the grill used to cook meat

paseo – avenue, promenade

patio de comidas – food court

peatonal – pedestrian mall

pehuén – the monkey-puzzle tree of southern South America

peña – club/bar that hosts informal folk music gatherings; performance at such a club

pensión – short-term budget accommodations in a family home, which may also have permanent lodgers

piropo – sexist remark, ranging from relatively innocuous to very offensive

pisco – white-grape brandy, Peruvian national drink; most frequently served as a pisco sour cocktail

Planalto – enormous plateau that covers much of southern Brazil

pollería – restaurant serving grilled chicken

por puesto – in Venezuela, shared taxi or minibus

posada – small family-owned guesthouse; term sometimes also used for a hotel; in Brazil, *pousada*

prato feito (Bra) – literally 'made plate' or 'plate of the day'; typically an enormous and very cheap, fixed-price meal

precordillera – foothills of the Andes

pucará – an indigenous Andean fortification

puna – Andean highlands, usually above 3000m

quebrada – ravine, normally dry

Quechua – indigenous language of the Andean highlands; 'Quichua' in Ecuador

quena – simple reed flute

quinoa – native Andean grain, the dietary equivalent of rice in the pre-Columbian era

rancho – rural house

recargo – surcharge; added by many businesses to credit-card transactions

reducción – in colonial Latin America, the concentration of native populations in central settlements, usually to aid political control or religious instruction; also known as *congregación*

refugio – rustic shelter in a national park or remote area

reggaeton – Caribbean-born popular music which combines Latin rhythms with rap

remise – in Argentina, taxi booked over the phone

residencial – budget accommodations, sometimes only seasonal; in general, *residenciales* are in buildings designed expressly for short-stay lodging

río – river; in Brazil, *rio*

rodoferroviária (Bra) – combined bus and train station

rodoviária (Bra) – bus station

ruta – route or highway

s/n – *sin número;* indicating a street address without a number

salar – salt lake or salt pan, usually in the high Andes or Argentine Patagonia

salsoteca – salsa club

salteña – meat and vegetable pasty, generally a spicier version of empanada

Semana Santa – celebrated all over South America, Holy Week, the week before Easter

Sendero Luminoso – Shining Path, Peru's Maoist terrorist group which led a guerrilla war in the late 1980s

serrano – inhabitant of the mountains

siesta – lengthy afternoon break for lunch and, occasionally, a nap

soroche – altitude sickness

Sranan Tongo – creole widely spoken in Suriname; also called Surinaams

suco (Bra) – fruit juice; fruit-juice bar

tasca – Spanish-style bar-restaurant

teleférico – cable car

telenovela – TV soap opera

tenedor libre – in Argentina, 'all-you-can-eat' buffet

tepui – flat-topped mountain; home to unique flora

termas – hot springs

terminal de ómnibus – bus station; also called *terminal terrestre*

tinto – red wine; in Colombia, small cup of black coffee

todo terreno – mountain bike

torrentismo – rappelling down a waterfall

totora – type of reed, used as a building material

vaquero – cowboy; in Brazil, *vaqueiro*

vicuña – wild relative of the domestic llama and alpaca, found only at high altitudes in the south-central Andes

yerba mate – 'Paraguayan tea' *(Ilex paraguariensis);* consumed regularly in Argentina, Paraguay, Uruguay and Brazil

zampoña – pan flute featured in traditional Andean music

zona franca – duty-free zone

Behind the Scenes

SEND US YOUR FEEDBACK

We love to hear from travelers – your comments keep us on our toes and help make our books better. Our well-traveled team reads every word on what you loved or loathed about this book. Although we cannot reply individually to postal submissions, we always guarantee that your feedback goes straight to the appropriate authors, in time for the next edition. Each person who sends us information is thanked in the next edition – the most useful submissions are rewarded with a selection of digital PDF chapters.

Visit **lonelyplanet.com/contact** to submit your updates and suggestions or to ask for help. Our award-winning website also features inspirational travel stories, news and discussions.

Note: We may edit, reproduce and incorporate your comments in Lonely Planet products such as guidebooks, websites and digital products, so let us know if you don't want your comments reproduced or your name acknowledged. For a copy of our privacy policy visit lonelyplanet.com/privacy.

OUR READERS

Many thanks to the travelers who used the last edition and wrote to us with helpful hints, useful advice and interesting anecdotes:

A Nimrod Aharon, Sebastián Arabito, Alon Armelin, Nicole Armitage, Alison Aspden, Eva Aymerich Mas **B** Olivier Baboulet, John Baile, Marie Baranger, Hannah Barron, Zoe Baumgart, Rob Bergen, Sebastian Biehl, Nicole Blaser, Steve Bogaerts, Ali Briggs, Annemiek Broer, Kathleen Brosnan, Paul Brown, Alexandra Buck, Niels Busch, Steve Buss **C** Lindsay Carlisle, Benjamin Carr, Marianna Castiaux, Nelson Chen, Pierre Chenier, C Chrobok, Samantha Chu, Matthew Clarkson, Tara Cloud, Mark Coady, Julie Copson, Stephanie Cox, David Crockett, Karen Crouch, Michyl Culos, Cori Cunningham **D** Juan David, David De Silva, Francisco Del Castillo, Vicet Del Paunet, Diogo Diniz, Susi Doegnitz, Cain Donovan **E** Philippe Eugster, Matt Evans **F** Laura Femino, Joras Ferwerda, Joan Finkle, Paul Forster, June Fujimoto **G** Michael Geertsen, Ali Grant, Rico Guler, Jessica Gulland **H** Jose Haasakker, Mathilde Hansen, Stefan Hey, Jeff Hopkins, Ruth Horwitz, Jaroslav Hruskovic, Lukas Huemer **I** Marco Ijmker, Dlae Ireland **J** Janghoi Jaramillo **K** Isla Kennedy, Shannon Kissane, Sharon Knowles, Jeremy Koehler, Yaniv Kriger **L** David Lederman, Graham Lee, Natalie Liles, Brigitte Lipman, Hayley Lyon **M** Heather Macleod, Kira Mavis, Lea Mayer, Jonathan Maytham, Shane Mccarthy, Robert Mckenzie, Fatima Menem, Alex Michaels, Raquel Miguel, Ina Johanne Mønsted Hunsballe, Yvonne Mos, Erik Mueller, Christian Muttoni **N** Matt Ng Wing Ho, Jenny Nicholson, Brian Nocella **O** Stephen O'regan **P** Adrian Palenchar, Dani Parry, Ronnie Parry, Caroline Pattinson, David James Pearson, Matt Pepe, Hendrik Pfaefflin, Gordon Pittendrigh, Maria Polak, Laura Poon, Michael Price, Ed Purkis **R** Koos Reitsma, Daniel Alejandro Rodriguez Cepeda, Vincenzo Romeo **S** Roc Salvans Buxo, Sven Schimpf, Anthony Schindler, Varoojan Sepanian, Danielle Shearing, Zia Sherrell, Sandra Shloznikov, Nolan Shulak, Brian Smith Hudson, Andrea Spirov, Warwick Sprawson, Linnea Stenström, Jasmine Stephenson, Barbara Strobl, Kenji Suzuki, Jan Szpetulski, **T** Maya Tanury, Joe Turner **V** Juan Valenzuela, Hans Van Kleef, Timmi Van Maldegem, Suzanne Verheij, Paolo Votino **W** Femke Waanders, David Waldmeier, HD Wardman, Carrie West, Joe Wheeler, Alan Wicks, Amos Wittenberg, Timo Würsch **Z** Asia Zabicka

AUTHOR THANKS

Regis St Louis

Many thanks to a talented team of coauthors for their dedication and hard work. In Ecuador, I'm grateful to the countless guides, expats and locals who shared tips and insight. Special thanks to John Potts in Quito; Marlon, Marcia, Tatiana and the rest of the Guayaquil gang; and cabin mate Alan Waterman and the entire Seaman cruisers and crew on the Galápagos. Heartfelt thanks to my family for making it all worthwhile.

Sandra Bao

Thanks to coordinating author Regis St Louis, coauthor Lucas Vidgen and commissioning editor Kathleen Munnelly. Along my travels, a shout out to Alejandro, Frances, Osvaldo, Miriam, Gustavo, Lucas, Alan, Madi, Jed and Sylvia – you all know who you are. Lots of love to my godmother Elsa Mallarini, and especially to husband Ben Greensfelder.

Greg Benchwick

Special thanks to Paul Smith, who updated the content for the South Central, Southeast, Amazon and Natural World sections, which I redacted from our *Bolivia* book for this edition. Stanford's Herbert Klein fact-checked our history coverage, Climbing South America's Jeff Sandifort helped us with climbing, and La Paz on Foot's Stephen Taranto reviewed trekking coverage. Huge props goes to the Lonely Planet team and the book's coordinating author. And love always to Alejandra and Violeta.

Celeste Brash

Thanks to my adventurous mum Jan, auntie Kem and uber travel buddy Teddiy Chierici. On the ground to Collin Edwards, Fernando Li, Ashley Holland, Gary, Milner, Rovin, Shonette, Guy, Kevin, Hilda Dominquez, Kayla Defreitus, Dr David Sing, Mano, Romano, Sudanu, Eric Kuiper at METS, Bryan at Zus & Zo, Orange Suriname, Paul and Joker and Anna. And, of course, to my husband and kids for being the best people in the world to come home to.

Gregor Clark

Thanks to the zillion Brazilians and shoestringers who helped me along the way, including Jacqueline, Peter, Andre, Paulo, Alex, Hector, Marcia, Gina, Alcino, Allan, Daniel, Natalia, Steve, Tom, Gaucho, Angela, Olivia, Laure, Kathleen and Jader. Extra special *abraços* to Gaen, Meigan and Chloe, who always make coming home the best part of the trip.

Alex Egerton

Big shouts go out to all the wonderful Colombians who contributed to the research, with special mention for Laura Cahnspeyer, Oscar, Urs, and Rainbow Nelson. Also thanks to Juan Lasso at VPT and to *Colombia 6* authors Mike Power and Mr Raub for producing such a fantastic base from which to work. At home much love to Mum, Julia and the boys, Nicholas and Olga.

Bridget Gleeson

Many thanks to Robin for introducing me to the magic of the Atacama. Thanks to the team at Fundación Altiplano in Arica, Lucia at Valle Hermoso, Magdalena at Sernatur, to my Chilean brother-in-law, Germán Parra, for introducing me to his culture, and to his family, especially Emelina Nanjari, for welcoming me into her home and improving my Spanish.

Beth Kohn

A big thanks to Kathleen Munnelly for signing me up, Regis St Louis for putting it all together and Bruce Evans for answering my questions. In-country credit goes to Ben Rodriguez, Brian Ellsworth and Isa Tovar, Steven Bodzin, Fabricio Mosegue Hidalgo, Ricardo Quijano, Francisco Álvarez, Miguel Bruggeman, Claudia Beckmann, Audrey at Le Petit Jardin, Isaac Salmeron, and Benedict Mander and Valentina. Home-front hugs to Claude Moller. The Venezuela chapter is dedicated to Luis Guillermo Quijano and his family.

Carolyn McCarthy

Heaps of gratitude goes out to the many Peruvian chefs and street vendors who played a key role in my contentment. I am also grateful for the friendship, advice and assistance of the South American Explorers, Daniel Fernandez Davila, Milton, Adam, Arturo Rojas, Jorge Riveros-Cayo, Edgar in Puno, Elizabeth Shumaker and Marco Palomino. Thanks also to the intrepid Peru authors and to my hard-working coordinator Regis – a chilled *pisco sour* is due.

Kevin Raub

First and foremost, thanks to my wife, Adriana Schmidt Raub, who always saves my ass on assignments in Brazil. At Lonely Planet, Kathleen Munnelly, and my partners in crime, Gregor Clark and Regis St Louis. On the road, Ian Papareskos, Roberta Rodrigues, Bebeto Le Garfs, Michael Smyth, Jeff Sobel, Eduardo Cruxen, Marília Nogueira, Maysa Provedello, Thiago Vitale, Isabel Tarrisse, Joel Souza, Gil Neto, Luciano and Osmeria at São Jorge, Nicholas Orosz and the Brazilian gringo, Mario Saraiva.

Paul Smith

Hugo del Castillo, Natalia Goldberg, Thomas and Sabine Vinke and Karina Atkinson were all really helpful in researching this edition. Thanks to all the team who worked on this book, especially Alison, Kathleen and Regis for their assistance. Special thanks to my fantastic family Carol and Shawn for their support as I spend yet more time away from home. This one is for mum, dad and Margie. Miss you all loads.

Lucas Vidgen

Thanks once again to the Argentines and Uruguayans for having such great countries to travel and work in. Specifically Victoria Toledo (La Rioja), Aïda Martínez (Montevideo), Ana Navarta (Córdoba), Ines Corbalan (Villa Gesell), Mariel Bango (Mardel), Ayelen Estanga (Bahía Blanca), Gabi Feroglio (Santa Fe), Cecilia Hauff (Formosa), Mariana Romero (Tucumán) and Charlie O'Malley and Adam Stern (Mendoza) – your collective wisdom, love for your country and willingness to help were phenomenal.

ACKNOWLEDGMENTS

Cover photograph: Machu Picchu, Peru, Gavin Hellier/AWL; Tango dancers, Buenos Aires, Argentina, Danita Delimont Stock/AWL; Macaw, Brazil, Lee Foster/LPI; Soccer game, Antofagasta, Chile, David Ryan/LPI

THIS BOOK

This 12th edition of Lonely Planet's *South America on a Shoestring* guidebook was researched and written by Regis St Louis (Coordinating Author, Ecuador), Sandra Bao (Argentina), Greg Benchwick (Bolivia), Celeste Brash (French Guiana, Guyana, Suriname), Gregor Clark (Brazil), Alex Egerton (Colombia), Bridget Gleeson (Chile), Beth Kohn (Venezuela), Carolyn McCarthy (Peru), Kevin Raub (Brazil), Paul Smith (Paraguay) and Lucas Vidgen (Argentina, Uruguay). The Bolivia chapter was adapted in part from research and writing by Paul Smith. The Chile chapter was adapted in part from research and writing by Carolyn McCarthy, Anja Mutić and Kevin Raub. The Peru chapter was adapted in part from research and writing by Carolina Miranda, Kevin Raub, Brendan Sainsbury and Luke Waterson. This guidebook was commissioned in Lonely Planet's Oakland office, and produced by the following:

Commissioning Editor Kathleen Munnelly

Coordinating Editors Bella Li, Branislava Vladisavljevic

Coordinating Cartographer Valentina Kremenchutskaya

Coordinating Layout Designer Mazzy Prinsep

Managing Editors Bruce Evans, Annelies Mertens

Managing Cartographers Alison Lyall, Adrian Persoglia

Managing Layout Designer Jane Hart

Assisting Editors Sarah Bailey, Carolyn Boicos, Paul Harding, Trent Holden, Gabrielle Innes, Kate Kiely, Pat Kinsella, Jenna Myers, Rosie Nicholson, Sally O'Brien, Mardi O'Connor, Charlotte Orr, Susan Paterson, Chris Pitts

Assisting Cartographer Julie Dodkins

Cover Research Brendan Dempsey

Internal Image Research Kylie McLaughlin

Thanks to Imogen Bannister, Ryan Evans, Larissa Frost, Genesys India, Jouve India, Trent Paton, Martine Power, Dianne Schallmeiner, Kerri-anne Southway, Gerard Walker, Juan Winata

ABBREVIATIONS

Arg	Argentina
Bol	Bolivia
Bra	Brazil
Chi	Chile
Col	Colombia
Ecu	Ecuador
FG	French Guiana
Guy	Guyana
Par	Paraguay
Per	Peru
Sur	Suriname
Uru	Uruguay
Ven	Venezuela

000 Map pages
000 Photo pages

000 Map pages
000 Photo pages

C

000 Map pages
000 Photo pages

D

E

000 Map pages
000 Photo pages

I

J

000 Map pages
000 Photo pages

000 Map pages
000 Photo pages

Q

R

S

000 Map pages
000 Photo pages

000 Map pages
000 Photo pages

V

W

000 Map pages
000 Photo pages

OUR STORY

A beat-up old car, a few dollars in the pocket and a sense of adventure. In 1972 that's all Tony and Maureen Wheeler needed for the trip of a lifetime – across Europe and Asia overland to Australia. It took several months, and at the end – broke but inspired – they sat at their kitchen table writing and stapling together their first travel guide, *Across Asia on the Cheap*. Within a week they'd sold 1500 copies. Lonely Planet was born.

Today, Lonely Planet has offices in Melbourne, London and Oakland, with more than 600 staff and writers. We share Tony's belief that 'a great guidebook should do three things: inform, educate and amuse'.

OUR WRITERS

Regis St Louis

Coordinating Author, Ecuador After his first trip to the Andes in 1999, Regis returned home, sold all his belongings and set off on a classic journey across Latin America. Since then, he's returned numerous times, logging thousands of miles on dodgy jungle and mountain roads. On his most recent trip he swam with sea lions in the Galápagos, cycled the scenic Baños-to-Puyo highway and thrashed a rental car on the back roads of Cotopaxi. Regis is the coordinating author of Lonely Planet's *Ecuador* and *Brazil* guides, and he has contributed to more than three dozen Lonely Planet titles. He lives in New York City.

Sandra Bao

Argentina Sandra is a Chinese-American born in Argentina who has traveled to around 60 countries – but now calls the beautiful Pacific Northwest home. She's still proud to be a *porteña*, however, and regularly returns to Argentina to investigate what the wildly fluctuating peso is doing. As well as writing sections of the Argentina chapter, over the last decade Sandra has contributed to a couple dozen Lonely Planet titles.

Read more about Sandra at:
lonelyplanet.com/memebers/sandrabao

Greg Benchwick

Bolivia Greg started his career in journalism as the managing editor of the world-famous *Bolivian Times*, covering everything from the war on drugs to human-rights abuses and the state of affairs in Bolivia's numerous bars and *discotecas*. Since then he's written dozens of guidebooks on countries throughout Latin America, interviewed Bolivian *campesinos* and *políticos* for the UN's International Fund for Agricultural Development, and continued on a path toward happiness and nonstop adventure.

Read more about Greg at:
lonelyplanet.com/memebers/gbenchwick

Celeste Brash

French Guiana, Guyana, Suriname This was Celeste's second trip to the Guianas and she's determined there will be a third. The down-to-earth adventure and rugged warmth remind her of her ex-home on an atoll in French Polynesia where she lived for 15 years. She currently resides in Portland, Oregon, and writes lots of other Lonely Planet guides (around 40 so far) as well as articles for publications ranging from *Islands Magazine* to the *LA Times*. Find her on the web at www.celestebrash.com.

OVER PAGE MORE WRITERS

Published by Lonely Planet Publications Pty Ltd
ABN 36 005 607 983
12th edition – Aug 2013
ISBN 978 1 74179 894 4

10 9 8 7 6 5 4 3 2 1
Printed in Singapore

Gregor Clark

Brazil A South American travel addict since 1990, Gregor Clark has traveled everywhere from Caracas to Tierra del Fuego, from the Galápagos to Machu Picchu to Easter Island. But Brazil remains his favorite country of all, thanks to the warmth, exuberance and graciousness of its people. Peak experiences on this trip included discovering Caraíva and Alter do Chão, returning to Jericoacoara and Lençóis, and finally reaching the Lençóis Maranhenses (a longstanding dream). Gregor contributes regularly to Lonely Planet's *Brazil* and *Argentina* guides.

Alex Egerton

Colombia A journalist by trade, Alex has been coming to Colombia for 15 years since falling in love with the country while on a mad six-week dash from Venezuela to Mexico. During that time he has learned to love *aguardiente*, climbed several of the country's majestic peaks and became a big fan of *tejo*, but he still can't dance salsa. When not on the road, Alex splits his time between Medellín and rural Nicaragua.

Bridget Gleeson

Chile Based in Buenos Aires, Bridget was just starting out as a travel writer when her sister fell in love with a Chilean. She's been crossing the Andes ever since to visit the Santiago branch of the family, learning how to mix the perfect *pisco sour* and prepare a proper *ceviche* along the way. She writes about Latin American food, wine and travel for Lonely Planet, *Budget Travel*, *Afar*, Jetsetter and BBC Travel. Follow her adventures at www.bridgetgleeson.com.

Read more about Bridget at:
lonelyplanet.com/memebers/bridgetgleeson

Beth Kohn

Venezuela An *aficionada* of Latin American rhythms and culture since her Miami childhood, Beth has claimed the window seat on buses throughout the Spanish-speaking world. During her third Lonely Planet sojourn to Venezuela, she was shooed out of the construction site of the new Simón Bolívar Mausoleum, just missed seeing a presidential candidate, and clocked untold hours crisscrossing the country in rattletrap *por puestos*. A resident of San Francisco, she's coauthored almost 20 books for Lonely Planet, including the *California*, *Mexico* and *Yosemite, Sequoia & Kings Canyon National Parks* guides. You can see more of her writing and photography at www.bethkohn.com.

Carolyn McCarthy

Peru Carolyn had her first major encounter with cumbia and palm reading on an early trip to Peru. For this trip, she sampled hundreds of Peruvian delicacies, climbed Huayna Picchu and checked into one medical clinic. Some of her other Lonely Planet titles include *Argentina, Panama, Yellowstone & Grand Teton National Parks, USA* and *Trekking in the Patagonian Andes*. Among other publications, she has written for *National Geographic*, *Outside* and *Boston Globe*. You can follow her Americas blog at www.carolynswildblueyonder.blogspot.com.

Kevin Raub

Brazil Kevin grew up in Atlanta and started his career as a music journalist in New York, working for *Men's Journal* and *Rolling Stone* magazines. He ditched the rock 'n' roll lifestyle for travel writing and moved to Brazil. Ever since, he's suffered from Bland Brazilian Beer Disease. Then he met the South. From Blumenau's German-influenced microbreweries to Porto Alegre's Dirty Old Man, Brazil's best boutique beer bar, he found *cerveja* salvation in the Brazilian south. This is Kevin's 22nd Lonely Planet guide. Find him at www.kevinraub.net.

Read more about Kevin at:
lonelyplanet.com/memebers/kraub

Paul Smith

Paraguay From an early age, and with a vague and naive ambition to be the next David Attenborough, Paul dreamed of exploring the remotest areas of the globe in search of wildlife, eventually settling in Paraguay in 2004. While researching this edition Paul came face to face with a jaguar in the Pantanal, witnessed a coup d'etat, was re-impressed by the power of water at the Itaipú Dam and learned about Jesuit cosmology.

Lucas Vidgen

Argentina, Uruguay Lucas was born in Australia but has been wandering around Latin America ever since he saved up the money for his first airfare. He's lived in Quito and Buenos Aires and came very close to renting an apartment in Montevideo. Lucas has contributed to a range of Lonely Planet titles, including various editions of the *Argentina* and *South America* guides. He currently lives in Quetzaltenango, Guatemala, where he publishes – and occasionally works on – XelaWho magazine (www.xelawho.com).

how to use this book

These symbols will help you find the listings you want:

- Sights
- Beaches
- Activities
- Courses
- Tours
- Festivals & Events
- Sleeping
- Eating
- Drinking
- Entertainment
- Shopping
- Information/Transport

These symbols give you the vital information for each listing:

- Telephone Numbers
- Opening Hours
- Parking
- Nonsmoking
- Air-Conditioning
- Internet Access
- Wi-Fi Access
- Swimming Pool
- Vegetarian Selection
- English-Language Menu
- Family-Friendly
- Pet-Friendly
- Bus
- Ferry
- Metro
- Subway
- Tram
- Train

Reviews are organised by author preference.

Look out for these icons:

TOP CHOICE Our author's recommendation

FREE No payment required

A green or sustainable option

Our authors have nominated these places as demonstrating a strong commitment to sustainability – for example by supporting local communities and producers, operating in an environmentally friendly way, or supporting conservation projects.

Map Legend

Sights
- Beach
- Buddhist
- Castle
- Christian
- Hindu
- Islamic
- Jewish
- Monument
- Museum/Gallery
- Ruin
- Winery/Vineyard
- Zoo
- Other Sight

Activities, Courses & Tours
- Diving/Snorkelling
- Canoeing/Kayaking
- Skiing
- Surfing
- Swimming/Pool
- Walking
- Windsurfing
- Other Activity/Course/Tour

Sleeping
- Sleeping
- Camping

Eating
- Eating

Drinking
- Drinking
- Cafe

Entertainment
- Entertainment

Shopping
- Shopping

Information
- Bank
- Embassy/Consulate
- Hospital/Medical
- Internet
- Police
- Post Office
- Telephone
- Toilet
- Tourist Information
- Other Information

Transport
- Airport
- Border Crossing
- Bus
- Cable Car/Funicular
- Cycling
- Ferry
- Monorail
- Parking
- Petrol Station
- Taxi
- Train/Railway
- Tram
- Underground Train Station
- Other Transport

Routes
- Tollway
- Freeway
- Primary
- Secondary
- Tertiary
- Lane
- Unsealed Road
- Plaza/Mall
- Steps
- Tunnel
- Pedestrian Overpass
- Walking Tour
- Walking Tour Detour
- Path

Geographic
- Hut/Shelter
- Lighthouse
- Lookout
- Mountain/Volcano
- Oasis
- Park
- Pass
- Picnic Area
- Waterfall

Population
- Capital (National)
- Capital (State/Province)
- City/Large Town
- Town/Village

Boundaries
- International
- State/Province
- Disputed
- Regional/Suburb
- Marine Park
- Cliff
- Wall

Hydrography
- River, Creek
- Intermittent River
- Swamp/Mangrove
- Reef
- Canal
- Water
- Dry/Salt/Intermittent Lake
- Glacier

Areas
- Beach/Desert
- Cemetery (Christian)
- Cemetery (Other)
- Park/Forest
- Sportsground
- Sight (Building)
- Top Sight (Building)